Bisel's

Pennsylvania Domestic Relations Lawsource®

The Collected Consolidated Pennsylvania and Federal Domestic Relations Statutes and Court Rules

2019 Mid-Year

By
ARTHUR S. ZANAN, ESQ.
Member of the Montgomery Bar

GEORGE T. BISEL COMPANY, INC.
710 S. WASHINGTON SQUARE

PHILADELPHIA PENNSYLVANIA

www.bisel.com

Judge's Chambers
Courtroom No. 2
Mercer County Courthouse
Mercer, Pennsylvania 16137

Copyright 1993, 1995, 1997, 1998, 1999, 2000, 2001, 2002, 2003, 2004, 2005, 2006, 2007, 2008, 2009, 2010, 2011, 2012, 2013, 2014, 2015, 2016, 2017, 2018

By

George T. Bisel Company, Inc.

Copyright 2019

By

George T. Bisel Company, Inc.

All Rights Reserved

The text of this publication, or any part thereof, may not be reproduced or transmitted in any form or by any means, electronic or mechanical, including photocopying, recording, storage in an information retrieval system, or otherwise, without the prior written permission of the publisher. The information contained herein is not intended to constitute legal advice generally or with respect to any particular set of facts or circumstances and should not be relied upon as such by the reader. Neither the author nor the publisher assume responsibility for errors or omissions as may be contained herein, the use of the information contained herein, or any damages arising or resulting from the use of the information contained herein. Although the publisher intends to update this material from time to time, neither the author nor the publisher assumes any obligation to do so and this material speaks only as of the date that research therefor was completed which necessarily preceded the publication date.

Printed in United States of America

Library of Congress Control Number: 92-74441

ISBN: 1-887024-20-4

HOW TO USE

First refer to main text herein, then check any current supplement, using same reference numbers. New material subsequent to publication of original text is contained in later supplements and text revisions. SINCE LAWS AND CODE REFERENCES CHANGE QUITE FREQUENTLY, ALWAYS CHECK THE TIMELINESS AND APPLICABILITY OF THE STATUTES AND CODE CONTAINED HEREIN.

FOR QUESTIONS ABOUT THIS PUBLICATION,
CALL TOLL FREE 1-800-247-3526

PREFACE

This Bisel Lawsource®, which replaces the 2018-Mid Year Edition, setting forth the collected Pennsylvania Consolidated Domestic Relations Statutes and related Pennsylvania Rules of Civil Procedure, with appropriate tables and a combined index, covers *Marriage; Adoption, Divorce; Support, Property and Contracts; Children and Minors;* and *Abuse of Family*. It brings together in one convenient publication the statutes and court rules relating to Pennsylvania Domestic Relations.

The format is designed to provide a convenient and practical one-stop source of the law and related rules in major areas of Pennsylvania practice, together with an index referencing both in one consolidated source.

The book is designed to be used as a reference work and a handbook. It is physically suited to fit handily into the practitioner's briefcase and will travel from office, to home and to the courthouse.

The reader may work with this book in two ways to assure quick access to the subject matter. First, you may access the book through the detailed Table of Contents, which follows the Domestic Relations Code, as enacted in Title 23 of the Pennsylvania Consolidated Statutes, and Domestic Relations Rules Of Procedure, set forth at Rules 1901, et al. Second, you may consult the detailed Index to locate your topic.

Other areas of the Pennsylvania law are contemplated utilizing the same format, and the Bisel Publishers welcome suggestions and comments in this regard, in order to help us direct our efforts into those areas the Bar values most. Should you wish to speak directly to a member of the Bisel editorial staff, please call toll free at 1-800-247-3526.

Supplementary revision is presently to take place bi-annually with a replacement revised volume. In this way, frequent revision will permit the removal of obsolete references to amended or repealed laws or rules on an on-going basis, and enable us to present a relevant and up-to-date product for ready reference.

This edition is current through Act 2019-5 and court rules amended through April 2019.

The Explanatory Notes and Comments that are included with the court rules have been prepared by the Civil Procedure Rules Committee. They appear in the text following the particular rules to which they relate. These Explanatory Notes and Comments are not part of the rules and have not been officially adopted or promulgated by the Supreme Court.

Special thanks must be extended to Gary J. Friedlander, Esq. for the time and energy he devoted to previous editions of this Lawsource®.

THE PUBLISHER

TABLE OF CONTENTS
(Condensed)

DOMESTIC RELATIONS CODE

Part		Chapter
I.	General Provisions	1
II.	Marriage	11
III.	Adoption	21
IV.	Divorce	31
V.	Support, Property and Contracts	41
VI.	Children and Minors	51
VII.	Abuse of Family	61
VIII.	Uniform Interstate Family Support	71
VIII-A.	Intrastate Family Support	81

PART I. GENERAL PROVISIONS

Chap.		Code Sec.
1.	Preliminary Provisions	101

PART II. MARRIAGE

Chap.		Code Sec.
11.	Preliminary Provisions	1101
13.	Marriage License	1301
15.	Marriage Ceremony	1501
17.	Miscellaneous Provisions Relating to Marriage	1701
19.	Abolition of Actions for Alienation of Affections and Breach of Promise to Marry	1901

PART III. ADOPTION

Chap.		Code Sec.
21.	Preliminary Provisions	2101
23.	Jurisdiction and Parties	2301
25.	Proceedings Prior to Petition to Adopt	2501
27.	Petition for Adoption	2701
29.	Decrees and Records	2901

PART IV. DIVORCE

Chap.		Code Sec.
31.	Preliminary Provisions	3101
33.	Dissolution of Marital Status	3301
35.	Property Rights	3501
37.	Alimony and Support	3701
39.	Mediation	3901

TABLE OF CONTENTS

PART V. SUPPORT, PROPERTY AND CONTRACTS

Chap.		Code Sec.
41.	General Provisions	4101
43.	Support Matters Generally	4301
45.	[Repealed]	
46.	Support of the Indigent	4601

PART VI. CHILDREN AND MINORS

Chap.		Code Sec.
51.	General Provisions	5101
52.	Uniform Child Abduction Prevention	5201
53.	Child Custody	5301
54.	Uniform Child Custody Jurisdiction and Enforcement	5401
55.	Liability of Tortious Acts of Children	5501
56.	Standby and Temporary Guardianship	5601
57.	Sex Trafficking and Missing and Abducted Children	5701

PART VII. ABUSE OF FAMILY

Chap.		Code Sec.
61.	Protection from Abuse	6101
63.	Child Protective Services	6301
65.	Newborn Protection	6501
67.	Domestic and Sexual Violence Victim Address Confidentiality	6701

PART VIII. UNIFORM INTERSTATE FAMILY SUPPORT

Chap.		Code Sec.
71.	General Provisions	7101
72.	Jurisdiction	7201
73.	Civil Provisions of General Application	7301
74.	Establishment of Support Order	7401
75.	Direct Enforcement of Order of Another State Without Registration	7501
76.	Enforcement and Modification of Support Order After Registration	7601
77.	Determination of Parentage	7701
78.	Interstate Rendition	7801
79.	Miscellaneous Provisions	7901

PART VIII-A. INTRASTATE FAMILY SUPPORT

Chap.		Code Sec.
81.	General Provisions	8101
82.	Jurisdiction	8201
83.	Civil Provision of General Application	8301
84.	Enforcement and Modification of Support Order After Registration	8401

DOMESTIC RELATIONS

MISCELLANEOUS PENNSYLVANIA DOMESTIC RELATIONS STATUTES

TITLE 18 - CRIMES CODE

Crimes and Offenses

PART II. DEFINITION OF SPECIFIC OFFENSES

ARTICLE B. OFFENSES INVOLVING DANGER TO THE PERSON

Chap.		Code Sec.
27.	Assault	2709 et seq.
29.	Kidnapping	2903 et seq.
31.	Sexual Offenses	
	Subchapter A. General Provisions	3101 et seq.
	Subchapter B. Definition of Offenses	3121 et seq.

ARTICLE D. OFFENSES AGAINST THE FAMILY

Chap.

43.	Offenses Against the Family	
	Subchapter A. Definition of Offenses Generally	4301 et seq.
	Subchapter B. Nonsupport (Repealed)	4321 et seq.

ARTICLE E. OFFENSES AGAINST PUBLIC ADMINISTRATION

Chap.

49.	Falsification and Intimidation	
	Subchapter A. Perjury and Falsification in Official Matters	4906.1
	Subchapter B. Victim and Witness Intimidation	4958

ARTICLE F. OFFENSES AGAINST PUBLIC ORDER AND DECENCY

Chap.

55.	Riot, Disorderly Conduct and Related Offenses	5504

ARTICLE G. MISCELLANEOUS OFFENSES

Chap.

61.	Firearms and Other Dangerous Articles	
63.	Minors	
	Subchapter C. Other Dangerous Articles	6312

TABLE OF CONTENTS

TITLE 20 - PROBATE, ESTATES AND FIDUCIARIES CODE

Sec.

§ 2106. Forfeiture.
§ 2203. Right of election; resident decedent.
§ 2507. Modification by circumstances.
§ 5605. Power of attorney not revoked until notice.
§ 5606. Proof of continuance of powers of attorney by affidavit.
§ 6111.1. Modification by divorce.
§ 6111.2. Effect of divorce on designation of beneficiaries.

TITLE 42 - JUDICIAL CODE

Chapter 19. Administrative Office of Pennsylvania Courts

Sec.		Code Sec.
1904.	Availability of Criminal Charge Information in Child Custody Proceedings	1904

Chapter 62A. Protections of Victims of Sexual Violence on Intimidation

Chapter 63. Juvenile Matters

Subchapter
- A. General Provisions.
- B. Jurisdiction and Custody.
- C. Procedures and Safeguards.
- D. Disposition of Children Generally.
- E. Dispositions Affecting Other Jurisdictions.

TITLE 43 - LABOR

Chapter 14. Unemployment Compensation

ARTICLE VII. PROTECTION OF RIGHTS AND COMPENSATION

§ 863.1. Child support intercept of unemployment compensation.

TITLE 51 - MILITARY AFFAIRS

Part II. Pennsylvania National Guard, Pennsylvania Guard and Militia

Subchapter
- D. Rights and Immunities.

§ 4109. Child custody proceedings during military deployment.

TITLE 54 - NAMES

Chapter 7. Judicial Change of Name

§ 704. Divorced person may resume prior name.

DOMESTIC RELATIONS

MISCELLANEOUS FEDERAL DOMESTIC RELATIONS STATUTES AND REGULATIONS—SELECTED PROVISIONS

Title 10. Armed Forces
Title 11. Bankruptcy Code
Title 18. Crimes and Criminal Procedure
Title 22. Foreign Relations and Intercourse
Title 26. Internal Revenue Code
Title 28. Judiciary and Judicial Procedure
Title 42. The Public Health and Welfare

The Hague Convention on the Civil Aspects of International Child Abduction

DOMESTIC RELATIONS RULES OF PROCEDURE

Part
- I. Rules of Civil Procedure Before Magisterial District Judges (Rules 1201–1211)
- II. Actions Pursuant to the Protection from Abuse Act (Rules 1901–1905)
- III. Actions for Support (Rules 1910.1–1910.50)
- IV. Actions for Custody of Minor Children (Rules 1915.1–1915.25)
- V. Actions of Divorce or for Annulment of Marriage (Rules 1920.1–1920.92)
- VI. Rules Relating to Domestic Relations Matters Generally (Rules 1930.1–1930.8)
- VII. Voluntary Mediation in Custody Actions (Rules 1940.1–1940.9)
- VIII. Actions Pursuant to the Protection of Victims of Sexual Violence or Intimidation Act (Rules 1951–1959)
- IX. Adoption (Orphans' Court Rules 15.1–15.9)
- X. Juvenile Rules (Dependency Rules 1100–1800)
- XI. Selected Pennsylvania Rules of Appellate Procedure (Fast Track Appeals)

DOMESTIC RELATIONS REGULATIONS

Chap.		Pa. Code
108.	Family Violence and TANF and GA	108.1–108.18
187.	Support From Relatives Not Living With the Client	187.21–187.84

DOMESTIC RELATIONS

TABLE OF CONTENTS

(Detailed)

DOMESTIC RELATIONS CODE

PART I. GENERAL PROVISIONS

Chapter 1. Preliminary Provisions
- § 101. Short title of title.
- § 102. Definitions.

PART II. MARRIAGE

Chapter 11. Preliminary Provisions
- § 1101. Short title of part.
- § 1102. Definitions.
- § 1103. Common-law marriage.
- § 1104. Forms.
- § 1105. Fees.
- § 1106. Records and statistics.

Chapter 13. Marriage License
- § 1301. Marriage license required.
- § 1302. Application for license.
- § 1303. Waiting period after application.
- § 1304. Restrictions on issuance of license.
- § 1305. Examination and tests for syphilis (Repealed).
- § 1306. Oral examination.
- § 1307. Issuance of license.
- § 1308. Judicial review of refusal to issue license.
- § 1309. Filing applications and consent certificates.
- § 1310. Duration and form of license.

Chapter 15. Marriage Ceremony
- § 1501. Form of marriage certificates.
- § 1502. Forms where parties perform ceremony.
- § 1503. Persons qualified to solemnize marriages.
- § 1504. Returns of marriages.

Chapter 17. Miscellaneous Provisions Relating to Marriage
- § 1701. Decree that spouse of applicant is presumed decedent.
- § 1702. Marriage during existence of former marriage.
- § 1703. Marriage within degree of consanguinity.
- § 1704. Marriage between persons of the same sex.

Chapter 19. Abolition of Actions for Alienation of Affections and Breach of Promise to Marry
- § 1901. Actions for alienation of affections abolished.
- § 1902. Actions for breach of promise to marry abolished.

TABLE OF CONTENTS

§ 1903. Purpose of chapter.
§ 1904. Filing or threatening to file actions prohibited.
§ 1905. Instruments executed in satisfaction of abolished claims prohibited.

PART III. ADOPTION

Chapter 21. Preliminary Provisions

§ 2101. Short title of part.
§ 2102. Definitions.

Chapter 23. Jurisdiction and Parties

Subchapter A. Jurisdiction

§ 2301. Court.
§ 2302. Venue.

Subchapter B. Parties

§ 2311. Who may be adopted.
§ 2312. Who may adopt.
§ 2313. Representation for child.

Chapter 25. Proceedings Prior to Petition to Adopt

Subchapter A. Voluntary Relinquishment

§ 2501. Relinquishment to agency.
§ 2502. Relinquishment to adult intending to adopt child.
§ 2503. Hearing.
§ 2504. Alternative procedure for relinquishment.
§ 2504.1. Confidentiality.
§ 2505. Counseling.

Subchapter B. Involuntary Termination

§ 2511. Grounds for involuntary termination.
§ 2512. Petition for involuntary termination.
§ 2513. Hearing.

Subchapter C. Decree of Termination

§ 2521. Effect of decree of termination.

Subchapter D. Reports and Investigation

§ 2530. Home study and preplacement report.
§ 2531. Report of intention to adopt.
§ 2532. Filing of report.
§ 2533. Report of intermediary.
§ 2534. Exhibits.
§ 2535. Investigation.

Subchapter E. Pennsylvania Adoption Cooperative Exchange

§ 2551. Definitions.
§ 2552. Pennsylvania Adoption Cooperative Exchange.
§ 2553. Registration of children.
§ 2554. Responsibilities of PACE.
§ 2555. Responsibilities of public and private agencies.
§ 2556. Related activities of agencies unaffected.
§ 2557. Regulations and staff.
§ 2558. Retroactive application of subchapter.

DOMESTIC RELATIONS

Chapter 27. Petition for Adoption
Subchapter A. Petition
§ 2701. Contents of petition for adoption.
§ 2702. Exhibits.

Subchapter B. Consents
§ 2711. Consents necessary to adoption.
§ 2712. Consents not naming adopting parents.
§ 2713. When other consents not required.
§ 2714. When consent of parent not required.

Subchapter C. Hearings
§ 2721. Notice of hearing.
§ 2722. Place of hearing.
§ 2723. Attendance at hearing.
§ 2724. Testimony and investigation.
§ 2725. Religious belief.

Subchapter D. Voluntary Agreement for Continuing Contact
§ 2731. Purpose of subchapter.
§ 2732. Definitions.
§ 2733. Parties to agreement.
§ 2734. Consent of a child.
§ 2735. Filing and approval of an agreement.
§ 2736. Failure to comply.
§ 2737. Modification of agreement.
§ 2738. Enforcement of agreement.
§ 2739. Discontinuance of agreement.
§ 2740. Procedures for facilitating and resolving agreements involving a county child welfare agency.
§ 2741. Counsel.
§ 2742. Costs.

Chapter 29. Decrees and Records
Subchapter A. General Provisions
§ 2901. Time of entry of decree of adoption.
§ 2902. Requirements and form of decree of adoption.
§ 2903. Retention of parental status.
§ 2904. Name of adoptee.
§ 2905. [Repealed]
§ 2906. Docket entries.
§ 2907. Certificate of adoption.
§ 2908. Foreign decree of adoption.
§ 2909. [Repealed]
§ 2910. Penalty for unauthorized disclosure.

Subchapter B. Records and Access to Information
§ 2911. Definitions.
§ 2912. Combined request for information.
§ 2913. Reasonable fees.
§ 2914. Immunity from liability.
§ 2915. Court and agency records.
§ 2916. Attorney records.

TABLE OF CONTENTS

Subchapter C. Information Registry
§ 2921. Establishment of registry.
§ 2922. Informational material.
§ 2923. Filing information with registry.
§ 2924. Who may request information from registry.
§ 2925. Providing information from registry.
§ 2926. Rules and regulations.

Subchapter D. Release of Information
§ 2931. Access to Information.
§ 2932. Nonidentifying Information.
§ 2933. Identifying Information.
§ 2934. Statement of Medical and Social History Information.
§ 2935. Confidentiality.
§ 2936. Refusal to Search.
§ 2937. Original Birth Record.
§ 2938. Rules and Regulations.

PART IV. DIVORCE

Chapter 31. Preliminary Provisions
§ 3101. Short title of part.
§ 3102. Legislative findings and intent.
§ 3103. Definitions.
§ 3104. Bases of jurisdiction.
§ 3105. Effect of agreement between parties.
§ 3106. Premarital agreements.

Chapter 33. Dissolution of Marital Status

Subchapter A. General Provisions
§ 3301. Grounds for divorce.
§ 3302. Counseling.
§ 3303. Annulment of void and voidable marriages.
§ 3304. Grounds for annulment of void marriages.
§ 3305. Grounds for annulment of voidable marriages.
§ 3306. Proceedings to determine marital status.
§ 3307. Defenses.
§ 3308. Action where defendant suffering from mental disorder.
§ 3309. General appearance and collusion.

Subchapter B. Procedure
§ 3321. Hearing by master.
§ 3322. Jury trial.
§ 3323. Decree of court.

Subchapter C. Attacks Upon Decrees
§ 3331. Limitations on attacks upon decrees.
§ 3332. Opening or vacating decrees.
§ 3333. Res judicata and estoppel.

Chapter 35. Property Rights
§ 3501. Definitions.
§ 3502. Equitable division of marital property.

DOMESTIC RELATIONS

§ 3503. Effect of divorce on property rights generally.
§ 3504. Disposition of property after termination of marriage.
§ 3505. Disposition of property to defeat obligations.
§ 3506. Statement of reasons for distribution.
§ 3507. Division of entireties property between divorced persons.
§ 3508. Conveyance of entireties property to divorced spouse.

Chapter 37. Alimony and Support

§ 3701. Alimony.
§ 3702. Alimony pendente lite, counsel fees and expenses.
§ 3703. Enforcement of arrearages.
§ 3704. Payment of support, alimony and alimony pendente lite.
§ 3705. Enforcement of foreign decrees.
§ 3706. Bar to alimony.
§ 3707. Effect of death of either party.

Chapter 39. Mediation

§ 3901. Mediation programs.
§ 3902. Fees and costs.
§ 3903. Review of programs.
§ 3904. Existing programs.

PART V. SUPPORT, PROPERTY AND CONTRACTS

Chapter 41. General Provisions

§ 4101. Liability for debts contracted before marriage.
§ 4102. Proceedings in case of debts contracted for necessaries.
§ 4103. (Reserved).
§ 4104. Right of married person to separate earnings.
§ 4105. Loans between married persons.
§ 4106. Construction of chapter.

Chapter 43. Support Matters Generally

Subchapter A. General Provisions

§ 4301. Scope of chapter.
§ 4302. Definitions.
§ 4303. Information to consumer reporting agency.
§ 4304. Cooperation of Commonwealth agencies. [Repealed 1996, Oct. 16, P.L. 706, No. 124, eff. in 60 days]
§ 4304.1. Cooperation of government and nongovernment agencies.
§ 4305. General administration of support matters.
§ 4306. Duties of Title IV-D attorney.
§ 4307. State income tax intercept.
§ 4308. Lottery winnings intercept.
§ 4308.1. Collection of overdue support from monetary awards.
§ 4309. Publication of delinquent support obligors.

Subchapter B. Support

§ 4321. Liability for support.
§ 4322. Support guideline.
§ 4323. Support of emancipated child.
§ 4324. Inclusion of spousal medical support.

TABLE OF CONTENTS

§ 4325. Payment of order of support.
§ 4326. Mandatory inclusion of child medical support.
§ 4327. Postsecondary educational costs.

Subchapter C. Proceedings Generally

§ 4341. Commencement of support actions or proceedings.
§ 4342. Expedited procedure.
§ 4343. Paternity.
§ 4344. Contempt for failure of obligor to appear.
§ 4345. Contempt for noncompliance with support order.
§ 4346. Contempt for noncompliance with visitation or partial custody order. [Repealed]
§ 4347. Security for attendance or performance.
§ 4348. Attachment of income.
§ 4349. Consolidation of proceedings.
§ 4350. Effect of appeal.
§ 4351. Costs and fees.
§ 4352. Continuing jurisdiction over support orders.
§ 4353. Duty to report.
§ 4354. Willful failure to pay support order.
§ 4355. Denial or suspension of licenses.

Subchapter D. Proceedings Against Entireties Property

§ 4361. Execution of support order against entireties property.
§ 4362. Plaintiff's share of proceeds of sale.
§ 4363. Trustee to distribute proceeds of sale.
§ 4364. Credit to plaintiff who purchases property.
§ 4365. Rights of divorced person in entireties property sold for support.
§ 4366. Other enforcement remedies preserved.

Subchapter E. Title IV-D Program and Related Matters

§ 4371. Definitions.
§ 4372. Establishment of Title IV-D program.
§ 4373. Administration of Title IV-D program.
§ 4374. State disbursement unit.
§ 4375. Access to records.
§ 4376. Central registry.
§ 4377. Power to expedite support cases.
§ 4378. Assistance recipients to seek support.
§ 4379. Cooperation required.
§ 4380. Enforcement of cooperation requirements.
§ 4381. Garnishment of wages of Commonwealth employees.

Subchapter F. New Hire Reporting

§ 4391. Definitions.
§ 4392. Employer reporting.
§ 4393. Use of information.
§ 4394. Guidelines.
§ 4395. Confidentiality.
§ 4396. Penalties.

Chapter 45. Reciprocal Enforcement of Support Orders (Repealed)

§ 4501–§ 4540 (Repealed).

DOMESTIC RELATIONS

Chapter 46. Support of the Indigent
- 4601. Scope.
- 4602. Definitions.
- 4603. Relatives' liability; procedure.
- 4604. Property liable for expenses.
- 4605. Recovery of money.
- 4606. Guardian.

PART VI. CHILDREN AND MINORS

Chapter 51. General Provisions
- § 5101. Attainment of full age.
- § 5102. Children declared to be legitimate.
- § 5103. Acknowledgment and claim of paternity.
- § 5104. Blood tests to determine paternity.
- § 5105. Fingerprinting of children.

Chapter 52. Uniform Child Abduction Prevention
- § 5201. Scope of chapter.
- § 5202. Definitions.
- § 5203. Cooperation and communication among courts.
- § 5204. Actions for abduction prevention measures.
- § 5205. Jurisdiction.
- § 5206. Contents of petition.
- § 5207. Factors to determine risk of abduction.
- § 5208. Provisions and measures to prevent abduction.
- § 5209. Warrant to take physical custody of child.
- § 5210. Duration of abduction prevention order.
- § 5211. Uniformity of application and construction.
- § 5212. Relation to Electronic Signatures in Global and National Commerce Act.

Chapter 53. Child Custody
- § 5321. Scope of chapter.
- § 5322. Definitions.
- § 5323. Award of custody.
- § 5324. Standing for any form of physical custody or legal custody.
- § 5325. Standing for partial physical custody and supervised physical custody.
- § 5326. Effect of adoption.
- § 5327. Presumption in cases concerning primary physical custody.
- § 5328. Factors to consider when awarding custody.
- § 5329. Consideration of criminal conviction.
- § 5329.1. Consideration of child abuse and involvement with protective services.
- § 5330. Consideration of criminal charge.
- § 5331. Parenting plan.
- § 5332. Informational programs.
- § 5333. Counseling as part of order.
- § 5334. Guardian ad litem for child.
- § 5335. Counsel for child.
- § 5336. Access to records and information.
- § 5337. Relocation.

TABLE OF CONTENTS

§ 5338. Modification of existing order.
§ 5339. Award of counsel fees, costs and expenses.
§ 5340. Court-appointed child custody health care or behavioral health practitioners.

Chapter 54. Uniform Child Custody Jurisdiction and Enforcement

Subchapter A. General Provisions

§ 5401. Short title of chapter.
§ 5402. Definitions.
§ 5403. Proceedings governed by other law.
§ 5404. Application to Native American tribes.
§ 5405. International application of chapter.
§ 5406. Effect of child custody determination.
§ 5407. Priority.
§ 5408. Notice to persons outside Commonwealth.
§ 5409. Appearance and limited immunity.
§ 5410. Communication between courts.
§ 5411. Taking testimony in another state.
§ 5412. Cooperation between courts; preservation of records.

Subchapter B. Jurisdiction

§ 5421. Initial child custody jurisdiction.
§ 5422. Exclusive, continuing jurisdiction.
§ 5423. Jurisdiction to modify determination.
§ 5424. Temporary emergency jurisdiction.
§ 5425. Notice; opportunity to be heard; joinder.
§ 5426. Simultaneous proceedings.
§ 5427. Inconvenient forum.
§ 5428. Jurisdiction declined by reason of conduct.
§ 5429. Information to be submitted to court.
§ 5430. Appearance of parties and child.

Subchapter C. Enforcement

§ 5441. Definitions.
§ 5442. Enforcement under Hague Convention.
§ 5443. Duty to enforce.
§ 5444. Temporary visitation.
§ 5445. Registration of child custody determination.
§ 5446. Enforcement of registered determination.
§ 5447. Simultaneous proceedings.
§ 5448. Expedited enforcement of child custody determination.
§ 5449. Service of petition and order.
§ 5450. Hearing and order.
§ 5451. Warrant to take physical custody of child.
§ 5452. Costs, fees and expenses.
§ 5453. Recognition and enforcement.
§ 5454. Appeals.
§ 5455. Role of prosecutor or public official.
§ 5456. Role of law enforcement.
§ 5457. Costs and expenses.

Subchapter D. Intrastate Application

§ 5471. Intrastate application.

DOMESTIC RELATIONS

Subchapter E. Miscellaneous Provisions
§ 5481. Application and construction.
§ 5482. Severability.

Chapter 55. Liability for Tortious Acts of Children
§ 5501. Definitions.
§ 5502. Liability of parents.
§ 5503. Establishing liability in criminal or juvenile proceedings.
§ 5504. Establishing liability in civil proceedings.
§ 5505. Monetary limits of liability.
§ 5506. Double recovery for same injury prohibited.
§ 5507. Indemnity or contribution from child prohibited.
§ 5508. Liability of parent not having custody or control of child.
§ 5509. Other liability of parent or child unaffected.

Chapter 56. Standby and Temporary Guardianship
Subchapter A. Preliminary Provisions
§ 5601. Short title of chapter.
§ 5602. Definitions.
§ 5603. Scope.

Subchapter B. General Provisions
§ 5611. Designation.
§ 5612. Petition for approval of a designation.
§ 5613. Authority of standby guardian.
§ 5614. Revocation.
§ 5615. Conflicting documents.
§ 5616. Bond.

Subchapter C. Temporary Guardianship
§ 5621. Designation.
§ 5622. Petition for approval of designation.
§ 5623. Authority of temporary guardian.
§ 5624. Period of temporary guardianship.
§ 5625. Termination of temporary guardianship.

Chapter 57. Sex Trafficking and Missing and Abducted Children
§ 5701. Definitions.
§ 5702. County responsibilities.
§ 5703. Law enforcement responsibilities.

PART VII. ABUSE OF FAMILY

Chapter 61. Protection from Abuse
§ 6101. Short title of chapter.
§ 6102. Definitions.
§ 6103. Jurisdiction.
§ 6104. Full faith and credit and foreign protection orders.
§ 6105. Responsibilities of law enforcement agencies.
§ 6106. Commencement of proceedings.
§ 6107. Hearings.
§ 6108. Relief.

TABLE OF CONTENTS

§ 6108.1. Return of relinquished firearms, other weapons and ammunition and additional relief.
§ 6108.2. Relinquishment for consignment sale, lawful transfer or safekeeping.
§ 6108.3. Relinquishment to third party for safekeeping.
§ 6108.4. Registry or database of firearm ownership.
§ 6108.5. Penalties for release of information.
§ 6108.6. Penalty for failure to secure firearms.
§ 6108.7. Order to seal record from public view.
§ 6109. Service of orders.
§ 6110. Emergency relief by minor judiciary.
§ 6111. Domestic violence counselor/advocate.
§ 6112. Disclosure of addresses.
§ 6113. Arrest for violation of order.
§ 6113.1. Private criminal complaints for violation of order or agreement.
§ 6114. Contempt for violation of order or agreement.
§ 6114.1. Civil contempt or modification for violation of an order or agreement.
§ 6115. Reporting abuse and immunity.
§ 6116. Confidentiality.
§ 6117. Procedure and other remedies.
§ 6118. Full faith and credit. [Repealed]
§ 6119. Immunity.
§ 6120. Inability to pay.
§ 6121. Warrantless searches.
§ 6122. Construction.

Chapter 63. Child Protective Services
Subchapter A. Preliminary Provisions

§ 6301. Short title of chapter.
§ 6302. Findings and purpose of chapter.
§ 6303. Definitions.
§ 6304. Exclusions from child abuse.
§ 6305. Electronic reporting.
§ 6306. Regulations.

Subchapter B. Provisions and Responsibilities for Reporting Suspected Child Abuse

§ 6311. Persons required to report suspected child abuse.
§ 6311.1. Privileged communications.
§ 6312. Persons encouraged to report suspected child abuse.
§ 6313. Reporting procedure.
§ 6314. Photographs, medical tests and X-rays of child subject to report.
§ 6315. Taking child into protective custody.
§ 6316. Admission to private and public hospitals.
§ 6317. Mandatory reporting and postmortem investigation of deaths.
§ 6318. Immunity from liability.
§ 6319. Penalties.
§ 6320. Protection from employment discrimination.

Subchapter C. Powers and Duties of Department

§ 6331. Establishment of Statewide database.
§ 6332. Establishment of Statewide toll-free telephone number.

DOMESTIC RELATIONS

§ 6333. Continuous availability of department.
§ 6334. Disposition of complaints received.
§ 6334.1. Responsibility for investigation.
§ 6335. Access to information in Statewide database.
§ 6336. Information in Statewide database.
§ 6337. Disposition and expunction of unfounded reports and general protective services reports.
§ 6338. Disposition of founded and indicated reports.
§ 6338.1. Expunction of information of perpetrator who was under 18 years of age when child abuse was committed.
§ 6339. Confidentiality of reports.
§ 6340. Release of information in confidential reports.
§ 6340.1. Exchange of information.
§ 6341. Amendment or expunction of information.
§ 6342. Studies of data in records.
§ 6343. Investigating performance of county agency.
§ 6343.1. Citizen review panels.
§ 6344. Employees having contact with children; adoptive and foster parents.
§ 6344.1. Information relating to certified or registered day-care home residents.
§ 6344.2. Volunteers having contact with children.
§ 6344.3. Continued employment or participation in program, activity or service.
§ 6344.4. Recertification.
§ 6345. Audits by Attorney General.
§ 6346. Cooperation of other agencies.
§ 6347. Reports to Governor and General Assembly.
§ 6348. Regulations.
§ 6349. Penalties.

Subchapter C.1 Students in Public and Private Schools

§ 6351. Definitions.
§ 6352. School employees.
§ 6353. Administration.
§ 6353.1. Investigation.
§ 6353.2. Responsibilities of county agency.
§ 6353.3. Information in Statewide central register.
§ 6353.4. Other provisions.

Subchapter C.2 Background Checks for Employment in Schools

§ 6354. Definitions.
§ 6355. Requirement.
§ 6356. Exceptions.
§ 6357. Fees.
§ 6358. Time limit for official clearance statement.

Subchapter D. Organization and Responsibilities of Child Protective Service

§ 6361. Organization for child protective services.
§ 6362. Responsibilities of county agency for child protective services.
§ 6363. County plan for protective services.
§ 6364. Purchasing services of other agencies.

TABLE OF CONTENTS

§ 6365. Services for prevention, investigation and treatment of child abuse.
§ 6366. Continuous availability to receive reports.
§ 6367. Reports to department and coroner.
§ 6368. Investigation of reports.
§ 6369. Taking child into protective custody.
§ 6370. Voluntary or court-ordered services; findings of child abuse.
§ 6371. Rehabilitative services for child and family.
§ 6372. Protecting well-being of children maintained outside home.
§ 6373. General protective services responsibilities of county agency.
§ 6374. Principles and goals of general protective services.
§ 6375. County agency requirements for general protective services.
§ 6376. Appeals with respect to general protective services.
§ 6377. Caseloads.
§ 6378. Purchase of services.

Subchapter E. Miscellaneous Provisions
§ 6381. Evidence in court proceedings.
§ 6382. Guardian ad litem for child in court proceedings (Repealed).
§ 6383. Education and training.
§ 6384. Legislative oversight.
§ 6385. Reimbursement to county agencies.
§ 6386. Notification to department and development of plan of safe care for children under one year of age.

Chapter 65. Newborn Protection
§ 6501. Short title of chapter.
§ 6502. Definitions.
§ 6503. Nonliability.
§ 6504. Health care providers accepting newborns.
§ 6504.1. Police officers accepting newborns.
§ 6504.2. Emergency services providers accepting newborns.
§ 6504.3. Incubators for newborns.
§ 6505. Reporting acceptance of newborns.
§ 6506. Failure to report acceptance of newborns.
§ 6507. Immunity.
§ 6508. Duty of hospital.
§ 6509. Duties of department.

Chapter 67. Domestic and Sexual Violence Victim Address Confidentiality
§ 6701. Short title of chapter.
§ 6702. Definitions.
§ 6703. Address Confidentiality Program.
§ 6704. Persons eligible to apply.
§ 6705. Application and certification process.
§ 6706. Cancellation, expiration and voluntary withdrawal.
§ 6707. Agency use of designated address.
§ 6708. Disclosure of actual address.
§ 6709. Waiver process.
§ 6710. Emergency disclosure.
§ 6711. Penalties.
§ 6712. Rules and regulations.
§ 6713. Civil immunity.

DOMESTIC RELATIONS

PART VIII. UNIFORM INTERSTATE FAMILY SUPPORT

Chapter 71. General Provisions

§ 7101. Short title of part.
§ 7101.1. Definitions.
§ 7102. Remedies cumulative (Repealed).
§ 7103. State tribunal and support enforcement agency.
§ 7104. Cumulative remedies.
§ 7105. Application of part to resident of foreign country and foreign support proceeding.

Chapter 72. Jurisdiction

Subchapter A. Extend Personal Jurisdiction

§ 7201. Bases for jurisdiction over nonresident.
§ 7202. Procedure when exercising jurisdiction over nonresident (Repealed).
§ 7202.1. Duration of personal jurisdiction.

Subchapter B. Proceedings Involving Two or More States

§ 7203. Initiating and responding tribunal of this State.
§ 7204. Simultaneous proceeding.
§ 7205. Continuing, exclusive jurisdiction to modify child support orders.
§ 7206. Continuing jurisdiction to enforce child support orders.

Subchapter C. Reconciliation of Multiple Orders

§ 7207. Determination of controlling child support order.
§ 7208. Multiple child support orders for two or more obligees.
§ 7209. Credit for payments.
§ 7210. Application of part to nonresident subject to personal jurisdiction.
§ 7211. Continuing exclusive jurisdiction to modify spousal support order.

Chapter 73. Civil Provisions of General Application

§ 7301. Proceedings under this part.
§ 7302. Action by minor parent.
§ 7303. Application of law of this State.
§ 7304. Duties of initiating tribunal.
§ 7305. Duties and powers of responding tribunal.
§ 7306. Inappropriate tribunal.
§ 7307. Duties of support enforcement agency.
§ 7308. Supervisory duty.
§ 7309. Private counsel.
§ 7310. Duties of department.
§ 7311. Pleadings and accompanying documents.
§ 7312. Nondisclosure of information in exceptional circumstances.
§ 7313. Costs and fees.
§ 7314. Limited immunity of petitioner.
§ 7315. Nonparentage as defense.
§ 7316. Special rules of evidence and procedure.
§ 7317. Communications between tribunals.
§ 7318. Assistance with discovery.
§ 7319. Receipt and disbursement of payments.

TABLE OF CONTENTS

Chapter 74. Establishment of Support Order or Determination of Parentage
- § 7401. Establishment of support order.
- § 7402. Proceeding to determine parentage.

Chapter 75. Enforcement of Support Order Without Registration
- § 7501. Employer's receipt of income-withholding order of another state.
- § 7501.1. Employer's compliance with income-withholding order of another state.
- § 7501.2. Compliance with multiple income-withholding orders.
- § 7501.3. Immunity from civil liability.
- § 7501.4. Penalties for noncompliance.
- § 7501.5. Contest by obligor.
- § 7502. Administrative enforcement of orders.

Chapter 76. Registration, Enforcement and Modification of Support Order After

Subchapter A. Registration and Enforcement of Support Order
- § 7601. Registration of order for enforcement.
- § 7602. Procedure to register order for enforcement.
- § 7603. Effect of registration for enforcement.
- § 7604. Choice of law.

Subchapter B. Contest of Validity or Enforcement
- § 7605. Notice of registration of order.
- § 7606. Procedure to contest validity or enforcement of registered support order.
- § 7607. Contest of registration or enforcement.
- § 7608. Confirmed order.

Subchapter C. Registration and Modification of Child Support Order of Another State
- § 7609. Procedure to register child support order of another state for modification.
- § 7610. Effect of registration for modification.
- § 7611. Modification of child support order of another state.
- § 7612. Recognition of order modified in another state.
- § 7613. Jurisdiction to modify child support order of another state when individual parties reside in this State.
- § 7614. Notice to issuing tribunal of modification.

Subchapter D. Registration and Modification of Foreign Child Support Order
- § 7615. Jurisdiction to modify child support order of a foreign country.
- § 7616. Procedure to register child support order of a foreign country for modification.

Chapter 77. Determination of Parentage (Repealed)
- § 7701. Proceeding to determine parentage (Repealed).

Chapter 77A. Support Proceeding Under Convention
- § 77A01. Definitions.
- § 77A02. Applicability.
- § 77A03. Relationship of department to United States central authority.

DOMESTIC RELATIONS

§ 77A04. Initiation by department of support proceeding under convention.
§ 77A05. Direct request.
§ 77A06. Registration of convention support order.
§ 77A07. Contest of registered convention support order.
§ 77A08. Recognition and enforcement of registered convention support order.
§ 77A09. Partial enforcement.
§ 77A10. Foreign support agreement.
§ 77A11. Modification of convention child support order.
§ 77A12. Personal information.
§ 77A13. Record in original language.

Chapter 78. Interstate Rendition.

§ 7801. Grounds for rendition.
§ 7802. Conditions of rendition.

Chapter 79. Miscellaneous Provisions

§ 7901. Uniformity of application and construction.
§ 7902. Transitional provisions.
§ 7903. Severability.

PART VIII-A. INTRASTATE FAMILY SUPPORT

Chapter 81. General Provisions

§ 8101. Short title of part and definitions.
§ 8102. Scope.
§ 8103. Remedies cumulative.

Chapter 82. Jurisdiction

§ 8201. Continuing, exclusive jurisdiction.
§ 8202. Recognition of support orders.
§ 8203. Credit for payments.

Chapter 83. Civil Provisions of General Application

§ 8301. Proceedings under this part.
§ 8302. Action by minor parent.
§ 8303. Duties of initiating tribunal.
§ 8304. Duties and powers of responding tribunal.
§ 8305. Inappropriate tribunal.
§ 8306. Duties of support enforcement agency.
§ 8307. Supervisory duty.
§ 8308. Private counsel.
§ 8309. Nondisclosure of information in exceptional circumstances.
§ 8310. Nonparentage not a defense.
§ 8311. Special rules of evidence and procedure.
§ 8312. Assistance with discovery.
§ 8313. Costs and fees.

Chapter 84. Enforcement and Modification of Support Order After Registration

Subchapter A. Registration of Support Order

§ 8401. Registration of order.
§ 8402. Procedure to register order.

TABLE OF CONTENTS

Subchapter B. Contest of Validity or Enforcement

§ 8411. Notice of registration of order.
§ 8412. Procedure to contest validity of registered order.
§ 8413. Contest of registration or enforcement.
§ 8414. Confirmed order.
§ 8415. Effect of a confirmed order.

MISCELLANEOUS PENNSYLVANIA DOMESTIC RELATIONS STATUTES

CRIMES CODE

Title 18
Crimes And Offenses

PART II. DEFINITION OF SPECIFIC OFFENSES

ARTICLE B. OFFENSES INVOLVING DANGER TO THE PERSON

Chapter 27. Assault

§ 2701. Simple assault.
§ 2702. Aggravated assault.
§ 2706. Terroristic threats.
§ 2709. Harassment.
§ 2709.1. Stalking.
§ 2711. Probable cause arrests in domestic violence cases.
§ 2714. Unauthorized administration of intoxicant.
§ 2718. Strangulation.

Chapter 29. Kidnapping

§ 2901. Kidnapping.
§ 2902. Unlawful restraint.
§ 2903. False imprisonment.
§ 2904. Interference with custody of children.
§ 2905. Interference with custody of committed persons.
§ 2906. Criminal coercion.
§ 2908. Missing children.
§ 2909. Concealment of whereabouts of a child.
§ 2910. Luring a child into a motor vehicle or structure.

Chapter 31. Sexual Offenses

Subchapter A. General Provisions

§ 3101. Definitions.
§ 3102. Mistake as to age.
§ 3103. Spouse relationships.
§ 3104. Evidence of victim's sexual conduct.
§ 3105. Prompt complaint.
§ 3106. Testimony of complainants.
§ 3107. Resistance not required.

DOMESTIC RELATIONS

Subchapter B. Definition of Offenses

§ 3121. Rape.
§ 3122. Statutory rape.
§ 3122.1. Statutory sexual assault.
§ 3123. Involuntary deviate sexual intercourse.
§ 3124. Voluntary deviate sexual intercourse.
§ 3124.2. Institutional sexual assault.
§ 3124.3. Sexual assault by sports official, volunteer or employee of nonprofit association.
§ 3125. Aggravated indecent assault.
§ 3126. Indecent assault.
§ 3127. Indecent exposure.
§ 3128. Spousal sexual assault.
§ 3129. Sexual intercourse with animal.
§ 3130. Conduct relating to sex offenders.

Subchapter C. Loss of Property Rights

§ 3141. General rule.

ARTICLE D. OFFENSES AGAINST THE FAMILY

Chapter 43. Offenses Against the Family

Subchapter A. Definition of Offenses Generally

§ 4301. Bigamy.
§ 4302. Incest.
§ 4303. Concealing death of child.
§ 4304. Endangering welfare of children.
§ 4305. Dealing in infant children.
§ 4306. Newborn protection.

Subchapter B. Nonsupport (Repealed)

§ 4321–§ 4324 (Repealed).

ARTICLE E. OFFENSES AGAINST PUBLIC ADMINISTRATION

Chapter 49. Falsification and Intimidation

Subchapter A. Perjury and Falsification in Official Matters

§ 4906.1. False reports of child abuse.

Subchapter B. Victims and Witness Intimidation

§ 4958. Intimidation, retaliation or obstruction in child abuse cases.

ARTICLE F. OFFENSES AGAINST PUBLIC ORDER AND DECENCY

§ 5504. Harassment and stalking by communication or address. [Repealed]

ARTICLE G. MISCELLANEOUS OFFENSES

Chapter 61. Firearms and Other Dangerous Articles

Subchapter A. Uniform Firearms Act

§ 6105. Persons not to possess, use, manufacture, control, sell or transfer firearms.

TABLE OF CONTENTS

§ 6105.2. Relinquishment of firearms and firearm licenses by convicted persons.
§ 6128. Abandonment of firearms, weapons or ammunition.

Chapter 63. Minors
Subchapter C. Other Dangerous Articles
§ 6301. Corruption of minors.
§ 6312. Sexual abuse of children.
§ 6321. Transmission of sexually explicit images by minor.

PROBATE, ESTATES AND FIDUCIARIES CODE
Title 20

§ 2106. Forfeiture.
§ 2203. Right of election; resident decedent.
§ 2507. Modification by circumstances.
§ 5605. Power of attorney not revoked until notice.
§ 5606. Proof of continuance of powers of attorney by affidavit.
§ 6111.1. Modification by divorce.
§ 6111.2. Effect of divorce on designation of beneficiaries.

JUDICIAL CODE
Title 42
Judiciary and Judiciary Act

Chapter 19. Administrative Office of Pennsylvania Courts
§ 1904. Availability of Criminal Charge Information in Child Custody Proceedings.

Chapter 62A. Protection of Victims of Sexual Violence or Intimidation
§ 62A01. Scope of chapter.
§ 62A02. Findings and purpose.
§ 62A03. Definitions.
§ 62A04. Responsibilities of law enforcement agencies.
§ 62A05. Commencement of proceedings.
§ 62A06. Hearings.
§ 62A07. Relief.
§ 62A08. (Reserved).
§ 62A09. Emergency relief by minor judiciary.
§ 62A10. Sexual assault counselor.
§ 62A11. Disclosure of addresses.
§ 62A12. Arrest for violation of order.
§ 62A13. Private criminal complaints for violation of order or agreement.
§ 62A14. Contempt for violation of order.
§ 62A15. Civil contempt or modification for violation of order or agreement.
§ 62A16. Confidentiality.
§ 62A17. Procedure and other remedies.
§ 62A18. Applicability.
§ 62A19. Inability to pay.
§ 62A20. Construction.

DOMESTIC RELATIONS

Chapter 63. Juvenile Matters

Subchapter A. General Provisions

§ 6301. Short title and purposes of chapter.
§ 6302. Definitions.
§ 6303. Scope of chapter.
§ 6304. Powers and duties of probation officers.
§ 6305. Masters.
§ 6306. Costs and expenses of care of child.
§ 6307. Inspection of court files and records.
§ 6308. Law enforcement records.
§ 6309. Juvenile history record information.
§ 6310. Parental participation.
§ 6311. Guardian ad litem for child in court proceedings.

Subchapter B. Jurisdiction and Custody

§ 6321. Commencement of proceedings.
§ 6322. Transfer from criminal proceedings.
§ 6323. Informal adjustment.
§ 6324. Taking into custody.
§ 6325. Detention of child.
§ 6326. Release or delivery to court.
§ 6327. Place of detention.

Subchapter C. Procedures and Safeguards

§ 6331. Release from detention or commencement of proceedings.
§ 6332. Informal hearing.
§ 6333. Subpoena.
§ 6334. Petition.
§ 6335. Release or holding of hearing.
§ 6336. Conduct of hearings.
§ 6336.1. Notice and hearing.
§ 6336.2. Use of restraints on children during court proceedings.
§ 6337. Right to counsel.
§ 6337.1. Right to counsel for children in dependency and delinquency proceedings.
§ 6338. Other basic rights.
§ 6339. Investigation and report.
§ 6340. Consent decree.
§ 6341. Adjudication.
§ 6342. Court-appointed special advocates.

Subchapter D. Disposition of Children Generally

§ 6351. Disposition of dependent child.
§ 6351.1. Authority of court upon petition to remove child from foster parent.
§ 6352. Disposition of delinquent child.
§ 6352.1. Treatment records.
§ 6353. Limitation on and change in place of commitment.
§ 6354. Effect of adjudication.
§ 6355. Transfer to criminal proceedings.
§ 6356 Disposition of mentally ill or mentally retarded child.
§ 6357. Rights and duties of legal custodian.
§ 6358. Assessment of delinquent children by the State Sexual Offenders Assessment Board.

TABLE OF CONTENTS

Subchapter E. Dispositions Affecting Other Jurisdictions
§ 6361. Disposition of nonresident child.
§ 6362. Disposition of resident child received from another state.
§ 6363. Ordering foreign supervision.
§ 6364. Supervision under foreign order.
§ 6365. Powers of foreign probation officers.

Subchapter F. Juvenile Court Judges' Commission
§ 6371. Definitions.
§ 6372. Juvenile Court Judges' Commission.
§ 6373. Powers and duties.
§ 6374. Power to make grants.
§ 6375. Funding.

Chapter 74. Collaboration Law Process
§ 7401 Short title and scope of chapter.
§ 7402. Definitions.
§ 7403. Beginning the collaborative law process.
§ 7404. Assessment and review.
§ 7405. Collaborative law participation agreement.
§ 7406 Concluding the collaborative law process.
§ 7407 Disqualification of collaborative attorney.
§ 7408. Disclosure of information.
§ 7409. Confidentiality.
§ 7410. Privilege.
§ 7411. Professional responsibility.

LABOR
Title 43

Chapter 14. Unemployment Compensation

ARTICLE VII. PROTECTION OF RIGHTS AND COMPENSATION
§ 863.1. Child support intercept of unemployment compensation.

MILITARY AFFAIRS
Title 51

PART II. PENNSYLVANIA NATIONAL GUARD, PENNSYLVANIA GUARD AND MILITIA

Subchapter D. Rights and Immunities
§ 4109. Child custody proceedings during military deployment.
§ 4110. Expedited or electronic hearing.

NAMES
Title 54

Chapter 7. Judicial Changes of Name
§ 701. Court approval required for change of name.
§ 702. Change by order of court.

DOMESTIC RELATIONS

§ 703. Effect on children.
§ 704. Divorcing and divorced person may resume prior name.
§ 704.1. Surviving spouse may resume prior name.
§ 705. Penalty for violation of chapter.

MISCELLANEOUS FEDERAL DOMESTIC RELATIONS STATUTES AND REGULATIONS— SELECTED PROVISIONS

Title 10.
Armed Forces

Chapter 71. Computation of Retired Pay

§ 1408. Payment of retired or retainer pay in compliance with court orders.

Chapter 73. Annuities Based on Retired or Retainer Pay

§ 1447. Definitions.
§ 1448. Application of Plan.
§ 1448a. Election to discontinue participation: one-year opportunity after second anniversary of commencement of payment of retired pay.
§ 1450. Payment of annuity: beneficiaries.
§ 1451. Amount of annuity.
§ 1452. Reduction in retired pay.
§ 1453. Recovery of amounts erroneously paid.
§ 1454. Correction of administrative errors.

Title 11.
Bankruptcy Code

§ 11 U.S.C. § 101. Definitions.
§ 11 U.S.C. § 362. Automatic stay.
§ 11 U.S.C. § 507. Priorities.
§ 11 U.S.C. § 522. Exemptions.
§ 11 U.S.C. § 523. Exceptions to discharge.
§ 11 U.S.C. § 541. Property of the estate.
§ 11 U.S.C. § 547. Preferences.
§ 11 U.S.C. § 704. Duties of trustee.
§ 11 U.S.C. § 1129. Confirmation of plan.

Title 18.
Crimes and Criminal Procedure

PART I. CRIMES

Chapter 11A. Child Support

§ 228. Failure to pay legal child support obligations.

Chapter 55. Kidnapping

§ 1204. International parental kidnapping.

Chapter 110A. Domestic Violence and Stalking

§ 2261. Interstate domestic violence.
§ 2261A. Stalking.
§ 2262. Interstate violation of protection order.

TABLE OF CONTENTS

§ 2263. Pretrial release of defendant.
§ 2264. Restitution.
§ 2265. Full faith and credit given to protection orders.
§ 2265A. Repeat offenders.
§ 2266. Definitions.

Title 22.
Foreign Relations and Intercourse

Chapter 4. Passports

§ 213. Application for passport; verification by oath of initial passport.
22 C.F.R. § 51.28 Minors.

Chapter 97. International Child Abduction Remedies

§ 9001. Findings and declarations.
§ 9002. Definitions.
§ 9003. Judicial remedies.
§ 9004. Provisional remedies.
§ 9005. Admissibility of documents.
§ 9006. United States Central Authority.
§ 9007. Costs and fees.
§ 9008. Collection, maintenance, and dissemination of information.
§ 9009. Office of Children's Issues.
§ 9010. Interagency coordinating group.
§ 9011. Authorization of appropriations.

Chapter 98. International Child Abduction Prevention and Return

§ 9101. Definitions.

Subchapter I. Department of State Actions

§ 9111. Annual Report.
§ 9112. Standards and assistance.
§ 9113. Bilateral procedures, including memoranda of understanding.
§ 9114. Report to congressional representatives.

Subchapter II. Actions By the Secretary of State

§ 9121. Response to international child abductions.
§ 9122. Actions by the Secretary of State in response to patterns of noncompliance in cases of international child abductions.
§ 9123. Consultations with foreign governments.
§ 9124. Waiver by the Secretary of State.
§ 9125. Termination of actions by the Secretary of State.

Subchapter III. Prevention of International Child Abduction

§ 9141. Authorization for judicial training on international parental child abduction.

Title 26.
Internal Revenue Code

Subtitle A.
Income Taxes

Chapter 1. Normal Taxes and Surtaxes
Subchapter B. Computation of Taxable Income

DOMESTIC RELATIONS

PART II. ITEMS SPECIFICALLY INCLUDED IN GROSS INCOME

§ 151. Allowance of deductions for personal exemptions.
§ 152. Dependent defined.
26 C.F.R. § 1.152-4 Special rule for a child of divorced or separated parents or parents who live apart.
§ 1041. Transfers of property between spouses or incident to divorce.
26 C.F.R. § 1.1041-1T Treatment of transfer of property between spouses or incident to divorce (temporary).
IRS Publication 504. Divorced or Separated Individuals (February 5, 2019).

Title 28.
Judiciary and Judicial Procedure
PART V. PROCEDURE

Chapter 115. Evidence; Documentary

§ 1738A. Full faith and credit given to child custody determinations.
§ 1738B. Full faith and credit for child support orders.
§ 1738C. Certain acts, records, and proceedings and the effect thereof.

Title 42.
The Public Health and Welfare

Chapter 7. Social Security

Subchapter IV. Grants to States for Aid and Services to Needy Families with Children and for Child-Welfare Services

PART D. CHILD SUPPORT AND ESTABLISHMENT OF PATERNITY

§ 651. Authorization of appropriations.
§ 652. Duties of Secretary.
§ 653. Federal Parent Locator Service.
§ 654. State plan for child and spousal support.
§ 655. Payments to States.
§ 656. Support obligation as obligation to State; amount; discharge in bankruptcy.
§ 657. Distribution of collected support.
§ 659. Consent by the United States to income withholding, garnishment, and similar proceedings for enforcement of child support and alimony obligations.
§ 659a. International support enforcement.
§ 660. Civil action to enforce child support obligations; jurisdiction of district courts.
§ 663. Use of Federal Parent Locator Service in connection with enforcement or determination of child custody in cases of parental kidnapping of child.
§ 664. Collection of past-due support from Federal tax refunds.
§ 665. Allotments from pay for child and spousal support owed by members of uniformed services on active duty.

TABLE OF CONTENTS

§ 666. Requirement of statutorily prescribed procedures to improve effectiveness of child support enforcement.
§ 667. State guidelines for child support awards.
§ 668. Encouragement of States to adopt simple civil process for voluntarily acknowledging paternity and a civil procedure for establishing paternity in contested cases.
§ 669. Collection and reporting of child support enforcement data.

Chapter 121. International Child Abduction Remedies Act [Transferred to Foreign Relations and Intercourse] (Title 22)

§§ 11601 to 11610. Transferred

Codification

Section 11601, Pub. L. 100–300, § 2, Apr. 29, 1988, 102 Stat. 437, which provided findings and declarations related to the International Child Abduction Remedies Act, was transferred to section 9001 of Title 22, Foreign Relations and Intercourse.

Section 11602, Pub. L. 100–300, § 3, Apr. 29, 1988, 102 Stat. 437, which provided definitions, was transferred to section 9002 of Title 22.

Section 11603, Pub. L. 100–300, § 4, Apr. 29, 1988, 102 Stat. 438, which related to judicial remedies, was transferred to section 9003 of Title 22.

Section 11604, Pub. L. 100–300, § 5, Apr. 29, 1988, 102 Stat. 439, which related to provisional remedies, was transferred to section 9004 of Title 22.

Section 11605, Pub. L. 100–300, § 6, Apr. 29, 1988, 102 Stat. 439, which related to admissibility of documents, was transferred to section 9005 of Title 22.

Section 11606, Pub. L. 100–300, § 7, Apr. 29, 1988, 102 Stat. 439; Pub. L. 105–277, div. G, title XXII, § 2213, Oct. 21, 1998, 112 Stat. 2681–812; Pub. L. 108–370, § 2, Oct. 25, 2004, 118 Stat. 1750, which related to the United States Central Authority, was transferred to section 9006 of Title 22.

Section 11607, Pub. L. 100–300, § 8, Apr. 29, 1988, 102 Stat. 440, which related to costs and fees, was transferred to section 9007 of Title 22.

Section 11608, Pub. L. 100–300, § 9, Apr. 29, 1988, 102 Stat. 440, which related to collection, maintenance, and dissemination of information, was transferred to section 9008 of Title 22.

Section 11608a, Pub. L. 106–113, div. B, § 1000(a)(7) [div. A, title II, § 201], Nov. 29, 1999, 113 Stat. 1536, 1501A–419, which related to the Office of Children's Issues, was transferred to section 9009 of Title 22.

Section 11609, Pub. L. 100–300, § 10, Apr. 29, 1988, 102 Stat. 441, which related to an interagency coordinating group, was transferred to section 9010 of Title 22.

Section 11610, Pub. L. 100–300, § 12, Apr. 29, 1988, 102 Stat. 442, which related to authorization of appropriations, was transferred to section 9011 of Title 22.

§§ 11611. Repealed. Pub. L. 113–150, title I, §101(e), Aug. 8, 2014, 128 Stat. 1815.

Section, Pub. L. 105–277, div. G, title XXVIII, § 2803, Oct. 21, 1998, 112 Stat. 2681–846; Pub. L. 106–113, div. B, § 1000(a)(7) [div. A, title II, § 202], Nov. 29, 1999, 113 Stat. 1536, 1501A–420; Pub. L. 107–228, div. A, title II, § 212, Sept. 30, 2002, 116 Stat. 1365, related to report on compliance with the Hague Convention on International Child Abduction.

DOMESTIC RELATIONS

THE HAGUE CONVENTION ON THE CIVIL ASPECTS OF INTERNATIONAL CHILD ABDUCTION

DOMESTIC RELATIONS RULES OF PROCEDURE

PART I. RULES OF CIVIL PROCEDURE BEFORE MAGISTERIAL DISTRICT JUDGES

EMERGENCY RELIEF FROM ABUSE, SEXUAL VIOLENCE OR INTIMIDATION

Pa.R.C.P.M.D.J.

1201. Applicability.
1202. Definitions.
1203. Limitation on Jurisdiction.
1204. Venue.
1205. Persons Who May Seek Emergency Relief.
1206. Commencement of Proceedings.
1207. Hearing.
1208. Findings and Protection Orders.
1209. Service and Execution of Emergency Protection Orders.
1210. Duration of Emergency Protection Orders.
1211. Certification to Court of Common Pleas.

PART II. PROTECTION FROM ABUSE

Pa.R.C.P.

1901. Definitions.
1901.1. Venue.
1901.2. Scheduling.
1901.3. Commencement of Action.
1901.4. Service and Registration of Order.
1901.5. Enforcement.
1901.6. Responsive Pleading Not Required.
1901.7. Decision. Post-Trial Relief.
1901.8. Modification or Discontinuance.
1902. [Renumbered as Rule 1901.3].
1903. [Renumbered as Rule 1901.4].
1904. [Renumbered as Rule 1901.6].
1905. Forms for Use in PFA Actions. Notice and Hearing. Petition, Temporary Protection Order. Final Protection Order.

New Protection From Abuse Forms in Multiple Languages

PART III. SUPPORT

Pa.R.C.P.

1910.1 Scope. Definitions.
1910.2 Venue.
1910.2-1 Procedures Pursuant to the Intrastate Family Support Act.
1910.3 Parties. Obligor. Obligee.
1910.4 Domestic Relations Section. Commencement of Action. No Filing Fees. Authorized Fees.
1910.5 Complaint. Order of Court.

TABLE OF CONTENTS

1910.6	Notification.
1910.7	Pleading by Defendant Not Required. Question of Jurisdiction or Venue or Statute of Limitations in Paternity.
1910.8	[Rescinded]
1910.9	Discovery.
1910.10	Alternative Hearing Procedures.
1910.11	Office Conference. Subsequent Proceedings. Order.
1910.12	Office Conference. Hearing. Record. Exceptions. Order.
1910.13	[Rescinded].
1910.13-1	Failure or Refusal to Appear Pursuant to Order of Court. Bench Warrant.
1910.13-2	Form of Request for Bench Warrant and Supporting Affidavit. Form of Bench Warrant.
1910.14	Defendant Leaving Jurisdiction. Security.
1910.15	Paternity.
1910.16	Support Order. Allocation. [Rescinded December 28, 2018].
1910.16-1	Amount of Support. Support Guidelines.
1910.16-2	Support Guidelines. Calculation of Monthly Net Income.
1910.16-3	Support Guidelines. Basic Child Support Schedule.
1910.16-3.1	Support Guidelines. High Income Cases.
1910.16-4	Support Guidelines. Calculation of Support Obligation. Formula.
1910.16-5	Support Guidelines. Deviation.
1910.16-6	Support Guidelines. Allocation. Basic Support Obligation. Additional Expenses.
1910.16-7	Support Guidelines. Awards of Child Support When There Are Multiple Families.
1910.17	Support Order. Effective Date. Change of Circumstances. Copies of Order. Priority of Distribution of Payments.
1910.18	Support Order. Subsequent Proceedings. Modification of Spousal Support or Alimony *Pendente Lite* Orders Entered Before January 1, 2019.
1910.19	Support. Modification, Termination, Guidelines as Substantial Change in Circumstances. Overpayments.
1910.20	Support Order. Enforcement. General.
1910.21	Support Order. Enforcement. Withholding of Income.
1910.21-1	[Renumbered as Rule 1910.25]
1910.21-2	[Renumbered as Rule 1910.25-1]
1910.21-3	[Renumbered as Rule 1910.25-2]
1910.21-4	[Renumbered as Rule 1910.25-3]
1910.21-5	[Renumbered as Rule 1910.25-4]
1910.21-6	[Renumbered as Rule 1910.25-5]
1910.21-7	[Renumbered as Rule 1910.25-6]
1910.22	Support Order. Enforcement. Liens Against Real Property.
1910.23	Support Order. Enforcement. Attachment of Assets Held by Financial Institutions.
1910.23-1	[Rescinded]
1910.23-2	[Rescinded]
1910.24	Support Order. Enforcement. Judgment for Arrearages. Petition to Correct Judgment. Execution.
1910.25	Enforcement. Support Order. Civil Contempt. Petition. Service. No Answer Required.
1910.25-1	Civil Contempt. Hearing by Court. Conference by Officer.

DOMESTIC RELATIONS

1910.25-2   Civil Contempt. Office Conference. Agreement. Alternative Procedures Upon Failure to Agree.
1910.25-3   Civil Contempt. Conference Summary. Order. Hearing *De Novo*.
1910.25-4   Civil Contempt. Alternative Procedure. Record Hearing. Report. Exceptions. Order.
1910.25-5   Civil Contempt. Contempt Order. Incarceration.
1910.25-6   Civil Contempt. No Post-Trial Relief.
1910.25-7   Indirect Criminal Contempt. Incarceration.
1910.26   Support Order. Enforcement. Stay of Proceedings. Special Relief.
1910.27   Form of Complaint. Order. Income Statements and Expense Statements. Health Insurance Coverage Information Form. Form of Support Order. Form Petition for Modification. Petition for Recovery of Support Overpayment.
1910.28   Order for Earnings and Health Insurance Information. Form of Earnings Report. Form of Health Insurance Coverage Information.
1910.29   Evidence in Support Matters.
1910.30   [Rescinded]
1910.31   [Rescinded]
1910.49   Acts of Assembly Not Suspended.
1910.50   Suspension of Acts of Assembly.

PART IV.   CUSTODY AND VISITATION
Pa.R.C.P.

1915.1   Scope. Definitions.
1915.2   Venue.
1915.3   Commencement of Action. Complaint. Order.
1915.3-1 Withdrawal of Pleading. Discontinuance of Action.
1915.3-2 Criminal Record or Abuse History.
1915.4   Prompt Disposition of Custody Cases.
1915.4-1 Alternative Hearing Procedures for Partial Custody Actions.
1915.4-2 Partial Custody. Office Conference. Hearing. Record. Exceptions. Order.
1915.4-3 Non-Record Proceedings. Trial.
1915.4-4 Pre-Trial Procedures.
1915.5   Question of Jurisdiction or Venue. No Responsive Pleading by Defendant Required. Counterclaim. Discovery.
1915.6   Joinder of Parties.
1915.7   Consent Order.
1915.8   Physical and Mental Examination of Persons.
1915.9   No Default Judgment.
1915.10   Decision. Order.
1915.11   Appointment of Attorney for Child. Interview of Child. Attendance of Child at Hearing or Conference.
1915.11.1 Parenting Coordination.
1915.11-2 Appointment of Guardian Ad Litem.
1915.12   Civil Contempt for Disobedience of Custody Order. Petition. Form of Petition. Service. Order.
1915.13   Special Relief.
1915.14   Disobedience of Order. Arrest. Contempt.
1915.15   Form of Complaint. Caption. Order. Petition to Modify a Custody Order.

TABLE OF CONTENTS

1915.16	Form of Order and Notice. Joinder. Intervention.
1915.17	Relocation. Notice and Counter-Affidavit.
1915.18	Form of Order Directing Expert Examination and Report.
1915.19	Form of Order Appointing Counsel for the Child.
1915.21	Form of Order Appointing Guardian Ad Litem.
1915.22	Form of Order Appointing Parenting Coordinator.
1915.23	Form the Summary and Recommendation of the Parenting Coordinator.
1915.24	Acts of Assembly Not Suspended.
1915.25	Suspension of Acts of Assembly.

PART V. DIVORCE AND ANNULMENT

Pa.R.C.P.

1920.1.	Definitions. Conformity to Civil Action
1920.2.	Venue
1920.3.	Commencement Action
1920.4.	Service
1920.5.	Warrant of Attorney
1920.6.	Multiple Actions. Priority. Stay
1920.7–1920.10.	[Blank]
1920.11.	Pleadings Allowed
1920.12.	Complaint
1920.13.	Pleading More Than One Cause of Action. Alternative Pleading
1920.14.	Answer. Denial. Affidavit Under Section 3301(d) of the Divorce Code
1920.15.	Counterclaim. Subsequent Petition
1920.16.	Severance of Actions and Claims
1920.17.	Discontinuance. Withdrawal of Complaint.
1920.21.	Bill of Particulars in Divorce or Annulment. Non Pros
1920.22.	Discovery [Rescinded]
1920.23–1920.30.	[Blank]
1920.31.	Joinder of Related Claims. Alimony. Counsel Fees. Costs and Expenses.
1920.32.	Joinder of Related Claims. Custody. Hearing by Court.
1920.33.	Joinder of Related Claims. Equitable Division. Enforcement.
1920.34.	Joinder of Parties.
1920.35–1920.40.	[Blank]
1920.41.	No Default Judgment.
1920.42.	Affidavit and Decree Under Section 3301(c) or 3301(d)(1) of the Divorce Code. Notice of Intention to Request Entry of Divorce Decree in Section 3301(c) and 3301(d)(1)(i) Divorces. Counter-Affidavit.
1920.43.	Special Relief.
1920.44.	Party Leaving Jurisdiction. Security.
1920.45.	Counseling.
1920.46.	Affidavit of Non-Military Service.
1920.47–1920.50.	[Blank]
1920.51.	Hearing by the Court. Appointment of Master. Notice of Hearing.
1920.52.	Hearing by Court. Decision. No Post-trial Relief. Decree.
1920.53.	Hearing by Master. Report.
1920.54.	Hearing by Master. Report. Related Claims.
1920.55.	Master's Report. Notice. Exceptions. Final Decree [Rescinded]

DOMESTIC RELATIONS

1920.55-1 Alternative Hearing Procedures for Matters Referred to a Master.
1920.55-2 Master's Report. Notice. Exceptions. Final Decree
1920.55-3 Master's Report. Notice. Hearing De Novo. Final Decree
1920.56. Support. Alimony Pendente Lite. Allocation of Order.
1920.57–1920.60. [Blank]
1920.61. Testimony Outside the County.
1920.62. Proceedings by Indigent Parties.
1920.63–1920.70. [Blank]
1920.71. Form of Notice.
1920.72. Form of Complaint. Affidavit Under Section 3301(c) or 3301(d) of the Divorce Code. Counter-Affidavit. Waiver of Notice of Intention to Request Decree Under § 3301(c)
1920.73. Notice of Intention to Request Entry of Divorce Decree. Praecipe to Transmit Record. Forms.
1920.74. Form of Motion for Appointment of Master. Order.
1920.75. Form of Inventory.
1920.76. Form of Divorce Decree.
1920.77–1920.90. [Blank].
1920.91. Suspension of Acts of Assembly.
1920.92. Effective Date. Pending Actions.

PART VI. RULES RELATING TO DOMESTIC RELATIONS MATTERS GENERALLY

Pa.R.C.P.

1930.1 Form of Caption. Confidential Information and Confidential Documents. Certification.
1930.2 No Post-Trial Practice. Motions for Reconsideration.
1930.3 Testimony by Electronic Means.
1930.4 Service of Original Process in Domestic Relations Matters.
1930.5 Discovery in Domestic Relations Matters.
1930.6 Paternity Actions. Scope. Venue. Commencement of Action.
1930.7 Status Conference.
1930.8 Self-Represented Party.
1930.9 Family Court Forms.
1931. Family Court Rules.

PART VII. RULES RELATING TO VOLUNTARY MEDIATION IN CUSTODY ACTIONS

Pa.R.C.P.

1940.1 Applicability of Rules to Mediation.
1940.2 Definitions.
1940.3 Order for Orientation Session and Mediation. Selection of Mediator.
1940.4 Minimum Qualifications of the Mediator.
1940.5 Duties of the Mediator. Role of the Mediator.
1940.6 Termination of Mediation.
1940.7 Mediator Compensation.
1940.8 Sanctions.
1940.9 Existing Mediation Programs.

TABLE OF CONTENTS

PART VIII. ACTIONS PURSUANT TO THE PROTECTION OF VICTIMS OF SEXUAL VIOLENCE OR INTIMITATION ACT

Pa.R.C.P.

1951. Definitions.
1952. Venue.
1953. Commencement of Action.
1954. Service of Original Process. Registration of Order. Service of Petition and Order. Fees.
1955. Enforcement.
1956. No Responsive Pleading Required.
1957. Decision. Post-Trial Relief.
1958. Discontinuance or Modification.
1959. Forms for Use in Protection of Victims of Sexual Violence or Intimidation Actions. Notice and Hearing. Petition. Temporary Protection Order. Final Protection Order.

PART IX. ADOPTION

Pa.O.C. Rule

15.1. Local Rules.
15.2. Voluntary Relinquishment to Agency.
15.3. Voluntary relinquishment to Adult Intending to Adopt Child.
15.4. Involuntary Termination of Parental Rights.
15.5. Adoption.
15.6. Notice to Persons; Method; Notice of Orphans' Court Proceedings Filed on Dependency Docket.
15.7. Impounding; Docket Entries; Reports; Privacy.
15.8. Registration of Foreign Adoption Decree.
15.9. Petition for Adoption of a Foreign-Born Child.

INDEX TO APPENDIX ORPHANS' COURT AND REGISTER OF WILLS FORMS

PART X. PENNSYLVANIA RULES OF JUVENILE COURT PROCEDURE

DEPENDENCY MATTERS

Introduction and Explanatory Reports

Chapter 11. General Provisions

Pa.R.J.C.P.

1100. Scope of Rules.
1101. Purpose and Construction.
1102. Citing the Juvenile Court Procedural Rules.

PART A. BUSINESS OF COURTS

1120. Definitions.
1121. Local Rules.
1122. Continuances.
1123. Subpoenas.

DOMESTIC RELATIONS

1124. Summons.
1126. Defects in Form, Content, or Procedure.
1127. Recording and Transcribing Juvenile Court Proceedings.
1128. Presence at Proceedings.
1129. Appearance by Advanced Communication Technology.
1130. Court Fees Prohibited for Advanced Communication Technology.
1133. Motion to Intervene.
1134. Proceedings *in Camera*.
1135. Captions.
1136. *Ex Parte* Communication.
1137. Public Discussion by Court Personnel of Pending Matters.
1140. Bench Warrants for Failure to Appear.

PART B(1). EXAMINATION AND TREATMENT OF CHILD

1145. Application or Motion for Examination and Treatment of a Child.
1146. Notice of Truancy Hearing.
1147. Educational Decision Maker.
1148. Educational Stability and Placement.
1149. Family Finding.

PART B(2). COUNSEL

1150. Attorneys—Appearances and Withdrawals.
1151. Assignment of Guardian *Ad Litem* and Counsel.
1152. Waiver of Counsel.
1154. Duties of Guardian *Ad Litem*.
1158. Assignment of Court Appointed Special Advocates.

PART C. RECORDS

PART C(1). ACCESS TO JUVENILE COURT RECORDS

1160. Inspection of the Official Court Record.

PART C(2). MAINTAINING RECORDS

1165. Design of Forms.
1166. Maintaining Records in the Clerk of Courts.
1167. Filings and Service of Court Orders and Notices.

PART D. MASTERS

1182. Qualifications of Juvenile Court Hearing Officer.
1185. Appointment to Cases.
1187. Authority of Juvenile Court Hearing Officer.
1190. Stipulations Before Juvenile Court Hearing Officer.
1191. Juvenile Court Hearing Officer's Findings and Recommendation to the Judge.

Chapter 12. Commencement of Proceedings, Emergency Custody, and Pre-Adjudicatory Placement

PART A. COMMENCING PROCEEDINGS

1200. Commencing Proceedings.
1201. Procedures for Protective Medical Custody.
1202. Procedures for Protective Custody by Police Officer, Juvenile Probation Officer, and County Agency.

TABLE OF CONTENTS

PART B. EMERGENCY CUSTODY
1210. Order for Protective Custody.

PART C. SHELTER CARE
1240. Shelter Care Application.
1241. Notification of Shelter Care Hearing.
1242. Shelter Care Hearing.
1243. Shelter Care Rehearings.

Chapter 13. Pre-Adjudicatory Procedures

PART A. VENUE
1300. Venue.
1302. Inter-County Transfer.

PART B. APPLICATION FOR PRIVATE PETITION
1320. Application to File a Private Petition.
1321. Hearing on Application for Private Petition.

PART C. PETITION
1330. Petition: Filing, Contents, Function, Aggravated Circumstances.
1331. Service of Petition.
1333. Separate Petitions and Consolidated Hearing.
1334. Amendment of Petition.
1335. Withdrawal of Petition.
1336. Re-Filing of the Petition After Withdrawal or Dismissal.

PART D. PROCEDURES FOLLOWING FILING OF PETITION
1340. Discovery and Inspection.
1342. Pre-Adjudicatory Conference.

PART D(1). MOTION PROCEDURES
1344. Motions and Answers.
1345. Filing and Service.

PART D(2). ADJUDICATORY SUMMONS AND NOTICE PROCEDURES
1360. Adjudicatory Summons.
1361. Adjudicatory Notice.
1363. Service of Summons.
1364. Failure to Appear on the Summons.

PART E. PRESERVATION OF TESTIMONY AND EVIDENCE
1380. Preservation of Testimony After Commencement of Proceedings.
1381. Preservation of Testimony by Video Recording.

DOMESTIC RELATIONS

Chapter 14. Adjudicatory Hearing
1401. Introduction to Chapter Fourteen.
1404. Prompt Adjudicatory Hearing.
1405. Stipulations.
1406. Adjudicatory Hearing.
1408. Findings on Petition.
1409. Adjudication of Dependency and Court Order.

Chapter 15. Dispositional Hearing

PART A. SUMMONS AND NOTICE OF THE DISPOSITIONAL HEARING
1500. Summons for the Dispositional Hearing.
1501. Dispositional Notice.

PART B. DISPOSITIONAL HEARING AND AIDS
1509. Aids in Disposition.
1510. Prompt Dispositional Hearing.
1511. Pre-Dispositional Statement.
1512. Dispositional Hearing.
1514. Dispositional Finding Before Removal from Home.
1515. Dispositional Order.
1516. Service of the Dispositional Order.

Chapter 16. Post-Dispositional Procedures

PART A. SUMMONS, NOTICE AND REPORTS
1600. Summons for the Permanency Hearing.
1601. Permanency Hearing Notice.
1604. Submission of Reports.

PART B(1). MODIFICATIONS
1606. Modification of Dependent Child's Placement.

PART B. PERMANENCY HEARING
1607. Regular Scheduling of Permanency Hearing.
1608. Permanency Hearing.
1609. Permanency Hearing Orders.
1610. Permanency Hearing for Children Over Eighteen.
1611. Permanency Hearing Orders for Children Over Eighteen.

PART C. POST-DISPOSITIONAL PROCEDURES
1613. [Reserved]
1616. Post-Dispositional Procedures; Appeals (Reserved).

PART D. CESSATION OR RESUMPTION OF COURT SUPERVISION OR JURISDICTION
1631. Termination of Court Supervision.
1634. Motion for Resumption of Jurisdiction.
1635. Hearing on Motion for Resumption of Jurisdiction.

TABLE OF CONTENTS

Chapter 17. Aggravated Circumstances
1701. Motion for Finding of Aggravated Circumstances.
1702. Filing of Motion for Finding of Aggravated Circumstances.
1705. Adjudication of Aggravated Circumstances.

Chapter 18. Suspensions
1800. Suspensions of Acts of Assembly.

PART XI. SELECTED PENNSYLVANIA RULES OF APPELLATE PROCEDURE

CHILDREN'S FAST TRACK APPEALS

ARTICLE I. PRELIMINARY PROVISIONS

CHAPTER 1. GENERAL PROVISIONS

IN GENERAL

Rule
102. Definitions.
127. Confidential Information and Confidential Documents. Certification.

ARTICLE II. APPELLATE PROCEDURE

CHAPTER 9. APPEALS FROM LOWER COURTS
904. Content of the Notice of Appeal.
905. Filing of Notice of Appeal.

CHAPTER 11. APPEALS FROM COMMONWEALTH COURT AND SUPERIOR COURT

PETITION FOR ALLOWANCE OF APPEAL
1112. Appeals by Allowance.
1113. Time for Petitioning for Allowance of Appeal.
1116. Answer to the Petition for Allowance of Appeal.
1123. Denial of Appeal; Reconsideration.

CHAPTER 19. PREPARATION AND TRANSMISSION OF RECORD AND RELATED MATTERS

RECORD ON APPEAL FROM LOWER COURT
1925. Opinion in Support of Order.
1931. Transmission of the Record.

DISPOSITION WITHOUT REACHING THE MERITS
1972. Dispositions on Motion.

CHAPTER 21. BRIEFS AND REPRODUCED RECORD

CONTENT OF BRIEFS
2113. Reply Brief.

DOMESTIC RELATIONS

CONTENT OF REPRODUCED RECORD
2154. Designation of Contents of Reproduced Record.

FORM OF BRIEFS AND REPRODUCED RECORD
2172. Covers.

FILING AND SERVICE
2185. Service and Filing of Briefs.

CHAPTER 25. POST-SUBMISSION PROCEEDINGS

APPLICATION FOR REARGUMENT
2542. Time for Application for Reargument. Manner of Filing.
2545. Answer to Application for Reargument.

REMAND OF RECORD
2572. Time for Remand of Record.

ARTICLE III. MISCELLANEOUS PROVISIONS

CHAPTER 37. BUSINESS OF THE COMMONWEALTH COURT

ARGUMENT BEFORE COURT EN BANC OR A PANEL
3723. Application for Reargument en Banc.

INTERNAL OPERATING PROCEDURES OF THE SUPERIOR COURT

CHILDREN'S FAST TRACK PROCEDURES
§ 65.14. Children's Fast Track and Other Family Fast Track Appeals.

MOTIONS PRACTICE
§ 65.21. Motions Review Subject to Single Judge Disposition.
§ 65.22. Motions Review Subject to Motions Panel Disposition.

DECISIONAL PROCEDURES
§ 65.31. Argument Sessions and Submit Panels.
§ 65.32. Daily List.
§ 65.42. Circulation and Voting in Children's Fast Track and Other Family Fast Track Appeals.

TRANSCRIPT ORDER FORM FOR CHILDREN'S FAST TRACK APPEALS ONLY
First Judicial District of Pennsylvania

TABLE OF CONTENTS

DOMESTIC REGULATIONS

CHAPTER 108. FAMILY VIOLENCE AND TANF AND GA GENERAL PROVISIONS

Sec.
- 108.1. Purpose.
- 108.2. Definitions.
- 108.3. Universal notification.
- 108.4. Written notification.
- 108.5. Individual notification.
- 108.6. Policy for applicants or recipients in immediate danger.
- 108.7. Requirements subject to waiver.
- 108.8. Claiming good cause based on domestic violence.
- 108.9. Time limits.
- 108.10. Verification.
- 108.11. Time frames for good cause waiver determinations based on domestic violence.
- 108.12. Notice of good cause waiver determinations based on domestic violence.
- 108.13. Review of waivers.
- 108.14. Safeguarding information.
- 108.15. Alternate address.
- 108.16. DRS responsibility for the FVI.
- 108.17. Agreement of Mutual Responsibility (AMR).
- 108.18. Referral for services.

CHAPTER 187. SUPPORT FROM RELATIVES NOT LIVING WITH THE CLIENT—Title 55 Pennsylvania Code (Public Welfare)

Support Provisions for Cash Assistance

Sec.
- 187.21. General policy.
- 187.22. Definitions.
- 187.23. Requirements.
- 187.24. [Reserved].
- 187.25. Notification to the applicant or recipient.
- 187.26. Noncooperation.
- 187.27. Waiver of cooperation for good cause.

Support Provisions for MA for the Categorically Needy

- 187.71. Policy.
- 187.73. Requirements.
- 187.74. Procedures.

Support Provisions for MA for the Medically Needy

- 187.81. Policy.
- 187.83. Requirements.
- 187.84. Procedures.

Consolidated Index

§ 1305. Examination and tests for syphilis (Repealed).

(a) General rule—

1997 Repeal Note. Section 1305 was repealed June 25, 1997, P.L.331, No.35, effectively immed.

§ 1306. Oral examination.

(a) General rule.—Each of the applicants for a marriage license shall appear in person and shall be examined under oath or affirmation as to:

(1) The legality of the contemplated marriage.

(2) Any prior marriage or marriages and its or their dissolution.

(3) The restrictions set forth in section 1304 (relating to restrictions on issuance of license).

(4) All the information required to be furnished on the application for license as prepared and approved by the department.

(b) Exception.—If an applicant is unable to appear in person because of his active military service, the applicant shall be permitted to forward an affidavit, which verifies all of the information required under subsection (a), to the issuing authority.

(c) Form.—The department shall develop and make available affidavit forms to be used by applicants under subsection (b).

(d) Definition.—As used in this section, the term "active military service" means active service in any of the armed services or forces of the United States or this Commonwealth.

2006 Amendment. Act 126 added subsecs. (a), (b), (c) and (d).

§ 1307. Issuance of license.

The marriage license shall be issued if it appears from properly completed applications on behalf of each of the parties to the proposed marriage that there is no legal objection to the marriage. Except as provided by section 1303(b) (relating to waiting period after application), the license shall not be issued prior to the third day following the date of the most recent of the two applications therefor.

§ 1308. Judicial review of refusal to issue license.

(a) Certifying proceedings to court.—If the issuance of a marriage license is refused, upon request of the applicants, the proceedings shall immediately be certified to the court without formality or expense to the applicants.

(b) Prompt hearing.—The application for a marriage license shall be heard by a judge of the court, without a jury, in court or in chambers at the earliest possible time.

§ 1309. Filing applications and consent certificates.

The applications for marriage licenses and consent certificates shall be immediately filed and docketed as public records.

§ 1310. Duration and form of license.

The marriage license shall not be valid for a longer period than 60 days from the date of issue and shall be in substantially the following form:

Commonwealth of Pennsylvania

                        ss: No. . . . .

County of (name)

To any person authorized by law to solemnize marriage:

You are hereby authorized to join together in holy state of matrimony, according to the laws of the Commonwealth of Pennsylvania, (name) and (name).

Given under my hand and seal of the Court of Common Pleas of (name), at (city, borough or town), on (date).

                                 Signed . . . .

                                        (Official Title)

CHAPTER 15

MARRIAGE CEREMONY

Sec.
1501. Form of marriage certificates.
1502. Forms where parties perform ceremony.
1503. Persons qualified to solemnize marriages.
1504. Returns of marriages.

Enactment. Chapter 15 was added December 19, 1990, P.L.1240, No.206, effective in 90 days.

§ 1501. Form of marriage certificates.

The marriage license shall have appended to it two certificates, numbered to correspond with the license (one marked original and one marked duplicate), which shall be in substantially the following form:

I hereby certify that on (date), at (city, borough or town), Pennsylvania, (name) and (name) were by me united in marriage, in accordance with license issued by the Court of Common Pleas of (name) numbered . . . .

Signed . . . .
(Title of person solemnizing marriage)
Address . . . .

Cross References. Section 1501 is referred to in section 1502 of this title.

§ 1502. Forms where parties perform ceremony.

(a) Declaration of authorization.—In all cases in which the parties intend to solemnize their marriage by religious ceremony without officiating clergy, the marriage shall not take place until their right so to do is certified in a declaration in substantially the following form:

Commonwealth of Pennsylvania

ss: No. . . . .

County of (name)

To (name) and (name)

Legal evidence having been furnished to me, in accordance with law, this certifies that I am satisfied that there is no legal impediment to you joining yourselves together in marriage.

Signed . . . .
(Official Title)

(b) Marriage certificates.—In lieu of the certificate set forth in section 1501 (relating to form of marriage certificates), there shall be appended to the declaration two certificates, numbered to correspond to the declaration, in the following form:

We hereby certify that on (date), we united ourselves in marriage, at (city, borough or town), County of (name), Pennsylvania, having first obtained from the Court of Common Pleas of (name) a declaration numbered . . . that the court was satisfied that there was no existing legal impediment to our so doing.

Signed . . . .
Signed . . . .

We, the undersigned, were present at the solemnization of the marriage of (name) and (name), as set forth in the foregoing certificate.

Signed . . . .
Signed . . . .

§ 1503. Persons qualified to solemnize marriages

(a) General rule.—The following are authorized to solemnize marriages between persons that produce a marriage license issued under this part:

(1) A justice, judge or magisterial district judge of this Commonwealth.

(2) A former or retired justice, judge or magisterial district judge of this Commonwealth who is serving as a senior judge or senior magisterial district judge as provided or prescribed by law; or not serving as a senior judge or senior magisterial district judge but meets the following criteria:

(i) has served as a magisterial district judge, judge or justice, whether or not continuously or on the same court, by election or appointment for an aggregate period equaling a full term of office;

(ii) has not been defeated for reelection or retention;

(iii) has not been convicted of, pleaded nolo contendere to or agreed to an Accelerated Rehabilitative Disposition or other probation without verdict program relative to any misdemeanor or felony offense under the laws of this Commonwealth or an equivalent offense under the laws of the United States or one of its territories or possessions, another state, the District of Columbia, the Commonwealth of Puerto Rico or a foreign nation;

(iv) has not resigned a judicial commission to avoid having charges filed or to avoid prosecution by Federal, State or local law enforcement agencies or by the Judicial Conduct Board;

(v) has not been removed from office by the Court of Judicial Discipline; and

(vi) is a resident of this Commonwealth.

(3) An active or senior judge or full-time magistrate of the District Courts of the United States for the Eastern, Middle or Western District of Pennsylvania.

(3.1) An active, retired or senior bankruptcy judge of the United States Bankruptcy Courts for the Eastern, Middle or Western District of Pennsylvania who is a resident of this Commonwealth.

(4) An active, retired or senior judge of the United States Court of Appeals for the Third Circuit who is a resident of this Commonwealth.

(5) A mayor of any city or borough of this Commonwealth.

(5.1) A former mayor of a city or borough of this Commonwealth who:

(i) has not been defeated for reelection;

(ii) has not been convicted of, pleaded nolo contendere to or agreed to an Accelerated Rehabilitative Disposition or other probation without verdict program relative to a misdemeanor or felony offense under the laws of this Commonwealth or an equivalent offense under the laws of the United States or any one of its possessions, another state, the District of Columbia, the Commonwealth of Puerto Rico or a foreign nation;

(iii) has not resigned the position of mayor to avoid having charges filed or to avoid prosecution by Federal, State or local law enforcement agencies;

(iv) has served as a mayor, whether continuously or not, by election for an aggregate of a full term in office; and

(v) is a resident of this Commonwealth.

(6) A minister, priest or rabbi of any regularly established church or congregation.

(b) Religious organizations.—Every religious society, religious institution or religious organization in this Commonwealth may join persons together in marriage when at least one of the persons is a member of the society, institution or organization, according to the rules and customs of the society, institution or organization.

(c) Marriage license needed to officiate.—No person or religious organization qualified to perform marriages shall officiate at a marriage ceremony without the parties having obtained a marriage license issued under this part.

1990, Dec. 19, P.L. 1240, No. 206 § 2, effective in 90 days. Amended 2000, June 22, P.L. 443, No. 59, § 1, imd. effective; 2004, Nov. 30, P.L. 1618, No. 207, § 6, effective Jan. 31, 2005; 2004, Dec. 1, P.L. 1777, No. 232, § 1, effective Jan. 31, 2005; 2009, July 14, P.L. 81, No. 18, § 1, imd. effective.

§ 1504. Returns of marriages.

(a) **General rule.**—The original marriage certificate shall be signed by the person solemnizing the marriage and given to the parties contracting the marriage. The duplicate certificate shall be signed by the person or by a member of the religious society, institution or organization solemnizing the marriage and returned for recording within ten days to the court which issued the license.

(b) **Marriage performed by parties.**—If the marriage was solemnized by the parties themselves, the original certificate shall be signed by the parties to the marriage, attested by two witnesses and retained by the parties contracting the marriage. The duplicate certificate shall be signed by the parties to the marriage, attested by the same two witnesses and returned for recording within ten days to the court issuing the license.

CHAPTER 17
MISCELLANEOUS PROVISIONS RELATING TO MARRIAGE

Sec.
1701. Decree that spouse of applicant is presumed decedent.
1702. Marriage during existence of former marriage.
1703. Marriage within degree of consanguinity.
1704. Marriage between persons of the same sex.

Enactment. Chapter 17 was added December 19, 1990, P.L.1240, No.206, effective in 90 days.

§ 1701. Decree that spouse of applicant is presumed decedent.

(a) **Finding of death.**—When the spouse of an applicant for a marriage license has disappeared or is absent from the place of residence of the spouse without being heard of after diligent inquiry, the court, aided by the report of a master if necessary, upon petition of the applicant for a marriage license, may make a finding and decree that the absentee is dead and the date of death if notice to the absentee has been given as provided in subsection (d) and either of the applicants is and for one year or more prior to the application has been a resident of this Commonwealth.

(b) **Presumption from absence.**—When the death of the spouse of an applicant for a marriage license is in issue, the unexplained absence from the last known place of residence and the fact that the absentee has been unheard of for seven years may be sufficient ground for finding that the absentee died seven years after the absentee was last heard from.

(c) **Exposure to specific peril.**—The fact that an absentee spouse was exposed to a specific peril of death may be a sufficient ground for finding that the absentee died less than seven years after the absentee was last heard from.

(d) **Notice to absentee.**—The court may require advertisement in any newspapers as the court, according to the circumstances of the case, deems advisable of the fact of the application for the marriage license, together with notice that, at a specified time and place, the court or a master appointed by the court will hear evidence concerning the alleged absence, including the circumstances and duration thereof.

(e) **Remarriage after decree of presumed death.**—Even though the absentee spouse declared to be presumed dead is in fact alive, the remarriage of the spouse who has obtained a license to marry and a decree of presumed death of the former spouse shall be valid for all purposes as though the former marriage had been terminated by divorce, and all property of the presumed decedent shall be administered and disposed of as provided by Title 20 (relating to decedents, estates and fiduciaries).

§ 1702. Marriage during existence of former marriage.

(a) **General rule.**—If a married person, during the lifetime of the other person with whom the marriage is in force, enters into a subsequent marriage pursuant to the requirements of this part and the parties to the marriage live together thereafter as husband and wife, and the subsequent marriage was entered into by one or both of the parties in good faith in the full belief that the former spouse was dead or that the former marriage has been annulled or terminated by a divorce, or without knowledge of the former marriage, they shall, after the impediment to their marriage has been removed by the death of the other party to the former marriage or by annulment or divorce, if they continue to live together as husband and wife in good faith on the part of one of them, be held to have been legally married from and immediately after the date of death or the date of the decree of annulment or divorce.

(b) **False rumor of death of spouse.**—Where a remarriage has occurred upon false rumor of the death of a former spouse in appearance wellfounded but there has been no decree of presumed death, the remarriage shall be void and subject to annulment by either party to the remarriage as provided by section 3304 (relating to grounds for annulment of void marriages), and the returning spouse shall have cause for divorce as provided in section 3301 (relating to grounds for divorce).

(c) Criminal penalties.—Where the remarriage was entered into in good faith, neither party to the remarriage shall be subject to criminal prosecution for bigamy.

§ 1703. Marriage within degree of consanguinity.

All marriages within the prohibited degrees of consanguinity as set forth in this part are voidable, but, when any of these marriages have not been dissolved during the lifetime of the parties, the unlawfulness of the marriage shall not be inquired into after the death of either of the parties to the marriage.

§ 1704. Marriage between persons of the same sex.

It is hereby declared to be the strong and longstanding public policy of this Commonwealth that marriage shall be between one man and one woman. A marriage between persons of the same sex which was entered into in another state or foreign jurisdiction, even if valid where entered into, shall be void in this Commonwealth.

1996 Amendment. Act 124 added section 1704.

CHAPTER 19
ABOLITION OF ACTIONS FOR ALIENATION OF AFFECTIONS AND BREACH OF PROMISE TO MARRY

Sec.
1901. Actions for alienation of affections abolished.
1902. Actions for breach of promise to marry abolished.
1903. Purpose of chapter.
1904. Filing or threatening to file actions prohibited.
1905. Instruments executed in satisfaction of abolished claims prohibited.

Enactment. Chapter 19 was added December 19, 1990, P.L.1240, No.206, effective in 90 days.

§ 1901. Actions for alienation of affections abolished.

(a) **General rule.**—All civil causes of action for alienation of affections of husband or wife are abolished.

(b) **Exception.**—Subsection (a) does not apply to cases where the defendant is a parent, brother or sister or a person formerly in loco parentis to the spouse of plaintiff.

§ 1902. Actions for breach of promise to marry abolished.

All causes of action for breach of contract to marry are abolished.

§ 1903. Purpose of chapter.

(a) **General rule.**—No act done within this Commonwealth shall give rise, either within or without this Commonwealth, to a cause of action abolished by this chapter.

(b) **Contract to marry.**—No contract to marry which is made within this Commonwealth shall give rise, either within or without this Commonwealth, to a cause of action for breach of the contract.

(c) **Intention of section.**—It is the intention of this section to fix the effect, status and character of such acts and contracts and to render them ineffective to support or give rise to any such causes of action, either within or without this Commonwealth.

§ 1904. Filing or threatening to file actions prohibited.

It is unlawful for a person, either as litigant or attorney, to file, cause to be filed, threaten to file or threaten to cause to be filed in a court in this Commonwealth any pleading or paper setting forth or seeking to recover upon any cause of action abolished or barred by this chapter whether the cause of action arose within or without this Commonwealth.

§ 1905. Instruments executed in satisfaction of abolished claims prohibited.

(a) **Contracts and instruments void.**—All contracts and instruments of every kind executed within this Commonwealth in payment, satisfaction, settlement or compromise of any claim or cause of action abolished or barred by this chapter, whether the claim or cause of action arose within or without this Commonwealth, are contrary to the public policy of this Commonwealth and void.

(b) **Execution and use prohibited.**—It is unlawful to cause, induce or procure a person to execute a contract or instrument proscribed by this chapter, or cause, induce or procure a person to give, pay, transfer or deliver any money or thing of value in payment, satisfaction, settlement or compromise of any such claim or cause of action, or to receive, take or accept any such money or thing of value in such payment, satisfaction, settlement or compromise.

(c) Actions to enforce prohibited.—It is unlawful to commence or cause to be commenced, either as litigant or attorney, in a court of this Commonwealth any proceeding or action seeking to enforce or recover upon a contract or instrument proscribed by this chapter, knowing it to be such, whether the contract or instrument was executed within or without this Commonwealth.

(d) Exceptions.—This section does not apply to the payment, satisfaction, settlement or compromise of any causes of action which are not abolished or barred by this chapter or to the bona fide holder in due course of a negotiable instrument.

PART III
ADOPTION

Chapter

21. Preliminary Provisions
23. Jurisdiction and Parties
25. Proceedings Prior to Petition to Adopt
27. Petition for Adoption
29. Decrees and Records

Enactment. Part III was added October 15, 1980, P.L.934, No.163, effective January 1, 1981.

Special Provisions in Appendix. See section 3 of Act 163 of 1980 in the appendix to this title for special provisions relating to the applicability of Part III to pending proceedings.

CHAPTER 21
PRELIMINARY PROVISIONS

Sec.

2101. Short title of part.
2102. Definitions.

Enactment. Chapter 21 was added October 15, 1980, P.L.934, No.163, effective January 1, 1981.

§ 2101. Short title of part.

This part shall be known and may be cited as the "Adoption Act."

§ 2102. Definitions.

The following words and phrases when used in this part shall have, unless the context clearly indicates otherwise, the meanings given to them in this section:

"Adoptee." An individual proposed to be adopted.

"Agency." Any incorporated or unincorporated organization, society, institution or other entity, public or voluntary, which may receive or provide for the care of children, supervised by the Department of Public Welfare and providing adoption services in accordance with standards established by the department.

"Clerk." The clerk of the division of the court of common pleas having jurisdiction over voluntary relinquishment, involuntary termination and adoption proceedings.

"Court." The court of common pleas.

"Intermediary." Any person or persons or agency acting between the parent or parents and the proposed adoptive parent or parents in arranging an adoption placement.

"Medical history information." Medical records and other information concerning an adoptee or an adoptee's natural family which is relevant to the adoptee's present or future health care or medical treatment. The term includes:

(1) otherwise confidential or privileged information provided that identifying contents have been removed pursuant to section 2909 (relating to medical history information); and

(2) information about the natural parents which may be relevant to a potential hereditary or congenital medical problem.

"Newborn child." A child who is six months of age or younger at the time of the filing of any petition pursuant to Chapter 25 (relating to proceedings prior to petition to adopt).

"Parent." Includes adoptive parent.

(June 23, 1982, P.L.617, No.174, eff. 60 days; May 21, 1992, P.L.228, No.34, eff. 60 days; Dec. 20, 1995, P.L.685, No.76, eff. 60 days)

1995 Amendment. Act 76 amended the def. of "medical history information."

1992 Amendment. Act 34 added the def. of "newborn child."

CHAPTER 23
JURISDICTION AND PARTIES

Subchapter

A. Jurisdiction
B. Parties

Enactment. Chapter 23 was added October 15, 1980, P.L.934, No.163, effective January 1, 1981.

SUBCHAPTER A
JURISDICTION

Sec.

2301. Court.
2302. Venue.

§ 2301. Court.

The court of common pleas of each county shall exercise through the appropriate division original jurisdiction over voluntary relinquishment, involuntary termination and adoption proceedings.

§ 2302. Venue.

Proceedings for voluntary relinquishment, involuntary termination and adoption may be brought in the court of the county:

  (1) Where the parent or parents or the adoptee or the person or persons who have filed a report of intention to adopt required by section 2531 (relating to report of intention to adopt) reside.

  (2) In which is located an office of an agency having custody of the adoptee or in the county where the agency having placed the adoptee is located.

  (3) With leave of court, in which the adoptee formerly resided.

SUBCHAPTER B
PARTIES

Sec.

2311. Who may be adopted.
2312. Who may adopt.
2313. Representation for child.

§ 2311. Who may be adopted.

Any individual may be adopted, regardless of his age or residence.

§ 2312. Who may adopt.

Any individual may become an adopting parent.

§ 2313. Representation for child.

  (a) **Child.**—The court shall appoint counsel to represent the child in an involuntary termination proceeding when the proceeding is being contested by one or both of the parents. The court may appoint counsel or a guardian ad litem to represent any child who has not reached the age of 18 years and is subject to any other proceeding under this part whenever it is in the best interests of the child. No attorney or law firm shall represent both the child and the adopting parent or parents.

(a.1) Parent.—The court shall appoint counsel for a parent whose rights are subject to termination in an involuntary termination proceeding if, upon petition of the parent, the court determines that the parent is unable to pay for counsel or if payment would result in substantial financial hardship.

(b) Payment of costs.—The court, in its discretion, may order all or part of the costs attendant to a proceeding under this part to be paid by the county wherein the case is heard, the adopting parents or apportioned to both, provided that if the adopting parents shall be ordered to bear all or a portion of the costs of this part that:

(1) the court may direct that the payment of the fees or a portion thereof may be paid by a court ordered schedule of payments extending beyond the date of the involuntary termination hearing; and

(2) the fee shall not exceed $150.

CHAPTER 25
PROCEEDINGS PRIOR TO PETITION TO ADOPT

Subchapter

- A. Voluntary Relinquishment
- B. Involuntary Termination
- C. Decree of Termination
- D. Reports and Investigation
- E. Pennsylvania Adoption Cooperative Exchange

Enactment. Chapter 25 was added October 15, 1980, P.L.934, No.163, effective January 1, 1981.

Cross References. Chapter 25 is referred to in section 2905 of this title.

SUBCHAPTER A
VOLUNTARY RELINQUISHMENT

Sec.

2501. Relinquishment to agency.
2502. Relinquishment to adult intending to adopt child.
2503. Hearing.
2504. Alternative procedure for relinquishment.
2504.1. Confidentiality.
2505. Counseling.

§ 2501. Relinquishment to agency.

(a) Petition.—When any child under the age of 18 years has been in the care of an agency for a minimum period of three days or, whether or not the agency has the physical care of the child, the agency has received a written notice of the present intent to transfer to it custody of the child, executed by the parent, the parent or parents of the child may petition the court for permission to relinquish forever all parental rights and duties with respect to their child.

(b) Consents.—The written consent of a parent or guardian of a petitioner who has not reached 18 years of age shall not be required. The consent of the agency to accept custody of the child until such time as the child is adopted shall be required.

Cross References. Section 2501 is referred to in sections 2503, 2521 of this title.

§ 2502. Relinquishment to adult intending to adopt child.

(a) Petition.—When any child under the age of 18 years has been for a minimum period of three days in the exclusive care of an adult or adults who have filed a report of intention to adopt required by section 2531 (relating to report of intention to adopt), the parent or parents of the child may petition the court for permission to relinquish forever all parental rights to their child.

(b) Consents.—The written consent of a parent or guardian of a petitioner who has not reached 18 years of age shall not be required. The adult or adults having care of the child shall file a separate consent to accept custody of the child.

2004 Amendment. Act 21 amended this section. Section 2 of Act 21 provided that the amendment of subsec. (a) shall apply to adoptions which are initiated on or after the effective date of Act 21.

Cross References. Section 2502 is referred to in sections 2503, 2521 of this title.

§ 2503. Hearing.

(a) General rule.—Upon presentation of a petition prepared pursuant to section 2501 (relating to relinquishment to agency) or section 2502 (relating to relinquishment to adult intending to adopt child), the court shall fix a time for hearing which shall not be less than ten days after filing of the petition. The petitioner must appear at the hearing.

(b) Notice.—

(1) At least ten days' notice of the hearing shall be given to the petitioner, and a copy of the notice shall be given to the other parent, to the putative father whose parental rights could be terminated pursuant to subsection (d) and to the parents or guardian of a petitioner who has not reached 18 years of age.

(2) The notice to the petitioner shall state the following:

"To: (insert petitioner's name)

A petition has been filed asking the court to put an end to all rights you have to your child (insert name of child). The court has set a hearing to consider ending your rights to your child. That hearing will be held in (insert place, giving reference to exact room and building number or designation) on (insert date) at (insert time). Your presence is required at the hearing. You have a right to be represented at the hearing by a lawyer. You should take this paper to your lawyer at once. If you do not have a lawyer or cannot afford one, go to or telephone the office set forth below to find out where you can get legal help.

(Name)......................
(Address)....................
....
(Telephone number)............"

(3) The copy of the notice which is given to the putative father shall state that his rights may also be subject to termination pursuant to subsection (d) if he fails to file either an acknowledgment of paternity or claim of paternity pursuant to section 5103 (relating to acknowledgment and claim of paternity) and fails to either appear at the hearing for the purpose of objecting to the termination of his rights or file a written objection to such termination with the court prior to the hearing.

(c) Decree.—After hearing, which shall be private, the court may enter a decree of termination of parental rights in the case of their relinquishment to an adult or a decree of termination of parental rights and duties, including the obligation of support, in the case of their relinquishment to an agency.

(d) Putative father.—If a putative father will not file a petition to voluntarily relinquish his parental rights pursuant to section 2501 (relating to relinquishment to agency) or 2502 (relating to relinquishment to adult intending to adopt child), has been given notice of the hearing being held pursuant to this section and fails to either appear at that hearing for the purpose of objecting to termination of his parental rights or file a written objection to such termination with the court prior to the hearing and has not filed an acknowledgment of paternity or claim of paternity pursuant to section 5103, the court may enter a decree terminating the parental rights of the putative father pursuant to subsection (c).

(e) Right to file personal and medical history information.—At the time the decree of termination is transmitted to the parent whose rights are terminated, the court shall advise that parent, in writing, of his or her continuing right to place and update personal and medical history information, whether or not the medical condition is in existence or discoverable at the time of adoption, on file with the court and with the Department of Public Welfare pursuant to Subchapter B of Chapter 29 (relating to records and access to information).

(June 23, 1982, P.L.617, No.174, eff. 60 days; May 21, 1992, P.L.228, No.34, eff. 60 days; Dec. 20, 1995, P.L.685, No.76, eff. 60 days; Oct. 27, 2010, P.L. 961, No. 101, eff. 180 days.)

2010 Amendment. Act 101 amended subsec. (e).

1995 Amendment. Act 76 amended subsec. (e).

1992 Amendment. Act 34 amended subsec. (b), (d) and added subsec. (e).

Cross References. Section 2503 is referred to in section 2505 of this title.

§ 2504. Alternative procedure for relinquishment.

(a) **Petition to confirm consent to adoption.**—If the parent or parents of the child have executed consents to an adoption, upon petition by the intermediary or, where there is no intermediary, by the adoptive parent, the court shall hold a hearing for the purpose of confirming a consent to an adoption upon expiration of the time periods under section 2711 (relating to consents necessary to adoption). The original consent or consents to the adoption shall be attached to the petition.

(b) **Hearing.**—Upon presentation of a petition filed pursuant to this section, the court shall fix a time for a hearing which shall not be less than ten days after filing of the petition. Notice of the hearing shall be by personal service or by registered mail or by such other means as the court may require upon the consenter and shall be in the form provided in section 2513(b) (relating to hearing). Notice of the hearing shall be given to the other parent or parents, to the putative father whose parental rights could be terminated pursuant to subsection (c) and to the parents or guardian of a consenting parent who has not reached 18 years of age. The notice shall state that the consenting parent's or putative father's rights may be terminated as a result of the hearing. After hearing, which shall be private, the court may enter a decree of termination of parental rights in the case of a relinquishment to an adult or a decree of termination of parental rights and duties, including the obligation of support, in the case of a relinquishment to an agency.

(c) **Putative father.**—If a putative father will not execute a consent to an adoption as required by section 2711, has been given notice of the hearing being held pursuant to this section and fails to either appear at that hearing for the purpose of objecting to termination of his parental rights or file a written objection to such termination with the court prior to the hearing and has not filed an acknowledgment of paternity or claim of paternity pursuant to section 5103 (relating to acknowledgment and claim of paternity), the court may enter a decree terminating the parental rights of the putative father pursuant to subsection (b).

(d) **Right to file personal and medical history information.**—At the time the decree of termination is transmitted to the parent, the court shall also advise, in writing, the parent whose rights have been terminated of his or her continuing right to place and update personal and medical history information, whether or not the medical condition is in existence or discoverable at the time of adoption, on file with the court and with the Department of Public Welfare pursuant to Subchapter B of Chapter 29 (relating to records and access to information).
(June 23, 1982, P.L.617, No.174, eff. 60 days; May 21, 1992, P.L.228, No.34, eff. 60 days; Dec. 20, 1995, P.L.685, No.76, eff. 60 days; March 24, 2004, P.L.159, No. 21, eff. May 24, 2004; Oct. 27, 2010, P.L. 961, No. 101, eff. 180 days.)

2010 Amendment. Act 101 amended subsec. (d).

2004 Amendment. Act 21 amended subsec. (a). Section 2 of Act 21 provided that the amendment of subsec. (a) shall apply to adoptions which are initiated on or after the effective date of Act 21.

1995 Amendment. Act 76 amended subsec. (d).

1992 Amendment. Act 34 amended subsec. (b), (c) and added subsec. (d).

Cross References. Section 2504 is referred to in section 2505 of this title.

§ 2504.1. Confidentiality.

The court shall take such steps as are reasonably necessary to assure that the identity of the adoptive parent or parents is not disclosed without their consent in any proceeding under this subchapter or Subchapter B (relating to involuntary termination). The Supreme Court may prescribe uniform rules under this section relating to such confidentiality.

1992 Amendment. Act 34 added sec. 2504.1.

§ 2505. Counseling.

(a) **List of counselors.**—Any hospital or other facility providing maternity care shall provide a list of available counselors and counseling services compiled pursuant to subsection (b) to its maternity patients who are known to be considering relinquishment or termination of parental rights pursuant to this part. The patient shall sign an acknowledgment of receipt of such list prior to discharge, a copy of which receipt shall be provided to the patient.

  (b) Compilation of list.—The court shall compile a list of qualified counselors and counseling services (including all adoption agencies) which are available to counsel natural parents within the county who are contemplating relinquishment or termination of parental rights pursuant to this part. Such list shall be distributed to every agency, hospital or other facility providing maternity care within the county and shall be made available upon request to any intermediary or licensed health care professional.

  (c) Court referral.—Prior to entering a decree of termination of parental rights pursuant to section 2503 (relating to hearing) or 2504 (relating to alternative procedure for relinquishment), if the parent whose rights are to be terminated is present in court, the court shall inquire whether he or she has received counseling concerning the termination and the alternatives thereto from an agency or from a qualified counselor listed by a court pursuant to subsection (b). If the parent has not received such counseling, the court may, with the parent's consent, refer the parent to an agency or qualified counselor listed by a court pursuant to subsection (b) for the purpose of receiving such counseling. In no event shall the court delay the completion of any hearing pursuant to section 2503 or 2504 for more than 15 days in order to provide for such counseling.

  (d) Application for counseling.—Any parent who has filed a petition to relinquish his or her parental rights, or has executed a consent to adoption, and is in need of counseling concerning the relinquishment or consent, and the alternatives thereto, may apply to the court for referral to an agency or qualified counselor listed by a court pursuant to subsection (b) for the purpose of receiving such counseling. The court, in its discretion, may make such a referral where it is satisfied that this counseling would be of benefit to the parent.

  (e) Counseling fund.—Except as hereinafter provided, each report of intention to adopt filed pursuant to section 2531 (relating to report of intention to adopt) shall be accompanied by a filing fee in the amount of $75 which shall be paid into a segregated fund established by the county. The county may also make supplemental appropriations to the fund. All costs of counseling provided pursuant to subsection (c) or (d) to individuals who are unable to pay for such counseling shall be paid from the fund. No filing fee may be exacted under this subsection with respect to the adoption of a special needs child who would be eligible for adoption assistance pursuant to regulations promulgated by the Department of Public Welfare. In addition, the court may reduce or waive the fee in cases of demonstrated financial hardship.

  1982 Amendment. Act 174 added section 2505.

  1992 Amendment. Act 34 amend subsec. (a), (b), and added subsec. (c), (d) and (e).

SUBCHAPTER B

INVOLUNTARY TERMINATION

Sec.

2511. Grounds for involuntary termination.
2512. Petition for involuntary termination.
2513. Hearing.

  Cross References. Subchapter B is referred to in section 2504.1 of this title; section 6351 of Title 42 (Judiciary and Judicial Procedure).

§ 2511. Grounds for involuntary termination.

  (a) General rule.—The rights of a parent in regard to a child may be terminated after a petition filed on any of the following grounds:

(1) The parent by conduct continuing for a period of at least six months immediately preceding the filing of the petition either has evidenced a settled purpose of relinquishing parental claim to a child or has refused or failed to perform parental duties.

(2) The repeated and continued incapacity, abuse, neglect or refusal of the parent has caused the child to be without essential parental care, control or subsistence necessary for his physical or mental well-being and the conditions and causes of the incapacity, abuse, neglect or refusal cannot or will not be remedied by the parent.

(3) The parent is the presumptive but not the natural father of the child.

(4) The child is in the custody of an agency, having been found under such circumstances that the identity or whereabouts of the parent is unknown and cannot be ascertained by diligent search and the parent does not claim the child within three months after the child is found.

(5) The child has been removed from the care of the parent by the court or under a voluntary agreement with an agency for a period of at least six months, the conditions which led to the removal or placement of the child continue to exist, the parent cannot or will not remedy those conditions within a reasonable period of time, the services or assistance reasonably available to the parent are not likely to remedy the conditions which led to the removal or placement of the child within a reasonable period of time and termination of the parental rights would best serve the needs and welfare of the child.

(6) In the case of a newborn child, the parent knows or has reason to know of the child's birth, does not reside with the child, has not married the child's other parent, has failed for a period of four months immediately preceding the filing of the petition to make reasonable efforts to maintain substantial and continuing contact with the child and has failed during the same four-month period to provide substantial financial support for the child.

(7) The parent is the father of a child conceived as a result of a rape or incest.

(8) The child has been removed from the care of the parent by the court or under a voluntary agreement with an agency, 12 months or more have elapsed from the date of removal or placement, the conditions which led to the removal or placement of the child continue to exist and termination of parental rights would best serve the needs and welfare of the child.

(9) The parent has been convicted of one of the following in which the victim was a child of the parent:

   (i) an offense under 18 Pa.C.S. Ch. 25 (relating to criminal homicide);

   (ii) a felony under 18 Pa.C.S. § 2702 (relating to aggravated assault);

   (iii) an offense in another jurisdiction equivalent to an offense in subparagraph (i) or (ii); or

   (iv) an attempt, solicitation or conspiracy to commit an offense in subparagraph (i), (ii) or (iii).

(10) The parent has been found by a court of competent jurisdiction to have committed sexual abuse against the child or another child of the parent based on a judicial adjudication as set forth in paragraph (1)(i), (ii), (iii) or (iv) or (4) of the definition of "founded report" in section 6303(a) (relating to definitions) where the judicial adjudication is based on a finding of "sexual abuse or exploitation" as defined in section 6303(a).

(11) The parent is required to register as a sexual offender under 42 Pa.C.S. Ch. 97 Subch. H (relating to registration of sexual offenders) or I (relating to continued registration of sexual offenders) or to register with a sexual offender registry in another jurisdiction or foreign country.

(b) Other considerations.—The court in terminating the rights of a parent shall give primary consideration to the developmental, physical and emotional needs and welfare of the child. The rights of a parent shall not be terminated solely on the basis of environmental factors such as inadequate housing, furnishings, income, clothing and medical care if found to be beyond the control of the parent. With respect to any petition filed pursuant to subsection (a)(1), (6) or (8), the court shall not consider any efforts by the parent to remedy the conditions described therein which are first initiated subsequent to the giving of notice of the filing of the petition.

(c) **Right to file personal and medical history information.**—At the time the decree of termination is transmitted to the parent whose rights have been terminated, the court shall advise the parent, in writing, of his or her continuing right to place and update personal and medical history information, whether or not the medical condition is in existence or discoverable at the time of adoption, on file with the court and with the Department of Public Welfare pursuant to Subchapter B of Chapter 29 (relating to records and access to information).

(May 21, 1992, P.L.228, No.34, eff. 60 days; Dec. 20, 1995, P.L.685, No.76; Apr. 4, 1996, P.L.58, No.20, eff. 60 days; Nov. 9, 2006, P.L.1358, No.146, eff. 180 days; Oct. 27, 2010, P.L.961, No.101, eff. 180 days; Oct. 28, 2016, P.L.966, No.115, eff. imd.; Feb. 21, 2018, P.L.27, No.10, eff. imd.; June 12, 2018, P.L.140, No.29, eff. imd.)

2018 Amendment. Act 10 amended subsec. (a)(11) and Act 29 reenacted subsec. (a)(11).

2016 Amendment. Act 115 added subsec. (a)(10) and (11).

2010 Amendment. Act 101 amended subsec. (c).

2006 Amendment. Act 146 added subsec. (a)(9).

1996 Amendment. Act 20 amended subsec. (a)(7).

1995 Amendment. Act 76 amended subsecs. (b) and (c) and added subsec. (a)(8). Section 7 of Act 76 provided that subsecs. (b) and (c) shall take effect in 60 days and, with regard to a child who has been removed from the care of the parent by the court or under a voluntary agreement with an agency prior to the effective date of Act 76, subsec. (a)(8) shall take effect 12 months after the effective date of Act 76.

References in Text. The Department of Public Welfare, referred to in this section, was redesignated as the Department of Human Services by Act 132 of 2014.

Cross References. Section 2511 is referred to in sections 2513, 2714 of this title; section 6302 of Title 42 (Judiciary and Judicial Procedure).

§ 2512. Petition for involuntary termination.

(a) **Who may file.**—A petition to terminate parental rights with respect to a child under the age of 18 years may be filed by any of the following:

(1) Either parent when termination is sought with respect to the other parent.

(2) An agency.

(3) The individual having custody or standing in loco parentis to the child and who has filed a report of intention to adopt required by section 2531 (relating to report of intention to adopt).

(4) An attorney representing a child or a guardian ad litem representing a child who has been adjudicated dependent under 42 Pa.C.S. § 6341(c) (relating to adjudication).

(b) **Contents.**—The petition shall set forth specifically those grounds and facts alleged as the basis for terminating parental rights. The petition filed under this section shall also contain an averment that the petitioner will assume custody of the child until such time as the child is adopted. If the petitioner is an agency it shall not be required to aver that an adoption is presently contemplated nor that a person with a present intention to adopt exists.

(c) **Father not identified.**—If the petition does not identify the father of the child, it shall state whether a claim of paternity has been filed under section 8303 (relating to claim of paternity).

1995 Amendment. Act 76 added subsec. (a)(4).

References in Text. Section 8303, referred to in this section, is repealed. The subject matter is now contained in section 5103.

Cross References. Section 2512 is referred to in sections 2513, 2521 of this title.

§ 2513. Hearing.

(a) **Time.**—The court shall fix a time for hearing on a petition filed under section 2512 (relating to petition for involuntary termination) which shall be not less than ten days after filing of the petition.

(b) **Notice.**—At least ten days' notice shall be given to the parent or parents, putative father, or parent of a minor parent whose rights are to be terminated, by personal service or by registered mail to his or their last known address or by such other means as the court may require. A copy of the notice shall be given in the same manner to the other parent, putative father or parent or guardian of a minor parent whose rights are to be terminated. A putative father shall include one who has filed a claim of paternity as provided in section 5103 (relating to acknowledgment and claim of paternity) prior to the institution of proceedings. The notice shall state the following:

"A petition has been filed asking the court to put an end to all rights you have to your child (insert name of child). The court has set a hearing to consider ending your rights to your child. That hearing will be held in (insert place, giving reference to exact room and building number or designation) on (insert date) at (insert time). You are warned that even if you fail to appear at the scheduled hearing, the hearing will go on without you and your rights to your child may be ended by the court without your being present. You have a right to be represented at the hearing by a lawyer. You should take this paper to your lawyer at once. If you do not have a lawyer or cannot afford one, go to or telephone the office set forth below to find out where you can get legal help.

(Name) . . . .
(Address) . . . .
. . . .
(Telephone number) . . . . "

(c) **Mother competent witness on paternity issue.**—The natural mother shall be a competent witness as to whether the presumptive or putative father is the natural father of the child.

(d) **Decree.**—After hearing, which may be private, the court shall make a finding relative to the pertinent provisions of section 2511 (relating to grounds for involuntary termination) and upon such finding may enter a decree of termination of parental rights. (June 23, 1982, P.L.617, No.174, eff. 60 days)

1982 Amendment. Act 174 amended subsec. (b).

1992 Amendment. Act 34 amended subsec. (b).

References in Text. Section 8303, referred to in this section, is repealed. The subject matter is now contained in section 5103.

Cross References. Section 2513 is referred to in sections 2503, 2504, 2714 of this title.

SUBCHAPTER C
DECREE OF TERMINATION

Sec.

2521. Effect of decree of termination.

§ 2521. Effect of decree of termination.

(a) **Adoption proceeding rights extinguished.**—A decree terminating all rights of a parent or a decree terminating all rights and duties of a parent entered by a court of competent jurisdiction shall extinguish the power or the right of the parent to object to or receive notice of adoption proceedings.

(b) **Award of custody.**—The decree shall award custody of the child to the agency or the person consenting to accept custody under section 2501 (relating to relinquishment to agency) or section 2502 (relating to relinquishment to adult intending to adopt child) or the petitioner in the case of a proceeding under section 2512 (relating to petition for involuntary termination).

(c) **Authority of agency or person receiving custody.**—An agency or person receiving custody of a child shall stand in loco parentis to the child and in such capacity shall have the authority, inter alia, to consent to marriage, to enlistment in the armed forces and to major medical, psychiatric and surgical treatment and to exercise such other authority concerning the child as a natural parent could exercise.

SUBCHAPTER D
REPORTS AND INVESTIGATION

Sec.
2530. Home study and preplacement report.
2531. Report of intention to adopt.
2532. Filing of report.
2533. Report of intermediary.
2534. Exhibits.
2535. Investigation.

§ 2530. Home study and preplacement report.

(a) **General rule.**—No intermediary shall place a child in the physical care or custody of a prospective adoptive parent or parents unless a home study containing a favorable recommendation for placement of a child with the prospective parent or parents has been completed within three years prior thereto and which has been supplemented within one year prior thereto. The home study shall be conducted by a local public child-care agency, an adoption agency or a licensed social worker designated by the court to perform such study.

(b) **Preplacement report.**—A preplacement report shall be prepared by the agency or person conducting the home study.

(1) The preplacement report shall set forth all pertinent information relating to the fitness of the adopting parents as parents.

(2) The preplacement report shall be based upon a study which shall include an investigation of the home environment, family life, parenting skills, age, physical and mental health, social, cultural and religious background, facilities and resources of the adoptive parents and their ability to manage their resources. The preplacement report shall also include the information required by section 6344(b) (relating to employees having contact with children; adoptive and foster parents).

(3) The preplacement report shall include a determination regarding the fitness of the adopting parents as parents.

(4) The preplacement report shall be dated and verified.

(c) **Interim placement.**—Where a home study required under this section is in process, but not yet completed, an intermediary may place a child in the physical care or custody of a prospective adoptive parent or parents if all of the following conditions are met:

(1) The intermediary has no reason to believe that the prospective adoptive parent or parents would not receive a favorable recommendation for placement as a result of the home study.

(2) The individual or agency conducting the home study assents to the interim placement.

(3) The intermediary immediately notifies the court of the interim placement and the identity of the individual or agency conducting the home study. If at any time prior to the completion of the home study the court is notified by the individual or agency conducting the home study that it withdraws its assent to the interim placement, the court may order the placement of the child in temporary foster care with an agency until a favorable recommendation for placement is received.

(May 21, 1992, P.L.228, No.34, eff. 60 days; Oct. 22, 2014, P.L.2529, No.153, eff. Dec. 31, 2014)

2014 Amendment. Act 153 amended subsec. (b)(2).

1992 Amendment. Act 34 added section 2530.

Cross References. Section 2530 is referred to in sections 2531, 2701 of this title.

§ 2531. Report of intention to adopt.

(a) **General rule.**—Every person now having or hereafter receiving or retaining custody or physical care of any child for the purpose or with the intention of adopting a child under the age of 18 years shall report to the court in which the petition for adoption will be filed.

(b) **Contents.**—The report shall set forth:

(1) The circumstances surrounding the persons receiving or retaining custody or physical care of the child, including the date upon which a preplacement investigation was concluded.

(2) The name, sex, racial background, age, date and place of birth and religious affiliation of the child.

(3) The name and address of the intermediary.

(4) An itemized accounting of moneys and consideration paid or to be paid to the intermediary.

(5) Whether the parent or parents whose parental rights are to be terminated have received counseling with respect to the termination and the alternatives thereto. If so, the report shall state the dates on which the counseling was provided and the name and address of the counselor or agency which provided the counseling.

(6) The name, address and signature of the person or persons making the report. Immediately above the signature of the person or persons intending to adopt the child shall appear the following statement:

I acknowledge that I have been advised or know and understand that the birth father or putative father may revoke the consent to the adoption of this child within 30 days after the later of the birth of the child or the date he has executed the consent to an adoption and that the birth mother may revoke the consent to an adoption of this child within 30 days after the date she has executed the consent.

(7) A copy of the preplacement report prepared pursuant to section 2530 (relating to home study and preplacement report).

When a person receives or retains custody or physical care of a child from an agency, the report shall set forth only the name and address of the agency, the circumstances surrounding such person receiving or retaining custody or physical care of the child and a copy of the preplacement report prepared pursuant to section 2530.

(c) **When report not required.**—No report shall be required when the child is the child, grandchild, stepchild, brother or sister of the whole or half blood, or niece or nephew by blood, marriage or adoption of the person receiving or retaining custody or physical care.

(June 23, 1982, P.L.617, No.174, eff. 60 days; May 21, 1992, P.L.228, No. 34, eff. 60 days; March 24, 2004, P.L.159, No. 21, eff. May 24, 2004.)

2004 Amendment. Act 21 amended subsec. (b).

1982 Amendment. Act 174 amended subsec. (b).

1992 Amendment. Act 34 amended subsec. 2531(b).

Cross References. Section 2531 is referred to in sections 2302, 2502, 2505, 2512, 2532, 2535, 2701, 2905 of this title.

§ 2532. Filing of report.

The report required by section 2531 (relating to report of intention to adopt) shall be filed within 30 days after the date of receipt of the custody or physical care of the child.

§ 2533. Report of intermediary.

(a) **General rule.**—Within six months after filing the report of intention to adopt, the intermediary who or which arranged the adoption placement of any child under the age of 18 years shall make a written report under oath to the court in which the petition for adoption will be filed and shall thereupon forthwith notify in writing the adopting parent or parents of the fact that the report has been filed and the date thereof.

(b) Contents.—The report shall set forth:

(1) The name and address of the intermediary.

(2) The name, sex, racial background, age, date and place of birth and religious affiliation of the child.

(3) The date of the placement of the child with the adopting parent or parents.

(4) The name, racial background, age, marital status as of the time of birth of the child and during one year prior thereto, and religious affiliation of the parents of the child.

(5) Identification of proceedings in which any decree of termination of parental rights, or parental rights and duties, with respect to the child was entered.

(6) The residence of the parents or parent of the child, if there has been no such decree of termination.

(7) A statement that all consents required by section 2711 (relating to consents necessary to adoption) are attached as exhibits or the basis upon which the consents are not required.

(8) An itemized accounting of moneys and consideration paid or to be paid to or received by the intermediary or to or by any other person or persons to the knowledge of the intermediary by reason of the adoption placement.

(9) A full description and statement of the value of all property owned or possessed by the child.

(10) A statement that no provision of any statute regulating the interstate placement of children has been violated with respect to the placement of the child.

(11) If no birth certificate or certification of registration of birth can be obtained, a statement of the reason therefor.

(12) A statement that medical history information was obtained and if not obtained, a statement of the reason therefor.

(c) Appropriate relief.—The court may provide appropriate relief where it finds that the moneys or consideration reported or reportable pursuant to subsection (b)(8) are excessive.

(d) Permissible reimbursement of expenses.—Payments made by the adoptive parents to an intermediary or a third party for reimbursement of the following expenses, calculated without regard to the income of the adoptive parents, are permissible and are not in violation of 18 Pa.C.S. § 4305 (relating to dealing in infant children):

(1) Medical and hospital expenses incurred by the natural mother for prenatal care and those medical and hospital expenses incurred by the natural mother and child incident to birth.

(2) Medical, hospital and foster care expenses incurred on behalf of the child prior to the decree of adoption.

(3) Reasonable expenses incurred by the agency or a third party for adjustment counseling and training services provided to the adoptive parents and for home studies or investigations.

(4) Reasonable administrative expenses incurred by the agency, to include overhead costs and attorney fees.

(June 23, 1982, P.L.617, No.174, eff. 60 days; Jan. 15, 1988, P.L.16, No.7, eff. imd.)

1988 Amendment. Act 7 added subsec. (d) and provided in section 2 of the act that Act 7 shall apply to expenses incurred for adoption decrees made after the effective date of Act 7, regardless of whether or not the expenses were incurred prior to or after the effective date of Act 7.

1982 Amendment. Act 174 amended subsec. (b) and added subsec. (c).

Cross References. Section 2533 is referred to in sections 2535, 2701, 2901 of this title.

§ 2534. Exhibits.

The report of the intermediary shall have attached to it the following exhibits:

(1) A birth certificate or certification of registration of birth of the child if it can be obtained.

(2) All consents to adoption required by section 2711 (relating to consents necessary to adoption).

(3) A certified copy of any decree of termination of parental rights or parental rights and duties made by a court other than the court in which the petition for adoption will be filed.

Cross References. Section 2534 is referred to in section 2702 of this title.

§ 2535. Investigation.

(a) General rule.—When a report required by section 2531 (relating to report of intention to adopt) has been filed, the court shall cause an investigation to be made and a report filed by a local public child care agency, a voluntary child care agency with its consent or an appropriate person designated by the court. In lieu of the investigation, the court may accept an investigation made by the agency which placed the child and the report of investigation in such cases may be incorporated into the report of the intermediary required by section 2533 (relating to report of intermediary).

(b) Matters covered.—The investigation shall cover all pertinent information regarding the child's eligibility for adoption and the suitability of the placement, including the physical, mental and emotional needs and welfare of the child, and the child's and the adopting parents' age, sex, health and racial, ethnic and religious background.

(c) Payment of costs.—The court may establish the procedure for the payment of investigation costs.

Cross References. Section 2535 is referred to in sections 2724, 2901, 2905, 6344 of this title.

SUBCHAPTER E
PENNSYLVANIA ADOPTION COOPERATIVE EXCHANGE

Sec.
2551. Definitions.
2552. Pennsylvania Adoption Cooperative Exchange.
2553. Registration of children.
2554. Responsibilities of PACE.
2555. Responsibilities of public and private agencies.
2556. Related activities of agencies unaffected.
2557. Regulations and staff.
2558. Retroactive application of subchapter.

Enactment. Subchapter E was added December 19, 1990, P.L.1240, No.206, effective in 90 days.

§ 2551. Definitions.

The following words and phrases when used in this subchapter shall have the meanings given to them in this section unless the context clearly indicates otherwise:

"Department." The Department of Public Welfare of the Commonwealth.

"PACE." The Pennsylvania Adoption Cooperative Exchange.

§ 2552. Pennsylvania Adoption Cooperative Exchange.

There shall be a Pennsylvania Adoption Cooperative Exchange in the Office of Children, Youth and Families of the Department of Public Welfare.

§ 2553. Registration of children.

(a) Mandatory registration.—PACE shall register and be responsible for the review and referral of children for whom parental rights have been terminated for 90 days and for whom no report of intention to adopt has been filed in the court of common pleas.

(b) Optional registration.—PACE may also register children where restoration to the biological family is neither possible nor appropriate, a petition to terminate parental rights has been filed and adoption is planned pending identification of an adoptive parent or parents. However, information about these children shall not be publicized without prior approval by the department, which shall ensure the anonymity of these children until such time as parental rights are terminated.

(c) Children excluded from registration.—A child for whom termination of parental rights is being appealed in a court shall not be registered with PACE as available for adoption. Identifying information of such children shall be forwarded to PACE by the agency, with reference to the specific reason for which the child is not to be placed on the listing service.

Cross References. Section 2553 is referred to in section 2555 of this title.

§ 2554. Responsibilities of PACE.

PACE shall be responsible for the following:

(1) Registration of adoptive parent applicants who have been approved by agencies.

(2) Accumulation and dissemination of statistical information regarding all children registered with PACE.

(3) Creation and administration of a public information program designed to inform potential adoptive parents of the need for adoptive homes for children registered with PACE.

(4) Preparation and distribution of a photographic listing service on children registered with PACE.

(5) Preparation of annual reports concerning functions of PACE regarding the children and the prospective parents listed with PACE. The reports shall be submitted annually to the Health and Welfare and Judiciary Committees of the House of Representatives, to the Public Health and Welfare and Judiciary Committees of the Senate and to the Governor.

(6) Coordination of its functions with other state, regional and national adoption exchanges.

§ 2555. Responsibilities of public and private agencies.

All public and licensed private child service agencies shall register all children with PACE for whom parental rights have been terminated for 90 days and for whom no report of intention to adopt has been filed in the court of common pleas. A public or licensed private agency may register other children as set forth in section 2553(b) (relating to registration of children).

§ 2556. Related activities of agencies unaffected.

This subchapter shall not be construed to limit or delay actions by agencies or institutions to arrange for adoptions or other related matters on their own initiative and shall not alter or restrict the duties, authority and confidentiality of the agencies and institutions in those matters.

§ 2557. Regulations and staff.

The department shall promulgate necessary regulations and shall hire the staff which is necessary to implement this subchapter.

§ 2558. Retroactive application of subchapter.

This subchapter shall apply retroactively to all children for whom:

(1) Parental rights have been terminated and for whom no report of intention to adopt has been filed in the court of common pleas.

(2) Restoration to the biological family is neither possible nor appropriate, a petition to terminate parental rights has been filed and adoption is planned pending identification of an adoptive parent or parents.

CHAPTER 27
PETITION FOR ADOPTION

Subchapter

A. Petition
B. Consents
C. Hearings
D. Voluntary Agreement for Continuing Contact

Enactment. Chapter 27 was added October 15, 1980, P.L.934, No.163, effective January 1, 1981.

SUBCHAPTER A
PETITION

Sec.

2701. Contents of petition for adoption.
2702. Exhibits.

§ 2701. Contents of petition for adoption.

A petition for adoption shall set forth:

(1) The full name, residence, marital status, age, occupation, religious affiliation and racial background of the adopting parent or parents and their relationship, if any, to the adoptee.

(2) That the reports under sections 2530 (relating to home study and preplacement report), 2531 (relating to report of intention to adopt) and 2533 (relating to report of intermediary) have been filed, if required.

(3) The name and address of the intermediary, if any.

(4) The full name of the adoptee and the fact and length of time of the residence of the adoptee with the adopting parent or parents.

(5) If there is no intermediary or if no report of the intermediary has been filed or if the adoptee is over the age of 18 years, all vital statistics and other information enumerated and required to be stated of record by section 2533, so far as applicable.

(6) If a change in name of the adoptee is desired, the new name.

(7) That all consents required by section 2711 (relating to consents necessary to adoption) are attached as exhibits or the basis upon which such consents are not required.

(8) That it is the desire of the petitioner or the petitioners that the relationship of parent and child be established between the petitioner or petitioners and the adoptee.

(9) If no birth certificate or certification of registration of birth can be obtained, a statement of the reason therefor and an allegation of the efforts made to obtain the certificate with a request that the court establish a date and place of birth at the adoption hearing on the basis of the evidence presented.

§ 2702. Exhibits.

The petition shall have attached to it the following exhibits:

(1) The consent or consents required by section 2711 (relating to consents necessary to adoption).

(2) If not already filed with a report of an intermediary, the exhibits enumerated in section 2534 (relating to exhibits).

SUBCHAPTER B
CONSENTS

Sec.

2711. Consents necessary to adoption.
2712. Consents not naming adopting parents.
2713. When other consents not required.
2714. When consent of parent not required.

§ 2711. Consents necessary to adoption.

(a) General rule.—Except as otherwise provided in this part, consent to an adoption shall be required of the following:

(1) The adoptee, if over 12 years of age.

(2) The spouse of the adopting parent, unless they join in the adoption petition.

(3) The parents or surviving parent of an adoptee who has not reached the age of 18 years.

(4) The guardian of an incapacitated adoptee.

(5) The guardian of the person of an adoptee under the age of 18 years, if any there be, or of the person or persons having the custody of the adoptee, if any such person can be found, whenever the adoptee has no parent whose consent is required.

(b) Husband of natural mother.—The consent of the husband of the mother shall not be necessary if, after notice to the husband, it is proved to the satisfaction of the court by evidence, including testimony of the natural mother, that the husband of the natural mother is not the natural father of the child. Absent such proof, the consent of a former husband of the natural mother shall be required if he was the husband of the natural mother at any time within one year prior to the birth of the adoptee.

(c) Validity of consent.—No consent shall be valid if it was executed prior to or within 72 hours after the birth of the child. A putative father may execute a consent at any time after receiving notice of the expected or actual birth of the child. Any consent given outside this Commonwealth shall be valid for purposes of this section if it was given in accordance with the laws of the jurisdiction where it was executed. A consent to an adoption may only be revoked as set forth in this subsection. The revocation of a consent shall be in writing and shall be served upon the agency or adult to whom the child was relinquished. The following apply:

(1) Except as otherwise provided in paragraph (3):

   (i) For a consent to an adoption executed by a birth father or a putative father, the consent is irrevocable more than 30 days after the birth of the child or the execution of the consent, whichever occurs later.

   (ii) For a consent to an adoption executed by a birth mother, the consent is irrevocable more than 30 days after the execution of the consent.

(2) An individual may not waive the revocation period under paragraph (1).

(3) Notwithstanding paragraph (1), the following apply:

   (i) An individual who executed a consent to an adoption may challenge the validity of the consent only by filing a petition alleging fraud or duress within the earlier of the following time frames:

      (A) Sixty days after the birth of the child or the execution of the consent, whichever occurs later.

      (B) Thirty days after the entry of the adoption decree.

(ii) A consent to an adoption may be invalidated only if the alleged fraud or duress under subparagraph (i) is proven by:
   (A) A preponderance of the evidence in the case of consent by a person 21 years of age or younger; or
   (B) clear and convincing evidence in all other cases.

(d) Contents of consent.—

(1) The consent of a parent of an adoptee under 18 years of age shall set forth the name, age and marital status of the parent, the relationship of the consenter to the child, the name of the other parent or parents of the child and the following:

I hereby voluntarily and unconditionally consent to the adoption of the above named child.

I understand that by signing this consent I indicate my intent to permanently give up all rights to this child.

I understand such child will be placed for adoption.

I understand I may revoke this consent to permanently give up all rights to this child by placing the revocation in writing and serving it upon the agency or adult to whom the child was relinquished.

If I am the birth father or putative father of the child, I understand that this consent to an adoption is irrevocable unless I revoke it within 30 days after either the birth of the child or my execution of the consent, whichever occurs later, by delivering a written revocation to (insert the name and address of the agency coordinating the adoption) or (insert the name and address of an attorney who represents the individual relinquishing parental rights or prospective adoptive parent of the child) or (insert the court of the county in which the voluntary relinquishment form was or will be filed).

If I am the birth mother of the child, I understand that this consent to an adoption is irrevocable unless I revoke it within 30 days after executing it by delivering a written revocation to (insert the name and address of the agency coordinating the adoption) or (insert the name and address of an attorney who represents the individual relinquishing parental rights or prospective adoptive parent of the child) or (insert the court of the county in which the voluntary relinquishment form was or will be filed).

I have read and understand the above and I am signing it as a free and voluntary act.

(2) The consent shall include the date and place of its execution and names and addresses and signatures of at least two persons who witnessed its execution and their relationship to the consenter.

2004 Amendment. Act 21 amended subsec. (c) and (d). Note: The amendment of 23 Pa.C.S. §§ 2502(a), 2504(a), 2531(b)(6) and 2711(c) and (d)(1) shall apply to adoptions which are initiated on or after the effective date of this section (May 24, 2004).

1982 Amendment. Act 174 added subsecs. (c) and (d).

1992 Amendment. Act 24 amended subsec. (a)(4). Act 34 amended subsecs. (c) and (d).

Cross References. Section 2711 is referred to in sections 2504, 2533, 2534, 2701, 2702 of this title.

§ 2712. Consents not naming adopting parents.

A consent to a proposed adoption meeting all the requirements of this part but which does not name or otherwise identify the adopting parent or parents shall be valid if it contains a statement that it is voluntarily executed without disclosure of the name or other identification of the adopting parent or parents.

§ 2713. When other consents not required.

The court, in its discretion, may dispense with consents other than that of the adoptee to a petition for adoption when:

(1) the adoptee is over 18 years of age; or

(2) the adoptee is under 18 years of age and has no parent living whose consent is required.

§ 2714. When consent of parent not required.

Consent of a parent to adoption shall not be required if a decree of termination with regard to such parent has been entered. When parental rights have not previously been terminated, the court may find that consent of a parent of the adoptee is not required if, after notice and hearing as prescribed in section 2513 (relating to hearing), the court finds that grounds exist for involuntary termination under section 2511 (relating to grounds for involuntary termination).

SUBCHAPTER C
HEARINGS

Sec.
2721. Notice of hearing.
2722. Place of hearing.
2723. Attendance at hearing.
2724. Testimony and investigation.
2725. Religious belief.

§ 2721. Notice of hearing.

The court shall fix a time and place for hearing. Notice of the hearing shall be given to all persons whose consents are required and to such other persons as the court shall direct. Notice to the parent or parents of the adoptee, if required, may be given by the intermediary or someone acting on his behalf. Notice shall be by personal service or by registered mail to the last known address of the person to be notified or in such other manner as the court shall direct.

§ 2722. Place of hearing.

The hearing shall be private or in open court as the court deems appropriate.

§ 2723. Attendance at hearing.

The adopting parent or parents and the adoptee must appear at and, if required, testify at the hearing under oath unless the court determines their presence is unnecessary. In addition, the court may require the appearance and testimony of all persons whose consents are required by this part and representatives of agencies or individuals who have acted as an intermediary if their appearance or testimony would be necessary or helpful to the court.

§ 2724. Testimony and investigation.

(a) **Testimony.**—The court shall hear testimony in support of the petition and such additional testimony as it deems necessary to inform it as to the desirability of the proposed adoption. It shall require a disclosure of all moneys and consideration paid or to be paid to any person or institution in connection with the adoption.

(b) **Investigation.**—The court may request that an investigation be made by a person or public agency or, with its consent, a voluntary agency, specifically designated by the court to verify the statements of the petition and such other facts that will give the court full knowledge of the desirability of the proposed adoption, or the court may rely in whole or in part upon a report earlier made under section 2535 (relating to investigation). In any case, the age, sex, health, social and economic status or racial, ethnic or religious background of the child or adopting parents shall not preclude an adoption but the court shall decide its desirability on the basis of the physical, mental and emotional needs and welfare of the child.

(c) Payment of investigation costs.—The court may establish a procedure for the payment of investigation costs by the petitioners or by such other persons as the court may direct.

§ 2725. Religious belief.

The intermediary may honor the preference of the natural parents as to the religious faith in which the adoptive parents intend to rear the adopted child. No person shall be denied the benefits of this part because of a religious belief in the use of spiritual means or prayer for healing.

SUBCHAPTER D
VOLUNTARY AGREEMENT FOR CONTINUING CONTACT

Sec.

2731. Purpose of subchapter.
2732. Definitions.
2733. Parties to agreement.
2734. Consent of a child.
2735. Filing and approval of an agreement.
2736. Failure to comply.
2737. Modification of agreement.
2738. Enforcement of agreement.
2739. Discontinuance of agreement.
2740. Procedures for facilitating and resolving agreements involving a county child welfare agency.
2741. Counsel.
2742. Costs.

§ 2731. Purpose of subchapter.

The purpose of this subchapter is to provide an option for adoptive parents and birth relatives to enter into a voluntary agreement for ongoing communication or contact that:

(1) is in the best interest of the child;

(2) recognizes the parties' interests and desires for ongoing communication or contact;

(3) is appropriate given the role of the parties in the child's life; and

(4) is subject to approval by the courts.

§ 2732. Definitions.

The following words and phrases when used in this subchapter shall have the meanings given to them in this section unless the context clearly indicates otherwise:

"Agency." A public or private entity, including a county agency, that:

(1) Is licensed, supervised or regulated by the Department of Public Welfare; and

(2) Provides adoption services.

"Agreement." A voluntary written agreement between an adoptive parent and a birth relative that is approved by a court and provides for continuing contact or communication between the child and the birth relative or between the adoptive parent and the birth relative as provided under this subchapter.

"Birth relative." A parent, grandparent, stepparent, sibling, uncle or aunt of the child's birth family, whether the relationship is by blood, marriage or adoption.

"Child." An individual who is under 18 years of age.

"County agency." A county children and youth social service agency established under section 405 of the act of June 24, 1937 (P.L.2017, No.396), known as the County Institution District Law, or its successor, and supervised by the Department of Public Welfare under Article IX of the act of June 13, 1967 (P.L.31, No.21), known as the Public Welfare Code.

"Department." The Department of Public Welfare of the Commonwealth.

§ 2733. Parties to agreement.

(a) **Prospective adoptive parents and birth relatives.**—A prospective adoptive parent of a child may enter into an agreement with a birth relative of the child to permit continuing contact or communication between the child and the birth relative or between the adoptive parent and the birth relative.

(b) **Guardians ad litem for siblings of adoptees.**—Where siblings have been freed for adoption through the termination of parental rights, following a dependency proceeding, and the prospective adoptive parent is not adopting all of the siblings, each such sibling who is under 18 years of age shall be represented by a guardian ad litem in the development of an agreement.

(c) **Notification.**—An agency or anyone representing the parties in an adoption shall provide notification to a prospective adoptive parent, a birth parent and a child who can be reasonably expected to understand that a prospective adoptive parent and a birth relative of a child have the option to enter into a voluntary agreement for continuing contact or communication.

(d) **Construction.**—Nothing in this chapter shall be construed to prohibit the parties from agreeing to mediation of an agreement at their own cost, including the modification of an agreement, before seeking a remedy from the court.

§ 2734. Consent of a child.

If the child is 12 years of age or older, an agreement made under this subchapter may not be entered into without the child's consent.

§ 2735. Filing and approval of an agreement.

(a) **General rule.**—An agreement shall be filed with the court that finalizes the adoption of the child.

(b) **Conditions for approval.**—The court shall approve the agreement if the court determines that:

(1) The agreement has been entered into knowingly and voluntarily by all parties. An affidavit made under oath must accompany the agreement affirmatively stating that the agreement was entered into knowingly and voluntarily and is not the product of coercion, fraud or duress. The affidavit may be executed jointly or separately.

(2) The agreement is in the best interest of the child. In making that determination, factors that the court may consider include, but are not limited to, the following:

(i) The length of time that the child has been under actual care, custody and control of a person other than a birth parent and the circumstances relating thereto.

(ii) The interaction and interrelationship of the child with birth relatives and other persons who routinely interact with the birth relatives and may significantly affect the child's best interests.

(iii) The adjustment to the child's home, school and community.

(iv) The willingness and ability of the birth relative to respect and appreciate the bond between the child and prospective adoptive parent.

(v) The willingness and ability of the prospective adoptive parent to respect and appreciate the bond between the child and the birth relative.

(vi) Any evidence of abuse or neglect of the child.

(c) **Legal effect.**—An agreement shall not be legally enforceable unless approved by the court.

§ 2736. Failure to comply.

Failure to comply with the terms of an agreement that has been approved by the court pursuant to this subchapter shall not be grounds for setting aside an adoption decree.

§ 2737. Modification of agreement.

(a) **General rule.**—Only the adoptive parent or a child who is 12 years of age or older may seek to modify an agreement by filing an action in the court that finalized the adoption.

(b) **Standard for modification.**—Before the court may enter an order modifying the agreement, it must find by clear and convincing evidence that modification serves the needs, welfare and best interest of the child.

§ 2738. Enforcement of agreement.

(a) **General rule.**—Any party to an agreement, a sibling or a child who is the subject of an agreement may seek to enforce an agreement by filing an action in the court that finalized the adoption.

(b) **Remedies.**—Any party to an agreement, a sibling or a child who is the subject of an agreement may request only specific performance in seeking to enforce an agreement and may not request monetary damages or modification of an agreement.

(c) **Requirements.**—For an agreement to be enforceable, it must be:

(1) In writing.

(2) Approved by the court on or before the date for any adoption decree.

(3) If the child is 12 years of age or older when the agreement is executed, the child must consent to the agreement at the time of its execution.

(d) **Prerequisites.**—Before the court may enter an order enforcing an agreement, it must find all of the following:

(1) The party seeking enforcement of the agreement is in substantial compliance with the agreement.

(2) By clear and convincing evidence, enforcement serves the needs, welfare and best interest of the child.

(e) **Cessation of enforceability.**—

(1) An agreement shall cease to be enforceable on the date the child turns 18 years of age unless the agreement otherwise stipulates or is modified by the court.

(2) The court issuing final approval of an agreement shall have continuing jurisdiction over enforcement of the agreement until the child turns 18 years of age, unless the agreement otherwise stipulates or is modified by the court.

(f) Exclusivity of remedy.—This section constitutes the exclusive remedy for enforcement of an agreement and no statutory or common law remedy shall be available for enforcement or damages in connection with an agreement.

§ 2739. Discontinuance of agreement.

(a) General rule.—A party to an agreement or a child that is at least 12 years of age or older may seek to discontinue an agreement by filing an action in the court that finalized the adoption.

(b) Standard for discontinuation.—Before the court may enter an order discontinuing an agreement, it must find by clear and convincing evidence that discontinuance serves the needs, welfare and best interest of the child.

§ 2740. Procedures for facilitating and resolving agreements involving a county child welfare agency.

(a) Department to develop procedures.—In termination of parental rights and adoption proceedings involving a county child welfare agency arising from a juvenile dependency case under 42 Pa.C.S. Ch. 63 (relating to juvenile matters), the department shall develop, in consultation with the Administrative Office of the Pennsylvania Courts and the Juvenile Courts Judges Commission, procedures to do the following:

(1) Facilitate the development of an agreement, when appropriate, before it is presented to the court.

(2) Resolve any requests to modify, enforce or discontinue an agreement consistent with the provisions of this subchapter.

(b) Requirements.—The procedures shall, among other provisions to be determined by the department, clearly inform the parties to and subject of an agreement how to seek modification, enforcement or discontinuance of an agreement that was approved by the court.

(c) Availability to county agencies.—The department shall make the procedures available to county agencies no later than 180 days after the effective date of this subchapter.

§ 2741. Counsel.

(a) General rule.—In proceedings under sections 2737 (relating to modification of agreement), 2738 (relating to enforcement of agreement) and 2739 (relating to discontinuance of agreement), parties shall not be entitled to court-appointed counsel.

(b) Guardians ad litem.—

(1) Notwithstanding the provisions of subsection (a), the court may appoint a guardian ad litem to represent the interests of a child in proceedings under sections 2737, 2738 and 2739 and a sibling under 18 years of age who seeks to enforce or to discontinue an agreement.

(2) When appointing a guardian ad litem under this subchapter, the court may appoint the same attorney who represents or has represented the child in any dependency proceedings or termination of parental rights proceedings.

§ 2742. Costs.

If the court finds that an action brought under section 2737 (relating to modification of agreement), 2738 (relating to enforcement of agreement) or 2739 (relating to discontinuance of agreement) was wholly insubstantial, frivolous or not advanced in good faith, the court may award attorney fees and costs to the prevailing parties.

CHAPTER 29
DECREES AND RECORDS

SUBCHAPTER A
GENERAL PROVISIONS

Sec.
2901. Time of entry of decree of adoption.
2902. Requirements and form of decree of adoption.
2903. Retention of parental status.
2904. Name of adoptee.
2905. [Repealed]
2906. Docket entries.
2907. Certificate of adoption.
2908. Foreign decree of adoption.
2909. [Repealed]
2910. Penalty for unauthorized disclosure.

Enactment. Chapter 29 was added October 15, 1980, P.L.934, No.163, effective January 1, 1981.

§ 2901. Time of entry of decree of adoption.

Unless the court for cause shown determines otherwise, no decree of adoption shall be entered unless the natural parent or parents' rights have been terminated, the investigation required by section 2535 (relating to investigation) has been completed, the report of the intermediary has been filed pursuant to section 2533 (relating to report of intermediary) and all other legal requirements have been met. If all legal requirements have been met, the court may enter a decree of adoption at any time.
(June 23, 1982, P.L.617, No.174, eff. 60 days)

§ 2902. Requirements and form of decree of adoption.

   (a) **General rule.**—If satisfied that the statements made in the petition are true, that the needs and welfare of the person proposed to be adopted will be promoted by the adoption and that all requirements of this part have been met, the court shall enter a decree so finding and directing that the person proposed to be adopted shall have all the rights of a child and heir of the adopting parent or parents and shall be subject to the duties of a child to him or them.

   (b) **Withdrawal or dismissal of petition.**—In any case in which the petition is withdrawn or dismissed, the court shall enter an appropriate order in regard to the custody of the child.

§ 2903. Retention of parental status.

Whenever a parent consents to the adoption of his child by his spouse, the parent-child relationship between him and his child shall remain whether or not he is one of the petitioners in the adoption proceeding.

§ 2904. Name of adoptee.

If requested by the petitioners, the decree may provide that the adoptee shall assume the name of the adopting parent or parents and any given first or middle names that may be chosen.

§ 2905. Impounding of proceedings and access to records. [Repealed]

2010 Amendment. Act 101 repealed this sec.

2004 Amendment. Act 148 amended subsec. (a).

1995 Amendment. Act 76 amended the heading of subsec. (d) and added subsec. (d)(3).

1992 Amendment. Act 34 amended subsecs. (a) and (d).

Cross References. Section 2905 is referred to in sections 2503, 2504, 2511, 2909 of this title.

§ 2906. Docket entries.

Upon the filing of any decree under this part, the clerk shall enter on the docket an entry showing the date of the decree. Information identifying the natural parents shall not be entered on the docket.

§ 2907. Certificate of adoption.

The clerk shall issue to the adopting parent or parents a certificate reciting that the court has granted the adoption. The certificate shall not disclose the name of any natural parent or the original name of the person adopted. The certificate shall be accepted in any legal proceedings in this Commonwealth as evidence of the fact that the adoption has been granted.

§ 2908. Foreign decree of adoption.

(a) Registration.—When a minor is adopted by a resident of this commonwealth and a final decree of adoption is made or entered in conformity with the laws of a foreign country, the adopting parent shall file a properly authenticated copy of the foreign decree of adoption, a copy of the child's visa and either the child's birth certificate or some form of birth identification with the clerk of the court in the county of residence of the parent. If the foreign decree of adoption is not in English, the adopting parent shall also file a certified English translation. If no birth certificate or birth identification can be obtained, the adopting parent shall include an affidavit stating the reason therefor.

(b) Foreign adoption registration form.—The court shall develop a foreign adoption registration form and instructions for its use. The adopting parent or parents shall sign the foreign adoption registration form indicating that they have read and understand the information provided.

(c) Contents of form.—

(1) The form shall include statements indicating that the foreign adoption may not be a full and final adoption if:

(i) Both parents, or just the sole parent if only one parent is adopting, were not present for the adoption hearing in the foreign country.

(ii) The foreign court did not enter a final adoption decree or its equivalent.

(iii) The child's visa is not the type that would afford the child full United States citizenship.

(2) The form shall notify the adopting parent or parents that an adoption decree may be obtained from the Commonwealth if the documents filed in subsection (a) are reviewed by the court and the court determines the foreign adoption was full and final.

(3) At the time of filing, a copy of the foreign decree of adoption and a certified English translation, if necessary, the child's visa and either the child's birth certificate or some form of birth identification shall be attached to the foreign registration form and submitted to the clerk of court.

(d) Foreign adoption review.—In cases where the court determines the foreign adoption was full and final, the court shall direct the clerk to enter upon the docket an entry showing the foreign court identification of the proceedings in that court and the date of the decree. The clerk shall issue to the parent a certificate of adoption as defined in section 2907 (relating to certificate of adoption). The clerk shall also send documentation to the department of health. no hearing shall be required prior to the issuance of the certificate of adoption and the parent shall not be required to obtain counsel.

(e) Readoption.—The court shall develop a standard petition, a standard court order and instructions for their use for occasions when a child must be readopted to finalize the adoption. The clerk shall provide the adopting parent with the standardized information.

(f) Records.—All documents required in subsection (a) as well as any other accompanying documents shall be kept in the files of the court as a permanent record and shall be withheld from inspection except on order of court granted upon cause shown. Information identifying the birth parents of the adoptee shall not be required. The clerk may charge a filing fee in accordance with the court's regular fee schedule as approved by the president judge.

2006 Amendment. Act 96 amended this sec., effective Sept. 5, 2006.

§ 2909. Medical history information. [Repealed]

2010 Amendment. Act 101 repealed this sec.

§ 2910. Penalty for unauthorized disclosure.

Any officer or employee of the court, other than a judge thereof, the Department of Health, the Department of Public Welfare or any agency who willfully discloses impounded or otherwise confidential information relating to an adoption, other than as expressly authorized and provided in this chapter, commits a misdemeanor of the third degree.

(Dec. 12, 1984, P.L.979, No.195, eff. 60 days; Dec. 20, 1995, P.L.685, No.76, eff. 60 days)

SUBCHAPTER B
RECORDS AND ACCESS TO INFORMATION

Sec.
2911. Definitions.
2912. Combined request for information.
2913. Reasonable fees.
2914. Immunity from liability.
2915. Court and agency records.
2916. Attorney records.

Enactment. Subchapter B was added October 27, 2010, P.L.961, No.101, effective in 180 days.

Cross References. Subchapter B is referred to in sections 2503, 2504, 2511 of this title.

§ 2911. Definitions.

The following words and phrases when used in this subchapter shall have the meanings given to them in this section unless the context clearly indicates otherwise:

"Agency records." All information collected by an agency relating to a birth family, an adoptive family and an adoptee.

"Authorization form." A form provided by the department on which an adoptee, an adoptive parent or a birth relative can authorize or prohibit the release of identifying information pursuant to the requirements of this chapter.

"Authorized representative." An individual who is appointed to conduct a search under this chapter and who has completed a standardized training program as required by the department under this chapter.

"Court records." All petitions, exhibits, reports, notes of testimony, decrees and other papers pertaining to a proceeding under this chapter or former statutes relating to adoption.

"Department." The Department of Public Welfare of the Commonwealth.

"Medical history information." Medical records and other information concerning an adoptee or an adoptee's birth family that is relevant to the present or future health care or medical treatment of the adoptee or the adoptee's birth family. The term includes, but is not limited to, the following:

(1) Otherwise confidential or privileged information, if identifying information has been removed under section 2925 (relating to providing information from registry).

(2) Information about the birth parents of a child that may concern a potential hereditary or congenital medical problem.

"**Noncertified copy of original birth record.**" A summary of original birth record, similar in form to a certified copy of an original birth record and consisting of only the names and ages of the birth parents, the date and county of the birth of the child and the name given to the child at birth.

"**Social history information.**" The term includes, but is not limited to, the following:

(1) Information about the adoptee and birth relatives of the adoptee, including economic, cultural and ethnic information.

(2) A developmental history of the adoptee, including the circumstances at birth, early development and subsequent age-appropriate task development.

(3) The social experiences of the adoptee, including abuse and neglect, out-of-home care and patterns of interpersonal relationships.

(4) The educational experiences of the adoptee, including the name of schools attended and dates of enrollment, academic performance, extracurricular activities and special interests.

(5) The current functioning of the adoptee, including behavioral patterns and relationships.

(6) The circumstances surrounding the adoption.

"**Summary of original birth record.**" (Deleted by amendment).

(Nov. 3, 2016, P.L.993, No.127, eff. imd.)

2016 Amendment. Act 127 added the def. of "noncertified copy of original birth record" and deleted the def. of "summary of original birth record."

References in Text. The Department of Public Welfare, referred to in this section, was redesignated as the Department of Human Services by Act 132 of 2014.

§ 2912. Combined request for information.

An individual authorized to receive both nonidentifying information and identifying information may file a single written request under Subchapter D (relating to release of information).

§ 2913. Reasonable fees.

Any court or agency may charge reasonable fees for services provided under this chapter.

§ 2914. Immunity from liability.

(a) **General rule.**—A person or agency, including the Commonwealth and any of its governmental subdivisions, that participates in good faith in providing services under this chapter has immunity from civil liability that may otherwise result by reason of an action or a failure to act under this chapter.

(b) **Presumption of good faith.**—For the purpose of a civil proceeding, the good faith of any person or agency that provides services pursuant to this chapter is presumed.

§ 2915. Court and agency records.

(a) **General rule.**—All court and agency records shall be maintained as a permanent record and withheld from inspection except as provided under this chapter.

(b) **Who may access court or agency records.**—Only the following are authorized to access court or agency records for the purpose of releasing nonidentifying or identifying information under this chapter:

(1) The court which finalized the adoption.

(2) The agency that coordinated the adoption.

(3) A successor agency authorized by the court which finalized the adoption.

(c) **Disposition of agency records upon closure.**—

(1) As soon as practicable, but not less than 30 days prior to the date on which an agency ceases to operate as a legal entity in this commonwealth, the agency shall, unless it has applied to operate as a new legal entity, notify the department of its intention to cease operating.

(2) Within this time period, the agency shall submit a plan to the department relating to the closure and transfer of case records to another agency. the plan shall be subject to approval by the department.

(3) In preparation for its closure and transfer of case records, the agency shall label its case records to identify the respective court that finalized an adoption or where a petition to terminate parental rights or to adopt has been filed.

(4) The department shall notify each court so identified by the agency of the name, address and telephone number of the agency to which case records have been transferred.

§ 2916. Attorney records.

An attorney representing a party to an adoption proceeding or acting as counsel or guardian ad litem for a child in a proceeding under this part may forward records and information relating to the child, the child's birth family and the adoptive family to the court which finalized the adoption, as established by general rule by the Supreme Court. Such records and information shall be treated as court records for purposes of this chapter.

SUBCHAPTER C
INFORMATION REGISTRY

Sec.

2921. Establishment of registry.
2922. Informational material.
2923. Filing information with registry.
2924. Who may request information from registry.
2925. Providing information from registry.
2926. Rules and regulations.

§ 2921. Establishment of registry.

The department shall do all of the following:

(1) Establish a Statewide confidential registry for the receipt, filing and retention of medical and social history information and authorization forms for all adoptions finalized or registered in this Commonwealth.

(2) Prescribe and distribute forms on which an adoptee, an adoptive parent and a birth parent may:

(i) Request identifying information or contact.

(ii) Authorize or refuse to authorize the release of identifying information or contact.

(iii) File and update information with the registry.

(3) Retain information filed with the registry as a permanent record.

(4) Disseminate the information pursuant to the requirements of this subchapter.

§ 2922. Informational material.

The department shall publicize the availability of the registry and the manner in which information may be filed with and obtained from the registry.

§ 2923. Filing information with registry.

An adoptee, an adoptive parent and a birth parent may at any time file and update medical and social history information with the registry on a form developed by the department.

§ 2924. Who may request information from registry.

The following individuals may request information from the registry:

(1) An adoptee who is at least 18 years of age.

(2) An adoptive parent of an adoptee who is under 18 years of age, adjudicated incapacitated or deceased.

(3) A legal guardian of an adoptee who is under 18 years of age or adjudicated incapacitated.

(4) A descendant of a deceased adoptee.

(5) The birth parent of an adoptee who is at least 21 years of age.

(6) A parent of a birth parent of an adoptee who is at least 21 years of age if the birth parent consents, is adjudicated incapacitated or is deceased.

(7) A birth sibling of an adoptee, if both the birth sibling and adoptee are at least 21 years of age, and:

   (i) the birth sibling remained in the custody of the birth parent and the birth parent consents, is deceased or adjudicated incapacitated;

   (ii) both the birth sibling and adoptee were adopted out of the same birth family; or

   (iii) the birth sibling was not adopted out of the birth family and did not remain in the custody of the birth parent.

§ 2925. Providing information from registry.

(a) Nonidentifying information.—Nonidentifying information, if available, shall be provided to the requester within 30 days of the request.

(b) Identifying information.—

(1) If an authorization form is on file, the department shall notify the requester within 30 days of the request whether information may be released.

(2) If there is no authorization on file, the department shall designate an authorized representative to:

   (i) Use reasonable efforts to locate the subject of the request.

   (ii) If the subject of the request is located, obtain written authorization from the subject before any information is released.

(c) Confidentiality of information.—In conducting a search, the court or agency shall ensure that no individual, other than a birth parent, is informed of the adoptee's existence and relationship to the birth parent.

(d) When inquiry not mandatory.—An authorized representative of the court or agency conducting a search may not make an inquiry which the representative reasonably believes may compromise the confidentiality relating to the relationship between the adoptee and a birth parent of the adoptee.

(e) Authorization form.—An authorization form allowing the release of identifying information may be withdrawn at any time by the individual who signed the authorization form.

(f) Editing information.—Before the release of information from the registry, the department shall remove any identifying information, unless authorized in writing by the subject of the information to release the identifying information.

§ 2926. Rules and regulations.

The department shall promulgate rules and regulations necessary to implement this subchapter. The department may request, but shall not require, an agency to submit medical and social history information for adoptions finalized or registered in this Commonwealth prior to the effective date of this subchapter.

SUBCHAPTER D
RELEASE OF INFORMATION

Sec.
2931. Access to Information.
2932. Nonidentifying Information.
2933. Identifying Information.
2934. Statement of Medical and Social History Information.
2935. Confidentiality.
2936. Refusal to Search.
2937. Original Birth Record.
2938. Rules and Regulations.

§ 2931. Access to Information.

(a) Who may access information.—The following individuals may file a written request for nonidentifying information or identifying information or contact with the court which finalized the adoption, the agency which coordinated the adoption or a successor agency:

(1) An adoptee who is at least 18 years of age.

(2) An adoptive parent of an adoptee who is:

(i) Under 18 years of age;

(ii) Adjudicated incapacitated and is 18 years of age or older; or

(iii) Deceased.

(3) A legal guardian of an adoptee who is under 18 years of age or adjudicated incapacitated.

(4) A descendant of a deceased adoptee.

(5) A birth parent of an adoptee who is 21 years of age or older.

(6) A parent of a birth parent of an adoptee who is 21 years of age or older, if the birth parent consents, is adjudicated incapacitated or is deceased.

(7) A birth sibling of an adoptee, if both the birth sibling and adoptee are 21 years of age or older and:

(i) The birth sibling remained in the custody of the birth parent and the birth parent consents, is deceased or adjudicated incapacitated;

(ii) Both the birth sibling and the adoptee were adopted out of the same birth family; or

(iii) The birth sibling was not adopted out of the birth family and did not remain in the custody of the birth parent.

(b) Who may be the subject of a request for information.—An individual enumerated under subsection (a) may request nonidentifying or identifying information regarding or contact with the following individuals:

(1) An adoptee who is 21 years of age or older.

(2) A birth parent of an adoptee.

(3) A parent of a birth parent of an adoptee who is 21 years of age or older, if the birth parent consents, is adjudicated incapacitated or is deceased.

(4) A birth sibling of an adoptee, if both the birth sibling and the adoptee are 21 years of age or older and:

(i) The birth sibling remained in the custody of the birth parent and the birth parent consents, is deceased or adjudicated incapacitated;

(ii) Both the birth sibling and the adoptee were adopted out of the same birth family; or

(iii) The birth sibling was not adopted out of the birth family and did not remain in the custody of the birth parent.

§ 2932. Nonidentifying Information.

(a) Notice of receipt of request.—When the court or agency receives a written request for nonidentifying information, it shall, within 30 days, notify the individual requesting the information of its receipt of the request.

(b) Furnishing nonidentifying information.—The court or agency shall, within 120 days, review its records and furnish to the requester any information concerning the adoption that will not compromise the confidentiality of the relationship between the adoptee and the adoptee's birth parent.

§ 2933. Identifying information.

(a) Notice of availability of records.—The court or agency shall, within 120 days of receiving a written request for identifying information or contact, do all of the following:

(1) Determine whether it has in its possession any records relating to the adoptee.

(2) Conduct a good faith search for identifying information, which search shall be commenced within 120 days. The search for information shall only be conducted by an authorized representative appointed by:

(i) The court in which the adoption was finalized;

(ii) The agency that coordinated the adoption;

(iii) A successor, by merger or acquisition, of the agency that coordinated the adoption; or

(iv) If neither the agency nor a successor exists, by an agency authorized by the court.

The authorized representative shall review the court and agency record for identifying information regarding the birth or adoptive family and shall determine whether an authorization form has been filed with the court or agency.

(3) Notify any other court or agency listed in its records of the existence of the request for identifying information.

(4) Ask any other court or agency listed in its records to advise if an authorization form has been filed.

(5) Contact the information registry established under Subchapter C (relating to information registry), advise the registry of the request for identifying information and ask whether an authorization form has been filed.

(6) Notify the requesting individual of its findings pursuant to this subsection.

(b) No authorization form.—If an applicable authorization form is not located, all of the following apply:

(1) The authorized representative shall use reasonable efforts to locate the subject of the search.

(2) If the subject of the search is located, the authorized representative shall obtain written authorization from the subject before any identifying information is released or contact between the parties is made.

(3) If the requester is an adoptee seeking the identity of a birth parent, the identity of a deceased birth parent may be disclosed.

(4) If the requester is an adoptee seeking the identity of both birth parents and only one birth parent agrees to the disclosure, only the information relating to that birth parent shall be disclosed.

(c) Withdrawal of authorization form.—An individual may withdraw the individual's authorization form at any time.

§ 2934. Statement of medical and social history information.

(a) **Filing places.**—A statement regarding medical and social history information may be filed with the following:

(1) The court that terminated parental rights.

(2) The court that finalized the adoption.

(3) The agency that coordinated the adoption.

(4) The information registry established under Subchapter C (relating to information registry).

(b) **Individuals authorized to file and request.**—The following individuals may at any time file, update and request a statement regarding medical and social history information:

(1) An adoptee who is 18 years of age or older.

(2) An adoptive parent or legal guardian of an adoptee who is under 18 years of age or adjudicated incapacitated.

(3) A descendant of a deceased adoptee.

(4) A birth parent.

(5) A legal guardian of an adjudicated incapacitated birth parent.

(6) A survivor of a deceased birth parent.

(c) **Maintenance of record.**—A statement regarding medical and social history information shall be maintained as a permanent record.

(d) **Forwarding statement.**—If a statement regarding medical and social history information is filed in the court that terminated parental rights, a copy of the statement shall be forwarded to the court that finalized the adoption and the information registry established under Subchapter C.

(e) **Notice of filing.**—

(1) Within 30 days of filing of a statement regarding medical and social history information, the court, agency or information registry shall give notice of its receipt to the individual who filed the statement.

(2) Within 120 days after a statement is filed, the court, agency or information registry shall give notice of the filing to the individual who is at least 21 years of age and whom the information is intended to benefit, if known or identified in its records.

(f) **Request for information.**—

(1) When the court or agency receives a written request for medical and social history information, it shall notify the requester within 120 days whether it possesses any medical and social history information relating to the adoption.

(2) Within 120 days of locating medical and social history information, the court or agency shall do the following:

(i) For nonidentifying information, review and furnish to the requester any medical and social history information that will not compromise the confidentiality of the relationship between the adoptee and the adoptee's birth parent.

(ii) For identifying information, if an authorization form is on file with the court, agency or information registry, furnish to the requester the available identifying information in its records.

(g) **No information or authorization form on file.**—If a court or agency receives a request for medical and social history information and finds that no such information is in its records or that no authorization form is on file, the court or agency shall do the following:

(1) Contact the subject of the request and ask that the subject:

(i) provide nonidentifying information for the benefit of the requester; or

(ii) file an authorization form.

(2) If the subject of the request cannot be located from information contained in the court records, appoint an authorized representative to use reasonable efforts to locate the subject.

(3) If nonidentifying information is provided by the subject of the request, provide the nonidentifying information to the requester.

(4) If an authorization form is filed, provide identifying information to the requester.

(h) Deceased birth parent.—If the requester is an adoptee seeking information about a birth parent and the birth parent is deceased, any information on file regarding the deceased birth parent may be disclosed.

§ 2935. Confidentiality.

(a) General rule.—In conducting a search, the court or agency shall ensure that no individual, other than a birth parent, is informed of the adoptee's existence and relationship to the birth parent of the adoptee.

(b) When inquiry not mandatory.—An authorized representative of the court or agency conducting a search may not make an inquiry which the representative reasonably believes may compromise the confidentiality relating to the relationship between the adoptee and a birth parent of the adoptee.

§ 2936. Refusal to search.

(a) Agency.—

(1) If an agency is satisfied that a request could cause physical or emotional harm to the requesting individual or others, the agency may decline to conduct a search to determine whether an individual will authorize the disclosure of identifying information or contact under this chapter.

(2) An agency may decline to commence or conduct a search required under this chapter if the requester fails to pay the reasonable costs associated with commencing or conducting the search.

(3)(i) An agency that declines to conduct a search shall refer the request to the court that finalized the adoption and inform the court of its reasons for declining the request.

(ii) The agency shall notify the requester of the referral and identify the court to which the referral was made.

(b) Court.—

(1) If a court is satisfied that a request could cause physical or emotional harm to the requesting individual or others, the court receiving a request for identifying information or contact may decline to perform a search.

(2) A court that declines to conduct a search shall inform the requesting individual of its decision in writing and of the procedures for appeal of that decision.

§ 2937. Original birth record.

(a) General rule.—Notwithstanding any other provision of law, an adoptee who is at least 18 years of age and who has graduated from high school, completed a General Educational Development program or has legally withdrawn from secondary schooling or, if the adoptee is deceased, the adoptee's descendants, may apply to the Department of Health for the adoptee's noncertified copy of original birth record. Subject to subsections (b) and (c), the Department of Health shall issue a noncertified copy of original birth record within 45 days of receipt of an application if the application complies with the requirements of subsection (d).

(b) Contact preference.—The Department of Health shall develop and, upon request, make available to each birth parent named on the original birth certificate a contact preference form on which the birth parent may state a preference regarding contact by an adoptee who is the birth child of the birth parent. Upon such request, the Department of Health shall also provide the birth parent with an updated medical history form, which shall be completed and returned, together with the completed contact preference form, by the birth parent to the Department of Health. The contact preference form shall provide the birth parent with options, in substantially the following form, from which the birth parent shall select one:

(1) I would like to be contacted. I have completed the contact preference form and an updated medical history form and am filing them with the Department of Health.

(2) I would prefer to be contacted only through an intermediary. I have completed the contact preference form and an updated medical history form and am filing them with the Department of Health.

(3) Do not contact me. I may change this preference by filling out another contact preference form. I have completed the contact preference form and an updated medical history form and am filing them with the Department of Health.

(c) **Redaction request form.**—A birth parent may request that the birth parent's name be redacted from a noncertified copy of original birth record issued to an adoptee in accordance with the following:

(1) The Department of Health shall prescribe a birth parent's name redaction request form. The form shall include all of the following:

(i) Information about the procedures and requirements for a birth parent to do either of the following:

(A) Have the form placed in the adoption file of the adoptee who is the birth child of the birth parent so that the birth parent's name is redacted from the noncertified copy of original birth record issued to the adoptee.

(B) Have the form removed from the adoption file of the adoptee if the birth parent later decides to permit the birth parent's name to be included on the noncertified copy of original birth record.

(ii) Provisions necessary for the Department of Health to be able to identify the adoption file of the adoptee to whom the form pertains.

(iii) A place for the birth parent to attest that the birth parent is the birth parent of the adoptee to whom the form pertains.

(2) The Department of Health shall make a birth parent's name redaction request form available upon request following the effective date of this subsection. The Department of Health shall accept a name redaction request form if all of the following apply:

(i) The form has been notarized.

(ii) The birth parent provides two items of identification of the birth parent.

(iii) If a medical history for the birth parent was not previously prepared, or the medical history was prepared but needs to be updated, the birth parent does the following, as appropriate:

(A) Completes a medical history form.

(B) Updates the birth parent's medical history information.

(iv) The Department of Health is satisfied that the form has been substantially completed.

(3) The Department of Health shall file an accepted name redaction request form in the adoption file of the adoptee to whom the form pertains.

(4) A birth parent may request at any time that the Department of Health remove the name redaction request form from the adoption file of the adoptee to whom the form pertains. The Department of Health shall remove the form if the birth parent provides the department all of the following:

(i) Two items of identification of the birth parent.

(ii) Information the Department of Health needs to be able to identify the adoption file of the adoptee to whom the form pertains.

(iii) A notarized attestation that the birth parent is the birth parent of the adoptee to whom the form pertains.

(5) A name redaction request form removed from an adoption file shall be destroyed.

(6) The Department of Health shall include on its Internet website information about birth parents' name redaction request forms. All of the following information shall be provided:

(i) The purpose of the form.

(ii) The procedures to be followed and requirements to be met for the Department of Health to accept the form.

(iii) The date when birth parents may begin to file the form with the Department of Health.

(iv) The procedures to be followed and requirements to be met for having the form removed from an adoption file.

(v) Any other information the Department of Health considers necessary.

(7) If the birth parent dies after submitting a name redaction request form, a noncertified copy of original birth record may be provided to the adoptee without redaction of the deceased birth parent's name.

(d) Application.—An application under subsection (a) shall be in a form acceptable to the Department of Health and shall include the following information:

(1) The adoptee's current name and name assumed at the time of adoption.

(2) The adoptee's address.

(3) The adoptee's age and date of birth.

(4) The adoptee's gender at birth.

(5) Proof of identification.

(6) The adoptee's telephone number.

(7) Any other information required by the Department of Health, but only to the extent the information is necessary for the Department of Health to verify the identity of the applicant, locate the relevant records or provide the adoptee's noncertified copy of original birth record to the adoptee.

(e) Application procedures.—The Department of Health shall develop policies and procedures necessary to comply with this section within 210 days of the effective date of this subsection.

(f) Fee.—The Department of Health may charge a fee for issuing a noncertified copy of original birth record as required by this section. The fee charged shall not exceed the fee for a certified copy of an original birth record provided in section 609-A of the act of April 9, 1929 (P.L.177, No.175), known as The Administrative Code of 1929.

(g) Construction.—Nothing in this section shall be construed to permit disclosure of an adoptee's birth record to the birth parents of an adoptee.
(Nov. 3, 2016, P.L.993, No.127, eff. imd.)

> **2016 Amendment.** Act 127 amended the entire section, effective immediately as to subsec. (e) and in one year as to the remainder of the section.

§ 2938. Rules and regulations.

The department shall promulgate rules and regulations implementing a standardized training program for court-appointed and agency-appointed authorized representatives conducting searches under this subchapter.

PART IV
DIVORCE

Chapter

31. Preliminary Provisions
33. Dissolution of Marital Status
35. Property Rights
37. Alimony and Support
39. Mediation

Enactment. Part IV was added December 19, 1990, P.L.1240, No.206, effective in 90 days.

Construction. See section 5 of Act 206 of 1990 in the appendix to this title for special provisions relating to construction of Divorce Code.

Cross References. Part IV is referred to in section 4106 of this title; sections 5948, 8127 of Title 42 (Judiciary and Judicial Procedure).

Actions of divorce or for annulment of marriage, see Pa.R.C.P. No.1920.1 et seq.

Note: The Official Comments provided throughout the Divorce Code were supplied by the Joint State Government Commission, and may be used to determine the intent of the Legislature. See 1 Pa.C.S. § 1939.

CHAPTER 31
PRELIMINARY PROVISIONS

Sec.

3101. Short title of part.
3102. Legislative findings and intent.
3103. Definitions.
3104. Bases of jurisdiction.
3105. Effect of agreement between parties.
3106. Premarital agreements.

Enactment. Chapter 31 was added December 19, 1990, P.L.1240, No.206, effective in 90 days.

§ 3101. Short title of part.

This part shall be known and may be cited as the Divorce Code.

§ 3102. Legislative findings and intent.

(a) **Policy.**—The family is the basic unit in society and the protection and preservation of the family is of paramount public concern. Therefore, it is the policy of the Commonwealth to:

(1) Make the law for legal dissolution of marriage effective for dealing with the realities of matrimonial experience.

(2) Encourage and effect reconciliation and settlement of differences between spouses, especially where children are involved.

(3) Give primary consideration to the welfare of the family rather than the vindication of private rights or the punishment of matrimonial wrongs.

(4) Mitigate the harm to the spouses and their children caused by the legal dissolution of the marriage.

(5) Seek causes rather than symptoms of family disintegration and cooperate with and utilize the resources available to deal with family problems.

(6) Effectuate economic justice between parties who are divorced or separated and grant or withhold alimony according to the actual need and ability to pay of the parties and insure a fair and just determination and settlement of their property rights.

(b) **Construction of part.**—The objectives set forth in subsection (a) shall be considered in construing provisions of this part and shall be regarded as expressing the legislative intent.

§ 3103. Definitions.

The following words and phrases when used in this part shall have the meanings given to them in this section unless the context clearly indicates otherwise:

"Alimony." An order for support granted by this Commonwealth or any other state to a spouse or former spouse in conjunction with a decree granting a divorce or annulment.

"Alimony pendente lite." An order for temporary support granted to a spouse during the pendency of a divorce or annulment proceeding.

"Convicted." Having been found guilty, having entered a plea of guilty or nolo contendere or having been accepted into Accelerated Rehabilitative Disposition.

"Divorce." Divorce from the bonds of matrimony.

"Grounds for divorce." The grounds enumerated in section 3301 (relating to grounds for divorce).

"Irretrievable breakdown." Estrangement due to marital difficulties with no reasonable prospect of reconciliation.

"Personal injury crime." An act that constitutes a misdemeanor or felony under any of the following, or criminal attempt, solicitation or conspiracy to commit any of the following:

18 Pa.C.S. Ch. 25 (relating to criminal homicide).

18 Pa.C.S. Ch. 27 (relating to assault).

18 Pa.C.S. Ch. 29 (relating to kidnapping).

18 Pa.C.S. Ch. 30 (relating to human trafficking).

18 Pa.C.S. Ch. 31 (relating to sexual offenses).

18 Pa.C.S. § 3301 (relating to arson and related offenses).

18 Pa.C.S. Ch. 37 (relating to robbery).

18 Pa.C.S. Ch. 49 Subch. B (relating to victim and witness intimidation).

75 Pa.C.S. § 3732 (relating to homicide by vehicle).

75 Pa.C.S. § 3742 (relating to accidents involving death or personal injury).

"Qualified professionals." Includes marriage counselors, psychologists, psychiatrists, social workers, ministers, priests, rabbis or other persons who, by virtue of their training and experience, are able to provide counseling.

"Separate and apart." Cessation of cohabitation, whether living in the same residence or not. In the event a complaint in divorce is filed and served, it shall be presumed that the parties commenced to live separate and apart not later than the date that the complaint was served.

"Spousal support." Care, maintenance and financial assistance.

(Nov. 29, 2004, P.L.1357, No.175, eff. 60 days; Apr. 21, 2016, P.L.166, No.24, eff. 60 days)

2016 Amendment. Act 24 added the defs. of "convicted" and "personal injury crime."

2004 Amendment. Act 175 amended the def. of "separate and apart." Section 5(1) of Act 175 provided that the amendment shall apply to complaints served before, on or after the effective date of par. (1).

Cross References. Section 3103 is referred to in section 5948 of Title 42 (Judiciary and Judicial Procedure).

§ 3104. Bases of jurisdiction.

(a) **Jurisdiction.**—The courts shall have original jurisdiction in cases of divorce and for the annulment of void or voidable marriages and shall determine, in conjunction with any decree granting a divorce or annulment, the following matters, if raised in the pleadings, and issue appropriate decrees or orders with reference thereto, and may retain continuing jurisdiction thereof:

(1) The determination and disposition of property rights and interests between spouses, including any rights created by any antenuptial, postnuptial or separation agreement and including the partition of property held as tenants by the entireties or otherwise and any accounting between them, and the order of any spousal support, alimony, alimony pendente lite, counsel fees or costs authorized by law.

(2) The future care, custody and visitation rights as to children of the marriage or purported marriage.

(3) Any support or assistance which shall be paid for the benefit of any children of the marriage or purported marriage.

(4) Any property settlement involving any of the matters set forth in paragraphs (1), (2) and (3) as submitted by the parties.

(5) Any other matters pertaining to the marriage and divorce or annulment authorized by law and which fairly and expeditiously may be determined and disposed of in such action.

(b) Residence and domicile of parties.—No spouse is entitled to commence an action for divorce or annulment under this part unless at least one of the parties has been a bona fide resident in this Commonwealth for at least six months immediately previous to the commencement of the action. Both parties shall be competent witnesses to prove their respective residence, and proof of actual residence within this Commonwealth for six months shall create a presumption of domicile within this Commonwealth.

(c) Powers of court.—The court has authority to entertain an action under this part notwithstanding the fact that the marriage of the parties and the cause for divorce occurred outside of this Commonwealth and that both parties were at the time of the occurrence domiciled outside this Commonwealth. The court also has the power to annul void or voidable marriages celebrated outside this Commonwealth at a time when neither party was domiciled within this Commonwealth.

(d) Foreign forum.—After the dissolution or annulment of a marriage in a foreign forum where a matter under subsection (a) has not been decided, a court of this Commonwealth shall have jurisdiction to determine a matter under subsection (a) to the fullest extent allowed under the Constitution of the United States.

(e) Venue.—A proceeding for divorce or annulment may be brought in the county:

(1) where the defendant resides;

(2) if the defendant resides outside of this Commonwealth, where the plaintiff resides;

(3) of matrimonial domicile, if the plaintiff has continuously resided in the county;

(4) prior to six months after the date of final separation and with agreement of the defendant, where the plaintiff resides or, if neither party continues to reside in the county of matrimonial domicile, where either party resides; or

(5) after six months after the date of final separation, where either party resides.

Note: **Suspension by Court Rule.** Section 3104(e) was suspended by Pennsylvania Rule of Civil Procedure No. 1920.91(1), as amended July 15, 1994, insofar as it applies to the practice and procedure in actions for divorce or annulment of marriage.

§ 3105. Effect of agreement between parties.

(a) Enforcement.—A party to an agreement regarding matters within the jurisdiction of the court under this part, whether or not the agreement has been merged or incorporated into the decree, may utilize a remedy or sanction set forth in this part to enforce the agreement to the same extent as though the agreement had been an order of the court except as provided to the contrary in the agreement.

(b) Certain provisions subject to modification.—A provision of an agreement regarding child support, visitation or custody shall be subject to modification by the court upon a showing of changed circumstances.

(c) Certain provisions not subject to modification.—In the absence of a specific provision to the contrary appearing in the agreement, a provision regarding the disposition of existing property rights and interests between the parties, alimony, alimony pendente lite, counsel fees or expenses shall not be subject to modification by the court.

§ 3106. Premarital agreements.

(a) General rule.—The burden of proof to set aside a premarital agreement shall be upon the party alleging the agreement to be unenforceable. A premarital agreement shall not be enforceable if the party seeking to set aside the agreement proves, by clear and convincing evidence, that:

(1) the party did not execute the agreement voluntarily; or

(2) the party, before execution of the agreement:

(i) was not provided a fair and reasonable disclosure of the property or financial obligations of the other party;

(ii) did not voluntarily and expressly waive, in writing, any right to disclosure of the property or financial obligations of the other party beyond the disclosure provided; and

(iii) did not have an adequate knowledge of the property or financial obligations of the other party.

(b) Definition.—As used in this section, the term "premarital agreement" means an agreement between prospective spouses made in contemplation of marriage and to be effective upon marriage.

Official Comment: Section 3106 is new. Currently, premarital agreements are governed by case law. In *Simeone v. Simeone,* 525 Pa. 392, 581 A.2d 162 (1990), the Supreme Court discarded the approach that had been followed since its 1968 decision in *Hillegass Estate,* 431 Pa. 144, 244 A.2d 672. The *Hillegass* approach upheld a prenuptial agreement if it either made a reasonable provision for the spouse or was entered into after full and fair disclosure of financial status. The Supreme Court's 1987 plurality decision in *In re Estate of Geyer,* 516 Pa. 492, 533 A.2d 423, stated that full and fair disclosure includes evidence that the parties are aware of the statutory rights they are relinquishing in the agreement. The *Simeone* decision rejected inquiry into whether a reasonable provision was made for a spouse and the parties' knowledge of their statutory rights and put premarital agreements on a par with other contracts, stating that they could be invalidated for fraud, misrepresentation or duress. It also recognized that because the parties to premarital agreements "stand in a relation of mutual confidence and trust," full and fair disclosure of the parties' financial positions is required.

Subsection (a) is modeled after section 6(a) of the Uniform Premarital Agreement Act and encompasses the approach of *Simeone.*

Section 6(a) of the Uniform Act provides that an agreement is not enforceable if the party challenging it did not execute it voluntarily, or if the agreement was unconscionable when executed and the challenging party did not receive and did not waive disclosure of the other party's property or financial obligations and could not reasonably have had adequate knowledge of such. Section 6(b) provides that where an agreement's modification or elimination of spousal support would cause a spouse to be eligible for public assistance, the court may award support to the extent necessary to avoid the eligibility.

While embracing the voluntary execution and disclosure provisions of the Uniform Act, subsection (a) does not adopt the unconscionability or public assistance provisions. Note that under the Uniform Act, lack of disclosure would render an agreement unenforceable only if the agreement were *also* unconscionable when executed.

Under subsection (a), the party seeking to set aside the agreement must prove that either the agreement was not executed voluntarily (paragraph (1)) *or* all the elements of paragraph (2) are met.

The definition of "premarital agreement" in subsection(b) is modeled after the definition in the Uniform Act.

2004 Amendment. Act 175 added this sec.

Note: The addition of 23 Pa.C.S. § 3106 shall apply to premarital agreements executed on or after the effective date of this paragraph (January 28, 2005).

CHAPTER 33

DISSOLUTION OF MARITAL STATUS

Subchapter
- A. General Provisions
- B. Procedure
- C. Attacks Upon Decrees

Enactment. Chapter 33 was added December 19, 1990, P.L.1240, No.206, effective in 90 days.

SUBCHAPTER A
GENERAL PROVISIONS

Sec.
3301. Grounds for divorce.
3302. Counseling.
3303. Annulment of void and voidable marriages.
3304. Grounds for annulment of void marriages.
3305. Grounds for annulment of voidable marriages.
3306. Proceedings to determine marital status.
3307. Defenses.
3308. Action where defendant suffering from mental disorder.
3309. General appearance and collusion.

§ 3301. Grounds for divorce.

(a) **Fault.**—The court may grant a divorce to the innocent and injured spouse whenever it is judged that the other spouse has:

(1) Committed willful and malicious desertion, and absence from the habitation of the injured and innocent spouse, without a reasonable cause, for the period of one or more years.

(2) Committed adultery.

(3) By cruel and barbarous treatment, endangered the life or health of the injured and innocent spouse.

(4) Knowingly entered into a bigamous marriage while a former marriage is still subsisting.

(5) Been sentenced to imprisonment for a term of two or more years upon conviction of having committed a crime.

(6) Offered such indignities to the innocent and injured spouse as to render that spouse's condition intolerable and life burdensome.

(b) **Institutionalization.**—The court may grant a divorce from a spouse upon the ground that insanity or serious mental disorder has resulted in confinement in a mental institution for at least 18 months immediately before the commencement of an action under this part and where there is no reasonable prospect that the spouse will be discharged from inpatient care during the 18 months subsequent to the commencement of the action. A presumption that no prospect of discharge exists shall be established by a certificate of the superintendent of the institution to that effect and which includes a supporting statement of a treating physician.

(c) **Mutual consent.**—

(1) The court may grant a divorce where it is alleged that the marriage is irretrievably broken and 90 days have elapsed from the date of commencement of

an action under this part and an affidavit has been filed by each of the parties evidencing that each of the parties consents to the divorce.

(2) The consent of a party shall be presumed where that party has been convicted of committing a personal injury crime against the other party.

(d) Irretrievable breakdown.—

(1) The court may grant a divorce where a complaint has been filed alleging that the marriage is irretrievably broken and an affidavit has been filed alleging that the parties have lived separate and apart for a period of at least one year and that the marriage is irretrievably broken and the defendant either:

(i) Does not deny the allegations set forth in the affidavit.

(ii) Denies one or more of the allegations set forth in the affidavit but, after notice and hearing, the court determines that the parties have lived separate and apart for a period of at least one year and that the marriage is irretrievably broken.

(2) If a hearing has been held pursuant to paragraph (1)(ii) and the court determines that there is a reasonable prospect of reconciliation, then the court shall continue the matter for a period not less than 90 days nor more than 120 days unless the parties agree to a period in excess of 120 days. During this period, the court shall require counseling as provided in section 3302 (relating to counseling). If the parties have not reconciled at the expiration of the time period and one party states under oath that the marriage is irretrievably broken, the court shall determine whether the marriage is irretrievably broken. If the court determines that the marriage is irretrievably broken, the court shall grant the divorce. Otherwise, the court shall deny the divorce.

(e) No hearing required in certain cases.—If grounds for divorce alleged in the complaint or counterclaim are established under subsection (c) or (d), the court shall grant a divorce without requiring a hearing on any other grounds.

(Apr. 21, 2016, P.L.166, No.24, eff. 60 days; Oct. 4, 2016, P.L.865, No. 102, eff. 60 days)

2016 Amendments. Act 24 amended subsec. (c) and Act 102 amended subsec. (d). Section 2 of Act 102 provided that the amendment of subsec. (d) shall apply to periods of living separate and apart that commence after the effective date of section 2.

Cross References. Section 3301 is referred to in sections 1702, 3103, 3302, 3307, 3323 of this title.

§ 3302. Counseling.

(a) Indignities.—Whenever indignities under section 3301(a)(6) (relating to grounds for divorce) is the ground for divorce, the court shall require up to a maximum of three counseling sessions where either of the parties requests it.

(b) Mutual consent.—Whenever mutual consent under section 3301(c) is the ground for divorce, the court shall require up to a maximum of three counseling sessions within the 90 days following the commencement of the action where either of the parties requests it.

(c) Irretrievable breakdown.—Whenever the court orders a continuation period as provided for irretrievable breakdown in section 3301(d)(2), the court shall require up to a maximum of three counseling sessions within the time period where either of the parties requests it or may require such counseling where the parties have at least one child under 16 years of age.

(d) Notification of availability of counseling.—Whenever section 3301(a)(6), (c) or (d) is the ground for divorce, the court shall, upon the commencement of an action under this part, notify both parties of the availability of counseling and, upon request, provide both parties a list of qualified professionals who provide such services.

(e) Choice of qualified professionals unrestricted.—The choice of a qualified professional shall be at the option of the parties, and the professional need not be selected from the list provided by the court.

(f) Report.—Where the court requires counseling, a report shall be made by the qualified professional stating that the parties did or did not attend.

(g) Exception.—Notwithstanding any other provision of law, in no case may the court require counseling over the objection of a party that has a protection from abuse order, enforceable under Chapter 61 (relating to protection from abuse) against the other party, or where that party was the victim of a personal injury crime for which the other party was convicted or has entered into an Accelerated Rehabilitative Disposition program as a result of conduct for which the other party was a victim.

(Apr. 21, 2016, P.L.166, No.24, eff. 60 days)

2016 Amendment. Act 24 added subsec. (g).

Cross References. Section 3302 is referred to in section 3301 of this title.

§ 3303. Annulment of void and voidable marriages.

(a) General rule.—In all cases where a supposed or alleged marriage has been contracted which is void or voidable under this title or under applicable law, either party to the supposed or alleged marriage may bring an action in annulment to have it declared void in accordance with the procedures provided by this part and prescribed by general rules.

(b) Common-law marriage.—In the case of a purported common-law marriage where a party was under 18 years of age, a parent or guardian of the minor may bring a declaratory judgment proceeding during the party's minority to have the marriage declared void.

Cross References. Section 3303 is referred to in section 3304 of this title.

§ 3304. Grounds for annulment of void marriages.

(a) General rule.—Where there has been no confirmation by cohabitation following the removal of an impediment, the supposed or alleged marriage of a person shall be deemed void in the following cases:

(1) Where either party at the time of such marriage had an existing spouse and the former marriage had not been annulled nor had there been a divorce except where that party had obtained a decree of presumed death of the former spouse.

(2) Where the parties to such marriage are related within the degrees of consanguinity prohibited by section 1304(e) (relating to restrictions on issuance of license).

(3) Where either party to such marriage was incapable of consenting by reason of insanity or serious mental disorder or otherwise lacked capacity to consent or did not intend to consent to the marriage.

(4) Where either party to a purported common-law marriage was under 18 years of age.

(b) Procedures.—In all cases of marriages which are void, the marriage may be annulled as set forth in section 3303 (relating to annulment of void and voidable marriages) or its invalidity may be declared in any collateral proceeding.

Cross References. Section 3304 is referred to in section 1702 of this title.

§ 3305. Grounds for annulment of voidable marriages.

(a) General rule.—The marriage of a person shall be deemed voidable and subject to annulment in the following cases:

(1) Where either party to the marriage was under 16 years of age unless the marriage was expressly authorized by the court.

(2) Where either party was 16 or 17 years of age and lacked the consent of parent or guardian or express authorization of the court and has not subsequently ratified the marriage upon reaching 18 years of age and an action for annulment is commenced within 60 days after the marriage ceremony.

(3) Where either party to the marriage was under the influence of alcohol or drugs and an action for annulment is commenced within 60 days after the marriage ceremony.

(4) Where either party to the marriage was at the time of the marriage and still is naturally and incurably impotent unless the condition was known to the other party prior to the marriage.

(5) Where one party was induced to enter into the marriage due to fraud, duress, coercion or force attributable to the other party and there has been no subsequent voluntary cohabitation after knowledge of the fraud or release from the effects of fraud, duress, coercion or force.

(b) Status of voidable marriage.—In all cases of marriages which are voidable, either party to the marriage may seek and obtain an annulment of the marriage but, until a decree of annulment is obtained from a court of competent jurisdiction, the marriage shall be valid. The validity of a voidable marriage shall not be subject to attack or question by any person if it is subsequently confirmed by the parties to the marriage or if either party has died.

§ 3306. Proceedings to determine marital status.

When the validity of a marriage is denied or doubted, either or both of the parties to the marriage may bring an action for a declaratory judgment seeking a declaration of the validity or invalidity of the marriage and, upon proof of the validity or invalidity of the marriage, the marriage shall be declared valid or invalid by decree of the court and, unless reversed upon appeal, the declaration shall be conclusive upon all persons concerned.

Cross References. Section 3306 is referred to in section 7541 of Title 42 (Judiciary and Judicial Procedure).

§ 3307. Defenses.

(a) General rule.—Existing common-law defenses are retained as to the grounds enumerated in section 3301(a) and (b) (relating to grounds for divorce). The defenses of condonation, connivance, collusion, recrimination and provocation are abolished as to the grounds enumerated in section 3301(c) and (d).

(b) Adultery.—In an action for divorce on the ground of adultery, it is a good defense and a perpetual bar against the action if the defendant alleges and proves, or if it appears in the evidence, that the plaintiff:

(1) has been guilty of like conduct;

(2) has admitted the defendant into conjugal society or embraces after the plaintiff knew of the fact;

(3) allowed the defendant's prostitution or received hire from it; or

(4) exposed the defendant to lewd company whereby the defendant became involved in the adultery.

§ 3308. Action where defendant suffering from mental disorder.

If a spouse is insane or suffering from serious mental disorder, an action may be commenced under this part against that spouse upon any ground for divorce or annulment.

§ 3309. General appearance and collusion.

The entry of a general appearance by, or in behalf of, a defendant does not constitute collusion. Collusion shall be found to exist only where the parties conspired to fabricate grounds for divorce or annulment, agreed to and did commit perjury or perpetrated fraud on the court. Negotiation and discussion of terms of property settlement and other matters arising by reason of contemplated divorce or annulment do not constitute collusion.

SUBCHAPTER B
PROCEDURE

Sec.
3321. Hearing by master.
3322. Jury trial.
3323. Decree of court.

§ 3321. Hearing by master.

The court may appoint a master to hear testimony on all or some issues, except issues of custody and paternity, and return the record and a transcript of the testimony together with a report and recommendation as prescribed by general rules, or a judge of the court in chambers may appoint a master to hold a nonrecord hearing and to make recommendations and return the same to the court, in which case either party may demand a hearing de novo before the court.

> **Note:** Suspension by Court Rule. Section 3321 was suspended by Pennsylvania Rule of Civil Procedure No. 1920.91, as amended July 15, 1994, insofar as it inhibits the appointment of masters in partial custody or visitation matters.
>
> **Cross References** Masters, see Pa.R.C.P. No. 1920.51 et seq.

§ 3322. Jury trial.

(a) Application for jury trial.—After service of the complaint in divorce or annulment on the defendant in the manner prescribed by general rules or entry of a general appearance for the defendant, if either of the parties desires any matter of fact that is affirmed by one and denied by the other to be tried by a jury, that party may take a rule upon the opposite party, to be allowed by a judge of the court, to show cause why the issues of fact set forth in the rule should not be tried by a jury, which rule shall be served upon the opposite party or counsel for the opposite party.

(b) Disposition of application.—Upon the return of the rule, after hearing, the court may discharge it, make it absolute or frame issues itself. Only the issues ordered by the court shall be tried. The rule shall not be made absolute when, in the opinion of the court, a trial by jury cannot be had without prejudice to the public morals.

§ 3323. Decree of court.

(a) General rule.—In all matrimonial causes, the court may either dismiss the complaint or enter a decree of divorce or annulment of the marriage.

(b) Contents of decree.—A decree granting a divorce or an annulment shall include, after a full hearing, where these matters are raised in any pleadings, an order determining and disposing of existing property rights and interests between the parties, custody, partial custody and visitation rights, child support, alimony, reasonable attorney fees, costs and expenses and any other related matters, including the enforcement of agreements voluntarily entered into between the parties. In the enforcement of the rights of any party to any of these matters, the court shall have all necessary powers, including, but not limited to, the power of contempt and the power to attach wages.

(c) Bifurcation.—(Deleted by amendment).

(c.1) Bifurcation.—With the consent of both parties, the court may enter a decree of divorce or annulment prior to the final determination and disposition of the matters provided for in subsection (b) if the court determines that doing so provides sufficient economic protections for any minor children of the marriage. In the absence of the consent of both parties, the court may enter a decree of divorce or annulment prior to the final determination and disposition of the matters provided for in subsection (b) if:

(1) grounds have been established as provided in subsection (g); and

(2) the moving party has demonstrated that:

(i) compelling circumstances exist for the entry of the decree of divorce or annulment; and

(ii) sufficient economic protections have been provided for the other party and any minor children of the marriage during the pendency of the disposition of the matters provided for in subsection (b).

(d) Substitution for deceased party.—If one of the parties dies after the decree of divorce has been entered, but prior to the final determination in such proceeding of the property rights and interests of the parties under this part, the personal representative of the deceased party shall be substituted as a party as provided by law and the action shall proceed.

(d.1) Death of a party.—In the event one party dies during the course of divorce proceedings, no decree of divorce has been entered and grounds have been established as provided in subsection (g), the parties' economic rights and obligations arising under the marriage shall be determined under this part rather than under 20 Pa.C.S. (relating to decedents, estates and fiduciaries).

(e) Costs.—The court may award costs to the party in whose favor the order or decree shall be entered or may order that each party shall pay their own costs or may order that costs be divided equitably as it shall appear just and reasonable.

(f) Equity power and jurisdiction of the court.—In all matrimonial causes, the court shall have full equity power and jurisdiction and may issue injunctions or other orders which are necessary to protect the interests of the parties or to effectuate the purposes of this part and may grant such other relief or remedy as equity and justice require against either party or against any third person over whom the court has jurisdiction and who is involved in or concerned with the disposition of the cause.

(g) Grounds established.—For purposes of subsections (c.1) and (d.1), grounds are established as follows:

(1) In the case of an action for divorce under section 3301(a) or (b) (relating to grounds for divorce), the court adopts a report of the master or makes its own findings that grounds for divorce exist.

(2) In the case of an action for divorce under section 3301(c), both parties have filed affidavits of consent or, if the presumption in section 3301(c)(2) is established, one party has filed an affidavit of consent.

(3) In the case of an action for divorce under section 3301(d), an affidavit has been filed and no counter-affidavit has been filed or, if a counter-affidavit has been filed denying the affidavit's averments, the court determines that the marriage is irretrievably broken and the parties have lived separate and apart for at least one year at the time of the filing of the affidavit.

(Nov. 29, 2004, P.L.1357, No.175, eff. 60 days; Apr. 21, 2016, P.L.166, No.24, eff. 60 days; Oct. 4, 2016, P.L.865, No. 102, eff. 60 days)

2016 Amendments. Act 24 amended subsec. (g)(2) and Act 102 amended subsecs. (c.2) and (g)(3). Section 2 of Act 102 provided that the amendment of subsec. (g)(3) shall apply to periods of living separate and apart that commence after the effective date of section 2.

2004 Amendment. Act 175 added subsecs. (c.1), (d.1) and (g) and deleted subsec. (c). See section 5(3), (4) and (5) of Act 175 in the appendix to this title for special provisions relating to applicability.

Cross References. Section 3323 is referred to in sections 2106, 2203, 2507, 6111.1, 6111.2 of Title 20 (Decedents, Estates and Fiduciaries).

SUBCHAPTER C
ATTACKS UPON DECREES

Sec.
3331. Limitations on attacks upon decrees.
3332. Opening or vacating decrees.
3333. Res judicata and estoppel.

§ 3331. Limitations on attacks upon decrees.

The validity of a decree of divorce or annulment issued by a court shall not be questioned, except by appeal, in any court or place in this Commonwealth after the death of either party to the proceeding. If it is shown that a party who subsequently attempts to question the validity of the decree had full knowledge of the facts and circumstances later complained of at the time of issuance of the decree or failed to take any action despite this knowledge within two years after the date of the decree, the party shall be barred from questioning the decree, and it shall be valid in all courts and places within this Commonwealth.

§ 3332. Opening or vacating decrees.

A motion to open a decree of divorce or annulment may be made only within the period limited by 42 Pa.C.S. § 5505 (relating to modification of orders) and not thereafter. The motion may lie where it is alleged that the decree was procured by intrinsic fraud or that there is new evidence relating to the cause of action which will sustain the attack upon its validity. A motion to vacate a decree or strike a judgment alleged to be void because of extrinsic fraud, lack of jurisdiction over the subject matter or a fatal defect apparent upon the face of the record must be made within five years after entry of the final decree. Intrinsic fraud relates to a matter adjudicated by the judgment, including perjury and false testimony, whereas extrinsic fraud relates to matters collateral to the judgment which have the consequence of precluding a fair hearing or presentation of one side of the case.

§ 3333. Res judicata and estoppel.

The validity of a divorce or annulment decree granted by a court having jurisdiction over the subject matter may not be questioned by a party who was subject to the personal jurisdiction of the court except by direct appeal provided or prescribed by law. A party who sought and obtained a decree, financed or agreed to its procurement, or accepted a property settlement, alimony pendente lite or alimony pursuant to the terms of the decree, or who remarries after the decree, or is guilty of laches, is barred from making a collateral attack upon the validity of the decree unless, by clear and convincing evidence, it is established that fraud by the other party prevented the making of a timely appeal from the divorce or annulment decree.

CHAPTER 35
PROPERTY RIGHTS

Sec.
3501. Definitions.
3502. Equitable division of marital property.
3503. Effect of divorce on property rights generally.
3504. Disposition of property after termination of marriage.
3505. Disposition of property to defeat obligations.
3506. Statement of reasons for distribution.
3507. Division of entireties property between divorced persons.
3508. Conveyance of entireties property to divorced spouse.

Enactment. Chapter 35 was added December 19, 1990, P.L.1240, No.206, effective in 90 days.

Cross References. Chapter 35 is referred to in section 3701 of this title.

§ 3501. Definitions.

(a) **General rule.**—As used in this chapter, "marital property" means all property acquired by either party during the marriage and the increase in value of any nonmarital property acquired pursuant to paragraphs (1) and (3) as measured and determined under subsection (a.1). However, marital property does not include:

(1) Property acquired prior to marriage or property acquired in exchange for property acquired prior to the marriage.

(2) Property excluded by valid agreement of the parties entered into before, during or after the marriage.

(3) Property acquired by gift, except between spouses, bequest, devise or descent or property acquired in exchange for such property.

(4) Property acquired after final separation until the date of divorce, except for property acquired in exchange for marital assets.

(5) Property which a party has sold, granted, conveyed or otherwise disposed of in good faith and for value prior to the date of final separation.

(6) Veterans' benefits exempt from attachment, levy or seizure pursuant to the act of September 2, 1958 (Public Law 85-857, 72 Stat. 1229), as amended, except for those benefits received by a veteran where the veteran has waived a portion of his military retirement pay in order to receive veterans' compensation.

(7) Property to the extent to which the property has been mortgaged or otherwise encumbered in good faith for value prior to the date of final separation.

(8) Any payment received as a result of an award or settlement for any cause of action or claim which accrued prior to the marriage or after the date of final separation regardless of when the payment was received.

Official Comment: A technical amendment is made to paragraph (3) to make it consistent with paragraph (1).

(a.1) **Measuring and determining the increase in value of nonmarital property.**—The increase in value of any nonmarital property acquired pursuant to subsection (a)(1) and (3) shall be measured from the date of marriage or later acquisition date to either the date of final separation or the date as close to the hearing on equitable distribution as possible, whichever date results in a lesser increase. Any decrease in value of the nonmarital property of a party shall be offset against any increase in value of the nonmarital property of that party. However, a decrease in value of the nonmarital property of a party shall not be offset against any increase in value of the nonmarital property of the other party or against any other marital property subject to equitable division.

Official Comment: Section 3501(a.1) is new. The first sentence of this subsection essentially codifies the decision in *Litmans v. Litmans,* 449 Pa. Super. 209, 673 A.2d 382 (1996), as it pertains to when to measure the increase in value of nonmarital property. Some discussion and uncertainty regarding this issue followed the Supreme Court's decision in *Solomon v. Solomon,* 531 Pa. 113, 611 A.2d 686 (1992), because of the Court's inclusion of footnote eleven in that opinion. The *Litmans* court found that the Supreme Court in footnote eleven of *Solomon* was referring "to a situation in which the increase in value of a nonmarital asset is determined as of the date of separation, there then ensues a long period of delay between separation and distribution, and the asset itself then *decreases* in value by the time of distribution. In such a case, footnote eleven would require the trial court to consider the 'change in value' of the nonmarital asset as a result of the delay." 673 A.2d at 395 (emphasis added). The *Litmans* court viewed *Solomon* footnote eleven as "mere dictum" since the Supreme Court did not remand *Solomon* to the lower court for a determination in accordance with the footnote. 673 A.2d at 394.

The offset language of the second sentence of subsection (a.1) ensures that only the net increase in value of all of a party's nonmarital property is considered part of the marital estate. To find the net increase in value, the increases in value of a party's nonmarital assets are offset by the decreases in value of that party's nonmarital assets. For example: A spouse enters a marriage with two nonmarital assets, each valued at $50 for a total of $100. During the marriage, one asset increases in value to $100 and the other decreases in value to $0, so that the total value of the nonmarital assets remains $100. Under existing law, there is an argument that there would be a $50 increase in value which would become marital property even though the total value of the nonmarital assets remained the same during the marriage. Some masters and trial courts have refused to consider decreases in nonmarital property as an offset against increases in other nonmarital property. Subsection (a.1) will specifically require such offset. Under subsection (a.1), the $50 increase in one asset would be offset by the $50 decrease in the other asset, and the resulting marital component of the nonmarital property would be $0.

The last sentence of subsection (a.1) is intended to ensure that where one party has a decrease in value in that party's nonmarital property, that decrease cannot be offset against any increase in value of nonmarital property of the other party or against the marital estate.

No distinction is made between consumption and decrease in value. Consumption may be addressed through the advocacy of counsel, and "malicious" consumption of an asset to avoid sharing it with the other spouse may be addressed under the dissipation factor in section 3502(a)(7) or under the court's equity powers in section 3323(f).

(b) Presumption.—All real or personal property acquired by either party during the marriage is presumed to be marital property regardless of whether title is held individually or by the parties in some form of co-ownership such as joint tenancy, tenancy in common or tenancy by the entirety. The presumption of marital property is overcome by a showing that the property was acquired by a method listed in subsection (a).

(c) Defined benefit retirement plans.—Notwithstanding subsections (a), (a.1) and (b):

(1) In the case of the marital portion of a defined benefit retirement plan being distributed by means of a deferred distribution, the defined benefit plan shall be allocated between its marital and nonmarital portions solely by use of a coverture fraction. The denominator of the coverture fraction shall be the number of months the employee spouse worked to earn the total benefit and the numerator shall be the number of such months during which the parties were married and not finally

separated. The benefit to which the coverture fraction is applied shall include all postseparation enhancements except for enhancements arising from postseparation monetary contributions made by the employee spouse, including the gain or loss on such contributions.

(2) In the case of the marital portion of a defined benefit retirement plan being distributed by means of an immediate offset, the defined benefit plan shall be allocated between its marital and nonmarital portions solely by use of a coverture fraction. The denominator of the coverture fraction shall be the number of months the employee spouse worked to earn the accrued benefit as of a date as close to the time of trial as reasonably possible and the numerator shall be the number of such months during which the parties were married and not finally separated. The benefit to which the coverture fraction is applied shall include all postseparation enhancements up to a date as close to the time of trial as reasonably possible except for enhancements arising from postseparation monetary contributions made by the employee spouse, including the gain or loss on such contributions.

Official Comment: New subsection (c) seeks to reverse *Berrington v. Berrington,* 534 Pa. 393, 633 A.2d 589 (1993), to adopt a coverture fraction methodology along the lines of *Holland v. Holland,* 403 Pa. Super. 116, 581 A.2d 58 (1991), and to include all postseparation enhancements except for postseparation monetary contributions by the employee spouse in the value of the pension. The new language codifies the result reached by Justices Flaherty, Cappy and Newman regarding the postseparation retirement enhancements in *Gordon v. Gordon,* 545 Pa. 391, 681 A.2d 732 (1996) (3-3 decision on this issue, affirming the Superior Court's exclusion of the enhancements from the marital estate). Three early retirement inducements were at issue in *Gordon.* The justices listed above opined that since no present efforts or contributions of the employee spouse were required to receive the supplemental retirement income and bonus inducements, they were includable in the marital estate. The third inducement was an annuity paid for partially by the employee spouse and partially by the employer. Justices Flaherty, Cappy and Newman would have included the portion of the annuity paid for by the employer in the marital estate.

Paragraph (c)(1) covers the deferred distribution of defined benefit retirement plans, and paragraph (c)(2) covers the immediate offset of such plans.

Where marital assets are sufficient to cover the nonemployee spouse's share of the pension, immediate offset is the preferred method of distribution. Where it is impracticable to use the immediate offset method, such as where the pension constitutes the bulk of the marital estate and the nonemployee spouse's share cannot be covered by other marital assets or where the pension has not yet vested, the distribution of the pension may be deferred.

2005 Amendment. Act 4 repealed section 5(7) of Act 2004-175.

2004 Amendment. Act 175 amended subsec. (a) and added subsecs. (a.1) and (c).

Note: The amendment or addition of 23 Pa.C.S. § 3501(a)(3) and (a.1) shall apply to all equitable distribution proceedings irrespective of whether the proceeding was commenced before, on or after the effective date of this paragraph (January 28, 2005).

The provisions of 23 Pa.C.S. § 3501(c) shall apply to all equitable distribution proceedings on or after the effective date of this section.

§ 3502. Equitable division of marital property.

(a) **General rule.**—Upon the request of either party in an action for divorce or annulment, the court shall equitably divide, distribute or assign, in kind or otherwise, the marital property between the parties without regard to marital misconduct in such percentages and in such manner as the court deems just after considering all relevant factors. The court may consider each marital asset or group of assets independently and apply a different percentage to each marital asset or group of assets. Factors which are relevant to the equitable division of marital property include the following:

(1) The length of the marriage.

(2) Any prior marriage of either party.

(3) The age, health, station, amount and sources of income, vocational skills, employability, estate, liabilities and needs of each of the parties.

(4) The contribution by one party to the education, training or increased earning power of the other party.

(5) The opportunity of each party for future acquisitions of capital assets and income.

(6) The sources of income of both parties, including, but not limited to, medical, retirement, insurance or other benefits.

(7) The contribution or dissipation of each party in the acquisition, preservation, depreciation or appreciation of the marital property, including the contribution of a party as homemaker.

(8) The value of the property set apart to each party.

(9) The standard of living of the parties established during the marriage.

(10) The economic circumstances of each party at the time the division of property is to become effective.

(10.1) The Federal, State and local tax ramifications associated with each asset to be divided, distributed or assigned, which ramifications need not be immediate and certain.

(10.2) The expense of sale, transfer or liquidation associated with a particular asset, which expense need not be immediate and certain.

(11) Whether the party will be serving as the custodian of any dependent minor children.

Official Comment: The two new sentences in the introductory language of subsection (a) clarify current statutory law to specifically authorize courts to consider each marital asset independently in equitable distribution and, in the appropriate case, to apply a different percentage to each marital asset. The phrase "or group of assets" indicates that the court need not determine a distribution percentage for each individual asset in a marital estate.

The "tax ramifications" language of current subsection (a)(10) became effective in February of 1988 as an amendment to former section 401(d)(10) of the 1980 Divorce Code. In an opinion that was not handed down until May of 1988, the Supreme Court held that "potential tax liability may be considered in valuing marital assets only where a taxable event has occurred as a result of the divorce or equitable distribution of property or is certain to occur within a time frame such that the tax liability can be reasonably predicted." *Hovis v. Hovis,* 518 Pa. 137, 541 A.2d 1378, 138081 (1988). However, the *Hovis* court quoted the *1980* version of former section 401(d)(10) and noted that "[t]he Pennsylvania statute does not list potential tax liability as a factor to be considered in making an equitable distribution award." 541 A.2d at 1380. Notwithstanding the legislative statement in the 1988 amendments, and perhaps because the *Hovis* opinion was handed down after the amendments had become effective (but clearly decided under preamendment law), lower court cases after *Hovis* have required tax ramifications to be immediate and certain in order for them to be considered in equitable distribution. New subsection (a)(10.1) seeks to change this interpretation by making clear that tax ramifications are relevant and need not be immediate and certain.

New subsection (a)(10.2) covers such expenses as brokerage commissions and the transfer tax on the sale of a house.

(b) Lien.—The court may impose a lien or charge upon property of a party as security for the payment of alimony or any other award for the other party.

(c) Family home.—The court may award, during the pendency of the action or otherwise, to one or both of the parties the right to reside in the marital residence.

(d) Life insurance.—The court may direct the continued maintenance and beneficiary designations of existing policies insuring the life or health of either party which were originally purchased during the marriage and owned by or within the effective control of either party. Where it is necessary to protect the interests of a party, the court may also direct the purchase of, and beneficiary designations on, a policy insuring the life or health of either party.

(e) Powers of the court.—If, at any time, a party has failed to comply with an order of equitable distribution, as provided for in this chapter or with the terms of an agreement as entered into between the parties, after hearing, the court may, in addition to any other remedy available under this part, in order to effect compliance with its order:

(1) enter judgment;

(2) authorize the taking and seizure of the goods and chattels and collection of the rents and profits of the real and personal, tangible and intangible property of the party;

(3) award interest on unpaid installments;

(4) order and direct the transfer or sale of any property required in order to comply with the court's order;

(5) require security to insure future payments in compliance with the court's order;

(6) issue attachment proceedings, directed to the sheriff or other proper officer of the county, directing that the person named as having failed to comply with the court order be brought before the court, at such time as the court may direct. If the court finds, after hearing, that the person willfully failed to comply with the court order, it may deem the person in civil contempt of court and, in its discretion, make an appropriate order, including, but not limited to, commitment of the person to the county jail for a period not to exceed six months;

(7) award counsel fees and costs;

(8) attach wages; or

(9) find the party in contempt.

Comment: The amendment to the definition of "separate and apart" establishes a rebuttable presumption designed to address the difficulty of proving a separation date, especially when the parties have not established different residences.

(f) Partial distribution.—The court, upon the request of either party, may at any stage of the proceedings enter an order providing for an interim partial distribution or assignment of marital property.

Official Comment: This amendment specifically authorizes the court to make interim equitable distribution awards, a power that was never intended to be proscribed but which some courts and commentators believe does not exist.

2004 Amendment. Act 175 amended subsec. (a) and added subsec. (f).

Note: The amendment or addition of 23 Pa.C.S. § 3502(a) introductory paragraph, (10.1) and (10.2) shall apply to all equitable distribution proceedings irrespective of whether the proceeding was commenced before, on or after the effective date of this paragraph (January 28, 2005).

The addition of 23 Pa.C.S. § 3502(f) shall apply to all divorce proceedings irrespective of whether the action was commenced before, on or after the effective date of this paragraph (January 28, 2005).

§ 3503. Effect of divorce on property rights generally.

Whenever a decree or judgment is granted which nullifies or absolutely terminates the bonds of matrimony, all property rights which are dependent upon the marital relation, except those which are vested rights, are terminated unless the court expressly provides otherwise in its decree. All duties, rights and claims accruing to either of the parties at any time theretofore in pursuance of the marriage shall cease, and the parties shall severally be at liberty to marry again as if they had never been married.

§ 3504. Disposition of property after termination of marriage.

Unless provided otherwise by the court, whenever a decree of divorce or annulment is entered by a court of competent jurisdiction, both parties whose marriage is terminated or affected shall have complete freedom of disposition as to their separate real and personal property and may mortgage, sell, grant, convey or otherwise encumber or dispose of their separate property, whether the property was acquired before, during or after converture, and neither need join in, consent to or acknowledge a deed, mortgage or instrument of the other.

§ 3505. Disposition of property to defeat obligations.

(a) **Preliminary relief.**—Where it appears to the court that a party is about to leave the jurisdiction of the court or is about to remove property of that party from the jurisdiction of the court or is about to dispose of, alienate or encumber property in order to defeat equitable distribution, alimony pendente lite, alimony, child and spousal support or a similar award, an injunction may issue to prevent the removal or disposition and the property may be attached as prescribed by general rules. The court may also issue a writ of ne exeat to preclude the removal.

(b) **Inventory of property.**—Both parties shall submit to the court an inventory and appraisement, which shall contain all of the following:

(1) A list of the property owned or possessed by either or both of them as of:

(i) the date of separation; and

(ii) thirty days prior to the date of hearing on equitable distribution.

(2) A list of the value of the property owned or possessed by either or both of them as of:

(i) the date of acquisition;

(ii) the date of separation; and

(iii) thirty days prior to the date of hearing on equitable distribution.

(3) A list of the liabilities of either or both of them as of 30 days prior to the date of hearing on equitable distribution, whether or not the liabilities are related to the property set forth in the inventory and appraisement.

(c) **Discovery.**—Discovery under this part shall be as provided for all other civil actions under the Pennsylvania Rules of Civil Procedure.

(d) **Constructive trust for undisclosed assets.**—If a party fails to disclose information required by general rule of the Supreme Court and in consequence thereof an asset or assets with a fair market value of $1,000 or more is omitted from the final distribution of property, the party aggrieved by the nondisclosure may at any time petition the court granting the award to declare the creation of a constructive trust as to all undisclosed assets for the benefit of the parties and their minor or dependent children, if any. The party in whose name the assets are held shall be declared the constructive trustee unless the court designates a different trustee, and the trust may include any terms and conditions the court may determine. The court shall grant the petition upon a finding of a failure to disclose the assets as required by general rule of the Supreme Court.

(e) **Encumbrance or disposition to third parties.**—An encumbrance or disposition of marital property to third persons who paid wholly inadequate consideration for the property may be deemed fraudulent and declared void.

(Nov. 29, 2004, P.L.1357, No.175, eff. 60 days)

2004 Amendment. Act 175 amended subsec. (d). Section 5(10) of Act 175 provided that the amendment shall apply to all equitable distribution proceedings irrespective of whether the proceeding was commenced before, on or after the effective date of par. (10).

Suspension by Court Rule. Section 3505(b) was suspended by Pennsylvania Rule of Civil Procedure No. 1920.91, as amended May 5, 1997, insofar as it applies to the practice and procedure in actions for divorce or annulment of marriage.

§ 3506. Statement of reasons for distribution.

In an order made under this chapter for the distribution of property, the court shall set forth the percentage of distribution for each marital asset or group of assets and the reason for the distribution ordered.

Official Comment: The amendment to this section conforms with the amendments made to section 3502(a).

2004 Amendment. Act 175 amended this sec.

Note: The amendment of 23 Pa.C.S. § 3506 shall apply to all orders made on or after the effective date of this paragraph (January 28, 2005).

§ 3507. Division of entireties property between divorced persons.

(a) General rule.—Whenever married persons holding property as tenants by entireties are divorced, they shall, except as otherwise provided by an order made under this chapter, thereafter hold the property as tenants in common of equal one-half shares in value, and either of them may bring an action against the other to have the property sold and the proceeds divided between them.

(b) Division of proceeds.—Except as provided in subsection (c), the proceeds of a sale under this section, after the payment of the expenses of sale, shall be equally divided between the parties.

(c) Liens.—The amount of any lien entered of record jointly against both of the parties, together with any interest due on the lien and docket costs, shall be deducted from the proceeds of sale and the amount of the liens entered of record against either of the parties, together with any interest due on the liens and docket costs, shall be deducted from the share of the party against whom the lien is filed and paid to the person or persons to whom the amount of the lien is due and payable.

(d) Record of divorce decree.—No decree of divorce shall be effective to change the existing law relating to liens upon property held by tenants by the entireties except a decree of divorce that is valid in this Commonwealth and not until the decree of divorce or a certified copy of the decree is recorded in the office of the recorder of deeds of the county where the property is situate. The decree shall be indexed in the grantor's index against each of the tenants by the entireties.

Saved from Suspension. Pennsylvania Rule of Civil Procedure No. 1910.49, as amended March 30, 1994, provided that section 3507 shall not be deemed suspended or affected by Rules 1910.1 through 1910.31 governing actions for support insofar as section 3507 provides for tenancy in common of property held by the entities after divorce.

§ 3508. Conveyance of entireties property to divorced spouse.

Whenever married persons have acquired real estate as tenants by entireties and thereafter are divorced, either former spouse, except as otherwise provided by an order made under this chapter, may convey to the other, without the joinder of the other, the grantor's interest in the real estate so that the grantee holds the real estate in fee simple, freed from all right, title and interest which the grantor had in the real estate as a tenant by the entireties.

CHAPTER 37
ALIMONY AND SUPPORT

Sec.
3701. Alimony.
3702. Alimony pendente lite, counsel fees and expenses.
3703. Enforcement of arrearages.
3704. Payment of support, alimony and alimony pendente lite.
3705. Enforcement of foreign decrees.
3706. Bar to alimony.
3707. Effect of death of either party.

Enactment. Chapter 37 was added December 19, 1990, P.L.1240, No.206, effective in 90 days.

§ 3701. Alimony.

(a) **General rule.**—Where a divorce decree has been entered, the court may allow alimony, as it deems reasonable, to either party only if it finds that alimony is necessary.

(b) **Factors relevant.**—In determining whether alimony is necessary and in determining the nature, amount, duration and manner of payment of alimony, the court shall consider all relevant factors, including:

(1) The relative earnings and earning capacities of the parties.

(2) The ages and the physical, mental and emotional conditions of the parties.

(3) The sources of income of both parties, but not limited to, medical, retirement, insurance or other benefits.

(4) The expectancies and inheritances of the parties.

(5) The duration of the marriage.

(6) The contribution by one party to the education, training or increased earning power of the other party.

(7) The extent to which the earning power, expenses or financial obligations of a party will be affected by reason of serving as the custodian of a minor child.

(8) The standard of living of the parties established during the marriage.

(9) The relative education of the parties and the time necessary to acquire sufficient education or training to enable the party seeking alimony to find appropriate employment.

(10) The relative assets and liabilities of the parties.

(11) The property brought to the marriage by either party.

(12) The contribution of a spouse as homemaker.

(13) The relative needs of the parties.

(14) The marital misconduct of either of the parties during the marriage. The marital misconduct of either of the parties from the date of final separation shall not be considered by the court in its determinations relative to alimony; except that the court shall consider the abuse of one party by the other party. As used in this paragraph "abuse" shall have the meaning given to it under section 6102 (relating to definitions).

(15) The Federal, State and local tax ramifications of the alimony award.

(16) Whether the party seeking alimony lacks sufficient property, including, but not limited to, property distributed under Chapter 35 (relating to property rights), to provide for the party's reasonable needs.

(17) Whether the party seeking alimony is incapable of self-support through appropriate employment.

(c) **Duration.**—The court in ordering alimony shall determine the duration of the order, which may be for a definite or an indefinite period of time which is reasonable under the circumstances.

(d) **Statement of reasons.**—In an order made under this section, the court shall set forth the reason for its denial or award of alimony and the amount thereof.

(e) **Modification and termination.**—An order entered pursuant to this section is subject to further order of the court upon changed circumstances of either party of a substantial and continuing nature whereupon the order may be modified, suspended, terminated or reinstituted or a new order made. Any further order shall apply only to payments accruing subsequent to the petition for the requested relief. Remarriage of the party receiving alimony shall terminate the award of alimony.

(f) **Status of agreement to pay alimony.**—Whenever the court approves an agreement for the payment of alimony voluntarily entered into between the parties, the agreement shall constitute the order of the court and may be enforced as provided in section 3703 (relating to enforcement of arrearages).

1998 Amendment. Act 36 amended subsec. (b)(14).

1997 Amendment. Act 58 amended subsec. (14).

Cross References. Section 3701 is referred to in section 3703 of this title.

§ 3702. Alimony pendente lite, counsel fees and expenses.

(a) **General rule.**—In proper cases, upon petition, the court may allow a spouse reasonable alimony pendente lite, spousal support and reasonable counsel fees and expenses. Reasonable counsel fees and expenses may be allowed pendente lite, and the court shall also have authority to direct that adequate health and hospitalization insurance coverage be maintained for the dependent spouse pendente lite.

(b) **Exception.**—Except where the court finds that an order for alimony pendente lite or spousal support is necessary to prevent manifest injustice, a party who has been convicted of committing a personal injury crime against the other party shall not be entitled to spousal support or alimony pendente lite. Any amount paid by the injured party after the commission of the offense but before the conviction of the other party shall be recoverable by the injured party upon petition.

(October 24, 2018, effective in 60 days).

2018 Amendment. Act 102 amended this sec.

1998 Amendment. Act 36 amended this sec.

1997 Amendment. Act 58 amended this sec.

Cross References. Section 3702 is referred to in section 3703 of this title.

§ 3703. Enforcement of arrearages.

If at any time a party is in arrears in the payment of alimony or alimony pendente lite as provided for in sections 3701 (relating to alimony) and 3702 (relating to alimony pendente lite, counsel fees and expenses), the court may, after hearing, in order to effect payment of the arrearages:

(1) Enter judgment.

(2) Authorize the taking and seizure of the goods and chattels and the collection of the rents and profits of the real estate of the party.

(3) Attach no more than 50% of the wages of the party.

(4) Award interest on unpaid installments.

(5) Require security to insure future payments.

(6) Issue attachment proceedings, directed to the sheriff or other proper officer of the county, directing that the person named as having failed to comply with the court order be brought before the court at such time as the court may direct. If the court finds, after hearing, that the named person willfully failed to comply with the court order, it may declare the person in civil contempt of court and in its

discretion make an appropriate order, including, but not limited to, commitment of the person to prison for a period not to exceed six months.

(7) Award counsel fees and costs.

Cross References. Section 3703 is referred to in section 3701 of this title.

§ 3704. Payment of support, alimony and alimony pendente lite.

When so ordered by the court, all payments of child and spousal support, alimony or alimony pendente lite shall be made to the domestic relations section of the court which issued the order or the domestic relations section of the court at the residence of the party entitled to receive the award. The domestic relations section shall keep an accurate record of all payments and shall notify the court immediately whenever a person subject to a payment order is 30 days in arrears of payment so that appropriate action may be taken to enforce the order of the court. The domestic relations section shall distribute the payments to the person entitled to them as soon as possible after receipt.

§ 3705. Enforcement of foreign decrees.

(a) **General rule.**—Whenever a person subject to a valid decree of a sister state or territory for the distribution of marital property or for the payment of alimony, temporary alimony or alimony pendente lite, or the property of that person is found within this Commonwealth, the obligee of the decree may petition the court where the obligor or the property of the obligor is found to register, adopt as its own and enforce the decree as a properly issued and authenticated decree of a sister state or territory. Upon registration and adoption, such relief and process for enforcement as is provided or prescribed by law in similar cases originally commenced in this Commonwealth shall be available. A copy of the decree and order shall be forwarded to the court of the state or territory which issued the original decree. The obligor shall have whatever defenses and relief are available to the obligor in the state or territory which issued the original decree and may question the jurisdiction of that court if not otherwise barred. Interest may be awarded on unpaid installments and security may be required to insure future payments as in cases originally commenced in this Commonwealth. Where property of the obligor, but not the person of the obligor, is found within this Commonwealth, there shall be jurisdiction quasi in rem, and, upon registration and adoption of the decree of the sister state or territory, relief and enforcement of the decree shall be available as in other proceedings which are quasi in rem.

(b) **Optional procedure.**—The right of a judgment creditor to proceed under 42 Pa.C.S. § 4306 (relating to enforcement of foreign judgments) or otherwise instead of proceeding under this section remains unimpaired.

§ 3706. Bar to alimony.

No petitioner is entitled to receive an award of alimony where the petitioner, subsequent to the divorce pursuant to which alimony is being sought, has entered into cohabitation with a person of the opposite sex who is not a member of the family of the petitioner within the degrees of consanguinity.

§ 3707. Effect of death of either party.

Upon the death of the payee party, the right to receive alimony pursuant to this chapter shall cease. Upon the death of the payor party, the obligation to pay alimony shall cease unless otherwise indicated in an agreement between the parties or an order of court.

CHAPTER 39
MEDIATION

Sec.

3901. Mediation programs.
3902. Fees and costs.
3903. Review of programs.
3904. Existing programs.

Enactment. Chapter 39 was added April 4, 1996, P.L.58, No.20, effective immediately.

§ 3901. Mediation programs.

(a) **Establishment.**—A court may establish a mediation program for actions brought under this part or Chapter 53 (relating to custody).

(b) **Issues subject to mediation.**—When a program has been established pursuant to subsection (a), the court may order the parties to attend an orientation session to explain the mediation process. Thereafter, should the parties consent to mediation, the court may order them to mediate such issues as it may specify.

(c) **Local rules.**—

(1) The court shall adopt local rules for the administration of the mediation program to include rules regarding qualifications of mediators, confidentiality and any other matter deemed appropriate by the court.

(2) The court shall not order an orientation session or mediation in a case where either party or child of either party is or has been a subject of domestic violence or child abuse at any time during the pendency of an action under this part or within 24 months preceding the filing of any action under this part.

(d) **Model guidelines.**—The Supreme Court shall develop model guidelines for implementation of this section and shall consult with experts on mediation and domestic violence in this Commonwealth in the development thereof. The effective date of this chapter shall not be delayed by virtue of this subsection.

§ 3902. Fees and costs.

(a) **Imposition of fee.**—A county in which the court has established a mediation program may impose an additional filing fee of up to $20 on divorce and custody complaints to be used to fund the mediation program.

(b) **Assessment of additional costs.**—The court may assess additional costs of mediation on either party.

§ 3903. Review of programs.

The Supreme Court shall monitor mediation programs established by courts of common pleas. The Supreme Court shall establish procedures for the evaluation of the effectiveness of the program.

§ 3904. Existing programs.

This chapter shall not affect any existing mediation program established in any judicial district pursuant to local rule.

PART V

SUPPORT, PROPERTY AND CONTRACTS

Chapter

41. General Provisions
43. Support Matters Generally
45. Reciprocal Enforcement of Support Orders [Repealed]
46. Support of the Indigent

Enactment. Part V was added October 30, 1985, P.L.264, No.66, effective in 90 days.

CHAPTER 41

GENERAL PROVISIONS

Sec.

4101. Liability for debts contracted before marriage.
4102. Proceedings in case of debts contracted for necessaries.
4103. (Reserved).
4104. Right of married person to separate earnings.
4105. Loans between married persons.
4106. Construction of chapter.

Enactment. Chapter 41 was added December 19, 1990, P.L.1240, No.206, effective in 90 days.

§ 4101. Liability for debts contracted before marriage.

(a) **General rule.**—A spouse is not liable for the debts of the other spouse contracted before marriage.

(b) **Liability of property unaffected.**—This chapter does not protect the property of a married person from liability for debts contracted by or in the name of the married person by any person authorized to so contract.

§ 4102. Proceedings in case of debts contracted for necessaries.

In all cases where debts are contracted for necessaries by either spouse for the support and maintenance of the family, it shall be lawful for the creditor in this case to institute suit against the husband and wife for the price of such necessaries and, after obtaining a judgment, have an execution against the spouse contracting the debt alone; and, if no property of that spouse is found, execution may be levied upon and satisfied out of the separate property of the other spouse.

§ 4103. (Reserved).

§ 4104. Right of married person to separate earnings.

Except as otherwise provided in this title, the separate earnings of any married person of this Commonwealth, whether these earnings are wages for labor, salary, property, business or otherwise, shall accrue to and enure to the separate benefit and use of that married person independently of the other spouse, and so as not to be subject to any legal claim of the other spouse. However, in any action in which the ownership of such property is in dispute, the person claiming such property shall be compelled, in the first instance, to show title and ownership in the property.

§ 4105. Loans between married persons.

A married person may loan the other spouse money from the separate estate of the married person and take in security therefor a judgment or mortgage against the property of the other spouse which shall be valid as otherwise provided by law.

§ 4106. Construction of chapter.

This chapter shall not be construed to affect Part IV (relating to divorce).

CHAPTER 43
SUPPORT MATTERS GENERALLY

Subchapter

A. General Provisions
B. Support
C. Proceedings Generally
D. Proceedings Against Entireties Property
E. Title IV-D Program and Related Matters
F. New Hire Reporting

Enactment. Chapter 43 was added October 30, 1985, P.L.264, No.66, effective in 90 days.

Cross References. Chapter 43 is referred to in sections 5603 and 6108 of this title.

Saved from Suspension. Pennsylvania Rule of Civil Procedure No. 1910.49, adopted November 7, 1988, provided that Chapter 43 shall not be deemed suspended or affected by Rules 1910.1 through 1910.31 governing actions for support.

SUBCHAPTER A
GENERAL PROVISIONS

Sec.

4301. Scope of chapter.
4302. Definitions.
4303. Information to consumer reporting agency.
4304. Cooperation of Commonwealth agencies. [Repealed. 1996, Oct. 16, P.L. 706, No. 124, eff. in 60 days]
4304.1. Cooperation of government and nongovernment agencies.
4305. General administration of support matters.
4306. Duties of Title IV-D attorney.
4307. State income tax intercept.
4308. Lottery winnings intercept.
4308.1. Collection of overdue support from monetary awards.
4309. Publication of delinquent support obligors.

§ 4301. Scope of chapter.

(a) **General rule.**—Actions or proceedings provided by this chapter are in addition to and not in substitution of actions or proceedings provided by unsuspended statutes where there is desertion or a failure to perform a duty to support.

(b) **Persons in institutions and foster homes.**—Matters relating to the support of persons living in public or private institutions or receiving foster home care and who are otherwise entitled to support under this chapter shall be determined by the court under the statutes pertaining to those institutions or foster homes.

§ 4302. Definitions.

The following words and phrases when used in this chapter shall have the meanings given to them in this section unless the context clearly indicates otherwise:

"Consumer reporting agency." As defined in section 630(f) of the Federal Fair Credit Reporting Act (Public Law 91-508, 15 U.S.C. § 1681a(f)).

"Department." The Department of Public Welfare of the Commonwealth.

"Employer." Includes an individual, partnership, association, corporation, trust, Federal agency, Commonwealth agency or political subdivision paying or obligated to pay income.

"Genetic tests." Includes any blood or tissue testing processes used to confirm or exclude parentage.

"**Government agency.**" Any agency of the Commonwealth including departments, boards, commissions, authorities, any political subdivisions or agency of such political subdivision or local or municipal authority or other local government unit or any court or related agency.

"**Income.**" Includes compensation for services, including, but not limited to, wages, salaries, bonuses, fees, compensation in kind, commissions and similar items; income derived from business; gains derived from dealings in property; interest; rents; royalties; dividends; annuities; income from life insurance and endowment contracts; all forms of retirement; pensions; income from discharge of indebtedness; distributive share of partnership gross income; income in respect of a decedent; income from an interest in an estate or trust; military retirement benefits; railroad employment retirement benefits; social security benefits; temporary and permanent disability benefits; worker's compensation; unemployment compensation; other entitlements to money or lump sum awards, without regard to source, including lottery winnings; income tax refunds; insurance compensation or settlements; awards or verdicts; and any form of payment due to and collectible by an individual regardless of source.

"**Judgment by operation of law.**" A judgment which exists without the need for any ministerial act and which arises out of the existence of facts readily verifiable from the domestic relations section's records. The existence of a valid support order and nonpayment of the order, together, create the judgment.

"**Labor organization.**" The term shall have the meaning given the term in section 2(5) of the National Labor Relations Act (49 Stat. 449, 29 U.S.C. § 151 et seq.) and shall include an entity used by the organization and an employer to carry out requirements of an agreement between the organization and the employer as set forth in section 8(f)(3) of the National Labor Relations Act.

"**Net income.**" Gross income minus taxes and any other deductions mandated by the employer as a condition of employment.

"**Obligee.**" The term shall have the meaning given in section 7101(b) (relating to short title of part and definitions).

"**Obligor.**" The term shall have the meaning given in section 7101(b) (relating to short title of part and definitions).

"**Order of support.**" Includes assistance imposed or imposable by law or by any court order, or by an agency administering a State Title IV-D program, whether temporary, final or subject to modification and whether incidental to a proceeding for divorce, separate maintenance, action for failure to support a child born out of wedlock or otherwise. The term includes an order for the support and maintenance of a child, including a child who has attained the age of majority or for the parent with whom the child is living, which provides for monetary support, health care, arrearages or reimbursement and which may include related costs and fees, interest and penalties, income withholding, attorney's fees and other relief.

"**Overdue support.**" Support which is delinquent under a payment schedule established by the court.

"**Past due support.**" Support included in an order of support which has not been paid.

"**State disbursement unit.**" The organizational unit established within the Department of Public Welfare responsible for collecting and disbursing support, as provided in section 4374 (relating to State disbursement unit).

"**Support.**" Care, maintenance and financial assistance.

1998 Amendment. Act 127 added the defs. of "overdue support" and "past due support."

1997 Amendment. Act 58 amended the defs. of "income" and "order of support," and added the defs. of "obligee," "obligor," "state disbursement unit."

1996 Amendment. Act 20 added the def. of "consumer reporting agency;" Act 124 added the def. of "government agency" and "labor organization," and amended the def. of "income."

1993 Amendment. Act 62 added the def. of "genetic tests."

1988 Amendment. Act 35 added the def. of "judgment by operation of law."

Cross References. Section 4302 is referred to in section 7501 of this title; sections 8102, 8533.1 of Title 24 (Education); sections 5102, 5953.1 of Title 71 (State Government).

1997 Amendment. Act 58 amended the defs. of "income" and "order of support," and added the defs. of "obligee," "obligor," "state disbursement unit."

§ 4303. Information to consumer reporting agency.

Information regarding the name and the amount of arrearages owed by an obligor shall be provided periodically to consumer reporting agencies whenever the obligor owes overdue support, subject to the following:

(1) The information shall be available only after the obligor owing the arrearages has been notified of the proposed action and given a period not to exceed 20 days to contest the accuracy of the information. The notice shall be as provided by local rule of the court of common pleas.

(2) Such information shall not be made available to:

(i) a consumer reporting agency which the department determines not to have sufficient capability to systematically and timely make accurate use of such information; or

(ii) an entity which has not furnished evidence satisfactory to the department that the entity is a consumer reporting agency. (Apr. 4, 1996, P.L. 58, No. 20, eff. imd.).

1997 Amendment. Act 58 amended this sec.

§ 4304. {Repealed}.

§ 4304.1. Cooperation of government and nongovernment agencies.

(a) Cooperation of government agencies.—Notwithstanding any other provision of law, including the provisions of section 731 of the act of April 9, 1929 (P.L. 343, No. 176), known as The Fiscal Code, all government agencies shall:

(1) At the request of the department, provide information, prescribed by the department regarding a person's wages, income, telephone numbers, addresses, Social Security numbers and date of birth, employer names, addresses and telephone numbers.

(2) Require the Social Security number of an individual who has one on any application for a professional or occupational license or certification; a permit; a driver's license including a commercial driver's license; a recreational license; or a marriage license. Collection of the Social Security number shall be performed in such manner as to protect its confidentiality. If the government agency uses another identifying number on the face of the application, the government agency shall advise the applicant and shall keep the Social Security number on file at the agency.

(3) Require the Social Security number of any individual subject to a divorce decree, support order, paternity determination or acknowledgment of paternity in all records relating to the matter. Collection of the Social Security number shall be kept confidential.

(4) Require the Social Security number of a deceased individual in records relating to the death, including the death certificate.

(b) Cooperation of labor organizations.—Labor organizations shall at the request of the department provide information in a form prescribed by the department regarding wages, income, telephone numbers, addresses, Social Security numbers and date of birth, employer names, addresses and telephone numbers.

(b.1) Cooperation of financial institutions.—Notwithstanding any other provision of law, all financial institutions doing business in this Commonwealth shall:

(1) Provide for each calendar quarter such identifying information, asset information and benefit information as the department may specify for any obligor who

owes past due support as identified by the department by name and Social Security number or other taxpayer identification number.

(2) Upon receipt of a notice of lien or seizure order from the domestic relations section or the department, encumber or surrender, as the case may be, identified assets of an obligor who is subject to a child support lien. The Supreme Court shall, by general rule, prescribe the form of the order. The financial institution shall remit to the domestic relations section or to the department the assets available in the account on the date of the receipt of the notice of lien or seizure order by the financial institution. Remittance by the financial institution shall be made within a reasonable period of time.

(b.2) Agreements between the department and financial institutions.—Notwithstanding any other provision of law, the department and any financial institution doing business in this Commonwealth are authorized to enter into agreements for the purpose of carrying out the provisions of subsection (b.1). The agreement may specify payment of a fee by the department to the financial institution to conduct the activities in accordance with subsection (b.1)(1) which shall not exceed actual and reasonable costs incurred by the financial institution.

(c) Penalty.—Following notice and hearing, the department may impose a civil penalty of up to $1,000 per violation upon any government agency, labor organization or financial institution which willfully fails to comply with a request by the department for information pursuant to this section.

(d) Confidentiality.—Any information provided or collected pursuant to this section shall be confidential and may be used by the department, the court or the domestic relations section solely for purposes of child and spousal support enforcement and, to the extent allowed by Federal law, for administration of public assistance programs. Any person, government agency, employer or agent of the department who divulges such information in a manner not provided in this section commits a misdemeanor of the third degree and, upon conviction, shall be sentenced to pay a fine of up to $1,000 per violation and costs and shall be subject to a term of imprisonment of not more than one year or both.

(d.1) Notification.—No financial institution shall be required to notify an obligor of a request for information by the department or the court under this section.

(e) Immunity.—A person, government agency, labor organization or financial institution providing information, encumbering or surrendering property pursuant to this section shall not be subject to civil or criminal liability to any person or entity. The department, a court, a domestic relations section or an authorized employee of such an entity requesting information under this section or ordering the seizure, encumbrance or surrender of an asset held by a financial institution shall not be subject to any civil or criminal liability. A financial institution shall not be subject to any civil or criminal liability for encumbering or surrendering assets of an obligor as required by this section. The immunity provided by this paragraph shall not apply to any person or agent of a government agency, labor organization or financial institution who knowingly supplies false information under this section.

(f) Data collection.—The department shall provide for the frequency and format, which may include automated data exchanges, for the collection of the information required in this section.

(g) Definitions.—As used in this section, the following words and phrases shall have the meanings given to them in this subsection:

"Account." A demand deposit account, checking or negotiable withdrawal order account, savings account, time deposit account or money market mutual fund account. The term does not include trust accounts, custodian accounts or accounts under 20 Pa.C.S. Ch. 53 (relating to the Pennsylvania Uniform Transfers to Minors Act).

"Asset information." Account balances, deposits, withdrawals, interest, investments, trusts, dividends, certificates of deposits and other asset information.

"Benefit information." Information regarding financial or health care benefits to which an individual may be entitled from government, an employer, an insurer or other source.

"Financial institution." A depository institution, as defined by section 3(c) of the Federal Deposit Insurance Act (64 Stat. 873, 12 U.S.C. § 1813(c)); an institution-affiliated party, as defined by section 3(u) of the Federal Deposit Insurance Act, a Federal credit union or State credit union, as defined in section 101 of the Federal Credit Union Act (48 Stat. 1216, 12 U.S.C. § 1752), including an institution-affiliated party of such a credit union, as defined in section 206(r) of the Federal Credit Union Act; and a benefit association, insurer, safe deposit company, money-market mutual fund or similar entity authorized to do business in this Commonwealth.

"Identifying information." Name, record address, Social Security number or other taxpayer identification number.

"Insurer." A foreign or domestic insurance company, association or exchange holding a certificate of authority under the act of May 17, 1921 (P.L. 682, No. 284), known as The Insurance Company Law of 1921; a risk-assuming preferred provider organization operating under section 630 of The Insurance Company Law of 1921; a health maintenance organization holding a certificate of authority under the act of December 29, 1972 (P.L. 1701, No. 364), known as the Health Maintenance Organization Act; a fraternal benefit society holding a certificate of authority under the act of December 14, 1992 (P.L. 835, No. 134), known as the Fraternal Benefit Societies Code; a hospital plan corporation holding a certificate of authority under 40 Pa.C.S. Ch. 61 (relating to hospital plan corporations); a professional health service plan corporation holding a certificate of authority under 40 Pa.C.S. Ch. 63 (relating to professional health service plan corporations); or a similar entity authorized to do insurance business in this Commonwealth.

1998 Amendment. Act 127 amended subsec. (a)(2) and (3).

1997 Amendment. Act 58 amended this sec.

1996 Amendment. Act 124 added sec. 4304.1.

§ 4305. General administration of support matters.

(a) Powers and duties.—Subject to any inconsistent general rules and to the supervision and direction of the court, the domestic relations section shall have the power and duty to:

(1) Process all complaints received under Pt. VIII (relating to uniform interstate family support) and Pt. VIII-A (relating to intrastate family support).

(2) Make such investigation as may be necessary.

(3) Take charge of any obligor before or after hearing, as may be directed by the court.

(4) Collect and pay over to the persons entitled thereto moneys received pursuant to support proceedings.

(5) Keep a full and complete record of all support proceedings, including orders of the court.

(6) Keep account of all payments made under order of court and promptly bring to the attention of the court and the district attorney any default in compliance with any order of court.

(6.1) In the case of a dispute as to the amount of an order of support proposed by the domestic relations section, issue a temporary order of support pending judicial determination. A temporary order of support under this paragraph may not be for less than the full amount of the proposed order of support being disputed.

(7) Make effective the orders of support entered.

(8) Furnish the court with such information and assistance as it may require and generally perform such services as it may direct relating to support proceedings.

(9) Inform both parties to a support action that guidelines as specified in section 4322 (relating to support guidelines) are available in the domestic relations section.

(10) Implement safeguards applicable to all confidential information received by the domestic relations section, in order to protect the privacy rights of the parties, including:

  (i) safeguards against unauthorized use or disclosure of information relating to proceedings or actions to establish paternity or to establish, modify or enforce support or to make or enforce a child custody determination;

  (ii) prohibitions against the release of information on the whereabouts of one party or the child to another party against whom a protective order with respect to the former party or the child has been entered; and

  (iii) prohibitions against the release of information on the whereabouts of one party or the child to another person if the domestic relations section has reason to believe that the release of the information may result in physical or emotional harm to the party or the child.

(11) Initiate judicial proceedings to void a fraudulent transfer or obtain a settlement from the transferee in the best interests of the child support obligee.

(b) Additional powers.—Subject to the supervision and direction of the court, but without the need for prior judicial order, the domestic relations section shall have the power to expedite the establishment and enforcement of support to:

(1) Order genetic testing for the purpose of paternity establishment pursuant to section 4343 (relating to paternity).

(2) Issue subpoenas against any entity within this Commonwealth, including for-profit, not-for-profit and governmental employers, to require production of information regarding the employment, compensation and benefits of any individual employed by the entity as an employee or contractor.

(3) Access records of all State and local government agencies, including the following:

  (i) vital statistic records, including records of marriage, birth and divorce;

  (ii) State and local tax and revenue records, including information on residence address, employer, income and assets;

  (iii) records of real and titled personal property;

  (iv) records of occupational and professional licenses;

  (v) records of the ownership and control of corporations, partnerships and other business entities;

  (vi) employment security records;

  (vii) records of agencies administering public assistance programs;

  (viii) motor vehicle registration and operator licensing records;

  (ix) probation and parole records; and

  (x) corrections records.

(4) Issue subpoenas for the records of public utilities and cable television companies with respect to individuals who are owed support, or against whom or with respect to whom a support obligation is sought, consisting of the names and addresses of the individuals or of their employers.

(5) Issue subpoenas for the records held by financial institutions with respect to individuals who are owed support, or against whom or with respect to whom a support obligation is sought.

(6) Issue subpoenas for financial or other information needed to establish, modify or enforce a support order.

(7) Issue orders directing an obligor or other payor to change the payee of a support order.

(8) Order income withholding pursuant to section 4348 (relating to attachment of income).

(9) Increase the amount of monthly support payments for the payment of arrearages, as may be provided by general rule or previous court order.

(10) Issue orders in cases where there is a support arrearage to secure assets to satisfy current support obligation and the arrearage by:

(i) Intercepting or seizing periodic or lump sum payments from a government agency, including unemployment compensation, workers' compensation and other benefits.

(ii) Intercepting or seizing judgments or settlements.

(iii) Attaching and seizing assets of the obligor held in financial institutions.

(iv) Attaching public and private retirement funds.

(v) Imposing liens on property.

(vi) Directing the sheriff to levy and sell other real or personal property.

(11) Transmit to another state a request for assistance in a case involving the enforcement of a support order and sufficient information to enable the state to which the request is transmitted to compare the information to the information in the data bases of the state. The transmittal shall serve as a certification of arrears and a certification that the state has complied with all procedural due process requirements applicable to the case.

(12) Respond to a request for assistance received from another state. The response shall confirm the receipt of the request, the action taken and the amount of support collected and specify any additional information or action required of the requesting tribunal to obtain enforcement of the child support obligation.

(c) **Civil penalty.**—In addition to initiating contempt proceedings, the domestic relations section may assess a civil administrative penalty of up to $1,000 per violation upon any person or entity which fails to comply with a subpoena or request for information under subsection (b)(2).

(d) **Due process and judicial review procedures.**—Subject to general rules which may be promulgated by the Supreme Court, each court shall establish due process and judicial review procedures for domestic relations sections exercising powers under this section.

(e) **Transmission of information.**—All information transmitted to this Commonwealth from another state for purposes of establishing or enforcing an order of support under this chapter may be transmitted electronically or by other methods.

1997 Amendment. Act 58 amended this sec.

§ 4306. Duties of Title IV-D attorney.

(a) **General rule.**—The county Title IV-D attorney shall at all times aid in the enforcement of the duty of child support and child and spousal support and shall cooperate with the domestic relations section in the presentation of complaints or in any proceeding designed to obtain compliance with any order of the court.

(b) **Representation of complainant.**—The district attorney, upon the request of the court or a Commonwealth or local public welfare official, shall represent any complainant in any proceeding under this subchapter.

(b.1) **Representation of Commonwealth.**—In matters relating to the establishment and enforcement of child support and child and spousal support, the Title IV-D interests of the Commonwealth shall be represented, where appropriate, by the county Title IV-D attorney in a proceeding for child support and child and spousal support.

(c) **Joinder of Department of Public Welfare.**—Whenever the record in any support action or proceeding indicates that the persons for whom support is sought have received public assistance from the Department of Public Welfare at any time since the initiation of the matter, the department may become a party to the action or proceeding by filing an entry of appearance. This entry of appearance may be entered without leave of court at any time and at any stage of the action or proceeding. (July 2, 1993, P.L.431, No.62, eff. imd.)

1997 Amendment. Act 58 amended this sec.

1993 Amendment. Section 7 of Act 62 provided that subsec. (c) shall apply to actions pending on the effective date of Act 62 under section 8(3) of Act 62.

§ 4307. State income tax intercept.

The department shall have the authority to implement a State income tax refund intercept program pursuant to section 466(a)(3) of the Social Security Act (Public Law 74-271, 42 U.S.C. § 666(a)(3)) when, in the judgment of the department, it is cost effective to do so.

1997 Amendment. Act 58 amended this sec.

§ 4308. Lottery winnings intercept.

(a) **Duty of Department of Revenue.**—In the case of any person winning more than $2,500 in the Pennsylvania State Lottery, the Department of Revenue shall request the department to make all reasonable efforts to determine if the winner is a delinquent support obligor prior to making any lottery winnings payment. If the winner is so found, the amount of any arrearages shall be deducted from the amount of lottery winnings and paid to the obligee in the manner provided in this title for the administration of support payments.

(b) **Duties of department.**—The department shall:

(1) Cause a search to be made periodically of the following:

(i) Its records relative to the Title IV-D Program.

(ii) Any information received from county domestic relations offices relative to arrearages of court-ordered child support.

(iii) Any information received from states with reciprocal enforcement of child support relative to arrearages of court-ordered child support.

(2) Furnish the Department of Revenue with the following information:

(i) The department identifier.

(ii) The obligor's full name and Social Security number.

(iii) The amount of the arrearage and the identifier of the court order which underlies it.

(3) Request the Department of Revenue to withhold from a lottery prizewinner the amount of any arrearage discovered pursuant to the provisions of paragraph (1).

(4) Request the Department of Revenue to pay over, whether in a lump sum or by installment, to the department that part of the prize which satisfies this arrearage and:

(i) Deduct from the amount received from the Department of Revenue any amount assigned to the department.

(ii) Pay over to the domestic relations section for distribution to the obligee of the child support court order the amount of prizewinnings which satisfies the arrearage owed to the obligee. This payment shall be made within 30 days of the date when the winnings are withheld.

(5) May, if prizewinnings are insufficient to satisfy the arrearages owed under the child support order, proceed as follows:

(i) It may collect as provided by law.

(ii) It may reinitiate the procedures set forth in this section if the obligor wins a subsequent lottery prize.

(6) Determine and set a fee which reflects the actual costs it and the Department of Revenue incur to administer this section, submit this calculation to the Department of Revenue for its approval, request the Department of Revenue to deduct the calculated amount from the amount to be paid to the prizewinner after the prizewinner's child support obligation has been fully satisfied and request that the deducted amount be divided between both departments based on the administrative expenses incurred by each.

(7) Within 30 days of the date the prize was won:

(i) Award the prizewinner the lottery prize winnings in whole or in part.

(ii) If applicable, notify the prizewinner that the prize or a portion thereof was used to satisfy arrearages owed for court-ordered child support.

(c) Notice.—The domestic relations section shall send a one-time notice to all obligors of existing orders informing them that arrearages may be intercepted as provided by this section.

(d) Right to review.—A lottery prizewinner whose prize is used to satisfy an obligation under this section may appeal to the department in accordance with 2 Pa.C.S. (relating to administrative law and procedure). The appeal shall be filed within 30 days after the prizewinner is notified by the Department of Revenue that the prize has been reduced or totally withheld to satisfy the prizewinner's outstanding arrearages for child support and related obligations.

(e) Rules and regulations.—The Department of Revenue and the department shall, in the manner provided by law, jointly promulgate the rules and regulations necessary to carry out this section.

1997 Amendment. Act 58 amended this sec.

1992 Amendment. Act 87 added Section 4308.

§ 4308.1. Collection of overdue support from monetary awards.

(a) General rule.—Overdue support shall be a lien by operation of law against the net proceeds of any monetary award, as defined herein, owed to an obligor, and distribution of any such award shall be stayed in an amount equal to the child support lien provided for under this section pending payment of the lien. except as provided in subsection (c) or (f), nothing in this section shall provide a basis for a paying agent or an insurer to delay payment of a settlement, verdict or judgment.

(b) General procedure.—Except as provided in subsection (f), before the prevailing party or beneficiary can receive the proceeds of a monetary award, the prevailing party or beneficiary shall provide his attorney with a statement made subject to 18 Pa.C.S. § 4904 (relating to unsworn falsification to authorities) that includes the prevailing party's or beneficiary's full name, mailing address, date of birth, and social security number. The prevailing party or beneficiary shall also provide his attorney with written documentation of arrears from the pennsylvania child support enforcement system website, or if no arrears exist, written documentation from the website indicating no arrears. The attorney shall obtain a copy of the prevailing party or beneficiary's statement and a lien report from the website at the time of the delivery of the release; the lien report shall be dated within 20 days of the date of the delivery of the release. In the event that there are arrears, the attorney shall make payment of any lien to the department's state disbursement unit from the net proceeds of any monetary award.

(c) Pro se actions.—If the prevailing party or beneficiary is not represented by an attorney, he shall provide the statement and written documentation of arrears or no arrears provided by subsection (b) or (d), to the insurer or other paying agent responsible for distribution of the monetary award who shall make payment of any lien, or disputed lien amount, as described in subsection (h), to the department's state disbursement unit from the net proceeds of any monetary award.

(d) Use of private judgment search companies.—In lieu of receiving the statement and written documentation of arrears or no arrears provided in subsections (b), (c) and (f), an attorney or insurer may use the services of a private judgment search company approved by the department, or an insurer may use the services of the child support enforcement lien program operated through a central reporting agency approved by the department. An attorney or insurer may deduct the fee for such a judgment search from any payment to the prevailing party or beneficiary.

(e) Immunity.—An attorney, insurer or other paying agent that makes distribution in accordance with a statement and the written documentation required under subsection (b), or the report of an approved private judgment search company under subsection (d), or an insurer which furnishes information and transmits funds under the child support enforcement lien program operated through a central reporting agency approved by the department, shall be immune from any civil, criminal, or administrative penalties for making an erroneous distribution. Nothing in this section shall give rise to a claim or cause of action against an attorney or an insurer by any person who asserts he is the intended obligee of the outstanding lien for child support.

(f) Workers' compensation awards.—With respect to any monetary award arising under the act of June 2, 1915 (p.l.736, No.338), known as the Workers' Compensation Act, or the Act of June 21, 1939 (p.l.566, No.284), known as the Pennsylvania Occupational Disease Act, no order providing for a payment shall be entered by the workers' compensation judge unless the prevailing party or beneficiary, who is a claimant under either or both of the acts, shall provide the judge with a statement made subject to 18 Pa.C.S. § 4904 (relating to unsworn falsification to authorities) that includes the full name, mailing address, date of birth and social security number for the prevailing party or beneficiary who is a claimant under either or both acts. The prevailing party or beneficiary, who is a claimant under either or both of the acts shall also provide the judge with either written documentation of arrears from the pennsylvania child support enforcement system website, or if no arrears exist, written documentation from the website indicating no arrears. The judge shall order payment of the lien for overdue support to the department's state disbursement unit from the net proceeds due the prevailing party or beneficiary who is a claimant under either or both acts.

(g) Exception.—This section shall not apply to any monetary award due to a prevailing party or beneficiary under 12 years of age or, in the case of an award under the Workers' Compensation Act or the Pennsylvania Occupational Disease Act, a claimant under 12 years of age.

(h) Escrow.—In the event that there is a dispute as to the amount of arrears owed by the prevailing party, beneficiary or claimant based on a mistake of fact, the amount in dispute shall be placed in escrow in the department's state disbursement unit by the prevailing party's or beneficiary's attorney and the escrowed funds shall not be distributed until the dispute is resolved. In such event, the distribution of the remaining net proceeds of the monetary award shall not be stayed. A mistake of fact, as used in this subsection, shall be limited to errors in the amount of arrearage or mistaken identity. Upon resolution of the dispute, the amount of arrears shall be paid to the department's state disbursement unit.

(i) Definitions.—As used in this section, the following words and phrases shall have the meanings given to them in this subsection:

"Monetary award." Any portion of a settlement paid as a lump sum negotiated in lieu of, or subsequent to the filing of a lawsuit for, or any civil judgment or civil arbitration award that is paid as a third party claim for bodily injury or death under a property and casualty insurance policy, or paid as a workers' compensation or occupational disease act award under a workers' compensation policy. The term includes self-insurers and also applies to property and casualty and workers compensation or occupational disease act policies which are issued by an insurer licensed or authorized to do business in this commonwealth. The term does not include a lump sum payable through a structured settlement annuity. The term shall apply only to those settlements, judgments, civil arbitrations, Workers' Compensation Act or the Pennsylvania Occupational Disease Act awards which are asserted and resolved in this Commonwealth.

"Net proceeds." Moneys in excess of $5,000 payable to a prevailing party or beneficiary, or in the case of an award under the Workers' Compensation Act or the Pennsylvania Occupational Disease Act, the claimant, after payment of attorney fees, witness fees, court costs, reasonable litigation expenses, documented unpaid expenses incurred for medical treatment causally related to the claim, any workers' compensation or occupational disease indemnity or medical payment, and payments to the medical assistance program under sections 1409 and 1412 of the act of June 13, 1967 (p.l.31, No.21), known as the public welfare code.

"Obligee." the term shall have the meaning provided under section 7101(b) (relating to short title of part and definitions).

"Obligor." The term shall have the meaning provided under section 7101(b).

"Overdue support." The term shall have the meaning provided under section 4302 (relating to definitions).

2006 Amendment. Act 109 added this sec., effective Sept. 5, 2006.

Editor Comment. This section requires all lawyers to certify that before a client receives a personal injury award or lump sum workers' comp award they do not owe back child support. This law effects all settlements, judgements, arbitration awards, workers' compensation awards with net proceeds in excess of $5,000.

This section allows the Department of Public Welfare to intercept lump sum monetary awards of settlements paid by insurers or workers' compensation to pay past due support.

The law requires plaintiffs' attorneys to obtain statements from their clients including personal information and the amount of any arrearages in child support. Attorneys are responsible for confirming with the Department of Public Welfare that there are no arrearages.

This obligation arises when the client will net more than $5,000 from any personal injury or workers' compensation settlement. Thus, if the client will receive less than $5,000 after a reduction of attorney's fees and costs, then the bill would not apply. If the client will net more than $5,000, then the bill applies to only the amount above $5,000 and not to the first $5,000.

There are a number of ways to obtain the amount of outstanding child support owed by the client:

1. Go to www.childsupport.state.pa.us and register to be able to conduct lien searches. This search will only give you the total amount of the current lien and not the lien payment history.
2. Use a professional judgement company to gather the information; or
3. Pay $25 to the local child support agency to do an audit.

If you determine that your client owes money. It must be paid directly to:

   PA SCDU
   PO BOX 69110
   Harrisburg, Pa 17106-9110

The check **must** include client's social security number or the PACSES (Case ID) number. The PACSES (Case ID) number can be obtained through the website above.

Forms:

STATEMENT CONCERNING CHILD SUPPORT ARREARS

I, _____, hereby certify that according to the Pennsylvania Child Support Enforcement System Website, that I currently owe $_____ in child support arrears as shown on the attached printout from the website.

If there are arrears owed, I acknowledge that the arrears constitute a lien against my personal injury or workers' compensation settlement or award.

I hereby acknowledge that my attorney is obligated by state law to pay the amount of the lien to Pennsylvania SCDU prior to the distribution of any settlement or award proceeds to me. I authorize my attorney to submit payment to SCDU of any lien amount for child support arrears as shown by the website printout.

Even if I dispute the amount of arrears shown on the website printout, I acknowledge that my attorney is obligated to submit the amount currently shown. I understand that I can then take steps to dispute the amount, but my attorney is not under any obligation to represent me in that dispute unless I hire him specifically for that purpose. My attorney's current representation of me in this personal injury or workers' compensation matter does not include representation concerning the dispute of child support arrears.

I understand that false statements herein are made subject to the penalties of 18 Pa. C.S.A. Section 4904, relating to unsworn falsification to authorities.

Printed name: _____

Address: _____

_____

Date of Birth: _____/_____/_____

SS#: _____-_____-_____

DATE:_____   _____
                                Signature

STATEMENT CONCERNING CHILD SUPPORT ARREARS

I, _____, hereby certify that I currently owe **$ 0.00** in child support arrears as evidenced by the attached printout from the Pennsylvania Child Support Enforcement System Website, which shows no records or results under my name.

I understand that false statements herein are made subject to the penalties of 18 Pa. C.S.A. Section 4904, relating to unsworn falsification to authorities.

Printed name: _____

Address: _____

_____

Date of Birth: _____/_____/_____

SS#: _____-_____-_____

DATE:_____   _____
                                Signature

§ 4309. Publication of delinquent support obligors.

   (a) **General rule.**—Any county, through its domestic relations section, may publish the names of delinquent support obligors who are in arrears 30 days or more in newspapers of general or special circulation in the county.

   (b) **Immunity.**—The county, its officials and newspapers shall be immune from any and all criminal and civil liability as a result of the publication of names and identities under subsection (a), unless the publication is a result of intentional misconduct by the county, its officials or newspapers.

(July 2, 1993, P.L.431, No.62, eff. 60 days)

   1993 Amendment. Act 62 added section 4309.

SUBCHAPTER B
SUPPORT

Sec.

4321. Liability for support.
4322. Support guideline.
4323. Support of emancipated child.
4324. Inclusion of spousal medical support.
4325. Payment of order of support.
4326. Mandatory inclusion of child medical support.
4327. Postsecondary educational costs.

Cross References. Actions for support, see Pa.R.C.P. No. 1910.1 et seq.

§ 4321. Liability for support.

Subject to the provisions of this chapter:

(1) Married persons are liable for the support of each other according to their respective abilities to provide support as provided by law.

(2) Parents are liable for the support of their children who are unemancipated and 18 years of age or younger.

(2.1) Paragraph (2) applies whether or not parental rights of the parent have been terminated due to a conviction for any of the following where the other parent is the victim and a child has been conceived as a result of the offense:

    (i) 18 Pa.C.S. § 3121 (relating to rape);

    (ii) 18 Pa.C.S. § 3122.1 (relating to statutory sexual assault);

    (iii) 18 Pa.C.S. § 3124.1 (relating to sexual assault) where the offense involved sexual intercourse;

    (iv) 18 Pa.C.S. § 3124.2 (relating to institutional sexual assault) where the offense involved sexual intercourse; or

    (v) 18 Pa.C.S. § 4302 (relating to incest) where the offense involved sexual intercourse.

Paternity of the child under this paragraph shall be established through voluntary acknowledgment of paternity or blood, genetic or other type of paternity test acceptable to the court. The cost of the testing shall be borne by the parent who was convicted of the offense.

(3) Parents may be liable for the support of their children who are 18 years of age or older.

(Oct. 1, 2015, P.L. ___, No. 40, eff. 60 days)

Note: The addition of 23 Pa.C.S. §§ 4321(2.1) and 5329 (b.1) shall apply to any action regarding custody of a child under 23 Pa.C.S. Ch. 43 or 53 that is filed on or after the effective date of this section.

§ 4322. Support guideline.

(a) **Statewide guideline.**—Child and spousal support shall be awarded pursuant to a Statewide guideline as established by general rule by the Supreme Court, so that persons similarly situated shall be treated similarly. The guideline shall be based upon the reasonable needs of the child or spouse seeking support and the ability of the obligor to provide support. In determining the reasonable needs of the child or spouse seeking support and the ability of the obligor to provide support, the guideline shall place primary emphasis on the net incomes and earning capacities of the parties, with allowable deviations for unusual needs, extraordinary expenses and other factors, such as the parties' assets, as warrant special attention. The guideline so developed shall be reviewed at least once every four years.

(b) Rebuttable presumption.—There shall be a rebuttable presumption, in any judicial or expedited process, that the amount of the award which would result from the application of such guideline is the correct amount of support to be awarded. A written finding or specific finding on the record that the application of the guideline would be unjust or inappropriate in a particular case shall be sufficient to rebut the presumption in that case, provided that the finding is based upon criteria established by the Supreme Court by general rule within one year of the effective date of this act.
(Dec. 20, 1989, P.L.654, No.81, eff. imd.)

<small>**Cross References.** Section 4322 is referred to in section 4305 of this title.</small>

§ 4323. Support of emancipated child.

(a) Emancipated child.—A court shall not order either or both parents to pay for the support of a child if the child is emancipated.

(b) Marital status of parents immaterial.—In making an order for the support of a child, no distinction shall be made because of the marital status of the parents.

§ 4324. Inclusion of spousal medical support.

In addition to periodic support payments, the court may require that an obligor pay a designated percentage of a spouse's reasonable and necessary health care expenses. If health care coverage is available through an obligor or obligee at no cost as a benefit of employment or at a reasonable cost, the court shall order an obligor or obligee to provide or extend health care coverage to a spouse. Upon failure of the obligor to make this payment or reimburse the spouse and after compliance with procedural due process requirement, the court shall treat the amount as arrearages.
(Dec. 4, 1992, P.L.757, No.114, eff. 90 days)

<small>**1992 Amendment.** Section 4(1) of Act 114 provided that the amendment of section 4324 shall apply to all support orders entered, reviewed or modified on or after the effective date of Act 114.

Cross References. Section 4324 is referred to in section 6108 of this title.</small>

§ 4325. Payment of order of support.

Unless procedures established by the department for the State disbursement unit provide otherwise, an order of support shall direct payment to be made payable to or payment to be made to the domestic relations section for transmission to the obligee or for transmission directly to a public body or public or private agency whenever the care, maintenance and assistance of the obligee is provided for by the public body or public or private agency.

<small>**1997 Amendment.** Act 58 amended this sec.</small>

§ 4326. Mandatory inclusion of child medical support.

(a) General rule.—In every proceeding to establish or modify an order which requires the payment of child support, the court shall ascertain the ability of each parent to provide medical support for the children of the parties, and the order shall include a requirement for medical support to be provided by either or both parents, provided that such medical support is accessible to the children.

(b) Noncustodial parent requirement.—If medical support is available at a reasonable cost to a noncustodial parent, the court shall require that the noncustodial parent provide such medical support to the children of the parties. In cases where there are two noncustodial parents having such medical support available, the court shall require one or both parents to provide medical support.

(c) Custodial parent requirement.—If medical support is available at a reasonable cost to a custodial parent, the court shall require that the custodial parent provide such medical support to the children of the parties, unless adequate medical support has already been provided through the noncustodial parent. In cases where the parents have shared custody of the child and medical support is available to both, the court shall require one or both parents to provide medical support, taking into account the financial ability of the parties and the extent of medical support available to each parent.

(d) **Additional requirement.**—If the court finds that medical support is not available to either parent at a reasonable cost, the court shall order either parent or both parents to obtain medical support for the parties' children which is available at reasonable cost.

(d.1) **Medical support notice.**—The department shall develop a medical support notice for use by the department or domestic relations section in accordance with procedures established by the department. The medical support notice shall comply with national standards established by the Federal Government for medical support notices. The department or domestic relations section shall send the medical support notice to the employer within two business days after the date of entry of an employee who is a new hire into the Commonwealth directory of new hires under section 4392 (relating to employer reporting).

(e) **Uninsured expenses.**—The court shall determine the amount of any deductible and copayments which each parent shall pay. In addition, the court may require that either parent or both parents pay a designated percentage of the reasonable and necessary uncovered health care expenses of the parties' children, including birth-related expenses incurred prior to the filing of the complaint. Upon request of the domestic relations section, the department shall provide to the domestic relations section all birth-related expenses which the department has incurred in cases it has referred to the domestic relations section for child support services.

(f) **Proof of insurance.**—Within 30 days after the entry of an order requiring a parent to provide health care coverage for a child or after any change in health care coverage due to a change in the parent's employment, the obligated parent shall submit to the other parent, or person having custody of the child, written proof that health care coverage has been obtained or that application for coverage has been made. Proof of coverage shall consist of at a minimum:

(1) The name of the health care coverage provider.

(2) Any applicable identification numbers.

(3) Any cards evidencing coverage.

(4) The address to which claims should be made.

(5) A description of any restrictions on usage, such as prior approval for hospital admissions, and the manner of obtaining approval.

(6) A copy of the benefit booklet or coverage contract.

(7) A description of all deductibles and copayments.

(8) Five copies of any claim forms.

(g) **Obligations of insurance companies.**—Every insurer doing business within this Commonwealth shall be obligated as follows:

(1) to permit the custodial parent or the provider, with the custodial parent's approval, to submit claims for covered services without the approval of the noncustodial parent and to make payment on such claims directly to such custodial parent, the provider or, in the case of Medical Assistance patients, to the department;

(2) to provide such information to the custodial parent as may be necessary to obtain benefits, including copies of benefit booklets, insurance contracts and claims information;

(3) if coverage is made available for dependents of the insured, to make such coverage available to the insured's children without regard to enrollment season restrictions, whether the child was born out of wedlock, whether the child is claimed as a dependent on the parent's Federal income tax return, whether the child resides in the insurer's service area, the amount of support contributed by a parent, the amount of time the child spends in the home or the custodial arrangements for the child;

(4) to permit the enrollment of children under court order upon application of the custodial parent, domestic relations section or the department within 30 days of receipt by the insurer of the order;

(4.1) not to disenroll or eliminate coverage of any child unless the insurer is provided satisfactory written evidence that a court order requiring coverage is no longer in effect or that the child is or will be enrolled in comparable health coverage through another insurer which will take effect no later than the effective date of such disenrollment;

(4.2) to receive, process and pay claims (whether or not on behalf of a child), including electronically submitted claims, submitted by the department within the time permitted by law without imposing any patient signature requirement or other requirement different from those imposed upon providers, agents or assignees of any insured individual;

(5) to provide the custodial parent who has complied with subsection (j) with the same notification of termination or modification of any health care coverage due to nonpayment of premiums or other reason as is provided to other insureds under the policy; and

(6) except as provided in paragraph (4.2), to not take into account the fact that any individual, whether or not a child, is eligible for or is being provided medical assistance when enrolling that individual or when making any payments for benefits to the individual or on the individual's behalf.

(h) Obligations of noninsurers.—To the maximum extent permitted by Federal law, the obligations of subsection (g) shall apply to noninsurers providing health care coverage within this Commonwealth, including health maintenance organizations, self-insured employee health benefit plans and any other entity offering a service benefit plan.

(h.1) Obligations of employers.—Every employer doing business within this Commonwealth shall be obligated as follows:

(1) in any case in which a parent is required by a court order to provide health coverage for a child and the parent is eligible for family health coverage, the employer shall permit the insured parent to enroll any child who is otherwise eligible without regard to any enrollment season restrictions;

(2) if the insured parent is enrolled but fails to make application to obtain coverage for such child, to enroll the child under the family coverage upon application by the child's other parent, the domestic relations section or the department;

(3) not to disenroll or eliminate coverage of any such child unless the employer is provided satisfactory written evidence that the court or administrative order is no longer in effect, the child is or will be enrolled in comparable health coverage which will take effect not later than the effective date of such disenrollment or the employer has eliminated family health coverage for all of its employees;

(4) to transfer health coverage for any child to the health coverage of the employer upon receipt of a medical support notice under subsection (d.1) issued by the department or a domestic relations section within 20 business days after the date of the notice; and

(5) to notify the domestic relations section whenever the insured parent's employment is terminated.

(i) Obligations of custodial parent.—The custodial parent shall comply with the insurer's existing claim procedures and present to the insurer one of the following documents:

(1) a copy of a court order as defined in subsection (l); or

(2) a release signed by the insured permitting the insurer to communicate directly with the custodial parent.

(j) **Enforcement of order.**—The employee's share, if any, of premiums for health coverage shall be deducted by the employer and paid to the insurer or other entity providing health care coverage. If an obligated parent fails to comply with the order to provide health care coverage for a child, fails to pay medical expenses for a child or receives payment from a third party for the cost of medical services provided to such child and fails to reimburse the custodial parent or provider of services, the court shall:

(1) If, after a hearing, the failure or refusal is determined to have been willful, impose the penalties of section 4345(a) (relating to contempt for noncompliance with support order).

(2) Enter an order for a sum certain against the obligated parent for the cost of medical care for the child and for any premiums paid or provided for the child during any period in which the obligated parent failed or refused to provide coverage. Failure to comply with an order under this paragraph shall be subject to section 4348 (relating to attachment of income).

(3) Upon failure of the obligated parent to make this payment or reimburse the custodial parent and after compliance with due process requirements, treat the amount as arrearages.

(k) **Enforcement against insurers.**—Any insurer or other entity which violates the obligations imposed upon it under subsection (g) or (h) shall be civilly liable for damages and may be adjudicated in contempt and fined by the court.

(l) **Definitions.**—As used in this section, the following words and phrases shall have the meanings given to them in this subsection:

"**Birth-related expenses.**" Costs of reasonable and necessary health care for the mother or child or both incurred before, during or after the birth of a child born in or out of wedlock which are the result of the pregnancy or birth and which benefit either the mother or child. Charges not related to the pregnancy or birth shall be excluded.

"**Child.**" A child to whom a duty of child support is owed.

"**Health care coverage.**" Coverage for medical, dental, orthodontic, optical, psychological, psychiatric or other health care services for a child. For the purposes of this section, medical assistance under Subarticle (f) of Article IV of the act of June 13, 1967 (P.L. 31, No. 21), known as the Public Welfare Code, shall not be considered health care coverage.

"**Insurer.**" A foreign or domestic insurance company, association or exchange holding a certificate of authority under the act of May 17, 1921 (P.L. 682, No. 284), known as The Insurance Company Law of 1921; a risk-assuming preferred provider organization operating under section 630 of The Insurance Company Law of 1921; a health maintenance organization holding a certificate of authority under the act of December 29, 1972 (P.L. 1701, No. 364), known as the Health Maintenance Organization Act; a fraternal benefit society holding a certificate of authority under the former act of December 14, 1992 (P.L. 835, No. 134), known as the Fraternal Benefit Societies Code; a hospital plan corporation holding a certificate of authority under 40 Pa.C.S. Ch. 61 (relating to hospital plan corporations); a professional health service plan corporation holding a certificate of authority under 40 Pa.C.S. Ch. 63 (relating to professional health services plan corporations); or a similar entity authorized to do insurance business in this Commonwealth.

"**Medical child support order.**" An order which relates to the child's right to receive certain health care coverage and which:

(1) includes the name and last known mailing address of the parent providing health care coverage and the name and last known mailing address of the child;

(2) includes a reasonable description of the type of coverage to be provided or includes the manner in which coverage is to be determined;

(3) designates the time period to which the order applies;

(4) if coverage is provided through a group health plan, designates each plan to which the order applies as of the date the order is written;

(4.1) requires that, if health care coverage is provided through the noncustodial parent's employer and that parent changes employment, the provisions of the order will remain in effect for the duration of the order and will automatically apply to the new employer. The new employer shall enroll the child in health care coverage without need for an amended order unless the noncustodial parent contests the enrollment; and

(5) includes the name and address of the custodial parent.

"**Medical support.**" Health care coverage, which includes coverage under a health insurance plan or government-subsidized health care coverage, including payment of costs of premiums, copayments, deductibles and capitation fees, and payment for medical expenses incurred on behalf of a child.

"**Reasonable cost.**" Cost of health care coverage that does not exceed 5% of the party's net monthly income and, if the obligor is to provide health care coverage, the cost of the premium when coupled with a cash child support obligation and other child support-related obligations does not exceed the amounts allowed by the Federal threshold set forth in the Consumer Credit Protection Act (Public Law 90-321, 15 U.S.C. § 1601 et seq.).

(1992, Dec. 4, P.L. 757, No. 114, § 2, effective in 90 days. Amended 1994, Dec. 16, P.L. 808, No. 150, § 1, imd. effective; 1997, Dec. 16, P.L. 549, No. 58, § 4, effective Jan. 1, 1998; 2001, Dec. 17, P.L. 942, No. 112, § 1, imd. effective; 2008, May 13, P.L. 144, No. 16, § 1, retroactive effective March 31, 2008). Section 5 of 2008, May 13, P.L. 144, No. 16, imd. effective, provides that "[t]he amendment of 23 Pa.C.S. § 4326, 4351, 4352 and 4374(c)(3) shall apply retroactively to March 31, 2008."

2008 Amendment. Act 2008-16—In subsec. (a), substituted "include a requirement for medical support to be provided by either or both parents, provided that such medical support is accessible to the children" for "provide health care coverage for each child as appropriate"; in subsec. (b), deleted "on an employment-related or other group basis" following "reasonable cost to a noncustodial parent"; in subsec. (c), deleted "on an employment-related or other group basis" following "reasonable cost to a custodial parent"; in subsec. (d), deleted "on an employment-related or other group basis" following "either parent at a reasonable cost"; in subsec. (l), in the definition of insurer, inserted "former", and added definitions of "medical support" and "reasonable cost"; and throughout subsecs. (a) to (d) and (l), substituted "medical support" for references to health care coverage.

2001 Amendment. Act 112 added subsec. (d.1) and amended subsec. (h.1).

1997 Amendment. Act 58 amended this sec.

1994 Amendment. Act 150 amended subsecs. (g), (h), (i), (j), (k) and (l) and added subsec. (h.1). Section 5 of Act 150 provided that the amendment of section 4326 shall apply to all actions pending on the effective date of Act 150.

1992 Amendment. Act 114 added section 4326. Section 4(1) of Act 114 provided that the addition of section 4326 shall apply to all support orders entered, reviewed or modified on or after the effective date of Act 114, and section 4(2) provided that section 4326(j) shall apply to support orders entered prior to the effective date of Act 114.

References in Text. Chapter 65 of Title 40 (Insurance), referred to in this section, is repealed. The subject matter is now contained in the act of December 14, 1992, P.L.835, No. 134, known as the Fraternal Benefit Societies Code.

Cross References. Section 4326 is referred to in sections 4348, 6108 of this title.

§ 4327. Postsecondary educational costs.

(a) **General rule.**—Where applicable under this section, a court may order either or both parents who are separated, divorced, unmarried or otherwise subject to an existing support obligation to provide equitably for educational costs of their child whether an application for this support is made before or after the child has reached 18 years of age. The responsibility to provide for postsecondary educational expenses is a shared responsibility between both parents. The duty of a parent to provide a postsecondary education for a child is not as exacting a requirement as the duty to provide food, clothing and shelter for a child of tender years unable to support himself. This authority shall extend to postsecondary education, including periods of undergraduate or vocational education after the child graduates from high school. An award for postsecondary educational costs may be entered only after the child or student has made reasonable efforts to apply for scholarships, grants and work-study assistance.

(b) Action to recover educational expenses.—An action to recover educational costs may be commenced:

(1) by the student if over 18 years of age; or

(2) by either parent on behalf of a child under 18 years of age, but, if the student is over 18 years of age, the student's written consent to the action must be secured.

(c) Calculation of educational costs.—In making an award under this section, the court shall calculate educational costs as defined in this section.

(d) Grants and scholarships.—The court shall deduct from the educational costs all grants and scholarships awarded to the student.

(e) Other relevant factors.—After calculating educational costs and deducting grants and scholarships, the court may order either parent or both parents to pay all or part of the remaining educational costs of their child. The court shall consider all relevant factors which appear reasonable, equitable and necessary, including the following:

(1) The financial resources of both parents.

(2) The financial resources of the student.

(3) The receipt of educational loans and other financial assistance by the student.

(4) The ability, willingness and desire of the student to pursue and complete the course of study.

(5) Any willful estrangement between parent and student caused by the student after attaining majority.

(6) The ability of the student to contribute to the student's expenses through gainful employment. The student's history of employment is material under this paragraph.

(7) Any other relevant factors.

(f) When liability may not be found.—A court shall not order support for educational costs if any of the following circumstances exist:

(1) Undue financial hardship would result to the parent.

(2) The educational costs would be a contribution for postcollege graduate educational costs.

(3) The order would extend support for the student beyond the student's twenty-third birthday. If exceptional circumstances exist, the court may order educational support for the student beyond the student's twenty-third birthday.

(g) Parent's obligation.—A parent's obligation to contribute toward the educational costs of a student shall not include payments to the other parent for the student's living expenses at home unless the student resides at home with the other parent and commutes to school.

(h) Termination or modification of orders.—Any party may request modification or termination of an order entered under this section upon proof of change in educational status of the student, a material change in the financial status of any party or other relevant factors.

(i) Applicability.—

(1) This act shall apply to all divorce decrees, support agreements, support orders, agreed or stipulated court orders, property settlement agreements, equitable distribution agreements, custody agreements and/or court orders and agreed to or stipulated court orders in effect on, executed or entered since, November 12, 1992.

(2) In addition, this act shall apply to all pending actions for support. This section shall not supersede or modify the express terms of a voluntary written marital settlement agreement or any court order entered pursuant thereto.

(j) **Definitions.**—As used in this section, the following words and phrases shall have the meanings given to them in this subsection:

"Educational costs." Tuition, fees, books, room, board and other educational materials.

"Postsecondary education." An educational or vocational program provided at a college, university or other postsecondary vocational, secretarial, business or technical school.

(July 2, 1993, P.L.431, No.62, eff. imd.)

> **1993 Amendment.** Act 62 added section 4327. See the preamble to Act 62.
>
> **Editor's Note:** In *Curtis v. Kline,* 542 Pa. 249, 666 A.2d (1995), the PA Supreme Court held that Act 62, 23 Pa.C.S. Sec. 4327, providing for post-secondary educational support, unconstitutionally classifies young adults according to the marital status of their parents. The Court held that sec. 4327 violates the equal protection clause of the Fourteenth Amendment and is thus unconstitutional. However, the PA legislature has not repealed section 4327, and therefore it continues to be included in the Domestic Relations Lawsource.

SUBCHAPTER C
PROCEEDINGS GENERALLY

Sec.
4341. Commencement of support actions or proceedings.
4342. Expedited procedure.
4343. Paternity.
4344. Contempt for failure of obligor to appear.
4345. Contempt for noncompliance with support order.
4346. Contempt for noncompliance with visitation or partial custody order.
4347. Security for attendance or performance.
4348. Attachment of income.
4349. Consolidation of proceedings.
4350. Effect of appeal.
4351. Costs and fees.
4352. Continuing jurisdiction over support orders.
4353. Duty to report.
4354. Willful failure to pay support order.
4355. Denial or suspension of licenses.

§ 4341. Commencement of support actions or proceedings.

(a) **Procedure.**—A support action or proceeding under this chapter shall be commenced in the manner prescribed by the Rules of Civil Procedure governing actions of support.

(b) **Standing.**—Any person caring for a child shall have standing to commence or continue an action for support of that child regardless of whether a court order has been issued granting that person custody of the child.

(c) **Jurisdiction.**—The court shall exercise Statewide jurisdiction over the parties to a proceeding under this chapter.

> **1997 Amendment.** Act 58 amended subsec. (a) and added subsecs. (b) and (c).

§ 4342. Expedited procedure.

(a) **General rule.**—The Supreme Court shall by general rule provide for expedited procedures for the determination of paternity and the determination and enforcement of support. The procedures shall include an office conference; a conference summary to the court by the hearing officer; an opportunity for the court to enter an order without hearing the parties; and an opportunity for the parties to demand a full hearing by the court.

(b) **Alternate procedure.**—The Supreme Court shall also provide an alternate expedited procedure which may be adopted by local rule of the courts of common pleas. The procedure shall include an office conference; an evidentiary hearing before a hearing officer who shall be an attorney; a transcript of the testimony; a report and recommendation to the court by the hearing officer; and an opportunity for the filing of exceptions with and argument before the court.

(c) **Long arm procedures.**—The Supreme Court shall by general rule establish procedures for the exercise of long arm jurisdiction to establish paternity and to establish and enforce support. Long arm jurisdiction shall be used in preference to proceedings under Part VIII (relating to uniform interstate family support) or VIII-A (relating to intrastate family support) unless it would be more effective to proceed otherwise. Long arm proceedings may be commenced or continued in any county where the plaintiff resides regardless of whether the parties maintained a family domicile in that county.

(d) **Jurisdiction over nonresident.**—(Deleted by amendment).

(e) **Default.**—The court shall enter a default order establishing paternity and enforcing support upon a showing that the defendant has been properly served and has not appeared.

(f) **Hearsay exception.**—For proceedings pursuant to this section, a verified petition, affidavit or document and a document incorporated by reference in any of them which would not be excluded under the hearsay rule if given in person is admissible in evidence if given under oath by a party or witness.

(g) **Payment record.**—A copy of the record of support payments certified as a true copy of the original by the custodian of the record is evidence of facts asserted in it and is admissible to show whether payments were made.

(h) **Bills.**—Copies of billing statements, bills for testing for parentage and for prenatal and postnatal health care of the mother and child furnished to the adverse party at least ten days before a court proceeding are admissible in evidence to prove the amount of the charges billed and to prove that the charges were reasonable, necessary and customary.

(i) **Transmission of documentary evidence.**—Documentary evidence transmitted to the domestic relations section by telephone, telecopier or other means which do not provide an original writing may not be excluded from evidence based on the means of transmission.

(j) **Testimony.**—In a proceeding under this part, a court may permit a party or witness to be deposed or to testify by telephone, audiovisual or other electronic means at a designated location.

(Mar. 25, 1988, P.L.296, No.35, eff. imd.; July 2, 1993, P.L.431, No.62, eff. imd.; Dec. 16, 1994, P.L.1286, No.150, eff. imd.; Apr. 4, 1996, P.L.58, No.20, eff. imd.; Dec. 16, 1997, P.L.549, No.58, eff. Jan. 1, 1998)

1997 Amendment. Act 58 added subsecs. (f), (g), (h), (i) and (j). Act 58 of 1997 was suspended by Pennsylvania Rule of Civil Procedure No. 1910.50(3), as amended May 31, 2000, insofar as it is inconsistent with Rule No.1910.20 relating to the availability of remedies for collection of past due and overdue support.

1996 Amendment. Act 20 amended subsec. (c) and deleted subsec. (d).

1994 Amendment. Act 150 amended subsec. (a) and added subsec. (e).

Suspension by Court Rule. Section 4342 was suspended by Pennsylvania Rule of Civil Procedure No. 1910.50(2), as amended May 31, 2000, insofar as it provides that long arm jurisdiction shall be used in preference to proceedings under Part VIII-A relating to intrastate family support actions.

Section 4342(f) was suspended by Pennsylvania Rule of Civil Procedure No. 1910.50(4), as amended May 31, 2000, insofar as it is inconsistent with Rule 1910.26 as it relates to record hearings in support actions.

§ 4343. Paternity.

(a) **Determination.**—Where the paternity of a child born out of wedlock is disputed, the determination of paternity shall be made by the court in a civil action without a jury. A putative father may not be prohibited from initiating a civil action to establish paternity. The burden of proof shall be by a preponderance of the evidence. Bills for pregnancy, childbirth, postnatal care related to the pregnancy and genetic testing are admissible as evidence without requiring third-party foundation testimony and shall constitute prima facie evidence of amounts incurred for such services or for testing on behalf of the child. If there is clear and convincing evidence of paternity on the basis of genetic tests or other evidence, the court shall, upon motion of a party, issue a temporary order of support pending the judicial resolution of a dispute regarding paternity. The Supreme Court shall provide by general rule for entry of a default order establishing paternity upon a showing of service of process on the defendant and a subsequent failure to appear for scheduled genetic testing.

(b) **Limitation of actions.**—

(1) An action or proceeding under this chapter to establish the paternity of a child born out of wedlock must be commenced within 18 years of the date of birth of the child.

(2) As of August 16, 1984, the requirement of paragraph (b)(1) shall also apply to any child for whom a paternity has not yet been established and any child for whom a paternity action was brought but dismissed because of a prior statute of limitations of less than 18 years.

(c) **Genetic tests.**—

(1) Upon the request of any party to an action to establish paternity, supported by a sworn statement from the party, the court or domestic relations section shall require the child and the parties to submit to genetic tests. The domestic relations section shall obtain an additional genetic test upon the request and advance payment by any party who contests the initial test.

(2) Genetic test results indicating a 99% or greater probability that the alleged father is the father of the child shall create a presumption of paternity which may be rebutted only by clear and convincing evidence that the results of the genetic tests are not reliable in that particular case.

(3) To ensure the integrity of the specimen and that the proper chain of custody has been maintained, the genetic tests of the biological mother, the child or children in question and the alleged father should be conducted by an established genetic-testing laboratory in the course of its regularly conducted business activity, and certified records should be issued. The certified records shall be admissible into evidence without further foundation, authentication or proof of accuracy if no objection is made within ten days prior to trial. The laboratory must be certified by either the American Association of Blood Banks or the American Association for Histocompatibility and Immunogenetics.

(4) If the court or domestic relations section orders genetic testing, the domestic relations section shall pay the cost of the test, subject to recoupment from the alleged father if paternity is established.

(5) A determination of paternity made by another state, whether through judicial proceedings, administrative proceedings or by acknowledgment of paternity, shall be given full faith and credit in the courts of this Commonwealth.

(6) A determination of nonpaternity made by another state with respect to a public assistance recipient shall not be binding upon the Department of Public Welfare unless the defendant shows that the department had actual notice of the

proceedings, including the date and time of any trial, and a fair opportunity to participate in all material proceedings through counsel of its own choice.

1997 Amendment. Act 58 amended this sec.

1994 Amendment. Act 150 amended subsec. 4343(c). The amendment shall apply to all actions pending on the effective date of this act.

Cross References. Paternity, acknowledgment or adjudication in support proceedings, see Pa.R.C.P. No.1910.15.

§ 4344. Contempt for failure of obligor to appear.

A person who willfully fails or refuses to appear in response to a duly served order or other process under this chapter may, as prescribed by general rule, be adjudged in contempt. Contempt shall be punishable by any one or more of the following:

(1) Imprisonment for a period not to exceed six months.

(2) A fine not to exceed $500.

(3) Probation for a period not to exceed six months.

Cross References. Section 4344 is referred to in section 4345 of this title.

§ 4345. Contempt for noncompliance with support order.

(a) **General rule.**—A person who willfully fails to comply with any order under this chapter, except an order subject to section 4344 (relating to contempt for failure of obligor to appear), may, as prescribed by general rule, be adjudged in contempt. Contempt shall be punishable by any one or more of the following:

(1) Imprisonment for a period not to exceed six months.

(2) A fine not to exceed $1,000.

(3) Probation for a period not to exceed one year.

(b) **Condition for release.**—An order committing a defendant to jail under this section shall specify the condition the fulfillment of which will result in the release of the obligor.

1996 Amendment. Act 1996-124 amended subsec. (a).

Cross References. Section 4345 is referred to in sections 4326, 4353 of this title. Civil contempt for willful failure to comply with support order, petition, hearing, and order, see Pa. R.C.P. No. 1910.21.

§ 4346. Contempt for noncompliance with visitation or partial custody order. [Repealed, Act 2010-112, Nov. 23, 2010, effective Jan. 22, 2011.]

2010 Amendment. Act 112 repealed this sec.

1998 Amendment. Act 127 amended subsec. (a).

1997 Amendment. Act 58 amended this sec.

§ 4347. Security for attendance or performance.

At any stage of the proceedings under this chapter, upon affidavit filed that the obligor is about to leave this Commonwealth or the judicial district or, where in the judgment of the court, the obligor has habitually failed to comply with court orders under this chapter, the court may, as prescribed by general rule, issue appropriate process directing that the obligor be brought before the court and may direct that the obligor give security to appear when directed by the court or to comply with any order of the court.

§ 4348. Attachment of income.

(a) **Existing and certain future orders.**—All orders of support existing as of the effective date of this provision, as well as all orders of support entered or modified after the effective date of this provision but before June 30, 1990, shall provide for mandatory attachment of income:

(1) if the obligor is in arrears in payment in an amount equal to or greater than one month's support obligation;

(2) at the request of the obligor;

(3) at the request of the obligee; or

(4) as of July 1, 1991, except as provided by subsection (b)(1) and (2).

(b) Future orders.—All orders of support entered or modified on or after July 1, 1990, shall, as part of the order, provide for the mandatory attachment of income unless:

(1) the obligor is not in arrears in payment in an amount equal to or greater of one month's support obligation; and

(2)(i) one of the parties demonstrates, and the court finds, that there is good cause not to require immediate income withholding; or

(ii) a written agreement is reached between the parties which provides for an alternative arrangement.

The court may, on its own motion, order the attachment of the obligor's income where the court has a reasonable basis to believe the obligor will not comply with the order of support. In making this determination, the court may consider evidence of the person's previous violations of orders entered in any jurisdiction or evidence that the obligor has attempted to conceal income or to transfer, convey or encumber property in order to reduce the obligor's support obligation. Attachment shall occur under this subsection without amendment to the order of support and, if arrearages occur, without the need for a judicial or administrative hearing.

(c) Assessment of penalty.—The court may impose a penalty of not more than 10% on any amount in arrears for 30 days or more if the court determines that the arrearage was willful.

(d) Arrearages.—If support arrearages exist at the time of the entry of the order, the order shall specify all of the following:

(1) To whom an arrearage is owed and the amount of the arrearage.

(2) The period of time for which the arrearage is calculated.

(3) The amount of periodic support to be applied to current support and the amount to be applied to arrearages.

(4) If support arrearages are owed to more than one obligee, how payments are to be divided and in which priority.

(5) A direction that all payments are to be credited to current support obligations first, with any payment in excess to be applied to arrearages.

(d.1) Insurance.—If an obligor or obligee is in violation of an order under section 4326(j)(3) (relating to mandatory inclusion of child medical support), the attachment shall be in favor of the appropriate provider of health care coverage.

(e) Attachment process.—

(1) The obligor shall be given notice of the attachment of his income. Such notice shall specify all of the following:

(i) The amount to be withheld on account of current support and on account of arrears.

(ii) That the order of attachment shall apply to current and future employers.

(iii) That the grounds for contesting the order of attachment shall be limited to mistakes of fact. Mistakes of fact shall be limited to errors in the amount of current support owed, errors in the amount of arrearage, an attachment in excess of the maximum amount set forth in subsection (g) or mistaken identity of the obligor.

(iv) That attachment has occurred or shall occur in all cases within ten days of the issuance of the notice.

(v) A notice of how and when the order may be contested.

(2) To contest the order, the obligor must appear before the domestic relations section no later than ten days after issuance of the notice, at which time it will

be determined if a mistake of fact has occurred. If so, the order shall be modified accordingly.

(f) **Request of obligor.**—The court shall also order the attachment of income where the obligor so requests.

(g) **Maximum amount.**—The maximum amount of any attachment under this section shall not exceed the limits set forth in the Consumer Credit Protection Act (Public Law 90-321, 15 U.S.C. § 1601 et seq.).

(h) **Termination.**—The court may order the termination of an order of attachment in any of the following instances:

(1) The support obligation has terminated and the total arrearages are paid.

(2) Where the payee cannot be located and it becomes impossible to forward payments.

(3) The result would be unconscionable.

(i) **Notice to employer.**—The employer of an obligor shall be given notice of the attachment as provided by the Rules of Civil Procedure governing support. This notice shall include reference to subsections (g), (k), (l), (n) and (o) and all of the following:

(1) The amount to be attached.

(2) That the attachment shall be implemented as soon as possible and no later than 14 days from the issuance of the notice to the employer.

(3) That the attachment payment must be sent to the domestic relations section or State disbursement unit, as appropriate, within seven business days of the date the obligor is paid.

(4) That the attachment order is binding upon the employer until further notice.

(5) That the employer may combine attachment payments into a single payment to the domestic relations section and separately identify the portions attributable to each obligor.

(6) That the employer must notify the domestic relations section when the obligor terminates employment and provide his last known address and the new employer's name and address, if known.

(j) **Effect of compliance by employer.**—Compliance by an employer with an order of attachment of income that is regular on its face operates as a discharge of the civil liability of the employer to the obligor as to that portion of the employment income of the obligor affected. An employer shall not be subject to criminal or civil liability to any individual or agency for conduct in compliance with the order. The employer may deduct from the income of the obligor a one-time fee of $50 for reimbursement of the expense in complying with the order. In no case shall the employer's reimbursement be deducted from the amount of the support order.

(k) **Effect of noncompliance by employer.**—

(1) An employer or officer or employee thereof who willfully fails to comply with an order of attachment under this chapter may, as prescribed by general rule, be adjudged in contempt and committed to jail or fined by the court.

(2) The employer shall be liable for any amount the employer willfully fails to withhold from income due an employee under an order of attachment of income and any amount which is withheld from such income but not forwarded to the domestic relations office.

(3) The court may, pursuant to general rule, attach funds or property of an employer.

(l) **Disciplinary action by employer prohibited.**—

(1) When an order of attachment on income withholding is about to be or has been entered, an employer or officer or employee thereof shall not use the attachment or possibility thereof as a basis, in whole or in part, for the refusal to employ or for

the discharge of an employee or for any disciplinary action against or demotion of an employee. In case of a violation of this subsection, the employer or officer or employee thereof may be adjudged in contempt and committed to jail or fined by the court.

(2) Any employee aggrieved by a violation of this subsection shall have the substantive right to bring an action for damages by reason of such violation in a court of competent jurisdiction.

(3) The department or a domestic relations section may impose a civil penalty of up to $1,000 per violation against any employer that willfully violates the provisions of this subsection or that willfully fails to withhold income or to pay such amounts to the State disbursement unit.

(m) Certify income.—Upon request of the domestic relations section, the employer shall report and certify the income of an employee.

(n) Bonding.—The court may attach forms of income other than wages, assets, including spendthrift trusts, and private, public, State, county and municipal pensions, and include bonding or other requirements in cases involving obligors whose income is from sources other than wages, in order to assure that support owed by obligors in this Commonwealth will be collected without regard to the types of these obligors' income or the nature of their income-producing activities.

(o) Priority of attachment.—(Deleted by amendment).

(p) Nonresidents.—Income attachment shall be available to obligees residing outside this Commonwealth where the income of the obligor is derived in this Commonwealth.

(q) Priority of attachment.—An order of attachment for support shall have priority over any attachment, execution, garnishment or wage assignment. The Supreme Court shall by general rule provide for priorities for withholding and allocating income withheld for multiple child support obligees received by an employer for the same obligor under this section and Chapter 75 (relating to direct enforcement of order of another state without registration).

(r) Information requests.—

(1) Upon the request of the department, a county domestic relations section or a child support agency of another state, any employer doing business within this Commonwealth, including a for-profit, not-for-profit or governmental employer, shall promptly provide information regarding the employment, compensation and benefits of any employee or contractor of the employer.

(2) In addition to any other remedy allowed by law, the department may impose a civil penalty of up to $1,000 per violation on an individual or entity that willfully fails to comply with a request for information under paragraph (1).

(Dec. 20, 1989, P.L.654, No.81, eff. imd.; Dec. 4, 1992, P.L.757, No.114, eff. 90 days; Oct. 16, 1996, P.L.706, No.124, eff. 60 days; Dec. 16, 1997, P.L.549, No.58, eff. Jan. 1, 1998; Dec. 15, 1998, P.L.963, No.127, eff. imd.; July 1, 2016, P.L.443, No.64, eff. 60 days)

2016 Amendment. Act 64 amended subsec. (j).

1998 Amendment. Act 127 added subsec. (r). Act 127 of 1998 was suspended by Pennsylvania Rule of Civil Procedure No. 1910.50(3), as amended May 31, 2000, insofar as it is inconsistent with Rule No. 1910.20 relating to the availability of remedies for collection of past due and overdue support.

1997 Amendment. Act 58 amended subsecs. (b), (e)(1) intro. par., (i) and (iv) and (2), (i)(3), (j) and (l)(1), deleted subsec. (o) and added subsecs. (l)(3) and (q). Act 58 of 1997 was suspended by Pennsylvania Rule of Civil Procedure No. 1910.50(3), as amended May 31, 2000, insofar as it is inconsistent with Rule No. 1910.20 relating to the availability of remedies for collection of past due and overdue support.

1992 Amendment. Act 114 added subsec. (d.1). Section 4(2) of Act 114 provided that subsec. (d.1) shall apply to support orders entered prior to the effective date of Act 114.

1989 Amendment. Act 81 amended subsecs. (a) and (b).

Cross References. Section 4348 is referred to in sections 4305, 4326, 7101, 7605, 8101 of this title.

§ 4349. Consolidation of proceedings.

In order to facilitate frequent and unimpeded contact between children and parents, a judge may consolidate with a support action or proceeding any proceeding commenced for visitation rights, sole or shared custody, temporary or permanent custody or any other matters pertaining to support authorized by law which fairly and expeditiously may be determined and disposed of in the support action or proceeding.

§ 4350. Effect of appeal.

An appeal from an order of support entered pursuant to this chapter shall not operate as a supersedeas unless so ordered by the court.

§ 4351. Costs and fees.

(a) General rule.—If an obligee prevails in a proceeding to establish paternity or to obtain a support order, the court may assess against the obligor filing fees, reasonable attorney fees and necessary travel and other reasonable costs and expenses incurred by the obligee and the obligee's witnesses. Attorney fees may be taxed as costs and shall be ordered to be paid directly to the attorney, who may enforce the order in the attorney's own name. Payment of support owed to the obligee shall have priority over fees, costs and expenses.

(a.1) Annual fee.—The Commonwealth shall impose a fee of $25 in each case in which an individual has never received assistance under Title IV-A of the Social Security Act (49 Stat. 620, 42 U.S.C. § 301 et seq.) and for whom the Commonwealth has collected at least $500 of support in a Federal fiscal year. The Commonwealth shall pay the $25 fee for those cases in which the annual collection is between $500 and $1,999.99. The $25 fee shall be collected from the custodial parent in cases where annual collections equal $2,000 or more.

(b) Lack of good cause for failure to pay on time.—If the court determines that the person subject to a child support order did not have good cause for failing to make child support payments on time, it may further assess costs and reasonable attorney fees incurred by the party seeking to enforce the order.

(1985, Oct. 30, P.L. 264, No. 66, § 1, effective in 90 days. Amended 1997, Dec. 1, P.L. 549, No. 58, § 8, effective Jan. 1, 1998; 2008, May 13, P.L. 144, No. 16, § 2, retroactive effective March 31, 2008). Section 5 of 2008, May 13, P.L. 144, No. 16, imd. effective, provides that "[t]he amendment of 23 Pa.C.S. § 4326, 4351, 4352 and 4374(c)(3) shall apply retroactively to March 31, 2008."

2008 Amendment. Act 2008-16 added subsec. (a.1).
1997 Amendment. Act 58 amended this sec.

§ 4352. Continuing jurisdiction over support orders.

(a) General rule.—The court making an order of support shall at all times maintain jurisdiction of the matter for the purpose of enforcement of the order and for the purpose of increasing, decreasing, modifying or rescinding the order unless otherwise provided by Part VIII (relating to uniform interstate family support) or VIII-A (relating to intrastate family support) without limiting the right of the obligee, or the department if it has an assignment or other interest, to institute additional proceedings for support in any county in which the obligor resides or in which property of the obligor is situated. The Supreme Court shall by general rule establish procedures by which each interested party shall be notified of all proceedings in which support obligations might be established or modified and shall receive a copy of any order issued in a case within 14 days after issuance of such order. A petition for modification of a support order may be filed at any time and shall be granted if the requesting party demonstrates a substantial change in circumstances.

(a.1) Automatic review.—Upon request of either parent, or automatically if there is an assignment under Title IV-A of the Social Security Act (49 Stat. 620, 42 U.S.C. § 301 et seq.), each order of support shall be reviewed at least once every three years from the date of establishment or the most recent review. The review shall be for the purpose of making any appropriate increase, decrease, modification or rescission of the order. During the review, taking into the account the best interest of the child involved, the court shall adjust the order, without requiring proof of a change in circumstances, by applying the Statewide guidelines or a cost-of-living adjustment in accordance with a formula developed by general rule. Automated methods, including automated matches with wage or State income tax data, may be used to identify the support orders eligible for review and implement appropriate adjustments.

(a.2) **Effect of incarceration.**—Incarceration, except incarceration for nonpayment of support, shall constitute a material and substantial change in circumstance that may warrant modification or termination of an order of support where the obligor lacks verifiable income or assets sufficient to enforce and collect amounts due.

(b) **Notice.**—Each party subject to an automatic child support review shall receive:

(1) thirty days' advance notice of the right of such party to request a review and adjustment of the order, except when the adjustment results from a cost-of-living adjustment or other automated adjustment;

(2) a copy of any order establishing, modifying or rescinding a child support obligation or, in the case of a denied petition for modification, a notice of determination that there should be no change in the amount of the child support order, within 14 days after issuance of such order or determination; and

(3) a 30-day period from the date of the notice of a cost-of-living adjustment or other automated adjustment to request an individual review and adjustment in accordance with the Statewide guideline.

(c) **Transfer of action.**—Where neither party to the action resides or is employed in the county wherein the support action was filed, the court may transfer the matter to any county wherein either party resides or where the defendant is regularly employed. If one of the parties resides outside of this Commonwealth, the action may be transferred to the county of residence or employment of the other party.

(d) **Arrears as judgments.**—On and after the date it is due, each and every support obligation shall constitute a judgment against the obligor by operation of law, with the full force, effect and attributes of a judgment of court, including the ability to be enforced, and shall be entitled as a judgment to full faith and credit in this or any other state. Overdue support obligations of this or any other state which are on record at the county domestic relations section shall constitute a lien by operation of law against all real property owned by the obligor within the county as provided in subsection (d.1). The department shall develop and implement a system for providing notice to the public of liens arising out of overdue support obligations. The system and its procedures shall ensure convenient access to lien information and shall address hours of access by the business community and the general public and access via modem or automated means. Thirty days after publication of notice in the Pennsylvania Bulletin that the system has been established, any lien on record shall constitute a lien against any real property in this Commonwealth owned by the obligor and shall also have the effect of a fully perfected security interest in personal property owned by the obligor in which a security interest can arise. The department shall consult with the Department of Transportation in the development of this system to enforce compliance with this subsection as it applies to liens on motor vehicles. The Supreme Court shall by general rule establish procedures for the recording of liens of other states at the county domestic relations section and for the enforcement of liens arising from overdue support without prior judicial notice or hearing. A bona fide good faith purchaser of personal property for value which is subject to a lien under this subsection acquires all title which the transferor had or had the power to transfer pursuant to 13 Pa.C.S. Ch. 24 (relating to title, creditors and good faith purchasers), and the obligee shall have all rights against such property which would be preserved to a fully perfected secured creditor under 13 Pa.C.S. Div. 9 (relating to secured transactions; sales of accounts, contract rights and chattel paper). The obligation for payment of arrears or overdue support shall terminate by operation of law when all arrears or overdue support has been paid.

(d.1) Real property liens.—

(1) Overdue support shall be a lien on real estate within the county in which the overdue support is on record at the county domestic relations section if:

(i) the underlying support action is pending in the county domestic relations section or is being enforced by the county domestic relations section;

(ii) notice of the existence of the support action is available to the public through a docket book or automated means; and

(iii) the county domestic relations section is able to determine the amount of overdue support by reference to its records and is able to provide the amount of the overdue support upon request.

(2) The priority and amount of a lien for overdue support shall be determined as follows:

(i) The date of the lien for purposes of determining priority shall be determined separately for each unpaid overdue support payment. The date shall be the later of:

(A) the date the obligor obtains a real property interest which may be subject to a lien;

(B) the date the overdue support becomes a lien under paragraph (1); or

(C) January 1, 1998.

(ii) The amount of the lien on any date shall be the amount of overdue support shown on that date in the records of the domestic relations section.

(3) Upon request of any person, the domestic relations section shall issue a written certification of the amount of overdue support owed by an individual as of the date of the certification and shall note on the docket the date of certification and the amount certified. The interests of any purchaser of real estate for value, mortgagee or other lienor that in good faith purchases the real estate or lends money on the security of the real estate and that records, within 30 days before or 60 days after the date of issuance of a certificate under this paragraph, a deed, mortgage or other encumbrance against the real estate shall not be subject to any lien for overdue support in excess of the amount shown on the certification.

(4) The amount of overdue support owed by an obligor and the name of the obligor shall be public information and shall be deemed a public record subject to the act of June 21, 1957 (P.L.390, No.212), referred to as the Right-to-Know Law.

(5) A lien arising from overdue support:

(i) shall automatically attach to after-acquired property owned by the obligor;

(ii) shall retain its priority without renewal or revival;

(iii) shall continue to encumber the property upon sale or other transfer;

(iv) shall not be divested upon a judicial sale or execution by a person with a lien with less priority;

(v) shall not attach to the interest of any other co-owner in the property;

(vi) shall expire 20 years after the due date of the last unsatisfied overdue support payment; and

(vii) may be released by the court as against abandoned or distressed real property at the request of a governmental unit in order to facilitate the property's sale and rehabilitation.

(6) The domestic relations section:

(i) shall satisfy the lien promptly upon payment but no later than 60 days following receipt of the payment;

(ii) may charge a fee not to exceed the lesser of its estimated cost of producing the report or $20 for the issuance of a lien certification or other written report of the overdue support obligations of an obligor;

(iii) shall provide to the prothonotary of the county the identity of obligors and amount of overdue support to be used to make the information available to the public. The information shall be updated at least monthly and shall be provided by a paper listing, diskette or any other electronic means until the Statewide system under subsection (d) is implemented; and

(iv) shall transmit at least every 60 days to credit bureaus directly or through the department reports and updates regarding the liens for overdue support.

(7) The domestic relations section or employees thereof shall not be liable for errors in the certification of amounts of overdue support or satisfaction of liens for overdue support except as provided in 42 Pa.C.S. § 8550 (relating to willful misconduct).

(8) Support may cease to be overdue if a revised payment schedule is established by the court, but any lien which has previously arisen against real estate shall remain in effect until paid or divested.

(9) Notwithstanding paragraphs (2) and (3), the interests of any person who recorded a deed, mortgage or other instrument creating an interest in or lien against real estate on or after January 1, 1998, and before the effective date of this subsection shall not be subject to a lien for any overdue support accruing on or after the date the deed, mortgage or other instrument creating the interest or lien was recorded.

(e) **Retroactive modification of arrears.**—No court shall modify or remit any support obligation, on or after the date it is due, except with respect to any period during which there is pending a petition for modification. If a petition for modification was filed, modification may be applied to the period beginning on the date that notice of such petition was given, either directly or through the appropriate agent, to the obligee or, where the obligee was the petitioner, to the obligor. However, modification may be applied to an earlier period if the petitioner was precluded from filing a petition for modification by reason of a significant physical or mental disability, misrepresentation of another party or other compelling reason and if the petitioner, when no longer precluded, promptly filed a petition. In the case of an emancipated child, arrears shall not accrue from and after the date of the emancipation of the child for whose support the payment is made.

(f) **Foreign support orders.**—(Deleted by amendment).

(g) **Notice to obligors and obligees.**—The domestic relations section shall mail notice to obligors and obligees of existing orders informing them that such orders may attain the status of a judgment by operation of law. The notice shall explain the nature of a judgment by operation of law and its effect. Further, the notice shall advise each party to a support proceeding of the party's duty to advise the domestic relations section of material changes in circumstance and of the necessity to promptly request a modification as soon as circumstances change.

(g.1) **Nondisclosure of certain information.**—If the court finds in an ex parte or other proceeding or if an existing order provides that the health, safety or liberty of a party or child would be unreasonably put at risk by the disclosure of identifying information, the court shall order that the address of the child or party or other identifying information not be disclosed in a pleading or other document filed in a proceeding under this part. Any court order under this subsection must be docketed in the domestic relations section.

(g.2) **Work activities.**—If an obligor owes overdue support with respect to any child receiving cash or medical assistance, the court shall upon motion of the department or domestic relations section order that overdue support be paid in accordance with a plan approved by the court or that the obligor participate in work activities approved by the department. Work activities include:

(1) Subsidized or unsubsidized public or private sector employment.

(2) Work experience programs.

(3) Work training programs.

(4) Community service programs.

(5) Job search requirements.

(6) Job readiness programs.

(7) Education directly related to employment.

(8) Attendance at secondary school.

(9) For a person who has not graduated high school, study leading to a high school diploma or equivalent.

(g.3) Voidable transfers.—The court may void any voidable transfer by the obligor pursuant to 12 Pa.C.S. Ch. 51 (relating to voidable transactions). It shall be a rebuttable presumption that a transfer by an obligor is voidable as to an obligee if the transfer was made for less than reasonably equivalent value and the transfer occurred after the initiation of a proceeding to establish or enforce support.

(h) Applicability.—This section applies to all support orders whether entered under this chapter or any other statute.

(Mar. 25, 1988, P.L.296, No.35, eff. imd.; Dec. 20, 1989, P.L.654, No.81, eff. imd.; Apr. 4, 1996, P.L.58, No.20, eff. imd.; Dec. 16, 1997, P.L.549, No.58, eff. Jan. 1, 1998; Dec. 15, 1998, P.L.963, No.127, eff. imd.; May 13, 2008, P.L.144, No.16, eff. imd.; Dec. 22, 2017, P.L.1249, No.78, eff. 60 days)

2017 Amendment. Act 78 amended subsec. (g.3). See section 7 of Act 78 in the appendix to this title for special provisions relating to applicability.

2008 Amendment. Act 16 amended subsec. (a.1) and added subsec. (a.2), retroactive to March 31, 2008.

1998 Amendment. Act 127 amended subsec. (d) and added subsec. (d.1). Section 15 of Act 127 provided that nothing in Act 127 shall impair the priority or validity of any lien recorded prior to the effective date of Act 127. Act 127 of 1998 was suspended by Pennsylvania Rule of Civil Procedure No. 1910.50(3), as amended May 31, 2000, insofar as it is inconsistent with Rule No. 1910.20 relating to the availability of remedies for collection of past due and overdue support.

1997 Amendment. Act 58 amended subsecs. (a), (b) and (d) and added subsecs. (a.1), (g.1), (g.2) and (g.3). Act 58 of 1997 was suspended by Pennsylvania Rule of Civil Procedure No. 1910.50(3), as amended May 31, 2000, insofar as it is inconsistent with Rule No. 1910.20 relating to the availability of remedies for collection of past due and overdue support.

1996 Amendment. Act 20 amended subsec. (a) and deleted subsec. (f).

Suspension by Court Rule. Section 4352(d) was suspended by Pennsylvania Rule of Civil Procedure No. 1910.50(5), as amended May 31, 2000, insofar as it is inconsistent with Rule 1910.22 providing that overdue support on public record at the domestic relations section constitutes a lien of record against all real property within the state of Pennsylvania which is owned by the obligor.

Section 4352(d.1) was suspended by Pennsylvania Rule of Civil Procedure No. 1910.50(6), as amended May 31, 2000, only insofar as subsection (d.1)(1) provides that the underlying support action shall either be pending at the county domestic relations section or shall be enforced by the county domestic relations section in order for a lien to arise to arise against real property located in that county.

References in Text. Division 9 of Title 13, referred to in subsec. (d), was repealed and added by the act of June 8, 2001 (P.L.123, No.18). Present Division 9 relates to secured transactions.

The act of June 21, 1957 (P.L.390, No.212), referred to as the Right-to-Know Law, referred to in subsec. (d.1)(4), was repealed by the act of February 14, 2008 (P.L.6, No.3), known as the Right-to-Know Law.

§ 4353. Duty to report.

(a) Notice of changes affecting support.—An individual who is a party to a support proceeding shall notify the domestic relations section, the department and the other parties in writing or by personal appearance within seven days of any material change in circumstances relevant to the level of support or the administration of the support order, including, but not limited to:

(1) change of employment; and

(2) change of personal address or change of address of any child receiving support.

(a.1) **Delivery.**—In any subsequent child support enforcement action between the parties, upon sufficient showing that due diligence has been made to ascertain the location of a party, the court or the department may deem due process requirements for notice and service of process to be met with respect to the party, upon delivery of written notice to the most recent residential address or employer address filed with the domestic relations section or the department pursuant to subsection (a).

(a.2) **Notice of location information.**—Each party to a support proceeding shall file with the domestic relations section and the department, and update as appropriate, information on the location and identity of the party, including Social Security number, residential and mailing addresses, telephone numbers, driver's license number and name, address and telephone number of employer.

(b) **Failure to give notice.**—Willful failure to comply with this section may be adjudged in contempt of court pursuant to section 4345 (relating to contempt for noncompliance with support order).

(Mar. 25, 1988, P.L.296, No.35, eff. imd.)

1997 Amendment. Act 58 amended this sec.

§ 4354. Willful failure to pay support order.

(a) **Offense defined.**—An individual who willfully fails to comply with a support order of a court of this Commonwealth when the individual has the financial ability to comply with the support order commits an offense.

(b) **Application.**—This section applies to all support cases, whether civil or criminal and whether the defendant is married, unmarried, separated or divorced.

(c) **Jurisdiction.**—Exclusive original jurisdiction of a proceeding under this section is vested in the courts of common pleas of this Commonwealth.

(d) **Grading.**—

(1) Except as otherwise provided for in paragraph (2), an offense under this section shall constitute a summary offense.

(2) An offense shall be graded a misdemeanor of the third degree if the individual convicted of the offense established residence outside this Commonwealth with the intention of not complying with the support order and either of the following apply:

(i) the offense is a second or subsequent offense under this section; or

(ii) the individual owes support in an amount equal to or greater than 12 months of the monthly support obligation.

(e) **Costs and expenses to be borne by individual.**—An individual convicted of an offense under this section who is apprehended outside this Commonwealth shall, in addition to any other sentence imposed, be sentenced to pay the costs and expenses of rendition.

(Mar. 25, 1988, P.L.296, No.35, eff. imd.; Oct. 9, 2008, P.L. 1384, No. 104, eff. in 60 days).

2008 Amendment. Act 104 added subsec. (d) and amended subsec. (a).

1988 Amendment. Act 35 added section 4354.

§ 4355. Denial or suspension of licenses.

(a) **General rule.**—Except as provided in subsection (d.1), where the domestic relations section or the department has been unable to attach the income of an obligor and the obligor owes support in an amount equal to or greater than three months of the monthly support obligation or where an individual has failed to comply with a visitation or partial custody order pursuant to section 4346 (relating to contempt for noncompliance) or an individual has failed, after appropriate notice, to comply with subpoenas or warrants relating to paternity or child support proceedings, the court, the domestic relations section or the department shall issue an order directing any licensing authority to:

(1) prohibit the issuance or renewal of a license of the obligor or other individual; or

(2) require the suspension of the license of the obligor or other individual.

(b) Notice to obligor or other individual.—

(1) Prior to the issuance of an order to suspend, nonrenew or deny a license, the obligor or other individual shall be given advance notice. The notice shall specify:

(i) The amount of arrears owed, if applicable.

(ii) How, when and where the notice can be contested.

(iii) That the grounds for contesting the notice shall be limited to mistakes of fact. Mistakes of fact shall be limited to errors in the amount of arrears owed or mistaken identity of the obligor.

(iv) That an order to the licensing authority to automatically suspend, nonrenew or deny the license will occur in all cases 30 days after issuance of the notice unless the arrearage is paid, a periodic payment schedule is approved by the court or the individual is excused from the failure to comply with the warrant or subpoena.

(2) The Supreme Court shall by general rule provide a procedure for the court or disciplinary board to deny, suspend or not renew the license of an attorney who owes past due support in a manner comparable to the procedures set forth in this section.

(c) Order.—

(1) Thirty days after the issuance of the notice, if the obligor has not paid the arrearage, entered into a court-approved periodic payment schedule or, if applicable, the obligor or other individual has not been excused from complying with the warrant or subpoena, the court, the domestic relations section or department shall direct or cause an order to be issued to the licensing authority to suspend or deny the issuance or renewal of a license. Upon receipt, the licensing authority shall immediately comply with the order or directive. The licensing authority shall have no authority to stay implementation of the order or to hold a hearing except in cases of mistaken identity.

(2) An order providing for a periodic payment schedule shall also provide that failure to comply with the schedule shall result in the immediate suspensions, nonrenewal or denial of the obligor's license.

(3) Subject to section 4377(c) (relating to appeals), to contest the order, the obligor or other individual must appear before the domestic relations section not later than ten days after issuance of the order. The grounds for contesting shall be limited to mistakes of fact. If, as determined by the domestic relations section, a mistake of fact has occurred, the action shall be modified accordingly within ten days.

(d) Reinstatement or issuance of license.—Where an order or directive has been issued pursuant to subsection (c) and the obligor has satisfied the arrearage, entered into a court approved payment plan or, if applicable, the obligor or other individual has been excused from the failure to comply with the subpoena or warrant, the court, the domestic relations section or the department shall order or direct the licensing authority to reinstate or issue the license to the obligor or other individual. Upon receipt of the order, the licensing authority shall reinstate or issue the license immediately, provided that the obligor or other individual meets any and all other requirements for issuance or reinstatement.

(d.1) Special procedures for operating privilege.—

(1) Where the domestic relations section or the department has been unable to attach the income of an obligor and the obligor owes support in an amount equal to or greater than three months of the monthly support obligation or where an individual has failed, after appropriate notice, to comply with subpoenas or war-

rants relating to paternity or child support proceedings, the court, the domestic relations section or the department may issue an order directing the Department of Transportation to:

(i) prohibit the issuance or renewal of a license of the obligor or other individual; or

(ii) require the suspension of the license of the obligor or other individual.

(2) Prior to the issuance of an order to suspend, nonrenew or deny a license, the obligor or other individual shall be given advance notice. The notice shall specify:

(i) The amount of arrears owed, if applicable.

(ii) How, when and where the notice can be contested.

(iii) That the grounds for contesting the notice shall be limited to mistakes of fact. Mistakes of fact shall be limited to errors in the amount of arrears owed or mistaken identity of the obligor.

(iv) That an order to the Department of Transportation to automatically suspend, nonrenew or deny the license will occur in all cases 30 days after issuance of the notice unless the arrearage is paid, a periodic payment schedule is approved by the court or the individual is excused from the failure to comply with the warrant or subpoena.

(3) Any order issued to the Department of Transportation pursuant to this section shall be issued as agreed upon by the department and the Department of Transportation. The order may be transmitted electronically or by other methods.

(4) Upon receipt of an order or directive from a court, the domestic relations section or the department authorizing the Department of Transportation to suspend the operating privilege of an obligor or other individual, the Department of Transportation shall immediately suspend the operating privilege of that obligor or other individual. Upon receipt of an order from the court or the domestic relations section or a directive from the department authorizing the Department of Transportation to restore the operating privilege of an obligor or other individual, the Department of Transportation shall immediately restore the operating privilege of that obligor or other individual if the person complies with the provisions of 75 Pa.C.S. § 1960 (relating to reinstatement of operating privilege or vehicle registration).

(5) An insurer may not increase premiums, impose a surcharge or rate penalty, make a driver record point assignment for automobile insurance or cancel or refuse to renew an automobile insurance policy on account of a suspension under this section.

(6) There shall be no right to appeal from a suspension under this section pursuant to 75 Pa.C.S. § 1550 (relating to judicial review). Subject to section 4377(c) (relating to power to expedite support cases), the sole remedy shall be to petition the court which entered the underlying support order resulting in the suspension, revocation or refusal to issue or renew the license.

(d.2) Special procedures for recreational licenses issued by Pennsylvania Game Commission.—

(1) Where the domestic relations section or the department has been unable to attach the income of an obligor and the obligor owes support in an amount equal to or greater than three months of the monthly support obligation, or where an individual has failed, after appropriate notice, to comply with subpoenas or warrants relating to paternity or child support proceedings, the court may issue an order directing the Pennsylvania Game Commission to prohibit the issuance or renewal of a recreational license of the obligor or other individual or to require the suspension of the recreational license of the obligor or other individual.

(2) Procedures for notice of suspension, nonrenewal or denial, issuance of the appropriate order and reinstatement or a recreational license shall be in accordance with subsections (b), (c) and (d).

(3) Upon receipt of an order from a court requiring the Pennsylvania Game Commission to refuse to issue or renew or to revoke or suspend the recreational license of the obligor or other individual, the Pennsylvania Game Commission shall immediately comply with the order. Upon receipt of an order from the court authorizing the Pennsylvania Game Commission to restore the recreational license of an obligor or other individual, the Pennsylania Game Commission shall immediately restore the recreational license of the obligor or other individual if the obligor or other individual complies with the provisions of 34 Pa.C.S. Ch. 27 (relating to hunting and furtaking licenses).

(4) There shall be no right to appeal from a refusal to issue or renew or from a revocation or suspension under this section, the sole remedy shall be to petition the court which entered the underlying support order which resulted in the revocation, suspension or refusal to issue or renew the recreational license.

(d.3) Special procedures for licenses issued by Pennsylvania Fish and Boat Commission.—

(1) Where the domestic relations section or the department has been unable to attach the income of an obligor and the obligor owes support in an amount equal to or greater than three months of the monthly support obligation, or where an individual has failed, after appropriate notice, to comply with subpoenas or warrants relating to paternity or child support proceedings, the court may issue an order directing the Pennsylvania Fish and Boat Commission to prohibit the issuance or renewal of a recreational license of the obligor or other individual or to require the suspension of the recreational license of the obligor or other individual.

(2) Procedures for notice of suspension, nonrenewal or denial, issuance of the appropriate order and reinstatement of a recreational license shall be in accordance with subsections (b), (c) and (d).

(3) Upon receipt of an order from a court requiring the Pennsylvania Fish and Boat Commission to refuse to issue or renew or to revoke or suspend the recreational license of the obligor or other individual, the Pennsylvania Fish and Boat Commission shall immediately comply with the order. Upon receipt of an order from the court authorizing the Pennsylvania Fish and Boat Commission to restore the recreational license of an obligor or other individual, the Pennsylvania Fish and Boat Commission shall immediately restore the recreational license of the obligor or other individual if the obligor or other individual complies with the provisions of 30 Pa.C.S. Ch. 27 (relating to fishing licenses).

(4) There shall be no right to appeal from a refusal to issue or renew or from a revocation or suspension under this section. The sole remedy shall be to petition the court which entered the underlying support order which resulted in the revocation, suspension or refusal to issue or renew the license.

(d.4) Implementation.—The department may promulgate regulations and issue directives to coordinate and carry out the provisions of this section.

(d.5) Construction.—This section shall supersede any conflicting provision in any other State law unless the provision specifically references this section and provides to the contrary.

(d.6) Immunity.—The court, the domestic relations section, the Department of Public Welfare, the Department of Transportation, the Pennsylvania Game Commission, the Pennsylvania Fish and Boat Commission or any employee of any of these entities or any person appointed by the Pennsylvania Game Commission or the Pennsylvania Fish and Boat Commission to issue licenses and permits pursuant to the applicable provisions of 30 Pa.C.S. (relating to fish) and 34 Pa.C.S. (relating to game) shall not be subject to civil or criminal liability for carrying out their duties under this section.

(e) Definitions.—As used in this section, the following words and phrases shall have the meanings given to them in this subsection:

"**License.**" A license, certificate, permit or other authorization to:

(1) engage in a profession, trade or business in this Commonwealth or a political subdivision or agency thereof; or

(2) operate a motor vehicle for personal or commercial purposes.

"**Licensing authority.**" Any entity of the Commonwealth, political subdivision or agency thereof which issues a license.

"**Operating privilege.**" The privilege to apply for and obtain a license to use as well as the privilege to use a vehicle on a highway as authorized under Title 75 (relating to vehicles).

"**Recreational license.**" A hunting or fishing license.

(July 2, 1993, P.L.431, No.62, eff. 60 days. Amended 1997, Dec. 16, P.L. 549, No. 58, eff. Jan. 1, 1998; 1998, Dec. 15, P.L. 963, No. 127, eff. imd.).

1998 Amendment. Act 127 amended subsec. (d.6).

1997 Amendment. Act 58 amended this sec.

1993 Amendment. Act 62 added section 4355.

Cross References. Section 4355 is referred to in sections 4346, 4377 of this title.

SUBCHAPTER D
PROCEEDINGS AGAINST ENTIRETIES PROPERTY

Sec.
4361. Execution of support order against entireties property.
4362. Plaintiff's share of proceeds of sale.
4363. Trustee to distribute proceeds of sale.
4364. Credit to plaintiff who purchases property.
4365. Rights of divorced person in entireties property sold for support.
4366. Other enforcement remedies preserved.

Enactment. Subchapter D was added December 19, 1990, P.L.1240, No.206, effective in 90 days.

§ 4361. Execution of support order against entireties property.

(a) **Entry of order.**—Whenever married persons hold real property by the entireties and one spouse secures an order of court against the other spouse for the support of the plaintiff spouse or of a child of both persons or the defendant or for the support of both the plaintiff spouse and child and a copy of the order has been certified to the court of common pleas of the county in this Commonwealth in which the property is situated, the order shall be entered in that court as a judgment with the same effect as if it has been recovered as a judgment of that court.

(b) **Execution on judgment.**—Execution may be issued on the judgment against the real property held by the entireties, and the property may be sold in the manner provided by law for the sale of real property on execution issued on a judgment. In any writs of execution on the judgment, the defendant shall not be entitled to the benefit of 42 Pa.C.S. Ch. 81 Subch. B (relating to exemptions from execution) or any other exemption statute.

(c) **Title of purchaser.**—The sale of real property under this section conveys to the purchaser or purchasers thereof a good and valid title to the property and vests in the purchaser or purchasers the entire title of both the married persons in the same manner and with the same effect as if both married persons had joined in the conveyance of the property.

§ 4362. Plaintiff's share of proceeds of sale.

(a) **General rule.**—The plaintiff spouse shall be entitled, out of the proceeds of this sale, to such sums of money as represents the share in the property, based on the proportionate part of the original purchase money furnished by the plaintiff spouse for the purchase of the property.

(b) **Petition to court.**—The plaintiff spouse may petition the court of common pleas of the county where the real property is situated, either before or after the sale of the property by execution, setting forth plaintiff's claim, and the court shall fix a date for a hearing on the petition.

(c) **Hearing and decree.**—After notice and hearing, the court shall make such decree as shall be proper. At the hearing, both spouses shall be competent witnesses.

Cross References. Section 4362 is referred to in section 4365 of this title.

§ 4363. Trustee to distribute proceeds of sale.

(a) **Appointment of trustee.**—The court shall, at the time of the hearing or thereafter, appoint a trustee who shall receive from the sheriff the proceeds of the sale of the property after the costs have been paid.

(b) **Disposition of proceeds.**—The trustee shall, out of the proceeds, pay to the plaintiff spouse the sum of money the court decreed as plaintiff's share in the property sold and also the sums of money, and interest thereon from the time the respective items making them up became due and payable, which are due and payable under the order of support. The trustee shall also pay to the plaintiff spouse any additional sums the plaintiff may be entitled to under any order of court for the support of plaintiff or the children of defendant.

§ 4364. Credit to plaintiff who purchases property.

(a) **General rule.**—If the plaintiff spouse becomes the purchaser at the execution sale, the plaintiff shall be entitled to a credit on the purchase price thereof for the sum of money found by the court to represent the plaintiff's share in the property and also for the sums of money due the plaintiff from the defendant under the order of support upon which the execution was issued at the time of the sale, together with interest on the sums due the plaintiff for support from the time the respective sums become due.

(b) **Allowance or assignment of credit.**—The credit shall be allowed the plaintiff by the sheriff or the plaintiff may assign the sums due the plaintiff to the purchaser of the property whereupon credit shall be given to the purchaser by the sheriff for the amount assigned.

§ 4365. Rights of divorced person in entireties property sold for support.

(a) **General rule.**—After the divorce of any spouse who is a tenant by the entireties of real property with the former spouse, the divorced spouse is entitled to all the rights and remedies provided in this subchapter for the collection of any sums of money ordered by a court to be paid to the divorced spouse for the support of the children of the former spouse as fully as if no divorce had occurred.

(b) **Proceeds of sale.**—Upon the sale of the real property for the collection of any sums of money due the divorced spouse under an order of court, the divorced spouse shall be entitled to receive therefrom such sum of money as represents the share of the divorced spouse in the property, as ordered by the court under section 4362 (relating to plaintiff's share of proceeds of sale), together with any sums which may be due to the divorced spouse under an order of support against the former spouse.

§ 4366. Other enforcement remedies preserved.

This subchapter and other provisions of this chapter do not remove from the plaintiff the rights to any other existing remedies to enforce a support order, including, but not limited to, the right of the plaintiff to institute proceedings against the real or personal property of the defendant.

SUBCHAPTER E
TITLE IV-D PROGRAM AND RELATED MATTERS

Sec.
4371. Definitions.
4372. Establishment of Title IV-D program.
4373. Administration of Title IV-D program.
4374. State disbursement unit.
4375. Access to records.
4376. Central registry.
4377. Power to expedite support cases.
4378. Assistance recipients to seek support.
4379. Cooperation required.
4380. Enforcement to cooperation requirements.
4381. Garnishment of wages of Commonwealth employees.

§ 4371. Definitions.

The following words and phrases when used in this subchapter shall have the meanings given to them in this section unless the context clearly indicates otherwise:

"Assistance." Cash assistance, medical assistance or designated services provided under Article IV of the act of June 13, 1967 (P.L. 31, No.21), known as the Public Welfare Code.

"Legally responsible relative." Effective January 1, 1997, a spouse and a parent for an unemancipated minor child.

"Secretary." The Secretary of Public Welfare of the Commonwealth.

§ 4372. Establishment of Title IV-D program.

(a) **Designation of Title IV-D agency.**—The department is the Title IV-D State agency. The department shall create a single and separate organizational unit which shall be responsible for developing and implementing, subject to the aproval of the secretary, a federally approved State plan for child support.

(b) **Implementation of Title IV-D requirements.**—The department shall construe and implement this subchapter in order to comply with Title IV-D of the Social Security Act (49 Stat. 620, 42 U.S.C. § 301 et seq.). The department shall take all steps necessary to implement a federally approved State plan for steps necessary to implement a federally approved State plan for child support. The department may issue regulations and orders necessary to implement a federally approved State plan for child support. The department may issue interim regulations if Federal law or regulations supersede existing statutes, regulations or court rules.

§ 4373. Administration of Title IV-D program.

(a) **Parent locator service.**—The department shall maintain a parent locator service for the purpose of establishing parentage, for establishing, setting the amount of, modifying or enforcing child support, establishing or enforcing visitation or custody orders, and locating legally responsible relatives. The locator services shall utilize all sources of information and legally available records. In addition, the department shall utilize the parent locator service of the Federal Government pursuant to Federal law and shall only make disclosures on information to individuals as provided by Federal law.

(b) **Cooperative agreements.**—The department shall undertake, either directly or pursuant to cooperative arrangements with appropriate counties, courts or law enforcement officials, including domestic relations sections, to do all of the following:

(1) Establish paternity of children with respect to whom assistance has been received.

(2) Secure support for children under paragraph (1) from a legally responsible relative.

(3) Determine whether the applicant or recipient is cooperating in good faith with matters set forth in section 4379 (relating to cooperation required).

(4) Notify the applicant or recipient of each noncooperation determination and the basis for such determination.

(5) Make available child support and paternity determination services to any individual not receiving assistance to the extent required by Federal law and upon application submitted to the department of forms provided by the department, the payment of any application fee established by the department and the agreement to pay costs in excess of any fee out of any recovery made by the department.

(c) **Incentive payments.**—The department shall make incentive payments to political subdivisions and other states consistent with Federal law whenever the political subdivision or other state enforces or collects support payable to the department.

§ 4374. State disbursement unit.

(a) **Establishment.**—The department shall establish and operate a State disbursement unit for collection and disbursement of payments on child support orders consistent with Federal law. The State disbursement unit shall also monitor support orders for enforcement action consistent with Federal law. At the option of the department, the domestic relations sections may be linked into the State disbursement unit and perform some or all of the functions thereof.

(b) **Collections and disbursements.**—The department may require that such collections and disbursements of support as the department may specify, including those related to persons not receiving public assistance, be processed through the State disbursement unit.

(1) The State disbursement unit shall use automated procedures, electronic processes and computer technology to the maximum extent feasible, efficient and economical for the collection and disbursement of support payments.

(2) If an employer is ordered to withhold income from more than one obligor to pay child support and employs 15 or more persons, the employer shall make payments to the State disbursement unit through electronic payment methods.

(3) If an employer has a history of two or more checks returned for nonsufficient funds, the employer shall make payments to the State disbursement unit through electronic funds transfer.

(4) An employer that is not required to make payments to the State disbursement unit in accordance with this subsection may voluntarily remit support payments through electronic funds transfer to the State disbursement unit.

(b.1) **Penalty.**—The department may impose a civil penalty of up to $1,000 per violation, following notice and hearing, upon an employer who willfully fails to comply with the electronic funds transfer payment provisions of this section.

(c) **Allocation of collections.**—Subject to subsections (d), (e), (f) and (f.1), support collected on behalf of a family shall be distributed as follows:

(1) In the case of a family receiving cash assistance from the Commonwealth:

(i) First, from the amount of current support collected, pass through to the assistance group the first $100 per month for one child or the first $200 per month for two or more children or the first $50 per month for spousal support, without decreasing the amount of cash assistance, provided, however, that in no event may any assistance group be paid more than one support pass-through payment per month.

(ii) Second, calculate the Federal Government's share of the remaining amount collected.

(iii) Third, pay the Federal Government's share and retain the remainder of the amount collected to reimburse the Commonwealth until the amount equals the amount of unreimbursed cash assistance paid to the assistance group.

(iv) Fourth, pay to the assistance group any amounts collected in excess of the amounts distributed or retained under subparagraphs (i), (ii) and (iii).

(2) In the case of a family that formerly received cash assistance from the Commonwealth:

(i) first, pay to the family the current support collected that does not exceed the court-ordered amount to be paid in the month; and

(ii) second, treat amounts collected in excess of the current support collected as arrearages and distribute as follows:

(A) In the case of arrearages that accrued after the family ceased to receive cash assistance from the Commonwealth and which are collected after October 1, 1998:

(I) first, pay the family up to the amount of arrearages that accrued after the family ceased to receive cash assistance from the Commonwealth;

(II) second, treat the balance as reimbursement of assistance in an amount not to exceed the total amount of unreimbursed cash assistance paid to the family and:

(a) pay an amount equal to the Federal share of the reimbursed amount to the Federal Government; and

(b) retain for the Commonwealth an amount equal to the non-Federal share of the reimbursed amount; and

(III) third, pay any remaining amount to the family.

(B) Deleted.

(C) In the case of arrearages that accrued before the family received cash assistance from the Commonwealth and which are collected after October 1, 1998:

(I) first, pay to the family up to the amount of arrearages that accrued before the family began to receive cash assistance from the Commonwealth;

(II) second, treat the balance as reimbursement of assistance in an amount not to exceed the total amount of unreimbursed cash assistance paid to the family and:

(a) pay an amount equal to the Federal share of the reimbursed amount to the Federal Government; and

(b) retain for the Commonwealth an amount equal to the non-Federal share of the reimbursed amount; and

(III) third, pay any remaining amount to the family.

(D) In the case of arrearages that accrued while the family received cash assistance from the Commonwealth:

(I) first, treat the amount collected as reimbursement of assistance in an amount not to exceed the total amount of unreimbursed cash assistance paid to the family and:

(a) pay an amount equal to the Federal share of the reimbursed amount to the Federal Government; and

(b) retain for the Commonwealth an amount equal to the non-Federal share of the reimbursed amount; and

(II) second, pay any remaining amount to the family.

(E) Notwithstanding clauses (A) through (C), the right to any support obligation assigned to the Commonwealth as a condition of receiving cash assistance in effect on September 30, 1997, shall remain assigned after that date.

(F) Except for amounts assigned to the Commonwealth under subsection (d), beginning October 1, 1998, any support arrearages collected shall be credited as follows:

 (I) first, to the period after the family ceased to receive assistance;

 (II) second, to the period before the family received assistance; and

 (III) third, to the period during which the family received assistance.

(3) In the case of a family that never received cash assistance from the Commonwealth, all support collections shall be paid to the family with the exception of the federally mandated $25 annual fee collected from the custodial parent as required under section 4351(a.1) (relating to costs and fees).

(d) Retention by Commonwealth.—

(1) Arrearages collected through use of the Internal Revenue Service Tax Refund Offset Program for a family receiving cash assistance shall be retained by the Commonwealth to the extent past due support has been assigned to the department as a condition of receiving assistance. Arrearages collected through use of the Internal Revenue Service Tax Refund Offset Program for a family that formerly received cash assistance shall first be applied to the monthly support obligation, and the balance shall be applied to arrears owed the family, including assignments of arrearages that accrued before the family received assistance from the Commonwealth and that were executed between October 1, 1997, and September 30, 2009. Any remaining arrearages shall be paid to the department. The department shall pay to the Federal Government the Federal share of the amounts so retained. In no event shall the total of amounts paid to the Federal Government and retained by the department exceed the total of the amount of cash assistance paid to the family by the Commonwealth. To the extent that the amounts collected exceed the amount retained, the department shall pay the excess to the family.

(2) Notwithstanding any other provision of law, the federally mandated $25 annual fee collected from the custodial parent as required under section 4351(a.1) shall be retained by the department.

(e) Child support, foster care children.—Notwithstanding the preceding provisions of this section, amounts collected by the department as child support for months in any period on behalf of a child for whom a public agency is making foster care maintenance payments under Part E of the Social Security Act (49 Stat. 620, 42 U.S.C. § 301 et seq.) shall:

 (1) be retained by the department to the extent necessary to reimburse the Commonwealth for foster care maintenance payments made with respect to the child during such period, with appropriate reimbursement to the Federal Government to the extent of its financial participation;

 (2) be paid to the public agency responsible for supervising the placement of the child to the extent that the amounts collected exceed the foster care maintenance payments made with respect to the child during such periods but not the amounts required by a court or administrative order to be paid as support on behalf of the child during such period; and the responsible agency may use the payment in the manner it determines will serve the best interests of the child, including setting such payments aside for the child's future needs or making all or part thereof available to the person responsible for meeting the child's day-to-day needs; and

 (3) be retained by the department if any portion of the amounts collected remains after making the payments required under paragraphs (1) and (2), to the extent that such portion is necessary to reimburse the Commonwealth for any past foster care maintenance payments or payments of cash assistance which were made with respect to the child and with respect to which past collections have not previously been retained.

Any balance shall be paid to the Commonwealth agency responsible for supervising the placement of the child for use by such agency in accordance with paragraph (2).

(f) Modification of distribution rules.—Notwithstanding any other provision of law, the department may modify the foregoing distribution rules when necessary to comply with Federal law.

(f.1) Distribution.—Notwithstanding any other provision of law, all child support arrears collected prior to October 1, 1998, shall be distributed in accordance with department procedures applying all of the provisions except subsection (b)(1) of section 457 of the Social Security Act (49 Stat. 620, 42 U.S.C. § 657) as in effect on August 21, 1996.

(g) Definitions.—The following words and phrases when used in this section shall have the meanings given to them in this subsection unless the context clearly indicates otherwise:

"Assistance group." The term shall have the meaning given in section 402 of the act of June 13, 1967 (P.L. 31, No. 21), [FN1] known as the Public Welfare Code.

"Family." The term shall include the child for whom support is received, the custodial parent living with the child and any other person in the same assistance group as the child.

(1997, Dec. 16, P.L. 549, No. 58, § 10, effective Jan. 1, 1998. Amended 1998, Dec. 15, P.L. 963, No. 127, § 6, imd. effective; 2006, July 7, P.L. 1055, No. 109, § 2, effective in 60 days [Sept. 5, 2006]; 2008, May 13, P.L. 144, No. 16, § 4). Section 5 of 2008, May 13, P.L. 144, No. 16, imd. effective, provides that "[t]he amendment of 23 Pa.C.S. § 4326, 4351, 4352 and 4374(c)(3) shall apply retroactively to March 31, 2008."

Section 6 of 2008, May 13, P.L. 144, No. 16, imd. effective, provides that "[t]his act shall take effect as follows:

"(1) The amendment of 23 Pa.C.S. § 4374(c)(1) and (d)(1) shall take effect October 1, 2008.

"(2) The amendment of 23 Pa.C.S. § 4378(b) shall take effect October 1, 2009.

"(3) The remainder of this act shall take effect immediately."

2008 Amendment. Act 2008-16, § 4, rewrote subsec. (c)(1); in subsec. (c)(3), inserted "with the exception of the federally mandated $25 annual fee collected from the custodial parent as required under section 4351(a.1) (relating to costs and fees)"; in subsec. (d), designated the existing text as par. (1) and therein, in the first sentence, inserted "for a family receiving cash assistance", and inserted new second and third sentences; and added subsec. (d)(2).

2006 Amendment. Act 109 amended subsec. (b) and added subsec. (b.1).

1998 Amendment. Act 127 amended subsec. (c) and added subsec. (f.1).

Note: The amendment of 23 Pa.C.S. § 4374 shall apply to all child support arrears collected on or after October 1, 1998.

§ 4375. Access to records.

(a) Access to be granted.—The secretary or his designees in writing shall have access to all records, and the department, in cooperation with all other agencies of the executive branch, shall establish a single uniform system of information clearance and retrieval. Information collected as a result of the use of tax records shall include the full name, residence or address, name and address of the employer, income and assets and the Social Security number of the noncustodial parent.

(b) Earnings records.—The Bureau of Employment Security shall provide the department with a statement of earnings clearance upon the request of the department.

(c) Motor vehicle registration information.—Upon request of the department, the Bureau of Motor Vehicles shall provide information as to all vehicles owned by the applicant or recipient.

§ 4376. Central registry.

(a) Central registry created.—A central registry of records shall be maintained in the department showing, as far as it is known, with respect to any absent parent against whom support is sought, all of the following:

(1) The full and true name of such parent together with any known aliases.

(2) The date and place of birth.

(3) Physical description

(4) Social Security number.

(5) Occupation and any special skills he may have.

(6) Military status and veterans administration or military service serial number.

(7) Last known address and the date thereof.

(8) The number of the driver's license.

(9) Any futher information that may be of assistance in locating the person or enforcing support.

(b) Information for registry.—To effectuate the purposes of this section, the department may request and shall receive from all boards or other agencies of this Commonwealth or any of its political subdivisions, and the same are authorized to provide, such assistance and data as will enable the Federal Government the department and other public agencies in this State or in other states to carry out their duties to locate absent parents for the support of their children. The data to be provided from tax records shall include the full name, residence or address, name and address of the employer, income and assets and the Social Security number of the noncustodial parent. The department shall utilize the parent locator service pursuant to establishment in the Department of Health and Human Services by filing in accordance with section 453 (b) of the Social Security Act (49 Stat. 620, 42 U.S.C. § 653(b)).

(c) Certain confidential records.—Notwithstanding any other provision of law, all State and local law enforcement agencies, the Board of Probation and Parole, the Department of Correction and the Department of Transportation shall upon request provide the department, any domestic relations section or any child support agency of the Federal Government or any state with such information regarding the location of an individual as may be contained in law enforcement, probation and parole, corrections, motor vehicle registration and operator licensing records.

(d) Limits on use—Any records established pursuant to the provisions of this section shall be available only to public welfare offices, district attorneys, probation department, domestic relations sections, Federal agencies and the agencies of other States conducting activities under Title IV-D of the Social Security Act, and courts having jurisdiction in support or abandonment proceedings or actions and only for the purposes for which the records have been established.

§ 4377. Power to expedite support cases.

(a) Administrative powers.—The department shall have Statewide jurisdiction to issue the following administrative orders to expedite the establishment and enforcement of support on behalf of any assistance recipient or nonrecipient receiving Title IV-D services:

(1) To order any individual to submit to genetic testing for the purpose of paternity establishment.

(2) To issue administrative supoenas against any entity within this Commonwealth, including for-profit, no-for-profit and governmental employers to require production of information regarding the employment, compensation and benefits of any individual employed by such entity as an employee or contractor.

(3) To access records of all State and local government agencies, including vital statistic records (including records of marriage, birth and divorce), State and local tax and revenue records (including information of residence address, employer, income and assets), records of real and titled personal property, records of occupational and professional licenses, records of the ownership and control of corporations, partnerships and other business entities, employment security records,

records of agencies administering public assistance programs, motor vehicle records, probation and parole records and corrections records.

(4) To issue administrative subpoenas for the records of public utilities and cable television companies with respect to individuals who owe or are owed support, or against whom or with respect to whom a support obligation is sought, consisting of the names and addresses of such individuals and the names and addresses of their employers.

(5) To issue administrative subpoenas for the records held by financial institutions with respect to individuals who owe or are owed support, or against whom or with respect to whom a support obligation is sought.

(6) To issue administrative subpoenas for financial or other information needed to establish, modify or enforce a support order.

(7) To issue orders directing an obligor or other payor to change the payee of a support order.

(8) To order income withholding.

(9) To increase the amount of monthly support payments for the payment of arrearages, as any be provided by general rule.

(10) To issue administrative orders in cases where there is a support arrearage to secure assets to satisfy any current support obligation and current support obligation and the arrearage by:

(i) Intercepting or seizing periodic or lump sum payments from a government agency, including unemployment compensation, workers' compensation and other benefits.

(ii) Intercepting or seizing judgements or settlements.

(iii) Attaching and seizing assets of the obligor held in financial institutions.

(iv) Attaching public and private retirement funds.

(v) Imposing liens on property.

(vi) Directing the sheriff to levy and sell other real or personal property.

(11) To transmit to another state, electronically or by other methods, a request for assistance in a case involving the enforcement of a support order sufficient information as will enable the state to which the request is transmitted to compare the information to the information in the data bases of the state. The transmittal shall serve as a certification of arrears and a certification that the state has complied with all procedural due process requirements applicable to the case.

(12) To respond to a request for assistance received from another state. The response, which may be transmitted electronically or by other methods, shall confirm the receipt of the request, the action taken and the amount of support collected and specify any additional information or action required of the requesting tribunal to obtain enforcement of the child support obligation.

(13) To prohibit the issuance or renewal of a license of an obligor or other individual under section 4355(a) (relating to denial or suspension of licenses) or to require the suspension of the license of an obligor or other individual pursuant to section 4355(d.1).

(b) Enforcement authority.—The department may administratively assess a civil penalty of up to $5,000 per violation upon any person or entity that fails to comply with an order, subpoena or request for information issued under subsection (a). The department may make application to any court of common pleas or to the Commonwealth Court for purposes of enforcing any subpoena or final administrative order.

(c) Appeals.—Any person aggrieved by an action of the department under this section shall have a right to appeal. An appeal of an action under subsection (a) shall be taken to an independent hearing officer designated by the department unless the appellant is challenging the validity or amount of the underlying support obligation, in which case the court having jurisdiction over the support obligation shall hear the appeal. An appeal from imposition of a civil penalty imposed under subsection (b) must be taken to the Bureau of Hearing and Appeals in the department. An appeal which is filed in the wrong tribunal shall be transferred to the correct tribunal. If no appeal is timely filed from the department action or under subsection (a) or (b), the department's action or order shall be final. An action or order of the department under this section shall remain in effect pending any appeal, unless stayed for good cause shown.

(d) **Immunity.**—The department and its employees shall be immune from civil or criminal liability for any good faith action taken under this section. The immunity provided by this subsection shall not apply to any individual who intentionally misuses the authority of the department for a purpose other than securing the lawful establishment or enforcement of support.

1998 Amendment. Act 127 added subsec. (a)(13).

§ 4378. Assistance recipients to seek support.

(a) **Seeking support required.**—Prior to authorization, every applicant for assistance whose circumstances include the reported absence of a legally responsible relative from the household or the presence of a putative father shall appear before the domestic relations section or other applicable division of the court of common pleas. Upon the request of a family court or domestic relations section, the secretary is authorized to waive the requirement of personal appearance before a family court or domestic relations section if another procedure would be as efficient and effective. Subject to Federal approval, only when necessary, assistance shall not be authorized by the department until it has been certified that the applicant has cooperated in determining paternity and enforcing support.

(Text of subsec. (b) effective until Oct. 1, 2009).

(b) **Assignment.**—Acceptance of assistance shall operate as an assignment to the department, by operation of law, of the assistance recipient's rights to receive support on his or her own behalf and on behalf of any family member with respect to whom the recipient is receiving assistance. Such assignment shall be effective only up to the amount of assistance received. The assignment shall take effect at the time that the recipient is determined to be eligible for assistance. Upon termination of assistance payments, the assignment of support rights shall terminate, provided that any amount of unpaid support obligations shall continue as an obligation to and collectible by the department to the extent of any unreimbursed assistance consistent with Federal law. Immediately upon receipt of notification from the department that a recipient has been determined to be eligible for assistance, the clerks of the appropriate courts of the Commonwealth shall transmit any and all support payments that they thereafter receive on behalf of such assistance recipients to the department. Such clerks shall continue transmitting such support payments until notified by the department that it is no longer necessary to do so. While the recipient is receiving assistance, any such support payments made to or on behalf of the assistance recipient shall be allocated to any amount due the department as assignee of the recipient's support rights consistent with Federal law. The assistance recipient shall be deemed to have appointed the department as his attorney-in-fact to endorse over to the department any and all drafts, checks, money orders or other negotiable instruments submitted for payment of support due during the time the recipient is receiving assistance on behalf of himself, herself or any family member.

(Text of subsec. (b) effective Oct. 1, 2009).

(b) **Assignment.**—Acceptance of assistance shall operate as an assignment to the department, by operation of law, of the assistance recipient's rights to receive support on his or her own behalf and on behalf of any family member with respect to whom the recipient is receiving assistance. Such assignment shall be effective only up to the amount of assistance received during the period that a family receives assistance. The assignment shall exclude arrears that accrued prior to receipt of assistance. The assignment shall take effect at the time that the recipient is determined to be eligible for assistance. Upon termination of assistance payments, the assignment of support rights shall terminate, provided that any amount of unpaid support obligations shall continue as an obligation to and collectible by the department to the extent of any unreimbursed assistance consistent with Federal law. Immediately upon receipt of notification from the department that a recipient has been determined to be eligible for assistance, the clerks of the appropriate courts of the Commonwealth shall transmit any and all support payments that they thereafter receive on behalf of such assistance recipients to the department. Such clerks shall continue transmitting such support payments until notified by the department that it is no longer necessary to do so. While the recipient is receiving assistance, any such support payments made to or on behalf of the assistance recipient shall be allocated to any amount due the department as assignee of the recipient's support rights consistent with Federal law. The assistance recipient shall be deemed to have appointed the department as his attorney-in-fact to endorse over to the department any and all drafts, checks, money orders or other negotiable instruments submitted for payment of support due during the time the recipient is receiving assistance on behalf of himself, herself or any family member.

(c) Standing.—An applicant or recipient shall have standing to commence an action to obtain support for any child with respect to whom the applicant or recipient claims assistance.

(1997, Dec. 16, P.L. 549, No. 58, § 10, effective Jan. 1, 1998. Amended 2008, May 13, P.L. 144, No. 16, § 4, effective Oct. 1, 2009).

> **2008 Amendment.** Act 2008-16 in subsec. (b), inserted "during the period that a family receives assistance. The assignment shall exclude arrears that accrued prior to receipt of assistance".

§ 4379. Cooperation required.

In accordance with a child support plan approved by the Federal Government, the department shall have the power and its duty shall be to:

(1) Require as a condition of eligibility for assistance that an applicant or recipient:

(i) Furnish his or her Social Security account number or to the extent permitted by Federal law, proof of making application for a Social Security account number if the applicant or recipient has no Social Security account number.

(ii) Assign to the department on forms provided by the department such support rights as the applicant or recipient may have individually or on behalf of any family member who is a part of the assistance group.

(iii) Cooperate with the department in establishing the paternity of a child with respect to whom assistance is claimed unless the department determines that the applicant or recipient has good cause for failing to do so.

(iv) Cooperate in obtraining support payments for such applicant or recipient and for a child with respect to whom such assistance is claimed or in obtaining any other payment or property due such applicant, recipient or such child unless the department determines that the applicant or recipient has good cause for failing to do so.

(2) Require cooperation in accordance with the following:

(i) Subject to Federal approval, only when necessary, cooperation shall include, but not be limited to taking the following actions:

(A) Identifying the parents of any child for whom assistance is sought or received, including appearing for scheduled genetic testing with the child and submitting to such testing.

(B) Keeping scheduled appointments with the department or domestic relations section.

(C) Providing truthful and accurate information and documents requested by the department or domestic relations section.

(D) Signing and returning any forms requested by the department or domestic relations section.

(E) Appearing as a witness and providing testimony at judicial and other hearings as requested by the domestic relations section.

(F) Paying to the department any support payment received directly from an absent parent after an assignment of support has been made.

(ii) Failure of the mother to identify by name the father of a child shall create a presumption of noncooperation which may be rebutted only by clear and convincing evidence.

(iii) Subject to Federal approval, if the applicant or recipient provides the names of two putative fathers subsequently excluded from paternity by genetic testing, the second excusion shall create a presumption of noncooperation, which may be rebutted only by clear and convincing evidence.

§ 4380. Enforcement of cooperation requirements.

(a) **Cooperation required.**—It is essential to the effective and responsible utilization of assistance funds that applicants and recipients who are caretakers of a child whose circumstances include the reported absence of a legally responsible relative from the household or presence of a putative fater, cooperate fully with the department and the court or domestic relations section in establishing paternity and in securing child support payments and in all matters set forth in section 4379 (relating to cooperation required).

(b) **Procedures.**—

(1) Upon application for assistance, each applicant or recipient shall be notified that his or her cooperation in the matters set forth in section 4379 shall be required as a condition of eligibility and that failure to cooperate will result in the termination of medical assistance and the reduction of the cash assistance allowance in an amount equal to no less than 25%, and may, if provided by departmental regulation, result in the imposition of protective payments for any child in whose behalf the applicant or recipient seeks assistance.

(2) If the department or domestic relations section, as applicable, determines that the applicant or recipient fails to cooperate as set forth in section 4379, unless the failure to cooperate was for good cause, the applicant or recipient shall be notified for the noncooperation determination and the basis for the noncooperation determination. The department shall notify the applicant or recipient in writing of the termination of medical assistance eligibility for the applicant or recipient, the reduction of the cash assistance allowance equal to not less than 25% and, if applicable, that protective payments will be imposed for any child so affected ten days after the date of notice. At the expiration of the ten-day period, the department shall impose the termination of medical assistance, the assistance allowance reduction and, if applicable, protective payments. Any hearing or appeal with respect to the notice of noncooperation issued by the department shall be conducted in accordance with the department's regulations governing an applicant's or a recipient's right to hearings.

(3) Subject to Federal approval, only when necessary, if after notice and opportunity for hearing the court or domestic relations section determines that the applicant or recipient failed to cooperate as set forth in section 4379 and lacked reasonable excuse for such failure, the court shall notify the applicant or recipient and the department of the basis of the noncooperation determination and order the department to impose a sanction for noncooperation. The

department shall issue a notice to the applicant or recipient to terminate medical assistance eligibility, reduce the assistance allowance by not less than 25% and, if applicable, impose a protective payment for any child so affected. The department shall implement the order of the court within ten days of receipt. Any hearing or appeals with respect to the recommendation and order of noncooperation directed by the court shall be conducted by the court in accordance with the Pennsylvania Rules of Civil Procedure as may be promulgated by the supreme Court governing actions for support. The decision to hold hearings for noncooperation cases shall be at the option of the court or domestic realtions section. If the court or domestic relations section chooses not to conduct the hearings on noncooperation, appropriate court or domestic relations section personnel shall be available to provide testimonial evidence by telephone testimony at the time and location set by the department for the departmental appeal hearing. A finding of noncooperation of an applicant or recipient shall not affect an obligor's duty to pay support.

§ 4381. Garnishment of wages of Commonwealth employees.

Notwithstanding any other provision of law, moneys due from or payable by the Commonwealth, including any agency, instrumentality or authority thereof, due to any individual shall be subject, in like manner and to the same extent as if the Commonwealth were a private person, to legal process brought for the enforcement against such individual of his legal obligations to provide support for a child or spouse.

SUBCHAPTER F
NEW HIRE REPORTING

Sec.
4391. Definitions.
4392. Employer reporting.
4393. Use of information.
4394. Guidelines.
4395. Confidentiality.
4396. Penalties.

§ 4391. Definitions.

The following words and phrases when used in this subchapter shall have the meanings given to them in this section unless the context clearly indicates otherwise:

"Date of hire." The first day an employee performs services for remuneration.

"Employee." An individual who is an employee within the meaning of Chapter 24 of the Internal Revenue Code of 1986 (Public Law 99-514, 26 U.S.C. § 3401 et seq.). The term shall not include an employee of a Federal or State agency performing intelligence or counter-intelligence functions if the head of the agency has determined that reporting the information required by this section with respect to the employee could endanger the safety of the employee or compromise an ongoing investigation or intelligence mission.

"Employer." The term has the meaning given in section 3401(d) of the Internal Revenue Code of 1986 (Public Law 99-514, 26 U.S.C. § 3401(d)) and includes any government agency and any labor organization.

"Newly hired employee." The term includes:

(1) a new employee; and

(2) a rehired former employee who was:

(i) laid off, furloughed, separated or granted leave without pay for more than 30 days; or

(ii) terminated from employment.

§ 4392. Employer reporting.

(a) General rule.—For purposes of enhancing child support enforcement activities, including the location of individuals, the establishment of paternity and the enforcement of child support obligations pursuant to this subchapter, a Commonwealth directory of new hires shall be established within the Department of Labor and Industry.

(b) Duty of employer.—Except as provided in subsection (c), each employer doing business in this Commonwealth shall provide the following information regarding a newly hired employee to the Commonwealth directory of new hires: name; home address; Social Security number; date of hire; the employer's name and address; the identifying number assigned to the employer under section 6109 of the Internal Revenue Code of 1986 (Public Law 99-514, 26 U.S.C. § 6109); and the name and telephone number of an employer contact. The information may be submitted on a form provided by the Department of Labor and Industry or by attaching the date of hire and name and telephone number of an employer contact to the W-4 form submitted for the newly hired employee. The information may be transmitted by first class mail, magnetically, electronically or by another method authorized by the directory of new hires.

(c) Employees in two or more states.—An employer that employs individuals in two or more states and that transmits reports magnetically or electronically may comply with subsection (b) by designating one of its offices located in a state in which the employer has employees to send the required report to the Commonwealth directory of new hires. An employer that transmits reports pursuant to this subsection shall notify the Commonwealth directory of new hires and the United States Secretary of Health and Human Services in writing as to which state such employer has designated to send the report required under subsection (b). If the Commonwealth is so designated, the employer shall transmit information in accordance with this subchapter, including the newly hired employee's state of hire, and shall comply with all procedures adopted under this subchapter.

(d) Time for submission.—The information required under subsection (b) shall be submitted by the employer to the Commonwealth directory of new hires no later than 20 days from the date of hire of a newly hired employee. In the case of a magnetic or electronic transmission of the information, the employer may comply by making two monthly transmissions not less than 12 days nor more than 16 days apart.

§ 4393. Use of information.

(a) Access to information.—The domestic relations sections and the department shall have access to all information required under this subchapter for purposes of locating individuals, establishing paternity and establishing, modifying and enforcing child support obligations. The domestic relations sections and the department may disclose such information to its employees, agents and contractors solely for the purposes set forth in this subsection.

(b) Department access to information.—The department shall have access to the information received by the Commonwealth directory of new hires for purposes of verifying eligibility for programs administered by the department.

(c) Other programs.—In addition to child support enforcement, the information received by the Commonwealth directory of new hires may be utilized by the Department of Labor and Industry for purposes of administering the workers' compensation and unemployment compensation programs, including fraud detection, and to develop labor market information for economic and work force development in this Commonwealth.

(d) National directory.—Information included in the Commonwealth directory of new hires shall be provided to the National Directory of New Hires and as otherwise required by Federal law.

§ 4394. Guidelines.

The Department of Labor and Industry shall develop guidelines for employers to use to determine if an individual qualifies as an employee under this subchapter.

§ 4395. Confidentiality.

All information received pursuant to this subchapter shall be confidential and shall be used only for the purpose set forth herein. A person commits a summary offense if he or she discloses information received pursuant to this subchapter to an unauthorized person or for an unauthorized purpose and shall be subject to a civil penalty of up to $250 per offense.

§ 4396. Penalties.

An employer that fails to report pursuant to this subchapter may be provided a written warning for the first violation and is subject to a civil penalty of up to $25 for each violation which is subsequent to the warning. The civil penalty shall be payable to the Department of Labor and Industry. If the failure to report, or the submission of a false report, is the result of a conspiracy between the employer and the employee, the employer shall be subject to a civil penalty of up to $500.

CHAPTER 45
RECIPROCAL ENFORCEMENT OF SUPPORT ORDERS
(Repealed)

1996 Repeal Note. Chapter 45 (§§ 4501–4540) was added October 30, 1985, P.L.264, No.66, and repealed April 4, 1996, P.L.58, No.20, effective immediately. The subject matter is now contained in Parts VIII and VIII-A of this title.

CHAPTER 46
SUPPORT OF THE INDIGENT

Sec.

4601. Scope.
4602. Definitions.
4603. Relatives' liability; procedure.
4604. Property liable for expenses.
4605. Recovery of money.
4606. Guardian.

Note: The Act of June 24, 1937 (P.L.2045, No.397), known as the Support Law, is repealed. Chapter 46 was added July 7, 2005, P.L. 196, No. 43, eff. immediately. However, Section 4 of 2005, July 7, P.L. 196, No. 43, imd. effective, provides that "[t]he addition of 23 Pa.C.S. Ch. 46 is a continuation of the act of June 24, 1937 (P.L. 2045, No. 397)[62 P.S. § 1971 et seq.], known as The Support Law.

§ 4601. Scope

This chapter relates to Support of Indigent Persons

2005 Amendment. Act 43 added this section.

§ 4602. Definitions.

The following words and phrases when used in this chapter shall have the meanings given to them in this section unless the context clearly indicates otherwise:

"Court." A Court of Common Pleas and the Philadelphia Municipal Court.

"Department." The Department of Public Welfare of the Commonwealth.

2005 Amendment. Act 43 added this section.

§ 4603. Relatives' liability; procedure.

(a) Liability.—

(1) Except as set forth in paragraph (2), all of the following individuals have the responsibility to care for and maintain or financially assist an indigent person, regardless of whether the indigent person is a public charge:

(i) The spouse of the indigent person.

(ii) A child of the indigent person.

(iii) A parent of the indigent person.

(2) Paragraph (1) does not apply in any of the following cases:

(i) If an individual does not have sufficient financial ability to support the indigent person.

(ii) A child shall not be liable for the support of a parent who abandoned the child and persisted in the abandonment for a period of ten years during the child's minority.

(b) Amount.—

(1) Except as set forth in paragraph (2), the amount of liability shall be set by the court in the judicial district in which the indigent person resides.

(2) For medical assistance for the aged other than public nursing home care, as provided in section 401 of the act of June 13, 1967 (P.L.31, No.21), known as the Public Welfare Code, the following apply:

(i) Except as set forth in subparagraph (ii), the amount of liability shall, during any 12-month period, be the lesser of:

(A) Six times the excess of the liable individual's average monthly income over the amount required for the reasonable support of the liable individual and other persons dependent upon the liable individual; or

(B) The cost of the medical assistance for the aged.

(ii) The department may, by reasonable regulations, adjust the liability under subparagraph (i), including complete elimination of the liability, at a cost to the commonwealth not exceeding those funds certified by the secretary of the budget as available for this purpose.

(c) Procedure.—A court has jurisdiction in a case under this section upon petition of:

(1) An indigent person; or

(2) Any other person or public body or public agency having any interest in the care, maintenance or assistance of such indigent person.

(d) Contempt.—

(1) If an individual liable for support under this section fails to comply with an order under this section, the court shall schedule a contempt hearing. At the hearing, if the court determines that the individual liable for support has intentionally failed to comply with the order, the court may hold the individual in contempt of court and may sentence the individual to up to six months imprisonment.

(2) This subsection applies regardless of whether the indigent person is confined in a public institution.

2005 Amendment. Act 43 added this section.

§ 4604. Property liable for expenses.

(a) General rule.—except as limited by subsection (c), the following apply:

(1) Subject to paragraph (2), the personal property of an indigent person shall be liable for the expenses incurred by a public body or public agency for the support, maintenance, assistance and burial of:

(i) The indigent person;

(ii) The spouse of the indigent person; and

(iii) Each unemancipated child of the indigent person.

(2) Paragraph (1) applies to personal property if:

(i) The property was owned during the time the expenses were incurred; or

(ii) During the time the expenses were incurred, there existed a cause of action which resulted in the ownership of the property.

(b) Suit.—

(1) A public body or public agency may sue the owner of property referred to in this subsection for money expended.

(2) Except as set forth in paragraph (3) or subsection (c), the following apply:

(i) A judgment obtained under this subsection shall be a lien upon the estate of the defendant and may be collected as other judgments.

(ii) A claim under this section shall have the force and effect against the real and personal estate of a deceased person as other debts of a descendant and shall be ascertained and recovered in the same manner.

(3) Paragraph (2)(i) does not apply to the real and personal property comprising the home and furnishings of the defendant.

(c) **Lien prohibited.**—Except pursuant to the judgment of a court on account of benefits incorrectly paid on behalf of an individual, no lien may be imposed against the real property which is the primary residence of any individual or of the individual's spouse on account of assistance paid or to be paid on the individual's behalf.

(d) **Lien against proceeds.**—In order to carry out the purposes of this section, the department shall have a first lien against the proceeds of any cause of action that existed during the time an individual, his spouse or his unemancipated children received cash assistance. Unless otherwise directed by the department, no payment or distribution shall be made to a claimant or claimant's designee of the proceeds of any action, claim or settlement where the department has an interest without first satisfying or assuring the satisfaction of the interest of the Commonwealth. Any person who, after receiving notice of the department's interest, knowingly fails to comply with this subsection shall be liable to the department; and the department may sue and recover from the person.

2005 Amendment. Act 43 added this section.

§ 4605. Recovery of money.

(a) **Recovery.**—Whenever any person shall become a public charge or receive public assistance, the public body or public agency caring for or furnishing the assistance to the person may sue for and recover any sum of money which is due the person.

(b) **Manner of suit.**—A suit under subsection (a) shall be brought in the name of the person for the use of the public body or public agency. Proof that the person to whom the money is due became a public charge, or was publicly assisted, shall be conclusive proof of the right to recover whatever may be legally due the person. If the amount due has been reduced to judgment, the public body or public agency may be substituted as plaintiff in the judgment. If the amount due is founded on an order or decree of a court, the public body or public agency shall have the right to recover the amount.

(c) **Self-support.**—If a person becomes self-supporting or supported by a relative or friend, any money recovered and not expended in the care or assistance of the person shall belong to the person. In the case of the person's death, money not expended for the person's care, assistance and burial shall belong to the person's estate.

2005 Amendment. Act 43 added this section.

§ 4606. Guardian.

(a) **Petition.**—Any public body or public agency caring for or assisting any indigent person may petition the court of common pleas, if the person is of full age, or the orphans' court, if the person is a minor, for a rule to show cause why the public body, public agency or some other person appointed by the court should not become the legal guardian of the person and property of the person. The petition shall have attached an inventory of the property of the person. The court shall schedule a hearing on the matter and shall serve notice of the hearing upon the person.

(b) **Order.**—After conducting a hearing pursuant to subsection (A), the court may issue an order constituting the public body, public agency or some other person, guardian of the person and the estate of the person, whether or not all of the estate was enumerated in the inventory provided under subsection (A). The proceedings and order shall be indexed in the name of the person pursuant to court rules.

(c) **Discharge.**—

(1) No person for whom a guardian has been appointed under this section shall be discharged from the guardianship until the person has petitioned the court for termination. The court may terminate the guardianship if it is satisfied that:

(i) The person has become able and willing to resume control of the person's own person and estate; and

(ii) The public body or public agency has been fully reimbursed for the expense of the person's care or assistance or that all of the person's estate has been expended for the reimbursement.

(2) The cost of the proceedings under this subsection shall be paid by the petitioner, unless otherwise ordered by the court.

(d) Leases permitted.—Under the supervision of the appropriate court, a guardian may lease the real estate of any person for a term of years and receive and apply the proceeds of the lease to defray the expenses incurred in the care or assistance and burial of the person. The balance of the proceeds shall be paid to the person upon termination of the guardianship or to the legal representatives of the person after the person's death.

2005 Amendment. Act 43 added this section.

Note: The addition of 23 Pa.C.S. Ch. 46 is a continuation of the act of June 24, 1937 (P.L.2045, No.397), known as the support law. The following apply:

(1) Except as otherwise provided in 23 Pa.C.S. Ch. 46, all activities initiated under the support law shall continue and remain in full force and effect and may be completed under 23 Pa.C.S. Ch. 46. Orders, regulations and decisions which were made under the support law and which are in effect on the effective date of section 2 of this act shall remain in full force and effect until revoked, vacated or modified under 23 Pa.C.S. Ch. 46. Contracts, obligations and agreements entered into under the support law are not affected nor impaired by the repeal of the support law.

(2) No provision of the support law which was suspended by order of the supreme court shall be revived by the addition of 23 Pa.C.S. Ch. 46.

(3) Except as set forth in paragraph (4), any difference in language between 23 Pa.C.S. Ch. 46 and the support law is intended only to conform to the style of the Pennsylvania consolidated statutes and is not intended to change or affect the legislative intent, judicial construction or administration and implementation of the support law.

(4) Paragraph (3) does not apply to the addition of 23 Pa.C.S. § 4604 (c) and (d).

(5) Any reference in a statute or a regulation to the support law shall be deemed a reference to 23 Pa.C.S. Ch. 46.

PART VI
CHILDREN AND MINORS

Chapter

51. General Provisions
52. Uniform Child Abduction Prevention
53. Custody
54. Uniform Child Custody Jurisdiction and Enforcement
55. Liability for Tortious Acts of Children
56. Standby Guardianship Act
57. Sex Trafficking and Missing and Abducted Children

Enactment. Part VI was added October 30, 1985, P.L.264, No.66, effective in 90 days.

Cross References. Part VI is referred to in section 5948 of Title 42 (Judiciary and Judicial Procedure).

CHAPTER 51
GENERAL PROVISIONS

Sec.

5101. Attainment of full age.
5102. Children declared to be legitimate.
5103. Acknowledgment and claim of paternity.
5104. Blood tests to determine paternity.
5105. Fingerprinting of Children.

Enactment. Chapter 51 was added December 19, 1990, P.L.1240, No.206, effective in 90 days.

§ 5101. Attainment of full age.

(a) **Age for entering into contracts.**—Any individual 18 years of age and older shall have the right to enter into binding and legally enforceable contracts and the defense of minority shall not be available to such individuals.

(b) **Age for suing and being sued.**—Except where otherwise provided or prescribed by law, an individual 18 years of age and older shall be deemed an adult and may sue and be sued as such.

§ 5102. Children declared to be legitimate.

(a) **General rule.**—All children shall be legitimate irrespective of the marital status of their parents, and, in every case where children are born out of wedlock, they shall enjoy all the rights and privileges as if they had been born during the wedlock of their parents except as otherwise provided in Title 20 (relating to decedents, estates and fiduciaries).

(b) **Determination of paternity.**—For purposes of prescribing benefits to children born out of wedlock by, from and through the father, paternity shall be determined by any one of the following ways:

(1) If the parents of a child born out of wedlock have married each other.

(2) If, during the lifetime of the child, it is determined by clear and convincing evidence that the father openly holds out the child to be his and either receives the child into his home or provides support for the child.

(3) If there is clear and convincing evidence that the man was the father of the child, which may include a prior court determination of paternity.

§ 5103. Acknowledgment and claim of paternity.

(a) **Acknowledgment of paternity.**—The father of a child born to an unmarried woman may file with the Department of Public Welfare, on forms prescribed by the department, an acknowledgment of paternity of the child which shall include the consent of the mother of the child, supported by her witnessed statement subject to 18 Pa.C.S. § 4904 (relating to unsworn falsification to authorities). In such case, the father shall have all the rights and duties as to the child which he would have had if he had been married to the mother at the time of the birth of the child, and the child shall have all the rights and duties as to the father which the child would have had if the father had been married to the mother at the time of birth. The hospital or other person accepting an acknowledgment of paternity shall provide written and oral notice, which may be through the use of video or audio equipment, to the birth mother and birth father of the alternatives to, the legal consequences of and the rights and responsibilities that arise from, signing the acknowledgement.

(b) **Claim of paternity.**—If the mother of the child fails or refuses to join in the acknowledgment of paternity provided for in subsection (a), the Department of Public Welfare shall index it as a claim of paternity. The filing and indexing of a claim of paternity shall not confer upon the putative father any rights as to the child except that the putative father shall be entitled to notice of any proceeding brought to terminate any parental rights as to the child.

(c) **Duty of hospital or birthing center.**—Upon the birth of a child to an unmarried woman, an agent of the hospital or birthing center where the birth occurred shall:

(1) Provide the newborn's birth parents with an opportunity to complete an acknowledgment of paternity. The completed, signed and witnessed acknowledgement shall be sent to the Department of Public Welfare. A copy shall be given to each of the birth parents. This acknowledgement shall contain:

(i) A signed, witnessed statement subject to 18 Pa.C.S. § 4904 (relating to unsworn falsification to authorities) by the birth mother consenting to the acknowledgment of paternity.

(ii) A signed, witnessed statement subject to 18 Pa.C.S. § 4904 by the birth father acknowledging his paternity.

(iii) A written explanation of the parental duties and parental rights which arise from signing such a statement.

(iv) The Social Security numbers and addresses of both birth parents.

(2) Provide written information, furnished by the department to the birth mother and birth father, which explains the benefits of having the child's paternity established, the availability of paternity establishment services and the availability of child support enforcement agencies.

(d) **Conclusive evidence.**—Notwithstanding any other provision of law, an acknowledgment of paternity shall constitute conclusive evidence of paternity without further judicial ratification in any action to establish support. The court shall give full faith and credit to an acknowledgment of paternity signed in another state according to its procedures.

(e) **Transfer.**—The Department of Health shall transfer to the Department of Public Welfare all acknowledgments or claims of paternity filed with the Department of Health under prior statutes.

(f) **Certifications.**—The Department of Public Welfare shall provide necessary certifications under Part III (relating to adoption) as to whether any acknowledgment or claim of paternity has been filed in regard to any child who is a prospective adoptive child.

(g) **Recission.**—

(1) Notwithstanding any other provision of law, a signed voluntary, witnessed acknowledgement of paternity subject to 18 Pa.C.S, § 4904 shall be considered a legal finding of paternity, subject to the right of any signatory to rescind the ackowledgment within the earlier of the following:

(i) sixty days; or

(ii) the date of an administrative or judicial proceeding relating to the child, including, but not limited to, a domestic relations section conference, or a proceeding to establish a support order in which the signatory is a party.

(2) After the expiration of the 60 days, an ackowledgment of paternity may be challenged in court only on the basis of fraud, duress or material mistake of fact, which must be established by the challenger through clear and convincing evidence. An order for support shall not be suspended during the period of challenge except for good cause shown.

(h) Penalties for noncompliance.—The department may impose a civil penalty of not to exceed $500 per day upon a hospital or birthing center which is not in compliance with the provisions of this section. A penalty under this subsection is subject to 2 Pa.C.S. Ch. 5 Subch. A (relating to practice and procedures of Commonwealth agencies) and Ch.7 Subch. A (relating to judicial review of Commonwealth agency action).

(i) Status of father.—The name of the father shall be included on the record of birth of the child of unmarried parents only if one of the following applies:

(1) The father and mother have signed a voluntary acknowledgement of paternity.

(2) A court or administrative agency of competent jurisdiction has issued an adjudication of paternity.

1998 Amendment. Act 127 amended subsec. (a).

1997 Amendment. Act 58 amended this sec.

1994 Amendment. Act 150 amended subsec. (a) and (b), and added subsec. (d), (e), and (f).

1993 Amendment. Act 62 added subsec. (c).

Cross References. Section 5103 is referred to in sections 2503, 2504, 2513 of this title.

Note. The provisions of this act are severable. If any provision of this act or its application to any person or circumstance is held invalid, the invalidity shall not affect other provisions or applications of this act which can be given effect without the invalid provision or application. The amendment of 23 Pa. C.S. §§ 4326, 4343 and 5103 shall apply to all actions pending on the effective date of this act.

§ 5104. Blood tests to determine paternity.

(a) Short title of section.—This section shall be known and may be cited as the Uniform Act on Blood Tests to Determine Paternity.

(b) Scope of section.—

(1) **Civil matters.**—This section shall apply to all civil matters.

(2) **Criminal proceedings.**—This section shall apply to all criminal proceedings subject to the following limitations and provisions:

(i) An order for the tests shall be made only upon application of a party or on the initiative of the court.

(ii) The compensation of the experts shall be paid by the party requesting the blood test or by the county, as the court shall direct.

(iii) The court may direct a verdict of acquittal upon the conclusions of all the experts under subsection (f). Otherwise, the case shall be submitted for determination upon all the evidence.

(iv) The refusal of a defendant to submit to the tests may not be used in evidence against the defendant.

(c) Authority for test.—In any matter subject to this section in which paternity, parentage or identity of a child is a relevant fact, the court, upon its own initiative or upon suggestion made by or on behalf of any person whose blood is involved, may or, upon motion of any party to the action made at a time so as not to delay the proceedings unduly, shall order the mother, child and alleged father to submit to blood tests. If any party refuses to submit to the tests, the court may resolve the question of paternity, parentage or identity of a child against the party or enforce its order if the rights of others and the interests of justice so require.

(d) **Selection of experts.**—The tests shall be made by experts qualified as examiners of blood types, who shall be appointed by the court. The experts shall be called by the court as witnesses to testify to their findings and shall be subject to cross-examination by the parties. Any party or person at whose suggestion the tests have been ordered may demand that other experts qualified as examiners of blood types perform independent tests under order of court, the results of which may be offered in evidence. The number and qualifications of experts shall be determined by the court.

(e) **Compensation of experts.**—The compensation of each expert witness appointed by the court shall be fixed at a reasonable amount. It shall be paid as the court shall order. Subject to general rules, the court may order that it be paid by the parties in such proportions and at such times as it shall prescribe or that the proportion of any party be paid by the county and that, after payment by the parties or the county, or both, all or part or none of it be taxed as costs in the action. Subject to general rules, the fee of an expert witness called by a party but not appointed by the court shall be paid by the party calling him, but shall not be taxed as costs in the action.

(f) **Effect of test results.**—If the court finds that the conclusions of all the experts as disclosed by the evidence based upon the tests are that the alleged father is not the father of the child, the question of paternity, parentage or identity of a child shall be resolved accordingly. If the experts disagree in their findings or conclusions, the question shall be submitted upon all the evidence.

(g) **Effect on presumption of legitimacy.**—The presumption of legitimacy of a child born during wedlock is overcome if the court finds that the conclusions of all the experts as disclosed by the evidence based upon the tests show that the husband is not the father of the child.

§ 5105. Fingerprinting of children.

Notwithstanding the provisions of 54 Pa.C.S. § 702(b) (relating to change by order of court), a child who is 12 years of age or younger shall not be required to submit a set of fingerprints for the purpose of a name change under 54 Pa.C.S. Ch. 7 (relating to judicial change of name).

1998 Amendment. Act 127 added section 5105.

Cross References. See Pa. R.C.P. 1910.15, 1930.6.

CHAPTER 52
UNIFORM CHILD ABDUCTION PREVENTION

Sec.

5201. Scope of chapter.
5202. Definitions.
5203. Cooperation and communication among courts.
5204. Actions for abduction prevention measures.
5205. Jurisdiction.
5206. Contents of petition.
5207. Factors to determine risk of abduction.
5208. Provisions and measures to prevent abduction.
5209. Warrant to take physical custody of child.
5210. Duration of abduction prevention order.
5211. Uniformity of application and construction.
5212. Relation to Electronic Signatures in Global and National Commerce Act.

Note: On January 22, 2014, Governor Corbett signed into law Act 2014-5, effective in 90 days. Act 2014-5 amends Title 23 (Domestic Relations) to provide for prevention of adoption of children. This legislation adds Chapter 52, Uniform Child Abduction Prevention, to provide guidance for courts to follow during custody disputes and divorce proceedings. This guidance is designed to help courts identify families at risk for child abduction and to provide methods to prevent the interstate or foreign abduction of children. The guidelines also allow a party to a child custody order to seek, through the petition process, a supplemental order establishing anti-child abduction measures as long as that party can demonstrate a heightened probability that abduction is possible. The legislation details what must be contained in any petition for anti-child abduction measures and lists the factors the court must consider in determining the risk of abduction.

Act 2010-112 amended Titles 23 (Domestic Relations) and 42 (Judiciary and Judicial Procedure) relating to child custody provisions within the Commonwealth in general, but did not address child custody issues related to a spouse abducting a child and moving them to a foreign country or another state. This legislation addresses these issues. Additionally, this legislation does the following:

- Allows for a court to order abduction prevention measures and issue a warrant to take physical custody of a child;
- Sets forth the contents of a petition for abduction prevention measures;
- Sets forth factors a court shall consider in determining whether there is a risk of abduction;
- Sets forth certain relevant information a court order must include, including requiring a party to post a bond so that if an abduction occurs the proceeds may be expended to locate the child; and
- Allows the court to issue a warrant to search relevant databases of the National Crime Information Center (NCIC) and similar state databases to determine if either the petitioner or respondent has a history of domestic violence, stalking, child abuse or neglect.

§ 5201. Scope of chapter.

This chapter relates to uniform child abduction prevention.

§ 5202. Definitions.

The following words and phrases when used in this chapter shall have the meanings given to them in this section unless the context clearly indicates otherwise:

"Abduction." The wrongful removal or wrongful retention of a child.

"Child." An unemancipated individual who is under 18 years of age.

"Child custody determination." Any judgment, decree or other order of a court providing for the legal custody, physical custody or visitation with respect to a child. The term includes a permanent, temporary, initial and modification order.

"Child custody proceeding." A proceeding in which legal custody, physical custody or visitation with respect to a child is at issue. The term includes a proceeding for divorce, dissolution of marriage, separation, neglect, abuse, dependency, guardianship, paternity, termination of parental rights or protection from domestic violence.

"Court." An entity authorized under the law of a state to establish, enforce or modify a child custody determination.

"Petition." A motion or its equivalent.

"Record." Information that is inscribed on a tangible medium or that is stored in an electronic or other medium and is retrievable in perceivable form.

"State." A state of the United States, the District of Columbia, Puerto Rico, the Virgin Islands or any territory or insular possession subject to the jurisdiction of the United States. The term includes a federally recognized Indian tribe or nation.

"Travel document." Records relating to a travel itinerary, including travel tickets, passes, reservations for transportation or accommodations. The term does not include a passport or visa.

"Wrongful removal." The taking of a child that breaches rights of custody or visitation given or recognized under the laws of this Commonwealth.

"Wrongful retention." The keeping or concealing of a child that breaches rights of custody or visitation given or recognized under the laws of this Commonwealth.

§ 5203. Cooperation and communication among courts.

Sections 5410 (relating to communication between courts), 5411 (relating to taking testimony in another state) and 5412 (relating to cooperation between courts; preservation of records) apply to cooperation and communications among courts in proceedings under this chapter.

§ 5204. Actions for abduction prevention measures.

(a) Court.—A court on its own motion may order abduction prevention measures in a child custody proceeding if the court finds that the evidence establishes a credible risk of abduction of the child.

(b) Party.—A party to a child custody determination or another individual or entity having a right under the laws of this Commonwealth or any other state to seek a child custody determination for the child may file a petition seeking abduction prevention measures to protect the child under this chapter.

(c) Prosecutors or public officials.—A prosecutor or public authority designated under section 5455 (relating to role of prosecutor or public official) may seek a warrant to take physical custody of a child under section 5209 (relating to warrant to take physical custody of child) or other appropriate prevention measures.

§ 5205. Jurisdiction.

(a) General rule.—A petition under this chapter may be filed only in a court that has jurisdiction to make a child custody determination with respect to the child at issue under Chapter 54 (relating to uniform child custody jurisdiction and enforcement).

(b) Emergency jurisdiction.—A court of this Commonwealth has temporary emergency jurisdiction under section 5424 (relating to temporary emergency jurisdiction) if the court finds a credible risk of abduction.

§ 5206. Contents of petition.

A petition under this chapter must be verified and include a copy of any existing child custody determination, if available. The petition must specify the risk factors for abduction, including the relevant factors described under section 5207 (relating to factors to determine risk of abduction). Subject to section 5429(e) (relating to information to be submitted to court), if reasonably ascertainable, the petition must contain:

(1) the name, date of birth and gender of the child;

(2) the customary address and current physical location of the child;

(3) the identity, customary address and current physical location of the respondent;

(4) a statement of whether a prior action to prevent abduction or domestic violence has been filed by a party or other individual or entity having custody of the child and the date, location and disposition of the action;

(5) a statement of whether a party to the proceeding has been arrested for a crime related to domestic violence, stalking or child abuse or neglect and the date, location and disposition of the case; and

(6) any other information required to be submitted to the court for a child custody determination under section 5429.

§ 5207. **Factors to determine risk of abduction.**

(a) **Evidence supporting risk.**—In determining whether there is a credible risk of abduction of a child, the court shall consider any evidence that the petitioner or respondent:

(1) has previously abducted or attempted to abduct the child;

(2) has threatened to abduct the child;

(3) has recently engaged in activities that may indicate a planned abduction, including:

(i) abandoning employment;

(ii) selling a primary residence;

(iii) terminating a lease;

(iv) closing bank or other financial management accounts, liquidating assets, hiding or destroying financial documents or conducting any unusual financial activities;

(v) applying for a passport or visa or obtaining travel documents for the respondent, a family member or the child; or

(vi) seeking to obtain the child's birth certificate or school or medical records;

(4) has engaged in domestic violence, stalking or child abuse or neglect;

(5) has refused to follow a child custody determination;

(6) lacks strong familial, financial, emotional or cultural ties to this Commonwealth or the United States;

(7) has strong familial, financial, emotional or cultural ties to another state or country;

(8) is likely to take the child to a country that:

(i) is not a party to the Hague Convention on the Civil Aspects of International Child Abduction and does not provide for the extradition of an abducting parent or for the return of an abducted child;

(ii) is a party to the Hague Convention on the Civil Aspects of International Child Abduction but:

(A) the Hague Convention on the Civil Aspects of International Child Abduction is not in force between the United States and that country;

(B) according to the most recent compliance report issued by the United States Department of State, is noncompliant; or

(C) lacks legal mechanisms for immediately and effectively enforcing a return order under the Hague Convention on the Civil Aspects of International Child Abduction;

(iii) poses a risk that the child's physical or emotional health or safety would be endangered in the country because of specific circumstances relating to the child or because of human rights violations committed against children;

(iv) has laws or practices that would:

(A) enable the respondent, without due cause, to prevent the petitioner from contacting the child;

(B) restrict the petitioner from freely traveling to or exiting from the country because of the petitioner's gender, nationality, marital status or religion; or

(C) restrict the child's ability legally to leave the country after the child reaches the age of majority because of a child's gender, nationality or religion;

(v) is included by the United States Department of State on a current list of state sponsors of terrorism;

(vi) does not have an official United States diplomatic presence in the country; or

(vii) is engaged in active military action or war, including a civil war, to which the child may be exposed;

(9) is undergoing a change in immigration or citizenship status that would adversely affect the respondent's ability to remain in the United States legally;

(10) has had an application for United States citizenship denied;

(11) has forged or presented misleading or false evidence on government forms or supporting documents to obtain or attempt to obtain a passport, a visa, travel documents, a Social Security card, a driver's license or other government-issued identification card or has made a misrepresentation to the United States Government;

(12) has used multiple names to attempt to mislead or defraud; or

(13) has engaged in any other conduct the court considers relevant to the risk of abduction.

(b) Good faith.—In the hearing on a petition under this chapter, the court shall consider any evidence that the respondent believed in good faith that the respondent's conduct was necessary to avoid imminent harm to the child or respondent and any other evidence that may be relevant to whether the respondent may be permitted to remove or retain the child.

§ 5208. Provisions and measures to prevent abduction.

(a) Contents of discretionary orders.—If a petition is filed under this chapter, the court may enter an order that must include:

(1) the basis for the court's exercise of jurisdiction;

(2) the manner in which notice and opportunity to be heard were given to the persons entitled to notice of the proceeding;

(3) a detailed description of each party's custody and visitation rights and residential arrangements for the child;

(4) a provision stating that a violation of the order may subject the party in violation to civil and criminal penalties; and

(5) identification of the child's country of habitual residence at the time of the issuance of the order.

(b) Abduction prevention orders.—

(1) If, at a hearing on a petition under this chapter or on the court's own motion, the court after reviewing the evidence finds a credible risk of abduction of the child, the court shall enter an abduction prevention order.

(2) The order must include the provisions required by subsection (a) and measures and conditions, including those in subsections (c), (d) and (e), that are reasonably calculated to prevent abduction of the child, giving due consideration to the custody and visitation rights of the parties.

(3) The court shall consider:

(i) the age of the child;

(ii) the potential harm to the child from an abduction;

(iii) the legal and practical difficulties of returning the child to the jurisdiction if abducted; and

(iv) the reasons for the potential abduction, including evidence of domestic violence, stalking or child abuse or neglect.

(c) Restrictions.—An abduction prevention order may include one or more of the following:

(1) an imposition of travel restrictions that require that a party traveling with the child outside a designated geographical area provide the other party with the following:

(i) the travel itinerary of the child;

(ii) a list of physical addresses and telephone numbers at which the child can be reached at specified times; and

(iii) copies of all travel documents;

(2) a prohibition of the respondent directly or indirectly:

(i) removing the child from this Commonwealth, the United States or another geographic area without permission of the court or the petitioner's written consent;

(ii) removing or retaining the child in violation of a child custody determination;

(iii) removing the child from school or a child-care or similar facility; or

(iv) approaching the child at any location other than a site designated for supervised visitation;

(3) a requirement that a party register the order in another state as a prerequisite to allowing the child to travel to that state;

(4) with regard to the child's passport:

(i) a direction that the petitioner place the child's name in the United States Department of State's Child Passport Issuance Alert Program;

(ii) a requirement that the respondent surrender to the court or the petitioner's attorney any United States or foreign passport issued in the child's name, including a passport issued in the name of both the parent and the child; and

(iii) a prohibition upon the respondent from applying on behalf of the child for a new or replacement passport or visa;

(5) as a prerequisite to exercising custody or visitation, a requirement that the respondent provide:

(i) to the United States Department of State Office of Children's Issues and the relevant foreign consulate or embassy, an authenticated copy of the order detailing passport and travel restrictions for the child;

(ii) to the court:

(A) proof that the respondent has provided the information in subparagraph (i); and

(B) an acknowledgment in a record from the relevant foreign consulate or embassy that no passport application has been made or passport issued on behalf of the child;

(iii) to the petitioner, proof of registration with the United States Embassy or other United States diplomatic presence in the destination country and with the Central Authority for the Hague Convention on the Civil Aspects of International Child Abduction, if that convention is in effect between the United States and the destination country, unless one of the parties objects; and

(iv) a written waiver under 5 U.S.C. § 552a (relating to records maintained on individuals), with respect to any document, application or other information pertaining to the child authorizing its disclosure to the court and the petitioner; and

(6) upon the petitioner's request, a requirement that the respondent obtain an order from the relevant foreign country containing terms identical to the child custody determination issued in the United States.

(d) Conditions on custody and visitation.—In an abduction prevention order, the court may impose conditions on the exercise of custody or visitation that:

(1) limit visitation or require that visitation with the child by the respondent be supervised until the court finds that supervision is no longer necessary and order the respondent to pay the costs of supervision;

(2) require the respondent to post a bond or provide other security in an amount sufficient to serve as a financial deterrent to abduction, the proceeds of which may be used to pay for the reasonable expenses of recovery of the child, including reasonable attorney fees and costs if there is an abduction; and

(3) require the respondent to obtain education on the potentially harmful effects to the child from abduction.

(e) Prevention of imminent abduction.—To prevent imminent abduction of a child, a court may:

(1) issue a warrant to take physical custody of the child under section 5209 (relating to warrant to take physical custody of child) or the laws of this Commonwealth other than this chapter;

(2) direct the use of law enforcement to take any action reasonably necessary to locate the child, obtain return of the child or enforce a custody determination under this chapter or the laws of this Commonwealth other than this chapter; or

(3) grant any other relief allowed under the laws of this Commonwealth other than this chapter.

(f) Cumulative remedies.—The remedies provided in this chapter are cumulative and do not affect the availability of other remedies to prevent abduction.

§ 5209. Warrant to take physical custody of child.

(a) Ex parte.—If a petition under this chapter contains allegations and the court finds that there is a credible risk that the child is imminently likely to be wrongfully removed, the court may issue an ex parte warrant to take physical custody of the child.

(b) Hearing.—The respondent on a petition under subsection (a) must be afforded an opportunity to be heard at the earliest possible time after the ex parte warrant is executed, but not later than the next judicial day unless a hearing on that date is impossible. In that event, the court shall hold the hearing on the first judicial day possible.

(c) Requirements.—An ex parte warrant under subsection (a) to take physical custody of a child must:

(1) Recite the facts upon which a determination of a credible risk of imminent wrongful removal of the child is based.

(2) Direct law enforcement officers to take physical custody of the child immediately.

(3) State the date and time for the hearing on the petition.

(4) Provide for the safe interim placement of the child pending further order of the court.

(d) Search of databases.—If feasible, before issuing a warrant and before determining the placement of the child after the warrant is executed, the court may order a search of the relevant databases of the National Crime Information Center system and similar state databases to determine if either the petitioner or respondent has a history of domestic violence, stalking or child abuse or neglect.

(e) **Service.**—The petition and warrant must be served on the respondent when or immediately after the child is taken into physical custody.

(f) **Enforcement.**—

(1) A warrant to take physical custody of a child, issued by this Commonwealth or another state, is enforceable throughout this Commonwealth.

(2) If the court finds that a less intrusive remedy will not be effective, it may authorize law enforcement officers to enter private property to take physical custody of the child. If required by exigent circumstances, the court may authorize law enforcement officers to make a forcible entry at any hour.

(g) **Fees and costs.**—If the court finds, after a hearing, that a petitioner sought an ex parte warrant under subsection (a) for the purpose of harassment or in bad faith, the court may award the respondent reasonable attorney fees, costs and expenses.

(h) **Other relief.**—This chapter does not affect the availability of relief allowed under the laws of this Commonwealth other than this chapter.

§ 5210. Duration of abduction prevention order.

An abduction prevention order remains in effect until the earliest of:

(1) the time stated in the order;

(2) the emancipation of the child;

(3) the child's attaining 18 years of age; or

(4) the time the order is modified, revoked, vacated or superseded by a court with jurisdiction under sections 5421 (relating to initial child custody jurisdiction), 5422 (relating to exclusive, continuing jurisdiction) and 5423 (relating to jurisdiction to modify determination) and applicable laws of this Commonwealth.

§ 5211. Uniformity of application and construction.

In applying and construing this chapter, consideration must be given to the need to promote uniformity of the law with respect to its subject matter among states that enact it.

§ 5212. Relation to Electronic Signatures in Global and National Commerce Act.

To the extent permitted by section 102 of the Electronic Signatures in Global and National Commerce Act (Public Law 106-229, 15 U.S.C. § 7002), this chapter may supersede provisions of that act.

(January 22, 2014, P.L. ___, No. 5, eff. in 90 days)

Pa.C.S.

CHAPTER 53
CHILD CUSTODY

Sec.

5321. Scope of chapter.
5322. Definitions.
5323. Award of custody.
5324. Standing for any form of physical custody or legal custody.
5325. Standing for partial physical custody and supervised physical custody.
5326. Effect of adoption.
5327. Presumption in cases concerning primary physical custody.
5328. Factors to consider when awarding custody.
5329. Consideration of criminal conviction.
5329.1. Consideration of child abuse and involvement with protective services.
5330. Consideration of criminal charge.
5331. Parenting plan.
5332. Informational programs.
5333. Counseling as part of order.
5334. Guardian ad litem for child.
5335. Counsel for child.
5336. Access to records and information.
5337. Relocation.
5338. Modification of existing order.
5339. Award of counsel fees, costs and expenses.
5340. Court-appointed child custody health care or behavioral health practitioners.

Note: On November 23, 2010, Governor Rendell signed into law Act 2010-112, effective in 60 days [January 22, 2011]. Act 2010-112 amends Titles 23 (Domestic Relations) and 42 (Judiciary and Judicial Procedure) relating to child custody provisions. The changes to Title 42 are technical in nature; however, changes to Title 23 differ from current law in numerous areas.

Section 4346 of Chapter 53 and Subchapter A headings and sections 5301 through 5315 of Title 23 are repealed and a new Chapter 53 is added. Definitions regarding custody have been added or amended to include qualifying language relating to the actual time spent with the child. The Act also amends the penalties for those failing to comply with a custody order and found in contempt. The Act lists a number of factors (more extensive than current law) which the court is to use, giving "weighted consideration" to those factors which affect the safety of the child, when determining custody and identifies the types of custody that the court may award if it is in the best interest of the child. A party who willfully fails to comply with a custody order may be adjudged in contempt and the act specifically lists penalties for such contempt.

The Act includes a variety of offenses to be considered by the court before making any order of custody and provides for initial evaluation and counseling when necessary. The Act expands on considerations of criminal convictions, adding some crimes not currently listed in law (such as driving under the influence and drug-related convictions).

The legislation identifies who may file an action for any form of physical custody or legal custody, including the right of individuals standing *in loco parentis*, and identifies the situations where grandparents and great-grandparents may file an action for partial physical custody or supervised physical custody. Guidelines for presumptions in custody cases are also outlined in the Act.

In a contested custody proceeding, the court may require the parties to submit parenting plans for the care and custody of the child to aid the court in resolving the custody dispute. The legislation includes the specific items to be addressed in such a plan. The court may on its own motion or the motion of a party appoint a guardian ad litem to represent the child in the action, including latitude for a non-lawyer appointed guardian ad litem, and the powers and duties of the guardian ad litem are listed. In addition, the court may appoint counsel to represent the child if the court determines that the appointment will assist in resolving the issues in the custody proceeding.

Finally, the legislation addresses relocation including: notice; time frames; counter-affidavit to object to a proposed relocation and the modification of a custody order; and the relocation factors the court shall consider to be given "weighted consideration" in determining whether to grant a proposed relocation.

The revisions regarding child custody matters set forth in Act 2010-112 consider recommendations from the Joint State Government Commission's Advisory Committee on Domestic Relations Law.

The Act takes effect on January 22, 2011. However, a proceeding under the former provisions of 23 Pa.C.S. Chapter 53 which was commenced before the effective date of Act 2010-112 [January 22, 2011] shall be governed by the law in effect at the time the proceeding was initiated.

§ 5321. Scope of chapter.

This chapter applies to disputes relating to child custody matters.

§ 5322. Definitions.

(a) **This chapter.**—The following words and phrases when used in this chapter shall have the meanings given to them in this subsection unless the context clearly indicates otherwise:

"**Abuse.**" As defined in section 6102 (relating to definitions).

"**Adult.**" An individual 18 years of age or older.

"**Agency.**" Any organization, society, institution, court facility or other entity which provides for the care of a child. The term does not include a county children and youth social service agency.

"**Child.**" An unemancipated individual under 18 years of age.

"Legal custody." The right to make major decisions on behalf of the child, including, but not limited to, medical, religious and educational decisions.

"**Parental duties.**" Includes meeting the physical, emotional and social needs of the child.

"**Partial physical custody.**" The right to assume physical custody of the child for less than a majority of the time.

"**Physical custody.**" The actual physical possession and control of a child.

"**Primary physical custody.**" The right to assume physical custody of the child for the majority of time.

"**Relocation.**" A change in a residence of the child which significantly impairs the ability of a nonrelocating party to exercise custodial rights.

"**Shared legal custody.**" The right of more than one individual to legal custody of the child.

"**Shared physical custody.**" The right of more than one individual to assume physical custody of the child, each having significant periods of physical custodial time with the child.

"**Sole legal custody.**" The right of one individual to exclusive legal custody of the child.

"**Sole physical custody.**" The right of one individual to exclusive physical custody of the child.

"**Supervised physical custody.**" Custodial time during which an agency or an adult designated by the court or agreed upon by the parties monitors the interaction between the child and the individual with those rights.

(b) **Other law.**—In a statutory provision other than in this chapter, when the term "visitation" is used in reference to child custody, the term may be construed to mean:

(1) partial physical custody;

(2) shared physical custody; or

(3) supervised physical custody.

§ 5323. Award of custody.

(a) Types of award.—After considering the factors set forth in section 5328 (relating to factors to consider when awarding custody), the court may award any of the following types of custody if it is in the best interest of the child:

(1) Shared physical custody.

(2) Primary physical custody.

(3) Partial physical custody.

(4) Sole physical custody.

(5) Supervised physical custody.

(6) Shared legal custody.

(7) Sole legal custody.

(b) Interim award.—The court may issue an interim award of custody to a party who has standing under section 5324 (relating to standing for any form of physical custody or legal custody) or 5325 (relating to standing for partial physical custody and supervised physical custody), in the manner prescribed by the Pennsylvania Rules of Civil Procedure governing special relief in custody matters.

(c) Notice.—Any custody order shall include notice of a party's obligations under section 5337 (relating to relocation).

(d) Reasons for award.—The court shall delineate the reasons for its decision on the record in open court or in a written opinion or order.

(e) Safety conditions.—After considering the factors under section 5328(a)(2), if the court finds that there is an ongoing risk of harm to the child or an abused party and awards any form of custody to a party who committed the abuse or who has a household member who committed the abuse, the court shall include in the custody order safety conditions designed to protect the child or the abused party.

(f) Enforcement.—In awarding custody, the court shall specify the terms and conditions of the award in sufficient detail to enable a party to enforce the court order through law enforcement authorities.

(g) Contempt for noncompliance with any custody order.—

(1) A party who willfully fails to comply with any custody order may, as prescribed by general rule, be adjudged in contempt. Contempt shall be punishable by any one or more of the following:

(i) Imprisonment for a period of not more than six months.

(ii) A fine of not more than $500.

(iii) Probation for a period of not more than six months.

(iv) An order for nonrenewal, suspension or denial of operating privilege under section 4355 (relating to denial or suspension of licenses).

(v) Counsel fees and costs.

(2) An order committing an individual to jail under this section shall specify the condition which, when fulfilled, will result in the release of that individual.

(h) Parties in same residence.—Parties living separate and apart in the same residence may seek relief under this chapter, but any custody order made under such a circumstance shall be effective only upon:

(1) one party physically vacating the residence; or

(2) an order awarding one party exclusive possession of the residence.

§ 5324. Standing for any form of physical custody or legal custody.

The following individuals may file an action under this chapter for any form of physical custody or legal custody:

(1) A parent of the child.

(2) A person who stands in loco parentis to the child.

(3) A grandparent of the child who is not in loco parentis to the child:

(i) whose relationship with the child began either with the consent of a parent of the child or under a court order;

(ii) who assumes or is willing to assume responsibility for the child; and

(iii) when one of the following conditions is met:

(A) the child has been determined to be a dependent child under 42 Pa.C.S. Ch. 63 (relating to juvenile matters);

(B) the child is substantially at risk due to parental abuse, neglect, drug or alcohol abuse or incapacity; or

(C) the child has, for a period of at least 12 consecutive months, resided with the grandparent, excluding brief temporary absences of the child from the home, and is removed from the home by the parents, in which case the action must be filed within six months after the removal of the child from the home.

(4) Subject to paragraph (5), an individual who establishes by clear and convincing evidence all of the following:

(i) The individual has assumed or is willing to assume responsibility for the child.

(ii) The individual has a sustained, substantial and sincere interest in the welfare of the child. In determining whether the individual meets the requirements of this subparagraph, the court may consider, among other factors, the nature, quality, extent and length of the involvement by the individual in the child's life.

(iii) Neither parent has any form of care and control of the child.

(5) Paragraph (4) shall not apply if:

(i) a dependency proceeding involving the child has been initiated or is ongoing; or

(ii) there is an order of permanent legal custody under 42 Pa.C.S. § 6351(a)(2.1) or (f.1)(3) (relating to disposition of dependent child).

(May 4, 2018, P.L.112, No.21, eff. 60 days).

Note: The addition of 23 Pa. C.S. Sect. 5324(4) and (5) shall apply to all custody proceedings irrespective of whether the proceeding was commenced before, on or after the effective date of this section.

2018 Amendment. Act 21 added pars. (4) and (5). Section 3 of Act 21 provided that the addition of pars. (4) and (5) shall apply to all custody proceedings irrespective of whether the proceeding was commenced before, on or after the effective date of this section.

Cross References. Section 5324 is referred to in sections 5323, 5325, 5326 of this title.

§ 5325. Standing for partial physical custody and supervised physical custody.

In addition to situations set forth in section 5324 (relating to standing for any form of physical custody or legal custody), grandparents and great-grandparents may file an action under this chapter for partial physical custody or supervised physical custody in the following situations:

(1) where the parent of the child is deceased, a parent or grandparent of the deceased parent may file an action under this section;

(2) where the relationship with the child began either with the consent of a parent of the child or under a court order and where the parents of the child:

(i) have commenced a proceeding for custody; and

(ii) do not agree as to whether the grandparents or great-grandparents should have custody under this section; or

(3) when the child has, for a period of at least 12 consecutive months, resided with the grandparent or great-grandparent, excluding brief temporary absences of the child from the home, and is removed from the home by the parents, an action must be filed within six months after the removal of the child from the home.

(May 4, 2018, P.L.112, No.21, eff. 60 days)

2018 Amendment. Act 21 amended par. (2).

Cross References. Section 5325 is referred to in sections 5323, 5326, 5328 of this title.

§ 5326. Effect of adoption.

Any rights to seek physical custody or legal custody rights and any custody rights that have been granted under section 5324 (relating to standing for any form of physical custody or legal custody) or 5325 (relating to standing for partial physical custody and supervised physical custody) to a grandparent or great-grandparent prior to the adoption of the child by an individual other than a stepparent, grandparent or great-grandparent shall be automatically terminated upon such adoption.

§ 5327. Presumption in cases concerning primary physical custody.

(a) Between parents.—In any action regarding the custody of the child between the parents of the child, there shall be no presumption that custody should be awarded to a particular parent.

(b) Between a parent and third party.—In any action regarding the custody of the child between a parent of the child and a nonparent, there shall be a presumption that custody shall be awarded to the parent. The presumption in favor of the parent may be rebutted by clear and convincing evidence.

(c) Between third parties.—In any action regarding the custody of the child between a nonparent and another nonparent, there shall be no presumption that custody should be awarded to a particular party.

§ 5328. Factors to consider when awarding custody

(a) Factors.—In ordering any form of custody, the court shall determine the best interest of the child by considering all relevant factors, giving weighted consideration to those factors which affect the safety of the child, including the following:

(1) Which party is more likely to encourage and permit frequent and continuing contact between the child and another party.

(2) The present and past abuse committed by a party or member of the party's household, whether there is a continued risk of harm to the child or an abused party and which party can better provide adequate physical safeguards and supervision of the child.

(2.1) The information set forth in section 5329.1(a) (relating to consideration of child abuse and involvement with protective services).

(3) The parental duties performed by each party on behalf of the child.

(4) The need for stability and continuity in the child's education, family life and community life.

(5) The availability of extended family.

(6) The child's sibling relationships.

(7) The well-reasoned preference of the child, based on the child's maturity and judgment.

(8) The attempts of a parent to turn the child against the other parent, except in cases of domestic violence where reasonable safety measures are necessary to protect the child from harm.

(9) Which party is more likely to maintain a loving, stable, consistent and nurturing relationship with the child adequate for the child's emotional needs.

(10) Which party is more likely to attend to the daily physical, emotional, developmental, educational and special needs of the child.

(11) The proximity of the residences of the parties.

(12) Each party's availability to care for the child or ability to make appropriate child-care arrangements.

(13) The level of conflict between the parties and the willingness and ability of the parties to cooperate with one another. A party's effort to protect a child from abuse by another party is not evidence of unwillingness or inability to cooperate with that party.

(14) The history of drug or alcohol abuse of a party or member of a party's household.

(15) The mental and physical condition of a party or member of a party's household.

(16) Any other relevant factor.

(b) Gender neutral.—In making a determination under subsection (a), no party shall receive preference based upon gender in any award granted under this chapter.

(c) Grandparents and great-grandparents.—

(1) In ordering partial physical custody or supervised physical custody to a party who has standing under section 5325(1) or (2)(relating to standing for partial physical custody and supervised physical custody), the court shall consider the following:

(i) the amount of personal contact between the child and the party prior to the filing of the action;

(ii) whether the award interferes with any parent-child relationship; and

(iii) whether the award is in the best interest of the child.

(2) In ordering partial physical custody or supervised physical custody to a parent's parent or grandparent who has standing under section 5325(3), the court shall consider whether the award:

(i) interferes with any parent-child relationship; and

(ii) is in the best interest of the child.

2010, Nov. 23, P.L. 1106, No. 112, § 2, effective in 60 days [Jan. 24, 2011]. Amended 2013, Dec. 18, P.L. 1167, No. 107, § 1, effective Jan. 1, 2014.

JT. ST. GOVT. COMM. COMMENT—2010

The factors under subsection (a) are not listed in order of preference. Subsection (a)(6) is intended to include full-blood siblings, half-blood siblings, step-siblings and adoptive siblings.

2013 Amendment. Act 107 added subsec. (a)(2.1). See section 6 of Act 107 in the appendix to this title for special provisions relating to applicability.

Cross References. Section 5328 is referred to in section 5323, 6340 of this title; section 6307 of Title 42 (Judiciary and Judicial Procedure).

§ 5329. Consideration of criminal conviction.

(a) Offenses.—Where a party seeks any form of custody, the court shall consider whether that party or member of that party's household has been convicted of or has pleaded guilty or no contest to any of the offenses in this section or an offense in another jurisdiction substantially equivalent to any of the offenses in this section. The court shall consider such conduct and determine that the party does not pose a threat of harm to the child before making any order of custody to that party when considering the following offenses:

18 Pa.C.S. Ch. 25 (relating to criminal homicide).

18 Pa.C.S. § 2702 (relating to aggravated assault).

18 Pa.C.S. § 2706 (relating to terroristic threats).

18 Pa.C.S. § 2709.1 (relating to stalking).

18 Pa.C.S. § 2901 (relating to kidnapping).

18 Pa.C.S. § 2902 (relating to unlawful restraint).

18 Pa.C.S. § 2903 (relating to false imprisonment).

18 Pa.C.S. § 2910 (relating to luring a child into a motor vehicle or structure).

18 Pa.C.S. § 3121 (relating to rape).

18 Pa.C.S. § 3122.1 (relating to statutory sexual assault).

18 Pa.C.S. § 3123 (relating to involuntary deviate sexual intercourse).

18 Pa.C.S. § 3124.1 (relating to sexual assault).

18 Pa.C.S. § 3125 (relating to aggravated indecent assault).

18 Pa.C.S. § 3126 (relating to indecent assault).

18 Pa.C.S. § 3127 (relating to indecent exposure).

18 Pa.C.S. § 3129 (relating to sexual intercourse with animal).

18 Pa.C.S. § 3130 (relating to conduct relating to sex offenders).

18 Pa.C.S. § 3301 (relating to arson and related offenses).

18 Pa.C.S. § 4302 (relating to incest).

18 Pa.C.S. § 4303 (relating to concealing death of child).

18 Pa.C.S. § 4304 (relating to endangering welfare of children).

18 Pa.C.S. § 4305 (relating to dealing in infant children).

18 Pa.C.S. § 5902(b) (relating to prostitution and related offenses).

18 Pa.C.S. § 5903(c) or (d) (relating to obscene and other sexual materials and performances).

18 Pa.C.S. § 6301 (relating to corruption of minors).

18 Pa.C.S. § 6312 (relating to sexual abuse of children).

18 Pa.C.S. § 6318 (relating to unlawful contact with minor).

18 Pa.C.S. § 6320 (relating to sexual exploitation of children).

Section 6114 (relating to contempt for violation of order or agreement).

The former 75 Pa.C.S. § 3731 (relating to driving under influence of alcohol or controlled substance).

75 Pa.C.S. Ch. 38 (relating to driving after imbibing alcohol or utilizing drugs).

Section 13(a)(1) of the act of April 14, 1972 (P.L.233, No.64), known as The Controlled Substance, Drug, Device and Cosmetic Act, to the extent that it prohibits the manufacture, sale or delivery, holding, offering for sale or possession of any controlled substance or other drug or device.

(b) Parent convicted of murder.—No court shall award custody, partial custody or supervised physical custody to a parent who has been convicted of murder under 18 Pa.C.S. § 2502(a) (relating to murder) of the other parent of the child who is the subject of the order unless the child is of suitable age and consents to the order.

(b.1) Parent convicted of certain sexual offenses.—

(1) Notwithstanding any provision of this chapter to the contrary and subject to paragraph (2), if a parent who is a victim of any of the offenses set forth in this paragraph objects, no court shall award any type of custody set forth in section 5323 (relating to award of custody) to the other parent of a child conceived as a result of any of the following offenses for which the other parent has been convicted:

18 Pa.C.S. § 3121.

18 Pa.C.S. § 3122.1.

18 Pa.C.S. § 3124.1, where the offense involved sexual intercourse.

18 Pa.C.S. § 3124.2 (relating to institutional sexual assault), where the offense involved sexual intercourse.

18 Pa.C.S. § 4302.

(2) A court may award any type of custody set forth in section 5323 to a parent who has been convicted of an offense under paragraph (1) if:

    (i) the parent who is a victim had an opportunity to address the court;

    (ii) the child is of suitable age and consents to the custody order; and

    (iii) the court determines the award is in the best interest of the child.

(3) Paternity of the child shall be established by voluntary acknowledgment of paternity or blood, genetic or other paternity testing acceptable to the court. The cost of the testing shall be borne by the parent who was convicted of the offense.

(c) Initial evaluation.—At the initial in-person contact with the court, the judge, conerence officer or other appointed individual shall perform an initial evaluation to determine whether the party or household member who committed an offense under subsection (a) poses a threat to the child and whether counseling is necessary. The initial evaluation shall not be conducted by a mental health professional. After the initial evaluation, the court may order further evaluation or counseling by a mental health professional if the court determines it is necessary.

(d) Counseling.—

(1) Where the court determines under subsection (c) that counseling is necessary, it shall appoint a qualified professional specializing in treatment relating to the particular offense to provide counseling to the offending individual.

(2) Counseling may include a program of treatment or individual therapy designed to rehabilitate the offending individual which addresses, but is not limited to, issues regarding physical and sexual abuse, the psychology of the offender and the effects of the offense on the victim.

(e) Subsequent evaluation.—

(1) At any time during or subsequent to the counseling under subsection (d), the court may require another evaluation to determine whether further counseling is necessary.

(2) If the court awards custody to a party who committed an offense under subsection (a) or who shares a household with an individual who committed an offense under subsection (a), the court may require subsequent evaluations on the rehabilitation of the offending individual and the well-being of the child subsequent to the order. If, upon review of a subsequent evaluation, the court determines that the offending individual poses a threat of physical, emotional or psychological harm to the child, the court may schedule a hearing to modify the custody order.

(f) Costs.—The court may order a party to pay all or part of the costs of the counseling and evaluations under this section.

(Apr. 12, 2012, P.L.241, No.32, eff. 60 days; Oct. 1, 2015, P.L.172, No.40, eff. 60 days; May 4, 2018, P.L.112, No.21, eff. 60 days)

    2018 Amendment. Act 21 amended subsec. (a) intro. par.

    2015 Amendment. Act 40 added subsec. (b.1). Section 3 of Act 40 provided that subsec. (b.1) shall apply to any action regarding custody of a child under Chapter 43 or 53 that is filed on or after the effective date of section 3.

    2012 Amendment. Act 32 amended subsec. (c).

    Cross References. Section 5329 is referred to in section 5330 of this title; section 1904 of Title 42 (Judiciary and Judicial Procedure).

§ 5329.1. Consideration of child abuse and involvement with protective services

(a) **Information sharing.**—In accordance with section 6340(a)(5.1) (relating to release of information in confidential reports), where a party seeks any form of custody subject to the examination of the parties, the court shall determine:

(1) With respect to child abuse under Chapter 63 (relating to child protective services) or a child who is a victim of a crime under 18 Pa.C.S. (relating to crimes and offenses) which would constitute abuse under Chapter 63:

(i) Whether the child is the subject of an indicated or founded report of child abuse.

(ii) Whether a party or a member of the party's household has been identified as the perpetrator in an indicated or founded report of child abuse.

(iii) The date and circumstances of the child abuse.

(iv) The jurisdiction where the child abuse investigation took place.

(2) With respect to child protective services or general protective services under Chapter 63:

(i) Whether a party or a member of a party's household has been provided services.

(ii) The type of services provided.

(iii) The circumstances surrounding the provision of services.

(iv) The status of services.

(v) The date the services were provided.

(vi) The jurisdiction where the services were provided.

(b) **Cooperation.**—The following apply:

(1) The Department of Public Welfare1 and the county children and youth social service agency shall fully cooperate with the court and assist the court in fulfilling its duties under this section.

(2) The Department of Public Welfare and the county children and youth social service agency shall fully cooperate with the governing authority in order to implement the provisions of this section.

(3) The governing authority shall develop procedures to implement the provisions of this section.

(4) As used in this subsection, the term "governing authority" shall have the meaning given to it in 42 Pa.C.S. § 102 (relating to definitions).

2013, Dec. 18, P.L. 1167, No. 107, § 2, effective Jan. 1, 2014.

2013 Amendment. Act 107 added section 5329.1. See section 6 of Act 107 in the appendix to this title for special provisions relating to applicability.

Cross References. Section 5329.1 is referred to in sections 5328, 6340 of this title; section 6307 of Title 42 (Judiciary and Judicial Procedure).

§ 5330. Consideration of criminal charge.

(a) **Expedited hearing.**—A party who has obtained information under 42 Pa.C.S. § 1904 (relating to availability of criminal charge information in child custody proceedings) or otherwise about a charge filed against the other party for an offense listed under section 5329(a) (relating to consideration of criminal conviction) may move for a temporary custody order or modification of an existing custody order. The court shall hold the hearing under this subsection in an expeditious manner.

(b) **Risk of harm.**—In evaluating any request under subsection (a), the court shall consider whether the party who is or has been charged with an offense set forth in section 5329(a) poses a risk of physical, emotional or psychological harm to the child.

(c) **No prejudice.**—Failure to either apply for information under 42 Pa.C.S. § 1904 or act under this section shall not prejudice any party in a custody proceeding.

§ 5331. **Parenting plan.**

(a) **Purpose.**—In a contested custody proceeding, the court may require the parties to submit parenting plans for the care and custody of the child to aid the court in resolving the custody dispute. A parenting plan and the position of a party as set forth in that parenting plan shall not be admissible as evidence by another party.

(b) **Contents.**—A parenting plan shall include the following:

(1) The schedule for personal care and control of the child, including parenting time, holidays and vacations.

(2) The education and religious involvement, if any, of the child.

(3) The health care of the child.

(4) Child-care arrangements.

(5) Transportation arrangements.

(6) A procedure by which proposed changes, disputes and alleged breaches of the custody order may be adjudicated or otherwise resolved through mediation, arbitration or other means.

(7) Any matter specified by the court.

(8) Any other matter that serves the best interest of the child.

(c) **Form.**—If the court orders the parties to propose a parenting plan, it shall be submitted to the court in substantially the following form:

CAPTION
PARENTING PLAN

This parenting plan involves the following child/children:

Child's Name	Age	Where does this child live?
1_____	_____	_____
2_____	_____	_____
3_____	_____	_____

If you have children not addressed by this parenting plan, name here:

Child's Name	Age	Where does this child live?
1_____	_____	_____
2_____	_____	_____
3_____	_____	_____

Legal Custody (who makes decisions about certain things):

Circle one

Diet	Both parties decide together / Plaintiff / Defendant
Religion	Both parties decide together / Plaintiff / Defendant
Medical Care	Both parties decide together / Plaintiff / Defendant
Mental Health Care	Both parties decide together / Plaintiff / Defendant
Discipline	Both parents decide together / Plaintiff / Defendant
Choice of School	Both parents decide together / Plaintiff / Defendant
Choice of Study	Both parents decide together / Plaintiff / Defendant
School Activities	Both parents decide together / Plaintiff / Defendant

Sports Activities   Both parents decide together / Plaintiff / Defendant
Additional items   Both parents decide together / Plaintiff / Defendant

Explain what process you will use to make decisions?

(For example, the parent confronted with or anticipating the choice will call the other parent when the choice presents itself, and the other parent must agree or disagree within 24 hours of any deadline)

_____

Physical Custody (where the child/children live)

The child's/children's residence is with _____

Describe which days and which times of the day the child/children will be with each person:

Sunday   Monday   Tuesday   Wednesday   Thursday   Friday   Saturday

_____

Describe where and when the child/children will be dropped off and/or picked up (day and time of day)?

Drop-Off

Where _____

When _____

_____

Pick-Up

Where _____

When _____

_____

If one of you doesn't show up, how long will the other wait?

_____

If there are any extraordinary costs (taxi, train, airplane, etc.), who will pay for which costs?

_____

HOLIDAYS

Where will the child/children stay?

HOLIDAY	YEAR A	YEAR B	EVERY YEAR
Martin Luther King Day			
President's Day			
Easter			
Memorial Day			
Fourth of July			
Labor Day			
Yom Kippur			
Rosh Hashanah			
Thanksgiving			
Vacation after Thanksgiving			
Christmas Vacation			

| Pa.C.S. | CHILD CUSTODY | 23 § 5331 |

Kwanzaa _____ _____ _____
New Year's Eve/Day _____ _____ _____
Spring Vacation _____ _____ _____
Easter Sunday _____ _____ _____
Child's Birthday _____ _____ _____
Mother's Day _____ _____ _____
Father's Day _____ _____ _____
Other _____ _____ _____
Other _____ _____ _____
Other _____ _____ _____
Summer Vacation Plans

_____

_____

Special Activities or School Activities

Will both of you attend?

Child's Name   Activity   If not, which of you will attend?
_____   _____   _____
_____   _____   _____
_____   _____   _____

Temporary changes to this parenting schedule

From time to time, one of you might want or need to rearrange the parenting time schedule due to work, family or other events. You can attempt to agree on these changes. If you cannot agree, the parent receiving the request will make the final decision.

The parent asking for the change will ask ___ in person ___ by letter/mail ___ by phone

No later than

___ 12 hours ___ 24 hours ___ 1 week ___ 1 month

The parent being asked for a change will reply

___ in person ___ by letter/mail ___ by phone

No later than

___ 12 hours ___ 24 hours ___ 1 week ___ 1 month

May parents contact one another? _____

When the child/children is/are with one of you, how may they contact the other parent?

_____

When and how may _____ contact the child?

_____

In the event that proposed changes, disputes or alleged breaches of this parenting plan and custody order are necessary or desired, the parties agree that such changes will be addressed by the following method (specify method of arbitration, mediation, court action, etc.):

_____

The following matter or matters as specified by the court:

_____

Other (Anything else you want to agree on)

_____

_____

Date _____

                                                             Signature of Mother

Date _____

                                                             Signature of Father

Date _____

                                                             Signature of Witness

§ 5332. Informational programs.

(a) Attendance.—The court may direct the parties to attend informational programs concerning parental duties.

(b) Process not delayed.—Subsequent proceedings and the entry of any order or decree shall not be delayed because of the lack of participation in any informational program by one of the parties.

(c) Costs.—The court may order a party to pay all or part of the costs of the informational programs under this section.

§ 5333. Counseling as part of order.

(a) Attendance.—The court may, as part of a custody order, require the parties to attend counseling sessions.

(b) Abuse.—In situations involving abuse, the court may order individual counseling for the abuser but may not order the parties to attend joint counseling.

(c) Verification.—Each party's participation in the counseling sessions shall be verified by the counselor.

(d) Costs.—The court may order a party to pay all or part of the costs of the counseling sessions under this section.

§ 5334. Guardian ad litem for child.

(a) Appointment.—The court may on its own motion or the motion of a party appoint a guardian ad litem to represent the child in the action. The court may assess the cost upon the parties or any of them or as otherwise provided by law. The guardian ad litem must be an attorney at law.

(b) Powers and duties.—The guardian ad litem shall be charged with representation of the legal interests and the best interests of the child during the proceedings and shall do all of the following:

(1) If appropriate to the child's age and maturity, meet with the child as soon as possible following the appointment and on a regular basis thereafter.

(2) On a timely basis, be given access to relevant court records, reports of examination of the parents or other custodian of the child and medical, psychological and school records.

(3) Participate in all proceedings.

(4) Conduct such further investigation necessary to ascertain relevant facts for presentation to the court.

(5) Interview potential witnesses, including the child's parents and caretakers, if any. The guardian ad litem may examine and cross-examine witnesses and present witnesses and evidence necessary to protect the best interests of the child.

(6) Make specific recommendations in a written report to the court relating to the best interests of the child, including any services necessary to address the child's needs and safety. The court shall make the written report part of the record so

that it may be reviewed by the parties. The parties may file with the court written comments regarding the contents of the report. The comments filed by the parties shall also become part of the record.

(7) Explain the proceedings to the child to the extent appropriate given the child's age, mental condition and emotional condition.

(8) Advise the court of the child's wishes to the extent that they can be ascertained and present to the court whatever evidence exists to support the child's wishes. When appropriate because of the age or mental and emotional condition of the child, determine to the fullest extent possible the wishes of the child and communicate this information to the court. A difference between the child's wishes under this paragraph and the recommendations under paragraph (6) shall not be considered a conflict of interest for the guardian ad litem.

(c) **Abuse.**—If substantial allegations of abuse of the child are made, the court shall appoint a guardian ad litem for the child if:

(1) counsel for the child is not appointed under section 5335 (relating to counsel for child); or

(2) the court is satisfied that the relevant information will be presented to the court only with such appointment.

(d) **Evidence subject to examination.**—A guardian ad litem may not testify except as authorized by Rule 3.7 of the Rules of Professional Conduct, but may make legal argument based on relevant evidence that shall be subject to examination by the parties.

(e) **Costs.**—The court may order a party to pay all or part of the costs of appointing a guardian ad litem under this section.

> Note: Suspended insofar as requires a guardian ad litem be an attorney, permits guardian ad litem to represent best interests and legal interests of child, provides guardian ad litem right to examine, cross-examine, present witnesses and evidence on behalf of child, prohibits guardian ad litem testifying. See, Pa.R.C.P. No. 1915.11-2 and Pa.R.C.P. No. 1915.25 (2013).

§ 5335. Counsel for child.

(a) **Appointment.**—The court may appoint counsel to represent the child if the court determines that the appointment will assist in resolving the issues in the custody proceeding. If a child has legal counsel and a guardian ad litem, counsel shall represent the legal interests of the child and the guardian ad litem shall represent the best interests of the child.

(b) **Abuse.**—Substantial allegations of abuse of the child constitute a reasonable basis for appointing counsel for the child.

(c) **Not subject to examination.**—Counsel appointed by the court for the child shall not be subject to examination unless such counsel testifies in the matter.

(d) **Costs.**—The court may order a party to pay all or part of the costs of appointing counsel for the child under this section.

§ 5336. Access to records and information.

(a) **General rule.**—Except as provided in subsections (b) and (c):

(1) A party granted sole or shared legal custody under section 5323 (relating to award of custody) shall be provided access to:

(i) the medical, dental, religious and school records of the child;

(ii) the address of the child and any other party; and

(iii) any other information that the court deems necessary or proper.

(2) Access to any records and information pertaining to the child may not be denied solely based upon a parent's physical custody schedule.

(3) Upon request, a parent, party or entity possessing any information set forth in paragraph (1) shall provide it to any party granted sole or shared legal custody.

(b) **Nondisclosure of confidential information.**—The court shall not order the disclosure of any of the following information to any parent or party granted custody:

(1) The address of a victim of abuse.

(2) Confidential information from an abuse counselor or shelter.

(3) Information protected under Chapter 67 (relating to domestic and sexual violence victim address confidentiality).

(4) Information independently protected from disclosure by the child's right to confidentiality under the act of July 9, 1976 (P.L.817, No.143), known as the Mental Health Procedures Act, or any other statute.

(c) **Other information.**—The court may determine not to release information set forth in subsection (a), in which case it shall state the reason for its denial on the record.

§ 5337. Relocation.

(a) **Applicability.**—This section applies to any proposed relocation.

(b) **General rule.**—No relocation shall occur unless:

(1) every individual who has custody rights to the child consents to the proposed relocation; or

(2) the court approves the proposed relocation.

(c) **Notice.**—

(1) The party proposing the relocation shall notify every other individual who has custody rights to the child.

(2) Notice, sent by certified mail, return receipt requested, shall be given no later than:

(i) the 60th day before the date of the proposed relocation; or

(ii) the tenth day after the date that the individual knows of the relocation, if:

(A) the individual did not know and could not reasonably have known of the relocation in sufficient time to comply with the 60-day notice; and

(B) it is not reasonably possible to delay the date of relocation so as to comply with the 60-day notice.

(3) Except as provided by section 5336 (relating to access to records and information), the following information, if available, must be included with the notice of the proposed relocation:

(i) The address of the intended new residence.

(ii) The mailing address, if not the same as the address of the intended new residence.

(iii) Names and ages of the individuals in the new residence, including individuals who intend to live in the new residence.

(iv) The home telephone number of the intended new residence, if available.

(v) The name of the new school district and school.

(vi) The date of the proposed relocation.

(vii) The reasons for the proposed relocation.

(viii) A proposal for a revised custody schedule.

(ix) Any other information which the party proposing the relocation deems appropriate.

(x) A counter-affidavit as provided under subsection (d)(1) which can be used to object to the proposed relocation and the modification of a custody order.

(xi) A warning to the nonrelocating party that if the nonrelocating party does not file with the court an objection to the proposed relocation within 30 days after receipt of the notice, that party shall be foreclosed from objecting to the relocation.

(4) If any of the information set forth in paragraph (3) is not known when the notice is sent but is later made known to the party proposing the relocation, then that party shall promptly inform every individual who received notice under this subsection.

(d) Objection to proposed relocation.—

(1) A party entitled to receive notice may file with the court an objection to the proposed relocation and seek a temporary or permanent order to prevent the relocation. The nonrelocating party shall have the opportunity to indicate whether he objects to relocation or not, and whether he objects to modification of the custody order or not. If the party objects to either relocation or modification of the custody order, a hearing shall be held as provided in subsection (g)(1). The objection shall be made by completing and returning to the court a counter-affidavit, which shall be verified subject to penalties under 18 Pa.C.S. § 4904 (relating to unsworn falsification to authorities), in substantially the following form:

COUNTER-AFFIDAVIT REGARDING RELOCATION

This proposal of relocation involves the following child/children:

Child's Name   Age   Currently residing at:
_____   _____   _____

Child's Name   Age   Currently residing at:
_____   _____   _____

Child's Name   Age   Currently residing at:
_____   _____   _____

I have received a notice of proposed relocation and

1. ___ I do not object to the relocation and I do not object to the modification of the custody order consistent with the proposal for revised custody schedule as attached to the notice.

2. ___ I do not object to the relocation, but I do object to modification of the custody order, and I request that a hearing be scheduled:

    a. ___ Prior to allowing (name of child/children) to relocate.

    b. ___ After the child/children relocate.

3. ___ I do object to the relocation and I do object to the modification of the custody order, and I further request that a hearing be held on both matters prior to the relocation taking place.

_____

I understand that in addition to checking (2) or (3) above, I must also file this notice with the court in writing and serve it on the other party by certified mail, return receipt requested. If I fail to do so within 30 days of my receipt of the proposed relocation notice, I shall be foreclosed from objecting to the relocation.

_____

I verify that the statements made in this counter-affidavit are true and correct. I understand that false statements herein are made subject to the penalties of 18 Pa.C.S. § 4904 (relating to unsworn falsification to authorities).

Date:

_____

(2) An objection made under this subsection shall be filed with the court within 30 days of receipt of the proposed relocation notice, and served on the other party by certified mail, return receipt requested.

(3) If notice of the proposed relocation has been properly given and no objection to the proposed relocation has been filed in court, then it shall be presumed that the nonrelocating party has consented to the proposed relocation.

(4) If a party who has been given proper notice does not file with the court an objection to the relocation within 30 days after receipt of the notice but later petitions the court for review of the custodial arrangements, the court shall not accept testimony challenging the relocation.

(e) Confirmation of relocation.—If no objection to the proposed relocation is filed under subsection (d), the party proposing the relocation shall file the following with the court prior to the relocation:

(1) an affidavit stating that the party provided notice to every individual entitled to notice, the time to file an objection to the proposed relocation has passed and no individual entitled to receive notice has filed an objection to the proposed relocation;

(2) Proof that proper notice was given in the form of a return receipt with the signature of the addressee and the full notice that was sent to the addressee.

(3) a petition to confirm the relocation and modify any existing custody order; and

(4) a proposed order containing the information set forth in subsection (c)(3).

(f) Modification of custody order.—If a counter-affidavit regarding relocation is filed with the court which indicates the nonrelocating party both has no objection to the proposed relocation and no objection to the modification of the custody order consistent with the proposal for revised custody schedule, the court may modify the existing custody order by approving the proposal for revised custody schedule submitted under section 5337(c)(viii), and shall specify the method by which its future modification can be made if desired by either party. If a counter-affidavit regarding relocation is filed with the court which indicates the nonrelocating party objects either to the proposed relocation or to the modification of the custody order consistent with the proposal for revised custody schedule, the court shall modify the existing custody order only after holding a hearing to establish the terms and conditions of the order pursuant to the relocation indicating the rights, if any, of the nonrelocating parties.

(g) Hearing.—

(1) Except as set forth in paragraph (3), the court shall hold an expedited full hearing on the proposed relocation after a timely objection has been filed and before the relocation occurs.

(2) Except as set forth in paragraph (3), the court may, on its own motion, hold an expedited full hearing on the proposed relocation before the relocation occurs.

(3) Notwithstanding paragraphs (1) and (2), if the court finds that exigent circumstances exist, the court may approve the relocation pending an expedited full hearing.

(4) If the court approves the proposed relocation, it shall:

(i) modify any existing custody order; or

(ii) establish the terms and conditions of a custody order.

(h) Relocation factors.—In determining whether to grant a proposed relocation, the court shall consider the following factors, giving weighted consideration to those factors which affect the safety of the child:

(1) The nature, quality, extent of involvement and duration of the child's relationship with the party proposing to relocate and with the nonrelocating party, siblings and other significant persons in the child's life.

(2) The age, developmental stage, needs of the child and the likely impact the relocation will have on the child's physical, educational and emotional development, taking into consideration any special needs of the child.

(3) The feasibility of preserving the relationship between the nonrelocating party and the child through suitable custody arrangements, considering the logistics and financial circumstances of the parties.

(4) The child's preference, taking into consideration the age and maturity of the child.

(5) Whether there is an established pattern of conduct of either party to promote or thwart the relationship of the child and the other party.

(6) Whether the relocation will enhance the general quality of life for the party seeking the relocation, including, but not limited to, financial or emotional benefit or educational opportunity.

(7) Whether the relocation will enhance the general quality of life for the child, including, but not limited to, financial or emotional benefit or educational opportunity.

(8) The reasons and motivation of each party for seeking or opposing the relocation.

(9) The present and past abuse committed by a party or member of the party's household and whether there is a continued risk of harm to the child or an abused party.

(10) Any other factor affecting the best interest of the child.

(i) Burden of proof.—

(1) The party proposing the relocation has the burden of establishing that the relocation will serve the best interest of the child as shown under the factors set forth in subsection (h).

(2) Each party has the burden of establishing the integrity of that party's motives in either seeking the relocation or seeking to prevent the relocation.

(j) Failure to provide reasonable notice.—The court may consider a failure to provide reasonable notice of a proposed relocation as:

(1) a factor in making a determination regarding the relocation;

(2) a factor in determining whether custody rights should be modified;

(3) a basis for ordering the return of the child to the nonrelocating party if the relocation has occurred without reasonable notice;

(4) sufficient cause to order the party proposing the relocation to pay reasonable expenses and counsel fees incurred by the party objecting to the relocation; and

(5) a ground for contempt and the imposition of sanctions against the party proposing the relocation.

(k) Mitigation.—Any consideration of a failure to provide reasonable notice under subsection (i) shall be subject to mitigation if the court determines that such failure was caused in whole, or in part, by abuse.

(l) Effect of relocation prior to hearing.—If a party relocates with the child prior to a full expedited hearing, the court shall not confer any presumption in favor of the relocation.

§ 5338. Modification of existing order.

(a) Best interest of the child.—Upon petition, a court may modify a custody order to serve the best interest of the child.

(b) Applicability.—Except as provided in 51 Pa.C.S. § 4109 (relating to child custody proceedings during military deployment), this section shall apply to any custody order entered by a court of this Commonwealth or any other state subject to the jurisdictional requirements set forth in Chapter 54 (relating to uniform child custody jurisdiction and enforcement).

2010, Nov. 23, P.L. 1106, No. 112, § 2, effective in 60 days [Jan. 24, 2011]. Amended 2012, April 12, P.L. 241, No. 32, § 1, effective in 60 days [June 11, 2012].

JT. ST. GOVT. COMM. COMMENT—2010

Subsection (a) codifies the standard used in *Karis v. Karis,* 518 Pa. 601, 544 A.2d 1328 (1988), where the Supreme Court held that "a petition for modification of a partial custody to shared custody order requires the court to inquire into the best interest of the child regardless of whether a 'substantial' change of circumstances has been shown." 518 Pa. at 607-8.

§ 5339. Award of counsel fees, costs and expenses.

Under this chapter, a court may award reasonable interim or final counsel fees, costs and expenses to a party if the court finds that the conduct of another party was obdurate, vexatious, repetitive or in bad faith.

§ 5340. Court-appointed child custody health care or behavioral health practitioners.

No party to a child custody matter in which the court has appointed a licensed health care or behavioral health practitioner to assist the court by conducting an examination or evaluation of the parties involved or making a recommendation concerning a child custody agreement or order may be permitted to file a complaint against the practitioner with the practitioner's State licensing board prior to the final agreement or order being issued and for 60 days thereafter. As used in this section, "licensed health care or behavioral health practitioner" means a person who is licensed, certified, accredited or otherwise regulated by the Commonwealth to provide health care or behavioral health services.

CHAPTER 54
UNIFORM CHILD CUSTODY JURISDICTION AND ENFORCEMENT

Subchapter

A. General Provisions
B. Jurisdiction
C. Enforcement
D. Intrastate Application
E. Miscellaneous Provisions

Enactment. Chapter 54 was added June 15, 2004, P.L.236, No.39, effective in 60 days.

SUBCHAPTER A
GENERAL PROVISIONS

Sec.

5401. Short title of chapter.
5402. Definitions.
5403. Proceedings governed by other law.
5404. Application to Native American tribes.
5405. International application of chapter.
5406. Effect of child custody determination.
5407. Priority.
5408. Notice to persons outside Commonwealth.
5409. Appearance and limited immunity.
5410. Communication between courts.
5411. Taking testimony in another state.
5412. Cooperation between courts; preservation of records.

§ 5401. Short title of chapter.

This chapter shall be known and may be cited as the Uniform Child Custody Jurisdiction and Enforcement Act.

§ 5402. Definitions.

The following words and phrases when used in this chapter shall have the meanings given to them in this section unless the context clearly indicates otherwise:

"Abandoned." Left without provision for reasonable and necessary care or supervision.

"Child." An individual who has not attained 18 years of age.

"Child custody determination." A judgment, decree or other order of a court providing for legal custody, physical custody or visitation with respect to a child. The term includes a permanent, temporary, initial and modification order. The term does not include an order relating to child support or other monetary obligation of an individual.

"Child custody proceeding." A proceeding in which legal custody, physical custody or visitation with respect to a child is an issue. The term includes a proceeding for divorce, separation, neglect, abuse, dependency, guardianship, paternity, termination of parental rights and protection from domestic violence, in which the issue may appear. The term does not include a proceeding involving juvenile delinquency, contractual emancipation or enforcement under Subchapter C (relating to enforcement).

"**Commencement.**" The filing of the first pleading in a proceeding.

"**Court.**" An entity authorized under the law of a state to establish, enforce or modify a child custody determination.

"**Home state.**" The state in which a child lived with a parent or a person acting as a parent for at least six consecutive months immediately before the commencement of a child custody proceeding. In the case of a child six months of age or younger, the term means the state in which the child lived from birth with any of the persons mentioned. A period of temporary absence of any of the mentioned persons is part of the period.

"**Initial determination.**" The first child custody determination concerning a particular child.

"**Issuing court.**" The court that makes a child custody determination for which enforcement is sought under this chapter.

"**Modification.**" A child custody determination that changes, replaces, supersedes or is otherwise made after a previous determination concerning the same child, whether or not it is made by the court that made the previous determination.

"**Person.**" An individual, corporation, business trust, estate, trust, partnership, limited liability company, association, joint venture, government or governmental subdivision, agency or instrumentality, public corporation or any other legal or commercial entity.

"**Person acting as a parent.**" A person, other than a parent, who:

(1) has physical custody of the child or has had physical custody for a period of six consecutive months, including any temporary absence, within one year immediately before the commencement of a child custody proceeding; and

(2) has been awarded legal custody by a court or claims a right to legal custody under the laws of this Commonwealth.

"**Physical custody.**" The physical care and supervision of a child.

"**State.**" A state of the United States, the District of Columbia, Puerto Rico, the United States Virgin Islands or any territory or insular possession subject to the jurisdiction of the United States.

"**Tribe.**" A Native American tribe or band, or Alaskan Native village, which is recognized by Federal law or formally acknowledged by a state.

"**Warrant.**" An order issued by a court authorizing law enforcement officers to take physical custody of a child.

§ 5403. Proceedings governed by other law.

This chapter does not govern an adoption proceeding or a proceeding pertaining to the authorization of emergency medical care for a child.

§ 5404. Application to Native American tribes.

(a) **Primacy of Indian Child Welfare Act.**—A child custody proceeding that pertains to a Native American child as defined in the Indian Child Welfare Act of 1978 (Public Law 95-608, 25 U.S.C. § 1901 et seq.) is not subject to this chapter to the extent that it is governed by the Indian Child Welfare Act of 1978.

(b) **Tribe treated as state.**—A court of this Commonwealth shall treat a tribe as if it were a state of the United States for the purpose of applying Subchapter B (relating to jurisdiction) and this subchapter.

(c) **Tribal custody determinations.**—A child custody determination made by a tribe under factual circumstances in substantial conformity with the jurisdictional standards of this chapter must be recognized and enforced under Subchapter C (relating to enforcement).

§ 5405. International application of chapter.

(a) Foreign country treated as state.—A court of this Commonwealth shall treat a foreign country as if it were a state of the United States for the purpose of applying Subchapter B (relating to jurisdiction) and this subchapter.

(b) Foreign custody determinations.—Except as otherwise provided in subsection (c), a child custody determination made in a foreign country under factual circumstances in substantial conformity with the jurisdictional standards of this chapter must be recognized and enforced under Subchapter C (relating to enforcement).

(c) Violation of human rights.—A court of this Commonwealth need not apply this chapter if the child custody law of a foreign country violates fundamental principles of human rights.

§ 5406. Effect of child custody determination.

A child custody determination made by a court of this Commonwealth that had jurisdiction under this chapter binds all persons who have been served in accordance with the laws of this Commonwealth or notified in accordance with section 5408 (relating to notice to persons outside Commonwealth) or who have submitted to the jurisdiction of the court and who have been given an opportunity to be heard. As to those persons, the determination is conclusive as to all decided issues of law and fact except to the extent the determination is modified.

§ 5407. Priority.

If a question of existence or exercise of jurisdiction under this chapter is raised in a child custody proceeding, the question, upon request of a party, must be given priority on the calendar and handled expeditiously.

§ 5408. Notice to persons outside Commonwealth.

(a) General rule.—Notice required for the exercise of jurisdiction when a person is outside this Commonwealth may be given in a manner prescribed by the laws of this Commonwealth for service of process or by the law of the state in which the service is made. Notice must be given in a manner reasonably calculated to give actual notice but may be by publication if other means are not effective.

(b) Proof of service.—Proof of service may be made in the manner prescribed by the laws of this Commonwealth or by the law of the state in which the service is made.

(c) Submission to jurisdiction.—Notice is not required for the exercise of jurisdiction with respect to a person who submits to the jurisdiction of the court.

Cross References. Section 5408 is referred to in sections 5406, 5425, 5430, 5445, 5448, 5450 of this title.

§ 5409. Appearance and limited immunity.

(a) General rule.—A party to a child custody proceeding, including a modification proceeding or a petitioner or respondent in a proceeding to enforce or register a child custody determination, is not subject to personal jurisdiction in this Commonwealth for another proceeding or purpose solely by reason of having participated or of having been physically present for the purpose of participating in the proceeding.

(b) Service.—A person who is subject to personal jurisdiction in this Commonwealth on a basis other than physical presence is not immune from service of process in this Commonwealth. A party present in this Commonwealth who is subject to the jurisdiction of another state is not immune from service of process allowable under the laws of that state.

(c) Acts committed while in this Commonwealth.—The immunity granted by subsection (a) does not extend to civil litigation based on acts unrelated to the participation in a proceeding under this chapter committed by an individual while present in this Commonwealth.

§ 5410. Communication between courts.

(a) **General rule.**—A court of this Commonwealth may communicate with a court in another state concerning a proceeding arising under this chapter.

(b) **Participation of parties.**—The court may allow the parties to participate in the communication. If the parties are not able to participate in the communication, they must be given the opportunity to present facts and legal arguments before a decision on jurisdiction is made.

(c) **Matters of cooperation between courts.**—Communication between courts on schedules, calendars, court records and similar matters may occur without informing the parties. A record need not be made of the communication.

(d) **Record.**—Except as otherwise provided in subsection (c), a record must be made of a communication under this section. The parties must be informed promptly of the communication and granted access to the record.

(e) **Definition.**—As used in this section, the term "record" means information that is inscribed on a tangible medium or that is stored in an electronic or other medium and is retrievable in perceivable form.

§ 5411. Taking testimony in another state.

(a) **General rule.**—In addition to other procedures available to a party, a party to a child custody proceeding may offer testimony of witnesses who are located in another state, including testimony of the parties and the child, by deposition or other means allowable in this Commonwealth for testimony taken in another state. The court on its own motion may order that the testimony of a person be taken in another state and may prescribe the manner in which and the terms upon which the testimony is taken.

(b) **Means and location.**—A court of this Commonwealth may permit an individual residing in another state to be deposed or to testify by telephone, audiovisual means or other electronic means before a designated court or at another location in that state. A court of this Commonwealth shall cooperate with courts of other states in designating an appropriate location for the deposition or testimony.

(c) **Transmission of documentary evidence.**—Documentary evidence transmitted from another state to a court of this Commonwealth by technological means that do not produce an original writing may not be excluded from evidence on an objection based on the means of transmission.

§ 5412. Cooperation between courts; preservation of records.

(a) **Assistance of another state.**—A court of this Commonwealth may request the appropriate court of another state to:

(1) hold an evidentiary hearing;

(2) order a person to produce or give evidence pursuant to procedures of that state;

(3) order that an evaluation be made with respect to the custody of a child involved in a pending proceeding;

(4) forward to the court of this Commonwealth a certified copy of the transcript of the record of the hearing, the evidence otherwise presented and any evaluation prepared in compliance with the request; and

(5) order a party to a child custody proceeding or any person having physical custody of the child to appear in the proceeding with or without the child.

(b) **Assistance to another state.**—Upon request of a court of another state, a court of this Commonwealth may hold a hearing, enter an order or forward transcripts, evidence and evaluations described in subsection (a).

(c) **Expenses.**—Travel and other necessary and reasonable expenses incurred under subsections (a) and (b) may be assessed against the parties according to the laws of this Commonwealth.

(d) **Preservation of records.**—A court of this Commonwealth shall preserve the pleadings, orders, decrees, records of hearings, evaluations and other pertinent records with respect to a child custody proceeding until the child attains 18 years of age. Upon appropriate request by a court or law enforcement official of another state, the court shall forward a certified copy of those records.

SUBCHAPTER B
JURISDICTION

Sec.
5421. Initial child custody jurisdiction.
5422. Exclusive, continuing jurisdiction.
5423. Jurisdiction to modify determination.
5424. Temporary emergency jurisdiction.
5425. Notice; opportunity to be heard; joinder.
5426. Simultaneous proceedings.
5427. Inconvenient forum.
5428. Jurisdiction declined by reason of conduct.
5429. Information to be submitted to court.
5430. Appearance of parties and child.

Cross References. Subchapter B is referred to in sections 5404, 5405, 5444, 5445, 5446, 5447, 5448, 5450, 5453 of this title.

§ 5421. Initial child custody jurisdiction.

(a) **General rule.**—Except as otherwise provided in section 5424 (relating to temporary emergency jurisdiction), a court of this Commonwealth has jurisdiction to make an initial child custody determination only if:

(1) this Commonwealth is the home state of the child on the date of the commencement of the proceeding, or was the home state of the child within six months before the commencement of the proceeding and the child is absent from this Commonwealth but a parent or person acting as a parent continues to live in this Commonwealth;

(2) a court of another state does not have jurisdiction under paragraph (1), or a court of the home state of the child has declined to exercise jurisdiction on the ground that this Commonwealth is the more appropriate forum under section 5427 (relating to inconvenient forum) or 5428 (relating to jurisdiction declined by reason of conduct), and:

(i) the child and the child's parents, or the child and at least one parent or a person acting as a parent, have a significant connection with this Commonwealth other than mere physical presence; and

(ii) substantial evidence is available in this Commonwealth concerning the child's care, protection, training and personal relationships;

(3) all courts having jurisdiction under paragraph (1) or (2) have declined to exercise jurisdiction on the ground that a court of this Commonwealth is the more appropriate forum to determine the custody of the child under section 5427 or 5428; or

(4) no court of any other state would have jurisdiction under the criteria specified in paragraph (1), (2) or (3).

(b) **Exclusive jurisdictional basis.**—Subsection (a) is the exclusive jurisdictional basis for making a child custody determination by a court of this Commonwealth.

(c) **Physical presence and personal jurisdiction unnecessary.**—Physical presence of or personal jurisdiction over a party or a child is not necessary or sufficient to make a child custody determination.

Cross References. Section 5421 is referred to in sections 5422, 5423, 5424, 5428 of this title.

§ 5422. Exclusive, continuing jurisdiction.

(a) **General rule.**—Except as otherwise provided in section 5424 (relating to temporary emergency jurisdiction), a court of this Commonwealth which has made a child custody determination consistent with section 5421 (relating to initial child custody jurisdiction) or section 5423 (relating to jurisdiction to modify determination) has exclusive, continuing jurisdiction over the determination until:

(1) a court of this Commonwealth determines that neither the child, nor the child and one parent, nor the child and a person acting as a parent have a significant connection with this Commonwealth and that substantial evidence is no longer available in this Commonwealth concerning the child's care, protection, training and personal relationships; or

(2) a court of this Commonwealth or a court of another state determines that the child, the child's parents and any person acting as a parent do not presently reside in this Commonwealth.

(b) **Modification where court does not have exclusive, continuing jurisdiction.**—A court of this Commonwealth which has made a child custody determination and does not have exclusive, continuing jurisdiction under this section may modify that determination only if it has jurisdiction to make an initial determination under section 5421.

Cross References. Section 5422 is referred to in sections 5423, 5424, 5428 of this title.

§ 5423. Jurisdiction to modify determination.

Except as otherwise provided in section 5424 (relating to temporary emergency jurisdiction), a court of this Commonwealth may not modify a child custody determination made by a court of another state unless a court of this Commonwealth has jurisdiction to make an initial determination under section 5421 (a)(1) or (2) (relating to initial child custody jurisdiction) and:

(1) the court of the other state determines it no longer has exclusive, continuing jurisdiction under section 5422 (relating to exclusive, continuing jurisdiction) or that a court of this Commonwealth would be a more convenient forum under section 5427 (relating to inconvenient forum); or

(2) a court of this Commonwealth or a court of the other state determines that the child, the child's parents and any person acting as a parent do not presently reside in the other state.

Cross References. Section 5423 is referred to in sections 5422, 5424, 5428 of this title.

§ 5424. Temporary emergency jurisdiction.

(a) **General rule.**—A court of this Commonwealth has temporary emergency jurisdiction if the child is present in this Commonwealth and the child has been abandoned or it is necessary in an emergency to protect the child because the child or a sibling or parent of the child is subjected to or threatened with mistreatment or abuse.

(b) **No previous custody determination or proceeding.**—If there is no previous child custody determination that is entitled to be enforced under this chapter and a child custody proceeding has not been commenced in a court of a state having jurisdiction under sections 5421 (relating to initial child custody jurisdiction) through 5423 (relating to jurisdiction to modify determination), a child custody determination made under this section remains in effect until an order is obtained from a court of a state having jurisdiction under sections 5421 through 5423. If a child custody proceeding has not been or is not commenced in a court of a state having jurisdiction under sections 5421 through 5423, a child custody determination made under this section becomes a final determination if it so provides and this Commonwealth becomes the home state of the child.

(c) **Previous custody determination or proceeding.**—If there is a previous child custody determination that is entitled to be enforced under this chapter or a child custody proceeding has been commenced in a court of a state having jurisdiction under sections 5421 through 5423, any order issued by a court of this Commonwealth under this section must specify in the order a period that the court considers adequate to allow the person seeking an order to obtain an order from the state having jurisdiction under sections 5421 through 5423. The order issued in this Commonwealth remains in effect until an order is obtained from the other state within the period specified or the period expires.

(d) **Mandatory communication between courts.**—A court of this Commonwealth which has been asked to make a child custody determination under this section, upon being informed that a child custody proceeding has been commenced in or a child custody determination has been made by a court of a state having jurisdiction under sections 5421 through 5423, shall immediately communicate with the other court. A court of this Commonwealth which is exercising jurisdiction pursuant to sections 5421 through 5423, upon being informed that a child custody proceeding has been commenced in or a child custody determination has been made by a court of another state under a statute similar to this section, shall immediately communicate with the court of that state to resolve the emergency, protect the safety of the parties and the child and determine a period for the duration of the temporary order.

Cross References. Section 5424 is referred to in sections 5421, 5422, 5423, 5426, 5428, 5450, 5454 of this title.

§ 5425. Notice; opportunity to be heard; joinder.

(a) **General rule.**—Before a child custody determination is made under this chapter, notice and an opportunity to be heard in accordance with the standards of section 5408 (relating to notice to persons outside Commonwealth) must be given to all persons entitled to notice under the laws of this Commonwealth as in child custody proceedings between residents of this Commonwealth, any parent whose parental rights have not been previously terminated and any person having physical custody of the child.

(b) **Lack of notice or opportunity to be heard.**—This chapter does not govern the enforceability of a child custody determination made without notice or any opportunity to be heard.

(c) **Joinder and intervention.**—The obligation to join a party and the right to intervene as a party in a child custody proceeding under this chapter are governed by the laws of this Commonwealth as in child custody proceedings between residents of this Commonwealth.

§ 5426. Simultaneous proceedings.

(a) **General rule.**—Except as otherwise provided in section 5424 (relating to temporary emergency jurisdiction), a court of this Commonwealth may not exercise its jurisdiction under this subchapter if, at the time of the commencement of the proceeding, a proceeding concerning the custody of the child has been commenced in a court of another state having jurisdiction substantially in conformity with this chapter, unless the proceeding has been terminated or is stayed by the court of the other state because a court of this Commonwealth is a more convenient forum under section 5427 (relating to inconvenient forum).

(b) **Stay; communication with other court.**—Except as otherwise provided in section 5424, a court of this Commonwealth, before hearing a child custody proceeding, shall examine the court documents and other information supplied by the parties pursuant to section 5429 (relating to information to be submitted to court). If the court determines that a child custody proceeding has been commenced in a court in another state having jurisdiction substantially in accordance with this chapter, the court of this Commonwealth shall stay its proceeding and communicate with the court of the other state. If the court of the state having jurisdiction substantially in accordance with this chapter does not determine that the court of this Commonwealth is a more appropriate forum, the court of this Commonwealth shall dismiss the proceeding.

(c) **Modification.**—In a proceeding to modify a child custody determination, a court of this Commonwealth shall determine whether a proceeding to enforce the determination has been commenced in another state. If a proceeding to enforce a child custody determination has been commenced in another state, the court may:

(1) stay the proceeding for modification pending the entry of an order of a court of the other state enforcing, staying, denying or dismissing the proceeding for enforcement;

(2) enjoin the parties from continuing with the proceeding for enforcement; or

(3) proceed with the modification under conditions it considers appropriate.

§ 5427. Inconvenient forum.

(a) **General rule.**—A court of this Commonwealth which has jurisdiction under this chapter to make a child custody determination may decline to exercise its jurisdiction at any time if it determines that it is an inconvenient forum under the circumstances and that a court of another state is a more appropriate forum. The issue of inconvenient forum may be raised upon motion of a party, the court's own motion or request of another court.

(b) **Factors.**—Before determining whether it is an inconvenient forum, a court of this Commonwealth shall consider whether it is appropriate for a court of another state to exercise jurisdiction. For this purpose, the court shall allow the parties to submit information and shall consider all relevant factors, including:

(1) whether domestic violence has occurred and is likely to continue in the future and which state could best protect the parties and the child;

(2) the length of time the child has resided outside this Commonwealth;

(3) the distance between the court in this Commonwealth and the court in the state that would assume jurisdiction;

(4) the relative financial circumstances of the parties;

(5) any agreement of the parties as to which state should assume jurisdiction;

(6) the nature and location of the evidence required to resolve the pending litigation, including testimony of the child;

(7) the ability of the court of each state to decide the issue expeditiously and the procedures necessary to present the evidence; and

(8) the familiarity of the court of each state with the facts and issues in the pending litigation.

(c) **Stay.**—If a court of this Commonwealth determines that it is an inconvenient forum and that a court of another state is a more appropriate forum, it shall stay the proceedings upon condition that a child custody proceeding be promptly commenced in another designated state and may impose any other condition the court considers just and proper.

(d) **Jurisdiction declined.**—A court of this Commonwealth may decline to exercise its jurisdiction under this chapter if a child custody determination is incidental to an action for divorce or another proceeding while still retaining jurisdiction over the divorce or other proceeding.

Cross References. Section 5427 is referred to in sections 5421, 5423, 5426, 5428 of this title.

§ 5428. Jurisdiction declined by reason of conduct.

(a) **General rule.**—Except as otherwise provided in section 5424 (relating to temporary emergency jurisdiction) or by other laws of this Commonwealth, if a court of this Commonwealth has jurisdiction under this chapter because a person seeking to invoke its jurisdiction has engaged in unjustifiable conduct, the court shall decline to exercise its jurisdiction unless:

(1) the parents and all persons acting as parents have acquiesced in the exercise of jurisdiction;

(2) a court of the state otherwise having jurisdiction under sections 5421 (relating to initial child custody jurisdiction) through 5423 (relating to jurisdiction to modify determination) determines that this Commonwealth is a more appropriate forum under section 5427 (relating to inconvenient forum); or

(3) no court of any other state would have jurisdiction under the criteria specified in sections 5421 through 5423.

(b) **Jurisdiction declined; remedy.**—If a court of this Commonwealth declines to exercise its jurisdiction pursuant to subsection (a), it may fashion an appropriate remedy to ensure the safety of the child and prevent a repetition of the unjustifiable conduct, including staying the proceeding until a child custody proceeding is commenced in a court having jurisdiction under sections 5421 through 5423.

(c) **Jurisdiction declined, expenses.**—If a court dismisses a petition or stays a proceeding because it declines to exercise its jurisdiction pursuant to subsection (a), it shall assess against the party seeking to invoke its jurisdiction necessary and reasonable expenses, including costs, communication expenses, attorney fees, investigative fees, expenses for witnesses, travel expenses and child care during the course of the proceedings unless the party from whom fees are sought establishes that the assessment would be clearly inappropriate. The court may not assess fees, costs or expenses against this Commonwealth unless authorized by law other than this chapter.

Cross References. Section 5428 is referred to in section 5421 of this title.

§ 5429. Information to be submitted to court.

(a) **General rule.**—Subject to the rules set forth in Chapter 53 (relating to child custody) providing for the confidentiality of procedures, addresses and other identifying information in a child custody proceeding, each party in its first pleading or in an attached affidavit shall give information, if reasonably ascertainable, under oath as to the child's present address or whereabouts, the places where the child has lived during the last five years and the names and present addresses of the persons with whom the child has lived during that period. The pleading or affidavit must state whether the party:

(1) has participated as a party or witness or in any other capacity in any other proceeding concerning the custody of or visitation with the child and, if so, identify the court, the case number and the date of the child custody determination, if any;

(2) knows of any proceeding that could affect the current proceeding, including proceedings for enforcement and proceedings relating to domestic violence, protective orders, termination of parental rights and adoptions, and, if so, identify the court, the case number and the nature of the proceeding; and

(3) knows the names and addresses of any person not a party to the proceeding who has physical custody of the child or claims rights of legal custody or physical custody of or visitation with the child and, if so, the names and addresses of those persons.

(b) **Stay.**—If the information required by subsection (a) is not furnished, the court, upon motion of a party or its own motion, may stay the proceeding until the information is furnished.

(c) **Additional information.**—If the declaration as to any of the items described in subsection (a)(1) through (3) is in the affirmative, the declarant shall give additional information under oath as required by the court. The court may examine the parties under oath as to details of the information furnished and other matters pertinent to the court's jurisdiction and the disposition of the case.

(d) **Duty to disclose other proceedings.**—Each party has a continuing duty to inform the court of any proceeding in this Commonwealth or any other state that could affect the current proceeding.

(e) **Identifying information.**—If a party alleges in an affidavit or a pleading under oath that the health, safety or liberty of a party or child would be jeopardized by disclosure of identifying information, the information must be sealed and may not be disclosed to the other party or the public unless the court orders the disclosure to be made after a hearing in which the court takes into consideration the health, safety or liberty of the party or child and determines that the disclosure is in the interest of justice.

Cross References. Section 5429 is referred to in sections 5426, 5445 of this title.

§ 5430. Appearance of parties and child.

(a) **General rule.**—In a child custody proceeding in this Commonwealth, the court may order a party to the proceeding who is in this Commonwealth to appear before the court in person with or without the child. The court may order any person who is in this Commonwealth and who has physical custody or control of the child to appear in person with the child.

(b) **Party outside this Commonwealth.**—If a party to a child custody proceeding whose presence is desired by the court is outside this Commonwealth, the court may order that a notice given pursuant to section 5408 (relating to notice to persons outside Commonwealth) include a statement directing the party to appear in person with or without the child and informing the party that failure to appear may result in a decision adverse to the party.

(c) **Personal safety.**—The court may enter any orders necessary to ensure the safety of the child and of any person ordered to appear under this section.

(d) **Expenses.**—If a party to a child custody proceeding who is outside this Commonwealth is directed to appear under subsection (b) or desires to appear personally before the court with or without the child, the court may require another party to pay reasonable and necessary travel and other expenses of the party so appearing and of the child.

SUBCHAPTER C
ENFORCEMENT

Sec.
5441. Definitions.
5442. Enforcement under Hague Convention.
5443. Duty to enforce.
5444. Temporary visitation.
5445. Registration of child custody determination.
5446. Enforcement of registered determination.
5447. Simultaneous proceedings.
5448. Expedited enforcement of child custody determination.
5449. Service of petition and order.
5450. Hearing and order.
5451. Warrant to take physical custody of child.

5452. Costs, fees and expenses.
5453. Recognition and enforcement.
5454. Appeals.
5455. Role of prosecutor or public official.
5456. Role of law enforcement.
5457. Costs and expenses.

Cross References. Subchapter C is referred to in sections 5402, 5404, 5405 of this title.

§ 5441. Definitions.

The following words and phrases when used in this subchapter shall have the meanings given to them in this section unless the context clearly indicates otherwise:

"Petitioner." A person who seeks enforcement of an order for return of a child under the Hague Convention on the Civil Aspects of International Child Abduction or enforcement of a child custody determination.

"Respondent." A person against whom a proceeding has been commenced for enforcement of an order for return of a child under the Hague Convention on the Civil Aspects of International Child Abduction or enforcement of a child custody determination.

§ 5442. Enforcement under Hague Convention.

Under this subchapter a court of this Commonwealth may enforce an order for the return of the child made under the Hague Convention on the Civil Aspects of International Child Abduction as if it were a child custody determination.

§ 5443. Duty to enforce.

(a) General rule.—A court of this Commonwealth shall recognize and enforce a child custody determination of a court of another state if the latter court exercised jurisdiction in substantial conformity with this chapter or the determination was made under factual circumstances meeting the jurisdictional standards of this chapter and the determination has not been modified in accordance with this chapter.

(b) Remedies.—A court of this Commonwealth may utilize any remedy available under other laws of this Commonwealth to enforce a child custody determination made by a court of another state. The remedies provided in this subchapter are cumulative and do not affect the availability of other remedies to enforce a child custody determination.

§ 5444. Temporary visitation.

(a) General rule.—A court of this Commonwealth which does not have jurisdiction to modify a child custody determination may issue a temporary order enforcing:

(1) a visitation schedule made by a court of another state; or

(2) the visitation provisions of a child custody determination of another state that does not provide for a specific visitation schedule.

(b) Time to obtain permanent change in visitation.—If a court of this Commonwealth makes an order under subsection (a)(2), it shall specify in the order a period that it considers adequate to allow the petitioner to obtain an order from a court having jurisdiction under the criteria specified in Subchapter B (relating to jurisdiction). The order remains in effect until an order is obtained from the other court or the period expires.

Cross References. Section 5444 is referred to in sections 5448 of this title.

§ 5445. Registration of child custody determination.

(a) General rule.—A child custody determination issued by a court of another state may be registered in this Commonwealth, with or without a simultaneous request for enforcement, by sending to the appropriate court in this Commonwealth:

(1) a letter or other document requesting registration;

(2) two copies, including one certified copy, of the determination sought to be registered and a statement under penalty of perjury that to the best of the knowledge and belief of the person seeking registration the order has not been modified; and

(3) except as otherwise provided in section 5429 (relating to information to be submitted to court), the name and address of the person seeking registration and any parent or person acting as a parent who has been awarded custody or visitation in the child custody determination sought to be registered.

(b) Duties of registering court.—On receipt of the documents required by subsection (a), the registering court shall:

(1) cause the determination to be filed as a foreign judgment, together with one copy of any accompanying documents and information, regardless of their form; and

(2) serve notice upon the persons named pursuant to subsection (a)(3) and provide them with an opportunity to contest the registration in accordance with this section.

(c) Notice.—The notice required by subsection (b)(2) must state that:

(1) a registered determination is enforceable as of the date of the registration in the same manner as a determination issued by a court of this Commonwealth;

(2) a hearing to contest the validity of the registered determination must be requested within 20 days after service of notice; and (3) failure to contest the registration will result in confirmation of the child custody determination and preclude further contest of that determination with respect to any matter that could have been asserted.

(d) Contest over validity of registered order.—A person seeking to contest the validity of a registered order must request a hearing within 20 days after service of the notice. At that hearing, the court shall confirm the registered order unless the person contesting registration establishes that:

(1) the issuing court did not have jurisdiction under Subchapter B (relating to jurisdiction);

(2) the child custody determination sought to be registered has been vacated, stayed or modified by a court having jurisdiction to do so under Subchapter B; or

(3) the person contesting registration was entitled to notice, but notice was not given in accordance with the standards of section 5408 (relating to notice to persons outside Commonwealth), in the proceedings before the court that issued the order for which registration is sought.

(e) Failure to contest.—If a timely request for a hearing to contest the validity of the registration is not made, the registration is confirmed as a matter of law and the person requesting registration and all persons served must be notified of the confirmation.

(f) Res judicata.—Confirmation of a registered order, whether by operation of law or after notice and hearing, precludes further contest of the order with respect to any matter that could have been asserted at the time of registration.

Cross References. Section 5445 is referred to in sections 5448, 5450 of this title.

§ 5446. Enforcement of registered determination.

(a) General rule.—A court of this Commonwealth may grant any relief normally available under the laws of this Commonwealth to enforce a registered child custody determination made by a court of another state.

(b) Modification.—A court of this Commonwealth shall recognize and enforce, but may not modify, except in accordance with Subchapter B (relating to jurisdiction), a registered child custody determination of a court of another state.

§ 5447. Simultaneous proceedings.

If a proceeding for enforcement under this subchapter is commenced in a court of this Commonwealth and the court determines that a proceeding to modify the determination is pending in a court of another state having jurisdiction to modify the determination under Subchapter B (relating to jurisdiction), the enforcing court shall immediately communicate with the modifying court. The proceeding for enforcement continues unless the enforcing court, after consultation with the modifying court, stays or dismisses the proceeding.

§ 5448. Expedited enforcement of child custody determination.

(a) Verification.—A petition under this subchapter must be verified. Certified copies of all orders sought to be enforced and of any order confirming registration must be attached to the petition. A copy of a certified copy of an order may be attached instead of the original.

(b) Petition.—A petition for enforcement of a child custody determination must state:

(1) whether the court that issued the determination identified the jurisdictional basis it relied upon in exercising jurisdiction and, if so, what the basis was;

(2) whether the determination for which enforcement is sought has been vacated, stayed or modified by a court whose decision must be enforced under this chapter and, if so, identify the court, the case number and the nature of the proceeding;

(3) whether any proceeding has been commenced that could affect the current proceeding, including proceedings relating to domestic violence, protective orders, termination of parental rights and adoptions and, if so, identify the court, the case number and the nature of the proceeding;

(4) the present physical address of the child and the respondent, if known;

(5) whether relief in addition to the immediate physical custody of the child and attorney fees is sought, including a request for assistance from law enforcement officials and, if so, the relief sought; and

(6) if the child custody determination has been registered and confirmed under section 5445 (relating to registration of child custody determination), the date and place of registration.

(c) Hearing.—Upon the filing of a petition, the court shall issue an order directing the respondent to appear in person with or without the child at a hearing and may enter any order necessary to ensure the safety of the parties and the child. The hearing must be held on the next judicial day after service of the order unless that date is impossible. In that event, the court shall hold the hearing on the first judicial day possible. The court may extend the date of hearing at the request of the petitioner.

(d) Contest over validity of custody determination.—An order issued under subsection (c) must state the time and place of the hearing and advise the respondent that at the hearing the court will order that the petitioner may take immediate physical custody of the child and the payment of fees, costs and expenses under section 5452 (relating to costs, fees and expenses) and may schedule a hearing to determine whether further relief is appropriate unless the respondent appears and establishes that:

(1) the child custody determination has not been registered and confirmed under section 5445 and that:

   (i) the issuing court did not have jurisdiction under Subchapter B (relating to jurisdiction);

   (ii) the child custody determination for which enforcement is sought has been vacated, stayed or modified by a court having jurisdiction to do so under Subchapter B; or

(iii) the respondent was entitled to notice, but notice was not given in accordance with the standards of section 5408 (relating to notice to persons outside Commonwealth), in the proceedings before the court that issued the order for which enforcement is sought; or

(2) the child custody determination for which enforcement is sought was registered and confirmed under section 5444 (relating to temporary visitation), but has been vacated, stayed or modified by a court of a state having jurisdiction to do so under Subchapter B.

Cross References. Section 5448 is referred to in section 5451 of this title.

§ 5449. Service of petition and order.

Except as otherwise provided in section 5451 (relating to warrant to take physical custody of child), the petition and order must be served by any method authorized by the laws of this Commonwealth upon respondent and any person who has physical custody of the child.

§ 5450. Hearing and order.

(a) **General rule.**—Unless the court issues a temporary emergency order pursuant to section 5424 (relating to temporary emergency jurisdiction), upon a finding that a petitioner is entitled to immediate physical custody of the child, the court shall order that the petitioner may take immediate physical custody of the child unless the respondent establishes that:

(1) the child custody determination has not been registered and confirmed under section 5445 (relating to registration of child custody determination) and that:

(i) the issuing court did not have jurisdiction under Subchapter B (relating to jurisdiction);

(ii) the child custody determination for which enforcement is sought has been vacated, stayed or modified by a court of a state having jurisdiction to do so under Subchapter B; or

(iii) the respondent was entitled to notice, but notice was not given in accordance with the standards of section 5408 (relating to notice to persons outside Commonwealth), in the proceedings before the court that issued the order for which enforcement is sought; or

(2) the child custody determination for which enforcement is sought was registered and confirmed under section 5445 but has been vacated, stayed or modified by a court of a state having jurisdiction to do so under Subchapter B.

(b) **Costs, fees and expenses.**—The court shall award the costs, fees and expenses authorized under section 5452 (relating to costs, fees and expenses) and may grant additional relief, including a request for the assistance of law enforcement officials, and set a further hearing to determine whether additional relief is appropriate.

(c) **Refusal to testify.**—If a party called to testify refuses to answer on the ground that the testimony may be self- incriminating, the court may draw an adverse inference from the refusal.

(d) **Spousal privilege unavailable.**—A privilege against disclosure of communications between spouses and a defense of immunity based on the relationship of husband and wife or parent and child may not be invoked in a proceeding under this subchapter.

§ 5451. Warrant to take physical custody of child.

(a) **General rule.**—Upon the filing of a petition seeking enforcement of a child custody determination, the petitioner may file a verified application for the issuance of a warrant to take physical custody of the child if the child is immediately likely to suffer serious physical harm or be removed from this Commonwealth.

(b) Petition.—If the court, upon the testimony of the petitioner or other witness, finds that the child is imminently likely to suffer serious physical harm or be removed from this Commonwealth, it may issue a warrant to take physical custody of the child. The petition must be heard on the next judicial day after the warrant is executed unless that date is impossible. In that event, the court shall hold the hearing on the first judicial day possible. The application for the warrant must include the statements required by section 5448(b) (relating to expedited enforcement of child custody determination).

(c) Warrant.—A warrant to take physical custody of a child must:

(1) recite the facts upon which a conclusion of imminent serious physical harm or removal from the jurisdiction is based;

(2) direct law enforcement officers to take physical custody of the child immediately; and

(3) provide for the placement of the child pending final relief.

(d) Time of service.—The respondent must be served with the petition, warrant and order immediately after the child is taken into physical custody.

(e) Enforcement.—A warrant to take physical custody of a child is enforceable throughout this Commonwealth. If the court finds on the basis of the testimony of the petitioner or other witness that a less intrusive remedy is not effective, it may authorize law enforcement officers to enter private property to take physical custody of the child. If required by exigent circumstances of the case, the court may authorize law enforcement officers to make a forcible entry at any hour.

(f) Appearance of child.—The court may impose conditions upon placement of a child to ensure the appearance of the child and the child's custodian.

Cross References. Section 5451 is referred to in section 5449 of this title.

§ 5452. Costs, fees and expenses.

(a) General rule.—The court shall award the prevailing party, including a state, necessary and reasonable expenses incurred by or on behalf of the party, including costs, communication expenses, attorney fees, investigative fees, expenses for witnesses, travel expenses and child care during the course of the proceedings, unless the party from whom fees or expenses are sought establishes that the award would be clearly inappropriate.

(b) Assessment against a state.—The court may not assess fees, costs or expenses against a state unless authorized by law other than this chapter.

Cross References. Section 5452 is referred to in sections 5448, 5450 of this title.

§ 5453. Recognition and enforcement.

A court of this Commonwealth shall accord full faith and credit to an order issued by another state and consistent with this chapter which enforces a child custody determination by a court of another state unless the order has been vacated, stayed or modified by a court having jurisdiction to do so under Subchapter B (relating to jurisdiction).

§ 5454. Appeals.

An appeal may be taken from a final order in a proceeding under this subchapter in accordance with expedited appellate procedures in other civil cases. Unless the court enters a temporary emergency order under section 5424 (relating to temporary emergency jurisdiction), the enforcing court may not stay an order enforcing a child custody determination pending appeal.

§ 5455. Role of prosecutor or public official.

(a) General rule.—In a case arising under this chapter or involving the Hague Convention on the Civil Aspects of International Child Abduction, the prosecutor or other appropriate public official may take any lawful action, including resort to a proceeding under this subchapter or any other available civil proceeding to locate a child, obtain the return of a child or enforce a child custody determination if there is:

(1) an existing child custody determination;

(2) a request to do so from a court in a pending child custody proceeding;

(3) a reasonable belief that a criminal statute has been violated; or

(4) a reasonable belief that the child has been wrongfully removed or retained in violation of the Hague Convention on the Civil Aspects of International Child Abduction.

(b) Authority.—A prosecutor or appropriate public official acting under this section acts on behalf of the court and may not represent any party.

Cross References. Sections 5455, 5456 is referred to in sections 5456, 5457 of this title.

§ 5456. Role of law enforcement.

At the request of a prosecutor or other appropriate public official acting under section 5455 (relating to role of prosecutor or public official), a law enforcement officer may take any lawful action reasonably necessary to locate a child or a party and assist a prosecutor or appropriate public official with responsibilities under section 5455.

Cross References. Section 5456 is referred to in section 5457 of this title.

§ 5457. Costs and expenses.

If the respondent is not the prevailing party, the court may assess against the respondent all direct expenses and costs incurred by the prosecutor or other appropriate public official and law enforcement officers under section 5455 (relating to role of prosecutor or public official) or 5456 (relating to role of law enforcement).

SUBCHAPTER D
INTRASTATE APPLICATION

Sec.

5471. Intrastate application.

§ 5471. Intrastate application.

The provisions of this chapter allocating jurisdiction and functions between and among courts of different states shall also allocate jurisdiction and functions between and among the courts of common pleas of this Commonwealth.

SUBCHAPTER E
MISCELLANEOUS PROVISIONS

Sec.

5481. Application and construction.
5482. Severability.

§ 5481. Application and construction.

In applying and construing this chapter, consideration must be given to the need to promote uniformity of the law with respect to its subject matter among states that enact it.

§ 5482. Severability.

If any provision of this chapter or its application to any person or circumstance is held invalid, the invalidity does not affect other provisions or applications of this chapter which can be given effect without the invalid provision or application, and to this end the provisions of this chapter are severable.

CHAPTER 55
LIABILITY FOR TORTIOUS ACTS OF CHILDREN

Sec.
5501. Definitions.
5502. Liability of parents.
5503. Establishing liability in criminal or juvenile proceedings.
5504. Establishing liability in civil proceedings.
5505. Monetary limits of liability.
5506. Double recovery for same injury prohibited.
5507. Indemnity or contribution from child prohibited.
5508. Liability of parent not having custody or control of child.
5509. Other liability of parents or child unaffected.

Enactment. Chapter 55 was added December 19, 1990, P.L. 1240, No.206, effective in 90 days.

§ 5501. Definitions.

The following words and phrases when used in this chapter shall have the meanings given to them in this section unless the context clearly indicates otherwise:

"**Child.**" An individual under 18 years of age.

"**Injury.**" Includes injury to the person and theft, destruction or loss of property.

"**Parent.**" Includes natural or adoptive parents.

"**Person.**" Includes government units and Federal agencies.

"**Tortious act.**" A willful tortious act resulting in injury.

§ 5502. Liability of parents.

Any parent whose child is found liable or is adjudged guilty by a court of competent jurisdiction of a tortious act shall be liable to the person who suffers the injury to the extent set forth in this chapter.

§ 5503. Establishing liability in criminal or juvenile proceedings.

(a) **General rule.**—In any criminal proceeding against a child and in any proceeding against a child under 42 Pa.C.S. Ch. 63 (relating to juvenile matters), the court shall ascertain the amount sufficient to fully reimburse any person who has suffered injury because of the tortious act of the child and direct the parents to make payment in the amount not to exceed the limitations set forth in section 5505 (relating to monetary limits of liability).

(b) **Noncompliance with direction of court.**—If the parents fail to comply with the direction of the court, the amount may be recovered in a civil action against the parents or either of them.

§ 5504. Establishing liability in civil proceedings.

(a) **Petition.**—If a judgment has been rendered against the child in a civil action for injury because of the tortious act of the child and the judgment has not been satisfied within a period of 30 days, the injured person may petition the court for a rule to show cause why judgment should not be entered against the parent.

(b) **Answer and trial.**—The parent may file an answer to the petition, and, if there is any dispute as to unlitigated facts, the case shall be set down for trial.

(c) **Judgment.**—If there is no dispute as to the unlitigated facts, the court shall authorize the entry of a judgment against the parent. In no case shall the judgment against the parent exceed the limitations set forth in section 5505 (relating to monetary limits of liability).

(d) **Action against parent.**—Notwithstanding any provision to the contrary, a victim of willful, tortious act of a child may initiate a civil action directly against the parent or parents of the child who committed the tortious act, for the purpose of receiving compensation for the injuries suffered, not to exceed the limitations set forth in section 5505.

(April 21, 1994, P.L.128, No.15, eff. 60 days)

1994 Amendment. Act 15 amended subsec. (d).

§ 5505. Monetary limits of liability.

(a) **General rule.**—Liability of the parents under this chapter shall be limited to:

(1) The sum of $1,000 for injuries suffered by any one person as a result of one tortious act or continuous series of tortious acts.

(2) The sum of $2,500 regardless of the number of persons who suffer injury as a result of one tortious act or continuous series of tortious acts.

(b) **Proceedings where loss exceed liability.**—In the event that actual loss as ascertained by the court or the judgment against the child exceeds $2,500, the parents shall be discharged from further liability by the payment of $2,500 into court. The court shall cause all aggrieved parties to submit itemized statements of loss in writing and shall make distribution proportionately, whether the claims be for injuries to the person or for theft, destruction or loss of property. The court may take testimony to assist it in making proper distribution and may appoint a master to accomplish this purpose. All costs and fees incurred in these proceedings shall be paid from the $2,500 paid into court.

(c) **Joint acts by children of same parent.**—The limitations on liability set forth in subsections (a) and (b) shall be applicable when two or more children of the same parent engage jointly in the commission of one tortious act or series of tortious acts.

(April 21, 1994, P.L.128, No.15, eff. 60 days)

1994 Amendment. Act 15 amended subsec. (a) and (b).

Cross References. Section 5505 is referred to in section 5503, 5504 of this title.

§ 5506. Double recovery for same injury prohibited.

In no case shall there be a double recovery for one injury. Any judgment against a child resulting from a tortious act for which a parent makes payment under this chapter shall be reduced by the amount paid by the parent.

§ 5507. Indemnity or contribution from child prohibited.

The parent shall have no right of indemnity or contribution against the child.

§ 5508. Liability of parent not having custody or control of child.

(a) **General rule.**—No liability may be imposed upon a parent under this chapter if, at the time of commission of the tortious act, the parent has neither custody of the child nor is entitled to custody of the child or if the child is institutionalized or emancipated.

(b) **Exception.**—No parent is absolved of liability due to the desertion of the child by the parent.

§ 5509. Other liability of parent or child unaffected.

The liability imposed upon parents by this chapter shall not limit the common-law liability of parents for damages caused by a child and shall be separate and apart from any liability which may be imposed upon the child.

CHAPTER 56
STANDBY AND TEMPORARY GUARDIANSHIP

Subchapter

A. Preliminary Provisions
B. General Provisions
C. Temporary Guardianship

Enactment. Chapter 56 was added November 24, 1998, P.L. 811, No. 103, effective in 60 days. The General Assembly finds and declares as follows:

(1) Existing law does not provide adequately for the needs of a parent who is terminally ill, or who is periodically incapable of caring for the needs of a minor due to the parent's incapacity or debilitation resulting from illness, and who desires to make long-term plans for the future of a minor without terminating or limiting in any way the parent's legal rights.

(2) It is the intent of the General Assembly to create an expeditious procedure which will enable a parent who is terminally ill or periodically incapable or debilitated to make long-term plans for a minor without terminating or limiting in any manner parental rights.

SUBCHAPTER A
PRELIMINARY PROVISIONS

Sec.

5601. Short title of chapter.
5602. Definitions.
5603. Scope.

§ 5601. Short title of chapter.

This chapter shall be known and may be cited as the Standby Guardianship Act.

§ 5602. Definitions.

The following words and phrases when used in this chapter shall have the meanings given to them in this section unless the context clearly indicates otherwise:

"Alternate." A person with all the rights, responsibilities and qualifications of a standby guardian who shall become a standby guardian only in the event that the currently designated standby guardian is unable or refuses to fulfill his obligation.

"Attending physician." A physician who has primary responsibility for the treatment and care of the designator. If physicians share responsibility, another physician is acting on the attending physician's behalf or no physician has primary responsibility, any physician who is familiar with the designator's medical condition may act as an attending physician under this chapter.

"Coguardian." A person who along with a parent shares physical or legal custody, or both, of a child.

"Consent." A written authorization signed by the designator in the presence of two witnesses who shall also sign the writing. The witnesses must be 18 years of age or older and not named in the designation.

"Court." Family Court Division or domestic relations section of a court of common pleas unless otherwise provided by local rules of court.

"Debilitation." A person's chronic and substantial inability as a result of a physically incapacitating disease or injury to care for a dependent minor.

"Designation." A written document naming the standby guardian or temporary guardian. A parent, a legal custodian or a legal guardian may designate an alternate standby guardian in the same writing.

"Designator." A parent, a legal custodian or a legal guardian who appoints a standby guardian or temporary guardian.

"Determination of debilitation." A written finding made by an attending physician which states that the designator suffers from a physically incapacitating disease or injury. No identification of the illness in question is required.

"Determination of incapacity." A written finding made by an attending physician which states the nature, extent and probable duration of the designator's mental or organic incapacity.

"Family member." A grandparent, aunt, uncle or adult sibling of a minor.

"Incapacity." A chronic and substantial inability, resulting from a mental or organic impairment, to understand the nature and consequences of decisions concerning the care of the designator's dependent minor and a consequent inability to care for the minor.

"Standby guardian." A person named by a designator to assume the duties of coguardian or guardian of a minor and whose authority becomes effective upon the incapacity, debilitation and consent, or death of the minor's parent.

"Temporary guardian." A family member, appointed by a court for a limited period as a guardian of the minor when the minor's custodial parent has entered a rehabilitation facility for treatment of drug or alcohol addiction or has been subject to emergency medical intervention due to abuse of drugs or alcohol.

"Triggering event." A specified occurrence stated in the designation which empowers a standby guardian to assume the powers, duties and responsibilities of guardian or coguardian.

(June 22, 2000, P.L.443, No.59, eff. 60 days; October 23, 2018, No. 88, eff. 60 days).

2018 Amendment. Act 88 amended the defs. of "designation" and "designator." and added the defs. of "family member" and "temporary guardian".

2000 Amendment. Act 59 amended the defs. of "designation" and "designator."

§ 5603. Scope.

The provisions of Chapter 53 (relating to custody) and 20 Pa.C.S. Ch. 25 (relating to wills) shall apply to standby guardians, coguardians, guardians, temporary guardians and any alternates unless otherwise specified in this chapter. Nothing in this chapter shall be construed to deprive any parent, custodial or noncustodial, of legal parental rights. Nothing in this chapter shall be construed to relieve any parent, custodial or noncustodial, of a duty to support a child under the provisions of Chapter 43 (relating to support matters generally).

(October 23, 2018, No. 88, eff. 60 days).

2018 Amendment. Act 88 amended this sec.

SUBCHAPTER B
GENERAL PROVISIONS

Sec.
5611. Designation.
5612. Petition for approval of a designation.
5613. Authority of standby guardian.
5614. Revocation.
5615. Conflicting documents.
5616. Bond.

§ 5611. Designation.

(a) **General rule.**—A custodial parent, a legal custodian or legal guardian may designate a standby guardian by means of a written designation unless the minor has another parent or adoptive parent:

(1) whose parental rights have not been terminated or relinquished;

(2) whose whereabouts are known; and

(3) who is willing and able to make and carry out the day-to-day child-care decisions concerning the minor.

(b) Exception where other parent consents.—Notwithstanding subsection (a), a parent, legal custodian or legal guardian may designate a standby guardian with the consent of the other parent.

(c) Contents.—

(1) A designation of a standby guardianship shall identify the custodial parent, legal custodian or legal guardian making the designation, the minor or minors, any other parent, the standby guardian and the triggering event or events upon which a named standby guardian shall become a coguardian or guardian. If desired, different standby guardians may be designated for different triggering events. The designation shall also include the signed consent of the standby guardian, and the signed consent of any other parent or an indication why the other parent's consent is not necessary.

(2) The designation shall be signed by the designating parent, legal custodian or legal guardian in the presence of two witnesses, who are 18 years of age or older and not otherwise named in the designation, who shall also sign the designation. If the parent, legal custodian or legal guardian is physically unable to sign the designation, the parent, legal custodian or legal guardian may direct another person not named in the designation to sign on the parent's, the legal custodian's or the legal guardian's behalf in the presence of the parent, legal custodian or legal guardian and the witnesses.

(3) A parent, legal custodian or legal guardian may also, but need not, designate an alternate in the designation.

(4) A designation may, but need not, be in the following form:

I (insert name of designator) do hereby appoint (insert name, address and telephone number of standby guardian) as the standby guardian of (insert name(s) of minor(s)) to take effect upon the occurrence of the following triggering event or events (insert specific triggering events).

I hereby revoke all former wills and codicils to the extent that there is a conflict between those formerly executed documents and this, my duly executed standby guardian designation.

I am the (insert designator's relationship to minor(s)) of (insert name(s) of minor(s)).

(Insert name(s) of minor(s)'s other parent(s)) is the father/mother of (insert name(s) of minor(s)).

His/her address is: _____

_____ (Check all that apply):

_____ He/she died on (insert date of death). _____ His/her parental rights were terminated or relinquished on (insert date of termination or relinquishment).

_____ His/her whereabouts are unknown. I understand that all living parents whose rights have not been terminated must be given notice of this designation pursuant to the Pennsylvania Rules of Civil Procedure or a petition to approve this designation may not be granted by the court.

_____ He/she is unwilling and unable to make and carry out day-to-day child-care decisions concerning the minor.

_____ He/she consents to this designation and has signed this form below.

By this designation I am granting (insert name of standby guardian) the authority to act for 60 days following the occurrence of the triggering event as a coguardian with me, or in the event of my death, as guardian of my minor child(ren).

Optional: I hereby nominate (insert name, address, and telephone number of alternate standby guardian) as the alternate standby guardian to assume the duties of the standby guardian named above in the event the standby guardian is unable or refuses to act as a standby guardian.

If I have indicated more than one triggering event, it is my intent that the triggering event which occurs first shall take precedence. If I have indicated "my death" as the triggering event, it is my intent that the person named in the designation to be standby guardian for my minor child(ren) in the event of my death shall be appointed as guardian of my minor child(ren) when I die.

It is my intention to retain full parental rights to the extent consistent with my condition and to retain the authority to revoke the standby guardianship if I so choose.

This designation is made after careful reflection, while I am of sound mind.

_____ _____
(Date) (Designator's signature)

_____ _____
(Witness's signature) (Witness's signature)

_____ _____
(Number and Street) (Number and Street)
(City, State and Zip Code) (City, State and Zip Code) (IF APPLICABLE): I (insert name of other parent) hereby consent to this designation.

_____ _____
(Date) (Signature of other parent)
(Address of other parent)

I, (insert name of standby guardian) hereby accept my nomination as standby guardian of (insert minor(s)'s name(s)), I understand that my rights and responsibilities toward the minor child(ren) named above will become effective upon the occurrence of the above-stated triggering event or events. I further understand that in order to continue caring for the child(ren), I must file a petition with the court within 60 days of the occurrence of the triggering event.

_____ _____
(Date) (Signature of standby guardian)

(June 22, 2000, P.L.443, No.59, eff. 60 days)

§ 5612. Petition for approval of a designation.

(a) General rule.—A petition for court approval of a designation under this chapter may be made at any time by filing with the court a copy of the designation. If the triggering event has not occurred on or before the time of filing, only the designator may file the petition. If the triggering event has occurred on or before the time of filing, the standby guardian named in the designation may file the petition and the petition shall also contain one of the following:

(1) A determination of the designator's incapacity.

(2) A determination of the designator's debilitation and the designator's signed and dated consent.

(3) A copy of the designator's death certificate.

(b) Notice.—

(1) The petitioner shall notify any person named in the designation within ten days of the filing of the petition and of any hearing thereon.

(2) If the petition alleges that a nondesignating parent cannot be located, that parent shall be notified in accordance with the notice provisions of the Pennsylvania

Rules of Civil Procedure in Custody Matters. No notice is necessary to a parent whose parental rights have previously been terminated or relinquished.

(c) **Jurisdiction.**—For purposes of determining jurisdiction under this chapter, the provisions of Chapter 54 (relating to uniform child custody jurisdiction and enforcement) shall apply.

(d) **Presumptions.**—In a proceeding for judicial appointment of a standby guardian, a designation shall constitute a rebuttable presumption that the designated standby guardian is capable of serving as coguardian or guardian. When the designator is the sole surviving parent, when the parental rights of any noncustodial parent have been terminated or relinquished or when all parties consent to the designation, there shall be a rebuttable presumption that entry of the approval order is in the best interest of the child. In any case, if the court finds entry of the approval order to be in the best interest of the child, the court shall enter an order approving the designation petition.

(e) **Approval without hearing.**—Approval of the designation without a hearing is permitted when the designator is the sole surviving parent, when the parental rights of any noncustodial parent have been terminated or relinquished or when all parties consent to entry of the approval order.

(f) **Hearing.**—In the event a hearing is required, it shall be conducted in accordance with the proceedings set forth in Chapters 53 (relating to custody) and 54.

(g) **Court appearance.**—The designator need not appear in court if the designator is medically unable to appear.

2004 Amendment. Act 39 amended subsec. (c) and (f).

Cross References. Section 5612 is referred to in sections 5613, 5614 of this title.

§ 5613. Authority of standby guardian.

(a) **General rule.**—The standby guardian shall have authority to act as coguardian or guardian upon the occurrence of the triggering event. The commencement of the standby guardian's authority to act as coguardian pursuant to: a determination of incapacity; a determination of debilitation and consent; or, the receipt of consent alone, shall not itself divest the designator of any parental rights, but shall confer upon the standby guardian concurrent or shared custody of the child. The commencement of the standby guardian's authority to act as guardian pursuant to the death of the designator shall not confer upon the standby guardian more than physical and legal custody of the child as defined in Ch. 53 (relating to custody). A coguardian shall assure frequent and continuing contact with and physical access to the child and shall further assure the involvement of the parent, to include, to the greatest extent possible, in the decision making on behalf of the child.

(b) **Effect of filing.**—The designator may file a petition for approval of a designation with the court at any time. If the petition is approved by the court before the occurrence of the triggering event, the standby guardian's authority will commence automatically upon the occurrence of the triggering event. No further petition or confirmation is necessary. If a designation has been made, but the petition for approval of the designation has not been filed and a triggering event had occurred, the standby guardian shall have temporary legal authority to act as a coguardian or guardian of the minor without the direction of the court for a period of 60 days. The standby guardian shall, within that period, file a petition for approval in accordance with section 5612 (relating to petition for approval of a designation). If no petition is filed within the specified 60 days, the standby guardian shall lose all authority to act as coguardian or guardian. If a petition is filed but the court does not act upon it within the 60-day period, the temporary legal authority to act as coguardian or guardian shall continue until the court orders otherwise.

(c) **Parental rights.**—The commencement of a coguardian's or guardian's authority under this subchapter may not, itself, divest a parent or legal guardian of any parental or guardianship rights.

(d) **Restored capacity.**—If a licensed physician determines that the designator has regained capacity, the coguardian's authority which commenced pursuant to the occurrence of a triggering event shall become inactive and the coguardian shall return to having no authority. Failure of a coguardian to comply with this provision and to immediately return the minor to the designator's care shall entitle the designator to an emergency hearing in a court of competent jurisdiction.

§ 5614. Revocation.

(a) **Prepetition.**—Prior to a petition being filed under section 5612 (relating to petition for approval of a designation) the designator may revoke a standby guardianship by simple destruction of the designation and notification of the revocation to the standby guardian.

(b) **Postpetition.**—After a petition has been filed, the designator may revoke a standby guardianship by:

(1) executing a written revocation;

(2) filing the revocation with the court; and

(3) notifying the persons named in the designation of the revocation in writing.

(c) **Unwritten revocation.**—Regardless of whether a petition has been filed, an unwritten revocation may be considered by the court if it can be proven by clear and convincing evidence.

§ 5615. Conflicting documents.

If a parent has appointed a testamentary guardian of the person or estate of a minor by will under 20 Pa.C.S. § 2519 (relating to testamentary guardian) and there is a conflict between that will and a duly executed written standby guardian designation, the document latest in date of execution shall prevail.

§ 5616. Bond.

In no event shall a standby guardian be required to post bond prior to the occurrence of the triggering event. The court may require a bond if the standby guardian is designated the coguardian or guardian of the estate of a minor but will not require a bond for the coguardianship or guardianship of the person of a minor.

SUBCHAPTER C
TEMPORARY GUARDIANSHIP

Sec.

5621. Designation.
5622. Petition for approval of a designation.
5623. Authority of temporary guardian.
5624. Period of temporary guardianship.
5625. Termination of temporary guardianship.

§ 5621. Designation.

(a) **General rule.**— Except as provided in subsection (b), a custodial parent may designate a temporary guardian by means of a written designation unless the minor has another parent or adoptive parent:

(1) whose parental rights have not been terminated or relinquished;

(2) whose whereabouts are known; and

(3) who is willing and able to make and carry out the day-to-day child-care decisions concerning the minor.

(b) **Exception where other parent consents.**—Notwithstanding subsection (a), a parent, legal custodian or legal guardian may designate a temporary guardian with the consent of the other parent.

(c) Contents.—

(1) A designation of a temporary guardianship shall identify the custodial parent, the minor or minors, any other parent, the temporary guardian and the triggering event or events upon which a named temporary guardian shall become a coguardian or guardian. The designation shall also include the signed consent of the temporary guardian and the signed consent of any other parent or an indication why the other parent's consent is not necessary.

(2) The designation shall be signed by the designating parent in the presence of two witnesses who are 18 years of age or older and not otherwise named in the designation, who shall also sign the designation.

(3) A parent may also but need not designate an alternate in the designation.

(4) A designation may but need not be in the following form:

_____ (Insert name of designator) do hereby appoint _____ (Insert name, address and telephone number of temporary guardian) as the temporary guardian of _____ (Insert name(s) of minor(s) to take effect upon _____ (Date).

I am the mother/father/other to_____
(Insert name(s) of minor(s)).

_____(Insert name(s) of other parent(s) of minor(s)) is the father/mother/other of _____ _____ Insert name(s) of minor(s)).

By this designation, I am granting _____
(insert name of temporary guardian) the authority to act for 90 days following the occurrence of _____ as a coguardian with me or as guardian of my minor child(ren).

It is my intention to retain full parental rights to the extent consistent with my condition and to retain the authority to revoke the temporary guardianship if I so choose.

This designation is made after careful reflection, while I am of sound mind.

_____   _____
(Date)   (Designator's signature)

_____   _____
(Witness's signature)   (Witness's signature)

_____   _____
(Number and Street)   (Number and Street)

_____   _____
(City, State and Zip Code) (City, State and Zip Code)

If applicable: I, _____, (Insert name of other parent) hereby consent to this designation.

_____   _____
(Date)   (Signature of other parent)

_____
(Address of other parent)

I, _____ (Insert name of temporary guardian), hereby accept my nomination as temporary guardian of _____ _____ (Insert minor(s)'s name(s)). I understand that my rights and responsibilities toward the minor child(ren) named above will become effective upon _____ (Date)

I further understand that in order to continue as temporary guardian for the child(ren), I must file a petition with the court of common pleas within 30 days of the order granting the petition for temporary guardianship.

_____   _____
       (Date)   (Signature of temporary guardian)

NOTARY SEAL

I hereby revoke the above temporary guardianship agreement.
_____ (Parent signature)
_____ (Date)

NOTARY SEAL

(October 23, 2018, No. 88, eff. 60 days)

2018 Amendment. Act 88 adopted this section.

§ 5622. Petition for approval of designation.

(a) General rule.—Except as provided in subsection (b), a petition for court approval of a designation under this chapter may be made when an individual who is a custodial parent of a minor has entered a rehabilitation facility for treatment of a drug or alcohol addiction or has been subject to emergency medical intervention due to abuse of drugs or alcohol by filing with the court a copy of the designation.

(b) Exception where designation has not been entered.—If a custodial parent has been subject to emergency medical intervention due to abuse of drugs or alcohol and a written designation has not been executed, a family member shall petition the court to hold a hearing to be designated temporary guardian. THE PETITION, WHICH SHALL REQUIRE THE NOTARIZED SIGNATURE OF THE PETITIONER, SHALL BE PROVIDED BY THE COURT IN THE FOLLOWING FORM:

PETITION FOR TEMPORARY GUARDIANSHIP WITHOUT CONSENT OF PARENT

I, _____(INSERT NAME, ADDRESS AND TELEPHONE NUMBER OF FAMILY MEMBER PETITIONING FOR TEMPORARY GUARDIANSHIP AND RELATIONSHIP TO MINOR), HEREBY DECLARE MY INTENT TO BE APPOINTED TEMPORARY GUARDIAN OF _____
_____ (INSERT NAME(S), ADDRESS(ES) AND TELEPHONE NUMBER(S) OF MINOR(S) FOR WHOM THE APPOINTMENT OF TEMPORARY GUARDIAN IS BEING SOUGHT) AS A RESULT OF EMERGENCY MEDICAL INTERVENTION RESULTING FROM ABUSE OF DRUGS OR ALCOHOL BY _____
_____ (INSERT NAME, ADDRESS AND TELEPHONE NUMBER), FATHER/MOTHER TO _____
_____ (INSERT NAME(S) OF MINOR(S)), ON_____ (INSERT APPROXIMATE DATE OF THE EVENT).

I HAVE NOTIFIED THE CHILD(REN)'S OTHER PARENT, _____
_____ INSERT NAME, ADDRESS AND TELEPHONE NUMBER), OF MY INTENT TO PETITION THIS COURT FOR TEMPORARY GUARDIANSHIP.

I UNDERSTAND THAT FILING THIS PETITION DOES NOT REVOKE THE PARENTAL RIGHTS OF THE MINOR'S PARENT(S) NOR DOES IT GRANT ME ANY PARENTAL RIGHTS.

I UNDERSTAND THAT MY RIGHTS AND RESPONSIBILITIES AS A TEMPORARY GUARDIAN TOWARD THE MINOR CHILD(REN) NAMED ABOVE WILL BECOME EFFECTIVE UPON THE COMPLETION OF A HEARING AND RENDERING OF A DECISION BY THE COURT.

I UNDERSTAND THAT FILING FEES AND OTHER COSTS ASSOCIATED WITH THESE PROCEEDINGS MAY BE WAIVED IF I DEMONSTRATE THE

FEES AND OTHER COSTS WOULD CONSTITUTE A FINANCIAL BURDEN TO ME AND MY FAMILY.

I HEREBY SWEAR OR AFFIRM THAT THE INFORMATION CONTAINED HEREIN IS TRUE AND CORRECT TO THE BEST OF MY KNOWLEDGE.

_____ _____
(Date) (Signature of Petitioner)

(c) Notice.—

(1) The court shall notify a person named in the designation within 10 days of the filing of the petition and of any hearing on the petition.

(2) If a designation has not been executed, the petitioner shall notify the custodial parent or parents, noncustodial parent or adoptive parent within 10 days of the filing of the petition and of any hearing on the petition.

(3) If the petition alleges that a noncustodial parent cannot be located, that parent shall be notified in accordance with the notice provisions of the Pennsylvania Rules of Civil Procedure in custody matters. No notice is necessary to a parent whose parental rights have previously been terminated or relinquished.

(d) Jurisdiction.—For purposes of determining jurisdiction under this chapter, the provisions of Chapter 54 (relating to uniform child custody jurisdiction and enforcement) shall apply.

(e) Presumptions.—In a proceeding for judicial appointment of a temporary guardian, a designation shall constitute a rebuttable presumption that the designated temporary guardian is capable of serving as coguardian or guardian. When the designator is the sole surviving parent and when the parental rights of any noncustodial parent have been terminated or relinquished or when all parties consent to the designation there shall be a rebuttable presumption that entry of the approval order is in the best interest of the child. In any case, if the court finds entry of the approval order to be in the best interests of the child, the court shall enter an order approving the designation petition.

(f) Approval without hearing.—Approval of the designation without a hearing is permitted when the designator is the sole surviving parent, when the parental rights of a noncustodial parent have been terminated or relinquished or when all parties consent to entry of the approval order.

(g) Hearing.—If a hearing is required, it shall be conducted in accordance with the proceedings under Chapters 53 (relating to child custody) and 54.

(h) Court appearance.—If a designation has not been executed and a petition for temporary guardianship has been filed with the court by a family member, the custodial parent and noncustodial parent or adoptive parent shall appear in court in order to consent to or oppose the designation. If notice has been given under subsection (c)(3) and a noncustodial parent does not appear in court, it is presumed that consent to the designation has been granted.

(i) Costs.—A court may waive filing fees and other costs upon application when the petitioner demonstrates the fees and other costs would constitute a financial burden upon the petitioner and the petitioner's family. There shall be a presumption of a financial burden if the income from all sources of the petitioner is less than 300% of the poverty level set by the Federal Government.

(October 23, 2018, No. 88, eff. 60 days)

2018 Amendment. Act 88 adopted this section.

§ 5623. Authority of temporary guardian.

(a) Authority.—

(1) The temporary guardian shall have the authority to act as coguardian or guardian upon a custodial parent entering into an alcohol or drug treatment facility or upon a court ordering the designation pursuant to hearing under subsection 5622(b) (relating to petition for approval of designation).

(2) The commencement of the temporary guardian's authority to act as coguardian shall not itself divest the custodial parent of parental rights but shall confer upon the temporary guardian concurrent or shared custody of the child.

(3) A coguardian shall assure frequent and continuing contact with and physical access to the child and shall further assure the involvement of the custodial parent, to the greatest extent possible, in the decision making on behalf of the child.

(4) The commencement of a temporary guardian's authority under this subchapter shall not itself divest a parent or legal guardian of parental or guardianship rights.

(b) Limitations on authority.—In addition to any other restrictions placed on a temporary guardian by the court, the temporary guardian may not:

(1) remove the minor or permit the minor to be removed from the United States either permanently or temporarily without the consent of the custodial parent and the approval of the court; or

(2) remove the minor from this Commonwealth absent a court order, which may only be issued after a hearing at which both parents and the minor shall have the right to be present.

(October 23, 2018, No. 88, eff. 60 days)

2018 Amendment. Act 88 adopted this section.

§ 5624. Period of temporary guardianship.

(a) Initial period.—Temporary guardianship under this subchapter shall be limited to not more than 90 days from entry of the order of temporary guardianship.

(b) Extension of guardianship.—Upon approval by the court or by written agreement of the temporary guardian and the parent who has entered a rehabilitation facility, temporary guardianship shall be extended for periods of up to 90 additional days.

(c) Total period.—The total period of guardianship under this section shall not exceed 365 days.

(October 23, 2018, No. 88, eff. 60 days)

2018 Amendment. Act 88 adopted this section.

§ 5625. Termination of temporary guardianship.

(a) Conditions.—A court shall terminate a temporary guardianship if any of the following exists:

(1) The custodial parent demonstrates the basis for the temporary guardianship no longer exists.

(2) The custodial parent and temporary guardian agree upon termination.

(3) The temporary guardian files a petition with the court seeking termination.

(4) Subject to subsection (b), a noncustodial or adoptive parent files a petition with the court seeking termination of the guardianship.

(5) The temporary guardian or an individual who resides with the temporary guardian commits an offense that results in the temporary guardian or an individual who resides with the temporary guardian being identified as a perpetrator as defined in section 6303 (relating to definitions).

(b) Mandatory considerations—Before terminating an order for temporary guardianship under subsection (a)(4), the court shall consider if termination of the temporary guardianship is in the best interests of the minor if the individual's parental rights were previously terminated.

(October 23, 2018, No. 88, eff. 60 days)

2018 Amendment. Act 88 adopted this section.

CHAPTER 57
SEX TRAFFICKING AND MISSING AND ABDUCTED CHILDREN

Sec.
5701. Definitions.
5702. County responsibilities.
5703. Law enforcement responsibilities.

Enactment. Chapter 57 was added December 28, 2015, P.L.559, No.94, effective January 1, 2016.

§ 5701. Definitions.

The following words and phrases when used in this chapter shall have the meanings given to them in this section unless the context clearly indicates otherwise:

"Child." An individual who is under 21 years of age and meets one of the following:

(1) The county agency is conducting an assessment of the need for services.

(2) The county agency is conducting an investigation of suspected child abuse of the child under Chapter 63 (relating to child protective services).

(3) The county agency is providing services to the child.

"County agency." As defined in section 6303 (relating to definitions).

"Department." The Department of Human Services of the Commonwealth.

"Law enforcement." The law enforcement agency which is responsible for investigating cases of missing children under 18 Pa.C.S. § 2908 (relating to missing children).

"Sex trafficking victim." As defined under section 475 of the Social Security Act (49 Stat. 620, 42 U.S.C. § 675).

§ 5702. County responsibilities.

(a) Report of possible sex trafficking victims.—A county agency shall report to law enforcement as soon as practicable, but in no case later than 24 hours after receiving information about a child who:

(1) the county agency has reasonable cause to suspect of being at risk of being a sex trafficking victim; or

(2) the county agency identifies as being a sex trafficking victim.

(b) Child missing from residence or abducted.—A county agency shall report to law enforcement and to the National Center for Missing and Exploited Children as soon as practicable but no later than 24 hours after receiving information about a child who is missing from the child's residence or is abducted.

(c) Report to department.—The county agency shall report annually to the department the total number of children who are sex trafficking victims. The report shall be submitted in the form and by the deadline prescribed by the department.

Cross References. Section 5702 is referred to in section 5703 of this title.

§ 5703. Law enforcement responsibilities.

When law enforcement receives information from a county agency about a child who is missing from the child's residence or is abducted under section 5702(b) (relating to county responsibilities), law enforcement shall enter the information into the National Crime Information Center database.

Pa.C.S.

PART VII
ABUSE OF FAMILY

Chapter

61. Protection from Abuse
63. Child Protective Services
65. Newborn Protection
67. Domestic and Sexual Violence Victim Address Confidentiality

Enactment. Part VII was added Dec. 19, 1990, P.L. 1240, No.206, effective in 90 days.

CHAPTER 61
PROTECTION FROM ABUSE

Sec.

6101. Short title of chapter.
6102. Definitions.
6103. Jurisdiction.
6104. Full faith and credit and foreign protection orders.
6105. Responsibilities of law enforcement agencies.
6106. Commencement of proceedings.
6107. Hearings.
6108. Relief.
6108.1. Return of relinquished firearms, other weapons and ammunition and additional relief.
6108.2. Relinquishment for consignment sale, lawful transfer or safekeeping.
6108.3. Relinquishment to third party for safekeeping.
6108.4. Registry or database of firearm ownership.
6108.5. Penalties for release of information.
6109. Service of orders.
6110. Emergency relief by minor judiciary.
6111. Domestic violence counselor/advocate.
6112. Disclosure of addresses.
6113. Arrest for violation of order.
6113.1. Private criminal complaints for violation of order or agreement.
6114. Contempt for violation of order or agreement.
6114.1. Civil contempt or modification for violation of an order or agreement.
6115. Reporting abuse and immunity.
6116. Confidentiality.
6117. Procedure and other remedies.
6118. Full faith and credit [Repealed].
6119. Immunity.
6120. Inability to pay.
6121. Warrantless searches.
6122. Construction.

Enactment. Chapter 61. was added December 19, 1990, P.L.1240, No.206, effective in 90 days.

Saved from Suspension. Pennsylvania Rule of Civil Procedure No. 1910.49, as amended March 30, 1994, provided that Chapter 61 shall not be deemed suspended or affected by Rules 1910.1 through 1910.31 governing actions for support.

Pennsylvania Rule of Civil Procedure No. 1915.24, as amended March 30, 1994, provided that Chapter 61 shall not be deemed suspended or affected by Rules 1915.1 through 1915.18 relating to actions for custody, partial custody and visitation of minor children.

Cross References. Chapter 61 is referred to in section 2711 of Title 18 (Crimes and Offenses); section 6105 of this title; sections 1126, 1725.1, 5924, 6302, 8127, 9711 of Title 42 (Judiciary and Judicial Procedure).

§ 6101. Short title of chapter.

This chapter shall be known and may be cited as the Protection from Abuse Act.

§ 6102. Definitions.

(a) **General rule.**—The following words and phrases when used in this chapter shall have the meanings given to them in this section unless the context clearly indicates otherwise:

"**Abuse.**" The occurrence of one or more of the following acts between family or household members, sexual or intimate partners or persons who share biological parenthood:

(1) Attempting to cause or intentionally, knowingly or recklessly causing bodily injury, serious bodily injury, rape, involuntary deviate sexual intercourse, sexual assault, statutory sexual assault, aggravated indecent assault, indecent assault or incest with or without a deadly weapon.

(2) Placing another in reasonable fear of imminent serious bodily injury.

(3) The infliction of false imprisonment pursuant to 18 Pa.C.S. § 2903 (relating to false imprisonment).

(4) Physically or sexually abusing minor children, including such terms as defined in Chapter 63 (relating to child protective services).

(5) Knowingly engaging in a course of conduct or repeatedly committing acts toward another person, including following the person, without proper authority, under circumstances which place the person in reasonable fear of bodily injury. The definition of this paragraph applies only to proceedings commenced under this title and is inapplicable to any criminal prosecutions commenced under Title 18 (relating to crimes and offenses).

"**Adult.**" An individual who is 18 years of age or older.

"**Appropriate law enforcement agency.**" The duly constituted municipal law enforcement agency that regularly provides primary police services to a political subdivision or, in the absence of any such municipal law enforcement agency, the Pennsylvania State Police installation that regularly provides primary police services to the political subdivision.

"**Certified copy.**" A paper copy of the original order of the issuing court endorsed by the appropriate clerk of that court or an electronic copy of the original order of the issuing court endorsed with a digital signature of the judge or appropriate clerk of that court. A raised seal on the copy of the order of the issuing court shall not be required.

"**Commercial armory.**" A for-profit entity which holds the appropriate Federal and State licenses to possess and secure firearms of third persons.

"**Comparable court.**" A foreign court that:

(1) has subject matter jurisdiction and is authorized to issue ex parte, emergency, temporary or final protection orders in that jurisdiction; and

(2) possessed jurisdiction over the parties when the protection order was issued in that jurisdiction.

"**Confidential communications.**" All information, whether written or spoken, transmitted between a victim and a domestic violence counselor or advocate in the course of the relationship. The term includes information received or given by the domestic violence counselor or advocate in the course of the relationship, as well as advice, reports, statistical data, memoranda or working papers, records or the like, given or made in the course of the relationship. The term also includes communications made by or to a linguistic interpreter assisting the victim, counselor or advocate in the course of the relationship.

"**Domestic violence counselor/advocate.**" An individual who is engaged in a domestic violence program, the primary purpose of which is the rendering of counseling or assistance to victims of domestic violence, who has undergone 40 hours of training.

"**Domestic violence program.**" A nonprofit organization or program whose primary purpose is to provide services to domestic violence victims which include, but are not limited to, crisis hotline; safe homes or shelters; community education; counseling systems intervention and interface; transportation, information and referral; and victim assistance.

"**Family or household members.**" Spouses or persons who have been spouses, persons living as spouses or who lived as spouses, parents and children, other persons related by consanguinity or affinity, current or former sexual or intimate partners or persons who share biological parenthood.

"**Firearm.**" Any weapon which is designed to or may readily be converted to expel any projectile by the action of an explosive or the frame or receiver of any such weapon as defined by 18 Pa.C.S. § 6105(i) (relating to persons not to possess, use, manufacture, control, sell or transfer firearms).

"**Foreign protection order.**" A protection order as defined by 18 U.S.C. § 2266 (relating to definitions) issued by a comparable court of another state, the District of Columbia, Indian tribe or territory, possession or commonwealth of the United States.

"**Hearing officer.**" A magisterial district judge, judge of the Philadelphia Municipal Court, arraignment court magistrate appointed under 42 Pa.C.S. § 1123 (relating to jurisdiction and venue), master appointed under 42 Pa.C.S. § 1126 (relating to masters) and master for emergency relief.

"**Master for emergency relief.**" A member of the bar of the Commonwealth appointed under section 6110(e) (relating to emergency relief by minor judiciary).

"**Minor.**" An individual who is not an adult.

"**Other weapon.**" Anything readily capable of lethal use and possessed under circumstances not manifestly appropriate for lawful uses which it may have. The term does not include a firearm.

"**Safekeeping permit.**" A permit issued by a sheriff allowing a person to take possession of any firearm, other weapon or ammunition that a judge ordered a defendant to relinquish in a protection from abuse proceeding.

"**Secure visitation facility.**" A court-approved visitation program offered in a facility with trained professional staff operated in a manner that safeguards children and parents from abuse and abduction.

"**Sheriff.**"

(1) Except as provided in paragraph (2), the sheriff of the county.

(2) In a city of the first class, the chief or head of the police department.

"**Victim.**" A person who is physically or sexually abused by a family or household member. For purposes of section 6116 (relating to confidentiality), a victim is a person against whom abuse is committed who consults a domestic violence counselor or advocate for the purpose of securing advice, counseling or assistance. The term shall also include persons who have a significant relationship with the victim and who seek advice, counseling or assistance from a domestic violence counselor or advocate regarding abuse of the victim.

"**Weapon.**" Anything readily capable of lethal use and possessed under circumstances not manifestly appropriate for lawful uses which it may have. The term includes a firearm which is not loaded or lacks a magazine, clip or other components to render it immediately operable and components which can readily be assembled into a weapon as defined by 18 Pa.C.S. § 907 (relating to possessing instruments of crime).

(b) **Other terms.**—Terms not otherwise defined in this chapter shall have the meaning given to them in 18 Pa.C.S. (relating to crimes and offenses).

(Oct. 6, 1994, P.L.574, No.85, eff. 60 days; Mar. 31, 1995, 1st Sp.Sess., P.L.985, No.10, eff. 60 days; June 22, 2001, P.L.576, No.39, eff. 60 days; Nov. 30, 2004, P.L.1618, No.207, eff. 60 days; Nov. 10, 2005, P.L.335, No.66, eff. 180 days; Oct. 9, 2008, P.L.1352, No.98, eff. 60 days; Oct. 12, 2018, P.L.519, No.79, eff. 180 days)

2018 Amendment. Act 79 added the defs. of "appropriate law enforcement agency" and "commercial armory" in subsec. (a). Act 79 shall apply to orders issued pursuant to 23 Pa.C.S. § 6108 on or after the effective date of section 11 of Act 79.

2008 Amendment. Act 98 amended the def. of "hearing officer" in subsec. (a). Section 10 of Act 98 provided that nothing in Act 98 shall be construed or deemed to provide arraignment court magistrates with retirement benefits or rights different from those availiable to bail commissioners immediately prior to the effective date of Act 98.

2005 Amendment. Act 66 amended the defs. of "confidential communications" and "hearing officer" and added the defs. of "firearm," "master for emergency relief," "other weapon," "safekeeping permit," "sheriff" and "weapon" in subsec. (a).

2004 Amendment. See section 29 of Act 207 in the appendix to this title for special provisions relating to construction of law.

2001 Amendment. Act 39 added the defs. of "certified copy," "comparable court" and "foreign protection order" in subsec. (a).

1995 Amendment. Act 10, 1st Sp.Sess., amended the def. of "abuse" in subsec. (a).

Cross References. Section 6102 is referred to in sections 3701, 5322, 6702, 6711 of this title; sections 2711, 2718, 6102, 6105 of Title 18 (Crimes and Offenses); sections 1726.2, 8127, 9720.8 of Title 42 (Judiciary and Judicial Procedure); section 304 of Title 53 (Municipalities Generally).

§ 6103. Jurisdiction

(a) **General rule.**—The court shall have jurisdiction over all proceedings under this chapter.

(b) **Effect of departure and nonresidence.**—The right of the plaintiff to relief under this chapter shall not be affected by either of the following:

(1) The plaintiff's leaving the residence or household to avoid further abuse.

(2) The defendant's absence from this Commonwealth or the defendant's nonresidence in this Commonwealth, provided that the court has personal jurisdiction over the defendant in accordance with 42 Pa.C.S. § 5322 (relating to bases of personal jurisdiction over persons outside this Commonwealth).

§ 6104. Full faith and credit and foreign protection orders.

(a) **General rule.**—A court shall recognize and enforce a valid foreign protection order issued by a comparable court. The validity of a foreign protection order shall only be determined by a court.

(b) **Affirmative defense.**—Failure by a comparable court to provide reasonable notice and opportunity to be heard shall be an affirmative defense to any charge or process filed seeking enforcement of a foreign protection order. A comparable court shall have complied with that court's notice requirements and shall have given the defendant the opportunity to be heard before the foreign order was issued. In the case of ex parte orders, the comparable court shall have complied with that court's notice requirements and have given the defendant an opportunity to be heard within a reasonable period of time after the order was issued, consistent with due process.

(c) **Invalid orders.**—A foreign protection order issued by a comparable court against a party who has filed a petition, complaint or other written pleading for a protection order is not valid and not entitled to full faith and credit if:

(1) no cross or counter petition, complaint or other written pleading was filed seeking the protection order; or

(2) a cross or counter petition, complaint or other written pleading was filed and the court did not make a specific finding that each party was entitled to a protection order.

(d) **Filing a foreign protection order.**—A plaintiff may file a certified copy of a foreign protection order with the prothonotary in any county within this Commonwealth where the plaintiff believes enforcement may be necessary. The following provisions shall apply:

(1) No costs or fees associated with filing a foreign protection order shall be assigned to the plaintiff, including the cost of obtaining certified copies of the order. Costs and fees associated with filing a foreign protection order may be assessed against the defendant.

(2) Upon filing of a foreign protection order, a prothonotary shall transmit, in a manner prescribed by the Pennsylvania State Police, a copy of the order to the Pennsylvania State Police registry of protection orders.

(3) Filing of a foreign protection order shall not be a prerequisite for service and enforcement.

(e) **Orders issued in another judicial district within this Commonwealth.**—The filing of an order issued in another judicial district within this Commonwealth is not required for enforcement purposes.

2005 Amendment. Act 66 added subsec. (d).

2001 Amendment. Act 39 added this sec.

§ 6105. Responsibilities of law enforcement agencies.

(a) **General rule.**—The police department of each municipal corporation, the Pennsylvania State Police and the sheriff of each county shall insure that all their officers, deputies and employees are familiar with the provisions of this chapter. Instruction concerning protection from abuse shall be made a part of the training curriculum for all trainee officers and deputies. All law enforcement agencies within this Commonwealth shall adopt a written domestic violence policy.

(b) **Notice of services and rights.**—Each law enforcement agency shall provide the abused person with oral and written notice of the availability of safe shelter and of domestic violence services in the community, including the hotline number for domestic violence services. The written notice, which shall be in English and Spanish and any additional language required by local rule of court, shall include the following statement:

"If you are the victim of domestic violence, you have the right to go to court and file a petition requesting an order for protection from domestic abuse pursuant to the Protection From Abuse Act (23 Pa.C.S. Ch. 61), which could include the following:

(1) An order restraining the abuser from further acts of abuse.

(2) An order directing the abuser to leave your household.

(3) An order preventing the abuser from entering your residence, school, business or place of employment.

(4) An order awarding you or the other parent temporary custody of or temporary visitation with your child or children.

(5) An order directing the abuser to pay support to you and the minor children if the abuser has a legal obligation to do so."

(c) **Mandatory report.**—Each law enforcement agency shall make an incident report, on a form prescribed by the Pennsylvania State Police, consistent with the report required by the Federal National Incident-Based Reporting System (NIBRS). The mandate for incident report completion shall not be operative until the Pennsylvania State Police have implemented NIBRS. The incident report may include the following:

(1) Names, addresses and telephone numbers of the victim, the accused, any witnesses and the caller.

(2) A second permanent address and telephone number for the victim, such as a close family member or a friend.

(3) A statement of the relationship between the victim and the accused.

(4) A narrative for the incident, including the date, time and whether the accused appeared intoxicated or under the influence of a controlled substance.

(5) What, if any, weapons were used or threatened to be used.

(6) A description of any injuries observed by the officer.

(7) A description of any injuries described by the victim but not observed by the officer and an indication that the injury was not observed.

(8) Documentation of any evidence that would tend to establish that a crime was committed.

(9) An indication of whether an arrest was made and the reason for electing not to arrest, whether there was a warrantless arrest, an arrest with a warrant or no arrest.

(10) Whether the accused actually was arrested or whether there is an outstanding arrest warrant.

(11) The crimes with which the accused was charged.

(12) If the accused was arrested and arraigned, whether bail was set and any conditions of bail imposed.

(13) If the officer did not arrest or seek an arrest warrant even though arrest was authorized, a detailed explanation of the reasons for the officer's decision not to arrest.

(14) The names and ages of any children present in the household and their address and telephone number if children were relocated.

(15) Notation of previous incidents of which the officer is personally aware.

(16) Notation of previous incidents reported by the victim or witnesses.

(17) If an officer was injured in the incident, the nature and circumstances of the injury.

(d) Notice of arrest.—All law enforcement agencies shall make reasonable efforts to notify any adult or emancipated minor protected by an order issued under this chapter of the arrest of the defendant for violation of an order as soon as possible. Unless the person cannot be located, notice of the arrest shall be provided not more than 24 hours after preliminary arraignment.

(e) Statewide registry.—

(1) The Pennsylvania State Police shall establish a Statewide registry of protection orders and shall maintain a complete and systematic record and index of all valid temporary and final court orders of protection, court-approved consent agreements and a foreign protection order filed pursuant to section 6104(d) (relating to full faith and credit and foreign protection orders). The Statewide registry shall include, but need not be limited to, the following:

(i) The names of the plaintiff and any protected parties.

(ii) The name and address of the defendant.

(iii) The relationship between the plaintiff and defendant.

(iv) The date the order was entered.

(v) The date the order expires.

(vi) The relief granted under sections 6108(a)(1), (2), (4), (6) and (7) (relating to relief) and 6110(a) (relating to emergency relief by minor judiciary).

(vii) The judicial district in which the order was entered.

(viii) Where furnished, the Social Security number and date of birth of the defendant.

(ix) Whether or not any or all firearms, other weapons or ammunition were ordered relinquished.

(2) The prothonotary shall send, on a form prescribed by the Pennsylvania State Police, a copy of the protection order or approved consent agreement to the Statewide registry of protection orders so that it is received within 24 hours of the entry of the order. Likewise, amendments to or revocation of an order shall

be transmitted by the prothonotary within 24 hours of the entry of the order for modification or revocation. The Pennsylvania State Police shall enter orders, amendments and revocations in the Statewide registry of protection orders within eight hours of receipt. Vacated or expired orders shall be purged from the registry.

(3) The registry of the Pennsylvania State Police shall be available at all times to inform courts, dispatchers and law enforcement officers of any valid protection order involving any defendant.

(4) When an order granting relief under section 6108(a)(7) has been entered by a court, such information shall be available to the Pennsylvania State Police for the purpose of conducting a criminal history records check in compliance with the applicable provisions of 18 Pa.C.S. Ch. 61 Subch. A (relating to Uniform Firearms Act).

(5) Information contained in the Statewide registry shall not be subject to access under the act of June 21, 1957 (P.L. 390, No. 212),[5] referred to as the Right-to-Know Law.

(f) Information concerning crimes of violence.—Each police department in a city, borough or township and the Pennsylvania State Police shall transmit to the Pennsylvania State Police, in a manner prescribed by the Pennsylvania State Police, the information specified in subsection (c) related to crimes of violence between family or household members.

(g) Annual report.—The Pennsylvania State Police shall annually compile and analyze the incident report data received and publish a Statewide report which includes aggregate, county and department-based statistical profiles. The Pennsylvania State Police shall transmit a copy of the annual report to the Governor, the General Assembly and each domestic violence program in this Commonwealth.

(h) Enforcement of foreign protection orders.—

(1) All foreign protection orders shall have the presumption of validity in this Commonwealth, and police officers shall make arrests for violations thereof in the same manner as set for violations of protection orders issued within this Commonwealth. Until a foreign order is declared to be invalid by a court, it shall be enforced by all law enforcement personnel in this Commonwealth.

(2) A police officer shall rely upon any copy of a foreign protection order which has been presented to the officer by any source and may verify the existence of a protection order consistent with the provisions of section 6113(a) (relating to arrest for violation of order). The fact that a foreign protection order has not been filed with a prothonotary or entered into the Pennsylvania State Police registry shall not be grounds for law enforcement to refuse to enforce the order.

(i) Immunity.—The following entities shall be immune from civil liability for good faith conduct in any action arising in connection with a court's finding that the foreign order is invalid or unenforceable:

(1) Law enforcement agencies and their agents and employees.

(2) County correctional and detention facilities and their agents and employees.

(3) Prothonotaries and their agents and employees.

2005 Amendment. Act 66 amended subsec. (e).
2001 Amendment. Act 39 amended subsec. (e) and added subsecs. (h) and (i).
1997 Amendment. Act 58 amended subsec. (e).
1994 Amendment. Act 85 amended sec. 6105.
Cross References. Section 6105 is referred to in sections 6104, 6106, 6109, 6114 of this title.

---

[5]65 P.S. § 66.1 et seq.

§ 6106. Commencement of proceedings.

(a) **General rule.**—An adult or an emancipated minor may seek relief under this chapter for that person or any parent, adult household member or guardian ad litem may seek relief under this chapter on behalf of minor children, or a guardian of the person of an adult who has been declared incompetent under 20 Pa.C.S. Ch. 51 Subch. B (relating to appointment of guardian) may seek relief on behalf of the incompetent adult, by filing a petition with the court alleging abuse by the defendant.

(a.1) **False reports.**—A person who knowingly gives false information to any law enforcement officer with the intent to implicate another under this chapter commits an offense under 18 Pa.C.S. § 4906 (relating to false reports to law enforcement authorities).

(a.2) **Notification of defendant's occupation.**—The plaintiff shall notify the court if the plaintiff has reason to believe that the defendant is a licensed firearms dealer, is employed by a licensed firearms dealer or manufacturer, is employed as a writer, researcher or technician in the firearms or hunting industry or is required to carry a firearm as a condition of employment.

(a.3) **Notification of need to protect plaintiff.**—The plaintiff shall notify the court anytime during the period commencing upon filing the petition and granting of an order or approving a consent agreement at a hearing held under section 6107(a) (relating to hearings) if the plaintiff has reason to believe the plaintiff's safety is at risk. In such a case, the court shall direct the Pennsylvania State Police, the municipal police or the sheriff to accompany the plaintiff to the plaintiff's residence to retrieve personal belongings or to accompany the plaintiff while the petition or order is served upon the defendant by the sheriff or competent adult, as set forth in the Pennsylvania Rules of Civil Procedure.

(a.4) **Notification regarding child abuse investigation.**—

(1) If the plaintiff has knowledge of a founded or indicated report of child abuse under Chapter 63 (relating to child protective services) involving the defendant, the petition shall include that information together with the name of the investigative agency.

(2) The notice of hearing and order shall include notice to the defendant that an order issued under this chapter may have an impact on the defendant under Chapter 63. The court shall develop procedures to implement the provisions of this paragraph.

(b) **Plaintiff fees not permitted.**—No plaintiff seeking relief under this chapter shall be charged any fees or costs associated with the filing, issuance, registration or service of a petition, motion, complaint, order or any other filing. Prohibited fees or costs shall include, but are not limited to, those associated with modifying, withdrawing, dismissing or certifying copies of a petition, motion, complaint, order or any other filing, as well as any judicial surcharge or computer system fee. No plaintiff seeking relief under this chapter shall be charged any fees or costs associated with filing a motion for reconsideration or an appeal from any order or action taken pursuant to this chapter. Nothing in this subsection is intended to expand or diminish the court's authority to enter an order pursuant to Pa.R.C.P. No. 1023.1 (relating to Scope. Signing of Documents. Representations to the Court. Violation).

(c) **Assessment of fees and costs against the defendant.**—When an order is granted pursuant to this chapter, fees and costs shall be assessed against the defendant. The court shall waive fees and costs upon a showing of good cause or when the court makes a finding that the defendant is not able to pay the costs. Nothing in this subsection is intended to expand or diminish the court's authority to enter an order pursuant to Pa.R.C.P. No. 1023.1.

(d) **Surcharge on order.**—When a protection order is granted under section 6107(a), other than pursuant to an agreement of the parties, a surcharge of $100 shall be assessed against the defendant. All moneys received from surcharges shall be distributed in the following order of priority:

(1) $25 shall be forwarded to the Commonwealth and shall be appropriated to the Pennsylvania State Police to establish and maintain the Statewide registry of protection orders provided for in section 6105.

(2) $50 shall be retained by the county and shall be used to carry out the provisions of this chapter as follows:

(i) $25 shall be used by the sheriff.

(ii) $25 shall be used by the court.

(3) $25 shall be forwarded to the Department of Public Welfare for use for victims of domestic violence in accordance with the provisions of section 2333 of the act of April 9, 1929 (P.L.177, No.175), known as The Administrative Code of 1929.

(d.1) Limitation.—The surcharge allocated under subsection (d)(1) and (3) shall be used to supplement and not to supplant any other source of funds received for the purpose of carrying out the provisions of this chapter.

(e) Court to adopt means of service.—The court shall adopt a means of prompt and effective service in those instances where the plaintiff avers that service cannot be safely effected by an adult individual other than a law enforcement officer or where the court so orders.

(f) Service by sheriff.—If the court so orders, the sheriff or other designated agency or individual shall serve the petition and order.

(g) Service of petition and orders.—The petition and orders shall be served upon the defendant, and orders shall be served upon the police departments and sheriff with appropriate jurisdiction to enforce the orders. Orders shall be promptly served on the police and sheriff. Failure to serve shall not stay the effect of a valid order.

(g.1) Service of original process of a foreign protection order.—No plaintiff or petitioner shall be charged any costs or fees associated with the service of original process of a foreign protection order. Costs or fees associated with the service of original process of a foreign protection order may be assessed against the defendant.

(h) Assistance and advice to plaintiff.—The courts and hearing officers shall:

(1) Provide simplified forms and clerical assistance in English and Spanish to help with the writing and filing of the petition for a protection order for an individual not represented by counsel.

(2) Provide the plaintiff with written and oral referrals, in English and Spanish, to the local domestic violence program, to the local legal services office and to the county bar association's lawyer referral service.

(Oct. 6, 1994, P.L.574, No.85, eff. 60 days; June 22, 2001, P.L.576, No.39, eff. 60 days; Nov. 10, 2005, P.L.335, No.66, eff. 180 days; Oct. 12, 2018, P.L.519, No.79, eff. 180 days; Oct. 24, 2018, P.L.649, No.92, eff. 180 days)

2018 Amendments. Act 79 amended subsec. (d) and added subsec. (a.3) and Act 92 added subsec. (a.4). Section 11 of Act 79 provided that Act 79 shall apply to orders issued pursuant to section 6108 on or after the effective date of section 11. Section 2(1) of Act 92 provided that the addition of subsec. (a.4) shall apply to an action under Chapter 61 filed on or after the effective date of section 2, and section 2(2) provided that the addition of subsec. (a.4) shall apply to a petition to modify or extend a protection from abuse order under Chapter 61 filed on or after the effective date of section 2.

2005 Amendment. Act 66 amended subsecs. (b), (c), (d), (g) and (g.1) and added subsecs. (a.2) and (d.1).

References in Text. The Department of Public Welfare, referred to in subsec. (d), was redesignated as the Department of Human Services by Act 132 of 2014.

Cross References. Section 6106 is referred to in sections 6107, 6108, 6110 of this title.

§ 6107. Hearings

(a) General rule.—Within ten business days of the filing of a petition under this chapter, a hearing shall be held before the court, at which the plaintiff must prove the allegation of abuse by a preponderance of the evidence. The court shall, at the time the defendant is given notice of the hearing, advise the defendant of the right to be represented by counsel, of the right to present evidence, of the right to compel attendance of witnesses, of the method by which witnesses may be compelled, of the possibility that any firearm, other weapon or ammunition owned and any firearm license possessed may be ordered temporarily relinquished, of the options for relinquishment of a firearm pursuant to this chapter, of the possibility that Federal or State law may prohibit the possession of firearms, including an explanation of 18 U.S.C. § 922(g)(8) (relating to unlawful acts) and 18 Pa.C.S. § 6105 (relating to persons not to possess, use, manufacture, control, sell or transfer firearms), and that any protection order granted by a court may be considered in any subsequent proceedings under this title. This notice shall be printed and delivered in a manner which easily attracts attention to its content and shall specify that child custody is one of the proceedings where prior protection orders may be considered.

(b) Temporary orders.—

(1) If a plaintiff petitions for temporary order for protection from abuse and alleges immediate and present danger of abuse to the plaintiff or minor children, the court shall conduct an ex parte proceeding.

(2) The court may enter such a temporary order as it deems necessary to protect the plaintiff or minor children when it finds they are in immediate and present danger of abuse. The order shall remain in effect until modified or terminated by the court after notice and hearing.

(3) In addition to any other relief, the court may, pursuant to section 6108 (relating to relief), direct that the defendant temporarily relinquish to the sheriff any firearms, other weapons or ammunition for the duration of the temporary order if the petition demonstrates any of the following:

(i) Abuse which involves a firearm or other weapon.

(ii) An immediate and present danger of abuse. In determining whether an immediate and present danger of abuse exists, the court shall consider a number of factors, including, but not limited to:

(A) Whether the temporary order of protection from abuse is not likely to achieve its purpose in the absence of such a condition.

(B) Whether the defendant has previously violated a protection from abuse order.

(C) Whether past or present abuse to the plaintiff or any of the plaintiff's minor children resulted in injury.

(D) Whether the abuse occurred in public.

(E) Whether the abuse includes:

(I) threats of abuse or suicide;

(II) killing or threatening to kill pets;

(III) an escalation of violence;

(IV) stalking or obsessive behavior;

(V) sexual violence; or

(VI) drug or excessive alcohol use.

(4) If the court orders the defendant to temporarily relinquish any firearm, other weapon or ammunition pursuant to paragraph (3), the defendant shall decide in what manner the defendant is going to relinquish any firearm, other weapon or ammunition listed in the order. Relinquishment may be to the sheriff pursuant to section 6108(a)(7) or to a third party for safekeeping pursuant to section 6108.3 (relating to relinquishment to third party for safekeeping).

(c) Continued hearings.—

(1) If a hearing under subsection (a) is continued and no temporary order is issued, the court may make ex parte temporary orders under subsection (b) as it deems necessary.

(2) If a hearing is scheduled to take place within three business days after a defendant is served under section 6106 (relating to commencement of proceedings), the court shall grant a continuance until the three business day-period has elapsed, if requested by the defendant.

(3) The court shall notify the defendant of the right to such continuance.

Cross References. Section 6107 is referred to in sections 6106, 6108 of this title. See Pa.R.C.P. No. 1903.

2018 Amendment. Act 79 added subsec. (a) and (c).

2005 Amendment. Act 66 amended subsecs. (a) and (b).

1997 Amendment. Act 58 amended subsec. (a).

1994 Amendment. Act 85 amended sec. 6107.

§ 6108. Relief.

(a) **General rule.**—Subject to subsection (a.1), the court may grant any protection order or approve any consent agreement to bring about a cessation of abuse of the plaintiff or minor children. The order or agreement may include:

(1) Directing the defendant to refrain from abusing the plaintiff or minor children.

(2) Granting possession to the plaintiff of the residence or household to the exclusion of the defendant by evicting the defendant or restoring possession to the plaintiff if the residence or household is jointly owned or leased by the parties, is owned or leased by the entireties or is owned or leased solely by the plaintiff.

(3) If the defendant has a duty to support the plaintiff or minor children living in the residence or household and the defendant is the sole owner or lessee, granting possession to the plaintiff of the residence or household to the exclusion of the defendant by evicting the defendant or restoring possession to the plaintiff or, with the consent of the plaintiff, ordering the defendant to provide suitable alternate housing.

(4) Awarding temporary custody of or establishing temporary visitation rights with regard to minor children. In determining whether to award temporary custody or establish temporary visitation rights pursuant to this paragraph, the court shall consider any risk posed by the defendant to the children as well as risk to the plaintiff. The following shall apply:

(i) A defendant shall not be granted custody, partial custody or unsupervised visitation where it is alleged in the petition, and the court finds after a hearing under this chapter, that the defendant:

(A) abused the minor children of the parties or poses a risk of abuse toward the minor children of the parties; or

(B) has been convicted of violating 18 Pa.C.S. § 2904 (relating to interference with custody of children) within two calendar years prior to the filing of the petition for protection order or that the defendant poses a risk of violating 18 Pa.C.S. § 2904.

(ii) Where the court finds after a hearing under this chapter that the defendant has inflicted abuse upon the plaintiff or a child, the court may require supervised custodial access by a third party. The third party must agree to be accountable to the court for supervision and execute an affidavit of accountability.

(iii) Where the court finds after a hearing under this chapter that the defendant has inflicted serious abuse upon the plaintiff or a child or poses a risk of abuse toward the plaintiff or a child, the court may:

(A) award supervised visitation in a secure visitation facility; or

(B) deny the defendant custodial access to a child.

(iv) If a plaintiff petitions for a temporary order under section 6107(b) (relating to hearings) and the defendant has partial, shared or full custody of the minor children of the parties by order of court or written agreement of the parties, the custody shall not be disturbed or changed unless the court finds that the defendant is likely to inflict abuse upon the children or to remove the children from the jurisdiction of the court prior to the hearing under section 6107(a). Where the defendant has forcibly or fraudulently removed any minor child from the care and custody of a plaintiff, the court shall order the return of the child to the plaintiff unless the child would be endangered by restoration to the plaintiff.

(v) Nothing in this paragraph shall bar either party from filing a petition for custody under Chapter 53 (relating to custody) or under the Pennsylvania Rules of Civil Procedure.

(vi) In order to prevent further abuse during periods of access to the plaintiff and child during the exercise of custodial rights, the court shall consider, and may impose on a custody award, conditions necessary to assure the safety of the plaintiff and minor children from abuse.

(5) After a hearing in accordance with section 6107(a), directing the defendant to pay financial support to those persons the defendant has a duty to support, requiring the defendant, under sections 4324 (relating to inclusion of medical support) and 4326 (relating to mandatory inclusion of child medical support), to provide health coverage for the minor child and spouse, directing the defendant to pay all of the unreimbursed medical expenses of a spouse or minor child of the defendant to the provider or to the plaintiff when he or she has paid for the medical treatment, and directing the defendant to make or continue to make rent or mortgage payments on the residence of the plaintiff to the extent that the defendant has a duty to support the plaintiff or other dependent household members. The support order shall be temporary, and any beneficiary of the order must file a complaint for support under the provisions of Chapters 43 (relating to support matters generally) and 45 (relating to reciprocal enforcement of support orders) within two weeks of the date of the issuance of the protection order. If a complaint for support is not filed, that portion of the protection order requiring the defendant to pay support is void. When there is a subsequent ruling on a complaint for support, the portion of the protection order requiring the defendant to pay support expires.

(6) Prohibiting the defendant from having any contact with the plaintiff or minor children, including, but not limited to, restraining the defendant from entering the place of employment or business or school of the plaintiff or minor children and from harassing the plaintiff or plaintiff's relatives or minor children.

(7) Prohibiting the defendant from acquiring or possessing any firearm for the duration of the order, ordering the defendant to temporarily relinquish to the sheriff or the appropriate law enforcement agency any firearms under the defendant's possession or control, and requiring the defendant to relinquish to the sheriff or the appropriate law enforcement agency any firearm license issued under section 6108.3 (relating to relinquishment to third party for safekeeping) or 18 Pa.C.S. § 6106 (relating to firearms not to be carried without a license) or 6109 (relating to licenses) the defendant may possess. The court may also order the defendant to relinquish the defendant's other weapons or ammunition that have been used or been threatened to be used in an incident of abuse against the plaintiff or the minor children. A copy of the court's order shall be transmitted to the chief or head of the appropriate law enforcement agency and to the sheriff of the county of which the defendant is a resident. When relinquishment is ordered, the following shall apply:

(i) (A) The court's order shall require the defendant to relinquish such firearms, other weapons, ammunition and any firearm license pursuant to the provisions of this chapter within 24 hours of service of a temporary order or the entry of a final order or the close of the next business day as necessary by closure of the sheriffs' offices, except for cause shown at the hearing, in which case the court shall specify the time for relinquishment of any or all of the defendant's firearms.

(B) A defendant subject to a temporary order requiring the relinquishment of firearms, other weapons or ammunition shall, in lieu of relinquishing specific firearms, other weapons or ammunition which cannot reasonably be retrieved within the time for relinquishment in clause (A) due to their current location, provide the sheriff or the appropriate law enforcement agency with an affidavit listing the firearms, other weapons or ammunition and their current location. If the defendant, within the time for relinquishment in clause (A), fails to provide the affidavit or fails to relinquish, pursuant to this chapter, any firearms, other weapons or ammunition ordered to be relinquished which are not specified in the affidavit, the sheriff or the appropriate law enforcement agency shall, at a minimum, provide immediate notice to the court, the plaintiff and appropriate law enforcement authorities. The defendant shall not possess any firearms, other weapons or ammunition specifically listed in the affidavit provided to the sheriff or the appropriate law enforcement agency pursuant to this clause for the duration of the temporary order.

(C) As used in this subparagraph, the term "cause" shall be limited to facts relating to the inability of the defendant to retrieve a specific firearm within 24 hours due to the current location of the firearm.

(ii) The court's order shall contain a list of any firearm, other weapon or ammunition ordered relinquished. Upon the entry of a final order, the defendant shall inform the court in what manner the defendant is going to relinquish any firearm, other weapon or ammunition ordered relinquished. Relinquishment may occur pursuant to section 6108.2 (relating to relinquishment for consignment sale, lawful transfer or safekeeping) or 6108.3 or to the sheriff or the appropriate law enforcement agency pursuant to this paragraph. Where the sheriff or the appropriate law enforcement agency is designated, the sheriff or the appropriate law enforcement agency shall secure custody of the defendant's firearms, other weapons or ammunition and any firearm license listed in the court's order for the duration of the order or until otherwise directed by court order. In securing custody of the defendant's relinquished firearms, the sheriff or the appropriate law enforcement agency shall comply with 18 Pa.C.S. § 6105(f)(4) (relating to persons not to possess, use, manufacture, control, sell or transfer firearms). In securing custody of the defendant's other weapons and ammunition, the sheriff or the appropriate law enforcement agency shall provide the defendant with a signed and dated written receipt which shall include a detailed description of the other weapon or ammunition and its condition. The court shall inform the defendant that firearms, other weapons or ammunition shall be deemed abandoned when the conditions under 18 Pa.C.S. § 6128(a) (relating to abandonment of firearms, weapons or ammunition) are satisfied and may then be disposed of in accordance with 18 Pa.C.S. § 6128.

(iii) The sheriff or the appropriate law enforcement agency shall provide the plaintiff with the name of the person to which any firearm, other weapon or ammunition was relinquished.

(iv) Unless the defendant has complied with subparagraph (i)(B) or section 6108.2 or 6108.3, if the defendant fails to relinquish any firearm, other weapon, ammunition or firearm license within 24 hours or upon the close of the next business day due to closure of sheriffs' or appropriate law enforcement agencies' offices or within the time ordered by the court upon cause being shown at the hearing, the sheriff or the appropriate law enforcement agency shall, at a minimum, provide immediate notice to the court, the plaintiff and appropriate law enforcement agencies, as appropriate.

(v) Any portion of any order or any petition or other paper which includes a list of any firearm, other weapon or ammunition ordered relinquished shall be kept in the files of the court as a permanent record thereof and withheld from public inspection except:

(A) upon an order of the court granted upon cause shown;

(B) as necessary, by law enforcement and court personnel; or

(C) after redaction of information listing any firearm, other weapon or ammunition.

(vi) As used in this paragraph, the term "defendant's firearms" shall, if the defendant is a licensed firearms dealer, only include firearms in the defendant's personal firearms collection pursuant to 27 CFR § 478.125a (relating to personal firearms collection).

(7.1) If the defendant is a licensed firearms dealer, ordering the defendant to follow such restrictions as the court may require concerning the conduct of his business, which may include ordering the defendant to relinquish any Federal or State license for the sale, manufacture or importation of firearms as well as firearms in the defendant's business inventory. In restricting the defendant pursuant to this paragraph, the court shall make a reasonable effort to preserve the financial assets of the defendant's business while fulfilling the goals of this chapter.

(8) Directing the defendant to pay the plaintiff for reasonable losses suffered as a result of the abuse, including medical, dental, relocation and moving expenses; counseling; loss of earnings or support; costs of repair or replacement of real or personal property damaged, destroyed or taken by the defendant or at the direction of the defendant; and other out-of-pocket losses for injuries sustained. In addition to out-of-pocket losses, the court may direct the defendant to pay reasonable attorney fees. An award under this chapter shall not constitute a bar to litigation for civil damages for injuries sustained from the acts of abuse giving rise to the award or a finding of contempt under this chapter.

(9) Directing the defendant to refrain from stalking or harassing the plaintiff and other designated persons as defined in 18 Pa.C.S. §§ 2709 (relating to harassment) and 2709.1 (relating to stalking).

(10) Granting any other appropriate relief sought by the plaintiff.

(a.1) Final order or agreement.—The following apply:

(1) Any final order must direct the defendant to refrain from abusing, harassing, stalking, threatening or attempting or threatening to use physical force against the plaintiff or minor children and must order that the defendant is subject to the firearms, other weapons or ammunition and firearms license prohibition relinquishment provisions under subsection (a)(7).

(2) A final agreement may direct the defendant to refrain from abusing, harassing, stalking, threatening or attempting or threatening to use physical force against the plaintiff or minor children and may order that the defendant is subject to the firearms, other weapons or ammunition and firearms license prohibition and relinquishment provisions under subsection (a)(7).

(b) Identifying information.—Any order issued under this section shall, where furnished by either party, specify the Social Security number and date of birth of the defendant.

(c) Mutual orders of protection.—Mutual orders of protection shall not be awarded unless both parties have filed timely written petitions, complied with service requirements under section 6106 (relating to commencement of proceedings) and are eligible for protection under this chapter. The court shall make separate findings and, where issuing orders on behalf of both petitioners, enter separate orders.

(d) Duration and amendment of order or agreement.—A protection order or approved consent agreement shall be for a fixed period of time not to exceed three years. The court may amend its order or agreement at any time upon subsequent petition filed by either party.

(e) Extension of protection orders.—

(1) An extension of a protection order may be granted:

(i) Where the court finds, after a duly filed petition, notice to the defendant and a hearing, in accordance with the procedures set forth in sections 6106 and 6107, that the defendant committed one or more acts of abuse subsequent to the entry of the final order or that the defendant engaged in a pattern or practice that indicates continued risk of harm to the plaintiff or minor child.

(ii) When a contempt petition or charge has been filed with the court or with a hearing officer in Philadelphia County, but the hearing has not occurred before the expiration of the protection order, the order shall be extended, at a minimum, until the disposition of the contempt petition and may be extended for another term beyond the disposition of the contempt petition.

(iii) If the plaintiff files a petition for an extension of the order and the defendant is or was incarcerated and will be released from custody in the next 90 days or has been released from custody within the past 90 days. The plaintiff does not need to show that the defendant committed one or more acts of abuse subsequent to the entry of the order or that the defendant engaged in a pattern or practice that indicates continued risk of harm to the plaintiff or minor children as set forth in subparagraph (i).

(2) Service of an extended order shall be made in accordance with section 6109 (relating to service of orders).

(3) There shall be no limitation on the number of extensions that may be granted.

(f) Support procedure.—The domestic relations section shall enforce any support award in a protection order where the plaintiff files a complaint for support under subsection (a)(5).

(g) Notice.—Notice shall be given to the defendant, in orders issued under this section, stating that violations of an order will subject the defendant to arrest under section 6113 (relating to arrest for violation of order) or contempt of court under section 6114 (relating to contempt for violation of order or agreement). Resumption of coresidency on the part of the plaintiff and defendant shall not nullify the provisions of the court order.

(h) Title to real property unaffected.—No order or agreement under this chapter shall in any manner affect title to any real property.

(i) Third parties and affidavits.—A court requiring relinquishment of firearms under this section shall provide for the hearing of petitions by third parties who request the return of a firearm relinquished by the defendant under subsection (a)(7). The following apply:

(1) A third party claiming to be the lawful owner of a firearm relinquished by the defendant under subsection (a)(7) may request the return of the firearm by providing proof of ownership and a sworn affidavit.

(2) The affidavit under paragraph (1) must affirm all of the following:

(i) The third party who is the lawful owner will not intentionally or knowingly return to the defendant the firearm or allow access to the firearm by the defendant.

(ii) The third party who is the lawful owner understands that violating subparagraph (i) constitutes a misdemeanor of the second degree under 18 Pa.C.S. Ch. 61 (relating to firearms and other dangerous articles).

(iii) If the third party who is the lawful owner is a family or household member of the defendant, any firearm returned under this section must be stored in a gun safe to which the defendant does not have access and will not be permitted to access, or stored in a location outside the third party's home to which the defendant does not have access.

(3) If the court orders the return of a firearm under this section, prior to the return of the firearm, the sheriff shall independently confirm that the person seeking relief under this section is legally eligible to possess firearms under Federal and State law. The sheriff shall conduct the background check as soon as practicable after the court enters an order under this section.

(June 23, 1993, P.L.124, No.28, eff. imd.; Oct. 6, 1994, P.L.574, No.85, eff. 60 days; Dec. 16, 1997, P.L.549, No.58, eff. 60 days; May 10, 2000, P.L.35, No.10, eff. imd.; Dec. 9, 2002, P.L.1759, No.218, eff. 60 days; Nov. 10, 2005, P.L.335, No.66, eff. 180 days; Oct. 12, 2018, P.L.519, No.79, eff. 180 days)

> **2018 Amendment.** Act 79 amended subsec. (a) intro. par. and (7) and added subsecs. (a.1), (e)(1)(iii) and (i). Act 79 shall apply to orders issued pursuant to 23 Pa.C.S. § 6108 on or after the effective date of section 11 of Act 79.
>
> **References in Text.** Chapter 45, referred to in subsec. (a)(5), was repealed by the act of April 4, 1996, P.L.58, No.20. The subject matter is now contained in Parts VIII and VIII-A of this title.
>
> Former Chapter 53 (Custody), referred to in this section, is repealed. The subject matter is now contained in Chapter 53 (Child Custody).
>
> **Cross References.** Section 6108 is referred to in sections 6105, 6107, 6108.2, 6108.3, 6108.5, 6108.7, 6110, 6113, 6117, 6120, 6303, 6711 of this title; sections 2709, 2709.1, 6105, 6106, 6128 of Title 18 (Crimes and Offenses).

§ 6108.1. Return of relinquished firearms, other weapons and ammunition and additional relief.

(a) **General rule.**—Any court order requiring the relinquishment of firearms, other weapons or ammunition shall provide for the return of the relinquished firearms, other weapons or ammunition to the defendant upon expiration of the order or dismissal of a petition for a protection from abuse order. The defendant may take custody of the firearms, other weapons and ammunition provided that the defendant is otherwise eligible to lawfully possess the relinquished items. The defendant shall not be required to pay any fees, costs or charges associated with the returns, whether those fees, costs or charges are imposed by the Pennsylvania State Police, any local law enforcement agency or any other entity, including a licensed importer, licensed manufacturer or licensed dealer in order to secure return of the relinquished firearms, other weapons or ammunition. The sheriff's or the appropriate law enforcement agency's office shall maintain a weapons return form that the defendant may fill out and return to the office once a temporary or final protection from abuse order has been dismissed or expires.

(a.1) **Conditions for return.**—The following conditions must be satisfied prior to the firearms, other weapons or ammunition being returned to the defendant:

(1) The firearms, other weapons or ammunition relinquished must not be evidence of a crime.

(2) The defendant or owner must not be otherwise prohibited by applicable Federal or State law, or another condition, including, but not limited to, bail, from taking possession of the firearms, other weapons or ammunition seized.

(3) The defendant or owner must have been given a clearance by the Pennsylvania State Police Instant Check System Unit or through the National Instant Criminal Background Check System (NICS), requested by the sheriff's office.

(a.2) **Notice to plaintiff.**—The plaintiff of the protection from abuse order shall be notified of the defendant's request to return the firearms, other weapons or ammunition.

(a.3) **Petition for return.**—If there is a determination under subsection (a.1) that the defendant is ineligible to regain possession of the firearms, other weapons or ammunition, the defendant or owner may file a petition appealing that determination and seeking their return. A copy of the petition must be served upon the plaintiff, sheriff and the district attorney.

(a.4) **Abandonment.**—Any firearms, other weapons or ammunition shall be deemed abandoned when the conditions under 18 Pa.C.S. § 6128(a) (relating to abandonment of firearms, weapons or ammunition) are satisfied and may then be disposed of in accordance with 18 Pa.C.S. § 6128.

(b) **Modification of court's order providing for return of relinquished firearm, other weapon or ammunition.**—Any other person may petition the court to allow for the return of that other person's firearms, other weapons and ammunition prior to the expiration of the court's order. The petition shall be served upon the plaintiff, and the plaintiff shall be given notice and an opportunity to be heard regarding that petition.

(1) (Deleted by amendment).

(2) (Deleted by amendment).

(c) Modification of court's order to provide for alternative means of relinquishing firearms, other weapons or ammunition.—The defendant may petition the court for modification of the order to provide for an alternative means of relinquishment in accordance with this chapter. The petition shall be served upon the plaintiff, and the plaintiff shall have an opportunity to be heard at the hearing as provided in subsection (d). Where the court orders a modification pursuant to this subsection providing for alternative means of relinquishment, the sheriff shall proceed as directed by the court.

(d) Hearing.—Within ten business days of the filing of any petition under this section, a hearing shall be held before the court.

(e) Definitions.—As used in this section, the following words and phrases shall have the meanings given to them in this subsection:

"**Other person.**" Any person, except the defendant, who is the lawful owner of a firearm, other weapon or ammunition relinquished pursuant to this chapter.

"**Safekeeping.**" The secure custody of a firearm, other weapon or ammunition ordered relinquished by an active protection from abuse order.

(Nov. 10, 2005, P.L.335, No.66, eff. 180 days; Oct. 12, 2018, P.L.519, No.79, eff. 180 days)

2018 Amendment. Act 79 amended subsecs. (a) and (b) and added subsecs. (a.1), (a.2), (a.3) and (a.4). Act 79 shall apply to orders issued pursuant to 23 Pa.C.S. § 6108 on or after the effective date of section 11 of Act 79.

2005 Amendment. Act 66 added section 6108.1.

Cross References. Section 6108.1 is referred to in section 6108.3 of this title; section 6105 of Title 18 (Crimes and Offenses).

§ 6108.2. Relinquishment for consignment sale, lawful transfer or safekeeping

(a) General rule.—Notwithstanding any other provision of law, a defendant who is the subject of a final protection from abuse order, which order provides for the relinquishment of firearms, other weapons or ammunition during the period of time the order is in effect, may, within the time frame specified in the order and in lieu of relinquishment to the sheriff or the appropriate law enforcement agency, relinquish to a dealer licensed pursuant to 18 Pa.C.S. § 6113 (relating to licensing of dealers) any firearms, other weapons or ammunition for consignment sale, lawful transfer or safekeeping. The dealer may charge the defendant a reasonable fee for accepting relinquishment and for storage of any firearms, other weapons or ammunition.

(b) Affidavit.—A defendant relinquishing firearms, other weapons or ammunition to a dealer pursuant to subsection (a) shall obtain an affidavit from the dealer on a form prescribed by the Pennsylvania State Police which shall include, at a minimum, the following:

(1) The caption of the case in which the protection from abuse order was issued.

(2) The name, address, date of birth and Social Security number of the defendant.

(3) A list of the firearms, other weapons or ammunition, including, if applicable, the manufacturer, model and serial number.

(4) The name and license number of the dealer licensed pursuant to 18 Pa.C.S. § 6113 and the address of the licensed premises.

(5) An acknowledgment that the firearms, other weapons or ammunition will not be returned to the defendant or sold or transferred to a person the dealer knows is a member of the defendant's household, while the defendant is the subject of an active protection from abuse order pursuant to section 6108, which order provides for the relinquishment of the firearm, other weapon or ammunition being returned, sold or transferred.

(6) An acknowledgment that the firearms, other weapons or ammunition, if sold or transferred, will be sold or lawfully transferred in compliance with 18 Pa.C.S. Ch. 61 (relating to firearms and other dangerous articles).

(c) Failure to provide affidavit.—A defendant relinquishing firearms, other weapons or ammunition to a dealer pursuant to subsection (a) shall, within the time frame specified in the order for relinquishing firearms, other weapons or ammunition, provide to the sheriff the affidavit obtained pursuant to subsection (b) and relinquish to the sheriff any firearms, other weapons or ammunition ordered to be relinquished which are not specified in the affidavit, in an affidavit provided in accordance with section 6108(a)(7)(i)(B) (relating to relief) or in an acknowledgment of receipt from a third party provided to the sheriff pursuant to section 6108.3 (relating to relinquishment to third party for safekeeping). If the defendant fails to comply with this subsection, the sheriff shall, at a minimum, provide immediate notice to the court, the plaintiff and appropriate law enforcement agencies.

(d) Form.—The Pennsylvania State Police shall develop and make available a form to be used by dealers to accept possession of firearms, other weapons and ammunition for consignment sale, lawful transfer or safekeeping pursuant to this section.

(e) Transfer upon entry of final order.—Upon entry of a final protection from abuse order issued pursuant to section 6108, a defendant who had relinquished firearms, other weapons or ammunition to the sheriff pursuant to a temporary order may request that the firearms, other weapons or ammunition be relinquished to a dealer for consignment sale, lawful transfer or safekeeping pursuant to this section. If the defendant can identify a licensed dealer willing to accept the firearms, other weapons or ammunition in compliance with this section, the court shall order the sheriff to transport the firearms, other weapons or ammunition to the licensed dealer at no cost to the defendant or the licensed dealer.

(f) Nondisclosure.—The affidavit obtained under subsection (c) shall not be subject to access under the act of June 21, 1957 (P.L. 390, No. 212), referred to as the Right-to-Know Law.

(g) Definitions.—As used in this section, the following words and phrases shall have the meanings given to them in this subsection:

"Safekeeping." The secure custody of firearms, other weapons or ammunition ordered relinquished by an active protection from abuse order.

"Sale or lawful transfer." Any sale or transfer to a person other than the defendant or a member of the defendant's household which is conducted in accordance with 18 Pa.C.S. Ch. 61 (relating to firearms and other dangerous articles).

2018 Amendment. Act 79 amended subsecs. (a) and (e).

2005 Amendment. Act 66 added sec. § 6108.2.

Cross References. Section 6108.2 is referred to in sections 6108, 6108.3 of this title; sections 6105, 6106 of Title 18.

§ 6108.3. Relinquishment to third party for safekeeping.

(a) General rule.—A defendant who is the subject of a protection from abuse order, which order provides for the relinquishment of firearms, other weapons or ammunition during the period of time the order is in effect, may, within the time frame specified in the order and in lieu of relinquishment to the sheriff, relinquish any firearms, other weapons or ammunition for safekeeping to a third party who meets the requirements of a third party under subsection (b)(3).

(b) Transfer to third party.—

(1) A defendant wishing to relinquish firearms, other weapons or ammunition to a third party pursuant to subsection (a) shall, within the time frame specified in the order for relinquishing firearms, other weapons and ammunition, report to the sheriff's office in the county where the order was entered along with the third party.

(2) Upon determination by the sheriff that the third party is not prohibited from possessing firearms, other weapons or ammunition pursuant to any Federal or State law and after the defendant and third party have executed the affidavits required under paragraph (3), the sheriff shall issue a safekeeping permit to the third party, which shall include, at a minimum, a list of the firearms, other weapons and ammunition which will be relinquished to the third party. The permit shall be issued at no cost to the third party or defendant. The permit shall require the third party to possess the defendant's firearms, other weapons and ammunition until the time that:

(i) the sheriff revokes the safekeeping permit pursuant to subsection (c)(1); or

(ii) the sheriff accepts return of the safekeeping permit pursuant to subsection (d).

(3) (i) A defendant wishing to relinquish firearms, other weapons or ammunition to a third party pursuant to subsection (a) shall, in the presence of the sheriff or the sheriff's designee, execute an affidavit on a form prescribed by the Pennsylvania State Police which shall include, at a minimum, the following:

(A) The caption of the case in which the protection from abuse order was issued.

(B) The name, address, date of birth and the Social Security number of the defendant.

(C) The name, address and date of birth of the third party.

(D) A list of the firearms, other weapons and ammunition which will be relinquished to the third party, including, if applicable, the manufacturer, model and serial number.

(E) An acknowledgment that the defendant will not take possession of any firearm, other weapon or ammunition relinquished to the third party until the sheriff accepts return of the safekeeping permit pursuant to subsection (d).

(F) A plain-language summary of 18 Pa.C.S. § 6105(a.1)(2) and (c)(6) (relating to persons not to possess, use, manufacture, control, sell or transfer firearms).

(G) A plain-language summary of 18 U.S.C. § 922(g)(8) (relating to unlawful acts).

(ii) A third party who will be accepting possession of firearms, other weapons and ammunition pursuant to subsection (a) shall, in the presence of the sheriff or the sheriff's designee, execute an affidavit on a form prescribed by the Pennsylvania State Police which shall include, at a minimum, the following:

(A) The caption of the case in which the protection from abuse order was issued.

(B) The name, address and date of birth of the defendant.

(C) The name, address, date of birth and the Social Security number of the third party.

(D) A list of the firearms, other weapons and ammunition which will be relinquished to the third party, including, if applicable, the manufacturer, model and serial number.

(E) An acknowledgment that no firearm, other weapon or ammunition relinquished to the third party will be returned to the defendant until the sheriff accepts return of the safekeeping permit pursuant to subsection (d).

(F) A plain-language summary of 18 Pa.C.S. §§ 6105(a.1)(5) and (c)(6), 6111(c) (relating to sale or transfer of firearms) and 6115 (relating to loans on, or lending or giving firearms prohibited).

(G) A plain-language summary of this section.

(H) An acknowledgment that the third party is not prohibited from possessing firearms, other weapons or ammunition pursuant to any Federal or State law.

(I) An acknowledgment that the third party is not subject to an active protection from abuse order.

(J) An acknowledgment that the defendant has never been the subject of a protection from abuse order issued on behalf of the third party.

(K) An acknowledgment that any firearms, other weapons and ammunition relinquished to the third party will be stored using a locking device as defined in paragraph (1) of the definition of "locking device" in 18 Pa.C.S. § 6142(f) (relating to locking device for firearms) or in a secure location to which the defendant does not have access.

(L) A detailed description of the third party liability pursuant to this section relating to civil liability.

(M) An acknowledgment that the third party shall inform the sheriff of any change of address for the third party within seven days of the change of address.

(N) An acknowledgment that the third party and the defendant are not family or household members.

(O) An acknowledgment that the third party is one of the following:

(I) An attorney at law, and further acknowledgment that the attorney at law and the defendant are in an attorney-client relationship. The attorney at law and the defendant shall sign a written agreement stating in substantially the following form: "Firearm(s) can be relinquished to the attorney at law upon the express, written condition that firearm(s) will be returned to the defendant, or otherwise transferred, only if in strict conformance with applicable law."

(II) A commercial armory, and further acknowledgment that the owner or operator of the commercial armory is not a family or household member of the defendant; the commercial armory is a secure storage facility designed to store firearms; the commercial armory possesses all Federal and State licenses to store firearms; and a form stating substantially the following: "Firearms can be relinquished to the commercial armory upon the express, written condition that firearm(s) will be returned, or transferred, to the defendant only in strict conformance with applicable law."

(4) The defendant shall, within the time frame specified in the order and in lieu of relinquishment to the sheriff, relinquish the firearms, other weapons and ammunition specified in the affidavits provided to the sheriff pursuant to paragraph (3) to the third party who has been issued a safekeeping permit pursuant to paragraph (2). Upon relinquishment of the firearms to the third party, the third party shall sign an acknowledgment of receipt on a form prescribed by the Pennsylvania State Police, which shall include, at a minimum, an acknowledgment that the firearms were relinquished to the third party within the time frame specified in the order.

(5) Within 24 hours of the issuance of the safekeeping permit issued to the third party pursuant to paragraph (2) or by close of the next business day as necessary

due to the closure of the sheriff's office, the defendant shall return the signed acknowledgment of receipt required under paragraph (4) to the sheriff in the county where the order was entered.

(6) If the defendant fails to provide the acknowledgment of receipt to the sheriff as required under paragraph (5), an affidavit prepared in accordance with section 6108(a)(7)(i)(B) (relating to relief), an affidavit under section 6108.2 (relating to relinquishment for consignment sale, lawful transfer or safekeeping) or fails to relinquish any firearms, other weapons or ammunition, the sheriff shall, at a minimum, provide immediate notice to the court, the plaintiff and appropriate law enforcement agencies.

(c) Revocation of safekeeping permit.—

(1) The sheriff shall revoke a third party's safekeeping permit and require the third party to relinquish to the sheriff any firearms, other weapons or ammunition which were relinquished to the third party by a defendant pursuant to subsection (a) upon determining or being notified that any of the following apply:

(i) A protection from abuse order has been entered against the third party.

(ii) The third party is prohibited from possessing firearms, other weapons or ammunition pursuant to any Federal or State law.

(iii) The defendant has been convicted of a violation of 18 Pa.C.S. Ch. 61 (relating to firearms and other dangerous articles) or any other offense involving the use of a firearm.

(iv) The defendant has been held in indirect criminal contempt for violating a provision of the protection from abuse order consistent with section 6108(a)(1), (2), (6), (7) or (9) (relating to relief).

(2) Upon revocation of a safekeeping permit, the sheriff shall seize the safekeeping permit and all of the defendant's firearms, other weapons and ammunition which were relinquished to the third party. If revocation of the safekeeping permit was:

(i) Required pursuant to paragraph (1)(i) or (ii), the sheriff shall notify the defendant that the firearms, other weapons and ammunition which were relinquished to the third party are in the sheriff's possession and that the defendant may report to the sheriff's office in order to relinquish the firearms, other weapons and ammunition to a subsequent third party pursuant to this section or to a licensed dealer pursuant to section 6108.2.

(ii) Required pursuant to paragraph (1)(iii) or (iv), the sheriff shall maintain possession of the firearms, other weapons and ammunition until the defendant is no longer prohibited from possessing firearms, other weapons and ammunition pursuant to any Federal or State law unless:

(A) the defendant has the firearms, other weapons and ammunition relinquished to a licensed dealer pursuant to section 6108.2; or

(B) the sheriff is directed to relinquish the firearms, other weapons and ammunition pursuant to a court order.

(d) Return of safekeeping permit.—

(1) Following expiration of a protection from abuse order, which order provided for the relinquishment of firearms, other weapons or ammunition, the defendant and the third party shall report to the sheriff's office to return the safekeeping permit. Upon a determination by the sheriff that the defendant is:

(i) Not prohibited from possessing firearms, other weapons and ammunition, the sheriff shall accept the return of the safekeeping permit, and the third party shall relinquish to the defendant all of the defendant's firearms, other weapons and ammunition which were relinquished to the third party pursuant to this section.

(ii) Prohibited from possessing a firearm, other weapon or ammunition pursuant to any Federal or State law, the sheriff shall accept return of the permit and seize from the third party all of the defendant's firearms, other weapons and ammunition which were relinquished to the third party pursuant to this section. The sheriff shall return to the defendant any firearm, other weapon or ammunition which the defendant is lawfully entitled to possess.

(2) Upon issuance of a court order pursuant to 18 Pa.C.S. §§ 6105(f)(2) or 6108.1(b) (relating to return of relinquished firearms, other weapons and ammunition and additional relief) which modifies a valid protection from abuse order by allowing the defendant to take possession of a firearm, other weapon or ammunition that had previously been ordered relinquished, the defendant and the third party shall report to the sheriff's office to return the safekeeping permit. The sheriff shall proceed as directed by the court order.

(3) If a third party wishes to relinquish the defendant's firearms, other weapons and ammunition prior to return of the safekeeping permit pursuant to paragraph (1), the sheriff shall accept return of the safekeeping permit and shall seize all of the defendant's firearms, other weapons and ammunition from the third party. The sheriff shall notify the defendant that the firearms, other weapons and ammunition which were relinquished to the third party are in the sheriff's possession and that the defendant may relinquish the firearms, other weapons and ammunition to a subsequent third party pursuant to this section or to a licensed dealer pursuant to section 6108.2.

(e) **Civil liability.**—A third party who intentionally or knowingly violates any of the provisions of this section shall, in addition to any other penalty prescribed in this chapter or 18 Pa.C.S. Ch. 61, be civilly liable to any person for any damages caused thereby and, in addition, shall be liable to any person for punitive damages in an amount not to exceed $5,000, and the court shall award a prevailing plaintiff a reasonable attorney fee as part of the costs.

(f) **Forms.**—The Pennsylvania State Police shall develop and make available:

(1) Forms to be used by sheriffs to issue safekeeping permits pursuant to subsection (b)(2).

(2) Affidavit forms and receipt forms to be used by defendants and third parties as required under subsection (b)(3) and (4).

(g) **Transfer upon final entry.**—A defendant who has previously relinquished firearms, other weapons or ammunition to the sheriff pursuant to a temporary order shall be permitted to have the firearms, other weapons and ammunition relinquished to a third party pursuant to this section following entry of a final protection from abuse order, which order provides for the relinquishment of firearms, other weapons or ammunition during the period of time the order is in effect.

(h) **Nondisclosure.**—All copies of the safekeeping permit issued under subsection (b)(2) retained by the sheriff and the affidavits and forms obtained under subsection (b)(3) and (4) shall not be subject to access under the act of June 21, 1957 (P.L.390, No.212), referred to as the Right-to-Know Law.

(i) **Definitions.**—As used in this section, the following words and phrases shall have the meanings given to them in this subsection:

"Safekeeping." The secure custody of firearms, other weapons or ammunition which were ordered relinquished by an active protection from abuse order.

"Third party." A person, other than the defendant, who:

(1) Is not a member of the defendant's household.

(2) Is not prohibited from possessing firearms pursuant to any Federal or State law.

(Nov. 10, 2005, P.L.335, No.66, eff. 180 days; Oct. 12, 2018, P.L.519, No.79, eff. 180 days)

2018 Amendment. Act 79 amended subsec. (a) and added susbsec. (b)(3)(ii)(N) and (O). Act 79 shall apply to orders issued pursuant to 23 Pa.C.S. § 6108 on or after the effective date of section 11 of Act 79.

2005 Amendment. Act 66 added section 6108.3.

References in Text. The act of June 21, 1957 (P.L.390, No.212), referred to as the Right-to-Know Law, referred to in subsec. (h), was repealed by the act of February 14, 2008 (P.L.6, No.3), known as the Right-to-Know Law.

Cross References. Section 6108.3 is referred to in sections 6107, 6108, 6108.2 of this title; sections 6105, 6105.2, 6106, 6115 of Title 18 (Crimes and Offenses).

§ 6108.4. Registry or database of firearm ownership

(a) **Confidentiality.**—Information retained to ensure compliance with this chapter and to document the return of firearms shall not be subject to access under the act of June 21, 1957 (P.L. 390, No. 212), referred to as the Right-to-Know Law.

2018 Amendment. Act 79 added this section.

(b) **Construction.**—Nothing in this chapter shall be construed to allow a government agency or law enforcement agency, or an agent or employee of either, or any other person or entity to create, maintain or operate a database or registry of firearm ownership within this Commonwealth. However, information may be retained to ensure compliance with this chapter and to document the return of firearms.

2005 Amendment. Act 66 added sec. § 6108.4.

§ 6108.5. Penalties for release of information

Any person who violates section 6108(a)(7)(v) (relating to relief) by releasing information with the intent and purpose of committing such violation commits a misdemeanor of the third degree.

2005 Amendment. Act 66 added sec. § 6108.5.

§ 6108.6. Penalty for failure to secure firearms.

In addition to any other penalty provided by 18 Pa.C.S. Ch. 61 subch. A (relating to uniform firearms act), a commercial armory which violates the provisions of this chapter regarding safekeeping shall forfeit all federal and state licenses related to firearms.

2018 Amendment. Act 79 added this section.

§ 6108.7. Order to seal record from public view.

(a) **General rule.**—Notwithstanding any other provision of this chapter, an individual who has entered into a consent agreement approved by the court under section 6108(a) (relating to relief) may petition the court for an order to seal the record of the of the individual from public view. The court may grant the order if the petitioner proves all of the following by clear and convincing evidence:

(1) The consent agreement for which the individual seeks relief under this section is the only such consent agreement to which the individual has ever been subject, and that, during the period in which the consent agreement was in effect, the individual did not violate an order or consent agreement under section 6108.

(2) A period of at least 10 years has elapsed since the expiration of the consent agreement.

(3) The individual has not been subject to another final protection from abuse order under section 6108.

(4) The individual has not been convicted of one of the following offenses where the victim is a family or household member:

(i) An offense set forth in 18 Pa.C.S. § 2711 (relating to probable cause arrests in domestic violence cases).

(ii) An offense equivalent to subparagraph (i) under the laws of the united states or one of its territories or possessions, another state, the District of Columbia, the commonwealth of Puerto Rico or a foreign nation.

(b) **Notice to District Attorney and plaintiff.—**

(1) The petitioner shall serve a copy of the petition under subsection (a) to the district attorney and to the plaintiff within 10 days of the filing of the petition.

(2) The district attorney and the plaintiff shall have an opportunity to be heard at the hearing.

(3) Within 30 days of receipt of notice, the district attorney or plaintiff may file objections to the petition.

(4) If no objection under paragraph (3) is timely filed, the court may grant the petition without further hearing if the requirements of this section have been met.

(5) As used in this subsection, the term "plaintiff" means the person who entered into the consent agreement with the defendant.

(c) **Notice to Prothonotary.**—Notice of an order to seal the individual's record from public view shall promptly be submitted to the prothonotary of the county holding the record. The prothonotary may not permit a member of the public from accessing the individual's record regarding the consent agreement. Nothing in this section shall be construed to limit access of the record of the individual by a criminal justice agency as defined in 18 Pa.C.S. § 9102 (relating to definitions).

2018 Amendment. Act 79 added this section.

§ 6109. Service of orders.

(a) **Issuance.**—A copy of an order under this chapter shall be issued to the plaintiff, the defendant and the police department with appropriate jurisdiction to enforce the order or agreement in accordance with the provisions of this chapter or as ordered by the court or hearing officer.

(b) **Placement in registry.**—Upon receipt of an order, the police department shall immediately place the order in a county registry of protection orders. The police department shall assure that the registry is current at all times and that orders are removed upon expiration thereof. County registries shall not be required when the Pennsylvania State Police registry provided for in section 6105(e) (relating to responsibilities of law enforcement agencies) is established and is fully operational.

1994 Amendment. Act 85 amended subsec. (b).

Cross References. Section 6109 is referred to in section 6108 of this title.

§ 6110. Emergency relief by minor judiciary.

(a) **General rule.**—When:

(1) in counties with less than four judges, the court is unavailable:

(i) from the close of business at the end of each day to the resumption of business the next morning;

(ii) from the end of the business week to the beginning of the business week; and

(iii) during the business day by reason of duties outside the county, illness or vacation;

(2) in counties with at least four judges, the court is unavailable:

(i) from the close of business at the end of each day to the resumption of business the next morning; and

(ii) from the end of the business week to the beginning of the business week;

a petition may be filed before a hearing officer who may grant relief in accordance with section 6108(a)(1), (2) and (6) or (1) and (6) (relating to relief) if the hearing officer deems it necessary to protect the plaintiff or minor children from abuse upon good cause shown in an ex parte proceeding. Immediate and present danger of abuse to the plaintiff or minor children shall constitute good cause for the purposes of this subsection.

(b) **Expiration of order.**—An order issued under subsection (a) shall expire at the end of the next business day the court deems itself available. The court shall schedule hearings on protection orders entered by hearing officers under subsection (a) and shall review and continue in effect protection orders that are necessary to protect the plaintiff or minor children from abuse until the hearing, at which time the plaintiff may seek a temporary order from the court.

(c) **Certification of order to court.**—An emergency order issued under this section and any documentation in support thereof shall be immediately certified to the court. The certification to the court shall have the effect of commencing proceedings under section 6106 (relating to commencement of proceedings) and invoking the other provisions of this chapter. If it is not already alleged in a petition for any emergency order, the plaintiff shall file a verified statement setting forth the abuse of defendant at least five days prior to the hearing. Service of the verified statement shall be made subject to section 6106.

(d) **Instructions regarding the commencement of proceedings.**—Upon issuance of an emergency order, the hearing officer shall provide the plaintiff instructions regarding the commencement of proceedings in the court of common pleas at the beginning of the next business day and regarding the procedures for initiating a contempt charge should the defendant violate the emergency order. The hearing officer shall also advise the plaintiff of the existence of programs for victims of domestic violence in the county or in nearby counties and inform the plaintiff of the availability of legal assistance without cost if the plaintiff is unable to pay for them.

(e) **Master for emergency relief.**—The president judge of a court of common pleas of a judicial district may, with the approval of the Administrative Office of Pennsylvania Courts, provide for the selection and appointment of a master for emergency relief on a full-time or part-time basis. The number of masters for emergency relief shall be fixed by the president judge with the approval of the Administrative Office of Pennsylvania Courts. The compensation of a master for emergency relief shall be fixed and paid by the county.

2005 Amendment. Act 66 added subsec. (e).

1994 Amendment. Act 85 amended subsec. (a) and (b).

1992 Amendment. Act 87 amended subsec. (a).

Cross References. Section 6110 is referred to in sections 6102, 6105 of this title; section 4137 of Title 42 (Judiciary and Judicial Procedure).

§ 6111. Domestic violence counselor/advocate.

A domestic violence counselor/advocate may accompany a party to any legal proceeding or hearing under this chapter.

1994 Amendment. Act 85 amended sect 6111.

§ 6112. Disclosure of addresses.

During the course of a proceeding under this chapter, the court or hearing officer may consider whether the plaintiff or plaintiff's family is endangered by disclosure of the permanent or temporary address of the plaintiff or minor children. Neither in the pleadings nor during proceedings or hearings under this chapter shall the court or hearing officer require disclosure of the address of a domestic violence program. Where the court concludes that the defendant poses a threat of continued danger to the plaintiff and where the plaintiff requests that his or her address, telephone number and information about whereabouts not be disclosed, the court shall enter an order directing that law enforcement agencies, human service agencies and school districts (both in which a plaintiff's child in custody of the plaintiff is or has been enrolled) shall not disclose the presence of the plaintiff or the child in the jurisdiction or district or furnish any address, telephone number or any other demographic information about the plaintiff and child except by further order of the court.

1994 Amendment. Act 85 amended sect 6112.

§ 6113. Arrest for violation of order

(a) **General rule.**—An arrest for violation of an order issued pursuant to this chapter or a foreign protection order may be without warrant upon probable cause whether or not the violation is committed in the presence of the police officer or sheriff in circumstances where the defendant has violated a provision of an order consistent with section 6108(a)(1), (2), (3), (4), (6), (7) or (9) (relating to relief). The police officer or sheriff may verify the existence of a protection order by telephone, radio or other electronic communication with the appropriate police department, Pennsylvania State

Police registry, protection order file or issuing authority. A police officer or sheriff shall arrest a defendant for violating an order issued under this chapter by a court within the judicial district, issued by a court in another judicial district within this Commonwealth or a foreign protection order issued by a comparable court.

(b) **Seizure of firearms, other weapons and ammunition.**—Subsequent to an arrest, the police officer or sheriff shall seize all firearms, other weapons and ammunition used or threatened to be used during the violation of the protection order or during prior incidents of abuse and any other firearms in the defendant's possession. As soon as it is reasonably possible, the arresting officer shall deliver the confiscated weapons firearms, other weapons and ammunition to the office of the sheriff. The sheriff shall maintain possession of the firearms, other weapons and ammunition until the court issues an order specifying the firearms, other weapons and ammunition to be relinquished and the persons to whom the firearms, other weapons and ammunition shall be relinquished.

(c) **Procedure following arrest.**—Subsequent to an arrest, the defendant shall be taken by the police officer or sheriff without unnecessary delay before the court in the judicial district where the contempt is alleged to have occurred. When that court is unavailable, the police officer or sheriff shall convey the defendant to a magisterial district judge designated as appropriate by local rules of court or, in the city of Pittsburgh, to a magistrate of the Pittsburgh Magistrates Court or, in counties of the first class, to the appropriate hearing officer. For purposes of procedure relating to arraignments for arrest for violation of an order issued under this chapter, the judges of Pittsburgh Magistrates Court shall be deemed to be magisterial district judges.

(d) **Preliminary arraignment.**—The defendant shall be afforded a preliminary arraignment without unnecessary delay.

(e) **Other emergency powers unaffected.**—This section shall not be construed to in any way limit any of the other powers for emergency relief provided in this chapter.

(f) **Hearing.**—A hearing shall be scheduled within ten days of the filing of the charge or complaint of indirect criminal contempt. The hearing and any adjudication shall not preclude a hearing on other criminal charges underlying the contempt, nor shall a hearing or adjudication on other criminal charges preclude a hearing on a charge of indirect criminal contempt.

2005 Amendment. Act 66 amended subsecs. (a), (b), and (c).

2004 Amendment. Act 207 amended subsec. (c).

2001 Amendment. Act 39 amended subsec. (a).

1994 Amendment. Act 85 amended subsec. (a), (c), (f) and (g).

Cross References. Section 6113 is referred to in sections 6105, 6108 and 6121 of this title.

§ 6113.1. Private criminal complaints for violation of order or agreement

(a) **General rule.**—A plaintiff may file a private criminal complaint against a defendant, alleging indirect criminal contempt for a noneconomic violation of any provision of an order or court-approved consent agreement issued under this chapter or a foreign protection order, with the court, the office of the district attorney or the magisterial district judge in the jurisdiction or county where the violation occurred, except that, in a city of the first class, a complaint may only be filed with the family division of the court of common pleas or the office of the district attorney.

(b) **Procedure service.**—Procedure for filing and service of a private criminal complaint shall be provided as set forth by local rule. No fees or costs associated with the prosecution of the private criminal complaint shall be assigned to the plaintiff at any stage of the proceeding, including, but not limited to, filing, service, failure to prosecute, withdrawal or dismissal. Nothing in this subsection is intended to expand or diminish the court's authority to enter an order pursuant to Pa.R.C.P. No. 1023.1 (relating to Scope. Signing of Documents. Representations to the Court. Violation).

(c) **Fees and costs.**—After a finding of indirect criminal contempt, fees and costs may be assessed against the defendant. The court shall waive fees and costs imposed pursuant to this chapter upon a showing of good cause or when the court makes a finding that the defendant is not able to pay the costs associated with the indirect criminal contempt action. Nothing in this subsection is intended to expand or diminish the court's authority to enter an order pursuant to Pa.R.C.P. No. 1023.1.

2005 Amendment. Act 66 amended subsec. (b) and added subsec. (c).

2004 Amendment. Act 207 amended subsec. (a).

2001 Amendment. Act 39 amended subsec. (a).

1994 Amendment. Act 85 added sect 6113.1.

§ 6114. Contempt for violation of order or agreement

(a) **General rule.**—Where the police, sheriff or the plaintiff have filed charges of indirect criminal contempt against a defendant for violation of a protection order issued under this chapter, a foreign protection order or a court-approved consent agreement, the court may hold the defendant in indirect criminal contempt and punish the defendant in accordance with law.

(a.1) **Jurisdiction.**—A court shall have jurisdiction over indirect criminal contempt charges for violation of a protection order issued pursuant to this chapter in the county where the violation occurred and in the county where the protection order was granted. A court shall have jurisdiction over indirect criminal contempt charges for violation of a foreign protection order in the county where the violation occurred.

(a.2) **Minor defendant.**—Any defendant who is a minor and who is charged with indirect criminal contempt for allegedly violating a protection from abuse order shall be considered to have committed an alleged delinquent act as that term is defined in 42 Pa.C.S. § 6302 (relating to definitions) and shall be treated as provided in 42 Pa.C.S. Ch. 63 (relating to juvenile matters).

(b) **Trial and punishment.**—

(1) A sentence for contempt under this chapter may include:

(i) (A) a fine of not less than $300 nor more than $1,000 and imprisonment up to six months; or

(B) a fine of not less than $300 nor more than $1,000 and supervised probation not to exceed six months; and

(ii) an order for other relief set forth in this chapter.

(2) All money received under this section shall be distributed in the following order of priority:

(i) $100 shall be forwarded to the Commonwealth and shall be appropriated to the Pennsylvania State Police to establish and maintain the Statewide registry of protection orders provided for in section 6105 (relating to responsibilities of law enforcement agencies).

(ii) $100 shall be retained by the county and shall be used to carry out the provisions of this chapter as follows:

(A) $50 shall be used by the sheriff.

(B) $50 shall be used by the court.

(iii) $100 shall be forwarded to the Department of Public Welfare for use for victims of domestic violence in accordance with the provisions of section 2333 of the act of April 9, 1929 (P.L. 177, No. 175), known as The Administrative Code of 1929.

(iv) Any additional money shall be forwarded to the Commonwealth and shall be used by the Pennsylvania State Police to establish and maintain the Statewide registry of protection orders provided for in section 6105.

(3) The defendant shall not have a right to a jury trial on a charge of indirect criminal contempt. However, the defendant shall be entitled to counsel.

(4) Upon conviction for indirect criminal contempt and at the request of the plaintiff, the court shall also grant an extension of the protection order for an additional term.

(5) Upon conviction for indirect criminal contempt, the court shall notify the sheriff of the jurisdiction which issued the protection order of the conviction.

(6) The minimum fine required by subsection (b)(1) allocated pursuant to subsection (b)(2)(i) and (iii) shall be used to supplement and not to supplant any other source of funds received for the purpose of carrying out the provisions of this chapter.

(c) Notification upon release.—The appropriate releasing authority or other official as designated by local rule shall use all reasonable means to notify the victim sufficiently in advance of the release of the offender from any incarceration imposed under subsection (b). Notification shall be required for work release, furlough, medical leave, community service, discharge, escape and recapture. Notification shall include the terms and conditions imposed on any temporary release from custody. The plaintiff must keep the appropriate releasing authority or other official as designated by local rule advised of contact information; failure to do so will constitute waiver of any right to notification under this section.

(d) Multiple remedies.—Disposition of a charge of indirect criminal contempt shall not preclude the prosecution of other criminal charges associated with the incident giving rise to the contempt, nor shall disposition of other criminal charges preclude prosecution of indirect criminal contempt associated with the criminal conduct giving rise to the charges.

2005 Amendment. Act 66 amended subsecs. (a), (a.1), (b).

2001 Amendment. Act 39 amended subsec. (a) and (a)(1).

1998 Amendment. Act 36 added subsec. (a.2).

1994 Amendment. Act 85 amended sect 6114.

Cross References. Section 6114 is referred to in section 6108 of this title; sections 4136, 4137 of Title 42 (Judiciary and Judicial Procedure).

§ 6114.1. Civil contempt or modification for violation of an order or agreement.

(a) General rule.—A plaintiff may file a petition for civil contempt with the issuing court alleging that the defendant has violated any provision of an order or court-approved agreement issued under this chapter or a foreign protection order.

(b) Civil contempt order.—Upon finding of a violation of a protection order or court-approved consent agreement issued under this chapter or a foreign protection order, the court, either pursuant to petition for civil contempt or on its own accord, may hold the defendant in civil contempt and constrain him in accordance with law.

(c) Sentencing.—A sentence for civil contempt under this chapter may include imprisonment until the defendant complies with provisions in the order or consent agreement or demonstrates the intent to do so, but in no case shall a term of imprisonment under this section exceed a period of six months.

(d) Jury trial and counsel.—The defendant shall not have a right to a jury trial; however, the defendant shall be entitled to counsel.

2001 Amendment. Act 39 amended subsecs. (a) and (b).

1994 Amendment. Act 85 added sect. 6114.1.

§ 6115. Reporting abuse and immunity.

(a) Reporting.—A person having reasonable cause to believe that a person is being abused may report the information to the local police department.

(b) Contents of report.—The report should contain the name and address of the abused person, information regarding the nature and extent of the abuse and information which the reporter believes may be helpful to prevent further abuse.

(c) Immunity.—A person who makes a report shall be immune from a civil or criminal liability on account of the report unless the person acted in bad faith or with malicious purpose.

§ 6116. Confidentiality.

Unless a victim waives the privilege in a signed writing prior to testimony or disclosure, a domestic violence counselor/advocate or a coparticipant who is present during domestic violence counseling/advocacy shall not be competent nor permitted to testify or to otherwise disclose confidential communications made to or by the counselor/advocate by or to a victim. The privilege shall terminate upon the death of the victim. Neither the domestic violence counselor/ advocate nor the victim shall waive the privilege of confidential communications by reporting facts of physical or sexual assault under Chapter 63 (relating to child protective services), a Federal or State mandatory reporting statute or a local mandatory reporting ordinance.

1994 Amendment. Act 85 amended sect. 6116.

Cross References. Section 6116 is referred to in section 6102 of this title.

§ 6117. Procedure and other remedies

(a) General rule.—Unless otherwise indicated in this chapter, a proceeding under this chapter shall be in accordance with applicable general rules and shall be in addition to any other available civil or criminal remedies. The plaintiff and the defendant may seek modification of an order issued under section 6108 (relating to relief) at any time during the pendency of an order. Except as otherwise indicated in this chapter, modification may be ordered after the filing of a petition for modification, service of the petition and a hearing on the petition.

(b) Remedies for bad faith.—Notwithstanding any other provision of law, upon finding that an individual commenced a proceeding under this chapter in bad faith, a court shall direct the individual to pay to the defendant actual damages and reasonable attorney fees. Failure to prove an allegation of abuse by a preponderance of the evidence shall not, by itself, result in a finding of bad faith.

2005 Amendment. Act 66 amended subsecs. (a) and (b).

1994 Amendment. Act 85 amended sect. 6117.

§ 6118. Full faith and credit. [Repealed].

2001 Amendment. Act 39 repealed this sec.

1994 Amendment. Act 85 added sect. 6118.

§ 6119. Immunity

(a) General rule.—Law enforcement agencies and their employees, including police officers and sheriffs, shall, except as provided in subsection (b), be immune from civil liability for actions taken in good faith to carry out their duties relating to the seizure and relinquishment of firearms, other weapons and ammunition as provided for in this chapter, except for gross negligence, intentional misconduct or reckless, willful or wanton misconduct.

(b) Exception.—Law enforcement agencies and their employees, including police officers and sheriffs, shall be liable to the lawful owner of confiscated, seized or relinquished firearms in accordance with 18 Pa.C.S. § 6105(f) (relating to persons not to possess, use, manufacture, control, sell or transfer firearms) and shall be liable to the lawful owner of confiscated, seized or relinquished other weapons or ammunition for any loss, damage or substantial decrease in the value of the other weapons or ammunition that is a direct result of a lack of reasonable care by the law enforcement agency or its employees.

2005 Amendment. Act 66 added this sec.

§ 6120. Inability to pay

(a) **Order for installment payments.**—Upon plea and proof that a person is without the financial means to pay a fine, a fee, economic relief ordered under section 6108(a)(8) (relating to relief) or a cost, a court may order payment of money owed in installments appropriate to the circumstances of the person and shall fix the amounts, times and manner of payment.

(b) **Use of credit cards.**—The treasurer of each county may allow the use of credit cards and bank cards in the payment of money owed under this chapter.

2005 Amendment. Act 66 added this sec.

§ 6121. Warrantless searches

Except as provided in section 6113 (relating to arrest for violation of order), nothing in this chapter shall authorize a warrantless search for firearms, other weapons or ammunition.

2005 Amendment. Act 66 added this sec.

§ 6122. Construction

Nothing in this chapter shall be construed to preclude an action for wrongful use of civil process pursuant to 42 Pa.C.S. Ch. 83 Subch. E (relating to wrongful use of civil proceedings) or criminal prosecution for a violation of 18 Pa.C.S. Ch. 49 (relating to falsification and intimidation).

2005 Amendment. Act 66 added this sec.

CHAPTER 63
CHILD PROTECTIVE SERVICES

Subchapter

A. Preliminary Provisions
B. Reporting Suspected Child Abuse
C. Powers and Duties of Department
D. Organization and Responsibilities of Child Protective Service
E. Miscellaneous Provisions

Enactment. Chapter 63 was added December 19, 1990, P.L.1240, No.206, effective in 90 days.

Cross References. Chapter 63 is referred to in section 6102, 6116 of this title; section 9121 of Title 18 (Crimes and Offenses); sections 5945, 6311, and 6342 of Title 42 (Judiciary and Judicial Procedure).

Saved from Suspension. Pennsylvania Rule of Civil Procedure No. 1915.24, as amended March 30, 1994, provided that Chapter 63 shall not be deemed suspended or affected by Rules 1915.1 through 1915.18 relating to actions for custody, partial custody and visitation of minor children.

SUBCHAPTER A
PRELIMINARY PROVISIONS

Sec.
6301. Short title of chapter.
6302. Findings and purpose of chapter.
6303. Definitions.
6304. Exclusions from child abuse.
6305. Electronic reporting.
6306. Regulations.

§ 6301. Short title of chapter.

This chapter shall be known and may be cited as the Child Protective Services Law.

§ 6302. Findings and purpose of chapter.

 (a) **Findings.**—Abused children are in urgent need of an effective child protective service to prevent them from suffering further injury and impairment.

 (b) **Purpose.**—It is the purpose of this chapter to encourage more complete reporting of suspected child abuse; to the extent permitted by this chapter, to involve law enforcement agencies in responding to child abuse; and to establish in each county protective services for the purpose of investigating the reports swiftly and competently, providing protection for children from further abuse and providing rehabilitative services for children and parents involved so as to ensure the child's well-being and to preserve, stabilize and protect the integrity of family life wherever appropriate or to provide another alternative permanent family when the unity of the family cannot be maintained. It is also the purpose of this chapter to ensure that each county children and youth agency establish a program of protective services with procedures to assess risk of harm to a child and with the capabilities to respond adequately to meet the needs of the family and child who may be at risk and to prioritize the response and services to children most at risk.

 (c) **Effect on rights of parents.**—This chapter does not restrict the generally recognized existing rights of parents to use reasonable supervision and control when raising their children.

1998 Amendment. Act 127 amended subsect (b), eff. March 1, 1999.

1994 Amendment. Act 151 amended subsect (a) and (b).

§ 6303. Definitions.

(a) General rule.--The following words and phrases when used in this chapter shall have the meanings given to them in this section unless the context clearly indicates otherwise:

"Accept for service." Decide on the basis of the needs and problems of an individual to admit or receive the individual as a client of the agency or as required by a court order entered under 42 Pa.C.S. Ch. 63 (relating to juvenile matters).

"Adult." An individual 18 years of age or older.

"Adult family member." A person 18 years of age or older who has the responsibility to provide care or services to an individual with an intellectual disability or chronic psychiatric disability.

"Bodily injury." Impairment of physical condition or substantial pain.

"Child." An individual under 18 years of age.

"Child-care services." Includes any of the following:

(1) Child day-care centers.

(2) Group day-care homes.

(3) Family child-care homes.

(4) Foster homes.

(5) Adoptive parents.

(6) Boarding homes for children.

(7) Juvenile detention center services or programs for delinquent or dependent children.

(8) Mental health services for children.

(9) Services for children with intellectual disabilities.

(10) Early intervention services for children.

(11) Drug and alcohol services for children.

(12) Day-care services or programs that are offered by a school.

(13) Other child-care services that are provided by or subject to approval, licensure, registration or certification by the department or a county social services agency or that are provided pursuant to a contract with the department or a county social services agency.

The term does not apply to services provided by administrative or other support personnel unless the administrative or other support personnel have direct contact with children.

"Child protective services." Those services and activities provided by the department and each county agency for child abuse cases.

"Children's advocacy center." A local public agency in this Commonwealth or a not-for-profit entity incorporated in this Commonwealth which:

(1) is tax exempt under section 501(c)(3) of the Internal Revenue Code of 1986 (Public Law 99-514, 26 U.S.C. § 501(c)(3)); and

(2) operates within this Commonwealth for the primary purpose of providing a child-focused, facility-based program dedicated to coordinating a formalized multidisciplinary response to suspected child abuse that, at a minimum, either onsite or through a partnership with another entity or entities, assists county agencies, investigative teams and law enforcement by providing services, including forensic interviews, medical evaluations, therapeutic interventions, victim support and advocacy, team case reviews and a system for case tracking.

"Cooperation with an investigation or assessment." Includes, but is not limited to, a school or school district which permits authorized personnel from the department or county agency to interview a student while the student is in attendance at school.

"County agency." The county children and youth social service agency established pursuant to section 405 of the act of June 24, 1937 (P.L.2017, No.396), known as the County Institution District Law, or its successor, and supervised by the department under Article IX of the act of June 13, 1967 (P.L.31, No.21), known as the Public Welfare Code.

"Department." The Department of Human Services of the Commonwealth.

"Direct contact with children." The care, supervision, guidance or control of children or routine interaction with children.

"Direct volunteer contact." The care, supervision, guidance or control of children and routine interaction with children.

"Education enterprise." An educational activity in this Commonwealth:

(1) for which college credits or continuing education units are awarded, continuing professional education is offered or tuition or fees are charged or collected; and

(2) that is sponsored by a corporation, entity or institution that is incorporated or authorized by other means in a state other than this Commonwealth and is approved and authorized to operate in this Commonwealth under 15 Pa.C.S. Pt. II Subpt. B (relating to business corporations) or C (relating to nonprofit corporations) and 24 Pa.C.S. Ch. 65 (relating to private colleges, universities and seminaries).

"Electronic technologies." The transfer of information in whole or in part by technology having electrical, digital, magnetic, wireless, optical, electromagnetic, photo-electronic or photo-optical systems, or similar capabilities. The term includes, but is not limited to, e-mail, Internet communication or other means of electronic transmission.

"Expunge." To strike out or obliterate entirely so that the expunged information may not be stored, identified or later recovered by any mechanical or electronic means or otherwise.

"Family child-care home." A residence where child day care is provided at any time to no less than four children and no more than six children who are not relatives of the caregiver.

"Family members." Spouses, parents and children or other persons related by consanguinity or affinity.

"Founded report." A child abuse report involving a perpetrator that is made pursuant to this chapter, if any of the following applies:

(1) There has been a judicial adjudication based on a finding that a child who is a subject of the report has been abused and the adjudication involves the same factual circumstances involved in the allegation of child abuse. The judicial adjudication may include any of the following:

(i) The entry of a plea of guilty or nolo contendere.

(ii) A finding of guilt to a criminal charge.

(iii) A finding of dependency under 42 Pa.C.S. § 6341 (relating to adjudication) if the court has entered a finding that a child who is the subject of the report has been abused.

(iv) A finding of delinquency under 42 Pa.C.S. § 6341 if the court has entered a finding that the child who is the subject of the report has been abused by the child who was found to be delinquent.

(2) There has been an acceptance into an accelerated rehabilitative disposition program and the reason for the acceptance involves the same factual circumstances involved in the allegation of child abuse.

(3) There has been a consent decree entered in a juvenile proceeding under 42 Pa.C.S. Ch. 63 (relating to juvenile matters), the decree involves the same factual circumstances involved in the allegation of child abuse and the terms and conditions of the consent decree include an acknowledgment, admission or finding that a child who is the subject of the report has been abused by the child who is alleged to be delinquent.

(4) A final protection from abuse order has been granted under section 6108 (relating to relief), when the child who is a subject of the report is one of the individuals protected under the protection from abuse order and:

(i) only one individual is charged with the abuse in the protection from abuse action;

(ii) only that individual defends against the charge;

(iii) the adjudication involves the same factual circumstances involved in the allegation of child abuse; and

(iv) the protection from abuse adjudication finds that the child abuse occurred.

"Founded report for school employee." (Deleted by amendment).

"General protective services." Those services and activities provided by each county agency for cases requiring protective services, as defined by the department in regulations.

"Health care facility." As defined in section 802.1 of the act of July 19, 1979 (P.L.130, No.48), known as the Health Care Facilities Act.

"Health care provider." A licensed hospital or health care facility or person who is licensed, certified or otherwise regulated to provide health care services under the laws of this Commonwealth, including a physician, podiatrist, optometrist, psychologist, physical therapist, certified nurse practitioner, registered nurse, nurse midwife, physician's assistant, chiropractor, dentist, pharmacist or an individual accredited or certified to provide behavioral health services.

"Immediate vicinity." An area in which an individual is physically present with a child and can see, hear, direct and assess the activities of the child.

"Independent contractor." An individual who provides a program, activity or service to an agency, institution, organization or other entity, including a school or regularly established religious organization, that is responsible for the care, supervision, guidance or control of children. The term does not apply to administrative or other support personnel unless the administrative or other support personnel have direct contact with children.

"Indicated report."

(1) Subject to paragraphs (2) and (3), a report of child abuse made pursuant to this chapter if an investigation by the department or county agency determines that substantial evidence of the alleged abuse by a perpetrator exists based on any of the following:

(i) Available medical evidence.

(ii) The child protective service investigation.

(iii) An admission of the acts of abuse by the perpetrator.

(2) A report may be indicated under paragraph (1)(i) or (ii) for any child who is the victim of child abuse, regardless of the number of alleged perpetrators.

(3) A report may be indicated under paragraph (1)(i) or (ii) listing the perpetrator as unknown" if substantial evidence of abuse by a perpetrator exists, but the department or county agency is unable to identify the specific perpetrator.

"Indicated report for school employee." (Deleted by amendment).

"Individual residing in the same home as the child." (Deleted by amendment).

"Institution of higher education." Any of the following:

(1) A community college which is an institution now or hereafter created pursuant to Article XIX-A of the act of March 10, 1949 (P.L.30, No.14), known as the Public School Code of 1949, or the act of August 24, 1963 (P.L.1132, No.484), known as the Community College Act of 1963.

(2) An independent institution of higher education which is an institution of higher education located in and incorporated or chartered by the Commonwealth, entitled to confer degrees as set forth in 24 Pa.C.S. § 6505 (relating to power to confer degrees) and entitled to apply to itself the designation "college," "university" or "seminary" as provided for by standards and qualifications prescribed by the State Board of Education under 24 Pa.C.S. Ch. 65.

(3) A State-owned institution.

(4) A State-related institution.

(5) An education enterprise.

"Intentionally." The term shall have the same meaning as provided in 18 Pa.C.S. § 302 (relating to general requirements of culpability).

"Knowingly." The term shall have the same meaning as provided in 18 Pa.C.S. § 302 (relating to general requirements of culpability).

"Law enforcement official." The term includes the following:

(1) The Attorney General.

(2) A Pennsylvania district attorney.

(3) A Pennsylvania State Police officer.

(4) A municipal police officer.

"Mandated reporter." A person who is required by this chapter to make a report of suspected child abuse.

"Matriculated student." A student who is enrolled in an institution of higher education and pursuing a program of study that results in a postsecondary credential, such as a certificate, diploma or degree.

"Near fatality." A child's serious or critical condition, as certified by a physician, where that child is a subject of the report of child abuse.

"Newborn." As defined in section 6502 (relating to definitions).

"Nonaccidental." (Deleted by amendment).

"Parent." A biological parent, adoptive parent or legal guardian.

"Perpetrator." A person who has committed child abuse as defined in this section. The following shall apply:

(1) The term includes only the following:

(i) A parent of the child.

(ii) A spouse or former spouse of the child's parent.

(iii) A paramour or former paramour of the child's parent.

(iv) A person 14 years of age or older and responsible for the child's welfare or having direct contact with children as an employee of child-care services, a school or through a program, activity or service.

(v) An individual 14 years of age or older who resides in the same home as the child.

(vi) An individual 18 years of age or older who does not reside in the same home as the child but is related within the third degree of consanguinity or affinity by birth or adoption to the child.

(vii) An individual 18 years of age or older who engages a child in severe forms of trafficking in persons or sex trafficking, as those terms are defined under section 103 of the Trafficking Victims Protection Act of 2000 (114 Stat. 1466, 22 U.S.C. § 7102).

(2) Only the following may be considered a perpetrator for failing to act, as provided in this section:

(i) A parent of the child.

(ii) A spouse or former spouse of the child's parent.

(iii) A paramour or former paramour of the child's parent.

(iv) A person 18 years of age or older and responsible for the child's welfare.

(v) A person 18 years of age or older who resides in the same home as the child.

"Person affiliated with." A person that directly or indirectly, through one or more intermediaries, controls, is controlled by or is under common control with a specified person.

"Person responsible for the child's welfare." A person who provides permanent or temporary care, supervision, mental health diagnosis or treatment, training or control of a child in lieu of parental care, supervision and control.

"Police department." A public agency of a political subdivision having general police powers and charged with making arrests in connection with the enforcement of criminal or traffic laws.

"Police officer." A full-time or part-time employee assigned to criminal or traffic law enforcement duties of a police department of a county, city, borough, town or township. The term also includes a member of the State Police Force.

"Police station." The station or headquarters of a police department or a Pennsylvania State Police station or headquarters.

"Private agency." A children and youth social service agency subject to the requirements of 55 Pa. Code Ch. 3680 (relating to administration and operation of a children and youth social service agency).

"Program, activity or service." Any of the following in which children participate and which is sponsored by a school or a public or private organization:

(1) A youth camp or program.

(2) A recreational camp or program.

(3) A sports or athletic program.

(4) A community or social outreach program.

(5) An enrichment or educational program.

(6) A troop, club or similar organization.

"Protective services." Those services and activities provided by the department and each county agency for children who are abused or are alleged to be in need of protection under this chapter.

"Recent act." Any act committed within two years of the date of the report to the department or county agency.

"Recent act or failure to act." Any act or failure to act committed within two years of the date of the report to the department or county agency.

"Recklessly." The term shall have the same meaning as provided in 18 Pa.C.S. § 302 (relating to general requirements of culpability).

"Resource family." A family which provides temporary foster or kinship care for children who need out-of-home placement and may eventually provide permanency for those children, including an adoptive family.

"Risk assessment." A Commonwealth-approved systematic process that assesses a child's need for protection or services based on the risk of harm to the child.

"Routine interaction." Regular and repeated contact that is integral to a person's employment or volunteer responsibilities.

"**Safety assessment.**" A Commonwealth-approved systematic process that assesses a child's need for protection or services, based on the threat to the safety of the child.

"**School.**" A facility providing elementary, secondary or postsecondary educational services. The term includes the following:

(1) Any school of a school district.

(2) An area vocational-technical school.

(3) A joint school.

(4) An intermediate unit.

(5) A charter school or regional charter school.

(6) A cyber charter school.

(7) A private school licensed under the act of January 28, 1988 (P.L.24, No.11), known as the Private Academic Schools Act.

(8) A private school accredited by an accrediting association approved by the State Board of Education.

(9) A nonpublic school.

(10) An institution of higher education.

(11) (Deleted by amendment).

(12) (Deleted by amendment).

(13) (Deleted by amendment).

(14) A private school licensed under the act of December 15, 1986 (P.L.1585, No.174), known as the Private Licensed Schools Act.

(15) The Hiram G. Andrews Center.

(16) A private residential rehabilitative institution as defined in section 914.1-A(c) of the Public School Code of 1949.

"**School employee.**" An individual who is employed by a school or who provides a program, activity or service sponsored by a school. The term does not apply to administrative or other support personnel unless the administrative or other support personnel have direct contact with children.

"**Secretary.**" The Secretary of Human Services of the Commonwealth.

"**Serious bodily injury.**" Bodily injury which creates a substantial risk of death or which causes serious permanent disfigurement or protracted loss or impairment of function of any bodily member or organ.

"**Serious mental injury.**" A psychological condition, as diagnosed by a physician or licensed psychologist, including the refusal of appropriate treatment, that:

(1) renders a child chronically and severely anxious, agitated, depressed, socially withdrawn, psychotic or in reasonable fear that the child's life or safety is threatened; or

(2) seriously interferes with a child's ability to accomplish age-appropriate developmental and social tasks.

"**Serious physical injury.**" (Deleted by amendment).

"**Serious physical neglect.**" Any of the following when committed by a perpetrator that endangers a child's life or health, threatens a child's well-being, causes bodily injury or impairs a child's health, development or functioning:

(1) A repeated, prolonged or egregious failure to supervise a child in a manner that is appropriate considering the child's developmental age and abilities.

(2) The failure to provide a child with adequate essentials of life, including food, shelter or medical care.

"**Sexual abuse or exploitation.**" Any of the following:

(1) The employment, use, persuasion, inducement, enticement or coercion of a child to engage in or assist another individual to engage in sexually explicit conduct, which includes, but is not limited to, the following:

(i) Looking at the sexual or other intimate parts of a child or another individual for the purpose of arousing or gratifying sexual desire in any individual.

(ii) Participating in sexually explicit conversation either in person, by telephone, by computer or by a computer-aided device for the purpose of sexual stimulation or gratification of any individual.

(iii) Actual or simulated sexual activity or nudity for the purpose of sexual stimulation or gratification of any individual.

(iv) Actual or simulated sexual activity for the purpose of producing visual depiction, including photographing, videotaping, computer depicting or filming.

This paragraph does not include consensual activities between a child who is 14 years of age or older and another person who is 14 years of age or older and whose age is within four years of the child's age.

(2) Any of the following offenses committed against a child:

(i) Rape as defined in 18 Pa.C.S. § 3121 (relating to rape).

(ii) Statutory sexual assault as defined in 18 Pa.C.S. § 3122.1 (relating to statutory sexual assault).

(iii) Involuntary deviate sexual intercourse as defined in 18 Pa.C.S. § 3123 (relating to involuntary deviate sexual intercourse).

(iv) Sexual assault as defined in 18 Pa.C.S. § 3124.1 (relating to sexual assault).

(v) Institutional sexual assault as defined in 18 Pa.C.S. § 3124.2 (relating to institutional sexual assault).

(vi) Aggravated indecent assault as defined in 18 Pa.C.S. § 3125 (relating to aggravated indecent assault).

(vii) Indecent assault as defined in 18 Pa.C.S. § 3126 (relating to indecent assault).

(viii) Indecent exposure as defined in 18 Pa.C.S. § 3127 (relating to indecent exposure).

(ix) Incest as defined in 18 Pa.C.S. § 4302 (relating to incest).

(x) Prostitution as defined in 18 Pa.C.S. § 5902 (relating to prostitution and related offenses).

(xi) Sexual abuse as defined in 18 Pa.C.S. § 6312 (relating to sexual abuse of children).

(xii) Unlawful contact with a minor as defined in 18 Pa.C.S. § 6318 (relating to unlawful contact with minor).

(xiii) Sexual exploitation as defined in 18 Pa.C.S. § 6320 (relating to sexual exploitation of children).

"**Student.**" An individual enrolled in a public or private school, intermediate unit or area vocational-technical school who is under 18 years of age.

"**Subject of the report.**" Any child, parent, guardian or other person responsible for the welfare of a child or any alleged or actual perpetrator in a report made to the department or a county agency under this chapter.

"**Substantial evidence.**" Evidence which outweighs inconsistent evidence and which a reasonable person would accept as adequate to support a conclusion.

"**Substantiated child abuse.**" Child abuse as to which there is an indicated report or founded report.

"**Under investigation.**" A child abuse report pursuant to this chapter which is being investigated to determine whether it is "founded," "indicated" or "unfounded."

"**Unfounded report.**" Any report made pursuant to this chapter unless the report is a "founded report" or an "indicated report."

(b) Child abuse.—(Deleted by amendment).

(b.1) Child abuse.—The term "child abuse" shall mean intentionally, knowingly or recklessly doing any of the following:

(1) Causing bodily injury to a child through any recent act or failure to act.

(2) Fabricating, feigning or intentionally exaggerating or inducing a medical symptom or disease which results in a potentially harmful medical evaluation or treatment to the child through any recent act.

(3) Causing or substantially contributing to serious mental injury to a child through any act or failure to act or a series of such acts or failures to act.

(4) Causing sexual abuse or exploitation of a child through any act or failure to act.

(5) Creating a reasonable likelihood of bodily injury to a child through any recent act or failure to act.

(6) Creating a likelihood of sexual abuse or exploitation of a child through any recent act or failure to act.

(7) Causing serious physical neglect of a child.

(8) Engaging in any of the following recent acts:

(i) Kicking, biting, throwing, burning, stabbing or cutting a child in a manner that endangers the child.

(ii) Unreasonably restraining or confining a child, based on consideration of the method, location or the duration of the restraint or confinement.

(iii) Forcefully shaking a child under one year of age.

(iv) Forcefully slapping or otherwise striking a child under one year of age.

(v) Interfering with the breathing of a child.

(vi) Causing a child to be present at a location while a violation of 18 Pa.C.S. § 7508.2 (relating to operation of methamphetamine laboratory) is occurring, provided that the violation is being investigated by law enforcement.

(vii) Leaving a child unsupervised with an individual, other than the child's parent, who the actor knows or reasonably should have known:

(A) Is required to register as a Tier II or Tier III sexual offender under 42 Pa.C.S. Ch. 97 Subch. H (relating to registration of sexual offenders), where the victim of the sexual offense was under 18 years of age when the crime was committed.

(B) Has been determined to be a sexually violent predator under 42 Pa.C.S. § 9799.24 (relating to assessments) or any of its predecessors.

(C) Has been determined to be a sexually violent delinquent child as defined in 42 Pa.C.S. § 9799.12 (relating to definitions).

(D) Has been determined to be a sexually violent predator under 42 Pa.C.S. § 9799.58 (relating to assessments) or has to register for life under 42 Pa.C.S. § 9799.55(b) (relating to registration).

(9) Causing the death of the child through any act or failure to act.

(10) Engaging a child in a severe form of trafficking in persons or sex trafficking, as those terms are defined under section 103 of the Trafficking Victims Protection Act of 2000 (114 Stat. 1466, 22 U.S.C. § 7102).

(c) Restatement of culpability.—Conduct that causes injury or harm to a child or creates a risk of injury or harm to a child shall not be considered child abuse if there is no evidence that the person acted intentionally, knowingly or recklessly when causing the injury or harm to the child or creating a risk of injury or harm to the child.

(d) **Child abuse exclusions.**—The term "child abuse" does not include any conduct for which an exclusion is provided in section 6304 (relating to exclusions from child abuse).

(Dec. 16, 1994, P.L.1292, No.151, eff. July 1, 1995; Mar. 31, 1995, 1st Sp.Sess., P.L.985, No.10, eff. 60 days; Dec. 9, 2002, P.L.1549, No.201, eff. 60 days; Nov. 29, 2004, P.L.1291, No.160, eff. 60 days; Nov. 9, 2006, P.L.1358, No.146, eff. 180 days; Nov. 29, 2006, P.L.1581, No.179, eff. 180 days; July 3, 2008, P.L.276, No.33, eff. 180 days; Dec. 18, 2013, P.L.1170, No.108, eff. Dec. 31, 2014; Dec. 18, 2013, P.L.1195, No.117, eff. Dec. 31, 2014; Dec. 18, 2013, P.L.1201, No.119, eff. Dec. 31, 2014; Jan. 22, 2014, P.L.6, No.4, eff. 90 days; Apr. 7, 2014, P.L.388, No.29, eff. Dec. 31, 2014; Apr. 15, 2014, P.L.417, No.33, eff. Dec. 31, 2014; May 14, 2014, P.L.645, No.44, eff. Dec. 31, 2014; May 14, 2014, P.L.653, No.45, eff. Dec. 31, 2014; July 2, 2014, P.L.843, No.91, eff. 60 days; Oct. 22, 2014, P.L.2529, No.153, eff. Dec. 31, 2014; July 1, 2015, P.L.94, No.15, eff. imd.; Oct. 28, 2016, P.L.966, No.115, eff. imd.; Feb. 21, 2018, P.L.27, No.10, eff. imd.; June 12, 2018, P.L.140, No.29, eff. imd.)

2018 Amendments. Act 10 amended the def. of "child abuse" in subsec. (b.1)(8)(vii) and Act 29 reenacted subsec. (b.1)(8)(vii).

2016 Amendment. Act 115 added par. (1)(vii) of the def. of "perpetrator" in subsec. (a) and added subsec. (b.1)(10).

2015 Amendment. Act 15 amended the defs. of "child-care services," "independent contractor," "perpetrator," "person responsible for the child's welfare," "program, activity or service," "school" and "school employee" and added the defs. of "adult family member," "direct volunteer contact," "education enterprise," "family child-care home," "immediate vicinity," "institution of higher education," "matriculated student" and "routine interaction" in subsec. (a).

2014 Amendments. Act 4 added the defs. of "health care provider" and "safety assessment" in subsec. (a), Act 29 amended the defs. of "child-care services" and added the defs. of "electronic technologies," "law enforcement official" and "mandated reporter" in subsec. (a), Act 33 amended the def. of "school employee" and added the defs. of "adult," "direct contact with children," "health care facility," "independent contractor," "mandated reporter," "person affiliated with," "program, activity or service" and "school" in subsec. (a), Act 44 amended the defs. of "bodily injury," "founded report," "general protective services," "near fatality" and "school employee," added the def. of "school" and deleted the defs. of "indicated report for school employee" and "individual residing in the same home as the child" in subsec. (a), Act 45 amended the defs. of "serious physical neglect" and "subject of the report" and deleted the def. of "founded report for school employee" in subsec. (a), Act 91 added the defs. of "police department," "police officer" and "police station" in subsec. (a) and Act 153 amended par. (13) of the def. of "child-care services" and the defs. of "child protective services," "cooperation with an investigation or assessment," "county agency," "department," "indicated report," "protective services," "recent act," "recent act or failure to act," "secretary" and "subject of the report" in subsec. (a). The amendments by Acts 29 and 33, adding the def. of "mandated reporter," are identical and have both been given effect in setting forth the text of "mandated reporter." The amendments by Acts 33 and 44, amending the def. of "school employee," are identical and have both been given effect in setting forth the text of "school employee."

2013 Amendments. Act 108 amended the defs. of "child," "founded report," "indicated report," "recent acts or omissions" and "sexual abuse or exploitation," added the defs. of "bodily injury," "intentionally," "knowingly," "parent," "recent act," "recklessly" and "serious physical neglect" and deleted the defs. of "nonaccidental" and "serious physical injury" in subsec. (a), added subsecs. (b.1), (c) and (d) and deleted subsec. (b), Act 117 amended the defs. of "perpetrator" and "person responsible for the child's welfare" in subsec. (a) and Act 119 added the def. of "child-care services" in subsec. (a).

2008 Amendment. Act 33 added the defs. of "children's advocacy center" and "substantiated child abuse."

2006 Amendments. Act 146 added the defs. of "near fatality" and "nonaccidental" in subsec. (a) and Act 179 amended the def. of "sexual abuse or exploitation" in subsec. (a).

2004 Amendment Act 160 added the defs. of "private agency" and "resource family" in subsec. (a).

2002 Amendment. Act 201 added the defs. of "child" and "newborn" in subsec. (a).

References in Text. The short title of the act of June 13, 1967, P.L.31, No.21, known as the Public Welfare Code, referred to in subsection (a), was amended by the act of December 28, 2015, P.L.500, No.92. The amended short title is now the Human Services Code.

Cross References. Section 6303 is referred to in sections 2511, 5701, 6340, 6368, 6502 of this title; sections 4306, 4958 of Title 18 (Crimes and Offenses); sections 62A05, 6302, 6336.1 of Title 42 (Judiciary and Judicial Procedure); section 4109 of Title 51 (Military Affairs); section 1905 of Title 75 (Vehicles).

§ 6304. Exclusions from child abuse.

(a) **Environmental factors.**—No child shall be deemed to be physically or mentally abused based on injuries that result solely from environmental factors, such as inadequate housing, furnishings, income, clothing and medical care, that are beyond the control of the parent or person responsible for the child's welfare with whom the child resides. This subsection shall not apply to any child-care service as defined in this chapter, excluding an adoptive parent.

(b) **Practice of religious beliefs.**—If, upon investigation, the county agency determines that a child has not been provided needed medical or surgical care because of sincerely held religious beliefs of the child's parents or relative within the third degree of consanguinity and with whom the child resides, which beliefs are consistent with those of a bona fide religion, the child shall not be deemed to be physically or mentally abused. In such cases the following shall apply:

(1) The county agency shall closely monitor the child and the child's family and shall seek court-ordered medical intervention when the lack of medical or surgical care threatens the child's life or long-term health.

(2) All correspondence with a subject of the report and the records of the department and the county agency shall not reference child abuse and shall acknowledge the religious basis for the child's condition.

(3) The family shall be referred for general protective services, if appropriate.

(4) This subsection shall not apply if the failure to provide needed medical or surgical care causes the death of the child.

(5) This subsection shall not apply to any child-care service as defined in this chapter, excluding an adoptive parent.

(c) **Use of force for supervision, control and safety purposes.**—Subject to subsection (d), the use of reasonable force on or against a child by the child's own parent or person responsible for the child's welfare shall not be considered child abuse if any of the following conditions apply:

(1) The use of reasonable force constitutes incidental, minor or reasonable physical contact with the child or other actions that are designed to maintain order and control.

(2) The use of reasonable force is necessary:

(i) to quell a disturbance or remove the child from the scene of a disturbance that threatens physical injury to persons or damage to property;

(ii) to prevent the child from self-inflicted physical harm;

(iii) for self-defense or the defense of another individual; or

(iv) to obtain possession of weapons or other dangerous objects or controlled substances or paraphernalia that are on the child or within the control of the child.

(d) **Rights of parents.**—Nothing in this chapter shall be construed to restrict the generally recognized existing rights of parents to use reasonable force on or against their children for the purposes of supervision, control and discipline of their children. Such reasonable force shall not constitute child abuse.

(e) **Participation in events that involve physical contact with child.**—An individual participating in a practice or competition in an interscholastic sport, physical education, a recreational activity or an extracurricular activity that involves physical contact with a child does not, in itself, constitute contact that is subject to the reporting requirements of this chapter.

(f) Child-on-child contact.—

(1) Harm or injury to a child that results from the act of another child shall not constitute child abuse unless the child who caused the harm or injury is a perpetrator.

(2) Notwithstanding paragraph (1), the following shall apply:

(i) Acts constituting any of the following crimes against a child shall be subject to the reporting requirements of this chapter:

(A) rape as defined in 18 Pa.C.S. § 3121 (relating to rape);

(B) involuntary deviate sexual intercourse as defined in 18 Pa.C.S. § 3123 (relating to involuntary deviate sexual intercourse);

(C) sexual assault as defined in 18 Pa.C.S. § 3124.1 (relating to sexual assault);

(D) aggravated indecent assault as defined in 18 Pa.C.S. § 3125 (relating to aggravated indecent assault);

(E) indecent assault as defined in 18 Pa.C.S. § 3126 (relating to indecent assault); and

(F) indecent exposure as defined in 18 Pa.C.S. § 3127 (relating to indecent exposure).

(ii) No child shall be deemed to be a perpetrator of child abuse based solely on physical or mental injuries caused to another child in the course of a dispute, fight or scuffle entered into by mutual consent.

(iii) A law enforcement official who receives a report of suspected child abuse is not required to make a report to the department under section 6334(a) (relating to disposition of complaints received), if the person allegedly responsible for the child abuse is a nonperpetrator child.

(g) Defensive force.—Reasonable force for self-defense or the defense of another individual, consistent with the provisions of 18 Pa.C.S. §§ 505 (relating to use of force in self-protection) and 506 (relating to use of force for the protection of other persons), shall not be considered child abuse.

(Dec. 18, 2013, P.L.1170, No.108, eff. Dec. 31, 2014)

2013 Amendment. Act 108 added section 6304.

Cross References. Section 6304 is referred to in section 6303 of this title.

§ 6305. Electronic reporting

(a) Departmental procedures.—The department shall establish procedures for the secure and confidential use of electronic technologies to transmit information under this chapter, including:

(1) the filing of reports and other required records, including those of the county agency; and

(2) the verification of records and signatures on forms.

(b) Confirmation of reports.—A confirmation by the department of the receipt of a report of suspected child abuse submitted electronically shall relieve the person making the report of making an additional oral or written report of suspected child abuse, subject to section 6313 (relating to reporting procedure).

(c) Effect on other law.—Nothing in this chapter shall be construed to supersede the act of December 16, 1999 (P.L. 971, No. 69), known as the Electronic Transactions Act. Any procedures developed by the department under this section shall comply with all applicable Federal and State laws regarding confidentiality of personally identifiable information.

2014, April 7, P.L. 388, No. 29, § 2, effective Dec. 31, 2014.

§ 6306. Regulations

The department shall promulgate regulations necessary to implement this chapter.
2014, April 7, P.L. 388, No. 29, § 2, effective Dec. 31, 2014.

SUBCHAPTER B
PROVISIONS AND RESPONSIBILITIES FOR REPORTING SUSPECTED CHILD ABUSE

Sec.
6311. Persons required to report suspect child abuse.
6311.1. Privileged communications.
6312. Persons encouraged to report suspected child abuse.
6313. Reporting procedure.
6314. Photographs, medical tests and X-rays of child subject to report.
6315. Taking child into protective custody.
6316. Admission to private and public hospitals.
6317. Mandatory reporting and postmortem investigation of deaths.
6318. Immunity from liability.
6319. Penalties.
6320. Protection from employment discrimination.

§ 6311. Persons required to report suspected child abuse.

(a) Mandated reporters.—The following adults shall make a report of suspected child abuse, subject to subsection (b), if the person has reasonable cause to suspect that a child is a victim of child abuse:

(1) A person licensed or certified to practice in any health-related field under the jurisdiction of the Department of State.

(2) A medical examiner, coroner or funeral director.

(3) An employee of a health care facility or provider licensed by the Department of Health, who is engaged in the admission, examination, care or treatment of individuals.

(4) A school employee.

(5) An employee of a child-care service who has direct contact with children in the course of employment.

(6) A clergyman, priest, rabbi, minister, Christian Science practitioner, religious healer or spiritual leader of any regularly established church or other religious organization.

(7) An individual paid or unpaid, who, on the basis of the individual's role as an integral part of a regularly scheduled program, activity or service, is a person responsible for the child's welfare or has direct contact with children.

(8) An employee of a social services agency who has direct contact with children in the course of employment.

(9) A peace officer or law enforcement official.

(10) An emergency medical services provider certified by the Department of Health.

(11) An employee of a public library who has direct contact with children in the course of employment.

(12) An individual supervised or managed by a person listed under paragraphs (1), (2), (3), (4), (5), (6), (7), (8), (9), (10), (11) and (13), who has direct contact with children in the course of employment.

(13) An independent contractor.

(14) An attorney affiliated with an agency, institution, organization or other entity, including a school or regularly established religious organization that is responsible for the care, supervision, guidance or control of children.

(15) A foster parent.

(16) An adult family member who is a person responsible for the child's welfare and provides services to a child in a family living home, community home for individuals with an intellectual disability or host home for children which are subject to supervision or licensure by the department under Articles IX and X of the act of June 13, 1967 (P.L.31, No.21), known as the Public Welfare Code.

(b) Basis to report.—

(1) A mandated reporter enumerated in subsection (a) shall make a report of suspected child abuse in accordance with section 6313 (relating to reporting procedure), if the mandated reporter has reasonable cause to suspect that a child is a victim of child abuse under any of the following circumstances:

(i) The mandated reporter comes into contact with the child in the course of employment, occupation and practice of a profession or through a regularly scheduled program, activity or service.

(ii) The mandated reporter is directly responsible for the care, supervision, guidance or training of the child, or is affiliated with an agency, institution, organization, school, regularly established church or religious organization or other entity that is directly responsible for the care, supervision, guidance or training of the child.

(iii) A person makes a specific disclosure to the mandated reporter that an identifiable child is the victim of child abuse.

(iv) An individual 14 years of age or older makes a specific disclosure to the mandated reporter that the individual has committed child abuse.

(2) Nothing in this section shall require a child to come before the mandated reporter in order for the mandated reporter to make a report of suspected child abuse.

(3) Nothing in this section shall require the mandated reporter to identify the person responsible for the child abuse to make a report of suspected child abuse.

(c) Staff members of institutions, etc.—Whenever a person is required to report under subsection (b) in the capacity as a member of the staff of a medical or other public or private institution, school, facility or agency, that person shall report immediately in accordance with section 6313 and shall immediately thereafter notify the person in charge of the institution, school, facility or agency or the designated agent of the person in charge. Upon notification, the person in charge or the designated agent, if any, shall facilitate the cooperation of the institution, school, facility or agency with the investigation of the report. Any intimidation, retaliation or obstruction in the investigation of the report is subject to the provisions of 18 Pa.C.S. § 4958 (relating to intimidation, retaliation or obstruction in child abuse cases). This chapter does not require more than one report from any such institution, school, facility or agency.

(d) Civil action for discrimination against person filing report.—(Deleted by amendment).

(Dec. 16, 1994, P.L.1292, No.151, eff. July 1, 1995; Nov. 29, 2006, P.L.1581, No.179, eff. 180 days; Apr. 15, 2014, P.L.414, No.32, eff. 60 days; Apr. 15, 2014, P.L.417, No.33, eff. Dec. 31, 2014; Apr. 15, 2014, P.L.425, No.34, eff. Dec. 31, 2014; May 14, 2014, P.L.645, No.44, eff. Dec. 31, 2014; Oct. 22, 2014, P.L.2529, No.153, eff. Dec. 31, 2014; July 1, 2015, P.L.94, No.15, eff. imd.)

2015 Amendment. Act 15 amended subsec. (a)(7) and (12) and added subsec. (a)(16).

2014 Amendments. Act 32 amended subsec. (a) and deleted subsec. (b), Act 33 amended subsecs. (a) and (c) and added subsec. (b), Act 34 deleted subsec. (d), Act 44 amended subsec. (c) and Act 153 amended subsec. (b)(1) intro. par. and added subsec. (a)(15). Act 33 overlooked the amendment by Act 32, but the amendments do not conflict in substance and have both been given effect in setting forth the text of subsec. (b). Act 44 overlooked the amendment by Act 33, but the amendments do not conflict in substance (except for the deletion of "assume the responsibility and," as to which Act 44 has been given effect) and have both been given effect in setting forth the text of subsec. (c).

Effective Date. Section 17 of Act 45 of 2014 provided that, notwithstanding section 4 of Act 32 of 2014, the amendment of subsecs. (a) and (b) shall take effect December 31, 2014.

Cross References. Section 6311 is referred to in sections 6313, 6318, 6320, 6340, 6340.1 of this title.

§ 6311.1. Privileged communications.

(a) General rule.—Subject to subsection (b), the privileged communications between a mandated reporter and a patient or client of the mandated reporter shall not:

(1) Apply to a situation involving child abuse.

(2) Relieve the mandated reporter of the duty to make a report of suspected child abuse.

(b) Confidential communications.—The following protections shall apply:

(1) Confidential communications made to a member of the clergy are protected under 42 Pa.C.S. § 5943 (relating to confidential communications to clergymen).

(2) Confidential communications made to an attorney are protected so long as they are within the scope of 42 Pa.C.S. §§ 5916 (relating to confidential communications to attorney) and 5928 (relating to confidential communications to attorney), the attorney work product doctrine or the rules of professional conduct for attorneys.

2014, April 15, P.L. 414, No. 32, § 2, effective Dec. 31, 2014.

§ 6312. Persons encouraged to report suspected child abuse.

Any person may make an oral or written report of suspected child abuse, which may be submitted electronically, or cause a report of suspected child abuse to be made to the department, county agency or law enforcement, if that person has reasonable cause to suspect that a child is a victim of child abuse.

1990, Dec. 19, P.L. 1240, No. 206, § 2, effective in 90 days. Amended 2014, April 15, P.L. 417, No. 33, § 2, effective Dec. 31, 2014.

§ 6313. Reporting procedure.

(a) Report by mandated reporter.—

(1) A mandated reporter shall immediately make an oral report of suspected child abuse to the department via the Statewide toll-free telephone number under section 6332 (relating to establishment of Statewide toll-free telephone number) or a written report using electronic technologies under section 6305 (relating to electronic reporting).

(2) A mandated reporter making an oral report under paragraph (1) of suspected child abuse shall also make a written report, which may be submitted electronically, within 48 hours to the department or county agency assigned to the case in a manner and format prescribed by the department.

(3) The failure of the mandated reporter to file the report under paragraph (2) shall not relieve the county agency from any duty under this chapter, and the county agency shall proceed as though the mandated reporter complied with paragraph (2).

(b) Contents of report.—A written report of suspected child abuse, which may be submitted electronically, shall include the following information, if known:

(1) The names and addresses of the child, the child's parents and any other person responsible for the child's welfare.

(2) Where the suspected abuse occurred.

(3) The age and sex of each subject of the report.

(4) The nature and extent of the suspected child abuse, including any evidence of prior abuse to the child or any sibling of the child.

(5) The name and relationship of each individual responsible for causing the suspected abuse and any evidence of prior abuse by each individual.

(6) Family composition.

(7) The source of the report.

(8) The name, telephone number and e-mail address of the person making the report.

(9) The actions taken by the person making the report, including those actions taken under section 6314 (relating to photographs, medical tests and X-rays of child subject to report), 6315 (relating to taking child into protective custody), 6316 (relating to admission to private and public hospitals) or 6317 (relating to mandatory reporting and postmortem investigation of deaths).

(10) Any other information required by Federal law or regulation.

(11) Any other information that the department requires by regulation.

(c), (d) Repealed by 2014, April 15, P.L. 417, No. 33, § 2, effective Dec. 31, 2014.

(e) Applicability of Mental Health Procedures Act.—Notwithstanding any other provision of law, a mandated reporter enumerated under 6311 (relating to persons required to report suspected child abuse) who makes a report of suspected child abuse pursuant to this section, or who makes a report of a crime against a child to law enforcement officials, shall not be in violation of the act of July 9, 1976 (P.L. 817, No. 143), known as the Mental Health Procedures Act, by releasing information necessary to complete the report.

1990, Dec. 19, P.L. 1240, No. 206, § 2, effective in 90 days. Amended 1994, Dec. 16, P.L. 1292, No. 151, § 3, effective July 1, 1995; 2014, April 15, P.L. 417, No. 33, § 2, effective Dec. 31, 2014; 2014, Oct. 22, P.L. 2529, No. 153, § 4, effective Dec. 31, 2014.

Cross References. Section 6313 is referred to in sections 6311, 6335, 6339, 6340, 6349, 6367 of this title.

§ 6314. Photographs, medical tests and X-rays of child subject to report.

A person or official required to report cases of suspected child abuse may take or cause to be taken photographs of the child who is subject to a report and, if clinically indicated, cause to be performed a radiological examination and other medical tests on the child. Medical summaries or reports of the photographs, X-rays and relevant medical tests taken shall be sent to the county agency at the time the written report is sent or within 48 hours after a report is made by electronic technologies or as soon thereafter as possible. The county agency shall have access to actual photographs or duplicates and X-rays and may obtain them or duplicates of them upon request. Medical summaries or reports of the photographs, X-rays and relevant medical tests shall be made available to law enforcement officials in the course of investigating cases pursuant to section 6340(a)(9) or (10) (relating to release of information in confidential reports).

1990, Dec. 19, P.L. 1240, No. 206, § 2, effective in 90 days. Amended 1994, Dec. 16, P.L. 1292, No. 151, § 3, effective July 1, 1995; 2014, April 15, P.L. 417, No. 33, § 2, effective Dec. 31, 2014.

§ 6315. Taking child into protective custody.

(a) General rule.—A child may be taken into protective custody:

(1) As provided by 42 Pa.C.S. § 6324 (relating to taking into custody).

(2) By a physician examining or treating the child or by the director, or a person specifically designated in writing by the director, of any hospital or other medical institution where the child is being treated if protective custody is immediately necessary to protect the child under this chapter.

(3) By a physician or the director, or a person specifically designated by the director, of a hospital pursuant to Chapter 65 (relating to newborn protection) if the child is a newborn.

(4) Subject to this section and after receipt of a court order, the county agency shall take a child into protective custody for protection from abuse. No county agency worker may take custody of the child without judicial authorization based on the merits of the situation.

(5) By a police officer at a police station under Chapter 65.

(6) By an emergency services provider on the grounds of an entity that employs or otherwise provides access to the emergency services provider under Chapter 65.

(b) Duration of custody.—No child may be held in protective custody for more than 24 hours unless the appropriate county agency is immediately notified that the child has been taken into custody and the county agency obtains an order from a court of competent jurisdiction permitting the child to be held in custody for a longer period. Each court shall insure that a judge is available 24 hours a day, 365 days a year to accept and decide the actions brought by a county agency under this subsection within the 24-hour period.

(c) Notice of custody.—

(1) Except as provided in paragraph (2), an individual taking a child into protective custody under this chapter shall immediately, and within 24 hours in writing, notify the parent, guardian or other custodian of the child of the whereabouts of the child, unless prohibited by court order, and the reasons for the need to take the child into protective custody and shall immediately notify the appropriate county agency in order that proceedings under 42 Pa.C.S. Ch. 63 (relating to juvenile matters) may be initiated, if appropriate.

(2) In the case of a newborn taken into protective custody pursuant to subsection (a)(3), the county agency shall within 24 hours make diligent efforts to notify a parent, guardian, custodian or other family member of the whereabouts of the newborn, unless prohibited by court order, and the reasons for the need to take the newborn into protective custody.

(d) Informal hearing.—In no case shall protective custody under this chapter be maintained longer than 72 hours without an informal hearing under 42 Pa.C.S. § 6332 (relating to informal hearing). If, at the hearing, it is determined that protective custody shall be continued and the child is alleged to be without proper parental care or control or is alleged to be a dependent child under 42 Pa.C.S. § 6302 (relating to definitions), the county agency shall within 48 hours file a petition with the court under 42 Pa.C.S. Ch. 63 alleging that the child is a dependent child.

(e) Place of detention.—No child taken into protective custody under this chapter may be detained during the protective custody except in an appropriate medical facility, foster home or other appropriate facility approved by the department for this purpose.

(f) Conference with parent or other custodian.—A conference between the parent, guardian or other custodian of the child taken into temporary protective custody pursuant to this section and the employee designated by the county agency to be responsible for the child shall be held within 48 hours of the time that the child is taken into custody for the purpose of:

(1) Explaining to the parent, guardian or other custodian the reasons for the temporary detention of the child and the whereabouts of the child, unless prohibited by court order.

(2) Expediting, wherever possible, the return of the child to the custody of the parent, guardian or other custodian where custody is no longer necessary.

(3) Explaining to the parent, guardian or other custodian the rights provided for under 42 Pa.C.S. §§ 6337 (relating to right to counsel) and 6338 (relating to other basic rights).

(Dec. 16, 1994, P.L.1292, No.151, eff. July 1, 1995; Dec. 9, 2002, P.L.1549, No.201, eff. 60 days; Apr. 15, 2014, P.L.417, No.33, eff. Dec. 31, 2014; July 2, 2014, P.L.843, No.91, eff. 60 days; Dec. 22, 2017, P.L.1219, No.68, eff. 60 days)

2017 Amendment. Act 68 added subsec. (a)(6).

2014 Amendments. Act 33 added subsec. (a)(4) and Act 91 added subsec. (a)(5).

2002 Amendment. Act 201 amended subsecs. (a) and (c).

Cross References. Section 6315 is referred to in sections 6313, 6316, 6318, 6375, 6504, 6504.1, 6504.2, 6508, 6509 of this title.

§ 6316. Admission to private and public hospitals.

(a) **General rule.**—Children appearing to suffer any physical or mental condition which may constitute child abuse shall be admitted to, treated and maintained in facilities of private and public hospitals on the basis of medical need and shall not be refused or deprived in any way of proper medical treatment and care.

(a.1) **Newborns.**—A newborn taken into protective custody pursuant to section 6315(a)(3) or (5) (relating to taking child into protective custody) shall be admitted to, treated and maintained in facilities of public and private hospitals on the basis of medical need and shall not be refused or deprived in any way of proper medical treatment and care. Once a newborn is taken into protective custody pursuant to section 6315(a)(3) or (5), the newborn shall be considered immediately eligible for Medicaid for payment of medical services provided. Until otherwise provided by court order, the county agency shall assume the responsibility for making decisions regarding the newborn's medical care.

(b) **Failure of hospital to admit child or newborn.**—The failure of a hospital to admit and properly treat and care for a child pursuant to subsection (a) or (a.1) shall be cause for the department to order immediate admittance, treatment and care by the hospital which shall be enforceable, if necessary, by the prompt institution of a civil action by the department. The child, through an attorney, shall also have the additional and independent right to seek immediate injunctive relief and institute an appropriate civil action for damages against the hospital.

1990, Dec. 19, P.L. 1240, No. 206, § 2, effective in 90 days. Amended 1994, Dec. 16, P.L. 1292, No. 151, § 3, effective July 1, 1995; 2002, Dec. 9, P.L. 1549, No. 201, § 4, effective in 60 days; 2014, July 2, P.L. 843, No. 91, § 4, effective in 60 days [Sept. 2, 2014].

§ 6317. Mandatory reporting and postmortem investigation of deaths.

A person or official required to report cases of suspected child abuse, including employees of a county agency, who has reasonable cause to suspect that a child died as a result of child abuse shall report that suspicion to the appropriate coroner or medical examiner. The coroner or medical examiner shall accept the report for investigation and shall report his finding to the police, the district attorney, the appropriate county agency and, if the report is made by a hospital, the hospital.

1990, Dec. 19, P.L. 1240, No. 206, § 2, effective in 90 days. Amended 1994, Dec. 16, P.L. 1292, No. 151, § 3, effective July 1, 1995; 2014, April 7, P.L. 388, No. 29, § 3, effective Dec. 31, 2014.

§ 6318. Immunity from liability.

(a) **General rule.**—A person, hospital, institution, school, facility, agency or agency employee acting in good faith shall have immunity from civil and criminal liability that might otherwise result from any of the following:

(1) Making a report of suspected child abuse or making a referral for general protective services, regardless of whether the report is required to be made under this chapter.

(2) Cooperating or consulting with an investigation under this chapter, including providing information to a child fatality or near-fatality review team.

(3) Testifying in a proceeding arising out of an instance of suspected child abuse or general protective services.

(4) Engaging in any action authorized under section 6314 (relating to photographs, medical tests and X-rays of child subject to report), 6315 (relating to taking child into protective custody), 6316 (relating to admission to private and public hospitals) or 6317 (relating to mandatory reporting and postmortem investigation of deaths).

(b) **Departmental and county agency immunity.**—An official or employee of the department or county agency who refers a report of suspected child abuse for general protective services to law enforcement authorities or provides services as authorized by this chapter shall have immunity from civil and criminal liability that might otherwise result from the action.

(c) **Presumption of good faith.**—For the purpose of any civil or criminal proceeding, the good faith of a person required to report pursuant to section 6311 (relating to persons required to report suspected child abuse) and of any person required to make a referral to law enforcement officers under this chapter shall be presumed.

(Dec. 16, 1994, P.L.1292, No.151, eff. July 1, 1995; Nov. 29, 2006, P.L.1581, No.179, eff. 60 days; July 3, 2008, P.L.276, No.33, eff. 180 days; Dec. 18, 2013, P.L.1201, No.119, eff. July 1, 2014).

§ 6319. Penalties.

(a) **Failure to report or refer.—**

(1) A person or official required by this chapter to report a case of suspected child abuse or to make a referral to the appropriate authorities commits an offense if the person or official willfully fails to do so.

(2) An offense under this section is a felony of the third degree if:

 (i) the person or official willfully fails to report;

 (ii) the child abuse constitutes a felony of the first degree or higher; and

 (iii) the person or official has direct knowledge of the nature of the abuse.

(3) An offense not otherwise specified in paragraph (2) is a misdemeanor of the second degree.

(4) A report of suspected child abuse to law enforcement or the appropriate county agency by a mandated reporter, made in lieu of a report to the department, shall not constitute an offense under this subsection, provided that the report was made in a good faith effort to comply with the requirements of this chapter.

(b) **Continuing course of action.**—If a person's willful failure under subsection (a) continues while the person knows or has reasonable cause to believe the child is actively being subjected to child abuse, the person commits a misdemeanor of the first degree, except that if the child abuse constitutes a felony of the first degree or higher, the person commits a felony of the third degree.

(c) **Multiple offenses.**—A person who commits a second or subsequent offense under subsection (a) commits a felony of the third degree, except that if the child abuse constitutes a felony of the first degree or higher, the penalty for the second or subsequent offenses is a felony of the second degree.

(d) **Statute of limitations.**—The statute of limitations for an offense under subsection (a) shall be either the statute of limitations for the crime committed against the minor child or five years, whichever is greater.

1990, Dec. 19, P.L. 1240, No. 206, § 2, effective in 90 days. Amended 2006, Nov. 29, P.L. 1581, No. 179, § 3, effective in 180 days [May 29, 2007]; 2014, April 15, P.L. 414, No. 32, § 3, effective Dec. 31, 2014.

§ 6320. Protection from employment discrimination.

(a) **Basis for relief.**—A person may commence an action for appropriate relief if all of the following apply:

   (1) The person is required to report under section 6311 (relating to persons required to report suspected child abuse) or encouraged to report under section 6312 (relating to persons encouraged to report suspected child abuse).

   (2) The person acted in good faith in making or causing the report of suspected child abuse to be made.

   (3) As a result of making the report of suspected child abuse, the person is discharged from employment or is discriminated against with respect to compensation, hire, tenure, terms, conditions or privileges of employment.

(b) **Applicability.**—This section does not apply to an individual making a report of suspected child abuse who is found to be a perpetrator because of the report or to any individual who fails to make a report of suspected child abuse as required under section 6311 and is subject to conviction under section 6319 (relating to penalties) for failure to report or to refer.

(c) **Location.**—An action under this section must be filed in the court of common pleas of the county in which the alleged unlawful discharge or discrimination occurred.

(d) **Relief.**—Upon a finding in favor of the plaintiff, the court may grant appropriate relief, which may include reinstatement of the plaintiff with back pay.

(e) **Departmental intervention.**—The department may intervene in an action commenced under this section.

2014, April 15, P.L. 425, No. 34, § 2, effective Dec. 31, 2014.

SUBCHAPTER C
POWERS AND DUTIES OF DEPARTMENT

Sec.
6331. Establishment of Statewide database.
6332. Establishment of Statewide toll-free telephone number.
6333. Continuous availability of department.
6334. Disposition of complaints received.
6334.1. Responsibility for investigation.
6335. Access to information in Statewide database.
6336. Information in Statewide database.
6337. Disposition and expunction of unfounded reports and general protective services reports.
6338. Disposition of founded and indicated reports.
6338.1. Expunction of information of perpetrator who was under 18 years of age when child abuse was committed.
6339. Confidentiality of reports.
6340. Release of information in confidential reports.
6340.1. Exchange of information.
6341. Amendment or expunction of information.
6342. Studies of data in records.
6343. Investigating performance of county agency.
6343.1. Citizen review panels.
6344. Employees having contact with children; adoptive and foster parents.
6344.1. Information relating to certified or registered day-care home residents.
6344.2. Volunteers having contact with children.

6344.3. Continued employment or participation in program, activity or service.
6344.4. Certification compliance.
6345. Audits by Attorney General.
6346. Cooperation of other agencies.
6347. Reports to Governor and General Assembly.
6348. Regulations.
6349. Penalties.

Cross References. Subchapter C is referred to in section 6313 of this title.

§ 6331. Establishment of Statewide database.

There shall be established in the department a Statewide database of protective services, which shall include the following, as provided by section 6336 (relating to information in Statewide database):

(1) Reports of suspected child abuse pending investigation.

(2) Reports with a status of pending juvenile court or pending criminal court action.

(3) Indicated and founded reports of child abuse.

(4) Unfounded reports of child abuse awaiting expunction.

(5) Unfounded reports accepted for services.

(6) Reports alleging the need for general protective services.

(7) General protective services reports that have been determined to be valid.

(8) Reports alleging the need for general protective services that have been determined invalid and are awaiting expunction.

(9) A family case record for all reports accepted for investigation, assessment or services.

(10) Information on reports made to the agency, but not accepted for investigation or assessment.

(11) False reports of child abuse pursuant to a conviction under 18 Pa.C.S. § 4906.1 (relating to false reports of child abuse) for the purpose of identifying and tracking patterns of intentionally false reports.

1990, Dec. 19, P.L. 1240, No. 206, § 2, effective in 90 days. Amended 1994, Dec. 16, P.L. 1292, No. 151, § 3, effective July 1, 1995; 2013, Dec. 18, P.L. 1201, No. 119, § 3, effective July 1, 2014; 2014, April 7, P.L. 388, No. 29, § 3.1, effective Dec. 31, 2014; 2014, May 14, P.L. 653, No. 45, § 2, effective Dec. 31, 2014.

Cross References. Section 6331 is referred to in sections 6334, 6353.2, 6353.3 of this title.

§ 6332. Establishment of Statewide toll-free telephone number.

(a) **General rule.**—The department shall establish a single Statewide toll-free telephone number that all persons, whether mandated by law or not, may use to report cases of suspected child abuse or children allegedly in need of general protective services. A county agency or law enforcement official shall use the Statewide toll-free telephone number or electronic technologies for determining the existence of reports of child abuse or general protective services reports in the Statewide database or reports under investigation.

(b) **Limitation on use.**—A county agency may only request and receive information pursuant to this subsection either on its own behalf because it has received a report of suspected child abuse or on behalf of a physician examining or treating a child or on behalf of the director or a person specifically designated in writing by the director of any hospital or other medical institution where a child is being treated, where the physician or the director or a person specifically designated in writing by the director suspects the child of being an abused child.

(c) **Posting Statewide toll-free telephone number in schools.**—All public and nonpublic schools that enroll students in grades kindergarten through 12 shall publicly display at each school campus a poster uniformly designed by the department that contains the Statewide toll-free telephone number for reporting suspected child abuse or neglect and any Statewide toll-free telephone number relating to school safety. The following apply:

(1) The poster shall be posted in a high-traffic, public area of the school that is readily accessible to and widely used by students.

(2) The department shall, in consultation with the Department of Education, design the poster, which shall:

(i) be 11 inches by 17 inches or larger;

(ii) display in bold print the Statewide toll-free telephone number for reporting suspected child abuse or neglect and any Statewide toll-free telephone number relating to school safety; and

(iii) include the department's publicly accessible Internet website that provides information and resources related to child protection.

(3) The department and the Department of Education shall make the poster available on their publicly accessible Internet websites to all public and nonpublic schools.

(d) **Posting Statewide toll-free telephone numbers in hospitals.**—All hospitals shall publicly display a poster that contains the Statewide toll-free telephone number for reporting suspected child abuse or neglect and any Statewide toll-free telephone number relating to school safety. The poster shall be 11 inches by 17 inches or larger and of a uniform design approved by the department in consultation with the Department of Health. The poster shall be posted in a high-traffic, public area of the emergency department of the hospital. The Statewide toll-free telephone numbers shall be printed in bold print. The poster shall also include the department's publicly accessible Internet website that provides information and resources related to child protection.

(Dec. 16, 1994, P.L.1292, No.151, eff. July 1, 1995; Apr. 7, 2014, P.L.388, No.29, eff. Dec. 31, 2014; June 28, 2018, P.L.375, No.54, eff. 60 days)

2018 Amendment. Act 54 added subsecs. (c) and (d).

2014 Amendment. Act 29 amended subsec. (a).

Cross References. Section 6332 is referred to in sections 6313, 6368 of this title.

§ 6333. Continuous availability of department.

The department shall be capable of receiving oral reports of child abuse, reports of children in need of general protective services, reports made by electronic technologies pursuant to this chapter and report summaries from county agencies. The department shall be capable of immediately identifying prior reports in the Statewide database and reports under investigation with a pending status and of monitoring the provision of child protective services 24 hours a day, seven days a week.

1990, Dec. 19, P.L. 1240, No. 206, § 2, effective in 90 days. Amended 1994, Dec. 16, P.L. 1292, No. 151, § 3, effective July 1, 1995; 2014, April 7, P.L. 388, No. 29, § 3.2, effective Dec. 31, 2014.

§ 6334. Disposition of complaints received.

(a) **Receipt of reports by county agencies and law enforcement.**—After ensuring the immediate safety of the child and any other child in the child's home, a county agency or law enforcement official that receives a report of suspected child abuse shall immediately notify the department of the report. If the report is an oral report by telephone, the county agency or law enforcement official shall attempt to collect as much of the information listed in section 6313(c) (relating to reporting procedure) as possible and shall submit the information to the department within 48 hours through a report in writing or by electronic technologies.

(b) **Receipt of reports by department and referral to county agency.**—The department shall immediately transmit an oral notice or a notice by electronic technologies to the county agency of the county where the suspected child abuse is alleged to have occurred. The notice shall contain the following information:

(1) That a report of suspected child abuse by a perpetrator has been received.

(2) The substance of the report.

(3) The existence in the Statewide database of a prior report or a current investigation or assessment concerning a subject of the report.

(c) **Receipt of reports by department and referral to law enforcement.**—If the department receives a report of suspected child abuse that also alleges that a criminal offense has been committed against the child, the department shall immediately transmit an oral notice or notice by electronic technologies to the appropriate law enforcement official in the county where the suspected child abuse is alleged to have occurred. The notice shall contain the following information, consistent with section 6340(a)(9) and (10) (relating to release of information in confidential reports):

(1) That a report of suspected child abuse has been received.

(2) The substance of the report.

(3) The existence in the Statewide database under section 6331 (relating to establishment of Statewide database) of a prior report or a current investigation or assessment concerning a subject of the report.

(d) **Notice of joint referrals.**—When a report is referred to the county agency under subsection (b) and is also referred to a law enforcement official under subsection (c), the notice shall include information as to the name and contact information of any persons receiving the referral, if known.

(e) **Jurisdictional overlap.**—If the residency of any subject of a report is a factor that requires the cooperation of more than one county agency, the department shall develop procedures to ensure the cooperation of those agencies in carrying out the requirements of this chapter.

(f) **Referral for services or investigation.**—If the report received does not suggest a need for protective services but does suggest a need for social services or other services or investigation, the department shall transmit the information to the county agency or other public agency for appropriate action. The information shall not be considered a child abuse report unless the agency to which the information was referred has reasonable cause to suspect after investigation that abuse occurred. If the agency has reasonable cause to suspect that abuse occurred, the agency shall notify the department, and the initial report shall be considered to have been a child abuse report.

(g) **Recording of pending reports.**—Upon receipt of a report of suspected child abuse, the department shall maintain a record of the complaint of suspected child abuse in the Statewide database. Upon receipt of a report under section 6353.2 (relating to responsibilities of county agency), the department shall maintain a record of the report in the Statewide database under section 6331.

(h) **Child abuse in another state where the victim child and the alleged perpetrator are residents of the Commonwealth.**—A report of suspected child abuse by a resident perpetrator occurring in another state shall be referred by the department to the county agency where the child resides in this Commonwealth and shall be investigated by the county agency as any other report of suspected child abuse by a perpetrator if the other state's child protective services agency cannot or will not investigate the report.

(i) **Child abuse in another state where only the alleged perpetrator is a resident of this Commonwealth.**—If suspected child abuse occurs in a jurisdiction other than this Commonwealth and only the alleged perpetrator is a resident of this Commonwealth, the report of suspected child abuse shall be referred to the county agency where the alleged perpetrator resides. The county agency shall do all of the following:

(1) Notify the children and youth social service agency of the jurisdiction in which the suspected child abuse occurred.

(2) If requested by the other agency, assist in investigating the suspected child abuse.

(j) Child abuse in another state where only the victim child is a resident of this Commonwealth.—A report of suspected child abuse occurring in another state where only the victim child resides in this Commonwealth and where the other state's child protective services agency cannot or will not investigate the report shall be assigned as a general protective services report to the county agency where the child resides.

(k) Copies of report.—A copy of a report of suspected child abuse under subsections (h), (i) and (j) shall be provided to the other state's child protective services agency and, if appropriate, to law enforcement officials where the incident occurred.

(l) Communication.—Reports and information under subsections (h), (i) and (j) shall be provided within seven calendar days of completion of the investigation.

1990, Dec. 19, P.L. 1240, No. 206, § 2, effective in 90 days. Amended 1994, Dec. 16, P.L. 1292, No. 151, § 3, effective July 1, 1995; 2005, July 7, P.L. 196, No. 43, § 2, imd. effective; 2014, April 7, P.L. 388, No. 29, § 3.2, effective Dec. 31, 2014.

Cross References. Section 6334 is referred to in sections 6335, 6336 of this title.

§ 6334.1. Responsibility for investigation.

The department shall establish procedures regarding the following different responses to address suspected child abuse and protective services depending on the person's allegedly committing the suspected child abuse or causing a child to be in need of protective services:

(1) If the suspected child abuse is alleged to have been committed by a perpetrator, the appropriate county agency shall investigate the allegation as provided in this chapter.

(2) If the suspected child abuse is alleged to have been committed by a perpetrator and the behavior constituting the suspected child abuse may include a violation of a criminal offense, the appropriate county agency and law enforcement officials shall jointly investigate the allegation through the investigative team established in section 6365(c) (relating to services for prevention, investigation and treatment of child abuse) and as provided in this chapter.

(3) If the suspected child abuse is alleged to have been committed by a person who is not a perpetrator and the behavior constituting the suspected child abuse may include a violation of a criminal offense, law enforcement officials where the suspected child abuse is alleged to have occurred shall be solely responsible for investigating the allegation.

(4) If a child is alleged to be in need of other protective services, the appropriate county agency shall assess the needs of the child as provided in this chapter.

2014, April 7, P.L. 388, No. 29, § 4, effective Dec. 31, 2014.

§ 6335. Access to information in Statewide database.

(a) Request for information.—A county agency or law enforcement official shall use the Statewide toll-free telephone number, or any manner prescribed by the department, to determine the existence of any prior reports involving a subject of the report. If the Statewide database contains information related to a report or a pending investigation or assessment concerning a subject of the report, the department shall immediately convey this information to the county agency or law enforcement official.

(b) **Verification of need.**—Information may be released under this section if a request for information is made orally or in writing and the department has done all of the following:

(1) Identified the requester, including electronic verification of the requester's identity.

(2) Determined whether the requester is authorized to obtain the information under this section.

(3) Provided notice to the requester that access and dissemination of the information is restricted as provided by this chapter.

(4) Obtained an affirmation by the requester that the request is within the scope of that person's official duties and the provisions of this chapter.

(c) **Use by county agency or law enforcement official.**—A county agency or law enforcement official may only request the information under subsection (a) for the purposes of investigating reports of child abuse, assessing allegations that a child is in need of general protective services, providing protective services to a child or investigating a crime against a child criminal offense. The following shall apply where information is requested pursuant to this section:

(1) A law enforcement official may use information contained in the Statewide database for the purpose of investigating a criminal offense as follows:

(i) Information regarding indicated and founded reports may be used for any purpose authorized by this chapter.

(ii) Information on all other reports may be used for the purposes of investigating a crime involving harm or threatened harm to a child, an alleged violation of section 6319 (relating to penalties for failure to report or to refer) or 6349 (relating to penalties) or an alleged violation of 18 Pa.C.S. § 4906.1 (relating to false reports of child abuse) or 4958 (relating to intimidation, retaliation or obstruction in child abuse cases).

(2) A county agency may use information contained in the Statewide database as follows:

(i) Information regarding indicated or founded reports may be used for any purpose authorized by this chapter.

(ii) Information on all other reports may be used for any purpose authorized by this chapter, except that information in reports that are not founded or indicated may not be used as evidence by the county agency when determining that a new report of suspected abuse is an indicated report.

(3) The department may use information contained in the Statewide database as follows:

(i) Information regarding indicated or founded reports may be used for any purpose authorized by this chapter.

(ii) Information on all other reports may be used for any purpose authorized by this chapter, except that information in reports that are not founded or indicated may not be used as evidence by the department when determining that a new report of suspected abuse is an indicated report.

(4) Information in the Statewide database may not be used for any purpose not authorized by this chapter.

(d) **Authorized releases for governmental functions.**—No person, other than an employee of the department in the course of official duties in connection with the responsibilities of the department under this chapter, shall have access to any information in the Statewide database except as provided under this section and the following:

(1) Section 6334 (relating to disposition of complaints received).

(2) Section 6340 (relating to release of information in confidential reports).

(3) Section 6342 (relating to studies of data in records).

(4) Section 6343 (relating to investigating performance of county agency).

(5) Section 6343.1 (relating to citizen review panels).

(6) Section 6347 (relating to reports to Governor and General Assembly).

(e) Certifications.—Information provided in response to inquiries under section 6344 (relating to employees having contact with children; adoptive and foster parents), 6344.1 (relating to information relating to certified or licensed child-care home residents) or 6344.2 (relating to volunteers having contact with children) shall not include unfounded reports of child abuse or reports related to general protective services and shall be limited to the following:

(1) Whether the person was named as a perpetrator of child abuse in a founded or indicated report.

(2) Whether there is an investigation pending in which the individual is an alleged perpetrator.

(3) The number, date of the incidents upon which the report is based and the type of abuse or neglect involved in any reports identified under paragraph (1).

(f) Electronic technologies.—Requests under this section may be made using electronic technologies if appropriate verification is made in accordance with subsection (b).

(Dec. 16, 1994, P.L.1292, No.151, eff. July 1, 1995; Dec. 15, 1998, P.L.963, No.127, eff. Mar. 1, 1999; Apr. 7, 2014, P.L.388, No.29, eff. Dec. 31, 2014; Oct. 22, 2014, P.L.2529, No.153, eff. Dec. 31, 2014; July 1, 2015, P.L.94, No.15, eff. imd.)

2015 Amendment. Act 15 amended subsec. (e).

§ 6336. Information in Statewide database.

(a) Information authorized.—The Statewide database shall include and shall be limited to the following information:

(1) The names, Social Security numbers, age, race, ethnicity and sex of the subjects of the reports.

(2) The date or dates and the nature and extent of the alleged instances that created the need for protective services.

(3) The home addresses of the subjects of the report.

(4) The county in which the alleged incidents that created the need for protective services occurred.

(5) Family composition.

(6) The name and relationship to the child in question and of other persons named in the report.

(7) Factors contributing to the need for protective services.

(8) The source of the report.

(9) Services planned or provided.

(10) If the report alleges child abuse, whether the report was determined to be founded, indicated or unfounded.

(11) If the report alleged the child was in need of general protective services, whether the report was valid or invalid.

(12) If the report was accepted for services and the reasons for the acceptance.

(13) If the report was not accepted for services, the reason the report was not accepted and whether the family was referred to other community services.

(14) Information obtained by the department in relation to a perpetrator's or school employee's request to release, amend or expunge information retained by the department or the county agency.

(15) The progress of any legal proceedings brought on the basis of the report of suspected child abuse.

(16) Whether a criminal investigation has been undertaken and the result of the investigation and of any criminal prosecution.

(17) In the case of an unfounded or invalid report, if it is later determined that the initial report was a false report, a notation to that effect regarding the status of the report.

(18) Unfounded reports of child abuse, limited to the information authorized under section 6337 (relating to disposition and expunction of unfounded reports and general protective services reports).

(19) Any additional information provided in section 6313(c) (relating to reporting procedure).

(20) Any additional demographic information that the department requires to comply with section 6342 (relating to studies of data in records).

(21) A family case record for each family accepted for investigation, assessment or services which shall be maintained consistent with regulatory requirements.

(22) With respect to cases that are not accepted for child abuse investigation or general protective services assessment or are referred to community services:

(i) The reason the report was not accepted.

(ii) Any information provided to the referral source or the family related to other services or option available to address the report.

(23) Any other information that is necessary to maintain the names of persons convicted of a violation under 18 Pa.C.S. § 4906.1 (relating to false reports of child abuse) or the names of persons who made a false report of the need for general protective services.

No information other than that permitted in this subsection shall be retained in the Statewide central register.

(b), (c) Deleted by 2014, April 7, P.L. 388, No. 29, § 5, effective Dec. 31, 2014.

1990, Dec. 19, P.L. 1240, No. 206, § 2, effective in 90 days. Amended 1994, Dec. 16, P.L. 1292, No. 151, § 3, effective July 1, 1995; 2014, April 7, P.L. 388, No. 29, § 5, effective Dec. 31, 2014.

Cross References. Section 6336 is referred to in section 6335, 6353.4 of this title.

§ 6337. Disposition and expunction of unfounded reports and general protective services reports.

(a) General rule.—When a report of suspected child abuse is determined by the appropriate county agency to be an unfounded report, the information concerning that report of suspected child abuse shall be maintained for a period of one year. Following the expiration of one year after the date the report was received by the department, the report shall be expunged from the Statewide database, as soon as possible, but no later than 120 days after the one-year period following the date the report was received by the department, and no information other than that authorized by subsection (b), which shall not include any identifying information on any subject of the report, shall be retained by the department. The expunction shall be mandated and guaranteed by the department.

(b) Absence of other determination.—If an investigation of a report of suspected child abuse conducted by the appropriate county agency pursuant to this chapter does not determine within 60 days of the date of the initial report of the instance of suspected child abuse that the report is a founded report, an indicated report or an unfounded report, or unless within that same 60-day period court action has been initiated and is responsible for the delay, the report shall be considered to be an unfounded report, and all information identifying the subjects of the report shall be expunged no later than 120 days following the expiration of one year after the date the report was received by the department. The agency shall advise the department that court action or an arrest has been initiated so that the Statewide database is kept current regarding the status of all legal proceedings and expunction is delayed.

(c) **Unfounded reports accepted for services.**—Information on an unfounded report shall be retained in the Statewide database if the county agency has accepted the family for services and the report of suspected child abuse is clearly identified as an unfounded report. The county agency shall notify the department immediately upon closure of the case, and the report shall be expunged as soon as possible, but no later than 120 days after the one-year period following the date the family case was closed. If the subject child of the unfounded report becomes 23 years of age prior to the closure of the family case, the unfounded report shall be expunged when the subject child reaches 23 years of age.

(d) **Expunction of valid general protective services reports.**—Information concerning valid general protective services reports shall be maintained in the Statewide database as follows:

(1) Reports that are assessed by the county agency and are determined to be valid, but are not accepted for services, shall be reported to the department and entered into the Statewide database. The reports shall be maintained for a period of ten years or until the youngest child identified in the most recent general protective services report attains 23 years of age, whichever occurs first. Following the expiration of ten years after the date the report was received by the department or until the youngest child identified in the most recent general protective services report attains 23 years of age, whichever occurs first, the report shall be expunged from the Statewide database as soon as possible, but no later than 120 days after the ten-year period following the date the report was received by the department or the youngest child identified in the most recent general protective services report attains 23 years of age, whichever occurs first.

(2) Reports that are assessed by the county agency and accepted for services shall be reported to the department, except as otherwise provided in subsection (f) (2), and entered into the Statewide database. The reports shall be maintained for a period of ten years after the closure of services by the county agency or until the youngest child identified in the most recent general protective services report attains 23 years of age, whichever occurs first. Following the expiration of ten years after the closure of services by the county agency or until the youngest child identified in the most recent general protective services report attains 23 years of age, whichever occurs first, the report shall be expunged from the Statewide database as soon as possible, but no later than 120 days after the ten-year period following the closure of services by the county agency or the youngest child identified in the most recent general protective services report attains 23 years of age, whichever occurs first.

(3) The expunction of information on general protective services under this subsection shall be mandated and guaranteed by the department.

(e) **Expunction of invalid general protective services reports.**—When a report alleging the need for general protective services is determined by the appropriate county agency to be an invalid report, the information concerning that report shall be maintained for a period of one year. Following the expiration of one year after the date the report was received by the department, the report shall be expunged as soon as possible, but no later than 120 days after the one-year period following the date the report was received by the department. The expunction shall be mandated and guaranteed by the department.

(f) **County agency records.**—Information concerning protective services reports shall be maintained by a county agency as follows:

(1) County agency records of protective services shall be used and maintained in a manner that is consistent with the use and maintenance of information in the

Statewide database, as provided under this chapter, except as otherwise provided in paragraph (2). If required under this chapter to amend or expunge information in the Statewide database, the department shall notify the appropriate county agency of the amendment or expungement within ten days. The county agency shall amend or expunge its records in a commensurate manner within ten days of receiving notification from the department.

(2) A county agency may maintain information regarding protective services reports that have been expunged in the Statewide database for access by the county agency to assist in future risk and safety assessments and research.

(Dec. 16, 1994, P.L.1292, No.151, eff. July 1, 1996; Dec. 15, 1998, P.L.963, No.127, eff. Mar. 1, 1999; Apr. 7, 2014, P.L.388, No.29, eff. Dec. 31, 2014; June 28, 2018, P.L.375, No.54, eff. 365 days)

2018 Amendment. Act 54 amended subsecs. (d) and (f). See section 3 of Act 54 in the appendix to this title for special provisions relating to expunction.

Cross References. Section 6337 is referred to in sections 6336, 6349 of this title.

§ 6338. Disposition of founded and indicated reports.

(a) **General rule.**—When a report of suspected child abuse is determined by the appropriate county agency to be a founded report or an indicated report, the status of the report shall be changed from pending to founded or indicated in the Statewide database. Notice of the determination that a report is a founded, indicated or unfounded report shall be made as provided in section 6368(f) (relating to investigation of reports).

(b) **Expunction of information when child attains 23 years of age.**—Except as provided in subsection (c), all information which identifies the subjects of founded and indicated child abuse reports shall be expunged when the subject child reaches the age of 23. The expunction shall be mandated and guaranteed by the department.

(c) **Retention of information.**—The Statewide database shall indefinitely retain the names of perpetrators of child abuse and school employees who are subjects of founded or indicated reports only if the individual's Social Security number or date of birth is known to the department. The entry in the Statewide database shall not include identifying information regarding other subjects of the report.

1990, Dec. 19, P.L. 1240, No. 206, § 2, effective in 90 days. Amended 1994, Dec. 16, P.L. 1292, No. 151, § 3, effective July 1, 1995; 2013, Dec. 18, P.L. 1170, No. 108, § 3, effective Dec. 31, 2014; 2014, April 7, P.L. 388, No. 29, § 5.1, effective Dec. 31, 2014; 2014, May 14, P.L. 653, No. 45, § 2, effective Dec. 31, 2014.

Cross References. Section 6338 is referred to in sections 6349, 6353.4 of this title.

§ 6338.1. Expunction of information of perpetrator who was under 18 years of age when child abuse was committed.

(a) **General rule.**—The name of a perpetrator who is the subject of an indicated report of child abuse and who was under 18 years of age when the individual committed child abuse shall be expunged from the Statewide database when the individual reaches 21 years of age or when five years have elapsed since the perpetrator's name was added to the database, whichever is later, if the individual meets all of the following:

(1) The individual has not been named as a perpetrator in any subsequent indicated report of child abuse and is not named as an alleged perpetrator in a child abuse report pending investigation.

(2) The individual has never been convicted or adjudicated delinquent following a determination by the court that the individual committed an offense under section 6344(c) (relating to employees having contact with children; adoptive and foster parents), and no proceeding is pending seeking such conviction or adjudication.

(3) The child abuse which resulted in the inclusion of the perpetrator's name in the database did not involve the use of a deadly weapon, as defined under 18 Pa.C.S. § 2301 (relating to definitions).

(b) Mandated expunction.—If the perpetrator meets all of the requirements under subsection (a), the expunction shall be mandated and guaranteed by the department.

(c) Nonapplicability.—The provisions of this section shall not apply to any of the following cases:

(1) A perpetrator who is the subject of a founded report of child abuse.

(2) A sexually violent delinquent child, as defined in 42 Pa.C.S. § 9799.12 (relating to definitions), who meets all of the following:

(i) Is required to register under 42 Pa.C.S. Ch. 97 Subch. H (relating to registration of sexual offenders).

(ii) Was found delinquent as a result of the same acts which resulted in the sexually violent delinquent child being named a perpetrator of child abuse.

(3) A juvenile offender, as defined in 42 Pa.C.S. § 9799.12, who meets all of the following:

(i) Is required to register under 42 Pa.C.S. Ch. 97 Subch. H as a result of an adjudication of delinquency for the same acts which resulted in the juvenile offender being named a perpetrator of child abuse.

(ii) Has not been removed from the Statewide Registry of Sexual Offenders pursuant to 42 Pa.C.S. § 9799.17 (relating to termination of period of registration for juvenile offenders).

(4) An individual who:

(i) Is required to register under 42 Pa.C.S. Ch. 97 Subch. H or I (relating to continued registration of sexual offenders) as a result of a criminal conviction for the same acts which resulted in the sexual offender being named a perpetrator of child abuse.

(ii) Has not completed the period of registration required under 42 Pa.C.S. Subch. H or I.

(Dec. 18, 2013, P.L.1195, No.117, eff. Dec. 31, 2014; May 14, 2014, P.L.653, No.45, eff. Dec. 31, 2014; Oct. 22, 2014, P.L.2529, No.153, eff. Dec. 31, 2014; Feb. 21, 2018, P.L.27, No.10, eff. imd.; June 12, 2018, P.L.140, No.29, eff. imd.)

2018 Amendments. Act 10 amended subsec. (c)(4) and Act 29 reenacted subsec. (c)(4).

2014 Amendments. Act 45 amended subsec. (a)(1) and Act 153 amended subsec. (a)(2).

2013 Amendment. Act 117 added section 6338.1.

Cross References. Section 6338.1 is referred to in section 6341 of this title.

§ 6339. Confidentiality of reports.

Except as otherwise provided in this subchapter or by the Pennsylvania Rules of Juvenile Court Procedure, reports made pursuant to this chapter, including, but not limited to, report summaries of child abuse and reports made pursuant to section 6313 (relating to reporting procedure) as well as any other information obtained, reports written or photographs or X-rays taken concerning alleged instances of child abuse in the possession of the department or a county agency shall be confidential.

1990, Dec. 19, P.L. 1240, No. 206, § 2, effective in 90 days. Amended 1994, Dec. 16, P.L. 1292, No. 151, § 3, effective July 1, 1995; 2014, April 7, P.L. 388, No. 29, § 5.2, effective Dec. 31, 2014; 2014, Oct. 22, P.L. ___, No. 153, § 7, effective Dec. 31, 2014.

Cross References. Section 6339 is referred to in section 6340 of this title.

Suspension by Court Rule. Section 6339 was suspended by Pennsylvania Rule of Juvenile Court Procedure No. 1800(9), adopted August 21, 2006, insofar as it is inconsistent with Rule 1340(B)(1)(e), which provides for the disclosure of reports if the reports are going to be used as evidence in a hearing to prove dependency of a child.

§ 6340. Release of information in confidential reports.

(a) **General rule.**—Reports specified in section 6339 (relating to confidentiality of reports) shall only be made available to:

(1) An authorized official of a county agency, of a Federal agency that has a need for such information to carry out its responsibilities under law to protect children from abuse and neglect or of an agency of another state that performs protective services analogous to those services performed by county agencies or the department in the course of the official's duties, multidisciplinary team members assigned to the case and duly authorized persons providing services pursuant to section 6370(a) (relating to voluntary or court-ordered services; findings of child abuse).

(2) A physician examining or treating a child or the director or a person specifically designated in writing by the director of any hospital or other medical institution where a child is being treated when the physician or the director or the designee of the director suspects the child of being an abused child or a child alleged to be in need of protection under this chapter.

(3) A guardian ad litem or court designated advocate for the child.

(4) An authorized official or agent of the department in accordance with department regulations or in accordance with the conduct of a performance audit as authorized by section 6343 (relating to investigating performance of county agency).

(5) A court of competent jurisdiction, including a magisterial district judge, a judge of the Philadelphia Municipal Court and a judge of the Pittsburgh Magistrates Court, pursuant to court order or subpoena in a criminal matter involving a charge of child abuse under section 6303(b) (relating to definitions). Disclosure through testimony shall be subject to the restrictions of subsection (c).

(5.1) A court of common pleas in connection with any matter involving custody of a child as set forth in sections 5328 (relating to factors to consider when awarding custody) and 5329.1 (relating to consideration of child abuse and involvement with protective services) or temporary guardianship of a child under Chapter 56 (relating to standby and temporary guardianship).

(6) A standing committee of the General Assembly, as specified in section 6384 (relating to legislative oversight).

(7) The Attorney General.

(8) Federal auditors if required for Federal financial participation in funding of agencies except that Federal auditors may not remove identifiable reports or copies thereof from the department or county agencies.

(9) Law enforcement officials of any jurisdiction, as long as the information is relevant in the course of investigating cases of:

(i) Homicide or other criminal offense set forth in section 6344(c) (relating to employees having contact with children; adoptive and foster parents), sexual abuse or exploitation, bodily injury or serious bodily injury caused by a perpetrator or nonperpetrator.

(ii) Child abuse other than that identified under subparagraph (i) by a nonperpetrator.

(iii) Repeated physical injury to a child under circumstances which indicate that the child's health, safety or welfare is harmed or threatened.

(iv) A missing child report.

(v) Severe forms of trafficking in persons or sex trafficking, as those terms are defined under section 103 of the Trafficking Victims Protection Act of 2000 (114 Stat. 1466, 22 U.S.C. § 7102).

(10) The district attorney's office or other law enforcement official, as set forth in county protocols for multidisciplinary investigative teams required in section 6365(c) (relating to services for prevention, investigation and treatment of child abuse), shall receive, immediately after the county agency has ensured the safety of

the child, reports of abuse according to regulations, from the department or county agency in which the initial report of suspected child abuse or initial inquiry into the report gives evidence that the abuse is:

(i) a criminal offense set forth under section 6344.3 (relating to grounds for denying employment or participation in program, activity or service), not including an offense under 18 Pa.C.S. § 4304 (relating to endangering welfare of children) or an equivalent crime under Federal law or law of another state; or

(ii) child abuse under section 6334.1 (relating to responsibility for investigation).

(11) Designated county officials, in reviewing the competence of the county agency or its employees pursuant to this chapter. Officials under this paragraph are limited to the following:

(i) The board of commissioners in counties other than counties of the first class.

(ii) Mayor in a city of the first class under the act of April 21, 1949 (P.L.665, No.155), known as the First Class City Home Rule Act.

(iii) An individual serving as a county chief executive as designated by a county home rule charter or optional plan form of government pursuant to the act of April 13, 1972 (P.L.184, No.62), known as the Home Rule Charter and Optional Plans Law.

(12) A mandated reporter of suspected child abuse under section 6311 (relating to persons required to report suspected child abuse) who made a report of abuse involving the subject child shall be limited to the following:

(i) Whether the child abuse report is indicated, founded or unfounded.

(ii) Any services provided, arranged for or to be provided by the county agency to protect the child.

(13) School administrators and child-care service employers, as provided under this paragraph. The following shall apply:

(i) If the alleged perpetrator is a school employee or child-care service employee, school administrators and child-care service employers shall receive notice of a pending allegation and the final status of the report following the investigation as to whether the report is indicated, founded or unfounded.

(ii) Information disclosed pursuant to this paragraph shall be provided to the school administrator or child-care service employer within ten days of the completion of the investigation.

(iii) If the perpetrator is a school employee, the notice of the final status of the report shall be sent to the Department of Education within ten days of the completion of the investigation.

(14) A prospective adoptive parent, approved by an adoption agency, when considering adopting an abused child in the custody of a county agency. The county agency having custody of the child and the adoption agency shall determine the scope and detail of information which must be provided so that the prospective parent may make an informed decision to adopt.

(15) Appropriate officials of another county or state regarding an investigation related to child abuse or protective services when a family has moved to that county or state. Reports under this paragraph shall include general protective service reports and related information. Reports and information under this paragraph shall be provided within seven calendar days. The department shall promulgate regulations as necessary to carry out the purposes of this paragraph.

(16) Members of citizen review panels convened pursuant to section 6343.1 (relating to citizen review panels), provided that such members shall not disclose to any

person or government official any identifying information about any specific child protective services case with respect to which the panel is provided information.

(17) A member of a child fatality or near fatality review team under section 6365(d).

(18) The Department of the Auditor General in conjunction with the performances of the duties designated to the Office of Auditor General, except that the Auditor General may not remove identifiable reports or copies thereof from the department or county agency.

(b) Release of information to subject.—Upon a written request, a subject of a report may receive a copy of all information, except that prohibited from being disclosed by subsection (c), contained in the Statewide database or in any report filed pursuant to section 6313 (relating to reporting procedure).

(c) Protecting identity.—Except for reports under subsection (a)(9) and (10) and in response to a law enforcement official investigating allegations of false reports under 18 Pa.C.S. § 4906.1 (relating to false reports of child abuse), the release of data by the department, county, institution, school, facility or agency or designated agent of the person in charge that would identify the person who made a report of suspected child abuse or who cooperated in a subsequent investigation is prohibited. Law enforcement officials shall treat all reporting sources as confidential informants.

(d) Exclusion of information.—Except as provided under section 6341(c.2)(4) (relating to amendment or expunction of information), information maintained in the Statewide database obtained from an investigating agency in relation to an appeal request shall not be released to any person except a department official. Information in the Statewide database or a confidential report provided under section 6341(c.2)(4) shall be subject to subsection (c).

(Dec. 16, 1994, P.L.1292, No.151, eff. July 1, 1995; Dec. 15, 1998, P.L.963, No.127; Nov. 30, 2004, P.L.1618, No.207, eff. 60 days; Nov. 9, 2006, P.L.1358, No.146, eff. 180 days; July 3, 2008, P.L.276, No.33, eff. 180 days; Dec. 18, 2013, P.L.1167, No.107, eff. Jan. 1, 2014; Apr. 7, 2014, P.L.388, No.29, eff. Dec. 31, 2014; Oct. 22, 2014, P.L.2529, No.153, eff. Dec. 31, 2014; July 1, 2015, P.L.94, No.15, eff. imd.; Oct. 28, 2016, P.L.966, No.115, eff. imd.; October 23, 2018, No. 88, eff. 60 days)

2018 Amendment. Act 88 amended subsec. (a)(5.1).

2016 Amendment. Act 115 added subsec. (a)(9)(v).

2015 Amendment. Act 15 added subsec. (a)(18).

2014 Amendments. Act 29 amended subsecs. (a)(9), (10), (12) and (13), (b), (c) and (d) and Act 153 amended subsecs. (a)(9)(i) and (c).

2013 Amendment. Act 107 amended subsec. (a)(5.1). See section 6 of Act 107 in the appendix to this title for special provisions relating to applicability.

2008 Amendment. Act 33 added subsec. (a)(17).

2006 Amendment. Act 146 amended subsec. (a)(1) and added subsec. (a)(16).

2004 Amendment. Act 207 amended subsec. (a)(5). See section 29 of Act 207 in the appendix to this title for special provisions relating to construction of law.

1998 Amendment. Act 127 amended subsec. (a)(5), (9) and (10) and added subsec. (a)(15), effective immediately as to subsec. (a)(5) and (15) and March 1, 1999, as to the remainder of the section.

References in Text. The act of April 13, 1972 (P.L.184, No.62), known as the Home Rule Charter and Optional Plans Law, referred to in subsec. (a), was repealed by the act of December 19, 1996 (P.L.1158, No.177). The subject matter is now contained in Subpart E of Part III of Title 53 (Municipalities Generally).

Cross References. Section 6340 is referred to in sections 5329.1, 6314, 6334, 6335, 6341, 6343, 6346, 6365, 6375 of this title.

§ 6340.1. Exchange of information.

(a) Certified medical practitioners.—In circumstances which negatively affect the medical health of a child, a certified medical practitioner shall, in a timely manner, provide the county agency with the following information when an assessment for general protective services or a child abuse investigation is being conducted or when the family has been accepted for services by a county agency:

(1) Relevant medical information known to the certified medical practitioner regarding the child's prior and current health.

(2) Information from a subsequent examination.

(3) Information regarding treatment of the child.

(4) Relevant medical information known regarding any other child in the child's household where such information may contribute to the assessment, investigation or provision of services by the county agency to the child or other children in the household.

(b) **Parental consent.**—Parental consent is not required for the certified medical practitioner to provide the information under subsection (a).

(c) **Request by certified medical practitioner.**—If requested by the child's primary care physician or a certified medical practitioner who is providing medical care to the child, the county agency, in order to ensure the proper medical care of the child, shall provide the following information as it pertains to circumstances which negatively affect the medical health of the child:

(1) The final status of any assessment of general protective services or an investigation of child abuse, if the report of child abuse is indicated or founded.

(2) Information on an unfounded report of child abuse if the certified medical practitioner made the report as a mandated reporter under section 6311 (relating to persons required to report suspected child abuse).

(3) If accepted for services, any service provided, arranged for or to be provided by the county agency.

(4) The identity of other certified medical practitioners providing medical care to the child to obtain the child's medical records to allow for coordination of care between medical practitioners.

(d) **Notification by county agency.**—In circumstances which negatively affect the medical health of a child, the county agency shall notify the certified medical practitioner who is the child's primary care provider, if known, of the following information:

(1) The final status of any assessment of general protective services or an investigation of child abuse, if the report of child abuse is indicated or founded.

(2) Information on an unfounded report of child abuse if the certified medical practitioner made the report as a mandated reporter under section 6311.

(3) If accepted for services, any service provided, arranged for or to be provided by the county agency.

2014, Oct. 22, P.L. 2876, No. 176, § 1, effective Dec. 31, 2014.

§ 6341. Amendment or expunction of information.

(a) **General rule.**—Notwithstanding section 6338.1 (relating to expunction of information of perpetrator who was under 18 years of age when child abuse was committed):

(1) At any time, the secretary may amend or expunge any record in the Statewide database under this chapter upon good cause shown and notice to the appropriate subjects of the report. The request shall be in writing in a manner prescribed by the department. For purposes of this paragraph, good cause shall include, but is not limited to, the following:

(i) Newly discovered evidence that an indicated report of child abuse is inaccurate or is being maintained in a manner inconsistent with this chapter.

(ii) A determination that the perpetrator in an indicated report of abuse no longer represents a risk of child abuse and that no significant public purpose would be served by the continued listing of the person as a perpetrator in the Statewide database.

(2) Any person named as a perpetrator, and any school employee named, in an indicated report of child abuse may, within 90 days of being notified of the status of the report, request an administrative review by, or appeal and request a hearing before, the secretary to amend or expunge an indicated report on the grounds that it is inaccurate or it is being maintained in a manner inconsistent with this chapter. The request shall be in writing in a manner prescribed by the department.

(3) Within 60 days of a request under paragraph (1) or a request for administrative review under paragraph (2), the department shall send notice of the secretary's decision.

(b) Review of grant of request.—If the secretary grants the request under subsection (a)(2), the Statewide database, appropriate county agency, appropriate law enforcement officials and all subjects shall be so advised of the decision. The county agency and any subject have 90 days in which to file an administrative appeal with the secretary. If an administrative appeal is received, the secretary or his designated agent shall schedule a hearing pursuant to Article IV of the act of June 13, 1967 (P.L. 31, No. 21), known as the Public Welfare Code, attending departmental regulations. If no administrative appeal is received within the designated time period, the Statewide database shall comply with the decision of the secretary and advise the county agency to amend or expunge the information in their records so that the records are consistent at both the State and local levels.

(c) Review of refusal of request.—Subject to subsection (c.1), if the secretary refuses a request under subsection (a)(1) or a request for administrative review under subsection (a)(2), or does not act within the prescribed time, the perpetrator or school employee shall have the right to appeal and request a hearing before the secretary to amend or expunge an indicated report on the grounds that it is inaccurate or it is being maintained in a manner inconsistent with this chapter. The request for hearing must be made within 90 days of notice of the decision. The appropriate county agency and appropriate law enforcement officials shall be given notice of the hearing. The burden of proof in the hearing shall be on the appropriate county agency. The department shall assist the county agency as necessary.

(c.1) Founded reports.—A person named as a perpetrator in a founded report of child abuse must provide to the department a court order indicating that the underlying adjudication that formed the basis of the founded report has been reversed or vacated.

(c.2) Hearing.—A person making an appeal under subsection (a)(2) or (c) shall have the right to a timely hearing to determine the merits of the appeal. A hearing shall be scheduled according to the following procedures:

(1) Within ten days of receipt of an appeal pursuant to this section, the department shall schedule a hearing on the merits of the appeal.

(2) The department shall make reasonable efforts to coordinate the hearing date with both the appellee and appellant.

(3) After reasonable efforts required by paragraph (2) have been made, the department shall enter a scheduling order, and proceedings before the Bureau of Hearings and Appeals shall commence within 90 days of the date the scheduling order is entered, unless all parties have agreed to a continuance. Proceedings and hearings shall be scheduled to be heard on consecutive days whenever possible, but if not on consecutive days, then the proceeding or hearing shall be concluded not later than 30 days from commencement.

(4) The department or county agency shall provide a person making an appeal with evidence gathered during the child abuse investigation within its possession that is relevant to the child abuse determination, subject to sections 6339 (relat-

ing to confidentiality of reports) and 6340 (relating to release of information in confidential reports).

(5) The department or county agency shall bear the burden of proving by substantial evidence that the report should remain categorized as an indicated report.

(c.3) **Prompt decision.**—The administrative law judge's or hearing officer's decision in a hearing under subsection (c.2) shall be entered, filed and served upon the parties within 45 days of the date upon which the proceeding or hearing is concluded unless, within that time, the tribunal extends the date for the decision by order entered of record showing good cause for the extension. In no event shall an extension delay the entry of the decision more than 60 days after the conclusion of the proceeding or hearing.

(c.4) **Notice of decision.**—Notice of the decision shall be made to the Statewide database, the appropriate county agency, any appropriate law enforcement officials and all subjects of the report, except for the abused child.

(d) **Stay of proceedings.**—Any administrative appeal proceeding pursuant to subsection (b) shall be automatically stayed upon notice to the department by either of the parties when there is a pending criminal proceeding or a dependency or delinquency proceeding pursuant to 42 Pa.C.S. Ch. 63 (relating to juvenile matters), including any appeal thereof, involving the same factual circumstances as the administrative appeal.

(e) **Order.**—The secretary or designated agent may make any appropriate order respecting the amendment or expunction of such records to make them accurate or consistent with the requirements of this chapter.

(f) **Notice of expunction.**—Written notice of an expunction of any child abuse record made pursuant to the provisions of this chapter shall be served upon the subject of the record who was responsible for the abuse or injury and the appropriate county agency. Except as provided in this subsection, the county agency, upon receipt of the notice, shall take appropriate, similar action in regard to the local child abuse records and inform, for the same purpose, the appropriate coroner if that officer has received reports pursuant to section 6367 (relating to reports to department and coroner). Whenever the county agency investigation reveals, within 60 days of receipt of the report of suspected child abuse, that the report is unfounded but that the subjects need services provided or arranged by the county agency, the county agency shall retain those records and shall specifically identify that the report was an unfounded report of suspected child abuse. An unfounded report regarding subjects who receive services shall be expunged no later than 120 days following the expiration of one year after the termination or completion of services provided or arranged by the county agency.

(g) **Reconsideration and appeal.**—Parties to a proceeding or hearing held under subsection (c.2) have 15 calendar days from the mailing date of the final order of the Bureau of Hearings and Appeals to request the secretary to reconsider the decision. Parties to a proceeding or hearing held under this section have 30 calendar days from the mailing date of the final order of the Bureau of Hearings and Appeals to perfect an appeal to Commonwealth Court. The filing for reconsideration shall not toll the 30 days provided.

1990, Dec. 19, P.L. 1240, No. 206, § 2, effective in 90 days. Amended 1994, Dec. 16, P.L. 1292, No. 151, § 3, effective July 1, 1995; 1998, Dec. 15, P.L. 963, No. 127, § 12, effective March 1, 1999; 2013, Dec. 18, P.L. 1170, No. 108, § 4, effective Dec. 31, 2014; 2013, Dec. 18, P.L. 1201, No. 119, § 4, effective Dec. 31, 2014; 2014, May 14, P.L. 653, No. 45, § 5, effective Dec. 31, 2014.

Cross References. Section 6341 is referred to in sections 6353.4, 6368, 6381 of this title.

§ 6342. Studies of data in records.

(a) **Studies.**—The department may conduct or authorize the conducting of studies of the data contained in the Statewide database and by county agencies and distribute the results of the studies. No study may contain the name or other information by which a subject of a report could be identified. The department may allow Federal auditors access to nonidentifiable duplicates of reports in the Statewide database if required for Federal financial participation in funding of agencies.

(b) **Data form.**—The department shall develop a data form to facilitate the collection of statistical and demographic information from a child fatality or near fatality review team and a county agency, which can be incorporated into a study conducted by the department.

1990, Dec. 19, P.L. 1240, No. 206, § 2, effective in 90 days. Amended 2008, July 3, P.L. 276, No. 33, § 2.1, effective in 180 days [Dec. 30, 2008]; 2014, April 7, P.L. 388, No. 29, § 5.2, effective Dec. 31, 2014.

Cross References. Section 6342 is referred to in sections 6335, 6336, 6341 of this title.

§ 6343. Investigating performance of county agency.

(a) **General rule.**—If, within 30 days from the date of an initial report of suspected child abuse, the appropriate county agency has not investigated the report and informed the department that the report is an indicated report or an unfounded report or unless within that same 30-day period the report is determined to be a founded report, the department shall have the authority to begin an inquiry into the performance of the county agency which inquiry may include a performance audit of the county agency as provided in subsection (b). On the basis of that inquiry, the department shall take appropriate action to require that the provisions of this chapter be strictly followed, which action may include, without limitation, the institution of appropriate legal action and the withholding of reimbursement for all or part of the activities of the county agency. The department shall determine in its review whether the county agency has sufficiently documented reasons why the investigation has not been completed in the 30-day period.

(b) **Performance audit.**—Notwithstanding any other provision of this chapter, the secretary or a designee of the secretary may direct, at their discretion, and after reasonable notice to the county agency, a performance audit of any activity engaged in pursuant to this chapter.

(c) **Department reviews and reports of child fatalities and near fatalities.**—

(1) The department shall conduct a child fatality and near fatality review and provide a written report on any child fatality or near fatality, if child abuse is suspected. The department shall summarize:

(i) the circumstances of the child's fatality or near fatality;

(ii) the nature and extent of its review;

(iii) statutory and regulatory compliance by the county agency in the county where:

(A) the fatality or near fatality occurred; and

(B) the child resided within the 16 months preceding the fatality or near fatality;

(iv) its findings; and

(v) recommendations for reducing the likelihood of future child fatalities and near fatalities resulting from child abuse.

(2) The department's child fatality or near fatality review shall be commenced immediately upon receipt of a report to the department that a child died or nearly died as a result of suspected child abuse. The department shall provide assistance and relevant information to the child fatality or near fatality review team and attempt to coordinate its fact-finding efforts and interviews with the team to avoid duplication. The department's child fatality or near fatality review and report shall be completed as soon as possible but no later than six months from receipt of the initial report of the child fatality or near fatality.

(3) Prior to completing its report, the department may release the following information to the public concerning a child who died or nearly died as a result of suspected or substantiated child abuse:

(i) The identity of the child, only in the case of a child's fatality.

(ii) If the child was in the custody of a public or private agency, the identity of the agency.

(iii) The identity of the public or private agency under contract with a county agency to provide services to the child and the child's family in the child's home prior to the child's death or near fatality.

(iv) A description of services provided under subparagraph (iii).

(v) The identity of the county agency that convened a child fatality or near fatality review team with respect to the child.

(4) Upon completion of the review and report, the department's child fatality or near fatality report shall be made available to the county agency, the child fatality or near fatality review team and designated county officials under section 6340(a)(11) (relating to release of information in confidential reports). The report shall be made available, upon request, to other individuals to whom confidential reports may be released, as specified by section 6340. The department's report shall be made available to the public, but identifying information shall be removed from the contents of the report except for disclosure of: the identity of a deceased child; if the child was in the custody of a public or private agency, the identity of the agency; the identity of the public or private agency under contract with a county agency to provide services to the child and the child's family in the child's home prior to the child's death or near fatality; and the identity of any county agency that convened a child fatality or near fatality review team in respect to the child. The report shall not be released to the public if the district attorney certifies that release of the report may compromise a pending criminal investigation or proceeding. Certification by the district attorney shall stay the release of the report for a period of 60 days, at which time the report shall be released unless a new certification is made by the district attorney.

1990, Dec. 19, P.L. 1240, No. 206, § 2, effective in 90 days. Amended 1994, Dec. 16, P.L. 1292, No. 151, § 3, effective July 1, 1995; 2008, July 3, P.L. 276, No. 33, § 3, effective in 180 days [Dec. 30, 2008]; 2014, May 14, P.L. 645, No. 44, § 2, effective Dec. 31, 2014.

Cross References. Section 6343 is referred to in section 6340, 6368 of this title.

§ 6343.1. Citizen review panels.

(a) **Establishment.**—The department shall establish a minimum of three citizen review panels. The department may designate a child fatality or near fatality review team under section 6365(d) (relating to services for prevention, investigation and treatment of child abuse) as a citizen review panel as long as the team has the capacity to perform as a citizen review panel.

(b) **Function.**—The panels shall examine all of the following:

(1) Policies, procedures and practices of State and local agencies and, where appropriate, specific cases to evaluate the extent to which State and local child protective services system agencies are effectively discharging their child protection responsibilities under section 106(b) of the Child Abuse Prevention and Treatment Act (Public Law 93-247, 42 U.S.C. § 5106a(b)).

(2) Other criteria the panel considers important to ensure the protection of children, including:

(i) a review of the extent to which the State and local child protective services system is coordinated with the foster care and adoption programs established under Part E of Title IV of the Social Security Act (49 Stat. 620, 42 U.S.C. § 670 et seq.); and

(ii) a review of child fatalities and near fatalities, including, but not limited to, a review of any child fatality or near fatality involving a child in the custody of a public or private agency where there is no report of suspected child abuse and the cause of death is neither the result of child abuse nor natural causes.

(c) **Membership.**—The panels shall be composed of volunteer members who represent the community, including members who have expertise in the prevention and treatment of child abuse and neglect.

(d) **Meetings.**—Each citizen review panel shall meet not less than once every three months.

(e) **Reports.**—The department shall issue an annual report summarizing the activities and recommendations of the panels and summarizing the department response to the recommendations.

2006, Nov. 9, P.L. 1358, No. 146, § 4, effective in 180 days [May 8, 2007]; 2008, July 9, P.L. 276, No.33, effective in 180 days.

2008 Amendment. Act 33 amended subsecs. (a) and (b).

2006 Amendment. Act 146 added this sec.

§ 6344. Employees having contact with children; adoptive and foster parents.

(a) **Applicability.**—Beginning December 31, 2014, this section applies to the following individuals:

(1) An employee of child-care services.

(2) A foster parent.

(3) A prospective adoptive parent.

(4) A self-employed provider of child-care services in a family child-care home.

(5)(i) Except as provided under subparagraph (ii), an individual 14 years of age or older who is applying for or holding a paid position as an employee with a program, activity or service, as a person responsible for the child's welfare or having direct contact with children.

(ii) If the program, activity or service is an internship, externship, work study, co-op or similar program, an adult applying for or holding a paid position with an employer that participates in the internship, externship, work study, co-op or similar program with a school and whom the employer and the school identify as the child's supervisor and the person responsible for the child's welfare while the child participates in the program with the employer. The adult identified under this subparagraph as the person responsible for the child's welfare is required to be in the immediate vicinity at regular intervals with the child during the program.

(6) Any individual seeking to provide child-care services under contract with a child-care facility or program.

(7) An individual 18 years of age or older who resides in the home of a foster parent for at least 30 days in a calendar year or who resides in the home of a prospective adoptive parent for at least 30 days in a calendar year.

(8) An individual 18 years of age or older who resides for at least 30 days in a calendar year in the following homes which are subject to supervision or licensure by the department under Articles IX and X of the act of June 13, 1967 (P.L.31, No.21), known as the Public Welfare Code:

(i) A family living home.

(ii) A community home for individuals with an intellectual disability.

(iii) A host home for children.

This paragraph does not include an individual with an intellectual disability or chronic psychiatric disability receiving services in a home.

(a.1) **School employees.**—This section shall apply to school employees as follows:

(1) School employees governed by the provisions of the act of March 10, 1949 (P.L.30, No.14), known as the Public School Code of 1949, shall be subject to the

provisions of section 111 of the Public School Code of 1949, except that this section shall apply with regard to the certification required under subsection (b)(2).

(2)(i) School employees not governed by the provisions of the Public School Code of 1949 shall be governed by this section.

(ii) This paragraph shall not apply to an employee of an institution of higher education whose direct contact with children, in the course of employment, is limited to either:

(A) prospective students visiting a campus operated by the institution of higher education; or

(B) matriculated students who are enrolled with the institution.

(iii) The exemption under subparagraph (ii)(B) shall not apply to students who are enrolled in a secondary school.

(a.2) **Minors.**—An individual between 14 and 17 years of age who applies for or holds a paid position as an employee who is a person responsible for the child's welfare or a person with direct contact with children through a program, activity or service prior to the commencement of employment or under section 6344.4 (relating to recertification) shall be required to submit only the information under subsection (b)(1) and (2) to an employer, administrator, supervisor or other person responsible for employment decisions, if the following apply:

(1) The individual has been a resident of this Commonwealth during the entirety of the previous 10-year period or, if not a resident of this Commonwealth during the entirety of the previous 10-year period, has received certification under subsection (b)(3) at any time since establishing residency in this Commonwealth and provides a copy of the certification to the employer.

(2) The individual and the individual's parent or legal guardian swear or affirm in writing that the individual is not disqualified from service under subsection (c) or has not been convicted of an offense similar in nature to those crimes listed in subsection (c) under the laws or former laws of the United States or one of its territories or possessions, another state, the District of Columbia, the Commonwealth of Puerto Rico or a foreign nation, or under a former law of this Commonwealth.

(a.3) **Exchange visitor.**—An individual in possession of a nonimmigrant visa issued pursuant to 8 U.S.C. § 1101(a)(15)(J) (relating to definitions) to an exchange visitor, commonly referred to as a "J-1" Visa, shall not be required to submit information under subsection (b) if all of the following apply:

(1) The individual is applying for or holds a paid position with a program, activity or service for a period not to exceed a total of 90 days in a calendar year.

(2) The individual has not been employed previously in this Commonwealth or another state, the District of Columbia or the Commonwealth of Puerto Rico.

(3) The individual swears or affirms in writing that the individual is not disqualified from service under subsection (c) or has not been convicted of an offense similar in nature to the crimes listed under subsection (c) under the laws or former laws of the United States or one of its territories or possessions, another state, the District of Columbia, the Commonwealth of Puerto Rico or a foreign nation, or under a former law of this Commonwealth.

(b) **Information to be submitted.**—An individual identified in subsection (a)(7) or (8) at the time the individual meets the description set forth in subsection (a)(7) or (8) and an individual identified in subsection (a)(1), (2), (3), (4), (5)(i) or (6), (a.1) or (a.2) prior to the commencement of employment or service or in accordance with section 6344.4 shall be required to submit the following information to an employer, administrator, supervisor or other person responsible for employment decisions or involved in the selection of volunteers:

(1) Pursuant to 18 Pa.C.S. Ch. 91 (relating to criminal history record information), a report of criminal history record information from the Pennsylvania State Police or a statement from the Pennsylvania State Police that the State Police central repository contains no such information relating to that person. The criminal history record information shall be limited to that which is disseminated pursuant to 18 Pa.C.S. § 9121(b)(2) (relating to general regulations).

(2) A certification from the department as to whether the applicant is named in the Statewide database as the alleged perpetrator in a pending child abuse investigation or as the perpetrator of a founded report or an indicated report.

(3) A report of Federal criminal history record information. The applicant shall submit a full set of fingerprints to the Pennsylvania State Police for the purpose of a record check, and the Pennsylvania State Police or its authorized agent shall submit the fingerprints to the Federal Bureau of Investigation for the purpose of verifying the identity of the applicant and obtaining a current record of any criminal arrests and convictions.

(b.1) Required documentation to be maintained and produced.—The employer, administrator, supervisor or other person responsible for employment decisions or acceptance of the individual to serve in any capacity identified in subsection (a)(1), (2), (3), (4), (5)(i) or (6), (a.1) or (a.2) shall maintain a copy of the required information and require the individual to submit the required documents prior to employment or acceptance to serve in any such capacity or as required in section 6344.4, except as allowed under subsection (m).

(b.2) Investigation.—An employer, administrator, supervisor or other person responsible for employment decisions shall require an applicant to submit the required documentation set forth in this chapter or as required in section 6344.4. An employer, administrator, supervisor or other person responsible for employment decisions that intentionally fails to require an applicant to submit the required documentation before the applicant's hiring or upon recertification commits a misdemeanor of the third degree.

(b.3) Volunteer certification prohibition.—An employer, administrator, supervisor or other person responsible for employment decisions is prohibited from accepting a certification that was obtained for volunteering purposes under section 6344.2 (relating to volunteers having contact with children).

(c) Grounds for denying employment or participation in program, activity or service.--

(1) In no case shall an administrator hire or approve an applicant where the department has verified that the applicant is named in the Statewide database as the perpetrator of a founded report committed within the five-year period immediately preceding verification pursuant to this section.

(2) In no case shall an administrator hire an applicant if the applicant's criminal history record information indicates the applicant has been convicted of one or more of the following offenses under Title 18 (relating to crimes and offenses) or an equivalent crime under Federal law or the law of another state:

Chapter 25 (relating to criminal homicide).

Section 2702 (relating to aggravated assault).

Section 2709.1 (relating to stalking).

Section 2901 (relating to kidnapping).

Section 2902 (relating to unlawful restraint).

Section 3121 (relating to rape).

Section 3122.1 (relating to statutory sexual assault).

Section 3123 (relating to involuntary deviate sexual intercourse).
Section 3124.1 (relating to sexual assault).
Section 3125 (relating to aggravated indecent assault).
Section 3126 (relating to indecent assault).
Section 3127 (relating to indecent exposure).
Section 4302 (relating to incest).
Section 4303 (relating to concealing death of child).
Section 4304 (relating to endangering welfare of children).
Section 4305 (relating to dealing in infant children).
A felony offense under section 5902(b) (relating to prostitution and related offenses).
Section 5903(c) or (d) (relating to obscene and other sexual materials and performances).
Section 6301 (relating to corruption of minors).
Section 6312 (relating to sexual abuse of children).
The attempt, solicitation or conspiracy to commit any of the offenses set forth in this paragraph.

(3) In no case shall an employer, administrator, supervisor or other person responsible for employment decisions hire or approve an applicant if the applicant's criminal history record information indicates the applicant has been convicted of a felony offense under the act of April 14, 1972 (P.L.233, No.64), known as The Controlled Substance, Drug, Device and Cosmetic Act, committed within the five-year period immediately preceding verification under this section.

(c.1) **Dismissal.**—If the information obtained pursuant to subsection (b) reveals that the applicant is disqualified from employment or approval pursuant to subsection (c), the applicant shall be immediately dismissed from employment or approval.

(d) **Prospective adoptive or foster parents.**—With regard to prospective adoptive or prospective foster parents, the following shall apply:

(1) In the course of causing an investigation to be made pursuant to section 2535(a) (relating to investigation), an agency or person designated by the court to conduct the investigation shall require prospective adoptive parents and any individual over the age of 18 years residing in the home to submit the information set forth in subsection (b) for review in accordance with this section. If a prospective adoptive parent, or any individual over 18 years of age residing in the home, has resided outside this Commonwealth at any time within the previous five-year period, the agency or person designated by the court shall require that person to submit a certification obtained within the previous one-year period from the Statewide central registry, or its equivalent in each state in which the person has resided within the previous five-year period, as to whether the person is named as a perpetrator of child abuse. If the certification shows that the person is named as a perpetrator of child abuse within the previous five-year period, the agency or person designated by the court shall forward the certification to the department for review. The agency or person designated by the court shall not approve the prospective adoptive parent if the department determines that the person is named as the equivalent of a perpetrator of a founded report of child abuse within the previous five-year period.

(2) In the course of approving a prospective foster parent, a foster family care agency shall require prospective foster parents and any individual over the age of 18 years residing in the home to submit the information set forth in subsection (b) for review by the foster family care agency in accordance with this section. If a prospective foster parent, or any individual over 18 years of age residing in the home, has resided outside this Commonwealth at any time within the previous five-year period, the foster family care agency shall require that person to submit

a certification obtained within the previous one-year period from the Statewide central registry, or its equivalent in each state in which the person has resided within the previous five-year period, as to whether the person is named as a perpetrator of child abuse. If the certification shows that the person is named as a perpetrator of child abuse within the previous five-year period, the foster family care agency shall forward the certification to the department for review. The foster family care agency shall not approve the prospective foster parent if the department determines that the person is named as the equivalent of a perpetrator of a founded report of child abuse within the previous five-year period. In addition, the foster family care agency shall consider the following when assessing the ability of applicants for approval as foster parents:

(i) The ability to provide care, nurturing and supervision to children.

(ii) Mental and emotional well-being. If there is a question regarding the mental or emotional stability of a family member which might have a negative effect on a foster child, the foster family care agency shall require a psychological evaluation of that person before approving the foster family home.

(iii) Supportive community ties with family, friends and neighbors.

(iv) Existing family relationships, attitudes and expectations regarding the applicant's own children and parent/child relationships, especially as they might affect a foster child.

(v) Ability of the applicant to accept a foster child's relationship with his own parents.

(vi) The applicant's ability to care for children with special needs.

(vii) Number and characteristics of foster children best suited to the foster family.

(viii) Ability of the applicant to work in partnership with a foster family care agency. This subparagraph shall not be construed to preclude an applicant from advocating on the part of a child.

(3) (Deleted by amendment).

(4) (Deleted by amendment).

(4.1) If a foster parent, prospective adoptive parent or an individual over 18 years of age residing in the home is arrested for or convicted of an offense that would constitute grounds for denying approval under this chapter or is named as a perpetrator in a founded or indicated report, the foster parent or prospective adoptive parent shall provide the foster family care agency or the agency listed to provide adoption services with written notice not later than 72 hours after the arrest, conviction or notification that the individual was named as a perpetrator in the Statewide database.

(5) Foster parents and prospective adoptive parents shall be required to report any other change in the family household composition within 30 days of the change for review by the foster family care agency or the agency listed to provide adoption services. If any individual over 18 years of age, who has resided outside this Commonwealth at any time within the previous five-year period, begins residing in the home of an approved foster family or a prospective adoptive family, that individual shall, within 30 days of beginning residence, submit to the foster family care agency or the agency listed to provide adoption services a certification obtained from the Statewide database, or its equivalent in each state in which the person has resided within the previous five-year period, as to whether the person is named as a perpetrator. If the certification shows that the person is named as a perpetrator within the previous five-year period, the foster family care agency or the agency listed to provide adoption services shall forward the certification to the department for review. If the department determines that the person is named as the equivalent of a perpetrator of a founded report within the previous five-year

period and the person does not cease residing in the home immediately, the county agency shall immediately seek court authorization to remove the foster child or children from the home. In emergency situations when a judge cannot be reached, the county agency shall proceed in accordance with the Pennsylvania Rules of Juvenile Court Procedure.

(6) In cases where foster parents knowingly fail to submit the material information required in paragraphs (4.1) and (5) and section 6344.4 such that it would disqualify them as foster parents, the county agency shall immediately seek court authorization to remove the foster child or children from the home. In emergency situations when a judge cannot be reached, the county agency shall proceed in accordance with the Pennsylvania Rules of Juvenile Court Procedure.

(7) An approved foster parent shall not be considered an employee for any purpose, including, but not limited to, liability, unemployment compensation, workers' compensation or other employee benefits provided by the county agency.

(8) The department shall require information based upon certain criteria for foster and adoptive parent applications. The criteria shall include, but not be limited to, information provided by the applicant or other sources in the following areas:

(i) Previous addresses within the last 10 years.

(ii) Criminal history background certification generated by the process outlined in this section.

(iii) Child abuse certification generated by the process outlined in this section.

(iv) Composition of the resident family unit.

(v) Protection from abuse orders filed by or against either parent, provided that such orders are accessible to the county or private agency.

(vi) Details of any proceedings brought in family court, provided that such records in such proceedings are accessible to the county or private agency.

(vii) Drug-related or alcohol-related arrests, if criminal charges or judicial proceedings are pending, and any convictions or hospitalizations within the last five years. If the applicant provides information regarding convictions or hospitalizations in that five-year period, then information on the prior five years shall be requested related to any additional convictions or hospitalizations.

(viii) Evidence of financial stability, including income verification, employment history, current liens and bankruptcy findings within the last 10 years.

(ix) Number of and ages of foster children and other dependents currently placed in the home.

(x) Detailed information regarding children with special needs currently living in the home.

(xi) Previous history as a foster parent, including number and types of children served.

(xii) Related education, training or personal experience working with foster children or the child welfare system.

(d.1) Establishment of a resource family registry

(1) The department shall establish a registry of resource family applicants.

(2) The foster family care agency or adoption agency shall register all resource family applicants on the resource family registry in accordance with subsection (d.2).

(3) The foster family care agency or adoption agency shall register all resource families that are approved on the effective date of this subsection within six months of the effective date of this subsection.

(4) Any resource family that is voluntarily registered on the foster parent registry shall be maintained on the resource family registry mandated under this section.

(d.2) Information in the resource family registry.

(1) The resource family registry shall include, but not be limited to, the following:

(i) The name, Social Security number, date of birth, sex, marital status, race and ethnicity of the applicants.

(ii) The date or dates of the resource family application.

(iii) The current and previous home addresses of the applicants.

(iv) The county of residence of the applicants.

(v) The name, date of birth, Social Security number and relationship of all household members.

(vi) The name, address and telephone number of all current and previous foster family care agency or adoption agency affiliations.

(vii) The foster family care agency or adoption agency disposition related to the approval or disapproval of the applicants and the date and basis for the disposition.

(viii) The type of care the resource family will provide.

(ix) The number of children that may be placed in the resource family home.

(x) The age, race, gender and level of special needs of children that may be placed in the resource family home.

(xi) The ability of the resource family to provide care for sibling groups.

(xii) The date and reason for any closure of the resource family home.

(xiii) The appeal activity initiated by a resource family applicant or an approved resource family and the basis for the appeal. This subparagraph shall not be construed to limit legitimate appeals.

(xiv) The status and disposition of all appeal-related activities. This subparagraph shall not be construed to limit legitimate appeals.

(2) The information maintained in the resource family registry may be released to the following individuals when the department has positively identified the individual requesting the information and the department, except in the case of subparagraphs (iii) and (iv), has inquired into whether and if it is satisfied that the individual has a legitimate need within the scope of the individual's official duties to obtain the information:

(i) An authorized official of a county or private agency, a Federal agency or an agency of another state who performs resource family approvals or the department in the course of the official's duties.

(ii) A guardian ad litem or court-designated advocate for a child. The information is limited to the information related to the resource family with whom the child resides.

(iii) A court of competent jurisdiction, including a district justice, a judge of the Municipal Court of Philadelphia or a judge of the Pittsburgh Magistrates Court, pursuant to court order or subpoena in a criminal matter involving a charge of child abuse under Chapter 63 (relating to child protective services).

(iv) A court of competent jurisdiction in connection with any matter involving custody of a child. The department shall provide to the court any files that the court considers relevant.

(v) The Attorney General.

(vi) Federal auditors, if required for Federal financial participation in funding of agencies, except that Federal auditors may not remove identifiable information or copies thereof from the department or county or private agencies.

(vii) Law enforcement agents of any jurisdiction, as long as the information is relevant in the course of investigating crimes involving the resource family.

(viii) Appropriate officials of a private agency or another county or state regarding a resource family that has applied to become a resource family for that agency, county or state.

(3) At any time and upon written request, a resource family may receive a copy of all information pertaining to that resource family contained in the resource family registry.

(d.3) Family living homes, community homes for individuals with an intellectual disability and host homes.—

(1) The following shall apply to an individual over 18 years of age residing in a family living home, a community home for individuals with an intellectual disability or a host home for children, which are subject to supervision or licensure by the department under Articles IX and X of the Public Welfare Code:

(i) If an individual is arrested for or convicted of an offense that would constitute grounds for denying approval under this chapter, or is named as a perpetrator in a founded or indicated report, the individual shall provide the agency with written notice not later than 72 hours after the arrest, conviction or notification that the individual was named as a perpetrator in the Statewide database.

(ii) The adult family member who is providing services to a child in the home shall be required to report any other change in the household composition within 30 days of the change for review by the agency. If any individual over 18 years of age, who has resided outside this Commonwealth at any time within the previous five-year period, begins residing in the home, that individual shall, within 30 days of beginning residence, submit to the agency a certification obtained from the Statewide database, or its equivalent in each state in which the individual has resided within the previous five-year period, as to whether the person is named as a perpetrator. If the certification shows that the person is named as a perpetrator within the previous five-year period, the agency shall forward the certification to the department for review.

(2) This subsection shall not apply to an individual with an intellectual disability or chronic psychiatric disability receiving services in a home.

(3) As used in this subsection, the term "agency" means a family living home agency, community home agency for individuals with an intellectual disability or a host home agency.

(e) Self-employed family child-care providers.—Self-employed family child-care providers who apply for a license with the department shall submit with their licensure application the information set forth under subsection (b) for review in accordance with this section.

(f) Submissions by operators of child-care services.—The department shall require persons seeking to operate child-care services to submit the information set forth in subsection (b) for review in accordance with this section.

(g) Regulations.—The department shall promulgate the regulations necessary to carry out this section. These regulations shall:

(1) Set forth criteria for unsuitability for employment in a child-care service in relation to criminal history record information which may include criminal history record information in addition to that set forth above. The criteria shall be reasonably related to the prevention of child abuse.

(2) Set forth sanctions for administrators who willfully hire applicants in violation of this section or in violation of the regulations promulgated under this section.

(h) Fees.—(Repealed).

(h.1) Form of payment.—Payment of the fee authorized under subsection (h) may be made by an individual or organization by check, money order, credit card or debit card.

(i) Time limit for certification.—The department shall comply with certification requests no later than 14 days from the receipt of the request.

(j) Voluntary certification of child caretakers.—The department shall develop a procedure for the voluntary certification of child caretakers to allow persons to apply to the department for a certificate indicating the person has met the requirements of subsection (b). The department shall also provide for the biennial recertification of child caretakers.

(k) Existing or transferred employees.—(Deleted by amendment).

(l) Temporary employees under special programs.—(Deleted by amendment).

(m) Provisional employees for limited periods.—Notwithstanding subsection (b), employers, administrators, supervisors or other persons responsible for employment decisions may employ applicants on a provisional basis for a single period not to exceed 90 days, if all of the following conditions are met:

(1) The applicant has applied for the information required under subsection (b) and the applicant provides a copy of the appropriate completed request forms to the employer, administrator, supervisor or other person responsible for employment decisions.

(2) The employer, administrator, supervisor or other person responsible for employment decisions has no knowledge of information pertaining to the applicant which would disqualify him from employment pursuant to subsection (c).

(3) The applicant swears or affirms in writing that he is not disqualified from employment pursuant to subsection (c) or has not been convicted of an offense similar in nature to those crimes listed in subsection (c) under the laws or former laws of the United States or one of its territories or possessions, another state, the District of Columbia, the Commonwealth of Puerto Rico or a foreign nation, or under a former law of this Commonwealth.

(4) If the information obtained pursuant to subsection (b) reveals that the applicant is disqualified from employment pursuant to subsection (c), the applicant shall be immediately dismissed by the employer, administrator, supervisor or other person responsible for employment decisions.

(5) The employer, administrator, supervisor or other person responsible for employment decisions requires that the applicant not be permitted to work alone with children and that the applicant work in the immediate vicinity of a permanent employee.

(n) Confidentiality.—The information provided and compiled under this section, including, but not limited to, the names, addresses and telephone numbers of applicants and foster and adoptive parents, shall be confidential and shall not be subject to the act of February 14, 2008 (P.L.6, No.3), known as the Right-to-Know Law. This information shall not be released except as permitted by the department through regulation.

(o) Use of information.—A foster family care agency may not approve a prospective foster parent if the prospective foster parent or an individual 18 years of age or older who resides for at least 30 days in a calendar year with the prospective foster parent meets either of the following:

(1) Is named in the Statewide database as the perpetrator of a founded report committed within the five-year period immediately preceding verification pursuant to this section.

(2) Has been found guilty of an offense listed in subsection (c).

(p) **Use of information.**—A prospective adoptive parent may not be approved if the prospective adoptive parent or an individual 18 years of age or older who resides for at least 30 days in a calendar year with the prospective adoptive parent meets either of the following:

(1) Is named in the Statewide database as the perpetrator of a founded report committed within the five-year period immediately preceding verification pursuant to this section.

(2) Has been found guilty of an offense listed in subsection (c).

(Dec. 16, 1994, P.L.1292, No.151, eff. July 1, 1995; Mar. 31, 1995, 1st Sp.Sess., P.L.985, No.10, eff. 60 days; Dec. 15, 1998, P.L.963, No.127, eff. Jan. 1, 1999; Dec. 17, 2001, P.L.942, No.112, eff. imd.; Dec. 9, 2002, P.L.1759, No.218, eff. 60 days; Nov. 29, 2004, P.L.1291, No.160, eff. 60 days; Nov. 29, 2006, P.L.1581, No.179, eff. 180 days; Dec. 18, 2007, P.L.469, No.73; Apr. 7, 2014, P.L.388, No.29, eff. Dec. 31, 2014; May 14, 2014, P.L.653, No.45, eff. Dec. 31, 2014; Oct. 22, 2014, P.L.2529, No.153, eff. Dec. 31, 2014; July 1, 2015, P.L.94, No.15, eff. imd.; Oct. 30, 2017, P.L.379, No.40, eff. imd.; June 28, 2018, P.L.375, No.54, eff. imd.)

2018 Amendment. Act 54 amended subsecs. (b) intro. par. and (b.1).

2017 Amendment. Act 40 repealed subsec. (h).

2015 Amendment. Act 15 amended subsecs. (a), (a.1), (b), (b.1), (b.2), (d)(4.1), (5), (6) and (8) and (e) and added subsecs. (a.2), (a.3), (b.3) and (d.3).

2014 Amendments. Act 29 amended subsecs. (b)(2), (o)(1) and (p)(1) and added subsec. (h.1), Act 45 amended subsecs. (b), (c) hdg. and (1), (o) and (p) and Act 153 amended the section heading and subsecs. (a), (b), (c)(3), (d)(5) and (6), (m), (n) and (p), added subsecs. (a.1), (b.1), (b.2), (c.1) and (d)(4.1) and deleted subsecs. (d)(3) and (4), (k) and (l).

2007 Amendment. Act 73 amended subsecs. (b), (d)(1), (2), (3), (4) and (5), (e), (f) and (k) and added subsec. (b.1), effective immediately as to subsec. (b.1), January 1, 2008, as to subsecs. (b) and (d)(1), (2), (3), (4) and (5) and July 1, 2008, as to subsecs. (e), (f) and (k).

2006 Amendment. Act 179 amended subsecs. (a) and (c)(1) and added subsecs. (o) and (p).

2004 Amendment. Act 160 amended subsecs. (d) and (g) and added subsecs. (d.1),(d.2) and (n).

2002 Amendment. Act 218 amended subsec. (c)(2).

2001 Amendment. Act 112 amended subsec. (h).

1998 Amendment. Act 127 amended subsecs. (b), (c) and (h).

Special Provisions in Appendix. See section 28 of Act 207 of 2004 in the appendix to this title for special provisions relating to applicability.

See section 6 of Act 33 of 2008 in the appendix to this title for special provisions relating to Department of Public Welfare reports.

See section 15 of Act 153 of 2014 in the appendix to this title for special provisions relating to study by Department of Human Services.

References in Text. Subsec. (a)(1), (2), (3), (4), (5) and (6), referred to in subsec. (b), do not exist.

The Statewide central registry, referred to in subsec. (d)(1) and (2), shall be deemed a reference to the Statewide database.

The short title of the act of June 13, 1967, P.L.31, No.21, known as the Public Welfare Code, referred to in subsections (a) and (d.3), was amended by the act of December 28, 2015, P.L.500, No.92. The amended short title is now the Human Services Code.

Subsec. (h), referred to in subsec. (h.1), was repealed by the act of October 30, 2017, P.L.379, No.40.

Cross References. Section 6344 is referred to in sections 2530, 6335, 6338.1, 6340, 6344.1, 6344.2, 6344.3, 6344.4, 6349, 6383 of this title; section 6351.1 of Title 42 (Judiciary and Judicial Procedure).

§ 6344.1. Information relating to certified or licensed child-care home residents.

(a) **General rule.**—In addition to the requirements of section 6344 (relating to employees having contact with children; adoptive and foster parents), an individual who applies to the department for a certificate of compliance or a license to provide child day care in a residence shall include criminal history record and child abuse record information required under section 6344(b) for every individual 18 years of age or older who resides in the home for at least 30 days in a calendar year.

(b) Required information.—Child abuse record information required under subsection (a) shall include certification by the department as to whether the applicant is named in the Statewide database as the perpetrator of a founded report or an indicated report.

(c) Effect on certification or licensure.—The department shall refuse to issue or renew a certificate of compliance or license or shall revoke a certificate of compliance or license if the day-care home provider or individual 18 years of age or older who has resided in the home for at least 30 days in a calendar year:

(1) is named in the Statewide database as the perpetrator of a founded report committed within the immediately preceding five-year period; or

(2) has been convicted of an offense enumerated in section 6344(c).

(d) Regulations.—The department shall promulgate regulations to administer this section.

(Nov. 29, 2006, P.L.1581, No.179, eff. 180 days; Apr. 7, 2014, P.L.388, No.29, eff. Dec. 31, 2014; May 14, 2014, P.L.653, No.45, eff. Dec. 31, 2014; Oct. 22, 2014, P.L.2529, No.153, eff. Dec. 31, 2014; July 1, 2015, P.L.94, No.15, eff. imd.)

2015 Amendment. Act 15 amended the section heading and subsecs. (a) and (c).

2014 Amendments. Act 29 amended subsecs. (b) and (c)(1), Act 45 amended subsec. (b) and Act 153 amended the section heading and subsecs. (a), (b) and (c).

2006 Amendment. Act 179 added section 6344.1.

Cross References. Section 6344.1 is referred to in section 6335 of this title.

§ 6344.2. Volunteers having contact with children.

(a) Applicability.—This section applies to an adult applying for or holding an unpaid position as a volunteer with a child-care service, a school or a program, activity or service, as a person responsible for the child's welfare or having direct volunteer contact with children and an individual identified under section 6344(a)(5)(ii) (relating to employees having contact with children; adoptive and foster parents).

(b) Investigation.—Employers, administrators, supervisors or other persons responsible for selection of volunteers shall require an applicant to submit to all requirements set forth in section 6344(b) except as provided in subsection (b.1). An employer, administrator, supervisor or other person responsible for selection of volunteers regarding an applicable prospective volunteer under this section that intentionally fails to require the submissions before approving that individual commits a misdemeanor of the third degree.

(b.1) Exception.—

(1) A person responsible for the selection of volunteers under this chapter shall require an applicable prospective volunteer prior to the commencement of service to submit only the information under section 6344(b)(1) and (2), if the following apply:

(i) The position the prospective volunteer is applying for is unpaid or the prospective volunteer is an individual identified under section 6344(a)(5)(ii).

(ii) The prospective volunteer has been a resident of this Commonwealth during the entirety of the previous 10-year period or, if not a resident of this Commonwealth during the entirety of the previous 10-year period, has received certification under section 6344(b)(3) at any time since establishing residency in this Commonwealth and provides a copy of the certification to the person responsible for the selection of volunteers.

(iii) The prospective volunteer swears or affirms in writing that the prospective volunteer is not disqualified from service pursuant to section 6344(c) or has not been convicted of an offense similar in nature to those crimes listed in section 6344(c) under the laws or former laws of the United States or one of its territories or possessions, another state, the District of Columbia, the Commonwealth of Puerto Rico or a foreign nation, or under a former law of this Commonwealth.

(2) If the information obtained pursuant to section 6344(b) reveals that the prospective volunteer applicant is disqualified from service pursuant to section 6344(c), the applicant shall not be approved for service.

(3) If all of the following apply, an individual shall not be required to obtain the certifications required under subsection (b):

(i) The individual is currently enrolled in a school.

(ii) The individual is not a person responsible for the child's welfare.

(iii) The individual is volunteering for an event that occurs on school grounds.

(iv) The event is sponsored by the school in which the individual is enrolled as a student.

(v) The event is not for children who are in the care of a child-care service.

(c) **Grounds for denial.**—Each prospective volunteer shall be subject to the requirements of section 6344(c).

(d) **Departmental treatment of information.**—Information provided and compiled under this section by the department shall be confidential and shall not be subject to the act of February 14, 2008 (P.L.6, No.3), known as the Right-to-Know Law. This information shall not be released except as permitted by the department through regulation. The department may charge a fee to conduct a certification as required by section 6344(b)(2) in accordance with the provisions of section 6344(h). The department shall promulgate regulations necessary to carry out this subsection.

(e) **Construction.**—(Deleted by amendment).

(f) **Nonresident volunteer certification.**—Employers, administrators, supervisors or other persons responsible for selection of volunteers may allow a volunteer to serve on a provisional basis not to exceed a total of 30 days in a calendar year if the volunteer is in compliance with the clearance standards under the law of the jurisdiction where the volunteer is domiciled. The nonresident volunteer must provide the employer, administrator, supervisor or other person responsible for selection of volunteers with documentation of certifications.

(g) **Waiver of fees for certain background certifications.**—The fees for certifications required under section 6344(b)(1) and (2) which a volunteer is required to submit under this section shall be waived, and the certifications shall be provided free of charge to the volunteer under the following conditions:

(1) The background certifications are necessary to comply with the requirements of subsection (b).

(2) The background certifications may not be used and shall not be valid to satisfy the requirements for employment under section 6344(b) or any other law for which a similar background check may be required.

(3) Background certifications shall only be provided free of charge to a volunteer once every 57 months.

(4) The volunteer swears or affirms, in writing, under penalty of 18 Pa.C.S. § 4904 (relating to unsworn falsification to authorities), the following:

(i) The background certifications are necessary to satisfy the requirements under subsection (b).

(ii) The volunteer has not received background certifications free of charge within the previous 57 months.

(iii) The volunteer understands that the certifications shall not be valid or used for any other purpose.

(h) Presumption of good faith.—For the purposes of criminal liability under this section, an employer, administrator, supervisor or other persons responsible for the selection of volunteers are presumed to have acted in good faith when identifying individuals required to submit certifications and maintain records as required by this section.

(Nov. 29, 2006, P.L.1581, No.179, eff. 60 days; May 14, 2014, P.L.653, No.45, eff. Dec. 31, 2014; Oct. 22, 2014, P.L.2529, No.153, eff. Dec. 31, 2014; July 1, 2015, P.L.94, No.15, eff. imd.; June 28, 2018, P.L.375, No.54, eff. imd.)

2018 Amendment. Act 54 amended subsecs. (a), (b) and (b.1)(1)(i).

2015 Amendment. Act 15 amended subsecs. (a), (b), (b.1) and (f), added subsecs. (g) and (h) and deleted subsec. (e).

2014 Amendments. Act 45 amended subsec. (b) and added subsec. (a.1) and Act 153 amended the entire section.

Cross References. Section 6344.2 is referred to in sections 6335, 6344, 6344.3, 6344.4 of this title.

§ 6344.3. Continued employment or participation in program, activity or service.

(a) (Reserved).

(b) (Reserved).

(c) (Reserved).

(d) (Reserved).

(e) **Noninterference with decisions.**—Nothing in this chapter shall be construed to otherwise interfere with the ability of an employer or person responsible for a program, activity or service to make employment, discipline or termination decisions or from establishing additional standards as part of the hiring or selection process for employees or volunteers.

(f) **Portability of certification.—**

(1) Subject to the restrictions under section 6344(b.3) (relating to employees having contact with children; adoptive and foster parents), if an individual's certifications are current under section 6344.4 (relating to recertification) and the individual completes an affirmation under paragraph (2), the individual may use the certifications as follows:

(i) to apply for employment as identified in section 6344 (relating to employees having contact with children; adoptive and foster parents);

(ii) to serve as an employee as identified in section 6344;

(iii) to apply as a volunteer under section 6344.2 (relating to volunteers having contact with children); and

(iv) to serve as a volunteer under section 6344.2.

(2) Prior to commencing employment or service, an individual must swear or affirm in writing that the individual has not been disqualified from employment or service under section 6344(c) or has not been convicted of an offense similar in nature to a crime listed in section 6344(c) under the laws or former laws of the United States or one of its territories or possessions, another state, the District of Columbia, the Commonwealth of Puerto Rico or a foreign nation, or under a former law of this Commonwealth.

(3) An employer, administrator, supervisor, other person responsible for employment decisions or other person responsible for the selection of volunteers shall make a determination of employment or volunteer matters based on a review of the information required under section 6344(b) prior to employment or acceptance to service in any such capacity and must maintain a copy of the required information.

(g) **Written notice of new arrest, conviction or substantiated child abuse.—**

(1) If an employee or volunteer subject to section 6344 (relating to employees having contact with children; adoptive and foster parents) or 6344.2 (relating to volunteers having contact with children) is arrested for or convicted of an offense that would constitute grounds for denying employment or participation in a program, activity or service under this chapter, or is named as a perpetrator in a founded or indicated report, the employee or volunteer shall provide the administrator or designee with written notice not later than 72 hours after the arrest, conviction or notification that the person has been listed as a perpetrator in the Statewide database.

(2) If the person responsible for employment decisions or the administrator of a program, activity or service has a reasonable belief that an employee or volunteer was arrested or convicted for an offense that would constitute grounds for denying employment or participation in a program, activity or service under this chapter, or was named as a perpetrator in a founded or indicated report, or the employee or volunteer has provided notice as required under this section, the person responsible for employment decisions or administrator of a program, activity or service shall immediately require the employee or volunteer to submit current information as required under subsection 6344(b). The cost of the information set forth in subsection 6344(b) shall be borne by the employing entity or program, activity or service.

(h) **Effect of noncompliance.—**An employee or volunteer who willfully fails to disclose information required by subsection (g)(1) commits a misdemeanor of the third degree and shall be subject to discipline up to and including termination or denial of employment or volunteer position.

(Oct. 22, 2014, P.L.2529, No.153, eff. Dec. 31, 2014; July 1, 2015, P.L.94, No.15, eff. imd.)

2015 Amendment. Act 15 amended subsecs. (e) and (f).

2014 Amendment. Act 153 added section 6344.3.

Special Provisions in Appendix. See section 15 of Act 153 of 2014 in the appendix to this title for special provisions relating to study by Department of Human Services.

Cross References. Section 6344.3 is referred to in section 6340 of this title.

§ 6344.4. Recertification.

New certifications shall be obtained in accordance with the following:

(1) Effective December 31, 2014:

(i) Except as provided in subparagraph (v), a person identified in section 6344 (relating to employees having contact with children; adoptive and foster parents) shall be required to obtain the certifications required by this chapter every 60 months.

(ii) School employees identified in section 6344(a.1)(1) shall be required to obtain reports under section 111 of the act of March 10, 1949 (P.L.30, No.14), known as the Public School Code of 1949, and under section 6344(b)(2) every 60 months.

(iii) Any person identified in section 6344 with a current certification issued prior to the effective date of this section shall be required to obtain the certifications required by this chapter within 60 months from the date of the person's oldest certification or, if the current certification is older than 60 months, within one year of the effective date of this section.

(iv) A person identified in section 6344 without a certification or who was previously not required to have a certification shall be required to obtain the certifications required by this chapter no later than December 31, 2015.

(2)(i) Effective August 25, 2015, a person identified in section 6344.2 (relating to volunteers having contact with children) shall be required to obtain the certifications required by this chapter every 60 months from the date of the person's most recent certification or, if the current certification is older than 60 months, within one year of the effective date of this section.

(ii) A person identified under section 6344.2 without a certification or who was previously not required to have a certification shall be required to obtain the certifications required by this chapter no later than July 1, 2016.

(3) For renewals of certification required under this chapter, the date for required renewal under this section shall be from the date of the oldest certification under section 6344(b).

(Oct. 22, 2014, P.L.2529, No.153, eff. Dec. 31, 2014; July 1, 2015, P.L.94, No.15, eff. imd.)

Special Provisions in Appendix. See section 15 of Act 153 of 2014 in the appendix to this title for special provisions relating to study by Department of Human Services.

Cross References. Section 6344.4 is referred to in sections 6344, 6344.3 of this title.

§ 6345. Audits by Attorney General.

The Attorney General shall conduct a mandated audit done randomly but at least once during each year on an unannounced basis to ensure that the expunction requirements of this chapter are being fully and properly conducted.

1994 Amendment. Act 151 amended sect 6345.

Cross References. Section 6345 is referred to in section 6335 of this title.

§ 6346. Cooperation of other agencies.

(a) **General rule.**—The secretary may request and shall receive from Commonwealth agencies, political subdivisions, an authorized agency or any other agency providing services under the local protective services plan any assistance and data that will enable the department and the county agency to fulfill their responsibilities properly, including law enforcement officials when assistance is needed in conducting an investigation or an assessment of safety or risk to the child. School districts shall cooperate with the department and the agency by providing them upon request with the information as is consistent with law.

(b) **Willful failure to cooperate.**—Any agency, school or facility or any person acting on behalf of an agency, school or facility that violates this section by willfully failing to cooperate with the department or a county agency when investigating a report of suspected child abuse or when assessing safety or risk to a child commits a misdemeanor of the third degree for a first violation and a misdemeanor of the second degree for subsequent violations.

(c) **Cooperation of county agency and law enforcement officials.**—Consistent with the provisions of this chapter, the county agency and law enforcement officials shall cooperate and coordinate, to the fullest extent possible, their efforts to respond to and investigate reports of suspected child abuse.

(d) **Advice to county agency.**—Whenever a report of suspected child abuse is referred from a county agency to a law enforcement official pursuant to section 6340(a)(9) and (10) (relating to release of information in confidential reports), as soon as possible, and without jeopardizing the criminal investigation or prosecution, the law enforcement official shall advise the county agency as to whether a criminal investigation has been undertaken and the results of the investigation and of any criminal prosecution. The county agency shall ensure that the information is referred to the Statewide database.

1990, Dec. 19, P.L. 1240, No. 206, § 2, effective in 90 days. Amended 1994, Dec. 16, P.L. 1292, No. 151, § 3, effective July 1, 1995; 1998, Dec. 15, P.L. 963, No. 127, § 12, effective March 1, 1999; 2014, April 7, P.L. 388, No. 29, § 7, effective Dec. 31, 2014; 2014, May 14, P.L. 653, No. 45, § 8, effective Dec. 31, 2014.

§ 6347. Reports to Governor and General Assembly.

(a) **General rule.**—No later than May 1 of every year, the secretary shall prepare and transmit to the Governor and the General Assembly a report on the operations of the Statewide database and protective services provided by county agencies. The report shall include a full statistical analysis of the reports of suspected child abuse made to the department and the reports of general protective services made to the department or county agencies, together with a report on the implementation of this chapter and its total cost to the Commonwealth, the evaluation of the secretary of services offered under this chapter and recommendations for repeal or for additional legislation to fulfill the purposes of this chapter. All such recommendations should contain an estimate of increased or decreased costs resulting therefrom. The report shall also include an explanation of services provided to children who were the subjects of founded or indicated reports while receiving child-care services. The department shall also describe its actions in respect to the perpetrators of the abuse.

(b) **Reports from county agencies.**—To assist the department in preparing its annual report and the quarterly reports required under subsection (c), each county agency shall submit a quarterly report to the department, including, at a minimum, the following information, on an aggregate basis, regarding general protective services and child protective services:

(1) The number of referrals received and referrals accepted.

(2) The number of children over whom the agency maintains continuing supervision.

(3) The number of cases which have been closed by the agency.

(4) The services provided to children and their families.

(5) A summary of the findings with nonidentifying information about each case of child abuse or neglect which has resulted in a child fatality or near fatality.

(c) **Quarterly reports.**—The department shall prepare and transmit to the Governor and the General Assembly a quarterly report that includes a summary of the findings with nonidentifying information about each case of child abuse or neglect that has resulted in a child fatality or near fatality. One of the quarterly reports may be included within the annual report required under subsection (a).

1990, Dec. 19, P.L. 1240, No. 206, § 2, effective in 90 days. Amended 1994, Dec. 16, P.L. 1292, No. 151, § 3, effective July 1, 1996; 2006, Nov. 9, P.L. 1358, No. 146, § 5, effective in 180 days [May 8, 2007]; 2014, April 7, P.L. 388, No. 29, § 7, effective Dec. 31, 2014; 2014, May 14, P.L. 653, No. 45, § 8, effective Dec. 31, 2014.

§ 6348. Regulations.

The department shall adopt regulations necessary to implement this chapter.

§ 6349. Penalties.

(a) **Failure to amend or expunge information.**—

(1) A person or official authorized to keep the records mentioned in section 6337 (relating to disposition and expunction of unfounded reports and general protective services reports) or 6338 (relating to disposition of founded and indicated reports) who willfully fails to amend or expunge the information when required commits a misdemeanor of the third degree for the first violation and a misdemeanor of the second degree for a second or subsequent violation.

(2) A person who willfully fails to obey a final order of the secretary or designated agent of the secretary to amend or expunge the summary of the report in the Statewide database or the contents of any report filed pursuant to section 6313 (relating to reporting procedure) commits a misdemeanor of the third degree.

(b) **Unauthorized release of information.**—A person who willfully releases or permits the release of any information contained in the Statewide database or the county agency records required by this chapter to persons or agencies not permitted by this chapter to receive that information commits a misdemeanor of the second degree.

Law enforcement officials shall insure the confidentiality and security of information under this chapter. A person, including a law enforcement official, who violates the provisions of this subsection shall, in addition to other civil or criminal penalties provided by law, be denied access to the information provided under this chapter.

(b.1) **Unauthorized access or use of information.**—A person who willfully accesses, attempts to access or uses information in the Statewide database for a purpose not authorized under this chapter commits a misdemeanor of the second degree. A person who uses information in the Statewide database for a purpose not authorized under this chapter with intent to harass, embarrass or harm another person commits a misdemeanor of the first degree.

(c) **Noncompliance with child-care personnel regulations.**—An administrator, or other person responsible for employment decisions in a child-care facility or program, who willfully fails to comply with the provisions of section 6344 (relating to employees having contact with children; adoptive and foster parents) commits a violation of this chapter and shall be subject to a civil penalty as provided in this subsection. The department shall have jurisdiction to determine violations of section 6344 and may, following a hearing, assess a civil penalty not to exceed $2,500. The civil penalty shall be payable to the Commonwealth.

(Dec. 16, 1994, P.L.1292, No.151, eff. July 1, 1995; Apr. 7, 2014, P.L.388, No.29, eff. Dec. 31, 2014; Oct. 22, 2014, P.L.2529, No.153, eff. Dec. 31, 2014)

2014 Amendments. Act 29 amended subsecs. (a) and (b), added subsec. (b.1) and carried without amendment subsec. (c) and Act 153 amended subsec. (c).

Cross References. Section 6349 is referred to in section 6335 of this title.

SUBCHAPTER C.1
STUDENTS IN PUBLIC AND PRIVATE SCHOOLS

Sec.
6351. Definitions.
6352. School employees.
6353. Administration.
6353.1. Investigation.
6353.2. Responsibilities of county agency.
6353.3. Information in Statewide central register.
6353.4. Other provisions.

Enactment. Subchapter C.1 was added December 16, 1994, P.L. 1292, No. 151, effective July 1, 1995.

Cross References. Subchapter C.1 is referred to in sections 6303, 6331, 6333, 6337, 6338, 6340, 6346, 6347 of this title.

§ 6351. Definitions.

The following words and phrases when used in this subchapter shall have the meanings given to them in this section unless the context clearly indicates otherwise:

"Administrator." The person responsible for the administration of a public or private school, intermediate unit or area vocational-technical school. The term includes an independent contractor.

1994, Dec. 16, P.L. 1292, No. 151, § 4, effective July 1, 1995.

REPEAL

Title 23 Pa.C.S.A. Ch. 63 Subch. C.1 §§ 6351 to 6353.4 are repealed effective Dec. 31, 2014, pursuant to 2014, May 14, P.L. 645, No. 44, §§ 3 to 6, and 2014, May 14, P.L. 653, No. 45, §§ 9 to 12. See generally, 23 Pa.C.S.A. § 6311.

§ 6352. School employees.

(a) Requirement.—

(1) Except as provided in paragraph (2), a school employee who has reasonable cause to suspect, on the basis of professional or other training and experience, that a student coming before the school employee in the employee's professional or official capacity is a victim of serious bodily injury or sexual abuse or sexual exploitation by a school employee shall immediately contact the administrator.

(2) If the school employee accused of seriously injuring or sexually abusing or exploiting a student is the administrator, the school employee who has reasonable cause to suspect, on the basis of professional or other training and experience, that a student coming before the school employee in the employee's professional or official capacity is a victim of serious bodily injury or sexual abuse or sexual exploitation shall immediately report to law enforcement officials and the district attorney under section 6353(a) (relating to administration). If an administrator is the school employee who suspects injury or abuse, the administrator shall make a report under section 6353(a).

(3) The school employee may not reveal the existence or content of the report to any other person.

(b) Immunity.—A school employee who refers a report under subsection (a) shall be immune from civil and criminal liability arising out of the report.

(c) Criminal penalty.—

(1) A school employee who willfully violates subsection (a) commits a summary offense.

(2) A school employee who, after being sentenced under paragraph (1), violates subsection (a) commits a misdemeanor of the third degree.

1994, Dec. 16, P.L. 1292, No. 151, § 4, effective July 1, 1995.

REPEAL

Title 23 Pa.C.S.A. Ch. 63 Subch. C.1 §§ 6351 to 6353.4 are repealed effective Dec. 31, 2014, pursuant to 2014, May 14, P.L. 645, No. 44, §§ 3 to 6, and 2014, May 14, P.L. 653, No. 45, §§ 9 to 12. See generally, 23 Pa.C.S. § 6311.

Cross References. Section 6352 is referred to in section 6353 of this title.

§ 6353. Administration.

(a) Requirement.—An administrator and a school employee governed by section 6352(a)(2) (relating to school employees) shall report immediately to law enforcement officials and the appropriate district attorney any report of serious bodily injury or sexual abuse or sexual exploitation alleged to have been committed by a school employee against a student.

(b) Report.—A report under subsection (a) shall include the following information:

(1) Name, age, address and school of the student.

(2) Name and address of the student's parent or guardian.

(3) Name and address of the administrator.

(4) Name, work and home address of the school employee.

(5) Nature of the alleged offense.

(6) Any specific comments or observations that are directly related to the alleged incident and the individuals involved.

(c) Immunity.—An administrator who makes a report under subsection (a) shall be immune from civil or criminal liability arising out of the report.

(d) Criminal penalty.—An administrator who willfully violates subsection (a) commits a misdemeanor of the third degree.

1994, Dec. 16, P.L. 1292, No. 151, § 4, effective July 1, 1995.

REPEAL

Title 23 Pa.C.S.A. Ch. 63 Subch. C.1 §§ 6351 to 6353.4 are repealed effective Dec. 31, 2014, pursuant to 2014, May 14, P.L. 645, No. 44, §§ 3 to 6, and 2014, May 14, P.L. 653, No. 45, §§ 9 to 12. See generally, 23 Pa.C.S. § 6311.

Cross References. Section 6353 is referred to in sections 6352, 6353.1 of this title.

§ 6353.1. Investigation.

(a) **General rule.**—Upon receipt of a report under section 6353 (relating to administration), an investigation shall be conducted by law enforcement officials, in cooperation with the district attorney, and a determination made as to what criminal charges, if any, will be filed against the school employee.

(b) **Referral to county agency.**—

(1) If local law enforcement officials have reasonable cause to suspect on the basis of initial review that there is evidence of serious bodily injury, sexual abuse or sexual exploitation committed by a school employee against a student, local law enforcement officials shall notify the county agency in the county where the alleged abuse or injury occurred for the purpose of the agency conducting an investigation of the alleged abuse or injury.

(2) To the fullest extent possible, law enforcement officials and the county agency shall coordinate their respective investigations. In respect to interviews with the student, law enforcement officials and the county agency shall conduct joint interviews. In respect to interviews with the school employee, law enforcement officials shall be given an opportunity to interview the school employee prior to the employee having any contact with the county agency.

(3) The county agency and law enforcement officials have the authority to arrange for photographs, medical tests or X-rays of a student alleged to have been abused or injured by a school employee. The county agency and law enforcement officials shall coordinate their efforts in this regard and, to the fullest extent possible, avoid the duplication of any photographs, medical tests or X-rays.

(4) Law enforcement officials and the county agency shall advise each other of the status and findings of their respective investigations on an ongoing basis.

1994, Dec. 16, P.L. 1292, No. 151, § 4, effective July 1, 1995.

REPEAL

Title 23 Pa.C.S. Ch. 63 Subch. C.1 §§ 6351 to 6353.4 are repealed effective Dec. 31, 2014, pursuant to 2014, May 14, P.L. 645, No. 44, §§ 3 to 6, and 2014, May 14, P.L. 653, No. 45, §§ 9 to 12. See generally, 23 Pa.C.S. § 6311.

Cross References. Section 6353.1 is referred to in section 6353.2 of this title.

§ 6353.2. Responsibilities of county agency.

(a) **Information for the pending complaint file.**—Immediately after receiving a report under section 6353.1 (relating to investigation), the county agency shall notify the department of the receipt of the report, which is to be filed in the pending complaint file as provided in section 6331(1) (relating to establishment of Statewide database). The oral report shall include the following information:

(1) The name and address of the student and the student's parent or guardian.

(2) Where the suspected abuse or injury occurred.

(3) The age and sex of the student.

(4) The nature and extent of the suspected abuse or injury.

(5) The name and home address of the school employee alleged to have committed the abuse or injury.

(6) The relationship of the student to the school employee alleged to have committed the abuse or injury.

(7) The source of the report to the county agency.

(8) The actions taken by the county agency, law enforcement officials, parents, guardians, school officials or other persons, including the taking of photographs, medical tests and X-rays.

(b) Investigation of reports.—Upon receipt of a report under section 6353.1, the county agency shall commence, within the time frames established in department regulations, an investigation of the nature, extent and cause of any alleged abuse or injury enumerated in the report. The county agency shall coordinate its investigation to the fullest extent possible with law enforcement officials as provided in section 6353.1(b).

(c) Completion of investigation.—The investigation by the county agency to determine whether the report is an indicated report for school employee or an unfounded report shall be completed within 60 days.

(d) Notice to subject of a report.—Prior to interviewing a subject of the report, the county agency shall orally notify the subject of the report of the existence of the report and the subject's rights under this chapter in regard to amendment or expungement. Within 72 hours following oral notification to the subject, the county agency shall give written notice to the subject. The notice may be reasonably delayed if notification is likely to threaten the safety of the student or the county agency worker, to cause the school employee to abscond or to significantly interfere with the conduct of a criminal investigation.

(e) Reliance on factual investigation.—The county agency may rely on a factual investigation of substantially the same allegations by a law enforcement officials to support the agency's finding. This reliance shall not relieve the county agency of its responsibilities relating to the investigation of reports under this subchapter.

(f) Notice to the department of the county agency's determination.—As soon as the county agency has completed its investigation, the county agency shall advise the department and law enforcement officials of its determination of the report as an indicated report for school employee or an unfounded report. Supplemental reports shall be made at regular intervals thereafter in a manner and form the department prescribes by regulation to the end that the department is kept fully informed and up-to-date concerning the status of the report.

1994, Dec. 16, P.L. 1292, No. 151, § 4, effective July 1, 1995. Amended 2013, Dec. 18, P.L. 1201, No. 119, § 5, effective July 1, 2014.

REPEAL

Title 23 Pa.C.S. Ch. 63 Subch. C.1 §§ 6351 to 6353.4 are repealed effective Dec. 31, 2014, pursuant to 2014, May 14, P.L. 645, No. 44, §§ 3 to 6, and 2014, May 14, P.L. 653, No. 45, §§ 9 to 12. See generally, 23 Pa.C.S. § 6311.

Cross References. Section 6353.2 is referred to in sections 6333, 6334, 6335 of this title.

§ 6353.3. Information in Statewide central register.

The Statewide central register established under section 6331 (relating to establishment of Statewide database) shall retain only the following information relating to reports of abuse or injury of a student by a school employee which have been determined to be a founded report for school employee or an indicated report for school employee:

(1) The names, Social Security numbers, age and sex of the subjects of the report.

(2) The home address of the subjects of the report.

(3) The date and the nature and extent of the alleged abuse or injury.

(4) The county and state where the abuse or injury occurred.

(5) Factors contributing to the abuse or injury.

(6) The source of the report.

(7) Whether the report is a founded or indicated report.

(8) Information obtained by the department in relation to the school employee's request to release, amend or expunge information retained by the department or the county agency.

(9) The progress of any legal proceedings brought on the basis of the report.

(10) Whether a criminal investigation has been undertaken and the result of the investigation and of any criminal prosecution.

1994, Dec. 16, P.L. 1292, No. 151, § 4, effective July 1, 1995. Amended 2013, Dec. 18, P.L. 1201, No. 119, § 5, effective July 1, 2014.

REPEAL

Title 23 Pa.C.S. Ch. 63 Subch. C.1 §§ 6351 to 6353.4 are repealed effective Dec. 31, 2014, pursuant to 2014, May 14, P.L. 645, No. 44, §§ 3 to 6, and 2014, May 14, P.L. 653, No. 45, §§ 9 to 12. See generally, 23 Pa.C.S. § 6311.

§ 6353.4. Other provisions.

The following provisions shall apply to the release and retention of information by the department and the county agency concerning reports of abuse or injury committed by a school employee as provided by this subchapter:

Section 6336(b) and (c) (relating to information in Statewide central register).

Section 6337 (relating to disposition of unfounded reports).

Section 6338(a) and (b) (relating to disposition of founded and indicated reports).

Section 6339 (relating to confidentiality of reports).

Section 6340 (relating to release of information in confidential reports).

Section 6341(a) through (f) (relating to amendment or expunction of information).

Section 6342 (relating to studies of data in records).

1994, Dec. 16, P.L. 1292, No. 151, § 4, effective July 1, 1995.

REPEAL

Title 23 Pa.C.S. Ch. 63 Subch. C.1 §§ 6351 to 6353.4 are repealed effective Dec. 31, 2014, pursuant to 2014, May 14, P.L. 645, No. 44, §§ 3 to 6, and 2014, May 14, P.L. 653, No. 45, §§ 9 to 12. See generally, 23 Pa.C.S. § 6311.

SUBCHAPTER C.2
BACKGROUND CHECKS FOR EMPLOYMENT IN SCHOOLS

Sec.

6354. Definitions.
6355. Requirement.
6356. Exceptions.
6357. Fees.
6358. Time limit for official clearance statement.

Enactment. Subchapter C.2 was added December 16, 1994, P.L. 1292, No. 151, effective July 1, 1996.

§ 6354. Definitions.

The following words and phrases when used in this subchapter shall have the meanings given to them in this section unless the context clearly indicates otherwise:

"Applicant." An individual who applies for a position as a school employee. The term includes an individual who transfers from one position as a school employee to another position as a school employee.

"Administrator." The person responsible for the administration of a public or private school, intermediate unit or area vocational-technical school. The term includes a person responsible for employment decisions in a school and an independent contractor.

1994, Dec. 16, P.L. 1292, No. 151, § 4, effective July 1, 1996.

REPEAL

Title 23 Pa.C.S. Ch. 63 Subch. C.2 §§ 6354 to 6358 are repealed effective Dec. 31, 2014, pursuant to 2014, May 14, P.L. 653, No. 45, §§ 13, 14. See generally, 23 Pa.C.S. § 6344.2 and 24 P.S. § 1-111.

§ 6355. Requirement.

(a) Investigation.—

(1) Except as provided in paragraph (2), an administrator shall require each applicant to submit an official clearance statement obtained from the department within the immediately preceding year as to whether the applicant is named as the perpetrator of an indicated or a founded report or is named as the individual responsible for injury or abuse in an indicated report for school employee or a founded report for school employee.

(2) The official clearance statement under paragraph (1) shall not be required for an applicant who:

(i) transfers from one position as a school employee to another position as a school employee of the same school district or of the same organization; and

(ii) has, prior to the transfer, already obtained the official clearance statement under paragraph (1).

(b) Grounds for denying employment.—Except as provided in section 6356 (relating to exceptions), an administrator shall not hire an applicant if the department verifies that the applicant is named as the perpetrator of a founded report or is named as the individual responsible for injury or abuse in a founded report for school employee. No individual who is a school employee on the effective date of this subchapter shall be required to obtain an official clearance statement under subsection (a)(1) as a condition of continued employment.

(c) Penalty.—An administrator who willfully violates this section shall be subject to an administrative penalty of $2,500. An action under this subsection is governed by 2 Pa.C.S. Ch. 5 Subch. A (relating to practice and procedure of Commonwealth agencies) and Ch. 7 Subch. A (relating to judicial review of Commonwealth agency action).

1994, Dec. 16, P.L. 1292, No. 151, § 4, effective July 1, 1996.

REPEAL

Title 23 Pa.C.S. Ch. 63 Subch. C.2 §§ 6354 to 6358 are repealed effective Dec. 31, 2014, pursuant to 2014, May 14, P.L. 653, No. 45, §§ 13, 14. See generally, 23 Pa.C.S. § 6344.2 and 24 P.S. § 1-111.

Cross References. Section 6355 is referred to in sections 6356, 6357, 6358 of this title.

§ 6356. Exceptions.

Section 6355 (relating to requirement) shall not apply to any of the following:

(1) A school employee who is:

(i) under 21 years of age;

(ii) participating in a job development or job training program; and

(iii) employed for not more than 90 days.

(2) A school employee hired on a provisional basis pending receipt of information under section 6355(a) if all of the following apply:

(i) The applicant demonstrates application for the official clearance statement under section 6355(a).

(ii) The applicant attests in writing by oath or affirmation that the applicant is not disqualified under section 6355(b).

(iii) The administrator has no knowledge of information which would disqualify the applicant under section 6355(b).

(iv) The provisional period does not exceed:

(A) 90 days for an applicant from another state; and

(B) 30 days for all other applicants.

(v) The hiring does not take place during a strike under the act of July 23, 1970 (P.L. 563, No. 195), known as the Public Employe Relations Act.

1994, Dec. 16, P.L. 1292, No. 151, § 4, effective July 1, 1996.

REPEAL

Title 23 Pa.C.S. Ch. 63 Subch. C.2 §§ 6354 to 6358 are repealed effective Dec. 31, 2014, pursuant to 2014, May 14, P.L. 653, No. 45, §§ 13, 14. See generally, 23 Pa.C.S. § 6344.2 and 24 P.S. § 1-111.

Cross References. Section 6356 is referred to in section 6355 of this title.

§ 6357. Fee.

The department may charge a fee of not more than $10 for the official clearance statement required under section 6355(a) (relating to requirement).

1994, Dec. 16, P.L. 1292, No. 151, § 4, effective July 1, 1996.

REPEAL

Title 23 Pa.C.S. Ch. 63 Subch. C.2 §§ 6354 to 6358 are repealed effective Dec. 31, 2014, pursuant to 2014, May 14, P.L. 653, No. 45, §§ 13, 14. See generally, 23 Pa.C.S. § 6344.2 and 24 P.S. § 1-111.

§ 6358. Time limit for official clearance statement.

The department shall comply with the official clearance statement requests under section 6355(a) (relating to requirement) within 14 days of receipt of the request.

1994, Dec. 16, P.L. 1292, No. 151, § 4, effective July 1, 1996.

REPEAL

Title 23 Pa.C.S. Ch. 63 Subch. C.2 §§ 6354 to 6358 are repealed effective Dec. 31, 2014, pursuant to 2014, May 14, P.L. 653, No. 45, §§ 13, 14. See generally, 23 Pa.C.S.A. § 6344.2 and 24 P.S. § 1-111.

SUBCHAPTER D

ORGANIZATION AND RESPONSIBILITIES OF CHILD PROTECTIVE SERVICE

Sec.
6361. Organization for child protective services.
6362. Responsibilities of county agency for child protective services.
6363. County plan for protective services.
6364. Purchasing services of other agencies.
6365. Services for prevention, investigation and treatment of child abuse.
6366. Continuous availability to receive reports.
6367. Reports to department and coroner.
6368. Investigation of reports.
6369. Taking child into protective custody.
6370. Voluntary or court-ordered services; findings of child abuse.

6371. Rehabilitative services for child and family.
6372. Protecting well-being of children maintained outside home.
6373. General protective services responsibilities of county agency.
6374. Principles and goals of general protective services.
6375. County agency requirements for general protective services.
6376. Appeals with respect to general protective services.
6377. Caseloads.
6378. Purchase of services.

§ 6361. Organization for child protective services.

(a) **Establishment.**—Every county agency shall make available child protective services within the agency. The department may waive the requirement that a county agency be the sole civil agency for receipt and investigation of reports pursuant to section 6362 (relating to responsibilities of county agency for child protective services) upon a showing by the county that:

(1) It is participating in a demonstration project for, or has become part of, an approved combined intake system for public human service agencies as permitted by department regulations. Nothing in this paragraph is intended to permit noncounty government agencies to participate in the receipt and investigation of the reports.

(2) The goals and objectives of this chapter will continue to be met if a waiver is granted.

If the department grants a waiver under this subsection, the county agency and its agents shall be bound by all other provisions of this chapter, including requirements concerning the maintenance and disclosure of confidential information and records.

(b) **Staff and organization.**—The county agency shall have a sufficient staff of sufficient qualifications to fulfill the purposes of this chapter and be organized in a way to maximize the continuity of responsibility, care and services of individual workers toward individual children and families. The department, by regulation, shall set forth staff-to-family ratios for the various activities required of the county agency under this chapter, including reports and investigations of suspected child abuse, risk assessment and the provision or monitoring of services to abused children and their families.

(c) **Functions authorized.**—The county agency staff shall perform those functions assigned to it by this chapter and such other functions as would further the purposes of this chapter.

1994 Amendment. Act 151 amended sect 6361.

Cross References. Section 6361 is referred to in sections 6362, 6364, 6375 of this title.

§ 6362. Responsibilities of county agency for child protective services.

(a) **General rule.**—The county agency shall be the sole civil agency responsible for receiving and investigating all reports of child abuse made pursuant to this chapter, specifically including, but not limited to, reports of child abuse in facilities operated by the department and other public agencies, for the purpose of providing protective services to prevent further abuses to children and to provide or arrange for and monitor the provision of those services necessary to safeguard and ensure the well-being and development of the child and to preserve and stabilize family life wherever appropriate.

(b) **Assumption of responsibility by department.**—When the suspected abuse has been committed by the county agency or any of its agents or employees, the department shall assume the role of the agency with regard to the investigation and directly refer the child for services.

(c) **Action by agencies for abuse by agents or employees.**—Where suspected child abuse has occurred and an employee or agent of the department or the county agency or a private or public institution is a subject of the report, the department, agency or institution shall be informed of the investigation so that it may take appropriate action.

(d) **Reliance on factual investigation.**—An agency charged by this section or section 6361 (relating to organization for child protective services) with investigating a report of child abuse may rely on a factual investigation of substantially the same allegations by a law enforcement agency to support the agency's finding. This reliance shall not, however, limit the duties imposed by section 6368(a) (relating to investigation of reports).

(e) **Risk assessment.**—Each county agency shall implement a State-approved risk assessment process in performance of its duties under this subchapter.

1994 Amendment. Act 151 amended subsec (a), (b) and (c), and added subsect (d) and (e).

(f) **Weekly face-to-face contacts.**—For those children assessed as being at high risk for abuse or neglect who are remaining in or returning to the home in which the abuse or neglect occurred, the county agency shall ensure that those children are seen at least once a week, either directly by a county agency worker or through purchase of service, until they are no longer assessed as being at high risk for abuse or neglect.

1999 Amendment. Act 50 added subsect (f).

Cross References. Section 6362 is referred to in sections 6361, 6364 of this title.

§ 6363. County plan for protective services.

The county agency shall include provisions for protective services in its annual plan as required by the act of June 13, 1967 (P.L. 31, No. 21), known as the Public Welfare Code.[7]

1994 Amendment. Act 151 amended sect 6363.

Cross References. Section 6363 is referred to in section 6364 of this title.

§ 6364. Purchasing services of other agencies.

Any other provision of law notwithstanding but consistent with sections 6361 (relating to organization for child protective services) and 6362 (relating to responsibilities of county agency for child protective services), the county agency, based upon the plan of services as provided in section 6363 (relating to county plan for protective services), may purchase and utilize the services of any appropriate public or private agency.

1994 Amendment. Act 151 amended sect 6364.

§ 6365. Services for prevention, investigation and treatment of child abuse.

(a) **Instruction and education.**—Each county agency shall make available among its services for the prevention and treatment of child abuse instruction and education for parenthood and parenting skills, protective and preventive social counseling, outreach and counseling services to prevent newborn abandonment, emergency caretaker services, emergency shelter care, emergency medical services and the establishment of self-help groups organized for the prevention and treatment of child abuse, part-day services, out-of-home placement services, therapeutic activities for child and family directed at alleviating conditions that present a risk to the safety and well-being of a child and any other services required by department regulations.

---

[7]62 P.S. § 101 et seq.

(b) **Multidisciplinary review team.**—The county agency shall make available among its services a multidisciplinary review team for the prevention, investigation and treatment of child abuse and shall convene the multidisciplinary review team at any time, but not less than annually:

(1) To review substantiated cases of child abuse, including responses by the county agency and other agencies providing services to the child.

(2) Where appropriate to assist in the development of a family service plan for the child.

(c) **Multidisciplinary investigative team.**—A multidisciplinary investigative team shall be used to coordinate child abuse investigations between county agencies and law enforcement. The county agency and the district attorney shall develop a protocol for the convening of multidisciplinary investigative teams for any case of child abuse by a perpetrator involving crimes against children which are set forth in section 6340(a)(9) and (10) (relating to release of information in confidential reports). The county multidisciplinary investigative team protocol shall include standards and procedures to be used in receiving and referring reports and coordinating investigations of reported cases of child abuse and a system for sharing the information obtained as a result of any interview. The protocol shall include any other standards and procedures to avoid duplication of fact-finding efforts and interviews to minimize the trauma to the child. The district attorney shall convene the multidisciplinary investigative team in accordance with the protocol. The multidisciplinary investigative team shall consist of those individuals and agencies responsible for investigating the abuse or for providing services to the child and shall at a minimum include a health care provider, county caseworker and law enforcement official.

(d) **Child fatality or near fatality review team and written report.**—

(1) A child fatality or near fatality review team shall be convened by a county agency in accordance with a protocol developed by the county agency, the department and the district attorney in a case when a child dies or nearly dies as a result of child abuse as to which there is an indicated report or when the county agency has not made a status determination within 30 days. The team may convene after a county agency makes a determination of an indicated report and shall convene no later than 31 days from the receipt of the oral report to the department of the suspected child abuse. A county agency in the county where the abuse occurred and in any county where the child resided within the 16 months preceding the fatality or near fatality shall convene a child fatality or near fatality review team. A team shall consist of at least six individuals who are broadly representative of the county where the team is established and who have expertise in prevention and treatment of child abuse. With consideration given to the circumstances of each case and availability of individuals to serve as members, the team may consist of the following individuals:

(i) A staff person from the county agency.

(ii) A member of the advisory committee of the county agency.

(iii) A health care professional.

(iv) A representative of a local school, educational program or child care or early childhood development program.

(v) A representative of law enforcement or the district attorney.

(vi) An attorney-at-law trained in legal representation of children or an individual trained under 42 Pa.C.S. § 6342 (relating to court-appointed special advocates).

(vii) A mental health professional.

(viii) A representative of a children's advocacy center that provides services to children in the county. The individual under this subparagraph must not be an employee of the county agency.

(ix) The county coroner or forensic pathologist.

(x) A representative of a local domestic violence program.

(xi) A representative of a local drug and alcohol program.

(xii) An individual representing parents.

(xiii) Any individual whom the county agency or child fatality or near fatality review team determines is necessary to assist the team in performing its duties.

(2) Members of the team shall be responsible for all of the following:

(i) Maintaining confidentiality of information under sections 6339 (relating to confidentiality of reports) and 6340.

(ii) Providing and discussing relevant case-specific information.

(iii) Attending and participating in all meetings and activities as required.

(iv) Assisting in the development of the report under paragraph (4)(v).

(3) The county agency, in accordance with the protocol and in consultation with the team, shall appoint an individual who is not an employee of the county agency to serve as chairperson.

(4) The team shall perform the following:

(i) Review the circumstances of the child's fatality or near fatality resulting from suspected or substantiated child abuse.

(ii) Review the delivery of services to the abused child and the child's family provided by the county agency and review services provided to the perpetrator by the county agency in each county where the child and family resided within the 16 months preceding the fatality or near fatality and the services provided to the child, the child's family and the perpetrator by other public and private community agencies or professionals. This subparagraph includes law enforcement, mental health services, programs for young children and children with special needs, drug and alcohol programs, local schools and health care providers.

(iii) Review relevant court records and documents related to the abused child and the child's family.

(iv) Review the county agency's compliance with statutes and regulations and with relevant policies and procedures of the county agency.

(v) Within 90 days of convening, submit a final written report on the child fatality or near fatality to the department and designated county officials under section 6340(a)(11). Within 30 days after submission of the report to the department, the report shall be made available, upon request, to other individuals to whom confidential reports may be released, as specified by section 6340. The report shall be made available to the public, but identifying information shall be removed from the contents of the report except for disclosure of: the identity of a deceased child; if the child was in the custody of a public or private agency, the identity of the agency; the identity of the public or private agency under contract with a county agency to provide services to the child and the child's family in the child's home prior to the child's death or near fatality; and the identity of any county agency that convened a child fatality or near fatality review team in respect to the child. The report shall not be released to the public if the district attorney certifies that release of the report may compromise a pending criminal investigation or proceeding. Certification by the district attorney shall stay the release of the report for a period of 60 days, at which time the report shall be released unless a new certification is made by the district attorney. The report shall include:

(A) Deficiencies and strengths in:

(i) compliance with statutes and regulations; and

(ii) services to children and families.

(B) Recommendations for changes at the State and local levels on:

(i) reducing the likelihood of future child fatalities and near fatalities directly related to child abuse and neglect;

(ii) monitoring and inspection of county agencies; and

(iii) collaboration of community agencies and service providers to prevent child abuse and neglect.

(d.1) Release by county agency.—Prior to completing its child fatality or near fatality report, the investigating county agency may release the following information to the public concerning a child who died or nearly died as a result of suspected or substantiated child abuse:

(1) The identity of the child, only in the case of a child's fatality.

(2) If the child was in the custody of a public or private agency, the identity of the agency.

(3) The identity of the public or private agency under contract with a county agency to provide services to the child and the child's family in the child's home prior to the child's death or near fatality.

(4) A description of services provided under paragraph (3).

(e) Response by department.—Within 45 days of receipt of a report of a child fatality or near fatality under subsection (d), the department shall review the findings and recommendations of the report and provide a written response to the county agency and the child fatality review team or near fatality review team. The department's response to the report of the child fatality or near fatality review team shall be made available, upon request, to other individuals to whom confidential reports may be released, as specified by section 6340. The department's response shall be made available to the public, but identifying information shall be removed from the contents of the response, except for disclosure of: the identity of a deceased child; if the child was in the custody of a public or private agency, the identity of the agency; the identity of the public or private agency under contract with a county agency to provide services to the child and the child's family in the child's home prior to the child's death or near fatality; and the identity of any county agency that convened a child fatality or near fatality review team in respect to the child. The response shall not be released to the public if the district attorney certifies that release of the response may compromise a pending criminal investigation or proceeding. Certification by the district attorney shall stay the release of the report for a period of 60 days, at which time the report shall be released unless a new certification is made by the district attorney.

(f) Construction.—The provisions of this section shall be construed to assist in the improvement of services designed to identify and prevent child abuse. The provisions shall not be construed to impede or interfere with criminal prosecutions of persons who have committed child abuse.

1990, Dec. 19, P.L. 1240, No. 206, § 2, effective in 90 days. Amended 1994, Dec. 16, P.L. 1292, No. 151, § 5, effective July 1, 1996; 1998, Dec. 15, P.L. 963, No. 127, § 12, effective March 1, 1999; 2002, Dec. 9, P.L. 1549, No. 201, § 5, effective in 60 days; 2008, July 3, P.L. 276, No. 33, § 5, effective in 180 days [Dec. 30, 2008]; 2013, Dec. 18, P.L. 1235, No. 123, § 1, effective in 90 days [March 18, 2014]; 2014, May 14, P.L. 645, No. 44, § 7, effective Dec. 31, 2014.

Cross References. Section 6365 is referred to in sections 6340, 6343.1, 6368, 6509 of this title.

§ 6366. Continuous availability to receive reports.

Each county agency shall receive 24 hours a day, seven days a week, all reports, both oral and written, of suspected child abuse in accordance with this chapter, the county plan for the provision of child protective services and the regulations of the department.

1994 Amendment. Act 151 amended sect 6366.

Cross References. Section 6366 is referred to in section 6344 of this title.

§ 6367. Reports to department and coroner.

(a) **Reports to department.**—Upon the receipt of each report of suspected child abuse made pursuant to this chapter, the county agency shall immediately transmit a child abuse report summary as provided in section 6313 (relating to reporting procedure) to the department. Supplemental reports shall be made at regular intervals thereafter in a manner and form the department prescribes by regulation to the end that the department is kept fully informed and up-to-date concerning the status of reports of child abuse.

(b) **Reports to coroner.**—The county agency shall give telephone notice and forward immediately a copy of reports made pursuant to this chapter which involve the death of a child to the appropriate coroner pursuant to section 6317 (relating to mandatory reporting and postmortem investigation of deaths).

(c) **Child deaths and near fatalities.**—A county agency shall immediately provide information to the department regarding its involvement with the child and with the child's parent, guardian or custodian when a child dies or nearly dies and child abuse is suspected. The county agency shall inform the department of any history of child protective or general protective services provided to the child prior to the child's death or near fatality and of services provided to other children of the child's parent, guardian or custodian by the county agency or by court order. The county agency shall inform the department if the child was in the agency's custody at the time of the child's death or near fatality. The county agency shall provide this information in writing on forms provided by the department within 48 hours of the oral report.

1990, Dec. 19, P.L. 1240, No. 206, § 2, effective in 90 days. Amended 1994, Dec. 16, P.L. 1292, No. 151, § 5, effective July 1, 1995; 2008, July 9, P.L. 276, No.33, effective in 180 days.

2008 Amendment. Act 33 added subsec. (c).

1994 Amendment. Act 151 amended sect 6367.

Cross References. Section 6367 is referred to in section 6341 of this title.

§ 6368. Investigation of reports.

(a) **Response to direct reports.**—Upon receipt of a report of suspected child abuse by a perpetrator from an individual, the county agency shall ensure the safety of the child and any other child in the child's home and immediately contact the department in accordance with the provisions of section 6334 (relating to disposition of complaints received).

(b) **Response to reports referred to county agency by department.**—Upon receipt of a report of suspected child abuse from the department, the county agency shall immediately commence an investigation and see the child within the following time frames:

(1) Immediately, if:

(i) emergency protective custody is required, has been or will be taken; or

(ii) it cannot be determined from the report whether emergency protective custody is needed.

(2) Within 24 hours of receipt of the report in all other cases.

(c) **Investigation.**—An investigation under this section shall include the following:

(1) A determination of the safety of or risk of harm to the child or any other child if each child continues to remain in the existing home environment.

(2) A determination of the nature, extent and cause of any condition listed in the report.

(3) Any action necessary to provide for the safety of the child or any other child in the child's household.

(4) The taking of photographic identification of the child or any other child in the child's household, which shall be maintained in the case file.

(5) Communication with the department's service under section 6332 (relating to establishment of Statewide toll-free telephone number).

(d) Investigative actions.—During the investigation, all of the following shall apply:

(1) The county agency shall provide or arrange for services necessary to protect the child while the agency is making a determination under this section.

(2) If the investigation indicates bodily injury, the county agency may require that a medical examination by a certified medical practitioner be performed on the child.

(3) Where there is reasonable cause to suspect that there is a history of prior or current abuse, the medical practitioner has the authority to arrange for further medical tests or the county agency has the authority to request further medical tests.

(4) The investigation shall include interviews with all subjects of the report, including the alleged perpetrator. If a subject of the report is not able to be interviewed or cannot be located, the county agency shall document its reasonable efforts to interview the subject and the reasons for its inability to interview the subject. The interview may be reasonably delayed if notice of the investigation has been delayed pursuant to subsection (m).

(e) Review of indicated reports.—A final determination that a report of suspected child abuse is indicated shall be approved by:

(1) the county agency administrator or a designee and reviewed by a county agency solicitor, when the county agency is investigating; or

(2) the secretary or a designee and reviewed by legal counsel for the department, when the department is investigating.

(f) Final determination.—Immediately upon conclusion of the child abuse investigation, the county agency shall provide the results of its investigation to the department in a manner prescribed by the department. Within three business days of receipt of the results of the investigation from the county agency, the department shall send notice of the final determination to the subjects of the report, other than the abused child. The determination shall include the following information:

(1) The status of the report.

(2) The perpetrator's right to request the secretary to amend or expunge the report.

(3) The right of the subjects of the report to services from the county agency.

(4) The effect of the report upon future employment opportunities involving children.

(5) The fact that the name of the perpetrator, the nature of the abuse and the final status of a founded or indicated report will be entered in the Statewide database, if the perpetrator's Social Security number or date of birth are known.

(6) The perpetrator's right to file an appeal of an indicated finding of abuse pursuant to section 6341 (relating to amendment or expunction of information) within 90 days of the date of notice.

(7) The perpetrator's right to a fair hearing on the merits on an appeal of an indicated report filed pursuant to section 6341.

(8) The burden on the investigative agency to prove its case by substantial evidence in an appeal of an indicated report.

(g) **Notice.**—Notice under subsection (f) shall constitute mailing of the final determination to the recipient's last known address. The determination is presumed received when not returned by the postal authorities as undeliverable. If the determination is returned as undeliverable, the entry in the Statewide database shall include information that the department was unable to provide notice. No further efforts to provide notice shall be required, except that the department shall resume reasonable efforts to provide notice if new information is received regarding the whereabouts of an individual who is entitled to receive notice under subsection (f).

(h) **Notice to mandated reporter.**—If a report was made by a mandated reporter under section 6313 (relating to reporting procedure), the department shall notify the mandated reporter who made the report of suspected child abuse of all of the following within three business days of the department's receipt of the results of the investigation:

(1) Whether the child abuse report is founded, indicated or unfounded.

(2) Any services provided, arranged for or to be provided by the county agency to protect the child.

(i) **Investigation concerning a school or child-care service employee.**—

(1) Upon notification that an investigation involves suspected child abuse by a school or child-care service employee, including, but not limited to, a service provider, independent contractor or administrator, the school or child-care service shall immediately implement a plan of supervision or alternative arrangement for the individual under investigation to ensure the safety of the child and other children who are in the care of the school or child-care service.

(2) The plan of supervision or alternative arrangement shall be approved by the county agency and kept on file with the agency until the investigation is completed.

(j) **Referral for investigation.**—If the complaint of suspected abuse is determined to be one that cannot be investigated under this chapter because the person accused of the abuse is not a perpetrator within the meaning of section 6303 (relating to definitions), but does suggest the need for investigation, the county agency shall immediately transmit the information to the appropriate law enforcement officials in accordance with the county protocols for multidisciplinary investigative teams required under section 6365(c) (relating to services for prevention, investigation and treatment of child abuse).

(k) **Need for social services.**—If the investigation determines that the child is being harmed by factors beyond the control of the parent or other person responsible for the child's welfare, the county agency shall promptly take all steps available to remedy and correct these conditions, including the coordination of social services for the child and the family or referral of the family to appropriate agencies for the provision of services.

(l) **Notice of investigation.**—

(1) Prior to interviewing a subject of a report, the county agency shall orally notify the subject, except for the alleged victim, who is about to be interviewed of the following information:

(i) The existence of the report.

(ii) The subject's rights under 42 Pa.C.S. §§ 6337 (relating to right to counsel) and 6338 (relating to other basic rights).

(iii) The subject's rights pursuant to this chapter in regard to amendment or expungement.

(iv) The subject's right to have an attorney present during the interview.

(2) Written notice shall be given to the subject within 72 hours following oral notification, unless delayed as provided in subsection (m).

(m) **Delay of notification.**—The notice under subsection (l)(2) may be reasonably delayed, subject to the following:

(1) If the notification is likely to:

(i) threaten the safety of a victim, a subject of the report who is not a perpetrator or the investigating county agency worker;

(ii) cause the perpetrator to abscond; or

(iii) significantly interfere with the conduct of a criminal investigation.

(2) The written notice shall be provided to all subjects of the report prior to the county agency reaching a finding on the validity of the report.

(n) **Completion of investigation.**—Investigations shall be completed in accordance with the following:

(1) Investigations to determine whether to accept the family for service and whether a report is founded, indicated or unfounded shall be completed within 60 days in all cases.

(2) If, due to the particular circumstances of the case, the county agency cannot complete the investigation within 30 days, the particular reasons for the delay shall be described in the child protective service record and made available to the department for purposes of determining whether either of the following occurred:

(i) The county agency strictly followed the provisions of this chapter.

(ii) The county agency is subject to action as authorized under section 6343 (relating to investigating performance of county agency).

(3) Where a petition has been filed under 42 Pa.C.S. Ch. 63 (relating to juvenile matters) alleging that a child is a dependent child, the county agency shall make all reasonable efforts to complete the investigation to enable the hearing on the petition to be held as required by 42 Pa.C.S. § 6335 (relating to release or holding of hearing).

(Dec. 16, 1994, P.L.1292, No.151, eff. July 1, 1996; Oct. 27, 2006, P.L.1192, No.126, eff. 60 days; Nov. 29, 2006, P.L.1581, No.179, eff. 180 days; Dec. 18, 2013, P.L.1170, No.108, eff. Dec. 31, 2014; Dec. 18, 2013, P.L.1235, No.123, eff. 90 days)

2013 Amendments. Act 108 added subsecs. (e), (f), (g) and (h) and Act 123 amended the entire section. Act 123 overlooked the amendment by Act 108, but the amendments do not conflict in substance and have both been given effect in setting forth the text of section 6368.

2006 Amendments. Section 3 of Act 126 provided that the Department of Public Welfare may promulgate rules and regulations to administer and enforce the amendment of section 6368 effected by Act 126.

1994 Amendment. See section 9 of Act 151 in the appendix to this title for special provisions relating to Department of Public Welfare study.

Cross References. Section 6368 is referred to in sections 6338, 6362 of this title.

§ 6369. Taking child into protective custody.

Pursuant to the provisions of section 6315 (relating to taking child into protective custody) and after receipt of a court order, the county agency shall take a child into protective custody for protection from abuse. No county agency worker may take custody of the child without judicial authorization based on the merits of the situation. 1990, Dec. 19, P.L. 1240, No. 206, § 2, effective in 90 days. Amended 1994, Dec. 16, P.L. 1292, No. 151, § 5, effective July 1, 1995.

REPEAL

23 Pa.C.S.A. § 6369 is repealed effective Dec. 31, 2014, pursuant to 2014, April 15, P.L. 417, No. 33, § 4.

§ 6370. Voluntary or court-ordered services; findings of child abuse.

(a) **General rule.**—Based on the investigation and evaluation conducted pursuant to this chapter, the county agency shall provide or contract with private or public agencies for the protection of the child at home whenever possible and those services necessary for adequate care of the child when placed in protective custody. Prior to offering these services to a family, the agency shall explain that it has no legal authority to compel the family to receive the services but may inform the family of the obligations and authority of the county agency to initiate appropriate court proceedings.

(b) Initiation of court proceeding.—

(1) In those cases in which an appropriate offer of service is refused and the county agency determines that the best interests of the child require court action, the county agency shall initiate the appropriate court proceeding. The county agency shall assist the court during all stages of the court proceeding in accordance with the purposes of this chapter.

(2)(i) If the county agency deems it appropriate in a dependency or delinquency proceeding, including an instance in which the alleged perpetrator has access or poses a threat to a child, the county agency may petition the court under 42 Pa.C.S. Ch. 63 (relating to juvenile matters) for a finding of child abuse.

(ii) If the court makes a specific finding that child abuse as defined by this chapter has not occurred, the county agency shall consider the court's finding to be a determination that the report of suspected abuse was an unfounded report. The county agency shall immediately notify the department of the change in the status of the report from an indicated report to an unfounded report. Upon notice, the department shall be responsible for expunging the indicated report consistent with the expunction requirements of this chapter.

(iii) If there is a determination that the subjects of the unfounded report need services provided or arranged by the county agency, the county agency may retain those records only if it specifically identifies the report as an unfounded report of suspected child abuse.

1994 Amendment. Act 151 amended sect 6370.

Cross References. Section 6370 is referred to in section 6340 of this title.

§ 6371. Rehabilitative services for child and family.

The county agency shall provide or arrange for and monitor rehabilitative services for children and their families on a voluntary basis or under a final or intermediate order of the court.

1994 Amendment. Act 151 amended sect 6371.

§ 6372. Protecting well-being of children maintained outside home.

The county agency shall be as equally vigilant of the status, well-being and conditions under which a child is living and being maintained in a facility other than that of a parent, custodian or guardian from which the child has been removed as the service is of the conditions in the dwelling of the parent, custodian or guardian. Where the county agency finds that the placement for any temporary or permanent custody, care or treatment is for any reason inappropriate or harmful in any way to the physical or mental well-being of the child, it shall take immediate steps to remedy these conditions including petitioning the court.

1994 Amendment. Act 151 amended sect 6372.

Cross References. Section 6372 is referred to in section 6344 of this title.

§ 6373. General protective services responsibilities of county agency.

(a) **Program objectives.—**Each county agency is responsible for administering a program of general protective services to children and youth that is consistent with the agency's objectives to:

(1) Keep children in their own homes, whenever possible.

(2) Prevent abuse, neglect and exploitation.

(3) Overcome problems that result in dependency.

(4) Provide temporary, substitute placement in a foster family home or residential childcare facility for a child in need of care.

(5) Reunite children and their families whenever possible when children are in temporary, substitute placement.

(6) Provide a permanent, legally assured family for a child in temporary, substitute care who cannot be returned to his own home.

(7) Provide services and care ordered by the court for children who have been adjudicated dependent.

(b) **Efforts to prevent need for removal from home.**—In its effort to assist the child and the child's parents, pursuant to Federal regulations, the county agency will make reasonable efforts prior to the placement of a child in foster care, to prevent or eliminate the need for removal of the child from his home, and to make it possible for the child to return to home.

(c) **Assistance in obtaining available benefits.**—The county agency shall aid the child and the family in obtaining benefits and services for which they may qualify under Federal, State and local programs.

(d) **Duplication of services.**—Except where ordered by the court in a proceeding brought under 42 Pa.C.S. Ch. 63 (relating to juvenile matters), a county agency shall not be required to duplicate services which are the statutory responsibility of any other agency.

§ 6374. Principles and goals of general protective services.

(a) **Primary purpose.**—The primary purpose of general protective services is to protect the rights and welfare of children so that they have an opportunity for healthy growth and development.

(b) **Assistance to parents.**—Implicit in the county agency's protection of children is assistance to parents in recognizing and remedying conditions harmful to their children and in fulfilling their parental duties more adequately.

§ 6375. County agency requirements for general protective services.

(a) **Duties of county agency.**—The county agency shall make available a program of general protective services within each agency. The county agency shall perform those functions assigned by this chapter and others that would further the purposes of this chapter. It shall have sufficient staff of sufficient qualifications to fulfill the purposes of this chapter and be organized in a way as to maximize the continuity of responsibility, care and service of individual workers toward individual children and families. The department by regulation shall set forth staff-to-family ratios for the receipt and assessment of reports of children in need of protective services and for the provision of services to neglected children and their families.

(b) **Organization of county agency.**—Each county agency shall be organized and staffed to ensure that the agency can provide intake for general protective services. Intake occurs when a report or referral is made to the agency or when a parent or person responsible for the child's welfare requests the assistance of the agency.

(c) **Assessment for services.—**

(1) Within 60 days of receipt of a report, an assessment shall be completed and a decision on whether to accept the family for service shall be made. The county agency shall provide or arrange for services necessary to protect the child during the assessment period.

(1.1) The county agency shall immediately notify the department upon the completion of the assessment whether the report was determined to be valid or invalid and whether the family was accepted for services or referred to community services.

(1.2) The county agency shall immediately notify the department upon the closure of services for a child or family that has been accepted for services.

(2) Each county agency shall implement a State-approved risk assessment process in performance of its duties.

(d) Receiving and assessing reports.—The county agency shall be the sole civil agency responsible for receiving and assessing all reports of children in need of protective services made pursuant to this chapter for the purpose of providing protective services to prevent abuse or neglect to children and to provide or arrange for and monitor the provision of those services necessary to safeguard and ensure the child's well-being and development and to preserve and stabilize family life wherever appropriate. The department may waive the receipt and assessment requirement pursuant to section 6361 (relating to organization for child protective services). Nothing in this subsection limits 42 Pa.C.S. § 6304 (relating to powers and duties of probation officers).

(e) Family service plan.—The county agency shall prepare a written family service plan in accordance with regulations adopted by the department.

(f) Types of services.—Each county agency shall make available for the prevention and treatment of child abuse and neglect: multidisciplinary teams, instruction and education for parenthood and parenting skills, protective and preventive social counseling, emergency caretaker services, emergency shelter care, emergency medical services, part-day services, out-of-home placement services, therapeutic activities for the child and family directed at alleviating conditions that present a risk to the safety and well-being of a child and any other services required by department regulations.

(g) Monitoring, evaluating and assessing.—The county agency shall frequently monitor the provision of services, evaluate the effectiveness of the services, conduct in-home visits and make a periodic assessment of the risk of harm to the child, which shall include maintaining an annually updated photograph of the child and verification of the identification of the child.

(h) Emergency coverage.—As part of its general protective services program, a county agency shall provide 24-hour-a-day emergency coverage and be accessible to the public.

(i) Protective custody.—Pursuant to section 6315 (relating to taking child into protective custody) and after receipt of a court order, the county agency shall take a child into protective custody to protect the child from abuse or further neglect. No county agency worker may take custody of a child without judicial authorization based on the merits of the situation.

(j) Court action.—If the county agency determines that protective services are in the best interest of a child and if an offer of those services is refused or if any other reason exists to warrant court action, the county agency shall initiate the appropriate court proceedings.

(k) Adjudication of dependency.—The county agency shall maintain its responsibility for petitioning the court when necessary for the adjudication of dependency of a child pursuant to 42 Pa.C.S. Ch. 63 (relating to juvenile matters).

(l) Assistance to court.—The county agency shall assist the court during all stages of a court proceeding in accordance with the purposes of this chapter.1

(m) Weekly face-to-face contacts.—For those children assessed under this section as being at high risk for abuse or neglect who are remaining in or returning to the home in which the abuse or neglect occurred, the county agency shall ensure that those children are seen at least once a week, either directly by a county agency worker or through purchase of service, until they are no longer assessed as being at high risk for abuse or neglect.

(n) Transfer of files between county agencies.—Whenever a county agency transfers to another county agency a file relating to a child who receives or is in need of protective services under this chapter, the file shall include any photographic identification and an annual photograph taken of the child.

(o) **Availability of information.**—Information related to reports of a child in need of general protective services shall be available to individuals and entities to the extent they are authorized to receive information under section 6340 (relating to release of information in confidential reports).

1994, Dec. 16, P.L. 1292, No. 151, § 6. Amended 1999, Nov. 24, P.L. 542, No. 50, § 1, effective in 60 days; 2006, Oct. 27, P.L. 1192, No. 126, § 2, effective in 60 days [Dec. 26, 2006]; 2013, Dec. 18, P.L. 1167, No. 107, § 4, effective Jan. 1, 2014; 2014, April 7, P.L. 388, No. 29, § 9, effective Dec. 31, 2014.

Cross References. Section 6375 is referred to in section 6334 of this title.

§ 6376. Appeals with respect to general protective services.

(a) **Right to appeal.**—A custodial parent or person who has primary responsibility for the welfare of a child may appeal the county agency's decision to accept the family for services. Written notice of this right, along with an explanation of the agency's decision, shall be given to the family within seven days of the decision to accept for service. The department has no authority to modify an order of a court of common pleas.

(b) **Receipt and grounds of appeal.**—Appeals must be received by the county agency within 45 days of the date when the notice was mailed to the custodial parent or person who has primary responsibility for the welfare of a child. Requests must be made on the grounds that the child is or is not at risk of abuse or neglect.

(c) **Review and decision and request for hearing.**—The county agency shall review the request and issue a written decision within 45 days of receipt of the appeal. If the agency denies the request, the custodial parent or person who has primary responsibility for the welfare of a child may request a hearing before the department. The request must be made within 45 days of the date of the county agency's decision.

(d) **Hearing.**—If a hearing is requested, the secretary or his designated agent shall schedule a hearing pursuant to Article IV of the act of June 13, 1967 (P.L. 31, No. 21), known as the Public Welfare Code,[8] and applicable department regulations. The burden of proof in the hearing shall be on the county agency. The department shall assist the county agency as necessary.

(e) **Order.**—The department is authorized and empowered to make any appropriate order regarding records to make them accurate or consistent with the requirements of this chapter.

(f) **Other appeals.**—Action by a custodial parent or person who has primary responsibility for the welfare of a child under this section does not preclude his right to exercise other appeals available through department regulations or the courts.

§ 6377. Caseloads.

The department by regulation shall set forth staff-to-family ratios for general protective services.

§ 6378. Purchase of services.

Except for the receipt and assessment of reports alleging a need for protective services, the county agency may purchase and utilize the services of any appropriate public or private agency. The department shall promulgate regulations establishing standards and qualifications of persons or agencies providing services for a county agency. The department may, by regulation, provide for the establishment of regional facilities or a regional coordination of licensed professional service providers to provide

---

[8]62 P.S. § 401 et seq.

county agencies with access to licensed physicians and psychologists, as required by this section.

SUBCHAPTER E
MISCELLANEOUS PROVISIONS

Sec.
6381. Evidence in court proceedings.
6382. Guardian ad litem for child in court proceedings [Repealed].
6383. Education and training.
6384. Legislative oversight.
6385. Reimbursement to county agencies.
6386. Notification to department and development of plan of safe care for children under one year of age.

§ 6381. Evidence in court proceedings.

(a) General rule.—In addition to the rules of evidence provided under 42 Pa.C.S. Ch. 63 (relating to juvenile matters), the rules of evidence in this section shall govern in child abuse proceedings in court or in any department administrative hearing pursuant to section 6341 (relating to amendment or expunction of information).

(b) Reports of unavailable persons.—Whenever a person required to report under this chapter is unavailable due to death or removal from the jurisdiction of the court, the written report of that person shall be admissible in evidence in any proceedings arising out of child abuse other than proceedings under Title 18 (relating to crimes and offenses). Any hearsay contained in the reports shall be given such weight, if any, as the court determines to be appropriate under all of the circumstances. However, any hearsay contained in a written report shall not of itself be sufficient to support an adjudication based on abuse.

(c) Privileged communications.—Except for privileged communications between a lawyer and a client and between a minister and a penitent, a privilege of confidential communication between husband and wife or between any professional person, including, but not limited to, physicians, psychologists, counselors, employees of hospitals, clinics, day-care centers and schools and their patients or clients, shall not constitute grounds for excluding evidence at any proceeding regarding child abuse or the cause of child abuse.

(d) Prima facie evidence of abuse.—Evidence that a child has suffered child abuse of such a nature as would ordinarily not be sustained or exist except by reason of the acts or omissions of the parent or other person responsible for the welfare of the child shall be prima facie evidence of child abuse by the parent or other person responsible for the welfare of the child.

(e) Child victims and witnesses.—In addition to the provisions of this section, any consideration afforded to a child victim or witness pursuant to 42 Pa.C.S. Ch. 59 Subch. D (relating to child victims and witnesses) in any prosecution or adjudication shall be afforded to a child in child abuse proceedings in court or in any department administrative hearing pursuant to section 6341.

(Dec. 16, 1994, P.L.1292, No.151, eff. July 1, 1995; Dec. 18, 2013, P.L.1170, No.108, eff. Dec. 31, 2014)

2013 Amendment. Act 108 added subsec. (e).

1994 Amendment. Act 151 amended subsecs. (a) and (d).

§ 6382. Guardian ad litem for child in court proceedings (Repealed).

2000 Repeal Note. Section 6382 was repealed May 10, 2000, P.L. 74, No. 18, effective in 60 days.

§ 6383. Education and training.

(a) Duties of department and county agencies.—The department and each county agency, both jointly and individually, shall conduct a continuing publicity and education program for the citizens of this Commonwealth aimed at the prevention of child abuse and child neglect, including the prevention of newborn abandonment, the identification of abused and neglected children and the provision of necessary ameliorative services to abused and neglected children and their families. The department and each county agency shall conduct an ongoing training and education program for local staff, persons required to make reports and other appropriate persons in order to familiarize those persons with the reporting and investigative procedures for cases of suspected child abuse and the rehabilitative services that are available to children and families. In addition, the department shall, by regulation, establish a program of training and certification for persons classified as protective services workers. The regulations shall provide for the grandfathering of all current permanent protective services workers as certified protective services workers. Upon request by the county agency and approval of the department, the agency may conduct the training of the county's protective services workers.

(a.1) Study by department.—The department shall conduct a study to determine the extent of the reporting of suspected child abuse in this Commonwealth where the reports upon investigation are determined to be unfounded and to be knowingly false and maliciously reported or it is believed that a minor was persuaded to make or substantiate a false and malicious report. The department shall submit the report to the Governor, General Assembly and Attorney General no later than June 1, 1996. The report shall include the department's findings and recommendations on how to reduce the incidence of knowingly false and malicious reporting.

(a.2) Information for mandated and permissive reporters.—

(1) In addition to the requirements of subsection (a), the department shall provide specific information related to the recognition and reporting of child abuse on its Internet website in forms, including, but not limited to, the following:

(i) Website content.

(ii) Printable booklets and brochures.

(iii) Educational videos.

(iv) Internet-based interactive training exercises.

(2) Information shall be pertinent to both mandated and permissive reporters and shall address topics, including, but not limited to:

(i) Conduct constituting child abuse under this chapter.

(ii) Persons classified as mandated reporters.

(iii) Reporting requirements and procedures.

(iv) The basis for making a report of suspected child abuse.

(v) Penalties for failure to report.

(vi) Background clearance requirements for individuals who work or volunteer with children.

(vii) Recognition of the signs and symptoms of child abuse.

(viii) Alternative resources to assist with concerns not related to child abuse.

(3) The department shall include the following with all certifications provided pursuant to section 6344(b)(2) (relating to employees having contact with children; adoptive and foster parents):

(i) Information that certain persons are required by law to report suspected child abuse.

(ii) The Internet address where the information and guidance required by this subsection can be obtained.

(iii) A telephone number and mailing address where guidance materials can be requested by individuals who cannot access the department's Internet website.

(4) The department shall implement this subsection within 180 days of the effective date of this subsection.

(b) Duties of Department of State.—

(1) The Department of State shall make training and educational programs and materials available for all professional licensing boards whose licensees are charged with responsibilities for reporting child abuse under this chapter with a program of distributing educational materials to all licensees.

(2) Each licensing board with jurisdiction over professional licensees identified as mandated reporters under this chapter shall promulgate regulations within one year of the effective date of this subsection on the responsibilities of mandated reporters. These regulations shall clarify that the provisions of this chapter take precedence over any professional standard that might otherwise apply in order to protect children from abuse.

(3) Each licensing board with jurisdiction over professional licensees identified as mandated reporters under this chapter shall:

(i) Require all persons applying for a license or certification issued by the licensing board to submit documentation acceptable to the licensing board of the completion of at least three hours of approved child abuse recognition and reporting training. Training shall address, but shall not be limited to, recognition of the signs of child abuse and the reporting requirements for suspected child abuse in this Commonwealth. Training shall be approved by the department. The training may occur as part of the continuing education requirement of the license.

(ii) Require all persons applying for the renewal of a license or certification issued by the licensing board to submit documentation acceptable to the licensing board of the completion of at least two hours of approved continuing education per licensure cycle. Continuing education shall address, but shall not be limited to, recognition of the signs of child abuse and the reporting requirements for suspected child abuse in this Commonwealth. Continuing education curricula shall be approved by the licensing board in consultation with the department. The two hours of continuing education on child abuse recognition and reporting shall be completed by each licensee as a portion of the total continuing education required for biennial license renewal.

(4) A licensing board with jurisdiction over professional licensees identified as mandated reporters under this chapter may exempt an applicant or licensee from the training or continuing education required by paragraph (3) if all of the following apply:

(i) The applicant or licensee submits documentation acceptable to the licensing board that the person has already completed child abuse recognition training.

(ii) The training was:

(A) required by section 1205.6 of the act of March 10, 1949 (P.L.30, No.14), known as the Public School Code of 1949, and the training program was approved by the Department of Education in consultation with the department; or

(B) required by the act of June 13, 1967 (P.L.31, No.21), known as the Public Welfare Code, and the training program was approved by the department.

(iii) The amount of training received equals or exceeds the amount of training or continuing education required by paragraph (3).

(5) Upon biennial renewal of a license, a licensing board shall provide to professional licensees under its jurisdiction identified as mandated reporters information related to mandatory reporting of child abuse and the reporting requirements of licensees.

(6) A professional licensee identified as a mandated reporter may apply to the licensing board with jurisdiction over the licensee for an exemption from the training or continuing education required by paragraph (3). A licensing board may exempt the licensee if the licensee submits documentation acceptable to the licensing board that the licensee should not be subject to the training or continuing education requirement.

(c) Training of persons subject to department regulation.—

(1) The following persons shall be required to meet the child abuse recognition and reporting training requirements of this subsection:

(i) Operators of institutions, facilities or agencies which care for children and are subject to supervision by the department under Article IX of the Public Welfare Code, and their employees who have direct contact with children.

(ii) Foster parents.

(iii) Operators of facilities and agencies which care for children and are subject to licensure by the department under Article X of the Public Welfare Code and their employees who have direct contact with children.

(iv) Caregivers in family child-care homes which are subject to licensure by the department under Article X of the Public Welfare Code and their employees who have direct contact with children.

(v) The adult family member who is a person responsible for the child's welfare and is providing services to a child in a family living home, a community home for individuals with an intellectual disability or a host home which is subject to supervision or licensure by the department under Articles IX and X of the Public Welfare Code.

(2) Within six months of the effective date of this subsection, operators and caregivers shall receive three hours of training prior to the issuance of a license or approval certificate and three hours of training every five years thereafter.

(3) Employees who have direct contact with children and foster parents shall receive three hours of training within six months of the issuance of a license or approval certificate and three hours of training every five years thereafter. New employees and new foster parents shall receive three hours of training within 90 days of hire or approval as a foster parent and three hours of training every five years thereafter.

(d) Definitions.—As used in this section, the following words and phrases shall have the meanings given to them in this subsection unless the context clearly indicates otherwise:

"Direct contact with children." The care, supervision, guidance or control of children or routine interaction with children.

"Operator." An executive or facility director. The term does not include a person who is not involved in managerial decisions related to the provision of services for or care of children with regard to any of the following:

(1) Personnel.

(2) Policy and procedures.

(3) Regulatory compliance.

(4) Services related to the general or medical care of children.

(5) Supervision of children.

(6) Safety of children.

(Dec. 16, 1994, P.L.1292, No.151; Dec. 9, 2002, P.L.1549, No.201, eff. 60 days; Apr. 15, 2014, P.L.411, No.31, eff. Dec. 31, 2014; Apr. 15, 2014, P.L.417, No.33, eff. Dec. 31, 2014; Oct. 22, 2014, P.L.2529, No.153, eff. Dec. 31, 2014; July 1, 2015, P.L.94, No.15, eff. imd.)

2015 Amendment. Act 15 amended subsec. (c)(1), (2) and (3).

2014 Amendments. Act 31 added subsecs. (b)(3), (4), (5) and (6), (c) and (d), Act 33 added subsec. (a.2) and Act 153 amended subsec. (a.2)(3). Section 2 of Act 31 provided that the amendment shall apply to persons applying for a license, certification, approval or registration, or for the renewal of a license, certification, approval or registration, on or after January 1, 2015.

2002 Amendment. Act 201 amended subsec. (a).

1994 Amendment. Section 10 of Act 151 provided that the amendment of subsec. (a) shall take effect July 1, 1996, and the remainder of the section shall take effect July 1, 1995.

Cross References. Section 6383 is referred to in section 6509 of this title.

§ 6384. Legislative oversight.

A committee of the Senate designated by the President pro tempore of the Senate and a committee of the House of Representatives designated by the Speaker of the House of Representatives, either jointly or separately, shall review the manner in which this chapter has been administered at the State and local level for the following purposes:

(1) Providing information that will aid the General Assembly in its oversight responsibilities.

(2) Enabling the General Assembly to determine whether the programs and services mandated by this chapter are effectively meeting the goals of this chapter.

(3) Assisting the General Assembly in measuring the costs and benefits of this program and the effects and side-effects of mandated program services.

(4) Permitting the General Assembly to determine whether the confidentiality of records mandated by this chapter is being maintained at the State and local level.

(5) Providing information that will permit State and local program administrators to be held accountable for the administration of the programs mandated by this chapter.

Cross References. Section 6384 is referred to in section 6340 of this title.

§ 6385. Reimbursement to county agencies.

The department shall certify in accordance with the needs-based budgeting provisions of Article VII of the act of June 13, 1967 (P.L. 31, No. 21), known as the Public Welfare Code,[9] a level of funds sufficient to meet the cost of services required by the provisions of this chapter which are reasonable and allowable as defined in Article VII.

1994 Amendment. Act 151 added section 6385.

Explanatory Note. Act 151 amended or added sections 6302 and 6303, the heading of Subchapter B of Chapter 63, sections 6311, 6313, 6314, 6315, 6316, 6317, 6318, 6331, 6332, 6333, 6334, 6335, 6336, 6337, 6338, 6339, 6340, 6341, 6343, 6344, 6345, 6346, 6347 and 6349, Subchapters C.1 and C.2, sections 6361, 6362, 6363, 6364, 6365, 6366, 6367, 6368, 6369, 6370, 6371, 6372, 6373, 6374, 6375, 6376, 6377, 6378, 6381, 6382, 6383 and 6385 of Title 23.

§ 6386. Notification to department and development of plan of safe care for children under one year of age.

(a) Notification to department.—For the purpose of assessing a child and the child's family for a plan of safe care, a health care provider shall immediately give notice or cause notice to be given to the department if the provider is involved in the delivery or care of a child under one year of age and the health care provider has determined, based on standards of professional practice, the child was born affected by:

(1) substance use or withdrawal symptoms resulting from prenatal drug exposure; or

(2) a Fetal Alcohol Spectrum Disorder.

---

[9] 62 P.S. § 701 et seq.

(i) (Deleted by amendment).

(ii) (Deleted by amendment).

(3) (Deleted by amendment).

(a.1) Notification not to constitute child abuse report.—The notification by a health care provider to the department and any transmittal to the county agency by the department shall not constitute a child abuse report.

(b) Safety or risk assessment.—(Deleted by amendment).

(b.1) Development of interagency protocols and plan of safe care.—The department, in collaboration with the Department of Health and the Department of Drug and Alcohol Programs, shall develop written protocols that include, but are not limited to:

(1) Definitions and evidence-based screening tools, based on standards of professional practice, to be utilized by health care providers to identify a child born affected by substance use or withdrawal symptoms resulting from prenatal drug exposure or a fetal alcohol spectrum disorder.

(2) Notification to the department that a child born affected by substance use or withdrawal symptoms resulting from prenatal drug exposure or a fetal alcohol spectrum disorder has been born and identified. Ongoing involvement of the county agency after taking into consideration the individual needs of the child and the child's parents and immediate caregivers may not be required.

(3) Collection of data to meet Federal and State reporting requirements.

(4) Identification, informed by an assessment of the needs of the child and the child's parents and immediate caregivers, of the most appropriate lead agency responsible for developing, implementing and monitoring a plan of safe care, informed by a multidisciplinary team meeting that is held prior to the child's discharge from the health care facility, which may include:

(i) public health agencies;

(ii) maternal and child health agencies;

(iii) home visitation programs;

(iv) substance use disorder prevention and treatment providers;

(v) mental health providers;

(vi) public and private children and youth agencies;

(vii) early intervention and developmental services;

(viii) courts;

(ix) local education agencies;

(x) managed care organizations and private insurers; and

(xi) hospitals and medical providers.

(5) Engagement of the child's parents and immediate caregivers in order to identify the need for access to treatment for any substance use disorder or other physical or behavioral health condition that may impact the safety, early childhood development and well-being of the child.

(c) County agency duties.—(Deleted by amendment).

(Nov. 9, 2006, P.L.1358, No.146, eff. 180 days; Jan. 22, 2014, P.L.6, No.4, eff. 90 days; July 1, 2015, P.L.94, No.15, eff. imd.; June 28, 2018, P.L.375, No.54, eff. Oct. 1, 2018).

CHAPTER 65
NEWBORN PROTECTION

Sec.
6501. Short title of chapter.
6502. Definitions.
6503. Nonliability.
6504. Health care providers accepting newborns.
6504.1. Police officers accepting newborns.
6504.2. Emergency services providers accepting newborns.
6504.3. Incubators for newborns.
6505. Reporting acceptance of newborns.
6506. Failure to report acceptance of newborns.
6507. Immunity.
6508. Duty of hospital.
6509. Duties of department.

Enactment. Chapter 65 was added December 9, 2002, P.L.1549, No.201, effective in 60 days.

Cross References. Chapter 65 is referred to in section 6315 of this title; section 4306 of Title 18 (Crimes and Offenses).

§ 6501. Short title of chapter.

This chapter shall be known and may be cited as the Newborn Protection Act.

§ 6502. Definitions.

The following words and phrases when used in this chapter shall have the meanings given to them in this section unless the context clearly indicates otherwise:

"Child abuse." Child abuse as defined in section 6303(b) (relating to definitions).

"County agency" or "agency." County agency as defined in section 6303(a) (relating to definitions).

"Department." The Department of Public Welfare of the Commonwealth.

"Emergency services provider." An emergency medical responder, emergency medical technician, advanced emergency medical technician or a paramedic as defined in 35 Pa.C.S. § 8103 (relating to definitions).

"Health care provider." A person who is licensed or certified by the laws of this Commonwealth to administer health care in the ordinary course of business or practice of a profession. For purposes of accepting a newborn as provided in section 6504(a)(1) (relating to accepting newborns) and for immunity provided pursuant to section 6507 (relating to immunity), the term includes administrative, managerial and security personnel and any other person employed by a hospital.

"Hospital." An institution having an organized medical staff which is primarily engaged in providing to inpatients, by or under the supervision of physicians, diagnostic and therapeutic services or rehabilitation services for the care or rehabilitation of people who are injured, disabled, pregnant, diseased, sick or mentally ill. The term includes facilities for the diagnosis and treatment of disorders within the scope of specific medical specialties, but not facilities caring exclusively for people with mental illness or those facilities primarily engaged in providing rehabilitation services or long-term care.

"Newborn." A child less than 28 days of age as reasonably determined by a physician.

"Police department." A public agency of a political subdivision having general police powers and charged with making arrests in connection with the enforcement of criminal or traffic laws.

"**Police officer.**" A full-time or part-time employee assigned to criminal or traffic law enforcement duties of a police department of a county, city, borough, town or township. The term also includes a member of the State Police Force.

"**Police station.**" The station or headquarters of a police department or a Pennsylvania State Police station or headquarters.

(July 2, 2014, P.L.843, No.91, eff. 60 days; Dec. 22, 2017, P.L.1219, No.68, eff. 60 days)

2017 Amendment. Act 68 added the def. of "emergency services provider."

2014 Amendment. Act 91 amended the def. of "health care provider" and added the defs. of "police department," "police officer" and "police station."

References in Text. The Department of Public Welfare, referred to in this section, was redesignated as the Department of Human Services by Act 132 of 2014.

Section 6303(b), referred to in the def. of "child abuse," was deleted by Act 108 of 2013.

Cross References. Section 6502 is referred to in section 6303 this title; section 4306 of Title 18 (Crimes and Offenses).

§ 6503. Nonliability.

A parent of a newborn shall not be criminally liable under any provision of Title 18 (relating to crimes and offenses) if the criteria set forth in 18 Pa.C.S. § 4306 (relating to newborn protection) are met.

§ 6504. Health care providers accepting newborns.

(a) General rule.—A health care provider at a hospital shall do all of the following relating to a newborn accepted under this chapter:

(1) Take the newborn into protective custody as provided in section 6315(a)(3) (relating to taking child into protective custody) or 6504.1(a)(2) (relating to police officers accepting newborns).

(2) Perform a medical evaluation as well as perform any act necessary to care for and protect the physical health and safety of the newborn.

(3) Notify the county agency and the local municipal police department or the Pennsylvania State Police where no municipal police jurisdiction exists as provided in section 6505 (relating to reporting acceptance of newborns).

(b) Accepting newborns.—When a health care provider accepts a newborn pursuant to this chapter, a parent, police officer or emergency services provider may provide a health care provider with information about the newborn's medical history and any identifying information.

(July 2, 2014, P.L.843, No.91, eff. 60 days; Dec. 22, 2017, P.L.1219, No.68, eff. 60 days)

2017 Amendment. Act 68 amended subsec. (b).

2014 Amendment. Act 91 amended the section heading and subsecs. (a)(1) and (b).

Cross References. Section 6504 is referred to in sections 6502, 6504.1, 6504.2 of this title.

§ 6504.1. Police officers accepting newborns.

(a) Duties.—A police officer at a police station shall do all of the following relating to a newborn accepted under this chapter:

(1) Take the newborn into protective custody under section 6315(a)(5) (relating to taking child into protective custody).

(2) Ensure the newborn is transported to a hospital and placed into the care of a health care provider under section 6504 (relating to health care providers accepting newborns).

(b) Information.—When a police officer accepts a newborn pursuant to this chapter, a parent may provide the police officer with information about the newborn's medical history and any identifying information.

2014, July 2, P.L. 843, No. 91, § 7, effective in 60 days [Sept. 2, 2014].

§ 6504.2. Emergency services providers accepting newborns.

(a) Duties.—In accepting a newborn under this chapter, an emergency services provider shall:

(1) take the newborn into protective custody as specified under section 6315(a)(6) (relating to taking child into protective custody); and

(2) ensure the newborn is transported to a hospital and placed into the care of a health care provider as specified under section 6504 (relating to health care providers accepting newborns).

(b) Medical history.—When an emergency services provider accepts a newborn under this chapter, a parent may provide the emergency services provider with information about the newborn's medical history and identifying information.

(c) Temporary signage.—An entity employing an emergency services provider accepting newborns under this chapter shall ensure its grounds or the grounds of an entity otherwise providing access to an emergency services provider clearly indicate, for a minimum of 18 months, that emergency services providers may accept newborns under section 6315(a) and 18 Pa.C.S. § 4306 (relating to newborn protection).

(Dec. 22, 2017, P.L.1219, No.68, eff. 60 days)

2017 Amendment. Act 68 added section 6504.2.

Cross References. Section 6504.2 is referred to in section 6505 of this title.

§ 6504.3. Incubators for newborns.

(a) Provision optional.—A hospital, police station or other entity employing or otherwise providing access to an emergency services provider may provide an incubator for the care of a newborn accepted under this chapter.

(b) Regulations.—The Department of Health shall promulgate regulations for providing an incubator under subsection (a). The regulations shall include all of the following:

(1) Sanitation standards for an incubator.

(2) Procedures to provide emergency care for an infant placed in an incubator.

(3) Manufacturing and manufacturer standards for an incubator.

(4) Design and function requirements for an incubator which shall include all of the following:

   (i) Installation of an incubator at a hospital, police station or other entity which employs or otherwise provides access to an emergency services provider.

   (ii) Allowance of an infant to be placed in the incubator anonymously by the parent.

   (iii) Locking an incubator after the parent places the infant in the incubator to prevent third parties from having access to the infant.

   (iv) Providing a controlled environment to protect and care for the infant.

   (v) Providing notice to the personnel of a hospital, police station or other entity which employs or otherwise provides access to an emergency services provider within 30 seconds of the infant being placed by the parent in the incubator.

   (vi) Triggering a 911 call if the personnel of a hospital, police station or other entity which employs or otherwise provides access to an emergency services provider does not respond within a reasonable amount of time under subparagraph (v).

(5) Operating policy, supervision and maintenance requirements for an incubator, including that only an emergency services provider at an entity that employs or otherwise provides access to the emergency services provider, a health care provider at a hospital or police officer at a police station may take an infant into protective custody in accordance with Chapter 63 (relating to child protective services).

(6) Qualifications to install an incubator.

(7) Procedures and forms for the free registration with the Department of Health of installers qualified to install incubators in accordance with this chapter.

(8) Procedures for the free registration with the Department of Health of an incubator installed in accordance with this chapter.

(9) The creation and installation of signs near an incubator to provide information to parents about how to use the incubators.

(10) Any other provisions deemed necessary by the Department of Health to ensure the safety of an infant and the safe use of an incubator by a parent.

(c) Notice.—The Department of Health shall publish notice in the Pennsylvania Bulletin of the promulgation of final regulations regarding incubators under subsection (b).

(Dec. 22, 2017, P.L.1219, No.68)

> **2017 Amendment.** Act 68 added section 6504.3. Section 7(1)(ii) of Act 68 provided that subsecs. (b) and (c) shall take effect immediately. Section 7(2) of Act 68 provided that subsec. (a) shall take effect 120 days after the publication in the Pennsylvania Bulletin of the promulgation of final regulations under 23 Pa.C.S. § 6504.3(c).

§ 6505. Reporting acceptance of newborns.

A health care provider at a hospital shall in all cases notify the county agency and the local municipal police department or the Pennsylvania State Police where no municipal police jurisdiction exists immediately by telephone regarding a newborn accepted by a hospital under this chapter. A written report shall be submitted to the county agency and local municipal police department or the Pennsylvania State Police within 48 hours after the oral report. This section applies in the case of a hospital accepting a newborn pursuant to sections 6504.1(a)(2) (relating to police officers accepting newborns) and 6504.2(a)(2) (relating to emergency services providers accepting newborns). For purposes of this section, the term "health care provider" shall include administrative, managerial and security personnel employed by a hospital.

(July 2, 2014, P.L.843, No.91, eff. 60 days; Dec. 22, 2017, P.L.1219, No.68, eff. 60 days)

> **Cross References.** Section 6505 is referred to in section 6504 of this title.

§ 6506. Failure to report acceptance of newborns.

A health care provider at a hospital who intentionally or knowingly fails to report the acceptance by a hospital of a newborn as required by this chapter commits a summary offense. A second or subsequent failure to report such acceptance is a misdemeanor of the third degree.

§ 6507. Immunity.

Except for a violation of section 6506 (relating to failure to report acceptance of newborns), no emergency services provider, entity that employs or otherwise provides access to an emergency services provider, hospital, health care provider at a hospital or police department, police officer or administrative or managerial personnel of a police department shall be subject to civil liability or criminal penalty solely by reason of complying with the provisions of this chapter.

(July 2, 2014, P.L.843, No.91, eff. 60 days; Dec. 22, 2017, P.L.1219, No.68, eff. 60 days)

> **Cross References.** Section 6507 is referred to in section 6502 of this title.

§ 6508. Duty of hospital.

A hospital shall insure that its officers, health care providers and employees are familiar with the provisions of this chapter, section 6315(a)(3) (relating to taking child into protective custody) and other applicable provisions of Chapter 63 (relating to child protective services) that relate to newborn protection and shall insure that the appropriate officers, health care providers and employees, as the case may be, receive educational materials provided by the department as established under section 6509 (relating to duties of department). Information concerning this chapter, section 6315(a)(3) and other applicable provisions of Chapter 63 that relate to newborn protection and regulations adopted by the department shall be made part of the training at each hospital. Each hospital shall adopt a written policy in accordance with the provisions of this chapter, section 6315(a)(3) and other applicable provisions of Chapter 63 that relate to newborn protection.

§ 6509. Duties of department.

The department shall provide educational materials for use by emergency services providers, entities which employ or otherwise provide access to emergency services providers, hospitals, health care providers, employees at hospitals and police officers regarding this chapter, section 6315(a)(3) (relating to taking child into protective custody) and other applicable provisions of Chapter 63 (relating to child protective services) that relate to newborn protection. The department shall promulgate such regulations as may be necessary to implement this chapter, section 6315(a)(3) and other applicable provisions of Chapter 63 that relate to newborn protection. The department shall also provide emergency services providers, entities which employ or otherwise provide access to emergency services providers, health care providers, hospitals, the Pennsylvania State Police and police departments with an informational pamphlet regarding this chapter, section 6315(a)(3) and other applicable provisions of Chapter 63 that relate to newborn protection which may be distributed to the public. In addition, the department shall comply with the provisions regarding infant abandonment in sections 6365 (relating to services for prevention, investigation and treatment of child abuse) and 6383 (relating to education and training). A report shall be made annually to the General Assembly on the number and disposition of newborns accepted in accordance with this chapter, section 6315(a)(3) and (5) and other applicable provisions of Chapter 63 that relate to newborn protection.

(July 2, 2014, P.L.843, No.91, eff. 60 days; Dec. 22, 2017, P.L.1219, No.68, eff. imd.)

Cross References. Section 6509 is referred to in section 6508 of this title.

CHAPTER 67
DOMESTIC AND SEXUAL VIOLENCE VICTIM ADDRESS CONFIDENTIALITY

Sec.

6701. Short title of chapter.
6702. Definitions.
6703. Address Confidentiality Program.
6704. Persons eligible to apply.
6705. Application and certification process.
6706. Cancellation, expiration and voluntary withdrawal.
6707. Agency use of designated address.
6708. Disclosure of actual address.
6709. Waiver process.
6710. Emergency disclosure.
6711. Penalties.
6712. Rules and regulations.
6713. Civil immunity.

Enactment. Chapter 67 was added November 30, 2004, P.L. ___, No. 188, effective in 180 days.

§ 6701. Short title of chapter.

This chapter shall be known and may be cited as the Domestic and Sexual Violence Victim Address Confidentiality Act.

§ 6702. Definitions.

The following words and phrases when used in this chapter shall have the meanings given to them in this section unless the context clearly indicates otherwise:

"Actual address." A residential address, school address or work address of an individual.

"Law enforcement agency." A police department of a city, borough, incorporated town or township, the Pennsylvania State Police, district attorneys' offices, and the Office of Attorney General.

"Office of Victim Advocate." The office established under section 301 of the act of November 24, 1998 (P.L.882, No.111), known as the Crime Victims Act, that is responsible for the address confidentiality program pursuant to this chapter.

"Program participant." A person certified by the Office of Victim Advocate as eligible to participate in the address confidentiality program established by this chapter.

"Substitute address." The official address of the Office of Victim Advocate or a confidential address designated by the Office of Victim Advocate.

"Victim of domestic violence." A person who is a victim as defined by section 6102 (relating to definitions).

"Victim of sexual assault." A victim of an offense enumerated in 18 Pa.C.S. §§ 3121 (relating to rape), 4302 (relating to incest), 6312 (relating to sexual abuse of children), 6318 (relating to unlawful contact with minor) and 6320 (relating to sexual exploitation of children).

"Victim of stalking." A victim of an offense enumerated in 18 Pa.C.S. § 2709.1 (relating to stalking).

§ 6703. Address Confidentiality Program.

(a) **Establishment.**—The Office of Victim Advocate shall establish a program to be known as the Address Confidentiality Program. Upon application and certification, persons eligible under section 6704 (relating to persons eligible to apply) shall receive a confidential, substitute address provided by the Office of Victim Advocate.

(b) Administration.—The Office of Victim Advocate shall forward all first class, registered and certified mail at no expense to a program participant within three business days. The Office of Victim Advocate may arrange to receive and forward other classes or kinds of mail at the program participant's expense.

(c) Notice.—Upon certification, the Office of Victim Advocate shall provide notice of participation and the program participant's substitute address to appropriate officials involved in an ongoing civil or criminal case in which a program participant is a victim, witness, plaintiff or defendant.

(d) Records.—All records relating to applicants and program participants are the property of the Office of Victim Advocate. These records, including program applications, participants' actual addresses and waiver proceedings, shall be kept confidential and shall not be subject to the provisions of the act of June 21, 1957 (P.L.390, No.212), referred to as the Right-to-Know Law, except that records may be released as specifically set forth in this chapter and to a district attorney to the extent necessary for the prosecution of conduct as set forth in section 6711 (relating to penalties).

§ 6704. Persons eligible to apply.

The following persons shall be eligible to apply to become program participants:

(1) A victim of domestic violence who files an affidavit with the Office of Victim Advocate stating the affiant's eligibility for a protection from abuse order and further stating that the affiant fears future violent acts by the perpetrator of the abuse.

(2) A victim of sexual assault who files an affidavit with the Office of Victim Advocate describing the perpetrator's violent actions or threatened violent actions toward the affiant and further stating that the affiant fears future violent acts by the perpetrator of the sexual violence.

(3) A victim of stalking who files an affidavit with the Office of Victim Advocate describing the perpetrator's course of conduct or repeated actions toward the affiant meeting the criteria enumerated in 18 Pa.C.S. § 2709.1 (relating to stalking) and further stating that the affiant fears future violent acts by the perpetrator of the stalking.

(4) A person who is a member of the same household as a program participant.

(5) A program participant who notifies the Office of Victim Advocate of the participant's intent to continue in the program prior to the expiration of certification.

§ 6705. Application and certification process.

(a) General rule.—A person must file an application with the Office of Victim Advocate on a form prescribed by the Office of Victim Advocate. The Office of Victim Advocate shall certify eligible applicants as program participants in accordance with the procedures outlined in subsection (b). Certification shall be valid for a period of three years following the date of certification unless the certification is withdrawn or canceled before the expiration of that period.

(b) Requirements for certification.—The Office of Victim Advocate shall certify an applicant as a program participant if:

(1) The applicant meets the eligibility requirements under section 6704 (relating to persons eligible to apply).

(2) The applicant designates the Office of Victim Advocate as an agent for the purpose of receiving service of process.

(3) The application contains the applicant's actual address and telephone number where the applicant can be contacted.

(4) The application contains a list of all pending civil and criminal proceedings, in which the applicant is a victim, witness, plaintiff or defendant and, if applicable, the applicant's involvement with State and county probation and parole.

(5) The application contains a statement signed by the applicant affirming that the information provided by the applicant is true to the best of the applicant's information, knowledge and belief.

(6) The application contains a statement signed by the applicant acknowledging that the applicant has a continuing duty to notify the Office of Victim Advocate of any change in the information provided to the Office of Victim Advocate in accordance with this chapter. The duty shall remain in effect for the duration of participation in the program.

(7) The application contains the date, the applicant's signature and the signature of any person who assisted in the preparation of the application.

§ 6706. Cancellation, expiration and voluntary withdrawal.

(a) **Cancellation.**—The Office of Victim Advocate shall cancel the certification of a program participant if:

(1) the program participant willingly provided false information on any portion of the application;

(2) the program participant failed to notify the Office of Victim Advocate within five days of a name change or an address change; or

(3) the program participant's mail is returned to the Office of Victim Advocate as nondeliverable.

(b) **Expiration.**—Certification as a program participant shall expire three years from the date on which an applicant was certified as a program participant. The Office of Victim Advocate shall send written notification of pending expiration to a program participant's last known actual address 30 days prior to the expiration of certification.

(c) **Withdrawal.**—A program participant may withdraw at any time by notifying the Office of Victim Advocate in writing.

(d) **Effect of cancellation, expiration or withdrawal.**—Notwithstanding cancellation, expiration or prior withdrawal from the program, all persons eligible to apply to become program participants may reapply for participation in the program.

§ 6707. Agency use of designated address.

State and local government agencies shall accept the substitute address designated on a valid program participation card issued to the program participant by the Office of Victim Advocate as the program participant's address except as follows:

(1) when the State or local government agency has been granted a waiver pursuant to section 6709 (relating to waiver process); or

(2) when the program participant is any of the following:

(i) a released offender complying with State or county probation or parole requirements; or

(ii) a convicted sexual offender who has fulfilled the offender's sentence but must register the offender's community residence as required under 42 Pa.C.S. Ch. 97 Subch. H (relating to registration of sexual offenders) or I (relating to continued registration of sexual offenders) or any similar registration requirement imposed by any other jurisdiction.

(Dec. 20, 2011, P.L.446, No.111, eff. one year; Feb. 21, 2018, P.L.27, No.10, eff. imd.; June 12, 2018, P.L.140, No.29, eff. imd.)

2018 Amendment. Act 10 amended section 6707 and Act 29 reenacted section 6707.

§ 6708. Disclosure of actual address.

The Office of Victim Advocate shall not disclose the actual address of a program participant except to any of the following:

(1) A State or local government agency when the State or local government agency has been granted a waiver by the Office of Victim Advocate and the disclosure is made pursuant to section 6709 (relating to waiver process).

(2) A person or agency when disclosure is determined by the Office of Victim Advocate to be required due to an emergency and the disclosure is made pursuant to section 6710 (relating to emergency disclosure).

(3) A person identified in an order of court directing the Office of Victim Advocate to disclose the program participant's actual address and disclosure is made pursuant to the court order.

§ 6709. Waiver process.

(a) Request for waiver.—A State or local government agency requesting disclosure of a program participant's actual address pursuant to this section shall make such a request in writing on agency letterhead and shall provide the Office of Victim Advocate with the following information:

(1) The name of the program participant for whom the agency seeks disclosure of the actual address.

(2) A statement, with explanation, setting forth the reason or reasons that the agency needs the program participant's actual address and a statement that the agency cannot meet its statutory or administrative obligations without disclosure of the program participant's actual address.

(3) A particular statement of facts showing that other methods to locate the program participant or the program participant's actual address have been tried and have failed or that the methods reasonably appear to be unlikely to succeed.

(4) A statement that the agency has adopted a procedure setting forth the steps the agency will take to protect the confidentiality of the program participant's actual address.

(b) Notice to program participant.—

(1) Except as provided in paragraph (3), the Office of Victim Advocate shall provide the program participant with notice of a request for waiver received pursuant to subsection (a) and to the extent possible, the program participant shall be afforded an opportunity to be heard regarding the request.

(2) Except as provided in paragraph (3), the Office of Victim Advocate shall provide the program participant with written notification whenever a waiver has been granted or denied pursuant to this section.

(3) No notice or opportunity to be heard shall be given to the program participant when the request for disclosure is made by a State or local law enforcement agency conducting a criminal investigation involving alleged criminal conduct by the program participant or when providing notice to the program participant would jeopardize an ongoing criminal investigation or the safety of law enforcement personnel.

(c) Review of request for waiver.—The Office of Victim Advocate shall promptly conduct a review of all requests received pursuant to this section. In conducting a review, the Office of Victim Advocate shall consider all information received pursuant to subsections (a) and (b) and any other appropriate information that the Office of Victim Advocate may require.

(d) Criteria for granting a request for waiver.—The Office of Victim Advocate shall grant a State or local government agency's request for waiver and release a program participant's actual address pursuant to this section if:

(1) the agency has a bona fide statutory or administrative need for the actual address;

(2) the actual address will only be used for the purpose stated in the request;

(3) other methods to locate the program participant or the program participant's actual address have been tried and have failed, or that such methods reasonably appear to be unlikely to succeed; and

(4) the agency has adopted a procedure for protecting the confidentiality of the actual address of the program participant.

(e) **Form of waiver.**—Upon granting a request for waiver pursuant to this section, the Office of Victim Advocate shall provide the State or local government agency receiving the waiver with a form containing:

(1) the program participant's actual address;

(2) a statement setting forth the permitted use of the actual address and the names or classes of persons permitted to have access to and use of the actual address;

(3) a statement that the agency receiving the waiver is required to limit access to and use of the actual address to the permitted use and persons set forth in the waiver; and

(4) the date on which the waiver expires, if the permitted use makes the expiration appropriate, after which the agency may no longer maintain, use or have access to the actual address.

(f) **Requirements of a State and local government agency receiving a waiver.**—A State or local government agency granted a waiver by the Office of Victim Advocate pursuant to this section shall:

(1) limit the use of the program participant's actual address to the purposes set forth in the waiver;

(2) limit the access to the program participant's actual address to the persons or classes of persons set forth in the waiver;

(3) cease to use and dispose of the program participant's actual address upon the expiration of the waiver; and

(4) except as otherwise set forth in the waiver, maintain the confidentiality of a program participant's actual address.

(g) **Denial of request for waiver.**—Upon denial of a State or local government agency's request for waiver, the Office of Victim Advocate shall provide prompt written notification to the agency stating that the agency's request has been denied and setting forth the specific reasons for the denial.

(h) **Filing of exceptions.**—A State or local government agency may file written exceptions with the Office of Victim Advocate no more than 15 days after written notification is provided pursuant to subsection (g). The exceptions shall restate the information contained in the request for waiver, state the grounds upon which the agency asserts that the request for waiver should be granted and specifically respond to the Office of Victim Advocate's specific reasons for denial.

(i) **Review of exceptions and determination.**—Unless the State or local government agency filing exceptions agrees otherwise, the Office of Victim Advocate shall make a final determination regarding the exceptions within 30 days after the filing of exceptions pursuant to subsection (h). Prior to making a final determination regarding the exceptions, the Office of Victim Advocate may request additional information from the agency or the program participant and conduct a hearing. If the final determination of the Office of Victim Advocate is that the denial of the agency's request for waiver was properly denied, the Office of Victim Advocate shall provide the agency with written notification of this final determination stating that the agency's request has again been denied and setting forth the specific reasons for the denial. If the final determination of the Office of Victim Advocate is that the denial of the agency's request for waiver has been improperly denied, the Office of Victim Advocate shall grant the agency's request for waiver in accordance with this section. The final determination of the Office of Victim Advocate shall be the final order of the Office of Victim Advocate.

(j) **Agency appeal of final determination.**—Within 30 days after notification that the Office of Victim Advocate has made a final determination affirming the denial of a State or local government agency's request for waiver, an agency may file a petition for review or any such other document as permitted or required by general court rules. The Office of Victim Advocate shall be given notice of any action commenced in accordance with this subsection or general rule and shall be afforded an opportunity to respond as permitted or required by general court rules.

(k) **Record on appeal.**—The record before any court hearing an agency appeal pursuant to subsection (j) shall consist of the State or local government agency's request for waiver, the Office of Victim Advocate's written response, the agency's exceptions, the hearing transcript, if any, and the Office of Victim Advocate's final determination.

(l) **Use of substitute address during certain periods.**—During any period of review, evaluation or appeal, the agency shall, to the extent possible, accept and use the program participant's substitute address.

(m) **Waiver.**—Nothing in this section shall be construed to prevent the Office of Victim Advocate from granting a waiver to a State or local government agency pursuant to this section upon receipt of a program participant's written consent to do so.

§ 6710. Emergency disclosure.

(a) **General rule.**—The Office of Victim Advocate shall establish a system to respond to requests for emergency disclosures that will provide for 24-hour access to a program participant's actual address.

(b) **Request for emergency disclosure.**—A government agency may request that the Office of Victim Advocate disclose a program participant's actual address through the system established pursuant to subsection (a). The Office of Victim Advocate shall disclose a program participant's actual address if the disclosure:

(1) will prevent physical harm to a program participant or to a program participant's family member; or

(2) is made to a law enforcement agency for law enforcement purposes and the circumstances warrant immediate disclosure.

(c) **Requirements for emergency disclosure.**—Prior to disclosing a program participant's actual address pursuant to this section, the Office of Victim Advocate shall require:

(1) verification of the requester's identity and the requester's employment with a government agency;

(2) verification of the stated reason for the request to adequately ensure that emergency disclosure is required pursuant to subsection (b);

(3) proof, to the satisfaction of the Office of Victim Advocate, that other methods to locate the program participant or the program participant's actual address have been tried and have failed or that the methods reasonably appear to be unlikely to succeed given the circumstances of the stated reason for the request;

(4) that the program participant's actual address only be used by the requester or the agency to the extent necessary to respond to the stated reason for the request;

(5) that the requester and the requester's agency maintain the confidentiality of the actual address of the program participant; and

(6) that the requester and the requester's agency agree to dispose of the program participant's actual address as soon as practicable after the circumstances surrounding the stated reason for the request no longer require emergency disclosure pursuant to this section.

§ 6711. Penalties.

(a) **False information.**—Any person who knowingly provides false information in regard to a material fact contained in any application made pursuant to section 6704 (relating to persons eligible to apply) or 6705 (relating to application and certification process) shall be subject to termination from the program and to criminal penalties under 18 Pa.C.S. § 4904 (relating to unsworn falsification to authorities).

(b) **Access by fraud or misrepresentation.**—

(1) Except as provided in paragraph (2), any person who intentionally, knowingly or recklessly attempts to gain access to or gains access to a program participant's actual address by fraud or misrepresentation commits a misdemeanor of the second degree. A second or subsequent violation of this paragraph shall be graded as a felony of the third degree.

(2) A first offense under paragraph (1) shall be graded as a felony of the third degree if it is committed by any person who has previously been convicted of a crime of violence involving the program participant under paragraph (1) or the program participant's family or household memberas defined in section 6102 (relating to definitions) including:

18 Pa.C.S. § 2701 (relating to simple assault);

18 Pa.C.S. § 2702 (relating to aggravated assault);

18 Pa.C.S. § 2705 (relating to recklessly endangering another person);

18 Pa.C.S. § 2709 (relating to harassment);

18 Pa.C.S. § 2709.1 (relating to stalking);

18 Pa.C.S. § 2901 (relating to kidnapping);

18 Pa.C.S. § 3121 (relating to rape);

18 Pa.C.S. § 3123 (relating to involuntary deviate sexual intercourse);

18 Pa.C.S. § 4954 (relating to protective orders); or

23 Pa.C.S. § 6108 (relating to relief).

(c) **Unauthorized use of disclosed actual address.**—A person who lawfully obtains a program participant's actual address pursuant to an exception contained in section 6708 (relating to disclosure of actual address) and who subsequently discloses or uses the actual address in a manner not authorized by this chapter commits a summary offense.

§ 6712. Rules and regulations.

The Office of Victim Advocate shall have the following duties in order to implement this chapter:

(1) The Office of Victim Advocate shall adopt and use guidelines, which shall be published in the Pennsylvania Bulletin. The guidelines shall not be subject to review under section 205 of the act of July 31, 1968 (P.L.769, No.240), referred to as the Commonwealth Documents Law, or the act of June 25, 1982 (P.L.633, No.181), known as the Regulatory Review Act.

(2) By July 1, 2006, the Office of Victim Advocate shall, in accordance with law, promulgate regulations to replace the guidelines under paragraph (1).

(3) The guidelines under paragraph (1) shall take effect in 180 days and expire on the earlier of the effective date of regulations promulgated under paragraph (2) or July 1, 2007.

§ 6713. Civil immunity.

Except for gross negligence, recklessness or intentional misconduct, the Office of Victim Advocate, law enforcement agencies and all agents, contractors and employees of the Office of Victim Advocate or a law enforcement agency shall be immune from civil liability in any action arising in connection with this chapter.

# PART VIII

UNIFORM INTERSTATE FAMILY SUPPORT

Chapter

71. General Provisions
72. Jurisdiction
73. Civil Provisions of General Application
74. Establishment of Support Order
75. Direct Enforcement of Order of Another State Without Registration
76. Enforcement and Modification of Support Order After Registration
77. Determination of Parentage (Repealed)
77A. Support Proceeding Under Convention
78. Interstate Rendition
79. Miscellaneous Provisions

Enactment. Part VIII was added April 4, 1996, P.L.58, No.20, effective immediately.

CHAPTER 71

GENERAL PROVISIONS

Sec.

7101. Short title of part.
7101.1. Definitions.
7102. Remedies cumulative (Repealed).
7103. State tribunal and support enforcement agency.
7104. Cumulative remedies.
7105. Application of part to resident of foreign country and foreign support proceeding.

Enactment. Chapter 71 was added April 4, 1996, P.L.58, No.20, effective immediately.

Cross References. Chapter 71 is referred to in sections 7105, 7613, 7210, 77A02 of this title.

§ 7101. Short title of part.

(a) **Short title of part.**—(Deleted by amendment).

(b) **Definitions.**—(Deleted by amendment).

This part shall be known and may be cited as the Uniform Interstate Family Support Act.

(Dec. 16, 1997, P.L.549, No.58, eff. Jan. 1, 1998; Dec. 28, 2015, P.L.559, No.94, eff. imd.)

2015 Amendment. Act 94 amended this section.

1997 Amendment. Act 58 amended the defs. of "income-withholding order," "initiating state," "responding state" and "state" in subsec. (b). Act 58 of 1997 was suspended by Pennsylvania Rule of Civil Procedure No. 1910.50(3), as amended May 31, 2000, insofar as it is inconsistent with Rule No. 1910.20 relating to the availability of remedies for collection of past due and overdue support.

References in Text. The Department of Public Welfare, referred to in this section, was redesignated as the Department of Human Services by Act 132 of 2014.

The Secretary of Public Welfare, referred to in this section, was redesignated as the Secretary of Human Services by Act 132 of 2014.

Cross References. Section 7101 is referred to in sections 4302, 4308.1 of this title.

§ 7101.1. Definitions.

Subject to additional definitions contained in subsequent provisions of this part which are applicable to specific provisions of this part, the following words and phrases when used in this part shall have the meanings given to them in this section unless the context clearly indicates otherwise:

"Child." An individual, whether over or under the age of majority, who is or is alleged to be owed a duty of support by the individual's parent or who is or is alleged to be the beneficiary of a support order directed to the parent.

"Child support order." A support order for a child, including a child who has attained the age of majority under the law of the issuing state or foreign country.

"Convention." The Convention on the International Recovery of Child Support and Other Forms of Family Maintenance, concluded at the Hague on November 23, 2007.

"Department." The Department of Human Services of the Commonwealth.

"Duty of support." An obligation imposed or imposable by law to provide support for a child, spouse or former spouse. The term includes an unsatisfied obligation to provide support.

"Foreign country." A country, including a political subdivision of a country other than the United States, which authorized the issuance of support orders and:

(1) has been declared under the law of the United States to be a foreign reciprocating country;

(2) has established a reciprocal arrangement for child support with this State as provided in section 7308 (relating to supervisory duty);

(3) has enacted a law or established procedures for the issuance and enforcement of support orders which are substantially similar to the procedures under this part; or

(4) in which the convention is in force with respect to the United States.

"Foreign support order." A support order of a foreign tribunal.

"Foreign tribunal." A court, administrative agency or quasi-judicial entity of a foreign country which is authorized to establish, enforce or modify support orders or to determine parentage of a child. The term includes a competent authority under the convention.

"Home state." The state or foreign country in which a child lived with a parent or a person acting as parent for at least six consecutive months immediately preceding the time of filing of a petition or comparable pleading for support and, if a child is less than six months old, the state or foreign country in which the child lived from birth with the parent or such person. A period of temporary absence of the parent or such person is counted as part of the six-month or other period.

"Income." The term includes earnings or other periodic entitlements to money from any source and any other property subject to withholding for support under the law of this State.

"Income-withholding order." An order or other legal process directed to an obligor's employer or other debtor, in accordance with section 4348 (relating to attachment of income), to withhold support from the income of the obligor.

"Initiating tribunal." The tribunal of a state or a foreign country from which a petition or comparable pleading is forwarded or in which a petition or comparable pleading is filed for forwarding to another state or foreign country.

"Issuing foreign country." The foreign country in which a tribunal issues a support order or a judgment determining parentage of a child.

"Issuing state." The state in which a tribunal issues a support order or a judgment determining parentage of a child.

"Issuing tribunal." The tribunal of a state or a foreign country that issues a support order or a judgment determining parentage of a child.

"**Law.**" The term includes decisional and statutory law and rules and regulations having the force of law.

"**Obligee.**" Any of the following:

(1) An individual to whom a duty of support is or is alleged to be owed or in whose favor a support order or a judgment determining parentage of a child has been issued.

(2) A foreign country, state or political subdivision to which the rights under a duty of support or support order have been assigned or which has independent claims based on financial assistance provided to an individual obligee in place of child support.

(3) An individual seeking a judgment determining parentage of the individual's child.

(4) The Department of Human Services.

(5) A person who is a creditor in a proceeding under Chapter 77A (relating to support proceeding under convention).

"**Obligor.**" An individual or the estate of a decedent that:

(1) owes or is alleged to owe a duty of support;

(2) is alleged but has not been adjudicated to be a parent of a child;

(3) is liable under a support order; or

(4) is a debtor in a proceeding under Chapter 77A (relating to support proceeding under convention).

"**Outside this State.**" A location in another state or a country other than the United States, whether or not the country is a foreign country.

"**Person.**" An individual, corporation, business trust, estate, trust, partnership, limited liability company, association, joint venture, public corporation, government or governmental subdivision or agency or instrumentality or any other legal or commercial entity.

"**Record.**" Information that is inscribed on a tangible medium or that is stored in an electronic or other medium and is retrievable in perceivable form.

"**Register.**" To record in a tribunal of this State a support order or judgment determining parentage of a child issued in another state or foreign country.

"**Registering tribunal.**" A tribunal in which a support order or judgment determining parentage of a child is registered.

"**Responding state.**" A state in which a petition or comparable pleading for support or to determine parentage of a child is filed or to which a petition or comparable pleading is forwarded for filing from another state or foreign country.

"**Responding tribunal.**" The authorized tribunal in a responding state or foreign country.

"**Secretary.**" The Secretary of Human Services of the Commonwealth.

"**Spousal support order.**" A support order for a spouse or former spouse of the obligor.

"**State.**" A state of the United States, the District of Columbia, Puerto Rico, the United States Virgin Islands or any territory or insular possession under the jurisdiction of the United States. The term includes an Indian nation tribe.

"**Support enforcement agency.**" A public official, governmental entity or private agency authorized to:

(1) seek enforcement of support orders or laws relating to the duty of support;

(2) seek establishment or modification of child support;

(3) request determination of parentage of a child;

(4) attempt to locate obligors or assets of an obligor; or

(5) request determination of the controlling child support order.

"Support order." A judgment, decree, order, decision or directive, whether temporary, final or subject to modification, issued in a state or a foreign country for the benefit of a child, spouse or former spouse, which provides for monetary support, health care, arrearages, retroactive support or reimbursement for financial assistance provided to an individual obligee in place of child support. The term may include related costs and fees, interest, income withholding, automatic adjustment, reasonable attorney fees and other relief.

"Tribunal." A court, administrative agency or quasi-judicial entity authorized to establish, enforce or modify support orders or to determine parentage.

"Tribunal of this State." A court of common pleas.

(Dec. 28, 2015, P.L.559, No.94, eff. imd.)

2015 Amendment. Act 94 added section 7101.1.

Cross References. Section 7101.1 is referred to in sections 7307, 77A01 of this title.

§ 7102. Remedies cumulative (Repealed).

2015 Repeal. Section 7102 was repealed December 28, 2015, P.L.559, No.94, effective immediately.

§ 7103. State tribunal and support enforcement agency.

(a) Tribunals.—The courts of common pleas are the tribunals of this State.

(b) Support enforcement agency.—The department's Bureau of Child Support Enforcement is the support enforcement agency of this State.

(Dec. 28, 2015, P.L.559, No.94, eff. imd.)

2015 Amendment. Act 94 added section 7103.

§ 7104. Cumulative remedies.

(a) Remedies.—Remedies provided by this part are cumulative and do not affect the availability of remedies under other law or the recognition of a foreign support order on the basis of comity.

(b) Limitations.—This part does not:

(1) provide the exclusive method of establishing or enforcing a support order under the law of this State; or

(2) grant a tribunal of this State jurisdiction to render judgment or issue an order relating to child custody or visitation in a proceeding under this part.

(Dec. 28, 2015, P.L.559, No.94, eff. imd.)

2015 Amendment. Act 94 added section 7104.

§ 7105. Application of part to resident of foreign country and foreign support proceeding.

(a) Applicability.—A tribunal of this State shall apply Chapter 71 (relating to general provisions), 72 (relating to jurisdiction), 73 (relating to civil provisions of general application), 74 (relating to establishment of support order or determination of parentage), 75 (relating to enforcement of support order without registration) or 76 (relating to registration, enforcement and modification of support order) and, as applicable, Chapter 77A (relating to support proceeding under convention), to a support proceeding involving any of the following:

(1) A foreign support order.

(2) A foreign tribunal.

(3) An obligee, obligor or child residing in a foreign country.

(b) Discretionary.—A tribunal of this State that is requested to recognize and enforce a support order on the basis of comity may apply the procedural and substantive provisions of Chapter 71, 72, 73, 74, 75 or 76.

(c) Limitations.—Chapter 77A applies only to a support proceeding under the convention. In a proceeding, if a provision of Chapter 77A is inconsistent with Chapter 71, 72, 73, 74, 75 or 76, Chapter 77A shall control.

(Dec. 28, 2015, P.L.559, No.94, eff. imd.)

2015 Amendment. Act 94 added section 7105.

CHAPTER 72
JURISDICTION

Subchapter

A. Extended Personal Jurisdiction
B. Proceedings Involving Two or More States or a Foreign Country
C. Reconciliation of Multiple Orders

Enactment. Chapter 72 was added April 4, 1996, P.L.58, No.20, effective immediately.

Cross References. Chapter 72 is referred to in section 7105, 7210, 7613 of this title.

SUBCHAPTER A
EXTENDED PERSONAL JURISDICTION

Sec.
7201. Bases for jurisdiction over nonresident.
7202. Procedure when exercising jurisdiction over nonresident (Repealed).
7202.1. Duration of personal jurisdiction.

§ 7201. Bases for jurisdiction over nonresident.

(a) **Jurisdiction.**—In a proceeding to establish or enforce a support order or to determine parentage of a child, a tribunal of this State may exercise personal jurisdiction over a nonresident individual or the individual's guardian or conservator if any of the following apply:

(1) The individual is personally served with a writ of summons, complaint or other appropriate pleading within this State.

(2) The individual submits to the jurisdiction of this State by consent in a record, by entering a general appearance or by filing a responsive document having the effect of waiving any contest to personal jurisdiction.

(3) The individual resided with the child in this State.

(4) The individual resided in this State and provided prenatal expenses or support for the child.

(5) The child resides in this State as a result of the acts or directives of the individual.

(6) The individual engaged in sexual intercourse in this State and the child may have been conceived by that act of intercourse.

(7) The individual acknowledged parentage of the child on a form filed with the department under section 5103 (relating to acknowledgment and claim of paternity).

(8) There is any other basis consistent with the constitutions of this State and the United States for the exercise of personal jurisdiction.

(b) **Modification.**—The bases of personal jurisdiction set forth in subsection (a) or in any other law of this State may not be used to acquire personal jurisdiction for a tribunal of this State to modify a child support order of another state unless the requirements of section 7611 (relating to modification of child support order of another state) are met or, in the case of a foreign support order, unless the requirements of section 7615 (relating to jurisdiction to modify child support order of a foreign country) are met.

(Dec. 28, 2015, P.L.559, No.94, eff. imd.)

Cross References. Section 7201 is referred to in sections 7611, 77A08 of this title.

§ 7202. Procedure when exercising jurisdiction over nonresident (Repealed).

2015 Repeal. Section 7202 was repealed December 28, 2015, P.L.559, No.94, effective immediately.

§ 7202.1. Duration of personal jurisdiction.

Personal jurisdiction acquired by a tribunal of this State in a proceeding under this part or other law of this State relating to a support order continues as long as a tribunal of this State has continuing exclusive jurisdiction to modify the tribunal's order or continuing jurisdiction to enforce the tribunal's order as provided by sections 7205 (relating to continuing, exclusive jurisdiction to modify child support orders), 7206 (relating to continuing jurisdiction to enforce child support orders) and 7211 (relating to continuing, exclusive jurisdiction to modify spousal support order).

(Dec. 28, 2015, P.L.559, No.94, eff. imd.)

2015 Amendment. Act 94 added section 7202.1.

SUBCHAPTER B
PROCEEDINGS INVOLVING TWO OR MORE STATES OR A FOREIGN COUNTRY

Sec.
7203. Initiating and responding tribunal of this State.
7204. Simultaneous proceedings.
7205. Continuing, exclusive jurisdiction to modify child support orders.
7206. Continuing jurisdiction to enforce child support orders.

Subchapter Heading. The heading of Subchapter B was amended December 28, 2015, P.L.559, No.94, effective immediately.

§ 7203. Initiating and responding tribunal of this State.

Under this part, a tribunal of this State may serve as an initiating tribunal to forward proceedings to a tribunal of another state and as a responding tribunal for proceedings initiated in another state or a foreign country.

(Dec. 28, 2015, P.L.559, No.94, eff. imd.)

§ 7204. Simultaneous proceedings.

(a) **Permissible.**—A tribunal of this State may exercise jurisdiction to establish a support order if the petition or comparable pleading is filed after a petition or comparable pleading is filed in another state or a foreign country only if all of the following apply:

(1) The petition or comparable pleading in this State is filed before the expiration of the time allowed in the other state or a foreign country for filing a responsive pleading challenging the exercise of jurisdiction by the other state or a foreign country.

(2) The contesting party timely challenges the exercise of jurisdiction in the other state or a foreign country.

(3) If relevant, this State is the home state of the child.

(b) **Impermissible.**—A tribunal of this State may not exercise jurisdiction to establish a support order if the petition or comparable pleading is filed before a petition or comparable pleading is filed in another state or a foreign country if all of the following apply:

(1) The petition or comparable pleading in the other state or a foreign country is filed before the expiration of the time allowed in this State for filing a responsive pleading challenging the exercise of jurisdiction by this State.

(2) The contesting party timely challenges the exercise of jurisdiction in this State.

(3) If relevant, the other state or a foreign country is the home state of the child.

(Dec. 28, 2015, P.L.559, No.94, eff. imd.)

§ 7205. Continuing, exclusive jurisdiction to modify child support orders.

(a) **Extent.**—A tribunal of this State that has issued a child support order consistent with the law of this State has and shall exercise continuing, exclusive jurisdiction to modify the child support order if the order is the controlling order and:

(1) at the time of the filing of a request for modification this State is the residence of the obligor, the individual obligee or the child for whose benefit the support order is issued; or

(2) even if this State is not the residence of the obligor, the individual obligee or the child for whose benefit the support order is issued, the parties consent in a record or in open court that the tribunal of this State may continue to exercise jurisdiction to modify the order.

(b) **Restriction.**—A tribunal of this State that has issued a child support order consistent with the law of this State may not exercise its continuing, exclusive jurisdiction to modify the order if:

(1) all of the parties who are individuals file consent in a record with the tribunal of this State that a tribunal of another state, that has jurisdiction over at least one of the parties who is an individual or that is located in the state of residence of the child, may modify the order and assume continuing, exclusive jurisdiction; or

(2) the order is not the controlling order.

(c) **Modification.**—(Deleted by amendment).

(d) **Faith and credit.**—If a tribunal of another state has issued a child support order under a law substantially similar to this part which modifies a child support order of a tribunal of this State, tribunals of this State shall recognize the continuing, exclusive jurisdiction of the tribunal of the other state.

(d.1) **Modification.**—A tribunal of this State that lacks continuing, exclusive jurisdiction to modify a child support order may serve as an initiating tribunal to request a tribunal of another state to modify a support order issued in that state.

(e) **Interim orders.**—A temporary support order issued ex parte or pending resolution of a jurisdictional conflict does not create continuing, exclusive jurisdiction in the issuing tribunal.

(f) **Duration and modification of spousal support orders.**—(Deleted by amendment).

(Dec. 16, 1997, P.L.549, No.58, eff. Jan. 1, 1998; Dec. 28, 2015, P.L.559, No.94, eff. imd.)

2015 Amendment. Act 94 amended this section.

1997 Amendment. Act 58 of 1997 was suspended by Pennsylvania Rule of Civil Procedure No. 1910.50(3), as amended May 31, 2000, insofar as it is inconsistent with Rule No. 1910.20 relating to the availability of remedies for collection of past due and overdue support.

Cross References. Section 7205 is referred to in sections 7202.1, 7207 of this title.

§ 7206. Continuing jurisdiction to enforce child support orders.

(a) **Initiating tribunal.**—A tribunal of this State that has issued a child support order consistent with the law of this State may serve as an initiating tribunal to request a tribunal of another state to enforce:

(1) the order, if the order is the controlling order and has not been modified by a tribunal of another state that assumed jurisdiction under a law substantially similar to this part; or

(2) a money judgment for arrears of support and interest on the order that accrued before a determination that an order of a tribunal of another state is the controlling order.

(b) **Responding tribunal.**—A tribunal of this State having continuing jurisdiction over a support order may act as a responding tribunal to enforce the order.

(c) **Lack of jurisdiction.**—(Deleted by amendment).

(Dec. 28, 2015, P.L.559, No.94, eff. imd.)

    Cross References. Section 7206 is referred to in sections 7202.1, 7207 of this title.

SUBCHAPTER C
RECONCILIATION OF MULTIPLE ORDERS

Sec.
7207. Determination of controlling child support order.
7208. Multiple child support orders for two or more obligees.
7209. Credit for payments.
7210. Application of part to nonresident subject to personal jurisdiction.
7211. Continuing, exclusive jurisdiction to modify spousal support order.

    Subchapter Heading. The heading of Subchapter C was amended December 16, 1997, P.L.549, No.58, effective January 1, 1998.

§ 7207. Determination of controlling child support order.

(a) **Single child support order.**—If a proceeding is brought under this part and only one tribunal has issued a child support order, the order of that tribunal controls and must be so recognized.

(a.1) **Multiple orders.**—If a proceeding is brought under this part and two or more child support orders have been issued by tribunals of this State, another state or a foreign country with regard to the same obligor and same child, a tribunal of this State having personal jurisdiction over both the obligor and the individual obligee shall apply the following rules and by order shall determine which order controls and must be recognized:

(1) If only one of the tribunals would have continuing, exclusive jurisdiction under this part, the order of that tribunal controls.

(2) If more than one of the tribunals would have continuing, exclusive jurisdiction under this part, an order issued by a tribunal in the current home state of the child controls and must be so recognized, but, if an order has not been issued in the current home state of the child, the order most recently issued controls and must be so recognized.

(3) If none of the tribunals would have continuing, exclusive jurisdiction under this part, the tribunal of this State shall issue a child support order, which controls.

(a.2) **Request to determine controlling order.**—If two or more child support orders have been issued for the same obligor and the same child, upon request of a party who is an individual or which is a support enforcement agency, a tribunal of this State having personal jurisdiction over both the obligor and the obligee who is an individual shall determine which order controls under subsection (a.1). The request may be filed with a registration for enforcement or registration for modification under Chapter 76 (relating to registration, enforcement and modification of support order) or may be filed as a separate proceeding. The request to determine which is the controlling order must be accompanied by a copy of every child support order in effect and the applicable record of payments. The requesting party shall give notice of the request to each party whose rights may be affected by the determination.

(b) Exclusive jurisdiction.—The tribunal that issued the controlling order under subsection (a), (a.1) or (a.2) is the tribunal that has continuing jurisdiction under section 7205 (relating to continuing, exclusive jurisdiction to modify child support orders) or 7206 (relating to continuing jurisdiction to enforce child support orders).

(c) Basis of order.—A tribunal of this State which determines by order the identity of the controlling order under subsection (a.1)(1) or (2) or (a.2) or which issues a new controlling order under subsection (a.1)(3) shall state all of the following in that order:

(1) The basis upon which the tribunal made its determination.

(2) The amount of prospective support, if any.

(3) The total amount of consolidated arrears and accrued interest, if any, under all of the orders after all payments made are credited under section 7209 (relating to credit for payments).

(d) Filing of copy of order.—Within 30 days after issuance of an order determining the identity of the controlling order, the party obtaining the determining order shall file a certified copy of it with each tribunal that issued or registered an earlier order of child support. A party or support enforcement agency that obtains a determining order and fails to file a certified copy is subject to appropriate sanctions by a tribunal in which the issue of failure to file arises. Failure to file a copy of the determining order does not affect the validity or enforceability of the controlling order.

(e) Recognition.—An order which has been determined to be the controlling order or a judgment for consolidated arrears of support and interest, if any, made under this section must be recognized in proceedings under this part.

(Dec. 16, 1997, P.L.549, No.58, eff. Jan. 1, 1998; Dec. 28, 2015, P.L.559, No.94, eff. imd.)

2015 Amendment. Act 94 amendede this section.

1997 Amendment. Act 58 of 1997 was suspended by Pennsylvania Rule of Civil Procedure No. 1910.50(3), as amended May 31, 2000, insofar as it is inconsistent with Rule No. 1910.20 relating to the availability of remedies for collection of past due and overdue support.

Cross References. Section 7207 is referred to in section 7611 of this title.

§ 7208. Multiple child support orders for two or more obligees.

In responding to registrations or petitions for enforcement of two or more child support orders in effect at the same time with regard to the same obligor and different individual obligees at least one of which was issued by a tribunal of another state or a foreign country, a tribunal of this State shall enforce those orders in the same manner as if the multiple orders had been issued by a tribunal of this State.

(Dec. 28, 2015, P.L.559, No.94, eff. imd.)

§ 7209. Credit for payments.

Amounts collected and credited for a particular period pursuant to a child support order issued by a tribunal of another state or a foreign country must be credited against the amounts accruing or accrued for the same period under a child support order for the same child issued by the tribunal of this State.

(Dec. 28, 2015, P.L.559, No.94, eff. imd.)

§ 7210. Application of part to nonresident subject to personal jurisdiction.

A tribunal of this State exercising personal jurisdiction over a nonresident in a proceeding under this part, under other law of this State relating to a support order or recognizing a foreign support order, may receive evidence from outside this State under section 7316 (relating to special rules of evidence and procedure), communicate with a tribunal outside this State pursuant to section 7317 (relating to communications between tribunals) and obtain discovery through a tribunal outside this State under section 7318 (relating to assistance with discovery). In all other respects, Chapter 71 (relating to general provisions), 72 (relating to jurisdiction), 73 (relating to civil provisions of general application), 74 (relating to establishment of support order or determination of parentage), 75 (relating to enforcement of support order without registration) or 76 (relating to registration, enforcement and modification of support order) do not apply, and the tribunal shall apply the procedural and substantive law of this State.

(Dec. 28, 2015, P.L.559, No.94, eff. imd.)

2015 Amendment. Act 94 added section 7210.

§ 7211. Continuing, exclusive jurisdiction to modify spousal support order.

(a) Modification.—A tribunal of this State issuing a spousal support order consistent with the law of this State has continuing, exclusive jurisdiction to modify the spousal support order throughout the existence of the support obligation.

(b) Prohibition.—A tribunal of this State may not modify a spousal support order issued by a tribunal of another state or a foreign country having continuing, exclusive jurisdiction over that order under the law of that state or foreign country.

(c) Tribunal.—A tribunal of this State that has continuing, exclusive jurisdiction over a spousal support order may serve as:

(1) an initiating tribunal to request a tribunal of another state to enforce the spousal support order issued in this State; or

(2) a responding tribunal to enforce or modify the spousal support order issued by the tribunal.

(Dec. 28, 2015, P.L.559, No.94, eff. imd.)

2015 Amendment. Act 94 added section 7211.

Cross References. Section 7211 is referred to in section 7202.1 of this title.

CHAPTER 73
CIVIL PROVISIONS OF GENERAL APPLICATION

Sec.
7301. Proceedings under this part.
7302. Action by minor parent.
7303. Application of lw of this State.
7304. Duties of initiating tribunal.
7305. Duties and powers of responding tribunal.
7306. Inappropriate tribunal.
7307. Duties of support enforcement agency.
7308. Supervisory duty.
7309. Private counsel.
7310. Duties of department.
7311. Pleadings and accompanying documents.
7312. Nondisclosure of information in exceptional circumstances.
7313. Costs and fees.
7314. Limited immunity of petitioner.
7315. Nonparentage as defense.
7316. Special rules of evidence and procedure.
7317. Communications between tribunals.
7318. Assistance with discovery.
7319. Receipt and disbursement of payments.

Enactment. Chapter 73 was added April 4, 1996, P.L.58, No.20, effective immediately.

Cross References. Chapter 73 is referred to in sections 7105, 7210, 7613, 77A02 of this title.

§ 7301. Proceedings under this part.

(a) **Scope.**—Except as otherwise provided in this part, this Chapter applies to all proceedings under this part.

(b) **Proceedings.**—(Deleted by amendment).

(c) **Commencement.**—An individual petitioner or a support enforcement agency may commence a proceeding authorized under this part by filing a petition in an initiating tribunal for forwarding to a responding tribunal or by filing a petition or a comparable pleading directly in a tribunal of another state or a foreign country which has or can obtain personal jurisdiction over the respondent.

(Dec. 28, 2015, P.L.559, No.94, eff. imd.)

Cross References. Section 7301 is referred to in section 7305 of this title.

§ 7302. Action by minor parent.

A minor parent or a guardian or other legal representative of a minor parent may maintain a proceeding on behalf of or for the benefit of the minor's child.

§ 7303. Application of law of this State.

Except as otherwise provided by this part, a responding tribunal of this State:

(1) shall apply the procedural and substantive law, including the rules on choice of law, generally applicable to similar proceedings originating in this State and may exercise all powers and provide all remedies available in those proceedings; and

(2) shall determine the duty of support and the amount payable in accordance with the law and support guidelines of this State.

§§ 7304. Duties of initiating tribunal.

(a) Copies of petition.—Upon the filing of a petition authorized by this part, an initiating tribunal of this State shall forward three copies of the petition and its accompanying documents:

(1) to the responding tribunal or appropriate support enforcement agency in the responding state; or

(2) if the identity of the responding tribunal is unknown, to the state information agency of the responding state with a request that they be forwarded to the appropriate tribunal and that receipt be acknowledged.

(b) Special circumstances.—

(1) If requested by the responding tribunal, a tribunal of this State shall issue a certificate or other document and make findings required by the law of the responding state.

(2) If the responding tribunal is in a foreign country, upon request, the tribunal of this State shall specify the amount of support sought, convert that amount into the equivalent amount in the foreign currency under applicable official or market exchange rates as publicly reported and provide other documents necessary to satisfy the requirements of the responding foreign tribunal.

(Dec. 16, 1997, P.L.549, No.58, eff. Jan. 1, 1998; Dec. 28, 2015, P.L.559, No.94, eff. imd.)

2015 Amendment. Act 94 amended subsec. (b).

1997 Amendment. Act 58 of 1997 was suspended by Pennsylvania Rule of Civil Procedure No. 1910.50(3), as amended May 31, 2000, insofar as it is inconsistent with Rule No. 1910.20 relating to the availability of remedies for collection of past due and overdue support.

§ 7305. Duties and powers of responding tribunal.

(a) Filing and notice.—If a responding tribunal of this State receives a petition or comparable pleading from an initiating tribunal or directly pursuant to section 7301(c) (relating to proceedings under this part), it shall cause the petition or pleading to be filed and notify the petitioner where and when it was filed.

(b) Action.—A responding tribunal of this State, to the extent otherwise not prohibited by law, may do any of the following:

(1) Establish or enforce a support order, modify a child support order, determine the controlling child support order or determine parentage of a child.

(2) Order an obligor to comply with a support order, specifying the amount and the manner of compliance.

(3) Order income withholding.

(4) Determine the amount of any arrearages and specify a method of payment.

(5) Enforce orders by civil or criminal contempt, or both.

(6) Set aside property for satisfaction of the support order.

(7) Place liens and order execution on the obligor's property.

(8) Order an obligor to keep the tribunal informed of the obligor's current residential address, e-mail address, telephone number, employer, address of employment and telephone number at the place of employment.

(9) Issue a bench warrant for an obligor who has failed after proper notice to appear at a hearing ordered by the tribunal and enter the bench warrant in any state and local computer systems for criminal warrants.

(10) Order the obligor to seek appropriate employment by specified methods.

(11) Award reasonable attorney fees and other fees and costs.

(12) Grant any other available remedy.

(c) Calculations.—A responding tribunal of this State shall include in a support order issued under this part or in the documents accompanying the order the calculations on which the support order is based.

(d) **Visitation.**—A responding tribunal of this State may not condition the payment of a support order issued under this part upon compliance by a party with provisions for visitation.

(e) **Notice.**—If a responding tribunal of this State issues an order under this part, the tribunal shall send a copy of the order to the petitioner and the respondent and to the initiating agency or tribunal, if any.

(f) **Foreign currency.**—If requested to enforce a support order, arrears or judgment or modify a support order stated in a foreign currency, a responding tribunal of this State shall convert the amount stated in the foreign currency to the equivalent amount in dollars under the applicable official or market exchange rates as publicly reported.

(Dec. 16, 1997, P.L.549, No.58, eff. Jan. 1, 1998; Dec. 28, 2015, P.L.559, No.94, eff. imd.)

2015 Amendment. Act 94 amended this section.

1997 Amendment. Act 58 of 1997 was suspended by Pennsylvania Rule of Civil Procedure No. 1910.50(3), as amended May 31, 2000, insofar as it is inconsistent with Rule No. 1910.20 relating to the availability of remedies for collection of past due and overdue support.

Cross References. Section 7305 is referred to in section 7401 of this title.

§ 7306. Inappropriate tribunal.

If a petition or comparable pleading is received by an inappropriate tribunal of this State, it shall forward the pleading and accompanying documents to an appropriate tribunal in this State or another state and notify the petitioner where and when the pleading was sent.

1997 Amendment. Act 58 amended this sec.

§ 7307. Duties of support enforcement agency.

(a) **General duty.**—In a proceeding under this part, a support enforcement agency of this State, upon request:

(1) Shall provide services to a petitioner residing in a state.

(2) Shall provide services to a petitioner requesting services through a central authority of a foreign country as defined in paragraph (1) or (4) of the definition of "foreign country" in section 7101.1 (relating to definitions).

(3) May provide services to a petitioner who is an individual not residing in a state.

(b) **Specific duties.**—A support enforcement agency that is providing services to the petitioner shall do all of the following:

(1) Take all steps necessary to enable an appropriate tribunal of this State, another state or a foreign country to obtain jurisdiction over the respondent.

(2) Request an appropriate tribunal to set a date, time and place for a hearing.

(3) Make a reasonable effort to obtain relevant information, including information as to income and property of the parties.

(4) Within two days, exclusive of Saturdays, Sundays and legal holidays, after receipt of a notice in a record from an initiating, responding or registering tribunal, send a copy of the notice to the petitioner.

(5) Within two days, exclusive of Saturdays, Sundays and legal holidays, after receipt of a communication in a record from the respondent or the respondent's attorney, send a copy of the communication to the petitioner.

(6) Notify the petitioner if jurisdiction over the respondent cannot be obtained.

(b.1) **Registration.**—A support enforcement agency of this State that requests registration of a child support order in this State for enforcement or for modification shall make reasonable efforts to do one of the following:

(1) Ensure that the order to be registered is the controlling order.

(2) If two or more child support orders exist and the identity of the controlling order has not been determined, ensure that a request for a determination is made in a tribunal having jurisdiction.

(b.2) Conversion.—A support enforcement agency of this State that requests registration and enforcement of a support order, arrears or judgment stated in a foreign currency shall convert the amounts stated in the foreign currency into the equivalent amounts in dollars under the applicable official or market exchange rates as publicly reported.

(b.3) Payment.—A support enforcement agency of this State shall request a tribunal of this State to issue a child support order and an income withholding order that redirect payment of current support, arrears and interest, if requested to do so by a support enforcement agency of another state under section 7319 (relating to receipt and disbursement of payments).

(c) Fiduciaries.—This part does not create or negate a relationship of attorney and client or other fiduciary relationship between a support enforcement agency or the attorney for the agency and the individual being assisted by the agency.

(Dec. 16, 1997, P.L.549, No.58, eff. Jan. 1, 1998; Dec. 28, 2015, P.L.559, No.94, eff. imd.)

2015 Amendment. Act 94 amended subsecs. (a), and (b), and added subsecs. (b.1), (b.2), and (b.3).

1997 Amendment. Act 58 of 1997 was suspended by Pennsylvania Rule of Civil Procedure No. 1910.50(3), as amended May 31, 2000, insofar as it is inconsistent with Rule No. 1910.20 relating to the availability of remedies for collection of past due and overdue support.

§ 7308. Supervisory duty.

(a) Secretary.—If the secretary determines that a support enforcement agency is neglecting or refusing to provide services to an individual, the secretary may order the agency to perform its duties under this part or may provide those services directly to the individual.

(b) Reciprocity.—The secretary may determine that a foreign country has established a reciprocal arrangement for child support with this State and take appropriate action for notification of the determination.

(Dec. 16, 1997, P.L.549, No.58, eff. Jan. 1, 1998; Dec. 28, 2015, P.L.559, No.94, eff. imd.)

2015 Amendment. Act 94 added subsecs. (a) and (b).

1997 Amendment. Act 58 of 1997 was suspended by Pennsylvania Rule of Civil Procedure No. 1910.50(3), as amended May 31, 2000, insofar as it is inconsistent with Rule No. 1910.20 relating to the availability of remedies for collection of past due and overdue support.

Cross References. Section 7308 is referred to in section 7101.1 of this title.

§ 7309. Private counsel.

An individual may employ private counsel to represent the individual in proceedings authorized by this part.

§ 7310. Duties of department.

(a) Designation.—The department is the State information agency under this part.

(b) Duties.—The department shall do all of the following:

(1) Compile and maintain a current list, including addresses, of the tribunals in this State which have jurisdiction under this part and any support enforcement agencies in this State and transmit a copy to the state information agency of every other state.

(2) Maintain a register of tribunals and support enforcement agencies received from other states.

(3) Forward to the appropriate tribunal in the place in this State in which the individual obligee or the obligor resides, or in which the obligor's property is

§ 7311   INTERSTATE FAMILY SUPPORT   Pa.C.S.

believed to be located, documents concerning a proceeding under this part received from another state or a foreign country.

(4) Obtain information concerning the location of the obligor and the obligor's property within this State not exempt from execution by such means as postal verification; Federal or State locator services; examination of telephone directories; requests for the obligor's address from employers; and examination of governmental records, including, to the extent not prohibited by other law, those relating to real property, vital statistics, law enforcement, taxation, motor vehicles, driver's licenses and Social Security.

(5) (Deleted by amendment).

(6) (Deleted by amendment).

(Dec. 16, 1997, P.L.549, No.58, eff. Jan. 1, 1998; Dec. 28, 2015, P.L.559, No.94, eff. imd.)

2015 Amendment. Act 94 amended subsect. (b).

1997 Amendment. Act 58 of 1997 was suspended by Pennsylvania Rule of Civil Procedure No. 1910.50(3), as amended May 31, 2000, insofar as it is inconsistent with Rule No. 1910.20 relating to the availability of remedies for collection of past due and overdue support.

§ 7311. Pleadings and accompanying documents.

(a) **Verification and content.**—In a proceeding under this part, a petitioner seeking to establish a support order to determine parentage of a child or to register and modify a support order of a tribunal of another state or a foreign country must file a petition. Unless otherwise ordered under section 7312 (relating to nondisclosure of information in exceptional circumstances), the petition or accompanying documents must provide, so far as known, the name, residential address and Social Security number of the obligor and the obligee or the parent and alleged parent and the name, sex, residential address, Social Security number and date of birth of each child for whose benefit support is sought or whose parentage is to be determined. Unless filed at the time of registration, the petition must be accompanied by a copy of any support order known to have been issued by another tribunal. The petition may include any other information that may assist in locating or identifying the respondent.

(b) **Relief.**—The petition must specify the relief sought. The petition and accompanying documents must conform substantially with the requirements imposed by the forms mandated by Federal law for use in cases filed by a support enforcement agency.

(Dec. 28, 2015, P.L.559, No.94, eff. imd.)

Cross References. Section 7311 is referred to in section 77A06 of this title.

§ 7312. Nondisclosure of information in exceptional circumstances.

If a party alleges in an affidavit or a pleading under oath that the health, safety or liberty of a party or child would be jeopardized by disclosure of the specific identifying information, the specific identifying information must be sealed and may not be disclosed to the other party or the public. After a hearing in which the tribunal takes into consideration the health, safety or liberty of the party or child, the tribunal may order disclosure of information that the tribunal determines to be in the interest of justice.

(Dec. 28, 2015, P.L.559, No.94, eff. imd.)

Cross References. Section 7312 is referred to in sections 7311, 7602 of this title.

§ 7313. Costs and fees.

(a) **Petitioner.**—The petitioner may not be required to pay a filing fee or other costs.

(b) **Obligor.**—If an obligee prevails, a responding tribunal of this State may assess against an obligor filing fees, reasonable attorney fees, other costs and necessary travel and other reasonable expenses incurred by the obligee and the obligee's witnesses. The tribunal may not assess fees, costs or expenses against the obligee or the support enforcement agency of either the initiating state or the responding state or foreign country except as provided by other law. Attorney fees may be taxed as costs and may be ordered paid directly to the attorney, who may enforce the order in the attorney's own name. Payment of support owed to the obligee has priority over fees, costs and expenses.

(c) **Dilatory actions.**—The tribunal shall order the payment of costs and reasonable attorney fees if it determines that a hearing was requested primarily for delay. In a proceeding under Chapter 76 (relating to registration, enforcement and modification of support order), a hearing is presumed to have been requested primarily for delay if a registered support order is confirmed or enforced without change.

(Dec. 28, 2015, P.L.559, No.94, eff. imd.)

§ 7314. Limited immunity of petitioner.

(a) **Jurisdiction over person.**—Participation by a petitioner in a proceeding before a responding tribunal, whether in person, by private attorney or through services provided by the support enforcement agency, does not confer personal jurisdiction over the petitioner in another proceeding.

(b) **Service.**—A petitioner is not amenable to service of civil process while physically present in this State to participate in a proceeding under this part.

(c) **Exception.**—The immunity granted by this section does not extend to civil litigation based on acts unrelated to a proceeding under this part committed by a party while present in this State to participate in the proceeding.

§ 7315. Nonparentage as defense.

A party whose parentage of a child has been previously determined by or pursuant to law may not plead nonparentage as a defense to a proceeding under this part.

§ 7316. Special rules of evidence and procedure.

(a) **Physical presence.**—The physical presence of a nonresident party who is an individual in a tribunal of this State is not required for the establishment, enforcement or modification of a support order or the rendition of a judgment determining parentage of a child.

(b) **Hearsay exception.**—A petition, affidavit or document, substantially complying with federally mandated forms, and a document incorporated by reference in any of them, not excluded under the hearsay rule if given in person, are admissible in evidence if given under penalty of perjury by a party or witness residing outside this State.

(c) **Payment record.**—A copy of the record of child support payments certified as a true copy of the original by the custodian of the record may be forwarded to a responding tribunal. The copy is evidence of facts asserted in it and is admissible to show whether payments were made.

(d) **Bills.**—Copies of bills for testing for parentage of a child and for prenatal and postnatal health care of the mother and child, furnished to the adverse party at least ten days before trial, are admissible in evidence to prove the amount of the charges billed and that the charges were reasonable, necessary and customary.

(e) **Transmission of documentary evidence.**—Documentary evidence transmitted from outside this State to a tribunal of this State by telephone, telecopier or other electronic means that do not provide an original record may not be excluded from evidence on an objection based on the means of transmission.

(f) **Testimony.**—In a proceeding under this part, a tribunal of this State may permit a party or witness residing outside this State to be deposed or to testify under penalty of perjury by telephone, audiovisual means or other electronic means at a designated tribunal or other location. A tribunal of this State shall cooperate with other tribunals in designating an appropriate location for the deposition or testimony.

(g) **Self-incrimination.**—If a party called to testify at a civil hearing refuses to answer on the ground that the testimony may be self-incriminating, the trier of fact may draw an adverse inference from the refusal.

(h) **Spousal communications.**—A privilege against disclosure of communications between spouses does not apply in a proceeding under this part.

(i) **Family immunity.**—The defense of immunity based on the relationship of husband and wife or parent and child does not apply in a proceeding under this part.

(j) **Parentage.**—A voluntary acknowledgment of paternity, certified as a true copy, is admissible to establish parentage of the child.

(Dec. 28, 2015, P.L.559, No.94, eff. imd.)

Cross References. Section 7316 is referred to in section 7210 of this title.

§ 7317. Communications between tribunals.

A tribunal of this State may communicate with a tribunal outside this State in a record or by telephone, e-mail or other means to obtain information concerning the laws; the legal effect of a judgment, decree or order of that tribunal; and the status of a proceeding. A tribunal of this State may furnish similar information by similar means to a tribunal outside this State.

(Dec. 28, 2015, P.L.559, No.94, eff. imd.)

Cross References. Section 7317 is referred to in section 7210 of this title.

§ 7318. Assistance with discovery.

A tribunal of this State may do all of the following:

(1) Request a tribunal outside this State to assist in obtaining discovery.

(2) Upon request, compel a person subject to its jurisdiction to respond to a discovery order issued by a tribunal outside this State.

(Dec. 28, 2015, P.L.559, No.94, eff. imd.)

Cross References. Section 7318 is referred to in section 7210 of this title.

§ 7319. Receipt and disbursement of payments.

(a) **Payments.**—A support enforcement agency or tribunal of this State shall disburse promptly any amounts received pursuant to a support order, as directed by the order. The agency or tribunal shall furnish to a requesting party or tribunal outside this State or of a foreign country a certified statement by the custodian of the record of the amounts and dates of all payments received.

(b) **Residency.**—If the obligor, the obligee who is an individual and the child do not reside in this State, upon request from the support enforcement agency of this State or another state, the support enforcement agency of this State or a tribunal of this State shall do all of the following:

(1) Direct that the support payment be made to the support enforcement agency in the state in which the obligee is receiving services.

(2) Issue and send to the obligor's employer a conforming income-withholding order or an administrative notice of change of payee, reflecting the redirected payments.

(c) **Certificated records.**—The support enforcement agency of this State receiving redirected payments from another state under a law similar to subsection (b) shall furnish to a requesting party or tribunal of the other state a certified statement by the custodian of the record of the amount and dates of all payments received.

(Dec. 28, 2015, P.L.559, No.94, eff. imd.)

Cross References. Section 7319 is referred to in section 7307 of this title.

CHAPTER 74

ESTABLISHMENT OF SUPPORT ORDER OR DETERMINATION OF PARENTAGE

Sec.
7401. Establishment of support order.
7402. Proceeding to determine parentage.

Chapter Heading. The heading of Chapter 74 was amended December 28, 2015, P.L.559, No.94, effective immediately.

Enactment. Chapter 74 was added April 4, 1996, P.L.58, No.20, effective immediately.

Cross References. Chapter 74 is referred to in sections 7613, 7105, 7210, 77A02 of this title.

§ 7401. Establishment of support order.

(a) **Jurisdiction.**—If a support order entitled to recognition under this part has not been issued, a responding tribunal of this State with personal jurisdiction over the parties may issue a support order if any of the following apply:

(1) The individual seeking the order resides outside this State.

(2) The support enforcement agency seeking the order is located outside this State.

(b) **Temporary orders.**—The tribunal may issue a temporary child support order if the tribunal determines that an order is appropriate and the individual ordered to pay is any of the following:

(1) A presumed father of the child.

(2) Petitioning to have his paternity adjudicated.

(3) Identified as the father of the child through genetic testing.

(4) An alleged father who has declined to submit to genetic testing.

(5) Shown by clear and convincing evidence to be the father of the child.

(6) An acknowledged father as provided by applicable state law.

(7) The mother of the child.

(8) An individual who has been ordered to pay child support in a previous proceeding and the order has not been reversed or vacated.

(c) **Relief.**—Upon finding, after notice and opportunity to be heard, that an obligor owes a duty of support, the tribunal shall issue a support order directed to the obligor and may issue other orders pursuant to section 7305 (relating to duties and powers of responding tribunal).

(Dec. 28, 2015, P.L.559, No.94, eff. imd.)

§ 7402. Proceeding to determine parentage.

A tribunal of this State authorized to determine parentage of a child may serve as a responding tribunal in a proceeding to determine parentage of a child brought under this part or a law or procedure substantially similar to this part.

(Dec. 28, 2015, P.L.559, No.94, eff. imd.)

2015 Amendment. Act 94 added section 7402.

CHAPTER 75
ENFORCEMENT OF SUPPORT ORDER WITHOUT REGISTRATION

Sec.
7501. Employer's receipt of income-withholding order of another state.
7501.1. Employer's compliance with income-withholding order of another state.
7501.2. Compliance with multiple income-withholding orders.
7501.3. Immunity from civil liability.
7501.4. Penalties for noncompliance.
7501.5. Contest by obligor.
7502. Administrative enforcement of orders.

Chapter Heading. The heading of Chapter 75 was amended December 28, 2015, P.L.559, No.94, effective immediately.

Enactment. Chapter 75 was added April 4, 1996, P.L.58, No.20, effective immediately.

Cross References. Chapter 75 is referred to in sections 4348, 7105, 7210, 7613, 77A02 of this title.

§ 7501. Employer's receipt of income-withholding order of another state.

An income-withholding order issued in another state may be sent by or on behalf of the obligee, or by the support enforcement agency, to the person or entity defined as the obligor's employer under section 4302 (relating to definitions) without first filing a petition or comparable pleading or registering the order with a tribunal of this State.
(Dec. 16, 1997, P.L.549, No.58, eff. Jan. 1, 1998; Dec. 28, 2015, P.L.559, No.94, eff. imd.)

2015 Amendment. Act 94 amended this section.

1997 Amendment. Act 58 of 1997 was suspended by Pennsylvania Rule of Civil Procedure No. 1910.50(3), as amended May 31, 2000, insofar as it is inconsistent with Rule No. 1910.20 relating to the availability of remedies for collection of past due and overdue support.

§ 7501.1. Employer's compliance with income-withholding order of another state.

(a) **Copy of order.**—Upon receipt of an income-withholding order, the obligor's employer shall immediately provide a copy of the order to the obligor.

(b) **Treatment of order.**—The employer shall treat an income-withholding order issued in another state which appears regular on its face as if it had been issued by a tribunal of this State.

(c) **Withholding and distribution of funds.**—Except as otherwise provided in subsection (d) and section 7501.2 (relating to compliance with multiple income-withholding orders) the employer shall withhold and distribute the funds as directed in the withholding order by complying with terms of the order which specify:

(1) the duration and amount of periodic payments of current child-support, stated as a sum certain;

(2) the person or agency designated to receive payments and the address to which the payments are to be forwarded;

(3) medical support, whether in the form of periodic cash payments, of a sum certain or order to the obligor to provide health insurance coverage for the child under a policy available through the obligor's employment;

(4) the amount of periodic payments of fees and costs for a support enforcement agency, the issuing tribunal, and the obligee's attorney, stated as sums certain; and

(5) the amount of periodic payments of arrearages and interest on arrearages, stated as sums certain.

(d) Compliance with law of obligor's place of employment.—An employer shall comply with the law of the state of the obligor's principal place of employment for withholding from income with respect to:

(1) the employer's fee for processing an income-withholding order;

(2) the maximum amount permitted to be withheld from the obligor's income; and

(3) the times within which the employer must implement the withholding order and forward the child support payment.

1997 Amendment. Act 58 added this sec.

§ 7501.2. Compliance with multiple income-withholding orders.

If an obligor's employer receives multiple income-withholding orders with respect to the earnings of the same obligor, the employer satisfies the terms of the multiple orders if the employer complies with the law of the state of the obligor's principal place of employment to establish the priorities for withholding and allocating income withheld for multiple child-support obligees.

1997 Amendment. Act 58 added this sec.

§ 7501.3. Immunity from civil liability.

An employer who complies with an income-withholding order issued in another state in accordance with this article is not subject to civil liability to an individual or agency with regard to the employer's withholding of child support from the obligor's income.

1997 Amendment. Act 58 added this sec.

§ 7501.4. Penalties for noncompliance.

An employer that willfully fails to comply with an income-withholding order issued in another state and received for enforcement is subject to the same penalties that may be imposed for noncompliance with an order issued by a tribunal of this State.

(Dec. 16, 1997, P.L.549, No.58, eff. Jan. 1, 1998; Dec. 28, 2015, P.L.559, No.94, eff. imd.)

2015 Amendment. Act 94 amended this section.

1997 Amendment. Act 58 of 1997 was suspended by Pennsylvania Rule of Civil Procedure No. 1910.50(3), as amended May 31, 2000, insofar as it is inconsistent with Rule No. 1910.20 relating to the availability of remedies for collection of past due and overdue support.

§ 7501.5. Contest by obligor.

An obligor may contest the validity or enforcement of an income-withholding order issued in another state and received directly by an employer in this State by registering the order in a tribunal of this State and filing a contest to that order as provided in Chapter 76 (relating to registration, enforcement and modification of support order) or otherwise contesting the order in the same manner as if the order had been issued by a tribunal of this State. The obligor shall give notice of the contest to:

(1) a support enforcement agency providing services to the obligee;

(2) each employer that has directly received an income-withholding order relating to the obligor; and

(3) the person or agency designated to receive payments in the income-withholding order or, if no person or agency is designated, to the obligee.

(Dec. 16, 1997, P.L.549, No.58, eff. Jan. 1, 1998; Dec. 28, 2015, P.L.559, No.94, eff. imd.)

2015 Amendment. Act 94 amended this section.

1997 Amendment. Act 58 of 1997 was suspended by Pennsylvania Rule of Civil Procedure No. 1910.50(3), as amended May 31, 2000, insofar as it is inconsistent with Rule No. 1910.20 relating to the availability of remedies for collection of past due and overdue support.

§ 7502. Administrative enforcement of orders.

(a) **Initiation.**—A party or support enforcement agency seeking to enforce a support order or an income-withholding order, or both, issued in another state or a support order issued by a foreign country may send the documents required for registering the order to a support enforcement agency of this State.

(b) **Procedure.**—Upon receipt of the documents, the support enforcement agency, without initially seeking to register the order, shall consider and, if appropriate, use any administrative procedure authorized by the law of this State to enforce a support order or an income-withholding order, or both. If the obligor does not contest administrative enforcement, the order need not be registered. If the obligor contests the validity or administrative enforcement of the order, the support enforcement agency shall register the order pursuant to this part.

(Dec. 28, 2015, P.L.559, No.94, eff. imd.)

2015 Amendment. Act 94 amended subsec. (a).

CHAPTER 76

REGISTRATION, ENFORCEMENT AND MODIFICATION OF SUPPORT ORDER

Subchapter

A. Registration for Enforcement of Support Order
B. Contest of Validity or Enforcement
C. Registration and Modification of Child Support Order of Another State
D. Registration and Modification of Foreign Child Support Order

Chapter Heading. The heading of Chapter 76 was amended December 28, 2015, P.L.559, No.94, effective immediately.

Enactment. Chapter 76 was added April 4, 1996, P.L.58, No.20, effective immediately.

Cross References. Chapter 76 is referred to in sections 7105, 7207, 7210, 7501.5, 77A02, 77A06, 7313, 8313 of this title.

SUBCHAPTER A

REGISTRATION AND ENFORCEMENT OF SUPPORT ORDER

Sec.

7601. Registration of order for enforcement.
7602. Procedure to register order for enforcement.
7603. Effect of registration for enforcement.
7604. Choice of law.

Subchapter Heading. The heading of Subchapter A was amended December 28, 2015, P.L.559, No.94, effective immediately.

Cross References. Subchapter A is referred to in sections 7609, 7616 of this title.

§ 7601. Registration of order for enforcement.

A support order or an income-withholding order issued in another state or a foreign support order may be registered in this State for enforcement.

(Dec. 28, 2015, P.L.559, No.94, eff. imd.)

2015 Amendment. Act 94 amended this section.

§ 7602. Procedure to register order for enforcement.

(a) **General rule.**—Except as otherwise provided in section 77A06 (relating to registration of convention support order), a support order or income-withholding order of another state or a foreign support order may be registered in this State by sending all of the following records to the appropriate tribunal in this State:

(1) A letter of transmittal to the tribunal requesting registration and enforcement.

(2) Two copies, including one certified copy, of the order to be registered, including any modification of the order.

(3) A sworn statement by the person requesting registration or a certified statement by the custodian of the records showing the amount of any arrearage.

(4) The name of the obligor and, if known:

(i) the obligor's address and Social Security number;

(ii) the name and address of the obligor's employer and any other source of income of the obligor; and

(iii) a description and the location of property of the obligor in this State not exempt from execution.

(5) Except as set forth in section 7312 (relating to nondisclosure of information in exceptional circumstances), the name and address of the obligee and, if applicable, the agency or person to whom support payments are to be remitted.

(b) **Docketing.**—On receipt of a request for registration, the registering tribunal shall file the order as an order of a tribunal of another state or a foreign support order, together with one copy of the documents and information, regardless of their form.

(c) **Simultaneous relief.**—A petition or comparable pleading seeking a remedy that must be affirmatively sought under other law of this State may be filed at the same time as the request for registration or later. The pleading must specify the grounds for the remedy sought.

(d) **Multiple orders.**—If two or more orders are in effect, the person requesting registration shall do all of the following:

(1) Furnish to the tribunal a copy of every support order asserted to be in effect in addition to the documents specified in this section.

(2) Specify the order alleged to be the controlling order, if any.

(3) Specify the amount of consolidated arrears, if any.

(e) **Request for determination.**—A request for a determination of which is the controlling order may be filed separately or with a request for registration and enforcement or for registration and modification. The person requesting registration shall give notice of the request to each party whose rights may be affected by the determination.

(Dec. 28, 2015, P.L.559, No.94, eff. imd.)

Cross References. Section 7602 is referred to in section 77A06 of this title.

§ 7603. Effect of registration for enforcement.

(a) **Procedure.**—A support order or income-withholding order issued in another state or a foreign support order is registered when the order is filed in the registering tribunal of this State.

(b) **Enforcement.**—A registered support order issued in another state or a foreign county is enforceable in the same manner and is subject to the same procedures as an order issued by a tribunal of this State.

(c) **Faith and credit.**—Except as otherwise provided in this chapter, a tribunal of this State shall recognize and enforce but may not modify a registered support order if the issuing tribunal had jurisdiction.

(Dec. 28, 2015, P.L.559, No.94, eff. imd.)

§ 7604. Choice of law.

(a) **General rule.**—Subject to subsection (d), the law of the issuing state or foreign country governs the following:

(1) The nature, extent, amount and duration of current payments under a registered support order.

(2) The computation and payment of arrearages and accrual of interest on the arrearages under the support order.

(3) The existence and satisfaction of other obligations under the support order.

(b) **Proceeding for arrearages.**—In a proceeding for arrearages under a registered support order, the statute of limitation under the laws of this State or of the issuing state or foreign country, whichever is longer, applies.

(c) **Procedures and remedies.**—A responding tribunal of this State shall apply the procedures and remedies of this State to enforce current support and collect arrearages and interest due on a support order of another state or a foreign country registered in this State.

(d) Controlling order.—After a tribunal of this State or another state determines which is the controlling order and issues an order consolidating arrearages, if any, a tribunal of this State shall prospectively apply the law of the state or foreign country issuing the controlling order, including the law on interest on arrearages, on current and future support and on consolidated arrearages.

(Dec. 28, 2015, P.L.559, No.94, eff. imd.)

Cross References. Section 7604 is referred to in section 7607 of this title.

SUBCHAPTER B
CONTEST OF VALIDITY OR ENFORCEMENT

Sec.
7605. Notice of registration of order.
7606. Procedure to contest validity or enforcement of registered support order.
7607. Contest of registration or enforcement.
7608. Confirmed order.

Cross References. Subchapter B is referred to in section 7609, 7616 of this title.

§ 7605. Notice of registration of order.

(a) **Requirement.**—When a support order or income-withholding order issued in another state or a foreign support order is registered, the registering tribunal of this State shall notify the nonregistering party. The notice must be accompanied by a copy of the registered order and the documents and relevant information accompanying the order.

(b) **Contents.**—The notice must inform the nonregistering party of all of the following:

(1) That a registered support order is enforceable as of the date of registration in the same manner as an order issued by a tribunal of this State.

(2) That a hearing to contest the validity or enforcement of the registered order must be requested within 20 days after notice unless the registered order is under section 77A07 (relating to contest of registered convention support order).

(3) That failure to contest the validity or enforcement of the registered order in a timely manner will result in confirmation of the order and enforcement of the order and the alleged arrearages.

(4) The amount of any alleged arrearages.

(b.1) **Multiple orders.**—If the registering party asserts that two or more orders are in effect, a notice must also do all the following:

(1) Identify the two or more orders and order alleged by the registering party to be the controlling order and the consolidated arrearages, if any.

(2) Notify the nonregistering party of the right to a determination of which is the controlling order.

(3) State that the procedure under subsection (b) applies to the determination of which is the controlling order.

(4) State that the failure to contest the validity or enforcement of the order alleged to be the controlling order in a timely manner may result in confirmation that the order is the controlling order.

(c) **Employer.**—Upon registration of an income-withholding order for enforcement, the support enforcement agency or the registering tribunal shall notify the obligor's employer pursuant to section 4348 (relating to attachment of income).

(Dec. 16, 1997, P.L.549, No.58, eff. Jan. 1, 1998; Dec. 28, 2015, P.L.559, No.94, eff. imd.)

Cross References. Section 7605 is referred to in section 7606 of this title.

2015 Amendment. Act 94 amended this section.

1997 Amendment. Act 58 of 1997 was suspended by Pennsylvania Rule of Civil Procedure No. 1910.50(3), as amended May 31, 2000, insofar as it is inconsistent with Rule No. 1910.20 relating to the availability of remedies for collection of past due and overdue support.

§ 7606. Procedure to contest validity or enforcement of registered support order.

(a) Action.—A nonregistering party seeking to contest the validity or enforcement of a registered support order in this State must request a hearing within the time required under section 7605 (relating to notice of registration of order). The nonregistering party may seek to vacate the registration, to assert any defense to an allegation of noncompliance with the registered order or to contest the remedies being sought or the amount of any alleged arrearages pursuant to section 7607 (relating to contest of registration or enforcement).

(b) Inaction.—If the nonregistering party fails to contest the validity or enforcement of the registered support order in a timely manner, the order is confirmed by operation of law.

(c) Hearing.—If a nonregistering party requests a hearing to contest the validity or enforcement of the registered support order, the registering tribunal shall schedule the matter for hearing and give notice to the parties of the date, time and place of the hearing.

(Dec. 16, 1997, P.L.549, No.58, eff. Jan. 1, 1998; Dec. 28, 2015, P.L.559, No.94, eff. imd.)

2015 Amendment. Act 94 amended this section.

1997 Amendment. Act 58 of 1997 was suspended by Pennsylvania Rule of Civil Procedure No. 1910.50(3), as amended May 31, 2000, insofar as it is inconsistent with Rule No. 1910.20 relating to the availability of remedies for collection of past due and overdue support.

§ 7607. Contest of registration or enforcement.

(a) Defenses.—A party contesting the validity or enforcement of a registered support order or seeking to vacate the registration has the burden of proving any of the following defenses:

(1) The issuing tribunal lacked personal jurisdiction over the contesting party.

(2) The order was obtained by fraud.

(3) The order has been vacated, suspended or modified by a later order.

(4) The issuing tribunal has stayed the order pending appeal.

(5) There is a defense under the law of this State to the remedy sought.

(6) Full or partial payment has been made.

(7) The statute of limitation under section 7604 (relating to choice of law) precludes enforcement of some or all of the arrearages.

(8) The alleged controlling order is not the controlling order.

(b) Relief.—If a party presents evidence establishing a full or partial defense under subsection (a), a tribunal may stay enforcement of a registered support order, continue the proceeding to permit production of additional relevant evidence and issue other appropriate orders. An uncontested portion of the registered support order may be enforced by all remedies available under the law of this State.

(c) Affirmance.—If the contesting party does not establish a defense under subsection (a) to the validity or enforcement of a registered support order, the registering tribunal shall issue an order confirming the order.

(Dec. 28, 2015, P.L.559, No.94, eff. imd.)

Cross References. Section 7607 is referred to in sections 7606, 77A07 of this title.

§ 7608. Confirmed order.

Confirmation of a registered support order, whether by operation of law or after notice and hearing, precludes further contest of the order with respect to any matter that could have been asserted at the time of registration.

(Dec. 28, 2015, P.L.559, No.94, eff. imd.)

Cross References. Section 7608 is referred to in section 77A07 of this title.

SUBCHAPTER C
REGISTRATION AND MODIFICATION OF CHILD SUPPORT ORDER OF ANOTHER STATE

Sec.
7609. Procedure to register child support order of another state for modification.
7610. Effect of registration for modification.
7611. Modification of child support order of another state.
7612. Recognition of order modified in another state.
7613. Jurisdiction to modify child support order of another state when individual parties reside in this State.
7614. Notice to issuing tribunal of modification.

Subchapter Heading. The heading of Subchapter C was amended December 28, 2015, P.L.559, No.94, effective immediately.

§ 7609. Procedure to register child support order of another state for modification.

A party or support enforcement agency seeking to modify or to modify and enforce a child support order issued in another state must register that order in this State in the same manner provided in Subchapter A (relating to registration for enforcement of support order) or B (relating to contest of validity or enforcement) if the order has not been registered. A petition for modification may be filed at the same time as a request for registration or later. The pleading must specify the grounds for modification.

(Dec. 28, 2015, P.L.559, No.94, eff. imd.)

§ 7610. Effect of registration for modification.

A tribunal of this State may enforce a child support order of another state registered for purposes of modification in the same manner as if the order had been issued by a tribunal of this State, but the registered support order may be modified only if the requirements of section 7611 (relating to modification of child support order of another state) or 7613 (relating to jurisdiction to modify child support order of another state when individual parties reside in this State) have been met.

(Dec. 28, 2015, P.L.559, No.94, eff. imd.)

§ 7611. Modification of child support order of another state.

(a) Authority.—After a child support order issued in another state has been registered in this State, the responding tribunal of this State may modify that order, upon petition, only if section 7613 (relating to jurisdiction to modify child support order of another state when individual parties reside in this State) does not apply and after notice and hearing it finds one of the following:

(1) The following requirements are met:

(i) the child, the individual obligee and the obligor do not reside in the issuing state;

(ii) a petitioner who is a nonresident of this State seeks modification; and

(iii) the respondent is subject to the personal jurisdiction of the tribunal of this State.

(2) This State is the residence of the child, or a party who is an individual is subject to the personal jurisdiction of the tribunal of this State; and all of the parties who are individuals have filed consents in a record in the issuing tribunal for a tribunal of this State to modify the support order and assume continuing, exclusive jurisdiction over the order.

(b) **General rule.**—Modification of a registered child support order is subject to the same requirements, procedures and defenses that apply to the modification of an order issued by a tribunal of this State, and the order may be enforced and satisfied in the same manner.

(c) **Restriction.**—A tribunal of this State may not modify any aspect of a child support order that may not be modified under the law of the issuing state, including the duration of the obligation of support. If two or more tribunals have issued child support orders for the same obligor and child, the order that controls and must be so recognized under section 7207 (relating to determination of controlling child support order) establishes the aspects of the support order which are not modifiable.

(c.1) **Modification.**—In a proceeding to modify a child support order, the law of the state that is determined to have issued the initial controlling order governs the duration of the obligation of support. The obligor's fulfillment of the duty of support established by that order precludes imposition of a further obligation of support by a tribunal of this State.

(d) **Continuing, exclusive jurisdiction.**—On issuance of an order by a tribunal of this State modifying a child support order issued in another state, a tribunal of this State becomes the tribunal of continuing, exclusive jurisdiction.

(e) **Filing.**—(Deleted by amendment).

(f) **Retained jurisdiction.**—Notwithstanding subsection (a), (b), (c) or (d) or section 7201(b) (relating to bases for jurisdiction over nonresident), a tribunal of this State retains jurisdiction to modify an order issued by a tribunal of this State if the following are met:

(1) One party resides in another state.

(2) The other party resides outside the United States.

(Dec. 28, 2015, P.L.559, No.94, eff. imd.)

Cross References. Section 7611 is referred to in sections 7201, 7615 of this title.

§ 7612. Recognition of order modified in another state.

If a child support order issued by a tribunal of this State is modified by a tribunal of another state which assumed jurisdiction under a law substantially similar to this part, all of the following are available to a tribunal of this State:

(1) A tribunal may enforce the order that was modified only as to arrears and interest accruing before the modification.

(2) (Deleted by amendment).

(3) A tribunal may provide appropriate relief for violations of that order which occurred before the effective date of the modification.

(4) A tribunal shall recognize the modifying order of the other state upon registration for the purpose of enforcement.

(Dec. 28, 2015, P.L.559, No.94, eff. imd.)

§ 7613. Jurisdiction to modify child support order of another state when individual parties reside in this State.

(a) **General rule.**—If all of the parties who are individuals reside in this State and the child does not reside in the issuing state, a tribunal of this State has jurisdiction to enforce and to modify the issuing state's child support order in a proceeding to register that order.

(b) Applicable law.—A tribunal of this State exercising jurisdiction under this section shall apply the provisions of Chapters 71 (relating to general provisions) and 72 (relating to jurisdiction), this Chapter and the procedural and substantive law of this State to the proceeding for enforcement or modification. Chapters 73 (relating to civil provisions of general application), 74 (relating to establishment of support order or determination of parentage), 75 (relating to enforcement of support order without registration), 77A (relating to support proceeding under convention) and 78 (relating to interstate rendition) do not apply.

(Dec. 28, 2015, P.L.559, No.94, eff. imd.)

Cross References. Section 7613 is referred to in section 7610 of this title.

§ 7614. Notice to issuing tribunal of modification.

Within 30 days after issuance of a modified child support order, the party obtaining the modification shall file a certified copy of the order with the issuing tribunal that had continuing, exclusive jurisdiction over the earlier order, and in each tribunal in which the party knows the earlier order had been registered. A party who obtains the order and fails to file a certified copy is subject to appropriate sanctions by a tribunal in which the issue of failure to file arises. The failure to file does not affect the validity or enforceability of the modified order of the new tribunal having continuing, exclusive jurisdiction.

SUBCHAPTER D
REGISTRATION AND MODIFICATION OF FOREIGN CHILD SUPPORT ORDER

Sec.
7615. Jurisdiction to modify child support order of a foreign country.
7616. Procedure to register child support order of a foreign country for modification.

Enactment. Subchapter D was added December 28, 2015, P.L.559, No.94, effective immediately.

§ 7615. Jurisdiction to modify child support order of a foreign country.

(a) Jurisdiction.—Except as otherwise provided under section 77A11 (relating to modification of convention child support order), if a foreign country lacks or refuses to exercise jurisdiction to modify a child support order issued by the foreign country under the foreign country's laws, a tribunal of this State may assume jurisdiction to modify the child support order and bind all individuals subject to the personal jurisdiction of the tribunal whether the consent to modification of a child support order otherwise required of the individual under section 7611 (relating to modification of child support order of another state) has been given or whether the individual seeking modification is a resident of this State or of a foreign country.

(b) Controlling order.—An order issued by a tribunal of this State modifying a foreign child support order under this section is the controlling order.

Cross References. Section 7615 is referred to in section 7201 of this title.

§ 7616. Procedure to register child support order of a foreign country for modification.

A party or support enforcement agency seeking to modify or to modify and enforce a foreign child support order not under the convention may register that order in this State under Subchapter A (relating to registration for enforcement of support order) or B (relating to contest of validity or enforcement) if the order has not been registered. A petition for modification may be filed at the same time as a request for registration or at another time. The petition must specify the grounds for modification.

CHAPTER 77

DETERMINATION OF PARENTAGE
(REPEALED)

2015 Repeal. Chapter 77 (§ 7701) was added April 4, 1996, P.L.58, No.20, and repealed December 28, 2015, P.L.559, No.94, effective immediately.

§ 7701. Proceeding to determine parentage (Repealed).

2015 Repeal. Section 7701 was repealed December 28, 2015, P.L.559, No.94, effective immediately.

CHAPTER 77A

SUPPORT PROCEEDING UNDER CONVENTION

Sec.
77A01. Definitions.
77A02. Applicability.
77A03. Relationship of department to United States central authority.
77A04. Initiation by department of support proceeding under convention.
77A05. Direct request.
77A06. Registration of convention support order.
77A07. Contest of registered convention support order.
77A08. Recognition and enforcement of registered convention support order.
77A09. Partial enforcement.
77A10. Foreign support agreement.
77A11. Modification of convention child support order.
77A12. Personal information.
77A13. Record in original language.

Enactment. Chapter 77A was added December 28, 2015, P.L.559, No.94, effective immediately.

Cross References. Chapter 77A is referred to in sections 7101.1, 7105, 7609, 7613, 7616 of this title.

§ 77A01. Definitions.

The following words and phrases when used in this chapter shall have the meanings given to them in this section unless the context clearly indicates otherwise:

"Application." A request under the convention by an obligee or obligor, or on behalf of a child, made through a central authority for assistance from another central authority.

"Central authority." The entity designated by the United States or a foreign country defined in paragraph (4) of the definition of "foreign country" in section 7101.1 (relating to definitions) to perform the functions specified in the convention.

"Convention support order." A support order of a tribunal of a foreign country defined in paragraph (4) of the definition of "foreign country" in section 7101.1.

"Direct request." A petition filed by an individual in a tribunal of this State in a proceeding involving an obligee, obligor or child residing outside the United States.

"Foreign central authority." The entity designated by a foreign country defined in paragraph (4) of the definition of "foreign country" in section 7101.1 to perform the functions specified in the convention.

"Foreign support agreement."

(1) An agreement for support in a record that:
  (i) is enforceable as a support order in the country of origin;
  (ii) has been:

(A) formally prepared or registered as an authentic instrument by a foreign tribunal; or

(B) authenticated by or concluded, registered, or filed with a foreign tribunal; and

(iii) may be reviewed and modified by a foreign tribunal.

(2) The term includes a maintenance arrangement or authentic instrument under the convention.

"United States central authority." The Secretary of the United States Department of Health and Human Services.

§ 77A02. Applicability.

This chapter applies only to a support proceeding under the convention. In a proceeding, if a provision of this chapter is inconsistent with Chapter 71 (relating to general provisions), 72 (relating to jurisdiction), 73 (relating to civil provisions of general application), 74 (relating to establishment of support order or determination of parentage), 75 (relating to enforcement of support order without registration) or 76 (relating to registration, enforcement and modification of support order), this chapter controls.

§ 77A03. Relationship of department to United States central authority.

The department is recognized as the agency designated by the United States central authority to perform specific functions under the convention.

§ 77A04. Initiation by department of support proceeding under convention.

(a) Duties.—In a support proceeding under this chapter, the department shall do all of the following:

(1) Transmit and receive applications.

(2) Initiate or facilitate the institution of a proceeding regarding an application in a tribunal of this State.

(b) Obligee support proceedings.—All of the following support proceedings are available to an obligee under the convention:

(1) Recognition or recognition and enforcement of a foreign support order.

(2) Enforcement of a support order issued or recognized in this State.

(3) Establishment of a support order if there is no existing order, including, if necessary, determination of parentage of a child.

(4) Establishment of a support order if recognition of a foreign support order is refused under section 77A08(b)(2), (4) or (9) (relating to recognition and enforcement of registered convention support order).

(5) Modification of a support order of a tribunal of this State.

(6) Modification of a support order of a tribunal of another state or a foreign country.

(c) Obligor support proceedings.—All of the following support proceedings are available under the convention to an obligor against which there is an existing support order:

(1) Recognition of an order suspending or limiting enforcement of an existing support order of a tribunal of this State.

(2) Modification of a support order of a tribunal of this State.

(3) Modification of a support order of a tribunal of another state or a foreign country.

(d) Prohibition.—A tribunal of this State may not require security, bond or deposit, however described, to guarantee the payment of costs and expenses in proceedings under the convention.

Cross References. Section 77A04 is referred to in section 77A08 of this title.

§ 77A05. Direct request.

(a) General rule.—A petitioner may file a direct request seeking:

(1) Establishment or modification of a support order or determination of parentage of a child. In the proceeding, the determination of parentage of a child under the law of this State applies.

(2) Recognition and enforcement of a support order or support agreement. In the proceeding, sections 77A06 (relating to registration of convention support order), 77A07 (relating to contest of registered convention support order), 77A08 (relating to recognition and enforcement of registered convention support order), 77A09 (relating to partial enforcement), 77A10 (relating to foreign support agreement), 77A11 (relating to modification of convention child support order), 77A12 (relating to personal information) and 77A13 (relating to record in original language) apply.

(b) Requirements.—In a direct request for recognition and enforcement of a convention support order or foreign support agreement, the following apply:

(1) A security, bond or deposit may not be required to guarantee the payment of costs and expenses.

(2) An obligee or obligor that, in the issuing country, has benefited from free legal assistance is entitled to benefit, at least to the same extent, from any free legal assistance provided for by the law of this State under the same circumstances.

(c) (Reserved).

(d) Assistance.—A petitioner filing a direct request is not entitled to assistance from the department.

(e) Application of other laws.—This chapter does not prevent the application of laws of this State that provide simplified, more expeditious rules regarding a direct request for recognition and enforcement of a foreign support order or foreign support agreement.

§ 77A06. Registration of convention support order.

(a) Registration required.—Except as otherwise provided in this chapter, a party who is an individual or a support enforcement agency seeking recognition of a convention support order shall register the order in this State as provided in Chapter 76 (relating to registration, enforcement and modification of support order).

(b) Documentation required.—Notwithstanding sections 7311 (relating to pleadings and accompanying documents) and 7602(a) (relating to procedure to register order for enforcement), a request for registration of a convention support order must be accompanied by the following:

(1) A complete text of the support order or an abstract of the support order prepared by the issuing foreign tribunal, which may be in the form recommended by the Hague Conference on Private International Law.

(2) A record stating that the support order is enforceable in the issuing country.

(3) If the respondent did not appear and was not represented in the proceedings in the issuing country, a record attesting, as appropriate, either that the respondent had proper notice of the proceedings and an opportunity to be heard or that the respondent had proper notice of the support order and an opportunity to be heard in a challenge or appeal on fact or law before a tribunal.

(4) A record showing the amount of arrears, if any, and the date the amount was calculated.

(5) A record showing a requirement for automatic adjustment of the amount of support, if any, and the information necessary to make the appropriate calculations.

(6) If necessary, a record showing the extent to which the applicant received free legal assistance in the issuing country.

(c) Recognition and partial enforcement.—A request for registration of a convention support order may seek recognition and partial enforcement of the order.

(d) Vacating registration.—A tribunal of this State may vacate the registration of a convention support order without the filing of a contest under section 77A07 (relating to contest of registered convention support order) only if, acting on its own motion, the tribunal finds that recognition and enforcement of the order would be manifestly incompatible with public policy.

(e) Notification.—The tribunal shall promptly notify the parties of the registration or the order vacating the registration of a convention support order.

Cross References. Section 77A06 is referred to in sections 7602, 77A05, 77A08 of this title.

§ 77A07. Contest of registered convention support order.

(a) Applicability.—Except as otherwise provided in this chapter, sections 7605 (relating to notice of registration of order), 7606 (relating to procedure to contest validity or enforcement of registered support order), 7607 (relating to contest of registration or enforcement) and 7608 (relating to confirmed order) apply to a contest of a registered convention support order.

(b) Time.—A party contesting a registered convention support order must file a contest:

(1) Not later than 30 days after notice of the registration if the contesting party resides in the United States.

(2) Not later than 60 days after notice of the registration if the contesting party does not reside in the United States.

(c) Failure to contest.—If the nonregistering party fails to contest the registered convention support order by the time specified in subsection (b), the order is enforceable.

(d) Basis of contest.—A contest of a registered convention support order may be based only on grounds set forth in section 77A08 (relating to recognition and enforcement of registered convention support order). The contesting party shall bear the burden of proof.

(e) Tribunal duties.—In a contest of a registered convention support order, a tribunal of this State:

(1) is bound by the findings of fact on which the foreign tribunal based its jurisdiction; and

(2) may not review the merits of the order.

(f) Notification of decision.—A tribunal of this State deciding a contest of a registered convention support order shall promptly notify the parties of its decision.

(g) Appeals.—A challenge or appeal does not stay the enforcement of a convention support order unless there are exceptional circumstances.

Cross References. Section 77A07 is referred to in sections 7605, 77A05, 77A06 of this title.

§ 77A08. Recognition and enforcement of registered convention support order.

(a) General rule.—Except as otherwise provided in subsection (b), a tribunal of this State shall recognize and enforce a registered convention support order.

(b) Refusal of recognition or enforcement.—The following grounds are the only grounds on which a tribunal of this State may refuse recognition and enforcement of a registered convention support order:

(1) Recognition and enforcement of the order is manifestly incompatible with public policy, including the failure of the issuing tribunal to observe minimum standards of due process, which include notice and an opportunity to be heard.

(2) The issuing tribunal lacked personal jurisdiction consistent with section 7201 (relating to bases for jurisdiction over nonresident).

(3) The order is not enforceable in the issuing country.

(4) The order was obtained by fraud in connection with a matter of procedure.

(5) A record transmitted in accordance with section 77A06 (relating to registration of convention support order) lacks authenticity or integrity.

(6) A proceeding between the same parties and having the same purpose is pending before a tribunal of this State and that proceeding was the first to be filed.

(7) The order is incompatible with a more recent support order involving the same parties and having the same purpose if the more recent support order is entitled to recognition and enforcement under this part in this State.

(8) Payment, to the extent alleged arrears have been paid in whole or in part.

(9) In a case in which the respondent did not appear and was not represented in the proceeding in the issuing foreign country:

(i) if the law of that country provides for prior notice of proceedings, the respondent did not have proper notice of the proceedings and an opportunity to be heard; or

(ii) if the law of that country does not provide for prior notice of the proceedings, the respondent did not have proper notice of the order and an opportunity to be heard in a challenge or appeal on fact or law before a tribunal.

(10) The order was made in violation of section 77A11 (relating to modification of convention child support order).

(c) Procedure in certain situations.—If a tribunal of this State does not recognize a convention support order under subsection (b)(2), (4) or (9):

(1) the tribunal may not dismiss the proceeding without allowing a reasonable time for a party to request the establishment of a new convention support order; and

(2) the department shall take all appropriate measures to request a child support order for the obligee if the application for recognition and enforcement was received under section 77A04 (relating to initiation by department of support proceeding under convention).

Cross References. Section 77A08 is referred to in sections 77A04, 77A05, 77A07, 77A11 of this title.

§ 77A09. Partial enforcement.

If a tribunal of this State does not recognize and enforce a convention support order in the order's entirety, the tribunal shall enforce any severable part of the order. An application or direct request may seek recognition and partial enforcement of a convention support order.

Cross References. Section 77A09 is referred to in section 77A05 of this title.

§ 77A10. Foreign support agreement.

(a) Recognition and enforcement.—Except as otherwise provided in subsections (c) and (d), a tribunal of this State shall recognize and enforce a foreign support agreement registered in this State.

(b) Documentation required.—An application or direct request for recognition and enforcement of a foreign support agreement must be accompanied by the following:

(1) A complete text of the foreign support agreement.

(2) A record stating that the foreign support agreement is enforceable as an order of support in the issuing country.

(c) Vacating registration.—A tribunal of this State may vacate the registration of a foreign support agreement only if, acting on its own motion, the tribunal finds that recognition and enforcement would be manifestly incompatible with public policy.

(d) Contested agreements.—In a contest of a foreign support agreement, a tribunal of this State may refuse recognition and enforcement of the agreement if it finds any of the following:

(1) Recognition and enforcement of the agreement is manifestly incompatible with public policy.

(2) The agreement was obtained by fraud or falsification.

(3) The agreement is incompatible with a support order involving the same parties and having the same purpose in this State, another state or a foreign country if the support order is entitled to recognition and enforcement under this part in this State.

(4) The record submitted under subsection (b) lacks authenticity or integrity.

(e) Suspension during appeal.—A proceeding for recognition and enforcement of a foreign support agreement must be suspended during the pendency of a challenge to or appeal of the agreement before a tribunal of another state or a foreign country.

Cross References. Section 77A10 is referred to in section 77A05 of this title.

§ 77A11. Modification of convention child support order.

(a) General rule.—A tribunal of this State may not modify a convention child support order if the obligee remains a resident of the foreign country where the support order was issued unless one of the following occurs:

(1) The obligee submits to the jurisdiction of a tribunal of this State, either expressly or by defending on the merits of the case without objecting to the jurisdiction at the first available opportunity.

(2) The foreign tribunal lacks or refuses to exercise jurisdiction to modify the support order or issue a new support order.

(b) Order not recognized.—If a tribunal of this State does not modify a convention child support order because the order is not recognized in this State, section 77A08(c) (relating to recognition and enforcement of registered convention support order) applies.

Cross References. Section 77A11 is referred to in sections 7615, 77A05, 77A08 of this title.

§ 77A12. Personal information.

Personal information gathered or transmitted under this chapter may be used only for the purposes for which the information was gathered or transmitted.

Cross References. Section 77A12 is referred to in section 77A05 of this title.

§ 77A13. Record in original language.

A record filed with a tribunal of this State under this part must be in the original language and, if not in English, must be accompanied by an English translation.

Cross References. Section 77A13 is referred to in section 77A05 of this title.

CHAPTER 78

INTERSTATE RENDITION

Sec.
7801. Grounds for rendition.
7802. Conditions of rendition.

Enactment. Chapter 78 was added April 4, 1996, P.L.58, No.20, effective immediately.

Cross References. Chapter 78 is referred to in section 7613 of this title.

§ 7801. Grounds for rendition.

(a) **Definition of Governor.**—For purposes of this chapter, "Governor" includes an individual performing the functions of Governor or the executive authority of a state covered by this part.

(b) **Authority of Governor.**—The Governor of this State may do either of the following:

(1) Demand that the Governor of another state surrender an individual found in the other state who is charged criminally in this State with having failed to provide for the support of an obligee.

(2) On the demand by the Governor of another state, surrender an individual found in this State who is charged criminally in the other state with having failed to provide for the support of an obligee.

(c) **Extended extradition.**—A provision for extradition of individuals not inconsistent with this part applies to the demand even if the individual whose surrender is demanded was not in the demanding state when the crime was allegedly committed and has not fled from the demanding state.

(Dec. 28, 2015, P.L.559, No.94, eff. imd.)

2015 Amendment. Act 94 amended subsec. (b).

§ 7802. Conditions of rendition.

(a) **Extradition to this State.**—Before making demand that the Governor of another state surrender an individual charged criminally in this State with having failed to provide for the support of an obligee, the Governor of this State may require a prosecutor of this State to demonstrate that at least 60 days previously the obligee had initiated proceedings for support pursuant to this part or that the proceeding would be of no avail.

(b) **Extradition from this State.**—If under this part or a law substantially similar to this part the Governor of another state makes a demand that the Governor of this State surrender an individual charged criminally in that state with having failed to provide for the support of a child or other individual to whom a duty of support is owed, the Governor may require a prosecutor to investigate the demand and report whether a proceeding for support has been initiated or would be effective. If it appears that a proceeding would be effective but has not been initiated, the Governor may delay honoring the demand for a reasonable time to permit the initiation of a proceeding.

(c) **Declining to honor demand.**—If a proceeding for support has been initiated and the individual whose rendition is demanded prevails, the Governor may decline to honor the demand. If the petitioner prevails and the individual whose rendition is demanded is subject to a support order, the Governor may decline to honor the demand if the individual is complying with the support order.

(Dec. 28, 2015, P.L.559, No.94, eff. imd.)

2015 Amendment. Act 94 amended subsec. (b).

CHAPTER 79
MISCELLANEOUS PROVISIONS

Sec.

7901. Uniformity of application and construction.

Enactment. Chapter 79 was added April 4, 1996, P.L.58, No.20, effective immediately.

§ 7901. Uniformity of application and construction.

In applying and construing this uniform part, consideration must be given to the need to promote uniformity of the law with respect to the law's subject matter among states which enact this uniform law.

(Dec. 28, 2015, P.L.559, No.94, eff. imd.)

§ 7902. Transitional provision.

This part applies to proceedings beginning on or after the effective date of this section to do any of the following:

(1) Establish a support order.

(2) Determine parentage of a child.

(3) Register, recognize, enforce or modify a prior support order, determination or agreement, whenever issued or entered.

(Dec. 28, 2015, P.L.559, No.94, eff. imd.)

2015 Amendment. Act 94 added section 7902.

§ 7903. Severability.

If any provision of this part or its application to any person or circumstance is held invalid, the invalidity does not affect other provisions or application of this part which can be given effect without the invalid provision or application, and to this end the provisions of this part are severable.

(Dec. 28, 2015, P.L.559, No.94, eff. imd.)

2015 Amendment. Act 94 added section 7903.

PART VIII-A
INTRASTATE FAMILY SUPPORT

Sec.
8101. Short title of part and definitions.
8102. Scope.
8103. Remedies cumulative.

Enactment. Part VIII-A was added April 4, 1996, P.L.58, No.20, effective immediately.

Applicability. Section 7 of Act 20 of 1996 provided that Act 20 shall apply to actions initiated on or after the effective date of Act 20.

CHAPTER 81
GENERAL PROVISIONS

Enactment. Chapter 81 was added April 4, 1996, P.L.58, No.20, effective immediately.

§ 8101. Short title of part and definitions.

(a) **Short title of part.**—This part shall be known and may be cited as the Intrastate Family Support Act.

(b) **Definitions.**—Subject to additional definitions contained in subsequent provisions of this part which are applicable to specific provisions of this part, the following words and phrases when used in this part shall have the meanings given to them in this section unless the context clearly indicates otherwise:

"**Child.**" An individual, whether over or under the age of majority, who is or is alleged to be owed a duty of support by the individual's parent or who is or is alleged to be the beneficiary of a support order directed to the parent.

"**Child support order.**" A support order for a child, including a child who has attained the age of majority.

"**Department.**" The Department of Public Welfare of the Commonwealth.

"**Duty of support.**" An obligation imposed or imposable by law to provide support for a child, spouse or former spouse. The term includes an unsatisfied obligation to provide support.

"**Income.**" The term includes earnings or other periodic entitlements to money from any source and any other property subject to withholding for support under the laws of this Commonwealth.

"**Income-withholding order.**" An order or other legal process directed to an obligor's employer or other debtor, in accordance with section 4348 (relating to attachment of income) to withhold support from the income of the obligor.

"**Initiating county.**" A county in which a proceeding under this part or a law substantially similar to this part, the Uniform Reciprocal Enforcement of Support Act or the Revised Uniform Reciprocal Enforcement of Support Act is filed for forwarding to a responding county.

"**Initiating tribunal.**" The authorized tribunal in an initiating county.

"**Issuing county.**" The county in which a tribunal issues a support order or renders a judgment determining parentage.

"**Issuing tribunal.**" The tribunal that issues a support order or renders a judgment determining parentage.

"**Law.**" The term includes decisional and statutory law and rules and regulations having the force of law.

"**Obligee.**" Any of the following:

(1) An individual to whom a duty of support is or is alleged to be owed or in whose favor a support order has been issued or a judgment determining parentage has been rendered.

(2) A political subdivision to which the rights under a duty of support or support order have been assigned or which has independent claims based on financial assistance provided to an individual obligee.

(3) An individual seeking a judgment determining parentage of the individual's child.

(4) The Department of Public Welfare.

"Obligor." An individual or the estate of a decedent that:

(1) owes or is alleged to owe a duty of support;

(2) is alleged but has not been adjudicated to be a parent of a child; or

(3) is liable under a support order.

"Register." To record a support order or judgment determining parentage in the office designated by a court of common pleas.

"Registering tribunal." A tribunal in which a support order is registered.

"Responding county." A county to which a proceeding is forwarded under this part.

"Responding tribunal." The authorized tribunal in a responding county.

"Secretary." The Secretary of Public Welfare of the Commonwealth.

"Spousal-support order." A support order for a spouse or former spouse of the obligor.

"Support enforcement agency." The department, a domestic relations section of a tribunal, a public official or a public agency authorized to seek:

(1) enforcement of support orders or laws relating to the duty of support;

(2) establishment or modification of child support;

(3) determination of parentage; or

(4) location of obligors or their assets.

"Support order." A judgment, decree or order, whether temporary, final or subject to modification, whether incidental to a pending divorce, for the benefit of a child, a spouse or a former spouse, which provides for monetary support, health care, arrearages or reimbursement. The term includes related costs and fees, interest, income withholding, attorney fees and other relief.

"Title IV-D attorney." The official in the appropriate county who, by statute, contract or appointment, has the duty to represent obligees in support actions brought in the county.

"Tribunal." A court of common pleas.

1997 Amendment. Act 58 amended the def. of "income-withholding order."

§ 8102. Scope.

This part applies to actions between parties from different counties in this Commonwealth. This part does not apply to actions under the Part VIII (relating to uniform interstate family support).

§ 8103. Remedies cumulative.

Remedies provided by this part are cumulative and do not affect the availability of remedies under other law. The procedures established by Pa.R.C.P. No. 1910.1 et seq. (relating to action for support) shall be used in preference to the procedures of this part unless any of the following applies:

(1) The tribunal or domestic relations section determines that use of this part is necessary for the effective establishment or enforcement of support because any of the following apply:

(i) After diligent effort, the obligee is unable to effect service upon the obligor.

(ii) It is not possible to enter an order against the obligor in the county where the obligee resides.

(iii) The obligor is already subject to an order for support in the case at bar or in any other case.

(2) The obligee requests proceedings under this part.

CHAPTER 82
JURISDICTION

Sec.
8201. Continuing, exclusive jurisdiction.
8202. Recognition of support orders.
8203. Credit for payments.

Enactment. Chapter 82 was added April 4, 1996, P.L.58, No.20, effective immediately.

§ 8201. Continuing, exclusive jurisdiction.

(a) **Extent.**—A tribunal issuing a support order has continuing, exclusive jurisdiction over a support order unless otherwise provided by Part VIII (relating to uniform interstate family support) or this part.

(b) **Faith and credit.**—A tribunal shall recognize the continuing, exclusive jurisdiction of another tribunal which has issued a support order.

§ 8202. Recognition of support orders.

(a) **Principles.**—If a proceeding is brought under this part and more than one support order has been issued in this Commonwealth with regard to the same obligation, a tribunal shall apply the following rules in determining which order to recognize for purposes of continuing, exclusive jurisdiction:

(1) If two or more tribunals have issued support orders for the same obligation and only one of the tribunals would have continuing, exclusive jurisdiction under this part, the order of that tribunal must be recognized.

(2) If two or more tribunals have issued support orders for the same obligation and more than one of the tribunals would have continuing, exclusive jurisdiction under this part, an order issued by a tribunal in the county where the obligee resides must be recognized, but, if an order has not been issued in the county where the obligee resides, the order most recently issued must be recognized.

(3) If two or more tribunals have issued support orders for the same obligation and none of the tribunals would have continuing, exclusive jurisdiction under this part, the tribunal may issue a support order which must be recognized.

(b) **Result.**—The tribunal that has issued an order recognized under subsection (a) is the tribunal having continuing, exclusive jurisdiction.

§ 8203. Credit for payments.

Amounts collected and credited for a particular period pursuant to a support order issued by one tribunal must be credited against the amounts accruing or accrued for the same period under a support order issued by another tribunal.

CHAPTER 83
CIVIL PROVISIONS OF GENERAL APPLICATION

Sec.
8301. Proceedings under this part.
8302. Action by minor parent.
8303. Duties of initiating tribunal.
8304. Duties and powers of responding tribunala.
8305. Inappropriate tribunal.
8306. Duties of support enforcement agency.
8307. Supervisory duty.
8308. Private counsel.
8309. Nondisclosure of information in exceptional circumstances.
8310. Nonparentage not a defense.
8311. Special rules of evidence and procedure.
8312. Assistance with discovery.
8313. Costs and fees.

Enactment. Chapter 83 was added April 4, 1996, P.L.58, No.20, effective immediately.

§ 8301. Proceedings under this part.

(a) **Scope.**—This part provides for the following proceedings:

(1) Establishment of an order for spousal support or child support.

(2) Registration of an order for spousal support or child support of another county for enforcement or modification pursuant to Chapter 84 (relating to enforcement and modification of support order after registration).

(b) **Commencement.**—An individual petitioner or a support enforcement agency must commence a proceeding authorized under this part by filing a petition or complaint in an initiating tribunal for forwarding to a responding tribunal or by filing a petition or complaint directly in a tribunal of another county which has or can obtain personal jurisdiction over the respondent.

Cross References. Section 8301 is referred to in section 8304 of this title.

§ 8302. Action by minor parent.

A minor parent or a guardian or other legal representative of a minor parent may maintain a proceeding on behalf of or for the benefit of the minor's child.

§ 8303. Duties of initiating tribunal.

Upon the filing of a petition or complaint authorized by this part, an initiating tribunal shall forward one copy of the petition or complaint and its accompanying documents to the responding tribunal.

§ 8304. Duties and powers of responding tribunal.

(a) **Filing and notice.**—If a responding tribunal receives a petition, a complaint or comparable pleading from an initiating tribunal or directly pursuant to section 8301(b) (relating to proceedings under this part), it shall file the pleading and notify the petitioner by first class mail where and when it was filed.

(b) **Action.**—A responding tribunal, to the extent otherwise authorized by law, may do any of the following:

(1) Exercise continuing, exclusive jurisdiction to issue or enforce a support order, modify a support order or render a judgment to determine parentage.

(2) Ordering an obligor to comply with a support order, specifying the amount and the manner of compliance.

(3) Order income withholding.

(4) Determine the amount of any arrearages and specify a method of payment.

(5) Enforce orders by civil or criminal contempt, or both.

(6) Set aside property for satisfaction of the support order.

(7) Place liens and order execution on the obligor's property.

(8) Order an obligor to keep the tribunal informed of the obligor's current residential address, telephone number, employer, address of employment and telephone number at place of employment.

(9) Issue a bench warrant for an obligor who has failed after proper notice to appear at a hearing ordered by the tribunal and enter the bench warrant in any state and local computer systems for criminal warrants.

(10) Order the obligor to seek appropriate employment by specified methods.

(11) Award reasonable attorney fees and other fees and costs.

(12) Issue a temporary child support order pending judicial resolution of a dispute regarding paternity if any of the following apply:

(i) The obligor has signed an acknowledgment of paternity.

(ii) The obligor has been determined under State law to be the parent.

(iii) There is clear and convincing evidence that the obligor is the child's parent.

(13) Grant any other available remedy.

(c) **Findings of fact.**—A responding tribunal shall include in a support order issued under this part or in the documents accompanying the order the findings of fact on which the support order is based.

(d) **Visitation.**—A responding tribunal may not condition the payment of a support order issued under this part upon compliance by a party with provisions for visitation.

(e) **Notice.**—If a responding tribunal issues an order under this part, the tribunal shall send a copy of the order by first class mail to the petitioner and the respondent and to the initiating tribunal, if any.

§ 8305. Inappropriate tribunal.

If a petition, complaint or comparable pleading is received by an inappropriate tribunal, it shall forward the pleading and accompanying documents to an appropriate tribunal and notify the petitioner by first class mail where and when the pleading was sent.

§ 8306. Duties of support enforcement agency.

(a) **General duty.**—A support enforcement agency upon request shall provide services to an obligee in a proceeding under this part.

(b) **Specific duties.**—A support enforcement agency that is providing services to the petitioner as appropriate shall do all of the following:

(1) Take all steps necessary to enable an appropriate tribunal to obtain jurisdiction over the respondent.

(2) Request an appropriate tribunal to set a date, time and place for a hearing.

(3) Make a reasonable effort to obtain all relevant information, including information as to income and property of the parties.

(4) Within two days, exclusive of Saturdays, Sundays and legal holidays, after receipts of a written notice from an initiating, responding or registering tribunal, send a copy of the notice by first class mail to the petitioner.

(5) Within two days, exclusive of Saturdays, Sundays and legal holidays, after receipt of a written communication from the respondent, send a copy of the communication by first class mail to the petitioner.

(6) Provide to the petitioner and respondent notice of all proceedings within two days, exclusive of Saturdays, Sundays, and legal holidays, of setting a date for proceedings pursuant to this part.

(7) Provide to the petitioner and respondent a copy of all recommendations and court orders, including findings of fact, within two days, exclusive of Saturdays, Sundays, and legal holidays, of issuing the recommendations or court order.

(8) Provide to the petitioner and respondent a copy of the court's procedure to file a demand for a de novo hearing or to file exception to the recommendation of the hearing officer.

(9) Notify the petitioner if jurisdiction over the respondent cannot be obtained.

(c) **Fiduciaries.**—This part does not create a relationship of attorney and client or other fiduciary relationship between a support enforcement agency or the attorney for the agency and the individual being assisted by the agency.

§ 8307. Supervisory duty.

If the secretary determines that a support enforcement agency is neglecting or refusing to provide services to an individual, the secretary may order the agency to perform its duties under this part or may provide those services directly to the individual.

1997 Amendment. Act 58 amended this sec.

§ 8308. Private counsel.

An individual may employ private counsel to represent the individual in proceedings authorized by this part.

§ 8309. Nondisclosure of information in exceptional circumstances.

Upon a finding, which may be made ex parte, that the health, safety or liberty of a party or child would be unreasonably put at risk by the disclosure of identifying information or if an existing order so provides, a tribunal shall order that the address of the child or party or other identifying information not be disclosed in a pleading or other document filed in a proceeding under this part.

§ 8310. Nonparentage not a defense.

A party whose parentage of a child has been previously determined by or pursuant to law may not plead nonparentage as a defense to a proceeding under this part.

§ 8311. Special rules of evidence and procedure.

(a) **Physical presence.**—The physical presence of the petitioner in a responding tribunal is not required for the establishment, enforcement or modification of a support order or the rendition of a judgment determining parentage.

(b) **Representation.**—The interests of the Commonwealth in establishing and enforcing support orders shall be represented, where appropriate, by the county Title IV-D attorney in a proceeding brought before the responding tribunal.

(c) **Hearsay exception.**—A verified petition, affidavit or document, and a document incorporated by reference in any of them, not excluded under the hearsay rule if given in person, is admissible in evidence if given under oath by a party or witness.

(d) **Payment record.**—A copy of the record of support payments certified as a true copy of the original by the custodian of the record may be forwarded to a responding tribunal. The copy is evidence of facts asserted in it and is admissible to show whether payments were made.

(e) **Bills.**—Copies of bills for testing for parentage and for prenatal and postnatal health care of the mother and child, furnished to the adverse party at least ten days before trial, are admissible in evidence to prove the amount of the charges billed and that the charges were reasonable, necessary and customary.

(f) Transmission of documentary evidence.—Documentary evidence transmitted to a tribunal by telephone, telecopier or other means that do not provide an original writing may not be excluded from evidence on an objection based on the means of transmission.

(g) Testimony.—In a proceeding under this part, a tribunal may permit a party or witness to be deposed or to testify by telephone, audiovisual means or other electronic means at a designated tribunal or other location. Tribunals shall cooperate in designating an appropriate location for the deposition or testimony.

§ 8312. Assistance with discovery.

A tribunal may do any of the following:

(1) Request another tribunal to assist in obtaining discovery.

(2) Upon request, compel a person over whom it has jurisdiction to respond to a discovery order issued by another tribunal.

§ 8313. Costs and fees.

(a) Prohibition.—The department or a support enforcement agency may not be required to pay a filing fee or other costs.

(b) Obligor.—If an obligee prevails, a responding tribunal may assess against an obligor filing fees, reasonable attorney fees, other costs and necessary travel and other reasonable expenses incurred by the obligee and the obligee's witnesses. The tribunal may not assess fees, costs or expenses against the department or against the support enforcement agency of either the initiating county or the responding county except as provided by other law. Attorney fees may be taxed as costs and may be ordered paid directly to the attorney, who may enforce the order in the attorney's own name. Payment of support owed to the obligee has priority over fees, costs and expenses.

(c) Dilatory actions.—Except as provided in subsection (a), the tribunal shall order the payment of costs and reasonable attorney fees if it determines that a hearing was requested primarily for delay. In a proceeding under Chapter 76 (relating to enforcement and modification of support order after registration), a hearing is presumed to have been requested primarily for delay if a registered support order is confirmed or enforced without change.

CHAPTER 84
ENFORCEMENT AND MODIFICATION OF SUPPORT ORDER AFTER REGISTRATION

Subchapter

A. Registration of Support Order
B. Contest of Validity or Enforcement
C. Reconciliation of Multiple Order

Enactment. Chapter 84 was added April 4, 1996, P.L.58, No.20, effective immediately.

Cross References. Chapter 84 is referred to in section 8301 of this title.

SUBCHAPTER A
REGISTRATION OF SUPPORT ORDER

Sec.

8401. Registration of order.
8402. Procedure to register order.

§ 8401. Registration of order.

A support order issued by a tribunal may be registered in any tribunal of competent jurisdiction.

§ 8402. Procedure to register order.

(a) General rule.—A support order may be registered by sending the following documents and information to the appropriate tribunal:

(1) A letter of transmittal to the tribunal requesting registration and enforcement.

(2) Two copies, including one certified copy, of the order to be registered, including any modification of the order.

(3) A sworn statement by the party seeking registration or a certified statement by the custodian of the records showing the amount of any arrearage.

(4) The name of the obligor and, if known:

   (i) the obligor's and Social Security number;

   (ii) the name and address of the obligor's employer and any other source of income of the obligor; and

   (iii) a description and the location of property of the obligor not exempt from execution.

(5) The name and address of the obligee and, if applicable, the agency or person to whom support payments are to be remitted.

(b) Docketing.—On receipt of a request for registration, the registering tribunal shall file the order as a foreign judgment, together with one copy of the documents and information, regardless of their form.

SUBCHAPTER B
CONTEST OF VALIDITY OR ENFORCEMENT

Sec.

8411. Notice of registration of order.
8412. Procedure to contest validity of registered order.

8413. Contest of registration or enforcement.
8414. Confirmed order.
8415. Effect of a confirmed order.

§ 8411. Notice of registration of order.

(a) Requirement.—If a support order or order issued by tribunal is registered, the registering tribunal shall notify the nonregistering party. Notice must be given by first class, certified or registered mail or by any means of personal service authorized by the law. The notice must be accompanied by a copy of the registered order and the documents and relevant information accompanying the order.

(b) Contents.—The notice must inform the nonregistering party of all of the following:

(1) A registered order is enforceable as of the date of registration in the same manner as an order issued by a tribunal.

(2) A hearing to contest the validity of the registered order must be requested within 20 days after the date of mailing or personal service of the notice.

(3) Failure to contest the validity of the registered order in a timely manner will result in confirmation of the order and enforcement of the order and the alleged arrearages and will preclude further contest of that order with respect to any matter that could have been asserted.

(4) The amount of any alleged arrearages.

§ 8412. Procedure to contest validity of registered order.

(a) Action.—A nonregistering party seeking to contest the validity of a registered order must request a hearing within 20 days after the date of mailing or personal service of notice of the registration. The nonregistering party may seek to vacate the registration or the amount of any alleged arrearages pursuant to section 8413 (relating to contest of registration or enforcement).

(b) Inaction.—If the nonregistering party fails to contest the validity of the registered order in a timely manner, the order is confirmed by operation of law.

(c) Hearing.—If a nonregistering party requests a hearing to contest the validity of the registered order, the registering tribunal shall schedule the matter for hearing and give notice to the parties by first class mail of the date, time and place of the hearing.

§ 8413. Contest of registration or enforcement.

(a) Defenses.—A party contesting the validity of a registered order or seeking to vacate the registration has the burden of proving one of the following defenses:

(1) The issuing tribunal lacked personal jurisdiction over the contesting party.

(2) The order was obtained by fraud.

(3) The order has been vacated, suspended or modified by a later order.

(4) The issuing tribunal has stayed the order pending appeal.

(5) Full payment has been made and there is no continuing support obligation.

(b) Relief.—If a party presents evidence establishing a full or partial defense under subsection (a), a tribunal may stay enforcement of the registered order, continue the proceeding to permit production of additional relevant evidence and issue other appropriate orders. An uncontested portion of the registered order may be enforced by all remedies available.

(c) Affirmance.—If the contesting party does not establish a defense under subsection (a) to the validity of the order, the registering tribunal shall issue an order confirming the order.

Cross References. Section 8413 is referred to in section 8412 of this title.

§ 8414. Confirmed order.

Confirmation of a registered order, whether by operation of law or after notice and hearing, precludes further contest of the order with respect to any matter that could have been asserted at the time of registration.

§ 8415. Effect of a confirmed order.

A confirmed order has the following effect:

(1) It confers continuing exclusive jurisdiction to the responding tribunal which registered the order.

(2) It eliminates the jurisdiction of the tribunal which issued the order or requested that the order be registered.

APPENDIX TO TITLE 23
DOMESTIC RELATIONS

Supplementary Provisions of Amendatory Statutes

1980, OCTOBER 15, P.L.934, NO.163

§ 3. Applicability.

This act shall apply to all proceedings begun after the effective date of this act. Proceedings in progress and not completed before the effective date of this act may be amended with leave of court after January 1, 1981 to conform to this act; otherwise, the proceedings shall be carried to their conclusion under the act of July 24, 1970 (P.L.620, No.208), known as the "Adoption Act."

> **Explanatory Note.** Act 163 added Parts III and IX of Title 23.

1990, DECEMBER 19, P.L.1240, NO.206

§ 5. Construction of Divorce Code.

The provisions of 23 Pa.C.S. Pt. IV (relating to divorce) shall apply to all cases, whether the cause for divorce or annulment arose prior or subsequent to the enactment of this act. The provisions of 23 Pa.C.S. Pt. IV shall not affect any suit or action pending on the effective date of the Divorce Code of 1980, but the suit or action may be proceeded with and concluded either under the laws in existence when the suit or action was instituted, notwithstanding the repeal of such laws, or, upon application granted, under the provisions of 23 Pa.C.S. Pt. IV. The provisions of 23 Pa.C.S. Pt. IV shall not apply to any case in which a decree has been rendered prior to the effective date of the Divorce Code of 1980. The provisions of 23 Pa.C.S. Pt. IV shall not affect any marital agreement executed prior to the effective date of the Divorce Code of 1980 or any amendment or modification thereto.

> **Explanatory Note.** Act 206 added Parts I, II, IV and VII, Chapters 41, 51 and 55, Subchapter E of Chapter 25 and Subchapter D of Chapter 43 of Title 23.

§ 6. Repeals.

* * *

(b) Nothing in this act shall repeal, modify or supplant section 7 of the act of February 12, 1988 (P.L.66, No.13), entitled "An act amending the act of April 2, 1980 (P.L.63, No.26), entitled !('An act consolidating, revising and amending the divorce and annulment laws of the Commonwealth and making certain repeals,' further providing for grounds for divorce, enforcement of foreign decrees, procedure, jurisdiction, marital property, relief and alimony; providing for agreements between parties; making editorial changes; and making a repeal."

* * *

1993, JULY 2, P.L.431, NO.62

Preamble

It is the intention of the General Assembly by enacting 23 Pa.C.S. § 4327 (relating to postsecondary educational costs) to codify the decision of the Superior Court in the case of Ulmer v. Sommerville, 200 Pa. Superior Ct. 640, 190 A.2d 182 (1963), and the subsequent line of cases interpreting Ulmer prior to the decision of the Pennsylvania Supreme Court in Blue v. Blue, 532 Pa. 521, 616 A.2d 628 (1992), decided on November 13, 1992.

Further, the General Assembly finds that it has a rational and legitimate governmental interest in requiring some parental financial assistance for a higher education for children of parents who are separated, divorced, unmarried or otherwise subject to an existing support obligation.

Explanatory Note. Act 62 amended or added sections 4302, 4306, 4309, 4327, 4342, 4355 and 5103 of Title 23.

1994, DECEMBER 16, P.L.1292, NO.151

§ 9. Department of Public Welfare study.

The Department of Public Welfare shall study the advisability of the adoption of a protocol for the screening of anonymous referrals of suspected child abuse which might include requiring some corroboration of the alleged abuse prior to the commencement of an appropriate investigation under 23 Pa.C.S. The Department of Public Welfare shall report its conclusions and recommendations to the General Assembly regarding anonymous referrals no later than June 1, 1996.

Explanatory Note. Act 151 amended or added sections 6302 and 6303, the heading of Subchapter B of Chapter 63, sections 6311, 6313, 6314, 6315, 6316, 6317, 6318, 6331, 6332, 6333, 6334, 6335, 6336, 6337, 6338, 6339, 6340, 6341, 6343, 6344, 6345, 6346, 6347 and 6349, Subchapters C.1 and C.2 and sections 6361, 6362, 6363, 6364, 6365, 6366, 6367, 6368, 6369, 6370, 6371, 6372, 6373, 6374, 6375, 6376, 6377, 6378, 6381, 6382, 6383 and 6385 of Title 23.

§ 10. Effective date.

This act shall take effect as follows:

(1)(i) The addition of 23 Pa.C.S. §§ 6362(e) and 6375(c)(2) shall take effect upon the effective date of regulations promulgated by the Department of Public Welfare to implement the provisions of this act or within three years from July 1, 1995, whichever is earlier.

(ii) Subparagraph (i) does not preclude the department from continuing to support the county agencies in the development of risk assessment processes prior to the adoption of regulations, as required under subparagraph (i).

(2)(i) The department shall promulgate regulations pertaining to general protective services as provided under this act no later than July 1, 1997.

(ii) Regulations pertaining to general protective services that have been adopted by the department under 55 Pa. Code Ch. 3480 (relating to Child Protective Services—General) shall remain in effect until regulations have been adopted pursuant to subparagraph (i).

* * *

1998, NOVEMBER 24, P.L.811, NO.103

Preamble

The General Assembly finds and declares as follows:

(1) Existing law does not provide adequately for the needs of a parent who is terminally ill or who is periodically incapable of caring for the needs of a minor due to the parent's incapacity or debilitation resulting from illness and who desires to make long-term plans for the future of a minor without terminating or limiting in any way the parent's legal rights.

(2) It is the intent of the General Assembly to create an expeditious procedure which will enable a parent who is terminally ill or periodically incapable or debilitated to make long-term plans for a minor without terminating or limiting in any manner parental rights.

Explanatory Note. Act 103 added Chapter 56 of Title 23.

2004, NOVEMBER 29, P.L.1357, NO.175

§ 5. Applicability.

This act shall apply as follows:

(1) The amendment of the definition of "separate and apart" in 23 Pa.C.S. § 3103 shall apply to complaints served before, on or after the effective date of this paragraph.

(2) The addition of 23 Pa.C.S. § 3106 shall apply to premarital agreements executed on or after the effective date of this paragraph.

(3) The amendment or addition of 23 Pa.C.S. § 3323(c) and (c.1) shall apply to bifurcation proceedings commenced on or after the effective date of this paragraph.

(4) The amendment or addition of 20 Pa.C.S. § 2203(a) and (c) and 23 Pa.C.S. § 3323(d.1) shall apply to the death of one of the parties on or after the effective date of this paragraph irrespective of whether the divorce proceeding was commenced before, on or after the effective date of this paragraph.

(5) The addition of 23 Pa.C.S. § 3323(g) shall apply to bifurcation proceedings commenced on or after the effective date of this paragraph and cases in which one of the parties dies on or after the effective date of this paragraph.

(6) The amendment or addition of 23 Pa.C.S. § 3501(a)(3) and (a.1) shall apply to all equitable distribution proceedings irrespective of whether the proceeding was commenced before, on or after the effective date of this paragraph.

(7) (Repealed).

(8) The amendment or addition of 23 Pa.C.S. § 3502(a) introductory paragraph, (10.1) and (10.2) shall apply to all equitable distribution proceedings irrespective of whether the proceeding was commenced before, on or after the effective date of this paragraph.

(9) The addition of 23 Pa.C.S. § 3502(f) shall apply to all divorce proceedings irrespective of whether the action was commenced before, on or after the effective date of this paragraph.

(10) The amendment of 23 Pa.C.S. § 3505(d) shall apply to all equitable distribution proceedings irrespective of whether the proceeding was commenced before, on or after the effective date of this paragraph.

(11) The amendment of 23 Pa.C.S. § 3506 shall apply to all orders made on or after the effective date of this paragraph.

Explanatory Note. Act 175 amended or added sections 3103, 3106, 3323, 3501, 3502, 3505 and 3506 of Title 23.

2004, NOVEMBER 30, P.L.1618, NO.207

§ 28. Applicability.

This act shall apply as follows:

(1) Except as otherwise provided in paragraph (2), any and all references in any other law to a "district judge" or "justice of the peace" shall be deemed to be references to a magisterial district judge.

(2) Paragraph (1) shall not apply to the provisions of 71 Pa.C.S.

Explanatory Note. Act 207 amended sections 102, 1503, 6102, 6113, 6113.1, and 6340 of Title 23.

§ 29. Construction of law.

Nothing in this act shall be construed or deemed to provide magisterial district judges with retirement benefits or rights that are different from those available to district justices or justices of the peace immediately prior to the effective date of this act. Nothing in this act shall be construed or deemed to provide senior magisterial district judges with retirement benefits or rights that are different from those available to senior district justices immediately prior to the effective date of this act.

2005, JULY 7, P.L. 196, NO.43

§ 4. Continuation of prior law.

The addition of 23 Pa.C.S. Ch. 46 is a continuation of the act of June 24, 1937 (P.L. 2045, No.397), known as The Support Law. The following apply:

(1) Except as otherwise provided in 23 Pa.C.S. Ch. 46, all activities initiated under The Support Law shall continue and remain in full force and effect and may be completed under 23 Pa.C.S. Ch. 46. Orders, regulations and decisions which were made under The Support Law and which are in effect on the effective date of section 2 of this act shall remain in full force and effect until revoked, vacated or modified under 23 Pa.C.S. Ch. 46. Contracts, obligations and agreements entered into under The Support Law are not affected nor impaired by the repeal of The support Law.

(2) No provision of The Support Law which was suspended by order of the Supreme Court shall be revived by the addition of 23 Pa.C.S. Ch. 46.

(3) Except as set forth in paragraph (4), any difference in language between 23 Pa.C.S. Ch. 46 and The Support Law is intended only to conform to the style of the Pennsylvania Consolidated Statutes and is not intended to change or affect the legislative intent, judicial construction or administration and implementation of The Support Law.

(4) Paragraph (3) does not apply to the addition of 23 Pa.C.S. § 4604(c) and (d).

(5) Any reference in a statute or a regulation to The Support Law shall be deemed a reference to 23 Pa.C.S. Ch. 46.

Explanatory Note. Act 43 amended or added Chapter 46 and section 6334 of Title 23.

2005, NOVEMBER 10, P.L.335, NO.66

Preamble

The General Assembly finds and declares as follows:

(1) The provisions of 23 Pa.C.S. Ch. 61 (relating to protection from abuse) are necessary and proper in that they further the Commonwealth's compelling State interest to protect victims of domestic violence from abuse.

(2) The Second Amendment to the Constitution of the United States and section 21 of Article I of the Constitution of Pennsylvania recognize a fundamental right to keep and bear arms.

(3) The limitation of firearm rights for the duration of a protection from abuse order as authorized by 23 Pa.C.S. Ch. 61 is a reasonable regulation, a valid exercise of the police power of the Commonwealth and furthers the compelling State interest to protect victims from abuse.

(4) As provided in 23 Pa.C.S. Ch. 61, a court may impose limitations on firearm rights prohibiting someone who has engaged in domestic violence from possessing firearms when the court deems it appropriate to do so in order to protect a victim.

Explanatory Note. Act 66 amended or added sections 6102, 6105, 6106, 6109 and 6115 of Title 18 and sections 6102, 6103, 6104, 6105, 6106, 6107, 6108, 6108.1, 6108.2, 6108.3, 6108.4, 6108.5, 6110, 6113, 6113.1, 6114, 6117, 6119, 6120, 6121 and 6122 of Title 23.

2008, JULY 9, P.L.276, NO.33

§ 6. Department of Public Welfare reports.

Within 12 months of the effective date of this section, the Department of Public Welfare shall submit a report to the Governor and General Assembly on implementation of child abuse and criminal history information requirements under the act of December 18, 2007 (P.L.469, No.73), entitled "An act amending Title 23 (Domestic Relations) of the Pennsylvania Consolidated Statutes, further providing for information relating to prospective child-care personnel." Information shall include, but not be limited to:

APPENDIX TO TITLE 23 Pa.C.S.

(1) A summary of the requirements of the act of December 18, 2007 (P.L.469, No.73), entitled "An act amending Title 23 (Domestic Relations) of the Pennsylvania Consolidated Statutes, further providing for information relating to prospective child-care personnel."

(2) The number of applicants for child-care services, day-care providers and foster and adoptive parents and adult persons who reside in their homes who are impacted by the requirements.

(3) Fees for Federal criminal history record checks.

(4) A description of the administrative process for the electronic transmission of fingerprints to the Federal Bureau of Investigation for Federal criminal history records.

(5) Any findings and recommendations.

Explanatory Note. Act 33 amended or added sections 6303, 6318, 6340, 6342, 6343, 6343.1, 6365 and 6367 of Title 23.

2013, DECEMBER 18, P.L.1167, NO.107
§ 6. Applicability.

The amendment or addition of 23 Pa.C.S. §§ 5328(a)(2.1), 5329.1, 6340(a)(5.1) and 6375(o) and 42 Pa.C.S. §§ 6307(a)(4.1) and (6.5) and 6308(a)(6) shall apply to:

(1) Any action regarding custody of a child under 23 Pa.C.S. Ch. 53 that is filed on or after the effective date of this section.

(2) Any petition to modify a custody order under 23 Pa.C.S. Ch. 53 that is filed on or after the effective date of this section.

Explanatory Note. Act 107 amended or added sections 5328, 5329.1, 6340 and 6375 of Title 23 and sections 6307 and 6308 of Title 42.

2014, OCTOBER 22, P.L.2529, NO.153
§ 15. Study by Department of Human Services.

The Department of Human Services, in conjunction with the Department of Education and the Pennsylvania Commission on Crime and Delinquency, shall conduct a study to analyze and make recommendations on employment bans for those having contact with children in this Commonwealth. The following apply:

(1) The study shall include recommendations on all of the following:

(i) Changes in permanent and temporary employment bans, which realign and make uniform the provisions of section 111 of the act of March 10, 1949 (P.L.30, No.14), known as the Public School Code of 1949, and 23 Pa.C.S. Ch. 63 with regard to employment bans, including the offenses relating to the welfare of a child to be included in any ban.

(ii) An appeals process.

(2) The Department of Human Services shall, by December 31, 2015, report the study's findings and recommendations to:

(i) The chairman and minority chairman of the Aging and Youth Committee of the Senate.

(ii) The chairman and minority chairman of the Public Health and Welfare Committee of the Senate.

(iii) The chairman and minority chairman of the Children and Youth Committee of the House of Representatives.

(iv) The chairman and minority chairman of the Health Committee of the House of Representatives.

Explanatory Note. Act 153 amended or added sections 2530, 6303, 6311, 6313, 6335, 6338.1, 6339, 6340, 6344, 6344.1, 6344.2, 6344.3, 6344.4, 6349, 6383 of Title 23 and sections 6351.1 of Title 42.

2017, DECEMBER 22, P.L.1249, NO.78

§ 7. **Applicability.**

This act shall apply as follows:

(1) This act shall apply to transfers made or obligations incurred on or after the effective date of this act.

(2) This act shall not apply to transfers made or obligations incurred before the effective date of this act.

(3) This act shall not apply to rights of action that have accrued before the effective date of this enacting legislation.

(4) For a purpose specified under this section, transfers are made and obligations are incurred at the time provided under 12 Pa.C.S. § 5106.

Explanatory Note. Act 78 amended, added or renumbered the heading of Chapter 51 and sections 5101, 5102, 5103, 5104, 5105, 5106, 5107, 5108, 5109, 5110, 5111, 5112, 5113 and 5114 of Title 12; section 4352 of Title 23.

2018, JUNE 28, P.L.375, NO.54

A report under 23 Pa.C.S. § 6337(d), which is due to be expunged from the Statewide database during the 365-day period following the enactment of this act, shall continue to be maintained in the Statewide database and shall be subject to the expunction provisions of 23 Pa.C.S. § 6337(d) on and after the effective date of the amendment of 23 Pa.C.S. § 6337(d).

Pa.C.S.

MISCELLANEOUS PENNSYLVANIA DOMESTIC RELATIONS STATUTES
(Amended Through April, 2019)

TITLE 18
CRIMES AND OFFENSES
(Crimes Code)

PART II. DEFINITION OF SPECIFIC OFFENSES
ARTICLE B. OFFENSES INVOLVING DANGER TO THE PERSON

Chapter 27. Assault

- § 2701. Simple assault.
- § 2702. Aggravated assault.
- § 2706. Terroristic threats.
- § 2709. Harassment.
- § 2709.1. Stalking.
- § 2711. Probable cause arrests in domestic violence cases.
- § 2714. Unauthorized administration of intoxicant.
- § 2718. Strangulation.

Chapter 29. Kidnapping

- § 2901. Kidnapping.
- § 2902. Unlawful restraint.
- § 2903. False imprisonment.
- § 2904. Interference with custody of children.
- § 2905. Interference with custody of committed persons.
- § 2906. Criminal coercion.
- § 2908. Missing children.
- § 2909. Concealment of whereabouts of a child.
- § 2910. Luring a child into a motor vehicle or structure.

Chapter 31. Sexual Offenses

Subchapter A. General Provisions

- § 3101. Definitions.
- § 3102. Mistake as to age.
- § 3103. Spouse relationships.
- § 3104. Evidence of victim's sexual conduct.
- § 3105. Prompt complaint.
- § 3106. Testimony of complainants.
- § 3107. Resistance not required.

Subchapter B. Definition of Offenses

- § 3121. Rape.
- § 3122. Statutory rape.
- § 3122.1. Statutory sexual assault.
- § 3123. Involuntary deviate sexual intercourse.
- § 3124. Voluntary deviate sexual intercourse.
- § 3124.2. Institutional sexual assault.
- § 3124.3. Sexual assault by sports official, volunteer or employee of nonprofit association.
- § 3125. Aggravated indecent assault.
- § 3126. Indecent assault.
- § 3127. Indecent exposure.
- § 3128. Spousal sexual assault.
- § 3129. Sexual intercourse with animal.
- § 3130. Conduct relating to sex offenders.

CRIMES AND OFFENSES

Subchapter C. Loss of PropertyRights
§ 3141. General rule.
§ 3142. Process and seizure (Repealed).
§ 3143. Custody of property (Repealed).
§ 3144. Disposal of property (Repealed).

ARTICLE D. OFFENSES AGAINST THE FAMILY
Chapter 43. Offenses Against the Family
Subchapter A. Definition of Offenses Generally
§ 4301. Bigamy.
§ 4302. Incest.
§ 4303. Concealing death of child.
§ 4304. Endangering welfare of children.
§ 4305. Dealing in infant children.
§ 4306. Newborn protection.

Subchapter B. Nonsupport (Repealed)
§ 4321–§ 4324 (Repealed).

ARTICLE E. OFFENSES AGAINST PUBLIC ADMINISTRATION
Chapter 49. Falsification and Intimidation
Subchapter A. Perjury and Falsification in Official Matters
§ 4906.1. False reports of child abuse.

Subchapter B. Victim and Witness Intimidation
§ 4958. Intimidation, retaliation or obstruction in child abuse cases.

ARTICLE F. OFFENSES AGAINST PUBLIC ORDER AND DECENCY
§ 5504. Harassment and stalking by communication or address. [Repealed].

ARTICLE G. MISCELLANEOUS OFFENSES
Chapter 63. Minors
Subchapter C. Other Dangerous Articles
§ 6301. Corruption of minors.
§ 6312. Sexual abuse of children.
§ 6321. Transmission of sexually explicit images by minor.

TITLE 20
PROBATE, ESTATES AND FIDUCIARIES CODE
§ 2106. Forfeiture.
§ 2203. Right of election; resident decedent.
§ 2507. Modification by circumstances.
§ 5605. Power of attorney not revoked until notice.
§ 5606. Proof of continuance of powers of attorney by affidavit.
§ 6111.1. Modification by divorce.
§ 6111.2. Effect of divorce on designation of beneficiaries.

TITLE 42
JUDICIARY AND JUDICIARY ACT
Chapter 19. Administrative Office of Pennsylvania Courts
§ 1904. Availability of criminal charge information in child custody proceedings.

Chapter 63. Juvenile Matters

Subchapter A. General Provisions

§ 6301. Short title and purposes of chapter.
§ 6302. Definitions.
§ 6303. Scope of chapter.
§ 6304. Powers and duties of probation officers.
§ 6305. Masters.
§ 6306. Costs and expenses of care of child.
§ 6307. Inspection of court files and records.
§ 6308. Law enforcement records.
§ 6309. Juvenile history record information.
§ 6310. Parental participation.
§ 6311. Guardian ad litem for child in court proceedings.

Subchapter B. Jurisdiction and Custody

§ 6321. Commencement of proceedings.
§ 6322. Transfer from criminal proceedings.
§ 6323. Informal adjustment.
§ 6324. Taking into custody.
§ 6325. Detention of child.
§ 6326. Release or delivery to court.
§ 6327. Place of detention.

Subchapter C. Procedures and Safeguards

§ 6331. Release from detention or commencement of proceedings.
§ 6332. Informal hearing.
§ 6333. Subpoena.
§ 6334. Petition.
§ 6335. Release or holding of hearing.
§ 6336. Conduct of hearings.
§ 6336.1. Notice and hearing.
§ 6336.2. Use of restraints on children during court proceedings.
§ 6337. Right to counsel.
§ 6337.1. Right to counsel for children in dependency and delinquency proceedings.
§ 6338. Other basic rights.
§ 6339. Investigation and report.
§ 6340. Consent decree.
§ 6341. Adjudication.
§ 6342. Court-appointed special advocates.

Subchapter D. Disposition of Children Generally

§ 6351. Disposition of dependent child.
§ 6351.1. Authority of court upon petition to remove child from foster parent.
§ 6352. Disposition of delinquent child.
§ 6352.1. Treatment records.
§ 6353. Limitation on and change in place of commitment.
§ 6354. Effect of adjudication.
§ 6355. Transfer to criminal proceedings.
§ 6356. Disposition of mentally ill or mentally retarded child.
§ 6357. Rights and duties of legal custodian.
§ 6358. Assessment of delinquent children by the State Sexual Offenders Assessment Board.

Subchapter E. Dispositions Affecting Other Jurisdictions

§ 6361. Disposition of dependent child.
§ 6362. Disposition of resident child received from another state.
§ 6363. Ordering foreign supervision.

CRIMES AND OFFENSES Pa.C.S.

§ 6364. Supervision under foreign order.
§ 6365. Powers of foreign probation officers.

Subchapter F. Juvenile Court Judges' Commission

§ 6371. Definitions.
§ 6372. Juvenile Court Judges' Commission.
§ 6373. Powers and duties.
§ 6374. Power to make grants.
§ 6375. Funding.

TITLE 43
LABOR

Chapter 14. Unemployment Compensation

ARTICLE VII. PROTECTION OF RIGHTS AND COMPENSATION

§ 863.1. Child support intercept of unemployment compensation.

TITLE 51
MILITARY AFFAIRS

PART II. PENNSYLVANIA NATIONAL GUARD, PENNSYLVANIA GUARD AND MILITIA

Subchapter D. Rights and Immunities

§ 4109. Child Custody Proceedings During Military Deployment.
§ 4110. Expedited or electronic hearing.

TITLE 54
NAMES

Chapter 7. Judicial Change of Name

§ 701. Court approval required for change of name.
§ 702. Change by order of court.
§ 703. Effect on children.
§ 704. Divorcing and divorced person may resume prior name.
§ 704.1. Surviving spouse may resume prior name.
§ 705. Penalty for violation of chapter.

MISCELLANEOUS PENNSYLVANIA DOMESTIC RELATIONS STATUTES

TITLE 18
CRIMES AND OFFENSES
(Crimes Code)

PART II
DEFINITION OF SPECIFIC OFFENSES

ARTICLE B
OFFENSES INVOLVING DANGER TO THE PERSON

CHAPTER 27
ASSAULT

Sec.

2701. Simple assault.

2702. Aggravated assault.
2706. Terroristic threats.
2709. Harrassment.
2709.1. Stalking.
2711. Probable cause arrests in domestic violence cases.
2714. Unauthorized administration of intoxicant.
2718. Strangulation.

§ 2701. Simple assault.

(a) Offense defined.—Except as provided under section 2702 (relating to aggravated assault), a person is guilty of assault if he:

(1) attempts to cause or intentionally, knowingly or recklessly causes bodily injury to another;

(2) negligently causes bodily injury to another with a deadly weapon;

(3) attempts by physical menace to put another in fear of imminent serious bodily injury; or

(4) conceals or attempts to conceal a hypodermic needle on his person and intentionally or knowingly penetrates a law enforcement officer or an officer or an employee of a correctional institution, county jail or prison, detention facility or mental hospital during the course of an arrest or any search of the person.

(b) Grading.—Simple assault is a misdemeanor of the second degree unless committed:

(1) in a fight or scuffle entered into by mutual consent, in which case it is a misdemeanor of the third degree; or

(2) against a child under 12 years of age by a person 18 years of age or older, in which case it is a misdemeanor of the first degree.

(Dec. 19, 1988, P.L.1275, No.158, eff. 60 days; June 22, 2001, P.L.605, No.48, eff. 60 days; Dec. 9, 2002, P.L.1391, No.172, eff. 60 days; Dec. 18, 2013, P.L.1198, No.118, eff. Jan. 1, 2014)

2013 Amendment. Act 118 amended subsecs. (a) and (b)(2).

Cross References. Section 2701 is referred to in sections 2709.1, 2711, 2712, 6105.1 of this title; section 6711 of Title 23 (Domestic Relations); section 4503 of Title 61 (Prisons and Parole).

§ 2702. Aggravated assault.

(a) Offense defined.—A person is guilty of aggravated assault if he:

(1) attempts to cause serious bodily injury to another, or causes such injury intentionally, knowingly or recklessly under circumstances manifesting extreme indifference to the value of human life;

(2) attempts to cause or intentionally, knowingly or recklessly causes serious bodily injury to any of the officers, agents, employees or other persons enumerated in subsection (c) or to an employee of an agency, company or other entity engaged in public transportation, while in the performance of duty;

(3) attempts to cause or intentionally or knowingly causes bodily injury to any of the officers, agents, employees or other persons enumerated in subsection (c), in the performance of duty;

(4) attempts to cause or intentionally or knowingly causes bodily injury to another with a deadly weapon;

(5) attempts to cause or intentionally or knowingly causes bodily injury to a teaching staff member, school board member or other employee, including a student employee, of any elementary or secondary publicly-funded educational institution, any elementary or secondary private school licensed by the Department of Education or any elementary or secondary parochial school while acting in the scope of his or her employment or because of his or her employment relationship to the school;

(6) attempts by physical menace to put any of the officers, agents, employees or other persons enumerated in subsection (c), while in the performance of duty, in fear of imminent serious bodily injury;

(7) uses tear or noxious gas as defined in section 2708(b) (relating to use of tear or noxious gas in labor disputes) or uses an electric or electronic incapacitation device against any officer, employee or other person enumerated in subsection (c) while acting in the scope of his employment;

(8) attempts to cause or intentionally, knowingly or recklessly causes bodily injury to a child less than six years of age, by a person 18 years of age or older; or

(9) attempts to cause or intentionally, knowingly or recklessly causes serious bodily injury to a child less than 13 years of age, by a person 18 years of age or older.

(b) Grading.—Aggravated assault under subsection (a)(1), (2) and (9) is a felony of the first degree. Aggravated assault under subsection (a)(3), (4), (5), (6), (7) and (8) is a felony of the second degree.

(c) Officers, employees, etc., enumerated.—The officers, agents, employees and other persons referred to in subsection (a) shall be as follows:

(1) Police officer.

(2) Firefighter.

(3) County adult probation or parole officer.

(4) County juvenile probation or parole officer.

(5) An agent of the Pennsylvania Board of Probation and Parole.

(6) Sheriff.

(7) Deputy sheriff.

(8) Liquor control enforcement agent.

(9) Officer or employee of a correctional institution, county jail or prison, juvenile detention center or any other facility to which the person has been ordered by the court pursuant to a petition alleging delinquency under 42 Pa.C.S. Ch. 63 (relating to juvenile matters).

(10) Judge of any court in the unified judicial system.

(11) The Attorney General.

(12) A deputy attorney general.

(13) A district attorney.

(14) An assistant district attorney.

(15) A public defender.

(16) An assistant public defender.

(17) A Federal law enforcement official.

(18) A State law enforcement official.

(19) A local law enforcement official.

(20) Any person employed to assist or who assists any Federal, State or local law enforcement official.

(21) Emergency medical services personnel.

(22) Parking enforcement officer.

(23) A magisterial district judge.

(24) A constable.

(25) A deputy constable.

(26) A psychiatric aide.

(27) A teaching staff member, a school board member or other employee, including a student employee, of any elementary or secondary publicly funded educational institution, any elementary or secondary private school licensed by the Department of Education or any elementary or secondary parochial school while acting in the scope of his or her employment or because of his or her employment relationship to the school.

(28) Governor.

(29) Lieutenant Governor.

(30) Auditor General.

(31) State Treasurer.

(32) Member of the General Assembly.

(33) An employee of the Department of Environmental Protection.

(34) An individual engaged in the private detective business as defined in section 2(a) and (b) of the act of August 21, 1953 (P.L.1273, No.361), known as The Private Detective Act of 1953.

(35) An employee or agent of a county children and youth social service agency or of the legal representative of such agency.

(36) A public utility employee or an employee of an electric cooperative.

(37) A wildlife conservation officer or deputy wildlife conservation officer of the Pennsylvania Game Commission.

(38) A waterways conservation officer or deputy waterways conservation officer of the Pennsylvania Fish and Boat Commission.

(d) Definitions.—As used in this section, the following words and phrases shall have the meanings given to them in this subsection:

"Electric or electronic incapacitation device." A portable device which is designed or intended by the manufacturer to be used, offensively or defensively, to temporarily immobilize or incapacitate persons by means of electric pulse or current, including devices operated by means of carbon dioxide propellant. The term does not include cattle prods, electric fences or other electric devices when used in agricultural, animal husbandry or food production activities.

"Emergency medical services personnel." The term includes, but is not limited to, doctors, residents, interns, registered nurses, licensed practical nurses, nurse aides, ambulance attendants and operators, paramedics, emergency medical technicians and members of a hospital security force while working within the scope of their employment.

(Oct. 1, 1980, P.L.689, No.139, eff. 60 days; Oct. 16, 1980, P.L.978, No.167, eff. 60 days; Dec. 11, 1986, P.L.1517, No.164, eff. 60 days; Feb. 2, 1990, P.L.6, No.4, eff. 60 days; July 6, 1995, P.L.238, No.27, eff. 60 days; Feb. 23, 1996, P.L.17, No.7, eff. 60 days; July 2, 1996, P.L.478, No.75, eff. 60 days; Dec. 21, 1998, P.L.1245, No.159, eff. 60 days; Nov. 6, 2002, P.L.1096, No.132, eff. 60 days; Nov. 29, 2004, P.L.1349, No.173, eff. 60 days; Nov. 30, 2004, P.L.1618, No.207, eff. 60 days; Oct. 24, 2012, P.L.1205, No.150, eff. 60 days; Dec. 18, 2013, P.L.1198, No.118, eff. Jan. 1, 2014)

2013 Amendment. Act 118 amended subsecs. (a)(6) and (7) and (b) and added subsec. (a)(8) and (9).

2012 Amendment. Act 150 amended subsec. (c).

2004 Amendments. See sections 28 and 29 of Act 207 in the appendix to this title for special provisions relating to applicability and construction of law.

Cross References. Section 2702 is referred to in sections 2701, 2703, 2709.1, 2711, 5702, 5708, 6105 of this title; sections 2511, 5329, 6344, 6711 of Title 23 (Domestic Relations); section 904 of Title 30 (Fish); section 905.1 of Title 34 (Game); sections 5551, 5552, 6302, 6307, 6308, 6336, 6355, 9714, 9717, 9718, 9719, 9802 of Title 42 (Judiciary and Judicial Procedure); section 702 of Title 54 (Names); section 7122 of Title 61 (Prisons and Parole).

§ 2706. Terroristic threats.

(a) Offense defined.—A person commits the crime of terroristic threats if the person communicates, either directly or indirectly, a threat to:

(1) commit any crime of violence with intent to terrorize another;

(2) cause evacuation of a building, place of assembly or facility of public transportation; or

(3) otherwise cause serious public inconvenience, or cause terror or serious public inconvenience with reckless disregard of the risk of causing such terror or inconvenience.

(b) Restitution.—A person convicted of violating this section shall, in addition to any other sentence imposed or restitution ordered under *42 Pa.C.S. § 9721(c)* (relating to sentencing generally), be sentenced to pay restitution in an amount equal to the cost of the evacuation, including, but not limited to, fire and police response; emergency medical service or emergency preparedness response; and transportation of an individual from the building, place of assembly or facility.

(c) Preservation of private remedies.—No judgment or order of restitution shall debar a person, by appropriate action, to recover from the offender as otherwise provided by law, provided that any civil award shall be reduced by the amount paid under the criminal judgment.

(d) Grading.—An offense under subsection (a) constitutes a misdemeanor of the first degree unless the threat causes the occupants of the building, place of assembly or facility of public transportation to be diverted from their normal or customary operations, in which case the offense constitutes a felony of the third degree.

(e) Definition.—As used in this section, the term "communicates" means, conveys in person or by written or electronic means, including telephone, electronic mail, Internet, facsimile, telex and similar transmissions.

§ 2709. Harassment.

(a) Offense defined.—A person commits the crime of harassment when, with intent to harass, annoy or alarm another, the person:

(1) strikes, shoves, kicks or otherwise subjects the other person to physical contact, or attempts or threatens to do the same;

(2) follows the other person in or about a public place or places;

(3) engages in a course of conduct or repeatedly commits acts which serve no legitimate purpose;

(4) communicates to or about such other person any lewd, lascivious, threatening or obscene words, language, drawings or caricatures;

(5) communicates repeatedly in an anonymous manner;

(6) communicates repeatedly at extremely inconvenient hours; or

(7) communicates repeatedly in a manner other than specified in paragraphs (4), (5) and (6).

(a.1) Cyber harassment of a child.—

(1) A person commits the crime of cyber harassment of a child if, with intent to harass, annoy or alarm, the person engages in a continuing course of conduct of making any of the following by electronic means directly to a child or by publication through an electronic social media service:

(i) seriously disparaging statement or opinion about the child's physical characteristics, sexuality, sexual activity or mental or physical health or condition; or

(ii) threat to inflict harm.

(2)(i) If a juvenile is charged with a violation of paragraph (1), the judicial authority with jurisdiction over the violation shall give first consideration to referring the juvenile charged with the violation to a diversionary program under Pa.R.J.C.P. No. 312 (relating to Informal Adjustment) or No. 370 (relating to Consent Decree). As part of the diversionary program, the judicial authority may order the juvenile to participate in an educational program which includes the legal and nonlegal consequences of cyber harassment.

 (ii) If the person successfully completes the diversionary program, the juvenile's records of the charge of violating paragraph (1) shall be expunged as provided for under section 9123 (relating to juvenile records).

(b) Stalking.—(Deleted by amendment).

(b.1) Venue.—

 (1) An offense committed under this section may be deemed to have been committed at either the place at which the communication or communications were made or at the place where the communication or communications were received.

 (2) Acts indicating a course of conduct which occur in more than one jurisdiction may be used by any other jurisdiction in which an act occurred as evidence of a continuing pattern of conduct or a course of conduct.

 (3) In addition to paragraphs (1) and (2), an offense under subsection (a.1) may be deemed to have been committed at the place where the child who is the subject of the communication resides.

(c) Grading.—

 (1) Except as provided under paragraph (3), an offense under subsection (a)(1), (2) or (3) shall constitute a summary offense.

 (2) An offense under subsection (a)(4), (5), (6) or (7) or (a.1) shall constitute a misdemeanor of the third degree.

 (3) The grading of an offense under subsection (a)(1), (2) or (3) shall be enhanced one degree if the person has previously violated an order issued under 23 Pa.C.S. § 6108 (relating to relief) involving the same victim, family or household member.

(d) False reports.—A person who knowingly gives false information to any law enforcement officer with the intent to implicate another under this section commits an offense under section 4906 (relating to false reports to law enforcement authorities).

(e) Application of section.—This section shall not apply to conduct by a party to a labor dispute as defined in the act of June 2, 1937 (P.L.1198, No.308), known as the Labor Anti-Injunction Act, or to any constitutionally protected activity.

(e.1) Course of conduct.—(Deleted by amendment).

(f) Definitions.—As used in this section, the following words and phrases shall have the meanings given to them in this subsection:

"Communicates." Conveys a message without intent of legitimate communication or address by oral, nonverbal, written or electronic means, including telephone, electronic mail, Internet, facsimile, telex, wireless communication or similar transmission.

"Course of conduct." A pattern of actions composed of more than one act over a period of time, however short, evidencing a continuity of conduct. The term includes lewd, lascivious, threatening or obscene words, language, drawings, caricatures or actions, either in person or anonymously. Acts indicating a course of conduct which occur in more than one jurisdiction may be used by any other jurisdiction in which an act occurred as evidence of a continuing pattern of conduct or a course of conduct.

"Emotional distress." A temporary or permanent state of mental anguish.

"Family or household member." Spouses or persons who have been spouses, persons living as spouses or who lived as spouses, parents and children, other persons related by consanguinity or affinity, current or former sexual or intimate partners or persons who share biological parenthood.

"Seriously disparaging statement or opinion." A statement or opinion which is intended to and under the circumstances is reasonably likely to cause substantial emotional distress to a child of the victim's age and which produces some physical manifestation of the distress.

(June 23, 1993, P.L.124, No.28, eff. imd.; Oct. 2, 1997, P.L.379, No.44, eff. 60 days; Dec. 15, 1999, P.L.915, No.59, eff. 60 days; Dec. 9, 2002, P.L.1759, No.218, eff. 60 days; Nov. 27, 2013, P.L.1061, No.91, eff. 60 days; July 10, 2015, P.L.140, No.26 eff. 60 days)

2015 Amendment. Act 26 amended subsecs. (c)(2) and (f) and added subsecs. (a.1) and (b.1)(3).

2013 Amendment. Act 91 amended subsec. (c) and added the def. of "family or household member" in subsec. (f).

2002 Amendment. See sections 9 and 10 of Act 218 in the appendix to this title for special provisions relating to references to section 2709 and references to section 5504.

Cross References. Section 2709 is referred to in sections 4954, 4955, 5708 of this title; section 3304 of Title 5 (Athletics and Sports); sections 6108, 6711 of Title 23 (Domestic Relations); sections 3573, 62A03 of Title 42 (Judiciary and Judicial Procedure).

§ 2709.1. Stalking.

(a) Offense defined.—A person commits the crime of stalking when the person either:

(1) engages in a course of conduct or repeatedly commits acts toward another person, including following the person without proper authority, under circumstances which demonstrate either an intent to place such other person in reasonable fear of bodily injury or to cause substantial emotional distress to such other person; or

(2) engages in a course of conduct or repeatedly communicates to another person under circumstances which demonstrate or communicate either an intent to place such other person in reasonable fear of bodily injury or to cause substantial emotional distress to such other person.

(b) Venue.—

(1) An offense committed under this section may be deemed to have been committed at either the place at which the communication or communications were made or at the place where the communication or communications were received.

(2) Acts indicating a course of conduct which occur in more than one jurisdiction may be used by any other jurisdiction in which an act occurred as evidence of a continuing pattern of conduct or a course of conduct.

(c) Grading.—

(1) Except as otherwise provided for in paragraph (2), a first offense under this section shall constitute a misdemeanor of the first degree.

(2) A second or subsequent offense under this section or a first offense under subsection (a) if the person has been previously convicted of a crime of violence involving the same victim, family or household member, including, but not limited to, a violation of section 2701 (relating to simple assault), 2702 (relating to aggravated assault), 2705 (relating to recklessly endangering another person), 2901 (relating to kidnapping), 3121 (relating to rape) or 3123 (relating to involuntary deviate sexual intercourse), an order issued under section 4954 (relating to protective orders) or an order issued under 23 Pa.C.S. § 6108 (relating to relief) shall constitute a felony of the third degree.

(d) False reports.—A person who knowingly gives false information to any law enforcement officer with the intent to implicate another under this section commits an offense under section 4906 (relating to false reports to law enforcement authorities).

(e) Application of section.—This section shall not apply to conduct by a party to a labor dispute as defined in the act of June 2, 1937 (P.L.1198, No.308), known as the Labor Anti-Injunction Act, or to any constitutionally protected activity.

(f) Definitions.—As used in this section, the following words and phrases shall have the meanings given to them in this subsection:

"Communicates." To convey a message without intent of legitimate communication or address by oral, nonverbal, written or electronic means, including telephone, electronic mail, Internet, facsimile, telex, wireless communication or similar transmission.

"Course of conduct." A pattern of actions composed of more than one act over a period of time, however short, evidencing a continuity of conduct. The term includes lewd, lascivious, threatening or obscene words, language, drawings, caricatures or actions, either in person or anonymously. Acts indicating a course of conduct which occur in more than one jurisdiction may be used by any other jurisdiction in which an act occurred as evidence of a continuing pattern of conduct or a course of conduct.

"Emotional distress." A temporary or permanent state of mental anguish.

"Family or household member." Spouses or persons who have been spouses, persons living as spouses or who lived as spouses, parents and children, other persons related by consanguinity or affinity, current or former sexual or intimate partners or persons who share biological parenthood.

2002 Amendment. Act 218 added section 2709.1.

Cross References. Section 2709.1 is referred to in sections 2711, 4954, 4955, 5708, 6105 of this title; section 3304 of Title 5 (Athletics and Sports); sections 5303, 6108, 6344 of Title 23 (Domestic Relations).

§ 2711. Probable cause arrests in domestic violence cases.

(a) General rule.—A police officer shall have the same right of arrest without a warrant as in a felony whenever he has probable cause to believe the defendant has violated section 2504 (relating to involuntary manslaughter), 2701 (relating to simple assault), 2702(a)(3), (4) and (5) (relating to aggravated assault), 2705 (relating to recklessly endangering another person), 2706 (relating to terroristic threats), 2709.1 (relating to stalking) or 2718 (relating to strangulation) against a family or household member although the offense did not take place in the presence of the police officer. A police officer may not arrest a person pursuant to this section without first observing recent physical injury to the victim or other corroborative evidence. For the purposes of this subsection, the term "family or household member" has the meaning given that term in 23 Pa.C.S. § 6102 (relating to definitions).

(b) Seizure of weapons.—The arresting police officer shall seize all weapons used by the defendant in the commission of the alleged offense.

(c) Bail.—

(1) A defendant arrested pursuant to this section shall be afforded a preliminary arraignment by the proper issuing authority without unnecessary delay. In no case shall the arresting officer release the defendant from custody rather than taking the defendant before the issuing authority.

(2) In determining whether to admit the defendant to bail, the issuing authority shall consider whether the defendant poses a threat of danger to the victim. In making a determination whether the defendant poses a threat of danger to the victim in cases under this section, the issuing authority may use a pretrial risk assessment tool as set forth in subsection (c.1). If the issuing authority makes such a determination, it shall require as a condition of bail that the defendant shall refrain from entering the residence or household of the victim and the victim's place of employment and shall refrain from committing any further criminal conduct against the victim and shall so notify the defendant thereof at the time the defendant is admitted to bail. Such condition shall expire at the time of the preliminary hearing or upon the entry or the denial of the protection of abuse order by the court, whichever occurs first. A violation of this condition may be punishable by the revocation of any form of pretrial release or the forfeiture of bail and the issuance of a bench

warrant for the defendant's arrest or remanding him to custody or a modification of the terms of the bail. The defendant shall be provided a hearing on this matter.

(c.1) Pretrial risk assessment tool.—The president judge of a court of common pleas may adopt a pretrial risk assessment tool for use by the court of common pleas or by the Philadelphia Municipal Court, the Pittsburgh Magistrates Court or magisterial district judges when acting as the issuing authority in cases under this section. The issuing authority may use the pretrial risk assessment tool to aid in determining whether the defendant poses a threat of danger to the victim. However, the pretrial risk assessment tool may not be the only means of determining whether to admit the defendant to bail. Nothing in this subsection shall be construed to conflict with the issuing authority's ability to determine whether to admit the defendant to bail under the Pennsylvania Rules of Criminal Procedure.

(c.2) Pennsylvania Commission on Sentencing.—The following apply to the Pennsylvania Commission on Sentencing:

(1) The commission shall develop a model pretrial risk assessment tool which may be used by the issuing authority in cases under this section, as set forth in subsection (c.1).

(2) Subject to any inconsistent rule of court, in order to ensure that the model pretrial risk assessment tool or other pretrial risk assessment tool adopted under this section is effective, accurate and free from racial or economic bias, prior to the adoption of the tool, the commission shall publish a report of validation using information from cases from the judicial district where the tool is to be utilized. The report shall be updated every two years.

(d) Notice of rights.—Upon responding to a domestic violence case, the police officer shall, orally or in writing, notify the victim of the availability of a shelter, including its telephone number, or other services in the community. Said notice shall include the following statement: "If you are the victim of domestic violence, you have the right to go to court and file a petition requesting an order for protection from domestic abuse pursuant to 23 Pa.C.S. Ch. 61 (relating to protection from abuse) which could include the following:

(1) An order restraining the abuser from further acts of abuse.

(2) An order directing the abuser to leave your household.

(3) An order preventing the abuser from entering your residence, school, business or place of employment.

(4) An order awarding you or the other parent temporary custody of or temporary visitation with your child or children.

(5) An order directing the abuser to pay support to you and the minor children if the abuser has a legal obligation to do so."

(Feb. 15, 1986, P.L.27, No.10, eff. 60 days; Dec. 19, 1990, P.L.1240, No.206, eff. 90 days; Dec. 20, 2000, P.L.728, No.101, eff. 60 days; Dec. 9, 2002, P.L.1759, No.218, eff. 60 days; Apr. 16, 2018, P.L.89, No.14)

2018 Amendment. Act 14 amended subsecs. (a) and (c)(2) and added subsecs. (c.1) and (c.2), effective in 60 days as to subsecs. (a), (c)(2), (c.1) and (c.2)(1) and two years as to subsec. (c.2)(2).

2002 Amendment. Act 218 amended subsec. (a).

1990 Amendment. Act 206 amended subsec. (d).

§ 2714. Unauthorized administration of intoxicant.

A person commits a felony of the third degree when, with the intent to commit an offense under section 3121(a)(4) (relating to rape), 3123(a)(4) (relating to involuntary deviate sexual intercourse), 3125(5) (relating to aggravated indecent assault) or 3126(a)(5) (relating to indecent assault), he or she substantially impairs the complainant's power to apprise or control his or her conduct by administering, without the knowledge of the complainant, drugs or other intoxicants.

1997 Amendment.—Act 65 added this sec.

§ 2718. Strangulation.

(a) Offense defined.—A person commits the offense of strangulation if the person knowingly or intentionally impedes the breathing or circulation of the blood of another person by:

(1) applying pressure to the throat or neck; or

(2) blocking the nose and mouth of the person.

(b) Physical injury.—Infliction of a physical injury to a victim shall not be an element of the offense. The lack of physical injury to a victim shall not be a defense in a prosecution under this section.

(c) Affirmative defense.—It shall be an affirmative defense to a charge under this section that the victim consented to the defendant's actions as provided under section 311 (relating to consent).

(d) Grading.—

(1) Except as provided in paragraph (2) or (3), a violation of this section shall constitute a misdemeanor of the second degree.

(2) A violation of this section shall constitute a felony of the second degree if committed:

(i) against a family or household member as defined in 23 Pa.C.S. § 6102 (relating to definitions);

(ii) by a caretaker against a care-dependent person; or

(iii) in conjunction with sexual violence as defined in 42 Pa.C.S. § 62A03 (relating to definitions) or conduct constituting a crime under section 2709.1 (relating to stalking) or Subchapter B of Chapter 30 (relating to prosecution of human trafficking).

(3) A violation of this section shall constitute a felony of the first degree if:

(i) at the time of commission of the offense, the defendant is subject to an active protection from abuse order under 23 Pa.C.S. Ch. 61 (relating to protection from abuse) or a sexual violence or intimidation protection order under 42 Pa.C.S. Ch. 62A (relating to protection of victims of sexual violence or intimidation) that covers the victim;

(ii) the defendant uses an instrument of crime as defined in section 907 (relating to possessing instruments of crime) in commission of the offense under this section; or

(iii) the defendant has previously been convicted of an offense under paragraph (2) or a substantially similar offense in another jurisdiction.

(e) Definitions.—As used in this section, the following words and phrases shall have the meanings given to them in this subsection unless the context clearly indicates otherwise:

"Care-dependent person." An adult who, due to physical or cognitive disability or impairment, requires assistance to meet his needs for food, shelter, clothing, personal care or health care.

"Caretaker." Any person who:

(1) Is an owner, operator, manager or employee of any of the following:

(i) A nursing home, personal care home, assisted living facility, private care residence or domiciliary home.

(ii) A community residential facility or intermediate care facility for a person with mental disabilities.

(iii) An adult daily living center.

(iv) A home health service provider whether licensed or unlicensed.

(v) An entity licensed under the act of July 19, 1979 (P.L.130, No.48), known as the Health Care Facilities Act.

(2) Provides care to a care-dependent person in the settings described under paragraph (1).

(3) Has an obligation to care for a care-dependent person for monetary consideration in the settings described under paragraph (1).

(4) Is an adult who resides with a care-dependent person and who has a legal duty to provide care or who has voluntarily assumed an obligation to provide care because of a familial relationship, contract or court order.

(5) Is an adult who does not reside with a care-dependent person but who has a legal duty to provide care or who has affirmatively assumed a responsibility for care or who has responsibility by contract or court order.

"Legal entity." An individual, partnership, unincorporated association, corporation or governing authority.

"Private care residence."

(1) A private residence:

(i) in which the owner of the residence or the legal entity responsible for the operation of the residence, for monetary consideration, provides or assists with or arranges for the provision of food, room, shelter, clothing, personal care or health care in the residence, for a period exceeding 24 hours, to fewer than four care-dependent persons who are not relatives of the owner; and

(ii) which is not required to be licensed as a long-term care nursing facility, as defined in section 802.1 of the Health Care Facilities Act.

(2) The term does not include:

(i) Domiciliary care as defined in section 2202-A of the act of April 9, 1929 (P.L.177, No.175), known as The Administrative Code of 1929.

(ii) A facility which provides residential care for fewer than four care-dependent adults and which is regulated by the Department of Human Services.

(Oct. 26, 2016, P.L.888, No.111, eff. 60 days)

2016 Amendment. Act 111 added section 2718.

CHAPTER 29
KIDNAPPING

Sec.
2901. Kidnapping.
2902. Unlawful restraint.
2903. False imprisonment.
2904. Interference with custody of children.
2905. Interference with custody of committed persons.
2906. Criminal coercion.
2908. Missing children.
2909. Concealment of whereabouts of a child.
2910. Luring a child into a motor vehicle or structure.

§ 2901. Kidnapping.

(a) Offense denied.—Except as provided in subsection (a.1), a person is guilty of kidnapping if he unlawfully removes another a substantial distance under the circumstances from the place where he is found, or if he unlawfully confines another for a substantial period in a place of isolation, with any of the following intentions:

(1) To hold for ransom or reward, or as a shield or hostage.

(2) To facilitate commission of any felony or flight thereafter.

(3) To inflict bodily injury on or to terrorize the victim or another.

(4) To interfere with the performance by public officials of any governmental or political function.

(a.1) Kidnapping of a minor.—A person is guilty of kidnapping of a minor if he unlawfully removes a person under 18 years of age a substantial distance under the circumstances from the place where he is found, or if he unlawfully confines a person under 18 years of age for a substantial period in a place of isolation, with any of the following intentions:

(1) To hold for ransom or reward, or as a shield or hostage.

(2) To facilitate commission of any felony or flight thereafter.

(3) To inflict bodily injury on or to terrorize the victim or another.

(4) To interfere with the performance by public officials of any governmental or political function.

(b) Grading.—The following apply:

(1) Kidnapping under subsection (a) is a felony of the first degree. A removal or confinement is unlawful within the meaning of subsection (a) if it is accomplished by force, threat or deception, or, in the case of an incapacitated person, if it is accomplished without the consent of a parent, guardian or other person responsible for general supervision of his welfare.

(2) Kidnapping under subsection (a.1) is a felony of the first degree. A removal or confinement is unlawful within the meaning of subsection (a.1) if it is accomplished by force, threat or deception, or, in the case of a person under 14 years of age, if it is accomplished without consent of a parent, guardian or other person responsible for general supervision of his welfare.

2011 Amendment. Act 111 amended this sec.

§ 2902. Unlawful restraint.

(a) Offense denied.—Except as provided under subsection (b) or (c), a person commits a misdemeanor of the first degree if he knowingly:

(1) restrains another unlawfully in circumstances exposing him to risk of serious bodily injury; or

(2) holds another in a condition of involuntary servitude.

(b) Unlawful restraint of a minor where offender is not victim's parent.— If the victim is a person under 18 years of age, a person who is not the victim's parent commits a felony of the second degree if he knowingly:

(1) restrains another unlawfully in circumstances exposing him to risk of serious bodily injury; or

(2) holds another in a condition of involuntary servitude.

(c) Unlawful restraint of minor where offender is victim's parent.— If the victim is a person under 18 years of age, a parent of the victim commits a felony of the second degree if he knowingly:

(1) restrains another unlawfully in circumstances exposing him to risk of serious bodily injury; or

(2) holds another in a condition of involuntary servitude.

(d) Definition.— As used in this section the term "parent" means a natural parent, stepparent, adoptive parent or guardian of a minor.

2011 Amendment. Act 111 amended this sec.

§ 2903. False imprisonment.

(a) Offense denied.— Except as provided under subsection (b) or (c), a person commits a misdemeanor of the second degree if he knowingly restrains another unlawfully so as to interfere substantially with his liberty.

(b) False imprisonment of a minor where offender is not victim's parent.— If the victim is a person under 18 years of age, a person who is not the victim's parent commits a felony of the second degree if he knowingly restrains another unlawfully so as to interfere substantially with his liberty.

(c) False imprisonment of a minor where offender is victim's parent.— If the victim is a person under 18 years of age, a parent of the victim commits a felony of the second degree if he knowingly restrains another unlawfully so as to interfere substantially with his liberty.

(d) Definition.— As used in this section the term "parent" means a natural parent, stepparent, adoptive parent or guardian of a minor.

2011 Amendment. Act 111 amended this sec.

§ 2904. Interference with custody of children.

(a) Offense defined.— A person commits an offense if he knowingly or recklessly takes or entices any child under the age of 18 years from the custody of its parent, guardian or other lawful custodian, when he has no privilege to do so.

(b) Defenses.— It is a defense that:

(1) the actor believed that his action was necessary to preserve the child from danger to its welfare; or

(2) the child, being at the time not less than 14 years old, was taken away at its own instigation without enticement and without purpose to commit a criminal offense with or against the child; or

(3) the actor is the child's parent or guardian or other lawful custodian and is not acting contrary to an order entered by a court of competent jurisdiction.

(c) Grading.— The offense is a felony of the third degree unless:

(1) the actor, not being a parent or person in equivalent relation to the child, acted with knowledge that his conduct would cause serious alarm for the safety of the child, or in reckless disregard of a likelihood of causing such alarm. In such cases, the offense shall be a felony of the second degree; or

(2) the actor acted with good cause for a period of time not in excess of 24 hours; and

   (i) the victim child is the subject of a valid order of custody issued by a court of this Commonwealth;

   (ii) the actor has been given either partial custody or visitation rights under said order; and

   (iii) the actor is a resident of this Commonwealth and does not remove the child from the Commonwealth.

In such cases, the offense shall be a misdemeanor of the second degree.

(July 9, 1984, P.L.661, No.138, eff. imd.)

1984 Amendment. Act 138 amended subsec. (c).

Cross References. Section 2904 is referred to in section 6108 of Title 23 (Domestic Relations).

§ 2905. Interference with custody of committed persons.

(a) Offense denied.—A person is guilty of a misdemeanor of the second degree if he knowingly or recklessly takes or entices any committed person away from lawful custody when he is not privileged to do so.

(b) Definition.—As used in this section, the term "committed person" means, in addition to anyone committed under judicial warrant, any orphan, neglected or delinquent child, mentally disabled person, or other dependent or incapacitated person entrusted to the custody of another by or through a recognized social agency or otherwise by authority of law.

§ 2906. Criminal coercion.

(a) Offense denied.—A person is guilty of criminal coercion, if, with intent unlawfully to restrict freedom of action of another to the detriment of the other, he threatens to:

   (1) commit any criminal offense;

   (2) accuse anyone of a criminal offense;

   (3) expose any secret tending to subject any person to hatred, contempt or ridicule; or

   (4) take or withhold action as an official, or cause an official to take or withhold action.

(b) Defense.—It is a defense to prosecution based on paragraphs (a)(2), (a)(3) or (a)(4) of this section that the actor believed the accusation or secret to be true or the proposed official action justified and that his intent was limited to compelling the other to behave in a way reasonably related to the circumstances which were the subject of the accusation, exposure or proposed official action, as by desisting from further misbehavior, making good a wrong done, refraining from taking any action or responsibility for which the actor believes the other disqualified.

(c) Grading.—Criminal coercion is a misdemeanor of the second degree unless the threat is to commit a felony or the intent of the actor is felonious, in which cases the offense is a misdemeanor of the first degree.

§ 2908. Missing children.

(a) Duties of law enforcement agencies.—Law enforcement agencies shall have the following duties with respect to missing children:

   (1) To investigate a report of a missing child immediately upon receipt of the report regardless of the age of the missing child or the circumstances surrounding the disappearance of the child. In no case shall law enforcement agencies impose a mandatory waiting period prior to commencing the investigation of a missing child.

(2) When conducting a missing child investigation, to record all information relevant to the missing child and the circumstances surrounding the disappearance of the missing child on the appropriate law enforcement investigative report.

(3) To make an entry into the Missing Persons File through the Commonwealth Law Enforcement Assistance Network (CLEAN) in accord with Pennsylvania State Police policy and procedures immediately upon receipt of sufficient identification information on the missing child.

(3.1) To make an entry into the Unidentified Persons File through Commonwealth Law Enforcement Assistance Network (CLEAN) in accord with Pennsylvania State Police policy and procedures immediately upon:

(i) taking custody of an unidentified living child, such as an infant, or a physically or mentally disabled child; or

(ii) discovering an unidentified deceased child.

(4) To insure timely cancellation of any entry made pursuant to this section where the missing child has returned or is located.

(a.1) Unidentified deceased children.—Law enforcement agencies and coroners shall, with respect to unidentified deceased children, have the duty to make an entry into the Unidentified Deceased Person File through the Commonwealth Law Enforcement Assistance Network (CLEAN) in accordance with Pennsylvania State Police policy and procedures immediately upon observing or receiving any descriptive information on an unidentified deceased child.

(b) Definition.—As used in this section the term "CHILD" means a person under 18 years of age.

§ 2909. Concealment of whereabouts of a child.

(a) Offense defined.—A person who removes a child from the child's known place of residence with the intent to conceal the child's whereabouts from the child's parent or guardian, unless concealment is authorized by court order or is a reasonable response to domestic violence or child abuse, commits a felony of the third degree. For purposes of this subsection, the term "removes" includes personally removing the child from the child's known place of residence, causing the child to be removed from the child's known place of residence, preventing the child from returning or being returned to the child's known place of residence and, when the child's parent or guardian has a reasonable expectation that the person will return the child, failing to return the child to the child's known place of residence.

(b) Application.—A person may be convicted under subsection (a) if either of the following apply:

(1) The acts that initiated the concealment occurred in this Commonwealth.

(2) The offender or the parent or guardian from whom the child is being concealed resides in this Commonwealth.

(Feb. 2, 1990, P.L.6, No.4, eff. 60 days)

1990 Amendment. Act 4 added section 2909.

§ 2910. Luring a child into a motor vehicle or structure.

(a) Offense.—Unless the circumstances reasonably indicate that the child is in need of assistance, a person who lures or attempts to lure a child into a motor vehicle or structure without the consent, express or implied, of the child's parent or guardian commits a misdemeanor of the first degree.

(b) Affirmative defense.—It shall be an affirmative defense to a prosecution under this section that the person lured or attempted to lure the child into the structure for a lawful purpose.

(c) Definitions.—As used in this section, the following words and phrases shall have the meanings given to them in this subsection:

"Motor vehicle." Every self-propelled device in, upon or by which any person or property is or may be transported or drawn on a public highway.

"Structure." A house, apartment building, shop, warehouse, barn, building, vessel, railroad car, cargo container, house car, trailer, trailer coach, camper, mine, floating home or other enclosed structure capable of holding a child, which is not open to the general public.

1990, Feb. 2, P.L. 6, No. 4, § 3, effective in 60 days. Amended 2005, Nov. 10, P.L. 330, No. 64, § 1, effective in 60 days [Jan. 9, 2006].

CHAPTER 31
SEXUAL OFFENSES

Subchapter

A. General Provisions
B. Definition of Offenses

Enactment. Chapter 31 was added December 6, 1972, P.L.1482, No.334, effective in six months.

SUBCHAPTER A
GENERAL PROVISIONS

Sec.
3101. Definitions
3102. Mistake as to age.
3103. Spouse relationships.
3104. Evidence of victim's sexual conduct.
3105. Prompt complaint.
3106. Testimony of complainants.
3107. Resistance not required.

§ 3101. Definitions.

Subject to additional definitions contained in subsequent provisions of this chapter which are applicable to specific provisions of this chapter, the following words and phrases when used in this chapter shall have, unless the context clearly indicates otherwise, the meanings given to them in this section:

"Deviate sexual intercourse." Sexual intercourse per os or per anus between human beings who are not husband and wife, except as provided in section 3128 (relating to spousal sexual assault), and any form of sexual intercourse with an animal. The term also includes penetration, however slight, of the genitals or anus of another person with a foreign object for any purpose other than good faith medical, hygienic or law enforcement procedures.

"Foreign object." Includes any physical object not a part of the actor's body.

"Indecent Contact." Any touching of the sexual or other intimate parts of the person for the purpose of arousing or gratifying sexual desire, in either person.

"Sexual intercourse." In addition to its ordinary meaning, includes intercourse per os or per anus, with some penetration however slight; emission is not required.

(Dec. 21, 1984, P.L.1210, No.230, eff. 60 days; Feb. 2, 1990, P.L.6, No.4, eff. 60 days)

§ 3102. Mistake as to age.

Whenever in this chapter the criminality of conduct depends on a child being below the age of 14 years, it is no defense that the actor did not know the age of the child, or reasonably believed the child to be the age of 14 years or older. When criminality depends on the child's being below a critical age other than 14 years, it is a defense for the actor to prove by a preponderance of the evidence that he reasonably believed the child to be above the critical age.

(May 18, 1976, P.L. 120, No.53, eff. 30 days)

§ 3103. Spouse relationships.

Except as provided in section 3128 (relating to spousal sexual assault), whenever in this chapter the definition of an offense excludes conduct with a spouse, the exclusion shall be deemed to extend to persons living as man and wife, regardless of the legal status of their relationship: Provided, however, That the exclusion shall be inoperative as respects spouses living in separate residences, or in the same residence but under terms of a written separation agreement or an order of a court of record. Where the definition of an offense excludes conduct with a spouse, this shall not preclude conviction of a spouse as accomplice in a sexual act which he or she causes another person, not within the exclusion, to perform.

(May 18, 1976, P.L.120, No.53, eff. 30 days; Dec. 21, 1984, P.L.1210, No.230, eff. 60 days)

§ 3104. Evidence of victim's sexual conduct.

(a) General rule.—Evidence of specific instances of the alleged victim's past sexual conduct, opinion evidence of the alleged victim's past sexual conduct, and reputation evidence of the alleged victim's past sexual conduct shall not be admissible in prosecutions under this chapter except evidence of the alleged victim's past sexual conduct with the defendant where consent of the alleged victim is at issue and such evidence is otherwise admissible pursuant to the rules of evidence.

(b) Evidentiary proceedings.—A defendant who proposes to offer evidence of the alleged victim's past sexual conduct pursuant to subsection (a) shall file a written motion and offer of proof at the time of the trial. If, at the time of trial, the court determines that the motion and offer of proof are sufficient on their faces, the court shall order an in camera hearing and shall make findings on the record as the relevance and admissibility of the proposed evidence pursuant to the standards set forth in subsection (a).

(May 18, 1976, P.L.120, No.53, eff. 30 days)

§ 3105. Prompt complaint.

Prompt reporting to public authority is not required in a prosecution under this chapter: Provided, however, That nothing in this section shall be construed to prohibit a defendant from introducing evidence of the alleged victim's failure to promptly report the crime if such evidence would be admissible pursuant to the rules of evidence.

(May 18, 1976, P.L.120, No.53, eff. 30 days)

§ 3106. Testimony of complainants.

The credibility of an alleged victim of an offense under this chapter shall be determined by the same standard as is the credibility of an alleged victim of any other crime. The testimony of a victim need not be corroborated in prosecutions under this chapter. In any prosecution before a jury for an offense under this chapter, no instructions shall be given cautioning the jury to view the alleged victim's testimony in any other way than that in which all victim's testimony is viewed.

(May 18, 1976, P.L.120, No.53, eff. 30 days)

1976 Amendment. Act 53 added present section 3106.

Prior Provisions. Former section 3106, relating to the same subject matter, was repealed November 21, 1973, P.L. 339, No.115, effective in 60 days.

§ 3107. Resistance not required.

The alleged victim need not resist the actor in prosecutions under this chapter: Provided, however, That nothing in this section shall be construed to prohibit a defendant from introducing evidence that the alleged victim consented to the conduct in question.

(May 18, 1976, P.L.120, No.53, eff. 30 days)

1976 Amendment. Act 53 added section 3107.

SUBCHAPTER B
DEFINITION OF OFFENSES

Sec.
3121. Rape
3122. Statutory rape.
3122.1. Statutory sexual assault.
3123. Involuntary deviate sexual intercourse.
3124. Voluntary deviate sexual intercourse.
3124.2. Institutional sexual assault.
3124.3. Sexual assault by sports official, volunteer or employee of nonprofit association.
3125. Aggravated indecent assault.
3126. Indecent assault.
3127. Indecent exposure.
3128. Spousal sexual assault.
3129. Sexual intercourse with animal.
3130. Conduct relating to sex offenders.

§ 3121. Rape.

(a) Offense defined.—A person commits a felony of the first degree when he or she engages in sexual intercourse with a complainant:

(1) By forcible compulsion.

(2) By threat of forcible compulsion that would prevent resistance by a person of reasonable resolution.

(3) Who is unconscious or where the person knows that the complainant is unaware that the sexual intercourse is occurring.

(4) Where the person has substantially impaired the complainant's power to appraise or control his or her conduct by administering or employing, without the knowledge of the complainant, drugs, intoxicants or other means for the purpose of preventing resistance.

(5) Who suffers from a mental disability which renders the complainant incapable of consent.

(6) Who is less than 13 years of age.

(b) Additional penalties.—In addition to the penalty provided for by subsection (a), a person may be sentenced to an additional term not to exceed ten years' confinement and an additional amount not to exceed $100,000 where the person engages in sexual intercourse with a complainant and has substantially impaired the complainant's power to appraise or control his or her conduct by administering or employing, without the knowledge of the complainant, any substance for the purpose of preventing resistance through the inducement of euphoria, memory loss and any other effect of this substance.

1997 Amendment. Act 65 amended this sec.

Cross References. Section 3121 is referred to in sections 3125, 5708 of this title; sections 5303, 6344 of Title 23 (Domestic Relations); sections 5552, 9717, 9718, 9729 of Title 42 (Judiciary and Judicial Procedure).

§ 3122. Statutory rape.

A person who is 18 years of age or older commits statutory rape, a felony of the second degree, when he engages in sexual intercourse with another person not his spouse who is less than 14 years of age.

(May 18, 1976, P.L.120, No.53, eff. 30 days)

Cross References. Section 3122 is referred to in section 3125 of this title; sections 5303, 6344 of Title 23 (Domestic Relations); sections 5552, 9729 of Title 42 (Judiciary and Judicial Procedure).

§ 3122.1. Statutory sexual assault.

(a) Felony of the second degree.—Except as provided in section 3121 (relating to rape), a person commits a felony of the second degree when that person engages in sexual intercourse with a complainant to whom the person is not married who is under the age of 16 years and that person is either:

　(1)　four years older but less than eight years older than the complainant; or

　(2)　eight years older but less than 11 years older than the complainant.

(b) Felony of the first degree.—A person commits a felony of the first degree when that person engages in sexual intercourse with a complainant under the age of 16 years and that person is 11 or more years older than the complainant and the complainant and the person are not married to each other.

§ 3123. Involuntary deviate sexual intercourse.

A person commits a felony of the first degree when he engages in deviate sexual intercourse with another person:

　(1)　by forcible compulsion;

　(2)　by threat of forcible compulsion that would prevent resistance by a person of reasonable resolution;

　(3)　who is unconscious;

　(4)　who is so mentally deranged or deficient that such person is incapable of consent; or

　(6)　who is less than 16 years of age.

Cross References. Section 3123 is referred to in sections 3124, 3125, 5708 of this title; sections 5303, 6344 of Title 23 (Domestic Relations); sections 5552, 9717, 9718, 9729 of Title 42 (Judiciary and Judicial Procedure).

§ 3124. Voluntary deviate sexual intercourse.

A person who engages in deviate sexual intercourse under circumstances not covered by section 3123 of this title (relating to involuntary deviate sexual intercourse) is guilty of a misdemeanor of the second degree.

Cross References. Section 3124 is referred to in section 5552 of Title 42 (Judiciary and Judicial Procedure).

§ 3124.2. Institutional sexual assault.

(a) General rule.—Except as provided under subsection (a.1) and in sections 3121 (relating to rape), 3122.1 (relating to statutory sexual assault), 3123 (relating to involuntary deviate sexual intercourse), 3124.1 (relating to sexual assault) and 3125 (relating to aggravated indecent assault), a person who is an employee or agent of the Department of Corrections or a county correctional authority, youth development center, youth forestry camp, State or county juvenile detention facility, other licensed residential facility serving children and youth, or mental health or mental retardation facility or institution commits a felony of the third degree when that person engages in sexual intercourse, deviate sexual intercourse or indecent contact with an inmate, detainee, patient or resident.

(a.1) Institutional sexual assault of a minor.—A person who is an employee or agent of the Department of Corrections or a county correctional authority, youth development center, youth forestry camp, State or county juvenile detention facility, other licensed residential facility serving children and youth or mental health or mental retardation facility or institution commits a felony of the third degree when that person engages in sexual intercourse, deviate sexual intercourse or indecent contact with an inmate, detainee, patient or resident who is under 18 years of age.

(a.2) Schools.—

(1) Except as provided in sections 3121, 3122.1, 3123, 3124.1 and 3125, a person who is a volunteer or an employee of a school or any other person who has direct contact with a student at a school commits a felony of the third degree when he engages in sexual intercourse, deviate sexual intercourse or indecent contact with a student of the school.

(2) As used in this subsection, the following terms shall have the meanings given to them in this paragraph:

(i) "Direct contact." Care, supervision, guidance or control.

(ii) "Employee."

(A) Includes:

(I) A teacher, a supervisor, a supervising principal, a principal, an assistant principal, a vice principal, a director of vocational education, a dental hygienist, a visiting teacher, a home and school visitor, a school counselor, a child nutrition program specialist, a school librarian, a school secretary the selection of whom is on the basis of merit as determined by eligibility lists, a school nurse, a substitute teacher, a janitor, a cafeteria worker, a bus driver, a teacher aide and any other employee who has direct contact with school students.

(II) An independent contractor who has a contract with a school for the purpose of performing a service for the school, a coach, an athletic trainer, a coach hired as an independent contractor by the Pennsylvania Interscholastic Athletic Association or an athletic trainer hired as an independent contractor by the Pennsylvania Interscholastic Athletic Association.

(B) The term does not include:

(I) A student employed at the school.

(II) An independent contractor or any employee of an independent contractor who has no direct contact with school students.

(iii) "School." A public or private school, intermediate unit or area vocational-technical school.

(iv) "Volunteer." The term does not include a school student.

(a.3) Child care.—Except as provided in sections 3121, 3122.1, 3123, 3124.1 and 3125, a person who is a volunteer or an employee of a center for children commits a felony of the third degree when he engages in sexual intercourse, deviate sexual intercourse or indecent contact with a child who is receiving services at the center.

(b) Definitions.—As used in this section, the following words and phrases shall have the meanings given to them in this subsection unless the context clearly indicates otherwise:

"Agent." A person who is assigned to work in a State or county correctional or juvenile detention facility, a youth development center, youth forestry camp, other licensed residential facility serving children and youth or mental health or mental retardation facility or institution, who is employed by any State or county agency or any person employed by an entity providing contract services to the agency.

"Center for children." Includes a child day-care center, group and family day-care home, boarding home for children, a center providing early intervention and drug and alcohol services for children or other facility which provides child-care services which are subject to approval, licensure, registration or certification by the

Department of Public Welfare or a county social services agency or which are provided pursuant to a contract with the department or a county social services agency. The term does not include a youth development center, youth forestry camp, State or county juvenile detention facility and other licensed residential facility serving children and youth.

§ 3124.3. Sexual assault by sports official, volunteer or employee of nonprofit association.

(a) **Sports official.**—Except as provided in section 3121 (relating to rape), 3122.1 (relating to statutory sexual assault), 3123 (relating to involuntary deviate sexual intercourse), 3124.1 (relating to sexual assault) and 3125 (relating to aggravated indecent assault), a person who serves as a sports official in a sports program of a nonprofit association or a for-profit association commits a felony of the third degree when that person engages in sexual intercourse, deviate sexual intercourse or indecent contact with a child under 18 years of age who is participating in a sports program of the nonprofit association or for-profit association.

(b) **Volunteer or employee of nonprofit association.**—Except as provided in sections 3121, 3122.1, 3123, 3124.1 and 3125, a volunteer or an employee of a nonprofit association having direct contact with a child under 18 years of age who participates in a program or activity of the nonprofit association commits a felony of the third degree if the volunteer or employee engages in sexual intercourse, deviate sexual intercourse or indecent contact with that child.

(c) **Definitions.**—As used in this section, the following words and phrases shall have the meanings given to them in this subsection unless the context clearly indicates otherwise:

"**Direct contact.**" Care, supervision, guidance or control.

"**Nonprofit association.**" As defined in 42 Pa.C.S. § 8332.1 (relating to manager, coach, umpire or referee and nonprofit association negligence standard).

"**Sports official.**" A person who supervises children participating in a sports program of a nonprofit association or a for-profit association, including, but not limited to, a coach, assistant coach, athletic trainer, team attendant, game manager, instructor or a person at a sports program who enforces the rules of a sporting event sponsored by a sports program of a nonprofit association or a for-profit association, including, but not limited to, an umpire or referee, whether receiving remuneration or holding the position as a volunteer.

"**Sports program.**" As defined in 42 Pa.C.S. § 8332.1 (relating to manager, coach, umpire or referee and nonprofit association negligence standard).

History. June 18, 2014, P.L. 741 2014 No. 56, § 2, eff. 8/17/2014.

§ 3125. Aggravated indecent assault.

Except as provided in sections 3121 (relating to rape), 3122 (relating to statutory rape) and 3123 (relating to involuntary deviate sexual intercourse), a person commits a felony of the second degree when he engages in penetration, however slight, of the genitals or anus of another with a part of the actor's body for any purpose other than good faith medical, hygienic or law enforcement procedures if:

(1) he does so without the consent of other person;

(2) he knows that the other person suffers from a mental disease or defect which renders him or her incapable of appraising the nature of his or her conduct;

(3) knows that the other person is unaware that the indecent contact is being committed;

(4) he has substantially impaired the other person's power to appraise or control his or her conduct by administering or employing, without the knowledge

of the other, drugs, intoxicants or other means for the purpose of preventing resistance;

(5) the other person is in custody of law or detained in a hospital or other institution and the actor has supervisory or disciplinary authority over him; or

(6) he is over 18 years of age and the other person is under 14 years of age.

(Feb. 2, 1990, P.L.6, No.4, eff. 60 days)

1990 Amendment. Act 4 added section 3125.

Prior Provisions. Former section 3125, which related to corruption of minors, was added December 6, 1972, P.L.1482, No.334, and repealed July 1, 1978, P.L.573, No. 104, effective in 60 days.

Cross References. Section 3125 is referred to in section 5552 of Title 42 (Judiciary and Judicial Procedure).

§ 3126. Indecent assault.

(a) **Offense defined.**—A person is guilty of indecent assault if the person has indecent contact with the complainant, causes the complainant to have indecent contact with the person or intentionally causes the complainant to come into contact with seminal fluid, urine or feces for the purpose of arousing sexual desire in the person or the complainant and:

(1) the person does so without the complainant's consent;

(2) the person does so by forcible compulsion;

(3) the person does so by threat of forcible compulsion that would prevent resistance by a person of reasonable resolution;

(4) the complainant is unconscious or the person knows that the complainant is unaware that the indecent contact is occurring;

(5) the person has substantially impaired the complainant's power to appraise or control his or her conduct by administering or employing, without the knowledge of the complainant, drugs, intoxicants or other means for the purpose of preventing resistance;

(6) the complainant suffers from a mental disability which renders [him or her] the complainant incapable of consent;

(7) the complainant is less than 13 years of age; or

(8) the complainant is less than 16 years of age and the person is four or more years older than the complainant and the complainant and the person are not married to each other.

(b) **Grading.**—Indecent assault shall be graded as follows:

(1) An offense under subsection(a)(1) or (8) is amisdemeanor of the second degree.

(2) An offense under subsection(a)(2), (3), (4), (5) or (6) is a misdemeanor of the first degree.

(3) An offense under subsection(a)(7) is a misdemeanor of the first degree unless any of the following apply, in which case it is a felony of the third degree:

(i) It is a second or subsequent offense.

(ii) There has been a course of conduct of indecent assault by the person.

(iii) The indecent assault was committed by touching the complainant's sexual or intimate parts with sexual or intimate parts of the person.

(iv) The indecent assault is committed by touching the person's sexual or intimate parts with the complainant's sexual or intimate parts.

2005 Amendment. Act 76 amended this sec.

Cross References. Section 3126 is referred to in sections 5303, 6344 of Title 23 (Domestic Relations); sections 5552, 9729 of Title 42 (Judiciary and Judicial Procedure).

§ 3127. Indecent exposure.

A person commits a misdemeanor of the second degree if, for the purpose of arousing or gratifying sexual desire of himself or of any person other than his spouse, he exposes his genitals under circumstances in which he knows his conduct is likely to cause affront or alarm.

Cross References. Section 3127 is referred to in section 6344 of Title 23 (Domestic Relations); section 5552 of Title 42 (Judiciary and Judicial Procedure).

§ 3128. Spousal sexual assault.

(a) Sexual assault.—A person commits a felony of the second degree when that person engages in sexual intercourse with that person's spouse:

(1) by forcible compulsion;

(2) by threat of forcible compulsion that would prevent resistance by a person of reasonable resolution; or

(3) who is unconscious.

(b) Involuntary spousal deviate sexual intercourse.—A person commits a felony of the second degree when that person engages in deviate sexual intercourse with that person's spouse:

(1) by forcible compulsion;

(2) by threat of forcible compulsion that would prevent resistance by a person of reasonable resolution; or

(3) who is unconscious.

(c) Crime to be reported.—The crime of spousal sexual assault shall be personally reported by the victim or her agent to a law enforcement agency having the requisite jurisdiction within 90 days of the commission of the offense.

(Dec. 21, 1984, P.L.1210, No.230, eff. 60 days)

1984 Amendment. Act 230 added section 3128.

Cross References. Section 3128 is referred to in sections 3101, 3103, 3121, 3209 of this title.

§ 3129. Sexual intercourse with animal.

A person who engages in any form of sexual intercourse with an animal commits a misdemeanor of the second degree.

1999 Amendment. Act 8 added this section.

§ 3130. Conduct relating to sex offenders.

(a) Offense defined.—A person commits a felony of the third degree if the person has reason to believe that a sex offender is not complying with or has not complied with the requirements of the sex offender's probation or parole, imposed by statute or court order, or with the registration requirements of 42 Pa.C.S. Ch. 97 Subch. H (relating to registration of sexual offenders) or I (relating to continued registration of sexual offenders), and the person, with the intent to assist the sex offender in eluding a law enforcement agent or agency that is seeking to find the sex offender to question the sex offender about, or to arrest the sex offender for, noncompliance with the requirements of the sex offender's probation or parole or the requirements of 42 Pa.C.S. Ch. 97 Subch. H or I:

(1) withholds information from or does not notify the law enforcement agent or agency about the sex offender's noncompliance with the requirements of parole, the requirements of 42 Pa.C.S. Ch. 97 Subch. H or I or, if known, the sex offender's whereabouts;

(2) harbors or attempts to harbor or assist another person in harboring or attempting to harbor the sex offender;

(3) conceals or attempts to conceal, or assists another person in concealing or attempting to conceal, the sex offender; or

(4) provides information to the law enforcement agent or agency regarding the sex offender which the person knows to be false.

(b) Definition.—As used in this section, the term "sex offender" means a person who is required to register with the Pennsylvania State Police pursuant to the provisions of 42 Pa.C.S. Ch. 97 Subch. H or I.

(Nov. 29, 2006, P.L.1567, No.178, eff. Jan. 1, 2007; Dec. 20, 2011, P.L.446, No.111, eff. one year; Feb. 21, 2018, P.L.27, No.10, eff. imd.; June 12, 2018, P.L.140, No.29, eff. imd.)

2018 Amendment. Act 29 reenacted section 3130.

2006 Amendment. See the preamble to Act 178 in the appendix to this title for special provisions relating to legislative intent.

Cross References. Section 3130 is referred to in section 5329 of Title 23 (Domestic Relations).

SUBCHAPTER C
LOSS OF PROPERTY RIGHTS

Sec.

3141. General rule.
3142. Process and seizure (Repealed).
3143. Custody of property (Repealed).
3144. Disposal of property(Repealed).

Enactment. Subchapter C was added November 29, 2006, P.L.1567, No.178, effective January 1, 2007.

Special Provisions in Appendix. See the preamble to Act 178 of 2006 in the appendix to this title for special provisions relating to legislative intent.

§ 3141. General rule.

A person:

(1) convicted under section 3121 (relating to rape), 3122.1 (relating to statutory sexual assault), 3123 (relating to involuntary deviate sexual intercourse), 3124.1 (relating to sexual assault), 3125 (relating to aggravated indecent assault) or 3126 (relating to indecent assault); or

(2) required to register with the Pennsylvania State Police under 42 Pa.C.S. Ch. 97 Subch. H (relating to registration of sexual offenders) or I (relating to continued registration of sexual offenders);

may be required to forfeit property rights in any property or assets used to implement or facilitate commission of the crime or crimes of which the person has been convicted. The forfeiture shall be conducted in accordance with 42 Pa.C.S. §§ 5803 (relating to asset forfeiture), 5805 (relating to forfeiture procedure), 5806 (relating to motion for return of property), 5807 (relating to restrictions on use), 5807.1 (relating to prohibition on adoptive seizures) and 5808 (relating to exceptions).

(Dec. 20, 2011, P.L.446, No.111, eff. one year; June 29, 2017, P.L.247, No.13, eff. July 1, 2017; Feb. 21, 2018, P.L.27, No.10, eff. imd.; June 12, 2018, P.L.140, No.29, eff. imd.)

2018 Amendment. Act 29 reenacted section 3141.

Cross References. Section 3141 is referred to in section 5803 of Title 42 (Judiciary and Judicial Procedure).

ARTICLE D
OFFENSES AGAINST THE FAMILY

Chapter

43. Offenses Against the Family

CHAPTER 43
OFFENSES AGAINST THE FAMILY

Subchapter

A. Definition of Offenses Generally
B. Nonsupport (Repealed)

Enactment. Chapter 43 was added December 6, 1972, P.L.1482, No.334, effective in six months.

SUBCHAPTER A
DEFINITION OF OFFENSES GENERALLY

Sec.

4301. Bigamy.
4302. Incest.
4303. Concealing death of child.
4304. Endangering welfare of children.
4305. Dealing in infant children.
4306. Newborn protection.

§ 4301. Bigamy.

(a) Bigamy.—A married person is guilty of bigamy, a misdemeanor of the second degree, if he contracts or purports to contract another marriage, unless at the time of the subsequent marriage:

(1) the actor believes that the prior spouse is dead;

(2) the actor and the prior spouse have been living apart for two consecutive years throughout which the prior spouse was not known by the actor to be alive; or

(3) a court has entered a judgment purporting to terminate or annul any prior disqualifying marriage, and the actor does not know that judgment to be invalid.

(b) Other party to bigamous marriage.—A person is guilty of bigamy if he contracts or purports to contract marriage with another knowing that the other is thereby committing bigamy.

§ 4302. Incest.

(a) General rule.—Except as provided under subsection (b), a person is guilty of incest, a felony of the second degree, if that person knowingly marries or cohabits or has sexual intercourse with an ancestor or descendant, a brother or sister of the whole or half blood or an uncle, aunt, nephew or niece of the whole blood.

(b) Incest of a minor.—A person is guilty of incest of a minor, a felony of the second degree, if that person knowingly marries, cohabits with or has sexual intercourse with a complainant who is an ancestor or descendant, a brother or sister of the whole or half blood or an uncle, aunt, nephew or niece of the whole blood and:

(1) is under the age of 13 years; or

(2) is 13 to 18 years of age and the person is four or more years older than the complainant.

(c) **Relationships.**—The relationships referred to in this section include blood relationships without regard to legitimacy, and relationship of parent and child by adoption.

§ 4303. Concealing death of child.

(a) **Offense defined.**—A person is guilty of a misdemeanor of the first degree if he or she endeavors privately, either alone or by the procurement of others, to conceal the death of his or her child, so that it may not come to light, whether it was born dead or alive or whether it was murdered or not.

(b) **Procedure.**—If the same indictment or information charges any person with the murder of his or her child, as well as with the offense of the concealment of the death, the jury may acquit or convict him or her of both offenses, or find him or her guilty of one and acquit him or her of the other.

§ 4304. Endangering welfare of children.

(1) A parent, guardian or other person supervising the welfare of a child under 18 years of age, or a person that employs or supervises such a person, commits an offense if he knowingly endangers the welfare of the child by violating a duty of care, protection or support.

(2) A person commits an offense if the person, in an official capacity, prevents or interferes with the making of a report of suspected child abuse under 23 Pa.C.S. Ch. 63 (relating to child protective services).

(3) As used in this subsection, the term "person supervising the welfare of a child" means a person other than a parent or guardian that provides care, education, training or control of a child.

(b) **Grading.**—

(1) Except as provided under paragraph (2), the following apply:

(i) An offense under this section constitutes a misdemeanor of the first degree(ii) If the actor engaged in a course of conduct of endangering the welfare of a child, the offense constitutes a felony of the third degree.

(iii) If, in the commission of the offense under subsection (a)(1), the actor created a substantial risk of death or serious bodily injury, the offense constitutes a felony of the third degree.

(iv) If the actor's conduct under subsection (a)(1) created a substantial risk of death or serious bodily injury and was part of a course of conduct, the offense constitutes a felony of the second degree.

(2) The grading of an offense under this section shall be increased one grade if, at the time of the commission of the offense, the child was under six years of age.

(c) **Counseling.**—A court shall consider ordering an individual convicted of an offense under this section to undergo counseling.

1972, Dec. 6, P.L. 1482, No. 334, § 1, effective June 6, 1973. Amended 1988, Dec. 19, P.L. 1275, No. 158, § 1, effective in 60 days; 1995, July 6, P.L. 251, No. 31, § 1, effective in 60 days; 2006, Nov. 29, P.L. 1581, No. 179, § 1, effective in 60 days [Jan. 29, 2007]; 2017, June 29, P.L. 246, No. 12, § 1, effective in 60 days [Aug. 28, 2017].

JT. ST. GOVT. COMM. COMMENT—1967

This section is derived from Section 230.4 of the Model Penal Code.

There is no similar provision in existing law. Section 727 of The Penal Code of 1939 (18 P.S. § 4727) covers neglect to maintain a child or abandonment of a child by a parent or person having custody; Section 728 (18 P.S. § 4728) punishes cruelty to minors. Section 726 (18 P.S. § 4726) punishes the abandonment by a parent of a child under seven (7) years of age; Section 641 (18 P.S. § 4641) makes it a crime for a person having custody of a child to employ such child for certain purposes; etc.

This section consolidates and simplifies the various provisions concerning crimes endangering the welfare of children. The offense involves the endangering of the physical or moral welfare of a child by an act or omission in violation of legal duty even though such legal duty does not itself carry a criminal sanction.

Penalty: Present law provides penalties ranging from 3 years or less. The maximum under the new provision would be 2 years.

§ 4305. Dealing in infant children.

A person is guilty of a misdemeanor of the first degree if he deals in humanity, by trading, bartering, buying, selling, or dealing in infant children.

Cross References. Section 4305 is referred to in section 5708 of this title; sections 2533, 6344 of Title 23 (Domestic Relations).

§ 4306. Newborn protection.

(a) General rule.—A parent of a newborn shall not be criminally liable for any violation of this title solely for leaving a newborn in the care of a hospital, a police officer at a police station pursuant to 23 Pa.C.S. Ch. 65 (relating to newborn protection) or an emergency services provider on the grounds of an entity employing the emergency services provider or otherwise providing access to the emergency services provider pursuant to 23 Pa.C.S. Ch. 65 if the following criteria are met:

(1) The parent expresses, either orally or through conduct, the intent to have the hospital, police officer or emergency services provider accept the newborn pursuant to 23 Pa.C.S. Ch. 65.

(2) The newborn is not a victim of child abuse or criminal conduct.

(a.1) Incubator.—A parent of a newborn shall not be criminally liable for any violation of this title solely for leaving a newborn in an incubator if the newborn is not a victim of child abuse or criminal conduct and the incubator is located:

(1) at a hospital;

(2) at a police station pursuant to 23 Pa.C.S. Ch. 65; or

(3) on the grounds of an entity employing the emergency services provider or otherwise providing access to the emergency services provider pursuant to 23 Pa.C.S. Ch. 65.

(b) Definitions.—As used in this section, the following words and phrases shall have the meanings given to them in this subsection unless the context clearly indicates otherwise:

"Child abuse." As defined in 23 Pa.C.S. § 6303(b.1) (relating to definitions).

"Emergency services provider." An emergency medical responder, emergency medical technician, advanced emergency medical technician or a paramedic as defined in 35 Pa.C.S. § 8103 (relating to definitions).

"Newborn." As defined in 23 Pa.C.S. § 6502 (relating to definitions).

"Police department." A public agency of a political subdivision having general police powers and charged with making arrests in connection with the enforcement of criminal or traffic laws.

"Police officer." A full-time or part-time employee assigned to criminal or traffic law enforcement duties of a police department of a county, city, borough, town or township. The term also includes a member of the State Police Force.

"Police station." The station or headquarters of a police department or a Pennsylvania State Police station or headquarters.

(Dec. 9, 2002, P.L.1549, No.201, eff. 60 days; July 2, 2014, P.L.843, No.91, eff. 60 days; Dec. 22, 2017, P.L.1219, No.68)

2017 Amendment. Section 7(2) of Act 68 provided that the addition of subsec. (a.1) shall take effect 120 days after the publication in the Pennsylvania Bulletin of the promulgation of final regulations under 23 Pa.C.S. § 6504.3(c).

2014 Amendment. Act 91 amended subsecs. (a) intro. par. and (1) and (b).

2002 Amendment. Act 201 added section 4306.

Cross References. Section 4306 is referred to in sections 6503, 6504.2 of Title 23 (Domestic Relations).

SUBCHAPTER B
NONSUPPORT
(REPEALED)

1985 Repeal Note. Subchapter B (§§ 4321-4324) was added December 6, 1972, P.L.1482, No.334, and repealed October 30, 1985, P.L.264, No.66, effective in 90 days. The subject matter is now contained in Chapter 43 of Title 23 (Domestic Relations).

ARTICLE E
OFFENSES AGAINST PUBLIC ADMINISTRATION

CHAPTER 49
FALSIFICATION AND INTIMIDATION

Subchapter

A. Perjury and Falsification in Official Matters
B. Victim and Witness Intimidation

Enactment. Chapter 49 was added December 6, 1972, P.L.1482, No.334, effective in six months.

Chapter Heading. The heading of Chapter 49 was amended December 4, 1980, P.L.1097, No.187, effective in 60 days.

Cross References. Chapter 49 is referred to in section 911 of this title; section 6122 of Title 23 (Domestic Relations); section 5508.3 of Title 53 (Municipalities Generally); section 6017 of Title 64 (Public Authorities and Quasi-Public Corporations).

SUBCHAPTER A
PERJURY AND FALSIFICATION IN OFFICIAL MATTERS

Sec.

4906.1. False reports of child abuse.

§ 4906.1. False reports of child abuse.

A person commits a misdemeanor of the second degree if the person intentionally or knowingly makes a false report of child abuse under 23 Pa.C.S. Ch. 63 (relating to child protective services) or intentionally or knowingly induces a child to make a false claim of child abuse under 23 Pa.C.S. Ch. 63.

(Dec. 18, 2013, P.L.1198, No.118, eff. Jan. 1, 2014)

2013 Amendment. Act 118 added section 4906.1.

Cross References. Section 4906.1 is referred to in section 6331 of Title 23 (Domestic Relations).

SUBCHAPTER B
VICTIM AND WITNESS INTIMIDATION

Sec.

4958. Intimidation, retaliation or obstruction in child abuse cases.

§ 4958. Intimidation, retaliation or obstruction in child abuse cases.

(a) **Intimidation.**—A person commits an offense if:

(1) The person has knowledge or intends that the person's conduct under paragraph (2) will obstruct, impede, impair, prevent or interfere with the making of a child abuse report or the conducting of an investigation into suspected child abuse under 23 Pa.C.S. Ch. 63 (relating to child protective services) or prosecuting a child abuse case.

(2) The person intimidates or attempts to intimidate any reporter, victim or witness to engage in any of the following actions:

(i) Refrain from making a report of suspected child abuse or not cause a report of suspected child abuse to be made.

(ii) Refrain from providing or withholding information, documentation, testimony or evidence to any person regarding a child abuse investigation or proceeding.

(iii) Give false or misleading information, documentation, testimony or evidence to any person regarding a child abuse investigation or proceeding.

(iv) Elude, evade or ignore any request or legal process summoning the reporter, victim or witness to appear to testify or supply evidence regarding a child abuse investigation or proceeding.

(v) Fail to appear at or participate in a child abuse proceeding or meeting involving a child abuse investigation to which the reporter, victim or witness has been legally summoned.

(b) Retaliation.—A person commits an offense if the person harms another person by any unlawful act or engages in a course of conduct or repeatedly commits acts which threaten another person in retaliation for anything that the other person has lawfully done in the capacity of a reporter, witness or victim of child abuse.

(b.1) Obstruction.—In addition to any other penalty provided by law, a person commits an offense if, with intent to prevent a public servant from investigating or prosecuting a report of child abuse under 23 Pa.C.S. Ch. 63, the person by any scheme or device or in any other manner obstructs, interferes with, impairs, impedes or perverts the investigation or prosecution of child abuse.

(c) Grading.—

(1) An offense under this section is a felony of the second degree if:

(i) The actor employs force, violence or deception or threatens to employ force, violence or deception upon the reporter, witness or victim or, with reckless intent or knowledge, upon any other person.

(ii) The actor offers pecuniary or other benefit to the reporter, witness or victim.

(iii) The actor's conduct is in furtherance of a conspiracy to intimidate or retaliate against the reporter, witness or victim.

(iv) The actor accepts, agrees or solicits another person to accept any pecuniary benefit to intimidate or retaliate against the reporter, witness or victim.

(v) The actor has suffered a prior conviction for a violation of this section or has been convicted under a Federal statute or statute of any other state of an act which would be a violation of this section if committed in this Commonwealth.

(2) An offense not otherwise addressed in paragraph (1) is a misdemeanor of the second degree.

(d) Definitions.—The following words and phrases when used in this section shall have the meanings given to them in this subsection unless the context clearly indicates otherwise:

"Child abuse." As defined in 23 Pa.C.S. § 6303(b.1) (relating to definitions).

"Mandated reporter." As defined in 23 Pa.C.S. § 6303(b)(b.1).

"Public servant." As defined in section 4501 (relating to definitions).

"Reporter." A person, including a mandated reporter, having reasonable cause to suspect that a child under 18 years of age is a victim of child abuse.

(Dec. 18, 2013, P.L.1198, No.118, eff. Jan. 1, 2014)

2013 Amendment. Act 118 added section 4958.

ARTICLE F
OFFENSES AGAINST PUBLIC ORDER AND DECENCY

CHAPTER 55
RIOT, DISORDERLY CONDUCT AND RELATED OFFENSES

§ 5504. **Harassment and stalking by communication or address. [Repealed]**

2002 Amendment. Act 218 repealed this sec.

2002 Repeal Note. Section 5504 was repealed December 9, 2002, P.L.1759, No.218, effective in 60 days.

ARTICLE G
MISCELLANEOUS OFFENSES

Chapter

63. Minors

CHAPTER 63
MINORS

Subchapter

C. Other Dangerous Articles

SUBCHAPTER C
OTHER DANGEROUS ARTICLES

Sec.

6301. Corruption of minors.
6312. Sexual abuse of children.
6321. Transmission of sexually explicit images by minor.

§ 6301. Corruption of minors.

(a) Offense defined.—

(1) Whoever, being of the age of 18 years and upwards, by any act corrupts or tends to corrupt the morals of any minor less than 18 years of age, or who aids, abets, entices or encourages any such minor in the commission of any crime, or who knowingly assists or encourages such minor in violating his or her parole or any order of court, commits a misdemeanor of the first degree.

(2) Any person who knowingly aids, abets, entices or encourages a minor younger than 18 years of age to commit truancy commits a summary offense. Any person who violates this paragraph within one year of the date of a first conviction under this section commits a misdemeanor of the third degree. A conviction under this paragraph shall not, however, constitute a prohibition under section 6105 (relating to persons not to possess, use, manufacture, control, sell or transfer firearms).

(b) Adjudication of delinquency unnecessary.—A conviction under the provisions of this section may be had whether or not the jurisdiction of any juvenile court has attached or shall thereafter attach to such minor or whether or not such minor has been adjudicated a delinquent or shall thereafter be adjudicated a delinquent.

(c) Presumptions.—In trials and hearings upon charges of violating the provisions of this section, knowledge of the minor's age and of the court's orders and decrees concerning such minor shall be presumed in the absence of proof to the contrary.

(d) Mistake as to age.—

(1) Whenever in this section the criminality of conduct depends upon the corruption of a minor whose actual age is under 16 years, it is no defense that the actor did not know the age of the minor or reasonably believed the minor to be older than 18 years.

(2) Whenever in this section the criminality of conduct depends upon the corruption of a minor whose actual age is 16 years or more but less than 18 years, it is a defense for the actor to prove by a preponderance of the evidence that he reasonably believed the minor to be 18 years or older.

1978, July 1, P.L. 573, No. 104, § 1, effective in 60 days. Amended 1996, July 11, P.L. 552, No. 98, § 4, effective in 60 days.

§ 6312. Sexual abuse of children.

(a) Deleted by 2009, July 14, P.L. 63, No. 15, § 1, effective in 60 days [Sept. 14, 2009].

(b) **Photographing, videotaping, depicting on computer or filming sexual acts.**—Any person who causes or knowingly permits a child under the age of 18 years to engage in a prohibited sexual act or in the simulation of such act is guilty of a felony of the second degree if such person knows, has reason to know or intends that such act may be photographed, videotaped, depicted on computer or filmed. Any person who knowingly photographs, videotapes, depicts on computer or films a child under the age of 18 years engaging in a prohibited sexual act or in the simulation of such an act is guilty of a felony of the second degree.

(c) **Dissemination of photographs, videotapes, computer depictions and films.**—

(1) Any person who knowingly sells, distributes, delivers, disseminates, transfers, displays or exhibits to others, or who possesses for the purpose of sale, distribution, delivery, dissemination, transfer, display or exhibition to others, any book, magazine, pamphlet, slide, photograph, film, videotape, computer depiction or other material depicting a child under the age of 18 years engaging in a prohibited sexual act or in the simulation of such act commits an offense.

(2) A first offense under this subsection is a felony of the third degree, and a second or subsequent offense under this subsection is a felony of the second degree.

(d) **Child pornography.**—

(1) Any person who intentionally views or knowingly possesses or controls any book, magazine, pamphlet, slide, photograph, film, videotape, computer depiction or other material depicting a child under the age of 18 years engaging in a prohibited sexual act or in the simulation of such act commits an offense.

(2) A first offense under this subsection is a felony of the third degree, and a second or subsequent offense under this subsection is a felony of the second degree.

(e) **Evidence of age.**—In the event a person involved in a prohibited sexual act is alleged to be a child under the age of 18 years, competent expert testimony shall be sufficient to establish the age of said person.

(e.1) **Mistake as to age.**—Under subsection (b) only, it is no defense that the defendant did not know the age of the child. Neither a misrepresentation of age by the child nor a bona fide belief that the person is over the specified age shall be a defense.

(f) **Exceptions.**—This section does not apply to any of the following:

(1) Any material that is viewed, possessed, controlled, brought or caused to be brought into this Commonwealth, or presented, for a bona fide educational, scientific, governmental or judicial purpose.

(2) Conduct prohibited under section 6321 (relating to transmission of sexually explicit images by minor), unless the conduct is specifically excluded by section 6321(d).

(3) An individual under 18 years of age who knowingly views, photographs, videotapes, depicts on a computer or films or possesses or intentionally views a visual depiction as defined in section 6321 of himself alone in a state of nudity as defined in section 6321.

(g) **Definitions.**—As used in this section, the following words and phrases shall have the meanings given to them in this subsection:

"Intentionally views." The deliberate, purposeful, voluntary viewing of material depicting a child under 18 years of age engaging in a prohibited sexual act or in the simulation of such act. The term shall not include the accidental or inadvertent viewing of such material.

"**Prohibited sexual act.**" Sexual intercourse as defined in section 3101 (relating to definitions), masturbation, sadism, masochism, bestiality, fellatio, cunnilingus, lewd exhibition of the genitals or nudity if such nudity is depicted for the purpose of sexual stimulation or gratification of any person who might view such depiction.

1977, Oct. 26, P.L. 212, No. 62, § 1, effective in 60 days. Amended 1988, Dec. 19, P.L. 1275, No. 158, § 3, effective in 60 days; 1995, March 31, P.L. 985, No. 10 (Spec. Sess. No. 1), § 11, effective in 60 days; 2002, Nov. 20, P.L. 1104, No. 134, § 1, effective in 60 days; 2009, July 14, P.L. 63, No. 15, § 1, effective in 60 days [Sept. 14, 2009]; Oct. 25, 2012 P.L. 1623, No. 198, eff. in 60 days [Dec. 24, 2012].

§ 6321. Transmission of sexually explicit images by minor.

(a) Summary offense.—Except as provided in section 6312 (relating to sexual abuse of children), a minor commits a summary offense when the minor:

(1) Knowingly transmits, distributes, publishes or disseminates an electronic communication containing a sexually explicit image of himself.

(2) Knowingly possesses or knowingly views a sexually explicit image of a minor who is 12 years of age or older.

(b) Misdemeanor of the third degree.—Except as provided in section 6312, a minor commits a misdemeanor of the third degree. when the minor knowingly transmits, distributes, publishes or disseminates an electronic communication containing a sexually explicit image of another minor who is 12 years of age or older.

(c) Misdemeanor of the second degree.—Except as provided in section 6312, a minor commits a misdemeanor of the second degree when, with the intent to coerce, intimidate, torment, harass or otherwise cause emotional distress to another minor, the minor:

(1) makes a visual depiction of any minor in a state of nudity without the knowledge and consent of the depicted minor; or

(2) transmits, distributes, publishes or disseminates a visual depiction of any minor in a state of nudity without the knowledge and consent of the depicted minor.

(d) Application of section.—This section shall not apply to the following:

(1) Conduct that involves images that depict sexual intercourse, deviate sexual intercourse or penetration, however slight, of the genitals or anus of a minor, masturbation, sadism, masochism or bestiality.

(2) Conduct that involves a sexually explicit image of a minor, if the image was taken, made, used or intended to be used for or in furtherance of a commercial purpose.

(e) Forfeiture.—Any electronic communication device used in violation of this section shall be subject to forfeiture to the Commonwealth and no property right shall exist in it.

(f) Diversionary program.—The magisterial district judge or any judicial authority with jurisdiction over the violation may refer shall give first consideration to referring a person charged with a violation of subsection (a) to a diversionary program under 42 Pa.C.S. § 1520 (relating to adjudication alternative program) and the Pennsylvania Rules of Criminal Procedure. As part of the diversionary program, the magisterial district judge or any judicial authority with jurisdiction over the violation may order the person to participate in an educational program which includes the legal and nonlegal consequences of sharing sexually explicit images. If the person successfully completes the diversionary program, the person's records of the charge of violating subsection (a) shall be expunged as provided for under Pa.R.C.P. No. 320 (relating to expungement upon successful completion of ARD program).

(g) Definitions.—As used in this section, the following words and phrases shall have the meanings given to them in this subsection unless the context clearly indicates otherwise:

"Disseminate." To cause or make an electronic or actual communication from one person, place or electronic communication device to two or more other persons, places or electronic communication devices.

"Distribute." To deliver or pass out.

"Electronic communication." As defined in section 5702 (relating to definitions).

"Knowingly possesses." The deliberate, purposeful, voluntary possession of a sexually explicit image of another minor who is 12 years of age or older. The term shall not include the accidental or inadvertent possession of such an image.

"Knowingly views." The deliberate, purposeful, voluntary viewing of a sexually explicit image of another minor who is 12 years of age or older. The term shall not include the accidental or inadvertent viewing of such an image.

"Minor." An individual under 18 years of age.

"Nudity." The showing of the human male or female genitals, pubic area or buttocks with less than a fully opaque covering, the showing of the female breast with less than a fully opaque covering of any portion thereof below the top of the nipple or the depiction of covered male genitals in a discernibly turgid state.

"Publish." To issue for distribution.

"Sexually explicit image." A lewd or lascivious visual depiction of a minor's genitals, pubic area, breast or buttocks or nudity, if such nudity is depicted for the purpose of sexual stimulation or gratification of any person who might view such nudity.

"Transmit." To cause or make an electronic communication from one person, place or electronic communication device to only one other person, place or electronic communication device.

"Visual depiction." A representation by picture, including, but not limited to, a photograph, videotape, film or computer image.

October 25, 2012, P.L. 1623, No. 198, effective in 60 days [Dec. 24, 2012].

TITLE 20
PROBATE, ESTATES AND FIDUCIARIES CODE

Sec.
2106. Forfeiture.
2203. Right of election; resident decedent.
2507. Modification by circumstances.
5605. Power of attorney not revoked until notice.
5606. Proof of continuance of powers of attorney by affidavit.
6111.1. Modification by divorce.
6111.2. Effect of divorce on designation of beneficiaries.

§ 2106. Forfeiture.

(a) Spouse's share.—

(1) A spouse who, for one year or upwards previous to the death of the other spouse, has willfully neglected or refused to perform the duty to support the other spouse, or who for one year or upwards has willfully and maliciously deserted the other spouse, shall have no right or interest under this chapter in the real or personal estate of the other spouse.

(2) A spouse shall have no right or interest under this chapter in the real or personal estate of the other spouse if:

(i) the other spouse dies domiciled in this Commonwealth during the course of divorce proceedings;

(ii) no decree of divorce has been entered pursuant to 23 Pa.C.S. § 3323 (relating to decree of court); and

(iii) grounds have been established as provided in 23 Pa.C.S. § 3323(g).

(b) Parent's share.—Any parent who, for one year or upwards previous to the death of the parent's minor or dependent child, has :

(1) failed to perform the duty to support the minor or dependent child or who, for one year, has deserted the minor or dependent child; or

(2) been convicted of one of the following offenses under Title 18:

section 4303 (relating to concealing death of child);

section 4304 (relating to endangering welfare of children);

section 6312 (relating to sexual abuse of children);

or an equivalent crime under Federal law or the law of another state involving his or her child;

shall have no right or interest under this chapter in the real or personal estate of the minor or dependent child. The determination under paragraph (1) shall be made by the court after considering the quality, nature and extent of the parent's contact with the child and the physical, emotional and financial support provided to the child.

(c) Slayer's share.—Any person who participates either as a principal or as an accessory before the fact in the wilful and unlawful killing of any person shall not in any way acquire property or receive any benefits as the result of such killing, but such property or benefits shall be distributed as provided in Chapter 88 of this code (relating to slayers).

(d) Surviving spouse as witness.—The surviving husband or wife shall be a competent witness as to all matters pertinent to the issue of forfeiture under this section.

1972, June 30, P.L. 508, No. 164, § 2, eff. July 1, 1972. Amended 1974, Dec. 10, P.L. 867, No. 293, § 5, imd. effective; 1976, July 9, P.L. 551, No. 135, § 5, imd. effective;

1984, March 7, P.L. 103, No. 21, § 1, imd. effective; 2000, Dec. 20, P.L. 838, No. 118, § 1, effective in 60 days; 2010, Oct. 27, P.L. 837, No. 85, effective in 60 days.

§ 2203. Right of election; resident decedent.

(a) **Property Subject to Election.**—Except as provided in subsection (c), when a married person domiciled in this commonwealth dies, his surviving spouse has a right to an elective share of one-third of the following property:

(1) Property passing from the decedent by will or intestacy.

(2) Income or use for the remaining life of the spouse of property conveyed by the decedent during the marriage to the extent that the decedent at the time of his death had the use of the property or an interest in or power to withdraw the income thereof.

(3) Property conveyed by the decedent during his lifetime to the extent that the decedent at the time of his death had a power to revoke the conveyance or to consume, invade or dispose of the principal for his own benefit.

(4) Property conveyed by the decedent during the marriage to himself and another or others with right of survivorship to the extent of any interest in the property that the decedent had the power at the time of his death unilaterally to convey absolutely or in fee.

(5) Survivorship rights conveyed to a beneficiary of an annuity contract to the extent it was purchased by the decedent during the marriage and the decedent was receiving annuity payments therefrom at the time of his death.

(6) Property conveyed by the decedent during the marriage and within one year of his death to the extent that the aggregate amount so conveyed to each donee exceeds $3,000, valued at the time of conveyance. In construing this subsection, a power in the decedent to withdraw income or principal, or a power in any person whose interest is not adverse to the decedent to distribute to or use for the benefit of the decedent any income or principal, shall be deemed to be a power in the decedent to withdraw so much of the income or principal as is subject to such power, even though such income or principal may be distributed only for support or other particular purpose or only in limited periodic amounts.

(b) **Property not subject to election.**—The provisions of subsection (a) shall not be construed to include any of the following except to the extent that they pass as part of the decedent's estate to his personal representative, heirs, legatees or devisees:

(1) Any conveyance made with the express consent or joinder of the surviving spouse.

(2) The proceeds of insurance, including accidental death benefits, on the life of the decedent.

(3) Interests under any broad-based nondiscriminatory pension, profit sharing, stock bonus, deferred compensation, disability, death benefit or other such plan established by an employer for the benefit of its employees and their beneficiaries.

(4) Property passing by the decedent's exercise or nonexercise of any power of appointment given by someone other than the decedent.

(c) **Nonapplicability.**—Pursuant to 23 Pa.C.S. § 3323(d.1) (relating to decree of court), this section shall not apply in the event a married person domiciled in this commonwealth dies during the course of divorce proceedings, no decree of divorce has been entered pursuant to 23 Pa.C.S. § 3323 and grounds have been established as provided in 23 Pa.C.S. § 3323(g).

§ 2507. Modification by circumstances.

Wills shall be modified upon the occurrence of any of the following circumstances, among others:

(1) Repealed by 1976, July 9, P.L. 551, No. 135, § 8, imd. effective.

(2) Divorce or pending divorce.—Any provision in a testator's will in favor of or relating to the testator's spouse shall become ineffective for all purposes unless it appears from the will that the provision was intended to survive a divorce, if the testator:

(i) is divorced from such spouse after making the will; or

(ii) dies domiciled in this Commonwealth during the course of divorce proceedings, no decree of divorce has been entered pursuant to 23 Pa.C.S. § 3323 (relating to decree of court) and grounds have been established as provided in 23 Pa.C.S. § 3323(g).

(3) Marriage.—If the testator marries after making a will, the surviving spouse shall receive the share of the estate to which he would have been entitled had the testator died intestate, unless the will shall give him a greater share or unless it appears from the will that the will was made in contemplation of marriage to the surviving spouse.

(4) Birth or adoption. If the testator fails to provide in his will for his child born or adopted after making his will, unless it appears from the will that the failure was intentional, such child shall receive out of the testator's property not passing to a surviving spouse, such share as he would have received if the testator had died unmarried and intestate owning only that portion of his estate not passing to a surviving spouse.

(5) Slaying. Any person who participates either as a principal or as an accessory before the fact in the wilful and unlawful killing of any person shall not in any way acquire property or receive any benefits as the result of the wilful and unlawful killing but such property or benefits shall be distributed as provided by Chapter 88 of this code (relating to slayers).

1972, June 30, P.L. 508, No. 164, § 2, eff. July 1, 1972. Amended 1992, Dec. 16, P.L. 1163, No. 152, § 3, imd. Effective; 2010, Oct. 27, P.L. 837, No. 85, effective in 60 days.

2010 Amendment. Act 85 amended this sec.

1992 Amendment. Act 152 amended pars. (2) and (3). Section 27(d) of Act 152 provided that the amendment of pars. (2) and (3) shall apply to the estates of decedents dying on or after the effective date of Act 152.

1976 Repeal Note. Act 135 replaced par. (1).

Cross References. Section 2507 is referred to in section 3153 of this title.

CHAPTER 56

POWERS OF ATTORNEY

Sec.
5601. General provisions.
5601.1. Powers of attorney presumed durable.
5601.2. Special rules for gifts (Repealed).
5601.3. Agent's duties.
5601.4. Authority that requires specific and general grant of authority.
5602. Form of power of attorney.
5603. Implementation of power of attorney.
5604. Durable powers of attorney.
5605. Power of attorney not revoked until notice.
5606. Proof of continuance of powers of attorney by affidavit.
5607. Corporate agent.
5608. Acceptance of and reliance upon power of attorney.
5608.1 Liability for refusal to accept power of attorney.
5608.2. Activities through employees.
5609. Compensation and reimbursement for expenses.
5610. Account.
5611. Validity.
5612. Principles of law and equity.
5613. Meaning and effect of power of attorney.
5614. Jurisdiction and venue.

Enactment. Present Chapter 56 was added February 18, 1982, P.L.45, No.26, effective immediately.

Special Provisions in Appendix. See section 21 of Act 79 of 2016 in the appendix to this title for special provisions relating to applicability.

Applicability. Section 13 of Act 26 of 1982 provided that Chapter 56 shall apply to all powers of attorney executed on or after the date of enactment of Act 26 and provided that nothing in Act 26 shall be construed to limit the effectiveness of powers of attorney in effect prior to the date of enactment of Act 26.

Prior Provisions. Former Chapter 56, which related to the same subject matter, was added December 10, 1974, P.L.899, No.295, and repealed February 18, 1982, P.L.45, No.26, effective immediately.

Cross References. Chapter 56 is referred to in sections 711, 5601, 7732 of this title section 2713 of Title 18 (Crimes and Offenses).

§ 5601. General provisions.

(a) General rule.—In addition to all other powers that may be delegated to an agent, any or all of the powers referred to in section 5602(a) (relating to form of power of attorney) may lawfully be granted in writing to an agent and, unless the power of attorney expressly directs to the contrary, shall be construed in accordance with the provisions of this chapter.

(b) Execution.—

(1) A power of attorney shall be dated, and it shall be signed by the principal by signature or mark, or by another individual on behalf of and at the direction of the principal if the principal is unable to sign but specifically directs another individual to sign the power of attorney.

(2) If the power of attorney is executed by mark or by another individual, then it shall be witnessed by two individuals, each of whom is 18 years of age or older. A witness shall not be the individual who signed the power of attorney on behalf of and at the direction of the principal.

(3) For a power of attorney executed on or after the effective date of this paragraph, the signature or mark of the principal, or the signature of another individual signing a power of attorney on behalf of and at the direction of the principal, shall be:

(i) Acknowledged before a notary public or other individual authorized by law to take acknowledgments. The notary public or other individual authorized by law to take acknowledgments shall not be the agent designated in the power of attorney.

(ii) Witnessed by two individuals, each of whom is 18 years of age or older. A witness shall not be the individual who signed the power of attorney on behalf of and at the direction of the principal, the agent designated in the power of attorney or the notary public or other person authorized by law to take acknowledgments before whom the power of attorney is acknowledged. Nothing in this section shall prohibit an acknowledgment of a power of attorney before a member of the bar of the Pennsylvania Supreme Court in the manner authorized by 42 Pa.C.S. § 327(a) (relating to oaths and acknowledgments) certified in the manner provided by 57 Pa.C.S. § 316(2.1) (relating to short form certificates) provided the attorney taking the acknowledgment does not act as one of the two witnesses required by this paragraph.

(c) **Notice.**—All powers of attorney shall include the following notice in capital letters at the beginning of the power of attorney. The notice shall be signed by the principal. In the absence of a signed notice, upon a challenge to the authority of an agent to exercise a power under the power of attorney, the agent shall have the burden of demonstrating that the exercise of this authority is proper.

NOTICE

The purpose of this power of attorney is to give the person you designate (your "agent") broad powers to handle your property, which may include powers to sell or otherwise dispose of any real or personal property without advance notice to you or approval by you.

This power of attorney does not impose a duty on your agent to exercise granted powers, but, when powers are exercised, your agent must use due care to act for your benefit and in accordance with this power of attorney.

Your agent may exercise the powers given here throughout your lifetime, even after you become incapacitated, unless you expressly limit the duration of these powers or you revoke these powers or a court acting on your behalf terminates your agent's authority.

Your agent must act in accordance with your reasonable expectations to the extent actually known by your agent and, otherwise, in your best interest, act in good faith and act only within the scope of authority granted by you in the power of attorney.

The law permits you, if you choose, to grant broad authority to an agent under power of attorney, including the ability to give away all of your property while you are alive or to substantially change how your property is distributed at your death. Before signing this document, you should seek the advice of an attorney at law to make sure you understand it.

A court can take away the powers of your agent if it finds your agent is not acting properly.

The powers and duties of an agent under a power of attorney are explained more fully in 20 Pa.C.S. Ch. 56.

If there is anything about this form that you do not understand, you should ask a lawyer of your own choosing to explain it to you.

I have read or had explained to me this notice and I understand its contents.

_____

_____   _____
(Principal)   (Date)

(d) **Acknowledgment executed by agent.**—An agent shall have no authority to act as agent under the power of attorney unless the agent has first executed and affixed to the power of attorney an acknowledgment in substantially the following form:

I, _____, have read the attached power of attorney and am the person identified as the agent for the principal. I hereby acknowledge that when I act as agent:

I shall act in accordance with the principal's reasonable expectations to the extent actually known by me and, otherwise, in the principal's best interest, act in good faith and act only within the scope of authority granted to me by the principal in the power of attorney.

_____

_____   _____
(Principal)   (Date)

(e) **Fiduciary relationship.**—(Deleted by amendment).

(e.1) **Limitation on applicability generally.**—

(1.1) Subsections (b)(3), (c) and (d) and section 5601.3 (relating to agent's duties) do not apply to:

(i) A power contained in an instrument used in a commercial transaction which authorizes an agency relationship.

(ii) A power to the extent it is coupled with an interest in the subject of the power, including a power given to or for the benefit of a creditor in connection with a loan or other credit transaction.

(iii) A power exclusively granted to facilitate transfer of stock, bonds and other assets.

(iv) A power:

(A) contained in the governing document for a corporation, partnership or limited liability company or other legal entity;

(B) authorized by the law that governs the internal affairs of a legal entity;

(C) by which a director, shareholder, partner, member or manager authorizes others to do things on behalf of the entity; or

(D) contained in a proxy or other delegation to exercise voting rights or management rights with respect to a legal entity.

(v) A warrant of attorney conferring authority to confess judgment.

(vi) A power given to a dealer as defined by the act of December 22, 1983 (P.L.306, No.84), known as the Board of Vehicles Act, when using the power in conjunction with a sale, purchase or transfer of a vehicle as authorized by 75 Pa.C.S. § 1119 (relating to application for certificate of title by agent).

(vii) A power created on a form prescribed by a Commonwealth agency, political subdivision or an authority or instrumentality of the Commonwealth or a political subdivision.

(2) Powers and powers of attorney exempted by this subsection need not be dated.

(3) Powers of attorney exempted by this subsection which are recorded in the office for the recorder of deeds under section 5602(c) shall be acknowledged before recording.

(e.2) **Limitation on applicability in health care and mental health care powers of attorney.**—Subsections (b)(3)(i), (c) and (d) and section 5601.3 do not apply to a power of attorney which exclusively provides for health care decision making or mental health care decision making.

(f) **Definitions.**—The following words and phrases when used in this chapter shall have the meanings given to them in this subsection unless the context clearly indicates otherwise:

"Agent." A person designated by a principal in a power of attorney to act on behalf of that principal.

"Good faith." Honesty in fact.

(Dec. 16, 1992, P.L.1163, No.152, eff. imd.; Oct. 12, 1999, P.L.422, No.39; May 16, 2002, P.L.330, No.50, eff. Apr. 12, 2000; Nov. 25, 2003, P.L.211, No.36, eff. 60 days; July 2, 2014, P.L.855, No.95; July 8, 2016, P.L.497, No.79, eff. Jan. 1, 2017; Oct. 4, 2016, P.L.867, No.103, eff. imd.)

2016 Amendments. Act 79 amended subsec. (b)(3) and Act 103 amended subsecs. (b)(3), (e.1) and (e.2), retroactive to January 1, 2015. The amendments of subsec. (b)(3) by Acts 79 and 103 do not conflict in substance and, under the provisions of 1 Pa.C.S. § 1954, have been merged in setting forth the text of subsec. (b)(3). See section 21 of Act 79 in the appendix to this title for special provisions relating to applicability.

2014 Amendment. Act 95 amended subsecs. (b), (c), (d), (e.1), (e.2) and (f) and deleted subsec. (e), effective immediately as to subsec. (f) and January 1, 2015, as to the remainder of the section. See section 9 of Act 95 in the appendix to this title for special provisions relating to application of law.

1999 Amendment. Act 39 amended the entire section, effective in six months as to subsecs. (c) and (d) and 60 days as to the remainder of the section. See section 13(1), (2), (3) and (8) of Act 39 in the appendix to this title for special provisions relating to applicability.

Cross References. Section 5601 is referred to in sections 5608.1, 5843 of this title.

§ 5601.1. Powers of attorney presumed durable.

Unless specifically provided otherwise in the power of attorney, all powers of attorney shall be durable as provided in section 5604 (durable powers of attorney).

1992, Dec. 16, P.L. 1163, No. 152, § 13, imd. effective.

§ 5601.2. Special rules for gifts (Repealed).

2014 Repeal. Section 5601.2 was repealed July 2, 2014, P.L.855, No.95, effective January 1, 2015.

§ 5601.3. Agent's duties.

(a) General rule.—Notwithstanding any provision in the power of attorney, an agent that has accepted appointment shall:

(1) Act in accordance with the principal's reasonable expectations to the extent actually known by the agent and, otherwise, in the principal's best interest.

(2) Act in good faith.

(3) Act only within the scope of authority granted in the power of attorney.

(b) Other duties.—Except as otherwise provided in the power of attorney, an agent that has accepted appointment shall:

(1) Act loyally for the principal's benefit.

(1.1) Keep the agent's funds separate from the principal's funds unless:

(i) the funds were not kept separate as of the date of the execution of the power of attorney; or

(ii) the principal commingles the funds after the date of the execution of the power of attorney and the agent is the principal's spouse.

(2) Act so as not to create a conflict of interest that impairs the agent's ability to act impartially in the principal's best interest.

(3) Act with the care, competence and diligence ordinarily exercised by agents in similar circumstances.

(4) Keep a record of all receipts, disbursements and transactions made on behalf of the principal.

(5) Cooperate with a person who has authority to make health care decisions for the principal to carry out the principal's reasonable expectations to the extent actually known by the agent and, otherwise, act in the principal's best interest.

(6) Attempt to preserve the principal's estate plan, to the extent actually known by the agent, if preserving the plan is consistent with the principal's best interest based on all relevant factors, including:

    (i) The value and nature of the principal's property.

    (ii) The principal's foreseeable obligations and need for maintenance.

    (iii) Minimization of taxes, including income, estate, inheritance, generation-skipping transfer and gift taxes.

    (iv) Eligibility for a benefit, program or assistance under a statute or regulation.

(c) Nonliability of agent.—

(1) An agent that acts in good faith shall not be liable to a beneficiary of the principal's estate plan for failure to preserve the plan.

(2) An agent that acts with care, competence and diligence for the best interest of the principal shall not be liable solely because the agent also benefits from the act or has an individual or conflicting interest in relation to the property or affairs of the principal.

(3) If an agent is selected by the principal because of special skills or expertise possessed by the agent or in reliance on the agent's representation that the agent has special skills or expertise, the special skills or expertise must be considered in determining whether the agent has acted with care, competence and diligence under the circumstances.

(4) Absent a breach of duty to the principal, an agent shall not be liable if the value of the principal's property declines.

(5) An agent that exercises authority to delegate to another person the authority granted by the principal or that engages another person on behalf of the principal shall not be liable for an act, error of judgment or default of that person if the agent exercises care, competence and diligence in selecting and monitoring the person.

(d) Disclosure of receipts, disbursements or transactions.—

(1) Except as otherwise provided in the power of attorney, an agent shall not be required to disclose receipts, disbursements or transactions conducted on behalf of the principal unless ordered by a court or requested by the principal, a guardian, conservator, another fiduciary acting for the principal, governmental agency having authority to protect the welfare of the principal or, upon the death of the principal, the personal representative or successor in interest of the principal's estate.

(2) Within 30 days of the request, the agent shall either comply with the request or provide a writing or other record substantiating the reason additional time is needed, in which case the agent shall comply with the request within an additional 30 days.

(July 2, 2014, P.L.855, No.95, eff. Jan. 1, 2015)

    2014 Amendment. Act 95 added section 5601.3. See section 9 of Act 95 in the appendix to this title for special provisions relating to application of law.

    Cross References. Section 5601.3 is referred to in section 5601 of this title.

§ 5601.4. Authority that requires specific and general grant of authority.

(a) General rule.—An agent under a power of attorney may do the following on behalf of the principal or with the principal's property only if the power of attorney expressly grants the agent the authority and exercise of the authority is not otherwise prohibited by another agreement or instrument to which the authority or property is subject:

(1) Create, amend, revoke or terminate an inter vivos trust other than as permitted under section 5602(a)(2), (3) and (7) (relating to form of power of attorney).

(2) Make a gift.

(3) Create or change rights of survivorship.

(4) Create or change a beneficiary designation.

(5) Delegate authority granted under the power of attorney.

(6) Waive the principal's right to be a beneficiary of a joint and survivor annuity, including a survivor benefit under a retirement plan.

(7) Exercise fiduciary powers that the principal has authority to delegate.

(8) Disclaim property, including a power of appointment.

(b) Limitation.—Notwithstanding a grant of authority to do an act described in subsection (a), unless the power of attorney otherwise provides, an agent that is not an ancestor, spouse or descendant of the principal may not exercise authority under a power of attorney to create in the agent, or in an individual to whom the agent owes a legal obligation of support, an interest in the principal's property, whether by gift, right of survivorship, beneficiary designation, disclaimer or otherwise.

(c) Scope of authority.—Subject to subsections (a), (b), (d) and (e), if a power of attorney grants to an agent authority to do all acts that a principal is authorized to perform, the agent has all of the powers which may be incorporated by reference pursuant to section 5602(a).

(d) Gifts.—Unless the power of attorney otherwise provides, a grant of authority to make a gift is subject to section 5603(a.1) (relating to implementation of power of attorney).

(e) Similar or overlapping subjects.—Subject to subsections (a), (b) and (d), if the subjects over which authority is granted in a power of attorney are similar or overlap, the broadest authority controls.

(f) Property.—Authority granted in a power of attorney is exercisable with respect to property that the principal has when the power of attorney is executed or acquires later, whether or not the property is located in this State and whether or not the authority is exercised or the power of attorney is executed in this State.

(g) Legal effect of agent's actions.—An act performed by an agent pursuant to a power of attorney has the same effect and inures to the benefit of and binds the principal and the principal's successors in interest as if the principal had performed the act.

(July 2, 2014, P.L.855, No.95, eff. Jan. 1, 2015)

2014 Amendment. Act 95 added section 5601.4. See section 9 of Act 95 in the appendix to this title for special provisions relating to application of law.

Cross References. Section 5601.4 is referred to in section 5603 of this title.

§ 5602. Form of power of attorney.

(a) Specification of powers.—A principal may, by inclusion of the language quoted in any of the following paragraphs or by inclusion of other language showing a similar intent on the part of the principal, empower an agent to do any or all of the following, each of which is defined in section 5603 (relating to implementation of power of attorney):

(1) "To make limited gifts."

(2) "To create a trust for my benefit."

(3) "To make additions to an existing trust for my benefit."

(4) "To claim an elective share of the estate of my deceased spouse."

(5) (Deleted by amendment).

(6) "To renounce fiduciary positions."

(7) "To withdraw and receive the income or corpus of a trust."

(8) "To authorize my admission to a medical, nursing, residential or similar facility and to enter into agreements for my care."
(9) "To authorize medical and surgical procedures."
(10) "To engage in real property transactions."
(11) "To engage in tangible personal property transactions."
(12) "To engage in stock, bond and other securities transactions."
(13) "To engage in commodity and option transactions."
(14) "To engage in banking and financial transactions."
(15) "To borrow money."
(16) "To enter safe deposit boxes."
(17) "To engage in insurance and annuity transactions."
(18) "To engage in retirement plan transactions."
(19) "To handle interests in estates and trusts."
(20) "To pursue claims and litigation."
(21) "To receive government benefits."
(22) "To pursue tax matters."
(23) "To make an anatomical gift of all or part of my body."

(a.1) Modification of authority.—A principal may modify the authority of an agent that is incorporated by reference as described in subsection (a).

(b) Appointment of agent and successor agent.—A principal may provide for:

(1) The appointment of more than one agent, who shall act jointly, severally or in any other combination that the principal may designate, but if there is no such designation, such agents shall only act jointly.

(1.1) The delegation of one or more powers by the agent to such person or persons as the agent may designate and on terms as the power of attorney may specify.

(2) The appointment of one or more successor agents who shall serve in the order named in the power of attorney, unless the principal expressly directs to the contrary.

(3) The delegation to an original or successor agent of the power to appoint his successor or successors.

(c) Filing and recording of power of attorney.—An originally executed power of attorney may be filed with the clerk of the orphans' court division of the court of common pleas in the county in which the principal resides, and, if it is acknowledged, it may be recorded in the office for the recording of deeds of the county of the principal's residence and of each county in which real property to be affected by an exercise of the power is located. A power of attorney executed in electronic form may be recorded in the same manner as a document subject to the act of July 5, 2012 (P.L.935, No.100), known as the Uniform Real Property Electronic Recording Act. The clerk of the orphans' court division or any office for the recording of deeds with whom the power has been filed may, upon request, issue certified copies of the power of attorney. Each such certified copy shall have the same validity and the same force and effect as if it were the original, and it may be filed of record in any other office of this Commonwealth (including, without limitation, the clerk of the orphans' court division or the office for the recording of deeds) as if it were the original.

(d) Copy of power of attorney.—Except for the purpose of filing or recording under subsection (c), a photocopy or electronically transmitted copy of an originally executed power of attorney has the same effect as the original.

(Dec. 16, 1992, P.L.1163, No.152, eff. imd.; Dec. 1, 1994, P.L.655, No.102, eff. 90 days; Oct. 12, 1999, P.L.422, No.39, eff. 60 days; July 2, 2014, P.L.855, No.95, eff. Jan. 1, 2015)

2014 Amendment. Act 95 amended subsecs. (a)(17) and (c), added subsecs. (a.1) and (d) and deleted subsec. (a)(5). See section 9 of Act 95 in the appendix to this title for special provisions relating to application of law.

1999 Amendment. See section 13(5) and (8) of Act 39 in the appendix to this title for special provisions relating to applicability.

1994 Amendment. Section 10 of Act 102 provided that the amendment shall apply beginning with the effective date of Act 102.

1992 Amendment. Section 27(e) of Act 152 provided that the amendments to subsecs. (a)(10), (11), (12), (13), (14), (15), (16), (17), (18), (19), (20), (21) and (22) and (b)(1.1) shall apply beginning with the effective date of Act 152.

Cross References. Section 5602 is referred to in sections 5601, 5601.4 of this title.

§ 5603. Implementation of power of attorney.

(a) **Power to make limited gifts.**—(Deleted by amendment).

(a.1) **Power to make limited gifts.**—(Deleted by amendment).

(b) **Power to create a trust.**—A power "to create a trust for my benefit" shall mean that the agent may execute a deed of trust, designating one or more persons (including the agent) as original or successor trustees and transfer to the trust any or all property owned by the principal as the agent may decide, subject to the following conditions:

(1) The income and corpus of the trust shall either be distributable to the principal or to the guardian of his estate, or be applied for the principal's benefit, and upon the principal's death, any remaining balance of corpus and unexpended income of the trust shall be distributed to the deceased principal's estate.

(2) The deed of trust may be amended or revoked at any time and from time to time, in whole or in part, by the principal or the agent, provided that any such amendment by the agent shall not include any provision which could not be included in the original deed.

(c) **Power to make additions to an existing trust.**—A power "to make additions to an existing trust for my benefit" shall mean that the agent, at any time or times, may add any or all of the property owned by the principal to any trust in existence when the power was created, provided that the terms of such trust relating to the disposition of the income and corpus during the lifetime of the principal are the same as those set forth in subsection (b). The agent and the trust and its beneficiaries shall be answerable as equity and justice may require to the extent that an addition to a trust is inconsistent with prudent estate planning or financial management for the principal or with the known or probable intent of the principal with respect to disposition of his estate.

(d) **Power to claim an elective share.**—A power "to claim an elective share of the estate of my deceased spouse" shall mean that the agent may elect to take against the will and conveyances of the principal's deceased spouse, disclaim any interest in property which the principal is required to disclaim as a result of such election, retain any property which the principal has the right to elect to retain, file petitions pertaining to the election, including petitions to extend the time for electing and petitions for orders, decrees and judgments in accordance with section 2211(c) and (d) (relating to determination of effect of election; enforcement), and take all other actions which the agent deems appropriate in order to effectuate the election: Provided, however, That the election shall be made only upon the approval of the court having jurisdiction of the principal's estate in accordance with section 2206 (relating to right of election personal to surviving spouse) in the case of a principal who is adjudicated an incapacitated person, or upon the approval of the court having jurisdiction of the deceased spouse's estate in the case of a principal who is not an incapacitated person.

(e) **Power to disclaim any interest in property.**—(Deleted by amendment).

(f) **Power to renounce fiduciary position.—**

(1) A power "to renounce fiduciary positions" shall mean that the agent may:

(i) renounce any fiduciary position to which the principal has been appointed; and

(ii) resign any fiduciary position in which the principal is then serving, and either file an accounting with a court of competent jurisdiction or settle on receipt and release or other informal method as the agent deems advisable.

(2) The term "fiduciary" shall be deemed to include, without limitation, an executor, administrator, trustee, guardian, agent or officer or director of a corporation.

(g) Power to withdraw and receive.—A power "to withdraw and receive the income or corpus of a trust" shall mean that the agent may:

(1) demand, withdraw and receive the income or corpus of any trust over which the principal has the power to make withdrawals;

(2) request and receive the income or corpus of any trust with respect to which the trustee thereof has the discretionary power to make distribution to or on behalf of the principal; and

(3) execute a receipt and release or similar document for the property received under paragraphs (1) and (2).

(h) Power to authorize admission to medical facility and power to authorize medical procedures.—(Deleted by amendment).

(i) Power to engage in real property transactions.—A power to "engage in real property transactions" shall mean that the agent may:

(1) Acquire or dispose of real property (including the principal's residence) or any interest therein, including, but not limited to, the power to buy or sell at public or private sale for cash or credit or partly for each; exchange, mortgage, encumber, lease for any period of time; give or acquire options for sales, purchases, exchanges or leases; buy at judicial sale any property on which the principal holds a mortgage.

(2) Manage, repair, improve, maintain, restore, alter, build, protect or insure real property; demolish structures or develop real estate or any interest in real estate.

(3) Collect rent, sale proceeds and earnings from real estate; pay, contest, protest and compromise real estate taxes and assessments.

(4) Release in whole or in part, assign the whole or a part of, satisfy in whole or in part and enforce any mortgage, encumbrance, lien or other claim to real property.

(5) Grant easements, dedicate real estate, partition and subdivide real estate and file plans, applications or other documents in connection therewith.

(6) In general, exercise all powers with respect to real property that the principal could if present.

(j) Power to engage in tangible personal property transactions.—A power to "engage in tangible personal property transactions" shall mean that the agent may:

(1) Buy, sell, lease, exchange, collect, possess and take title to tangible personal property.

(2) Move, store, ship, restore, maintain, repair, improve, manage, preserve and insure tangible personal property.

(3) In general, exercise all powers with respect to tangible personal property that the principal could if present.

(k) Power to engage in stock, bond and other securities transactions.—A power to "engage in stock, bond and other securities transactions" shall mean that the agent may:

(1) Buy or sell (including short sales) at public or private sale for cash or credit or partly for cash all types of stocks, bonds and securities; exchange, transfer, hypothecate, pledge or otherwise dispose of any stock, bond or other security.

(2) Collect dividends, interest and other distributions.

(3) Vote in person or by proxy, with or without power of substitution, either discretionary, general or otherwise, at any meeting.

(4) Join in any merger, reorganization, consolidation, dissolution, liquidation, voting-trust plan or other concerted action of security holders and make payments in connection therewith.

(5) Hold any evidence of the ownership of any stock, bond or other security belonging to the principal in the name of a nominee selected by the agent.

(6) Deposit or arrange for the deposit of securities in a clearing corporation as defined in Division 8 of Title 13 (relating to investment securities).

(7) Receive, hold or transfer securities in book-entry form.

(8) In general, exercise all powers with respect to stocks, bonds and securities that the principal could if present.

(l) Power to engage in commodity and option transactions.—A power to "engage in commodity and option transactions" shall mean that the agent may:

(1) Buy, sell, exchange, assign, convey, settle and exercise commodities future contracts and call and put options on stocks and stock indices traded on a regulated options exchange and collect and receipt for all proceeds of any such transactions.

(2) Establish or continue option accounts for the principal with any securities of a futures broker.

(3) In general, exercise all powers with respect to commodity and option transactions that the principal could if present.

(m) Power to engage in banking and financial transactions.—A power to "engage in banking and financial transactions" shall mean that the agent may:

(1) Sign checks, drafts, orders, notes, bills of exchange and other instruments ("items") or otherwise make withdrawals from checking, savings, transaction, deposit, loan or other accounts in the name of the principal and endorse items payable to the principal and receive the proceeds in cash or otherwise.

(2) Open and close such accounts in the name of the principal, purchase and redeem savings certificates, certificates of deposit or similar instruments in the name of the principal and execute and deliver receipts for any funds withdrawn or certificates redeemed.

(3) Deposit any funds received for the principal in accounts of the principal.

(4) Do all acts regarding checking, savings, transaction, deposit, loan or other accounts, savings certificates, certificates of deposit or similar instruments, the same as the principal could do if personally present.

(5) Sign any tax information or reporting form required by Federal, State or local taxing authorities, including, but not limited to, any Form W-9 or similar form.

(6) In general, transact any business with a banking or financial institution that the principal could if present.

(n) Power to borrow money.—A power to "borrow money" shall mean that the agent may borrow money and pledge or mortgage any properties that the principal owns as a security therefor.

(o) Power to enter safe deposit boxes.—A power to "enter safe deposit boxes" shall mean that the agent may enter any safe deposit box in the name of the principal; add to or remove the contents of such box, open and close safe deposit boxes in the name of the principal; however, the agent shall not deposit or keep in any safe deposit box of the principal any property in which the agent has a personal interest.

(p) Power to engage in insurance and annuity transactions.—A power to "engage in insurance and annuity transactions" shall mean that the agent may:

(1) Purchase, continue, renew, convert or terminate any type of insurance (including, but not limited to, life, accident, health, disability or liability insurance)

or annuity and pay premiums and collect benefits and proceeds under insurance policies and annuity contracts.

(2) Exercise nonforfeiture provisions under insurance policies and annuity contracts.

(3) In general, exercise all powers with respect to insurance and annuities that the principal could if present, provided, however, that the agent shall have no power to create or change a beneficiary designation unless authorized in accordance with section 5601.4 (relating to authority that requires specific and general grant of authority).

(q) Power to engage in retirement plan transactions.—A power to "engage in retirement plan transactions" shall mean that the agent may contribute to, withdraw from and deposit funds in any type of retirement plan (including, but not limited to, any tax qualified or nonqualified pension, profit sharing, stock bonus, employee savings and retirement plan, deferred compensation plan or individual retirement account), select and change payment options for the principal, make roll-over contributions from any retirement plan to other retirement plans and, in general, exercise all powers with respect to retirement plans that the principal could if present, provided, however, that the agent shall have no power to create or change a beneficiary designation unless authorized in accordance with section 5601.4.

(r) Power to handle interests in estates and trusts.—A power to "handle interests in estates and trusts" shall mean that the agent may receive a bequest, devise, gift or other transfer of real or personal property to the principal in the principal's own right or as a fiduciary for another and give full receipt and acquittance therefor or a refunding bond therefor; approve accounts of any estate, trust, partnership or other transaction in which the principal may have an interest; enter into any compromise and release in regard thereto; and receive on behalf of the principal all notices and reports required by section 7780.3 (relating to duty to inform and report) or permitted by section 7785(a) (relating to limitation of action against trustee).

(s) Power to pursue claims and litigation.—A power to "pursue claims and litigation" shall mean that the agent may:

(1) Institute, prosecute, defend, abandon, arbitrate, compromise, settle or otherwise dispose of, and appear for the principal in, any legal proceedings before any tribunal regarding any claim relating to the principal or to any property interest of the principal.

(2) Collect and receipt for any claim or settlement proceeds; waive or release rights of the principal; employ and discharge attorneys and others on such terms (including contingent fee arrangements) as the agent deems appropriate.

(3) In general, exercise all powers with respect to claims and litigation that the principal could if present.

(t) Power to receive government benefits.—A power to "receive government benefits" shall mean that the agent may prepare, sign and file any claim or application for Social Security, unemployment, military service or other government benefits; collect and receipt for all government benefits or assistance; and, in general, exercise all powers with respect to government benefits that the principal could if present.

(u) Power to pursue tax matters.—A power to "pursue tax matters" shall mean that the agent may:

(1) Prepare, sign, verify and file any tax return on behalf of the principal, including, but not limited to, joint returns and declarations of estimated tax; examine and copy all the principal's tax returns and tax records.

(2) Sign an Internal Revenue Service power of attorney form.

(3) Represent the principal before any taxing authority; protest and litigate tax assessments; claim, sue for and collect tax refunds; waive rights and sign all documents required to settle, pay and determine tax liabilities; sign waivers extending the period of time for the assessment of taxes or tax deficiencies.

(4) In general, exercise all powers with respect to tax matters that the principal could if present.

(u.1) Power to make anatomical gift.—(Deleted by amendment).

(u.2) Power to operate a business or entity.—A power "to operate a business or entity" shall mean that the agent may:

(1) Continue or participate in the operation of any business or other entity in which the principal holds an interest, whether alone or with others, by making and implementing decisions regarding its financing, operations, employees and all other matters pertinent to the business or entity.

(2) Change the form of ownership of the business or entity to a corporation, partnership, limited liability company or other entity, and initiate or take part in a corporate reorganization, including a merger, consolidation, dissolution or other change in organizational form.

(3) Compensate an agent actively managing, supervising or engaging in the operation of a business or entity, as appropriate, from the principal's assets or from the business or entity, provided that the compensation is reasonably based upon the actual responsibilities assumed and performed.

(4) In general, exercise all powers with respect to operating a business or entity that the principal could if present.

(u.3) Power to provide for personal and family maintenance.—

(1) A power "to provide for personal and family maintenance" shall mean that the agent may provide for the health, education, maintenance and support, in order to maintain the customary standard of living of the principal's spouse and the following individuals, whether living when the power of attorney is executed or later born:

(i) The principal's minor children.

(ii) Other individuals legally entitled to be supported by the principal.

(iii) The individuals whom the principal has customarily supported and intends to support.

(2) In acting under this subsection, the agent shall:

(i) Take into account the long-term needs of the principal.

(ii) Consider any independent means available to those individuals apart from the support provided by the principal.

(3) Authority with respect to personal and family maintenance is in addition to and not limited by authority that an agent may or may not have with respect to gifts under this chapter.

(v) Powers generally.—

(1) All powers described in this section shall be exercisable with respect to any matter in which the principal is in any way interested at the giving of the power of attorney or thereafter and whether arising in this Commonwealth or elsewhere.

(2) A principal may, in a power of attorney, modify any power described in this section.

(April 16, 1992, P.L.108, No.24, eff. 60 days; Dec. 16, 1992, P.L.1163, No.152, eff. imd.; Dec. 1, 1994, P.L.655, No.102, eff. 90 days; Oct. 12, 1999, P.L.422, No.39, eff. 60 days; Oct. 27, 2010, P.L.837, No.85, eff. 60 days; July 2, 2014, P.L.855, No.95, eff. Jan. 1, 2015; July 8, 2016, P.L.497, No.79, eff. Jan. 1, 2017; Oct. 4, 2016, P.L.867, No.103, eff. imd.)

2016 Amendments. Act 79 amended subsecs. (d) and (r), added subsecs. (u.2) and (u.3) and deleted subsecs. (a.1), (h) and (u.1) and Act 103 amended subsec. (d), retroactive to January 1, 2015. The amendments of subsec. (d) by Acts 79 and 103 do not conflict in substance and, under the provisions of 1 Pa.C.S. § 1954, have been merged in setting forth the text of subsec. (d). Section 21(2)(ii) of Act

79 provided that the amendment of subsec. (r) shall apply to all powers of attorney executed before, on or after the effective date of section 21(2)(ii).

2014 Amendment. Act 95 amended subsecs. (k)(4), (p), (q) and (v), added subsec. (a.1) and deleted subsecs. (a) and (e). See section 9 of Act 95 in the appendix to this title for special provisions relating to application of law.

Cross References. Section 5603 is referred to in sections 2206, 5602 of this title.

§ 5604. Durable powers of attorney

(a) Definition.—A durable power of attorney is a power of attorney by which a principal designates another his agent in writing. The authority conferred shall be exercisable notwithstanding the principal's subsequent disability or incapacity. A principal may provide in the power of attorney that the power shall become effective at a specified future time or upon the occurrence of a specified contingency, including the disability or incapacity of the principal.

(b) Durable power of attorney not affected by disability or lapse of time.— All acts done by an agent pursuant to a durable power of attorney during any period of disability or incapacity of the principal have the same effect and inure to the benefit of and bind the principal and his successors in interest as if the principal were competent and not disabled. Unless the power of attorney states a time of termination, it is valid notwithstanding the lapse of time since its execution.

(c) Relation of agent to court-appointed guardian.—

(1) If, following execution of a durable power of attorney, the principal becomes an incapacitated person and a guardian is appointed for his estate, the agent is accountable to the guardian as well as to the principal.

(2) A principal may nominate, by a durable power of attorney, the guardian of his estate or of his person for consideration by the court if incapacity proceedings for the principal's estate or person are thereafter commenced. The court shall make its appointment in accordance with the principal's most recent nomination in a durable power of attorney except for good cause or disqualification.

(3) In its guardianship order and determination of a person's incapacity, the court shall determine whether and the extent to which the incapacitated person's durable power of attorney remains in effect.

(d) Discovery of information and records regarding actions of agent.—

(1) If the agency acting pursuant to the act of November 6, 1987 (P.L.381, No.79), known as the Older Adults Protective Services Act, is denied access to records necessary for the completion of a proper investigation of a report or a client assessment and service plan or the delivery of needed services in order to prevent further abuse, neglect, exploitation or abandonment of the older adult principal reported to be in need of protective services, the agency may petition the court of common pleas for an order requiring the appropriate access when either of the following conditions applies:

(i) the older adult principal has provided written consent for confidential records to be disclosed and the agent denies access; or

(ii) the agency can demonstrate that the older adult principal has denied or directed the agent to deny access to the records because of incompetence, coercion, extortion or justifiable fear of future abuse, neglect, exploitation or abandonment.

(2) This petition may be filed in the county wherein the agent resides or has his principal place of business or, if a nonresident, in the county wherein the older adult principal resides. The court, after reasonable notice to the agent and to the older adult principal, may conduct a hearing on the petition.

(3) Upon the failure of the agent to provide the requested information, the court may make and enforce such further orders.

(4) A determination to grant or deny an order, whether in whole or in part, shall not be considered a finding regarding the competence, capacity or impairment of the older adult principal, nor shall the granting or denial of an order preclude the availability of other remedies involving protection of the person or estate of the older adult principal or the rights and duties of the agent.

(e) **Definitions.**—As used in this section, the following words and phrases shall have the meanings given to them in this subsection:

"Abandonment." As that term is defined in the act of November 6, 1987 (P.L.381, No.79), known as the Older Adults Protective Services Act.

"Abuse." As that term is defined in the act of November 6, 1987 (P.L.381, No.79), known as the Older Adults Protective Services Act.

"Agency." As that term is defined in the act of November 6, 1987 (P.L.381, No.79), known as the Older Adults Protective Services Act, except that in cities of the first class the term shall mean the Department of Aging.

"Exploitation." As that term is defined in the act of November 6, 1987 (P.L.381, No.79), known as the Older Adults Protective Services Act.

"Neglect." As that term is defined in the act of November 6, 1987 (P.L.381, No.79), known as the Older Adults Protective Services Act.

"Older adult principal." A principal who is 60 years of age or older.

(Apr. 16, 1992, P.L.108, No.24, eff. 60 days; Dec. 16, 1992, P.L.1163, No.152, eff. imd.; Oct. 12, 1999, P.L.422, No.39, eff. 60 days; Dec. 20, 2000, P.L.978, No.137, eff. imd.; July 8, 2016, P.L.497, No.79, eff. Jan. 1, 2017; Oct. 4, 2016, P.L.867, No.103, eff. imd.)

2016 Amendments. Act 79 amended subsec. (c)(1) and added subsec. (c)(3) and Act 103 amended subsec. (c)(1), retroactive to January 1, 2015. The amendments of subsec. (c)(1) by Acts 79 and 103 do not conflict in substance and, under the provisions of 1 Pa.C.S. § 1954, have been merged in setting forth the text of subsec. (c)(1). See section 21 of Act 79 in the appendix to this title for special provisions relating to applicability.

2000 Amendment. Act 137 added subsecs. (d) and (e).

1999 Amendment. See section 13(8) of Act 39 in the appendix to this title for special provisions relating to applicability.

1992 Amendments. See section 21 of Act 24 in the appendix to this title for special provisions relating to applicability. See section 27(b) of Act 152 in the appendix to this title for special provisions relating to applicability.

Cross References. Section 5604 is referred to in sections 2206, 5601.1, 6202 of this title.

§ 5605. Power of attorney not revoked until notice

(a) **Death of principal.**—The death of a principal who has executed a written power of attorney, durable or otherwise, shall not revoke or terminate the agency as to the agent or other person, who, without actual knowledge of the death of the principal, acts in good faith under the power. Any action so taken, unless otherwise invalid or unenforceable, shall bind successors in interest of the principal.

(b) **Disability or incapacity of principal.**—The disability or incapacity of a principal who has previously executed a written power of attorney which is not a durable power shall not revoke or terminate the agency as to the agent or other person, who, without actual knowledge of the disability or incapacity of the principal, acts in good faith under the power. Any action so taken, unless otherwise invalid or unenforceable, shall bind the principal and his successors in interest.

(c) **Filing a complaint in divorce.**—If a principal designates his spouse as his agent and thereafter either the principal or his spouse files an action in divorce, the designation of the spouse as agent shall be revoked as of the time the action was filed, unless it appears from the power of attorney that the designation was intended to survive such an event.

1982, Feb. 18, P.L. 45, No. 26, § 9, imd. effective. Amended 1992, Dec. 16, P.L. 1163, No. 152, § 17, imd. effective; 1999, Oct. 12, P.L. 422, No. 39, § 10, effective in 60 days.

§ 5606. Proof of continuance of powers of attorney by affidavit

As to acts undertaken in good faith reliance thereon, an affidavit executed by the agent under a power of attorney stating that he did not have at the time of exercise of the power actual knowledge of the termination of the power by revocation, death or, if applicable, disability or incapacity or the filing of an action in divorce and that, if applicable, the specified future time or contingency has occurred, is conclusive proof of the nonrevocation or nontermination of the power at that time and conclusive proof that the specified time or contingency has occurred. The agent shall furnish an affidavit to a person relying upon the power of attorney on demand; however, good faith reliance on the power shall protect the person who acts without an affidavit. If the exercise of the power of attorney requires execution and delivery of any instrument which is recordable, the affidavit when authenticated for record is likewise recordable. This section does not affect any provision in a power of attorney for its termination by expiration of time or occurrence of an event other than express revocation or a change in the principal's capacity.

1982, Feb. 18, P.L. 45, No. 26, § 9, imd. effective. Amended 1992, Dec. 16, P.L. 1163, No. 152, § 18, imd. effective; 1999, Oct. 12, P.L. 422, No. 39, § 10, effective in 60 days.

§ 5607. Corporate agent

A bank and trust company or a trust company authorized to act as a fiduciary in this Commonwealth and acting as an agent pursuant to a power of attorney, or appointed by another who possesses such a power, shall have the powers, duties and liabilities set forth in section 3321 (relating to nominee registration; corporate fiduciary as agent; deposit of securities in a clearing corporation; book-entry securities).

1982, Feb. 18, P.L. 45, No. 26, § 9, imd. effective. Amended 1999, Oct. 12, P.L. 422, No. 39, § 10, effective in 60 days.

§ 5608. Acceptance of and reliance upon power of attorney.

(a) **Third party liability.**—(Deleted by amendment).

(b) **Third party immunity.**—(Deleted by amendment).

(c) **Genuineness.**—A person who in good faith accepts a power of attorney without actual knowledge that a signature or mark of any of the following are not genuine may, without liability, rely upon the genuineness of the signature or mark of:

(1) The principal.

(2) A person who signed the power of attorney on behalf of the principal and at the direction of the principal.

(3) A witness.

(4) A notary public or other person authorized by law to take acknowledgments.

(d) **Immunity.**—A person who in good faith accepts a power of attorney without actual knowledge of any of the following may, without liability, rely upon the power of attorney as if the power of attorney and agent's authority were genuine, valid and still in effect and the agent had not exceeded and had properly exercised the authority that:

(1) The power of attorney is void, invalid or terminated.

(2) The purported agent's authority is void, invalid or terminated.

(3) The agent is exceeding or improperly exercising the agent's authority.

(e) **Request for information.**—A person who is asked to accept a power of attorney may request and, without liability, rely upon without further investigation:

(1) An agent's certification under penalty of perjury of any factual matter concerning the principal, agent or power of attorney or an affidavit under section 5606 (relating to proof of continuance of powers of attorney by affidavit).

(2) An English translation of the power of attorney, if the power of attorney contains, in whole or in part, language other than English.

(3) An opinion of counsel relating to whether the agent is acting within the scope of the authority granted by the power of attorney if the person making the request provides in writing or other record the reason for the request.

(f) Additional request for information.—A person who has accepted a power of attorney, whether or not the person has a certification or an opinion of counsel under subsection (e) or an affidavit under section 5606, and has acted upon it by allowing the agent to exercise authority granted under the power of attorney, shall not be precluded from requesting at later times a certification or an opinion of counsel under this subsection, subsection (e) or an affidavit under section 5606 with regard to any further exercise of authority by the agent under the power of attorney.

(g) English translation.—An English translation or an opinion of counsel requested under this section shall be at the principal's expense, unless the request is made more than seven business days after the power of attorney or any revision or addition to a power of attorney:

(1) is presented for acceptance; or

(2) after being previously accepted by a person, is presented to exercise a power not previously exercised by the agent in a transaction with that person.

(h) Limitations.—Except as otherwise provided by law, nothing in this section shall in itself:

(1) validate a forged instrument conveying an interest in real property;

(2) provide that the recording of a forged instrument gives constructive notice of a conveyance of an interest in real property; or

(3) limit the liability of an insurer, indemnitor or guarantor of contractual obligations to indemnify, hold harmless or defend a person who accepts or relies upon a power of attorney.

(Dec. 16, 1992, P.L.1163, No.152, eff. imd.; Oct. 12, 1999, P.L.422, No.39, eff. 60 days; July 2, 2014, P.L.855, No.95, eff. imd.)

2014 Amendment. See section 9 of Act 95 in the appendix to this title for special provisions relating to application of law.

1999 Amendment. See section 13(8) of Act 39 in the appendix to this title for special provisions relating to applicability.

1992 Amendment. Section 27(e) of Act 152 provided that section 5608 shall apply beginning with the effective date of Act 152.

Cross References. Section 5608 is referred to in sections 5608.1, 5608.2 of this title.

§ 5608.1. Liability for refusal to accept power of attorney.

(a) Acceptance required.—Except as provided under subsections (b) and (d):

(1) A person shall either:

(i) accept a power of attorney; or

(ii) request one of the following:

(A) an affidavit under section 5606 (relating to proof of continuance of powers of attorney by affidavit); or

(B) a certification, translation or an opinion of counsel under section 5608(e) (relating to acceptance of and reliance upon power of attorney);

not later than seven business days after presentation of the power of attorney for acceptance.

(2) If a person requests a certification, a translation, an affidavit under section 5606 or an opinion of counsel under section 5608(e), the person shall accept the power of attorney not later than five business days after receipt of the certification, translation, affidavit or opinion of counsel or unless the information provided by the certification, translation, affidavit or opinion of counsel provides a substantial basis for making a further request under section 5606 or 5608(e).

(3) A person may not require an additional or different form of power of attorney for authority granted in the power of attorney presented.

(b) Acceptance not required.—A person may not be required to accept a power of attorney if any of the following applies:

(1) The person is not otherwise required to engage in a transaction with the principal in the same circumstances.

(2) Engaging in a transaction with the agent or the principal in the same circumstances would be inconsistent with any provisions of this chapter, including:

(i) the failure of the power of attorney to be executed in the manner required under section 5601(b) (relating to general provisions); and

(ii) circumstances in which an agent has no authority to act because of the absence of an acknowledgment as provided under section 5601(d), except as provided under section 5601(e.1) or (e.2).

(3) Engaging in a transaction with the agent in the same circumstances would be inconsistent with any other law or regulation.

(4) The person has actual knowledge of the termination of the agent's authority or of the power of attorney before exercise of the power.

(5) A request for a certification, a translation, an affidavit under section 5606 or an opinion of counsel under section 5608(e) is refused, including a certification, an affidavit or an opinion of counsel requested to demonstrate that the exercise of authority pursuant to a power of attorney is proper without the notice provided for under section 5601(c), except as provided under section 5601(e.1) or (e.2).

(6) The person in good faith believes that the power of attorney is not valid or the agent does not have the authority to perform the act requested, whether or not a certification, a translation, an affidavit under section 5606 or an opinion of counsel under section 5608(e) has been requested or provided.

(7) The person makes a report to the local protective services agency under section 302 of the act of November 6, 1987 (P.L.381, No.79), known as the Older Adults Protective Services Act, stating a good faith belief that the principal may be subject to physical or financial abuse, neglect, exploitation or abandonment by the agent or someone acting for or with the agent.

(8) The person has actual knowledge that another person has made a report to the local protective services agency under section 302 of the Older Adults Protective Services Act stating a good faith belief that the principal may be subject to physical or financial abuse, neglect, exploitation or abandonment by the agent or someone acting for or with the agent.

(c) Violation.—A person who refuses, in violation of this section, to accept a power of attorney shall be subject to:

(1) Civil liability for pecuniary harm to the economic interests of the principal proximately caused by the person's refusal to comply with the instructions of the agent designated in the power of attorney.

(2) A court order mandating acceptance of the power of attorney.

(d) Nonapplicability.—The requirements and penalties of this section shall not apply to:

(1) a power of attorney subject to the laws of another state or jurisdiction; or

(2) a power of attorney prescribed by a government or governmental subdivision, agency or instrumentality for a governmental purpose.

(July 2, 2014, P.L.855, No.95, eff. imd.)

    2014 Amendment. Act 95 added section 5608.1. See section 9 of Act 95 in the appendix to this title for special provisions relating to application of law.

    Cross References. Section 5608.1 is referred to in section 5608.2 of this title.

§ 5608.2. Activities through employees.

For the purposes of sections 5608 (relating to acceptance of and reliance upon power of attorney) and 5608.1 (relating to liability for refusal to accept power of attorney), the following shall apply:

(1) A person who conducts activities through employees shall be considered to be without actual knowledge of a fact relating to a power of attorney, a principal or an agent, if the employee conducting the transaction involving the power of attorney is without knowledge of the fact.

(2) An employee has knowledge of a fact if the employee has actual knowledge of the fact or acts with conscious disregard or willful ignorance regarding the existence of the fact.

(July 2, 2014, P.L.855, No.95, eff. imd.)

    2014 Amendment. Act 95 added section 5608.2. See section 9 of Act 95 in the appendix to this title for special provisions relating to application of law.

§ 5609. Compensation and reimbursement for expenses

(a) **Compensation.**—In the absence of a specific provision to the contrary in the power of attorney, the agent shall be entitled to reasonable compensation based upon the actual responsibilities assumed and performed.

(b) **Reimbursement for expenses.**—An agent shall be entitled to reimbursement for actual expenses advanced on behalf of the principal and to reasonable expenses incurred in connection with the performance of the agent's duties.

1999, Oct. 12, P.L. 422, No. 39, § 11, effective in 60 days.

§ 5610. Account

An agent shall file an account of his administration whenever directed to do so by the court and may file an account at any other time. All accounts shall be filed in the office of the clerk in the county where the principal resides.

1999, Oct. 12, P.L. 422, No. 39, § 11, effective in 60 days.

§ 5611. Validity.

A power of attorney executed in or under the laws of another state or jurisdiction shall be valid in this Commonwealth if, when the power of attorney was executed, the execution complied with:

(1) the law of the jurisdiction indicated in the power of attorney and, in the absence of an indication of jurisdiction, the law of the jurisdiction in which the power of attorney was executed; or

(2) the requirements for a military power of attorney under 10 U.S.C. § 1044(b) (relating to legal assistance).

(Oct. 12, 1999, P.L.422, No.39, eff. 60 days; July 2, 2014, P.L.855, No.95, eff. imd.)

    2014 Amendment. See section 9 of Act 95 in the appendix to this title for special provisions relating to application of law.

    1999 Amendment. Act 39 added section 5611. See section 13(8) of Act 39 in the appendix to this title for special provisions relating to applicability.

§ 5612. Principles of law and equity.

Unless displaced by a provision of this chapter, the principles of law and equity supplement this chapter.

(July 2, 2014, P.L.855, No.95, eff. imd.)

2014 Amendment. Act 95 added section 5612. See section 9 of Act 95 in the appendix to this title for special provisions relating to application of law.

20 Pa.C.S. § 6111.1 Modification by divorce or pending divorce.

Any provision in a conveyance which was revocable by a conveyor at the time of the conveyor's death and which was to take effect at or after the conveyor's death in favor of or relating to the conveyor's spouse shall become ineffective for all purposes unless it appears in the governing instrument that the provision was intended to survive a divorce, if the conveyor:

(1) is divorced from such spouse after making the conveyance; or

(2) dies domiciled in this Commonwealth during the course of divorce proceedings, no decree of divorce has been entered pursuant to 23 Pa.C.S. § 3323 (relating to decree of court) and grounds have been established as provided in 23 Pa.C.S. § 3323(g).

(Apr. 18, 1978, P.L.42, No.23, eff. 60 days; Dec. 16, 1992, P.L.1163, No.152, eff. imd.; 2010 Oct. 27, P.L. 837, No. 85, effective in 60 days)

2010 Amendment. Act 85 amended this sec.

1992 Amendment. Section 27(d) of Act 152 provided that the amendment of section 6111.1 shall apply to the estates of decedents dying on or after the effective date of Act 152.

20 Pa.C.S. § 6111.2 Effect of divorce or pending divorce on designation of beneficiaries.

(a) Applicability.—This section is applicable if an individual:

(1) is domiciled in this Commonwealth;

(2) designates the individual's spouse as beneficiary of the individual's life insurance policy, annuity contract, pension or profit-sharing plan or other contractual arrangement providing for payments to the spouse; and

(3) either:

(i) at the time of the individual's death is divorced from the spouse; or

(ii) dies during the course of divorce proceedings, no decree of divorce has been entered pursuant to 23 Pa.C.S. § 3323 (relating to decree of court) and grounds have been established as provided in 23 Pa.C.S. § 3323(g).

(b) General rule.—Any designation described in subsection (a)(2) in favor of the individual's spouse or former spouse that was revocable by the individual at the individual's death shall become ineffective for all purposes and shall be construed as if the spouse or former spouse had predeceased the individual, unless it appears the designation was intended to survive the divorce based on:

(1) the wording of the designation;

(2) a court order;

(3) a written contract between the individual and the spouse or former spouse; or

(4) a designation of a former spouse as a beneficiary after the divorce decree has been issued.

(c) Liability.—

(1) Unless restrained by court order, no insurance company, pension or profit-sharing plan trustee or other obligor shall be liable for making payments to a spouse or former spouse which would have been proper in the absence of this section.

(2) Any spouse or former spouse to whom payment is made shall be answerable to anyone prejudiced by the payment.

(Dec. 16, 1992, P.L.1163, No.152, eff. imd.; Dec. 1, 1994, P.L.655, No.102, eff. 60 days; 2010 Oct. 27, P.L. 837, No. 85, effective in 60 days))

2010 Amendment. Act 85 amended this sec.

TITLE 42
JUDICIARY AND JUDICIARY ACT
(Judicial Code)

Chapter 19. Administrative Office of Pennsylvania Courts
§ 1904. Availability of Criminal Charge Information in Child Custody Proceedings.

Chapter 63. Juvenile Matters
Subchapter A. General Provisions
§ 6301. Short title and purposes of chapter.
§ 6302. Definitions.
§ 6303. Scope of chapter.
§ 6304. Powers and duties of probation officers.
§ 6305. Masters.
§ 6306. Costs and expenses of care of child.
§ 6307. Inspection of court files and records.
§ 6308. Law enforcement records.
§ 6309. Juvenile history record information.
§ 6310. Parental participation.
§ 6311. Guardian ad litem for child in court proceedings.

Subchapter B. Jurisdiction and Custody
§ 6321. Commencement of proceedings.
§ 6322. Transfer from criminal proceedings.
§ 6323. Informal adjustment.
§ 6324. Taking into custody.
§ 6325. Detention of child.
§ 6326. Release or delivery to court.
§ 6327. Place of detention.

Subchapter C. Procedures and Safeguards
§ 6331. Release from detention or commencement of proceedings.
§ 6332. Informal hearing.
§ 6333. Subpoena.
§ 6334. Petition.
§ 6335. Release or holding of hearing.
§ 6336. Conduct of hearings.
§ 6336.1. Notice and hearing.
§ 6337. Right to counsel.
§ 6337.1. Right to counsel for children in dependency and delinquency proceedings.
§ 6338. Other basic rights.
§ 6339. Investigation and report.
§ 6340. Consent decree.
§ 6341. Adjudication.
§ 6342. Court-appointed special advocates.

Subchapter D. Disposition of Children Generally
§ 6351. Disposition of dependent child.
§ 6351.1. Authority of court upon petition to remove child from foster parent.
§ 6352. Disposition of delinquent child.

§ 6352.1. Treatment records.
§ 6353. Limitation on and change in place of commitment.
§ 6354. Effect of adjudication.
§ 6355. Transfer to criminal proceedings.
§ 6356. Disposition of mentally ill or mentally retarded child.
§ 6357. Rights and duties of legal custodian.
§ 6358. Assessment of delinquent children by the State Sexual Offenders Assessment Board.

Subchapter E. Dispositions Affecting Other Jurisdictions

§ 6361. Disposition of nonresident child.
§ 6362. Disposition of resident child received from another state.
§ 6363. Ordering foreign supervision.
§ 6364. Supervision under foreign order.
§ 6365. Powers of foreign probation officers.

§ 1904. Availability of criminal charge information in child custody proceedings.

(a) **Establishment of criminal charge information system.**—The Administrative Office shall establish and maintain an information system to enable a parent who is a party to a custody proceeding or order to have access to information about the criminal charges filed against the other parent to the custody proceeding or order. The criminal charge information that shall be available for access under this section is limited to the information requested by those parents involved in a custody proceeding or order and for which an application has been filed and verified for access as provided for in this section.

(b) **Criminal charges enumerated.**—The criminal charge information that shall be available on the information system shall be limited to the offenses listed in 23 Pa.C.S. § 5329(a) (relating to consideration of criminal conviction).

(c) **Application for access to criminal charge information.**—To obtain information about charges covered in 23 Pa.C.S. § 5329(a), a parent who has been awarded custody or partial custody or who is a party to a custody proceeding must file an application for access to the information with the office of the prothonotary in the county where the proceeding or order was filed.

(1) A person who knowingly gives false information with the intent to gain information provided for under this section commits an offense under 18 Pa.C.S. § 4904(a) (relating to unsworn falsification to authorities).

(2) The application must be filed with the prothonotary by one of the following methods:

(i) In person, at the office of the prothonotary, by the parent who is filing the application. The applicant must have a valid form of photoidentification available for the inspection of the prothonotary.

(ii) By mailing a notarized application using first class mail.

(iii) By including the application with the original complaint, initial response or any other pleading or motion filed with the prothonotary.

(3) The Administrative Office shall develop the application for access to the criminal charge information system. The following information shall be included in the application:

(i) Docket number of original court filing.

(ii) Date of filing.

(iii) Date of birth of all children involved in the custody proceeding or order.

(iv) A personal access code.

(v) A notice to the parent that additional information relating to criminal history record information is available, as provided for in 18 Pa.C.S. Ch. 91 (relating to criminal history record information).

(vi) A statement verifying that:

(A) the person who is filing for access to the criminal charge information system is the actual person listed on the application;

(B) to the best of the applicant's knowledge and belief, all the information included in the application is true and correct; and

(C) the applicant is a party to the custody proceeding or order that is listed on the application.

(vii) A warning as to the penalty under 18 Pa.C.S. § 4904.

(viii) Any additional information that it is determined to be necessary to expedite the verification of the application and to provide access to the system, as determined by the Administrative Office.

(4) Applications shall be made available through county prothonotaries.

(d) Verification of application.—The prothonotary shall verify and transmit the application to the Administrative Office within six business days.

(1) Verification consists of checking court records to determine whether there exists an active custody proceeding or valid custody order remaining in effect.

(2) The Administrative Office shall determine how the application is to be transmitted.

(e) Access.—

(1) Except as provided in this subsection, the charge information system shall be accessible by telephone during regular business hours to parents who have filed a verified application and have been entered into the system. Information relating to the regular business hours of the Administrative Office shall be included with the application.

(2) The Administrative Office may interrupt the system for necessary maintenance, the processing and updating of information and the removal of names upon the termination of a custody order.

(3) Personal access codes shall remain valid until the youngest child involved in the custody proceeding or order reaches the age of 18.

(f) Time for providing access.—The Administrative Office shall provide for access to the criminal charge information system for each qualified individual within one business day of its receipt of the application. Access to the criminal charge information system shall be provided by a telephone service which requires an established fee to be paid by the caller at a cost not to exceed 50¢ per minute.

(g) Funds generated.—Funds transmitted to the Administrative Office under sections 1725(c)(2) (relating to the establishment of fee and charges) and 1725.1(a.1) (relating to costs) for the implementation of this section and telephone tolls collected under subsection (f) shall be utilized in the following order of priority:

(1) To annually operate the system under this section.

(2) To build a surplus fund of $50,000 to deal with emergencies and computer upgrading, in the operation of the system under this section.

(3) To repay to the General Fund appropriations made to operate the system under this section.

(4) To the General Fund for use under section 2333(b) of the act of April 9, 1929 (P.L. 177, No. 175), known as the Administrative Code of 1929.

(h) Information available to parent.—

(1) After applying and qualifying to obtain the criminal charge information provided by the system, a parent may request information by telephone as to whether the other parent has been charged with any offense listed in 23 Pa.C.S. § 5329(a).

(2) The parent shall also be entitled to criminal history record information as provided for in 18 Pa.C.S. Ch. 91; and the parent shall be informed of the availability.

(3) Criminal charge information shall be retained on the system for the period of time as provided for the retention of criminal charges and records under 18 Pa.C.S. Ch. 91 and then only until the youngest child involved in the custody proceeding or order reaches 18 years of age. At no time shall information be retained on the system beyond what is permitted under 18 Pa.C.S. Ch. 91.

(i) Information available to counsel and the court.—Information available under this act shall be available to counsel for either parent and to judges who are presiding over custody proceedings involving either parent.

(j) Imposition of cost prohibited.—No cost shall be assessed for applying for or acquiring information under this section, except:

(1) The cost of telephone toll charges shall be assessed.

(2) Costs shall be assessed as provided for in 18 Pa.C.S. Ch. 91.

(k) Disclosure restricted.—The contents of all applications and the inquiries made by all parents shall be confidential and shall only be disclosed as authorized in this section.

(l) Definition.—As used in this section, the term "parent" means a party to a custody proceeding who has been granted custody, partial custody or visitation with a child or who is a party to a custody proceeding.

1996, Oct. 7, P.L. 691, No. 119, § 4, effective in 120 days; 2010, Nov. 23, P.L. 1106, No. 112, effective in 60 days [Jan. 22, 2011].

2010 Amendment. Act 85 amended this sec.

1996 Amendment. Act 119 added section 1904.

Cross References. Section 1904 is referred to in sections 1725, 1725.1 of Title 42; section 5303 of Title 23 (Domestic Relations).

Note:

The *Jen & Dave Program* is a 24-hour telephone service providing criminal charge information on parties involved in child custody cases. Administered by the Administrative Office of Pennsylvania Courts, the *Jen & Dave Program* is the first centralized automated system for providing criminal charge information to individuals involved in custody cases. To apply for access to the *Jen & Dave Program*, a party must complete an application, which is available from all County Prothonotary Offices in Pennsylvania or which is available online at: www.jendaveprogram.us

After the application is verified and registered in the system, a party may call the following telephone number to learn if another party has been charged with specific criminal offenses in Pennsylvania: 1-900-226-3120.

Although there is no application fee, each call costs $.50 a minute, with a three-minute, $1.50 minimum charge. The average length of a call with one reportable charge is four minutes and will cost $2.00. The *Jen & Dave Program* only provides information on charges that have been filed after a party registers in the system. For more information on the *Jen & Dave Program*, you may call the Help Desk at: 866-536-3283.

TITLE 42
JUDICIARY AND JUDICIAL PROCEDURE

PART VI
ACTIONS, PROCEEDINGS AND OTHER MATTERS GENERALLY

CHAPTER 62A
PROTECTION OF VICTIMS OF SEXUAL VIOLENCE OR INTIMIDATION

Sec.
62A01. Scope of chapter.
62A02. Findings and purpose.
62A03. Definitions.
62A04. Responsibilities of law enforcement agencies.
62A05. Commencement of proceedings.
62A06. Hearings.
62A07. Relief.
62A08. (Reserved).
62A09. Emergency relief by minor judiciary.
62A10. Sexual assault counselor.
62A11. Disclosure of addresses.
62A12. Arrest for violation of order.
62A13. Private criminal complaints for violation of order or agreement.
62A14. Contempt for violation of order.
62A15. Civil contempt or modification for violation of order or agreement.
62A16. Confidentiality.
62A17. Procedure and other remedies.
62A18. Applicability.
62A19. Inability to pay.
62A20. Construction.

Enactment. Chapter 62A was added March 21, 2014, P.L.365, No.25, effective July 1, 2015.

Cross References. Chapter 62A is referred to in section 6302 of this title.

§ 62A01. Scope of chapter.
This chapter relates to protection of victims of sexual violence or intimidation.

§ 62A02. Findings and purpose.
The General Assembly finds and declares that:

(1) Sexual violence is the most heinous crime against a person other than murder.

(2) Sexual violence and intimidation can inflict humiliation, degradation and terror on the victim.

(3) According to the Department of Justice, someone is sexually assaulted every two minutes in the United States.

(4) Rape is recognized as one of the most underreported crimes, and studies indicate that only one in three rapes is reported to law enforcement.

(5) Victims of sexual violence and intimidation desire safety and protection from future interactions with their offender, regardless of whether they seek criminal prosecution.

(6) This chapter provides the victim with a civil remedy requiring the offender to stay away from the victim, as well as other appropriate relief.

§ 62A03. Definitions.

The following words and phrases when used in this chapter shall have the meanings given to them in this section unless the context clearly indicates otherwise:

"Adult." An individual who is 18 years of age or older.

"Certified copy." A paper copy of the original order of the issuing court endorsed by the appropriate clerk of that court or an electronic copy of the original order of the issuing court endorsed with a digital signature of the judge or appropriate clerk of that court, regardless of whether or not there is a raised seal on the copy of the order of the issuing court.

"Confidential communications." As defined in section 5945.1 (relating to confidential communications with sexual assault counselors).

"Coparticipant." As defined in section 5945.1 (relating to confidential communications with sexual assault counselors).

"Court." The court or magisterial district judge having jurisdiction over the matter under and exercised as provided in this title or as otherwise provided or prescribed by law.

"Family or household members." Spouses or persons who have been spouses, persons living as spouses or who lived as spouses, parents and children, other persons related by consanguinity or affinity, current or former sexual or intimate partners or persons who share biological parenthood.

"Hearing officer." A magisterial district judge, judge of the Philadelphia Municipal Court, bail commissioner appointed under section 1123 (relating to jurisdiction and venue), master appointed under section 1126 (relating to masters) or master for emergency relief.

"Intimidation." Conduct constituting a crime under either of the following provisions between persons who are not family or household members:

18 Pa.C.S. § 2709(a)(4), (5), (6) or (7) (relating to harassment) where the conduct is committed by a person 18 years of age or older against a person under 18 years of age.

18 Pa.C.S. § 2709.1 (relating to stalking) where the conduct is committed by a person 18 years of age or older against a person under 18 years of age.

"Master for emergency relief." A member of the bar of the Commonwealth appointed under section 62A09(e) (relating to emergency relief by minor judiciary).

"Minor." An individual who is not an adult.

"Plaintiff." An individual who applies for a protection order, either for the benefit of that individual or on behalf of another individual.

"Protection order" or **"order."** An order issued under this chapter designed to protect a victim of sexual violence or intimidation.

"Rape crisis center." As defined in section 5945.1 (relating to confidential communications with sexual assault counselors).

"Sexual assault counselor." As defined in section 5945.1 (relating to confidential communications with sexual assault counselors).

"Sexual violence." Conduct constituting a crime under any of the following provisions between persons who are not family or household members:

18 Pa.C.S. Ch. 31 (relating to sexual offenses), except 18 Pa.C.S. §§ 3129 (relating to sexual intercourse with animal) and 3130 (relating to conduct relating to sex offenders).

18 Pa.C.S. § 4304 (relating to endangering welfare of children) if the offense involved sexual contact with the victim.

18 Pa.C.S. § 6301(a)(1)(ii) (relating to corruption of minors).

18 Pa.C.S. § 6312(b) (relating to sexual abuse of children).

18 Pa.C.S. § 6318 (relating to unlawful contact with minor).

18 Pa.C.S. § 6320 (relating to sexual exploitation of children).

"Sheriff." The sheriff of a county or, in a city of the first class, the chief or head of the police department.

"Victim." A person who is the victim of sexual violence or intimidation.

§ 62A04. Responsibilities of law enforcement agencies.

(a) **General rule.**—The police department of each municipal corporation, the Pennsylvania State Police and the sheriff of each county shall ensure that all their officers, deputies and employees are familiar with the provisions of this chapter. Instruction concerning orders shall be made a part of the training curriculum for all trainee officers and deputies. All law enforcement agencies shall adopt a written policy regarding orders issued under this chapter.

(b) **Notice of arrest.**—The police department of each municipal corporation and the Pennsylvania State Police shall make reasonable efforts to notify any person protected by an order issued under this chapter of the arrest of the defendant for violation of an order as soon as possible. Unless the person cannot be located, notice of the arrest shall be provided not more than 24 hours after preliminary arraignment.

(c) **Statewide registry.**—

(1) A complete and systematic record and index of all valid temporary and final orders issued under this chapter shall be entered and maintained in the database established and maintained by the Pennsylvania State Police pursuant to 23 Pa.C.S. § 6105(e) (relating to responsibilities of law enforcement agencies).

(2) With respect to orders issued under this chapter, the Statewide registry shall include, but need not be limited to, the following:

(i) The names of the plaintiff and the victim, if the victim is not the same individual as the plaintiff.

(ii) The name of other designated persons protected by the order under section 62A07(b) (relating to relief).

(iii) The name and address of the defendant.

(iv) The date the order was entered.

(v) The date the order expires.

(vi) The relief granted under sections 62A07 and 62A09 (relating to emergency relief by minor judiciary).

(vii) The judicial district in which the order was entered.

(viii) Where furnished, the Social Security number and date of birth of the defendant.

(3) The prothonotary shall send, on a form prescribed by the Pennsylvania State Police, a copy of an order to the Statewide registry so that it is received within 24 hours of the entry of the order. An amendment to or revocation of an order shall be transmitted by the prothonotary within 24 hours of the entry of the order for modification or revocation. The Pennsylvania State Police shall enter orders, amendments and revocations in the Statewide registry within eight hours of receipt. Vacated or expired orders shall be purged from the registry.

(4) The registry of the Pennsylvania State Police shall be available at all times to inform courts, dispatchers and law enforcement officers of any valid order involving any defendant.

(5) Information contained in the Statewide registry relating to orders shall not be subject to access under the act of February 14, 2008 (P.L.6, No.3), known as the Right-to-Know Law.

Cross References. Section 62A04 is referred to in section 62A05 of this title.

§ 62A05. Commencement of proceedings.

(a) **General rule.**—An adult or emancipated minor may seek relief under this chapter for that person or any parent, adult household member or guardian ad litem may seek relief under this chapter on behalf of a minor child, or the guardian of the person of an adult who has been declared incapacitated under 20 Pa.C.S. Ch. 55 (relating to incapacitated persons) may seek relief on behalf of an incapacitated adult, by filing a petition with the court alleging the need for protection from the defendant with respect to sexual violence or intimidation.

(a.1) **False reports.**—A person who knowingly gives false information to a law enforcement officer with intent to implicate another under this chapter commits an offense under 18 Pa.C.S. § 4906 (relating to false reports to law enforcement authorities).

(b) **No prepayment of fees.**—The petition shall be filed and service shall be made without the prepayment of fees.

(c) **Assessment of fees and costs.**—

(1)(i) No plaintiff seeking relief under this chapter shall be charged any fees or costs associated with the filing, issuance, registration or service of a petition, motion, complaint, order or any other filing. Prohibited fees or costs shall include, but are not limited to, those associated with modifying, withdrawing, dismissing or certifying copies of a petition, motion, complaint, order or any other filing, as well as any judicial surcharge or computer system fee.

(ii) No plaintiff seeking relief under this chapter shall be charged any fees or costs associated with filing a motion for reconsideration or an appeal from any order or action taken under this chapter.

(2) When an order is granted under this chapter, fees and costs shall be assessed against the defendant. The court shall waive fees and costs upon a showing of good cause or when the court makes a finding that the defendant is not able to pay the fees and costs.

(3) Nothing in this section is intended to expand or diminish the court's authority to enter an order under Pa.R.C.P. No.1023.1 (relating to Scope. Signing of Documents. Representations to the Court. Violation.).

(c.1) **Surcharge on order.**—When an order is granted under section 62A06 (relating to hearings), a surcharge of $100 shall be assessed against the defendant. All moneys received from surcharges shall be distributed in the following order of priority:

(1) Twenty-five dollars shall be forwarded to the Commonwealth and shall be used by the Pennsylvania State Police to establish and maintain the Statewide registry of protection orders provided for in section 62A04(c) (relating to responsibilities of law enforcement agencies).

(2) Fifty dollars shall be retained by the county and shall be used to carry out the provisions of this chapter as follows:

(i) Twenty-five dollars shall be used by the sheriff.

(ii) Twenty-five dollars shall be used by the court.

(3) Twenty-five dollars shall be forwarded to the Department of Public Welfare for use for victims of sexual assault in accordance with the provisions of section 2333 of the act of April 9, 1929 (P.L.177, No.175), known as The Administrative Code of 1929.

(4) The surcharge allocated under paragraphs (1) and (3) shall be used to supplement and not to supplant any other source of funds received for the purpose of carrying out the provisions of this chapter.

(d) Service.—

(1) The court shall adopt a means of prompt and effective service. If the court so orders, the sheriff or another court-designated agency or individual shall serve the petition and protection order. Under no circumstances shall the plaintiff be obligated to serve the petition or protection order.

(2) The petition and order shall be served upon the defendant.

(3) Within two business days, the order shall be served upon the police department, sheriff and district attorney in the jurisdiction where the order was entered.

(4) A certified copy of the order shall be issued to the plaintiff.

(5) In the case of a minor victim of sexual violence, a copy of the petition and order shall be served upon the county agency and the Department of Public Welfare. For purposes of this subparagraph, the term "county agency" shall be as defined in 23 Pa.C.S. § 6303 (relating to definitions).

(6) A copy of the order shall be issued as otherwise ordered by the court or hearing officer.

(7) Failure to serve the police department, sheriff or district attorney's office shall not stay the effect of a valid order.

(e) Assistance and advice to plaintiff.—The courts and hearing officers shall:

(1) Provide simplified forms and clerical assistance in English and Spanish to help with the writing and filing of the petition for an order for an individual not represented by counsel.

(2) Provide the plaintiff with written and oral referrals, in English and Spanish, to local sexual assault services in the case of sexual violence and to the local legal services office and to the county bar association's lawyer referral service in the case of sexual violence or intimidation.

(f) Effect of departure and nonresidence.—The right of the plaintiff to relief under this chapter shall not be affected by the defendant's absence from this Commonwealth or the defendant's nonresidence in this Commonwealth, provided that the court has personal jurisdiction over the defendant in accordance with section 5322 (relating to bases of personal jurisdiction over persons outside this Commonwealth).

References in Text. The Department of Public Welfare, referred to in this section, was redesignated as the Department of Human Services by Act 132 of 2014.

Cross References. Section 62A05 is referred to in sections 62A07, 62A09 of this title.

§ 62A06. Hearings.

(a) General rule.—Within ten business days of the filing of a petition under this chapter, a hearing shall be held before the court where the plaintiff must:

(1) assert that the plaintiff or another individual, as appropriate, is a victim of sexual violence or intimidation committed by the defendant; and

(2) prove by preponderance of the evidence that the plaintiff or another individual, as appropriate, is at a continued risk of harm from the defendant.

(a.1) Right to counsel.—The court shall, at the time the defendant is given notice of the hearing, advise the defendant of the right to be represented by counsel. The notice shall be printed and delivered in a manner that easily attracts attention to its contents.

(b) Temporary orders.—If a plaintiff seeks a temporary order for protection from an immediate and present danger, the court shall conduct an ex parte proceeding. The court may enter a temporary order as it deems necessary to protect the plaintiff or another individual, as appropriate, when it finds the plaintiff or another individual is in immediate and present danger from the defendant. The temporary order shall remain in effect until modified or terminated by the court after notice and hearing.

(c) **Continued hearings.**—If a hearing under subsection (a) is continued and no temporary order is issued, the court may make ex parte temporary orders under subsection (b), as it deems necessary.

Cross References. Section 62A06 is referred to in sections 62A05, 62A07 of this title.

§ 62A07. Relief.

(a) **Order or consent agreement.**—The court may issue an order or approve a consent agreement to protect the plaintiff or another individual, as appropriate, from the defendant.

(b) **General rule.**—An order or a consent agreement may include:

(1) Prohibiting the defendant from having any contact with the victim, including, but not limited to, restraining the defendant from entering the victim's residence, place of employment, business or school. This may include prohibiting indirect contact through third parties and also prohibiting direct or indirect contact with other designated persons.

(2) Granting any other appropriate relief sought by the plaintiff.

(c) **Duration and amendment of order or agreement.**—A protection order or an approved consent agreement shall be for a fixed period of time not to exceed 36 months. The court may amend its order or agreement at any time upon subsequent petition filed by either party.

(d) **Extension of protection orders.**—

(1) An extension of an order may be granted:

(i) Where the court, after a duly filed petition, notice to the defendant and a hearing, in accordance with the procedures set forth in sections 62A05 (relating to commencement of proceedings) and 62A06 (relating to hearings), finds that the extension is necessary because the defendant engaged in one or more acts or finds some other circumstances that, in the discretion of the court, demonstrate a continued risk of harm to the victim.

(ii) When a contempt petition or charge has been filed with the court or, in a county of the first class, a hearing officer, but the hearing has not occurred before the expiration of the protection order, the order shall be extended, at a minimum, until the disposition of the contempt petition.

(2) Service of an extended order shall be made in accordance with section 62A05(d).

(3) There shall be no limitation on the number of extensions that may be granted.

(e) **Notice.**—Notice shall be given to the defendant stating that violations of the order will subject the defendant to arrest under section 62A12 (relating to arrest for violation of order) or contempt of court under section 62A14 (relating to contempt for violation of order).

(f) **Incarceration.**—When the defendant is or was incarcerated and will be released from custody in the next 90 days or has been released from custody within the past 90 days, a plaintiff does not need to show that the defendant engaged in one or more acts that indicate a continued risk of harm to the victim in order to obtain an extension or a subsequent protection order under this chapter.

(g) **Identifying information.**—Any order issued under this chapter shall, when furnished by either party, specify the Social Security number and date of birth of the defendant.

Cross References. Section 62A07 is referred to in sections 62A04, 62A09, 62A12, 62A17 of this title.

§ 62A08. (Reserved).

§ 62A09. Emergency relief by minor judiciary.

(a) **General rule.**—When:

(1) in counties with fewer than four judges, the court is unavailable:

(i) from the close of business at the end of each day to the resumption of business the next morning;

(ii) from the end of the business week to the beginning of the business week; and

(iii) during the business day by reason of duties outside the county, illness or vacation; or

(2) in counties with at least four judges, the court is unavailable:

(i) from the close of business at the end of each day to the resumption of business the next morning; and

(ii) from the end of the business week to the beginning of the business week;

a petition may be filed before a hearing officer who may grant relief in accordance with section 62A07 (relating to relief) if the hearing officer deems it necessary to protect the victim upon good cause shown in an ex parte proceeding. Immediate and present danger posed by the defendant to the victim shall constitute good cause for the purposes of this subsection.

(b) Expiration of order.—An order issued under subsection (a) shall expire at the end of the next business day the court deems itself available. The court shall schedule hearings on orders entered by hearing officers under subsection (a) and shall review and continue in effect orders that are necessary to protect the plaintiff or another individual, as appropriate, until the hearing, at which time the plaintiff may seek a temporary order from the court.

(c) Certification of order to court.—An emergency order issued under this section and any documentation in support thereof shall be immediately certified to the court. The certification to the court shall have the effect of commencing proceedings under section 62A05 (relating to commencement of proceedings) and invoking the other provisions of this chapter. If it is not already alleged in a petition for an emergency order, the plaintiff shall file a verified statement setting forth the reasons for the need for protection at least five days prior to the hearing. Service of the verified statement shall be made subject to section 62A05(d).

(d) Instructions regarding the commencement of proceedings.—Upon issuance of an emergency order, the hearing officer shall provide the plaintiff instructions regarding the commencement of proceedings in the court at the beginning of the next business day and regarding the procedures for initiating a contempt charge should the defendant violate the emergency order. The hearing officer shall also advise the plaintiff of the existence of rape crisis centers in the county or in nearby counties in the case of sexual violence and inform the plaintiff of the availability of legal assistance without cost if the plaintiff is unable to pay for them in the case of sexual violence or intimidation.

(e) Master of emergency relief.—The president judge of a court of common pleas of a judicial district may, with the approval of the Administrative Office of Pennsylvania Courts, provide for the selection and appointment of a master for emergency relief on a full-time or part-time basis. The number of masters for emergency relief shall be fixed by the president judge with the approval of the Administrative Office of Pennsylvania Courts. The compensation of a master for emergency relief shall be fixed and paid by the county.

Cross References. Section 62A09 is referred to in sections 62A03, 62A04 of this title.

§ 62A10. Sexual assault counselor.

A sexual assault counselor may accompany and provide assistance to a plaintiff in any legal proceeding or hearing under this chapter which relates to sexual violence.

§ 62A11. Disclosure of addresses.

(a) General rule.—During the course of a proceeding under this chapter, the court or hearing officer may consider whether the plaintiff or victim, as appropriate, is endangered by disclosure of the permanent or temporary address of the plaintiff or victim. The court shall consider the wishes of the plaintiff regarding the disclosure of the address. Neither in the pleadings nor during proceedings or hearings under this chapter shall the court or hearing officer require disclosure of the address of a rape crisis center or the plaintiff or victim, as appropriate.

(b) **Order.**—Where the court concludes that the defendant poses a continued risk of harm to the victim and where the plaintiff requests that the address, telephone number and information about the victim's whereabouts not be disclosed, the court shall enter an order directing that law enforcement agencies, human service agencies and school districts shall not disclose the presence of the victim in the jurisdiction or district or furnish any address, telephone number or any other demographic information about the victim except by further order of the court.

§ 62A12. Arrest for violation of order.

(a) **General rule.**—An arrest for a violation of an order issued under this chapter may be without warrant upon probable cause, whether or not the violation is committed in the presence of the police officer or sheriff, in circumstances where the defendant has violated a provision of an order consistent with section 62A07 (relating to relief). The police officer or sheriff may verify the existence of an order by telephone, radio or other electronic communication with the appropriate police department, Pennsylvania State Police registry or issuing authority. A police officer or sheriff shall arrest a defendant for violating an order by a court within the judicial district or issued by a court in another judicial district within this Commonwealth.

(b) **Procedure following arrest.—**

(1) Subsequent to an arrest, the defendant shall be taken by the police officer or sheriff without unnecessary delay before the court in the judicial district where the contempt is alleged to have occurred.

(2) When that court is unavailable, the police officer or sheriff shall convey the defendant to a magisterial district judge designated as appropriate by local rules of court or, in counties of the first class, to the appropriate hearing officer.

(c) **Preliminary arraignment.**—The defendant shall be afforded a preliminary arraignment without unnecessary delay.

(d) **Other emergency powers unaffected.**—This section shall not be construed to in any way limit any of the other powers for emergency relief provided under this chapter.

(e) **Hearing.**—A hearing shall be scheduled within ten business days of the filing of the charge or complaint of indirect criminal contempt. The hearing and any adjudication shall not preclude a hearing on other criminal charges underlying the contempt, nor shall a hearing or adjudication on other criminal charges preclude a hearing on a charge of indirect criminal contempt.

Cross References. Section 62A12 is referred to in section 62A07 of this title.

§ 62A13. Private criminal complaints for violation of order or agreement.

(a) **General rule.**—A plaintiff may file a private criminal complaint against a defendant, alleging indirect criminal contempt for a violation of any provision of an order or court-approved consent agreement issued under this chapter, with the court, the office of the district attorney or the magisterial district judge in the jurisdiction or county where the violation occurred, except that in a county of the first class, a complaint may only be filed with the family division of the court of common pleas or the office of district attorney.

(b) **Procedure service.—**

(1) Procedure for filing and service of a private criminal complaint shall be provided as set forth by local rule.

(2) Nothing in this subsection is intended to expand or diminish the court's authority to enter an order pursuant to Pa.R.C.P. No.1023.1 (relating to Scope. Signing of Documents. Representations to the Court. Violation.).

(c) Fees and costs.—

(1) No fees or costs associated with the prosecution of the private criminal complaint shall be assigned to the plaintiff, including, but not limited to, filing, service, failure to prosecute, withdrawal or dismissal.

(2)(i) After a finding of indirect criminal contempt, fees and costs may be assigned against the defendant.

(ii) The court shall waive fees and costs imposed under this chapter upon a showing of good cause or if the court makes a finding that the defendant is not able to pay the costs associated with the indirect criminal contempt action.

(3) Nothing in this subsection shall be construed to expand or diminish the court's authority to enter an order under Pa.R.C.P. No.1023.1.

§ 62A14. Contempt for violation of order.

(a) General rule.—Where the police department, sheriff or the plaintiff has filed charges of indirect criminal contempt against a defendant for violation of an order or court-approved consent agreement entered into under this chapter, the court may hold the defendant in indirect criminal contempt and punish the defendant in accordance with law.

(b) Jurisdiction.—A court shall have jurisdiction over indirect criminal contempt charges for violation of a protection order in the county where the violation occurred and in the county where the order was granted.

(c) Minor defendant.—Any defendant who is a minor and who is charged with indirect criminal contempt for allegedly violating a protection order related to sexual violence shall be considered to have committed an alleged delinquent act as that term is defined in section 6302 (relating to definitions) and shall be treated as provided in Chapter 63 (relating to juvenile matters).

(d) Trial and punishment.—

(1) Notwithstanding section 4136(a) (relating to rights of persons charged with certain indirect criminal contempts), the defendant shall not have the right to a jury trial on the charge of indirect criminal contempt; however, the defendant shall be entitled to counsel.

(2) A sentence for indirect criminal contempt under this chapter may include:

(i) A fine of not less than $300 nor more than $1,000 and imprisonment for a period not exceeding six months.

(ii) A fine of not less than $300 nor more than $1,000 and supervised probation for a period not exceeding six months.

(iii) An order for any other relief provided for under this chapter.

(3) Upon conviction for indirect criminal contempt and at the request of the plaintiff, the court shall also grant an extension of the protection order for an additional term.

(4) Upon conviction for indirect criminal contempt, the court shall notify the sheriff of the jurisdiction which issued the protection order of the conviction.

(5) All moneys received under this section shall be distributed in the following order of priority:

(i) One hundred dollars shall be forwarded to the Commonwealth and shall be used by the Pennsylvania State Police to establish and maintain the State-wide registry of protection orders provided for in section 62A04(c) (relating to responsibilities of law enforcement agencies).

(ii) One hundred dollars shall be retained by the county and shall be used to carry out the provisions of this chapter as follows:

    (A) Fifty dollars shall be used by the sheriff.

    (B) Fifty dollars shall be used by the court.

(iii) One hundred dollars shall be forwarded to the Department of Public Welfare for use for victims of sexual assault in accordance with the provisions of section 2333 of the act of April 9, 1929 (P.L.177, No.175), known as The Administrative Code of 1929.

(iv) Any additional money shall be distributed in the manner under subparagraph (i).

(e) Notification upon release.—

(1) The appropriate releasing authority or other official as designated by local rule shall use all reasonable means to notify the victim sufficiently in advance of the release of the offender from any incarceration imposed under subsection (d). Notification shall be required for work release, furlough, medical leave, community service, discharge, escape and recapture. Notification shall include the terms and conditions imposed on any temporary release from custody.

(2) The plaintiff must keep the appropriate releasing authority or other official as designated by local rule advised of contact information; failure to do so will constitute waiver of any right to notification under this section.

(f) Multiple remedies.—Disposition of a charge of indirect criminal contempt shall not preclude the prosecution of other criminal charges associated with the incident giving rise to the contempt, nor shall disposition of other criminal charges preclude prosecution of indirect criminal contempt associated with the criminal conduct giving rise to the charges.

    References in Text. The Department of Public Welfare, referred to in this section, was redesignated as the Department of Human Services by Act 132 of 2014.

    Cross References. Section 62A14 is referred to in section 62A07 of this title.

§ 62A15. Civil contempt or modification for violation of order or agreement.

(a) General rule.—A plaintiff may file a petition for civil contempt with the issuing court alleging that the defendant has violated any provision of an order or court- approved consent agreement entered into under this chapter.

(b) Civil contempt order.—Upon finding of a violation of a protection order or court-approved consent agreement issued under this chapter, the court, either pursuant to petition for civil contempt or on its own accord, may hold the defendant in civil contempt and constrain the defendant in accordance with law.

(c) Sentencing.—A sentence for civil contempt under this chapter may include imprisonment until the defendant complies with provisions of the order or court-approved consent agreement or demonstrates the intent to do so, but in no case shall a term of imprisonment under this section exceed a period of six months.

(d) Jury trial and counsel.—Notwithstanding section 4136(a) (relating to rights of persons charged with certain indirect criminal contempts), the defendant shall not have a right to a jury trial; however, the defendant shall be entitled to counsel.

§ 62A16. Confidentiality.

(a) Nature of privilege.—

(1) Unless a victim of sexual violence who consults a sexual assault counselor for the purpose of securing advice, counseling or assistance waives the privilege in a signed writing prior to testimony or disclosure, a sexual assault counselor or a coparticipant who is present during sexual assault counseling or advocacy shall not be competent nor permitted to testify, release the records of or to otherwise disclose

confidential communications made to or by the counselor by or to the victim. The privilege shall terminate upon the death of the victim.

(2) Neither the sexual assault counselor nor the victim shall waive the privilege of confidential communications by reporting facts of physical or sexual violence under 23 Pa.C.S. Ch. 63 (relating to child protective services), a Federal or State mandatory reporting statute or a local mandatory reporting ordinance.

(b) Scope.—The provisions of this section applicable to the victim of sexual violence shall also apply to a person who seeks advice, counseling or assistance from a sexual assault counselor regarding the victim.

§ 62A17. Procedure and other remedies.

(a) General rule.—Unless otherwise indicated under this chapter, a proceeding under this chapter shall be in accordance with applicable general rules and shall be in addition to any other available civil or criminal remedies. The plaintiff and the defendant may seek modification of a protection order issued under section 62A07 (relating to relief) at any time during the pendency of the order. Except as otherwise provided in this chapter, modification may be ordered after the filing of a petition for modification, service of the petition and a hearing on the petition.

(b) Remedies for bad faith.—Notwithstanding any other provision of law, upon finding that an individual commenced a proceeding under this chapter in bad faith, a court shall direct the individual to pay to the defendant actual damages and reasonable attorney fees. Failure to prove an allegation of continued risk of harm by a preponderance of the evidence shall not, by itself, result in a finding of bad faith.

§ 62A18. Applicability.

The provisions of the following acts relating to victims who are protected by an order issued under 23 Pa.C.S. Ch. 61 (relating to protection from abuse) shall apply also to victims who are protected by an order issued under this chapter:

(1) The act of November 24, 1998 (P.L.882, No.111), known as the Crime Victims Act.

(2) 23 Pa.C.S. Ch. 67 (relating to domestic and sexual violence victim address confidentiality).

§ 62A19. Inability to pay.

(a) Order for installment payments.—Upon plea and proof that a person is without the financial means to pay a fine, a fee or a cost, a court may order payment of money owed in installments appropriate to the circumstances of the person and shall fix the amounts, times and manner of payment.

(b) Electronic payment.—The treasurer of each county may allow the use of credit cards and bank cards in the payment of money owed under this chapter.

§ 62A20. Construction.

Nothing in this chapter shall be construed to preclude an action for wrongful use of civil process in accordance with Subchapter E of Chapter 83 (relating to wrongful use of civil proceedings) or criminal prosecution for a violation of 18 Pa.C.S. Ch. 49 (relating to falsification and intimidation).

CHAPTER 63
JUVENILE MATTERS

Subchapter

A. General Provisions
B. Jurisdiction and Custody
C. Procedures and Safeguards
D. Disposition of Children Generally
E. Dispositions Affecting Other Jurisdictions

Enactment. Chapter 63 was added July 9, 1976, P.L.586, No.142, effective 60 days from the date of final enactment of the act of April 28, 1978 (P.L.202, No.53).

Save from Suspension. Pennsylvania Rule of Civil Procedure No. 1915.24, readopted and amended November 8, 1982, provided that Chapter 63 shall not be deemed suspended or affected by Rules 1915.1 through 1915.25 governing actions for custody, partial custody and visitation of minor children.

Cross References. Chapter 63 is referred to in sections 1123, 1515, 4402, 4416, 5986, 62A14, 6403, 6408, 9799.27, 9799.28 of this title; sections 2702, 6305, 9121 of Title 18 (Crimes and Offenses); sections 2740, 5324, 5503, 6114, 6303, 6315, 6341, 6368, 6370, 6373, 6375, 6381 of Title 23 (Domestic Relations); section 922 of Title 34 (Game); section 4104 of Title 61 (Prisons and Parole); sections 1532, 3804 of Title 75 (Vehicles).

SUBCHAPTER A
GENERAL PROVISIONS

Sec.

6301. Short title and purposes of chapter.
6302. Definitions.
6303. Scope of chapter.
6304. Powers and duties of probation officers.
6305. Masters.
6306. Costs and expenses of care of child.
6307. Inspection of court files and records.
6308. Law enforcement records.
6309. Juvenile history record information.
6310. Parental participation.
6311. Guardian ad litem for child in court proceedings.

§ 6301. Short title and purposes of chapter.

(a) Short title.—This chapter shall be known and may be cited as the "Juvenile Act."

(b) Purposes.—This chapter shall be interpreted and construed as to effectuate the following purposes:

(1) To preserve the unity of the family whenever possible or to provide another alternative permanent family when the unity of the family cannot be maintained.

(1.1) To provide for the care, protection, safety and wholesome mental and physical development of children coming within the provisions of this chapter.

(2) Consistent with the protection of the public interest, to provide for children committing delinquent acts programs of supervision, care and rehabilitation which provide balanced attention to the protection of the community, the imposition of accountability for offenses committed and the development of competencies to enable children to become responsible and productive members of the community.

(3) To achieve the foregoing purposes in a family environment whenever possible, separating the child from parents only when necessary for his welfare, safety or health or in the interests of public safety, by doing all of the following:

(i) employing evidence-based practices whenever possible and, in the case of a delinquent child, by using the least restrictive intervention that is consistent with the protection of the community, the imposition of accountability for offenses committed and the rehabilitation, supervision and treatment needs of the child; and

(ii) imposing confinement only if necessary and for the minimum amount of time that is consistent with the purposes under paragraphs (1), (1.1) and (2).

(4) To provide means through which the provisions of this chapter are executed and enforced and in which the parties are assured a fair hearing and their constitutional and other legal rights recognized and enforced.

(Nov. 17, 1995, 1st Sp.Sess., P.L.1127, No.33, eff. 120 days; Dec. 15, 1998, P.L.949, No.126, eff. Jan. 1, 1999, Oct. 25, 2012, P.L. 1655, No. 204, eff. 60 days).

2012 Amendment. Act 204 amended subsec. (b).

1998 Amendment. Act 126 amended subsec. (b).

Cross References. Section 6301 is referred to in section 6352 of this title.

§ 6302. Definitions.

The following words and phrases when used in this chapter shall have, unless the context clearly indicates otherwise, the meanings given to them in this section:

"Age-appropriate or developmentally appropriate." The following:

(1) activities or items that are generally accepted as suitable for children of the same chronological age or level of maturity or that are determined to be developmentally appropriate for a child based on the development of cognitive, emotional, physical and behavioral capacities that are typical for an age or age group; and

(2) in the case of a specific child, activities or items that are suitable for the child based on the developmental stages attained by the child with respect to the cognitive, emotional, physical and behavioral capacities of the child.

"Aggravated circumstances." Any of the following circumstances:

(1) The child is in the custody of a county agency and either:

(i) the identity or whereabouts of the parents is unknown and cannot be ascertained and the parent does not claim the child within three months of the date the child was taken into custody; or

(ii) the identity or whereabouts of the parents is known and the parents have failed to maintain substantial and continuing contact with the child for a period of six months.

(2) The child or another child of the parent has been the victim of physical abuse resulting in serious bodily injury, sexual violence or aggravated physical neglect by the parent.

(3) The parent of the child has been convicted of any of the following offenses where the victim was a child:

(i) criminal homicide under 18 Pa.C.S. Ch. 25 (relating to criminal homicide);

(ii) a felony under 18 Pa.C.S. § 2702 (relating to aggravated assault), 3121 (relating to rape), 3122.1 (relating to statutory sexual assault), 3123 (relating to involuntary deviate sexual intercourse), 3124.1 (relating to sexual assault) or 3125 (relating to aggravated indecent assault).

(iii) A misdemeanor under 18 Pa.C.S. § 3126 (relating to indecent assault).

(iv) An equivalent crime in another jurisdiction.

(4) The attempt, solicitation or conspiracy to commit any of the offenses set forth in paragraph (3).

(5) The parental rights of the parent have been involuntarily terminated with respect to a child of the parent.

(6) The parent of the child is required to register as a sexual offender under Subchapter H of Chapter 97 (relating to registration of sexual offenders) or to register with a sexual offender registry in another jurisdiction or foreign country.

"Aggravated physical neglect." Any omission in the care of a child which results in a life-threatening condition or seriously impairs the child's functioning.

"Assessment." An individualized examination of a child to determine the child's psychosocial needs and problems, including the type and extent of any mental health, substance abuse or co-occurring mental health and substance abuse disorders and recommendations for treatment. The term includes, but is not limited to, a drug and alcohol, psychological and psychiatric evaluation, records review, clinical interview and the administration of a formal test and instrument.

"Board." The State Sexual Offenders Assessment Board.

"Caregiver." A person with whom the child is placed in an out-of-home placement, including a resource family or an individual designated by a county agency or private agency. The resource family is the caregiver for any child placed with them.

"Child." An individual who:

(1) is under the age of 18 years;

(2) is under the age of 21 years who committed an act of delinquency before reaching the age of 18 years; or

(3) is under the age of 21 years and was adjudicated dependent before reaching the age of 18 years, who has requested the court to retain jurisdiction and who remains under the jurisdiction of the court as a dependent child because the court has determined that the child is:

(i) completing secondary education or an equivalent credential;

(ii) enrolled in an institution which provides postsecondary or vocational education;

(iii) participating in a program actively designed to promote or remove barriers to employment;

(iv) employed for at least 80 hours per month; or

(v) incapable of doing any of the activities described in subparagraph (i), (ii), (iii) or (iv) due to a medical or behavioral health condition, which is supported by regularly updated information in the permanency plan of the child.

"County agency." The term as defined in 23 Pa.C.S. § 6303 (relating to definitions).

"Court." The court of common pleas.

"Court-appointed special advocate" or "CASA." An individual appointed by the court to participate as an advocate for a child who is dependent or alleged to be dependent.

"Custodian." A person other than a parent or legal guardian, who stands in loco parentis to the child, or a person to whom legal custody of the child has been given by order of a court.

"Delinquent act."

(1) The term means an act designated a crime under the law of this Commonwealth, or of another state if the act occurred in that state, or under Federal law, or an act which constitutes indirect criminal contempt under Chapter 62A (relating to protection of victims of sexual violence or intimidation) with respect to sexual violence or 23 Pa.C.S. Ch. 61 (relating to protection from abuse) or the failure of

a child to comply with a lawful sentence imposed for a summary offense, in which event notice of the fact shall be certified to the court.

(2) The term shall not include:

(i) The crime of murder.

(ii) Any of the following prohibited conduct where the child was 15 years of age or older at the time of the alleged conduct and a deadly weapon as defined in 18 Pa.C.S. § 2301 (relating to definitions) was used during the commission of the offense which, if committed by an adult, would be classified as:

(A) Rape as defined in 18 Pa.C.S. § 3121 (relating to rape).

(B) Involuntary deviate sexual intercourse as defined in 18 Pa.C.S. § 3123 (relating to involuntary deviate sexual intercourse).

(C) Aggravated assault as defined in 18 Pa.C.S. § 2702(a)(1) or (2) (relating to aggravated assault).

(D) Robbery as defined in 18 Pa.C.S. § 3701(a)(1)(i), (ii) or (iii) (relating to robbery).

(E) Robbery of motor vehicle as defined in 18 Pa.C.S. § 3702 (relating to robbery of motor vehicle).

(F) Aggravated indecent assault as defined in 18 Pa.C.S. § 3125 (relating to aggravated indecent assault).

(G) Kidnapping as defined in 18 Pa.C.S. § 2901 (relating to kidnapping).

(H) Voluntary manslaughter.

(I) An attempt, conspiracy or solicitation to commit murder or any of these crimes as provided in 18 Pa.C.S. §§ 901 (relating to criminal attempt), 902 (relating to criminal solicitation) and 903 (relating to criminal conspiracy).

(iii) Any of the following prohibited conduct where the child was 15 years of age or older at the time of the alleged conduct and has been previously adjudicated delinquent of any of the following prohibited conduct which, if committed by an adult, would be classified as:

(A) Rape as defined in 18 Pa.C.S. § 3121.

(B) Involuntary deviate sexual intercourse as defined in 18 Pa.C.S. § 3123.

(C) Robbery as defined in 18 Pa.C.S. § 3701(a)(1)(i), (ii) or (iii).

(D) Robbery of motor vehicle as defined in 18 Pa.C.S. § 3702.

(E) Aggravated indecent assault as defined in 18 Pa.C.S. § 3125.

(F) Kidnapping as defined in 18 Pa.C.S. § 2901.

(G) Voluntary manslaughter.

(H) An attempt, conspiracy or solicitation to commit murder or any of these crimes as provided in 18 Pa.C.S. §§ 901, 902 and 903.

(iv) Summary offenses.

(v) A crime committed by a child who has been found guilty in a criminal proceeding for other than a summary offense.

"Delinquent child." A child ten years of age or older whom the court has found to have committed a delinquent act and is in need of treatment, supervision or rehabilitation.

"Dependent child." A child who:

(1) is without proper parental care or control, subsistence, education as required by law, or other care or control necessary for his physical, mental, or emotional health, or morals. A determination that there is a lack of proper parental care or control may be based upon evidence of conduct by the parent, guardian or other

custodian that places the health, safety or welfare of the child at risk, including evidence of the parent's, guardian's or other custodian's use of alcohol or a controlled substance that places the health, safety or welfare of the child at risk;

    (2) has been placed for care or adoption in violation of law;

    (3) has been abandoned by his parents, guardian, or other custodian;

    (4) is without a parent, guardian, or legal custodian;

    (5) while subject to compulsory school attendance is habitually and without justification truant from school;

    (6) has committed a specific act or acts of habitual disobedience of the reasonable and lawful commands of his parent, guardian or other custodian and who is ungovernable and found to be in need of care, treatment or supervision;

    (7) has committed a delinquent act or crime, other than a summary offense, while under the age of ten years;

    (8) has been formerly adjudicated dependent, and is under the jurisdiction of the court, subject to its conditions or placements and who commits an act which is defined as ungovernable in paragraph (6);

    (9) has been referred pursuant to section 6323 (relating to informal adjustment), and who commits an act which is defined as ungovernable in paragraph (6); or

    (10) is born to a parent whose parental rights with regard to another child have been involuntarily terminated under 23 Pa.C.S. § 2511 (relating to grounds for involuntary termination) within three years immediately preceding the date of birth of the child and conduct of the parent poses a risk to the health, safety or welfare of the child.

"Facility designed or operated for the benefit of delinquent children." A facility that either identifies itself by charter, articles of incorporation or program description as solely for delinquent children.

"Out-of-home placement." A setting that provides 24-hour substitute care for a child away from the child's parents or guardians and for whom the county agency has placement care and responsibility. The term includes resource family homes and supervised settings in which a child is living and, for a child who has attained 18 years of age, a supervised setting in which the individual is living independently. The term does not include secure facilities, facilities operated primarily for the detention of children who have been adjudicated delinquent, accredited psychiatric residential treatment facilities or hospitals.

"Private agency." An entity that provides out-of-home placement services to children under a contract with a county agency.

"Protective supervision." Supervision ordered by the court of children found to be dependent.

"Reasonable and prudent parent standard." The standard, characterized by careful and sensible parental decisions that maintain the health, safety and best interests of a child while encouraging the emotional and developmental growth of the child, that a caregiver must use when determining whether to allow a child in an out-of-home placement under the responsibility of the county agency to participate in extracurricular, enrichment, cultural and social activities.

"Resource family." As defined under section 3 of the act of November 22, 2005 (P.L.404, No.73), known as the Resource Family Care Act.

"Screening." A process, regardless of whether it includes the administration of a formal instrument, that is designed to identify a child who is at increased risk of having mental health, substance abuse or co-occurring mental health and substance abuse disorders that warrant immediate attention, intervention or more comprehensive assessment.

"Serious bodily injury." Bodily injury which creates a substantial risk of death or which causes serious, permanent disfigurement or protracted loss or impairment of the function of any bodily member or organ.

"Sexual violence." Rape, indecent contact as defined in 18 Pa.C.S. § 3101 (relating to definitions), incest or using, causing, permitting, persuading or coercing the child to engage in a prohibited sexual act as defined in 18 Pa.C.S. § 6312(a) (relating to sexual abuse of children) or a simulation of a prohibited sexual act for the purpose of photographing, videotaping, depicting on computer or filming involving the child.

"Shelter care." Temporary care of a child in physically unrestricted facilities. A facility approved by the Department of Public Welfare to provide shelter care may be located in the same building as a facility approved to provide secure detention services provided that children receiving shelter care services are segregated from the children receiving secure detention services as required by the department.

(Apr. 28, 1978, P.L.202, No.53, eff. 60 days; Dec. 11, 1986, P.L.1521, No.165, eff. 60 days; Mar. 15, 1995, 1st Sp.Sess., P.L.972, No.6, eff. 60 days; Nov. 17, 1995, 1st Sp.Sess., P.L.1127, No.33, eff. 120 days; June 18, 1998, P.L.640, No.84, eff. 60 days; Dec. 15, 1998, P.L.949, No.126, eff. Jan. 1, 1999; Dec. 15, 1998, P.L.978, No.128, eff. 60 days; Dec. 20, 2000, P.L.946, No.129, eff. 60 days; Aug. 14, 2003, P.L.97, No.21, eff. 180 days; Oct. 9, 2008, P.L.1396, No.109, eff. 60 days; July 5, 2012, P.L.880, No.91, eff. imd.; Oct. 25, 2012, P.L.1655, No.204, eff. imd.; March 21, 2014, P.L.365, No.25, eff. July 1, 2015; Dec. 28, 2015, P.L.559, No.94, eff. Jan. 1, 2016; Oct. 28, 2016, P.L.966, No.115, eff. imd.; June 28, 2018, P.L.361, No.49, eff. 60 days)

2018 Amendment. Act 49 amended the def. of "delinquent act."

2016 Amendment. Act 115 added par. (6) of the def. of "aggravated circumstances."

2015 Amendment. Act 94 added the defs. of "age-appropriate or developmentally appropriate," "caregiver," "out-of-home placement," "private agency," "reasonable and prudent parent standard" and "resource family."

2012 Amendments. Act 91 amended par. (3) of the def. of "child" and Act 204 amended par. (7) of the def. of "dependent child."

2012 Correction. Incorrect language was added to the def. of "aggravated circumstances" in 2012. The correct version of the def. appears in this title.

2008 Amendment. Act 109 added the defs. of "assessment" and "screening."

2003 Amendment. Act 21 added the def. of "board."

2000 Amendment. Act 129 amended the def. of "shelter care" and added the def. of "facility designed or operated for the benefit of delinquent children."

1998 Amendments. Act 126 amended the def. of "dependent child" and added the defs. of "aggravated circumstances," "aggravated physical neglect," "county agency," "serious bodily injury" and "sexual violence" and Act 128 added the def. of "court-appointed special advocate" or "CASA."

1995 Amendment. Section 8 of Act 33, 1st Sp.Sess., provided that Act 33 shall apply to all delinquent acts committed on or after the effective date of Act 33.

Care of Dependent Children. Section 31 of Act 53 of 1978 limits the liability of counties for costs of operating new shelter care programs for dependent children classified under paragraph (6) of the definition of "dependent child."

References in Text. The Department of Public Welfare, referred to in this section, was redesignated as the Department of Human Services by Act 132 of 2014.

Cross References. Section 6302 is referred to in sections 62A14, 6303, 6311, 6322, 6323, 6327, 6351, 6355, 6402 of this title; sections 6114, 6315 of Title 23 (Domestic Relations).

§ 6303. Scope of chapter.

(a) **General rule.**—This chapter shall apply exclusively to the following:

(1) Proceedings in which a child is alleged to be delinquent or dependent.

(2) Transfers under section 6322 (relating to transfer from criminal proceedings).

(3) Proceedings arising under Subchapter E (relating to dispositions affecting other jurisdictions).

(4) Proceedings under the Interstate Compact on Juveniles, as set forth in section 731 of the act of June 13, 1967 (P.L.31, No.21), known as the Public Welfare Code.

(5) Proceedings in which a child is charged with a summary offense arising out of the same episode or transaction involving a delinquent act for which a petition alleging delinquency is filed under this chapter. The summary offense shall be included in any petition regarding the accompanying delinquent act. Upon finding a child to have committed a summary offense, the court may utilize any disposition available to the minor judiciary where a child is found to have committed a summary offense, including a finding of guilt on the summary offense.

(b) Minor judiciary.—No child shall be detained, committed or sentenced to imprisonment by a magisterial district judge or a judge of the minor judiciary unless the child is charged with an act set forth in paragraph (2)(i), (ii), (iii) or (v) of the definition of "delinquent act" in section 6302 (relating to definitions).

(c) Summary offenses generally.—In addition to the provisions of subsection (a)(5) and notwithstanding the exclusion of summary offenses generally from the definition of "delinquent act" under section 6302, the provisions of sections 6307 (relating to inspection of court files and records) and 6336(d) (relating to conduct of hearings), insofar as section 6336(d) relates to the exclusion of the general public from the proceedings, shall apply to proceedings involving a child charged with a summary offense when the proceedings are before a judge of the minor judiciary, the Philadelphia Municipal Court or a court of common pleas.

(Apr. 28, 1978, P.L.202, No.53, eff. 60 days; Mar. 31, 1995, 1st Sp.Sess., P.L.983, No.9, eff. 60 days; Mar. 29, 1996, P.L.51, No.17, eff. imd.; Nov. 30, 2004, P.L.1618, No.207, eff. 60 days; Oct. 25, 2012, P.L.1655, No.204, eff. 90 days; Sept. 27, 2014, P.L.2482, No.138, eff. 60 days)

2014 Amendment. Act 138 amended subsec. (c).

2004 Amendment. Act 207 amended subsec. (b). See sections 28 and 29 of Act 207 in the appendix to this title for special provisions relating to applicability and construction of law.

Suspension by Court Rule. Subsection (b) was suspended by Pennsylvania Rule of Juvenile Court Procedure No. 800(8), amended December 30, 2005, insofar as it is inconsistent with Rule 210 relating to arrest warrants.

References in Text. Section 731 of the act of June 13, 1967 (P.L.31, No.21), known as the Public Welfare Code, referred to in subsec. (a), was repealed by the act of July 2, 2004 (P.L.468, No.54). The subject matter is now contained the Interstate Compact for Juveniles Act.

Cross References. Section 6303 is referred to in section 6336 of this title.

§ 6304. Powers and duties of probation officers.

(a) General rule.—For the purpose of carrying out the objectives and purposes of this chapter, and subject to the limitations of this chapter or imposed by the court, a probation officer shall:

(1) Make investigations, reports, and recommendations to the court.

(2) Receive and examine complaints and charges of delinquency or dependency of a child for the purpose of considering the commencement of proceedings under this chapter.

(3) Supervise and assist a child placed on probation or in his protective supervision or care by order of the court or other authority of law.

(4) Make appropriate referrals to other private or public agencies of the community if their assistance appears to be needed or desirable.

(5) Take into custody and detain a child who is under his supervision or care as a delinquent or dependent child if the probation officer has reasonable cause to believe that the health or safety of the child is in imminent danger, or that he may abscond or be removed from the jurisdiction of the court, or when ordered by the court pursuant to this chapter or that he violated the conditions of his probation.

(6) Perform all other functions designated by this chapter or by order of the court pursuant thereto.

(a.1) Authority to search.—

(1) Probation officers may search the person and property of children:

(i) under their supervision as delinquent children or pursuant to a consent decree in accordance with this section;

(ii) taken into custody pursuant to subsection (a) and section 6324 (relating to taking into custody); and

(iii) detained pursuant to subsection (a) and section 6325 (relating to detention of child) or during the intake process pursuant to subsection (a) and section 6331 (relating to release from detention or commencement of proceedings) and in accordance with this section.

(2) Nothing in this section shall be construed to permit searches or seizures in violation of the Constitution of the United States or section 8 of Article I of the Constitution of Pennsylvania.

(3) No violation of this section shall constitute an independent ground for suppression of evidence in any proceeding.

(4)(i) A personal search of a child may be conducted by any probation officer:

(A) If there is a reasonable suspicion to believe that the child possesses contraband or other evidence of violations of the conditions of supervision.

(B) When a child is transported or taken into custody.

(C) When a child enters or leaves a detention center, institution or other facility for alleged or adjudicated delinquent children.

(ii) A property search may be conducted by any probation officer if there is reasonable suspicion to believe that the real or other property in the possession of or under the control of the child contains contraband or other evidence of violations of the conditions of supervision.

(iii) Prior approval of a supervisor shall be obtained for a property search absent exigent circumstances or unless the search is being conducted by a supervisor. No prior approval shall be required for a personal search.

(iv) A written report of every property search conducted without prior approval shall be prepared by the probation officer who conducted the search and filed in the child's case record. The exigent circumstances shall be stated in the report.

(v) The child may be detained if he is present during a property search. If the child is not present during a property search, the probation officer in charge of the search shall make a reasonable effort to provide the child with notice of the search, including a list of the items seized, after the search is completed.

(vi) The existence of reasonable suspicion to search shall be determined in accordance with constitutional search and seizure provisions as applied by judicial decision. In accordance with that case law, the following factors, where applicable, may be taken into account:

(A) The observations of officers.

(B) Information provided by others.

(C) The activities of the child.

(D) Information provided by the child.

(E) The experience of the probation officer with the child.

(F) The experience of probation officers in similar circumstances.

(G) The prior delinquent and supervisory history of the offender.

(H) The need to verify compliance with the conditions of supervision.

(b) Foreign jurisdictions.—Any of the functions specified in subsection (a) may be performed in another jurisdiction if authorized by the court of this Commonwealth and permitted by the laws of the other jurisdiction.

(c) Definitions.—As used in this section, the following words and phrases shall have the meanings given to them in this subsection:

"Conditions of supervision." A term or condition of a child's supervision, whether imposed by the court or a probation officer, including compliance with all requirements of Federal, State and local law.

"Contraband." An item that a child is not permitted to possess under the conditions of supervision, including an item whose possession is forbidden by any Federal, State or local law.

"Court." The court of common pleas or a judge thereof.

"Exigent circumstances." The term includes, but is not limited to, reasonable suspicion that contraband or other evidence of violations of the conditions of supervision might be destroyed or suspicion that a weapon might be used.

"Personal search." A warrantless search of a child's person, including, but not limited to, the child's clothing and any personal property which is in the possession, within the reach or under the control of the child.

"Probation officer." A probation officer appointed or employed by a court or by a county probation department.

"Property search." A warrantless search of real property, vehicle or personal property which is in the possession or under the control of a child.

"Supervisor." An individual acting in a supervisory or administrative capacity.

§ 6304.1. Summary offenses.

(a) Review.—

(1) Upon notice being certified to the court that a child has failed to comply with a lawful sentence imposed for a summary offense, a probation officer shall review the complaints and charges of delinquency pursuant to section 6304 (relating to powers and duties of probation officers) for the purpose of considering the commencement of proceedings under this chapter.

(2) A proceeding commenced under the review in this subsection is a separate action from the underlying summary conviction. For the purposes of proceedings commenced under this section, failure to comply with a lawful sentence imposed for a summary offense is an alleged delinquent act.

(3) Any reference to the underlying summary conviction is solely for the purpose of the certification from the magisterial district judge to the court of common pleas that the juvenile was convicted of the summary offense and failed to comply under section 4132(2) (relating to attachment and summary punishment for contempts).

(b) Administration of money.—Any money subsequently paid by the child pursuant to the disposition of the charges shall be administered and disbursed in accordance with written guidelines adopted by the president judge of the court of common pleas. The court may direct that any portion of the money received from the child shall be deposited into a restitution fund established by the president judge of the court of common pleas pursuant to section 6352(a)(5) (relating to disposition of delinquent child).

(Nov. 30, 2004, P.L.1703, No.217, eff. imd.; June 28, 2018, P.L.361, No.49, eff. 60 days)

2018 Amendment. Act 49 amended subsec. (a).

2004 Amendment. Act 217 added section 6304.1.

§ 6305. Masters.

(a) General rule.—The governing authority may promulgate rules for the selection and appointment of masters on a full-time or part-time basis. A master shall be a member of the bar of this Commonwealth. The number and compensation of masters shall be fixed by the governing authority, and their compensation shall be paid by the county.

(b) Hearings before masters.—The court of common pleas may direct that hearings in any case or class of cases be conducted in the first instance by the master in the manner provided in this chapter. Before commencing the hearing the master shall inform the parties who have appeared that they are entitled to have the matter heard by a judge. If a party objects, the hearing shall be conducted by a judge.

(c) Recommendations of masters.—Upon the conclusion of a hearing before a master, he shall transmit written findings and recommendations for disposition to the judge. Prompt written notice and copies of the findings and recommendations shall be given to the parties to the proceeding.

(d) Rehearing before judge.—A rehearing before the judge may be ordered by the judge at any time upon cause shown. Unless a rehearing is ordered, the findings and recommendations become the findings and order of the court when confirmed in writing by the judge.

§ 6306. Costs and expenses of care of child.

The costs and expenses of the care of the child shall be paid as provided by sections 704.1 and 704.2 of the act of June 13, 1967 (P.L. 31, No. 21), known as the "Public Welfare Code."

§ 6307. Inspection of court files and records.

(a) General rule.—All files and records of the court in a proceeding under this chapter are open to inspection only by:

(1) The judges, officers and professional staff of the court.

(2 The parties to the proceeding and their counsel and representatives, but the persons in this category shall not be permitted to see reports revealing the names of confidential sources of information contained in social reports, except at the discretion of the court.

(3) A public or private agency or institution providing supervision or having custody of the child under order of the court.

(4) A court and its probation and other officials or professional staff and the attorney for the defendant for use in preparing a presentence report in a criminal case in which the defendant is convicted and who prior thereto had been a party to a proceeding under this chapter.

(4.1) A court in determining custody, as provided in 23 Pa.C.S. §§ 5328 (relating to factors to consider when awarding custody) and 5329.1 (relating to consideration of child abuse and involvement with protective services).

(5) A judge or issuing authority for use in determining bail, provided that such inspection is limited to orders of delinquency adjudications and dispositions and petitions relating thereto, orders resulting from disposition review hearings and histories of bench warrants and escapes.

(6) The Administrative Office of Pennsylvania Courts.

(6.1) The judges, officers and professional staff of courts of other jurisdictions when necessary for the discharge of their official duties.

(6.2) Officials of the Department of Corrections or a State Correctional Institution or other penal institution to which an individual who was previously adjudicated delinquent in a proceeding under this chapter has been committed, but the persons in this category shall not be permitted to see reports revealing the names of confidential sources of information contained in social reports, except at the discretion of the court.

(6.3) A parole board, court or county probation official in considering an individual's parole or in exercising supervision over any individual who was previously adjudicated delinquent in a proceeding under this chapter, but the persons in this category shall not be permitted to see reports revealing the names of confidential sources of information contained in social reports, except at the discretion of the court.

(6.4) The board for use in completing assessments.

(6.5) The Department of Public Welfare for use in determining whether an individual named as the perpetrator of an indicated report of child abuse should be expunged from the Statewide database.

(7) With leave of court, any other person or agency or institution having a legitimate interest in the proceedings or in the work of the unified judicial system.

(b) Public availability.—

(1) (Deleted by amendment).

(1.1) The contents of court records and files concerning a child shall not be disclosed to the public unless any of the following apply:

(i) The child has been adjudicated delinquent by a court as a result of an act or acts committed when the child was 14 years of age or older and the conduct would have constituted one or more of the following offenses if committed by an adult:

(A) Murder.

(B) Voluntary manslaughter.

(C) Aggravated assault as defined in 18 Pa.C.S. § 2702(a)(1) or (2) (relating to aggravated assault).

(D) Sexual Assault as defined in 18 Pa.C.S. § 3124.1 (relating to sexual assault).

(E) Aggravated indecent assault as defined in 18 Pa.C.S. § 3125 (relating to aggravated indecent assault).

(F) Arson as defined in 18 Pa.C.S. § 3301(a)(1) (relating to arson and related offenses).

(G) Burglary as a felony in the first degree as defined in 18 Pa.C.S. § 3502(c)(1) (relating to burglary).

(H) Involuntary deviate sexual intercourse.

(I) Kidnapping.

(J) Rape.

(K) Robbery as defined in 18 Pa.C.S. § 3701(a)(1)(i), (ii) or (iii) (relating to robbery).

(L) Robbery of motor vehicle.

(M) Violation of 18 Pa.C.S. Ch. 61 (relating to firearms and other dangerous articles).

(N) Attempt or conspiracy to commit any of the offenses in this subparagraph.

(ii) A petition alleging delinquency has been filed alleging that the child has committed an act or acts subject to a hearing pursuant to section 6336(e) (relating to conduct of hearings) and the child previously has been adjudicated delinquent by a court as a result of an act or acts committed when the child was 14 years of age or older and the conduct would have constituted one or more of the following offenses if committed by an adult:

(A) Murder.

(B) Voluntary manslaughter.

(C) Aggravated assault as defined in 18 Pa.C.S. § 2702(a)(1) or (2).

(D) Sexual Assault as defined in 18 Pa.C.S. § 3124.1.

(E) Aggravated indecent assault as defined in 18 Pa.C.S. § 3125.

(F) Arson as defined in 18 Pa.C.S. § 3301(a)(1).

(G) Burglary as a felony in the first degree as defined in 18 Pa.C.S. § 3502(c)(1).

(H) Involuntary deviate sexual intercourse.

(I) Kidnapping.

(J) Rape.

(K) Robbery as defined in 18 Pa.C.S. § 3701(a)(1)(i), (ii) or (iii).

(L) Robbery of motor vehicle.

(M) Violation of 18 Pa.C.S. Ch. 61.

(N) Attempt or conspiracy to commit any of the offenses in this subparagraph.

(2) If the conduct of the child meets the requirements for disclosure as set forth in paragraph (1.1), then the court shall disclose the name, age and address of the child, the offenses charged and the disposition of the case. The judge who adjudicates a child delinquent shall specify the particular offenses and counts thereof which the child is found to have committed, and such information shall be inserted on any court or law enforcement records or files disclosed to the public as provided for in this section or in section 6308(b)(2) (relating to law enforcement records).

(c) Summary offenses.—The provisions of this section shall apply to proceedings involving a child charged with a summary offense when the proceedings are before a judge of the minor judiciary, the Philadelphia Municipal Court or a court of common pleas.

(Feb. 22, 1995, 1st Sp.Sess., P.L.959, No.1, eff. imd.; Dec. 20, 2000, P.L.946, No.129, eff. 60 days; Dec. 9, 2002, P.L.1705, No.215, eff. 60 days; Aug. 14, 2003, P.L.97, No.21, eff. 180 days; July 7, 2006, P.L.378, No.81, eff. 7 days; Oct. 25, 2012, P.L.1655, No.204, eff. 90 days; Dec. 18, 2013, P.L.1167, No.107, eff. Jan. 1, 2014; Sept. 27, 2014, P.L.2482, No.138, eff. 60 days; June 28, 2018, P.L.402, No.56, eff. 365 days)

2018 Amendment. Act 56 amended subsec. (b). See Act 56 in the appendix to this title for special provisions relating to findings and declarations.

2014 Amendment. Act 138 amended subsec. (c).

2013 Amendment. Act 107 added subsec. (a)(4.1) and (6.5). See section 6 of Act 107 in the appendix to this title for special provisions relating to applicability.

2006 Amendment. Section 5 of Act 81 provided that Act 81 shall apply to all actions instituted on or after the effective date of Act 81.

References in Text. The Department of Public Welfare, referred to in this section, was redesignated as the Department of Human Services by Act 132 of 2014.

Cross References. Section 6307 is referred to in sections 6303, 6336.1 of this title.

§ 6308. Law enforcement records.

(a) **General rule.**—Law enforcement records and files concerning a child shall be kept separate from the records and files of arrests of adults. Unless a charge of delinquency is transferred for criminal prosecution under section 6355 (relating to transfer to criminal proceedings), the interest of national security requires, or the court otherwise orders in the interest of the child, the records and files shall not be open to public inspection or their contents disclosed to the public except as provided in subsection (b); but inspection of the records and files is permitted by:

(1) The court having the child before it in any proceeding.

(2) Counsel for a party to the proceeding.

(3) The officers of institutions or agencies to whom the child is committed.

(4) Law enforcement officers of other jurisdictions when necessary for the discharge of their official duties.

(5) A court in which the child is convicted of a criminal offense for the purpose of a presentence report or other dispositional proceeding, or by officials of penal institutions and other penal facilities to which he is committed, or by a parole board in considering his parole or discharge or in exercising supervision over him.

(6) The Department of Public Welfare for use in determining whether an individual named as the perpetrator of an indicated report of child abuse should be expunged from the Statewide database.

(b) Public availability.—

(1) (Deleted by amendment).

(1.1) The contents of law enforcement records and files concerning a child shall not be disclosed to the public unless any of the following apply:

(i) The child has been adjudicated delinquent by a court as a result of an act or acts committed when the child was 14 years of age or older and the conduct would have constituted one or more of the following offenses if committed by an adult:

(A) Murder.

(B) Voluntary manslaughter.

(C) Aggravated assault as defined in 18 Pa.C.S. § 2702(a)(1) or (2) (relating to aggravated assault).

(D) Sexual Assault as defined in 18 Pa.C.S. § 3124.1 (relating to sexual assault).

(E) Aggravated indecent assault as defined in 18 Pa.C.S. § 3125 (relating to aggravated indecent assault).

(F) Arson as defined in 18 Pa.C.S. § 3301(a)(1) (relating to arson and related offenses).

(G) Burglary as a felony in the first degree as defined in 18 Pa.C.S. § 3502(c)(1) (relating to burglary).

(H) Involuntary deviate sexual intercourse.

(I) Kidnapping.

(J) Rape.

(K) Robbery as defined in 18 Pa.C.S. § 3701(a)(1)(i), (ii) or (iii) (relating to robbery).

(L) Robbery of motor vehicle.

(M) Violation of 18 Pa.C.S. Ch. 61 (relating to firearms and other dangerous articles).

(N) Attempt or conspiracy to commit any of the offenses in this subparagraph.

(ii) A petition alleging delinquency has been filed alleging that the child has committed an act or acts subject to a hearing pursuant to section 6336(e) (relating to conduct of hearings) and the child previously has been adjudicated delinquent by a court as a result of an act or acts committed when the child was 14 years of age or older and the conduct would have constituted one or more of the following offenses if committed by an adult:

(A) Murder.

(B) Voluntary manslaughter.

(C) Aggravated assault as defined in 18 Pa.C.S. § 2702(a)(1) or (2).

(D) Sexual Assault as defined in 18 Pa.C.S. § 3124.1.

(E) Aggravated indecent assault as defined in 18 Pa.C.S. § 3125.

(F) Arson as defined in 18 Pa.C.S. § 3301(a)(1).

(G) Burglary as a felony in the first degree as defined in 18 Pa.C.S. § 3502(c)(1).

(H) Involuntary deviate sexual intercourse.

(I) Kidnapping.

(J) Rape.

(K) Robbery as defined in 18 Pa.C.S. § 3701(a)(1)(i), (ii) or (iii).

(L) Robbery of motor vehicle.

(M) Violation of 18 Pa.C.S. Ch. 61.

(N) Attempt or conspiracy to commit any of the offenses in this subparagraph.

(2) If the conduct of the child meets the requirements for disclosure as set forth in paragraph (1.1), then the law enforcement agency shall disclose the name, age and address of the child, the offenses charged and the disposition of the case.

(c) Fingerprints and photographs.—

(1) Law enforcement officers shall have the authority to take or cause to be taken the fingerprints or photographs, or both, of any child who is alleged to have committed an act designated as a misdemeanor or felony under the laws of this Commonwealth or of another state if the act occurred in that state or under Federal law. If a child is found to be a delinquent child pursuant to section 6341 (relating to adjudication) on the basis of an act designated as a misdemeanor or felony or the child's case is transferred for criminal prosecution pursuant to section 6355, the law enforcement agency that alleged the child to be a delinquent child shall take or cause to be taken the fingerprints and photographs of the child, if not previously taken pursuant to this case, and ensure that these records are forwarded to the central repository pursuant to section 6309(c) (relating to juvenile history record information). If a child was alleged to be delinquent by other than a law enforcement agency, the court shall direct the juvenile probation department to ensure that the delinquent child's fingerprints and photographs are taken by a law enforcement agency.

(2) Fingerprint and photographic records may be disseminated to law enforcement officers of other jurisdictions, the Pennsylvania State Police and the Federal Bureau of Investigation and may be used for investigative purposes.

(3) Fingerprints and photographic records of children shall be kept separately from adults and shall be immediately destroyed upon notice of the court as provided under section 6341(a) (relating to adjudication) by all persons and agencies having these records if the child is not adjudicated delinquent or not found guilty in a criminal proceeding for reason of the alleged acts.

(d) Pennsylvania State Police registry.—

(1) The contents of law enforcement records and files concerning a child shall not be disclosed to the public except if the child is 14 years of age or older at the time of the alleged conduct and if any of the following apply:

(i) The child has been adjudicated delinquent by a court as a result of any offense enumerated in 18 Pa.C.S. § 6105 (relating to persons not to possess, use, manufacture, control, sell or transfer firearms).

(ii) A petition alleging delinquency has been filed by a law enforcement agency alleging that the child has committed any offense enumerated in 18 Pa.C.S. § 6105 and the child previously has been adjudicated delinquent by a court as a result of an act or acts which included the elements of one of such crimes.

(iii) (Deleted by amendment).

(2) (Repealed).

(Apr. 28, 1978, P.L.202, No.53, eff. 60 days; Feb. 29, 1980, P.L.36, No.12, eff. 60 days; June 26, 1981, P.L.123, No.41, eff. 60 days; Dec. 11, 1986, P.L.1521, No.165, eff. 60 days; Dec. 22, 1989, P.L.727, No.99, eff. imd.; Mar. 15, 1995, 1st Sp.Sess., P.L.972, No.6, eff. 60 days; June 13, 1995, 1st Sp.Sess., P.L.1024, No.17, eff. 120 days; Nov. 22, 1995, P.L.621, No.66, eff. imd.; May 22, 1996, P.L.300, No.46, eff. imd.; Jan. 27, 1998, P.L.20, No.3, eff. 60 days; Nov. 29, 2004, P.L.1364, No.176, eff. imd.; July 7, 2006, P.L.378, No.81, eff. 7 days; Dec. 18, 2013, P.L.1167, No.107, eff. Jan. 1, 2014; June 28, 2018, P.L.402, No.56, eff. 365 days)

2018 Amendment. Act 56 amended subsec. (b). See Act 56 in the appendix to this title for special provisions relating to findings and declarations.

2013 Amendment. Act 107 added subsec. (a)(6). See section 6 of Act 107 in the appendix to this title for special provisions relating to applicability.

2006 Amendment. Section 5 of Act 81 provided that Act 81 shall apply to all actions instituted on or after the effective date of Act 81.

1998 Amendment. Act 3 amended subsec. (c)(1).

1996 Amendment. Act 46 deleted subsec. (d)(1)(iii).

1995 Repeal. Act 66 repealed subsec. (d)(1)(i) and (ii) in part and repealed subsec. (d)(2). The repealed provisions have been deleted from the text.

1995 Amendments. Act 6, 1st Sp.Sess., amended the entire section and Act 17, 1st Sp.Sess., added subsec. (d). See the preamble to Act 17 in the appendix to this title for special provisions relating to legislative purpose.

References in Text. The Department of Public Welfare, referred to in this section, was redesignated as the Department of Human Services by Act 132 of 2014.

Cross References. Section 6308 is referred to in sections 6307, 6309 of this title; section 6111.1 of Title 18 (Crimes and Offenses).

§ 6309. Juvenile history record information.

(a) Applicability of Criminal History Record Information Act.—Except for 18 Pa.C.S. §§ 9105 (relating to other criminal justice information), 9112(a) and (b) (relating to mandatory fingerprinting), 9113 (relating to disposition reporting by criminal justice agencies) and 9121(b) (relating to general regulations), the remaining provisions of 18 Pa.C.S. Ch. 91 (relating to criminal history record information) shall apply to all alleged delinquents and adjudicated delinquents whose fingerprints and photographs are taken pursuant to section 6308(c) (relating to law enforcement records) and to any juvenile justice agency which collects, maintains, disseminates or receives juvenile history record information. The disclosure to the public of the contents of law enforcement records and files concerning a child shall be governed by section 6308(b).

(b) Central repository.—The Pennsylvania State Police shall establish a Statewide central repository of fingerprints, photographs and juvenile history record information of alleged delinquents and adjudicated delinquents whose fingerprints and photographs are taken pursuant to section 6308(c).

(c) Fingerprints and photographs.—The arresting authority shall ensure that the fingerprints and photographs of alleged and adjudicated delinquents whose fingerprints and photographs have been taken by the arresting authority pursuant to section 6308(c) are forwarded to the central repository as required by the Pennsylvania State Police.

(d) Disposition reporting.—The division or judge of the court assigned to conduct juvenile hearings shall, within seven days after disposition of a case where the child has been alleged to be delinquent, notify the arresting authority of the disposition of the case. The disposition of cases where a child has been alleged to be delinquent, including the disposition of cases resulting in an adjudication of delinquency, shall be provided to the Pennsylvania State Police for inclusion in the central repository as determined by the Administrative Office of Pennsylvania Courts in consultation with the Juvenile Court Judges' Commission. In addition, the Juvenile Court Judges' Commission shall be provided with information pertaining to the cases of children who have been alleged to be delinquent as the commission determines necessary to fulfill its responsibilities under section 6373 (relating to powers and duties).

(e) **Definitions.**—As used in this section, the following words and phrases shall have the meanings given to them in this subsection:

"Criminal history record information." In addition to the meaning in 18 Pa.C.S. § 9102 (relating to definitions), the term includes the meaning of juvenile history record information as defined in this subsection.

"Juvenile history record information." Information collected pursuant to this section concerning alleged delinquents and adjudicated delinquents whose fingerprints and photographs are taken pursuant to section 6308(c) and arising from an allegation of delinquency, consisting of identifiable descriptions, dates and notations of arrests or other delinquency charges and any adjudication of delinquency or preadjudication disposition other than dismissal arising therefrom. This information shall also include the last known location and the juvenile court jurisdiction status of each adjudicated delinquent. Juvenile history record information shall not include intelligence information, investigative information, treatment information, including medical and psychiatric information, caution indicator information, modus operandi information, wanted persons information, stolen property information, missing persons information, employment history information, personal history information or presentence investigation information.

(Dec. 11, 1986, P.L.1521, No.165, eff. 60 days; Mar. 15, 1995, 1st Sp.Sess., P.L.972, No.6, eff. 60 days; Nov. 17, 1995, 1st Sp.Sess., P.L.1115, No.30, eff. 60 days; May 22, 1996, P.L.300, No.46, eff. imd.; Dec. 20, 2000, P.L.946, No.129, eff. 60 days; Sept. 27, 2014, P.L.2482, No.138, eff. 60 days)

2014 Amendment. Act 138 amended subsecs. (d) and (e).

Cross References. Section 6309 is referred to in section 6308 of this title.

§ 6310. Parental participation.

(a) **General rule.**—In any proceeding under this chapter, a court may order a parent, guardian or custodian to participate in the treatment, supervision or rehabilitation of a child, including, but not limited to, community service, restitution, counseling, treatment and education programs.

(b) **Presence at proceedings.**—The court may, when the court determines that it is in the best interests of the child, order a parent, guardian or custodian of a child to be present at and to bring the child to any proceeding under this chapter.

(c) **Contempt.**—A person who, without good cause, fails to comply with an order issued under this section may be found in contempt of court. The court may issue a bench warrant for any parent, guardian or custodian who, without good cause, fails to appear at any proceeding.

(d) **Intent.**—The General Assembly hereby declares that every parent, guardian or custodian of a child who is the subject of a proceeding under this chapter and a court-ordered program under this chapter should attend the proceeding and participate fully in the program.

(e) **Limitation.**—Nothing in this section shall be construed to create a right of a child to have his parent, guardian or custodian present at a proceeding under this chapter or participate in a court-ordered program.

§ 6311. Guardian ad litem for child in court proceedings.

(a) **Appointment.**—When a proceeding, including a master's hearing, has been initiated alleging that the child is a dependent child under paragraph (1), (2), (3), (4) or (10) of the definition of "dependent child" in section 6302 (relating to definitions), the court shall appoint a guardian ad litem to represent the legal interests and the best interests of the child. The guardian ad litem must be an attorney at law.

(b) Powers and duties.—The guardian ad litem shall be charged with representation of the legal interests and the best interests of the child at every stage of the proceedings and shall do all of the following:

(1) Meet with the child as soon as possible following appointment pursuant to section 6337 (relating to right to counsel) and on a regular basis thereafter in a manner appropriate to the child's age and maturity.

(2) On a timely basis, be given access to relevant court and county agency records, reports of examination of the parents or other custodian of the child pursuant to this chapter and medical, psychological and school records.

(3) Participate in all proceedings, including hearings before masters, and administrative hearings and reviews to the degree necessary to adequately represent the child.

(4) Conduct such further investigation necessary to ascertain the facts.

(5) Interview potential witnesses, including the child's parents, caretakers and foster parents, examine and cross-examine witnesses, and present witnesses and evidence necessary to protect the best interests of the child.

(6) At the earliest possible date, be advised by the county agency having legal custody of the child of:

(i) any plan to relocate the child or modify custody or visitation arrangements, including the reasons therefor, prior to the relocation or change in custody or visitation; and

(ii) any proceeding, investigation or hearing under 23 Pa.C.S. Ch. 63 (relating to child protective services) or this chapter directly affecting the child.

(7) Make specific recommendations to the court relating to the appropriateness and safety of the child's placement and services necessary to address the child's needs and safety.

(8) Explain the proceedings to the child to the extent appropriate given the child's age mental condition and emotional condition.

(9) Advise the court of the child's wishes to the extent that they can be ascertained and present to the court whatever evidence exists to support the child's wishes. When appropriate because of the age or mental and emotional condition of the child, determine to the fullest extent possible the wishes of the child and communicate this information to the court. A difference between the child's wishes under this paragraph and the recommendations under paragraph (7) shall not be considered a conflict of interest for the guardian ad litem.

SUBCHAPTER B
JURISDICTION AND CUSTODY

Sec.
6321. Commencement of proceedings.
6322. Transfer from criminal proceedings.
6323. Informal adjustment.
6324. Taking into custody.
6325. Detention of child.
6326. Release or delivery to court.
6327. Place of detention.

§ 6321. Commencement of proceedings.

(a) **General rule.**—A proceeding under this chapter may be commenced:

(1) By transfer of a case as provided in section 6322 (relating to transfer from criminal proceedings).

(2) By the court accepting jurisdiction as provided in section 6362 (relating to disposition of resident child received from another state) or accepting supervision of a child as provided in section 6364 (relating to supervision under foreign order).

(2.1) By taking a child into custody in accordance with the provisions of section 6324 (relating to taking into custody).

(3) The other cases by the filing of a petition as provided in this chapter. The petition and all other documents in the proceeding shall be entitled "In the interest of ...., a minor," and shall be captioned and docketed as provided by general rule.

(b) **Venue.**—A proceeding under this chapter may be commenced:

(1) In the county in which the child resides.

(2) If delinquency is alleged, in the county in which the acts constituting the alleged delinquency occurred.

(3) If dependency is alleged, in the county in which the child is present when it is commenced.

(c) **Transfer to another court within this Commonwealth.**—

(1) If the child resides in a county of this Commonwealth and the proceeding is commenced in a court of another county, the court, on motion of a party or on its own motion made after the adjudicatory hearing or at any time prior to final disposition, may transfer the proceeding to the county of the residence of the child for further action. Like transfers may be made if the residence of the child changes during the proceeding. The proceeding may be transferred if the child has been adjudicated delinquent and other proceedings involving the child are pending in the court of the county of his residence.

(2) Certified copies of all legal and social documents and records pertaining to the case on file with the court shall accompany the transfer.

§ 6322. Transfer from criminal proceedings.

(a) **General rule.**—Except as provided in 75 Pa.C.S. § 6303 (relating to rights and liabilities of minors) or in the event the child is charged with murder or any of the offenses excluded by paragraph (2)(ii) or (iii) of the definition of "delinquent act" in section 6302 (relating to definitions) or has been found guilty in a criminal proceeding, if it appears to the court in a criminal proceeding that the defendant is a child, this chapter shall immediately become applicable, and the court shall forthwith halt further criminal proceedings, and, where appropriate, transfer the case to the division or a judge of the court assigned to conduct juvenile hearings, together with a copy of the accusatory pleading and other papers, documents, and transcripts of testimony relating to the case. If it appears to the court in a criminal proceeding charging murder or any of the offenses excluded by paragraph (2)(ii) or (iii) of the definition of "delinquent act" in section 6302, that the defendant is a child, the case may similarly be transferred and the provisions of this chapter applied. In determining whether to transfer a case charging murder or any of the offenses excluded from the definition of "delinquent act" in section 6302, the child shall be required to establish by a preponderance of the evidence that the transfer will serve the public interest. In determining whether the child has so established that the transfer will serve the public interest, the court shall consider the factors contained in section 6355(a)(4)(iii) (relating to transfer to criminal proceedings).

(b) Order.—If the court finds that the child has met the burden under subsection (a), the court shall make findings of fact, including specific references to the evidence, and conclusions of law in support of the transfer order. If the court does not make its finding within 20 days of the hearing on the petition to transfer the case, the defendant's petition to transfer the case shall be denied by operation of law.

(c) Expedited review of transfer orders.—The transfer order shall be subject to the same expedited review applicable to orders granting or denying release or modifying the conditions of release prior to sentence, as provided in Rule 1762 of the Pennsylvania Rules of Appellate Procedure.

(d) Effect of transfer order.—Where review of the transfer order is not sought or where the transfer order is upheld the defendant shall be taken forthwith to the probation officer or to a place of detention designated by the court or released to the custody of his parent, guardian, custodian, or other person legally responsible for him, to be brought before the court at a time to be designated. The accusatory pleading may serve in lieu of a petition otherwise required by this chapter, unless the court directs the filing of a petition.

(e) Transfer of convicted criminal cases.—If in a criminal proceeding, the child is found guilty of a crime classified as a misdemeanor, and the child and the attorney for the Commonwealth agree to the transfer, the case may be transferred for disposition to the division or a judge of the court assigned to conduct juvenile hearings.

§ 6323. Informal adjustment.

(a) General rule.—

(1) Before a petition is filed, the probation officer or other officer of the court designated by it, subject to its direction, shall, in the case of a dependent child where the jurisdiction of the court is premised upon the provisions of paragraph (1), (2), (3), (4), (5) or (7) of the definition of "dependent child" in section 6302 (relating to definitions) and if otherwise appropriate, refer the child and his parents to any public or private social agency available for assisting in the matter. Upon referral, the agency shall indicate its willingness to accept the child and shall report back to the referring officer within three months concerning the status of the referral.

(2) Similarly, the probation officer may in the case of a delinquent child, or a dependent child where the jurisdiction of the court is permitted under paragraph (6) of the definition of "dependent child" in section 6302, refer the child and his parents to an agency for assisting in the matter.

(3) The agency may return the referral to the probation officer or other officer for further informal adjustment if it is in the best interests of the child.

(b) Counsel and advice.—Such social agencies and the probation officer or other officer of the court may give counsel and advice to the parties with a view to an informal adjustment if it appears:

(1) counsel and advice without an adjudication would be in the best interest of the public and the child;

(2) the child and his parents, guardian, or other custodian consent thereto with knowledge that consent is not obligatory; and

(3) in the case of the probation officer or other officer of the court, the admitted facts bring the case within the jurisdiction of the court.

(c) Limitation on duration of counsel and advice.—The giving of counsel and advice by the probation or other officer of the court shall not extend beyond six months from the day commenced unless extended by an order of court for an additional period not to exceed three months.

(d) **No detention authorized.**—Nothing contained in this section shall authorize the detention of the child.

(e) **Privileged statements.**—An incriminating statement made by a participant to the person giving counsel or advice and in the discussions or conferences incident thereto shall not be used against the declarant over objection in any criminal proceeding or hearing under this chapter.

(f) **Terms and conditions.**—The terms and conditions of an informal adjustment may include payment by the child of reasonable amounts of money as costs, fees or restitution, including a supervision fee and contribution to a restitution fund established by the president judge of the court of common pleas pursuant to section 6352(a)(5) (relating to disposition of delinquent child).

2004 Amendment. Act 217 added subsec (f).

§ 6324. Taking into custody.

A child may be taken into custody:

(1) Pursuant to an order of the court under this chapter. Prior to entering a protective custody order removing a child from the home of the parent, guardian or custodian, the court must determine that to allow the child to remain in the home is contrary to the welfare of the child.

(2) Pursuant to the laws of arrest.

(3) By a law enforcement officer or duly authorized officer of the court if there are reasonable grounds to believe that the child is suffering from illness or injury or is in imminent danger from his surroundings, and that his removal is necessary.

(4) By a law enforcement officer or duly authorized officer of the court if there are reasonable grounds to believe that the child has run away from his parents, guardian, or other custodian.

(5) By a law enforcement officer or duly authorized officer of the court if there are reasonable grounds to believe that the child has violated conditions of his probation.

§ 6325. Detention of child.

A child taken into custody shall not be detained or placed in shelter care prior to the hearing on the petition unless his detention or care is required to protect the person or property of others or of the child or because the child may abscond or be removed from the jurisdiction of the court or because he has no parent, guardian, or custodian or other person able to provide supervision and care for him and return him to the court when required, or an order for his detention or shelter care has been made by the court pursuant to this chapter.

§ 6326. Release or delivery to court.

(a) **General rule.**—A person taking a child into custody, with all reasonable speed and without first taking the child elsewhere, shall:

(1) notify the parent, guardian or other custodian of the apprehension of the child and his whereabouts;

(2) release the child to his parents, guardian, or other custodian upon their promise to bring the child before the court when requested by the court, unless his detention or shelter care is warranted or required under section 6325 (relating to detention of child); or

(3) bring the child before the court or deliver him to a detention or shelter care facility designated by the court or to a medical facility if the child is believed to suffer from a serious physical condition or illness which requires prompt treat-

ment. He shall promptly give written notice, together with a statement of the reason for taking the child into custody, to a parent, guardian, or other custodian and to the court.

Any temporary detention or questioning of the child necessary to comply with this subsection shall conform to the procedures and conditions prescribed by this chapter and other provisions of law.

(b) Detention in police lockup generally prohibited.—Unless a child taken into custody is alleged to have committed a crime or summary offense or to be in violation of conditions of probation or other supervision following an adjudication of delinquency, the child may not be detained in a municipal police lockup or cell or otherwise held securely within a law enforcement facility or structure which houses an adult lockup. A child shall be deemed to be held securely only when physically detained or confined in a locked room or cell or when secured to a cuffing rail or other stationary object within the facility.

(c) Detention in police lockup under certain circumstances.—A child alleged to have committed a crime or summary offense or to be in violation of conditions of probation or other supervision following an adjudication of delinquency may be held securely in a municipal police lockup or other facility which houses an adult lockup only under the following conditions:

(1) the secure holding shall only be for the purpose of identification, investigation, processing, releasing or transferring the child to a parent, guardian, other custodian, or juvenile court or county children and youth official, or to a shelter care or juvenile detention center;

(2) the secure holding shall be limited to the minimum time necessary to complete the procedures listed in paragraph (1), but in no case may such holding exceed six hours; and

(3) if so held, a child must be separated by sight and sound from incarcerated adult offenders and must be under the continuous visual supervision of law enforcement officials or facility staff.

(d) Conditions of detention.—Notwithstanding other provisions of law, a child held in nonsecure custody in a building or facility which houses an adult lockup may be so held only under the following conditions:

(1) the area where the child is held is an unlocked multipurpose area which is not designated or used as a secure detention area or is not part of a secure detention area; or, if the area is a secure booking or similar area, it is used only for processing purposes;

(2) the child is not physically secured to a cuffing rail or other stationary object during the period of custody in the facility;

(3) the area is limited to providing nonsecure custody only long enough for the purposes of identification, investigation, processing or release to parents or for arranging transfer to another agency or appropriate facility; and

(4) the child must be under continuous visual supervision by a law enforcement officer or other facility staff during the period of nonsecure custody.

(e) Reports regarding children held in custody.—Law enforcement agencies shall provide information and reports regarding children held in secure and nonsecure custody under subsections (c) and (d) as requested by the Pennsylvania Commission on Crime and Delinquency.

(f) Enforcement of undertaking to produce child.—If a parent, guardian, or other custodian, when requested, fails to bring the child before the court as provided in subsection (a), the court may issue its warrant directing that the child be taken into custody and brought before the court.

§ 6327. Place of detention.

(a) **General rule.**—A child alleged to be delinquent may be detained only in:

(1) A licensed foster home or a home approved by the court.

(2) A facility operated by a licensed child welfare agency or one approved by the court.

(3) A detention home, camp, center or other facility for delinquent children which is under the direction or supervision of the court or other public authority or private agency, and is approved by the Department of Public Welfare.

(4) Any other suitable place or facility, designated or operated by the court and approved by the Department of Public Welfare.

Under no circumstances shall a child be detained in any facility with adults, or where the child is apt to be abused by other children.

(b) **Report by correctional officer of receipt of child.**—The official in charge of a jail or other facility for the detention of adult offenders or persons charged with crime shall inform the court immediately if a person who is or appears to be under the age of 18 years is received at the facility and shall bring him before the court upon request or deliver him to a detention or shelter care facility designated by the court.

(c) **Detention in jail prohibited.**—It is unlawful for any person in charge of or employed by a jail knowingly to receive for detention or to detain in the jail any person whom he has or should have reason to believe is a child unless, in a criminal proceeding, the child has been charged with or has been found guilty of an act set forth in paragraph (2)(i), (ii), (iii) or (v) of the definition of "delinquent act" in section 6302 (relating to definitions).

(c.1) **Detention of child.**—

(1) A child who is subject to criminal proceedings having been charged with an act set forth under paragraph (2)(i), (ii) or (iii) of the definition of "delinquent act" in section 6302, who has not been released on bail and who may seek or is seeking transfer to juvenile proceedings under section 6322 (relating to transfer from criminal proceedings) may be detained in a secure detention facility approved by the Department of Public Welfare for the detention of alleged and adjudicated delinquent children if the attorney for the Commonwealth has consented to and the court has ordered the detention.

(2) Secure detention ordered under this subsection shall not affect a child's eligibility for or ability to post bail.

(3) For a child held in secure detention under this subsection, the court shall order the immediate transfer of the child to the county jail if any of the following apply:

(i) The court determines that the child is no longer seeking transfer under section 6322.

(ii) The court denies the motion filed under section 6322.

(iii) The child attains 18 years of age. This subparagraph does not apply if:

(A) the court has granted the motion filed under section 6322; or

(B) the child is otherwise under order of commitment to the secure detention facility pursuant to the jurisdiction of the court in a delinquency matter.

(d) **Transfer of child subject to criminal proceedings.**—If a case is transferred for criminal prosecution the child may be transferred to the appropriate officer or detention facility in accordance with the law governing the detention of persons charged with crime. The court in making the transfer may order continued detention as a juvenile pending trial if the child is unable to provide bail.

(e) **Detention of dependent child.**—A child alleged to be dependent may be detained or placed only in a Department of Public Welfare approved shelter care facility as stated in subsection (a)(1), (2) and (4), and shall not be detained in a jail or other facility intended or used for the detention of adults charged with criminal offenses, but may be detained in the same shelter care facilities with alleged or adjudicated delinquent children.

(f) **Development of approved shelter care programs.**—The Department of Public Welfare shall develop or assist in the development in each county of this Commonwealth approved programs for the provision of shelter care for children needing these services who have been taken into custody under section 6324 (relating to taking into custody) and for children referred to or under the jurisdiction of the court.

(Apr. 28, 1978, P.L.202, No.53, eff. 60 days; June 14, 1991, P.L.68, No.9, eff. 60 days; Mar. 29, 1996, P.L.51, No.17, eff. imd.; Dec. 20, 2000, P.L.946, No.129, eff. 60 days; Oct. 27, 2010, P.L.949, No.96, eff. imd.)

2010 Amendment. Act 96 added subsec. (c.1). Section 4(2) of Act 96 provided that subsec. (c.1) shall apply to a criminal proceeding commenced on or after the effective date of section 4(2).

2000 Amendment. Act 129 amended subsec. (e).

1996 Amendment. Act 17 amended subsec. (c).

1991 Amendment. Act 9 amended subsec. (f).

1978 Amendment. Act 53 amended subsec. (a), relettered subsec. (c) to (d), amended and relettered subsec. (d) to (e) and added subsecs. (c) and (f).

See sections 23, 25, 27 and 28 of Act 53 of 1978 in the appendix to this title for special provisions relating to confinement of children with adults, confinement of children in jails, required county detention services and regional detention facilities.

SUBCHAPTER C
PROCEDURES AND SAFEGUARDS

Sec.
6331. Release from detention or commencement of proceedings.
6332. Informal hearing.
6333. Subpoena.
6334. Petition.
6335. Release or holding of hearings.
6336. Conduct of hearings.
6336.1. Notice and hearing.
6336.2. Use of restraints on children during court proceedings.
6337. Right to counsel.
6337.1. Rights to counsel for children in dependency and delinquency proceedings.
6338. Other basic rights.
6339. Investigation and report.
6340. Consent decree.
6341. Adjudication.
6342. Court-appointed special advocates.

§ 6331. Release from detention or commencement of proceedings.

If a child is brought before the court or delivered to a detention or shelter care facility designated by the court, the intake or other authorized officer of the court shall immediately make an investigation and release the child unless it appears that his detention or shelter care is warranted or required under section 6325 (relating to detention of child). The release of the child shall not prevent the subsequent filing of a petition as provided in this chapter. If he is not so released, a petition shall be promptly made and presented to the court within 24 hours or the next court business day of the admission of the child to detention or shelter care.

§ 6332. Informal hearing.

(a) **General rule.**—An informal hearing shall be held promptly by the court or master and not later than 72 hours after the child is placed in detention or shelter care to determine whether his detention or shelter care is required under section 6325 (relating to detention of child), whether to allow the child to remain in the home would be contrary to the welfare of the child and, if the child is alleged to be delinquent, whether probable cause exists that the child has committed a delinquent act. Reasonable notice thereof, either oral or written, stating the time, place, and purpose of the hearing shall be given to the child and if they can be found, to his parents, guardian, or other custodian. Prior to the commencement of the hearing the court or master shall inform the parties of their right to counsel and to appointed counsel if they are needy persons, and of the right of the child to remain silent with respect to any allegations of delinquency. If the child is alleged to be a dependent child, the court or master shall also determine whether reasonable efforts were made to prevent such placement or, in the case of an emergency placement where services were not offered and could not have prevented the necessity of placement, whether this level of effort was reasonable due to the emergency nature of the situation, safety considerations and circumstances of the family.

(b) **Rehearing.**—If the child is not so released and a parent, guardian or other custodian has not been notified of the hearing, did not appear or waive appearance at the hearing, and files his affidavit showing these facts, the court or master shall rehear the matter without unnecessary delay and order release of the child, unless it appears from the hearing that his detention or shelter care is required under section 6325.

§ 6333. Subpoena.

(a) **General rule.**—Upon application of a child, parent, guardian, custodian, probation officer, district attorney, or other party to the proceedings, the court, master, or the clerk of the court shall issue, or the court or master may on its own motion issue, subpoenas requiring attendance and testimony of witnesses and production of papers at any hearing under this chapter.

(b) **Copy to parents, guardians and custodians.—**

(1) A copy of the subpoena requiring attendance and testimony of a witness who is under 18 years of age shall be issued to the parent, guardian or other custodian of the witness in addition to the issuance of the subpoena for the witness.

(2) The court may waive issuance of the copy under paragraph (1) for cause shown in a specific case.

(Oct. 9, 2008, P.L.1352, No.98, eff. 60 days)

§ 6334. Petition.

(a) **Contents of petition.**—A petition, which shall be verified and may be on information and belief, may be brought by any person including a law enforcement officer. It shall set forth plainly:

(1) The facts which bring the child within the jurisdiction of the court and this chapter, with a statement that it is in the best interest of the child and the public that the proceeding be brought and, if delinquency is alleged, that the child is in need of treatment, supervision or rehabilitation.

(2) The name, age, and residence address, if any, of the child on whose behalf the petition is brought.

(3) The names and residence addresses, if known to the petitioner, of the parents, guardian, or custodian of the child and of the spouse, if any, of the child. If none of his parents, guardian, or custodian resides or can be found within this Commonwealth, or if their respective places of residence address are unknown, the name of any known adult relative residing within the county, or if there be none, the known adult relative residing nearest to the location of the court.

(4) If the child is in custody and, if so, the place of his detention and the time he was taken into custody.

(b) Aggravated circumstances.—

(1) An allegation that aggravated circumstances exist may be brought:

(i) in a petition for dependency with regard to a child who is alleged to be a dependent child; or

(ii) in a petition for a permanency hearing with regard to a child who has been determined to be a dependent child.

(2) The existence of aggravated circumstances may be alleged by the county agency or the child's attorney. If the county agency reasonably believes that aggravated circumstances exist, it shall file the appropriate petition as soon as possible but no later than 21 days from the determination by the county agency that aggravated circumstances exist.

(3) A petition for dependency or a permanency hearing that alleges aggravated circumstances shall include a statement of the facts the county agency or the child's attorney intends to prove to support the allegation. A criminal conviction shall not be required to allege the existence of aggravated physical neglect or physical abuse resulting in serious bodily injury or sexual violence committed by the parent.

§ 6335. Release or holding of hearing.

(a) General rule.—After the petition has been filed alleging the child to be dependent or delinquent, the court shall fix a time for hearing thereon, which, if the child is in detention or shelter care shall not be later than ten days after the filing of the petition. Except as provided in subsection (f), if the hearing is not held within such time, the child shall be immediately released from detention or shelter care. A child may be detained or kept in shelter care for an additional single period not to exceed ten days where:

(1) the court determines at a hearing that:

(i) evidence material to the case is unavailable;

(ii) due diligence to obtain such evidence has been exercised; and

(iii) there are reasonable grounds to believe that such evidence will be available at a later date; and

(2) the court finds by clear and convincing evidence that:

(i) the life of the child would be in danger;

(ii) the community would be exposed to a specific danger; or

(iii) the child will abscond or be removed from the jurisdiction of the court.

The court shall direct the issuance of a summons to the parents, guardian, or other custodian, a guardian ad litem, and any other persons as appear to the court to be proper or necessary parties to the proceeding, requiring them to appear before the court at the time fixed to answer the allegations of the petition. The summons shall also be directed to the child if he is 14 or more years of age or is alleged to be a delinquent. A copy of the petition shall accompany the summons.

(b) Personal appearance.—The court may endorse upon the summons an order:

(1) Directing the parents, guardian, or other custodian of the child to appear personally at the hearing.

(2) Directing the person having the physical custody or control of the child to bring the child to the hearing.

(c) **Warrant of arrest.**—If it appears from affidavit filed or from sworn testimony before the court that the conduct, condition, or surroundings of the child are endangering his health or welfare or those of others, or that he may abscond or be removed from the jurisdiction of the court or will not be brought before the court notwithstanding the service of the summons, the court may issue a warrant of arrest.

(d) **From.**—A summons and warrant of arrest shall be in such form and shall be served as prescribed by general rules.

(e) **Waiver of service.**—A party, other than the child, may waive service of summons by written stipulation or by voluntary appearance at the hearing. If the child is present at the hearing, his counsel, with the consent of the parent, guardian, or other custodian, or guardian ad litem, may waive service of summons in his behalf.

(f) **Limitations on release.**—The child shall not be released from detention or shelter care under authority of subsection (a) if the failure to hold a hearing within ten days after the filing of the petition is the result of delay caused by the child. Delay caused by the child shall include, but not be limited to:

(1) Delay caused by the unavailability of the child or his attorney.

(2) Delay caused by any continuance granted at the request of the child or his attorney.

(3) Delay caused by the unavailability of a witness resulting from conduct by or on behalf of the child.

At the conclusion of any court proceeding in which the scheduled hearing is not held, the court shall state on the record whether the failure to hold the hearing resulted from delay caused by the child. Where the court determines that failure to hold a hearing is the result of delay caused by the child, the child may continue to be held in detention or shelter care. However, the additional period of detention shall not exceed ten days, provided that such detention may be continued by the court for successive ten-day intervals.

§ 6336. Conduct of hearings.

(a) **General rule.**—Hearings under this chapter shall be conducted by the court without a jury, in an informal but orderly manner, and separate from other proceedings not included in section 6303 (relating to scope of chapter).

(b) **Functions of district attorney.**—The district attorney, upon request of the court, shall present the evidence in support of the petition and otherwise conduct the proceedings on behalf of the Commonwealth.

(c) **Record.**—If requested by the party or ordered by the court the proceedings shall be recorded by appropriate means. If not so recorded, full minutes of the proceedings shall be kept by the court.

(d) **Proceeding in camera.**—Except in hearings to declare a person in contempt of court and in hearings as specified in subsection (e), the general public shall be excluded from hearings under this chapter. Only the parties, their counsel, witnesses, the victim and counsel for the victim, other persons accompanying a party or a victim for his or her assistance, and any other person as the court finds have a proper interest in the proceeding or in the work of the court shall be admitted by the court. The court may temporarily exclude the child from the hearing except while allegations of his delinquency are being heard.

(e) **Open proceedings.**—The general public shall not be excluded from any hearings under this chapter:

(1) Pursuant to a petition alleging delinquency where the child was 14 years of age or older at the time of the alleged conduct and the alleged conduct would be considered a felony if committed by an adult.

(2) Pursuant to a petition alleging delinquency where the child was 12 years of age or older at the time of the alleged conduct and where the alleged conduct would have constituted one or more of the following offenses if committed by an adult:

(i) Murder.

(ii) Voluntary manslaughter.

(iii) Aggravated assault as defined in 18 Pa.C.S. § 2702(a)(1) or (2) (relating to aggravated assault).

(iv) Arson as defined in 18 Pa.C.S. § 3301(a)(1) (relating to arson and related offenses).

(v) Involuntary deviate sexual intercourse.

(vi) Kidnapping.

(vii) Rape.

(viii) Robbery as defined in 18 Pa.C.S. § 3701(a)(1)(i), (ii) or (iii) (relating to robbery).

(ix) Robbery of motor vehicle.

(x) Attempt or conspiracy to commit any of the offenses in this paragraph.

Notwithstanding anything in this subsection, the proceedings shall be closed upon and to the extent of any agreement between the child and the attorney for the Commonwealth.

(f) Discretion of court.—The court at any disposition proceeding under subsection (e) shall have discretion to maintain the confidentiality of mental health, medical or juvenile institutional documents or juvenile probation reports.

(g) Summary offenses.—The provisions of subsection (d), insofar as subsection (d) relates to the exclusion of the general public from the proceedings, shall apply to proceedings involving a child charged with a summary offense when the proceedings are before a judge of the minor judiciary, the Philadelphia Municipal Court or a court of common pleas.

(h) Adjudication alternative.—The magisterial district judge may refer a child charged with a summary offense to an adjudication alternative program under section 1520 (relating to adjudication alternative program) and the Pennsylvania Rules of Criminal Procedure.

(Dec. 11, 1986, P.L.1521, No.165, eff. 60 days; Apr. 6, 1995, 1st Sp.Sess., P.L.997, No.11, eff. 60 days; Oct. 25, 2012, P.L.1655, No.204, eff. 90 days; Sept. 27, 2014, P.L.2482, No.138, eff. 60 days)

2014 Amendment. Act 138 amended subsec. (g).

2012 Amendment. Act 204 added subsecs. (g) and (h).

Suspension by Court Rule. Subsection (c) was suspended by Pennsylvania Rule of Juvenile Court Procedure No. 800(3), amended December 30, 2005, insofar as it is inconsistent with Rule 127(A) relating to recording and transcribing juvenile court proceedings.

Subsection (c) was suspended by Pennsylvania Rule of Juvenile Court Procedure No. 1800(2), adopted August 21, 2006, insofar as it is inconsistent with Rules 1127(A) and 1242(B)(2) relating to recording and transcribing juvenile court proceedings and general conduct of shelter care hearing.

Cross References. Section 6336 is referred to in sections 6303, 6307, 6308 of this title.

§ 6336.1. Notice and hearing.

(a) General rule.—The court shall direct the county agency or juvenile probation department to provide the child's foster parent, preadoptive parent or relative providing care for the child with timely notice of the hearing. The court shall provide the child's foster parent, preadoptive parent or relative providing care for the child the right to be heard at any hearing under this chapter. Unless a foster parent, preadoptive parent or relative providing care for a child has been awarded legal custody pursuant to section 6357 (relating to rights and duties of legal custodian), nothing in this section shall give the foster parent, preadoptive parent or relative providing care for the child legal standing in the matter being heard by the court.

(b) Permanency hearings.—

(1) Prior to a permanency hearing under section 6351(e) (relating to disposition of dependent child), a child's foster parent or parents, preadoptive parent or relative providing care for the child may submit to the court a report in regard to the child's adjustment, progress and condition.

(2) The county agency shall notify the foster parent or parents, preadoptive parent or relative providing care for the child of the right to submit a report under this subsection to the court on a form under paragraph (3). The county agency shall provide the foster parent or parents, preadoptive parent or relative providing care for the child with information identifying the name of the judge or officer of the court, along with mailing address, to whom the report is to be submitted.

(3) The Department of Public Welfare shall develop a form for use by a foster parent or parents, preadoptive parent or relative providing care for the child, including, but not limited to, the following information:

(i) Date of completion.

(ii) Name and address of child.

(iii) Name and address of foster parent or parents, preadoptive parent or relative providing care for the child. The information under this subparagraph shall be considered confidential except at the discretion of the court.

(iv) Name of primary caseworker and agency.

(v) Description of child's adjustment in the home.

(vi) Description of child's interaction with foster parent or parents, preadoptive parent or relative providing care and with family members of individuals referred to in this subparagraph.

(vii) Description of child's interaction with others.

(viii) Evaluation of child's respect for property.

(ix) Description of physical and emotional condition of child.

(x) Description of child's interaction with the primary caseworker.

(xi) Description of caseworker's interaction with the child and foster parent or parents, preadoptive parent or relative providing care for the child and with family members of individuals referred to in this paragraph.

(xii) Description of educational status, grades, attendance and behavior of child in school or child's experience in a child day-care setting or early childhood development program.

(xiii) Description of child's experience involving visitation with birth parents, specifying if visitation is supervised or unsupervised and any significant events which occurred.

(xiv) Opinion on overall adjustment, progress and condition of the child.

(xv) Other concerns, comments or recommendations.

(4) The report shall be reviewed by the court and is subject to review by other persons and agencies under sections 6307 (relating to inspection of court files and records) and 6342(d)(1) (relating to court-appointed special advocates).

(5) A county agency or a private agency as defined under 23 Pa.C.S. § 6303 (relating to definitions) shall not take any retaliatory action against a foster parent, preadoptive parent or relative for any information, comments or concerns provided in good faith in a report under this subsection. This paragraph shall not be construed to prevent any agency from taking any action if the report contains information that

the foster parent, preadoptive parent or relative has engaged in any conduct that is contrary to any regulation or law or is not in the child's best interest.

2008 Amendment. Act 109 amended subsec. (a) and added subsec. (b).

2007 Amendment. Act 76 amended this sec.

§ 6336.2. Use of restraints on children during court proceedings.

(a) Use of restraints.—Except as provided for in subsection (b), restraints such as handcuffs, chains, shackles, irons or straitjackets shall be removed prior to the commencement of a court proceeding.

(b) Exception.—Restraints may be used during a court proceeding if the court determines on the record, after providing the child with an opportunity to be heard, that they are necessary:

(1) to prevent physical harm to the child or another person;

(2) to prevent disruptive courtroom behavior, evidenced by a history of behavior that created potentially harmful situations or presented substantial risk of physical harm; or

(3) to prevent the child, evidenced by an escape history or other relevant factors, from fleeing the courtroom.

(May 29, 2012, P.L.570, No.56, eff. 60 days)

2012 Amendment. Act 56 added section 6336.2.

§ 6337. Right to counsel.

Except as provided under this section and in section 6311 (relating to guardian ad litem for child in court proceedings), a party is entitled to representation by legal counsel at all stages of any proceedings under this chapter and if he is without financial resources or otherwise unable to employ counsel, to have the court provide counsel for him. If a party other than a child appears at a hearing without counsel the court shall ascertain whether he knows of his right thereto and to be provided with counsel by the court if applicable. The court may continue the proceeding to enable a party to obtain counsel. Except as provided under section 6337.1 (relating to right to counsel for children in dependency and delinquency proceedings), counsel must be provided for a child. If the interests of two or more parties may conflict, separate counsel shall be provided for each of them.

(May 10, 2000, P.L.74, No.18, eff. 60 days; Apr. 9, 2012, P.L.223, No.23, eff. 60 days)

Suspension by Court Rule. Section 6337 was suspended by Pennsylvania Rule of Juvenile Court Procedure No. 800(5), amended December 30, 2005, insofar as it is inconsistent with Rule 152 relating to waiver of counsel.

Section 6337 was suspended by Pennsylvania Rule of Juvenile Court Procedure No. 1800(4), adopted August 21, 2006, insofar as it is inconsistent with Rule 1152 relating to waiver of counsel.

Cross References. Section 6337 is referred to in section 6311 of this title; sections 6315, 6368 of Title 23 (Domestic Relations).

§ 6337.1. Right to counsel for children in dependency and delinquency proceedings.

(a) Children in dependency proceedings.—Legal counsel shall be provided for a child who is alleged or has been found to be a dependent child in accordance with the Pennsylvania Rules of Juvenile Court Procedure.

(b) Children in delinquency proceedings.—

(1) In delinquency cases, all children shall be presumed indigent. If a child appears at any hearing without counsel, the court shall appoint counsel for the child prior to the commencement of the hearing. The presumption that a child is indigent may be rebutted if the court ascertains that the child has the financial resources to

retain counsel of his choice at his own expense. The court may not consider the financial resources of the child's parent, guardian or custodian when ascertaining whether the child has the financial resources to retain counsel of his choice at his own expense.

(2) Although a child alleged to be delinquent may appear with counsel at the intake conference conducted by a juvenile probation officer following the submission of a written allegation, counsel shall not be mandatory at the proceeding.

(3) Notwithstanding paragraph (1), a child who is 14 years of age or older may waive the right to counsel if the court has determined that the waiver is knowingly, intelligently and voluntarily made after having conducted a colloquy with the child on the record, in accordance with the Pennsylvania Rules of Juvenile Court Procedure, and the hearing for which waiver is sought is not one of the following:

(i) An informal detention or shelter hearing under section 6332 (relating to informal hearing).

(ii) A hearing to consider transfer to criminal proceedings under section 6355 (relating to transfer to criminal proceedings).

(iii) A hearing to consider evidence on the petition or accept an admission to an alleged delinquent act under section 6341 (relating to adjudication).

(iv) A hearing to consider evidence as to whether the child is in need of treatment, supervision or rehabilitation under section 6341.

(v) A disposition hearing under section 6341 or 6352 (relating to disposition of delinquent child).

(vi) A hearing to modify or revoke probation or other disposition entered under section 6352.

(4) The court may assign stand-by counsel if the child waives counsel at any hearing.

(5) If a child waives counsel for any hearing, the waiver shall only apply to that hearing and the child may revoke the waiver of counsel at any time. At any subsequent hearing, the child shall be informed of the right to counsel.

(Apr. 9, 2012, P.L.223, No.23, eff. 60 days)

2012 Amendment. Act 23 added section 6337.1.

§ 6338. Other basic rights.

(a) **General rule.**—A party is entitled to the opportunity to introduce evidence and otherwise be heard in his own behalf and to cross-examine witnesses.

(b) **Self-incrimination.**—A child charged with a delinquent act need not be a witness against or otherwise incriminate himself. An extrajudicial statement, if obtained in the course of violation of this chapter or which could be constitutionally inadmissible in a criminal proceeding, shall not be used against him. Evidence illegally seized or obtained shall not be received over objection to establish the allegations made against him. A confession validly made by a child out of court at a time when the child is under 18 years of age shall be insufficient to support an adjudication of delinquency unless it is corroborated by other evidence.

(c) **Statements and information obtained during screening or assessment.—**

(1) No statements, admissions or confessions made by or incriminating information obtained from a child in the course of a screening or assessment that is undertaken in conjunction with any proceedings under this chapter, including, but not limited to, that which is court ordered, shall be admitted into evidence against the child on the issue of whether the child committed a delinquent act under this chapter or on the issue of guilt in any criminal proceeding.

(2) The provisions of paragraph (1) are in addition to and do not override any existing statutory and constitutional prohibition on the admission into evidence in

delinquency and criminal proceedings of information obtained during screening, assessment or treatment.

2008 Amendment. Act 109 added subsec. (c).

§ 6339. Investigation and report.

(a) General rule.—If the allegations of a petition are admitted by a party or notice of hearing under section 6355 (relating to transfer to criminal proceedings) has been given, the court, prior to the hearing on need for treatment or disposition, may direct that a social study and report in writing to the court be made by an officer of the court or other person designated by the court, concerning the child, his family, his environment, and other matters relevant to disposition of the case. If the allegations of the petition are not admitted and notice of a hearing under section 6355 has not been given, the court shall not direct the making of the study and report until after the court has held a hearing on the petition upon notice of hearing given pursuant to this chapter and the court has found that the child committed a delinquent act or is a dependent child.

(b) Physical and mental examinations and treatment.—During the pendency of any proceeding the court may order the child to be examined at a suitable place by a physician or psychologist and may also order medical or surgical treatment of a child who is suffering from a serious physical condition or illness which in the opinion of a licensed physician requires prompt treatment, even if the parent, guardian, or other custodian has not been given notice of a hearing, is not available, or without good cause informs the court of his refusal to consent to the treatment.

§ 6340. Consent decree.

(a) General rule.—At any time after the filing of a petition and before the entry of an adjudication order, the court may, on motion of the district attorney or of counsel for the child, suspend the proceedings, and continue the child under supervision in his own home, under terms and conditions negotiated with the probation services and agreed to by all parties affected. The order of the court continuing the child under supervision shall be known as a consent decree.

(b) Objection.—Where the child or the district attorney objects to a consent decree, the court shall proceed to findings, adjudication and disposition.

(c) Duration of decree.—A consent decree shall remain in force for six months unless the child is discharged sooner by probation services with the approval of the court. Upon application of the probation services or other agency supervising the child, made before expiration of the six-month period, a consent decree may be extended by the court for an additional six months.

(c.1) Terms and conditions.—Consistent with the protection of the public interest, the terms and conditions of a consent decree may include payment by the child of reasonable amounts of money as costs, fees or restitution, including a supervision fee and contribution to a restitution fund established by the president judge of the court of common pleas pursuant to section 6352(a)(5) (relating to disposition of delinquent child), and shall, as appropriate to the circumstances of each case, include provisions which provide balanced attention to the protection of the community, accountability for offenses committed and the development of competencies to enable the child to become a responsible and productive member of the community.

(d) Reinstatement of petition.—If prior to discharge by the probation services or expiration of the consent decree, a new petition is filed against the child, or the child otherwise fails to fulfill express terms and conditions of the decree, the petition under which the child was continued under supervision may, in the discretion of the district attorney following consultation with the probation services, be reinstated and the child held accountable as if the consent decree had never been entered.

(e) **Effect of decree.**—A child who is discharged by the probation services, or who completes a period of supervision without reinstatement of the original petition, shall not again be proceeded against in any court for the same offense alleged in the petition or an offense based upon the same conduct.

2004 Amendment. Act 217 amended subsec. (c.1).

§ 6341. Adjudication.

(a) **General rule.**—After hearing the evidence on the petition the court shall make and file its findings as to whether the child is a dependent child. If the petition alleges that the child is delinquent, within seven days of hearing the evidence on the petition, the court shall make and file its findings whether the acts ascribed to the child were committed by him. This time limitation may only be extended pursuant to the agreement of the child and the attorney for the Commonwealth. The court's failure to comply with the time limitations stated in this section shall not be grounds for discharging the child or dismissing the proceeding. If the court finds that the child is not a dependent child or that the allegations of delinquency have not been established it shall dismiss the petition and order the child discharged from any detention or other restriction theretofore ordered in the proceeding. For cases involving allegations of delinquency where fingerprints or photographs or both have been taken by a law enforcement agency and where it is determined that acts ascribed to the child were not committed by him, the court shall direct that those records be immediately destroyed by law enforcement agencies.

(b) **Finding of delinquency.**—If the court finds on proof beyond a reasonable doubt that the child committed the acts by reason of which he is alleged to be delinquent it shall enter such finding on the record and shall specify the particular offenses, including the grading and counts thereof which the child is found to have committed. The court shall then proceed immediately or at a postponed hearing, which shall occur not later than 20 days after such finding if the child is in detention or not more than 60 days after such finding if the child is not in detention, to hear evidence as to whether the child is in need of treatment, supervision or rehabilitation, as established by a preponderance of the evidence, and to make and file its findings thereon. This time limitation may only be extended pursuant to the agreement of the child and the attorney for the Commonwealth. The court's failure to comply with the time limitations stated in this section shall not be grounds for discharging the child or dismissing the proceeding. In the absence of evidence to the contrary, evidence of the commission of acts which constitute a felony shall be sufficient to sustain a finding that the child is in need of treatment, supervision or rehabilitation. If the court finds that the child is not in need of treatment, supervision or rehabilitation it shall dismiss the proceeding and discharge the child from any detention or other restriction theretofore ordered.

(b.1) **School notification.**—

(1) Upon finding a child to be a delinquent child, the court shall, through the juvenile probation department, provide the following information to the building principal or his or her designee of any public, private or parochial school in which the child is enrolled:

(i) Name and address of the child.

(ii) The delinquent act or acts which the child was found to have committed.

(iii) A brief description of the delinquent act or acts.

(iv) The disposition of the case.

(2) If the child is adjudicated delinquent for an act or acts which if committed by an adult would be classified as a felony, the court, through the juvenile probation department, shall additionally provide to the building principal or his or her designee relevant information contained in the juvenile probation or treatment reports pertaining to the adjudication, prior delinquent history and the supervision plan of the delinquent child.

(3) Notwithstanding any provision set forth herein, the court or juvenile probation department shall have the authority to share any additional information regarding the delinquent child under its jurisdiction with the building principal or his or her designee as deemed necessary to protect public safety or to enable appropriate treatment, supervision or rehabilitation of the delinquent child.

(4) Information provided under this subsection is for the limited purposes of protecting school personnel and students from danger from the delinquent child and of arranging appropriate counseling and education for the delinquent child. The building principal or his or her designee shall inform the child's teacher of all information received under this subsection. Information obtained under this subsection may not be used for admissions or disciplinary decisions concerning the delinquent child unless the act or acts surrounding the adjudication took place on or within 1,500 feet of the school property.

(5) Any information provided to and maintained by the building principal or his or her designee under this subsection shall be transferred to the building principal or his or her designee of any public, private or parochial school to which the child transfers enrollment.

(6) Any information provided to the building principal or his or her designee under this subsection shall be maintained separately from the child's official school record. Such information shall be secured and disseminated by the building principal or his or her designee only as appropriate in paragraphs (4) and (5).

(b.2) Evidence on the finding of delinquency.—

(1) No statements, admissions or confessions made by or incriminating information obtained from a child in the course of a screening or assessment that is undertaken in conjunction with any proceedings under this chapter, including, but not limited to, that which is court ordered, shall be admitted into evidence against the child on the issue of whether the child committed a delinquent act under this chapter or on the issue of guilt in any criminal proceeding.

(2) The provisions of paragraph (1) are in addition to and do not override any existing statutory and constitutional prohibition on the admission into evidence in delinquency and criminal proceedings of information obtained during screening, assessment or treatment.

(c) Finding of dependency.—If the court finds from clear and convincing evidence that the child is dependent, the court shall proceed immediately or at a postponed hearing, which shall occur not later than 20 days after adjudication if the child has been removed from his home, to make a proper disposition of the case.

(c.1) Aggravated circumstances.—If the county agency or the child's attorney alleges the existence of aggravated circumstances and the court determines that the child is dependent, the court shall also determine if aggravated circumstances exist. If the court finds from clear and convincing evidence that aggravated circumstances exist, the court shall determine whether or not reasonable efforts to prevent or eliminate the need for removing the child from the home or to preserve and reunify the family shall be made or continue to be made and schedule a hearing as required in section 6351(e)(3) (relating to disposition of dependent child).

(d) Evidence on issue of disposition.—

(1)(i) In disposition hearings under subsections (b) and (c) all evidence helpful in determining the questions presented, including oral and written reports, may be received by the court and relied upon to the extent of its probative value even though not otherwise competent in the hearing on the petition.

(ii) Subparagraph (i) includes any screening and assessment examinations ordered by the court to aid in disposition, even though no statements or admissions made during the course thereof may be admitted into evidence against the child on the issue of whether the child committed a delinquent act.

(2) The parties or their counsel shall be afforded an opportunity to examine and controvert written reports so received and to cross-examine individuals making the reports. Sources of information given in confidence need not be disclosed.

(e) **Continued hearings.**—On its motion or that of a party the court may continue the hearings under this section for a reasonable period, within the time limitations imposed by this section, to receive reports and other evidence bearing on the disposition or the need for treatment, supervision or rehabilitation. In this event the court shall make an appropriate order for detention of the child or his release from detention subject to supervision of the court during the period of the continuance. In scheduling investigations and hearings the court shall give priority to proceedings in which a child is in detention or has otherwise been removed from his home before an order of disposition has been made.

(Apr. 28, 1978, P.L.202, No.53, eff. 60 days; Mar. 15, 1995, 1st Sp.Sess., P.L.972, No.6, eff. 60 days; Nov. 17, 1995, 1st Sp.Sess., P.L.1115, No.30, eff. 60 days; Dec. 15, 1998, P.L.949, No.126, eff. Jan. 1, 1999; May 10, 2000, P.L.74, No.18, eff. 60 days; Dec. 9, 2002, P.L.1705, No.215, eff. 60 days; Oct. 9, 2008, P.L.1396, No.109, eff. 60 days; June 28, 2018, P.L.361, No.49, eff. 60 days)

2018 Amendment Act 49 amended subsec. (b).

2008 Amendment. Act 109 amended subsec. (d) and added subsec. (b.2).

2000 Amendment. Act 18 amended subsecs. (a), (b) and (e). Section 5(1) of Act 18 provided that Act 18 shall apply to proceedings initiated on or after the effective date of Act 18.

1998 Amendment. Act 126 added subsec. (c.1).

1995 Amendments. Act 6, 1st Sp.Sess., amended subsec. (a) and Act 30, 1st Sp.Sess., added subsec. (b.1).

1978 Amendment. Act 53 amended subsecs. (a), (b) and (c).

Cross References. Section 6341 is referred to in sections 6308, 6337.1, 9799.19, 9799.23 of this title; section 6105 of Title 18 (Crimes and Offenses); sections 2512, 6303 of Title 23 (Domestic Relations).

§ 6342. Court-appointed special advocates.

(a) **General rule.**—The court may appoint or discharge a CASA at any time during a proceeding or investigation regarding dependency under this chapter.

(b) **Immunity.**—A court-appointed special advocate shall be immune from civil liability for actions taken in good faith to carry out the duties of the CASA under this chapter except for gross negligence, intentional misconduct or reckless, willful or wanton misconduct.

(c) **Qualifications.**—Prior to appointment a CASA shall:

(1) Be 21 years of age or older.

(2) Successfully pass screening requirements, including criminal history and child abuse background checks.

(3) Successfully complete the training requirements established under subsection (f) and by the court of common pleas of the county where the CASA will serve.

(d) **Powers and duties.**—Following appointment by the court, the CASA shall:

(1) have full access to and review all records, including records under 23 Pa.C.S. Ch. 63 (relating to child protective services) relating to the child and other information, unless otherwise restricted by the court;

(2) interview the child and other appropriate persons as necessary to develop its recommendations;

(3) receive reasonable prior notice of all hearings, staff meetings, investigations or other proceedings relating to the child;

(4) receive reasonable prior notice of the movement of the child from one placement to another placement, the return of a child to the home, the removal of a child from the home or any action that materially affects the treatment of the child;

(5) submit written reports to the court to assist the court in determining the disposition best suited to the health, safety and welfare of the child; and

(6) submit copies of all written reports and recommendations to all parties and any attorney of a party.

(e) Confidentiality.—All records and information received under this section shall be confidential and only used by the CASA in the performance of his duties.

(f) Standards.—The Juvenile Court Judges' Commission established under the act of December 21, 1959 (P.L. 1962, No. 717), entitled "An act providing for the creation and operation of the Juvenile Court Judges' Commission in the Department of Justice; prescribing its powers and duties; and making an appropriation," shall develop standards governing the qualifications and training of court-appointed special advocates.

SUBCHAPTER D
DISPOSITION OF CHILDREN GENERALLY

Sec.

6351. Disposition of dependent child.
6351.1. Authority of court upon petition to remove child from foster parent.
6352. Disposition of delinquent child.
6352.1. Treatment records.
6353. Limitation on and change in place of commitment.
6354. Effect of adjudication.
6355. Transfer to criminal proceedings.
6356. Disposition of mentally ill or mentally retarded child.
6357. Rights and duties of legal custodian.
6358. Assessment of delinquent children by the State Sexual Offenders Assessment Board

§ 6351. Disposition of dependent child.

(a) General rule.—If the child is found to be a dependent child the court may make any of the following orders of disposition best suited to the safety, protection and physical, mental, and moral welfare of the child:

(1) Permit the child to remain with his parents, guardian, or other custodian, subject to conditions and limitations as the court prescribes, including supervision as directed by the court for the protection of the child.

(2) Subject to conditions and limitations as the court prescribes transfer temporary legal custody to any of the following:

(i) Any individual resident within or without this Commonwealth, including any relative, who, after study by the probation officer or other person or agency designated by the court, is found by the court to be qualified to receive and care for the child.

(ii) An agency or other private organization licensed or otherwise authorized by law to receive and provide care for the child.

(iii) A public agency authorized by law to receive and provide care for the child.

(2.1) Subject to conditions and limitations as the court prescribes, transfer permanent legal custody to an individual resident in or outside this Commonwealth, including any relative, who, after study by the probation officer or other person or agency designated by the court, is found by the court to be qualified to receive and care for the child. A court order under this paragraph may set forth the temporary visitation rights of the parents. The court shall refer issues related to support and continuing visitation by the parent to the section of the court of common pleas that regularly determines support and visitation.

(3) Without making any of the foregoing orders transfer custody of the child to the juvenile court of another state if authorized by and in accordance with section 6363 (relating to ordering foreign supervision).

(b) Required preplacement findings.—Prior to entering any order of disposition under subsection (a) that would remove a dependent child from his home, the court shall enter findings on the record or in the order of court as follows:

(1) that continuation of the child in his home would be contrary to the welfare, safety or health of the child; and

(2) whether reasonable efforts were made prior to the placement of the child to prevent or eliminate the need for removal of the child from his home, if the child has remained in his home pending such disposition; or

(3) if preventive services were not offered due to the necessity for an emergency placement, whether such lack of services was reasonable under the circumstances; or

(4) if the court has previously determined pursuant to section 6332 (relating to informal hearing) that reasonable efforts were not made to prevent the initial removal of the child from his home, whether reasonable efforts are under way to make it possible for the child to return home; and

(5) if the child has a sibling who is subject to removal from his home, whether reasonable efforts were made prior to the placement of the child to place the siblings together or whether such joint placement is contrary to the safety or well-being of the child or sibling.

The court shall not enter findings under paragraph (2), (3) or (4) if the court previously determined that aggravated circumstances exist and no new or additional reasonable efforts to prevent or eliminate the need for removing the child from the home or to preserve and reunify the family are required.

(b.1) Visitation for child and sibling.—If a sibling of a child has been removed from his home and is in a different placement setting than the child, the court shall enter an order that ensures visitation between the child and the child's sibling no less than twice a month, unless a finding is made that visitation is contrary to the safety or well-being of the child or sibling.

(c) Limitation on confinement.—Unless a child found to be dependent is found also to be delinquent he shall not be committed to or confined in an institution or other facility designed or operated for the benefit of delinquent children.

(d) County programs.—Every county of this Commonwealth shall develop programs for children under paragraph (5) or (6) of the definition of "dependent child" in section 6302 (relating to definitions).

(e) Permanency hearings.—

(1) The court shall conduct a permanency hearing for the purpose of determining or reviewing the permanency plan of the child, the date by which the goal of permanency for the child might be achieved and whether placement continues to be best suited to the safety, protection and physical, mental and moral welfare of the child. In any permanency hearing held with respect to the child, the court shall consult

with the child regarding the child's permanency plan, including the child's desired permanency goal, in a manner appropriate to the child's age and maturity. If the court does not consult personally with the child, the court shall ensure that the views of the child regarding the permanency plan have been ascertained to the fullest extent possible and communicated to the court by the guardian ad litem under section 6311 (relating to guardian ad litem for child in court proceedings) or, as appropriate to the circumstances of the case by the child's counsel, the court-appointed special advocate or other person as designated by the court.

(2) If the county agency or the child's attorney alleges the existence of aggravated circumstances and the court determines that the child has been adjudicated dependent, the court shall then determine if aggravated circumstances exist. If the court finds from clear and convincing evidence that aggravated circumstances exist, the court shall determine whether or not reasonable efforts to prevent or eliminate the need for removing the child from the child's parent, guardian or custodian or to preserve and reunify the family shall be made or continue to be made and schedule a hearing as provided in paragraph (3).

(3) The court shall conduct permanency hearings as follows:

(i) Within six months of:

(A) the date of the child's removal from the child's parent, guardian or custodian for placement under section 6324 (relating to taking into custody) or 6332 or pursuant to a transfer of temporary legal custody or other disposition under subsection (a)(2), whichever is the earliest; or

(B) each previous permanency hearing until the child is returned to the child's parent, guardian or custodian or removed from the jurisdiction of the court.

(ii) Within 30 days of:

(A) an adjudication of dependency at which the court determined that aggravated circumstances exist and that reasonable efforts to prevent or eliminate the need to remove the child from the child's parent, guardian or custodian or to preserve and reunify the family need not be made or continue to be made;

(B) a permanency hearing at which the court determined that aggravated circumstances exist and that reasonable efforts to prevent or eliminate the need to remove the child from the child's parent, guardian or custodian or to preserve and reunify the family need not be made or continue to be made and the permanency plan for the child is incomplete or inconsistent with the court's determination;

(C) an allegation that aggravated circumstances exist regarding a child who has been adjudicated dependent, filed under section 6334(b) (relating to petition); or

(D) a petition alleging that the hearing is necessary to protect the safety or physical, mental or moral welfare of a dependent child.

(iii) If the court resumes jurisdiction of the child pursuant to subsection (j), permanency hearings shall be scheduled in accordance with applicable law until court jurisdiction is terminated, but no later than when the child attains 21 years of age.

(f) Matters to be determined at permanency hearing.—At each permanency hearing, a court shall determine all of the following:

(1) The continuing necessity for and appropriateness of the placement.

(2) The appropriateness, feasibility and extent of compliance with the permanency plan developed for the child.

(3) The extent of progress made toward alleviating the circumstances which necessitated the original placement.

(4) The appropriateness and feasibility of the current placement goal for the child.

(5) The likely date by which the placement goal for the child might be achieved.

(5.1) Whether reasonable efforts were made to finalize the permanency plan in effect.

(6) Whether the child is safe.

(7) If the child has been placed outside the Commonwealth, whether the placement continues to be best suited to the safety, protection and physical, mental and moral welfare of the child.

(8) The services needed to assist a child who is 14 years of age or older to make the transition to successful adulthood.

(8.1) Whether the child continues to meet the definition of "child" and has requested that the court continue jurisdiction pursuant to section 6302 if the child is between 18 and 21 years of age.

(8.2) That a transition plan has been presented in accordance with section 475 of the Social Security Act (49 Stat. 620, 42 U.S.C. § 675(5)(H)).

(9) If the child has been in placement for at least 15 of the last 22 months or the court has determined that aggravated circumstances exist and that reasonable efforts to prevent or eliminate the need to remove the child from the child's parent, guardian or custodian or to preserve and reunify the family need not be made or continue to be made, whether the county agency has filed or sought to join a petition to terminate parental rights and to identify, recruit, process and approve a qualified family to adopt the child unless:

(i) the child is being cared for by a relative best suited to the physical, mental and moral welfare of the child;

(ii) the county agency has documented a compelling reason for determining that filing a petition to terminate parental rights would not serve the needs and welfare of the child; or

(iii) the child's family has not been provided with necessary services to achieve the safe return to the child's parent, guardian or custodian within the time frames set forth in the permanency plan.

(10) If a sibling of a child has been removed from his home and is in a different placement setting than the child, whether reasonable efforts have been made to place the child and the sibling of the child together or whether such joint placement is contrary to the safety or well-being of the child or sibling.

(11) If the child has a sibling, whether visitation of the child with that sibling is occurring no less than twice a month, unless a finding is made that visitation is contrary to the safety or well-being of the child or sibling.

(12) If the child has been placed with a caregiver, whether the child is being provided with regular, ongoing opportunities to participate in age-appropriate or developmentally appropriate activities. In order to make the determination under this paragraph, the county agency shall document the steps it has taken to ensure that:

(i) the caregiver is following the reasonable and prudent parent standard; and

(ii) the child has regular, ongoing opportunities to engage in age-appropriate or developmentally appropriate activities. The county agency shall consult with the child regarding opportunities to engage in such activities.

For children placed in foster care on or before November 19, 1997, the county agency shall file or join a petition for termination of parental rights under this subsection in accordance with section 103(c)(2) of the Adoption and Safe Families Act of 1997 (Public Law 105-89, 111 Stat. 2119).

(f.1) Additional determination.—Based upon the determinations made under subsection (f) and all relevant evidence presented at the hearing, the court shall determine one of the following:

(1) If and when the child will be returned to the child's parent, guardian or custodian in cases where the return of the child is best suited to the safety, protection and physical, mental and moral welfare of the child.

(2) If and when the child will be placed for adoption, and the county agency will file for termination of parental rights in cases where return to the child's parent, guardian or custodian is not best suited to the safety, protection and physical, mental and moral welfare of the child.

(3) If and when the child will be placed with a legal custodian in cases where the return to the child's parent, guardian or custodian or being placed for adoption is not best suited to the safety, protection and physical, mental and moral welfare of the child.

(4) If and when the child will be placed with a fit and willing relative in cases where return to the child's parent, guardian or custodian, being placed for adoption or being placed with a legal custodian is not best suited to the safety, protection and physical, mental and moral welfare of the child.

(5) If and when the child will be placed in another planned permanent living arrangement which is approved by the court, the following shall apply:

(i) The child must be 16 years of age or older.

(ii) The county agency shall identify at least one significant connection with a supportive adult willing to be involved in the child's life as the child transitions to adulthood, or document that efforts have been made to identify a supportive adult.

(iii) The county agency shall document:

(A) A compelling reason that it would not be best suited to the safety, protection and physical, mental and moral welfare of the child to be returned to the child's parent, guardian or custodian, to be placed for adoption, to be placed with a legal custodian or to be placed with a fit and willing relative.

(B) Its intensive, ongoing and, as of the date of the hearing, unsuccessful efforts to return the child to the child's parent, guardian or custodian or to be placed for adoption, to be placed with a legal custodian or to be placed with a fit and willing relative.

(C) Its efforts to utilize search technology to find biological family members for the child.

(iv) The court shall:

(A) Ask the child about the desired permanency goal for the child.

(B) Make a judicial determination explaining why, as of the date of the hearing, another planned permanent living arrangement is the best permanency plan for the child.

(C) Provide compelling reasons why it continues not to be in the best interests of the child to return to the child's parent, guardian or custodian, be placed for adoption, be placed with a legal custodian or be placed with a fit and willing relative.

(D) Make findings that the significant connection is identified in the permanency plan or that efforts have been made to identify a supportive adult, if no one is currently identified.

(f.2) Evidence.—Evidence of conduct by the parent that places the health, safety or welfare of the child at risk, including evidence of the use of alcohol or a controlled substance that places the health, safety or welfare of the child at risk, shall be presented to the court by the county agency or any other party at any disposition or permanency hearing whether or not the conduct was the basis for the determination of dependency.

(g) Court order.—On the basis of the determination made under subsection (f.1), the court shall order the continuation, modification or termination of placement or other disposition which is best suited to the safety, protection and physical, mental and moral welfare of the child.

(h) Certain hearings discretionary.—(Deleted by amendment).

(i) Assignment to orphans' court.—A judge who adjudicated the child dependent or who has conducted permanency hearings or other dependency proceedings involving the child may be assigned to the orphans' court division for the purpose of hearing proceedings relating to any of the following:

(1) Involuntary termination of parental rights of a parent of the dependent child under 23 Pa.C.S. Ch. 25 Subch. B (relating to involuntary termination).

(2) A petition to adopt the dependent child.

(j) Resumption of jurisdiction.—At any time prior to a child reaching 21 years of age, a child may request the court to resume dependency jurisdiction if:

(1) the child continues to meet the definition of "child" pursuant to section 6302; and

(2) dependency jurisdiction was terminated:

(i) within 90 days prior to the child's 18th birthday; or

(ii) on or after the child's 18th birthday, but before the child turns 21 years of age.

(Apr. 28, 1978, P.L.202, No.53, eff. 60 days; Dec. 15, 1986, P.L.1598, No.177, eff. 60 days; July 11, 1996, P.L.607, No.104, eff. 60 days; Dec. 15, 1998, P.L.949, No.126, eff. Jan. 1, 1999; Dec. 9, 2002, P.L.1705, No.215, eff. 60 days; Dec. 18, 2007, P.L.484, No.76, eff. Jan. 1, 2008; Nov. 23, 2010, P.L.1140, No.115, eff. 60 days; July 5, 2012, P.L.880, No.91, eff. imd.; Dec. 28, 2015, P.L.559, No.94, eff. Jan. 1, 2016)

2015 Amendment. Act 94 amended subsecs. (e)(1), (f)(8) and (f.1)(5) and added par. (f)(12). See section 30 of Act 94 of 2015 in the appendix to this title for special provisions relating to duties of Department of Human Services.

2012 Amendment. Act 91 added subsecs. (e)(3)(iii), (f)(8.1) and (8.2) and (j).

2010 Amendment. Act 115 amended subsec. (b) and added subsecs. (b.1) and (f)(10) and (11).

Care of Dependent Children. Section 31 of Act 53 of 1978 limits the liability of counties for costs of operating new shelter care programs for dependent children classified under paragraph (6) of the definition of "dependent child" in 42 Pa.C.S. § 6302.

Suspension by Court Rule. Section 6351(e)(3)(i)(B) was suspended by Pennsylvania Rule of Juvenile Court Procedure No. 1800(12), amended September 16, 2009, insofar as it is inconsistent with Rule 1607 relating to regular scheduling of permanency hearings.

Cross References. Section 6351 is referred to in sections 6336.1, 6341, 6351.1, 6352, 6352.1, 6357 of this title.

§ 6351.1. Authority of court upon petition to remove child from foster parent.

(a) Order required.—Notwithstanding sections 6324 (relating to taking into custody) and 6351(a) (relating to disposition of dependent child), if a county agency petitions the court for removal of a child because the foster parent has been convicted of an offense set forth in 23 Pa.C.S. § 6344(c) (relating to employees having contact with children; adoptive and foster parents), the court shall immediately enter an order removing the child from the foster parent.

(b) Limitation on placement.—If a court enters an order under subsection (a), the following apply:

(1) Except as set forth in paragraph (2), the court may, under section 6351(a), enter an order of disposition best suited to the child's safety; protection; and physical, mental and moral welfare.

(2) Notwithstanding section 6351(a), if the court finds that the foster parent has been convicted of an offense set forth in 23 Pa.C.S. § 6344(c), the court has no authority to place or return the child to the foster parent who was named in the petition filed by the county agency under subsection (a).

(Oct. 31, 2003, P.L.200, No.31, eff. 60 days; Oct. 22, 2014, P.L.2529, No.153, eff. Dec. 31, 2014)

2014 Amendment. Act 153 amended subsec. (a).

2003 Amendment. Act 31 added section 6351.1. Section 3 of Act 31 provided that section 6351.1 shall apply to petitions filed on or after the effective date of section 3.

§ 6352. Disposition of delinquent child.

(a) General rule.—If the child is found to be a delinquent child the court may make any of the following orders of disposition determined to be consistent with the protection of the public interest and best suited to the child's treatment, supervision, rehabilitation and welfare, which disposition shall, as appropriate to the individual circumstances of the child's case, provide balanced attention to the protection of the community, the imposition of accountability for offenses committed and the development of competencies to enable the child to become a responsible and productive member of the community:

(1) Any order authorized by section 6351 (relating to disposition of dependent child).

(2) Placing the child on probation under supervision of the probation officer of the court or the court of another state as provided in section 6363 (relating to ordering foreign supervision), under conditions and limitations the court prescribes.

(3) Committing the child to an institution, youth development center, camp, or other facility for delinquent children operated under the direction or supervision of the court or other public authority and approved by the Department of Public Welfare.

(4) If the child is 12 years of age or older, committing the child to an institution operated by the Department of Public Welfare.

(5) Ordering payment by the child of reasonable amounts of money as fines, costs, fees or restitution as deemed appropriate as part of the plan of rehabilitation considering the nature of the acts committed and the earning capacity of the child, including a contribution to a restitution fund. The president judge of the court of common pleas shall establish a restitution fund for the deposit of all contributions to the restitution fund which are received or collected. The president judge of the court of common pleas shall promulgate written guidelines for the administration of the fund. Disbursements from the fund shall be made, subject to the written guidelines and the limitations of this chapter, at the discretion of the president judge and used to reimburse crime victims for financial losses resulting from delinquent acts. For an order made under this subsection, the court shall retain jurisdiction until there has been full compliance with the order or until the delinquent child attains 21 years of age. Any restitution order which remains unpaid at the time the child attains 21 years of age shall continue to be collectible under section 9728 (relating to collection of restitution, reparation, fees, costs, fines and penalties).

(6) An order of the terms of probation may include an appropriate fine considering the nature of the act committed or restitution not in excess of actual damages caused by the child which shall be paid from the earnings of the child received through participation in a constructive program of service or education

acceptable to the victim and the court whereby, during the course of such service, the child shall be paid not less than the minimum wage of this Commonwealth. In ordering such service, the court shall take into consideration the age, physical and mental capacity of the child and the service shall be designed to impress upon the child a sense of responsibility for the injuries caused to the person or property of another. The order of the court shall be limited in duration consistent with the limitations in section 6353 (relating to limitation on and change in place of commitment) and in the act of May 13, 1915 (P.L.286, No.177), known as the Child Labor Law. The court order shall specify the nature of the work, the number of hours to be spent performing the assigned tasks, and shall further specify that as part of a plan of treatment and rehabilitation that up to 75% of the earnings of the child be used for restitution in order to provide positive reinforcement for the work performed.

In selecting from the alternatives set forth in this section, the court shall follow the general principle that the disposition imposed should provide the means through which the provisions of this chapter are executed and enforced consistent with section 6301(b) (relating to purposes) and when confinement is necessary, the court shall impose the minimum amount of confinement that is consistent with the protection of the public and the rehabilitation needs of the child.

(b) Limitation on place of commitment.—A child shall not be committed or transferred to a penal institution or other facility used primarily for the execution of sentences of adults convicted of a crime.

(c) Required statement of reasons.—Prior to entering an order of disposition under subsection (a), the court shall state its disposition and the reasons for its disposition on the record in open court, together with the goals, terms and conditions of that disposition. If the child is to be committed to out-of-home placement, the court shall also state the name of the specific facility or type of facility to which the child will be committed and its findings and conclusions of law that formed the basis of its decision consistent with subsection (a) and section 6301, including the reasons why commitment to that facility or type of facility was determined to be the least restrictive placement that is consistent with the protection of the public and best suited to the child's treatment, supervision, rehabilitation and welfare.

(Apr. 28, 1978, P.L.202, No.53, eff. 60 days; May 12, 1995, 1st Sp.Sess., P.L.1006, No.13, eff. 60 days; Nov. 17, 1995, 1st Sp.Sess., P.L.1127, No.33, eff. 120 days; Nov. 30, 2004, P.L.1703, No.217, eff. imd.; Apr. 3, 2012, P.L.222, No.22, eff. imd.)

2012 Amendment. Act 22 added subsec. (c).

2004 Amendment. Act 217 amended subsec. (a)(5).

1995 Amendments. Act 13, 1st Sp.Sess, amended subsec. (a)(5) and Act 33, 1st Sp.Sess., amended subsec. (a). Section 8 of Act 33, 1st Sp.Sess., provided that Act 33 shall apply to all delinquent acts committed on or after the effective date of Act 33.

Cross References. Section 6352 is referred to in sections 6304.1, 6323, 6337.1, 6340, 6352.1, 6358, 6403, 9728, 9795.4, 9799.12, 9799.15, 9799.16, 9799.17, 9799.19, 9799.24, 9799.31, 9799.34 of this title.

§ 6352.1. Treatment records.

Notwithstanding any other provision of law, drug and alcohol treatment records or related information regarding a child who is alleged or who has been found to be dependent or delinquent, or the child's parent, shall be released to the county agency, court or juvenile probation officer upon the consent of the child or the child's parent or upon an order of the court. The disclosure of drug and alcohol treatment records under this section shall be obtained or ordered in a manner that is consistent with the procedures, limitations and criteria set forth in regulations adopted by the Department of Health and Human Services relating to the confidentiality of drug and alcohol treatment records. The county agency, court or juvenile probation officer shall only use the records to carry out the purposes of this chapter and shall not release the records to any other person. The court may order the participation of the county agency or juvenile probation officer in the development of a treatment plan for the child as necessary to protect the health, safety or welfare of the child, to include discussions with the individual, facility or program providing treatment and the child or the child's parent in furtherance of a disposition under section 6351 (relating to disposition of dependent child) or 6352 (relating to disposition of delinquent child).

§ 6353. Limitation on and change in place of commitment.

(a) **General rule.**—No child shall initially be committed to an institution for a period longer than four years or a period longer than he could have been sentenced by the court if he had been convicted of the same offense as an adult, whichever is less. The initial commitment may be extended for a similar period of time, or modified, if the court finds after hearing that the extension or modification will effectuate the original purpose for which the order was entered. The child shall have notice of the extension or modification hearing and shall be given an opportunity to be heard. The committing court shall review each commitment every six months and shall hold a disposition review hearing at least every nine months.

(b) **Transfer to other institution.**—After placement of the child, and if his progress with the institution warrants it, the institution may seek to transfer the child to a less secure facility, including a group home or foster boarding home. The institution shall give the committing court written notice of all requests for transfer and shall give the attorney for the Commonwealth written notice of a request for transfer from a secure facility to another facility. If the court, or in the case of a request to transfer from a secure facility, the attorney for the Commonwealth, does not object to the request for transfer within ten days after the receipt of such notice, the transfer may be effectuated. If the court, or in the case of a request to transfer from a secure facility, the attorney for the Commonwealth, objects to the transfer, the court shall hold a hearing within 20 days after objecting to the transfer for the purpose of reviewing the commitment order. The institution shall be notified of the scheduled hearing, at which hearing evidence may be presented by any interested party on the issue of the propriety of the transfer. If the institution seeks to transfer to a more secure facility the child shall have a full hearing before the committing court. At the hearing, the court may reaffirm or modify its commitment order.

(c) **Notice of available facilities and services.**—Immediately after the Commonwealth adopts its budget, the Department of Public Welfare shall notify the courts and the General Assembly, for each Department of Public Welfare region, of the available:

(1) Secure beds for the serious juvenile offenders.

(2) General residential beds for the adjudicated delinquent child.

(3) The community-based programs for the adjudicated delinquent child.

If the population at a particular institution or program exceeds 110% of capacity, the department shall notify the courts and the General Assembly that intake to that institution or program is temporarily closed and shall make available equivalent services to children in equivalent facilities.

§ 6354. Effect of adjudication.

(a) **General rule.**—An order of disposition or other adjudication in a proceeding under this chapter is not a conviction of crime and does not impose any civil disability ordinarily resulting from a conviction or operate to disqualify the child in any civil service application or appointment.

(b) **Effect in subsequent judicial matters.**—The disposition of a child under this chapter may only be used against him:

(1) in dispositional proceedings after conviction for the purposes of a presentence investigation and report if the child was adjudicated delinquent;

(2) in a subsequent juvenile hearing, whether before or after reaching majority;

(3) if relevant, where he has put his reputation or character in issue in a civil matter; or

(4) in a criminal proceeding, if the child was adjudicated delinquent for an offense, the evidence of which would be admissible if committed by an adult.

§ 6355. Transfer to criminal proceedings.

(a) General rule.—After a petition has been filed alleging delinquency based on conduct which is designated a crime or public offense under the laws, including local ordinances, of this Commonwealth, the court before hearing the petition on its merits may rule that this chapter is not applicable and that the offense should be prosecuted, and transfer the offense, where appropriate, to the division or a judge of the court assigned to conduct criminal proceedings, for prosecution of the offense if all of the following exist:

(1) The child was 14 or more years of age at the time of the alleged conduct.

(2) A hearing on whether the transfer should be made is held in conformity with this chapter.

(3) Notice in writing of the time, place, and purpose of the hearing is given to the child and his parents, guardian, or other custodian at least three days before the hearing.

(4) The court finds:

(i) that there is a prima facie case that the child committed the delinquent act alleged;

(ii) that the delinquent act would be considered a felony if committed by an adult;

(iii) that there are reasonable grounds to believe that the public interest is served by the transfer of the case for criminal prosecution. In determining whether the public interest can be served, the court shall consider the following factors:

(A) the impact of the offense on the victim or victims;

(B) the impact of the offense on the community;

(C) the threat to the safety of the public or any individual posed by the child;

(D) the nature and circumstances of the offense allegedly committed by the child;

(E) the degree of the child's culpability;

(F) the adequacy and duration of dispositional alternatives available under this chapter and in the adult criminal justice system; and

(G) whether the child is amenable to treatment, supervision or rehabilitation as a juvenile by considering the following factors:

(I) age;

(II) mental capacity;

(III) maturity;

(IV) the degree of criminal sophistication exhibited by the child;

(V) previous records, if any;

(VI) the nature and extent of any prior delinquent history, including the success or failure of any previous attempts by the juvenile court to rehabilitate the child;

(VII) whether the child can be rehabilitated prior to the expiration of the juvenile court jurisdiction;

(VIII) probation or institutional reports, if any;

(IX) any other relevant factors; and

(iv) that there are reasonable grounds to believe that the child is not committable to an institution for the mentally retarded or mentally ill.

(b) Chapter inapplicable following transfer.—The transfer terminates the applicability of this chapter over the child with respect to the delinquent acts alleged in the petition.

(c) Transfer at request of child.—The child may request that the case be transferred for prosecution in which event the court may order this chapter not applicable.

(d) Effect of transfer from criminal proceedings.—No hearing shall be conducted where this chapter becomes applicable because of a previous determination by the court in a criminal proceeding.

(e) Murder and other excluded acts.—Where the petition alleges conduct which if proven would constitute murder, or any of the offenses excluded by paragraph (2)(ii) or (iii) of the definition of "delinquent act" in section 6302 (relating to definitions), the court shall require the offense to be prosecuted under the criminal law and procedures, except where the case has been transferred pursuant to section 6322 (relating to transfer from criminal proceedings) from the division or a judge of the court assigned to conduct criminal proceedings.

(f) Transfer action interlocutory.—The decision of the court to transfer or not to transfer the case shall be interlocutory.

(g) Burden of proof.—The burden of establishing by a preponderance of evidence that the public interest is served by the transfer of the case to criminal court and that a child is not amenable to treatment, supervision or rehabilitation as a juvenile shall rest with the Commonwealth unless the following apply:

(1)(i) a deadly weapon as defined in 18 Pa.C.S. § 2301 (relating to definitions) was used and the child was 14 years of age at the time of the offense; or

(ii) the child was 15 years of age or older at the time of the offense and was previously adjudicated delinquent of a crime that would be considered a felony if committed by an adult; and

(2) there is a prima facie case that the child committed a delinquent act which, if committed by an adult, would be classified as rape, involuntary deviate sexual intercourse, aggravated assault as defined in 18 Pa.C.S. § 2702(a)(1) or (2) (relating to aggravated assault), robbery as defined in 18 Pa.C.S. § 3701(a)(1)(i), (ii) or (iii) (relating to robbery), robbery of motor vehicle, aggravated indecent assault, kidnapping, voluntary manslaughter, an attempt, conspiracy or solicitation to commit any of these crimes or an attempt to commit murder as specified in paragraph (2)(ii) of the definition of "delinquent act" in section 6302.

If either of the preceding criteria are met, the burden of establishing by a preponderance of the evidence that retaining the case under this chapter serves the public interest and that the child is amenable to treatment, supervision or rehabilitation as a juvenile shall rest with the child.

§ 6356. Disposition of mentally ill or mentally retarded child.

If, at a dispositional hearing of a child found to be a delinquent or at any hearing, the evidence indicates that the child may be subject to commitment or detention under the provisions of the act of October 20, 1966 (3rd Sp.Sess., P.L. 96, No. 6), known as the "Mental Health and Mental Retardation Act of 1966," or the act of July 9, 1976 (P.L. 817, No. 143), known as the "Mental Health Procedures Act," the court shall proceed under the provisions of the appropriate statute.

§ 6357. Rights and duties of legal custodian.

A custodian to whom legal custody has been given by the court under this chapter has the right to the physical custody of the child, the right to determine the nature of the care and treatment of the child, including ordinary medical care and the right and duty to provide for the care, protection, training, and education, and the physical, mental, and moral welfare of the child. An award of legal custody shall be subject to the conditions and limitations of the order and to the remaining rights and duties of the parents or guardian of the child as determined by the court. The court may award legal custody under this section on a temporary basis to an individual or agency under section 6351(a)(2) (relating to disposition of dependent child) or permanent basis to an individual under section 6351(a)(2.1).

§ 6358. Assessment of delinquent children by the State Sexual Offenders Assessment Board.

(a) **General rule.**—A child who has been found to be delinquent for an act of sexual violence which if committed by an adult would be a violation of 18 Pa.C.S. § 3121 (relating to rape), 3123 (relating to involuntary deviate sexual intercourse), 3124.1 (relating to sexual assault), 3125 (relating to aggravated indecent assault), 3126 (relating to indecent assault) or 4302 (relating to incest) who is committed to an institution or other facility pursuant to section 6352 (relating to disposition of delinquent child) and who remains in any such institution or facility as a result of that adjudication of delinquency upon attaining 20 years of age shall be subject to an assessment by the board.

(b) **Duty of probation officer.**—Ninety days prior to the 20th birthday of the child, the probation officer shall have the duty to notify the board of the status of the delinquent child and the institution or other facility where the child is presently committed. The probation officer shall assist the board in obtaining access to the child and any information required by the board to perform the assessment, including, but not limited to, the child's official court record and complete juvenile probation file.

(b.1) **Notification to board.**—The probation officer shall, within five days of the effective date of this subsection, notify the board of any child whose age precludes compliance with subsection (b) provided the child has not yet attained 21 years of age.

(c) **Assessment.**—The board shall conduct an assessment, which shall include the board's determination of whether or not the child is in need of commitment for involuntary treatment due to a mental abnormality as defined in section 6402 (relating to definitions) or a personality disorder, either of which results in serious difficulty in controlling sexually violent behavior. Upon the completion of the assessment pursuant to this section, the board shall provide the assessment to the court. In no case shall the board file the assessment later than 90 days after the child's 20th birthday unless notification of the board was delayed under subsection (b.1), in which case the assessment shall be filed no later than 180 days after the child's 20th birthday.

(d) **Duty of court.**—The court shall provide a copy of the assessment by the board to the probation officer, the district attorney, county solicitor or designee and the child's attorney.

(e) **Dispositional review hearing.**—Where the board has concluded that the child is in need of involuntary treatment pursuant to the provisions of Chapter 64 (relating to court-ordered involuntary treatment of certain sexually violent persons), the court shall conduct a hearing at which the county solicitor or a designee, the probation officer and the child's attorney are present. The court shall consider the assessment, treatment information and any other relevant information regarding the delinquent child at the dispositional review hearing pursuant to section 6353 (relating to limitation on and change in place of commitment), which shall be held no later than 180 days before the 21st birthday of the child. Where the submission of the report was delayed pursuant to subsection (c), the dispositional review hearing shall be held no later than 90 days before the 21st birthday of the child.

(f) **Subsequent proceeding.**—If, at the conclusion of the dispositional review hearing required in subsection (e), the court finds there is a prima facie case that the child is in need of involuntary treatment under the provisions of Chapter 64, the court shall direct that the county solicitor or a designee file a petition to initiate proceedings under the provisions of that chapter.

(Aug. 14, 2003, P.L.97, No.21, eff. 180 days; Dec. 20, 2011, P.L.446, No.111, eff. one year; July 5, 2012, P.L.880, No.91, eff. Dec. 20, 2012)

2012 Amendment. Act 91 amended subsec. (a).

2011 Amendment. Act 111 amended subsecs. (a) and (b).

2003 Amendment. Act 21 added section 6358.

Cross References. Section 6358 is referred to in sections 6403, 9795.4, 9799.24 of this title.

SUBCHAPTER E
DISPOSITIONS AFFECTING OTHER JURISDICTIONS

Sec.
6361. Disposition of nonresident child.
6362. Disposition of resident child received from another state.
6363. Ordering foreign supervision.
6364. Supervision under foreign order.
6365. Powers of foreign probation officers.

§ 6361. Disposition of nonresident child.

(a) General rule.—If the court finds that a child who has been adjudged to have committed a delinquent act or to be dependent is or is about to become a resident of another state which has adopted the Uniform Juvenile Court Act, or a substantially similar law which includes provisions corresponding to this section and section 6362 (relating to disposition of resident child received from another state), the court may defer hearing on need of treatment and disposition and request by any appropriate means the appropriate court of the county or parish of the residence or prospective residence of the child to accept jurisdiction of the child.

(b) Change of residence under court order.—If the child becomes a resident of another state while on probation or under protective supervision under order of a court of this Commonwealth, the court may request the court of the state in which the child has become a resident to accept jurisdiction of the child and to continue his probation or protective supervision.

(c) Procedure for transfer.—Upon receipt and filing of an acceptance the court of this Commonwealth shall transfer custody of the child to the accepting court and cause him to be delivered to the person designated by that court to receive his custody. It also shall provide the accepting court with certified copies of the order adjudging the child to be a delinquent, or dependent child, of the order of transfer, and if the child is on probation or under protective supervision under order of the court, of the order of disposition. It also shall provide the accepting court with a statement of the facts found by the court of this Commonwealth and any recommendations and other information or documents it considers of assistance to that court in making a disposition of the case or in supervising the child on probation or otherwise.

(d) Effect of transfer to accepting court.—Upon compliance with subsection (c) the jurisdiction of the court of this Commonwealth over the child is terminated.

§ 6362. Disposition of resident child received from another state.

(a) General rule.—If a juvenile court of another state which has adopted the Uniform Juvenile Court Act, or a substantially similar law which includes provisions corresponding to section 6361 (relating to disposition of nonresident child) and this section, requests a court of this Commonwealth to accept jurisdiction of a child found by the requesting court to have committed a delinquent act or to be an unruly or dependent child, and the court of this Commonwealth finds, after investigation that the child is, or is about to become, a resident of a county for which the court is established, the court shall promptly and not later than 14 days after receiving the request issue its acceptance in writing to the requesting court and direct its probation officer or other person designated by it to take physical custody of the child from the requesting court and bring him before the court of this Commonwealth or make other appropriate provisions for his appearance before the court.

(b) **Hearing on further disposition.**—Upon the filing of certified copies of the orders of the requesting court:

(1) determining that the child committed a delinquent act or is an unruly or dependent child; and

(2) committing the child to the jurisdiction of the court of this Commonwealth; the court of this Commonwealth shall immediately fix a time for a hearing on the need for treatment, supervision or rehabilitation and disposition of the child or on the continuance of any probation or protective supervision.

(c) **Further proceedings.**—The hearing and notice thereof and all subsequent proceedings are governed by this chapter. The court may make any order of disposition permitted by the facts and this chapter. The orders of the requesting court are conclusive that the child committed the delinquent act or is an unruly or dependent child and of the facts found by the court in making the orders. If the requesting court has made an order placing the child on probation or under protective supervision, a like order shall be entered by the court of this Commonwealth.

§ 6363. Ordering foreign supervision.

(a) **General rule.**—Subject to the provisions of this chapter governing dispositions and to the extent that funds are available the court may place a child in the custody of a suitable person in another state. On obtaining the written consent of a juvenile court of another state which has adopted the Uniform Juvenile Court Act or a substantially similar law, which includes provisions corresponding to this section and section 6364 (relating to supervision under foreign order), the court of this Commonwealth may order that the child be placed under the supervision of a probation officer or other appropriate official designated by the accepting court. One certified copy of the order shall be sent to the accepting court and another filed with the clerk of the requesting court of this Commonwealth.

(b) **Costs and expenses.**—The reasonable cost of the supervision, including the expenses of necessary travel, shall be borne initially by the county of the requesting court of this Commonwealth. Upon receiving a certified statement signed by the judge of the accepting court of the cost incurred by the supervision the court of this Commonwealth shall certify if it so appears that the sum so stated was reasonably incurred and file it with the county for payment. The county shall thereupon make payment of the sum approved to the appropriate officials of the county or parish of the accepting court.

§ 6364. Supervision under foreign order.

(a) **General rule.**—Upon receiving a request of a juvenile court of another state which has adopted the Uniform Juvenile Court Act, or a substantially similar law which includes provisions corresponding to section 6363 (relating to ordering foreign supervision) and this section to provide supervision of a child under the jurisdiction of that court, a court of this Commonwealth may issue its written acceptance to the requesting court and designate its probation or other appropriate officer who is to provide supervision, stating the probable cost per day therefor.

(b) **Supervision and report.**—Upon the receipt and filing of a certified copy of the order of the requesting court placing the child under the supervision of the officer so designated the officer shall arrange for the reception of the child from the requesting court, provide supervision pursuant to the order and this chapter, and report thereon from time to time together with any recommendations he may have to the requesting court.

(c) **Costs and expenses.**—The court of this Commonwealth from time to time shall certify to the requesting court the cost of supervision that has been incurred and request payment therefor from the appropriate officials of the county or parish of the requesting court to the county of the accepting court.

(d) **Termination of supervision.**—The court of this Commonwealth at any time may terminate supervision by notifying the requesting court. In that case, or if the supervision is terminated by the requesting court, the probation officer supervising the child shall return the child to a representative of the requesting court authorized to receive him.

§ 6365. Powers of foreign probation officers.

If a child has been placed on probation or protective supervision by a juvenile court of another state which has adopted the Uniform Juvenile Court Act or a substantially similar law which includes provisions corresponding to this section, and the child is in this Commonwealth with or without the permission of that court, the probation officer of that court or other person designated by that court to supervise or take custody of the child has all the powers and privileges in this Commonwealth with respect to the child as given by this chapter to like officers or persons of this Commonwealth including the right of visitation, counseling, control, and direction, taking into custody, and returning to that state.

SUBCHAPTER F
JUVENILE COURT JUDGES' COMMISSION

§ 6371. Definitions.

The following words and phrases when used in this subchapter shall have the meanings given to them in this section unless the context clearly indicates otherwise:

"Commission." The Juvenile Court Judges' Commission created pursuant to section 6372(a) (relating to Juvenile Court Judges' Commission).

"Commissioner." A member appointed to the Juvenile Court Judges' Commission pursuant to section 6372(b) (relating to Juvenile Court Judges' Commission).

2007, Dec. 4, P.L. 427, No. 64, § 1, imd. effective.

§ 6372. Juvenile Court Judges' Commission.

(a) **Establishment.**—There is hereby established in the Office of General Counsel the Juvenile Court Judges' Commission.

(b) **Composition.**—The commission shall consist of nine judges who shall be appointed by the Governor from a list of judges, serving in the juvenile courts, selected and submitted by the Chief Justice of Pennsylvania.

(c) **Tenure.**—Of the first nine appointees to the commission, three shall serve for three years, three for two years and three for one year. After the initial term, the term for all members shall be three years.

(d) **Officers.**—The commission shall annually select one of its members as chairman and one member as secretary.

(e) **Staff.**—The chairman, with the approval of the majority of the commission, may appoint and fix the compensation of assistants, clerks and stenographers as he deems necessary to enable the commission to perform its powers and duties. During his term of employment, no assistant shall engage, directly or indirectly, in the practice of law in any juvenile court in this Commonwealth.

(f) Staff compensation.—The compensation of the assistants, clerks and stenographers shall be fixed within limitations fixed by the Executive Board and shall be eligible to apply for membership in the State Employees' Retirement System.

(g) Meetings.—Each year there shall be quarterly meetings of the commission and such additional meetings as the chairman shall deem necessary. Each commissioner attending the meetings shall be paid only his necessary expenses incurred in attending the meetings. Five members of the commission shall constitute a quorum at meetings.

2007, Dec. 4, P.L. 427, No. 64, § 1, imd. effective.

§ 6373. Powers and duties.

The commission shall have the power and is required to do the following:

(1) Advise the juvenile court judges of this Commonwealth in all matters pertaining to the proper care and maintenance of delinquent and dependent children.

(2) Examine the administrative methods and judicial procedure used in juvenile courts throughout this Commonwealth, establish standards and make recommendations on the same to the courts presiding over juvenile proceedings within this Commonwealth.

(3) Examine the personnel practices and employment standards used in probation offices in this Commonwealth, establish standards and make recommendations on the same to courts presiding over juvenile proceedings within this Commonwealth.

(4) Collect and analyze data to identify trends and to determine the effectiveness of programs and practices to ensure the reasonable and efficient administration of the juvenile court system, make recommendations concerning evidence-based programs and practices to judges, the Administrative Office of Pennsylvania Courts and other appropriate entities and post related information on the commission's publicly accessible Internet website.

(May 17, 2012, P.L.261, No.42, eff. 60 days)

2012 Amendment. Act 42 amended par. (4).

§ 6374. Power to make grants.

The commission shall have the power, and its duty shall be to make annual grants to political subdivisions for the development and improvement of probation services for juveniles.

2007, Dec. 4, P.L. 427, No. 64, § 1, imd. effective.

§ 6375. Funding.

The General Assembly shall annually appropriate such sums as it deems to be necessary for the operation and expenses of the commission.

2007, Dec. 4, P.L. 427, No. 64, § 1, imd. effective.

CHAPTER 74

COLLABORATIVE LAW PROCESS

Sec.
7401. Short title and scope of chapter.
7402. Definitions.
7403 Beginning the collaborative law process.
7404. Assessment and review.
7405. Collaborative law participation agreement.
7406. Concluding the collaborative law process.
7407. Disqualification of collaborative attorney.
7408. Disclosure of information.
7409. Confidentiality.
7410. Privilege.
7411. Professional responsibility.

Enactment. Chapter 74 was added June 28, 2018, P.L.381, No.55, effective in 60 days.

Applicability. See section 1 of Act 55 of 2018 in the appendix to this title for special provisions relating to findings and declarations.

§ 7401. Short title and scope of chapter.

(a) Short title.—This chapter shall be known and may be cited as the Collaborative Law Act.

(b) Scope.—This chapter shall apply to a collaborative law process between family members and arising from a participation agreement that meets the requirements of section 7405 (relating to collaborative law participation agreement).

§ 7402. Definitions.

The following words and phrases when used in this chapter shall have the meanings given to them in this section unless the context clearly indicates otherwise:

"Collaborative communication." A statement or question that concerns the collaborative law process or a collaborative matter and that occurs after the parties sign a collaborative law participation agreement but before the collaborative law process is concluded. The term does not include a written settlement agreement that is signed by all parties to the agreement.

"Collaborative law process." A procedure to resolve a claim, transaction, dispute or issue without intervention by a tribunal, in which procedure all parties sign a collaborative law participation agreement, all parties are represented by counsel and counsel is disqualified from representing the parties in a proceeding before a tribunal.

"Collaborative matter." A dispute, transaction, claim or issue for resolution that is described in a participation agreement concerning any of the following:

   (1) Marriage, divorce and annulment.
   (2) Property distribution, usage and ownership.
   (3) Child custody, visitation and parenting time.
   (4) Parentage.
   (5) Alimony, alimony pendente lite, spousal support and child support.
   (6) Prenuptial, marital and postnuptial agreements.
   (7) Adoption.
   (8) Termination of parental rights.
   (9) A matter arising under 20 Pa.C.S. (relating to decedents, estates and fiduciaries).

(10) A matter arising under 15 Pa.C.S. Pt. II (relating to corporations).

"Family members." All of the following:

(1) Spouses and former spouses.

(2) Parents and children, including individuals acting in loco parentis.

(3) Individuals currently or formerly cohabiting.

(4) Other individuals related by consanguinity or affinity.

"Nonparty participant." A person other than a party or a party's attorney that participates in the collaborative law process. The term may include, but is not limited to, support persons, mental health professionals, financial neutrals and potential parties.

"Party." A person that signs a collaborative law participation agreement and whose consent is necessary to resolve a collaborative matter.

"Person." An individual, corporation, business trust, estate, trust, partnership, limited liability company, association, joint venture, public corporation, government or governmental subdivision, agency or instrumentality or any other legal or commercial entity.

"Proceeding." A judicial, administrative, arbitral or other adjudicative process before a tribunal.

"Related matter." A matter involving the same parties, dispute, transaction, claim or issue as a collaborative matter.

"Tribunal." A court, arbitrator, administrative agency or other body acting in an adjudicative capacity that has jurisdiction to render a binding decision directly affecting a party's interests in a matter.

§ 7403. Beginning the collaborative law process.

(a) Voluntariness.—Participation in a collaborative law process is voluntary and may not be compelled by a tribunal. A party may terminate the collaborative law process at any time with or without cause.

(b) Commencement.—A collaborative law process shall begin when the parties sign a collaborative law participation agreement. Parties to a proceeding pending before a tribunal may enter into a collaborative law process to resolve a matter related to the proceeding.

§ 7404. Assessment and review.

(a) General assessment.—Before entering into a collaborative law participation agreement, a prospective party shall:

(1) Assess factors the prospective party's attorney reasonably believes relate to whether the collaborative law process is appropriate for the matter and for the parties, including a prospective party or nonparty participant's history, if any, of violent or threatening behavior.

(2) Review information that the attorney reasonably believes is sufficient for the prospective party to make an informed decision about the material benefits and risks of a collaborative law process, as compared with other alternatives.

(b) Threatening or violent behavior.—

(1) Before a prospective party signs a collaborative law participation agreement, an attorney shall inquire whether the prospective party has a history of threatening or violent behavior toward any party or nonparty participant who will be part of the collaborative law process.

(2) If an attorney learns or reasonably believes, before commencing or at any point in the collaborative law process, that a party or prospective party has engaged in or has a history of threatening or violent behavior toward any other party or

nonparty participant, the attorney may not begin or continue the collaborative law process unless the party or prospective party:

    (i) Requests beginning or continuing the collaborative law process.

    (ii) Indicates that the safety of all parties to the collaborative law process can be protected adequately during the collaborative law process.

(c) Private cause of action.—An attorney's failure to protect a party under this section shall not give rise to a private cause of action against the attorney.

§ 7405. Collaborative law participation agreement.

(a) Requirements.—A collaborative law participation agreement must:

(1) Be in writing.

(2) Be signed by the parties.

(3) State the parties' intention to resolve a collaborative matter through a collaborative law process.

(4) Describe the nature and scope of the collaborative matter.

(5) Identify the attorney who represents each party in the collaborative law process.

(6) Include a statement that the representation of each attorney is limited to the collaborative law process and that the attorneys are disqualified from representing any party or nonparty participant in a proceeding related to a collaborative matter, consistent with this chapter.

(b) Optional provisions.—Parties may include in a collaborative law participation agreement additional provisions not inconsistent with this chapter or other applicable law, including, but not limited to:

(1) An agreement concerning confidentiality of collaborative communications.

(2) An agreement that part or all of the collaborative law process will not be privileged in a proceeding.

(3) The scope of voluntary disclosure.

(4) The role of nonparty participants.

(5) The retention and role of nonparty experts.

(6) The manner and duration of a collaborative law process under sections 7403 (relating to beginning the collaborative law process) and 7406 (relating to concluding the collaborative law process).

(c) Nonconforming agreements.—This chapter shall apply to an agreement that does not meet the requirements of subsection (a) if:

(1) The agreement indicates an intent to enter into a collaborative law participation agreement.

(2) The agreement is signed by all parties.

(3) A tribunal determines that the parties intended to and reasonably believed that they were entering into a collaborative law agreement subject to the requirements of this chapter.

§ 7406. Concluding the collaborative law process.

(a) General rule.—A collaborative law process shall be concluded by:

(1) Resolution of the collaborative matter, as evidenced by a signed record.

(2) Resolution of a part of the collaborative matter and agreement by all parties that the remaining parts of the collaborative matter will not be resolved in the collaborative law process, as evidenced by a signed record.

(3) Termination under subsection (b).

(4) A method specified in the collaborative law participation agreement.

(b) Termination.—A collaborative law process shall be terminated when:

(1) A party gives written notice to all parties that the collaborative law process is terminated.

(2) A party begins or resumes a pending proceeding before a tribunal related to a collaborative matter without the agreement of all parties.

(3) Except as provided in subsection (c), a party discharges the party's attorney or the attorney withdraws from further representation of a party. An attorney who is discharged or withdraws shall give prompt written notice to all parties and nonparty participants.

(c) Continuation.—Notwithstanding the discharge or withdrawal of a collaborative attorney, a collaborative law process shall continue if, not later than 30 days after the date that the notice under subsection (b)(3) is sent, the unrepresented party engages a successor attorney and the participation agreement is amended to identify the successor attorney.

§ 7407. Disqualification of collaborative attorney.

(a) Rule.—

(1) Except as provided in subsection (b), an attorney who represents a party in a collaborative law process and any law firm or government agency with which the attorney is associated shall be disqualified from representing any party or nonparty participant in a proceeding related to the collaborative matter.

(2) Requesting the approval of a settlement agreement by a tribunal shall be considered part of the collaborative law process and not a related proceeding.

(b) Exception.—Disqualification under subsection (a) shall not operate to prevent a collaborative attorney from seeking or defending an emergency order to protect the health, safety or welfare of a party or a family member.

§ 7408. Disclosure of information.

During the collaborative law process, parties shall provide timely, full, candid and informal disclosure of information related to the collaborative matter without formal discovery, and shall update promptly previously disclosed information that has materially changed.

§ 7409. Confidentiality.

A collaborative law communication shall be confidential to the extent provided by the laws of this Commonwealth or as specified in the collaborative law participation agreement.

§ 7410. Privilege.

(a) General rule.—Except as otherwise provided in this section, a collaborative communication is privileged, may not be compelled through discovery and shall not be admissible as evidence in an action or proceeding. Evidence that is otherwise admissible and subject to discovery shall not become inadmissible or protected from discovery solely because of its disclosure or use in a collaborative law process.

(b) Waiver.—

(1) A party may waive a privilege belonging to the party only if all parties waive the privilege and, in the case of a communication by a nonparty participant, only if the nonparty participant and all parties waive the privilege.

(2) If a party discloses a privileged collaborative communication that prejudices another party, the disclosing party waives the right to assert a privilege under this section to the extent necessary for the party prejudiced to respond to the disclosure or representation.

(c) Nonapplicability.—Privilege under subsection (a) shall not apply to:

(1) A communication that is not subject to the privilege by agreement of the parties according to the terms of a participation agreement.

(2) A communication that is made during a session of a collaborative law process that is open, or required by law to be open, to the public.

(3) A communication sought, obtained or used to:

(i) threaten or plan to inflict bodily injury, commit or attempt to commit a crime; or

(ii) conceal ongoing criminal activity.

(d) Exceptions.—The following exceptions apply to the privilege under subsection (a):

(1) A communication sought or offered to prove or disprove facts relating to a claim or complaint of professional misconduct or malpractice or a fee dispute.

(2) A communication sought or offered to prove facts relating to the abuse, neglect, abandonment or exploitation of a child or abuse of an adult.

(3) A communication sought or offered in a criminal proceeding or in an action to enforce, void, set aside or modify a settlement agreement where a tribunal or court of competent jurisdiction finds that the evidence is not otherwise available and the need for the evidence substantially outweighs the interest in protecting the privilege.

(e) Limitation.—

(1) If a collaborative communication is subject to an exception under subsection (d), only the part of the collaborative communication necessary for the application of the exception may be disclosed or admitted.

(2) Disclosure or admission of evidence under subsection (d) does not make the evidence or any other collaborative communication discoverable or admissible for any other purpose.

(f) Construction.—This section shall not be construed to affect the scope of another applicable privilege under State law or rule of court.

§ 7411. Professional responsibility.

This chapter shall not affect the professional responsibility obligations and standards applicable to an attorney or other person professionally licensed or certified under State law.

(June 28, 2018, P.L. 381, No. 55, effective in 60 days).

TITLE 43
LABOR

CHAPTER 14
UNEMPLOYMENT COMPENSATION

ARTICLE VII
PROTECTION OF RIGHTS AND COMPENSATION

§ 863.1. Child support intercept of unemployment compensation.

Notwithstanding any other provisions of this or any other act:

(a) An individual filing a new claim for unemployment compensation shall, at the time of filing such claim, be required to disclose whether he owes child support obligations as defined in subsection (h).

(b) Information that the individual has been determined to be eligible for unemployment compensation shall be provided to state or local child support enforcement agencies enforcing such obligation.

(c) The Department of Labor and Industry shall deduct and withhold from any unemployment compensation payable to an individual that owes child support obligations as defined under subsection (h):

(1) the amount specified by the individual to be deducted and withheld under this subsection if neither paragraph (2) nor (3) is applicable;

(2) the amount (if any) determined pursuant to an agreement submitted to the department under section 454(20)(B)(i) of the Social Security Act by the State or local child support enforcement agency, unless paragraph (3) is applicable; or

(3) any amount otherwise required to be so deducted and withheld from such unemployment compensation pursuant to legal process (as defined in section 462(e) of the Social Security Act).

(d) Any amount deducted and withheld under subsection (c) shall be paid to the appropriate State or local child support enforcement agency.

(e) Any amount deducted and withheld under subsection (c) shall for all purposes be treated as if it were paid to the individual as unemployment compensation and paid by such individual to the State or local child support enforcement agency in satisfaction of the individual's child support obligations.

(f) For purposes of subsections (a) through (e), the term "unemployment compensation" means any compensation payable under the State law (including amounts payable pursuant to an agreement under any federal law providing for compensation, assistance, or allowances with respect to unemployment).

(g) Deductions will be made pursuant to this section only if appropriate arrangements have been made for reimbursement by the State or local child support enforcement agency for the administrative costs incurred by the department under this section which are attributable to child support obligations being enforced by the State or local child support enforcement agency.

(h) The term "child support obligations" is defined for purposes of these provisions as including only obligations which are being enforced pursuant to a plan described in section 454 of the Social Security Act which has been approved by the Secretary of Health and Human Services under Part D of Title IV of the Social Security Act.

(i) The term "State or local child support enforcement agency" as used in these provisions means any agency of a State or political subdivision thereof operating pursuant to a plan described in subsection (h).

1936, Second Ex.Sess., Dec. 5, P.L.(1937) 2897, art. VII, § 703.1, added 1981, Oct. 22, P.L. 301, No. 106, § 5, effective Oct. 1, 1982.

TITLE 51
MILITARY AFFAIRS

PART II
PENNSYLVANIA NATIONAL GUARD, PENNSYLVANIA GUARD AND MILITIA

SUBCHAPTER D
RIGHTS AND IMMUNITIES

§ 4109. Child custody proceedings during military deployment.

   (a) **Restriction on change of custody.**—If a petition for change of custody of a child of an eligible servicemember is filed with any court in this Commonwealth while the eligible servicemember is deployed in support of a contingency operation, no court may enter an order modifying or amending any previous judgment or order, or issue a new order, that changes the custody arrangement for that child that existed as of the date of the deployment of the eligible servicemember, except that a court may enter a temporary custody order if it is in the best interest of the child.

   (a.1) **Temporary assignment to family members.**—If an eligible servicemember has received notice of deployment in support of a contingency operation, a court may issue a temporary order to an eligible servicemember who has rights to a child under 23 Pa.C.S. § 5323 (relating to award of custody) or former 23 Pa.C.S. Ch. 53 Subch. A (relating to general provisions), including a temporary order to temporarily assign custody rights to family members of the servicemember. In the case of temporary assignment of rights to family members of the servicemember, the following shall apply:

   (1) The servicemember may petition the court for a temporary order to temporarily assign custody rights to family members of the servicemember. The servicemember shall be joined in the petition by the family members to whom the servicemember is seeking to assign temporary custody rights. The petition shall include a proposed revised custody schedule for care of the child by the family members. The proposed revised custody schedule may not include custody rights which exceed the rights granted to a servicemember set forth in the order in effect at the time of the filing of the petition to grant temporary custody rights to family members.

   (2) The court may issue a temporary order with a revised custody schedule as proposed by the servicemember and the family members or another revised custody schedule as the court deems appropriate, if the court finds that a temporary assignment of custody rights to family members of the servicemember is in the best interest of the child. In no case shall a temporary order granting custody rights to the family members of a servicemember exceed the custody rights granted to the servicemember set forth in the order in effect at the time of the filing of the petition to assign temporary custody rights to family members.

   In the case of any other temporary order issued under this subsection, the court may issue a temporary order if it is in the best interest of the child.

   (b) **Completion of deployment.**—In any temporary custody order entered under subsection (a) or (a.1), a court shall require that, upon the return of the eligible servicemember from deployment in support of a contingency operation, the custody order that was in effect immediately preceding the date of the deployment of the eligible servicemember is reinstated.

   (c) **Exclusion of military service from determination of child's best interest.**—If a petition for the change of custody of the child of an eligible servicemember who was deployed in support of a contingency operation is filed after the end of the deployment, no court may consider the absence of the eligible servicemember by reason of that deployment in determining the best interest of the child.

(d) **Failure to appear due to military deployment.**—The failure of an eligible servicemember to appear in court due to deployment in support of a contingency operation shall not, in and of itself, be sufficient to justify a modification of a custody order if the reason for the failure to appear is the eligible servicemember's active duty in support of a contingency operation.

(e) **Relationship to other laws.**—Notwithstanding any other provision of law, the provisions of this section shall be applied with regard to child custody issues related to eligible servicemembers deployed in support of contingency operations.

(f) **Definitions.**—As used in this section, the following words and phrases shall have the meanings given to them in this subsection:

"**Contingency operation.**" A military operation that:

(1) is designated by the Secretary of Defense as an operation in which members of the armed forces are or may become involved in military actions, operations or hostilities against an enemy of the United States or against an opposing military force; or

(2) results in the call or order to, or retention on, active duty of members of the uniformed services under 10 U.S.C. § 688 (relating to retired members: authority to order to active duty; duties), 12301(a) (relating to reserve components generally), 12302 (relating to Ready Reserve), 12304 (relating to Selected Reserve and certain Individual Ready Reserve members; order to active duty other than during war or national emergency), 12305 (relating to authority of President to suspend certain laws relating to promotion, retirement, and separation) or 12406 (relating to National Guard in Federal service: call) or any other provision of 10 U.S.C. during a war or during a national emergency declared by the President or Congress.

"**Eligible servicemember.**" A member of the Pennsylvania National Guard or a member of an active or reserve component of the Armed Forces of the United States who is serving on active duty, other than active duty for training, for a period of 30 or more consecutive days, in support of a contingency operation.

"**Family members.**" As defined in 23 Pa.C.S. § 6303 (relating to definitions).

2008, Oct. 9, P.L. 1522, No. 127, § 2, effective in 60 days [Dec. 8, 2008]. Amended 2012, April 12, P.L. 241, No. 32, § 2, effective in 60 days [June 11, 2012].

Cross References. Section 4109 is referred to in section 4110 of this title; section 5338 of Title 23 (Domestic Relations).

§ 4110. Expedited or electronic hearing.

(a) **Expedited hearing.**—Upon motion of an eligible servicemember who has received notice of deployment in support of a contingency operation, the court shall, for good cause shown, hold an expedited hearing in custody matters instituted under section 4109 (relating to child custody proceedings during military deployment) when the military duties of the eligible servicemember have a material effect on the eligible servicemember's ability, or anticipated ability, to appear in person at a regularly scheduled hearing.

(b) **Electronic hearing.**—Upon motion of an eligible servicemember who has received notice of deployment in support of a contingency operation, the court shall, upon reasonable advance notice and for good cause shown, allow the eligible servicemember to present testimony and evidence by electronic means in custody matters instituted under section 4109 when the military duties of the eligible servicemember have a material effect on the eligible servicemember's ability to appear in person at a regularly scheduled hearing.

(c) **Definitions.**—As used in this section, the following words and phrases shall have the meanings given to them in this subsection unless the context clearly indicates otherwise:

"Contingency operation." As defined in section 4109 (relating to child custody proceedings during military deployment).

"Electronic means." Includes communication by telephone, video conference or the Internet.

"Eligible servicemember." As defined in section 4109 (relating to child custody proceedings during military deployment).

"Matter." As defined in 42 Pa.C.S. § 102 (relating to definitions).

(Apr. 12, 2012, P.L.241, No.32, eff. 60 days)

2012 Amendment. Act 32 added section 4110.

TITLE 54
NAMES

Chapter 7. Judicial Change of Name

§ 701. Court approval required for change of name.
§ 702. Change by order of court.
§ 703. Effect on children.
§ 704. Divorcing and divorced person may resume prior name.
§ 704.1. Surviving spouse may resume prior name.
§ 705. Penalty for violation of chapter.

§ 701. Court approval required for change of name.

 (a) General rule.—Except as set forth in subsection 13 (b), it shall be unlawful for any person to assume a name 14 different from the name by which such person is and has been known, unless such change in name is made pursuant to proceedings in court in accordance with subsection (a.1).

 (a.1) Procedure.—

 (1) An individual must file a petition in the court of common pleas of the county in which the individual resides. If a petitioner is married, the petitioner's spouse may join as a party petitioner, in which event, upon compliance with the provisions of this subsection, the spouse shall also be entitled to the benefits of this subsection.

 (2) The petition must set forth all of the following:

 (i) The intention to change the petitioner's name.

 (ii) The reason for the name change.

 (iii) The current residence of petitioner.

 (iv) Any residence of the petitioner for the five years prior to the date of the petition.

 (v) If the petitioner requests the court proceed under paragraph (3)(iii).

 (3) Upon filing of the petition, the court shall do all of the following:

 (i) Set a date for a hearing on the petition. The hearing shall be held not less than one month nor more than three months after the petition is filed.

 (ii) Except as provided in subparagraph (iii), by order, direct that notice be given of the filing of the petition and of the date set for the hearing on the petition and that the notice be treated as follows:

 (A) Published in two newspapers of general circulation in the county where the petitioner resides or a county contiguous to that county. One of the publications may be in the official paper for the publication of legal notices in the county.

 (B) Given to any nonpetitioning parent of a child whose name may be affected by the proceedings.

 (iii) If the court finds that the notice required in subparagraph (ii) would jeopardize the safety of the person seeking the name change or his or her child or ward, the notice required shall be waived by order of the court. Upon granting the request to waive any notice requirement, the court shall seal the file. In all cases filed under this paragraph, whether or not the name change petition is granted, there shall be no public access to any court record of the name change petition, proceeding or order, unless the name change is granted but the file is not sealed. The records shall only be opened by order of the court in which the petition was granted based upon a showing of good cause or at the applicant's request.

(4) At the hearing, the following apply:

(i) Any person having lawful objection to the change of name may appear and be heard.

(ii) The petitioner must present to the court all of the following:

(A) Proof of publication of the notice under paragraph (3)(ii), unless petitioner requested the court proceed under paragraph (3)(iii) and the court granted the request.

(B) An official search of the proper offices of the county where petitioner resides and of any other county where petitioner has resided within five years prior to filing the petition showing that there are no judgments, decrees of record or other similar matters against the petitioner. This clause may be satisfied by a certificate given by a corporation authorized by law to make the search under this clause.

(5) The court may enter a decree changing the name as petitioned if the court is satisfied after the hearing that there is no lawful objection to the granting of the petition.

(b) Informal change of name.—Notwithstanding subsection (a), a person may at any time adopt and use any name if such name is used consistently, nonfraudulently and exclusively. The adoption of such name shall not, however, be in contravention of the prohibitions contained in section 702(c) (relating to change by order of court).

2004 Amendment. Act 214 amended subsec. (a).

§ 702. Change by order of court.

(a) General rule.—The court of common pleas of any county may by order change the name of any person resident in the county.

(b) Procedure.—Prior to entry of an order of approval of change of name, all of the following shall apply:

(1) The court must forward to the Pennsylvania State Police a duplicate copy of the application for change of name and a set of the person's fingerprints. The person applying for the change of name is responsible for costs under this paragraph.

(2) The Pennsylvania State Police shall use the fingerprints to determine if the person is subject to 18 Pa.C.S. Ch. 91 (relating to criminal history record information).

(3) The Pennsylvania State Police shall:

(i) if the person is subject to 18 Pa.C.S. Ch. 91, note the name change on the person's criminal history record information; or

(ii) if the person is not subject to 18 Pa.C.S. Ch. 91, destroy the fingerprints.

(4) Within 60 days of receipt of the material under paragraph (1), the Pennsylvania State Police shall certify to the court what action has been taken under paragraph (3).

(5) The procedure in this subsection shall not apply to proceedings involving:

(i) An election to resume a prior surname pursuant to section 704 (relating to divorced person may resume prior name).

(ii) Name changes involving minor children in adoption proceedings [pursuant to 23 Pa.C.S. § 2904 (relating to name of adoptee)].

(iii) A name change involving a minor child whose name is being changed pursuant to section 703 (relating to effect on children) or because of the change of name of the child's parent.

(c) Convicted felons.—

(1) The court may order a change of name for a person convicted of a felony, subject to provisions of paragraph (2), if:

(i) at least two calendar years have elapsed from the date of completion of a person's sentence and that person is not subject to the probation or parole jurisdiction of any court, county probation agency or the Pennsylvania Board of Probation and Parole; or

(ii) the person has been pardoned.

(2) The court may not order a change of name for a person convicted of murder, voluntary manslaughter, rape, involuntary deviate sexual intercourse, statutory sexual assault, sexual assault, aggravated indecent assault, robbery as defined in 18 Pa.C.S. § 3701(a)(1)(i) (relating to robbery), aggravated assault as defined in 18 Pa.C.S. § 2702(a)(1) or (2) (relating to aggravated assault), arson as defined in 18 Pa.C.S. § 3301(a) (relating to arson and related offenses), kidnapping or robbery of a motor vehicle or criminal attempt, criminal conspiracy or criminal solicitation to commit any of the offenses listed above or an equivalent crime under the laws of this Commonwealth in effect at the time of the commission of that offense or an equivalent crime in another jurisdiction.

(3) The court shall notify the Office of Attorney General, the Pennsylvania State Police and the office of the distict attorney of the county in which the person resides when a change of name for a person convicted of a felony has been ordered. The Pennsylvania State Police, upon receipt of this notice, shall include the change of name information in the central repository as provided for in 18 Pa.C.S. Ch. 91 (relating to criminal history record information).

2004 Amendment. Act 214 amended subsec. (b).

§ 703. Effect on children.

(a) General rule.—Whenever an order is made under this chapter changing the surname of anyone who is at the time thereof the parent of a minor child or adopted minor child, then under the care of such parent, the new surname of such parent shall, unless otherwise ordered by the court, thereafter be borne likewise by such minor child.

(b) Further change on attaining majority.—Any minor child whose surname has been changed pursuant to subsection (a) upon attaining majority shall also be entitled to the benefits of section 702 (relating to change by order of court).

1982, Dec. 16, P.L. 1309, No. 295, § 2, effective in 90 days.

§ 704. Divorcing and divorced person may resume prior name.

(a) General rule.—Any person who is a party in a divorce action may, at any time prior to or subsequent to the entry of the divorce decree, resume any prior surname used by him or her by filing a written notice to such effect in the office of the prothonotary of the county in which the divorce action was filed or the decree of divorce was entered, showing the caption and docket number of the proceeding in divorce.

(b) Foreign decrees.—Where a divorced person has been the subject of a decree of divorce granted in a foreign jurisdiction, a certified copy of such foreign divorce decree may be filed with the prothonotary of the county where the person resides and, thereafter, the notice specified in subsection (a) may be filed with reference to such decree.

2005 Amendment. Act 18 amended subsec. (a) and (b).

2000 Amendment. Act 92 amended subsec. (a).

Cross References. Section 704 is referred to in section 702 of this title.

§ 704.1. Surviving spouse may resume prior name.

A surviving spouse may, at any time, resume any prior surname used by him or her by filing a written notice to such effect in the office of the prothonotary of the county where the surviving spouse resides, accompanied by a certificate of death for the decedent. In counties where there is no prothonotary, the notice shall be filed in the office that performs the functions of the offices of prothonotary as provided for in the act of August 9, 1955 (P.L.323, No.130), known as The County Code.

§ 705. Penalty for violation of chapter.

Any person violating the provisions of this chapter for purpose of avoiding payment of taxes or other debts commits a summary offense.

1982, Dec. 16, P.L. 1309, No. 295, § 2, effective in 90 days.

U.S.C.

MISCELLANEOUS FEDERAL DOMESTIC RELATIONS STATUTES AND REGULATIONS—SELECTED PROVISIONS

(Amended Through April, 2019)

Title 10.
Armed Forces

Chapter 71. Computation of Retired Pay

§ 1408. Payment of retired or retainer pay in compliance with court orders.

Chapter 73. Annuities Based on Retired or Retainer Pay

§ 1447. Definitions.
§ 1448. Application of Plan.
§ 1448a. Election to discontinue participation: one-year opportunity after second anniversary of commencement of payment of retired pay.
§ 1450. Payment of annuity: beneficiaries.
§ 1451. Amount of annuity.
§ 1452. Reduction in retired pay.
§ 1453. Recovery of amounts erroneously paid.
§ 1454. Correction of administrative errors.

Title 11.
Bankruptcy Code

§ 11 U.S.C. § 101.   Definitions.
§ 11 U.S.C. § 362.   Automatic stay.
§ 11 U.S.C. § 507.   Priorities.
§ 11 U.S.C. § 522.   Exemptions.
§ 11 U.S.C. § 523.   Exceptions to discharge.
§ 11 U.S.C. § 541.   Property of the estate.
§ 11 U.S.C. § 547.   Preferences.
§ 11 U.S.C. § 704.   Duties of trustee.
§ 11 U.S.C. § 1129. Confirmation of plan.

Title 18.
Crimes and Criminal Procedure

PART I. CRIMES

Chapter 11A. Child Support

§ 228. Failure to pay legal child support obligations.

Chapter 55. Kidnapping

§ 1204. International parental kidnapping.

Chapter 110A. Domestic Violence and Stalking

§ 2261.   Interstate domestic violence.
§ 2261A. Stalking.
§ 2262.   Interstate violation of protection order.
§ 2263.   Pretrial release of defendant.
§ 2264.   Restitution.
§ 2265.   Full faith and credit given to protection orders.
§ 2265A. Repeat offenders.
§ 2266.   Definitions.

FEDERAL STATUTES U.S.C.

Title 22.
Foreign Relations and Intercourse

Chapter 4. Passports

§ 213. Application for passport; verification by oath of initial passport.
22 C.F.R. § 51.28 Minors.

Chapter 97. International Child Abduction Remedies

§ 9001. Findings and declarations.
§ 9002. Definitions.
§ 9003. Judicial remedies.
§ 9004. Provisional remedies.
§ 9005. Admissibility of documents.
§ 9006. United States Central Authority.
§ 9007. Costs and fees.
§ 9008. Collection, maintenance, and dissemination of information.
§ 9009. Office of Children's Issues.
§ 9010. Interagency coordinating group.
§ 9011. Authorization of appropriations.

Chapter 98. International Child Abduction Prevention and Return

§ 9101. Definitions.

Subchapter I. Department of State Actions

§ 9111. Annual Report.
§ 9112. Standards and assistance.
§ 9113. Bilateral procedures, including memoranda of understanding.
§ 9114. Report to congressional representatives.

Subchapter II. Actions By the Secretary of State

§ 9121. Response to international child abductions.
§ 9122. Actions by the Secretary of State in response to patterns of noncompliance in cases of international child abductions.
§ 9123. Consultations with foreign governments.
§ 9124. Waiver by the Secretary of State.
§ 9125. Termination of actions by the Secretary of State.

Subchapter III. Prevention of International Child Abduction

§ 9141. Authorization for judicial training on international parental child abduction.

Title 26.
Internal Revenue Code

Subtitle A.
Income Taxes

Chapter 1. Normal Taxes and Surtaxes
Subchapter B. Computation of Taxable Income

PART II. ITEMS SPECIFICALLY INCLUDED IN GROSS INCOME

§ 71. Alimony and separate maintenance payments.

| U.S.C. | PROCEDURE |

26 C.F.R. §1.71-1 Alimony and separate maintenance payments; income to wife or former wife.
26 C.F.R. §1.71-1T Alimony and separate maintenance payments (temporary).
§ 151. Allowance of deductions for personal exemptions.
§ 152. Dependent defined.
26 C.F.R. § 1.152-4 Special rule for a child of divorced or separated parents or parents who live apart.
§ 215. Alimony, etc., payments.
26 C.F.R. § 1.215-1 Periodic alimony, etc., payments.
26 C.F.R. § 1.215-1T Alimony, etc., payments (temporary).
§ 1041. Transfers of property between spouses or incident to divorce.
26 C.F.R. § 1.1041-1T Treatment of transfer of property between spouses or incident to divorce (temporary).
§ 6013. Joint returns of income tax by husband and wife.

26 C.F.R.
§ 1.6015–0. Table of contents.
§ 1.6015–1. Relief from joint and several liability on a joint return.
§ 1.6015–2. Relief from liability applicable to all qualifying joint filers.
§ 1.6015–3. Allocation of deficiency for individuals who are no longer married, are legally separated, or are not members of the same household.
§ 1.6015–4. Equitable relief.
§ 1.6015–5. Time and manner for requesting relief.
§ 1.6015–6. Nonrequesting spouse's notice and opportunity to participate in administrative proceedings.
§ 1.6015–7. Tax Court review.
§ 1.6015–8. Applicable liabilities.
§ 1.6015–9. Effective date.

Title 28.
Judiciary and Judicial Procedure

PART V. PROCEDURE

Chapter 115. Evidence; Documentary
§ 1738A. Full faith and credit given to child custody determinations.
§ 1738B. Full faith and credit for child support orders.
§ 1738C. Certain acts, records, and proceedings and the effect thereof.

Title 42.
The Public Health and Welfare

Chapter 7. Social Security

Subchapter IV. Grants to States for Aid and Services to Needy Families with Children and for Child-Welfare Services

PART D. CHILD SUPPORT AND ESTABLISHMENT OF PATERNITY

§ 651. Authorization of appropriations.
§ 652. Duties of Secretary.

§ 653.	Federal Parent Locator Service.
§ 654.	State plan for child and spousal support.
§ 655.	Payments to States.
§ 656.	Support obligation as obligation to State; amount; discharge in bankruptcy.
§ 657.	Distribution of collected support.
§ 659.	Consent by the United States to income withholding, garnishment, and similar proceedings for enforcement of child support and alimony obligations.
§ 659a.	International support enforcement.
§ 660.	Civil action to enforce child support obligations; jurisdiction of district courts.
§ 663.	Use of Federal Parent Locator Service in connection with enforcement or determination of child custody in cases of parental kidnapping of child.
§ 664.	Collection of past-due support from Federal tax refunds.
§ 665.	Allotments from pay for child and spousal support owed by members of uniformed services on active duty.
§ 666.	Requirement of statutorily prescribed procedures to improve effectiveness of child support enforcement.
§ 667.	State guidelines for child support awards.
§ 668.	Encouragement of States to adopt simple civil process for voluntarily acknowledging paternity and a civil procedure for establishing paternity in contested cases.
§ 669.	Collection and reporting of child support enforcement data.

Chapter 121. International Child Abduction Remedies Act

11601.	Findings and declarations.
11602.	Definitions.
11603.	Judicial remedies.
11604.	Provisional remedies.
11605.	Admissibility of documents.
11606.	United States Central Authority.
11607.	Costs and fees.
11608.	Collection, maintenance, and dissemination of information.
11608a.	Office of children's issues.
11609.	Interagency coordinating group.
11610.	Authorization of appropriations.
11611.	Report on compliance with the Hague Convention on International Child Abduction.

The Hague Convention on the Civil Aspects
of International Child Abduction

TITLE 10

ARMED FORCES

CHAPTER 71

COMPUTATION OF RETIRED PAY

§ 1408. **Payment of retired or retainer pay in compliance with court orders.**

(a) **Definitions.**—In this section:

(A) any court of competent jurisdiction of any State, the District of Columbia, the Commonwealth of Puerto Rico, Guam, American Samoa, the Virgin Islands, the Northern Mariana Islands, and the Trust Territory of the Pacific Islands;

(B) any court of the United States (as defined in section 451 of title 28) having competent jurisdiction;

(C) any court of competent jurisdiction of a foreign country with which the United States has an agreement requiring the United States to honor any court order of such country; and

(D) any administrative or judicial tribunal of a State competent to enter orders for support or maintenance (including a State agency administering a program under a State plan approved under part D of title IV of the Social Security Act), and, for purposes of this subparagraph, the term "State" includes the District of Columbia, the Commonwealth of Puerto Rico, the Virgin Islands, Guam, and American Samoa.

(2) The term "court order" means a final decree of divorce, dissolution, annulment, or legal separation issued by a court, or a court ordered, ratified, or approved property settlement incident to such a decree (including a final decree modifying the terms of a previously issued decree of divorce, dissolution, annulment, or legal separation, or a court ordered, ratified, or approved property settlement incident to such previously issued decree), or a support order, as defined in section 453(p) of the Social Security Act (42 U.S.C. 653(p)), which—

(A) is issued in accordance with the laws of the jurisdiction of that court;

(B) provides for—

(i) payment of child support (as defined in section 459(i)(2) of the Social Security Act (42 U.S.C. 659(i)(2)));

(ii) payment of alimony (as defined in section 459(i)(3) of the Social Security Act (42 U.S.C. 659(i)(3))); or

(iii) division of property (including a division of community property); and

(C) in the case of a division of property, specifically provides for the payment of an amount, expressed in dollars or as a percentage of disposable retired pay, from the disposable retired pay of a member to the spouse or former spouse of that member.

(3) The term "final decree" means a decree from which no appeal may be taken or from which no appeal has been taken within the time allowed for taking such appeals under the laws applicable to such appeals, or a decree from which timely appeal has been taken and such appeal has been finally decided under the laws applicable to such appeals.

(4) (A) The term "disposable retired pay" means the total monthly retired pay to which a member is entitled less amounts which—

(i) are owed by that member to the United States for previous overpayments of retired pay and for recoupments required by law resulting from entitlement to retired pay;

(ii) are deducted from the retired pay of such member as a result of forfeitures of retired pay ordered by a court-martial or as a result of a waiver of retired pay required by law in order to receive compensation under title 5 or title 38;

(iii) in the case of a member entitled to retired pay under chapter 61 of this title, are equal to the amount of retired pay of the member under that chapter computed using the percentage of the member's disability on the date when the member was retired (or the date on which the member's name was placed on the temporary disability retired list); or

(iv) are deducted because of an election under chapter 73 of this title to provide an annuity to a spouse or former spouse to whom payment of a portion of such member's retired pay is being made pursuant to a court order under this section.

(B) For purposes of subparagraph (A), in the case of a division of property as part of a final decree of divorce, dissolution, annulment, or legal separation that becomes final prior to the date of a member's retirement, the total monthly retired pay to which the member is entitled shall be—

(i) in the case of a member not described in clause (ii), the amount of retired pay to which the member would have been entitled using the member's retired pay base and years of service on the date of the decree of divorce, dissolution, annulment, or legal separation, as computed under section 1406 or 1407 of this title, whichever is applicable, increased by the sum of the cost-of-living adjustments that—

(I) would have occurred under section 1401a(b) of this title between the date of the decree of divorce, dissolution, annulment, or legal separation and the time of the member's retirement using the adjustment provisions under section 1401a of this title applicable to the member upon retirement; and

(II) occur under 1401a of this title after the member's retirement; or

(ii) in the case of a member who becomes entitled to retired pay pursuant to chapter 1223 of this title, the amount of retired pay to which the member would have been entitled using the member's retired pay base and creditable service points on the date of the decree of divorce, dissolution, annulment, or legal separation, as computer under chapter 1223 of this title, increased by the sum of the cost-of-living adjustments as described in clause (i) that apply with respect to the member.

(5) The term "member" includes a former member entitled to retired pay under section 12731 of this title.

(6) The term "spouse or former spouse" means the husband or wife, or former husband or wife, respectively, of a member who, on or before the date of a court order, was married to that member.

(7) The term "retired pay" includes retainer pay.

(b) Effective Service of Process.—For the purposes of this section—

(1) service of a court order is effective if—

(A) an appropriate agent of the Secretary concerned designated for receipt of service of court orders under regulations prescribed pursuant to subsection (i) or, if no agent has been so designated, the Secretary concerned, is personally served or is served by facsimile or electronic transmission or by mail;

(B) the court order is regular on its face;

(C) the court order or other documents served with the court order identify the member concerned and include, if possible, the social security number of such member; and

(D) the court order or other documents served with the court order certify that the rights of the member under the Servicemembers Civil Relief Act (50 U.S.C. 3901 et seq.) were observed; and

(2) a court order is regular on its face if the order—

(A) is issued by a court of competent jurisdiction;

(B) is legal in form; and

(C) includes nothing on its face that provides reasonable notice that it is issued without authority of law.

(c) Authority for court to treat retired pay as property of the member and spouse.—

(1) Subject to the limitations of this section, a court may treat disposable retired pay payable to a member for pay periods beginning after June 25, 1981, either as property solely of the member or as property of the member and his spouse in accordance with the law of the jurisdiction of such court. A court may not treat retired pay as property in any proceeding to divide or partition any amount of retired pay of a member as the property of the member and the member's spouse or former spouse if a final decree of divorce, dissolution, annulment, or legal separation (including a court ordered, ratified, or approved property settlement incident to such decree) affecting the member and the member's spouse or former spouse (A) was issued before June 25, 1981, and (B) did not treat (or reserve jurisdiction to treat) any amount of retired pay of the member as property of the member and the member's spouse or former spouse.

(2) Notwithstanding any other provision of law, this section does not create any right, title, or interest which can be sold, assigned, transferred, or otherwise disposed of (including by inheritance) by a spouse or former spouse. Payments by the Secretary concerned under subsection (d) to a spouse or former spouse with respect to a division of retired pay as the property of a member and the member's spouse under this subsection may not be treated as amounts received as retired pay for service in the uniformed services.

(3) This section does not authorize any court to order a member to apply for retirement or retire at a particular time in order to effectuate any payment under this section.

(4) A court may not treat the disposable retired pay of a member in the manner described in paragraph (1) unless the court has jurisdiction over the member by reason of (A) his residence, other than because of military assignment, in the territorial jurisdiction of the court, (B) his domicile in the territorial jurisdiction of the court, or (C) his consent to the jurisdiction of the court.

(d) Payments by Secretary concerned to (or for benefit of) spouse or former spouse.—

(1) After effective service on the Secretary concerned of a court order providing for the payment of child support or alimony or, with respect to a division of property, specifically providing for the payment of an amount of the disposable retired pay from a member to the spouse or a former spouse of the member, the Secretary shall make payments (subject to the limitations of this section) from the disposable retired pay of the member to the spouse or former spouse (or for the benefit of such spouse or former spouse to a State disbursement unit established pursuant to section 454B of the Social Security Act or other public payee designated by a State, in accordance with part D of title IV of the Social Security Act, as directed by court order, or as otherwise directed in accordance with such part D) in an amount sufficient to satisfy the amount of child support and alimony set forth in the court order and, with respect to a division of property, in the amount of disposable retired pay specifically provided for in the court order. In the case of a spouse or former spouse who, pursuant to section 408(a)(3) of the Social Security Act (42 U.S.C. 608(a)(4)),[2] assigns to a State the rights of the spouse or former spouse to receive support, the Secretary concerned may make the child support payments referred to in the preceding sentence to that State in amounts consistent with that assignment of rights. In the case of a member entitled to receive retired pay on the date of the effective service of the court order, such payments shall begin not later than 90 days after the date of effective service. In the case of a member not entitled to receive retired pay on the date of the effective service of the court order, such payments shall begin not later than 90 days after the date on which the member first becomes entitled to receive retired pay.

(2) If the spouse or former spouse to whom payments are to be made under this section was not married to the member for a period of 10 years or more during which the member performed at least 10 years of service creditable in determining the member's eligibility for retired pay, payments may not be made under this section to the extent that they include an amount resulting from the treatment by the court under subsection (c) of disposable retired pay of the member as property of the member or property of the member and his spouse.

(3) Payments under this section shall not be made more frequently than once each month, and the Secretary concerned shall not be required to vary normal pay and disbursement cycles for retired pay in order to comply with a court order.

(4) Payments from the disposable retired pay of a member pursuant to this section shall terminate in accordance with the terms of the applicable court order, but not later than the date of the death of the member or the date of the death of the spouse or former spouse to whom payments are being made, whichever occurs first.

(5) If a court order described in paragraph (1) provides for a division of property (including a division of community property) in addition to an amount of child support or alimony or the payment of an amount of disposable retired pay as the result of the court's treatment of such pay under subsection (c) as property of the member and his spouse, the Secretary concerned shall pay (subject to the limitations of this section) from the disposable retired pay of the member to the spouse or former spouse of the member, any part of the amount payable to the spouse or former spouse under the division of property upon effective service of a final court order of garnishment of such amount from such retired pay.

(6) In the case of a court order for which effective service is made on the Secretary concerned on or after August 22, 1996, and which provides for payments from the disposable retired pay of a member to satisfy the amount of child support set forth in the order, the authority provided in paragraph (1) to make payments from the disposable retired pay of a member to satisfy the amount of child support set forth in a court order shall apply to payment of any amount of child support arrearages set forth in that order as well as to amounts of child support that currently become due.

(7) (A) The Secretary concerned may not accept service of a court order that is an out-of-State modification, or comply with the provisions of such a court order, unless the court issuing that order has jurisdiction in the manner specified in subsection (c)(4) over both the member and the spouse or former spouse involved.

(B) A court order shall be considered to be an out-of-State modification for purposes of this paragraph if the order—

(i) modifies a previous court order under this section upon which payments under this subsection are based; and

(ii) is issued by a court of a State other than the State of the court that issued the previous court order.

(8) A division of property award computed as a percentage of a member's disposable retired pay shall be increased by the same percentage as any cost-of-living adjustment made under section 1401a after the member's retirement.

(e) Limitations.—

(1) The total amount of the disposable retired pay of a member payable under all court orders pursuant to subsection (c) may not exceed 50 percent of such disposable retired pay.

(2) In the event of effective service of more than one court order which provide for payment to a spouse and one or more former spouses or to more than one former spouse, the disposable retired pay of the member shall be used to satisfy (subject to the limitations of paragraph (1)) such court orders on a first-come, first-served basis. Such court orders shall be satisfied (subject to the limitations of paragraph

(1)) out of that amount of disposable retired pay which remains after the satisfaction of all court orders which have been previously served.

(3) (A) In the event of effective service of conflicting court orders under this section which assert to direct that different amounts be paid during a month to the same spouse or former spouse of the same member, the Secretary concerned shall—

(i) pay to that spouse from the member's disposable retired pay the least amount directed to be paid during that month by any such conflicting court order, but not more than the amount of disposable retired pay which remains available for payment of such court orders based on when such court orders were effectively served and the limitations of paragraph (1) and subparagraph (B) of paragraph (4);

(ii) retain an amount of disposable retired pay that is equal to the lesser of—

(I) the difference between the largest amount required by any conflicting court order to be paid to the spouse or former spouse and the amount payable to the spouse or former spouse under clause (i); and

(II) the amount of disposable retired pay which remains available for payment of any conflicting court order based on when such court order was effectively served and the limitations of paragraph (1) and subparagraph (B) of paragraph (4); and

(iii) pay to that member the amount which is equal to the amount of that member's disposable retired pay (less any amount paid during such month pursuant to legal process served under section 459 of the Social Security Act (42 U.S.C. 659) and any amount paid during such month pursuant to court orders effectively served under this section, other than such conflicting court orders) minus—

(I) the amount of disposable retired pay paid under clause (i); and

(II) the amount of disposable retired pay retained under clause (ii).

(B) The Secretary concerned shall hold the amount retained under clause (ii) of subparagraph (A) until such time as that Secretary is provided with a court order which has been certified by the member and the spouse or former spouse to be valid and applicable to the retained amount. Upon being provided with such an order, the Secretary shall pay the retained amount in accordance with the order.

(4) (A) In the event of effective service of a court order under this section and the service of legal process pursuant to section 459 of the Social Security Act (42 U.S.C. 659), both of which provide for payments during a month from the same member, satisfaction of such court orders and legal process from the retired pay of the member shall be on a first-come, first-served basis. Such court orders and legal process shall be satisfied out of moneys which are subject to such orders and legal process and which remain available in accordance with the limitations of paragraph (1) and subparagraph (B) of this paragraph during such month after the satisfaction of all court orders or legal process which have been previously served.

(B) Notwithstanding any other provision of law, the total amount of the disposable retired pay of a member payable by the Secretary concerned under all court orders pursuant to this section and all legal processes pursuant to section 459 of the Social Security Act (42 U.S.C. 659) with respect to a member may not exceed 65 percent of the amount of the retired pay payable to such member that is considered under section 462 of the Social Security Act (42 U.S.C. 662) to be remuneration for employment that is payable by the United States.

(5) A court order which itself or because of previously served court orders provides for the payment of an amount which exceeds the amount of disposable retired pay available for payment because of the limit set forth in paragraph (1), or which, because of previously served court orders or legal process previously served under section 459 of the Social Security Act (42 U.S.C. 659), provides for payment of an amount that exceeds the maximum amount permitted under paragraph (1) or sub-

paragraph (B) of paragraph (4), shall not be considered to be irregular on its face solely for that reason. However, such order shall be considered to be fully satisfied for purposes of this section by the payment to the spouse or former spouse of the maximum amount of disposable retired pay permitted under paragraph (1) and subparagraph (B) of paragraph (4).

(6) Nothing in this section shall be construed to relieve a member of liability for the payment of alimony, child support, or other payments required by a court order on the grounds that payments made out of disposable retired pay under this section have been made in the maximum amount permitted under paragraph (1) or subparagraph (B) of paragraph (4). Any such unsatisfied obligation of a member may be enforced by any means available under law other than the means provided under this section in any case in which the maximum amount permitted under paragraph (1) has been paid and under section 459 of the Social Security Act (42 U.S.C. 659) in any case in which the maximum amount permitted under subparagraph (B) of paragraph (4) has been paid.

(f) Immunity of officers and employees of United States.—

(1) The United States and any officer or employee of the United States shall not be liable with respect to any payment made from retired pay to any member, spouse, or former spouse pursuant to a court order that is regular on its face if such payment is made in accordance with this section and the regulations prescribed pursuant to subsection (i).

(2) An officer or employee of the United States who, under regulations prescribed pursuant to subsection (i), has the duty to respond to interrogatories shall not be subject under any law to any disciplinary action or civil or criminal liability or penalty for, or because of, any disclosure of information made by him in carrying out any of his duties which directly or indirectly pertain to answering such interrogatories.

(g) Notice to member of service of court order on Secretary concerned.—

A person receiving effective service of a court order under this section shall, as soon as possible, but not later than 30 days after the date on which effective service is made, send a written notice of such court order (together with a copy of such order) to the member affected by the court order at his last known address.

(h) Benefits for dependents who are victims of abuse by members losing right to retired pay.—

(1) (A) If, in the case of a member or former member of the armed forces referred to in paragraph (2)(A), a court order provides (in the manner applicable to a division of property) for the payment of an amount from the disposable retired pay of that member or former member (as certified under paragraph (4)) to an eligible spouse or former spouse of that member or former member, the Secretary concerned, beginning upon effective service of such court order, shall pay that amount in accordance with this subsection to such spouse or former spouse.

(B) If, in the case of a member or former member of the armed forces referred to in paragraph (2)(A), a court order provides for the payment as child support of an amount from the disposable retired pay of that member or former member (as certified under paragraph (4)) to an eligible dependent child of the member or former member, the Secretary concerned, beginning upon effective service of such court order, shall pay that amount in accordance with this subsection to such dependent child.

(2) A spouse or former spouse, or a dependent child, of a member or former member of the armed forces is eligible to receive payment under this subsection if—

(A) the member or former member, while a member of the armed forces and after becoming eligible to be retired from the armed forces on the basis of years of service, has eligibility to receive retired pay terminated as a result of misconduct while a member involving abuse of a spouse or dependent child (as defined in regulations prescribed by the Secretary of Defense or, for the Coast Guard when it is not operating as a service in the Navy, by the Secretary of Homeland Security);

(B) in the case of eligibility of a spouse or former spouse under paragraph (1)(A), the spouse or former spouse—

(i) was the victim of the abuse and was married to the member or former member at the time of that abuse; or

(ii) is a natural or adopted parent of a dependent child of the member or former member who was the victim of the abuse; and

(C) in the case of eligibility of a dependent child under paragraph (1)(B), the other parent of the child died as a result of the misconduct that resulted in the termination of retired pay.

(3) The amount certified by the Secretary concerned under paragraph (4) with respect to a member or former member of the armed forces referred to in paragraph (2)(A) shall be deemed to be the disposable retired pay of that member or former member for the purposes of this subsection.

(4) Upon the request of a court or an eligible spouse or former spouse, or an eligible dependent child, of a member or former member of the armed forces referred to in paragraph (2)(A) in connection with a civil action for the issuance of a court order in the case of that member or former member, the Secretary concerned shall determine and certify the amount of the monthly retired pay that the member or former member would have been entitled to receive as of the date of the certification—

(A) if the member or former member's eligibility for retired pay had not been terminated as described in paragraph (2)(A); and

(B) if, in the case of a member or former member not in receipt of retired pay immediately before that termination of eligibility for retired pay, the member or former member had retired on the effective date of that termination of eligibility.

(5) A court order under this subsection may provide that whenever retired pay is increased under section 1401a of this title (or any other provision of law), the amount payable under the court order to the spouse or former spouse, or the dependent child, of a member or former member described in paragraph (2)(A) shall be increased at the same time by the percent by which the retired pay of the member or former member would have been increased if the member or former member were receiving retired pay.

(6) Notwithstanding any other provision of law, a member or former member of the armed forces referred to in paragraph (2)(A) shall have no ownership interest in, or claim against, any amount payable under this section to a spouse or former spouse, or to a dependent child, of the member or former member.

(7) (A) If a former spouse receiving payments under this subsection with respect to a member or former member referred to in paragraph (2)(A) marries again after such payments begin, the eligibility of the former spouse to receive further payments under this subsection shall terminate on the date of such marriage.

(B) A person's eligibility to receive payments under this subsection that is terminated under subparagraph (A) by reason of remarriage shall be resumed in the event of the termination of that marriage by the death of that person's spouse or by annulment or divorce. The resumption of payments shall begin as of the first day of the month in which that marriage is so terminated. The monthly amount of the payments shall be the amount that would have been paid if the continuity of the payments had not been interrupted by the marriage.

(8) Payments in accordance with this subsection shall be made out of funds in the Department of Defense Military Retirement Fund established by section 1461 of this title or, in the case of the Coast Guard, out of funds appropriated to the Department of Homeland Security for payment of retired pay for the Coast Guard.

(9) (A) A spouse or former spouse of a member or former member of the armed forces referred to in paragraph (2)(A), while receiving payments in accordance with this subsection, shall be entitled to receive medical and dental care, to use commissary and exchange stores, and to receive any other benefit that a spouse or a former spouse of a retired member of the armed forces is entitled to receive on the basis of being a spouse or former spouse, as the case may be, of a retired member of the armed forces in the same manner as if the member or former member referred to in paragraph (2)(A) was entitled to retired pay.

(B) A dependent child of a member or former member referred to in paragraph (2)(A) who was a member of the household of the member or former member at the time of the misconduct described in paragraph (2)(A) shall be entitled to receive medical and dental care, to use commissary and exchange stores, and to have other benefits provided to dependents of retired members of the armed forces in the same manner as if the member or former member referred to in paragraph (2)(A) was entitled to retired pay.

(C) If a spouse or former spouse or a dependent child eligible or entitled to receive a particular benefit under this paragraph is eligible or entitled to receive that benefit under another provision of law, the eligibility or entitlement of that spouse or former spouse or dependent child to such benefit shall be determined under such other provision of law instead of this paragraph.

(10) (A) For purposes of this subsection, in the case of a member of the armed forces who has been sentenced by a court-martial to receive a punishment that will terminate the eligibility of that member to receive retired pay if executed, the eligibility of that member to receive retired pay may, as determined by the Secretary concerned, be considered terminated effective upon entry of judgment under section 860c of this title (article 60c of the Uniform Code of Military Justice).

(B) If each form of the punishment that would result in the termination of eligibility to receive retired pay is later remitted, set aside, or mitigated to a punishment that does not result in the termination of that eligibility, a payment of benefits to the eligible recipient under this subsection that is based on the punishment so vacated, set aside, or mitigated shall cease. The cessation of payments shall be effective as of the first day of the first month following the month in which the Secretary concerned notifies the recipient of such benefits in writing that payment of the benefits will cease. The recipient may not be required to repay the benefits received before that effective date (except to the extent necessary to recoup any amount that was erroneous when paid).

(11) In this subsection, the term "dependent child", with respect to a member or former member of the armed forces referred to in paragraph (2)(A), means an unmarried legitimate child, including an adopted child or a stepchild of the member or former member, who—

(A) is under 18 years of age;

(B) is incapable of self-support because of a mental or physical incapacity that existed before becoming 18 years of age and is dependent on the member or former member for over one-half of the child's support; or

(C) if enrolled in a full-time course of study in an institution of higher education recognized by the Secretary of Defense for the purposes of this subparagraph, is under 23 years of age and is dependent on the member or former member for over one-half of the child's support.

(i) Certification date.—It is not necessary that the date of a certification of the authenticity or completeness of a copy of a court order for child support received by the Secretary concerned for the purposes of this section be recent in relation to the date of receipt by the Secretary.

(j) **Regulations.**—The Secretaries concerned shall prescribe uniform regulations for the administration of this section.

(k) **Relationship to other laws.**—In any case involving an order providing for payment of child support (as defined in section 459(i)(2) of the Social Security Act) by a member who has never been married to the other parent of the child, the provisions of this section shall not apply, and the case shall be subject to the provisions of section 459 of such Act.

(l) **Garnishment to satisfy a judgment rendered for physically, sexually, or emotionally abusing a child.**—

(1) Subject to paragraph (2), any payment of retired pay that would otherwise be made to a member shall be paid (in whole or in part) by the Secretary concerned to another person if and to the extent expressly provided for in the terms of a child abuse garnishment order.

(2) A court order providing for the payment of child support or alimony or, with respect to a division of property, specifically providing for the payment of an amount of the disposable retired pay from a member to the spouse or a former spouse of the member, shall be given priority over a child abuse garnishment order. The total amount of the disposable retired pay of a member payable under a child abuse garnishment order shall not exceed 25 percent of the member's disposable retired pay.

(3) In this subsection, the term "court order" includes a child abuse garnishment order.

(4) In this subsection, the term "child abuse garnishment order" means a final decree issued by a court that—

(A) is issued in accordance with the laws of the jurisdiction of that court; and

(B) provides in the nature of garnishment for the enforcement of a judgment rendered against the member for physically, sexually, or emotionally abusing a child.

(5) for purposes of this subsection, a judgment rendered for physically, sexually, or emotionally abusing a child is any legal claim perfected through a final enforceable judgment, which claim is based in whole or in part upon the physical, sexual, or emotional abuse of an individual under 18 years of age, whether or not that abuse is accompanied by other actionable wrongdoing, such as sexual exploitation or gross negligence.

(6) if the Secretary concerned is served with more than one court order with respect to the retired pay of a member, the disposable retired pay of the member shall be available to satisfy such court orders on a first-come, first-served basis, subject to the order of precedence specified in paragraph (2), with any such process being satisfied out of such monies as remain after the satisfaction of all such processes which have been previously served.

(7) the Secretary concerned shall not be required to vary normal pay and disbursement cycles for retired pay in order to comply with a child abuse garnishment order.

(Added Pub. L. 97–252, title X, § 1002(a), Sept. 8, 1982, 96 Stat. 730; amended Pub. L. 98–525, title VI, § 643(a)–(d), Oct. 19, 1984, 98 Stat. 2547; Pub. L. 99–661, div. A, title VI, § 644(a), Nov. 14, 1986, 100 Stat. 3887; Pub. L. 100–26, §§ 3(3), 7(h)(1), Apr. 21, 1987, 101 Stat. 273, 282; Pub. L. 101–189, div. A, title VI, § 653(a)(5), title XVI, § 1622(e)(6), Nov. 29, 1989, 103 Stat. 1462, 1605; Pub. L. 101–510, div. A, title V, § 555(a)–(d), (f), (g), Nov. 5, 1990, 104 Stat. 1569, 1570; Pub. L. 102–190, div. A, title X, § 1061(a)(7), Dec. 5, 1991, 105 Stat. 1472; Pub. L. 102–484, div. A, title VI, § 653(a), Oct. 23, 1992, 106 Stat. 2426; Pub. L. 103–160, div. A, title V, § 555(a), (b), title XI, § 1182(a)(2), Nov. 30, 1993, 107 Stat. 1666, 1771; Pub. L. 104–106, div. A, title XV, § 1501(c)(16), Feb. 10, 1996, 110 Stat. 499; Pub. L. 104–193, title III, §§ 362(c),

363(c)(1)–(3), Aug. 22, 1996, 110 Stat. 2246, 2249; Pub. L. 104–201, div. A, title VI, § 636, Sept. 23, 1996, 110 Stat. 2579; Pub. L. 105–85, div. A, title X, § 1073(a)(24), (25), Nov. 18, 1997, 111 Stat. 1901; Pub. L. 107–107, div. A, title X, § 1048(c)(9), Dec. 28, 2001, 115 Stat. 1226; Pub. L. 107–296, title XVII, § 1704(b)(1), Nov. 25, 2002, 116 Stat. 2314; Pub. L. 108–189, § 2(c), Dec. 19, 2003, 117 Stat. 2866; Pub. L. 109–163, div. A, title VI, § 665(a), Jan. 6, 2006, 119 Stat. 3317; Pub. L. 111–84, div. A, title X, § 1073(a)(15), Oct. 28, 2009, 123 Stat. 2473; Pub. L. 114–328, div. A, title VI, § 641(a), title X, § 1081(b)(2)(B), Dec. 23, 2016, 130 Stat. 2164, 2418; Pub. L. 115–91, div. A, title V, §§ 531(m), 534(a), title VI, § 624(a), Dec. 12, 2017, 131 Stat. 1386, 1390, 1429.)

CHAPTER 73
ANNUITIES BASED ON RETIRED OR RETAINER PAY

§ 1447. Definitions.

In this subchapter:

(1) **Plan.**— The term "Plan" means the Survivor Benefit Plan established by this subchapter.

(2) **Standard annuity.**— The term "standard annuity" means an annuity provided by virtue of eligibility under section 1448(a)(1)(A) of this title.

(3) **Reserve-component annuity.**— The term "reserve-component annuity" means an annuity provided by virtue of eligibility under section 1448(a)(1)(B) of this title.

(4) **Retired pay.**— The term "retired pay" includes retainer pay paid under section 8330 of this title.

(5) **Reserve-component retired pay.**— The term "reserve-component retired pay" means retired pay under chapter 1223 of this title (or under chapter 67 of this title as in effect before the effective date of the Reserve Officer Personnel Management Act).

(6) **Base amount.**—The term "base amount" means the following:

(A) **Full amount under standard annuity.**—In the case of a person who dies after becoming entitled to retired pay, such term means the amount of monthly retired pay (determined without regard to any reduction under section 1409(b)(2) or 1415(b)(1)(B) of this title) to which the person—

(i) was entitled when he became eligible for that pay; or

(ii) later became entitled by being advanced on the retired list, performing active duty, or being transferred from the temporary disability retired list to the permanent disability retired list.

(B) **Full amount under -component annuity.**—In the case of a person who would have become eligible for reserve-component retired pay but for the fact that he died before becoming 60 years of age, such term means the amount of monthly retired pay for which the person would have been eligible—

(i) if he had been 60 years of age on the date of his death, for purposes of an annuity to become effective on the day after his death in accordance with a designation made under section 1448(e) of this title; or

(ii) upon becoming 60 years of age (if he had lived to that age), for purposes of an annuity to become effective on the 60th anniversary of his birth in accordance with a designation made under section 1448(e) of this title.

(C) **Reduced amount.**—Such term means any amount less than the amount otherwise applicable under subparagraph (A) or (B) with respect to an annuity provided under the Plan but which is not less than $300 and which is designated by the person (with the concurrence of the person's spouse, if required under section 1448(a)(3) of this title) providing the annuity on or before—

(i) the first day for which he becomes eligible for retired pay, in the case of a person providing a standard annuity, or

(ii) the end of the 90-day period beginning on the date on which he receives the notification required by section 12731(d) of this title that he has completed the years of service required for eligibility for reserve-component retired pay, in the case of a person providing a reserve-component annuity.

(7) **Widow.**—The term "widow" means the surviving wife of a person who, if not married to the person at the time he became eligible for retired pay—

(A) was married to him for at least one year immediately before his death; or

(B) is the mother of issue by that marriage.

(8) **Widower.**—The term "widower" means the surviving husband of a person who, if not married to the person at the time she became eligible for retired pay—

(A) was married to her for at least one year immediately before her death; or

(B) is the father of issue by that marriage.

(9) **Surviving spouse.**— The term "surviving spouse" means a widow or widower.

(10) **Former spouse.**— The term "former spouse" means the surviving former husband or wife of a person who is eligible to participate in the Plan.

(11) **Dependent child.**—

(A) **In general.**—The term "dependent child" means a person who—

(i) is unmarried;

(ii) is (I) under 18 years of age, (II) at least 18, but under 22, years of age and pursuing a full-time course of study or training in a high school, trade school, technical or vocational institute, junior college, college, university, or comparable recognized educational institution, or (III) incapable of self-support because of a mental or physical incapacity existing before the person's eighteenth birthday or incurred on or after that birthday, but before the person's twenty-second birthday, while pursuing such a full-time course of study or training; and

(iii) is the child of a person to whom the Plan applies, including (I) an adopted child, and (II) a stepchild, foster child, or recognized natural child who lived with that person in a regular parent-child relationship.

(B) **Special rules for college students.**— For the purpose of subparagraph (A), a child whose twenty-second birthday occurs before July 1 or after August 31 of a calendar year, and while regularly pursuing such a course of study or training, is considered to have become 22 years of age on the first day of July after that birthday. A child who is a student is considered not to have ceased to be a student during an interim between school years if the interim is not more than 150 days and if the child shows to the satisfaction of the Secretary of Defense that the child has a bona fide intention of continuing to pursue a course of study or training in the same or a different school during the school semester (or other period into which the school year is divided) immediately after the interim.

(C) **Foster children.**— A foster child, to qualify under this paragraph as the dependent child of a person to whom the Plan applies, must, at the time of the death of that person, also reside with, and receive over one-half of his support from, that person, and not be cared for under a social agency contract. The temporary absence of a foster child from the residence of that person, while a student as described in this paragraph, shall not be considered to affect the residence of such a foster child.

(12) **Court.**—The term "court" has the meaning given that term by section 1408(a)(1) of this title.

(13) **Court order.**—

(A) **In general.**—The term "court order" means a court's final decree of divorce, dissolution, or annulment or a court ordered, ratified, or approved property settlement incident to such a decree (including a final decree modifying the terms of a previously issued decree of divorce, dissolution, annulment, or legal separation, or of a court ordered, ratified, or approved property settlement agreement incident to such previously issued decree).

(B) **Final decree.**—The term "final decree" means a decree from which no appeal may be taken or from which no appeal has been taken within the time allowed for the taking of such appeals under the laws applicable to such appeals, or a decree from which timely appeal has been taken and such appeal has been finally decided under the laws applicable to such appeals.

(C) **Regular on its face.**— The term "regular on its face", when used in connection with a court order, means a court order that meets the conditions prescribed in section 1408(b)(2) of this title.

(Added Pub. L. 92–425, § 1(3), Sept. 21, 1972, 86 Stat. 706; amended Pub. L. 94–496, § 1(1), Oct. 14, 1976, 90 Stat. 2375; Pub. L. 95–397, title II, § 201, Sept. 30, 1978, 92 Stat. 843; Pub. L. 96–402, § 2, Oct. 9, 1980, 94 Stat. 1705; Pub. L. 97–252, title X, § 1003(a), Sept. 8, 1982, 96 Stat. 735; Pub. L. 98–94, title IX, § 941(c)(1), Sept. 24, 1983, 97 Stat. 653; Pub. L. 99–145, title VII, §§ 719(1), (2), 721(b), Nov. 8, 1985, 99 Stat. 675, 676; Pub. L. 99–348, title III, § 301(a)(1), July 1, 1986, 100 Stat. 702; Pub. L. 99–661, div. A, title XIII, § 1343(a)(8)(A), Nov. 14, 1986, 100 Stat. 3992; Pub. L. 100–180, div. A, title XII, § 1231(17), Dec. 4, 1987, 101 Stat. 1161; Pub. L. 101–189, div. A, title XIV, § 1407(a)(1)–(3), Nov. 29, 1989, 103 Stat. 1588; Pub. L. 101–510, div. A, title XIV, § 1484(l)(4)(C)(i), Nov. 5, 1990, 104 Stat. 1720; Pub. L. 103–337, div. A, title XVI, § 1671(d), Oct. 5, 1994, 108 Stat. 3014; Pub. L. 104–201, div. A, title VI, § 634, Sept. 23, 1996, 110 Stat. 2551; Pub. L. 115–91, div. A, title VI, § 622(a), Dec. 12, 2017, 131 Stat. 1428; Pub. L. 115–232, div. A, title VIII, § 809(a), Aug. 13, 2018, 132 Stat. 1840.)

§ 1448. **Application of Plan.**

(a) **General rules for participation in the Plan.**—

(1) **Name of Plan; eligible participants.**—The program established by this subchapter shall be known as the Survivor Benefit Plan. The following persons are eligible to participate in the Plan:

(A) Persons entitled to retired pay.

(B) Persons who would be eligible for reserve-component retired pay but for the fact that they are under 60 years of age.

(2) **Participants in the Plan.**—The Plan applies to the following persons, who shall be participants in the Plan:

(A) **Standard annuity participants.**—A person who is eligible to participate in the Plan under paragraph (1)(A) and who is married or has a dependent child when he becomes entitled to retired pay, unless he elects (with his spouse's concurrence, if required under paragraph (3)) not to participate in the Plan before the first day for which he is eligible for that pay.

(B) **Reserve-component annuity participants.**—A person who (i) is eligible to participate in the Plan under paragraph (1)(B), and (ii) is married or has a dependent child when he is notified under section 12731(d) of this title that he has completed the years of service required for eligibility for reserve-component retired pay, unless the person elects (with his spouse's concurrence, if required under paragraph (3)) not to participate in the Plan before the end of the 90-day period beginning on the date on which he receives that notification.

A person who elects under subparagraph (B) not to participate in the Plan remains eligible, upon reaching 60 years of age and otherwise becoming entitled to retired pay, to participate in the Plan in accordance with eligibility under paragraph (1)(A).

(3) **Elections.**—

(A) **Spousal consent for certain elections respecting standard annuity.**—A married person who is eligible to provide a standard annuity may not without the concurrence of the person's spouse elect—

(i) not to participate in the Plan;

(ii) to provide an annuity for the person's spouse at less than the maximum level; or

(iii) to provide an annuity for a dependent child but not for the person's spouse.

(B) **Spousal consent for certain elections respecting reserve-component annuity.**—A married person who is eligible to provide a reserve-component annuity may not without the concurrence of the person's spouse elect—

(i) not to participate in the Plan;

(ii) to designate under subsection (e)(2) the effective date for commencement of annuity payments under the Plan in the event that the member dies before becoming 60 years of age to be the 60th anniversary of the member's birth (rather than the day after the date of the member's death);

(iii) to provide an annuity for the person's spouse at less than the maximum level; or

(iv) to provide an annuity for a dependent child but not for the person's spouse.

(C) **Exception when spouse unavailable.**—A person may make an election described in subparagraph (A) or (B) without the concurrence of the person's spouse if the person establishes to the satisfaction of the Secretary concerned—

(i) that the spouse's whereabouts cannot be determined; or

(ii) that, due to exceptional circumstances, requiring the person to seek the spouse's consent would otherwise be inappropriate.

(D) **Construction with former spouse election provisions.**—This paragraph does not affect any right or obligation to elect to provide an annuity for a former spouse (or for a former spouse and dependent child) under subsection (b)(2).

(E) **Notice to spouse of election to provide former spouse annuity.**—If a married person who is eligible to provide a standard annuity elects to provide an annuity for a former spouse (or for a former spouse and dependent child) under subsection (b)(2), that person's spouse shall be notified of that election.

(4) **Irrevocability of elections.—**

(A) **Standard annuity.**—An election under paragraph (2)(A) is irrevocable if not revoked before the date on which the person first becomes entitled to retired pay.

(B) **Reserve-component annuity.**—An election under paragraph (2)(B) is irrevocable if not revoked before the end of the 90-day period referred to in that paragraph.

(5) **Participation by person marrying after retirement, etc.—**

(A) **Election to participate in Plan.**—A person who is not married and has no dependent child upon becoming eligible to participate in the Plan but who later marries or acquires a dependent child may elect to participate in the Plan.

(B) **Manner and time of election.**—Such an election must be written, signed by the person making the election, and received by the Secretary concerned within one year after the date on which that person marries or acquires that dependent child.

(C) **Limitation on revocation of election.**—Such an election may not be revoked except in accordance with subsection (b)(3).

(D) **Effective date of election.**—The election is effective as of the first day of the first calendar month following the month in which the election is received by the Secretary concerned.

(E) **Designation if RCSBP election.**—In the case of a person providing a reserve-component annuity, such an election shall include a designation under subsection (e).

(6) **Election out of Plan by person with spouse coverage who remarries.—**

(A) **General rule.—**A person—

(i) who is a participant in the Plan and is providing coverage under the Plan for a spouse (or a spouse and child);

(ii) who does not have an eligible spouse beneficiary under the Plan; and

(iii) who remarries,

may elect not to provide coverage under the Plan for the person's spouse.

(B) **Effect of election on retired pay.—**If such an election is made, reductions in the retired pay of that person under section 1452 of this title shall not be made.

(C) **Terms and conditions of election.—**An election under this paragraph—

(i) is irrevocable;

(ii) shall be made within one year after the person's remarriage; and

(iii) shall be made in such form and manner as may be prescribed in regulations under section 1455 of this title.

(D) **Notice to spouse.—**If a person makes an election under this paragraph—

(i) not to participate in the Plan;

(ii) to provide an annuity for the person's spouse at less than the maximum level; or

(iii) to provide an annuity for a dependent child but not for the person's spouse,

the person's spouse shall be notified of that election.

(E) **Construction with former spouse election provisions.—**This paragraph does not affect any right or obligation to elect to provide an annuity to a former spouse under subsection (b).

(b) **Insurable interest and former spouse coverage.—**

(1) **Coverage for person with insurable interest.—**

(A) **General rule.—**A person who is not married and does not have a dependent child upon becoming eligible to participate in the Plan may elect to provide an annuity under the Plan to a natural person with an insurable interest in that person. In the case of a person providing a reserve-component annuity, such an election shall include a designation under subsection (e).

(B) **Termination of coverage.—**An election under subparagraph (A) for a beneficiary who is not the former spouse of the person providing the annuity may be terminated. Any such termination shall be made by a participant by the submission to the Secretary concerned of a request to discontinue participation in the Plan, and such participation in the Plan shall be discontinued effective on the first day of the first month following the month in which the request is received by the Secretary concerned. Effective on such date, the Secretary concerned shall discontinue the reduction being made in such person's retired pay on account of participation in the Plan or, in the case of a person who has been required to make deposits in the Treasury on account of participation in the Plan, such person may discontinue making such deposits effective on such date.

(C) **Form for discontinuation.—**A request under subparagraph (B) to discontinue participation in the Plan shall be in such form and shall contain such information as may be required under regulations prescribed by the Secretary of Defense.

(D) **Withdrawal of request for discontinuation.**—The Secretary concerned shall furnish promptly to each person who submits a request under subparagraph (B) to discontinue participation in the Plan a written statement of the advantages and disadvantages of participating in the Plan and the possible disadvantages of discontinuing participation. A person may withdraw the request to discontinue participation if withdrawn within 30 days after having been submitted to the Secretary concerned.

(E) **Consequences of discontinuation.**—Once participation is discontinued, benefits may not be paid in conjunction with the earlier participation in the Plan and premiums paid may not be refunded. Participation in the Plan may not later be resumed except through a qualified election under paragraph (5) of subsection (a) or under subparagraph (G) of this paragraph.

(F) **Vitiation of election by disability retiree who dies of disability-related cause.**—If a member retired after November 23, 2003, under chapter 61 of this title dies within one year after the date on which the member is so retired and the cause of death is related to a disability for which the member was retired under that chapter (as determined under regulations prescribed by the Secretary of Defense)—

(i) an election made by the member under paragraph (1) to provide an annuity under the Plan to any person other than a dependent of that member (as defined in section 1072(2) of this title) is vitiated; and

(ii) the amounts by which the member's retired pay was reduced under section 1452 of this title shall be refunded and paid to the person to whom the annuity under the Plan would have been paid pursuant to such election.

(G) **Election of new beneficiary upon death of previous beneficiary.**—

(i) **Authority for election.**—If the reason for discontinuation in the Plan is the death of the beneficiary, the participant in the Plan may elect a new beneficiary. Any such beneficiary must be a natural person with an insurable interest in the participant. Such an election may be made only during the 180-day period beginning on the date of the death of the previous beneficiary.

(ii) **Procedures.**—Such an election shall be in writing, signed by the participant, and made in such form and manner as the Secretary concerned may prescribe. Such an election shall be effective the first day of the first month following the month in which the election is received by the Secretary.

(iii) **Vitiation of election by participant who dies within two years of election.**—If a person providing an annuity under a election under clause (i) dies before the end of the two-year period beginning on the effective date of the election—

(I) the election is vitiated; and

(II) the amount by which the person's retired pay was reduced under section 1452 of this title that is attributable to the election shall be paid in a lump sum to the person who would have been the deceased person's beneficiary under the vitiated election if the deceased person had died after the end of such two-year period.

(2) **Former spouse coverage upon becoming a participant in the Plan.**—

(A) **General rule.**—A person who has a former spouse upon becoming eligible to participate in the Plan may elect to provide an annuity to that former spouse.

(B) **Effect of former spouse election on spouse or dependent child.**—In the case of a person with a spouse or a dependent child, such an election prevents payment of an annuity to that spouse or child (other than a child who is a beneficiary under an election under paragraph (4)), including payment under subsection (d).

(C) **Designation if more than one former spouse.**—If there is more than one former spouse, the person shall designate which former spouse is to be provided the annuity.

(D) **Designation if RCSBP election.**—In the case of a person providing a reserve-component annuity, such an election shall include a designation under subsection (e).

(3) **Former spouse coverage by persons already participating in Plan.**—

(A) **Election of coverage.**—

(i) **Authority for election.**—A person—

(I) who is a participant in the Plan and is providing coverage for a spouse or a spouse and child (even though there is no beneficiary currently eligible for such coverage), and

(II) who has a former spouse who was not that person's former spouse when that person became eligible to participate in the Plan,

may (subject to subparagraph (B)) elect to provide an annuity to that former spouse.

(ii) **Termination of previous coverage.**—Any such election terminates any previous coverage under the Plan.

(iii) **Manner and time of election.**—Any such election must be written, signed by the person making the election, and received by the Secretary concerned within one year after the date of the decree of divorce, dissolution, or annulment.

(B) **Limitation on election.**—A person may not make an election under subparagraph (A) to provide an annuity to a former spouse who that person married after becoming eligible for retired pay unless—

(i) the person was married to that former spouse for at least one year, or

(ii) that former spouse is the parent of issue by that marriage.

(C) **Irrevocability, etc.**—An election under this paragraph may not be revoked except in accordance with section 1450(f) of this title. This paragraph does not provide the authority to change a designation previously made under subsection (e).

(D) **Notice to spouse.**—If a person who is married makes an election to provide an annuity to a former spouse under this paragraph, that person's spouse shall be notified of the election.

(E) **Effective date of election.**—An election under this paragraph is effective as of—

(i) the first day of the first month following the month in which the election is received by the Secretary concerned; or

(ii) in the case of a person required (as described in section 1450(f)(3)(B) of this title) to make the election by reason of a court order or filing the date of which is after October 16, 1998, the first day of the first month which begins after the date of that court order or filing.

(4) **Former spouse and child coverage.**—A person who elects to provide an annuity for a former spouse under paragraph (2) or (3) may, at the time of the election, elect to provide coverage under that annuity for both the former spouse and a dependent child, if the child resulted from the person's marriage to that former spouse.

(5) **Disclosure of whether election of former spouse coverage is required.**—A person who elects to provide an annuity to a former spouse under paragraph (2) or (3) shall, at the time of making the election, provide the Secretary

concerned with a written statement (in a form to be prescribed by that Secretary and signed by such person and the former spouse) setting forth—

(A) whether the election is being made pursuant to the requirements of a court order; or

(B) whether the election is being made pursuant to a written agreement previously entered into voluntarily by such person as a part of, or incident to, a proceeding of divorce, dissolution, or annulment and (if so) whether such voluntary written agreement has been incorporated in, or ratified or approved by, a court order.

(6) Special needs trusts for sole benefit of certain dependent children.— A person who has established a supplemental or special needs trust under subparagraph (A) or (C) of section 1917(d)(4) of the Social Security Act (42 U.S.C. 1396p(d)(4)) for the sole benefit of a dependent child considered disabled under section 1614(a)(3) of that Act (42 U.S.C. 1382c(a)(3)) who is incapable of self-support because of mental or physical incapacity may elect to provide an annuity to that supplemental or special needs trust.

(7) Effect of death of former spouse beneficiary.—

(A) **Termination of participation in Plan.—**A person who elects to provide an annuity to a former spouse under paragraph (2) or (3) and whose former spouse subsequently dies is no longer a participant in the Plan, effective on the date of death of the former spouse.

(B) **Authority for election of new spouse beneficiary.—**If a person's participation in the Plan is discontinued by reason of the death of a former spouse beneficiary, the person may elect to resume participation in the Plan and to elect a new spouse beneficiary as follows:

(i) **Married on the date of death of former spouse.—**A person who is married at the time of the death of the former spouse beneficiary may elect to provide coverage to that person's spouse. Such an election must be received by the Secretary concerned within one year after the date of death of the former spouse beneficiary.

(ii) **Marriage after death of former spouse beneficiary.—**A person who is not married at the time of the death of the former spouse beneficiary and who later marries may elect to provide spouse coverage. Such an election must be received by the Secretary concerned within one year after the date on which that person marries.

(C) **Effective date of election.—**The effective date of election under this paragraph shall be as follows:

(i) An election under subparagraph (B)(i) is effective as of the first day of the first calendar month following the death of the former spouse beneficiary.

(ii) An election under subparagraph (B)(ii) is effective as of the first day of the first calendar month following the month in which the election is received by the Secretary concerned.

(D) **Level of coverage.—**A person making an election under subparagraph (B) may not reduce the base amount previously elected.

(E) **Procedures.—**An election under this paragraph shall be in writing, signed by the participant, and made in such form and manner as the Secretary concerned may prescribe.

(F) **Irrevocability.—**An election under this paragraph is irrevocable.

(c) Persons on temporary disability retired list.—The application of the Plan to a person whose name is on the temporary disability retired list terminates when his name is removed from that list and he is no longer entitled to disability retired pay.

(d) Coverage for survivors of members who die on active duty.—

(1) Surviving spouse annuity.—Except as provided in paragraph (2)(B), the Secretary concerned shall pay an annuity under this subchapter to the surviving spouse of—

(A) a member who dies while on active duty after—

(i) becoming eligible to receive retired pay;

(ii) qualifying for retired pay except that the member has not applied for or been granted that pay; or

(iii) completing 20 years of active service but before the member is eligible to retire as a commissioned officer because the member has not completed 10 years of active commissioned service; or

(B) a member not described in subparagraph (A) who dies in line of duty while on active duty.

(2) Dependent children.—

(A) Annuity when no eligible surviving spouse.—In the case of a member described in paragraph (1), the Secretary concerned shall pay an annuity under this subchapter to the member's dependent children under subsection (a)(2) or (a)(4) of section 1450 of this title as applicable.

(B) Optional annuity when there is an eligible surviving spouse.—In the case of a member described in paragraph (1) who dies after October 7, 2001, and for whom there is a surviving spouse eligible for an annuity under paragraph (1), the Secretary may pay an annuity under this subchapter to the member's dependent children under subsection (a)(3) or (a)(4) of section 1450 of this title, if applicable, instead of paying an annuity to the surviving spouse under paragraph (1), if the Secretary concerned, in consultation with the surviving spouse, determines it appropriate to provide an annuity for the dependent children under this paragraph instead of an annuity for the surviving spouse under paragraph (1).

(3) Mandatory former spouse annuity.—If a member described in paragraph (1) is required under a court order or spousal agreement to provide an annuity to a former spouse upon becoming eligible to be a participant in the Plan or has made an election under subsection (b) to provide an annuity to a former spouse, the Secretary—

(A) may not pay an annuity under paragraph (1) or (2); but

(B) shall pay an annuity to that former spouse as if the member had been a participant in the Plan and had made an election under subsection (b) to provide an annuity to the former spouse, or in accordance with that election, as the case may be, if the Secretary receives a written request from the former spouse concerned that the election be deemed to have been made in the same manner as provided in section 1450(f)(3) of this title.

(4) Priority.—An annuity that may be provided under this subsection shall be provided in preference to an annuity that may be provided under any other provision of this subchapter on account of service of the same member.

(5) Computation.—The amount of an annuity under this subsection is computed under section 1451(c) of this title.

(6) Deemed election.—

(A) Annuity for dependent.—In the case of a member described in paragraph (1) who dies after November 23, 2003, the Secretary concerned may, if no other annuity is payable on behalf of the member under this subchapter, pay an annuity to a natural person who has an insurable interest in such member as if the annuity were elected by the member under subsection (b)(1). The Secretary concerned may pay such an annuity under this paragraph only in the case of a person who is a dependent of that member (as defined in section 1072(2) of this title).

(B) **Computation of annuity.**—An annuity under this subparagraph shall be computed under section 1451(b) of this title as if the member had retired for total disability on the date of death with reductions as specified under section 1452(c) of this title, as applicable to the ages of the member and the natural person with an insurable interest.

(e) **Designation for commencement of reserve-component annuity.**—In any case in which a person is required to make a designation under this subsection, the person shall designate whether, in the event he dies before becoming 60 years of age, the annuity provided shall become effective on—

(1) the day after the date of his death; or

(2) the 60th anniversary of his birth.

(f) **Coverage of survivors of persons dying when or before eligible to elect reserve-component annuity.**—

(1) **Surviving spouse annuity.**—The Secretary concerned shall pay an annuity under this subchapter to the surviving spouse of a person who—

(A) is eligible to provide a reserve-component annuity and dies—

(i) before being notified under section 12731(d) of this title that he has completed the years of service required for eligibility for reserve-component retired pay; or

(ii) during the 90-day period beginning on the date he receives notification under section 12731(d) of this title that he has completed the years of service required for eligibility for reserve-component retired pay if he had not made an election under subsection (a)(2)(B) to participate in the Plan; or

(B) is a member of a reserve component not described in subparagraph (A) and dies from an injury or illness incurred or aggravated in the line of duty during inactive-duty training.

(2) **Dependent children annuity.**—

(A) **Annuity when no eligible surviving spouse.**—In the case of a person described in paragraph (1), the Secretary concerned shall pay an annuity under this subchapter to the dependent children of that person under section 1450(a)(2) of this title as applicable.

(B) **Optional annuity when there is an eligible surviving spouse.**—The Secretary may pay an annuity under this subchapter to the dependent children of a person described in paragraph (1) under section 1450(a)(3) of this title, if applicable, instead of paying an annuity to the surviving spouse under paragraph (1), if the Secretary concerned, in consultation with the surviving spouse, determines it appropriate to provide an annuity for the dependent children under this paragraph instead of an annuity for the surviving spouse under paragraph (1).

(3) **Mandatory former spouse annuity.**—If a person described in paragraph (1) is required under a court order or spousal agreement to provide an annuity to a former spouse upon becoming eligible to be a participant in the Plan or has made an election under subsection (b) to provide an annuity to a former spouse, the Secretary—

(A) may not pay an annuity under paragraph (1) or (2); but

(B) shall pay an annuity to that former spouse as if the person had been a participant in the Plan and had made an election under subsection (b) to provide an annuity to the former spouse, or in accordance with that election, as the case may be, if the Secretary receives a written request from the former spouse concerned that the election be deemed to have been made in the same manner as provided in section 1450(f)(3) of this title.

(4) Computation.—The amount of an annuity under this subsection is computed under section 1451(c) of this title.

(5) Deemed election to provide an annuity for dependent.—Paragraph (6) of subsection (d) shall apply in the case of a member described in paragraph (1) who dies after November 23, 2003, when no other annuity is payable on behalf of the member under this subchapter.

(g) Election to increase coverage upon remarriage.—

   (1) Election.—A person—

   (A) who is a participant in the Plan and is providing coverage under subsection (a) for a spouse or a spouse and child, but at less than the maximum level; and

   (B) who remarries,

may elect, within one year of such remarriage, to increase the level of coverage provided under the Plan to a level not in excess of the current retired pay of that person.

   (2) Payment required.—Such an election shall be contingent on the person paying to the United States the amount determined under paragraph (3) plus interest on such amount at a rate determined under regulations prescribed by the Secretary of Defense.

   (3) Amount to be paid.—The amount referred to in paragraph (2) is the amount equal to the difference between—

   (A) the amount that would have been withheld from such person's retired pay under section 1452 of this title if the higher level of coverage had been in effect from the time the person became a participant in the Plan; and

   (B) the amount of such person's retired pay actually withheld.

   (4) Manner of making election.—An election under paragraph (1) shall be made in such manner as the Secretary shall prescribe and shall become effective upon receipt of the payment required by paragraph (2).

   (5) Disposition of payments.—A payment received under this subsection by the Secretary of Defense shall be deposited into the Department of Defense Military Retirement Fund. Any other payment received under this subsection shall be deposited in the Treasury as miscellaneous receipts.

(Added Pub.L. 92-425, § 1(3), Sept. 21, 1972, 86 Stat. 707; amended Pub.L. 94-496, § 1(2), Oct. 14, 1976, 90 Stat. 2375; Pub.L. 95-397, Title II, § 202, Sept. 30, 1978, 92 Stat. 844; Pub.L. 97-252, Title X, § 1003(b), Sept. 8, 1982, 96 Stat. 735; Pub.L. 97-295, § 1(18), Oct. 12, 1982, 96 Stat. 1290; Pub.L. 98-94, Title IX, § 941 (a)(1), (2), (c)(2), Sept. 24, 1983, 97 Stat. 652, 653; Pub.L. 99-145, Title V, § 513(b), Title VII, §§ 712(a), 713(a), 715, 716(a), 719(3), (8)(A), 721(a), Nov. 8, 1985, 99 Stat. 628, 670, 671, 673 to 676; Pub.L. 99-661, Div. A, Title VI, §§ 641(b)(1), 642(a), Title XIII, § 1343(a)(8)(B), Nov. 14, 1986, 100 Stat. 3885, 3886, 3992; Pub.L. 101-189, Div. A, Title XIV, § 1407(a)(2), (3), Nov. 29, 1989, 103 Stat. 1588; Pub.L. 103-337, Div. A, Title VI, § 638, Title XVI, § 1671(d)(2), Oct. 5, 1994, 108 Stat. 2791, 3015; Pub.L. 104-201, Div. A, Title VI, § 634, Sept. 23, 1996, 110 Stat. 2553; Pub.L. 105-85, Div. A, Title X, § 1073(a)(27), Nov. 18, 1997, 111 Stat. 1901; Pub.L. 105-261, Div. A, Title VI, § 643(a), Oct. 17, 1998, 112 Stat. 2047; Pub.L. 106-65, Div. A, Title X, § 1066(a) (12), Oct. 5, 1999, 113 Stat. 771; Pub.L. 106-398, § 1 [Div. A, Title VI, § 655(a) to (c)(3), Title X, § 1087(a)(10)], Oct. 30, 2000, 114 Stat. 1654, 1654A-165, 1654A-166, 1654A-290; Pub.L. 107-107, Div. A, Title VI, § 642(a), (c)(1), Dec. 28, 2001, 115 Stat. 1151, 1152; Pub.L. 108-136, Div. A, Title VI, §§ 644(a), (b), 645(a), (b)(1), (c), Nov. 24, 2003, 117 Stat. 1517; Pub.L. 108-375, Div. A, Title X, § 1084(d)(10), Oct. 28, 2004, 118 Stat. 2061; Pub.L. 109-364, Div. A, Title VI, §§ 643(a), 644(a), Title X, § 1071(a)(8), Oct. 17, 2006, 120 Stat. 2260, 2261, 2398; Pub.L. 113-291, Div. A, Title

VI, § 624(a)(2)(B), Dec. 19, 2014, 128 Stat. 3403; Pub.L. 114-92, Div. A, Title VI, § 641(a), Nov. 25, 2015, 129 Stat. 852; Pub.L. 114-328, Div. A, Title VI, § 642(b), (c), Dec. 23, 2016, 130 Stat. 2165.)

§ 1448a. Election to discontinue participation: one-year opportunity after second anniversary of commencement of payment of retired pay.

(a) Authority.—A participant in the Plan may, subject to the provisions of this section, elect to discontinue participation in the Plan at any time during the one-year period beginning on the second anniversary of the date on which payment of retired pay to the participant commences.

(b) Concurrence of spouse.—

(1) **Concurrence required.**—A married participant may not (except as provided in paragraph (2)) make an election under subsection (a) without the concurrence of the participant's spouse.

(2) **Exceptions.**—A participant may make such an election without the concurrence of the participant's spouse by establishing to the satisfaction of the Secretary concerned that one of the conditions specified in section 1448(a)(3)(C) of this title exists.

(3) **Form of concurrence.**—The concurrence of a spouse under paragraph (1) shall be made in such written form and shall contain such information as may be required under regulations prescribed by the Secretary of Defense.

(c) Limitation on election when former spouse coverage in effect.—The limitation set forth in section 1450(f)(2) of this title applies to an election to discontinue participation in the Plan under subsection (a).

(d) Withdrawal of election to discontinue.—Section 1448(b)(1)(D) of this title applies to an election under subsection (a).

(e) Consequences of discontinuation.—Section 1448(b)(1)(E) of this title applies to an election under subsection (a).

(f) Notice to affected beneficiaries.—The Secretary concerned shall notify any former spouse or other natural person previously designated under section 1448(b) of this title of an election to discontinue participation under subsection (a).

(g) Effective date of election.—An election under subsection (a) is effective as of the first day of the first calendar month following the month in which the election is received by the Secretary concerned.

(h) Inapplicability of irrevocability provisions.—Paragraphs (4)(B) and (5)(C) of section 1448(a) of this title do not apply to prevent an election under subsection (a).

§ 1450. Payment of annuity: beneficiaries

(a) In General.—Effective as of the first day after the death of a person to whom section 1448 of this title applies (or on such other day as that person may provide under subsection (j)), a monthly annuity under section 1451 of this title shall be paid to the person's beneficiaries under the Plan, as follows:

(1) **Surviving spouse or former spouse.**—The eligible surviving spouse or the eligible former spouse.

(2) **Surviving children.**—The surviving dependent children in equal shares, if the eligible surviving spouse or the eligible former spouse is dead, dies, or otherwise becomes ineligible under this section.

(3) **Dependent children.**—The dependent children in equal shares if the person to whom section 1448 of this title applies (with the concurrence of the person's

spouse, if required under section 1448(a)(3) of this title) elected to provide an annuity for dependent children but not for the spouse or former spouse.

(4) **Special needs trusts for sole benefit of certain dependent children.—** Notwithstanding subsection (i), a supplemental or special needs trust established under subparagraph (A) or (C) of section 1917(d)(4) of the Social Security Act (42 U.S.C. 1396p(d)(4)) for the sole benefit of a dependent child considered disabled under section 1614(a)(3) of that Act (42 U.S.C. 1382c(a)(3)) who is incapable of self-support because of mental or physical incapacity.

(5) **Natural person designated under "insurable interest" coverage.—** The natural person designated under section 1448(b)(1) of this title, unless the election to provide an annuity to the natural person has been changed as provided in subsection (f).

(b) **Termination of annuity for death, remarriage before age 55, etc.—**

(1) **General rule.—** An annuity payable to the beneficiary terminates effective as of the first day of the month in which eligibility is lost.

(2) **Termination of annuity upon death or remarriage before age 55.—** An annuity for a surviving spouse or former spouse shall be paid to the surviving spouse or former spouse while the surviving spouse or former spouse is living or, if the surviving spouse or former spouse remarries before reaching age 55, until the surviving spouse or former spouse remarries.

(3) **Effect of termination of subsequent marriage before age 55.—** If the surviving spouse or former spouse remarries before reaching age 55 and that marriage is terminated by death, annulment, or divorce, payment of the annuity shall be resumed effective as of the first day of the month in which the marriage is so terminated. However, if the surviving spouse or former spouse is also entitled to an annuity under the Plan based upon the marriage so terminated, the surviving spouse or former spouse may not receive both annuities but must elect which to receive.

(c) **Offset for amount of dependency and indemnity compensation.—**

(1) **Required offset.—** If, upon the death of a person to whom section 1448 of this title applies, the surviving spouse or former spouse of that person is also entitled to dependency and indemnity compensation under section 1311(a) of title 38, the surviving spouse or former spouse may be paid an annuity under this section, but only in the amount that the annuity otherwise payable under this section would exceed that compensation.

(2) **Effective date of offset.—** A reduction in an annuity under this section required by paragraph (1) shall be effective on the date of the commencement of the period of payment of such dependency and indemnity compensation under title 38.

(3) **Limitation on recoupment of offset amount.—** Any amount subject to offset under this subsection that was previously paid to the surviving spouse or former spouse shall be recouped only to the extent that the amount paid exceeds any amount to be refunded under subsection (e). In notifying a surviving spouse or former spouse of the recoupment requirement, the Secretary shall provide the spouse or former spouse—

(A) a single notice of the net amount to be recouped or the net amount to be refunded, as applicable, under this subsection or subsection (e);

(B) a written explanation of the statutory requirements for recoupment of the offset amount and for refund of any applicable amount deducted from retired pay;

(C) a detailed accounting of how the offset amount being recouped and retired pay deduction amount being refunded were calculated; and

(D) contact information for a person who can provide information about the offset recoupment and retired pay deduction refund processes and answer questions the surviving spouse or former spouse may have about the requirements, processes, or amounts.

(d) Limitation on payment of annuities when coverage under civil service retirement elected.—If, upon the death of a person to whom section 1448 of this title applies, that person had in effect a waiver of that person's retired pay for the purposes of subchapter III of chapter 83 of title 5 or chapter 84 of such title, an annuity under this section shall not be payable unless, in accordance with section 8339(j) or 8416(a) of title 5, that person notified the Office of Personnel Management that he did not desire any spouse surviving him to receive an annuity under section 8341(b) or 8442(a) of that title.

(e) Refund of amounts deducted from retired pay or CRSC when DIC offset is applicable.—

(1) **Full refund when DIC greater than SBP annuity.**—If an annuity under this section is not payable because of subsection (c), any amount deducted from the retired pay or combat-related special compensation of the deceased under section 1452 of this title shall be refunded to the surviving spouse or former spouse.

(2) **Partial refund when SBP annuity reduced by DIC.**— If, because of subsection (c), the annuity payable is less than the amount established under section 1451 of this title, the annuity payable shall be recalculated under that section. The amount of the reduction in the retired pay required to provide that recalculated annuity shall be computed under section 1452 of this title, and the difference between the amount deducted before the computation of that recalculated annuity and the amount that would have been deducted on the basis of that recalculated annuity shall be refunded to the surviving spouse or former spouse.

(f) Change in election of insurable interest or former spouse beneficiary.—

(1) **Authorized changes.—**

(A) **Election in favor of or child.**—A person who elects to provide an annuity to a person designated by him under section 1448(b) of this title may, subject to paragraph (2), change that election and provide an annuity to his spouse or dependent child.

(B) **Notice.**— The Secretary concerned shall notify the former spouse or other natural person previously designated under section 1448(b) of this title of any change of election under subparagraph (A).

(C) **Procedures, effective date, etc.**—Any such change of election is subject to the same rules with respect to execution, revocation, and effectiveness as are set forth in section 1448(a)(5) of this title (without regard to the eligibility of the person making the change of election to make such an election under that section). Notwithstanding the preceding sentence, a change of election under this subsection to provide an annuity to a spouse instead of a former spouse may (subject to paragraph (2)) be made at any time after the person providing the annuity remarries without regard to the time limitation in section 1448(a)(5)(B) of this title.

(2) **Limitation on change in beneficiary when coverage in effect.**—A person who, incident to a proceeding of divorce, dissolution, or annulment, is required by a court order to elect under section 1448(b) of this title to provide an annuity to a former spouse (or to both a former spouse and child), or who enters into a written agreement (whether voluntary or required by a court order) to make such an election, and who makes an election pursuant to such order or agreement, may not change that election under paragraph (1) unless, of the following requirements, whichever are applicable in a particular case are satisfied:

(A) **In a case in which the election is required by a court order, or in which an agreement to make the election has been incorporated in or ratified or approved by a court order, the person—**

(i) furnishes to the Secretary concerned a certified copy of a court order which is regular on its face and which modifies the provisions of all previous court orders relating to such election, or the agreement to make such election, so as to permit the person to change the election; and

(ii) certifies to the Secretary concerned that the court order is valid and in effect.

(B) In a case of a written agreement that has not been incorporated in or ratified or approved by a court order, the person—

(i) furnishes to the Secretary concerned a statement, in such form as the Secretary concerned may prescribe, signed by the former spouse and evidencing the former spouse's agreement to a change in the election under paragraph (1); and

(ii) certifies to the Secretary concerned that the statement is current and in effect.

(3) Required former spouse election to be deemed to have been made.—

(A) Deemed election upon request by former spouse.—If a person described in paragraph (2) or (3) of section 1448(b) of this title is required (as described in subparagraph (B)) to elect under section 1448(b) of this title to provide an annuity to a former spouse and such person then fails or refuses to make such an election, such person shall be deemed to have made such an election if the Secretary concerned receives the following:

(i) Request from former spouse.—A written request, in such manner as the Secretary shall prescribe, from the former spouse concerned requesting that such an election be deemed to have been made.

(ii) Copy of court order or other official statement.—Either—

(I) a copy of the court order, regular on its face, which requires such election or incorporates, ratifies, or approves the written agreement of such person; or

(II) a statement from the clerk of the court (or other appropriate official) that such agreement has been filed with the court in accordance with applicable State law.

(B) Persons required to make election.—A person shall be considered for purposes of subparagraph (A) to be required to elect under section 1448(b) of this title to provide an annuity to a former spouse if—

(i) the person enters, incident to a proceeding of divorce, dissolution, or annulment, into a written agreement to make such an election and the agreement (I) has been incorporated in or ratified or approved by a court order, or (II) has been filed with the court of appropriate jurisdiction in accordance with applicable State law; or

(ii) the person is required by a court order to make such an election.

(C) Time limit for request by former spouse.— An election may not be deemed to have been made under subparagraph (A) in the case of any person unless the Secretary concerned receives a request from the former spouse of the person within one year of the date of the court order or filing involved.

(D) Effective date of deemed election.— An election deemed to have been made under subparagraph (A) shall become effective on the day referred to in section 1448(b)(3)(E) (ii) of this title.

(4) Former spouse coverage may be required by court order.— A court order may require a person to elect (or to enter into an agreement to elect) under section 1448(b) of this title to provide an annuity to a former spouse (or to both a former spouse and child).

(g) **Limitation on changing or revoking elections.—**

(1) **In general.—**An election under this section may not be changed or revoked.

(2) **Exceptions.—**Paragraph (1) does not apply to—

(A) a revocation of an election under section 1449(b) of this title; or

(B) a change in an election under subsection (f).

(h) **Treatment of annuities under other laws.—**Except as provided in section 1451 of this title, an annuity under this section is in addition to any other payment to which a person is entitled under any other provision of law. Such annuity shall be considered as income under laws administered by the Secretary of Veterans Affairs.

(i) **Annuities exempt from certain legal process.—** Except as provided in subsection (a)(4) or (l)(3)(B), an annuity under this section is not assignable or subject to execution, levy, attachment, garnishment, or other legal process.

(j) **Effective date of reserve-component annuities.—**

(1) **Persons making section 1448(e) designation.—**A reserve-component annuity shall be effective in accordance with the designation made under section 1448(e) of this title by the person providing the annuity.

(2) **Persons dying before making section 1448(e) designation.—**An annuity payable under section 1448(f) of this title shall be effective on the day after the date of the death of the person upon whose service the right to the annuity is based.

(k) **Adjustment of spouse or former spouse annuity upon loss of dependency and indemnity compensation.—**

(1) **Readjustment if beneficiary 55 years of age or more.—**If a surviving spouse or former spouse whose annuity has been adjusted under subsection (c) subsequently loses entitlement to dependency and indemnity compensation under section 1311(a) of title 38 because of the remarriage of the surviving spouse, or former spouse, and if at the time of such remarriage the surviving spouse or former spouse is 55 years of age or more, the amount of the annuity of the surviving spouse or former spouse shall be readjusted, effective on the effective date of such loss of dependency and indemnity compensation, to the amount of the annuity which would be in effect with respect to the surviving spouse or former spouse if the adjustment under subsection (c) had never been made.

(2) **Repayment of amounts previously refunded.—**

(A) **General rule.—** A surviving spouse or former spouse whose annuity is readjusted under paragraph (1) shall repay any amount refunded under subsection (e) by reason of the adjustment under subsection (c).

(B) **Interest required if repayment not a lump sum.—** If the repayment is not made in a lump sum, the surviving spouse or former spouse shall pay interest on the amount to be repaid. Such interest shall commence on the date on which the first such payment is due and shall be applied over the period during which any part of the repayment remains to be paid.

(C) **Manner of repayment; rate of interest.—** The manner in which such repayment shall be made, and the rate of any such interest, shall be prescribed in regulations under section 1455 of this title.

(D) **Deposit of amounts repaid.—** An amount repaid under this paragraph (including any such interest) received by the Secretary of Defense shall be deposited into the Department of Defense Military Retirement Fund. Any other amount repaid under this paragraph shall be deposited into the Treasury as miscellaneous receipts.

(l) **Participants in the plan who are missing.—**

(1) **Authority to presume death of missing participant.—**

(A) **In general.—**Upon application of the beneficiary of a participant in the Plan who is missing, the Secretary concerned may determine for purposes of this subchapter that the participant is presumed dead.

(B) Participant who is missing.—A participant in the Plan is considered to be missing for purposes of this subsection if—

(i) the retired pay of the participant has been suspended on the basis that the participant is missing; or

(ii) in the case of a participant in the Plan who would be eligible for reserve-component retired pay but for the fact that he is under 60 years of age, his retired pay, if he were entitled to retired pay, would be suspended on the basis that he is missing.

(C) Requirements applicable to presumption of death.—Any such determination shall be made in accordance with regulations prescribed under section 1455 of this title. The Secretary concerned may not make a determination for purposes of this subchapter that a participant who is missing is presumed dead unless the Secretary finds that—

(i) the participant has been missing for at least 30 days; and

(ii) the circumstances under which the participant is missing would lead a reasonably prudent person to conclude that the participant is dead.

(2) Commencement of annuity.— Upon a determination under paragraph (1) with respect to a participant in the Plan, an annuity otherwise payable under this subchapter shall be paid as if the participant died on the date as of which the retired pay of the participant was suspended.

(3) Effect of person not being dead.—

(A) Termination of annuity.—If, after a determination under paragraph (1), the Secretary concerned determines that the participant is alive—

(i) any annuity being paid under this subchapter by reason of this subsection shall be terminated; and

(ii) the total amount of any annuity payments made by reason of this subsection shall constitute a debt to the United States.

(B) Collection from participant of annuity amounts erroneously paid.—A debt under subparagraph (A)(ii) may be collected or offset—

(i) from any retired pay otherwise payable to the participant;

(ii) if the participant is entitled to compensation under chapter 11 of title 38, from that compensation; or

(iii) if the participant is entitled to any other payment from the United States, from that payment.

(C) Collection from beneficiary.— If the participant dies before the full recovery of the amount of annuity payments described in subparagraph (A)(ii) has been made by the United States, the remaining amount of such annuity payments may be collected from the participant's beneficiary under the Plan if that beneficiary was the recipient of the annuity payments made by reason of this subsection.

(m) Special survivor indemnity allowance.—

(1) Provision of allowance.—The Secretary concerned shall pay a monthly special survivor indemnity allowance under this subsection to the surviving spouse or former spouse of a member of the uniformed services to whom section 1448 of this title applies if—

(A) the surviving spouse or former spouse is entitled to dependency and indemnity compensation under section 1311(a) of title 38;

(B) except for subsection (c) of this section, the surviving spouse or former spouse is eligible for an annuity by reason of a participant in the Plan under subsection (a)(1) of section 1448 of this title or by reason of coverage under subsection (d) or (f) of such section; and

(C) the eligibility of the surviving spouse or former spouse for an annuity as described in subparagraph (B) is affected by subsection (c) of this section.

(2) **Amount of payment.**—Subject to paragraph (3), the amount of the allowance paid to an eligible survivor under paragraph (1) for a month shall be equal to—

(A) for months during fiscal year 2009, $50;

(B) for months during fiscal year 2010, $60;

(C) for months during fiscal year 2011, $70;

(D) for months during fiscal year 2012, $80;

(E) for months during fiscal year 2013, $90;

(F) for months during fiscal year 2014, $150;

(G) for months during fiscal year 2015, $200;

(H) for months during fiscal year 2016, $275;

(I) for months from October 2016 through November 2018, $310; and

(J) for months after November 2018, the amount determined in accordance with paragraph (6).

(3) **Limitation.**— The amount of the allowance paid to an eligible survivor under paragraph (1) for any month may not exceed the amount of the annuity for that month that is subject to offset under subsection (c).

(4) **Status of payments.**— An allowance paid under this subsection does not constitute an annuity, and amounts so paid are not subject to adjustment under any other provision of law.

(5) **Source of funds.**— The special survivor indemnity allowance shall be paid from amounts in the Department of Defense Military Retirement Fund established under section 1461 of this title.

(6) **Cost-of-living adjustments after November 2018.**—

(A) **In general.**— Whenever retired pay is increased for a month under section 1401a of this title (or any other provision of law), the amount of the allowance payable under paragraph (1) for that month shall also be increased.

(B) **Amount of increase.**—With respect to an eligible survivor of a member of the uniformed services, the increase for a month shall be—

(i) the amount payable pursuant to paragraph (2) for months during the preceding 12-month period; plus

(ii) an amount equal to a percentage of the amount determined pursuant to clause (i), which percentage is the percentage by which the retired pay of the member would have increased for the month, as described in subparagraph (A), if the member was alive (and otherwise entitled to such pay).

(C) **Rounding down.**— The monthly amount of an allowance payable under this subsection, if not a multiple of $1, shall be rounded to the next lower multiple of $1.

(D) **Public notice on amount of allowance payable.**— Whenever an increase in the amount of the allowance payable under paragraph (1) is made pursuant to this paragraph, the Secretary of Defense shall publish the amount of the allowance so payable by reason of such increase, including the months for which payable.

(Added Pub. L. 92–425, § 1(3), Sept. 21, 1972, 86 Stat. 708; amended Pub. L. 94–496, § 1(3), (4), Oct. 14, 1976, 90 Stat. 2375; Pub. L. 95–397, title II, §§ 203, 207(b), (c), Sept. 30, 1978, 92 Stat. 845, 848; Pub. L. 97–22, § 11(a)(3), July 10, 1981, 95 Stat. 137; Pub. L. 97–252, title X, § 1003(c), (d), Sept. 8, 1982, 96 Stat. 736; Pub. L. 98–94, title IX, § 941(a)(3), (c)(3), Sept. 24, 1983, 97 Stat. 653; Pub. L. 98–525, title VI, §§ 642(b), 644, Oct. 19, 1984, 98 Stat. 2546, 2548; Pub. L. 99–145, title VII, §§ 713(b), 717, 718,

719(4)–(6), (8)(A), 722, 723(a), (b)(1), title XIII, § 1303(a)(11), Nov. 8, 1985, 99 Stat. 672, 674–677, 739; Pub. L. 99–661, div. A, title VI, §§ 641(a), (b)(2), (3), 643(a), title XIII, § 1343(a)(8)(C), Nov. 14, 1986, 100 Stat. 3885, 3886, 3992; Pub. L. 100–26, § 3(3), Apr. 21, 1987, 101 Stat. 273; Pub. L. 100–180, div. A, title VI, § 636(a), Dec. 4, 1987, 101 Stat. 1106; Pub. L. 100–224, § 5(b)(1), Dec. 30, 1987, 101 Stat. 1538; Pub. L. 101–189, div. A, title XIV, § 1407(a)(2)–(4), title XVI, § 1621(a)(1), Nov. 29, 1989, 103 Stat. 1588, 1602; Pub. L. 103–337, div. A, title X, § 1070(e)(3), Oct. 5, 1994, 108 Stat. 2859; Pub. L. 104–201, div. A, title VI, § 634, Sept. 23, 1996, 110 Stat. 2561; Pub. L. 105–85, div. A, title VI, § 642(a), Nov. 18, 1997, 111 Stat. 1799; Pub. L. 105–261, div. A, title VI, § 643(b), Oct. 17, 1998, 112 Stat. 2048; Pub. L. 106–398, § 1 [[div. A], title VI, § 655(c)(4)], Oct. 30, 2000, 114 Stat. 1654, 1654A–166; Pub. L. 110–181, div. A, title VI, §§ 643(a), 644, Jan. 28, 2008, 122 Stat. 157, 158; Pub. L. 110–417, [div. A], title VI, § 631(a), Oct. 14, 2008, 122 Stat. 4492; Pub. L. 111–31, div. B, title II, § 201, June 22, 2009, 123 Stat. 1857; Pub. L. 112–239, div. A, title VI, § 641(b), Jan. 2, 2013, 126 Stat. 1783; Pub. L. 113–291, div. A, title VI, § 624(a)(1), (2)(A), Dec. 19, 2014, 128 Stat. 3403; Pub. L. 114–328, div. A, title VI, §§ 642(d), 643(c)(2), 646, Dec. 23, 2016, 130 Stat. 2165, 2166, 2168; Pub. L. 115–91, div. A, title VI, § 621, Dec. 12, 2017, 131 Stat. 1427; Pub. L. 115–232, div. A, title VI, § 622(a), (b), Aug. 13, 2018, 132 Stat. 1799.)

§ 1451. Amount of annuity

(a) **Computation of annuity for a spouse, former spouse, or child.—**

(1) **Standard annuity.**—In the case of a standard annuity provided to a beneficiary under section 1450(a) of this title (other than under section 1450(a)(5)), the monthly annuity payable to the beneficiary shall be determined as follows:

(A) **Beneficiary under 62 years of age.**—If the beneficiary is under 62 years of age or is a dependent child when becoming entitled to the annuity, the monthly annuity shall be the amount equal to 55 percent of the base amount.

(B) **Beneficiary 62 years of age or older.—**

(i) **General rule.**—If the beneficiary (other than a dependent child) is 62 years of age or older when becoming entitled to the annuity, the monthly annuity shall be the amount equal to the product of the base amount and the percent applicable to the month, as follows:

(I) For a month before October 2005, the applicable percent is 35 percent.

(II) For months after September 2005 and before April 2006, the applicable percent is 40 percent.

(III) For months after March 2006 and before April 2007, the applicable percent is 45 percent.

(IV) For months after March 2007 and before April 2008, the applicable percent is 50 percent.

(V) For months after March 2008, the applicable percent is 55 percent.

(ii) **Rule if beneficiary eligible for social security offset computation.**— If the beneficiary is eligible to have the annuity computed under subsection (e) and if computation of the annuity under that subsection is more favorable to the beneficiary than computation under clause (i), the annuity shall be computed under that subsection rather than under clause (i).

(2) **Reserve-component annuity.**—In the case of a reserve-component annuity provided to a beneficiary under section 1450(a) of this title (other than under section 1450(a)(5)), the monthly annuity payable to the beneficiary shall be determined as follows:

(A) **Beneficiary under 62 years of age.**—If the beneficiary is under 62 years of age or is a dependent child when becoming entitled to the annuity, the monthly annuity shall be the amount equal to a percentage of the base amount that—

(i) is less than 55 percent; and

(ii) is determined under subsection (f).

(B) Beneficiary 62 years of age or older.—

(i) **General rule.**—If the beneficiary (other than a dependent child) is 62 years of age or older when becoming entitled to the annuity, the monthly annuity shall be the amount equal to a percentage of the base amount that—

(I) is less than the percent specified under subsection (a)(1)(B)(i) as being applicable for the month; and

(II) is determined under subsection (f).

(ii) Rule if beneficiary eligible for social security offset computation.— If the beneficiary is eligible to have the annuity computed under subsection (e) and if, at the time the beneficiary becomes entitled to the annuity, computation of the annuity under that subsection is more favorable to the beneficiary than computation under clause (i), the annuity shall be computed under that subsection rather than under clause (i).

(b) Insurable interest beneficiary.—

(1) Standard annuity.— In the case of a standard annuity provided to a beneficiary under section 1450(a)(5) of this title, the monthly annuity payable to the beneficiary shall be the amount equal to 55 percent of the retired pay of the person who elected to provide the annuity after the reduction in that pay in accordance with section 1452(c) of this title.

(2) Reserve-component annuity.—In the case of a reserve-component annuity provided to a beneficiary under section 1450(a)(5) of this title, the monthly annuity payable to the beneficiary shall be the amount equal to a percentage of the retired pay of the person who elected to provide the annuity after the reduction in such pay in accordance with section 1452(c) of this title that—

(A) is less than 55 percent; and

(B) is determined under subsection (f).

(3) Computation of reserve-component annuity when participant dies before age 60.—For the purposes of paragraph (2), a person—

(A) who provides an annuity that is determined in accordance with that paragraph;

(B) who dies before becoming 60 years of age; and

(C) who at the time of death is otherwise entitled to retired pay, shall be considered to have been entitled to retired pay at the time of death. The retired pay of such person for the purposes of such paragraph shall be computed on the basis of the rates of basic pay in effect on the date on which the annuity provided by such person is to become effective in accordance with the designation of such person under section 1448(e) of this title.

(c) Annuities for survivors of certain persons dying during a period of special eligibility for SBP.—

(1) In general.—In the case of an annuity provided under section 1448(d) or 1448(f) of this title, the amount of the annuity shall be determined as follows:

(A) Beneficiary under 62 years of age.—If the person receiving the annuity is under 62 years of age or is a dependent child when the member or former member dies, the monthly annuity shall be the amount equal to 55 percent of the retired pay to which the member or former member would have been entitled if the member or former member had been entitled to that pay when he died determined as follows:

(i) In the case of an annuity provided under section 1448(d) or 1448(f) of this title (other than in a case covered by clause (ii) or (iii)), such retired pay shall be computed as if the member had been retired under section 1201 of this title on the date of the member's death with a disability rated as total.

(ii) In the case of an annuity provided under section 1448(d)(1)(A) of this title by reason of the death of a member not in line of duty, such retired pay shall be computed based upon the member's years of active service when he died.

(iii) In the case of an annuity provided under section 1448(f)(1)(A) of this title by reason of the death of a member or former member not in line of duty, such retired pay shall be computed based upon the member or former member's years of service when he died computed under section 12733 of this title.

(B) **Beneficiary 62 years of age or older.—**

(i) **General rule.—**If the person receiving the annuity (other than a dependent child) is 62 years of age or older when the member or former member dies, the monthly annuity shall be the amount equal to the applicable percent of the retired pay to which the member or former member would have been entitled as determined under subparagraph (A). The percent applicable for a month under the preceding sentence is the percent specified under subsection (a)(1)(B)(i) as being applicable for that month.

(ii) **Rule if beneficiary eligible for social security offset computation.—**If the beneficiary is eligible to have the annuity computed under subsection (e) and if computation of the annuity under that subsection is more favorable to the beneficiary than computation under clause (i), the annuity shall be computed under that subsection rather than under clause (i).

(2) **DIC offset.—**An annuity computed under paragraph (1) that is paid to a surviving spouse shall be reduced by the amount of dependency and indemnity compensation to which the surviving spouse is entitled under section 1311(a) of title 38. Any such reduction shall be effective on the date of the commencement of the period of payment of such compensation under title 38.

(3) **Servicemembers not yet granted retired pay.—**In the case of an annuity provided by reason of the service of a member described in clause (ii) or (iii) of section 1448(d)(1)(A) of this title who first became a member of a uniformed service before September 8, 1980, the retired pay to which the member would have been entitled when he died shall be determined for purposes of paragraph (1) based upon the rate of basic pay in effect at the time of death for the grade in which the member was serving at the time of death, unless (as determined by the Secretary concerned) the member would have been entitled to be retired in a higher grade.

(4) **Rate of to be used in computing annuity.—**In the case of an annuity paid under section 1448(f) of this title by reason of the service of a person who first became a member of a uniformed service before September 8, 1980, the retired pay of the person providing the annuity shall for the purposes of paragraph (1) be computed on the basis of the rates of basic pay in effect on the effective date of the annuity.

(d) **Reduction of annuities at Age 62.—**

(1) **Reduction required.—**The annuity of a person whose annuity is computed under subparagraph (A) of subsection (a)(1), (a)(2), or (c)(1) shall be reduced on the first day of the month after the month in which the person becomes 62 years of age.

(2) **Amount of annuity as reduced.—**

(A) **Computation of annuity.—**Except as provided in subparagraph (B), the reduced amount of the annuity shall be the amount of the annuity that the person would be receiving on that date if the annuity had initially been computed under subparagraph (B) of that subsection.

(B) **Savings provision for beneficiaries eligible for social security offset computation.—**In the case of a person eligible to have an annuity computed under subsection (e) and for whom, at the time the person becomes 62 years of age, the annuity computed with a reduction under subsection (e)(3) is more favorable than the annuity with a reduction described in subparagraph (A), the reduction in the annuity shall be computed in the same manner as a reduction under subsection (e)(3).

(e) **Savings Provision for Certain Beneficiaries.—**

(1) **Persons covered.—**The following beneficiaries under the Plan are eligible to have an annuity under the Plan computed under this subsection:

(A) A beneficiary receiving an annuity under the Plan on October 1, 1985, as the surviving spouse or former spouse of the person providing the annuity.

(B) A spouse or former spouse beneficiary of a person who on October 1, 1985—

(i) was a participant in the Plan;

(ii) was entitled to retired pay or was qualified for that pay except that he had not applied for and been granted that pay; or

(iii) would have been eligible for reserve-component retired pay but for the fact that he was under 60 years of age.

(2) **Amount of annuity.—**Subject to paragraph (3), an annuity computed under this subsection is determined as follows:

(A) **Standard annuity.—**In the case of the beneficiary of a standard annuity, the annuity shall be the amount equal to 55 percent of the base amount.

(B) **Reserve-component annuity.—**In the case of the beneficiary of a reserve-component annuity, the annuity shall be the percentage of the base amount that—

(i) is less than 55 percent; and

(ii) is determined under subsection (f).

(C) **Beneficiaries of persons dying during a period of special eligibility for SBP.—** In the case of the beneficiary of an annuity under section 1448(d) or 1448(f) of this title, the annuity shall be the amount equal to 55 percent of the retired pay of the person providing the annuity (as that pay is determined under subsection (c)).

(3) **Social security offset.—**An annuity computed under this subsection shall be reduced by the lesser of the following:

(A) **Social security computation.—**The amount of the survivor benefit, if any, to which the surviving spouse (or the former spouse, in the case of a former spouse beneficiary who became a former spouse under a divorce that became final after November 29, 1989) would be entitled under title II of the Social Security Act (42 U.S.C. 401 et seq.) based solely upon service by the person concerned as described in section 210(l)(1) of such Act (42 U.S.C. 410(l)(1)) and calculated assuming that the person concerned lives to age 65.

(B) **Maximum amount of reduction.—**40 percent of the amount of the monthly annuity as determined under paragraph (2).

(4) **Special rules for social security offset computation.—**

(A) **Treatment of deductions made on account of work.—** For the purpose of paragraph (3), a surviving spouse (or a former spouse, in the case of a person who becomes a former spouse under a divorce that becomes final after November 29, 1989) shall not be considered as entitled to a benefit under title II of the Social Security Act (42 U.S.C. 401 et seq.) to the extent that such benefit has been offset by deductions under section 203 of such Act (42 U.S.C. 403) on account of work.

(B) **Treatment of certain periods for which social security refunds are made.—**In the computation of any reduction made under paragraph (3), there shall be excluded any period of service described in section 210(l)(1) of the Social Security Act (42 U.S.C. 410(l)(1))—

(i) which was performed after December 1, 1980; and

(ii) which involved periods of service of less than 30 continuous days for which the person concerned is entitled to receive a refund under section 6413(c) of the Internal Revenue Code of 1986 of the social security tax which the person had paid.

(f) Determination of percentages applicable to computation of reserve component annuities.—The percentage to be applied in determining the amount of an annuity computed under subsection (a)(2), (b)(2), or (e)(2)(B) shall be determined under regulations prescribed by the Secretary of Defense. Such regulations shall be prescribed taking into consideration the following:

(1) The age of the person electing to provide the annuity at the time of such election.

(2) The difference in age between such person and the beneficiary of the annuity.

(3) Whether such person provided for the annuity to become effective (in the event he died before becoming 60 years of age) on the day after his death or on the 60th anniversary of his birth.

(4) Appropriate group annuity tables.

(5) Such other factors as the Secretary considers relevant.

(g) Adjustments to Annuities.—

(1) Periodic adjustments for cost-of-living.—

(A) Increases in annuities when increased.—Whenever retired pay is increased under section 1401a of this title (or any other provision of law), each annuity that is payable under the Plan shall be increased at the same time.

(B) Percentage of increase.—The increase shall, in the case of any annuity, be by the same percent as the percent by which the retired pay of the person providing the annuity would have been increased at such time if the person were alive (and otherwise entitled to such pay).

(C) Certain reductions to be disregarded.—The amount of the increase shall be based on the monthly annuity payable before any reduction under section 1450(c) of this title or under subsection (c)(2).

(2) Rounding down.—The monthly amount of an annuity payable under this subchapter, if not a multiple of $1, shall be rounded to the next lower multiple of $1.

(h) Adjustments to base amount.—

(1) Periodic adjustments for cost-of-living.—

(A) Increases in base amount when retired pay increased.—Whenever retired pay is increased under section 1401a of this title (or any other provision of law), the base amount applicable to each participant in the Plan shall be increased at the same time.

(B) Percentage of increase.—The increase shall be by the same percent as the percent by which the retired pay of the participant is so increased.

(2) Recomputation at age 62.—When the retired pay of a person who first became a member of a uniformed service on or after August 1, 1986, and who is a participant in the Plan is recomputed under section 1410 of this title upon the person's becoming 62 years of age, the base amount applicable to that person shall be recomputed (effective on the effective date of the recomputation of such retired pay under section 1410 of this title) so as to be the amount equal to the amount of the base amount that would be in effect on that date if increases in such base amount under paragraph (1) had been computed as provided in paragraph (2) of section 1401a(b) of this title (rather than under paragraph (3) of that section).

(3) **Disregarding of retired pay reductions for retirement of certain members before 30 years of service.**—Computation of a member's retired pay for purposes of this section shall be made without regard to any reduction under section 1409(b)(2) of this title.

(i) **Recomputation of annuity for certain beneficiaries.**—In the case of an annuity under the Plan which is computed on the basis of the retired pay of a person who would have been entitled to have that retired pay recomputed under section 1410 of this title upon attaining 62 years of age, but who dies before attaining that age, the annuity shall be recomputed, effective on the first day of the first month beginning after the date on which the member or former member would have attained 62 years of age, so as to be the amount equal to the amount of the annuity that would be in effect on that date if increases under subsection (h)(1) in the base amount applicable to that annuity to the time of the death of the member or former member, and increases in such annuity under subsection (g)(1), had been computed as provided in paragraph (2) of section 1401a(b) of this title (rather than under paragraph (3) of that section).

(Added Pub. L. 92–425, § 1(3), Sept. 21, 1972, 86 Stat. 709; amended Pub. L. 94–496, § 1(4), Oct. 14, 1976, 90 Stat. 2375; Pub. L. 95–397, title II, § 204, Sept. 30, 1978, 92 Stat. 846; Pub. L. 96–402, § 3, Oct. 9, 1980, 94 Stat. 1705; Pub. L. 97–22, § 11(a)(4), July 10, 1981, 95 Stat. 137; Pub. L. 98–94, title IX, § 922(a)(14)(B), Sept. 24, 1983, 97 Stat. 642; Pub. L. 98–525, title VI, § 641(a), Oct. 19, 1984, 98 Stat. 2545; Pub. L. 99–145, title VII, § 711(a), (b), Nov. 8, 1985, 99 Stat. 666, 670; Pub. L. 99–348, title III, § 301(a)(2), (b), (c), July 1, 1986, 100 Stat. 702; Pub. L. 99–661, div. A, title VI, § 642(b), title XIII, § 1343(a)(8)(D), Nov. 14, 1986, 100 Stat. 3886, 3992; Pub. L. 100–26, § 7(h)(1), Apr. 21, 1987, 101 Stat. 282; Pub. L. 100–224, § 3(a), (c), Dec. 30, 1987, 101 Stat. 1537; Pub. L. 100–456, div. A, title VI, § 652(a), Sept. 29, 1988, 102 Stat. 1991; Pub. L. 101–189, div. A, title XIV, §§ 1403(a), 1407(a)(5)–(8), (b)(1), Nov. 29, 1989, 103 Stat. 1579, 1588, 1589; Pub. L. 103–337, div. A, title X, § 1070(e)(4), Oct. 5, 1994, 108 Stat. 2859; Pub. L. 104–201, div. A, title VI, § 634, Sept. 23, 1996, 110 Stat. 2566; Pub. L. 105–85, div. A, title X, § 1073(a)(28), Nov. 18, 1997, 111 Stat. 1901; Pub. L. 106–65, div. A, title VI, § 643(a)(1), Oct. 5, 1999, 113 Stat. 663; Pub. L. 107–107, div. A, title VI, § 642(b), (c)(2), Dec. 28, 2001, 115 Stat. 1152; Pub. L. 107–314, div. A, title X, § 1062(a)(6), Dec. 2, 2002, 116 Stat. 2650; Pub. L. 108–375, div. A, title VI, § 644(a), Oct. 28, 2004, 118 Stat. 1960; Pub. L. 114–328, div. A, title VI, § 642(a), Dec. 23, 2016, 130 Stat. 2164; Pub. L. 115–91, div. A, title X, § 1081(a)(25), Dec. 12, 2017, 131 Stat. 1595.)

§ 1452. Reduction in retired pay

(a) **Spouse and former spouse annuities.**—

(1) **Required reduction in retired pay.**—Except as provided in subsection (b), the retired pay, other than retired pay received as a lump sum under section 1415(b)(1)(A) of this title, of a participant in the Plan who is providing spouse coverage (as described in paragraph (5)) shall be reduced as follows:

(A) **Standard annuity.**—If the annuity coverage being provided is a standard annuity, the reduction shall be as follows:

(i) **Disability and nonregular service retirees.**— In the case of a person who is entitled to retired pay under chapter 61 or chapter 1223 of this title, the reduction shall be in whichever of the alternative reduction amounts is more favorable to that person.

(ii) **Members as of enactment of flat-rate reduction.**— In the case of a person who first became a member of a uniformed service before March 1, 1990, the reduction shall be in whichever of the alternative reduction amounts is more favorable to that person.

(iii) **New entrants after enactment of flat-rate reduction.**— In the case of a person who first becomes a member of a uniformed service on or after March 1, 1990, and who is entitled to retired pay under a provision of law other than chapter 61 or chapter 1223 of this title, the reduction shall be in an amount equal to 6½ percent of the base amount.

(iv) **Alternative reduction amounts.**—For purposes of clauses (i) and (ii), the alternative reduction amounts are the following:

(I) **Flat-rate reduction.**—An amount equal to 6½ percent of the base amount.

(II) **Amount under pre-flat-rate reduction.**—An amount equal to 2½ percent of the first $337 (as adjusted after November 1, 1989, under paragraph (4)) of the base amount plus 10 percent of the remainder of the base amount.

(B) **Reserve-component annuity.**—If the annuity coverage being provided is a reserve-component annuity, the reduction shall be in whichever of the following amounts is more favorable to that person:

(i) **Flat-rate reduction.**—An amount equal to 6½ percent of the base amount plus an amount determined in accordance with regulations prescribed by the Secretary of Defense as a premium for the additional coverage provided through reserve-component annuity coverage under the Plan.

(ii) **Amount under pre-flat-rate reduction.**—An amount equal to 2½ percent of the first $337 (as adjusted after November 1, 1989, under paragraph (4)) of the base amount plus 10 percent of the remainder of the base amount plus an amount determined in accordance with regulations prescribed by the Secretary of Defense as a premium for the additional coverage provided through reserve-component annuity coverage under the Plan.

(2) **Additional reduction for coverage.**—If there is a dependent child as well as a spouse or former spouse, the amount prescribed under paragraph (1) shall be increased by an amount prescribed under regulations of the Secretary of Defense.

(3) **No reduction when no beneficiary.**—The reduction in retired pay prescribed by paragraph (1) shall not be applicable during any month in which there is no eligible spouse or former spouse beneficiary.

(4) **Periodic adjustments.**—

(A) **Adjustments for increases in rates of basic pay.**—Whenever there is an increase in the rates of basic pay of members of the uniformed services effective on or after October 1, 1985, the amounts under paragraph (1) with respect to which the percentage factor of 2½ is applied shall be increased by the overall percentage of such increase in the rates of basic pay. The increase under the preceding sentence shall apply only with respect to persons whose retired pay is computed based on the rates of basic pay in effect on or after the date of such increase in rates of basic pay.

(B) **Adjustments for retired pay COLAS.**—In addition to the increase under subparagraph (A), the amounts under paragraph (1) with respect to which the percentage factor of 2½ is applied shall be further increased at the same time and by the same percentage as an increase in retired pay under section 1401a of this title effective on or after October 1, 1985. Such increase under the preceding sentence shall apply only with respect to a person who initially participates in the Plan on a date which is after both the effective date of such increase under section 1401a and the effective date of the rates of basic pay upon which that person's retired pay is computed.

(5) **Spouse coverage described.**—For the purposes of paragraph (1), a participant in the Plan who is providing spouse coverage is a participant who—

(A) has (i) a spouse or former spouse, or (ii) a spouse or former spouse and a dependent child; and

(B) has not elected to provide an annuity to a person designated by him under section 1448(b)(1) of this title or, having made such an election, has changed his election in favor of his spouse under section 1450(f) of this title.

(b) Child-only annuities.—

(1) **Required reduction in retired pay.**—The retired pay, other than retired pay received as a lump sum under section 1415(b)(1)(A) of this title, of a participant in the Plan who is providing child-only coverage (as described in paragraph (4)) shall be reduced by an amount prescribed under regulations by the Secretary of Defense.

(2) **No reduction when no child.**—There shall be no reduction in retired pay under paragraph (1) for any month during which the participant has no eligible dependent child.

(3) **Special rule for certain RCSBP participants.**—In the case of a participant in the Plan who is participating in the Plan under an election under section 1448(a)(2)(B) of this title and who provided child-only coverage during a period before the participant becomes entitled to receive retired pay, the retired pay of the participant shall be reduced by an amount prescribed under regulations by the Secretary of Defense to reflect the coverage provided under the Plan during the period before the participant became entitled to receive retired pay. A reduction under this paragraph is in addition to any reduction under paragraph (1) and is made without regard to whether there is an eligible dependent child during a month for which the reduction is made.

(4) **Child-only coverage defined.**—For the purposes of this subsection, a participant in the Plan who is providing child-only coverage is a participant who has a dependent child and who—

(A) does not have an eligible spouse or former spouse; or

(B) has a spouse or former spouse but has elected to provide an annuity for dependent children only.

(c) Reduction for insurable interest coverage.—

(1) **Required reduction in retired pay.**—The retired pay, other than retired pay received as a lump sum under section 1415(b)(1)(A) of this title, of a person who has elected to provide an annuity to a person designated by him under section 1450(a)(5) of this title shall be reduced as follows:

(A) **Standard annuity.**—In the case of a person providing a standard annuity, the reduction shall be by 10 percent plus 5 percent for each full five years the individual designated is younger than that person.

(B) **Reserve component annuity.**—In the case of a person providing a reserve-component annuity, the reduction shall be by an amount prescribed under regulations of the Secretary of Defense.

(2) **Limitation on total reduction.**—The total reduction under paragraph (1) may not exceed 40 percent.

(3) **Duration of reduction.**—The reduction in retired pay prescribed by this subsection shall continue during the lifetime of the person designated under section 1450(a)(5) of this title or until the person receiving retired pay changes his election under section 1450(f) of this title.

(4) **Rule for computation.**—Computation of a member's retired pay for purposes of this subsection shall be made without regard to any reduction under section 1409(b)(2) or 1415(b)(1)(B) of this title.

(5) **Rule for designation of new insurable interest beneficiary following death of beneficiary.**—The Secretary of Defense shall prescribe in regulations premiums which a participant making an election under section 1448(b)(1)(G) of this title shall be required to pay for participating in the Plan pursuant to that election. The total amount of the premiums to be paid by a participant under the regulations shall be equal to the sum of the following:

(A) The total additional amount by which the retired pay of the participant would have been reduced before the effective date of the election if the original beneficiary (i) had not died and had been covered under the Plan through the date of the election, and (ii) had been the same number of years younger than the participant (if any) as the new beneficiary designated under the election.

(B) Interest on the amounts by which the retired pay of the participant would have been so reduced, computed from the dates on which the retired pay would have been so reduced at such rate or rates and according to such methodology as the Secretary of Defense determines reasonable.

(C) Any additional amount that the Secretary determines necessary to protect the actuarial soundness of the Department of Defense Military Retirement Fund against any increased risk for the fund that is associated with the election.

(d) Deposits to cover periods when retired pay not paid or not sufficient.—

(1) Required deposits.—If a person who has elected to participate in the Plan has been awarded retired pay and is not entitled to that pay for any period, that person must deposit in the Treasury the amount that would otherwise have been deducted from his pay for that period, except to the extent that the required deduction is made pursuant to paragraph (2).

(2) Deduction from combat-related special compensation when not adequate.—In the case of a person who has elected to participate in the Plan and who has been awarded both retired pay and combat-related special compensation under section 1413a of this title, if a deduction from the person's retired pay for any period cannot be made in the full amount required, there shall be deducted from the person's combat-related special compensation in lieu of deduction from the person's retired pay the amount that would otherwise have been deducted from the person's retired pay for that period.

(3) Deposits not required when participant on active duty.—Paragraphs (1) and (2) do not apply to a person with respect to any period when that person is on active duty under a call or order to active duty for a period of more than 30 days.

(e) Deposits not required for certain participants in CSRS and FERS.—When a person who has elected to participate in the Plan waives that person's retired pay for the purposes of subchapter III of chapter 83 of title 5 or chapter 84 of such title, that person shall not be required to make the deposit otherwise required by subsection (d) as long as that waiver is in effect unless, in accordance with section 8339(j) or 8416(a) of title 5, that person has notified the Office of Personnel Management that he does not desire a spouse surviving him to receive an annuity under section 8341(b) or 8442(a) of title 5.

(f) Refunds of deductions not allowed.—

(1) General rule.—A person is not entitled to refund of any amount deducted from retired pay or combat-related special compensation under this section.

(2) Exceptions.—Paragraph (1) does not apply—

(A) in the case of a refund authorized by section 1450(e) of this title; or

(B) in case of a deduction made through administrative error.

(g) Discontinuation of participation by participants whose surviving spouses will be entitled to DIC.—

(1) Discontinuation.—

(A) Conditions.—Notwithstanding any other provision of this subchapter but subject to paragraphs (2) and (3), a person who has elected to participate in the Plan and who is suffering from a service-connected disability rated by the Secretary of Veterans Affairs as totally disabling and has suffered from such disability while so rated for a continuous period of 10 or more years (or, if so rated for a lesser period, has suffered from such disability while so rated for a continuous period of not less than 5 years from the date of such person's last discharge or release from active duty) may discontinue participation in the Plan by submitting to the Secretary concerned a request to discontinue participation in the Plan.

(B) **Effective date.**—Participation in the Plan of a person who submits a request under subparagraph (A) shall be discontinued effective on the first day of the first month following the month in which the request under subparagraph (A) is received by the Secretary concerned. Effective on such date, the Secretary concerned shall discontinue the reduction being made in such person's retired pay on account of participation in the Plan or, in the case of a person who has been required to make deposits in the Treasury on account of participation in the Plan, such person may discontinue making such deposits effective on such date.

(C) **Form for request for discontinuation.**—Any request under this paragraph to discontinue participation in the Plan shall be in such form and shall contain such information as the Secretary concerned may require by regulation.

(2) **Consent of beneficiaries required.**—A person described in paragraph (1) may not discontinue participation in the Plan under such paragraph without the written consent of the beneficiary or beneficiaries of such person under the Plan.

(3) **Information on plan to be provided by Secretary concerned.**—

(A) **Information to be provided promptly to participant.**—The Secretary concerned shall furnish promptly to each person who files a request under paragraph (1) to discontinue participation in the Plan a written statement of the advantages of participating in the Plan and the possible disadvantages of discontinuing participation.

(B) **Right to withdraw discontinuation request.**—A person may withdraw a request made under paragraph (1) if it is withdrawn within 30 days after having been submitted to the Secretary concerned.

(4) **Refund of deductions from retired pay or CRSC.**—Upon the death of a person described in paragraph (1) who discontinued participation in the Plan in accordance with this subsection, any amount deducted from the retired pay or combat-related special compensation of that person under this section shall be refunded to the person's surviving spouse.

(5) **Resumption of participation in Plan.**—

(A) **Conditions for resumption.**—A person described in paragraph (1) who discontinued participation in the Plan may elect to participate again in the Plan if—

(i) after having discontinued participation in the Plan the Secretary of Veterans Affairs reduces that person's service-connected disability rating to a rating of less than total; and

(ii) that person applies to the Secretary concerned, within such period of time after the reduction in such person's service-connected disability rating has been made as the Secretary concerned may prescribe, to again participate in the Plan and includes in such application such information as the Secretary concerned may require.

(B) **Effective date of resumed coverage.**—Such person's participation in the Plan under this paragraph is effective beginning on the first day of the month after the month in which the Secretary concerned receives the application for resumption of participation in the Plan.

(C) **Resumption of contributions.**—When a person elects to participate in the Plan under this paragraph, the Secretary concerned shall begin making reductions in that person's retired pay, or require such person to make deposits in the Treasury under subsection (d), as appropriate, effective on the effective date of such participation under subparagraph (B).

(h) **Increases in reduction with increases in retired pay.**—

(1) **General rule.**—Whenever retired pay is increased under section 1401a of this title (or any other provision of law), the amount of the reduction to be made

under subsection (a) or (b) in the retired pay of any person shall be increased at the same time and by the same percentage as such retired pay is so increased.

(2) Coordination when payment of increase in retired pay is delayed by law.—

(A) In general.—Notwithstanding paragraph (1), when the initial payment of an increase in retired pay under section 1401a of this title (or any other provision of law) to a person is for a month that begins later than the effective date of that increase by reason of the application of subsection (b)(2)(B) of such section (or section 631(b) of Public Law 104–106 (110 Stat. 364)), then the amount of the reduction in the person's retired pay shall be effective on the date of that initial payment of the increase in retired pay rather than the effective date of the increase in retired pay.

(B) Delay not to affect computation of annuity.—Subparagraph (A) may not be construed as delaying, for purposes of determining the amount of a monthly annuity under section 1451 of this title, the effective date of an increase in a base amount under subsection (h) of such section from the effective date of an increase in retired pay under section 1401a of this title to the date on which the initial payment of that increase in retired pay is made in accordance with subsection (b)(2)(B) of such section.

(i) Recomputation of reduction upon recomputation of retired pay.—Whenever the retired pay of a person who first became a member of a uniformed service on or after August 1, 1986, and who is a participant in the Plan is recomputed under section 1410 of this title upon the person's becoming 62 years of age, the amount of the reduction in such retired pay under this section shall be recomputed (effective on the effective date of the recomputation of such retired pay under section 1410 of this title) so as to be the amount equal to the amount of such reduction that would be in effect on that date if increases in such retired pay under section 1401a(b) of this title, and increases in reductions in such retired pay under subsection (h), had been computed as provided in paragraph (2) of section 1401a(b) of this title (rather than under paragraph (3) of that section).

(j) Coverage Paid Up at 30 Years and Age 70.—Effective October 1, 2008, no reduction may be made under this section in the retired pay of a participant in the Plan for any month after the later of—

(1) the 360th month for which the participant's retired pay is reduced under this section; and

(2) the month during which the participant attains 70 years of age.

(Added Pub. L. 92–425, § 1(3), Sept. 21, 1972, 86 Stat. 710; amended Pub. L. 94–496, § 1(4), (5), Oct. 14, 1976, 90 Stat. 2375; Pub. L. 95–397, title II, § 205, Sept. 30, 1978, 92 Stat. 847; Pub. L. 96–402, § 4, Oct. 9, 1980, 94 Stat. 1706; Pub. L. 97–22, § 11(a) (3), (5), July 10, 1981, 95 Stat. 137; Pub. L. 99–145, title VII, §§ 714(a), 719(7), (8), 723(b)(2), Nov. 8, 1985, 99 Stat. 672, 675–677; Pub. L. 99–348, title III, § 301(a)(3), July 1, 1986, 100 Stat. 702; Pub. L. 99–661, div. A, title XIII, § 1343(a)(8)(E), Nov. 14, 1986, 100 Stat. 3992; Pub. L. 100–224, § 3(b), Dec. 30, 1987, 101 Stat. 1537; Pub. L. 101–189, div. A, title XIV, §§ 1402(a)–(c), 1407(a)(9), title XVI, § 1621(a)(1), Nov. 29, 1989, 103 Stat. 1577, 1578, 1589, 1602; Pub. L. 101–510, div. A, title XIV, § 1484(l) (4)(C)(ii), Nov. 5, 1990, 104 Stat. 1720; Pub. L. 103–337, div. A, title VI, § 637(a), Oct. 5, 1994, 108 Stat. 2790; Pub. L. 104–201, div. A, title VI, §§ 634, 635(a), Sept. 23, 1996, 110 Stat. 2572, 2579; Pub. L. 105–85, div. A, title X, § 1073(a)(29), Nov. 18, 1997, 111 Stat. 1901; Pub. L. 105–261, div. A, title VI, § 641, Oct. 17, 1998, 112 Stat. 2045; Pub. L. 106–65, div. A, title VI, § 643(a)(2), Oct. 5, 1999, 113 Stat. 663; Pub. L. 109–364, div. A, title VI, § 643(b), Oct. 17, 2006, 120 Stat. 2260; Pub. L. 112–239, div. A, title VI, § 641(a), Jan. 2, 2013, 126 Stat. 1782; Pub. L. 114–328, div. A, title VI, § 643(a), (b), Dec. 23, 2016, 130 Stat. 2165, 2166; Pub. L. 115–91, div. A, title VI, § 622(b), title X, § 1081(a)(26), Dec. 12, 2017, 131 Stat. 1428, 1595.)

§ 1453. Recovery of amounts erroneously paid

(a) Recovery.—In addition to any other method of recovery provided by law, the Secretary concerned may authorize the recovery of any amount erroneously paid to a person under this subchapter by deduction from later payments to that person.

(b) Authority to waive recovery.—Recovery of an amount erroneously paid to a person under this subchapter is not required if, in the judgment of the Secretary concerned—

(1) there has been no fault by the person to whom the amount was erroneously paid; and

(2) recovery of such amount would be contrary to the purposes of this subchapter or against equity and good conscience.

§ 1454. Correction of administrative errors

(a) Authority.—The Secretary concerned may, under regulations prescribed under section 1455 of this title, correct or revoke any election under this subchapter when the Secretary considers it necessary to correct an administrative error.

(b) Finality.—Except when procured by fraud, a correction or revocation under this section is final and conclusive on all officers of the United States.

TITLE 11

BANKRUPTCY CODE—SELECTED PROVISIONS

§ 11 U.S.C. § 101. Definitions.

In this title the following definitions shall apply: . . .

(5) The term "claim" means—

(A) right to payment, whether or not such right is reduced to judgment, liquidated, unliquidated, fixed, contingent, matured, unmatured, disputed, undisputed, legal, equitable, secured, or unsecured; or

(B) right to an equitable remedy for breach of performance if such breach gives rise to a right to payment, whether or not such right to an equitable remedy is reduced to judgment, fixed, contingent, matured, unmatured, disputed, undisputed, secured, or unsecured. . . .

(14A) The term "domestic support obligation" means a debt that accrues before, on, or after the date of the order for relief in a case under this title, including interest that accrues on that debt as provided under applicable nonbankruptcy law notwithstanding any other provision of this title, that is—

(A) owed to or recoverable by—

(i) a spouse, former spouse, or child of the debtor or such child's parent, legal guardian, or responsible relative; or

(ii) a governmental unit;

(B) in the nature of alimony, maintenance, or support (including assistance provided by a governmental unit) of such spouse, former spouse, or child of the debtor or such child's parent, without regard to whether such debt is expressly so designated;

(C) established or subject to establishment before, on, or after the date of the order for relief in a case under this title, by reason of applicable provisions of—

(i) a separation agreement, divorce decree, or property settlement agreement;

(ii) an order of a court of record; or

(iii) a determination made in accordance with applicable nonbankruptcy law by a governmental unit; and

(D) not assigned to a nongovernmental entity, unless that obligation is assigned voluntarily by the spouse, former spouse, child of the debtor, or such child's parent, legal guardian, or responsible relative for the purpose of collecting the debt.

Comment: *Definition of Domestic Support Obligation.* A definition of "domestic support obligation: is added to section 101. The definition is largely coextensive with debts that are currently nondischargeable under section 523(a)(5) as alimony, maintenance or support, but includes debts that accrue after the petition and includes support debts that from their inception are owed to a governmental unit.

§ 11 U.S.C. § 362. Automatic stay.

* * * *

(b) The filing of a petition under section 301, 302, or 303 of this title, or of an application under section 5(a) (3) of the Securities Investor Protection Act of 1970, does not operate as a stay—

(1) under subsection (a) of this section, of the commencement or continuation of a criminal action or proceeding against the debtor;

(2) under subsection (a)—

(A) of the commencement or continuation of a civil action or proceeding—

(i) for the establishment of paternity;

(ii) for the establishment or modification of an order for domestic support obligations;

(iii) concerning child custody or visitation;

(iv) for the dissolution of a marriage, except to the extent that such proceeding seeks to determine the division of property that is property of the estate; or

(v) regarding domestic violence;

(B) of the collection of a domestic support obligation from property that is not property of the estate;

(C) with respect to the withholding of income that is property of the estate or property of the debtor for payment of a domestic support obligation under a judicial or administrative order or a statute;

(D) of the withholding, suspension, or restriction of a driver's license, a professional or occupational license, or a recreational license, under State law, as specified in section 466(a)(16) of the Social Security Act;

(E) of the reporting of overdue support owed by a parent to any consumer reporting agency as specified in section 466(a)(7) of the Social Security Act;

* * * *

(d) On request of a party in interest and after notice and a hearing, the court shall grant relief from the stay provided under subsection (a) of this section, such as by terminating, annulling, modifying, or conditioning such stay—

(1) for cause, including the lack of adequate protection of an interest in property of such party in interest;

(2) with respect to a stay of an act against property under subsection (a) of this section, if—

(A) the debtor does not have an equity in such property; and

(B) such property is not necessary to an effective reorganization;

* * * *

Comment: *Automatic Stay.* Additional exceptions to the automatic stay are created for commencement or continuation of proceedings concerning child custody, domestic violence, and divorce, to the extent the divorce proceeding does not involve division of property that is property of the estate; withholding of income to pay a domestic support obligation pursuant to a judicial or administrative order or a statute; interception of tax refunds for domestic support obligations; withholding of licenses from debtors who do not pay support obligations; reporting of credit reporting agencies of debtors who do not pay support; interception of tax refunds to collect support; and enforcement of medical support obligations.

§ 11 U.S.C. § 507. Priorities.

(a) The following expenses and claims have priority in the following order:

(1) First:

(A) Allowed unsecured claims for domestic support obligations that, as of the date of the filing of the petition in a case under this title, are owed to or recoverable by a spouse, former spouse, or child of the debtor, or such child's parent, legal guardian, or responsible relative, without regard to whether the claim is filed by such person or is filed by a governmental unit on behalf of such person, on the condition that funds received under this paragraph by a governmental unit under this title after the date of the filing of the petition shall be applied and distributed in accordance with applicable nonbankruptcy law.

(B) Subject to claims under subparagraph (A), allowed unsecured claims for domestic support obligations that, as of the date of the filing of the petition, are assigned by a spouse, former spouse, child of the debtor, or such child's parent, legal guardian, or responsible relative to a governmental unit (unless such obligation is assigned voluntarily by the spouse, former spouse, child, parent, legal guardian, or responsible relative of the child for the purpose of collecting the debt) or are owed directly to or recoverable by a governmental unit under applicable nonbankruptcy law, on the condition that funds received under this paragraph by a governmental unit under this title after the date of the filing of the petition be applied and distributed in accordance with applicable nonbankruptcy law.

(C) If a trustee is appointed or elected under section 701, 702, 703, 1104, 1202, or 1302, the administrative expenses of the trustee allowed under paragraphs (1)(A), (2), and (6) of section 503(b) shall be paid before payment of claims under subparagraphs (A) and (B), to the extent that the trustee administers assets that are otherwise available for the payment of such claims.

* * * *

Comment: *Priority of Domestic Support Obligations.* Domestic support obligations are first in priority among unsecured debts. Among such obligations, those owed to spouse, former spouse or child of a debtor are given a higher priority than those that are assigned. Administrative expenses of a trustee are paid prior to domestic support obligations to the extent those expenses are incurred in administering assets to pay those obligations.

§ 11 U.S.C. § 522. Exemptions.

(a) In this section—

(1) "dependent" includes spouse, whether or not actually dependent; and

(2) "value" means fair market value as of the date of the filing of the petition or, with respect to property that becomes property of the estate after such date, as of the date such property becomes property of the estate.

(b)(1) Notwithstanding section 541 of this title, an individual debtor may exempt from property of the estate the property listed in either paragraph (2) or, in the alternative, paragraph (3) of this subsection. In joint cases filed under section 302 of this title and individual cases filed under section 301 or 303 of this title by or against debtors who are husband and wife, and whose estates are ordered to be jointly administered under Rule 1015(b) of the Federal Rules of Bankruptcy Procedure, one debtor may not elect to exempt property listed in paragraph (2) and the other debtor elect to exempt property listed in paragraph (3) of this subsection. If the parties cannot agree on the alternative to be elected, they shall be deemed to elect paragraph (2), where such election is permitted under the law of the jurisdiction where the case is filed.

(2) Property listed in this paragraph is property that is specified under subsection (d), unless the State law that is applicable to the debtor under paragraph (3)(A) specifically does not so authorize.

* * * *

(c) Unless the case is dismissed, property exempted under this section is not liable during or after the case for any debt of the debtor that arose, or that is determined under section 502 of this title as if such debt had arisen, before the commencement of the case, except—

(1) a debt of a kind specified in paragraph (1) or (5) of section 523(a) (in which case, notwithstanding any provision of applicable nonbankruptcy law to the contrary, such property shall be liable for a debt of a kind specified in section 523(a)(5));

* * * *

(d) The following property may be exempted under subsection (b)(2) of this section:

(10) The debtor's right to receive— * * * *

(D) alimony, support, or separate maintenance, to the extent reasonably necessary for the support of the debtor and any dependent of the debtor;

Comment: *Exemptions.* All property exempted by the debtor is liable for domestic support obligations, even if such property would not have been liable for such obligations under applicable nonbankruptcy law.

§ 11 U.S.C. § 523. Exceptions to discharge.

(a) A discharge under section 727, 1141, 1228(a), 1228(b), or 1328(b) of this title does not discharge an individual debtor from any debt— * * * *

(5) for a domestic support obligation; * * * *

(15) to a spouse, former spouse, or child of the debtor and not of the kind described in paragraph (5) that is incurred by the debtor in the course of a divorce or separation or in connection with a separation agreement, divorce decree or other order of a court of record, or a determination made in accordance with State or territorial law by a governmental unit;

Comment: *Dischargeability of Family-Related Obligations.* All domestic support obligations are nondischargeable. All marital property settlement obligations not in the nature of support are nondischargeable under section 523(a)(15). The bankruptcy court no longer has exclusive jurisdiction over the dischargeability of such debts.

§ 11 U.S.C. § 541. Property of the estate.

(a) The commencement of a case under section 301, 302, or 303 of this title creates an estate. Such estate is comprised of all the following property, wherever located and by whomever held: . . .

(5) Any interest in property that would have been property of the estate if such interest had been an interest of the debtor on the date of the filing of the petition, and that the debtor acquires or becomes entitled to acquire within 180 days after such date— . . .

(B) as a result of a property settlement agreement with the debtor's spouse, or of an interlocutory or final divorce decree; . . .

§ 11 U.S.C. § 547. Preferences.

* * * *

(c) The trustee may not avoid under this section a transfer— * * * *

(7) to the extent such transfer was a bona fide payment of a debt for a domestic support obligation;

Comment: *Preferences.* A preference cannot be avoided to the extent the transfer was in payment of a domestic support obligation.

§ 11 U.S.C. § 704. Duties of trustee.

(a) The trustee shall— * * * *

(10) if with respect to the debtor there is a claim for a domestic support obligation, provide the applicable notice specified in subsection (c); . . .

(c)(1) In a case described in subsection (a)(10) to which subsection (a)(10) applies, the trustee shall—

(A)(i) provide written notice to the holder of the claim described in subsection (a)(10) of such claim and of the right of such holder to use the services of the State child support enforcement agency established under sections 464 and 466 of the Social Security Act for the State in which such holder resides, for assistance in collecting child support during and after the case under this title;

    (ii) include in the notice provided under clause (i) the address and telephone number of such State child support enforcement agency; and

    (iii) include in the notice provided under clause (i) an explanation of the rights of such holder to payment of such claim under this chapter;

(B)(i) provide written notice to such State child support enforcement agency of such claim; and

    (ii) include in the notice provided under clause (i) the name, address, and telephone number of such holder; and

(C) at such time as the debtor is granted a discharge under section 727, provide written notice to such holder and to such State child support enforcement agency of—

    (i) the granting of the discharge;

    (ii) the last recent known address of the debtor;

    (iii) the last recent known name and address of the debtor's employer; and

    (iv) the name of each creditor that holds a claim that—

        (I) is not discharged under paragraph (2), (4), or (14A) of section 523(a); or

        (II) was reaffirmed by the debtor under section 524(c).

(2)(A) The holder of a claim described in subsection (a)(10) or the State child support enforcement agency of the State in which such holder resides may request from a creditor described in paragraph (1)(C)(iv) the last known address of the debtor.

(B) Notwithstanding any other provision of law, a creditor that makes a disclosure of a last known address of a debtor in connection with a request made under subparagraph (A) shall not be liable by reason of making such disclosure.

Comment: *Chapter 7 Trustee Notices to Domestic Support Obligees.* The chapter 7, 11, 12, or 13 trustee must provide notice to any holder of a claim for a domestic support obligation of the availability of state child support enforcement agency services and an explanation of the rights of the holder to payment of the claim under chapter 7. The trustee must also provide notice to the state child support enforcement agency of the name, address, and telephone number of the holder of the domestic support obligation claim. In addition, at the time a discharge is granted, the trustee must provide notice to the claim holder and state child support enforcement agency of the granting of the discharge, the last known address of the debtor, the last known name and address of the debtor's employer, and the name of each creditor holding a claim that was reaffirmed. The holder of a domestic support obligation may request the debtor's address from such creditors whose debts have not been discharged or reaffirmed and the creditor may supply that information.

§ 11 U.S.C. § 1129. Confirmation of plan.

(a) The court shall confirm a plan only if all of the following requirements are met: * * * *

(14) If the debtor is required by a judicial or administrative order, or by statute, to pay a domestic support obligation, the debtor has paid all amounts payable under such order or such statute for such obligation that first become payable after the date of the filing of the petition.

Comment: *Confirmation, Dismissal, and Discharge in Chapter 11, 12, and 13 Cases.* The standards for confirmation of a plan in chapter 11, 12, and 13 cases are amended to include the debtor's payment of domestic support obligations that first become payable after the filing of the petition. A chapter 12 or chapter 13 plan that does not pay in full priority domestic support obligations that have been assigned may not be confirmed over the objection of a domestic support creditor unless the plan applies all of the debtor's projected disposable income to plan payments for five years. Grounds for dismissal of a chapter 12 or chapter 13 case are amended to include failure to pay domestic support obligations that first become payable after the filing of the petition. A full compliance chapter 12 or chapter 13 discharge for a debtor who is required by a judicial or administrative order or by statute to pay a domestic support obligation cannot be entered unless the debtor certifies that all payments due on such obligation have been paid, except to the extent the plan did not require payment of prepetition obligations.

TITLE 18
CRIMES AND CRIMINAL PROCEDURE

PART I
CRIMES

CHAPTER 11A
CHILD SUPPORT

§ 228. **Failure to pay legal child support obligations.**

(a) **Offense.**—Any person who—

(1) willfully fails to pay a support obligation with respect to a child who resides in another State, if such obligation has remained unpaid for a period longer than 1 year, or is greater than $5,000;

(2) travels in interstate or foreign commerce with the intent to evade a support obligation, if such obligation has remained unpaid for a period longer than 1 year, or is greater than $5,000; or

(3) willfully fails to pay a support obligation with respect to a child who resides in another State, if such obligation has remained unpaid for a period longer than 2 years, or is greater than $10,000; shall be punished as provided in subsection (c).

(b) **Presumption.**—The existence of a support obligation that was in effect for the time period charged in the indictment or information creates a rebuttable presumption that the obligor has the ability to pay the support obligation for that time period.

(c) **Punishment.**—The punishment for an offense under this section is—

(1) in the case of a first offense under subsection (a)(1), a fine under this title, imprisonment for not more than 6 months, or both; and

(2) in the case of an offense under paragraph (2) or (3) of subsection (a), or a second or subsequent offense under subsection (a)(1), a fine under this title, imprisonment for not more than 2 years, or both.

(d) **Mandatory restitution.**—Upon a conviction under this section, the court shall order restitution under section 3663A in an amount equal to the total unpaid support obligation as it exists at the time of sentencing.

(e) **Venue.**—With respect to an offense under this section, an action may be inquired of and prosecuted in a district court of the United States for—

(1) the district in which the child who is the subject of the support obligation involved resided during a period during which a person described in subsection (a) (referred to in this subsection as an "obligor") failed to meet that support obligation;

(2) the district in which the obligor resided during a period described in paragraph (1); or

(3) any other district with jurisdiction otherwise provided for by law.

(f) **Definitions.**—As used in this section—

(1) the term "Indian tribe" has the meaning given that term in section 102 of the Federally Recognized Indian Tribe List Act of 1994 (25 U.S.C. 479a);

(2) the term "State" includes any State of the United States, the District of Columbia, and any commonwealth, territory, or possession of the United States; and

(3) the term "support obligation" means any amount determined under a court order or an order of an administrative process pursuant to the law of a State or of an Indian tribe to be due from a person for the support and maintenance of a child or of a child and the parent with whom the child is living.

CHAPTER 55

KIDNAPPING

§ 1204. **International parental kidnapping.**

(a) Whoever removes a child from the United States, or attempts to do so, or retains a child (who has been in the United States) outside the United States with intent to obstruct the lawful exercise of parental rights shall be fined under this title or imprisoned not more than 3 years, or both.

(b) As used in this section—

(1) the term "child" means a person who has not attained the age of 16 years; and

(2) the term "parental rights", with respect to a child, means the right to physical custody of the child—

(A) whether joint or sole (and includes visiting rights); and

(B) whether arising by operation of law, court order, or legally binding agreement of the parties.

(c) It shall be an affirmative defense under this section that—

(1) the defendant acted within the provisions of a valid court order granting the defendant legal custody or visitation rights and that order was obtained pursuant to the Uniform Child Custody Jurisdiction Act or the Uniform Child Custody Jurisdiction and Enforcement Act and was in effect at the time of the offense;

(2) the defendant was fleeing an incidence or pattern of domestic violence; or

(3) the defendant had physical custody of the child pursuant to a court order granting legal custody or visitation rights and failed to return the child as a result of circumstances beyond the defendant's control, and the defendant notified or made reasonable attempts to notify the other parent or lawful custodian of the child of such circumstances within 24 hours after the visitation period had expired and returned the child as soon as possible.

(d) This section does not detract from The Hague Convention on the Civil Aspects of International Parental Child Abduction, done at The Hague on October 25, 1980.

CHAPTER 110A

DOMESTIC VIOLENCE AND STALKING

§ 2261. Interstate domestic violence.

(a) Offenses.—

(1) Travel or conduct of offender.—A person who travels in interstate or foreign commerce or enters or leaves Indian country or is present within the special maritime and territorial jurisdiction of the United States with the intent to kill, injure, harass, or intimidate a spouse, intimate partner, or dating partner, and who, in the course of or as a result of such travel or presence, commits or attempts to commit a crime of violence against that spouse, intimate partner, or dating partner, shall be punished as provided in subsection (b).

(2) Causing travel of victim.—A person who causes a spouse, intimate partner, or dating partner to travel in interstate or foreign commerce or to enter or leave Indian country by force, coercion, duress, or fraud, and who, in the course of, as a result of, or to facilitate such conduct or travel, commits or attempts to commit a crime of violence against that spouse, intimate partner, or dating partner, shall be punished as provided in subsection (b).

(b) Penalties.—A person who violates this section or section 2261A shall be fined under this title, imprisoned-

(1) for life or any term of years, if death of the victim results;

(2) for not more than 20 years if permanent disfigurement or life threatening bodily injury to the victim results;

(3) for not more than 10 years, if serious bodily injury to the victim results or if the offender uses a dangerous weapon during the offense;

(4) as provided for the applicable conduct under chapter 109A if the offense would constitute an offense under chapter 109A (without regard to whether the offense was committed in the special maritime and territorial jurisdiction of the United States or in a Federal prison); and

(5) for not more than 5 years, in any other case,

or both fined and imprisoned.

(6) Whoever commits the crime of stalking in violation of a temporary or permanent civil or criminal injunction, restraining order, no-contact order, or other order described in section 2266 of title 18, United States Code, shall be punished by imprisonment for not less than 1 year.

(Added Pub. L. 103–322, title IV, § 40221(a), Sept. 13, 1994, 108 Stat. 1926; amended Pub. L. 104–201, div. A, title X, § 1069(b)(1), (2), Sept. 23, 1996, 110 Stat. 2656; Pub. L. 106–386, div. B, title I, § 1107(a), Oct. 28, 2000, 114 Stat. 1497; Pub. L. 109–162, title I, §§ 114(b), 116(a), 117(a), Jan. 5, 2006, 119 Stat. 2988, 2989; Pub. L. 113–4, title I, § 107(a), Mar. 7, 2013, 127 Stat. 77.)

§ 2261A. Stalking.

Whoever—

(1) travels in interstate or foreign commerce or is present within the special maritime and territorial jurisdiction of the United States, or enters or leaves Indian country, with the intent to kill, injure, harass, intimidate, or place under surveillance with intent to kill, injure, harass, or intimidate another person, and in the course of, or as a result of, such travel or presence engages in conduct that—

(A) places that person in reasonable fear of the death of, or serious bodily injury to—

(i) that person;

(ii) an immediate family member (as defined in section 115) of that person;

(iii) a spouse or intimate partner of that person; or

(iv) the pet, service animal, emotional support animal, or horse of that person; or

(B) causes, attempts to cause, or would be reasonably expected to cause substantial emotional distress to a person described in clause (i), (ii), or (iii) of subparagraph (A); or

(2) with the intent to kill, injure, harass, intimidate, or place under surveillance with intent to kill, injure, harass, or intimidate another person, uses the mail, any interactive computer service or electronic communication service or electronic communication system of interstate commerce, or any other facility of interstate or foreign commerce to engage in a course of conduct that—

(A) places that person in reasonable fear of the death of or serious bodily injury to a person, a pet, a service animal, an emotional support animal, or a horse described in clause (i), (ii), (iii), or (iv) of paragraph (1)(A); or

(B) causes, attempts to cause, or would be reasonably expected to cause substantial emotional distress to a person described in clause (i), (ii), or (iii) of paragraph (1)(A), shall be punished as provided in section 2261(b) of this title.

(Added Pub. L. 104–201, div. A, title X, §1069(a), Sept. 23, 1996, 110 Stat. 2655; amended Pub. L. 106–386, div. B, title I, §1107(b)(1), Oct. 28, 2000, 114 Stat. 1498; Pub. L. 109–162, title I, §114(a), Jan. 5, 2006, 119 Stat. 2987; Pub. L. 113–4, title I, §107(b), Mar. 7, 2013, 127 Stat. 77; Pub. L. 115–334, title XII, §12502(a)(1), Dec. 20, 2018, 132 Stat. 4982.)

§ 2262. Interstate violation of protection order.

(a) Offenses.—

(1) Travel or conduct of offender.—A person who travels in interstate or foreign commerce, or enters or leaves Indian country or is present within the special maritime and territorial jurisdiction of the United States, with the intent to engage in conduct that violates the portion of a protection order that prohibits or provides protection against violence, threats, or harassment against, contact or communication with, or physical proximity to, another person or the pet, service animal, emotional support animal, or horse of that person, or that would violate such a portion of a protection order in the jurisdiction in which the order was issued, and subsequently engages in such conduct, shall be punished as provided in subsection (b).

(2) Causing travel of victim.—A person who causes another person to travel in interstate or foreign commerce or to enter or leave Indian country by force, coercion, duress, or fraud, and in the course of, as a result of, or to facilitate such conduct or travel engages in conduct that violates the portion of a protection order that prohibits or provides protection against violence, threats, or harassment against, contact or communication with, or physical proximity to, another person or the pet, service animal, emotional support animal, or horse of that person, or that would violate such a portion of a protection order in the jurisdiction in which the order was issued, shall be punished as provided in subsection (b).

(b) Penalties.—A person who violates this section shall be fined under this title, imprisoned—

(1) for life or any term of years, if death of the victim results;

(2) for not more than 20 years if permanent disfigurement or life threatening bodily injury to the victim results;

(3) for not more than 10 years, if serious bodily injury to the victim results or if the offender uses a dangerous weapon during the offense;

(4) as provided for the applicable conduct under chapter 109A if the offense would constitute an offense under chapter 109A (without regard to whether the offense was committed in the special maritime and territorial jurisdiction of the United States or in a Federal prison); and

(5) for not more than 5 years, in any other case, including any case in which the offense is committed against a pet, service animal, emotional support animal, or horse, or both fined and imprisoned.

(Added Pub. L. 103–322, title IV, §40221(a), Sept. 13, 1994, 108 Stat. 1927; amended Pub. L. 104–201, div. A, title X, §1069(b)(2), Sept. 23, 1996, 110 Stat. 2656; Pub. L. 104–294, title VI, §605(d), Oct. 11, 1996, 110 Stat. 3509; Pub. L. 106–386, div. B, title I, §1107(c), Oct. 28, 2000, 114 Stat. 1498; Pub. L. 109–162, title I, §117(b), Jan. 5, 2006, 119 Stat. 2989; Pub. L. 113–4, title I, §107(c), Mar. 7, 2013, 127 Stat. 78; Pub. L. 115–334, title XII, §12502(a)(2), Dec. 20, 2018, 132 Stat. 4982.)

§ 2263. Pretrial release of defendant.

In any proceeding pursuant to section 3142 for the purpose of determining whether a defendant charged under this chapter shall be released pending trial, or for the purpose of determining conditions of such release, the alleged victim shall be given an opportunity to be heard regarding the danger posed by the defendant.

§ 2264. Restitution.

(a) In general.—Notwithstanding section 3663 or 3663A, and in addition to any other civil or criminal penalty authorized by law, the court shall order restitution for any offense under this chapter.

(b) Scope and nature of order.—

(1) **Directions.**—The order of restitution under this section shall direct the defendant to pay the victim (through the appropriate court mechanism) the full amount of the victim's losses as determined by the court pursuant to paragraph (2).

(2) **Enforcement.**—An order of restitution under this section shall be issued and enforced in accordance with section 3664 in the same manner as an order under section 3663A.

(3) **Definition.**—For purposes of this subsection, the term "full amount of the victim's losses" includes any costs incurred by the victim for—

 (A) medical services relating to physical, psychiatric, or psychological care;

 (B) physical and occupational therapy or rehabilitation;

 (C) necessary transportation, temporary housing, and child care expenses;

 (D) lost income;

 (E) attorneys' fees, plus any costs incurred in obtaining a civil protection order; and

 (F) any other losses suffered by the victim as a proximate result of the offense.

(4) **Order mandatory.**—(A) The issuance of a restitution order under this section is mandatory.

 (B) A court may not decline to issue an order under this section because of—

 (i) the economic circumstances of the defendant; or

 (ii) the fact that a victim has, or is entitled to, receive compensation for his or her injuries from the proceeds of insurance or any other source.

(c) Victim defined.—For purposes of this section, the term "victim" means the individual harmed as a result of a commission of a crime under this chapter, including, in the case of a victim who is under 18 years of age, incompetent, incapacitated, or deceased, the legal guardian of the victim or representative of the victim's estate, another family member, or any other person appointed as suitable by the court, but in no event shall the defendant be named as such representative or guardian.

§ 2265. Full faith and credit given to protection orders.

(a) **Full Faith and Credit.**—Any protection order issued that is consistent with subsection (b) of this section by the court of one State, Indian tribe, or territory (the issuing State, Indian tribe, or territory) shall be accorded full faith and credit by the court of another State, Indian tribe, or territory (the enforcing State, Indian tribe, or territory) and enforced by the court and law enforcement personnel of the other State, Indian tribal government or Territory 1 as if it were the order of the enforcing State or tribe.

(b) **Protection Order.**—A protection order issued by a State, tribal, or territorial court is consistent with this subsection if—

(1) such court has jurisdiction over the parties and matter under the law of such State, Indian tribe, or territory; and

(2) reasonable notice and opportunity to be heard is given to the person against whom the order is sought sufficient to protect that person's right to due process. In the case of ex parte orders, notice and opportunity to be heard must be provided within the time required by State, tribal, or territorial law, and in any event within a reasonable time after the order is issued, sufficient to protect the respondent's due process rights.

(c) **Cross or Counter Petition.**—A protection order issued by a State, tribal, or territorial court against one who has petitioned, filed a complaint, or otherwise filed a written pleading for protection against abuse by a spouse or intimate partner is not entitled to full faith and credit if—

(1) no cross or counter petition, complaint, or other written pleading was filed seeking such a protection order; or

(2) a cross or counter petition has been filed and the court did not make specific findings that each party was entitled to such an order.

(d) **Notification and Registration.**—

(1) **Notification.**—A State, Indian tribe, or territory according full faith and credit to an order by a court of another State, Indian tribe, or territory shall not notify or require notification of the party against whom a protection order has been issued that the protection order has been registered or filed in that enforcing State, tribal, or territorial jurisdiction unless requested to do so by the party protected under such order.

(2) **No prior registration or filing as prerequisite for enforcement.**—Any protection order that is otherwise consistent with this section shall be accorded full faith and credit, notwithstanding failure to comply with any requirement that the order be registered or filed in the enforcing State, tribal, or territorial jurisdiction.

(3) **Limits on internet publication of registration information.**—A State, Indian tribe, or territory shall not make available publicly on the Internet any information regarding the registration, filing of a petition for, or issuance of a protection order, restraining order or injunction, restraining order, or injunction in either the issuing or enforcing State, tribal or territorial jurisdiction, if such publication would be likely to publicly reveal the identity or location of the party protected under such order. A State, Indian tribe, or territory may share court-generated and law enforcement-generated information contained in secure, governmental registries for protection order enforcement purposes.

(e) **Tribal Court Jurisdiction.**—For purposes of this section, a court of an Indian tribe shall have full civil jurisdiction to issue and enforce protection orders involving any person, including the authority to enforce any orders through civil contempt proceedings, to exclude violators from Indian land, and to use other appropriate mecha-

nisms, in matters arising anywhere in the Indian country of the Indian tribe (as defined in section 1151) or otherwise within the authority of the Indian tribe.
(Added Pub. L. 103–322, title IV, § 40221(a), Sept. 13, 1994, 108 Stat. 1930; amended Pub. L. 106–386, div. B, title I, § 1101(b)(4), Oct. 28, 2000, 114 Stat. 1493; Pub. L. 109–162, title I, § 106(a)–(c), Jan. 5, 2006, 119 Stat. 2981, 2982; Pub. L. 109–271, § 2(n), Aug. 12, 2006, 120 Stat. 754; Pub. L. 113–4, title IX, § 905, Mar. 7, 2013, 127 Stat. 124.)

§ 2265A. Repeat offenders

(a) Maximum Term of Imprisonment.—The maximum term of imprisonment for a violation of this chapter after a prior domestic violence or stalking offense shall be twice the term otherwise provided under this chapter.

(b) Definition.—For purposes of this section—

(1) the term "prior domestic violence or stalking offense" means a conviction for an offense—

(A) under section 2261, 2261A, or 2262 of this chapter; or

(B) under State or tribal law for an offense consisting of conduct that would have been an offense under a section referred to in subparagraph (A) if the conduct had occurred within the special maritime and territorial jurisdiction of the United States, or in interstate or foreign commerce; and

(2) the term "State" means a State of the United States, the District of Columbia, or any commonwealth, territory, or possession of the United States.

(Added Pub. L. 109–162, title I, § 115, Jan. 5, 2006, 119 Stat. 2988; amended Pub. L. 113–4, title IX, § 906(c), Mar. 7, 2013, 127 Stat. 125.)

§ 2266. Definitions.

In this chapter:

(1) Bodily injury.—The term "bodily injury" means any act, except one done in self-defense, that results in physical injury or sexual abuse.

(2) Course of conduct.—The term "course of conduct" means a pattern of conduct composed of 2 or more acts, evidencing a continuity of purpose.

(3) Enter or leave Indian country.—The term "enter or leave Indian country" includes leaving the jurisdiction of 1 tribal government and entering the jurisdiction of another tribal government.

(4) Indian country.—The term "Indian country" has the meaning stated in section 1151 of this title.

(5) Protection order.—The term "protection order" includes—

(A) any injunction, restraining order, or any other order issued by a civil or criminal court for the purpose of preventing violent or threatening acts or harassment against, sexual violence, or contact or communication with or physical proximity to, another person, including any temporary or final order issued by a civil or criminal court whether obtained by filing an independent action or as a pendente lite order in another proceeding so long as any civil or criminal order was issued in response to a complaint, petition, or motion filed by or on behalf of a person seeking protection; and

(B) any support, child custody or visitation provisions, orders, remedies or relief issued as part of a protection order, restraining order, or injunction pursuant to State, tribal, territorial, or local law authorizing the issuance of protection orders, restraining orders, or injunctions for the protection of victims of domestic violence, sexual assault, dating violence, or stalking.

(6) Serious bodily injury.—The term "serious bodily injury" has the meaning stated in section 2119(2).

(7) **Spouse or intimate partner.**—The term "spouse or intimate partner" includes—

(A) for purposes of—

(i) sections other than 2261A—

(I) a spouse or former spouse of the abuser, a person who shares a child in common with the abuser, and a person who cohabits or has cohabited as a spouse with the abuser; or

(II) a person who is or has been in a social relationship of a romantic or intimate nature with the abuser, as determined by the length of the relationship, the type of relationship, and the frequency of interaction between the persons involved in the relationship; and

(ii) section 2261A—

(I) a spouse or former spouse of the target of the stalking, a person who shares a child in common with the target of the stalking, and a person who cohabits or has cohabited as a spouse with the target of the stalking; or

(II) a person who is or has been in a social relationship of a romantic or intimate nature with the target of the stalking, as determined by the length of the relationship, the type of the relationship, and the frequency of interaction between the persons involved in the relationship.1

(B) any other person similarly situated to a spouse who is protected by the domestic or family violence laws of the State or tribal jurisdiction in which the injury occurred or where the victim resides.

(8) **State.**—The term "State" includes a State of the United States, the District of Columbia, and a commonwealth, territory, or possession of the United States.

(9) **Travel in interstate or foreign commerce.**—The term "travel in interstate or foreign commerce" does not include travel from 1 State to another by an individual who is a member of an Indian tribe and who remains at all times in the territory of the Indian tribe of which the individual is a member.

(10) **Dating partner.**—The term "dating partner" refers to a person who is or has been in a social relationship of a romantic or intimate nature with the abuser. The existence of such a relationship is based on a consideration of—

(A) the length of the relationship; and

(B) the type of relationship; and

(C) the frequency of interaction between the persons involved in the relationship.

(11) **Pet.**—The term "pet" means a domesticated animal, such as a dog, cat, bird, rodent, fish, turtle, or other animal that is kept for pleasure rather than for commercial purposes.

(12) **Emotional support animal.**—The term "emotional support animal" means an animal that is covered by the exclusion specified in section 5.303 of title 24, Code of Federal Regulations (or a successor regulation), and that is not a service animal.

(13) **Service animal.**—The term "service animal" has the meaning given the term in section 36.104 of title 28, Code of Federal Regulations (or a successor regulation).

(Added Pub. L. 103–322, title IV, §40221(a), Sept. 13, 1994, 108 Stat. 1931; amended Pub. L. 106–386, div. B, title I, §1107(d), Oct. 28, 2000, 114 Stat. 1499; Pub. L. 109–162, title I, §§106(d), 116(b), Jan. 5, 2006, 119 Stat. 2982, 2988; Pub. L. 109–271, §2(c), (i), Aug. 12, 2006, 120 Stat. 752; Pub. L. 115–334, title XII, §12502(a)(4), Dec. 20, 2018, 132 Stat. 4983.)

TITLE 22
FOREIGN RELATIONS AND INTERCOURSE

CHAPTER 4
PASSPORTS

§ 213. Application for passport; verification by oath of initial passport.

Before a passport is issued to any person by or under authority of the United States such person shall subscribe to and submit a written application which shall contain a true recital of each and every matter of fact which may be required by law or by any rules authorized by law to be stated as a prerequisite to the issuance of any such passport. If the applicant has not previously been issued a United States passport, the application shall be duly verified by his oath before a person authorized and empowered by the Secretary of State to administer oaths.

CHAPTER 97

INTERNATIONAL CHILD ABDUCTION REMEDIES

Sec.
9001. Findings and declarations.
9002. Definitions.
9003. Judicial remedies.
9004. Provisional remedies.
9005. Admissibility of documents.
9006. United States Central Authority.
9007. Costs and fees.
9008. Collection, maintenance, and dissemination of information.
9009. Office of Children's Issues.
9010. Interagency coordinating group.
9011. Authorization of appropriations.

§ 9001. Findings and declarations.

(a) Findings

The Congress makes the following findings:

(1) The international abduction or wrongful retention of children is harmful to their well-being.

(2) Persons should not be permitted to obtain custody of children by virtue of their wrongful removal or retention.

(3) International abductions and retentions of children are increasing, and only concerted cooperation pursuant to an international agreement can effectively combat this problem.

(4) The Convention on the Civil Aspects of International Child Abduction, done at The Hague on October 25, 1980, establishes legal rights and procedures for the prompt return of children who have been wrongfully removed or retained, as well as for securing the exercise of visitation rights. Children who are wrongfully removed or retained within the meaning of the Convention are to be promptly returned unless one of the narrow exceptions set forth in the Convention applies. The Convention provides a sound treaty framework to help resolve the problem of international abduction and retention of children and will deter such wrongful removals and retentions.

(b) Declarations

The Congress makes the following declarations:

(1) It is the purpose of this chapter to establish procedures for the implementation of the Convention in the United States.

(2) The provisions of this chapter are in addition to and not in lieu of the provisions of the Convention.

(3) In enacting this chapter the Congress recognizes—

(A) the international character of the Convention; and

(B) the need for uniform international interpretation of the Convention.

(4) The Convention and this chapter empower courts in the United States to determine only rights under the Convention and not the merits of any underlying child custody claims.

(Pub. L. 100–300, § 2, Apr. 29, 1988, 102 Stat. 437.)

Codification

Section was formerly classified to section 11601 of Title 42, The Public Health and Welfare.

§ 9002. Definitions.

For the purposes of this chapter—

(1) the term "applicant" means any person who, pursuant to the Convention, files an application with the United States Central Authority or a Central Authority of any other party to the Convention for the return of a child alleged to have been wrongfully removed or retained or for arrangements for organizing or securing the effective exercise of rights of access pursuant to the Convention;

(2) the term "Convention" means the Convention on the Civil Aspects of International Child Abduction, done at The Hague on October 25, 1980;

(3) the term "Parent Locator Service" means the service established by the Secretary of Health and Human Services under section 653 of title 42;

(4) the term "petitioner" means any person who, in accordance with this chapter, files a petition in court seeking relief under the Convention;

(5) the term "person" includes any individual, institution, or other legal entity or body;

(6) the term "respondent" means any person against whose interests a petition is filed in court, in accordance with this chapter, which seeks relief under the Convention;

(7) the term "rights of access" means visitation rights;

(8) the term "State" means any of the several States, the District of Columbia, and any commonwealth, territory, or possession of the United States; and

(9) the term "United States Central Authority" means the agency of the Federal Government designated by the President under section 9006(a) of this title.

(Pub. L. 100–300, § 3, Apr. 29, 1988, 102 Stat. 437.)

Codification

Section was formerly classified to section 11602 of Title 42, The Public Health and Welfare.

§ 9003. Judicial remedies.

(a) Jurisdiction of courts

The courts of the States and the United States district courts shall have concurrent original jurisdiction of actions arising under the Convention.

(b) Petitions

Any person seeking to initiate judicial proceedings under the Convention for the return of a child or for arrangements for organizing or securing the effective exercise of rights of access to a child may do so by commencing a civil action by filing a petition for the relief sought in any court which has jurisdiction of such action and which is authorized to exercise its jurisdiction in the place where the child is located at the time the petition is filed.

(c) Notice

Notice of an action brought under subsection (b) shall be given in accordance with the applicable law governing notice in interstate child custody proceedings.

(d) Determination of case

The court in which an action is brought under subsection (b) shall decide the case in accordance with the Convention.

(e) Burdens of proof

(1) A petitioner in an action brought under subsection (b) shall establish by a preponderance of the evidence—

(A) in the case of an action for the return of a child, that the child has been wrongfully removed or retained within the meaning of the Convention; and

(B) in the case of an action for arrangements for organizing or securing the effective exercise of rights of access, that the petitioner has such rights.

(2) In the case of an action for the return of a child, a respondent who opposes the return of the child has the burden of establishing—

(A) by clear and convincing evidence that one of the exceptions set forth in article 13b or 20 of the Convention applies; and

(B) by a preponderance of the evidence that any other exception set forth in article 12 or 13 of the Convention applies.

(f) Application of Convention

For purposes of any action brought under this chapter—

(1) the term "authorities", as used in article 15 of the Convention to refer to the authorities of the state of the habitual residence of a child, includes courts and appropriate government agencies;

(2) the terms "wrongful removal or retention" and "wrongfully removed or retained", as used in the Convention, include a removal or retention of a child before the entry of a custody order regarding that child; and

(3) the term "commencement of proceedings", as used in article 12 of the Convention, means, with respect to the return of a child located in the United States, the filing of a petition in accordance with subsection (b) of this section.

(g) Full faith and credit

Full faith and credit shall be accorded by the courts of the States and the courts of the United States to the judgment of any other such court ordering or denying the return of a child, pursuant to the Convention, in an action brought under this chapter.

(h) Remedies under Convention not exclusive

The remedies established by the Convention and this chapter shall be in addition to remedies available under other laws or international agreements.

(Pub. L. 100–300, § 4, Apr. 29, 1988, 102 Stat. 438.)

Codification

Section was formerly classified to section 11603 of Title 42, The Public Health and Welfare.

§ 9004. Provisional remedies.

(a) Authority of courts

In furtherance of the objectives of article 7(b) and other provisions of the Convention, and subject to the provisions of subsection (b) of this section, any court exercising jurisdiction of an action brought under section 9003(b) of this title may take or cause to be taken measures under Federal or State law, as appropriate, to protect the well-being of the child involved or to prevent the child's further removal or concealment before the final disposition of the petition.

(b) Limitation on authority

No court exercising jurisdiction of an action brought under section 9003(b) of this title may, under subsection (a) of this section, order a child removed from a person having physical control of the child unless the applicable requirements of State law are satisfied.

(Pub. L. 100–300, § 5, Apr. 29, 1988, 102 Stat. 439.)

Codification

Section was formerly classified to section 11604 of Title 42, The Public Health and Welfare.

§ 9005. Admissibility of documents.

With respect to any application to the United States Central Authority, or any petition to a court under section 9003 of this title, which seeks relief under the Convention, or any other documents or information included with such application or petition or provided after such submission which relates to the application or petition, as the case may be, no authentication of such application, petition, document, or information shall be required in order for the application, petition, document, or information to be admissible in court.

(Pub. L. 100–300, § 6, Apr. 29, 1988, 102 Stat. 439.)

Codification

Section was formerly classified to section 11605 of Title 42, The Public Health and Welfare.

§ 9006. United States Central Authority.

(a) Designation

The President shall designate a Federal agency to serve as the Central Authority for the United States under the Convention.

(b) Functions

The functions of the United States Central Authority are those ascribed to the Central Authority by the Convention and this chapter.

(c) Regulatory authority

The United States Central Authority is authorized to issue such regulations as may be necessary to carry out its functions under the Convention and this chapter.

(d) Obtaining information from Parent Locator Service

The United States Central Authority may, to the extent authorized by the Social Security Act [42 U.S.C. 301 et seq.], obtain information from the Parent Locator Service.

(e) Grant authority

The United States Central Authority is authorized to make grants to, or enter into contracts or agreements with, any individual, corporation, other Federal, State, or local agency, or private entity or organization in the United States for purposes of accomplishing its responsibilities under the Convention and this chapter.

(f) Limited liability of private entities acting under the direction of the United States Central Authority

(1) Limitation on liability

Except as provided in paragraphs (2) and (3), a private entity or organization that receives a grant from or enters into a contract or agreement with the United States Central Authority under subsection (e) of this section for purposes of assisting the United States Central Authority in carrying out its responsibilities and functions under the Convention and this chapter, including any director, officer, employee, or agent of such entity or organization, shall not be liable in any civil action sounding in tort for damages directly related to the performance of such responsibilities and functions as defined by the regulations issued under subsection (c) of this section that are in effect on October 1, 2004.

(2) Exception for intentional, reckless, or other misconduct

The limitation on liability under paragraph (1) shall not apply in any action in which the plaintiff proves that the private entity, organization, officer, employee, or agent described in paragraph (1), as the case may be, engaged in intentional misconduct or acted, or failed to act, with actual malice, with reckless disregard to a substantial risk of causing injury without legal justification, or for a purpose unrelated to the performance of responsibilities or functions under this chapter.

(3) Exception for ordinary business activities

The limitation on liability under paragraph (1) shall not apply to any alleged act or omission related to an ordinary business activity, such as an activity involving general administration or operations, the use of motor vehicles, or personnel management.

(Pub. L. 100–300, § 7, Apr. 29, 1988, 102 Stat. 439; Pub. L. 105–277, div. G, title XXII, § 2213, Oct. 21, 1998, 112 Stat. 2681–812; Pub. L. 108–370, § 2, Oct. 25, 2004, 118 Stat. 1750.)

Codification

Section was formerly classified to section 11606 of Title 42, The Public Health and Welfare.

§ 9007. Costs and fees.

(a) Administrative costs

No department, agency, or instrumentality of the Federal Government or of any State or local government may impose on an applicant any fee in relation to the administrative processing of applications submitted under the Convention.

(b) Costs incurred in civil actions

(1) Petitioners may be required to bear the costs of legal counsel or advisors, court costs incurred in connection with their petitions, and travel costs for the return of the child involved and any accompanying persons, except as provided in paragraphs (2) and (3).

(2) Subject to paragraph (3), legal fees or court costs incurred in connection with an action brought under section 9003 of this title shall be borne by the petitioner unless they are covered by payments from Federal, State, or local legal assistance or other programs.

(3) Any court ordering the return of a child pursuant to an action brought under section 9003 of this title shall order the respondent to pay necessary expenses incurred by or on behalf of the petitioner, including court costs, legal fees, foster home or other care during the course of proceedings in the action, and transportation costs related to the return of the child, unless the respondent establishes that such order would be clearly inappropriate.

(Pub. L. 100–300, § 8, Apr. 29, 1988, 102 Stat. 440.)

Codification

Section was formerly classified to section 11607 of Title 42, The Public Health and Welfare.

§ 9008. Collection, maintenance, and dissemination of information.

(a) In general

In performing its functions under the Convention, the United States Central Authority may, under such conditions as the Central Authority prescribes by regulation, but subject to subsection (c), receive from or transmit to any department, agency, or instrumentality of the Federal Government or of any State or foreign government, and receive from or transmit to any applicant, petitioner, or respondent, information necessary to locate a child or for the purpose of otherwise implementing the Convention with respect to a child, except that the United States Central Authority—

(1) may receive such information from a Federal or State department, agency, or instrumentality only pursuant to applicable Federal and State statutes; and

(2) may transmit any information received under this subsection notwithstanding any provision of law other than this chapter.

(b) Requests for information

Requests for information under this section shall be submitted in such manner and form as the United States Central Authority may prescribe by regulation and shall be accompanied or supported by such documents as the United States Central Authority may require.

(c) Responsibility of government entities

Whenever any department, agency, or instrumentality of the United States or of any State receives a request from the United States Central Authority for information authorized to be provided to such Central Authority under subsection (a), the head of such department, agency, or instrumentality shall promptly cause a search to be made of the files and records maintained by such department, agency, or instrumentality in order to determine whether the information requested is contained in any such files or records. If such search discloses the information requested, the head of such department, agency, or instrumentality shall immediately transmit such information to the United States Central Authority, except that any such information the disclosure of which—

(1) would adversely affect the national security interests of the United States or the law enforcement interests of the United States or of any State; or

(2) would be prohibited by section 9 of title 13;

shall not be transmitted to the Central Authority. The head of such department, agency, or instrumentality shall, immediately upon completion of the requested search, notify the Central Authority of the results of the search, and whether an exception set forth in paragraph (1) or (2) applies. In the event that the United States Central Authority receives information and the appropriate Federal or State department, agency, or instrumentality thereafter notifies the Central Authority that an exception set forth in paragraph (1) or (2) applies to that information, the Central Authority may not disclose that information under subsection (a).

(d) Information available from Parent Locator Service

To the extent that information which the United States Central Authority is authorized to obtain under the provisions of subsection (c) can be obtained through the Parent Locator Service, the United States Central Authority shall first seek to obtain such information from the Parent Locator Service, before requesting such information directly under the provisions of subsection (c) of this section.

(e) Recordkeeping

The United States Central Authority shall maintain appropriate records concerning its activities and the disposition of cases brought to its attention.

(Pub. L. 100–300, § 9, Apr. 29, 1988, 102 Stat. 440.)

Codification

Section was formerly classified to section 11608 of Title 42, The Public Health and Welfare.

§ 9009. Office of Children's Issues.

(a) Director requirements

The Secretary of State shall fill the position of Director of the Office of Children's Issues of the Department of State (in this section referred to as the "Office") with an individual of senior rank who can ensure long-term continuity in the management and policy matters of the Office and has a strong background in consular affairs.

(b) Case officer staffing

Effective April 1, 2000, there shall be assigned to the Office of Children's Issues of the Department of State a sufficient number of case officers to ensure that the average caseload for each officer does not exceed 75.

(c) Embassy contact

The Secretary of State shall designate in each United States diplomatic mission an employee who shall serve as the point of contact for matters relating to international abductions of children by parents. The Director of the Office shall regularly inform the designated employee of children of United States citizens abducted by parents to that country.

(d) Reports to parents

(1) In general

Except as provided in paragraph (2), beginning 6 months after November 29, 1999, and at least once every 6 months thereafter, the Secretary of State shall report to each parent who has requested assistance regarding an abducted child overseas. Each such report shall include information on the current status of the abducted child's case and the efforts by the Department of State to resolve the case.

(2) Exception

The requirement in paragraph (1) shall not apply in a case of an abducted child if—

(A) the case has been closed and the Secretary of State has reported the reason the case was closed to the parent who requested assistance; or

(B) the parent seeking assistance requests that such reports not be provided.

(Pub. L. 106–113, div. B, § 1000(a)(7) [div. A, title II, § 201], Nov. 29, 1999, 113 Stat. 1536, 1501A-419).

Codification

Section was enacted as part of the Admiral James W. Nance and Meg Donovan Foreign Relations Authorization Act, Fiscal Years 2000 and 2001, and not as part of the International Child Abduction Remedies Act which comprises this chapter.

Section was formerly classified to section 11608a of Title 42, The Public Health and Welfare.

§ 9010. Interagency coordinating group.

The Secretary of State, the Secretary of Health and Human Services, and the Attorney General shall designate Federal employees and may, from time to time, designate private citizens to serve on an interagency coordinating group to monitor the operation of the Convention and to provide advice on its implementation to the United States Central Authority and other Federal agencies. This group shall meet from time to time at the request of the United States Central Authority. The agency in which the United States Central Authority is located is authorized to reimburse such private citizens for travel and other expenses incurred in participating at meetings of the interagency coordinating group at rates not to exceed those authorized under subchapter I of chapter 57 of title 5 for employees of agencies.

(Pub. L. 100–300, § 10, Apr. 29, 1988, 102 Stat. 441.)

Codification

Section was formerly classified to section 11609 of Title 42, The Public Health and Welfare.

§ 9011. Authorization of appropriations.

There are authorized to be appropriated for each fiscal year such sums as may be necessary to carry out the purposes of the Convention and this chapter.

(Pub. L. 100–300, § 12, Apr. 29, 1988, 102 Stat. 442.)

Codification

Section was formerly classified to section 11610 of Title 42, The Public Health and Welfare.

CHAPTER 98

INTERNATIONAL CHILD ABDUCTION PREVENTION AND RETURN

Sec.

9101. Definitions.

Subchapter I. Department of State Actions

9111. Annual Report.
9112. Standards and assistance.
9113. Bilateral procedures, including memoranda of understanding.
9114. Report to congressional representatives.

Subchapter II. Actions By the Secretary of State

9121. Response to international child abductions.
9122. Actions by the Secretary of State in response to patterns of noncompliance in cases of international child abductions.
9123. Consultations with foreign governments.
9124. Waiver by the Secretary of State.
9125. Termination of actions by the Secretary of State.

Subchapter III. Prevention of International Child Abduction

9141. Authorization for judicial training on international parental child abduction.

§ 9101. Definitions.

In this chapter:

(1) Abducted child

The term "abducted child" means a child who is the victim of international child abduction.

(2) Abduction

The term "abduction" means the alleged wrongful removal of a child from the child's country of habitual residence, or the wrongful retention of a child outside such country, in violation of a left-behind parent's custodial rights, including the rights of a military parent.

(3) Abduction case

The term "abduction case" means a case that—

(A) has been reported to the Central Authority of the United States by a left-behind parent for the resolution of an abduction; and

(B) meets the criteria for an international child abduction under the Hague Abduction Convention, regardless of whether the country at issue is a Convention country.

(4) Access case

The term "access case" means a case involving an application filed with the Central Authority of the United States by a parent seeking rights of access.

(5) Annual Report

The term "Annual Report" means the Annual Report on International Child Abduction required under section 9111 of this title.

(6) Application

The term "application" means—

(A) in the case of a Convention country, the application required pursuant to article 8 of the Hague Abduction Convention;

(B) in the case of a bilateral procedures country, the formal document required, pursuant to the provisions of the applicable arrangement, to request the return of an abducted child or to request rights of access, as applicable; and

(C) in the case of a non-Convention country, the formal request by the Central Authority of the United States to the Central Authority of such country requesting the return of an abducted child or for rights of contact with an abducted child.

(7) Appropriate congressional committees

The term "appropriate congressional committees" means the Committee on Foreign Relations of the Senate and the Committee on Foreign Affairs of the House of Representatives.

(8) Bilateral procedures

The term "bilateral procedures" means any procedures established by, or pursuant to, a bilateral arrangement, including a Memorandum of Understanding between the United States and another country, to resolve abduction and access cases, including procedures to address interim contact matters.

(9) Bilateral procedures country

The term "bilateral procedures country" means a country with which the United States has entered into bilateral procedures, including Memoranda of Understanding, with respect to child abductions.

(10) Central Authority

The term "Central Authority" means—

(A) in the case of a Convention country, the meaning given such term in article 6 of the Hague Abduction Convention;

(B) in the case of a bilateral procedures country, the official entity designated by the government of the bilateral procedures country within the applicable memorandum of understanding pursuant to section 9113(b)(1) of this title to discharge the duties imposed on the entity; and

(C) in the case of a non-Convention country, the foreign ministry or other appropriate authority of such country.

(11) Child

The term "child" means an individual who has not attained 16 years of age.

(12) Convention country

The term "Convention country" means a country for which the Hague Abduction Convention has entered into force with respect to the United States.

(13) Hague Abduction Convention

The term "Hague Abduction Convention" means the Convention on the Civil Aspects of International Child Abduction, done at The Hague October 25, 1980.

(14) Interim contact

The term "interim contact" means the ability of a left-behind parent to communicate with or visit an abducted child during the pendency of an abduction case.

(15) Left-behind parent

The term "left-behind parent" means an individual or legal custodian who alleges that an abduction has occurred that is in breach of rights of custody attributed to such individual.

(16) Non-Convention country

The term "non-Convention country" means a country in which the Hague Abduction Convention has not entered into force with respect to the United States.

(17) Overseas military dependent child

The term "overseas military dependent child" means a child whose habitual residence is the United States according to United States law even though the child is residing outside the United States with a military parent.

(18) Overseas military parent

The term "overseas military parent" means an individual who—

(A) has custodial rights with respect to a child; and

(B) is serving outside the United States as a member of the United States Armed Forces.

(19) Pattern of noncompliance

(A) In general

The term "pattern of noncompliance" means the persistent failure—

(i) of a Convention country to implement and abide by provisions of the Hague Abduction Convention;

(ii) of a non-Convention country to abide by bilateral procedures that have been established between the United States and such country; or

(iii) of a non-Convention country to work with the Central Authority of the United States to resolve abduction cases.

(B) Persistent failure

Persistent failure under subparagraph (A) may be evidenced in a given country by the presence of 1 or more of the following criteria:

(i) Thirty percent or more of the total abduction cases in such country are unresolved abduction cases.

(ii) The Central Authority regularly fails to fulfill its responsibilities pursuant to—

(I) the Hague Abduction Convention; or

(II) any bilateral procedures between the United States and such country.

(iii) The judicial or administrative branch, as applicable, of the national government of a Convention country or a bilateral procedures country fails to regularly implement and comply with the provisions of the Hague Abduction Convention or bilateral procedures, as applicable.

(iv) Law enforcement authorities regularly fail to enforce return orders or determinations of rights of access rendered by the judicial or administrative authorities of the government of the country in abduction cases.

(20) Rights of access

The term "rights of access" means the establishment of rights of contact between a child and a parent seeking access in Convention countries—

(A) by operation of law;

(B) through a judicial or administrative determination; or

(C) through a legally enforceable arrangement between the parties.

(21) Rights of custody

The term "rights of custody" means rights of care and custody of a child, including the right to determine the place of residence of a child, under the laws of the country in which the child is a habitual resident—

(A) attributed to an individual or legal custodian; and

(B) arising—

(i) by operation of law; or

(ii) through a judicial or administrative decision; or

(iii) through a legally enforceable arrangement between the parties.

(22) Rights of interim contact

The term "rights of interim contact" means the rights of contact between a child and a left-behind parent, which has been provided as a provisional measure while an abduction case is pending, under the laws of the country in which the child is located—

(A) by operation of law; or

(B) through a judicial or administrative determination; or

(C) through a legally enforceable arrangement between the parties.

(23) Unresolved abduction case

(A) In general

Subject to subparagraph (B), the term "unresolved abduction case" means an abduction case that remains unresolved for a period that exceeds 12 months after the date on which the completed application for return of the child is submitted for determination to the judicial or administrative authority, as applicable, in the country in which the child is located.

(B) Resolution of case

An abduction case shall be considered to be resolved if—

(i) the child is returned to the country of habitual residence, pursuant to the Hague Abduction Convention or other appropriate bilateral procedures, if applicable;

(ii) the judicial or administrative branch, as applicable, of the government of the country in which the child is located has implemented, and is complying with, the provisions of the Hague Abduction Convention or other bilateral procedures, as applicable;

(iii) the left-behind parent reaches a voluntary arrangement with the other parent;

(iv) the left-behind parent submits a written withdrawal of the application or the request for assistance to the Department of State;

(v) the left-behind parent cannot be located for 1 year despite the documented efforts of the Department of State to locate the parent; or

(vi) the child or left-behind parent is deceased.

(Pub. L. 113–150, § 3, Aug. 8, 2014, 128 Stat. 1809.)

Findings; Sense of Congress; Purposes

Pub. L. 113–150, § 2, Aug. 8, 2014, 128 Stat. 1807, provided that:

"(a) Findings.—Congress finds the following:

"(1) Sean Goldman, a United States citizen and resident of New Jersey, was abducted from the United States in 2004 and separated from his father, David Goldman, who spent nearly 6 years battling for the return of his son from Brazil before Sean was finally returned to Mr. Goldman's custody on December 24, 2009.

"(2) The Department of State's Office of Children's Issues, which serves as the Central Authority of the United States for the purposes of the 1980 Hague Convention on the Civil Aspects of International Child Abduction (referred to in this Act [see Short Title note above] as the 'Hague Abduction Convention'), has received thousands of requests since 2007 for assistance in the return to the United States of children who have been wrongfully abducted by a parent or other legal guardian to another country.

"(3) For a variety of reasons reflecting the significant obstacles to the recovery of abducted children, as well as the legal and factual complexity involving such cases, not all cases are reported to the Central Authority of the United States.

"(4) More than 1,000 outgoing international child abductions are reported every year to the Central Authority of the United States, which depends solely on proactive reporting of abduction cases.

"(5) Only about one-half of the children abducted from the United States to countries with which the United States enjoys reciprocal obligations under the Hague Abduction Convention are returned to the United States.

"(6) The United States and other Convention countries have expressed their desire, through the Hague Abduction Convention, 'to protect children internationally from the harmful effects of their wrongful removal or retention and to establish procedures to ensure their prompt return to the State of their habitual residence, as well as to secure protection for rights of access.'

"(7) Compliance by the United States and other Convention countries depends on the actions of their designated central authorities, the performance of their judicial systems as reflected in the legal process and decisions rendered to enforce or effectuate the Hague Abduction Convention, and the ability and willingness of their law enforcement authorities to ensure the swift enforcement of orders rendered pursuant to the Hague Abduction Convention.

"(8) According to data from the Department of State, approximately 40 percent of abduction cases involve children taken from the United States to countries with which the United States does not have reciprocal obligations under the Hague Abduction Convention or other arrangements relating to the resolution of abduction cases.

"(9) According to the Department of State's April 2010 Report on Compliance with the Hague Convention on the Civil Aspects of International Child Abduction, 'parental child abduction jeopardizes the child and has substantial long-term consequences for both the child and the left-behind parent.'

"(10) Few left-behind parents have the extraordinary financial resources necessary—

"(A) to pursue individual civil or criminal remedies in both the United States and a foreign country, even if such remedies are available; or

"(B) to engage in repeated foreign travel to attempt to obtain the return of their children through diplomatic or other channels.

"(11) Military parents often face additional complications in resolving abduction cases because of the challenges presented by their military obligations.

"(12) In addition to using the Hague Abduction Convention to achieve the return of abducted children, the United States has an array of Federal, State, and local law enforcement, criminal justice, and judicial tools at its disposal to prevent international abductions.

"(13) Federal agencies tasked with preventing international abductions have indicated that the most effective way to stop international child abductions is while they are in progress, rather than after the child has been removed to a foreign destination.

"(14) Parental awareness of abductions in progress, rapid response by relevant law enforcement, and effective coordination among Federal, State, local, and international stakeholders are critical in preventing such abductions.

"(15) A more robust application of domestic tools, in cooperation with international law enforcement entities and appropriate application of the Hague Abduction Convention could—

"(A) discourage some parents from attempting abductions;

"(B) block attempted abductions at ports of exit; and

"(C) help achieve the return of more abducted children.

"(b) Sense of Congress.—It is the sense of Congress that the United States should set a strong example for other Convention countries in the timely location and prompt resolution of cases involving children abducted abroad and brought to the United States.

"(c) Purposes.—The purposes of this Act are—

"(1) to protect children whose habitual residence is the United States from wrongful abduction;

"(2) to assist left-behind parents in quickly resolving cases and maintaining safe and predictable contact with their child while an abduction case is pending;

"(3) to protect the custodial rights of parents, including military parents, by providing the parents, the judicial system, and law enforcement authorities with the information they need to prevent unlawful abduction before it occurs;

"(4) to enhance the prompt resolution of abduction and access cases;

"(5) to detail an appropriate set of actions to be undertaken by the Secretary of State to address persistent problems in the resolution of abduction cases;

"(6) to establish a program to prevent wrongful abductions; and

"(7) to increase interagency coordination in preventing international child abduction by convening a working group composed of presidentially appointed and Senate confirmed officials from the Department of State, the Department of Homeland Security, and the Department of Justice."

SUBCHAPTER I
DEPARTMENT OF STATE ACTIONS

§ 9111. Annual Report.

(a) In general

Not later than April 30 of each year, the Secretary of State shall submit to the appropriate congressional committees an Annual Report on International Child Abduction. The Secretary shall post the Annual Report to the publicly accessible website of the Department of State.

(b) Contents

Each Annual Report shall include—

(1) a list of all countries in which there were 1 or more abduction cases, during the preceding calendar year, relating to a child whose habitual residence is the United States, including a description of whether each such country—

(A) is a Convention country;

(B) is a bilateral procedures country;

(C) has other procedures for resolving such abductions; or

(D) adheres to no protocols with respect to child abduction;

(2) for each country with respect to which there were 5 or more pending abduction cases, during the preceding year, relating to a child whose habitual residence is the United States—

(A) the number of such new abduction and access cases reported during the preceding year;

(B) for Convention and bilateral procedures countries—

(i) the number of abduction and access cases that the Central Authority of the United States transmitted to the Central Authority of such country; and

(ii) the number of abduction and access cases that were not submitted by the Central Authority to the judicial or administrative authority, as applicable, of such country;

(C) the reason for the delay in submission of each case identified in subparagraph (B)(ii) by the Central Authority of such country to the judicial or administrative authority of that country;

(D) the number of unresolved abduction and access cases, and the length of time each case has been pending;

(E) the number and percentage of unresolved abduction cases in which law enforcement authorities have—

(i) not located the abducted child;

(ii) failed to undertake serious efforts to locate the abducted child; and

(iii) failed to enforce a return order rendered by the judicial or administrative authorities of such country;

(F) the total number and the percentage of the total number of abduction and access cases, respectively, resolved during the preceding year;

(G) recommendations to improve the resolution of abduction and access cases; and

(H) the average time it takes to locate a child;

(3) the number of abducted children whose habitual residence is in the United States and who were returned to the United States from—

(A) Convention countries;

(B) bilateral procedures countries;

(C) countries having other procedures for resolving such abductions; or

(D) countries adhering to no protocols with respect to child abduction;

(4) a list of Convention countries and bilateral procedures countries that have failed to comply with any of their obligations under the Hague Abduction Convention or bilateral procedures, as applicable, with respect to the resolution of abduction and access cases;

(5) a list of countries demonstrating a pattern of noncompliance and a description of the criteria on which the determination of a pattern of noncompliance for each country is based;

(6) information on efforts by the Secretary of State to encourage non-Convention countries—

(A) to ratify or accede to the Hague Abduction Convention;

(B) to enter into or implement other bilateral procedures, including memoranda of understanding, with the United States; and

(C) to address pending abduction and access cases;

(7) the number of cases resolved without abducted children being returned to the United States from Convention countries, bilateral procedures countries, or other non-Convention countries;

(8) a list of countries that became Convention countries with respect to the United States during the preceding year; and

(9) information about efforts to seek resolution of abduction cases of children whose habitual residence is in the United States and whose abduction occurred before the Hague Abduction Convention entered into force with respect to the United States.

(c) Exceptions

Unless a left-behind parent provides written permission to the Central Authority of the United States to include personally identifiable information about the parent or the child in the Annual Report, the Annual Report may not include any personally identifiable information about any such parent, child, or party to an abduction or access case involving such parent or child.

(d) Additional sections

Each Annual Report shall also include—

(1) information on the number of unresolved abduction cases affecting military parents;

(2) a description of the assistance offered to such military parents;

(3) information on the use of airlines in abductions, voluntary airline practices to prevent abductions, and recommendations for best airline practices to prevent abductions;

(4) information on actions taken by the Central Authority of the United States to train domestic judges in the application of the Hague Abduction Convention; and

(5) information on actions taken by the Central Authority of the United States to train United States Armed Forces legal assistance personnel, military chaplains, and military family support center personnel about—

(A) abductions;

(B) the risk of loss of contact with children; and

(C) the legal means available to resolve such cases.

(e) Omitted

(f) Notification to Congress on countries in noncompliance

(1) In general

The Secretary of State shall include, in a separate section of the Annual Report, the Secretary's determination, pursuant to the provisions under section 9122(b) of this title, of whether each country listed in the report has engaged in a pattern of noncompliance in cases of child abduction during the preceding 12 months.

(2) Contents

The section described in paragraph (1)—

(A) shall identify any action or actions described in section 9122(d) of this title (or commensurate action as provided in section 9122(e) of this title) that have been taken by the Secretary with respect to each country;

(B) shall describe the basis for the Secretary's determination of the pattern of noncompliance by each country;

(C) shall indicate whether noneconomic policy options designed to resolve the pattern of noncompliance have reasonably been exhausted, including the consultations required under section 9123 of this title.

(Pub. L. 113–150, title I, § 101, Aug. 8, 2014, 128 Stat. 1813.)

Codification

Section is comprised of section 101 of Pub. L. 113–150. Subsec. (e) of section 101 of Pub. L. 113–150 repealed section 11611 of Title 42, The Public Health and Welfare.

§ 9112. Standards and assistance.

The Secretary of State shall—

(1) ensure that United States diplomatic and consular missions abroad—

(A) maintain a consistent reporting standard with respect to abduction and access cases;

(B) designate at least 1 senior official in each such mission, at the discretion of the Chief of Mission, to assist left-behind parents from the United States who are visiting such country or otherwise seeking to resolve abduction or access cases; and

(C) monitor developments in abduction and access cases; and

(2) develop and implement written strategic plans for engagement with any Convention or non-Convention country in which there are 5 or more cases of international child abduction.

(Pub. L. 113–150, title I, § 102, Aug. 8, 2014, 128 Stat. 1815.)

§ 9113. Bilateral procedures, including memoranda of understanding.

(a) Development

(1) In general

Not later than 180 days after August 8, 2014, the Secretary of State shall initiate a process to develop and enter into appropriate bilateral procedures, including memoranda of understanding, as appropriate, with non-Convention countries that are unlikely to become Convention countries in the foreseeable future, or with Convention countries that have unresolved abduction cases that occurred before the Hague Abduction Convention entered into force with respect to the United States or that country.

(2) Prioritization

In carrying out paragraph (1), the Secretary of State shall give priority to countries with significant abduction cases and related issues.

(b) Elements

The bilateral procedures described in subsection (a) should include provisions relating to—

(1) the identification of—

(A) the Central Authority;

(B) the judicial or administrative authority that will promptly adjudicate abduction and access cases;

(C) the law enforcement agencies; and

(D) the implementation of procedures to ensure the immediate enforcement of an order issued by the authority identified pursuant to subparagraph (B) to return an abducted child to a left-behind parent, including by—

  (i) conducting an investigation to ascertain the location of the abducted child;

  (ii) providing protection to the abducted child after such child is located; and

  (iii) retrieving the abducted child and making the appropriate arrangements for such child to be returned to the child's country of habitual residence;

(2) the implementation of a protocol to effectuate the return of an abducted child identified in an abduction case not later than 6 weeks after the application with respect to the abduction case has been submitted to the judicial or administrative authority, as applicable, of the country in which the abducted child is located;

(3) the implementation of a protocol for the establishment and protection of the rights of interim contact during pendency of abduction cases; and

(4) the implementation of a protocol to establish periodic visits between a United States embassy or consular official and an abducted child, in order to allow the official to ascertain the child's location and welfare.

(Pub. L. 113–150, title I, § 103, Aug. 8, 2014, 128 Stat. 1815.)

§ 9114. Report to congressional representatives.

(a) Notification

The Secretary of State shall submit written notification to the Member of Congress and Senators, or Resident Commissioner or Delegate, as appropriate, representing the legal residence of a left-behind parent if such parent—

(1) reports an abduction to the Central Authority of the United States; and

(2) consents to such notification.

(b) Timing

At the request of any person who is a left-behind parent, including a left-behind parent who previously reported an abduction to the Central Authority of the United States before August 8, 2014, the notification required under subsection (a) shall be provided as soon as is practicable.

(Pub. L. 113–150, title I, § 104, Aug. 8, 2014, 128 Stat. 1816.)

SUBCHAPTER II
ACTIONS BY THE SECRETARY OF STATE

§ 9121. Response to international child abductions.

(a) United States policy

It is the policy of the United States—

(1) to promote the best interest of children wrongfully abducted from the United States by—

(A) establishing legal rights and procedures for their prompt return; and

(B) ensuring the enforcement of reciprocal international obligations under the Hague Abduction Convention or arrangements under bilateral procedures;

(2) to promote the timely resolution of abduction cases through 1 or more of the actions described in section 9122 of this title; and

(3) to ensure appropriate coordination within the Federal Government and between Federal, State, and local agencies involved in abduction prevention, investigation, and resolution.

(b) Actions by the Secretary of State in response to unresolved cases

(1) Determination of action by the Secretary of State

For each abduction or access case relating to a child whose habitual residence is in the United States that remains pending or is otherwise unresolved on the date that is 12 months after the date on which the Central Authority of the United States submits such case to a foreign country, the Secretary of State shall determine whether the government of such foreign country has failed to take appropriate steps to resolve the case. If the Secretary of State determines that such failure occurred, the Secretary should, as expeditiously as practicable—

(A) take 1 or more of the actions described in subsections (d) and (e) of section 9122 of this title; and

(B) direct the Chief of Mission in that foreign country to directly address the resolution of the case with senior officials in the foreign government.

(2) Authority for delay of action by the Secretary of State

The Secretary of State may delay any action described in paragraph (1) if the Secretary determines that an additional period of time, not to exceed 1 year, will substantially assist in resolving the case.

(3) Report

If the Secretary of State delays any action pursuant to paragraph (2) or decides not to take an action described in subsection (d) or (e) of section 9122 of this title after making the determination described in paragraph (1), the Secretary, not later than 15 days after such delay or decision, shall provide a report to the appropriate congressional committees that details the reasons for delaying action or not taking action, as appropriate.

(4) Congressional briefings

At the request of the appropriate congressional committees, the Secretary of State shall provide a detailed briefing, including a written report, if requested, on actions taken to resolve a case or the cause for delay.

(c) Implementation

(1) In general

In carrying out subsection (b), the Secretary of State should—

(A) take 1 or more actions that most appropriately respond to the nature and severity of the governmental failure to resolve the unresolved abduction case; and

(B) seek, to the fullest extent possible—

(i) to initially respond by communicating with the Central Authority of the country; and

(ii) if clause (i) is unsuccessful, to target subsequent actions—

(I) as narrowly as practicable, with respect to the agencies or instrumentalities of the foreign government that are responsible for such failures; and

(II) in ways that respect the separation of powers and independence of the judiciary of the country, as applicable.

(2) Guidelines for actions by the Secretary of State

In addition to the guidelines under paragraph (1), the Secretary of State, in determining whether to take 1 or more actions under paragraphs (5) through (7) of section 9122(d) of this title or section 9122(e) of this title, shall seek to minimize any adverse impact on—

(A) the population of the country whose government is targeted by the action or actions;

(B) the humanitarian activities of United States and nongovernmental organizations in the country; and

(C) the national security interests of the United States.

(Pub. L. 113–150, title II, § 201, Aug. 8, 2014, 128 Stat. 1817.)

§ 9122. Actions by the Secretary of State in response to patterns of noncompliance in cases of international child abductions.

(a) Response to a pattern of noncompliance

It is the policy of the United States—

(1) to oppose institutional or other systemic failures of foreign governments to fulfill their obligations pursuant to the Hague Abduction Convention or bilateral procedures, as applicable, to resolve abduction and access cases;

(2) to promote reciprocity pursuant to, and in compliance with, the Hague Abduction Convention or bilateral procedures, as appropriate; and

(3) to directly engage with senior foreign government officials to most effectively address patterns of noncompliance.

(b) Determination of countries with patterns of noncompliance in cases of international child abduction

(1) Annual review

Not later than April 30 of each year, the Secretary of State shall—

(A) review the status of abduction and access cases in each foreign country in order to determine whether the government of such country has engaged in a pattern of noncompliance during the preceding 12 months; and

(B) report such determination pursuant to section 9111(f) of this title.

(2) Determinations of responsible parties

The Secretary of State shall seek to determine the agencies or instrumentalities of the government of each country determined to have engaged in a pattern of noncompliance under paragraph (1)(A) that are responsible for such pattern of noncompliance—

(A) to appropriately target actions in response to such noncompliance; and

(B) to engage with senior foreign government officials to effectively address such noncompliance.

(c) Actions by the Secretary of State with respect to a country with a pattern of noncompliance

(1) In general

Not later than 90 days (or 180 days in case of a delay under paragraph (2)) after a country is determined to have been engaged in a pattern of noncompliance under subsection (b)(1)(A), the Secretary of State shall—

(A) take 1 or more of the actions described in subsection (d);

(B) direct the Chief of Mission in that country to directly address the systemic problems that led to such determination; and

(C) inform senior officials in the foreign government of the potential repercussions related to such designation.

(2) Authority for delay of actions by the Secretary of State

The Secretary shall not be required to take action under paragraph (1) until the expiration of a single, additional period of up to 90 days if, on or before the date on which the Secretary of State is required to take such action, the Secretary determines and certifies to the appropriate congressional committees that such additional period is necessary—

(A) for a continuation of negotiations that have been commenced with the government of a country described in paragraph (1) in order to bring about a cessation of the pattern of noncompliance by such country;

(B) for a review of corrective action taken by a country after the designation of such country as being engaged in a pattern of noncompliance under subsection (b)(1)(A); or

(C) in anticipation that corrective action will be taken by such country during such 90-day period.

(3) Exception for additional action by the Secretary of State

The Secretary of State shall not be required to take additional action under paragraph (1) with respect to a country determined to have been engaged in a persistent pattern of noncompliance if the Secretary—

(A) has taken action pursuant to paragraph (5), (6), or (7) of subsection (d) with respect to such country in the preceding year and such action continues to be in effect;

(B) exercises the waiver under section 9124 of this title and briefs the appropriate congressional committees; or

(C) submits a report to the appropriate congressional committees that—

(i) indicates that such country is subject to multiple, broad-based sanctions; and

(ii) describes how such sanctions satisfy the requirements under this subsection.

(4) Report to Congress

Not later than 90 days after the submission of the Annual Report, the Secretary shall submit a report to Congress on the specific actions taken against countries determined to have been engaged in a pattern of noncompliance under this section.

(d) Description of actions by the Secretary of State in Hague Abduction Convention countries

Except as provided in subsection (f), the actions by the Secretary of State referred to in this subsection are—

(1) a demarche;

(2) an official public statement detailing unresolved cases;

(3) a public condemnation;

(4) a delay or cancellation of 1 or more bilateral working, official, or state visits;

(5) the withdrawal, limitation, or suspension of United States development assistance in accordance with section 116 of the Foreign Assistance Act of 1961 (22 U.S.C. 2151n);

(6) the withdrawal, limitation, or suspension of United States security assistance in accordance with section 502B of the Foreign Assistance Act of 1961 (22 U.S.C. 2304);

(7) the withdrawal, limitation, or suspension of assistance to the central government of a country pursuant to chapter 4 of part II of the Foreign Assistance Act of 1961 (22 U.S.C. 2346 et seq.; relating to the Economic Support Fund); and

(8) a formal request to the foreign country concerned to extradite an individual who is engaged in abduction and who has been formally accused of, charged with, or convicted of an extraditable offense.

(e) Commensurate action

(1) In general

Except as provided in subsection (f), the Secretary of State may substitute any other action authorized by law for any action described in subsection (d) if the Secretary determines that such action—

(A) is commensurate in effect to the action substituted; and

(B) would substantially further the purposes of this chapter.

(2) Notification

If commensurate action is taken pursuant to this subsection, the Secretary shall submit a report to the appropriate congressional committees that—

(A) describes such action;

(B) explains the reasons for taking such action; and

(C) specifically describes the basis for the Secretary's determination under paragraph (1) that such action—

(i) is commensurate with the action substituted; and

(ii) substantially furthers the purposes of this chapter.

(f) Resolution

The Secretary of State shall seek to take all appropriate actions authorized by law to resolve the unresolved case or to obtain the cessation of such pattern of noncompliance, as applicable.

(g) Humanitarian exception

Any action taken pursuant to subsection (d) or (e) may not prohibit or restrict the provision of medicine, medical equipment or supplies, food, or other life-saving humanitarian assistance.

(Pub. L. 113–150, title II, § 202, Aug. 8, 2014, 128 Stat. 1818.)

§ 9123. Consultations with foreign governments.

As soon as practicable after the Secretary of State makes a determination under section 9121 of this title in response to a failure to resolve unresolved abduction cases or the Secretary takes an action under subsection (d) or (e) of section 9122 of this title, based on a pattern of noncompliance, the Secretary shall request consultations with the government of such country regarding the situation giving rise to such determination.

(Pub. L. 113–150, title II, § 203, Aug. 8, 2014, 128 Stat. 1820.)

§ 9124. Waiver by the Secretary of State.

(a) In general

Subject to subsection (b), the Secretary of State may waive the application of any of the actions described in subsections (d) and (e) of section 9122 of this title with respect to a country if the Secretary determines and notifies the appropriate congressional committees that—

(1) the government of such country—

(A) has satisfactorily resolved the abduction cases giving rise to the application of any of such actions; or

(B) has ended such country's pattern of noncompliance; or

(2) the national security interest of the United States requires the exercise of such waiver authority.

(b) Congressional notification

Not later than the date on which the Secretary of State exercises the waiver authority under subsection (a), the Secretary shall—

(1) notify the appropriate congressional committees of such waiver; and

(2) provide such committees with a detailed justification for such waiver, including an explanation of the steps the noncompliant government has taken—

(A) to resolve abductions cases; or

(B) to end its pattern of noncompliance.

(c) Publication in Federal Register

Subject to subsection (d), the Secretary of State shall ensure that each waiver determination under this section—

(1) is published in the Federal Register; or

(2) is posted on the Department of State website.

(d) Limited disclosure of information

The Secretary of State may limit the publication of information under subsection (c) in the same manner and to the same extent as the President may limit the publication of findings and determinations described in section 2414(c) of this title, if the Secretary determines that the publication of such information would be harmful to the national security of the United States and would not further the purposes of this chapter.

(Pub. L. 113–150, title II, § 204, Aug. 8, 2014, 128 Stat. 1821.)

§ 9125. Termination of actions by the Secretary of State.

Any specific action taken under this Act or any amendment made by this Act with respect to a foreign country shall terminate on the date on which the Secretary of State submits a written certification to Congress that the government of such country—

(1) has resolved any unresolved abduction case that gave rise to such specific action; or

(2) has taken substantial and verifiable steps to correct such country's persistent pattern of noncompliance that gave rise to such specific action, as applicable.

(Pub. L. 113–150, title II, § 205, Aug. 8, 2014, 128 Stat. 1821.)

SUBCHAPTER III

PREVENTION OF INTERNATIONAL CHILD ABDUCTION

§ 9141. Authorization for judicial training on international parental child abduction.

(a) In general

The Secretary of State, subject to the availability of appropriations, shall seek to provide training, directly or through another government agency or nongovernmental organizations, on the effective handling of parental abduction cases to the judicial and administrative authorities in countries—

(1) in which a significant number of unresolved abduction cases are pending; or

(2) that have been designated as having a pattern of noncompliance under section 9122(b) of this title.

(b) Strategy requirement

Not later than 180 days after August 8, 2014, the President shall submit a strategy to carry out the activities described in subsection (a) to—

(1) the Committee on Foreign Relations of the Senate;

(2) the Committee on Foreign Affairs of the House of Representatives;

(3) the Committee on Appropriations of the Senate; and

(4) the Committee on Appropriations of the House of Representatives.

(c) Authorization of appropriations

(1) In general

There is authorized to be appropriated to the Secretary of State $1,000,000 for each of the fiscal years 2015 and 2016 to carry out subsection (a).

(2) Use of funds

Amounts appropriated for the activities set forth in subsection (a) shall be used pursuant to the authorization and requirements under this section.

(Pub. L. 113–150, title III, § 302, Aug. 8, 2014, 128 Stat. 1822.)

22 CFR § 51.28

§ 51.28. Minors.

(a) Minors under age 16.

(1) Personal appearance. Minors under 16 years of age applying for a passport must appear in person, unless the personal appearance of the minor is specifically excused by a senior passport authorizing officer, pursuant to guidance issued by the Department. In cases where personal appearance is excused, the person(s) executing the passport application on behalf of the minor shall appear in person and verify the application by oath or affirmation before a person authorized by the Secretary to administer oaths or affirmations, unless these requirements are also excused by a senior passport authorizing officer pursuant to guidance issued by the Department.

(2) Execution of passport application by both parents or by each legal guardian. Except as specifically provided in this section, both parents or each of the minor's legal guardians, if any, whether applying for a passport for the first time or for a renewal, must execute the application on behalf of a minor under age 16 and provide documentary evidence of parentage or legal guardianship showing the minor's name, date and place of birth, and the names of the parent or parents or legal guardian.

(3) Execution of passport application by one parent or legal guardian. A passport application may be executed on behalf of a minor under age 16 by only one parent or legal guardian if such person provides:

(i) A notarized written statement or affidavit from the non-applying parent or legal guardian, if applicable, consenting to the issuance of the passport, or

(ii) Documentary evidence that such person is the sole parent or has sole custody of the minor. Such evidence includes, but is not limited to, the following:

(A) A birth certificate providing the minor's name, date and place of birth and the name of only the applying parent;

(B) A Consular Report of Birth Abroad of a Citizen of the United States of America or a Certification of Report of Birth of a United States Citizen providing the minor's name, date and place of birth and the name of only the applying parent;

(C) A copy of the death certificate for the non-applying parent or legal guardian;

(D) An adoption decree showing the name of only the applying parent;

(E) An order of a court of competent jurisdiction granting sole legal custody to the applying parent or legal guardian containing no travel restrictions inconsistent with issuance of the passport; or, specifically authorizing the applying parent or legal guardian to obtain a passport for the minor, regardless of custodial arrangements; or specifically authorizing the travel of the minor with the applying parent or legal guardian;

(F) An order of a court of competent jurisdiction terminating the parental rights of the non-applying parent or declaring the non-applying parent or legal guardian to be incompetent.

(G) An order of a court of competent jurisdiction providing for joint legal custody or requiring the permission of both parents or the court for important decisions will be interpreted as requiring the permission of both parents or the court, as appropriate. Notwithstanding the existence of any such court order, a passport may be issued when compelling humanitarian or emergency reasons relating to the welfare of the minor exist.

(4) Execution of passport application by a person acting in loco parentis.

(i) A person may apply in loco parentis on behalf of a minor under age 16 by submitting a notarized written statement or a notarized affidavit from both parents or each legal guardian, if any, specifically authorizing the application.

(ii) If only one parent or legal guardian provides the notarized written statement or notarized affidavit, the applicant must provide documentary evidence that an application may be made by one parent or legal guardian, consistent with § 51.28(a)(3).

(5) Exigent or special family circumstances. A passport may be issued when only one parent, legal guardian or person acting in loco parentis executes the application, in cases of exigent or special family circumstances.

(i) "Exigent circumstances" are defined as time-sensitive circumstances in which the inability of the minor to obtain a passport would jeopardize the health and safety or welfare of the minor or would result in the minor being separated from the rest of his or her traveling party. "Time sensitive" generally means that there is not enough time before the minor's emergency travel to obtain either the required consent of both parents/legal guardians or documentation reflecting a sole parent's/legal guardian's custody rights.

(ii) "Special family circumstances" are defined as circumstances in which the minor's family situation makes it exceptionally difficult for one or both of the parents to execute the passport application; and/or compelling humanitarian circumstances where the minor's lack of a passport would jeopardize the health, safety, or welfare of the minor; or, pursuant to guidance issued by the Department, circumstances in which return of a minor to the jurisdiction of his or her home state or habitual residence is necessary to permit a court of competent jurisdiction to adjudicate or enforce a custody determination. A passport issued due to such special family circumstances may be limited for direct return to the United States in accordance with § 51.60(e).

(iii) A parent, legal guardian, or person acting in loco parentis who is applying for a passport for a minor under age 16 under this paragraph must submit a written statement with the application describing the exigent or special family circumstances he or she believes should be taken into consideration in applying an exception.

(iv) Determinations under § 51.28(a)(5) must be made by a senior passport authorizing officer pursuant to guidance issued by the Department.

(6) Nothing contained in this section shall prohibit any Department official adjudicating a passport application filed on behalf of a minor from requiring an applicant to submit other documentary evidence deemed necessary to establish the applying adult's entitlement to obtain a passport on behalf of a minor under the age of 16 in accordance with the provisions of this regulation.

(b) Minors 16 years of age and above.

(1) A minor 16 years of age and above applying for a passport must appear in person and may execute the application for a passport on his or her own behalf unless the personal appearance of the minor is specifically excused by a senior passport authorizing officer pursuant to guidance issued by the Department, or unless, in the judgment of the person before whom the application is executed, it is not advisable for the minor to execute his or her own application. In such case, it must be executed by a parent or legal guardian of the minor, or by a person in loco parentis, unless the personal appearance of the parent, legal guardian or person in loco parentis is excused by the senior passport authorizing officer pursuant to guidance issued by the Department.

(2) The passport authorizing officer may at any time require a minor 16 years of age and above to submit the notarized consent of a parent, a legal guardian, or a person in loco parentis to the issuance of the passport.

(c) Rules applicable to all minors—

(1) Objections. At any time prior to the issuance of a passport to a minor, the application may be disapproved and a passport may be denied upon receipt of a

written objection from a parent or legal guardian of the minor, or from another party claiming authority to object, so long as the objecting party provides sufficient documentation of his or her custodial rights or other authority to object.

(2) An order from a court of competent jurisdiction providing for joint legal custody or requiring the permission of both parents or the court for important decisions will be interpreted as requiring the permission of both parents or the court as appropriate.

(3) The Department will consider a court of competent jurisdiction to be a U.S. state or federal court or a foreign court located in the minor's home state or place of habitual residence.

(4) The Department may require that conflicts regarding custody orders, whether domestic or foreign, be settled by the appropriate court before a passport may be issued.

(5) Access by parents and legal guardians to passport records for minors. Either parent or any legal guardian of a minor may upon written request obtain information regarding the application for and issuance of a passport to a minor, unless the requesting parent's parental rights have been terminated by an order of a court of competent jurisdiction, a copy of which has been provided to the Department. The Department may deny such information to a parent or legal guardian if it determines that the minor objects to disclosure and the minor is 16 years of age or older or if the Department determines that the minor is of sufficient age and maturity to invoke his or her own privacy rights.

TITLE 26

INTERNAL REVENUE CODE

SUBTITLE A
INCOME TAXES

CHAPTER 1
NORMAL TAXES AND SURTAXES

SUBCHAPTER B
COMPUTATION OF TAXABLE INCOME

PART II
ITEMS SPECIFICALLY INCLUDED IN GROSS INCOME

§ 151. Allowance of deductions for personal exemptions
Effective: December 22, 2017

(a) **Allowance of deductions.**—In the case of an individual, the exemptions provided by this section shall be allowed as deductions in computing taxable income.

(b) **Taxpayer and spouse.**—An exemption of the exemption amount for the taxpayer; and an additional exemption of the exemption amount for the spouse of the taxpayer if a joint return is not made by the taxpayer and his spouse, and if the spouse, for the calendar year in which the taxable year of the taxpayer begins, has no gross income and is not the dependent of another taxpayer.

(c) **Additional exemption for dependents.**—An exemption of the exemption amount for each individual who is a dependent (as defined in section 152) of the taxpayer for the taxable year.

(d) **Exemption amount.**—For purposes of this section—

(1) **In general.**—Except as otherwise provided in this subsection, the term "exemption amount" means $2,000.

(2) **Exemption amount disallowed in case of certain dependents.**—In the case of an individual with respect to whom a deduction under this section is allowable to another taxpayer for a taxable year beginning in the calendar year in which the individual's taxable year begins, the exemption amount applicable to such individual for such individual's taxable year shall be zero.

(3) **Phaseout.**—

(A) **In general.**—In the case of any taxpayer whose adjusted gross income for the taxable year exceeds the applicable amount in effect under section 68(b), the exemption amount shall be reduced by the applicable percentage.

(B) **Applicable percentage.**—For purposes of subparagraph (A), the term "applicable percentage" means 2 percentage points for each $2,500 (or fraction thereof) by which the taxpayer's adjusted gross income for the taxable year exceeds the applicable amount in effect under section 68(b). In the case of a married individual filing a separate return, the preceding sentence shall be applied by substituting "$1,250" for "$2,500". In no event shall the applicable percentage exceed 100 percent.

(C) **Coordination with other provisions.**—The provisions of this paragraph shall not apply for purposes of determining whether a deduction under this section with respect to any individual is allowable to another taxpayer for any taxable year.

[(D) Redesignated (C)]

[(E) Repealed. Pub.L. 112-240, Title I, § 101(b)(2)(B)(i)(III), Jan. 2, 2013, 126 Stat. 2317]

[(F) Repealed. Pub.L. 112-240, Title I, § 101(b)(2)(B)(i)(III), Jan. 2, 2013, 126 Stat. 2317]

(4) Inflation adjustment.—Except as provided in paragraph (5), in the case of any taxable year beginning in a calendar year after 1989, the dollar amount contained in paragraph (1) shall be increased by an amount equal to—

(A) such dollar amount, multiplied by

(B) the cost-of-living adjustment determined under section 1(f)(3) for the calendar year in which the taxable year begins, by substituting "calendar year 1988" for "calendar year 2016" in subparagraph (A)(ii) thereof.

(5) Special rules for taxable years 2018 through 2025.—In the case of a taxable year beginning after December 31, 2017, and before January 1, 2026—

(A) **Exemption amount.**—The term "exemption amount" means zero.

(B) **References.**—For purposes of any other provision of this title, the reduction of the exemption amount to zero under subparagraph (A) shall not be taken into account in determining whether a deduction is allowed or allowable, or whether a taxpayer is entitled to a deduction, under this section.

(e) Identifying information required.—No exemption shall be allowed under this section with respect to any individual unless the TIN of such individual is included on the return claiming the exemption.

(Aug. 16, 1954, c. 736, 68A Stat. 42; Pub.L. 91-172, Title VIII, § 801(a)(1), (b)(1), (c)(1), (d)(1), Title IX, § 941(b), Dec. 30, 1969, 83 Stat. 675, 726; Pub.L. 92-178, Title II, § 201(a)(1), (b)(1), (c), Dec. 10, 1971, 85 Stat. 510, 511; Pub.L. 94-455, Title XIX, § 1901(a)(23), Oct. 4, 1976, 90 Stat. 1767; Pub.L. 95-600, Title I, § 102(a), Nov. 6, 1978, 92 Stat. 2771; Pub.L. 97-34, Title I, § 104(c), Aug. 13, 1981, 95 Stat. 189; Pub.L. 98-369, Title IV, § 426(a), July 18, 1984, 98 Stat. 804; Pub.L. 99-514, Title I, § 103, Title XVIII, § 1847(b)(3), Oct. 22, 1986, 100 Stat. 2102, 2856; Pub.L. 100-647, Title VI, § 6010(a), Nov. 10, 1988, 102 Stat. 3691; Pub.L. 101-508, Title XI, §§ 11101(d)(1)(F), 11104(a), Nov. 5, 1990, 104 Stat. 1388-405, 1388-407; Pub.L. 102-318, Title V, § 511, July 3, 1992, 106 Stat. 300; Pub.L. 103-66, Title XIII, §§ 13201(b)(3)(G), 13205, Aug. 10, 1993, 107 Stat. 459, 462; Pub.L. 104-188, Title I, §§ 1615(a)(1), 1702(a)(2), Aug. 20, 1996, 110 Stat. 1853, 1868; Pub.L. 106-554, § 1(a)(7) [Title III, § 306(a)], Dec. 21, 2000, 114 Stat. 2763, 2763A-634; Pub.L. 107-16, Title I, § 102(a), June 7, 2001, 115 Stat. 44; Pub.L. 107-147, Title IV, §§ 412(b), 417(6), Mar. 9, 2002, 116 Stat. 53, 56; Pub.L. 108-311, Title II, § 206, Oct. 4, 2004, 118 Stat. 1176; Pub.L. 112-240, Title I, § 101(b)(2)(B), Jan. 2, 2013, 126 Stat. 2317; Pub.L. 115-97, Title I, §§ 11002(d)(1)(Q), 11041(a), Dec. 22, 2017, 131 Stat. 2060, 2082.)

§ 152. Dependent defined

Effective: December 22, 2017

(a) In general.—For purposes of this subtitle, the term "dependent" means—

(1) a qualifying child, or

(2) a qualifying relative.

(b) Exceptions.—For purposes of this section—

(1) Dependents ineligible.—If an individual is a dependent of a taxpayer for any taxable year of such taxpayer beginning in a calendar year, such individual shall be treated as having no dependents for any taxable year of such individual beginning in such calendar year.

(2) Married dependents.—An individual shall not be treated as a dependent of a taxpayer under subsection (a) if such individual has made a joint return with the individual's spouse under section 6013 for the taxable year beginning in the calendar year in which the taxable year of the taxpayer begins.

(3) Citizens or nationals of other countries.—

(A) In general.—The term "dependent" does not include an individual who is not a citizen or national of the United States unless such individual is a resident of the United States or a country contiguous to the United States.

(B) Exception for adopted child.—Subparagraph (A) shall not exclude any child of a taxpayer (within the meaning of subsection (f)(1)(B)) from the definition of "dependent" if—

(i) for the taxable year of the taxpayer, the child has the same principal place of abode as the taxpayer and is a member of the taxpayer's household, and

(ii) the taxpayer is a citizen or national of the United States.

(c) Qualifying child.—For purposes of this section—

(1) In general.—The term "qualifying child" means, with respect to any taxpayer for any taxable year, an individual—

(A) who bears a relationship to the taxpayer described in paragraph (2),

(B) who has the same principal place of abode as the taxpayer for more than one-half of such taxable year,

(C) who meets the age requirements of paragraph (3),

(D) who has not provided over one-half of such individual's own support for the calendar year in which the taxable year of the taxpayer begins, and

(E) who has not filed a joint return (other than only for a claim of refund) with the individual's spouse under section 6013 for the taxable year beginning in the calendar year in which the taxable year of the taxpayer begins.

(2) Relationship.—For purposes of paragraph (1)(A), an individual bears a relationship to the taxpayer described in this paragraph if such individual is—

(A) a child of the taxpayer or a descendant of such a child, or

(B) a brother, sister, stepbrother, or stepsister of the taxpayer or a descendant of any such relative.

(3) Age requirements.—

(A) In general.—For purposes of paragraph (1)(C), an individual meets the requirements of this paragraph if such individual is younger than the taxpayer claiming such individual as a qualifying child and—

(i) has not attained the age of 19 as of the close of the calendar year in which the taxable year of the taxpayer begins, or

(ii) is a student who has not attained the age of 24 as of the close of such calendar year.

(B) Special rule for disabled.—In the case of an individual who is permanently and totally disabled (as defined in section 22(e)(3)) at any time during such calendar year, the requirements of subparagraph (A) shall be treated as met with respect to such individual.

(4) Special rule relating to 2 or more who can claim the same qualifying child.—

(A) In general.—Except as provided in subparagraphs (B) and (C), if (but for this paragraph) an individual may be claimed as a qualifying child by 2 or more taxpayers for a taxable year beginning in the same calendar year, such individual shall be treated as the qualifying child of the taxpayer who is—

(i) a parent of the individual, or

(ii) if clause (i) does not apply, the taxpayer with the highest adjusted gross income for such taxable year.

(B) **More than 1 parent claiming qualifying child.**—If the parents claiming any qualifying child do not file a joint return together, such child shall be treated as the qualifying child of—

(i) the parent with whom the child resided for the longest period of time during the taxable year, or

(ii) if the child resides with both parents for the same amount of time during such taxable year, the parent with the highest adjusted gross income.

(C) **No parent claiming qualifying child.**—If the parents of an individual may claim such individual as a qualifying child but no parent so claims the individual, such individual may be claimed as the qualifying child of another taxpayer but only if the adjusted gross income of such taxpayer is higher than the highest adjusted gross income of any parent of the individual.

(d) **Qualifying relative.**—For purposes of this section—

(1) **In general.**—The term "qualifying relative" means, with respect to any taxpayer for any taxable year, an individual—

(A) who bears a relationship to the taxpayer described in paragraph (2),

(B) whose gross income for the calendar year in which such taxable year begins is less than the exemption amount (as defined in section 151(d)),

(C) with respect to whom the taxpayer provides over one-half of the individual's support for the calendar year in which such taxable year begins, and

(D) who is not a qualifying child of such taxpayer or of any other taxpayer for any taxable year beginning in the calendar year in which such taxable year begins.

(2) **Relationship.**—For purposes of paragraph (1)(A), an individual bears a relationship to the taxpayer described in this paragraph if the individual is any of the following with respect to the taxpayer:

(A) A child or a descendant of a child.

(B) A brother, sister, stepbrother, or stepsister.

(C) The father or mother, or an ancestor of either.

(D) A stepfather or stepmother.

(E) A son or daughter of a brother or sister of the taxpayer.

(F) A brother or sister of the father or mother of the taxpayer.

(G) A son-in-law, daughter-in-law, father-in-law, mother-in-law, brother-in-law, or sister-in-law.

(H) An individual (other than an individual who at any time during the taxable year was the spouse, determined without regard to section 7703, of the taxpayer) who, for the taxable year of the taxpayer, has the same principal place of abode as the taxpayer and is a member of the taxpayer's household.

(3) **Special rule relating to multiple support agreements.**—For purposes of paragraph (1)(C), over one-half of the support of an individual for a calendar year shall be treated as received from the taxpayer if—

(A) no one person contributed over one-half of such support,

(B) over one-half of such support was received from 2 or more persons each of whom, but for the fact that any such person alone did not contribute over one-half of such support, would have been entitled to claim such individual as a dependent for a taxable year beginning in such calendar year,

(C) the taxpayer contributed over 10 percent of such support, and

(D) each person described in subparagraph (B) (other than the taxpayer) who contributed over 10 percent of such support files a written declaration (in such manner and form as the Secretary may by regulations prescribe) that such person will not claim such individual as a dependent for any taxable year beginning in such calendar year.

(4) Special rule relating to income of handicapped dependents.—

(A) In general.—For purposes of paragraph (1)(B), the gross income of an individual who is permanently and totally disabled (as defined in section 22(e)(3)) at any time during the taxable year shall not include income attributable to services performed by the individual at a sheltered workshop if—

(i) the availability of medical care at such workshop is the principal reason for the individual's presence there, and

(ii) the income arises solely from activities at such workshop which are incident to such medical care.

(B) Sheltered workshop defined.—For purposes of subparagraph (A), the term "sheltered workshop" means a school—

(i) which provides special instruction or training designed to alleviate the disability of the individual, and

(ii) which is operated by an organization described in section 501(c)(3) and exempt from tax under section 501(a), or by a State, a possession of the United States, any political subdivision of any of the foregoing, the United States, or the District of Columbia.

(5) Special rules for support.—

(A) In general.—For purposes of this subsection—

(i) payments to a spouse of alimony or separate maintenance payments shall not be treated as a payment by the payor spouse for the support of any dependent, and

(ii) in the case of the remarriage of a parent, support of a child received from the parent's spouse shall be treated as received from the parent.

(B) Alimony or separate maintenance payment.—For purposes of subparagraph (A), the term "alimony or separate maintenance payment" means any payment in cash if—

(i) such payment is received by (or on behalf of) a spouse under a divorce or separation instrument (as defined in section 121(d)(3)(C)),

(ii) in the case of an individual legally separated from the individual's spouse under a decree of divorce or of separate maintenance, the payee spouse and the payor spouse are not members of the same household at the time such payment is made, and

(iii) there is no liability to make any such payment for any period after the death of the payee spouse and there is no liability to make any payment (in cash or property) as a substitute for such payments after the death of the payee spouse.

(e) Special rule for divorced parents, etc.—

(1) In general.—Notwithstanding subsection (c)(1)(B), (c)(4), or (d)(1)(C), if—

(A) a child receives over one-half of the child's support during the calendar year from the child's parents—

(i) who are divorced or legally separated under a decree of divorce or separate maintenance,

(ii) who are separated under a written separation agreement, or

(iii) who live apart at all times during the last 6 months of the calendar year, and—

(B) such child is in the custody of 1 or both of the child's parents for more than one-half of the calendar year, such child shall be treated as being the qualifying child or qualifying relative of the noncustodial parent for a calendar year if the requirements described in paragraph (2) or (3) are met.

(2) Exception where custodial parent releases claim to exemption for the year.—For purposes of paragraph (1), the requirements described in this paragraph are met with respect to any calendar year if—

(A) the custodial parent signs a written declaration (in such manner and form as the Secretary may by regulations prescribe) that such custodial parent will not claim such child as a dependent for any taxable year beginning in such calendar year, and

(B) the noncustodial parent attaches such written declaration to the noncustodial parent's return for the taxable year beginning during such calendar year.

(3) Exception for certain pre-1985 instruments.—

(A) **In general.**—For purposes of paragraph (1), the requirements described in this paragraph are met with respect to any calendar year if—

(i) a qualified pre-1985 instrument between the parents applicable to the taxable year beginning in such calendar year provides that the noncustodial parent shall be entitled to any deduction allowable under section 151 for such child, and

(ii) the noncustodial parent provides at least $600 for the support of such child during such calendar year.

For purposes of this subparagraph, amounts expended for the support of a child or children shall be treated as received from the noncustodial parent to the extent that such parent provided amounts for such support.

(B) **Qualified pre-1985 instrument.**—For purposes of this paragraph, the term "qualified pre-1985 instrument" means any decree of divorce or separate maintenance or written agreement—

(i) which is executed before January 1, 1985,

(ii) which on such date contains the provision described in subparagraph (A)(i), and

(iii) which is not modified on or after such date in a modification which expressly provides that this paragraph shall not apply to such decree or agreement.

(4) Custodial parent and noncustodial parent.—For purposes of this subsection—

(A) **Custodial parent.**—The term "custodial parent" means the parent having custody for the greater portion of the calendar year.

(B) **Noncustodial parent.**—The term "noncustodial parent" means the parent who is not the custodial parent.

(5) Exception for multiple-support agreement.—This subsection shall not apply in any case where over one-half of the support of the child is treated as having been received from a taxpayer under the provision of subsection (d)(3).

(6) Special rule for support received from new spouse of parent.—For purposes of this subsection, in the case of the remarriage of a parent, support of a child received from the parent's spouse shall be treated as received from the parent.

(f) Other definitions and rules.—For purposes of this section—

(1) Child defined.—

(A) **In general.**—The term "child" means an individual who is—

(i) a son, daughter, stepson, or stepdaughter of the taxpayer, or

(ii) an eligible foster child of the taxpayer.

(B) **Adopted child.**—In determining whether any of the relationships specified in subparagraph (A)(i) or paragraph (4) exists, a legally adopted individual of the taxpayer, or an individual who is lawfully placed with the taxpayer for legal adoption by the taxpayer, shall be treated as a child of such individual by blood.

(C) **Eligible foster child.**—For purposes of subparagraph (A)(ii), the term "eligible foster child" means an individual who is placed with the taxpayer by an authorized placement agency or by judgment, decree, or other order of any court of competent jurisdiction.

(2) **Student defined.**—The term "student" means an individual who during each of 5 calendar months during the calendar year in which the taxable year of the taxpayer begins—

(A) is a full-time student at an educational organization described in section 170(b)(1)(A)(ii), or

(B) is pursuing a full-time course of institutional on-farm training under the supervision of an accredited agent of an educational organization described in section 170(b)(1)(A)(ii) or of a State or political subdivision of a State.

(3) **Determination of household status.**—An individual shall not be treated as a member of the taxpayer's household if at any time during the taxable year of the taxpayer the relationship between such individual and the taxpayer is in violation of local law.

(4) **Brother and sister.**—The terms "brother" and "sister" include a brother or sister by the half blood.

(5) **Special support test in case of students.**—For purposes of subsections (c)(1)(D) and (d)(1)(C), in the case of an individual who is—

(A) a child of the taxpayer, and

(B) a student,

amounts received as scholarships for study at an educational organization described in section 170(b)(1)(A)(ii) shall not be taken into account.

(6) **Treatment of missing children.**—

(A) **In general.**—Solely for the purposes referred to in subparagraph (B), a child of the taxpayer—

(i) who is presumed by law enforcement authorities to have been kidnapped by someone who is not a member of the family of such child or the taxpayer, and

(ii) who had, for the taxable year in which the kidnapping occurred, the same principal place of abode as the taxpayer for more than one-half of the portion of such year before the date of the kidnapping,

shall be treated as meeting the requirement of subsection (c)(1)(B) with respect to a taxpayer for all taxable years ending during the period that the child is kidnapped.

(B) **Purposes.**—Subparagraph (A) shall apply solely for purposes of determining—

(i) the deduction under section 151(c),

(ii) the credit under section 24 (relating to child tax credit),

(iii) whether an individual is a surviving spouse or a head of a household (as such terms are defined in section 2), and

(iv) the earned income credit under section 32.

(C) **Comparable treatment of certain qualifying relatives.**—For purposes of this section, a child of the taxpayer—

(i) who is presumed by law enforcement authorities to have been kidnapped by someone who is not a member of the family of such child or the taxpayer, and

(ii) who was (without regard to this paragraph) a qualifying relative of the taxpayer for the portion of the taxable year before the date of the kidnapping, shall be treated as a qualifying relative of the taxpayer for all taxable years ending during the period that the child is kidnapped.

(D) Termination of treatment.—Subparagraphs (A) and (C) shall cease to apply as of the first taxable year of the taxpayer beginning after the calendar year in which there is a determination that the child is dead (or, if earlier, in which the child would have attained age 18).

(7) Cross references.—

For provision treating child as dependent of both parents for purposes of certain provisions, see sections 105(b), 132(h)(2)(B), and 213(d)(5).

(Aug. 16, 1954, c. 736, 68A Stat. 43; Aug. 9, 1955, c. 693, § 2, 69 Stat. 626; Pub.L. 85-866, Title I, § 4(a) to (c), Sept. 2, 1958, 72 Stat. 1607; Pub.L. 86-376, § 1(a), Sept. 23, 1959, 73 Stat. 699; Pub.L. 90-78, § 1, Aug. 31, 1967, 81 Stat. 191; Pub.L. 91-172, Title IX, § 912(a), Dec. 30, 1969, 83 Stat. 722; Pub.L. 92-580, § 1(a), Oct. 27, 1972, 86 Stat. 1276; Pub.L. 94-455, Title XIX, §§ 1901(a)(24), (b)(7)(B), (8)(A), 1906(b)(13)(A), Title XXI, § 2139(a), Oct. 4, 1976, 90 Stat. 1767, 1794, 1834, 1932; Pub.L. 98-369, Div. A, Title IV, §§ 423(a), 482(b)(2), July 18, 1984, 98 Stat. 799, 848; Pub.L. 99-514, Title I, § 104(b)(1)(B), (3), Title XIII, § 1301(j)(8), Oct. 22, 1986, 100 Stat. 2104, 2105, 2658; Pub.L. 108-311, Title II, § 201, Oct. 4, 2004, 118 Stat. 1169; Pub.L. 109-135, Title IV, § 404(a), Dec. 21, 2005, 119 Stat. 2632; Pub.L. 110-351, Title V, § 501(a), (b), (c)(2), Oct. 7, 2008, 122 Stat. 3979, 3980; Pub.L. 115-97, Title I, § 11051(b)(3)(B), Dec. 22, 2017, 131 Stat. 2089.)

26 C.F.R. § 1.152-4

§ 1.152-4. Special rule for a child of divorced or separated parents or parents who live apart.

(a) **In general.** A taxpayer may claim a dependency deduction for a child (as defined in section 152(f)(1)) only if the child is the qualifying child of the taxpayer under section 152(c) or the qualifying relative of the taxpayer under section 152(d). Section 152(c)(4)(B) provides that a child who is claimed as a qualifying child by parents who do not file a joint return together is treated as the qualifying child of the parent with whom the child resides for a longer period of time during the taxable year or, if the child resides with both parents for an equal period of time, of the parent with the higher adjusted gross income. However, a child is treated as the qualifying child or qualifying relative of the noncustodial parent if the custodial parent releases a claim to the exemption under section 152(e) and this section.

(b) **Release of claim by custodial parent—(1) In general.** Under section 152(e)(1), notwithstanding section 152(c)(1)(B), (c)(4), or (d)(1)(C), a child is treated as the qualifying child or qualifying relative of the noncustodial parent (as defined in paragraph (d) of this section) if the requirements of paragraphs (b)(2) and (b)(3) of this section are met.

(2) **Support, custody, and parental status—(i) In general.** The requirements of this paragraph (b)(2) are met if the parents of the child provide over one-half of the child's support for the calendar year, the child is in the custody of one or both parents for more than one-half of the calendar year, and the parents—

(A) Are divorced or legally separated under a decree of divorce or separate maintenance;

(B) Are separated under a written separation agreement; or

(C) Live apart at all times during the last 6 months of the calendar year whether or not they are or were married.

(ii) **Multiple support agreement.** The requirements of this paragraph (b)(2) are not met if over one-half of the support of the child is treated as having been received from a taxpayer under section 152(d)(3).

(3) **Release of claim to child.** The requirements of this paragraph (b)(3) are met for a calendar year if—

(i) The custodial parent signs a written declaration that the custodial parent will not claim the child as a dependent for any taxable year beginning in that calendar year and the noncustodial parent attaches the declaration to the noncustodial parent's return for the taxable year; or

(ii) A qualified pre-1985 instrument, as defined in section 152(e)(3)(B), applicable to the taxable year beginning in that calendar year, provides that the noncustodial parent is entitled to the dependency exemption for the child and the noncustodial parent provides at least $600 for the support of the child during the calendar year.

(c) **Custody.** A child is in the custody of one or both parents for more than one-half of the calendar year if one or both parents have the right under state law to physical custody of the child for more than one-half of the calendar year.

(d) **Custodial parent—(1) In general.** The custodial parent is the parent with whom the child resides for the greater number of nights during the calendar year, and the noncustodial parent is the parent who is not the custodial parent. A child is treated as residing with neither parent if the child is emancipated under state law. For purposes of this section, a child resides with a parent for a night if the child sleeps—

(i) At the residence of that parent (whether or not the parent is present); or

(ii) In the company of the parent, when the child does not sleep at a parent's residence (for example, the parent and child are on vacation together).

(2) **Night straddling taxable years.** A night that extends over two taxable years is allocated to the taxable year in which the night begins.

(3) **Absences.** (i) Except as provided in paragraph (d)(3)(ii) of this section, for purposes of this paragraph (d), a child who does not reside (within the meaning of paragraph (d)(1) of this section) with a parent for a night is treated as residing with the parent with whom the child would have resided for the night but for the absence.

(ii) A child who does not reside (within the meaning of paragraph (d)(1) of this section) with a parent for a night is treated as not residing with either parent for that night if it cannot be determined with which parent the child would have resided or if the child would not have resided with either parent for the night.

(4) **Special rule for equal number of nights.** If a child is in the custody of one or both parents for more than one-half of the calendar year and the child resides with each parent for an equal number of nights during the calendar year, the parent with the higher adjusted gross income for the calendar year is treated as the custodial parent.

(5) **Exception for a parent who works at night.** If, in a calendar year, due to a parent's nighttime work schedule, a child resides for a greater number of days but not nights with the parent who works at night, that parent is treated as the custodial parent. On a school day, the child is treated as residing at the primary residence registered with the school.

(e) **Written declaration—(1) Form of declaration—(i) In general.** The written declaration under paragraph (b)(3)(i) of this section must be an unconditional release of the custodial parent's claim to the child as a dependent for the year or years for which the declaration is effective. A declaration is not unconditional if the custodial parent's release of the right to claim the child as a dependent requires the satisfaction of any condition, including the noncustodial parent's meeting of an obligation such as the payment of support. A written declaration must name the noncustodial parent to whom the exemption is released. A written declaration must specify the year or years for which it is effective. A written declaration that specifies all future years is treated as specifying the first taxable year after the taxable year of execution and all subsequent taxable years.

(ii) **Form designated by IRS.** A written declaration may be made on Form 8332, Release/Revocation of Release of Claim to Exemption for Child by Custodial Parent, or successor form designated by the IRS. A written declaration not on the form designated by the IRS must conform to the substance of that form and must be a document executed for the sole purpose of serving as a written declaration under this section. A court order or decree or a separation agreement may not serve as a written declaration.

(2) **Attachment to return.** A noncustodial parent must attach a copy of the written declaration to the parent's return for each taxable year in which the child is claimed as a dependent.

(3) **Revocation of written declaration—(i) In general.** A parent may revoke a written declaration described in paragraph (e)(1) of this section by providing written notice of the revocation to the other parent. The parent revoking the written declaration must make reasonable efforts to provide actual notice to the other parent. The revocation may be effective no earlier than the taxable year that begins in the first calendar year after the calendar year in which the parent revoking the written declaration provides, or makes reasonable efforts to provide, the written notice.

(ii) **Form of revocation.** The revocation may be made on Form 8332, Release/Revocation of Release of Claim to Exemption for Child by Custodial Parent, or successor form designated by the IRS whether or not the written declaration was made on a form designated by the IRS. A revocation not on that form must conform to the substance of the form and must be a document executed for the sole purpose of serving as a revocation under this section. The revocation must specify the year or years for which the revocation is effective. A revocation that specifies all future years is treated as specifying the first taxable year after the taxable year the revocation is executed and all subsequent taxable years.

(iii) **Attachment to return.** The parent revoking the written declaration must attach a copy of the revocation to the parent's return for each taxable year for which the parent claims a child as a dependent as a result of the revocation. The parent revoking the written declaration must keep a copy of the revocation and evidence of delivery of the notice to the other parent, or of the reasonable efforts to provide actual notice.

(4) **Ineffective declaration or revocation.** A written declaration or revocation that fails to satisfy the requirements of this paragraph (e) has no effect.

(5) **Written declaration executed in a taxable year beginning on or before July 2, 2008.** A written declaration executed in a taxable year beginning on or before July 2, 2008, that satisfies the requirements for the form of a written declaration in effect at the time the written declaration is executed, will be treated as meeting the requirements of paragraph (e)(1) of this section. Paragraph (e)(3) of this section applies without regard to whether a custodial parent executed the written declaration in a taxable year beginning on or before July 2, 2008.

(f) **Coordination with other sections.** If section 152(e) and this section apply, a child is treated as the dependent of both parents for purposes of sections 105(b), 132(h)(2)(B), and 213(d)(5).

(g) **Examples.** The provisions of this section are illustrated by the following examples that assume, unless otherwise provided, that each taxpayer's taxable year is the calendar year, one or both of the child's parents provide over one-half of the child's support for the calendar year, one or both parents have the right under state law to physical custody of the child for more than one-half of the calendar year, and the child otherwise meets the requirements of a qualifying child under section 152(c) or a qualifying relative under section 152(d). In addition, in each of the examples, no qualified pre-1985 instrument or multiple support agreement is in effect. The examples are as follows:

Example 1. (i) B and C are the divorced parents of Child. In 2009, Child resides with B for 210 nights and with C for 155 nights. B executes a Form 8332 for 2009 releasing B's right to claim Child as a dependent for that year, which C attaches to C's 2009 return.

(ii) Under paragraph (d) of this section, B is the custodial parent of Child in 2009 because B is the parent with whom Child resides for the greater number of nights in 2009. Because the requirements of paragraphs (b)(2) and (3) of this section are met, C may claim Child as a dependent.

Example 2. The facts are the same as in Example 1 except that B does not execute a Form 8332 or similar declaration for 2009. Therefore, section 152(e) and this section do not apply. Whether Child is the qualifying child or qualifying relative of B or C is determined under section 152(c) or (d).

Example 3. (i) D and E are the divorced parents of Child. Under a custody decree, Grandmother has the right under state law to physical custody of Child from January 1 to July 31, 2009.

(ii) Because D and E do not have the right under state law to physical custody of Child for over one-half of the 2009 calendar year, under paragraph (c) of this section, Child is not in the custody of one or both parents for over one-half of the calendar year. Therefore, section 152(e) and this section do not apply, and whether Child is the qualifying child or qualifying relative of D, E, or Grandmother is determined under section 152(c) or (d).

Example 4. (i) The facts are the same as in Example 3, except that Grandmother has the right to physical custody of Child from January 1 to March 31, 2009, and, as a result, Child resides with Grandmother during this period. D and E jointly have the right to physical custody of Child from April 1 to December 31, 2009. During this period, Child resides with D for 180 nights and with E for 95 nights. D executes a

Form 8332 for 2009 releasing D's right to claim Child as a dependent for that year, which E attaches to E's 2009 return.

(ii) Under paragraph (c) of this section, Child is in the custody of D and E for over one-half of the calendar year, because D and E have the right under state law to physical custody of Child for over one-half of the calendar year.

(iii) Under paragraph (d)(3)(ii) of this section, the nights that Child resides with Grandmother are not allocated to either parent. Child resides with D for a greater number of nights than with E during the calendar year and, under paragraph (d)(1) of this section, D is the custodial parent.

(iv) Because the requirements of paragraphs (b)(2) and (3) of this section are met, section 152(e) and this section apply, and E may claim Child as a dependent.

Example 5. (i) The facts are the same as in Example 4, except that D is away on military service from April 10 to June 15, 2009, and September 6 to October 20, 2009. During these periods Child resides with Grandmother in Grandmother's residence. Child would have resided with D if D had not been away on military service. Grandmother claims Child as a dependent on Grandmother's 2009 return.

(ii) Under paragraph (d)(3)(i) of this section, Child is treated as residing with D for the nights that D is away on military service. Because the requirements of paragraphs (b)(2) and (3) of this section are met, section 152(e) and this section apply, and E, not Grandmother, may claim Child as a dependent.

Example 6. F and G are the divorced parents of Child. In May of 2009, Child turns age 18 and is emancipated under the law of the state where Child resides. Therefore, in 2009 and later years, F and G do not have the right under state law to physical custody of Child for over one-half of the calendar year, and Child is not in the custody of F and G for over one-half of the calendar year. Section 152(e) and this section do not apply, and whether Child is the qualifying child or qualifying relative of F or G is determined under section 152(c) or (d).

Example 7. (i) The facts are the same as in Example 6, except that Child turns age 18 and is emancipated under state law on August 1, 2009, resides with F from January 1, 2009, through May 31, 2009, and resides with G from June 1, 2009, through December 31, 2009. F executes a Form 8332 releasing F's right to claim Child as a dependent for 2009, which G attaches to G's 2009 return.

(ii) Under paragraph (c) of this section, Child is in the custody of F and G for over one-half of the calendar year.

(iii) Under paragraph (d)(1) of this section, Child is treated as not residing with either parent after Child's emancipation. Therefore, Child resides with F for 151 nights and with G for 61 nights. Because the requirements of paragraphs (b)(2) and (3) of this section are met, section 152(e) and this section apply, and G may claim Child as a dependent.

Example 8. H and J are the divorced parents of Child. Child generally resides with H during the week and with J every other weekend. Child resides with J in H's residence for 10 consecutive nights while H is hospitalized. Under paragraph (d)(1)(i) of this section, Child resides with H for the 10 nights.

Example 9. K and L, who are separated under a written separation agreement, are the parents of Child. In August 2009, K and Child spend 10 nights together in a hotel while on vacation. Under paragraph (d)(1)(ii) of this section, Child resides with K for the 10 nights that K and Child are on vacation.

Example 10. M and N are the divorced parents of Child. On December 31, 2009, Child attends a party at M's residence. After midnight on January 1, 2010, Child travels to N's residence, where Child sleeps. Under paragraph (d)(1) of this section, Child resides with N for the night of December 31, 2009, to January 1, 2010, because Child sleeps at N's residence that night. However, under paragraph (d)(2) of this section, the night of December 31, 2009, to January 1, 2010, is allocated to taxable year 2009 for purposes of determining whether Child resides with M or N for a greater number of nights in 2009.

Example 11. O and P, who never married, are the parents of Child. In 2009, Child spends alternate weeks residing with O and P. During a week that Child is residing with O, O gives Child permission to spend a night at the home of a friend. Under paragraph (d)(3)(i) of this section, the night Child spends at the friend's home is treated as a night that Child resides with O.

Example 12. The facts are the same as in Example 11, except that Child also resides at summer camp for 6 weeks. Because Child resides with each parent for alternate weeks, Child would have resided with O for 3 weeks and with P for 3 weeks of the period that Child is at camp. Under paragraph (d)(3)(i) of this section, Child is treated as residing with O for 3 weeks and with P for 3 weeks.

Example 13. The facts are the same as in Example 12, except that Child does not spend alternate weeks residing with O and P, and it cannot be determined whether Child would have resided with O or P for the period that Child is at camp. Under paragraph (d)(3)(ii) of this section, Child is treated as residing with neither parent for the 6 weeks.

Example 14. (i) Q and R are the divorced parents of Child. Q works from 11 PM to 7 AM Sunday through Thursday nights. Because of Q's nighttime work schedule, Child resides with R Sunday through Thursday nights and with Q Friday and Saturday nights. Therefore, in 2009, Child resides with R for 261 nights and with Q for 104 nights. Child spends all daytime hours when Child is not in school with Q and Q's address is registered with Child's school as Child's primary residence. Q executes a Form 8332 for 2009 releasing Q's right to claim Child as a dependent for that year, which R attaches to R's 2009 return.

(ii) Under paragraph (d) of this section, Q is the custodial parent of Child in 2009. Child resides with R for a greater number of nights than with Q due to Q's nighttime work schedule, and Child spends a greater number of days with Q. Therefore, paragraph (d)(5) of this section applies rather than paragraph (d)(1) of this section. Because the requirements of paragraphs (b)(2) and (3) of this section are met, R may claim Child as a dependent.

Example 15. (i) In 2009, S and T, the parents of Child, execute a written separation agreement. The agreement provides that Child will live with S and that T will make monthly child support payments to S. In 2009, Child resides with S for 335 nights and with T for 30 nights. S executes a letter declaring that S will not claim Child as a dependent in 2009 and in subsequent alternate years. The letter contains all the information requested on Form 8332, does not require the satisfaction of any condition such as T's payment of support, and has no purpose other than to serve as a written declaration under section 152(e) and this section. T attaches the letter to T's return for 2009 and 2011.

(ii) In 2010, T fails to provide support for Child, and S executes a Form 8332 revoking the release of S's right to claim Child as a dependent for 2011. S delivers a copy of the Form 8332 to T, attaches a copy of the Form 8332 to S's tax return for 2011, and keeps a copy of the Form 8332 and evidence of delivery of the written notice to T.

(iii) T may claim Child as a dependent for 2009 because S releases the right to claim Child as a dependent under paragraph (b)(3) of this section by executing the letter, which conforms to the requirements of paragraph (e)(1) of this section, and T attaches the letter to T's return in accordance with paragraph (e)(2) of this section. In 2010, S revokes the release of the claim in accordance with paragraph (e)(3) of this section, and the revocation takes effect in 2011, the taxable year that begins in the first calendar year after S provides written notice of the revocation to T. Therefore, in 2011, section 152(e) and this section do not apply, and whether Child is the qualifying child or qualifying relative of S or T is determined under section 152(c) or (d).

Example 16. The facts are the same as Example 15, except that the letter expressly states that S releases the right to claim Child as a dependent only if T is current in the payment of support for Child at the end of the calendar year. The letter does not qualify as a written declaration under paragraph (b)(3) of this section because S's agreement not to claim Child as a dependent is conditioned on T's payment of support and, under paragraph (e)(1)(i) of this section, a written declaration must be unconditional. Therefore, section 152(e) and this section do not apply, and whether Child is the qualifying child or qualifying relative of S or T for 2009 as well as 2011 is determined under section 152(c) or (d).

Example 17. (i) U and V are the divorced parents of Child. Child resides with U for more nights than with V in 2009 through 2011. In 2009, U provides a written statement to V declaring that U will not claim Child as a dependent, but the statement does not specify the year or years it is effective. V attaches the statement to V's returns for 2009 through 2011.

(ii) Because the written statement does not specify a year or years, under paragraph (e)(1) of this section, it is not a written declaration that conforms to the substance of Form 8332. Under paragraph (e)(4) of this section, the statement has no effect. Section 152(e) and this section do not apply, and whether Child is the qualifying child or qualifying relative of U or V is determined under section 152(c) or (d).

Example 18. (i) W and X are the divorced parents of Child. In 2009, Child resides solely with W. The divorce decree requires X to pay child support to W and requires W to execute a Form 8332 releasing W's right to claim Child as a dependent. W fails to sign a Form 8332 for 2009, and X attaches an unsigned Form 8332 to X's return for 2009.

(ii) The order in the divorce decree requiring W to execute a Form 8332 is ineffective to allocate the right to claim Child as a dependent to X. Furthermore, under paragraph (e)(1) of this section, the unsigned Form 8332 does not conform to the substance of Form 8332, and under paragraph (e)(4) of this section, the Form 8332 has no effect. Therefore, section 152(e) and this section do not apply, and whether Child is the qualifying child or qualifying relative of W or X is determined under section 152(c) or (d).

(iii) If, however, W executes a Form 8332 for 2009, and X attaches the Form 8332 to X's return, then X may claim Child as a dependent in 2009.

Example 19. (i) Y and Z are the divorced parents of Child. In 2003, Y and Z enter into a separation agreement, which is incorporated into a divorce decree, under which Y, the custodial parent, releases Y's right to claim Child as a dependent for all future years. The separation agreement satisfies the requirements for the form of a written declaration in effect at the time it is executed. Z attaches a copy of the separation agreement to Z's returns for 2003 through 2009.

(ii) Under paragraph (e)(1)(ii) of this section, a separation agreement may not serve as a written declaration. However, under paragraph (e)(5) of this section, a written declaration executed in a taxable year beginning on or before July 2, 2008, that satisfies the requirements for the form of a written declaration in effect at the time the written declaration is executed, will be treated as meeting the requirements of paragraph (e)(1) of this section. Therefore, the separation agreement may serve as the written declaration required by paragraph (b)(3)(i) of this section for 2009, and Z may claim Child as a dependent in 2009 and later years.

Example 20. (i) The facts are the same as in Example 19, except that in 2009 Y executes a Form 8332 revoking the release of Y's right to claim Child as a dependent for 2010. Y complies with all the requirements of paragraph (e)(3) of this section.

(ii) Although Y executes the separation agreement releasing Y's right to claim Child as a dependent in a taxable year beginning on or before July 2, 2008, under paragraph (e)(5) of this section, Y's execution of the Form 8332 in 2009 is effective to revoke the release. Therefore, section 152(e) and this section do not apply in 2010, and whether Child is the qualifying child or qualifying relative of Y or Z is determined under section 152(c) or (d).

(h) Effective/applicability date. This section applies to taxable years beginning after July 2, 2008.

§ 1041. Transfers of property between spouses or incident to divorce

(a) General rule.—No gain or loss shall be recognized on a transfer of property from an individual to (or in trust for the benefit of)—

(1) a spouse, or

(2) a former spouse, but only if the transfer is incident to the divorce.

(b) Transfer treated as gift; transferee has transferor's basis.—In the case of any transfer of property described in subsection (a)—

(1) for purposes of this subtitle, the property shall be treated as acquired by the transferee by gift, and

(2) the basis of the transferee in the property shall be the adjusted basis of the transferor.

(c) Incident to divorce.—For purposes of subsection (a)(2), a transfer of property is incident to the divorce if such transfer—

(1) occurs within 1 year after the date on which the marriage ceases, or

(2) is related to the cessation of the marriage.

(d) Special rule where spouse is nonresident alien.—Subsection (a) shall not apply if the spouse (or former spouse) of the individual making the transfer is a nonresident alien.

(e) Transfers in trust where liability exceeds basis.—Subsection (a) shall not apply to the transfer of property in trust to the extent that—

(1) the sum of the amount of the liabilities assumed, plus the amount of the liabilities to which the property is subject, exceeds

(2) the total of the adjusted basis of the property transferred.

Proper adjustment shall be made under subsection (b) in the basis of the transferee in such property to take into account gain recognized by reason of the preceding sentence.

26 C.F.R. § 1.1041-1T

§ 1.1041-1T. **Treatment of transfer of property between spouses or incident to divorce (temporary).**

Q-1: How is the transfer of property between spouses treated under section 1041?

A-1: Generally, no gain or loss is recognized on a transfer of property from an individual to (or in trust for the benefit of) a spouse or, if the transfer is incident to a divorce, a former spouse. The following questions and answers describe more fully the scope, tax consequences and other rules which apply to transfers of property under section 1041.

(a) **Scope of section 1041 in general.**

Q-2: Does section 1041 apply only to transfers of property incident to divorce?

A-2: No. Section 1041 is not limited to transfers of property incident to divorce. Section 1041 applies to any transfer of property between spouses regardless of whether the transfer is a gift or is a sale or exchange between spouses acting at arm's length (including a transfer in exchange for the relinquishment of property or marital rights or an exchange otherwise governed by another nonrecognition provision of the Code). A divorce or legal separation need not be contemplated between the spouses at the time of the transfer nor must a divorce or legal separation ever occur.

Example 1. A and B are married and file a joint return. A is the sole owner of a condominium unit. A sale or gift of the condominium from A to B is a transfer which is subject to the rules of section 1041.

Example 2. A and B are married and file separate returns. A is the owner of an independent sole proprietorship, X Company. In the ordinary course of business, X Company makes a sale of property to B. This sale is a transfer of property between spouses and is subject to the rules of section 1041.

Example 3. Assume the same facts as in example (2), except that X Company is a corporation wholly owned by A. This sale is not a sale between spouses subject to the rules of section 1041. However, in appropriate circumstances, general tax principles, including the step-transaction doctrine, may be applicable in recharacterizing the transaction.

Q-3: Do the rules of section 1041 apply to a transfer between spouses if the transferee spouse is a nonresident alien?

A-3: No. Gain or loss (if any) is recognized (assuming no other nonrecognition provision applies) at the time of a transfer of property if the property is transferred to a spouse who is a nonresident alien.

Q-4: What kinds of transfers are governed by section 1041?

A-4: Only transfers of property (whether real or personal, tangible or intangible) are governed by section 1041. Transfers of services are not subject to the rules of section 1041.

Q-5: Must the property transferred to a former spouse have been owned by the transferor spouse during the marriage?

A-5: No. A transfer of property acquired after the marriage ceases may be governed by section 1041.

(b) **Transfer incident to the divorce.**

Q-6: When is a transfer of property incident to the divorce?

A-6: A transfer of property is incident to the divorce in either of the following 2 circumstances—

(1) The transfer occurs not more than one year after the date on which the marriage ceases, or

(2) The transfer is related to the cessation of the marriage.

Thus, a transfer of property occurring not more than one year after the date on which the marriage ceases need not be related to the cessation of the marriage to qualify for section 1041 treatment. (See A-7 for transfers occurring more than one year after the cessation of the marriage.)

Q-7: When is a transfer of property related to the cessation of the marriage?

A-7: A transfer of property is treated as related to the cessation of the marriage if the transfer is pursuant to a divorce or separation instrument, as defined in section 71(b)(2), and the transfer occurs not more than 6 years after the date on which the marriage ceases. A divorce or separation instrument includes a modification or amendment to such decree or instrument. Any transfer not pursuant to a divorce or separation instrument and any transfer occurring more than 6 years after the cessation of the marriage is presumed to be not related to the cessation of the marriage. This presumption may be rebutted only by showing that the transfer was made to effect the division of property owned by the former spouses at the time of the cessation of the marriage. For example, the presumption may be rebutted by showing that (a) the transfer was not made within the one- and six-year periods described above because of factors which hampered an earlier transfer of the property, such as legal or business impediments to transfer or disputes concerning the value of the property owned at the time of the cessation of the marriage, and (b) the transfer is effected promptly after the impediment to transfer is removed.

Q-8: Do annulments and the cessations of marriages that are void *ab initio* due to violations of state law constitute divorces for purposes of section 1041?

A-8: Yes.

(c) Transfers on behalf of a spouse.

Q-9: May transfers of property to third parties on behalf of a spouse (or former spouse) qualify under section 1041?

A-9: Yes. There are three situations in which a transfer of property to a third party on behalf of a spouse (or former spouse) will qualify under section 1041, provided all other requirements of the section are satisfied. The first situation is where the transfer to the third party is required by a divorce or separation instrument. The second situation is where the transfer to the third party is pursuant to the written request of the other spouse (or former spouse). The third situation is where the transferor receives from the other spouse (or former spouse) a written consent or ratification of the transfer to the third party. Such consent or ratification must state that the parties intend the transfer to be treated as a transfer to the nontransferring spouse (or former spouse) subject to the rules of section 1041 and must be received by the transferor prior to the date of filing of the transferor's first return of tax for the taxable year in which the transfer was made. In the three situations described above, the transfer of property will be treated as made directly to the nontransferring spouse (or former spouse) and the nontransferring spouse will be treated as immediately transferring the property to the third party. The deemed transfer from the nontransferring spouse (or former spouse) to the third party is not a transaction that qualifies for nonrecognition of gain under section 1041. This A-9 shall not apply to transfers to which § 1.1041-2 applies.

(d) Tax consequences of transfers subject to section 1041.

Q-10: How is the transferor of property under section 1041 treated for income tax purposes?

A-10: The transferor of property under section 1041 recognizes no gain or loss on the transfer even if the transfer was in exchange for the release of marital rights or other consideration. This rule applies regardless of whether the transfer is of property separately owned by the transferor or is a division (equal or unequal) of community property. Thus, the result under section 1041 differs from the result in *United States* v. Davis, 370 U.S. 65 (1962).

Q-11: How is the transferee of property under section 1041 treated for income tax purposes?

A-11: The transferee of property under section 1041 recognizes no gain or loss upon receipt of the transferred property. In all cases, the basis of the transferred property in the hands of the transferee is the adjusted basis of such property in the hands of the transferor immediately before the transfer. Even if the transfer is a bona fide sale, the transferee does not acquire a basis in the transferred property equal to the transferee's cost (the fair market value). This carryover basis rule applies whether the adjusted basis of the transferred property is less than, equal to, or greater than its fair market value at the time of transfer (or the value of any consideration provided by the transferee) and applies for purposes of determining loss as well as gain upon the subsequent disposition of the property by the transferee. Thus, this rule is different from the rule applied in section 1015(a) for determining the basis of property acquired by gift.

Q-12: Do the rules described in A-10 and A-11 apply even if the transferred property is subject to liabilities which exceed the adjusted basis of the property?

A-12: Yes. For example, assume A owns property having a fair market value of $10,000 and an adjusted basis of $1,000. In contemplation of making a transfer of this property incident to a divorce from B, A borrows $5,000 from a bank, using the property as security for the borrowing. A then transfers the property to B and B assumes, or takes the property subject to, the liability to pay the $5,000 debt. Under section 1041, A recognizes no gain or loss upon the transfer of the property, and the adjusted basis of the property in the hands of B is $1,000.

Q-13: Will a transfer under section 1041 result in a recapture of investment tax credits with respect to the property transferred?

A-13: In general, no. Property transferred under section 1041 will not be treated as being disposed of by, or ceasing to be section 38 property with respect to, the transferor. However, the transferee will be subject to investment tax credit recapture if, upon or after the transfer, the property is disposed of by, or ceases to be section 38 property with respect to, the transferee. For example, as part of a divorce property settlement, B receives a car from A that has been used in A's business for two years and for which an investment tax credit was taken by A. No part of A's business is transferred to B and B's use of the car is solely personal. B is subject to recapture of the investment tax credit previously taken by A.

(e) Notice and recordkeeping requirement with respect to transactions under section 1041.

Q-14: Does the transferor of property in a transaction described in section 1041 have to supply, at the time of the transfer, the transferee with records sufficient to determine the adjusted basis and holding period of the property at the time of the transfer and (if applicable) with notice that the property transferred under section 1041 is potentially subject to recapture of the investment tax credit?

A-14: Yes. A transferor of property under section 1041 must, at the time of the transfer, supply the transferee with records sufficient to determine the adjusted basis and holding period of the property as of the date of the transfer. In addition, in the case of a transfer of property which carries with it a potential liability for investment tax credit recapture, the transferor must, at the time of the transfer, supply the transferee with records sufficient to determine the amount and period of such potential liability. Such records must be preserved and kept accessible by the transferee.

(f) Property settlements—effective dates, transitional periods and elections.

Q-15: When does section 1041 become effective?

A-15: Generally, section 1041 applies to all transfers after July 18, 1984. However, it does not apply to transfers after July 18, 1984 pursuant to instruments in effect on or before July 18, 1984. (See A-16 with respect to exceptions to the general rule.)

Q-16: Are there any exceptions to the general rule stated in A-15 above?

A-16: Yes. Two transitional rules provide exceptions to the general rule stated in A-15. First, section 1041 will apply to transfers after July 18, 1984 under instruments that were in effect on or before July 18, 1984 if both spouses (or former spouses) elect to have section 1041 apply to such transfers. Second, section 1041 will apply to all transfers after December 31, 1983 (including transfers under instruments in effect on or before July 18, 1984) if both spouses (or former spouses) elect to have section 1041 apply. (See A-18 relating to the time and manner of making the elections under the first or second transitional rule.)

Q-17: Can an election be made to have section 1041 apply to some, but not all, transfers made after December 31, 1983, or some but not all, transfers made after July 18, 1984 under instruments in effect on or before July 18, 1984?

A-17: No. Partial elections are not allowed. An election under either of the two elective transitional rules applies to all transfers governed by that election whether before or after the election is made, and is irrevocable.

(g) Property settlements—time and manner of making the elections under section 1041.

Q-18: How do spouses (or former spouses) elect to have section 1041 apply to transfers after December 31, 1983, or to transfers after July 18, 1984 under instruments in effect on or before July 18, 1984?

A-18: In order to make an election under section 1041 for property transfers after December 31, 1983, or property transfers under instruments that were in effect on or before July 18, 1984, both spouses (or former spouses) must elect the application of the rules of section 1041 by attaching to the transferor's first filed income tax return for the taxable year in which the first transfer occurs, a statement signed by both spouses (or former spouses) which includes each spouse's social security number and is in substantially the form set forth at the end of this answer.

In addition, the transferor must attach a copy of such statement to his or her return for each subsequent taxable year in which a transfer is made that is governed by the transitional election. A copy of the signed statement must be kept by both parties.

The election statements shall be in substantially the following form:

In the case of an election regarding transfers after 1983:

Section 1041 Election

The undersigned hereby elect to have the provisions of section 1041 of the Internal Revenue Code apply to all qualifying transfers of property after December 31, 1983. The undersigned understand that section 1041 applies to all property transferred between spouses, or former spouses incident to divorce. The parties further understand that the effects for Federal income tax purposes of having section 1041 apply are that (1) no gain or loss is recognized by the transferor spouse or former spouse as a result of this transfer; and (2) the basis of the transferred property in the hands of the transferee is the adjusted basis of the property in the hands of the transferor immediately before the transfer, whether or not the adjusted basis of the transferred property is less than, equal to, or greater than its fair market value at the time of the transfer. The undersigned understand that if the transferee spouse or former spouse disposes of the property in a transaction in which gain is recognized, the amount of gain which is taxable may be larger than it would have been if this election had not been made.

In the case of an election regarding preexisting decrees:

Section 1041 Election

The undersigned hereby elect to have the provisions of section 1041 of the Internal Revenue Code apply to all qualifying transfers of property after July 18, 1984 under any instrument in effect on or before July 18, 1984. The undersigned understand that section 1041 applies to all property transferred between spouses, or former spouses incident to the divorce. The parties further understand that the effects for Federal income tax purposes of having section 1041 apply are that (1) no gain or loss is recognized by the transferor spouse or former spouse as a result of this transfer; and (2) the basis of the transferred property in the hands of the transferee is the adjusted basis of the property in the hands of the transferor immediately before the transfer, whether or not the adjusted basis of the transferred property is less than, equal to, or greater than its fair market value at the time of the transfer. The undersigned understand that if the transferee spouse or former spouse disposes of the property in a transaction in which gain is recognized, the amount of gain which is taxable may be larger than it would have been if this election had not been made.

IRS Publication 504. Divorced or Separated Individuals
(February 5, 2019)

Department of the Treasury
Internal Revenue Service

Publication 504
Cat. No. 15006I

Divorced or Separated Individuals

For use in preparing
2018 Returns

Get forms and other information faster and easier at:
- *IRS.gov* (English)
- *IRS.gov/Spanish* (Español)
- *IRS.gov/Chinese* (中文)
- *IRS.gov/Korean* (한국어)
- *IRS.gov/Russian* (Русский)
- *IRS.gov/Vietnamese* (TiếngViệt)

Feb 05, 2019

Contents

Future Developments	1
What's New	2
Reminders	2
Introduction	2
Filing Status	3
Married Filing Jointly	4
Married Filing Separately	5
Head of Household	6
Dependents	8
Exemptions	8
Qualifying Child or Qualifying Relative	8
Children of Divorced or Separated Parents (or Parents Who Live Apart)	9
Qualifying Child of More Than One Person	11
Alimony	13
General Rules	14
Certain Rules for Instruments Executed After 1984	15
Alimony Requirements	15
Recapture of Alimony	17
Instruments Executed Before 1985	18
Qualified Domestic Relations Order	18
Individual Retirement Arrangements	19
Property Settlements	19
Transfer Between Spouses	20
Gift Tax on Property Settlements	21
Gift Tax Return	22
Sale of Jointly-Owned Property	22
Costs of Getting a Divorce	23
Tax Withholding and Estimated Tax	23
Community Property	23
Community Income	23
Alimony (Community Income)	25
How To Get Tax Help	26
Index	28

Future Developments

For the latest information about developments related to Pub. 504, such as legislation enacted after this publication was published, go to *IRS.gov/Pub504*.

What's New

Forms 1040A and 1040EZ no longer available. Form 1040 has been redesigned for 2018 to include reporting previously done on Forms 1040A and 1040EZ. Filers of these forms will now file Form 1040. Despite this change, some forms and publications that were released in 2017 or early 2018 (for example, Form W-2) may still reference Form 1040A or 1040-EZ. Please disregard those references.

The redesigned Form 1040 now has six new numbered schedules in addition to the existing schedules such as Schedule A.

Many people will only need to file Form 1040 and none of the new numbered schedules. However, if your return is more complicated (for example, if you claim certain deductions or credits or owe additional taxes), you will need to complete one or more of the new numbered schedules.

For information about the redesigned Form 1040 or tax law changes affecting Form 1040 for the 2018 tax year, go to *IRS.gov/Form1040*.

Personal exemption suspended. The personal exemption deduction for you, your spouse, or a dependent has been suspended for tax years 2018 through 2025.

Divorce or separation agreements after 2018. Amounts paid as alimony or separate maintenance payments under a divorce or separation agreement executed, or changed, after 2018 won't be deductible by the payer. Such amounts also won't be includible in the income of the recipient.

ITIN renewals for certain spouses and dependents residing outside of the United States. Generally, an individual taxpayer identification number (ITIN) that hasn't been included on a U.S. federal tax return at least once for tax years 2015, 2016, or 2017, and ITINs assigned before 2013, must be renewed to avoid delays in processing your tax return. However, spouses and dependents residing outside of the United States who could've been claimed in previous years for the personal exemption and no other benefit don't need to renew their ITINs, unless they anticipate being claimed for a different tax benefit or if they file their own tax return. For more information, visit *IRS.gov/ITIN*.

Community property. Several states have enacted laws that allow residents (and in some cases nonresidents) to elect to treat certain income and property as community property. For details, see *Community property states*, later.

Reminders

Health care law. Under the health care law, you must have qualifying health care coverage, qualify for an exemption from qualifying health care coverage, or make a shared responsibility payment. Your divorce or separation may affect your responsibilities under the health care law. For details, see *Health care law considerations*.

Relief from joint liability. In some cases, one spouse may be relieved of joint liability for tax, interest, and penalties on a joint tax return. For more information, see *Relief from joint liability* under *Married Filing Jointly*.

Social security numbers for dependents. You must include on your tax return the taxpayer identification number (generally, the social security number (SSN)) of every dependent you claim. See *Dependents*, later.

Using and getting an ITIN. The ITIN is entered wherever an SSN is requested on a tax return. If you're required to include another person's SSN on your return and that person doesn't have and can't get an SSN, enter that person's ITIN. The IRS will issue an ITIN to a nonresident or resident alien who doesn't have and isn't eligible to get an SSN. To apply for an ITIN, file Form W-7, Application for IRS Individual Taxpayer Identification Number, with the IRS. Allow 7 weeks for the IRS to notify you of your ITIN application status (9 to 11 weeks if you submit the application during peak processing periods (January 15 through April 30) or if you're filing from overseas). If you haven't received your ITIN at the end of that time, you can call the IRS to check the status of your application. For more information, go to *IRS.gov/FormW7*.

Change of address. If you change your mailing address, be sure to notify the IRS. You can use Form 8822, Change of Address.

Change of name. If you change your name, be sure to notify the Social Security Administration using Form SS-5, Application for a Social Security Card.

Change of withholding. If you have been claiming a withholding exemption for your spouse, and you divorce or legally separate, you must give your employer a new Form W-4, Employee's Withholding Allowance Certificate, within 10 days after the divorce or separation.

Photographs of missing children. The IRS is a proud partner with the *National Center for Missing & Exploited Children® (NCMEC)*. Photographs of missing children selected by the Center may appear in this publication on pages that would otherwise be blank. You can help bring these children home by looking at the photographs and calling 1-800-THE-LOST (1-800-843-5678) if you recognize a child.

Introduction

This publication explains tax rules that apply if you are divorced or separated from your spouse. It covers general filing information and can help you choose your filing status. It also can help you decide which benefits you are entitled to claim.

The publication also discusses payments and transfers of property that often occur as a result of divorce and how you must treat them on your tax return. Examples include alimony, child support, other court-ordered payments, property settlements, and transfers of individual retirement arrangements. In addition, this publication also explains deductions allowed for some of the costs of obtaining a divorce and how to handle tax withholding and estimated tax payments.

The last part of the publication explains special rules that may apply to persons who live in community property states.

Comments and suggestions. We welcome your comments about this publication and your suggestions for future editions.

You can send us comments through IRS.gov/FormComments. Or you can write to:

Internal Revenue Service
Tax Forms and Publications
1111 Constitution Ave. NW, IR-6526
Washington, DC 20224

Although we can't respond individually to each comment received, we do appreciate your feedback and will consider your comments as we revise our tax forms, instructions, and publications.

Ordering forms and publications. Visit IRS.gov/FormsPubs to download forms and publications. Otherwise, you can go to IRS.gov/OrderForms to order current and prior-year forms and instructions. Your order should arrive within 10 business days.

Tax questions. If you have a tax question not answered by this publication, check IRS.gov and How To Get Tax Help at the end of this publication.

Useful Items

You may want to see:

Publications

- ❏ **501** Dependents, Standard Deduction, and Filing Information
- ❏ **544** Sales and Other Dispositions of Assets
- ❏ **555** Community Property
- ❏ **590-A** Contributions to Individual Retirement Arrangements (IRAs)
- ❏ **590-B** Distributions from Individual Retirement Arrangements (IRAs)
- ❏ **971** Innocent Spouse Relief
- ❏ **974** Premium Tax Credit

Forms (and Instructions)

- ❏ **8332** Release/Revocation of Release of Claim to Exemption for Child by Custodial Parent
- ❏ **8379** Injured Spouse Allocation
- ❏ **8857** Request for Innocent Spouse Relief

See How To Get Tax Help near the end of this publication for information about getting publications and forms.

Filing Status

Your filing status is used in determining whether you must file a return, your standard deduction, and the correct tax. It also may be used in determining whether you can claim certain other deductions and credits. The filing status you can choose depends partly on your marital status on the last day of your tax year.

Marital status. If you are unmarried, your filing status is single or, if you meet certain requirements, head of household or qualifying widow(er). If you are married, your filing status is either married filing a joint return or married filing a separate return. For information about the single and qualifying widow(er) filing statuses, see Pub. 501, Dependents, Standard Deduction, and Filing Information.

Unmarried persons. You are unmarried for the whole year if either of the following applies.

- You have obtained a final decree of divorce or separate maintenance by the last day of your tax year. You must follow your state law to determine if you are divorced or legally separated.

    Exception. If you and your spouse obtain a divorce in one year for the sole purpose of filing tax returns as unmarried individuals, and at the time of divorce you intend to remarry each other and do so in the next tax year, you and your spouse must file as married individuals.

- You have obtained a decree of annulment, which holds that no valid marriage ever existed. You must file amended returns (Form 1040X, Amended U.S. Individual Income Tax Return) for all tax years affected by the annulment that aren't closed by the statute of limitations. The statute of limitations generally doesn't end until 3 years (including extensions) after the date you file your original return or within 2 years after the date you pay the tax. On the amended return you will change your filing status to single or, if you meet certain requirements, head of household.

Married persons. You are married for the whole year if you are separated but you haven't obtained a final decree of divorce or separate maintenance by the last day of your tax year. An interlocutory decree isn't a final decree. However, individuals who have entered into a registered domestic partnership, civil union, or other similar relationship that isn't called a marriage under state (or foreign) law aren't married for federal tax purposes. For more information, see Pub. 501.

Same-sex marriage. For federal tax purposes, the marriage of a same-sex couple is treated the same as the marriage of a man to a woman. However, individuals who have entered into a registered domestic partnership, civil union, or other similar relationship that isn't considered a marriage under state law aren't considered married for federal tax purposes.

Exception. If you live apart from your spouse, under certain circumstances, you may be considered unmarried and can file as head of household. See *Head of Household*, later.

Health care law considerations. Under the health care law, you must have qualifying health care coverage, qualify for an exemption from qualifying health care coverage, or make a shared responsibility payment.

Qualifying health care coverage (also called minimum essential coverage) includes:

- Most coverage through government-sponsored programs (including Medicaid coverage, Medicare parts A or C, the Children's Health Insurance Program (CHIP), certain benefits for veterans and their families, TRICARE, and health coverage for Peace Corps volunteers);
- Most types of employer-sponsored coverage;
- Grandfathered health plans; and
- Other health coverage the Department of Health and Human Services designates as minimum essential coverage.

Your divorce or separation may impact your responsibilities under the health care law in the following ways.

- **Special Marketplace Enrollment Period.** If you lose your health insurance coverage due to divorce, you are still required to have coverage for every month of the year for yourself and the dependents you can claim on your tax return. Losing coverage through a divorce is considered a qualifying life event that allows you to enroll in health coverage through the Health Insurance Marketplace during a Special Enrollment Period.
- **Changes in Circumstances.** If you purchase health insurance coverage through the Health Insurance Marketplace, you may get advance payments of the premium tax credit in 2018. If you do, you should report changes in circumstances to your Marketplace throughout the year. Changes to report include a change in marital status, a name change, and a change in your income or family size. By reporting changes, you will help make sure that you get the proper type and amount of financial assistance. This also will help you avoid getting too much or too little credit in advance.
- **Shared Policy Allocation.** If you divorced or are legally separated during the tax year and are enrolled in the same qualified health plan, you and your former spouse must allocate policy amounts on your separate tax returns to figure your premium tax credit and reconcile any advance payments made on your behalf. The Instructions for Form 8962, Premium Tax Credit, has more information about the Shared Policy Allocation.

Married Filing Jointly

If you are married, you and your spouse can choose to file a joint return. If you file jointly, you both must include all your income, deductions, and credits on that return. You can file a joint return even if one of you had no income or deductions.

 If both you and your spouse have income, you usually should figure your tax on both a joint return and separate returns (using the filing status of married filing separately) to see which gives the two of you the lower combined tax.

Nonresident alien. To file a joint return, at least one of you must be a U.S. citizen or resident alien at the end of the tax year. If either of you was a nonresident alien at any time during the tax year, you can file a joint return only if you agree to treat the nonresident spouse as a resident of the United States. This means that your combined worldwide incomes are subject to U.S. income tax. These rules are explained in Pub. 519, U.S. Tax Guide for Aliens.

Signing a joint return. Both you and your spouse generally must sign the return, or it won't be considered a joint return.

Joint and individual liability. Both you and your spouse may be held responsible, jointly and individually, for the tax and any interest or penalty due on your joint return. This means that one spouse may be held liable for all the tax due even if all the income was earned by the other spouse.

Divorced taxpayers. If you are divorced, you are jointly and individually responsible for any tax, interest, and penalties due on a joint return for a tax year ending before your divorce. This responsibility applies even if your divorce decree states that your former spouse will be responsible for any amounts due on previously filed joint returns.

Relief from joint liability. In some cases, a spouse may be relieved of the tax, interest, and penalties on a joint return. You can ask for relief no matter how small the liability.

There are three types of relief available.

- Innocent spouse relief.
- Separation of liability, which applies to joint filers who are divorced, widowed, legally separated, or who haven't lived together for the 12 months ending on the date election of this relief is filed.
- Equitable relief.

Married persons who live in community property states, but who didn't file joint returns, also may qualify for relief from liability for tax attributable to an item of community income or for equitable relief. See *Relief from liability for tax attributable to an item of community income*, later, under *Community Property*.

Each kind of relief has different requirements. You must file Form 8857 to request relief under any of these categories. Pub. 971 explains these kinds of relief and who may qualify for them. You also can find information on our website at IRS.gov.

Tax refund applied to spouse's debts. The overpayment shown on your joint return may be used to pay the past-due amount of your spouse's debts. This includes your spouse's federal tax, state income tax, child or spousal support payments, or a federal nontax debt, such as a student loan. You can get a refund of your share of the overpayment if you qualify as an injured spouse.

Injured spouse. You are an injured spouse if you file a joint return and all or part of your share of the overpayment was, or is expected to be, applied against your spouse's past-due debts. An injured spouse can get a refund for his or her share of the overpayment that would otherwise be used to pay the past-due amount.

To be considered an injured spouse, you must:

1. Have made and reported tax payments (such as federal income tax withheld from wages or estimated tax payments), or claimed a refundable tax credit, such as the earned income credit or additional child tax credit on the joint return, and

2. Not be legally obligated to pay the past-due amount.

If the injured spouse's permanent home is in a community property state, then the injured spouse must only meet (2). For more information, see Pub. 555.

If you are an injured spouse, you must file Form 8379 to have your portion of the overpayment refunded to you. Follow the instructions for the form.

If you haven't filed your joint return and you know that your joint refund will be offset, file Form 8379 with your return. You should receive your refund within 14 weeks from the date the paper return is filed or within 11 weeks from the date the return is filed electronically.

If you filed your joint return and your joint refund was offset, file Form 8379 by itself. When filed after offset, it can take up to 8 weeks to receive your refund. Don't attach the previously filed tax return, but do include copies of all Forms W-2, Wage and Tax Statement, and W-2G, Certain Gambling Winnings, for both spouses and any Forms 1099 that show income tax withheld.

 An injured spouse claim is different from an innocent spouse relief request. An injured spouse uses Form 8379 to request an allocation of the tax overpayment attributed to each spouse. An innocent spouse uses Form 8857 to request relief from joint liability for tax, interest, and penalties on a joint return for items of the other spouse (or former spouse) that were incorrectly reported on or omitted from the joint return. For information on innocent spouses, see Relief from joint liability, earlier.

Married Filing Separately

If you and your spouse file separate returns, you should each report only your own income, deductions, and credits on your individual return. You can file a separate return even if only one of you had income.

Community or separate income. If you live in a community property state and file a separate return, your income may be separate income or community income for income tax purposes. For more information, see *Community Income* under *Community Property*, later.

Separate liability. If you and your spouse file separately, you each are responsible only for the tax due on your own return.

Itemized deductions. If you and your spouse file separate returns and one of you itemizes deductions, the other spouse can't use the standard deduction and also should itemize deductions.

Dividing itemized deductions. You may be able to claim itemized deductions on a separate return for certain expenses that you paid separately or jointly with your spouse. See Table 1.

Separate returns may give you a higher tax. Some married couples file separate returns because each wants to be responsible only for his or her own tax. There is no joint liability. But in almost all instances, if you file separate returns, you will pay more combined federal tax than you would with a joint return. This is because the following special rules apply if you file a separate return.

1. Your tax rate generally is higher than it would be on a joint return.

2. Your exemption amount for figuring the alternative minimum tax is half of that allowed on a joint return.

3. You can't take the credit for child and dependent care expenses in most cases, and the amount you can exclude from income under an employer's dependent care assistance program is limited to $2,500 (instead of $5,000 on a joint return). If you are legally separated or living apart from your spouse, you may be able to file a separate return and still take the credit. See Pub. 503 for more information.

4. You can't take the earned income credit.

5. You can't take the exclusion or credit for adoption expenses in most cases.

6. You can't exclude the interest from qualified savings bonds that you used for higher education expenses.

7. If you lived with your spouse at any time during the tax year:

    a. You can't claim the credit for the elderly or the disabled, and

    b. You will have to include in income a higher percentage (up to 85%) of any social security or equivalent railroad retirement benefits you received.

8. The following credits and deductions are reduced at income levels that are half those for a joint return.

    a. The child tax credit.

    b. The retirement savings contributions credit.

9. Your capital loss deduction limit is $1,500 (instead of $3,000 on a joint return).

Table 1. **Itemized Deductions on Separate Returns**

This table shows itemized deductions you can claim on your married filing separate return whether you paid the expenses separately with your own funds or jointly with your spouse.

Caution: If you live in a community property state, these rules don't apply. See Community Property.

IF you paid ...	AND you ...	THEN you can deduct on your separate federal return ...
medical expenses	paid with funds deposited in a joint checking account in which you and your spouse have an equal interest	half of the total medical expenses, subject to certain limits, unless you can show that you alone paid the expenses.
state income tax	file a separate state income tax return	the state income tax you alone paid during the year.
	file a joint state income tax return and you and your spouse are jointly and individually liable for the full amount of the state income tax	the state income tax you alone paid during the year.
	file a joint state income tax return and you are liable for only your own share of state income tax	the smaller of: • the state income tax you alone paid during the year, or • the total state income tax you and your spouse paid during the year multiplied by the following fraction. The numerator is your gross income and the denominator is your combined gross income.
property tax	paid the tax on property held as tenants by the entirety	the property tax you alone paid.
mortgage interest	paid the interest on a qualified home[1] held as tenants by the entirety	the mortgage interest you alone paid.
casualty loss	have a casualty loss[2] resulting from a federally declared disaster on a home you own as tenants by the entirety	half of the loss, subject to the deduction limits. Neither spouse may report the total casualty loss.

[1] For more information on a qualified home and deductible mortgage interest, see Pub. 936, Home Mortgage Interest Deduction.

[2] For more information on casualty losses, see Pub. 547, Casualties, Disasters and Thefts.

10. If your spouse itemizes deductions, you can't claim the standard deduction. If you can claim the standard deduction, your basic standard deduction is half the amount allowed on a joint return.

11. You can't take the credit for higher education expenses (American opportunity and lifetime learning credits), the deduction for student loan interest, or the tuition and fees deduction.

Joint return after separate returns. If either you or your spouse (or both of you) file a separate return, you generally can change to a joint return within 3 years from the due date (not including extensions) of the separate return or returns. This applies to a return either of you filed claiming married filing separately, single, or head of household filing status. Use Form 1040X to change your filing status.

Separate returns after joint return. After the due date of your return, you and your spouse can't file separate returns if you previously filed a joint return.

Exception. A personal representative for a decedent can change from a joint return elected by the surviving spouse to a separate return for the decedent. The personal representative has 1 year from the due date (including extensions) of the joint return to make the change.

Head of Household

Filing as head of household has the following advantages.

- You can claim the standard deduction even if your spouse files a separate return and itemizes deductions.
- Your standard deduction is higher than is allowed if you claim a filing status of single or married filing separately.
- Your tax rate usually will be lower than it is if you claim a filing status of single or married filing separately.
- You may be able to claim certain credits (such as the dependent care credit and the earned income credit) you can't claim if your filing status is married filing separately.

- Income limits that reduce your child tax credit and your retirement savings contributions credit, for example, are higher than the income limits if you claim a filing status of married filing separately.

Requirements. You may be able to file as head of household if you meet all the following requirements.

- You are unmarried or "considered unmarried" on the last day of the year.
- You paid more than half the cost of keeping up a home for the year.
- A "qualifying person" lived with you in the home for more than half the year (except for temporary absences, such as school). However, if the "qualifying person" is your dependent parent, he or she doesn't have to live with you. See *Special rule for parent*, later, under *Qualifying person*.

Considered unmarried. You are considered unmarried on the last day of the tax year if you meet all the following tests.

- You file a separate return. A separate return includes a return claiming married filing separately, single, or head of household filing status.
- You paid more than half the cost of keeping up your home for the tax year.
- Your spouse didn't live in your home during the last 6 months of the tax year. Your spouse is considered to live in your home even if he or she is temporarily absent due to special circumstances. See *Temporary absences*, later.
- Your home was the main home of your child, stepchild, or foster child for more than half the year. (See *Qualifying person*, later, for rules applying to a child's birth, death, or temporary absence during the year.)
- You must be able to claim the child as a dependent. However, you meet this test if you can't claim the child as a dependent only because the noncustodial parent can claim the child. The general rules for claiming a dependent are shown in Table 3.

 If you were considered married for part of the year and lived in a community property state (one of the states listed later under Community Property), special rules may apply in determining your income and expenses. See Pub. 555 for more information.

Nonresident alien spouse. If your spouse was a nonresident alien at any time during the tax year, and you haven't chosen to treat your spouse as a resident alien, you are considered unmarried for head of household purposes. However, your spouse isn't a qualifying person for head of household purposes. You must have another qualifying person and meet the other requirements to file as head of household.

Keeping up a home. You are keeping up a home only if you pay more than half the cost of its upkeep for the year. This includes rent, mortgage interest, real estate taxes, insurance on the home, repairs, utilities, and food eaten in the home. This doesn't include the cost of clothing, education, medical treatment, vacations, life insurance, or transportation for any member of the household.

Qualifying person. Table 2 shows who can be a qualifying person. Any person not described in Table 2 isn't a qualifying person.

Generally, the qualifying person must live with you for more than half of the year.

Special rule for parent. If your qualifying person is your father or mother, you may be eligible to file as head of household even if your father or mother doesn't live with you. However, you must be able to claim your father or mother as a dependent. Also, you must pay more than half the cost of keeping up a home that was the main home for the entire year for your father or mother.

You are keeping up a main home for your father or mother if you pay more than half the cost of keeping your parent in a rest home or home for the elderly.

Death or birth. If the person for whom you kept up a home was born or died in 2018, you still may be able to file as head of household. If the person is your qualifying child, the child must have lived with you for more than half the part of the year he or she was alive. If the person is anyone else, see Pub. 501.

Temporary absences. You and your qualifying person are considered to live together even if one or both of you are temporarily absent from your home due to special circumstances such as illness, education, business, vacation, military service, or detention in a juvenile facility. It must be reasonable to assume that the absent person will return to the home after the temporary absence. You must continue to keep up the home during the absence.

Kidnapped child. You may be eligible to file as head of household even if the child who is your qualifying person has been kidnapped. You can claim head of household filing status if all the following statements are true.

- The child is presumed by law enforcement authorities to have been kidnapped by someone who isn't a member of your family or the child's family.
- In the year of the kidnapping, the child lived with you for more than half the part of the year before the kidnapping.
- In the year of the child's return, the child lived with you for more than half the part of the year following the date of the child's return.
- You would have qualified for head of household filing status if the child hadn't been kidnapped.

This treatment applies for all years until the earliest of:

1. The year the child is returned,
2. The year there is a determination that the child is dead, or
3. The year the child would have reached age 18.

Table 2. **Who Is a Qualifying Person Qualifying You To File as Head of Household?**[1]

Caution. *See the text of this publication for the other requirements you must meet to claim head of household filing status.*

IF the person is your ...	AND ...	THEN that person is ...
qualifying child (such as a son, daughter, or grandchild who lived with you more than half the year and meets certain other tests)[2]	he or she is single	a qualifying person, whether or not you can claim the person as a dependent.
	he or she is married and you can claim him or her as a dependent	a qualifying person.
	he or she is married and you can't claim him or her as a dependent	not a qualifying person.[3]
qualifying relative[4] who is your father or mother	you can claim him or her as a dependent[5]	a qualifying person.[6]
	you can't claim him or her as a dependent	not a qualifying person.
qualifying relative[4] other than your father or mother (such as a grandparent, brother, or sister who meets certain tests)	he or she lived with you more than half the year, and he or she is related to you in one of the ways listed under *Relatives who don't have to live with you* in Pub. 501 and you can claim him or her as a dependent[5]	a qualifying person.
	he or she didn't live with you more than half the year	not a qualifying person.
	he or she isn't related to you in one of the ways listed under *Relatives who don't have to live with you* in Pub. 501 and is your qualifying relative only because he or she lived with you all year as a member of your household	not a qualifying person.
	you can't claim him or her as a dependent	not a qualifying person.

[1] A person can't qualify more than one taxpayer to use the head of household filing status for the year.

[2] See Table 3 for the tests that must be met to be a qualifying child. **Note.** If you are a noncustodial parent, the term "qualifying child" for head of household filing status doesn't include a child who is your qualifying child only because of the rules described under *Children of Divorced or Separated Parents (or Parents Who Live Apart)*, later. If you are the custodial parent and those rules apply, the child generally is your qualifying child for head of household filing status even though you can't claim the child as a dependent.

[3] This person is a qualifying person if the only reason you can't claim them as a dependent is because you can be claimed as a dependent on someone else's return.

[4] See Table 3 for the tests that must be met to be a qualifying relative.

[5] If you can claim a person as a dependent only because of a multiple support agreement, that person isn't a qualifying person. See *Multiple Support Agreement* in Pub. 501.

[6] See *Special rule for parent*.

For more information on filing as head of household, see Pub. 501.

Dependents

Exemptions

The personal exemption deduction for dependents has been suspended for tax years 2018 through 2025.

Qualifying Child or Qualifying Relative

The term "dependent" means:
- A qualifying child, or
- A qualifying relative.

Table 3 shows the tests that must be met to be either a qualifying child or qualifying relative, plus the additional requirements for claiming a dependent. For detailed information, see Pub. 501.

IRS DIVORCED OR SEPARATED INDIVIDUALS PUBLICATION 504

Table 3. Overview of the Rules for Claiming a Dependent

Caution. This table is only an overview of the rules. For details, see Pub. 501.

- You can't claim any dependents if you, or your spouse if filing jointly, could be claimed as a dependent by another taxpayer.
- You can't claim a married person who files a joint return as a dependent unless that joint return is filed only to claim a refund of withheld income tax or estimated tax paid.
- You can't claim a person as a dependent unless that person is a U.S. citizen, U.S. resident alien, U.S. national, or a resident of Canada or Mexico.[1]
- You can't claim a person as a dependent unless that person is your **qualifying child** or **qualifying relative.**

Tests To Be a Qualifying Child	Tests To Be a Qualifying Relative
1. The child must be your son, daughter, stepchild, foster child, brother, sister, half brother, half sister, stepbrother, stepsister, or a descendant of any of them.	1. The person can't be your qualifying child or the qualifying child of anyone else.
2. The child must be (a) under age 19 at the end of the year and younger than you (or your spouse if filing jointly), (b) under age 24 at the end of the year, a student, and younger than you (or your spouse if filing jointly), or (c) any age if permanently and totally disabled.	2. The person either (a) must be related to you in one of the ways listed under *Relatives who don't have to live with you* in Pub. 501 or (b) must live with you all year as a member of your household[2] (and your relationship must not violate local law).
3. The child must have lived with you for more than half of the year.[2]	3. The person's gross income for the year must be less than $4,150.[3]
4. The child must not have provided more than half of his or her own support for the year.	4. You must provide more than half of the person's total support for the year.[4]
5. The child isn't filing a joint return for the year (unless that joint return is filed only to claim a refund of withheld income tax or estimated tax paid).	A person isn't a qualifying relative unless he or she meets items (1) through (4).
A child isn't a qualifying child unless he or she meets items (1) through (5).	
If the child meets the rules to be a qualifying child of more than one person, only one person can actually treat the child as a qualifying child. See *Qualifying Child of More Than One Person*, later, to find out which person is the person entitled to claim the child as a qualifying child.	

[1] An exception exists for certain adopted children.
[2] Exceptions exist for temporary absences, children who were born or died during the year, children of divorced or separated parents (or parents who live apart), and kidnapped children.
[3] An exception exists for persons who are disabled and have income from a sheltered workshop.
[4] Exceptions exist for multiple support agreements, children of divorced or separated parents (or parents who live apart), and kidnapped children. See Pub. 501.

TIP *You may be entitled to a child tax credit for each qualifying child who was under age 17 at the end of the year if you claimed that child as a dependent. If you can't claim the child tax credit for a child who is an eligible dependent, you may be able to claim the credit for other dependents instead. See the Form 1040 instructions for details.*

Children of Divorced or Separated Parents (or Parents Who Live Apart)

In most cases, because of the residency test (see item 3 under *Tests To Be a Qualifying Child* in Table 3), a child of divorced or separated parents is the qualifying child of the custodial parent. However, the child will be treated as the qualifying child of the noncustodial parent if the rule for children of divorced or separated parents (or parents who live apart) (discussed next) applies.

Children of divorced or separated parents (or parents who live apart). A child will be treated as the qualifying child of his or her noncustodial parent if all four of the following statements are true.

1. The parents:
   a. Are divorced or legally separated under a decree of divorce or separate maintenance,

Publication 504 (2018) Page 9

b. Are separated under a written separation agreement, or
   c. Lived apart at all times during the last 6 months of the year, whether or not they are or were married.
2. The child received over half of his or her support for the year from the parents.
3. The child is in the custody of one or both parents for more than half of the year.
4. Either of the following applies.
   a. The custodial parent signs a written declaration, discussed later, that he or she won't claim the child as a dependent for the year, and the noncustodial parent attaches this written declaration to his or her return. (If the decree or agreement went into effect after 1984, see *Divorce decree or separation agreement that went into effect after 1984 and before 2009*, or *Post-2008 divorce decree or separation agreement*, later.)
   b. A pre-1985 decree of divorce or separate maintenance or written separation agreement that applies to 2018 states that the noncustodial parent can claim the child as a dependent, the decree or agreement wasn't changed after 1984 to say the noncustodial parent can't claim the child as a dependent, and the noncustodial parent provides at least $600 for the child's support during the year. See *Child support under pre-1985 agreement*, later.

Custodial parent and noncustodial parent. The custodial parent is the parent with whom the child lived for the greater number of nights during the year. The other parent is the noncustodial parent.

If the parents divorced or separated during the year and the child lived with both parents before the separation, the custodial parent is the one with whom the child lived for the greater number of nights during the rest of the year.

A child is treated as living with a parent for a night if the child sleeps:

- At that parent's home, whether or not the parent is present, or
- In the company of the parent, when the child doesn't sleep at a parent's home (for example, the parent and child are on vacation together).

Equal number of nights. If the child lived with each parent for an equal number of nights during the year, the custodial parent is the parent with the higher adjusted gross income.

December 31. The night of December 31 is treated as part of the year in which it begins. For example, the night of December 31, 2018, is treated as part of 2018.

Emancipated child. If a child is emancipated under state law, the child is treated as not living with either parent. See *Examples 5* and *6*.

Absences. If a child wasn't with either parent on a particular night (because, for example, the child was staying at a friend's house), the child is treated as living with the parent with whom the child normally would have lived for that night, except for the absence. But if it can't be determined with which parent the child normally would have lived or if the child wouldn't have lived with either parent that night, the child is treated as not living with either parent that night.

Parent works at night. If, due to a parent's nighttime work schedule, a child lives for a greater number of days but not nights with the parent who works at night, that parent is treated as the custodial parent. On a school day, the child is treated as living at the primary residence registered with the school.

Example 1—child lived with one parent greater number of nights. You and your child's other parent are divorced. In 2018, your child lived with you 210 nights and with the other parent 155 nights. You are the custodial parent.

Example 2—child is away at camp. In 2018, your daughter lives with each parent for alternate weeks. In the summer, she spends 6 weeks at summer camp. During the time she is at camp, she is treated as living with you for 3 weeks and with her other parent, your ex-spouse, for 3 weeks because this is how long she would have lived with each parent if she hadn't attended summer camp.

Example 3—child lived same number of days with each parent. Your son lived with you 180 nights during the year and lived the same number of nights with his other parent, your ex-spouse. Your adjusted gross income is $40,000. Your ex-spouse's adjusted gross income is $25,000. You are treated as your son's custodial parent because you have the higher adjusted gross income.

Example 4—child is at parent's home but with other parent. Your son normally lives with you during the week and with his other parent, your ex-spouse, every other weekend. You become ill and are hospitalized. The other parent lives in your home with your son for 10 consecutive days while you are in the hospital. Your son is treated as living with you during this 10-day period because he was living in your home.

Example 5—child emancipated in May. When your son turned age 18 in May 2018, he became emancipated under the law of the state where he lives. As a result, he isn't considered in the custody of his parents for more than half of the year. The special rule for children of divorced or separated parents (or parents who live apart) doesn't apply.

Example 6—child emancipated in August. Your daughter lives with you from January 1, 2018, until May 31, 2018, and lives with her other parent, your ex-spouse, from June 1, 2018, through the end of the year. She turns 18 and is emancipated under state law on August 1, 2018. Because she is treated as not living with either parent beginning on August 1, she is treated as living with you the greater number of nights in 2018. You are the custodial parent.

Written declaration. The custodial parent must use either Form 8332 or a similar statement (containing the same information required by the form) to make a written declaration to release a claim to an exemption for a child to the noncustodial parent. Although the exemption amount is zero for tax year 2018, this release allows the noncustodial parent to claim the child tax credit, additional child tax credit, and credit for other dependents, if applicable, for the child. The noncustodial parent must attach a copy of the form or statement to his or her tax return each year the custodial parent releases his or her claims.

The release can be for 1 year, for a number of specified years (for example, alternate years), or for all future years, as specified in the declaration.

 Form 8332 doesn't apply to other tax benefits, such as the earned income credit, dependent care credit, or head of household filing status. See Pub. 501.

Divorce decree or separation agreement that went into effect after 1984 and before 2009. If the divorce decree or separation agreement went into effect after 1984 and before 2009, the noncustodial parent may be able to attach certain pages from the decree or agreement instead of Form 8332. The decree or agreement must state all three of the following.

1. The noncustodial parent can claim the child as a dependent without regard to any condition, such as payment of support.
2. The custodial parent won't claim the child as a dependent for the year.
3. The years for which the noncustodial parent, rather than the custodial parent, can claim the child as a dependent.

The noncustodial parent must attach all of the following pages of the decree or agreement to his or her return.

- The cover page (write the other parent's SSN on this page).
- The pages that include all of the information identified in items (1) through (3) above.
- The signature page with the other parent's signature and the date of the agreement.

Post-2008 divorce decree or separation agreement. If the decree or agreement went into effect after 2008, a noncustodial parent claiming a child as a dependent can't attach pages from a divorce decree or separation agreement instead of Form 8332. The custodial parent must sign either a Form 8332 or a similar statement. The only purpose of this statement must be to release the custodial parent's claim to an exemption. The noncustodial parent must attach a copy to his or her return. The form or statement must release the custodial parent's entitlement to claim the child without any conditions. For example, the release must not depend on the noncustodial parent paying support.

 The noncustodial parent must attach the required information even if it was filed with a return in an earlier year.

Revocation of release of claim to an exemption. The custodial parent can revoke a release of claim to an exemption that he or she previously released to the noncustodial parent. For the revocation to be effective for 2018, the custodial parent must have given (or made reasonable efforts to give) written notice of the revocation to the noncustodial parent in 2017 or earlier. The custodial parent can use Part III of Form 8332 for this purpose and must attach a copy of the revocation to his or her return for each tax year he or she claims the child as a dependent as a result of the revocation.

Remarried parent. If you remarry, the support provided by your new spouse is treated as provided by you.

Child support under pre-1985 agreement. All child support payments actually received from the noncustodial parent under a pre-1985 agreement are considered used for the support of the child.

Example. Under a pre-1985 agreement, the noncustodial parent provides $1,200 for the child's support. This amount is considered support provided by the noncustodial parent even if the $1,200 was actually spent on things other than support.

Parents who never married. This rule for divorced or separated parents also applies to parents who never married and lived apart at all times during the last 6 months of the year.

Alimony. Payments to your spouse that are includible in his or her gross income as either alimony, separate maintenance payments, or similar payments from an estate or trust, aren't treated as a payment for the support of a dependent.

Qualifying Child of More Than One Person

 If your qualifying child isn't a qualifying child of anyone else, this topic doesn't apply to you and you don't need to read about it. This is also true if your qualifying child isn't a qualifying child of anyone else except your spouse with whom you plan to file a joint return.

 If a child is treated as the qualifying child of the noncustodial parent under the rules for Children of divorced or separated parents (or parents who live apart), earlier, see Applying the tiebreaker rules to divorced or separated parents (or parents who live apart), later.

Sometimes, a child meets the relationship, age, residency, support, and joint return tests to be a qualifying child of more than one person. (For a description of these tests, see list items 1 through 5 under *Tests To Be a Qualifying Child* in Table 3). Although the child meets the conditions to be a qualifying child of each of these persons, only one person can actually claim the child as a qualifying child to take the following tax benefits (provided the person is eligible).

1. The child tax credit, the credit for other dependents, and the additional child tax credit.
2. Head of household filing status.
3. The credit for child and dependent care expenses.
4. The exclusion from income for dependent care benefits.
5. The earned income credit.

In other words, you and the other person can't agree to divide these tax benefits between you.

Tiebreaker rules. To determine which person can treat the child as a qualifying child to claim these tax benefits, the following tiebreaker rules apply.

- If only one of the persons is the child's parent, the child is treated as the qualifying child of the parent.
- If the parents file a joint return together and can claim the child as a qualifying child, the child is treated as the qualifying child of the parents.
- If the parents don't file a joint return together but both parents claim the child as a qualifying child, the IRS will treat the child as the qualifying child of the parent with whom the child lived for the longer period of time during the year. If the child lived with each parent for the same amount of time, the IRS will treat the child as the qualifying child of the parent who had the higher adjusted gross income (AGI) for the year.
- If no parent can claim the child as a qualifying child, the child is treated as the qualifying child of the person who had the highest AGI for the year.
- If a parent can claim the child as a qualifying child but no parent claims the child, the child is treated as the qualifying child of the person who had the highest AGI for the year, but only if that person's AGI is higher than the highest AGI of any of the child's parents who can claim the child. If the child's parents file a joint return with each other, this rule can be applied by dividing the parents' total AGI evenly between them. See Pub. 501 for details.

Subject to these tiebreaker rules, you and the other person may be able to choose which of you claims the child as a qualifying child.

You may be able to qualify for the earned income credit under the rules for taxpayers without a qualifying child if you have a qualifying child for the earned income credit who is claimed as a qualifying child by another taxpayer. For more information, see Pub. 596.

Example 1—separated parents. You, your husband, and your 10-year-old son lived together until August 1, 2018, when your husband moved out of the household. In August and September, your son lived with you. For the rest of the year, your son lived with your husband, the boy's father. Your son is a qualifying child of both you and your husband because your son lived with each of you for more than half the year and because he met the relationship, age, support, and joint return tests for both of you. At the end of the year, you and your husband still weren't divorced, legally separated, or separated under a written separation agreement, so the rule for children of divorced or separated parents (or parents who live apart) doesn't apply.

You and your husband will file separate returns. Your husband agrees to let you treat your son as a qualifying child. This means, if your husband doesn't claim your son as a qualifying child, you can claim your son as a dependent and treat him as a qualifying child for the child tax credit and exclusion for dependent care benefits, if you qualify for each of those tax benefits. However, you can't claim head of household filing status because you and your husband didn't live apart the last 6 months of the year. And, as a result of your filing status being married filing separately, you can't claim the earned income credit or the credit for child and dependent care expenses.

Example 2—separated parents claim same child. The facts are the same as in *Example 1* except that you and your husband both claim your son as a qualifying child. In this case, only your husband will be allowed to treat your son as a qualifying child. This is because, during 2018, the boy lived with him longer than with you. If you claimed the child tax credit for your son, the IRS will disallow your claim to the child tax credit. If you don't have another qualifying child or dependent, the IRS also will disallow your claim to the exclusion for dependent care benefits. In addition, because you and your husband didn't live apart the last 6 months of the year, your husband can't claim head of household filing status. And, as a result of his filing status being married filing separately, he can't claim the earned income credit or the credit for child and dependent care expenses.

Applying the tiebreaker rules to divorced or separated parents (or parents who live apart). If a child is treated as the qualifying child of the noncustodial parent under the rules for children of divorced or separated parents (or parents who live apart) described earlier, only the noncustodial parent can claim the child tax credit or the credit for other dependents for the child. However, the custodial parent, if eligible, or other eligible person can claim the child as a qualifying child for head of household filing status, the credit for child and dependent care expenses, the exclusion for dependent care benefits, and the earned income credit. If the child is the qualifying child of more than one person for those tax benefits, the tiebreaker rules determine which person can treat the child as a qualifying child.

Example 1. You and your 5-year-old son lived all year with your mother, who paid the entire cost of keeping up the home. Your AGI is $10,000. Your mother's AGI is $25,000. Your son's father doesn't live with you or your son.

Under the rules for children of divorced or separated parents (or parents who live apart), your son is treated as the qualifying child of his father, who can claim the child tax credit for the child if he meets all the requirements to do so. Because of this, you can't claim the child tax credit for your son. However, your son's father can't claim your son as a qualifying child for head of household filing status, the credit for child and dependent care expenses, the exclusion for dependent care benefits, or the earned income credit.

You and your mother didn't have any child care expenses or dependent care benefits, but the boy is a qualifying child of both you and your mother for head of household filing status and the earned income credit because he meets the relationship, age, residency, support, and joint return tests for both you and your mother. (Note: The support test doesn't apply for the earned income credit.) However, you agree to let your mother claim your son. This means she can claim him for head of household filing status and the earned income credit if she qualifies for each and if you don't claim him as a qualifying child for the earned income credit. (You can't claim head of household filing status because your mother paid the entire cost of keeping up the home.)

Example 2. The facts are the same as in *Example 1* except that your AGI is $25,000 and your mother's AGI is $21,000. Your mother can't claim your son as a qualifying child for any purpose because her AGI isn't higher than yours.

Example 3. The facts are the same as in *Example 1* except that you and your mother both claim your son as a qualifying child for the earned income credit. Your mother also claims him as a qualifying child for head of household filing status. You, as the child's parent, will be the only one allowed to claim your son as a qualifying child for the earned income credit. The IRS will disallow your mother's claim to the earned income credit and head of household filing status unless she has another qualifying child.

Alimony

Alimony is a payment to or for a spouse or former spouse under a divorce or separation instrument. It doesn't include voluntary payments that aren't made under a divorce or separation instrument.

Alimony is deductible by the payer, and the recipient must include it in income. Although this discussion generally is written for the payer of the alimony, the recipient also can use the information to determine whether an amount received is alimony.

Note. Amounts paid as alimony or separate maintenance payments under a divorce or separation agreement executed after 2018 won't be deductible by the payer. Such amounts also won't be includible in the income of the recipient.

To be alimony, a payment must meet certain requirements. There are some differences between the requirements that apply to payments under instruments executed after 1984 and to payments under instruments executed before 1985. The general requirements that apply to payments regardless of when the divorce or separation instrument was executed and the specific requirements that apply to post-1984 instruments (and, in certain cases, some pre-1985 instruments) are discussed in this publication. See *Instruments Executed Before 1985*, later, if you are looking for information on where to find the specific requirements that apply to pre-1985 instruments.

Spouse or former spouse. Unless otherwise stated, the term "spouse" includes former spouse.

Divorce or separation instrument. The term "divorce or separation instrument" means:

- A decree of divorce or separate maintenance or a written instrument incident to that decree,
- A written separation agreement, or
- A decree or any type of court order requiring a spouse to make payments for the support or maintenance of the other spouse. This includes a temporary decree, an interlocutory (not final) decree, and a decree of alimony pendente lite (while awaiting action on the final decree or agreement).

Invalid decree. Payments under a divorce decree can be alimony even if the decree's validity is in question. A divorce decree is valid for tax purposes until a court having proper jurisdiction holds it invalid.

Amended instrument. An amendment to a divorce decree may change the nature of your payments. Amendments aren't ordinarily retroactive for federal tax purposes. However, a retroactive amendment to a divorce decree correcting a clerical error to reflect the original intent of the court generally will be effective retroactively for federal tax purposes.

Example 1. A court order retroactively corrected a mathematical error under your divorce decree to express the original intent to spread the payments over more than 10 years. This change also is effective retroactively for federal tax purposes.

Example 2. Your original divorce decree didn't fix any part of the payment as child support. To reflect the true intention of the court, a court order retroactively corrected the error by designating a part of the payment as child support. The amended order is effective retroactively for federal tax purposes.

Amendments on treatment of alimony received. Alimony and separate maintenance payments you receive aren't included in your income if you entered into a divorce or separation agreement before 2019 and the agreement is changed after December 31, 2018, to expressly provide that alimony received isn't included in your income.

Deducting alimony paid. Generally you can deduct alimony you paid, whether or not you itemized deductions on your return. However, you can't deduct alimony paid under an agreement that is executed after 2018.

You must use Form 1040 to deduct alimony you paid. You can't use Form 1040NR. Enter the amount of alimony

IRS DIVORCED OR SEPARATED INDIVIDUALS   PUBLICATION 504

you paid on Schedule 1 (Form 1040), line 31a. In the space provided on line 31b, enter your recipient's SSN or ITIN.

If you paid alimony to more than one person, enter the SSN or ITIN of one of the recipients. Show the SSN or ITIN and amount paid to each other recipient on an attached statement. Enter your total payments on line 31a.

If you don't provide your spouse's SSN or ITIN, you may have to pay a $50 penalty and your deduction may be disallowed.

Reporting alimony received. Report alimony you received as income on Schedule 1 (Form 1040), line 11, or on Schedule NEC (Form 1040NR), line 12. You can't use Form 1040NR-EZ.

Note. Don't include in income alimony you receive under an agreement executed after 2018, or an agreement executed before 2019 if the agreement is changed after 2018 to expressly provide that alimony received isn't included in your income.

You must give the person who paid the alimony your SSN or ITIN. If you don't, you may have to pay a $50 penalty.

Withholding on nonresident aliens. If you are a U.S. citizen or resident alien and you pay alimony to a nonresident alien spouse, you may have to withhold income tax at a rate of 30% on each payment. However, many tax treaties provide for an exemption from withholding for alimony payments. For more information, see Pub. 515, Withholding of Tax on Nonresident Aliens and Foreign Entities.

General Rules

The following rules apply to alimony regardless of when the divorce or separation instrument was executed.

Payments not alimony. Not all payments under a divorce or separation instrument are alimony. Alimony doesn't include:

- Child support,
- Noncash property settlements,
- Payments that are your spouse's part of community income, as explained later under *Community Property*,
- Payments to keep up the payer's property, or
- Use of the payer's property.

Example. Under your written separation agreement, your spouse lives rent-free in a home you own and you must pay the mortgage, real estate taxes, insurance, repairs, and utilities for the home. Because you own the home and the debts are yours, your payments for the mortgage, real estate taxes, insurance, and repairs aren't alimony. Neither is the value of your spouse's use of the home.

If they qualify, you may be able to deduct the payments for utilities as alimony. Your spouse must report them as income. If you itemize deductions, you can deduct the real estate taxes and, if the home is a qualified home, you also can include the interest on the mortgage in figuring your deductible interest. However, if your spouse owned the home, see *Example 2* under *Payments to a third party* later. If you owned the home jointly with your spouse, see Table 4. For more information, see Pub. 936, Home Mortgage Interest Deduction.

Child support. To determine whether a payment is child support, see the discussion under *Certain Rules for Instruments Executed After 1984*, later. If your divorce or separation agreement was executed before 1985, see the 2004 revision of Pub. 504 available at *IRS.gov/FormsPubs*.

Underpayment. If both alimony and child support payments are called for by your divorce or separation instrument, and you pay less than the total required, the payments apply first to child support and then to alimony.

Example. Your divorce decree calls for you to pay your former spouse $200 a month ($2,400 ($200 x 12) a year) as child support and $150 a month ($1,800 ($150 x 12) a year) as alimony. If you pay the full amount of $4,200 ($2,400 + $1,800) during the year, you can deduct $1,800 as alimony and your former spouse must report $1,800 as alimony received. If you pay only $3,600 during the year, $2,400 is child support. You can deduct only $1,200 ($3,600 − $2,400) as alimony and your former spouse must report $1,200 as alimony received.

Payments to a third party. Cash payments, checks, or money orders to a third party on behalf of your spouse under the terms of your divorce or separation instrument can be alimony, if they otherwise qualify. These include payments for your spouse's medical expenses, housing costs (rent, utilities, etc.), taxes, tuition, etc. The payments are treated as received by your spouse and then paid to the third party.

Example 1. Under your divorce decree, you must pay your former spouse's medical and dental expenses. If the payments otherwise qualify, you can deduct them as alimony on your return. Your former spouse must report them as alimony received and can include them in figuring deductible medical expenses.

Example 2. Under your separation agreement, you must pay the real estate taxes, mortgage payments, and insurance premiums on a home owned by your spouse. If they otherwise qualify, you can deduct the payments as alimony on your return, and your spouse must report them as alimony received. Your spouse may be able to deduct the real estate taxes and home mortgage interest, subject to the limitations on those deductions. See the Instructions for Schedule A (Form 1040). However, if you owned the home, see the example under *Payments not alimony*, earlier. If you owned the home jointly with your spouse, see Table 4.

Table 4. Expenses for a Jointly-Owned Home

Use the table below to find how much of your payment is alimony and how much you can claim as an itemized deduction.

IF you must pay all of the ...	AND your home is ...	THEN you can deduct and your spouse (or former spouse) must include as alimony ...	AND you can claim as an itemized deduction ...
mortgage payments (principal and interest)	jointly owned	half of the total payments	half of the interest as interest expense (if the home is a qualified home).[1]
real estate taxes and home insurance	held as tenants in common	half of the total payments	half of the real estate taxes[2] and none of the home insurance.
	held as tenants by the entirety or in joint tenancy	none of the payments	all of the real estate taxes and none of the home insurance.

[1] Your spouse (or former spouse) can deduct the other half of the interest if the home is a qualified home.
[2] Your spouse (or former spouse) can deduct the other half of the real estate taxes.

Life insurance premiums. Alimony includes premiums you must pay under your divorce or separation instrument for insurance on your life to the extent your spouse owns the policy.

Payments for jointly-owned home. If your divorce or separation instrument states that you must pay expenses for a home owned by you and your spouse or former spouse, some of your payments may be alimony. See Table 4.

However, if your spouse owned the home, see Example 2 under Payments to a third party, earlier. If you owned the home, see the example under Payments not alimony, earlier.

Certain Rules for Instruments Executed After 1984

The following rules for alimony apply to payments under divorce or separation instruments executed after 1984.

Exception for instruments executed before 1985. There are two situations where the rules for instruments executed after 1984 apply to instruments executed before 1985.

1. A divorce or separation instrument executed before 1985 and then modified after 1984 to specify that the after-1984 rules will apply.
2. A temporary divorce or separation instrument executed before 1985 and incorporated into, or adopted by, a final decree executed after 1984 that:
   a. Changes the amount or period of payment, or
   b. Adds or deletes any contingency or condition.

For the rules for alimony payments under pre-1985 instruments not meeting these exceptions, see the 2004 revision of Pub. 504 available at IRS.gov/FormsPubs.

Example 1. In November 1984, you and your former spouse executed a written separation agreement. In February 1985, a decree of divorce was substituted for the written separation agreement. The decree of divorce didn't change the terms for the alimony you pay your former spouse. The decree of divorce is treated as executed before 1985. Alimony payments under this decree aren't subject to the rules for payments under instruments executed after 1984.

Example 2. The facts are the same as in Example 1 except that the decree of divorce changed the amount of the alimony. In this example, the decree of divorce isn't treated as executed before 1985. The alimony payments are subject to the rules for payments under instruments executed after 1984.

Alimony Requirements

A payment to or for a spouse under a divorce or separation instrument is alimony if the spouses don't file a joint return with each other and all the following requirements are met.

- The payment is in cash.
- The instrument doesn't designate the payment as not alimony.
- The spouses aren't members of the same household at the time the payments are made. This requirement applies only if the spouses are legally separated under a decree of divorce or separate maintenance.
- There is no liability to make any payment (in cash or property) after the death of the recipient spouse.

- The payment isn't treated as child support.

Each of these requirements is discussed next.

Cash payment requirement. Only cash payments, including checks and money orders, qualify as alimony. The following don't qualify as alimony.

- Transfers of services or property (including a debt instrument of a third party or an annuity contract).
- Execution of a debt instrument by the payer.
- The use of the payer's property.

Payments to a third party. Cash payments to a third party under the terms of your divorce or separation instrument can qualify as cash payments to your spouse. See *Payments to a third party* under *General Rules*, earlier.

Also, cash payments made to a third party at the written request of your spouse may qualify as alimony if all the following requirements are met.

- The payments are in lieu of payments of alimony directly to your spouse.
- The written request states that both spouses intend the payments to be treated as alimony.
- You receive the written request from your spouse before you file your return for the year you made the payments.

Payments designated as not alimony. You and your spouse can designate that otherwise qualifying payments aren't alimony. You do this by including a provision in your divorce or separation instrument that states the payments aren't deductible as alimony by you and are excludable from your spouse's income. For this purpose, any instrument (written statement) signed by both of you that makes this designation and that refers to a previous written separation agreement is treated as a written separation agreement (and therefore a divorce or separation instrument). If you are subject to temporary support orders, the designation must be made in the original or a later temporary support order.

Your spouse can exclude the payments from income only if he or she attaches a copy of the instrument designating them as not alimony to his or her return. The copy must be attached each year the designation applies.

Spouses can't be members of the same household. Payments to your spouse while you are members of the same household aren't alimony if you are legally separated under a decree of divorce or separate maintenance. A home you formerly shared is considered one household, even if you physically separate yourselves in the home.

You aren't treated as members of the same household if one of you is preparing to leave the household and does leave no later than 1 month after the date of the payment.

Exception. If you aren't legally separated under a decree of divorce or separate maintenance, a payment under a written separation agreement, support decree, or other court order may qualify as alimony even if you are members of the same household when the payment is made.

Liability for payments after death of recipient spouse. If any part of payments you make must continue to be made for any period after your spouse's death, that part of your payments isn't alimony whether made before or after the death. If all of the payments would continue, then none of the payments made before or after the death are alimony.

The divorce or separation instrument doesn't have to expressly state that the payments cease upon the death of your spouse if, for example, the liability for continued payments would end under state law.

Example. You must pay your former spouse $10,000 in cash each year for 10 years. Your divorce decree states that the payments will end upon your former spouse's death. You also must pay your former spouse or your former spouse's estate $20,000 in cash each year for 10 years. The death of your spouse wouldn't end these payments under state law.

The $10,000 annual payments may qualify as alimony. The $20,000 annual payments that don't end upon your former spouse's death aren't alimony.

Substitute payments. If you must make any payments in cash or property after your spouse's death as a substitute for continuing otherwise qualifying payments before the death, the otherwise qualifying payments aren't alimony. To the extent that your payments begin, accelerate, or increase because of the death of your spouse, otherwise qualifying payments you made may be treated as payments that weren't alimony. Whether or not such payments will be treated as not alimony depends on all the facts and circumstances.

Example 1. Under your divorce decree, you must pay your former spouse $30,000 annually. The payments will stop at the end of 6 years or upon your former spouse's death, if earlier.

Your former spouse has custody of your minor children. The decree provides that if any child is still a minor at your spouse's death, you must pay $10,000 annually to a trust until the youngest child reaches the age of majority. The trust income and corpus (principal) are to be used for your children's benefit.

These facts indicate that the payments to be made after your former spouse's death are a substitute for $10,000 of the $30,000 annual payments. Of each of the $30,000 annual payments, $10,000 isn't alimony.

Example 2. Under your divorce decree, you must pay your former spouse $30,000 annually. The payments will stop at the end of 15 years or upon your former spouse's death, if earlier. The decree provides that if your former spouse dies before the end of the 15-year period, you must pay the estate the difference between $450,000 ($30,000 × 15) and the total amount paid up to that time. For example, if your spouse dies at the end of the tenth year, you must pay the estate $150,000 ($450,000 − $300,000).

These facts indicate that the lump-sum payment to be made after your former spouse's death is a substitute for the full amount of the $30,000 annual payments. None of the annual payments are alimony. The result would be the same if the payment required at death were to be discounted by an appropriate interest factor to account for the prepayment.

Child support. A payment that is specifically designated as child support or treated as specifically designated as child support under your divorce or separation instrument isn't alimony. The amount of child support may vary over time. Child support payments aren't deductible by the payer and aren't taxable to the payee.

Specifically designated as child support. A payment will be treated as specifically designated as child support to the extent that the payment is reduced either:

- On the happening of a contingency relating to your child, or
- At a time that can be clearly associated with the contingency.

A payment may be treated as specifically designated as child support even if other separate payments are specifically designated as child support.

Contingency relating to your child. A contingency relates to your child if it depends on any event relating to that child. It doesn't matter whether the event is certain or likely to occur. Events relating to your child include the child's:

- Becoming employed,
- Dying,
- Leaving the household,
- Leaving school,
- Marrying, or
- Reaching a specified age or income level.

Clearly associated with a contingency. Payments that would otherwise qualify as alimony are presumed to be reduced at a time clearly associated with the happening of a contingency relating to your child only in the following situations.

1. The payments are to be reduced not more than 6 months before or after the date the child will reach 18, 21, or local age of majority.
2. The payments are to be reduced on two or more occasions that occur not more than 1 year before or after a different one of your children reaches a certain age from 18 to 24. This certain age must be the same for each child, but need not be a whole number of years.

In all other situations, reductions in payments aren't treated as clearly associated with the happening of a contingency relating to your child.

Either you or the IRS can overcome the presumption in the two situations above. This is done by showing that the time at which the payments are to be reduced was determined independently of any contingencies relating to your children. For example, if you can show that the period of alimony payments is customary in the local jurisdiction, such as a period equal to one-half of the duration of the marriage, you can overcome the presumption and may be able to treat the amount as alimony.

Recapture of Alimony

If your alimony payments decrease or end during the first 3 calendar years, you may be subject to the recapture rule. If you are subject to this rule, you have to include in income (in the third year) part of the alimony payments you previously deducted. Your spouse can deduct (in the third year) part of the alimony payments he or she previously included in income.

The 3-year period starts with the first calendar year you make a payment qualifying as alimony under a decree of divorce or separate maintenance or a written separation agreement. Don't include any time in which payments were being made under temporary support orders. The second and third years are the next 2 calendar years, whether or not payments are made during those years.

The reasons for a reduction or end of alimony payments that can require a recapture include:

- A change in your divorce or separation instrument,
- A failure to make timely payments,
- A reduction in your ability to provide support, or
- A reduction in your spouse's support needs.

When to apply the recapture rule. You are subject to the recapture rule in the third year if the alimony you pay in the third year decreases by more than $15,000 from the second year or the alimony you pay in the second and third years decreases significantly from the alimony you pay in the first year.

When you figure a decrease in alimony, don't include the following amounts.

- Payments made under a temporary support order.
- Payments required over a period of at least 3 calendar years that vary because they are a fixed part of your income from a business or property, or from compensation for employment or self-employment.
- Payments that decrease because of the death of either spouse or the remarriage of the spouse receiving the payments before the end of the third year.

How to figure and report the recapture. Both you and your spouse can use Worksheet 1 to figure recaptured alimony.

Including the recapture in income. If you must include a recapture amount in income, show it on Schedule 1 (Form 1040), line 11 ("Alimony received"). Cross out "received" and enter "recapture." On the dotted line next to the amount, enter your spouse's last name and SSN or ITIN.

Deducting the recapture. If you can deduct a recapture amount, show it on Schedule 1 (Form 1040), line 31a

Worksheet 1. Recapture of Alimony   *Keep for Your Records*

Note. *Don't enter less than -0- on any line.*

1. Alimony paid in **2nd year** .... 1. _____
2. Alimony paid in **3rd year** .... 2. _____
3. Floor 3. $15,000
4. Add lines 2 and 3 .... 4. _____
5. Subtract line 4 from line 1. If zero or less, enter -0- .... 5. _____
6. Alimony paid in **1st year** .... 6. _____
7. Adjusted alimony paid in **2nd year** (line 1 minus line 5) .... 7. _____
8. Alimony paid in **3rd year** .... 8. _____
9. Add lines 7 and 8 .... 9. _____
10. Divide line 9 by 2 .... 10. _____
11. Floor 11. $15,000
12. Add lines 10 and 11 .... 12. _____
13. Subtract line 12 from line 6 .... 13. _____
14. **Recaptured alimony.** Add lines 5 and 13 .... *14. _____

* If you deducted alimony paid, report this amount as income on Schedule 1 (Form 1040), line 11.
If you reported alimony received, deduct this amount on Schedule 1 (Form 1040), line 31a.

("Alimony paid"). Cross out "paid" and enter "recapture." In the space provided, enter your spouse's SSN or ITIN.

Example. You pay your former spouse $50,000 alimony the first year, $39,000 the second year, and $28,000 the third year. In the third year, you report $1,500 as income on Schedule 1 (Form 1040), line 11, and your former spouse reports $1,500 as a deduction on Schedule 1 (Form 1040), line 31a. (See the worksheet that was completed for this example.)

Instruments Executed Before 1985

Information on pre-1985 instruments was included in this publication through 2004. If you need the 2004 revision, please visit *IRS.gov/FormsPubs*.

Qualified Domestic Relations Order

A qualified domestic relations order (QDRO) is a judgment, decree, or court order (including an approved property settlement agreement) issued under a state's domestic relations law that:

- Recognizes someone other than a participant as having a right to receive benefits from a qualified retirement plan (such as most pension and profit-sharing plans) or a tax-sheltered annuity;

- Relates to payment of child support, alimony, or marital property rights to a spouse, former spouse, child, or other dependent of the participant; and

- Specifies certain information, including the amount or part of the participant's benefits to be paid to the participant's spouse, former spouse, child, or other dependent.

Benefits paid to a child or other dependent. Benefits paid under a QDRO to the plan participant's child or other dependent are treated as paid to the participant. For information about the tax treatment of benefits from retirement plans, see Pub. 575, Pension and Annuity Income.

Benefits paid to a spouse or former spouse. Benefits paid under a QDRO to the plan participant's spouse or former spouse generally must be included in the spouse's or former spouse's income. If the participant contributed to the retirement plan, a prorated share of the participant's cost (investment in the contract) is used to figure the taxable amount.

The spouse or former spouse can use the special rules for lump-sum distributions if the benefits would have been treated as a lump-sum distribution had the participant received them. For this purpose, consider only the balance to the spouse's or former spouse's credit in determining whether the distribution is a total distribution. See *Lump-Sum Distributions* in Pub. 575 for information about the special rules.

Worksheet 1. **Recapture of Alimony—Illustrated**

Note. *Don't enter less than -0- on any line.*						
1. Alimony paid in **2nd year**			1.	$39,000		
2. Alimony paid in **3rd year**	2.	28,000				
3. Floor	3.	$15,000				
4. Add lines 2 and 3			4.	43,000		
5. Subtract line 4 from line 1. If zero or less, enter -0-					5.	-0-
6. Alimony paid in **1st year**			6.	50,000		
7. Adjusted alimony paid in **2nd year** (line 1 minus line 5)	7.	39,000				
8. Alimony paid in **3rd year**	8.	28,000				
9. Add lines 7 and 8	9.	67,000				
10. Divide line 9 by 2	10.	33,500				
11. Floor	11.	$15,000				
12. Add lines 10 and 11			12.	48,500		
13. Subtract line 12 from line 6					13.	1,500
14. **Recaptured alimony.** Add lines 5 and 13					*14.	1,500

* If you deducted alimony paid, report this amount as income on Schedule 1 (Form 1040), line 11.
If you reported alimony received, deduct this amount on Schedule 1 (Form 1040), line 31a.

Rollovers. If you receive an eligible rollover distribution under a QDRO as the plan participant's spouse or former spouse, you may be able to roll it over tax free into a traditional individual retirement arrangement (IRA) or another qualified retirement plan.

For more information on the tax treatment of eligible rollover distributions, see Pub. 575.

Individual Retirement Arrangements

The following discussions explain some of the effects of divorce or separation on traditional individual retirement arrangements (IRAs). Traditional IRAs are IRAs other than Roth or SIMPLE IRAs.

Spousal IRA. If you get a final decree of divorce or separate maintenance by the end of your tax year, you can't deduct contributions you make to your former spouse's traditional IRA. You can deduct only contributions to your own traditional IRA.

IRA transferred as a result of divorce. The transfer of all or part of your interest in a traditional IRA to your spouse or former spouse, under a decree of divorce or separate maintenance or a written instrument incident to the decree, isn't considered a taxable transfer. Starting from the date of the transfer, the traditional IRA interest transferred is treated as your spouse's or former spouse's traditional IRA.

IRA contribution and deduction limits. All taxable alimony you receive under a decree of divorce or separate maintenance is treated as compensation for the contribution and deduction limits for traditional IRAs.

For more information about IRAs, including Roth IRAs, see Pub. 590-A and Pub. 590-B.

Property Settlements

Generally, there is no recognized gain or loss on the transfer of property between spouses, or between former spouses if the transfer is because of a divorce. You may, however, have to report the transaction on a gift tax return. See *Gift Tax on Property Settlements*, later. If you sell property that you own jointly to split the proceeds as part of your property settlement, see *Sale of Jointly-Owned Property*, later.

Transfer Between Spouses

Generally, no gain or loss is recognized on a transfer of property from you to (or in trust for the benefit of):

- Your spouse, or
- Your former spouse, but only if the transfer is incident to your divorce.

This rule applies even if the transfer was in exchange for cash, the release of marital rights, the assumption of liabilities, or other consideration.

Exceptions to nonrecognition rule. This rule doesn't apply in the following situations.

- Your spouse or former spouse is a nonresident alien.
- Certain transfers in trust, discussed later.
- Certain stock redemptions under a divorce or separation instrument or a valid written agreement that are taxable under applicable tax law, as discussed in Regulations section 1.1041-2.

Property subject to nonrecognition rule. The term "property" includes all property whether real or personal, tangible or intangible, or separate or community. It includes property acquired after the end of your marriage and transferred to your former spouse. It doesn't include services.

Health savings account (HSA). If you transfer your interest in an HSA to your spouse or former spouse under a divorce or separation instrument, it isn't considered a taxable transfer. After the transfer, the interest is treated as your spouse's HSA.

Archer medical savings account (MSA). If you transfer your interest in an Archer MSA to your spouse or former spouse under a divorce or separation instrument, it isn't considered a taxable transfer. After the transfer, the interest is treated as your spouse's Archer MSA.

Individual retirement arrangement (IRA). The treatment of the transfer of an interest in an IRA as a result of divorce is similar to that just described for the transfer of an interest in an HSA and an Archer MSA. See IRA transferred as a result of divorce, earlier, under Individual Retirement Arrangements.

Incident to divorce. A property transfer is incident to your divorce if the transfer:

- Occurs within 1 year after the date your marriage ends, or
- Is related to the end of your marriage.

A divorce, for this purpose, includes the end of your marriage by annulment or due to violations of state laws.

Related to end of marriage. A property transfer is related to the end of your marriage if both of the following conditions apply.

- The transfer is made under your original or modified divorce or separation instrument.
- The transfer occurs within 6 years after the date your marriage ends.

Unless these conditions are met, the transfer is presumed not to be related to the end of your marriage. However, this presumption won't apply if you can show that the transfer was made to carry out the division of property owned by you and your spouse at the time your marriage ended. For example, the presumption won't apply if you can show that the transfer was made more than 6 years after the end of your marriage because of business or legal factors which prevented earlier transfer of the property and the transfer was made promptly after those factors were taken care of.

Transfers to third parties. If you transfer property to a third party on behalf of your spouse (or former spouse, if incident to your divorce), the transfer is treated as two transfers.

- A transfer of the property from you to your spouse or former spouse.
- An immediate transfer of the property from your spouse or former spouse to the third party.

You don't recognize gain or loss on the first transfer. Instead, your spouse or former spouse may have to recognize gain or loss on the second transfer.

For this treatment to apply, the transfer from you to the third party must be one of the following.

- Required by your divorce or separation instrument.
- Requested in writing by your spouse or former spouse.
- Consented to in writing by your spouse or former spouse. The consent must state that both you and your spouse or former spouse intend the transfer to be treated as a transfer from you to your spouse or former spouse subject to the rules of Internal Revenue Code section 1041. You must receive the consent before filing your tax return for the year you transfer the property.

 This treatment doesn't apply to transfers to which Regulations section 1.1041-2 (certain stock redemptions) applies.

Transfers in trust. If you make a transfer of property in trust for the benefit of your spouse (or former spouse, if incident to your divorce), you generally don't recognize any gain or loss.

However, you must recognize gain or loss if, incident to your divorce, you transfer an installment obligation in trust for the benefit of your former spouse. For information on the disposition of an installment obligation, see Pub. 537, Installment Sales.

You also must recognize as gain on the transfer of property in trust the amount by which the liabilities assumed by the trust, plus the liabilities to which the property is subject, exceed the total of your adjusted basis in the transferred property.

Example. You own property with a fair market value of $12,000 and an adjusted basis of $1,000. You transfer the property in trust for the benefit of your spouse. The trust didn't assume any liabilities. The property is subject to a $5,000 liability. Your recognized gain is $4,000 ($5,000 − $1,000).

Reporting income from property. You should report income from property transferred to your spouse or former spouse as shown in Table 5.

For information on the treatment of interest on transferred U.S. savings bonds, see chapter 1 of Pub. 550, Investment Income and Expenses.

 When you transfer property to your spouse (or former spouse, if incident to your divorce), you must give your spouse sufficient records to determine the adjusted basis and holding period of the property on the date of the transfer. If you transfer investment credit property with recapture potential, you also must provide sufficient records to determine the amount and period of the recapture.

Tax treatment of property received. Property you receive from your spouse (or former spouse, if the transfer is incident to your divorce) is treated as acquired by gift for income tax purposes. Its value isn't taxable to you.

Basis of property received. Your basis in property received from your spouse (or former spouse, if incident to your divorce) is the same as your spouse's adjusted basis. This applies for determining either gain or loss when you later dispose of the property. It applies whether the property's adjusted basis is less than, equal to, or greater than either its value at the time of the transfer or any consideration you paid. It also applies even if the property's liabilities are more than its adjusted basis.

This rule generally applies to all property received after July 18, 1984, under a divorce or separation instrument in effect after that date. It also applies to all other property received after 1983 for which you and your spouse (or former spouse) made a "section 1041 election" to apply this rule. For information about how to make that election, see Temporary Regulations section 1.1041-1T(g).

Example. Karen and Don owned their home jointly. Karen transferred her interest in the home to Don as part of their property settlement when they divorced last year. Don's basis in the interest received from Karen is her adjusted basis in the home. His total basis in the home is their joint adjusted basis.

Property received before July 19, 1984. Your basis in property received in settlement of marital support rights before July 19, 1984, or under an instrument in effect before that date (other than property for which you and your spouse (or former spouse) made a "section 1041 election") is its fair market value when you received it.

Example. Larry and Gina owned their home jointly before their divorce in 1983. That year, Gina received Larry's interest in the home in settlement of her marital support rights. Gina's basis in the interest received from Larry is the part of the home's fair market value proportionate to that interest. Her total basis in the home is that part of the fair market value plus her adjusted basis in her own interest.

Property transferred in trust. If the transferor recognizes gain on property transferred in trust, as described earlier under Transfers in trust, the trust's basis in the property is increased by the recognized gain.

Example. Your spouse transfers property in trust, recognizing a $4,000 gain. Your spouse's adjusted basis in the property was $1,000. The trust's basis in the property is $5,000 ($1,000 + $4,000).

Gift Tax on Property Settlements

The federal gift tax doesn't apply to most transfers of property between spouses, or between former spouses because of divorce. The transfers usually qualify for one or more of the exceptions explained in this discussion. However, if your transfer of property doesn't qualify for an exception, or qualifies only in part, you must report it on a gift tax return. See Gift Tax Return, later.

For more information about the federal gift tax, see Estate and Gift Taxes in Pub. 559, Survivors, Executors, and Administrators, and Form 709 and its instructions.

Exceptions

Your transfer of property to your spouse or former spouse isn't subject to gift tax if it meets any of the following exceptions.

- It is made in settlement of marital support rights.
- It qualifies for the marital deduction.
- It is made under a divorce decree.
- It is made under a written agreement, and you are divorced within a specified period.
- It qualifies for the annual exclusion.

Settlement of marital support rights. A transfer in settlement of marital support rights isn't subject to gift tax to the extent the value of the property transferred isn't more than the value of those rights. This exception doesn't apply to a transfer in settlement of dower, curtesy, or other marital property rights.

Marital deduction. A transfer of property to your spouse before receiving a final decree of divorce or separate maintenance isn't subject to gift tax. However, this exception doesn't apply to:

- Transfers of certain terminable interests, or
- Transfers to your spouse if your spouse isn't a U.S. citizen.

Transfer under divorce decree. A transfer of property under the decree of a divorce court having the power to prescribe a property settlement isn't subject to gift tax. This exception also applies to a property settlement

Table 5. Property Transferred Pursuant to Divorce

The tax treatment of items of property transferred from you to your spouse or former spouse pursuant to your divorce is shown below.

IF you transfer ...	THEN you ...	AND your spouse or former spouse ...	FOR more information, see ...
income-producing property (such as an interest in a business, rental property, stocks, or bonds)	include on your tax return any profit or loss, rental income or loss, dividends, or interest generated or derived from the property during the year until the property is transferred	reports any income or loss generated or derived after the property is transferred.	Pub. 550, Investment Income and Expenses. (See *Ownership transferred* under *U. S. Savings Bonds* in chapter 1.)
interest in a passive activity with unused passive activity losses	can't deduct your accumulated unused passive activity losses allocable to the interest	increases the adjusted basis of the transferred interest by the amount of the unused losses.	Pub. 925, Passive Activity and At-Risk Rules.
investment credit property with recapture potential	don't have to recapture any part of the credit	may have to recapture part of the credit if he or she disposes of the property or changes its use before the end of the recapture period.	Form 4255, Recapture of Investment Credit.
interests in nonstatutory stock options and nonqualified deferred compensation	don't include any amount in gross income upon the transfer	includes an amount in gross income when he or she exercises the stock options or when the deferred compensation is paid or made available to him or her.	

agreed on before the divorce if it was made part of or approved by the decree.

Transfer under written agreement. A transfer of property under a written agreement in settlement of marital rights or to provide a reasonable child support allowance isn't subject to gift tax if you are divorced within the 3-year period beginning 1 year before and ending 2 years after the date of the agreement. This exception applies whether or not the agreement is part of or approved by the divorce decree.

Annual exclusion. The first $15,000 of gifts of present interests to each person during 2018 isn't subject to gift tax. The annual exclusion is $152,000 for transfers to a spouse who isn't a U.S. citizen provided the gift would otherwise qualify for the gift tax marital deduction if the donee were a U.S. citizen.

Present interest. A gift is considered a present interest if the donee has unrestricted rights to the immediate use, possession, and enjoyment of the property or income from the property.

Gift Tax Return

Report a transfer of property subject to gift tax on Form 709. Generally, Form 709 is due April 15 following the year of the transfer.

Transfer under written agreement. If a property transfer would be subject to gift tax except that it is made under a written agreement, and you don't receive a final decree of divorce by the due date for filing the gift tax return, you must report the transfer on Form 709 and attach a copy of your written agreement. The transfer will be treated as not subject to the gift tax until the final decree of divorce is granted, but no longer than 2 years after the effective date of the written agreement.

Within 60 days after you receive a final decree of divorce, send a certified copy of the decree to the IRS office where you filed Form 709.

Sale of Jointly-Owned Property

If you sell property that you and your spouse own jointly, you must report your share of the recognized gain or loss on your income tax return for the year of the sale. Your share of the gain or loss is determined by your state law governing ownership of property. For information on reporting gain or loss, see Pub. 544.

Sale of home. If you sold your main home, you may be able to exclude up to $250,000 (up to $500,000 if you and your spouse file a joint return) of gain on the sale. For more information, including special rules that apply to separated and divorced individuals selling a main home, see Pub. 523, Selling Your Home.

Costs of Getting a Divorce

You can't deduct legal fees and court costs for getting a divorce. In addition, you can't deduct legal fees paid for tax advice in connection with a divorce and legal fees to get alimony or fees you pay to appraisers, actuaries, and accountants for services in determining your correct tax or in helping to get alimony.

Other Nondeductible expenses. You can't deduct the costs of personal advice, counseling, or legal action in a divorce. These costs aren't deductible, even if they are paid, in part, to arrive at a financial settlement or to protect income-producing property.

You also can't deduct legal fees you pay for a property settlement. However, you can add it to the basis of the property you receive. For example, you can add the cost of preparing and filing a deed to put title to your house in your name alone to the basis of the house.

Finally, you can't deduct fees you pay for your spouse or former spouse, unless your payments qualify as alimony. (See *Payments to a third party* under *Alimony*, earlier.) If you have no legal responsibility arising from the divorce settlement or decree to pay your spouse's legal fees, your payments are gifts and may be subject to the gift tax.

Tax Withholding and Estimated Tax

When you become divorced or separated, you usually will have to file a new Form W-4 with your employer to claim your proper withholding allowances. If you receive alimony, you may have to make estimated tax payments.

 If you don't pay enough tax either through withholding or by making estimated tax payments, you will have an underpayment of estimated tax and you may have to pay a penalty. If you don't pay enough tax by the due date of each payment, you may have to pay a penalty even if you are due a refund when you file your tax return.

For more information, see Pub. 505, Tax Withholding and Estimated Tax.

Joint estimated tax payments. If you and your spouse made joint estimated tax payments for 2018 but file separate returns, either of you can claim all of your payments, or you can divide them in any way on which you both agree. If you can't agree, the estimated tax you can claim equals the total estimated tax paid times the tax shown on your separate return for 2018, divided by the total of the tax shown on your 2018 return and your spouse's 2018 return. You may want to attach an explanation of how you and your spouse divided the payments.

If you claim any of the payments on your tax return, enter your spouse's or former spouse's SSN in the space provided on Form 1040. If you were divorced and remarried in 2018, enter your present spouse's SSN in that space and enter your former spouse's SSN, followed by "DIV" to the left of Schedule 5 (Form 1040), line 66.

Community Property

If you are married and your domicile (permanent legal home) is in a community property state, special rules determine your income. Some of these rules are explained in the following discussions. For more information, see Pub. 555.

Community property states. Community property states include:

- Arizona,
- California,
- Idaho,
- Louisiana,
- Nevada,
- New Mexico,
- Texas,
- Washington, and
- Wisconsin.

Community Income

If your domicile is in a community property state during any part of your tax year, you may have community income. Your state law determines whether your income is separate or community income. If you and your spouse file separate returns, you must report half of any income described by state law as community income and all of your separate income, and your spouse must report the other half of any community income plus all of his or her separate income. Each of you can claim credit for half the income tax withheld from community income.

Community Property Laws Disregarded

The following discussions are situations where special rules apply to community property.

Certain community income not treated as community income by one spouse. Community property laws may not apply to an item of community income that you received but didn't treat as community income. You will be responsible for reporting all of it if:

- You treat the item as if only you are entitled to the income, and
- You don't notify your spouse of the nature and amount of the income by the due date for filing the return (including extensions).

Relief from liability for tax attributable to an item of community income. You aren't responsible for the tax on an item of community income if all five of the following conditions exist.

1. You didn't file a joint return for the tax year.
2. You didn't include an item of community income in gross income on your separate return.
3. The item of community income you didn't include is one of the following.
   a. Wages, salaries, and other compensation your spouse (or former spouse) received for services he or she performed as an employee.
   b. Income your spouse (or former spouse) derived from a trade or business he or she operated as a sole proprietor.
   c. Your spouse's (or former spouse's) distributive share of partnership income.
   d. Income from your spouse's (or former spouse's) separate property (other than income described in (a), (b), or (c)). Use the appropriate community property law to determine what is separate property.
   e. Any other income that belongs to your spouse (or former spouse) under community property law.
4. You establish that you didn't know of, and had no reason to know of, that community income.
5. Under all facts and circumstances, it wouldn't be fair to include the item of community income in your gross income.

Equitable relief from liability for tax attributable to an item of community income. To be considered for equitable relief from liability for tax attributable to an item of community income, you must meet all of the following conditions.

1. You timely filed your claim for relief.
2. You and your spouse (or former spouse) didn't transfer assets to one another as a part of a fraudulent scheme. A fraudulent scheme includes a scheme to defraud the IRS or another third party, such as a creditor, former spouse, or business partner.
3. Your spouse (or former spouse) didn't transfer property to you for the main purpose of avoiding tax or the payment of tax.
4. You didn't knowingly participate in the filing of a fraudulent joint return.

5. The income tax liability from which you seek relief is attributable (either in full or in part) to an item of your spouse (or former spouse) or an unpaid tax resulting from your spouse's (or former spouse's) income. If the liability is partially attributable to you, then relief can only be considered for the part of the liability attributable to your spouse (or former spouse). The IRS will consider granting relief regardless of whether the understated tax, deficiency, or unpaid tax is attributable (in full or in part) to you if any of the following exceptions apply.

   a. The item is attributable or partially attributable to you solely due to the operation of community property law. If you meet this exception, that item will be considered attributable to your spouse (or former spouse) for purposes of equitable relief.
   b. If the item is titled in your name, the item is presumed to be attributable to you. However, you can rebut this presumption based on the facts and circumstances.
   c. You didn't know, and had no reason to know, that funds intended for the payment of tax were misappropriated by your spouse (or former spouse) for his or her benefit. If you meet this exception, the IRS will consider granting equitable relief although the unpaid tax may be attributable in part or in full to your item, and only to the extent the funds intended for payment were taken by your spouse (or former spouse).
   d. You establish that you were the victim of spousal abuse or domestic violence before the return was filed, and that, as a result of the prior abuse, you didn't challenge the treatment of any items on the return for fear of your spouse's (or former spouse's) retaliation. If you meet this exception, relief will be considered even though the understated tax or unpaid tax may be attributable in part or in full to your item.
   e. The item giving rise to the understated tax or deficiency is attributable to you, but you establish that your spouse's (or former spouse's) fraud is the reason for the erroneous item.

Requesting relief. For information on how and when to request relief from liabilities arising from community property laws, see *Community Property Laws* in Pub. 971.

Spousal agreements. In some states spouses may enter into an agreement that affects the status of property or income as community or separate property. Check your state law to determine how it affects you.

Spouses living apart all year. If you are married at any time during the calendar year, special rules apply for reporting certain community income. You must meet **all** the following conditions for these special rules to apply.

1. You and your spouse lived apart all year.
2. You and your spouse didn't file a joint return for a tax year beginning or ending in the calendar year.

3. You and/or your spouse had earned income for the calendar year that is community income.

4. You and your spouse haven't transferred, directly or indirectly, any of the earned income in (3) between yourselves before the end of the year. Don't take into account transfers satisfying child support obligations or transfers of very small amounts or value.

If all these conditions exist, you and your spouse must report your community income as explained in the following discussions. See also *Certain community income not treated as community income by one spouse*, earlier.

Earned income. Treat earned income that isn't trade or business or partnership income as the income of the spouse who performed the services to earn the income. Earned income is wages, salaries, professional fees, and other pay for personal services.

Earned income doesn't include amounts paid by a corporation that are a distribution of earnings and profits rather than a reasonable allowance for personal services rendered.

Trade or business income. Treat income and related deductions from a trade or business that isn't a partnership as those of the spouse carrying on the trade or business.

Partnership income or loss. Treat income or loss from a trade or business carried on by a partnership as the income or loss of the spouse who is the partner.

Separate property income. Treat income from the separate property of one spouse as the income of that spouse.

Social security benefits. Treat social security and equivalent railroad retirement benefits as the income of the spouse who receives the benefits.

Other income. Treat all other community income, such as dividends, interest, rents, royalties, or gains, as provided under your state's community property law.

Example. George and Sharon were married throughout the year but didn't live together at any time during the year. Both domiciles were in a community property state. They didn't file a joint return or transfer any of their earned income between themselves. During the year their incomes were as follows:

	George	Sharon
Wages	$20,000	$22,000
Consulting business	5,000	
Partnership		10,000
Dividends from separate property	1,000	2,000
Interest from community property	500	500
Totals	$26,500	$34,500

Under the community property law of their state, all the income is considered community income. (Some states treat income from separate property as separate income—check your state law.) Sharon didn't take part in George's consulting business.

Ordinarily, on their separate returns they would each report $30,500, half the total community income of $61,000 ($26,500 + $34,500). But because they meet the four conditions listed earlier under *Spouses living apart all year*, they must disregard community property law in reporting all their income (except the interest income) from community property. They each report on their returns only their own earnings and other income, and their share of the interest income from community property. George reports $26,500 and Sharon reports $34,500.

Other separated spouses. If you and your spouse are separated but don't meet the four conditions discussed earlier under *Spouses living apart all year*, you must treat your income according to the laws of your state. In some states, income earned after separation but before a decree of divorce continues to be community income. In other states it is separate income.

Ending the Marital Community

When the marital community ends as a result of divorce or separation, the community assets (money and property) are divided between the spouses. Each spouse is taxed on half the community income for the part of the year before the community ends. However, see *Spouses living apart all year*, earlier. Income received after the community ended is separate income, taxable only to the spouse to whom it belongs.

An absolute decree of divorce or annulment ends the marital community in all community property states. A decree of annulment, even though it holds that no valid marriage ever existed, usually doesn't nullify community property rights arising during the "marriage." However, you should check your state law for exceptions.

A decree of legal separation or of separate maintenance may or may not end the marital community. The court issuing the decree may terminate the marital community and divide the property between the spouses.

A separation agreement may divide the community property between you and your spouse. It may provide that this property, along with future earnings and property acquired, will be separate property. This agreement may end the community.

In some states, the marital community ends when the spouses permanently separate, even if there is no formal agreement. Check your state law.

Alimony (Community Income)

Payments that may otherwise qualify as alimony aren't deductible by the payer if they are the recipient spouse's part of community income. They are deductible by the payer as alimony and taxable to the recipient spouse only to the extent they are more than that spouse's part of community income.

Example. You live in a community property state. You are separated but the special rules explained earlier under *Spouses living apart all year* don't apply. Under a written agreement, you pay your spouse $12,000 of your $20,000 total yearly community income. Your spouse receives no other community income. Under your state law, earnings of a spouse living separately and apart from the other spouse continue as community property.

On your separate returns, each of you must report $10,000 of the total community income. In addition, your spouse must report $2,000 as alimony received. You can deduct $2,000 as alimony paid.

 Alimony or separate maintenance payments under a divorce or separation agreement executed after 2018 won't be deductible by the payer. Such amounts also won't be includible in the income of the recipient if received under an agreement executed after 2018.

How To Get Tax Help

If you have questions about a tax issue, need help preparing your tax return, or want to download free publications, forms, or instructions, go to IRS.gov and find resources that can help you right away.

Tax reform. Major tax reform legislation impacting individuals, businesses, and tax-exempt entities was enacted in the Tax Cuts and Jobs Act on December 22, 2017. Go to *IRS.gov/TaxReform* for information and updates on how this legislation affects your taxes.

Preparing and filing your tax return. Find free options to prepare and file your return on IRS.gov or in your local community if you qualify.

The Volunteer Income Tax Assistance (VITA) program offers free tax help to people who generally make $55,000 or less, persons with disabilities, and limited-English-speaking taxpayers who need help preparing their own tax returns. The Tax Counseling for the Elderly (TCE) program offers free tax help for all taxpayers, particularly those who are 60 years of age and older. TCE volunteers specialize in answering questions about pensions and retirement-related issues unique to seniors.

You can go to IRS.gov to see your options for preparing and filing your return which include the following.

- **Free File.** Go to *IRS.gov/FreeFile* to see if you qualify to use brand-name software to prepare and *e-file* your federal tax return for free.
- **VITA.** Go to *IRS.gov/VITA*, download the free IRS2Go app, or call 800-906-9887 to find the nearest VITA location for free tax return preparation.

- **TCE.** Go to *IRS.gov/TCE*, download the free IRS2Go app, or call 888-227-7669 to find the nearest TCE location for free tax return preparation.

 Getting answers to your tax questions. On IRS.gov, get answers to your tax questions anytime, anywhere.

- Go to *IRS.gov/Help* for a variety of tools that will help you get answers to some of the most common tax questions.
- Go to *IRS.gov/ITA* for the Interactive Tax Assistant, a tool that will ask you questions on a number of tax law topics and provide answers. You can print the entire interview and the final response for your records.
- Go to *IRS.gov/Pub17* to get Pub. 17, Your Federal Income Tax for Individuals, which features details on tax-saving opportunities, 2018 tax changes, and thousands of interactive links to help you find answers to your questions. View it online in HTML, as a PDF, or download it to your mobile device as an eBook.
- You may also be able to access tax law information in your electronic filing software.

Getting tax forms and publications. Go to *IRS.gov/Forms* to view, download, or print all of the forms and publications you may need. You can also download and view popular tax publications and instructions (including the 1040 instructions) on mobile devices as an eBook at no charge. Or you can go to *IRS.gov/OrderForms* to place an order and have forms mailed to you within 10 business days.

Access your online account (individual taxpayers only). Go to *IRS.gov/Account* to securely access information about your federal tax account.

- View the amount you owe, pay online, or set up an online payment agreement.
- Access your tax records online.
- Review the past 24 months of your payment history.
- Go to *IRS.gov/SecureAccess* to review the required identity authentication process.

Using direct deposit. The fastest way to receive a tax refund is to combine direct deposit and IRS *e-file*. Direct deposit securely and electronically transfers your refund directly into your financial account. Eight in 10 taxpayers use direct deposit to receive their refund. The IRS issues more than 90% of refunds in less than 21 days.

Refund timing for returns claiming certain credits. The IRS can't issue refunds before mid-February 2019 for returns that claimed the earned income credit (EIC) or the additional child tax credit (ACTC). This applies to the entire refund, not just the portion associated with these credits.

Getting a transcript or copy of a return. The quickest way to get a copy of your tax transcript is to go to *IRS.gov/Transcripts*. Click on either "Get Transcript Online" or "Get

Transcript by Mail" to order a copy of your transcript. If you prefer, you can:

- Order your transcript by calling 800-908-9946, or
- Mail Form 4506-T or Form 4506T-EZ (both available on IRS.gov).

Using online tools to help prepare your return. Go to *IRS.gov/Tools* for the following.

- The *Earned Income Tax Credit Assistant* (*IRS.gov/ EITCAssistant*) determines if you're eligible for the EIC.
- The *Online EIN Application* (*IRS.gov/EIN*) helps you get an employer identification number.
- The *IRS Withholding Calculator* (*IRS.gov/W4App*) estimates the amount you should have withheld from your paycheck for federal income tax purposes and can help you perform a "paycheck checkup."
- The *First Time Homebuyer Credit Account Look-up* (*IRS.gov/HomeBuyer*) tool provides information on your repayments and account balance.
- The *Sales Tax Deduction Calculator* (*IRS.gov/ SalesTax*) figures the amount you can claim if you itemize deductions on Schedule A (Form 1040), choose not to claim state and local income taxes, and you didn't save your receipts showing the sales tax you paid.

Resolving tax-related identity theft issues.

- The IRS doesn't initiate contact with taxpayers by email or telephone to request personal or financial information. This includes any type of electronic communication, such as text messages and social media channels.
- Go to *IRS.gov/IDProtection* for information.
- If your SSN has been lost or stolen or you suspect you're a victim of tax-related identity theft, visit *IRS.gov/IdentiityTheft* to learn what steps you should take.

Checking on the status of your refund.

- Go to *IRS.gov/Refunds*.
- The IRS can't issue refunds before mid-February 2019 for returns that claimed the EIC or the ACTC. This applies to the entire refund, not just the portion associated with these credits.
- Download the official IRS2Go app to your mobile device to check your refund status.
- Call the automated refund hotline at 800-829-1954.

Making a tax payment. The IRS uses the latest encryption technology to ensure your electronic payments are safe and secure. You can make electronic payments online, by phone, and from a mobile device using the IRS2Go app. Paying electronically is quick, easy, and faster than mailing in a check or money order. Go to *IRS.gov/Payments* to make a payment using any of the following options.

- *IRS Direct Pay*: Pay your individual tax bill or estimated tax payment directly from your checking or savings account at no cost to you.
- **Debit or credit card:** Choose an approved payment processor to pay online, by phone, and by mobile device.
- **Electronic Funds Withdrawal:** Offered only when filing your federal taxes using tax return preparation software or through a tax professional.
- **Electronic Federal Tax Payment System:** Best option for businesses. Enrollment is required.
- **Check or money order:** Mail your payment to the address listed on the notice or instructions.
- **Cash:** You may be able to pay your taxes with cash at a participating retail store.

What if I can't pay now? Go to *IRS.gov/Payments* for more information about your options.

- Apply for an *online payment agreement* (*IRS.gov/ OPA*) to meet your tax obligation in monthly installments if you can't pay your taxes in full today. Once you complete the online process, you will receive immediate notification of whether your agreement has been approved.
- Use the *Offer in Compromise Pre-Qualifier* (*IRS.gov/ OIC*) to see if you can settle your tax debt for less than the full amount you owe.

Checking the status of an amended return. Go to *IRS.gov/WMAR* to track the status of Form 1040X amended returns. Please note that it can take up to 3 weeks from the date you mailed your amended return for it to show up in our system and processing it can take up to 16 weeks.

Understanding an IRS notice or letter. Go to *IRS.gov/ Notices* to find additional information about responding to an IRS notice or letter.

Contacting your local IRS office. Keep in mind, many questions can be answered on IRS.gov without visiting an IRS Tax Assistance Center (TAC). Go to *IRS.gov/ LetUsHelp* for the topics people ask about most. If you still need help, IRS TACs provide tax help when a tax issue can't be handled online or by phone. All TACs now provide service by appointment so you'll know in advance that you can get the service you need without long wait times. Before you visit, go to *IRS.gov/TACLocator* to find the nearest TAC, check hours, available services, and appointment options. Or, on the IRS2Go app, under the Stay Connected tab, choose the Contact Us option and click on "Local Offices."

Watching IRS videos. The IRS Video portal (*IRSVideos.gov*) contains video and audio presentations for individuals, small businesses, and tax professionals.

IRS DIVORCED OR SEPARATED INDIVIDUALS PUBLICATION 504

Getting tax information in other languages. For taxpayers whose native language isn't English, we have the following resources available. Taxpayers can find information on IRS.gov in the following languages.

- _Spanish_ (_IRS.gov/Spanish_).
- _Chinese_ (_IRS.gov/Chinese_).
- _Vietnamese_ (_IRS.gov/Vietnamese_).
- _Korean_ (_IRS.gov/Korean_).
- _Russian_ (_IRS.gov/Russian_).

The IRS TACs provide over-the-phone interpreter service in over 170 languages, and the service is available free to taxpayers.

The Taxpayer Advocate Service (TAS) Is Here To Help You

What is TAS?

TAS is an **independent** organization within the IRS that helps taxpayers and protects taxpayer rights. Their job is to ensure that every taxpayer is treated fairly and that you know and understand your rights under the _Taxpayer Bill of Rights_.

How Can You Learn About Your Taxpayer Rights?

The Taxpayer Bill of Rights describes 10 basic rights that all taxpayers have when dealing with the IRS. Go to _TaxpayerAdvocate.IRS.gov_ to help you understand _what these rights mean to you_ and how they apply. These are **your** rights. Know them. Use them.

What Can TAS Do For You?

TAS can help you resolve problems that you can't resolve with the IRS. And their service is free. If you qualify for their assistance, you will be assigned to one advocate who will work with you throughout the process and will do everything possible to resolve your issue. TAS can help you if:

- Your problem is causing financial difficulty for you, your family, or your business;
- You face (or your business is facing) an immediate threat of adverse action; or
- You've tried repeatedly to contact the IRS but no one has responded, or the IRS hasn't responded by the date promised.

How Can You Reach TAS?

TAS has offices _in every state, the District of Columbia, and Puerto Rico_. Your local advocate's number is in your local directory and at _TaxpayerAdvocate.IRS.gov/Contact-Us_. You can also call them at 877-777-4778.

How Else Does TAS Help Taxpayers?

TAS works to resolve large-scale problems that affect many taxpayers. If you know of one of these broad issues, please report it to them at _IRS.gov/SAMS_.

TAS also has a website, _Tax Reform Changes_, which shows you how the new tax law may change your future tax filings and helps you plan for these changes. The information is categorized by tax topic in the order of the IRS Form 1040. Go to _TaxChanges.us_ for more information.

Low Income Taxpayer Clinics (LITCs)

LITCs are independent from the IRS. LITCs represent individuals whose income is below a certain level and need to resolve tax problems with the IRS, such as audits, appeals, and tax collection disputes. In addition, clinics can provide information about taxpayer rights and responsibilities in different languages for individuals who speak English as a second language. Services are offered for free or a small fee. To find a clinic near you, visit _TaxpayerAdvocate.IRS.gov/LITCmap_ or see IRS Pub. 4134, _Low Income Taxpayer Clinic List_.

Index To help us develop a more useful index, please let us know if you have ideas for index entries. See "Comments and Suggestions" in the "Introduction" for the ways you can reach us.

A
Absence, temporary 7
Address, change of 2
Aliens (_See_ Nonresident aliens)
Alimony 11, 18
   Community income 25
   Deductibility 13
   Defined 13
   Inclusion in income 13
Annual exclusion, gift tax 22

Annulment decrees:
   Absolute decree 25
   Amended return required 3
   Considered unmarried 3
Archer MSA 20
Assistance (_See_ Tax help)

B
Basis:
   Property received in settlement 21

Benefits paid under QDROs 18
Birth of dependent 7

C
Change of address 2
Change of name 2
Change of withholding 2
Child custody 10
Children:
   Birth of child:

Head of household, qualifying person to file as 7
Claiming parent, when child is head of household 7
Custody of 10
Death of child:
 Head of household, qualifying person to file as 7
Photographs of missing children 2
Child support:
 Alimony, difference from 14
 Clearly associated with contingency 17
 Contingency relating to child 17
 Payment specifically designated as 17
Child support under pre-1985 agreement 11
Community income 23–26
Community property 23–26
 (*See also* Community income)
 Ending the marital community 25
 Laws disregarded 23
 States 23
Costs of getting divorce:
 Nondeductible, generally 23
 Nondeductible expenses 23
 Other nondeductible expenses 23
Custody of child 10

D
Death of dependent 7
Death of recipient spouse. 15
Debts of spouse:
 Refund applied to 5
Deductions:
 Alimony paid 13
 Alimony recapture 17
 Limits on IRAs 19
 Marital 21
Dependents:
 Qualifying child 8
 Qualifying child (Table 3) 9
 Qualifying relative 8
 Qualifying relative (Table 3) 9
 Social security numbers 2
Divorce decrees:
 Absolute decree 25
 Amended 13
 Defined for purposes of alimony 13
 Invalid 13
 Unmarried persons 3
Divorced parents 9
 Child custody 10
Domestic relations orders (*See* Qualified domestic relations orders (QDROs))
Domicile 23

E
Earned income 25
Equitable relief (*See* Relief from joint liability)
Estimated tax 23
 Joint payments 23
Exemptions:
 Suspended through 2025 2

F
Filing status 3
 Head of household 7
Form 1040:
 Deducting alimony paid before 2018 13
 Reporting alimony received 14
Form 1040X:
 Annulment, decree of 3
Form 8332:
 Release of claims to an exemption to noncustodial parent 11
Form 8379:
 Injured spouse 5
Form 8857:
 Innocent spouse relief 4
Former spouse:
 Defined for purposes of alimony 13
Form W-4:
 Withholding 23
Form W-7:
 Individual taxpayer identification number (ITIN) 2

G
Gift tax 21, 22

H
Head of household 6
Health care law 2
Health savings accounts (HSAs) 20
Home owned jointly:
 Alimony payments for 15
 Sale of 23
HSAs (Health savings accounts) 20

I
Identification number 2
Identity theft 27
Income 23
 (*See also* Community income)
 Alimony received 14
Individual retirement arrangements (IRAs) 19
Individual taxpayer identification numbers (ITINs):
 Processing 2
 Renewal 2
Injured spouse 5
Innocent spouse relief 4
Insurance premiums 15
Invalid decree 13
IRAs (Individual retirement arrangements) 19
Itemized deductions on separate returns 5
ITINs (Individual taxpayer identification numbers) 2

J
Joint liability:
 Relief from 2, 4
Jointly-owned home:
 Alimony payments for 15
 Sale of 22, 23
Joint returns 4
 Change from separate return 6
 Change to separate return 6
 Divorced taxpayers 4
 Joint and individual liability 4
 Relief from joint liability 4
 Signing 4

K
Kidnapped child:
 Head of household status and 7

L
Liability for taxes (*See* Relief from joint liability)
Life insurance premiums as alimony 15

M
Marital community, ending 25
Marital status 3
Married persons 3
Medical savings accounts (MSAs) 20
Missing children, photographs of 2
Mortgage payments as alimony 15
MSAs (Medical savings accounts) 20

N
Name, change of 2
Nondeductible expenses 23
Nonresident aliens:
 Joint returns 4
 Withholding 14

IRS DIVORCED OR SEPARATED INDIVIDUALS PUBLICATION 504

P
Parent:
   Head of household, claim for 7
Parents, divorced or separated 9
Property settlements 19–23
Publications (*See* Tax help)

Q
Qualified domestic relations orders (QDROs) 18
Qualifying child, tests for claiming (Table 3) 9
Qualifying person, head of household 7
   Table 2 8
Qualifying relative, tests for claiming (Table 3) 9

R
Recapture of alimony 17
Refunds:
   Spouse debts, applied to 5
Release of exemption to noncustodial parent 11
Relief from joint liability 2, 4
Relief from separate return liability:
   Community income 24
Reporting requirements:
   Alimony received 14
Returns:
   Amended return required 3
   Joint (*See* Joint returns)
   Separate (*See* Separate returns)
Revocation of release of claim to an exemption 11

Rollovers 19

S
Sales of jointly-owned property 22
Section 1041 election 21
Separated parents 9
Separate maintenance decrees 3, 13, 25
Separate returns 5
   Change to or from joint return 6
   Community or separate income 5
   Itemized deductions 5
   Relief from liability 24
   Separate liability 5
   Tax consequences 5
Separation agreements 25
   Defined for purposes of alimony 13
Separation of liability (*See* Relief from joint liability)
Settlement of property (*See* Property settlements)
Social security benefits 25
Social security numbers (SSNs):
   Alimony recipient's number required 14
   Dependents 2
Spousal IRA 19
Spouse:
   Defined for purposes of alimony 13
   Refund applied to debts 5
Statute of limitations:
   Amended return 3
   Injured spouse allocation 5

T
Tables and figures:
   Property transferred pursuant to divorce (Table 5) 22
   Qualifying person for head of household (Table 2) 8
   Rules for claiming dependents (Table 3) 9
Tax help 26
Taxpayer identification numbers:
   Processing 2
   Renewal 2
Tax withholding (*See* Withholding)
Third parties:
   Alimony payments to 14, 16
   Property settlements, transfers to 20
Tiebreaker rules 12

U
Underpayment of alimony 14
Unmarried persons 3

W
What's New 2
Withholding:
   Change of 2, 23
   Nonresident aliens 14
Worksheets:
   Recapture of alimony (Worksheet 1) 17

TITLE 28
JUDICIARY AND JUDICIAL PROCEDURE

PART V
PROCEDURE

CHAPTER 115
EVIDENCE; DOCUMENTARY

§ 1738A. Full faith and credit given to child custody determinations.

(a) The appropriate authorities of every State shall enforce according to its terms, and shall not modify except as provided in subsections (f), (g), and (h) of this section, any custody determination or visitation determination made consistently with the provisions of this section by a court of another State.

(b) As used in this section, the term—

(1) "child" means a person under the age of eighteen;

(2) "contestant" means a person, including a parent or grandparent, who claims a right to custody or visitation of a child;

(3) "custody determination" means a judgment, decree, or other order of a court providing for the custody of a child, and includes permanent and temporary orders, and initial orders and modifications;

(4) "home State" means the State in which, immediately preceding the time involved, the child lived with his parents, a parent, or a person acting as parent, for at least six consecutive months, and in the case of a child less than six months old, the State in which the child lived from birth with any of such persons. Periods of temporary absence of any of such persons are counted as part of the six-month or other period;

(5) "modification" and "modify" refer to a custody or visitation determination which modifies, replaces, supersedes, or otherwise is made subsequent to, a prior custody or visitation determination concerning the same child, whether made by the same court or not;

(6) "person acting as a parent" means a person, other than a parent, who has physical custody of a child and who has either been awarded custody by a court or claims a right to custody;

(7) "physical custody" means actual possession and control of a child;

(8) "State" means a State of the United States, the District of Columbia, the Commonwealth of Puerto Rico, or a territory or possession of the United States; and

(9) "visitation determination" means a judgment, decree, or other order of a court providing for the visitation of a child and includes permanent and temporary orders and initial orders and modifications.

(c) A child custody or visitation determination made by a court of a State is consistent with the provisions of this section only if—

(1) such court has jurisdiction under the law of such State; and

(2) one of the following conditions is met:

(A) such State (i) is the home State of the child on the date of the commencement of the proceeding, or (ii) had been the child's home State within six months before the date of the commencement of the proceeding and the child is absent from such State because of his removal or retention by a contestant or for other reasons, and a contestant continues to live in such State;

(B) (i) it appears that no other State would have jurisdiction under subparagraph (A), and (ii) it is in the best interest of the child that a court of such State assume jurisdiction because (I) the child and his parents, or the child and at least one contestant, have a significant connection with such State other than mere physical presence in such State, and (II) there is available in such State substantial evidence concerning the child's present or future care, protection, training, and personal relationships;

(C) the child is physically present in such State and (i) the child has been abandoned, or (ii) it is necessary in an emergency to protect the child because the child, a sibling, or parent of the child has been subjected to or threatened with mistreatment or abuse;

(D) (i) it appears that no other State would have jurisdiction under subparagraph (A), (B), (C), or (E), or another State has declined to exercise jurisdiction on the ground that the State whose jurisdiction is in issue is the more appropriate forum to determine the custody or visitation of the child, and (ii) it is in the best interest of the child that such court assume jurisdiction; or

(E) the court has continuing jurisdiction pursuant to subsection (d) of this section.

(d) The jurisdiction of a court of a State which has made a child custody or visitation determination consistently with the provisions of this section continues as long as the requirement of subsection (c)(1) of this section continues to be met and such State remains the residence of the child or of any contestant.

(e) Before a child custody or visitation determination is made, reasonable notice and opportunity to be heard shall be given to the contestants, any parent whose parental rights have not been previously terminated and any person who has physical custody of a child.

(f) A court of a State may modify a determination of the custody of the same child made by a court of another State, if—

(1) it has jurisdiction to make such a child custody determination; and

(2) the court of the other State no longer has jurisdiction, or it has declined to exercise such jurisdiction to modify such determination.

(g) A court of a State shall not exercise jurisdiction in any proceeding for a custody or visitation determination commenced during the pendency of a proceeding in a court of another State where such court of that other State is exercising jurisdiction consistently with the provisions of this section to make a custody or visitation determination.

(h) A court of a State may not modify a visitation determination made by a court of another State unless the court of the other State no longer has jurisdiction to modify such determination or has declined to exercise jurisdiction to modify such determination.

§ 1738B. Full faith and credit for child support orders.

(a) **General rule.**—The appropriate authorities of each State—

(1) shall enforce according to its terms a child support order made consistently with this section by a court of another State; and

(2) shall not seek or make a modification of such an order except in accordance with subsections (e), (f), and (i).

(b) **Definitions.**—In this section:

(1) The term "child" means—

(A) a person under 18 years of age; and

(B) a person 18 or more years of age with respect to whom a child support order has been issued pursuant to the laws of a State.

(2) The term "child's State" means the State in which a child resides.

(3) The term "child's home State" means the State in which a child lived with a parent or a person acting as parent for at least 6 consecutive months immediately preceding the time of filing of a petition or comparable pleading for support and, if a child is less than 6 months old, the State in which the child lived from birth with any of them. A period of temporary absence of any of them is counted as part of the 6-month period.

(4) The term "child support" means a payment of money, continuing support, or arrearages or the provision of a benefit (including payment of health insurance, child care, and educational expenses) for the support of a child.

(5) The term "child support order"—

(A) means a judgment, decree, or order of a court requiring the payment of child support in periodic amounts or in a lump sum; and

(B) includes—

(i) a permanent or temporary order; and

(ii) an initial order or a modification of an order.

(6) The term "contestant" means—

(A) a person (including a parent) who—

(i) claims a right to receive child support;

(ii) is a party to a proceeding that may result in the issuance of a child support order; or

(iii) is under a child support order; and

(B) a State or political subdivision of a State to which the right to obtain child support has been assigned.

(7) The term "court" means a court or administrative agency of a State that is authorized by State law to establish the amount of child support payable by a contestant or make a modification of a child support order.

(8) The term "modification" means a change in a child support order that affects the amount, scope, or duration of the order and modifies, replaces, supersedes, or otherwise is made subsequent to the child support order.

(9) The term "State" means a State of the United States, the District of Columbia, the Commonwealth of Puerto Rico, the territories and possessions of the United States, and Indian country (as defined in section 1151 of title 18).

(c) Requirements of child support orders.—A child support order made by a court of a State is made consistently with this section if—

(1) a court that makes the order, pursuant to the laws of the State in which the court is located and subsections (e), (f), and (g)—

(A) has subject matter jurisdiction to hear the matter and enter such an order; and

(B) has personal jurisdiction over the contestants; and

(2) reasonable notice and opportunity to be heard is given to the contestants.

(d) Continuing jurisdiction.—A court of a State that has made a child support order consistently with this section has continuing, exclusive jurisdiction over the order if the State is the child's State or the residence of any individual contestant unless the court of another State, acting in accordance with subsections (e) and (f), has made a modification of the order.

(e) Authority to modify orders.—A court of a State may modify a child support order issued by a court of another State if—

(1) the court has jurisdiction to make such a child support order pursuant to subsection (i); and

(2)(A) the court of the other State no longer has continuing, exclusive jurisdiction of the child support order because that State no longer is the child's State or the residence of any individual contestant; or

(B) each individual contestant has filed written consent with the State of continuing, exclusive jurisdiction for a court of another State to modify the order and assume continuing, exclusive jurisdiction over the order.

(f) Recognition of child support orders.—If 1 or more child support orders have been issued with regard to an obligor and a child, a court shall apply the following rules in determining which order to recognize for purposes of continuing, exclusive jurisdiction and enforcement:

(1) If only 1 court has issued a child support order, the order of that court must be recognized.

(2) If 2 or more courts have issued child support orders for the same obligor and child, and only 1 of the courts would have continuing, exclusive jurisdiction under this section, the order of that court must be recognized.

(3) If 2 or more courts have issued child support orders for the same obligor and child, and more than 1 of the courts would have continuing, exclusive jurisdiction under this section, an order issued by a court in the current home State of the child must be recognized, but if an order has not been issued in the current home State of the child, the order most recently issued must be recognized.

(4) If 2 or more courts have issued child support orders for the same obligor and child, and none of the courts would have continuing, exclusive jurisdiction under this section, a court having jurisdiction over the parties shall issue a child support order, which must be recognized.

(5) The court that has issued an order recognized under this subsection is the court having continuing, exclusive jurisdiction under subsection (d).

(g) Enforcement of modified orders.—A court of a State that no longer has continuing, exclusive jurisdiction of a child support order may enforce the order with respect to nonmodifiable obligations and unsatisfied obligations that accrued before the date on which a modification of the order is made under subsections (e) and (f).

(h) Choice of law.—

(1) In general.—In a proceeding to establish, modify, or enforce a child support order, the forum State's law shall apply except as provided in paragraphs (2) and (3).

(2) Law of state of issuance of order.—In interpreting a child support order including the duration of current payments and other obligations of support, a court shall apply the law of the State of the court that issued the order.

(3) Period of limitation.—In an action to enforce arrears under a child support order, a court shall apply the statute of limitation of the forum State or the State of the court that issued the order, whichever statute provides the longer period of limitation.

(i) Registration for modification.—If there is no individual contestant or child residing in the issuing State, the party or support enforcement agency seeking to modify, or to modify and enforce, a child support order issued in another State shall register that order in a State with jurisdiction over the nonmovant for the purpose of modification.

(Added Pub. L. 103–383, § 3(a), Oct. 20, 1994, 108 Stat. 4064; amended Pub. L. 104–193, title III, § 322, Aug. 22, 1996, 110 Stat. 2221; Pub. L. 105–33, title V, § 5554, Aug. 5, 1997, 111 Stat. 636; Pub. L. 113–183, title III, § 301(f)(2), Sept. 29, 2014, 128 Stat. 1944.)

Congressional Findings and Declaration of Purpose

Pub. L. 103–383, § 2, Oct. 20, 1994, 108 Stat. 4063, provided that:

"(a) **Findings.**—The Congress finds that—

"(1) there is a large and growing number of child support cases annually involving disputes between parents who reside in different States;

"(2) the laws by which the courts of different jurisdictions determine their authority to establish child support orders are not uniform;

"(3) those laws, along with the limits imposed by the Federal system on the authority of each State to take certain actions outside its own boundaries—

"(A) encourage noncustodial parents to relocate outside the States where their children and the custodial parents reside to avoid the jurisdiction of the courts of such States, resulting in an increase in the amount of interstate travel and communication required to establish and collect on child support orders and a burden on custodial parents that is expensive, time consuming, and disruptive of occupations and commercial activity;

"(B) contribute to the pressing problem of relatively low levels of child support payments in interstate cases and to inequities in child support payments levels that are based solely on the noncustodial parent's choice of residence;

"(C) encourage a disregard of court orders resulting in massive arrearages nationwide;

"(D) allow noncustodial parents to avoid the payment of regularly scheduled child support payments for extensive periods of time, resulting in substantial hardship for the children for whom support is due and for their custodians; and

"(E) lead to the excessive relitigation of cases and to the establishment of conflicting orders by the courts of various jurisdictions, resulting in confusion, waste of judicial resources, disrespect for the courts, and a diminution of public confidence in the rule of law; and

"(4) among the results of the conditions described in this subsection are—

"(A) the failure of the courts of the States to give full faith and credit to the judicial proceedings of the other States;

"(B) the deprivation of rights of liberty and property without due process of law;

"(C) burdens on commerce among the States; and

"(D) harm to the welfare of children and their parents and other custodians.

"(b) **Statement of policy.**—In view of the findings made in subsection (a), it is necessary to establish national standards under which the courts of the various States shall determine their jurisdiction to issue a child support order and the effect to be given by each State to child support orders issued by the courts of other States.

"(c) **Purposes.**—The purposes of this Act [enacting this section and provisions set out as a note under section 1 of this title] are—

"(1) to facilitate the enforcement of child support orders among the States;

"(2) to discourage continuing interstate controversies over child support in the interest of greater financial stability and secure family relationships for the child; and

"(3) to avoid jurisdictional competition and conflict among State courts in the establishment of child support orders."

§ 1738C. Certain acts, records, and proceedings and the effect thereof.

No State, territory, or possession of the United States, or Indian tribe, shall be required to give effect to any public act, record, or judicial proceeding of any other State, territory, possession, or tribe respecting a relationship between persons of the same sex that is treated as a marriage under the laws of such other State, territory, possession, or tribe, or a right or claim arising from such relationship.

TITLE 42

THE PUBLIC HEALTH AND WELFARE

CHAPTER 7
SOCIAL SECURITY

SUBCHAPTER IV
GRANTS TO STATES FOR AID AND SERVICES TO NEEDY FAMILIES WITH CHILDREN AND FOR CHILD-WELFARE SERVICES

PART D
CHILD SUPPORT AND ESTABLISHMENT OF PATERNITY

§ 651. Authorization of appropriations.

For the purpose of enforcing the support obligations owed by noncustodial parents to their children and the spouse (or former spouse) with whom such children are living, locating noncustodial parents, establishing paternity, obtaining child and spousal support, and assuring that assistance in obtaining support will be available under this part to all children (whether or not eligible for assistance under a state program funded under part A of this subchapter) for whom such assistance is requested, there is hereby authorized to be appropriated for each fiscal year a sum sufficient to carry out the purposes of this part.

§ 652. Duties of Secretary.

(a) Establishment of separate organizational unit; duties

The Secretary shall establish, within the Department of Health and Human Services a separate organizational unit, under the direction of a designee of the Secretary, who shall report directly to the Secretary and who shall—

(1) establish such standards for State programs for locating noncustodial parents, establishing paternity, and obtaining child support and support for the spouse (or former spouse) with whom the noncustodial parent's child is living as he determines to be necessary to assure that such programs will be effective;

(2) establish minimum organizational and staffing requirements for State units engaged in carrying out such programs under plans approved under this part;

(3) review and approve State plans for such programs;

(4)(A) review data and calculations transmitted by State agencies pursuant to section 654(15)(B) of this title on State program accomplishments with respect to performance indicators for purposes of subsection (g) of this section and section 658a of this title;

(B) review annual reports submitted pursuant to section 654(15)(A) of this title and, as appropriate, provide to the State comments, recommendations for additional or alternative corrective actions, and technical assistance; and

(C) conduct audits, in accordance with the Government auditing standards of the Comptroller General of the United States—

(i) at least once every 3 years (or more frequently, in the case of a State which fails to meet the requirements of this part concerning performance standards and reliability of program data) to assess the completeness, reliability, and security of the data and the accuracy of the reporting systems used in calculating performance indicators under subsection (g) of this section and section 658a of this title;

(ii) of the adequacy of financial management of the State program operated under the State plan approved under this part, including assessments of—

(I) whether Federal and other funds made available to carry out the State program are being appropriately expended, and are properly and fully accounted for; and

(II) whether collections and disbursements of support payments are carried out correctly and are fully accounted for; and

(iii) for such other purposes as the Secretary may find necessary;

(5) assist States in establishing adequate reporting procedures and maintain records of the operations of programs established pursuant to this part in each State, and establish procedures to be followed by States for collecting and reporting information required to be provided under this part, and establish uniform definitions (including those necessary to enable the measurement of State compliance with the requirements of this part relating to expedited processes) to be applied in following such procedures;

(6) maintain records of all amounts collected and disbursed under programs established pursuant to the provisions of this part and of the costs incurred in collecting such amounts;

(7) provide technical assistance to the States to help them establish effective systems for collecting child and spousal support and establishing paternity, and specify the minimum requirements of an affidavit to be used for the voluntary acknowledgment of paternity which shall include the social security number of each parent and, after consultation with the States, other common elements as determined by such designee;

(8) receive applications from States for permission to utilize the courts of the United States to enforce court orders for support against noncustodial parents and, upon a finding that (A) another State has not undertaken to enforce the court order of the originating State against the noncustodial parent within a reasonable time, and (B) that utilization of the Federal courts is the only reasonable method of enforcing such order, approve such applications;

(9) operate the Federal Parent Locator Service established by section 653 of this title;

(10) not later than three months after the end of each fiscal year, beginning with the year 1977, submit to the Congress a full and complete report on all activities undertaken pursuant to the provisions of this part, which report shall include, but not be limited to, the following:

(A) total program costs and collections set forth in sufficient detail to show the cost to the States and the Federal Government, the distribution of collections to families, State and local governmental units, and the Federal Government; and an identification of the financial impact of the provisions of this part, including—

(i) the total amount of child support payments collected as a result of services furnished during the fiscal year to individuals receiving services under this part;

(ii) the cost to the States and to the Federal Government of so furnishing the services; and

(iii) the number of cases involving families—

(I) who became ineligible for assistance under State programs funded under part A of this subchapter during a month in the fiscal year; and

(II) with respect to whom a child support payment was received in the month;

(B) costs and staff associated with the Office of Child Support Enforcement;

(C) the following data, separately stated for cases where the child is receiving assistance under a State program funded under part A of this subchapter (or foster care maintenance payments under part E of this subchapter), or formerly received such assistance or payments and the State is continuing to collect support assigned to it pursuant to section 608(a)(3) of this title or under section 671(a)(17) or 1396k of this title, and for all other cases under this part:

(i) the total number of cases in which a support obligation has been established in the fiscal year for which the report is submitted;

(ii) the total number of cases in which a support obligation has been established;

(iii) the number of cases in which support was collected during the fiscal year;

(iv) the total amount of support collected during such fiscal year and distributed as current support;

(v) the total amount of support collected during such fiscal year and distributed as arrearages;

(vi) the total amount of support due and unpaid for all fiscal years; and

(vii) the number of child support cases filed in each State in such fiscal year, and the amount of the collections made in each State in such fiscal year, on behalf of children residing in another State or against parents residing in another State;

(D) the status of all State plans under this part as of the end of the fiscal year last ending before the report is submitted, together with an explanation of any problems which are delaying or preventing approval of State plans under this part;

(E) data, by State, on the use of the Federal Parent Locator Service, and the number of locate requests submitted without the noncustodial parent's social security account number;

(F) the number of cases, by State, in which an applicant for or recipient of assistance under a State program funded under part A of this subchapter has refused to cooperate in identifying and locating the noncustodial parent and the number of cases in which refusal so to cooperate is based on good cause (as determined by the State);

(G) data, by State, on use of the Internal Revenue Service for collections, the number of court orders on which collections were made, the number of paternity determinations made and the number of parents located, in sufficient detail to show the cost and benefits to the States and to the Federal Government;

(H) the major problems encountered which have delayed or prevented implementation of the provisions of this part during the fiscal year last ending prior to the submission of such report; and

(I) compliance, by State, with the standards established pursuant to subsections (h) and (i) of this section; and

(11) not later than October 1, 1996, after consulting with the State directors of programs under this part, promulgate forms to be used by States in interstate cases for—

(A) collection of child support through income withholding;

(B) imposition of liens; and

(C) administrative subpoenas.

(b) Certification of child support obligations to Secretary of the Treasury for collection

The Secretary shall, upon the request of any State having in effect a State plan approved under this part, certify to the Secretary of the Treasury for collection pursuant to the provisions of section 6305 of the Internal Revenue Code of 1986 the amount of any child support obligation (including any support obligation with respect to the parent who is living with the child and receiving assistance under the State program funded under part A of this subchapter) which is assigned to such State or is undertaken to be collected by such State pursuant to section 654(4) of this title. No amount may be certified for collection under this subsection except the amount of the delinquency under a court or administrative order for support and upon a showing by the State that such State has made diligent and reasonable efforts to collect such amounts utilizing its own collection mechanisms, and upon an agreement that the State will reimburse the Secretary of the Treasury for any costs involved in making the collection. All reimbursements shall be credited to the appropriation accounts which bore all or part of the costs involved in making the collections. The Secretary after consultation with the Secretary of the Treasury may, by regulation, establish criteria for accepting amounts for collection and for making certification under this subsection including imposing such limitations on the frequency of making such certifications under this subsection.

(c) Payment of child support collections to States

The Secretary of the Treasury shall from time to time pay to each State for distribution in accordance with the provisions of section 657 of this title the amount of each collection made on behalf of such State pursuant to subsection (b) of this section.

(d) Child support management information system

(1) Except as provided in paragraph (3), the Secretary shall not approve the initial and annually updated advance automated data processing planning document, referred to in section 654(16) of this title, unless he finds that such document, when implemented, will generally carry out the objectives of the management system referred to in such subsection, and such document—

(A) provides for the conduct of, and reflects the results of, requirements analysis studies, which include consideration of the program mission, functions, organization, services, constraints, and current support, of, in, or relating to, such system,

(B) contains a description of the proposed management system referred to in section 654(16) of this title, including a description of information flows, input data, and output reports and uses,

(C) sets forth the security and interface requirements to be employed in such management system,

(D) describes the projected resource requirements for staff and other needs, and the resources available or expected to be available to meet such requirements,

(E) contains an implementation plan and backup procedures to handle possible failures,

(F) contains a summary of proposed improvement of such management system in terms of qualitative and quantitative benefits, and

(G) provides such other information as the Secretary determines under regulation is necessary.

(2)(A) The Secretary shall through the separate organizational unit established pursuant to subsection (a) of this section, on a continuing basis, review, assess, and inspect the planning, design, and operation of, management information systems referred to in section 654(16) of this title, with a view to determining whether, and to what extent, such systems meet and continue to meet requirements imposed under paragraph (1) and the conditions specified under section 654(16) of this title.

(B) If the Secretary finds with respect to any statewide management information system referred to in section 654(16) of this title that there is a failure substantially to comply with criteria, requirements, and other undertakings, prescribed by the advance automated data processing planning document theretofore approved by the Secretary with respect to such system, then the Secretary shall suspend his approval of such document until there is no longer any such failure of such system to comply with such criteria, requirements, and other undertakings so prescribed.

(3) The Secretary may waive any requirement of paragraph (1) or any condition specified under section 654(16) of this title, and shall waive the single statewide system requirement under sections 654(16) and 654a of this title, with respect to a State if—

(A) the State demonstrates to the satisfaction of the Secretary that the State has or can develop an alternative system or systems that enable the State—

(i) for purposes of section 609(a)(8) of this title, to achieve the paternity establishment percentages (as defined in subsection (g)(2) of this section) and other performance measures that may be established by the Secretary;

(ii) to submit data under section 654(15)(B) of this title that is complete and reliable;

(iii) to substantially comply with the requirements of this part; and

(iv) in the case of a request to waive the single statewide system requirement, to—

(I) meet all functional requirements of sections 654(16) and 654a of this title;

(II) ensure that calculation of distributions meets the requirements of section 657 of this title and accounts for distributions to children in different families or in different States or sub-State jurisdictions, and for distributions to other States;

(III) ensure that there is only one point of contact in the State which provides seamless case processing for all interstate case processing and coordinated, automated intrastate case management;

(IV) ensure that standardized data elements, forms, and definitions are used throughout the State;

(V) complete the alternative system in no more time than it would take to complete a single statewide system that meets such requirement; and

(VI) process child support cases as quickly, efficiently, and effectively as such cases would be processed through a single statewide system that meets such requirement;

(B)(i) the waiver meets the criteria of paragraphs (1), (2), and (3) of section 1315(c) of this title; or

(ii) the State provides assurances to the Secretary that steps will be taken to otherwise improve the State's child support enforcement program; and

(C) in the case of a request to waive the single statewide system requirement, the State has submitted to the Secretary separate estimates of the total cost of a single statewide system that meets such requirement, and of any such alternative system or systems, which shall include estimates of the cost of developing and completing the system and of operating and maintaining the system for 5 years, and the Secretary has agreed with the estimates.

(e) Technical assistance to States

The Secretary shall provide such technical assistance to States as he determines necessary to assist States to plan, design, develop, or install and provide for the security of, the management information systems referred to in section 654(16) of this title.

(f) Regulations

The Secretary shall issue regulations to require that State agencies administering the child support enforcement program under this part enforce medical support included as part of a child support order whenever health care coverage is available to the noncustodial parent at a reasonable cost. A State agency administering the program under this part may enforce medical support against a custodial parent if health care coverage is available to the custodial parent at a reasonable cost, notwithstanding any other provision of this part. Such regulation shall also provide for improved information exchange between such State agencies and the State agencies administering the State medicaid programs under subchapter XIX of this chapter with respect to the availability of health insurance coverage. For purposes of this part, the term "medical support" may include health care coverage, such as coverage under a health insurance plan (including payment of costs of premiums, co-payments, and deductibles) and payment for medical expenses incurred on behalf of a child.

(g) Performance standards for State paternity establishment programs

(1) A State's program under this part shall be found, for purposes of section 609(a)(8) of this title, not to have complied substantially with the requirements of this part unless, for any fiscal year beginning on or after October 1, 1994, its paternity establishment percentage for such fiscal year is based on reliable data and (rounded to the nearest whole percentage point) equals or exceeds—

(A) 90 percent;

(B) for a State with a paternity establishment percentage of not less than 75 percent but less than 90 percent for such fiscal year, the paternity establishment percentage of the State for the immediately preceding fiscal year plus 2 percentage points;

(C) for a State with a paternity establishment percentage of not less than 50 percent but less than 75 percent for such fiscal year, the paternity establishment percentage of the State for the immediately preceding fiscal year plus 3 percentage points;

(D) for a State with a paternity establishment percentage of not less than 45 percent but less than 50 percent for such fiscal year, the paternity establishment percentage of the State for the immediately preceding fiscal year plus 4 percentage points;

(E) for a State with a paternity establishment percentage of not less than 40 percent but less than 45 percent for such fiscal year, the paternity establishment percentage of the State for the immediately preceding fiscal year plus 5 percentage points; or

(F) for a State with a paternity establishment percentage of less than 40 percent for such fiscal year, the paternity establishment percentage of the State for the immediately preceding fiscal year plus 6 percentage points.

In determining compliance under this section, a State may use as its paternity establishment percentage either the State's IV–D paternity establishment percentage (as defined in paragraph (2)(A)) or the State's statewide paternity establishment percentage (as defined in paragraph (2)(B)).

(2) For purposes of this section—

(A) the term "IV–D paternity establishment percentage" means, with respect to a State for a fiscal year, the ratio (expressed as a percentage) that the total number of children—

(i) who have been born out of wedlock,

(ii)(I) except as provided in the last sentence of this paragraph, with respect to whom assistance is being provided under the State program funded under part A of this subchapter in the fiscal year or, at the option of the State, as of the end of such year, or (II) with respect to whom services are being provided under the State's plan approved under this part in the fiscal year or, at the option of the State, as of the end of such year pursuant to an application submitted under section 654(4)(A)(ii) of this title, and

(iii) the paternity of whom has been established or acknowledged,

bears to the total number of children born out of wedlock and (except as provided in such last sentence) with respect to whom assistance was being provided under the State program funded under part A of this subchapter as of the end of the preceding fiscal year or with respect to whom services were being provided under the State's plan approved under this part as of the end of the preceding fiscal year pursuant to an application submitted under section 654(4)(A)(ii) of this title;

(B) the term "statewide paternity establishment percentage" means, with respect to a State for a fiscal year, the ratio (expressed as a percentage) that the total number of minor children—

(i) who have been born out of wedlock, and

(ii) the paternity of whom has been established or acknowledged during the fiscal year,

bears to the total number of children born out of wedlock during the preceding fiscal year; and

(C) the term "reliable data" means the most recent data available which are found by the Secretary to be reliable for purposes of this section.

For purposes of subparagraphs (A) and (B), the total number of children shall not include any child with respect to whom assistance is being provided under the State program funded under part A of this subchapter by reason of the death of a parent unless paternity is established for such child or any child with respect to whom an applicant or recipient is found by the State to qualify for a good cause or other exception to cooperation pursuant to section 654(29) of this title.

(3)(A) The Secretary may modify the requirements of this subsection to take into account such additional variables as the Secretary identifies (including the percentage of children in a State who are born out of wedlock or for whom support has not been established) that affect the ability of a State to meet the requirements of this subsection.

(B) The Secretary shall submit an annual report to the Congress that sets forth the data upon which the paternity establishment percentages for States for a fiscal year are based, lists any additional variables the Secretary has identified under subparagraph (A), and describes State performance in establishing paternity.

(h) Prompt State response to requests for child support assistance

The standards required by subsection (a)(1) of this section shall include standards establishing time limits governing the period or periods within which a State must accept and respond to requests (from States, jurisdictions thereof, or individuals who apply for services furnished by the State agency under this part or with respect to whom an assignment pursuant to section 608(a)(3) of this title is in effect) for assistance in establishing and enforcing support orders, including requests to locate noncustodial parents, establish paternity, and initiate proceedings to establish and collect child support awards.

(i) Prompt State distribution of amounts collected as child support

The standards required by subsection (a)(1) of this section shall include standards establishing time limits governing the period or periods within which a State must distribute, in accordance with section 657 of this title, amounts collected as child support pursuant to the State's plan approved under this part.

(j) Training of Federal and State staff, research and demonstration programs, and special projects of regional or national significance

Out of any money in the Treasury of the United States not otherwise appropriated, there is hereby appropriated to the Secretary for each fiscal year an amount equal to 1 percent of the total amount paid to the Federal Government pursuant to a plan approved under this part during the immediately preceding fiscal year (as determined on the basis of the most recent reliable data available to the Secretary as of the end of the third calendar quarter following the end of such preceding fiscal year) or the amount appropriated under this paragraph 1 for fiscal year 2002, whichever is greater, which shall be available for use by the Secretary, either directly or through grants, contracts, or interagency agreements, for—

(1) information dissemination and technical assistance to States, training of State and Federal staff, staffing studies, and related activities needed to improve programs under this part (including technical assistance concerning State automated systems required by this part); and

(2) research, demonstration, and special projects of regional or national significance relating to the operation of State programs under this part.

The amount appropriated under this subsection shall remain available until expended.

(k) Denial of passports for nonpayment of child support

(1) If the Secretary receives a certification by a State agency in accordance with the requirements of section 654(31) of this title that an individual owes arrearages of child support in an amount exceeding $2,500, the Secretary shall transmit such certification to the Secretary of State for action (with respect to denial, revocation, or limitation of passports) pursuant to paragraph (2).

(2) The Secretary of State shall, upon certification by the Secretary transmitted under paragraph (1), refuse to issue a passport to such individual, and may revoke, restrict, or limit a passport issued previously to such individual.

(3) The Secretary and the Secretary of State shall not be liable to an individual for any action with respect to a certification by a State agency under this section.

(l) Facilitation of agreements between State agencies and financial institutions

The Secretary, through the Federal Parent Locator Service, may aid State agencies providing services under State programs operated pursuant to this part and financial institutions doing business in two or more States in reaching agreements regarding the receipt from such institutions, and the transfer to the State agencies, of information that may be provided pursuant to section 666(a)(17)(A)(i) of this title, except that any State that, as of July 16, 1998, is conducting data matches pursuant to section 666(a)(17)(A)(i) of this title shall have until January 1, 2000, to allow the Secretary to obtain such information from such institutions that are operating in the State. For purposes of section 3413(d) of title 12, a disclosure pursuant to this subsection shall be considered a disclosure pursuant to a Federal statute.

(m) Comparisons with insurance information

(1) In general

The Secretary, through the Federal Parent Locator Service, may—

(A) compare information concerning individuals owing past-due support with information maintained by insurers (or their agents) concerning insurance claims, settlements, awards, and payments; and

(B) furnish information resulting from the data matches to the State agencies responsible for collecting child support from the individuals.

(2) Liability

An insurer (including any agent of an insurer) shall not be liable under any Federal or State law to any person for any disclosure provided for under this subsection, or for any other action taken in good faith in accordance with this subsection.

(n) Compliance with multilateral child support conventions

The Secretary shall use the authorities otherwise provided by law to ensure the compliance of the United States with any multilateral child support convention to which the United States is a party.

(o) Data exchange standards for improved interoperability

(1) Designation

The Secretary shall, in consultation with an interagency work group established by the Office of Management and Budget and considering State government perspectives, by rule, designate data exchange standards to govern, under this part—

(A) necessary categories of information that State agencies operating programs under State plans approved under this part are required under applicable Federal law to electronically exchange with another State agency; and

(B) Federal reporting and data exchange required under applicable Federal law.

(2) Requirements

The data exchange standards required by paragraph (1) shall, to the extent practicable—

(A) incorporate a widely accepted, non-proprietary, searchable, computer-readable format, such as the eXtensible Markup Language;

(B) contain interoperable standards developed and maintained by intergovernmental partnerships, such as the National Information Exchange Model;

(C) incorporate interoperable standards developed and maintained by Federal entities with authority over contracting and financial assistance;

(D) be consistent with and implement applicable accounting principles;

(E) be implemented in a manner that is cost-effective and improves program efficiency and effectiveness; and

(F) be capable of being continually upgraded as necessary.

(3) Rule of construction

Nothing in this subsection shall be construed to require a change to existing data exchange standards found to be effective and efficient.

(Aug. 14, 1935, ch. 531, title IV, § 452, as added Pub. L. 93–647, § 101(a), Jan. 4, 1975, 88 Stat. 2351; amended Pub. L. 95–30, title V, § 504(a), May 23, 1977, 91 Stat. 163; Pub. L. 96–265, title IV, §§ 402(a), 405(c), (d), June 9, 1980, 94 Stat. 462, 464, 465; Pub. L. 96–272, title III, § 301(b), June 17, 1980, 94 Stat. 527; Pub. L. 97–35, title XXIII, § 2332(b), Aug. 13, 1981, 95 Stat. 861; Pub. L. 97–248, title I, § 175(a)(1), Sept. 3, 1982, 96 Stat. 403; Pub. L. 98–369, div. B, title VI, § 2663(c)(12), (j)(2)(B)(viii), July 18, 1984, 98 Stat. 1166, 1170; Pub. L. 98–378, §§ 4(b), 9(a)(1), 13(a), (b), 16, Aug. 16, 1984, 98 Stat. 1312, 1316, 1319, 1321; Pub. L. 99–514, § 2, Oct. 22, 1986, 100 Stat. 2095; Pub. L. 100–203, title IX, § 9143(a), Dec. 22, 1987, 101 Stat. 1330–322; Pub. L. 100–485, title I, §§ 111(a), 121(a), 122(a), 123(b), (d), Oct. 13, 1988, 102 Stat. 2348, 2351-2353; Pub. L. 101–239, title X, § 10403(a)(1)(B)(i), Dec. 19, 1989, 103 Stat. 2487; Pub. L. 103–66, title XIII, § 13721(a), Aug. 10, 1993, 107 Stat. 658; Pub. L. 103–432, title II, § 213, Oct. 31, 1994, 108 Stat. 4461; Pub. L. 104–35, § 1(b), Oct. 12, 1995, 109 Stat. 294; Pub. L. 104–193, title I, § 108(c)(2)–(9), title III, §§ 301(c)(1), (2), 316(e)(1), 324(a), 331(b), 341(b), formerly 341(c), 342(b), 343(a), 345(a), 346(a), 370(a)(1), 395(d)(1)(B), Aug. 22, 1996, 110 Stat. 2165, 2200, 2215, 2223, 2230, 2232-2234, 2237, 2238, 2251, 2259; Pub. L. 104–208, div. A, title I, § 101(e) [title II, § 215], Sept. 30, 1996, 110 Stat. 3009–233, 3009-255; Pub. L. 105–33, title V, §§ 5513(a)(1), (2), 5540, 5541(a), 5556(c), Aug. 5, 1997, 111 Stat. 619, 630, 637; Pub. L. 105–200, title I, § 102(a), title II, § 201(e)(1)(A), title IV, §§ 401(c)(2), 406(b), 407(b), July 16, 1998, 112 Stat. 647, 657, 662, 671, 672; Pub. L. 106–169, title IV, § 401(f), Dec. 14, 1999, 113 Stat. 1858; Pub. L. 109–171, title VII, §§ 7303(a), 7304, 7306(a), 7307(a)(2)(A)(i), (b), (c), Feb. 8, 2006, 120 Stat. 145-147; Pub. L. 113–183, title III, §§ 301(a)(1), 304(a), Sept. 29, 2014, 128 Stat. 1943, 1947.)

Regulations

Pub. L. 113–183, title III, § 304(b), Sept. 29, 2014, 128 Stat. 1947, provided that: "The Secretary of Health and Human Services shall issue a proposed rule within 24 months after the date of the enactment of this section [Sept. 29, 2014]. The rule shall identify federally required data exchanges, include specification and timing of exchanges to be standardized, and address the factors used in determining whether and when to standardize data exchanges. It should also specify State implementation options and describe future milestones."

Pub. L. 100–485, title I, § 122(b), Oct. 13, 1988, 102 Stat. 2351, provided that: "Not later than 180 days after the date of the enactment of this Act [Oct. 13, 1988], the Secretary of Health and Human Services shall issue a notice of proposed rulemaking with respect to the standards required by the amendment made by subsection (a) [amending this section], and, after allowing not less than 60 days for public comment, shall issue final regulations not later than the first day of the 10th month to begin after such date of enactment."

Implementation of Performance Standards for State Paternity Establishment Programs

Pub. L. 100–485, title I, § 111(f)(3), Oct. 13, 1988, 102 Stat. 2350, provided that: "The Secretary of Health and Human Services shall collect the data necessary to implement the requirements of section 452(g) of the Social Security Act [42 U.S.C. 652(g)] (as added by subsection (a) of this section) and may, in carrying out the requirement of determining a State's paternity establishment percentage for the fiscal year 1988, compute such percentage on the basis of data collected with respect to the last quarter of such fiscal year (or, if such data are not available, the first quarter of the fiscal year 1989) if the Secretary determines that data for the full year are not available."

Requests for Child Support Assistance; Advisory Committee; Promulgation of Regulations

Pub. L. 100–485, title I, § 121(b), Oct. 13, 1988, 102 Stat. 2351, provided that:

"(1) Not later than 60 days after the date of the enactment of this Act [Oct. 13, 1988], the Secretary of Health and Human Services shall establish an advisory committee. The committee shall include representatives of organizations representing State governors, State welfare administrators, and State directors of programs under part D of title IV of the Social Security Act [42 U.S.C. 651 et seq.]. The Secretary shall consult with the advisory committee before issuing any regulations with respect to the standards required by the amendment made by subsection (a) [amending this section] (including regulations regarding what constitutes an adequate response on the part of a State to the request of an individual, State, or jurisdiction).

"(2) Not later than 180 days after the date of the enactment of this Act, the Secretary of Health and Human Services shall issue a notice of proposed rulemaking with respect to the standards required by the amendment made by subsection (a), and, after allowing not less than 60 days for public comment, shall issue final regulations not later than the first day of the 10th month beginning after such date of enactment."

Supplemental Report To Be Submitted to Congress Not Later Than June 30, 1977

Pub. L. 95–30, title V, § 504(c), May 23, 1977, 91 Stat. 164, directed the Secretary of Health, Education, and Welfare to submit to Congress, not later than June 30, 1977, a special supplementary report with respect to activities undertaken pursuant to part D of title IV of the Social Security Act (42 U.S.C. 651 et seq.).

§ 653. Federal parent locator service.

(a) Establishment; purpose

(1) The Secretary shall establish and conduct a Federal Parent Locator Service, under the direction of the designee of the Secretary referred to in section 652(a) of this title, which shall be used for the purposes specified in paragraphs (2) and (3).

(2) For the purpose of establishing parentage or establishing, setting the amount of, modifying, or enforcing child support obligations, the Federal Parent Locator Service shall obtain and transmit to any authorized person specified in subsection (c) of this section—

(A) information on, or facilitating the discovery of, the location of any individual—

(i) who is under an obligation to pay child support;

(ii) against whom such an obligation is sought;

(iii) to whom such an obligation is owed; or

(iv) who has or may have parental rights with respect to a child,

including the individual's social security number (or numbers), most recent address, and the name, address, and employer identification number of the individual's employer;

(B) information on the individual's wages (or other income) from, and benefits of, employment (including rights to or enrollment in group health care coverage); and

(C) information on the type, status, location, and amount of any assets of, or debts owed by or to, any such individual.

(3) For the purpose of enforcing any Federal or State law with respect to the unlawful taking or restraint of a child, or making or enforcing a child custody or visitation determination, as defined in section 663(d)(1) of this title, the Federal Parent Locator Service shall be used to obtain and transmit the information specified in section 663(c) of this title to the authorized persons specified in section 663(d)(2) of this title.

(b) Disclosure of information to authorized persons

(1) Upon request, filed in accordance with subsection (d) of this section, of any authorized person, as defined in subsection (c) of this section for the information described in subsection (a)(2) of this section, or of any authorized person, as defined in section 663(d)(2) of this title for the information described in section 663(c) of this title, the Secretary shall, notwithstanding any other provision of law, provide through the Federal Parent Locator Service such information to such person, if such information—

(A) is contained in any files or records maintained by the Secretary or by the Department of Health and Human Services; or

(B) is not contained in such files or records, but can be obtained by the Secretary, under the authority conferred by subsection (e) of this section, from any other department, agency, or instrumentality of the United States or of any State,

and is not prohibited from disclosure under paragraph (2).

(2) No information shall be disclosed to any person if the disclosure of such information would contravene the national policy or security interests of the United States or the confidentiality of census data. The Secretary shall give priority to requests made by any authorized person described in subsection (c)(1) of this section. No information shall be disclosed to any person if the State has notified the Secretary that the State has reasonable evidence of domestic violence or child abuse and the disclosure of such information could be harmful to the custodial parent or the child of such parent, provided that—

(A) in response to a request from an authorized person (as defined in subsection (c) of this section and section 663(d)(2) of this title), the Secretary shall advise the authorized person that the Secretary has been notified that there is reasonable evidence of domestic violence or child abuse and that information can only be disclosed to a court or an agent of a court pursuant to subparagraph (B); and

(B) information may be disclosed to a court or an agent of a court described in subsection (c)(2) of this section or section 663(d)(2)(B) of this title, if—

(i) upon receipt of information from the Secretary, the court determines whether disclosure to any other person of that information could be harmful to the parent or the child; and

(ii) if the court determines that disclosure of such information to any other person could be harmful, the court and its agents shall not make any such disclosure.

(3) Information received or transmitted pursuant to this section shall be subject to the safeguard provisions contained in section 654(26) of this title.

(c) "Authorized person" defined

As used in subsection (a) of this section, the term "authorized person" means—

(1) any agent or attorney of any State or Indian tribe or tribal organization (as defined in subsections (e) and (l) of section 450b of title 25), having in effect a plan approved under this part, who has the duty or authority under such plans to seek to recover any amounts owed as child and spousal support (including, when authorized under the State plan, any official of a political subdivision);

(2) the court which has authority to issue an order or to serve as the initiating court in an action to seek an order against a noncustodial parent for the support and maintenance of a child, or any agent of such court;

(3) the resident parent, legal guardian, attorney, or agent of a child (other than a child receiving assistance under a State program funded under part A of this subchapter) (as determined by regulations prescribed by the Secretary) without regard to the existence of a court order against a noncustodial parent who has a duty to support and maintain any such child;

(4) a State agency that is administering a program operated under a State plan under subpart 1 of part B of this subchapter, or a State plan approved under subpart 2 of part B of this subchapter or under part E of this subchapter; and

(5) an entity designated as a Central Authority for child support enforcement in a foreign reciprocating country or a foreign treaty country for purposes specified in section 659a(c)(2) of this title.

(d) Form and manner of request for information

A request for information under this section shall be filed in such manner and form as the Secretary shall by regulation prescribe and shall be accompanied or supported by such documents as the Secretary may determine to be necessary.

(e) Compliance with request; search of files and records by head of any department, etc., of United States; transmittal of information to Secretary; reimbursement for cost of search; fees

(1) Whenever the Secretary receives a request submitted under subsection (b) of this section which he is reasonably satisfied meets the criteria established by subsections (a), (b), and (c) of this section, he shall promptly undertake to provide the information requested from the files and records maintained by any of the departments, agencies, or instrumentalities of the United States or of any State.

(2) Notwithstanding any other provision of law, whenever the individual who is the head of any department, agency, or instrumentality of the United States receives a request from the Secretary for information authorized to be provided by the Secretary under this section, such individual shall promptly cause a search to be made of the files and records maintained by such department, agency, or instrumentality with a view to determining whether the information requested is contained in any such files or records. If such search discloses the information requested, such individual shall immediately transmit such information to the Secretary, except that if any information is obtained the disclosure of which would contravene national policy or security interests of the United States or the confidentiality of census data,

such information shall not be transmitted and such individual shall immediately notify the Secretary. If such search fails to disclose the information requested, such individual shall immediately so notify the Secretary. The costs incurred by any such department, agency, or instrumentality of the United States or of any State in providing such information to the Secretary shall be reimbursed by him in an amount which the Secretary determines to be reasonable payment for the information exchange (which amount shall not include payment for the costs of obtaining, compiling, or maintaining the information). Whenever such services are furnished to an individual specified in subsection (c)(3) of this section, a fee shall be charged such individual. The fee so charged shall be used to reimburse the Secretary or his delegate for the expense of providing such services.

(3) The Secretary of Labor shall enter into an agreement with the Secretary to provide prompt access for the Secretary (in accordance with this subsection) to the wage and unemployment compensation claims information and data maintained by or for the Department of Labor or State employment security agencies.

(f) Arrangements and cooperation with State and tribal agencies

The Secretary, in carrying out his duties and functions under this section, shall enter into arrangements with State and tribal agencies administering State and tribal plans approved under this part for such State and tribal agencies to accept from resident parents, legal guardians, or agents of a child described in subsection (c)(3) of this section and to transmit to the Secretary requests for information with regard to the whereabouts of noncustodial parents and otherwise to cooperate with the Secretary in carrying out the purposes of this section.

(g) Reimbursement for reports by State agencies

The Secretary may reimburse Federal and State agencies for the costs incurred by such entities in furnishing information requested by the Secretary under this section in an amount which the Secretary determines to be reasonable payment for the information exchange (which amount shall not include payment for the costs of obtaining, compiling, or maintaining the information).

(h) Federal Case Registry of Child Support Orders

(1) In general

Not later than October 1, 1998, in order to assist States in administering programs under State plans approved under this part and programs funded under part A of this subchapter, and for the other purposes specified in this section, the Secretary shall establish and maintain in the Federal Parent Locator Service an automated registry (which shall be known as the "Federal Case Registry of Child Support Orders"), which shall contain abstracts of support orders and other information described in paragraph (2) with respect to each case and order in each State case registry maintained pursuant to section 654a(e) of this title, as furnished (and regularly updated), pursuant to section 654a(f) of this title, by State agencies administering programs under this part.

(2) Case and order information

The information referred to in paragraph (1) with respect to a case or an order shall be such information as the Secretary may specify in regulations (including the names, social security numbers or other uniform identification numbers, and State case identification numbers) to identify the individuals who owe or are owed support (or with respect to or on behalf of whom support obligations are sought to be established), and the State or States which have the case or order. Beginning not later than October 1, 1999, the information referred to in paragraph (1) shall include the names and social security numbers of the children of such individuals.

(3) Administration of Federal tax laws

The Secretary of the Treasury shall have access to the information described in paragraph (2) for the purpose of administering those sections of the Internal

Revenue Code of 1986 which grant tax benefits based on support or residence of children.

(i) National Directory of New Hires

(1) In general

In order to assist States in administering programs under State plans approved under this part and programs funded under part A of this subchapter, and for the other purposes specified in this section, the Secretary shall, not later than October 1, 1997, establish and maintain in the Federal Parent Locator Service an automated directory to be known as the National Directory of New Hires, which shall contain the information supplied pursuant to section 653a(g)(2) of this title.

(2) Data entry and deletion requirements

(A) In general

Information provided pursuant to section 653a(g)(2) of this title shall be entered into the data base maintained by the National Directory of New Hires within two business days after receipt, and shall be deleted from the data base 24 months after the date of entry.

(B) 12-month limit on access to wage and unemployment compensation information

The Secretary shall not have access for child support enforcement purposes to information in the National Directory of New Hires that is provided pursuant to section 653a(g)(2)(B) of this title, if 12 months has elapsed since the date the information is so provided and there has not been a match resulting from the use of such information in any information comparison under this subsection.

(C) Retention of data for research purposes

Notwithstanding subparagraphs (A) and (B), the Secretary may retain such samples of data entered in the National Directory of New Hires as the Secretary may find necessary to assist in carrying out subsection (j)(5) of this section.

(3) Administration of Federal tax laws

The Secretary of the Treasury shall have access to the information in the National Directory of New Hires for purposes of administering section 32 of the Internal Revenue Code of 1986, or the advance payment of the earned income tax credit under section 3507 of such Code, and verifying a claim with respect to employment in a tax return.

(4) List of multistate employers

The Secretary shall maintain within the National Directory of New Hires a list of multistate employers that report information regarding newly hired employees pursuant to section 653a(b)(1)(B) of this title, and the State which each such employer has designated to receive such information.

(j) Information comparisons and other disclosures

(1) Verification by Social Security Administration

(A) In general

The Secretary shall transmit information on individuals and employers maintained under this section to the Social Security Administration to the extent necessary for verification in accordance with subparagraph (B).

(B) Verification by SSA

The Social Security Administration shall verify the accuracy of, correct, or supply to the extent possible, and report to the Secretary, the following information supplied by the Secretary pursuant to subparagraph (A):

    (i) The name, social security number, and birth date of each such individual.

    (ii) The employer identification number of each such employer.

(2) Information comparisons

For the purpose of locating individuals in a paternity establishment case or a case involving the establishment, modification, or enforcement of a support order, the Secretary shall—

(A) compare information in the National Directory of New Hires against information in the support case abstracts in the Federal Case Registry of Child Support Orders not less often than every 2 business days; and

(B) within 2 business days after such a comparison reveals a match with respect to an individual, report the information to the State agency responsible for the case.

(3) Information comparisons and disclosures of information in all registries for subchapter IV program purposes

To the extent and with the frequency that the Secretary determines to be effective in assisting States to carry out their responsibilities under programs operated under this part, part B, or part E and programs funded under part A of this subchapter, the Secretary shall—

(A) compare the information in each component of the Federal Parent Locator Service maintained under this section against the information in each other such component (other than the comparison required by paragraph (2)), and report instances in which such a comparison reveals a match with respect to an individual to State agencies operating such programs; and

(B) disclose information in such components to such State agencies.

(4) Provision of new hire information to the Social Security Administration

The National Directory of New Hires shall provide the Commissioner of Social Security with all information in the National Directory.

(5) Research

The Secretary may provide access to data in each component of the Federal Parent Locator Service maintained under this section and to information reported by employers pursuant to section 653a(b) of this title for research purposes found by the Secretary to be likely to contribute to achieving the purposes of part A of this subchapter or this part, but without personal identifiers.

(6) Information comparisons and disclosure for enforcement of obligations on Higher Education Act loans and grants

(A) Furnishing of information by the Secretary of Education

The Secretary of Education shall furnish to the Secretary, on a quarterly basis or at such less frequent intervals as may be determined by the Secretary of Education, information in the custody of the Secretary of Education for comparison with information in the National Directory of New Hires, in order to obtain the information in such directory with respect to individuals who—

(i) are borrowers of loans made under title IV of the Higher Education Act of 1965 [20 U.S.C. 1070 et seq., 42 U.S.C. 2751 et seq.] that are in default; or

(ii) owe an obligation to refund an overpayment of a grant awarded under such title.

(B) Requirement to seek minimum information necessary

The Secretary of Education shall seek information pursuant to this section only to the extent essential to improving collection of the debt described in subparagraph (A).

(C) **Duties of the Secretary**

(i) **Information comparison; disclosure to the Secretary of Education**

The Secretary, in cooperation with the Secretary of Education, shall compare information in the National Directory of New Hires with information in the custody of the Secretary of Education, and disclose information in that Directory to the Secretary of Education, in accordance with this paragraph, for the purposes specified in this paragraph.

(ii) **Condition on disclosure**

The Secretary shall make disclosures in accordance with clause (i) only to the extent that the Secretary determines that such disclosures do not interfere with the effective operation of the program under this part. Support collection under section 666(b) of this title shall be given priority over collection of any defaulted student loan or grant overpayment against the same income.

(D) **Use of information by the Secretary of Education**

The Secretary of Education may use information resulting from a data match pursuant to this paragraph only—

(i) for the purpose of collection of the debt described in subparagraph (A) owed by an individual whose annualized wage level (determined by taking into consideration information from the National Directory of New Hires) exceeds $16,000; and

(ii) after removal of personal identifiers, to conduct analyses of student loan defaults.

(E) **Disclosure of information by the Secretary of Education**

(i) **Disclosures permitted**

The Secretary of Education may disclose information resulting from a data match pursuant to this paragraph only to—

(I) a guaranty agency holding a loan made under part B of title IV of the Higher Education Act of 1965 [20 U.S.C. 1071 et seq.] on which the individual is obligated;

(II) a contractor or agent of the guaranty agency described in subclause (I);

(III) a contractor or agent of the Secretary; and

(IV) the Attorney General.

(ii) **Purpose of disclosure**

The Secretary of Education may make a disclosure under clause (i) only for the purpose of collection of the debts owed on defaulted student loans, or overpayments of grants, made under title IV of the Higher Education Act of 1965 [20 U.S.C. 1070 et seq., 42 U.S.C. 2751 et seq.].

(iii) **Restriction on redisclosure**

An entity to which information is disclosed under clause (i) may use or disclose such information only as needed for the purpose of collecting on defaulted student loans, or overpayments of grants, made under title IV of the Higher Education Act of 1965.

(F) **Reimbursement of HHS costs**

The Secretary of Education shall reimburse the Secretary, in accordance with subsection (k)(3) of this section, for the additional costs incurred by the Secretary in furnishing the information requested under this subparagraph.

(7) Information comparisons for housing assistance programs

(A) Furnishing of information by HUD

Subject to subparagraph (G), the Secretary of Housing and Urban Development shall furnish to the Secretary, on such periodic basis as determined by the Secretary of Housing and Urban Development in consultation with the Secretary, information in the custody of the Secretary of Housing and Urban Development for comparison with information in the National Directory of New Hires, in order to obtain information in such Directory with respect to individuals who are participating in any program under—

(i) the United States Housing Act of 1937 (42 U.S.C. 1437 et seq.);

(ii) section 1701q of title 12;

(iii) section 1715l(d)(3), 1715l(d)(5), or 1715z–1 of title 12;

(iv) section 8013 of this title; or

(v) section 1701s of title 12.

(B) Requirement to seek minimum information

The Secretary of Housing and Urban Development shall seek information pursuant to this section only to the extent necessary to verify the employment and income of individuals described in subparagraph (A).

(C) Duties of the Secretary

(i) Information disclosure

The Secretary, in cooperation with the Secretary of Housing and Urban Development, shall compare information in the National Directory of New Hires with information provided by the Secretary of Housing and Urban Development with respect to individuals described in subparagraph (A), and shall disclose information in such Directory regarding such individuals to the Secretary of Housing and Urban Development, in accordance with this paragraph, for the purposes specified in this paragraph.

(ii) Condition on disclosure

The Secretary shall make disclosures in accordance with clause (i) only to the extent that the Secretary determines that such disclosures do not interfere with the effective operation of the program under this part.

(D) Use of information by HUD

The Secretary of Housing and Urban Development may use information resulting from a data match pursuant to this paragraph only—

(i) for the purpose of verifying the employment and income of individuals described in subparagraph (A); and

(ii) after removal of personal identifiers, to conduct analyses of the employment and income reporting of individuals described in subparagraph (A).

(E) Disclosure of information by HUD

(i) Purpose of disclosure

The Secretary of Housing and Urban Development may make a disclosure under this subparagraph only for the purpose of verifying the employment and income of individuals described in subparagraph (A).

(ii) Disclosures permitted

Subject to clause (iii), the Secretary of Housing and Urban Development may disclose information resulting from a data match pursuant to this paragraph only to a public housing agency, the Inspector General of the Department of Housing and Urban Development, and the Attorney General in connection with the administration of a program described in subparagraph (A). Information obtained by the Secretary of Housing and Urban Development pursuant to this paragraph shall not be made available under section 552 of title 5.

(iii) **Conditions on disclosure**

Disclosures under this paragraph shall be—

(I) made in accordance with data security and control policies established by the Secretary of Housing and Urban Development and approved by the Secretary;

(II) subject to audit in a manner satisfactory to the Secretary; and

(III) subject to the sanctions under subsection (l)(2) of this section.

(iv) **Additional disclosures**

(I) **Determination by Secretaries**

The Secretary of Housing and Urban Development and the Secretary shall determine whether to permit disclosure of information under this paragraph to persons or entities described in subclause (II), based on an evaluation made by the Secretary of Housing and Urban Development (in consultation with and approved by the Secretary), of the costs and benefits of disclosures made under clause (ii) and the adequacy of measures used to safeguard the security and confidentiality of information so disclosed.

(II) **Permitted persons or entities**

If the Secretary of Housing and Urban Development and the Secretary determine pursuant to subclause (I) that disclosures to additional persons or entities shall be permitted, information under this paragraph may be disclosed by the Secretary of Housing and Urban Development to a private owner, a management agent, and a contract administrator in connection with the administration of a program described in subparagraph (A), subject to the conditions in clause (iii) and such additional conditions as agreed to by the Secretaries.

(v) **Restrictions on redisclosure**

A person or entity to which information is disclosed under this subparagraph may use or disclose such information only as needed for verifying the employment and income of individuals described in subparagraph (A), subject to the conditions in clause (iii) and such additional conditions as agreed to by the Secretaries.

(F) **Reimbursement of HHS costs**

The Secretary of Housing and Urban Development shall reimburse the Secretary, in accordance with subsection (k)(3) of this section, for the costs incurred by the Secretary in furnishing the information requested under this paragraph.

(G) **Consent**

The Secretary of Housing and Urban Development shall not seek, use, or disclose information under this paragraph relating to an individual without the prior written consent of such individual (or of a person legally authorized to consent on behalf of such individual).

(8) **Information comparisons and disclosure to assist in administration of unemployment compensation programs**

(A) **In general**

If, for purposes of administering an unemployment compensation program under Federal or State law, a State agency responsible for the administration of such program transmits to the Secretary the names and social security account numbers of individuals, the Secretary shall disclose to such State agency information on such individuals and their employers maintained in the National Directory of New Hires, subject to this paragraph.

(B) Condition on disclosure by the Secretary

The Secretary shall make a disclosure under subparagraph (A) only to the extent that the Secretary determines that the disclosure would not interfere with the effective operation of the program under this part.

(C) Use and disclosure of information by State agencies

(i) In general

A State agency may not use or disclose information provided under this paragraph except for purposes of administering a program referred to in subparagraph (A).

(ii) Information security

The State agency shall have in effect data security and control policies that the Secretary finds adequate to ensure the security of information obtained under this paragraph and to ensure that access to such information is restricted to authorized persons for purposes of authorized uses and disclosures.

(iii) Penalty for misuse of information

An officer or employee of the State agency who fails to comply with this subparagraph shall be subject to the sanctions under subsection (l)(2) of this section to the same extent as if such officer or employee was an officer or employee of the United States.

(D) Procedural requirements

State agencies requesting information under this paragraph shall adhere to uniform procedures established by the Secretary governing information requests and data matching under this paragraph.

(E) Reimbursement of costs

The State agency shall reimburse the Secretary, in accordance with subsection (k)(3) of this section, for the costs incurred by the Secretary in furnishing the information requested under this paragraph.

(9) Information comparisons and disclosure to assist in Federal debt collection

(A) Furnishing of information by the Secretary of the Treasury

The Secretary of the Treasury shall furnish to the Secretary, on such periodic basis as determined by the Secretary of the Treasury in consultation with the Secretary, information in the custody of the Secretary of the Treasury for comparison with information in the National Directory of New Hires, in order to obtain information in such Directory with respect to persons—

(i) who owe delinquent nontax debt to the United States; and

(ii) whose debt has been referred to the Secretary of the Treasury in accordance with section 3711(g) of title 31.

(B) Requirement to seek minimum information

The Secretary of the Treasury shall seek information pursuant to this section only to the extent necessary to improve collection of the debt described in subparagraph (A).

(C) Duties of the Secretary

(i) Information disclosure

The Secretary, in cooperation with the Secretary of the Treasury, shall compare information in the National Directory of New Hires with information provided by the Secretary of the Treasury with respect to persons described in subparagraph (A) and shall disclose information in such Directory regarding such persons to the Secretary of the Treasury in accordance with this paragraph, for the purposes specified in this paragraph. Such comparison of information shall not be considered a matching program as defined in section 552a of title 5.

(ii) Condition on disclosure

The Secretary shall make disclosures in accordance with clause (i) only to the extent that the Secretary determines that such disclosures do not interfere with the effective operation of the program under this part. Support collection under section 666(b) of this title shall be given priority over collection of any delinquent Federal nontax debt against the same income.

(D) Use of information by the Secretary of the Treasury

The Secretary of the Treasury may use information provided under this paragraph only for purposes of collecting the debt described in subparagraph (A).

(E) Disclosure of information by the Secretary of the Treasury

(i) Purpose of disclosure

The Secretary of the Treasury may make a disclosure under this subparagraph only for purposes of collecting the debt described in subparagraph (A).

(ii) Disclosures permitted

Subject to clauses (iii) and (iv), the Secretary of the Treasury may disclose information resulting from a data match pursuant to this paragraph only to the Attorney General in connection with collecting the debt described in subparagraph (A).

(iii) Conditions on disclosure

Disclosures under this subparagraph shall be—

(I) made in accordance with data security and control policies established by the Secretary of the Treasury and approved by the Secretary;

(II) subject to audit in a manner satisfactory to the Secretary; and

(III) subject to the sanctions under subsection (l)(2) of this section.

(iv) Additional disclosures

(I) Determination by Secretaries

The Secretary of the Treasury and the Secretary shall determine whether to permit disclosure of information under this paragraph to persons or entities described in subclause (II), based on an evaluation made by the Secretary of the Treasury (in consultation with and approved by the Secretary), of the costs and benefits of such disclosures and the adequacy of measures used to safeguard the security and confidentiality of information so disclosed.

(II) Permitted persons or entities

If the Secretary of the Treasury and the Secretary determine pursuant to subclause (I) that disclosures to additional persons or entities shall be permitted, information under this paragraph may be disclosed by the Secretary of the Treasury, in connection with collecting the debt described in subparagraph (A), to a contractor or agent of either Secretary and to the Federal agency that referred such debt to the Secretary of the Treasury for collection, subject to the conditions in clause (iii) and such additional conditions as agreed to by the Secretaries.

(v) Restrictions on redisclosure

A person or entity to which information is disclosed under this subparagraph may use or disclose such information only as needed for collecting the debt described in subparagraph (A), subject to the conditions in clause (iii) and such additional conditions as agreed to by the Secretaries.

(F) Reimbursement of HHS costs

The Secretary of the Treasury shall reimburse the Secretary, in accordance with subsection (k)(3) of this section, for the costs incurred by the Secretary in furnishing the information requested under this paragraph. Any such costs paid by the Secretary of the Treasury shall be considered costs of implementing section 3711(g) of title 31 in accordance with section 3711(g)(6) of title 31 and may be paid from the account established pursuant to section 3711(g)(7) of title 31.

(10) Information comparisons and disclosure to assist in administration of supplemental nutrition assistance program benefits

(A) In general

If, for purposes of administering a supplemental nutrition assistance program under the Food and Nutrition Act of 2008 [7 U.S.C. 2011 et seq.], a State agency responsible for the administration of the program transmits to the Secretary the names and social security account numbers of individuals, the Secretary shall disclose to the State agency information on the individuals and their employers maintained in the National Directory of New Hires, subject to this paragraph.

(B) Condition on disclosure by the Secretary

The Secretary shall make a disclosure under subparagraph (A) only to the extent that the Secretary determines that the disclosure would not interfere with the effective operation of the program under this part.

(C) Use and disclosure of information by State agencies

(i) In general

A State agency may not use or disclose information provided under this paragraph except for purposes of administering a program referred to in subparagraph (A).

(ii) Information security

The State agency shall have in effect data security and control policies that the Secretary finds adequate to ensure the security of information obtained under this paragraph and to ensure that access to such information is restricted to authorized persons for purposes of authorized uses and disclosures.

(iii) Penalty for misuse of information

An officer or employee of the State agency who fails to comply with this subparagraph shall be subject to the sanctions under subsection (l)(2) to the same extent as if the officer or employee were an officer or employee of the United States.

(D) Procedural requirements

State agencies requesting information under this paragraph shall adhere to uniform procedures established by the Secretary governing information requests and data matching under this paragraph.

(E) Reimbursement of costs

The State agency shall reimburse the Secretary, in accordance with subsection (k)(3), for the costs incurred by the Secretary in furnishing the information requested under this paragraph.

(11) Information comparisons and disclosures to assist in administration of certain veterans benefits

(A) Furnishing of information by Secretary of Veterans Affairs

Subject to the provisions of this paragraph, the Secretary of Veterans Affairs shall furnish to the Secretary, on such periodic basis as determined by the Secretary of Veterans Affairs in consultation with the Secretary, information in the custody of the Secretary of Veterans Affairs for comparison with information in the National Directory of New Hires, in order to obtain information in such Directory with respect to individuals who are applying for or receiving—

(i) needs-based pension benefits provided under chapter 15 of title 38 or under any other law administered by the Secretary of Veterans Affairs;

(ii) parents' dependency and indemnity compensation provided under section 1315 of title 38;

(iii) health care services furnished under subsections (a)(2)(G), (a)(3), or (b) of section 1710 of title 38; or

(iv) compensation paid under chapter 11 of title 38 at the 100 percent rate based solely on unemployability and without regard to the fact that the disability or disabilities are not rated as 100 percent disabling under the rating schedule.

(B) Requirement to seek minimum information

The Secretary of Veterans Affairs shall seek information pursuant to this paragraph only to the extent necessary to verify the employment and income of individuals described in subparagraph (A).

(C) Duties of the Secretary

(i) Information disclosure

The Secretary, in cooperation with the Secretary of Veterans Affairs, shall compare information in the National Directory of New Hires with information provided by the Secretary of Veterans Affairs with respect to individuals described in subparagraph (A), and shall disclose information in such Directory regarding such individuals to the Secretary of Veterans Affairs, in accordance with this paragraph, for the purposes specified in this paragraph.

(ii) Condition on disclosure

The Secretary shall make disclosures in accordance with clause (i) only to the extent that the Secretary determines that such disclosures do not interfere with the effective operation of the program under this part.

(D) Use of information by Secretary of Veterans Affairs

The Secretary of Veterans Affairs may use information resulting from a data match pursuant to this paragraph only—

(i) for the purposes specified in subparagraph (B); and

(ii) after removal of personal identifiers, to conduct analyses of the employment and income reporting of individuals described in subparagraph (A).

(E) Reimbursement of HHS costs

The Secretary of Veterans Affairs shall reimburse the Secretary, in accordance with subsection (k)(3), for the costs incurred by the Secretary in furnishing the information requested under this paragraph.

(F) Consent

The Secretary of Veterans Affairs shall not seek, use, or disclose information under this paragraph relating to an individual without the prior written consent of such individual (or of a person legally authorized to consent on behalf of such individual).

(G) Expiration of authority

The authority under this paragraph shall be in effect as follows:

(i) During the period beginning on December 26, 2007, and ending on November 18, 2011.

(ii) During the period beginning on September 30, 2013, and ending 180 days after that date.

(k) Fees

(1) For SSA verification

The Secretary shall reimburse the Commissioner of Social Security, at a rate negotiated between the Secretary and the Commissioner, for the costs incurred by the Commissioner in performing the verification services described in subsection (j) of this section.

(2) For information from State directories of new hires

The Secretary shall reimburse costs incurred by State directories of new hires in furnishing information as required by section 653a(g)(2) of this title, at rates which the Secretary determines to be reasonable (which rates shall not include payment for the costs of obtaining, compiling, or maintaining such information).

(3) For information furnished to State and Federal agencies

A State or Federal agency that receives information from the Secretary pursuant to this section or section 652(m) of this title shall reimburse the Secretary for costs incurred by the Secretary in furnishing the information, at rates which the Secretary determines to be reasonable (which rates shall include payment for the costs of obtaining, verifying, maintaining, and comparing the information).

(l) Restriction on disclosure and use

(1) In general

Information in the Federal Parent Locator Service, and information resulting from comparisons using such information, shall not be used or disclosed except as expressly provided in this section, subject to section 6103 of the Internal Revenue Code of 1986.

(2) Penalty for misuse of information in the National Directory of New Hires

The Secretary shall require the imposition of an administrative penalty (up to and including dismissal from employment), and a fine of $1,000, for each act of unauthorized access to, disclosure of, or use of, information in the National Directory of New Hires established under subsection (i) of this section by any officer or employee of the United States or any other person who knowingly and willfully violates this paragraph.

(m) Information integrity and security

The Secretary shall establish and implement safeguards with respect to the entities established under this section designed to—

(1) ensure the accuracy and completeness of information in the Federal Parent Locator Service; and

(2) restrict access to confidential information in the Federal Parent Locator Service to authorized persons, and restrict use of such information to authorized purposes.

(n) Federal Government reporting

Each department, agency, and instrumentality of the United States shall on a quarterly basis report to the Federal Parent Locator Service the name and social security number of each employee and the wages paid to the employee during the previous quarter, except that such a report shall not be filed with respect to an employee of a department, agency, or instrumentality performing intelligence or counterintelligence functions, if the head of such department, agency, or instrumentality has determined that filing such a report could endanger the safety of the employee or compromise an ongoing investigation or intelligence mission.

(o) Use of set-aside funds

Out of any money in the Treasury of the United States not otherwise appropriated, there is hereby appropriated to the Secretary for each fiscal year an amount equal to 2 percent of the total amount paid to the Federal Government pursuant to a plan approved under this part during the immediately preceding fiscal year (as determined on the basis of the most recent reliable data available to the Secretary as of the end of the third calendar quarter following the end of such preceding fiscal year) or the amount appropriated under this paragraph 1 for fiscal year 2002, whichever is greater, which shall be available for use by the Secretary, either directly or through grants, contracts, or interagency agreements, for operation of the Federal Parent Locator Service under this section, to the extent such costs are not recovered through user fees. Amounts appropriated under this subsection shall remain available until expended.

(p) "Support order" defined

As used in this part, the term "support order" means a judgment, decree, or order, whether temporary, final, or subject to modification, issued by a court or an administrative agency of competent jurisdiction, for the support and maintenance of a child, including a child who has attained the age of majority under the law of the issuing State, or of the parent with whom the child is living, which provides for monetary support, health care, arrearages, or reimbursement, and which may include related costs and fees, interest and penalties, income withholding, attorneys' fees, and other relief.

(Aug. 14, 1935, ch. 531, title IV, § 453, as added Pub. L. 93–647, § 101(a), Jan. 4, 1975, 88 Stat. 2353; amended Pub. L. 97–35, title XXIII, § 2332(c), Aug. 13, 1981, 95 Stat. 862; Pub. L. 98–369, div. B, title VI, § 2663(c)(13), (j)(2)(B)(ix), July 18, 1984, 98 Stat. 1166, 1170; Pub. L. 98–378, §§ 17, 19(a), Aug. 16, 1984, 98 Stat. 1321, 1322; Pub. L. 100–485, title I, § 124(a), Oct. 13, 1988, 102 Stat. 2353; Pub. L. 104–193, title I, § 108(c)(10), title III, §§ 316(a)–(f), 345(b), 366, 395(d)(1)(C), (2)(A), Aug. 22, 1996, 110 Stat. 2166, 2214-2216, 2237, 2250, 2259; Pub. L. 104–208, div. A, title I, § 101(e) [title II, § 215], Sept. 30, 1996, 110 Stat. 3009–233, 3009-255; Pub. L. 105–33, title V, §§ 5534(a), 5535, 5541(b), 5543, 5553, 5556(c), Aug. 5, 1997, 111 Stat. 627, 629-631, 636, 637; Pub. L. 105–34, title X, § 1090(a)(2), Aug. 5, 1997, 111 Stat. 961; Pub. L. 105–89, title I, § 105, Nov. 19, 1997, 111 Stat. 2120; Pub. L. 105–200, title IV, §§ 402(a), (b), 410(d), July 16, 1998, 112 Stat. 668, 669, 673; Pub. L. 106–113, div. B, § 1000(a)(5) [title III, § 303(a), (b)], Nov. 29, 1999, 113 Stat. 1536, 1501A-304, 1501A-306; Pub. L. 108–199, div. G, title II, § 217(a), Jan. 23, 2004, 118 Stat. 394; Pub. L. 108–295, § 3, Aug. 9, 2004, 118 Stat. 1091; Pub. L. 108–447, div. H, title VI, § 643, Dec. 8, 2004, 118 Stat. 3283; Pub. L. 109–171, title VII, §§ 7305, 7306(b), Feb. 8, 2006, 120 Stat. 145, 146; Pub. L. 109–250, § 2, July 27, 2006, 120 Stat. 652; Pub. L. 110–157, title III, § 301(a), Dec. 26, 2007, 121 Stat. 1833; Pub. L. 110–234, title IV, § 4002(b)(1)(A), (B), (2)(V), May 22, 2008, 122 Stat. 1095–1097; Pub. L. 110–246, § 4(a), title IV, § 4002(b)(1)(A), (B), (2)(V), June 18, 2008, 122 Stat. 1664, 1857, 1858; Pub. L. 110–351, title I, § 105, Oct. 7, 2008, 122 Stat. 3957; Pub. L. 112–37, § 17(b), Oct. 5, 2011, 125 Stat. 398; Pub. L. 113–37, § 3(a), Sept. 30, 2013, 127 Stat. 525; Pub. L. 113–79, title IV, § 4030(p), Feb. 7, 2014, 128 Stat. 815; Pub. L. 113–183, title III, §§ 301(a)(2), (b), 302(a), (c), Sept. 29, 2014, 128 Stat. 1943, 1945, 1946.)

§ 654. State plan for child and spousal support.

A State plan for child and spousal support must—

(1) provide that it shall be in effect in all political subdivisions of the State;

(2) provide for financial participation by the State;

(3) provide for the establishment or designation of a single and separate organizational unit, which meets such staffing and organizational requirements as the Secretary may by regulation prescribe, within the State to administer the plan;

(4) provide that the State will—

(A) provide services relating to the establishment of paternity or the establishment, modification, or enforcement of child support obligations, as appropriate, under the plan with respect to—

(i) each child for whom (I) assistance is provided under the State program funded under part A of this subchapter, (II) benefits or services for foster care maintenance are provided under the State program funded under part E of this subchapter, (III) medical assistance is provided under the State plan approved under subchapter XIX of this chapter, or (IV) cooperation is required pursuant to section 2015(l)(1) of title 7, unless, in accordance with paragraph (29), good cause or other exceptions exist;

(ii) any other child, if an individual applies for such services with respect to the child (except that, if the individual applying for the services resides in a foreign reciprocating country or foreign treaty country, the State may opt to require the individual to request the services through the Central Authority for child support enforcement in the foreign reciprocating country or the foreign treaty country, and if the individual resides in a foreign country that is not a foreign reciprocating country or a foreign treaty country, a State may accept or reject the application); and

(B) enforce any support obligation established with respect to—

(i) a child with respect to whom the State provides services under the plan; or

(ii) the custodial parent of such a child;

(5) provide that (A) in any case in which support payments are collected for an individual with respect to whom an assignment pursuant to section 608(a)(3) of this title is effective, such payments shall be made to the State for distribution pursuant to section 657 of this title and shall not be paid directly to the family, and the individual will be notified on a monthly basis (or on a quarterly basis for so long as the Secretary determines with respect to a State that requiring such notice on a monthly basis would impose an unreasonable administrative burden) of the amount of the support payments collected, and (B) in any case in which support payments are collected for an individual pursuant to the assignment made under section 1396k of this title, such payments shall be made to the State for distribution pursuant to section 1396k of this title, except that this clause shall not apply to such payments for any month after the month in which the individual ceases to be eligible for medical assistance;

(6) provide that—

(A) services under the plan shall be made available to residents of other States on the same terms as to residents of the State submitting the plan;

(B)(i) an application fee for furnishing such services shall be imposed on an individual, other than an individual receiving assistance under a State program funded under part A or E of this subchapter, or under a State plan approved under subchapter XIX of this chapter, or who is required by the State to cooperate with the State agency administering the program under this part pursuant to subsection (l) or (m) of section 2015 of title 7, and shall be paid by the individual applying for such services, or recovered from the absent parent, or paid by the State out of its own funds (the payment of which from State funds shall not be considered as an administrative cost of the State for the operation of the plan, and shall be considered income to the program), the amount of which (I) will not exceed $25 (or such higher or lower amount (which shall be uniform for all States) as the Secretary may determine to be appropriate for any fiscal year to reflect increases or decreases in administrative costs), and (II) may vary among such individuals on the basis of ability to pay (as determined by the State); and

(ii) in the case of an individual who has never received assistance under a State program funded under part A and for whom the State has collected at least $500 of support, the State shall impose an annual fee of $25 for each case in which services are furnished, which shall be retained by the State from support collected on behalf of the individual (but not from the first $500 so collected), paid by the individual applying for the services, recovered from the absent parent, or paid by the State out of its own funds (the payment of which from State funds shall not be considered as an administrative cost of the State for the operation of the plan, and the fees shall be considered income to the program);

(C) a fee of not more than $25 may be imposed in any case where the State requests the Secretary of the Treasury to withhold past-due support owed to or on behalf of such individual from a tax refund pursuant to section 664(a)(2) of this title;

(D) a fee (in accordance with regulations of the Secretary) for performing genetic tests may be imposed on any individual who is not a recipient of assistance under a State program funded under part A of this subchapter; and

(E) any costs in excess of the fees so imposed may be collected—

(i) from the parent who owes the child or spousal support obligation involved; or

(ii) at the option of the State, from the individual to whom such services are made available, but only if such State has in effect a procedure whereby all persons in such State having authority to order child or spousal support are informed that such costs are to be collected from the individual to whom such services were made available;

(7) provide for entering into cooperative arrangements with appropriate courts and law enforcement officials and Indian tribes or tribal organizations (as defined in subsections (e) and (l) of section 450b of title 25) (A) to assist the agency administering the plan, including the entering into of financial arrangements with such courts and officials in order to assure optimum results under such program, and (B) with respect to any other matters of common concern to such courts or officials and the agency administering the plan;

(8) provide that, for the purpose of establishing parentage, establishing, setting the amount of, modifying, or enforcing child support obligations, or making or enforcing a child custody or visitation determination, as defined in section 663(d)(1) of this title the agency administering the plan will establish a service to locate parents utilizing—

(A) all sources of information and available records; and

(B) the Federal Parent Locator Service established under section 653 of this title,

and shall, subject to the privacy safeguards required under paragraph (26), disclose only the information described in sections 653 and 663 of this title to the authorized persons specified in such sections for the purposes specified in such sections;

(9) provide that the State will, in accordance with standards prescribed by the Secretary, cooperate with any other State—

(A) in establishing paternity, if necessary;

(B) in locating a noncustodial parent residing in the State (whether or not permanently) against whom any action is being taken under a program established under a plan approved under this part in another State;

(C) in securing compliance by a noncustodial parent residing in such State (whether or not permanently) with an order issued by a court of competent jurisdiction against such parent for the support and maintenance of the child or children or the parent of such child or children with respect to whom aid is being provided under the plan of such other State;

(D) in carrying out other functions required under a plan approved under this part; and

(E) not later than March 1, 1997, in using the forms promulgated pursuant to section 652(a)(11) of this title for income withholding, imposition of liens, and issuance of administrative subpoenas in interstate child support cases;

(10) provide that the State will maintain a full record of collections and disbursements made under the plan and have an adequate reporting system;

(11)(A) provide that amounts collected as support shall be distributed as provided in section 657 of this title; and

(B) provide that any payment required to be made under section 656 or 657 of this title to a family shall be made to the resident parent, legal guardian, or caretaker relative having custody of or responsibility for the child or children;

(12) provide for the establishment of procedures to require the State to provide individuals who are applying for or receiving services under the State plan, or who are parties to cases in which services are being provided under the State plan—

(A) with notice of all proceedings in which support obligations might be established or modified; and

(B) with a copy of any order establishing or modifying a child support obligation, or (in the case of a petition for modification) a notice of determination that there should be no change in the amount of the child support award, within 14 days after issuance of such order or determination;

(13) provide that the State will comply with such other requirements and standards as the Secretary determines to be necessary to the establishment of an effective program for locating noncustodial parents, establishing paternity, obtaining support orders, and collecting support payments and provide that information requests by parents who are residents of other States be treated with the same priority as requests by parents who are residents of the State submitting the plan;

(14)(A) comply with such bonding requirements, for employees who receive, disburse, handle, or have access to, cash, as the Secretary shall by regulations prescribe;

(B) maintain methods of administration which are designed to assure that persons responsible for handling cash receipts shall not participate in accounting or operating functions which would permit them to conceal in the accounting records the misuse of cash receipts (except that the Secretary shall by regulations provide for exceptions to this requirement in the case of sparsely populated areas where the hiring of unreasonable additional staff would otherwise be necessary);

(15) provide for—

(A) a process for annual reviews of and reports to the Secretary on the State program operated under the State plan approved under this part, including such information as may be necessary to measure State compliance with Federal requirements for expedited procedures, using such standards and procedures as are required by the Secretary, under which the State agency will determine the extent to which the program is operated in compliance with this part; and

(B) a process of extracting from the automated data processing system required by paragraph (16) and transmitting to the Secretary data and calculations concerning the levels of accomplishment (and rates of improvement) with respect to applicable performance indicators (including paternity establishment percentages) to the extent necessary for purposes of sections 652(g) and 658a of this title;

(16) provide for the establishment and operation by the State agency, in accordance with an (initial and annually updated) advance automated data processing planning document approved under section 652(d) of this title, of a statewide automated data processing and information retrieval system meeting the requirements of section 654a of this title designed effectively and efficiently to assist management in the administration of the State plan, so as to control, account for, and monitor all the factors in the support enforcement collection and paternity determination process under such plan;

(17) provide that the State will have in effect an agreement with the Secretary entered into pursuant to section 663 of this title for the use of the Parent Locator Service established under section 653 of this title, and provide that the State will accept and transmit to the Secretary requests for information authorized under the provisions of the agreement to be furnished by such Service to authorized persons, will impose and collect (in accordance with regulations of the Secretary) a fee sufficient to cover the costs to the State and to the Secretary incurred by reason of such requests, will transmit to the Secretary from time to time (in accordance with such regulations) so much of the fees collected as are attributable to such costs to the Secretary so incurred, and during the period that such agreement is in effect will otherwise comply with such agreement and regulations of the Secretary with respect thereto;

(18) provide that the State has in effect procedures necessary to obtain payment of past-due support from overpayments made to the Secretary of the Treasury as set forth in section 664 of this title, and take all steps necessary to implement and utilize such procedures;

(19) provide that the agency administering the plan—

(A) shall determine on a periodic basis, from information supplied pursuant to section 508 of the Unemployment Compensation Amendments of 1976, whether any individuals receiving compensation under the State's unemployment compensation law (including amounts payable pursuant to any agreement under any Federal unemployment compensation law) owe child support obligations which are being enforced by such agency; and

(B) shall enforce any such child support obligations which are owed by such an individual but are not being met—

(i) through an agreement with such individual to have specified amounts withheld from compensation otherwise payable to such individual and by submitting a copy of any such agreement to the State agency administering the unemployment compensation law; or

(ii) in the absence of such an agreement, by bringing legal process (as defined in section 659(i)(5) of this title) to require the withholding of amounts from such compensation;

(20) provide, to the extent required by section 666 of this title, that the State (A) shall have in effect all of the laws to improve child support enforcement effectiveness which are referred to in that section, and (B) shall implement the procedures which are prescribed in or pursuant to such laws;

(21)(A) at the option of the State, impose a late payment fee on all overdue support (as defined in section 666(e) of this title) under any obligation being enforced under this part, in an amount equal to a uniform percentage determined by the State (not less than 3 percent nor more than 6 percent) of the overdue support, which shall be payable by the noncustodial parent owing the overdue support; and

(B) assure that the fee will be collected in addition to, and only after full payment of, the overdue support, and that the imposition of the late payment fee shall not directly or indirectly result in a decrease in the amount of the support which is paid to the child (or spouse) to whom, or on whose behalf, it is owed;

(22) in order for the State to be eligible to receive any incentive payments under section 658a of this title, provide that, if one or more political subdivisions of the State participate in the costs of carrying out activities under the State plan during any period, each such subdivision shall be entitled to receive an appropriate share (as determined by the State) of any such incentive payments made to the State for such period, taking into account the efficiency and effectiveness of the activities carried out under the State plan by such political subdivision;

(23) provide that the State will regularly and frequently publicize, through public service announcements, the availability of child support enforcement services under the plan and otherwise, including information as to any application fees for such services and a telephone number or postal address at which further information may be obtained and will publicize the availability and encourage the use of procedures for voluntary establishment of paternity and child support by means the State deems appropriate;

(24) provide that the State will have in effect an automated data processing and information retrieval system—

(A) by October 1, 1997, which meets all requirements of this part which were enacted on or before October 13, 1988; and

(B) by October 1, 2000, which meets all requirements of this part enacted on or before August 22, 1996, except that such deadline shall be extended by 1 day for each day (if any) by which the Secretary fails to meet the deadline imposed by section 344(a)(3) of the Personal Responsibility and Work Opportunity Reconciliation Act of 1996;

(25) provide that if a family with respect to which services are provided under the plan ceases to receive assistance under the State program funded under part A of this subchapter, the State shall provide appropriate notice to the family and continue to provide such services, subject to the same conditions and on the same basis as in the case of other individuals to whom services are furnished under the plan, except that an application or other request to continue services shall not be required of such a family and paragraph (6)(B) shall not apply to the family;

(26) have in effect safeguards, applicable to all confidential information handled by the State agency, that are designed to protect the privacy rights of the parties, including—

(A) safeguards against unauthorized use or disclosure of information relating to proceedings or actions to establish paternity, or to establish, modify, or enforce support, or to make or enforce a child custody determination;

(B) prohibitions against the release of information on the whereabouts of 1 party or the child to another party against whom a protective order with respect to the former party or the child has been entered;

(C) prohibitions against the release of information on the whereabouts of 1 party or the child to another person if the State has reason to believe that the release of the information to that person may result in physical or emotional harm to the party or the child;

(D) in cases in which the prohibitions under subparagraphs (B) and (C) apply, the requirement to notify the Secretary, for purposes of section 653(b)(2) of this title, that the State has reasonable evidence of domestic violence or child abuse against a party or the child and that the disclosure of such information could be harmful to the party or the child; and

(E) procedures providing that when the Secretary discloses information about a parent or child to a State court or an agent of a State court described in section 653(c)(2) or 663(d)(2)(B) of this title, and advises that court or agent that the Secretary has been notified that there is reasonable evidence of domestic violence or child abuse pursuant to section 653(b)(2) of this title, the court shall determine whether disclosure to any other person of information received from the Secretary could be harmful to the parent or child and, if the court determines that disclosure to any other person could be harmful, the court and its agents shall not make any such disclosure;

(27) provide that, on and after October 1, 1998, the State agency will—

(A) operate a State disbursement unit in accordance with section 654b of this title; and

(B) have sufficient State staff (consisting of State employees) and (at State option) contractors reporting directly to the State agency to—

(i) monitor and enforce support collections through the unit in cases being enforced by the State pursuant to paragraph (4) (including carrying out the automated data processing responsibilities described in section 654a(g) of this title); and

(ii) take the actions described in section 666(c)(1) of this title in appropriate cases;

(28) provide that, on and after October 1, 1997, the State will operate a State Directory of New Hires in accordance with section 653a of this title;

(29) provide that the State agency responsible for administering the State plan—

(A) shall make the determination (and redetermination at appropriate intervals) as to whether an individual who has applied for or is receiving assistance under the State program funded under part A of this subchapter, the State program under part E of this subchapter, the State program under subchapter XIX of this chapter, or the supplemental nutrition assistance program, as defined under section 2012(l) of title 7, is cooperating in good faith with the State in establishing the paternity of, or in establishing, modifying, or enforcing a support order for, any child of the individual by providing the State agency with the name of, and such other information as the State agency may require with respect to, the noncustodial parent of the child, subject to good cause and other exceptions which—

(i) in the case of the State program funded under part A of this subchapter, the State program under part E of this subchapter, or the State program under subchapter XIX of this chapter shall, at the option of the State, be defined, taking into account the best interests of the child, and applied in each case, by the State agency administering such program; and

(ii) in the case of the supplemental nutrition assistance program, as defined under section 2012(l) of title 7, shall be defined and applied in each case under that program in accordance with section 2015(l)(2) of title 7;

(B) shall require the individual to supply additional necessary information and appear at interviews, hearings, and legal proceedings;

(C) shall require the individual and the child to submit to genetic tests pursuant to judicial or administrative order;

(D) may request that the individual sign a voluntary acknowledgment of paternity, after notice of the rights and consequences of such an acknowledgment, but may not require the individual to sign an acknowledgment or otherwise relinquish the right to genetic tests as a condition of cooperation and eligibility for assistance under the State program funded under part A of this subchapter, the State program under part E of this subchapter, the State program under subchapter XIX of this chapter, or the supplemental nutrition assistance program, as defined under section 2012(l) of title 7; and

(E) shall promptly notify the individual and the State agency administering the State program funded under part A of this subchapter, the State agency administering the State program under part E of this subchapter, the State agency administering the State program under subchapter XIX of this chapter, or the State agency administering the supplemental nutrition assistance program, as defined under section 2012(l) of title 7, of each such determination, and if noncooperation is determined, the basis therefor;

(30) provide that the State shall use the definitions established under section 652(a)(5) of this title in collecting and reporting information as required under this part;

(31) provide that the State agency will have in effect a procedure for certifying to the Secretary, for purposes of the procedure under section 652(k) of this title,

determinations that individuals owe arrearages of child support in an amount exceeding $2,500, under which procedure—

(A) each individual concerned is afforded notice of such determination and the consequences thereof, and an opportunity to contest the determination; and

(B) the certification by the State agency is furnished to the Secretary in such format, and accompanied by such supporting documentation, as the Secretary may require;

(32)(A) provide that any request for services under this part by a foreign reciprocating country, a foreign treaty country, or a foreign country with which the State has an arrangement described in section 659a(d) of this title shall be treated as a request by a State;

(B) provide, at State option, notwithstanding paragraph (4) or any other provision of this part, for services under the plan for enforcement of a spousal support order not described in paragraph (4)(B) entered by such a country (or subdivision); and

(C) provide that no applications will be required from, and no costs will be assessed for such services against, the foreign reciprocating country, foreign treaty country, or foreign individual (but costs may at State option be assessed against the obligor);

(33) provide that a State that receives funding pursuant to section 628 of this title and that has within its borders Indian country (as defined in section 1151 of title 18) may enter into cooperative agreements with an Indian tribe or tribal organization (as defined in subsections (e) and (l) of section 450b of title 25), if the Indian tribe or tribal organization demonstrates that such tribe or organization has an established tribal court system or a Court of Indian Offenses with the authority to establish paternity, establish, modify, or enforce support orders, or to enter support orders in accordance with child support guidelines established or adopted by such tribe or organization, under which the State and tribe or organization shall provide for the cooperative delivery of child support enforcement services in Indian country and for the forwarding of all collections pursuant to the functions performed by the tribe or organization to the State agency, or conversely, by the State agency to the tribe or organization, which shall distribute such collections in accordance with such agreement; and

(34) include an election by the State to apply section 657(a)(2)(B) of this title or former section 657(a)(2)(B) of this title (as in effect for the State immediately before the date this paragraph first applies to the State) to the distribution of the amounts which are the subject of such sections and, for so long as the State elects to so apply such former section, the amendments made by subsection (b)(1) of section 7301 of the Deficit Reduction Act of 2005 shall not apply with respect to the State, notwithstanding subsection (e) of such section 7301.

The State may allow the jurisdiction which makes the collection involved to retain any application fee under paragraph (6)(B) or any late payment fee under paragraph (21). Nothing in paragraph (33) shall void any provision of any cooperative agreement entered into before August 22, 1996, nor shall such paragraph deprive any State of jurisdiction over Indian country (as so defined) that is lawfully exercised under section 1322 of title 25.

(Aug. 14, 1935, ch. 531, title IV, § 454, as added Pub. L. 93–647, § 101(a), Jan. 4, 1975, 88 Stat. 2354; amended Pub. L. 94–88, title II, § 208(b), (c), Aug. 9, 1975, 89 Stat. 436; Pub. L. 95–30, title V, § 502(a), May 23, 1977, 91 Stat. 162; Pub. L. 96–265, title IV, § 405(b), June 9, 1980, 94 Stat. 463; Pub. L. 96–611, § 9(a), Dec. 28, 1980, 94 Stat. 3571; Pub. L. 97–35, title XXIII, §§ 2331(b), 2332(d), 2333(a), (b), 2335(a), Aug. 13, 1981, 95 Stat. 860, 862, 863; Pub. L. 97–248, title I, §§ 171(a), (b)(1), 173(a), Sept. 3, 1982, 96 Stat. 401, 403; Pub. L. 98–369, div. B, title VI, § 2663(c)(14), (j)(2)(B)(x), July 18, 1984, 98 Stat. 1166, 1170; Pub. L. 98–378, §§ 3(a), (c)–(f), 5(b), 6(a),

11(b)(1), 12(a), (b), 14(a), 21(d), Aug. 16, 1984, 98 Stat. 1306, 1310, 1311, 1314, 1318, 1319, 1320, 1324; Pub. L. 100–203, title IX, §§ 9141(a)(2), 9142(a), Dec. 22, 1987, 101 Stat. 1330–321; Pub. L. 100–485, title I, §§ 104(a), 111(c), 123(a), (d), Oct. 13, 1988, 102 Stat. 2348, 2349, 2352, 2353; Pub. L. 104–35, § 1(a), Oct. 12, 1995, 109 Stat. 294; Pub. L. 104–193, title I, § 108(c)(11), (12), title III, §§ 301(a), (b), 302(b)(2), 303(a), 304(a), 312(a), 313(a), 316(g)(1), 324(b), 332, 333, 342(a), 343(b), 344(a)(1), (4), 370(a)(2), 371(b), 375(a), (c), 395(d)(1)(D), (2)(B), Aug. 22, 1996, 110 Stat. 2166, 2199, 2204, 2205, 2207, 2209, 2218, 2223, 2230, 2233, 2234, 2236, 2252, 2254, 2256, 2259, 2260; Pub. L. 105–33, title V, §§ 5531(a), 5542(c), 5545, 5546(a), 5548, 5552, 5556(b), Aug. 5, 1997, 111 Stat. 625, 631, 633, 635, 637; Pub. L. 106–169, title IV, § 401(g), (h), Dec. 14, 1999, 113 Stat. 1858; Pub. L. 109–171, title VII, §§ 7301(b)(1)(C), 7303(b), 7310(a), Feb. 8, 2006, 120 Stat. 143, 145, 147; Pub. L. 110–234, title IV, §§ 4002(b)(1)(A), (B), (2)(V), 4115(c)(2)(H), May 22, 2008, 122 Stat. 1095–1097, 1110; Pub. L. 110–246, § 4(a), title IV, §§ 4002(b)(1)(A), (B), (2)(V), 4115(c)(2)(H), June 18, 2008, 122 Stat. 1664, 1857, 1858, 1871; Pub. L. 113–79, title IV, § 4030(v), Feb. 7, 2014, 128 Stat. 815; Pub. L. 113–183, title III, § 301(c), Sept. 29, 2014, 128 Stat. 1943.)

§ 655. Payments to States.

(a) Amounts payable each quarter

(1) From the sums appropriated therefor, the Secretary shall pay to each State for each quarter an amount—

(A) equal to the percent specified in paragraph (2) of the total amounts expended by such State during such quarter for the operation of the plan approved under section 654 of this title,

(B) equal to the percent specified in paragraph (3) of the sums expended during such quarter that are attributable to the planning, design, development, installation or enhancement of an automatic data processing and information retrieval system (including in such sums the full cost of the hardware components of such system); and

(C) equal to 66 percent of so much of the sums expended during such quarter as are attributable to laboratory costs incurred in determining paternity, and

(D) equal to 66 percent of the sums expended by the State during the quarter for an alternative statewide system for which a waiver has been granted under section 652(d)(3) of this title, but only to the extent that the total of the sums so expended by the State on or after July 16, 1998, does not exceed the least total cost estimate submitted by the State pursuant to section 652(d)(3)(C) of this title in the request for the waiver; except that no amount shall be paid to any State on account of amounts expended from amounts paid to the State under section 658a of this title or to carry out an agreement which it has entered into pursuant to section 663 of this title. In determining the total amounts expended by any State during a quarter, for purposes of this subsection, there shall be excluded an amount equal to the total of any fees collected or other income resulting from services provided under the plan approved under this part.

(2) The percent applicable to quarters in a fiscal year for purposes of paragraph (1)(A) is—

(A) 70 percent for fiscal years 1984, 1985, 1986 and 1987,

(B) 68 percent for fiscal years 1988 and 1989, and

(C) 66 percent for fiscal year 1990 and each fiscal year thereafter.

(3)(A) The Secretary shall pay to each State, for each quarter in fiscal years 1996 and 1997, 90 percent of so much of the State expenditures described in paragraph (1)(B) as the Secretary finds are for a system meeting the requirements specified in section 654(16) of this title (as in effect on September 30, 1995) but limited to the amount approved for States in the advance planning documents of such States submitted on or before September 30, 1995.

(B)(i) The Secretary shall pay to each State or system described in clause (iii), for each quarter in fiscal years 1996 through 2001, the percentage specified in clause (ii) of so much of the State or system expenditures described in paragraph (1)(B) as the Secretary finds are for a system meeting the requirements of sections 654(16) and 654a of this title.

(ii) The percentage specified in this clause is 80 percent.

(iii) For purposes of clause (i), a system described in this clause is a system that has been approved by the Secretary to receive enhanced funding pursuant to the Family Support Act of 1988 (Public Law 100-485; 102 Stat. 2343) for the purpose of developing a system that meets the requirements of sections 654(16) (as in effect on and after September 30, 1995) and 654a of this title, including systems that have received funding for such purpose pursuant to a waiver under section 1315(a) of this title.

(4)(A)(i) If—

(I) the Secretary determines that a State plan under section 654 of this title would (in the absence of this paragraph) be disapproved for the failure of the State to comply with a particular subparagraph of section 654(24) of this title, and that the State has made and is continuing to make a good faith effort to so comply; and

(II) the State has submitted to the Secretary a corrective compliance plan that describes how, by when, and at what cost the State will achieve such compliance, which has been approved by the Secretary, then the Secretary shall not disapprove the State plan under section 654 of this title, and the Secretary shall reduce the amount otherwise payable to the State under paragraph (1)(A) of this subsection for the fiscal year by the penalty amount.

(ii) All failures of a State during a fiscal year to comply with any of the requirements referred to in the same subparagraph of section 654(24) of this title shall be considered a single failure of the State to comply with that subparagraph during the fiscal year for purposes of this paragraph.

(B) In this paragraph:

(i) The term "penalty amount" means, with respect to a failure of a State to comply with a subparagraph of section 654(24) of this title—

(I) 4 percent of the penalty base, in the case of the first fiscal year in which such a failure by the State occurs (regardless of whether a penalty is imposed under this paragraph with respect to the failure);

(II) 8 percent of the penalty base, in the case of the second such fiscal year;

(III) 16 percent of the penalty base, in the case of the third such fiscal year;

(IV) 25 percent of the penalty base, in the case of the fourth such fiscal year; or

(V) 30 percent of the penalty base, in the case of the fifth or any subsequent such fiscal year.

(ii) The term "penalty base" means, with respect to a failure of a State to comply with a subparagraph of section 454(24) during a fiscal year, the amount otherwise payable to the State under paragraph (1)(A) of this subsection for the preceding fiscal year.

(C)(i) The Secretary shall waive a penalty under this paragraph for any failure of a State to comply with section 654(24)(A) of this title during fiscal year 1998 if—

(I) on or before August 1, 1998, the State has submitted to the Secretary a request that the Secretary certify the State as having met the requirements of such section;

(II) the Secretary subsequently provides the certification as a result of a timely review conducted pursuant to the request; and

(III) the State has not failed such a review.

(ii) If a State with respect to which a reduction is made under this paragraph for a fiscal year with respect to a failure to comply with a subparagraph of section 654(24) of this title achieves compliance with such subparagraph by the beginning of the succeeding fiscal year, the Secretary shall increase the amount otherwise payable to the State under paragraph (1)(A) of this subsection for the succeeding fiscal year by an amount equal to 90 percent of the reduction for the fiscal year.

(iii) The Secretary shall reduce the amount of any reduction that, in the absence of this clause, would be required to be made under this paragraph by reason of the failure of a State to achieve compliance with section 654(24)(B) of this title during the fiscal year, by an amount equal to 20 percent of the amount of the otherwise required reduction, for each State performance measure described in section 658a(b)(4) of this title with respect to which the applicable percentage under section 658a(b)(6) of this title for the fiscal year is 100 percent, if the Secretary has made the determination described in section 658a(b)(5)(B) of this title with respect to the State for the fiscal year.

(D) The Secretary may not impose a penalty under this paragraph against a State with respect to a failure to comply with section 654(24)(B) of this title for a fiscal year if the Secretary is required to impose a penalty under this paragraph against the State with respect to a failure to comply with section 654(24)(A) of this title for the fiscal year.

(5)(A)(i) If—

(I) the Secretary determines that a State plan under section 654 of this title would (in the absence of this paragraph) be disapproved for the failure of the State to comply with subparagraphs (A) and (B)(i) of section 654(27) of this title, and that the State has made and is continuing to make a good faith effort to so comply; and

(II) the State has submitted to the Secretary, not later than April 1, 2000, a corrective compliance plan that describes how, by when, and at what cost the State will achieve such compliance, which has been approved by the Secretary, then the Secretary shall not disapprove the State plan under section 654 of this title, and the Secretary shall reduce the amount otherwise payable to the State under paragraph (1)(A) of this subsection for the fiscal year by the penalty amount

(ii) All failures of a State during a fiscal year to comply with any of the requirements of section 654b of this title shall be considered a single failure of the State to comply with subparagraphs (A) and (B)(i) of section 654(27) of this title during the fiscal year for purposes of this paragraph.

(B) In this paragraph:

(i) The term "penalty amount" means, with respect to a failure of a State to comply with subparagraphs (A) and (B)(i) of section 654(27) of this title—

(I) 4 percent of the penalty base, in the case of the 1st fiscal year in which such a failure by the State occurs (regardless of whether a penalty is imposed in that fiscal year under this paragraph with respect to the failure), except as provided in subparagraph (C)(ii) of this paragraph;

(II) 8 percent of the penalty base, in the case of the 2nd such fiscal year;

(III) 16 percent of the penalty base, in the case of the 3rd such fiscal year;

(IV) 25 percent of the penalty base, in the case of the 4th such fiscal year; or

(V) 30 percent of the penalty base, in the case of the 5th or any subsequent such fiscal year.

(ii) The term "penalty base" means, with respect to a failure of a State to comply with subparagraphs (A) and (B)(i) of section 654(27) of this title during a fiscal year, the amount otherwise payable to the State under paragraph (1)(A) of this subsection for the preceding fiscal year.

(C)(i) The Secretary shall waive all penalties imposed against a State under this paragraph for any failure of the State to comply with subparagraphs (A) and (B)(i) of section 654(27) of this title if the Secretary determines that, before April 1, 2000, the State has achieved such compliance.

(ii) If a State with respect to which a reduction is required to be made under this paragraph with respect to a failure to comply with subparagraphs (A) and (B)(i) of section 654(27) of this title achieves such compliance on or after April 1, 2000, and on or before September 30, 2000, then the penalty amount applicable to the State shall be 1 percent of the penalty base with respect to the failure involved.

(D) The Secretary may not impose a penalty under this paragraph against a State for a fiscal year for which the amount otherwise payable to the State under paragraph (1)(A) of this subsection is reduced under paragraph (4) of this subsection for failure to comply with section 654(24)(A) of this title.

(b) Estimate of amounts payable; installment payments

(1) Prior to the beginning of each quarter, the Secretary shall estimate the amount to which a State will be entitled under subsection (a) of this section for such quarter, such estimates to be based on (A) a report filed by the State containing its estimate of the total sum to be expended in such quarter in accordance with the provisions of such subsection, and stating the amount appropriated or made available by the State and its political subdivisions for such expenditures in such quarter, and if such amount is less than the State's proportionate share of the total sum of such estimated expenditures, the source or sources from which the difference is expected to be derived, and (B) such other investigation as the Secretary may find necessary.

(2) Subject to subsection (d) of this section, the Secretary shall then pay, in such installments as he may determine, to the State the amount so estimated, reduced or increased to the extent of any overpayment or underpayment which the Secretary determines was made under this section to such State for any prior quarter and with respect to which adjustment has not already been made under this subsection.

(3) Upon the making of any estimate by the Secretary under this subsection, any appropriations available for payments under this section shall be deemed obligated.

(c) Repealed. Pub.L. 97-248, Title I, § 174(b), Sept. 3, 1982, 96 Stat. 403

(d) State reports

Notwithstanding any other provision of law, no amount shall be paid to any State under this section for any quarter, prior to the close of such quarter, unless for the period consisting of all prior quarters for which payment is authorized to be made to such State under subsection (a) of this section, there shall have been submitted by the State to the Secretary, with respect to each quarter in such period (other than the last two quarters in such period), a full and complete report (in such form and manner and containing such information as the Secretary shall prescribe or require) as to the amount of child support collected and disbursed and all expenditures with respect to which payment is authorized under subsection (a) of this section.

(e) Special project grants for interstate enforcement; appropriations

(1) In order to encourage and promote the development and use of more effective methods of enforcing support obligations under this part in cases where either the children on whose behalf the support is sought or their noncustodial parents do not reside in the State where such cases are filed, the Secretary is authorized to make grants, in such amounts and on such terms and conditions as the Secretary determines to be appropriate, to States which propose to undertake new or innovative methods of support collection in such cases and which will use the proceeds of such grants to carry out special projects designed to demonstrate and test such methods.

(2) A grant under this subsection shall be made only upon a finding by the Secretary that the project involved is likely to be of significant assistance in carrying out the purpose of this subsection; and with respect to such project the Secretary may waive any of the requirements of this part which would otherwise be applicable, to such extent and for such period as the Secretary determines is necessary or desirable in order to enable the State to carry out the project.

(3) At the time of its application for a grant under this subsection the State shall submit to the Secretary a statement describing in reasonable detail the project for which the proceeds of the grant are to be used, and the State shall from time to time thereafter submit to the Secretary such reports with respect to the project as the Secretary may specify.

(4) Amounts expended by a State in carrying out a special project assisted under this section shall be considered, for purposes of section 658(b) of this title (as amended by section 5(a) of the Child Support Enforcement Amendments of 1984), to have been expended for the operation of the State's plan approved under section 654 of this title.

(5) There is authorized to be appropriated the sum of $7,000,000 for fiscal year 1985, $12,000,000 for fiscal year 1986, and $15,000,000 for each fiscal year thereafter, to be used by the Secretary in making grants under this subsection.

(f) Direct Federal funding to Indian tribes and tribal organizations

The Secretary may make direct payments under this part to an Indian tribe or tribal organization that demonstrates to the satisfaction of the Secretary that it has the capacity to operate a child support enforcement program meeting the objectives of this part, including establishment of paternity, establishment, modification, and enforcement of support orders, and location of absent parents. The Secretary shall promulgate regulations establishing the requirements which must be met by an Indian tribe or tribal organization to be eligible for a grant under this subsection.

§ 656. Support obligation as obligation to State; amount; discharge in bankruptcy.

(a) Collection processes

(1) The support rights assigned to the State or secured on behalf of a child receiving foster care maintenance payments shall constitute an obligation owed to such State by the individual responsible for providing such support. Such obligation shall be deemed for collection purposes to be collectible under all applicable State and local processes pursuant to section 608(a)(3) of this title.

(2) The amount of such obligation shall be—

(A) the amount specified in a court order which covers the assigned support rights, or

(B) if there is no court order, an amount determined by the State in accordance with a formula approved by the Secretary.

(3) Any amounts collected from a noncustodial parent under the plan shall reduce, dollar for dollar, the amount of his obligation under subparagraphs (A) and (B) of paragraph (2).

(b) Nondischargeability

A debt (as defined in section 101 of Title 11) owed under State law to a State (as defined in such section) or municipality (as defined in such section) that is in the nature of support and that is enforceable under this part is not released by a discharge in bankruptcy under Title 11.

§ 657. Distribution of collected support.

(a) In general

Subject to subsections (d) and (e) of this section, an amount collected on behalf of a family as support by a State pursuant to a plan approved under this part shall be distributed as follows:

(1) Families receiving assistance

In the case of a family receiving assistance from the State, the State shall—

(A) pay to the Federal Government the Federal share of the amount so collected; and

(B) retain, or distribute to the family, the State share of the amount so collected.

In no event shall the total of the amounts paid to the Federal Government and retained by the State exceed the total of the amounts that have been paid to the family as assistance by the State.

(2) Families that formerly received assistance

In the case of a family that formerly received assistance from the State:

(A) Current support payments

To the extent that the amount so collected does not exceed the amount required to be paid to the family for the month in which collected, the State shall distribute the amount so collected to the family.

(B) Payments of arrearages

To the extent that the amount so collected exceeds the amount required to be paid to the family for the month in which collected, the State shall distribute the amount so collected as follows:

(i) Distribution of arrearages that accrued after the family ceased to receive assistance

(I) Pre-October 1997

Except as provided in subclause (II), the provisions of this section as in effect and applied on the day before August 22, 1996 (other then subsection (b)(1) (as so in effect)), shall apply with respect to the distribution of support arrearages that—

(aa) accrued after the family ceased to receive assistance, and

(bb) are collected before October 1, 1997.

(II) Post-September 1997

With respect to the amount so collected on or after October 1, 1997 (or before such date, at the option of the State)—

(aa) In general

The State shall first distribute the amount so collected (other than any amount described in clause (iv)) to the family to the extent necessary to satisfy any support arrearages with respect to the family that accrued after the family ceased to receive assistance from the State.

(bb) Reimbursement of governments for assistance provided to the family

After the application of division (aa) and clause (ii)(II)(aa) with respect to the amount so collected, the State shall retain the State share of the amount so collected, and pay to the Federal Government the Federal share (as defined in subsection (c)(2) of this section) of the amount so collected, but only to the extent necessary to reimburse amounts paid to the family as assistance by the State.

(cc) Distribution of the remainder to the family

To the extent that neither division (aa) nor division (bb) applies to the amount so collected, the State shall distribute the amount to the family.

(ii) Distribution of arrearages that accrued before the family received assistance

(I) Pre-October 2000

Except as provided in subclause (II), the provisions of this section as in effect and applied on August 21, 1996 (other than subsection (b)(1) (as so in effect)), shall apply with respect to the distribution of support arrearages that—

(aa) accrued before the family received assistance, and

(bb) are collected before October 1, 2000.

(II) Post-September 2000

Unless, based on the report required by paragraph (5), the Congress determines otherwise, with respect to the amount so collected on or after October 1, 2000 (or before such date, at the option of the State)—

(aa) In general

The State shall first distribute the amount so collected (other than any amount described in clause (iv)) to the family to the extent necessary to satisfy any support arrearages with respect to the family that accrued before the family received assistance from the State.

(bb) Reimbursement of governments for assistance provided to the family

After the application of clause (i)(II)(aa) and division (aa) with respect to the amount so collected, the State shall retain the State share of the amount so collected, and pay to the Federal Government the Federal share (as defined in subsection (c)(2) of this section) of the amount so collected, but only to the extent necessary to reimburse amounts paid to the family as assistance by the State.

(cc) Distribution of the remainder to the family

To the extent that neither division (aa) nor division (bb) applies to the amount so collected, the State shall distribute the amount to the family.

(iii) Distribution of arrearages that accrued while the family received assistance

In the case of a family described in this subparagraph, the provisions of paragraph (1) shall apply with respect to the distribution of support arrearages that accrued while the family received assistance.

(iv) Amounts collected pursuant to section 664

Notwithstanding any other provision of this section, any amount of support collected pursuant to section 664 of this title shall be retained by the State to the extent past-due support has been assigned to the State as a condition of receiving assistance from the State, up to the amount necessary to reimburse the State for amounts paid to the family as assistance by the State. The State shall pay to the Federal Government the Federal share of the amounts so retained. To the extent the amount collected pursuant to section 664 of this title exceeds the amount so retained, the State shall distribute the excess to the family.

(v) Ordering rules for distributions

For purposes of this subparagraph, unless an earlier effective date is required by this section, effective October 1, 2000, the State shall treat any support arrearages collected, except for amounts collected pursuant to section 664 of this title, as accruing in the following order:

(I) To the period after the family ceased to receive assistance.

(II) To the period before the family received assistance.

(III) To the period while the family was receiving assistance.

(3) Families that never received assistance

In the case of any other family, the State shall distribute to the family the portion of the amount so collected that remains after withholding any fee pursuant to section 654(6)(B)(ii) of this title.

(4) Families under certain agreements

In the case of an amount collected for a family in accordance with a cooperative agreement under section 654(33) of this title, distribute the amount so collected pursuant to the terms of the agreement.

(5) Study and report

Not later than October 1, 1999, the Secretary shall report to the Congress the Secretary's findings with respect to—

(A) whether the distribution of post-assistance arrearages to families has been effective in moving people off of welfare and keeping them off of welfare;

(B) whether early implementation of a pre-assistance arrearage program by some States has been effective in moving people off of welfare and keeping them off of welfare;

(C) what the overall impact has been of the amendments made by the Personal Responsibility and Work Opportunity Reconciliation Act of 1996 with respect to child support enforcement in moving people off of welfare and keeping them off of welfare; and

(D) based on the information and data the Secretary has obtained, what changes, if any, should be made in the policies related to the distribution of child support arrearages.

(6) State option for applicability

Notwithstanding any other provision of this subsection, a State may elect to apply the rules described in clauses (i)(II), (ii)(II), and (v) of paragraph (2)(B) to support arrearages collected on and after October 1, 1998, and, if the State makes such an election, shall apply the provisions of this section, as in effect and applied on the day before August 22, 1996, other than subsection (b)(1) (as so in effect), to amounts collected before October 1, 1998.

(b) Continuation of assignments

Any rights to support obligations, assigned to a State as a condition of receiving assistance from the State under part A of this subchapter and in effect on September 30, 1997 (or such earlier date, on or after August 22, 1996, as the State may choose), shall remain assigned after such date.

(c) Definitions

As used in subsection (a) of this section:

(1) Assistance

The term "assistance from the State" means—

(A) assistance under the State program funded under part A of this subchapter or under the State plan approved under part A of this subchapter (as in effect on August 21, 1996); and

(B) foster care maintenance payments under the State plan approved under part E of this subchapter.

(2) Federal share

The term "Federal share" means that portion of the amount collected resulting from the application of the Federal medical assistance percentage in effect for the fiscal year in which the amount is distributed.

(3) Federal medical assistance percentage

The term "Federal medical assistance percentage" means—

(A) 75 percent, in the case of Puerto Rico, the Virgin Islands, Guam, and American Samoa; or

(B) the Federal medical assistance percentage (as defined in section 1396d(b) of this title, as such section was in effect on September 30, 1995) in the case of any other State.

(4) State share

The term "State share" means 100 percent minus the Federal share.

(d) Gap payments not subject to distribution under this section

At State option, this section shall not apply to any amount collected on behalf of a family as support by the State (and paid to the family in addition to the amount of assistance otherwise payable to the family) pursuant to a plan approved under this part if such amount would have been paid to the family by the State under section 602(a)(28) of this title, as in effect and applied on the day before August 21, 1996.

(e) Foster care maintenance payments

Notwithstanding the preceding provisions of this section, amounts collected by a State as child support for months in any period on behalf of a child for whom a public agency is making foster care maintenance payments under part E of this subchapter (42 U.S.C. 670 et seq.)—

(1) shall be retained by the State to the extent necessary to reimburse it for the foster care maintenance payments made with respect to the child during such period (with appropriate reimbursement of the Federal Government to the extent of its participation in the financing);

(2) shall be paid to the public agency responsible for supervising the placement of the child to the extent that the amounts collected exceed the foster care maintenance payments made with respect to the child during such period but not the amounts required by a court or administrative order to be paid as support on behalf of the child during such period; and the responsible agency may use the payments in the manner it determines will serve the best interests of the child, including setting such payments aside for the child's future needs or making all or a part thereof available to the person responsible for meeting the child's day-to-day needs; and

(3) shall be retained by the State, if any portion of the amounts collected remains after making the payments required under paragraphs (1) and (2), to the extent that such portion is necessary to reimburse the State (with appropriate reimbursement to the Federal Government to the extent of its participation in the financing) for any past foster care maintenance payments (or payments of assistance under the State program funded under part A of this subchapter (42 U.S.C. 601 et seq.)) which were made with respect to the child (and with respect to which past collections have not previously been retained); and any balance shall be paid to the State agency responsible for supervising the placement of the child, for use by such agency in accordance with paragraph (2).

§ 659. Consent by the United States to income withholding, garnishment, and similar proceedings for enforcement of child support and alimony obligations.

(a) Consent to support enforcement

Notwithstanding any other provision of law (including section 407 of this title and section 5301 of Title 38), effective January 1, 1975, moneys (the entitlement to which is based upon remuneration for employment) due from, or payable by, the United States or the District of Columbia (including any agency, subdivision, or instrumentality thereof) to any individual, including members of the Armed Forces of the United States, shall be subject, in like manner and to the same extent as if the United States or the District of Columbia were a private person, to withholding in accordance with State law enacted pursuant to subsections (a)(1) and (b) of section 666 of this title and regulations of the Secretary under such subsections, and to any other legal process brought, by a State agency administering a program under a State plan approved under this part or by an individual obligee, to enforce the legal obligation of the individual to provide child support or alimony.

(b) Consent to requirements applicable to private person

With respect to notice to withhold income pursuant to subsection (a)(1) or (b) of section 666 of this title, or any other order or process to enforce support obligations against an individual (if the order or process contains or is accompanied by sufficient data to permit prompt identification of the individual and the moneys involved), each governmental entity specified in subsection (a) of this section shall be subject to the same requirements as would apply if the entity were a private person, except as otherwise provided in this section.

(c) Designation of agent; response to notice or process

(1) Designation of agent

The head of each agency subject to this section shall—

(A) designate an agent or agents to receive orders and accept service of process in matters relating to child support or alimony; and

(B) annually publish in the Federal Register the designation of the agent or agents, identified by title or position, mailing address, and telephone number.

(2) Response to notice or process

If an agent designated pursuant to paragraph (1) of this subsection receives notice pursuant to State procedures in effect pursuant to subsection (a)(1) or (b) of section 666 of this title, or is effectively served with any order, process, or interrogatory, with respect to an individual's child support or alimony payment obligations, the agent shall—

(A) as soon as possible (but not later than 15 days) thereafter, send written notice of the notice or service (together with a copy of the notice or service) to the individual at the duty station or last-known home address of the individual;

(B) within 30 days (or such longer period as may be prescribed by applicable State law) after receipt of a notice pursuant to such State procedures, comply with all applicable provisions of section 666 of this title; and

(C) within 30 days (or such longer period as may be prescribed by applicable State law) after effective service of any other such order, process, or interrogatory, withhold available sums in response to the order or process, or answer the interrogatory.

(d) Priority of claims

If a governmental entity specified in subsection (a) of this section receives notice or is served with process, as provided in this section, concerning amounts owed by an individual to more than 1 person—

(1) support collection under section 666(b) of this title must be given priority over any other process, as provided in section 666(b)(7) of this title;

(2) allocation of moneys due or payable to an individual among claimants under section 666(b) of this title shall be governed by section 666(b) of this title and the regulations prescribed under such section; and

(3) such moneys as remain after compliance with paragraphs (1) and (2) shall be available to satisfy any other such processes on a first-come, first-served basis, with any such process being satisfied out of such moneys as remain after the satisfaction of all such processes which have been previously served.

(e) No requirement to vary pay cycles

A governmental entity that is affected by legal process served for the enforcement of an individual's child support or alimony payment obligations shall not be required to vary its normal pay and disbursement cycle in order to comply with the legal process.

(f) Relief from liability

(1) Neither the United States, nor the government of the District of Columbia, nor any disbursing officer shall be liable with respect to any payment made from moneys due or payable from the United States to any individual pursuant to legal process regular on its face, if the payment is made in accordance with this section and the regulations issued to carry out this section.

(2) No Federal employee whose duties include taking actions necessary to comply with the requirements of subsection (a) of this section with regard to any individual shall be subject under any law to any disciplinary action or civil or criminal liability or penalty for, or on account of, any disclosure of information made by the employee in connection with the carrying out of such actions.

(g) Regulations

Authority to promulgate regulations for the implementation of this section shall, insofar as this section applies to moneys due from (or payable by)—

(1) the United States (other than the legislative or judicial branches of the Federal Government) or the government of the District of Columbia, be vested in the President (or the designee of the President);

(2) the legislative branch of the Federal Government, be vested jointly in the President pro tempore of the Senate and the Speaker of the House of Representatives (or their designees), and

(3) the judicial branch of the Federal Government, be vested in the Chief Justice of the United States (or the designee of the Chief Justice).

(h) Moneys subject to process

(1) In general

Subject to paragraph (2), moneys payable to an individual which are considered to be based upon remuneration for employment, for purposes of this section—

(A) consist of—

(i) compensation payable for personal services of the individual, whether the compensation is denominated as wages, salary, commission, bonus, pay, allowances, or otherwise (including severance pay, sick pay, and incentive pay);

(ii) periodic benefits (including a periodic benefit as defined in section 428(h)(3) of this title) or other payments—

(I) under the insurance system established by subchapter II of this chapter;

(II) under any other system or fund established by the United States which provides for the payment of pensions, retirement or retired pay, annuities, dependents' or survivors' benefits, or similar amounts payable on account of personal services performed by the individual or any other individual;

(III) as compensation for death under any Federal program;

(IV) under any Federal program established to provide "black lung" benefits; or

(V) by the Secretary of Veterans Affairs as compensation for a service-connected disability paid by the Secretary to a former member of the Armed Forces who is in receipt of retired or retainer pay if the former member has waived a portion of the retired or retainer pay in order to receive such compensation;

(iii) worker's compensation benefits paid or payable under Federal or State law;

(iv) benefits paid or payable under the Railroad Retirement System, and

(v) special benefits for certain World War II veterans payable under subchapter VIII of this chapter [42 U.S.C. § 1001 et seq.]; but

(B) do not include any payment—

(i) by way of reimbursement or otherwise, to defray expenses incurred by the individual in carrying out duties associated with the employment of the individual;

(ii) as allowances for members of the uniformed services payable pursuant to chapter 7 of Title 37, as prescribed by the Secretaries concerned (defined by section 101(5) of Title 37) as necessary for the efficient performance of duty; or

(iii) of periodic benefits under title 38, United States Code, except as provided in subparagraph (A)(ii)(V).

(2) Certain amounts excluded

In determining the amount of any moneys due from, or payable by, the United States to any individual, there shall be excluded amounts which—

(A) are owed by the individual to the United States;

(B) are required by law to be, and are, deducted from the remuneration or other payment involved, including Federal employment taxes, and fines and forfeitures ordered by court-martial;

(C) are properly withheld for Federal, State, or local income tax purposes, if the withholding of the amounts is authorized or required by law and if amounts withheld are not greater than would be the case if the individual claimed all dependents to which he was entitled (the withholding of additional amounts pursuant to section 3402(i) of the Internal Revenue Code of 1986 may be permitted only when the individual presents evidence of a tax obligation which supports the additional withholding);

(D) are deducted as health insurance premiums;

(E) are deducted as normal retirement contributions (not including amounts deducted for supplementary coverage); or

(F) are deducted as normal life insurance premiums from salary or other remuneration for employment (not including amounts deducted for supplementary coverage).

(i) Definitions

For purposes of this section—

(1) United States

The term "United States" includes any department, agency, or instrumentality of the legislative, judicial, or executive branch of the Federal Government, the United States Postal Service, the Postal Regulatory Commission, any Federal corporation created by an Act of Congress that is wholly owned by the Federal Government, and the governments of the territories and possessions of the United States.

(2) Child support

The term "child support", when used in reference to the legal obligations of an individual to provide such support, means amounts required to be paid under a judgment, decree, or order, whether temporary, final, or subject to modification, issued by a court or an administrative agency of competent jurisdiction, for the support and maintenance of a child, including a child who has attained the age of majority under the law of the issuing State, or a child and the parent with whom the child is living, which provides for monetary support, health care, arrearages or reimbursement, and which may include other related costs and fees, interest and penalties, income withholding, attorney's fees, and other relief.

(3) Alimony

(A) In general

The term "alimony", when used in reference to the legal obligations of an individual to provide the same, means periodic payments of funds for the support and maintenance of the spouse (or former spouse) of the individual, and (subject to and in accordance with State law) includes separate maintenance, alimony pendente lite, maintenance, and spousal support, and includes attorney's fees, interest, and court costs when and to the extent that the same are expressly made recoverable as such pursuant to a decree, order, or judgment issued in accordance with applicable State law by a court of competent jurisdiction.

(B) Exceptions

Such term does not include—

(i) any child support; or

(ii) any payment or transfer of property or its value by an individual to the spouse or a former spouse of the individual in compliance with any community property settlement, equitable distribution of property, or other division of property between spouses or former spouses.

(4) Private person

The term "private person" means a person who does not have sovereign or other special immunity or privilege which causes the person not to be subject to legal process.

(5) Legal process

The term "legal process" means any writ, order, summons, or other similar process in the nature of garnishment—

(A) which is issued by—

(i) a court or an administrative agency of competent jurisdiction in any State, territory, or possession of the United States;

(ii) a court or an administrative agency of competent jurisdiction in any foreign country with which the United States has entered into an agreement which requires the United States to honor the process; or

(iii) an authorized official pursuant to an order of such a court or an administrative agency of competent jurisdiction or pursuant to State or local law; and

(B) which is directed to, and the purpose of which is to compel, a governmental entity which holds moneys which are otherwise payable to an individual to make a payment from the moneys to another party in order to satisfy a legal obligation of the individual to provide child support or make alimony payments.

§ 659a. International support enforcement.

(a) Authority for declarations

(1) Declaration

The Secretary of State, with the concurrence of the Secretary of Health and Human Services, is authorized to declare any foreign country (or a political subdivision thereof) to be a foreign reciprocating country if the foreign country has established, or undertakes to establish, procedures for the establishment and enforcement of duties of support owed to obligees who are residents of the United States, and such procedures are substantially in conformity with the standards prescribed under subsection (b) of this section.

(2) Revocation

A declaration with respect to a foreign country made pursuant to paragraph (1) may be revoked if the Secretaries of State and Health and Human Services determine that—

(A) the procedures established by the foreign country regarding the establishment and enforcement of duties of support have been so changed, or the foreign country's implementation of such procedures is so unsatisfactory, that such procedures do not meet the criteria for such a declaration; or

(B) continued operation of the declaration is not consistent with the purposes of this part.

(3) Form of declaration

A declaration under paragraph (1) may be made in the form of an international agreement, in connection with an international agreement or corresponding foreign declaration, or on a unilateral basis.

(b) Standards for foreign support enforcement procedures

(1) Mandatory elements

Support enforcement procedures of a foreign country which may be the subject of a declaration pursuant to subsection (a)(1) of this section shall include the following elements:

(A) The foreign country (or political subdivision thereof) has in effect procedures, available to residents of the United States—

(i) for establishment of paternity, and for establishment of orders of support for children and custodial parents; and

(ii) for enforcement of orders to provide support to children and custodial parents, including procedures for collection and appropriate distribution of support payments under such orders.

(B) The procedures described in subparagraph (A), including legal and administrative assistance, are provided to residents of the United States at no cost.

(C) An agency of the foreign country is designated as a Central Authority responsible for—

(i) facilitating support enforcement in cases involving residents of the foreign country and residents of the United States; and

(ii) ensuring compliance with the standards established pursuant to this subsection.

(2) Additional elements

The Secretary of Health and Human Services and the Secretary of State, in consultation with the States, may establish such additional standards as may be considered necessary to further the purposes of this section.

(c) Designation of United States Central Authority

It shall be the responsibility of the Secretary of Health and Human Services to facilitate support enforcement in cases involving residents of the United States and residents of foreign reciprocating countries or foreign treaty countries, by activities including—

(1) development of uniform forms and procedures for use in such cases;

(2) notification of foreign reciprocating countries and foreign treaty countries of the State of residence of individuals sought for support enforcement purposes, on the basis of information provided by the Federal Parent Locator Service; and

(3) such other oversight, assistance, and coordination activities as the Secretary may find necessary and appropriate.

(d) Effect on other laws

States may enter into reciprocal arrangements for the establishment and enforcement of support obligations with foreign countries that are not foreign reciprocating countries or foreign treaty countries, to the extent consistent with Federal law.

(e) References

In this part:

(1) Foreign reciprocating country

The term "foreign reciprocating country" means a foreign country (or political subdivision thereof) with respect to which the Secretary has made a declaration pursuant to subsection (a).

(2) Foreign treaty country

The term "foreign treaty country" means a foreign country for which the 2007 Family Maintenance Convention is in force.

(3) 2007 Family Maintenance Convention

The term "2007 Family Maintenance Convention" means the Hague Convention of 23 November 2007 on the International Recovery of Child Support and Other Forms of Family Maintenance.

(Aug. 14, 1935, ch. 531, title IV, § 459A, as added Pub. L. 104–193, title III, § 371(a), Aug. 22, 1996, 110 Stat. 2252; amended Pub. L. 113–183, title III, § 301(d), Sept. 29, 2014, 128 Stat. 1944.)

§ 660. Civil action to enforce child support obligations; jurisdiction of district courts.

The district courts of the United States shall have jurisdiction, without regard to any amount in controversy, to hear and determine any civil action certified by the Secretary of Health and Human Services under section 652(a)(8) of this title. A civil action under this section may be brought in any judicial district in which the claim arose, the plaintiff resides, or the defendant resides.

§ 663. Use of Federal Parent Locator Service in connection with enforcement or determination of child custody in cases of parental kidnapping of child.

(a) Agreements with States for use of Federal Parent Locator Service

The Secretary shall enter into an agreement with every State under which the services of the Federal Parent Locator Service established under section 653 of this title shall be made available to each State for the purpose of determining the whereabouts of any parent or child when such information is to be used to locate such parent or child for the purpose of—

(1) enforcing any State or Federal law with respect to the unlawful taking or restraint of a child; or

(2) making or enforcing a child custody or visitation determination.

(b) Requests from authorized persons for information

An agreement entered into under subsection (a) of this section shall provide that the State agency described in section 654 of this title will, under procedures prescribed by the Secretary in regulations, receive and transmit to the Secretary requests from authorized persons for information as to (or useful in determining) the whereabouts of any parent or child when such information is to be used to locate such parent or child for the purpose of—

(1) enforcing any State or Federal law with respect to the unlawful taking or restraint of a child; or

(2) making or enforcing a child custody or visitation determination.

(c) Information which may be disclosed

Information authorized to be provided by the Secretary under subsection (a), (b), (e), or (f) of this section shall be subject to the same conditions with respect to disclosure as information authorized to be provided under section 653 of this title, and a request for information by the Secretary under this section shall be considered to be a request for information under section 653 of this title which is authorized to be provided under such section. Only information as to the most recent address and place of employment of any parent or child shall be provided under this section.

(d) "Custody determination" and "authorized person" defined

For purposes of this section—

(1) the term "custody or visitation determination" means a judgment, decree, or other order of a court providing for the custody or visitation of a child, and includes permanent and temporary orders, and initial orders and modification;

(2) the term "authorized person" means—

(A) any agent or attorney of any State having an agreement under this section, who has the duty or authority under the law of such State to enforce a child custody or visitation determination;

(B) any court having jurisdiction to make or enforce such a child custody or visitation determination, or any agent of such court; and

(C) any agent or attorney of the United States, or of a State having an agreement under this section, who has the duty or authority to investigate, enforce, or bring a prosecution with respect to the unlawful taking or restraint of a child.

(e) Agreements on use of Federal Parent Locator Service with United States Central Authority under Convention on the Civil Aspects of International Child Abduction

The Secretary shall enter into an agreement with the Central Authority designated by the President in accordance with section 11606 of this title, under which the services of the Federal Parent Locator Service established under section 653 of this title shall be made available to such Central Authority upon its request for the purpose of locating any parent or child on behalf of an applicant to such Central Authority within the meaning of section 11602(1) of this title. The Federal Parent Locator Service shall charge no fees for services requested pursuant to this subsection.

(f) Agreement to assist in locating missing children under Parent Locator Service

The Secretary shall enter into an agreement with the Attorney General of the United States, under which the services of the Federal Parent Locator Service established under section 653 of this title shall be made available to the Office of Juvenile Justice and Delinquency Prevention upon its request to locate any parent or child on behalf of such Office for the purpose of—

(1) enforcing any State or Federal law with respect to the unlawful taking or restraint of a child, or

(2) making or enforcing a child custody or visitation determination.

The Federal Parent Locator Service shall charge no fees for services requested pursuant to this subsection.

U.S.C.   SOCIAL SECURITY   42 § 664

§ 664. Collection of past-due support from Federal tax refunds.

(a) Procedures applicable; distribution

(1) Upon receiving notice from a State agency administering a plan approved under this part that a named individual owes past-due support which has been assigned to such State pursuant to section 608(a)(3) or section 671(a)(17) of this title, the Secretary of the Treasury shall determine whether any amounts, as refunds of Federal taxes paid, are payable to such individual (regardless of whether such individual filed a tax return as a married or unmarried individual). If the Secretary of the Treasury finds that any such amount is payable, he shall withhold from such refunds an amount equal to the past-due support, shall concurrently send notice to such individual that the withholding has been made (including in or with such notice a notification to any other person who may have filed a joint return with such individual of the steps which such other person may take in order to secure his or her proper share of the refund), and shall pay such amount to the State agency (together with notice of the individual's home address) for distribution in accordance with section 657 of this title. This subsection may be executed by the disbursing official of the Department of the Treasury.

(2)(A) Upon receiving notice from a State agency administering a plan approved under this part that a named individual owes past-due support which such State has agreed to collect under paragraph (4)(A)(ii) or (32) of section 654 of this title, and that the State agency has sent notice to such individual in accordance with paragraph (3)(A), the Secretary of the Treasury shall determine whether any amounts, as refunds of Federal taxes paid, are payable to such individual (regardless of whether such individual filed a tax return as a married or unmarried individual). If the Secretary of the Treasury finds that any such amount is payable, he shall withhold from such refunds an amount equal to such past-due support, and shall concurrently send notice to such individual that the withholding has been made, including in or with such notice a notification to any other person who may have filed a joint return with such individual of the steps which such other person may take in order to secure his or her proper share of the refund. The Secretary of the Treasury shall pay the amount withheld to the State agency, and the State shall pay to the Secretary of the Treasury any fee imposed by the Secretary of the Treasury to cover the costs of the withholding and any required notification. The State agency shall, subject to paragraph (3)(B), distribute such amount to or on behalf of the child to whom the support was owed in accordance with section 657 of this title. This subsection may be executed by the Secretary of the Department of the Treasury or his designee.

(B) This paragraph shall apply only with respect to refunds payable under section 6402 of the Internal Revenue Code of 1986 after December 31, 1985.

(3)(A) Prior to notifying the Secretary of the Treasury under paragraph (1) or (2) that an individual owes past-due support, the State shall send notice to such individual that a withholding will be made from any refund otherwise payable to such individual. The notice shall also (i) instruct the individual owing the past-due support of the steps which may be taken to contest the State's determination that past-due support is owed or the amount of the past-due support, and (ii) provide information, as may be prescribed by the Secretary of Health and Human Services by regulation in consultation with the Secretary of the Treasury, with respect to procedures to be followed, in the case of a joint return, to protect the share of the refund which may be payable to another person.

(B) If the Secretary of the Treasury determines that an amount should be withheld under paragraph (1) or (2), and that the refund from which it should be withheld is based upon a joint return, the Secretary of the Treasury shall notify the State that the withholding is being made from a refund based upon a joint return, and shall furnish to the State the names and addresses of each taxpayer filing such joint return. In the case of a withholding under paragraph

(2), the State may delay distribution of the amount withheld until the State has been notified by the Secretary of the Treasury that the other person filing the joint return has received his or her proper share of the refund, but such delay may not exceed six months.

(C) If the other person filing the joint return with the named individual owing the past-due support takes appropriate action to secure his or her proper share of a refund from which a withholding was made under paragraph (1) or (2), the Secretary of the Treasury shall pay such share to such other person. The Secretary of the Treasury shall deduct the amount of such payment from amounts subsequently payable to the State agency to which the amount originally withheld from such refund was paid.

(D) In any case in which an amount was withheld under paragraph (1) or (2) and paid to a State, and the State subsequently determines that the amount certified as past-due support was in excess of the amount actually owed at the time the amount withheld is to be distributed to or on behalf of the child, the State shall pay the excess amount withheld to the named individual thought to have owed the past-due support (or, in the case of amounts withheld on the basis of a joint return, jointly to the parties filing such return).

(b) Regulations; contents, etc.

(1) The Secretary of the Treasury shall issue regulations, approved by the Secretary of Health and Human Services, prescribing the time or times at which States must submit notices of past-due support, the manner in which such notices must be submitted, and the necessary information that must be contained in or accompany the notices. The regulations shall be consistent with the provisions of subsection (a) (3) of this section, shall specify the minimum amount of past-due support to which the offset procedure established by subsection (a) of this section may be applied, and the fee that a State must pay to reimburse the Secretary of the Treasury for the full cost of applying the offset procedure, and shall provide that the Secretary of the Treasury will advise the Secretary of Health and Human Services, not less frequently than annually, of the States which have furnished notices of past-due support under subsection (a) of this section, the number of cases in each State with respect to which such notices have been furnished, the amount of support sought to be collected under this subsection by each State, and the amount of such collections actually made in the case of each State. Any fee paid to the Secretary of the Treasury pursuant to this subsection may be used to reimburse appropriations which bore all or part of the cost of applying such procedure.

(2) In the case of withholdings made under subsection (a)(2) of this section, the regulations promulgated pursuant to this subsection shall include the following requirements:

(A) The withholding shall apply only in the case where the State determines that the amount of the past-due support which will be owed at the time the withholding is to be made, based upon the pattern of payment of support and other enforcement actions being pursued to collect the past-due support, is equal to or greater than $500. The State may limit the $500 threshold amount to amounts of past-due support accrued since the time that the State first began to enforce the child support order involved under the State plan, and may limit the application of the withholding to past-due support accrued since such time.

(B) The fee which the Secretary of the Treasury may impose to cover the costs of the withholding and notification may not exceed $25 per case submitted.

(c) "Past-due support" defined

In this part the term "past-due support" means the amount of a delinquency, determined under a court order, or an order of an administrative process established under State law, for support and maintenance of a child (whether or not a minor), or of a child (whether or not a minor) and the parent with whom the child is living.

(Aug. 14, 1935, ch. 531, title IV, § 464, as added Pub. L. 97–35, title XXIII, § 2331(a), Aug. 13, 1981, 95 Stat. 860; amended Pub. L. 98–378, §§ 11(d), 21(a)–(c), Aug. 16, 1984, 98 Stat. 1318, 1322-1324; Pub. L. 99–514, § 2, title XVIII, § 1883(b)(8), Oct. 22, 1986, 100 Stat. 2095, 2917; Pub. L. 101–508, title V, § 5011(a), (b), Nov. 5, 1990, 104 Stat. 1388–220; Pub. L. 104–134, title III, § 31001(v)(2), Apr. 26, 1996, 110 Stat. 1321–375; Pub. L. 104–193, title III, § 302(b)(1), Aug. 22, 1996, 110 Stat. 2204; Pub. L. 105–33, title V, §§ 5513(a)(4), 5531(b), 5532(i)(1), Aug. 5, 1997, 111 Stat. 620, 626, 627; Pub. L. 109–171, title VII, § 7301(f)(1), Feb. 8, 2006, 120 Stat. 144; Pub. L. 113–183, title III, § 301(e), Sept. 29, 2014, 128 Stat. 1944.)

§ 665. Allotments from pay for child and spousal support owed by members of uniformed services on active duty.

(a) Mandatory allotment; notice upon failure to make; amount of allotment; adjustment or discontinuance; consultation

(1) In any case in which child support payments or child and spousal support payments are owed by a member of one of the uniformed services (as defined in section 101(3) of Title 37) on active duty, such member shall be required to make allotments from his pay and allowances (under chapter 13 of Title 37) as payment of such support, when he has failed to make periodic payments under a support order that meets the criteria specified in section 1673(b)(1)(A) of Title 15 and the resulting delinquency in such payments is in a total amount equal to the support payable for two months or longer. Failure to make such payments shall be established by notice from an authorized person (as defined in subsection (b) of this section) to the designated official in the appropriate uniformed service. Such notice (which shall in turn be given to the affected member) shall also specify the person to whom the allotment is to be payable. The amount of the allotment shall be the amount necessary to comply with the order (which, if the order so provides, may include arrearages as well as amounts for current support), except that the amount of the allotment, together with any other amounts withheld for support from the wages of the member, as a percentage of his pay from the uniformed service, shall not exceed the limits prescribed in sections 1673(b) and (c) of Title 15. An allotment under this subsection shall be adjusted or discontinued upon notice from the authorized person.

(2) Notwithstanding the preceding provisions of this subsection, no action shall be taken to require an allotment from the pay and allowances of any member of one of the uniformed services under such provisions (A) until such member has had a consultation with a judge advocate of the service involved (as defined in section 801(13) of Title 10), or with a judge advocate (as defined in section 801(11) of such title) in the case of the Coast Guard, or with a legal officer designated by the Secretary concerned (as defined in section 101(5) of Title 37) in any other case, in person, to discuss the legal and other factors involved with respect to the member's support obligation and his failure to make payments thereon, or (B) until 30 days have elapsed after the notice described in the second sentence of paragraph (1) is given to the affected member in any case where it has not been possible, despite continuing good faith efforts, to arrange such a consultation.

(b) "Authorized person" defined

For purposes of this section the term "authorized person" with respect to any member of the uniformed services means—

(1) any agent or attorney of a State having in effect a plan approved under this part who has the duty or authority under such plan to seek to recover any amounts owed by such member as child or child and spousal support (including, when authorized under the State plan, any official of a political subdivision); and

(2) the court which has authority to issue an order against such member for the support and maintenance of a child, or any agent of such court.

(c) Regulations

The Secretary of Defense, in the case of the Army, Navy, Air Force, and Marine Corps, and the Secretary concerned (as defined in section 101(5) of Title 37) in the case of each of the other uniformed services, shall each issue regulations applicable to allotments to be made under this section, designating the officials to whom notice of failure to make support payments, or notice to discontinue or adjust an allotment, should be given, prescribing the form and content of the notice and specifying any other rules necessary for such Secretary to implement this section.

§ 666. Requirement of statutorily prescribed procedures to improve effectiveness of child support enforcement.

(a) Types of procedures required

In order to satisfy section 654(20)(A) of this title, each State must have in effect laws requiring the use of the following procedures, consistent with this section and with regulations of the Secretary, to increase the effectiveness of the program which the State administers under this part:

(1)(A) Procedures described in subsection (b) of this section for the withholding from income of amounts payable as support in cases subject to enforcement under the State plan.

(B) Procedures under which the income of a person with a support obligation imposed by a support order issued (or modified) in the State before January 1, 1994, if not otherwise subject to withholding under subsection (b) of this section, shall become subject to withholding as provided in subsection (b) of this section if arrearages occur, without the need for a judicial or administrative hearing.

(2) Expedited administrative and judicial procedures (including the procedures specified in subsection (c) of this section) for establishing paternity and for establishing, modifying, and enforcing support obligations. The Secretary may waive the provisions of this paragraph with respect to one or more political subdivisions within the State on the basis of the effectiveness and timeliness of support order issuance and enforcement or paternity establishment within the political subdivision (in accordance with the general rule for exemptions under subsection (d) of this section).

(3) Procedures under which the State child support enforcement agency shall request, and the State shall provide, that for the purpose of enforcing a support order under any State plan approved under this part—

(A) any refund of State income tax which would otherwise be payable to a noncustodial parent will be reduced, after notice has been sent to that noncustodial parent of the proposed reduction and the procedures to be followed to contest it (and after full compliance with all procedural due process requirements of the State), by the amount of any overdue support owed by such noncustodial parent;

(B) the amount by which such refund is reduced shall be distributed in accordance with section 657 of this title in the case of overdue support assigned to a State pursuant to section 608(a)(3) or 671(a)(17) of this title, or, in any other case, shall be distributed, after deduction of any fees imposed by the State to cover the costs of collection, to the child or parent to whom such support is owed; and

(C) notice of the noncustodial parent's social security account number (or numbers, if he has more than one such number) and home address shall be furnished to the State agency requesting the refund offset, and to the State agency enforcing the order.

(4) Liens

Procedures under which—

(A) liens arise by operation of law against real and personal property for amounts of overdue support owed by a noncustodial parent who resides or owns property in the State; and

(B) the State accords full faith and credit to liens described in subparagraph (A) arising in another State, when the State agency, party, or other entity seeking to enforce such a lien complies with the procedural rules relating to recording or serving liens that arise within the State, except that such rules may not require judicial notice or hearing prior to the enforcement of such a lien.

(5) Procedures concerning paternity establishment

  (A) Establishment process available from birth until age 18

    (i) Procedures which permit the establishment of the paternity of a child at any time before the child attains 18 years of age.

    (ii) As of August 16, 1984, clause (i) shall also apply to a child for whom paternity has not been established or for whom a paternity action was brought but dismissed because a statute of limitations of less than 18 years was then in effect in the State.

  (B) Procedures concerning genetic testing

    (i) Genetic testing required in certain contested cases

  Procedures under which the State is required, in a contested paternity case (unless otherwise barred by State law) to require the child and all other parties (other than individuals found under section 654(29) of this title to have good cause and other exceptions for refusing to cooperate) to submit to genetic tests upon the request of any such party, if the request is supported by a sworn statement by the party—

      (I) alleging paternity, and setting forth facts establishing a reasonable possibility of the requisite sexual contact between the parties; or

      (II) denying paternity, and setting forth facts establishing a reasonable possibility of the nonexistence of sexual contact between the parties.

    (ii) Other requirements

  Procedures which require the State agency, in any case in which the agency orders genetic testing—

      (I) to pay costs of such tests, subject to recoupment (if the State so elects) from the alleged father if paternity is established; and

      (II) to obtain additional testing in any case if an original test result is contested, upon request and advance payment by the contestant.

  (C) Voluntary paternity acknowledgment

    (i) Simple civil process

  Procedures for a simple civil process for voluntarily acknowledging paternity under which the State must provide that, before a mother and a putative father can sign an acknowledgment of paternity, the mother and the putative father must be given notice, orally, or through the use of video or audio equipment, and in writing, of the alternatives to, the legal consequences of, and the rights (including, if 1 parent is a minor, any rights afforded due to minority status) and responsibilities that arise from, signing the acknowledgment.

    (ii) Hospital-based program

  Such procedures must include a hospital-based program for the voluntary acknowledgment of paternity focusing on the period immediately before or after the birth of a child.

    (iii) Paternity establishment services

      (I) State-offered services

  Such procedures must require the State agency responsible for maintaining birth records to offer voluntary paternity establishment services.

      (II) Regulations

(aa) Services offered by hospitals and birth record agencies

The Secretary shall prescribe regulations governing voluntary paternity establishment services offered by hospitals and birth record agencies.

(bb) Services offered by other entities

The Secretary shall prescribe regulations specifying the types of other entities that may offer voluntary paternity establishment services, and governing the provision of such services, which shall include a requirement that such an entity must use the same notice provisions used by, use the same materials used by, provide the personnel providing such services with the same training provided by, and evaluate the provision of such services in the same manner as the provision of such services is evaluated by, voluntary paternity establishment programs of hospitals and birth record agencies.

(iv) Use of paternity acknowledgment affidavit

Such procedures must require the State to develop and use an affidavit for the voluntary acknowledgment of paternity which includes the minimum requirements of the affidavit specified by the Secretary under section 652(a)(7) of this title for the voluntary acknowledgment of paternity, and to give full faith and credit to such an affidavit signed in any other State according to its procedures.

(D) Status of signed paternity acknowledgment

(i) Inclusion in birth records

Procedures under which the name of the father shall be included on the record of birth of the child of unmarried parents only if—

(I) the father and mother have signed a voluntary acknowledgment of paternity; or

(II) a court or an administrative agency of competent jurisdiction has issued an adjudication of paternity.

Nothing in this clause shall preclude a State agency from obtaining an admission of paternity from the father for submission in a judicial or administrative proceeding, or prohibit the issuance of an order in a judicial or administrative proceeding which bases a legal finding of paternity on an admission of paternity by the father and any other additional showing required by State law.

(ii) Legal finding of paternity

Procedures under which a signed voluntary acknowledgment of paternity is considered a legal finding of paternity, subject to the right of any signatory to rescind the acknowledgment within the earlier of—

(I) 60 days; or

(II) the date of an administrative or judicial proceeding relating to the child (including a proceeding to establish a support order) in which the signatory is a party.

(iii) Contest

Procedures under which, after the 60-day period referred to in clause (ii), a signed voluntary acknowledgment of paternity may be challenged in court only on the basis of fraud, duress, or material mistake of fact, with the burden of proof upon the challenger, and under which the legal responsibilities (including child support obligations) of any signatory arising from the acknowledgment may not be suspended during the challenge, except for good cause shown.

(E) Bar on acknowledgment ratification proceedings

Procedures under which judicial or administrative proceedings are not required or permitted to ratify an unchallenged acknowledgment of paternity.

(F) Admissibility of genetic testing results

Procedures—

(i) requiring the admission into evidence, for purposes of establishing paternity, of the results of any genetic test that is—

(I) of a type generally acknowledged as reliable by accreditation bodies designated by the Secretary; and

(II) performed by a laboratory approved by such an accreditation body;

(ii) requiring an objection to genetic testing results to be made in writing not later than a specified number of days before any hearing at which the results may be introduced into evidence (or, at State option, not later than a specified number of days after receipt of the results); and

(iii) making the test results admissible as evidence of paternity without the need for foundation testimony or other proof of authenticity or accuracy, unless objection is made.

(G) Presumption of paternity in certain cases

Procedures which create a rebuttable or, at the option of the State, conclusive presumption of paternity upon genetic testing results indicating a threshold probability that the alleged father is the father of the child.

(H) Default orders

Procedures requiring a default order to be entered in a paternity case upon a showing of service of process on the defendant and any additional showing required by State law.

(I) No right to jury trial

Procedures providing that the parties to an action to establish paternity are not entitled to a trial by jury.

(J) Temporary support order based on probable paternity in contested cases

Procedures which require that a temporary order be issued, upon motion by a party, requiring the provision of child support pending an administrative or judicial determination of parentage, if there is clear and convincing evidence of paternity (on the basis of genetic tests or other evidence).

(K) Proof of certain support and paternity establishment costs

Procedures under which bills for pregnancy, childbirth, and genetic testing are admissible as evidence without requiring third-party foundation testimony, and shall constitute prima facie evidence of amounts incurred for such services or for testing on behalf of the child.

(L) Standing of putative fathers

Procedures ensuring that the putative father has a reasonable opportunity to initiate a paternity action.

(M) Filing of acknowledgments and adjudications in State registry of birth records

Procedures under which voluntary acknowledgments and adjudications of paternity by judicial or administrative processes are filed with the State registry of birth records for comparison with information in the State case registry.

(6) Procedures which require that a noncustodial parent give security, post a bond, or give some other guarantee to secure payment of overdue support, after notice has been sent to such noncustodial parent of the proposed action and of the procedures to be followed to contest it (and after full compliance with all procedural due process requirements of the State).

(7) Reporting arrearages to credit bureaus

(A) In general

Procedures (subject to safeguards pursuant to subparagraph (B)) requiring the State to report periodically to consumer reporting agencies (as defined in section 1681a(f) of Title 15) the name of any noncustodial parent who is delinquent in the payment of support, and the amount of overdue support owed by such parent.

(B) Safeguards

Procedures ensuring that, in carrying out subparagraph (A), information with respect to a noncustodial parent is reported—

(i) only after such parent has been afforded all due process required under State law, including notice and a reasonable opportunity to contest the accuracy of such information; and

(ii) only to an entity that has furnished evidence satisfactory to the State that the entity is a consumer reporting agency (as so defined).

(8)(A) Procedures under which all child support orders not described in subparagraph (B) will include provision for withholding from income, in order to assure that withholding as a means of collecting child support is available if arrearages occur without the necessity of filing application for services under this part.

(B) Procedures under which all child support orders which are initially issued in the State on or after January 1, 1994, and are not being enforced under this part will include the following requirements:

(i) The income of a noncustodial parent shall be subject to withholding, regardless of whether support payments by such parent are in arrears, on the effective date of the order; except that such income shall not be subject to withholding under this clause in any case where (I) one of the parties demonstrates, and the court (or administrative process) finds, that there is good cause not to require immediate income withholding, or (II) a written agreement is reached between both parties which provides for an alternative arrangement.

(ii) The requirements of subsection (b)(1) of this section (which shall apply in the case of each noncustodial parent against whom a support order is or has been issued or modified in the State, without regard to whether the order is being enforced under the State plan).

(iii) The requirements of paragraphs (2), (5), (6), (7), (8), (9), and (10) of subsection (b) of this section, where applicable.

(iv) Withholding from income of amounts payable as support must be carried out in full compliance with all procedural due process requirements of the State.

(9) Procedures which require that any payment or installment of support under any child support order, whether ordered through the State judicial system or through the expedited processes required by paragraph (2), is (on and after the date it is due)—

(A) a judgment by operation of law, with the full force, effect, and attributes of a judgment of the State, including the ability to be enforced,

(B) entitled as a judgment to full faith and credit in such State and in any other State, and

(C) not subject to retroactive modification by such State or by any other State;

except that such procedures may permit modification with respect to any period during which there is pending a petition for modification, but only from the date that notice of such petition has been given, either directly or through the appropriate agent, to the obligee or (where the obligee is the petitioner) to the obligor.

(10) Review and adjustment of support orders upon request

(A) 3-year cycle

(i) In general

Procedures under which every 3 years (or such shorter cycle as the State may determine), upon the request of either parent or if there is an assignment under part A of this subchapter, the State shall with respect to a support order being enforced under this part, taking into account the best interests of the child involved—

(I) review and, if appropriate, adjust the order in accordance with the guidelines established pursuant to section 667(a) of this title if the amount of the child support award under the order differs from the amount that would be awarded in accordance with the guidelines;

(II) apply a cost-of-living adjustment to the order in accordance with a formula developed by the State; or

(III) use automated methods (including automated comparisons with wage or State income tax data) to identify orders eligible for review, conduct the review, identify orders eligible for adjustment, and apply the appropriate adjustment to the orders eligible for adjustment under any threshold that may be established by the State.

(ii) Opportunity to request review of adjustment

If the State elects to conduct the review under subclause (II) or (III) of clause (i), procedures which permit either party to contest the adjustment, within 30 days after the date of the notice of the adjustment, by making a request for review and, if appropriate, adjustment of the order in accordance with the child support guidelines established pursuant to section 667(a) of this title.

(iii) No proof of change in circumstances necessary in 3-year cycle review

Procedures which provide that any adjustment under clause (i) shall be made without a requirement for proof or showing of a change in circumstances.

(B) Proof of substantial change in circumstances necessary in request for review outside 3-year cycle

Procedures under which, in the case of a request for a review, and if appropriate, an adjustment outside the 3-year cycle (or such shorter cycle as the State may determine) under clause (i), the State shall review and, if the requesting party demonstrates a substantial change in circumstances, adjust the order in accordance with the guidelines established pursuant to section 667(a) of this title.

(C) Notice of right to review

Procedures which require the State to provide notice not less than once every 3 years to the parents subject to the order informing the parents of their right to request the State to review and, if appropriate, adjust the order pursuant to this paragraph. The notice may be included in the order.

(11) Procedures under which a State must give full faith and credit to a determination of paternity made by any other State, whether established through voluntary acknowledgment or through administrative or judicial processes.

(12) Locator information from interstate networks

Procedures to ensure that all Federal and State agencies conducting activities under this part have access to any system used by the State to locate an individual for purposes relating to motor vehicles or law enforcement.

(13) Recording of social security numbers in certain family matters

Procedures requiring that the social security number of—

(A) any applicant for a professional license, driver's license, occupational license, recreational license, or marriage license be recorded on the application;

(B) any individual who is subject to a divorce decree, support order, or paternity determination or acknowledgment be placed in the records relating to the matter; and

(C) any individual who has died be placed in the records relating to the death and be recorded on the death certificate.

For purposes of subparagraph (A), if a State allows the use of a number other than the social security number to be used on the face of the document while the social security number is kept on file at the agency, the State shall so advise any applicants.

(14) High-volume, automated administrative enforcement in interstate cases

(A) In general

Procedures under which—

(i) the State shall use high-volume automated administrative enforcement, to the same extent as used for intrastate cases, in response to a request made by another State to enforce support orders, and shall promptly report the results of such enforcement procedure to the requesting State;

(ii) the State may, by electronic or other means, transmit to another State a request for assistance in enforcing support orders through high-volume, automated administrative enforcement, which request—

(I) shall include such information as will enable the State to which the request is transmitted to compare the information about the cases to the information in the data bases of the State; and

(II) shall constitute a certification by the requesting State—

(aa) of the amount of support under an order the payment of which is in arrears; and

(bb) that the requesting State has complied with all procedural due process requirements applicable to each case;

(iii) if the State provides assistance to another State pursuant to this paragraph with respect to a case, neither State shall consider the case to be transferred to the caseload of such other State (but the assisting State may establish a corresponding case based on such other State's request for assistance); and

(iv) the State shall maintain records of—

(I) the number of such requests for assistance received by the State;

(II) the number of cases for which the State collected support in response to such a request; and

(III) the amount of such collected support.

(B) High-volume automated administrative enforcement

In this part, the term "high-volume automated administrative enforcement", in interstate cases, means, on request of another State, the identification by a State, through automated data matches with financial institutions and other entities where assets may be found, of assets owned by persons who owe child support in other States, and the seizure of such assets by the State, through levy or other appropriate processes.

(15) Procedures to ensure that persons owing overdue support work or have a plan for payment of such support

Procedures under which the State has the authority, in any case in which an individual owes overdue support with respect to a child receiving assistance under a State program funded under part A of this subchapter, to issue an order or to request that a court or an administrative process established pursuant to State law issue an order that requires the individual to—

(A) pay such support in accordance with a plan approved by the court, or, at the option of the State, a plan approved by the State agency administering the State program under this part; or

(B) if the individual is subject to such a plan and is not incapacitated, participate in such work activities (as defined in section 607(d) of this title) as the court, or, at the option of the State, the State agency administering the State program under this part, deems appropriate.

(16) Authority to withhold or suspend licenses

Procedures under which the State has (and uses in appropriate cases) authority to withhold or suspend, or to restrict the use of driver's licenses, professional and occupational licenses, and recreational and sporting licenses of individuals owing overdue support or failing, after receiving appropriate notice, to comply with subpoenas or warrants relating to paternity or child support proceedings.

(17) Financial institution data matches

(A) In general

Procedures under which the State agency shall enter into agreements with financial institutions doing business in the State—

(i) to develop and operate, in coordination with such financial institutions, and the Federal Parent Locator Service in the case of financial institutions doing business in two or more States, a data match system, using automated data exchanges to the maximum extent feasible, in which each such financial institution is required to provide for each calendar quarter the name, record address, social security number or other taxpayer identification number, and other identifying information for each noncustodial parent who maintains an account at such institution and who owes past-due support, as identified by the State by name and social security number or other taxpayer identification number; and

(ii) in response to a notice of lien or levy, encumber or surrender, as the case may be, assets held by such institution on behalf of any noncustodial parent who is subject to a child support lien pursuant to paragraph (4).

(B) Reasonable fees

The State agency may pay a reasonable fee to a financial institution for conducting the data match provided for in subparagraph (A)(i), not to exceed the actual costs incurred by such financial institution.

(C) Liability

A financial institution shall not be liable under any Federal or State law to any person—

(i) for any disclosure of information to the State agency under subparagraph (A)(i);

(ii) for encumbering or surrendering any assets held by such financial institution in response to a notice of lien or levy issued by the State agency as provided for in subparagraph (A)(ii); or

(iii) for any other action taken in good faith to comply with the requirements of subparagraph (A).

(D) Definitions

For purposes of this paragraph—

(i) Financial institution

The term "financial institution" has the meaning given to such term by section 669a(d)(1) of this title.

(ii) Account

The term "account" means a demand deposit account, checking or negotiable withdrawal order account, savings account, time deposit account, or money-market mutual fund account.

(18) Enforcement of orders against paternal or maternal grandparents

Procedures under which, at the State's option, any child support order enforced under this part with respect to a child of minor parents, if the custodial parent of such child is receiving assistance under the State program under part A of this subchapter, shall be enforceable, jointly and severally, against the parents of the noncustodial parent of such child.

(19) Health care coverage

Procedures under which—

(A) effective as provided in section 401(c)(3) of the Child Support Performance and Incentive Act of 1998, all child support orders enforced pursuant to this part shall include a provision for medical support for the child to be provided by either or both parents, and shall be enforced, where appropriate, through the use of the National Medical Support Notice promulgated pursuant to section 401(b) of the Child Support Performance and Incentive Act of 1998 (and referred to in section 609(a)(5)(C) of the Employee Retirement Income Security Act of 1974 in connection with group health plans covered under title I of such Act, in section 401(e) of the Child Support Performance and Incentive Act of 1998 in connection with State or local group health plans, and in section 401(f) of such Act in connection with church group health plans);

(B) unless alternative coverage is allowed for in any order of the court (or other entity issuing the child support order), in any case in which a parent is required under the child support order to provide such health care coverage and the employer of such parent is known to the State agency—

(i) the State agency uses the National Medical Support Notice to transfer notice of the provision for the health care coverage of the child to the employer;

(ii) within 20 business days after the date of the National Medical Support Notice, the employer is required to transfer the Notice, excluding the severable employer withholding notice described in section 401(b)(2)(C) of the Child Support Performance and Incentive Act of 1998, to the appropriate plan providing any such health care coverage for which the child is eligible;

(iii) in any case in which the parent is a newly hired employee entered in the State Directory of New Hires pursuant to section 653a(e) of this title, the State agency provides, where appropriate, the National Medical Support Notice, together with an income withholding notice issued pursuant to subsection (b) of this section, within two days after the date of the entry of such employee in such Directory; and

(iv) in any case in which the employment of the parent with any employer who has received a National Medical Support Notice is terminated, such employer is required to notify the State agency of such termination; and

(C) any liability of the obligated parent to such plan for employee contributions which are required under such plan for enrollment of the child is effectively subject to appropriate enforcement, unless the obligated parent contests such enforcement based on a mistake of fact.

Notwithstanding section 654(20)(B) of this title, the procedures which are required under paragraphs (3), (4), (6), (7), and (15) need not be used or applied in cases where the State determines (using guidelines which are generally available within the State and which take into account the payment record of the noncustodial parent, the availability of other remedies, and other relevant considerations) that such use or application would not carry out the purposes of this part or would be otherwise inappropriate in the circumstances.

(b) Withholding from income of amounts payable as support

The procedures referred to in subsection (a)(1)(A) of this section (relating to the withholding from income of amounts payable as support) must provide for the following:

(1) In the case of each noncustodial parent against whom a support order is or has been issued or modified in the State, and is being enforced under the State plan, so much of such parent's income must be withheld, in accordance with the succeeding provisions of this subsection, as is necessary to comply with the order and provide for the payment of any fee to the employer which may be required under paragraph (6)(A), up to the maximum amount permitted under section 1673(b) of Title 15. If there are arrearages to be collected, amounts withheld to satisfy such arrearages, when added to the amounts withheld to pay current support and provide for the fee, may not exceed the limit permitted under such section 1673(b), but the State need not withhold up to the maximum amount permitted under such section in order to satisfy arrearages.

(2) Such withholding must be provided without the necessity of any application therefor in the case of a child (whether or not eligible for assistance under a State program funded under part A of this subchapter) with respect to whom services are already being provided under the State plan under this part, and must be provided in accordance with this subsection on the basis of an application for services under the State plan in the case of any other child in whose behalf a support order has been issued or modified in the State. In either case such withholding must occur without the need for any amendment to the support order involved or for any further action (other than those actions required under this part) by the court or other entity which issued such order.

(3)(A) The income of a noncustodial parent shall be subject to such withholding, regardless of whether support payments by such parent are in arrears, in the case of a support order being enforced under this part that is issued or modified on or after the first day of the 25th month beginning after October 13, 1988, on the effective date of the order; except that such income shall not be subject to such withholding under this subparagraph in any case where (i) one of the parties demonstrates, and the court (or administrative process) finds, that there is good cause not to require immediate income withholding, or (ii) a written agreement is reached between both parties which provides for an alternative arrangement.

(B) The income of a noncustodial parent shall become subject to such withholding, in the case of income not subject to withholding under subparagraph (A), on the date on which the payments which the noncustodial parent has failed to make under a support order are at least equal to the support payable for one month or, if earlier, and without regard to whether there is an arrearage, the earliest of—

(i) the date as of which the noncustodial parent requests that such withholding begin,

(ii) the date as of which the custodial parent requests that such withholding begin, if the State determines, in accordance with such procedures and standards as it may establish, that the request should be approved, or

(iii) such earlier date as the State may select.

(4)(A) Such withholding must be carried out in full compliance with all procedural due process requirements of the State, and the State must send notice to each noncustodial parent to whom paragraph (1) applies—

(i) that the withholding has commenced; and

(ii) of the procedures to follow if the noncustodial parent desires to contest such withholding on the grounds that the withholding or the amount withheld is improper due to a mistake of fact.

(B) The notice under subparagraph (A) of this paragraph shall include the information provided to the employer under paragraph (6)(A).

(5) Such withholding must be administered by the State through the State disbursement unit established pursuant to section 654b of this title, in accordance with the requirements of section 654b of this title.

(6)(A)(i) The employer of any noncustodial parent to whom paragraph (1) applies, upon being given notice as described in clause (ii), must be required to withhold from such noncustodial parent's income the amount specified by such notice (which may include a fee, established by the State, to be paid to the employer unless waived by such employer) and pay such amount (after deducting and retaining any portion thereof which represents the fee so established) to the State disbursement unit within 7 business days after the date the amount would (but for this subsection) have been paid or credited to the employee, for distribution in accordance with this part. The employer shall withhold funds as directed in the notice, except that when an employer receives an income withholding order issued by another State, the employer shall apply the income withholding law of the State of the obligor's principal place of employment in determining—

(I) the employer's fee for processing an income withholding order;

(II) the maximum amount permitted to be withheld from the obligor's income;

(III) the time periods within which the employer must implement the income withholding order and forward the child support payment;

(IV) the priorities for withholding and allocating income withheld for multiple child support obligees; and

(V) any withholding terms or conditions not specified in the order.

An employer who complies with an income withholding notice that is regular on its face shall not be subject to civil liability to any individual or agency for conduct in compliance with the notice.

(ii) The notice given to the employer shall be in a standard format prescribed by the Secretary, and contain only such information as may be necessary for the employer to comply with the withholding order.

(iii) As used in this subparagraph, the term "business day" means a day on which State offices are open for regular business.

(B) Methods must be established by the State to simplify the withholding process for employers to the greatest extent possible, including permitting any employer to combine all withheld amounts into a single payment to each appropriate agency or entity (with the portion thereof which is attributable to each individual employee being separately designated).

(C) The employer must be held liable to the State for any amount which such employer fails to withhold from income due an employee following receipt by such employer of proper notice under subparagraph (A), but such employer shall not be required to vary the normal pay and disbursement cycles in order to comply with this paragraph.

(D) Provision must be made for the imposition of a fine against any employer who—

(i) discharges from employment, refuses to employ, or takes disciplinary action against any noncustodial parent subject to income withholding required by this subsection because of the existence of such withholding and the obligations or additional obligations which it imposes upon the employer; or

(ii) fails to withhold support from income or to pay such amounts to the State disbursement unit in accordance with this subsection.

(7) Support collection under this subsection must be given priority over any other legal process under State law against the same income.

(8) For purposes of subsection (a) of this section and this subsection, the term "income" means any periodic form of payment due to an individual, regardless of source, including wages, salaries, commissions, bonuses, worker's compensation, disability, payments pursuant to a pension or retirement program, and interest.

(9) The State must extend its withholding system under this subsection so that such system will include withholding from income derived within such State in cases where the applicable support orders were issued in other States, in order to assure that child support owed by noncustodial parents in such State or any other State will be collected without regard to the residence of the child for whom the support is payable or of such child's custodial parent.

(10) Provision must be made for terminating withholding.

(11) Procedures under which the agency administering the State plan approved under this part may execute a withholding order without advance notice to the obligor, including issuing the withholding order through electronic means.

(c) Expedited procedures

The procedures specified in this subsection are the following:

(1) Administrative action by State agency

Procedures which give the State agency the authority to take the following actions relating to establishment of paternity or to establishment, modification, or enforcement of support orders, without the necessity of obtaining an order from any other judicial or administrative tribunal, and to recognize and enforce the authority of State agencies of other States to take the following actions:

(A) Genetic testing

To order genetic testing for the purpose of paternity establishment as provided in subsection (a)(5) of this section.

(B) Financial or other information

To subpoena any financial or other information needed to establish, modify, or enforce a support order, and to impose penalties for failure to respond to such a subpoena.

(C) Response to State agency request

To require all entities in the State (including for-profit, nonprofit, and governmental employers) to provide promptly, in response to a request by the State agency of that or any other State administering a program under this part, information on the employment, compensation, and benefits of any individual employed by such entity as an employee or contractor, and to sanction failure to respond to any such request.

(D) Access to information contained in certain records

To obtain access, subject to safeguards on privacy and information security, and subject to the nonliability of entities that afford such access under this subparagraph, to information contained in the following records (including automated access, in the case of records maintained in automated data bases):

(i) Records of other State and local government agencies, including—

(I) vital statistics (including records of marriage, birth, and divorce);

(II) State and local tax and revenue records (including information on residence address, employer, income and assets);

(III) records concerning real and titled personal property;

(IV) records of occupational and professional licenses, and records concerning the ownership and control of corporations, partnerships, and other business entities;

(V) employment security records;

(VI) records of agencies administering public assistance programs;

(VII) records of the motor vehicle department; and

(VIII) corrections records.

(ii) Certain records held by private entities with respect to individuals who owe or are owed support (or against or with respect to whom a support obligation is sought), consisting of—

(I) the names and addresses of such individuals and the names and addresses of the employers of such individuals, as appearing in customer records of public utilities and cable television companies, pursuant to an administrative subpoena authorized by subparagraph (B); and

(II) information (including information on assets and liabilities) on such individuals held by financial institutions.

(E) Change in payee

In cases in which support is subject to an assignment in order to comply with a requirement imposed pursuant to part A of this subchapter, part E of this subchapter, or section 1396k of this title, or to a requirement to pay through the State disbursement unit established pursuant to section 654b of this title, upon providing notice to obligor and obligee, to direct the obligor or other payor to change the payee to the appropriate government entity.

(F) Income withholding

To order income withholding in accordance with subsections (a)(1)(A) and (b).

(G) Securing assets

In cases in which there is a support arrearage, to secure assets to satisfy any current support obligation and the arrearage by—

(i) intercepting or seizing periodic or lump-sum payments from—

(I) a State or local agency, including unemployment compensation, workers' compensation, and other benefits; and

(II) judgments, settlements, and lotteries;

(ii) attaching and seizing assets of the obligor held in financial institutions;

(iii) attaching public and private retirement funds; and

(iv) imposing liens in accordance with subsection (a)(4) of this section and, in appropriate cases, to force sale of property and distribution of proceeds.

(H) Increase monthly payments

For the purpose of securing overdue support, to increase the amount of monthly support payments to include amounts for arrearages, subject to such conditions or limitations as the State may provide.

Such procedures shall be subject to due process safeguards, including (as appropriate) requirements for notice, opportunity to contest the action, and opportunity for an appeal on the record to an independent administrative or judicial tribunal.

(2) Substantive and procedural rules

The expedited procedures required under subsection (a)(2) of this section shall include the following rules and authority, applicable with respect to all proceedings to establish paternity or to establish, modify, or enforce support orders:

(A) Locator information; presumptions concerning notice

Procedures under which—

(i) each party to any paternity or child support proceeding is required (subject to privacy safeguards) to file with the State case registry upon entry of an order, and to update as appropriate, information on location and identity of the party, including social security number, residential and mailing addresses, telephone number, driver's license number, and name, address, and telephone number of employer; and

(ii) in any subsequent child support enforcement action between the parties, upon sufficient showing that diligent effort has been made to ascertain the location of such a party, the court or administrative agency of competent jurisdiction shall deem State due process requirements for notice and service of process to be met with respect to the party, upon delivery of written notice to the most recent residential or employer address filed with the State case registry pursuant to clause (i).

(B) Statewide jurisdiction

Procedures under which—

(i) the State agency and any administrative or judicial tribunal with authority to hear child support and paternity cases exerts statewide jurisdiction over the parties; and

(ii) in a State in which orders are issued by courts or administrative tribunals, a case may be transferred between local jurisdictions in the State without need for any additional filing by the petitioner, or service of process upon the respondent, to retain jurisdiction over the parties.

(3) Coordination with ERISA

Notwithstanding subsection (d) of section 514 of the Employee Retirement Income Security Act of 1974 (relating to effect on other laws), nothing in this subsection shall be construed to alter, amend, modify, invalidate, impair, or supersede subsections (a), (b), and (c) of such section 514 as it applies with respect to any procedure referred to in paragraph (1) and any expedited procedure referred to in paragraph (2), except to the extent that such procedure would be consistent with the requirements of section 206(d)(3) of such Act (relating to qualified domestic relations orders) or the requirements of section 609(a) of such Act (relating to qualified medical child support orders) if the reference in such section 206(d)(3) to a domestic relations order and the reference in such section 609(a) to a medical child support order were a reference to a support order referred to in paragraphs (1) and (2) relating to the same matters, respectively.

(d) Exemption of States

If a State demonstrates to the satisfaction of the Secretary, through the presentation to the Secretary of such data pertaining to caseloads, processing times, administrative costs, and average support collections, and such other data or estimates as the Secretary may specify, that the enactment of any law or the use of any procedure or procedures required by or pursuant to this section will not increase the effectiveness and efficiency of the State child support enforcement program, the Secretary may exempt the State, subject to the Secretary's continuing review and to termination of the exemption should circumstances change, from the requirement to enact the law or use the procedure or procedures involved.

(e) "Overdue support" defined

For purposes of this section, the term "overdue support" means the amount of a delinquency pursuant to an obligation determined under a court order, or an order of an administrative process established under State law, for support and maintenance of a minor child which is owed to or on behalf of such child, or for support and maintenance of the noncustodial parent's spouse (or former spouse) with whom the child is living if and to the extent that spousal support (with respect to such spouse or former spouse) would be included for purposes of section 654(4) of this title. At the option of the State, overdue support may include amounts which otherwise meet the definition in the first sentence of this subsection but which are owed to or on behalf of a child who is not a minor child. The option to include support owed to children who are not minors shall apply independently to each procedure specified under this section.

(f) Uniform Interstate Family Support Act

In order to satisfy section 654(20)(A) of this title, on and after January 1, 1998, each State must have in effect the Uniform Interstate Family Support Act, as approved by the American Bar Association on February 9, 1993, and as in effect on August 22, 1996, including any amendments officially adopted as of such date by the National Conference of Commissioners on Uniform State Laws.

(g) Laws voiding fraudulent transfers

In order to satisfy section 454(20)(A), each State must have in effect—

(1)(A) the Uniform Fraudulent Conveyance Act of 1981;

(B) the Uniform Fraudulent Transfer Act of 1984; or

(C) another law, specifying indicia of fraud which create a prima facie case that a debtor transferred income or property to avoid payment to a child support creditor, which the Secretary finds affords comparable rights to child support creditors; and

(2) procedures under which, in any case in which the State knows of a transfer by a child support debtor with respect to which such a prima facie case is established, the State must—

(A) seek to void such transfer; or

(B) obtain a settlement in the best interests of the child support creditor.

§ 667. State guidelines for child support awards.

(a) Establishment of guidelines; method

Each State, as a condition for having its State plan approved under this part, must establish guidelines for child support award amounts within the State. The guidelines may be established by law or by judicial or administrative action, and shall be reviewed at least once every 4 years to ensure that their application results in the determination of appropriate child support award amounts.

(b) Availability of guidelines; rebuttable presumption

(1) The guidelines established pursuant to subsection (a) of this section shall be made available to all judges and other officials who have the power to determine child support awards within such State.

(2) There shall be a rebuttable presumption, in any judicial or administrative proceeding for the award of child support, that the amount of the award which would result from the application of such guidelines is the correct amount of child support to be awarded. A written finding or specific finding on the record that the application of the guidelines would be unjust or inappropriate in a particular case, as determined under criteria established by the State, shall be sufficient to rebut the presumption in that case.

(c) Technical assistance to States; State to furnish Secretary with copies

The Secretary shall furnish technical assistance to the States for establishing the guidelines, and each State shall furnish the Secretary with copies of its guidelines.

§ 668. Encouragement of States to adopt simple civil process for voluntarily acknowledging paternity and a civil procedure for establishing paternity in contested cases.

In the administration of the child support enforcement program under this part, each State is encouraged to establish and implement a civil procedure for establishing paternity in contested cases.

§ 669. Collection and reporting of child support enforcement data.

(a) In general

With respect to each type of service described in subsection (b) of this section, the Secretary shall collect and maintain up-to-date statistics, by State, and on a fiscal year basis, on—

(1) the number of cases in the caseload of the State agency administering the plan approved under this part in which the service is needed; and

(2) the number of such cases in which the service has actually been provided.

(b) Types of services

The statistics required by subsection (a) shall be separately stated with respect to paternity establishment services and child support obligation establishment services.

(c) Types of service recipients

The statistics required by subsection (a) shall be separately stated with respect to—

(1) recipients of assistance under a State program funded under part A or of payments or services under a State plan approved under part E; and

(2) individuals who are not such recipients.

(d) Rule of interpretation

For purposes of subsection (a)(2) of this section, a service has actually been provided when the task described by the service has been accomplished.

CHAPTER 121

INTERNATIONAL CHILD ABDUCTION REMEDIES ACT

§§ 11601 to 11610. Transferred.

Codification

Section 11601, Pub. L. 100–300, § 2, Apr. 29, 1988, 102 Stat. 437, which provided findings and declarations related to the International Child Abduction Remedies Act, was transferred to section 9001 of Title 22, Foreign Relations and Intercourse.

Section 11602, Pub. L. 100–300, § 3, Apr. 29, 1988, 102 Stat. 437, which provided definitions, was transferred to section 9002 of Title 22.

Section 11603, Pub. L. 100–300, § 4, Apr. 29, 1988, 102 Stat. 438, which related to judicial remedies, was transferred to section 9003 of Title 22.

Section 11604, Pub. L. 100–300, § 5, Apr. 29, 1988, 102 Stat. 439, which related to provisional remedies, was transferred to section 9004 of Title 22.

Section 11605, Pub. L. 100–300, § 6, Apr. 29, 1988, 102 Stat. 439, which related to admissibility of documents, was transferred to section 9005 of Title 22.

Section 11606, Pub. L. 100–300, § 7, Apr. 29, 1988, 102 Stat. 439; Pub. L. 105–277, div. G, title XXII, § 2213, Oct. 21, 1998, 112 Stat. 2681–812; Pub. L. 108–370, § 2, Oct. 25, 2004, 118 Stat. 1750, which related to the United States Central Authority, was transferred to section 9006 of Title 22.

Section 11607, Pub. L. 100–300, § 8, Apr. 29, 1988, 102 Stat. 440, which related to costs and fees, was transferred to section 9007 of Title 22.

Section 11608, Pub. L. 100–300, § 9, Apr. 29, 1988, 102 Stat. 440, which related to collection, maintenance, and dissemination of information, was transferred to section 9008 of Title 22.

Section 11608a, Pub. L. 106–113, div. B, § 1000(a)(7) [div. A, title II, § 201], Nov. 29, 1999, 113 Stat. 1536, 1501A-419, which related to the Office of Children's Issues, was transferred to section 9009 of Title 22.

Section 11609, Pub. L. 100–300, § 10, Apr. 29, 1988, 102 Stat. 441, which related to an interagency coordinating group, was transferred to section 9010 of Title 22.

Section 11610, Pub. L. 100–300, § 12, Apr. 29, 1988, 102 Stat. 442, which related to authorization of appropriations, was transferred to section 9011 of Title 22.

§ 11611. Repealed. Pub. L. 113–150, title I, § 101(e), Aug. 8, 2014, 128 Stat. 1815 .

Section, Pub. L. 105–277, div. G, title XXVIII, § 2803, Oct. 21, 1998, 112 Stat. 2681–846; Pub. L. 106–113, div. B, § 1000(a)(7) [div. A, title II, § 202], Nov. 29, 1999, 113 Stat. 1536, 1501A-420; Pub. L. 107–228, div. A, title II, § 212, Sept. 30, 2002, 116 Stat. 1365, related to report on compliance with the Hague Convention on International Child Abduction.

THE HAGUE CONVENTION

THE HAGUE CONVENTION ON THE CIVIL ASPECTS OF INTERNATIONAL CHILD ABDUCTION

Official English Text:

The States signatory to the present Convention,

Firmly convinced that the interests of children are of paramount importance in matters relating to their custody, Desiring to protect children internationally from the harmful effects of their wrongful removal or retention and to establish procedures to ensure their prompt return to the State of their habitual residence, as well as to secure protection for rights of access,

Have resolved to conclude a Convention to this effect, and have agreed upon the following provisions—

CHAPTER I—SCOPE OF THE CONVENTION

Article 1

The objects of the present Convention are—

a) to secure the prompt return of children wrongfully removed to or retained in any Contracting State; and

b) to ensure that rights of custody and of access under the law of one Contracting State are effectively respected in other Contracting States.

Article 2

Contracting States shall take all appropriate measures to secure within their territories the implementation of the objects of the Convention. For this purpose they shall use the most expeditious procedures available.

Article 3

The removal or the retention of a child is to be considered wrongful where—

a) it is in breach of rights of custody attributed to a person, an institution or any other body, either jointly or alone, under the law of the State in which the child was habitually resident immediately before the removal or retention; and

b) at the time of removal or retention those rights were actually exercised, either jointly or alone, or would have been so exercised but for the removal or retention.

The rights of custody mentioned in sub-paragraph a above, may arise in particular by operation of law or by reason of a judicial or administrative decision, or by reason of an agreement having legal effect under the law of that State.

Article 4

The Convention shall apply to any child who was habitually resident in a Contracting State immediately before any breach of custody or access rights. The Convention shall cease to apply when the child attaint the age of 16 years.

Article 5

For the purposes of this Convention—

a) `rights of custody' shall include rights relating to the care of the person of the child and, in particular, the right to determine the child's place of residence;

b) `rights of access' shall include the right to take a child for a limited period of time to a place other than the child's habitual residence.

CHAPTER II—CENTRAL AUTHORITIES

Article 6

A Contracting State shall designate a Central Authority to discharge the duties which are imposed by the Convention upon such authorities.

Federal States, States with more than one system of law or States having autonomous territorial organizations shall be free to appoint more than one Central Authority and to specify the territorial extent of their powers. Where a State has appointed more than one Central Authority, it shall designate the Central Authority to which applications may be addressed for transmission to the appropriate Central Authority within that State.

Article 7

Central Authorities shall co-operate with each other and promote co-operation amongst the competent authorities in their respective States to secure the prompt return of children and to achieve the other objects of this Convention.

In particular, either directly or through any intermediary, they shall take all appropriate measures—

a) to discover the whereabouts of a child who has been wrongfully removed or retained;

b) to prevent further harm to the child or prejudice to interested parties by taking or causing to be taken provisional measures;

c) to secure the voluntary return of the child or to bring about an amicable resolution of the issues;

d) to exchange, where desirable, information relating to the social background of the child;

e) to provide information of a general character as to the law of their State in connection with the application of the Convention;

f) to initiate or facilitate the institution of judicial or administrative proceedings with a view to obtaining the return of the child and, in a proper case, to make arrangements for organizing or securing the effective exercise of rights of access;

g) where the circumstances so require, to provide or facilitate the provision of legal aid and advice, including the participation of legal counsel and advisers;

h) to provide such administrative arrangements as may be necessary and appropriate to secure the safe return of the child;

i) to keep other each other informed with respect to the operation of this Convention and, as far as possible, to eliminate any obstacles to its application.

CHAPTER III—RETURN OF CHILDREN

Article 8

Any person, institution or other body claiming that a child has been removed or retained in breach of custody rights may apply either to the Central Authority of the child's habitual residence or to the Central Authority of any other Contracting State for assistance in securing the return of the child.

The application shall contain—

a) information concerning the identity of the applicant, of the child and of the person alleged to have removed or retained the child;

b) where available, the date of birth of the child;

c) the grounds on which the applicant's claim for return of the child is based;

d) all available information relating to the whereabouts of the child and the identity of the person with whom the child is presumed to be.

The application may be accompanied or supplemented by—

e) an authenticated copy of any relevant decision or agreement;

f) a certificate or an affidavit emanating from a Central Authority, or other competent authority of the State of the child's habitual residence, or from a qualified person, concerning the relevant law of that State;

g) any other relevant document.

THE HAGUE CONVENTION

Article 9

If the Central Authority which receives an application referred to in Article 8 has reason to believe that the child is in another Contracting State, it shall directly and without delay transmit the application to the Central Authority of that Contracting State and inform the requesting Central Authority, or the applicant, as the case may be.

Article 10

The Central Authority of the State where the child is shall take or cause to be taken all appropriate measures in order to obtain the voluntary return of the child.

Article 11

The judicial or administrative authorities of Contracting States shall act expeditiously in proceedings for the return of children.

If the judicial or administrative authority concerned has not reached a decision within six weeks from the date of commencement of the proceedings, the applicant or the Central Authority of the requested State, on its own initiative or if asked by the Central Authority of the requesting State, shall have the right to request a statement of the reasons for the delay. If a reply is received by the Central Authority of the requested State, that Authority shall transmit the reply to the Central Authority of the requesting State, or to the applicant, as the case may be.

Article 12

Where a child has been wrongfully removed or retained in terms of Article 3 and, at the date of the commencement of the proceedings before the judicial or administrative authority of the Contracting State where the child is, a period of less than one year has elapsed from the date of the wrongful removal or retention, the authority concerned shall order the return of the child forthwith.

The judicial or administrative authority, even where the proceedings have been commenced after the expiration of the period of one year referred to in the preceding paragraph, shall also order the return of the child, unless it is demonstrated that the child is now settled in its new environment.

Where the judicial or administrative authority in the requested State has reason to believe that the child has been taken to another State, it may stay the proceedings or dismiss the application for the return of the child.

Article 13

Notwithstanding the provisions of the preceding Article, the judicial or administrative authority of the requested State is not bound to order the return of the child if the person, institution or other body which opposes its return establishes that—

a) the person, institution or other body having the care of the person of the child was not actually exercising the custody rights at the time of removal or retention, or had consented to or subsequently acquiesced in the removal of retention; or

b) there is a grave risk that his or her return would expose the child to physical or psychological harm or otherwise place the child in an intolerable situation.

The judicial or administrative authority may also refuse to order the return of the child if it finds that the child objects to being returned and has attained an age and degree of maturity at which it is appropriate to take account of its views.

In considering the circumstances referred to in this Article, the judicial and administrative authorites shall take into account the information relating to the social background of the child provided by the Central Authority or other competent authority of the child's habitual residence.

Article 14

In ascertaining whether there has been a wrongful removal of retention within the meaning of Article 3, the judicial or administrative authorities of the requested State may take notice directly of the law of, and of judicial or administrative decisions, formally recognized or not in the State of the habitual residence of the child, without recourse to the specific procedures for the proof of that law or for the recognition of foreign decisions which would otherwise be applicable.

Article 15

The judicial or administrative authorities of a Contracting State may, prior to the making of an order for the return of the child, request that the applicant obtain from the authorities of the State of the habitual residence of the child a decision or other determination that the removal or retention was wrongful within the meaning of Article 3 of the Convention, where such a decision or determination may be obtained in that State. The Central Authorities of the Contracting States shall so far as practicable assist applicants to obtain such a decision or determination.

Article 16

After receiving notice of a wrongful removal or retention of a child in the sense of Article 3, the judicial or administrative authorities of the Contracting State to which the child has been removed or in which it has been retained shall not decide on the merits of rights of custody until it has been determined that the child is not to be returned under this Convention or unless an application under the Convention is not lodged within a reasonable time following receipt of the notice.

Article 17

The sole fact that a decision relating to custody has been given in or is entitled to recognition in the requested State shall not be a ground for refusing to return a child under this Convention, but the judicial or administrative authorities of the requested State may take account of the reasons for that decision in applying this Convention.

Article 18

The provisions of this Chapter do not limit the power of a judicial or administrative authority to order the return of the child at any time.

Article 19

A decision under this Convention concerning the return of the child shall not be taken to be determination on the merits of any custody issue.

Article 20

The return of the child under the provision of Article 12 may be refused if this would not be permitted by the fundamental principles of the requested State relating to the protection of human rights and fundamental freedoms.

CHAPTER VI—RIGHTS OF ACCESS

Article 21

An application to make arrangements for organizing or securing the effective exercise of rights of access may be presented to the Central Authorities of the Contracting States in the same way as an application for the return of a child.

The Central Authorities are bound by the obligations of co-operation which are set forth in Article 7 to promote the peaceful enjoyment of access rights and the fulfillment of any conditions to which the exercise of such rights may be subject. The central Authorities shall take steps to remove, as far as possible, all obstacles to the exercise of such rights. The Central Authorities, either directly or through intermediaries, may initiate or assist in the institution of proceedings with a view to organizing or protecting these rights and securing respect for the conditions to which the exercise of these rights may be subject.

Article 22

No security, bond or deposit, however described, shall be required to guarantee the payment of costs and expenses in the judicial or administrative proceedings falling within the scope of this Convention.

THE HAGUE CONVENTION

Article 23

No legalization or similar formality may be required in the context of this Convention.

Article 24

Any application, communication or other document sent to the Central Authority of the requested State shall be in the original language, and shall be accompanied by a translation into the official language or one of the official languages of the requested State or, where that is not feasible, a translation into French or English.

However, a Contracting State may, by making a reservation in accordance with Article 42, object to the use of either French or English, but not both, in any application, communication or other document sent to its Central Authority.

Article 25

Nationals of the Contracting States and persons who are habitually resident within those States shall be entitled in matters concerned with the application of this Convention to legal aid and advice in any other Contracting State on the same conditions as if they themselves were nationals of and habitually resident in that State.

Article 26

Each Central Authority shall bear its own costs in applying this Convention.

Central Authorities and other public services of Contracting States shall not impose any charges in relation to applications submitted under this Convention. In particular, they may not require any payment from the applicant towards the costs and expenses of the proceedings or, where applicable, those arising from the participation of legal counsel or advisers. However, they may require the payment of the expenses incurred or to be incurred in implementing the return of the child.

However, a Contracting State may, by making a reservation in accordance with Article 42, declare that it shall not be bound to assume any costs referred to in the preceding paragraph resulting from the participation of legal counsel or advisers or from court proceedings, except insofar as those costs may be covered by its system of legal aid and advice.

Upon ordering the return of a child or issuing an order concerning rights of access under this Convention, the judicial or administrative authorities may, where appropriate, direct the person who removed or retained the child, or who prevented the exercise of rights of access, to pay necessary expenses incurred by or on behalf of the applicant, including travel expenses, any costs incurred or payments made for locating the child, the costs of legal representation of the applicant, and those of returning the child.

Article 27

When it is manifest that the requirements of this Convention are not fulfilled or that the application is otherwise not well founded, a Central Authority is not bound to accept the application. In that case, the Central Authority shall forthwith inform the applicant or the Central Authority through which the application was submitted, as the case may be, of its reasons.

Article 28

A Central Authority may require that the application be accompanied by a written authorization empowering it to act on behalf of the applicant, or to designate a representative so to act.

Article 29

This Convention shall not preclude any person, institution or body who claims that there has been a breach of custody or access rights within the meaning of Article 3 or 21 from applying directly to the judicial or administrative authorities of a Contracting State, whether or not under the provisions of this Convention.

FEDERAL STATUTES

Article 30

Any application submitted to the Central Authorities or directly to the judicial or administrative authorities of a Contracting State in accordance with the terms of this Convention, together with documents and any other information appended thereto or provided by a Central Authority, shall be admissible in the courts or administrative authorities of the Contracting States.

Article 31

In relation to a State which in matters of custody of children has two or more systems of law applicable in different territorial units —

a) any reference to habitual residence in that State shall be construed as referring to habitual residence in a territorial unit of that State;

b) any reference to the law of the State of habitual residence shall be construed as referring to the law of the territorial unit in that State where the child habitually resides.

Article 32

In relation to a State which in matters of custody of children has two or more systems of law applicable to different categories of persons, any reference to the law of that State shall be construed as referring to the legal system specified by the law of that State.

Article 33

A State within which different territorial units have their own rules of law in respect of custody of children shall not be bound to apply this Convention where a State with a unified system of law would not be bound to do so.

Article 34

This Convention shall take priority in matters within its scope over the Convention of 5 October 1961 concerning the powers of authorities and the law applicable in respect of the protection of minors, as between Parties to both Conventions. Otherwise the present Convention shall not restrict the application of an international instrument in force between the State of origin and the State addressed or other law of the State addressed for the purposes of obtaining the return of a child who has been wrongfully removed or retained or of organizing access rights.

Article 35

This Convention shall apply as between Contracting States only to wrongful removals or retentions occurring after its entry into force in those States.

Where a declaration has been made under Article 39 or 40, the reference in the preceding paragraph to a Contracting State shall be taken to refer to the territorial unit or units in relation to which this Convention applies.

Article 36

Nothing in this Convention shall prevent two or more Contracting State, in order to limit the restrictions to which the return of the child may be subject, from agreeing among themselves to derogate from any provision of this Convention which may imply such a restriction.

CHAPTER VI—FINAL CLAUSES

Article 37

The Convention shall be open for signature by the States which were Members of the Hague Conference on Private International Law at the time of its Fourteenth Session.

It shall be ratified, accepted or approved and the instruments of ratification, acceptance or approval shall be deposited with the Ministry of Foreign Affairs of the Kingdom of the Netherlands.

THE HAGUE CONVENTION

Article 38

Any other State may accede to the Convention. The instrument of accession shall be deposited with the Ministry of Foreign Affairs of the Kingdom of the Netherlands.

The Convention shall enter into force for a State acceding to it on the first day of the third calendar month after the deposit of its instrument of accession.

The accession will have effect only as regards the relations between the acceding State and such Contracting States as will have declared their acceptance of the accession. Such a declaration will also have to be made by any Member State ratifying, accepting or approving the Convention after an accession. Such declaration shall be deposited at the Ministry of Foreign Affairs of the Kingdom of the Netherlands; this Ministry shall forward, through diplomatic channels, a certified copy to each of the Contracting States.

The Convention will enter into force as between the acceding State and the State that has declared its acceptance of the accession on the first day of the third calendar month after the deposit of the declaration of acceptance.

Article 39

Any State may, at the time of signature, ratification, acceptance, approval or accession, declare that the Convention shall extend to all the territories for the international relations of which it is responsible, or to one or more of them. Such a declaration shall take effect at the time the Convention enters into force for that State.

Such declaration, as well as any subsequent extension, shall be notified to the Ministry of Foreign Affairs of the Kingdom of the Netherlands.

Article 40

If a Contracting State has two or more territorial units in which different systems of law are applicable in relation to matters dealt with in this Convention, it may at the time of signature, ratification, acceptance, approval or accession declare that this Convention shall extend to all its territorial units or only to one or more of them and may modify this declaration by submitting another declaration at any time.

Any such declaration shall be notified to the Ministry of Foreign Affairs of the Kingdom of the Netherlands and shall state expressly the territorial units to which the Convention applies.

Article 41

Where a Contracting State has a system of government under which executive, judicial and legislative powers are distributed between central and other authorities within that State, its signature or ratification, acceptance or approval of, or accession to this Convention, or its making of any declaration in terms of Article 40 shall carry no implication as to the internal distribution of powers within that State.

Article 42

Any State may, not later than the time of ratification, acceptance, approval or accession, or at the time of making a declaration in terms of Article 39 or 40, make one or both of the reservations provided for in Article 24 and Article 26, third paragraph. No other reservations shall be permitted.

Any State may at any time withdraw a reservation it has made. The withdraw shall be notified to the Ministry of Foreign Affairs of the Kingdom of the Netherlands. The reservation shall cease to have effect on the first day of the third calendar month after the notification referred to in the preceding paragraph.

Article 43

The Convention shall enter into force on the first day of the third calendar month after the deposit of the third instrument of ratification, acceptance, approval or accession referred to in Articles 37 and 38.

FEDERAL STATUTES

Thereafter the Convention shall enter into force—

1 for each State ratifying, accepting, approving or acceding to it subsequently, on the first day of the third calendar month after the deposit of its instrument of ratification, acceptance, approval or accession;

2 for any territory or territorial unit to which the Convention has been extended in conformity with Article 39 or 40, on the first day of the third calendar month after the notification referred to in that Article.

Article 44

The Convention shall remain in force for five years form the date of its entry into force in accordance with the first paragraph of Article 43 even for States which subsequently have ratified, accepted, approved it or acceded to it.

If there has been no denunciation, it shall be renewed tacitly every five years.

Any denunciation shall be notified to the Ministry of Foreign Affairs of the Kingdom of the netherlands at least six months before the expiry of the five year period. It may be limited to certain of the territories or territorial units to which the Convention applies.

The denunciation shall have effect only as regards the State which has notified it. The Convention shall remain in force for the other Contracting States.

Article 45

The Ministry of Foreign Affairs of the Kingdom of the Netherlands shall notify the States Members of the Conference, and the States which have acceded in accordance with Article 38, of the following—

1—the signatures and ratifications, acceptances and approvals referred to in Article 37;

2—the accession referred to in Article 38;

3—the date on which the Convention enters into force in accordance with Article 43;

4—the extensions referred to in Article 39;

5—the declarations referred to in Articles 38 and 40;

6—the reservations referred to in Article 24 and Article 26, third paragraph, and the withdrawls referred to in Article 42;

7—the denunciation referred to in Article 44.

In witness whereof the undersigned, being duly authorized thereto, have signed this Convention.

Done at The Hague, on the 25th day of October, 1980, in the English and French languages, both texts being equally authentic, in a single copy which shall be deposited in the archives of the Government of the Kingdom of the Netherlands, and of which a certified copy shall be sent, through diplomatic channels, to each of the States Members of the Hague Conference on Private International Law at the date of its Fourteenth Session.

THE HAGUE CONVENTION

STATUS TABLE

28: Convention of 25 October 1980 on the Civil Aspects of International Child Abduction

Entry into force: 1-XII-1983

Last update: 27-VII-2016
Number of Contracting States to this Convention: 95

Members

Members of the Organisation

States	S[1]	R/A/S[2]	Type[3]	EIF[4]	EXT[5]	Auth[6]	Res/D/N[7]
Albania		4-V-2007	A*	1-VIII-2007		1	Res
Andorra		6-IV-2011	A*	1-VII-2011		1	Res
Argentina	28-I-1991	19-III-1991	R	1-VI-1991		1	D
Armenia		1-III-2007	A*	1-VI-2007		1	Res
Australia	29-X-1986	29-X-1986	R	1-I-1987		1	D
Austria	12-V-1987	14-VII-1988	R	1-X-1988		1	
Belarus		12-I-1998	A*	1-IV-1998		1	Res
Belgium	11-I-1982	9-II-1999	R	1-V-1999		1	
Bosnia and Herzegovina		23-VIII-1993	Su	6-III-1992		1	
Brazil		19-X-1999	A*	1-I-2000		1	Res
Bulgaria		20-V-2003	A*	1-VIII-2003		1	Res
Burkina Faso		25-V-1992	A*	1-VIII-1992		1	
Canada	25-X-1980	2-VI-1983	R	1-XII-1983	13	1	D,Res
Chile		23-II-1994	A*	1-V-1994		1	D
China, People's Republic of			C			2	D,N
Costa Rica		9-XI-1998	A*	1-II-1999		1	
Croatia		23-IV-1993	Su	1-XII-1991		1	
Cyprus		4-XI-1994	A*	1-II-1995		1	
Czech Republic	28-XII-1992	15-XII-1997	R	1-III-1998		1	Res

725

FEDERAL STATUTES

Denmark	17-IV-1991	17-IV-1991	R	1-VII-1991	1	1		D,Res
Ecuador		22-I-1992	A*	1-IV-1992		1		
Estonia		18-IV-2001	A*	1-VII-2001		1		Res
Finland	25-V-1994	25-V-1994	R	1-VIII-1994		1		Res
France	25-X-1980	16-IX-1982	R	1-XII-1983		1		Res,D
Georgia		24-VII-1997	A*	1-X-1997		1		
Germany	9-IX-1987	27-IX-1990	R	1-XII-1990		1		D,Res
Greece	25-X-1980	19-III-1993	R	1-VI-1993		1		Res
Hungary		7-IV-1986	A*	1-VII-1986		1		
Iceland		14-VIII-1996	A*	1-XI-1996		1		Res
Ireland	23-V-1990	16-VII-1991	R	1-X-1991		1		
Israel	4-IX-1991	4-IX-1991	R	1-XII-1991		1		Res
Italy	2-III-1987	22-II-1995	R	1-V-1995		1		
Japan	24-I-2014	24-I-2014	R	1-IV-2014		1		Res
Korea, Republic of		13-XII-2012	A*	1-III-2013		1		D,Res
Latvia		15-XI-2001	A*	1-II-2002		1		Res
Lithuania		5-VI-2002	A*	1-IX-2002		1		Res
Luxembourg	18-XII-1984	8-X-1986	R	1-I-1987		1		Res
Malta		26-X-1999	A*	1-I-2000		1		
Mauritius		23-III-1993	A*	1-VI-1993		1		Res
Mexico		20-VI-1991	A*	1-IX-1991		1		
Monaco		12-XI-1992	A*	1-II-1993		1		Res
Montenegro		1-III-2007	Su	3-VI-2006		1		
Morocco		9-III-2010	A*	1-VI-2010		1		
Netherlands	11-IX-1987	12-VI-1990	R	1-IX-1990	1	1		D,Res
New Zealand		31-V-1991	A*	1-VIII-1991		1		Res
Norway	9-I-1989	9-I-1989	R	1-IV-1989		1		Res

THE HAGUE CONVENTION

Panama		2-II-1994	A*	1-V-1994		1	Res
Paraguay		13-V-1998	A*	1-VIII-1998		1	
Peru		28-V-2001	A*	1-VIII-2001		1	
Philippines		16-III-2016	A*	1-VI-2016		1	D
Poland		10-VIII-1992	A*	1-XI-1992		1	Res
Portugal	22-VI-1982	29-IX-1983	R	1-XII-1983		1	
Republic of Moldova		10-IV-1998	A*	1-VII-1998		1	Res
Romania		20-XI-1992	A*	1-II-1993		1	
Russian Federation		28-VII-2011	A*	1-X-2011		1	Res
Serbia		29-IV-2001	Su	27-IV-1992		1	
Singapore		28-XII-2010	A*	1-III-2011		1	Res
Slovakia	28-XII-1992	7-XI-2000	R	1-II-2001		1	Res
Slovenia		22-III-1994	A*	1-VI-1994		1	
South Africa		8-VII-1997	A*	1-X-1997		1	Res
Spain	7-II-1986	16-VI-1987	R	1-IX-1987		1	
Sri Lanka		28-IX-2001	A*	1-XII-2001		1	Res
Sweden	22-III-1989	22-III-1989	R	1-VI-1989		1	Res
Switzerland	25-X-1980	11-X-1983	R	1-I-1984		1	
The former Yugoslav Republic of Macedonia		20-IX-1993	Su	1-XII-1991		1	
Turkey	21-I-1998	31-V-2000	R	1-VIII-2000		1	Res
Ukraine		2-VI-2006	A*	1-IX-2006		1	D
United Kingdom of Great Britain and Northern Ireland	19-XI-1984	20-V-1986	R	1-VIII-1986	7	1	N,Res
United States of America	23-XII-1981	29-IV-1988	R	1-VII-1988		1	Res

FEDERAL STATUTES

Uruguay		16-XI-1999	A*	1-II-2000	1	
Venezuela	16-X-1996	16-X-1996	R	1-I-1997	1	Res
Zambia		26-VIII-2014	A*	1-XI-2014	1	

1) S = Signature
2) R/A/Su = Ratification, Accession or Succession
3) Type = R: Ratification;

    A: Accession;
    A*: Accession giving rise to an acceptance procedure; click on A* for details of acceptances of the accession;
    C: Continuation;
    Su: Succession;
    Den: denunciation;

4) EIF = Entry into force
5) EXT = Extensions of application
6) Authorities per Convention = Designation of Authorities
7) Res/D/N = Reservations, declarations or notifications

THE HAGUE CONVENTION

STATUS TABLE

28: Convention of 25 October 1980 on the Civil Aspects of International Child Abduction

Entry into force: 1-XII-1983

Last update: 27-VII-2016
Number of Contracting States to this Convention: 95

Non-Members

Non-Member States of the Organisation

States	S[1]	R/A/S[2]	Type[3]	EIF[4]	EXT[5]	Auth[6]	Res/D/N[7]
Bahamas		1-X-1993	A*	1-I-1994		1	
Belize		22-VI-1989	A*	1-IX-1989		1	Res
Bolivia		13-VII-2016	A	1-X-2016			D,Res
Colombia		13-XII-1995	A*	1-III-1996		1	
Dominican Republic		11-VIII-2004	A*	1-XI-2004		1	
El Salvador		5-II-2001	A*	1-V-2001		1	D,Res
Fiji		16-III-1999	A*	1-VI-1999		1	
Gabon		6-XII-2010	A*	1-III-2011			
Guatemala		6-II-2002	A*	1-V-2002		1	Res
Guinea		7-XI-2011	A*	1-II-2012		1	
Honduras		20-XII-1993	A*	1-III-1994		1	Res
Iraq		21-III-2014	A*	1-VI-2014			
Kazakhstan		3-VI-2013	A*	1-IX-2013		1	Res
Lesotho		18-VI-2012	A*	1-IX-2012		1	
Nicaragua		14-XII-2000	A*	1-III-2001		1	
Saint Kitts and Nevis		31-V-1994	A*	1-VIII-1994		1	Res
San Marino		14-XII-2006	A*	1-III-2007		1	D

FEDERAL STATUTES

Seychelles	27-V-2008	A*	1-VIII-2008	1	
Thailand	14-VIII-2002	A*	1-XI-2002	1	Res
Trinidad and Tobago	7-VI-2000	A*	1-IX-2000	1	
Turkmenistan	29-XII-1997	A*	1-III-1998	1	
Uzbekistan	31-V-1999	A*	1-VIII-1999	1	Res
Zimbabwe	4-IV-1995	A*	1-VII-1995	1	Res

1) S = Signature
2) R/A/Su = Ratification, Accession or Succession
3) Type = R: Ratification;

    A: Accession;
    A*: Accession giving rise to an acceptance procedure; click on A* for details of acceptances of the accession;
    C: Continuation;
    Su: Succession;
    Den: denunciation;

4) EIF = Entry into force
5) EXT = Extensions of application
6) Authorities per Convention = Designation of Authorities
7) Res/D/N = Reservations, declarations or notifications

THE HAGUE CONVENTION

OUTLINE

HAGUE CHILD ABDUCTION CONVENTION

The *Convention of 25 October 1980 on the Civil Aspects of International Child Abduction*

Introduction

Although international child abduction is not a new problem, the incidence of such abductions continue to grow with the ease of international travel, the increase in bi-cultural marriages and the rise in the divorce rate. International child abductions have serious consequences for both the child and the left-behind parent. The child is removed, not only from contact with the other parent, but also from his or her home environment and transplanted to a culture with which he or she may have had no prior ties. International abductors move the child to another State with a different legal system, social structure, culture and, often, language. These differences, plus the physical distance generally involved, can make locating, recovering and returning internationally abducted children complex and problematic.

The *Convention of 25 October 1980 on the Civil Aspects of International Child Abduction* seeks to combat parental child abduction by providing a system of co-operation between Central Authorities and a rapid procedure for the return of the child to the country of the child's habitual residence.

The return mechanism

The principal object of the Convention, aside from protecting rights of access, is to protect children from the harmful effects of cross-border abductions (and wrongful retentions) by providing a procedure designed to bring about the prompt return of such children to the State of their habitual residence.[1] The Convention is based on a presumption that, save in exceptional circumstances, the wrongful removal or retention of a child across international boundaries is not in the interests of the child,[2] and that the return of the child to the State of the habitual residence will promote his or her interests by vindicating the right of the child to have contact with both parents,[3] by supporting continuity in the child's life,[4] and by ensuring that any determination of the issue of custody or access is made by the most appropriate court having regard to the likely availability of relevant evidence. The principle of prompt return also serves as a deterrent to abductions and wrongful removals, and this is seen by the Convention to be in the interests of children generally. The return order is designed to restore the status quo which existed before the wrongful removal or protection, and to deprive the wrongful parent of any advantage that might otherwise be gained by the abduction.

A return order is not a custody determination. It is simply an order that the child be returned to the jurisdiction which is most appropriate to determine custody and access. It is clearly stated in Article 19 that a return decision is not a decision on the merits of any custody issue. It is this which justifies the requirement in Article 12 that the return order be made "forthwith", and of Article 16 that a court dealing with an abduction case is not permitted to decide on "the merits of rights of custody" until it has been decided that there exists a reason for not ordering return, or the application is not lodged within a reasonable time.

The requirements to be met by an applicant for a return order are strict. He / she must establish:

---

[1] See Article 1.

[2] Preamble. And see Article 11 of the *United Nations Convention on the Rights of the Child* (UNCRC), which is quoted in the text below.

[3] See UNCRC Article 9.3:
"States Parties shall respect the right of the child who is separated from one or both parents to maintain personal relations and direct contact with both parents on a regular basis, except if it is contrary to the child's best interests."

[4] See UNCRC, Article 8, quoted below in the text.

May 2014

FEDERAL STATUTES

that the child was habitually residing in the other State; that the removal or retention of the child constituted a breach of custody rights attributed by the law of that State; and that the applicant was actually exercising those rights at the time of the wrongful removal or retention.

Once the applicant has established a *prima facie* case under Article 3 *b*, there remains the possibility of the application being rejected under Article 13 if consent or subsequent acquiescence to the removal can be shown, or there is a grave risk that return would expose the child to physical or psychological harm or otherwise place the child in an intolerable situation. Also under Article 13 the objections of the child, if he/she has attained sufficient age and maturity, may be a basis for refusal. Article 12 gives a discretion not to return a child if the application was made a year after the removal or retention and the child is now settled in his / her new environment. Finally, under Article 20 return may be refused if this would not be permitted by the fundamental rules relating to the protection of human rights and fundamental freedoms of the State addressed.

Co-operation

As is usual among the Hague Children's Conventions, Central Authorities in each Contracting State are given an integral role as the focus for administrative co-operation in achieving child protection. Central Authorities in each country provide assistance in locating the child and in achieving, if possible, a voluntary return of the child or an amicable resolution of the issues. They also co-operate to prevent further harm to the child by initiating or helping to initiate proceedings for the return of the child, and by making necessary administrative arrangements to secure the child's safe return. Article 21 also gives the Central Authorities obligations to promote the peaceful enjoyment of access rights and to take steps to remove, as far as possible, obstacles to the exercise of such rights.

Significant post-Convention work has also been carried out on the 1980 Abduction Convention. A Special Commission for the Monitoring and Review of the Operation of the 1980 Abduction Convention has been set up and meets every few years to discuss developments. In addition, the Hague Conference has produced several Guides to Good Practice for the implementation and operation of the Convention and provides other resources such as a database of case law (INCADAT) and of statistics (INCASTAT) relating to international child abduction.

Protecting children and their rights

While pre-dating the CRC, the 1980 Hague Convention in part implements CRC Articles 11[5] and 35;[6] it helps to give effect to the fundamental rights of the child, such as those expressed in CRC Articles 9.3[7] and 10.2,[8] and has been found in a number of court decisions in different parts of the world to be consistent with national Constitutions, as well as regional and international human rights instruments.

The UN Committee on the Rights of the Child recommends CRC States to become Party to the 1980 Hague Convention as a means by which CRC Article 11 may be practically implemented.[9] The 1980 Hague Convention has contributed to resolving thousands of abduction cases and has

---

[5] CRC Article 11: "1. States Parties shall take measures to combat the illicit transfer and non-return of children abroad. 2. To this end, States Parties shall promote the conclusion of bilateral or multilateral agreements or accession to existing agreements."

[6] CRC Article 35: "States Parties shall take all appropriate national, bilateral and multilateral measures to prevent the abduction, the sale of or traffic in children for any purpose or in any form."

[7] CRC Article 9.3: "States Parties shall respect the right of the child who is separated from one or both parents to maintain personal relations and direct contact with both parents on a regular basis, except if it is contrary to the child's best interests."

[8] CRC Article 10.2: "A child whose parents reside in different States shall have the right to maintain on a regular basis, save in exceptional circumstances, personal relations and direct contacts with both parents. [. . .]"

[9] *See, e.g.,* Concluding Observations of the Committee on the Rights of the Child: South Africa, 23/02/2000, CRC/C/15/Add.122 (Concluding Observations/Comments), para. 40: "The Committee notes the efforts of the State party to address the situation of the sale, trafficking and abduction of children, including the adoption of the Hague Convention on Civil Aspects of International Child Abduction, into domestic legislation. . . ." *See also* Implementation Handbook for the Convention on the Rights of the Child, United Nations Children's Fund, prepared for UNICEF by Rachel Hodgkin and Peter Newell, UNICEF 2002, at 153-58.

THE HAGUE CONVENTION

served as a deterrent to many others through the clarity of its message (abduction is harmful to children, who have a right to contact with both parents) and through the simplicity of its central remedy (the return order). With currently more than 90 Contracting States, the 1980 Hague Convention can be viewed as one of the most successful family law instruments to be completed under the auspices of the Hague Conference on Private International Law.

The operation of the 1980 Hague Convention has been further strengthened by complementing provisions in the *Convention of 19 October 1996 on Jurisdiction, Applicable Law, Recognition, Enforcement and Co-operation in Respect of Parental Responsibility and Measures for the Protection of Children.*

The Child Abduction Section on the website of the Hague Conference contains the latest information about the status of the 1980 Convention, and the contact details of Central Authorities. For this, and much more information about the 1980 Convention, see < www.hcch.net >.

DOMESTIC RELATIONS RULES OF PROCEDURE
(Amended Through April, 2019)

PART

I. Rules of Civil Procedure Before Magisterial District Judges (Rules 1201–1211)
II. Actions Pursuant to the Protection From Abuse Act (Rules 1901–1905)
III. Actions for Support (Rules 1910.1–1910.50)
IV. Actions for Custody of Minor Children (Rules 1915.1–1915.25)
V. Actions of Divorce or for Annulment of Marriage (Rules 1920.1–1920.92)
VI. Rules Relating to Domestic Relations Matters Generally (Rules 1930.1–1930.8)
VII. Voluntary Mediation in Custody Actions (Rules 1940.1–1940.9)
VIII. Actions Pursuant to the Protection of Victims of Sexual Violence or Intimidation Act (Rules 1951–1959)
IX. Adoption (Orphans' Court Rules 15.1–15.9)
X. Juvenile Rules (Dependency Rules 1100–1800)
XI. Selected Pennsylvania Rules of Appellate Procedure (Fast Track Appeals)

I. Pennsylvania Rules of Civil Procedure Before Magisterial District Judges

Chapter 1200. Actions for Emergency Protective Relief (Rules 1201–1211)

RULE

Final Report–Recommendation 2-2015, Minor Court Rules Committee
Final Report–Recommendation 3-2016, Minor Court Rules Committee
1201. Applicability
1202. Definitions
1203. Limitation on Jurisdiction
1204. Venue
1205. Persons Who May Seek Emergency Relief
1206. Commencement of Proceedings
1207. Hearing
1208. Findings and Protection Orders
1209. Service and Execution of Emergency Protection Orders.
1210. Duration of Emergency Protection Orders
1211. Certification to Court of Common Pleas

RULES OF CIVIL PROCEDURE

FINAL REPORT[1]

Recommendation 2-2015, Minor Court Rules Committee

Amendment of Rules 206, 1201-1209, and of the Official Notes to Rules 112, 215, 1210-1211 of the Pennsylvania Rules of Civil Procedure before Magisterial District Judges

PROTECTIVE ORDERS FOR VICTIMS OF SEXUAL VIOLENCE OR INTIMIDATION

I. Introduction

The Minor Court Rules Committee ("Committee") recommended amendments to Rules 206, 1201-1209, and to the Official Notes to Rules 112, 215, 1210-1211 of the Pennsylvania Rules of Civil Procedure before Magisterial District Judges ("Rules"). The amendments establish procedures for protective orders sought for victims of sexual violence or intimidation, as provided for in recent legislation.

II. Background and Discussion

The Committee learned of enacted legislation that permits a victim of sexual violence or intimidation to petition a court for protection from a defendant. See 42 Pa.C.S. §§ 62A01-62A20 ("Act"). The Act provides for emergency protective orders for victims of sexual violence and intimidation, in much the same manner as existing emergency protection from abuse orders. The new law takes effect July 1, 2015.

After comparing the provisions of the Act with the Protection from Abuse Act, 23 Pa.C.S. §§ 6101-6122, as well as current Rules 1201-1211, the Committee drafted and recommended amendments to the rules to incorporate the new protective order provisions within existing Rules 1201-1211.

III. Rule Changes

The Committee recommended amending Rules 1201-1211 and the corresponding Official Notes to add references to the new emergency protective orders, add required definitions and statutory references, and make the rules gender neutral. The Committee also recommended deleting the first sentence of the Official Note to Rule 1206, indicating that the "plaintiff is apt to be in an excited state," as the Committee did not find the observation to be helpful. The Committee also recommended revising the last clause of Rule 1207 to more closely mirror the statutory requirements for nondisclosure of the location of a victim, and adding a sentence to the Official Note to Rule 1207 indicating that nothing in the rule is intended to preclude a magisterial district judge from making a proper determination regarding venue. The Committee also recommended amending Rule 1209 to include service provisions specific to the new emergency protective orders.

Additionally, the Committee recommended updating and adding cross-references to Rule 206, as well as the Official Note to Rule 112. The Committee also recommended adding cross-references to the Official Notes to Rules 215 and 1207 to clarify that the use of advanced communication technology is permitted in hearings on petitions for protective orders.

---

[1]. The Committee's Final Report should not be confused with the Official Notes to the Rules. Also, the Supreme Court of Pennsylvania does not adopt the Committee's Official Notes or the contents of the explanatory Final Reports.

RULES OF CIVIL PROCEDURE

FINAL REPORT[1]

Recommendation 3-2016, Minor Court Rules Committee

Amendment of Rules 1201, 1205-1206 and 1208, and of the Official Note to Rule 206 of the Pennsylvania Rules of Civil Procedure before Magisterial District Judges

EMERGENCY PROTECTIVE ORDERS IN CONNECTION WITH CLAIMS OF SEXUAL VIOLENCE OR INTIMIDATION

I. Introduction

The Minor Court Rules Committee ("Committee") recommended amendments to Rules 1201, 1205-1206 and 1208, and to the Official Note to Rule 206 of the Pennsylvania Rules of Civil Procedure before Magisterial District Judges ("Rules"). The amendments clarify the nature of the emergency relief available in connection with claims of sexual violence or intimidation, as provided for in recent legislation.

II. Background and Discussion

In 2014, the Committee learned of enacted legislation that permits a victim of sexual violence or intimidation to petition a court for protection from a defendant. See Act of Mar. 21, 2014, P.L. 365, No. 25, 42 Pa.C.S. §§ 62A01-62A20 ("Act"). The Act provides for emergency protective orders in connection with claims of sexual violence and intimidation, in much the same manner as existing emergency protection from abuse orders. The new law took effect July 1, 2015.

The Committee compared the provisions of the Act with the Protection From Abuse Act, 23 Pa.C.S. §§ 6101-6122, as well as current Rules 1201-1211, and drafted and recommended amendments to incorporate the new protective order provisions within existing Rules 1201-1211. The Court adopted the recommendation on June 29, 2015, and it took effect on July 1, 2015.[2]

After the adoption of the rule changes, the Committee was queried whether the allegation of harm required by the petition was stricter than that required by the Act. Specifically, the emergency petition contained a provision that "[e]mergency relief from sexual violence or intimidation is required because there is immediate and present danger of sexual violence or intimidation by the defendant to me and the above listed minor (child)(children)(incapacitated person)."

The Act's general provision on commencement of proceedings provides that a person may seek relief "by filing a petition with the court alleging the need for protection from the defendant with respect to sexual violence or intimidation." 42 Pa.C.S. § 62A05(a). Additionally, the provision of the Act addressing emergency relief by the minor judiciary provides that a hearing officer may grant relief "if the hearing officer deems it necessary to protect the victim upon good cause shown in an ex parte proceeding. Immediate and present danger posed by the defendant to the victim shall constitute good cause for the purposes of this subsection." 42 Pa.C.S. § 62A09(a).

Upon further examination of the Act, the Committee agreed that its intent was to provide protection in connection with claims of sexual violence or intimidation, and that the protection granted is not be limited to providing protection from further

---

[1]. The Committee's Final Report should not be confused with the Official Notes to the Rules. Also, the Supreme Court of Pennsylvania does not adopt the Committee's Official Notes or the contents of the explanatory Final Reports.

[2]. Order, see No. 387 Magisterial Rules Docket (June 29, 2015).

RULES OF CIVIL PROCEDURE

acts of sexual violence or intimidation. Applying a narrow reading of 42 Pa.C.S. § 62A05(a), and requiring an allegation of immediate and present danger of further sexual violence or intimidation, could have the unintended consequence of denying protective relief to a person who may not fear further sexual violence or intimidation by the defendant, but rather bodily injury or death. The Committee agreed that the showing required by 42 Pa.C.S. § 62A09(a), "[i]mmediate and present danger" is the appropriate standard for emergency protective relief under the Act.

III. Rule Changes

The amendments clarify that the protective relief is in connection with claims of sexual violence and intimidation, and is not specifically protection from further sexual violence or intimidation. In Rules 1201, 1205-1206 and 1208, additional subparagraphs have been added to distinguish relief available under the Protection From Abuse Act, set forth in the Domestic Relations Code, 23 Pa.C.S. § 6101-6122, from relief available in connection with claims of sexual violence and intimidation under the Act. The Official Note to Rule 206 is amended to clarify that the general relief available under the Act is for victims of sexual violence or intimidation, and not specifically relief from further sexual violence or intimidation. Additionally, while the content of the petition and order forms are not contained within the Rules, those forms are being modified consistent with the changes described above.

Rule 1201. Applicability

The rules in this chapter apply to the exercise by a hearing officer of jurisdiction under:

(1) Section 6110 of the Protection From Abuse Act, 23 Pa.C.S. § 6110, granting emergency relief from abuse, and

(2) Section 62A09 of Title 42, 42 Pa.C.S. § 62A09, granting emergency relief in connection with claims of sexual violence or intimidation.

> **Official Note:** *See* the Protection From Abuse Act set forth in the Domestic Relations Code, 23 Pa.C.S. §§ 6101-6122, and 42 Pa.C.S. §§ 62A01-62A20.
>
> The court of common pleas of each judicial district is responsible to ensure that a judge or magisterial district judge "is available on a 24-hour-a-day, 365-day-a-year basis to accept and decide on petitions for an emergency court order under" the Older Adult Protective Services Act. 35 P.S. § 10225.307. Actions commenced under the Older Adult Protective Services Act are governed by statute and local procedures, not by these rules.
>
> This chapter was amended in 2015 to provide procedural rules for protective orders sought for victims of sexual violence or intimidation. See 42 Pa.C.S. §§ 62A01-62A20.
>
> **Source:** *The provisions of this Rule 1201 amended March 27, 1992, effective immediately, 22 Pa.B. 1900; amended November 2, 2001, effective February 1, 2002, 31 Pa.B. 6385; amended July 7, 2006, effective immediately, 36 Pa.B. 3810; amended June 29, 2015, effective July 1, 2015, 45 Pa.B. 3811; amended October 28, 2016, effective December 31, 2016, 46 Pa.B. 7165.*

Rule 1202. Definitions

As used in this chapter:

(1) "abuse" means the occurrence of one or more of the following acts between family or household members, sexual or intimate partners or persons who share biological parenthood:

(a) attempting to cause or intentionally, knowingly or recklessly causing bodily injury, serious bodily injury, rape, involuntary deviate sexual intercourse, sexual assault, statutory sexual assault, aggravated indecent assault, indecent assault or incest with or without a deadly weapon.

(b) placing another in reasonable fear of imminent serious bodily injury.

(c) the infliction of false imprisonment pursuant to 18 Pa.C.S. § 2903 (relating to false imprisonment).

(d) physically or sexually abusing minor children, including such terms as defined in Chapter 63 of the Domestic Relations Code (relating to child protective services).

(e) knowingly engaging in a course of conduct or repeatedly committing acts toward another person, including following the person, without proper authority, under circumstances which place the person in reasonable fear of bodily injury. This definition applies only to proceedings commenced under the Domestic Relations Code and is inapplicable to any criminal prosecutions commenced under Title 18 (relating to crimes and offenses).

(2) "adult" means an individual who is 18 years of age or older.

(3) "court" means:

(a) the court of common pleas of the judicial district in which the office of the hearing officer taking action under these rules is located in actions brought under the Protection from Abuse Act, 23 Pa.C.S. §§ 6101-6122, or

(b) the court or magisterial district judge having jurisdiction over the matter in actions brought pursuant to Section 62A09 of Title 42, 42 Pa.C.S. § 62A09 (providing for protection of victims of sexual violence or intimidation).

(4) "family or household members" means spouses or persons who have been spouses, persons living as spouses or who lived as spouses, parents and children, other persons related by consanguinity or affinity, current or former sexual or intimate partners or persons who share biological parenthood.

(5) "hearing officer" means a magisterial district judge, judge of the Philadelphia Municipal Court, arraignment court magistrate appointed under 42 Pa.C.S. § 1123 (relating to jurisdiction and venue), master appointed under 42 Pa.C.S. § 1126 (relating to masters), and master for emergency relief appointed under 23 Pa.C.S. § 6110(e) or 42 Pa.C.S. § 62A09(e) (relating to master for emergency relief).

(6) "intimidation" means conduct constituting a crime under either of the following provisions between persons who are not family or household members:

(a) 18 Pa.C.S. § 2709(a)(4), (5), (6) or (7) (relating to harassment) where the conduct is committed by a person 18 years of age or older against a person under 18 years of age.

(b) 18 Pa.C.S. § 2709.1 (relating to stalking) where the conduct is committed by a person 18 years of age or older against a person under 18 years of age.

(7) "minor" means an individual who is not an adult.

(8) "sexual violence" means conduct constituting a crime under any of the following provisions between persons who are not family or household members:

(a) 18 Pa.C.S. Ch. 31 (relating to sexual offenses), except 18 Pa.C.S. §§ 3129 (relating to sexual intercourse with animal) and 3130 (relating to conduct relating to sex offenders).

(b) 18 Pa.C.S. § 4304 (relating to endangering welfare of children) if the offense involved sexual contact with the victim.

(c) 18 Pa.C.S. § 6301(a)(1)(ii) (relating to corruption of minors).

(d) 18 Pa.C.S. § 6312(b) (relating to sexual abuse of children).

(e) 18 Pa.C.S. § 6318 (relating to unlawful contact with minor).

(f) 18 Pa.C.S. § 6320 (relating to sexual exploitation of children).

(9) "victim" means a person who is a victim of abuse, sexual violence or intimidation.

Note: These definitions are largely derived from 23 Pa.C.S. § 6102 and 42 Pa.C.S. § 62A03.

Adopted March 24, 1977, imd. effective. Amended June 30, 1982, effective 30 days after July 17, 1982; March 27, 1992, imd. effective; Nov. 2, 2001, effective Feb. 1, 2002; Jan. 6, 2005, effective Jan. 29, 2005; July 7, 2006, imd. effective; June 29, 2015, effective July 1, 2015.

Rule 1203. Limitation on Jurisdiction

The hearing officer may grant relief under these rules only when the court is unavailable to do so pursuant to the provisions of:

(1) Section 6110 of the Protection From Abuse Act, 23 Pa.C.S. § 6110,

(2) 42 Pa.C.S. § 62A09 (providing for protection of victims of sexual violence or intimidation), or

(3) local rule of court.

Note: The limitation in this rule is taken from Section 6110 of the Protection From Abuse Act, 23 Pa.C.S. § 6110, and 42 Pa.C.S. § 62A09.

This rule recognizes and reaffirms the existing practice in many counties. The availability of each court to grant necessary emergency relief will vary greatly, both during the business and non-business day; therefore, it was deemed desirable to permit each court to promulgate such rules as would best serve its specific needs in providing for efficient implementation of emergency relief measures.

Adopted March 24, 1977, imd. effective. Amended June 30, 1982, effective 30 days after July 17, 1982; March 27, 1992, imd. effective; Nov. 2, 2001, effective Feb. 1, 2002; June 29, 2015, effective July 1, 2015.

Explanatory Comment—1992

Rule 1203 reflects the expansion in the jurisdiction of Hearing Officers to receive petitions filed for emergency relief and to grant such petitions resulting from the most recent amendments to the Protection from Abuse Act.

Under the previous provisions of the Act, Hearing Officers retained jurisdiction to grant relief only when the court was unavailable from the close of business at the end of the week to the resumption of business at the beginning of the week. However, 23 Pa.C.S.A., Section 6110(a) increases the jurisdiction of Hearing Officers to grant petitions during the business day, in counties with less than four judges when the court is unavailable during the business day by reason of duties outside the county, illness or vacation; and to grant petitions during the end of each day to the resumption of business the next morning or from the end of the business week to the beginning of the next business week, in counties with at least four judges when the court deems itself unavailable during said periods.

Furthermore, the Rule provides that Hearing Officers may also entertain emergency petitions and grant relief during those times as established by the local rules of court of their respective judicial districts.

The Note to Rule 1203 recognizes that the availability of Hearing Officers to entertain petitions and to grant relief is dependent upon the number of judges in the judicial district, the existence of certain conditions as specified in the Act, and the particular needs of the judicial district. Hence, the Note permits the judicial districts to promulgate local rules in order to implement the provisions of the Act. The Note also recognizes and reaffirms those practices which govern the availability of Hearing Officers to grant emergency petitions and which have already been adopted by the various judicial districts through local rule.

Rule 1204. Venue

A. Except as provided in subdivision B, a proceeding for emergency relief may be brought in a magisterial district within the county in which

    (1) the plaintiff resides, either temporarily or permanently, or

    (2) the abuse, sexual violence or intimidation occurred.

B. If the relief sought includes possession of the residence or household to the exclusion of the defendant, the action may be brought only in a magisterial district within the county in which the residence or household is located.

Note: This rule is consistent with Pa.R.C.P. No. 1901.1 and provides the necessary flexibility to a plaintiff who may have to flee the county of permanent residence to escape further abuse. This rule is intended to provide maximum flexibility to a plaintiff to use a convenient forum to seek an emergency protective order. However, where practicable, plaintiffs should give preference to filing in the magisterial district in which the plaintiff resides, either temporarily or permanently, or in the magisterial district in which the abuse occurred. A proceeding is considered to have been brought in a magisterial district even if it is before a hearing officer serving temporarily in that district, or before a hearing officer who has been invested by local rule with temporary county-wide jurisdiction.

Subdivision B of this rule only applies to actions brought pursuant to Section 6110 of the Protection From Abuse Act, 23 Pa.C.S. § 6110.

Adopted March 24, 1977, imd. effective. Amended June 30, 1982, effective 30 days after July 17, 1982; March 27, 1992, imd. effective; Nov. 2, 2001, effective Feb. 1, 2002; June 29, 2015, effective July 1, 2015.

Explanatory Comment—1992

In order to implement the provisions of the Protection from Abuse Act relative to the availability of Hearing Officers, many judicial districts have enacted local rules of court which grant jurisdiction and venue throughout the county to a single Hearing Officer, especially during the evening and weekend periods as a practical matter. The Note to Rule 1204 recognizes this practice pursuant to the authority of president judges to insure the continuous availability of at least one District Justice within the judicial district--(Refer to Pa.R.Crim.P. 23).

Rule 1205. Persons Who May Seek Emergency Relief

A. In actions brought pursuant to Section 6110 of the Protection From Abuse Act, 23 Pa.C.S. § 6110, an adult or an emancipated minor may seek emergency relief from abuse for himself or herself. Also, any parent, adult household member or guardian ad litem may seek emergency relief from abuse on behalf of minor children. In addition, a guardian of the person of an incapacitated person as defined in 20 Pa.C.S. § 5501 may seek emergency relief on behalf of the incapacitated person.

B. In actions brought pursuant to Section 62A09 of Title 42, 42 Pa.C.S. § 62A09 (providing for protection in connection with claims of sexual violence and intimidation), an adult or emancipated minor may seek emergency relief for himself or herself. Also, any parent, adult household member or guardian ad litem may seek emergency relief on behalf of a minor child. In addition, a guardian of the person of an incapacitated person as defined in 20 Pa.C.S. § 5501 may seek emergency relief on behalf of the incapacitated person.

Official Note: This rule is derived from Section 6106 of the Protection From Abuse Act, 23 Pa.C.S. § 6106, as well as 42 Pa.C.S. § 62A05.

The filings required by this rule are subject to the Case Records Public Access Policy of the Unified Judicial System of Pennsylvania. See Rule 217.

Source: *The provisions of this Rule 1205 amended March 27, 1992, effective immediately, 22 Pa.B. 1900; amended November 2, 2001, effective February 1, 2002, 31 Pa.B. 6385; amended June 29, 2015, effective July 1, 2015, 45 Pa.B. 3811; amended October 28, 2016, effective December 31, 2016, 46 Pa.B. 7165; amended June 1, 2018, eff. July 1, 2018.*

Explanatory Comment—1992

As a result of the amendments to the Protection from Abuse Act, 23 Pa.C.S.A., Section 6106(a), a guardian of the person of an adult who has been declared incompetent under 20 Pa.C.S.Ch. 51 Subch. B. (relating to appointment of guardian) may also seek relief on behalf of the incompetent adult through the filing of a petition. Rule 1205 incorporates this provision of the Act.

Rule 1206. Commencement of Proceedings

A. A proceeding for emergency relief

(1) from abuse, or

(2) in connection with claims of sexual violence or intimidation

shall be commenced by the filing of a petition by the plaintiff with the hearing officer on a form that shall be prescribed by the State Court Administrator. The petition shall be signed by the plaintiff and shall set forth the names and addresses of the plaintiff and the defendant and the names, addresses and ages of any person on whose behalf the plaintiff is seeking relief. The plaintiff shall also allege in the petition, in general terms, the cause for seeking emergency relief.

B. Upon issuance of an emergency order, the hearing officer shall provide the plaintiff with instructions regarding the commencement of proceedings in the court of common pleas and regarding the procedures for initiating a contempt charge should the defendant violate the emergency order. The hearing officer shall also advise the plaintiff of the existence of rape crisis centers in the county or in nearby counties in the case of sexual violence, as well as programs for victims of domestic or sexual violence in the county or in nearby counties and inform the plaintiff of the availability of legal assistance without cost if the plaintiff is unable to pay therefor.

C. The petition shall be filed and service shall be made without prepayment of costs.

Official Note: Paragraph B is added to assure compliance with the requirement of Section 6110(d) of the Protection From Abuse Act, 23 Pa.C.S. § 6110(d), as well as 42 Pa.C.S. § 62A09(d). Practice varies among the judicial districts as to what procedures the plaintiff must follow to continue in effect a protection order in the court of common pleas upon the certification of an emergency protection order to the court of common pleas. The hearing officer should provide clear instructions to the plaintiff as to what must be done to continue in effect the protection order in the court of common pleas. *See* Rule 1210 and Note and Rule 1211 and Note. Paragraph C is derived from Section 6106(b) of the Protection From Abuse Act, 23 Pa.C.S. § 6106(b), as well as 42 Pa.C.S. § 62A05(b), and reflects the practice when a temporary order is issued at the common pleas level.

The filings required by this rule are subject to the Case Records Public Access Policy of the Unified Judicial System of Pennsylvania. See Rule 217.

Source: *The provisions of this Rule 1206 amended March 27, 1992, effective immediately, 22 Pa.B. 1900; amended November 2, 2001, effective February 1, 2002, 31 Pa.B. 6385; amended June 29, 2015, effective July 1, 2015, 45 Pa.B. 3811; amended October 28, 2016, effective December 31, 2016, 46 Pa.B. 7165; amended June 1, 2018, eff. July 1, 2018.*

Explanatory Comment—1992

The responsibilities of Hearing Officers to the plaintiff have been increased as a result of the amendments to the Protection from Abuse Act, 23 Pa.C.S.A., Section 6110(d). When issuing an emergency order, Hearing Officers must advise the plaintiff of the existence of programs for victims of domestic violence in the county or in nearby counties and they must inform the plaintiff of the availability of legal assistance without cost if the plaintiff is unable to pay for them. Rule 1206, through the inclusion of Subdivision B, conforms the Rule to this particular statutory provision; and the amendment to the Note simply provides the justification for Subdivision B, i.e., to assure compliance with the Title 23 provisions of the Protection from Abuse Act.

Rule 1207. Hearing

As soon as possible after the filing of the petition, the hearing officer shall hold an ex parte hearing thereon. The plaintiff may present witnesses at the hearing. Neither in the petition nor during a hearing shall the hearing officer require disclosure of the address of a domestic violence program, a rape crisis center, or the plaintiff or victim, as appropriate.

Note: The hearing is ex parte, and the emergency order issued by the hearing officer as a result of the hearing is of short duration. *See* 23 Pa.C.S. § 6110(a)-(b), 42 Pa.C.S. § 62A09(a)-(b). Accordingly, there are no provisions in these rules for notice to the defendant prior to the hearing. The hearing need not be held at the office of the hearing officer. *See* Rule 215 (permitting the use of advanced communication technology in any civil action or proceeding governed by the Rules of Civil Procedure for Magisterial District Judges.) The last phrase was added to ensure compliance with Section 6112 of the Act, 23 Pa.C.S. § 6112 and 42 Pa.C.S. § 62A11. Nothing in the last phrase is intended to preclude a magisterial district judge from determining that venue is proper pursuant to Rule 1204.

Adopted March 24, 1977, imd. effective. Amended June 30, 1982, effective 30 days after July 17, 1982; March 27, 1992, imd. effective; Nov. 2, 2001, effective Feb. 1, 2002; June 29, 2015, effective July 1, 2015.

Explanatory Comment—1992

Under the provisions of 23 Pa.C.S.A., Section 6112, the Hearing Officer may consider whether the plaintiff or plaintiff's family is endangered by disclosure of the permanent or temporary address of the plaintiff or minor children. The statute further provides that neither in the pleading nor during proceedings or hearings under the chapter shall the Hearing Officer require disclosure of the address of a domestic violence program.

Hence, Rule 1207 reflects this provision of the Protection from Abuse Act by providing that plaintiff's witness need not be compelled to disclose the permanent or temporary residence of the plaintiff or minor children; and the amendment to the Note simply provides the justification for the amendment, i.e., to assure compliance with the Title 23 provisions of the Act.

Rule 1208. Findings and Protection Orders

A.(1) If the hearing officer, upon good cause shown, finds it necessary to protect the plaintiff or minor children from abuse the hearing officer may grant relief in accordance with Section 6110(a) of the Protection From Abuse Act, 23 Pa.C.S. § 6110(a), and make any protection orders necessary to effectuate that relief. Immediate and present danger of abuse to the plaintiff or minor children shall constitute good cause.

(2) If the hearing officer, upon good cause shown, finds it necessary to protect the plaintiff or another individual in connection with claims of sexual violence or intimidation, the hearing officer may grant relief in accordance with 42 Pa.C.S. § 62A09(a), and make any protection orders necessary to effectuate that relief. Immediate and present danger posed by the defendant to the plaintiff or another individual shall constitute good cause.

B. The hearing officer shall enter on the petition form the findings and any protection orders made or other action taken.

Official Note: Subparagraph A(1) of this rule permits the hearing officer to grant limited relief in accordance with 23 Pa.C.S. § 6108(a)(1), (2) and (6) or (1) and (6). Subparagraph A(2) of this rule permits the hearing officer to grant limited relief to plaintiffs in accordance with 42 Pa.C.S. § 62A07(b).

Source: *The provisions of this Rule 1208 amended March 27, 1992, effective immediately, 22 Pa.B. 1900; amended November 2, 2001, effective February 1, 2002, 31 Pa.B. 6385; amended June 29, 2015, effective July 1, 2015, 45 Pa.B. 3811; amended October 28, 2016, effective December 31, 2016, 46 Pa.B. 7165.*

Explanatory Comment—1992

Hearing Officers' authority to grant relief under the Act has been enlarged under 23 Pa.C.S.A., Section 6108. In accordance with the provisions of the Act, the court may grant any protection order or approve any consent agreement to bring about a cessation of abuse of the plaintiff or minor children. The order or agreement may include the following:

(a)(1) Directing the defendant to refrain from abusing the plaintiff or minor children.

(a)(2) Granting possession to the plaintiff of the residence or household to the exclusion of the defendant by evicting the defendant or restoring possession to the plaintiff when the residence or household is jointly owned or leased by the parties, is owned or leased by the entireties or is owned or leased solely by the plaintiff.

(a)(3) When the defendant has a duty to support the plaintiff or minor children living in the residence or household and the defendant is the sole owner or lessee, granting possession to the plaintiff of the residence or household to the exclusion of the defendant by evicting the defendant or restoring possession to the plaintiff or, by consent agreement, allowing the defendant to provide suitable alternate housing.

Therefore, Rule 1208 incorporates the additional relief remedies available to the Hearing Officer.

Rule 1209. Service and Execution of Emergency Protection Orders

A. The hearing officer shall provide to the plaintiff a copy of a protection order made under Rule 1208. The hearing officer or, when necessary, the plaintiff shall immediately deliver a service copy of any protection order made under Rule 1208 to a police officer, police department, sheriff or certified constable for service upon the defendant and execution. After making reasonable effort, if the executing officer is unable to serve the protection order upon the defendant in a timely fashion, the executing officer shall leave a service copy of the petition form containing the order with the police department with jurisdiction over the area in which the plaintiff resides for service upon the defendant, and shall advise such police department that the order could not be served.

B. When a protection order is issued under Rule 1208 in accordance with 42 Pa.C.S. § 62A09(a), the hearing officer shall:

(1) within two business days, serve the order upon the police department, sheriff and district attorney in the jurisdiction where the order was entered, and

(2) in the case of a minor victim of sexual violence, serve a copy of the petition and order upon the county agency (as defined by 23 Pa.C.S. § 6303) and the Department of Human Services.

Note: The hearing officer should provide the plaintiff with at least one copy of a protection order, but more than one copy may be needed. For example, the plaintiff may wish to serve the order upon multiple police departments when the plaintiff lives and works in different police jurisdictions, etc. If it is necessary for the plaintiff to deliver the protection order to the executing officer, the hearing officer should make sure that the plaintiff fully understands the process and what must be done to have the order served upon the defendant. The hearing officer should make every effort to have the protection order served by a law enforcement officer in a timely fashion. The Rule requires that if the executing officer is unable to serve the protection order in a timely fashion, the executing officer shall leave a service copy of the order with the police department with jurisdiction over the area in which the plaintiff resides. This was thought advisable so that the local police would have a service copy in case they would be called to the plaintiff's residence should the defendant return there. Due to the emergency nature of these protection orders and the fact that to be meaningful they must be served and executed at night or on a weekend, the hearing officer should have the authority to use police officers as well as sheriffs and certified constables to serve and execute these orders. Protection orders issued under Rule 1208 in accordance with 42 Pa. C.S. § 62A09 (providing for protection of victims of sexual violence or intimidation) are subject to additional service requirements. *See* Section 6109(a) of the Protection From Abuse Act, 23 Pa.C.S. § 6109(a), and 42 Pa.C.S. § 62A05(d).

Service shall be made without prepayment of costs. *See* Rule 1206(C).

Service of protection orders upon the defendant at the time of execution may not be possible under some circumstances.

Adopted March 24, 1977, imd. effective. Amended June 30, 1982, effective 30 days after July 17, 1982; March 27, 1992, imd. effective; Nov. 2, 2001, effective Feb. 1, 2002; June 29, 2015, effective July 1, 2015.

Rule 1210. Duration of Emergency Protection Orders

Protection orders issued under Rule 1208 shall expire at the end of the next business day the court deems itself available.

Note: This rule is derived from Section 6110(b) of the Protection From Abuse Act, 23 Pa.C.S. § 6110(b), as well as 42 Pa.C.S. § 62A09(b). Practice varies among the judicial districts as to what procedures the plaintiff must follow to continue in effect a protection order in the court of common pleas upon the certification of an emergency protection order to the court of common pleas. The hearing officer should provide clear instructions to the plaintiff as to what must be done to continue in effect the protection order in the court of common pleas. *See* Rule 1206 and Note, and Rule 1211 and Note.

Adopted March 24, 1977, imd. effective. Amended March 27, 1992, imd. effective; Nov. 2, 2001, effective Feb. 1, 2002; June 29, 2015, effective July 1, 2015.

Explanatory Comment—1992

Initially, the Protection from Abuse Act provided that emergency orders issued by Hearing Officers were to expire at the resumption of business of the court at the beginning of the week or within 72 hours, whichever occurs sooner. This language has been simplified under 23 Pa.C.S.A., Section 6110(b) to provide that said orders expire as of the resumption of business of the court at the beginning of the next business day. Rule 1210 incorporates this simplification.

Rule 1211. Certification to Court of Common Pleas

A. Any protection order issued under Rule 1208, together with any documentation in support thereof, shall immediately be certified to the court of common pleas by the hearing officer.

B. Certification under subdivision A of this Rule shall be accomplished by sending to the prothonotary of the court by first class mail or messenger a certified copy of the petition form containing the order, with any supporting documentation attached.

> **Note:** Certification under subdivision A of this rule is required by Section 6110(c) of the Protection From Abuse Act, 23 Pa.C.S. § 6110(c), as well as 42 Pa.C.S. § 62A09(c). This rule is also consistent with Pa.R.C.P. Nos. 1901.3(b) and 1953(b), which permit commencement of an action by filing with the prothonotary a certified copy of an emergency protection order. However, practice varies among the judicial districts as to how the protection order is continued in effect after it is certified to the court of common pleas. For example, some judicial districts may require that the plaintiff appear in person to continue the action in the court of common pleas. Others may automatically commence an action in the court of common pleas upon receipt of a certified copy of the emergency order from the hearing officer. *See* Rule 1206 and Note, and Rule 1210 and Note.
>
> Depending on local practice, the plaintiff or the plaintiff's representative may act as a messenger under subdivision B of this rule.

Adopted March 24, 1977, imd. effective. Amended June 30, 1982, effective 30 days after July 17, 1982; March 27, 1992, imd. effective; Nov. 2, 2001, effective Feb. 1, 2002; June 29, 2015, effective July 1, 2015.

II. Actions Pursuant to the Protection From Abuse Act
(Amended Through April, 2019)

Rules 1901-1905

RULE
1901. Definitions
1901.1 Venue
1901.2 Scheduling
1901.3 Commencement of Action
1901.4 Service and Registration of Order
1901.5 Enforcement
1901.6 Responsive Pleading Not Required
1901.7 Decision. Post-Trial Relief
1901.8 Modification or Discontinuance.
1905. Forms for Use in PFA Actions. Notice and Hearing. Petition, Temporary Protection Order. Final Protection Order.

Rule 1901. Definitions

As used in this chapter:

Act—Protection From Abuse Act No. 206 approved December 19, 1990, 23 Pa.C.S. § 6101 et seq.

Action—A proceeding for protection from abuse defined in § 6102 of the Act.

Court—The court of common pleas.

Emergency Order—An order entered by a hearing officer, who is a person meeting the definition set forth at 23 Pa.C.S. § 6102.

Fees—Any costs associated with the filing, issuance, registration, service or appeal of a Protection From Abuse matter, including any foreign protection order.

Master for Emergency Relief—An attorney, admitted to the practice of law by the Supreme Court of Pennsylvania and appointed pursuant to 23 Pa.C.S. § 6110(e), to hear petitions for emergency protection from abuse.

Temporary Order—An ex parte order entered by the court pursuant to 23 Pa.C.S. § 6107.

Explanatory Comment—2006

The 2005 amendments to the Protection From Abuse Act, Act 66 of 2005, authorize two methods to secure emergency protection from abuse orders. The first is through a magisterial district judge and the other is through a master for emergency relief. In order for a county to exercise the master for emergency relief option, the county must assume the costs of the master and the Administrative Office of Pennsylvania Courts must approve the master's selection and appointment. 23 Pa.C.S. § 6110 (e).

The 2005 amendments to the Protection From Abuse Act also prohibit the assessment of fees or costs against the plaintiff or petitioner. This prohibition includes fees related to filing, serving, registering or appealing a protection from abuse petition or order. 23 Pa.C.S. §§ 6104 (d)(1), 6106(b) and (g.1) and 6113.1(b).

Rule 1901.1 Venue

(a) Except as provided in subdivision (b), an action for protection from abuse may be brought in a county in which

(1) the plaintiff resides, either temporarily or permanently, or is employed, or

(2) the defendant may be served, or

(3) the abuse occurred.

(b) If the relief sought includes possession of the residence or household to the exclusion of the defendant, the action shall be brought only in the county in which the residence or household is located.

(c) An action for indirect criminal contempt may be filed in, and heard by, the court in the county in which the order was issued or where the violation occurred.

Explanatory Comment—1991

The statute and rules governing actions for protection from abuse formerly contained no provision for venue. Recommendation No. 84 of the Civil Procedural Rules Committee proposed a new rule to fill that void and the rule has been adopted as Rule 1901.1

Subdivision (a) provides for venue in the following counties: (1) the county in which the abuse occurred, (2) the county in which the defendant may be served, (3) the county in which the plaintiff resides, either permanently or temporarily, and (4) the county in which the plaintiff is employed. These are the counties with which the plaintiff has the most significant contacts and the greatest interest in remaining free from abuse. The county of temporary residence is included because an abused person may have to flee the county of permanent residence to escape further abuse.

The rule imposes limited venue when the relief sought includes the sole possession of the residence or household. In that instance, the action must be brought in the county in which the residence or household is located.

Explanatory Comment—2006

The 2005 amendments to the Protection From Abuse Act grant jurisdiction over indirect criminal contempt complaints in either the county in which the order was issued or the county where the violation occurred. This rule allows for flexible and immediate enforcement of protection from abuse orders. With this amendment, indirect criminal contempt jurisdiction is parallel to prosecution for stalking and harassment. 23 Pa.C.S. § 6114 (a.1).

Rule 1901.2. Scheduling

Each judicial district shall establish times when the court will hear temporary Protection From Abuse matters.

Rule 1901.3. Commencement of Action

(a) Except as provided in subdivision (b), an action shall be commenced by presenting to the court or filing with the prothonotary a petition setting forth the alleged abuse by the defendant. The petition shall be substantially

Rule 1901.4   ACTIONS UNDER PROTECTION FROM ABUSE

in the form set forth in Rule 1905(b) and shall have as its first page the Notice of Hearing and Order set forth in Rule 1905(a).

(b) An action may be commenced by filing with the prothonotary a certified copy of an emergency order entered pursuant to 23 Pa.C.S.A. § 6110, including orders issued by masters for emergency relief.

(c) Any fees associated with this action shall not be charged to the plaintiff.

(c) The master for emergency relief shall follow the procedures set forth in the Pennsylvania Rules of Civil Procedure Governing Actions and Proceedings Before Magisterial District Judges for emergency relief under the Protection From Abuse Act.

> *Note:* See Pa.R.C.P. No. 1930.1(b). This rule may require attorneys or unrepresented parties to file confidential documents and documents containing confidential information that are subject to the *Case Records Public Access Policy of the Unified Judicial System of Pennsylvania.*

Adopted March 9, 1977, effective April 10, 1977. Amended March 30, 1994, effective July 1, 1994. Renumbered from Rule 1902 and amended March 9, 1998, effective July 1, 1998. Amended May 2, 2006, effective May 9, 2006; Jan. 5, 2018, effective Jan. 6, 2018; June 1, 2018, effective on July 1, 2018.

Rule 1901.4.   Service and Registration of Order

(a) Service of the petition and temporary order shall be in accordance with Rule 1930.4.

(b) An Affidavit of Service substantially in the form set forth in Rule 1905(d) shall be filed with the prothonotary.

(c) Upon the filing of a protection order with the prothonotary, the prothonotary shall transmit a copy of the order to the State Police PFA Registry in the manner prescribed by the Pennsylvania State Police.

Official Note: This provision also applies to an order denying a plaintiff's request for a final protection order.

(d) No fee shall be charged to the plaintiff or petitioner for service of any protection from abuse order or pleading or for the registration, filing or service of any foreign protection order.

Explanatory Comment—1997

Subdivision (c) reflects the prothonotary's role in ensuring that all protection orders reach the new statewide PFA Registry. Pursuant to the 1994 amendments to the Protection From Abuse Act, the Pennsylvania State Police Department is mandated to establish this registry for all protection orders issued or registered in the commonwealth. Once it becomes fully operational, it will be available at all times to inform law enforcement officers, dispatchers and courts of the existence and terms of protection orders. The registry represents a major improvement in the manner in which protections orders are registered and verified by not only eliminating the need to register the order in every county where the victim believes enforcement is necessary, but also enabling the police to immediately verify the order for purposes of enforcement. In order to ensure that the information in the registry remains current, subdivision (c) requires the prothonotary to transmit all protection orders issued or registered in the commonwealth, including temporary, final, modified and consent orders, as well as any orders withdrawing, extending or denying the plaintiff's request for a protection order.

Explanatory Comment—2006

New subdivision (d) reflects the prohibition against charging fees to the plaintiff, even those related to foreign protection orders, as set forth in the 2005 amendments to the Protection From Abuse Act. 23 Pa.C.S. § 6106(b) and (g.1).

Amended February 10, 2015, effective March 12, 2015.

Rule 1901.5. Enforcement

(a) When an arrest is made for violation of an order, a complaint for indirect criminal contempt shall be completed and signed by either a police officer, the sheriff or the plaintiff. When the complaint is filed by a police officer or sheriff, neither the plaintiff's presence nor signature is required.

(b) If an arrest is not effected, a complaint for indirect criminal contempt may be completed and signed by the plaintiff pursuant to 23 Pa.C.S. § 6113.1.

Explanatory Comment—2006

The 2005 amendments to the Protection From Abuse Act authorize the sheriff to arrest the defendant for violations of a protection from abuse order. In addition, the sheriff is authorized to exercise a search and seizure of any firearm, other weapon and ammunition subsequent to arrest. 23 Pa.C.S. § 6113(a) and (b).

Rule 1901.6. Responsive Pleading Not Required

The defendant is not required to file an answer or other responsive pleading to the petition or the certified order, and all averments not admitted shall be deemed denied.

Note: For procedures as to the time and manner of hearings and issuance of orders, see 23 Pa.C.S. § 6107. For provisions as to the scope of relief available, see 23 Pa.C.S. § 6108. For provisions as to contempt for violation of an order, see 23 Pa.C.S. § 6114.

See Pa.R.C.P. No. 1930.1(b). This rule may require attorneys or unrepresented parties to file confidential documents and documents containing confidential information that are subject to the *Case Records Public Access Policy of the Unified Judicial System of Pennsylvania.*

Adopted March 9, 1977, effective April 10, 1977. Amended March 30, 1994, effective July 1, 1994. Renumbered from Rule 1904, March 9, 1998, effective July 1, 1998. Amended May 2, 2006, effective May 9, 2006; Jan. 5, 2018, effective Jan. 6, 2018; June 1, 2018, effective July 1, 2018.

Rule 1901.7. Decision. Post-trial relief

(a) The decision of the court may consist of only general findings of abuse but shall dispose of all claims for relief. The court's final order shall be rendered substantially in the form set forth in Rule 1905(e).

(b) No motion for post-trial relief may be filed to the final order.

Note: The procedure relating to Motions for Reconsideration is set forth in Rule 1930.2.

(c) If a final protection from abuse order directs the defendant to pay support to the plaintiff for the benefit of the plaintiff and/or a child, the plaintiff must file a complaint for support with the domestic relations section within two weeks of the date of the order or the support provisions of the order shall lapse automatically. If the plaintiff timely files with the domestic

Rule 1901.8 ACTIONS UNDER PROTECTION FROM ABUSE

relations section, the support provisions of the final protection from abuse order shall remain in effect until a support order is entered.

(d) The custody provisions of a Protection From Abuse order are temporary. Either party may initiate custody proceedings pursuant to the custody statute at 23 Pa.C.S. § 5321 et seq. Any valid custody order entered after the final Protection From Abuse order supersedes the custody provisions in paragraph 5 of the Protection From Abuse order.

Adopted March 9, 1977, effective April 10, 1977. Amended Oct. 19, 1983, effective Jan. 1, 1984; March 30, 1994, effective July 1, 1994. Renumbered from Rule 1905 and amended March 9, 1998, effective July 1, 1998. Amended May 9, 2005, imd. effective; May 2, 2006, effective May 9, 2006; Feb. 10, 2015, effective March 12, 2015.

Explanatory Comment—1977

New Rules 1901, et seq. promulgated March 9, 1977 and effective 15 days after publication in the *Pennsylvania Bulletin* implement the Protection From Abuse Act No. 218 of 1976 which became effective December 6, 1976.

The Act introduces a new civil remedy authorizing protective orders to bring about cessation of abuse of the plaintiff or minor children, which relief includes, inter alia, exclusion of the errant spouse from the household, the award of temporary custody and visitation rights with regard to minor children and support.

The Act also authorizes temporary ex parte orders when the exigency of the situation requires immediate relief before process can be served on a defendant.

Jurisdiction is also conferred on the magisterial district judges over the weekend if and when a judge of the court of common pleas is not available, but any temporary order of a magisterial district judge expires at the resumption of business of the common pleas court at the beginning of the week or within seventy-two (72) hours, whichever occurs first. The magisterial district judge is required immediately to certify his or her order to the common pleas court and the certification under the Act has the effect of commencing a proceeding in the common pleas court and invoking the other provisions of the Act.

Section 9 of the Act provides that all proceedings shall be in accordance with Rules of Civil Procedure and shall be in addition to any other available civil or criminal remedies.

Explanatory Comment—2005

Act 207-2004 amended numerous titles of the *Pennsylvania Consolidated Statutes* changing the title of "district justice" to "magisterial district judge." The amendments to Rule 1901.7's Explanatory Comment--1977 reflect the change in title, make the comment gender-neutral and delete outdated material.

Rule 1901.8. Modification or Discontinuance

(a) In cases in which a temporary protection order has not yet been granted or has been denied, a plaintiff in a protection from abuse action who wishes to discontinue the action may file a praecipe to discontinue, pursuant to Pa.R.C.P. 229, prior to the final order hearing. The party may also request the discontinuance by oral motion at a hearing.

(b) In cases in which a temporary protection order has been granted, a plaintiff in a protection from abuse action who wishes to vacate the temporary order and discontinue the action shall either file a petition with the court prior to the final order hearing or make the request by oral motion at the final order hearing.

(c) If either party seeks a modification after a final judgment has been entered in a protection from abuse action, the party shall petition the court to modify the final order. The court shall enter an order granting or denying the petition following an appearance by the petitioner before the court.

Adopted June 25, 2013, effective July 25, 2013.

Explanatory Comment—2013

Jurisdictions across the commonwealth have adopted varying procedures and processes for the withdrawal, discontinuance and modification of protection from abuse actions. This rule provides a uniform process that comports with the requirements of 23 Pa.C.S. §§ 6107(b)(2) (related to hearings), 6117 (related to procedure and other remedies) and *Commonwealth v. Charnik*, 921 A.2d 1214 (Pa. Super. 2007). These requirements, when read together, require a different procedure for withdrawal, discontinuance and modification at various stages in a protection from abuse proceeding.

After a final protection order is entered, and no motion to reconsider or appeal is filed, the court no longer retains jurisdiction to vacate that order. *Charnik*, 921 A.2d at 1217. The court does, however, have jurisdiction to modify a protection from abuse order at any time after the filing of a petition for modification, service of the petition and a hearing on the petition. 23 Pa.C.S. § 6117. Thus, a party may request that the court modify the order to expire at an earlier date if the party does not want the order to remain in effect.

Rule 1905. Forms For Use in PFA Actions. Notice and Hearing. Petition. Temporary Protection Order. Final Protection Order

(a) The Notice of Hearing and Order required by Pa.R.C.P. No. 1901.3 shall be substantially in the following form:

(Caption)

NOTICE OF HEARING AND ORDER

YOU HAVE BEEN SUED IN COURT. If you wish to defend against the claims set forth in the following papers, you must appear at the hearing scheduled herein. If you fail to do so, the case may proceed against you and a FINAL order may be entered against you granting the relief requested in the petition. In particular, you may be evicted from your residence, prohibited from possessing any firearm, other weapon, ammunition, or any firearm license, and lose other important rights, including custody of your children. A protection order granted by a court may be considered in subsequent proceedings under Title 23 (Domestic Relations) of the Pennsylvania Consolidated Statutes, including child custody proceedings under Chapter 53 (relating to custody) and Child Protective Services Law proceedings under Chapter 63 (related to juvenile matters).

A hearing on the matter is scheduled for the____day of_____, 20_____, at_____.m., in Courtroom _____at_____ Courthouse, _____Pennsylvania.

If an order of protection has been entered, you MUST obey the order until it is modified or terminated by the court after notice and hearing. If you disobey this order, the police or sheriff may arrest you. Violation of this order may subject you to a charge of indirect criminal contempt under 23 Pa.C.S. § 6114. Violation may also subject you to prosecution and criminal penalties under the Pennsylvania Crimes Code. Under federal law, 18 U.S.C. § 2265, this order is enforceable anywhere in the United States, tribal lands, U.S. Territories, and the Commonwealth of Puerto Rico. If you travel out-

Rule 1905   ACTIONS UNDER PROTECTION FROM ABUSE

side of the state and intentionally violate this order, you may be subject to federal criminal proceedings under the Violence Against Women Act, 18 U.S.C. §§ 2261-2262.

If this order directs you to relinquish any firearm, other weapon, ammunition, or any firearm license to the sheriff or the appropriate law enforcement agency, you may do so upon service of this order. As an alternative, you may relinquish any firearm, other weapon, or ammunition listed herein to a third party provided you and the third party first comply with all requirements to obtain a safekeeping permit. 23 Pa.C.S. § 6108.3. You must relinquish any firearm, other weapon, ammunition, or any firearm license listed in the order no later than 24 hours after service of the order. If, due to their current location, firearms, other weapons, or ammunition cannot reasonably be retrieved within the time for relinquishment, you must provide an affidavit to the sheriff or the appropriate law enforcement agency listing the firearms, other weapons, or ammunition and their current location no later than 24 hours after service of the order. Failure to timely relinquish any firearm, other weapon, ammunition, or any firearm license shall result in a violation of this order and may result in criminal conviction under the Uniform Firearms Act, 18 Pa.C.S. § 6105.

NOTICE: Even if this order does not direct you to relinquish firearms, you may be subject to federal firearms prohibitions and federal criminal penalties under 18 U.S.C. § 922(g)(8) or state firearms prohibitions and state criminal penalties under 18 Pa.C.S. § 6105.

YOU HAVE THE RIGHT TO HAVE A LAWYER REPRESENT YOU AT THE HEARING, HOWEVER, THE COURT WILL NOT APPOINT A LAWYER FOR YOU. YOU HAVE THE RIGHT TO PRESENT EVIDENCE AT THE HEARING, INCLUDING SUBPOENAING WITNESSES TO TESTIFY ON YOUR BEHALF.

YOU SHOULD TAKE THIS PAPER TO YOUR LAWYER AT ONCE. IF YOU DO NOT HAVE A LAWYER, GO TO OR TELEPHONE THE OFFICE SET FORTH BELOW. THIS OFFICE CAN PROVIDE YOU WITH INFORMATION ABOUT HIRING A LAWYER. IF YOU CANNOT AFFORD TO HIRE A LAWYER, THIS OFFICE MAY BE ABLE TO PROVIDE YOU WITH INFORMATION ABOUT AGENCIES THAT MAY OFFER LEGAL SERVICES TO ELIGIBLE PERSONS AT A REDUCED FEE OR NO FEE. IF YOU CANNOT FIND A LAWYER, YOU MAY HAVE TO PROCEED WITHOUT ONE.

County Lawyer Referral Service

[insert Street Address]

[insert City, State, and ZIP]

[insert Phone Number]

(b) The petition in an action filed pursuant to the Act shall be substantially in the following form, but the first page (paragraphs 1 through 4), following the Notice of Hearing and Order, shall be exactly as set forth in this rule:

PETITION FOR PROTECTION   IN THE COURT OF COMMON PLEAS
FROM ABUSE   OF _____ COUNTY,
                                PENNSYLVANIA NO. _____

1. PLAINTIFF

_____

First   Middle   Last   Plaintiff's DOB

Plaintiff's Address:

☐ Plaintiff's address is confidential or ☐ Plaintiff's address is:

_____

V.

Pa. R.C.P.   Rule 1905

2. DEFENDANT

First   Middle   Last   Suffix

Defendant's Address:

DEFENDANT IDENTIFIERS
DOB _____ HEIGHT _____
SEX _____ WEIGHT _____
RACE _____ EYES _____

CAUTION: HAIR _____

☐ Weapon Involved   SSN _____

☐ Weapon Present on the Property   DRIVER'S LICENSE # _____

☐ Weapon Requested Relinquished   EXP DATE _____ STATE _____

Defendant's place of employment is: _____

☐ Check here if you have reason to believe that Defendant is a licensed firearms dealer; employed by a licensed firearms dealer or manufacturer; employed as a writer, researcher or technician in the firearms or hunting industry; or is required to carry a firearm as a condition of employment.

3. I am filing this Petition on behalf of: ☐ Myself and/or ☐ Another Person

If you checked "myself", please answer all questions referring to yourself as "Plaintiff". If you ONLY checked "another person", please answer all questions referring to that person as the "Plaintiff", and provide your name and address here, as filer, unless confidential.

Filer's Name: _____

First   Middle   Last   Suffix

☐ Filer's address is confidential or ☐ Filer's address is:

_____

If you checked "Another Person", indicate your relationship with Plaintiff:

☐ parent of minor Plaintiff(s)

☐ applicant for appointment as guardian ad litem of minor Plaintiff(s)

☐ adult household member with minor Plaintiff(s)

☐ court appointed guardian of incompetent Plaintiff(s)

4. Name(s) of all persons, including minor child/ren who seek protection from abuse:

_____

_____

5. Indicate the relationship between Plaintiff and Defendant:

CHECK ALL THAT APPLY:

    ☐ spouse or former spouse of Defendant

    ☐ parent of a child with Defendant

    ☐ current or former sexual or intimate partner with Defendant

    ☐ child of Plaintiff

Rule 1905 ACTIONS UNDER PROTECTION FROM ABUSE

  ☐ child of Defendant
  ☐ family member related by blood (consanguinity) to Defendant
  ☐ family member related by marriage or affinity to Defendant
  ☐ sibling (person who shares parenthood) of Defendant
  ☐ Check here if Defendant is 17 years old or younger.

6. Have Plaintiff and Defendant been involved in any of the following court actions? ☐ Divorce ☐ Custody ☐ Support ☐ Protection From Abuse
   If you checked any of the above, briefly indicate when and where the case was filed and the court number, if known: _____
   _____

7. Has Defendant been involved in any criminal court action? _____
   _____
   If you answered Yes, is Defendant currently on probation? _____

   Has Defendant been determined to be a perpetrator in a founded or indicated report under the Child Protective Services Law, 23 Pa.C.S. §§ 6301—6386? _____
   If you answered Yes, what county's court or child protective services agency issued the founded or indicated report?_____

8. Plaintiff and Defendant are the parents of the following minor child/ren:
   Name(s)   Age(s)   who reside at (list address unless confidential)
   _____   _____   _____
   _____   _____   _____

9. If Plaintiff and Defendant are parents of any minor child/ren together, is there an existing court order regarding their custody? _____
   If you answered "Yes", describe the terms of the order (e.g., primary, shared, legal and/or physical custody):
   _____

   If you answered "Yes", in what county and state was the order issued?
   _____

   If you are now seeking an order of child custody as part of this petition, list the following information:
   (a) Where has each child resided during the past five years?

Child's name	Person(s) child lived with	Address, unless confidential	When
_____	_____	_____	_____
_____	_____	_____	_____
_____	_____	_____	_____

   (b) List any other persons who are known to have or claim a right to custody of each child listed above.

Name	Address	Basis of Claim
_____	_____	_____
_____	_____	_____
_____	_____	_____

10. The following other minor child/ren presently live with Plaintiff:

Pa. R.C.P.   Rule 1905

Name(s)	Age(s)	Plaintiff's relationship to child/ren

11. The facts of the most recent incident of abuse are as follows:

    Approximate Date: _____
    Approximate Time: _____
    Place: _____

    Describe in detail what happened, including any physical or sexual abuse, threats, injury, incidents of stalking, medical treatment sought, and/or calls to law enforcement (attach additional sheets of paper if necessary): ___

    _____

12. If Defendant has committed prior acts of abuse against Plaintiff or the minor child/ren, describe these prior incidents, including any threats, injuries, or incidents of stalking, and indicate approximately when such acts of abuse occurred (attach additional sheets of paper if necessary):

    _____
    _____

13. (a) Has Defendant used or threatened to use any firearms or other weapons against Plaintiff or the minor child/ren? If so, please describe the use or threatened use below and list on Attachment A to Petition, which is incorporated by reference into this petition, any firearms, other weapons, or ammunition Defendant used or threatened to use against Plaintiff or the minor child/ren:_____

    _____
    _____
    _____
    _____

    (b) Other than the firearms, other weapons, or ammunition Defendant used or threatened to use against Plaintiff or the minor child/ren, does Defendant, to the best of your knowledge or belief, own or possess any additional firearm, other weapon, ammunition, or any firearm license?

    (c) If the answer to (b) above is "yes," list any additional firearm, other weapon, or ammunition owned by or in the possession of Defendant on Attachment A to Petition, which is incorporated by reference into this petition.

    (d) Plaintiff (check one) ☐ DOES ☐ DOES NOT request that the court order Defendant to relinquish firearms, other weapons, or ammunition listed on Attachment A to Petition. If Plaintiff does seek relinquishment, identify on Attachment A to Petition the firearms, other weapons, or ammunition Plaintiff requests the court to order Defendant to relinquish.

14. Identify the sheriff, police department, or law enforcement agency in the area in which Plaintiff lives that should be provided with a copy of the protection order:

    _____
    _____

Rule 1905   ACTIONS UNDER PROTECTION FROM ABUSE

15. There is an immediate and present danger of further abuse from Defendant.

CHECK THE FOLLOWING BOXES ONLY IF THEY APPLY TO YOUR CASE AND PROVIDE THE REQUESTED INFORMATION

☐ Plaintiff is asking the court to evict and exclude Defendant from the following residence: _____

☐ owned by (list owners, if known): _____
☐ rented by (list all names, if known): _____
☐ Defendant owes a duty of support to Plaintiff or the minor child/ren:
☐ Plaintiff has suffered out-of-pocket financial losses as a result of the abuse described above. Those losses are: _____

FOR THE REASONS SET FORTH ABOVE, I REQUEST THAT THE COURT ENTER A TEMPORARY ORDER, AND AFTER HEARING, A FINAL ORDER THAT WOULD DO THE FOLLOWING (CHECK ALL FORMS OF RELIEF REQUESTED):

☐ A. Restrain Defendant from abusing, harassing, stalking, threatening, or attempting or threatening to use physical force against Plaintiff or the minor child/ren in any place where Plaintiff or the child/ren may be found.

☐ B. Evict/exclude Defendant from Plaintiff's residence and prohibit Defendant from attempting to enter any temporary or permanent residence of Plaintiff.

☐ C. Require Defendant to provide Plaintiff or the minor child/ren with other suitable housing.

☐ D. Award Plaintiff temporary custody of the minor child/ren and place the following restrictions on contact between Defendant and the child/ren: _____

☐ E. Prohibit Defendant from having any contact with Plaintiff or the minor child/ren, in person, by telephone, or in writing, personally or through third persons, including but not limited to any contact at Plaintiff's school, business, or place of employment, except as the court may find necessary with respect to partial custody with the minor child/ren.

☐ F. Prohibit Defendant from having any contact with Plaintiff's relatives and Plaintiff's children listed in this petition, except as the court may find necessary with respect to partial custody with the minor child/ren. The following persons are Plaintiff's relatives or family and household members that Plaintiff believes require protection from stalking and harassment by Defendant.

Name	Address (optional)	Relationship to Plaintiff

Pa. R.C.P. Rule 1905

☐ G. Order Defendant to temporarily relinquish the firearms, other weapons, or ammunition listed on Attachment A to Petition, under Defendant's control, or in Defendant's possession, or any firearm license to the sheriff or the appropriate law enforcement agency.

☐ H. Prohibit Defendant from acquiring or possessing firearms for the duration of the order.

☐ I. Order Defendant to pay temporary support for Plaintiff or the minor child/ren, including medical support and ☐ payment of the rent or mortgage on the residence.

☐ J. Direct Defendant to pay Plaintiff for the reasonable financial losses suffered as the result of the abuse, to be determined at the hearing.

☐ K. Order Defendant to pay the costs of this action, including filing and service fees.

☐ L. Order Defendant to pay Plaintiff's reasonable attorney's fees.

☐ M. Order the following additional relief, not listed above:

_____
_____
_____
_____

☐ N. Grant such other relief as Plaintiff requests or the court deems appropriate.

☐ O. Order the police, sheriff, or other law enforcement agency to serve Defendant with a copy of this petition, any order issued, and the order for hearing. Plaintiff will inform the designated authority of any addresses, other than Defendant's residence, where Defendant can be served.

☐ P. Direct the Pennsylvania State Police, the municipal police, or the sheriff to accompany Plaintiff to his or her residence to retrieve personal belongings or accompany Plaintiff while the petition or order is served on Defendant, if Plaintiff has reason to believe his or her safety is at risk.

VERIFICATION

I verify that I am the petitioner as designated in the present action and that the facts and statements contained in the above Petition are true and correct to the best of my knowledge. I understand that any false statements are made subject to the penalties of 18 Pa.C.S. § 4904, relating to unsworn falsification to authorities.

_____
Signature

_____
Date

(Caption)

ATTACHMENT A TO PETITION FIREARMS, OTHER WEAPONS, OR AMMUNITION INVENTORY

I, _____, Plaintiff in this Protection From Abuse Action, hereby

(a) state that Defendant used or threatened to use the following firearms, other weapons, or ammunition against Plaintiff or the minor child/ren (include addresses or locations, if known, such as "front seat of blue truck," "gun cabinet," "bedroom closet," etc.):

Rule 1905   ACTIONS UNDER PROTECTION FROM ABUSE

Firearm/Other Weapon/Ammunition   Location
1.
2.
3.
4.
5.

(b) state that Defendant, to the best of my knowledge or belief, owns or possesses the following firearms, other weapons, or ammunition not set forth in (a) above (include addresses or locations if, known):

Firearm/Other Weapon/Ammunition   Location
1.
2.
3.
4.
5.

(c) request that the court order Defendant to relinquish the following firearms, other weapons, or ammunition (include addresses or locations, if known):

Firearm/Other Weapon/Ammunition   Location
1.
2.
3.
4.
5.

☐ All firearms, other weapons, and ammunition owned or possessed by Defendant. If more space is needed, more sheets may be attached to this document.

Name _____ Date _____

Notice: This attachment will be withheld from public inspection in accordance with 23 Pa.C.S. § 6108(a)(7)(v).

> *Official Note: See* Pa.R.C.P. No. 1930.1(b). This rule may require attorneys or unrepresented parties to file confidential documents and documents containing confidential information that are subject to the Case Records Public Access Policy of the Unified Judicial System of Pennsylvania.

(c) The Temporary Order of Court, or any continued, amended, or modified Temporary Order of Court, entered pursuant to the Act shall be substantially in the following form, but the first page shall be exactly as set forth in this rule:

TEMPORARY PROTECTION   IN THE COURT OF COMMON PLEAS
FROM ABUSE ORDER   OF _____ COUNTY,
☐ Amended Order   PENNSYLVANIA NO. _____
☐ Continued Order

PLAINTIFF

_____
First   Middle   Last   Plaintiff's DOB

Pa. R.C.P.   Rule 1905

Name(s) of all protected persons, including minor child/ren and DOB:
_____
_____

            V.

DEFENDANT

First	Middle	Last	Suffix

Defendant's Address: DEFENDANT IDENTIFIERS
_____   DOB _____   HEIGHT _____
_____   SEX _____   WEIGHT _____
_____   RACE _____   EYES _____
_____   HAIR _____

CAUTION: SSN _____
☐ Weapon Involved   DRIVER'S LICENSE # _____
☐ Weapon Present on the Property   EXP DATE _____ STATE _____
☐ Weapon Ordered Relinquished

The Court Hereby Finds: That it has jurisdiction over the parties and subject matter, and the Defendant will be provided with reasonable notice and opportunity to be heard.

The Court Hereby Orders:

☐ Defendant shall not abuse, harass, stalk, threaten, or attempt or threaten to use physical force against any of the above persons in any place where they might be found.

☐ Except for such contact with the minor child/ren as may be permitted under Paragraph 5 of this order, Defendant shall not contact Plaintiff, or any other person protected under this order, by telephone or by any other means, including through third persons.

☐ Additional findings of this order are set forth below.

Order Effective Date _____ Order Expiration Date _____

NOTICE TO THE DEFENDANT

Defendant is hereby notified that failure to obey this order may result in arrest as set forth in 23 Pa.C.S. § 6113 and that violation of the order may result in a charge of indirect criminal contempt as set forth in 23 Pa.C.S. § 6114. Consent of Plaintiff to Defendant's return to the residence shall not invalidate this order, which can only be changed or modified through the filing of appropriate court papers for that purpose. 23 Pa.C.S. § 6108 (g). If Defendant is required to relinquish any firearms, other weapons, ammunition or any firearm license, those items must be relinquished to the sheriff or the appropriate law enforcement agency within 24 hours of the service of this order. As an alternative, Defendant may relinquish any firearm, other weapon or ammunition listed herein to a third party provided Defendant and the third party first comply with all requirements to obtain a safekeeping permit. If, due to their current location, firearms, other weapons, or ammunition cannot reasonably be retrieved within the time for relinquishment, Defendant shall provide an affidavit to the sheriff or the appropriate law enforcement

Rule 1905 ACTIONS UNDER PROTECTION FROM ABUSE

agency listing the firearms, other weapons, or ammunition and their current location no later than 24 hours after the service of this order. Defendant is further notified that violation of this order may subject him/her to state charges and penalties under the Pennsylvania Crimes Code under 18 Pa.C.S. § 6105 and to federal criminal charges and penalties under 18 U.S.C. § 922(g)(8) and the Violence Against Women Act, 18 U.S.C. §§ 2261-2262.

AND NOW, this ___ day of _____, 20__, upon consideration of the attached Petition for Protection From Abuse, the court hereby enters the following Temporary Order:

☐ Plaintiff's request for a Temporary Protection Order is denied.

☐ Plaintiff's request for a Temporary Protection Order is granted.

☐ 1. Defendant shall not abuse, harass, stalk, threaten, or attempt or threaten to use physical force against any of the above persons in any place where they might be found.

☐ 2. Defendant is evicted and excluded from the residence at [NONCONFIDENTIAL ADDRESS FROM WHICH DEFENDANT IS EXCLUDED] or any other permanent or temporary residence where Plaintiff or any other person protected under this order may live. Plaintiff is granted exclusive possession of the residence. Defendant shall have no right or privilege to enter or be present on the premises of Plaintiff or any other person protected under this order.

☐ 3. Except for such contact with the minor child/ren as may be permitted under Paragraph 5 of this order, Defendant is prohibited from having ANY CONTACT with Plaintiff, or any other person protected under this order, either directly or indirectly, at any location, including but not limited to any contact at Plaintiff's school, business, or place of employment. Defendant is specifically ordered to stay away from the following locations for the duration of this order: _____

☐ 4. Except for such contact with the minor child/ren as may be permitted under Paragraph 5 of this order, Defendant shall not contact Plaintiff, or any other person protected under this order, by telephone or by any other means, including through third persons.

☐ 5. CUSTODY.

☐ There is a current custody order as to the child/ren of the parties:

_____
(county court)   (docket number)

☐ THIS ORDER SHALL NOT SUPERSEDE THE CURRENT CUSTODY ORDER.

☐ THIS ORDER SUPERSEDES ANY PRIOR ORDER RELATING TO CHILD CUSTODY.

☐ Until the final hearing, all contact between Defendant and the child/ren shall be limited to the following: _____

☐ Pending the outcome of the final hearing in this matter, Plaintiff is awarded temporary custody of the following minor child/ren: _____

The local law enforcement agency in the jurisdiction where the child/ren are located shall ensure that the child/ren are placed in the care and control of the Plaintiff in accordance with the terms of this order.

☐ 6. FIREARMS, OTHER WEAPONS, OR AMMUNITION RESTRICTIONS.

Check all that apply:

☐ Defendant is prohibited from possessing or acquiring any firearms for the duration of this order.

☐ Defendant shall relinquish to the sheriff or the appropriate law enforcement agency the following firearm licenses owned or possessed by Defendant:

_____

☐ Defendant is directed to relinquish to the sheriff or the appropriate law enforcement agency any firearm, other weapon, or ammunition listed in Attachment A to Temporary Order, which is incorporated herein by reference, under Defendant's control or in Defendant's possession.

Defendant may relinquish any firearms, other weapons, or ammunition to the sheriff or the appropriate law enforcement agency. As an alternative, Defendant may relinquish firearms, other weapons, or ammunition to a third party provided Defendant and the third party first comply with all the requirements to obtain a safekeeping permit. Defendant must relinquish any firearm, other weapon, ammunition, or firearm license ordered to be relinquished no later than 24 hours after service of this order. If, due to their current location, firearms, other weapons, or ammunition cannot reasonably be retrieved within the time for relinquishment, Defendant shall provide to the sheriff or the appropriate law enforcement agency an affidavit listing the firearms, other weapons, or ammunition and their current location no later than 24 hours after service of this order. Failure to timely relinquish any firearm, other weapon, ammunition, or any firearm license shall result in a violation of this order and may result in criminal conviction under the Uniform Firearms Act, 18 Pa.C.S. § 6105.

☐ 7. The following additional relief is granted:

☐ Defendant is prohibited from stalking, as defined in 18 Pa.C.S. § 2709.1, or harassing, as defined in 18 Pa.C.S. § 2709, the following family and household members of Plaintiff:

Name	Address (optional)	Relationship to Plaintiff

☐ Other relief:

_____
_____
_____
_____

☐ 8. The Pennsylvania State Police, the municipal police, or the sheriff shall accompany Plaintiff to his or her residence to retrieve personal belongings or accompany Plaintiff while the petition or order is served on Defendant.

☐ 9. A certified copy of this order shall be provided to the sheriff or police department where Plaintiff resides and any other agency specified hereafter: [insert name of agency]

Rule 1905 ACTIONS UNDER PROTECTION FROM ABUSE

☐ 10. THIS ORDER SUPERSEDES ANY PRIOR PROTECTION FROM ABUSE ORDER OBTAINED BY THE SAME PLAINTIFF AGAINST THE SAME DEFENDANT.

☐ 11. THIS ORDER APPLIES IMMEDIATELY TO DEFENDANT AND SHALL REMAIN IN EFFECT UNTIL [insert expiration date] OR UNTIL OTHERWISE MODIFIED OR TERMINATED BY THIS COURT AFTER NOTICE AND HEARING.

NOTICE TO THE DEFENDANT

Defendant is hereby notified that failure to obey this order may result in arrest as set forth in 23 Pa.C.S. § 6113 and that violation of the order may result in a charge of indirect criminal contempt as set forth in 23 Pa.C.S. § 6114. Consent of Plaintiff to Defendant's return to the residence shall not invalidate this order, which can only be changed or modified through the filing of appropriate court papers for that purpose. 23 Pa.C.S. § 6108(g). If Defendant is required to relinquish any firearms, other weapons, ammunition, or any firearm license, those items must be relinquished to the sheriff or the appropriate law enforcement agency within 24 hours of the service of this order. As an alternative, Defendant may relinquish any firearm, other weapon, or ammunition listed herein to a third party provided Defendant and the third party first comply with all requirements to obtain a safekeeping permit. If, due to their current location, firearms, other weapons, or ammunition cannot reasonably be retrieved within the time for relinquishment, Defendant shall provide an affidavit to the sheriff or the appropriate law enforcement agency listing the firearms, other weapons, or ammunition and their current location no later than 24 hours after the service of this order. Defendant is further notified that violation of this order may subject him/her to state charges and penalties under the Pennsylvania Crimes Code under 18 Pa.C.S. § 6105 and to federal criminal charges and penalties under 18 U.S.C. § 922(g)(8) and the Violence Against Women Act, 18 U.S.C. §§ 2261-2262.

NOTICE TO SHERIFF, POLICE AND LAW ENFORCEMENT OFFICIALS

This order shall be enforced by the police department or sheriff who has jurisdiction over Plaintiff's residence OR any location where a violation of this order occurs OR where Defendant may be located. If Defendant violates Paragraphs 1 through 6 of this order, Defendant shall be arrested on the charge of indirect criminal contempt. An arrest for violation of this order may be made without warrant, based solely on probable cause, whether or not the violation is committed in the presence of a police officer or sheriff.

Subsequent to an arrest, the law enforcement officer or sheriff shall seize all firearms, other weapons, or ammunition in Defendant's possession which were used or threatened to be used during the violation of the protection order or during prior incidents of abuse and any other firearms in Defendant's possession. Any firearm, other weapon, ammunition, or any firearm license must be delivered to the sheriff or the appropriate law enforcement agency, which sheriff or agency shall maintain possession of the firearms, other weapons, or ammunition until further order of this court, unless the weapon(s) are evidence of a crime, in which case, they shall remain with the law enforcement agency whose officer or sheriff made the arrest.

BY THE COURT:

_____
Judge

_____
Date

Pa. R.C.P. Rule 1905

(Caption)
ATTACHMENT A TO TEMPORARY ORDER FIREARMS, OTHER WEAPONS AND AMMUNITION INVENTORY

It is hereby ordered that Defendant relinquish the following firearms, other weapons, or ammunition to the sheriff or the appropriate law enforcement agency:

Firearm/Other Weapon/Ammunition   Location

1.
2.
3.
4.
5.
6.
7.
8.
9.
10.

☐ All firearms, other weapons and ammunition owned or possessed by the defendant.

BY THE COURT:

_____
Judge

_____
Date

Notice: This attachment will be withheld from public inspection in accordance with 23 Pa.C.S. § 6108(a)(7)(v).

(d) The form of the Affidavit of Service in a Protection From Abuse matter shall be substantially in the following form:

(Caption)
AFFIDAVIT OF SERVICE

I, _____, the undersigned, hereby state that I served a copy of the Notice of Hearing and Order, Petition and Temporary Order in the above-captioned action upon Defendant by handing the papers to _____ at the following address: _____ on the __ day of _____, 20__, at approximately __ o'clock __.m.

I verify that the statements made in this Affidavit are true and correct. I understand that false statements herein are made subject to the penalties of 18 Pa.C.S.A. § 4904, relating to unsworn falsification to authorities.

(Signature) _____

(Title) _____

(Address) _____

(Date) _____

THIS FORM MUST BE COMPLETED AND SIGNED BY THE PERSON WHO SERVES THE DEFENDANT WITH THE NOTICE OF HEARING AND ORDER,

Rule 1905   ACTIONS UNDER PROTECTION FROM ABUSE

PETITION AND TEMPORARY ORDER. IT MUST BE FILED WITH THE PROTHONOTARY OR BROUGHT TO THE COURT ON THE HEARING DATE.

(e) The Final Order of Court, or any amended, modified or extended Final Order of Court, entered pursuant to the Act shall be substantially in the following form, but the first page must be exactly as set forth in this rule:

FINAL PROTECTION FROM ABUSE ORDER
☐ Extended Order
☐ Amended Order

IN THE COURT OF COMMON PLEAS OF _____ COUNTY, PENNSYLVANIA NO. _____

PLAINTIFF

_____
First   Middle   Last   Plaintiff's DOB

Name(s) of all protected persons, including minor child/ren and DOB:
_____
_____
_____

V.

DEFENDANT

_____
First   Middle   Last   Suffix

Defendant's Address:
_____
_____
_____
_____

DEFENDANT IDENTIFIERS
DOB _____ HEIGHT _____
SEX _____ WEIGHT _____
RACE _____ EYES _____
HAIR _____

CAUTION:
☐ Weapon Involved
☐ Weapon Present on the Property
☐ Weapon Ordered Relinquished

SSN _____
DRIVER'S LICENSE # _____
EXP DATE _____ STATE _____

The Court Hereby Finds: That it has jurisdiction over the parties and subject matter, and the Defendant has been provided with reasonable notice and opportunity to be heard.

The Court Hereby Orders:

☐ Defendant shall not abuse, harass, stalk, threaten, or attempt or threaten to use physical force against any of the above persons in any place where they might be found.

☐ Except as provided in Paragraph 5 of this order, Defendant shall not contact Plaintiff, or any other person protected under this order, by telephone or by any other means, including through third persons.

☐ Additional findings of this order are set forth below.

Order Effective Date _____ Order Expiration Date _____

Pa. R.C.P.   Rule 1905

NOTICE TO THE DEFENDANT

Defendant is hereby notified that failure to obey this order may result in arrest as set forth in 23 Pa.C.S. § 6113 and that violation of the order may result in a charge of indirect criminal contempt as set forth in 23 Pa.C.S. § 6114. Violation may also subject you to prosecution and criminal penalties under the Pennsylvania Crimes Code. A violation of this order may result in the revocation of the safekeeping permit, which will require the immediate relinquishment of your firearms, other weapons, or ammunition to the sheriff or the appropriate law enforcement agency. Plaintiff's consent to contact by Defendant shall not invalidate this order which can only be modified by further order of court. 23 Pa.C.S. § 6108(g).

This order is enforceable in all fifty (50) States, the District of Columbia, Tribal Lands, U.S. Territories and the Commonwealth of Puerto Rico under the Violence Against Women Act, 18 U.S.C. § 2265. If you travel outside of the State and intentionally violate this order, you may be subject to federal criminal proceedings under that Act. 18 U.S.C §§ 2261-2262. If you possess a firearm or any ammunition while this order is in effect, you may be charged with a federal criminal offense even if this Pennsylvania order does not expressly prohibit you from possessing firearms or ammunition under 18 U.S.C. § 922(g)(8) or state criminal offenses and state criminal penalties under 18 Pa.C.S. § 6105.

CHECK ALL THAT APPLY:

Plaintiff or Protected Person(s) is/are:

☐ spouse or former spouse of Defendant

☐ parent of a child with Defendant

☐ current or former sexual or intimate partner with Defendant

☐ child of Plaintiff

☐ child of Defendant

☐ family member related by blood (consanguinity) to Defendant

☐ family member related by marriage or affinity to Defendant

☐ sibling (person who shares parenthood) of Defendant

Defendant was served in accordance with Pa.R.C.P. No. 1930.4 and provided notice of the time, date, and location of the hearing scheduled in this matter.

AND NOW, this ___ day of _____, 20___, the court having jurisdiction over the parties and the subject-matter, it is ORDERED, ADJUDGED, and DECREED as follows:

This order is entered (check one) ☐ by agreement ☐ by agreement without an admission,☐ after a hearing and decision by the court ☐ after a hearing at which Defendant was not present, despite proper service being made ☐ by default. Without regard as to how the order was entered, this is a final order of court subject to full enforcement pursuant to the Protection From Abuse Act.

Note: Space is provided to allow for 1) the court's general findings of abuse; 2) inclusion of the terms under which the order was entered (e.g., that the order was entered with the consent of the parties, or that Defendant, though properly served, failed to appear for the hearing, or the reasons why the plaintiff's request for a final PFA order was denied); or 3) information that may be helpful to law enforcement (e.g., whether a firearm or other weapon was involved in the incident of abuse or whether Defendant is believed to be armed and dangerous).

☐ Plaintiff's request for a final protection order is denied.

Rule 1905 ACTIONS UNDER PROTECTION FROM ABUSE

OR

☐ Plaintiff's request for a final protection order is granted.

☐ 1. Defendant shall not abuse, stalk, harass, threaten, or attempt or threaten to use physical force against Plaintiff or any other protected person in any place where they might be found.

☐ 2. Defendant is completely evicted and excluded from the residence at (NONCONFIDENTIAL ADDRESS FROM WHICH DEFENDANT IS EXCLUDED) or any other residence where Plaintiff or any other person protected under this order may live. Exclusive possession of the residence is granted to Plaintiff. Defendant shall have no right or privilege to enter or be present on the premises of Plaintiff or any other person protected under this order.

☐ On [insert date and time], Defendant may enter the residence to retrieve his/her clothing and other personal effects, provided that Defendant is in the company of a law enforcement officer or sheriff when such retrieval is made and [insert any other conditions] _____

☐ 3. Except as provided in Paragraph 5 of this order, Defendant is prohibited from having ANY CONTACT with Plaintiff, either directly or indirectly, or any other person protected under this order, at any location, including but not limited to any contact at Plaintiff's school, business, or place of employment. Defendant is specifically ordered to stay away from the following locations for the duration of this order.

☐ 4. Except as provided in Paragraph 5 of this order, Defendant shall not contact Plaintiff, either directly or indirectly, or any other person protected under this order, by telephone or by any other means, including through third persons.

☐ 5. Temporary custody of the minor children, [NAMES OF THE CHILDREN SUBJECT TO THE PROVISION OF THIS PARAGRAPH] shall be as follows:

Check all that apply:

☐ STATE TO WHOM PRIMARY PHYSICAL CUSTODY IS AWARDED, STATE TERMS OF PARTIAL CUSTODY, IF ANY.

_____

_____

☐ There is a current custody order as to the children of the parties:

_____

(county court) (docket number)

☐ A custody petition is pending.

☐ A hearing is scheduled for _____ (date, time and location)

☐ THIS ORDER SHALL NOT SUPERSEDE THE CURRENT CUSTODY ORDER.

☐ THIS ORDER SHALL NOT SUPERSEDE THE CURRENT CUSTODY ORDER.

The custody provisions of Paragraph 5 of this order are temporary. Either party may initiate custody proceedings pursuant to the custody statute at 23 Pa.C.S. §§ 5321—5340. Any valid custody order entered after the final Protection From Abuse order supersedes the custody provisions of this order.

☐ 6. FIREARMS, OTHER WEAPONS, OR AMMUNITION RESTRICTIONS

Check all that apply:

☐ Defendant is prohibited from possessing or acquiring any firearms for the duration of this order.

☐ Defendant shall relinquish to the sheriff or the appropriate law enforcement agency the following firearm licenses owned or possessed by Defendant: _____

☐ Defendant may relinquish any firearms, other weapons, or ammunition to the sheriff or the appropriate law enforcement agency. As an alternative, Defendant may either relinquish firearms, other weapons, or ammunition to a third party provided Defendant and the third party first comply with all the requirements to obtain a safekeeping permit, or relinquish firearms, other weapons, or ammunition to a licensed firearms dealer for consignment sale, lawful transfer, or safekeeping pursuant to 23 Pa.C.S. § 6108.2(e). Defendant must relinquish any firearm, other weapon, ammunition, or firearm license ordered to be relinquished no later than 24 hours after service of this order. Failure to timely relinquish any firearm, other weapon, ammunition, or any firearm license ordered to be relinquished shall result in a violation of this order and may result in criminal conviction under the Uniform Firearms Act, 18 Pa.C.S. § 6105.

☐ 7. Any firearm delivered to the sheriff or the appropriate law enforcement agency or transferred to a licensed firearm dealer or a qualified third party, who satisfies the procedural and substantive requirements to obtain a safekeeping permit issued under 23 Pa.C.S. § 6108.3 pursuant to this order or the temporary order, shall not be returned to Defendant until further order of court or as otherwise provided by law.

☐ 8. The Pennsylvania State Police, the municipal police, or the sheriff shall accompany Plaintiff to his or her residence to retrieve personal belongings.

☐ 9. The following additional relief is granted as authorized by § 6108 of the Act:

☐ Defendant is prohibited from stalking, as defined in 18 Pa.C.S. § 2709.1, or harassing, as defined in 18 Pa.C.S. § 2709, the following family and household members of Plaintiff:

Name	Address (optional)	Relationship to Plaintiff

☐ Other relief: _____

_____

_____

_____

_____

☐ 10. Defendant is directed to pay temporary support for: [INSERT THE NAMES OF THE PERSONS FOR WHOM SUPPORT IS TO BE PAID] as follows: [INSERT AMOUNT, FREQUENCY AND OTHER TERMS AND CONDITIONS OF THE SUPPORT ORDER]. This order for support shall remain in effect until a final support order is entered by this court. However, this order shall lapse automatically if Plaintiff does not file a complaint for support with the Domestic Relations Section of the court within two weeks of the date of this order. The amount of this temporary order does not necessarily

Rule 1905 ACTIONS UNDER PROTECTION FROM ABUSE

reflect Defendant's correct support obligation, which shall be determined in accordance with the guidelines at the support hearing. Any adjustments in the final amount of support shall be credited, retroactive to this date, to the appropriate party.

11. ☐ (a) The costs of this action are imposed on Defendant.

☐ (b) Because this order followed a contested proceeding, or a hearing at which Defendant was not present, despite being served with a copy of the petition, temporary order and notice of the date, time and place of the hearing, Defendant is ordered to pay an additional $100 surcharge to the court, which shall be distributed in the manner set forth in 23 Pa.C.S. § 6106(d).

☐ (c) Upon a showing of good cause or a finding that Defendant is unable to pay, the costs of this action are waived.

☐ 12. Defendant shall pay $ ___ to Plaintiff by (insert date) as compensation for Plaintiff's out-of-pocket losses, which are as follows: _____

_____

An installment schedule is ordered as follows: _____

_____

OR

☐ Plaintiff is granted leave to present a petition, with appropriate notice to Defendant, to [INSERT THE NAME OF THE JUDGE OR COURT TO WHICH THE PETITION SHOULD BE PRESENTED] requesting recovery of out-of-pocket losses. The petition shall include an exhibit itemizing all claimed out-of-pocket losses, copies of all bills and estimates of repair, and an order scheduling a hearing. No fee shall be required by the prothonotary's office for the filing of this petition.

☐ 13. THIS ORDER SUPERSEDES ANY PRIOR PROTECTION FROM ABUSE ORDER OBTAINED BY THE SAME PLAINTIFF AGAINST THE SAME DEFENDANT.

14. All provisions of this order shall expire:

Check one

☐ in [INSERT DAYS, MONTHS OR YEARS] on [INSERT EXPIRATION DATE]

☐ in three years, on [INSERT EXPIRATION DATE]

NOTICE TO DEFENDANT

DEFENDANT IS HEREBY NOTIFIED THAT FAILURE TO OBEY THIS ORDER MAY RESULT IN ARREST AS SET FORTH IN 23 PA.C.S. § 6113 AND THAT VIOLATION OF THE ORDER MAY RESULT IN A CHARGE OF INDIRECT CRIMINAL CONTEMPT AS SET FORTH IN 23 PA.C.S. § 6114. VIOLATION MAY ALSO SUBJECT YOU TO PROSECUTION AND CRIMINAL PENALTIES UNDER THE PENNSYLVANIA CRIMES CODE. A VIOLATION OF THIS ORDER MAY RESULT IN THE REVOCATION OF THE SAFEKEEPING PERMIT, WHICH WILL REQUIRE THE IMMEDIATE RELINQUISHMENT OF YOUR FIREARMS, OTHER WEAPONS, AND AMMUNITION TO THE SHERIFF OR THE APPROPRIATE LAW ENFORCEMENT AGENCY. PLAINTIFF'S CONSENT TO CONTACT BY DEFENDANT SHALL NOT INVALIDATE THIS ORDER, WHICH CAN ONLY BE MODIFIED BY FURTHER ORDER OF COURT. 23 PA.C.S. § 6108(g).

THIS ORDER IS ENFORCEABLE IN ALL FIFTY (50) STATES, THE DISTRICT OF COLUMBIA, TRIBAL LANDS, U.S. TERRITORIES, AND THE COMMONWEALTH OF PUERTO RICO UNDER THE VIOLENCE AGAINST WOMEN ACT, 18 U.S.C. § 2265. IF YOU TRAVEL OUTSIDE OF THE STATE

Pa. R.C.P.   Rule 1905

AND INTENTIONALLY VIOLATE THIS ORDER, YOU MAY BE SUBJECT TO FEDERAL CRIMINAL PROCEEDINGS UNDER THAT ACT. 18 U.S.C. §§ 2261-2262. IF YOU POSSESS A FIREARM OR ANY AMMUNITION WHILE THIS ORDER IS IN EFFECT, YOU MAY BE CHARGED WITH A FEDERAL CRIMINAL OFFENSE EVEN IF THIS PENNSYLVANIA ORDER DOES NOT EXPRESSLY PROHIBIT YOU FROM POSSESSING FIREARMS OR AMMUNITION UNDER 18 U.S.C. § 922(g)(8) OR STATE CRIMINAL OFFENSES AND STATE CRIMINAL PENALTIES UNDER 18 PA.C.S. § 6105.

NOTICE TO SHERIFF, POLICE AND LAW ENFORCEMENT OFFICIALS

The police and sheriff who have jurisdiction over Plaintiff's residence OR any location where a violation of this order occurs OR where Defendant may be located, shall enforce this order. The court shall have jurisdiction over any indirect criminal contempt proceeding, either in the county where the violation occurred or where this protective order was entered. An arrest for violation of Paragraphs 1 through 7 of this order may be without warrant, based solely on probable cause, whether or not the violation is committed in the presence of the police or any sheriff. 23 Pa.C.S. § 6113.

Subsequent to an arrest, and without the necessity of a warrant, the police officer or sheriff shall seize all firearms, other weapons, and ammunition in Defendant's possession that were used or threatened to be used during the violation of the protection order or during prior incidents of abuse and any other firearms in Defendant's possession. The [insert the appropriate name or title] shall maintain possession of the firearms, other weapons, or ammunition until further order of this court.

When Defendant is placed under arrest for violation of the order, Defendant shall be taken to the appropriate authority or authorities before whom Defendant is to be arraigned. A "Complaint for Indirect Criminal Contempt" shall then be completed and signed by the police officer, sheriff, OR Plaintiff. Plaintiff's presence and signature are not required to file the complaint.

If sufficient grounds for violation of this order are alleged, Defendant shall be arraigned, bond set, if appropriate, and both parties given notice of the date of the hearing.

BY THE COURT:

_____
Judge

_____
Date

This order was entered pursuant to the consent of Plaintiff and Defendant:

_____
(Plaintiff's signature)

_____
(Defendant's signature)

(Caption)

ATTACHMENT A TO FINAL ORDER FIREARMS, OTHER WEAPONS AND AMMUNITION INVENTORY

It is hereby ordered that Defendant relinquish the following firearms, other weapons, and ammunition to the sheriff or the appropriate law enforcement agency:

Rule 1905 ACTIONS UNDER PROTECTION FROM ABUSE

Firearm/Other Weapon/Ammunition   Location
1.
2.
3.
4.
5.
6.
7.
8.
9.
10.

☐ All firearms, other weapons, and ammunition owned or possessed by Defendant.

BY THE COURT:

_____

Judge

_____

Date

Notice: This attachment will be withheld from public inspection in accordance with 23 Pa.C.S. § 6108(a)(7)(v).

Adopted March 9, 1998, effective July 1, 1998. Amended March 2, 2000, imd. effective; June 2, 2000, imd. effective; Oct. 27, 2000, imd. effective; Oct. 31, 2002, imd. effective; March 18, 2004, effective June 16, 2004; May 2, 2006, effective May 9, 2006; Feb. 6, 2007, effective May 7, 2007; Aug. 13, 2008, effective Nov. 11, 2008; Feb. 10, 2015, effective March 12, 2015; Jan. 5, 2018, effective Jan. 6, 2018; June 1, 2018, effective July 1, 2018; March 5, 2019, effective April 10, 2019.

Explanatory Comment—1997

The use of standardized forms provides uniformity and is also critical to the enforcement of protection orders both inside and outside of the Commonwealth. These forms are substantially based on those proposed by members of the Pennsylvania Coalition Against Domestic Violence and have been further refined to accommodate the litigants' need for simplicity, the court's need for flexibility and law enforcements' need for certain identifying information necessary to enforce the protection order.

The forms must be used so that all protection orders can be properly registered with the statewide PFA Registry and the federal Protection Order File (POF) established by the National Crime Information Center (NCIC) for the collection of information that is necessary for nationwide enforcement of protection orders. Entering a protection order into the Registry and NCIC file enables law enforcement to immediately verify the existence and terms of the order. It is important, therefore, that all protection orders be registered with these two files. To this end, the forms capture all of the information that is required for data entry and the form orders are further structured to present that information in the order and sequence that is most helpful to the various law enforcement agencies responsible for entering the information into the files. Once the information reaches the Registry and is accepted by the NCIC file, it becomes immediately accessible to law enforcement agencies, dispatchers and courts throughout the country.

The provisions in the form petition and orders reflect the most common forms of relief available under the Protection From Abuse Act. Plenty of space, however, is provided for the plaintiff to request additional relief, and for courts to fashion appropriate relief, based on the individual circumstances of the litigants. Since all of the provisions will not necessarily apply in every case, the forms adopt a checkbox method that requires the user to affirmatively check only those provisions which are applicable to his or her situation.

In cases where a provision is generally applicable but its terms do not correspond precisely to the relief being requested or granted, the user should not check the standard provision but instead should use the blank spaces provided in the forms to specify the relief. For example, while the final order contains a standard provision permitting the defendant to retrieve personal belongings only in the company of a police officer, there may be more suitable methods of retrieval available in some cases. If so, then the plaintiff or court should use the blank spaces provided in the form petition or order (rather than the standard provision) to specify the alternative manner of retrieval.

Explanatory Comment—2000

Paragraph 2 of the final order has been amended to enable courts to include additional conditions for the retrieval of personalty by the defendant in a section of the final order which permits arrest without a warrant if the conditions are violated. Paragraph 9 of the final order has been amended to require the filing of a support complaint within two weeks, rather than fifteen days, of the entry of a final order under the Protection From Abuse Act to prevent the automatic lapse of any temporary support provisions included in the order. This change is consistent with the statutory provisions at 23 Pa.C.S.A. § 6108(a)(5).

Explanatory Comment—2006

The Notice to Defend in subdivision (a) was amended to include three notice requirements of the 2005 Protection From Abuse Act amendments, Act 66 of 2005. 23 Pa.C.S.A. § 6107(a). The amendments provide that sheriffs may arrest defendants for violations of protective orders. The notice also advises the defendant that if firearms, other weapons or ammunition cannot reasonably be retrieved within the required time, the defendant must provide the sheriff with an affidavit listing the firearms, other weapons and ammunition and their current location within 24 hours. Pa.C.S.A. § 6108(a)(7)(i)(B). In addition, defendants have the option to turn firearms, other weapons and ammunition over to a qualified third party instead of the sheriff, and federal firearms prohibitions and penalties are more clearly stated.

The 2005 amendments to the Protection From Abuse Act require several changes to the form petition at subdivision (b). The plaintiff is required to inform the court if the defendant works in a job that requires the handling of firearms. This provision was included to allow courts to exercise appropriate discretion when a defendant is exempt from federal firearm prohibitions and penalties. It also directs the court to "make a reasonable effort to preserve the financial assets of the defendant's business while fulfilling the goals" of the Protection From Abuse Act. 23 Pa.C.S.A. § 6108(a)(7.1). Federal law prohibits possession of firearms and penalizes defendants who possess them if they are subject to an order prohibiting abuse, stalking or harassment. However, certain law enforcement officials are exempt from this prohibition and penalty. Under 18 U.S.C. § 925(a)(1), a person performing an official duty on behalf of the federal, state or local law enforcement agency may possess a firearm as long as the officer is required to possess the firearm in his or her official capacity. The Bureau of Alcohol, Tobacco and Firearms requires the official possession of the firearm to be authorized by statute, regulation or official department policy. The new notice requirement is found in 23 Pa.C.S.A. § 6106(a.2).

Paragraph 14 of the form petition was amended to address the manner in which the firearms and other weapons were used against the plaintiff or minor children and to remove the listing of firearms in the petition itself. The amended statute prohibits public access to any list or inventory of the defendant's firearms, other weapons or ammunition. Thus, a separate Attachment A is included at the end of the petition for purposes of listing the firearms, other weapons and ammunition at issue. This will allow the prothonotary to more easily redact the list from public access, while at the same time permitting the court, the parties and law enforcement agencies to enforce the order. 23 Pa.C.S.A. § 6108 (a)(7)(v). Section 6108(a)(7) of the Protection From Abuse Act provides for relinquishment of other weapons and ammunition only if they have been used or threatened to be used in an act of abuse. Paragraph 14 and Attachment A to Petition balance the court's need to be advised of firearms, other weapons and ammunition used or threatened to be used in an act of abuse or available to the defendant with the plaintiff's right to decline to seek relinquishment of some or all of those firearms, other weapons and ammunition.

The form petition also was amended to address the court's authority to order the defendant to relinquish any and all firearms, whether they were used or threatened to be used in an act of abuse or not. Any one of several circumstances authorizes the court to grant this relief, including, but not limited to, abuse involving a firearm or weapon or an immediate and present danger of abuse. The amended statute provides the court with multiple examples of what may constitute proof of immediate and present danger for the purposes of ordering the relinquishment of any or all of the defendant's firearms. 23 Pa.C.S.A. § 6107(b) (3). Finally, the form addresses the court's authority to order the defendant to relinquish other weapons and ammunition which were used or threatened to be used in an act of abuse.

The form temporary order retains a space for the defendant's Social Security number. Pursuant to 23 Pa.C.S.A. § 6108(b), "[a]ny order issued under this section shall, where furnished by either party, specify the Social Security number and date of birth of the defendant."

In subdivisions (c) and (e), paragraph three in the form temporary and final orders is amended to clarify that even indirect contact with a protected person may be prohibited. This clarification reflects the Pennsylvania Supreme Court's holding in *Commonwealth v. Baker*, 564 Pa. 192, 766 A.2d 328 (2001), that the order must be "definite, clear, specific and leave no doubt or uncertainty in the mind of the person to whom it was addressed of the prohibited conduct."

The amendments to paragraph 5 of the form temporary and final orders are consistent with the statutory provisions of the Protection From Abuse Act relating to custody. *See* 23 Pa.C.S.A. § 6108(a)(4).

The 2005 amendments to the Protection From Abuse Act provide that the court may order the defendant to relinquish ammunition and firearm licenses, in addition to firearms and other weapons. 23 Pa.C.S.A. §§ 6108(a)(7) and (7.1). These items were added to paragraph six of the temporary and final order forms, the notices to the defendant and the notices to the sheriff, police and law enforcement.

The amendments to paragraph six of the form orders also provide the court with discretion to place certain restrictions on firearms possession or to completely proscribe firearms possession. The amended paragraphs and the notices to the defendant inform the parties that if the defendant is ordered to relinquish firearms, weapons or ammunition, they must be relinquished to the sheriff or, in the alternative, they may be relinquished to a third party who complies with the substantive and procedural requirements for a third party safekeeping permit.

23 Pa.C.S.A. §§ 6107(a), 6108.3. Upon entry of a final order, the defendant may also relinquish firearms, other weapons or ammunition to a licensed firearms dealer. No matter which option Defendant chooses, if firearms and weapons are ordered to be relinquished, any firearm license ordered to be relinquished must be relinquished to the sheriff. The aforementioned items may be relinquished at the time of service, but no later than 24 hours after service unless, with regard to firearms, other weapons or ammunition, they cannot reasonably be retrieved due to their location. 23 Pa.C.S.A. § 6108(a)(7)(i). The notice to the defendant in the final order was expanded to advise the defendant that violation of the order may result in the revocation of the third-party safekeeping permit.

Paragraph seven of the final order form was amended to reflect 23 Pa.C.S.A. § 6108.1(a) and other statutory provisions concerning the return of firearms.

Paragraph ten of the final order form was amended to reflect the statute's prohibition against charging the plaintiff fees or costs related to filing, service, registration or appeal in any Protection From Abuse matter. A new subparagraph (b) in paragraph ten of the final order reflects the 2005 amendments to the Protection From Abuse Act which increased the surcharge a court may order a defendant to pay when an action is contested and directs the disbursement of the collected surcharges. 23 Pa.C.S.A. § 6106(d).

Paragraph fourteen of the final order form was amended to reflect the increased period of protection the court may grant. The maximum period of protection was increased from eighteen months to three years.

The amended notice to the sheriff, police and law enforcement in the final order clarifies that the defendant may be arrested anywhere a violation occurs, and that the court has jurisdiction to hear the issue of indirect criminal contempt either where the order was issued or where the violation occurred. With this amendment, jurisdiction for indirect criminal contempt is parallel to prosecution for stalking and harassment. 23 Pa.C.S. A. § 6114(a.1). The notice also makes it clear that a search and seizure of firearms may occur without a warrant when incident to arrest. 23 Pa.C.S.A. §§ 6113(b) and 6121.

Other amendments to the order forms reflect that the sheriff is authorized to arrest for violations of the order under the Protection From Abuse Act. 23 Pa.C.S.A. § 6113. The references to a protective order superseding provisions of a prior custody order were moved to paragraph five, which deals with custody, in both the temporary and final orders.

Explanatory Comment—2008

The Protection From Abuse petition form, temporary order form and final order form are being modified to conform to the model template used in Project Passport. Project Passport was designed to improve recognition and enforcement of protection orders within and between states and tribes by encouraging states and tribes to adopt a recognizable first page for protection orders. Use of the model template is supported by the National Center for State Courts and the National American Indian Court Judges Association.

The critical aspects of the model template for the first page are common data elements jointly identified by multi-disciplinary teams. Using a recognizable first page for protection orders with this essential data readily available and easily recognizable on a protection order, particularly on "foreign protection orders," helps strengthen the safety net for domestic violence survivors and their children by offering greater consistency in the issuance and enforcement of protection orders.

Implementation of the model first page for Project Passport requires several changes to the Pennsylvania Protection From Abuse petition, temporary order and final order forms. The petition form caption, as well as the plaintiff's or filer's name, relationship to the plaintiff, names and dates of birth of the protected persons, plaintiff's address, defendant's address, social security number, place of

Rule 1905   ACTIONS UNDER PROTECTION FROM ABUSE

employment, and age, were moved to the Project Passport first page. The petition paragraphs are also renumbered. On the temporary order and final order forms, the captions and the defendant's name, date of birth and social security number, as well as the names of the plaintiff and protected persons and dates of birth, were moved to the Project Passport first page. The Project Passport first page for the petition and temporary and final orders all include physical identifiers for the defendant and an indication if weapons were involved, present on the property or relinquished. The first page of the final order also includes the effective and expiration dates of the protection order and the notice to the defendant.

Pa. R.C.P. **Rule 1905**

New Protection From Abuse Forms in Multiple Languages

Forms allowing Pennsylvanians to file for protection from abuse are now available in a variety of languages, the state Supreme Court announced, in an effort to give equal access to justice to non-English-speaking families facing domestic violence. The translation of these documents mandated by Rule 1905 of the Rules of Civil Procedure under the Protection from Abuse Act, 23 Pa. C.S.A. §6101 et. seq., into the eleven most commonly encountered languages in the Pennsylvania court system was possible through a grant from the Stop Violence Against Women program, which operates under the Pennsylvania Commission on Crime and Delinquency.

More than a dozen forms involved in the PFA process are now available online in Arabic, Simplified Chinese, French and Spanish, as well as six other widely spoken non-English languages. Posted online to provide easy access, the forms are an important part of civil court proceedings, and failure to understand and complete them properly can delay or invalidate proceedings. The documents are in a bilingual format with the left-hand column in English, and the right-hand side in the foreign language.

The forms include the initial petition for protection from abuse and weapons attachment, the notice of hearing and order, the temporary protection order form and its weapons attachment, service affidavit, the final protection order form and its weapons attachment, and the notice to vacate and subpoena form.

The postings also include four forms used exclusively by the Philadelphia courts, which have a slightly different filing and service process than the rest of the state. The Philadelphia forms consist of an intake form, service instructions, information sheet and assessment instructions.

http://www.pacourts.us/Forms/BilingualPFAForms.htm

III. Actions for Support
(Amended Through April, 2019)

Rules 1910.1–1910.50

RULE

1910.1	Scope. Definitions.
1910.2	Venue. Transfer of Action.
1910.2-1	Procedures Pursuant to the Intrastate Family Support Act.
1910.3	Parties. Obligor. Obligee
1910.4	Domestic Relations Section. Commencement of Action. No Filing Fees. Authorized Fees.
1910.5	Complaint. Order of Court.
1910.6	Notification.
1910.7	Pleading by Defendant Not Required. Question of Jurisdiction or Venue or Statute of Limitations in Paternity.
1910.8	Rescinded.
1910.9	Discovery.
1910.10	Alternative Hearing Procedures.
1910.11	Office Conference. Subsequent Proceedings. Order.
1910.12	Office Conference. Hearing. Record. Exceptions. Order.
1910.13	[Rescinded].
1910.13-1	Failure or Refusal to Appear Pursuant to Order of Court. Bench Warrant.
1910.13-2	Form of Request for Bench Warrant and Supporting Affidavit. Form of Bench Warrant.
1910.14	Defendant Leaving Jurisdiction. Security.
1910.15	Paternity.
1910.16	Support Order. Allocation. [Rescinded Dec. 28, 2018].
1910.16-1	Amount of Support. Support Guidelines.
1910.16-2	Support Guidelines. Calculation of Monthly Net Income.
1910.16-3	Support Guidelines. Basic Child Support Schedule.
1910.16-3.1	Support Guidelines. High Income Cases.
1910.16-4	Support Guidelines. Calculation of Support Obligation. Formula.
1910.16-5	Support Guidelines. Deviation.
1910.16-6	Support Guidelines. Basic Support Obligation. Additional Expenses Allocation.
1910.16-7	Support Guidelines. Awards of Child Support When There are Multiple Families.
1910.17	Support Order. Effective Date. Change of Circumstances. Copies of Order. Priority of Distribution of Payments.
1910.18	Support Order. Subsequent Proceedings. Modification of Spousal Support or Alimony *Pendente Lite* Orders Entered Before January 1, 2019
1910.19	Support Modification. Termination. Guidelines as Substantial Change in Circumstances. Overpayments.
1910.20	Support Order. Enforcement. General.
1910.21	[Rescinded].
1910.21-1	[Renumbered as Rule 1910.25].
1910.21-2	[Renumbered as Rule 1910.25-1].

Pa. R.C.P.

1910.21–3 [Renumbered as Rule 1910.25–2].
1910.21–4 [Renumbered as Rule 1910.25–3].
1910.21–5 [Renumbered as Rule 1910.25–4].
1910.21–6 [Renumbered as Rule 1910.25–5].
1910.21–7 [Renumbered as Rule 1910.25–6].
1910.22 Support Order. Enforcement. Liens Against Real Property.
1910.23 Support Order. Enforcement. Attachment of Assets Held by Financial Institutions.
1910.23–1 [Rescinded].
1910.23–2 [Rescinded].
1910.24 Support Order. Enforcement. Judgment for Arrearages. Petition to Correct Judgment. Execution.
1910.25 Enforcement. Support Order. Civil Contempt. Petition. Service. No Answer Required.
1910.25–1 Civil Contempt. Hearing by Court. Conference by Officer.
1910.25–2 Civil Contempt. Office Conference. Agreement. Alternative Procedures Upon Failure to Agree.
1910.25–3 Civil Contempt. Conference Summary. Order. Hearing De Novo.
1910.25–4 Civil Contempt. Alternative Procedure. Record Hearing. Report. Exceptions. Order.
1910.25–5 Civil Contempt. Contempt Order. Incarceration.
1910.25–6 Civil Contempt. No Post-Trial Relief.
1910.25–7 Indirect Criminal Contempt. Incarceration.
1910.26 Support Order. Enforcement. Stay of Proceedings. Special Relief.
1910.27 Form of Complaint. Order. Income Statements and Expense Statements. Health Insurance Coverage Information Form. Form of Support Order. Form Petition for Modification. Petition for Recovery of Support Overpayment.
1910.28 Order for Earnings and Health Insurance Information. Form of Earnings Report. Form of Health Insurance Coverage Information.
1910.29 Evidence in Support Matters.
1910.30 [Rescinded].
1910.31 [Rescinded].
1910.49 Acts of Assembly Not Suspended.
1910.50 Suspension of Acts of Assembly.

Explanatory Comment—1981

Introduction

The family courts have recently become the focus of increased attention by society in general and the legal community in particular. This attention is due to several factors. Increased filings for divorce, spouse and child support, and custody have resulted from rapidly changing social values. Federal funding of programs such as the IV–D program in spouse and child support has caused authorities to review judicial procedures and the processing of family court matters.

The importance of the procedures to enforce the duty of support was highlighted by Senate Report No. 93–1356 relating to the Social Services Amendments of 1974, P.L. 93–647, enacting Title IV–D of the Social Security Act; 1974 U.S. Code Congressional and Administrative News, pp. 8133, 8145:

"The problem of welfare in the United States is, to a considerable extent, a problem of the nonsupport of children by their absent parents. Of the 11 mil-

ACTIONS FOR SUPPORT

lion recipients who are now receiving Aid to Families With Dependent Children (AFDC), 4 out of every 5 are on the rolls because they have been deprived of the support of a parent who has absented himself from the home."

However, the Senate Report found that "the enforcement of child support obligations is not an area of jurisprudence about which this country can be proud", page 8146.

The IV–D program was enacted to improve enforcement. The Senate Report describes the legislation, page 8134:

"The Committee bill includes a number of features designed to assure an effective program of child support. The Committee bill leaves basic responsibility for child support and establishment of paternity to the State but it envisions a far more active role on the part of the Federal Government in monitoring and evaluating State programs, in providing technical assistance, and, in certain instances, in undertaking to give direct assistance to the States in locating absent parents and obtaining support payments from them.

"States would be required to have effective programs for the collection of support and the establishment of paternity; Federal matching for these efforts would be increased from the present 50 percent to 75 percent but States not complying with the requirements would face a penalty in the form of reduced Federal matching funds for Aid to Families With Dependent Children.

"Access to support collection services would be available to families not on welfare as well as to those on welfare."

The Rules are designed to provide family courts with a basic procedure to deal effectively with an area of law characterized by (1) its great importance to the parties, (2) the necessity for a just and equitable result, and (3) a tremendous volume for the courts of counties both large and small, metropolitan and rural. However, Rules of Civil Procedure alone will not guarantee an expeditious and just procedure in the absence of efficient court administration and the cooperation of both the bench and the bar.

Many people feel that support should be a civil action only and not a subject matter for the criminal law. The decriminalization of support is a matter of substantive law which involves serious questions of policy for determination by the legislature. It is not a matter to be resolved by procedural rules.

Statewide rules of the Supreme Court governing actions for support are generally required for two principal reasons. First, a number of counties have reviewed their procedures in support actions and have promulgated local rules containing diverse procedures. Basic procedural rights as a matter of policy should apply to litigants throughout the Commonwealth. The increased emphasis upon family law matters requires a modern, expeditious and uniform procedure to be employed in all counties. Second, the concept of a unified judicial system, as contained in the Constitution of 1968, and a system of statewide practice of law require a uniformity of procedure throughout the Commonwealth.

The Rules governing the action of support significantly affect several aspects of support procedure:

First, these Rules apply to a contract or agreement for support if the contract or agreement provides that it may be enforced by an action under these Rules. Thus the enforcement provisions of a support action will now become available in an action upon such a contract or agreement.

Second, in two instances specified in Rule 1910.6(b), service of process may be made in a county of the Commonwealth other than the county in which the action was commenced. This provision will have substantial impact by providing an alternative to the statutory intercounty proceedings in the situations specified. Also, Rule 1910.6(c) recognizes that within the limits prescribed by that Rule a plaintiff may serve a defendant outside the Commonwealth pursuant to

Rule 2079(c) governing nonresident defendants and Section 5323 of the Judicial Code, relating to service of process upon persons outside the Commonwealth. Alternatively, the plaintiff may proceed under Section 6741 et seq. of the Judicial Code, the Revised Uniform Reciprocal Enforcement of Support Act (1968) (RURESA).

Third, the Rules introduce a "diversionary procedure" into actions for support. In every case, the parties must appear before a domestic relations officer for a conference. If the parties agree on the need for an order and the amount, the domestic relations officer will prepare as part of his report an order embodying the agreement for submission to the court. If the parties cannot agree, the court can, after consideration of the recommendation, nevertheless enter an appropriate order, subject to the right of either party to demand a hearing de novo before the court. A local option permanent master hearing procedure in lieu of de novo hearing procedure is also provided.

Fourth, Rule 1910.15 includes a procedure when the paternity of a child is in issue. This Rule implements Act No. 1978–46, which made the action to determine paternity a civil action.

Fifth, the cumbersome five-step procedure to obtain an adjudication of contempt upon violation of a support order is eliminated. An adjudication of contempt may be had upon petition, notice and hearing.

Finally, the Rules provide a number of forms for use in the action. A noteworthy innovation is the deletion of the usual form of verification requiring an oath and its replacement with a statement that it is made subject to the penalties of Section 4904 of the Crimes Code, 18 Pa.C.S. § 4904, relating to unsworn falsification to authorities.

A detailed analysis of the Rules follows.

[See Explanatory Comments under specific rules]

Rule 1910.1. Scope. Definitions.

(a) Except as provided by subdivision (b), the rules of this chapter govern all civil actions or proceedings brought in the court of common pleas to enforce a duty of support, or an obligation to pay alimony pendente lite.

Official Note: A duty of support is imposed by the following statutes: 23 Pa.C.S. § 4321 and Section 3 of the Support Law of June 24, 1937, P. L. 2045, 62 P. S. § 1973 (repealed) now Act 43-2005, July 7, 2005, P. L. 196. The procedure under the rules of this chapter implements Chapter 43 of Part V of the Domestic Relations Code, Title 23 of the Consolidated Statutes, 23 Pa.C.S. § 4301 et seq., relating to support proceedings. The procedure under these rules provides an alternative to the intrastate and interstate procedures under Parts VIII and VIII-A of the Domestic Relations Code, 23 Pa.C.S. §§ 7101 et seq. and 8101 et seq. For alimony and alimony pendente lite, see Sections 3701 and 3702 of the Divorce Code, 23 Pa.C.S. §§ 3701, 3702.

Official Note: Long arm jurisdiction is available in support actions brought pursuant to these rules per 23 Pa.C.S. § 4342(c).

(b) The rules of this chapter shall not govern

(1) an action or proceeding for support based upon a contract or agreement which provides that it may not be enforced by an action in accordance with these rules,

(2) an application for a temporary order of support and other relief pursuant to the Protection from Abuse Act of December 19, 1990, P. L. 1240, No. 206, 23 Pa.C.S. § 6101 et seq. or

(3) an action for support of an indigent brought pursuant to Chapter 46 of the Domestic Relations Code, 23 Pa.C.S. § 4601 et seq.

Official Note: Where a contract or agreement provides that it cannot be enforced in accordance with the rules, actions upon a contract or agreement for support are to be heard by the court and not a conference officer or hearing officer under Rules 1910.11 or 1910.12. However, such actions should be expedited and given preference in court listings.

(c) As used in this chapter, unless the context of a rule indicates otherwise, the following terms shall have the following meanings:

"Conference officer," the person who conducts an office conference pursuant to Rule 1910.11.

"Hearing officer," the person who conducts a hearing on the record and makes recommendations to the court pursuant to Rule 1910.12.

"Overdue support," the amount of delinquent support equal to or greater than one month's support obligation which accrues after entry or modification of a support order as the result of obligor's nonpayment of that order.

"Past due support," the amount of support which accrues prior to entry or modification of a support order as the result of retroactivity of that order. When nonpayment of the order causes overdue support to accrue, any and all amounts of past due support owing under the order shall convert immediately to overdue support and remain as such until paid in full.

"Suspend," eliminate the effect of a support order for a period of time.

"Terminate," end not only the support order, but the support obligation as well.

"Trier of fact," the judge, hearing officer, or conference officer who makes factual determinations.

"Vacate," declare a particular support order null and void, as if it were never entered.

Adopted April 23, 1981, effective July 22, 1981. Amended Nov. 7, 1988, effective Jan. 1, 1989; March 30, 1994 and April 15, 1994, effective July 1, 1994; Dec. 8, 1994, effective July 1, 1995; May 31, 2000, effective July 1, 2000; January 22, 2007, effective immediately.

Explanatory Comment—1994

Nothing in this rule should be interpreted to eliminate the distinctions between spousal support and alimony pendente lite which are established by case law.

Alimony pendente lite must be distinguished from permanent alimony for purposes of this rule. The rule applies only to alimony pendente lite. The procedure for obtaining permanent alimony is governed by Section 3702 of the Divorce Code, 23 Pa.C.S. § 3702, and Rules of Civil Procedure 1920.1 et seq. Agreements for alimony approved by the court in connection with actions for divorce under Section 3701 of the Divorce Code are deemed to be court orders enforceable under Section 3703 of the Code.

Section 3105(a) of the Divorce Code provides that all agreements relating to matters under the code, whether or not merged or incorporated into the decree, are to be treated as orders for purposes of enforcement unless the agreement provides otherwise. Subdivision (b)(1) is amended to conform to the statute.

There is considerable diversity in the terminology used throughout the rules, and in the various counties, to describe the individuals who conduct conferences and hearings pursuant to the support rules. The addition of subdivision (c) to the rules standardizes terminology and eliminates the confusion which results from individual counties using inconsistent terms to refer to persons performing the same function. All references in the rules to conference or hearing officers have been amended to conform to the terminology set forth in subdivision (c).

In an effort to further standardize the terminology used in support matters, the additional terms are defined.

Explanatory Comment—2000

Act 1998-127 technically amended Act 1997-58 to define and differentiate between past due and overdue support to clarify that only overdue support constitutes a lien by operation of law against the obligor's real or personal property. 23 Pa.C.S. § 4302 now defines overdue support as "support which is delinquent under a payment schedule established by the court." Past due support is defined as "support included in an order of support which has not been paid."

The definitions of past due and overdue support in this rule do not substantively change the legislative definitions. They merely elaborate on them in terms which are more familiar and helpful to the bench and bar. Specifically, past due support consists of the purely retroactive arrearages which accumulate between the date of the filing of the complaint or petition for modification and the date of the hearing and entry of the initial or modified support order. Overdue support refers to the delinquent arrearages which accrue after entry of the order due to the obligor's failure to pay support pursuant to the order.

These definitions are important for determining the remedies available for collecting support arrearages. Pursuant to 23 Pa.C.S. § 4352(d), only overdue support (delinquent arrearages) constitutes a lien by operation of law against the obligor's property. Conversely, past due support (retroactive arrears) does not operate as a lien against this property as long as the obligor remains current on the support order.

Rule 1910.20 extends this legislative distinction between overdue and past due support to the following remedies available to collect support: (1) consumer agency reporting under 23 Pa.C.S. § 4303; (2) suspension of licenses under 23 Pa.C.S. § 4355; and (3) the full range of new collection remedies under 23 Pa.C.S. § 4305(b)(10). Accordingly, these remedies are available only to collect overdue support. They are not available to collect past due support as long as the obligor remains current on the order. If, however, the obligor subsequently defaults on the support order, Rule 1910.20(c) provides that any past due support still owing under the order immediately becomes overdue support subject to the full range of collection remedies. It remains overdue support until collected in full.

Pursuant to Rule 1910.20(c), all overdue support, including past due support which has converted to overdue support, remains subject to Act 58 remedies until paid in full. Any repayment plan subsequently agreed to by the parties, or ordered by the court pursuant to a contempt proceeding (including any arrearage component), does not preclude the use of these remedies for collecting overdue support more quickly, whenever feasible.

In cases involving past due support only, the obligee is not entirely without remedy in the event that additional income or assets of the obligor are discovered after the hearing which would enable collection of past due support more quickly. In these cases, identification of those income sources or assets provides a basis for modification pursuant to Rule 1910.19. Modification includes increasing the rate of repayment on past due support and, if appropriate, ordering that the past due support be paid in full. In these cases, the obligee may also petition the court for special relief pursuant to Rule 1910.26 to have the income or assets frozen and seized pending the petition for modification in order to secure payment of past due support.

Explanatory Comment—2007

Act 43-2005, July 7, 2005, P. L. 196, repealed the Act of June 24, 1937 (P. L. 2045, No. 397), known as The Support Law and added Chapter 46 to the Domestic Relations Code, 23 Pa.C.S. § 4601 et seq. Section 4 of Act 43-2005 states that the addition of Chapter 46 is a continuation of the Act of June 24, 1937 (P. L. 2045, No. 397). Chapter 46 addresses the responsibility of certain family members to maintain indigent relatives, whether or not the indigent person is a public charge. New subdivision (b)(3) clarifies that the support rules and guidelines do not apply to actions brought under Chapter 46 of the Domestic Relations Code.

Rule 1910.2 Venue. Transfer of Action.

(a) An action may be brought in

(1) the county in which the defendant resides, or

(2) the county in which the defendant is regularly employed, or

(3) the county in which the plaintiff resides and that county is the county in which the last marital domicile was located and in which the plaintiff has continued to reside, or

(4) the county in which the child resides if the relief sought includes child support.

(b) Where jurisdiction is acquired over the defendant pursuant to the long arm statute, 23 Pa.C.S. § 4342(c), the action may be brought in the county where the plaintiff resides.

Note: 23 Pa.C.S. § 7201 sets forth the specific bases for long arm jurisdiction over a nonresident defendant.

(c) If, at the time of the filing of the action, there is a divorce or custody action pending between the parties in an appropriate court in another county, the court upon good cause shown may transfer the support action to that county.

(d) For the convenience of the parties and witnesses the court may transfer an action to the appropriate court of any other county where the action could have been brought at the time of transfer.

Note: The standards for transfer of an action for the convenience of parties and witnesses are the same as the standards under Rule 1006(d).

(e) A support order may be enforced in accordance with the Uniform Interstate Family Support Act, 23 Pa.C.S. § 7101 et seq., if the defendant resides outside the Commonwealth, or in accordance with the Intrastate Family Support Act, 23 Pa.C.S. § 8101 et seq., if the defendant resides in another county within the Commonwealth.

Adopted April 23, 1981, effective July 22, 1981. Amended June 20, 1986, effective Jan. 1, 1986; Nov. 7, 1988, effective Jan. 1, 1989; Dec. 8, 1994, effective July 1, 1995; Dec. 18, 1999, effective Jan. 1, 1999; Oct. 31, 2002, effective immediately.

Explanatory Comment—1999

Under the former rule, venue in support matters was in the county where the defendant lived or worked, or in the county where the plaintiff lived if that county was the last family domicile. The amended Rule expands the circumstances under which venue lies in the county in which plaintiff resides. If the action is one for spousal and child support or child support only, plaintiff may bring the action in the county in which the child resides regardless of whether that county was the last family domicile. It is important to note, however, that the court may always permit a party or witness to testify by telephone, audiovisual or other electronic means at specially designated locations. 23 Pa.C.S. § 4342(j).

If plaintiff seeks spousal support only, then venue continues to lie in plaintiff's county only if that county wsa also the last marital domicile.

Rule 1910.2–1. Procedures Pursuant to the Intrastate Family Support Act

(a) The court in the county in which the complaint for support is filed shall retain and process the case for so long as all of the following conditions are met:

(1) there is proper venue pursuant to Rule 1910.2;

(2) the defendant-obligor's mailing address is known;

(3) sufficient information is known about the defendant-obligor's employment to enable the court to issue an earnings subpoena; and

(4) the obligee consents.

Note: A support action should be maintained in the county in which the obligee and/or the child(ren) reside and should not involve a second county unless the county of residence is unable to obtain service on the defendant-obligor or obtain information regarding the defendant-obligor's employment. However, the obligee is permitted to request that the case proceed under the Intrastate Family Support Act (IFSA) in accordance with 23 Pa. C.S. § 8103.

If the venue requirements are met, the court in the obligee's county of residence should attempt to retain the case if there already is an order that county against the same defendant-obligor in this or another child/spousal support case or if the defendant-obligor is incarcerated.

(b) If courts in two or more counties must be involved in the establishment and enforcement of an obligation for support:

(1) the case must proceed pursuant to the Intrastate Family Support Act; and

(2) venue shall follow the defendant-obligor in order to maintain the availability of statutory enforcement remedies.

Explanatory Comment—2002

Upon receipt of an Intrastate Family Support Act ("IFSA") complaint, the responding court shall accept the complaint and its original filing date.

Rule 1910.3   ACTIONS FOR SUPPORT

The obligee in an IFSA action is not required to be physically present in the responding court at any proceedings to establish, enforce or modify a support order, or to make a determination of paternity. 23 Pa. C.S. §8311(f) and (g) permits documentary evidence and testimony to be transmitted or obtained through the use of electronic media. In the event that additional information is required from the obligee, the responding court must notify the obligee as to the information needed and the acceptable means of providing it, and offer the obligee the assistance and use of the initiating court's staff and/or facilities to transmit such information. Telephonic hearings are authorized by Rule 1930.3 to accommodate out-of-county parties in both IFSA and locally-filed cases with the approval of the court upon good cause shown. The responding court must provide legal representation for an out-of-county obligee, where necessary, unless the obligee elects to be represented by private counsel.

(c) A support order shall not be registered in another county unless;

(1) requested to the obligee, or

(2) necessary to maintain an order for support, to obtain payment of the support obligation or to consolidate multiple cases involving the same defendant-obligor.

(d) Only one support order shall be charging against a defendant-obligor for the same spouse and/or child(ren) at one time.

Explanatory Comment—2002

If the obligee no longer resides in the initiating county, the initiating court may close its case after the following steps have been completed: 1) sending a copy of its docket file to the court in the obligee's new county of residence; 2) notifying the obligee and responding court, if applicable, of when and where the case was transferred; and 3) receiving from the court in the new county of residence acknowledgment of its receipt of the docket file and assumption of the initiating role.

If the defendant-obligor no longer resides in Pennsylvania or is employed outside the commonwealth, and the responding court cannot enforce the order or subpoena earnings or income information, the responding court must consider registration of the case under the provisions of the Uniform Interstate Family Support Act (UIFSA).

Rule 1910.3.   Parties. Obligor. Obligee

(a) An action may be brought

    (1) by a person, including a minor parent or a minor spouse, to whom a duty of support is owing, or

    (2) on behalf of a minor child by a person having custody of the child, without appointment as guardian ad litem, or

    (3) on behalf of a minor child by a person caring for the child regardless of whether a court order has been issued granting that person custody of the child, or

    (4) by a public body or private agency having an interest in the case, maintenance or assistance of a person to whom a duty of support is owing, or

    (5) by a parent, guardian or public or private agency on behalf of an unemancipated child over eighteen years of age to whom a duty of support is owing, or

(6) by any person who may owe a duty of support to a child or spouse. If the person to whom a duty of support may be owed does not appear, the action may be dismissed without prejudice for the petitioner to seek further relief from the court.

(b) The trier of fact shall enter an appropriate order based upon the evidence presented, without regard to which party initiated the support action, filed a modification petition or filed a petition for recovery of support overpayment. The determination of which party will be the obligee and which will be the obligor will be made by the trier of fact based upon the respective incomes of the parties, consistent with the support guidelines and existing law, and the custodial arrangements at the time of the initial or subsequent conference, hearing or trial. If supported by the evidence, the party named as the defendant in the initial pleading may be deemed to be the obligee, even if that party did not file a complaint for support. The provisions of this subdivision do not apply to parties seeking spousal support or alimony pendente lite. Parties seeking spousal support or alimony pendente lite must assert a claim in an appropriate pleading with proper notice served upon the other party.

(1) In general, the party who has primary custody of the children shall be the obligee of a child support order.

(2) When the parties share custody of the children equally, the party with the higher income shall be the obligor as provided in Rule 1910.16-4(c)(2).

Adopted April 23, 1981, effective July 22, 1981. Amended March 2, 2000, imd. effective; Oct. 30, 2001, imd. effective; Aug. 26, 2011, effective Nov. 1, 2011; November 5, 2012, effective December 5, 2012.

Explanatory Comment—1999

New subdivision (c) incorporates 23 Pa.C.S. § 4341(b) to confer standing on any person who is caring for a child to seek support on behalf of that child even though there is no court order granting legal or physical custody to that person. The statutory provision effectively overrules *Larson v. Diveglia*, 700 A.2d 931 (Pa. 1997), which held to the contrary.

Subdivision (e) is amended to eliminate the requirement of consent when the child is over 18 years of age. This requirement was originally intended only for applicable child support actions for higher educational support, which actions were abolished by *Curtis v. Kline*, 666 A.2d 265 (Pa. 1995). This rule also is intended to apply to children who are unemancipated by reason of physical or mental disability, consistent with 23 Pa.C.S. § 4321(3) as interpreted by case law.

Explanatory Comment—2011

A new category has been added in subdivision (a) to allow a party who may not have primary custody of the parties' child or who may owe a duty of support to a spouse to initiate a support action in which an appropriate order may be entered. In some cases, the obligor may want to start paying spousal support or alimony pendente lite to the obligee as soon as possible to avoid the accumulation of retroactive arrears, but § 71 of the Internal Revenue Code provides that payments to a spouse or ex-spouse must be pursuant to an order or a divorce or separation instrument to receive alimony tax treatment. Thus, any payments made prior to the entry of a support order will not be deductible by the obligor. This provision is intended to allow an obligor to commence the process by which he or she may pay support earlier.

A new subdivision (b) has been added to clarify that in all initial and subsequent child support actions, the trier of fact may enter a support order against either party, without regard to which party filed the complaint or petition for modification. This facilitates judicial economy, and relieves the parties from incurring additional filing fees, losing time from work or family, losing retroactivity and having to wait for a new proceeding to be scheduled. It enables the trier of fact to base the order on the facts and circumstances at the time of the proceeding, which may be different than at the time of filing.

Rule 1910.4 Domestic Relations Section. Commencement of Action. No Filing Fees. Authorized Fees

(a) Each court of common pleas shall have a domestic relations section that shall be the filing office for pleadings and documents for child support, spousal support, and alimony *pendente lite* actions.

(b) A party shall commence actions for child support and spousal support by filing a complaint in the domestic relations section. A party shall commence an action for alimony *pendente lite* by filing a complaint in the domestic relations section if a divorce complaint has been filed with the prothonotary.

Note: See Pa.R.C.P. No. 1910.27(a) for the form of the complaint.

See Pa.R.C.P. No. 1930.1(b). To the extent this rule applies to actions not governed by other legal authority regarding confidentiality of information and documents in support actions or

that attorneys or unrepresented parties file support-related confidential information and documents in non-support actions (e.g., divorce, custody), the *Case Records Public Access Policy of the Unified Judicial System of Pennsylvania* shall apply.

See the Pennsylvania Department of Human Services Child Support Program for e-services, including filing for support or requesting a modification of an existing support order at *https://www.humanservices.state.pa.us/csws/*.

See Pa.R.C.P. No. 1920.31(a)(2) regarding the filing of alimony pendente lite actions in the domestic relations section.

(c) The domestic relations section shall not require payment of a filing fee to commence or modify an action.

(d) Unless authorized by statute, a judicial district shall not impose additional fees in actions for child support, spousal support, and alimony *pendente lite*. The domestic relations section shall collect fees through the Pennsylvania Child Support Enforcement System (PACSES).

Note: The statutorily authorized fees in actions for child support, spousal support, and alimony *pendente lite* include the genetic testing fee, the federally mandated annual fee, and fees associated with statewide court operations referenced in 204 Pa. Code § 29.351.

Adopted April 23, 1981, effective July 22, 1981. Amended May 31, 2000, effective July 1, 2000; Jan. 5, 2018, effective Jan. 6, 2018; June 1, 2018, effective July 1, 2018; July 30, 2018, effective January 1, 2019.

Rule 1910.5. Complaint. Order Of Court.

(a) The complaint shall be substantially in the form provided by Rule 1910.27(a).

(b) The complaint shall not contain a notice to defend or be endorsed with a notice to plead.

Official Note: Neither Rule 1018.1 nor Rule 1361 applies to a complaint in an action for support.

(c) An order shall be attached at the front of the complaint directing the defendant to appear before an officer for a conference at the time and place directed by the court. The order shall be substantially in the form provided by Rule 1910.27(b) and must include notice that a child support order may be entered against either party without regard to which party initiated the action.

Official Note: For service of original process in support matters, see Rule 1930.4.

The provisions of Rule 1910.5 amended May 31, 2000, effective July 1, 2000; amended August 26, 2011, effective November 1, 2011.

Rule 1910.6 Notification

Parties to a support action and their attorneys shall be provided notice of all proceedings in which support obligations might be established or modified. Notice must be provided at least 20 days prior to the proceeding. The parties and their attorneys shall also be provided with a copy of any order issued in the support action within 14 days after issuance of the order. If there is no activity in a support action for a period of three years, the domestic relations section shall send a notice to each of the parties' attorneys advising each attorney that his or her appearance in the support action shall be deemed to be withdrawn unless the attorney objects within thirty (30) days of the date the notice is mailed to the attorney. An attorney representing a party in a support action shall not be deemed to be representing that party in any other action, nor shall a withdrawal of appearance in a support action be deemed to be a withdrawal of appearance for the party in any other proceeding.

Explanatory Comment—2000

Rule 1910.6 implements 23 Pa.C.S. § 4352(b)(2) to require that parties to a support action be notified in advance of all support and modification proceedings and that they be furnished with a copy of any order entered in those proceedings within 14 days of issuance of the order.

Adopted May 31, 2000, effective July 1, 2000; Oct. 30, 2001, eff. imd.

Rule 1910.7 Pleading by Defendant Not Required. Question of Jurisdiction or Venue or Statute of Limitations in Paternity

(a) An answer or other responsive pleading by the defendant shall not be required, but if the defendant elects to file a pleading, the domestic relations office conference required by the order of court shall not be delayed.

Rule 1910.8   ACTIONS FOR SUPPORT

Note: See Pa.R.C.P. No. 1930.1(b). To the extent this rule applies to actions not governed by other legal authority regarding confidentiality of information and documents in support actions or that attorneys or unrepresented parties file support-related confidential information and documents in non-support actions (e.g., divorce, custody), the Case Records Public Access Policy of the Unified Judicial System of Pennsylvania shall apply.

(b) If defendant raises a question of jurisdiction or venue or in paternity cases the defense of the statute of limitations, the court shall promptly dispose of the question and may, in an appropriate case, stay the domestic relations office conference.

Adopted April 23, 1981, effective July 22, 1981. Amended Jan. 5, 2018, effective Jan. 6, 2018; June 1, 2018, effective July 1, 2018.

Explanatory Comment—1981

The pleading required by the Rules is minimal. Only one pleading is required, the complaint. The technicalities of pleading are avoided by providing a form of complaint in Rule 1910.26(a).

Under subdivision (a), the defendant may but is not required to plead to the complaint. All averments may be disputed by the defendant at the domestic relations office conference. An attorney who wishes to deny averments of the complaint by filing an answer may do so. However, the domestic relations office conference is not to be delayed to permit the filing of an answer.

A defendant who wishes to object to venue or jurisdiction or to raise the statute of limitations in paternity cases should do so as promptly as possible. Such preliminary issues should be disposed of by the court as expeditiously as possible.

The domestic relations office conference should not be stayed pending resolution of these questions except by court order in an unusual case. The interest in the prompt listing of support cases outweighs any benefit to be gained by the stay of the conference in most cases.

Rule 1910.8   Rescinded

Rescinded Dec. 18, 1999, effective Jan. 1, 1999.

Note: The provisions in this Rule now appear in Rule 1910.2(d) through (f).

Rule 1910.9   Discovery

(a) Except as provided in Rule 1910.11(j) and Rule 1910.12(c), there shall be no discovery in an action for support unless authorized by special order of court.

Note: The rule relating to discovery in domestic relations matters generally is Rule 1930.5.

(b) Where a party is employed, the court shall ascertain the party's earnings and may enter an order directing the employer to furnish earnings information to the court as provided by Rule 1910.28.

Adopted April 23, 1981, effective July 22, 1981; amended May 5, 1997, effective July 1, 1997; March 2, 2000, imd. effective; May 31, 2000, effective July 1, 2000.

Explanatory Comment—1997

Subdivision (a) is amended to permit discovery in accordance with R.C.P. 4001 et seq. in any support matter where a separate listing has been obtained under

Rules 1910.11(j) and 1910.12(c). In all other support matters discovery is permitted only by leave of court. Cases should not be listed separately in order to obtain discovery, nor should a support hearing be used to conduct discovery. Instead, the court should grant leave to engage in discovery in the few support cases which are not listed separately and in which discovery is warranted.

Subdivision (b) authorizes the court to obtain earnings and health insurance information from the employer of either party to a support action, using the forms provided in Rule 1910.28.

Rule 1910.10. Alternative Hearing Procedures.

(a) The action shall proceed as prescribed by Pa.R.C.P. No. 1910.11 unless the court by local rule adopts the alternative hearing procedure of Pa.R.C.P. No. 1910.12.

(b) The president judge or the administrative judge of Family Division of each county shall certify that all support proceedings in that county are conducted in accordance with either Pa.R.C.P. No. 1910.11 or Pa.R.C.P. No. 1910.12. The certification shall be filed with the Domestic Relations Procedural Rules Committee, and shall be substantially in the following form:

I hereby certify that _____ County conducts its support proceedings in accordance with Pa.R.C.P.No. ___.

_____

(PRESIDENT JUDGE) (ADMINISTRATIVE JUDGE)

Note: For a complete list of the Alternative Hearing Procedures for each county: http://www.pacourts.us/courts/supreme-court/committees/rules-committees/domestic-relations-procedural-rules-committee.

Explanatory Comment

In accordance with Pa.R.C.P. No. 1910.10, a judicial district may opt for one of two procedures for support matters; the procedure selected is then certified by the president judge or administrative judge to the Domestic Relations Procedural Rules Committee as prescribed in subdivision (b). Subdivision (b) was added in response to requests from appellate court judges who find that it is often difficult to determine the rule with which the actual support procedure is intended to comply. Subsequently, a judicial district may, at any time, change its support procedure by filing a new certification with the staff of the Domestic Relations Procedural Rules Committee indicating the rule according to which support matters will proceed. However, a judicial district may, by local rule, permit interstate actions to proceed directly to a hearing officer or judge without a conference.

The procedure set forth in Pa.R.C.P. No. 1910.11 provides for a conference before a conference officer, a conference summary and entry of an interim order for support calculated in accordance with the guidelines, and a right to demand a hearing de novo before a judge. The hearing must be held and the final order entered within 60 days of the written demand for hearing.

The alternate procedure, as set forth in Pa.R.C.P. No. 1910.12, provides for a conference before a conference officer, a record hearing before a hearing officer, and issuance of a report and recommendation to which exceptions may be filed within ten days. The court must hear argument and enter a final order within 60 days of the filing of exceptions.

In lieu of continuing the practice of including in the Note a 67–county list identifying the hearing procedure selected by the local county court, the list can now be found on the Domestic Relations Procedural Rules Committee website.

Rule 1910.11 ACTIONS FOR SUPPORT

Adopted April 23, 1981, effective July 22, 1981. Amended March 30, 1994, effective July 1, 1994; Sept. 5, 1995, effective Jan. 1, 1996; Oct. 27, 2000, imd. effective; Oct. 30, 2001, imd. effective; Oct. 11, 2002, imd. effective; July 30, 2003, imd. effective; Jan. 12, 2010, effective May 12, 2010; Sept. 16, 2013, effective Oct. 16, 2013; October 13, 2015, effective Jan. 1, 2016; October 14, 2016, effective December 1, 2016.

Rule 1910.11. Office Conference. Subsequent Proceedings. Order.

(a) Office Conferencel

(1) A conference officer shall conduct the office conference.

(2) A lawyer serving as a conference officer employed by, or under contract with, a judicial district or appointed by the court shall not practice family law before a conference officer, hearing officer, permanent or standing master, or judge of the same judicial district.

Note: Conference officers preside at office conferences under Pa.R.C.P. No. 1910.11. Hearing officers preside at hearings under Pa.R.C.P. No. 1910.12. The appointment of masters to hear actions in divorce or for annulment of marriage is authorized by Pa.R.C.P. No. 1920.51.

(b) If a party fails to appear at the conference as directed by the court, the conference may proceed.

(c) At the conference, the parties shall provide to the conference officer the following documents:

- the most recently filed individual federal income tax returns, including all schedules, W-2s, and 1099s;
- the partnership or business tax returns with all schedules, including K-1, if the party is self-employed or a principal in a partnership or business entity;
- pay stubs for the preceding six months;
- verification of child care expenses;
- child support, spousal support, alimony pendente lite, or alimony orders or agreements for other children or former spouses;
- proof of available medical coverage; and
- an Income Statement and, if necessary, an Expense Statement on the forms provided in Pa.R.C.P. No. 1910.27(c) and completed as set forth in subdivisions (c)(1) and (2).

Note: See Pa.R.C.P. No. 1930.1(b). To the extent this rule applies to actions not governed by other legal authority regarding confidentiality of information and documents in support actions or that attorneys or unrepresented parties file support-related confidential information and documents in non-support actions (e.g., divorce, custody), the *Case Records Public Access Policy of the Unified Judicial System of Pennsylvania* shall apply.

(1) The parties shall provide the conference officer with a completed:

(i) Income Statement as set forth in Pa.R.C.P. No. 1910.27(c)(1) in all support cases, including high-income cases under Pa.R.C.P. No. 1910.16-3.1; and

(ii) Expense Statement as set forth in Pa.R.C.P. No. 1910.27(c)(2)(A), if a party:

(A) claims that unusual needs and unusual fixed expenses may warrant a deviation from the guideline support amount pursuant to Pa.R.C.P. No. 1910.16-5; or

(B) seeks expense apportionment pursuant to Pa.R.C.P. No. 1910.16-6.

(2) For high-income support cases as set forth in Pa.R.C.P. No. 1910.16-3.1, the

(d) Conference Officer Recommendation.

(1) The conference officer shall calculate and recommend a guideline support amount to the parties.

(2) If the parties agree on a support amount at the conference, the conference officer shall:

(i) prepare a written order consistent with the parties' agreement and substantially in the form set forth in Pa.R.C.P. No. 1910.27(e), which the parties shall sign; and

(ii) submit to the court the written order along with the conference officer's recommendation for approval or disapproval.

(iii) The court may enter the order in accordance with the agreement without hearing from the parties.

(3) In all cases in which one or both parties are unrepresented, the parties must provide income information to the domestic relations section so that a guidelines calculation can be performed.

(4) In cases in which both parties are represented by counsel, the parties shall not be obligated to provide income information and the domestic relations section shall not be required to perform a guidelines calculation if the parties have reached an agreement about the amount of support and the amount of contribution to additional expenses.

(e) At the conclusion of the conference or not later than 10 days after the conference, the conference officer shall prepare a conference summary and furnish copies to the court and to both parties. The conference summary shall state:

(1) the facts upon which the parties agree;

(2) the contentions of the parties with respect to facts upon which they disagree; and

(3) the conference officer's recommendation; if any, of

(i) the amount of support and by and for whom the support shall be paid; and

(ii) the effective date of any order.

(f) If an agreement for support is not reached at the conference, the court, without hearing the parties, shall enter an interim order calculated in accordance with the guidelines and substantially in the form set forth in Rule 1910.27(e). Each party shall be provided, either in person at the time of the conference or by mail, with a copy of the interim order and written notice that any party may, within twenty days after the date of receipt or the date of the mailing of the interim order, whichever occurs first, file a written demand with the domestic relations section for a hearing before the court.

(g) A demand for a hearing before the court shall not stay the interim order entered under subdivision (f) unless the court so directs.

(h) If no party demands a hearing before the court within the twenty day period, the interim order shall constitute a final order.

(i) If a demand is filed, there shall be a hearing de novo before the court. The domestic relations section shall schedule the hearing and give notice to the parties. The court shall hear the case and enter a final order substantially in the form set forth in Rule 1910.27(e) within sixty days from the date of the written demand for hearing.

(j)(1) Promptly after receipt of the notice of the scheduled hearing, a party may move the court for a separate listing where:

(i) there are complex questions of law, fact or both; or

(ii) the hearing will be protracted; or

(iii) the orderly administration of justice requires that the hearing be listed separately.

(2) If the motion for separate listing is granted, discovery shall be available in accordance with Rule 4001 et seq.

Note: The rule relating to discovery in domestic relations matters generally is Rule 1930.5.

(k) No motion for post-trial relief may be filed to the final order of support.

Adopted April 23, 1981, effective July 22, 1981. Amended October 19, 1983, effective January 1, 1984. November 7, 1988, effective January 1, 1989; September 29, 1989, effective October 15, 1989; March 30, 1994, effective July 1, 1994; December 2, 1994, effective March 1, 1995; September 8, 1995, effective January 1, 1996; May 5, 1997, effective July 1, 1997; May 31, 2000, effective July 1, 2000; August 8, 2006, immediately effective; November 8, 2006, effective February 6, 2007; October 30, 2007, immediately effective; January 12, 2010, effective May 12, 2010; August 26, 2011, effective November 1, 2011; December 23, 2011, effective January 31, 2012; July 2, 2014, effective August 1, 2014; March 4, 2015, effective April 3, 2015; January 5, 2018, effective January 6, 2018; June 1, 2018, effective July 1, 2018; December 28, 2018, effective January 1, 2019.

Explanatory Comment—1994

The domestic relations office conference provided by Rule 1910.11 constitutes the heart of the support procedure. There are two primary advantages to the inclusion of a conference. First, in many cases the parties will agree upon an amount of support and a final order will be prepared, to be entered by the court, thus dispensing with a judicial hearing. Second, those cases which do go to hearing can proceed more quickly because the necessary factual information has already been gathered by the conference officer.

Subdivision (a)(2) prohibits certain officers of the court from practicing family law before fellow officers of the same court. These officers are the conference officer who is an attorney (Rule 1910.11), the hearing officer (Rule 1910.12), and the standing or permanent master who is employed by the court (Rule 1920.51). The amendments are not intended to apply to the attorney who is appointed occasionally to act as a master in a divorce action.

Subdivision (e)(3) makes clear that even if the parties agree on an amount of support, the conference officer is still empowered to recommend to the court that the agreement be disapproved. This provision is intended to protect the destitute spouse who might out of desperation agree to an amount of support that is unreasonably low or which would in effect bargain away the rights of the children. The officer's disapproval of the agreement serves to prevent an inadequate order being entered unwittingly by the court.

The provision for an interim order in subdivision (f) serves two purposes. First, it ensures that the obligee will receive needed support for the period during which the judicial determination is sought. Second, it eliminates the motive of delay in seeking a judicial determination.

Because the guidelines are income driven, the trier of fact has little need for the expense information required in the Income and Expense Statement. Therefore in guideline cases, the rule no longer requires that expense information be provided. If a party feels that there are expenses so extraordinary that they merit consideration by the trier of fact, that party is free to provide the information. In cases decided according to Melzer v. Witsberger, 505 Pa. 462, 480 A.2d 991 (1984), living expenses are properly considered, and therefore must be presented on the Income and Expense Statement.

Explanatory Comment—1995

Rule 1910.11(e) is amended to eliminate the need for a party to request a copy of the conference summary.

Because the court is required to enter a guideline order on the basis of the conference officer's recommendation, there is no need for (g)(2), which provided for a hearing before the court where an order was not entered within five days of the conference. It is eliminated accordingly.

Pursuant to subdivision (g), support payments are due and owing under the interim order which continues in effect until the court enters a final order after the hearing de novo. The provision for an interim order serves two purposes. First, it ensures that the obligee will receive needed support for the period during which the judicial determination is sought. Second, it eliminates the motive of delay in seeking a judicial determination. Therefore, the plaintiff and the dependent children are not prejudiced by allowing the court sixty days, rather than the original forty-five, in which to enter its final order.

Explanatory Comment—2006

The time for filing a written demand for a hearing before the court has been expanded from ten to twenty days. The purpose of this amendment is to provide ample opportunity for litigants and counsel to receive notice of the entry of the order, to assure Commonwealth-wide consistency in calculation of time for filing and to conform to applicable general civil procedural rules.

The amendments reflect the separated Income Statement and Expense Statements in Rule 1910.27(c).

Explanatory Comment—2010

When the parties' combined net income exceeds $ 30,000 per month, calculation of child support, spousal support and alimony pendente lite shall be pursuant to Rule 1910.16-3.1. Rule 1910.16-2(e) has been amended to eliminate the application of *Melzer v. Witsberger*, 505 Pa. 462, 480 A.2d 991 (1984), in high income child support cases.

Explanatory Comment—2011

The rule has been amended to require that income information be provided in all cases, unless both parties are represented in reaching an agreement, so that a guidelines calculation can be performed. The guidelines create a rebuttable presumption that the amount calculated pursuant to them is the correct amount, so there should be a calculation in every case. If parties agree to receive or to pay an order other than the guideline amount, they should know what that amount is so that they can enter an agreement knowingly. If both parties are represented by counsel, it is assumed that their entry into the agreement for an amount other than a guidelines amount is knowing as it is counsels' responsibility to advise the parties. In addition, part of the mandatory quadrennial review of the support guidelines mandates a study of the number of cases in which the support amount ordered varies from the amount that would result from a guidelines calculation. Federal regulations presume that if a large percentage of cases vary from the guideline amount, then the guidelines are not uniform statewide..

Rule 1910.12. Office Conference. Hearing. Record. Exceptions. Order

(a) There shall be an office conference as provided by Rule 1910.11(a) through (d). The provisions of Rule 1910.11(d)(3) and (4) regarding income information apply in cases proceeding pursuant to Rule 1910.12.

(b)(1) At the conclusion of a conference attended by both parties, if an agreement for support has not been reached, and the conference and hearing are not scheduled on the same day, the court, without hearing the parties, shall enter an interim order calculated in accordance with the guidelines and substantially in the form set forth in Rule 1910.27(e), and the parties shall be given notice of the date, time and place of a hearing. A record hearing shall be conducted by a hearing officer who must be a lawyer.

(2) If either party, having been properly served, fails to attend the conference, the court may enter an interim order calculated in accordance with the guidelines and substantially in the form set forth in Rule 1910.27(e). Within twenty days after the date of receipt or the date of mailing of the interim order, whichever occurs first, either party may demand a hearing before a hearing officer. If no hearing is requested, the order shall become final.

(3) Any lawyer serving as a hearing officer employed by, or under contract with, a judicial district or appointed by the court shall not practice family law before a conference officer, hearing officer, permanent or standing master, or judge of the same judicial district.

Note: Conference officers preside at office conferences under Rule 1910.11. Hearing officers preside at hearings under Rule 1910.12. The appointment of masters to hear actions in divorce or for annulment of marriage is authorized by Rule 1920.51.

(c)(1) Except as provided in subdivision (c)(2), promptly after conclusion of the conference, a party may move the court for a separate listing of the hearing where:

(i) there are complex questions of law, fact or both; or

(ii) the hearing will be protracted; or

(iii) the orderly administration of justice requires that the hearing be listed separately.

(2) Where the conference and hearing are scheduled on the same day, all requests for separate listing must be presented to the court at least seven days prior to the scheduled court date.

(3) If the motion for separate listing is granted, discovery shall be available in accordance with Rule 4001 et seq.

Note: The rule relating to discovery in domestic relations matters generally is Rule 1930.5.

(d) The hearing officer shall receive evidence, hear argument and, not later than 20 days after the close of the record, file with the court a report containing a recommendation with respect to the entry of an order of support. The report may be in narrative form stating the reasons for the recommendation and shall include a proposed order substantially in the form set forth in Rule 1910.27(e) stating:

(1) the amount of support calculated in accordance with the guidelines;

(2) by and for whom it shall be paid; and

(3) the effective date of the order.

(e) The court, without hearing the parties, shall enter an interim order consistent with the proposed order of the hearing officer. Each party shall be provided, either in person at the time of the hearing or by mail, with a copy of the interim order and written notice that any party may, within twenty days after the date of receipt or the date of mailing of the order, whichever occurs first, file with the domestic relations section written exceptions to the report of the hearing officer and interim order.

> **Note:** Objections to the entry of an interim order consistent with the proposed order may be addressed pursuant to Rule 1910.26.

(f) Within twenty days after the date of receipt or the date of mailing of the report by the hearing officer, whichever occurs first, any party may file exceptions to the report or any part thereof, to rulings on objections to evidence, to statements or findings of facts, to conclusions of law, or to any other matters occurring during the hearing. Each exception shall set forth a separate objection precisely and without discussion. Matters not covered by exceptions are deemed waived unless, prior to entry of the final order, leave is granted to file exceptions raising those matters. If exceptions are filed, any other party may file exceptions within twenty days of the date of service of the original exceptions.

(g) If no exceptions are filed within the twenty-day period, the interim order shall constitute a final order.

(h) If exceptions are filed, the interim order shall continue in effect. The court shall hear argument on the exceptions and enter an appropriate final order substantially in the form set forth in Rule 1910.27(e) within sixty days from the date of the filing of exceptions to the interim order. No motion for post-trial relief may be filed to the final order.

Adopted April 23, 1981, effective July 22, 1981. Amended Oct. 19, 1983, effective Jan. 1, 1984; March 23, 1987, effective July 1, 1987; Nov. 7, 1988, effective Jan. 1, 1989; Sept. 29, 1989, effective Oct. 15, 1989; March 30, 1994, effective July 1, 1994; Sept. 8, 1995, effective Jan. 1, 1996; May 5, 1997, effective July 1, 1997; May 31, 2000, effective July 1, 2000; Aug. 8, 2006, imd. effective; Aug. 26, 2011, effective Nov. 1, 2011; Dec. 23, 2011, effective Jan. 31, 2012; July 2, 2014, effective August 1, 2014; March 4, 2015, effective April 3, 2015.

Explanatory Comment—1995

Language is added to subdivision (b) to acknowledge that the conference and hearing can be held the same day, and to provide for the immediate entry of an interim order in judicial districts where the hearing occurs at a later date. New subdivision (b)(2) permits entry of a guideline order after a conference which the defendant, though properly served, fails to attend. New subdivision (c)(2) is intended to prevent delays in the hearing of complex cases by requiring that requests for separate listing be made at least seven days in advance where the conference and hearing are scheduled on the same day.

In addition, the phrase "record hearing" in subdivision (a) replaces the reference to a "stenographic record" in recognition of the variety of means available to create a reliable record of support proceedings.

Amended subdivision (e) allows an interim order to be entered and served on the parties at the conclusion of the hearing, rather than after the expiration of the exceptions period as was true under the old rule. In addition, the amended subdivision requires that the interim order include language advising the parties of their right to file exceptions within ten days of the date of the order.

Support payments are due and owing under the interim order which continues in effect until the court enters a final order after considering the parties' exceptions. Therefore, extension of the deadline for entering the final order by fifteen days does not prejudice the persons dependent upon payment of the support.

Explanatory Comment—2006

The time for filing exceptions has been expanded from ten to twenty days. The purpose of this amendment is to provide ample opportunity for litigants and counsel to receive notice of the entry of the order, to assure Commonwealth-wide consistency in calculation of time for filing and to conform to applicable general civil procedural rules.

Rule 1910.13 Disobedience of Order of Court. Arrest. Contempt [Rescinded]

Rescinded March 30, 1994, effective July 1, 1994.

Rule 1910.13-1. Failure or Refusal to Appear Pursuant to Order of Court. Bench Warrant

(a) If a party fails to appear at a conference and/or hearing as directed by order of court, the court may issue a bench warrant for the arrest of the party if it finds

(1) following a hearing on the record that the party had actual notice that the party was ordered to attend the conference and/or hearing, or

(2) upon the affidavit of a hearing officer or conference officer that

(i) the order of court scheduling the conference and/or hearing was served by ordinary mail with the return address of the domestic relations section appearing thereon, that the mail was not returned to the domestic relations section within fifteen days after mailing, and that, at a date after the order of court was mailed, the domestic relations section has verified through the U.S. Postal Service or by electronic means that mail for the party was being delivered at the address to which the court order was mailed; or

(ii) the party signed a receipt indicating acceptance of a copy of the court order; or

(iii) an employee of the court handed a copy of the order to the party; or

(iv) a competent adult handed a copy of the court order to the party, and filed an affidavit of service.

Official Note: See Rule 76 for the definition of "competent adult."

The support statute, at 23 Pa.C.S.A. § 4353(a), requires parties to a support proceeding to notify the domestic relations section within seven days of a change of personal address. Pursuant to 23 Pa.C.S.A. § 4353(a.1), the court may deem due process service requirements to have been met upon delivery of written notice to the most recent address the party filed with the domestic relations section.

(b) The request for a bench warrant shall be made by the domestic relations office within sixty days following the party's failure to appear. The request shall be in the form provided by Rule 1910.13-2(b), and shall include the hearing officer or conference officer's certification that the party has not appeared for any domestic relations matter involving the same parties since the date the party failed to appear.

(c) Upon appearance in court by a party on the matter underlying the bench warrant, the bench warrant shall be vacated forthwith and the notice shall be given to all computer networks into which the bench warrant has been entered.

(d) When a bench warrant is executed, the case is to proceed in accordance with the following procedures.

(1) When an individual is arrested pursuant to a bench warrant, he or she shall be taken without unnecessary delay for a hearing on the bench warrant. The hearing shall be conducted by the judicial officer who issued the bench warrant, or, another judicial officer designated by the president judge or by the president judge's designee to conduct bench warrant hearings. As used in this rule, "judicial officer" is limited to the common pleas court judge who issued the bench warrant, or common pleas court judge designated by the president judge or by the president judge's designee to conduct bench warrant hearings.

(2) In the discretion of the judicial officer, the bench warrant hearing may be conducted using two-way simultaneous audio-visual communication.

(3) When the individual is arrested in the county of issuance, and the bench warrant hearing cannot be conducted promptly after the arrest, the individual shall be lodged in the county jail pending the hearing. The authority in charge of the county jail promptly shall notify the sheriff's office and the director of the domestic relations section that the individual is being held pursuant to the bench warrant.

(4) When the individual is arrested outside the county of issuance, the authority in charge of the county jail in the arresting county promptly shall notify the proper authorities in the county of issuance that the individual is being held pursuant to the bench warrant.

(5) The bench warrant hearing shall be conducted without unnecessary delay after the individual is lodged in the jail of the county of issuance of that bench warrant. The individual shall not be detained without a hearing on the bench warrant longer than 72 hours, or the close of the next business day if the 72 hours expires on a non-business day.

(6) At the conclusion of the bench warrant hearing following the disposition of the matter, the judicial officer immediately shall vacate the bench warrant.

(7) If a bench warrant hearing is not held within the time limits in paragraph (d)(5), the bench warrant shall expire by operation of law.

Adopted March 30, 1994, effective July 1, 1994. Amended May 14, 1999, effective July 1, 1999; Nov. 8, 2006, effective Feb. 6, 2007; July 30, 2010, effective immediately.

Explanatory Comment—1994

In 1988, Section 4342 of the Domestic Relations Code, 23 Pa. C.S. § 4342, was amended to require establishment of procedures for expedited contempt in support. Those procedures are set forth in new Rules 1910.13-1, 1910.13-2, and 1910.21-1 through 1910.21-7.

Former Rule 1910.13 provided for the issuance of a bench warrant for failure of a person to obey a court order other than an order for support. It is replaced with new Rule 1910.13-1 which sets forth detailed procedures for the issuance of a bench warrant, and new Rule 1910.13-2 which provides the associated forms. The new rules apply only to a party who fails to appear at a support conference or hearing as directed by an order of court.

An individual arrested pursuant to a bench warrant can be incarcerated for a period not to exceed seventy-two hours prior to hearing as set forth in new Rule 1910.13-1(d). Under the old rules, if the court was unavailable at the time of arrest, the individual could not be held. Therefore, law enforcement officials were unable to execute bench warrants in the evenings or on weekends, when their efforts were most likely to be successful. By limiting the possible period of incarceration to seventy-two hours, new Rule 1910.13-1(d) balances the need to bring parties before the court with the desire to avoid lengthy pre-hearing detention. Bail can be set by the court where appropriate, providing additional protection for the respondent.

Explanatory Comment—1999

The rules of civil procedure governing service of original process and other legal papers have used the term "competent adult." In certain circumstances, the term has been used with the restrictive language "who is not a party to the action."

The Supreme Court of Pennsylvania has amended Definition Rule 76 by adding the following definition: "'competent adult' means an individual eighteen years of age or older who is neither a party to the action nor an employee or a relative of a party." In view of this new definition, the rules of civil procedure which used the term "competent adult who is not a party to the action" have been amended by deleting as unnecessary the restrictive language "who is not a party to the action." These rules using the term "competent adult" will be governed by the new definition. The rules which used the term "competent adult" without the restrictive language have been amend by deleting the word "competent," thus continuing to permit service by an adult without further restriction.

Explanatory Comment—2006

Beginning in 2006, bench warrants issued for failure to obey a court order to appear in a support matter will be available through the Judicial Network ("JNET") system. JNET expands the capacity of law enforcement officers throughout the commonwealth to be informed of outstanding bench warrants issued by both the criminal and civil courts. The Supreme Court of Pennsylvania has promulgated new Pa.R.Crim.P. 150, effective August 1, 2006, which sets forth the procedure related to criminal bench warrants. The amendments to Rule 1910.13-1 and 1910-13-2 track the new criminal procedural rule so that bench warrant procedures will be uniform throughout the commonwealth. For additional information see the Criminal Procedural Rules Committee's Final Report explaining new Pa.R.Crim.P. 150, published with the promulgation order at 36 Pa. B. 184 (January 14, 2006).

Rule 1910.13–2 Form of Request for Bench Warrant and Supporting Affidavit. Form of Bench Warrant

(a) Request for a bench warrant pursuant to Rule 1910.13–1 shall be in substantially the following form and shall be attached to the Bench Warrant form set forth in subdivision (b) of this rule:

(CAPTION)
REQUEST FOR BENCH WARRANT AND
SUPPORTING AFFIDAVIT

1. _____ did not appear for a conference and/or hearing in the Court of Common Pleas of _____ County on the _____ day of _____, 20__, which was scheduled by an order of court compelling this person's appearance, a copy of which is attached to this request.

2. The party received the order of court scheduling the conference and/or hearing in the following manner:

☐ (a) The order of court (i) was served upon the party by ordinary mail with the return address of the court thereon; (ii) the mail was not returned to the court within fifteen (15) days after mailing; and (iii) at a date after the order of court was mailed, the United States Postal Service has verified that mail for the party was being delivered at the address to which the court order was mailed.

☐ (b) The party signed a receipt indicating acceptance of the court order.

☐ (c) An employee of the court handed a copy of the court order to the party. The employee's affidavit of service is attached.

☐ (d) A competent adult handed a copy of the court order to the party. The adult's affidavit of service is attached.

3. ☐ This request for Bench Warrant is made within sixty days following the party's failure to appear for the conference and/or hearing; and

☐ I have reviewed the records of the Court and the Domestic Relations Office concerning this case, and attest that the party has not appeared for any domestic relations matter involving the same parties since the date upon which the party failed to appear in violation of the attached order of court.

4. In my capacity as hearing officer or conference officer, I request that the attached Bench Warrant be issued against the party named on account of the party's failure to appear for a scheduled conference and/or hearing in violation of an order of court.

The records of the Domestic Relations Section show that:
☐ the party owes support arrearages in the amount of $_____.
☐ the party has failed to appear for _____ hearings relating to this case.

I verify that the statements made in this affidavit are true and correct. I understand that false statements herein are made subject to the penalties of 18 Pa.C.S. § 4904 relating to unsworn falsification to authorities.

DATE: _____ _____
                                          NAME/OFFICIAL TITLE

Rule 1910.13–2   **ACTIONS FOR SUPPORT**

(b) The Bench Warrant entered by a court pursuant to Rule 1910.13–1 shall be in substantially the following form, and shall be attached to the Request for Bench Warrant form set forth in subdivision (a) of this rule:

(CAPTION)
BENCH WARRANT

AND NOW, this _____ day of _____, 20 ____, the Sheriff of _____ County, or any constable, or police officer, or other law enforcement officer is hereby ordered to take _____, residing at _____, into custody for appearance before this Court.

This bench warrant is issued because it appears that the (plaintiff) (defendant) has failed to appear, after notice, before the court for a scheduled conference and/or hearing.

We command you, the arresting officer, forthwith to convey and deliver the party into the custody of the Court of Common Pleas of _____ County, at

_____
(address)

_____
(city)

Pennsylvania, for a hearing.

DESCRIPTIVE INFORMATION

Social Security # _____ Sex ____ D.O.B. ____ Age ____

Height ____ Weight ____ Race ____ Eyes ____ Hair ____

   Distinguishing features (scars, tattoos, facial hair, disability, etc.)

_____

_____

Alias _____

Telephone _____

You are further commanded that if the court is unavailable, the party may be held in the County Jail until the court is opened for business, at which time the party shall be promptly conveyed and delivered into the custody of the court at

_____
(address)

_____
(city)

Pennsylvania, for hearing.

The authority in charge of the county jail shall notify the sheriff's office and the director of the domestic relations section forthwith that the party is being held pursuant to the bench warrant.

Under no circumstances may the party be held in the county jail of the county that issued this bench warrant for more than seventy-two hours or the close of the next business day if the 72 hours expires on a non-business day. See Pa.R.Crim.P 150(A)(5).

Bail in this matter shall be set as follows:

☐ No bail.

☐ Bail to be set in the amount of _____.

Official Note: Standards for setting bail are set forth in Rule of Criminal Procedure 525.

BY THE COURT:

JUDGE

Adopted March 30, 1994, effective July 1, 1994. Amended May 14, 1999, effective July 1, 1999; Amended Oct. 30, 2001, eff. imd.; Amended May 9, 2005, eff. imd.; November 8, 2006, effective February 6, 2007.

[See Explanatory Comment—1994 following Rule 1910.13–1]

Explanatory Comment—2005

Act 207-2004 amended numerous titles of the Pennsylvania Consolidated Statutes changing the title of "district justice" to "magisterial district judge." The amendments to Rule 1910.13-2 reflect the change in title.

Rule 1910.14 Defendant Leaving Jurisdiction. Security

At any stage of the proceeding, upon affidavit that the defendant is about to leave the jurisdiction, the court may issue appropriate process directing that the defendant be brought before the court at such time as the court may direct. At that time the court may direct that the defendant give security, with one or more sureties, to appear when directed by the court or to comply with any order of court.

Adopted April 23, 1981, effective July 22, 1981.

Explanatory Comment—1981

Rule 1910.14 is a stylistic restatement of Section 6707(a) of the Judicial Code. The present practice is continued without change.

Rule 1910.15 Paternity

(a) **Acknowledgment of Paternity.** If the action seeks support for a child born out of wedlock and the alleged father is named as defendant, the defendant may acknowledge paternity in a verified writing. The conference officer shall advise the parties that pursuant to Section 5103(d) of Title 23 of the Pennsylvania Consolidated Statutes an acknowledgment constitutes conclusive evidence of defendant's paternity without further judicial ratification in any action to establish support. Upon defendant's execution of the written acknowledgment, the action shall proceed as in other actions for support.

(b) Genetic Testing. If the defendant appears but does not execute an acknowledgment of paternity at the conference:

(1) The court shall enter an order directing the parties to appear for genetic testing. The order must advise the defendant that his failure to appear for the testing will result in entry of an order finding that he is the father of the child. The order must also advise the plaintiff that her failure to appear for testing may result in sanctions, including entry of an order dismissing the paternity action without prejudice.

(2) The conference officer shall advise and provide written notice to the parties that they may enter into a written stipulation whereby both agree to submit to genetic testing for the purpose of resolving finally the issue of paternity. If the test results indicate a 99% or higher probability of paternity, the defendant shall be stipulated to be the biological father of the child and the case referred for a child support conference. If the test results indicate an exclusion, the action shall be dismissed. The written stipulation constitutes a waiver of the right to a hearing on the genetic testing or trial on the issue of paternity.

(3) The conference officer shall advise and provide written notice to the parties that if they do not enter into a written stipulation and the test results do not indicate an exclusion, there will be a hearing regarding genetic testing or trial before a judge without a jury on the issue of paternity in accordance with the procedures set forth in subdivision (d) of this Rule.

(c) Estoppel and Presumption of Paternity. If either party or the court raises the issue of estoppel or the issue of whether the presumption of paternity is applicable, the court shall dispose promptly of the issue and may stay the order for genetic testing until the issue is resolved.

(d) Post-Testing Procedures.

(1) The results of the genetic tests shall be provided in writing to counsel for the parties or, if unrepresented, to the parties themselves.

(2) If the results of the genetic tests resolve the issue of paternity pursuant to the stipulation of the parties, a paternity order shall be entered and served on the parties. If the defendant is excluded, the action shall be dismissed. If the defendant is stipulated to be the biological father, the action shall proceed as in other actions for support.

(3) If the results of the genetic tests do not resolve the issue of paternity pursuant to the stipulation of the parties but the test results indicate a 99% or more probability of paternity, the court shall issue a rule against the defendant to show cause why an order should not be entered finding him to be the father. The rule shall advise the defendant that pursuant to 23 Pa.C.S. § 4343 his defense is limited to a showing by clear and convincing evidence that the results of the genetic tests are not reliable. The rule shall direct that an answer be filed within 20 days after service of the rule on the defendant. The answer shall state the material facts which constitute this defense. Any allegation of fact which does not appear of record must be verified.

If an answer is not timely filed, the court shall enter an order finding paternity and refer the action to conference and hearing as in other actions for support. If an answer is filed raising a disputed issue of material fact relating to the reliability of the genetic testing, the case shall be listed promptly for expedited hearing before a judge. The burden of proof at the hearing is on the defendant and is limited to proof by clear and convincing evidence that the results of the genetic tests are not reliable.

(4) If the results of the genetic tests do not resolve the issue of paternity and the test results indicate less than a 99% probability of paternity, the case shall be promptly listed for expedited trial before a judge.

(5) If, after a hearing or trial, the decision is for the defendant on the issue of paternity, a final order shall be entered by the court dismissing the action as to the child. If the decision is against the defendant on the issue of paternity, an interlocutory order shall be entered by the court finding paternity. The court may enter an interim order for child support at that time and shall refer the action to conference and hearing as in other actions for support.

(e) **Failure to Appear.** If defendant fails to appear as ordered for a conference, hearing or trial, or for genetic tests, the court shall, upon proof of service on the defendant, enter an order establishing paternity. The court may also enter an interim order for child support at that time and shall refer the action to conference and hearing as in other actions for support.

(f) **Appeal of Paternity Order.** An order establishing paternity is not an appealable order. The issue of paternity may be included in an appeal from the final order of child support.

Adopted April 23, 1981, effective July 22, 1981. Amended Oct. 19, 1983, effective Jan. 1, 1984; March 30, 1994, effective July 1, 1994; March 24, 1997, effective July 1, 1997; May 31, 2000, effective July 1, 2000.

Explanatory Comment—2000

Rule 1910.15 is amended generally to reflect the elimination of jury trials in paternity actions. It has also been reorganized so that it more logically follows the six ways in which paternity may be established: 1) by voluntary acknowledgment under subdivision (a); 2) in the absence of an acknowledgment, by stipulation of the parties to be bound by the genetic test results under subdivision (b); 3) by estoppel under subdivision (c); 4) by operation of law or presumption under subdivision (c); 5) by a hearing regarding the reliability of genetic testing or a trial before a judge on the issue of paternity upon receipt of the test results under subdivision (d); or 6) by failing to appear for the initial conference, genetic testing, trial or hearing, which results in entry of a default order establishing paternity under subdivision (e).

Subdivision (d)(3) is new. In cases where there is no voluntary acknowledgment or stipulation by the parties, but the genetic test results reveal a 99% or higher probability of paternity, the Rule establishes expedited hearing procedures for resolving paternity prior to a full evidentiary trial before a judge. These procedures borrow heavily from the rule to show cause procedures set forth in Rules 206.1 through 206.7 except that 1) the plaintiff is not required to petition the court to have the rule issued and 2) the court must issue the rule whenever the test results indicate a 99% or higher probability of paternity. The burden is on the defendant to return the rule by filing an answer within 20 days of service. Pursuant to 23 Pa.C.S. § 4343(c)(2), his defense is limited to showing by clear and convincing evidence that the test results are not reliable.

The standard forms which were formerly required by this Rule to be used in paternity actions have been rescinded in light of the statewide implementation of the Pennsylvania Child Support Enforcement System (PACSES). All courts are now required to use the standard forms which appear on the PACSES system to the extent they are consistent with the Rules of Civil Procedure.

Rule 1910.16 Rescinded Dec. 28, 2018, Effective Jan. 1, 2019

Adopted April 23, 1981, effective July 22, 1981. Amended November 7, 1988, effective January 1, 1989; September 29, 1989, effective October 1, 1989; March 30, 1994, effective July 1, 1994; July 30, 2018, effective January 1, 2019; Rescinded, December 28, 2018, effective January 1, 2019.

Rule 1910.16-1. Amount of Support. Support Guidelines

(a) Applicability of the Support Guidelines.

(1) Except as provided in subdivision (3), the support guidelines determine the amount of support that a spouse or parent should pay based on the parties' combined monthly net income, as defined in Pa.R.C.P. No. 1910.16-2, and the number of persons being supported.

(2) If a person caring for or having custody of a minor child, who does not have a duty of support to the minor child, initiates a child support action as provided in Pa.R.C.P. No. 1910.3:

(i) the complaint shall identify the parent(s) as defendant(s);

(ii) in determining the basic child support amount, the monthly net income for the individual initiating the action shall not be considered in the support calculation by the trier of fact;

(iii) the parents' monthly net incomes shall be combined to determine the basic child support amount, which shall be apportioned based on the parents' respective monthly net incomes consistent with Pa.R.C.P. No. 1910.16-4. The parents shall pay the obligee their proportionate share of the basic child support amount as a separate obligor; and

(iv) as with other support actions, the trier of fact may make adjustments or deviations consistent with the support guidelines based on the evidence presented by the parties.

Example 1. The parents have one child, who is in the custody of the maternal grandmother. Maternal grandmother initiates a support action against the parents. Mother's monthly net income is $ 3,000 and Father's monthly net income is $ 2,000 for a combined monthly net income of $ 5,000. For purposes of the child support calculation, maternal grandmother's income is irrelevant and not part of the calculation. The basic child support obligation for one child at a combined monthly net income of $ 5,000 is $ 990 per month. Mother's percentage share of the combined monthly net income is 60% ($ 3,000/$ 5,000) and Father's percentage share of the combined monthly net income is 40% ($ 2,000/$ 5,000). Mother's preliminary monthly share of the child support obligation is $ 594 ($ 990 x 60%) and Father's preliminary monthly share of the child support obligation is $ 396 ($ 990 x 40%). Maternal grandmother is the obligee with Mother and Father as separate obligors owing $ 594 and $ 396 respectively to the maternal grandmother.

(3) In actions in which the plaintiff is a public body or private agency pursuant to Pa.R.C.P. No. 1910.3, the amount of the order shall be calculated under the guidelines based upon each obligor's monthly net income, as defined in Pa.R.C.P. No. 1910.16-2, with the public or private entity's income as zero. In such cases, each parent shall be treated as a separate

obligor and the parent's obligation will be based upon his or her own monthly net income without regard to the income of the other parent.

(i) The amount of basic child support owed to other children not in placement shall be deducted from each parent's monthly net income before calculating support for the child or children in placement, including the amount of direct support the guidelines assume will be provided by the custodial parent.

Example 2. Mother and Father have three children and do not live in the same household. Mother has primary custody of two children and monthly net income of $ 2,000 per month. Father's monthly net income is $ 3,000. The parties' third child is in foster care placement. Pursuant to the schedule in Pa.R.C.P. No. 1910.16-3, the basic child support amount for the two children with Mother is $ 1,415. As Father's income is 60% of the parties' combined monthly net income, his basic support obligation to Mother is $ 849 per month. The guidelines assume that Mother will provide $ 566 per month in direct expenditures to the two children in her home. The agency/obligee brings an action against each parent for the support of the child in placement. Father/obligor's income will be $ 2,151 for purposes of this calculation ($ 3,000 less $ 849 in support for the children with Mother). As the agency/obligee's income is zero, Father's support for the child in placement will be 100% of the schedule amount of basic support for one child at the $ 2,151 income level, or $ 509 per month. Mother/obligor's income will be $ 1,434 for purposes of this calculation ($ 2,000 less $ 566 in direct support to the children in her custody). Her support obligation will be 100% of the schedule amount for one child at that income level, or $ 348 per month.

Example 3. Mother and Father have two children in placement. Father owes child support of $ 500 per month for two children of a former marriage. At the same income levels as in Example 2, Father's income for determining his obligation to the children in placement would be $ 2,500 ($ 3,000 less $ 500 support for two children of prior marriage). His obligation to the agency would be $ 849 per month (100% of the schedule amount for two children at the $ 2,500 per month income level). Mother's income would not be diminished as she owes no other child support. She would owe $ 686 for the children in placement (100% of the schedule amount for two children at the $ 2,000 income level).

(ii) If the parents reside in the same household, their respective obligations to the children who remain in the household and are not in placement shall be calculated according to the guidelines, with the parent having the higher income as the obligor, and the calculated support amount shall be deducted from the parents' monthly net incomes for purposes of calculating support for the child(ren) in placement.

Example 4. Mother and Father have four children, two of whom are in placement. Mother's monthly net income is $ 4,000 and Father's is $ 3,000. The basic support amount for the two children in the home is $ 1,660, according to the schedule in Pa.R.C.P. No. 1910.16-3. As Mother's income is 57% of the parties' combined monthly net incomes, her share would be $ 946, and Father's 43% share would be $ 714. Mother's income for purposes of calculating support for the two children in placement would be $ 3,054 ($ 4,000 less $ 946). She would pay 100% of the basic child support at that income level, or $ 1,032, for the children in placement. Father's income would be $ 2,286 ($ 3,000 less $ 714) and his obligation to the children in placement would be $ 784.

(iii) In the event that the combined amount the parents are required to pay exceeds the cost of placement, the trier of fact shall deviate the support amount downward to reduce each parent's obligation in proportion to his or her share of the combined obligation.

(4) The support of a spouse or child is a priority obligation so that a party is expected to meet this obligation by adjusting his or her other expenditures.

(b) Support Amount. The support amount (child support, spousal support or alimony *pendente lite*) awarded pursuant to the Pa.R.C.P. Nos. 1910.11 and 1910.12 procedures must be determined in accordance with the support guidelines, which consist of the guidelines expressed as the child support schedule in Pa.R.C.P. No. 1910.16-3, the Pa.R.C.P. No. 1910.16-4 formulas, and the operation of the guidelines as set forth in these rules.

(c) Spousal Support and Alimony Pendente Lite.

(1) Spousal support and alimony *pendente lite* orders must not be in effect simultaneously.

(2) In determining a spousal support or alimony *pendente lite* award's duration, the trier-of-fact shall consider the marriage's duration, i.e., the date of marriage to the date of final separation.

(d) Rebuttable Presumption. If the trier-of-fact determines that a party has a duty to pay support, there is a rebuttable presumption that the guideline-calculated support amount is the correct support amount.

(1) The presumption is rebutted if the trier-of-fact concludes in a written finding or states on the record that the guideline support amount is unjust or inappropriate.

(2) The trier-of-fact shall consider the children's and parties' special needs and obligations, and apply the Pa.R.C.P. No. 1910.16-5 deviation factors, as appropriate.

(e) Guidelines Review. The guidelines must be reviewed at least every four years to ensure that their application determines appropriate support amounts.

Adopted September 6, 1989, effective September 30, 1989. Amended January 27, 1993, immediately effective; December 8, 1998, effective April 1, 1999; October 27, 2000, immediately effective; August 20, 2003, immediately effective September 27, 2005, effective in four months. [January 27, 2006]; January 12, 2010, effective May 12, 2010; April 9, 2013, effective August 9, 2013; February 10, 2017, effective May 1, 2017; August 3, 2017, effective October 1, 2017; December 28, 2018, effective January 1, 2019.

Explanatory Comment—2003

New subdivision (2) is intended to clarify in particular the calculation of child support when a child is in a foster care or institutional placement and not in the custody of either parent.

Explanatory Comment—2010

Introduction. Pennsylvania law requires that child and spousal support be awarded pursuant to a statewide guideline. 23 Pa.C.S. § 4322(a). That statute further provides that the guideline shall be "established by general rule by the Supreme Court, so that persons similarly situated shall be treated similarly." Id.

Pursuant to federal law, The Family Support Act of 1988 (P.L. 100-485, 102 Stat. 2343 (1988), all states are required to have statewide child support guidelines. Federal regulations, 45 C.F.R. § 302.56, further require that the guidelines be reviewed at least once every four years and that such reviews include an assessment of the most recent economic data on child-rearing costs and a review of data from case files to assure that deviations from the guidelines are limited.

The Pennsylvania statute also requires a review of the support guidelines every four years. 23 Pa.C.S.A. § 4322(a).

The Domestic Relations Procedural Rules Committee of the Supreme Court of Pennsylvania began the mandated review process in 2007. The committee was assisted in its work by Jane Venohr, Ph.D., an economist with the Center for Policy Research, under contract between the Pennsylvania Department of Public Welfare and Policy Studies, Inc. As a result of the review, the committee recommended to the Supreme Court several amendments to the statewide guidelines.

A. *Income Shares Model.* Pennsylvania's child support guidelines are based upon the Income Shares Model. That model was developed under the Child Support Guidelines Project funded by the U.S. Office of Child Support Enforcement and administered by the National Center for State Courts. The Guidelines Project Advisory Group recommended the Income Shares Model for state guidelines. At present, 37 states use the Income Shares Model as a basis for their child support guidelines.

The Income Shares Model is based upon the concept that the child of separated, divorced or never-married parents should receive the same proportion of parental income that she or he would have received if the parents lived together. A number of authoritative economic studies provide estimates of the average amount of household expenditures for children in intact households. These studies show that the proportion of household spending devoted to children is directly related to the level of household income and to the number of the children. The basic support amounts reflected in the schedule in Rule 1910.16-3 represent average marginal expenditures on children for food, housing, transportation, clothing and other miscellaneous items that are needed by children and provided by their parents, including the first $ 250 of unreimbursed medical expenses incurred annually per child.

1. *Economic Measures.* The support schedule in Rule 1910.16-3 is based upon child-rearing expenditures measured by David M. Betson, Ph.D., Professor of Economics, University of Notre Dame. Dr. Betson's measurements were developed for the U.S. Department of Health and Human Services for the explicit purpose of assisting states with the development and revision of child support guidelines. Dr. Betson's research also was used in developing the prior schedule, effective in January 2006. Dr. Betson updates his estimates using data from the Consumer Expenditure Survey conducted by the U.S. Bureau of Labor Statistics. In the current schedule, those figures were converted to 2008 price levels using the Consumer Price Index.

2. *Source of Data.* The estimates used to develop the schedule are based upon national data. The specific sources of the data are the periodic Consumer Expenditure Surveys. Those national surveys are used because they are the most detailed available source of data on household expenditures. The depth and quality of this information is simply not available at the state level and would be prohibitively costly to gather.

The U.S. Department of Agriculture's Center for Nutrition Policy and Promotion ("CNPP") also develops economic estimates for the major categories of child-rearing expenditures. Although the committee reviewed these estimates, it is aware of only one state that relies upon the CNPP estimates as a basis for its child support schedule, and even that state makes certain adjustments.

B. *Statutory Considerations.* The Pennsylvania statute, 23 Pa.C.S.A. § 4322(a), provides:

Child and spousal support shall be awarded pursuant to a Statewide guideline as established by general rule by the Supreme Court, so that persons similarly situated shall be treated similarly. The guideline shall be based upon the reasonable needs of the child or spouse seeking support and the ability of the obligor to provide support. In determining the reasonable needs of the child or spouse seeking support and the ability of the obligor to provide support, the guideline shall place primary emphasis on the net incomes and earning capacities of the parties, with allowable deviations for unusual needs, extraordinary expenses and other factors, such as the parties' assets, as warrant special attention. The guideline so developed shall be reviewed at least once every four years.

1. *Reasonable Needs and Reasonable Ability to Provide Support.* The guidelines make financial support of a child a primary obligation and assume that parties with similar net incomes will have similar reasonable and necessary expenses. After the basic needs of the parents have been met, the child's needs shall receive priority. The guidelines assume that if the obligor's net income is at the poverty level, he or she is barely able to provide for his or her own basic needs. In those cases, therefore, the entry of a minimal order may be appropriate after considering the party's living expenses. In some cases, it may not be appropriate to enter a support order at all. In most cases, however, a party's living expenses are not relevant in determining his or her support obligation. Rather, as the statute requires, the obligation is based upon the reasonable needs of a dependent spouse or child and the reasonable ability of the obligor to pay.

2. *Net Income.* The guidelines use the net incomes of the parties. Each parent is required to contribute to a share of the child's reasonable needs in proportion to that parent's share of the combined net income. The custodial parent makes these contributions through direct expenditures for food, shelter, clothing, transportation and other reasonable needs. The non-custodial parent makes contributions through periodic support payments to the custodial parent. Rule 1910.16-2(d) has been amended to clarify the provisions relating to income and earning capacity.

3. *Allowable Deviations.* The guidelines are designed to treat similarly situated parents, spouses and children in the same manner. However, when there are unavoidable differences, deviations must be made from the guidelines. Failure to deviate from these guidelines by considering a party's actual expenditures where there are special needs and special circumstances constitutes a misapplication of the guidelines.

C. **Child Support Schedule**. The child support schedule in Rule 1910.16-3 has been amended to reflect updated economic data, as required by federal and state law, to ensure that children continue to receive adequate levels of support. The support amounts in the schedule have been expanded to apply to a combined net monthly income of $ 30,000 and remain statistically valid. The economic data support the revised schedule.

D. **Self-Support Reserve ("SSR")**. The amended schedule also incorporates an increase in the "Self-Support Reserve" or "SSR" from $ 748 per month to $ 867 per month, the 2008 federal poverty level for one person. Formerly designated as the "Computed Allowance Minimum" or "CAM," the Self-Support Reserve, as it is termed in most other states' guidelines, is intended to assure that low-income obligors retain sufficient income to meet their own basic needs, as well as to maintain the incentive to continue employment. The SSR is built into the schedule in Rule 1910.16-3 and adjusts the basic support obligation to prevent the obligor's net income from falling below $ 867 per month. Because the schedule in Rule 1910.16-3 applies to child support only, Rule 1910.16-2(e)(1)(B) provides for a similar adjustment in spousal support and alimony pendente lite cases to assure that the obligor retains a minimum of $ 867 per month.

E. **Shared Custody**. In creating the new schedule, the amounts of basic child support were first increased to reflect updated economic data, including 2008 price levels. Next, the amounts of basic child support were adjusted to incorporate into the schedule the assumption that the children spend 30% of the time with the obligor and that the obligor makes direct expenditures on their behalf during that time. That does not mean that the entire schedule was reduced by 30%.

Only those variable expenditures, such as food and entertainment, that fluctuate based upon parenting time were adjusted.

The calculation in Rule 1910.16-4(c) reduces an obligor's support obligation further if the obligor spends significantly more time with the children. The revised schedule assumes that the obligor has 30% parenting time. The obligor will receive an additional 10% reduction in the amount of support owed at 40% parenting time, increasing incrementally to a 20% reduction at 50% parenting time. This method may still result in a support obligation even if custody of the children is equally shared. In those cases, the rule provides for a maximum obligation which may reduce the obligation so that the obligee does not receive a larger portion of the parties' combined income than the obligor.

F. *Child Care Expenses*. Rule 1910.16-6(a) was amended in 2006 to provide that child care expenses incurred by both parties shall be apportioned between the parties in recognition of the fact that a non-custodial parent also may incur such expenses during his or her custodial periods with the children.

G. S*pousal Support and Alimony Pendente Lite*. Subdivision (c) has been amended to require the court to consider the duration of the marriage in determining the duration of a spousal support or alimony pendente lite award. The language was moved from Rule 1910.16-5 which deals with deviation. The primary purpose of this provision is to prevent the unfairness that arises in a short-term marriage when the obligor is required to pay support over a substantially longer period of time than the parties were married and there is little or no opportunity for credit for these payments at the time of equitable distribution.

H. Other Amendments. All of the examples in the guidelines have been updated to reflect the changes to the basic child support schedule. Prior explanatory comments have been deleted or revised and incorporated into new comments.

Explanatory Comment—2013

The schedule of basic child support has been updated to reflect newer economic data. The schedule was prepared by Jane Venohr, Ph.D., the economist who assisted in the last guideline review using the same methodology. It includes an increase in the Self-Support Reserve to $ 931 per month, the 2012 federal poverty level for one person.

Explanatory Comment—2017

Pursuant to Pa.R.C.P. No. 1910.3(a), a person having custody of a child or caring for a child may initiate a support action against the child's parent(s). Previously, this rule only addressed when a public body or private agency had custody of a child but was silent with regard to an individual third party, e.g., grandparent, seeking support. The rule has been amended by adding a new subdivision (a)(2) and renumbering the previous (a)(2) to (a)(3). In addition, an example illustrating the new (a)(2) calculation has been included.

Subdivision (a)(2) excludes the income of the third party/obligee, as that person does not have a duty of support to the child; instead, the rule uses the combined monthly net income of the parents to determine the basic child support amount, which is then apportioned between the parents consistent with their respective percentage of the combined monthly net income in the same manner as a parent vs. parent support action. However, under this rule, each parent would be a separate obligor, would pay the obligee their proportionate share under a separate support order, and would be subject to separate enforcement proceedings. Under (a)(2), the exclusion of the third party's income is consistent with Pa.R.C.P. No. 1910.16-2(b)(2)(ii) as that rule relates to an action for support by a third party against a surviving parent in which the child receives a Social Security derivative benefit due to the death of the other parent.

In accordance with Pa.R.C.P. No. 1910.16-6(c), payment of the first $ 250 of unreimbursed medical expenses per year per child is applicable to third party/obligees in support actions governed by (a)(2). The first $ 250 of unreimbursed medical expenses is built into the Basic Child Support Schedule.

In accordance with Pa.R.C.P. No. 1910.16-6(c), payment of the first $250 of unreimbursed medical expenses per year per child is applicable to third party/obligees in support actions governed by (a)(2). The first $250 of unreimbursed medical expenses is built into the Basic Child Support Schedule.

Rule 1910.16-2. Support Guidelines. Calculation of Monthly Net Income

Generally, the support amount awarded is based on the parties' monthly net income.

(a) *Monthly Gross Income.* Monthly gross income is ordinarily based on at least a six-month average of a party's income. The support law, 23 Pa.C.S. § 4302, defines the term "income" and includes income from any source. The statute lists many types of income including, but not limited to:

 (1) wages, salaries, bonuses, fees, and commissions;

 (2) net income from business or dealings in property;

 (3) interest, rents, royalties, and dividends;

 (4) pensions and all forms of retirement;

 (5) income from an interest in an estate or trust;

 (6) Social Security disability benefits, Social Security retirement benefits, temporary and permanent disability benefits, workers' compensation, and unemployment compensation;

 (7) alimony if, in the trier-of-fact's discretion, inclusion of part or all of it is appropriate; and

Note: In determining the appropriateness of including alimony in gross income, the trier-of-fact shall consider whether the party receiving the alimony must include the amount received as gross income when filing his or her federal income taxes. If the alimony is not includable in the party's gross income for federal income tax purposes, the trier-of-fact may include in the party's monthly net income the alimony received, as appropriate. *See* Pa.R.C.P. No. 1910.16-2(c)(2)(ii).

Since the reasons for ordering payment of alimony vary, the appropriateness of including it in the recipient's gross income must also vary. For example, if the obligor is paying $ 1,000 per month in alimony for the express purpose of financing the obligee's college education, it would be inappropriate to consider that alimony as income from which the obligee could provide child support. However, if alimony is intended to finance the obligee's general living expenses, inclusion of the alimony as income is appropriate.

 (8) other entitlements to money or lump sum awards, without regard to source, including:

  (i) lottery winnings;

  (ii) income tax refunds;

  (iii) insurance compensation or settlements;

  (iv) awards and verdicts; and

(v) payments due to and collectible by an individual regardless of source.

Note: The trier-of-fact determines the most appropriate method for imputing lump-sum awards as income for purposes of establishing or modifying the party's support obligation. These awards may be annualized or averaged over a shorter or longer period depending on the case's circumstances. The trier-of-fact may order all or part of the lump sum award escrowed to secure the support obligation during that period.

The trier-of-fact shall not include income tax refunds in a party's income, if the trier-of-fact factored in the tax refund when calculating the party's actual tax obligation and monthly net income.

(b) *Treatment of Public Assistance, SSI Benefits, Social Security Payments to a Child Due to a Parent's Death, Disability or Retirement and Foster Care Payments.*

(1) *Public Assistance and SSI Benefits.* Neither public assistance nor Supplemental Security Income (SSI) benefits shall be included as income for determining support.

(2) *Child's Social Security Derivative Benefits.*

(i) If a child is receiving Social Security derivative benefits due to a parent's retirement or disability:

(A) The trier-of-fact shall determine the basic child support amount as follows:

(I) add the child's benefit to the monthly net income of the party who receives the child's benefit;

(II) calculate the parties' combined monthly net income, including the child's benefit;

(III) determine the basic child support amount set forth in the Pa.R.C.P. No. 1910.16-3 schedule; and

(IV) apportion the basic child support amount between the parties based on the party's percentage of the combined monthly net income.

(B) If the obligee receives the child's benefit, the trier-of-fact shall deduct the child's benefit from the basic support obligation of the party whose retirement or disability created the child's benefit.

(C) If the obligor receives the child's benefit, the trier-of-fact shall not deduct the child's benefit from the obligor's basic support obligation, even if the obligor's retirement or disability created the child's benefit. To illustrate for the parties the impact of the obligor receiving the benefit instead of the obligee, the domestic relations section shall provide the parties with two calculations theoretically assigning the benefit to each household.

(D) The trier-of-fact shall allocate the additional expenses in Pa.R.C.P. No. 1910.16-6 based on the parties' monthly net incomes without considering the child's benefit.

(E) In equally shared custody cases, the party with the higher monthly net income, excluding the child's benefit, is the obligor.

(ii) If a child is receiving Social Security derivative benefits due to a parent's death:

(A) The trier-of-fact shall determine the surviving parent's basic child support amount as follows:

(I) The non-parent obligee's monthly net income shall include only those funds the obligee is receiving on the child's behalf, including the Social Security derivative benefit.

(II) If the surviving-parent obligor receives the Social Security derivative benefit, the benefit shall be added to the parent's monthly net income to calculate child support.

(3) *Foster Care Payments.* If either party to a support action is a foster parent and/or is receiving payments from a public or private agency for the care of a child who is not his or her biological or adoptive child, those payments shall not be included in the income of the foster parent or other caretaker for purposes of calculating child support for the foster parent's or other caretaker's biological or adoptive child.

Example 1. The obligor has monthly net income of $ 2,000. The obligee's monthly net income is $ 1,500 and the obligee, as primary custodial parent of the parties' two children, receives $ 700 per month in Social Security derivative benefits on behalf of the children as a result of the obligor's disability. Add the children's benefit to the obligee's income, which now is $ 2,200 per month. At the parties' combined monthly net income of $ 4,200, the amount of basic child support for two children is $ 1,301. As the obligor's income is 48% of the parties' combined monthly net income, the obligor's preliminary share of the basic support obligation is $ 624. However, because the obligor's disability created the children's Social Security derivative benefits that the obligee is receiving, the obligor's obligation is reduced by the amount of the benefit, $ 700. As the support amount cannot be less than zero, the obligor's support obligation is $ 0 per month. If it were the obligee's disability that created the benefit, the obligor's support obligation would remain $ 624. If the obligor were receiving the children's benefit as a result of the obligor's retirement or disability, the obligor's income would include the amount of the benefit and total $ 2,700, or 64% of the parties' combined monthly net income. The obligor's share of the basic support obligation would then be $ 833 and would not be reduced by the amount of the children's benefit because the obligor, not the obligee, is receiving the benefit. Therefore, the obligor's support obligation is less if the obligee is receiving the benefit created by the obligor.

Example 2. Two children live with Grandmother who receives $ 800 per month in Social Security death benefits for the children as a result of Father's death. Grandmother also receives $ 500 per month from a trust established by Father for the benefit of the children. Grandmother is employed and earns $ 2,000 net per month. Grandmother seeks support from the children's mother, who earns $ 2,000 net per month. For purposes of calculating Mother's support obligation, Grandmother's income will be $ 1,300, the amount she receives on behalf of the children in Social Security derivative benefits and the income from the trust. (If Mother were receiving the benefit on behalf of the children it would be added to her income such that Mother's income would be $ 2,800 and Grandmother's income would be $ 500.) Therefore, Mother's and Grandmother's combined monthly net incomes total $ 3,300. The basic support amount at the $ 3,300 income level for two children is $ 1,115. As Mother's income of $ 2,000 is 61% of the parties' combined income of $ 3,300, her portion of the basic support obligation is $ 680. Since Mother's retirement or disability did not generate the child's derivative benefit, the benefit amount is not subtracted from her portion of the basic support amount and Mother owes Grandmother $ 680. If Grandmother was not receiving the children's derivative benefits or income from the trust, her income for purposes of calculating Mother's child support obligation would be zero, and Mother would pay 100% of the basic support amount because Grandmother has no duty to support the children.

Note: Care must be taken to distinguish Social Security from Supplemental Security Income (SSI) benefits. Social Security benefits are income pursuant to subdivision (a) of this rule.

(c) *Monthly Net Income.*

(1) Unless these rules provide otherwise, the trier-of-fact shall deduct only the following items from monthly gross income to arrive at monthly net income:

(i) federal, state, and local income taxes;

(ii) unemployment compensation taxes and Local Services Taxes (LST);

(iii) F.I.C.A. payments (Social Security, Medicare and Self-Employment taxes) and non-voluntary retirement payments;

(iv) mandatory union dues; and

(v) alimony paid to the other party.

(2) In computing a spousal support or alimony *pendente lite* obligation, the trier-of-fact shall:

(i) deduct from the obligor's monthly net income child support, spousal support, alimony *pendente lite,* or alimony amounts paid to children and former spouses, who are not part of this action; and

(ii) include in a party's monthly net income alimony *pendente lite* or alimony received from a former spouse that was not included in the party's gross income, as provided in subdivision (a).

Note: Since the reasons for ordering payment of alimony vary, the appropriateness of including it in the recipient's monthly net income must also vary. For example, if the obligor is paying $ 1,000 per month in alimony for the express purpose of financing the obligee's college education, it would be inappropriate to consider that alimony as income from which the obligee could provide child support. However, if alimony is intended to finance the obligee's general living expenses, inclusion of the alimony as income is appropriate.

(d) *Reduced or Fluctuating Income.*

(1) *Voluntary Reduction of Income.* When either party voluntarily assumes a lower paying job, quits a job, leaves employment, changes occupations or changes employment status to pursue an education, or is fired for cause, there generally will be no effect on the support obligation.

(2) *Involuntary Reduction of, and Fluctuations in, Income.* No adjustments in support payments will be made for normal fluctuations in earnings. However, appropriate adjustments will be made for substantial continuing involuntary decreases in income, including but not limited to the result of illness, lay-off, termination, job elimination or some other employment situation over which the party has no control unless the trier of fact finds that such a reduction in income was willfully undertaken in an attempt to avoid or reduce the support obligation.

(3) *Seasonal Employees.* Support orders for seasonal employees, such as construction workers, shall ordinarily be based upon a yearly average.

(4) *Earning Capacity.* If the trier of fact determines that a party to a support action has willfully failed to obtain or maintain appropriate employment, the trier of fact may impute to that party an income equal to the party's earning capacity. Age, education, training, health, work

experience, earnings history and child care responsibilities are factors which shall be considered in determining earning capacity. In order for an earning capacity to be assessed, the trier of fact must state the reasons for the assessment in writing or on the record. Generally, the trier of fact should not impute an earning capacity that is greater than the amount the party would earn from one full-time position. Determination of what constitutes a reasonable work regimen depends upon all relevant circumstances including the choice of jobs available within a particular occupation, working hours, working conditions and whether a party has exerted substantial good faith efforts to find employment.

(e) *Net Income Affecting Application of the Support Guidelines.*

(1) *Low-Income Cases.*

(i) If the obligor's monthly net income and corresponding number of children fall into the shaded area of the schedule set forth in Pa.R.C.P. No. 1910.16-3, the basic child support obligation shall be calculated initially by using the obligor's monthly net income only. For example, if the obligor has monthly net income of $ 1,100, the presumptive support amount for three children is $ 110 per month. This amount is determined directly from the schedule in Pa.R.C.P. No. 1910.16-3. Next, the obligor's child support obligation is calculated by using the parties' combined monthly net incomes and the appropriate formula in Pa.R.C.P. No. 1910.16-4. The lower of the two calculated amounts shall be the obligor's basic child support obligation.

Example 1. The parties have two children. The obligor has monthly net income of $ 1,500, which falls into the shaded area of the schedule for two children. Using only the obligor's monthly net income, the amount of support for two children would be $ 472. Next, calculate support using the parties' combined monthly net incomes. The obligee has monthly net income of $ 2,500 so the combined monthly net income of the parties is $ 4,000. The basic child support amount at that income level for two children is $ 1,269. As the obligor's income is 38% of the combined monthly net income of the parties, the obligor's share of the basic support amount is $ 482. As the amount of support the obligor would pay using only the obligor's income is less than the amount calculated using the parties' combined monthly net incomes, the lower amount would be awarded, and the obligor's basic child support obligation would be $ 472.

(ii) In computing a basic spousal support or alimony *pendente lite* obligation, the presumptive support amount shall not reduce the obligor's monthly net income below the Self-Support Reserve of $ 981 per month.

Example 2. If the obligor earns $ 1,000 per month and the obligee earns $ 300 per month, the formula in Pa.R.C.P. No. 1910.16-4(a)(1)(Part B) would result in a support obligation of $ 213 per month (($ 1,000 x 33%) or $ 333 minus ($ 300 x 40%) or $ 120 for a total of $ 213). Since this amount leaves the obligor with only $ 787 per month, it must be adjusted so that the obligor retains at least $ 981 per month. The presumptive minimum spousal support amount, therefore, is $ 19 per month in this case.

(iii) If the obligor's monthly net income is $ 981 or less, the trier-of-fact may award support only after consideration of the parties' actual financial resources and living expenses.

(2) *High-Income Cases.* If the parties' combined monthly net income exceeds $ 30,000 per month, child support, spousal support, and alimony *pendente lite* calculations shall be pursuant to Pa.R.C.P. No. 1910.16-3.1.

Note: *See Hanrahan v. Bakker*, 186 A.3d 958 (Pa. 2018).

(f) *Child Tax Credit.* **In order to maximize the total income available to the parties and children, the trier-of-fact may award, as appropriate, the federal child tax credit to the non-custodial parent, or to either parent in cases of equally shared custody, and order the other party to execute the waiver required by the Internal Revenue Code, 26 U.S.C. § 152(e). The tax consequences associated with the federal child tax credit must be considered in calculating the party's monthly net income available for support.**

Adopted December 8, 1998, effective April 1, 1999. Amended October 27, 2000, immediately effective; October 30, 2001, immediately effective; November 9, 2004, immediately effective; September 27, 2005, effective in four months. [January 27, 2006]; January 5, 2010, immediately effective; January 12, 2010, effective May 12, 2010; August 26, 2011, effective September 30, 2011; November 5, 2012, effective December 5, 2012; April 9, 2013, effective August 9, 2013; April 29, 2015, effective July 1, 2015; February 10, 2017, effective May 1, 2017; February 9, 2018, effective April 1, 2018; December 28, 2018, effective January 1, 2019.

Explanatory Comment—2010

Subdivision (a) addresses gross income for purposes of calculating the support obligation by reference to the statutory definition at 23 Pa.C.S. § 4322. Subdivision (b) provides for the treatment of public assistance, SSI benefits, Social Security derivative benefits, and foster care payments.

Subdivision (c) sets forth the exclusive list of the deductions that may be taken from gross income in arriving at a party's net income. When the cost of health insurance premiums is treated as an additional expense subject to allocation between the parties under Pa.R.C.P. No. 1910.16-6, it is not deductible from gross income. However, part or all of the cost of health insurance premiums may be deducted from the obligor's gross income pursuant to Pa.R.C.P. No. 1910.16-6(b) in cases in which the obligor is paying the premiums and the obligee has no income or minimal income. Subdivision (c) relates to spousal support or alimony *pendente lite* awards when there are multiple families. In these cases, a party's monthly net income must be reduced to account for his or her child support obligations, as well as any pre-existing spousal support, alimony *pendente lite* or alimony obligations being paid to former spouses who are not the subject of the support action.

Subdivision (d) has been amended to clarify the distinction between voluntary and involuntary changes in income and the imputing of earning capacity. Statutory provisions at 23 Pa.C.S. § 4322, as well as case law, are clear that a support obligation is based upon the ability of a party to pay, and that the concept of an earning capacity is intended to reflect a realistic, rather than a theoretical, ability to pay support. Amendments to subdivision (d) are intended to clarify when imposition of an earning capacity is appropriate.

Subdivision (e) has been amended to reflect the updated schedule in Pa.R.C.P. No. 1910.16-3 and the increase in the Self-Support Reserve ("SSR"). The schedule now applies to all cases in which the parties' combined monthly net income is $ 30,000 or less. The upper income limit of the prior schedule was only $ 20,000. The support amount at each income level of the schedule also has changed, so the examples in Pa.R.C.P. No. 1910.16-2 were revised to be consistent with the new support amounts.

The SSR is intended to assure that obligors with low incomes retain sufficient income to meet their basic needs and to maintain the incentive to continue employment. When the obligor's monthly net income or earning capacity falls into the shaded area of the schedule, the basic child support obligation can be derived directly from the schedule in Pa.R.C.P. No. 1910.16-3. There is no need to use the formula in Pa.R.C.P. No. 1910.16-4 to calculate the obligor's support obligation because the SSR keeps the amount of the obligation the same regardless of the obligee's income. The obligee's income may be a relevant factor, however, in determining whether to deviate from the basic guideline obligation pursuant to Pa.R.C.P. No. 1910.16-5 and in considering whether to require the obligor to contribute to any additional expenses under Pa.R.C.P. No. 1910.16-6.

Since the schedule in Pa.R.C.P. No. 1910.16-3 sets forth basic child support only, subdivision (e)(1)(ii) is necessary to reflect the operation of the SSR in spousal support and alimony *pendente lite* cases. It adjusts the basic guideline obligation, which would otherwise be calculated under the formula in Pa.R.C.P. No. 1910.16-4, so that the obligor's income does not fall below the SSR amount in these cases.

Previously, the SSR required that the obligor retain at least $ 748 per month. The SSR now requires that the obligor retain income of at least $ 867 per month, an amount equal to the 2008 federal poverty level for one person. When the obligor's monthly net income is less than $ 867, subdivision (e)(1)(iii) provides that the trier-of-fact must consider the parties' actual living expenses before awarding support. The guidelines assume that at this income level the obligor is barely able to meet basic personal needs. In these cases, therefore, entry of a minimal order may be appropriate. In some cases, it may not be appropriate to order support at all.

The schedule at Pa.R.C.P. No. 1910.16-3 sets forth the presumptive amount of basic child support to be awarded. If the circumstances warrant, the trier-of-fact may deviate from that amount under Pa.R.C.P. No. 1910.16-5 and may also consider a party's contribution to additional expenses, which are typically added to the basic amount of support under Pa.R.C.P. No. 1910.16-6. If, for example, the obligor earns only $ 900 per month but is living with his or her parents, or has remarried and is living with a fully-employed spouse, the trier-of-fact may consider an upward deviation under Pa.R.C.P. No. 1910.16-5(b)(3) or may order the party to contribute to the additional expenses under Pa.R.C.P. No. 1910.16-6. Consistent with the goals of the SSR, however, the trier-of-fact should ensure that the overall support obligation leaves the obligor with sufficient income to meet basic personal needs and to maintain the incentive to continue working so that support can be paid.

Subdivision (e) also has been amended to eliminate the application of *Melzer v. Witsberger*, 480 A.2d 991 (Pa. 1984), in high-income child support cases. In cases in which the parties' combined net monthly income exceeds $ 30,000, child support will be calculated in accordance with the three-step process in Pa.R.C.P. No. 1910.16-3.1(a).

Explanatory Comment—2013

The SSR has been increased to $ 931, the 2012 federal poverty level for one person. Subdivision (e) has been amended to require that when the obligor's income falls into the shaded area of the basic child support schedule in Pa.R.C.P. No. 1910.16-3, two calculations must be performed. One calculation uses only the obligor's income and the other is a regular calculation using both parties' incomes, awarding the lower amount to the obligee. The two-step process is intended to address those cases in which the obligor has minimal income and the obligee's income is substantially greater.

Explanatory Comment—2015

The rule has been amended to provide that a party's support obligation will be reduced by the child's Social Security derivative benefit amount if that party's retirement or disability created the benefit and the benefit is being paid to the household in which the child primarily resides or the obligee in cases of equally shared custody. In most cases, payment of the benefit to the obligee's household will increase the resources available to the child and the parties. The rule is intended to encourage parties to direct that the child's benefits be paid to the obligee.

Rule 1910.16-3. Support Guidelines. Basic Child Support Schedule.

The following schedule represents the amounts spent on children of intact families by combined monthly net income and number of children. Combined monthly net income is on the schedule's vertical axis and the number of children is on the schedule's horizontal axis. This schedule determines the basic child support obligation. Unless these rules provide otherwise, the obligor's share of the basic support obligation shall be computed using either the formula set forth in Pa.R.C.P. No. 1910.16-4(a)(1)(Part C) or (2)(Part I).

Rule 1910.16-3   ACTIONS FOR SUPPORT

Monthly Basic Child Support Schedule

COMBINED MONTHLY NET INCOME	ONE CHILD	TWO CHILDREN	THREE CHILDREN	FOUR CHILDREN	FIVE CHILDREN	SIX CHILDREN
1000	17	17	18	18	18	18
1050	62	63	64	64	65	66
1100	107	108	110	111	112	113
1150	152	154	156	157	159	161
1200	197	199	202	204	206	208
1250	242	245	248	250	253	256
1300	287	290	294	297	300	303
1350	325	336	340	343	347	351
1400	336	381	386	390	394	398
1450	348	427	432	436	441	446
1500	360	472	478	483	488	493
1550	372	518	524	529	535	541
1600	383	555	570	576	582	588
1650	395	571	616	622	629	636
1700	407	588	662	669	676	683
1750	418	605	708	715	723	731
1800	430	621	730	762	770	778
1850	441	638	748	808	817	826
1900	452	654	767	855	864	873
1950	464	670	786	878	911	921
2000	475	686	805	899	958	968
2050	487	703	824	920	1005	1016
2100	498	719	843	941	1035	1063

Monthly Basic Child Support Schedule

COMBINED MONTHLY NET INCOME	ONE CHILD	TWO CHILDREN	THREE CHILDREN	FOUR CHILDREN	FIVE CHILDREN	SIX CHILDREN
2150	509	735	861	962	1058	1111
2200	521	751	880	983	1081	1158
2250	532	768	899	1004	1105	1201
2300	543	784	918	1025	1128	1226
2350	555	800	937	1046	1151	1251
2400	566	816	956	1067	1174	1276
2450	578	832	974	1088	1197	1301
2500	589	849	993	1109	1220	1326
2550	600	865	1012	1131	1244	1352
2600	612	882	1032	1153	1268	1378
2650	623	898	1052	1175	1292	1404
2700	635	915	1071	1197	1316	1431
2750	647	932	1091	1218	1340	1457
2800	658	949	1111	1240	1364	1483
2850	670	965	1130	1262	1389	1509
2900	681	982	1150	1284	1413	1536
2950	693	999	1169	1306	1437	1562
3000	704	1015	1189	1328	1461	1588
3050	716	1032	1209	1350	1485	1614
3100	727	1049	1228	1372	1509	1641
3150	739	1065	1248	1394	1534	1667
3200	751	1082	1268	1416	1558	1693
3250	762	1099	1287	1438	1582	1719

Rule 1910.16-3

Monthly Basic Child Support Schedule

COMBINED MONTHLY NET INCOME	ONE CHILD	TWO CHILDREN	THREE CHILDREN	FOUR CHILDREN	FIVE CHILDREN	SIX CHILDREN
3300	774	1115	1307	1460	1606	1745
3350	782	1127	1320	1475	1622	1763
3400	791	1140	1333	1489	1638	1781
3450	800	1152	1347	1504	1655	1799
3500	809	1164	1360	1519	1671	1817
3550	818	1176	1373	1534	1687	1834
3600	827	1188	1387	1549	1704	1852
3650	836	1200	1400	1564	1720	1870
3700	845	1212	1413	1579	1737	1888
3750	853	1224	1427	1594	1753	1905
3800	862	1236	1440	1608	1769	1923
3850	868	1245	1450	1620	1782	1937
3900	873	1253	1460	1630	1793	1949
3950	879	1261	1469	1641	1805	1962
4000	884	1269	1479	1652	1817	1975
4050	890	1277	1488	1662	1829	1988
4100	895	1285	1498	1673	1840	2001
4150	900	1293	1508	1684	1852	2013
4200	906	1301	1517	1695	1864	2026
4250	911	1309	1527	1705	1876	2039
4300	917	1317	1536	1716	1888	2052
4350	922	1325	1545	1726	1899	2064
4400	928	1333	1555	1736	1910	2076

Pa. R.C.P.   Rule 1910.16-3

Monthly Basic Child Support Schedule

COMBINED MONTHLY NET INCOME	ONE CHILD	TWO CHILDREN	THREE CHILDREN	FOUR CHILDREN	FIVE CHILDREN	SIX CHILDREN
4450	934	1341	1564	1747	1921	2088
4500	940	1349	1573	1757	1932	2100
4550	946	1357	1582	1767	1943	2113
4600	952	1365	1591	1777	1955	2125
4650	957	1373	1600	1787	1966	2137
4700	963	1381	1609	1797	1977	2149
4750	969	1389	1618	1807	1988	2161
4800	975	1397	1627	1817	1999	2173
4850	979	1403	1633	1824	2006	2181
4900	983	1407	1637	1828	2011	2186
4950	986	1411	1641	1833	2016	2191
5000	990	1415	1644	1837	2020	2196
5050	993	1419	1648	1841	2025	2201
5100	996	1423	1652	1845	2030	2206
5150	1000	1427	1656	1850	2034	2211
5200	1003	1431	1660	1854	2039	2217
5250	1007	1436	1663	1858	2044	2222
5300	1010	1440	1667	1862	2049	2227
5350	1014	1445	1672	1868	2055	2234
5400	1018	1451	1679	1876	2063	2243
5450	1022	1457	1686	1883	2072	2252
5500	1027	1463	1693	1891	2080	2261
5550	1031	1469	1700	1899	2089	2270

Rule 1910.16-3   ACTIONS FOR SUPPORT

Monthly Basic Child Support Schedule

COMBINED MONTHLY NET INCOME	ONE CHILD	TWO CHILDREN	THREE CHILDREN	FOUR CHILDREN	FIVE CHILDREN	SIX CHILDREN
5600	1036	1475	1707	1906	2097	2279
5650	1040	1481	1714	1914	2105	2289
5700	1044	1487	1720	1922	2114	2298
5750	1049	1493	1727	1929	2122	2307
5800	1053	1499	1734	1937	2131	2316
5850	1057	1505	1741	1945	2139	2325
5900	1062	1511	1748	1952	2148	2334
5950	1066	1517	1755	1960	2156	2343
6000	1071	1523	1761	1968	2164	2353
6050	1075	1529	1768	1975	2173	2362
6100	1079	1536	1775	1983	2181	2371
6150	1085	1542	1783	1992	2191	2381
6200	1090	1549	1791	2000	2200	2392
6250	1095	1556	1798	2009	2210	2402
6300	1100	1563	1806	2017	2219	2412
6350	1105	1570	1814	2026	2228	2422
6400	1110	1577	1821	2034	2238	2432
6450	1115	1584	1829	2043	2247	2443
6500	1120	1591	1836	2051	2256	2453
6550	1125	1598	1844	2060	2266	2463
6600	1130	1605	1852	2068	2275	2473
6650	1135	1612	1859	2077	2285	2483
6700	1140	1619	1867	2085	2294	2494

Monthly Basic Child Support Schedule

COMBINED MONTHLY NET INCOME	ONE CHILD	TWO CHILDREN	THREE CHILDREN	FOUR CHILDREN	FIVE CHILDREN	SIX CHILDREN
6750	1145	1625	1875	2094	2303	2504
6800	1151	1632	1882	2103	2313	2514
6850	1156	1639	1890	2111	2322	2524
6900	1160	1646	1898	2120	2332	2535
6950	1165	1653	1906	2129	2342	2546
7000	1170	1660	1914	2138	2352	2556
7050	1175	1667	1922	2147	2361	2567
7100	1180	1674	1930	2156	2371	2578
7150	1185	1681	1938	2165	2381	2588
7200	1190	1687	1946	2173	2391	2599
7250	1195	1694	1954	2182	2401	2609
7300	1199	1701	1962	2191	2410	2620
7350	1204	1708	1970	2200	2420	2631
7400	1209	1715	1978	2209	2430	2641
7450	1214	1722	1986	2218	2440	2652
7500	1219	1729	1994	2227	2450	2663
7550	1224	1736	2002	2236	2459	2673
7600	1229	1743	2010	2245	2469	2684
7650	1233	1749	2017	2253	2478	2694
7700	1238	1756	2024	2261	2487	2704
7750	1243	1762	2032	2269	2496	2714
7800	1248	1769	2039	2278	2505	2723
7850	1253	1776	2046	2286	2514	2733

Rule 1910.16-3 — ACTIONS FOR SUPPORT

Monthly Basic Child Support Schedule

COMBINED MONTHLY NET INCOME	ONE CHILD	TWO CHILDREN	THREE CHILDREN	FOUR CHILDREN	FIVE CHILDREN	SIX CHILDREN
7900	1257	1782	2054	2294	2523	2743
7950	1262	1789	2061	2302	2532	2753
8000	1267	1795	2068	2310	2541	2762
8050	1272	1802	2076	2319	2550	2772
8100	1276	1808	2083	2327	2559	2782
8150	1281	1815	2090	2335	2568	2792
8200	1286	1822	2098	2343	2577	2802
8250	1291	1828	2105	2351	2586	2811
8300	1296	1835	2112	2359	2595	2821
8350	1300	1841	2120	2368	2604	2831
8400	1305	1848	2127	2376	2613	2841
8450	1310	1854	2134	2384	2622	2850
8500	1315	1861	2142	2392	2631	2860
8550	1320	1868	2149	2400	2640	2870
8600	1324	1874	2156	2408	2649	2880
8650	1329	1881	2164	2417	2659	2890
8700	1334	1888	2172	2426	2669	2901
8750	1339	1895	2181	2436	2679	2912
8800	1344	1902	2189	2445	2689	2923
8850	1349	1909	2197	2454	2699	2934
8900	1353	1916	2205	2463	2710	2945
8950	1358	1923	2214	2473	2720	2956
9000	1363	1930	2222	2482	2730	2967

Monthly Basic Child Support Schedule

COMBINED MONTHLY NET INCOME	ONE CHILD	TWO CHILDREN	THREE CHILDREN	FOUR CHILDREN	FIVE CHILDREN	SIX CHILDREN
9050	1368	1937	2230	2491	2740	2978
9100	1373	1944	2238	2500	2750	2990
9150	1378	1951	2247	2509	2760	3001
9200	1383	1958	2255	2519	2771	3012
9250	1387	1965	2263	2528	2781	3023
9300	1392	1972	2271	2537	2791	3034
9350	1397	1979	2280	2546	2801	3045
9400	1402	1986	2288	2556	2811	3056
9450	1407	1993	2296	2565	2821	3067
9500	1412	2000	2304	2574	2831	3078
9550	1417	2007	2313	2583	2842	3089
9600	1421	2014	2321	2593	2852	3100
9650	1426	2020	2328	2601	2861	3110
9700	1428	2024	2332	2605	2866	3115
9750	1431	2027	2336	2609	2870	3120
9800	1433	2031	2340	2614	2875	3125
9850	1436	2034	2344	2618	2880	3130
9900	1438	2038	2347	2622	2884	3135
9950	1441	2041	2351	2626	2889	3140
10000	1443	2044	2355	2630	2894	3145
10050	1445	2048	2359	2635	2898	3150
10100	1448	2051	2363	2639	2903	3155
10150	1450	2055	2366	2643	2908	3160

Rule 1910.16-3   ACTIONS FOR SUPPORT

Monthly Basic Child Support Schedule

COMBINED MONTHLY NET INCOME	ONE CHILD	TWO CHILDREN	THREE CHILDREN	FOUR CHILDREN	FIVE CHILDREN	SIX CHILDREN
10200	1453	2058	2370	2647	2912	3166
10250	1455	2061	2374	2652	2917	3171
10300	1458	2065	2378	2656	2922	3176
10350	1460	2068	2382	2660	2926	3181
10400	1463	2072	2385	2664	2931	3186
10450	1465	2075	2389	2669	2936	3191
10500	1468	2079	2393	2673	2940	3196
10550	1470	2082	2397	2677	2945	3201
10600	1473	2085	2401	2681	2950	3206
10650	1475	2089	2404	2686	2954	3211
10700	1479	2094	2410	2692	2961	3219
10750	1483	2100	2416	2699	2969	3227
10800	1487	2105	2422	2706	2976	3235
10850	1491	2111	2428	2713	2984	3243
10900	1495	2116	2434	2719	2991	3251
10950	1499	2122	2441	2726	2999	3260
11000	1504	2127	2447	2733	3006	3268
11050	1508	2133	2453	2740	3014	3276
11100	1512	2138	2459	2746	3021	3284
11150	1516	2144	2465	2753	3029	3292
11200	1520	2149	2471	2760	3036	3300
11250	1524	2155	2477	2767	3043	3308
11300	1528	2160	2483	2774	3051	3316

Monthly Basic Child Support Schedule

COMBINED MONTHLY NET INCOME	ONE CHILD	TWO CHILDREN	THREE CHILDREN	FOUR CHILDREN	FIVE CHILDREN	SIX CHILDREN
11350	1532	2166	2489	2780	3058	3324
11400	1536	2171	2495	2787	3066	3333
11450	1540	2177	2501	2794	3073	3341
11500	1545	2182	2507	2801	3081	3349
11550	1549	2188	2513	2808	3088	3357
11600	1553	2193	2520	2814	3096	3365
11650	1557	2199	2526	2821	3103	3373
11700	1561	2204	2532	2828	3111	3381
11750	1565	2210	2538	2835	3118	3389
11800	1569	2215	2544	2841	3126	3398
11850	1573	2221	2550	2848	3133	3406
11900	1577	2226	2556	2855	3141	3414
11950	1582	2232	2563	2863	3149	3423
12000	1586	2239	2570	2871	3158	3433
12050	1591	2245	2577	2879	3167	3442
12100	1595	2251	2585	2887	3176	3452
12150	1600	2258	2592	2895	3185	3462
12200	1604	2264	2600	2904	3194	3472
12250	1609	2271	2607	2912	3203	3482
12300	1613	2277	2614	2920	3212	3492
12350	1618	2283	2622	2928	3221	3501
12400	1622	2290	2629	2937	3230	3511
12450	1627	2296	2636	2945	3239	3521

Rule 1910.16-3 ACTIONS FOR SUPPORT

Monthly Basic Child Support Schedule

COMBINED MONTHLY NET INCOME	ONE CHILD	TWO CHILDREN	THREE CHILDREN	FOUR CHILDREN	FIVE CHILDREN	SIX CHILDREN
12500	1631	2303	2644	2953	3248	3531
12550	1636	2309	2651	2961	3257	3541
12600	1640	2316	2658	2969	3266	3551
12650	1645	2322	2666	2978	3275	3560
12700	1649	2328	2673	2986	3285	3570
12750	1654	2335	2681	2994	3294	3580
12800	1659	2341	2688	3002	3303	3590
12850	1663	2348	2695	3011	3312	3600
12900	1668	2354	2703	3019	3321	3610
12950	1672	2360	2710	3027	3330	3619
13000	1677	2367	2717	3035	3339	3629
13050	1681	2373	2725	3044	3348	3639
13100	1686	2380	2732	3052	3357	3649
13150	1690	2386	2739	3060	3366	3659
13200	1695	2392	2747	3068	3375	3669
13250	1699	2399	2754	3076	3384	3678
13300	1704	2405	2762	3085	3393	3688
13350	1708	2412	2769	3093	3402	3698
13400	1713	2418	2776	3101	3411	3708
13450	1717	2424	2784	3109	3420	3718
13500	1722	2431	2791	3118	3429	3728
13550	1726	2437	2798	3126	3438	3737
13600	1731	2444	2806	3134	3447	3747

Monthly Basic Child Support Schedule

COMBINED MONTHLY NET INCOME	ONE CHILD	TWO CHILDREN	THREE CHILDREN	FOUR CHILDREN	FIVE CHILDREN	SIX CHILDREN
13650	1735	2450	2813	3142	3456	3757
13700	1740	2457	2820	3150	3465	3767
13750	1745	2463	2828	3159	3475	3777
13800	1749	2469	2835	3167	3484	3787
13850	1754	2476	2843	3175	3493	3797
13900	1758	2482	2850	3183	3502	3806
13950	1763	2489	2857	3192	3511	3816
14000	1766	2493	2863	3198	3517	3823
14050	1770	2498	2868	3203	3524	3830
14100	1773	2503	2873	3209	3530	3837
14150	1776	2507	2878	3215	3536	3844
14200	1780	2512	2883	3221	3543	3851
14250	1783	2517	2889	3227	3549	3858
14300	1786	2521	2894	3232	3556	3865
14350	1790	2526	2899	3238	3562	3872
14400	1793	2531	2904	3244	3568	3879
14450	1797	2535	2909	3250	3575	3886
14500	1800	2540	2915	3256	3581	3893
14550	1803	2545	2920	3261	3588	3900
14600	1807	2549	2925	3267	3594	3907
14650	1810	2554	2930	3273	3600	3914
14700	1814	2558	2935	3279	3607	3921
14750	1817	2563	2941	3285	3613	3927

Rule 1910.16-3   **ACTIONS FOR SUPPORT**

Monthly Basic Child Support Schedule

COMBINED MONTHLY NET INCOME	ONE CHILD	TWO CHILDREN	THREE CHILDREN	FOUR CHILDREN	FIVE CHILDREN	SIX CHILDREN
14800	1820	2568	2946	3290	3620	3934
14850	1824	2572	2951	3296	3626	3941
14900	1827	2577	2956	3302	3632	3948
14950	1830	2582	2961	3308	3639	3955
15000	1834	2586	2967	3314	3645	3962
15050	1837	2591	2972	3320	3651	3969
15100	1841	2596	2977	3325	3658	3976
15150	1844	2600	2982	3331	3664	3983
15200	1847	2605	2987	3337	3671	3990
15250	1851	2610	2993	3343	3677	3997
15300	1854	2614	2998	3349	3683	4004
15350	1858	2619	3003	3354	3690	4011
15400	1861	2624	3008	3360	3696	4018
15450	1864	2628	3013	3366	3703	4025
15500	1868	2633	3019	3372	3709	4032
15550	1871	2638	3024	3378	3715	4039
15600	1874	2642	3029	3383	3722	4046
15650	1878	2647	3034	3389	3728	4053
15700	1881	2652	3039	3395	3735	4059
15750	1885	2656	3045	3401	3741	4066
15800	1888	2661	3050	3407	3747	4073
15850	1891	2666	3055	3412	3754	4080
15900	1895	2670	3060	3418	3760	4087

Monthly Basic Child Support Schedule

COMBINED MONTHLY NET INCOME	ONE CHILD	TWO CHILDREN	THREE CHILDREN	FOUR CHILDREN	FIVE CHILDREN	SIX CHILDREN
15950	1898	2675	3065	3424	3767	4094
16000	1902	2679	3071	3430	3773	4101
16050	1905	2684	3076	3436	3779	4108
16100	1908	2689	3081	3442	3786	4115
16150	1912	2693	3086	3447	3792	4122
16200	1915	2698	3091	3453	3798	4129
16250	1918	2703	3097	3459	3805	4136
16300	1922	2707	3102	3465	3811	4143
16350	1925	2712	3107	3471	3818	4150
16400	1929	2717	3112	3476	3824	4157
16450	1932	2721	3117	3482	3830	4164
16500	1935	2726	3123	3488	3837	4171
16550	1939	2731	3128	3494	3843	4178
16600	1942	2735	3133	3500	3850	4184
16650	1946	2740	3138	3505	3856	4191
16700	1949	2745	3143	3511	3862	4198
16750	1952	2749	3149	3517	3869	4205
16800	1956	2754	3154	3523	3875	4212
16850	1959	2759	3159	3529	3882	4219
16900	1963	2763	3164	3534	3888	4226
16950	1966	2768	3169	3540	3894	4233
17000	1969	2773	3175	3546	3901	4240
17050	1973	2777	3180	3552	3907	4247

Rule 1910.16-3   **ACTIONS FOR SUPPORT**

Monthly Basic Child Support Schedule

COMBINED MONTHLY NET INCOME	ONE CHILD	TWO CHILDREN	THREE CHILDREN	FOUR CHILDREN	FIVE CHILDREN	SIX CHILDREN
17100	1976	2782	3185	3558	3913	4254
17150	1979	2787	3190	3564	3920	4261
17200	1983	2791	3195	3569	3926	4268
17250	1986	2796	3201	3575	3933	4275
17300	1990	2801	3206	3581	3939	4282
17350	1993	2805	3211	3587	3945	4289
17400	1996	2810	3216	3593	3952	4296
17450	2000	2814	3221	3598	3958	4303
17500	2003	2819	3227	3604	3965	4310
17550	2007	2824	3232	3610	3971	4316
17600	2010	2828	3237	3616	3977	4323
17650	2013	2833	3242	3622	3984	4330
17700	2017	2838	3247	3627	3990	4337
17750	2020	2842	3253	3633	3997	4344
17800	2023	2847	3258	3639	4003	4351
17850	2027	2852	3263	3645	4009	4358
17900	2030	2856	3268	3651	4016	4365
17950	2034	2861	3273	3656	4022	4372
18000	2037	2866	3279	3662	4028	4379
18050	2040	2870	3284	3668	4035	4386
18100	2044	2875	3289	3674	4041	4393
18150	2047	2880	3294	3680	4048	4400
18200	2051	2884	3299	3685	4054	4407

Pa. R.C.P. Rule 1910.16-3

Monthly Basic Child Support Schedule

COMBINED MONTHLY NET INCOME	ONE CHILD	TWO CHILDREN	THREE CHILDREN	FOUR CHILDREN	FIVE CHILDREN	SIX CHILDREN
18250	2054	2889	3305	3691	4060	4414
18300	2057	2894	3310	3697	4067	4421
18350	2061	2898	3315	3703	4073	4428
18400	2064	2903	3320	3709	4080	4435
18450	2067	2908	3325	3715	4086	4441
18500	2071	2912	3331	3720	4092	4448
18550	2074	2917	3336	3726	4099	4455
18600	2078	2922	3341	3732	4105	4462
18650	2081	2926	3346	3738	4112	4469
18700	2084	2931	3351	3744	4118	4476
18750	2088	2935	3357	3749	4124	4483
18800	2091	2940	3362	3755	4131	4490
18850	2095	2945	3367	3761	4137	4497
18900	2098	2949	3372	3767	4143	4504
18950	2101	2954	3377	3773	4150	4511
19000	2105	2959	3383	3778	4156	4518
19050	2108	2963	3388	3784	4163	4525
19100	2112	2968	3393	3790	4169	4532
19150	2115	2973	3398	3796	4175	4539
19200	2118	2977	3403	3802	4182	4546
19250	2122	2982	3409	3807	4188	4553
19300	2125	2987	3414	3813	4195	4560
19350	2128	2991	3419	3819	4201	4566

Rule 1910.16-3   **ACTIONS FOR SUPPORT**

Monthly Basic Child Support Schedule

COMBINED MONTHLY NET INCOME	ONE CHILD	TWO CHILDREN	THREE CHILDREN	FOUR CHILDREN	FIVE CHILDREN	SIX CHILDREN
19400	2132	2996	3424	3825	4207	4573
19450	2135	3001	3429	3831	4214	4580
19500	2139	3005	3435	3837	4220	4587
19550	2142	3010	3440	3842	4227	4594
19600	2145	3015	3445	3848	4233	4601
19650	2149	3019	3450	3854	4239	4608
19700	2152	3024	3455	3860	4246	4615
19750	2156	3029	3461	3866	4252	4622
19800	2159	3033	3466	3871	4259	4629
19850	2162	3038	3471	3877	4265	4636
19900	2166	3043	3476	3883	4271	4643
19950	2169	3047	3481	3889	4278	4650
20000	2172	3052	3487	3895	4284	4657
20050	2176	3056	3492	3900	4290	4664
20100	2179	3061	3497	3906	4297	4671
20150	2183	3066	3502	3912	4303	4678
20200	2186	3070	3507	3918	4310	4685
20250	2189	3075	3513	3924	4316	4692
20300	2193	3080	3518	3929	4322	4698
20350	2196	3084	3523	3935	4329	4705
20400	2200	3089	3528	3941	4335	4712
20450	2203	3094	3533	3947	4342	4719
20500	2206	3098	3539	3953	4348	4726

Pa. R.C.P. **Rule 1910.16-3**

Monthly Basic Child Support Schedule

COMBINED MONTHLY NET INCOME	ONE CHILD	TWO CHILDREN	THREE CHILDREN	FOUR CHILDREN	FIVE CHILDREN	SIX CHILDREN
20550	2210	3103	3544	3959	4354	4733
20600	2213	3108	3549	3964	4361	4740
20650	2216	3112	3554	3970	4367	4747
20700	2220	3117	3559	3976	4374	4754
20750	2223	3122	3565	3982	4380	4761
20800	2227	3126	3570	3988	4386	4768
20850	2230	3131	3575	3993	4393	4775
20900	2233	3136	3580	3999	4399	4782
20950	2237	3140	3585	4005	4405	4789
21000	2240	3145	3591	4011	4412	4796
21050	2244	3150	3596	4017	4418	4803
21100	2247	3154	3601	4022	4425	4810
21150	2250	3159	3606	4028	4431	4817
21200	2254	3164	3611	4034	4437	4823
21250	2257	3168	3617	4040	4444	4830
21300	2261	3173	3622	4046	4450	4837
21350	2264	3177	3627	4051	4457	4844
21400	2267	3182	3632	4057	4463	4851
21450	2271	3187	3637	4063	4469	4858
21500	2274	3191	3643	4069	4476	4865
21550	2277	3196	3648	4075	4482	4872
21600	2281	3201	3653	4080	4489	4879
21650	2284	3205	3658	4086	4495	4886

Rule 1910.16-3   **ACTIONS FOR SUPPORT**

Monthly Basic Child Support Schedule

COMBINED MONTHLY NET INCOME	ONE CHILD	TWO CHILDREN	THREE CHILDREN	FOUR CHILDREN	FIVE CHILDREN	SIX CHILDREN
21700	2288	3210	3663	4092	4501	4893
21750	2291	3215	3669	4098	4508	4900
21800	2294	3219	3674	4104	4514	4907
21850	2298	3224	3679	4110	4520	4914
21900	2301	3229	3684	4115	4527	4921
21950	2305	3233	3689	4121	4533	4928
22000	2308	3238	3695	4127	4540	4935
22050	2311	3243	3700	4133	4546	4942
22100	2315	3247	3705	4139	4552	4949
22150	2318	3252	3710	4144	4559	4955
22200	2321	3257	3715	4150	4565	4962
22250	2325	3261	3721	4156	4572	4969
22300	2328	3266	3726	4162	4578	4976
22350	2332	3271	3731	4168	4584	4983
22400	2335	3275	3736	4173	4591	4990
22450	2338	3280	3741	4179	4597	4997
22500	2342	3285	3747	4185	4604	5004
22550	2345	3289	3752	4191	4610	5011
22600	2349	3294	3757	4197	4616	5018
22650	2352	3299	3762	4202	4623	5025
22700	2355	3303	3767	4208	4628	5031
22750	2359	3307	3771	4212	4633	5036
22800	2362	3311	3775	4216	4638	5041

Monthly Basic Child Support Schedule

COMBINED MONTHLY NET INCOME	ONE CHILD	TWO CHILDREN	THREE CHILDREN	FOUR CHILDREN	FIVE CHILDREN	SIX CHILDREN
22850	2365	3315	3779	4220	4642	5046
22900	2369	3319	3783	4224	4647	5051
22950	2372	3323	3787	4229	4652	5056
23000	2375	3328	3792	4233	4656	5061
23050	2378	3332	3796	4237	4661	5066
23100	2382	3336	3800	4241	4665	5071
23150	2385	3340	3804	4246	4670	5076
23200	2388	3344	3808	4250	4675	5081
23250	2392	3348	3812	4254	4679	5087
23300	2395	3352	3816	4258	4684	5092
23350	2398	3356	3820	4262	4689	5097
23400	2402	3360	3824	4267	4693	5102
23450	2405	3365	3828	4271	4698	5107
23500	2408	3369	3833	4275	4703	5112
23550	2412	3373	3837	4279	4707	5117
23600	2415	3377	3841	4284	4712	5122
23650	2418	3381	3845	4288	4717	5127
23700	2422	3385	3849	4292	4721	5132
23750	2425	3389	3853	4296	4726	5137
23800	2428	3393	3857	4300	4730	5142
23850	2432	3397	3861	4305	4735	5147
23900	2435	3401	3865	4309	4740	5152
23950	2438	3406	3869	4313	4744	5157

Rule 1910.16-3   ACTIONS FOR SUPPORT

Monthly Basic Child Support Schedule

COMBINED MONTHLY NET INCOME	ONE CHILD	TWO CHILDREN	THREE CHILDREN	FOUR CHILDREN	FIVE CHILDREN	SIX CHILDREN
24000	2441	3410	3874	4317	4749	5162
24050	2445	3414	3878	4322	4754	5167
24100	2448	3418	3882	4326	4758	5172
24150	2451	3422	3886	4330	4763	5177
24200	2455	3426	3890	4334	4768	5182
24250	2458	3430	3894	4338	4772	5187
24300	2461	3434	3898	4343	4777	5192
24350	2465	3438	3902	4347	4782	5198
24400	2468	3442	3906	4351	4786	5203
24450	2471	3447	3910	4355	4791	5208
24500	2475	3451	3914	4359	4795	5213
24550	2478	3455	3919	4364	4800	5218
24600	2481	3459	3923	4368	4805	5223
24650	2485	3463	3927	4372	4809	5228
24700	2488	3467	3931	4376	4814	5233
24750	2491	3471	3935	4381	4819	5238
24800	2495	3475	3939	4385	4823	5243
24850	2498	3479	3943	4389	4828	5248
24900	2501	3484	3947	4393	4833	5253
24950	2504	3488	3951	4397	4837	5258
25000	2508	3492	3955	4402	4842	5263
25050	2511	3496	3960	4406	4846	5268
25100	2514	3500	3964	4410	4851	5273

Pa. R.C.P.   **Rule 1910.16-3**

Monthly Basic Child Support Schedule

COMBINED MONTHLY NET INCOME	ONE CHILD	TWO CHILDREN	THREE CHILDREN	FOUR CHILDREN	FIVE CHILDREN	SIX CHILDREN
25150	2518	3504	3968	4414	4856	5278
25200	2521	3508	3972	4419	4860	5283
25250	2524	3512	3976	4423	4865	5288
25300	2528	3516	3980	4427	4870	5293
25350	2531	3520	3984	4431	4874	5298
25400	2534	3525	3988	4435	4879	5303
25450	2538	3529	3992	4440	4884	5308
25500	2541	3533	3996	4444	4888	5314
25550	2544	3537	4000	4448	4893	5319
25600	2548	3541	4005	4452	4898	5324
25650	2551	3545	4009	4457	4902	5329
25700	2554	3549	4013	4461	4907	5334
25750	2558	3553	4017	4465	4911	5339
25800	2561	3557	4021	4469	4916	5344
25850	2564	3562	4025	4473	4921	5349
25900	2567	3566	4029	4478	4925	5354
25950	2571	3570	4033	4482	4930	5359
26000	2574	3574	4037	4486	4935	5364
26050	2577	3578	4041	4490	4939	5369
26100	2581	3582	4046	4494	4944	5374
26150	2584	3586	4050	4499	4949	5379
26200	2587	3590	4054	4503	4953	5384
26250	2591	3594	4058	4507	4958	5389

Rule 1910.16-3 ACTIONS FOR SUPPORT

Monthly Basic Child Support Schedule

COMBINED MONTHLY NET INCOME	ONE CHILD	TWO CHILDREN	THREE CHILDREN	FOUR CHILDREN	FIVE CHILDREN	SIX CHILDREN
26300	2594	3598	4062	4511	4962	5394
26350	2597	3603	4066	4516	4967	5399
26400	2601	3607	4070	4520	4972	5404
26450	2604	3611	4074	4524	4976	5409
26500	2607	3615	4078	4528	4981	5414
26550	2611	3619	4082	4532	4986	5419
26600	2614	3623	4086	4537	4990	5424
26650	2617	3627	4091	4541	4995	5430
26700	2621	3631	4095	4545	5000	5435
26750	2624	3635	4099	4549	5004	5440
26800	2627	3640	4103	4554	5009	5445
26850	2630	3644	4107	4558	5014	5450
26900	2634	3648	4111	4562	5018	5455
26950	2637	3652	4115	4566	5023	5460
27000	2640	3656	4119	4570	5027	5465
27050	2644	3660	4123	4575	5032	5470
27100	2647	3664	4127	4579	5037	5475
27150	2650	3668	4132	4583	5041	5480
27200	2654	3672	4136	4587	5046	5485
27250	2657	3676	4140	4592	5051	5490
27300	2660	3681	4144	4596	5055	5495
27350	2664	3685	4148	4600	5060	5500
27400	2667	3689	4152	4604	5065	5505

Pa. R.C.P. Rule 1910.16-3

Monthly Basic Child Support Schedule

COMBINED MONTHLY NET INCOME	ONE CHILD	TWO CHILDREN	THREE CHILDREN	FOUR CHILDREN	FIVE CHILDREN	SIX CHILDREN
27450	2670	3693	4156	4608	5069	5510
27500	2674	3697	4160	4613	5074	5515
27550	2677	3701	4164	4617	5079	5520
27600	2680	3705	4168	4621	5083	5525
27650	2684	3709	4173	4625	5088	5530
27700	2687	3713	4177	4629	5092	5535
27750	2690	3718	4181	4634	5097	5541
27800	2693	3722	4185	4638	5102	5546
27850	2697	3726	4189	4642	5106	5551
27900	2700	3730	4193	4646	5111	5556
27950	2703	3734	4197	4651	5116	5561
28000	2707	3738	4201	4655	5120	5566
28050	2710	3742	4205	4659	5125	5571
28100	2713	3746	4209	4663	5130	5576
28150	2717	3750	4213	4667	5134	5581
28200	2720	3754	4218	4672	5139	5586
28250	2723	3759	4222	4676	5143	5591
28300	2727	3763	4226	4680	5148	5596
28350	2730	3767	4230	4684	5153	5601
28400	2733	3771	4234	4689	5157	5606
28450	2737	3775	4238	4693	5162	5611
28500	2740	3779	4242	4697	5167	5616
28550	2743	3783	4246	4701	5171	5621

Rule 1910.16-3   ACTIONS FOR SUPPORT

Monthly Basic Child Support Schedule

COMBINED MONTHLY NET INCOME	ONE CHILD	TWO CHILDREN	THREE CHILDREN	FOUR CHILDREN	FIVE CHILDREN	SIX CHILDREN
28600	2747	3787	4250	4705	5176	5626
28650	2750	3791	4254	4710	5181	5631
28700	2753	3796	4259	4714	5185	5636
28750	2756	3800	4263	4718	5190	5641
28800	2760	3804	4267	4722	5195	5646
28850	2763	3808	4271	4727	5199	5651
28900	2766	3812	4275	4731	5204	5657
28950	2770	3816	4279	4735	5208	5662
29000	2773	3820	4283	4739	5213	5667
29050	2776	3824	4287	4743	5218	5672
29100	2780	3828	4291	4748	5222	5677
29150	2783	3832	4295	4752	5227	5682
29200	2786	3837	4299	4756	5232	5687
29250	2790	3841	4304	4760	5236	5692
29300	2793	3845	4308	4764	5241	5697
29350	2796	3849	4312	4769	5246	5702
29400	2800	3853	4316	4773	5250	5707
29450	2803	3857	4320	4777	5255	5712
29500	2806	3861	4324	4781	5259	5717
29550	2810	3865	4328	4786	5264	5722
29600	2813	3869	4332	4790	5269	5727
29650	2816	3874	4336	4794	5273	5732
29700	2819	3878	4340	4798	5278	5737

Monthly Basic Child Support Schedule

COMBINED MONTHLY NET INCOME	ONE CHILD	TWO CHILDREN	THREE CHILDREN	FOUR CHILDREN	FIVE CHILDREN	SIX CHILDREN
29750	2823	3882	4345	4802	5283	5742
29800	2826	3886	4349	4807	5287	5747
29850	2829	3890	4353	4811	5292	5752
29900	2833	3894	4357	4815	5297	5757
29950	2836	3898	4361	4819	5301	5762
30000	2839	3902	4365	4824	5306	5768

Adopted September 6, 1989, eff. September 30, 1989; amended Oct. 25, 1989, eff. Oct. 25, 1989; amended Jan. 27, 1993, eff. imd.; amended July 15, 1994, eff. Sept. 1, 1994; amended Dec. 7, 1998, eff. April 1, 1999; amended Oct. 27, 2000, eff. imd., amended Sept. 27, 2005, eff. in 4 months; amended Jan. 12, 2010, eff. May 12, 2010; amended April 9, 2013, eff. Aug. 9, 2013; Feb. 10, 2017, eff. May 1, 2017; December 28, 2018, effective January 1, 2019.

Explanatory Comment—2010

The basic child support schedule has been amended to reflect updated economic data. The schedule has been expanded to include all cases in which the parties' combined net monthly income is $30,000 or less. It also reflects an increase in the Self-Support Reserve to $867, the 2008 poverty level for one person. The schedule was further adjusted to incorporate an assumption that the children spend 30% of the time with the obligor.

Explanatory Comment—2013

The basic child support schedule has been amended to reflect updated economic data. It also reflects an increase in the Self-Support Reserve to $931, the 2012 poverty level for one person, which has been incorporated into the schedule.

Rule 1910.16-3.1. Support Guidelines. High Income Cases.

(a) *Child Support Formula.* If the parties' combined monthly net income exceeds $ 30,000, the following three-step process shall be applied to calculate the parties' respective child support obligations. The support amount calculated pursuant to this three-step process shall not be less than the support amount that would have been awarded if the parties' combined monthly net income was $ 30,000. The calculated amount is the presumptive minimum support amount.

   (1) The following formula shall be applied as a preliminary analysis in calculating the basic child support amount apportioned between the parties according to their respective monthly net incomes:

One child: $ 2,839 +8.6 of combined monthly net income above $ 30,000.

Two children: $ 3,902 +11.8 of combined monthly net income above $ 30,000.

Three children: $ 4,365 +12.9 of combined monthly net income above $ 30,000.

Four children: $ 4,824 +14.6 of combined monthly net income above $ 30,000.

Five children: $ 5,306 +16.1 of combined monthly net income above $ 30,000.

Six children: $ 5,768 +17.5 of combined monthly net income above $ 30,000;

   (2) The trier-of-fact shall apply the formulas in Pa.R.C.P. No. 1910.16-4(a)(1)(Part D) and (Part E) or (2)(Part II) and (Part III), adjusting for substantial or shared custody pursuant to Pa.R.C.P. No. 1910.16-4(c) and allocating additional expenses pursuant to Pa.R.C.P. No. 1910.16-6, as appropriate;

   (3) The trier-of-fact shall consider the factors in Pa.R.C.P. No. 1910.16-5 in making a final child support award and shall make findings of fact on the record or in writing. After considering the factors in Pa.R.C.P. No. 1910.16-5, the trier-of-fact may adjust the amount calculated pursuant to subdivisions (1) and (2), subject to the presumptive minimum.

(b) *Spousal Support and Alimony Pendente Lite.* In cases in which the parties' combined monthly net income exceeds $ 30,000, the trier-of-fact shall apply the formula in either Pa.R.C.P. No. 1910.16-4(a)(1)(Part B) or (2)(Part IV) as a preliminary analysis in calculating spousal support or alimony *pendente lite*. In determining the final spousal support or alimony *pendente lite* amount and duration, the trier-of-fact shall consider the factors in Pa.R.C.P. No. 1910.16-5 and shall make findings of fact on the record or in writing.

Adopted January 12, 2010, effective May 12, 2010. Amended August 26, 2011, effective September 30, 2011; April 9, 2013, effective August 9, 2013; February 10, 2017, effective May 1, 2017; December 28, 2018, effective January 1, 2019.

Explanatory Comment—2010

Pa.R.C.P. No. 1910.16-3.1 is intended to bring all child support cases under the guidelines and treat similarly situated parties similarly. Thus, high-income child support cases no longer will be decided pursuant to *Melzer v. Witsberger*, 480 A.2d 991 (Pa. 1984). Economic data support the basic child support schedule up to combined net incomes of $ 30,000 per month. Above that amount, economic data are not readily available. Thus, for cases in which the parties' combined monthly net income is above $ 30,000, the formula first applies a fixed percentage to calculate the support amount. The formula is an extrapolation of the available economic data to high-income cases. Spousal support and alimony pendente lite awards in high-income cases are preliminarily calculated pursuant to the formulas in either Pa.R.C.P. No. 1910.16-4(a)(1)(Part B) or (2)(Part IV). However, in both high-income child support and spousal support and high-income child support and alimony *pendente lite* cases, the trier-of-fact is required to consider the factors in Pa.R.C.P. No. 1910.16-5 before entering a final order and to make findings of fact on the record or in writing. Pursuant to Pa.R.C.P. No. 1910.11(c)(2), in all high-income cases, the parties must submit an Income Statement and the Expense Statement at Pa.R.C.P. No. 1910.27(c)(2)(B) to enable the trier-of-fact to consider the factors in Pa.R.C.P. No. 1910.16-5.

Explanatory Comment—2011

The rule has been amended to clarify that the provisions of Pa.R.C.P. No. 1910.16-4(c), regarding support adjustments if the obligor has substantial or shared custody, apply in high-income cases. Previously, when high-income cases were decided pursuant to *Melzer v. Witsberger*, 480 A.2d 991 (Pa. 1984), case law held that because the time and resources each parent provided to a child were factored into the *Melzer* formula, the substantial or shared parenting time reductions did not apply to cases decided pursuant to *Melzer*. *See, e.g., Sirio v. Sirio*, 951 A.2d 1188 (Pa. Super. 2008); Bulgarelli v. Bulgarelli, 934 A.2d 107 (Pa. Super. 2007). As *Melzer* no longer applies to calculate support in high-income cases, the prohibition against substantial or shared parenting time reductions in such cases is no longer applicable.

Rule 1910.16-4. Support Guidelines. Calculation of Support Obligation. Formula

(a) The trier-of-fact shall use either the subdivision (1) or subdivision (2) formula to calculate the obligor's share of basic child support, either from the schedule in Pa.R.C.P. No. 1910.16-3 or the formula in Pa.R.C.P. No. 1910.16-3.1(a), as well as spousal support and alimony *pendente lite* obligations. In high-income cases, the trier-of-fact shall use either the subdivision (1)(Part B) or subdivision (2)(Part IV) formula, as appropriate, as a preliminary analysis in the calculation of spousal support or alimony *pendente lite* obligations.

(1) The formula in Parts A through E is for an order entered on or after January 1, 2019, or for a modification of an order entered before January 1, 2019 that includes spousal support or alimony *pendente lite* in which the amendments to the Internal Revenue Code made by Section 11051 of the Tax Cuts and Jobs Act of 2017 (Pub. L. No. 115-97) expressly apply.

Note: Section 11051 of the Tax Cuts and Jobs Act of 2017 (Pub. L. No. 115-97) amended the Internal Revenue Code by repealing the alimony deduction—the amount of spousal support, alimony *pendente lite*, and alimony paid or received—from the payor's gross income and the alimony inclusion into the payee's gross income. *See* subdivision (2) for a modification of an order entered before January 1, 2019 that includes spousal support or alimony *pendente lite* in which the amendments to the Internal Revenue Code made by Tax Cuts and Jobs Act of 2017 (Pub. L. No. 115-97) do not apply to the modification.

PART A. CALCULATION OF MONTHLY NET INCOME

	OBLIGOR	OBLIGEE
1. Total Gross Income Per Pay Period (See Pa.R.C.P. No. 1910.16-2(a))	_____	_____
2. Deductions (See Pa.R.C.P. No. 1910.16-2(c))	(_____)	(_____)
3. Net Income (line 1 minus line 2)	_____	_____
4. Conversion to Monthly Net Income (if pay period is other than monthly)	_____	_____

Rule 1910.16-4   ACTIONS FOR SUPPORT

PART B. SPOUSAL SUPPORT OR ALIMONY PENDENTE LITE

	WITHOUT DEPENDENT CHILDREN	WITH DEPENDENT CHILDREN
5. Obligors Monthly Net Income (line 4)	_____	_____
6. Obligors child support, pousal support, alimony pendente lite or alimony obligations to children or former spouses who are not part of this action, if any. (See Pa.R.C.P. No. 1910.16-2(c)(2))	(_____)	(_____)
7. Obligors Net Income available for spousal support or alimony *pendente lite* (line 5 minus line 6)	_____	_____
8. Obligors Net Income percentage for spousal support or alimony pendente lite	x _____33%	x _____25%
9. Obligors proportionate share of spousal support or alimony pendente lite (line 7 multiplied by line 8)	_____	_____
10. Obligees Monthly Net Income (line 4)	_____	_____
11. Obligees Net Income percentage for spousal support or alimony pendente lite	x _____40%	x _____30%
12. Obligees proportionate share of spousal support or alimony pendente lite (line 10 multiplied by line 11)	_____	_____
13. Preliminary Monthly Spousal Support or Alimony Pendente Lite amount (line 9 minus line 12—if the result is less than zero, enter a zero on line 13)	_____	
14. Adjustments for Part E Additional Expenses (See Pa.R.C.P. No. 1910.16-6)	_____	
15. Total Monthly Spousal Support or Alimony Pendente Lite Amount (line 13 plus or minus line 14, as appropriate)	_____	

PART C. BASIC CHILD SUPPORT

	OBLIGOR	OBLIGEE
16. Monthly Net Income (line 4 and add the child's monthly Social Security Disability or Retirement Derivative benefit amount, if any, to the Monthly Net Income of the party receiving the benefit pursuant to Pa.R.C.P. No. 1910.16-2(b)(2)(i) or (ii))	_____	_____
17. Preliminary Monthly Spousal Support or Alimony Pendente Lite amount, if any. (line 13)	(_____)	+_____
18. Adjusted Monthly Net Income (for obligor, line 16 minus line 17; for obligee, line 16 plus line 17)	_____	_____

19. Combined Monthly Net Income
    (obligors' line 18 plus obligees line 18) _____

20. Basic Child Support Obligation
    (determined from child support
    schedules in Pa.R.C.P. No. 1910.16-3
    based on the number of children
    and line 19) _____

21. Net Income expressed as a _____% _____%
    percentage of Combined Monthly
    Net Income (line 18 divided by line
    19 and multiplied by 100)

22. Preliminary Monthly Basic Child _____ _____
    Support Obligation (line 20
    multiplied by line 21)

23. Childs Social Security Derivative _____ _____
    Disability or Retirement Benefit. (if
    the benefits are paid to the obligee,
    enter the benefit amount on the line
    for the party whose retirement or
    disability created the child's benefit
    pursuant to Pa.R.C.P. No. 1910.16-2(b))

24. Adjusted Monthly Basic Child _____ _____
    Support Obligation (line 22 minus
    line 23—if the result is less than
    zero, enter a zero on line 24)

PART D. SUBSTANTIAL OR SHARED PHYSICAL CUSTODY ADJUSTMENT, IF APPLICABLE (See subdivision (c))

25. a. Percentage of time obligor spends _____%
       with children (divide number of
       overnights with the obligor by 365
       and multiply by 100)

    b. Subtract 30% (_____30%)

    c. Difference (line 25a minus line 25b) _____%

    d. Obligors Adjusted Percentage _____%
       Share of the Basic Monthly Support
       Obligation (line 21 minus line 25c)

    e. Obligors Preliminary Adjusted _____
       Basic Monthly Support Obligation
       (line 20 multiplied by line 25d)

    f. Further adjustment, if necessary _____
       under subdivision (c)(2)

    g. Obligors Adjusted Basic Child _____
       Support Amount

PART E. ADDITIONAL EXPENSES (See Pa.R.C.P. No. 1910.16-6)

26. a. Obligors Share of Child Care _____
       Expenses

    b. Obligors Share of Health _____
       Insurance Premium (if the
       obligee is paying the premium)

    c. Obligees Share of the Health (_____)
       Insurance Premium (if the obligor
       is paying the premium)

    d. Obligors Share of Unreimbursed _____
       Medical Expenses

    e. Other Additional Expenses _____

Rule 1910.16-4 ACTIONS FOR SUPPORT

    f. Total Additional Expenses (add lines 26a, b, d, and e, then subtract line 26c) _____

27. Obligors Total Monthly Support Obligation (line 24 or 25g plus line 26f, if applicable) _____

(2) The formula in Parts I through IV is for a modification of an order entered before January 1, 2019 that includes spousal support or alimony *pendente lite*.

    Note: *See* subdivision (1) for an order entered on or after January 1, 2019, or for a modification of an order entered before January 1, 2019 that includes spousal support or alimony *pendente lite* in which the amendments to the Internal Revenue Code made by Tax Cuts and Jobs Act of 2017 (Pub. L. No. 115-97) expressly apply to the modification.

PART I. BASIC CHILD SUPPORT

	OBLIGOR	OBLIGEE
1. Total Gross Income Per Pay Period (See Pa.R.C.P. No. 1910.16-2(a))	_____	_____
2. Deductions (See Pa.R.C.P. No. 1910.16-2(c))	(_____)	(_____)
3. Net Income (line 1 minus line 2)	_____	_____
4. Conversion to Monthly Amount (if pay period is other than monthly) Include the child's monthly Social Security derivative benefit amount, if any, in the monthly net income of the party receiving the benefit pursuant to Pa.R.C.P. No. 1910.16-2(b)(2)(i) or (ii).	_____	_____
5. Combined Total Monthly Net Income (obligor's line 4 plus obligee's line 4)	_____	
6. Basic Child Support Obligation (determined from schedule at Pa.R.C.P. No. 1910.16-3 based on number of children and line 5)	_____	
7. Net Income Expressed as a Percentage Share of Income (divide line 4 by line 5 and multiply by 100)	_____ %	_____ %
8. Each Party's Preliminary Monthly Share of the Basic Child Support Obligation (multiply line 6 and 7)	_____	_____
9. Childs Social Security Derivative Disability or Retirement Benefit (if the benefits are paid to the obligee, enter the benefit amount on the line for the party whose retirement or disability created the child's benefit)	_____	_____
10. Each Party's Adjusted Monthly Share of the Basic Child Support Obligation (line 8 minus line 9—if the result is less than zero, enter a zero on line 10)	_____	_____

Pa. R.C.P.   **Rule 1910.16-4**

PART II. SUBSTANTIAL OR SHARED PHYSICAL CUSTODY ADJUSTMENT, IF APPLICABLE (*See* Subdivision (c))

11. a. Percentage of Time Obligor Spends with Children (divide number of overnights with the obligor by 365 and multiply by 100)   _____ %

    b. Subtract 30%   (_____%)

    c. Obligors Adjusted Percentage Share of the Basic Monthly Support Obligation (subtract result of calculation in line 11b from line 7)   _____ %
   _____ %

    d. Obligors Preliminary Adjusted Share of the Basic Monthly Support Obligation (multiply line 11c and line 6)   _____

    e. Further adjustment, if necessary under subdivision (c)(2)   _____

    f. Obligors Adjusted Share of the Basic Child Support Amount (Total of line 11d and line 11e)   _____

PART III. ADDITIONAL EXPENSES (See Pa.R.C.P. No. 1910.16-6)

12. a. Obligor's Share of Child Care Expenses   _____

    b. Obligor's Share of Health Insurance Premium (if the obligee is paying the premium)   _____

    c. Obligees Share of the Health Insurance Premium (if the obligor is paying the premium)   (_____)

    d. Obligors Share of Unreimbursed Medical Expenses   _____

    e. Other Additional Expenses   _____

    f. Total Additional Expenses (add lines 12a, b, d, and e, then subtract line 12c)   _____

13. Obligors Total Monthly Support Obligation (add line 10 or 11f and line 12f, if applicable)   _____

PART IV. SPOUSAL SUPPORT OR APL
            With Dependent Children

14. Obligor's Monthly Net Income (line 4)   _____

15. Obligors Support, Alimony *Pendente Lite* or Alimony Obligations, to Children or Former Spouses who are not part of this action, if any (See Pa.R.C.P. No. 1910.16-2(c)(2))   (_____)

16. Obligees Monthly Net Income (line 4)   (_____)

17. Difference (line 14 minus lines 15 and 16)   _____

18. Obligors Total Monthly Child Support Obligation without Part II Substantial or Shared Custody Adjustment, if any (Obligors line 10 plus line 12(f) (_____)
19. Difference (line 17 minus line 18) _____
20. Multiply by 30% x _____ 30
21. Monthly Spousal Support or APL Amount (line 19 multiplied by line 20) _____

Without Dependent Children

22. Obligors Monthly Net Income (line 4) _____
23. Obligors Support, Alimony *Pendente Lite* or Alimony Obligations to Children or Former Spouses who are not part of this action, if any (Pa.R.C.P. No. 1910.16-2(c)(2)) (_____)
24. Less Obligee's Monthly Net Income (Line 4) (_____)
25. Difference (line 22 minus lines 23 and 24) _____
26. Multiply by 40% x _____ 40%
27. Preliminary Monthly Spousal Support or APL amount (line 25 multiplied by line 26) _____
28. Adjustments for Other Expenses (See Pa.R.C.P. No. 1910.16-6) (line 12f) _____
29. Total Monthly Spousal Support or APL amount (line 27 plus or minus line 28, as appropriate) _____

(b) *Order For More Than Six Children.* When there are more than six children who are the subject of a single order, the child support obligation shall be calculated as follows. First, determine the appropriate amount of support for six children under the guidelines. Using the same income figures, subtract the support amount for five children from the amount for six children. Multiply the difference by the number of children in excess of six and add the resulting amount to the guideline amount for six children.

(c) *Substantial or Shared Physical Custody.*

(1) When the children spend 40% or more of their time during the year with the obligor, a rebuttable presumption arises that the obligor is entitled to a reduction in the basic support obligation to reflect this time. This rebuttable presumption also applies in high income cases decided pursuant to Rule 1910.16-3.1. Except as provided in subsection (2) below, the reduction shall be calculated pursuant to the formula set forth in Part II of subdivision (a) of this rule. For purposes of this provision, the time spent with the children shall be determined by the number of overnights they spend during the year with the obligor.

Example. If the obligor and the obligee have monthly net incomes of $ 5,000 and $ 2,300, respectively, their combined child support obligation is $ 1,701 for two children. Using the income shares formula in Part I, the obligor's share of this obligation is 68%, or $ 1,157. If the children spend 40% of their time with the obligor, the formula in Part II applies to reduce his or her percentage share of the combined support obligation to 58%, or $ 987. If the children spend 45% of their time with the obligor, his or her percentage share of the combined obligation is reduced to 53%, or $ 902. If the children spend equal time with both parents, the obligor's percentage share is reduced to 48%, or $ 816.

(2) Without regard to which parent initiated the support action, when the children spend equal time with their parents, the Part II formula cannot be applied unless the obligor is the parent with the higher income. An order shall not be entered requiring the parent with the lower income to pay basic child support to the parent with the higher income. However, this subdivision shall not preclude the entry of an order requiring the parent with less income to contribute to additional expenses pursuant to Pa.R.C.P. No. 1910.16-6. Based upon the evidence presented, the trier of fact may enter an order against either party without regard to which party initiated the action. If the parties share custody equally and the support calculation results in the obligee receiving a larger share of the parties' combined income, then the court shall adjust the support obligation so that the combined monthly net income is allocated equally between the two households. In those cases, spousal support or alimony *pendente lite* shall not be awarded.

Example 1. Mother and Father have monthly net incomes of $ 3,000 and $ 2,700, respectively. Mother has filed for support for the parties' two children with whom the parties share time equally. As the parties have equal custody and Mother has the higher income, Mother cannot be the obligee. Although Mother initiated the support action, she would be the obligor. Pursuant to the basic child support schedule in Pa.R.C.P. No. 1910.16-3, the support amount for two children at the parties' combined monthly net income level is $ 1,487 per month. Mother's share is 53% of that amount, or $ 788. Father's share is 47%, or $ 699. Application of lines 11a and 11b of the Part II formula results in a 20% reduction in support when the obligor has 50% custody of the children. Mother's adjusted percentage share of the basic support amount is 33% (53%-20%=33%). Her adjusted share of the basic support amount is $ 491 (33% of $ 1,487). However, as this amount would result in Father having a greater share of the parties' combined monthly net income ($ 3,191 vs. $ 2,509), Mother's support obligation would be adjusted to $ 150 per month to allocate the parties' combined monthly net income equally between the two households and would be the presumptive amount of basic support payable to Father under these circumstances.

Example 2. If the obligor and the obligee have monthly net incomes of $ 3,000 and $ 2,500, respectively, then their combined child support obligation for two children is $ 1,463. The obligor's share of this obligation is 55%, or $ 805 ($ 1,463 x 55%). If the children spend equal time with the parents, the formula in Part II results in a support obligation of $ 512 ($ 1,463 x 35%) payable to the obligee. Since this amount results in the obligee having monthly net income of $ 3,012 and the obligor having monthly net income of $ 2,488, the obligor's support obligation would be adjusted to $ 250 to equalize the combined monthly net income between the parties' households and would be the presumptive amount of basic support payable to the obligee under these circumstances.

(d) *Divided or Split Physical Custody. When Each Party Owes Child Support to the Other Party. Varied Partial or Shared Custodial Schedules.*

(1) Divided or Split Physical Custody. *When Each Party Owes Child Support to the Other Party.* When calculating a child support obligation and each party owes child support to the other party as a result of the custodial arrangement, the court shall offset the parties' respective child support obligations and award the net difference to the obligee as child support.

Rule 1910.16-4   ACTIONS FOR SUPPORT

Example 1. If the parties have three children, one child resides with Mother and two children reside with Father, and their monthly net incomes are $ 4000 and $ 2,000 respectively, Mother's child support obligation is calculated using the schedule in Pa.R.C.P. No. 1910.16-3 for two children at the parties' combined monthly net income of $ 6,000. The amount of basic child support to be apportioned between the parties is $ 1,523. As Mother's income is 67% of the parties' combined monthly net income, Mother's support obligation for the two children living with Father is $ 1,020. Father's child support obligation is calculated using the schedule in Pa.R.C.P. No. 1910.16-3 for one child at the parties' combined monthly net income of $ 6,000. The amount of basic child support to be apportioned between the parties is $ 1,071. Father's support obligation for the child living with Mother is $ 353. Subtracting $ 353 from $ 1,020 produces a net basic support amount of $ 667 payable to Father as child support.

Example 2. If the parties have two children, one child resides with Mother and the parties share custody (50%—50%) of the other child, and the parties' monthly net incomes are as set forth in Example 1. The child support obligation is calculated using the schedule in Pa.R.C.P. No. 1910.16-3 for the one child primarily residing with Mother at the parties' combined monthly net income of $ 6,000, the amount of basic child support to be apportioned between the parties is $ 1,071. Father's income is 33% of the parties' combined monthly net income, and the support obligation for the child living with Mother is $ 353. For Mother's obligation for the child with the 50%—50% shared custody arrangement, using the schedule in Pa.R.C.P. No. 1910.16-3 for one child at the parties' combined monthly net income of $ 6,000, the amount of basic child support to be apportioned between the parties is $ 1,071. Mother's proportionate share of the combined monthly net incomes is 67%, but it is reduced to 47% after applying the shared parenting time adjustment for 50% custody under subdivision (c). Mother's child support obligation for the shared custody child is $ 503 ($ 1,071 x 47%). As Mother's obligation is greater than Father's obligation, Father is the obligee and receives the net of the two obligations by subtracting $ 353 from $ 503, or $ 150.

(2) Varied Partial or Shared Custodial Schedules. When the parties have more than one child and each child spends either (a) different amounts of partial or shared custodial time with the party with the higher income or (b) different amounts of partial custodial time with the party with the lower income, the trier of fact shall add the percentage of time each child spends with that party and divide by the number of children to determine the party's percentage of custodial time. If the average percentage of custodial time the children spend with the party is 40% or more, the provisions of subdivision (c) apply.

Example 1. The parties have two children and one child spends 50% of the time with Mother, who has the higher income, and the other child spends 20% of the time with Mother. Add those percentages together and divide by the number of children (50% plus 20% = 70% divided by 2 children = 35% average time with Mother). Pursuant to subdivision (c), Mother does not receive a reduction in the support order for substantial parenting time.

Example 2. The parties have three children. Two children spend 50% of the time with Mother, who has the higher income, and the third child spends 30% of the time with Mother. Add the percentages of custodial time for all three children together and divide by the number of children (50% plus 50% plus 30% = 130% divided by three children = 43.33% average percentage of time with Mother). Pursuant to subdivision (c), Mother receives a reduction in the support order for substantial parenting time.

Example 3. The parties have three children, Mother has primary custody (60%—40%) of one child, Father has primary custody (60%—40%) of one child, and the parties share custody (50%—50%) of the third child. The parties' monthly net incomes are $ 2,500 (Mother) and $ 2,000 (Father). As a result of the custodial arrangement, Father owes support for the child in the primary custody of Mother and Mother owes support for the child in the primary custody of Father and for the child shared equally between the parties. Father's child support obligation is calculated using the schedule in Pa.R.C.P. No. 1910.16-3 for one child at the parties' combined monthly net income of $ 4,500. The amount of basic child support to be apportioned between the parties is $ 940. Father's proportionate share of the combined monthly net incomes is 44%, but is reduced to 34% after applying the shared parenting time adjustment for 40% custody under subdivision (c). Father's child support obligation for this child is $ 320 ($ 940 x 34%). Mother's child support obligation is calculated using the schedule in Pa.R.C.P. No. 1910.16-3 for two children at the parties' combined monthly net income of $ 4,500. The amount of basic child support to be apportioned between the parties is $ 1,349. Mother has varying partial or shared custody of the two children (40% and 50%). Under subdivision (d)(2), the custodial time is averaged or in this case 45%. Mother's proportionate share of the combined monthly net incomes is 56%, but it is reduced to 41% after applying the shared parenting time adjustment for 45% custody under subdivision (c). Mother's child support obligation for these children is $ 553 ($ 1,349 x 41%). Offsetting the support amounts consistent with subdivision (d)(1), Mother's obligation is greater than Father's obligation, and Father is the obligee receiving the net of the two obligations by subtracting $ 320 from $ 553, or $ 233.

Note: In cases with more than one child and varied partial or shared custodial schedules, it is not appropriate to perform a separate calculation for each child and offset support amounts as that method does not consider the incremental increases in support for more than one child built into the schedule of basic child support.

(3) When calculating a combined child support and spousal or alimony *pendente lite* obligation and one or more children reside with each party, the court shall offset the obligor's spousal and child support obligation with the obligee's child support obligation and award the net difference to the obligee as spousal and child support. If one or more of the children resides with each party then, in calculating the spousal support or alimony *pendente lite* obligation, the court shall deduct from the obligor's income both the support owed for the child or children residing with the obligee, as well as the direct support the obligor provides to the child or children living with the obligor, calculated in accordance with the guidelines as if the child or children were not living with the obligor.

(e) *Support Obligations When Custodial Parent Owes Spousal Support.* If children are residing with the spouse (custodial parent) obligated to pay spousal support or alimony *pendente lite* and the other spouse (non-custodial parent) has a legal obligation to support the children, the guideline spousal support or alimony *pendente lite* amount is determined by offsetting the non-custodial parent's child support amount and the custodial parent's spousal support or alimony *pendente lite* amount, and awarding the net difference either to the non-custodial parent as spousal support/alimony *pendente lite* or to the custodial parent as child support as the circumstances warrant. The calculation is a five-step process:

(1) Calculate the custodial parent's spousal support or alimony *pendente lite* obligation to the non-custodial parent based on the parties' monthly net incomes using the "without dependent children" formula in either Pa.R.C.P. No. 1910.16-4(a)(1)(Part B) or (2)(Part IV), as appropriate.

(2) Recalculate the parties' monthly net incomes by adjusting for the spousal support or alimony *pendente lite* payment paid or received in (1).

(3) Using the recomputed monthly net incomes from (2), calculate the non-custodial parent's child support obligation to the custodial parent.

(4) The final support amount is the difference calculated in (1) and (3).

   (i) If the amount in (1) is greater than the amount in (3), the final amount is spousal support or alimony *pendente lite* payable to the non-custodial parent.

   (ii) If the amount in (1) is less than the amount in (3), the final amount is child support payable to the custodial parent.

(5) If the proceeding is a modification of an order entered before January 1, 2019 that has federal tax consequences associated with spousal support or alimony *pendente lite* payments and the final order is spousal support or alimony *pendente lite* as in (4)(i), the offset spousal support or alimony *pendente lite* amount is federally taxable, and the trier-of-fact may deviate the final order due to the tax effect, as appropriate.

Note: *See* Pa.R.C.P. No. 1910.16-4.

Adopted December 8, 1998, effective April 1, 1999. Amended March 2, 2000, immediately effective; October 27, 2000, immediately effective; June 5, 2001, immediately effective; October 30, 2001, immediately effective; September 24, 2002, immediately effective; November 9, 2004, immediately effective; May 17, 2005, immediately effective; September 27, 2005, effective in four months. [January 27, 2006]; January 12, 2010, effective May 12, 2010, July 8, 2010, effective September 6, 2010; August 3, 2011, effective in 30 days [September 2, 2011]; August 26, 2011, effective September 30, 2011; January 31, 2012, effective February 28, 2012; April 9, 2013, effective August 9, 2013; July 2, 2014, effective August 1, 2014; September 25, 2014, effective October 25, 2014; April 29, 2015, effective July 1, 2015; October 14, 2016, effective January 1, 2017; February 10, 2017, effective May 1, 2017; February 9, 2018, effective April 1, 2018; July 30, 2018, effective January 1, 2019; December 28, 2018, effective January 1, 2019.

Explanatory Comment—2005

Pa.R.C.P. No. 1910.16-4(a) sets forth the income shares formula used to establish the support obligation. Subdivision (b) provides the method for calculating support for seven or more children as the basic support schedule in Pa.R.C.P. No. 1910.16-3 sets forth the presumptive amount of support for up to six children.

Subdivision (c) sets forth the method for calculating the presumptive amount of support in cases where the children spend 40% or more of their time during the year with the obligor. When there is equal time sharing, subdivision (2) reduces the support obligation further so that the obligor does not pay more than is necessary to equalize the parties' combined monthly net income between the two households. Subdivision (3) expressly excludes SSR cases from the application of this rule. Since the SSR already reduces support to a minimal level, a further reduction should not be given for the amount of time spent with the children.

Subdivision (d) relates to the calculation of support in divided or split custody cases. It retains the existing method for offsetting the parties' respective support obligations when one or more of the children resides with each party.

Subdivision (e) governs spousal support obligations when the custodial parent owes spousal support. It has not been amended, other than to update the example to be consistent with the new schedule at Pa.R.C.P. No. 1910.16-3.

Explanatory Comment—2010

The basic support schedule incorporates an assumption that the children spend 30% of the time with the obligor and that the obligor makes direct expenditures on their behalf during that time. Variable expenditures, such as food and entertainment, that fluctuate based upon parenting time were adjusted in the schedule to build in the assumption of 30% parenting time. Upward deviation should be considered in cases in which the obligor has little or no contact with the children. However, an upward deviation may not be appropriate if an obligor has infrequent overnight contact with the child, but provides meals and entertainment during daytime contact. Fluctuating expenditures should be considered rather than the extent of overnight time. A downward deviation may be appropriate when the obligor incurs substantial fluctuating expenditures during parenting time but has infrequent overnights with the children.

The calculation in Pa.R.C.P. No. 1910.16-4(c) reduces an obligor's support obligation further if the obligor spends significantly more time with the children. The obligor will receive an additional 10% reduction in the amount of support owed at 40% parenting time, increasing incrementally to a 20% reduction at 50% parenting time. This method still may result in a support obligation even if custody of the children is equally shared. In those cases, the rule provides for a maximum obligation so that the obligee does not receive a larger portion of the parties' combined monthly net income than the obligor.

Rule 1910.16–5 Support Guidelines. Deviation

(a) Deviation. If the amount of support deviates from the amount of support determined by the guidelines, the trier of fact shall specify, in writing or on the record, the guideline amount of support, and the reasons for, and findings of fact justifying, the amount of the deviation.

Official Note: The deviation applies to the amount of the support obligation and not to the amount of income.

(b) Factors. In deciding whether to deviate from the amount of support determined by the guidelines, the trier of fact shall consider:

(1) unusual needs and unusual fixed obligations;

(2) other support obligations of the parties;

(3) other income in the household;

(4) ages of the children;

(5) the relative assets and liabilities of the parties;

(6) medical expenses not covered by insurance;

(7) standard of living of the parties and their children;

(8) in a spousal support or alimony pendente lite case, the duration of the marriage from the date of marriage to the date of final separation; and

(9) other relevant and appropriate factors, including the best interests of the child or children.

Explanatory Comment—2010

The provisions of subdivision (c), which provided that the court must consider the duration of the parties' marriage in determining the duration of an award of spousal support or alimony pendente lite, were moved to new Rule 1910.16-1(c)(2). The duration of the marriage, from the date of marriage to the date of final separation, remains a factor to consider in determining whether or not deviation from the amount of the award is warranted.

Explanatory Comment—2005

Rule 1910.16-5 sets forth the factors for deviation from the presumptive amount of support. Subdivision (c) and subsection (b)(8) permit the court to consider the length of the marriage in determining the amount and duration of a spousal support or alimony pendente lite award. The primary purpose of these provisions is to prevent the unfairness that arises in a short-term marriage when the obligor is required to pay support over a substantially longer period of time than the parties were married and there is little or no opportunity for credit for these payments at the time of equitable distribution.

Adopted December 8, 1998, effective April 1, 1999; Amended, September 24, 2003, imd. Effective; September 27, 2005, effective in 4 months [Jan. 27, 2006]; amended January 12, 2010, effective in 120 days [May 12, 2010].

Rule 1910.16-6. Support Guidelines. Basic Support Obligation. Adjustments. Additional Expenses Allocation

The trier-of-fact may allocate between the parties the additional expenses in subdivisions (a)—(e). If a basic support order is inappropriate under the facts of the case, the trier-of-fact may allocate between the parties the additional expenses.

Except for the subdivisions (b)(4) and (e) expenses, the trier-of-fact shall calculate the parties' proportionate share of the additional expenses after adjusting the parties' monthly net income by the monthly spousal support or alimony *pendente lite* amount received or paid, and then dividing each party's adjusted monthly net income by the parties' combined monthly net income. However, the trier-of-fact shall not adjust the parties' monthly net incomes when apportioning the expenses in child support only cases.

(a) Child care expenses. The trier-of-fact shall allocate reasonable child care expenses paid by the parties, if necessary to maintain employment or appropriate education in pursuit of income. The trier-of-fact may order that the obligor's share is added to his or her basic support obligation, paid directly to the service provider, or paid directly to the obligee. When a party is receiving a child care subsidy through the Department of Human Services, the expense allocated between the parties is the amount actually paid by the party receiving the subsidy.

Example. Mother has primary custody of the parties' two children and Father has partial custody. Mother's monthly net income is $ 2,000 and Father's is $ 3,500. At their combined income level of $ 5,500, the basic monthly child support from the schedule in Pa.R.C.P. No. 1910.16-3 is $ 1,463 for two children. As Father's income is 64% of the parties' combined monthly net income, his share is $ 936. Mother incurs child care expenses of $ 400 per month and Father incurs $ 100 of such expenses per month. The total child care expenses, $ 500, will be apportioned between the parties, with Father paying 64%, or $ 320. As Father is already paying $ 100 for child care while the children are in his partial custody, he would pay the remaining $ 220 to Mother for a total child support obligation of $ 1,156 ($ 936 + $ 220 = $ 1,156).

(1) Documentation of the child care expenses shall be provided to the other party within a reasonable period of time after receipt unless the service provider invoices the parties separately for their proportionate

share of the expense. Allocation of expenses for which documentation is not timely provided to the other party shall be within the discretion of the court.

(2) Except as provided in subdivision (3), the total child care expenses shall be reduced to reflect the amount of the federal child care tax credit available to the eligible party, whether or not the credit is actually claimed by that party, up to the maximum annual cost allowable under the Internal Revenue Code.

(3) The federal child care tax credit shall not be used to reduce the child care expenses subject to allocation between the parties if the eligible party is not qualified to receive the credit.

(b) Health Insurance Premiums.

(1) The trier-of-fact shall allocate the health insurance premiums paid by the parties, including the premium attributable to the party paying the premium, provided that a statutory duty of support is owed to the party or child covered by the health insurance.

(i) If the party paying the health insurance premium is the obligor, the obligee's share is deducted from the obligor's basic support amount.

(ii) If the obligee is paying the health insurance premium, the obligor's share is added to his or her basic support amount.

(iii) An allocation of health insurance premiums between the parties shall also include health insurance that is provided and paid by a third-party resident of either party's household (e.g., step-parent) for a child who is the subject of the support order.

(2) The trier-of-fact shall not allocate employer-paid premiums or premiums paid for a party, person, or child to whom no statutory duty of support is owed.

(i) If the parties present evidence of the excluded premium's actual amount—the amount attributed to a party, person, or child not owed a statutory duty of support—the trier-of-fact shall deduct the actual amount excluded from the total premium before allocating the health insurance premium between the parties.

(ii) If the parties do not present evidence of the excluded premium's actual amount, the trier-of-fact shall calculate the excluded amount as follows:

(A) determine the premium's cost per person by dividing the total premium by the number of persons covered under the policy;

(B) multiply the cost per person by the number of persons who are not owed a statutory duty of support, or are not parties to, or the subject of, the support action; and

(C) the resulting amount is excluded from allocation.

Example 1. If the parties are separated, but not divorced, and Husband pays $ 200 per month toward the cost of a health insurance policy provided through his employer which covers himself, Wife, the parties' child, and two additional children from a previous marriage, the portion of the premium attributable to the additional two children, if not otherwise verifiable or known with reasonable ease and certainty, is calculated by dividing $ 200 by five persons and then multiplying the resulting amount of $ 40 per person by the two additional children, for a total of $ 80 to be excluded from allocation. Deduct this amount from the total cost of the premium to arrive at the portion of the premium to be allocated between the parties—$ 120. Since Husband is paying the premium, and spouses have a statutory duty to support one another pursuant to 23 Pa.C.S. § 4321, Wife's percentage share of the $ 120 is deducted from Husband's support obligation. If Wife had been providing the coverage, then Husband's percentage share would be added to his basic support obligation.

Example 2. If the parties are divorced and Father pays $ 200 per month toward the cost of a health insurance policy provided through his employer which covers himself, the parties' child and two additional children from a previous marriage, the portion of the premium attributable to Father and the two additional children will not be allocated between the parties. Thus, using the same calculations in Example 1, the amount of the premium attributable to Father and the two other children is $ 150 ($ 200 premium divided among four covered persons equals $ 50 per person multiplied by three) and that amount is deducted from the total cost of the premium, leaving $ 50 ($ 200 - $ 150 = $ 50) to be allocated between the parties.

Example 3. The parties are divorced and Mother is the obligee of a child support order. Father, the obligor, pays $ 200 per month toward the cost of a health insurance policy provided by his employer that covers himself and the parties' child. Mother pays $ 400 per month for her employer-sponsored health insurance that covers only herself. The amount of the premium Father pays to cover the parties' child, $ 100 ($ 200 premium divided between two covered persons, Father and the child), will be allocated between the parties in proportion to their respective incomes. The portion of the premium that covers Father will not be allocated because the parties are no longer married and he is not owed a duty of support by Mother. The premium Mother pays to provide her own coverage will not be allocated because the parties are no longer married and she is not owed a duty of support by Father.

(3) Pursuant to 23 Pa.C.S. § 4326(a), in every support proceeding, the court must ascertain each parent's ability to provide medical support for the parties' children and the support "order shall include a requirement for medical support to be provided by either or both parents, provided that such medical support is accessible to the children."

(i) The obligor bears the initial responsibility of providing health care coverage for the children if it is available at a reasonable cost. "Reasonable cost" to an obligor shall be defined as an amount that does not exceed 5% of the obligor's net monthly income and, when added to the amount of basic child support plus additional expenses the obligor is ordered to pay, does not exceed 50% of the obligor's net monthly income. If the obligee is providing the coverage, the reasonable amount of the obligor's share shall be defined as an amount that does not exceed 5% of the obligor's net monthly income and, when added to the amount of basic child support plus additional expenses the obligor is ordered to pay, does not exceed 50% of the obligor's net monthly income.

(ii) Unless health care coverage for the parties' children is provided by the obligee or a third party, the court shall issue the National Medical Support Notice required by 23 Pa.C.S. § 4326(d.1) to the obligor's employer in response to notification that the obligor is employed. The notice shall direct the employer to enroll the children of the obligor who are the subject of the support proceeding if the coverage is available at a reasonable cost to the obligor. However, the notice shall direct that enrollment shall not occur earlier than 25 days from the date of the National Medical Support Notice to allow the obligor time to object. Concurrent with the issuance of the National Medical Support Notice, the court shall provide notice to the obligor setting forth the process to object to the enrollment based upon unreasonable cost, mistake of fact or availability of alternative health care coverage for the children. If there is more than one employer-provided health care coverage option, the obligor shall select the plan, subject to the obligee's right to seek a court order designating a different option.

(iii) Absent the availability of health care coverage to the obligor for the parties' children at a reasonable cost, the court shall order the obligee to provide health care coverage for the children if it is available at a reasonable cost. "Reasonable cost" to the obligee shall be defined as an amount not to exceed 5% of the obligee's net monthly income.

(iv) If health care coverage is not available to either party at a reasonable cost, the court may order the custodial parent to apply for government-sponsored coverage, such as the Children's Health Insurance Program ("CHIP"), with any co-premium or other cost apportioned between the parties in proportion to their respective net monthly incomes.

(v) Within thirty days after the entry of the support order, the party ordered to provide health care coverage shall provide written proof to the other party that medical insurance has been obtained, including insurance cards and all other materials set forth in the form order in Rule 1910.27(e). There shall be a continuing obligation to provide the other party and the court with proof of any changes in coverage.

(vi) The court shall give preference to health care coverage that is readily accessible to the child, as defined by geographic coverage area, access to local treatment providers or other relevant factors.

Note: The maximum amount of any attachment for child and medical support is set forth by the federal Consumer Credit Protection Act (Public Law 90-321, Section 303(b); 15 U.S.C. § 1601 et seq.).

(4) In cases in which the obligor is paying the cost of health insurance coverage and the obligee has no income or minimal income such that the obligor will bear 90% or more of the proportional share of the cost of the health insurance premiums, the trier of fact may, as fairness requires, deduct part or all of the cost of the premiums actually paid by the obligor to provide coverage for the other party or the children from the obligor's gross income to determine net income for support purposes. If such a deduction is taken from the obligor's gross income, then the allocation of premium costs as set forth in (b)(1) above shall not be applied.

Note: Subdivision (b) of this rule does not apply to Medical Assistance. See 23 Pa.C.S. § 4326(1). The 2005 amendments to Rule 1910.16-6(b)(1) and (2) clarify that the portion of the insurance premium covering the party carrying the insurance cannot be allocated between the parties if there is no statutory duty of support owed to that party by the other party. See Maher v. Maher, 575 Pa. 181, 835 A.2d 1281 (2003) and 23 Pa.C.S. § 4321.

(c) **Unreimbursed Medical Expenses.** The trier-of-fact shall allocate the obligee's or children's unreimbursed medical expenses. However, the trier-of-fact shall not allocate unreimbursed medical expenses incurred by a party who is not owed a statutory duty of support by the other party. The trier-of-fact may order that the obligor's expense share is added to his or her basic support obligation, paid directly to the health care provider, or paid directly to the obligee.

(1) For purposes of this subdivision, medical expenses are annual unreimbursed medical expenses in excess of $250 per person. Medical expenses include insurance co-payments and deductibles and all expenses incurred

for reasonably necessary medical services and supplies, including but not limited to surgical, dental and optical services, and orthodontia. Medical expenses do not include cosmetic, chiropractic, psychiatric, psychological or other services unless specifically directed in the order of court.

Note: While cosmetic, chiropractic, psychiatric, psychological or other expenses are not required to be apportioned between the parties, the court may apportion such expenses that it determines to be reasonable and appropriate under the circumstances.

(2) An annual limitation may be imposed when the burden on the obligor would otherwise be excessive.

(3) Annual expenses pursuant to this subdivision (c), shall be calculated on a calendar year basis. In the year in which the initial support order is entered, or in any period in which support is being paid that is less than a full year, the $ 250 threshold shall be pro-rated. Documentation of unreimbursed medical expenses that either party seeks to have allocated between the parties shall be provided to the other party not later than March 31 of the year following the calendar year in which the final bill was received by the party seeking allocation. For purposes of subsequent enforcement, unreimbursed medical bills need not be submitted to the domestic relations section prior to March 31. Allocation of unreimbursed medical expenses for which documentation is not timely provided to the other party shall be within the discretion of the court.

(4) If the trier of fact determines that out-of-network medical expenses were not obtained due to medical emergency or other compelling factors, the court may decline to assess any of such expenses against the other party.

Note: If the trier of fact determines that the obligee acted reasonably in obtaining services which were not specifically set forth in the order of support, payment for such services may be ordered retroactively.

(d) **Private School Tuition. Summer Camp. Other Needs.** Expenditures for needs outside the scope of typical child-rearing expenses, e.g., private school tuition, summer camps, have not been factored into the Basic Child Support Schedule.

(1) If a party incurs an expense for a need not factored into the Basic Child Support Schedule and the trier-of-fact determines the need and expense are reasonable, the trier-of-fact shall allocate the expense. The trier-of-fact may order that the obligor's expense share is added to his or her basic support obligation, paid directly to the service provider, or paid directly to the obligee.

(2) Documentation of the expenses allocated under (d)(1) shall be provided to the other party not later than March 31 of the year following the calendar year in which the invoice was received unless the service provider invoices the parties separately for their proportionate share of the expense. For purposes of subsequent enforcement, these expenses need not be submitted to the domestic relations section prior to March 31. Allocation of expenses for which documentation is not timely provided to the other party shall be within the discretion of the court.

(e) **Mortgage Payment.** The guidelines assume that the spouse occupying the marital residence will be solely responsible for the mortgage payment, real estate taxes, and homeowners' insurance. Similarly, the trier-of-fact will assume that the party occupying the marital residence will be paying the items listed unless the recommendation specifically provides otherwise.

(1) If the obligee is living in the marital residence and the mortgage payment exceeds 25% of the obligee's monthly net income (including amounts of spousal support, alimony pendente lite, and child support), the trier-of-fact may direct the obligor to assume up to 50% of the excess amount as part of the total support amount.

(2) If the obligor is occupying the marital residence and the mortgage payment exceeds 25% of the obligor's monthly net income (less any amount of spousal support, alimony pendente lite, and child support the obligor is paying), the trier-of-fact may downwardly adjust the obligor's support amount.

(3) This rule shall not be applied after a final resolution of the outstanding economic claims in the parties' divorce action.

(4) For purposes of this subdivision, the term "mortgage" shall include first mortgages, real estate taxes, and homeowners' insurance and may include subsequent mortgages, home equity loans, and other marital obligations secured by the marital residence.

Adopted December 8, 1998, effective April 1, 1999. Amended October 27, 2000, immediately effective; June 5, 2001, immediately effective; October 30, 2001, immediately effective; October 31, 2002, immediately effective; July 30, 2003, immediately effective; September 24, 2003, immediately effective; November 9, 2004, immediately effective; May 17, 2005, immediately effective; September 27, 2005, effective in four months. [January 27, 2006]; October 17, 2006, immediately effective; August 13, 2008, effective October 12, 2008; December 8, 2009, immediately effective: January 12, 2010, effective May 12, 2010; July 8, 2010, effective September 6, 2010 August 26, 2011, effective September 30, 2011; April 9, 2013, effective August 9, 2013; May 14, 2014, effective June 13, 2014; March 12, 2015, effective April 11, 2015; February 10, 2017, effective May 1, 2017; June 23, 2017, effective October 1, 2017; December 28, 2018, effective January 1, 2019.

Explanatory Comment—2004

Subdivision (a), relating to the federal child care tax credit, has been amended to reflect recent amendments to the Internal Revenue Code, 26 U.S.C. § 21. By generally referencing the Tax Code, rather than incorporating current Code provisions in the rule, further amendments will be incorporated into the support calculation.

Explanatory Comment—2005

Pa.R.C.P. No. 1910.16-6 governs the treatment of additional expenses that warrant an adjustment to the basic support obligation.

Subdivision (a) relates to child care expenses. Subdivision (a) has been amended to require that child care expenses incurred by either party are to be allocated between the parties in proportion to their respective net incomes. Subsection (a)(1), relating to the federal child care tax credit, was amended in 2004 to reflect recent amendments to the Internal Revenue Code. 26 U.S.C. § 21. By referring to the Tax Code in general, rather than incorporating current Code provisions in the rule, any further amendments will be incorporated into the support calculation. Since the tax credit may be taken only against taxes owed, it cannot be used when the eligible parent does not incur sufficient tax liability to fully realize the credit. For this reason, subsection (2) provides that no adjustment to the total child care expenses may be made if the eligible parent does not qualify to receive the credit.

Subdivision (b) addresses health insurance premiums. The cost of the premiums is generally treated as an additional expense to be allocated between the parties in proportion to their net incomes. Subdivision (b)(1) of the rule permits allocation of the entire premium, including the portion of the premium covering the party carrying the insurance, when the insurance benefits the other party and/or the children. Subdivision (b)(2) clarifies that, in calculating the amount of the health care premium to be allocated between the parties, subdivision (b)(1) requires the inclusion of that portion of the health insurance premium covering the party who is paying the premium, so long as there is a statutory duty of support owed to that party, but not the portion of the premium attributable to non-parties and children who are not the subjects of the support order. Subdivision (b)(2) provides for proration of the premium when the health insurance covers other persons who are not subject to the support action or owed a statutory duty of support. Subdivision (b) also permits an alternative method for dealing with the cost of health insurance premiums in certain circumstances. While, in general, the cost of the premiums will be treated as an additional expense to be allocated between the parties in proportion to their net incomes, in cases in which the obligee has no income or minimal income, subsection (4) authorizes the trier-of-fact to reduce the obligor's gross income for support purposes by some or all of the amount of the health insurance premiums. This is to avoid the result under a prior rule in which the entire cost of health insurance would have been borne by the obligor, with no resulting reduction in the amount of support he or she would otherwise be required to pay under the support guidelines. The goal of this provision is to encourage and facilitate the maintenance of health insurance coverage for dependents by giving the obligor a financial incentive to maintain health insurance coverage.

Subdivision (c) deals with unreimbursed medical expenses. Since the first $ 250 of medical expenses per year per child is built into the basic guideline amount in the child support schedule, only medical expenses in excess of $ 250 per year per child are subject to allocation under this rule as an additional expense to be added to the basic support obligation. The same is true with respect to spousal support so that the obligee-spouse is expected to assume the first $ 250 per year of these expenses and may seek contribution under this rule only for unreimbursed expenses which exceed $ 250 per year. The definition of "medical expenses" includes insurance co-payments, deductibles and orthodontia and excludes chiropractic services.

Subdivision (d) governs apportionment of private school tuition, summer camp and other unusual needs not reflected in the basic guideline amounts of support. The rule presumes allocation in proportion to the parties' net incomes consistent with the treatment of the other additional expenses.

Subdivision (e) provides for the apportionment of mortgage expenses. It defines "mortgage" to include the real estate taxes and homeowners' insurance. While real estate taxes and homeowners' insurance must be included if the trier-of-fact applies the provisions of this subdivision, the inclusion of second mortgages, home equity loans and other obligations secured by the marital residence is within the trier-of-fact's discretion based upon the circumstances of the case.

Explanatory Comment—2006

A new introductory sentence in Pa.R.C.P. No. 1910.16-6 clarifies that additional expenses contemplated in the rule may be allocated between the parties even if the parties' respective incomes do not warrant an award of basic support. Thus, even if application of either formula Pa.R.C.P. No. 1910.16-4 results in a basic support obligation of zero, the trier-of-fact may enter a support order allocating between the parties any or all of the additional expenses addressed in this rule.

The amendment of subdivision (e) recognizes that the obligor may be occupying the marital residence and that, in particular circumstances, justice and fairness may warrant an adjustment in his or her support obligation.

Explanatory Comment—2008

Federal and state statutes require clarification to subdivision (b) to ensure that all court orders for support address the children's ongoing need for medical care.

In those instances where the children's health care needs are paid by the state's medical assistance program, and eligibility for the Children's Health Insurance Program ("CHIP") is denied due to the minimal income of the custodial parent, the obligor remains required to enroll the parties' children in health insurance that is, or may become, available that is reasonable in cost.

Government-sponsored health care plans represent a viable alternative to the often prohibitive cost of health insurance obtainable by a parent. Except for very low income children, every child is eligible for CHIP, for which the parent with primary physical custody must apply and which is based on that parent's income. A custodial parent may apply for CHIP by telephone or on the Internet. While co-premiums or co-pays increase as the custodial parent's income increases, such costs are generally modest and should be apportioned between the parties. Moreover, health care coverage obtained by the custodial parent generally yields more practical results, as the custodial parent resides in the geographic coverage area, enrollment cards are issued directly to the custodial parent, and claims may be submitted directly by the custodial parent.

Explanatory Comment—2010

Subdivision (e), relating to mortgages on the marital residence, has been amended to clarify that the rule cannot be applied after a final order of equitable distribution has been entered. To the extent that Isralsky v. Isralsky, 824 A.2d 1178 (Pa. Super. 2003), holds otherwise, it is superseded. At the time of resolution of the parties' economic claims, the former marital residence will either have been awarded to one of the parties or otherwise addressed.

Explanatory Comment—2018

The amendments provide for an adjustment to the parties' monthly net incomes prior to determining the percentage each party pays toward the expenses set forth in Pa.R.C.P. No. 1910.16-6. Previously, the Rules of Civil Procedure apportioned the enumerated expenses in Pa.R.C.P. No. 1910.16-6(a)-(d), with the exception of subdivision (c)(5), between the parties based on the parties' respective monthly net incomes as calculated pursuant to Pa.R.C.P. No. 1910.16-2. This apportionment did not consider the amount of support paid by the obligor or received by the obligee. The amended rule adjusts the parties' monthly net incomes, upward or downward, by the spousal support/APL amount paid or received by that party prior to apportioning the expenses. This methodology is not new to the Rules of Civil Procedure. In Pa.R.C.P. No. 1910.16-6(c)(5)(rescinded), the parties' monthly net incomes in spousal support/APL-only cases were similarly adjusted prior to the apportionment of unreimbursed medical expenses. Likewise, Pa.R.C.P. No. 1910.16-6(e) considers the parties' monthly net income after the receipt or payment of the support obligation for purposes of determining a mortgage deviation. As the new procedure adopts the methodology in former subdivision (c)(5), that subdivision has been rescinded as delineating the spousal support only circumstance is unnecessary.

Lastly, the amendment consolidates Pa.R.C.P. No. 1910.16-6(b)(1), (2), and (2.1)

Rule 1910.16–7 Support Guidelines. Awards of Child Support When There are Multiple Families

(a) When the total of the obligor's basic child support obligations equals 50% or less of his or her monthly net income, there will be no deviation from the guideline amount of support on the ground of the existence of a new family.

Example: If the obligor requests a reduction of support for one child of the first marriage on the basis that there is a new child of the second intact marriage, and the relevant monthly net incomes are $2,500 for the obligor, $500 for the former spouse and $1,300 for the current spouse, then the request for a reduction will be denied because the total support obligation of $1,153 ($584 for the first child and $569 for the second child) is less than half of the obligor's monthly net income.

(b) When the total of the obligor's basic support obligations exceeds 50% of his or her monthly net income, the court may consider a proportional reduction of these obligations. Since, however, the goal of the guidelines is to treat each child equitably, a first or later family shall not receive preference, and the court shall not divide the guideline amount for all of the obligor's children among the households in which those children live.

Example 1. The obligor is sued for support of an out of wedlock child. The obligor is already paying support for two children of the first marriage, and has an intact second marriage with one child. The relevant monthly net incomes are $3,800 for the obligor, $1,100 for the former spouse, $0 for the current spouse and $1,500 for the parent of the new child. The obligor's basic support obligations to each family are $1,097 for the two children of the first marriage, $862 for the one child of the second marriage, and $727 for the one child out of wedlock for a total support obligation of $2,686. Since the total of these obligations exceeds 50% of the obligor's monthly net income of $3,800 per month, the court may consider a proportional reduction of all of the orders.

Example 2. The obligor is sued for support of three children of a second marriage. There is already an order in effect for two children of the first marriage. The relevant monthly net incomes are $2,500 for the obligor, $0 for the first spouse and $500 for the second spouse. The obligor's basic support obligations to each family are $849 for the two children of the first marriage and $987 for the three children of the second marriage for a total support obligation of $1,836. Since this total obligation leaves the obligor with only $664 on which to live, the orders are too high as the obligor must be left with a Self-Support Reserve of $981. However, reducing the order for three children while leaving the existing order intact would give preference to the first family, contrary to the rule. Therefore, both orders must be reduced proportionally.

Example 3. The obligor is sued by three obligees to establish orders for three children. The monthly net income for the obligor and for each obligee is $1,500. The court would determine that the obligor's basic support obligation for each child is $352 for a total obligation of $1,056 for three children. It would be incorrect to determine the guideline amount for three children, in this case $1,189, and then divide that amount among the three children. Due to the total support amount exceeding 50% of the obligor's monthly net income, the support orders should be reduced proportionately consistent with subdivision (b) and ensure the obligor retains the Self-Support Reserve of $981 consistent with Pa.R.C.P. No. 1910.16-2(e).

(c) For purposes of this rule, the presumptive amount of the obligor's basic support obligation is calculated using only the basic guideline amounts of support, as determined from the formula in Pa.R.C.P. No. 1910.16-4, and does not include any additional expenses that may be added to these amounts pursuant to Pa.R.C.P. No. 1910.16-6. In calculating the presumptive amount of the obligor's basic support obligation, the court should ensure that the obligor retains at least $981 per month consistent with Pa.R.C.P. No. 1910.16-2(e).

Example 1. Assume that the obligor is paying $566 per month support for one child of the first marriage, plus an additional $200 per month for child care expenses. The obligor requests a reduction in this support obligation on the basis that there is one new child of the second intact marriage. The relevant incomes are $2,400 for the obligor and $0 for both the former and current spouses. The obligor's request for a reduction should be denied because the total of the basic guideline obligations for both children is only $1,132 ($566 for each child) and does not exceed 50% of the obligor's monthly net income. A reduction should not be given on the basis that the obligor's contribution to child care expenses for the first child results in an overall support obligation of $1,332 which exceeds 50% of the obligor's monthly net income. Thus, the presumptive amount of basic support for the two children is still $1,132 ($566 for each child). The court must then consider the deviation factors under Pa.R.C.P. No. 1910.16-5 and the parties' respective contributions to additional expenses under Pa.R.C.P. No. 1910.16-6 in arriving at an appropriate amount of total support for each child.

Example 2. Assume that the obligor is paying $360 per month support for one child of the first marriage. The obligor has one new child of the second intact marriage. The relevant incomes are $1,500 for the obligor and $0 for the former and current spouses. A reduction should not be given on the basis of the obligor's new child because the total of the basic guideline obligations for both children is only $720 ($360 for each child) and this amount does not exceed 50% of the obligor's monthly net income. Since, however, this amount leaves the obligor with only $780 per month, the court should proportionally reduce the support obligations so that the obligor retains $981 per month. Thus, the presumptive amount of basic support for the two children is $519 ($259.50 for each child). The court must then consider the deviation factors under Pa.R.C.P. No. 1910.16-5 and the parties' respective contributions to additional expenses under Pa.R.C.P. No. 1910.16-6 in arriving at an appropriate amount of total support for each child.

Adopted Dec. 8, 1998, effective April 1, 1999. Amended Oct. 30, 2001, imd. effective; Oct. 31, 2002, imd. effective; Sept. 27, 2005, effective in 4 months [Jan. 27, 2006]; Aug. 13, 2008, effective Oct. 12, 2008; Jan. 12, 2010, effective May 12, 2010; April 9, 2013, effective Aug. 9, 2013; Sept. 25, 2014, effective Oct. 25, 2014; Feb. 10, 2017, effective May 1, 2017; Feb. 9, 2018, effective April 1, 2018.

Explanatory Comment—2005

Rule 1910.16-7 has been amended to reflect the updated schedule at Rule 1910.16-3 and the increase in the Self-Support Reserve ("SSR"), formerly the CAM, to $748 per month. This rule sets forth the calculation of child support obligations in the context of multiple families. Awards of spousal support in this context are addressed in Rule 1910.16-2(c)(2).

In determining whether the total support obligations exceed 50% of the obligor's net income to warrant a proportionate reduction of the child support orders, subdivision (c) clarifies that the total consists only of the basic amounts of child support, as derived from the income shares formula in Rule 1910.16-4, and does not include additional expenses that may be added to these basic amounts under Rule 1910.16-6. As the first example illustrates, no reduction should be given

Rule 1910.17   ACTIONS FOR SUPPORT

if the basic support obligations do not exceed 50% of the obligor's net monthly income even though his or her contribution to additional expenses may result in an overall obligation exceeding this percentage of income. As the second example illustrates, however, in low income cases it may be necessary to adjust the child support obligations proportionally even though they do not exceed 50% of the obligor's net income. This is consistent with the goals of the SSR to ensure that the obligor retains sufficient income to maintain the incentive to work so that he or she can support all of the children.

Subdivision (c) also emphasizes that the initial amounts which are calculated for purposes of determining whether a proportional reduction is warranted are only presumptive amounts of child support. They are subject to upward or downward adjustment under Rules 1910.16-5 and 1910.16-6 relating to deviation and additional child-related expenses which are typically added to the basic obligation. This is intended only to emphasize that the establishment of appropriate support obligations for children of different families involves the same considerations as the establishment of a support obligation for a child or children of a single family.

Explanatory Comment—2010

Rule 1910.16-7 has been amended to reflect the updated schedule in Rule 1910.16-3 and the increase in the Self-Support Reserve to $867 per month, the 2008 federal poverty level for one person. The distribution priorities formerly in subdivision (d) have been moved to Rule 1910.17(d) to clarify that these priorities apply to all support orders, not just those involving multiple families.

Explanatory Comment—2013

Rule 1910.16-7 has been amended to reflect the updated schedule in Rule 1910.16-3 and the increase in the Self-Support Reserve to $931 per month, the 2012 federal poverty level for one person.

Rule 1910.17. Support Order. Effective Date. Change Of Circumstances. Copies Of Order. Priority Of Distribution Of Payments

(a) An order of support shall be effective from the date of the filing of the complaint or petition for modification unless the order specifies otherwise. In a child support case, if a change in custody occurs after the date of filing, but before a domestic relations conference is held, the trier of fact shall enter a charging order going forward in favor of the primary custodian that shall be effective from the date of the change in custody. The trier of fact also may enter a retroactive arrears order in favor of the party who was the primary custodian at the time of filing. Such an order may address the period from the date of filing to the date of the change in custody. However, a modification of an existing support order may be retroactive to a date preceding the date of filing if the petitioner was precluded from filing a petition for modification by reason of a significant physical or mental disability, misrepresentation of another party or other compelling reason and if the petitioner, when no longer precluded, promptly filed a petition.

Example: **Mother has primary custody of the children and files for child support. Two months later, Father becomes the primary custodian. One** month after the change in custody, a support conference is held. Father will be the obligee on a charging order that is retroactive to the date he became the primary custodian. However, an order also may be entered with Mother as the obligee for the two-month period from the date of filing to the date of the change in custody.

> **Note:** The order must direct payment to be made payable to or payment to be made to the State Collection and Disbursement Unit for transmission to the obligee. See 23 Pa.C.S. § 4325. Subdivision (a) was amended in 2005 to include the statutory provision at 23 Pa.C.S. § 4352(e) that authorizes the court to enter a modified order that is effective to a date prior to the date on which the petition for modification was filed in certain circumstances. To the effect that the holding in *Kelleher v. Bush, 832 A.2d 483 (Pa. Super. Ct. 2003),* is inconsistent, it is superseded. See 23 Pa.C.S. § 4352(e) for additional provisions. Every order of support must contain an immediate or conditional order for the attachment of income. See Rule 1910.21.

(b) The order shall notify the obligee and the obligor that each is under a continuing obligation to inform the domestic relations section in writing or by personal appearance and all other parties in writing within seven days of any material change in circumstances relevant to the level of support or the administration of the support order, including but not limited to, loss or change of income or employment and change of personal address or change of address of any child receiving support. The order shall also notify the parties that if a party willfully fails to inform the domestic relations section of the required information, the court may adjudge the party to be in contempt of court pursuant to Rules 1910.25 through 1910.25-6 and may order the party to be punished by one or more of the following: jail, fine or probation.

(c) A copy of the support order shall be provided to each party to the action and to the party's attorney, if any, pursuant to Rule 440.

(d) The priorities for distribution of payments and/or collections from the obligor, without regard to the source of the funds or method of collection, are as follows:

   (1) monthly current child support.

   (2) medical, child care or other court-ordered child support-related expenses.

   (3) monthly ordered amount toward child support arrears.

   (4) monthly current spousal support or alimony pendente lite.

   (5) remaining child support arrears.

   (6) monthly ordered amount toward spousal support or alimony pendente lite arrears.

   (7) remaining spousal support or alimony pendente lite arrears.

   (8) court costs and fees.

Amended Nov. 7, 1988, effective Jan. 1, 1989;Nov. 22, 1994, effectiveJan.1, 1995;May 31, 2000, effective July 1, 2000; May 17, 2005, effective immediately; Jan. 12, 2010, effective May 12, 2010; August 26, 2011, effective Nov. 1, 2011; July 30, 2018, effective Jan. 1, 2019.

Explanatory Comment—2010

Subdivision (d) has moved from Pa.R.C.P. No. 1910.16-7 and expanded for clarification. It addresses the priority of the distribution of payments and collections in all cases, not just those involving multiple families. However, collections realized through the interception of federal tax returns by the Internal Revenue Service are subject to federal distribution priorities. *See* 45 CFR § 303.72(h). An unallocated order for child support and spousal support or child support and alimony *pendente lite* has the same priority as a child support order.

Rule 1910.18. Support Order. Subsequent Proceedings. Modification of Spousal Support or Alimony *Pendente Lite* Orders Entered Before January 1, 2019.

(a) Subsequent support order modification or termination proceedings pursuant to Pa.R.C.P. No. 1910.19 shall be brought in the court that entered the order. If the action has been transferred pursuant to Pa.R.C.P. No. 1910.2 following the entry of a support order, subsequent proceedings shall be brought in the court to which the action was transferred.

(b) Subsequent support order enforcement proceedings pursuant to Pa.R.C.P. No. 1910.20 may be brought in the court that entered the support order or the court to which the order has been transferred.

(c) Subdivision (a) shall not limit the plaintiff's right to institute additional support proceedings in a county of proper venue.

(d) Unless a modification provides that the Internal Revenue Code, as amended by the Tax Cuts and Jobs Act of 2017 (Pub. L. No. 115-97), expressly applies, an order entered before January 1, 2019 that includes spousal support or alimony pendente lite is governed by the Pa.R.C.P. No. 1910.16-4(a)(2)(Part IV) formula.

Note: *See* Pa.R.C.P. No. 1910.16-4(a)(1)(Part B) or (2)(Part IV), as relevant.

Adopted April 23, 1981, effective July 22, 1981. Amended December 18, 1999, effective January 1, 1999; amended December 28, 2018, effective January 1, 2019.

Explanatory Comment—1998

Rule 1910.18 clarifies the question of jurisdiction which arises where parties wish to proceed for termination, modification or enforcement in counties other than the county which entered the order. Section 6710 of the Judicial Code provides that the county which entered the original order continues to retain jurisdiction for termination, modification or enforcement. Section 6710 also provides that this shall not limit the right of the plaintiff to "institute additional proceedings" in any county where the defendant resides or where his or her property is located. Additionally, Rule 1910.2(g) permits enforcement of a support order in accordance with the Intrastate Family Support Act, 23 Pa.C.S. § 8101 et seq., if the defendant resides in another county within the Commonwealth.

There will be instances where the parties no longer reside in the original county. In this situation, Rule 1910.18 permits a party to seek transfer of the entire matter under Rule 1910.2 and authorizes the transferee county to modify, terminate or enforce the order. There may be other instances where the parties retain some connection with the county which entered the order but circumstances require the enforcement of the order in another county. In such a case, the plaintiff, without an order of court may transfer the support order and seek enforcement under the Uniform Intrastate Family Support Act or the Transfer of Judgment Rule 3001 et seq.

Rule 1910.19. Support. Modification. Termination. Guidelines as Substantial Change in Circumstances. Overpayments

(a) A petition for modification or termination of an existing support order shall specifically aver the material and substantial change in circumstances upon which the petition is based. A new guideline amount resulting from new or revised support guidelines may constitute a material and substantial change in circumstances. The existence of additional income, income sources or assets identified through automated methods or otherwise may also constitute a material and substantial change in circumstances.

(b) The procedure upon the petition shall be in accordance with Rule 1910. 10 et seq. After a party has filed a petition for modification of a child support order, the petition may not be withdrawn unless both parties consent or with leave of court. A petition for modification of spousal support or alimony pendente lite may be withdrawn without the consent of the other party or leave of court.

(c) Pursuant to a petition for modification, the trier-of-fact may modify or terminate the existing support order in any appropriate manner based on the evidence presented without regard to which party filed the petition for modification. If the trier-of-fact finds that there has been a material and substantial change in circumstances, the order may be increased or decreased based on the parties' respective monthly net incomes, consistent with the support guidelines, existing law, and Pa.R.C.P. No. 1910.18(d), and the party's custodial time with the child at the time the modification petition is heard.

(d) All charging orders for spousal support and alimony pendente lite shall terminate upon the death of the payee spouse.

(e) Within six months prior to the date a child who is the subject of a child support order reaches eighteen (18) years of age, the domestic relations section shall issue an emancipation inquiry and notice to the obligee, with a copy to the obligor, seeking the following information:

(1) confirmation of the child's date of birth, date of graduation or withdrawal from high school;

(2) whether the child has left the obligee's household and, if so, the date of departure;

(3) the existence of any agreement between the parties requiring payments for the benefit of the child after the child has reached age eighteen (18) or graduated from high school; and

(4) any special needs of the child which may be a basis for continuing support for that child beyond the child's eighteenth birthday or graduation from high school, whichever is last to occur.

The notice shall advise the obligee that if the inquiry is not returned within thirty (30) days of mailing or if there is no agreement or the child does not have any special needs, the charging order may be modified or terminated by the court. In order to avoid overpayment, when no other children are subjects of the child support order and the obligee either does not return the emancipation inquiry within thirty (30) days of its mailing or does not assert grounds for continuing support for the child, then the domestic relations section shall administratively terminate the child support charging order without further proceedings on the last to occur of the date the last child reaches age eighteen (18) or graduates from high school. Termination of the charging order shall not affect any arrears accrued through the date of termination. The court shall have the authority to enter an order requiring the obligor to pay on arrears in an amount equal to the amount of the charging order until all arrears are paid.

If the order applies to another child or children and/or the obligee asserts that there is an agreement between the parties or that a child has special needs requiring continued support, then the domestic relations section may schedule a conference prior to the child's attaining age 18 or graduating from high school to determine if the charging order should be modified.

(f) Upon notice to the obligee, with a copy to the obligor, explaining the basis for the proposed modification or termination, the court may modify or terminate a charging order for support and remit any arrears, all without prejudice, when it appears to the court that:

(1) the order is no longer able to be enforced under state law; or

(2) the obligor is unable to pay, has no known income or assets and there is no reasonable prospect that the obligor will be able to pay in the foreseeable future.

The notice shall advise the obligee to contact the domestic relations section within 60 days of the date of the mailing of the notice if the obligee wishes to contest the proposed modification or termination. If the obligee objects, the domestic relations section shall schedule a conference to provide the obligee the opportunity to contest the proposed action. If the obligee does not respond to the notice or object to the proposed action, the court shall have the authority to modify or terminate the order and remit any arrears, without prejudice.

(g) Overpayments.

(1) *Order in Effect.* If there is an overpayment in an amount in excess of two months of the monthly support obligation and a charging order remains in effect, after notice to the parties as set forth below, the domestic relations section shall reduce the charging order by 20% or an amount sufficient to retire the overpayment by the time the charging order is terminated. The notice shall advise the parties to contact the domestic relations section within 30 days of the date of the mailing of the notice if either or both of them wishes to contest the proposed reduction of the charging order. If either party objects, the domestic relations section shall schedule a conference to provide the objecting party the opportunity to contest the proposed action. If neither party responds to the notice or objects to the proposed action, the domestic relations section shall have the authority to reduce the charging order.

(2) *Order Terminated.* If there is an overpayment in any amount and there is no charging order in effect, within one year of the termination of the charging order, the former obligor may file a petition with the domestic relations section seeking recovery of the overpayment. A copy shall be served upon the former obligee as original process. The domestic relations section shall schedule a conference on the petition, which shall be conducted consistent with the rules governing support actions. The domestic relations section shall have the authority to enter an order against the former obligee for the amount of the overpayment in a monthly amount to be determined by the trier of fact after consideration of the former obligee's ability to pay.

(h) **Modification of a Support Order with Child Support and Spousal Support or Child Support and Alimony Pendente Lite Entered Before January 1, 2019.**

(1) In a subsequent modification proceeding of an order awarding child support and spousal support or child support and alimony pendente lite, as provided in Pa.R.C.P. No. 1910.18(d), the trier-of-fact may on its own motion or upon the motion of a party:

(i) make an unallocated award in favor of the spouse and one or more children; or

(ii) state the support amount allocable to the spouse and to each child.

(2) The trier-of-fact shall clearly state whether the order is allocated or unallocated even if the child support and spousal support or child support and alimony pendente lite amounts are delineated in the order.

(i) If the order is allocated, the Pa.R.C.P. No. 1910-16.4(a)(2)(Part IV) formula determines the spousal support amount.

(A) As the formula assumes an unallocated order, if the order's allocation utilizing the formula is inequitable, the trier-of-fact may adjust the order, as appropriate.

(B) In making an adjustment, the trier-of-fact shall consider the federal income tax consequences.

(C) If the parties are in higher income brackets, the income tax considerations are likely to be a more significant factor in determining a support amount.

(ii) If the order is unallocated or the order is for spousal support or alimony pendente lite only, the trier-of-fact shall not consider the federal income tax consequences.

Note: *See* 23 Pa.C.S. § 4348(d) for additional matters that must be specified in a support order if arrearages exist when the order is entered.

(3) A support award for a spouse and children is taxable to the obligee while an award for the children only is not. Consequently, in certain situations, an award only for the children will be more favorable to the obligee than an award to the spouse and children. In this situation, the trier-of-fact should utilize the method that provides the greatest benefit to the obligee.

(4) If the obligee's monthly net income is equal to or greater than the obligor's monthly net income, the guideline amount for spouse and children is identical to the guideline amount for children only. Therefore, in cases involving support for spouse and children, whenever the obligee's monthly net income is equal to or greater than the obligor's monthly net income, the guideline amount indicated shall be attributed to child support only.

(5) Unallocated child support and spousal support or child support and alimony *pendente lite* orders shall terminate upon the obligee's death.

(6) In the event that the obligor defaults on an unallocated order, the trier-of-fact shall allocate the order for child support collection pursuant to the Internal Revenue Service income tax refund intercept program or for registration and enforcement of the order in another jurisdiction under the Uniform Interstate Family Support Act, 23 Pa.C.S. §§ 7101—7903. The trier-of-fact shall provide the parties with notice of allocation.

Note: This provision is necessary to comply with various state and federal laws relating to child support enforcement. It is not intended to affect an unallocated order's tax consequences.

Rule 1910.19   ACTIONS FOR SUPPORT

(7) **An unallocated child support and spousal support or child support and alimony pendente lite order is a final order as to the claims covered in the order.**

(8) **Motions for post-trial relief cannot be filed to the final order.**

Note: The procedure relating to Motions for Reconsideration is set forth in Pa.R.C.P. No. 1930.2.

Subdivision (h) incorporates Pa.R.C.P. No. 1910.16 (rescinded) and Pa.R.C.P. No. 1910.16-4(f)(rescinded) for subsequent modification proceedings due to the enactment of the Tax Cuts and Jobs Act of 2017 (Pub. L. No. 115-97).

Adopted April 23, 1981, effective July 22, 1981. Amended January 27, 1993, immediately effective; December 2, 1994, effective March 1, 1995; May 31, 2000, effective July 1, 2000; June 5, 2001, immediately effective; October 11, 2002, immediately effective; May 19, 2006, immediately effective; August 26, 2011, effective November 1, 2011; September 19, 2011, effective October 31, 2011; November 5, 2012, effective December 5, 2012; December 28, 2018, effective January 1, 2019.

Explanatory Comment—1981

Subdivision (a) sets forth a rule of pleading. It requires the petition for modification or termination to aver "specifically" the reasons for the relief sought. Modification of a prior order requires a "material and substantial change in circumstances." This change in circumstances should be alleged specifically.

Subdivision (b) requires that a petition for modification or termination follow the same procedure as an original complaint. The Rule recognizes that the domestic relations office conference may serve the same beneficial purposes that it serves in an original proceeding. These benefits, settlement or, if there is no settlement, the assembly of all necessary information will aid the court in the prompt disposition of these petitions.

Explanatory Comment—1993

Existence of Guidelines as Substantial Change in Circumstances. In its opinion in Newman v. Newman, 409 Pa. Super. Ct. 108, 597 A.2d 684 (1991), the Superior Court held that enactment of the guidelines does not constitute a substantial change in circumstance which could serve as the basis for modification of a support order. The amended rule allows the trier of fact to consider new or revised rules as a change in circumstances where the change in the guidelines, either by itself or in combination with other factors, is material and substantial.

Explanatory Comment—2000

The Pennsylvania Child Support Enforcement System (PACSES) is electronically linked to a variety of governmental and private agencies and institutions. This linkage enables PACSES to immediately locate and identify an obligor's income, income sources and assets. Rule 1910.19 is amended to provide that their identification through these automated methods provides a basis for modifying both the current support obligation and the rate of repayment on either past due or overdue support. Identification through means other than PACSES continues to provide the same basis for modification.

While identification of income sources or assets provides a basis for modification, this rule is not intended to prevent a court from ordering that the income or assets be frozen and seized under Rule 1910.26 pending the hearing on the petition for modification. Such relief remains available under Rule 1910.26 governing appropriate interim or special relief. See Rule 1910.1 Explanatory Comment. Nor is this rule intended to affect the court's ability to seize income or assets under Rule 1910.20 to secure an overdue support obligation.

Explanatory Comment—2002

Although support orders do not terminate automatically, many obligors are unaware of the necessity of filing a petition to terminate a child support order when the child becomes emancipated. As a result, old orders have continued to charge long after the subject child has become an adult. New subdivision (e) is intended to address this problem by giving the obligee notice of a proposed modification or termination of the order and the opportunity to object. If no objection is made, or if the obligee fails to respond with a reason to continue the order, the rule gives the court the authority to terminate or modify the charging order, depending upon whether or not other children are covered under the order.

Explanatory Comment—2006

New subdivision (f) addresses an increasing multiplicity of circumstances in which the continued existence of a court-ordered obligation of support is inconsistent with rules or law. An obligor with no known assets whose sole source of income is Supplemental Security Income or cash assistance cannot be ordered to pay support under Rule 1910.16-2. Likewise, an obligor with no verifiable income or assets whose institutionalization, incarceration or long-term disability precludes the payment of support renders the support order unenforceable and uncollectible, diminishing the perception of the court as a source of redress and relief. Often, the obligor is unable or unaware of the need to file for a modification or termination, or the parties abandon the action. In those circumstances, the courts are charged with managing dockets with no viable outcomes. Both the rules and the federal guidelines for child support under Title IV-D of the Social Security Act provide for circumstances under which a support order shall not be entered or under which a child support case may be closed. Subdivision (f) expands the authority of the courts to respond to case management issues brought about by changes in circumstances of the parties of which the courts become aware through the expansion of automated interfaces and data exchanges.

Rule 1910.20 Support Order. Enforcement. General

(a) A support order shall be enforced by income withholding as required by law in the manner provided by Rule 1910.21.

(b) Upon the obligor's failure to comply with a support order, the order may also be enforced by any one or all of the following remedies:

(1) pursuant to Rule 1910.21, and without further hearing or prior notice to the obligor, increasing the amount of monthly support payments for payment of the overdue support at a rate to be determined by the court; withholding or seizing periodic or lump sum payments of income from a government agency, including unemployment compensation, social security, retirement or disability benefits and any other benefits; withholding or seizing periodic or lump sum payments of income from insurance carriers or privately-insured employers, including workers' compensation benefits; withholding or seizing judgments or settlements; and withholding or seizing public and private retirement funds in pay status;

(2) pursuant to Rule 1910.22, imposing liens on real property;

(3) pursuant to Rule 1910.23, attaching and seizing assets of the obligor held in financial institutions;

(4) pursuant to Rule 1910.24, reducing and executing a judgment against the obligor;

(5) pursuant to Rules 1910.25 through 1910.25-6, initiating contempt proceedings;

(6) reporting the amount of overdue support to consumer reporting agencies in the manner prescribed by 23 Pa.C.S. § 4303;

(7) when the obligor owes overdue support in an amount of three months or more, suspending occupational, commercial/driver's and recreational licenses in the manner prescribed by 23 Pa.C.S. § 4355.

These remedies are cumulative and not alternative.

(c) For purposes of this Rule, overdue support remains subject to the remedies set forth in subdivision (b) of this Rule until paid in full. Except as provided in 23 Pa.C.S. § 4355 for suspension of licenses, neither a repayment schedule subsequently agreed to by the parties nor an order of court establishing such a schedule precludes the use of these remedies for collecting overdue support more quickly, whenever feasible.

Adopted April 23, 1981, effective July 22, 1981. Amended Nov. 7, 1988, effective Jan. 1, 1989; March 30, 1994, effective July 1, 1994; May 31, 2000, effective July 1, 2000.

Explanatory Comment—2000

Subdivision (a) continues to reflect the use of mandatory income withholding as the primary tool for enforcement of a support obligation. Withholding is applicable to all forms of income, not merely wages, as the term "income" is broadly defined in 23 Pa.C.S. § 4302. Rule 1910.21 prescribes the procedures for withholding income.

Subdivision (b) is new and reflects the availablity of the new enforcement remedies set forth in Act 58–1997, 23 Pa.C.S. § 4305(b)(10). Consistent with the definitions of past due and overdue support, these remedies are restricted to cases involving overdue support, i.e., the delinquent support arrearages which accumulate as the result of nonpayment of a support order. They may not be used to collect past due support more quickly so long as the obligor remains current on all provisions of the support order, including repayment of past due support. If, however, the obligor subsequently defaults on the support order, subdivision (c) of this rule and the definitions in Rule 1910.1 make it clear that any past due support still owing under the order immediately converts to overdue support and remains overdue support subject to these remedies until collected in full.

Under the new enforcement rules, an obligor essentially has one opportunity to remain current on his or her support obligation so that Act 58 remedies will not apply to permit collection of the past due support arrearages more quickly than the rate at which he or she is repaying those arrearages under the support order. If, however, the obligor defaults in his or her payment of the order, Rule 1910.20 converts the past due support to overdue support and causes Act 58 remedies to become available to collect all of the overdue support until it is paid in full. It remains subject to these remedies until paid in full despite the existence of any later agreement by the parties or court order providing otherwise.

For example, assume a support order is entered requiring the obligor to pay $100 per month in current support and an additional $25 per month on past due support of $400. So long as obligor remains current on the total monthly payment of $125 per month, the past due support of $400 does not operate as a lien on the obligor's real property. Nor will it be collected more quickly through the court's automatic increase of income withholding, seizure of lump-sum forms of income, attachment of the obligor's bank accounts, or reduction of the past due support to a judgment of record for levy and execution on obligor's property in accordance with these Rules. However, subsequent identification of additional income sources or assets provides a basis for increasing the support order under Rule 1910.19 and freezing such income or assets under Rule 1910.26(b).

If, however, the obligor defaults on the support order in any respect (including his or her failure to pay the $25 per month on the past due support), the $400 of past due support immediately becomes overdue support under the definitions set forth in 23 Pa.C.S. § 4302 and Rule 1910.1. It becomes a lien on real property and is also subject to increased withholding, attachment of assets and all of the other remedies available for collecting overdue support as quickly as possible. In addition, it remains overdue support subject to these remedies until paid in full. Even if, therefore, the obligor subsequently agreed to repayment of this amount in larger monthly installments, or an order were entered pursuant to a contempt proceeding for larger installments. Act 58 remedies remain available to collect the $400 whenever additional income or assets are subsequently located and can be used to satisfy the obligation more quickly. This is the case even though at the time of identification the obligor may still be current on the agreement or contempt order.

Subdivision (b) of this rule restricts consumer agency reporting and suspension of licenses to cases involving overdue support. The actual procedures for reporting and license suspension, however, continue to be governed by statute rather than rule. See 23 Pa. C.S. §§ 4303 and 4355.

Rule 1910.20 does not address the collection of support through IRS intercept, Pennsylvania state tax intercept, lottery winnings or any other remedies which may be authorized by federal or state law but are not specifically listed in this rule.

Rule 1910.21   Support Order. Enforcement. Withholding of Income

(a) *Immediate Income Withholding.* **Every order of court shall contain an immediate order for the withholding of income unless (1) there is no overdue support owing under the order and (2) either the court finds there is good cause not to require immediate income withholding or the parties agree in writing to an alternative arrangement.**

(b) *Initiated Income Withholding.* **If there is no immediate income withholding pursuant to subdivision (a), and nonpayment of the support order causes overdue support to accrue, the court shall enter an order for the immediate withholding of income.**

(c) *Order for Withholding.* **An order for income withholding must include a provision directing that no commutation or compromise and release of worker's compensation benefits, severance pay or any payment in lieu thereof shall be paid to the defendant until the order for withholding is dissolved by further order of court.**

(d) *Service on Employer.*

   (1) **The order for income withholding shall be served upon the obligor's employer. The employer shall pay to the State Collection and Disbursement Unit the full amount set forth in the order and may deduct from the balance due the obligor an amount authorized by law for clerical work and expense involved in complying with the order. Upon termination of the obligor's employment, the employer shall notify the domestic relations section of the termination, the obligor's last known address, and the name and address of the obligor's new employer, if known.**

   (2) **Upon willful failure to obey an order for income withholding, the employer, or an officer or employee of the employer, may be held in contempt and subject to other remedies provided by law.**

Rule 1910.21   ACTIONS FOR SUPPORT

Note: 23 Pa.C.S. § 4348(k)(1) provides that contempt is punishable by jail or fine. 23 Pa.C.S. § 4348(k)(2) provides that the employer is liable for any amount which the employer willfully fails to withhold or for any amount withheld but not forwarded to the domestic relations section. 23 Pa.C.S. § 4348(k)(3) provides that the court may attach funds or property of an employer.

(e) *Notice to Obligor. Objections.* **A notice of entry of an order for income withholding shall be served on the obligor. The obligor may object to the order in writing or by personal appearance before the county domestic relations section within ten days after issuance of the notice. The grounds for an objection are limited to the following mistakes of fact: (i) no overdue support exists under the order or there is a mistake in the amount of overdue support; (ii) there is a mistake in the identity of the obligor; or (iii) the amount being withheld exceeds the maximum amount which may be withheld under the federal Consumer Credit Protection Act, 15 U.S.C. § 1673. If a mistake of fact has occurred, the order shall be modified accordingly.**

(f) *Income Withholding When the Obligor Defaults on Support Order.*

    (1) **When an obligor is subject to an order for income withholding and payment is received from the employer within 15 days from the date upon which the obligor's obligation would be considered overdue (i.e. the date upon which delinquent support is equal to one month's support obligation), the payment shall be considered timely and any past due support shall not be converted to overdue support or subject to automated enforcement mechanisms.**

    (2) **When nonpayment of the support order by the obligor causes overdue support to accrue, the court may increase the order for income withholding until the overdue support is paid in full. The court may also direct the employer to withhold any periodic or lump sum distributions of income which may be payable to the obligor in addition to regular income until further order of court.**

(g) *Priority of Income Withholding.* **If there are multiple support obligations in effect against the income of the obligor, the court shall allocate among the obligees the amount of income available for withholding, giving priority to current child support, child support-related expenses and child support arrears to the limit provided by law and stating the priority of payment to the obligee.**

(h) *Termination of Order for Income Withholding.* **An order for income withholding shall continue until dissolved by the court as provided by law.**

Amended Aug. 13, 2008, eff. Oct. 12, 2008.

Official Note: Pursuant to 23 Pa.C.S. § 4348(h), an order for income withholding may be terminated when (1) the support obligation has terminated and the total arrears are paid; (2) the payee cannot be located and it becomes impossible to forward payments; or (3) the result would be unconscionable. The order may also be terminated administratively by the domestic relations section.

Explanatory Comment—2000

1. Rule 1910.21 continues to implement the requirements of mandatory income withholding under 23 Pa.C.S. § 4348(b) in all support cases except those in which there is no overdue support and either the parties agree to an alternative arrangement or the court finds good cause for not requiring such withholding. Consistent with Act 1997-58, advance notice to the obligor is no longer required before the court may issue an order for income withholding. Notice is

now provided concurrently with issuance of the order to the obligor's employer under subdivision (e).

2. This rule continues to apply to the withholding of "income," not merely wages. Income is broadly defined in 23 Pa.C.S. § 4302 as including "compensation for services, including, but not limited to, wages, salaries, bonuses, fees, compensation in kind, commissions and similar items; income derived from business; gains derived from dealings in property; interest; rents; royalties; dividends; annuities; income from life insurance and endowment contracts; all forms of retirement; pensions; income from discharge of indebtedness; distributive share of partnership gross income; income with respect of a decedent; income from an interest in an estate or trust; military retirement benefits; railroad employment retirement benefits; social security benefits; temporary and permanent disability benefits; worker's compensation; unemployment compensation; other entitlements to money or lump sum awards, without regard to source, including lottery winnings, income tax refunds, insurance compensation or settlements; awards or verdicts; and any form of payment due to and collectible by an individual regardless of source."

The Consumer Credit Protection Act, 15 U.S.C. § 1673, sets forth the limitations on monetary withholding. It is important to note, however, that these federal limitations apply only to an obligor's wages or earnings, as those terms are defined in the Consumer Credit Protection Act, and do not apply to any additional forms of income set forth in 23 Pa.C.S. § 4302.

3. The term "employer" is broadly defined in 23 Pa.C.S. § 4302 as including an individual, partnership, association, corporation, trust, federal agency, commonwealth agency or political subdivision paying or obligated to pay income.

4. Subdivision (c) requires all orders for income withholding to include a provision directing the employer to withhold any income which may be payable to the obligor at the end of the employment relationship. This provision contemplates forms of income payable to obligor "in lieu of" regular income as a direct result of the end of the employment relationship—*e.g.,* lump-sum commutations of workers' compensation benefits, severance pay, golden parachutes, or any form of income payable in lieu of the regular stream of income which had been used during the course of employment to secure the monthly support obligation.

5. Subdivision (f) differs in scope and purpose from subdivision (c). Subdivision (f) applies only in cases involving overdue support, and permits the court to increase the rate of income withholding until the overdue support is paid in full. It also allows the court to order the employer to withhold all forms of income which may be owing and payable to the obligor "in addition to" regular income—*e.g.,* bonuses, proceeds from the exercise of stock options or any other kinds of income which are periodically payable during the course of employment.

6. Subdivision (g) incorporates former Rule 1910.22(e) relating to income withholding for multiple support obligations. The provision is amended only to establish the priority of collecting child support before spousal support in cases where the maximum amount of income which can be withheld under the Consumer Credit Protection Act is not sufficient to cover all of the obligor's support obligations in full. In those cases, the income must be allocated first to meet all of the obligor's child support obligations before it may be used to satisfy any of the obligor's spousal support obligations. The portion of the obligation which cannot be satisfied through income withholding will have to be collected through other available means of enforcement.

Explanatory Comment—2008

New subdivision 1910.21(f)(1) is intended to address circumstances in which an employer timely withholds income from an obligor pursuant to an income withholding order, but a delay occurs in receipt of the funds by the State

Collection and Disbursement Unit. In those cases, it would be inappropriate to consider the obligor's payment as untimely and convert past due support to overdue support because an obligor subject to an income withholding order has no control over the timing of the transmission of the funds from the employer. This new rule addresses solely timing issues by providing a 15-day grace period. It does not apply to obligors who are not subject to an order for income withholding.

Rule 1910.21–1   Renumbered as Rule 1910.25

Rule 1910.21–2   Renumbered as Rule 1910.25–1

Rule 1910.21–3   Renumbered as Rule 1910.25–2

Rule 1910.21–4   Renumbered as Rule 1910.25–3

Rule 1910.21–5   Renumbered as Rule 1910.25–4

Rule 1910.21–6   Renumbered as Rule 1910.25–5

Rule 1910.21–7   Renumbered as Rule 1910.25–6

Rule 1910.22   Support Order. Enforcement. Liens Against Real Property

(a) An overdue support obligation of this or any other state which is on record at the domestic relations section shall constitute a lien of record by operation of law against the obligor's real property located in Pennsylvania. When the overdue obligation arises in another state, it shall be transmitted to the Department of Public Welfare Central Registry. Upon receipt and verification of the amount owed, the Central Registry shall notify the appropriate domestic relations section which shall enter the amount owed in its records.

(b) A person seeking certification of a lien of record arising from overdue support owed by an obligor shall submit a written request for certification to the domestic relations section. The request must include the obligor's full name, date of birth and social security number, if known. Within two business days, the domestic relations section shall provide written certification of the amount of overdue support owed as of the date of certification and shall enter the amount and date of certification on the docket.

Note: Rule 76 defines "person" as including a corporation, partnership and association as well as a natural person.

(c) The domestic relations section shall provide a copy of the written certification to the parties. Either party may object to the certification in writing or by personal appearance before the domestic relations section. The grounds for an objection are limited to the following: (1) no overdue support exists under the support order or there is a mistake in the certified amount of overdue support; (2) there is a mistake in the identity of the obligor; or (3) the lien cannot attach to the property as a matter of law. Pending a court's disposition of the objection, the certification shall remain in full force and effect unless stayed by the court for good cause shown.

(d) Payment of the certified amount of overdue support shall constitute a satisfaction thereof and the domestic relations section shall record the amount of payment on the docket.

Former Rule 1910.22 rescinded and new rule adopted May 31, 2000, effective July 1, 2000.

Explanatory Comment—2000

New Rule 1910.22 implements 23 Pa.C.S. § 4352(d) as amended by Act 1997–58 and Act 1998–127. Under prior law, the existence of overdue support created only a judgment by operation of law against the obligor. The judgment did not, however, operate as a lien against the property until and unless, either at the direction of the court or upon praecipe of the party, the court certified the overdue support and entered it of record at the prothonotary's office. Pursuant to § 4352(d), as amended, the existence of overdue support not only creates a judgment by operation of law against the obligor, it also creates a lien by operation of law against the obligor's real property. The practical effect of this amendment is that certification by the court is no longer required to create the lien on real property. It is the existence of overdue support, not its judicial certification, which creates the lien on real property. The lien also extends to any and all real property owned by the obligor which is located in Pennsylvania.

While the existence of overdue support creates an automatic lien on real property, it does not create an automatic lien against an obligor's personal property. Nor does it have the effect of a fully perfected security interest in such property until the Department of Public Welfare establishes a statewide system for providing public notice of liens on such property. To the extent, however, that overdue support continues to operate as a judgment by operation of law against the obligor, it may still also be reduced to a judgment of record and satisfied through levy and execution on both real and personal property in the manner prescribed in Rule 1910.24.

1. Subdivision (a) requires that the overdue support be "of record" at the domestic relations section. Overdue support becomes a matter of record at the time it is automatically recorded into the PACSES computer system. Since statewide implementation of PACSES means that every domestic relations section in Pennsylvania now has equal access to all information relating to overdue support obligations, no additional paperwork in or by the county is necessary for a lien on real property to become of record for purposes of giving the lien statewide effect against the obligor's real property.

When the overdue support obligation arises in another state but is forwarded for enforcement in Pennsylvania, the originating state must initially forward it to the Department of Public Welfare Central Registry. The Central Registry will verify the amount owed and transmit the information to the appropriate domestic relations section. The domestic relations section must then enter this amount in its records. This recording creates the "lien of record" making the foreign obligation enforceable as a lien against any and all real property owned by obligor which is located in Pennsylvania.

2. While certification of overdue support is no longer necessary to create the lien on real property, certification is necessary for purposes of satisfying and removing the lien from the property prior to refinancing or sale of the property. Subdivisions (b) through (d) prescribe the procedures for obtaining this written certification. The effect of certification on the rights and liabilities of the parties involved in the actual refinancing or sales transaction is set forth in 23 Pa.C.S. § 4352(d.1)(3).

3. Subdivision (c) sets forth the limited grounds for objecting to the imposition of a lien on real property. The third ground for objection is that the property is exempt from attachment as a matter of law. This objection contemplates property held by the obligor and his or her spouse as tenants by the entireties.

4. 23 Pa.C.S. § 4352(d.1)(2) through (9) establish the priorities of liens against real property. Pursuant to 23 Pa.C.S. § 4352(d.1)(2)(i)(B), moreover, any overdue support existing on the effective date of this rule which becomes a lien on property in another county solely by virtue of the promulgation of this rule shall have priority against the property in the other county only from the effective date of this rule.

Rule 1910.23 Support Order. Enforcement. Attachment of Assets Held by Financial Institutions

(a) Upon identification of an obligor's assets held by a financial institution, the court shall, upon certification of the overdue support owed by the obligor, enter an immediate order prohibiting the release of those assets until further order of court. The order shall be served on the financial institution in the manner prescribed by Rules 400 through 406 governing service of original process or by registered mail, return receipt requested or by electronic service upon the request of the financial institution. Service by mail is complete upon the return of the registered mail receipt personally signed by the financial institution or other evidence of service satisfactory to the court. Service of the order on the financial institution shall attach the asset up to the amount of the overdue support until further order of court.

(b) The domestic relations section shall provide written notification of the attachment to the obligor. The obligor and any joint owner of the account who has been notified by the financial institution may object to the attachment in writing or by personal appearance before the domestic relations section within 30 days after issuance of the notice. The grounds for an objection are limited to the following: (1) no overdue support exists under the support order or there is a mistake in the certified amount of overdue support; (2) there is a mistake in the identity of the obligor; or (3) the account is not subject to attachment as a matter of law.

(c) If no objection is made within 30 days after notice was issued, the court shall, upon proof that obligor was properly served with notice of the attachment, enter an order seizing the assets up to the amount of overdue support owed. The order shall be served on the financial institution and a copy of the order provided to both parties.

Adopted May 31, 2000, effective July 1, 2000; amended January 25, 2013, eff. Feb. 24, 2013.

Explanatory Comment—2000

Rule 1910.23 implements 23 Pa.C.S. § 4305(b)(10)(iii) authorizing the attachment and seizure of an obligor's assets held in financial institutions. A "financial institution" is defined in 23 Pa.C.S. § 4304.1(g) and includes any bank, federal or state credit union, insurer, safe deposit company or money-market mutual fund authorized to do business in Pennsylvania.

Subdivision (b) of this rule sets forth the three limited grounds for objecting to an attachment of assets under this rule. The third ground for objection—that the assets are not subject to attachment as a matter of law—chiefly contemplates assets held by the obligor and his or her spouse as tenants by the entireties. Other examples include assets being held in an escrow or trust account in the name of the obligor as the escrowee or trustee.

Rule 1910.23–1. [Rescinded]

Rescinded May 31, 2000, effective July 1, 2000.

Rule 1910.23–2. [Rescinded]

Rescinded May 31, 2000, effective July 1, 2000.

Rule 1910.24 Support Order. Enforcement. Judgment for Arrearages. Petition to Correct Judgment. Execution

(a) On and after the date it is due, overdue support shall constitute a judgment against the obligor as provided by law. The prothonotary shall enter the judgment of record upon the proper docket and in the judgment index either at the direction of the court or upon praecipe of a party or the domestic relations section. The judgment must be accompanied by a written certification showing that obligor owes overdue support pursuant to an order of court.

(b) A petition to correct the judgment shall be limited to the following grounds: (1) no overdue support exists under the support order or (2) there is a mistake in the amount of overdue support. The petition initially shall be determined before a conference officer or hearing officer in the same manner as an original proceeding for support. Except as provided by order of court, the filing of a petition to correct a judgment shall not stay the proceedings.

> **Note:** It is important to note that the petition to strike or open a judgment used in civil practice is not adopted here.

(c) The judgment may be enforced against the obligor's real or personal property as provided by Rules 3001 through 3011, governing transfer of judgments, and Rules 3101 through 3149, governing enforcement of judgments for the payment of money.

> **Note:** See Section 8104 of the Judicial Code, 42 Pa.C.S., § 8104, which imposes a duty upon a judgment creditor who has received satisfaction of a judgment, upon written request and tender of the fee, to enter satisfaction in the office of the clerk of court (the prothonotary) in which the judgment is outstanding.

Former Rule 1910.24 rescinded and new rule adopted May 31, 2000, effective July 1, 2000.

Explanatory Comment—2000

Rule 1910.24 incorporates former Rules 1910.23-1 and 1910.23-2 prescribing the procedures for reducing overdue support to a judgment of record against the obligor and for petitioning to have the judgment corrected in the event the amount of overdue support is incorrect. Although 23 Pa.C.S. § 4352(d) states that "a support obligation" constitutes a judgment by operation of law, subdivision (a) states that only overdue support constitutes a judgment by operation of law. This is in accordance with Welz v. Stump, 403 Pa. Super. 93, 588 A.2d 47 (1991) which holds that a judgment cannot be entered against the obligor for past due support when the support order specifically provides for repayment of the past due support in monthly installments and the obligor is in compliance with the order.

A judgment entered of record does not arise simply when a support obligation becomes due and remains unpaid. Nor does it arise merely upon the court's determination of the amount of arrears as of a particular date. Rather, the court must specifically direct that the judgment in the specified amount be entered of record. The prothonotary must then enter the judgment in the proper docket and judgment index in order to create the notice of the judgment. Only after the judgment has been properly entered of record is the judgment enforceable under the general rules of civil procedure governing garnishment and execution against the obligor's real or personal property.

Rule 1910.24's authorized use of the prothonotary to enforce a judgment does not in any way limit the authority of the domestic relations section to issue writs and orders pursuant to 23 Pa.C.S. § 4305(b).

Rule 1910.25. Enforcement. Support Order. Civil Contempt. Petition. Service. No Answer Required

(a) Upon failure to comply with an order of support, a petition for civil contempt

(1) may be filed by the obligee at any time, or

(2) shall be filed by the domestic relations section

(i) immediately upon the accrual of arrearages in any amount for fifteen days where it is known at the outset that income cannot be attached; or

(ii) immediately upon learning that an order for income withholding pursuant to Rule 1910.21 has been ineffective, or within twenty days of failure to comply with the order of support, whichever is earlier.

Official Note: Except as provided in 23 Pa.C.S. § 4355 relating to suspension of licenses, an order entered pursuant to a contempt proceeding which establishes a rate of repayment on overdue support does not preclude the use of other remedies under Title 23 or these Rules for collecting overdue support more quickly, whenever feasible.

(b) The petition shall begin with an order of court in substantially the following form:

(CAPTION)

ORDER OF COURT

Legal proceedings have been brought against you alleging that you have disobeyed an order of court for support.

Pa. R.C.P. Rule 1910.25

(1) A critical issue in the contempt proceeding is your ability to pay and comply with the terms of the support order. If you wish to defend against the claim set forth in the following pages, you may, but are not required to, file in writing with the court your defenses or objections.

(2) You, _____, Respondent, must appear in person in court on _____ (day and date) at _____ (a.m./p.m.) in (court) room _____, _____ (address).

IF YOU DO NOT APPEAR IN PERSON, THE COURT MAY ISSUE A WARRANT FOR YOUR ARREST AND YOU MAY BE COMMITTED TO JAIL.

(3) If the court finds that you have willfully failed to comply with its order for support, you may be found to be in contempt of court and committed to jail, fined or both.

You will have the opportunity to disclose income, other financial information and any relevant personal information at the conference/hearing so that the court can determine if you have the ability to pay. You may also tell the court about any unusual expenses that may affect your ability to pay. You may fill out the enclosed Income Statement and Expense Statement forms and submit them to the court.

At the conference/hearing, the contempt petition may be dismissed, new and/or modified purge conditions may be imposed, or the judge may order you to jail. If the obligee fails to appear, the court will proceed with the case and enter an appropriate order.

YOU ARE REQUIRED TO BRING:

Your most recent pay stub for any and all employers

Payroll address, phone number, fax number and contact person

Proof of medical coverage

Any other documentation relevant to your case and the issue of contempt as stated in the petition, including the completed Income Statement and Expense Statement forms. For example, other documentation that may be relevant includes documents related to claims for unemployment compensation, workers' compensation and Social Security benefits.

BY THE COURT

DATE OF ORDER: _____   _____
                                              Judge

YOU SHOULD TAKE THIS PAPER TO YOUR LAWYER AT ONCE. IF YOU DO NOT HAVE A LAWYER, GO TO OR TELEPHONE THE OFFICE SET FORTH BELOW. THIS OFFICE CAN PROVIDE YOU WITH INFORMATION ABOUT HIRING A LAWYER. IF YOU CANNOT AFFORD TO HIRE A LAWYER, THIS OFFICE MAY BE ABLE TO PROVIDE YOU WITH INFORMATION ABOUT AGENCIES THAT MAY OFFER LEGAL SERVICES TO ELIGIBLE PERSONS AT A REDUCED FEE OR NO FEE.

_____
(Name)

_____
(Address)

_____
(Telephone Number)

Rule 1910.25–1   ACTIONS FOR SUPPORT

Official Note: Neither Rule 1018.1 (Notice to Defend) nor Rule 1361 (Notice to Plead) apply to a petition for enforcement of support.

(c) **The petition shall aver the facts alleged to constitute the failure to comply with the support order. The petition shall set forth the amount of support arrearages, if any, as provided by the domestic relations section. Unless specially ordered by the court, no answer to the petition is required.**

(d) **The petition shall be served upon the respondent**

(1) **by ordinary mail with the return address of the domestic relations section appearing thereon; or**

(2) **by any form of mail which requires the respondent to sign a receipt; or**

(3) **by a competent adult; or**

Official Note: See Rule 76 for the definition of "competent adult."

(4) **pursuant to special order of court. A respondent who attends the conference and/or hearing in person shall be deemed to have been served.**

(e) **The court may issue a bench warrant as provided by Rule 1910.13-1 for failure of the respondent to appear.**

(f) **The respondent shall be advised in the Order/Notice to Appear that his or her present ability to pay is a critical issue in the contempt proceeding. The respondent shall be provided with Income and Expense Statements to demonstrate financial ability to pay. At the hearing, the respondent shall be provided the opportunity to respond to any questions about his or her financial status. The trier of fact shall issue an express finding that the respondent does or does not have the present ability to pay.**

Adopted March 30, 1994, effective July 1, 1994. Amended May 14, 1999, effective July 1, 1999. Renumbered from Rule 1910.21-1 and amended May 31, 2000, effective July 1, 2000. Amended March 18, 2004, effective June 16, 2004; November 30, 2012, effective December 30, 2012.

Explanatory Comment—2012

The amendments to the form in subdivision (b) and new subdivision (f) are intended to assure compliance with the U.S. Supreme Court's decision in *Turner v. Rogers*, 131 S. Ct. 2507 (2011). In that case, the Court held that counsel need not automatically be appointed for indigent support obligors facing incarceration in civil contempt proceedings. The Court held that the due process clause of the Fourteenth Amendment to the U.S. Constitution does not require that counsel be provided where the obligee is not represented by counsel and the state provides alternative procedural safeguards including adequate notice of the importance of the ability to pay, a fair opportunity to present, and to dispute, relevant information, and express court findings as to the obligor's ability to pay.

Rule 1910.25–1   Civil Contempt. Hearing by Court. Conference by Officer

(a) **After service of the petition and order of court upon the respondent, there shall be**

(1) an office conference conducted by a conference officer, as provided by Rule 1910.25-2, or (2) an immediate hearing by the court, if permitted by the court.

(b) If, at any time during a contempt proceeding, including proceedings under 1910.25-2, 1910.25-3 and 1910.25-4, the hearing officer or conference officer determines that the failure to comply with the support order is willful and there is present ability to comply, the petition for contempt shall be heard by the court for consideration of incarceration and other appropriate sanctions.

Note: The determination required by subdivision (b) shall be made by a conference officer in counties adopting the procedure of Rule 1910.25-3 (conference and hearing de novo) or by a hearing officer in counties adopting the alternative procedure of Rule 1910.25-4 (record hearing and exceptions).

Courts should strive to hear these cases promptly, on the same day if possible.

Adopted March 30, 1994, effective July 1, 1994. Renumbered from Rule 1910.21-2 and amended May 31, 2000, effective July 1, 2000.

Rule 1910.25–2 Civil Contempt. Office Conference. Agreement. Alternative Procedures Upon Failure to Agree

(a) The office conference shall be conducted by a conference officer.

(b) The conference officer may make a recommendation to the parties as to the disposition of the proceedings.

(c) If an agreement is reached at the conference, the conference officer shall prepare a written order in conformity with the agreement for signature by the parties and submission to the court. The court may enter the order in accordance with the agreement without hearing the parties.

(d) If an agreement is not reached, the procedure shall be as prescribed by Rule 1910.25-3 unless the court by local rule adopts the alternative procedure of Rule 1910.25-4.

Adopted March 30, 1994, effective July 1, 1994. Renumbered from Rule 1910.21-3 and amended May 31, 2000, effective July 1, 2000.

[See Explanatory Comment—1994 following Rule 1910.13-1]

Rule 1910.25–3 Civil Contempt. Conference Summary. Order. Hearing De Novo

(a) If an agreement is not reached, the conference officer shall, at the conclusion of the conference or shortly thereafter, prepare a conference summary and furnish copies to the court and to all parties. The conference summary shall state:

(1) the facts upon which the parties agree,

(2) the contentions of the parties with respect to facts upon which they disagree, and

(3) the conference officer's recommendation whether

(i) the respondent has willfully failed to comply with the order for support,

(ii) the respondent should be held in contempt, and

(iii) sanctions or purge conditions should be imposed against the respondent.

Note: The sanction of imprisonment may be imposed only following an evidentiary hearing before a judge. See Rule 1910.25-5(a).

(b) The court, without hearing the parties, may enter an appropriate order after consideration of the conference summary. Each party shall be provided with a copy of the order and written notice that any party may, within twenty days after the date of receipt or the date of the mailing of the order, whichever occurs first, file a written demand with the domestic relations section for a hearing before the court.

(c) A demand for a hearing before the court shall stay the contempt order.

(d) If the court does not enter an order under Rule 1910.25-2(c) or subdivision (b) of this rule within five days of the conference, or if an order is entered and a demand for a hearing before the court is filed, there shall be a hearing de novo before the court. The domestic relations section shall schedule the hearing and give notice to the parties. The hearing de novo shall be held no later than seventy-five days after the date the petition for contempt was filed.

(e) The court shall not be precluded from conducting a hearing on the petition for contempt on the same day as the office conference.

Note: Every effort should be made to ensure that these cases are heard promptly, on the same day if possible.

Adopted March 30, 1994, effective July 1, 1994. Renumbered from Rule 1910.21-4 and amended May 31, 2000, effective July 1, 2000; Amended, June 11, 2007, effective immediately.

[See Explanatory Comment—1994 following Rule 1910.13-1]

Rule 1910.25–4 Civil Contempt. Alternative Procedure. Record Hearing. Report. Exceptions. Order

(a) At the conclusion of the conference if an agreement has not been reached, the parties shall be given notice of the date, time, and place of a hearing if the conference and hearing have not been scheduled for the same date. The hearing on the record shall be conducted by a hearing officer who must be a lawyer.

Note: Every effort should be made to ensure that cases are heard promptly, on the same day if possible.

(b) The hearing officer shall receive evidence, hear argument and file with the court a report containing a proposed order. A copy of the report shall be furnished to all parties at the conclusion of the hearing. The report may be in narrative form and shall include the officer's recommendation with respect to the following matters, together with the reasons therefor:

(1) whether the respondent has willfully failed to comply with the order for support,

(2) whether the respondent should be held in contempt, and

(3) whether sanctions or purge conditions should be imposed against the respondent.

Note: The sanction of imprisonment may be imposed only following an evidentiary hearing before the judge. See Rule 1910.25-5(a).

(c) Within twenty days after the conclusion of the hearing, any party may file exceptions to the report or any part thereof, to rulings on objections, to statements or findings of fact, to conclusions of law, or to any other matters occurring during the hearing. Each exception shall set forth a separate objection precisely and without discussion. Matters not covered by exceptions are deemed waived unless, prior to the entry of the order, leave is granted to file exceptions raising those matters.

(d) If no exceptions are filed within the twenty-day period, the court shall review the report and, if approved, enter an order.

(e) If exceptions are filed, the court shall, no later than seventy-five days after the date the petition for contempt was filed, hear argument on the exceptions or hold a hearing de novo. The court shall enter an appropriate order.

Adopted March 30, 1994, effective July 1, 1994. Renumbered from Rule 1910.21-5 and amended May 31, 2000, effective July 1, 2000; Amended, June 11, 2007, effective immediately.

[See Explanatory Comment—1994 following Rule 1910.13-1]

Rule 1910.25-5. Civil Contempt. Contempt Order. Incarceration

(a) No respondent may be incarcerated as a sanction for contempt without an evidentiary hearing before a judge.

(b) The court shall make a finding, on the record, as to whether the respondent, based upon the evidence presented at the hearing, does or does not have the present ability to pay the court-ordered amount of support.

(c) An order committing a respondent to jail for civil contempt of a support order shall specify the conditions the fulfillment of which will result in the release of the respondent.

Official Note: The time periods set forth in Rules 1910.25 through 1910.25-6 are for the benefit of the plaintiff, and not for the defendant. The goal is the prompt initiation of contempt proceedings because of the importance of ongoing support payments. The time periods in no way limit the right of either the domestic relations section or the plaintiff to proceed with a contempt action.

Adopted March 30, 1994, effective July 1, 1994. Renumbered from 1910.21-6 and amended May 31, 2000, effective July 1, 2000. Amended June 11, 2007, imd. effective; November 30, 2012, effective December 30, 2012.

[See Explanatory Comment—1994 following Rule 1910.13-1]

Rule 1910.25–6 Civil Contempt. No Post-Trial Relief

No motions for post trial relief shall be filed to any orders entered pursuant to Rules 1910.25 through 1910.25-6.

Adopted March 30, 1994, effective July 1, 1994. Renumbered from Rule 1910.21-7 and amended May 31, 2000, effective July 1, 2000.

Rule 1910.25–7 Indirect Criminal Contempt. Incarceration.

In addition to any other remedy available to the court, the court may order the respondent to obtain employment with income that can be verified and is subject to income attachment. If the respondent willfully fails to comply with an order to obtain such employment, the court may commit the respondent to jail upon adjudication for indirect criminal contempt, provided the respondent is afforded all of the procedural safeguards available to criminal defendants.

Explanatory Comment—2007

Parental support of children is a fundamental requirement of law and public policy. Absent an inability to maintain employment or acquire other income or assets, sanction in the form of incarceration may be imposed by the court to compel compliance and provide an incentive to obey the law. The contempt process, which should be used as a last resort, is necessary to impose coercive sanctions upon those obligors whose circumstances provide no recourse to the court to compel payment or a good faith effort to comply. Appellate opinions have made it clear that an obligor who is in civil contempt cannot be incarcerated without the present ability to fulfill the conditions the court imposes for release. However, the courts also have noted that recalcitrant obligors may be imprisoned for indirect criminal contempt if afforded the proper procedural safeguards. See *Godfrey v. Godfrey*, 894 A.2d 776 (Pa. Super. 2006); *Hyle v. Hyle*, 868 A.2d 601 (Pa. Super. 2005).

Rule 1910.26 Support Order. Enforcement. Stay of Proceedings. Special Relief

(a) An action for support or a support order may be stayed only by a special order of court upon a showing of compelling circumstances following notice and hearing or upon agreement of the parties in writing.

(b) At any time after the filing of the complaint, the court may on application issue a preliminary or special injunction, appoint a temporary receiver, order the seizure of property, dispose of seized property or grant other appropriate interim or special relief.

Adopted May 31, 2000, effective July 1, 2000.

Explanatory Comment—2000

New Rule 1910.26 merely consolidates into one rule the provisions formerly found in Rules 1910.24 and 1910.25.

Subdivision (a) continues to reflect the existing policy of eliminating delay and procedural impediments to the receipt of support. The routine granting of a stay of proceedings would defeat this policy and have a disastrous effect upon a destitute obligee and child. Thus, a stay of an action for support or of a support order may only be granted (1) upon a special order of court following notice and hearing or (2) upon written agreement of the parties.

Subdivision (b) continues to reflect the availability of special relief. Sections 1 and 2 of the Act 1907, 48 P.S. §§ 131 and 132, authorize the bringing of an action at law or in equity to enforce the duty of support. These sections are suspended by these Rules insofar as they provide practice and procedure for an action of support. However, equitable remedies may still be useful in a case which warrants them. Illustrations are the enjoining of a resident trustee from disbursing funds to a defendant beneficiary outside the Commonwealth or to an improvident defendant or obtaining satisfaction from a spendthrift trust. The Rule contains a broad provision empowering the court to provide special relief where appropriate. It may also be used to freeze and seize income or assets to secure past due support when appropriate. See Rule 1910.1 and Rule 1910.20 Explanatory Comments.

Rule 1910.27. Form of Complaint. Order. Income Statements and Expense Statements. Health Insurance Coverage Information Form. Form of Support Order. Form Petition for Modification. Petition for Recovery of Support Overpayment

(a) The complaint in an action for support shall be substantially in the following form:

(Caption)

COMPLAINT FOR SUPPORT

1. **Plaintiff resides at** _____,
(Street) (City) (Zip Code)
_____ **County. Plaintiff's Social Security Number is**
_____, **and date of birth is** _____.

2. **Defendant resides at** _____,
(Street) (City) (Zip Code)
_____ **County. Defendant's Social Security Number is**
_____, **and date of birth is** _____.

3. (a) **Plaintiff and Defendant were married on** _____, **at**
(Date)
_____.
(City) (State)
(b) **Plaintiff and Defendant were separated on** _____.
(Date)
(c) **Plaintiff and Defendant were divorced on** _____,
(Date)
at _____.
(City) (State)

Rule 1910.27   ACTIONS FOR SUPPORT

4. Plaintiff and Defendant are the parents of the following children:

   (a) Born of the Marriage:

   Name   Birth Date   Age   Residence
   _____   _____   ____   _____
   _____   _____   ____   _____

   (b) Born out of Wedlock:

   Name   Birth Date   Age   Residence
   _____   _____   ____   _____
   _____   _____   ____   _____

5. Plaintiff seeks to pay support or receive support for the following persons:
   _____.

6. (a) Plaintiff is (not) receiving public assistance in the amount of
   $ _____ per _____ for the support of _____
   _____.
              (Name(s))

   (b) Plaintiff is receiving additional income in the amount of
   $ _____ from _____.
                                      (Name(s))

7. A previous support order was entered against the [ ] plaintiff
   [ ] defendant on _____ in an action at _____
                     (Date)
   _____ in the amount of $ _____
   (Court, term and docket number)
   for the support of _____.
                                (Name(s))
   There are (no) arrearages in the amount of $ _____.
   The order has (not) been terminated.

8. [ ] Plaintiff [ ] Defendant last received support from the other
   party in the amount of $ _____ on _____.
                                                  (Date)

WHEREFORE, Plaintiff requests that an order be entered on behalf of the aforementioned child(ren) and/or spouse for reasonable support and medical coverage.

_____
(Date)   Plaintiff or Attorney for Plaintiff

I verify that the statements made in this Complaint are true and correct, I understand that false statements herein are made subject to the penalties of 18 Pa.C.S. § 4904, relating to unsworn falsification to authorities.

_____
Date   Plaintiff

NOTICE

Guidelines for child and spousal support, and for alimony pendente lite have been prepared by the court of common pleas and are available for inspection in the office of the Domestic Relations Section,

Pa. R.C.P.   Rule 1910.27

(Address)

Note: See Pa.R.C.P. No. 1930.1(b). To the extent this rule applies to actions not governed by other legal authority regarding confidentiality of information and documents in support actions or that attorneys or unrepresented parties file support-related confidential information and documents in non-support actions (e.g., divorce, custody), the *Case Records Public Access Policy of the Unified Judicial System of Pennsylvania* shall apply.

(b) The order to be attached at the front of the complaint in subdivision (a) shall be substantially in the following form:

(Caption)

ORDER OF COURT

Plaintiff, _____ and _____, defendant, are ordered to appear at _____ before _____ _____, a conference officer of the Domestic Relations Section, on the _____ day of _____, 20____, at _____.M., for a conference, after which the officer may recommend that an order for support be entered against you.

You are further ordered to bring to the conference

(1) a true copy of your most recent Federal Income Tax Return, including W-2s, as filed,

(2) your pay stubs for the preceding six months,

(3) the Income Statement and the appropriate Expense Statement, if required, attached to this order, completed as required by Rule 1910.11(c),

(4) verification of child care expenses, and

(5) proof of medical coverage which you may have, or may have available to you. If you fail to appear for the conference or to bring the required documents, the court may issue a warrant for your arrest and/or enter an interim support order. If paternity is an issue, the court shall enter an order establishing paternity.

(6) If a physician has determined that a medical condition affects your ability to earn income you must obtain a Physician Verification Form from the domestic relations section, sign it, have it completed by your doctor, and bring it with you to the conference..

THE TRIER OF FACT SHALL ENTER AN APPROPRIATE CHILD SUPPORT ORDER BASED UPON THE EVIDENCE PRESENTED, WITHOUT REGARD TO WHICH PARTY INITIATED THE SUPPORT ACTION. THE DETERMINATION OF WHICH PARTY WILL BE THE OBLIGEE AND WHICH WILL BE THE OBLIGOR WILL BE MADE BY THE TRIER OF FACT BASED UPON THE RESPECTIVE INCOMES OF THE PARTIES, CONSISTENT WITH THE SUPPORT GUIDELINES AND EXISTING LAW, AND THE CUSTODIAL ARRANGEMENTS AT THE TIME OF THE INITIAL OR SUBSEQUENT CONFERENCE, HEARING, OR TRIAL. IF SUPPORTED BY THE EVIDENCE, THE PARTY NAMED AS THE DEFENDANT IN THE INITIAL PLEADING MAY BE DEEMED TO BE THE OBLIGEE, EVEN IF THAT PARTY DID NOT FILE A COMPLAINT FOR SUPPORT.

Date of Order:

_____

J.

Rule 1910.27   **ACTIONS FOR SUPPORT**

YOU HAVE THE RIGHT TO A LAWYER, WHO MAY ATTEND THE CONFERENCE AND REPRESENT YOU. IF YOU DO NOT HAVE A LAWYER, GO TO OR TELEPHONE THE OFFICE SET FORTH BELOW. THIS OFFICE CAN PROVIDE YOU WITH INFORMATION ABOUT HIRING A LAWYER.

IF YOU CANNOT AFFORD TO HIRE A LAWYER, THIS OFFICE MAY BE ABLE TO PROVIDE YOU WITH INFORMATION ABOUT AGENCIES THAT MAY OFFER LEGAL SERVICES TO ELIGIBLE PERSONS AT A REDUCED FEE OR NO FEE.

_____
(Name)

_____
(Address)

_____
(Telephone Number)

AMERICANS WITH DISABILITIES ACT OF 1990

The Court of Common Pleas of _____ County is required by law to comply with the Americans with Disabilities Act of 1990. For information about accessible facilities and reasonable accommodations available to disabled individuals having business before the court, please contact our office. All arrangements must be made at least 72 hours prior to any hearing or business before the court. You must attend the scheduled conference or hearing.

(c) The Income Statements and Expense Statements to be attached to the order in subdivision (b) shall be substantially in the following form:

(1) *Income Statements.* This form must be filled out in all cases.

Note: *See* Pa.R.C.P. No. 1930.1(b).To the extent this rule applies to actions not governed by other legal authority regarding confidentiality of information and documents in support actions or that attorneys or unrepresented parties file support-related confidential information and documents in non-support actions (e.g., divorce, custody), the *Case Records Public Access Policy of the Unified Judicial System of Pennsylvania* shall apply.

_____

v.

_____

No.

_____

THIS FORM MUST BE FILLED OUT

(If you are self-employed or if you are salaried by a business of which you are owner in whole or in part, you must also fill out the Supplemental Income Statement which appears below.)

INCOME STATEMENT OF

(Name)   (PACSES Number)

_____

I verify that the statements made in this Income Statement are true and correct. I understand that false statements herein are made subject to the penalties of 18 Pa.C.S.A. § 4904 relating to unsworn falsification to authorities.

Pa. R.C.P.   Rule 1910.27

Date:
_____

_____

Plaintiff or Defendant
INCOME
Employer:_____
Address:_____
Type of Work: _____
Payroll Number: _____
Pay Period (weekly, biweekly, etc); _____
Gross Pay per Pay Period: $ _____
Itemized Payroll Deductions: _____
Federal Withholding $ _____
FICA   _____
Local Wage Tax   _____
State Income Tax   _____
Mandatory Retirement   _____
Union Dues

                                                 _____
                                                 _____
                                                 _____
Health Insurance   _____
Other (specify)   _____

_____   _____

_____   _____
Net Pay per Pay Period: $ _____
Other Income:

	Week	Month	Year
	(Fill in Appropriate Column)		
Interest	$ _____	$ _____	$ _____
Dividends	_____	_____	_____
Pension Distributions	_____	_____	_____
Annuity	_____	_____	_____
Social Security	_____	_____	_____
Rents	_____	_____	_____
Royalties	_____	_____	_____
	_____	_____	_____
	_____	_____	_____
Unemployment Comp.	_____	_____	_____

Rule 1910.27   **ACTIONS FOR SUPPORT**

    Workers Comp.   _____   _____   _____
    Employer Fringe Benefits   _____   _____   _____
    Other

_____   _____   _____   _____
    Total $ _____ $ _____ $ _____
TOTAL INCOME $ _____

PROPERTY OWNED

	Description	Value	Ownership*		
			H	W	J
Checking accounts	_____	$ _____	__	__	__
Savings accounts	_____	_____	__	__	__
Credit Union	_____	_____	__	__	__
Stocks/bonds	_____	_____	__	__	__
Real Estate	_____	_____	__	__	__
Other	_____	_____	__	__	__
	Total	$ _____			

INSURANCE

	Company	Policy No.	Coverage*		
			H	W	C
Hospital					
Blue Cross	_____	_____	__	__	__
Other	_____	_____	__	__	__
Medical					
Blue Shield	_____	_____	__	__	__
Other	_____	_____	__	__	__
Health/Accident	_____	_____	__	__	__
Disability Income	_____	_____	__	__	__
Dental	_____	_____	__	__	__
Other	_____	_____	__	__	__

* H = Husband; W = Wife; J = Joint; C = Child

SUPPLEMENTAL INCOME STATEMENT

(a) This form is to be filled out by a person (check one):
    ☐ (1) who operates a business or practices a profession, or
    ☐ (2) who is a member of a partnership or joint venture, or
    ☐ (3) who is a shareholder in and is salaried by a closed corporation or similar entity.

Pa. R.C.P. **Rule 1910.27**

(b) Attach to this statement a copy of the following documents relating to the partnership, joint venture, business, profession, corporation or similar entity:

   (1) the most recent Federal Income Tax Return, and

   (2) the most recent Profit and Loss Statement.

(c) Name of business:

_____

Address and Telephone Number:

_____

_____

(d) Nature of business

   (check one)

   ☐ (1) partnership

   ☐ (2) joint venture

   ☐ (3) profession

   ☐ (4) closed corporation

   ☐ (5) other

(e) Name of accountant, controller or other person in charge of financial records:

_____

(f) Annual income from business: _____

   (1) How often is income received? _____

   (2) Gross income per pay period: _____

   (3) Net income per pay period: _____

   (4) Specified deductions, if any: _____

(2) *Expense Statements.* An Expense Statement is not required in cases that can be determined pursuant to the guidelines unless a party avers unusual needs and expenses that may warrant a deviation from the guideline amount of support pursuant to Pa.R.C.P. No. 1910.16-5 or seeks an apportionment of expenses pursuant to Pa.R.C.P. No. 1910.16-6. See Pa.R.C.P. No. 1910.11(c)(1). Child support is calculated under the guidelines based upon the monthly net incomes of the parties, with additional amounts ordered as necessary to provide for child care expenses, health insurance premiums, unreimbursed medical expenses, mortgage payments, and other needs, contingent upon the obligor's ability to pay. The Expense Statement in subparagraph (A) shall be utilized if a party is claiming that he or she has unusual needs and unusual fixed expenses that may warrant deviation or adjustment in a case determined under the guidelines. In child support, spousal support, and alimony *pendente lite* cases calculated pursuant to Pa.R.C.P. No. 1910.16-3.1 and in divorce cases involving claims for alimony, counsel fees, or costs and expenses pursuant to Pa.R.C.P. No. 1920.31(a), the parties shall complete the Expense Statement in subparagraph (B).

   Note: *See* Pa.R.C.P. No. 1930.1(b). To the extent this rule applies to actions not governed by other legal authority regarding confidentiality of information and documents in support actions or that attorneys or unrepresented parties file support-related confidential information and documents in non-support actions (e.g., divorce, custody), the *Case Records Public Access Policy of the Unified Judicial System of Pennsylvania* shall apply.

Rule 1910.27 ACTIONS FOR SUPPORT

(A) Guidelines Expense Statement. If the combined monthly net income of the parties is $30,000 or less, it is not necessary to complete this form unless a party is claiming unusual needs and expenses that may warrant a deviation from the guideline amount of support pursuant to Rule 1910.16-5 or seeks an apportionment of expenses pursuant to Rule 1910.16-6. At the conference, each party must provide receipts or other verification of expenses claimed on this statement. The Guidelines Expense Statement shall be substantially in the following form.

EXPENSE STATEMENT OF

_____
(Name)(PACSES Number)

I verify that the statements made in this Expense Statement are true and correct. I understand that false statements herein are made subject to the penalties of 18 Pa. C.S.A. § 4904 relating to unsworn falsification to authorities.

Date: _____   _____
                          Plaintiff or Defendant

	Weekly	Monthly	Yearly
	(Fill in Appropriate Column)		
Mortgage (including real estate taxes and homeowner's insurance) or Rent	$ _____	$ _____	$ _____
Health Insurance Premiums	_____	_____	_____
Unreimbursed Medical Expenses:			
Doctor	_____	_____	_____
Dentist	_____	_____	_____
Orthodontist	_____	_____	_____
Hospital	_____	_____	_____
Medicine	_____	_____	_____
Special Needs (glasses, braces, orthopedic devices, therapy)	_____	_____	_____
Child Care	_____	_____	_____
Private school	_____	_____	_____
Parochial school	_____	_____	_____
Loans/Debts	_____	_____	_____
Support of Other Dependents:			
Other child support	_____	_____	_____
Alimony payments	_____	_____	_____
Other: (Specify)	_____	_____	_____
Total	$ _____	$ _____	$ _____

(B) Expense Statement for Cases Pursuant to Rule 1910.16-3.1 and Rule 1920.31. No later than five business days prior to the conference, the parties shall exchange this form, along with receipts or other verification of the

Pa. R.C.P.   Rule 1910.27

expenses set forth on this form. Failure to comply with this provision may result in an appropriate order for sanctions and/or the entry of an interim order based upon the information provided.

EXPENSE STATEMENT OF

_____
(Name)(PACSES Number)

I verify that the statements made in this Expense Statement are true and correct. I understand that false statements herein are made subject to the penalties of 18 Pa. C.S.A. § 4904 relating to unsworn falsification to authorities.

Date: _____   _____
                                     Plaintiff or Defendant

EXPENSES	Monthly Total	Monthly Children	Monthly Parent
HOME			
Mortgage or Rent	_____	_____	_____
Maintenance	_____	_____	_____
Lawn Care	_____	_____	_____
2nd Mortgage	_____	_____	_____
UTILITIES			
Electric	_____	_____	_____
Gas	_____	_____	_____
Oil	_____	_____	_____
Telephone	_____	_____	_____
Cell Phone	_____	_____	_____
Water	_____	_____	_____
Sewer	_____	_____	_____
Cable TV	_____	_____	_____
Internet	_____	_____	_____
Trash/Recycling	_____	_____	_____
TAXES			
Real Estate	_____	_____	_____
Personal Property	_____	_____	_____
INSURANCE			
Homeowners/Renters	_____	_____	_____
Automobile	_____	_____	_____
Life	_____	_____	_____
Accident/Disability	_____	_____	_____
Excess Coverage	_____	_____	_____
Long-Term Care	_____	_____	_____

Rule 1910.27 **ACTIONS FOR SUPPORT**

AUTOMOBILE
  Lease or Loan Payments _____ _____ _____
  Fuel _____ _____ _____
  Repairs _____ _____ _____
  Memberships _____ _____ _____

MEDICAL
  Medical Insurance _____ _____ _____
  Doctor _____ _____ _____
  Dentist _____ _____ _____
  Hospital _____ _____ _____
  Medication _____ _____ _____
  Counseling/Therapy _____ _____ _____
  Orthodontist _____ _____ _____
  Special Needs (glasses, etc.) _____ _____ _____

EDUCATION
  Tuition _____ _____ _____
  Tutoring _____ _____ _____
  Lessons _____ _____ _____
  Other _____ _____ _____

PERSONAL
  Debt Service _____ _____ _____
  Clothing _____ _____ _____
  Groceries _____ _____ _____
  Haircare _____ _____ _____
  Memberships _____ _____ _____

MISCELLANEOUS
  Child Care _____ _____ _____
  Household Help _____ _____ _____
  Summer Camp _____ _____ _____
  Papers/Books/Magazines _____ _____ _____
  Entertainment _____ _____ _____
  Pet Expenses _____ _____ _____
  Vacations _____ _____ _____
  Gifts _____ _____ _____
  Legal Fees/Prof. Fees _____ _____ _____
  Charitable contributions _____ _____ _____
  Children's Parties _____ _____ _____
  Children's Allowances _____ _____ _____
  Other Child Support _____ _____ _____
  Alimony payments _____ _____ _____

Pa. R.C.P.   Rule 1910.27

TOTAL MONTHLY EXPENSES

(d) The form used to obtain information relating to health insurance coverage from a party shall be in substantially the following form:

(Caption)
HEALTH INSURANCE COVERAGE INFORMATION
REQUIRED BY THE COURT
This form must be completed and returned to the domestic relations section.

IF YOU FAIL TO PROVIDE THE INFORMATION REQUESTED, THE COURT MAY FIND THAT YOU ARE IN CONTEMPT OF COURT.

Do you provide insurance coverage for the dependents named below? (Check each type of insurance which you provide).

Type of Coverage

Full Name SS #	Hospital-ization	Medical	Dental	Eye	Prescription	Other
_____	☐	☐	☐	☐	☐	☐
_____	☐	☐	☐	☐	☐	☐
_____	☐	☐	☐	☐	☐	☐
_____	☐	☐	☐	☐	☐	☐
_____	☐	☐	☐	☐	☐	☐
_____	☐	☐	☐	☐	☐	☐

Note: Before forwarding the form to the party, the domestic relations section should fill in the names and Social Security numbers of the dependents about whom the information is sought.

Provide the following information for all types of insurance you maintain, whether or not any of the above-named dependents is covered at this time:

Insurance company (provider):

_____

Group #:   Plan #:   Policy #:

_____   _____   _____

Effective coverage date: Type of coverage:

_____   _____

Employee cost of coverage for dependents:

_____

Insurance company (provider):

_____

Group #:   Plan #:   Policy #:

_____   _____   _____

Rule 1910.27 ACTIONS FOR SUPPORT

Effective coverage date: _____ Type of coverage: _____

_____ _____

Employee cost of coverage for dependents:

_____

Insurance company (provider):

_____

Group #: _____ Plan #: _____ Policy #: _____

_____ _____ _____

Effective coverage date: _____ Type of coverage: _____

_____ _____

Employee cost of coverage for dependents:

_____

If the above-named dependents are not currently covered by insurance, please state the earliest date coverage could be provided.

_____

   (e) The form of a support order shall be substantially as follows:

(Caption)
(FINAL) (TEMPORARY) (MODIFIED)
ORDER OF COURT

AND NOW, _____, based upon the Court's determination that Payee's monthly net income is $____, and Payor's monthly net income is $_____, it is hereby ordered that the Payor pay to the Domestic Relations Section, Court of Common Pleas, _____ Dollars ($_____.___) a month payable (WEEKLY/BI-WEEKLY/SEMI-MONTHLY/MONTHLY) as follows: . Arrears set at $_____ as of _____ are due in full IMMEDIATELY. Contempt proceedings, credit bureau reporting and tax refund offset certification will not be initiated, and judgment will not be entered, as long as payor pays $_____ on arrears on each payment date. Failure to make each payment on time and in full will cause all arrears to become subject to immediate collection by all of the means listed above.

For the support of: _____

_____
_____
_____
_____
_____

Said money to be turned over by the domestic relations section to: _____

_____
_____

Pa. R.C.P.   Rule 1910.27

Payments must be made (STATE ACCEPTABLE FORMS OF PAYMENT). All checks and money orders must be made payable to (NAME OF ENTITY TO WHOM CHECKS SHOULD BE MADE PAYABLE) and mailed to (NAME OF OFFICE) at (MAILING ADDRESS). Each payment must bear your (FILE/CASE/FOLIO/DOMESTIC RELATIONS) number in order to be processed. Do not send cash by mail.

Unreimbursed medical expenses are to be paid _____% by defendant and _____% by plaintiff. (PLAINTIFF/DEFENDANT/NEITHER) to provide medical insurance coverage. Within 30 days after the entry of this order, the party ordered to provide medical insurance shall submit to the other party written proof that medical insurance coverage has been obtained or that application for coverage has been made. Proof of coverage shall consist, at a minimum, of: 1) the name of the health care coverage provider(s); 2) any applicable identification numbers; 3) any cards evidencing coverage; 4) the address to which claims should be made; 5) a description of any restrictions on usage, such as prior approval for hospital admissions, and the manner of obtaining approval; 6) a copy of the benefit booklet or coverage contract; 7) a description of all deductibles and co-payments; and 8) five copies of any claim forms.

PARTIES MUST WITHIN SEVEN DAYS INFORM THE DOMESTIC RELATIONS SECTION AND THE OTHER PARTIES, IN WRITING, OF ANY MATERIAL CHANGE IN CIRCUMSTANCES RELEVANT TO THE LEVEL OF SUPPORT OR THE ADMINISTRATION OF THE SUPPORT ORDER, INCLUDING, BUT NOT LIMITED TO, LOSS OR CHANGE OF INCOME OR EMPLOYMENT AND CHANGE OF PERSONAL ADDRESS OR CHANGE OF ADDRESS OF ANY CHILD RECEIVING SUPPORT. *A PARTY WHO WILLFULLY FAILS TO REPORT A MATERIAL CHANGE IN CIRCUMSTANCE MAY BE ADJUDGED IN CONTEMPT OF COURT, AND MAY BE FINED OR IMPRISONED.*

PENNSYLVANIA LAW PROVIDES THAT ALL SUPPORT ORDERS SHALL BE REVIEWED AT LEAST ONCE EVERY THREE (3) YEARS IF SUCH A REVIEW IS REQUESTED BY ONE OF THE PARTIES. IF YOU WISH TO REQUEST A REVIEW AND ADJUSTMENT OF YOUR ORDER, YOU MUST DO THE FOLLOWING: AN UNREPRESENTED PERSON WHO WANTS TO MODIFY (ADJUST) A SUPPORT ORDER SHOULD (insert instructions for local domestic relations section).

ALIMONY PENDENTE LITE, INCLUDING UNALLOCATED ORDERS FOR CHILD AND SPOUSAL SUPPORT OR CHILD SUPPORT AND ALIMONY PENDENTE LITE, SHALL TERMINATE UPON THE DEATH OF THE PAYEE.

A MANDATORY INCOME ATTACHMENT WILL ISSUE UNLESS THE DEFENDANT IS NOT IN ARREARS IN PAYMENT IN AN AMOUNT EQUAL TO OR GREATER THAN ONE MONTH'S SUPPORT OBLIGATION AND (1) THE COURT FINDS THAT THERE IS GOOD CAUSE NOT TO REQUIRE IMMEDIATE INCOME WITHHOLDING; OR (2) A WRITTEN AGREEMENT IS REACHED BETWEEN THE PARTIES WHICH PROVIDES FOR AN ALTERNATE ARRANGEMENT.

DELINQUENT ARREARAGE BALANCES MAY BE REPORTED TO CREDIT AGENCIES. ON AND AFTER THE DATE IT IS DUE, EACH UNPAID SUPPORT PAYMENT SHALL CONSTITUTE A JUDGMENT AGAINST YOU.

IT IS FURTHER ORDERED that, upon payor's failure to comply with this order, payor may be arrested and brought before the Court for a Contempt hearing; payor's wages, salary, commissions, and/or income may be attached in accordance with law; this Order will be increased without further hearing to $_____ a month until all arrearages are paid in full. Payor is responsible for court costs and fees.

Rule 1910.27 ACTIONS FOR SUPPORT

Copies delivered to parties

_____
(INDICATE DATE DELIVERED).

Consented:

_____ _____
Plaintiff   Plaintiff's Attorney

_____ _____
Defendant   Defendant's Attorney

BY THE COURT:

_____
J.

(f) A petition for modification of support shall be in substantially the following form:

(Caption)

PETITION FOR MODIFICATION OF AN EXISTING SUPPORT ORDER

1. The petition of _____ respectfully represents that on _____, 19_____, an Order of Court was entered for the support of _____
_____. A true and correct copy of the order is attached to this petition.

2. Petitioner is entitled to _____ * of this Order because of the following material and substantial change(s) in circumstance:

_____
_____
_____

* Fill in the relief sought, i.e. increase, decrease, modification, termination, suspension, vacation

WHEREFORE, Petitioner requests that the Court modify the existing order for support.

_____
(Attorney for Petitioner)(Petitioner)

I verify that the statements made in this complaint are true and correct. I understand that false statements herein are made subject to the penalties of 18 Pa.C.S. § 4904 relating to unsworn falsification to authorities.

_____ _____
Date   Petitioner

(g) The order to be attached at the front of the petition for modification set forth in subdivision (f) shall be in substantially the following form:

(Caption)

ORDER OF COURT

You, _____, Respondent, have been sued in Court to modify an existing support order. You are ordered to appear in person at _____ on _____ at ___ _____.M., for a conference/hearing and to remain until dismissed

Pa. R.C.P. Rule 1910.27

by the Court. If you fail to appear as provided in this Order, an Order for Modification may be entered against you.

You are further ordered to bring to the conference

(1) a true copy of your most recent Federal Income Tax Return, including W-2s, as filed,

(2) your pay stubs for the preceding six months,

(3) the Income Statement and appropriate Expense Statement, if required, attached to this order, completed as required by Rule 1910.11(c),

(4) verification of child care expenses, and

(5) proof of medical coverage which you may have, or may have available to you.

(6) If a physician has determined that a medical condition affects your ability to earn income you must obtain a Physician Verification Form from the domestic relations section, sign it, have it completed by your doctor, and bring it with you to the conference.

THE TRIER OF FACT MAY INCREASE, DECREASE OR TERMINATE THE EXISTING ORDER BASED UPON THE EVIDENCE PRESENTED. AN ORDER MAY BE ENTERED AGAINST EITHER PARTY WITHOUT REGARD TO WHICH PARTY FILED THE MODIFICATION PETITION.

Date of Order:

_____

_____

J.

YOU HAVE THE RIGHT TO A LAWYER, WHO MAY ATTEND THE CONFERENCE AND REPRESENT YOU. IF YOU DO NOT HAVE A LAWYER, GO TO OR TELEPHONE THE OFFICE SET FORTH BELOW. THIS OFFICE CAN PROVIDE YOU WITH INFORMATION ABOUT HIRING A LAWYER. IF YOU CANNOT AFFORD TO HIRE A LAWYER, THIS OFFICE MAY BE ABLE TO PROVIDE YOU WITH INFORMATION ABOUT AGENCIES THAT MAY OFFER LEGAL SERVICES TO ELIGIBLE PERSONS AT A REDUCED FEE OR NO FEE.

_____

(Name)

_____

(Address)

_____

(Telephone Number)

AMERICANS WITH DISABILITIES ACT OF 1990

The Court of Common Pleas of _____ County is required by law to comply with the Americans with Disabilities Act of 1990. For information about accessible facilities and reasonable accommodations available to disabled individuals having business before the court, please contact our office. All arrangements must be made at least 72 hours prior to any hearing or business before the court. You must attend the scheduled conference or hearing.

   (h) A petition for recovery of a support overpayment when a support order remains in effect shall be in substantially the following form:

Rule 1910.27   **ACTIONS FOR SUPPORT**

(Caption)
PETITION FOR RECOVERY OF SUPPORT
OVERPAYMENT IN ACTIVE CASE.

1. Obligor and Obligee are parties in a support action at the docket number captioned above.

2. There is an overpayment owing to Obligor in an amount in excess of two months of the monthly support obligation.

Wherefore, Obligor requests that, pursuant to Pa.R.C.P. No. 1910.19(g)(1), the charging order be reduced by 20% or an amount sufficient to retire the overpayment by the time the charging order is terminated.

_____   _____
(Date)   (Petitioner or Attorney for Petitioner)

I verify that the statements in this petition are true and correct to the best of my knowledge, information and belief. I understand that false statements herein are made subject to the penalties of 18 Pa.C.S. § 4904 relating to unsworn falsification to authorities.

_____   _____
(Date)   (Petitioner signature)

  (i) A petition for recovery of a support overpayment when a support order has been terminated shall be in substantially the following form:

(Caption)
PETITION FOR RECOVERY OF SUPPORT OVERPAYMENT
IN CLOSED CASE.

1. Plaintiff is an adult individual residing at:

_____
_____

2. Defendant is an adult individual residing at:

_____
_____

3. Plaintiff and defendant were parties in a prior support action that was terminated by order dated _____ at docket number ___.

4. There is an overpayment owing to the instant plaintiff.

Wherefore, the plaintiff requests that, pursuant to Pa.R.C.P. No. 1910.19(g)(2), an order be entered against the defendant and in favor of the plaintiff in the amount of the overpayment.

_____   _____
(Date)   (Petitioner or Attorney for Petitioner)

I verify that the statements in this petition are true and correct to the best of my knowledge, information and belief. I understand that false statements herein are made subject to the penalties of 18 Pa.C.S. § 4904 relating to unsworn falsification to authorities.

_____   _____
(Date)   (Petitioner signature)

Pa. R.C.P.   **Rule 1910.27**

(j) The order to be attached at the front of the petition for recovery of support overpayment in closed case set forth in subdivision (i) shall be in substantially the following form:

(Caption)
ORDER OF COURT

You, _____, defendant, are ordered to appear at _____ before _____, a conference officer of the Domestic Relations Section, on the ___ day of _____, 20 ___, at _____.M., for a conference, after which the officer may recommend that an order for the recovery of a support overpayment be entered against you.

You are further ordered to bring to the conference

(1) a true copy of your most recent federal income tax return, including W-2s, as filed,

(2) your pay stubs for the preceding six months, and

(3) the Income Statement and the appropriate Expense Statement, if you are claiming that you have unusual needs or unusual fixed obligations.

Date of Order:_____   _____

                                                                 J.

YOU HAVE THE RIGHT TO A LAWYER, WHO MAY ATTEND THE CONFERENCE AND REPRESENT YOU. IF YOU DO NOT HAVE A LAWYER, GO TO OR TELEPHONE THE OFFICE SET FORTH BELOW. THIS OFFICE CAN PROVIDE YOU WITH INFORMATION ABOUT HIRING A LAWYER.

IF YOU CANNOT AFFORD TO HIRE A LAWYER, THIS OFFICE MAY BE ABLE TO PROVIDE YOU WITH INFORMATION ABOUT AGENCIES THAT MAY OFFER LEGAL SERVICES TO ELIGIBLE PERSONS AT A REDUCED FEE OR NO FEE.

_____
(Name)

_____
(Address)

_____
(Telephone Number)

AMERICANS WITH DISABILITIES ACT OF 1990

The Court of Common Pleas of _____ County is required by law to comply with the Americans with Disabilities Act of 1990. For information about accessible facilities and reasonable accommodations available to disabled individuals having business before the court, please contact our office. All arrangements must be made at least 72 hours prior to any hearing or business before the court. You must attend the scheduled conference or hearing.

Adopted April 23, 1981, effective July 22, 1981. Amended March 23, 1987, effective July 1, 1987; Nov. 7, 1988, effective Jan. 1, 1989; March 30, 1994, effective July 1, 1994; Dec. 2, 1994, effective March 1, 1995; March 24, 1997, effective July 1, 1997. Renumbered from 1910.26 May 31, 2000, effective July 1, 2000. Amended June 5, 2001, imd. effective; June 24, 2002, imd. effective; March 18, 2004, effective June 16, 2004; Nov. 8, 2006, effective Feb. 6, 2007; Aug. 13, 2008, effective Oct. 12, 2008; Jan. 12, 2010, effective May 12, 2010; Aug. 26, 2011, effective Nov. 1, 2011; Nov. 5, 2012, effective Dec. 5, 2012; Nov. 30, 2012, effective

Rule 1910.27 ACTIONS FOR SUPPORT

Dec. 30, 2012; Sept. 25, 2014, effective Oct. 25, 2014; Jan. 5, 2018, effective Jan. 6, 2018; June 1, 2018, effective July 1, 2018.

Explanatory Comment—1994

The support complaint and Income and Expense Statements contain a verification which states that the documents are subject to the penalties of the Crimes Code relating to unsworn falsification to authorities. A notary public is not needed.

Explanatory Comment—2006

Rule 1910.27(c) is amended to separate income and expense information and to elicit the expense information relevant in cases that fall within the guidelines, as well as those that do not. In cases which can be determined under the guidelines, no expense information need be provided unless a party is claiming unusual needs and expenses that may warrant a deviation pursuant to Rule 1910.16-5 or an apportionment of expenses pursuant to Rule 1910.16-6. If a party is claiming such expenses, the form at subsection (c)(2)(A) should be submitted. A separate expense form for cases in which the parties' combined monthly net income exceeds $20,000 is set forth at subsection (c)(2)(B).

Rule 1910.11(c) was amended, effective in March 1995, to provide that only income and extraordinary expenses need be shown on the Income and Expense Statement in cases which can be determined pursuant to the guidelines. The Explanatory Comment--1994 explained the rationale for the amendment.

Nevertheless, because space for both income and expense information was provided on the same form Income and Expense Statement, parties often needlessly expended time and effort to provide expense information that was not relevant at the conference. The amendments are intended to clarify and simplify the submission of expense information.

Explanatory Comment—2010

When the combined net monthly income of the parties exceeds $30,000, the case will be decided pursuant to Rule 1910.16-3.1 and the Income Statement and the Expense Statement at Rule 1910.27(c)(2)(B) must be submitted.

Explanatory Comment—2012

The form complaint for support in subdivision (a) has been amended to accommodate cases initiated pursuant to Rule 1910.3(a)(6). Because a support order may be entered against either party without regard to which party initiated the support action pursuant to Rule 1910.3(b), a party who believes that he or she may owe a duty of support may use the complaint form to initiate the action even if he or she ultimately is determined to be the obligor. In active charging support cases in which there is an overpayment in an amount in excess of two months of the monthly support obligation and the domestic relations section fails to reduce the charging order automatically to recoup the overpayment pursuant to Rule 1910.19(g)(1), the obligor may file a petition for recovery as set forth in subdivision (h) above. A separate form petition has been added in subdivision (i) by which a former support obligor may seek recovery of an overpayment in any amount in terminated cases pursuant to Rule 1910.19(g)(2).

Pa. R.C.P. Rule 1910.28

Rule 1910.28 Order for Earnings and Health Insurance Information. Form of Earnings Report. Form of Health Insurance Coverage Information

(a) The order for earnings and health insurance information shall be in substantially the following form:

(Caption)

ORDER FOR EARNINGS REPORT, HEALTH
INSURANCE INFORMATION AND SUBPOENA

TO: _____

TO: _____

TO: _____

AND NOW, this _____ day of _____, 20_____, since it appears that _____ (name of employee) is employed by you, and it is necessary that the Court obtain earnings and health insurance information relating to the above-named individual in order to adjudicate a matter of support, IT IS HEREBY ORDERED AND DECREED that you supply the Court with the information required by the enclosed Earnings Report and Health Insurance Coverage Report and file them with the Court within fifteen (15) days of the date of this order.

If you fail to supply the information required by this Order, a subpoena will issue requiring you to attend Court and bring the material with you, or other appropriate sanctions will be imposed by the Court.

BY THE COURT:

_____
J.

(b) The employer shall file an Earnings Report substantially in the following form:

Employer: _____   Re: Name _____
          _____   Social Security No. _____
                                   Support Action No. _____

EARNINGS REPORT

To the Employer:

Furnish earnings information for the above-named employee for each pay period during the last six months. It is preferred that you attach a photocopy of your records containing the earnings information requested. Attach a copy of the employee's most recent W-2 Form.

Payroll Number: _____

Nature of Employment: _____

Rule 1910.28   **ACTIONS FOR SUPPORT**

Payroll Period Ending									
Date of Pay									
Gross Pay									
Deductions									
Fed. Withholding									
Social Security									
Local Wage Tax									
State Income Tax									
Retirement									
Savings Bonds									
Credit Union									
Life Insurance									
Health Insurance									
Other (Specify)									
_____									
_____									
Net Pay									
Hours Worked									

I verify that the statements made in this Earnings Report are true and correct. I understand that false statements herein are made subject to the penalties of 18 Pa.C.S. § 4904 relating to unsworn falsification to authorities.

Date: _____ Signed by: _____

                                              Position: _____

  (c) The form which the employer uses to report health insurance coverage information shall be substantially as follows:

    Note: The information requested in the following report may be provided by an employer on its own form, for example, as a computer print out.

(Caption)

HEALTH INSURANCE COVERAGE REPORT

  This information must be completed and returned within 15 days. Failure to comply may result in issuance of a subpoena or other appropriate sanctions.

Employee's Name: _____

Employee's Social Security #: _____

Does the employer make medical, dental, eye care, prescription or other insurance coverage available to the employee? Yes ☐ No ☐

Name the dependents covered under the employee's insurance, and indicate which types of coverage they have through your company.

Pa. R.C.P.   Rule 1910.28

Full Name	SS #	Type of Coverage					
		Hospitalization	Medical	Dental	Eye	Prescription	Other
_____		☐	☐	☐	☐	☐	☐
_____		☐	☐	☐	☐	☐	☐
_____		☐	☐	☐	☐	☐	☐
_____		☐	☐	☐	☐	☐	☐
_____		☐	☐	☐	☐	☐	☐
_____		☐	☐	☐	☐	☐	☐

Provide the information indicated for each type of insurance which is available to the employee, whether or not any of the above-named dependents are covered at this time:

Insurance company (provider): _____
Group #: _____ Plan #: _____ Policy #: _____
Effective coverage date: _____ Type of coverage: _____
Cost of coverage for dependents: _____

Insurance company (provider): _____
Group #: _____ Plan #: _____ Policy #: _____
Effective coverage date: _____ Type of coverage: _____
Cost of coverage for dependents: _____

Insurance company (provider): _____
Group #: _____ Plan #: _____ Policy #: _____
Effective coverage date: _____ Type of coverage: _____
Cost of coverage for dependents: _____

Insurance company (provider): _____
Group #: _____ Plan #: _____ Policy #: _____
Effective coverage date: _____ Type of coverage: _____
Cost of coverage for dependents: _____

If the above-named dependents are not currently covered by insurance, please state the earliest date coverage could be provided. _____

PLEASE PROVIDE FORMS NECESSARY TO ADD DEPENDENTS, AS THE EMPLOYEE MAY BE ORDERED TO PROVIDE COVERAGE FOR THEM.

I verify that the statements made in this Health Insurance Coverage Information form are true and correct. I understand that false statements herein are made subject to the penalties of 18 Pa.C.S. § 4904 relating to unsworn falsification to authorities.

Date: _____   Signature: _____
                   Title: _____

Adopted April 23, 1981, effective July 22, 1981. Amended March 23, 1987, effective July 1, 1987; Dec. 2, 1994, effective March 1, 1995. Renumbered from Rule 1910.27 and former Rule 1910.28 rescinded May 31, 2000, effective July 1, 2000; Sept. 24, 2002, effective immed.

Rule 1910.29. Evidence in Support Matters.

(a) *Record Hearing.* Except as provided in this rule, the Pennsylvania Rules of Evidence shall be followed in all record hearings conducted in an action for support. A verified petition, affidavit or document, and any document incorporated by reference therein which would not be excluded under the hearsay rule if given in person shall be admitted into evidence if (1) at least 20 days' written notice of the intention to offer them into evidence was given to the adverse party accompanied by a copy of each document to be offered; (2) the other party does not object to their admission into evidence; and (3) the evidence is offered under oath by the party or witness. An objection must be in writing and served on the proponent of the document within 10 days of the date of service of the notice of intention to offer the evidence. When an objection is properly made, the Pennsylvania Rules of Evidence shall apply to determine the admissibility of the document into evidence.

(b) *Medical Evidence.*

(1) *Non-Record Proceeding.* In a non-record hearing, if a physician has determined that a medical condition affects a party's ability to earn income and that party obtains a Physician Verification Form from the domestic relations section, has it completed by the party's physician and submits it at the conference, it may be considered by the conference officer. If a party is receiving Social Security disability or workers' compensation benefits, the party shall submit copies of the disability or workers' compensation determination in lieu of the Physician Verification Form.

(2) *Record Proceeding.* If the matter proceeds to a record hearing and the party wishes to introduce the completed Physician Verification Form into evidence, he or she must serve the form on the other party not later than 20 days after the conference. The other party may file and serve an objection to the introduction of the form within 10 days of the date of service. If an objection is made and the physician testifies, the trier of fact shall have the discretion to allocate the costs of the physician's testimony between the parties. If there is no objection, the form may be admitted into evidence without the testimony of the physician. In the event that the record hearing is held sooner than 30 days after the conference, the trier of fact may provide appropriate relief, such as granting a continuance to the objecting party.

(3) The Physician Verification Form shall be substantially in the following form:

IN THE COURT OF COMMON PLEAS OF _____ COUNTY

Member Name:

Docket Number:

PACSES Case Number:

Other State ID Number:

PHYSICIAN VERIFICATION FORM

TO BE COMPLETED BY THE TREATING PHYSICIAN

Physician's name: _____

Physician's license number _____

Pa. R.C.P.   Rule 1910.29

Nature of patient's sickness or injury:

_____

_____

_____

Date of first treatment:_____

Date of most recent treatment:_____

Frequency of treatments:_____

Medication:_____

The patient has had a medical condition that affects his or her ability to earn income from: _____ through _____

If the patient is unable to work, when should the patient be able to return to work?

Will there be limitations? _____

_____

Remarks: _____

_____

Date: _____

Signature of Treating Physician: _____

Physician's address: _____

_____

Physician's telephone number: _____

I authorize my physician to release the above information to the _____ County Domestic Relations Section.

Patient's signature: _____ Date: _____

Former Rule 1910.29 rescinded and new rule adopted May 31, 2000, effective July 1, 2000; November 30, 2012, effective December 30, 2012.

Explanatory Comment—2000

23 Pa.C.S. §4342(f) creates a hearsay exception in support actions to permit a verified petition, affidavit or document and a document incorporated by reference in any of them to be admitted into evidence if it would not otherwise be excluded as hearsay if given in person and it is admitted under oath by a party or witness to the support action. Rule 1910.29 requires that notice of the documents to be admitted be given to the other party prior to the hearing. It also sets forth the procedures for raising an objection to the admission of those documents.

If the requisite 20-day notice is given and there is no objection, the document must be admitted into evidence under this rule and 23 Pa.C.S. §4342(f). In the event an objection is timely made, the rules of evidence apply to determine the document's ultimate admissibility.

Rule 1910.29 is not intended to affect 23 Pa.C.S. §4342(g) and (h) relating to admissibility of payment records, billing statements and bills for genetic testing and prenatal and postnatal health care of the mother and child. Those documents are admissible into evidence without advance notice for the limited purposes which are expressly set forth in those statutory provisions.

Rule 1910.30. [Rescinded]

Rescinded May 31, 2000, effective July 1, 2000.

Rule 1910.31. [Rescinded]

Rescinded May 31, 2000, effective July 1, 2000.

Rule 1910.49 Acts of Assembly not Suspended

The rules governing an action for support shall not be deemed to suspend or affect the following Acts or parts of Acts of Assembly:

(1) Chapter 43 of Title 23 of the Consolidated Statutes, 23 Pa.C.S. § 4301 et seq., relating to support matters generally;

(2) Chapter 45 of Title 23 of the Consolidated Statutes, 23 Pa.C.S. § 4501 et seq., except § 4533, known as the Revised Uniform Reciprocal Enforcement of Support Act (1968);

(3) Section 1 of the Act of June 11, 1913, P.L. 468, 48 P.S. § 133, relating to execution of a support order against real property owned by the entireties.

(4) Sections 1 to 5 of the Act of May 24, 1923, P.L. 446, 48 P.S. §§ 137–141, only insofar as the Act authorizes execution against real estate held by the entireties;

(5) The Act of December 19, 1990, P.L. 1240, No. 206, 23 Pa.C.S. § 3507, insofar as it provides for tenancy in common of property held by the entireties after divorce; and

Note: See the Divorce Code as to equitable distribution of property in divorce actions.

(6) The Act of December 19, 1990, P.L. 1240, No. 206, 23 Pa.C.S. § 6101, known as the Protection From Abuse Act.

Note: The Protection from Abuse Act provides a procedure to obtain a temporary order of support in addition to other relief.

Adopted Nov. 7, 1988, effective Jan. 1, 1989. Amended March 30, 1994, effective July 1, 1994.

Explanatory Comment—1994

Rule 1910.49 specifically saves from suspension the new support law enacted by Act 66. The amendments to the rules are intended to supplement the statute and an attorney prosecuting a support action will be required to be familiar with both the statute and the rules.

Rule 1910.50. Suspension of Acts of Assembly

The following Acts or parts of Acts of Assembly are suspended insofar as they apply to the practice and procedure in an action for support:

(1) Section 3 of the Support Law of June 24, 1937, P.L. 2045, 62 P.S. § 1973, insofar as it provides a procedure to enforce the liability of relatives for the support of an indigent person; and

(2) Section 4 of Act 1996-20, 23 Pa.C.S. § 4342, insofar as it provides that long arm jurisdiction shall be used in preference to proceedings under Part VIII-A relating to intrastate family support actions;

(3) Act Nos. 1997-58 and 1998-127 insofar as they are inconsistent with Rule 1910.20 relating to the availability of remedies for collection of past due and overdue support;

(4) Section 4 of Act 1997-58, 23 Pa.C.S. § 4342(f), insofar as it is inconsistent with Rule 1910.29 as it relates to record hearings in support actions;

(5) Section 4 of Act 1998-127, 23 Pa.C.S. § 4352(d), insofar as it is inconsistent with Rule 1910.22 providing that overdue support on public record at the domestic relations section constitutes a lien of record against all real property within the state of Pennsylvania which is owned by the obligor;

(6) Section 4 of Act 1998-127, 23 Pa.C.S. § 4352(d.1), only insofar as subsection (1) of that provision provided that the underlying support action shall either be pending at the county domestic relations section or shall be enforced by the county domestic relations section in order for a lien to arise against real property located in that county; and

(7) All Acts or parts of Acts of Assembly inconsistent with these rules to the extent of such inconsistency.

Adopted Nov. 7, 1988, effective Jan. 1, 1989. Amended Dec. 18, 1998, effective Jan. 1, 1999; May 31, 2000, effective July 1, 2000; November 30, 2012, effective December 30, 2012.

Explanatory Comment—1998

Insofar as long arm jurisdiction is an issue that arises only in the context of interstate cases in which the defendant resides outside of the Commonwealth, the language in 23 Pa.C.S. §4342(c) implying that it has relevance to intrastate support cases is suspended.

IV. Actions for Custody of Minor Children
(Amended Through April, 2019)

Rules 1915.1-1915.25

RULE

Rule	
1915.1	Scope. Definitions.
1915.2	Venue.
1915.3	Commencement of Action. Complaint. Order.
1915.3-1	Withdrawal of Pleading. Discontinuance of Action.
1915.3-2	Criminal Record or Abuse History.
1915.4	Prompt Disposition of Custody Cases.
1915.4-1	Alternative Hearing Procedures for Partial Custody Actions.
1915.4–2	Partial Custody. Office Conference. Hearing. Record. Exceptions. Order.
1915.4–3	Non-Record Proceedings. Trial.
1915.4-4	Pre-Trial Procedures.
1915.5	Question of Jurisdiction or Venue. No Responsive Pleading by Defendant Required. Counterclaim. Discovery.
1915.6	Joinder of Parties.
1915.7	Consent Order.
1915.8	Physical and Mental Examination of Persons.
1915.9	No Default Judgment.
1915.10	Decision. Order.
1915.11	Appointment of Attorney for Child. Interview of Child. Attendance of Child at Hearing or Conference.
1915.11-1	Parenting Coordination.
1915.11-2	Appointment of Guardian Ad Litem.
1915.12	Civil Contempt for Disobedience of Custody Order. Petition. Form of Petition. Service. Order.
1915.13	Special Relief.
1915.14	Disobedience of Order. Arrest. Contempt.
1915.15	Form of Complaint. Caption. Order. Petition to Modify a Custody Order.
1915.16	Form of Order and Notice. Joinder. Intervention.
1915.17	Relocation. Notice and Counter-Affidavit.
1915.18	Form of Order Directing Expert Examination and Report.
1915.19	Form of Order Appointing Counsel for the Child.
1915.21	Form of Order Appointing Guardian Ad Litem.
1915.22	Form of Order Appointing Parenting Coordinator.
1915.23	Form of the Summary and Recommendation of Parenting Coordinator.
1915.24	Acts of Assembly Not Suspended.
1915.25	Suspension of Acts of Assembly.

ACTIONS FOR CUSTODY, PARTIAL CUSTODY AND VISITATION OF MINOR CHILDREN

Explanatory Comment—1981

Introduction

In an era of legislative and judicial activism, the law of custody has not remained untouched. In the procedural context, the legislature has enacted the Uniform Child

Custody Jurisdiction Act and has extended, in general, its provisions to intrastate proceedings. At the same time, "the Pennsylvania Superior Court, in its continuing redefinition and refinement of the adversarial and judicial functions essential to child-custody disputes, has drawn up a catalog of criteria whose imposition removes that area of law from the realm of caprice."

(Hon. Lawrence W. Kaplan, "The Child Advocate in Custody Litigation," as published in *The Changing Direction of Child Custody Litigation: The Modern Approach,* PBI publication No. 1980–140, p. 86.)

It is in furtherance of the legislative and judicial objective of the appropriate and prompt disposition of custody disputes that these rules governing the custody, partial custody and visitation of minor children are promulgated.

Effective Date

Order of the Supreme Court, Eastern District, June 25, 1982, extended the effective date on Rules 1915.1 to 1915.25 to January 1, 1983.

Rule 1915.1 Scope. Definitions

(a) These rules govern the practice and procedure in all actions for legal and physical custody of minor children, including habeas corpus proceedings and claims for custody asserted in an action of divorce.

Note: The term custody includes shared legal custody, sole legal custody, partial physical custody, primary physical custody, shared physical custody, sole physical custody and supervised physical custody. See 23 Pa.C.S. § 5322(a). Rule 1920.32(a) provides that when a claim for custody is joined with the action of divorce, the practice and procedure governing the claim for custody shall be in accordance with these rules.

(b) As used in this chapter, unless the context of a rule indicates otherwise, the following terms shall have the following meanings:

"action," all proceedings for legal and physical custody and proceedings for modification of prior orders of any court;

"child," an unemancipated individual under 18 years of age;

"conference officer," an individual who presides over an office conference pursuant to Pa.R.C.P. No. 1915.4-2(a) or the initial non-record proceeding under Pa.R.C.P. No. 1915.4-3(a). For purposes of these rules, a conciliator is synonymous with a conference officer;

"custody," the legal right to keep, control, guard, care for, and preserve a child and includes the terms "legal custody," "physical custody," and "shared custody;"

"hearing officer," a lawyer who conducts a record hearing on partial custody cases pursuant to Pa.R.C.P. No. 1915.4-2(b);

"home county," the county in which the child lived with either or both parents, a person acting as a parent, or in an institution for at least six consecutive months immediately preceding the filing of the action, and in the case of a child less than six months old, the county in which the child lived from birth with any of the persons mentioned. A period of temporary absence of the child from the physical custody of the parent, institution, or person acting as parent shall not affect the six-month or other period;

"*in loco parentis,*" a person who puts himself or herself in the situation of a lawful parent by assuming the obligations incident to the parental relationship without going through the formality of a legal adoption. The status of *in loco parentis* embodies two ideas: (1) the assumption of a parental status; and (2) the discharge of parental duties;

Note: *See A.S. v. I.S.,* 130 A.3d 763, 766 n.3 (Pa. 2015).

"legal custody," the right to make major decisions on behalf of the child, including, but not limited to, medical, religious, and educational decisions;

"mediator," an individual qualified under Pa.R.C.P. No. 1940.4 and who assists custody litigants independently from the procedures set forth in Pa.R.C.P. Nos. 1915.1—1915.25 by engaging the litigants in the alternative dispute principles in Pa.R.C.P. No. 1940.2 to resolve custody matters in whole or in part;

"mediation," the confidential process by which a neutral mediator assists the parties in attempting to reach a mutually acceptable agreement on issues arising in a custody action. Mediation is not a court proceeding; rather, it is an independent, non-record proceeding in lieu of court involvement for the purpose of assisting the parties to address the child's best interest. An agreement reached by the parties must be based on the voluntary decisions of the parties and not the decision of the mediator. The agreement may resolve all or only some of the disputed issues. The parties are required to mediate in good faith, but are not compelled to reach an agreement. While mediation is an alternative means of conflict resolution, it is not a substitute for the benefit of legal advice. The participants in mediation shall be limited to the parties to the custody action, primarily the child's parents and persons acting as parents. Except as provided in Pa.R.C.P. No. 1940.5(c), non-parties, including children, grandparents, and the parties' attorneys, shall not participate in the mediation.

"non-record proceeding," the initial office conference set forth in Pa.R.C.P. No. 1915.4-3. Mediation, as outlined in Pa.R.C.P. No. 1940.1—1940.9, shall not be construed as a non-record proceeding;

"partial physical custody," the right to assume physical custody of the child for less than a majority of the time;

"person acting as a parent," a person other than a parent, including an institution, who has physical custody of a child and who has either been awarded custody by a court or claims a right to custody. *See also* the definition of *in loco parentis*;

"physical custody," the actual physical possession and control of a child;

"primary physical custody," the right to assume physical custody of the child for the majority of time;

"relocation," a change in a residence of the child that significantly impairs the ability of a non-relocating party to exercise custodial rights;

"shared legal custody," the right of more than one individual to legal custody of the child;

"shared physical custody," the right of more than one individual to assume physical custody of the child, each having significant periods of physical custodial time with the child;

"sole legal custody," the right of one individual to exclusive legal custody of the child;

"sole physical custody," the right of one individual to exclusive physical custody of the child; and

"supervised physical custody," custodial time during which an agency or an adult designated by the court or agreed upon by the parties monitors the interaction between the child and the individual with those rights.

Note: The term "supervised visitation" in the prior statute has been replaced by the term "supervised physical custody."

The definitions of the terms of the various forms of legal custody and physical custody are taken from 23 Pa.C.S. § 5322(a).

For additional definitions, see the Uniform Child Custody Jurisdiction and Enforcement Act, 23 Pa.C.S. § 5402.

Adopted Dec. 10, 1981, effective July 1, 1982; effective date extended to Jan. 1, 1983 by order of June 25, 1982. Readopted and amended Nov. 8, 1982, effective Jan. 1, 1983; March 30, 1994, effective July 1, 1994; Nov. 19, 2008, imd. effective; Aug. 1, 2013, effective Sept. 3, 2013; Feb. 8, 2018, effective April 1, 2018.

Rule 1915.2 Venue

(a) An action may be brought in any county

(1) (i) which is the home county of the child at the time of commencement of the proceeding, or

(ii) which had been the child's home county within six months before commencement of the proceeding and the child is absent from the county but a parent or person acting as parent continues to live in the county; or

(2) when the court of another county does not have venue under subdivision (1), and the child and the child's parents, or the child and at least one parent or a person acting as a parent, have a significant connection with the county other than mere physical presence and there is available within the county substantial evidence concerning the child's protection, training and personal relationships; or

(3) when all counties in which venue is proper pursuant to subdivisions (1) and (2) have found that the court before which the action is pending is the more appropriate forum to determine the custody of the child; or

(4) when it appears that venue would not be proper in any other county under prerequisites substantially in accordance with paragraph (1), (2) or (3); or

(5) when the child is present in the county and has been abandoned or it is necessary in an emergency to protect the child because the child or a sibling or parent of the child is subjected to or threatened with mistreatment or abuse.

(b) Physical presence of the child or a party, while desirable, is not necessary or sufficient to make a child custody determination except as provided in subdivision (a)(5) above.

(c) The court at any time may transfer an action to the appropriate court of any other county where the action could originally have been brought or could be brought if it determines that it is an inconvenient forum under the circumstances and the court of another county is the more appropriate forum. It shall be the duty of the prothonotary of the court in which the action is pending to forward to the prothonotary of the county to which the action is transferred certified copies of the docket entries, process, pleadings and other papers filed in the action. The costs and fees of the petition for transfer and the removal of the record shall be paid by the petitioner in the first instance to be taxable as costs in the case.

Official Note: Under the Uniform Child Custody Jurisdiction and Enforcement Act, 23 Pa.C.S.A. § 5401 et seq., the court may decline to exercise its jurisdiction in a particular action despite the action having been brought in a county of proper venue. Section 5426 of the act, relating to simultaneous proceedings in other courts, provides for the mandatory refusal by the court to exercise its jurisdiction in an action. Section 5427 of the act, relating to inconvenient forum, and § 5428 of the act, relating to jurisdiction declined by reason of conduct, provide for the discretionary refusal by the court to exercise its jurisdiction.

Explanatory Comment—2008

Subdivision (a) of Rule 1915.2 incorporates the categories of jurisdiction for initial custody determinations and temporary emergency proceedings in the Uniform Child Custody Jurisdiction and Enforcement Act at 23 Pa.C.S.A. §§ 5421 and 5424 as the venue provisions for these rules, restating them in rule form without change in substance. Subdivision (a) follows the policy of § 5471 of the Uniform Child Custody Jurisdiction and Enforcement Act, which provides that the provisions of the act "allocating jurisdiction and functions between and among courts of different states shall also allocate jurisdiction and functions between and among courts of common pleas of this Commonwealth."

Subdivision (b), relating to the effect of the physical presence of the child or a party within a county, follows § 5421(c) without substantial change.

Subdivision (c) follows the inconvenient forum provisions of 23 Pa.C.S.A. § 5427.

Rule 1915.3. Commencement of Action. Complaint. Order

(a) **Except as provided by subdivision (c), an action shall be commenced by filing a verified complaint substantially in the form provided by Pa.R.C.P. No. 1915.15(a).**

Note: See Pa.R.C.P. No. 1930.1(b). This rule may require attorneys or unrepresented parties to file confidential documents and documents containing confidential information that are subject to the *Case Records Public Access Policy of the Unified Judicial System of Pennsylvania.*

(b) **An order shall be attached to the complaint directing the defendant to appear at a time and place specified. The order shall be substantially in the form provided by Rule 1915.15(b).**

Note: See § 5430(d) of the Uniform Child Custody Jurisdiction and Enforcement Act, 23 Pa.C.S. § 5430(d), relating to costs and expenses for appearance of parties and child, and 23 Pa.C.S. § 5471, relating to intrastate application of the Uniform Child Custody Jurisdiction and Enforcement Act.

(c) **A claim for custody which is joined with an action of divorce shall be asserted in the complaint or a subsequent petition, which shall be substantially in the form provided by Rule 1915.15(a).**

Note: Rule 1920.13(b) provides that claims which may be joined with an action of divorce shall be raised by the complaint or a subsequent petition.

(d) **If the mother of the child is not married and the child has no legal or presumptive father, then a putative father initiating an action for custody must file a claim of paternity pursuant to 23 Pa.C.S. § 5103 and attach a copy to the complaint in the custody action.**

Note: If a putative father is uncertain of paternity, the correct procedure is to commence a civil action for paternity pursuant to the procedures set forth at Rule 1930.6.

(e) **A grandparent who is not in loco parentis to the child and is seeking physical and/or legal custody of a grandchild pursuant to 23 Pa.C.S. § 5323 must plead, in paragraph 9 of the complaint set forth at Rule 1915.15(a), facts establishing standing under § 5324(3). A grandparent or great-grandparent seeking partial physical custody or supervised physical custody must plead, in paragraph 9 of the complaint, facts establishing standing pursuant to 23 Pa.C.S. § 5325.**

(f) An unemancipated minor parent may commence, maintain or defend an action for custody of the minor parent's child without the requirement of the appointment of a guardian for the minor parent.

Adopted Dec. 10, 1981, effective July 1, 1982; effective date extended to Jan. 1, 1983 by order of June 25, 1982. Readopted Nov. 8, 1982, effective Jan. 1, 1983. Amended Oct. 30, 2001, imd. effective; Oct. 31, 2002, imd. effective; Nov. 19, 2008, imd. effective; Aug. 1, 2013, effective Sept. 3, 2013; July 20, 2015, effective Sept. 1, 2015; Jan. 5, 2018, effective Jan. 6, 2018; June 1, 2018, effective July 1, 2018.

Rule 1915.3-1. Withdrawal of Pleading. Discontinuance of Action

(a) Withdrawal of Pleading. A custody pleading cannot be withdrawn after the issuance of a scheduling order or notice of conference regarding claims made in the pleading except

   (1) by leave of court after notice to the non-moving party, or

   (2) by written agreement of the parties.

(b) Discontinuance of a Custody Action.

   (1) A custody action may be discontinued by praecipe only upon a verified statement by the moving party that the complaint has not been served.

   (2) A custody action cannot be discontinued after the complaint has been served except

   (A) by leave of court after notice to the non-moving party, or

   (B) by written agreement of the parties.

Adopted June 25, 2013, effective July 25, 2013.

Rule 1915.3-2. Criminal Record or Abuse History

(a) *Criminal Record or Abuse History Verification.* A party must file and serve with the complaint, any petition for modification, any counterclaim, any petition for contempt or any count for custody in a divorce complaint or counterclaim a verification regarding any criminal record or abuse history of that party and anyone living in that party's household. The verification shall be substantially in the form set forth in subdivision (c) below. The party must attach a blank verification form to a complaint, counterclaim or petition served upon the other party. Although the party served need not file a responsive pleading pursuant to Rule 1915.5, he or she must file with the court a verification regarding his or her own criminal record or abuse history and that of anyone living in his or her household on or before the initial in-person contact with the court (including, but not limited to, a conference with a conference officer or judge or conciliation, depending upon the procedure in the judicial district) but not later than 30 days after service of the complaint or petition. A party's failure to file a Criminal Record or Abuse History Verification may result in sanctions against that party. Both parties shall file and serve updated verifications five days prior to trial.

(b) *Initial Evaluation.* At the initial in-person contact with the court, the judge, conference officer, conciliator or other appointed individual shall perform an initial evaluation to determine whether the existence of a criminal or abuse history of either party or a party's household member poses a threat to the child and whether counseling is necessary. The initial evaluation

Rule 1915.3-2 ACTIONS FOR CUSTODY, VISITATION

required by 23 Pa.C.S. § 5329(c) shall not be conducted by a mental health professional. After the initial evaluation, the court may order further evaluation or counseling by a mental health professional if the court determines it is necessary. Consistent with the best interests of the child, the court may enter a temporary custody order on behalf of a party with a criminal history or a party with a household member who has a criminal history, pending the party's or household member's evaluation and/or counseling.

> *Note:* The court shall consider evidence of criminal record or abusive history presented by the parties. There is no obligation for the court to conduct an independent investigation of the criminal record or abusive history of either party or members of their household. The court should not consider ARD or other diversionary programs. When determining whether a party or household member requires further evaluation or counseling, or whether a party or household member poses a threat to a child, the court should give consideration to the severity of the offense, the age of the offense, whether the victim of the offense was a child or family member and whether the offense involved violence.

(c) *Verification.* The verification regarding criminal or abuse history shall be substantially in the following form:

(Caption)

CRIMINAL RECORD / ABUSE HISTORY VERIFICATION

I _____, hereby swear or affirm, subject to penalties of law including 18 Pa.C.S. § 4904 relating to unsworn falsification to authorities that:

1. Unless indicated by my checking the box next to a crime below, neither I nor any other member of my household have been convicted or pled guilty or pled no contest or was adjudicated delinquent where the record is publicly available pursuant to the Juvenile Act, 42 Pa.C.S. § 6307 to any of the following crimes in Pennsylvania or a substantially equivalent crime in any other jurisdiction, including pending charges:

Check all that apply	Crime	Self	Other household member	Date of conviction, guilty plea, no contest plea or pending charges	Sentence
☐	18 Pa.C.S. Ch. 25 (relating to criminal homicide)	☐	☐	_____	_____
☐	18 Pa.C.S. § 2702 (relating to aggravated assault)	☐	☐	_____	_____
☐	18 Pa.C.S. § 2706 (relating to terroristic threats)	☐	☐	_____	_____
☐	18 Pa.C.S. § 2709.1 (relating to stalking)	☐	☐	_____	_____
☐	18 Pa.C.S. § 2901 (relating to kidnapping)	☐	☐	_____	_____
☐	18 Pa.C.S. § 2902 (relating to unlawful restraint)	☐	☐	_____	_____
☐	18 Pa.C.S. § 2903 (relating to false imprisonment)	☐	☐	_____	_____

Pa. R.C.P. Rule 1915.3-2

☐ 18 Pa.C.S. § 2910 ☐ ☐ _____ _____
(relating to luring a child into a motor vehicle or structure)

☐ 18 Pa.C.S. § 3121 ☐ ☐ _____ _____
(relating to rape)

☐ 18 Pa.C.S. § 3122.1 ☐ ☐ _____ _____
(relating to statutory sexual assault)

☐ 18 Pa.C.S. § 3123 ☐ ☐ _____ _____
(relating to involuntary deviate sexual intercourse)

☐ 18 Pa.C.S. § 3124.1 ☐ ☐ _____ _____
(relating to sexual assault)

☐ 18 Pa.C.S. § 3125 ☐ ☐ _____ _____
(relating to aggravated indecent assault)

☐ 18 Pa.C.S. § 3126 ☐ ☐ _____ _____
(relating to indecent assault)

☐ 18 Pa.C.S. § 3127 ☐ ☐ _____ _____
(relating to indecent exposure)

☐ 18 Pa.C.S. § 3129 ☐ ☐ _____ _____
(relating to sexual intercourse with animal)

☐ 18 Pa.C.S. § 3130 ☐ ☐ _____ _____
(relating to conduct relating to sex offenders)

☐ 18 Pa.C.S. § 3301 ☐ ☐ _____ _____
(relating to arson and related offenses)

☐ 18 Pa.C.S. § 4302 ☐ ☐ _____ _____
(relating to incest)

☐ 18 Pa.C.S. § 4303 ☐ ☐ _____ _____
(relating to concealing death of child)

☐ 18 Pa.C.S. § 4304 ☐ ☐ _____ _____
(relating to endangering welfare of children)

☐ 18 Pa.C.S. § 4305 ☐ ☐ _____ _____
(relating to dealing in infant children)

☐ 18 Pa.C.S. § 5902(b) ☐ ☐ _____ _____
(relating to prostitution and related offenses)

☐ 18 Pa.C.S. § 5903(c) or (d) ☐ ☐ _____ _____
(relating to obscene and other sexual materials and performances)

☐ 18 Pa.C.S. § 6301 ☐ ☐ _____ _____
(relating to corruption of minors)

Rule 1915.3-2 ACTIONS FOR CUSTODY, VISITATION

☐	18 Pa.C.S. § 6312 (relating to sexual abuse of children)	☐	☐	————	———
☐	18 Pa.C.S. § 6318 (relating to unlawful contact with minor)	☐	☐	————	———
☐	18 Pa.C.S. § 6320 (relating to sexual exploitation of children)	☐	☐	————	———
☐	23 Pa.C.S. § 6114 (relating to contempt for violation of protection order or agreement)	☐	☐	————	———
☐	Driving under the influence of drugs or alcohol	☐	☐	————	———
☐	Manufacture, sale, delivery, holding, offering for sale or possession of any controlled substance or other drug or device	☐	☐	————	———

2. Unless indicated by my checking the box next to an item below, neither I nor any other member of my household have a history of violent or abusive conduct, or involvement with a Children & Youth agency, including the following:

Check all that apply		Self	Other household member	Date
☐	A finding of abuse by a Children & Youth Agency or similar agency in Pennsylvania or similar statute in another jurisdiction	☐	☐	———
☐	Abusive conduct as defined under the Protection from Abuse Act in Pennsylvania or similar statute in another jurisdiction	☐	☐	———
☐	Involvement with a Children & Youth Agency or similar agency in Pennsylvania or another jurisdiction. Where?:	☐	☐	———
☐	Other: _____	☐	☐	———

3. Please list any evaluation, counseling or other treatment received following conviction or finding of abuse:

_____
_____

4. If any conviction above applies to a household member, not a party, state that person's name, date of birth and relationship to the child.

_____
_____

5. If you are aware that the other party or members of the other party's household has or have a criminal record/abuse history, please explain:

_____
_____

I verify that the information above is true and correct to the best of my knowledge, information or belief. I understand that false statements herein are made subject to the penalties of 18 Pa.C.S. § 4904 relating to unsworn falsification to authorities.

_____
Signature

_____
Printed Name

Adopted Aug. 1, 2013, effective Sept. 3, 2013. Amended May 14, 2014, effective June 13, 2014; July 20, 2015, effective Sept. 1, 2015.

Rule 1915.4. Prompt Disposition of Custody Cases

(a) Initial Contact With the Court. Depending upon the procedure in the judicial district, the parties' initial in-person contact with the court (including, but not limited to a conference with a conference officer pursuant to Rule 1915.4-2, a conference with a judge, conciliation, mediation and/or class/seminar) shall be scheduled to occur not later than 45 days from the filing of a complaint or petition.

(b) Listing Trials Before the Court. Depending upon the procedure in the judicial district, within 180 days of the filing of the complaint either the court shall automatically enter an order scheduling a trial before a judge or a party shall file a praecipe, motion or request for trial, except as otherwise provided in this subdivision. If it is not the practice of the court to automatically schedule trials and neither party files a praecipe, motion or request for trial within 180 days of filing of the pleading, the court shall, sua sponte or on motion of a party, dismiss the matter unless a party has been granted an extension for good cause shown, or the court finds that dismissal is not in the best interests of the child. The extension shall not exceed 60 days beyond the 180 day limit. A further reasonable extension may be granted by the court upon agreement of the parties or when the court finds, on the record, compelling circumstances for a further reasonable extension. If an extension is granted and, thereafter, neither party files a praecipe, motion or request for trial within the time period allowed by the extension, the court shall, sua sponte or on the motion of a party, dismiss the matter unless the court finds that dismissal is not in the best interests of the child. A motion to dismiss, pursuant to this rule, shall be filed and served upon the opposing party. The opposing party shall have 20 days from the date of service to file an objection. If no objection is filed, the court shall dismiss the case. Prior to a sua sponte dismissal, the court shall notify the parties of an intent to dismiss the case unless an objection is filed within 20 days of the date of the notice.

(c) Trial. Trials before a judge shall commence within 90 days of the date the scheduling order is entered. Trials and hearings shall be scheduled to be heard on consecutive days whenever possible but, if not on consecutive days, then the trial or hearing shall be concluded not later than 45 days from commencement.

(d) Prompt Decisions. The judge's decision shall be entered and filed within 15 days of the date upon which the trial is concluded unless, within that time, the court extends the date for such decision by order entered of record showing good cause for the extension. In no event shall an extension delay the entry of the court's decision more than 45 days after the conclusion of trial.

(e) **Emergency or Special Relief.** Nothing in this rule shall preclude a party from seeking, nor a court from ordering, emergency or interim special relief at any time after the commencement of the action.

Official Note: For service of original process in custody, partial custody and visitation matters, see Rule 1930.4.

Rescinded June 20, 1985 effective Jan. 1, 1986. Note amended Oct. 2, 1995, effective Jan. 1, 1996. Replaced by new rule; amended June 25, 2013, effective July 25, 2013.

Explanatory Comment—2000

A new rule requiring prompt custody trials was recommended by a special committee established by the Pennsylvania Superior Court. That committee concluded that the interests of children who are the subjects of custody litigation would best be served by a requirement that the litigation be concluded within specific time frames.

Rule 1915.4-1. Alternative Hearing Procedures for Partial Custody Actions

(a) A custody action shall proceed as prescribed by Pa.R.C.P. No. 1915.4-3 unless the court, by local rule, adopts the alternative hearing procedure authorized by Pa.R.C.P. No. 1915.4-2 pursuant to which an action for partial custody may be heard by a hearing officer, except as provided in subdivision (b).

(b) Promptly after the parties' initial contact with the court as set forth in Pa.R.C.P. No. 1915.4(a), a party may move the court for a hearing before a judge, rather than a hearing officer, in an action for partial custody where:

(1) there are complex questions of law, fact or both; or

(2) the parties certify to the court that there are serious allegations affecting the child's welfare.

(c) The president judge or the administrative judge of the family division of each county shall certify that custody proceedings generally are conducted in accordance with either Pa.R.C.P. No. 1915.4-2 or Pa.R.C.P. No. 1915.4-3. The certification shall be filed with the Domestic Relations Procedural Rules Committee of the Supreme Court of Pennsylvania and shall be substantially in the following form:

I hereby certify that _____ County conducts its custody proceedings in accordance with Pa.R.C.P. No. ___.

(President Judge)

(Administrative Judge)

Note: For a complete list of the Alternative Hearing Procedures for each county: http://www.pacourts.us/courts/supreme-court/committees/rules-committees/domestic-relations-procedural-rules-committee.

Adopted July 15, 1994, effective Jan. 1, 1995. Amended Nov. 30, 2000, effective March 1, 2001; Oct. 30, 2007, imd. effective; April 8, 2008, imd. effective; Aug. 1, 2013, effective Sept. 3, 2013; Nov. 18, 2014, effective Dec. 18, 2014; October 14, 2016, effective December 1, 2016.

Explanatory Comment

These rules provide an optional procedure for using hearing officers in partial custody cases. The procedure is similar to the one provided for support cases in Pa.R.C.P. No. 1910.12: a conference, record hearing before a hearing officer and argument on exceptions before a judge. The terms "conference officer" and "hearing officer" have the same meaning here as in the support rules.

It is important to note that use of the procedure prescribed in Pa.R.C.P. Nos. 1915.4–1 and 1915.4–2 is optional rather than mandatory. Counties which prefer to have all partial custody cases heard by a judge may continue to do so.

These procedures are not intended to replace or prohibit the use of any form of mediation or conciliation. On the contrary, they are intended to be used in cases which are not resolved through the use of less adversarial means.

The intent of the 2007 amendments to Pa.R.C.P. Nos. 1915.4–1 and 1915.4–2, and Pa.R.C.P. No. 1915–4.3, was to clarify the procedures in record and non-record custody proceedings. When the first proceeding is non-record, no exceptions are required and a request for a de novo hearing may be made.

In lieu of continuing the practice of including in the Note a 67–county list identifying the hearing procedure selected by the local county court, the list can now be found on the Domestic Relations Procedural Rules Committee website.

Rule 1915.4-2. Partial Custody. Office Conference. Hearing Record. Exceptions. Order

(a) *Office Conference.*

(1) The office conference shall be conducted by a conference officer.

(2) If the respondent fails to appear at the conference before the conference officer as directed by the court, the conference may proceed without the respondent.

(3) The conference officer may make a recommendation to the parties relating to partial custody or supervised physical custody of the child or children. If an agreement for partial custody or supervised physical custody is reached at the conference, the conference officer shall prepare a written order in conformity with the agreement for signature by the parties and submission to the court together with the officer's recommendation for approval or disapproval. The court may enter an order in accordance with the agreement without hearing the parties.

(4) At the conclusion of the conference, if an agreement relating to partial custody or supervised physical custody has not been reached, the parties shall be given notice of the date, time and place of a hearing before a hearing officer, which may be the same day, but in no event shall be more than forty-five days from the date of the conference.

(b) *Hearing.*

(1) The hearing shall be conducted by a hearing officer who must be a lawyer, and a record shall be made of the testimony. A hearing officer who is a lawyer employed by, or under contract with, a judicial district or appointed by the court shall not practice family law before a conference officer, hearing officer, permanent or standing master, or judge of the same judicial district.

(2) The hearing officer shall receive evidence and hear argument. The hearing officer may recommend to the court that the parties and/or the

subject child or children submit to examination and evaluation by experts pursuant to Rule 1915.8.

(3) Within ten days of the conclusion of the hearing, the hearing officer shall file with the court and serve upon all parties a report containing a recommendation with respect to the entry of an order of partial custody or supervised physical custody. The report may be in narrative form stating the reasons for the recommendation and shall include a proposed order, including a specific schedule for partial custody or supervised physical custody.

(4) Within twenty days after the date the hearing officer's report is mailed or received by the parties, whichever occurs first, any party may file exceptions to the report or any part thereof, to rulings on objections to evidence, to statements or findings of fact, to conclusions of law, or to any other matters occurring during the hearing. Each exception shall set forth a separate objection precisely and without discussion. Matters not covered by exceptions are deemed waived unless, prior to entry of the final order, leave is granted to file exceptions raising those matters. If exceptions are filed, any other party may file exceptions within twenty days of the date of service of the original exceptions.

(5) If no exceptions are filed within the twenty-day period, the court shall review the report and, if approved, enter a final order.

(6) If exceptions are filed, the court shall hear argument on the exceptions within forty-five days of the date the last party files exceptions, and enter an appropriate final order within fifteen days of argument. No motion for Post-Trial Relief may be filed to the final order.

Adopted July 15, 1994, effective Jan. 1, 1995. Amended Nov. 30, 2000, effective March 1, 2001; Aug. 8, 2006, imd. effective; Oct. 30, 2007, imd. effective; Aug. 1, 2013, effective Sept. 3, 2013; March 4, 2015, effective April 3, 2015.

Explanatory Comment—2006

The time for filing exceptions has been expanded from ten to twenty days. The purpose of this amendment is to provide ample opportunity for litigants and counsel to receive notice of the entry of the order, to assure Commonwealth-wide consistency in calculation of time for filing and to conform to applicable general civil procedural rules.

Rule 1915.4-3. Non-Record Proceedings. Trial

(a) *Non-Record Proceedings.* In judicial districts utilizing an initial non-record proceeding, *i.e.*, office conference, if an agreement is not finalized by the conclusion of the proceeding, the conference officer shall promptly notify the court that the matter should be listed for trial. A lawyer employed by, or under contract with, a judicial district or appointed by the court to serve as a conference officer to preside over a non-record proceeding shall not practice family law before a conference officer, hearing officer, permanent or standing master, or judge of the same judicial district.

(b) *Trial.* The trial before the court shall be *de novo*. The court shall hear the case and render a decision within the time periods set forth in Pa.R.C.P. No. 1915.4.

Adopted Oct. 30, 2007, imd. effective. Amended Aug. 1, 2013, effective Sept. 3, 2013; March 4, 2015, effective April 3, 2015; Feb. 8, 2018, effective April 1, 2018.

Explanatory Comment—2018

The amendment to this rule, in conjunction with the amendment to Pa.R.C.P. No. 1915.1, standardizes terminology used in the custody process and identifies court personnel by title and in some cases qualifications. Of note, the term "mediator," which had been included in the rule, has been omitted and is specifically defined in Pa.R.C.P. No. 1915.1.

As in the support rules, custody conference officers preside over conferences and hearing officers preside over hearings. Regardless of the individual's title, presiding over a conference or a hearing triggers the family law attorney practice preclusion in this rule and in Pa.R.C.P. No. 1915.4-2(b) in the case of a hearing officer. Mediators, as defined in Pa.R.C.P. No. 1915.1 and as qualified in Pa.R.C.P. No. 1940.4, do not preside over custody conferences or hearings; rather, mediators engage custody litigants in alternative dispute resolution methods pursuant to Chapter 1940 of the Rules of Civil Procedure and, as such, the preclusion from practicing family law in the same judicial district in which an attorney/mediator is appointed is inapplicable.

Rule 1915.4-4. Pre-Trial Procedures

A pre-trial conference in an initial custody or modification proceeding shall be scheduled before a judge at the request of a party or sua sponte by the court and the procedure shall be as set forth in this rule. If a party wishes to request a pre-trial conference, the praecipe set forth in subdivision (g) shall be filed. The scheduling of a pre-trial conference shall not stay any previously scheduled proceeding unless otherwise ordered by the court.

(a) The praecipe may be filed at any time after a custody conciliation or conference with a conference officer unless a pre-trial conference has already been scheduled or held. The pre-trial conference may be scheduled at any time, but must be scheduled at least 30 days prior to trial.

(b) Not later than five days prior to the pre-trial conference, each party shall file a pre-trial statement with the prothonotary's office and serve a copy upon the court and the other party or counsel of record. The pre-trial statement shall include the following matters, together with any additional information required by special order of the court:

(1) the name and address of each expert whom the party intends to call at trial as a witness;

(2) the name and address of each witness the party intends to call at trial and the relationship of that witness to the party. Inclusion of a witness on the pre-trial statement constitutes an affirmation that the party's counsel or the self-represented party has communicated with the witness about the substance of the witness's testimony prior to the filing of the pretrial statement; and

(3) a proposed order setting forth the custody schedule requested by the party.

In addition to the above items included in the pre-trial statement, any reports of experts and other proposed exhibits shall be included as part of the pre-trial statement served upon the other party or opposing counsel, but not included with the pre-trial statement served upon the court.

Note: *See* Pa.R.C.P. No. 1930.1(b). This rule may require attorneys or unrepresented parties to file confidential documents and documents containing confidential information that are subject to the *Case Records Public Access Policy of the Unified Judicial System of Pennsylvania.*

(c) If a party fails to file a pre-trial statement or otherwise comply with the requirements of subdivision (b), the court may make an appropriate order under Pa.R.C.P. No. 4019(c)(2) and (4) governing sanctions.

(d) Unless otherwise ordered by the court, the parties may amend their pre-trial statements at any time, but not later than seven days before trial.

(e) At the pre-trial conference, the following shall be considered:
   (1) issues for resolution by the court;
   (2) unresolved discovery matters;
   (3) any agreements of the parties;
   (4) issues relating to expert witnesses;
   (5) settlement and/or mediation of the case;

(6) such other matters as may aid in the disposition of the case; and

(7) if a trial date has not been scheduled, it shall be scheduled at the pre-trial conference.

(f) The court shall enter an order following the pre-trial conference detailing the agreements made by the parties as to any of the matters considered, limiting the issues for trial to those not disposed of by agreement and setting forth the schedule for further action in the case. Such order shall control the subsequent course of the action unless modified at trial to prevent manifest injustice.

(g) The praecipe for pre-trial conference shall be substantially in the following form:

(Caption)

PRAECIPE FOR PRE-TRIAL CONFERENCE

To the Prothonotary:

Please schedule a pre-trial conference in the above-captioned custody matter pursuant to Pa.R.C.P. No. 1915.4-4.

The parties' initial in-person contact with the court (conference with a conference officer or judge, conciliation or mediation) occurred on _____.

Plaintiff/Defendant/Attorney for Plaintiff/Defendant

Adopted June 25, 2013, effective July 25, 2013. Amended October 28, 2015, effective January 1, 2016; Jan. 5, 2018, effective Jan. 6, 2018; June 1, 2018, effective July 1, 2018.

Explanatory Comment

In 2013, the Domestic Relations Procedural Rules Committee (the "Committee") recognized there was a wide disparity in pre-trial procedures in custody cases among the various judicial districts. By adopting this rule, the Supreme Court established uniform state-wide pre-trial procedures in custody cases. With an eye toward reducing custody litigation, the rule encourages early preparation and court involvement for purposes of expedited resolutions. The rule was based upon the pretrial procedures in divorce cases as set forth in Pa.R.C.P. No. 1920.33(b). The rule does not affect, however, the First Judicial District's practice of conducting a pre-trial conference upon the filing of a motion for a protracted or semi-protracted trial.

In 2015, the Committee expressed concern the rule as previously adopted by the Supreme Court allowed for an interpretation contrary to the intent of the rule. The Committee proposed and the Court adopted an amendment to the rule to clarify the rule's mandate as it relates to witnesses. As a goal of any pre-trial conference is to settle the case, in whole or in part, the Committee believed a best practice in reaching that goal is having a thorough knowledge of the case, including the substance of anticipated witness testimony. As amended, the rule plainly states that counsel or a self-represented party is required to discuss with the witness their testimony prior to including the witness on the pre-trial statement.

Unlike Pa.R.C.P. No. 1920.33(b), the rule does not require inclusion of a summary of the witness's testimony in the pre-trial statement; but rather, an affirmation by counsel or self-represented party that there was actual communication with each witness about the witness's testimony. With the additional information from witnesses, counsel, self-represented parties and the trial court can better engage in more fruitful settlement discussions at the pre-trial conference.

Rule 1915.5. Question of Jurisdiction, Venue or Standing. No Responsive Pleading by Defendant Required. Counterclaim. Discovery.

(a) **A party must raise any question of jurisdiction of the person or venue, and may raise any question of standing, by preliminary objection filed within twenty days of service of the pleading to which objection is made or at the time of hearing, whichever first occurs. No other pleading shall be required, but if one is filed it shall not delay the hearing.**

Official Note: The court may raise at any time a question of (1) jurisdiction over the subject matter of the action or (2) the exercise of its jurisdiction pursuant to § 5426 of the Uniform Child Custody Jurisdiction and Enforcement Act, relating to simultaneous proceedings in other courts, § 5427, relating to inconvenient forum, and § 5428, relating to jurisdiction declined by reason of conduct. The Uniform Child Custody Jurisdiction and Enforcement Act, 23 Pa.C.S. § 5407, provides that, upon request of a party, an action in which a question of the existence or exercise of jurisdiction is raised shall be given calendar priority and handled expeditiously.

(b) **A party may file a counterclaim asserting the right of custody, partial custody or visitation within twenty days of service of the complaint upon that party or at the time of hearing, whichever first occurs. The claim shall be in the same form as a complaint as required by Rule 1915.3.**

(c) **There shall be no discovery unless authorized by special order of court.**

Official Note: The rule relating to discovery in domestic relations matters generally is Rule 1930.5.

Adopted Dec. 10, 1981, effective July 1, 1982; effective date extended to Jan. 1, 1983 by order of June 25, 1982. Readopted Nov. 8, 1982, effective Jan. 1, 1983; amended March 30, 1994, effective July 1, 1994; May 5, 1997, effective July 1, 1997; Nov. 19, 2008, imd. effective; Aug. 1, 2013, effective Sept. 3, 2013; July 7, 2014, effective August 6, 2014.

Explanatory Comment—1994

Under subdivision (a), the defendant may but is not required to plead to the complaint. All averments may be disputed by the defendant at the custody hearing. An attorney who wished to file another pleading may do so. However, the action is not to be delayed to permit its filing.

Rule 1915.6. Joinder of Parties

(a)(1) If the court learns from the pleadings or any other source that a parent whose parental rights have not been previously terminated or a person who has physical custody of the child is not a party to the action, it shall order that the person be joined as a party. Such person shall be served with a copy of all prior pleadings and notice of the joinder substantially in the form prescribed by Rule 1915.16(a).

(2) The person joined must file any objection to the order of joinder within twenty days after notice of the order.

(3) The person joined may file a counterclaim asserting a right to physical or legal custody in the form required for a complaint by Rule 1915.3. A copy of the counterclaim shall be served upon all other parties to the action as provided by Rule 440.

(b) If the court learns from the pleadings or any other source that any other person who claims to have custodial rights with respect to the child is not a party to the action, it shall order that notice be given to that person of the pendency of the action and of the right to intervene therein. The notice shall be substantially in the form prescribed by Rule 1915.16(b).

Adopted Dec. 10, 1981, effective July 1, 1982; effective date extended to Jan. 1, 1983 by order of June 25, 1982. Readopted Nov. 8, 1982, effective Jan. 1, 1983; amended March 30, 1994, effective July 1, 1994; Nov. 19, 2008, imd. effective; Aug. 1, 2013, effective Sept. 3, 2013.

Explanatory Comment—1994

The position taken by the rules is that a person in physical custody of the child and a parent whose parental rights have not been terminated are necessary parties to a custody determination. While it may be desirable to have other persons who claim custody rights as parties to the action, their joinder is not a prerequisite to a custody determination.

Rule 1915.7. Consent Order

If an agreement for custody is reached and the parties desire a consent order to be entered, they shall note their agreement upon the record or shall submit to the court a proposed order bearing the written consent of the parties or their counsel.

Note: See Pa.R.C.P. No. 1930.1(b). This rule may require attorneys or unrepresented parties to file confidential documents and documents containing confidential information that are subject to the *Case Records Public Access Policy of the Unified Judicial System of Pennsylvania.*

Adopted Dec. 10, 1981, effective July 1, 1982; effective date extended to Jan. 1, 1983 by order of June 25, 1982. Readopted and amended Nov. 8, 1982, effective Jan. 1, 1983. Amended Aug. 1, 2013, effective Sept. 3, 2013; Jan. 5, 2018, effective Jan. 6, 2018; June 1, 2018, effective July 1, 2018.

Explanatory Comment—1981

As in other types of litigation, determination of an action through agreement of the parties is a desirable goal. However, the power of the parties to enter into an agreement is not absolute. In Com. ex rel. Veihdeffer v. Veihdeffer, 235 Pa.Super. 447, 344 A.2d 613, 614 (1975), the Superior Court stated:

It is well settled that an agreement between the parties as to custody is not controlling but should be given weight taking into consideration all the circumstances. . . . A child cannot be made the subject of a contract with the same force and effect as if it were a mere chattel has long been established law.

If the parties seek to have their agreement incorporated into a consent order, Rule 1915.7 provides two methods of presenting the agreement to the court. The first is by noting the agreement on the record. The second is by submitting to the court a proposed order bearing the written consent of the parties. Whichever method is used, however, the parties must be present before the court unless the court directs otherwise. The child affected by the order need be present only if the court so directs.

Rule 1915.8. Physical and Mental Examination of Persons

(a) The court may order the child(ren) and/or any party to submit to and fully participate in an evaluation by an appropriate expert or experts. The order, which shall be substantially in the form set forth in Rule 1915.18, may be made upon the court's own motion, upon the motion of a party with reasonable notice to the person to be examined, or by agreement of the parties. The order shall specify the place, manner, conditions and scope of the examination and the person or persons by whom it shall be made and to whom distributed. In entering an order directing an evaluation pursuant to this rule, the court shall consider all appropriate factors including the following, if applicable:

(1) the allocation of the costs, including insurance coverage, if any, attendant to the undertaking of the evaluation and preparation of the resultant report and court testimony of any appointed expert;

(2) the execution of appropriate authorizations and/or consents to facilitate the examination;

(3) any deadlines imposed regarding the completion of the examination and payment of costs;

(4) the production of any report and of underlying data to counsel and/or any unrepresented party upon the completion of the examination; and

(5) any additional safeguards that are deemed appropriate as a result of the alleged presence of domestic violence and/or child abuse.

(b) Unless otherwise directed by the court, the expert shall deliver to the court, to the attorneys of record for the parties, to any unrepresented party, and to the guardian ad litem and/or counsel for the child, if any, copies of any reports arising from the evaluation setting out the findings, results of all tests made, diagnosis and conclusions. No reports shall be filed of record or considered evidence unless and until admitted by the court. Any report which is prepared at the request of a party, with or without a court order, and which a party intends to introduce at trial, must be delivered to the court and the other party at least thirty days before trial. If the report or any information from the evaluator is provided to the court, the evaluator shall be subject to cross-examination by all counsel and any unrepresented party without regard to who obtains or pays for the evaluation.

(c) If a party refuses to obey an order of court made under subdivision (a) of this rule, the court may make an order refusing to allow the disobedient party to support or oppose designated claims or defenses, prohibiting the party from introducing in evidence designated documents, things or testimony, prohibiting the party from introducing evidence of physical or mental condition, or making such other order as is just. The willful failure or refusal of a party to comply with an order entered pursuant to this rule may also give rise to a finding of contempt and the imposition of such sanctions as may be deemed appropriate by the court, including, but not limited to, an adverse inference against the non-complying party.

(d) A petition for contempt alleging failure to comply with an order entered pursuant to subdivision (a) of this rule shall be treated in an expedited manner.

Adopted Dec. 10, 1981, effective July 1, 1982; effective date extended to Jan. 1, 1983 by order of June 25, 1982. Readopted Nov. 8, 1982, effective Jan. 1, 1983. Amended May 16, 1994, effective July 1, 1994; May 23, 2007, effective Aug. 1, 2007; August 2, 2010, effective immediately.

Explanatory Comment—2007

This rule addresses the process for any number of expert evaluations a court may order in a custody case, including, but not limited to, physical, mental health, custody and/or drug and alcohol evaluations, and/or home studies. Since the initial promulgation of this rule in 1981, the frequency of utilizing professionals as expert witnesses in child custody litigation has increased considerably. In appropriate cases, evaluations have served as a means to provide the court with a full and complete record and to facilitate settlement of the litigation.

The proposed revisions to Rule 1915.8 are intended to afford the trial court and the parties a more flexible and case-sensitive means of determining the scope and parameters of a physical and/or mental examination, including deadlines, costs, underlying data, and access. In many instances, the previous sixty-day deadline was impractical and ignored. While some cases demanded that the evaluation be completed in less than 60 days, others demanded far more time than that. The revisions to this rule also specifically permit the trial court to draw an adverse inference from one party's failure to comply with an order pursuant to this rule.

Rule 1915.9 No Default Judgment

No judgment may be entered by default or on the pleadings.

Adopted Dec. 10, 1981, effective July 1, 1982; effective date extended to Jan. 1, 1983 by order of June 25, 1982. Readopted Nov. 8, 1982, effective Jan. 1, 1983 and applied to pending actions.

Explanatory Note—1981

An order of custody, partial custody or visitation may be obtained in several ways. If the parties reach an agreement, they may seek a consent order pursuant to Rule 1915.7. If they do not reach an agreement and contest the right to the relief sought, the court will enter an order after a hearing pursuant to Rule 1915.10.

Rule 1915.9 governs two additional situations. The first is where there is no appearance by the defendant. In such a case, there is both no consent with respect to the relief sought but also no contest. The rule provides that there shall be no judgment entered by default.

The second is where the parties seek judgment as a matter of law, i.e., on the pleadings. While any action will probably involve questions of law, the determination of the best interest of a child is never a purely legal determination. Rather, a multitude of factual determinations is required. Thus the rule provides that there shall be no judgment entered on the pleadings.

Rule 1915.10. Decision. Order

(a) The court may make the decision before the testimony has been transcribed. The court shall state the reasons for its decision either on the record in open court, in a written opinion, or in the order.

(b) The terms of the order shall be sufficiently specific to enforce the order. The court's decision shall include safety provisions designed to protect an endangered party or a child in any case in which the court has found that either is at risk of harm.

(c) Any custody order shall include notice of a party's obligations pursuant to 23 Pa.C.S. § 5337 dealing with a party's intention to relocate with a minor child.

(d) No motion for post-trial relief may be filed to an order of legal or physical custody.

Adopted Dec. 10, 1981, effective July 1, 1982; effective date extended to Jan. 1, 1983 by order of June 25, 1982. Readopted and amended Nov. 8, 1982, effective Jan. 1, 1983. Amended Oct. 19, 1983, effective Jan. 1, 1984; Nov. 7, 1988, effective Jan. 1, 1989; Aug. 1, 2013, effective Sept. 3, 2013.

Explanatory Comment—2013

The custody statute, at 23 Pa.C.S. § 5323(d), requires the court to delineate the reasons for its decision on the record in open court or in a written opinion or order. Subdivision (b) further defines and reinforces the requirements found in 23 Pa.C.S. § 5323(e). Examples of safety provisions include, but are not limited to: supervised physical custody, supervised or neutral custody exchange location, neutral party presence at custody exchange, telephone or computer-facilitated contact with the child, no direct contact between the parties, third-party contact for cancellations, third-party transportation and designating secure, neutral location for a child's passport. The statute, at 23 Pa.C.S. § 5323, requires that any custody order must include notice of a party's obligations when there is a proposed relocation under 23 Pa.C.S. § 5337. Rule 1915.17 also addresses relocation.

Rule 1915.11. Appointment of Attorney for Child. Inteview of Child. Attendance of Child at Hearing or Conference

(a) The court may on its own motion, or the motion of a party, appoint an attorney to represent the child in the action. Counsel for the child shall represent the child's legal interests and zealously represent the child as any other client in an attorney-client relationship. Counsel for the child shall not perform the role of a guardian ad litem or best interests attorney. The court may assess the cost of the child's attorney upon the parties such proportions as the court deems appropriate or as otherwise provided by law. The order appointing an attorney to represent the child shall be in substantially the form set forth in Pa.R.C.P. No. 1915.19.

(b) The court may interview a child, whether or not the child is the subject of the action, in open court or in chambers. The interview shall be conducted in the presence of the attorneys and, if permitted by the court, the parties. The attorneys shall have the right to interview the child under the supervision of the court. The interview shall be part of the record.

(c) Unless otherwise directed by the court, the child who is the subject of the action shall not be required to attend a hearing before the court or a conference.

Note: A party may bring a child to a conference or hearing but, in the absence of an order of court, is not required to do so.

Adopted Dec. 10, 1981, effective July 1, 1982; effective date extended to Jan. 1, 1983 by order of June 25, 1982. Readopted Nov. 8, 1982, effective Jan. 1, 1983. Amended April 29, 1991, effective July 1, 1991; Aug. 1, 2013, effective Sept. 3, 2013; May 18, 2016, effective July 1, 2016.

Explanatory Comment--1991

Rule 1915.15(b) provides a form of order to appear at a conference or hearing in an action for custody, partial custody or visitation of minor children. Prior to its recent amendment, the form required that one or more children who are the subject of the action attend the hearing or conference.

However, the presence of a child in court is not always necessary or desirable. The experience may be traumatic and disruptive. Consequently, the child should not be required to attend a hearing or conference in every case. When the presence of a child is required and the custodial party does not voluntarily bring the child, the court may issue an order for the child's attendance.

Subdivision (c) has been added to Rule 1915.11 to provide that, in the absence of an order of court, a child who is the subject of the action need not be brought to a conference or a hearing before the court. The form of order to appear provided by Rule 1915.15(b) has been revised to implement this policy.

Rule 1915.11-1. Parenting Coordination

If a judicial district implements a parenting coordination program, the court shall maintain a roster of qualified individuals to serve as parenting coordinators and establish the hourly rate at which parenting coordinators shall be compensated. The parenting coordinator shall attempt to resolve issues arising out of the custody order by facilitating an agreement between the parties and, if unable to reach an agreement, recommend a resolution to the court.

(a) *Appointment of a Parenting Coordinator.*

(1) After a final custody order has been entered, a judge may appoint a parenting coordinator to resolve parenting issues in cases involving repeated or intractable conflict between the parties affecting implementation of the final custody order. A parenting coordinator should not be appointed in every case. The appointment may be made on the motion of a party or the court's motion.

(2) Unless the parties consent and appropriate safety measures are in place to protect the participants, including the parenting coordinator and other third parties, a parenting coordinator shall not be appointed if:

(i) the parties to the custody action have a parotection from abuse order in effect;

(ii) the court makes a finding that a party has been the victim of domestic violence perpetrated by a party to the custody action, either during the pendency of the custody action or within 36 months preceding the filing of the custody action; or

(iii) the court makes a finding that a party to the custody action has been the victim of a personal injury crime, as defined in 23 Pa.C.S. § 3103, which was perpetrated by a party to the custody action.

(iv) If a party objects to the appointment of a parenting coordinator based on an allegation that the party has been the victim of domestic violence perpetrated by a party to the custody action, the court shall have a hearing on the issue and may consider abuse occurring beyond the 36 months provided in subdivision (a)(2)(ii).

(3) The appointment of a parenting coordinator shall be for a specified period, which shall not exceed 12 months. A party may petition the court for an extension of the appointment or the court in its discretion may extend the appointment for an additional period.

(4) If the parenting coordinator seeks to withdraw from service in a case, the parenting coordinator shall petition the court and provide a copy of the petition to the parties or the parties' attorneys.

(5) The parenting coordinator shall set forth in a separate written agreement with the parties:

(i) the amount of any retainer;

(ii) the hourly rate to be charged;

(iii) the process for invoices and payment for services;

(iv) information on the parenting coordination process; and

(v) provide a signed copy of the agreement to the parties before initiating any services.

(b) *Qualifications of the Parenting Coordinator.*

(1) A parenting coordinator shall be licensed to practice in the Commonwealth of Pennsylvania as either an attorney or a mental health professional with a master's degree or higher. At a minimum, the parenting coordinator shall have:

(i) practiced family law for five years or have five years of professional post-degree experience in psychiatry, psychology, counseling, family therapy, or other comparable behavioral or social science field; and

(ii) specialized training by a provider approved or certified by the American Psychological Association, Pennsylvania Psychological Association, American Bar Association, Pennsylvania Bar Association, Pennsylvania Bar Institute, or American Academy of Matrimonial Lawyers. The training shall include:

(A) five hours in the parenting coordination process;

(B) ten hours of family mediation;

(C) five hours of training in domestic violence; and

(D) in each two-year period after the initial appointment, ten continuing education credits on any topic related to parenting coordination with a minimum of two hours on domestic violence.

(2) An attorney or a mental health professional seeking an appointment as a parenting coordinator:

(i) shall sign an affidavit attesting that he or she has met the qualifications outlined in (b)(1);

(ii) shall submit the affidavit to the president judge or administrative judge of the judicial district where the parenting coordinator is seeking appointment; and

(iii) after submission of the initial affidavit, a parenting coordinator shall submit a new affidavit every two years attesting that he or she continues to meet the qualifications for a parenting coordinator outlined in (b)(1).

(c) **Appointment Order.** The parenting coordinator's authority as delineated in subdivision (d) shall be included in the order appointing the parenting coordinator, which shall be substantially in the form set forth in Pa.R.C.P. No. 1915.22.

(d) **Scope of Authority of the Parenting Coordinator.** The parenting coordinator shall have the authority to recommend resolutions to the court on issues related to the custody order if the parties are unable to reach an agreement.

(1) To implement the custody order and resolve related parenting issues about which the parties cannot agree, the parenting coordinator is authorized to recommend resolutions to the court about issues that include, but are not limited to:

(i) places and conditions for custodial transitions between households;

(ii) temporary variation from the custodial schedule for a special event or particular circumstance;

(iii) school issues, apart from school selection;

(iv) the child(ren)'s participation in recreation, enrichment, and extracurricular activities, including travel;

(v) child-care arrangements;

(vi) clothing, equipment, toys, and personal possessions of the child(ren);

(vii) information exchanges (e.g., school, health, social) between the parties and communication with or about the child(ren);

(viii) coordination of existing or court-ordered services for the child(ren) (e.g., psychological testing, alcohol or drug monitoring/testing, psychotherapy, anger management);

(ix) behavioral management of the child(ren); and

(x) other related custody issues that the parties mutually have agreed in writing to submit to the parenting coordinator, which are not excluded in subdivision (d)(2).

(2) The following issues are excluded from the parenting coordinator's scope of authority:

(i) a change in legal custody as set forth in the custody order;

(ii) a change in primary physical custody as set forth in the custody order;

(iii) except as set forth in subdivision (d)(1)(ii), a change in the court-ordered custody schedule that reduces or expands the child(ren)'s time with a party;

(iv) a change in the residence (relocation) of the child(ren);

(v) determination of financial issues, other than allocation of the parenting coordinator's fees as set forth in subdivision (g)(1);

(vi) major decisions affecting the health, education, or religion of the child(ren); and

(vii) other issues limited by the appointing judge.

(3) Unless the parties consent, the parenting coordinator shall not contact collateral sources or speak with the child(ren) and to effectuate this provision, the parties shall execute releases, as necessary, authorizing the parenting coordinator to communicate with the appropriate individuals. Any communication with the collateral sources or child-(ren) shall be limited to the issue(s) currently before the parenting coordinator.

(e) Communications. No Testimony.

(1) Communication between the parties or the parties' attorneys and the parenting coordinator is not confidential.

(2) A party or a party's attorney may communicate in writing with the parenting coordinator, but shall contemporaneously send a copy of the written communication to the other party or the other party's attorney. Documents, recordings, or other material that one party gives to the parenting coordinator shall be promptly made available to the other party or the other party's attorney for inspection and copying.

(3) The parties and their attorneys may receive, but not initiate, oral ex parte communication with the parenting coordinator. A parenting coordinator may initiate oral communication with a party or party's attorney, but shall promptly advise the other party or the other party's attorney of the communication.

(4) Communication between the parenting coordinator and the court shall be in writing and copies of the written communication shall be sent contemporaneously to the parties or the parties' attorneys.

(5) A party cannot compel the testimony of a parenting coordinator without an order of court.

(f) Recommendations. Objecting to the Recommendation. Judicial Review. Record Hearing.

(1) The parenting coordinator shall provide to the parties notice and an opportunity to be heard on the issues.

(2) The parenting coordinator's recommendation shall be in writing on the Summary and Recommendation of the Parenting Coordinator form set forth in Pa.R.C.P. No. 1915.23 and sent to the court for review within two days after hearing from the parties on the issues. The parenting coordinator shall serve a copy of the Summary and Recommendation on the parties or the parties' attorneys.

(3) A party objecting to the recommendation shall file a petition for a record hearing before the court within five days of service of the Summary and Recommendation of the Parenting Coordinator form. The petition must specifically state the issues to be reviewed and include a demand for a record hearing. A copy of the recommendation shall be attached to the petition. In accordance with Pa.R.C.P. No. 440, the objecting party shall serve the petition on the other party or the other party's attorney and the parenting coordinator.

(4) If the parties do not file an objection within five days of service of the parenting coordinator's recommendation, the court shall:

(i) approve the recommendation;

(ii) approve the recommendation in part and conduct a record hearing on issues not approved;

(iii) remand the recommendation to the parenting coordinator for more specific information; or

(iv) not approve the recommendation and conduct a record hearing on the issues.

(5) As soon as practical, the court shall conduct a record hearing on the issues specifically set forth in the petition. The court shall render a decision within the time set forth in Pa.R.C.P. No. 1915.4(d).

(6) If a party makes a timely objection, the recommendation shall become an interim order of court pending further disposition by the court.

(g) Fees.

(1) The appointing judge shall allocate between the parties the fees of the parenting coordinator. The parenting coordinator may reallocate the fees, subject to the approval of the court, if one party has caused a disproportionate need for the services of the parenting coordinator.

(2) To limit the financial burden on the parties, a parenting coordinator should meet with the parties only upon a request of a party to resolve an issue about which the parties disagree.

(3) Waiver of fees or reduced fees. Judicial districts implementing a parenting coordination program shall effectuate a policy or program by local rule so that indigent or low-income parties may participate in the parenting coordination program at a reduced fee or no fee.

Adopted August 9, 2018, effective March 1, 2019.

Rule 1915.11-2. Appointment of Guardian Ad Litem

(a) The court may, on its own motion or the motion of a party, appoint a guardian ad litem to represent the best interests of the child in a custody action. The guardian ad litem shall be a licensed attorney or licensed mental health professional. The guardian ad litem shall not act as the child's counsel or represent the child's legal interests. Prior to appointing a guardian ad litem, the court shall make a finding that the appointment is necessary to assist the court in determining the best interests of the child.

(b) The court may order either or both parties to pay all or part of the costs of appointing a guardian ad litem.

(c) The guardian ad litem shall file of record and provide copies of any reports prepared by the guardian ad litem to each party and the court not later than 20 days prior to trial. The admissibility of the report shall be determined at the hearing. Prior to disclosure to the parties of confidential information prohibited by 23 Pa.C.S. § 5336, the court shall make a determination of whether the information may be disclosed. The guardian ad litem shall attend all proceedings and be prepared to testify. The guardian ad litem shall be subject to cross-examination if called to testify by either party or the court.

(d) The order appointing a guardian ad litem shall be in substantially the form set forth in Rule 1915.21.

Official Note: 23 Pa.C.S. § 5334 is suspended insofar as it (1) requires that a guardian ad litem be an attorney, (2) permits the guardian ad litem to represent both the best interests and legal interests of the child, (3) provides the guardian ad litem the right to examine, cross-examine, present witnesses and present evidence on behalf of the child, and (4) prohibits the guardian ad litem from testifying.

Adopted Aug. 1, 2013, effective Sept. 3, 2013.

Pa. R.C.P.   Rule 1915.12

Rule 1915.12. Civil Contempt for Disobedience of Custody Order. Petition. Form of Petition. Service. Order

(a) A petition for civil contempt shall begin with a notice and order to appear in substantially the following form:

NOTICE AND ORDER TO APPEAR

Legal proceedings have been brought against you alleging you have willfully disobeyed an order of court for custody.

If you wish to defend against the claim set forth in the following pages, you may but are not required to file in writing with the court your defenses or objections.

Whether or not you file in writing with the court your defenses or objections, you must appear in person in court on _____ (Day and Date), at _____.M. (Time), in Courtroom _____, _____ (Address).

IF YOU DO NOT APPEAR IN PERSON, THE COURT MAY ISSUE A WARRANT FOR YOUR ARREST.

If the court finds that you have willfully failed to comply with its order, you may be found to be in contempt of court and committed to jail, fined or both.

YOU SHOULD TAKE THIS PAPER TO YOUR LAWYER AT ONCE. IF YOU DO NOT HAVE A LAWYER, GO TO OR TELEPHONE THE OFFICE SET FORTH BELOW. THIS OFFICE CAN PROVIDE YOU WITH INFORMATION ABOUT HIRING A LAWYER.

IF YOU CANNOT AFFORD TO HIRE A LAWYER, THIS OFFICE MAY BE ABLE TO PROVIDE YOU WITH INFORMATION ABOUT AGENCIES THAT MAY OFFER LEGAL SERVICES TO ELIGIBLE PERSONS AT A REDUCED FEE OR NO FEE.

                                   _____
                                   (Name)

                                   _____
                                   (Address)

                                   _____
                                   (Telephone Number)

                                   BY THE COURT:

                                   _____
                                                                                       J.

Date: _____

(b) The petition shall allege the facts which constitute willful failure to comply with the custody order, a copy of which shall be attached to the petition.

(c) The petition shall be in substantially the following form:

Rule 1915.13   ACTIONS FOR CUSTODY, VISITATION

(Caption)

PETITION FOR CIVIL CONTEMPT FOR DISOBEDIENCE
OF CUSTODY ORDER

The Petition of _____, respectfully represents:

1. That on _____, Judge _____ entered an Order awarding (Petitioner) (Respondent) (shared legal custody) (sole legal custody) (partial physical custody) (primary physical custody) (shared physical custody) (sole physical custody) (supervised physical custody) of the minor child(ren)

(NAME(S) OF CHILD(REN))

A true and correct copy of the order is attached to this petition.

2. Respondent has willfully failed to abide by the order in that

3. Petitioner has attached the Criminal Record/Abuse History Verification form required pursuant to Pa.R.C.P. No. 1915.3-2.

WHEREFORE, Petitioner requests that Respondent be held in contempt of court.

_____
(Attorney for Petitioner) (Petitioner)

I verify that the statements made in this petition are true and correct. I understand that false statements herein are made subject to the penalties of 18 Pa.C.S. § 4904 relating to unsworn falsification to authorities.

_____   _____
Date   Petitioner

(d) The petition shall be served upon the respondent by personal service or regular mail. No answer to the petition shall be required. If service is by mail, the hearing on the petition shall not be held sooner than seven days after mailing of the petition unless the court for cause shown orders an earlier hearing. If the respondent fails to appear, the court shall continue the hearing and may order personal service by the sheriff or constable, or alternative service as accepted by the court, of the petition and notice of a new hearing date, or the court may issue a bench warrant for production of the respondent in court and not for imprisonment.

(e) After hearing, an order committing a respondent to jail for contempt of a custody order shall specify the condition which must be fulfilled to obtain release of the respondent.

Note: See the Uniform Child Custody Jurisdiction and Enforcement Act, 23 Pa.C.S. §§ 5443 and 5445, relating to registration and enforcement of custody decrees of another state, and 23 Pa.C.S. § 5471, relating to intrastate application of the Uniform Child Custody Jurisdiction and Enforcement Act.

Adopted Dec. 10, 1981, effective July 1, 1982. Effective date extended to Jan. 1, 1983 by order of June 25, 1982. Readopted and amended Nov. 8, 1982, effective Jan. 1, 1983. Amended Dec. 2, 1994, effective March 1, 1995; March 18, 2004, effective June 16, 2004; Nov. 19, 2008, imd. effective; Aug. 1, 2013, effective Sept. 3, 2013; July 20, 2015, effective September 1, 2015.

Rule 1915.13. Special Relief

At any time after commencement of the action, the court may on application or its own motion grant appropriate interim or special relief. The relief may include, but is not limited to, the award of temporary legal or physical custody; the issuance of appropriate process directing that a child or a party or person having physical custody of a child be brought before the court; and a direction that a person post security to appear with the child when directed by the court or to comply with any order of the court.

Official Note: This rule supplies relief formerly available by habeas corpus for production of the child.

Adopted Dec. 10, 1981, effective July 1, 1982; effective date extended to Jan. 1, 1983 by order of June 25, 1982. Readopted Nov. 8, 1982, effective Jan. 1, 1983. Amended Aug. 1, 2013, effective Sept. 3, 2013.

Explanatory Comment—1981

Rule 1915.13 contains a broad provision empowering the court to provide special relief where appropriate. In a custody proceeding, such special relief might include relief in the nature of a writ of ne exeat, directing the parties not to leave the jurisdiction and not to remove the child from the jurisdiction.

The rule catalogs several types of relief which might be granted, including the entry of a temporary order of custody, partial custody or visitation. The rule specifically provides that the power of the court to grant special relief shall not be limited to the types of relief cataloged.

Rule 1915.14. Disobedience of Order. Arrest. Contempt

If a person disobeys an order of court other than a custody order, the court may issue a bench warrant for the arrest of the person and if the disobedience is willful may, after hearing, adjudge the person to be in contempt.

Official Note: For disobedience of a custody order, see Rule 1915.12.

Adopted Dec. 10, 1981, effective July 1, 1982; effective date extended to Jan. 1, 1983 by order of June 25, 1982. Readopted Nov. 8, 1982, effective Jan. 1, 1983. Amended Aug. 1, 2013, effective Sept. 3, 2013.

Rule 1915.15. Form of Complaint. Caption. Order. Petition to Modify a Custody Order

(a) The complaint in an action for custody shall be substantially in the following form:

(Caption)

COMPLAINT FOR CUSTODY

1. The plaintiff is _____, residing at _____ (Street) _____ (City)_____ (Zip Code) _____ (County)

2. The defendant is _____, residing at _____ (Street) _____ (City) _____ (Zip Code) _____ (County)

3. Plaintiff seeks (shared legal custody) (sole legal custody) (partial physical custody) (primary physical custody) (shared physical custody) (sole physical custody) (supervised physical custody) of the following child(ren):

Rule 1915.15   ACTIONS FOR CUSTODY, VISITATION

Name	Present Residence	Age
_____	_____	_____
_____	_____	_____
_____	_____	_____

The child (was)(was not) born out of wedlock.

The child is presently in the custody of _____, (Name) who resides at _____ (Street) _____ (City) _____ (State).

During the past five years, the child has resided with the following persons and at the following addresses:

(List All Persons)	(List All Addresses)	(Dates)
_____	_____	_____
_____	_____	_____
_____	_____	_____

A parent of the child is _____ currently residing at _____
This parent is (married) (divorced) (single).
A parent of the child is _____, currently residing at _____.
This parent is (married) (divorced) (single).

4. The relationship of plaintiff to the child is that of _____. The plaintiff currently resides with the following persons:

Name	Relationship
_____	_____
_____	_____

5. The relationship of defendant to the child is that of _____.
The defendant currently resides with the following persons:

Name	Relationship
_____	_____
_____	_____

6. Plaintiff (has) (has not) participated as a party or witness, or in another capacity, in other litigation concerning the custody of the child in this or another court. The court, term and number, and its relationship to this action is: _____

Plaintiff (has) (has no) information of a custody proceeding concerning the child pending in a court of this Commonwealth or any other state. The court, term and number, and its relationship to this action is: _____

Plaintiff (knows) (does not know) of a person not a party to the proceedings who has physical custody of the child or claims to have custodial rights with respect to the child. The name and address of such person is: _____

7. The best interest and permanent welfare of the child will be served by granting the relief requested because (set forth facts showing that the

Pa. R.C.P.   Rule 1915.15

granting of the relief requested will be in the best interest and permanent welfare of the child: _____

8. Each parent whose parental rights to the child have not been terminated and the person who has physical custody of the child have been named as parties to this action. All other persons, named below, who are known to have or claim a right to custody of the child will be given notice of the pendency of this action and the right to intervene:

Name	Address	Basis of Claim
_____	_____	_____
_____	_____	_____

9. (a) If the plaintiff is a grandparent who is not in loco parentis to the child and is seeking physical and/or legal custody pursuant to 23 Pa.C.S. § 5323, you must plead facts establishing standing pursuant to 23 Pa.C.S. § 5324(3).

_____

(b) If the plaintiff is a grandparent or great-grandparent who is seeking partial physical custody or supervised physical custody pursuant to 23 Pa.C.S. § 5325, you must plead facts establishing standing pursuant to § 5325.

_____

(c) If the plaintiff is a person seeking physical and/or legal custody pursuant to 23 Pa.C.S. § 5324(2) as a person who stands in loco parentis to the child, you must plead facts establishing standing.

_____

10. Plaintiff has attached the Criminal Record/Abuse History Verification form required pursuant to Pa.R.C.P. No. 1915.3-2.

Wherefore, plaintiff requests the court to grant (shared legal custody) (sole legal custody) (partial physical custody) (primary physical custody) (shared physical custody) (sole physical custody) (supervised physical custody) of the child.

_____
Attorney for Plaintiff

I verify that the statements made in this Complaint are true and correct. I understand that false statements herein are made subject to the penalties of 18 Pa.C.S. § 4904 relating to unsworn falsification to authorities.

_____
Plaintiff

Note: The form of complaint is appropriate if there is one plaintiff and one defendant and if the custody of one child is sought, or if the custody of several children is sought and the information required by paragraphs 3 to 7 is identical for all of the children. If there are multiple parties, the complaint should be appropriately adapted to accommodate them. If the custody of several children is sought and the information

Rule 1915.15   ACTIONS FOR CUSTODY, VISITATION

required is not identical for all of the children, the complaint should contain a separate paragraph for each child.

See Pa.R.C.P. No. 1930.1(b). This rule may require attorneys or unrepresented parties to file confidential documents and documents containing confidential information that are subject to the Case Records *Public Access Policy of the Unified Judicial System of Pennsylvania.*

(b) A petition to modify a custody order shall be substantially in the following form:

(Caption)

PETITION FOR MODIFICATION OF A CUSTODY ORDER

1. Petitioner is _____ and resides at _____.

2. Respondent is _____ and resides at _____.

3. Petitioner respectfully represents that on _____, 20 ___ an Order of Court was entered for (shared legal custody) (sole legal custody) (partial physical custody) (primary physical custody) (shared physical custody) (sole physical custody) (supervised physical custody). A true and correct copy of the Order is attached.

4. This Order should be modified because: _____
_____.

5. Petitioner has attached the Criminal Record/Abuse History Verification form required pursuant to Pa.R.C.P. No. 1915.3-2.

WHEREFORE, Petitioner requests that the Court modify the existing Order because it will be in the best interest of the child(ren).

_____
(Attorney for Petitioner) (Petitioner)

I verify that the statements made in this petition are true and correct. I understand that false statements herein are made subject to the penalties of 18 Pa.C.S. § 4904 relating to unsworn falsification to authorities.

_____   _____
        Date   Petitioner

Note: *See* Pa.R.C.P. No. 1930.1(b). This rule may require attorneys or unrepresented parties to file confidential documents and documents containing confidential information that are subject to the Case Records *Public Access Policy of the Unified Judicial System of Pennsylvania.*

(c) The order to be attached at the front of the complaint or petition for modification shall be substantially in the following form:

(Caption)

ORDER OF COURT

You, _____, (defendant) (respondent), have been sued in court to (OBTAIN)(MODIFY) (shared legal custody) (sole legal custody) (partial physical

Pa. R.C.P. Rule 1915.15

custody) (primary physical custody) (shared physical custody) (sole physical custody) (supervised physical custody) of the child(ren):

You are ordered to appear in person at _____(Address), on _____(Day and Date), at _____(Time), ____.M., for

☐ a conciliation or mediation conference.

☐ a pretrial conference.

☐ a hearing before the court.

If you fail to appear as provided by this order, an order for custody may be entered against you or the court may issue a warrant for your arrest.

You must file with the court a verification regarding any criminal record or abuse history regarding you and anyone living in your household on or before the initial in-person contact with the court (including, but not limited to, a conference with a conference officer or judge or conciliation) but not later than 30 days after service of the complaint or petition.

No party may make a change in the residence of any child which significantly impairs the ability of the other party to exercise custodial rights without first complying with all of the applicable provisions of 23 Pa.C.S. § 5337 and Pa.R.C.P. No. 1915.17 regarding relocation.

YOU SHOULD TAKE THIS PAPER TO YOUR LAWYER AT ONCE. IF YOU DO NOT HAVE A LAWYER, GO TO OR TELEPHONE THE OFFICE SET FORTH BELOW. THIS OFFICE CAN PROVIDE YOU WITH INFORMATION ABOUT HIRING A LAWYER. IF YOU CANNOT AFFORD TO HIRE A LAWYER, THIS OFFICE MAY BE ABLE TO PROVIDE YOU WITH INFORMATION ABOUT AGENCIES THAT MAY OFFER LEGAL SERVICES TO ELIGIBLE PERSONS AT A REDUCED FEE OR NO FEE.

_____
(Name)

_____
Address

_____
(Telephone)

AMERICANS WITH DISABILITIES ACT OF 1990

The Court of Common Pleas of _____ County is required by law to comply with the Americans with Disabilities Act of 1990. For information about accessible facilities and reasonable accommodations available to disabled individuals having business before the court, please contact our office. All arrangements must be made at least 72 hours prior to any hearing or business before the court. You must attend the scheduled conference or hearing.

BY THE COURT:

Date: _____

_____
J.

Adopted Dec. 10, 1981, effective July 1, 1982; effective date extended to Jan. 1, 1983 by order of June 25, 1982. Readopted and amended Nov. 8, 1982, effective Jan. 1, 1983. Amended April 29, 1991, effective July 1, 1991; Dec. 2, 1994, effective March 1, 1995; March 2, 2000, imd. effective; March 18, 2004, effective June 16, 2004; Nov. 19, 2008, imd. effective; Aug. 1, 2013, effective Sept. 3, 2013; July 20, 2015, effective September 1, 2015; May 18, 2016, effective July 1, 2016; Jan. 5, 2018, effective Jan. 6, 2018; June 1, 2018, effective July 1, 2018.

Rule 1915.16   ACTIONS FOR CUSTODY, VISITATION

Explanatory Comment—2008

In an effort to promote uniformity of practice throughout the Commonwealth, several forms are included in the rules. Two aspects of these forms are worthy of mention. First, much of the information which must be set forth in the complaint is required by the Uniform Child Custody Jurisdiction and Enforcement Act, 23 Pa.C.S.A. § 5429. Second, the complaint is verified by use of a statement that it is subject to the penalties of the Crimes Code relating to unsworn falsification to authorities. A notary public is not needed.

Rule 1915.16. Form of Order and Notice. Joinder. Intervention

(a) The order and notice joining a party in an action under Rule 1915.6(a) shall be substantially in the following form:

(Caption)

ORDER AND NOTICE

A complaint has been filed in the Court of Common Pleas of _____ County concerning custody of the following child(ren): _____.

The Court has learned you may have a legal interest in custody of the child(ren) named.

A hearing will be held in Courtroom ___ of the Court of Common Pleas, _____ (Address), on _____ (Day and Date), at _____ (Time), ___.M. If you wish to protect any legal interest you may have or wish to present evidence to the Court on those matters, you should appear at the place and time and on the date above.

If you have the child(ren) in your possession or control, you must appear and bring them to the Courthouse with you.

If you wish to claim a right of custody, you may file a counterclaim.

If you fail to appear as provided by this order or to bring the child(ren), an order for custody may be entered against you or the Court may issue a warrant for your arrest.

YOU SHOULD TAKE THIS PAPER TO YOUR LAWYER AT ONCE. IF YOU DO NOT HAVE A LAWYER, GO TO OR TELEPHONE THE OFFICE SET FORTH BELOW. THIS OFFICE CAN PROVIDE YOU WITH INFORMATION ABOUT HIRING A LAWYER.

IF YOU CANNOT AFFORD TO HIRE A LAWYER, THIS OFFICE MAY BE ABLE TO PROVIDE YOU WITH INFORMATION ABOUT AGENCIES THAT MAY OFFER LEGAL SERVICES TO ELIGIBLE PERSONS AT A REDUCED FEE OR NO FEE.

_____

(Name)

_____

Address

_____

(Telephone)

Pa. R.C.P.   Rule 1915.16

AMERICANS WITH DISABILITIES ACT OF 1990

The Court of Common Pleas of _____ County is required by law to comply with the Americans with Disabilities Act of 1990. For information about accessible facilities and reasonable accommodations available to disabled individuals having business before the court, please contact our office. All arrangements must be made at least 72 hours prior to any hearing or business before the court.

BY THE COURT:

Date: _____   _____

J.

(b) The order for notice of the pendency of the action and the right to intervene required by Rule 1915.6(b) shall be substantially in the following form:

(Caption)
ORDER AND NOTICE

A complaint has been filed in the Court of Common Pleas of _____ County concerning custody of the following child(ren): _____.

The Court has learned you claim custodial rights with respect to the child(ren) named.

A hearing will be held in courtroom ___ of the Court of Common Pleas, _____ (Address), on _____ (Day and Date), at _____ (Time), ___.M. If you wish to assert your claim to custodial rights with respect to the child(ren) or wish to present evidence to the Court on those matters, you should petition the Court, on or before the above date, for leave to intervene in the proceedings.

YOU SHOULD TAKE THIS PAPER TO YOUR LAWYER AT ONCE. IF YOU DO NOT HAVE A LAWYER, GO TO OR TELEPHONE THE OFFICE SET FORTH BELOW. THIS OFFICE CAN PROVIDE YOU WITH INFORMATION ABOUT HIRING A LAWYER. IF YOU CANNOT AFFORD TO HIRE A LAWYER, THIS OFFICE MAY BE ABLE TO PROVIDE YOU WITH INFORMATION ABOUT AGENCIES THAT MAY OFFER LEGAL SERVICES TO ELIGIBLE PERSONS AT A REDUCED FEE OR NO FEE.

_____
(Name)

_____
Address

_____
(Telephone)

AMERICANS WITH DISABILITIES ACT OF 1990

The Court of Common Pleas of _____ County is required by law to comply with the Americans with Disabilities Act of 1990. For information about accessible facilities and reasonable accommodations available to disabled individuals having business before the court, please contact our office. All arrangements must be made at least 72 hours prior to any hearing or business before the court.

BY THE COURT:

Date: _____   _____

J.

Rule 1915.17   ACTIONS FOR CUSTODY, VISITATION

Adopted Dec. 10, 1981, effective July 1, 1982; effective date extended to Jan. 1, 1983 by order of June 25, 1982. Readopted Nov. 8, 1982, effective Jan. 1, 1983. Amended Dec. 2, 1994, effective March 1, 1995; March 18, 2004, effective June 16, 2004; Aug. 1, 2013, effective Sept. 3, 2013.

Rule 1915.17. Relocation. Notice and Counter-Affidavit

(a) A party proposing to change the residence of a child which significantly impairs the ability of a non-relocating party to exercise custodial rights must notify every other person who has custodial rights to the child and provide a counter-affidavit by which a person may agree or object. The form of the notice and counter-affidavit are set forth in subdivisions (i) and (j) below. The notice shall be sent by certified mail, return receipt requested, addressee only or pursuant to Pa.R.A.P. No. 1930.4, no later than the sixtieth day before the date of the proposed change of residence or other time frame set forth in 23 Pa.C.S. § 5337(c)(2).

(b) If the other party objects to the proposed change in the child's residence, that party must serve the counter-affidavit on the party proposing the change by certified mail, return receipt requested, addressee only, or pursuant to Pa.R.C.P. No. 1930.4 within 30 days of receipt of the notice required in subdivision (a) above. If there is an existing child custody case, the objecting party also shall file the counter-affidavit with the court.

(c) If no objection to a proposed change of a child's residence is timely served after notice, the proposing party may change the residence of the child and such shall not be considered a "relocation" under statute or rule.

(d) The procedure in any relocation case shall be expedited. There shall be no requirement for parenting education or mediation prior to an expedited hearing before a judge.

(e) If the party proposing the relocation seeks an order of court, has served a notice of proposed relocation as required by 23 Pa.C.S. § 5337, has not received notice of objection to the move and seeks confirmation of relocation, the party proposing the relocation shall file:

    (1) a complaint for custody and petition to confirm relocation, when no custody case exists, or

    (2) a petition to confirm relocation when there is an existing custody case and

    (3) a proposed order including the information set forth at 23 Pa.C.S. § 5337(c)(3).

(f) If the party proposing the relocation has received notice of objection to the proposed move after serving a notice of proposed relocation as required by 23 Pa.C.S. § 5337 et seq., the party proposing relocation shall file:

    (1) a complaint for custody or petition for modification, as applicable;

    (2) a copy of the notice of proposed relocation served on the non-relocating party;

    (3) a copy of the counter-affidavit indicating objection to relocation; and

    (4) a request for a hearing.

(g) If the non-relocating party has been served with a notice of proposed relocation and the party proposing relocation has not complied with subdivision (f) above, the non-relocating party may file:

Pa. R.C.P. Rule 1915.17

    (1) a complaint for custody or petition for modification, as applicable;
    (2) a counter-affidavit as set forth in 23 Pa.C.S. § 5337(d)(1), and
    (3) a request for a hearing.

(h) If a non-relocating party has not been served with a notice of proposed relocation and seeks an order of court preventing relocation, the non-relocating party shall file:

    (1) a complaint for custody or petition for modification, as applicable;
    (2) a statement of objection to relocation; and
    (3) a request for a hearing.

    (i) The notice of proposed relocation shall be substantially in the following form:

(Caption)

NOTICE OF PROPOSED RELOCATION

You, _____, are hereby notified that _____ (party proposing relocation) _____ proposes to relocate with the following minor child(ren):

_____.

To object to the proposed relocation, you must complete the attached counter-affidavit and serve it on the other party by certified mail, return receipt requested, addressee only, or pursuant to Pa.R.C.P. No. 1930.4 within 30 days of receipt of this notice. If there is an existing child custody case, you also must file the counter-affidavit with the court. If you do not object to the proposed relocation within 30 days, the party proposing relocation has the right to relocate and may petition the court to approve the proposed relocation and to modify any effective custody orders or agreements. FAILURE TO OBJECT WITHIN 30 DAYS WILL PREVENT YOU FROM OBJECTING TO THE RELOCATION ABSENT EXIGENT CIRCUMSTANCES.

Address of the proposed new residence:

_____

☐ *Check here if the address is confidential pursuant to 23 Pa.C.S. § 5336(b).*

Mailing address of intended new residence (if not the same as above)

_____

☐ *Check here if the address is confidential pursuant to 23 Pa.C.S. § 5336(b).*

Names and ages of the individuals who intend to reside at the new residence:

Name   Age

_____

_____

_____

_____

☐ *Check here if the information is confidential pursuant to 23 Pa.C.S. § 5336(b) or (c).*

Home telephone number of the new residence:

Rule 1915.17 ACTIONS FOR CUSTODY, VISITATION

☐ *Check here if the information is confidential pursuant to 23 Pa.C.S. § 5336(b) or (c).*

Name of the new school district and school the child(ren) will attend after relocation:

_____

☐ *Check here if the information is confidential pursuant to 23 Pa.C.S. § 5336(b) or (c).*

Date of the proposed relocation:

☐ *Check here if the information is confidential pursuant to 23 Pa.C.S. § 5336(b) or (c).*

Reasons for the proposed relocation:

_____
_____
_____

☐ *Check here if the information is confidential pursuant to 23 Pa.C.S. § 5336(b) or (c).*

Proposed modification of custody schedule following relocation:

_____
_____
_____
_____

Other information:

_____

YOU SHOULD TAKE THIS PAPER TO YOUR LAWYER AT ONCE. IF YOU DO NOT HAVE A LAWYER, GO TO OR TELEPHONE THE OFFICE SET FORTH BELOW. THIS OFFICE CAN PROVIDE YOU WITH INFORMATION ABOUT HIRING A LAWYER.

IF YOU CANNOT AFFORD TO HIRE A LAWYER, THIS OFFICE MAY BE ABLE TO PROVIDE YOU WITH INFORMATION ABOUT AGENCIES THAT MAY OFFER LEGAL SERVICES TO ELIGIBLE PERSONS AT A REDUCED FEE OR NO FEE.

_____
_____

Note: See Pa.R.C.P. No. 1930.1(b). This rule may require attorneys or unrepresented parties to file confidential documents and documents containing confidential information that are subject to the Case Records Public Access Policy of the Unified Judicial System of Pennsylvania.

(j) **The counter-affidavit that must be served with the relocation notice shall be substantially in the following form as set forth in 23 Pa.C.S.§ 5337(d):**

Pa. R.C.P.   Rule 1915.17

(Caption)

COUNTER-AFFIDAVIT REGARDING RELOCATION

This proposal of relocation involves the following child/children:

Child's Name	Age	Currently residing at:
Child's Name	Age	Currently residing at:
Child's Name	Age	Currently residing at:

I have received a notice of proposed relocation and (*check all that apply*):

1. ☐ I do not object to the relocation

2. ☐ I do not object to the modification of the custody order consistent with the proposal for modification set forth in the notice.

3. ☐ I do not object to the relocation, but I do object to modification of the custody order.

4. ☐ I plan to request that a hearing be scheduled by filing a request for hearing with the court:

    a. ☐ Prior to allowing (name of child/children) to relocate.

    b. ☐ After the child/children relocate.

5. ☐ I do object to the relocation

6. ☐ I do object to the modification of the custody order.

I understand that in addition to objecting to the relocation or modification of the custody order above, I must also serve this counter-affidavit on the other party by certified mail, return receipt requested, addressee only, or pursuant to Pa.R.C.P. No. 1930.4, and, if there is an existing custody case, I must file this counter-affidavit with the court. If I fail to do so within 30 days of my receipt of the proposed relocation notice, I understand that I will not be able to object to the relocation at a later time.

    I verify that the statements made in this counter-affidavit are true and correct. I understand that false statements herein are made subject to the penalties of 18 Pa.C.S. § 4904 (relating to unsworn falsification to authorities).

_____   _____

        (Date)   (Signature)

Rule 1915.18   ACTIONS FOR CUSTODY, VISITATION

Note: See Pa.R.C.P. No. 1930.1(b). This rule may require attorneys or unrepresented parties to file confidential documents and documents containing confidential information that are subject to the Case Records Public Access Policy of the Unified Judicial System of Pennsylvania.

Adopted Aug. 1, 2013, effective Sept. 3, 2013. Amended July 20, 2015, effective September 1, 2015; Jan. 5, 2018, effective Jan. 6, 2018; June 1, 2018, effective, July 1, 2018.

Rule 1915.18. Form of Order Directing Expert Examination and Report

The order of court directing expert evaluation in a custody matter pursuant to Pa.R.C.P.No. 1915.8 shall be substantially in the following form:

(Caption)

ORDER OF COURT

AND NOW, this ___ day of ___, 20__, it is hereby ORDERED, that:

1. The evaluator [ ] shall be _____ or [ ] will be selected by the parties.

2. The evaluator shall conduct a

[ ] Physical Evaluation

[ ] Psychological Evaluation

[ ] Custody Evaluation

[ ] Drug and/or Alcohol Evaluation

[ ] Home Study

[ ] Other (Specify) _____

3. The evaluator [ ] shall [ ] shall not make specific recommendations for legal and physical custody. If the evaluator makes specific recommendations, the evaluator shall state the specific reasons for the recommendations.

4. The parties shall participate fully with the evaluator on a timely basis, including retaining the evaluator upon appropriate terms, scheduling appointments, paying promptly, participating in all sessions and in appropriate testing recommended by the evaluator and executing any reasonable consents relating to themselves and their children.

[ ] 5. If the evaluation is a medical necessity, the service may be covered by insurance. If so, both parties shall promptly cooperate to maximize the use of available insurance coverage, if any, and to notify the other party of the result. The [ ] plaintiff [ ] defendant shall submit the costs to his or her insurance first. The cost of the unreimbursed portion of the evaluation shall preliminarily be allocated between the parties with the plaintiff paying ___ % and the defendant paying ___ % without prejudice to the ultimate apportionment of such costs by subsequent agreement of the parties or order of court.

[ ] 6. The cost of the evaluation shall be borne by the county, subject to reimbursement by ___.

7. The cost for the evaluator's time for depositions and/or testimony for hearing shall be [ ] allocated ___% to the plaintiff and ___% to the defendant or [ ] paid by the party seeking the testimony.

[ ] 8. The evaluator may consult with and/or interview any person the evaluator reasonably believes can provide relevant information, including other experts and/or fact witnesses.

[ ] 9. The evaluator may utilize the services of another qualified professional (e.g. to perform additional services) without court approval.

[ ] 10. Subject to the applicable rules of evidence, the evaluator's file (including notes, exhibits, correspondence, test interpretations and, to the extent it is not a violation of copyright law or applicable professional rules, raw test data) shall promptly be made available to counsel for the parties.

[ ] 11. Provided that the parties cooperate on a timely basis, the evaluator shall deliver his or her report to counsel for the parties, any unrepresented party, the guardian *ad litem* and/or counsel for the child, if any, and to the court at least ___ days prior to the first day of trial. The report shall not be filed of record.

[ ] 12. Prior to and/or subsequent to the submission of the evaluator's written report, counsel for the parties shall not be permitted to communicate with the evaluator as to substantive issues, without the consent or direct participation of counsel for the other party.

13. If the report or any information from the evaluator is provided to the court, the evaluator shall be subject to cross examination by all counsel and any unrepresented party regardless of who obtains or pays for the services of the evaluator.

14. The evaluator shall be provided with a copy of this order.

15. The evaluator's report shall not be inappropriately disseminated.

[ ] 16. Other provisions:_____

FAILURE TO COMPLY WITH THE TERMS OF THIS ORDER MAY RESULT IN FINES, IMPRISONMENT OR OTHER SANCTIONS.

BY THE COURT:

_____
J.

Adopted May 16, 1994, effective July 1, 1994. Amended May 23, 2007, effective Aug. 1, 2007; Aug. 2, 2010, imd. effective; Jan. 5, 2018, effective Jan. 6, 2018.

Rule 1915.19. Form of Order Appointing Counsel for the Child

The order appointing an attorney to represent a child in a child custody action pursuant to Rule 1915.11 shall be in substantially the following form:

(Caption)

ORDER OF COURT

AND NOW, THIS _____ day of _____, 20 _____, it is hereby ordered as follows:

Pursuant to Pa.R.C.P. No. 1915.11, is appointed as attorney for the minor child _____ (D.O.B. _____) in connection with the civil proceedings related to the custody of the minor child.

Counsel for the child shall zealously represent the legal interests of the child as any other client in an attorney-client relationship and shall not act as the child's guardian ad litem or best interests attorney. The child's attorney shall not be called to testify and communications between the child's attorney and the child shall be privileged, consistent with the attorney-client relationship.

It is ordered and decreed that all relevant schools, police departments, hospitals and social service agencies including home and school agencies who have records, reports and/or information pertaining to the child relevant to the custody of the child, shall allow the child's attorney access to all files and records in its possession, custody or control and shall cooperate in responding to all relevant inquires. These files/records may include but are not limited to medical, psychological or psychiatric charts including evaluations and progress notes and records, X-rays, photographs, tests, test evaluations, intake and discharge summaries, police records, and school records including report cards, educational assessments and educational plans, relevant to this custody dispute and/or relevant to any special needs or requirements of the child. The child's attorney shall have the right to copy any part of the files and records maintained in connection with the child.

It is further ordered and decreed that the child's attorney shall be permitted to see and speak with the child, and family, medical and/or social service providers connected with this case, and take all steps appropriate to and consistent with this order.

The fees for the child's attorney shall be paid as follows:

_____

This appointment shall terminate upon the entry of a final order resolving the petition pending as of the date of this order or as provided in subsequent order of court.

BY THE COURT:

_____ J.

Adopted Aug. 1, 2013, effective Sept. 3, 2013.

Rule 1915.21. Form of Order Appointing Guardian Ad Litem

The order appointing a guardian ad litem in a child custody action pursuant to Rule 1915.11-2 shall be in substantially the following form:

(Caption)
ORDER OF COURT

AND NOW, THIS _____ day of _____, 20 _____, it is hereby ordered as follows:

Pursuant to Pa.R.C.P. No. 1915.11-2, _____ is appointed as guardian ad litem for the minor child _____ (D.O.B. _____) in connection with the civil proceedings related to the custody of the minor child.

The child's guardian ad litem shall represent the best interests of the child. The guardian ad litem shall not act as the child's attorney or represent the child's legal interests.

It is ordered and decreed that all relevant schools, police departments, hospitals and social service agencies including home and school agencies who have records, reports and/or information pertaining to the child relevant to the custody of the child, shall allow the guardian ad litem access to all files and records in its possession, custody or control and shall cooperate in responding to all relevant inquires. These files/records may include but are not limited to medical, psychological or psychiatric charts including evaluations and progress notes and records, X-rays, photographs, tests, test evaluations, intake and discharge summaries, police records, and school records including report cards, educational assessments and educational plans, relevant to this custody dispute and/or relevant to any special needs or requirements of the child. The guardian ad litem shall have the right to copy any part of the files and records maintained in connection with the child.

It is further ordered and decreed that the guardian ad litem shall be permitted to see and speak with the child, and family, medical and/or social service providers connected with this case, and take all steps appropriate to and consonant with this order.

The guardian ad litem shall provide copies of any reports prepared by the guardian ad litem to each party, or to their counsel, and to the court not later than 20 days prior to trial. The guardian ad litem shall attend all proceedings and be prepared to testify. The guardian ad litem shall be subject to cross-examination if called to testify by either party or the court.

The fees for the guardian ad litem shall be paid as follows:

_____

This appointment shall terminate upon the entry of a final order resolving the petition pending as of the date of this order or as provided in subsequent order of court.

BY THE COURT:

_____

J.

Adopted Aug. 1, 2013, effective Sept. 3, 2013.

Rule 1915.22 Form of Order Appointing Parenting Coordinator

The order appointing a parenting coordinator pursuant to Pa.R.C.P. No. 1915.11-1 shall be in substantially the following form:

(Caption)
ORDER OF COURT

AND NOW, this_____ day of _____, 20 ___, it is hereby ordered as follows:

1. APPOINTMENT AND TERM:

Pursuant to Pa.R.C.P. No. 1915.11-1, _____is appointed as the parties' parenting coordinator for a term of months (not exceeding 12 months).

Legal counsel for ,or either party, if unrepresented, shall provide copies of all orders, pleadings and custody evaluations in this case to the parenting coordinator within ten (10) days of the date of this order.

2. ROLE OF THE PARENTING COORDINATOR:

(a) The parenting coordinator shall attempt to resolve issues arising out of the custody order by facilitating an agreement between the parties and, if unable to reach an agreement, recommend a resolution to the court.

(b) The parenting coordinator shall not function as the attorney, advocate, counselor, or psychotherapist for the parties, the parties' child(ren), or family. However, the parenting coordinator is permitted and encouraged to facilitate communication and agreement between the parties when conflicts arise and shall always act in a manner conducive to the best interests of the child(ren).

3. PARENTING COORDINATOR'S SCOPE OF AUTHORITY:

To implement the custodial arrangement set forth in the custody order and resolve related parenting issues about which the parties cannot agree, the parenting coordinator is authorized to recommend resolutions to the court about issues that include, but are not limited to:

(a) places and conditions for transitions between households;

(b) temporary variation from the schedule for a special event or particular circumstance;

(c) school issues, apart from school selection;

(d) the child(ren)'s participation in recreation, enrichment, and extracurricular activities, including travel;

(e) child-care arrangements;

(f) clothing, equipment, toys, and personal possessions of the child(ren);

(g) information exchanges (e.g., school, health, social) and communication with or about the child(ren);

(h) coordination of existing or court-ordered services for the child(ren)   (e.g., psychological testing, alcohol or drug monitoring/testing, psychotherapy, anger management);

(i) behavioral management of the child(ren); and

(j) other related custody issues that the parties mutually have agreed in writing to submit to the parenting coordinator, which are not excluded in Paragraph 4.

4. EXCLUSIONS FROM PARENTING COORDINATOR'S AUTHORITY:

(a) The following specific issues are excluded from the parenting coordinator's scope of authority:

(1) a change in legal custody as set forth in the custody order;

(2) a change in primary physical custody set forth in the custody order;

(3) other than as set forth in Paragraph 3(b), a change in the court-ordered custody schedule that reduces or expands the child(ren)'s time with a party;

(4) a change in the residence (relocation) of the child(ren);

(5) determination of financial issues, other than allocation of the parenting coordinator's fees as set forth in Pa.R.C.P. 1915.11-1(g)(1);

(6) major decisions affecting the health, education, or religion of the child(ren); and

(7) Other:_____

(b) Unless the parties consent, the parenting coordinator shall not contact collateral sources or speak with the child(ren). The parties shall execute releases, as necessary, authorizing the parenting coordinator to communicate with the appropriate individuals. Any communication with the collateral sources or child(ren) shall be limited to the issue(s) currently before the parenting coordinator.

5. COMMUNICATIONS:

(a) The parenting coordinator shall determine the protocol of all communications, interviews, and sessions, including who shall attend the sessions (including the children), and whether the sessions will be conducted in person or by other means. The protocols should include measures addressing the safety of all participants.

(b) Communication between the parties or their attorneys and the parenting coordinator is not confidential.

(c) The parties and their attorneys shall have the right to receive, but not initiate, oral ex parte communication with the parenting coordinator. The parenting coordinator shall promptly advise the other party or the other party's attorney of the communication. A party or a party's attorney may communicate in writing with the parenting coordinator, but shall contemporaneously send a copy of the written communication to the other party or the other party's attorney. Documents, recordings, or other material that one party gives to the parenting coordinator must be promptly made available to the other party or the other party's attorney for inspection and copying.

(d) Communication between the parenting coordinator and the court shall be in writing and copies of the written communication shall be sent contemporaneously to the parties or the parties' attorneys.

(e) A party cannot compel the testimony of a parenting coordinator without an order of court.

6. PARENTING COORDINATION PROCESS:

(a) The parenting coordinator shall provide to the parties notice and an opportunity to be heard on the issues.

(b) The parenting coordinator's recommendation shall be in writing on the Summary and Recommendation of the Parenting Coordinator form set forth in Pa.R.C.P. No. 1915.23 and sent to the court for review within two days after hearing from the parties on the issues. The parenting coordinator shall serve a copy of the Summary and Recommendation on the parties or the parties' attorneys.

(c) A party objecting to the recommendation shall file a petition for a record hearing before the court within five days of service of the Summary and Recommendation of the Parenting Coordinator form. The petition must specifically state the issues to be reviewed and include a demand for a record hearing. A copy of the recommendation shall be attached to the petition. In accordance with Pa.R.C.P. No. 440, the objecting party shall serve the petition upon the other party or the party's attorney and the parenting coordinator.

7. RECORD HEARING:

(a) If the parties do not file an objection within five days of service of the parenting coordinator's recommendation, the court shall:

(1) approve the recommendation;

(2) approve the recommendation in part and conduct a record hearing on issues not approved;

(3) remand the recommendation to the parenting coordinator for more specific information; or

(4) not approve the recommendation and conduct a record hearing on the issues.

Rule 1915.23   ACTIONS FOR CUSTODY, VISITATION

(b) As soon as practical, the court shall conduct a record hearing on the issues specifically set forth in the petition. The court shall render a decision within the time set forth in Pa.R.C.P. No. 1915.4(d).

(c) If a party makes a timely objection, the recommendation shall become an interim order of court pending further disposition by the court.

8. ALLOCATION OF FEES:

(a) The parties will share the obligation to pay the fees of the parenting coordinator as follows: __% Mother, __% Father, __% Third party. Fees may be reallocated by the court or the parenting coordinator if a party has disproportionately caused the need for the services of the parenting coordinator.

(b) The judicial district's established hourly rate for parenting coordinators shall be set forth in a separate written agreement entered into between the parties and the parenting coordinator.

(c) The parties will pay a joint retainer to the parenting coordinator in the percentages set forth above in an amount to be set forth in a separate agreement between the parties and the parenting coordinator. After each session, or at least once monthly, the parenting coordinator shall provide the parties with an invoice of charges incurred. The retainer may be replenished as services are rendered. Funds remaining at the conclusion of the parenting coordinator's appointment shall be returned to the parties.

9. TERMINATION/WITHDRAWAL OF PARENTING COORDINATOR:

(a) The parties may not terminate the parenting coordinator's services without court approval.

(b) A party seeking the termination of the parenting coordinator's services shall serve the other party or the party's attorney and parenting coordinator with a copy of the petition for termination.

(c) If the parenting coordinator seeks to withdraw from service in a case, the parenting coordinator shall petition the court and provide a copy of the petition to the parties or the parties' attorneys.

10. APPEAL:

If there is an appeal of the underlying custody order or this order, then this order shall be stayed during the pendency of the appeal.

                               BY THE COURT:

                                                          J.

Adopted August 9, 2018, effective March 1, 2019

Rule 1915.23   Form of the Summary and Recommendation of the Parenting Coordinator.

The recommendation of the parenting coordinator shall be in writing and shall be in substantially the following form:

(Caption)
SUMMARY AND RECOMMENDATION OF
THE PARENTING COORDINATOR

The undersigned, the duly appointed parenting coordinator in the above-captioned matter, pursuant to the Order of Court dated _____, 20__, after

Pa. R.C.P. Rule 1915.23

submission of the issue described below and after providing the parties with an opportunity to heard on the issue, the parenting coordinator sets forth the following:

SUMMARY OF THE ISSUE(S)

1. Description of the issue(s):

___

2. The respective parties' position on the issue(s):

___

RECOMMENDATION

___

Within five days of the date set forth below, a party may object to this recommendation by filing a petition with the court and requesting a record hearing before the judge as set forth in Pa.R.C.P. No. 1915.11-1(f)(3).

The undersigned parenting coordinator certifies that this Summary and Recommendation of the Parenting Coordinator has been served on the court and the parties or the parties' attorneys on the date set forth below

_____   _____
Date   Parenting Coordinator

ORDER OF COURT

JUDICIAL REVIEW OF PARENTING COORDINATOR'S RECOMMENDATION

[ ] The Recommendation is approved.

[ ] The Recommendation is approved in part. The issue(s) not approved by the court is/are:_____
and a record hearing is scheduled for _____, 20__ at _____ a.m./p.m. before the undersigned.

[ ] The Recommendation is remanded to the parenting coordinator for additional information on the following issue(s):_____

[ ] The Recommendation is not approved and a record hearing on the issue(s) is scheduled for _____, 20__ at _____ a.m./p.m. before the under signed.

BY THE COURT:

_____
J.

Adopted August 9, 2018, effective March 1, 2019.

Rule 1915.24 Acts of Assembly Not Suspended

The following Acts or parts of Acts of Assembly shall not be deemed suspended or affected:

(1) Chapter 63 of the Judicial Code, 42 Pa.C.S. § 6301 et seq., known as the Juvenile Act;

(2) Section 5341 et seq. of the Domestic Relations Code, 23 Pa.C.S. § 5341 et seq., known as the Uniform Child Custody Jurisdiction Act, except to the extent suspended by Rule 1915.25 governing Suspension of Acts of Assembly;

(3) The Act of December 19, 1990, No. 206, 23 Pa.C.S. § 6301 et seq., known as the Child Protective Services Law;

(4) The Act of October 7, 1976, No. 218, as amended, 23 Pa.C.S. § 6101 et seq., known as the Protection From Abuse Act; and

(5) Chapter 53, Subchapter A of Title 23 of the Consolidated Statutes, 23 Pa.C.S. § 5301 et seq., setting forth general custody provisions.

Adopted Dec. 10, 1981, effective July 1, 1982; effective date extended to Jan. 1, 1983 by Order of June 25, 1982. Readopted and amended Nov. 8, 1982, effective Jan. 1, 1983 and applied to pending actions; amended Nov. 7, 1988, effective Jan. 1, 1989; March 30, 1994, effective July 1, 1994.

Rule 1915.25. Suspension of Acts of Assembly

Section 5351 of the Domestic Relations Code, 23 Pa.C.S. § 5351, of the Uniform Child Custody Jurisdiction Act, relating to additional parties, is suspended insofar as it provides for the joinder of a person not a party who claims to have custody or visitation rights with respect to the child.

> **Official Note:** Rule 1915.6(b) provides that a person not a party who claims to have custody or visitation rights with respect to the child shall be given notice of the pendency of the proceedings and of the right to intervene.

23 Pa.C.S. § 5334 is suspended insofar as it (1) requires that a guardian ad litem be an attorney, (2) permits the guardian ad litem to represent both the best interests and legal interests of the child, (3) provides the guardian ad litem the right to examine, cross-examine, present witnesses and present evidence on behalf of the child, and (4) prohibits the guardian ad litem from testifying.

Adopted Dec. 10, 1981, effective July 1, 1982; effective date extended to Jan. 1, 1983 by order of June 25, 1982. Readopted Nov. 8, 1982, effective Jan. 1, 1983. Amended March 30, 1994, effective July 1, 1994; Aug. 1, 2013, effective Sept. 3, 2013.

V. Actions of Divorce or for Annulment of Marriage

(Amended Through April, 2019)

Rules 1920.1–1920.92

RULE

1920.1	Definitions. Conformity to Civil Action.
1920.2	Venue.
1920.3	Commencement of Action.
1920.4	Service.
1920.5	Warrant of Attorney.
1920.6	Multiple Actions. Priority. Stay.
1920.7 to 1920.10	[Blank].
1920.11	Pleadings Allowed.
1920.12	Complaint.
1920.13	Pleading More Than One Cause of Action. Alternative Pleading.
1920.14	Answer. Denial. Affidavit Under Section 3301(d) of the Divorce Code.
1920.15	Counterclaim. Subsequent Petition.
1920.16	Severance of Actions and Claims.
1920.17	Discontinuance. Withdrawal of Complaint.
1920.21	Bill of Particulars in Divorce or Annulment. Non Pros.
1920.22	Discovery.
1920.23 to 1920.30	[Blank].
1920.31	Joinder of Related Claims. Alimony. Counsel Fees. Costs and Expenses.
1920.32	Joinder of Related Claims. Custody. Hearing by Court.
1920.33	Joinder of Related Claims. Equitable Division. Enforcement.
1920.34	Joinder of Parties.
1920.35 to 1920.40	[Blank].
1920.41	No Default Judgment.
1920.42	Affidavit and Decree Under Section 3301(c) or 3301(d)(1) of the Divorce Code. Notice of Intention to Request Entry of Divorce Decree in Section 3301(d)(1)(i) Divorces. Counter–Affidavit.
1920.43	Special Relief.
1920.44	Party Leaving Jurisdiction. Security.
1920.45	Counseling.
1920.46	Affidavit of Non-Military Service.
1920.47 to 1920.50	[Blank].
1920.51	Hearing by the Court. Appointment of Master. Notice of Hearing.
1920.52	Hearing by Court. Decision. No Post-trial Relief. Decree.
1920.53	Hearing by Master. Report.
1920.54	Hearing by Master. Report. Related Claims.
1920.55	Master's Report. Notice. Exceptions. Final Decree. [Rescinded]
1920.55-1	Alternative Hearing Procedures for Matters Referred to a Master.
1920.55-2	Master's Report. Notice. Exceptions. Final Decree.

Rule 1920.1   ACTIONS OF DIVORCE, ANNULMENT

1920.55-3   Master's Report. Notice. Hearing De Novo. Final Decree.
1920.56   Support. Alimony Pendente Lite. Allocation of Order.
1920.57 to 1920.60   [Blank].
1920.61   Testimony Outside the County.
1920.62   Proceedings by Indigent Parties.
1920.63 to 1920.70   [Blank].
1920.71   Form of Notice.
1920.72   Form of Complaint. Affidavit Under Section 3301(c) or 3301(d) of the Divorce Code.
1920.73   Notice of Intention to Request Entry of Divorce Decree. Praecipe to Transmit Record. Forms.
1920.74   Form of Motion for Appointment of Master. Order.
1920.75   Form of Inventory.
1920.76   Form of Divorce Decree.
1920.77 to 1920.90   [Blank].
1920.91   Suspension of Acts of Assembly.
1920.92   Effective Date. Pending Actions.

COURT RULES

ACTIONS OF DIVORCE OR FOR ANNULMENT OF MARRIAGE

Explanatory Comment—1993

Introduction

On April 2, 1980, the General Assembly enacted the Divorce Code of 1980, effective July 1, 1980. New Rules 1920.1 et seq. were promulgated June 27, 1980, effective July 1, to implement the new Code. The Civil Procedural Rules Committee was unable to submit the rules to the bench and bar for comment prior to their adoption, due to the short period of time between the enactment of the Code and its effective date.

Since promulgation of the new rules, the Committee has received numerous suggestions for amendment of the rules from the bench and bar. Local procedures have developed which warrant inclusion in the rules as statewide practices. Other diverse local practices have developed under the new state rules, rendering the multicounty practice of law burdensome.

In view of these developments, the Supreme Court has promulgated amendments to the rules governing the action of divorce or for annulment of marriage. The following commentary [see Explanatory Note—1983 after amended rules] summarizes the amendments.

Rule 1920.1 Definitions. Conformity to Civil Action

(a) As used in this chapter action, an action of divorce or an action for annulment of marriage, which may include the ancillary claims that may be joined with the action of divorce or for annulment under the Divorce Code, except as otherwise provided in these rules;

"custody," includes partial custody;

"divorce," divorce from the bonds of matrimony or dissolution of a civil union;

"marital property rights" means those rights created solely by Section 3501 of the Divorce Code; and

"nonmarital property rights" means all property rights other than marital property rights.

(b) Except as otherwise provided in this chapter, the procedure in the action shall be in accordance with the rules relating to a civil action.

> Note: See Section 3104 of the Divorce Code for the ancillary claims that may be joined in a divorce action, except as otherwise provided in these rules.
>
> See Pa.R.C.P. No. 1920.31(a)(2) as to raising claims for child support, spousal support, and alimony pendente lite.
>
> The definition of divorce has been expanded to include civil unions. See Neyman v. Buckley, 153 A.3d 1010 (Pa. Super. 2016).

Adopted June 27, 1980, effective July 1, 1980. Amended December 16, 1983, effective July 1, 1984; March 30, 1994, effective July 1, 1994; July 30, 2018, effective January 1, 2019.

Rule 1920.2 Venue

(a) The action, except a claim for custody, may be brought only in the county

(1) in which the plaintiff or the defendant resides, or

(2) upon which the parties have agreed

(i) in a writing which shall be attached to the complaint, or

(ii) by participating in the proceeding.

> Note: Rule 1920.2 governs the venue of related claims, except a claim for custody, when joined with an action of divorce or for annulment. Venue in an action for custody is governed by Rule 1915.2.
>
> See Rule 1006(d) for the transfer of an action for the convenience of parties and witnesses.
>
> Under subdivision (a)(2), the agreement of the parties is an independent basis for venue and is not a waiver of improper venue.

(b) The record shall establish compliance with the venue requirement of subdivision (a) prior to the entry of the decree.

(c) Notwithstanding any agreement of the parties, if neither the plaintiff nor the defendant has resided in the county at any time during the pendency of the action, the court, upon its own motion and for its own convenience, may transfer the action to the appropriate court of any other county where the action originally could have been brought.

Adopted June 27, 1980, effective July 1, 1980. Amended Jan. 28, 1983, effective July 1, 1983; Feb. 7, 1989, effective July 1, 1989.

Explanatory Comment—1994

The rule permits choice of venue where the parties both consent either by a writing attached to the complaint or by participation in the proceedings. The rule does not specify what participation is required to show consent. However, entering an appearance in order to file a preliminary objection to venue is not participation for purposes of subdivision (a)(2)(ii) 1920.2.

Rule 1920.3 Commencement of Action

An action shall be commenced by filing a complaint with the prothonotary.

Adopted June 27, 1980, effective July 1, 1980.

Rule 1920.4 Service

(a) Service of original process and proof of service in an action pursuant to this chapter shall be in accordance with Rule 1930.4.

(b) Service of the complaint in the manner provided by Rule 1930.4 shall constitute service of process with respect to any claim which may under the Divorce Code be joined with an action of divorce or for annulment.

(c) In an action under Section 3301(d) of the Divorce Code, if no appearance has been entered and plaintiff avers that defendant cannot be located after diligent search, the court may waive service of the affidavit.

(d) The defendant may accept service of the complaint as provided by Rule 1930.4. Acceptance of service shall not be deemed collusive.

Former rule rescinded and new rule adopted Oct. 2, 1995, effective Jan. 1, 1996.

Rule 1920.5 Warrant of Attorney

No attorney shall be required to file a record a warrant of attorney from a party in the action.

Adopted Jan. 28, 1983, effective July 1, 1983 and applied to pending actions.

Explanatory Note—1983

Local practice under the Divorce Code varies with respect to the necessity of filing a warrant of attorney by the defendant. Some counties require it and others do not.

There is no requirement under the Rules of Civil Procedure that a warrant of attorney be filed in any action at law or in equity. There appears to be no reason why the warrant should be required in the action of divorce. Therefore, new Rule 1920.5 provides a uniform state practice of not requiring the filing of a warrant in a divorce action.

Rule 1920.6 Multiple Actions. Priority. Stay

(a) If, within ninety days of service of the complaint, a second action is brought in another county and one of the two counties is the county in which the last family domicile was located and in which one of the parties continues to reside, the court of the county of the last family domicile shall determine, based upon the purposes of the Divorce Code, which of the two actions shall be stayed and which shall proceed. If neither action was brought in the county of the last family domicile and in which one of the parties continues to reside, the court in which the first action was brought shall make the determination.

(b) If a second action is brought in another county more than ninety days after service of the complaint in the first action, the second action shall be stayed until the conclusion of the first action.

Adopted Feb. 7, 1989, effective July 1, 1989.

Explanatory Comment—1989

The Domestic Relations Committee has been apprised of the situation in which each party to a divorce brings an action in a different county. The two actions proceed simultaneously with the court of neither county deferring to the other. This results in a waste of judicial manpower and facilities as well as added burdens and expense to the parties.

Rule 1920.6 resolves the problem of multiple actions. If a second action is brought within ninety days after service of the complaint in the first action, the court of the county of the last family domicile and in which one of the parties continues to reside is empowered to make the determination of which action is to proceed. The bases upon which the court is to make the determination are the purposes of the Divorce Code. If there is no county of last marital domicile or neither party resides in such county, then the court of the county in which the first action was instituted is to make the determination.

Where the second action is commenced more than ninety days after service of the first complaint, the rule provides for the first action to proceed and the second action to be stayed.

Rules 1920.7 to 1920.10   [Blank]

Rule 1920.11   Pleadings Allowed

The pleadings in an action shall be limited to those authorized by Rule 1017, a bill of particulars, a petition authorized by the Divorce Code and an answer thereto.

Official Note: For limitations as to judgment by default or on the pleadings, see Rule 1920.41.

Adopted June 27, 1980, effective July 1, 1980.

Rule 1920.12   Complaint

(a) Except as provided by subdivision (b), the plaintiff shall set forth in the complaint as to the cause of action of divorce or for annulment

(1) the names of the plaintiff and defendant and, if either party is a minor or incompetent, a statement to that effect and the name and address of such party's guardian, if any;

(2) the residence of the plaintiff;

(3) the last known residence and present whereabouts of the defendant, or that the plaintiff has no knowledge thereof, and in that case the names and addresses of near relatives and other persons who would be likely to know the present residence and whereabouts of the defendant;

(4) an averment that the plaintiff, defendant or both have resided in the Commonwealth for at least six months immediately previous to the commencement of the action;

(5) the date and place of marriage;

(6) the ground on which the action is based, stated substantially in the language of the Divorce Code;

(7) whether there has been any prior action of divorce or for annulment of marriage between the parties in this or any other jurisdiction and if so the caption, court, term and number thereof, the date commenced, the grounds therefor and the present status if pending or the final disposition thereof;

(8) in an action under Section 3301(a)(6), 3301(c) or 3301(d) of the Divorce Code, an averment that the plaintiff has been advised of the availability of counseling and that the plaintiff may have the right to request that the court require the parties to participate in counseling; and

(9) a prayer for relief.

(b) The complaint in an action based upon Section 3301(c) or (d) of the Divorce Code shall be substantially in the form prescribed by Rule 1920.72(a).

(c) Every complaint shall begin with a notice substantially in the form prescribed by Rule 1920.71.

Adopted June 27, 1980, effective July 1, 1980. Amended Jan. 28, 1983, effective July 1, 1983 and applied to pending actions; March 30, 1994, effective July 1, 1994.

Explanatory Comment—1994

Three revisions were made to this rule in 1983. First, the need to state the nationalities of the parties under (a)(3) was eliminated as irrelevant. Second, (a)(4) was revised to require a statement that either or both parties have resided in the Commonwealth for at least six months, replacing the requirement that the complaint allege the length of time the parties have resided within the Commonwealth. Third, new subdivision (a)(8) was added to include an acknowledgement that plaintiff has been advised of the availability of counseling.

Rule 1920.13 Pleading More Than One Cause of Action. Alternative Pleading

(a) The plaintiff may state in the complaint one or more grounds for divorce and may join in the alternative a cause of action for annulment.

(b) Except as otherwise provided in these rules, the plaintiff may:

(1) join as separate counts in the complaint the ancillary claims that may be joined with an action of divorce or for annulment under the Divorce Code;

(2) amend the complaint to include the ancillary claims;

(3) file to the same term and number a separate supplemental complaint or complaints limited to the ancillary claims; or

(4) file to the same term and number a subsequent petition raising the ancillary claims.

(c) The court may order reasonable counsel fees and costs and expenses pending final disposition of any claim.

Note: See Pa.R.C.P. No. 1930.1(b). This rule may require attorneys or unrepresented parties to file confidential documents and documents containing confidential information that are subject to the Case Records Public Access Policy of the Unified Judicial System of Pennsylvania.

See Pa.R.C.P. No. 1920.31(a)(2) as to raising claims for child support, spousal support, and alimony *pendente lite*.

See Pa.R.C.P. No. 1910.26(b) for interim or special relief for support and alimony *pendente lite* actions proceeding through the domestic relations section.

Adopted June 27, 1980, effective July 1, 1980. Amended January 5, 2018, effective January 6, 2018; July 30, 2018, effective January 1, 2019.

Rule 1920.14 Answer. Denial. Affidavit Under Section 3301(d) of the Divorce Code.

(a) The averments in the complaint as to the divorce or annulment, all other claims which may be joined under the Divorce Code and any petition for special relief under these rules shall be deemed denied unless admitted by an answer. Notwithstanding the foregoing, the court may require a response to a petition for special relief.

(b) The averments of the affidavit under Section 3301(d) of the Divorce Code shall be deemed admitted unless denied by counteraffidavit.

Official Note: See Rule 1920.72(d) for the form of counteraffidavit.

Explanatory Comment—1994

Subdivision (b) requires that the averments of the plaintiff's affidavit under Section 3301(d) of the Divorce Code be denied by counteraffidavit. If the defendant fails to file a counteraffidavit, all allegations are deemed admitted.

Explanatory Comment—2007

Subdivision (a) has been amended to clarify that the averments in a petition for special relief in a divorce or annulment action are deemed to be denied unless admitted by an answer.

The provisions of this Rule 1920.14 adopted June 27, 1980, effective July 1, 1980; amended January 28, 1983, effective July 1, 1983. 677; amended November 7, 1988, effective January 1, 1989; amended March 30, 1994, effective July 1, 1994; amended April 11, 2007, effective immediately.

Rule 1920.15 Counterclaim. Subsequent Petition

(a) The defendant may state a cause of action of divorce or for annulment in an answer under the heading "Counterclaim".

(b) Except as otherwise provided in these rules, the defendant may:

(1) join as separate counts in the counterclaim the ancillary claims that may be joined with an action of divorce or for annulment under the Divorce Code; or

(2) file to the same term and number a subsequent petition raising the ancillary claims that may be joined with an action of divorce or for annulment under the Divorce Code.

(c) The averments in the counterclaim shall be deemed denied unless admitted by an answer.

Note: See Pa.R.C.P. No. 1920.31, which requires the joinder of certain related claims under penalty of waiver. A claim for alimony must be raised before the entry of a final decree of divorce or annulment.

See Pa.R.C.P. No. 1920.31(a)(2) as to raising claims for child support, spousal support, and alimony *pendente lite*.

See Pa.R.C.P. No. 1930.1(b). This rule may require attorneys or unrepresented parties to file confidential documents and documents containing confidential information that are subject to the *Case* Records Public Access Policy of the Unified Judicial System of Pennsylvania.

Adopted June 27, 1980, effective July 1, 1980. Amended January 28, 1983, effective July 1, 1983; January 5, 2018, effective January 6, 2018; July 30, 2018, effective January 1, 2019.

Explanatory Comment—1983

The deletion of the words «also» and «other» from subdivision (b) makes clear that claims which may be joined with an action of divorce may be raised by the defendant either in a counterclaim or by a subsequent petition.

The note to Rule 1920.15 is revised to delete a reference to Rule 1920.33 relating to waiver of claims for the equitable distribution of marital property. As promulgated, Rule 1920.33 does not govern the subject matter of waiver of claims. Thus a revision of the note was warranted.

Rule 1920.16 Severance of Actions and Claims

The court, in furtherance of convenience or to avoid prejudice, may on its own motion or on motion of any party order a separate trial of any cause of action or claim or of any number of causes of action or claims.

Adopted June 27, 1980, effective July 1, 1980.

Rule 1920.17. Discontinuance. Withdrawal of Complaint

(a) **The plaintiff may withdraw the divorce complaint and discontinue the divorce action by praecipe that includes a certification that:**

(1) **no ancillary claims or counterclaims have been asserted by either party; and**

(2) **grounds for divorce have not been established.**

(b) **A party may withdraw a claim of equitable distribution only:**

(1) **by written consent of both parties filed with the court, or**

(2) **after filing and serving on the other party a written notice that the party intends to withdraw the claim of equitable distribution 20 days after service of the notice.**

(c) **The notice required in subdivision (b) above shall be substantially in the following form:**

(Caption)

NOTICE OF INTENTION TO WITHDRAW CLAIM FOR
EQUITABLE DISTRIBUTION

TO: _____

(PLAINTIFF) (DEFENDANT)

(Plaintiff) (Defendant) intends to withdraw (his) (her) pending claim for equitable distribution of property twenty days after the service of this notice. Unless you have already filed with the court a written claim for equitable distribution, you should do so within twenty days of the service of this notice, or you may lose the right to assert a claim for equitable distribution. If a decree

in divorce is entered and you have not filed a claim for equitable distribution, you will forever lose the right to equitable distribution of property.

YOU SHOULD TAKE THIS PAPER TO YOUR LAWYER AT ONCE. IF YOU DO NOT HAVE A LAWYER, GO TO OR TELEPHONE THE OFFICE SET FORTH BELOW. THIS OFFICE CAN PROVIDE YOU WITH INFORMATION ABOUT HIRING A LAWYER. IF YOU CANNOT AFFORD TO HIRE A LAWYER, THIS OFFICE MAY BE ABLE TO PROVIDE YOU WITH INFORMATION ABOUT AGENCIES THAT MAY OFFER LEGAL SERVICES TO ELIGIBLE PERSONS AT A REDUCED FEE OR NO FEE.

(Name)

(Address)

(Telephone)

(d) In the event one party dies during the course of the divorce proceeding, no decree of divorce has been entered and grounds for divorce have been established, neither the complaint nor economic claims can be withdrawn except by the consent of the surviving spouse and the personal representative of the decedent. If there is no agreement, the economic claims shall be determined pursuant to the Divorce Code. If no personal representative has been appointed within one year of the decedent's death, then, upon motion of the surviving party, the court may allow the withdrawal or dismissal of the complaint and/or any pending economic claims.

   Note: To the extent that *Tosi v. Kizis*, 85 A.3d 585 (Pa. Super. 2014) holds that 23 Pa.C.S. § 3323(d.1) does not prevent the plaintiff in a divorce action from discontinuing the divorce action following the death of the defendant after grounds for divorce have been established, it is superseded.

Adopted May 6, 2015, effective July 1, 2015.

Rule 1920.21 Bill of Particulars in Divorce or Annulment. Non Pros

(a) The prothonotary on praecipe filed within such time as not to delay the trial shall enter a rule as of course upon the party seeking a divorce under Section 3301(a) or (b) of the Divorce Code or an annulment to file a bill of particulars as to such cause of action.

(b) If a bill of particulars is not filed within twenty days after service of the rule or within such further time as the court may allow, the prothonotary upon praecipe shall enter a judgment of non pros against the defaulting party with respect to the cause of action for divorce under Section 3301(a) or (b) of the Divorce Code, or the cause of action for annulment.

(c) No answer to a bill of particulars is required.

Adopted June 27, 1980, effective July 1, 1980. Amended Jan. 28, 1983, effective July 1, 1983 and applied to pending actions; amended April 8, 1992, effective July 1, 1992.

Explanatory Comment—1992

   The requirement in subdivision (a) that the praecipe be filed "within such time as not to delay the trial" is intended to promote prompt disposition of divorce and annulment matters, and make more difficult use of the bill of particulars as a delay tactic.

The rule is revised to bring the statutory citations into conformity with the codification of the Divorce Code under Act 1990–206, and to make absolutely clear that a non pros for failure to file a bill of particulars is available only with regard to a cause of action in annulment or in divorce filed pursuant to Section 3301(a) or 3301(b) of the Divorce Code. Should the Complaint include grounds for divorce under Section 3301(c) or 3301(d) the party may continue to prosecute the divorce action notwithstanding the non pros under Section 3301(a) or 3301(b).

Rule 1920.22   Discovery [Rescinded]

Official Note: The rule relating to discovery in domestic relations matters generally is Rule 1930.5. Rescinded May 5, 1997, effective July 1, 1997.

Rules 1920.23 to 1920.30   [Blank]

Rule 1920.31.   Joinder of Related Claims. Alimony. Counsel Fees. Costs and Expenses

(a)(1) **If a party has raised a claim for alimony, counsel fees, or costs and expenses, the parties shall file a true copy of the most recent federal income tax return, pay stubs for the preceding six months, a completed Income Statement in the form required by Pa.R.C.P. No. 1910.27(c)(1), and a completed Expense Statement in the form required by Pa.R.C.P. No. 1910.27(c)(2)(B). A party may not file a motion for the appointment of a master or a request for court action regarding alimony, counsel fees, or costs and expenses until at least 30 days following the filing of that party's tax returns, Income Statement, and Expense Statement. The other party shall file the tax returns, Income Statement, and Expense Statement within 20 days of service of the moving party's documents.**

> **Note:** See Pa.R.C.P. No. 1930.1(b). This rule may require attorneys or unrepresented parties to file confidential documents and documents containing confidential information that are subject to the *Case Records Public Access Policy of the Unified Judicial System of* Pennsylvania.

(2) **A divorce complaint shall not include claims for child support, spousal support, and alimony** *pendente lite*. **Instead, claims for child support, spousal support, and alimony** *pendente lite* **shall be raised in the domestic relations section by filing a complaint pursuant to Pa.R.C.P. No. 1910.4.**

(3) **If a party fails to file the documents as required by subdivision (a)(1), the court on motion may make an appropriate order under Pa.R.C.P. No. 4019 governing sanctions.**

> (b)1) Orders for alimony may be enforced as provided by the rules governing actions for support and divorce, and in the Divorce Code.

Note: *See, inter alia,* Section 3323(b) of the Divorce Code relating to enforcement of the rights of any party under a decree, Section 3505(a) of the Divorce Code relating to an injunction against disposition of property pending suit, and Section 3703 of the Divorce Code relating to the collection of arrearages.

(2) When so ordered by the court, payments for alimony shall be made to the domestic relations section of the court that issued the order.

(c) The failure to claim spousal support, alimony, alimony pendente lite, counsel fees, and costs and expenses prior to the entry of a final decree of divorce or annulment shall be deemed a waiver of those claims, unless the court expressly provides otherwise in its decree. The failure to claim child support before the entry of a final decree of divorce or annulment shall not bar a separate and subsequent action.

(d) Upon entry of a decree in divorce, an existing order for spousal support shall be deemed an order for alimony pendente lite if any economic claims remain pending.

Adopted June 27, 1980, effective July 1, 1980. Amended January 28, 1983, effective July 1, 1983; May 17, 1991, effective July 1, 1991; March 30, 1994, effective July 1, 1994; December 2, 1994, effective March 1, 1995; April 21, 1995, effective July 1, 1995; August 17, 1995, immediately effective; May 31, 2000, effective July 1, 2000; November 8, 2006, effective February 6, 2007; October 30, 2007, immediately effective; May 6, 2015, effective July 1, 2015; January 5, 2018, effective January 6, 2018; July 30, 2018, effective January 1, 2019.

Explanatory Comment—2018

As amended, Pa.R.C.P. No. 1920.31 precludes parties from raising claims for child support, spousal support, and alimony *pendente lite* as counts in a divorce action. Instead, parties shall file those claims in the domestic relations section as a separate action from the divorce. The amendment of this rule is not intended to affect the legal distinction between spousal support and alimony *pendente lite*.

Rule 1920.32 Joinder of Related Claims. Custody. Hearing by Court

(a) Claims for custody of children shall be heard by the court. The practice and procedure with respect to these claims shall follow the practice and procedure governing custody.

(b) The failure to claim custody of minor children prior to the entry of a final decree shall not bar subsequent claims for custody.

Adopted June 27, 1980, effective July 1, 1980.

Rule 1920.33. Joinder of Related Claims. Equitable Division. Enforcement

(a) If a pleading or petition raises a claim for equitable division of marital property under Section 3502 of the Divorce Code, the parties shall file and serve on the other party an inventory, which shall include the information in subdivisions (1) through (3) and shall be substantially in the form set forth in Pa.R.C.P. No. 1920.75. Within 20 days of service of the moving party's inventory, the non-moving party shall file an inventory. A party may not file a motion for the appointment of a master or a request for court action regarding equitable division until at least 30 days following the filing of that party's inventory.

Note: *See* Pa.R.C.P. No. 1930.1(b). This rule may require attorneys or unrepresented parties to file confidential documents and documents containing confidential information that are subject to the *Case Records Public Access Policy of the Unified Judicial System of Pennsylvania.*

The inventory shall set forth as of the date of separation:

(1) a specific description of the marital assets which either or both parties have a legal or equitable interest, individually or jointly with another person, the name of the co-owners, if applicable, and the marital liabilities, which either party incurred individually or jointly with another person, and the name of any co-debtors, if applicable;

(2) a specific description of the assets or liabilities claimed to be non-marital and the basis for such claim; and

(3) the estimated value of the marital and non-marital assets and the amount due for each marital and non-marital liability.

Note: Subdivision (c) provides for sanctions for failure to file an inventory as required by subdivision (a). An inventory may be incomplete if a party lacks comprehensive knowledge of the assets and liabilities involved in the claim for equitable division. Consequently, the rule does not contemplate that a party will be precluded from presenting testimony or offering evidence as to assets or liabilities omitted from the inventory. The omission may be remedied by inclusion of the omitted information in the pre-trial statement required by subdivision (b).

(b) Within the time required by order of court or written directive of the master or, if none, at least 60 days before the scheduled hearing on the claim for equitable division, the parties shall file and serve upon the other party a pre-trial statement. The pre-trial statement shall include the following matters, together with any additional information required by special order of the court:

(1) a list of assets, which may be in chart form, specifying:

(i) the marital assets:

a. the value;

b. the date of the valuation;

c. the value of any non-marital portion;

d. the facts and documentation upon which the party relies to support the valuation; and

e. any liens or encumbrances associated with the asset.

(ii) The non-marital assets:

a. the value;

b. the date of the valuation;

c. the facts and documentation upon which the party relies to support the valuation; and

d. any liens or encumbrances associated with the asset.

(2) the name and address of the expert witness(es) the party intends to call at trial. A report of each expert witness listed shall be attached to the pre-trial statement. The report shall describe the expert's qualifications and experience, state the substance of the facts and opinions to which the expert is expected to testify and summarize the grounds for each opinion;

(3) the name, address, and a short summary of the testimony of the witnesses, other than the party, whom the party intends to call at trial;

(4) a list of exhibits that the party expects to offer into evidence. Exhibits not exceeding three pages shall be attached to the pre-trial statement and shall have an identifying exhibit number affixed to or incorporated

into the document, and exhibits exceeding three pages shall be described specifically and shall have an exhibit number in the description;

(5) the party's gross income from all sources, payroll deductions, net income, and the party's most recent state and federal income tax returns and pay stubs;

(6) if the party intends to offer testimony as to his or her expenses, an Expense Statement in the form required by Pa.R.C.P. No. 1910.27(c)(2)(B);

(7) if there is a claim for counsel fees, the amount of fees to be charged, the basis for the charge, and a detailed itemization of the services rendered;

(8) the description and value of disputed tangible personal property, specifically the personalty contemplated by item number 25 of the form in Pa.R.C.P. No. 1920.75, the method of valuing each item, and the evidence, including documentation, to be offered in support of the valuation;

(9) a list of liabilities, which may be in chart form, specifying:

(i) The marital liabilities:
  a. amount of liability;
  b. date of the valuation;
  c. amount of any non-marital portion;
  d. the facts and documentation upon which the party relies to support the valuation; and
  e. amount, if any, of payments made on the liabilities after the date of separation.

(ii) The non-marital liabilities:
  a. amount of the liability;
  b. date of the valuation; and
  c. the facts and documentation upon which the party relies to support the valuation.

(10) a proposed resolution of the economic issues raised in the pleadings.

Note: *See* Pa.R.C.P. No. 1930.1(b). This rule may require attorneys or unrepresented parties to file confidential documents and documents containing confidential information that are subject to the *Case Records Public Access Policy of the Unified Judicial System of Pennsylvania*.

(c) If a party fails to file either an inventory, as required by subdivision (a), or a pre-trial statement as required by subdivision (b), the court may make an appropriate order under Pa.R.C.P. No. 4019(c) governing sanctions.

(d) (1) A party who fails to comply with a requirement of subdivision (b) may be barred from offering testimony or introducing evidence in support of or in opposition to claims for the matters omitted.

(2) A party may be barred from offering testimony or introducing evidence that is inconsistent with or goes beyond the fair scope of the information set forth in the pre-trial statement.

(e) An order entered by the court pursuant to Section 3502 of the Divorce Code may be enforced as provided by the rules governing actions for support and divorce and in the Divorce Code.

Adopted May 17, 1991, effective July 1, 1991. Amended Nov. 8, 2006, effective Feb. 6, 2007; May 6, 2015, effective July 1, 2015; June 10, 2016, effective Oct. 1, 2016; Jan. 5, 2018, effective Jan. 6, 2018; June 1, 2018, effective July 1, 2018.

Explanatory Comment—1994

23 Pa.C.S. § 3105(a) states that an agreement is enforceable by any means available pursuant to the Divorce Code for enforcement of an order, as though the agreement were an order of court, except as otherwise provided in the agreement. Thus, although Rule 1920.33 refers only to enforcement of orders, it also applies to enforcement of agreements.

Rule 1920.34 Joinder of Parties

At any stage of an action, the court may order the joinder of any additional person who could have joined or been joined in the action and may stay the proceedings in whole or in part until such person has been joined. The action may proceed although such person has not been made a party if jurisdiction over that person cannot be obtained and that person is not an indispensable party to the action.

> **Note:** The joinder of persons other than husband and wife may be essential in claims for child custody where neither has custody or custody is claimed by others, or where persons other than the parties have an interest in property which is the subject matter of a distribution.
>
> The intervention in an action by a person not a party is governed by Rule 2326 et seq.

Adopted June 27, 1980, effective July 1, 1980. Amended March 30, 1994, effective July 1, 1994.

Rules 1920.35 to 1920.40 [Blank]

Rule 1920.41 No Default Judgment

No judgment may be entered by default or on the pleadings.

Adopted June 27, 1980, effective July 1, 1980.

Rule 1920.42. Affidavit and Decree Under § 3301(c) or § 3301(d)(1) of the Divorce Code. Notice of Intention to Request Entry of Divorce Decree in § 3301(c) and § 3301(d)(1)(i) Divorces. Counter-Affidavit

(a) If a complaint has been filed requesting a divorce on the ground of irretrievable breakdown and

   (1) both parties have filed an affidavit under § 3301(c) of the Divorce Code substantially in the form prescribed by Rule 1920.72(b), or

   (2) either party has filed a § 3301(d) affidavit under § 3301(d) of the Divorce Code substantially in the form prescribed by Rule 1920.72(d) and

has served it upon the other party along with a form counter-affidavit and the other party has admitted or failed to deny the averments of the § 3301(d) affidavit, the prothonotary on praecipe in the form prescribed by Rule 1920.73(b) shall transmit the record to the court, which shall review the record and enter the appropriate decree. No master shall be appointed.

(b) The affidavit required by § 3301(c) of the Divorce Code must have been executed

(1) ninety days or more after both filing and service of the complaint, and

(2) within thirty days of the date the affidavit was filed.

(c) An affidavit of consent may be withdrawn only with leave of court.

(d)(1) Except as provided in (e), no decree shall be entered by the court under § 3301(c) or § 3301(d)(1)(i) of the Divorce Code unless a notice of intention to request entry of divorce decree, substantially in the form prescribed by Rule 1920.73(a), was mailed or delivered to the attorney of record of the party against whom the decree is to be entered or, if there is no attorney of record, to the party, along with a form counter-affidavit if none has been filed, at least twenty days prior to the date of the filing of the praecipe to transmit the record. A copy of the praecipe, which shall state the date and manner of service of the notice, shall be attached.

(2) The affidavit required under § 3301(d) of the Divorce Code shall be filed with the prothonotary and served upon the other party, along with a form counter-affidavit. The moving party must wait a minimum of 20 days after service of the § 3301(d) affidavit before serving the Notice of Intention to File Praecipe to Transmit the Record and another form counter-affidavit or filing the waiver of notice pursuant to Rule 1920.72(c).

(e) Notice of intention to request entry of divorce decree shall not be required prior to entry of a divorce decree

(1) where the parties have executed and filed with the prothonotary a waiver of notice substantially in the form set forth in Rule 1920.72(c); or

(2) under § 3301(d) where the court finds that no appearance has been entered on defendant's behalf and that defendant cannot be located after diligent search.

Note: This counter-affidavit will be filed only if the party against whom the decree is to be entered has not previously denied the allegations of the other party's affidavit or has not previously claimed economic relief by counterclaim or petition.

Adopted Nov. 7, 1988, effective Jan. 1, 1989. Amended May 17, 1991, effective July 1, 1991; Sept. 11, 1995, effective Jan. 1, 1996; April 10, 1997, effective July 1, 1997; March 2, 2000, imd. effective; May 6, 2015, effective July 1, 2015.

Explanatory Comment—1994

Rule 1920.42 was revised in 1988 to add new subdivision (c) which imposes a requirement that the plaintiff notify the defendant or defendant's attorney, if represented, of the intention to request entry of a divorce decree in an action under Section 3301(d)(1)(i) of the Divorce Code. In such an action the defendant has not actively participated in the proceedings and may be unaware that the court is about to enter a decree which will cut off certain economic rights unless a claim is promptly asserted. The requirement of notice is not extended to actions in which the defendant has actively participated by filing an affidavit of consent under Section 3301(c) of the Divorce Code or by contesting the plaintiff's affidavit under Section 3301(d)(1)(ii).

In addition, subparagraph (2) of subsection (c) requires that an unrepresented defendant also be served with a form counteraffidavit contained in Rule

1920.72(d). The defendant can use this form to deny the allegations contained in the plaintiff's affidavit or to claim economic relief.

Explanatory Comment—1995

The rule is amended to require the same notice prior to entry of the decree in a § 3301(c) divorce as was previously required in a proceeding under § 3301(d). This notice is already required by local rule in many counties, and is adopted in a general rule to further standardize practice.

The requirement in new subdivision (c) that a party obtain leave of court before withdrawing an affidavit of consent is included to ensure orderly process, including notice to the other party and the court. The committee notes that the law is unsettled as to whether a court has the authority to refuse leave to withdraw an affidavit of consent.

Rule 1920.43 Special Relief

(a) At any time after the filing of the complaint, on petition setting forth facts entitling the party to relief, the court may, upon such terms and conditions as it deems just, including the filing of security,

(1) issue preliminary or special injunctions necessary to prevent the removal, disposition, alienation or encumbering of real or personal property in accordance with Rule 1531(a), (c), (d) and (e); or

(2) order the seizure or attachment of real or personal property; or

(3) grant other appropriate relief.

Official Note: See Section 3505 of the Divorce Code relating to injunction against disposition of property pending suit.

(b) Where property ordered attached is in the possession of a garnishee, the practice and procedure shall conform as nearly as may be to Rules 3111 to 3113 and Rules 3142 to 3145 governing attachment execution. Judgment shall not be entered against a garnishee except by order of the court.

Adopted June 27, 1980, effective July 1, 1980. Amended March 30, 1994, effective July 1, 1994.

Rule 1920.44 Party Leaving Jurisdiction. Security

At any stage of the proceeding, upon affidavit that a party is about to leave the jurisdiction, the court may issue appropriate process directing that the party be brought before the court at such time as the court may direct. At that time, the court may direct that the party give security, with one or more sureties, to appear when directed by the court or to comply with any order of court.

Adopted June 27, 1980, effective July 1, 1980.

Rule 1920.45 Counseling

(a) When counseling is provided for in the Divorce Code, the parties shall be notified of the availability of counseling as prescribed by Rules 1920.12(a)(8) and 1920.71.

(b) The court shall maintain and make available to all parties in the prothonotary's office a list of qualified professionals who provide counseling services.

Official Note: Section 3103 of the Divorce Code defines the term "qualified professionals."

(c)(1) When the ground for divorce is under Section 3301(c) of the Divorce Code and counseling is requested by either party, the counseling must be completed within ninety days after filing the complaint.

Note: See Section 3302(b) of the Divorce Code providing for the ninety-day period.

(2) When the ground for divorce is under Section 3301(d) of the Divorce Code and the court orders counseling, it must be completed within one hundred twenty days unless the parties agree to a longer period.

Note: See Section 3301(d)(2) of the Divorce Code providing for a period "not less than 90 days nor more than 120 days . . ."

(d) If the action for divorce has been referred to a master and there is a request for counseling pursuant to the Divorce Code, the master, without leave of court, may require counseling and continue the hearing pending the counselor's report.

Official Note: See Section 3302 of the Divorce Code for the instances in which counseling may be requested or required.

Adopted June 27, 1980, effective July 1, 1980. Amended Jan. 28, 1983, effective July 1, 1983 and applied to pending actions; March 30, 1994, effective July 1, 1994.

Explanatory Note—1983

Subdivision (a) as originally promulgated provided for the court to notify the parties of the availability of counseling. However, the rule did not specify the method of notification and diverse local practices developed.

Subdivision (a) as revised specifies that the parties shall be notified of the availability of counseling as provided by Rules 1920.12(a)(8) and 1920.71. The plaintiff acknowledges notification of the availability of counseling by an allegation in the complaint. See Rule 1920.12(a)(8), supra. The defendant is notified of the availability of counseling by a paragraph in the notice to defend the claim rights provided by Rule 1920.71, infra.

The revision to subdivision (b) provides for the court to maintain and make available to all parties a list of marriage counselors. The list is to be maintained in the prothonotary's office rather than the office of the domestic relations section.

Rule 1920.46 Affidavit of Non-Military Service

If the defendant fails to appear in the action, the plaintiff shall file an affidavit regarding military service with the motion for appointment of a master, prior to a trial by the court, or with the plaintiff's affidavit required by Rule 1920.42(a)(2).

Official Note: The Servicemembers Civil Relief Act, 50 App. U.S.C.A. § 521, requires that in cases in which the defendant does not make an appearance, the plaintiff must file an affidavit of non-military service before the court may enter judgment. If the defendant is in the military service and an attorney has not entered an appearance on behalf of the defendant, no judgment may be entered until the court appoints an attorney to represent the defendant and protect his or her interest.

Rule 1920.42(a)(2) governs an action for divorce under Section 3301(d)(1)(i) of the Divorce Code.

Explanatory Comment—2003

35 P.S. § 450.602 previously required a certificate of each divorce or annulment decreed in the commonwealth to be transmitted to the Vital Statistics Division of the Commonwealth of Pennsylvania Department of Health. The statute was amended October 30, 2001, P.L. 826, No. 82, § 1, effective in 60 days, to require that the prothonotary submit a monthly statistical summary of divorces and annulments, rather than individual forms for each decree. Thus, subdivision (a) of Rule 1920.46, requiring the filing of the vital statistics form, is no longer necessary. Former subdivision (b) now comprises the entirety of the rule and the title has been amended to reflect that the rule applies only to the affidavit regarding military service.

Rules 1920.47 to 1920.50   [Blank]

Rule 1920.51.   Hearing by the Court. Appointment of Master. Notice of Hearing

(a) (1) The court may hear the testimony or, upon motion of a party or of the court, the court may appoint a master to hear the actions and ancillary claims specified in subdivision (a)(2)(i) and issue a report and recommendation. The order of appointment shall specify the actions and ancillary claims that are referred to the master.

(2)(i) The court may appoint a master in an action of divorce under Section 3301(a), (b), and (d)(1)(ii) of the Divorce Code, an action for annulment, and the ancillary claims for alimony, equitable division of marital property, partial custody, counsel fees, and costs and expenses, or any aspect of those actions or claims.

(ii) If there are no claims other than divorce, no master may be appointed to determine grounds for divorce if either party has asserted grounds for divorce pursuant to § 3301(c) or § 3301(d)(1)(i) of the Divorce Code. A master may be appointed to hear ancillary economic claims in a divorce action pursuant to § 3301(c) or § 3301(d) of the Divorce Code. The master may be appointed to hear ancillary economic claims prior to the entry of a divorce decree if grounds for divorce have been established.

(iii) No master may be appointed in a claim for legal, physical or shared custody or paternity.

Note: Section 3321 of the Divorce Code, 23 Pa.C.S. § 3321, prohibits the appointment of a master as to the claims of custody and paternity.

(3) The motion for the appointment of a master and the order shall be substantially in the form prescribed by Rule 1920.74.

(4) A permanent or standing master employed by, or under contract with, a judicial district or appointed by the court shall not practice family law before a conference officer, hearing officer, permanent or standing master, or judge of the same judicial district.

Note: Hearing conference officers preside at office conferences under Rule 1910.11. Hearing officers preside at hearings under Rule 1910.12. The appointment of masters to hear actions in divorce or for annulment of marriage is authorized by Rule 1920.51.

(b) Written notice of the hearing shall be given to each attorney of record by the master. If a master has not been appointed, the prothonotary, clerk or other officer designated by the court shall give the notice.

(c) If no attorney has appeared of record for a party, notice of the hearing shall be given to the party by the master, or if a master has not been appointed, by the prothonotary, clerk or other officer designated by the court, as follows:

(1) to the plaintiff, by ordinary mail to the address on the complaint;

(2) to the defendant,

(i) if service of the complaint was made other than pursuant to special order of court, by ordinary mail to the defendant's last known address; or

(ii) if service of the complaint was made pursuant to special order of court, (a) by sending a copy of the notice by ordinary mail to the persons, if any, named in the investigation affidavit, likely to know the present whereabouts of the defendant; and (b) by sending a copy by registered mail to the defendant's last known address.

Note: Under Rule 76, registered mail includes certified mail.

(d) Advertising of notice of the hearing shall not be required.

(e) Proof of notice shall be filed of record.

Note: Consistent with Section 3301(e) of the Divorce Code as amended, these rules contemplate that if a divorce decree may be entered under the no fault provisions of §§ 3301(c) or (d), a divorce decree will be entered on these grounds and no hearing shall berequired on any other grounds.

Adopted June 27, 1980, effective July 1, 1980. Amended January 28, 1983, effective July 1, 1983; September 29, 1989, effective October 15, 1989; May 17, 1991, effective July 1, 1991; March 30, 1994, effective July 1, 1994; July 15, 1994, effective January 1, 1995; September 11, 1995, effective January 1, 1996; July 8, 2010, effective September 6, 2010; March 4, 2015, effective April 3, 2015; July 30, 2018, effective January 1, 2019.

Explanatory Comment—1994

While subdivision (a)(2)(ii) clearly prohibits appointment of a master to determine a divorce claim brought under §§ 3301(c) or 3301(d), the provision does permit a master to hear claims which are joined with the divorce action.

The rule is amended to conform with proposed new Rules 1915.4-1 and 1915.4-2, and to remove the implied prohibition against the use of hearing officers in partial custody or visitation cases.

Explanatory Comment—2010

The rule is amended to clarify the role of the master in a divorce case when either party has asserted grounds for divorce pursuant to § 3301(c) or § 3301(d) of the Divorce Code. The rule had been interpreted in some jurisdictions as requiring the entry of a bifurcated decree before a master could be appointed to hear economic claims.

Rule 1920.52. Hearing by Court. Decision. No Post-Trial Relief. Decree

(a) In claims involving:

(1) marital property;

(2) enforcement of marital agreements;

(3) alimony; or

(4) a contested action of divorce or for annulment,

the order of the court shall state the reasons for its decision. A motion for post-trial relief may not be filed to orders with the actions or claims enumerated in this subdivision.

(b) In claims involving:

(1) paternity;

(2) custody;

(3) counsel fees;

(4) costs and expenses;

(5) an uncontested action of divorce or annulment; or

(6) protection from abuse, the order of the court may set forth only general findings. A motion for post-trial relief may not be filed to orders with the actions or claims enumerated in this subdivision.

Note: The procedure relating to motions for reconsideration is set forth in Rule 1930.2.

(c) The court need not determine all claims at one time but may enter a decree adjudicating a specific claim or claims. However, unless by agreement of the parties, no bifurcated decree of divorce shall be entered except as set forth in 23 Pa.C.S.A. § 3323(c.1). In any bifurcated decree entered by the court without the agreement of the parties, the court shall state with specificity the compelling circumstances that exist for the entry of the decree and the economic provisions sufficient to protect the non-moving party.

(d) In all cases the court shall enter a decree separately adjudicating each claim raised.

Adopted March 30, 1994, effective July 1, 1994. Amended May 31, 2000, effective July 1, 2000; amended July 8, 2010, effective in 60 days. [September 6, 2010]; amended July 30, 2018, effective January 1, 2019.

Explanatory Comment—2010

The Divorce Code was amended in 2004 to make it more difficult for the court to enter a bifurcated divorce decree absent the agreement of the parties. Section 3323(c.1) became effective on January 28, 2005 and limits the circumstances in which the court may enter a bifurcated decree, requiring the establishment of grounds for divorce, compelling circumstances for the entry of the decree and sufficient economic protections for the non-moving party.

Rule 1920.53 Hearing by Master. Report

In an action for divorce or annulment which has been referred to a master, the master's report shall include findings of fact, conclusions of law and a recommended disposition of the case.

(a) The findings of fact shall include

(1) the method and date of service of process,

(2) the manner and date of service of the notice of the master's hearing or the master's efforts to notify the defendant,

(3) the date and place of marriage,

(4) information relating to any prior marriage of either party and proof of dissolution of such prior marriage,

(5) the residences of the parties at the time of the marriage and subsequent thereto, the actual length of time the parties have resided in the Commonwealth, and whether the residence requirement of Section 3104(b) of the Divorce Code has been met,

(6) the age and occupation of each party,

(7) the name and age of each child of the parties, if any, and with whom each resides,

(8) the grounds upon which the action is based,

(9) defenses to the action, if any, and

(10) whether the divorce should be granted on the basis of the complaint or the counterclaim, if filed.

(b) The conclusions of law shall include a discussion of the law as it relates to the facts, as well as the legal conclusions reached by the master.

(c) The report shall include the master's recommendation that the divorce or annulment be granted or denied. If divorce or annulment is recommended, the master shall attach a proposed decree.

Former rule rescinded and new rule adopted Sept. 11, 1995, effective Jan. 1, 1996.

Rule 1920.54. Hearing by Master. Report. Related Claims

(a) If claims for counsel fees and costs and expenses have been referred to a master pursuant to Pa.R.C.P. No. 1920.51(a), the master's report shall contain a separate section captioned "Counsel Fees and Costs and Expenses". The report may be in a narrative form stating the reasons for the recommendation and shall include a proposed order stating:

(1) the amount;

(2) by and for whom it shall be paid; and

(3) the effective date of the order.

(b) If a claim for alimony has been referred to a master, the report shall contain a separate action captioned "Alimony." The report shall conform to the requirements of subdivision (a) and, in addition, shall set forth

(1) the findings required by Section 3701(a) of the Divorce Code,

(2) the relevant factors considered under Section 3701(b) of the Divorce Code,

(3) the nature, amount, duration and manner of payment of alimony, if any, and

(4) the reason or reasons for the recommended denial or award of alimony.

(c) If a claim for the determination and distribution of existing property rights and interests between the parties has been referred to a master, the report shall contain a separate section captioned "Division of Property." The section shall be divided into two parts,

Rule 1920.55

(1) one captioned "Marital Property," listing all property to be designated as such and including a proposed equitable distribution thereof with a discussion of the relevant factors considered under Section 3502(a) of the Divorce Code; and

(2) one captioned "Nonmarital Property," listing all property to be designated as such.

Adopted June 27, 1980, effective July 1, 1980. Amended March 30, 1994, effective July 1, 1994; November 8, 2006, effective February 6, 2007; May 6, 2015, effective July 1, 2015; July 30, 2018, effective January 1, 2019.

Rule 1920.55 Master's Report. Notice. Exceptions. Final Decree [Rescinded]

Rescinded Sept. 11, 1995, effective Jan. 1, 1996.

Rule 1920.55-1. Alternative Hearing Procedures for Matters Referred to a Master.

(a) Matters referred to a master for hearing shall proceed as prescribed by Pa.R.C.P. No. 1920.55-2 unless the court by local rule adopts the alternative procedure of Pa.R.C.P. No. 1920.55-3.

(b) The president judge or the administrative judge of Family Division of each county shall certify that all divorce proceedings which are referred to a master in that county are conducted in accordance with either Pa.R.C.P. No. 1920.55-2 or Pa.R.C.P. No. 1920.55-3. The certification shall be filed with the Domestic Relations Procedural Rules Committee and shall be substantially in the following form:

I hereby certify that _____ County conducts its divorce proceedings that are referred to a master in accordance with Pa.R.C.P. No. _____.

_____ _____
(PRESIDENT JUDGE)   (ADMINISTRATIVE JUDGE)

Note: For a complete list of the Alternative Hearing Procedures for each county: http://www.pacourts.us/courts/supreme–court/committees/rules–committees/domestic–relations–procedural–rules–committee.

Explanatory Comment

The 1995 amendments created alternative procedures for appeal from the recommendation of a master in divorce. Pa.R.C.P. No. 1920.55–1 states that, if the court chooses to appoint a master, the exceptions procedure set forth in proposed Pa.R.C.P. No. 1920.55–2 will be used unless the court has, by local rule, adopted the alternative procedure of proposed Pa.R.C.P. No. 1920.55–3.

In lieu of continuing the practice of including in the Note a 67–county list identifying the hearing procedure selected by the local county court, the list can now be found on the Domestic Relations Procedural Rules Committee website.

The provisions of rule 1920.55-1 adopted September 11, 1995, effective January 1, 1996; amended March 16, 2011, effective immediately; amended October 14, 2016, effective December 2016.

Rule 1920.55-2. Master's Report. Notice. Exceptions. Final Decree

(a) After conclusion of the hearing, the master shall:

(1) file the record and the report within;

(i) twenty days in uncontested actions or;

(ii) thirty days from the last to occur of the receipt of the transcript by the master or close of the record in contested actions; and

(2) immediately serve upon counsel for each party, or, if unrepresented, upon the party, a copy of the report and recommendation and written notice of the right to file exceptions.

(b) Within twenty days of the date of receipt or the date of mailing of the master's report and recommendation, whichever occurs first, any party may file exceptions to the report or any part thereof, to rulings on objections to evidence, to statements or findings of fact, to conclusions of law, or to any other matters occurring during the hearing. Each exception shall set forth a separate objection precisely and without discussion. Matters not covered by exceptions are deemed waived unless, prior to entry of the final decree, leave is granted to file exceptions raising those matters.

(c) If exceptions are filed, any other party may file exceptions within twenty days of the date of service of the original exceptions. The court shall hear argument on the exceptions and enter a final decree.

(d) If no exceptions are filed, the court shall review the report and, if approved, shall enter a final decree.

(e) No Motion for Post-Trial Relief may be filed to the final decree.

Adopted Sept. 11, 1995, effective Jan. 1, 1996. Amended Aug. 8, 2006, imd. effective; May 6, 2015, effective July 1, 2015.

Explanatory Comment—1995

The proposed amendments create alternative procedures for appeal from the recommendation of a master in divorce. Rule 1920.55-1 states that, if the court chooses to appoint a master, the exceptions procedure set forth in proposed Rule 1920.55-2 will be used unless the court has, by local rule, adopted the alternative procedure of proposed Rule 1920.55-3.

Explanatory Comment—2006

The time for filing exceptions has been expanded from ten to twenty days. The purpose of this amendment is to provide ample opportunity for litigants and counsel to receive notice of the report and recommendation, to assure Commonwealth-wide consistency in calculation of time for filing and to conform to applicable general civil procedural rules.

Rule 1920.55-3 Master's Report. Notice. Hearing De Novo. Final Decree

(a) No record shall be made of the hearing in proceedings held pursuant to this rule.

(b) After the conclusion of hearing, the master shall:

(1) file the report within;

(i) twenty days in uncontested actions or;

(ii) thirty days in contested actions; and

(2) immediately serve upon counsel for each party, or, if unrepresented, upon the party, a copy of the report and recommendation, and written notice of the right to demand a hearing de novo.

(c) Within twenty days of the date the master's report is mailed or received, whichever occurs first, any party may file a written demand for a hearing de novo. If a demand is filed, the court shall hold a hearing de novo and enter a final decree.

(d) If no demand for de novo hearing is filed within the twenty-day period, the court shall review the report and recommendation and, if approved, shall enter a final decree.

(e) No Motion for Post-Trial Relief may be filed to the final decree.

Adopted Sept. 11, 1995, effective Jan. 1, 1996; August 8, 2006, eff. imd.

Explanatory Comment—2006

The time for filing exceptions has been expanded from ten to twenty days. The purpose of this amendment is to provide ample opportunity for litigants and counsel to receive notice of the report and recommendation, to assure commonwealth-wide consistency in calculation of time for filing and to conform to applicable general civil procedural rules.

Explanatory Comment—1995

The amendments create alternative procedures for appeal from the recommendation of a master in divorce. Rule 1920.55-1 states that, if the court chooses to appoint a master, the exceptions procedure set forth in Rule 1920.55-2 will be used unless the court has, by local rule, adopted the alternative procedure of Rule 1920.55-3.

Rule 1920.56 [Rescinded]

Rescinded July 30, 2018, effective January 1, 2019.

Adopted Sept. 29, 1989, effective Oct. 1, 1989; July 30, 1018, effective January 1, 2018.

Rules 1920.57 to 1920.60 [Blank]

Rule 1920.61 Testimony Outside the County

On motion of a party and upon such terms as it may order, the court may authorize and direct the master to take testimony of witnesses within any other county of the Commonwealth or in any other state or territory subject to the jurisdiction of the United States, or in any foreign country.

Adopted June 27, 1980, effective July 1, 1980.

Rule 1920.62 Proceedings by Indigent Parties

The procedures set forth in Rule 240 are incorporated herein, and shall govern proceedings by indigent parties in divorce and annulment.

Former rule rescinded and new rule adopted April 19, 1995, effective July 1, 1995.

Pa. R.C.P.   Rule 1920.71

Explanatory Comment—1995

The procedure for obtaining leave to proceed in forma pauperis in divorce and annulment matters as set forth in rescinded Rule 1920.62 was considerably less detailed than the procedure set forth in Rule 240, and did not prescribe a form petition for leave to proceed in forma pauperis. Practice is simplified by rescinding old Rule 1920.62 and directing indigent litigants in divorce and annulment matters to use the procedure and form petition set forth in Rule 240.

Rules 1920.63 to 1920.70   [Blank]

Rule 1920.71.   Form of Notice

The notice required by Rule 1920.12(c) shall be substantially in the following form:

NOTICE TO DEFEND AND CLAIM RIGHTS

You have been sued in court. If you wish to defend against the claims set forth in the following pages, you must take prompt action. You are warned that if you fail to do so, the case may proceed without you and a decree of divorce or annulment may be entered against you by the court. A judgment may also be entered against you for any other claim or relief requested in these papers by the plaintiff. You may lose money or property or other rights important to you, including custody of your children.

When the ground for the divorce is indignities or irretrievable breakdown of the marriage, you may request marriage counseling. A list of marriage counselors is available in the Office of the Prothonotary at _____

(Room Number—Address)

IF YOU DO NOT FILE A CLAIM FOR ALIMONY, DIVISION OF PROPERTY, LAWYER'S FEES OR EXPENSES BEFORE A DIVORCE OR ANNULMENT IS GRANTED, YOU MAY LOSE THE RIGHT TO CLAIM ANY OF THEM.

YOU SHOULD TAKE THIS PAPER TO YOUR LAWYER AT ONCE. IF YOU DO NOT HAVE A LAWYER, GO TO OR TELEPHONE THE OFFICE SET FORTH BELOW. THIS OFFICE CAN PROVIDE YOU WITH INFORMATION ABOUT HIRING A LAWYER.

IF YOU CANNOT AFFORD TO HIRE A LAWYER, THIS OFFICE MAY BE ABLE TO PROVIDE YOU WITH INFORMATION ABOUT AGENCIES THAT MAY OFFER LEGAL SERVICES TO ELIGIBLE PERSONS AT A REDUCED FEE OR NO FEE.

_____

(Name)

_____

(Address)

_____

(Telephone Number)

Adopted June 27, 1980, effective July 1, 1980. Amended Jan. 28, 1983, effective July 1, 1983; March 18, 2004, effective June 16, 2004; May 6, 2015, effective July 1, 2015.

Explanatory Comment—1983

The notice to defend and claim rights has been revised in two respects. First, a new paragraph has been added advising the defendant that he may request marriage counseling when the divorce is based upon certain grounds. This provision implements Rule 1920.45(a) which requires that notice be given to the parties of the availability of counseling.

In addition, the paragraph of the notice advising that certain claims are waived if not made prior to the entry of the divorce decree has been revised stylistically.

Rule 1920.72. Form of Complaint. Affidavit Under § 3301(c) or 3301(d) of the Divorce Code. Counter-affidavit. Waiver of Notice of Intention to Request Decree Under § 3301(c) and § 3301(d)

(a) The complaint in an action of divorce under § 3301(c) or 3301(d) shall begin with the Notice to Defend and Claim Rights required by Rule 1920.71 and shall be substantially in the following form:

(Caption)

COMPLAINT UNDER SECTION 3301(c) OR 3301(d) OF THE DIVORCE CODE

1. Plaintiff is _____ (Name), who currently resides at _____ (Address), _____ (City), _____ (County), _____ (State), since _____ (Date).

2. Defendant is _____ (Name), who currently resides at _____ (Address), _____ (City), _____ (County), _____ (State), since _____ (Date).

3. _____ (Plaintiff and/or Defendant) has/have been a bona fide resident(s) in the Commonwealth for at least six months immediately previous to the filing of this Complaint.

4. The plaintiff and defendant were married on _____ (Date) at _____ (City), _____ (State/County).

5. There have been no prior actions of divorce or for annulment between the parties except _____.

6. The marriage is irretrievably broken.

7. Plaintiff has been advised that counseling is available and that plaintiff may have the right to request that the court require the parties to participate in counseling.

Pa. R.C.P. Rule 1920.72

8. Plaintiff requests the court to enter a decree of divorce.

I verify that the statements made in this Complaint are true and correct. I understand that false statements herein are made subject to the penalties of 18 Pa.C.S. § 4904, relating to unsworn falsification to authorities.

_____
Plaintiff

Date: _____

_____
Attorney for Plaintiff

(b) The affidavit of consent required by § 3301(c) of the Divorce Code and Rule 1920.42(a)(1) shall be substantially in the following form:

(Caption)

AFFIDAVIT OF CONSENT

1. A complaint in divorce under § 3301(c) of the Divorce Code was filed on _____ .
 Date

2. The marriage of plaintiff and defendant is irretrievably broken and ninety days have elapsed from the date of filing and service of the Complaint.

3. I consent to the entry of a final decree of divorce after service of notice of intention to request entry of the decree.

I verify that the statements made in this affidavit are true and correct. I understand that false statements herein are made subject to the penalties of 18 Pa.C.S. § 4904 relating to unsworn falsification to authorities.

Date: _____

_____
(PLAINTIFF)(DEFENDANT)

(c) The waiver permitted by Rule 1920.42(e) shall be in substantially the following form:

(Caption)

WAIVER OF NOTICE OF INTENTION TO REQUEST ENTRY OF
A DIVORCE DECREE UNDER § 3301(c) AND § 3301(d) OF THE
DIVORCE CODE

1. I consent to the entry of a final decree of divorce without notice.

2. I understand that I may lose rights concerning alimony, division of property, lawyer's fees or expenses if I do not claim them before a divorce is granted.

3. I understand that I will not be divorced until a divorce decree is entered by the Court and that a copy of the decree will be sent to me immediately after it is filed with the prothonotary.

I verify that the statements made in this affidavit are true and correct. I understand that false statements herein are made subject to the penalties of 18 Pa.C.S. § 4904 relating to unsworn falsification to authorities.

Date: _____

_____
(PLAINTIFF)(DEFENDANT)

(d) The affidavit required by § 3301(d) of the Divorce Code and Pa.R.C.P. No. 1920.42(a)(2) shall be substantially in the following form:

Rule 1920.72   ACTIONS OF DIVORCE, ANNULMENT

(Caption)

NOTICE

If you wish to deny any of the statements set forth in this affidavit, you must file a counter-affidavit within 20 days after this affidavit has been served on you or the statements will be admitted.

AFFIDAVIT UNDER SECTION 3301(d) OF THE DIVORCE CODE

1. The parties to this action separated on _____.

2. Check either (a) or (b):

☐ (a) The date of separation was prior to December 5, 2016, and the parties have continued to live separate and apart for a period of at least two years.

☐ (b) The date of separation was on or after December 5, 2016, and the parties have continued to live separate and apart for a period of at least one year.

3. The marriage is irretrievably broken.

4. I understand that I may lose rights concerning alimony, division of property, lawyer's fees or expenses if I do not claim them before a divorce is granted.

I verify that the statements made in this affidavit are true and correct. I understand that false statements herein are made subject to the penalties of 18 Pa.C.S. § 4904 relating to unsworn falsification to authorities.

Date: _____   _____
                                                                      (PLAINTIFF)(DEFENDANT)

(e)(1) The counter-affidavit prescribed by Pa.R.C.P. No. 1920.42(d)(2) for a divorce under § 3301(c) of the Divorce Code shall be substantially in the following form:

(Caption)

COUNTER-AFFIDAVIT UNDER § 3301(c) OF THE DIVORCE CODE

I wish to claim economic relief which may include alimony, division of property, lawyer's fees or expenses or other important rights.

I understand that I must file my economic claims with the prothonotary in writing and serve them on the other party. If I fail to do so before the date set forth on the Notice of Intention to Request Divorce Decree, the divorce decree may be entered without further notice to me, and I shall be unable thereafter to file any economic claims.

I verify that the statements made in this counter-affidavit are true and correct. I understand that false statements herein are made subject to the penalties of 18 Pa.C.S. § 4904, relating to unsworn falsification to authorities.

Date: _____   _____
                                                                      (PLAINTIFF)(DEFENDANT)

NOTICE: IF YOU DO NOT WISH TO CLAIM ECONOMIC RELIEF, YOU SHOULD NOT FILE THIS COUNTER-AFFIDAVIT.

(2) The counter-affidavit prescribed by § 3301(d) of the Divorce Code and Pa.R.C.P. No. 1920.42(d)(2) shall be substantially in the following form:

Pa. R.C.P.   Rule 1920.72

(Caption)

COUNTER-AFFIDAVIT UNDER § 3301(d) OF THE DIVORCE CODE

1. Check either (a) or (b):

☐ (a) I do not oppose the entry of a divorce decree.

☐ (b) I oppose the entry of a divorce decree because:

(Check (i), (ii), (iii) or all):

☐ (i) The parties to this action have not lived separate and apart for the required separation period: two years for parties that separated prior to December 5, 2016, and one year for parties that separated on or after December 5, 2016.

☐ (ii) The marriage is not irretrievably broken.

☐ (iii) There are economic claims pending.

(2) Check (a), (b) or (c):

☐ (a) I do not wish to make any claims for economic relief. I understand that I may lose rights concerning alimony, division of property, lawyer's fees or expenses if I do not claim them before a divorce is granted.

☐ (b) I wish to claim economic relief which may include alimony, division of property, lawyer's fees or expenses or other important rights.

I UNDERSTAND THAT IN ADDITION TO CHECKING (b) ABOVE, I MUST ALSO FILE ALL OF MY ECONOMIC CLAIMS WITH THE PROTHONOTARY IN WRITING AND SERVE THEM ON THE OTHER PARTY. IF I FAIL TO DO SO BEFORE THE DATE SET FORTH ON THE NOTICE OF INTENTION TO REQUEST DIVORCE DECREE, THE DIVORCE DECREE MAY BE ENTERED WITHOUT FURTHER NOTICE TO ME, AND I SHALL BE UNABLE THEREAFTER TO FILE ANY ECONOMIC CLAIMS.

☐ (c) Economic claims have been raised and are not resolved.

I verify that the statements made in this counter-affidavit are true and correct. I understand that false statements herein are made subject to the penalties of 18 Pa.C.S. § 4904, relating to unsworn falsification to authorities.

Date: _____   _____

                                                              (PLAINTIFF)(DEFENDANT)

NOTICE: IF YOU DO NOT WISH TO OPPOSE THE ENTRY OF A DIVORCE DECREE AND YOU DO NOT WISH TO MAKE ANY CLAIM FOR ECONOMIC RELIEF, YOU SHOULD NOT FILE THIS COUNTER-AFFIDAVIT.

Adopted June 27, 1980, effective July 1, 1980. Amended Jan. 28, 1983, effective July 1, 1983; March 23, 1987, effective July 1, 1987; Nov. 7, 1988, effective Jan. 1, 1989; May 17, 1991, effective July 1, 1991; March 30, 1994, effective July 1, 1994; Sept. 11, 1995, effective Jan. 1, 1996; April 10, 1997, effective July 1, 1997; March 2, 2000, imd. effective; May 6, 2015, effective July 1, 2015; Nov. 18, 2016, effective Dec. 5, 2016.

Explanatory Comment—1994

The forms set forth in Rule 1920.72 are intended to promote uniform practice throughout the Commonwealth. Additional forms are set forth at 1920.73 through 1920.76.

The reference in subdivision (d) to the parties living separate and apart for three years is corrected to reflect the current statutory requirement of two years.

Explanatory Comment—2016

Act 102 of 2016 (the Act) amended the Divorce Code by reducing the separation period required by § 3301(d) from two years to one year for parties separating after the Act's effective date: December 5, 2016. The Act provides that the one-year separation period is only applicable to married persons separating after the effective date of the Act. However, the current two-year separation period remains applicable to married persons that separated prior to the effective date of the Act. As such, the current forms could not be amended merely by substituting one-year for two-year on the affidavit and counter-affidavit in Pa.R.C.P. No. 1920.72(d) and (e)(2), respectively. Instead, the current forms have been amended to delineate when the parties separated vis-à-vis the Act's effective date. Therefore, a party alleging a date of separation prior to December 5, 2016, should proceed under a two-year separation period. A party alleging a date of separation on or after December 5, 2016 should proceed under a one-year separation period.

Rule 1920.73. Notice of Intention to Request Entry of Divorce Decree. Praecipe to Transmit Record. Forms

(a)(1) The notice of the intention to request entry of divorce decree prescribed by Rule 1920.42(d) shall be substantially in the following form if there is an attorney of record:

(Caption)

NOTICE OF INTENTION TO REQUEST ENTRY OF DIVORCE DECREE

TO: _____

(PLAINTIFF) (DEFENDANT)

_____ (PLAINTIFF) (DEFENDANT) intends to file with the court the attached Praecipe to Transmit Record on or after _____, 20____ requesting that a final decree in divorce be entered.

_____

Attorney for (Plaintiff) (Defendant)

(2)(i) The notice of the intention to request entry of a § 3301(c) divorce decree prescribed by Rule 1920.42(d) shall be substantially in the following form if there is no attorney of record:

(Caption)

NOTICE OF INTENTION TO REQUEST ENTRY OF
§ 3301(c) DIVORCE DECREE

TO: _____

(PLAINTIFF) (DEFENDANT)

You have signed a § 3301(c) affidavit consenting to the entry of a divorce decree. Therefore, on or after _____, 20____, the other party can request the court to enter a final decree in divorce.

Pa. R.C.P.   Rule 1920.73

Unless you have already filed with the court a written claim for economic relief, you must do so by the date in the paragraph above, or the court may grant the divorce and you will lose forever the right to ask for economic relief. The filing of the form counter-affidavit alone does not protect your economic claims.

YOU SHOULD TAKE THIS PAPER TO YOUR LAWYER AT ONCE. IF YOU DO NOT HAVE A LAWYER, GO TO OR TELEPHONE THE OFFICE SET FORTH BELOW. THIS OFFICE CAN PROVIDE YOU WITH INFORMATION ABOUT HIRING A LAWYER. IF YOU CANNOT AFFORD TO HIRE A LAWYER, THIS OFFICE MAY BE ABLE TO PROVIDE YOU WITH INFORMATION ABOUT AGENCIES THAT MAY OFFER LEGAL SERVICES TO ELIGIBLE PERSONS AT A REDUCED FEE OR NO FEE.

_____
(Name)

_____
(Address)

_____
(Telephone)

Official Note: The above lines are to be completed with the name, address and telephone number of the officer, organization, agency or person designated by the court in accordance with Rule 1018.1(c).

The date to be inserted in the first paragraph of the notice must be at least twenty days after the date on which the notice was mailed or delivered.

(ii) **The notice of the intention to request entry of § 3301(d) divorce decree prescribed by Rule 1920.42(d) shall be substantially in the following form if there is no attorney of record:**

(Caption)

NOTICE OF INTENTION TO REQUEST ENTRY OF
§ 3301(d) DIVORCE DECREE

TO: _____
      (PLAINTIFF) (DEFENDANT)

You have been sued in an action for divorce. You have failed to answer the complaint or file a counter-affidavit to the § 3301(d) affidavit. Therefore, on or after _____, 20____, the other party can request the court to enter a final decree in divorce.

If you do not file with the prothonotary of the court an answer with your signature notarized or verified or a counter-affidavit by the above date, the court can enter a final decree in divorce. A counter-affidavit which you may file with the prothonotary of the court is attached to this notice.

Unless you have already filed with the court a written claim for economic relief, you must do so by the above date or the court may grant the divorce and you will lose forever the right to ask for economic relief. The filing of the form counter-affidavit alone does not protect your economic claims.

YOU SHOULD TAKE THIS PAPER TO YOUR LAWYER AT ONCE. IF YOU DO NOT HAVE A LAWYER, GO TO OR TELEPHONE THE OFFICE SET FORTH BELOW. THIS OFFICE CAN PROVIDE YOU WITH INFORMATION ABOUT HIRING A LAWYER. IF YOU CANNOT AFFORD TO HIRE A LAW-

Rule 1920.73 ACTIONS OF DIVORCE, ANNULMENT

YER, THIS OFFICE MAY BE ABLE TO PROVIDE YOU WITH INFORMATION ABOUT AGENCIES THAT MAY OFFER LEGAL SERVICES TO ELIGIBLE PERSONS AT A REDUCED FEE OR NO FEE.

_____
(Name)

_____
(Address)

_____
(Telephone)

Official Note: The above lines are to be completed with the name, address and telephone number of the officer, organization, agency or person designated by the court in accordance with Rule 1018.1(c).

The date to be inserted in the first paragraph of the notice must be at least twenty days after the date on which the notice was mailed or delivered.

(b) The praecipe to transmit the record prescribed by Rule 1920.42 shall be in substantially the following form:

(Caption)

PRAECIPE TO TRANSMIT RECORD

To the Prothonotary:

Transmit the record, together with the following information, to the court for entry of a divorce decree:

1. Ground for divorce: irretrievable breakdown under § (3301(c)) and § (3301(d)(1)) of the Divorce Code. (Strike out inapplicable section).

2. Date and manner of service of the complaint: _____.

3. Complete either paragraph (a) or (b).

(a) Date of execution of the affidavit of consent required by § 3301(c) of the Divorce Code: by plaintiff ____; by defendant _____.

(b)(1) Date of execution of the affidavit required by § 3301(d) of the Divorce Code: _____;

(2) Date of filing and service of the § 3301(d) affidavit upon the opposing party: _____.

4. Related claims pending: _____.

5. Complete either (a) or (b).

(a) Date and manner of service of the notice of intention to file praecipe a copy of which is attached:

(b) Date plaintiff's Waiver of Notice was filed with the prothonotary: _____

Date defendant's Waiver of Notice was filed with the prothonotary:

_____
(Attorney for) (Plaintiff) (Defendant)

Pa. R.C.P.   Rule 1920.74

Adopted Jan. 28, 1983, effective July 1, 1983. Amended Nov. 7, 1988, effective Jan. 1, 1989; March 30, 1994, effective July 1, 1994; April 10, 1997, effective July 1, 1997; March 2, 2000, imd. effective; Oct. 11, 2002, imd. effective; March 18, 2004, effective June 16, 2004; July 8, 2010, effective in 60 days [September 6, 2010].

Explanatory Comment—1983

New Forms.

Four new forms have been added to the rules to promote uniformity of practice. The praecipe to transmit record prescribed by Rule 1920.73 and the motion for appointment of master prescribed by Rule 1920.74 require specified information to facilitate the court's disposition of the matter.

Rule 1920.75 prescribes a form of inventory and appraisement. The form contains the information required by Rule 1920.33(a). In addition, the form contains a list of assets which are commonly found in cases involving distribution of property as well as a list of liabilities. Assets and liabilities involved in a particular case must be checked on the lists. The lists will serve as a convenient guide for the attorney preparing the inventory and appraisement.

The final form is a decree prescribed by Rule 1920.76. The language of the decree has been shortened, simplified and modernized. The second paragraph of the decree preserves the rights of the parties with respect to claims made but not disposed of prior to the entry of the final decree. The claims so preserved must be specifically set forth in the decree.

Explanatory Comment—1988

Rule 1920.73 is amended by adding new subdivision (a) which prescribes two form notices of intention to request entry of divorce decree. The first form of notice, contained in paragraph (a)(1), is directed to the defendant's attorney of record. If an attorney has entered an appearance on behalf of the defendant, this shorter form of notice is given only to the attorney. Paragraph (a)(2) provides a more detailed notice directed to the defendant himself when there is no attorney of record. In this instance, the notice advises the unrepresented defendant of the possible consequences of his failure to act promptly with respect to contesting the divorce or asserting economic claims. In addition, attached to the notice to an unrepresented defendant will be the form counteraffidavit required by Rule 1920.42(c)(2) and contained in Rule 1920.72(d) so that a defendant who wishes to oppose the divorce or to assert economic claims at this time readily may do so.

Rule 1920.74   Form of Motion for Appointment of Master. Order

(a) The motion for appointment of a master shall be substantially in the following form:

(Caption)

MOTION FOR APPOINTMENT OF MASTER

_____**(Plaintiff) (Defendant), moves the court to appoint a master with respect to the following claims:**

( ) Divorce   ( ) **Division of Marital Property**

( ) Annulment   ( ) **Counsel Fees**

( ) Alimony   ( ) **Cost and Expenses**

and in support of the motion states:

Rule 1920.74 ACTIONS OF DIVORCE, ANNULMENT

(1) Discovery (is) (is not) complete as to the claim(s) for which the appointment of a master is requested.

(2) The non-moving party (has) (has not) appeared in the action (personally) (by his attorney, _____ , Esquire).

(3) The statutory ground(s) for divorce (is) (are) _____ .

(4) Delete the inapplicable paragraph(s):

   (a) The action is not contested.

   (b) An agreement has been reached with respect to the following claims: _____

   (c) The action is contested with respect to the following claims: _____ .

(5) The action (involves) (does not involve) complex issues of law or fact.

(6) The hearing is expected to take _____ (hours) (days).

(7) Additional information, if any, relevant to the motion: _____

Date: _____

                                                  Attorney for (Plaintiff)
                                                              (Defendant)

(b) The order appointing a master shall be substantially in the following form:

(Caption)

ORDER APPOINTING MASTER

AND NOW, _____, 20_____, _____, Esquire, is appointed master with respect to the following claims: _____.

BY THE COURT:
_____

MOVING PARTY	NON-MOVING PARTY
Name:	Name:s
Attorney's Name:	Attorney's Name:
Attorney's Address:	Attorney's Address:
Attorney's Telephone #:	Attorney's Telephone #:
Attorney's E-Mail:	Attorney's E-Mail:

Pa. R.C.P. Rule 1920.75

Party's Address and Telephone # if not represented by counsel:

Party's Address and Telephone # if not represented by counsel:

Note: It is within the discretion of the court to determine the point at which a master should be appointed in a case. The court may appoint a master to deal with discovery issues.

Adopted January 28, 1983, effective July 1, 1983 and applied to pending actions; amended October 31, 2002, effective immediately; July 30, 2018, effective January 1, 2019.

Explanatory Comment—1983

See Explanatory Comment following Rule 1920.73.

Rule 1920.75. Form of Inventory

The inventory required by Pa.R.C.P. No. 1920.33(a) shall be substantially in the following form:

(Caption)
INVENTORY
OF

(Plaintiff) (Defendant) files the following inventory of all property owned or possessed by either party at the date of separation and all property transferred within the preceding three years.

(Plaintiff) (Defendant) verifies that the statements made in this inventory are true and correct. (Plaintiff) (Defendant) understands that false statements herein are made subject to the penalties of 18 Pa.C.S. § 4904 relating to unsworn falsification to authorities.

(Plaintiff) (Defendant)

ASSETS OF PARTIES

(Plaintiff) (Defendant) marks on the list below those items applicable to the case at bar and itemizes the assets on the following pages.

( ) 1. Real property
( ) 2. Motor vehicles
( ) 3. Stocks, bonds, securities and options
( ) 4. Certificates of deposit
( ) 5. Checking accounts, cash
( ) 6. Savings accounts, money market and savings certificates
( ) 7. Contents of safe deposit boxes
( ) 8. Trusts
( ) 9. Life insurance policies (indicate face value, cash surrender value and current beneficiaries)
( ) 10. Annuities
( ) 11. Gifts

Rule 1920.75   ACTIONS OF DIVORCE, ANNULMENT

( ) 12. Inheritances
( ) 13. Patents, copyrights, inventions, royalties
( ) 14. Personal property outside the home
( ) 15. Business (list all owners, including percentage of ownership, and officer/director positions held by a party with company)
( ) 16. Employment termination benefits—severance pay, worker's compensation claim/award
( ) 17. Profit sharing plans
( ) 18. Pension plans (indicate employee contribution and date plan vests)
( ) 19. Retirement plans, Individual Retirement Accounts
( ) 20. Disability payments
( ) 21. Litigation claims (matured and unmatured)
( ) 22. Military/V.A. benefits
( ) 23. Education benefits
( ) 24. Accounts receivable, including loans and mortgages payable to a party
( ) 25. Household furnishings and personalty (include as a total category and attach itemized list if distribution of such assets is in dispute)
( ) 26. Other

MARITAL PROPERTY

(Plaintiff) (Defendant) lists all marital property in which either or both spouses have a legal or equitable interest individually or with any other person as of the date of separation:

Item Number	Description of Property	Names of all Owners	Estimated Value at Date of Separation

NON-MARITAL PROPERTY

(Plaintiff) (Defendant) lists all property in which a spouse has a legal or equitable interest which is claimed to be excluded from marital property:

Item Number	Description of Property	Reason for Exclusion	Estimated Value at Date of Marriage	Estimated Value at Date of Separation

PROPERTY TRANSFERRED

Item Number	Description of Property	Date of Transfer	Consideration	Person to Whom Transferred	Estimated Value at Date of Separation

LIABILITIES

Item Number	Description of Property	Names of all Creditors	Names of all Debtors	Estimated Amount at Date of Separation

Note: *See* Pa.R.C.P. No. 1930.1(b). This rule may require attorneys or unrepresented parties to file confidential documents and documents containing confidential information that are subject to the *Case Records Public Access Policy of the Unified Judicial System of Pennsylvania: Case Records of the Appellate and Trial Courts*.

Adopted Jan. 28, 1983, effective July 1, 1983. Amended May 17, 1991, effective July 1, 1991; May 6, 2015, effective July 1, 2015; Jan. 5, 2018, effective Jan. 6, 2018; June 1, 2018, effective July 1, 2018.

Explanatory Comment—1983

See Explanatory Comment following Rule 1920.73.

Rule 1920.76 Form of Divorce Decree

The decree of divorce shall be substantially in the following form:

(Caption)

DECREE

AND NOW, _____, 19_____, it is ordered and decreed that _____, plaintiff, and _____, defendant, are divorced from the bonds of matrimony.

The court retains jurisdiction of any claims raised by the parties to this action for which a final order has not yet been entered.

Any existing spousal support order shall hereafter be deemed an order for alimony pendente lite if any economic claims remain pending.

BY THE COURT:

_____

J.

Official Note: The court may add any other provisions which it deems necessary.

Adopted Jan. 28, 1983, effective July 1, 1983 and applied to pending actions. Amended Nov. 7, 1988, effective Jan. 1, 1989; Dec. 2, 1994, effective March 1, 1995.

Explanatory Comment—1988

The amendment to Rule 1920.76 revises the form of divorce decree so that the court will no longer be required to list the claims as to which a final order has not been entered at the time of entry of the final divorce decree. Rather, the decree will simply state that the court retain jurisdiction over unresolved issues.

Rules 1920.77 to 1920.90 [Blank]

Rule 1920.91 Suspension of Acts of Assembly

The following Acts of Assembly are suspended insofar as they apply to the practice and procedure in actions for divorce or annulment of marriage to the extent hereinafter set forth:

(1) **Section 3104(e) of the Domestic Relations Code, 23 Pa.C.S. § 3104(e), absolutely;**

Official Note: Suspended Section 3104(e) of the Divorce Code prescribes venue in actions of divorce or for annulment of marriage. Venue in such actions is prescribed by Rule of Civil Procedure 1920.2.

(2) **Section 3505(b) of the Domestic Relations Code, 23 Pa.C.S. § 3505(b), absolutely;**

Note: Suspended Section 3505(b) of the Divorce Code requires the submission to the court of an inventory and appraisement of property. Rule of Civil Procedure 1920.33(a) supplants this provision by requiring parties seeking the distribution of property to file an inventory while subdivision (b) of the rule requires the filing of a pre-trial statement.

(3) **Section 3321 of the Domestic Relations Code, 23 Pa.C.S. § 3321, insofar as it prohibits the appointment of masters in partial custody or visitation matters.**

Official Note: Suspended Section 3321 of the Divorce Code states that the court may appoint a master to hear testimony on all issues relating to a divorce except custody or paternity.

(4) **And all other Acts or parts of Acts of Assembly inconsistent with these rules to the extent of such inconsistency.**

Adopted June 27, 1980, effective July 1, 1980. Amended Feb. 7, 1989, effective July 1, 1989; May 17, 1991, effective July 1, 1991; July 15, 1994, effective Jan. 1, 1995; May 5, 1997, effective July 1, 1997.

Explantory Comment—1989

Rule 1920.91 is amended to suspend two provisions of the Act of February 12, 1988, No. 13, which amended the Divorce Code. The suspended provisions provided for venue and discovery in actions for divorce or annulment. Venue in actions of divorce or for annulment of marriage is prescribed by Rule 1920.2, while discovery in these actions is prescribed by Rule 1920.22.

[See Explanatory Comment—1991 following Rule 1920.31]

Rule 1920.92 Effective Date. Pending Actions

These rules shall become effective July 1, 1980. They shall not affect any suit or action pending on that date, but the case may be proceeded with and concluded under the rules in existence when such suit or action was instituted notwithstanding their rescission by this order, unless, upon application granted, the court orders that the action proceed under the Divorce Code and these rules.

Adopted June 27, 1980, effective July 1, 1980.

VI. Rules Relating to Domestic Relations Matters Generally

(Amended Through April, 2019)

Rules 1930.1–1931

RULE

1930.1	Form of Caption. Confidential Information and Confidential Documents. Certification
1930.2	No Post-Trial Practice. Motions for Reconsideration.
1930.3	Testimony by Electronic Means.
1930.4	Service of Original Process in Domestic Relations Matters.
1930.5	Discovery in Domestic Relations Matters.
1930.6	Paternity Actions. Scope. Venue. Commencement of Action.
1930.7	Status Conference.
1930.8	Self-Represented Party.
1930.9	Family Court Forms.
1931	Family Court Rules.

Rule 1930.1 Form of Caption. Confidential Information and Confidential Documents. Certification

(a) The form of the caption in all domestic relations matters shall be substantially in the following form:

In the Court of Common Pleas of _____ County, Pennsylvania

A. Litigant,
           Plaintiff   )
vs.   ) No. (Docket Number)
B. Litigant,
           Defendant)

(Title of Pleading)

> **Note:** As domestic relations matters are no longer quasi-criminal, the phrase "Commonwealth ex rel." shall not be used in the caption of any domestic relations matter.

(b) Unless public access is otherwise constrained by applicable authority, any attorney, or any party if unrepresented, who files a document pursuant to these rules with the prothonotary's office shall comply with the requirements of Sections 7.0 and 8.0 of the Case Records *Public Access Policy of the Unified Judicial System of Pennsylvania* (Policy) including a certification of compliance with the Policy and, as necessary, a Confidential Information Form, unless otherwise specified by rule or order of court, or a Confidential Document Form in accordance with the Policy.

> **Note:** Applicable authority includes but is not limited to statute, procedural rule, or court order. The Case Records *Public Access Policy of the Unified Judicial System of Pennsylvania* (Policy) can be found on the website of the Supreme Court of Pennsylvania at http://www.pacourts.us/public-records. Sections 7.0(D) and 8.0(D) of the Policy provide that the certification shall be in substantially the following form:

I certify that this filing complies with the provisions of the Case Records *Public Access Policy of the Unified Judicial System of Pennsylvania* that require filing confidential information and documents differently than non-confidential information and documents.

The Confidential Information Form and the Confidential Document Form can be found at http://www.pacourts.us/public-records. In lieu of the Confidential Information Form, Section 7.0(C) of the Policy provides for a court to adopt a rule or order permitting the filing of a document in two versions, a "Redacted Version" and an "Unredacted Version."

Adopted Dec. 2, 1994, effective March 1, 1995. Amended Jan. 5, 2018, effective Jan. 6, 2018; June 1, 2018, effective July 1, 2018.

Rule 1930.2 No Post–Trial Practice. Motions for Reconsideration

(a) There shall be no motions for post-trial relief in any domestic relations matter, including Protection of Victims of Sexual Violence or Intimidation matters.

Note: See Pa.R.C.P. No. 1957.

(b) A party aggrieved by the decision of the court may file a motion for reconsideration in accordance with Pa.R.A.P 1701(b)(3). If the court does not grant the motion for reconsideration within the time permitted, the time for filing a notice of appeal will run as if the motion for reconsideration had never been presented to the court.

Note: Pennsylvania Rule of Appellate Procedure 903 states that the Notice of Appeal shall be filed within 30 days after the entry of the order from which the appeal is taken, except as otherwise set forth in that rule.

(c) The court shall render its reconsidered decision within 120 days of the date the motion for reconsideration is granted, except as set forth in subdivision (e). If the court's decision is not rendered within 120 days, the motion shall be deemed denied.

(d) If the court does not enter a reconsidered decision within 120 days, the time for filing a notice of appeal will begin to run anew from the date of entry of the reconsidered decision or from the 121st day after the motion for reconsideration was granted.

(e) If the court grants the motion for reconsideration and files its order within the 30–day appeal period, the court may issue an order during the applicable 120–day period directing that additional testimony be taken. If the court issues an order for additional testimony, the reconsidered decision need not be rendered within 120 days, and the time for filing a notice of appeal will run from the date the reconsidered decision is rendered.

[Adopted March 30, 1994, effective July 1, 1994. Amended October 6, 2016, eff. January 1, 2017.]

Explanatory Comment—1994

All post-trial practice in domestic relations cases is abolished by this rule. In order to allow the trial court to take a second look at a case before it is appealed to the Superior Court, the rule allows a request for reconsideration to be filed in accordance with Appellate Rule 1701(b)(3). The aim of these rules is to ensure that domestic cases are moved as quickly as possible toward a final resolution, and thus the requirement of Appellate Rule 1701 that the motion for reconsideration be filed and granted within the thirty day appeal period is adopted here. If the motion for reconsideration is granted, the time for filing the notice of appeal is tolled. However, if it is not granted, there is no extension of the appeal period, so that the matter proceeds without delay.

If the court grants the motion for reconsideration, it has 120 days in which to enter a reconsidered decision. The appeal period begins to run anew upon the entry of the reconsidered decision, or on the 121st day if the decision is not entered within the 120 day period. The time limit does not apply where the court determines that it is necessary to take additional testimony. In that event, the time for filing a notice of appeal begins to run anew when the reconsidered decision is entered.

Rule 1930.3 Testimony by Electronic Means

With the approval of the court upon good cause shown, a party or witness may be deposed or testify by telephone, audiovisual or other electronic means at a designated location in all domestic relations matters.

Adopted Dec. 8, 1994, effective July 1, 1995. Amended May 31, 2000, effective July 1, 2000.

Explanatory Comment—2000

This rule is amended to implement 23 Pa.C.S. § 4342(j) which sets forth the various electronic methods that may be used to take testimony in an action for support. It also extends these methods to all domestic relations matters.

Rule 1930.4. Service of Original Process in Domestic Relations Matters

(a) *Persons Who May Serve.* Original process in all domestic relations matters, including Protection of Victims of Sexual Violence or Intimidation matters, may be served by the sheriff or a competent adult:

(1) by handing a copy to the defendant;

(2) by handing a copy:

(i) at the residence of the defendant to an adult member of the family with whom the defendant resides; but if no adult member of the family is found, then to an adult person in charge of such residence;

(ii) at the residence of the defendant to the clerk or manager of the hotel, inn, apartment house, boarding house or other place of lodging at which the defendant resides;

(iii) at any office or usual place of business of the defendant to the defendant's agent or to the person for the time being in charge; or

(3) pursuant to special order of court.

Note: See Pa.R.C.P. No. 76 for the definition of "competent adult." Original process served on an incarcerated person in a domestic relations action must also include notice of any hearing in such action and specific notice of the incarcerated individual's right to apply to the court for a writ of habeas corpus ad testificandum to enable him or her to participate in the hearing. The writ is available if an incarcerated individual wishes to testify as provided by statute or rule, or if the incarcerated individual's testimony is sought by another. Vanaman v. Cowgill, 526 A.2d 1226 (Pa. Super. 1987). See 23

Pa.C.S. § 4342(j) and Pa.R.C.P. No. 1930.3. In determining whether a writ of habeas corpus ad testificandum should be issued, a court must weigh the factors set forth in Salemo v. Salemo, 554 A.2d 563 (Pa. Super. 1989).

(b) *Service in Protection From Abuse and Protection of Victims of Sexual Violence or Intimidation Matters.* **If personal service cannot be completed within 48 hours after a Protection From Abuse or a Protection of Victims of Sexual Violence or Intimidation petition is filed, the court may authorize alternative service by special order as set forth in subdivision (a)(3), including, but not limited to, service by mail pursuant to subdivision (c) of this rule.**

(c) *Service by Mail.*

(1) **Except in Protection from Abuse and Protection of Victims of Sexual Violence or Intimidation matters, original process in all domestic relations matters may be served by mailing the original process, a notice or order to appear, if required, and other orders or documents, as necessary, to the defendant's last known address by both regular and certified mail.**

(i) **Delivery of the certified mail shall be restricted to the addressee only and a return receipt shall be requested.**

(ii) **If the certified mail is refused by the defendant, but the regular mail is not returned within 15 days, service may be deemed complete.**

(iii) **If the mail is returned with notation by the postal authorities that it was unclaimed, service shall be made by another means pursuant to these rules.**

(2) **In Protection from Abuse and Protection of Victims of Sexual Violence or Intimidation matters, original process may be served by mail pursuant to this rule, if authorized by the court under subdivision (a)(3).**

Note: Nothing in this rule is intended to preclude a judicial district from utilizing the United States Postal Service's return receipt electronic option, or any similar service that electronically provides a return receipt, when using certified mail, return receipt requested.

(d) *Acceptance of Service.* **In lieu of service pursuant to this rule, the defendant or the defendant's authorized agent may accept service of original process as set forth in Pa.R.C.P. No. 402(b).**

(e) *Service Within the Commonwealth.* **Original process shall be served on a defendant located within the Commonwealth within 30 days of the filing of the original process.**

(f) *Service Outside of the Commonwealth.* **Original process shall be served on a defendant located outside the Commonwealth within 90 days of the filing of the original process:**

(1) **by any means authorized by this rule;**

(2) **in the manner provided by the law of the jurisdiction in which defendant will be served;**

(3) **in the manner provided by treaty; or**

(4) **as directed by the foreign authority in response to a letter rogatory or request.**

In Protection from Abuse matters, a defendant outside of the Commonwealth must be personally served with original process Service may be made either in accordance with subdivisions (a) and (b) governing personal service or as provided for by the law in the jurisdiction where the defendant resides or is located. If personal service cannot be completed within 48 hours after

the filing of the original process, service outside of the Commonwealth may be made by other means authorized by this rule.

   Note: Sections 5323 and 5329(2) of the Judicial Code, 42 Pa.C.S. §§ 5323 and 5329(2), provide additional alternative procedures for service outside the Commonwealth. For Protection from Abuse matters, personal service outside of the Commonwealth must be attempted first before service can be made by certified and regular mail or by other means prescribed in subsection (f) for out-of-state service.

   (g) *Reinstatement of Original Process.* If service is not made as required by subdivision (e) or (f), the prothonotary shall reinstate the original process upon praecipe accompanied by the original process, or praecipe indicating that the original process has been lost or destroyed accompanied by a substituted original process.

   (1) Original process may be reinstated at any time and any number of times. A new party defendant may be named in a reinstated original process.

   (2) Reinstated original process shall be served as required by subdivision (e) or (f).

   (h) Proof of Service.
     (1) Proof of service shall state:
       (i) the date and time of service;
       (ii) the place of service;
       (iii) the manner in which service was made;
       (iv) the identity of the person served; and
       (v) other facts necessary for the court to determine whether proper service has been made.
     (2) Original Process Served.
       (i) Personal Service Pursuant to Subdivision (a).
         (A) The person serving the original process shall complete a proof of service.
         (B) If a person other than a sheriff serves the original process, the proof of service shall be by an affidavit.
         (C) The proof of service shall be filed in the appropriate filing office within 10 days of the date of service.
       (ii) Service by Mail Pursuant to Subdivision (c).
         (A) Proof of service by mail shall be by an affidavit that includes the certified mail return receipt signed by the defendant except as set forth in (B).
         (B) If the defendant has refused to accept the certified mail, the proof of service shall include the returned envelope with the notation that the defendant refused to accept delivery and an affidavit stating that the regular mail was not returned within 15 days after mailing.
         (C) The proof of service shall be filed in the appropriate filing office within 10 days of the date the defendant signed the certified mail return re-ceipt or after the passage of time set forth in subdivision (c)(1)(ii).
       (iii) Acceptance of Service Pursuant to Subdivision (d).
         (A) If the defendant or the defendant's authorized agent accepts service of the original process as set forth in subdivision (d), the defendant or the defendant's authorized agent shall sign an Acceptance of Service.
         (B) The Acceptance of Service shall be filed in the appropriate filing office within 10 days of accepting service.

Official Note: See Pa.R.C.P. No. 402(b) for the prescribed form document.

(3) **Original Process Not Served.**

(i) **If the defendant cannot be served within the time allowed in subdivision (e) or (f), the person attempting service shall complete a proof of no service promptly.**

(ii) **If a person other than a sheriff attempts service of the original process, the proof of no service shall be by an affidavit stating with particularity the efforts made to effect service.**

(iii) **The proof of no service shall be filed in the appropriate filing office within 10 days of the expiration of time allowed for service in subdivision (e) or (f).**

Official Note: See Pa.R.C.P. No. 1910.4(a). The Domestic Relations Section is the filing office for child support, spousal support and alimony pendente lite cases.

See Pennsylvania Rule of Professional Conduct 7.3(b)(4). The timing of an attorney's solicitation of a prospective client in actions governed by the Family Court Rules, *see* Pa.R.C.P. No. 1931(a), and actions pursuant to the Protection of Victims of Sexual Violence or Intimidation Act, *see* 42 Pa.C.S. §§ 62A03—62A20, is restricted until proof of service appears on the docket.

(i) *Appearance at Hearing or Conference.* **A party appearing for the hearing or conference will be deemed to have been served.**

Adopted Oct. 2, 1995, effective Jan. 1, 1996. Amended March 9, 1998, effective July 1, 1998; May 14, 1999, effective July 1, 1999; Oct. 11, 2002, imd. effective; Aug. 8, 2006, imd. effective; March 4, 2014, effective April 3, 2014; March 4, 2015, effective April 3, 2015; October 6, 2016, effective January 1, 2017; September 12, 2018, effective September 28, 2018.

Explanatory Comment—1995

This new rule replaces the numerous rules which previously governed service of process in domestic relations matters.

Rule 1930.5 Discovery in Domestic Relations Matters

(a) **There shall be no discovery in a simple support, custody, Protection from Abuse, or Protection of Victims of Sexual Violence or Intimidation proceedings unless authorized by order of court.**

(b) **Discovery shall be available without leave of court in accordance with Pa.R.C.P. Nos. 4001- 4025 in alimony, equitable distribution, counsel fee and expense, and complex support proceedings.**

Adopted May 5, 1997, effective July 1, 1997; amended March 9, 1998, effective July 1, 1998, March 2, 2000, effective immediately; June 5, 2001, effective immediately; October 6, 2016, effective January 1, 2017.

Explanatory Comment—2000

Subdivision (b) has been amended to clarify that the adjective "complex" applies only to a support proceeding.

Explanatory Comment—1997

Whether a support case is complex is to be determined by motion before the court for a separate listing pursuant to Rules 1910.11(j)(1) and 1910.12(c)(1). It is not necessary, however, to have a case listed separately on grounds of complexity of factual or legal issues in order to engage in discovery. If discovery is needed in a support case which does not require a separate listing, the court should grant leave to engage in it.

Rule 1930.6   Paternity Actions. Scope. Venue. Commencement of Actions

(a)   This rule shall govern the procedure by which a putative father may initiate a civil action to establish paternity and seek genetic testing. Such an action shall not be permitted if an order already has been entered as to the paternity, custody, or support of the child, or if a support or custody action to which the putative father is a party is pending.

(b)   An action may be brought only in the county in which the defendant or the child(ren) reside.

(c)   An action shall be commenced by filing a verified complaint to establish paternity and for genetic testing substantially in the form set forth in subdivision (1). The complaint shall have as its first page the Notice of Hearing and Order set forth in subdivision (2).

Note: See Pa.R.C.P. No. 1930.1(b). This rule may require attorneys or unrepresented parties to file confidential documents and documents containing confidential information that are subject to the Case Records *Public Access Policy of the Unified Judicial System of Pennsylvania.*

(1)   The complaint filed in a civil action to establish paternity shall be substantially in the following form:

(Caption)

COMPLAINT TO ESTABLISH PATERNITY AND FOR
GENETIC TESTING

Plaintiff, _____, requests genetic testing to establish paternity pursuant to 23 Pa. C.S. § 4343 and in support of that request states that:

1. Plaintiff is an adult individual who resides at _____

2. Defendant is an adult individual who resides at

3. Defendant is the natural mother and Plaintiff believes that he may be the natural father of the following child(ren):

Child's Name   Date of Birth

4. The above-named children reside at the following address with the following individuals:

Address   Person(s) Living with Child   Relationship to Child

Rule 1930.6   **DOMESTIC RELATIONS MATTERS**

    5. Defendant was/was not married at the time the child(ren) was/were conceived or born.

    6. Defendant is/is not now married. If married, spouse's name: _____

---

    7. There is/is not a custody, support or other action involving the paternity of the above-named child(ren) now pending in any jurisdiction. Identify any such actions by caption and docket number _____

    8. There has/has not been a determination by any court as to the paternity of the child(ren) in any prior support, custody, divorce or any other action. If so, identify the action by caption and docket number _____

    9. Plaintiff agrees to pay all costs associated with genetic testing directly to the testing facility in accordance with the procedures established by that facility.

_____Wherefore, Plaintiff requests that the court order Defendant to submit to genetic testing and to make the child(ren) available for genetic testing.

  I verify that the statements made in this complaint are true and correct to the best of my knowledge, information and belief. I understand that false statements herein are made subject to the penalties of 18 Pa. C.S. § 4904 relating to unsworn falsification to authorities.

                                      _____
                                                Petitioner

    (2) The Notice of Hearing and Order required by this rule shall be substantially in the following form:

                                                  (Caption)

                                  NOTICE OF HEARING AND ORDER

YOU HAVE BEEN SUED IN COURT. If you wish to defend against the claims set forth in the following papers, you must appear at the hearing scheduled below. If you fail to do so, the case may proceed against you and a final order may be entered against you granting the relief requested by the plaintiff.

Plaintiff and Defendant are directed to appear on the _____ day of _____, 20__ at __.m. in courtroom _____ for a hearing on Plaintiff's request for genetic testing. If you fail to appear as ordered, the court may enter an order in your absence requiring you and your child(ren) to submit to genetic tests.

YOU SHOULD TAKE THIS PAPER TO YOUR LAWYER AT ONCE. IF YOU DO NOT HAVE A LAWYER, GO TO OR TELEPHONE THE OFFICE SET FORTH BELOW. THIS OFFICE CAN PROVIDE YOU WITH INFORMATION ABOUT HIRING A LAWYER. IF YOU CANNOT AFFORD TO HIRE A LAWYER, THIS OFFICE MAY BE ABLE TO PROVIDE YOU WITH INFORMATION ABOUT AGENCIES THAT MAY OFFER LEGAL SERVICES TO ELIGIBLE PERSONS AT A REDUCED FEE OR NO FEE.

                (name)
            _____

                (address)
            _____

                (telephone number)
            _____

Americans with Disabilities Act of 1990

The Court of Common Pleas of _____ County is required by law to comply with the Americans with Disabilities Act of 1990. For information about accessible facilities and reasonable accommodations available to disabled individuals having business before the court, please contact our office. All arrangements must be made at least 72 hours prior to any hearing or business before the court. You must attend the scheduled conference or hearing.

(d) Service. Service of original process and proof of service in a civil action to establish paternity shall be in accordance with Rule 1930.4.

(e) At the hearing, the judge will determine whether or not the plaintiff is legally entitled to genetic testing and, if so, will issue an order directing the defendant and the child(ren) to submit to genetic testing, the cost of which shall be borne by the plaintiff.

Adopted June 15, 2001, imd. effective. Amended June 24, 2002, imd. effective; March 18, 2004, effective June 16, 2004; Jan. 5, 2018, effective Jan. 6, 2018; June 1, 2018, effective July 1, 2018.

Explanatory Comment—2001

Where the paternity of a child born out-of-wedlock is disputed, 23 Pa.C.S. § 4343 provides that the court shall make the determination of paternity in a civil action without a jury. That statutory provision also states, "A putative father may not be prohibited from initiating a civil action to establish paternity." Rule 1930.6 governs the procedures by which a putative father may initiate a civil action to establish paternity outside the context of a support or custody proceeding.

Rule 1930.7. Status Conference

At any time in the proceedings, the court, the court's designee or the master, *sua sponte* or upon application of any party, may hold a status conference, in person or by any other means permitted by these rules, with counsel or with counsel and the parties in order to review the case status and expedite the litigation.

Adopted August 18, 2006, effective immediately.

Rule 1930.8. Self-Represented Party

(a) A party representing himself or herself shall enter a written appearance which shall state an address, which need not be his or her home address, where the party agrees that pleadings and other legal papers may be served, and a telephone number through which the party may be contacted. The entry of appearance may include a facsimile number as provided by Pa.R.C.P. No. 1012.

(b) A self-represented party is under a continuing obligation to provide current contact information to the court, to other self-represented parties, and to attorneys of record.

(c) When a party has an attorney of record, the party may assert his or her self-representation by:

(1) Filing a written entry of appearance and directing the prothonotary/court clerk to remove the name of his or her counsel of record with contemporaneous notice to said counsel, or

(2) Filing an entry of appearance with the withdrawal of appearance signed by his or her attorney of record.

(d) The self-represented party shall provide a copy of the entry of appearance to all self-represented parties and attorneys of record.

(e) The assertion of self-representation shall not delay any stage of the proceeding.

(f) The entry of appearance of a self-represented party shall be substantially in the following form:

[CAPTION]
ENTRY OF APPEARANCE OF SELF-REPRESENTED PARTY
PURSUANT TO Pa.R.C.P. No. 1930.8

I, _____, Plaintiff or Defendant (circle one), represent myself in the within action.

REMOVAL OR WITHDRAWAL OF COUNSEL OF RECORD (If Applicable)

__ Remove _____, Esq., as my attorney of record.

__ Withdraw my appearance for the filing party.

Esq. (Print name)   ID#

SIGNATURE   DATE:

I understand that I am under a continuing obligation to provide current contact information to the court, to other self-represented parties, and to attorneys of record.

All pleadings and legal papers can be served on me at the address listed below, which may or may not be my home address pursuant to Rule 1930.8:

Print Name

Signature   Telephone number

Address   FAX

City, State, Zip Code   Date

THE PARTY FILING THIS ENTRY OF APPEARANCE MUST PROVIDE NOTICE BY SENDING A COPY TO ALL PARTIES AND ATTORNEYS, INCLUDING THE ATTORNEY REMOVED FROM THE CASE.

Note: This form cannot be used when filing for support through the Department of Public Welfare Bureau of Child Support Enforcement's E-Services program. An entry of appearance form is available on the E-Services site for individuals filing through that program.

Adopted June 5, 2013, effective July 5, 2013. Amended March 4, 2015, effective April 3, 2015.

Explanatory Comment—2013

Withdrawal of appearance by counsel of record without the entry of appearance by a self-represented party is governed by Pa.R.C.P. No. 1012. Service of original process in domestic relations matters is governed by Pa.R.C.P. No. 1930.4. Service of legal papers other than original process is governed by Pa.R.C.P. No. 440.

Rule 1930.9. Family Court Forms.

Forms adopted by the Supreme Court of Pennsylvania and included in the Pennsylvania Rules of Civil Procedure relating to the practice and procedure of domestic relations matters shall be accepted for filing in all jurisdictions. Some of these forms may be maintained for public access at a website designated by the Supreme Court of Pennsylvania.

> **Official Note:** Pa.R.C.P. No. 205.2 provides: "No pleading or other legal paper that complies with the Pennsylvania Rules of Civil Procedure shall be refused for filing by the prothonotary based on a requirement of a local rule of civil procedure or judicial administration . . ."

Adopted June 16, 2014, effective July 16, 2014.

Rule 1931. Family Court Rules.

(a) Actions Governed by These Rules:

(1) Divorce, Annulment, Dissolution of Marriage.

(i) Equitable Distribution.

(ii) Alimony/Alimony Pendente Lite.

(iii) Counsel Fees, Costs and Expenses.

(2) Child Custody.

(i) Legal Custody.

(ii) Physical Custody.

(iii) Partial Custody/Visitation.

(3) Support.

(i) Child Support.

(ii) Spousal Support.

(iii) Modification and Enforcement.

(4) Paternity.

(5) Protection From Abuse.

(b) Commencement of Action.

(1) *Unified Family Court Docketing.* All actions under these Family Court Rules which involve identical parties shall be entered on the court's docket under the same primary case number. Additional letters or numbers may be added parenthetically to specify the type of action, judge assigned or other identifying information.

(2) *Custody Agreements.* If, at a support proceeding, it appears that resolution of custody issues will facilitate compliance with the child support order, the conference officer, hearing officer or master may provide the parties with a form custody complaint and form custody agreement, along with information as to where to file the completed documents, the filing fee and how to contact the lawyers referral service. The support conference officer, hearing officer or master shall not participate in custody negotiations, preparation of the forms or provide legal advice.

(c) Consolidation of Family Court Matters.

(1) *General Rule.* Two or more actions under these Family Court Rules involving the same parties and common questions of law and/or fact shall be consolidated for hearing or trial unless the court determines that it is inappropriate or impractical to do so.

(2) *Trial Continuity.* Trials before a judge or hearings before a master shall be scheduled to be heard on consecutive days or within a ten (10) day period. If not completed within the time allotted, the trial or hearing shall be concluded within ninety (90) days of the date of the commencement of the trial or hearing, unless a shorter time frame is required by statute or another procedural rule.

(3) *Prompt Decisions.*

(i) Except as provided in subdivision (ii) below, in any matter brought under these Family Court Rules, a decision by a conference officer, master or judge shall be entered, filed and served upon counsel for the parties, or any party not represented by counsel, not later than thirty (30) days after the conference, hearing or trial concludes, unless a shorter time frame is required by statute or another procedural rule.

(ii) The time for entering and filing a decision may be extended if, within thirty (30) days of the conclusion of the conference, hearing or trial, the court extends the date for such decision by order entered of record showing good cause for the extension. In no event shall an extension delay entry of the decision more than sixty (60) days after the conclusion of the conference, hearing or trial.

(d) Continuing Education for Family Court Personnel.

(1) *Program Development.* Courses of instruction that include, at a minimum, the following topics shall be developed or approved by the Administrative Office of Pennsylvania Courts (AOPC):

(i) The substantive law and procedural aspects of the areas of law governed by these Family Court Rules;

(ii) Domestic violence;

(iii) Child development;

(iv) Family dynamics;

(v) Addictions and treatments;

(vi) Asset valuation;

(vii) Community resources.

(2) *Initial Training.* Within one (1) year of assignment to cases governed by these Family Court Rules, each master, hearing officer, conciliator, mediator and other court personnel designated by the president or administrative judge of each judicial district shall successfully complete the coursework developed or approved by the AOPC.

(3) *Continuing Education.* Each master, hearing officer, conciliator, mediator and other court personnel designated by the president or administrative judge who is assigned to cases governed by these Family Court Rules shall successfully complete six (6) hours of continuing education developed or approved by the AOPC each calendar year following the calendar year in which the initial training was completed.

(4) *Compliance.* The AOPC shall monitor compliance with the educational requirements of this rule.

Explanatory Comment 2002

This new rule is suspended in all judicial districts except the First (Philadelphia), Fifth (Allegheny County), Twenty-third (Berks County) and Forty-fifth (Lackawanna County) Judicial Districts until further order of the Supreme Court of Pennsylvania.

(December 17, 2002, effective immediately in the First, Fifth, Twenty-Third and Forty-Fifth Judicial Districts).

VII. Rules Relating to Voluntary Mediation in Custody Actions
(Amended Through April, 2019)

Rules 1940.1–1940.9

RULE

1940.1	Applicability of Rules to Mediation.
1940.2	Definitions.
1940.3	Order for Orientation Session and Mediation. Selection of Mediator.
1940.4	Minimum Qualifications of the Mediator.
1940.5	Duties of the Mediator. Role of the Mediator.
1940.6	Termination of Mediation.
1940.7	Mediator Compensation.
1940.8	Sanctions.
1940.9	Existing Mediation Programs.

Explanatory Comment—1999
Introduction

In recent years, the use of mediation as a means for alternative dispute resolution of custody and visitation cases has received widespread attention from legislators, judges, attorneys and mental health professionals. As two noted mediation experts observed: "[c]ourts are ill-equipped to mandate particular visitation schedules and custodial arrangements, the wisdom of which depend on the situations of the parents and children rather than on legal rules." Nancy G. Rogers & Craig A. McEwen, Mediation Law Policy Practice 230 (1989). Many share this frustration with the adversarial system and a growing body of research suggests that mediation may be the more satisfactory and desirable means of conflict resolution in these cases. Mediation offers more flexibility both in terms of the subject matter that may be discussed during mediation and the range of solutions available to the parties. Effective mediation also assists the parties in shaping their own framework for future discussion and resolution of conflicts that arise following separation and divorce.

In 1996, the Pennsylvania legislature amended the Divorce Code, Act No. 20-1996, § 2, codified at 23 Pa.C.S. §§ 3901-3904, to encourage local courts to establish voluntary mediation programs for divorce and custody cases. The following Rules of Civil Procedure are intended to govern custody cases only. They set forth the procedures for referring cases to mediation, minimum mediator qualifications, the duties of the mediator, the procedures for terminating mediation as well as sanctions for noncompliance with these rules. These are all areas in which statewide uniformity of practice and procedure is essential to successful mediation in Pennsylvania. These rules are flexibly designed to encourage the establishment of mediation programs.

Pursuant to 23 Pa.C.S. § 3903, the Supreme Court is directed to monitor and evaluate the overall effectiveness of mediation programs statewide. At present, the Domestic Relations Procedural Rules Committee is working on the development of uniform statewide reporting requirements and evaluation forms. Reporting is necessary to assess the overall effectiveness of mediation as an alternative to litigation and it will eventually be required. The current lack of reporting requirements, however, should not be a cause for delay in the establishment of mediation programs or the implementation of statewide mediation rules.

These rules do not address confidentiality and privilege in the context of mediation. Those issues are goverened by 42 Pa.C.S. § 5949, and the Committee concluded that to address them further in the rules would confuse rather than clarify any legal issues arising from the statutory language.

Rule 1940.1 Applicability of Rules to Mediation

The rules in this chapter shall apply to all court-established custody mediation programs and to any court-ordered mediation of individual custody cases.

Explanatory Comment—1999

23 Pa.C.S. § 3901 authorizes a court to establish a mediation program for both divorce and custody cases. At the present time, these rules apply only to court-connected mediation of custody cases because most, if not all, court-connected mediation programs that have been established for domestic relations, are limited to mediation of custody disputes. If, in the future, these programs expand to include mediation of divorce issues, these rules will be revised accordingly.

These rules do not apply to private mediation, which may be agreed to by the parties and conducted independent of the custody proceeding. They do apply, however, whenever the court refers a custody case for mediation, regardless of whether the referral is made to a formal program established and operated by the court or to a less formal arrangement between courts and mediators such as a court-approved list of mediators or, in the absence of such a list, to individual mediators appointed by the court to mediate particular cases.

Rule 1940.2 Definitions

As used in this Chapter, the following terms shall have the following meanings:

"Mediation," the confidential process by which a neutral mediator assists the parties in attempting to reach a mutually acceptable agreement on issues arising in a custody action. Mediation is not a court proceeding; rather, it is an independent, non-record proceeding in lieu of court involvement for the purpose of assisting the parties to address the child's best interest. An agreement reached by the parties must be based on the voluntary decisions of the parties and not the decision of the mediator. The agreement may resolve all or only some of the disputed issues. The parties are required to mediate in good faith but are not compelled to reach an agreement. While mediation is an alternative means of conflict resolution, it is not a substitute for the benefit of legal advice. The participants in mediation shall be limited to the parties to the custody action, primarily the child's parents and persons acting as parents. Except as provided in Pa.R.C.P. No. 1940.5(c), non-parties, including children, grandparents, and the parties' attorneys, shall not participate in the mediation.

Note: *See* Pa.R.C.P. No. 1915.1 for the definition of a person acting as a parent.

"Memorandum of Understanding," the written document prepared by a mediator that contains and summarizes the resolution reached by the parties during mediation. A Memorandum of Understanding is primarily for the benefit of the parties and is not legally binding on either party.

"Orientation Session," the initial process of educating the parties on the mediation process so that they can make an informed choice about continued participation in mediation. This process may be mandated by the court and may be structured to include either group or individual sessions. An orientation session may also include an educational program for parents and children on the process of divorce and separation and the benefits of mediation in resolving custody disputes.

Adopted Oct. 28, 1999, imd. effective. Amended Feb. 8, 2018, effective April 1, 2018.

Explanatory Comment—1999

The definitions of "orientation session" and "mediation" follow the legislative distinction between the initial orientation session, which the court may order the parties to attend, and actual mediation of the issues in dispute by the parties, which may be ordered only upon the parties' agreement. See 23 Pa.C.S. § 3901(b). The purpose of the orientation session is to educate the parties on the availability of mediation, the advantages and disadvantages of mediation, and the process of mediation so that the parties can make an informed decision about whether they wish to proceed further with mediation.

The definition of mediation set forth in this rule is not intended to restrict, expand or otherwise modify the statutory definition of mediation in 42 Pa.C.S. § 5949(c) relating to confidentiality. The statutory provision defines mediation for the purpose of determining when confidentiality and privilege attach to communications made or documents submitted during a mediation session.

Rule 1940.3 Order for Orientation Session and Mediation. Selection of Mediator

(a) Except as provided in (b), the court may order the parties to attend an orientation session at any time upon motion by a party, stipulation of the parties, or the court's own initiative.

(b) The court may not order an orientation session if a party or a child of either party is or has been the subject of domestic violence or child abuse either during the pendency of the action or within 24 months preceding the filing of the action.

Official Note: See also Rule 1940.6(a)(4) requiring termination of mediation when the mediator finds that the proceeding is "inappropriate" for mediation. The mediator has a continuing ethical obligation, consistent with Rule 1940.4(b), during the mediation to screen for abuse and to terminate the mediation in the event he or she determines that the abuse renders the case unsuitable for mediation.

(c) Following the orientation session and with the consent of the parties, the court may refer the parties to mediation. The mediation may address any issues agreed to by the parties unless limited by court order.

Explanatory Comment—1999

Rule 1940.3 describes the circumstances under which a case may be referred to mediation. Consistent with 23 Pa.C.S. § 3901(c)(2), it prohibits the referral of any case involving past or present domestic violence or abuse because of the substantial imbalance of negotiating power that exists between the parties. The parties themselves, however, may always agree to mediation. Although each court may devise its own procedures for screening these cases, screening must occur prior to referral of a case to the orientation session.

Rule 1940.4 Minimum Qualifications of the Mediator

(a) A mediator must have at least the following qualifications:

(1) a bachelor's degree and practical experience in law, psychiatry, psychology, counseling, family therapy or any comparable behavioral or social science field;

(2) successful completion of basic training in domestic and family violence or child abuse and a divorce and custody mediation program approved by the Association for Conflict Resolution, American Bar Association, American Academy of Matrimonial Lawyers or Administrative Office of Pennsylvania Courts:

(3) mediation professional liability insurance; and

(4) additional mediation training consisting of a minimum of 4 mediated cases totaling 10 hours under the supervision of a mediator who has complied with subdivisions (1) through (3) above and is approved by the court to supervise other mediators.

(b) The mediator shall comply with the ethical standards of the mediator profession as well as those of his or her primary profession and complete at least 20 hours of continuing education every two years in topics related to family mediation.

(c) A post-graduate student enrolled in a state or federally accredited educational institution in the disciplines of law, psychiatry, psychology, counseling, family therapy or any comparable behavioral or social science field may mediate with direct and actual supervision by a qualified mediator.

Explanatory Comment—1999

Mediator qualifications are a key component of any successful mediation program. This rule sets forth the *minimum* qualifications that a mediator must have in order to participate in court-connected mediation. Local courts may impose additional, more stringent qualifications.

In addition to a bachelor's degree and practical experience, a mediator must have basic training in a program approved by one of the organizations listed in subdivision (a)(2). While these are the organizations which have been recommended by mediators and other trained professionals, the Domestic Relations Procedural Rules Committee and the Administrative Office of Pennsylvania Courts may, from time to time, propose to the Court that additional organizations be added to this list. Subdivision (a)(3) of the rule requires the mediator to have his or her own professional liability insurance. Prior to mediating independently, subdivision (a)(4) of the rule requires that the mediator co-mediate at least four cases under the supervision of a court-connected mediator.

Rule 1940.5 Duties of the Mediator. Role of the Mediator

(a) As part of the orientation session, the mediator must inform the parties in writing of the following:

(1) the costs of mediation;

Note: Pa.R.C.P. No. 240 sets forth the procedures for obtaining leave to proceed *in forma pauperis* when the parties do not have the financial resources to pay the costs of litigation. This rule applies to court-connected mediation services as well, so that parties without sufficient resources may file a petition seeking a waiver or reduction of the costs of mediation.

(2) the process of mediation;

(3) that the mediator does not represent either or both of the parties;

(4) the nature and extent of any relationships with the parties and any personal, financial, or other interests that could result in a bias or conflict of interest;

(5) that mediation is not a substitute for the benefit of independent legal advice; and

(6) that the parties should obtain legal assistance for drafting any agreement or for reviewing any agreement drafted by the other party.

(b) When mediating a custody dispute, the mediator shall ensure that the parties consider fully the best interests of the child or children.

(c) With the consent of the parties, the mediator may meet with the parties' children or invite other persons to participate in the mediation.

(d) The role of the mediator is to assist the parties in identifying the issues, reducing misunderstandings, clarifying priorities, exploring areas of compromise, and finding points of agreement.

Adopted Oct. 28, 1999, imd. effective. Amended Feb. 8, 2018, effective April 1, 2018.

Explanatory Comment—1999

Rule 1940.5 sets forth the mediator's responsibilities to the parties. Subdivision (c) permits the participation of third persons with the consent of both parties. Such persons would include attorneys, other family members, mental health professionals or any other person who may be of assistance in resolving the disputed issues.

Rule 1940.6 Termination of Mediation

(a) Mediation shall terminate upon the earliest of the following circumstances to occur:

(1) a determination by the mediator that the parties are unable to reach a resolution regarding all of the issues subject to mediation;

(2) a determination by the mediator that the parties have reached a resolution regarding all of the issues subject to mediation;

(3) a determination by the mediator that the parties have reached a partial resolution and that further mediation will not resolve the remaining issues subject to mediation; or

(4) a determination by the mediator that the proceedings are inappropriate for mediation.

(b) If the parties reach a complete or partial resolution, the mediator shall, within 14 days, prepare and transmit to the parties a Memorandum of Understanding. At the request of a party, the mediator shall also transmit a copy of the Memorandum of Understanding to the party's counsel.

(c) If no resolution is reached during mediation, the mediator shall, within 14 days, report this in writing to the court, without further explanation.

Explanatory Comment—1999

This rule sets forth the circumstances for termination of mediation. Subdivision (a)(4) reflects the mediator's continuing ethical obligation, consistent with Rule

1940.4(b), to screen for domestic violence, substance abuse and any other factors, which make the case unsuitable for mediation.

Subdivision (b) requires the mediator to prepare a Memorandum of Understanding, as that term is defined in Rule 1940.2.

Reducing the parties' resolution to a binding and enforceable agreement is accomplished either by the parties' attorneys or, if not represented, the parties themselves, but in no event is the mediator responsible for drafting the parties' agreement. Court approval of the final agreement is not necessary for the purpose of enforcing it to the same extent as a court order.

Rule 1940.7 Mediator Compensation

Mediators shall be compensated for their services at a rate to be established by each court.

Explanatory Comment—1999

Mediator compensation is necessary to establish and maintain a quality mediation program. Presently, however, the absence of a statewide office for alternative dispute resolution means that each court must develop and secure its own funds for the mediation program. Because the availability of such funds varies significantly from court to court, each court may establish its own rate and method of compensation at this time, provided that the fees are structured so that all parties are assured equal access to mediation services. As Pennsylvania moves in the direction of a unified judicial system, a statewide fee schedule setting forth uniform fee standards may eventually be established for mediation compensation.

Rule 1940.8 Sanctions

On its own motion or a party's motion, the court may impose sanctions against any party or attorney who fails to comply or causes a party not to comply with these mediation rules. Sanctions may include an award of mediation costs and attorney fees, including those reasonably incurred in pursuing the sanctions.

Official Note: To the extent court orders are employed to direct parties regarding mediation, contempt proceedings may also be instituted to enforce these orders.

Rule 1940.9 Existing Mediation Programs

These rules shall not affect any existing mediation program established in any judicial district pursuant to local rule prior to October 29, 1999. However, any changes or amendments to any existing program shall be consistent with these rules.

Adopted October 27, 2000, effective immediately

Explanatory Comment—2000

This new rule is consistent with 23 Pa. C.S. § 3904.

VIII. Actions Pursuant to the Protection of Victims of Sexual Violence or Intimidation Act
(Amended Through April, 2019)

Rules 1951–1959

RULE
1951. Definitions
1952. Venue
1953. Commencement of Action
1954. Service of Original Process. Registration of Order. Service of Petition and Order. Fees
1955. Enforcement
1956. No Responsive Pleading Required
1957. Decision. Post-Trial Relief
1958. Discontinuance or Modification
1959. Forms for Use in Protection of Victims of Sexual Violence or Intimidation Actions. Notice and Hearing. Petition. Temporary Protection Order. Final Protection Order

Rule 1951. Definitions

As used in this chapter:

the Act—Act of Mar. 21, 2014, P.L. 365, No. 25 relating to the protection of victims of sexual violence or intimidation, 42 Pa.C.S. §§ 62A01–62A20.

action—a proceeding for protection from sexual violence or intimidation as defined in § 62A03 of the Act.

court—the court of common pleas.

emergency order—an order entered by a hearing officer, who is a person satisfying the definition set forth in 42 Pa.C.S. § 62A03.

fees—any fees or costs, including but not limited to the filing, issuance, registration, service or appeal of a protection action under the Act, including any foreign protection order.

temporary order or temporary protection order—an *ex parte* order entered by the court pursuant to 42 Pa.C.S. § 62A06(b).

plaintiff—an individual who applies for a protection order, either for the benefit of that individual or on behalf of another individual.

protection order or order—an order issued under the Act.

Adopted June 29, 2015, effective July 1, 2015.

Rule 1952. Venue

(a) An action for protection of victims of sexual violence or intimidation may be brought in a county where:

(1) the plaintiff resides, either temporarily or permanently;

(2) the plaintiff is employed;

(3) the defendant may be served; or

(4) the sexual violence or intimidation occurred.

(b) An action for indirect criminal contempt may be filed in, and heard by, the court in the county where the order was issued or the violation occurred.

Adopted June 29, 2015, effective July 1, 2015.

Rule 1953. Commencement of Action

(a) Except as provided in subdivision (b), an action shall be commenced by filing with the prothonotary a petition alleging the need for protection from the defendant with respect to sexual violence or intimidation. The petition shall be identical in content to the form set forth in Pa.R.C.P. No. 1959(b) and shall have the Notice of Hearing and Order set forth in Pa.R.C.P. No. 1959(a) as the first page(s).

(b) If an emergency order has been entered pursuant to 42 Pa.C.S. § 62A09, an action shall be commenced by filing with the prothonotary the certified emergency order and any documentation in support.

(c) Any fees associated with this action shall not be charged to the plaintiff.

> **Note:** *See* Pa.R.C.P. No. 1930.1(b). This rule may require attorneys or unrepresented parties to file confidential documents and documents containing confidential information that are subject to the Case Records *Public Access Policy of the Unified Judicial System of Pennsylvania.*

Adopted June 29, 2015, effective July 1, 2015. Amended Jan. 5, 2018, effective Jan. 6, 2018; June 1, 2018, effective July 1, 2018.

Rule 1954. Service of Original Process. Registration of Order. Service of Petition and Order. Fees

(a) Service of the petition or certified emergency order, the notice and order scheduling the hearing and any temporary order in a protection of victims of sexual violence and intimidation action shall be in accordance with Pa.R.C.P. No. 1930.4 and consistent with the rules for service in protection from abuse matters.

(b) An Affidavit of Service, substantially in the form set forth in Pa.R.C.P. No. 1959(d), shall be filed with the prothonotary.

(c) Within 24 hours of entry of a protection order under the Act, the prothonotary shall transmit a copy of the order to the Pennsylvania State Police Statewide Registry in the manner prescribed by the Pennsylvania State Police.

(d) If a petition alleges an act of sexual violence perpetrated on a minor child, the prothonotary shall serve a copy of the petition and any protection order entered under the Act to the Department of Human Services of the Commonwealth and the county children and youth social service agency in the jurisdiction where the order was entered.

(e) Within two business days of any protection order under the Act being entered, the prothonotary shall serve a copy of the order to the police department, sheriff and district attorney in the jurisdiction where the order was entered.

(f) No fee shall be charged to the plaintiff for service of any protection order or pleading or for the registration, filing and service of any foreign protection order.

Adopted June 29, 2015, effective July 1, 2015.

Rule 1955. Enforcement

A plaintiff may file a private criminal complaint against a defendant alleging indirect criminal contempt for a violation of any provision of a protection order or agreement with the court, the Office of the District Attorney or the magisterial district judge in the jurisdiction or county where the violation occurred. However, in a county of the first class, a complaint may be filed only with the Family Division of the Court of Common Pleas or the Office of the District Attorney.

   Note: See 42 Pa.C.S. § 62A13.

Adopted June 29, 2015, effective July 1, 2015.

Rule 1956. No Responsive Pleading Required

No pleading need be filed in response to the petition or the certified emergency order. All averments not admitted shall be deemed denied.

Adopted June 29, 2015, effective July 1, 2015.

Rule 1957. Decision. Post-Trial Relief

(a) The decision of the court may consist of only general findings of sexual violence and/or intimidation, but shall dispose of all claims for relief. The court's final order shall be rendered identical in content to the form set forth in Pa.R.C.P. No. 1959(e).

(b) No motion for post-trial relief may be filed to the final order.

Adopted June 29, 2015, effective July 1, 2015.

Rule 1958. Discontinuance or Modification

(a) In cases in which a temporary protection order has not yet been granted or has been denied, a plaintiff in a protection of victims of sexual violence or intimidation action, who wishes to discontinue the action, may file a praecipe to discontinue, pursuant to Pa.R.C.P. No. 229, prior to the final order hearing. The plaintiff also may request the discontinuance by oral motion at a hearing.

(b) In cases in which a temporary protection order has been granted, a plaintiff who wishes to vacate the temporary order and discontinue the action shall either file a petition with the court prior to the final order hearing or make the request by oral motion at the final order hearing.

(c) If either party seeks a modification after a final protection order has been entered, the party shall petition the court to modify the final order. Modification may be ordered after the filing and service of the petition and a hearing on the petition pursuant to 42 Pa.C.S. § 62A17.

Adopted June 29, 2015, effective July 1, 2015.

Rule 1959. Forms for Use in Protection of Victims of Sexual Violence or Intimidation Actions. Notice and Hearing. Petition. Temporary Protection Order. Final Protection Order

(a) The Notice of Hearing and Order required by Pa.R.C.P. No. 1953 shall be identical in content to the following form:

(Caption)

NOTICE OF HEARING AND ORDER

YOU HAVE BEEN SUED IN COURT. If you wish to defend against the claims set forth in the following papers, you must appear at the hearing scheduled herein. If you fail to appear, the case may proceed against you and a FINAL order may be entered against you granting the relief requested in the petition.

A hearing on the matter is scheduled for the _____ day of _____, 20 ___ at _____ _.m. in Courtroom _____ at _____ Courthouse, _____, Pennsylvania.

If a temporary protection order has been entered, you MUST obey the order until it is modified or terminated by the court after notice and a hearing. If you disobey that order, the police or sheriff may arrest you. A violation of this order may subject you to a charge of indirect criminal contempt. A violation may also subject you to prosecution and criminal penalties under the Pennsylvania Crimes Code. Under 18 U.S.C. § 2265, an order entered by the court may be enforceable in all fifty (50) States, the District of Columbia, Tribal Lands, U.S. Territories and the Commonwealth of Puerto Rico. If you travel outside of the state and intentionally violate this order, you may be subject to federal criminal proceedings under the Violence Against Women Act, 18 U.S.C. § 2262.

YOU SHOULD TAKE THIS PAPER TO YOUR LAWYER IMMEDIATELY. YOU HAVE THE RIGHT TO HAVE A LAWYER REPRESENT YOU AT THE HEARING. THE COURT WILL NOT, HOWEVER, APPOINT A LAWYER FOR YOU. IF YOU DO NOT HAVE A LAWYER, GO TO OR CALL THE OFFICE SET FORTH BELOW. THIS OFFICE CAN PROVIDE YOU WITH INFORMATION ABOUT HIRING A LAWYER. IF YOU CANNOT AFFORD TO HIRE A LAWYER, THIS OFFICE MAY BE ABLE TO PROVIDE YOU WITH INFORMATION ABOUT AGENCIES THAT MAY OFFER LEGAL SERVICES TO ELIGIBLE PERSONS AT A REDUCED FEE OR NO FEE. IF YOU CANNOT FIND A LAWYER, YOU MAY HAVE TO PROCEED WITHOUT ONE.

County Lawyer Referral Service
(insert Street Address)
(insert City, State, and ZIP)
(insert Phone Number)

AMERICANS WITH DISABILITIES ACT OF 1990

The Court of Common Pleas of _____ County is required by law to comply with the Americans with Disabilities Act of 1990. For information about accessible facilities and reasonable accommodations available to disabled

Pa. R.C.P. Rule 1959

individuals having business before the court, please contact our office. All arrangements must be made at least 72 hours prior to any hearing or business before the court. You must attend the scheduled conference or hearing.

BY THE COURT:

_____
Judge

_____
Date

(b) The petition in an action filed pursuant to the Act shall be identical in content to the following form:

(Caption)

PETITION FOR PROTECTION OF VICTIMS OF

☐ SEXUAL VIOLENCE
☐ SEXUAL VIOLENCE AGAINST A MINOR CHILD
☐ INTIMIDATION

1. Plaintiff:

_____
First   Middle   Last Name

Plaintiff's Address: _____

☐ Plaintiff's address is confidential pursuant to 42 Pa.C.S. § 62A11.

Plaintiff's Date of Birth: _____

I am filing this petition on behalf of ☐ myself or ☐ another person.

If you checked "myself," please answer all questions referring to yourself as "Plaintiff." If you checked "another person," please answer all questions referring to that person as "Plaintiff," and provide your name and address below.

Name: _____

Address: _____

If you checked "another person," indicate your relationship to the plaintiff:

_____

2. Defendant:

_____

DEFENDANT IDENTIFIERS

First	Middle	Last Name	DOB	HEIGHT
			SEX	WEIGHT
			RACE	EYES

1023

Rule 1959 PROTECTION OF VICTIMS

Defendant's Address:

HAIR

SSN

DRIVERS LICENSE #

EXP DATE   STATE

3. Name(s) of other designated person(s) under 42 Pa.C.S. § 62A07(b)(1):

4. Is there a relationship between Plaintiff and Defendant? _____. If yes, what is the relationship?

5. Have Plaintiff and Defendant been involved in any other legal proceedings? If so, state when and where the case was filed and the court docket number, if known:

6. Has Defendant been involved in any criminal proceedings?

If you answered Yes, is Defendant currently on probation or parole?

7. (a) The facts of the most recent incident of sexual violence are as follows:
Approximate Date: _____
Approximate Time: _____
Place: _____

Describe in detail what happened, including any physical or sexual abuse, threats, injury, incidents of stalking, medical treatment sought, and/or calls to law enforcement (attach additional sheets of paper if necessary):

(b) The facts of the most recent incident of intimidation are as follows:
Approximate Date: _____
Approximate Time: _____
Place: _____

Describe in detail what happened, including medical treatment sought, and/or calls to law enforcement (attach additional sheets of paper if necessary):

Pa. R.C.P.   Rule 1959

8. If Defendant has committed prior acts of sexual violence or intimidation against Plaintiff, describe these prior incidents, and indicate approximately when such acts occurred (attach additional sheets of paper if necessary):

_____

_____

9. Identify the sheriff, police department, or other law enforcement agency in the area in which Plaintiff lives that should be provided with a copy of the protection order:

_____

10. Is Plaintiff in immediate and present danger from Defendant? If so, please describe:

_____

FOR THE REASONS SET FORTH ABOVE, I REQUEST THAT THE COURT ENTER A TEMPORARY ORDER AND, AFTER A HEARING, A FINAL ORDER THAT WOULD INCLUDE ALL OF THE FOLLOWING RELIEF (CHECK ALL FORMS OF RELIEF REQUESTED):

☐ A. Restrain Defendant from having any contact with the victim, including, but not limited to, entering the victim's residence, place of employment, business, or school.

☐ B. Prohibit indirect contact through third parties.

☐ C. Prohibit direct or indirect contact with other designated persons.

☐ D. Order Defendant to pay the fees of this action.

☐ E. Order the following additional relief, not listed above:

_____

_____

_____

☐ F. Grant such other relief as the court deems appropriate, including, but not limited to, issuing an order under 42 Pa.C.S. § 62A11(b) related to the non-disclosure of the victim's address, telephone number, whereabouts or other demographic information.

☐ G. Order the police, sheriff or other law enforcement agency to serve the Defendant with a copy of this petition, any order issued, and the order for the hearing. Plaintiff will inform the designated authority of any addresses, other than Defendant's residence, where Defendant can be served.

VERIFICATION

I verify that the statements made in this petition are true and correct to the best of my knowledge. I understand that false statements herein are made subject to the penalties of 18 Pa.C.S. § 4904, relating to unsworn falsification to authorities.

_____

Signature

_____

Date

Rule 1959   **PROTECTION OF VICTIMS**

Note: *See* Pa.R.C.P. No. 1930.1(b). This rule may require attorneys or unrepresented parties to file confidential documents and documents containing confidential information that are subject to the Case Records *Public Access Policy of the Unified Judicial System of Pennsylvania.*

(c) The Temporary Order of Court, or any continued, amended or modified Temporary Order of Court, entered pursuant to the Act shall be identical in content to the following form:

(Caption)
TEMPORARY ORDER FOR PROTECTION OF VICTIMS OF
- SEXUAL VIOLENCE
- SEXUAL VIOLENCE AGAINST A MINOR CHILD
- INTIMIDATION

Plaintiff:

_____

    First   Middle   Last Name

Plaintiff's Address: _____

☐ Plaintiff's address is confidential pursuant to 42 Pa.C.S. § 62A11.

Defendant:

_____

DEFENDANT IDENTIFIERS

First	Middle	Last Name	DOB	HEIGHT
			SEX	WEIGHT
			RACE	EYES
Defendant's Address:			HAIR	
			SSN	
			DRIVERS LICENSE #	
			EXP DATE	STATE

AND NOW, this _____ day of _____, 20 ___, upon consideration of the attached Petition for Protection of Victims of Sexual Violence or Intimidation, the court hereby enters the following Temporary Order:

☐ Plaintiff's request for a Temporary Protection Order is denied.

☐ Plaintiff's request for a Temporary Protection Order is granted.

Pa. R.C.P. Rule 1959

1. The following person is protected under this order:

2. Defendant is:

☐ A. Restrained from having any contact with the victim, including, but not limited to, entering the victim's residence, place of employment, business, or school.

☐ B. Prohibited from indirect contact with the victim through third parties.

☐ C. Prohibited from direct or indirect contact with the following designated persons:

☐ 3. Additional relief, including, but not limited to, issuing an order under 42 Pa.C.S. § 62A11(b) related to the non-disclosure of the victim's address, telephone number, whereabouts or other demographic information:

☐ 4. A certified copy of this order shall be provided to the sheriff or police department where Plaintiff resides and any other agency specified (insert name of agency):

☐ 5. THIS ORDER SUPERSEDES ANY PRIOR PROTECTION OF VICTIMS OF SEXUAL VIOLENCE OR INTIMIDATION ORDER OBTAINED BY THE SAME PLAINTIFF AGAINST THE SAME DEFENDANT.

☐ 6. THIS ORDER APPLIES IMMEDIATELY TO THE DEFENDANT AND SHALL REMAIN IN EFFECT UNTIL _____ (insert expiration date) OR UNTIL OTHERWISE MODIFIED OR TERMINATED BY THIS COURT AFTER NOTICE AND A HEARING.

NOTICE TO THE DEFENDANT

Defendant is hereby notified that violation of this order may result in arrest for indirect criminal contempt. Under 18 U.S.C. § 2265, an order entered by the court may be enforceable in all fifty (50) States, the District of Columbia, Tribal Lands, U.S. Territories and the Commonwealth of Puerto Rico. If you travel outside of the state and intentionally violate this order, you may be subject to federal criminal proceedings under the Violence Against Women Act, 18 U.S.C. § 2262. Consent of Plaintiff shall not invalidate this order, which can only be changed or modified through the filing of appropriate court papers for that purpose. 42 Pa.C.S. § 62A17. Defendant is further notified that violation of this order may subject him/her to prosecution and criminal penalties under the Pennsylvania Crimes Code.

NOTICE TO SHERIFF, POLICE AND
LAW ENFORCEMENT OFFICIALS

The police department and sheriff who have jurisdiction over Plaintiff's residence, the location where a violation of this order occurs, or where Defendant may be located, shall enforce this order. The court shall have jurisdiction over any indirect criminal contempt proceeding, either in the county where the violation occurred or where this protective order was entered. An arrest for violation of paragraphs 2 and 3 of this order may be without warrant, based solely on probable cause, whether or not the violation is committed in the presence of the police or any sheriff. 42 Pa.C.S. § 62A12.

When Defendant is placed under arrest for violation of the order, Defendant shall be taken to the appropriate authority or authorities before whom Defendant is to be arraigned. A "Complaint for Indirect Criminal Contempt" shall then be completed and signed by the police officer, sheriff or Plaintiff. Plaintiff's presence and signature are not required to file the complaint.

If sufficient grounds for violation of this order are alleged: (1) Defendant shall be arraigned; (2) bond set, if appropriate; and (3) both parties shall be given notice of the date of the hearing.

BY THE COURT:

_____
Judge

_____
Date

(d) The form of the Affidavit of Service in a proceeding under the Act shall be substantially in the following form:

(Caption)

AFFIDAVIT OF SERVICE

I, _____, the undersigned, hereby state that I served a copy of the Notice of Hearing and Order, Petition and Temporary Order in the above-captioned action upon Defendant by handing the papers to _____ at the following address: _____ on the _____ day of _____, 20___, at approximately _____ o'clock _.m.

I verify that the statements made in this Affidavit are true and correct. I understand that false statements herein are made subject to the penalties of 18 Pa.C.S. § 4904, relating to unsworn falsification to authorities.

_____
(Signature)

_____
(Title)

_____
(Address)

_____
(Date)

THIS FORM MUST BE COMPLETED AND SIGNED BY THE PERSON WHO SERVES THE DEFENDANT WITH THE NOTICE OF HEARING AND ORDER, PETITION AND TEMPORARY ORDER. IT MUST BE FILED WITH THE PROTHONOTARY OR BROUGHT TO THE COURT ON THE HEARING DATE.

Pa. R.C.P. **Rule 1959**

(e) The Final Order of Court, or any amended, modified or extended Final Order of Court, entered pursuant to the Act shall be identical in content to the following form:

(Caption)

FINAL ORDER FOR PROTECTION OF VICTIMS OF

- SEXUAL VIOLENCE
- SEXUAL VIOLENCE AGAINST A MINOR CHILD
- INTIMIDATION

Plaintiff:

_____
      First   Middle   Last Name

Plaintiff's Address: _____

☐ Plaintiff's address is confidential pursuant to 42 Pa.C.S. § 62A11.

Defendant:

_____

DEFENDANT IDENTIFIERS

First	Middle	Last Name	DOB	HEIGHT
			SEX	WEIGHT
			RACE	EYES
Defendant's Address:			HAIR	
			SSN	
			DRIVERS LICENSE #	
			EXP DATE	STATE

The court hereby finds that it has jurisdiction over the parties and the subject matter and that Defendant has been provided with reasonable notice and opportunity to be heard.

Defendant was served in accordance with Pa.R.C.P. No. 1954(a) and provided notice of the time, date and location of the hearing scheduled in this matter.

Order Effective Date: _____ Order Expiration Date: _____

Rule 1959   PROTECTION OF VICTIMS

☐ AND NOW, this _____ day of _____, 20 ___, upon consideration of the attached Petition for Protection of Victims of Sexual Violence or Intimidation, the court hereby enters the following Final Order:

It is ORDERED, ADJUDGED AND DECREED as follows:

This order is entered (check one) ☐ by agreement; ☐ by agreement without an admission; ☐ after a hearing and decision by the court; ☐ after a hearing at which Defendant was not present, despite proper service being made; ☐ by default. Without regard as to how the order was entered, this is a final order of court subject to full enforcement pursuant to the Protection of Victims of Sexual Violence or Intimidation Act.

☐ Plaintiff's request for a final protection order is denied.

OR

☐ Plaintiff's request for a final protection order is granted.

1. The following person is protected under this order:

_____

2. Defendant is:

☐ A. Restrained from having any contact with the victim, including, but not limited to, entering the victim's residence, place of employment, business or school.

☐ B. Prohibited from indirect contact with the victim through third parties.

☐ C. Prohibited from direct or indirect contact with the following designated persons:

_____

☐ D. Ordered to pay the fees of this action.

☐ 3. Additional relief, including, but not limited to, issuing an order under 42 Pa.C.S. § 62A11(b) related to the non-disclosure of the victim's address, telephone number, whereabouts or other demographic information:

_____

_____

_____

_____

☐ 4. Because this order followed a contested proceeding, or a hearing at which Defendant was not present, despite being served with a copy of the petition, temporary order and notice of the date, time and place of the hearing, Defendant is ordered to pay an additional $100 surcharge to the court, which shall be distributed in the manner set forth in 42 Pa.C.S. § 62A05(c.1).

☐ 5. THIS ORDER SUPERSEDES ANY PRIOR PROTECTION OF VICTIMS OF SEXUAL VIOLENCE OR INTIMIDATION ORDER OBTAINED BY THE SAME PLAINTIFF AGAINST THE SAME DEFENDANT.

NOTICE TO THE DEFENDANT

Defendant is hereby notified that violation of this order may result in arrest for indirect criminal contempt. Under 18 U.S.C. § 2265, an order entered by the court may be enforceable in all fifty (50) States, the District of Columbia, Tribal Lands, U.S. Territories and the Commonwealth of Puerto Rico. If you travel outside of the state and intentionally violate this order, you may be subject to federal criminal proceedings under the Violence Against Women Act, 18 U.S.C. § 2262. Consent of Plaintiff shall not invalidate this order, which can only be changed or modified through the filing of appropriate court papers for that purpose. 42 Pa.C.S. § 62A17. Defendant is further notified that violation of this order may subject him/her to prosecution and criminal penalties under the Pennsylvania Crimes Code.

NOTICE TO SHERIFF, POLICE AND LAW ENFORCEMENT OFFICIALS

The police department and sheriff who have jurisdiction over Plaintiff's residence, the location where a violation of this order occurs, or where Defendant may be located, shall enforce this order. The court shall have jurisdiction over any indirect criminal contempt proceeding, either in the county where the violation occurred or where this protective order was entered. An arrest for violation of paragraphs 2 and 3 of this order may be without warrant, based solely on probable cause, whether or not the violation is committed in the presence of the police or any sheriff. 42 Pa.C.S. § 62A12.

When Defendant is placed under arrest for violation of the order, Defendant shall be taken to the appropriate authority or authorities before whom Defendant is to be arraigned. A "Complaint for Indirect Criminal Contempt" shall then be completed and signed by the police officer, sheriff or Plaintiff. Plaintiff's presence and signature are not required to file the complaint.

If sufficient grounds for violation of this order are alleged: (1) Defendant shall be arraigned; (2) bond set, if appropriate; and (3) both parties shall be given notice of the date of the hearing.

BY THE COURT:

_____

Judge

_____

Date

If a Final Order of Court is entered pursuant to the consent of the plaintiff and the defendant, both shall sign the order along with their counsel, if any:

_____

(Plaintiff's signature)   **(Defendant's signature)**

_____

(Plaintiff's attorney's signature)   **(Defendant's attorney's signature)**

   Note: Pa.R.C.P. No. 1959(a), (b), (c), and (e) utilize the phrase "shall be identical in content" in reference to the form documents provided under those subparagraphs, which include the Notice of Hearing, the Petition for Protection of Victims of Sexual Violence or Intimidation, the Temporary Order, and the Final Order. In using "shall be identical in content" rather than the more usual phrase "shall be substantially in the following form," the intent of the rule is to ensure only the relevant information and relief authorized under the Act is incorporated into any third-party generated form document while allowing for stylistic differences as to format and layout.

   Adopted June 29, 2015, effective July 1, 2015. Amended Oct. 27, 2016, effective in 60 days (Dec. 27, 2016); Jan. 5, 2018, effective Jan. 6, 2018; June 1, 2018, effective July 1, 2018.

IX. Supreme Court Orphans' Court Rules
(Amended Through April, 2019)

Supreme Court Orphans' Court Rules—Adoptions

Rules 15.1–15.9

RULE
- 15.1. Local Rules
- 15.2. Voluntary Relinquishment to Agency
- 15.3. Voluntary Relinquishment to Adult Intending to Adopt Child
- 15.4. Involuntary Termination of Parental Rights
- 15.5. Adoption
- 15.6. Notice to Persons; Method; Notice of Orphans' Court Proceedings Filed on Dependency Docket
- 15.7. Impounding; Docket Entries; Reports; Privacy
- 15.8. Registration of Foreign Adoption Decree
- 15.9. Petition for Adoption of a Foreign Born Child

Rule 15. Adoptions[1]

Rule 15.1. Local Rules

The practice and procedure with respect to adoptions shall be as provided by Act of Assembly and to the extent not inconsistent therewith shall conform either with the pertinent general rule or special order of the local Orphans' Court or, in the absence thereof, with this Rule 15.

Adopted Nov. 24, 1975, effective Jan. 1, 1976.

Rule 15.2. Voluntary Relinquishment to Agency[2]

(a) **Petition.** A petition under Section 301 of the Adoption Act to relinquish parental rights and duties with respect to a child who has been in the care of an Agency shall include the following allegations:

(1) the name, address, age, racial background and religious affiliation of each petitioner;

(2) the information required in subparagraph (1) as to any parent who is not a petitioner, including the father of a child born out of wedlock, if he has been identified, unless the court, for cause shown, determines such information is not essential;

(3) the marital status of the mother as of the time of birth of the child and during one year prior thereto and, if the mother has ever been married, the name of her husband or husbands and her maiden name;

---

[1] See the Adoption Act of 1970, P.L. 620, 1 P.S. 101 et seq. As to adoption jurisdiction in the Orphans' Court Division in all counties other than Philadelphia, see Secs. 711(7) and 713, PEF Code, 20 Pa.C.S. Secs. 711(7) and 713.

[2] For the rights of a father of a child born out of wedlock, see Stanley v. Illinois, 92 S.Ct. 1208, 405 U.S. 645, 31 L.Ed.2d 551, 1972.

(4) the name, age, date of birth, racial background, sex and religious affiliation of the child;

(5) the name and address of the Agency having care of the child;

(6) the date when the child was placed with the Agency;

(7) when the child is born out of wedlock, whether the mother and the father of the child intend to marry;

(8) the reasons for seeking relinquishment;

(9) that each petitioner understands the petition, has considered the alternatives, and has executed the petition voluntarily to promote what the petitioner believes to be in petitioner's and the child's best interests.

(b) Exhibits. The petition shall have attached to it the following exhibits:

(1) the joinder of a parent who is not a petitioner or his or her waiver of all interest in the child, if either is obtainable;

(2) a birth certificate or certification of registration of birth of the child;

(3) the written consent of a parent or guardian of a petitioner who has not reached 18 years of age;

(4) the joinder of the Agency having care of the child and its consent to accept custody of the child until such time as the child is adopted.

(c) Notice and Hearing. If a parent, including the parent of a child born out of wedlock, has not relinquished, his or her duties in and to the child or joined in the other parent's petition hereunder, then notice of the hearing on the petition to relinquish rights and duties shall be given to the first referred to parent as provided in Rule 15.6. A parent may waive in writing the right to such notice. Each petitioner and each person whose joinder or consent is attached to the petition shall be examined under oath at the hearing unless executed by the court.

Adopted Nov. 24, 1975, effective Jan. 1, 1976.

Rule 15.3. Voluntary Relinquishment to Adult Intending to Adopt Child

(a) Petition. A petition under Section 302 of the Adoption Act to relinquish parental rights with respect to a child who has been in the exclusive care of an adult or adults who have filed a Report of Intention to Adopt shall include the allegations required under subparagraphs (1), (2), (3), (4), (7), (8) and (9) of Rule 15.2(a) and (1) the date when the Report of Intention to Adopt was filed; (2) the date when the child was placed with the adult or adults;

(b) Exhibits. The petition shall have attached to it the first three exhibits specified in Rule 15.2(b) and (1) the separate consent of the adult or adults to accept custody of the child.

(c) Notice and Hearing. If a parent, including the parent of a child born out of wedlock, has not relinquished his or her rights in the child or joined in the petition hereunder, then notice of the hearing on a parent's petition to relinquish rights shall be given to the first referred to parent as provided in Rule 15.6. A parent may waive in writing the right to such notice. Each petitioner and each person whose joinder or consent is attached to the petititon shall be examined under oath at the hearing unless excused by the court.

Adopted Nov. 24, 1975, effective Jan. 1, 1976.

Rule 15.4. Involuntary Termination of Parental Rights[3]

(a) *Petition.* A petition for involuntary termination of parental rights under Sections 311 and 312 of the Adoption Act shall include the following allegations:

(1) the name and address of the petitioner and his or her standing;

(2) the name, age, date of birth, racial background, sex and religious affiliation of the child;

(3) the name, address, age, racial background and religious affiliation of the parent or parents, including the father of a child born out of wedlock, if he has been identified;

(4) the marital status of the mother as of the time of birth of the child and during one year prior thereto and, if the mother has ever been married, the name of her husband or husbands and her maiden name;

(5) the date when the child was placed in the care of the petitioner;

(6) facts constituting grounds for the involuntary termination under Section 311 of the Adoption Act, and a reference to the applicable subsection or subsections;

(7) whether either parent of the child is entitled to the benefits of the Soldiers' and Sailors' Civil Relief Act of 1940, as amended, (50 U.S.C.A. § 501 et seq.);

(8) that the petitioner will assume custody of the child until such time as the child is adopted.

(b) *Exhibits.* The petition shall have attached to it the following exhibits:

(1) a birth certificate or certification of registration of birth of the child;

(2) the joinder of a parent of a petitioner who is under the age of 18, unless excused by the court.

(c) *Guardian ad Litem.*

(1) When the termination of the parental rights of a parent who has not attained the age of 18 years is sought, unless the court finds the parent is already adequately represented, the court shall appoint a guardian ad litem to represent the parent. The appointment of a guardian ad litem may be provided for in the preliminary order attached to the petition for involuntary termination of parental rights.

(2) The decree appointing a guardian ad litem shall give the name, date of birth and address (if known) of the individual whom the guardian ad litem is to represent and the proceedings and period of time for which the guardian ad litem shall act.

(d) *Notice and Hearing.* Notice of the hearing on the petition shall be given, in accordance with Rule 15.6 hereof, to the parent or parents whose rights are sought to be terminated, including the parent of a child born out of wedlock, to any intermediary named in a Report of Intention to Adopt, if one has been filed, and to the guardian of the person or guardian ad litem of any parent or parents who is or are under the age of 18 years. Each petitioner, each person whose joinder or consent is attached to the petition and

---

[3]For the rights of a father of a child born out of wedlock, see Stanley v. Illinois, 92 S.Ct. 1208, 405 U.S. 645, 31 L.Ed.2d 551, 1972.

any intermediary named in a Report of Intention to Adopt shall be examined under oath at the hearing unless they are excused by the court.

Adopted Nov. 24, 1976, effective Jan. 1, 1976.

Rule 15.5. Adoption[4]

(a) Petition. The petition shall contain all declarations and information required by Section 401 of the Adoption Act and any additional information required by local rules.

(b) Notice or Consent—Parents of Child. Notice as provided by Rule 15.6 shall be given to each parent unless

(1) he or she consented in writing to the adoption and waived notice of hearing, or

(2) he or she has voluntarily relinquished his or her parental rights in a proceeding under Rule 15.2 or Rule 15.3, or

(3) his or her parental rights have been involuntarily terminated in a proceeding under Rule 15.4.

(c) Investigation. A petition for adoption shall be subject to investigation as prescribed by local rules. The investigation report shall cover the matters alleged in the petition, any other matters that may affect the welfare of the child, and the information required by Sections 335 and 424 of the Adoption Act.

(d) Disclosure of Fee and Costs. At the hearing there shall be offerred in evidence a report, certified by counsel for the petitioner, setting forth the amount of fees and expenses paid or to be paid to counsel, and any other fees, costs and expenses paid or to be paid to an intermediary or any other person or institution, in connection with the adoption.

(e) Adult—Change of Name. When the person to be adopted is over the age of 18 years and desires to assume the surname of the adopting parent or parents, evidence showing compliance with the law relating to change of name must be introduced before a decree will be made.[5]

Adopted Nov. 24, 1975, effective Jan. 1, 1976.

Rule 15.6. Notice to Persons; Method; Notice of Orphans' Court Proceedings Filed on Dependency Docket.

(a) Notice to every person to be notified shall be by personal service, service at his or her residence on an adult member of the household, or by registered or certified mail to his or her last known address. If such service is unobtainable and the registered mail is returned undelivered, then:

---

[4] For the rights of a father of a child born out of wedlock, see Stanley v. Illinois, 92 S.Ct. 1208, 405 U.S. 645, 31 L.Ed.2d 551, 1972.
[5] Act of April 18, 1923, P.L. 75, as amended, 54 P.S. 1 et seq.

(1) no further notice shall be required in proceedings under Rules 15.2 or 15.3, and

(2) in proceedings under Rules 15.4 and 15.5, further notice by publication or otherwise shall be given if required by general rule or special order of the local Orphans' Court. If, after reasonable investigation, the identity of a person to be notified is unknown, notice to him or her shall not be required.

(b) When a child is in the legal custody of a county agency:

(1) Within seven (7) days of the filing of a petition to terminate parental rights under Rules 15.2 or 15.4, or a petition to confirm consent under 23 Pa.C.S. § 2504, or a petition to adopt under Rule 15.5, the county agency shall file a praecipe with the clerk of the court where the child was declared dependent using the caption of the dependency proceeding, notifying the clerk of the name of the petition filed and the date of filing in substantially the form approved by the Supreme Court.

(2) Within seven (7) days of receiving the Court's disposition of the petitions described in subparagraph (b)(1), the county agency shall file a praecipe with the clerk of the court where the child was declared dependent using the caption of the dependency proceeding, notifying the clerk of the disposition of the petition and the date of the order in substantially the form approved by the Supreme Court.

(3) If a notice of appeal from an order described in subparagraph (b)(2) is filed, then within seven (7) days of service of the notice of appeal, the county agency shall file a praecipe with the clerk of the court where the child was declared dependent using the caption of the dependency proceeding, notifying the clerk of the appeal and the date of filing in substantially the form approved by the Supreme Court.

(4) Within seven (7) days of receiving the appellate court's disposition of the appeal described in subparagraph (b)(3), the county agency shall file a praecipe with the clerk of the court where the child was declared dependent using the caption of the dependency proceeding, notifying the clerk of the disposition of the appeal and the date of the decision in substantially the form approved by the Supreme Court.

Explanatory Comment

This Rule was amended in 2013 to add paragraph (b). The purpose of the amendment was to provide a procedure for collecting data concerning children who have been declared dependent under the Juvenile Act and placed in the custody of the county agency. The information is entered into the Common Pleas Case Management System-Dependency Module to comply with reporting requirements and to monitor dependent children in the foster care system. Unlike a "notice," as used in paragraph (a), the county agency is not required to serve the praecipe upon the parties to the dependency, termination, or adoption proceeding. The definition of "county agency" as used in this Rule is that contained in Pa.R.J.C.P. 1120. Where used in this Rule, "Orphans' Court" includes the Family Court division of the First Judicial District. *See* 20 Pa.C.S. § 713.

Pursuant to Rule 1.3 (Forms), the Court has approved forms for state-wide practice to comply with the requirements of paragraph (b). These forms can be found in the Appendix to these Rules.

Adopted Nov. 24, 1975, eff. Jan. 1, 1976; amended March 19, 2013, eff. April 19, 2013.

Pa. O.C. Rules   Rule 15.6

IN THE COURT OF COMMON PLEAS
_____ COUNTY PENNSYLVANIA
JUVENILE COURT DIVISION
(FAMILY COURT DIVISION in Philadelphia County)

In the Interest   : Docket No.: CP-_____DP-_____-20___
of _____, a Minor :
   [Initials of Minor]   :
                           :
Date of Birth _____ :

TO CLERK OF _____:
             [Title of Clerk Maintaining Dependency Docket][1]

Please kindly record the following in the CPCMS – Dependency Module:

I hereby notify you that the following has been filed on __[DATE OF FILING]__ with the Orphans' Court in _____[NAME]_____ County concerning the above-child:

☐ A petition to relinquish parental rights of __[INITIALS OF PARENT(S) NAMED IN THE PETITION]__.

☐ A petition to terminate parental rights of __[INITIALS OF PARENT(S) NAMED IN THE PETITION]__.

☐ A petition to confirm consent of __[INITIALS OF PARENT(S) NAMED IN THE PETITION]__.

☐ A petition for adoption.

   Date: _____   _____
                                             On behalf of: [County Agency]

IN THE COURT OF COMMON PLEAS
_____ COUNTY PENNSYLVANIA
JUVENILE COURT DIVISION
(FAMILY COURT DIVISION in Philadelphia County)

In the Interest   : Docket No.: CP-_____DP-_____-20___
of _____, a Minor :
   [Initials of Minor]   :
                           :
Date of Birth _____ :

TO CLERK OF _____:
             [Title of Clerk Maintaining Dependency Docket][2]

Please kindly record the following in the CPCMS – Dependency Module:

---

[1] In the First Judicial District (i.e., Philadelphia County), this Clerk will be the Clerk of the Family Court division; in the Fifth Judicial District (i.e., Allegheny County), this Clerk will be personnel at the Department of Records for the Civil/Family division; and in most of the other counties, the Clerk will be the Clerk of the Juvenile Court division.

[2] In the First Judicial District (i.e., Philadelphia County), this Clerk will be the Clerk of the Family Court division; in the Fifth Judicial District (i.e., Allegheny County), this Clerk will be personnel at the Department of Records for the Civil/Family division; and in most of the other counties, the Clerk will be the Clerk of the Juvenile Court division.

Rule 15.6   **ADOPTIONS**

I hereby notify you that the following has been entered on ___[DATE OF FILING]___ by the Orphans' Court in _____[NAME]_____ County concerning the above-child:

☐ An order granting denying (circle one) the petition to relinquish parental rights of [INITIALS OF PARENT(S) NAMED IN THE PETITION].

☐ An order granting denying (circle one) the petition to terminate parental rights of [INITIALS OF PARENT(S) NAMED IN THE PETITION].

☐ An order granting denying (circle one) the petition to confirm consent of [INITIALS OF PARENT(S) NAMED IN THE PETITION].

☐ With the above-order relinquishing or terminating parental rights or confirming the consent of the parent(s), the child is available for adoption.
              Do not check if at least one parent still has parental rights.

☐ An order granting denying (circle one) the petition for adoption.

Date: _____   _____
                                                      On behalf of: [County Agency]

IN THE COURT OF COMMON PLEAS
_____ COUNTY PENNSYLVANIA
JUVENILE COURT DIVISION
(FAMILY COURT DIVISION in Philadelphia County)

In the Interest   :   Docket No.: CP-_____DP-_____-20___

of _____, a Minor   :
    [Initials of Minor]
                                        :

Date of Birth _____   :

TO CLERK OF _____:
                 [Title of Clerk Maintaining Dependency Docket][3]

Please kindly record the following in the CPCMS – Dependency Module:

I hereby notify you that the following has been filed on _____[DATE]_____ concerning the above-child from the following Orphans' Court order:

☐ An order granting denying (circle one) the petition to relinquish parental rights of [INITIALS OF PARENT(S) NAMED IN THE PETITION].

☐ An order granting denying (circle one) the petition to terminate parental rights of [INITIALS OF PARENT(S) NAMED IN THE PETITION].

☐ An order granting denying (circle one) the petition to confirm consent of [INITIALS OF PARENT(S) NAMED IN THE PETITION].

☐ An order granting denying (circle one) the petition for adoption.

Date: _____   _____
                                                      On behalf of: [County Agency]

---

[3]In the First Judicial District (i.e., Philadelphia County), this Clerk will be the Clerk of the Family Court division; in the Fifth Judicial District (i.e., Allegheny County), this Clerk will be personnel at the Department of Records for the Civil/Family division; and in most of the other counties, the Clerk will be the Clerk of the Juvenile Court division.

Pa. O.C. Rules   Rule 15.8

IN THE COURT OF COMMON PLEAS
_____ COUNTY PENNSYLVANIA
JUVENILE COURT DIVISION
(FAMILY COURT DIVISION in Philadelphia County)

In the Interest   :   Docket No.: CP-_____DP-_____-20___

of _____ , a Minor :

       [Initials of Minor]   :

                                           :

Date of Birth _____   :

TO CLERK OF _____:

                 [Title of Clerk Maintaining Dependency Docket][4]

Please kindly record the following in the CPCMS – Dependency Module:

I hereby notify you that the appeal from the Orphans' Court order concerning the above-child has been disposed on _____[DATE]_____ in the following manner:

☐ Quashed   ☐ Affirmed   ☐ Reversed   ☐ Vacated & Remanded

☐ Other: _____

     Date: _____   _____

                                                 On behalf of: [County Agency]

Rule 15.7. Impounding; Docket Entries; Reports; Privacy

(a) All proceedings shall be impounded, docket entries made, report made to the Department of Public Welfare, and certificates of adoption issued as provided in Sections 505, 506, 507 and 508, respectively, of the Adoption Act, 23 Pa.C.S. § 2101, et seq.

(b) The name or names of the natural parents and the name or names of the child before adoption shall not be entered on any docket which is subject to public inspection.

(c) No decision under the Adoption Act of any hearing judge or appellate court publicly reported or in any other way made available to the public by the court shall disclose the identity of the individual parties.

Official Note: For confidentiality requirements on appeal, see Pa.R.A.P. 3901.

Adopted Nov. 24, 1975, effective Jan. 1, 1976; amended March 3, 1999, effective immediately.

Rule 15.8. Registration of Foreign Adoption Decree

(a) Adopting parent(s) may petition the Court of Common Pleas in the county of their residence to register a foreign adoption decree so that it will be given full and final effect in this Commonwealth. The Petition and Final

---

[4]In the First Judicial District (i.e., Philadelphia County), this Clerk will be the Clerk of the Family Court division; in the Fifth Judicial District (i.e., Allegheny County), this Clerk will be personnel at the Department of Records for the Civil/Family division; and in most of the other counties, the Clerk will be the Clerk of the Juvenile Court division.

Decrees shall be in substantially the form approved by the Supreme Court. See Appendix of Forms to these Rules.

(1) As part of the Petition to Register Foreign Adoption Decree, a child's name may be changed from that appearing on the foreign adoption decree if the child is younger than twelve (12) years of age.

(b) A foreign adoption decree previously registered or otherwise finalized by a Court of this Commonwealth or of any other state may not be registered subsequently in another Court of this Commonwealth.

(c) If the Court of Common Pleas determines that the foreign adoption decree can be registered, the Court shall sign the Final Decree and shall direct the Clerk of the appropriate Court to enter the date of the foreign adoption decree and identify the foreign court on the docket. The Clerk shall send Form No. HD01273F, Certificate of Adoption of a Foreign-Born Child, and Form No. HD01275F, Statement of Citizenship and Residency, to the Department of Health, Division of Vital Records, along with a copy of U.S. Government Form N-560, Certificate of Citizenship, and/or a copy of the child's United States passport, if either or both documents have been provided by the adopting parent(s). The Clerk shall issue to the adopting parent(s) a certificate of adoption in accordance with Section 2907 of the Adoption Act. See 23 Pa.C.S. § 2907.

(d) If the Court of Common Pleas determines that the foreign adoption decree cannot be registered, the adopting parent(s) shall proceed as applicable under the provisions set forth in the Adoption Act, 23 Pa.C.S. §§ 2101 *et seq.*, Pa.O.C. Rule 15.9 (specific to the adoption of a foreign born child), and local rules of court.

(e) Adopting parent(s) who are eligible to register the foreign adoption decree under this Rule may, for any reason, proceed under Pa.O.C. Rule 15.9.

> **Explanatory Note:** Pursuant to 23 Pa.C.S. § 2908(b), as amended by Act 96 of 2006, a set of forms, consisting of a Petition to Register Foreign Adoption Decree, Final Decrees approving and denying the Petition, and detailed Instructions for the *pro se* petitioner (s) are set forth in the Appendix to these Rules.

The Petition should be filed with the Clerk of the Orphans' Court Division, except in Philadelphia County, where it should be filed with the Clerk of the Family Court Division. The Petition and accompanying documents, including the Final Decree, are confidential and should be impounded and withheld from public inspection as provided in the Adoption Act, 23 Pa. C.S. §§ 2905, 2906, 2907 and 2908(f) and Pa.O.C. Rule 15.7.

The Clerk shall make available to petitioner(s) the necessary Department of Health, Division of Vital Records forms: Form No. HD01273F, Certificate of Adoption of a Foreign-Born Child; and Form No. HD01275F, Statement of Citizenship and Residency.

A change of name from that appearing on the foreign adoption decree is permitted without the need to comply with the procedures of 54 Pa.C.S. § 702 if the child is younger than twelve (12) years of age. Cf. 23 Pa.C.S. § 2711(a)(1). If the foreign born adopted child is twelve (12) years of age or older, then the child and parent(s) would need to follow the procedures set forth in 54 Pa.C.S. § 702 and would not be foreclosed by 54 Pa.C.S. § 702(b)(5)(ii) because the name change petition would not be in connection with any adoption proceeding as the foreign adoption is full and final and therefore completed.

A foreign born child who has been issued an IR-2, IR-3 or IH-3 United States visa has had the adoption proceeding fully completed in the foreign country and the foreign adoption decree only needs to be registered here to be given the full force and effect of an adoption decree issued by this Commonwealth. However, situations may arise that necessitate proceeding under Pa.O.C.

Pa. O.C. Rules   Rule 15.8

Rule 15.9 even though the foreign born child has been issued an IR-2, IR-3 or IH-3 United States visa, such as the inclusion of an incorrect birth year on the foreign adoption decree, or other personal family reasons. Proceeding under Pa.O.C. Rule 15.9 is permitted; Pa.O.C. Rule 15.8 is not the exclusive means to obtain a Pennsylvania adoption decree and birth certificate for a foreign born adopted child.

Only one court, whether in this Commonwealth or another state, should exercise jurisdiction over the foreign adoption decree. Thus, if the foreign adoption decree has been registered or otherwise finalized in another state court, the adopting parent(s) need not and should not register the foreign adoption decree in this Commonwealth under this Rule. In similar fashion, if the foreign adoption decree has been registered in this Commonwealth, and thereafter, another petitioner in this Commonwealth seeks to adopt this child, the subsequent proceeding will be a standard proceeding under the applicable provisions of the Adoption Act, 23 Pa. C.S. §§ 2101 et seq. Such a situation could occur when the child is to be adopted by a step-parent after divorce or death of the original adopting parent(s), or when, after termination of parental rights, the child is to be adopted by different adopting parent(s).

If the Court determines that the foreign adoption is not a full and final adoption because the foreign born child has been issued an IH-4 or IR-4 visa, the adopting parent(s) shall proceed under subdivision (d) of this Rule. See also Pa.O.C. Rule 15.9.

IN THE COURT OF COMMON PLEAS
_____ COUNTY, PENNSYLVANIA
ORPHANS' COURT DIVISION
(FAMILY COURT DIVISION IN PHILADELPHIA COUNTY)
IN RE: FOREIGN ADOPTION OF _____
FILE NO. _____
PETITION TO REGISTER FOREIGN
ADOPTION DECREE
PURSUANT TO 23 PA. C.S. § 2908

1. Petitioner(s), the Adopting Parent(s) of the above-named adopted child, is/are

_____

2. Petitioner(s) reside(s) in _____County, Pennsylvania, at

_____
(Street Address)

_____
(City, State, Zip)

3. Has any other court in this Commonwealth or in any other state reviewed, registered, finalized or otherwise assumed jurisdiction over the foreign adoption decree being registered here:

(circle one) Yes No

If yes, please provide the name of the court, the state and county, what was previously presented to the court and the resulting decision from the court: (Attach all court decrees).

_____

_____

_____

Rule 15.8 ADOPTIONS

_____
_____

    4. The full name of the adopted child at birth as listed on the foreign birth certificate, if available, was _____.

    5. The full name of the adopted child as written on the foreign adoption decree is

_____

    6. The full name of the adopted child as he or she is to be known from this time forward is

_____

    7. The date of birth of the adopted child is _____.
    8. The date of the foreign adoption decree is _____.
    9. The type of United States visa issued to the adopted child is:
(circle one) IR-2, IR-3, IH-3, IR-4, IH-4
   10. The following documents are attached to this Petition:
      a. Copy of child's birth certificate or other birth identification issued by country of birth; if none, an Affidavit of parent(s) stating why none is available.
      b. Copy of Decree of Adoption issued by foreign government; if Decree is not in English, an English translation certified by the translator to be correct.
      c. Copy of adopted child's United States visa.
      d. Pennsylvania Department of Health, Division of Vital Records Form No. HD01273F, Certificate of Adoption of a Foreign-Born Child with Parts 1 and 2 (and Part 3, if applicable) completed.
      e. Pennsylvania Department of Health, Division of Vital Records Form No. HD01275F, Statement of Citizenship and Residency.
      f. A copy of U.S. Government Form N-560, Certificate of Citizenship, and/or a copy of the child's United States passport, if either or both documents are available.

WHEREFORE, Petitioner(s) request(s) that this Court enter a Decree authorizing the registration and docketing of the attached Foreign Adoption Decree with the Clerk of the appropriate Court and decreeing that _____
_____ *Name of child as written on Foreign Adoption Decree)*
shall henceforth be known as _____
_____ *(Child's name from this time forward)* and shall have all the rights of a child and heir of the Petitioner(s).

                                      _____
                                      Signature of Adopting Parent*

                                      _____
                                      Signature of Adopting Parent

_____

Daytime telephone no. for Adopting Parent(s)

VERIFICATION TO PETITION TO REGISTER FOREIGN ADOPTION DECREE PURSUANT TO 23 PA. C.S. § 2908

    I/We, _____, verify that I/we am/are the Petitioner(s) named in the foregoing Petition, that I/we have read and understand the information set forth in the Instructions to the Petition to Register Foreign Adoption Decree, and that the

_____

*When there are two adopting parents, both must sign.

Pa. O.C. Rules   Rule 15.8

facts set forth in the foregoing Petition are true and correct to the best of my/our knowledge, information and belief. I/We further verify that all documents attached to this Petition are true and correct copies of the originals. I/We understand that false statements made herein are subject to the penalties of 18 Pa. C.S. § 4904 relating to unsworn falsification to authorities.

Date: _____

_____
Signature of Adopting Parent

_____
Signature of Adopting Parent

IN THE COURT OF COMMON PLEAS
_____ COUNTY, PENNSYLVANIA
ORPHANS' COURT DIVISION
(FAMILY COURT DIVISION in Philadelphia County)
IN RE: FOREIGN ADOPTION OF _____
ADOPTION NO. _____

FINAL DECREE

    AND NOW, this _____ day of _____, 20____, it is hereby ORDERED and DECREED that the Petition of _____ *(Adopting Parent(s))* to Register Foreign Adoption Decree is GRANTED and that this Court authorizes the registration and docketing of the Foreign Adoption Decree entered on _____ *(Date of Foreign Adoption Decree)* by _____ *(Foreign Country)* in _____. *(Name of Foreign Court)*

    It is FURTHER ORDERED and DECREED that the above Foreign Adoption Decree shall be enforceable as if this Court had entered the Decree and that henceforth this child _____ *Name of child as written on Foreign Adoption Decree)* shall be known as _____ *(Child's name from this time forward)* and shall have all the rights of a child and heir of _____ _____. *(Adopting Parent(s))*

BY THE COURT:

_____
J.

IN THE COURT OF COMMON PLEAS
_____ COUNTY, PENNSYLVANIA
ORPHANS' COURT DIVISION
(FAMILY COURT DIVISION in Philadelphia County)
IN RE: FOREIGN ADOPTION OF _____
ADOPTION NO. _____

FINAL DECREE

    AND NOW, this _____ day of _____, 20____, it is hereby ORDERED and DECREED that the Petition of _____ *(Adopting Parent(s))* to Register Foreign Adoption Decree is DENIED.

BY THE COURT:

_____
J.

Rule 15.8 ADOPTIONS

INSTRUCTIONS FOR FILING PETITION TO REGISTER FOREIGN ADOPTION DECREE PURSUANT TO 23 PA.C.S. § 2908

When a child is adopted in conformity with the laws of a foreign country, the adopting parent(s) may register the Foreign Adoption Decree so that the Decree is considered full and final, enforceable as if entered pursuant to the Pennsylvania Adoption Act, and a Pennsylvania birth certificate can be obtained.

Adopting parent(s) seeking to register the Foreign Adoption Decree must:

1. Complete, sign and date the Petition to Register Foreign Adoption Decree and Verification. *If a Foreign Adoption Decree shows that there are two adopting parents, both parent(s) must execute the Petition to Register Foreign Adoption Decree.*

2. Attach the following documents to the Petition:

☐ A copy of the Foreign Adoption Decree;

☐ A copy of the child's birth certificate. If no birth certificate was issued, a copy of any other birth identification issued by the country of birth should be attached. If no birth certificate or birth identification can be obtained, an Affidavit stating the reason should be submitted;

☐ A copy of the child's United States visa;

☐ An English translation of all documents not in English, with a verification by the translator that all translations are true and correct;

☐ Pennsylvania Department of Health, Division of Vital Records Form No. HD01273F, Certificate of Adoption of a Foreign-Born Child with Parts 1 and 2 (and Part 3, if applicable) completed;

☐ Pennsylvania Department of Health, Division of Vital Records Form No. HD01275F, Statement of Citizenship and Residency;

☐ If available, a copy of U. S. Government Form N-560 and/or a copy of the child's U.S. passport.

3. The Petition to Register with the attachments should be filed with the Clerk of the Orphans' Court Division of the Court of Common Pleas in the county in which the adopting parent(s) reside(s), except for Philadelphia County resident(s), who must file with the Family Court Division. A filing fee will be charged in accordance with the fee schedule of the county court.

After the Petition to Register is filed, it will be submitted to the Court for review. If the Petition to Register and accompanying documents establish that the foreign adoption of the child is full and final, the Court will enter a Decree directing the registration of the Foreign Adoption Decree. The Clerk of the appropriate Court will then issue a certificate of adoption and transmit to the Department of Health, Division of Vital Records Forms HD01273F and HD01275F, and if provided by the adopting parent(s), a copy of U.S. Government Form N-560 and/or a copy of the child's United States passport.

If the Court cannot determine that the foreign adoption is full and final, it will enter a Decree denying the Petition. In that case, it will be necessary to proceed under Pa.O.C. Rule 15.9.

Some of the following are reasons why a foreign adoption may not be a full and final adoption eligible for registration:

☐ both adopting parents were not present for the adoption hearing in the foreign country and the foreign country is not a Hague Convention country; or

☐ the sole adopting parent was not present at the adoption hearing in the foreign country and the foreign country is not a Hague Convention country; or

☐ the foreign court did not enter a final adoption Decree or Order or its equivalent; or

☐ the child's United States visa is not the type that affords the child full United States citizenship.

If the child has an IH-4 or IR-4 United States visa, it will be necessary to proceed under Pa.O.C. Rule 15.9.

Rule 15.9. Petition for Adoption of a Foreign Born Child

(a) *General Rule.* Adopting parent(s) who are residents of the Commonwealth may petition the Court of Common Pleas in any county as provided in Section 2302 of the Adoption Act (see 23 Pa. C.S. §2302) to proceed with an adoption of their foreign born child who has entered the United States pursuant to an IR-2, IR-3, IH-3, IR-4 or IH-4 United States visa.

(b) *Required Documents.* The following documents shall be filed in the following order with the Clerk of the appropriate division of the Common Pleas Court:

 (1) Preliminary Decree;

 (2) Final Decree;

 (3) Petition for Adoption of a Foreign Born Child;

 (4) Copy of United States visa;

 (5) Reports of investigations, home studies, preplacement and postplacement;

 (6) Copy of birth certificate of foreign born child (if available), with translation;

 (7) Copy of any other relevant foreign decrees and/or documents with translations;

 (8) Consents of any person and/or agency having custody and/or legal and/or physical rights to the child;

 (9) Report of Intermediary (if an intermediary agency was involved);

 (10) Verifications signed by petitioner(s), intermediary and translator(s) stating that facts set forth are true and correct, copies are true and correct copies of originals, that the English translation of foreign documents is accurate, and that false statements are subject to the penalties of 18 Pa. C.S. § 4904;

 (11) Pennsylvania Department of Health, Division of Vital Records Form No. HD01273F, Certificate of Adoption of a Foreign-Born Child with Parts 1 and 2 (and Part 3, if applicable) completed;

 (12) Pennsylvania Department of Health, Division of Vital Records Form No. HD01275F, Statement of Citizenship and Residency; and

 (13) A copy of U.S. Government Form N-560, Certificate of Citizenship, and/or a copy of the child's United States passport, if either or both documents are available.

(c) *Form of Documents:* The Preliminary Decree, Final Decree, Petition for Adoption of a Foreign Born Child, Report of Intermediary (if applicable), and verifications referenced in subparagraph (b)(10) above shall be in substantially the form approved by the Supreme Court. See Appendix of Forms to these Rules.

Rule 15.9   ADOPTIONS

(d) *Judicial Review and Hearing*

(1) *Scope of Review.* The Petition and accompanying documents filed under this Rule shall be subject to review by the Court as prescribed by the Pennsylvania Adoption Act, 23 Pa.C.S. §§ 2101 et seq., Pennsylvania Orphans' Court Rules and local rules of court.

(2) *Home Study and Investigation.* The Court may rely in whole or in part upon a home study containing information required by Section 2530(b) of the Adoption Act and an investigative report containing information required by Section 2535(b) of the Adoption Act previously commissioned in the foreign adoption proceeding without regard to when such reports were prepared. See 23 Pa. C.S. §§ 2530, 2535. The Court may in its discretion require additional reports and investigations to be made in accordance with the Pennsylvania Adoption Act, Pennsylvania Orphans' Court Rules and local rules of court.

(3) *Original Documents, Decrees and Translations.* All original documents, decrees and translations must be available for review by the Court upon request.

(4) *Pre-adoption Requirements.* In order to grant an adoption, the Court must be satisfied that the pre-adoption requirements set forth in Sections 2530-2535 of the Adoption Act have been met. See 23 Pa.C.S. §§ 2530-2535. If the adopting parent(s) were Pennsylvania residents at the time that the United States visa was issued to the foreign born child, the Court may accept an IH or IR United States visa as proof that the pre-adoption requirements have been met.

(5) *Proof that the Child is an Orphan.* In order to grant an adoption, the Court must be satisfied that the child to be adopted is an orphan. The Court may accept the child's IH or IR United States visa as proof that the foreign born child is an orphan.

(6) *Hearing.* The Court shall schedule a hearing to allow for testimony pursuant to Sections 2721-2724 of the Adoption Act. See 23 Pa.C.S. §§ 2721-2724. Petitioner(s) and the child to be adopted shall appear at the hearing. The Court may in its discretion require the presence of additional persons, including a representative of the intermediary.

(e) *Disclosure of Fees and Costs.* Prior to or at the hearing, a report shall be filed setting forth the amount of fees, expenses and costs paid or to be paid to counsel, the intermediary and/or any other person or agency in connection with the adoption of the foreign born child. The Court may request an itemization of any of the amount(s) reported.

(f) *Final Decree.* After the hearing, the Court shall determine if the adoption of the foreign born child can be granted, and if so, the Court shall enter a decree as provided in Section 2902 of the Adoption Act. See 23 Pa.C.S. § 2902.

(g) *Clerk of the Appropriate Court.* Upon the filing of a decree granting the adoption under this Rule, the Clerk of the appropriate Court shall enter the decree and date of the decree on the docket. The Clerk shall send Form No. HD01273F, Certificate of Adoption of a Foreign-Born Child, and Form No. HD01275F, Statement of Citizenship and Residency, to the Department of Health, Division of Vital Records, along with a copy of U.S. Government Form N-560, Certificate of Citizenship, and/or a copy of the child's United States passport, if either or both documents have been provided by the adopting parent(s). The Clerk shall issue to the adopting parent(s) a certificate of adoption in accordance with Section 2907 of the Adoption Act. See 23 Pa.C.S. § 2907.

(h) *Only One Court May Assume Jurisdiction.* A parent shall not proceed under this Rule if the foreign adoption has been registered or otherwise finalized by a Court of this Commonwealth or any other state.

Explanatory Note: Pursuant to 23 Pa.C.S. § 2908(e), as amended by Act 96 of 2006, a set of forms, consisting of a Petition for Adoption of a Foreign Born Child, Report of Intermediary, Verification of Translator, Preliminary Decree, and Final Decree are set forth in the Appendix to these Rules.

In most instances, the adopting parent(s) of a foreign born child who has entered the United States with an IR-2, IR-3 or IH-3 United States visa will not need to proceed under Pa.O.C. Rule 15.9, but can register the foreign adoption decree pursuant to Pa.O.C. Rule 15.8. Situations may arise, though, that necessitate proceeding under this Rule, such as the inclusion of an incorrect birth year on the foreign adoption decree, or other personal family reasons. In these situations, adopting parent(s) of a foreign born child entering the United States with an IR-2, IR-3, or IH-3 United States visa may proceed under Pa.O.C. Rule 15.9; however, adopting parent(s) should be advised by counsel of the additional costs, additional documentation required, and the delay caused by the need for a hearing.

If a foreign born child has entered the United States with an IH-4 or IR-4 United States visa, the adopting parent(s) must proceed under Pa.O.C. Rule 15.9 because the adoption of their foreign born child was not finalized in the country of the child's birth.

Only one state court, whether in this Commonwealth or another state, should exercise jurisdiction over the registration of the foreign adoption decree or the completion of the adoption initiated in the native country of the foreign born child. Thus, if the adoption has been finalized or the foreign adoption decree has been registered in another state court or in another court within this Commonwealth, the adopting parent(s) need not and should not proceed under this Rule. In similar fashion, if the adoption of the foreign born child has been finalized in this Commonwealth, and thereafter, another petitioner seeks to adopt this child, the subsequent proceeding will be a standard proceeding under the applicable provisions of the Adoption Act, 23 Pa.C.S. §§ 2101 et seq. Such a situation could occur when the child is to be adopted by a step-parent after divorce or death of the original adopting parent(s), or when, after termination of parental rights, the child is to be adopted by different adopting parent(s).

The documents referenced in Pa.O.C Rule 15.9 should be filed with the Clerk of the Orphans' Court Division, except in Philadelphia County, where they should be filed with the Clerk of the Family Court Division. The Petition and accompanying documents under this Rule, including the decree granting the adoption, are confidential and should be impounded and withheld from public inspection as provided in the Adoption Act, 23 Pa. C.S. §§ 2905 et seq. and Pa.O.C. Rule 15.7.

The Clerk shall make available to the petitioner(s) the necessary Department of Health, Division of Vital Records forms: Form No. HD01273F, Certificate of Adoption of a Foreign-Born Child; and Form No. HD01275F, Statement of Citizenship and Residency.

IN THE COURT OF COMMON PLEAS OF _____ COUNTY, PENNSYLVANIA
ORPHANS' COURT DIVISION
(FAMILY COURT DIVISION in Philadelphia County)
IN RE: ADOPTION OF _____ (initials only)
ADOPTION NO. _____

PRELIMINARY DECREE

AND NOW, this _____ day of _____, 20____, upon consideration of the within Petition and on the motion of _____, Esquire, attorney for

Rule 15.9 ADOPTIONS

Petitioner(s) or _____, Pro Se, a hearing thereon is fixed for _____ in _____ before the Honorable _____ at _____ am/pm.

Notice shall be given to the following persons and or entities having any legal and/or physical rights to the child:

1. NAME
   ADDRESS
   _____
   RELATIONSHIP

2. NAME
   ADDRESS
   _____
   RELATIONSHIP

3. NAME
   ADDRESS
   _____
   RELATIONSHIP

BY THE COURT:

_____
J.

IN THE COURT OF COMMON PLEAS OF _____ COUNTY, PENNSYLVANIA
ORPHANS' COURT DIVISION
(FAMILY COURT DIVISION in Philadelphia County)
IN RE: ADOPTION OF _____ (initials only)
ADOPTION NO. _____

FINAL DECREE

AND NOW, this ____ day of _____, 20____, upon consideration of the within Petition and after the hearing thereon, the Court having made an investigation to verify the statements of the Petition and other facts to give the Court full knowledge as to the desirability of the proposed adoption; and the Court, being satisfied, finds that the statements made in the Petition are true, that the needs and welfare of the child proposed to be adopted will be promoted by this adoption, and that all requirements of the Adoption Act have been met, it is hereby ORDERED, ADJUDGED and DECREED that this child, _____ *(Name of child as written on Foreign Decree)* is hereby adopted, shall be known as _____ *(Child's name from this time forward)* and shall have all the rights of a child and heir of _____. *(Adopting Parent(s))*, and shall be subject to the duties of a child to said adopting parent(s).

BY THE COURT:

_____
J.

Pa. O.C. Rules Rule 15.9

IN THE COURT OF COMMON PLEAS OF
_____ COUNTY, PENNSYLVANIA
ORPHANS' COURT DIVISION
(FAMILY COURT DIVISION in Philadelphia County)
IN RE: ADOPTION OF _____ (initials only)
ADOPTION NO. _____

PETITION FOR ADOPTION OF A FOREIGN BORN CHILD

To the Honorable, the Judge of said Court:

The Petition of _____ *(Name(s) of Adopting Parent(s))* under 23 Pa. C.S. §§ 2701 and 2908 respectfully states that:

1. At least one of the Petitioners filing this Petition is a resident of the Commonwealth of Pennsylvania and has resided in this Commonwealth since_____. *(Provide at least month and year)*

2. No other court in this Commonwealth or in any other state has reviewed, registered, finalized or otherwise assumed jurisdiction over the adoption of this child, except as follows: _____

__ *(Provide name of court, county and state)*

Explain the proceeding previously initiated and the resulting decision from the court: (Attach all court decrees).

_____

_____

_____

_____

3. Petitioner(s) desire(s) to adopt this child known as _____, *(Name of child as written on Foreign Decree)* and intend that such child shall be treated as one of (his/her/their) heirs and hereby declare(s) that (he/she/they) will perform all the duties of parent(s) to him/her.

4. The child has entered the United States pursuant to a United States visa. A true and correct copy of the United States visa is attached as an exhibit to this Petition. The United States visa was issued as an:

(Please circle one) IR-2, IR-3, IH-3, IR-4 or IH-4

5. a) The child's full name as shown on the United States visa is

_____

b) The full birth name of the child as listed on the foreign birth certificate (if available) is

_____

c) The full name of the child as it appears on the foreign decree is

_____

d) The full name of the child as he/she is to be known from this time forward is

_____

6. The child has resided with Petitioner(s) for the following length of time

Rule 15.9 ADOPTIONS

7. Information concerning the Petitioner(s), the adopting parent(s), is as follows:
    a) Adopting Father:
        1) Full name _____
        2) Residence _____
        3) Marital status _____
        4) Age _____
        5) Occupation _____
        6) Religious affiliation _____
        7) Racial background _____
        8) Relationship to adoptee by blood or marriage, if any _____
        9) Daytime telephone no. _____
    b) Adopting Mother:
        1) Full name _____
        2) Residence _____
        3) Marital status _____
        4) Age _____
        5) Occupation _____
        6) Religious affiliation _____
        7) Racial background _____
        8) Relationship to adoptee by blood or marriage, if any _____
        9) Daytime telephone no. _____
8. The following reports, as applicable, have been completed as of the dates set forth below. A true and correct copy of each of these reports is attached as an exhibit to this Petition.
    a) Report of Intermediary described in 23 Pa. C.S. § 2533
    _____

    b) Home Study and/or Preplacement Reports described in 23 Pa. C.S. § 2530
    _____

    c) Investigation Reports described in 23 Pa. C.S. § 2535
    _____

    d) Postplacement Reports, if any
    _____

9. Information concerning the intermediary agency, if any, is as follows:

_____
Name of agency

_____
Address

_____
Telephone no.

_____
County where office is located

Pa. O.C. Rules   Rule 15.9

10. If there is no report of an intermediary, the following information is being provided by the Petitioner(s) as to the adoptee child:

    a) Sex _____

    b) Racial background _____

    c) Age _____

    d) Birth date _____

    e) Birthplace _____

    f) Places of residence since birth _____

    g) Religious affiliation _____

    h) A full statement of the value of all property owned or possessed by the child, if any _____

    i) State whether medical history information was obtained, and if not, explain why not _____

11. If there is no report of an intermediary, and the adoptee child is under 18 years of age, provide the following information as to the birth mother, if known:

    a) Name _____

    b) Residence or last known address _____

    c) Racial background _____

    d) Age _____

    e) Marital status as of the time of the birth of child _____

    f) Marital status during one year prior to birth of child _____

    g) Religious affiliation _____

    h) Birth mother's parental rights were terminated by decree of _____ dated _____

12. If there is no report of an intermediary, and the adoptee child is under 18 years of age, provide the following information as to the birth father, if known:

    a) Name _____

    b) Residence or last known address _____

    c) Racial background _____

    d) Age _____

    e) Marital status as of the time of the birth of child _____

    f) Marital status during one year prior to birth of child _____

    g) Religious affiliation _____

    h) Birth father's parental rights were terminated by decree of _____ dated _____

13. If there is no report of an intermediary, attach a copy of the birth certificate. If no birth certificate or other birth identification issued by the country of birth can be obtained, a statement of the reason and a detailed explanation of the efforts made to obtain the certificate are required and attached as an exhibit to this Petition.

Rule 15.9 ADOPTIONS

14. If there is no report of an intermediary, attach copies of any foreign decrees and/or documents concerning this adoption, including any decree terminating the parental rights of birth mother and/or birth father, if needed, with an English translation for those decrees and/or documents not in English, certified by a translator to be true and correct translations of the foreign decrees and/or documents.

15. If there is no report of an intermediary, attach all consents required by Section 2711 of the Adoption Code, 23 Pa. C.S. § 2711. If consents are not required, explain

_____
_____
_____
_____

16. Attach Pennsylvania Department of Health, Division of Vital Records Form No. HD01273F, Certificate of Adoption of a Foreign-Born Child with Parts 1 and 2 (and Part 3, if applicable) completed.

17. Attach Pennsylvania Department of Health, Division of Vital Records Form No. HD01275F, Statement of Citizenship and Residency.

18. Attach a copy of U.S. Government Form N-560, Certificate of Citizenship, and/or a copy of the child's United States passport, if either or both documents are available.

19. It is the desire of the Petitioner(s) that the relationship of parent and child be established between the Petitioner(s) and the adoptee child.

WHEREFORE, Petitioner(s) pray your Honorable Court to enter a Final Decree that the child proposed to be adopted shall have all the rights of a child and heir of Petitioner(s) and Petitioner(s) shall be subject to the duties as parent(s) of such child, and that the child's name shall henceforth be _____.

DATE: _____

_____
Signature of Adopting Parent*

_____
Signature of Adopting Parent

_____
_____
_____
_____

(If represented, counsel's name, address, and telephone number)

VERIFICATION TO PETITION FOR ADOPTION OF A FOREIGN BORN CHILD

I/We, _____, verify that I/we are the Petitioner(s) named in the foregoing Petition and that the facts set forth therein are true and correct to the best of my/our knowledge, information and belief. I/We further verify that all documents attached to this Petition are true and correct copies of the originals. I/We understand

---

*When there are two adopting parents, both must sign.

Pa. O.C. Rules   Rule 15.9

that false statements herein are made subject to the penalties of 18 Pa. C.S. § 4904 relating to unsworn falsification to authorities.

DATE: _____

_____
Signature of Adopting Parent

_____
Signature of Adopting Parent

IN THE COURT OF COMMON PLEAS OF _____ COUNTY, PENNSYLVANIA
ORPHANS' COURT DIVISION
(FAMILY COURT DIVISION in Philadelphia County)
IN RE: ADOPTION OF _____ (initials only)
ADOPTION NO. _____

REPORT OF THE INTERMEDIARY IN THE ADOPTION OF A FOREIGN BORN CHILD

The report of the agency, _____, as intermediary, under 23 Pa. C.S. § 2533, states as follows:

1. Intermediary's address
   _____

   Intermediary's telephone no.
   _____

   County where office is located:
   _____

2. The facts as to the adoptee child are:
   a) Name _____
   b) Sex _____
   c) Racial background _____
   d) Age _____
   e) Birth date _____
   f) Birthplace _____
   g) Religious affiliation _____

3. Date of the placement of the child with the Petitioner(s), adopting parent(s),
   _____

4. If known, the facts as to the birth mother are:
   a) Name _____
   b) Residence or last known address _____
   c) Racial background _____
   d) Age _____
   e) Marital status as of the time of the birth of child _____
   f) Marital status during one year prior to birth of child _____
   g) Religious affiliation _____
   h) Birth mother's parental rights were terminated by decree of _____
      _____ dated _____

5. If known, the facts as to the birth father are:
   a) Name _____
   b) Residence or last known address _____
   c) Racial background _____
   d) Age _____
   e) Marital status as of the time of the birth of child _____
   f) Marital status during one year prior to birth of child _____
   g) Religious affiliation _____
   h) Birth father's parental rights were terminated by decree of ____
   _____ dated _____

6. All consents required by 23 Pa. C.S. § 2711 are attached to this Report as exhibits or are not required for the following reasons, provide explanation:
_____
_____

7. a) A true and correct copy of the birth certificate or a registration of the birth by the country of birth is attached to this Report as an exhibit. If no birth certificate or other birth identification issued by the country of birth can be obtained, a statement of the reason and a detailed explanation of the efforts made to obtain the certificate are attached as exhibits to this Report.

   b) Attach copies of any foreign decrees and/or documents concerning this adoption, including any decree terminating the parental rights of birth mother and/or birth father, with an English translation for those decrees and/or documents not in English, certified by a translator to be true and correct translations of the decrees and/or documents.

8. Attach a verified list of itemized fees and/or expenses paid or to be paid to or received by the intermediary and/or any other person or persons to the knowledge of the intermediary by reason of the adoption placement.

9. A full description and statement of the value of all property owned or possessed by the child, if any, is as follows:
_____
_____

10. No provision of any act regulating the interstate placement of children has been violated with respect to the placement of the child.

11. The child's medical history information was obtained and is available, except as follows:
_____
_____

DATE: _____

                         Signature
                         (Type name of signor, title, and name of agency)

Pa. O.C. Rules   Rule 15.9

VERIFICATION TO REPORT OF INTERMEDIARY

I, _____, *Title* verify that I am of _____
_____ *(Name of Agency)* and I am authorized to take this verification on its behalf, and that the facts set forth in the foregoing Report are true and correct to the best of my knowledge, information and belief. I further verify that all documents attached to this Report are true and correct copies of the originals. I understand that false statements herein are made subject to the penalties of 18 Pa. C.S. § 4904 relating to unsworn falsification to authorities.

DATE: _____

_____
Signature

VERIFICATION OF TRANSLATOR

I, _____, verify that I am a licensed translator and that all translations of the foreign documents which are attached to this Petition are true and correct English translations of the originals. I understand that false statements herein are made subject to the penalties of 18 Pa. C.S. § 4904 relating to unsworn falsification to authorities.

DATE: _____

_____
Signature

INDEX TO APPENDIX
ORPHANS' COURT AND REGISTER OF WILLS FORMS ADOPTED BY SUPREME COURT PURSUANT TO Pa. O.C. Rule 1.3

F. Foreign Adoption Forms
  1. *Registration Forms—Pa.O.C. Rule 15.8*
     a. Petition to Register Foreign Adoption Decree
     b. Final Decree—Granted
     c. Final Decree—Denied
     d. Instructions for Filing Petition
  2. *Completion of Foreign Adoption Forms—Pa.O.C. Rule 15.9*
     a. Preliminary Decree
     b. Final Decree
     c. Petition for Adoption of a Foreign Born Child
     d. Report of the Intermediary
     e. Verification of Translator
        - Rule 15.6(b)(1) Form—Notification of the filing of a petition
        - Rule 15.6(b)(2) Form—Notification of the entry of an Order from Orphans' Court
        - Rule 15.6(b)(3) Form—Notification of an appeal from an Orphans' Court Order
        - Rule 15.6(b)(4) Form—Notification of the entry of an Order disposing of an appeal

X. Juvenile Rules

PART I. RULES OF JUVENILE COURT PROCEDURE
(Amended Through April, 2019)

Dependency Matters

CHAPTER 11
GENERAL PROVISIONS

1100. Scope of Rules
1101. Purpose and Construction
1102. Citing the Juvenile Court Procedural Rules

PART A
BUSINESS OF COURTS

1120. Definitions
1121. Local Rules
1122. Continuances
1123. Subpoenas
1124. Summons
1126. Defects in Form, Content, or Procedure
1127. Recording and Transcribing Juvenile Court Proceedings
1128. Presence at Proceedings
1129. Appearance by Advanced Communication Technology
1130. Court Fees Prohibited for Advanced Communication Technology
1133. Motion to Intervene
1134. Proceedings *In Camera*
1135. Captions
1136. *Ex Parte* Communication
1137. Public Discussion by Court Personnel of Pending Matters
1140. Bench Warrants for Failure to Appear

PART B(1)
EDUCATION AND HEALTH OF CHILD

1145. Application or Motion for Examination and Treatment of a Child
1146. Notice of Truancy Hearing.
1147. Educational Decision Maker.
1148. Educational Stability and Placement.
1149. Family Finding.

PART B(2)
COUNSEL

1150. Attorneys—Appearances and Withdrawals
1151. Assignment of Guardian *ad litem* & Counsel
1152. Waiver of Counsel
1154. Duties of Guardian *ad litem*
1158. Assignment of CASA

PART C
RECORDS

PART C(1)
ACCESS TO JUVENILE COURT RECORDS

1160. Inspection of Juvenile Court File/Records

PART C(2)
MAINTAINING RECORDS

1165. Design of Forms
1166. Maintaining Records in the Clerk of Courts
1167. Filings and Service of Court Orders and Notices

PART D
MASTERS

1182. Qualifications of Juvenile Court Hearing Officer
1185. Appointment to Cases
1187. Authority of Juvenile Court Hearing Officer
1190. Stipulations Before Juvenile Court Hearing Officer
1191. Juvenile Court Hearing Officer's Findings and Recommendation to the Judge

CHAPTER 12
COMMENCEMENT OF PROCEEDINGS, EMERGENCY CUSTODY, AND PRE-ADJUDICATORY PLACEMENT

PART A
COMMENCING PROCEEDINGS

1200. Commencing Proceedings
1201. Procedures for Protective Medical Custody
1202. Procedures for Protective Custody by Police and County Agency

PART B
EMERGENCY CUSTODY

1210. Order for Protective Custody

PART C
SHELTER CARE

1240. Shelter Care Application
1241. Notification of Shelter Care Hearing
1242. Shelter Care Hearing
1243. Shelter Care Rehearing

Pa. R.J.C.P.

CHAPTER 13
PRE-ADJUDICATORY PROCEDURES

PART A
VENUE

1300. Venue
1302. Inter-County Transfer

PART B
APPLICATION FOR PRIVATE PETITION

1320. Application to File a Private Petition
1321. Hearing on Application for Private Petition

PART C
PETITION

1330. Petition: Filing, Contents, Function, Aggravated Circumstances
1331. Service of Petition
1333. Separate Petitions and Consolidated Hearing
1334. Amendment of Petition
1335. Withdrawal of Petition
1336. Re-filing of the Petition After Withdrawal or Dismissal

PART D
PROCEDURES FOLLOWING FILING OF PETITION

1340. Discovery and Inspection
1342. Pre-Adjudicatory Conference.

PART D(1)
MOTION PROCEDURES

1344. Motions and Answers
1345. Filing and Service

PART D(2)
ADJUDICATORY SUMMONS AND NOTICE PROCEDURES

1360. Adjudicatory Summons
1361. Adjudicatory Notice
1363. Service of Summons
1364. Failure to Appear on the Summons

Pa. R.J.C.P.

PART E
PRESERVATION OF TESTIMONY AND EVIDENCE

1380. Preservation of Testimony After Commencement of Proceedings
1381. Preservation of Testimony by Video Recording

CHAPTER 14
ADJUDICATORY HEARING

1401. Introduction to Chapter Fourteen
1404. Prompt Adjudicatory Hearing
1405. Stipulations
1406. Adjudicatory Hearing
1408. Findings on Petition
1409. Adjudication of Dependency & Court Order

CHAPTER 15
DISPOSITIONAL HEARING

PART A
SUMMONS AND NOTICE OF THE DISPOSITIONAL HEARING

1500. Summons for the Dispositional Hearing
1501. Dispositional Notice

PART B
DISPOSITIONAL HEARING AND AIDS

1509. Aids in Disposition
1510. Prompt Dispositional Hearing
1511. Pre-Dispositional Statement
1512. Dispositional Hearing
1514. Dispositional Finding Before Removal From Home
1515. Dispositional Order
1516. Service of Dispositional Order

CHAPTER 16
POST-DISPOSITIONAL PROCEDURES

PART A
SUMMONS, NOTICE, AND REPORTS

1600. Summons for the Permanency Hearing
1601. Permanency Hearing Notice
1604. Submission of Reports

PART B(1)
MODIFICATIONS

1606. Modification of Dependent Child's Placement

Pa. R.J.C.P.

PART (B)(2)
PERMANENCY HEARING

1607. Regular Scheduling of Permanency Hearing
1608. Permanency Hearing
1609. Permanency Hearing Orders
1610. Permanency Hearing for Children Over Eighteen.
1611. Permanency Hearing Orders for Children Over Eighteen.

PART (C)
TERMINATION & POST-DISPOSITIONAL PROCEDURES

1613. Termination of Court Supervision
1616. Post-Dispositional Procedures; Appeals [RESERVED]

PART D. CESSATION OR RESUMPTION OF COURT SUPERVISION OR JURISDICTION

1631. Termination of Court Supervision.
1634. Motion for Resumption of Jurisdiction.
1635. Hearing on Motion for Resumption of Jurisdiction.

CHAPTER 17
AGGRAVATED CIRCUMSTANCES

1701. Motion for Finding of Aggravated Circumstances
1702. Filing of Motion for Finding of Aggravated Circumstances
1705. Adjudication of Aggravated Circumstances

CHAPTER 18
SUSPENSIONS

1800. Suspensions of Acts of Assembly

CHAPTER 11
GENERAL PROVISIONS

1100. Scope of Rules
1101. Purpose and Construction
1102. Citing the Juvenile Court Procedural Rules

Rule 1100. Scope of Rules

A. These rules shall govern dependency proceedings in all courts. Unless otherwise specifically provided, these rules shall not apply to orphans' court, domestic relations and delinquency proceedings.

B. Each of the courts exercising dependency jurisdiction, as provided in the Juvenile Act, 42 Pa.C.S. § 6301 et seq., may adopt local rules of procedure in accordance with Rule 1121.

Comment

The Pennsylvania Rules of Juvenile Court Procedure are split into two categories: delinquency matters and dependency matters. All delinquency matters are governed by Chapters One through Ten (Rules 100 - 1099). All dependency matters are governed by Chapters Eleven through Twenty (Rules 1100 - 2099).

Unless specifically provided in these rules, the Pennsylvania Rules of Civil Procedure and the Pennsylvania Rules of Criminal Procedure do not apply to dependency proceedings commenced pursuant to Rule 1200 and 42 Pa.C.S. § 6301 et seq.

These rules govern proceedings when the Juvenile Act vests jurisdiction in the Court of Common Pleas. *See* 42 Pa.C.S. §§ 6321 and 6302.

Each judicial district may promulgate local rules that follow the requirements of Rule 1121 and Pa.R.J.A. 103.

Official Note: Rule 1100 adopted August, 21, 2006, effective February 1, 2007. Amended May 12, 2008, effective immediately.

Committee Explanatory Reports:

Final Report explaining the provisions of Rule 1100 published with the Court's Order at 36 Pa.B. 5571 (September 2, 2006). Final Report explaining the amendments to Rule 1100 published with the Court's Order at 38 Pa.B. 2360 (May 12, 2008).

Rule 1101. Purpose and Construction

A. These rules are intended to provide for the just determination of every dependency proceeding.

B. These rules establish uniform practice and procedure for courts exercising jurisdiction as provided in the Juvenile Act, 42 Pa.C.S. § 6301 *et seq.*, and shall be construed to secure uniformity and simplicity in procedure, fairness in administration, and the elimination of unjustifiable expense and delay.

C. These rules shall be interpreted and construed to effectuate the purposes stated in the Juvenile Act, 42 Pa.C.S. § 6301(b).

D. To the extent practicable, these rules shall be construed in consonance with the rules of statutory construction.

Official Note: Rule 1101 adopted August, 21, 2006, effective February 1, 2007.

Pa. R.J.C.P. — Rule 1102

Committee Explanatory Reports:

Final Report explaining the provisions of Rule 1101 published with the Court's Order at 36 Pa.B. 5571 (September 2, 2006).

Rule 1102. Citing the Juvenile Court Procedural Rules

All juvenile court procedural rules adopted by the Supreme Court of Pennsylvania under the authority of Article V § 10(c) of the Constitution of Pennsylvania, adopted April 23, 1968, shall be known as the Pennsylvania Rules of Juvenile Court Procedure and shall be cited as "Pa.R.J.C.P."

Comment

The authority for rule-making is granted to the Supreme Court by Article V § 10(c) of the Pennsylvania Constitution, which states in part, "[t]he Supreme Court shall have the power to prescribe general rules governing practice, procedure and the conduct of all courts . . . if such rules are consistent with this Constitution and neither abridge, enlarge nor modify the substantive rights of any litigant, nor affect the right of the General Assembly to determine the jurisdiction of any court or justice of the peace, nor suspend nor alter any statute of limitation or repose. All laws shall be suspended to the extent that they are inconsistent with rules prescribed under these provisions."

Official Note: Rule 1102 adopted August, 21, 2006, effective February 1, 2007.

Committee Explanatory Reports:

Final Report explaining the provisions of Rule 1102 published with the Court's Order at 36 Pa.B. 5571 (September 2, 2006).

PART A
BUSINESS OF COURTS

1120. Definitions
1121. Local Rules
1122. Continuances
1123. Subpoenas
1124. Summons
1126. Defects in Form, Content, or Procedure
1127. Recording and Transcribing Juvenile Court Proceedings
1128. Presence at Proceedings
1129. Appearance by Advanced Communication Technology
1130. Court Fees Prohibited for Advanced Communication Technology
1133. Motion to Intervene
1134. Proceedings In Camera
1135. Captions
1136. Ex Parte Communication
1137. Public Discussion by Court Personnel of Pending Matters
1140. Bench Warrants for Failure to Appear

Rule 1120. Definitions.

ADULT is any person, other than a child, eighteen years old or older.

ADVANCED COMMUNICATION TECHNOLOGY is any communication equipment that is used as a link between parties in physically separate locations and includes, but is not limited to, systems providing for two-way simultaneous audio-visual communication, closed circuit television, telephone and facsimile equipment, and electronic mail.

AGE-APPROPRIATE OR DEVELOPMENTALLY-APPROPRIATE is used to describe the: 1) activities or items that are generally accepted as suitable for children of the same chronological age or level of maturity or that are determined to be developmentally appropriate for a child, based on the development of cognitive, emotional, physical, and behavioral capacities that are typical for an age or age group; or 2) in the case of a specific child, activities or items that are suitable based on the developmental stages attained by the child with respect to the cognitive, emotional, physical, and behavioral capacities of the child.

AGGRAVATED CIRCUMSTANCES are those circumstances specifically defined pursuant to the Juvenile Act, 42 Pa.C.S. § 6302.

CAREGIVER is a person with whom the child is placed in an out-of-home placement, including a resource family or individual designated by a county agency or private agency. The resource family is the caregiver for any child placed with them.

CHILD is a person who:

1) is under the age of eighteen and is the subject of the dependency petition; or

2) is under the age of twenty-one; and

    a) was adjudicated dependent before reaching the age of eighteen;

    b) has requested the court to retain jurisdiction; and

    c) who remains under the jurisdiction of the court or for whom jurisdiction has been resumed as a dependent child because the court has determined that the child is one of the following:

        i) completing secondary education or an equivalent credential;

        ii) enrolled in an institution which provides postsecondary or vocational education;

        iii) participating in a program actively designed to promote or remove barriers to employment;

        iv) employed for at least eighty hours per month; or

        v) incapable of doing any of the activities as prescribed above in (2)(c)(i)-(iv) due to a medical or behavioral health condition, which is supported by regularly updated information in the permanency plan for the child.

CLERK OF COURTS is that official in each judicial district who has the responsibility and function under state law or local practice to maintain the official court record and docket, without regard to that person's official title. A party to the proceedings shall not function as the clerk of courts.

COPY is an exact duplicate of an original document, including any required signatures, produced through mechanical or electronic means and includes, but is not limited to, copies reproduced by transmission using facsimile equipment, or by scanning into and printing out of a computer.

COUNTY AGENCY is the county children and youth social service agency established pursuant to the County Institution District Law, 62 P.S. § 2305

(1937) or established through the county commissioners in the judicial districts where the County Institution District Law was abolished, 16 P.S. §§ 2161 and 2168, and supervised by the Department of Public Welfare[1] pursuant to the Public Welfare Code, 62 P.S. § 901 et seq.

COURT is the Court of Common Pleas, a court of record, which is assigned to hear dependency matters. Court shall include juvenile court hearing officers when they are permitted to hear cases under these rules. Juvenile court shall have the same meaning as court.

DILIGENT EFFORTS are the comprehensive and ongoing efforts made to identify and locate adult relatives and kin for a child until the permanency goal is achieved.

EDUCATIONAL DECISION MAKER is a responsible adult appointed by the court to make decisions regarding a child's education when the child has no guardian or the court has limited the guardian's right to make such decisions for the child. The educational decision maker acts as the child's representative concerning all matters regarding education unless the court specifically limits the authority of the educational decision maker.

FAMILY FINDING is the ongoing diligent efforts of the county agency, or its contracted providers, to search for and identify adult relatives and kin, and engage them in the county agency's social service planning and delivery of services, including gaining commitment from relatives and kin to support a child or guardian receiving county agency services.

FAMILY SERVICE PLAN is the document in which the county agency sets forth the service objectives for a family and services to be provided to a family by the county agency.

GUARDIAN is any parent, custodian, or other person who has legal custody of a child, or person designated by the court to be a temporary guardian for purposes of a proceeding.

HEALTH CARE is care related to any medical need including physical, mental, and dental health. This term is used in the broadest sense to include any type of health need.

JUDGE is a judge of the Court of Common Pleas.

JUVENILE COURT HEARING OFFICER is an attorney with delegated authority to preside over and make recommendations for dependency matters. Juvenile court hearing officer has the same meaning as master as used pursuant to 42 Pa.C.S. § 6301 et seq.

JUVENILE PROBATION OFFICER is a person who has been appointed by the court or employed by a county's juvenile probation office, and who has been properly commissioned by being sworn in as an officer of the court to exercise the powers and duties set forth in Rule 195, the Juvenile Act, and the Child Protective Services Law.

KIN is a relative of the child through blood or marriage, godparent of the child as recognized through an organized church, a member of the child's tribe or clan, or someone who has a significant positive relationship with the child or the child's family.

KINSHIP CARE is the full-time nurturing and protection of a child who is separated from the child's guardian and placed in the home of a caregiver who has an existing relationship with the child and/or the child's family.

LAW ENFORCEMENT OFFICER is any person who is by law given the power to enforce the law when acting within the scope of that person's employment.

MEDICAL FACILITY is any hospital, urgent care facility, psychiatric or psychological ward, drug and alcohol detoxification or rehabilitation program, or any other similar facility designed to treat a child medically or psychologically.

MINOR is any person under the age of eighteen.

OFFICIAL COURT RECORD is the juvenile court file maintained by the clerk of courts which contains all court orders, court notices, docket entries, filed documents, evidence admitted into the record, and other court designated documents in each case.

PARTY is a person or the county agency who has standing to participate in the proceedings but nothing in these Rules confers standing upon a person.

PERMANENCY PLAN is a comprehensive plan that will result in a permanent home for the child.

PETITION is a formal document by which a child is alleged to be dependent.

PETITIONER is any person, who signs or verifies, and files a petition.

POLICE OFFICER is any person, who is by law given the power to arrest when acting within the scope of that person's employment.

PROCEEDING is any stage in the dependency process occurring once a shelter care application has been submitted or a petition has been filed.

PROTECTIVE CUSTODY is when a child is taken into custody for protection as an alleged dependent child pursuant to the Juvenile Act, 42 Pa.C.S. § 6301 et seq. or custody may be assumed pursuant to 23 Pa.C.S. § 6315.

REASONABLE AND PRUDENT PARENT STANDARD is the standard, characterized by careful and sensible parental decisions that maintain the health, safety, and best interests of a child while encouraging the emotional and developmental growth of the child, that a caregiver must use when determining whether to allow a child to participate in extracurricular, enrichment, cultural, and social activities.

RECORDING is the means to provide a verbatim account of a proceeding through the use of a court stenographer, audio recording, audio-visual recording, or other appropriate means.

SHELTER CARE FACILITY is a physically unrestricted facility that provides temporary care of a child and is approved by the Department of Public Welfare.

VERIFICATION is a written statement made by a person that the information provided is true and correct to that person's personal knowledge, information, or belief and that any false statements are subject to the penalties of the Crimes Code, 18 Pa.C.S. § 4904, relating to unsworn falsification to authorities.

Comment

In 2013, the definition of "child" was expanded to include those children who have requested the court to resume jurisdiction after juvenile court supervision had been previously terminated. This rule change followed the changes to the definition of "child" in the Juvenile Act pursuant to Act of July 5, 2012 (P.L. 880, No. 91). *See* 42 Pa.C.S. § 6302.

A party to the proceedings is not to function as the clerk of courts. Because the clerk of courts maintains the official court record, this person is to remain neutral and unbiased by having no personal connection to the proceedings. The county agency is a party to the proceeding and is not to function as the "Clerk of Courts."

The definition of "Clerk of Courts" should not necessarily be interpreted to mean the office of clerk of courts as set forth in 42 Pa.C.S. § 102, but instead refers to that official who maintains the official court record and docket regardless of the person's official title in each judicial district. It is to be determined locally which official is to maintain these records and the associated docket.

The county institution districts, as used in the definition of "county agency," in counties of the fourth, fifth, sixth, seventh, and eighth classes were abolished pursuant to 16 P.S. § 2161. It is the county commissioners' duties in the counties of those classes to provide the children and youth social service agency with the necessary services for the agency to provide care for the child. See 16 P.S. § 2168.

Under the term "court," to determine if juvenile court hearing officers are permitted to hear cases, see Rule 1187.

An "educational decision maker" is to be appointed by court order. The scope of the appointment is limited to decisions regarding the child's education. The educational decision maker acts as the child's spokesperson on all matters regarding education unless the court specifically limits the authority of the educational decision maker. The educational decision maker holds educational and privacy rights as the child's guardian for purposes of 20 U.S.C. § 1232g and 34 C.F.R. § 99.3. *See also* Rule 1147(C) for the duties and responsibilities of an educational decision maker.

The definition of "family finding" is derived from 62 P.S. § 1302.

Diligence is to include utilizing reasonable resources available when engaging in family finding, never ceasing efforts until multiple relatives and kin are identified, and going beyond basic searching tools by exploring alternative tools and methodologies. "Diligent efforts" is to include, but not limited to, interviews with immediate and extended family and kin, genograms, eco-mapping, case mining, cold calls, and specialized computer searches.

It is insufficient to complete only a basic computer search or attempt to contact known relatives at a last-known address or phone number.

For multiple resources efforts that may be utilized, see Commonwealth of Pennsylvania, Department of Public Welfare, Office of Children, Youth and Families Bulletin, No. 3130-12-03, issued May 11, 2012, effective July 1, 2013; Seneca Family Finding, which may be found at www.familyfinding.org, or Legal Services Initiative, diligent search packet, Statewide Adoption and Permanency Network, which may be found at www.diakon-swan.org.

Supporting a child under the definition of "family finding" means any type of aid, including but not limited to emotional, financial, physical, or psychological aid.

See also 62 P.S. § 1301 *et seq.* and 42 U.S.C. § 675 (Fostering Connections) to comply with state and federal regulations.

For the family service plan, see 55 Pa. Code § 3130.61.

"Health care" includes, but is not limited to, routine physical check-ups and examinations; emergency health care; surgeries; exploratory testing; psychological exams, counseling, therapy and treatment programs; drug and alcohol treatment; support groups; routine eye examinations and procedures; teeth cleanings, fluoride treatments, fillings, preventative dental treatments, root canals, and other dental surgeries; and any other examination or treatment relating to any physical, mental, and dental needs of the child.

A "juvenile probation officer" is an officer of the court. "Properly commissioned" as used in the definition of a juvenile probation officer includes the swearing in under oath or affirmation and receipt of a document, certificate, or order of the court memorializing the authority conferred upon the juvenile probation officer by the court.

A properly commissioned juvenile probation officer is vested with all the powers and duties set forth in 42 Pa.C.S. § 6304, and the power to take a child into protective custody as a duly authorized officer of the court pursuant to 42 Pa.C.S.

§ 6324 unless the President Judge has limited such authority pursuant to Rule 195. *See also* 23 Pa.C.S. § 6315.

The definition of "law enforcement officer" does not give the power of arrest to any person who is not otherwise given that power by law.

The "official court record" is to contain all court orders, court notices, docket entries, filed documents, evidence admitted into the record, and other court designated documents in each case. The court may also designate any document to be a part of the record. It does not include items contained in county agency's records unless they are made a part of the official record by being filed with the clerk of courts.

The term "petitioner" may include any person; however, if the person is not the county agency, an application to file a petition pursuant to Rule 1320 is to be made. If the court, after a hearing, grants the application, the applicant may file a petition.

The definition of "proceeding" includes all formal stages once a shelter care application has been submitted or a petition has been filed, including all subsequent proceedings until supervision is terminated pursuant to Rule 1613.

Official Note: Rule 1120 adopted August 21, 2006, effective February 1, 2007. Amended March 19, 2009, effective June 1, 2009. Amended December 24, 2009, effective immediately. Amended April 21, 2011, effective July 1, 2011. Amended April 29, 2011, effective July 1, 2011. Amended May 20, 2011, effective July 1, 2011. Amended June 24, 2013, effective January 1, 2014. Amended October 21, 2013, effective December 1, 2013. Amended July 28, 2014, effective September 29, 2014. Amended July 13, 2015, effective October 1, 2015. Amended December 9, 2015, effective January 1, 2016. Amended April 6, 2017, effective September 1, 2017.

Rule 1121. Local Rules.

The requirements for the promulgation and amendment of local procedural rules for dependency proceedings are set forth in Pennsylvania Rule of Judicial Administration 103(d).

Comment

Effective August 1, 2016, Pennsylvania Rule of Judicial Administration 103 was amended to consolidate and include all local rulemaking requirements. Accordingly, the rulemaking requirements under Pa.R.J.C.P. 1121 for the promulgation and amendment of local procedural rules for dependency proceedings were rescinded and replaced. All local rules previously promulgated in accordance with the requirements of Pa.R.J.C.P. 1121 prior to rescission of this rule remain effective upon compilation and publication pursuant to Pa.R.J.A. No. 103(d)(7).

Official Note: Rule 1121 adopted August, 21, 2006, effective February 1, 2007. Amended December 12, 2008, effective immediately. Amended January 11, 2010, effective March 1, 2010. Rescinded and replaced June 28, 2016, effective August 1, 2016.

Committee Explanatory Reports:

Final Report explaining the provisions of Rule 1121 published with the Court's Order at 36 Pa.B. 5571 (September 2, 2006).

Final Report explaining the amendments to Rule 1121 published with the Court's Order at 38 Pa.B. 7080 (December 27, 2008).

Final Report explaining the amendments to Rule 1121 published with the Courts Order at 40 Pa.B. 518 (January 23, 2010).

Final Report explaining the rescission and replacement of Rule 1121 published with the Court's Order at 46 Pa.B. 3808 (July 16, 2016).

Rule 1122. Continuances

A. **Generally.** In the interests of justice, the court may grant a continuance on its own motion or the motion of any party. On the record, the court shall identify the moving party and state its reasons for granting or denying the continuance.

B. **Notice and rescheduling.** If a continuance is granted, all persons summoned to appear shall be notified of the date, place, and time of the rescheduled hearing.

Comment

Whenever possible, continuances should not be granted when they could be deleterious to the safety or well-being of a party. The interests of justice require the court to look at all the circumstances, effectuating the purposes of the Juvenile Act, 42 Pa.C.S. § 6301, in determining whether a continuance is appropriate.

A party seeking a continuance should notify the court and opposing counsel as soon as possible. Whenever possible, given the time constraints, notice should be written.

Under paragraph (B), if a person is summoned to appear and the case is continued, the party is presumed to be under the scope of the original summons and a new summons is not necessary.

See Rules 1344 and 1345 for motion and filing procedures.

See In re Anita H., 351 Pa.Super. 342, 505 A.2d 1014 (1986).

Official Note: Rule 1122 adopted August, 21, 2006, effective February 1, 2007.

Committee Explanatory Reports:

Final Report explaining the provisions of Rule 1122 published with the Court's Order at 36 Pa.B. 5571 (September 2, 2006).

Rule 1123. Subpoenas

A. **Contents.** A subpoena in a dependency case shall:
   1) order the witness named to appear before the court at the date, time, and place specified;
   2) order the witness to bring any items identified or described;
   3) state on whose behalf the witness is being ordered to testify; and
   4) state the identity, address, and phone number of the person who applied for the subpoena.
B. **Service.**
   1) **Method of Service.** A subpoena shall be served upon a witness by:
      a) in-person delivery;
      b) registered or certified mail, return receipt requested; or
      c) first-class mail.
C. **Duration.** A subpoena shall remain in force until the end of a proceeding.
D. **Bench Warrant.** If any subpoenaed person fails to appear for the hearing and the court finds that sufficient notice was given, the judge may issue a bench warrant pursuant to Rule 1140.

E. Parental notification.
  1) Generally. If a witness is a minor, the witness's guardian shall be:
     a) notified that the minor has been subpoenaed; and
     b) provided with a copy of the subpoena.
  2) Exception. Upon prior court approval and good cause shown, a subpoena may be served upon a minor without such notification to the guardian. If and when necessary, request for such prior court approval may be obtained *ex parte*.

Comment

A subpoena is used to order a witness to appear and a summons is issued to bring a party to the proceeding.

A *subpoena duces tecum* is to set forth with particularity, the documents, records, or other papers to be produced at the hearing. The items sought are to be relevant to the proceedings. See Rule 1340 on discovery, *In re J.C.*, 412 Pa.Super. 369, 603 A.2d 627 (1992), and *In re A.H.*, 763 A.2d 873 (Pa. Super. Ct. 2000) for production of documents necessary to prepare for a hearing.

Prior to issuing a bench warrant for a minor, the judge should determine if the guardian of the witness was served. Nothing in these rules gives the guardians of witnesses legal standing in the matter being heard by the court or creates a right for witnesses to have their guardians present. In addition, lack of required notice to the guardian does not prevent the minor witness from testifying. See Rule 1140 for procedures on bench warrants.

For power to compel attendance, see 42 Pa.C.S. § 6333. Nothing in this rule prohibits the court from holding a contempt hearing. See *In re Crawford*, 360 Pa.Super. 36, 519 A.2d 978 (1987) for punishment of contempt (children). See also *In re Griffin*, 456 Pa.Super. 440, 690 A.2d 1192 (1997) (foster parents), *Janet D. v. Carros*, 240 Pa.Super. 291, 362 A.2d 1060 (1976) (county agency), and *In re Rose*, 161 Pa.Super. 204, 54 A.2d 297 (1947) (parents) for additional guidance on contempt for other parties.

Any person may file a motion to quash the subpoena for a witness and/or for requested items. The court is to rule on the motion prior to the production of the witness or the items.

Official Note: Rule 1123 adopted August, 21, 2006, effective February 1, 2007. Amended May 12, 2008, effective immediately. Amended March 19, 2009, effective June 1, 2009. Amended September 16, 2009, effective immediately.

Committee Explanatory Reports:

Final Report explaining the provisions of Rule 1123 published with the Court's Order at 36 Pa.B. 5571 (September 2, 2006). Final Report explaining the amendments to Rule 1123 published with the Court's Order at 38 Pa.B. 2360 (May 24, 2008). Final Report explaining the amendments to Rule 1123 published with the Court's Order at 39 Pa.B. 1614 (April 4, 2009). Final Report explaining the amendments to Rule 1123 published with the Court's Order at 39 Pa.B. 5544 (September 26, 2009).

Rule 1124. Summons

A. Requirements of the summons. The summons shall:
  1) be in writing;
  2) set forth the date, time, and place of the hearing;

3) instruct the parties about the right to counsel; and
   4) give a warning stating that the failure to appear for the hearing may result in arrest.
B. Method of Service. The summons shall be served:
   1) in-person; or
   2) by certified mail, return receipt and first-class mail.
C. Exception to service. If service cannot be accomplished pursuant to paragraph (B), the party may move for a special order directing the method of service. The motion shall be accompanied by an affidavit stating the nature and extent of the investigation which has been made to determine the whereabouts of the person sought to be served and the reasons why service can not be made.
D. Bench Warrant. If any summoned person fails to appear for the hearing and the court finds that sufficient notice was given, the judge may issue a bench warrant pursuant to Rule 1140.

Comment

A subpoena is used to order a witness to appear and a summons is issued to bring a party to the proceeding.

In paragraph (D), this rule provides that a summoned person is to fail to appear and the court is to find that sufficient notice was given before a bench warrant may be issued. The Juvenile Act, 42 Pa.C.S. § 6335(c), which provides for the issuance of arrest warrants if the child may abscond or may not attend or be brought to a hearing, is suspended to the extent that it conflicts with this rule. *See* Rule 1800 for suspensions.

See Rules 1360(A), 1500(A), and 1600(A) for service of the parties for a proceeding.

See Rule 1140 for procedures on bench warrants.

Official Note: Rule 1124 adopted August 21, 2006, effective February 1, 2007. Amended March 19, 2009, effective June 1, 2009.

Committee Explanatory Reports:

Final Report explaining the provisions of Rule 1124 published with the Court's Order at 36 Pa.B. 5571 (September 2, 2006). Final Report explaining the amendments to Rule 1124 published with the Court's Order at 39 Pa.B. 1614(April 4, 2009).

Rule 1126. Defects in Form, Content, or Procedure

A child shall not be released, nor shall a case be dismissed, because of a defect in the form or content of the pleading or a defect in the procedures of these rules, unless the party raises the defect prior to the commencement of the adjudicatory hearing, and the defect is prejudicial to the rights of a party.

Comment

A petition, emergency custody authorization form, shelter care application, or warrant may be amended at any time to remedy any defect in form or content. The court may also issue another remedy as interests of justice require. Nothing in this rule is to prevent the filing of a new emergency custody authorization form, a new or amended petition, or the reissuance of process.

Official Note: Rule 1126 adopted August, 21, 2006, effective February 1, 2007.

Committee Explanatory Reports:

Final Report explaining the provisions of Rule 1126 published with the Court's Order at 36 Pa.B. 5571 (September 2, 2006).

Rule 1127. Recording and Transcribing Juvenile Court Proceedings

A. **Recording.** There shall be a recording of all dependency proceedings, including proceedings conducted by juvenile court hearing officers, except as provided in Rule 1242(B)(2).

B. **Transcribing.** Upon the motion of any party, upon its own motion, or as required by law, the court shall order the record to be transcribed.

C. **Modifying.** At any time before an appeal is taken, the court may correct or modify the record in the same manner as is provided by Rule 1926 of the Pennsylvania Rules of Appellate Procedure.

Comment

Some form of record or transcript is necessary to permit meaningful consideration of claims of error and effective appellate review. *In re J.H.*, 788 A.2d 1006 (Pa. Super. 2001). *See, e.g.*, Pa.R.A.P. 1922, 1923, 1924; *Commonwealth v. Fields*, 387 A.2d 83 (Pa. 1978); *Commonwealth v. Shields*, 383 A.2d 844 (Pa. 1978). This rule is intended to provide a mechanism to ensure appropriate recording and transcribing of court proceedings. Pursuant to Rule 1800, 42 Pa.C.S. § 6336(c) was suspended only to the extent that all proceedings are to be recorded, except as provided in Rule 1242 (B)(2). Full minutes are not recordings. This change was to effectuate effective appellate review.

The rule is intended to apply to all dependency proceedings and to ensure all proceedings are recorded, including proceedings before juvenile court hearing officers, except for shelter care hearings.

Paragraph (B) of the rule is intended to authorize courts to require transcription of only such portions of the record, if any, as are needed to review claims of error.

Paragraph (C) provides a method for correcting and modifying transcripts before an appeal is taken by incorporating Pa.R.A.P. 1926, which otherwise applies only after an appeal has been taken. It is intended that the same standards and procedures apply both before and after appeal.

Official Note: Rule 1127 adopted August 21, 2006, effective February 1, 2007. Amended April 6, 2017, effective September 1, 2017.

Rule 1128. Presence at Proceedings

A. **General Rule.** All parties shall be present at any proceeding unless the exceptions of paragraph (B) apply.

B. **Exceptions.**

1) **Absence from proceedings.** The court may proceed in the absence of a party upon good cause shown except that in no case shall a hearing occur in the absence of a child's attorney. If a child has a guardian ad litem and legal counsel, both attorneys shall be present.

2) **Exclusion from proceedings.** A party may be excluded from a proceeding only for good cause shown. If a party is so excluded, counsel for the party shall be permitted to be present.

C. **Advanced Communication Technology.** A child or guardian may appear by utilizing advanced communication technology pursuant to Rule 1129.

D. **Order appearance.** The court may order any person having the physical custody or control of a child to bring the child to any proceeding.

Comment

In no case is a proceeding to occur in the absence of the child's attorney. The court has discretion whether to proceed if the court finds that a party received proper notice of the hearing and has willfully failed to appear.

Requiring the child's attorney to be present pursuant to paragraph (B)(2) protects the child's interest if the proceeding is conducted in the child's absence. However, unless good cause is shown, a child should appear in court. It is important that all children, including infants, appear in court so the court can observe the interaction between the caregiver and child and observe the child's development and health.

Ensuring a child appears in court on a regular basis is critical because the court oversees the child and is to ensure his or her care, protection, safety, and wholesome mental and physical development. However, the court may ask that the child be removed from the courtroom during sensitive testimony.

See *In re Adoption of S.B.B. and E.P.R.*, 372 Pa.Super. 456, 539 A.2d 883 (1988).

Nothing in these rules creates a right of a child to have his or her guardian present. *See* 42 Pa.C.S. §§ 6310, 6335(b), 6336.1.

Official Note: Rule 1128 adopted August, 21, 2006, effective February 1, 2007. Amended April 21, 2011, effective July 1, 2011.

Committee Explanatory Reports:

Final Report explaining the provisions of Rule 1128 published with the Court's Order at 36 Pa.B. 5599 (September 2, 2006). Final Report explaining the amendments to Rule 1128 published with the Court's Order at 41 Pa.B. 2319 (May 7, 2011).

Rule 1129. Appearance by Advanced Communication Technology

A. **Generally.**
   1) The child, guardian, or a witness may appear at a proceeding by utilizing advanced communication technology pursuant to Rules 1140, 1242, 1406, 1512, and 1608.
   2) At a minimum, the child shall appear in person at least every six months unless as otherwise provided by Rule 1128.

B. **Counsel.**
   1) The child or guardian shall be permitted to confer with counsel before entering into an agreement to appear utilizing advanced communication technology.
   2) The child or guardian shall be permitted to communicate fully and confidentially with counsel immediately prior to and during the proceeding.

Comment

Paragraph (A) requires that every child is to appear in person at least every six months. There may be instances in which the child is excused from attending pursuant to Rule 1128.

This rule is not intended to compel the use of advanced communication technology but rather permit appearance by telephone or by a system providing two-way simultaneous audio-visual communication. Advanced communication technology may be utilized for the convenience for witnesses; efficient use of resources; or when a party or witness has an illness, is incarcerated, or is otherwise in a remote location. *See* Rules 1140, 1242, 1406, 1512, and 1608 for specific requirements for the use of advanced communication technology.

Additionally, special care is to be taken when utilizing advanced communication technology to prevent disclosure of sensitive information to unauthorized persons and entities or to prevent a breach of confidentiality between a party and the party's attorney.

Pursuant to paragraph (B)(1), the child or guardian is to be permitted to confer with counsel prior to agreeing to a proceeding utilizing advanced communication technology. Counsel includes legal counsel and/or the guardian *ad litem*. Pursuant to paragraph (B)(2), the child or guardian is permitted to confer with counsel privately prior to and during the proceedings. The child is to be afforded all the same rights as if the hearing was held with all parties present in the courtroom.

Official Note: Rule 1129 adopted April 21, 2011, effective July 1, 2011.

Committee Explanatory Reports:

Final Report explaining the amendments to Rule 1129 published with the Court's Order at 41 Pa.B. 2319 (May 7, 2011).

Rule 1130. Court Fees Prohibited for Advanced Communication Technology

The court shall not impose any fees upon any party or witness for utilizing advanced communication technology.

Comment

See March 13, 2002 Order of the Supreme Court of Pennsylvania (No. 241 Judicial Administration; Doc. No. 1) which provides that no fees shall be imposed against a defendant in a criminal proceeding for the utilization of advanced communication technology.

Official Note: Rule 1130 adopted April 21, 2011, effective July 1, 2011.

Committee Explanatory Reports:

Final Report explaining the amendments to Rule 1130 published with the Court's Order at 41 Pa.B. 2319 (May 7, 2011).

Rule 1133. Motion to Intervene

A. Contents. The motion to intervene shall include:

1) the name and address of the person moving to intervene;
2) the relationship of the intervening person to the child;
3) the contact between the child and the intervening person;
4) the grounds on which intervention is sought; and
5) the request sought.

B. **Action by court.** Upon the filing of a motion to intervene and after a hearing, the court shall enter an order granting or denying the motion.

Comment

Under paragraph (B), a motion may be denied if, among other reasons, there are insufficient grounds for the motion, the interest of the movant is already adequately represented, the motion for intervention was unduly delayed, or the intervention will unduly delay or prejudice the adjudication of dependency or the rights of the parties.

To move for intervention in a dependency case, a person is to show that the interest is substantial, direct, and immediate. *See, e.g., South Whitehall Township Police Serv. v. South Whitehall Township*, 521 Pa. 82, 555 A.2d 793 (1989).

Standing is conferred upon a person if the person cares for or controls the child or is accused of abusing the child. *In re J.P.*, 832 A.2d 492 (Pa. Super. Ct. 2003); *In re L.J.*, 456 Pa.Super. 685, 691 A.2d 520 (1997). *See* 23 Pa. C.S. § 5313 for grandparent intervention. *See also R.M. v. Baxter*, 565 Pa. 619, 777 A.2d 446 (2001) (grandparent standing); *Mitch v. Bucks Co. Children and Youth Social Service Agency*, 383 Pa.Super. 42, 556 A.2d 419 (1989) (prospective adoptive parent standing); *In re M.K.*, 431 Pa.Super. 198, 636 A.2d 198 (1994) (alleged abuser standing). For distinction between foster parent and prospective adoptive parent standing, see *In re N.S.*, 845 A.2d 884 (Pa. Super. Ct. 2004).

A non-custodial parent may intervene in a dependency petition filed by a third party to protect the child from being adjudicated dependent and placed in the custody of the Commonwealth. *In re Anita H.*, 351 Pa.Super. 342, 505 A.2d 1014 (1986).

See also In re Michael Y., 365 Pa.Super. 488, 530 A.2d 115 (1987) and *In re R.T. & A.T.*, 405 Pa.Super. 156, 592 A.2d 55 (1991) for additional parties to proceedings.

See Rule 1344 for motions and Rule 1345 for service.

Official Note: Rule 1133 adopted August, 21, 2006, effective February 1, 2007.

Committee Explanatory Reports:

Final Report explaining the provisions of Rule 1133 published with the Court's Order at 36 Pa.B. 5571 (September 2, 2006).

Rule 1134. Proceedings *In Camera*

Upon motion by any party or on the court's own motion, in camera proceedings are to be recorded and each party's attorney shall be present.

Comment

See In re Leslie H., 329 Pa.Super. 453, 478 A.2d 876 (1984).

If a party is not represented, the court is to make reasonable efforts to protect the due process rights of the party.

Official Note: Rule 1134 adopted August, 21, 2006, effective February 1, 2007.

Rule 1135. Captions

All court documents and orders shall contain a caption that includes the following:

1) "In the Interest of (the child's name);"
2) the child's case docket number; and
3) the name of the court.

Official Note: Rule 1135 adopted August, 21, 2006, effective February 1, 2007.

Rule 1136. *Ex Parte* Communication

A. Unless otherwise authorized by law, no person shall communicate with the court in any way regarding matters pending before the court unless all parties:

(1) are present or have been copied if the communication is written or in electronic form; or

(2) have waived their presence or right to receive the communication.

B. If the court receives any ex parte communication, the court shall inform all parties of the communication and its content.

Comment

No *ex parte* communications with the court are to occur. Communications should include all parties, such as the filing of a motion, or conducting a conference or a hearing.

Attorneys are bound by the Rules of Professional Conduct. *See* Rules of Professional Conduct Rule 3.5(b). Judges are bound by the Code of Judicial Conduct. *See* Code of Judicial Conduct Rule 2.9.

Attorneys and judges understand the impropriety of *ex parte* communications regarding matters pending before the court but many participants are not attorneys or judges. This rule ensures that all parties have received the same information that is being presented to the court so that it may be challenged or supplemented.

Administrative matters are not considered *ex parte* communications.

Note: Rule 1136 adopted April 29, 2011, effective July 1, 2011. Amended April 29, 2016, effective immediately.

Rule 1137. Public Discussion by Court Personnel of Pending Matters

All court personnel including, among others, court clerks, bailiffs, tipstaffs, sheriffs, and court stenographers, are prohibited from disclosing to any person, without authorization from the court, information relating to a pending dependency case that is not part of the court record otherwise available to the public or not part of the record in an open proceeding. This rule specifically prohibits the divulgence of information concerning arguments and proceedings that are closed proceedings, held in chambers, or otherwise outside the presence of the public.

Official Note: Rule 1130 adopted August, 21, 2006, effective February 1, 2007. Renumbered Rule 1137 and amended April 21, 2011, effective July 1, 2011.

Committee Explanatory Reports:

Final Report explaining the provisions of Rule 1130 published with the Court's Order at 36 Pa.B. 5571 (September 2, 2006). Final Report explaining the renumbering of 1130 to 1137 published with the Court's Order at 41 Pa.B. 2319 (May 7, 2011).

Rule 1140. Bench Warrants for Failure to Appear

A. Assuance of warrant.

(1) Before a bench warrant may be issued by a judge, the judge shall find that the subpoenaed or summoned person received sufficient notice of the hearing and failed to appear.

(2) For the purpose of a bench warrant, a judge may not find notice solely based on first-class mail service.

(3) The judge shall not issue an arrest warrant for a dependent child who absconds.

B. Party.

(1) Where to take the party.

(a) When a party is taken into custody pursuant to a bench warrant, the party shall be taken without unnecessary delay to the judge who issued the warrant or a judge designated by the President Judge to hear bench warrants.

(b) If the party is not brought before a judge, the party shall be released unless the warrant specifically orders detention of the party.

(c) If the warrant specifically orders detention of a party, the party shall be detained pending a hearing.

(i) Minor. If the party is a minor, the party shall be detained in a shelter care facility or other placement as deemed appropriate by the judge.

(ii) Adult. If the party is an adult, the witness shall be detained at the county jail.

(2) Prompt hearing.

(a) If a party is detained pursuant to a specific order in the bench warrant, the party shall be brought before the judge who issued the warrant, a judge designated by the President Judge to hear bench warrants, or an out-of-county judge pursuant to paragraph (B)(4) within seventy-two hours.

(b) If the party is not brought before a judge within this time, the party shall be released.

(3) Notification of guardian. If a party is a child and is taken into custody pursuant to a bench warrant, the arresting officer shall immediately notify the child's guardian of the child's whereabouts and the reasons for the issuance of the bench warrant.

(4) Out-of-county custody.

(a) If a party is taken into custody pursuant to a bench warrant in a county other than the county of issuance, the county of issuance shallbe notified immediately.

(b) Arrangements to transport the party shall be made immediately.

(c) If transportation cannot be arranged immediately, then the party shall be taken without unnecessary delay to a judge of the county where the party is found.

(d) The judge will identify the party as the subject of the warrant, decide whether detention is warranted, and order that arrangements be made to transport the party to the county of issuance.

(5) Time requirements. The time requirements of Rules 1242, 1404, 1510, and 1607 shall be followed.

C. Witnesses.

(1) Where to take the witness.

(a) When a witness is taken into custody pursuant to a bench warrant, the witness shall be taken without unnecessary delay to the judge who issued the warrant or a judge designated by the President Judge to hear bench warrants.

(b) If the witness is not brought before a judge, the witness shall be released unless the warrant specifically orders detention of the witness.

(c) A motion for detention as a witness may be filed anytime before or after the issuance of a bench warrant. The judge may order detention of the witness pending a hearing.

(i) Minor. If a detained witness is a minor, the witness shall be detained in a shelter care facility or other placement as deemed appropriate by the judge.

(ii) Adult. If a detained witness is an adult, the witness shall be detained at the county jail.

(2) Prompt hearing.

(a) If a witness is detained pursuant to paragraph (C)(1)(c) or brought back to the county of issuance pursuant to paragraph (C)(4)(f), the witness shall be brought before the judge by the next business day.

(b) If the witness is not brought before a judge within this time, the witness shall be released.

(3) Notification of Guardian. If a witness who is taken into custody pursuant to a bench warrant is a minor, the arresting officer shall immediately notify the witness's guardian of the witness's whereabouts and the reasons for the issuance of the bench warrant.

(4) Out-of-county custody.

(a) If a witness is taken into custody pursuant to a bench warrant in a county other than the county of issuance, the county of issuance shall be notified immediately.

(b) The witness shall be taken without unnecessary delay and within the next business day to a judge of the county where the witness is found.

(c) The judge will identify the witness as the subject of the warrant, decide whether detention as a witness is warranted, and order that arrangements be made to transport the witness to the county of issuance.

(d) Arrangements to transport the witness shall be made immediately.

(e) If transportation cannot be arranged immediately, the witness shall be released unless the warrant or other order of court specifically orders detention of the witness.

(i) Minor. If the witness is a minor, the witness may be detained in an out-of-county shelter care facility or other placement as deemed appropriate by the judge.

(ii) **Adult.** If the witness is an adult, the witness may be detained in an out-of-county jail.

(f) If detention is ordered, the witness shall be brought back to the county of issuance within seventy-two hours from the execution of the warrant.

(g) If the time requirements of this paragraph are not met, the witness shall be released.

D. **Advanced Communication Technology.** A court may utilize advanced communication technology pursuant to Rule 1129 unless good cause is shown otherwise.

E. **Return & Execution of the Warrant for Parties and Witnesses.**

(1) The bench warrant shall be executed without unnecessary delay.

(2) The bench warrant shall be returned to the judge who issued the warrant or to the judge designated by the President Judge to hear bench warrants.

(3) When the bench warrant is executed, the arresting officer shall immediately execute a return of the warrant with the judge.

(4) Upon the return of the warrant, the judge shall vacate the bench warrant.

Comment

Pursuant to paragraph (A), the judge is to ensure that the person received sufficient notice of the hearing and failed to attend. The judge may order that the person be served in-person or by certified mail, return receipt. The judge may rely on first-class mail service if additional evidence of sufficient notice is presented. For example, testimony that the person was told in person about the hearing is sufficient notice. Before issuing a bench warrant, the judge should determine if the guardian was notified.

Under Rule 1800, 42 Pa.C.S. § 6335(c) was suspended only to the extent that it is inconsistent with this rule. Under paragraph (A)(1), the judge is to find a subpoenaed or summoned person failed to appear and sufficient notice was given to issue a bench warrant. The fact that the party or witness may abscond or may not attend or be brought to a hearing is not sufficient evidence for a bench warrant. The normal rules of procedure in these rules are to be followed if a child is detained. See Chapter Twelve.

Paragraph (A)(3) does not preclude the issuance of a bench warrant for a case in which the child is subject to the jurisdiction of the dependency and delinquency court, see Rule 141 (Bench Warrants for Absconders), or an order for protective custody. Nor does the paragraph preclude judicial inquiry into efforts to locate a missing dependent child.

In paragraphs (B)(1)(c)(i), (C)(1)(c)(i), & (C)(4)(e)(i), "other placement as deemed appropriate by the judge" does not include a detention facility if a child is only alleged to be dependent because the use of detention facilities for dependent children is strictly prohibited. See 42 Pa.C.S. § 6302 & 6327(e).

Under paragraphs (B)(2) and (B)(4), a party taken into custody pursuant to a bench warrant is to have a hearing within seventy-two hours regardless of where the party is found. See Rule 1242(D).

Pursuant to paragraph (B)(4), the party may be detained out-of-county until transportation arrangements can be made.

Pursuant to paragraph (C)(4)(b), a witness is to be brought before an out-of-county judge by the next business day unless the witness can be brought before the judge who issued the bench warrant within this time. When the witness is transported back to the county of issuance within seventy-two hours of the execution of the bench warrant, the witness is to be brought before the judge who issued the bench warrant by the next business day. See paragraph (C)(4)(f).

Pursuant to paragraph (E)(4), the bench warrant is to be vacated after the return of the warrant is executed so the party or witness is not taken into custody on the same warrant if the party or witness is released. "Vacated" is to denote that the bench warrant has been served, dissolved, executed, dismissed, canceled, returned, or any other similar language used by the judge to terminate the warrant. The bench warrant is no longer in effect once it has been vacated.

See 42 Pa.C.S. § 4132 for punishment of contempt for children and witnesses.

Throughout these rules, the "child" is the subject of the dependency proceedings. When a witness or another party is under the age of eighteen, the witness or party is referred to as a "minor." When "minor" is used, it may include a child. This distinction is made to differentiate between children who are alleged dependents and other minors who are witnesses. See also Rule 1120 for the definitions of "child" and "minor."

Rule 1140 adopted March 19, 2009, effective June 1, 2009. Amended April 21, 2011, effective July 1, 2011. Amended April 23, 2018, effective July 1, 2018.

PART B(1)
EDUCATION AND HEALTH OF CHILD

1145. Application or Motion for Examination and Treatment of a Child
1146. Notice of Truancy Hearing.
1147. Educational Decision Maker.
1148. Educational Stability and Placement.
1149. Family Finding.

Rule 1145. Application or Motion for Examination and Treatment of a Child

A. **Pre-petition treatment.** Prior to the filing of a dependency petition, an application to the court may be made to treat a child when prompt treatment is necessary.

B. **Post-petition examination and treatment.** After a petition has been filed, a motion for examination and treatment of a child may be filed.

Comment

The term "application" is used in paragraph (A) of this rule. An application is to be made to the court if there is no formal court action pending. Once a dependency petition is filed, a motion, as provided in paragraph (B), is the proper course of action for seeking examination and treatment of a child. All parties are notified and copied on all motions. The procedures of Rule 1344 are to be followed. *See* Rule 1344.

It should be noted that paragraph (A) only relates to treatment of a child when prompt treatment is necessary.

Pursuant to 42 Pa.C.S. § 6339(b), the court may order the child to be examined at a suitable place by a physician or psychologist and may also order medical or surgical treatment of a child who is suffering from a serious physical condition or illness, which in the opinion of a licensed physician, requires prompt treatment, even if the guardian has not been given notice of a hearing, is not available, or without good cause informs the court of his refusal to consent to the treatment. 42 Pa.C.S. § 6339(b). In addition, 42 Pa.C.S. § 6357 provides a custodian to whom legal custody has been given by the court has the right to the physical custody of the child, the right to determine the nature of the care and treatment of the child, including ordinary medical care and the right and duty to provide for the care, protection, training, and education, and the physical, mental, and moral welfare of the child. An award of legal custody shall be subject to the conditions and limitations of the order and to the remaining rights and duties of the parents or guardian of the child as determined by the court. 42 Pa.C.S. § 6357.

If a child has been adjudicated dependent, the court may order that the county agency participate in the treatment plan of the child as necessary to protect the health, safety, or welfare of the child, including discussions with the individual, facility, or program providing treatment, and the child or the child's guardian in furtherance of the disposition. 42 Pa.C.S. § 6352.1.

Under paragraph (B), if the legal custodian is the county agency, the county agency is to comply with the regulations of 55 Pa. Code §§ 3130.91 and 3680.52.

Official Note: Rule 1145 adopted August, 21, 2006, effective February 1, 2007.

Committee Explanatory Reports:

Final Report explaining the provisions of Rule 1145 published with the Court's Order at 36 Pa.B. 5571 (September 2, 2006).

Rule 1146. Notice of Truancy Hearing.

Upon receiving written notice of a hearing regarding a citation or complaint for truancy against a child or a person in parental relation pursuant to 24 P.S. § 13-1333.1 when the child is the subject of a dependency proceeding, the county agency shall serve a copy of the notice upon the dependency court and parties.

Comment

Pursuant to 24 P.S. § 13-1333.2(b)(1), the court in which a truancy citation or complaint is filed shall provide the county agency with written notice of the hearing. For definition of "person in parental relation," see 24 P.S. § 13-1326.

The President Judge may adopt local rules coordinating jurisdiction and proceedings between the judge of the court where the citation or complaint was filed and the dependency court judge. Coordination may include, but is not limited to, the entry of an order staying the truancy proceeding for further consideration by the dependency court.

Official Note: Rule 1146 adopted December 21, 2018, effective May 1, 2019.

Committee Explanatory Reports:

Final Report explaining the provisions of Rule 1146 published with the Court's Order at 49 Pa.B. 610 (February 9, 2019).

Rule 1147. Educational Decision Maker.

A. *Generally.* **At any proceeding or upon motion, the court shall appoint an educational decision maker for the child if it determines that:**

  1) the child has no guardian; or

2) the court, after notice to the guardian and an opportunity for the guardian to be heard, has made a determination that it is in the child's best interest to limit the guardian's right to make decisions regarding the child's education.

B. *Notice of hearings.* The educational decision maker shall receive notice of all proceedings.

C. *Duties and responsibilities.* The educational decision maker shall:

1) make appropriate inquiries and take appropriate actions to ensure that:

 a) issues concerning the child's educational stability are addressed;

 b) school discipline matters are addressed;

 c) the child is receiving appropriate education that will allow the child to meet state standards, including any necessary services concerning special education in the least restrictive environment, or remedial services;

 d) the child, who is fourteen years of age or older, is receiving the necessary educational services to transition to successful adulthood;

 e) the child, who is receiving services concerning special education, is engaged in transition planning with the school entity beginning no later than the school year in which the child turns fourteen; and

 f) the child, who is aging out of care within ninety days, has a transition plan that addresses the child's educational needs, and if applicable, the plan is coordinated with the child's transition planning concerning special education under the Individuals with Disabilities Education Act.

2) address the child's educational needs by:

 a) meeting with the child at least once and as often as necessary to make decisions regarding education that are in the child's best interests;

 b) participating in special education and other meetings, and making decisions regarding all matters affecting the child's educational needs in a manner consistent with the child's best interests;

 c) making any specific recommendations to the court relating to:

  i) the timeliness and appropriateness of the child's educational placement;

  ii) the timeliness and appropriateness of the child's transitional planning; and

  iii) services necessary to address the child's educational needs;

 d) appearing and testifying at court hearings when necessary; and

 e) having knowledge and skills that ensure adequate representation of the child.

Comment

A child in dependent care is to have a clearly identified, legally authorized educational decision maker. This is a particular concern for highly mobile children whose caregivers may change and whose guardian may be unavailable. An educational decision maker's responsibilities may include, but are not limited to: ensuring educational stability as mandated by 42 U.S.C. §§ 675(1)(G) and 11431 *et seq.*; ensuring prompt enrollment in a new school as required pursuant to 22 Pa. Code § 11.11(b); facilitating access to a full range of school programs;

advocating for the child in school discipline matters; ensuring meaningful transition planning as required by 42 Pa.C.S. § 6351 and 42 U.S.C. § 675(5)(H); and for a child eligible for special education, ensuring access to appropriate services including transition planning beginning no later than age fourteen. *See* 24 P.S. §§ 13-1371, 13-1372, 20 U.S.C. §§ 1400 *et seq. See* paragraph (A) and (C).

An educational decision maker appointed pursuant to this rule who represents a child who is also adjudicated delinquent is to review Rule 147.

A court is not to appoint an educational decision maker if there is a parent, guardian, or other authorized person (*e.g.*, foster parent, relative with whom the child lives or surrogate parent appointed under the IDEA) who is competent, willing, and available to make decisions regarding the child's education and who is acting in the child's best interest regarding all educational matters. *See* Individuals with Disabilities Education Act ("IDEA"), 20 U.S.C. §§ 1400 *et seq.* (2004). A court should limit the authority of a parent to make decisions regarding education only to the extent necessary to protect the child's interest and can reinstate the parent or change the educational decision maker at any time.

Unless limited by the court in its appointment order, an educational decision maker: 1) is responsible for making all decisions concerning education, including special education, for the child; and 2) can consent to or prohibit the release of information from the child's school records as a parent in accordance with the Family Educational Rights and Privacy Act, 20 U.S.C. § 1232g and 34 C.F.R. § 99.3 (1974). The educational decision maker may be a family member, a family friend, a mentor, a foster parent, a former foster parent, a Court Appointed Special Advocate, or, if an educational decision maker for special education is not needed, a child welfare professional. Except as otherwise provided by the IDEA, it is within the discretion of the court to appoint an educational decision maker and whom to appoint. In all cases, however, an educational decision maker appointed by the court should be familiar with a child's educational rights or is to agree to be trained regarding these issues.

If the child is or may be eligible for special education, an educational decision maker is to be appointed in accordance with the standards and procedures set forth in federal and state laws concerning special education. See IDEA, 20 U.S.C. §§ 1400, 1401(23), and 1415(b)(2); 34 C.F.R. §§ 300.30, 300.45, and 300.519. The IDEA recognizes a court's authority to appoint persons to make decisions concerning special education for a child. However, such decision makers cannot be the State or employees of any agency that is involved in the education or care of the child. 34 C.F.R. § 300.519(c), (d)(2)(i).

The educational decision maker should refer to the Fostering Connections to Success and Increasing Adoptions Act of 2008 (P.L. 110-351) and the McKinney-Vento Homeless Assistance Act, 42 U.S.C. §§ 11431 *et seq.* (1989) for guidance in educational stability. Specifically, the educational decision maker is to: a) ensure the right to remain in the same school regardless of a change in placement when it is in the child's best interest; b) facilitate immediate enrollment in a new school when a school change is in the child's best interest; and c) ensure that school proximity is considered in all placement changes, 42 U.S.C. §§ 675(1)(G) and 11431 *et seq.*

The educational decision maker is to also ensure: a) that the child receives an appropriate education, including, as applicable, any necessary special education, early intervention, or remedial services; see 24 P.S. §§ 13-1371, 13-1372, 55 Pa. Code § 3130.87, 20 U.S.C. §§ 1400 *et seq.*; b) that the child receives educational services necessary to support the child's transition to successful adulthood if the child is fourteen or older pursuant to 42 Pa.C.S. § 6351(F)(8); and c) that the educational decision maker participates in the development of a transition plan that addresses the child's educational needs pursuant to 42 U.S.C. § 675(5)(H) if the child will age out of care within ninety days.

The authority of the court to appoint an educational decision maker is derived from the broad powers of the court to issue orders that "provide for the care, protection, safety, and wholesome mental and physical development of children." 42 Pa.C.S. § 6301(b)(1.1). The IDEA also requires that each child who is eligible for special education has an active parent or other identified person who can participate in the process concerning special education. *See* IDEA, 20 U.S.C. §§ 1401(23) and 1415(b)(2); 34 C.F.R. §§ 300.30, 300.45, and 300.519.

Official Note: Rule 1147 adopted April 29, 2011, effective July 1, 2011. Amended December 21, 2018, effective May 1, 2019.

Committee Explanatory Reports:

Final Report explaining the provisions of Rule 1147 published with the Court's Order at 41 Pa.B. 2413 (May 14, 2011).

Final Report explaining the amendments to Rule 1147 published with the Court's Order at 49 Pa.B. 610 (February 9, 2019).

Rule 1148. Educational Stability and Placement.

A. *General Rule.* **Any order resulting in the placement of a child or a change in placement shall address the educational stability of the child.**

B. *School of Origin.* **A child in placement shall remain in their school of origin unless the court finds remaining in the school of origin is not in the child's best interest. If the court finds that it is not in the best interest of the child to remain in the school of origin, then the court may order the child to be enrolled in another school that best meets the child's needs.**

C. *Another School.* **If a court orders the child to be enrolled in another school pursuant to paragraph (B), then the child shall attend a public school unless the court finds that a public school is not in the best interest of the child.**

Comment

This rule is intended to apply at any point in a dependency proceeding when the child is in placement, including pre-dispositional placement and post-dispositional modification of a dependent child's placement. This rule is intended to complement rather than supersede the requirements of Rule 1512(D)(1)(i).

In paragraph (B), the best interest determination should be based on factors including the appropriateness of the current educational setting considering the child's needs and the proximity of the school of origin relative to the placement location. This paragraph is not intended to usurp the administrative process contemplated by the Elementary and Secondary Education Act of 1965, as amended, 20 U.S.C. § 6311(g)(1)(E). This paragraph is intended to facilitate educational stability while the child remains under the jurisdiction of the Juvenile Court and to codify the presumption that a child is to remain in their school of origin absent evidence that it is not in the child's best interest to do so.

In paragraph (C), circumstances indicating that it may not be in the best interest for the child to attend a public school include the security and safety of the child and treatment needs. Paragraph (C) is intended to codify the presumption that a child is to attend public school while in placement absent evidence demonstrating that it is not in the best interest of the child to do so. The bundling of residential services and educational services should not be permitted without a court order authorizing such.

A court may consider an Individualized Education Program, Service Agreement, or administrative determination in making findings pursuant to this Rule.

Official Note: Rule 1148 adopted December 21, 2018, effective May 1, 2019.

Committee Explanatory Reports:

Final Report explaining the provisions of Rule 1148 published with the Court's Order at 49 Pa.B. 610 (February 9, 2019).

Rule 1149. Family Finding.

A. *Court's inquiry and determination.*

    1) **The court shall inquire as to the efforts made by the county agency to comply with the family finding requirements pursuant to 62 P.S. § 1301 et seq.**

    2) **The court shall place its determinations on the record as to whether the county agency has reasonably engaged in family finding.**

B. *Discontinued family finding.* Family finding may be discontinued only if, after a hearing, the court has made a specific determination that:

    1) continued family finding no longer serves the best interests of the child;

    2) continued family finding is a threat to the child's safety; or

    3) the child is in a preadoptive placement and the court proceedings to adopt the child have been commenced pursuant to 23 Pa.C.S. Part III (relating to adoption).

C. *Resuming family finding.* The county agency shall resume family finding when the court determines that resuming family finding:

    1) **is best suited to the safety, protection and physical, mental, and moral welfare of the child; and**

    2) does not pose a threat to the child's safety.

Comment

Pursuant to paragraph (A), efforts by the county agency may include, but are not limited to whether the county agency is or will be: a) searching for and locating adult relatives and kin; b) identifying and building positive connections between the child and the child's relatives and kin; c) when appropriate: i) supporting the engagement of relatives and kin in social service planning and delivery of services; and ii) creating a network of extended family support to assist in remedying the concerns that led to the child becoming involved with the county agency; d) when possible, maintaining family connections; and e) when in the best interests of the child and when possible, keeping siblings together in care.

The extent to which the county agency is involved in the case when a child is still in the home is dependent on several variables and specific to each case. In some instances, the county agency is more involved and actively engaged in family finding because the child needs support services or could be removed from the home. The search in these instances is used to find resources to help keep the child in the home by preventing removal, or to find resources if removal becomes necessary.

See 62 P.S. § 1301 for legislative intent regarding family finding and promotion of kinship care.

Family finding is required for every child when a child is accepted for services by the county agency. *See* 62 P.S. § 1302. It is best practice to find as many kin as possible for each child. These kin may help with care or support for the child. The county agency should ask the guardian, the child, and siblings about relatives or other adults in the child's life, including key supporters of the child or guardians.

Specific evidence should be provided indicating the steps taken to locate and engage relatives and kin. *See* Comment to Rule 1120 regarding diligent efforts considerations for locating relatives and kin. When considering the method by which relatives and kin are engaged in service planning and delivery, courts and the parties are encouraged to be creative. Strategies of engagement could include, but are not limited to, inviting relatives and kin to: 1) be involved in a family group decision making conference, family team conferencing, or other family meetings aimed at developing or supporting the family service plan; 2) assist with visitation; 3) assist with transportation; 4) provide respite or child care services; or 5) provide actual kinship care.

Pursuant to paragraph (A)(2), the court is to place its determinations on the record as to whether the county has reasonably engaged in family finding. The level of reasonableness is to be determined by the length of the case and time the county agency has had to begin or continue the process. For example, at the shelter care hearing, the county agency should at least ask the question whether there is family or kin available as a resource. The initial removal of the child is the most critical time in the case. Potential trauma should be considered and ameliorated by family finding efforts as much as possible. Phone calls at this time are reasonable. However, at the dispositional or permanency hearings, the county agency has had more time to engage in a more thorough diligent search as discussed *infra*. *See also* Rule 1120 and its Comment.

The court's inquiry and determination regarding family finding should be made at each stage of the case, including, but not limited to the entry of an order for protective custody, shelter care hearing, adjudicatory hearing, dispositional hearing, and permanency hearing. *See* Rules 1210, 1242, 1408, 1409, 1512, 1514, 1515, 1608, 1609, 1610, and 1611, and their Comments.

Paragraph (B)(3) is meant to include notice of intent to adopt, petition to adopt, or voluntary relinquishment of parental rights, or consent to adopt.

Note: Rule 1149 adopted July 13, 2015, effective October 1, 2015.

PART B(2)
COUNSEL

1150. **Attorneys—Appearances and Withdrawals**
1151. **Assignment of Guardian *ad litem* & Counsel**
1152. **Waiver of Counsel**
1154. **Duties of Guardian *ad litem***
1158. **Assignment of CASA**

Rule 1150. Attorneys—Appearances and Withdrawals

A. **Appearances.**
   1) The Guardian *ad litem* and counsel for each party, except under paragraph (A)(3), shall file an entry of appearance with the clerk of

courts promptly after being retained and serve a copy on all other parties.

    a) If a firm name is entered, the name of the individual lawyer who is designated as being responsible for the conduct of the case shall be entered.

    b) The entry of appearance shall include the attorney's address, phone number, and attorney ID number.

2) When counsel is appointed pursuant to Rule 1151 (Assignment of Counsel), the filing of the appointment order shall enter the appearance of appointed counsel.

3) The president judge of each judicial district may enter an order stating that the specified Solicitor's appearance is automatically entered in every dependency case unless another attorney's appearance is entered pursuant to paragraph (A)(1).

B. **Duration.** Once an appearance is entered or the court assigns counsel for the child, counsel shall represent the child until the closing of the dependency case, including any proceeding upon direct appeal and permanency review, unless permitted to withdraw pursuant to paragraph (C).

C. **Withdrawals.**

1) Upon motion, counsel shall be permitted to withdraw only:

    a) by order of the court for good cause shown; or

    b) if new counsel has entered an appearance in accordance with paragraph (A).

2) A motion to withdraw shall be:

    a) filed with the clerk of courts, and a copy concurrently served on the other parties' attorneys, or the party, if unrepresented; or

    b) made orally on the record in open court in the presence of the parties.

Comment

Paragraph (A)(3) allows the Solicitor to be automatically entered in the record as counsel for the agency. The order is to include the attorney's address, phone number, and attorney ID number.

Under paragraph (C), withdrawal is presumed when a court's jurisdiction is terminated because the child reaches the age of twenty-one. *See* 42 Pa.C.S. § 6302.

Under paragraph (C)(1)(a), a court can terminate an attorney's representation if there is good cause shown. The court should allow an attorney to withdraw from a case for good cause if the standards for termination of representation, as provided for in the Rules of Professional Conduct 1.16, are met.

Under paragraph (C)(1)(b), because the county agency will be on notice of the identity of the new attorney, the agency should comply with the discovery requirements of Rule 1340.

Under paragraph (C)(2), counsel is to file a motion to withdraw in all cases. Counsel's obligation to represent a party, whether as retained or appointed counsel, remains until leave to withdraw is granted by the court. *See e.g., Com. v. Librizzi*, 810 A.2d 692 (Pa. Super. Ct. 2002). The court is to make a determination of the status of the case before permitting counsel to withdraw. Although there are many factors considered by the court in determining whether there is good cause to permit the withdrawal of counsel, when granting leave, the court should determine if new counsel needs to be appointed, and that the change in attorneys will not delay the proceedings or prejudice the party, particularly concerning time limits.

See Rule 1167 for service of court orders.

See the Comment to Rule 1634 for assisting children in filing resumption of jurisdiction motions. It is best practice for the court to appoint the guardian ad litem or legal counsel who was previously assigned to the child as legal counsel in the re-opened case. If there are extenuating circumstances preventing the attorney from representing the child, the attorney should make this known at the time of the filing of the motion for resumption of jurisdiction so the court can assign a new attorney.

See also Rule 1613 for termination of court supervision.

For admission pro hac vice, see Pa.B.A.R. 301.

Official Note: Rule 1150 adopted August, 21, 2006, effective February 1, 2007. Amended October 21, 2013, effective December 1, 2013. Amended December 10, 2013, effective February 10, 2014.

Committee Explanatory Reports:

Final Report explaining the provisions of Rule 1150 published with the Court's Order at 36 Pa.B. 5571 (September 2, 2006). Final Report explaining the amendments to Rule 1150 published with the Court's Order at 43 Pa.B. - (November 2, 2013). Final Report explaining the amendments to Rule 1150 published with the Court's Order at 43 Pa.B 7547 (December 28, 2013).

Rule 1151. Assignment of Guardian *Ad Litem* & Counsel

A. Guardian *ad litem* for child. The court shall assign a guardian *ad litem* to represent the legal interests and the best interests of the child if a proceeding has been commenced pursuant to Rule 1200 alleging a child to be dependent who:

1) is without proper parental care or control, subsistence, education as required by law, or other care or control necessary for the physical, mental or emotional health, or morals;

2) has been placed for care or adoption in violation of law;

3) has been abandoned by parents, guardian, or other custodian;

4) is without a parent, guardian or legal custodian; or

5) is born to a parent whose parental rights with regard to another child have been involuntarily terminated under 23 Pa.C.S. § 2511 (relating to grounds for involuntary termination) within three years immediately preceding the date of birth of the child and conduct of the parent poses a risk to the health, safety, or welfare of the child.

B. Counsel for child. The court shall appoint legal counsel for a child:

1) if a proceeding has been commenced pursuant to Rule 1200 alleging a child to be dependent who:

a) while subject to compulsory school attendance is habitually and without justification truant from school;

b) has committed a specific act or acts of habitual disobedience of the reasonable and lawful commands of the child's guardian and

who is ungovernable and found to be in need of care, treatment, or supervision;
- c) is under the age of ten years and has committed a delinquent act;
    - d) has been formerly adjudicated dependent, and is under the jurisdiction of the court, subject to its conditions or placements and who commits an act which is defined as ungovernable in paragraph (B)(1)(b);
    - e) has been referred pursuant to section 6323 (relating to informal adjustment), and who commits an act which is defined as ungovernable in paragraph (B)(1)(b); or 2) upon order of the court; or
- f) has filed a motion for resumption of jurisdiction pursuant to Rule 1634

C. Counsel and Guardian *ad litem* for child. If a child has legal counsel and a guardian *ad litem*, counsel shall represent the legal interests of the child and the guardian *ad litem* shall represent the best interests of the child.

D. Time of appointment.
  1) Child in custody. The court shall appoint a guardian *ad litem* or legal counsel immediately after a child is taken into protective custody and prior to any proceeding.
  2) Child not in custody. If the child is not in custody, the court shall appoint a guardian *ad litem* or legal counsel for the child when a dependency petition is filed.

E. Counsel for other parties. If counsel does not enter an appearance for a party, the court shall inform the party of the right to counsel prior to any proceeding. If counsel is requested by a party in any case, the court shall assign counsel for the party if the party is without financial resources or otherwise unable to employ counsel. Counsel shall be appointed prior to the first court proceeding.

Comment

See 42 Pa.C.S. §§ 6302, 6311, and 6337.

The guardian *ad litem* for the child may move the court for appointment as legal counsel and assignment of a separate guardian *ad litem* when, for example, the information that the guardian *ad litem* possesses gives rise to the conflict and can be used to the detriment of the child. To the extent 42 Pa.C.S. § 6311(b)(9) is inconsistent with this rule, it is suspended. *See* Rule 1800. *See also* Pa.R.P.C. 1.7 and 1.8.

Pursuant to paragraph (B)(1)(f), the court is to appoint legal counsel when a motion for resumption of jurisdiction has been filed. It is best practice to appoint the guardian ad litem or legal counsel who was previously assigned to the child as legal counsel.

Under paragraph (C), legal counsel represents the legal interests of the child and the guardian *ad litem* represents the best interests of the child.

Nothing in these rules anticipates that a guardian *ad litem* for an adult is to be appointed by these rules. For appointment of a guardian of the person, see 20 Pa.C.S. § 5501 *et seq.* and Pa.O.C. Rules 14.2 - 14.5.

Pursuant to paragraph (E), the court is to inform all parties of the right to counsel if they appear at a hearing without counsel. If a party is without financial resources or otherwise unable to employ counsel, the court is to appoint counsel prior to the proceeding. Because of the nature of the proceedings, it is extremely important that every "guardian" has an attorney. Therefore, the court is to encourage the child's guardian to obtain counsel. Pursuant to Rule 1120, a guardian is any parent, custodian, or other person who has legal custody of a child, or person designated by the court to be a temporary guardian for purposes of a proceeding. *See* Pa.R.J.C.P. 1120.

Official Note: Rule 1151 adopted August, 21, 2006, effective February 1, 2007. Amended February 20, 2007, effective immediately. Amended May 12, 2008, effective immediately. Amended April 29, 2011, effective July 1, 2011. Amended October 21, 2013, effective December 1, 2013.

Committee Explanatory Reports:

Final Report explaining the provisions of Rule 1151 published with the Court's Order at 36 Pa.B. 5571 (September 2, 2006). Final Report explaining the amendments to this rule published with the Court's Order at 37 Pa.B. 1123 (March 10, 2007). Final Report explaining the amendments to Rule 1151 published with the Court's Order at 38 Pa.B. 2360 (May 12, 2008). Final Report explaining the amendments to Rule 1151 published with the Court's Order at 41 Pa.B. 2430 (May 14, 2011). Final Report explaining the amendments to Rule 1151 published with the Court's Order at 43 Pa.B. - (November 2, 2013).

Rule 1152. Waiver of Counsel

A. **Children.**
   1) **Guardian ad litem.** A child may not waive the right to a guardian *ad litem.*
   2) **Legal Counsel.** A child may waive legal counsel if:
      a) the waiver is knowingly, intelligently, and voluntarily made; and
      b) the court conducts a colloquy with the child on the record.
B. **Other parties.** Except as provided in paragraph (A), a party may waive the right to counsel if:
   1) the waiver is knowingly, intelligently, and voluntarily made; and
   2) the court conducts a colloquy with the party on the record.
C. **Stand-by counsel.** The court may assign stand-by counsel if a party waives counsel at any proceeding or stage of a proceeding.
D. **Notice and revocation of waiver.** If a party waives counsel for any proceeding, the waiver only applies to that proceeding, and the party may revoke the waiver of counsel at any time. At any subsequent proceeding, the party shall be informed of the right to counsel.

Comment

Under paragraph (A), a child may not waive the right to a guardian *ad litem.* The right of waiver to legal counsel belongs to the child, not the guardian. *See* Rule 1800, which suspends 42 Pa.C.S. § 6337, which provides that counsel must be provided unless the guardian is present and waives counsel for the child.

It is recommended that, at a minimum, the court ask questions to elicit the following information in determining a knowing, intelligent, and voluntary waiver of counsel:

1) Whether the party understands the right to be represented by counsel;

2) Whether the party understands the nature of the dependency allegations and the elements of each of those allegations;

3) Whether the party is aware of the dispositions and placements that may be imposed by the court, including foster care placement and adoption;

4) Whether the party understands that if he or she waives the right to counsel, he or she will still be bound by all the normal rules of procedure and that counsel would be familiar with these rules;

5) Whether the party understands that counsel may be better suited to defend the dependency allegations; and

6) Whether the party understands that the party has many rights that, if not timely asserted, may be lost permanently; and if errors occur and are not timely objected to, or otherwise timely raised by the party, the ability to correct these errors may be lost permanently.

Official Note: Rule 1152 adopted August, 21, 2006, effective February 1, 2007.

Committee Explanatory Reports:

Final Report explaining the provisions of Rule 1152 published with the Court's Order at 36 Pa.B. 5571 (September 2, 2006).

Rule 1154. Duties of Guardian *Ad Litem*

A guardian *ad litem* shall:

(1) Meet with the child as soon as possible following assignment pursuant to Rule 1151 and on a regular basis thereafter in a manner appropriate to the child's age and maturity;

(2) On a timely basis, be given access to relevant court and county agency records, reports of examination of the guardians or the child, and medical, psychological, and school records;

(3) Participate in all proceedings, including hearings before juvenile court hearing officers, and administrative hearings and reviews to the degree necessary to adequately represent the child;

(4) Conduct such further investigation necessary to ascertain the facts;

(5) Interview potential witnesses, including the child's guardians, caretakers, and foster parents, examine and cross-examine witnesses, and present witnesses and evidence necessary to protect the best interests of the child;

(6) At the earliest possible date, be advised by the county agency having legal custody of the child of:

 (a) any plan to relocate the child or modify custody or visitation arrangements, including the reasons, prior to the relocation or change in custody or visitation; and

 (b) any proceeding, investigation, or hearing under the Child Protective Services Law, 23 Pa.C.S. § 6301 *et seq.* or the Juvenile Act, 42 Pa.C.S. § 6301 *et seq.*, directly affecting the child;

(7) Make any specific recommendations to the court relating to the appropriateness and safety of the child's placement and services necessary to address the child's needs and safety, including the child's educational, health care, and disability needs;

(8) Explain the proceedings to the child to the extent appropriate given the child's age, mental condition, and emotional condition; and

(9) Advise the court of the child's wishes to the extent that they can be ascertained and present to the court whatever evidence exists to support the child's wishes. When appropriate because of the age or mental and emotional condition of the child, determine to the fullest extent possible the wishes of the child and communicate this information to the court.

Comment

If there is a conflict of interest between the duties of the guardian *ad litem* pursuant to paragraphs (7) and (9), the guardian *ad litem* for the child may move the court for appointment as legal counsel and assignment of a separate guardian *ad litem* when, for example, the information that the guardian *ad litem* possesses gives rise to the conflict and can be used to the detriment of the child. If there is not a conflict of interest, the guardian *ad litem* represents the legal interests and best interests of the child at every stage of the proceedings. 42 Pa.C.S. § 6311(b). To the extent 42 Pa.C.S. § 6311(b)(9) is inconsistent with this rule, it is suspended. *See* Rules 1151 and 1800. *See also* Pa.R.P.C. 1.7 and 1.8.

"Legal interests" denotes that an attorney is to express the child's wishes to the court regardless of whether the attorney agrees with the child's recommendation. "Best interests" denotes that a guardian *ad litem* is to express what the guardian *ad litem* believes is best for the child's care, protection, safety, and wholesome physical and mental development regardless of whether the child agrees.

Pursuant to paragraph (7), the guardian *ad litem* is to make specific recommendations to the court regarding the appropriateness of the child's placement, giving consideration to the proximity and appropriateness of the child's school. *See* 42 Pa.C.S. § 6311(b)(7) and 42 U.S.C. § 675(1)(G). Inquiries into the child's education should include the right to: 1) educational stability, including the right to remain in the same school regardless of a change in placement when in the child's best interest and the right to immediate enrollment when a school change is in the child's best interest, 42 U.S.C. §§ 675(1)(G) and 11431 *et seq.*; 2) an educational decision maker pursuant to Rule 1147, 42 Pa.C.S. § 6301, 20 U.S.C. § 1439(a)(5), and 34 C.F.R. § 300.519; 3) an appropriate education, including any necessary special education, early intervention, or remedial services, 24 P.S. §§ 13-1371 and 13-1372, 55 Pa. Code § 3130.87, and 20 U.S.C. § 1400 *et seq.*; 4) the educational services necessary to support the child's transition to independent living, 42 Pa.C.S. § 6351 if a child is sixteen or older; and 5) a transition plan that addresses the child's educational needs, 42 U.S.C. § 675(5)(H), if the child will age out of care in the next ninety days.

See In re S.J., 906 A.2d 547, 551 (Pa. Super. Ct. 2006) (citing *In re Tameka M.*, 525 Pa. 348, 580 A.2d 750 (1990)), for issues addressing a child's mental and moral welfare.

Pursuant to paragraph (7), the guardian *ad litem* is to make specific recommendations to the court regarding the appropriateness of the child's placement, giving consideration to meeting the child's needs concerning health care and disability. Inquiries into the child's health should include the right of: 1) the child to receive timely and medically appropriate screenings and health care services, 55 Pa. Code §§ 3700.51 and 3800.32, 42 U.S.C. § 1396d(r); and 2) a child with disabilities to receive necessary accommodations, 42 U.S.C. § 12132, 28 C.F.R. § 35.101 *et seq.*, Section 504 of the Rehabilitation Act of 1973, *as amended*, 29 U.S.C. § 794 and implementing regulations at 45 C.F.R. § 84.1 *et seq.*

The guardian *ad litem* may be appointed as the educational decision maker. If the guardian *ad litem* is not the educational decision maker, the guardian *ad litem* is to coordinate efforts and consult with the educational decision maker. See Rule 1147 for duties of the educational decision maker.

Official Note: Rule 1154 adopted August 21, 2006, effective February 1, 2007. Amended April 29, 2011, effective July 1, 2011. Amended April 6, 2017, effective September 1, 2017.

Rule 1158. Assignment of Court Appointed Special Advocates

A court appointed special advocate shall follow the duties as set forth in the Juvenile Act, 42 Pa.C.S. § 6342(d) and in the Juvenile Court Judges' Commission's Juvenile Court Standards, 37 Pa. Code, Chapter 200.

Official Note: Rule 1158 adopted August, 21, 2006, effective February 1, 2007.

PART C
RECORDS

PART C(1)
ACCESS TO JUVENILE COURT RECORDS

1160. Inspection of Official Court Record

Rule 1160. Inspection of the Official Court Record

The official court record is only open to inspection by:

1) The judges, officers, and professional staff of the court;

2) The parties to the proceeding and their counsel and representatives, but the persons in this category shall not be permitted to see reports revealing the names of confidential sources of information contained in social reports, except at the discretion of the court;

3) A public or private agency or institution providing supervision or having custody of the child under order of the court;

4) A court, its probation officers, other officials or professional staff, and the attorney for the defendant for use in preparing a presentence report in a criminal case in which the defendant is convicted and who prior thereto had been a party to a proceeding under the Juvenile Act, 42 Pa.C.S. § 6301 *et seq.*;

5) The Administrative Office of Pennsylvania Courts;

6) The judges, officers, and professional staff of courts of other jurisdictions when necessary for the discharge of their official duties;

7) Officials of the Department of Corrections, a State Correctional Institution, or other penal institution to which an individual, who was previously adjudicated delinquent in a proceeding under the Juvenile Act, 42 Pa.C.S. § 6301 *et seq.*, has been committed, but the persons

in this category shall not be permitted to see reports revealing the names of confidential sources of information contained in social reports, except at the discretion of the court;

8) A parole board, court, or county probation official in considering an individual's parole or in exercising supervision over any individual who was previously adjudicated delinquent in a proceeding under the Juvenile Act, 42 Pa.C.S. § 6301 *et seq.*, but the persons in this category shall not be permitted to see reports revealing the names of confidential sources of information contained in social reports, except at the discretion of the court.

9) The State Sexual Offenders Assessment Board for use in completing assessments; and

10) With leave of court, any other person or agency or institution having a legitimate interest in the proceedings or in the work of the unified judicial system.

Comment

See the Juvenile Act, 42 Pa.C.S. § 6307, for the statutory provisions on inspection of all files and records of the court in a proceeding.

Persons specified in 23 Pa.C.S. § 6340 as having access to reports may qualify as persons having a legitimate interest in the proceedings under paragraph (10). *See* 23 Pa.C.S. § 6340.

This rule is meant to include the contents of the official court record as described in Rule 1166, which does not include agency records.

Official Note: Rule 1160 adopted August 21, 2006, effective February 1, 2007. Amended December 24, 2009, effective immediately.

Committee Explanatory Reports:

Final Report explaining the provisions of Rule 1160 published with the Court's Order at 36 Pa.B. 5571 (September 2, 2006). Final Report explaining the amendments to Rule 1160 published with the Court's Order at 40 Pa.B. 222 (January 9, 2010).

PART C(2)
MAINTAINING RECORDS

1165. Design of Forms
1166. Maintaining Records in the Clerk of Courts
1167. Filings and Service of Court Orders and Notices

Rule 1165. Design of Forms

The Court Administrator of Pennsylvania, in consultation with the Juvenile Court Procedural Rules Committee, shall design and publish forms necessary to implement these rules.

Comment

The purpose of the unified judicial system can be further achieved by creating uniform forms to implement a particular rule.

Official Note: Rule 1165 adopted August, 21, 2006, effective February 1, 2007.

Committee Explanatory Reports:

Final Report explaining the provisions of Rule 1165 published with the Court's Order at 36 Pa.B. 5571 (September 2, 2006).

Rule 1166. Maintaining Records in the Clerk of Courts

A. **Generally.** The juvenile court file is the official court record and shall contain all original records, papers, and orders filed, copies of all court notices, and docket entries. These records shall be maintained by the clerk of courts and shall not be taken from the custody of the clerk of courts without order of the court.

B. **Docket entries.** The clerk of courts shall maintain a list of docket entries: a chronological list, in electronic or written form, of documents and entries in the official court record and of all proceedings in the case. The clerk of courts shall make docket entries at the time the information is made known to the clerk.

C. **Contents of docket entries.** The docket entries shall include, at a minimum, the following information:

(1) the child's name, address, date of birth, if known;

(2) the guardian's name, address, if known;

(3) the names and addresses of all attorneys who have appeared or entered an appearance, the date of the entry of appearance(s), and the date of any withdrawal of appearance(s);

(4) notations concerning all papers filed with the clerk, including all court notices, appearances, motions, orders, findings and adjudications, dispositions, permanency reviews, and adoptions, briefly showing the nature and title, if any, of each paper filed, writ issued, and motion made, and the substance of each order or disposition of the court and of the returns showing execution of process;

(5) notations concerning motions made orally or orders issued orally in the courtroom when directed by the court;

(6) a notation of every judicial proceeding, continuance, and disposition;

(7) the location of exhibits made part of the record during the proceedings; and

(8)(a) the date of receipt in the clerk's office of the order or court notice;

(b) the date appearing on the order or court notice; and

(c) the date and manner of service of the order or court notice; and

(9) all other information required by Rule 1345.

Comment

This rule sets forth the mandatory contents of the list of docket entries and the official court record. This is not intended to be an exhaustive list of what is required to be recorded in the docket entries. The judicial districts may require additional information to be recorded in a case or in all cases.

The list of docket entries is a running record of all information related to any action in a dependency case in the court of common pleas of the clerk's county, such as dates of filings, of orders, and of court proceedings, including hearings conducted by juvenile court hearing officers. Nothing in this rule is intended to preclude the use of automated or other electronic means for time-stamping or making docket entries.

This rule applies to all proceedings in the court of common pleas, including hearings conducted by juvenile court hearing officers, at any stage of the dependency case.

This rule is not intended to include items contained in the county agency records or reports.

The practice in some counties of creating the list of docket entries only if an appeal is taken is inconsistent with this rule.

The requirement of paragraph (C)(3) that all attorneys and their addresses be recorded makes certain there is a record of all attorneys who have appeared for any party in the case. The requirement also ensures that attorneys are served as required by Rules 1167 and 1345. *See also* Rule 1345(C) concerning certificates of service.

In those cases in which the attorney has authorized receiving service by facsimile transmission or electronic means, the docket entry required by paragraph (C)(3) is to include the facsimile number or electronic address.

Paragraph (C)(5) recognizes that occasionally resolution of oral motions presented in open court should be reflected in the docket, such as motions and orders.

Official Note: Rule 1166 adopted August 21, 2006, effective February 1, 2007. Amended December 24, 2009, effective immediately. Amended April 6, 2017, effective September 1, 2017.

Rule 1167. Filings and Service of Court Orders and Notices

A. **Filings.**
   1) All orders and court notices shall be transmitted promptly to the clerk of courts for filing. Upon receipt by the clerk of courts, the order or court notice shall be time-stamped promptly with the date of receipt.
   2) All orders and court notices shall be filed in the official court record.
B. Service.
   1) A copy of any order or court notice shall be served promptly on each party's attorney, and the party, if unrepresented.
   2) The clerk of courts shall serve the order or court notice, unless the president judge has promulgated a local rule designating service to be by the court or its designee.
   3) Methods of service. Service shall be:
      a) in writing by:
         i) personal delivery to the party's attorney, and if unrepresented, the party;
         ii) mailing a copy to the party's attorney or leaving a copy for the attorney at the attorney's office;
         iii) in those judicial districts that maintain in the courthouse assigned boxes for counsel to receive service, leaving a copy for the attorney in the attorney's box;
         iv) sending a copy to an unrepresented party by first class mail addressed to the party's place of business, residence, or detention;

v) sending a copy by facsimile transmission or other electronic means if the party's attorney, and if unrepresented, the party has filed written request for this method of service or has included a facsimile number or an electronic address on a prior legal paper filed in the case;

vi) delivery to the party's attorney, and if unrepresented, the party by carrier service; or b) orally in open court on the record.

C. Unified Practice. Any local rule that is inconsistent with the provisions of this rule is prohibited, including any local rule requiring a person to file or serve orders or court notices.

Comment

Court notices, as used in this rule, are communications that ordinarily are issued by a judge or the court administrator concerning, for example, calendaring or scheduling, including proceedings requiring the party's presence.

A facsimile number or electronic address set forth on the letterhead is not sufficient to authorize service by facsimile transmission or other electronic means under paragraph (B)(3)(a)(v). The authorization for service by facsimile transmission or other electronic means under this rule is valid only for the duration of the case. A separate authorization is to be filed in each case by the party, if unrepresented, or by the attorney who wants to receive documents by this method of service.

Nothing in this rule is intended to preclude the use of automated or other electronic means for the transmission of the orders or court notices between the judge, court administrator, and clerk of courts, or for time-stamping.

Official Note: Rule 1167 adopted August 21, 2006, effective February 1, 2007. Amended December 24, 2009, effective immediately.

Committee Explanatory Reports:

Final Report explaining the provisions of Rule 1167 published with the Court's Order at 36 Pa.B. 5571 (September 2, 2006). Final Report explaining the amendments to Rule 1167 published with the Court's Order at 40 Pa.B. 222 (January 9, 2010).

PART D
MASTERS

1182. Qualifications of Juvenile Court Hearing Officer
1185. Appointment to Cases
1187. Authority of Juvenile Court Hearing Officer
1190. Stipulations Before Juvenile Court Hearing Officer
1191. Juvenile Court Hearing Officer's Findings and Recommendation to the Judge

Rule 1182. Qualifications of Juvenile Court Hearing Officer

A. Education, Experience, and Training. To preside as a juvenile court hearing officer over cases governed by the Juvenile Act, 42 Pa.C.S. § 6301 *et seq.*, an individual shall:

(1) be a member, in good standing, of the bar of this Commonwealth;

   (2) have been licensed to practice law for at least five consecutive years; and

   (3) have completed six hours of instruction, approved by the Pennsylvania Continuing Legal Education Board prior to hearing cases, which specifically addresses all of the following topics:

     (a) the Juvenile Act;

     (b) the Pennsylvania Rules of Juvenile Court Procedure;

     (c) the Child Protective Services Law;

     (d) evidence rules and methodology; and

     (e) child and adolescent development.

B. Continuing Education. Upon meeting the requirements of paragraph (A)(3), a juvenile court hearing officer shall thereafter complete six hours of instruction from a course(s) designed by the Office of Children and Families in the Courts, in juvenile dependency law, policy, or related social science research every two years.

C. Compliance.

   (1) A juvenile court hearing officer shall sign an affidavit attesting that he or she has met the requirements of this rule.

   (2) Prior to presiding as a juvenile court hearing officer, the attorney shall send the affidavit to the President Judge or his or her designee of each judicial district where the attorney is seeking to preside as a juvenile court hearing officer.

   (3) After submission of the initial affidavit pursuant to paragraph (C)(2), juvenile court hearing officers shall submit a new affidavit every two years attesting that the continuing education requirements of paragraph (B) have been met.

Comment

Pursuant to paragraphs (A)(1) & (2), juvenile court hearing officers are to be in good standing and have at least five consecutive years of experience as an attorney. It is best practice to have at least two years of experience in juvenile law.

Pursuant to paragraph (A)(3), the initial training program(s) is to be approved by the Pennsylvania Continuing Legal Education Board (Board). The program may be one course or multiple courses with at least six hours of instruction, equivalent to at least six CLE credits. When the Board is approving courses designed to address the requirements of this rule, it should consult with the Office of Children and Families in the Courts to ensure proper course requirements are being met. Additionally, for this initial training course(s), training already provided by the Office of Children and Families in the Courts or the Juvenile Court Judges' Commission may meet the requirements of this Rule.

For continuing education under paragraph (B), juvenile court hearing officers are to attend six hours of instruction from a course or multiple courses designed by the Office of Children and Families in the Courts. This is to ensure uniform training among juvenile court hearing officers.

These requirements are additional requirements to the Pa.R.C.L.E. because they mandate specific training in juvenile dependency law. However, the credit hours received do count towards the total maximum required under Pa.R.C.L.E. 105.

Pursuant to paragraph (C), a juvenile court hearing officer is to certify to the court that the requirements of this rule have been met prior to presiding as a juvenile court hearing officer, and submit new affidavits every two years thereafter.

Official Note: Rule 1182 adopted September 11, 2014, amended July 13, 2015, effective August 1, 2017. Amended April 6, 2017, effective September 1, 2017.

Explanatory Report

Modifications have been made to clarify that new Rules 182 and 1182 were not intended to be drafted as a prospective requirement but a requirement applying to all masters, including current masters. To accommodate any confusion caused by these rules, the new rules are now effective August 1, 2017.

Rule 1185. Appointment to Cases

A. **Appointment.** If necessary to assist the juvenile court judge, the president judge or his or her designee may appoint juvenile court hearing officers to hear designated dependency matters.

B. **Prohibited practice.** Juvenile court hearing officers shall not engage in practice before the juvenile court in the same judicial district where they preside over dependency matters.

Comment

Under paragraph (A), the president judge of each judicial district may restrict the classes of cases to be heard by the juvenile court hearing officer, in addition to the restrictions of Rule 1187. *See* 42 Pa.C.S. § 6305(b) and Rule 1187.

Official Note: Rule 1185 adopted August 21, 2006, effective February 1, 2007. Amended April 6, 2017, effective September 1, 2017.

Rule 1187. Authority of Juvenile Court Hearing Officer

A. **No authority.** A juvenile court hearing officer shall not have the authority to:

   (1) preside over:

      (a) termination of parental rights hearings;

      (b) adoptions;

      (c) any hearing in which any party seeks to establish a permanency goal of adoption or change the permanency goal to adoption;

   (2) enter orders for emergency or protective custody pursuant to Rules 1200 and 1210;

   (3) issue warrants; and

   (4) issue contempt orders.

B. **Right to hearing before judge.**

   (1) Prior to the commencement of any proceeding, the juvenile court hearing officer shall inform all parties of the right to have the matter heard by a judge. If a party objects to having the matter heard by the juvenile court hearing officer, the case shall proceed before the judge.

   (2) If a party objects to having the matter heard by the juvenile court hearing officer pursuant to paragraph (B)(1), the juvenile court hearing officer or the court's designee for scheduling cases shall immediately schedule a hearing before the judge. The time requirements of these rules shall apply.

Rule 1190   JUVENILE COURT PROCEDURE

Comment

A juvenile court hearing officer's authority is limited under this rule. To implement this rule, Rule 1800 suspends 42 Pa.C.S. § 6305(b) only to the extent that juvenile court hearing officers may not hear all classes of cases.

Under paragraph (A)(1)(c), once the permanency goal has been approved for adoption by a judge, all subsequent reviews or hearings may be heard by the juvenile court hearing officer unless a party objects pursuant to paragraph (B).

Under paragraph (A)(3), nothing is intended to limit the juvenile court hearing officer's ability, in a proper case before the juvenile court hearing officer, to recommend to the court that a warrant be issued. This includes arrest, bench, and search warrants.

Concerning the provisions of paragraph (B), see 42 Pa.C.S. § 6305(b).

Under paragraph (B)(2), it should be determined whenever possible before the date of the hearing whether there will be an objection to having the matter heard before a juvenile court hearing officer. If it is anticipated that there will be an objection, the case is to be scheduled in front of the judge, rather than the juvenile court hearing officer to prevent continuances and delays in the case.

See Rule 1127 for recording of proceedings before a juvenile court hearing officer.

Official Note: Rule 1187 adopted August 21, 2006, effective February 1, 2007. Amended April 6, 2017, effective September 1, 2017.

Rule 1190. Stipulations Before Juvenile Court Hearing Officer

A. **Types of cases.** Juvenile court hearing officers may accept stipulations in any classes of cases that they are permitted to hear pursuant to Rule 1187.

B. **Requirements.** The stipulation requirements of Rule 1405 shall be followed.

Comment

Under paragraph (A), a juvenile court hearing officer may accept stipulations in those permissible classes of cases pursuant to Rule 1187. In addition, the president judge of each judicial district may further restrict the classes of cases. *See* Rule 1185.

The court is to receive corroborating evidence, in addition to the stipulated facts, to make an independent determination that a child is dependent. *See* Rule 1405 and its *Comment*.

Official Note: Rule 1190 adopted August 21, 2006, effective February 1, 2007. Amended April 6, 2017, effective September 1, 2017.

Rule 1191. Juvenile Court Hearing Officer's Findings and Recommendation to the Judge

A. **Announcement of Findings and Recommendation.** At the conclusion of the hearing, the juvenile court hearing officer shall announce in open court on the record, the juvenile court hearing officer's findings and recommendation to the judge.

B. **Submission of Papers and Contents of Recommendation.** Within two business days of the hearing, the juvenile court hearing officer shall submit specific findings and a recommendation to the juvenile court judge. If requested, a copy of the findings and recommendation shall be given to any party.

C. **Challenge to Recommendation.** A party may challenge the juvenile court hearing officer's recommendation by filing a motion with the clerk of courts within three days of receipt of the recommendation. The motion shall request a rehearing by the judge and aver reasons for the challenge.

D. **Judicial Action.** Within seven days of receipt of the juvenile court hearing officer's findings and recommendation, the judge shall review the findings and recommendation of the juvenile court hearing officer and:

   (1) accept the recommendation by order;

   (2) reject the recommendation and issue an order with a different disposition;

   (3) send the recommendation back to the juvenile court hearing officer for more specific findings; or

   (4) conduct a rehearing.

Comment

The juvenile court may promulgate a form for juvenile court hearing officers to use. The findings and recommendation may take the form of a court order to be adopted by the court.

If a party contests the juvenile court hearing officer's decision, the copy of the findings and recommendation may be used as an attachment in a motion for a rehearing in front of the judge.

The juvenile court hearing officer's decision is subject to approval of the judge. When the judge, in rejecting the juvenile court hearing officer's recommendation, modifies a factual determination, a rehearing is to be conducted. The judge may reject the juvenile court hearing officer's findings and enter a new finding or disposition without a rehearing if there is no modification of factual determinations. *See In re Perry*, 459 A.2d 789 (Pa. Super. 1983).

Nothing in this rule prohibits the court from modifying conclusions of law made by the juvenile court hearing officer.

Official Note: Rule 1191 adopted August 21, 2006, effective February 1, 2007. Amended April 6, 2017, effective September 1, 2017.

Rule 1200   JUVENILE COURT PROCEDURE

CHAPTER 12
COMMENCEMENT OF PROCEEDINGS, EMERGENCY CUSTODY, AND PRE-ADJUDICATORY PLACEMENT

PART A
COMMENCING PROCEEDINGS

1200. Commencing Proceedings
1201. Procedures for Protective Medical Custody
1202. Procedures for Protective Custody by Police and County Agency

PART B
EMERGENCY CUSTODY

1210. Order for Protective Custody

PART C
SHELTER CARE

1240. Shelter Care Application
1241. Notification of Shelter Care Hearing
1242. General Conduct of Shelter Care Proceeding
1243. Shelter Care Rehearing

PART A
COMMENCING PROCEEDINGS

1200. Commencing Proceedings
1201. Procedures for Protective Medical Custody
1202. Procedures for Protective Custody by Police and County Agency

Rule 1200. Commencing Proceedings

Dependency proceedings within a judicial district shall be commenced by:
1) the filing of a dependency petition;
2) the submission of an emergency custody application;
3) the taking of the child into protective custody pursuant to a court order or statutory authority;
4) the court accepting jurisdiction of a resident child from another state;
5) the court accepting supervision of child pursuant to another state's order; or
6) the filing of a motion for resumption of jurisdiction pursuant to Rule 1634.

Comment

See 42 Pa.C.S. §§ 6321, 6324, 23 Pa.C.S. §§ 6315, 6369, 62 P.S. § 761.

If a county agency has custody of a child under a voluntary placement agreement and custody will exceed thirty days, dependency proceedings are to be commenced by the filing of a petition by the thirtieth day. A dependency petition is to be filed if a guardian requests return of the child and the county agency refuses to return the child. A dependency petition is to be filed at the time of refusal of return by the county agency. *See* 55 Pa. Code § 3130.65 for provisions on voluntary agreements.

For procedures on protective medical custody, see Rule 1201. For procedures on protective custody by police and the county agency, see Rule 1202.

For proceedings that have already been commenced in another judicial district, see Rule 1302 for inter-county transfer of the case.

For resumption of jurisdiction, see Rules 1634 and 1635 & 42 Pa.C.S. §§ 6302 and 6351(j).

The clerk of courts and the county agency should have form motions available for children who want to file for resumption of juvenile court jurisdiction. These forms are available at http://www.pacourts.us/Forms/dependency.htm.

The clerk of courts or county agency is to assist any child who requests assistance in completing the form and the clerk of courts is to accept all filings for resumption of juvenile court jurisdiction regardless of whether the motions meet the standard for legal filings or there are objections by other parties. This is to ensure these children have easy access to the court. *See also* Rule 1126.

Official Note: Rule 1200 adopted August, 21, 2006, effective February 1, 2007. Amended October 21, 2013, effective December 1, 2013.

Committee Explanatory Reports:

Final Report explaining the provisions of Rule 1200 published with the Court's Order at 36 Pa.B. 5571 (September 2, 2006). Final Report explaining the amendments to Rule 1200 published with the Court's Order at 43 Pa.B. - (November 2, 2013).

Rule 1201. Procedures for Protective Medical Custody

When a physician examining or treating a child, a director, or a person specifically designated in writing by the director, of any hospital or other medical institution takes a child into custody pursuant to Rule 1200, the following provisions shall apply:

a) Notice.

1) The person taking the child into custody shall notify the guardian and the county agency of:

a) the whereabouts of the child, unless disclosure is prohibited by court order; and

b) the reasons for taking the child into custody.

2) Notice may be oral. The notice shall be reduced to writing within twenty-four hours.

b) Duration of custody. No child may be held in protective custody in a hospital or other medical institution for more than twenty-four hours unless the appropriate county agency is immediately notified that the child has been taken into custody and the county agency obtains an order permitting the child to be held in custody for a longer period. The president judge of each judicial district shall ensure that a judge is available twenty-four hours a day, every day of the year to accept and decide actions brought by the county agency within the twenty-four hour period.

Rule 1202 JUVENILE COURT PROCEDURE

Comment

Notice to the county agency under paragraph (A) is to insure that appropriate proceedings are commenced. Notice may be oral but is to be reduced to writing within twenty-four hours.

A child taken into protective custody is to be placed during the protective custody in an appropriate medical facility, foster home, or other appropriate facility approved by the Department of Public Welfare for this purpose.

A conference between the guardian of the child taken into protective custody and the employee designated by the county agency to be responsible for the child should be held within forty-eight hours of the time that the child is taken into custody for the purpose of: 1) explaining to the guardian the reasons for the temporary detention of the child and the whereabouts of the child, unless disclosure is prohibited by court order; 2) expediting, whenever possible, the return of the child to the custody of the guardian when protective custody is no longer necessary; and 3) explaining to the guardian the rights provided for by 42 Pa.C.S. §§ 6337, 6338.

See In re J.R.W., 428 Pa.Super. 597, 631 A.2d 1019 (1993) and 23 Pa.C.S. § 6315.

Official Note: Rule 1201 adopted August, 21, 2006, effective February 1, 2007.

Committee Explanatory Reports:

Final Report explaining the provisions of Rule 1201 published with the Court's Order at 36 Pa.B. 5571 (September 2, 2006).

Rule 1202. Procedures for Protective Custody by a Police Juvenile Probation Officer, and County Agency

A. Protective custody.

   1) No court order.

      a) A police officer or a juvenile probation officer may take a child into protective custody pursuant to Rule 1200 if there are reasonable grounds to believe that the child is suffering from illness or injury or is in imminent danger from the surroundings and removal is necessary.

      b) Without unnecessary delay, but no more than twenty-four hours after a child is taken into custody, an application for a protective custody order shall be made to provide temporary emergency supervision of a child pending a hearing pursuant to Rule 1242. The president judge of each judicial district shall ensure that a judge is available twenty-four hours a day, every day of the year to accept and decide actions brought by the county agency within the twenty-four hour period.

   2) Court order.

      a) A police officer, juvenile probation officer, or county agency may obtain a protective custody order removing a child from the home pursuant to Rule 1210 if the court finds that remaining in the home is contrary to the welfare and the best interests of the child.

      b) Pursuant to 23 Pa.C.S. § 6315 and after a court order, the county agency shall take the child into protective custody for protection from abuse. No county agency may take custody of the child without judicial authorization based on the merits of the situation.

B. **Notice.**
1) **In all cases, the person taking the child into custody immediately shall notify the guardian and the county agency of:**
   a) **the whereabouts of the child, unless disclosure is prohibited by court order; and**
   b) **the reasons for taking the child into custody.**
2) **Notice may be oral. The notice shall be reduced to writing within twenty-four hours.**
C. **Placement. A child shall be placed in an appropriate shelter care facility or receive other appropriate care pending a shelter care hearing pursuant to Rule 1242.**

Comment

A properly commissioned juvenile probation officer has the authority to take a child into protective custody as a duly authorized officer of the court pursuant to 42 Pa.C.S. § 6324 unless the President Judge has limited such authority pursuant to Rule 195. *See also* 23 Pa.C.S. § 6315.

Under paragraph (A)(1)(a) & (A)(2)(a), the police officer's or juvenile probation officer's duty is to protect the child and remove the child safely. A police officer or juvenile probation officer may bring the child to the county agency for supervision of the child pending a court order that should be given immediately. The police officer's or juvenile probation officer's duty is to take a child into protective custody if there are reasonable grounds to believe that the child is suffering from illness or injury or is in imminent danger from his or her surroundings, and that protective custody is necessary, whereas the county agency's duty is to supervise the child and find an appropriate placement for the child when necessary. Only a police officer or juvenile probation officer may take custody of the child without a court order. *See* Rule 1800 for suspension of 42 Pa.C.S. § 6324, which provides that law enforcement officers may take a child into custody.

Paragraph (B) is to ensure that if the guardian is not present when the child is removed, the guardian knows the whereabouts of the child and the reasons the child is taken into custody. If the person removing the child is not a caseworker, the county agency is to be notified to commence proceedings in juvenile court.

Under paragraph (C), a child taken into protective custody is to be placed during the protective custody in an appropriate shelter care facility or receive other appropriate care.

A conference between the guardian of the child taken into protective custody and the employee designated by the county agency to be responsible for the child should be held within forty-eight hours of the time that the child is taken into custody for the purpose of: 1) explaining to the guardian the reasons for the temporary detention of the child and the whereabouts of the child, unless disclosure is prohibited by court order; 2) expediting, whenever possible, the return of the child to the custody of the guardian when protective custody is no longer necessary; and 3) explaining to the guardian the rights provided for by 42 Pa.C.S. §§ 6337, 6338.

See 42 Pa.C.S. §§ 6324 & 6326 and 23 Pa.C.S. § 6369.

Official Note: Rule 1202 adopted August, 21, 2006, effective February 1, 2007. Amended May 20, 2011, effective July 1, 2011.

Committee Explanatory Reports:

Final Report explaining the provisions of Rule 1202 published with the Court's Order at 36 Pa.B. 5571 (September 2, 2006). Final Report explaining the amendments to Rule 1202 published with the Court's Order at 41 Pa.B. 2839 (June 4, 2011).

PART B
EMERGENCY CUSTODY

1210. Order for Protective Custody

Rule 1210. Order for Protective Custody

   A. *Application of order.* The application for a court order of protective custody may be orally made; however, the request shall be reduced to writing within twenty-four hours. The request shall set forth reasons for the need of protective custody.

   B. *Finding of court.*

   (1) A child may be taken into protective custody by court order when the court determines that removal of the child is necessary for the welfare and best interests of the child.

   (2) At the time the court issues a protective custody order, the court shall inquire as to whether family finding efforts pursuant to Rule 1149 have been initiated by the county agency.

   (3) The order may initially be oral, provided that it is reduced to writing within twenty-four hours or the next court business day.

   C. *Law enforcement.* The court may authorize a search of the premises by law enforcement or the county agency so that the premises may be entered into without authorization of the owner for the purpose of taking a child into protective custody.

   D. *Contents of order.* The court order shall include:

   (1) the name of the child sought to be protected;

   (2) the date of birth of the child, if known;

   (3) the whereabouts of the child, if known;

   (4) the names and addresses of the guardians;

   (5) the reasons for taking the child into protective custody;

   (6) a finding whether reasonable efforts were made to prevent placement of the child;

   (7) a finding whether the reasons for keeping the child in shelter care and that remaining in the home is ontrary to the welfare and best interests of the child; and.

   (8) findings and orders related to the requirements of Rule 1149 regarding family finding.

   E. *Execution of order.* The court shall specify:

   (1) the limitations of the order;

   (2) the manner in which the order is to be executed; and

   (3) who shall execute the order.

Comment

See 42 Pa.C.S. § 6324 for statutory provisions concerning taking into custody.

For a discussion of the due process requirements for taking a child into emergency custody, see *Patterson v. Armstrong County Children and Youth Services*, 141 F. Supp. 2d 512 (W.D. Pa. 2001).

The court is to determine whether reasonable efforts, including services and family finding efforts, were made to prevent placement or in the case of an emergency placement where services were not offered and could not have prevented the necessity of placement, whether this level of effort was reasonable due to the emergency nature of the situation, safety considerations and circumstances of the family. 42 Pa.C.S. § 6332.

See also In re Petition to Compel Cooperation with Child Abuse Investigation, 875 A.2d 365 (Pa. Super. Ct. 2005).

Pursuant to paragraph (D)(8), the county agency should be looking for family and kin as a resource to aid and assist the family to prevent removal of the child from the home. When removal of the child is necessary, placement with family and kin will help reduce the potential trauma of the removal from the home. *See* Rule 1149 regarding family finding requirements.

Note: Rule 1210 adopted August 21, 2006, effective February 1, 2007. Amended July 13, 2015, effective October 1, 2015.

PART C
SHELTER CARE

1240. Shelter Care Application
1241. Notification of Shelter Care Hearing
1242. Shelter Care Hearing
1243. Shelter Care Rehearing

Rule 1240. Shelter Care Application

A. *Filings.* A shelter care application may be oral or in writing. If oral, within twenty-four hours of exercising protective custody pursuant to Rule 1210, the county agency shall file a written shelter care application.

B. *Application contents.* Every shelter care application shall set forth:

   (1)   the name of the applicant;

   (2)   the name, date of birth, and address of the child, if known;

   (3)   the name and address of the child's guardian, or if unknown, the name and address of the nearest adult relative;

   (4)   the date that the child was taken into custody;

   (5)   a concise statement of facts in support of the allegation of dependency;

   (6)   a statement detailing family finding efforts and:

      (a)   the reasonable efforts made to prevent placements; and

      (b)   why there are no less restrictive alternatives available;

   (7)   a verification by the applicant that the facts set forth in the petition are true and correct to the applicant's personal knowledge, information, or belief, and that any false statements are subject to the penalties of the Crimes Code, 18 Pa.C.S. § 4904, relating to unsworn falsification to authorities;

   (8)   the signature of the applicant and the date of the execution of the application; and

   (9)   the whereabouts of the child unless the county agency has determined it would pose a risk to the safety of the child or the guardian, or disclosure is prohibited by the court.

Comment

In lieu of a shelter care application, the county agency may file a petition as set forth in Rule 1330.

Pursuant to paragraph (B)(6), the application is to contain a statement detailing the reasonable efforts made to prevent placement and the specific reasons why there are no less restrictive alternatives available. This statement may include information such as: 1) the circumstances of the case; 2) family finding efforts made by the county agency; 3) contact with family members or other kin; 4) the child's educational, health care, and disability needs; and 5) any need for emergency actions.

See Rule 1149 regarding family finding requirements.

The primary focus of the shelter care application is to assert that protective custody is needed and the child should remain in the custody of the county agency. A shelter care hearing is to be held within seventy-two hours of taking the child into protective custody. *See* Rule 1242(D).

Note: Rule 1240 adopted August 21, 2006, effective February 1, 2007. Amended April 29, 2011, effective July 1, 2011. Amended July 13, 2015, effective October 1, 2015.

Rule 1241. Notification of Shelter Care Hearing

A. **Generally. The applicant for the shelter care hearing shall notify the following persons of the date, time, and place of the shelter care hearing:**
   1) **the child;**
   2) **the guardian(s) of the child;**
   3) **the attorney for the child;**
   4) **the attorney(s) for the guardian(s);**
   5) **the attorney for the county agency;**
   6) **the county agency; and**
   7) **any other appropriate person.**

B. **Counsel. The guardian of the child shall be notified of the right to counsel immediately after a child is taken into protective custody and before a shelter care hearing.**

Comment

Notice should be as timely as possible. Because there is a seventy-two hour time restriction, notice may be oral. Every possible attempt to notify all parties is to be made. It is not sufficient to notify only one guardian. All guardians are to be notified. *See In re M.L.*, 562 Pa. 646, 757 A.2d 849 (2000).

The hearing may go forward if a guardian is not present. However, if a guardian has not been notified, a rehearing is to be ordered under Rule 1243 upon submission of an affidavit by the guardian.

The court is to direct the county agency to provide the child's foster parent, preadoptive parent or relative providing care for the child with timely notice of the hearing. *See* 42 Pa.C.S. § 6336.1.

If a court appointed special advocate is involved in the case, the court appointed special advocate is to be notified as any other appropriate person pursuant to paragraph (A)(7).

Official Note: Rule 1241 adopted August, 21, 2006, effective February 1, 2007.

Committee Explanatory Reports:

Final Report explaining the provisions of Rule 1241 published with the Court's Order at 36 Pa.B. 5571 (September 2, 2006).

Rule 1242. Shelter Care Hearing

A. *Informing of rights.* Upon commencement of the hearing, the court shall ensure that:

   (1) a copy of the shelter care application is provided to the parties; and

   (2) all parties are informed of the right to counsel.

B. *Manner of hearing.*

   (1) *Conduct.* The hearing shall be conducted in an informal but orderly manner.

   (2) *Recording.* If requested, or if ordered by the court, the hearing shall be recorded by appropriate means. If not so recorded, full minutes of the hearing shall be kept.

   (3) *Testimony and evidence.* All evidence helpful in determining the questions presented, including oral or written reports, may be received by the court and relied upon to the extent of its probative value even though not competent in the hearing on the petition. The child's attorney, the guardian, if unrepresented, and the attorney for the guardian shall be afforded an opportunity to examine and controvert written reports so received.

   (4) *Advanced Communication Technology.* Upon good cause shown, a court may utilize advanced communication technology pursuant to Rule 1129.

C. *Findings.* The court shall determine whether:

   (1) there are sufficient facts in support of the shelter care application;

   (2) the county agency has reasonably engaged in family finding;

   (3) custody of the child is warranted after consideration of the following factors:

      (a) remaining in the home would be contrary to the welfare and best interests of the child;

      (b) reasonable efforts were made by the county agency to prevent the child's placement;

      (c) the child's placement is the least restrictive placement that meets the needs of the child, supported by reasons why there are no less restrictive alternatives available; and

      (d) the lack of efforts was reasonable in the case of an emergency placement where services were not offered;

   (4) a person, other than the county agency, submitting a shelter care application, is a party to the proceedings; and

   (5) there are any special needs of the child that have been identified and that the court deems necessary to address while the child is in shelter care.

D. *Prompt hearing.* The court shall conduct a hearing within seventy-two hours of taking the child into protective custody. The parties shall not be permitted to waive the shelter care hearing.

E. *Court order.* At the conclusion of the shelter care hearing, the court shall enter a written order setting forth:

(1) its findings pursuant to paragraph (C);

(2) any conditions placed upon any party;

(3) any orders regarding family finding pursuant to Rule 1149;

(4) any orders for placement or temporary care of the child;

(5) any findings or orders necessary to ensure the stability and appropriateness of the child's education, and when appropriate, the court shall appoint an educational decision maker pursuant to Rule 1147;

(6) any findings or orders necessary to identify, monitor, and address the child's needs concerning health care and disability, if any, and if parental consent cannot be obtained, authorize evaluations and treatment needed; and

(7) any orders of visitation.

Comment

Pursuant to paragraph (B)(4), it is expected that the parties be present. Only upon good cause shown should advanced communication technology be utilized.

Pursuant to paragraph (C), the court is to make a determination that the evidence presented with the shelter care application under Rule 1240 is supported by sufficient facts. After this determination, the court is to determine whether the custody of the child is warranted by requiring a finding that: 1) remaining in the home would be contrary to the health and welfare of the child; 2) reasonable efforts were made by the county agency to prevent the placement of the child; 3) the child was placed in the least restrictive placement available; and 4) if the child was taken into emergency placement without services being offered, the lack of efforts by the county agency was reasonable. Additionally, the court is to state the reasons why there are no less restrictive alternatives available.

Family finding is to be initiated prior to the shelter care hearing. *See Comment* to Rule 1149 as to level of reasonableness.

Pursuant to paragraph (C)(2), the court is to make a determination whether the county agency has reasonably engaged or is to engage in family finding in the case. The county agency will be required to report its diligent family finding efforts at subsequent hearings. *See* Rule 1149 for requirements of family finding. *See also* Rules 1408(2), 1512(D)(1)(h), 1514(A)(4), 1608(D)(1)(h), and 1610(D) and their *Comments* for the court's findings as to the county agency's satisfaction of the family finding requirements and Rules 1210(D), 1409(C) and 1609(D) and *Comments* to Rules 1408, 1409, 1512, 1514, 1515, 1608, 1609, 1610, and 1611 on the court's orders.

Pursuant to paragraph (C)(4), the court is to determine whether or not a person is a proper party to the proceedings. Regardless of the court's findings on the party status, the court is to determine if the application is supported by sufficient evidence.

Under paragraph (D), the court is to ensure a timely hearing. Nothing in paragraph (D) is intended to preclude the use of stipulations or agreements among the parties, subject to court review and acceptance at the shelter care hearing.

See 42 Pa.C.S. § 6332.

Pursuant to paragraph (E), the court is to enter a written order. It is important that the court address any special needs of the child while the child is in shelter care. The child's attorney or the county agency is to present any educational, health care, and disability needs to the court, if known at the time of the hearing. These needs may include a child's educational stability, needs concerning early intervention, remedial services, health care, and disability. If the court determines a child is in need of an educational decision maker, the court is to appoint an educational decision maker pursuant to Rule 1147.

The court's order should address the child's educational stability, including the right to an educational decision maker. The order should address the child's right to: 1) educational stability, including the right to: a) remain in the same school regardless of a change in placement when it is in the child's best interest; b) immediate enrollment when a school change is in the child's best interest; and c) have school proximity considered in all placement changes, 42 U.S.C. §§ 675(1)(G) and 11431 et seq.; 2) an educational decision maker pursuant to Rule 1147, 42 Pa. C.S. § 6301, 20 U.S.C. § 1439(a)(5), and 34 C.F.R. § 300.519; 3) an appropriate education, including any necessary special education, early intervention, or remedial services pursuant to 24 P.S. §§ 13-1371 and 13-1372, 55 Pa. Code § 3130.87, and 20 U.S.C. § 1400 et seq.; 4) the educational services necessary to support the child's transition to independent living pursuant to 42 Pa.C.S. § 6351 if the child is sixteen or older; and 5) a transition plan that addresses the child's educational needs pursuant to 42 U.S.C. § 675(5)(H) if the child will age out of care within ninety days.

When addressing the child's health and disability needs, the court's order should address the right of: 1) a child to receive timely and medically appropriate screenings and health care services, 55 Pa. Code § 3800.32 and 42 U.S.C. § 1396d(r); and 2) a child with disabilities to receive necessary accommodations, 42 U.S.C. § 12132, 28 C.F.R. § 35.101 et seq., Section 504 of the Rehabilitation Act of 1973, *as amended*, 29 U.S.C. § 794, and implementing regulations at 45 C.F.R. § 84.1 et seq.

Pursuant to the Juvenile Act, the court has authority to order a physical or mental examination of a child and medical or surgical treatment of a minor, who is suffering from a serious physical condition or illness which requires prompt treatment in the opinion of a physician. The court may order the treatment even if the guardians have not been given notice of the pending hearing, are not available, or without good cause inform the court that they do not consent to the treatment. 42 Pa.C.S. § 6339(b).

Nothing in this rule prohibits informal conferences, narrowing of issues, if necessary, and the court making appropriate orders to expedite the case. The shelter care hearing may be used as a vehicle to discuss the matters needed and narrow the issues. The court is to ensure a timely adjudicatory hearing is held.

See 42 Pa.C.S. § 6339 for orders of physical and mental examinations and treatment.

See Rule 1330(A) for filing of a petition.

Official Note: Rule 1242 adopted August 21, 2006, effective February 1, 2007. Amended April 21, 2011, effective July 1, 2011. Amended April 29, 2011, effective July 1, 2011. Amended July 13, 2015, effective October 1, 2015. Amended May 16, 2017, effective July 1, 2017.

Rule 1243. Shelter Care Rehearings

A. **Mandatory Rehearing. If the guardian submits an affidavit to the county agency alleging that the guardian was not notified of the shelter care hearing and that the guardian did not appear or waive appearance at the shelter care hearing, a rehearing shall be held within seventy-two hours of the submission of the affidavit.**

B. **Discretionary Rehearing. The court may grant a rehearing upon request of a party or on its own motion.**

Rule 1243   JUVENILE COURT PROCEDURE

C. **Forum. The judge, who heard the original shelter care hearing or adopted the findings of the juvenile court hearing officer, shall hold the rehearing, unless the judge assigns the case to a juvenile court hearing officer.**

Comment

See 42 Pa.C.S. § 6332(b).

Under paragraph (A), upon receiving an affidavit, the county agency is to schedule a rehearing, forward the affidavit to the proper person to schedule a rehearing, or submit the affidavit to the court for rescheduling.

Under paragraph (C), only a judge may hold a rehearing, unless the judge orders a juvenile court hearing officer to hear the case.

Note: *Rule 1243 adopted August 21, 2006, effective February 1, 2007. Amended April 6, 2017, effective September 1, 2017.*

Pa. R.J.C.P.

CHAPTER 13
PRE-ADJUDICATORY PROCEDURES

PART A
VENUE

1300. Venue
1302. Inter-County Transfer

PART B
APPLICATION FOR PRIVATE PETITION

1320. Application to File a Private Petition
1321. Hearing on Application for Private Petition

PART C
PETITION

1330. Petition: Filing, Contents, Function, Aggravated Circumstances
1331. Service of Petition
1333. Separate Petitions and Consolidated Hearing
1334. Amendment of Petition
1335. Withdrawal of Petition
1336. Re-filing of the Petition After Withdrawal or Dismissal

PART D
PROCEDURES FOLLOWING FILING OF PETITION

1340. Discovery and Inspection
1342. Pre-Adjudicatory Conference.

PART D(1)
MOTION PROCEDURES

1344. Motions and Answers
1345. Filing and Service

PART D(2)
ADJUDICATORY SUMMONS AND NOTICE PROCEDURES

1360. Adjudicatory Summons
1361. Adjudicatory Notice
1363. Service of Summons
1364. Failure to Appear on the Summons

PART E
PRESERVATION OF TESTIMONY AND EVIDENCE

1380. Preservation of Testimony After Commencement of Proceedings
1381. Preservation of Testimony by Video Recording

Rule 1300   JUVENILE COURT PROCEDURE

PART A
VENUE

1300. Venue
1302. Inter-County Transfer

Rule 1300. Venue

A.   **Generally.** A dependency proceeding shall be commenced in:
     1) the county in which the child is present; or
     2) the child's county of residence.

B.   **Change of venue.** For the convenience of parties and witnesses, the court, upon its own motion or motion of any party, may transfer an action to the appropriate court of any county where the action could originally have been brought or could be brought at the time of filing the motion to change venue.

C.   **Transmission of all records.** If there is a change of venue pursuant to paragraph (B):
     1) the transferring court shall transfer certified copies of all documents, reports, and summaries in the child's official court record to the receiving court; and
     2) The county agency of the transferring court shall transfer all its records to the county agency where venue has been transferred.

Comment

See 42 Pa.C.S. § 6321.

For procedures regarding motions and answers, see Rule 1344. In addition to the procedures for service of orders under Rule 1167, an order changing venue is to be served upon the new county agency and the receiving court so they may begin proceedings in the receiving county.

Official Note: Rule 1300 adopted August 21, 2006, effective February 1, 2007. Amended December 24, 2009, effective immediately.

Committee Explanatory Reports:

Final Report explaining the provisions of Rule 1300 published with the Court's Order at 36 Pa.B. 5571 (September 2, 2006). Final Report explaining the amendments to Rule 1300 published with the Court's Order at 40 Pa.B. 222 (January 9, 2010).

Rule 1302. Inter-County Transfer

A.   **Transfer.** A court may transfer a case to another county at any time.

B.   **Transmission of official court record.** If the case is transferred pursuant to paragraph (A):
     1) the transferring court shall transfer certified copies of all documents, reports, and summaries in the child's official court record to the receiving court; and
     2) the county agency of the transferring court shall transfer all its records to the county agency where jurisdiction has been transferred.

Pa. R.J.C.P.   Rule 1320

Comment

See 42 Pa.C.S. § 6321.

Official Note: Rule 1302 adopted August 21, 2006, effective February 1, 2007. Amended December 24, 2009, effective immediately.

Committee Explanatory Reports:

Final Report explaining the provisions of Rule 1302 published with the Court's Order at 36 Pa.B.5571 (September 2, 2006). Final Report explaining the amendments to Rule 1302 published with the Court's Order at 40 Pa.B. 222 (January 9, 2010).

PART B
APPLICATION FOR PRIVATE PETITION

1320. Application to File a Private Petition
1321. Hearing on Application for Private Petition

Rule 1320. Application to File a Private Petition

A. Application contents. Any person, other than the county agency, may present an application to file a private petition with the court. The application shall include the following information:

(1) the name of the person applying for a petition;

(2) the name of the alleged dependent child;

(3) the relationship of the person presenting this application to the child and to any other parties;

(4) if known, the following:

   (a) the date of birth and address of the child;

   (b) the name and address of the child's guardian, or the name and address of the nearest adult relative;

   (c) if a child is Native American, the child's Native American history or affiliation with a tribe;

   (d) a statement, including court file numbers where possible, of pending juvenile or family court proceedings and prior or present juvenile or family court orders relating to the child;

(5) a concise statement of facts in support of the allegations for which the application for a petition has been filed;

(6) a statement that the applying person has reported the circumstances underlying this application to the county agency or a reason for not having reported the circumstances underlying the application;

(7) a verification by the person making the application that the facts set forth in the application are true and correct to the person's personal knowledge, information, or belief, and that any false statements are subject to the penalties of the Crimes Code, 18 Pa.C.S. §4904, relating to unsworn falsification to authorities; and

(8) the signature of the person and the date of the execution of the application for a petition.

B. Notice to County Agency. Upon receipt of an application, the court shall provide a copy of the application to the county agency. The county agency shall thereafter receive notice of the hearing.

Rule 1321   JUVENILE COURT PROCEDURE

Comment

Any person, other than the county agency, shall first file an application to file a petition under this Rule. Rule 1800 suspends 42 Pa.C.S. § 6334 to the extent it is inconsistent with this Rule.

See Rule 1321 for hearing on application.

This rule is not intended to preclude the county agency from seeking to intervene and participate in the hearing on the application. See Rule 1133 (Motion to Intervene).

Note: *Rule 1320 adopted August 21, 2006, effective February 1, 2007. Amended May 12, 2008, effective immediately. Amended May 16, 2017, effective July 1, 2017.*

Rule 1321. Hearing on Application for Private Petition

A. **Hearing.** The court shall conduct a hearing within fourteen days of the presentation of the application for a petition to determine:
   (1) if there are sufficient facts alleged to support a petition of dependency; and
   (2) whether the person applying for the petition is a proper party to the proceedings.

B. **Findings.**
   (1) If the court finds sufficient facts to support a petition of dependency, then the applicant may file a petition pursuant to Rule 1330.
   (2) If the court finds the person making the application for a petition is a proper party to the proceedings, then the person shall be afforded all rights and privileges given to a party pursuant to law.

C. **Joinder.** Following grant of an application under this rule, the county agency shall be joined as a party in any further proceedings upon filing and service of a private petition pursuant to Rules 1330 and 1331.

Comment

Under paragraph (A), at a hearing, the court is to determine if: 1) there are sufficient facts alleged to support a petition of dependency; and 2) the applying person is a proper party to the proceedings. A petition of dependency may go forward whether or not the applying person is determined to be a party to the proceedings.

If a child is in custody, the hearing under paragraph (A) may be combined with the shelter care hearing pursuant to Rule 1242.

Official Note: Rule 1321 adopted August 21, 2006, effective February 1, 2007. Amended May 16, 2017, effective July 1, 2017.

PART C
PETITION

1330. Petition: Filing, Contents, Function, Aggravated Circumstances
1331. Service of Petition
1333. Separate Petitions and Consolidated Hearing
1334. Amendment of Petition
1335. Withdrawal of Petition

1336. Re-filing of the Petition After Withdrawal or Dismissal

Rule 1330. Petition: Filing, Contents, Function, Aggravated Circumstances

A. *Filings.*

(1) A dependency petition may be filed at any time; however, if a child is taken into custody, the requirements of paragraph (A)(2) shall be met.

(2) Within twenty-four hours of the shelter care hearing, the county agency shall file a dependency petition with the clerk of courts when:

   (a) the child remains in protective custody pursuant to Rule 1201, 1202 or 1210; or

   (b) the child is not in protective custody but it is determined at a shelter care hearing pursuant to Rule 1242 that the filing of a dependency petition is appropriate.

B. *Petition contents.* Every petition shall set forth plainly:

(1) the name of the petitioner;

(2) the name, date of birth, and address of the child, if known;

(3) the name and address of the child's guardian, or if unknown, the name and address of the nearest adult relative;

(4) if a child is Native American, the child's Native American history or affiliation with a tribe;

(5) a statement that:

   (a) it is in the best interest of the child and the public that the proceedings be brought;

   (b) the child is or is not currently under the supervision of the county agency;

(6) a statement detailing family finding efforts and, if the county agency is seeking placement:

   (a) the reasonable efforts made to prevent placement; and

   (b) why there are no less restrictive alternatives available;

(7) a concise statement of facts in support of the allegations for which the petition has been filed;

   (a) facts for each allegation shall be set forth separately;

   (b) the relevant statute or code section shall be set forth specifically for each allegation;

(8) a verification by the petitioner that the facts set forth in the petition are true and correct to the petitioner's personal knowledge, information, or belief, and that any false statements are subject to the penalties of the Crimes Code, 18 Pa.C.S. § 4904, relating to unsworn falsification to authorities;

(9) the signature of the petitioner and the date of the execution of the petition; and

(10) the whereabouts of the child unless disclosure is prohibited by court order and if taken into custody, the date and time thereof.

C. *Aggravated circumstances.* A motion for finding of aggravated circumstances may be brought in the petition pursuant to Rule 1701(A).

Comment

Petitions should be filed without unreasonable delay.

Under paragraph (A)(2), a petition is to be filed twenty-four hours after the shelter care hearing if the requirements of (A)(2)(a) and (b) are met. Rule 1800 suspends 42 Pa.C.S. § 6331 only as to the time requirement of when a petition is to be filed.

Additionally, paragraph (A)(2) requires that the county agency file a petition. Any other person, other than the county agency, is to file an application to file a petition under Rule 1320. Rule 1800 suspends 42 Pa.C.S. § 6334, which provides any person may file a petition.

For the safety or welfare of a child or a guardian, the court may order that the addresses of the child or a guardian not be disclosed to specified individuals.

Pursuant to paragraph (B)(6), when the county agency is seeking placement, the petition is to include the reasonable efforts made to prevent placement, including efforts for family finding, and why there are no less restrictive alternatives available. *See* Rule 1149 for family finding requirements. *See also* Rule 1242(C)(2)&(3)(b)&(c) and *Comments* to Rules 1242, 1409, 1515, 1608, 1609, 1610, and 1611 for reasonable efforts determinations.

If a petition is filed after the county agency has discontinued family finding for non-court cases, the county agency is to aver reasons for the discontinuance in the petition. *See* 62 P.S. § 1302.2(a).

A motion for finding of aggravated circumstances may be brought in a dependency petition. *See* Rule 1701(A). If aggravated circumstances are determined to exist after the filing of a petition, a written motion is to be filed pursuant to Rules 1701 and 1344.

The aggravated circumstances, as defined by 42 Pa.C.S. § 6302, are to be specifically identified in the motion for finding of aggravated circumstances.

Note: Rule 1330 adopted August 21, 2006, effective February 1, 2007. Amended July 13, 2015, effective October 1, 2015.

Rule 1331. Service of Petition

A. **Copy.** Upon the filing of a petition, a copy of the petition shall be served promptly upon the child, the child's guardian, the child's attorney, the guardian's attorney, the attorney for the county agency, and the county agency.

B. **Method of Service.**
   1) **Child and guardian.** The petition shall be served upon the child and all of the child's guardians by:
      a) certified mail, return receipt requested and first-class mail; or
      b) delivery in-person.
   2) **Attorneys and the county agency.** The petition shall be served upon the attorneys and county agency by:
      a) first-class mail;
      b) delivery in-person; or
      c) another agreed upon alternative method.

C. **Proof of service.** An affidavit of service shall be filed prior to the adjudicatory hearing.

Comment

Under paragraph (B)(1), if a parent is not the child's custodial guardian, the parent is to also receive service of the petition. *See* Rule 1120 for definition of "guardian."

Alternative methods of services that may be utilized under paragraph (B)(2)(c) could be electronic transmission, facsimile, county agency inter-office mail, and other similar methods.

Official Note: Rule 1331 adopted August, 21, 2006, effective February 1, 2007.

Committee Explanatory Reports:

Final Report explaining the provisions of Rule 1331 published with the Court's Order at 36 Pa.B. 5571 (September 2, 2006).

Rule 1333. Separate Petitions and Consolidated Hearing

A. **A separate petition for dependency shall be filed for each child alleged to be dependent.**

B. **If there are multiple petitions filed alleging the dependency of siblings, there shall be a reference in each petition to the sibling's petition.**

C. **Petitions alleging the dependency of siblings shall be consolidated for one hearing, unless otherwise ordered by the court.**

Official Note: Rule 1333 adopted August, 21, 2006, effective February 1, 2007.

Committee Explanatory Reports:

Final Report explaining the provisions of Rule 1333 published with the Court's Order at 36 Pa.B. 5571 (September 2, 2006).

Rule 1334. Amendment of Petition

A. Amendment.
   1) Mandatory. The court shall allow a petition to be amended when there is a defect in:
      a) form;
      b) the description of the allegations;
      c) the description of any person or property; or
      d) the date alleged.
   2) Discretionary. Absent prejudice to any party, the court may allow a petition to be amended if the petition alleges a different set of events or allegations, where the elements or matters of proof by any party are materially different from the elements or matters of proof to the allegation originally petitioned.

B. Continuance. Upon amendment, the court may:
   1) grant a continuance of the adjudicatory hearing; or
   2) order other relief as is necessary in the interests of justice.

Comment

If a petition is amended, a continuance may be appropriate to allow a party to prepare adequately. For continuances, see Rule 1122.

Official Note: Rule 1334 adopted August, 21, 2006, effective February 1, 2007.

Committee Explanatory Reports:

Final Report explaining the provisions of Rule 1334 published with the Court's Order at 36 Pa.B. 5571 (September 2, 2006).

Rule 1335. Withdrawal of Petition

The attorney for the county agency may withdraw the petition. The withdrawal shall be filed with the clerk of courts.

Comment

See Rule 1345 for the procedures on filings and service.

Official Note: Rule 1335 adopted August, 21, 2006, effective February 1, 2007.

Committee Explanatory Reports:

Final Report explaining the provisions of Rule 1335 published with the Court's Order at 36 Pa.B. 5571 (September 2, 2006).

Rule 1336. Re-Filing of the Petition After Withdrawal or Dismissal

A. **Re-filing.** A petition may be re-filed after the petition has been withdrawn pursuant to Rule 1335 or dismissed by the court.

B. **Motion for dismissal.** The court may entertain a motion by any party to dismiss the re-filed petition.

Comment

If a petition is re-filed, the procedures of Rule 1330 are to be followed. It may be necessary to have a shelter care hearing under the procedures of Rule 1242.

Official Note: Rule 1336 adopted August, 21, 2006, effective February 1, 2007.

Committee Explanatory Reports:

Final Report explaining the provisions of Rule 1336 published with the Court's Order at 36 Pa.B. 5571 (September 2, 2006).

PART D

PROCEDURES FOLLOWING FILING OF PETITION

1340. Discovery and Inspection
1342. Pre-Adjudicatory Conference.

Rule 1340. Discovery and Inspection

A. **Informal.** Before any party can seek any disclosure or discovery under these rules, the parties or their counsel shall make a good faith effort to resolve all questions of discovery, and to provide information required or requested under these rules as to which there is no dispute. When there are items requested by one party that the other party has refused to disclose, the demanding party may make an appropriate motion to the court. Such motion shall be made as soon as possible prior to the hearing. In such motion, the party shall state that a good faith effort to discuss the requested material has taken place and proved unsuccessful. Nothing in this rule shall delay the disclosure of any items agreed upon by the parties pending resolution of any motion for discovery.

B. Mandatory disclosure.

  1) By the county agency. In all cases, on request by a party and subject to any protective order which the county agency might obtain under this rule, the county agency shall disclose to a party, all of the following requested items or information, provided they are material to the instant case. The county agency shall, when applicable, permit a party to inspect and copy or photograph such items:

      a) the name and last known address of each witness to the occurrence that forms the basis of allegations of dependency unless disclosure is prohibited by law;

      b) the name and last known address of each witness who did not witness the occurrence but is expected to testify;

      c) copies of any written statements made by any party or witness unless disclosure is prohibited by law;

      d) any results or reports of scientific tests or expert opinions that are within the possession or control of the county agency that the county agency intends to use as evidence at a hearing;

      e) any police reports, records of prior county agency involvement, or records of current or prior reports involving the Child Protective Services Law, 23 Pa.C.S. § 6301 *et seq.*, that the county agency intends to use as evidence at a hearing;

      f) if any physical or mental condition of a party is in controversy, any physical or mental examinations, including oral or written reports that a party intends to use as evidence at the hearing;

      g) any tangible objects, including documents, photographs, or other tangible evidence unless disclosure is prohibited by law;

      h) the names, addresses, and curriculum vitae of any expert witness that a party intends to call at a hearing and the subject matter about which each expert witness is expected to testify, and a summary of the grounds for each opinion to be offered; and

      i) any other evidence that is material to adjudication, disposition, dispositional review, or permanency unless disclosure is prohibited by law, and is within the possession or control of the county agency;

  2) By all other parties. All other parties shall provide discovery to the county agency and all other parties and shall disclose, all of the following requested items or information that the party intends to use at a hearing, provided they are material to the instant case unless disclosure is prohibited by law. The party shall, when applicable, permit the county agency to inspect and copy or photograph such items:

a) the names and last known addresses of each witness who is expected to testify;
b) copies of any written statements made by any party or witness;
c) any tangible objects, including documents, photographs, or other tangible evidence;
d) the names, addresses, and curriculum vitae of any expert witness that a party intends to call at a hearing and the subject matter about which each expert witness is expected to testify, and a summary of the grounds for each opinion to be offered; and
e) any other evidence that a party intends to introduce at a hearing.

C. Discretionary. Upon motion of any party for discovery, the court may order any discovery upon a showing that the evidence is material to the preparation of the case and that the request is reasonable.

D. Continuing Duty to Disclose. If, prior to or during a hearing, either party discovers additional evidence or material previously requested or ordered to be disclosed by it, which is subject to discovery or inspection under this rule, or the identity of an additional witness or witnesses, such party promptly shall notify the opposing party or the court of the additional evidence, material, or witness.

E. Remedy. If at any time during the course of the proceedings it is brought to the attention of the court that a party has failed to comply with this rule, the court may order such party to permit discovery or inspection, may grant a continuance, or may prohibit such party from introducing evidence or witnesses not disclosed, or it may enter such other order as it deems just under the circumstances.

F. Protective orders. Upon a sufficient showing, the court may at any time order that the discovery or inspection be denied, restricted, or deferred, or make such other order as is appropriate to protect the best interests of the child. Upon motion of any party, the court may permit the showing to be made, in whole or in part, in the form of a written statement to be inspected by the court. If the court enters an order granting relief, the entire text of the statement shall be sealed and preserved in the records of the court to be made available to the appellate court(s) in the event of an appeal.

G. Work Product. Disclosure shall not be required of legal research or of records, correspondence, reports, or memoranda to the extent that they contain the opinions, theories, or conclusions of the attorney for a party, or members of their legal staffs.

Comment

Discovery under this rule applies to discovery for the adjudicatory hearing, dispositional hearing, dispositional review hearings, or permanency hearings of dependency proceedings governed by the Juvenile Act. *See* Rule 1100 for scope of rules. *See* Rule 1123 for production of documents pursuant to a *subpoena duces tecum*. *See also In re A.H.*, 763 A.2d 873 (Pa. Super. Ct. 2000).

The purpose of paragraph (A) is to encourage an informal discovery process. Only when the informal process fails and there is a genuine dispute as to discovery, should a motion to compel discovery be made. Motions may be oral or written, see Rule 1344.

The items listed in paragraph (B) are to be disclosed to ensure a party has the ability to prepare adequately for the hearing. *See In re J.C.*, 412 Pa.Super. 369, 603 A.2d 627 (1992).

See Rule 1800 for suspension of 23 Pa.C.S. § 6339, which provides for the confidentiality of reports made pursuant to the Child Protective Services Law, 23 Pa.C.S. § 6301 *et seq.*, which is suspended only insofar as the Law is inconsistent with Rule 1340(B)(1)(e), which provides for the disclosure of such reports if the reports are going to be used as evidence in a hearing to prove dependency of a child. It is important to note that this section is only suspended if the reports are going to be used as evidence during a hearing. If the reports are not going to be used, the confidentiality requirements of 23 Pa.C.S. § 6339 still apply. In addition, confidential sources are protected and the name of the source does not have to be disclosed. *See* 23 Pa.C.S. § 6340 (c) for protection of confidential sources reporting allegations of abuse under the Child Protective Services Law. 23 Pa.C.S. § 6301 *et seq.*

Under paragraph (C), the following are examples of evidence that may be material to the preparation of the case, but the list is not meant to be exhaustive: 1) domestic violence treatment records; 2) drug and alcohol treatment records; 3) mental health records; 4) medical records; 5) any other evidence specifically identified, provided the requesting party can additionally establish that its disclosure would be in the interests of justice, including any information concerning any person involved in the case who has received either valuable consideration, or an oral or written promise or contract for valuable consideration, for information concerning the case, or for the production of any work describing the case, or for the right to depict the character of the person in connection with his or her involvement in the case. Items listed in this paragraph are subject to rules of confidentiality and this rule is not intended to subrogate those rules.

Under paragraph (C), the court has discretion, upon motion, to order an expert who is expected to testify at a hearing to prepare a report. However, these provisions are not intended to require a prepared report in every case. The court should determine, on a case-by-case basis, whether a report should be prepared. For example, a prepared report ordinarily would not be necessary when the expert is known to the parties and testifies about the same subject on a regular basis. On the other hand, a report might be necessary if the expert is not known to the parties or is going to testify about a new or controversial technique.

It is intended that the remedies provided in paragraph (E) apply equally to all parties, as the interests of justice require.

The provision for a protective order, paragraph (F), does not confer upon any party any right of appeal not presently afforded by law.

In addition to information requested under this rule, an attorney has the right to inspect all court records and files. *See* Rule 1160.

Official Note: Rule 1340 adopted August, 21, 2006, effective February 1, 2007.

Committee Explanatory Reports:

Final Report explaining the provisions of Rule 1340 published with the Court's Order at 36 Pa.B. 5571 (September 2, 2006).

Rule 1342. Pre-Adjudicatory Conference

A. **Scope of conference.** At any time after the filing of a petition, upon motion, or upon its own motion, the court may order the parties to appear before it for a conference.

B. **Objections.** The parties shall have the right to record an objection to rulings of the court during the conference.

C. **Record.** The court shall place on the record the agreements or objections made by the parties and rulings made by the court as to any of the matters considered in the pre-adjudicatory conference. Such order shall control the subsequent proceedings unless modified at the adjudicatory hearing to prevent injustice.

Comment

This rule does not prevent other forms of pre-adjudicatory conferences. A judge may order a pre-adjudicatory conference between parties without the judge's presence at the conference to discuss preliminary matters.

Under paragraph (A), the court may consider: (1) the terms and procedures for pre-adjudicatory discovery and inspection; (2) the simplification or stipulation of factual issues, including admissibility of evidence; (3) the qualification of exhibits as evidence to avoid unnecessary delay; (4) the number of witnesses who are to give testimony of a cumulative nature; (5) whether expert witnesses will be called; (6) whether the hearing will be scheduled in front of the juvenile court hearing officer or judge; and (7) such other matters as may aid in the disposition of the proceeding.

Official Note: Rule 1342 adopted August 21, 2006, effective February 1, 2007. Amended April 6, 2017, effective September 1, 2017.

PART D(1)
MOTION PROCEDURES

1344. Motions and Answers
1345. Filing and Service

Rule 1344. Motions and Answers

A. **Generally.** All motions and answers shall be made orally on the record or in writing. An answer to a motion is not required unless ordered by the court or otherwise provided in these rules. Failure to answer shall not constitute an admission of the well-pleaded facts alleged in the motion.

B. **Filings by attorneys.** If a party is represented by an attorney, the attorney shall make or file all motions and answers.

C. **Requirements for motions.** All motions shall comply with the following requirements:

   1) The person making a written motion shall sign the motion. The signature shall constitute a certification that the motion is made in good faith. An oral motion shall be made on the record and the oral motion shall constitute a certification that the motion is made in good faith.

   2) The motion shall state with particularity the grounds for the motion, the facts that support each ground, and the types of relief or order requested.

   3) If the motion sets forth facts that do not already appear of record in the case, a verification shall be included or an oral statement shall be given that the facts set forth in the motion are true and correct to the movant's personal knowledge, information, or belief.

4) If the motion is written, a certificate of service as required by Rule 1345(C) shall be included.
D. **Requirements for answers.** All answers, including those that are required either by court order or otherwise required by these rules, shall comply with the following requirements:
   1) The person making the answer shall sign the answer or shall reply to the motion on the record. The signature or oral answer on the record shall constitute a certification that the answer is being made in good faith.
   2) The answer shall meet the allegations of the motion and shall specify the type of relief, order, or other action sought.
   3) If the answer sets forth facts that do not already appear of record in the case, a verification shall be included or an oral answer shall include a statement that the facts set forth in the answer are true and correct to the respondent's personal knowledge, information, or belief.
   4) If the answer is written, a certificate of service as required by Rule 1345(C) shall be included.
E. **Alternative relief.** Any motion may request such alternative relief as may be appropriate.

Comment

Under paragraph (A), oral motions and answers are permitted because of the emphasis on prompt disposition in juvenile court. Answers to written motions may be made orally if the answer complies with the requirements of this rule.

Under paragraphs (C)(4) and (D)(4), a certificate of service is required for all written motions and answers. *See* Rule 1345(B) for service of documents and Rule 1345(C) for certificates of service.

Official Note: Rule 1344 adopted August, 21, 2006, effective February 1, 2007.

Committee Explanatory Reports:

Final Report explaining the provisions of Rule 1344 published with the Court's Order at 36 Pa.B. 5571 (September 2, 2006).

Rule 1345. Filing and Service

A. **Filings.**
   1) **Generally.** Except as otherwise provided in these rules, all written motions, and any notice or document for which filing is required, shall be filed with the clerk of courts.
   2) **Clerk of courts' duties.** Except as provided in paragraph (A)(3), the clerk of courts shall docket a written motion, notice, or document when it is received and record the time of filing in the docket. The clerk of courts promptly shall transmit a copy of these papers to such person as may be designated by the court.
   3) **Filings by represented parties.** In any case in which a party is represented by an attorney, if the party submits for filing a written motion, notice, or document that has not been signed by the party's attorney, the clerk of courts shall not file the motion, notice, or document in the child's official court record or make a docket entry, but shall forward it promptly to the party's attorney.

Rule 1345   JUVENILE COURT PROCEDURE

    4) Method of filing. Filing may be accomplished by:
       a) personal delivery to the clerk of courts; or
       b) mail addressed to the clerk of courts, provided, however, that filing by mail shall be timely only when actually received by the clerk within the time fixed for filing.

B.   Service.
    1) Generally. The party filing the document shall serve the other party concurrently with the filing.
    2) Method of service to parties. Service on the parties shall be by:
       a) personal delivery of a copy to a party's attorney, or, if unrepresented, the party; or
       b) mailing a copy to a party's attorney or leaving a copy for the attorney at the attorney's office; or
       c) in those judicial districts that maintain in the courthouse assigned boxes for counsel to receive service, leaving a copy for the attorney in the attorney's box; or
       d) sending a copy to an unrepresented party by first class mail addressed to the party's place of residence.

C.   Proof of service. All documents that are filed and served pursuant to this rule shall include a certificate of service.

Comment

See Rule 1166 for maintaining records in the clerk of courts.

Under paragraph (A)(2), the court is to designate a court official to process motions and other matters for appropriate scheduling and resolution.

Under paragraph (B)(1), the party filing a document is required to serve the other party.

This rule does not affect court orders, which are to be served upon each party's attorney and the guardian, if unrepresented, by the clerk of courts as provided in Rule 1167.

For service of petitions, see Rule 1331.

Official Note: Rule 1345 adopted August 21, 2006, effective February 1, 2007. Amended December 24, 2009, effective immediately.

Committee Explanatory Reports:

Final Report explaining the provisions of Rule 1345 published with the Court's Order at 36 Pa.B. 5571 (September 2, 2006). Final Report explaining the amendments to Rule 1345 published with the Court's Order at 40 Pa.B. 222 (January 9, 2010).

PART D(2)

ADJUDICATORY SUMMONS AND NOTICE PROCEDURES

1360. Adjudicatory Summons
1361. Adjudicatory Notice
1363. Service of Summons
1364. Failure to Appear on the Summons

Rule 1360. Adjudicatory Summons

A. Summons. The court shall issue a summons compelling all parties to appear for the adjudicatory hearing.

B. Order appearance. The court may order the person having the physical custody or control of the child to bring the child to the hearing.

C. Requirements. The summons shall:

1) be in writing;

2) set forth the date, time, and place of the adjudicatory hearing;

3) instruct the child and the guardian about their rights to counsel, and if the child's guardian is without financial resources or otherwise unable to employ counsel, the right to assigned counsel;

4) give a warning stating that the failure to appear for the hearing may result in arrest; and

5) include a copy of the petition unless the petition has been previously served.

Comment

Section 6335 of the Juvenile Act provides that the court is to direct the issuance of a summons to the parent, guardian, or other custodian, a guardian *ad litem,* and any other persons as appear to the court to be proper and necessary parties to the proceedings. It also provides for ordering the person having the physical custody or control of the child to bring the child to the proceeding. 42 Pa.C.S. § 6335. Pursuant to Rule 1361, all parents and relatives providing care for the child are to receive notice of the hearing. Under paragraph (A), the custodial guardian is to receive a summons.

Other persons may be subpoenaed to appear for the hearing. *See* 42 Pa.C.S. § 6333.

Section 6335(a) of the Juvenile Act requires a copy of the petition to accompany the summons. 42 Pa.C.S. § 6335(a). Under paragraph (C)(5), a petition is to be included with the summons and served pursuant to Rule 1363 unless the petition has already been served pursuant to Rule 1331. See Rule 1800 for suspension of 42 Pa.C.S. § 6335, only to the extent that it conflicts with this rule.

See Rule 1128 for presence at proceedings. *See* Rule 1124 for general summons procedures.

Official Note: Rule 1360 adopted August, 21, 2006, effective February 1, 2007.

Committee Explanatory Reports:

Final Report explaining the provisions of Rule 1360 published with the Court's Order at 36 Pa.B. 5571 (September 2, 2006).

Rule 1361. Adjudicatory Notice

The court shall give notice of the adjudicatory hearing to:

1) the attorney for the county agency;

2) the child's attorney;

3) the guardian's attorney;

4) the parents, child's foster parent, preadoptive parent, or relative providing care for the child;

5) the county agency;
6) the court appointed special advocate, if assigned; and
7) any other persons as directed by the court.

Comment

All parties are to receive a summons pursuant to Rule 1360.

Official Note: Rule 1361 adopted August, 21, 2006, effective February 1, 2007.

Committee Explanatory Reports:

Final Report explaining the provisions of Rule 1361 published with the Court's Order at 36 Pa.B. 5571 (September 2, 2006).

Rule 1363. Service of Summons

A. Method of Service. The summons shall be served:
1) in-person; or
2) by certified mail, return receipt and first-class mail.

B. Time of Service.
1) Child in custody. If the child is in protective custody, the summons shall be served no less than seven days prior to the adjudicatory hearing.
2) Child not in custody. If the child is not in protective custody, the summons shall be served no less than fourteen days prior to the adjudicatory hearing.

C. Proof of service. Affidavit of service shall be filed prior to the adjudicatory hearing.

D. Efforts Made to Serve. In the absence of an affidavit of service under paragraph (C), the serving party shall advise the court of what efforts were made to notify a person. The court may proceed to a hearing upon a showing of reasonable efforts to locate and notify all persons pursuant to Rule 1360.

Comment

Pursuant to Rule 1360, all parties are to be served a summons. Pursuant to Rule 1361, the attorneys, the parents, child's foster parent, preadoptive parent, and relative providing care for the child are to receive notice.

A copy of the petition is to be included with the summons unless the petition has already been served pursuant to Rule 1331. *See* Rule 1360 (C)(5).

Official Note: Rule 1363 adopted August, 21, 2006, effective February 1, 2007.

Committee Explanatory Reports:

Final Report explaining the provisions of Rule 1363 published with the Court's Order at 36 Pa.B. 5571 (September 2, 2006).

Rule 1364. Failure to Appear on the Summons

If any summoned person fails to appear for the adjudicatory hearing and the court finds that sufficient notice was given, the judge may issue a bench warrant pursuant to Rule 1140.

Comment

See Rule 1140 for issuance of a bench warrant.

Official Note: Rule 1364 adopted August 21, 2006, effective February 1, 2007. Amended March 19, 2009, effective June 1, 2009.

Committee Explanatory Reports:

Final Report explaining the provisions of Rule 1364 published with the Court's Order at 36 Pa.B. 5571 (September 2, 2006). Final Report explaining the amendments to Rule 1364 published with the Court's Order at 39 Pa.B. 1614 (April 4, 2009).

PART E
PRESERVATION OF TESTIMONY AND EVIDENCE

1380. Preservation of Testimony After Commencement of Proceedings
1381. Preservation of Testimony by Video Recording

Rule 1380. Preservation of Testimony After Commencement of Proceedings

A. By Court Order.
   (1) At any time after the commencement of proceedings, upon motion of any party, and after notice and hearing, the court may order the taking and preserving of the testimony of any witness who may be unavailable for the adjudicatory hearing or for any other proceeding, or when due to exceptional circumstances, it is in the interests of justice that the witness' testimony be preserved;
   (2) The court shall state on the record the grounds on which the order is based;
   (3) The court's order shall specify the time and place for the taking of the testimony, the manner in which the testimony shall be recorded and preserved, and the procedures for custody of the recorded testimony;
   (4) The testimony shall be taken in the presence of the court, all parties and their attorneys, unless otherwise ordered; and
   (5) The court shall rule on the admissibility of the preserved testimony if it is offered into evidence at the adjudicatory hearing or other judicial proceeding.

B. By Agreement of the Parties.
   (1) At any time after the commencement of proceedings, the testimony of any witness may be taken and preserved upon the express written agreement of all parties;
   (2) The agreement shall specify the time and place for taking the testimony, the manner in which the testimony shall be recorded and preserved, and the procedures for custody of the recorded testimony;
   (3) The testimony shall be taken in the presence of all parties and their attorneys unless they otherwise agree;
   (4) The agreement shall be filed with the clerk of courts pursuant to Rule 1345(A); and

(5) **The court shall rule on the admissibility of the preserved testimony if it is offered into evidence at the adjudicatory hearing or other judicial proceeding.**

Comment

This rule is intended to provide the means by which testimony may be preserved for use at a current or subsequent stage in the proceedings, which includes the taking of a deposition during the adjudicatory hearing to be used at a later stage of the adjudicatory hearing.

When testimony is to be preserved by video recording, see also Rule 1381.

This rule does not address the admissibility of the preserved testimony. The court is to decide all questions of admissibility. *See* Pa.R.E. 104(a).

"May be unavailable," as used in paragraph (A)(1), is intended to include situations in which the court has reason to believe that the witness will be unable to be present or to testify at the adjudicatory hearing or other proceedings, such as when the witness is dying, or will be out of the jurisdiction and therefore cannot be effectively served with a subpoena, or is elderly, frail, or demonstrates the symptoms of mental infirmity or dementia, or may become incompetent to testify for any other legally sufficient reason.

Under paragraph (A)(4), the court should preside over the taking of testimony. The court, however, may order that testimony be taken and preserved without the court's presence when exigent circumstances exist or the location of the witness renders the court's presence impracticable. Furthermore, nothing in this rule is intended to preclude the parties, their attorneys, and the court from agreeing on the record that the court need not be present. Paragraph (B)(3) permits the parties and their attorneys to determine among themselves whether the court should be present during the taking of testimony. That determination should be made a part of the written agreement required by paragraph (B)(1).

Nothing in this rule is intended to preclude the parties from waiving their presence during the taking of testimony.

The means by which the testimony is recorded and preserved are within the discretion of the court under paragraph (A) and the parties under paragraph (B), and may include the use of electronic or photographic techniques such as videotape or digital video diskette. There are, however, additional procedural requirements for preservation of testimony by video recording mandated by Rule 1381.

The party on whose motion testimony is taken should normally have custody of and be responsible for safeguarding the preserved testimony. That party should also promptly provide a copy of the preserved testimony to the other parties. Additionally, this rule is not intended to conflict with the requirements of the Pennsylvania Rules of Judicial Administration. For reporting and transcripts by court-employed reporters, see Pa.R.J.A. Nos. 4001-4016.

When testimony is taken under this rule, the proceeding should afford the parties full opportunity to examine and cross-examine the witness. Counsel should not reserve objections at the time of the adjudicatory hearing.

For the definition of "court," see Rule 1120

Official Note: Rule 1380 adopted August 21, 2006, effective February 1, 2007. Amended November 16, 2016, effective January 1, 2017.

Committee Explanatory Reports:

Final Report explaining the provisions of Rule 1380 published with the Court's Order at 36 Pa.B. 5571 (September 2, 2006).

Rule 1381. Preservation of Testimony by Video Recording

A. When the testimony of a witness is taken and preserved pursuant to Rule 1380 by means of video recording, the testimony shall be recorded simultaneously by a stenographer.

B. The following technical requirements shall be made part of the court order required by Rule 1380(A) or the written agreement provided in Rule 1380(B):

1) The video recording shall begin with a statement on camera that includes: a) the operator's name and business address; b) the name and address of the operator's employer; c) the date, time, and place of the video recording; d) the caption of the case; e) the name of the witness; f) the party on whose behalf the witness is testifying; and g) the nature of the judicial proceedings for which the testimony is intended;

2) The court and the persons shall identify themselves on camera;

3) The witness shall be sworn on camera;

4) If the length of the testimony requires the use of more than one video recording, the end of each video recording and the beginning of each succeeding video recording shall be announced on camera;

5) At the conclusion of the witness' testimony, a statement shall be made on camera that the testimony is concluded. A statement shall also be made concerning the custody of the video recording(s);

6) Statements concerning stipulations, exhibits, or other pertinent matters may be made at any time on camera;

7) The video recording shall be timed by a digital clock on camera that continually shows the hour, minute, and second of the testimony;

8) All objections and the reasons for them shall be made on the record. When the court presides over the video recording of testimony, the court's rulings on objections shall also be made on the record;

9) When the court does not preside over the video recording of testimony, the video recording operator shall keep a log of each objection, referenced to the time each objection is made. All rulings on objections shall be made before the video recording is shown at any judicial proceeding; and

10) The original video recording shall not be altered.

Comment

This rule provides the basic technical requirements for taking and preserving testimony by video recording under Rule 1380. The list of requirements is not intended to be exhaustive. Rather, it is recommended that all recording by video be carefully planned and executed, and that in addition to complying with the basic requirements, each court order or written agreement for the video recording of testimony be tailored to the nature of the case and the needs of the persons.

Generally, the camera should focus on the witness to the extent practicable.

Under paragraph (B)(9), the court may rule on objections by either reviewing pertinent sections of the video recording, aided by the video operator's log, or by reviewing the stenographic transcript required by paragraph (A).

Any editing procedure ordered by the court or agreed upon by the persons may be used as long as it comports with current technology and does not alter the original video recording. Paragraph (B)(10) is intended to insure preservation of the original video, thereby providing for those situations in which a dispute arises over editing procedures.

This rule authorizes the use of video recording devices only for the preservation of testimony under Rule 1380. It is not intended to affect other rules governing recording devices.

Official Note: Rule 1381 adopted August, 21, 2006, effective February 1, 2007.

Committee Explanatory Reports:

Final Report explaining the provisions of Rule 1381 published with the Court's Order at 36 Pa.B. 5571 (September 2, 2006).

CHAPTER 14
ADJUDICATORY HEARING

1401. Introduction to Chapter Fourteen
1404. Prompt Adjudicatory Hearing
1405. Stipulations
1406. Adjudicatory Hearing
1408. Findings on Petition
1409. Adjudication of Dependency & Court Order

Rule 1401. Introduction to Chapter Fourteen

Under these rules and the Juvenile Act, 42 Pa.C.S. § 6301 *et seq.*, a determination for each case requires separate and distinct findings. First, the court is to hold an adjudicatory hearing, governed by Rule 1406 or accept stipulations, governed by Rule 1405. Second, after hearing the evidence or accepting the stipulations, the court is to make specific findings on the petition as to each allegation pursuant to Rule 1408, stating with particularity the allegations proven by clear and convincing evidence. Third, after entering its findings, the court is to determine if the child is dependent, pursuant to Rule 1409. If aggravated circumstances are alleged, the court is to determine if aggravated circumstances exist, pursuant to Rule 1705. After the court has made these findings and if the court finds that the child is dependent, the court is to hold a dispositional hearing as provided for in Rule 1512 and is to enter a dispositional order under Rule 1515. Nothing in these rules precludes the court from making these determinations at the same proceeding as long as the requirements of each rule are followed.

Official Note: Rule 1401 adopted August, 21, 2006, effective February 1, 2007.

Committee Explanatory Reports:

Final Report explaining the provisions of Rule 1401 published with the Court's Order at 36 Pa.B. 5571 (September 2, 2006).

Rule 1404. Prompt Adjudicatory Hearing

A. **Child in custody.** If a child has been removed from the home, an adjudicatory hearing shall be held within ten days of the filing of the petition.

B. **Child not in custody.** If a child has not been removed from the home, the adjudicatory hearing shall be held as soon as practical but within forty-five days of the filing of the petition.

Official Note: Rule 1404 adopted August, 21, 2006, effective February 1, 2007.

Committee Explanatory Reports:

Final Report explaining the provisions of Rule 1404 published with the Court's Order at 36 Pa.B. 5571 (September 2, 2006).

Rule 1405. Stipulations

A. **Agreements.** At any time after the filing of a petition, any party may present stipulations or agreements by all parties to the court in writing or orally on the record to any or all of the following:

   1) Findings of fact to be deemed admitted by the parties;

   2) A statement of the parties' agreement for placement;

   3) A statement of the parties' agreement for visitation;

   4) Time frame within which the stipulation shall be in effect;

   5) Time frame within which court shall review compliance; or

   6) Any other stipulation or agreement found to be appropriate by the court.

B. **Court action.** The court shall decide whether to accept the stipulations.

   1) Court accepts stipulations.

      a) **Stipulation to all allegations.** If the court accepts the stipulations to all the allegations, the court shall:

         i) take additional testimony as necessary to make an independent determination of dependency; and

         ii) enter its findings pursuant to Rule 1408 and an adjudication of dependency pursuant to Rule 1409.

      b) **Stipulations to some allegations or agreements for disposition.** If the parties agree to some allegations or placement, visitation, or other disposition resolutions, the court shall hold an adjudicatory hearing as to the remaining contested allegations in the petition pursuant to Rule 1406, followed by its finding on the petition pursuant to Rule 1408 and an adjudication of dependency pursuant to Rule 1409.

   2) **Court rejects stipulations.** If the court rejects the stipulations, the court shall proceed with an adjudicatory hearing pursuant to Rule 1406, followed by its findings on the petition pursuant to Rule 1408 and an adjudication of dependency pursuant to Rule 1409.

Comment

If all parties do not agree to all the allegations in the petition, the court is to hold an adjudicatory hearing as to the remaining allegations pursuant to Rule 1406.

Under paragraph (B)(2), the court may reject the stipulations and proceed to an adjudication of dependency pursuant to Rule 1406.

The court is to make an independent determination that a child is dependent. Before accepting the stipulation the judge is to be satisfied that the facts are credible and solidly based and not the product of speculation as to what the child may do in the future. *In re Mark T.*, 296 Pa.Super. 533, 442 A.2d 1179 (1982). Furthermore, to be accepted by the court, such stipulation is to be joined by all the parties. If accepted by the court, the stipulation has evidentiary value and may be considered alone or in conjunction with other evidence. The judge is to consider all of the evidence presented as well as the relevant law to arrive at a reasoned decision regarding dependency. *In re Michael Y.*, 365 Pa.Super. 488, 530 A.2d 115 (1987). *See In re A.S.*, 406 Pa.Super. 466, 594 A.2d 714 (1991) and 42 Pa.C.S. § 6341.

Official Note: Rule 1405 adopted August, 21, 2006, effective February 1, 2007.

Committee Explanatory Reports:

Final Report explaining the provisions of Rule 1405 published with the Court's Order at 36 Pa.B. 5571 (September 2, 2006).

Rule 1406. Adjudicatory Hearing

A. **Manner of hearing.** The court shall conduct the adjudicatory hearing in an informal but orderly manner.
  1) **Notification.** Prior to commencing the proceedings, the court shall ascertain:
     a) whether notice requirements pursuant to Rules 1360 and 1361 have been met; and
     b) whether unrepresented parties have been informed of the right to counsel pursuant to 42 Pa.C.S. § 6337.
  2) **Advanced Communication Technology.** Upon good cause shown, a court may utilize advanced communication technology pursuant to Rule 1129.
B. **Recording.** The adjudicatory hearing shall be recorded.
C. **Evidence.** Each party shall be given the opportunity to:
  1) introduce evidence;
  2) present testimony; and
  3) to cross-examine any witness.

Comment

Due process requires that the litigants receive notice of the issues before the court and an opportunity to present their case in relation to those issues. *In re M.B.*, 356 Pa.Super. 257, 514 A.2d 599 (1986), *aff'd*, 517 Pa. 459, 538 A.2d 495 (1988).

Pursuant to paragraph (A)(2), it is expected that the parties be present. Only upon good cause shown should advanced communication technology be utilized. A full record of the hearing is to be kept. *In re J.H.*, 788 A.2d 1006 (Pa. Super. Ct. 2001). *See* also 42 Pa.C.S. § 6336.

Under paragraph (B), notes of testimony should be provided to counsel for a party upon good cause shown. The court may place conditions of release on the notes of testimony. When an appeal is taken, the record is to be transcribed pursuant to Pa.R.A.P. 1922. *See* Pa.R.A.P. 1911 for request of transcript. Under paragraph (C), the court is to receive evidence from all interested parties and from objective, disinterested witnesses. The judge's findings should be supported by a full discussion of the evidence. *See In Re Clouse*, 244 Pa.Super. 396, 368 A.2d 780 (1976).

For application of the Rules of Evidence, see Pa.R.E. 101. *See* Rule 1136 for *ex parte* communications.

Official Note: Rule 1406 adopted August, 21, 2006, effective February 1, 2007. Amended April 21, 2011, effective July 1, 2011. Amended April 29, 2011, effective July 1, 2011.

Committee Explanatory Reports:

Final Report explaining the provisions of Rule 1406 published with the Court's Order at 36 Pa.B. 5571 (September 2, 2006). Final Report explaining the amendments to Rule 1406 published with the Court's Order at 41 Pa.B. 2319 (May 7, 2011). Final Report explaining the amendments to Rule 1406 published with the Court's Order at 41 Pa.B. 2413 (May 14, 2011).

Rule 1408. Findings on Petition

The court shall enter findings, within seven days of hearing the evidence on the petition or accepting stipulated facts by the parties:

(1) by specifying which, if any, allegations in the petition were proved by clear and convincing evidence; and

(2) its findings as to whether the county agency has reasonably engaged in family finding as required pursuant to Rule 1149.

Comment

The court is to specify which allegations in the petition are the bases for the finding of dependency.

Pursuant to paragraph (2), the court is to make a determination whether the county agency has reasonably engaged in family finding in the case. The county agency will be required to report its diligent family finding efforts at subsequent hearings. *See* Rule 1149 for requirements of family finding. *See also* Rules 1210(D)(8), 1242(E)(3), 1512(D)(1)(h), 1514(A)(4), 1608(D)(1)(h), and 1610(D) and their *Comments* for the court's findings as to the county agency's satisfaction of the family finding requirements and Rules 1242(E)(3), 1409(C), 1609(D), and 1611(C) and *Comments* to Rules 1242, 1409, 1512, 1514, 1515, 1608, 1609, 1610, and 1611 on the court's orders.

Note: Rule 1408 adopted August 21, 2006, effective February 1, 2007. Amended July 13, 2015, effective October 1, 2015.

Rule 1409. Adjudication of Dependency and Court Order

A. *Adjudicating the child dependent.* **Once the court has made its findings under Rule 1408, the court shall enter an order whether the child is dependent.**

(1) *Dependency.* **If the court finds from clear and convincing evidence that the child is dependent, the court shall proceed to a dispositional hearing under Rule 1512.**

(2) *No dependency.* **If the court finds the child not to be dependent or the court finds a parent ready, willing, and able to provide proper parental care or control, the court shall:**

(a) dismiss the petition;

(b) order the child to be discharged from custody and any restrictions ordered in the proceedings; and

(c) enter an order identifying individual(s) who will have the legal and physical custody until such order is modified by further order of the court.

B. *Timing.*

(1) *Child in custody.* If a child is removed from the home, the court shall enter an adjudication of dependency within seven days of the adjudicatory hearing and enter its findings pursuant to Rule 1408.

(2) *Child not in custody.* If a child is not removed from the home and if the court fails to enter an order of dependency, the court shall hold a status hearing every thirty days.

C. *Court order.* The court shall include the following in its court order:

(1) A statement pursuant to paragraph (A):

(a) as to whether the court finds the child to be dependent from clear and convincing evidence;

(b) including the specific factual findings that form the bases of the court's decision;

(c) including any legal determinations made; and

(2) Any orders directing the removal of a child from the home or change in the current residential status, including:

(a) orders as to placement; or

(b) visitation; or

(c) change in custody; and

(3) Any orders as to any aids in disposition that may assist in the preparation of the dispositional hearing, including orders regarding family finding.

Comment

Before the court can find a child to be dependent, there must be clear and convincing evidence in support of the petition. The burden of proof is on the petitioner. The court's inquiry is to be comprehensive and its findings are to be supported by specific findings of fact and a full discussion of the evidence. *In re LaRue*, 244 Pa.Super. 218, 366 A.2d 1271 (1976). *See also In re Frank W.D., Jr.*, 315 Pa.Super. 510, 462 A.2d 708 (1983); *In re Clouse*, 244 Pa.Super. 396, 368 A.2d 780 (1976). The evidence must support that the child is dependent. *In the Matter of DeSavage*, 241 Pa.Super. 174, 360 A.2d 237 (1976). The court is not free to apply the best interest of the child standard as the requirements of the Juvenile Act, 42 Pa.C.S. § 6341(c), require clear and convincing evidence that the child is dependent is the proper standard. *In re Haynes*, 326 Pa. Super. 311, 473 A.2d 1365 (1983). A child, whose non-custodial parent is ready, willing, and able to provide adequate care for the child, cannot be found dependent on the basis of lacking proper parental care and control. *In re M.L.*, 562 Pa. 646, 757 A.2d 849 (2000). A trial court has the authority to transfer custody or modify custody to the child's non-custodial parent without a finding of dependency if sufficient evidence of dependency would have existed but for the availability of the non-custodial parent. *In re Justin S.*, 375 Pa.Super. 88, 543 A.2d 1192 (1988).

The court is to specify which allegations in the petition are the bases for the finding of dependency pursuant to Rule 1408. The court is to make an adjudication of dependency based upon the allegations in the petition, not on alternative grounds. Due process and fundamental fairness require adequate notice of the allegations to afford a reasonable opportunity to prepare a defense. *In re R.M.*, 567 Pa. 646, 790 A.2d 300 (2002).

Under paragraph (B), if a child is removed from the home, a finding of dependency is to be made within seven days.

Under paragraph (C)(3), aids in disposition may include, but are not limited to, any services, investigations, evaluations, studies, treatment plans, and any other appropriate reports that may aid the court in making its determination at the dispositional hearing. *See* 42 Pa.C.S. § 6339 for orders of a social study or physical and mental examinations and treatment.

See also 42 Pa.C.S. §§ 6341 & 6302.

Pursuant to paragraph (C)(3), when making its determination for reasonable efforts made by the county agency, the court is to consider the extent to which the county agency has fulfilled its obligation pursuant to Rule 1149 regarding family finding. *See also* Rules 1242(C)(2) & (3)(b) & (c) and 1330(B)(6) and *Comments* to Rules 1242, 1330, 1515, 1608, 1609, 1610, and 1611 for reasonable efforts determinations.

If the requirements of Rule 1149 regarding family finding have not been met, the court is to make necessary orders to ensure compliance by enforcing this legislative mandate. *See* 62 P.S. § 1301 *et seq. See also* Rules 1242(E)(3) and 1609(D) and *Comments* to Rules 1242, 1408, 1512, 1514, 1515, 1608, 1609, 1610, and 1611.

Note: Rule 1409 adopted August 21, 2006, effective February 1, 2007. Amended July 13, 2015, effective October 1, 2015.

CHAPTER 15
DISPOSITIONAL HEARING

PART A
SUMMONS AND NOTICE OF THE DISPOSITIONAL HEARING

1500. **Summons for the Dispositional Hearing**
1501. **Dispositional Notice**

PART B
DISPOSITIONAL HEARING AND AIDS

1509. **Aids in Disposition**
1510. **Prompt Dispositional Hearing**
1511. **Pre-Dispositional Statement**
1512. **Dispositional Hearing**
1514. **Dispositional Finding Before Removal From Home**
1515. **Dispositional Order**
1516. **Service of Dispositional Order**

Rule 1500. Summons for the Dispositional Hearing

A. **Summons.** The court may issue a summons compelling any party to appear for the dispositional hearing.

B. Order appearance. The court may order the person having the physical custody or control of the child to bring the child to the hearing.

C. Requirements. The general summons procedures of Rule 1124 shall be followed.

Comment

Section 6335 of the Juvenile Act provides that the court is to direct the issuance of a summons to the parent, guardian, or other custodian, a guardian *ad litem,* and any other persons as appear to the court to be proper and necessary parties to the proceedings. 42 Pa.C.S. § 6335(a).

Other persons may be subpoenaed to appear for the hearing. *See* 42 Pa.C.S. § 6333.

Official Note: Rule 1500 adopted August, 21, 2006, effective February 1, 2007.

Committee Explanatory Reports:

Final Report explaining the provisions of Rule 1500 published with the Court's Order at 36 Pa.B. 5571 (September 2, 2006).

Rule 1501. Dispositional Notice

The court or its designee shall give notice of the dispositional hearing to:
1) all parties;
2) the attorney for the county agency;
3) the child's attorney
4) the guardian's attorney;
5) the parents, child's foster parent, preadoptive parent, or relative providing care for the child;
6) the court appointed special advocate, if assigned;
7) the educational decision maker, if applicable; and
8) any other persons as directed by the court.

Official Note: Rule 1501 adopted August, 21, 2006, effective February 1, 2007. Amended April 29, 2011, effective July 1, 2011.

Committee Explanatory Reports:

Final Report explaining the provisions of Rule 1501 published with the Court's Order at 36 Pa.B. 5571 (September 2, 2006). Final Report explaining the amendments to Rule 1501 published with the Court's Order at 41 Pa.B. 2413 (May 14, 2011).

Rule 1509. Aids in Disposition

A. Examinations. The court may order the child, parent, guardian, or other person being considered as a dispositional placement resource to undergo any examination permitted by law, as it deems appropriate to aid in the decision for disposition.

B. Experts. Experts may be utilized during the dispositional hearing. Discovery pursuant to Rule 1340 shall occur prior to the dispositional hearing.

C. **Family Service Plan or Permanency Plan.** If the county agency has completed a family service plan or permanency plan, it shall be given to all parties immediately and submitted to the court upon request.

Comment

Section 6341(e) of the Juvenile Act requires the court to receive reports and other evidence bearing on the disposition. *In re McDonough,* 287 Pa.Super. 326, 430 A.2d 308 (1981).

For discovery rules for the dispositional hearing, see Rule 1340 and its *Comments.*

Because of time constraints, a family service plan might not be prepared prior to the original dispositional hearing. If the family service plan has been prepared, all parties are to receive the plan to prepare for the dispositional hearing. In all cases, the family service plan is to be completed by the county agency within sixty days of accepting a family for service. *See* 55 Pa. Code § 3130.61.

Official Note: Rule 1509 adopted August, 21, 2006, effective February 1, 2007.

Committee Explanatory Reports:

Final Report explaining the provisions of Rule 1509 published with the Court's Order at 36 Pa.B. 5571 (September 2, 2006).

Rule 1510. Prompt Dispositional Hearing

If the child has been removed from the home, the dispositional hearing shall be held no later than twenty days after the findings on the petition under Rule 1408.

Comment

For continuances, see 42 Pa.C.S. § 6341(e).

Official Note: Rule 1510 adopted August, 21, 2006, effective February 1, 2007.

Committee Explanatory Reports:

Final Report explaining the provisions of Rule 1510 published with the Court's Order at 36 Pa.B. 5571 (September 2, 2006).

Rule 1511. Pre-Dispositional Statement

The petitioner shall state its recommended disposition in a pre-dispositional statement. The statement shall be filed with the court at least three days prior to the dispositional hearing.

Comment

This statement may be included in other court documents, such as, the family service plan or petition.

Official Note: Rule 1511 adopted August, 21, 2006, effective February 1, 2007.

Committee Explanatory Reports:

Final Report explaining the provisions of Rule 1511 published with the Court's Order at 36 Pa.B. 5571 (September 2, 2006).

Rule 1512. Dispositional Hearing

A. *Manner of hearing.* The court shall conduct the dispositional hearing in an informal but orderly manner.

(1) *Evidence.* The court shall receive any oral or written evidence which is helpful in determining disposition, including evidence that was not admissible at the adjudicatory hearing.

(2) *Opportunity to be heard.* Before deciding disposition, the court shall give the parent, child's foster parent, preadoptive parent, relative providing care for the child and court appointed special advocate, if assigned, an opportunity to make a statement.

(3) *Advanced Communication Technology.* Upon good cause shown, a court may utilize advanced communication technology pursuant to Rule 1129.

B. *Recording.* The dispositional hearing shall be recorded.

C. *Duties of the court.* The court shall determine on the record whether the parties have been advised of the following:

(1) the right to file an appeal;

(2) the time limits for an appeal; and

(3) the right to counsel to prepare the appeal.

D. *Court's findings.* The court shall enter its findings and conclusions of law into the record and enter an order pursuant to Rule 1515.

(1) On the record in open court, the court shall state:

(a) its disposition;

(b) the reasons for its disposition;

(c) the terms, conditions, and limitations of the disposition;

(d) the name of any person or the name, type, category, or class of agency, licensed organization, or institution that shall provide care, shelter, and supervision of the child;

(e) whether any evaluations, tests, counseling, or treatments are necessary;

(f) the permanency plan for the child;

(g) the services necessary to achieve the permanency plan;

(h) whether the county agency has reasonably satisfied the requirement of Rule 1149 regarding family finding, and if not, the findings and conclusions of the court on why the requirements have not been met by the county agency;

(i) any findings necessary to ensure the stability and appropriateness of the child's education, and when appropriate, the court shall appoint an educational decision maker pursuant to Rule 1147;

(j) any findings necessary to identify, monitor, and address the child's needs concerning health care and disability, if any, and if parental consent cannot be obtained, authorize evaluations and treatment needed; and

(k) a visitation schedule, including any limitations.

(2) The court shall state on the record in open court or enter into the record through the dispositional order, findings pursuant to Rule 1514, if the child is placed.

Comment

To the extent practicable, the judge or juvenile court hearing officer that presided over the adjudicatory hearing for a child should preside over the dispositional hearing for the same child.

Paragraph (A)(2) does not infringe on the right to call witnesses to testify, in addition to those specified individuals. *See* Rule 1123 for subpoenaing a witness.

Pursuant to paragraph (A)(3), it is expected that the parties be present. Only upon good cause shown should advanced communication technology be utilized.

Pursuant to paragraph (C), the court is to advise the parties of their appellate rights orally in the courtroom on the record. The court is to explain the right to appointed counsel for an appeal if a party is without counsel, and without the financial resources or otherwise unable to employ counsel. *See* 42 Pa.C.S. § 6337; *see also* Rule 1150(B) for duration of counsel and Rule 1151 for assignment of counsel.

All the findings made in open court are to be placed in writing through the court's dispositional order pursuant to Rule 1515. Nothing in this rule is intended to preclude the court from further explaining its findings in its dispositional order. In addition to the findings pursuant to paragraph (D), *see* Rule 1514 for dispositional findings before removal from the home.

Pursuant to paragraph (D)(1)(f), the court is to determine the permanency plan for the child. A permanency plan should include two plans or goals: the primary plan and the secondary or concurrent plan.

The primary plan is the comprehensive plan developed to achieve the permanency goal. The secondary or concurrent plan is developed and initiated so that if the primary plan is not fulfilled, timely permanency for the child may still be achieved. These two plans are to be simultaneously addressed by the county agency.

Rule 1608 mandates permanency hearings at least every six months. It is best practice to have three-month hearings to ensure permanency is achieved in a timely fashion and the court is informed of the progress of the case. *See Comment* to Rule 1608.

Pursuant to paragraph (D)(1)(h), the court is to determine whether the county agency has reasonably satisfied the requirements of Rule 1149 regarding family finding. If the county agency has failed to meet the diligent family finding efforts requirements of Rule 1149, the court is to utilize its powers to enforce this legislative mandate. *See* 62 P.S. § 1301 *et seq. See also* Rules 1210(D)(8), 1242(E)(3), 1409(C), 1609(D), and 1611(C) and *Comments* to Rules 1242, 1408, 1409, 1514, 1515, 1608, 1609, 1610, and 1611.

Pursuant to paragraph (D)(1)(i), the court is to address the child's educational stability, including the right to an educational decision maker, 42 Pa.C.S. § 6301, 20 U.S.C. § 1439(a)(5), and 34 C.F.R. § 300.519. The court's findings should address the child's right to: 1) educational stability, including the right to: a) remain in the same school regardless of a change in placement when it is in the child's best interest; b) immediate enrollment when a school change is in the child's best interest; and c) have school proximity considered in all placement changes, 42 U.S.C. §§ 675(1)(G) and 11431 *et seq.*; 2) an educational decision maker pursuant to Rule 1147, 42 Pa.C.S. § 6301, 20 U.S.C. § 1439(a)(5), and 34 C.F.R. § 300.519; 3) an appropriate education, including any necessary special education, early intervention, or remedial services pursuant to 24 P.S. §§ 13-1371 and 13-1372, 55 Pa. Code § 3130.87, and 20 U.S.C. § 1400 *et seq.*; 4) the educational services necessary to support the child's transition to independent living pursuant to 42 Pa.C.S. § 6351 if the child is sixteen or older; and 5) a transition plan that addresses the child's educational needs pursuant to 42 U.S.C. § 675(5)(H) if the child will age out of care within ninety days.

Pursuant to paragraph (D)(1)(j), the court is to address the child's needs concerning health care and disability. The court's findings should address the right of: 1) a child to receive timely and medically appropriate screenings and health care services pursuant to 55 Pa. Code §§ 3700.51 and 3800.32, and 42 U.S.C. § 1396d(r); 2) a child to a transition plan that addresses the child's health care needs, and includes specific options for how the child can obtain health insurance after leaving care pursuant to 42 U.S.C. § 675(5)(H) if the child will age out of care within 90 days; and 3) a child with disabilities to receive necessary accommodations pursuant to 42 U.S.C. § 12132; 28 C.F.R. § 35.101 *et seq.*, Section 504 of the Rehabilitation Act of 1973, *as amended*, 29 U.S.C. § 794, and implementing regulations at 45 C.F.R. § 84.1 *et seq.* In addition, the court is to ensure progress and compliance with the child's case plan for the ongoing oversight and coordination of health care services under 42 U.S.C. § 622(b)(15).

Pursuant to the Juvenile Act, the court has authority to order a physical or mental examination of a child and medical or surgical treatment of a minor, who is suffering from a serious physical condition or illness which requires prompt treatment in the opinion of a physician. The court may order the treatment even if the guardians have not been given notice of the pending hearing, are not available, or without good cause inform the court that they do not consent to the treatment. 42 Pa.C.S. § 6339(b).

Pursuant to paragraph (D)(1)(k), the court is to include siblings in its visitation schedule. *See* 42 U.S.C. § 671(a)(31), which requires reasonable efforts be made to place siblings together unless it is contrary to the safety or well-being of either sibling and that frequent visitation be assured if joint placement cannot be made.

See Rule 1127 for recording and transcribing of proceedings.

See Rule 1136 for *ex parte* communications.

Official Note: Rule 1512 adopted August 21, 2006, effective February 1, 2007. Amended April 21, 2011, effective July 1, 2011. Amended April 29, 2011, effective July 1, 2011. Amended July 13, 2015, effective October 1, 2015. Amended April 6, 2017, effective September 1, 2017.

Rule 1514. Dispositional Finding Before Removal From Home

A. *Required findings*. Prior to entering a dispositional order removing a child from the home, the court shall state on the record in open court the following specific findings:

(1) Continuation of the child in the home would be contrary to the welfare, safety, or health of the child;

(2) The child's placement is the least restrictive placement that meets the needs of the child, supported by reasons why there is no less restrictive alternative available;

(3) If the child has a sibling who is subject to removal from the home, whether reasonable efforts were made prior to the placement of the child to place the siblings together or whether such joint placement is contrary to the safety or well-being of the child or sibling;

(4) The county agency has reasonably satisfied the requirements of Rule 1149 regarding family finding; and

(5) One of the following:

(a) Reasonable efforts were made prior to the placement of the child to prevent or eliminate the need for removal of the child from the home, if the child has remained in the home pending such disposition; or

(b) If preventive services were not offered due to the necessity for emergency placement, whether such lack of services was reasonable under the circumstances; or

(c) If the court previously determined that reasonable efforts were not made to prevent the initial removal of the child from the home, whether reasonable efforts are under way to make it possible for the child to return home.

B. *Aggravated circumstances.* If the court has previously found aggravated circumstances to exist and that reasonable efforts to remove the child from the home or to preserve and reunify the family are not required, a finding under paragraphs (A)(5)(a) through (c) is not necessary.

Comment

See 42 Pa.C.S. § 6351(b).

Pursuant to paragraph (A)(3), the court is to utilize reasonable efforts in placing siblings together unless it is contrary to the safety or well-being of a child or sibling. 42 U.S.C. § 675 (Fostering Connections).

Pursuant to paragraph (A)(4), the court is to determine whether the county agency has reasonably satisfied the requirements of Rule 1149 regarding family finding. If the county agency has failed to meet the diligent family finding efforts requirements of Rule 1149, the court is to utilize its powers to enforce this legislative mandate. *See* 62 P.S. § 1301 *et seq. See also* Rules 1210(D)(8), 1242(E)(3), 1409(C), 1609(D), and 1611(C) and *Comments* to Rules 1242, 1408, 1409, 1512, 1515, 1608, 1609, 1610, and 1611.

Note: Rule 1514 adopted August 21, 2006, effective February 1, 2007. Amended April 29, 2011, effective July 1, 2011. Amended July 13, 2015, effective October 1, 2015.

Rule 1515. Dispositional Order

A. *Generally.* When the court enters a disposition, the court shall issue a written order, which provides that the disposition is best suited to the safety, protection, and physical, mental, and moral welfare of the child. The order shall include:

(1) any findings pursuant to Rules 1512(D) and 1514;

(2) the date of the order; and

(3) the signature and printed name of the judge entering the order.

B. *Transfer of custody.* If the court decides to transfer custody of the child to a person or agency found to be qualified to provide care, shelter, and supervision of the child, the dispositional order shall include:

(1) the name and address of such person or agency, unless the court determines disclosure is inappropriate;

(2) the limitations of the order, including the type of custody granted; and

(3) any visitation rights.

C. *Guardian.* The dispositional order shall include any conditions, limitations, restrictions, and obligations imposed upon the guardian.

Comment

See 42 Pa.C.S. §§ 6310, 6351.

When issuing a dispositional order, the court should issue an order that is "best suited to the safety, protection, and physical, mental, and moral welfare of the child." 42 Pa.C.S. § 6351(a). *See In re S.J.*, 906 A.2d 547, 551 (Pa. Super. Ct. 2006) (citing *In re Tameka M.*, 525 Pa. 348, 580 A.2d 750 (1990)), for issues addressing a child's mental and moral welfare.

When making its determination for reasonable efforts made by the county agency, the court is to consider the extent to which the county agency has fulfilled its obligation pursuant to Rule 1149 regarding family finding. *See also* Rules 1240(B)(6), 1242(C)(2) & (3)(b) & (c), and 1330(B)(6) and *Comments* to Rules 1242, 1330, 1409, 1608, 1609, 1610, and 1611 for reasonable efforts determinations.

If the requirements of Rule 1149 regarding family finding have not been met, the court is to make necessary orders to ensure compliance by enforcing this legislative mandate. *See* 62 P.S. § 1301 *et seq. See also* Rules 1210(D)(8), 1242(E)(3), 1409(C), 1609(D), and 1611(C) and *Comments* to Rules 1242, 1408, 1409, 1512, 1514, 1608, 1609, 1610, and 1611. 45 C.F.R § 1356.21 provides a specific foster care provider may not be placed in a court order to be in compliance with and receive funding through the Federal Financial Participation.

Dispositional orders should comport in substantial form and content to the model orders to receive funding under the federal Adoption and Safe Families Act (ASFA) of 1997 (P.L. 105-89). The model forms are also in compliance with Title IV-B and Title IV-E of the Social Security Act. For model orders, see http://www.pacourts.us/forms/dependency-forms.

See In re Tameka M., 525 Pa. 348, 580 A.2d 750 (1990).

Note: Rule 1515 adopted August 21, 2006, effective February 1, 2007. Amended April 29, 2011, effective July 1, 2011. Amended July 13, 2015, effective October 1, 2015.

Rule 1516. Service of the Dispositional Order

Upon entry of the disposition, the court shall issue a dispositional order and the order shall be served promptly upon all parties, their attorneys, and any other person as directed by the court.

Official Note: Rule 1516 adopted August, 21, 2006, effective February 1, 2007.

Committee Explanatory Reports:

Final Report explaining the provisions of Rule 1516 published with the Court's Order at 36 Pa.B. 5571 (September 2, 2006).

CHAPTER 16
POST-DISPOSITIONAL PROCEDURES

PART A
SUMMONS, NOTICE, AND REPORTS

1600. Summons for the Permanency Hearing
1601. Permanency Hearing Notice
1604. Submission of Reports

PART B(1)
MODIFICATIONS

1606. Modification of Dependent Child's Placement

PART (B)(2)
PERMANENCY HEARING

1607. Regular Scheduling of Permanency Hearing
1608. Permanency Hearing
1609. Permanency Hearing Orders
1610. Permanency Hearing for Children Over Eighteen
1611. Permanency Hearing Orders for Children Over Eighteen

PART (C)
POST-DISPOSITIONAL PROCEDURES

1613. [Reserved]
1616. Post-Dispositional Procedures; Appeals [RESERVED]

PART (D)
CESSATION OR RESUMPTION OF COURT SUPERVISION OR JURISDICTION

1631. Termination of Court Supervision
1634. Motion for Resumption of Jurisdiction
1635. Hearing on Motion for Resumption of Jurisdiction

PART A
SUMMONS AND NOTICE

Rule 1600. Summons for the Permanency Hearing

A. **Summons.** At least fifteen days prior to the permanency hearing, the court may issue a summons compelling any party to appear for the permanency hearing.
B. **Order appearance.** The court may order the person having the physical custody or control of the child to bring the child to the hearing.
C. **Requirements.** The general summons procedures of Rule 1124 shall be followed.

Comment

Section 6335 of the Juvenile Act provides that the court is to direct the issuance of a summons to the parent, guardian, or other custodian, a guardian *ad litem*, and any other persons as appear to the court to be proper and necessary parties to the proceedings. 42 Pa.C.S. § 6335(a).

Other persons may be subpoenaed to appear for the hearing. *See* 42 Pa.C.S. § 6333.

Official Note: Rule 1600 adopted August, 21, 2006, effective February 1, 2007.

Committee Explanatory Reports:

Final Report explaining the provisions of Rule 1600 published with the Court's Order at 36 Pa.B. 5571 (September 2, 2006).

Rule 1601. Permanency Hearing Notice

A. At least fifteen days prior to the hearing, the court or its designee shall give notice of the permanency hearing to:
   1) all parties;
   2) the attorney for the county agency;
   3) the child's attorney
   4) the guardian's attorney;
   5) the parents, child's foster parent, preadoptive parent, or relative providing care for the child;
   6) the court appointed special advocate, if assigned;
   7) the educational decision maker, if applicable; and
   8) any other persons as directed by the court.
B. If a party intends to request a goal change from reunification, then either the notice shall state this purpose or the party shall give separate notice of the intended goal change in accordance with paragraph (A).

Comment

Given the significance of discontinuing the goal of reunification, the requirement of paragraph (B) is to ensure that parties, counsel, and interested persons have notice of the purpose of the hearing and are able to prepare for and attend the hearing.

April 1601 adopted August 21, 2006, effective February 1, 2007. Amended April 29, 2011, effective July 1, 2011. Amended May 17, 20, 18, effective October 1, 2018.

Rule 1604. Submission of Reports

A. **Generally.**
   1) **A foster parent, preadoptive parent, or relative providing care for a child may submit a report regarding the child's adjustment, progress, and condition for review by the court.**
   2) **The report shall be submitted to the court designee at least seven days prior to the permanency hearing.**
B. **Designation by President Judge.** The President Judge of each judicial district shall appoint a designee, other than a judge or party, to receive these reports.

C. Duties of the County Agency. Upon placement of the child with a foster parent, preadoptive parent, or relative providing care for a child, the county agency shall inform such person of:
   1) the right to submit a report;
   2) the name and address of the court designee who shall receive the reports; and
   3) the requirement to submit the report at least seven days prior to the permanency hearing.
D. Duties of Designee. Within one business day of receiving the report, the court designee shall:
   1) file a copy of the report with the clerk of courts; and
   2) distribute copies to the judge, attorneys, parties, and if appointed, the court-appointed special advocate.
E. Examination of Report. Pursuant to Rule 1608(C), the court shall examine this report and consider its contents as it would consider any other evidence in the case.

Comment

The county agency is to provide the form designed by the Department of Public Welfare to the foster parent, preadoptive parent, or relative providing care for the child. *See* 42 Pa.C.S. § 6336.1(b).

See also 42 Pa.C.S. § 6341(d).

Pursuant to paragraph (E), the court is to examine this report and consider it contents as it would consider any other evidence. Evidence is to be properly entered into the record before the court will consider it. Evidence submitted directly to the court is considered an *ex parte* communication and is strictly prohibited. *See* Rule 1136 on *ex parte* communications.

Official Note: Rule 1604 adopted December 18, 2009, effective immediately. Amended April 29, 2011, effective July 1, 2011.

Committee Explanatory Reports:

Final Report explaining the provisions of Rule 1604 published with the Court's Order at 40 Pa.B. 21 (January 2, 2010). Final Report explaining the amendments to Rule 1604 published with the Court's Order at 41 Pa.B. 2434 (May 14, 2011).

PART B(1)
MODIFICATIONS

1606. Modification of Dependent Child's Placement

Rule 1606. Modification of Dependent Child's Placement

A. County agency's duties.
   1) Emergencies.
      a) Only in an emergency when a judge cannot be reached, a child may be placed temporarily in a shelter care facility or other appropriate care.

b) The county agency immediately shall notify the court and all parties of any change made due to the emergency.

c) The county agency shall file a motion or stipulation for modification of the dispositional order by the next business day of the child's placement in a shelter care facility or other appropriate care.

2) Non-emergent cases. In all other cases, the county agency shall seek approval of the court for a change in the child's placement prior to the removal of the child from the placement by the filing of a motion or a stipulation for modification of the dispositional order.

B. Contents of the motion. The motion for modification of the dispositional order shall include:

1) the specific reasons for the necessity of change to the order;
2) the proposed placement;
3) the current location of the child;
4) the manner in which any educational, health care, and disability needs of the child will be addressed;
5) an averment as to whether each party concurs or objects to the proposal, including the child's wishes if ascertainable; and
6) the signatures of all the parties.

C. Objections. If a party objects to proposed modification of the dispositional order, the objections shall be filed no later than three days after the filing of the motion for modification of the child's placement.

D. Court's duties. Once the county agency has requested approval from the court to modify a child's placement or after an emergency change in placement has already taken place, the court may:

1) schedule a prompt hearing to determine whether there will be a modification of the child's placement;
2) enter an appropriate order to modify the child's placement; or
3) enter an order denying the motion.

Comment

This rule is intended to address changes in the child's placement. Brief temporary removals for hospitalization, respite situations, visitations, or other matters when a child will be returned to the same placement are not covered under this rule.

Pursuant to paragraph (A)(1), if there must be a change in the placement of the child due to an emergent situation, the county agency may temporarily place a child in a shelter-care facility or other appropriate care pending the filing of a motion for modification of the dispositional order. The county agency immediately is to notify the court and all parties of the change made and file a motion or stipulation by the next business day.

Pursuant to paragraph (A)(2), in all other cases, the court is to make a decision prior to the child being removed from the placement. Stability for the child is critical. Multiple placements can add to a child's trauma. A child should not be shuffled from home to home out of convenience for a foster parent, relative, or other person caring for the child.

Official Note: Rule 1606 adopted April 29, 2011, effective July 1, 2011.

Committee Explanatory Reports:

Final Report explaining the provisions of Rule 1606 published with the Court's Order at 41 Pa.B. 2430 (May 14, 2011).

PART (B)(2)
PERMANENCY HEARING

Rule 1607. Regular Scheduling of Permanency Hearings

A. Thirty days. The court shall conduct permanency hearings within thirty days of:
   1) an adjudication of dependency at which the court determined that aggravated circumstances exist and that reasonable efforts to prevent or eliminate the need to remove the child from the child's guardian or to preserve and reunify the family need not be made or continue to be made;
   2) a permanency hearing at which the court determined that aggravated circumstances exist and that reasonable efforts to prevent or eliminate the need to remove the child from the child's guardian or to preserve and reunify the family need not be made or continue to be made and the permanency plan for the child is incomplete or inconsistent with the court's determination;
   3) an allegation that aggravated circumstances exist regarding a child who has been adjudicated dependent; or
   4) a motion alleging that the hearing is necessary to protect the safety or physical, mental, or moral welfare of a dependent child.

B. Six months. The court shall conduct a permanency hearing within six months of:
   1) the date of the child's removal from the child's guardian for placement pursuant to 42 Pa. C.S. §§ 6324 or 6332, or pursuant to a transfer of legal custody, or other disposition pursuant to Rule 1515, whichever is earliest; or
   2) each previous permanency hearing until the child is removed from the jurisdiction of the court pursuant to Rule 1613.

Comment

See 42 Pa.C.S. § 6351(e)(3).

Paragraph (A) provides when permanency hearings are to be held within thirty days. If the requirements of paragraph (A) do not apply, the court is to hold a permanency hearing every six months in every case until the child is removed from the jurisdiction of the court pursuant to paragraph (B). This includes cases when the child is not removed from the home or the child was removed and subsequently returned to the guardian, but the child is under the court's supervision.

See Rule 1800(11).

Official Note: Rule 1607 adopted August 21, 2006, effective February 1, 2007. Amended September 16, 2009, effective immediately.

Committee Explanatory Reports:

Final Report explaining the provisions of Rule 1607 published with the Court's Order at 36 Pa.B. 5571 (September 2, 2006). Final Report explaining the amendments to Rule 1607 published with the Court's Order at 39 Pa.B. 5546 (September 26, 2009).

Rule 1608. Permanency Hearing

A. *Purpose and timing of hearing.* For every case, the court shall conduct a permanency hearing at least every six months for purposes of determining or reviewing:

(1) the permanency plan of the child;

(2) the date by which the goal of permanency for the child might be achieved; and

(3) whether the placement continues to be best suited to the safety, protection, and physical, mental, and moral welfare of the child.

B. *Recording.* The permanency hearing shall be recorded.

C. *Evidence.*

(1) Any evidence helpful in determining the appropriate course of action, including evidence that was not admissible at the adjudicatory hearing, shall be presented to the court.

(2) If a report was submitted pursuant to Rule 1604, the court shall review and consider the report as it would consider all other evidence.

D. *Court's findings.*

(1) *Findings at all Six-Month Hearings.* At each permanency hearing, the court shall enter its findings and conclusions of law into the record and enter an order pursuant to Rule 1609. On the record in open court, the court shall state:

(a) the appropriateness of the placement;

(b) the appropriateness, feasibility, and extent of compliance with the permanency plan developed for the child;

(c) the appropriateness and feasibility of the current permanency goal for the child provided that, at no time may a goal be changed from reunification unless notice has been provided in accordance with Rule1601(B);

(d) the likely date by which the permanency goal for the child might be achieved;

(e) whether reasonable efforts were made to finalize the permanency plan in effect;

(f) whether the county agency has made services available to theguardian, and if not, why those services have not been made available;

(g) the continued appropriateness of the permanency plan and the concurrent plan;

(h) whether the county agency has satisfied the requirements of Rule 1149 regarding family finding, and if not, the findings and conclusions of the court on why the requirements have not been met by the county agency;

(i) whether the child is safe;

(j) if the child has been placed outside the Commonwealth, whether the placement continues to be best suited to the safety, protection, and physical, mental, and moral welfare of the child;

(k) the services needed to assist a child who is fourteen years of age or older to make the transition to a successful adulthood, including:

(i) the specific independent living services or instructions that are currently being provided by the county agency or private provider;

(ii) the areas of need in independent living instruction that have been identified by the independent living assessment completed pursuant to the Chafee Act, *42 U.S.C. § 671 et seq.*;

(iii) the independent living services that the child will receive prior to the next permanency review hearing;

(iv) whether the child is in the least restrictive, most family-like setting that will enable him to develop independent living skills;

(v) the efforts that have been made to develop and maintain connections with supportive adults regardless of placement type;

(vi) whether the child is making adequate educational progress to graduate from high school or whether the child is enrolled in another specified educational program that will assist the child in achieving self-sufficiency;

(vii) the job-readiness services that have been provided to the child and the employment/career goals that have been established; (viii) whether the child has physical health or behavioral health needs that will require continued services into adulthood; and

(ix) the steps being taken to ensure that the youth will have stable housing or living arrangements when discharged from care;

(l) any educational, health care, and disability needs of the child and the plan to ensure those needs are met;

(m) if a sibling of a child has been removed from the home and is in a different setting than the child, whether reasonable efforts have been made to place the child and sibling of the child together or whether such joint placement is contrary to the safety or well-being of the child or sibling;

(n) if the child has a sibling, whether visitation of the child with that sibling is occurring no less than twice a month, unless a finding is made that visitation is contrary to the safety or well-being of the child or sibling;

(o) whether sufficient steps have been taken by the county agency to ensure the caregiver is exercising the reasonable and prudent parent standard;

(p) whether sufficient steps have been taken by the county agency to ensure the child has been provided regular, ongoing opportunities to engage in age-appropriate or developmentally-appropriate activities, including:

(i) consulting the child in an age-appropriate or developmentally-appropriate manner about the opportunities to participate in activities; and

(ii) identifying and addressing any barriers to participation; and

(q) whether the visitation schedule for the child with the child's guardian is adequate, unless a finding is made that visitation is contrary to the safety or well-being of the child.

(2) *Another Planned Permanent Living Arrangement (APPLA) for Children Sixteen Years of Age or Older.* APPLA shall not be utilized for any child under the age of sixteen. At each permanency hearing for a child who is sixteen years or older and has a permanency goal of APPLA, the following additional considerations, inquiry, and findings shall be made by the court:

(a) Court's APPLA Considerations. Before making its findings pursuant to paragraph (D)(2)(c), the court shall consider evidence, which is obtained as of the date of the hearing, and entered into the record concerning:

(i) the intensive, ongoing, and unsuccessful efforts made to:

(A) return the child home; or

(B) secure a placement for the child with a fit and willing relative, a legal guardian, or an adoptive parent;

(ii) the specific services, including the use of search technology and social media to find biological family members and kin, as well as permanency services that have been provided to the child that serve as the intensive ongoing, and unsuccessful efforts to achieve reunification, adoption, or placement with a guardian or a fit and willing relative;

(iii) the full name of at least one identified supportive adult with whom the child has significant connections;

(iv) how each identified supportive adult has formalized the connection with the child;

(v) the specific services that will be provided by the agency to support and maintain the connection between the child and identified supportive adult(s); and

(vi) the specific planned, permanent placement or living arrangement for the child that will provide the child with stability.

(b) Court's Inquiry of Child's Desired Permanency Outcome. Before making its findings pursuant to paragraph (D)(2)(c), the court shall ask the child about the child›s desired permanency outcome.

(c) Court's APPLA Findings. After making all the findings of paragraph (D)(1) and before assigning the permanency goal of APPLA, at each subsequent permanency hearing, based upon the considerations and inquiry provided in paragraph (D)(2)(a)&(b) and any other evidence deemed appropriate by the court, the court shall state in open court on the record the following:

(i) reasons why APPLA continues to be the best permanency plan for the child; and

(ii) compelling reasons why it continues not to be in the best interests of the child to:

(A) return home;

(B) be placed for adoption;

(C) be placed with a legal guardian;

(D) be placed with a fit and willing relative; and

(iii) the full name of at least one identified supportive adult with whom the child has significant connections.

(3) *Additional findings for fifteen of last twenty-two months.* If the child has been in placement for fifteen of the last twenty-two months, the court may direct the county agency to file a petition to terminate parental rights.

E. *Advanced Communication Technology.* Upon good cause shown, a court may utilize advanced communication technology pursuant to Rule 1129.

F. *Family Service Plan or Permanency Plan.*

(1) The county agency shall review the family service plan or permanency plan at least every six months, including all family finding efforts pursuant to Rule 1149.

(2) The family service plan or permanency plan shall identify which relatives and kin were included in its development and the method of that inclusion.

(3) If the plan is modified, the county agency shall follow the filing and service requirements pursuant to Rule 1345.

(4) The parties and when requested, the court, shall be provided with the modified plan at least fifteen days prior to the permanency hearing.

(3) *Additional findings for fifteen of last twenty-two months.* If the child has been in placement for fifteen of the last twenty-two months, the court may direct the county agency to file a petition to terminate parental rights.

E. *Advanced Communication Technology.* Upon good cause shown, a court may utilize advanced communication technology pursuant to Rule 1129.

F. *Family Service Plan or Permanency Plan.*

(1) The county agency shall review the family service plan or permanency plan at least every six months, including all family finding efforts pursuant to Rule 1149.

(2) The family service plan or permanency plan shall identify which relatives and kin were included in its development and the method of that inclusion.

(3) If the plan is modified, the county agency shall follow the filing and service requirements pursuant to Rule 1345.

(4) The parties and when requested, the court, shall be provided with the modified plan at least fifteen days prior to the permanency hearing.

Comment

See 42 Pa.C.S. §§ 6341, 6351.

Permanency planning is a concept whereby children are not relegated to the limbo of spending their childhood in foster homes, but instead, dedicated effort is made by the court and the county agency to rehabilitate and reunite the family in a reasonable time, and failing in this, to free the child for adoption. *In re M.B.*, 674 A.2d 702, 704 (Pa. Super. 1996) (quoting *In re Quick, 559 A.2d 42* (Pa. 1989)).

To the extent practicable, the judge or juvenile court hearing officer who presided over the adjudicatory and original dispositional hearing for a child should preside over the permanency hearing for the same child.

Pursuant to paragraph (A), courts are to conduct a permanency hearing every six months. Courts are strongly encouraged to conduct more frequent permanency hearings, such as every three months, when possible.

The court may schedule a three-month hearing or conference. At the three-month hearing, the court should ensure that: 1) services ordered at the dispositional hearing pursuant to Rule 1512 are put into place by the county agency; 2) the guardian who is the subject of the petition is given access to the services ordered; 3) the guardian is cooperating with the court-ordered services; and 4) a concurrent plan is developed if the primary plan may not be achieved.

A three-month hearing or conference is considered best practice for dependency cases and is highly recommended. The court should not wait until six months has elapsed to determine if the case is progressing. Time to achieve permanency is critical in dependency cases. In order to seek reimbursement under Title IV-E of the Social Security Act, 42 U.S.C. § 601 *et seq.*, a full permanency hearing is to be conducted every six months, including required findings and conclusions of law on the record pursuant to paragraph (D).

In addition to the permanency hearing contemplated by this rule, courts may also conduct additional and/or more frequent intermittent review hearings or status conferences that address specific issues based on the circumstances of the case and assist the court in ensuring timely permanency.

Every child should have a concurrent plan, which is a secondary plan to be pursued if the primary permanency plan for the child cannot be achieved. *See Comment* to Rule 1512. For example, the primary plan may be reunification with the guardian. If the guardian does not substantially comply with the requirements of the court-ordered services, subsidized legal guardianship may be utilized as the concurrent plan. Because of time requirements, the concurrent plan is to be in place so that permanency may be achieved in a timely manner.

Paragraph (D)(1)(c) is intended to provide adequate notice and the opportunity to be heard when a goal is being changed from reunification. If the court intends to change the child's goal from reunification without a prior notice provided by a party pursuant to Rule 1601(B), then the court shall direct the county agency to provide such notice in accordance with Rule 1601(B).

Pursuant to paragraph (D)(1)(h), the court is to determine whether the county agency has reasonably satisfied the requirements of Rule 1149 regarding family finding, including the location and engagement of relatives and kin at least every six months, prior to each permanency hearing. If the county agency has failed to meet the diligent family finding efforts requirements of Rule 1149, the court is to utilize its powers to enforce this legislative mandate. *See* 62 P.S. § 1301 *et seq.*; *see also* Rules 1210(D)(8), 1242(E)(3), 1409(C), 1609(D), and 1611(C) and *Comments* to Rules 1242, 1408, 1409, 1512, 1514, 1515, 1609, and 1611.

When making its determination for reasonable efforts made by the county agency, the court is to consider family finding. *See also* Rules 1240(B)(6), 1242(C)(2) & (3)(b) & (c) and 1330(B)(6) and *Comments* to Rules 1242, 1330, 1409, 1515, 1609, and 1611 for reasonable efforts determinations.

See 42 U.S.C. § 675(5)(A)-(I) for development of a transition plan pursuant to paragraph (D)(1)(k).

Pursuant to paragraph (D)(1)(o), the county agency is to testify and enter evidence into the record on how it took sufficient steps to ensure the caregiver is exercising the reasonable and prudent parent standard. For the definition of "caregiver" and the "reasonable and prudent parent standard," see Rule 1120. Pursuant to paragraph (D)(1)(p), when documenting its steps taken, the county agency is to include how it consulted with the child in an age-appropriate or developmentally-appropriate manner about the opportunities of the child to participate in activities. For the definition of "age-appropriate or developmentally-appropriate," see Rule 1120. These additions have been made to help dependent children have a sense of normalcy in their lives. These children should be able to participate in extracurricular, enrichment, cultural, and social activities without having to consult caseworkers and ask the court's permission many days prior to the event. *See also* Preventing Sex Trafficking and Strengthening Families Act (P.L. 113-183), 42 U.S.C. §§ 675 and 675a (2014).

Pursuant to paragraph (D)(2), there are additional considerations, inquiries, and findings when the court conducts a permanency hearing for a child, who is sixteen years of age or older and has a permanency plan of APPLA. APPLA should only be utilized as a permanency plan when all other alternatives have been exhausted. Even after exhaustive efforts have been made, the county agency should identify at least one supportive adult to be involved in the life of the child. Diligent efforts to search for relatives, guardians, adoptive parents, or kin are to be utilized. *See* Rule 1149 on family finding. Independent living services should also be addressed. Under paragraph (D)(2)(a)(i)(B), a fit and willing relative may include adult siblings.

Pursuant to paragraph (D)(2)(b), the court is to engage the child in conversation to ascertain the child's desired permanency outcome. The conversation is to be between the child and the court, not the guardian *ad litem* answering for the child.

After all the requirements of paragraph (D)(1) and (D)(2)(a) and (b) have been made, the court is to state in open court on the record the specific reasons why APPLA continues to be the best permanency plan for the child, the compelling reasons why it continues not to be in the best interests of the child to return home or be placed for adoption, with a legal guardian, or with a fit and willing relative, and the full name of at least one identified supportive adult with whom the child has significant connections. *See* paragraph (D)(2)(c). The standards of this rule make choosing the plan of APPLA difficult to ensure that it is the last alternative available for the child. Additionally, this rule requires the court to state its finding in open court on the record. If the court takes a case under advisement, it is to continue the hearing until it is ready to make these findings. The time requirements of the Rules are to be followed when taking a case under advisement.

Pursuant to paragraph (D)(3), a "petition to terminate parental rights" is a term of art used pursuant to 23 Pa.C.S. § 2511 and Pa.O.C. Rule 15.4 to describe the motion terminating parental rights. This does not refer to the "petition" as defined in Pa.R.J.C.P. 1120.

The court is to move expeditiously towards permanency. A goal change motion may be filed at any time.

A President Judge may allow Common Pleas Judges to "wear multiple hats" during a proceeding by conducting a combined hearing on dependency and Orphans' Court matters. *See* 42 Pa.C.S. § 6351(i); *see also In re Adoption of S.E.G., 901 A.2d 1017 (Pa. 2006),* where involuntary termination occurred prior to a goal change by the county agency.

For family service plan requirements, see 55 Pa. Code §§ 3130.61 and 3130.63.

See Rule 1136 regarding *ex parte* communications.

See Rule 1610 for permanency hearing for children over the age of eighteen.

Rule 1608 adopted August 21, 2006, effective February 1, 2007. Amended December 18, 2009, effective immediately. Amended April 21, 2011, effective July 1, 2011. Amended April 29, 2011, effective July 1, 2011. Amended October 21, 2013, effective December 1, 2013. Amended July 13, 2015, effective October 1, 2015. Amended December 9, 2015, effective January 1, 2016. Amended, June 14, 2016, effective August 1, 2016. Amended April 6, 2017, effective September 1, 2017. Amended May 17, 2018, effective October 1, 2018.

Rule 1609. Permanency Hearing Orders

A. *Court order.* After every permanency hearing, the court shall issue a written order, which provides whether the permanency plan is best suited to the safety, protection, and physical, mental, and moral welfare of the child.

B. *Determination made.* The court's order shall reflect a determination made pursuant to Rule 1608(D).

C. *Transfer of custody.* If the court decides to transfer custody of the child to a person found to be qualified to provide care, shelter, and supervision of the child, the permanency order shall include:

(1) the name and address of such person unless disclosure is prohibited by court order;

(2) the limitations of the order, including the type of custody granted; and

(3) any temporary visitation rights of parents.

D. *Orders on family finding.*

(1) The court order shall indicate whether family finding efforts made by the county agency were reasonable;

(2) If the family finding efforts were not reasonable, the court shall order the county agency to engage in family finding prior to the next permanency hearing;

E. *Orders concerning education.*

(1) The court's order shall address the stability and appropriateness of the child's education; and

(2) When appropriate, the court shall appoint an educational decision maker pursuant to Rule 1147.

F. *Orders concerning health care and disability.*

(1) The court's order shall identify, monitor, and address the child's needs concerning health care and disability; and

(2) The court's orders shall authorize evaluations and treatment if parental consent cannot be obtained.

G. *Guardians.* The permanency order shall include any conditions, limitations, restrictions, and obligations imposed upon the guardian.

Comment

When issuing a permanency order, the court should issue an order that is "best suited to the safety, protection, and physical, mental, and moral welfare of the child." 42 Pa.C.S. § 6351(a). See *In re S.J.,* 906 A.2d 547, 551 (Pa. Super. Ct. 2006) (citing *In re Tameka M.*, 525 Pa. 348, 580 A.2d 750 (1990)), for issues addressing a child's mental and moral welfare.

Pursuant to paragraph (D), when making its determination for reasonable efforts made by the county agency, the court is to consider the extent to which the county agency has fulfilled its obligation pursuant to Rule 1149 regarding family finding. *See also* Rules 1240(B)(6), 1242(C)(2) & (3)(b) & (c), and 1330(B)(6) and *Comments* to Rules 1242, 1330, 1409, 1515, 1608, 1610, and 1611 for reasonable efforts determinations.

If the requirements of Rule 1149 regarding family finding have not been met, the court is to make necessary orders to ensure compliance by enforcing this legislative mandate. *See* 62 P.S. § 1301 *et seq. See also* Rules 1210(D)(8), 1242(E)(3), and 1409(C) and *Comments* to Rules 1242, 1408, 1409, 1512, 1514, 1515, 1608, 1610, and 1611.

Pursuant to paragraph (E), the court's order is to address the child's educational stability, including the right to an educational decision maker. The order should address the child's right to: 1) educational stability, including the right to: a) remain in the same school regardless of a change in placement when it is in the child's best interest; b) immediate enrollment when a school change is in the child's best interest; and c) have school proximity considered in all placement changes, 42 U.S.C. §§ 675(1)(G) and 11431 *et seq.*; 2) an educational decision maker pursuant to Rule 1147, 42 Pa.C.S. § 6301, 20 U.S.C. § 1439(a)(5), and 34 C.F.R. § 300.519; 3) an appropriate education, including any necessary special education, early intervention, or remedial services pursuant to 24 P. S. §§ 13-1371 and 13-1372, 55 Pa. Code § 3130.87, and 20 U.S.C. § 1400 *et seq.*; 4) the educational services necessary to support the child's transition to independent living pursuant to 42 Pa.C.S. § 6351 if the child is sixteen or older; and 5) a transition plan that addresses the child's educational needs pursuant to 42 U.S.C. § 675(5)(H) if the child will age out of care within ninety days.

Pursuant to paragraph (F), the court's order is to address the child's needs concerning health care and disability. The order should address the right of: 1) a child to receive timely and medically appropriate screenings and health care services pursuant to 55 Pa. Code §§ 3700.51 and 3800.32 and 42 U.S.C. § 1396d(r);

2) a child to a transition plan that addresses the child's health care needs, and includes specific options for how the child can obtain health insurance after leaving care pursuant to 42 U.S.C. § 675(5)(H) if the child will age out of care within ninety days; and 3) a child with disabilities to receive necessary accommodations pursuant to 42 U.S.C. § 12132; 28 C.F.R. § 35.101 et seq., Section 504 of the Rehabilitation Act of 1973, *as amended*, 29 U.S.C. § 794, and implementing regulations at 45 C.F.R. § 84.1 et seq. In addition, the court is to ensure progress and compliance with the child's case plan for the ongoing oversight and coordination of health care services under 42 U.S.C. § 622(b)(15).

Pursuant to the Juvenile Act, the court has authority to order a physical or mental examination of a child and medical or surgical treatment of a minor, who is suffering from a serious physical condition or illness which requires prompt treatment in the opinion of a physician. The court may order the treatment even if the guardians have not been given notice of the pending hearing, are not available, or without good cause inform the court that they do not consent to the treatment. 42 Pa.C.S. § 6339(b).

See Rule 1611 for permanency hearing orders for children over the age of eighteen.

Note: Rule 1609 adopted August 21, 2006, effective February 1, 2007. Amended April 29, 2011, effective July 1, 2011. Amended October 21, 2013, effective December 1, 2013. Amended July 13, 2015, effective October 1, 2015.

Rule 1610. Permanency Hearing for Children Over Eighteen

A. *Purpose and timing of hearing.* For every case for children over the age of eighteen, the court shall conduct a permanency hearing at least every six months for purposes of determining:

(1) whether the child continues to meet the definition of child under Rule 1120 and has requested the court to retain dependency jurisdiction;

(2) whether the transition plan of the child is consistent with Rule 1631(E)(2);

(3) the date by which the goal of permanency for the child might be achieved; and

(4) whether the placement continues to be best suited to the safety, protection, and physical, mental, and moral welfare of the child.

B. *Recording.* The permanency hearing shall be recorded.

C *Evidence.* Any evidence helpful in determining the appropriate course of action, including evidence that was not admissible at the adjudicatory hearing, shall be presented to the court.

D. *Court's findings.* At the permanency hearing, the court shall enter its findings and conclusions of law into the record and enter an order pursuant to Rule 1611. The court shall make a determination whether the county agency has satisfied the requirements of Rule 1149 regarding family finding, and if not, the findings and conclusions of the court on why the requirements have not been met by the county agency.

Comment

See 42 Pa.C.S. §§ 6341, 6351.

To the extent practicable, the judge or juvenile court hearing officer who presided over the adjudicatory and original dispositional hearing for a child should preside over the permanency hearings for the same child. In resumption of jurisdiction cases, to the extent practicable, the judge or juvenile court hearing officer who presided over the original case should preside over the re-opened case.

Pursuant to paragraph (A), courts are to conduct a permanency hearing every six months. Courts are strongly encouraged to conduct more frequent permanency hearings, such as every three months, when possible.

A three-month hearing or conference is considered best practice for dependency cases and is highly recommended. The court should not wait until six months has elapsed to determine if the transition plan is progressing. Time to achieve permanency is critical in dependency cases. In order to seek reimbursement under Title IV-E of the Social Security Act, 42 U.S.C. § 601 *et seq.*, a full permanency hearing is to be conducted every six months.

In addition to the permanency hearing contemplated by this rule, courts may also conduct additional and/or more frequent intermittent review hearings or status conferences, which address specific issues based on the circumstances of the case, and which assist the court in ensuring timely transition.

See 42 U.S.C. § 675 (5)(A)-(H) for development of a transition plan.

See Rule 1128 regarding presence at proceedings and Rule 1136 regarding *ex parte* communications.

Pursuant to paragraph (D), the court is to determine whether the county agency has reasonably satisfied the requirements of Rule 1149 regarding family finding, including the location and engagement of relatives and kin at least every six months, prior to each permanency hearing. If the county agency has failed to meet the diligent family finding efforts requirements of Rule 1149, the court is to utilize its powers to enforce this legislative mandate. *See* 62 P.S. § 1301 *et seq. See also* Rules 1210(D)(8), 1242(E)(3), 1409(C), 1609(D), and 1611(C) and *Comments* to Rules 1242, 1408, 1409, 1512, 1514, 1515, 1608, 1609, and 1611.

When making its determination for reasonable efforts made by the county agency, the court is to consider family finding. *See also* Rules 1240(B)(6), 1242(C)(2)&(3)(b)&(c) and 1330(B)(6) and *Comments* to Rules 1242, 1330, 1409, 1515, 1608, 1609, and 1611 for reasonable efforts determinations.

When the court has resumed jurisdiction pursuant to Rule 1635, the court is to schedule regular permanency hearings. The county agency is to develop a new transition plan for the child.

Official Note: Adopted October 21, 2013, effective December 1, 2013. Amended July 13, 2015, effective October 1, 2015. Amended April 6, 2017, effective September 1, 2017.

Rule 1611. Permanency Hearing Orders for Children Over Eighteen

A. *Court order.* After every permanency hearing for children over the age of eighteen, the court shall issue a written order, which provides whether the transition plan is best suited to the safety, protection, and physical, mental, and moral welfare of the child.

B. *Determinations made.* The court's order shall reflect the determinations made pursuant to Rule 1610(D).

C. *Orders on family finding.*

(1) The court order shall indicate whether family finding efforts made by the county agency were reasonable;

(2) If the family finding efforts were not reasonable, the court shall order the county agency to engage in family finding prior to the next permanency hearing;

D. *Orders concerning education.* The court's order shall address the stability and appropriateness of the child's education, if applicable, including whether an educational decision maker is appropriate.

E. *Orders concerning health care and disability.*

(1) The court's order shall identify, monitor, and address the child's needs concerning health care and disability; and

(2) The court's orders may authorize evaluations and treatment.

Comment

When issuing a permanency order, the court should issue an order that is "best suited to the safety, protection, and physical, mental, and moral welfare of the child." 42 Pa.C.S. § 6351(a). See *In re S.J.*, 906 A.2d 547, 551 (Pa. Super. Ct. 2006)(citing *In re Tameka M.*, 525 Pa. 348, 580 A.2d 750 (1990)), for issues addressing a child's mental and moral welfare.

Pursuant to paragraph (C), when making its determination for reasonable efforts made by the county agency, the court is to consider the extent to which the county agency has fulfilled its obligation pursuant to Rule 1149 regarding family finding. *See also* Rules 1240(B)(6), 1242(C)(2)&(3)(b)&(c), and 1330(B)(6) and *Comments* to Rules 1242, 1330, 1409, 1515, 1608, 1609, and 1610 for reasonable efforts determinations.

If the requirements of Rule 1149 regarding family finding have not been met, the court is to make necessary orders to ensure compliance by enforcing this legislative mandate. *See* 62 P.S. § 1301 *et seq. See also* Rules 1210(D)(8), 1242(E)(3), and 1409(C) and *Comments* to Rules 1242, 1408, 1409, 1512, 1514, 1515, 1608, 1609, and 1610.

Pursuant to paragraph (D), the court's order is to address the child's educational stability, including the right to an educational decision maker. The intent of this paragraph is to ensure that the inquiry regarding the appointment of an educational decision maker is considered. Federal and state law requires educational decision makers until the age of twenty-one if an educational decision maker is necessary. *See Comment* to Rule 1609(E) and 34 C.F.R. § 300.320(c).

Pursuant to paragraph (E), the court's order is to address the child's needs concerning health care and disability. *See Comment* to Rule 1609(F).

Note: Adopted October 21, 2013, effective December 1, 2013. Amended July 13, 2015, effective October 1, 2015.

PART C
POST-DISPOSITIONAL PROCEDURES

1613. [Reserved]

Rule 1613. [Reserved]

Comment

This rule was renumbered from Rule 1613 to Rule 1631 on October 21, 2013. See Rule 1631.

Rule 1616. Post-Dispositional Procedures; Appeals [Reserved]

PART D
CESSATION OR RESUMPTION OF COURT SUPERVISION OR JURISDICTION

1631. Termination of Court Supervision.
1634. Motion for Resumption of Jurisdiction.
1635. Hearing on Motion for Resumption of Jurisdiction.

Rule 1631. Termination Of Court Supervision

A. Concluding Supervision. Any party, or the court on its own motion, may move for the termination of supervision when court-ordered services from the county agency are no longer needed and:

1) the child has remained with the guardian and the circumstances which necessitated the dependency adjudication have been alleviated;

2) the child has been reunified with the guardian and the circumstances which necessitated the dependency adjudication and placement have been alleviated;

3) the child has been placed with a ready, willing, and able parent who was not previously identified by the county agency;

4) the child has been adopted and services from the county agency are no longer needed;

5) the child has been placed in the custody of a permanent legal custodian and services from the county agency are no longer needed;

6) the child has been placed in the physical and legal custody of a fit and willing relative and services from the county agency are no longer needed;

7) the child has been placed in another living arrangement intended to be permanent and services from the county agency are no longer needed and a hearing has been held pursuant to paragraph (E) for a child who is age eighteen or older;

8) the child has been adjudicated delinquent and services from the county agency are no longer needed because all dependency issues have been resolved;

9) the child has been emancipated by the court;

10) the child is eighteen years of age or older and a hearing has been held pursuant to paragraph (E);

11) the child has died;

12) a court in another county of this Commonwealth has accepted jurisdiction; or

13) a court in another state has accepted jurisdiction.

B. Ready, willing, and able parent. When services from the county agency are no longer necessary because the court has determined that the child is not dependent pursuant to paragraph (A)(3) because a non-custodial parent has been found by the court to be able and available, the court shall enter an order awarding custody to that parent and the court order shall have the effect and be docketed as a decision entered pursuant to the Pa.R.C.P.

C. Objection. Any party may object to a motion under paragraph (A) and request a hearing.

D. Hearing. If objections have been made under paragraph (C), the court shall hold a hearing and give each party an opportunity to be heard before the court enters its final order.

E. Children eighteen years of age or older.
  1) Before the court can terminate its supervision of a child who is eighteen years of age or older, a hearing shall be held at least ninety days prior to the child turning eighteen years of age.
  2) Prior to the hearing, the child shall have the opportunity to make decisions about the transition plan and confer with the county agency about the details of the plan. The county agency shall provide the transition plan to the court and the plan shall, at a minimum, include:
      a) the specific plans for housing;
      b) a description of the child's source of income;
      c) the specific plans for pursuing educational or vocational training goals;
      d) the child's employment goals and whether the child is employed;
      e) a description of the health insurance plan that the child is expected to obtain and any continued health or behavioral health needs of the child;
      f) a description of any available programs that would provide mentors or assistance in establishing positive adult connections;
      g) verification that all vital identification documents and records have been provided to the child;
      h) a description of any other needed support services; and
      i) notice to the child that the child can request resumption of juvenile court jurisdiction until the child turns twenty-one years of age if specific conditions are met.
  3) At the hearing, the court shall review the transition plan for the child. If the court is not satisfied that the requirements of paragraph (E)(2) have been met, a subsequent hearing shall be scheduled.
  4) The court shall not terminate its supervision of the child without approving an appropriate transition plan, unless the child, after an appropriate transition plan has been offered, is unwilling to consent to the supervision and the court determines termination is warranted.

F. Cessation of services. When all of the above listed requirements have been met, the court may discharge the child from its supervision and close the case.

Comment

For procedures on motions, see Rule 1344. For procedures on the dispositional order, see Rule 1515.

For guidelines under paragraph (A), see 42 Pa.C.S. §§ 6301(b) & 6351(f.1).

Pursuant to paragraph (A)(8), if a child has been adjudicated delinquent, the court may terminate court supervision unless dependency is necessary for placement. In re Deanna S., 422 Pa.Super. 439, 619 A.2d 758 (1993). The court may also decide to retain dependency jurisdiction regardless of the delinquency adjudication because the child still needs dependency services.

If dependency issues have not been resolved, the case should be kept open and services ordered. The court should ensure that services are not discontinued solely because the child was adjudicated delinquent. The county agency and the juvenile probation are to collaborate on the case and resolve all outstanding issues. If a child is in a delinquency placement, the court is to ensure that the county agency and the juvenile probation office have collaborated to ensure appropriate services are in place.

For procedures on emancipation pursuant to paragraph (A)(9), see Berks County Children and Youth Services v. Rowan, 428 Pa.Super. 448, 631 A.2d 615 (1993). See also, 22 Pa.Code § 11.11, 55 Pa.Code § 145.62.

Pursuant to paragraph (A)(10), a child who was adjudicated dependent prior to reaching the age of eighteen and who, while engaged in a course of instruction or treatment, requests the court to retain jurisdiction until the course has been completed, may remain in the course of instruction or treatment until the age of twenty-one. 42 Pa.C.S. § 6302. See also, 55 Pa.Code §§ 3130.5 & 3130.87; In re S.J., 906 A.2d 547 (Pa. Super. Ct. 2006).

The court may not terminate jurisdiction solely because the dependent child is a runaway. In re Deanna S., 422 Pa.Super. 439, 619 A.2d 758 (1993).

A child whose non-custodial parent is ready, willing, and able to provide adequate care for the child may not be found dependent. In re M.L., 562 Pa. 646, 757 A.2d 849 (2000). See paragraph (B). Paragraph (B) does not apply to resumption of jurisdiction cases.

Pursuant to 42 Pa.C.S. § 6351(a)(2.1), a court may transfer permanent legal custody to a person found by the court to be qualified to receive and care for the child. 42 Pa.C.S. § 6351(a)(2.1). See also Justin S., 375 Pa.Super. 88, 543 A.2d 1192 (1988).

Pursuant to paragraph (E)(2), the county agency is to assist the child and provide all the support necessary in developing a transition plan. See 42 U.S.C. § 675 (5)(A)-(H).

Pursuant to paragraph (E)(3), the court is to approve a transition plan that is suitable for the child and that has been personalized at the direction of the child.

If the court has resumed jurisdiction pursuant to Rule 1635, a new transition plan is to be developed for the child. Before the court can terminate supervision, the requirements of paragraph (E) are to be followed. In no case is a juvenile over twenty-one to remain under juvenile court supervision. See Rule 1635(E). See also Rule 1635(E) for termination of juvenile court jurisdiction if the court denies the motion for resumption of jurisdiction.

Official Note: Rule 1613 adopted August, 21, 2006, effective February 1, 2007. Amended July 29, 2009, effective immediately. Amended April 29, 2011, effective July 1, 2011. Amended October 21, 2013 and renumbered from Rule 1613 to Rule 1631, effective December 1, 2013.

Committee Explanatory Reports:

Final Report explaining the provisions of Rule 1613 published with the Court's Order at 36 Pa.B. 5571 (September 2, 2006). Final Report explaining the amendments to Rule 1613 published with the Court's Order at 39 Pa.B. 4887 (August 15, 2009). Final Report explaining the amendments to Rule 1613 published with the Court's Order at 41 Pa.B. 2430 (May 14, 2011). Final Report explaining the amendments to Rule 1631 published with the Court's Order at 43 Pa.B. - (November 2, 2013).

Rule 1634. Motion for Resumption of Jurisdiction.

A. **Venue.** A motion to resume jurisdiction shall be filed with the court that terminated court supervision of the child pursuant to Rule 1631.

B. **Contents.** The motion for resumption of jurisdiction shall aver:
   1) dependency jurisdiction was previously terminated:
      a) within ninety days prior to the child's eighteenth birthday; or
      b) on or after the child's eighteenth birthday; and
   2) the child:
      a) is under twenty-one years of age;
      b) was adjudicated dependent prior to turning eighteen years of age;
      c) has requested the court to resume jurisdiction; and
      d) is:
         i) completing secondary education or an equivalent credential;
         ii) enrolled in an institution which provides postsecondary or vocational education;
         iii) participating in a program actively designed to promote or prevent barriers to employment;
         iv) employed for at least eighty hours per month; or
         v) incapable of doing any of the activities as prescribed in paragraphs (B)(2)(d)(i)-(iv) due to a medical or behavioral health condition, which is supported by regularly updated information in the permanency plan for the child;
   3) whether the child would like his or her guardian or other interested adult involved in the court proceedings;
   4) that a verification has been signed by the child attesting the above requirements have been met; and
   5) whether an expedited hearing for placement and services is being requested due to the child's current living arrangement.

C. **Service.** A copy of the motion shall be served upon:
   1) the county agency;
   2) the attorney for the county agency;
   3) the child;
   4) the child's attorney; and
   5) the guardian or other interested adult if the child requesting resumption of jurisdiction would like the guardian or other interested adult involved in the case as averred in paragraph (B)(3).

Comment

A motion to resume jurisdiction can be filed by the child, county agency, or attorney for the child.

At the request of the child, if the county agency or previous attorney is approached by the child concerning the court reopening the child's case, the county agency or attorney is to assist the child in the filing of the motion.

Pursuant to paragraph (A), the motion is to be filed in the county that terminated juvenile court jurisdiction. If the juvenile has moved to another county, the juvenile may request the court to transfer jurisdiction pursuant to Rule 1302 at any time after the filing of the motion to resume jurisdiction, including prior to the hearing on the motion. See Rules 1302 and 1635.

If the child does not have an attorney at the time of the filing of the motion, the court is to assign legal counsel pursuant to Rule 1151 and immediately order service of the motion to resume jurisdiction on the child's attorney. It is best practice to appoint the guardian ad litem or legal counsel who was previously assigned to the child as legal counsel. See Rule 1151.

If the child is the party filing the motion, the President Judge of each judicial district is to designate a person to serve the other parties for the child. If the county agency or attorney is filing the motion, they should serve the other parties.

If the child has averred that the child desires the involvement of a guardian or other interested adult in their case, this person is to be served with the motion and given notice of any subsequent hearings if the court orders such involvement. Notice does not confer standing upon the guardian or other interested adult. See Rule 1635(B)(5) and Comment.

See 42 Pa.C.S. §§ 6302 & 6351(j).

See also Rule 1300 for change of venue and Rule 1302 for inter-county transfer of the case.

Official Note: Adopted October 21, 2013, effective December 1, 2013.

Committee Explanatory Reports:

Final Report explaining the provisions of Rule 1634 published with the Court's Order at 43 Pa.B. - (November 2, 2013).

Rule 1635. Hearing on Motion for Resumption of Jurisdiction

A. *Time for hearing.* Within thirty days of receiving a motion for resumption of jurisdiction, the court shall conduct a hearing to determine whether it will resume juvenile court jurisdiction.

B. *Notice.* Notice of the date, time, place, and purpose of the hearing shall be given to:

(1) the county agency;

(2) the attorney for the county agency;

(3) the child;

(4) the child's attorney;

(5) any other persons, including the guardian or other interested adult, as directed by the court.

C. *Hearing.* At the hearing, the court shall state its findings and conclusions of law on the record in open court as to whether:

(1) dependency jurisdiction was previously terminated:

(a) within ninety days prior to the child's eighteenth birthday; or

(b) on or after the child's eighteenth birthday but before the child turns twenty-one years of age; and

(2) the child continues to meet the definition of child pursuant to 42 Pa.C.S. § 6302 because the child:

    (a) is under twenty-one years of age;

    (b) was adjudicated dependent prior to turning eighteen years of age;

    (c) has requested the court to resume jurisdiction; and

    (d) is:

        (i) completing secondary education or an equivalent credential;

        (ii) enrolled in an institution which provides postsecondary or vocational education;

        (iii) participating in a program actively designed to promote or prevent barriers to employment;

        (iv) employed for at least eighty hours per month; or

        (v) incapable of doing any of the activities as prescribed in paragraphs (C)(2)(d)(i)-(iv) due to a medical or behavioral health condition, which is supported by regularly updated information in the permanency plan for the child;

(3) reasonable efforts were made by the county agency to prevent the return of the child to juvenile court jurisdiction unless, due to the child's immediate need for assistance, such lack of efforts was reasonable;

(4) it will exercise jurisdiction pursuant to 42 Pa.C.S. § 6351(j) because it is best suited to the protection and physical, mental, and moral welfare of the child;

(5) a guardian or other interested adult should be involved in the child's case;

(6) there are any health or educational needs of the child; and

(7) the county agency has developed an appropriate transition plan.

D. *Orders.*

(1) After a hearing, the court shall enter an order granting or denying the motion to resume juvenile court jurisdiction.

(2) If the court resumes jurisdiction, the court shall order:

    (a) that resumption of jurisdiction is best suited to the protection and physical, mental, and moral welfare of the child;

    (b) any findings as to the transition plan for the child;

    (c) regular scheduling of permanency hearings pursuant to Rule 1608;

    (d) any designations of custody and/or placement of the child; and

    (e) any evaluations, tests, or treatments for the health and educational needs of the child.

E. *Termination of court supervision in resumption cases.*

(1) Once the goals in the transition plan have been accomplished for a child which, at a minimum, includes the requirements pursuant to Rule 1631(E)(2), or the child has refused to cooperate with the plan, a party may move for termination of court supervision pursuant to Rule 1631.

(2) In no event shall a child remain under juvenile court supervision once the child has turned twenty-one years of age.

F. *Advanced Communication Technology.* The provisions of Rule 1129 shall apply to this proceeding.

Rule 1635 JUVENILE COURT PROCEDURE

Comment

The court may decide whether a guardian or other interested adult will participate in the child's case. The court is to consider the preferences of the child when making an order for participation. *See* Rule 1634(B)(3) for notation of child's preference and 42 Pa.C.S. § 6310 for guardian involvement. Notice or invitation to participate does not confer standing upon the guardian or other interested adult.

See 42 Pa.C.S. §§ 6302 & 6351(j).

A juvenile court hearing officer may conduct these hearings. *See* Rule 1187.

If the court resumes jurisdiction, the county agency is to engage in family finding unless presently or previously discontinued pursuant to Rule 1149(B). *See* Rules 1608(D)(1)(h) and 1610(D)(court findings at permanency hearing whether the county agency has satisfied the requirements of Rule 1149 regarding family finding). If family finding was previously discontinued, the county agency may seek to resume family finding efforts pursuant to Rule 1149(C).

Adopted October 21, 2013, effective December 1, 2013. Amended July 13, 2015, effective October 1, 2015. Amended April 6, 2017, effective September 1, 2017.

CHAPTER 17
AGGRAVATED CIRCUMSTANCES

1701. Motion for Finding of Aggravated Circumstances
1702. Filing of Motion for Finding of Aggravated Circumstances
1705. Adjudication of Aggravated Circumstances

Rule 1701. Motion for Finding of Aggravated Circumstances

A. **Dependency Petitions.** A motion for finding of aggravated circumstances may be included in a dependency petition pursuant to Rule 1330.

B. **Motion for Aggravated Circumstances.** If it is determined that aggravated circumstances exist after the filing of the petition, a request for a finding of aggravated circumstances shall be made by motion pursuant to Rule 1344. The motion shall be written.

Comment

See 42 Pa.C.S. §§ 6302, 6334(b).

Under paragraph (B), all motions for a finding of aggravated circumstances are to be written. Oral motions under Rule 1344 do not apply to motions for finding of aggravated circumstances.

The aggravated circumstances, as defined by 42 Pa.C.S. § 6302, are to be specifically identified in the motion for finding of aggravated circumstances.

Official Note: Rule 1701 adopted August, 21, 2006, effective February 1, 2007.

Committee Explanatory Reports:

Final Report explaining the provisions of Rule 1701 published with the Court's Order at 36 Pa.B. 5571 (September 2, 2006).

Rule 1702. Filing of Motion for Finding of Aggravated Circumstances

A motion for finding of aggravated circumstances shall be filed with the clerk of courts by the county agency as soon as possible but no later than twenty-one days from the determination by the county agency that aggravated circumstances exist.

Comment

See 42 Pa.C.S. § 6334(b).

Official Note: Rule 1702 adopted August, 21, 2006, effective February 1, 2007.

Committee Explanatory Reports:

Final Report explaining the provisions of Rule 1702 published with the Court's Order at 36 Pa.B. 5571 (September 2, 2006).

Rule 1705. Adjudication of Aggravated Circumstances

A. Finding after adjudication of dependency. After a finding of dependency pursuant to Rule 1409, the court shall determine if aggravated circumstances exist.

B. Reasonable efforts. If the court finds aggravated circumstances exist, the court shall determine whether reasonable efforts to prevent or eliminate the need for removing the child from the home or to preserve and reunify the family shall be made or continue to be made and the court shall proceed to a dispositional hearing under Rule 1512.

C. Court order. If the court finds that reasonable efforts pursuant to paragraph (B) were made, the court shall include a statement in its order to that effect.

Comment

Under paragraph (A), the court is to find a child dependent before determining if aggravated circumstances exist. See 42 Pa.C.S. § 6341(c.1). The petition may be amended to include aggravated circumstances pursuant to Rule 1330(C).

A statement as to whether reasonable efforts were made under paragraph (B) are to be included in the court order under Rule 1409(C).

Official Note: Rule 1705 adopted August, 21, 2006, effective February 1, 2007.

Committee Explanatory Reports:

Final Report explaining the provisions of Rule 1705 published with the Court's Order at 36 Pa.B. 5571 (September 2, 2006).

CHAPTER 18
SUSPENSIONS

Rule 1800. Suspensions of Acts of Assembly

This rule provides for the suspension of the following Acts of Assembly that apply to dependency proceedings only:

(1) The Act of July 9, 1976, P.L. 586, No. 142, § 2, 42 Pa.C.S. § 6335(c), which provides for the issuance of arrest warrants if the child may abscond or may not attend or be brought to a hearing, is suspended only insofar as the Act is inconsistent with Rules 1124, 1140, and 1364, which require a summoned person to fail to appear and the court to find that sufficient notice was given.

(2) The Act of July 9, 1976, P.L. 586, No. 142, § 2, 42 Pa.C.S. § 6336(c), which provides that if a proceeding is not recorded, full minutes shall be kept by the court, is suspended only insofar as the Act is inconsistent with Rules 1127(A) & 1242(B)(2), which require all proceedings to be recorded, except for shelter care hearings.

(3) The Act of July 9, 1976, P.L. 586, No. 142, § 2, 42 Pa.C.S. § 6311(b)(9), which provide that there is not a conflict of interest for the guardian *ad litem* in communicating the child's wishes and the recommendation relating to the appropriateness and safety of the child's placement and services necessary to address the child's needs and safety, is suspended only insofar as the Act is inconsistent with Rules 1151 and 1154, which allows for appointment of separate legal counsel and a guardian *ad litem* when the guardian *ad litem* determines there is a conflict of interest between the child's legal interest and best interest.

(4) The Act of July 9, 1976, P.L. 586, No. 142, § 2, 42 Pa.C.S. § 6337, which provides that counsel must be provided unless the guardian is present and waives counsel for the child, is suspended only insofar as the Act is inconsistent with Rule 1152, which does not allow a guardian to waive the child's right to counsel and a child may not waive the right to a guardian *ad litem*.

(5) The Act of July 9, 1976, P.L. 586, No. 142, § 2, 42 Pa.C.S. § 6305(b), which provides that the court may direct hearings in any case or classes of cases be conducted by the juvenile court hearing officer, is suspended only insofar as the Act is inconsistent with Rule 1187, which allows juvenile court hearing officers to hear only specific classes of cases.

(6) The Act of July 9, 1976, P.L. 586, No. 142, § 2, 42 Pa.C.S. § 6324, which authorizes law enforcement officers to take a child into custody, is suspended only insofar as the Act is inconsistent with Rule 1202, which provides for police officers and juvenile probation officers taking a child into custody.

(7) The Act of July 9, 1976, P.L. 586, No. 142, § 2, 42 Pa.C.S. § 6331, which provides for the filing of a petition with the court within twenty-four hours or the next business day of the admission of the child to shelter care, is suspended only insofar as the Act is inconsistent with the filing of a petition within twenty-four hours or the next business day from the shelter care hearing if the child is in protective custody under Rules 1242 and 1330(A).

(8) The Act of July 9, 1976, P.L. 586, No. 142, § 2, 42 Pa.C.S. § 6334, which provides that any person may bring a petition, is suspended only insofar as the Act is inconsistent with Rules 1320, 1321, and 1330, which provide

that the county agency may file a petition and any other person shall file an application to file a petition.

(9) The Act of December 19, 1990, P.L. 1240, No. 206, § 2, 23 Pa.C.S. § 6339, which provides for the confidentiality of reports made pursuant to the Child Protective Services Law, 23 Pa.C.S. § 6301 *et seq.*, is suspended only insofar as the Law is inconsistent with Rule 1340(B)(1)(e), which provides for the disclosure of such reports if the reports are going to be used as evidence in a hearing to prove dependency of a child.

(10) The Act of July 9, 1976, P.L. 586, No. 142, § 2, 42 Pa.C.S. § 6335, which provides that a copy of the petition is to accompany a summons, is suspended only insofar as the Act is inconsistent with Rule 1360, which provides that the summons is to include a copy of the petition unless the petition has been previously served.

(11) The Act of July 9, 1976, P.L. 586, No. 142, § 2, 42 Pa.C.S. § 6336.1(b)(2), which provides that the foster parent or parents, preadoptive parent or relative providing care for the child has a right to submit a report to the court, is suspended only insofar as the Act is inconsistent with Rule 1604, which requires the report to be submitted to a court designee who files the report and submits it to the judge, attorneys, parties, and if appointed, a court appointed special advocate.

(12) The Act of July 9, 1976, P.L. 586, No. 142, § 2, 42 Pa.C.S. § 6351(e)(3)(i)(B), which provides for permanency hearings within six months of each previous permanency hearing until the child is returned home or removed from the jurisdiction of the court, is suspended only insofar as the Act is inconsistent with Rule 1607, which requires permanency hearings in all cases until the child is removed from the jurisdiction of the court.

Comment

The authority for suspension of Acts of Assembly is granted to the Supreme Court by Article V § 10(c) of the Pennsylvania Constitution. *See also* Rule 1102.

Official Note: Rule 1800 adopted August 21, 2006, effective February 1, 2007. Amended March 19, 2009, effective June 1, 2009. Amended September 16, 2009, effective immediately. Amended April 29, 2011, effective July 1, 2011. Amended May 20, 2011, effective July 1, 2011. Amended April 6, 2017, effective September 1, 2017.

Part XI. Selected Pennsylvania Rules of Appellate Procedure
(Amended Through April, 2019)

CHILDREN'S FAST TRACK APPEALS

ARTICLE I
PRELIMINARY PROVISIONS

CHAPTER 1
GENERAL PROVISIONS

IN GENERAL

Rule 102. Definitions

Subject to additional definitions contained in subsequent provisions of these rules which are applicable to specific provisions of these rules, the following words and phrases when used in these rules shall have, unless the context clearly indicates otherwise, the meanings given to them in this rule:

Action.—Any action or proceeding at law or in equity.

Argument.—Where required by the context, the term includes submission on briefs.

Administrative Office.—The Administrative Office of Pennsylvania Courts.

Appeal.—Any petition or other application to a court for review of subordinate governmental determinations. The term includes an application for certiorari under 42 Pa.C.S. § 934 (writs of certiorari) or under any other provision of law. Where required by the context, the term includes proceedings on petition for review.

Note: Under these rules a "subordinate governmental determination" includes an order of a lower court. The definition of "government unit" includes courts, and the definition of "determination" includes action or inaction by (and specifically--an order entered by) a court or other government unit. In general any appeal now extends to the whole record, with like effect as upon an appeal from a judgment entered upon the verdict of a jury in an action at law and the scope of review of an order on appeal is not limited as on broad or narrow certiorari. See 42 Pa.C.S. § 5105(d) (scope of appeal).

Appellant.—Includes petitioner for review.

Appellate court.—The Supreme Court, the Superior Court or the Commonwealth Court.

Appellee.—Includes a party named as respondent in a petition for review.

Application.—Includes a petition or a motion.

Appropriate security.—Security which meets the requirements of Rule 1734 (appropriate security).

Rule 102   Pa. R.App.P.

Children's fast track appeal.—Any appeal from an order involving dependency, termination of parental rights, adoptions, custody or paternity. See 42 Pa.C.S. §§ 6301 et seq.; 23 Pa.C.S. §§ 2511 et seq.; 23 Pa.C.S. §§ 2101 et seq.; 23 Pa.C.S. §§ 5301 et seq.; 23 Pa.C.S. §§ 5102 et seq.

Clerk.—Includes prothonotary.

Counsel.—Counsel of record.

Determination.—Action or inaction by a government unit which action or inaction is subject to judicial review by a court under Section 9 of Article V of the Constitution of Pennsylvania or otherwise. The term includes an order entered by a government unit.

Docket Entries.—Includes the schedule of proceedings of a government unit.

General rule.—A rule or order promulgated by or pursuant to the authority of the Supreme Court.

Government unit.—The Governor and the departments, boards, commissions, officers, authorities and other agencies of the Commonwealth, including the General Assembly and its officers and agencies and any court or other officer or agency of the unified judicial system, and any political subdivision or municipal or other local authority or any officer or agency of any such political subdivision or local authority. The term includes a board of arbitrators whose determination is subject to review under 42 Pa.C.S. § 763(b) (awards of arbitrators).

Judge.—Includes a justice of the Supreme Court.

Lower court.—The court from which an appeal is taken or to be taken. With respect to matters arising under Chapter 17 (effect of appeals; supersedeas and stays), the term means the trial court from which the appeal was first taken.

Matter.—Action, proceeding or appeal. The term includes a petition for review.

Order.—Includes judgment, decision, decree, sentence and adjudication.

Petition for allowance of appeal.—(a) A petition under Rule 1112 (appeals to the Supreme Court by allowance); or (b) a statement pursuant to Rule 2119(f) (discretionary aspects of sentence). See 42 Pa. C.S. § 9781.

Petition for permission to appeal.—A petition under Rule 1311 (interlocutory appeals by permission).

Petition for review.—A petition under Rule 1511 (manner of obtaining judicial review of governmental determinations).

President judge.—When applied to the Supreme Court, the term means the Chief Justice of Pennsylvania.

Proof of service.—Includes acknowledgment of service endorsed upon a pleading.

Quasijudicial order.—An order of a government unit, made after notice and opportunity for hearing, which is by law reviewable solely upon the record made before the government unit, and not upon a record made in whole or in part before the reviewing court.

Reargument.—Includes, in the case of applications for reargument under Chapter 25 (post-submission proceedings), reconsideration and rehearing.

Reconsideration.—Includes reargument and rehearing.

Rule 127

Reproduced record.—That portion of the record which has been reproduced for use in an appellate court. The term includes any supplemental reproduced record.

Rule of court.—A rule promulgated by a court regulating practice or procedure before the promulgating court.

Verified statement.—A document filed with a clerk under these rules containing statements of fact and a statement by the signatory that it is made subject to the penalties of 18 Pa.C.S. § 4904 (unsworn falsification to authorities).

> **Note:** Based on 42 Pa.C.S. § 102 (definitions). The definition of "determination" is not intended to affect the scope of review provided by 42 Pa.C.S. § 5105(d) (scope of appeal) or other provision of law.

Adopted Nov. 5, 1975, effective July 1, 1976. Amended June 23, 1976, effective July 1, 1976; Dec. 11, 1978, effective Dec. 30, 1978; Sept. 10, 2008, effective Dec. 1, 2008; Jan. 13, 2009, effective as to appeals filed 60 days or more after adoption; May 28, 2014, effective July 1, 2014.

Rule 127. Confidential Information and Confidential Documents. Certification

(a) Unless public access is otherwise constrained by applicable authority, any attorney or any unrepresented party who files a document pursuant to these rules shall comply with the requirements of Sections 7.0 and 8.0 of the *Public Access Policy of the Unified Judicial System of Pennsylvania Case Records* ("Public Access Policy"). In accordance with the Policy, the filing shall include a certification of compliance with the Policy and, as necessary, a Confidential Information Form, unless otherwise specified by rule or order of court, or a Confidential Document Form.

(b) Unless an appellate court orders otherwise, case records or documents that are sealed by a court, government unit, or other tribunal shall remain sealed on appeal.

> *Note:* Paragraph (a)—"Applicable authority" includes but is not limited to statute, procedural rule, or court order. *The Public Access Policy of the Unified Judicial System of Pennsylvania Case Records* ("Public Access Policy") can be found at http://www.pacourts.us/public-records. Sections 7.0(D) and 8.0(D) of the Public Access Policy provide that the certification shall be in substantially the following form:
>
>> I certify that this filing complies with the provisions of the *Case Records Policy of the Unified Judicial System of Pennsylvania* that require filing confidential information and documents differently than non-confidential information and documents.
>
> Appropriate forms can be found at http://www.pacourts.us/public-records. Pursuant to Section 7.0(C) of the Policy, a court may adopt a rule or order that permits, in lieu of a Confidential Information Form, the filing of a document in two versions, that is, a "Redacted Version" and an "Unredacted Version." For certification of the Reproduced Record and Supplemental Reproduced Record in compliance with the Public Access Policy, see Pa.R.A.P. 2152, 2156, 2171, and accompanying notes.
>
> **Paragraph (b)**—Once a document is sealed, it shall remain sealed on appeal unless the appellate court orders, either *sua sponte* or on application, that the case record or document be opened.

Adopted Jan. 5, 2018, effective Jan. 6, 2018; Amended June 1, 1018, eff. July 1, 2018.

ARTICLE II
APPELLATE PROCEDURE

CHAPTER 9
APPEALS FROM LOWER COURTS

Rule 904. Content of the Notice of Appeal.

(a) *Form.*— Except as otherwise prescribed by this rule, the notice of appeal shall be in substantially the following form:

COURT OF COMMON PLEAS
OF _____ COUNTY

A.B., Plaintiff :
v.
C.D., Defendant :

Docket or File No. _____
Offense Tracking Number _____

NOTICE OF APPEAL

Notice is hereby given that C.D., defendant above named, hereby appeals to the (Supreme) (Superior) (Commonwealth) Court of Pennsylvania from the order entered in this matter on the _____ day of _____, 20____. This order has been entered in the docket as evidenced by the attached copy of the docket entry.

(S) _____
_____(Address and telephone number)

(b) *Caption.*—The parties shall be stated in the caption as they stood upon the record of the trial court at the time the appeal was takenn.

(c) *Request for transcript.*—The request for transcript contemplated by Pa.R.A.P. 1911 or a statement signed by counsel that either there is no verbatim record of the proceedings or the complete transcript has been lodged of record shall accompany the notice of appeal, but the absence of or defect in the request for transcript shall not affect the validity of the appeal.

(d) *Docket entry.*—The notice of appeal shall include a statement that the order appealed from has been entered on the docket. A copy of the docket entry showing the entry of the order appealed from shall be attached to the notice of appeal.

(e) *Content in criminal cases.*—When the Commonwealth takes an appeal pursuant to Pa.R.A.P. 311(d), the notice of appeal shall include a certification by counsel that the order will terminate or substantially handicap the prosecution.

(f) *Content in children's fast track appeals.*—In a children's fast track appeal the notice of appeal shall include a statement advising the appellate court that the appeal is a children's fast track appeal.

Official Note: The Offense Tracking Number (OTN) is required only in an appeal in a criminal proceeding. It enables the Administrative Office of the Pennsylvania Courts to collect and forward to the Pennsylvania State Police information pertaining to the disposition of all criminal cases as provided by the Criminal History Record Information Act, 18 Pa.C.S. § 9101 *et seq.*

The notice of appeal must include a statement that the order appealed from has been entered on the docket. The appellant does not need to certify that the order has been reduced to judgment. This omission does not eliminate the requirement of reducing an order to judgment before there is a final appealable order where required by applicable practice or case law.

With respect to paragraph (e), in *Commonwealth v. Dugger*, 486 A.2d 382, 386 (Pa. 1985), the Supreme Court held that the Commonwealth's certification that an order will terminate or substantially handicap the prosecution is not subject to review as a prerequisite to the Superior Court's review of the merits of the appeal. The principle in *Dugger* has been incorporated in and superseded by Pa.R.A.P. 311(d). *Commonwealth v. Dixon*, 907 A.2d 468, 471 n.8 (Pa. 2006). Thus, the need for a detailed analysis of the effect of the order, formerly necessarily a part of the Commonwealth's appellate brief, has been eliminated.

A party filing a cross-appeal should identify it as a cross-appeal in the notice of appeal to assure that the prothonotary will process the cross-appeal with the initial appeal. *See also* Pa.R.A.P. 2113, 2136, and 2185 regarding briefs in cross-appeals and Pa.R.A.P. 2322 regarding oral argument in multiple appeals

Adopted Nov. 5, 1975, effective July 1, 1976. Amended June 23, 1976, effective July 1, 1976; Dec. 11, 1978, effective Dec. 30, 1978; April 26, 1982, effective retroactive to July 15, 1981; Dec. 16, 1983, effective Jan. 1, 1984; Dec. 10, 1986, effective Jan. 31, 1987; July 7, 1997, effective in 60 days; Oct. 18, 2002, effective Dec. 2, 2002; Jan. 13, 2009, effective as to appeals filed 60 days or more after adoption; Dec. 14, 2015, effective April 1, 2016.

Explanatory Comment—2002

See Comment following Pa.R.A.P., Rule 511.

Rule 905. Filing of Notice of Appeal.

(a) *Filing with clerk.*

(1) Two copies of the notice of appeal, the order for transcript, if any, and the proof of service required by Rule 906 (service of notice of appeal), shall be filed with the clerk of the trial court. If the appeal is to the Supreme Court, the jurisdictional statement required by Rule 909 shall also be filed with the clerk of the trial court.

(2) If the appeal is a children's fast track appeal, the concise statement of errors complained of on appeal as described in Rule 1925(a)(2) shall be filed with the notice of appeal and served in accordance with Rule 1925(b)(1).

(3) Upon receipt of the notice of appeal the clerk shall immediately stamp it with the date of receipt, and that date shall constitute the date when the appeal was taken, which date shall be shown on the docket.

(4) If a notice of appeal is mistakenly filed in an appellate court, or is otherwise filed in an incorrect office within the unified judicial system, the clerk shall immediately stamp it with the date of receipt and transmit it to the clerk of the court which entered the order appealed from, and upon payment of an additional filing fee the notice of appeal shall be deemed filed in the trial court on the date originally filed.

(5) A notice of appeal filed after the announcement of a determination but before the entry of an appealable order shall be treated as filed after such entry and on the day thereof.

(b) *Transmission to appellate court.* The clerk shall immediately transmit to the prothonotary of the appellate court named in the notice of appeal a copy of the notice of appeal showing the date of receipt, the related proof of service and a receipt showing collection of any docketing fee in the appellate court required under Subdivision (c). If the appeal is a children's fast track appeal, the clerk shall stamp the notice of appeal with a "Children's Fast Track" designation in red ink, advising the appellate court that the appeal is a children's fast track appeal and shall transmit to the prothonotary of the appellate court named in the notice of appeal the concise statement of errors complained of on appeal required by Subdivision (a)(2) of this rule. The clerk shall also transmit with such papers:

1. a copy of any order for transcript;

2. a copy of any verified statement, application or other document filed under Rule 551 through Rule 561 relating to *in forma pauperis;* and

3. if the appeal is to the Supreme Court, the jurisdictional statement required by Rule 909.

(c) *Fees.* The appellant upon filing the notice of appeal shall pay any fees therefor (including docketing fees in the appellate court) prescribed by Chapter 27 (fees and costs in appellate courts and on appeal).

> **Official Note:** Insofar as the clerk or prothonotary of the lower court is concerned, the notice of appeal is for all intents and purposes a writ in the nature of certiorari in the usual form issued out of the appellate court named therein and returnable thereto within the time prescribed by Chapter 19 (preparation and transmission of record and related matters).
>
> To preserve a mailing date as the filing date for an appeal as of right from an order of the Commonwealth Court, see Rule 1101(b).

* * * * *

CHAPTER 11
APPEALS FROM COMMONWEALTH COURT AND SUPERIOR COURT
PETITION FOR ALLOWANCE OF APPEAL

Rule 1112. Appeals by Allowance.

(a) *General rule.*—An appeal may be taken by allowance under 42 Pa.C.S. § 724(a) (allowance of appeals from Superior and Commonwealth Courts) from any final order of the Commonwealth Court, not appealable under Rule 1101 (appeals as of right from the Commonwealth Court), or from any final order of the Superior Court.

(b) *Definition. Final order.*—A final order of the Superior Court or Commonwealth Court is any order that concludes an appeal, including an order that remands an appeal, in whole or in part, unless the appellate court remands and retains jurisdiction.

(c) *Petition for allowance of appeal.—*

(1) Allowance of an appeal from a final order of the Superior Court or the Commonwealth Court may be sought by filing a petition for allowance of appeal with the Prothonotary of the Supreme Court within the time allowed by Rule 1113 (time for petitioning for allowance of appeal), with proof of service on all other parties to the matter in the appellate court below.

(2) If the petition for allowance of appeal is transmitted to the Prothonotary of the Supreme Court by means of first class, express, or priority United States Postal Service mail, the petition shall be deemed received by the

prothonotary for the purposes of Rule 121(a) (filing) on the date deposited in the United States mail, as shown on a United States Postal Service Form 3817 Certificate of Mailing or other similar United States Postal Service form from which the date of deposit can be verified. The certificate of mailing or other similar Postal Service form from which the date of deposit can be verified shall be cancelled by the Postal Service, shall show the docket number of the matter in the appellate court below and shall be either enclosed with the petition or separately mailed to the prothonotary.

(3) Upon actual receipt of the petition for allowance of appeal the Prothonotary of the Supreme Court shall immediately stamp it with the date of actual receipt. That date, or the date of earlier deposit in the United States mail as prescribed in this subdivision, shall constitute the date when allowance of appeal was sought, which date shall be shown on the docket. The Prothonotary of the Supreme Court shall immediately note the Supreme Court docket number upon the petition for allowance of appeal and give written notice of the docket number assignment in person or by first class mail to the prothonotary of the appellate court below who shall note on the docket that a petition for allowance of appeal has been filed to the petitioner and to the other persons named in the proof of service accompanying the petition.

(4) In a children's fast track appeal, the Prothonotary of the Supreme Court shall stamp the petition for allowance of appeal with a "Children's Fast Track" designation in red ink, advising the Supreme Court that the petition for allowance of appeal is a children's fast track appeal.

(d) *Reproduced record.*—One copy of the reproduced record, if any, in the appellate court below shall be lodged with the Prothonotary of the Supreme Court at the time the petition for allowance of appeal is filed therein. A party filing a cross-petition for allowance of appeal from the same order need not lodge any reproduced record in addition to that lodged by petitioner.

(e) *Fee.*—The petitioner upon filing the petition for allowance of appeal shall pay any fee therefor prescribed by Chapter 27 (fees and costs in appellate courts and on appeal).

(f) *Entry of appearance.*—Upon the filing of the petition for allowance of appeal the Prothonotary of the Supreme Court shall note on the record as counsel for the petitioner the name of his or her counsel, if any, set forth in or endorsed upon the petition for allowance of appeal, and, as counsel for other parties, counsel, if any, named in the proof of service. The Prothonotary shall upon praecipe of any such counsel for other parties, filed at any time within 30 days after filing of the petition, strike off or correct the record of appearance. Thereafter a counsel's appearance for a party may not be withdrawn without leave of court unless another lawyer has entered or simultaneously enters an appearance for the party.

Official Note: Based on 42 Pa.C.S. § 724(a) (allowance of appeals from Superior and Commonwealth Courts). The notation on the docket by the Prothonotary of the Superior Court or Commonwealth Court of the filing of a petition for allowance of appeal renders universal the rule that the appeal status of any order may be discovered by examining the docket of the court in which it was entered.

The United States Postal Service form may be in substantially the following form:

* * * * *

The transmittal should be taken *unsealed* to the Post Office, the Form 3817 Certificate of Mailing or other similar United States Postal Service form from which the date of deposit can be verified should be obtained, cancelled, and attached to the petition, and the envelope should only then be sealed. Alternately, the cancelled Form 3817 or other similar United States Postal Service form from which the date of deposit can be verified can be submitted to the prothonotary under separate cover with clear identification of the filing to which it relates.

It is recommended that the petitioner obtain a duplicate copy of the Form 3817 or other similar United States Postal Service form from which the date of deposit can be verified as evidence of mailing. Since the Post Office is technically the filing office for the purpose of this rule a petition which was mailed in accordance with this rule and which is subsequently lost in the mail will nevertheless toll the time for petitioning for allowance of appeal. However, counsel will be expected to follow up on a mail filing by telephone inquiry to the appellate prothonotary where written notice of the docket number assignment is not received in due course.

With regard to subdivision (f) and withdrawal of appearance without leave of the appellate court, counsel may nonetheless be subject to trial court supervision pursuant to Pa.R.Crim.P. 904 (Entry of Appearance and Appointment of Counsel; *In Forma Pauperis*).

With respect to appearances by new counsel following the initial docketing of appearances pursuant to Subdivision (f) of this rule, please note the requirements of Rule 120.

Rule 1113. Time for Petitioning for Allowance of Appeal.

(a) *General rule.*—Except as otherwise prescribed by this rule, a petition for allowance of appeal shall be filed with the Prothonotary of the Supreme Court within 30 days after the entry of the order of the Superior Court or the Commonwealth Court sought to be reviewed.

(1) If a timely application or reargument is filed in the Superior Court or Commonwealth Court by any party, the time for filing a petition for allowance of appeal for all parties shall run from the entry of the order denying reargument or from the entry of the decision on reargument, whether or not that decision amounts to a reaffirmation of the prior decision.

(2) Unless the Superior Court or the Commonwealth Court acts on the application for reargument within 60 days after it is filed the court shall no longer consider the application, it shall be deemed to have been denied and the prothonotary of the appellate court shall forthwith enter an order denying the application and shall immediately give written notice in person or by first class mail of entry of the order denying the application to each party who has appeared in the appellate court. A petition for allowance of appeal filed before the disposition of such an application for reargument shall have no effect. A new petition for allowance of appeal must be filed within the prescribed time measured from the entry of the order denying or otherwise disposing of such an application for reargument.

(3) In a children's fast track appeal, unless the Superior Court acts on the application for reargument within 45 days after it is filed the court shall no longer consider the application, it shall be deemed to have been denied and the Prothonotary of the Superior Court shall forthwith enter an order denying the application and shall immediately give written notice in person or by first class mail of entry of the order denying the application to each party who has appeared in the appellate court. A petition for allowance of appeal filed before the disposition of such an application for reargument shall have no effect. A new petition for allowance of appeal must be filed within the prescribed time measured from the entry of the order denying or otherwise disposing of such an application for reargument.

(b) *Cross petitions.*—Except as otherwise prescribed in Subdivision (c) of this rule, if a timely petition for allowance of appeal is filed by a party, any other party may file a petition for allowance of appeal within 14 days of the date on which the first petition for allowance of appeal was filed, or within the time otherwise prescribed by this rule, whichever period last expires.

(c) *Special provisions.*—Notwithstanding any other provision of this rule, a petition for allowance of appeal from an order in any matter arising under any of the following shall be filed within ten days after the entry of the order sought to be reviewed:

(1) Pennsylvania Election Code.

(2) Local Government Unit Debt Act or any similar statute relating to the authorization of public debt.

Official Note: See note to Rule 903 (time for appeal).

A party filing a cross petition for allowance of appeal pursuant to Subdivision (b) should identify it as a cross petition to assure that the prothonotary will process the cross petition with the initial petition. See also Rule 511 (cross appeals), Rule 2136 (Briefs in Cases Involving Cross Appeals) and Rule 2322 (Cross and Separate Appeals).

Rule 1116. Answer to the Petition for Allowance of Appeal.

(a) *General rule.* Except as otherwise prescribed by this rule, within 14 days after service of a petition for allowance of appeal an adverse party may file an answer. The answer shall be deemed filed on the date of mailing if first class, express, or priority United States Postal Service mail is utilized. The answer need not be set forth in numbered paragraphs in the manner of a pleading, shall set forth any procedural, substantive or other argument or ground why the order involved should not be reviewed by the Supreme Court, and shall comply with Pa.R.A.P. 1115(a).7. No separate motion to dismiss a petition for allowance of appeal will be received. A party entitled to file an answer under this rule who does not intend to do so shall, within the time fixed by these rules for filing an answer, file a letter stating that an answer to the petition for allowance of appeal will not be filed. The failure to file an answer will not be construed as concurrence in the request for allowance of appeal.

(b) *Children's fast track appeals.* In a children's fast track appeal, within 10 days after service of a petition for allowance of appeal, an adverse party may file an answer.

(c) *Length.* An answer to a petition for allowance of appeal shall not exceed 9,000 words. An answer that does not exceed 20 pages when produced by a word processor or typewriter shall be deemed to meet the 9,000 word limit. In all other cases, the attorney or the unrepresented filing party shall include a certification that the answer complies with the word count limit. The certificate may be based on the word count of the word processing system used to prepare the answer.

(d) *Supplementary matter.* The cover of the answer, pages containing the table of contents, table of citations, proof of service, signature block and anything appended to the answer shall not count against the word count limitations of this rule.

(e) *Certificate of compliance with Case Records Public Access Policy of the Unified Judicial System of Pennsylvania.* An answer to a petition for allowance of appeal shall contain the certificate of compliance required by Pa.R.A.P. 127.

Note: This rule and Pa.R.A.P. 1115 contemplate that the petition and answer will address themselves to the heart of the issue, such as whether the Supreme Court ought to exercise its discretion to allow an appeal, without the need to comply with the formalistic pattern of numbered averments in the petition and correspondingly numbered admissions and denials in the response. While such a formalistic format is appropriate when factual issues are being framed in a trial court (as in the petition for review under Chapter 15) such a format interferes with the clear narrative exposition necessary to outline succinctly the case for the Supreme Court in the allocatur context.

Adopted Nov. 5, 1975, effective July 1, 1976. Amended June 23, 1976, effective July 1, 1976; Sept. 10, 2008, effective Dec. 1, 2008; Jan. 13, 2009, effective as to appeals filed 60 days or more after adoption; Dec. 30, 2014, effective in 60 days; Jan. 5, 2018, effective Jan. 6, 2018; June 1, 2018, eff. July 1, 2018.

Rule 1123. Denial of Appeal; Reconsideration.

(a) *Denial.* If the petition for allowance of appeal is denied the Prothonotary of the Supreme Court shall immediately give written notice in person or by first class mail of the entry of the order denying the appeal to each party who has appeared in the Supreme Court. After the expiration of the time allowed by paragraph (b) of this rule for the filing of an application for reconsideration of denial of a petition for allowance of appeal, if no application for reconsideration is filed, the Prothonotary of the Supreme Court shall notify the prothonotary of the appellate court below of the denial of the petition.

(b) *Reconsideration.* Applications for reconsideration of denial of allowance of appeal are not favored and will be considered only in the most extraordinary circumstances. An application for reconsideration of denial of a petition for allowance of appeal shall be filed with the Prothonotary of the Supreme Court within fourteen days after entry of the order denying the petition for allowance of appeal. In a children's fast track appeal, the application for reconsideration of denial of a petition for allowance of appeal shall be filed with the Prothonotary of the Supreme Court within 7 days after entry of the order denying the petition for allowance of appeal. Any application filed under this paragraph must comport with the following:

(1) Briefly and distinctly state grounds which are confined to intervening circumstances of substantial or controlling effect.

(2) Be supported by a certificate of counsel to the effect that it is presented in good faith and not for delay. Counsel must also certify that the application is restricted to the grounds specified under subparagraph (b)(1).

(3) Contain the certificate of compliance required by Pa.R.A.P. 127.

No answer to an application for reconsideration will be received unless requested by the Supreme Court. Second or subsequent applications for reconsideration, and applications for reconsideration which are out of time under this rule, will not be received.

(c) *Manner of filing.* If the application for reconsideration is transmitted to the prothonotary of the appellate court by means of first class, express, or priority United States Postal Service mail, the application shall be deemed received by the prothonotary for the purposes of Pa.R.A.P. 121(a) (filing) on the date deposited in the United States mail as shown on a United States

Postal Service Form 3817 Certificate of Mailing, or other similar United States Postal Service form from which the date of deposit can be verified. The certificate of mailing or other similar Postal Service form from which the date of deposit can be verified shall be cancelled by the Postal Service, shall show the docket number of the matter in the court in which reconsideration is sought, and shall be enclosed with the application or separately mailed to the prothonotary. Upon actual receipt of the application, the prothonotary shall immediately stamp it with the date of actual receipt. That date, or the date of earlier deposit in the United States mail as prescribed in this paragraph, shall constitute the date when application was sought, which date shall be shown on the docket.

Adopted Nov. 5, 1975, effective July 1, 1976. Amended May 16, 1996, effective July 1, 1996; Sept. 10, 2008, effective Dec. 1, 2008; Jan. 13, 2009, effective as to appeals filed 60 days or more after adoption; Jan. 5, 2018, effective Jan. 6, 2018.

CHAPTER 19
PREPARATION AND TRANSMISSION OF RECORD AND RELATED MATTERS
RECORD ON APPEAL FROM LOWER COURT

Rule 1925. Opinion in Support of Order.

(a) *Opinion in support of order.*

(1) *General rule.*—Except as otherwise prescribed by this rule, upon receipt of the notice of appeal, the judge who entered the order giving rise to the notice of appeal, if the reasons for the order do not already appear of record, shall forthwith file of record at least a brief opinion of the reasons for the order, or for the rulings or other errors complained of, or shall specify in writing the place in the record where such reasons may be found.

If the case appealed involves a ruling issued by a judge who was not the judge entering the order giving rise to the notice of appeal, the judge entering the order giving rise to the notice of appeal may request that the judge who made the earlier ruling provide an opinion to be filed in accordance with the standards above to explain the reasons for that ruling.

(2) *Children's fast track appeals.*—In a children's fast track appeal:

(i) The concise statement of errors complained of on appeal shall be filed and served with the notice of appeal required by Rule 905. See Pa. R.A.P. 905(a)(2).

(ii) Upon receipt of the notice of appeal and the concise statement of errors complained of on appeal required by Rule 905(a)(2), the judge who entered the order giving rise to the notice of appeal, if the reasons for the order do not already appear of record, shall within 30 days file of record at least a brief opinion of the reasons for the order, or for the rulings or other errors complained of, which may, but need not, refer to the transcript of the proceedings.

(3) *Appeals arising under the Pennsylvania Code of Military Justice.*—In an appeal arising under the Pennsylvania Code of Military Justice, the concise statement of errors complained of on appeal shall be filed and served with the notice of appeal. See Pa.R.A.P. 4004(b).

(b) *Direction to file statement of errors complained of on appeal; instructions to the appellant and the trial court.*—If the judge entering the order giving rise to the notice of appeal ("judge") desires clarification of the errors complained of on appeal, the judge may enter an order directing the appellant to file of record in the trial court and serve on the judge a concise statement of the errors complained of on appeal ("Statement").

(1) *Filing and service.*—Appellant shall file of record the Statement and concurrently shall serve the judge. Filing of record and service on the judge shall be in person or by mail as provided in Pa.R.A.P. 121(a) and shall be complete on mailing if appellant obtains a United States Postal Service Form 3817, Certificate of Mailing, or other similar United States Postal Service form from which the date of deposit can be verified in compliance with the requirements set forth in Pa.R.A.P. 1112(c). Service on parties shall be concurrent with filing and shall be by any means of service specified under Pa.R.A.P. 121(c).

(2) *Time for filing and service.*—The judge shall allow the appellant at least 21 days from the date of the order's entry on the docket for the filing and service of the Statement. Upon application of the appellant and for good cause shown, the judge may enlarge the time period initially specified or permit an amended or supplemental Statement to be filed. Good cause includes, but is not limited to, delay in the production of a transcript necessary to develop the Statement so long as the delay is not attributable to a lack of diligence in ordering or paying for such transcript by the party or counsel on appeal. In extraordinary circumstances, the judge may allow for the filing of a Statement or amended or supplemental Statement nunc pro tunc.

(3) *Contents of order.*—The judge's order directing the filing and service of a Statement shall specify:

(i) the number of days after the date of entry of the judge's order within which the appellant must file and serve the Statement;

(ii) that the Statement shall be filed of record;

(iii) that the Statement shall be served on the judge pursuant to paragraph (b)(1);

(iv) that any issue not properly included in the Statement timely filed and served pursuant to subdivision (b) shall be deemed waived.

(4) *Requirements; waiver.*

(i) The Statement shall set forth only those rulings or errors that the appellant intends to challenge.

(ii) The Statement shall concisely identify each ruling or error that the appellant intends to challenge with sufficient detail to identify all pertinent issues for the judge. The judge shall not require the citation to authorities; however, appellant may choose to include pertinent authorities in the Statement.

(iii) The judge shall not require appellant or appellee to file a brief, memorandum of law, or response as part of or in conjunction with the Statement.

(iv) The Statement should not be redundant or provide lengthy explanations as to any error. Where non-redundant, non-frivolous issues are set forth in an appropriately concise manner, the number of errors raised will not alone be grounds for finding waiver.

(v) Each error identified in the Statement will be deemed to include every subsidiary issue contained therein which was raised in the trial

Rule 1925

court; this provision does not in any way limit the obligation of a criminal appellant to delineate clearly the scope of claimed constitutional errors on appeal.

(vi) If the appellant in a civil case cannot readily discern the basis for the judge's decision, the appellant shall preface the Statement with an explanation as to why the Statement has identified the errors in only general terms. In such a case, the generality of the Statement will not be grounds for finding waiver.

(vii) Issues not included in the Statement and/or not raised in accordance with the provisions of this paragraph (b)(4) are waived.

(c) *Remand.*

(1) An appellate court may remand in either a civil or criminal case for a determination as to whether a Statement had been filed and/or served or timely filed and/or served.

(2) Upon application of the appellant and for good cause shown, an appellate court may remand in a civil case for the filing nunc pro tunc of a Statement or for amendment or supplementation of a timely filed and served Statement and for a concurrent supplemental opinion.

(3) If an appellant in a criminal case was ordered to file a Statement and failed to do so, such that the appellate court is convinced that counsel has been per se ineffective, the appellate court shall remand for the filing of a Statement nunc pro tunc and for the preparation and filing of an opinion by the judge.

(4) In a criminal case, counsel may file of record and serve on the judge a statement of intent to file an Anders/McClendon brief in lieu of filing a Statement. If, upon review of the Anders/McClendon brief, the appellate court believes that there are arguably meritorious issues for review, those issues will not be waived; instead, the appellate court may remand for the filing of a Statement, a supplemental opinion pursuant to Rule 1925(a), or both. Upon remand, the trial court may, but is not required to, replace appellant's counsel.

(d) *Opinions in matters on petition for allowance of appeal.*—Upon receipt of notice of the filing of a petition for allowance of appeal under Rule 1112(c) (appeals by allowance), the appellate court below which entered the order sought to be reviewed, if the reasons for the order do not already appear of record, shall forthwith file of record at least a brief statement, in the form of an opinion, of the reasons for the order.

Note: *Subdivision (a)* The 2007 amendments clarify that a judge whose order gave rise to the notice of appeal may ask a prior judge who made a ruling in question for the reasons for that judge's decision. In such cases, more than one judge may issue separate Rule 1925(a) opinions for a single case. It may be particularly important for a judge to author a separate opinion if credibility was at issue in the pretrial ruling in question. See, e.g., *Commonwealth v. Yogel*, 307 Pa. Super. 241, 243-44, 453 A.2d 15, 16 (1982). At the same time, the basis for some pre-trial rulings will be clear from the order and/or opinion issued by the judge at the time the ruling was made, and there will then be no reason to seek a separate opinion from that judge under this rule. See, e.g., Pa.R. Crim.P. 581(I). Likewise, there will be times when the prior judge may explain the ruling to the judge whose order has given rise to the notice of appeal in sufficient detail that there will be only one opinion under Rule 1925(a), even though there are multiple rulings at issue. The time period for transmission of the record is specified in Pa.R.A.P. 1931, and that rule was concurrently amended to expand the time period for the preparation of the opinion and transmission of the record.

Rule 1925   **Pa. R.App.P.**

Subdivision (b) This subdivision permits the judge whose order gave rise to the notice of appeal ("judge") to ask for a statement of errors complained of on appeal ("Statement") if the record is inadequate and the judge needs to clarify the errors complained of. The term "errors" is meant to encourage appellants to use the Statement as an opportunity to winnow the issues, recognizing that they will ultimately need to be refined to a statement that will comply with the requirements of Pa.R.A.P. 2116. Nonetheless, the term "errors" is intended in this context to be expansive, and it encompasses all of the reasons the trial court should not have reached its decision or judgment, including, for example, those that may not have been decisions of the judge, such as challenges to jurisdiction.

Paragraph (b)(1) This paragraph maintains the requirement that the Statement be both filed of record in the trial court and served on the judge. Service on the judge may be accomplished by mail or by personal service. The date of mailing will be considered the date of filing and of service upon the judge only if counsel obtains a United States Postal Service form from which the date of mailing can be verified, as specified in Pa.R.A.P. 1112(c). Counsel is advised to retain date-stamped copies of the postal forms (or pleadings if served by hand), in case questions arise later as to whether the Statement was timely filed or served on the judge.

Paragraph (b)(2) This paragraph extends the time period for drafting the Statement from 14 days to at least 21 days, with the trial court permitted to enlarge the time period or to allow the filing of an amended or supplemental Statement upon good cause shown. In *Commonwealth v. Mitchell*, 588 Pa. 19, 41, 902 A.2d 430, 444 (2006), the Court expressly observed that a Statement filed "after several extensions of time" was timely. An enlargement of time upon timely application might be warranted if, for example, there was a serious delay in the transcription of the notes of testimony or in the delivery of the order to appellate counsel. A trial court should enlarge the time or allow for an amended or supplemental Statement when new counsel is retained or appointed. A supplemental Statement may also be appropriate when the ruling challenged was so non-specific—e.g., "Motion Denied"—that counsel could not be sufficiently definite in the initial Statement.

In general, nunc pro tunc relief is allowed only when there has been a breakdown in the process constituting extraordinary circumstances. See, e.g., *In re Canvass of Absentee Ballots of Nov. 4, 2003 Gen. Election*, 577 Pa. 231, 248-49, 843 A.2d 1223, 1234 (2004) ("We have held that fraud or the wrongful or negligent act of a court official may be a proper reason for holding that a statutory appeal period does not run and that the wrong may be corrected by means of a petition filed nunc pro tunc.") Courts have also allowed nunc pro tunc relief when "non-negligent circumstances, either as they relate to appellant or his counsel" occasion delay. *McKeown v. Bailey*, 731 A.2d 628, 630 (Pa. Super. 1999). However, even when there is a breakdown in the process, the appellant must attempt to remedy it within a "very short duration" of time. Id.; *Amicone v. Rok*, 839 A.2d 1109, 1113 (Pa. Super. 2003) (recognizing a breakdown in process, but finding the delay too long to justify nunc pro tunc relief).

Paragraph (b)(3) This paragraph specifies what the judge must advise appellants when ordering a Statement.

Paragraph (b)(4) This paragraph sets forth the parameters for the Statement and explains what constitutes waiver. It should help counsel to comply with the concise-yet-sufficiently-detailed requirement and avoid waiver under either *Lineberger v. Wyeth*, 894 A.2d 141, 148-49 (Pa. Super. 2006) or *Kanter v. Epstein*, 866 A.2d 394, 400-03 (Pa. Super. 2004), allowance of appeal denied, 584 Pa. 678, 880 A.2d 1239 (2005), cert. denied sub nom. *Spector Gadon & Rosen, P.C. v. Kanter*, 546 U.S. 1092 (2006). The paragraph explains that the Statement should be sufficiently specific to allow the judge to draft the opinion required under 1925(a), and it provides that the number of issues alone will not constitute waiver—so long as the issues set forth are non-redundant and non-frivolous. It allows appellants to rely on the fact that subsidiary issues will be deemed included if the overarching issue is identified and if all of the issues have been properly preserved in the trial court. This provision has been taken

Rule 1925

from the United States Supreme Court rules. See Sup. Ct. R. 14(1). This paragraph does not in any way excuse the responsibility of an appellant who is raising claims of constitutional error to raise those claims with the requisite degree of specificity. This paragraph also allows—but does not require—an appellant to state the authority upon which the appellant challenges the ruling in question, but it expressly recognizes that a Statement is not a brief and that an appellant shall not file a brief with the Statement. This paragraph also recognizes that there may be times that a civil appellant cannot be specific in the Statement because of the non-specificity of the ruling complained of on appeal. In such instances, civil appellants may seek leave to file a supplemental Statement to clarify their position in response to the judge's more specific Rule 1925(a) opinion.

Subdivision (c) The appellate courts have the right under the Judicial Code to "affirm, modify, vacate, set aside or reverse any order brought before it for review, and may remand the matter and direct the entry of such appropriate order, or require such further proceedings to be had as may be just under the circumstances." 42 Pa.C.S. § 706. The following additions to the rule are based upon this statutory authorization.

Paragraph (c)(1) This paragraph applies to both civil and criminal cases and allows an appellate court to seek additional information—whether by supplementation of the record or additional briefing—if it is not apparent whether an initial or supplemental Statement was filed and/or served or timely filed and/or served.

Paragraph (c)(2) This paragraph allows an appellate court to remand a civil case to allow an initial, amended, or supplemental Statement and/or a supplemental opinion. See also 42 Pa.C.S. § 706.

Paragraph (c)(3) This paragraph allows an appellate court to remand in criminal cases only when the appellant has completely failed to respond to an order to file a Statement. It is thus narrower than (c)(2), above. Prior to these amendments of this rule, the appeal was quashed if no timely Statement was filed or served; however, because the failure to file and serve a timely Statement is a failure to perfect the appeal, it is presumptively prejudicial and "clear" ineffectiveness. See, e.g., *Commonwealth v. Halley*, 582 Pa. 164, 172, 870 A.2d 795, 801 (2005); *Commonwealth v. West*, 883 A.2d 654, 657 (Pa. Super. 2005). Direct appeal rights have typically been restored through a post-conviction relief process, but when the ineffectiveness is apparent and per se, the court in West recognized that the more effective way to resolve such per se ineffectiveness is to remand for the filing of a Statement and opinion. See *West*, 883 A.2d at 657. The procedure set forth in West is codified in paragraph (c)(3). As the West court recognized, this rationale does not apply when waiver occurs due to the improper filing of a Statement. In such circumstances, relief may occur only through the post-conviction relief process and only upon demonstration by the appellant that, but for the deficiency of counsel, it was reasonably probable that the appeal would have been successful. An appellant must be able to identify per se ineffectiveness to secure a remand under this section, and any appellant who is able to demonstrate per se ineffectiveness is entitled to a remand. Accordingly, this paragraph does not raise the concerns addressed in *Johnson v. Mississippi*, 486 U.S. 578, 588-89 (1988) (observing that where a rule has not been consistently or regularly applied, it is not—under federal law—an adequate and independent state ground for affirming petitioner's conviction.)

Paragraph (c)(4) This paragraph clarifies the special expectations and duties of a criminal lawyer. Even lawyers seeking to withdraw pursuant to the procedures set forth in *Anders v. California*, 386 U.S. 738 (1967) and *Commonwealth v. McClendon*, 495 Pa. 467, 434 A.2d 1185 (1981) are obligated to comply with all rules, including the filing of a Statement. See *Commonwealth v. Myers*, 897 A.2d 493, 494-96 (Pa. Super. 2006); *Commonwealth v. Ladamus*, 896 A.2d 592, 594 (Pa. Super. 2006). However, because a lawyer will not file an *Anders/McClendon* brief without concluding that there are no non-frivolous issues to raise on appeal, this amendment allows a lawyer to file, in lieu of a Statement, a representation that no errors have been raised because the lawyer is (or intends to be) seeking to withdraw under *Anders/McClendon*. At that point, the appellate court will reverse or remand for a supplemental Statement and/or opinion if it finds potentially non-frivolous issues during its constitutionally required review of the record.

Subdivision (d) was formerly (c). The text has not been revised, except to update the reference to Pa.R.A.P. 1112(c).

The 2007 amendments attempt to address the concerns of the bar raised by cases in which courts found waiver: (a) because the Statement was too vague; or (b) because the Statement was so repetitive and voluminous that it did not enable the judge to focus on the issues likely to be raised on appeal. See, e.g., *Lineberger v. Wyeth*, 894 A.2d 141, 148-49 (Pa. Super. 2006); *Kanter v. Epstein*, 866 A.2d 394, 400-03 (Pa. Super. 2004), allowance of appeal denied, 584 Pa. 678, 880 A.2d 1239 (2005), cert. denied sub nom. *Spector Gadon & Rosen, P.C. v. Kanter*, 546 U.S. 1092 (2006). Courts have also cautioned, however, "against being too quick to find waiver, claiming that Rule 1925(b) statements are either too vague or not specific enough." *Astorino v. New Jersey Transit Corp.*, 912 A.2d 308, 309 (Pa. Super. 2006).

While conciseness and vagueness are very case-specific inquiries, certain observations may be helpful. First, the Statement is only the first step in framing the issues to be raised on appeal, and the requirements of Pa.R.A.P. 2116 are even more stringent. Thus, the Statement should be viewed as an initial winnowing. Second, when appellate courts have been critical of sparse or vague Statements, they have not criticized the number of issues raised but the paucity of useful information contained in the Statement. Neither the number of issues raised nor the length of the Statement alone is enough to find that a Statement is vague or non-concise enough to constitute waiver. See *Astorino v. New Jersey Transit Corp.*, 912 A.2d 308, 309 (Pa. Super. 2006). The more carefully the appellant frames the Statement, the more likely it will be that the judge will be able to articulate the rationale underlying the decision and provide a basis for counsel to determine the advisability of appealing that issue. Thus, counsel should begin the winnowing process when preparing the Statement and should articulate specific rulings with which the appellant takes issue and why. Nothing in the rule requires an appellant to articulate the arguments within a Statement. It is enough for an appellant—except where constitutional error must be raised with greater specificity—to have identified the rulings and issues that comprise the putative trial court errors.

Adopted Nov. 5, 1975, effective July 1, 1976. Amended May 16, 1979, effective 120 days after June 2, 1979; Dec. 30, 1987, effective Jan. 16, 1988; May 10, 2007, effective 60 days after adoption; Jan. 13, 2009, effective as to appeals filed 60 days or more after adoption; Nov. 15, 2013, effective in 30 days; March 18, 2014, effective April 18, 2014.

Rule 1931. Transmission of the Record.

(a) *Time for transmission.*

(1) *General rule.*—Except as otherwise prescribed by this rule, the record on appeal, including the transcript and exhibits necessary for the determination of the appeal, shall be transmitted to the appellate court within 60 days after the filing of the notice of appeal. If an appeal has been allowed or if permission to appeal has been granted, the record shall be transmitted as provided by Pa.R.A.P. 1122 (allowance of appeal and transmission of record) or by Pa.R.A.P. 1322 (permission to appeal and transmission of record), as the case may be. The appellate court may shorten or extend the time prescribed by this paragraph for a class or classes of cases.

(2) *Children's fast track appeals.*—In a children's fast track appeal, the record on appeal, including the transcript and exhibits necessary for the determination of the appeal, shall be transmitted to the appellate court within 30 days after the filing of the notice of appeal. If an appeal has been allowed or if permission to appeal has been granted, the record shall

Rule 1931

be transmitted as provided by Pa.R.A.P. 1122 (allowance of appeal and transmission of record) or by Pa.R.A.P. 1322 (permission to appeal and transmission of record), as the case may be.

(b) *Duty of trial court.*—After a notice of appeal has been filed the judge who entered the order appealed from shall comply with Pa.R.A.P. 1925 (opinion in support of order), shall cause the official court reporter to comply with Pa.R.A.P. 1922 (transcription of notes of testimony) or shall otherwise settle a statement of the evidence or proceedings as prescribed by this chapter, and shall take any other action necessary to enable the clerk to assemble and transmit the record as prescribed by this rule.

(c) *Duty of clerk to transmit the record.*—When the record is complete for purposes of the appeal, the clerk of the lower court shall transmit it to the prothonotary of the appellate court. The clerk of the lower court shall number the documents comprising the record and shall transmit with the record a list of the documents correspondingly numbered and identified with sufficient specificity to allow the parties on appeal to identify each document and whether it is marked as confidential, so as to determine whether the record on appeal is complete. Any Confidential Information Forms and the "Unredacted Version" of any pleadings, documents, or other legal papers where a "Redacted Version" was also filed shall be separated either physically or electronically and transmitted to the appellate court. Whatever is confidential shall be labeled as such. If any case records or documents were sealed in the lower court, the list of documents comprising the record shall specifically identify such records or documents as having been sealed in the lower court. Documents of unusual bulk or weight and physical exhibits other than documents shall not be transmitted by the clerk unless he or she is directed to do so by a party or by the prothonotary of the appellate court. A party must make advance arrangements with the clerk for the transportation and receipt of exhibits of unusual bulk or weight. Transmission of the record is effected when the clerk of the lower court mails or otherwise forwards the record to the prothonotary of the appellate court. The clerk of the lower court shall indicate, by endorsement on the face of the record or otherwise, the date upon which the record is transmitted to the appellate court.

(d) *Service of the list of record documents.*—The clerk of the lower court shall, at the time of the transmittal of the record to the appellate court, mail a copy of the list of record documents to all counsel of record, or if unrepresented by counsel, to the parties at the address they have provided to the clerk. The clerk shall note on the docket the giving of such notice.

(e) *Multiple appeals.*—Where more than one appeal is taken from the same order, it shall be sufficient to transmit a single record, without duplication.

(f) *Inconsistency between list of record documents and documents actually transmitted.*—If the clerk of the lower court fails to transmit to the appellate court all of the documents identified in the list of record documents, such failure shall be deemed a breakdown in processes of the court. Any omission shall be corrected promptly pursuant to Pa.R.A.P. 1926 (correction or modification of the record) and shall not be the basis for any penalty against a party.

> **Note:** Pa.R.A.P. 1926 (correction or modification of the record) provides the means to resolve any disagreement between the parties as to what should be included in the record on appeal.

Adopted Nov. 5, 1975, effective July 1, 1976. Amended June 23, 1976, effective July 1, 1976; Dec. 11, 1978, effective Dec. 30, 1978; April 1, 2004, effective June 1, 2004; May 10,

2007, effective 60 days after adoption; Jan. 13, 2009, effective as to appeals filed 60 days or more after adoption; May 9, 2013, effective to appeals and petitions for review filed 30 days after adoption; Jan. 5, 2018, effective Jan. 6, 2018.

Explanatory Comment—1976

This provision makes clear that in multiple appeals only one original record need be transmitted.

Explanatory Comment—2004

It is hoped that the 2004 amendment to Rule 1931 will alleviate the potential waiver problem which results when counsel is unable to ascertain whether the entire record in a particular case has been transmitted to the appellate court for review. The rule change is intended to assist counsel in his or her responsibility under the Rules of Appellate Procedure to provide a full and complete record for effective appellate review. See *Commonwealth v. Williams*, 552 Pa. 451, 715 A.2d 1101 (1998) ("The fundamental tool for appellate review is the official record of what happened at trial, and appellate courts are limited to considering only those facts that have been duly certified in the record on appeal."); *Commonwealth v. Wint*, 1999 Pa.Super. 81, 730 A.2d 965 (1999) ("Appellant has the responsibility to make sure that the record forwarded to an appellate court contains those documents necessary to allow a complete and judicious assessment of the issues raised on appeal."). In order to facilitate counsel's ability to monitor the contents of the original record which is transmitted from the trial court to the appellate court, new subdivision (d) requires that a copy of the list of record documents be mailed to all counsel of record, or to the parties themselves if unrepresented, and that the giving of such notice be noted on the record. Thereafter, in the event that counsel discovers that anything material to either party has been omitted from the certified record, such omission can be corrected pursuant to Pa.R.A.P. 1926.

DISPOSITION WITHOUT REACHING THE MERITS

Rule 1972. Dispositions on Motion.

(a) Except as otherwise prescribed by this rule, subject to Rule 123 (applications for relief), any party may move:

(1) To transfer the record of the matter to another court because the matter should have been commenced in, or the appeal should have been taken to, such other court. See Rule 741 (waiver of objections to jurisdiction).

(2) To transfer to another appellate court under Rule 752 (transfers between Superior and Commonwealth Courts).

(3) To dismiss for want of jurisdiction in the unified judicial system of this Commonwealth.

(4) To dismiss for mootness.

(5) To dismiss for failure to preserve the question below, or because the right to an appeal has been otherwise waived. See Rule 302 (requisites for reviewable issue) and Rule 1551(a) (review of quasijudicial orders).

(6) To continue generally or to quash because the appellant is a fugitive.

(7) To quash for any other reason appearing on the record.

Any two or more of the grounds specified in this rule may be joined in the same motion. Unless otherwise ordered by the appellate court, a motion under this rule shall not relieve any party of the duty of filing his or her briefs and reproduced records within the time otherwise prescribed therefor. The court may grant or refuse the motion, in whole or in part; may postpone consideration thereof until argument of the case on the merits; or may make such other order as justice may require.

(b) In a children's fast track appeal, a dispositive motion filed under Paragraphs (a)(1), (a)(2), (a)(5), (a)(6) or (a)(7) of this rule shall be filed within 10 days of the filing of the statement of errors complained of on appeal required by Rule 905(a)(2), or within 10 days of the lower court's filing of a Rule 1925(a)(2) opinion, whichever period expires last, unless the basis for seeking to quash the appeal appears on the record subsequent to the time limit provided herein, or except upon application and for good cause shown.

Official Note: Based on former Supreme Court Rule 33 and former Superior Court Rule 25.

As to Paragraph (6) see, e.g. *Commonwealth v. Galloway,* 460 Pa. 309, 333 A.2d 741 (1975) (continuing generally), *Commonwealth v. Barron,* 237 Pa. Super. 369, 352 A.2d 84 (1975) (quashing). Rule 1933 (record for preliminary hearing in appellate court) makes clear the right of a moving party to obtain immediate transmission of as much of the record as may be necessary for the purposes of a motion under this rule. See Rule 123(c) (speaking applications).

CHAPTER 21
BRIEFS AND REPRODUCED RECORD
CONTENT OF BRIEFS

Rule 2113. Reply Brief.

(a) *General rule.*—In accordance with Pa.R.A.P. 2185(a) (time for serving and filing briefs), the appellant may file a brief in reply to matters raised by appellee's brief or in any *amicus curiae* brief and not previously addressed in appellant's brief. If the appellee has cross appealed, the appellee may file a similarly limited reply brief. A reply brief shall contain the certificates of compliance required by Pa.R.A.P. 127 and 2135(d).

(b) *Response to draft or plan.*—A reply brief may be filed as prescribed in Pa.R.A.P. 2134 (drafts or plans).

(c) *Other briefs.*—No further briefs may be filed except with leave of court.

Note: An appellant now has a general right to file a reply brief. The scope of the reply brief is limited, however, in that such brief may only address matters raised by appellee and not previously addressed in appellant's brief. No subsequent brief may be filed unless authorized by the court.

The length of a reply brief is set by Pa.R.A.P. 2135 (length of briefs). The due date for a reply brief is found in Pa.R.A.P. 2185(a) (service and filing of briefs).

Where there are cross appeals, the deemed or designated appellee may file a similarly limited reply brief addressing issues in the cross appeal. *See also* Pa.R.A.P. 2136 (briefs in cases involving cross appeals).

The 2011 amendment to paragraph (a) authorized an appellant to address in a reply brief matters raised in *amicus curiae* briefs. Before the 2011 amendment, the rule permitted the appellant to address in its reply brief only matters raised in the appellee's brief. The 2011 amendment did not change the requirement that the reply brief must not address matters previously addressed in the appellant's principal brief.

Rule 2154 — Pa. R.App.P.

Adopted Nov. 5, 1975, effective July 1, 1976. Amended June 23, 1976, effective July 1, 1976; Dec. 30, 1987, effective Jan. 16, 1988; Oct. 18, 2002, effective Dec. 2, 2002; Jan. 13, 2009, effective as to appeals filed 60 days or more after adoption; Oct. 3, 2011, effective in 30 days [Nov. 2, 2011]; Jan. 5, 2018, effective Jan. 6, 2018.

Explanatory Comment—2002

See Comment following Pa.R.A.P., Rule 511.

CONTENT OF REPRODUCED RECORD

Rule 2154. Designation of Contents of Reproduced Record.

(a) *General rule.*—Except when the appellant has elected to proceed under Subdivision (b) of this rule, or as otherwise provided in Subdivision (c) of this rule, the appellant shall not later than 30 days before the date fixed by or pursuant to Rule 2185 (service and filing of briefs) for the filing of his or her brief, serve and file a designation of the parts of the record which he or she intends to reproduce and a brief statement of issues which he or she intends to present for review. If the appellee deems it necessary to direct the particular attention of the court to parts of the record not designated by the appellant, the appellee shall, within ten days after receipt of the designations of the appellant, serve and file a designation of those parts. The appellant shall include in the reproduced record the parts thus designated. In designating parts of the record for reproduction, the parties shall have regard for the fact that the entire record is always available to the court for reference and examination and shall not engage in unnecessary designation.

(b) *Large records.*—If the appellant shall so elect, or if the appellate court has prescribed by rule of court for classes of matters or by order in specific matters, preparation of the reproduced record may be deferred until after the briefs have been served. Where the appellant desires thus to defer preparation of the reproduced record, the appellant shall, not later than the date on which his or her designations would otherwise be due under Subdivision (a), serve and file notice that he or she intends to proceed under this subdivision. The provisions of Subdivision (a) shall then apply, except that the designations referred to therein shall be made by each party at the time his or her brief is served, and a statement of the issues presented shall be unnecessary.

(c) *Children's fast track appeals.*

(1) In a children's fast track appeal, the appellant shall not later than 23 days before the date fixed by or pursuant to Rule 2185 (service and filing of briefs) for the filing of his or her brief, serve and file a designation of the parts of the record which he or she intends to reproduce and a brief statement of issues which he or she intends to present for review. If the appellee deems it necessary to direct the particular attention of the court to parts of the record not designated by the appellant, the appellee shall, within 7 days after receipt of the designations of the appellant, serve and file a designation of those parts. The appellant shall include in the reproduced record the parts thus designated. In designating parts of the record for reproduction, the parties shall have regard for the fact that the entire record is always available to the court for reference and examination and shall not engage in unnecessary designation.

(2) In a children's fast track appeal, the provisions of Subdivision (b) shall not apply.

Official Note: Based in part upon former Supreme Court Rule 44, former Superior Court Rule 36 and former Commonwealth Court Rule 88. The prior statutory practice required the lower court or the appellate court to resolve disputes concerning the contents of the reproduced record prior to reproduction. The statutory practice was generally recognized as wholly unsatisfactory and has been abandoned in favor of deferral of the issue to the taxation of costs phase. The uncertainty of the ultimate result on the merits provides each party with a significant incentive to be reasonable, thus creating a self-policing procedure.

Of course, parties proceeding under either procedure may by agreement omit the formal designations and accelerate the preparation of a reproduced record containing the material which the parties have agreed should be reproduced.

See Rule 2189 for procedure in cases involving the death penalty.

Explanatory Note—1979

The principal criticism of the new Appellate Rules has been the provisions for deferred preparation of the reproduced record, and the resulting procedure for the filing of advance copies of briefs (since the page citations to the reproduced record pages are not then available) followed by the later preparation and filing of definitive briefs with citations to the reproduced record pages. It has been argued that in the typical state court appeal the record is quite small, with the result that the pre-1976 practice of reproducing the record in conjunction with the preparation of appellant's definitive brief is entirely appropriate and would ordinarily be followed if the rules did not imply a preference for the deferred method. The Committee has been persuaded by these comments, and the rules have been redrafted to imply that the deferred method is a secondary method particularly appropriate for longer records.

FORM OF BRIEFS AND REPRODUCED RECORD

Rule 2172. Covers.

(a) *Briefs and Petitions for Allowance of or Permission to Appeal.*—On the front cover of the brief there shall appear the following:

(1) the name of the appellate court in which the matter is to be heard;

(2) the docket number of the case in the appellate court;

(3) the caption of the case in the appellate court, as prescribed by these rules;

(4) title of the filing, such as "Brief for Appellant" or "Brief for Respondent." If the reproduced record is bound with the brief, the title shall so indicate, for example "Brief for Appellant and Reproduced Record," or "Brief for Appellee and Supplemental Reproduced Record," such as the case may be;

(5) designation of the order appealed from such as "Appeal from the Order of" the court from which the appeal is taken, with the docket number therein. On appeals from the Superior Court or the Commonwealth Court its docket number shall be given, followed by a statement as to whether it affirmed, reversed or modified the order of the court or tribunal of first instance, giving also the name of the latter and the docket number, if any, of the case therein;

(6) the names of counsel, giving the office address and telephone number of the one upon whom it is desired notices shall be served.

(b) *Children's fast track appeals.*—In a children's fast track appeal, the front cover shall include a statement advising the appellate court that the appeal is a children's fast track appeal.

(c) *Reproduced record.*—If the reproduced record is bound separately, the cover thereof shall be the same as provided in Subdivision (a), except that in place of the information set forth in Paragraph (a)(4) of this rule there shall appear "Reproduced Record" or "Supplemental Reproduced Record", as the case may be.

(d) *Repetition in body of document.*—Unless expressly required by these rules, none of the material set forth in Subdivisions (a) through (c) shall be repeated in the brief or reproduced record.

(e) *Cover stock.*—The covers of all briefs and reproduced records must be so light in color as to permit writing in ink thereon to be easily read and so firm in texture that the ink will not run.

> **Official Note:** Based on former Supreme Court Rules 35C and 36, former Superior Court Rules 27C and 28, and former Commonwealth Court Rule 82, without change in substance except that Paragraph (a)(4) is clarified by eliminating the "Appeal of . . ." heading, which would not conform to the caption on the notice of appeal, and Subdivision (d) is extended to the Commonwealth Court.

FILING AND SERVICE

Rule 2185. Service and Filing of Briefs.

(a) *Time for serving and filing briefs.*

(1) *General rule.*— Except as otherwise provided by this rule, the appellant shall serve and file appellant's brief not later than the date fixed pursuant to Subdivision (b) of this rule, or within 40 days after the date on which the record is filed, if no other date is so fixed. The appellee shall serve and file appellee's brief within 30 days after service of appellant's brief and reproduced record if proceeding under Rule 2154(a). A party may serve and file a reply brief permitted by these rules within 14 days after service of the preceding brief but, except for good cause shown, a reply brief must be served and filed so as to be received at least three days before argument. In cross appeals, the second brief of the deemed or designated appellant shall be served and filed within 30 days of service of the deemed or designated appellee's first brief. Except as prescribed by Rule 2187(b) (advance text of briefs), each brief shall be filed not later than the last day fixed by or pursuant to this rule for its service. Briefs shall be deemed filed on the date of mailing if first class, express, or priority United States Postal Service mail is utilized.

(2) *Children's fast track appeals.*

(i) In a children's fast track appeal, the appellant shall serve and file appellant's brief within 30 days after the date on which the record is filed, if no other date is so fixed. The appellee shall serve and file appellee's brief within 21 days after service of appellant's brief and reproduced record. A party may serve and file a reply brief permitted by these rules within 7 days after service of the preceding brief but, except for good cause shown, a reply brief must be served and filed so as to be received at least 3 days before argument. In cross appeals, the second brief of the deemed or designated appellant shall be served and filed within 21 days of service of the deemed or designated appellee's first brief. Briefs shall be deemed filed on the date of mailing if first class, express, or priority United States Postal Service mail is utilized.

(ii) In a children's fast track appeal, the provisions of Subdivisions (b) and (c) of this Rule shall not apply.

(b) *Notice of deferred briefing schedule.*—When the record is filed the prothonotary of the appellate court shall estimate the date on which the matter will be argued before or submitted to the court, having regard for the nature of the case and the status of the calendar of the court. If the prothonotary determines that the matter will probably not be reached by the court for argument or submission within 30 days after the latest date on which the last brief could be filed under the usual briefing schedule established by these rules, the prothonotary shall fix a specific calendar date as the last date for the filing of the brief of the appellant in the matter, and shall give notice thereof as required by these rules. The date so fixed by the prothonotary shall be such that the latest date on which the last brief in the matter could be filed under these rules will fall approximately 30 days before the probable date of argument or submission of the matter.

(c) *Definitive copies.*—If the record is being reproduced pursuant to Rule 2154(b) (large records) the brief served pursuant to Subdivision (a) of this rule may be typewritten or page proof copies of the brief, with appropriate references to pages of the parts of the original record involved. Within 14 days after the reproduced record is filed each party who served briefs in advance form under this subdivision shall serve and file definitive copies of his or her brief or briefs containing references to the pages of the reproduced record in place of or in addition to the initial references to the pages of the parts of the original record involved (see Rule 2132 (references in the briefs to the record)). No other changes may be made in the briefs as initially served, except that typographical errors may be corrected.

Official Note: The 2002 amendment recognizes that in cross appeals the deemed or designated appellant's second brief is more extensive than a reply brief and, therefore may require more than 14 days to prepare. See Rule 2136 (briefs in cases involving cross appeals).

CHAPTER 25
POST-SUBMISSION PROCEEDINGS
APPLICATION FOR REARGUMENT

Rule 2542. Time for Application for Reargument. Manner of Filing.

(a) *Time.*

(1) *General rule.*— Except as otherwise prescribed by this rule, an application for reargument shall be filed with the prothonotary within 14 days after entry of the judgment or other order involved.

(2) *Children's fast track appeals.*—In a children's fast track appeal, an application for reargument shall be filed with the prothonotary within 7 days after entry of the judgment or other order involved.

(b) *Manner of Filing.*—If the application for reargument is transmitted to the prothonotary of the appellate court by means of first class, express, or priority United States Postal Service mail, the application shall be deemed received by the prothonotary for the purposes of Rule 121(a) (filing) on the date deposited in the United States mail as shown on a United States Postal Service Form 3817 Certificate of Mailing or other similar United States Postal Service form from which the date of deposit can be verified. The certificate of mailing or similar Postal Service form from which the date of deposit can be verified shall be cancelled by the Postal Service, shall show the docket number of the matter in the court in which reargument is sought and shall be enclosed with the application or separately mailed to the prothonotary. Upon actual receipt of the application, the prothonotary shall immediately stamp it with the date of actual receipt. That date, or the date of earlier deposit in the United States mail as prescribed in this subdivision, shall constitute the date when application was sought, which date shall be shown on the docket.

Official Note: Former Supreme Court Rule 64, former Superior Court Rules 55 and 58 and former Commonwealth Court Rule 113A required the application for reargument to be filed within ten days of the entry of the order. Under Rule 105(b) (enlargement of time) the time for seeking reargument may be enlarged by order, but no order of the Superior Court or of the Commonwealth Court, other than an actual grant of reargument meeting the requirements of Rule 1701(b)(3) (authority of lower court or agency after appeal), will have the effect of postponing the finality of the order involved under Rule 1113 (time for petitioning for allowance of appeal).

The 1986 amendment provided that an application shall be deemed received on the date deposited in the United States mail as shown on a United States Postal Service Form 3817 Certificate of Mailing.

* * * * *

Rule 2545. Answer to Application for Reargument.

(a) *General rule.*—Except as otherwise prescribed by this rule, within 14 days after service of an application for reargument, an adverse party may file an answer. The answer shall be deemed filed on the date of mailing if first class, express, or priority United States Postal Service mail is utilized. The answer need not be set forth in numbered paragraphs in the manner of a pleading. The answer shall set forth any procedural, substantive or other argument or ground why the court should not grant reargument. The answer shall contain the certificate of compliance required by Pa.R.A.P. 127. No separate motion to dismiss an application for reargument will be received. A party entitled to file an answer under this rule who does not intend to do so shall, within the time fixed by these rules for filing an answer, file a letter stating that an answer to the application for reargument will not be filed. The failure to file an answer will not be construed as concurrence in the request for reargument.

(b) *Children's fast track appeals.*—In a children's fast track appeal, within 7 days after service of an application for reargument, an adverse party may file an answer. The answer shall be deemed filed on the date of mailing if first class, express, or priority United States Postal Service mail is utilized. The answer need not be set forth in numbered paragraphs in the manner of a pleading. The answer shall set forth any procedural, substantive or other argument or ground why the court should not grant reargument. The answer shall contain the certificate of compliance required by Pa.R.A.P. 127.No separate motion to dismiss an application for reargument will be received. A party entitled to file an answer under this rule who does not intend to do so shall, within the time fixed by these rules for filing an answer, file a letter stating that an answer to the application for reargument will not be filed. The failure to file an answer will not be construed as concurrence in the request for reargument.

Adopted Nov. 5, 1975, effective July 1, 1976. Amended Dec. 11, 1978, effective Dec. 30, 1978; May 16, 1979, effective 120 days after June 2, 1979; Feb. 27, 1980, effective March 15, 1980; April 26, 1982, effective 120 days after May 15, 1982; Dec. 10, 1986, effective Jan. 31, 1987; Sept. 10, 2008, effective Dec. 1, 2008; Jan. 13, 2009, effective as to appeals filed 60 days or more after adoption; Jan. 5, 2018, effective Jan. 6, 2018.

REMAND OF RECORD

Rule 2572. Time for Remand of Record.

(a) *General rule.*—Except as provided in paragraphs (b) or (c), the record shall be remanded after the entry of the judgment or other final order of the appellate court possessed of the record.

(1) *Supreme Court orders.*—The time for the remand of the record following orders of the Supreme Court shall be

(i) Seven days after expiration of the time for filing an appeal or petition for writ of *certiorari* to the United States Supreme Court in cases in which the death penalty has been imposed, and

(ii) 14 days in all other cases.

(2) *Intermediate Appellate Court orders.*—The record shall be remanded to the court or other government unit from which it was certified at the expiration of 30 days after the entry of the judgment or other final order of the appellate court possessed of the record.

(b) *Effect of pending post-decision applications on remand.*—Remand is stayed until disposition of: (1) an application for reargument; (2) any other application affecting the order; or (3) a petition for allowance of appeal from the order. The court possessed of the record shall remand 30 days after either the entry of a final order or the disposition of all post-decision applications, whichever is later.

(c) *Stay of remand pending United States Supreme Court Review* Upon application, the Supreme Court of Pennsylvania may stay remand of the record pending review in the Supreme Court of the United States. The Supreme Court Prothonotary shall notify the court having possession of the record of the application and of disposition of the application. The stay shall not exceed 90 days unless the period is extended for cause shown. If a stay is granted and the Clerk of the Supreme Court of the United States notifies the Supreme Court of Pennsylvania that the party that obtained the stay has filed a jurisdictional statement or a petition for a writ of *certiorari*, the stay shall continue until final disposition by the Supreme Court of the United States. Upon the filing in the Supreme Court of Pennsylvania of a copy of an order of the Supreme Court of the United States dismissing the appeal or denying the petition for a writ of *certiorari*, the record shall be remanded immediately.

(d) *Security.*—Appropriate security in an adequate amount may be required as a condition to the grant or continuance of a stay of remand of the record.

(e) *Docket entry of remand.*—The prothonotary of the appellate court shall note on the docket the date on which the record is remanded and give written notice to all parties of the date of remand.

> **Official Note:** This rule keeps the movement of the record to a minimum and decreases the risks associated with the physical movement of the record. The 2017 amendment clarifies that an application for stay of the remand of the record pending United States Supreme Court review should be filed in the Pennsylvania Supreme Court.

Amended February 14, 2017, effective April 1, 2017.

ARTICLE III
MISCELLANEOUS PROVISIONS

CHAPTER 37
BUSINESS OF THE COMMONWEALTH COURT

ARGUMENT BEFORE COURT EN BANC OR A PANEL

Rule 3723. Application for Reargument en Banc.

In cases argued before a single judge, as in petitions for review of determinations of government units which are determined in whole or in part upon the record made before the court, or in cases argued before a panel of judges, the court, at any time on its own initiative before its order becomes final, or upon application for reargument pursuant to these rules, may allow reargument before the court en banc. Such action will be taken only for compelling and persuasive reasons.

> **Official Note:** Based on former Commonwealth Court Rule 43. The time for applying for reargument is increased from ten to 14 days. See Rule 2542(a)(1) (time for application for reargument).

INTERNAL OPERATING PROCEDURES OF THE SUPERIOR COURT

CHILDREN'S FAST TRACK PROCEDURES

§ 65.14. **Children's Fast Track and Other Family Fast Track Appeals.**

A. In accordance with Pa.R.A.P. 102, revised in 2009, and in accordance with a program first established in this court in 2000, the court shall expedite handling of appeals involving parent-child relationships as follows:

1. Children's Fast Track: All cases involving dependency, termination of parental rights, adoption, custody, or paternity shall be designated as Children's Fast Track in the Superior Court.

2. Other Family Fast Track: Central Legal Staff in its discretion may expedite other appeals involving the parent-child relationship. Such cases shall be designated "Other Family Fast Track."

B. For all cases designated as Children's Fast Track or Other Family Fast Track, primary responsibility for monitoring the receipt of the record shall rest with the Central Legal Staff.

1. Upon receipt of an appeal that has been designated Children's Fast Track appeal by the trial court and/or the parties, the Prothonotary shall forward a letter from the President Judge of the Superior Court to the trial court judge, with copies to the clerk of the lower court, counsel for the parties or to the parties themselves if they are proceeding pro se, and Central Legal Staff. The letter shall stress the importance of the trial court's duty to send the record to the Superior Court in a timely manner, and shall stress the Superior Court's internal operating policy with respect to extensions of time for briefing, as set forth in I.O.P. 65.21 B.2.

2. In all cases designated Other Family Fast Track by the Superior Court, the Central Legal Staff shall forward the letter from the President Judge as set forth in the preceding paragraph B.1.

3. Upon receipt of an appeal that has not been designated Children's Fast Track by the trial court or the parties, the Prothonotary or Central Legal Staff may designate the appeal as a Children's Fast Track appeal if the circumstances so warrant. In such a case, the procedures set forth in paragraph B.1. or B.2. above will apply.

The provisions of this § 65.14 adopted March 16, 2009, effective immediately

MOTIONS PRACTICE

§ 65.21. Motions Review Subject to Single Judge Disposition.

* * * * *

B All petitions for extension of time shall be referred by the Prothonotary to the motions judge. Such petitions should be acted upon as soon as possible unless the motions judge feels an answer is necessary.

1. Petitions for extension shall be granted only on cause shown and in any event the filing of the brief is required, particularly in criminal cases, even though the right to argue is lost. Central Legal Staff shall be notified of the filing of the motion and the disposition. However, if the petition for extension is accompanied by a substantive motion, such as a motion to quash, remand, or withdraw, Central Legal Staff shall review the motion in an expeditious manner pursuant to the procedures set forth in Section 65.21(C) herein. Whenever an order is entered granting a petition for extension of time, and the order provides that no further extensions will be granted, any subsequent petition for extension of time shall be referred by the Prothonotary to the judge who issued the original order.

2. Notwithstanding any contrary procedures set forth above, all petitions for extension of time to file a brief in cases designated Children's Fast Track or Other Family Fast Track, upon receipt by the Prothonotary, shall be sent to Central Legal Staff for processing. All such petitions shall be presented to a motions judge for disposition within three days of receipt of the petition by Central Legal Staff. Petitions for extension of time to file a brief in Children's Fast Track or Other Family Fast Track cases shall be granted only upon a showing of good cause and extraordinary circumstances. Generalities such as the purpose of the motion is not for delay or that counsel is too busy will not constitute either good cause or extraordinary circumstances. Extensions

for time should rarely be granted, and when granted should rarely be for a period in excess of seven days.

* * * * *

§ 65.22. Motions Review Subject to Motions Panel Disposition.

* * * * *

B. After a motion subject to this Rule has been filed with the Prothonotary's office, the Prothonotary shall forward the motion to Central Legal Staff which shall prepare and circulate to the motions panel a legal memorandum and recommendation.

1. Votes thereon shall be due three weeks from the date on which the motion and accompanying documents are sent by Central Legal Staff, unless the case has been designated Children's Fast Track or Other Family Fast Track.

2. Votes on cases which have been identified as Children's Fast Track or Other Family Fast Track shall be due two weeks from the date on which the motion and accompanying documents are sent by Central Legal Staff.

* * * * *

DECISIONAL PROCEDURES

§ 65.31. Argument Sessions and Submit Panels.

A. Argument sessions shall be held in the cities of Harrisburg, Philadelphia, and Pittsburgh. Special argument sessions may be scheduled in other locations by decision of the President Judge. Argument sessions shall begin at 9:30 a.m. unless otherwise designated.

B. Submit panels shall be governed by I.O.P. 65.36.

C. The Prothonotary shall give Children's Fast Track and Other Family Fast Track cases priority in listing before argued and submit panels, and may schedule special sessions of the court at any time that the unlisted and eligible number of Children's Fast Track plus Other Family Fast Track cases which cannot be listed before a scheduled argued or submitted panel within thirty days exceeds six in any district.

§ 65.32. Daily List.

* * * * *

B. A case shall be ready and available for assignment to a daily list on the date on which the appellee's brief is due, regardless of whether the brief has been filed, unless the case has been designated Children's Fast Track or Other Family Fast Track. Cases designated as Children's Fast Track or Other Family Fast Track shall be eligible for listing before an argument panel at the time that the brief for the appellant is filed.

§ 65.42. Circulation and Voting in Children's Fast Track and Other Family Fast Track Appeals.

Notwithstanding any contrary procedures set forth above, panels shall give priority in both circulation of and voting on proposed decisions, first in Children's Fast Track cases, and then in Other Family Fast Track cases.

TRANSCRIPT ORDER FORM
FOR CHILDREN'S FAST TRACK APPEALS ONLY

First Judicial District of Pennsylvania
Court Reporter, Digital Recording & Interpreter Administration
215-683-8000
Fax **with Notice of Appeal** immediately to:
215-683-8005
Attention: Paul Meronyck

Court Reporters and/or Digital Recording

Caption:	Docket #:

Hearing/Trial Date:	Courtroom #:	Judge:

Type of Hearing: (This form is to be used ONLY for a hearing type listed below)

☐ Termination of Parental Rights   ☐ Dependency   ☐ Adoption   ☐ Custody   ☐ Paternity

Requesting Judge:	Phone #:	Fax #:

Date of Request:

☐ Court Reporter

☐ Digital Recording

<u>Administrative use only:</u>

Date Received: _____   Initials: _____

Date notification was given to Reporter/Transcriptionist: _____

Date e-mail notification sent to Judge: _____   Initials: _____

08-10A

DOMESTIC RELATIONS REGULATIONS
Pennsylvania Code—Title 55

CHAPTER 108. FAMILY VIOLENCE AND TANF AND GA

GENERAL PROVISIONS

Sec.
108.1.	Purpose.
108.2.	Definitions.
108.3.	Universal notification.
108.4.	Written notification.
108.5.	Individual notification.
108.6.	Policy for applicants or recipients in immediate danger.
108.7.	Requirements subject to waiver.
108.8.	Claiming good cause based on domestic violence.
108.9.	Time limits.
108.10.	Verification.
108.11.	Time frames for good cause waiver determinations based on domestic violence.
108.12.	Notice of good cause waiver determinations based on domestic violence.
108.13.	Review of waivers.
108.14.	Safeguarding information.
108.15.	Alternate address.
108.16.	DRS responsibility for the FVI.
108.17.	Agreement of Mutual Responsibility (AMR).
108.18.	Referral for services.

§ 108.1. Purpose.

This chapter establishes rules and policies that apply to victims of domestic violence who are applicants for or recipients of TANF or GA cash assistance. These policies reflect the Department's commitment to address domestic violence among welfare recipients and are based on the Department's election of the FVO, authorized under Federal law.

§ 108.2. Definitions.

The following words and terms, when used in this chapter, have the following meanings, unless the context clearly indicates otherwise:

DRS—Domestic Relations Section—The section of a court of common pleas responsible for establishing and enforcing support orders.

Domestic violence—One or more of the following:

(i) Physical acts that resulted in, or threatened to result in, physical injury to the individual.

(ii) Sexual abuse.

(iii) Sexual activity involving a dependent child.

(iv) Being forced as the caretaker relative of a dependent child to engage in nonconsensual sexual acts or activities.

(v) Threats or attempts of physical or sexual abuse.

(vi) Mental abuse.

(vii) Neglect or deprivation of medical care.

FVI—Family violence indicator—A marker placed on Department and DRS records to indicate one or more individuals in the file are victims of domestic violence.

FVO—Family violence option—An optional provision in section 402(a)(7) of the Social Security Act (42 U.S.C.A. § 602(a)(7)), regarding eligible states; State plan, under which a state may elect to identify individuals with a history of domestic violence, refer them for counseling and supportive services and, upon a showing of good cause, waive one or more program requirements for these individuals.

Federal parent locator database—A National computer location system operated by the Federal Office of Child Support Enforcement, to assist states in locating noncustodial parents, putative fathers and custodial parties for the establishment of paternity and child support obligations, as well as the enforcement and modification of orders for child support, custody and visitation.

PACSES—Pennsylvania Automated Child Support Enforcement System—Pennsylvania's single Statewide automated data processing and information retrieval system for child support enforcement under Title IV-D of the Social Security Act (42 U.S.C.A. §§ 651—669b).

Work and work-related activities—Activities set forth in Chapter 165 (relating to Road to Economic Self-Sufficiency through Employment and Training (RESET) Program).

Work and work-related activity requirements—Requirements set forth in Chapter 165.

§ 108.3. Universal notification.

The Department will provide applicants and recipients with information about:

(1) Policies and procedures relating to domestic violence.

(2) Referrals to domestic violence services.

(3) Good cause waivers of certain TANF and GA program requirements.

(4) Specific information about program requirements if a waiver is not requested.

(5) Safeguards that may help the individual safely comply with program requirements, including placement of an FVI as defined in § 108.2 (relating to definitions) on Department and DRS files and other confidentiality protections.

(6) Opportunities to participate as a volunteer in work or work-related activities, including education and training, and to receive supportive services, under §§ 165.31 and 165.41 (relating to RESET participation requirements; and eligibility for special allowances for supportive services) if the individual receives a good cause waiver.

§ 108.4. Written notification.

The Department will provide applicants and recipients with written notification of the information described in § 108.3 (relating to universal notification).

§ 108.5. Individual notification.

(a) The Department will provide applicants with written notification of the right to claim good cause based on domestic violence.

(b) The Department will provide recipients who have not previously disclosed domestic violence with written notification of the right to claim good cause based on domestic violence as follows:

(1) Prior to referral to the DRS.

(2) When the Department has reason to believe a family or household member has been subjected to or is at risk of further domestic violence.

(3) Prior to imposing a sanction for noncooperation with child support requirements according to § 187.26 (relating to noncooperation).

(4) When compliance with work requirements as defined in § 108.2 (relating to definitions) is discussed according to § 165.51 (relating to compliance review) and prior to imposing a sanction for noncooperation with work requirements according to § 165.61 (relating to sanctions).

(5) Prior to denying, terminating, reducing or suspending benefits due to failure to comply with a TANF or GA program requirement.

(c) The Department will provide a recipient who has previously disclosed domestic violence with written notification of the right to claim good cause based on domestic violence according to subsection (b)(1)—(5), unless the recipient notifies the Department in writing that written notification of this right would place the recipient at risk of further domestic violence.

(d) Written notification must include an explanation of:

(1) The availability of referrals for assistance for victims of domestic violence.

(2) The availability of and procedures for requesting a good cause waiver of certain TANF or GA program requirements based on domestic violence.

(3) The confidentiality protections.

(e) The Department will provide oral notification to applicants and recipients of the right to claim good cause based on domestic violence as follows:

(1) At the application and renewal interviews.

(2) Prior to a referral to the DRS.

(3) When the Department has reason to believe a family or household member has been subjected to or is at risk of further domestic violence.

(4) At a compliance review under § 165.51 in which the recipient participates.

§ 108.6. Policy for applicants or recipients in immediate danger.

If an applicant or recipient is in immediate danger, the Department will:

(1) Provide a private space to allow the applicant or recipient to call a domestic violence hotline, if requested.

(2) Offer the applicant or recipient help in making arrangements for emergency shelter, medical care, transportation, child care and work.

§ 108.7. Requirements subject to waiver.

(a) The policies set forth in §§ 108.8—108.13 apply to good cause waivers of requirements for support cooperation, work, time limits, teen parents, verification and other TANF and GA program requirements, based on domestic violence.

(b) The Department may not waive the following TANF or GA program requirements except as provided in subsection (c):

(1) Minor child under § 145.41 (relating to policy).

(2) Specified relative under § 151.41 (relating to policy).

(3) Income under § 183.5 (relating to income verification).

(4) Resources under § 177.1 (relating to general requirements).

(5) Citizenship under § 149.23 (relating to requirements).

(6) Deprivation under § 153.41 (relating to policy).

(7) Enumeration under § 155.2 (relating to general).

(8) Identity under § 125.1 (relating to policy).

(9) Criminal status under sections 432(9) and 481.1 of the Public Welfare Code (62 P. S. §§ 432(9) and 481.1) regarding eligibility; false statements; investigations; and penalty.

(10) Residency under § 147.23 (relating to requirements).

(11) GA categorical eligibility requirement under § 141.61 (relating to policy).

(12) Signature on required forms, such as the application for benefits and authorization for release of information form under § 125.1.

(13) Permanent sanction under § 165.61 (relating to sanctions).

(14) Application for and cooperation in establishing eligibility for potential income under section 432.21(a) of the Public Welfare Code (62 P. S. § 432.21(a)) regarding requirement that certain Federal benefits be the primary source of assistance.

(c) The Department will determine whether to approve a request to waive one or more requirements in subsection (b)(3)—(14) on a case-by-case basis.

§ 108.8. Claiming good cause based on domestic violence.

(a) An individual may request a good cause waiver of a TANF or GA program requirement based on past, present or risk of further domestic violence, as defined in § 108.2 (relating to definitions).

(b) The Department will grant a good cause waiver of a TANF or GA program requirement if compliance with the program requirement would result in one of the following:

(1) Making it more difficult for the individual or family member to escape domestic violence.

(2) Placing the individual or family member at risk of further domestic violence.

(3) Unfairly penalizing the individual or family member because of domestic violence.

(c) The Department may grant a good cause waiver regardless of whether the alleged abuser is in the household.

§ 108.9. Time limits.

(a) An applicant or recipient may receive up to 12 months of TANF cash assistance that do not count towards the 60-month TANF time limit according to § 141.41(d) (relating to policy) based on past, present or risk of further domestic violence to the individual or family member. The months need not be sequential.

(b) Individuals may receive Extended TANF, as defined in § 141.52 (relating to definitions), if the individual or family member is or has been a victim of domestic violence or is at risk of further domestic violence according to § 141.53 (relating to eligibility based on domestic violence).

(c) Individuals may be eligible for cash assistance under this section regardless of whether the alleged abuser is in the household.

§ 108.10. Verification.

(a) An individual who requests a good cause waiver of a TANF or GA program requirement based on domestic violence shall complete the verification form provided by the Department.

(b) The Department will provide the verification form, in person or by mail, to an individual who requests the form and will instruct the individual to provide verification that may include one of the following:

(1) Law enforcement records.

(2) Court records.

(3) Medical or treatment records, or both.

(4) Social services records.

(5) Child protective services records.

(6) Third party verification from a public or private organization or an individual with knowledge of the circumstances including:

(i) A domestic violence service provider.

(ii) A medical, psychological or social services provider.

(iii) A law enforcement professional.

(iv) A legal representative.

(v) An acquaintance, friend, relative, or neighbor of the claimant, or other individual.

(c) If the individual cannot safely obtain verification described in subsection (b), the individual may affirm on the verification form provided by the Department that the individual cannot safely comply with a TANF or GA program requirement due to domestic violence.

(d) When an individual claims good cause based on domestic violence, the Department may not:

(1) Contact the alleged abuser.

(2) Require the individual to obtain a Protection from Abuse Order.

§ 108.11. Time frames for good cause waiver determinations based on domestic violence.

The Department will make a good cause waiver determination within 15 calendar days from the date the claim was initiated by the applicant or recipient.

§ 108.12. Notice of good cause waiver determinations based on domestic violence.

(a) The Department will provide written notice to the individual of its determination regarding the good cause waiver request.

(b) If the Department grants the waiver request, the notice will:

(1) State the program requirement being waived.

(2) Explain the duration of the waiver. If the Department is uncertain of the duration of the need for the waiver, the notice will explain that the waiver will remain in effect as long as necessary, subject to review every 6 months.

(c) If the Department denies the waiver request, the notice will:

(1) State which program requirements are not waived and the basis for the determination.

(2) State the legal authority for the denial.

(3) Explain the right to appeal.

(4) State what additional verification or information is needed to substantiate good cause and the time frame in which the information shall be provided.

(5) Explain that the individual shall comply with the program requirement for which the waiver was requested.

(d) The Department will follow the notice requirements in §§ 125.1 and 133.4 (relating to policy; and procedures).

§ 108.13. Review of waivers.

When the Department determines that a waiver of a TANF or GA program requirement based on domestic violence is appropriate, it will grant the waiver for as long as necessary, subject to review every 6 months as follows:

(1) An individual who verified domestic violence under § 108.10(b) (relating to verification) need not provide new or additional verification at the 6-month review if circumstances have not changed since the waiver was initially granted or since the last 6-month review.

(2) An individual who affirmed domestic violence under § 108.10(c) may provide verification under § 108.10(b) for the waiver to continue.

(3) An individual who affirmed domestic violence but remains unable to provide verification under § 108.10(b) may again affirm domestic violence on the verification form provided by the Department under § 108.10(c). The individual may receive a waiver for an additional 6 months.

(4) An individual who remains unable to provide verification under § 108.10(b) after 12 months may have the waiver continue by affirming domestic violence under § 108.10(c), subject to approval by the Department on a case-by-case basis. The individual's waiver and benefits will continue pending the Department's decision. If the waiver is approved, the individual may, if necessary, continue to affirm at each subsequent 6-month redetermination.

§ 108.14. Safeguarding information.

(a) Unless required by law or pursuant to the individual's written authorization, the Department may not disclose or release the following information about an applicant, recipient or family member who has disclosed domestic violence, has a Protection from Abuse Order or is at risk of further domestic violence by the disclosure of information:

(1) The residential address, the name and address of the individual's employer, education, training, or work program or other work activity, the name and address of the children's school and the identity and location of child care or medical providers.

(2) Whether the individual or family member is living in a domestic violence shelter and location of the shelter.

(3) The amount of benefits received by the individual or family member.

(b) The individual's written authorization must be provided on a form approved by the Department. The form may be provided to the individual in person or by mail. The form must include the name of the requestor, the information requested and the purpose of the request.

(c) The Department will place an FVI, as defined in § 108.2 (relating to definitions), on the electronic and paper files of an individual or family member who has disclosed domestic violence, has a Protection from Abuse Order or is at risk of further physical or emotional harm by the disclosure of confidential information.

§ 108.15. Alternate address.

(a) A victim of domestic violence may use an alternate mailing address if one of the following applies:

(1) The individual has applied for or received a good cause waiver based on domestic violence.

(2) The individual is at risk of further domestic violence.

(3) The individual is a participant in the Address Confidentiality Program administered by the Pennsylvania Office of Victim Advocate, under 37 Pa. Code Chapter 802 (relating to The Domestic and Sexual Violence Address Confidentiality Program).

(b) The Department will ask an individual who discloses domestic violence, has applied for or received a good cause waiver or is at risk of domestic violence, whether it is safe to send mail to the home address or whether it would be safer to send mail to an alternate address.

§ 108.16. DRS responsibility for the FVI.

(a) The Department will instruct the DRS to place an FVI in PACSES, as defined in § 108.2 (relating to definitions), for an individual who receives cash assistance and discloses domestic violence.

(1) For individuals who make a personal appearance at the DRS and request an FVI be placed in their files, the DRS shall place the FVI in PACSES.

(2) For individuals in counties in which a personal appearance at the DRS is waived, the Department will electronically inform the DRS that a FVI was placed on the automated client information system and directs DRS to place the FVI on PACSES.

(b) If the FVI is placed on the file:

(1) The DRS will not disclose information according to § 108.14 (relating to safeguarding information).

(2) The DRS and other Department staff will not access a DRS file unless access to the file is needed in the performance of their duties.

(3) The DRS will transmit the FVI to the Federal parent locator database as defined in § 108.2.

§ 108.17. Agreement of Mutual Responsibility (AMR).

(a) To ensure confidentiality, the Department will not record information about domestic violence on the AMR, as defined in § 123.22 (relating to definitions).

(b) If the Department has waived a TANF or GA program requirement based on domestic violence, the Department will identify the specific requirement that is being waived on the AMR. The AMR will not include the basis for the waiver.

(c) The AMR serves as the domestic violence service plan in accordance with 45 CFR 260.55 (relating to what are the additional requirements for Federal recognition of good cause domestic violence waivers).

§ 108.18. Referral for services.

When an applicant or recipient discloses domestic violence or requests a referral to domestic violence services, the Department will provide the individual with names, phone numbers and information about the services of local domestic violence agencies, which may include shelter, safety planning and counseling.

# CHAPTER 187. SUPPORT FROM RELATIVES NOT LIVING WITH THE CLIENT

TANF PROGRAM

The Department of Public Welfare (Department), by this order, adopts the amendments to read as set forth in Annex A. The statutory authority for this rulemaking is sections 201(2) and 403(b) of the Public Welfare Code (62 P. S. §§ 201(2) and 403(b)) (code); the Support Law (62 P. S. §§ 1971–1977); Titles I and III of the Personal Responsibility and Work Opportunity Reconciliation Act of 1996 (Pub. L. No. 104-193) (PRWORA), creating the Temporary Assistance for Needy Families (TANF) Program, and amending 42 U.S.C.A. §§ 601–619, 651–669(b) and 1396u-1; section 5543 of the Balanced Budget Act of 1997 (Pub. L. No. 105-33) (42 U.S.C.A. § 653(p)); section 1902(a)(10)(A) and (C) of the Social Security Act (42 U.S.C.A. § 1396a(a)(10)(A) and (C)); the Federal TANF regulations in 45 CFR 260.10–265.10; and the Domestic Relations Code, 23 Pa.C.S. §§ 4301–4381, 5103, 7101–7901 and 8101–8418.

Notice of proposed rulemaking was published at 31 Pa.B. 5875 (October 20, 2001).

Need for Amendments

The purpose of this final-form rulemaking is to codify regulations based upon landmark Federal and State welfare reform legislation that emphasizes personal responsibility, work and self-sufficiency. Specifically, TANF and the Domestic Relations Code transformed welfare from an unlimited entitlement to a temporary support system. The new regulations reflect the legislative intent to promote self-sufficiency. Changes, including more substantial work requirements and increased financial incentives for working welfare recipients, illustrate this refocus of welfare. Moreover, the Domestic Relations Code contains revised provisions requiring cooperation with the Child Support Enforcement Program (established under Title IV-D of the Social Security Act) as a condition of eligibility for cash assistance, and a new support pass-through program. Implementation of child support cooperation provisions is another key component to assure an income source for needy families seeking to achieve self-sufficiency. This final-form rulemaking provides numerous supports and incentives to assist employable individuals in their quest for financial independence. These supports and incentives include waivers of various program requirements for victims of domestic violence, a 50% earned income disregard, exclusion of educational savings accounts and special allowances, such as child care and transportation expenses, to support training, education and work.

Scope

This final-form rulemaking codifies the basic TANF program. This final-form rulemaking affects applicants and recipients of TANF assistance, General Assistance (GA) and Medical Assistance (MA). Certain provisions regarding employment and training also affect Food Stamp recipients.

Grounded in the legislative directive in the Domestic Relations Code that work is essential to self-sufficiency, this final-form rulemaking incorporates statutory work and work-related requirements and sanctions for willful noncompliance with these requirements. At the same time, the Department recognizes that some individuals have significant obstacles that hinder their ability to work. Depending on the nature and extent of these obstacles, an individual may be exempt or excused from work and work-related requirements for good cause, and receive appropriate supportive services. These requirements and benefits associated with employment and training are embodied in the Department's Road to Economic Self-Sufficiency Through

Pa. Code: Ch. 187 SUPPORT FROM RELATIVES

Employment and Training (RESET) program, established by the Domestic Relations Code.

This final-form rulemaking also reflects changes involving good cause waivers of child support cooperation requirements for victims of domestic violence. The Department elected to adopt the Family Violence Option (FVO) (42 U.S.C.A. § 602(a)(7); 45 CFR 260.50–260.59) in 1997, and implemented many FVO provisions in a Notice of Rule Change (NORC) published at 30 Pa.B. 2957 (June 10, 2000). In doing so, the Department demonstrated a commitment to help victims of domestic violence become self-sufficient without compromising their safety.

Further, to ensure that the Department's final-form rulemaking is consistent with its policy and TANF State Plans, this final-form rulemaking includes other changes to existing regulations. For example, the Department amended various provisions to exclude educational assistance as income or a resource. In addition, the Department has incorporated its revised good cause policy for education and training in this final-form rulemaking. These and other changes required applicable amendments to regulations governing TANF-related and GA-related MA.

Finally, this final-form rulemaking incorporates the Federal 60-month time limit for TANF assistance and specifies how that time accrues. This final-form rulemaking also clarifies exceptions to the 60-month limit. The definition of "family" also reflects a clarification regarding application of the time limit policy for certain specified relatives. For assistance that extends beyond the 60-month limit, the Department has proposed a separate rulemaking at 32 Pa.B. 431 (January 26, 2002). The Department refers to those benefits as "Extended TANF." The Department intends to publish final rulemaking for Extended TANF following adoption of this final-form rulemaking. In the interim, TANF individuals who reach the 60-month limit will continue to receive TANF assistance if they are otherwise eligible. In the following comment/response section of this Preamble, the Department's time limit policy is discussed in greater detail.

Summary of Public Comments and Changes

Written comments, suggestions and objections were solicited within a 30-day comment period after the publication date of the proposed rulemaking. The Department received 18 public comments. Commentators included: citizens, advocates, the Minority Chairperson of the Senate Public Health and Welfare Committee, the Minority Chairperson of the House Health and Human Services Committee and the Independent Regulatory Review Commission (IRRC).

The Department has carefully reviewed and considered each comment and thanks the individuals and organizations who commented on the proposed rulemaking. The following is a summary of the comments received during the public comment period and the Department's responses.

* * *

Good cause for not cooperating in obtaining support or establishing paternity § 187.25(a) and (b). Oral notification of right to claim good cause.

Comment: Commentators requested that the Department revise § 187.25(a) (relating to notification to the applicant or recipient) to include detailed oral notification of an individual's right to claim good cause for not cooperating in obtaining support or establishing paternity.

Response: The Department concurs, and has revised this section (and § 187.25(b)) accordingly.

§ 187.27(b) and (c). Proof of good cause—use of the terms "corroboration" and "corroborative evidence."

Comment: Commentators suggested that the Department replace "corroboration" and "corroborative evidence" with "verification."

Response: The Department concurs, and has revised § 187.27(b) and (c) (relating to waiver of cooperation for good cause) as requested. In addition, the Department has replaced "corroborated" with "verified."

§ 187.27(b)(1)(iv). Verification of good cause—medical records.

Comment: Commentators suggested that § 187.27(b)(1)(iv) contains burdensome verification requirements and does not comport with other verification requirements for victims of domestic violence. They suggested that the Department delete this subparagraph.

Response: The Department has considered this comment and does not agree that verification requirements in this subparagraph are burdensome. This subparagraph is simply permissive; a victim of domestic violence is not required to produce medical records to verify her claim. Section 187.27(b)(1)(iv) applies to an individual who wishes to use medical records to verify a good cause claim, whether she is claiming good cause as a victim of domestic violence, incest or rape. Therefore, this provision is not inconsistent with other verification requirements for victims of domestic violence.

§ 187.27(b)(1)(v). Scope of good cause circumstances.

Comment: Commentators suggested that § 187.27(b)(1)(v) does not recite the full scope of good cause circumstances set forth in § 187.27(a)(4) (relocated to § 187.22 (relating to definitions) in this final-form rulemaking). They also asked the Department to delete the phrase "indicate that the putative father, noncustodial parent or absent spouse might inflict harm on the individual or family member as specified under subsection (a)(4)" from § 187.27(b)(1)(v), and replace it with "verify domestic violence as defined at subsection (a)(4)."

Response: The Department does not agree that § 187.27(b)(1)(v) should recite examples of good cause. This provision involves only verification of good cause. However, the Department has revised this provision by replacing the quoted language as suggested, and cross referencing § 187.22, the relevant provision.

§ 187.27(b)(1)(vi) and (2). Prohibition on contacting abuser.

Comment: Commentators suggested that the Department relocate the following sentence in § 187.27(b)(1)(vi): "The CAO may not contact the putative father or noncustodial parent to verify good cause in a domestic violence situation." They suggested moving the sentence to § 187.27(b)(2), which describes the CAO's role in assisting with verification.

Response: The Department concurs, and has moved this sentence to § 187.27(b)(2). In addition, the Department has revised the sentence as follows: "The CAO may not contact the putative father or noncustodial parent to verify good cause based on a claim of domestic violence."

§ 187.27(b)(1)(vii). Person completing good cause waiver form.

Comment: Commentators suggested that the Department revise § 187.27(b)(1)(vii) to clarify that the CAO will complete the Verification of Good Cause Based on Domestic Violence Form with the individual.

Response: The Department concurs, and has revised this section as recommended.

Pa. Code: Ch. 187   SUPPORT FROM RELATIVES

§§ 187.27(c)(3) and 187.23(d)(4). Expiration of waivers.

Comment: Commentators suggested that the Department revise § 187.23(d)(4) (relating to requirements) and § 187.27(c)(3) to specify that a good cause waiver may last as long as necessary, subject to a review every 6 months. They questioned the wisdom of establishing an expiration date for a good cause waiver.

Response: The Department concurs and has deleted reference to expiration of the waiver in § 187.27(c)(3), and in § 187.23(d)(4) the Department clarified that the good cause waiver may last as long as the good cause exists.

§ 187.27(c)(4). Review of good cause.

Comment: Commentators suggested that the Department revise § 187.27(c)(4) to clarify that a good cause waiver will not be reviewed more often than every 6 months. They recommended that the Department delete the last sentence in § 187.27(c)(4), which specifies that the review may be earlier if the circumstances warranting good cause change or the CAO granted the good cause waiver for a shorter period.

Response: The Department has revised this section as recommended. However, this revision does not preclude the Department from reviewing the good cause waiver before the usual 6-month review period. For example, if the CAO authorizes assistance for a mother and her children in February, but she receives a good cause waiver in May, the CAO would likely review good cause at her regular redetermination in August. Thereafter, the CAO would review good cause every 6 months, at each redetermination.

§ 187.27(c)(4)(i). Verification requirements after initial good cause waiver.

Comment: Commentators suggested that § 187.27(c) (4)(i) is unduly burdensome for victims of domestic violence. They suggested that an individual with a good cause waiver based on documentation or third-party statements should not be required to submit additional verification for future waivers, if her circumstances have not changed. They requested that the Department revise the provision by deleting the requirement that these individuals submit a Verification of Good Cause Based on Domestic Violence Form completed by a person trained in domestic violence.

Response: The Department concurs, and has revised this section as recommended.

§§ 187.23(b)(1)(i), 187.27(b)(1)(vii)(B), (C), (3) and (c)(4)(ii). Miscellaneous Chapter 187 revisions.

Comment: Two commentators submitted an attachment to their written comments consisting of suggested minor edits to the sections noted previously.

Response: The Department has revised all but one of these sections as suggested. The Department does not agree that the phrase "without good cause" should be inserted after the phrase "minor child" in § 187.23(b)(1)(i) (regarding identifying the father of an unemancipated minor). Section 187.23(b)(1)(i) simply follows section 4379(2)(ii) of the Domestic Relations Code (relating to cooperation required), which states that failure of the mother to identify the child's father shall create a presumption of noncooperation. As section 4379(2)(ii) of the Domestic Relations Code illustrates, the General Assembly did not intend to obviate this presumption with a showing of good cause. Rather, under section 4380(b)(2) of the Domestic Relations Code (relating to enforcement of cooperation requirements), if the mother does not rebut this presumption, good cause excuses her noncooperation. However, the Department agrees that because it elected the FVO, in cases involving domestic violence, the cooperation requirement is altogether waived. In these cases, the CAO need not determine if the mother cooperated with this requirement.

* * *

§ 187.22. Definition of "budget group."

Comment: Commentators suggested that the Department revise the definition of "budget group" in § 187.22. They disputed that all siblings should be included in the budget group, including children for whom support or other income is paid. They noted that the Federal mandatory budget group requirement was eliminated when AFDC was repealed in 1996. One commentator questioned whether this definition discourages support from a noncustodial parent if that support must be included in the budget group income in determining eligibility.

Response: The Department does not agree that the definition of budget group should be revised as suggested. As the Department explained in its initial TANF State Plan, published at 27 Pa.B. 342 (January 18, 1997), many of the rules and procedures under which the Department administered the former AFDC program will remain in effect under the new TANF program. This includes the definition of "budget group" in §§ 141.42 and 187.22 and the policy for grant groups and filing units in § 171.21.

The Department's rationale for leaving the definition of "budget group" intact is premised on the explicit legislative purpose of public assistance: to enable needy individuals who lack sufficient means of support to become self-sufficient. See sections 401, 405.1, 432 and 432.12 of the code. Mindful of the need to allocate finite social welfare resources to the most needy, the Department requires individuals to first turn to other sources of income and resources before resorting to public assistance. To ensure that scarce public funds are preserved for the most needy, other financial sources are considered in determining a family's actual need for government benefits. Other financial sources include income, such as support, attributed to a sibling residing with a recipient child.

Finally, the Department does not agree with the commentator's suggestion that noncustodial parents may be inclined to withhold support if the regulation is not revised as requested. Pennsylvania law plainly requires parents to support their minor dependent children. See section 4321 of the Domestic Relations Code (relating to liability for support). The Department's definition of "budget group" does not affect this obligation.

§ 187.23(b)(6) and (c)(6). Assignment of support.

Comment: Commentators suggested that the Department revise § 187.23(b)(6) and (c)(6) to state that support received or anticipated to be received directly from the payor after assignment of support is not always required to be paid to the Department. They explained that in the initial month of application for TANF, any support received or anticipated to be received is counted in determining the amount of assistance, subject to a $50 disregard.

Response: The Department does not agree that § 187.23(b)(6) and (c)(6) should be revised as requested. However, the Department has revised § 183.32 to reflect the revised procedures for handling support payments received in the initial month of assistance.

With the conversion of the computer systems of the county domestic relations sections to the Statewide automated child support system of the Pennsylvania Child Support Enforcement System, assignment of support to the Department is immediate upon authorization of assistance. Prior to authorization, support paid to an applicant is not assigned to the Department, but is counted in determining the amount of assistance for the initial month. Because assignment is immediate upon authorization, any support received after this time must be reimbursed to the Department, as section 4379(2)(i)(F) of the Domestic Relations Code specifically mandates. Section 187.23(b)(6) and (c)(6) simply follows section 4379(2)(i)(F) of the Domestic Relations Code. The Department does not intend to deviate from this statute.

* * *

SUPPORT PROVISIONS FOR CASH ASSISTANCE

Sec.
187.21. General Policy.
187.22. Definitions.
187.23. Requirements.
187.24. [Reserved].
187.25. Notification to the applicant or recipient.
187.26. Noncooperation.
187.27. Waiver of cooperation for good cause.

§ 187.21. General policy.

Legal bases for support requirements. The Support Law (62 P. S. §§ 1971–1977) provides authority to the courts to order or direct support to needy individuals from LRR upon petition from the needy individual or the Department. The Public Welfare Code (62 P. S. §§ 101–1503) requires the Department to grant assistance only to those individuals who apply for and meet all conditions of eligibility. By law, then, LRRs will be a potential resource to individuals applying for or receiving assistance. The Support Law (62 P. S. §§ 1971–1977), 23 Pa.C.S. §§ 4301–5104 and 7101–8415, and the Public Welfare Code (62 P. S. §§ 101–1503) mesh to make it mandatory to explore and develop the resource that an LRR may provide to an individual. Under the child support program, support collection and paternity determination services will also be made available upon request to individuals who are not applying for or receiving assistance. The domestic relations section in each county has been designated to process requests for support services.

§ 187.22. Definitions.

The following words and terms, when used in this chapter, have the following meanings, unless the context clearly indicates otherwise:

Arrears—Past due and unpaid support.

BCSE—Bureau of Child Support Enforcement—The organizational unit in this Commonwealth responsible for supervising the State Plan for Child Support Enforcement under Title IV-D of the Social Security Act (42 U.S.C.A. §§ 651—669b).

Budget group—One or more related or unrelated individuals who occupy a common residence or would occupy a common residence if they were not homeless and whose needs and eligibility are considered together in determining eligibility for cash assistance under one category of assistance.

CAO—County assistance office—The local office of the Department responsible for the determination of eligibility for cash, Food Stamps and MA Programs.

Cash assistance allowance—The monthly family size allowance, reduced by the net income of the budget group. The family size allowance is described under § 175.23(a) (relating to requirements).

DRS—Domestic Relations Section—The division of a court of common pleas responsible for establishing and enforcing support orders.

Establishing paternity—The process that determines the legal father of a child.

LRR—Legally responsible relative—The spouse, including common-law, of the applicant or recipient of cash assistance, or the biological or adoptive parent of an unemancipated minor child for whom cash assistance is sought or received.

Obtaining support—Establishing, modifying or enforcing a support order.

Support—A judgment, decree or order whether temporary, final or subject to modification, imposed or imposable by a court or an administrative agency of competent jurisdiction for the support and maintenance of a child or spouse, or both, which provides for monetary support, health care, arrears or reimbursement, and which may include other relief.

Unemancipated minor child—An individual who is under 18 years of age, or an individual 18 years of age or older but under 21 years of age, who has not graduated from high school, is not married and is in the care and control of a parent or caretaker.

§ 187.23. Requirements.

(a) *Applicability*. This chapter applies to applicants for and recipients of cash assistance if there is: The reported absence of a parent from the home of an unemancipated minor child; a putative father for an unemancipated minor child; or a spouse absent from the home. The absence of a parent from the home is determined according to the requirements under § 153.44(a) (relating to procedures).

(b) *Cooperation requirements for child support*. As a condition of eligibility for cash assistance, every applicant or recipient seeking or receiving cash assistance on behalf of an unemancipated minor child shall cooperate in establishing paternity of an unemancipated minor child with respect to whom assistance is sought and cooperate in obtaining support from an LRR for the unemancipated minor child, unless the applicant or recipient establishes good cause for failing to do so. Cooperation includes taking the following actions:

(1) Identifying the parents of an unemancipated minor child for whom assistance is sought or received, including appearing for scheduled genetic testing with the child and submitting to the testing.

(i) Failure of the mother to identify by name the father of an unemancipated minor child shall create a presumption of noncooperation which may be rebutted only by clear and convincing evidence.

(ii) If the applicant or recipient provides the names of two putative fathers subsequently excluded from paternity by genetic testing, the second exclusion shall create a presumption of noncooperation, which may be rebutted only by clear and convincing evidence.

(2) Keeping scheduled appointments with the Department or the DRS.

(3) Providing truthful and accurate information and documents requested by the Department or the DRS.

(i) When the whereabouts of a parent or putative father are unknown, the applicant or recipient will be required to take whatever steps are appropriate to the individual circumstances to locate the missing parent or putative father. This may include contacting relatives and friends for information about the whereabouts of the parent or putative father or giving consent to the CAO to contact other agencies, relatives and other individuals, or possible employers and similar resources.

(ii) The CAO will provide whatever help is appropriate to the individual circumstances of the applicant or recipient to assist in locating the missing parent or putative father and supplement the efforts of the applicant or recipient by checking appropriate governmental records.

(iii) Together, the CAO and the applicant or recipient will plan and agree on the specific steps to be taken to locate the missing parent or putative father. Assistance will be authorized or continued on the agreement of the applicant or recipient to take the specific steps within the time set for doing so.

(4) Signing and returning any forms requested by the Department or the DRS.

(5) Appearing as a witness and providing testimony at judicial and other hearings as requested by the DRS.

(6) Paying to the Department any support payment received directly from an absent parent after an assignment of support has been made.

(c) *Cooperation criteria for spousal support.* As a condition of eligibility for cash assistance, every applicant or recipient seeking or receiving cash assistance on behalf of himself and for whom there is an absent spouse shall cooperate in obtaining support unless the applicant or recipient establishes good cause for failing to do so. Cooperation includes the following:

(1) Naming the absent spouse.

(2) Keeping scheduled appointments with the Department or the DRS.

(3) Providing truthful and accurate information and documents requested by the Department or the DRS.

(i) When the whereabouts of a spouse is unknown, the applicant or recipient shall take whatever steps are appropriate to the individual circumstances to locate the missing spouse. This may include contacting relatives and friends for information about the whereabouts of the spouse or giving consent to the CAO to contact other agencies, relatives and other individuals or possible employers and similar resources.

(ii) The CAO will provide whatever help is appropriate to the individual circumstances of the applicant or recipient to assist in locating the missing spouse and supplement the efforts of the applicant or recipient by checking appropriate governmental records.

(iii) Together, the CAO staff and the applicant or recipient will plan and agree on the specific steps to be taken to locate the missing spouse. Assistance will be authorized or continued on the agreement of the applicant or recipient to take the specific steps within the time set for doing so.

(4) Signing and returning any forms requested by the Department or the DRS.

(5) Appearing as a witness and providing testimony at judicial and other hearings as requested by the DRS.

(6) Paying to the Department any support payment received directly from an absent spouse after an assignment of support has been made.

(d) *Cooperation prior to authorization.* Except as provided in paragraphs (3) and (4), every applicant or recipient of cash assistance shall cooperate in establishing paternity and obtaining support. The applicant or recipient shall:

(1) Appear before the DRS or other applicable division of the court of common pleas and provide to the CAO certification from the DRS of cooperation by the applicant or recipient of cash assistance in establishing paternity and in obtaining support.

(2) Cooperate with the procedures established for the county when a waiver of the personal appearance requirement is in place. The Secretary is authorized to waive the personal appearance requirement under paragraph

(1) if another procedure would be as effective and efficient and a family court or DRS requests a waiver.

(3) In the case of a newborn, cooperate with the requirements under § 133.23(b)(4)(v) (relating to requirements).

(4) File a good cause claim. The cooperation requirements are waived from the time a good cause claim is filed until the CAO, court of common pleas or DRS makes a determination on the claim. If the CAO, court of common pleas or DRS determines that good cause exists, the cooperation requirements are waived as long as the good cause exists.

(e) *Assignment of support rights.* Acceptance of cash assistance shall operate as an assignment to the Department, by operation of law, of the assistance recipient's rights to receive support, on the recipient's own behalf and on behalf of any family member with respect to whom the recipient is receiving cash assistance. The assignment shall be effective only up to the amount of assistance received. The assignment shall take effect at the time that the individual is determined to be eligible for assistance. Upon termination of assistance payments, the assignment of support rights shall terminate, provided that any amount of unpaid support obligations shall continue as an obligation to and collectible by the Department to the extent of any unreimbursed assistance consistent with Federal law.

§ 187.24. (Reserved).

§ 187.25. Notification to the applicant or recipient.

(a) *Cash assistance sought or received for an unemancipated minor child.* Before requiring cooperation under § 187.23(b) (relating to requirements), the CAO will provide oral and written notice of the cooperation requirements to the applicant or recipient. The oral and written notice will advise the applicant or recipient of the following:

(1) The potential benefits that the unemancipated minor child may derive from the cooperation of the applicant or recipient in establishing paternity and obtaining support.

(2) Cooperation is a condition of eligibility.

(3) Failure to cooperate without good cause will result in the reduction of the cash assistance allowance by 25%.

(4) The right to claim good cause, good cause circumstances, proving the good cause claim, and the good cause determination under § 187.27 (relating to waiver of cooperation for good cause).

(5) The CAO will waive the cooperation requirements when the CAO, the court of common pleas or the DRS determines that good cause exists.

(6) A finding of noncooperation of an applicant or recipient does not affect the LRR's duty to pay support.

(b) *Cash assistance sought or received for a spouse.* Before requiring cooperation under § 187.23(c), the CAO will provide oral and written notice to the applicant or recipient of the cooperation requirements and the right to claim good cause. The oral and written notice will advise the applicant or recipient of the information specified in subsection (a).

§ 187.26. Noncooperation.

(a) *Determination of noncooperation by the CAO, court of common pleas or DRS.* The CAO, court or DRS may make the determination of whether an applicant or recipient refused to cooperate without good cause. The court of common pleas of each county will have the option of hearing appeals from any determination of its DRS that an applicant or recipient has not cooperated in accordance with § 187.23 (relating to requirements). If the court declines to exercise the option to hold hearings on the appeals, the procedures in subsection (b) apply. If the CAO determines noncooperation without good cause, the procedures in subsection (c) apply. Subsection (c) (1) applies to applicants. Subsection (c)(2) applies to recipients. The procedures in subsection (c)(1) or (2) also apply when the court declines to hold the noncooperation hearing. If the court, after notice and an opportunity to be heard, determines that the applicant or recipient refused to cooperate without good cause, the Department will implement the court's order, as specified in subsection (d).

(b) If the court or the DRS determines that the applicant or recipient has failed to cooperate, without good cause, with § 187.23, the court or the DRS will provide notice of any noncooperation determination to the CAO along with notice of its decision to opt not to hold a hearing on noncooperation. Appropriate court personnel shall be made available to provide testimonial evidence by telephone testimony at the time and location set by the Department for the Departmental appeal hearing. Upon receipt of the notice from the court or the DRS, the CAO shall proceed in accordance with subsection (c)(1) or (2) depending upon whether the individual is an applicant for or recipient of assistance.

(c) If the CAO determines that the applicant or recipient has failed to cooperate, without good cause, with § 187.23, or upon receipt of a notice of a noncooperation determination by the court or DRS under subsection (b), the CAO will:

(1) In the case of an applicant:

(i) Provide notice to the applicant of the noncooperation determination, the basis for the noncooperation determination and the reduction of the cash assistance allowance by 25% effective upon authorization of assistance.

(ii) Provide notice to the applicant of the right to appeal to the Department's Bureau of Hearings and Appeals under Chapter 275 (relating to appeal and fair hearing and administrative disqualification hearings).

(iii) Authorize the cash assistance allowance reduced by 25% effective upon authorization of assistance.

(iv) Authorize the full cash assistance allowance if so ordered as a result of a decision rendered by the Bureau of Hearings and Appeals, as a result of a good cause claim initiated by the applicant, or as a result of the applicant cooperating with the support requirements.

(2) In the case of a recipient:

(i) Provide notice to the recipient of the noncooperation determination, the basis for the noncooperation determination, and the reduction of the cash assistance allowance by 25% 10 days after the date of the notice.

(ii) Provide notice to the recipient of the right to appeal to the Bureau of Hearings and Appeals under Chapter 275.

(iii) Authorize the reduction of the cash assistance allowance by 25% effective 10 days after the date of the notice, unless the recipient has invoked his right to a hearing and has filed an appeal within the 10-day period. If the recipient has invoked his right to a fair hearing within the 10-day period, cash assistance will not be reduced pending a decision in the hearing.

(iv) Initiate recovery of the assistance granted pending the fair hearing if the Department action is sustained.

(d) *Determination of noncooperation by the court.* A hearing or appeal with respect to the recommendation order of noncooperation directed by the court or DRS will be conducted by the court in accordance with the 231 Pa. Code (relating to rules of civil procedure).

(1) Upon receipt of a court order issued by a court of common pleas, the CAO will implement the order within 10 days of receipt. The CAO will:

(i) Provide notice to the applicant or recipient of the court order and the cash assistance allowance reduction by 25%.

(ii) Provide notice to the applicant or recipient of the right to appeal to the Bureau of Hearings and Appeals under Chapter 275 and that the right of appeal to the Bureau of Hearings and Appeals does not include appeal of a court order in which noncooperation has been determined by the court. The right to appeal in this instance to the Bureau of Hearings and Appeals under Chapter 275 is restricted to the calculation of the assistance allowance.

(iii) For an applicant, authorize the cash assistance allowance reduced by 25% effective upon authorization of assistance. For a recipient, the CAO will reduce the cash assistance allowance by 25% effective 10 days after the date of the notice, unless the recipient has invoked his right to a hearing and has filed an appeal within the 10-day period. If the recipient has invoked his right to a fair hearing within the 10-day period, the cash assistance allowance will not be reduced pending a decision in the hearing.

(2) If the court order directs the Department to rescind the sanction for noncooperation, the Department will implement the order immediately upon receipt.

§ 187.27. Waiver of cooperation for good cause.

(a) *Good cause circumstances.* Cooperation requirements may be waived for good cause. Requirements for granting a good cause waiver based on a claim of domestic violence, as defined in § 108.2 (relating to definitions), may be provided under §§ 108.7 and 108.8 (relating to requirements subject to waiver; and claiming good cause based on domestic violence). Other good cause circumstances include the following:

(1) The child was conceived as a result of incest or rape.

(2) Legal proceedings for the adoption of the child are pending before a court.

(3) The applicant or recipient of cash assistance is currently being assisted by a public or licensed private social agency to resolve the issue of whether to keep the child or relinquish the child for adoption and the discussions have not progressed for more than 3 months.

(b) *Proving the good cause claim.* The applicant or recipient of cash assistance shall provide relevant verification.

(1) A good cause claim may be verified with the following types of evidence:

(i) A birth certificate or medical or law enforcement records which indicate that the child was conceived as the result of incest or rape.

(ii) Court documents or other records which indicate that legal proceedings for adoption are pending.

(iii) A written statement from a public or licensed private social agency that the applicant or recipient is being assisted by the agency to resolve the issue of whether to relinquish the child for adoption.

(iv) Medical records which indicate emotional health history and present emotional health status of the applicant or recipient or the child for whom support would be sought; or, written statements from a mental health professional indicating a diagnosis or prognosis concerning the emotional health of the applicant or recipient or the child for whom support would be sought. Supportive evidence submitted from a mental health professional will be defined as statements written by individuals who have obtained licensure or certification, if applicable, or have received a degree in defined areas of mental health including psychiatry, social work, psychology, nursing, occupational therapy or recreational therapy.

(v) Court, medical, criminal, child protective services, social services, psychological or law enforcement records.

(vi) Statements from individuals other than the applicant or recipient with knowledge of the good cause circumstances, including a domestic violence service provider, a medical, psychological or social service provider, a law enforcement professional, a legal representative, an acquaintance, friend, relative or neighbor of the claimant or other individual.

(2) When the applicant or recipient initiates a claim of good cause, the Department, court or the DRS may provide help with obtaining verification. If requested by the applicant or recipient, the Department, court or DRS will provide help in securing the needed evidence by advising how to obtain specific documents that may be available and by undertaking to obtain specific documents the applicant or recipient is not able to obtain.

(3) An applicant or recipient shall provide verification of the good cause claim, as specified under paragraph (1)(iv)—(vi), within 30 days from the date the claim is made, except when the applicant or recipient cannot otherwise provide verification of the good cause claim as specified in paragraph (1)(vii)(C).

(i) In the case of an applicant, assistance will be authorized no later than 30 days following application when the applicant is claiming good cause and verification is not readily available or pending from a third party.

(ii) In the case of a recipient, the CAO will continue assistance if verification is not provided within 30 days and the delay is due to a third party.

(c) *Good cause determination.* The court or the DRS will make a determination within 45 days from the day the claim was initiated by the applicant or recipient of cash assistance. The Department will make a determination within 15-calendar days from the date the claim was initiated by the applicant or recipient. The Department, court or the DRS may approve additional days for the determination to be completed.

(1) If the CAO makes a determination on a good cause claim, the CAO will notify the applicant or recipient of cash assistance in writing of the final determination regarding the claim of good cause and the basis therefore and of the right to appeal under Chapter 275 (relating to appeal and fair hearing and administrative disqualification hearings). If the good cause claim is denied, neither the Department nor the Bureau of Child Support Enforcement will attempt to establish paternity or obtain support for at least 30 days after the individual has been informed orally and in writing of the denial of the good cause claim.

(2) If the court of common pleas or DRS makes a determination on a good cause claim, the DRS will notify the applicant or recipient of cash assistance and the CAO of the final determination and the basis therefore and of the right to appeal under Chapter 275.

(3) When the CAO, court of common pleas or the DRS approve a waiver of the cooperation requirement based on a claim of good cause, the DRS will not attempt to establish paternity or obtain support.

(4) When good cause is determined to exist, the Department will review the circumstances upon which the good cause determination is based, at least every 6 months. If the good cause waiver was granted based on verification, no additional verification is required if circumstances have not changed since approval of the initial waiver.

SUPPORT PROVISIONS FOR MA FOR THE CATEGORICALLY NEEDY

Sec.
187.71. Policy.
187.73. Requirements.
187.74. Procedures.

§ 187.71. Policy.

Support from LRR's.–Legally responsible relatives will be limited to the spouse of the applicant and the natural or adoptive parent or parents of an unemancipated minor child. However, there will be no relative responsibility by the relatives of the following children for MA purposes:

(1) Adoptive or natural parents of a child, regardless of age, adopted under the provisions of the act of June 13, 1967 (P. L. 31, No. 21) (62 P. S. §§ 771–774) known as the Adoption Opportunities Act. The adoptive parents of children adopted under the provisions of the Adoption Opportunities Act will be issued a "Certificate of Subsidized Adoption" card, CY 931, by the Child Welfare Office, which will be sufficient proof of adoption under the terms of this act.

(2) Parents of a child, 18 to 21 years of age, when the child receives MA services in the MH/MR facility.

(3) Parents of a child, regardless of age, or a spouse when the child or spouse is receiving SSI payments. The parent or spouse will be liable in determining MA eligibility and payment until the child or spouse receives SSI benefits, at which time, the child or spouse will be categorically needy on the basis of SSI eligibility and there will be no further relative liability for MA purposes.

§ 187.73. Requirements.

The requirements of § 187.23 (relating to requirements) will apply as modified by § 187.71 (relating to policy).

§ 187.74. Procedures.

(a) For nonapplicant spouse and the natural or adoptive parent or parents of an unemancipated minor child living with the applicant, PA Manual 175 and § 183.64 (relating to income averaging), the method of arriving at assistance, will apply.

(b) For the spouse of an applicant and the natural or adoptive parent or parents of an unemancipated minor child not living with the applicant, the following method will be used to determine financial ability to support:

(1) The dependents living with the spouse/parent will be determined. Minor children under 18 will always be included. Other persons will be included if they are without income of their own or the spouse/parent requests their income be added to his income.

(2) Total net income of the spouse/parent including that of his dependents whose income must be taken into account will be determined. Net income from self-employment or business is profit before tax deductions. Net income from other employment is gross less $20 per month for work expenses.

(3) The amount the LRR is paying for the support of his spouse or his minor child or children outside his home will be deducted.

(4) The appropriate figure from the following income scale will be selected and subtracted from the total net income:

No. of Persons Dependent Upon LRR's Income	1	2	3	4	5	6	Each Additional Person
Net Monthly Income	$173	$260	$317	$373	423	$459	Add $54

(5) The appropriate fraction will be applied to the remainder:

(i) $1/2$ when the assistance unit includes one legal dependent.

(ii) $2/3$ when the assistance unit includes two legal dependents.

(iii) $3/4$ when the assistance unit includes three or more legal dependents.

(6) The expected contribution will be the resulting figure or the total allowances for the persons for whom the LRR is legally responsible, whichever is lesser.

(c) The total allowances for the person or persons for whom the relative is legally responsible will be the difference between the family size allowances with the person or persons in the assistance unit, excluding special needs allowances, and what the allowances would be if the person or persons were not included in the assistance unit. When it has been determined that an LRR is financially able to provide support, the client will be expected to either contact the LRR directly to arrange for the amount of the expected contribution or to give consent for the County Office to contact the LRR. If the expected contribution from the relative is secured, it will become available to the client. Court action will be required in accordance with the procedures in § 187.24 (relating to procedures) whenever the following occur:

(1) The total amount of the expected contribution is not secured.

(2) The client is unwilling to contact the LRR directly and objects to the Department contacting the LRR.

(d) Assistance will be continued until the court makes a decision. Any amount that the LRR is actually contributing will be considered income available to the client.

SUPPORT PROVISIONS FOR MA FOR THE MEDICALLY NEEDY

Sec.
187.81. Policy.
187.83. Requirements.
187.84. Procedures.

§ 187.81. Policy.

Support from LRR's.—Policy regarding support from the LRR's will be as follows:

(1) Legally responsible relatives will be limited to the spouse of the applicant and the natural or adoptive parent or parents of an unemancipated minor child. However, there will be no relative responsibility by the relatives of the following children for MA purposes:

(i) Adoptive or natural parents of a child, regardless of age, adopted under the provisions of the act of June 13, 1967 (P. L. 31, No. 21) (62 P. S. §§ 771–774) known as the Adoption Opportunities Act. The adoptive parents of children adopted under the provisions of the the Adoption Opportunities Act will be issued a "Certificate of Subsidized Adoption" card, CY 931, by the Child Welfare Office, which will be sufficient proof of adoption under the terms of this act.

(ii) Parents of a child, 18 to 21 years of age, when the child received MA services in a MH/MR facility.

(iii) Parents of a child, regardless of age, or a spouse when the child or spouse is receiving SSI payments. The parent or spouse will be liable in determining MA eligibility and payment until the child or spouse received SSI benefits, at which time the child or spouse will be categorically needy on the basis of SSI eligibility and there will be no further relative liability for MA purposes.

(2) A finding of financial ability to contribute to the applicant group will be made for each such relative except that a relative over 60 years of age will be excluded.

(3) Parent will include the father of a child born out of wedlock only if paternity has been legally established.

(4) The court alone will have the authority to decide that a spouse or parent must provide support and to what extent. If there is an existing court order, or, where appropriate, the Revenue Agent has determined the amount to be paid, no further determination will be needed. The amount of the order that is being paid will be considered as the income of the person.

(5) For cases where there is no existing order, or where an established court order is not being met, the Department has developed regulations for determining the amount a spouse or parent might be expected to contribute towards meeting the cost of the MA care received.

(6) The findings of the Department on the financial ability of a spouse or parent will be exclusively for the purpose of determining the amount of the monthly income in excess of the amount the Department believes is reasonable for the support of himself and others dependent on him.

(7) If the applicant is otherwise eligible and if an immediate finding cannot be made of the financial ability of a legally responsible relative to help meet the medical care costs of his spouse or unemancipated minor children, the client will be eligible for medical assistance for a temporary period, not to exceed such time as a decision can be reached as to the availability of funds from the legally responsible relative.

(8) A determination of ability to support will be made at each redetermination. If it is necessary to determine the LRR's ability to pay before 6 months have passed since the last application of redetermination, the amount the LRR has already paid or has obligated himself to pay since the contribution was last determined will be deducted from the amount arrived at in § 187.84 (relating to procedures) to determine the amount by which the LRR continues to be a resource. If the case was referred to the Claim Settlement Area Office for court action, before the County Office makes a new determination of ability to support and the amount of support expected, it will request the Area Office to report the amount collected and any other pertinent information.

(9) The liability of a parent for children receiving MA services in a mental health or mental retardation facility will be limited to children under 18 years of age.

§ 187.83. Requirements.

Requirements for seeking support from LRR.—Requirements for seeking support from LRR will be as follows:

(1) **Information about the financial circumstances of the LRR.**—The statement of the client that the circumstances of the LRR are one of the following will be acceptable verification that the LRR is financially unable to help, and his financial ability will not need to be determined:

(i) The relative has six or more dependents, including the LRR himself.

(ii) The relative is unemployed or receiving assistance other than SBP.

(iii) The earning capacity of the relative is so limited because of physical or mental handicap that there is little likelihood of his ever having enough income to help meet the costs of MA.

(iv) The occupation of the relative and the prevailing wage rates for that type of work indicate that there is little likelihood of his having enough income to help meet the cost of MA.

(v) The relative is a housewife without income.

(vi) The LRR is missing.

(2) **Missing LRR's.**—No efforts will be made to locate a missing LRR if the client states that the current location of the relative is unknown.

§ 187.84. Procedures.

(a) **Determination of expected contribution.**—The contribution expected from a spouse or from a parent of an unemancipated minor child will be determined as follows:

(1) The allowable dependents living with the spouse parent will be determined. Dependents that may be included are as follows:

(i) Minor children for whom the LRR is legally responsible.

(ii) Other legal dependent without income.

(iii) Other legal dependent with income, providing the LRR so requests.

(2) Total net income of the spouse parent and his dependents will be determined. Net income from self-employment or business is profit before tax deductions. Net income from other employment is gross income less $20 per month for work expenses. Income earned under Title I of the Economic Opportunity Act of 1964 (42 U.S.C.A. §§ 2711—2756b) will not be included.

(3) The following will be deducted from the total determined in paragraph (2).

(i) The amount the LRR is paying for the support of a person not living with him, and for whom he or his wife is legally responsible.

(ii) The amount the LRR is contributing towards the support of spouse or child.

(4) If the spouse or parent is an SBP recipient, $85 will be deducted from the monthly income.

(5) The appropriate figure will be selected from the following income scale and subtracted from the total net income:

No. of Persons Dependent Upon Relative's Income (Including the Relative)	1	2	3	4	5	6
Net Monthly Income	$230	$340	$400	$460	$520	$580

(6) Six times the resulting figure will be considered to be available for meeting the cost of MA.

(b) **Waiver of expected contribution.**—When an LRR has been determined able to contribute according to subsection (a), and it appears unsound, unreasonable, or impracticable to expect the LRR to make the determined contribution, the situation will be presented to the Executive Director or his delegate for a decision as to whether the expected contribution is to be waived. The fact that the scale in subsection (a) does not reflect current living costs will not of itself be a sound basis for waiver. A waiver will be made for a specified period. The basis of the waiver as well as the time period specified will be recorded in the notes section of the Form PA 743 or Form 743-R.

(c) **Court action.**—The county office will refer a case for court action under the following conditions:

(1) **Legally responsible relative refuses to acknowledge liability for support.**—A legally responsible relative who refuses to acknowledge liability for support will be as follows:

(i) An LRR will be considered as refusing to acknowledge liability for support in the following cases:

(A) The LRR fails to provide information about his financial circumstances within 15 days of the date of the request for the information.

(B) The LRR is found to be financially able to contribute but advises the county office that he will not pay or that he will pay only part of the expected contribution.

(ii) In either of the circumstances in clauses (A) and (B), an otherwise eligible client will be found eligible for MA, counting as an available resource only the amount the LRR has agreed to pay. The county office will refer the case to the Claim Settlement Area Office on a Form PA 173-M for collection from the LRR by court action if necessary in accordance with the following:

(A) If the first invoice paid is for inpatient hospital care, hospital-home care, or private nursing home care, the referral will be made at that time.

(B) If the invoices paid are for services other than the three listed in clause (A), then the referral will be made at the end of the quarterly period covered by the identification card. The amount to be collected will be the sum of the invoices paid during that period up to the amount of the expected contribution.

(iii) The LRR's listed on the Form PA 173-M will be only those who refuse to acknowledge liability for support. If the Form PA 173-M indicates that the county office has not computed the amount of the expected contribution, claim settlement will determine the amount of the expected contribution in accordance with subsection (a).

(2) **Legally responsible relative agrees to contribute.**—When an LRR agrees to contribute, the expected amount will be counted as another available resource in determining eligibility for MA.

APPENDIX A. [Reserved]

APPENDIX B. [Reserved]

INDEX

References are to Sections of the Pennsylvania Domestic Relations Code, Pennsylvania Crimes Code, Pennsylvania Judicial Code, Pennsylvania Domestic Relations Court Rules, and Selected Federal Statutes, Court Rules, and Regulations

—A—

Abandoned
Defined, child custody jurisdiction, § 5402

Absence and Absentees
Marriage, presumption of death, § 1701

Abuse of Persons
Abuse, as defined, protection from abuse, § 6102
Alimony, divorce, § 3701
Child abuse, defined, child protective services, § 6303
Child Protective Services, generally, this index
Custody, § 5322
Generally, Rule 1901 et seq.
Hearings by court, decision and post-trial relief, Rule 1920.52
Protection from Abuse, see generally, this index
Service of process, Rule 1930.4
Sexual abuse, defined, child protective services, § 6303

Accident and Health Insurance
Coverage, forms, Rule 1910.27

Accord and Satisfaction
Liens and encumbrances, enforcement of support orders, Rule 1910.22
Marriage, instruments executed in satisfaction of abolished claims, prohibition, § 1905

Account
Definitions, disclosure, cooperation, § 4304.1

Accounts and Accounting
Divorce, determination and distribution of property, Rule 1920.33
Forms, 1920.75

Acknowledgement
Paternity, support actions, Rule 1910.15, 1910.28
Paternity, § 5103

Actions and Proceedings
Adoption, this index
Alienation of affections, abolition, § 1901
Alternate procedure, § 4342
Attendance, interstate family support enforcement, § 7316
Attorneys, private counsel, interstate family support enforcement, § 7309
Bonds or security, attendance or performance, § 4347
Commencement, § 4341
Consolidation, § 4349
Costs, § 4351
  Interstate family support enforcement, § 7313
Defenses, nonparentage, interstate family support enforcement, § 7315
Educational expenses, § 4327
Entireties property, support order execution against, § 4361 et seq.
Evidence, interstate family support enforcement, § 7316
Expedited procedure, § 4342
Fees, interstate family support enforcement, § 7313
Initiating tribunal, interstate family support enforcement, powers and duties, § 7304
Interstate family support enforcement, § 7301 et seq.
Joinder, public welfare department, § 4306
Minor parents, intrastate family support enforcement, § 8302
Breach of promise to marry, abolition, § 1902
Child protective services
  Evidence, § 6381
  Guardian ad litem for child, § 6382
Custody or visitation of minors, Rule 1915.1

1225

INDEX

References are to Sections of the Pennsylvania Domestic Relations Code, Pennsylvania Crimes Code, Pennsylvania Judicial Code, Pennsylvania Domestic Relations Court Rules, and Selected Federal Statutes, Court Rules, and Regulations

Actions and Proceedings—Cont'd
Hospitals, failure to admit child abuse victims, § 6316
Parental liability for torts, § 5501 et seq.
Protection from abuse, commencement, § 6106; Rule 1901 et seq.
Tortious acts of children, establishing liability of parent
    Civil proceedings, § 5504
    Criminal or juvenile proceedings, § 5503

Address
Changes, support order, Rule 1910.17
Disclosure, § 4352
Notice, § 4353
Protection from abuse, disclosure, § 6112

Addicts
Chemically Dependent Persons, generally, this index

Administration
Support matters, § 4305

Admissibility of Evidence
Evidence, generally, this index

Admissions
Judgments and Decrees, generally, this index

Adopted Children
Custody, exception, § 5314

Adoptees
Defined, adoption, § 2102
Names, adoption, § 2904

Adoption
    Generally, § 2101 et seq.; Pa O.C. Rule 15.1, et seq.
Abuse of children
    Parental rights termination, § 2511
Access to records, § 2905
Accumulation of information concerning registered children, § 2554
Actions and proceedings, § 2301 et seq.
    Impoundment, § 2905
    Proceedings prior to petition to adopt, § 2501 et seq.
Administration
    Public information programs, § 2554
Adopted children, custody, exception, § 5314
Adoptees
    Defined, § 2102
    Name, § 2904

Adoption—Cont'd
Adults, voluntary relinquishment of child to adult intending to adopt, § 2502
Age,
    Consent, § 2711
Agents and agencies
    Application of law, § 2556
    Child custody, parental rights termination, § 2511
    Child service agencies, duties, § 2555
    Defined, § 2102
    Voluntary relinquishment to, § 2501
Alternative procedure for voluntary relinquishment, § 2504
Anonymity, natural parents, medical history information, § 2905
Appeal and review, foreign adoptions, § 2908
Appearance, petition for adoption, hearing, § 2723
Attendance, petition for adoption, hearing, § 2723
Attorney fees,
    Counsel for representation, § 2313
    Intermediary, reimbursement, § 2533
Attorneys, appointment for child, § 2313
Birth certificates,
    Identity of natural parents, § 2905
    Reports, intermediaries, § 2534
Certificate of adoption, § 2907
Child service agencies, duties, § 2555
Children and minors
    Children 12 years of age or over, consent required, § 2734
    Guardians ad litem for child and sibling, § 2741
    Representation, § 2313
    Voluntary relinquishment to an adult intending to adopt, § 2502
Clerk, defined, § 2102
Confidential or privileged information,
    Disclosure, penalty, § 2910
    Foreign decrees and companion documents, § 2908
    Identity of adoptive parents, § 2504.1
    Natural parents identity, § 2905
    Records, § 2905
Confidential information, disclosure, penalty, § 2910
Confidential or privileged information, release, § 2935

1226

INDEX

References are to Sections of the Pennsylvania Domestic Relations Code, Pennsylvania Crimes Code, Pennsylvania Judicial Code, Pennsylvania Domestic Relations Court Rules, and Selected Federal Statutes, Court Rules, and Regulations

Adoption—Cont'd
Consents, petition for adoption, § 2711 et seq.
  Consents not naming adopting parents, § 2712
  Discretion, dispensing with consents other than adoptee's, § 2713 Guardians, § 2711
  Identification,
    Adopting parents, nondisclosure, § 2712
    Natural parents, § 2905
  Necessary consents, § 2711
  Parental rights termination decree already entered, § 2714
  Parents of adoptees, §§ 2711, 2905
  Petitions, § 2702
  Relinquishment, of parental rights,
    Adults who are intending to adopt and have custody, § 2502
    Agency, § 2501
  Reports, intermediaries, § 2534
  Spouse of adopting parent, § 2711
  When consent of parent not required, § 2714
  When other consents not required, § 2713
Contested hearing, appointment of counsel, § 2313
Costs,
  Attorney fees, § 2313
  Investigations, § 2535, 2724
Counseling, voluntary relinquishment, § 2505
Court referrals, counseling services, § 2905
Courts
  Defined, § 2102
  Jurisdiction, § 2301
Creation, public information programs, § 2554
Crimes and offenses, unauthorized disclosure, § 2910
Decree terminating parental rights, § 2521
Decree of adoption, § 2901 et seq.
  Dockets, entries, § 2906
  Foreign decrees, § 2908
  Form, § 2902

Adoption—Cont'd
  Names, adoptee, § 2904
  Requirements, § 2902
  Time of entry, § 2901
Decree of termination, effect, § 2521
Definitions, § 2102
Disclosure,
  Foreign decrees and companion documents, § 2908
  Identity of natural parents, § 2905
  Records, § 2905
Disclosure, unauthorized disclosure, penalty, § 2910
Discretion of court,
  Contacting natural parents, § 2905
  Dispensing with consents other than adoptees, § 2713
Dissemination, statistical information concerning registered children, § 2554
Dockets, entries, § 2906
Duress or coercion, § 2711
Eligibility to adopt, § 2312
Evidence,
  Certificates of adoption, § 2907
  Hearings, § 2724
Exclusions, § 2724
  Children with parental rights terminated excluded from registration, § 2553
Exhibits,
  Confidentiality, § 2905
  Petitions, § 2702
  Reports, intermediaries, § 2534
Expenses and expenditures, intermediary, reimbursement, § 2533
Files and filing, reports, intention to adopt, § 2532
Fines and penalties, unauthorized disclosure, § 2910
Foreign adoption registration procedure, Pa.O.C. Rule 15.8
Foreign decrees, § 2908
Forms, decree of adoption, § 2902
Foster care, expenses and expenditures, intermediary, reimbursement,
Grandparents, visitation, § 5314
Grounds, involuntary termination, § 2511
Guardian ad litem, appointment, § 2313
Guardians, consent, § 2711
Hearings, § 2721, et seq.
  Alternatives, § 2504
  Appearance, § 2723

INDEX

References are to Sections of the Pennsylvania Domestic Relations Code, Pennsylvania Crimes Code, Pennsylvania Judicial Code, Pennsylvania Domestic Relations Court Rules, and Selected Federal Statutes, Court Rules, and Regulations

Adoption—Cont'd
  Attorneys appointed, § 2313
  Evidence, § 2724
  Involuntary termination, § 2513
  Notice, § 2721
  Petition for adoption
    Attendance, § 2723
    Investigation, § 2724
    Location, § 2722
    Notice, § 2721
    Religious beliefs, § 2725
    Testimony, § 2724
  Private hearings, § 2722
  Home studies prior to adoption, § 2530
  Voluntary relinquishment, § 2503
  Hospitals, appointment of counseling, § 2505
  Husband and wife, consent, spouse of adopting parent, § 2711
  Identification,
    Adopting parents, consents not disclosing, § 2712
  Impounding proceedings § 2905
  Inspection and inspectors,
    Foreign decrees and companion documents, § 2908
    Records, § 2905
  Intention to adopt, report, § 2531
    Filing, § 2532
    Investigation, § 2535
  Intermediaries
    Defined, § 2102
    Reports, § 2533
      Exhibits, § 2534
  Investigations
    Petition for adoption, hearing, § 2724
    Report of intention to adopt, § 2535
  Involuntary termination
    Confidentiality, identity of adoptive parents, § 2504.1
    Grounds, § 2511
    Hearing, § 2513
    Petition, § 2512
  Judgments and decrees, § 2901
    Confidentiality, § 2905
    Docket entries, § 2906
      Foreign decrees, § 2908
    Foreign decrees, § 2908
    Form, § 2902
    Relinquishment, parental rights, § 2503

Adoption—Cont'd
  Termination of parental rights, § 2513
    Certified copies of decrees, reports, intermediaries, § 2534
    Effect of decrees, § 2521
    Time, § 2901
  Jurisdiction
    Court, § 2301
    Venue, § 2302
  Mail and mailing, certified or registered mail, notice,
    Hearings, § 2721
    Parental right termination hearings, § 2513
  Medical care and treatment, expenses and expenditures, intermediary, reimbursement, § 2533
  Medical history information, § 2909
    Defined, § 2102
  Names,
    Adoptees, § 2904
    Retention of parental names, § 2903
  Necessary consents, § 2711
  Neglect of children, parental rights termination, § 2511
  Notice,
    Adoptee, § 2904
    Parent having lost rights, § 2521
    Parental rights,
      Relinquishment hearings, § 2503
      Termination hearings, § 2513
    Petition for adoption, hearing, § 2721
  Parental consent, § 2711
  Parental rights,
    Guardian ad litem, appointment, § 2313
    Retention, parents consenting to adoption by spouse, § 2903
  Parental status, retention, § 2903
  Parents
    Adoptive parents, confidentiality of identity, § 2504.1
    Defined, § 2102
    Petition for adoption, consents
      Consents not naming adopting parents, § 2712
      When consent of parent not required, § 2714
      When other consents not required, § 2713

INDEX

References are to Sections of the Pennsylvania Domestic Relations Code, Pennsylvania Crimes Code, Pennsylvania Judicial Code, Pennsylvania Domestic Relations Court Rules, and Selected Federal Statutes, Court Rules, and Regulations

Adoption—Cont'd
Parties
    Representation for child, § 2313
    Who may adopt, § 2312
    Who may be adopted, § 2311
Pennsylvania Adoption Cooperative Exchange, generally, this index
Personal and Medical History, § 2503, § 2504
Personal information, right to file, involuntary termination, § 2511
Petition for adoption, § 2701 et seq.
    Consents, § 2711 et seq.
        Consents not naming adopting parents, § 2712
        Necessary consents, § 2711
        When consent of parent not required, § 2714
        When other consents not required, § 2713
    Content, § 2701
    Exhibits, § 2702
    Hearings, § 2721 et seq.
        Attendance, § 2723
        Investigation, § 2724
        Location, § 2722
        Notice, § 2721
        Religious belief, § 2725
        Testimony, § 2724
    Proceedings prior to, § 2501 et seq.
Petition for involuntary termination, § 2512
Private child service agencies, duties, § 2555
Private hearings, § 2722
Proceedings prior to petition to adopt, § 2501 et seq.
Process, service of process, hearings, notice, § 2721
Prospective adoptive parents, information, § 6344
Public child service agencies, duties, § 2555
Public information programs, creation and administration, § 2554
Putative father, alternative procedure for relinquishment, § 2504
Records, access, § 2905
Registration,
    Adoptive parent applicants, § 2554
    Children with parental rights terminated, § 2553
Release of information, § 2931

Adoption—Cont'd
Religious beliefs, petition for adoption, hearing, § 2725
Relinquishment of parental rights, § 2501 et seq.
    Adults intending to adopt and having custody, § 2502
    Agencies, parent relinquishing to agency, § 2501
    Consent, § 2501
        Adults intending to adopt and having custody, § 2502
    Hearing, § 2503
    Venue, § 2302
Reports, § 2531 et seq.
    Confidentiality, § 2905
    Home studies prior to adoption, § 2530
    Identity of natural parents, § 2905
    Intention to adopt, § 2531
        Filing, § 2532
        Investigation, § 2535
    Intermediaries, § 2533
        Exhibits, § 2534
    Listed children and prospective adoptive parents, § 2554
    Voluntary or local public child care agency or appropriate person, § 2535
Representation for child, § 2313
Retention of parental status, § 2903
Short title of law, § 2101
Termination, decree, effect, § 2521
Termination of parental rights, § 2511 et seq.
    Attorney, appointment for child, § 2313
    Grounds, § 2511
    Hearings, § 2513
    Petition, § 2512
    Venue, § 2302
Testimony, petition for adoption, hearing, § 2724
Time,
    Decrees, § 2901
Validity, consent, § 2711
Unauthorized disclosure, penalty, § 2910
Venue, § 2302
Voluntary relinquishment, § 2501 et seq.
    Alternative procedure for relinquishment, § 2504
    Confidentiality, identity of adoptive parents, § 2504.1
    Counseling, § 2505

INDEX

References are to Sections of the Pennsylvania Domestic Relations Code, Pennsylvania Crimes Code, Pennsylvania Judicial Code, Pennsylvania Domestic Relations Court Rules, and Selected Federal Statutes, Court Rules, and Regulations

Adoption—Cont'd
    Hearing, § 2503
    Relinquishment to adult intending to adopt child, § 2502, Pa. O.C. Rule 15.3
    Relinquishment to agency, § 2501
    Witnesses, petition for adoption, hearing, § 2724
    Who may adopt, § 2312
    Who may be adopted, § 2311
    Witnesses, competency of mother, presumptive or putative father's status as natural father, § 2513

Adoption Act
Generally, § 2101 et seq.

Adultery
Divorce,
    Defense, § 3307
    Grounds, § 3301

Advocates
Domestic violence counselor-advocate
    Defined, protection from abuse, § 6102
    Protection from abuse, § 6111

Affections
Alienation of Affections, generally, this index

Affidavits
Acknowledgment of paternity, § 5103
Annulment of marriage, service, Rule 1920.4
Child custody proceedings, required information, § 5350
Counteraffidavits, Rules 1920.42, 1920.72
Counter-affidavits regarding relocation of child, § 5337
Divorce or annulment actions, Rules 1920.14, 1920.42, 1920.46, 1920.72
Divorce,
    Mutual consent to divorce, § 3301
Domestic violence actions,
    Insufficient funds for filing fees, § 6106
Firearms, relinquishment to dealer, protection from abuse, § 6108.2
Paternity acknowledgment, § 5103

Affirmations
Oaths and Affirmations, generally, this index

Age
Annulment of marriage, marital property division factor, § 3502
Children and minors, attainment of full age, § 5101
Divorce,
    Marital property division factor, § 3502
    Party ages, alimony necessity factor, § 3701

Agencies
Adoption, voluntary relinquishment to, § 2501
Child protective services
    Cooperation, § 6346
    Purchasing services of other agencies, § 6364
Defined, adoption, § 2102
Law enforcement agencies, protection from abuse, responsibilities, § 6105
Pennsylvania Adoption Cooperative Exchange
    Related activities unaffected, § 2556
    Responsibilities, § 2555
State Agencies, generally, this index
Support of persons, parties, Rule 1910.3

Agreements
Contracts, generally, this index
Defined, adoption, voluntary agreement for continuing contact, § 2732
Effect, § 3105, Rule 1910.11
Postsecondary education, expenses, applicability, § 4327
Premarital agreements, § 3106

Alcoholics and Intoxicated Persons
Annulment of marriage,
    Voidable marriages, parties who are under alcohol influence, grounds for annulment, § 3305
Marriage,
    Restrictions on marriage license issuance, § 1304

Alienation of Affections
Actions abolished, § 1901
Filing or threatening actions prohibited, § 1904
Instruments executed in satisfaction of abolished claims prohibited, § 1905
Purpose of law, § 1903

INDEX

References are to Sections of the Pennsylvania Domestic Relations Code, Pennsylvania Crimes Code, Pennsylvania Judicial Code, Pennsylvania Domestic Relations Court Rules, and Selected Federal Statutes, Court Rules, and Regulations

Alimony
Generally, § 3701 et seq.; Rule 1910.1 et seq.
Abuse, alimony necessary factors, § 3701
Age,
    Alimony necessity factor, § 3701
Agreements to pay alimony, status, § 3701
Allocation, Rule 1920.56
Alternative hearing procedures, Rule 1910.10
Answers, contempt petitions, Rule 1910.25
Arrearages, enforcement, § 3703
Arrest, bench warrant,
    Contempt petitions, Rule 1910.21-1
    Failure or refusal to appear, Rules 1910.13-1, 1910.13-2
Assets of parties, alimony necessity factor, § 3701
Attorney fees,
    Pendente lite alimony awards, § 3702
Bar to alimony, § 3706
Change of circumstances, court order modification or termination, § 3701
Civil procedure rules, Rule 1910.1 et seq.
Commencement of action, Rule 1910.4
Complaint, Rules 1910.4, 1910.5
Conferences,
    Contempt petitions, Rules 1910.25-1, 1910.25-2
    Failure or refusal to appear, arrest bench warrant, Rules 1910.13-1, 1910.13-2
    Summary, contempt petitions, Rule 1910.21-4
Contempt, Rule 1910.25 et seq.
Contempt, arrearages enforcement, § 3703
Death of parties, effect, § 3707
Defendant, pleading, Rule 1910.7
Defined, § 3103
Dependency tax exemption, Rule 1910.16-2
Discovery, Rules 1910.9, 1920.22, 1930.5
Disposition of property to defeat alimony, attachment, § 3505
Distributions, domestic relations section of court, § 3704
Divorce or annulment actions, Rules 1920.31, 1920.56

Alimony—Cont'd
Domicile and residence, venue, Rule 1910.2
Duration of marriage, alimony necessity factor, § 3701
Earnings of parties, alimony necessity factor, § 3701
Educational contribution of one party to other, alimony necessity factor, § 3701
Emotional conditions of parties, alimony necessity factor, § 3701
Employability of parties, alimony necessity factor, § 3701
Enforcement of arrearages, § 3703
Exceptions, contempt petition hearing report, Rule 1910.25-4
Expectancies of divorced parties, alimony necessity factor, § 3701
Expenses and expenditures,
    Pendente lite alimony awards, § 3702
Factors determining necessity of alimony, § 3701
Federal tax ramifications, alimony necessity factor, § 3701
Fee, filing complaint, Rule 1910.4
Filing pendente lite claim as count in divorce, Rule 1920.31
Financial Records, disclosure, Rule 1920.31
Foreign decrees, enforcement, § 3705
Gross income, computation, Rule 1910.16-2
Hearings,
    Contempt petitions, Rule 1910.25-1
    Record hearing, Rule 1910.25-4
    Decision and post-trial relief, Rule 1920.52
    Failure or refusal to appear, arrest bench warrant, Rules 1910.13-1, 1910.13-2
Homemaker contribution of spouse, alimony necessity factor, § 3701
Incarceration, contempt, Rule 1910.25-5
Income, computation, Rule 1910.16-2
Income tax-federal, 26 C.F.R. § 1.71-1, 26 C.F.R. § 1.71-1T
Inheritances, divorced parties, alimony necessity factor, § 3701
Insurance benefits of divorced parties, § 3701

INDEX

References are to Sections of the Pennsylvania Domestic Relations Code, Pennsylvania Crimes Code, Pennsylvania Judicial Code, Pennsylvania Domestic Relations Court Rules, and Selected Federal Statutes, Court Rules, and Regulations

Alimony—Cont'd
Interest awards, unpaid alimony installments, arrearages enforcement, § 3703
Joinder of related claims, Rule 1920.31
Judgments and decrees,
  Arrearages enforcement, § 3703
Jurisdiction, § 3104
Liabilities of parties, alimony necessity factor, § 3701
Liens and encumbrances, § 3502
Local tax ramifications, alimony necessity factor, § 3701
Marital misconduct of parties, alimony necessity factor, § 3701
Masters, appointment, Rule 1920.51
Medical income sources of divorced parties, alimony necessity factor, § 3701
Mental conditions of parties, alimony necessity factor, § 3701
Modification of court order, § 3701
Monthly gross income, computation, Rule 1910.16-2
Necessity of alimony, determination, § 3701
Notice, hearings, contempt petition, Rules 1910.25-3, 1910.25-4
Obligations to pay, termination, death of payor party, § 3707
Orders, contempt, Rule 1910.25-5
  Petition conferences, Rule 1910.25-2
Orders; payment allocation, Rules 1920.31, 1920.56
Parties, Rule 1910.3
Pendente lite, Rule 1920.56
  Alimony, § 3702
  Arrearages, enforcement, § 3703
    Court order, § 3323
    Foreign decrees, the enforcement, § 3705
    Payments to domestic relations section of court § 3704
Petitions, contempt, Rule 1910.25
Petitions,
  Pendente lite alimony, § 3702
Physical condition of parties, alimony necessity factor, § 3701
Post-trial relief, contempt orders, Rule 1910.25-6
Property contributions of parties, alimony necessity factor, § 3701

Alimony—Cont'd
Property holdings of parties, alimony necessity factor, § 3701
Reasons for award or denial of alimony, § 3701
Reinstatement of court order, § 3701
Relative assets and liabilities of parties, alimony necessity factor, § 3701
Remarriage of party receiving alimony, award termination, § 3701
Reports, contempt petition hearings, Rule 1910.25-4
Retirement income of the divorced parties, alimony necessity factor, § 3701
Self-support capabilities of parties, alimony necessity factor, § 3701
Special relief, Rule 1920.43
Standard of living, alimony necessity factor, § 3701
State tax ramifications, alimony necessity factor, § 3701
Stay of proceedings, contempt petition, request for hearings, Rule 1910.25-4
Summary, conference contempt petitions, Rule 1910.25-3
Tax exemptions, dependency tax, Rule 1910.16-2
Temporary alimony, foreign decrees, enforcement, § 3705
Termination of alimony rights, death of parties, § 3707
Termination of court order, § 3701
Transfer of actions, Rule 1910.8
Venue, Rule 1910.2
Wage attachment, alimony enforcement, § 3703
Waiver, failure to claim, Rule 1920.31

Alimony Pendente Lite
Generally, Rule 1920.56
Arrearages, enforcement, § 3703
Foreign decrees, enforcement, § 3705

Allocation
Support order, Rules 1910.16, 1920.56

Alternative Hearings
Procedures, Rule 1910.10

Alternative Pleading
See Pleadings

Amendment or Modification
Support actions, Rules 1910.17, 1910.19, 1910.27

INDEX

References are to Sections of the Pennsylvania Domestic Relations Code, Pennsylvania Crimes Code, Pennsylvania Judicial Code, Pennsylvania Domestic Relations Court Rules, and Selected Federal Statutes, Court Rules, and Regulations

Americans with Disabilities Act
Notice, compliance, Rules 1910.26, 1915.15, 1915.16

Annulment of Marriage
Affidavits
    Military service, Rule 1920.46
    Service, Rule 1920.4
Age,
    Common-law marriages, under age, grounds for annulment, § 3304
    Marital property division factor, § 3502
    Underage parties, voidable marriage, grounds for annulment, § 3305
Alcohol,
    Party under influence, grounds for annulment, § 3305
Alimony pendente lite,
    Court order, § 3323
Answer, Rule 1920.14-1920.15
Appearance, general appearance, § 33 of nine
Applications,
    Jury trial, § 3322
Armed Forces, annuities, 10 U.S.C. § 1448
Attachment,
    Marital property division enforcement, § 3502
    Property being disposed of to defeat obligations, § 3505
    Wage attachment, marital property division enforcement, § 3502
Attorney fees,
    Court order, § 3323
    Marital property division enforcement, court award, § 3502
    Rules 1920.13, 1920.31, 1920.52
Bifurcation of proceedings, § 3323
Child custody, marital property division factor, § 3502
Coercion, induced marriage, grounds for annulment, § 3305
Collusion, § 3309
Commencement of action, Rule 1920.3
Common-law marriages, § 3303
Complaint, Rules 1920.3, 1920.12-1920.13
Complaint dismissal, § 3323
Consanguinity, marriages within prohibited degrees of, grounds for annulment, § 3304

Annulment of Marriage—Cont'd
Consent incapability, grounds for annulment, § 3304
Conspiracy, fabricated grounds for annulment, § 3309
Contempt,
    Marital property division enforcement, § 3502
Costs,
    Award, Rules 1920.13, 1920.52
    Court order, § 3323
    Marital property division enforcement, court award, § 3502
    Waiver, failure to claim, Rule 1920.31
Counseling, Rule 1920.45
Counterclaim, Rule 1920.15
De novo hearing, party right, § 3321
Death of party,
    Subsequent attack upon annulment decree, § 3331
Decrees, § 3323
    Effect on property rights, § 3503
    Estoppel, § 3333
    Limitations on attacks on decrees, § 3331
    Opening decree, motion, § 3332
    Res judicata, § 3333
    Vacating decree, motion, § 3332
Default judgments, Rule 1920.41
Degrees of consanguinity, marriages within the prohibited degrees, grounds for annulment, § 3304
Devises, marital property status, § 3501
Discovery,
    Property of parties, § 3505
Discovery, Rule 1920.22, 1930.5
    Financial records, disclosure, Rule 1920.31
    Property, inventory and appraisal, Rule 1920.33
Dismissal of complaint, § 3323
Disposition of property after termination of marriage, § 3504
Distribution of marital property, statement of reasons, § 3506
Division of costs, § 3323
Division of marital property, equitable division, § 3502
Domicile and residence,
    Parties, prerequisites, § 3104

INDEX

References are to Sections of the Pennsylvania Domestic Relations Code, Pennsylvania Crimes Code, Pennsylvania Judicial Code, Pennsylvania Domestic Relations Court Rules, and Selected Federal Statutes, Court Rules, and Regulations

Annulment of Marriage—Cont'd
Drugs,
    Parties under influence, grounds for annulment, § 3305
Duress, induced marriage, grounds for annulment, § 3305
Earning power increase contributions to other party, marital property division factor, § 3502
Economic circumstances of parties, marital property division factor, § 3502
Educational contributions to other party, marital property division factor, § 3502
Employability, marital property division factor, § 3502
Equitable division of marital property, § 3502
Equity power of court, § 3323
Estoppel, decree of annulment, § 3333
Evidence,
    New evidence, motion to open or vacate decree, § 3332
    Presumptions,
        Property acquisitions, marital property status, § 3501
Expenses and expenditures,
    Court order, § 3323
Fabricated grounds, collusion, § 3309
Factors,
    Equitable division of marital property, § 3502
Family home,
    Residing in by parties during pendency of action, court award, § 3502
Force, induced marriage, grounds for annulment, § 3305
Former marriage not terminated, grounds for annulment, § 3304
Forms
    Complaints, Rule 1920.12
    Inventories, § 3505, Rule 1920.75
    Master, appointment, Rule 1920.74
    Notice to defend, Rule 1920.71
Fraud,
    Collusion, § 3309
    Decree procurement by intrinsic fraud, motion to open or vacate, § 3332
    Inducement of marriage, grounds for annulment, § 3305
Gifts, marital property status, § 3501

Annulment of Marriage—Cont'd
Grounds,
    Determination of jurisdiction, § 3104
    Void marriages annulment, § 3304
    Voidable marriages, § 3305
Guardian consent lacking, underage parties, grounds for annulment, § 3305
Health,
    Marital property division factor, § 3502
Hearing by master, § 3321
Hearings, Rule 1920.51
    Court, Rule 1920.52
    Masters, Rule 1920.53 et seq.
    Notice, Rule 1920.51
Homemaker contributions, marital property division factor, § 3502
Impotency, grounds for annulment, § 3305
Incapability of consenting, grounds for annulment, § 3304
Income,
    Amount and sources, marital property division factor, § 3502
Indigent parties, proceedings by, Rule 1920.62
Injunction, § 3323
    Disposition of property to defeat obligations, § 3505
Inventory of property, § 3505, Rule 1920.75
Joinder
    Parties, Rule 1920.34
    Related claims, Rule 1920.31 et seq.
Judgments and decrees, Rule 1920.52
    Exceptions, Rule 1920.55-2
    Final decree, Rule 1920.55
    Non pros, bill of particulars, failure to file, Rule 1920.21
    Report of master, 1920.53 et seq.
Jurisdiction, §§ 3104, 3323
Jury trial, § 3322
Laches, collateral attack on decree, § 3333
Length of marriage, marital property division factor, § 3502
Liabilities of parties, marital property division factor, § 3502
Limitation of actions,
    Attacks upon annulment decrees, § 3331

INDEX

References are to Sections of the Pennsylvania Domestic Relations Code, Pennsylvania Crimes Code, Pennsylvania Judicial Code, Pennsylvania Domestic Relations Court Rules, and Selected Federal Statutes, Court Rules, and Regulations

Annulment of Marriage—Cont'd
Marital property, § 3501 et seq.
  Court powers, equitable distribution issues, § 3502
  Defined, § 3501
  Equitable distribution,
    Disposition of property to defeat equitable distribution, attachment, § 3505
  Equitable division, § 3502
  Statement of reasons for distribution, § 3506
Master, hearing, § 3321
Masters
  Appointment, Rule 1920.51
    Forms, Rule 1920.74
    Hearings, Rule 1920.53 et seq.
    Reports, hearings, Rule 1920.53 et seq.
    Witnesses, testimony outside county, Rule 1920.61
Medical income source, marital property division factor, § 3502
Mentally ill persons,
  Commencement of action against mentally ill spouse, § 3308
  Consent incapability, grounds for annulment, § 3304
Military service, affidavits, Rule 1920.46
Motions,
  Decrees, opening or vacating, § 3332
Multiple Actions,
  Stay of proceedings, Rule 1920.6
Notices
  Counseling, Rule 1920.45
  Hearing, Rule 1920.51
Parental consent lacking, underage parties, grounds for annulment, § 3305
Pending actions, Rule 1920.92
Pleading, Rule 1920.11 et seq.
Postnuptial agreements, the marital property status, § 3501
Post-trial relief, Rule 1930.2
Premarital agreements, burden of proof, § 3106
Prenuptial agreements, marital property status, § 3501
Prior marriages, marital property division factor, § 3502
Procedures,
  Void marriage annulments, § 3304

Annulment of Marriage—Cont'd
Prohibited consanguinity degrees, marriages within, grounds for annulment, § 3304
Property,
  Disposition after termination of marriage, § 3504
  Disposition to defeat obligations, § 3505
  Inventory of property, parties, § 3505
Property rights, § 3501 et seq.
  Inventory and appraisal, Rule 1920.33
Protection of party interest, temporary order, § 3323
Ratification of marriage, underage parties, § 3305
Reconsideration motions, Rule 1930.2
Reports, masters report, Rule 1920.53 et seq.
Retirement income source, marital property division factor, § 3502
Sales,
  Court ordered sales, marital property distribution enforcement, § 3502
  Disposition of property after termination of marriage, § 3504
Serious mental disorder, consent incapability, grounds for annulment, § 3304
Service, Rule 1930.4
  Plaintiff affidavit, Rule 1920.4
Severance of actions and claims, Rule 1920.16
Special relief, Rule 1920.43
Standard of living, marital property division factor, § 3502
Station in life, marital property division factor, § 3502
Status of voidable marriages, § 3305
Statute of limitations, § 3331
Termination,
  Disposition of property after termination of marriage, § 3504
  Property rights dependent on marital relationship, § 3503
Transfers,
  Court ordered transfers of property, marital property distribution enforcement, § 3502

INDEX

References are to Sections of the Pennsylvania Domestic Relations Code, Pennsylvania Crimes Code, Pennsylvania Judicial Code, Pennsylvania Domestic Relations Court Rules, and Selected Federal Statutes, Court Rules, and Regulations

Annulment of Marriage—Cont'd
Trusts and trustees,
　Constructive trusts, undisclosed assets of parties, § 3505
Vacating decrees, motion, § 3332
Value, property set apart to each party, marital property division factor, § 3502
Venue, § 3104
Venue, Rule 1920.2
Vital Statistics, reports, Rule 1920.46
Vocation skills, marital property division factor, § 3502
Void marriages, §§ 1702, 3302, 3303
　Grounds for annulment, § 3304
Voidable marriages, § 3303
　Grounds for annulment, § 3305
Warrant of attorney, Rule 1920.5
Witnesses, testimony outside county, masters, Rule 1920.61

Answers
Contempt petition, support and alimony, Rule 1910.25
Custody, Rule 1915.5
Divorce or annulment actions, Rule 1920.14, 1920.43
Support, Rule 1910.7
Visitation, Rule 1915.5

Antenuptial Agreements
Divorce, rights determination and disposition, jurisdiction, § 3104

Appeal and Review
Adoption, foreign adoption, § 2908
Annulment of marriage, Rule 1920.55-1
Marriage licenses, refusal, § 1308
Paternity, Rule 1910.15
Support, effect, § 4308, 4350, 4377

Appeals
Child custody jurisdiction, enforcement, § 5454
Divorce actions, recommendations of master, alternative hearing procedures, Rule 1920.55-1 et seq.
Support of persons, conference officer report, Rule 1910.12

Appearance
Adoption, petition for adoption, hearing, § 2723
Child custody jurisdiction
　Foreign states, orders, § 5360
　Parties and child, § 5352
Divorce, § 3309

Appearance—Cont'd
Domestic relations matters, deemed service, Rule 1930.4
Paternity, failure to appear, Rule 1910.15
Support
　Contempt, failure of obligor to appear, § 4344
　Security for attendance or performance, § 4347

Appellate Procedure
Children's fast track appeals, PA R.A.P. 102-3723
Internal operating procedures of the Superior Court, § 65.14–65.42

Application of Law
Child custody jurisdiction
　International application, § 5365
　Intrastate application, § 5364
Pennsylvania Adoption Cooperative Exchange, retroactive application, § 2558

Applications
Marriage licenses, § 1302
　Filing, § 1309

Applications, Petitions, and Requests
Custody, partial custody and visitation actions, disobedience of custody order, Rule 1915.12
Divorce or annulment actions, Rule 1920.15

Appointment
Attorneys, custody, partial custody and visitation actions, Rule 1915.11
Masters, Rules 1558, 1920.51, 1920.74

Appraisal and Appraisers
Annulment of marriage,
　Inventoried property of parties, § 3505
Divorce,
　Inventoried property of parties, § 3505
Divorce or annulment actions, Rule 1920.75

Arbitration and Award
Attorney fees, bed conduct of other party, custody proceedings, § 5339
Overdue support, collection from monetary awards, § 4308.1

Armed Forces (See Military Forces)
Divorce or annulment actions, military service, Rule 1920.46

INDEX

References are to Sections of the Pennsylvania Domestic Relations Code, Pennsylvania Crimes Code, Pennsylvania Judicial Code, Pennsylvania Domestic Relations Court Rules, and Selected Federal Statutes, Court Rules, and Regulations

Arraignment
Domestic violence arrests, preliminary arraignment, § 6113

Arrearages
Child medical support, § 4326
Conflict of laws, § 7604
Delinquent obligors, names, publication, § 4309
Disclosure, consumer reporting agencies, § 4303
Divorce, alimony, attorney fees, etc., enforcement, § 3703
Execution of judgment, Rule 1910.24
Fines and penalties, § 4348
Income tax refund intercept program, § 4307
Information to consumer credit bureau, § 4303
Intrastate family support enforcement, § 8411
Judgments and decrees, § 4352; Rule 1910.24
Limitations of actions, § 7604
Monetary awards, collections, § 4308.1
Periodic payment schedules, professional or occupational licenses, § 4355
Professions and occupations, licenses and permits, denial, § 4355
Reports, consumer reporting agencies, § 4303
State lottery prize interception, § 4308
Support actions, Rules 1910.24, § 4374

Arrest
Alimony, bench warrant, Rule 1910.25
Bench warrants,
　Contempt petitions, Rule 1910.25
　Disobedience, court orders, Rule 1910.25
　Failure or refusal to appear, Rule 1910.13-1; Rule 1910.13-2
Conferences, failure or refusal to appear, Rule 1910.13-1; Rule 1910.13-2
Custody, partial custody and visitation actions, Rule 1915.14
Disobedience of orders, Rules 1910.13, 1915.14
Hearings, failure or refusal to appear, Rule 1910.13-1; Rule 1910.13-2
Protection from abuse, violation of orders, § 6113
Support actions, Rules 1910.13-1, 1910.13-2, 1910.25

Arrest—Cont'd
Visitation, disobedience of court order, Rule 1915.14
Warrants, § 5451

Asset Information
Definitions, disclosure, cooperation, § 4304.1

Assets
Substantial change in circumstance, Rule 1910.19

Assignment
Credit rights of purchasing plaintiff spouse, § 4364
Child medical support, insurance, § 4348
Compensation and salaries, § 4348
Disposition of property to defeat support obligations, divorce or annulment, § 3505
Enforcement of support orders, § 4348; Rule 1910.20
Financial institutions, Rule 1910.23
Orders, financial institutions, Rule 1910.23
Payments, § 4305

Attachment Orders
Forms, Rule 1910.31
Notice, judgments and decrees, Rule 1910.30

Attachment
Alimony enforcement, wage attachment, § 3703
Annulment of marriage, this index
Compensation and salaries,
　Marital property division enforcement, divorce or annulment proceedings, § 3502
Divorce,
　Special relief, Rule 1920.43
Form, Rule 1910.31
Support, income, § 4348
Support actions, Rules 1910.20-1910.22, 1910.29-1910.31

Attendance
Petition for adoption, hearings, § 2723
Support, security for attendance or performance, § 4347

Attorney General
Child protective services, audits, § 6345
Powers and duties, support enforcement agencies, § 7308

INDEX

References are to Sections of the Pennsylvania Domestic Relations Code, Pennsylvania Crimes Code, Pennsylvania Judicial Code, Pennsylvania Domestic Relations Court Rules, and Selected Federal Statutes, Court Rules, and Regulations

Attorneys Fees
Adoption,
    Appointment of counsel, § 2313
    Intermediary, reimbursement, § 2533
Agreements, § 3105
Alimony,
    Pendente lite alimony awards, § 3702
Custody proceedings, bad conduct of other party, § 5339
Divorce, fees, § 3702
Domestic violence, § 6117
Entitlement, § 3702
Enforcement of arrearages, § 3703
Intrastate family support enforcement, § 8313
Jurisdiction, § 3104
Marital property division enforcement, court award, § 3502
Mediation, custody, sanctions, Rule 1940.8
Support, intrastate family support enforcement, § 8313
Weapons, domestic violence, § 6108.3

Attorneys
Adoption, appointment of counsel for child, § 2313
Appointment, custody, partial custody and visitation actions, Rule 1915.11
Arrearages, discipline, § 4355
Children and minors, parental rights termination, the appointment of counsel, § 2313

Attorneys Fees—Cont'd
Conference officers, support of persons conferences, Rule 1910.11
Custody, appointment for minors, Rule 1915.11
District attorneys, support matters, duties, § 4306
Divorce fees, § 3702
    Enforcement of arrearages, § 3703
Divorce or annulment actions, Rules 1920.5, 1920.13, 1920.31, 1920.52
Fees
    divorce or annulment actions, Rules 1920.31, 1920.52
Hearing officers, partial custody and visitation, restrictions on practice, Rule 1915.4-2, Rule 1910.12
Interstate family support enforcement, § 7309
Intrastate family support enforcement, § 8309
Powers and duties, § 4306
Private counsel, intrastate family support enforcement, § 8308
Support of persons, hearing officers, Rule 1910.11-1910.12, § 4355
Visitation, appointment for minors, Rule 1915.11
Warrant of attorney, divorce or annulment actions, Rule 1920.5

Audits and Auditing
Child protective services, Attorney General, § 6345

—B—

Bankruptcy, § 3502
Selected Bankruptcy Code provisions, 11 U.S.C. § 101, et seq.

Barbarous Treatment
Divorce, life or health endangerment, grounds for divorce, § 3301

Behavioral Health Practitioners
Custody matters, court appointment for child, § 5340

Benefit Information
Definitions, disclosure, cooperation, § 4304.1

Bequest
Marital property status, § 3501

Bifurcation
Proceedings, § 3323, 3502

Bigamy
Divorce, grounds for divorce, § 3301

Bill of Particulars
Divorce or annulment actions, Rule 1920.3, 1920.21

Birth Certificates, § 5103

Birth Related Expenses
Definitions, child medical support, § 4326

Blood Tests
Paternity, determination, § 5104, Rule 1930.6

INDEX

References are to Sections of the Pennsylvania Domestic Relations Code, Pennsylvania Crimes Code, Pennsylvania Judicial Code, Pennsylvania Domestic Relations Court Rules, and Selected Federal Statutes, Court Rules, and Regulations

Bond or Security
Custody of minor children, Rule 1915.13
Divorce or annulment of marriage actions, party leaving jurisdiction, Rule 1920.44
Support, security for attendance or performance, § 4347

Breakdown in Marriage
Irretrievable breakdown, grounds for, § 3301

Breach of Promise to Marry
Actions abolished, § 1902
    Filing or threatening actions prohibited, § 1904

Breach of Promise to Marry—Cont'd
Instruments executed in satisfaction of abolished claims prohibited, § 1905
Purpose of law, § 1903
Attendance or performance, support proceedings, § 4347
Defendant leaving jurisdiction, Rule 1910.14

Burden of Proof
Custody, proposed relocation of child, § 5337
Premarital agreements, § 3106

Bureaus
Consumer credit bureaus, information to, support, § 4303

—C—

Caption
Domestic relations, form, Rule 1930.1

Casualty Insurance
Arrearages, collections, § 4308.1

Central Registers
Statewide central register. Child Protective Services, this index

Ceremonies
Marriage, this index

Certificates and Certification
Adoption, § 2907
Child protective services plans, local plans, § 6363
Domestic violence,
    Emergency court orders, § 6110
Laboratories,
    Paternity proceeding genetic test results, § 4343
Liens and encumbrances, enforcement, Rule 1910.22
Marriage certificates, form, § 1501
    Ceremonies performed by parties, § 1502
Marriage licenses, consent certificates, filing, § 1309

Certified Copies
Child custody jurisdiction, custody decrees, § 5358

Change of Address
Support actions, Rule 1910.17

Change of Name (See Names)

Chemically Dependent Persons
Alcoholics and Intoxicated Persons, generally, this index
Annulment of marriage,
    Parties under influence of drugs, voidable marriage, grounds for annulment, § 3305
Marriage,
    Restrictions on marriage license issuance, § 1304

Child Abduction
Remedies for international child abduction, 42 U.S.C. § 11601, et seq.

Child Abduction Prevention
    Generally, § 5201 et seq.
Abduction prevention orders
    Contents of, § 5208
    Duration, § 5210
Actions for abduction prevention measures, § 5204
Custody, restrictions on, § 5208
Definitions, § 5202
Discretionary court orders, contents of, § 5208
Factors to determine risk of abduction, § 5207
Jurisdiction, § 5205
Petitions, contents of, § 5206
Petitions, filing, § 5205
Physical custody of child, warrant to take, § 5204, 5209

INDEX

References are to Sections of the Pennsylvania Domestic Relations Code, Pennsylvania Crimes Code, Pennsylvania Judicial Code, Pennsylvania Domestic Relations Court Rules, and Selected Federal Statutes, Court Rules, and Regulations

Child Abduction Prevention—Cont'd
Travel, restrictions on, § 5208
Visitation, restrictions on, § 5208

Child Abuse
Child Protective Services, generally, this index
Defined, child protective services, § 6303
Protection from Abuse, see generally, this index

Child Custody Jurisdiction
    Generally, § 5401 et seq.
Appeals, § 5454
Appearance and limited immunity, § 5409
Appearance of parties and child, § 5430
Application and construction, § 5481
Application to Native American tribes, § 5404
Child custody determination, effective, § 5406
Communication between courts, § 5410
Cooperation between courts, § 5212
Costs and expenses, § 5457
Costs, fees and expenses, § 5452
Cooperation between courts; preservation of records, § 5412
Definitions, § 5402, § 5441
Duty to enforce, § 5443
Effect of child custody determination, § 5406
Enforcement of registered determination, § 5446
Enforcement under Hague Convention, § 5442
Exclusive, continuing jurisdiction, § 5422
Expedited enforcement of child custody determination, § 5448
Hearing and order, § 5450
Inconvenient forum, § 5427
Information to be submitted to court, § 5429
Initial child custody jurisdiction, § 5421
International application of chapter, § 5405
Intrastate application, § 5471
Joinder, § 5425
Jurisdiction declined by reason of conduct, § 5428
Jurisdiction to modify determination, § 5423
Marital property division factor, § 3502
Notice; opportunity to be heard; joinder, § 5425

Child Custody Jurisdiction—Cont'd
Notice to persons outside Commonwealth, § 5408
Priority, § 5407
Proceedings governed by other law, § 5403
Recognition and enforcement, § 5453
Registration of child custody determination, § 5445
Role of law enforcement, § 5456
Role of prosecutor or public official, § 5455
Service of petition and order, § 5449
Severability, § 5482
Short title of chapter, § 5401
Simultaneous proceedings, § 5426, § 5447
Taking testimony in another state, § 5411
Temporary emergency jurisdiction, § 5424
Temporary visitation, § 5444
Warrant to take physical custody of child, § 5451

Child Medical Support
Requirement, § 4326

Child Protective Services
    Generally, § 6301 et seq., 6361
Abuse
    Child abuse
        Defined, § 6303
        Reporting suspected abuse, § 6311 et seq.
        Services for prevention and treatment of, §§ 6365, 6362
    Sexual abuse, defined, § 6303
Actions and proceedings
    Evidence, § 6381
    Guardian ad litem for child, § 6382
Admission of child to hospital, reporting suspected child abuse, § 6316
Agencies
    Cooperation, § 6346
    Counties, general protective services, requirements, § 6375
    Purchasing the services of other agencies, § 6364
Amendment of information, § 6341
Attorney General, audits, § 6345
Audits by Attorney General, § 6345
Availability of department, § 6333
    Continuous availability to receive reports, § 6366

INDEX

References are to Sections of the Pennsylvania Domestic Relations Code, Pennsylvania Crimes Code, Pennsylvania Judicial Code, Pennsylvania Domestic Relations Court Rules, and Selected Federal Statutes, Court Rules, and Regulations

Child Protective Services—Cont'd
Child abuse
  Defined, § 6303
  Reporting suspected abuse, § 6311 et seq.
  Services for prevention and treatment of, § 6365
Child-care personnel, information relating to, § 6344
Child-care services, defined, § 6303
Children and minors
  Guardian ad litem for child in court proceedings, § 6382
  Protecting well-being of child maintained outside home, § 6372
  Rehabilitative services for child and family, § 6371
  Services for protection of child at home or in custody, § 6370
  Taking into protective custody, § 6369
Citizen review panels, § 6340, § 6343.1
Complaints
  Disposition, § 6334
  Pending complaint file
    Establishment, § 6331
    Information in, § 6335
Confidential information
  Release, § 6340
  Reports, § 6339
Continuous availability of department, § 6333
  Receipt of reports, § 6366
Cooperation
  Cooperation with an investigation, defined, § 6303
  Other agencies, § 6346
Coroners, reports to, § 6367
County agencies, defined, § 6303
County plans, § 6363
Court proceedings
  Evidence, § 6381
  Guardian ad litem for child, § 6382
Custody
  Child abuse, consideration of when awarding, § 5329.1
  Protective custody, taking child into, § 6369, § 6375
    Reporting suspected child abuse, § 6315
  Services for protection of child at home or in custody, § 6370
Data in records, studies, § 6342
Deaths, reporting and postmortem investigation, reporting suspected child abuse, § 6317

Child Protective Services—Cont'd
Defined, § 6303
Definitions, § 6303
Department, defined, § 6303
Department of Public Welfare
  Availability, § 6333
    Continuous availability to receive reports, § 6366
  Powers and duties, § 6331 et seq.
  Reports to, § 6367
Disposition
  Complaints received, § 6334
  Founded reports, § 6338
  Indicated reports, § 6338
  Unfounded reports, § 6337
Education, § 6383
Emergency services, § 6375
Employees
  Child-care personnel, information relating to, § 6344
  Violations, penalty, § 6349
Evidence in court proceedings, § 6381
Expunge, defined, § 6303
Expungement of information, § 6341
Failure to report suspected child abuse, penalty, § 6319
Families
  Family members, defined, § 6303
  Rehabilitative services for child and family, § 6371, 6375
Files and filing, pending complaint file
  Establishment, § 6331
  Information in, § 6335
Fines and penalties
  Failure to report suspected child abuse, § 6319
  Information and personnel violations, § 6349
Founded reports
  Defined, § 6303
  Disposition, § 6338
General protective services, § 6373
  Appeals, § 6376
  Caseloads, § 6377
  County agency requirements, § 6375
  Defined, § 6303
  Goals, § 6374
  Hearings, § 6376
  Principles, § 6374
  Purchasing services of other agencies, § 6378
Goals, general protective services, § 6374
General Assembly
  Annual reports to, § 6347
  Legislative oversight, § 6384

INDEX

References are to Sections of the Pennsylvania Domestic Relations Code, Pennsylvania Crimes Code, Pennsylvania Judicial Code, Pennsylvania Domestic Relations Court Rules, and Selected Federal Statutes, Court Rules, and Regulations

Child Protective Services—Cont'd
Governor, annual reports to, § 6347
Guardian ad litem for child in court proceedings, § 6382
Hearings, § 6376
Homes
    Protecting well-being of child maintained outside home, § 6372
    Services for protection of child at home or in custody, § 6370
Hospitals, admission of child to, reporting suspected child abuse, § 6316
Immunity from liability, reporting suspected child abuse, § 6318
Indicated reports
    Defined, § 6303
    Disposition, § 6338
Information
    Amendment, sealing or expungement, § 6341
    Confidential reports, release, § 6340
    Family day-care home residents, § 6344.1
    Pending complaint file, information in, § 6335
    Prospective child-care personnel, § 6344
    Release and retention
        Students in public and private schools, § 6353.4
    Release of information in confidential reports, § 6340
    Statewide central register, information in, § 6336
    Violations, penalty, § 6349
Injuries, serious bodily injury, defined, confidential information, § 6340
Investigations
    Cooperation with an investigation, defined, § 6303
    Deaths, reporting suspected child abuse, § 6317
    Newborn children, § 6504
    Performance of child protective services, § 6343, 6365
    Reports, § 6368
    Under investigation, defined, § 6303
Legislative oversight, § 6384
Liability, immunity, reporting suspected child abuse, § 6318
Local plans, § 6363
Mandatory reporting of infants born and identified as being affected by illegal substance abuse, § 6386

Child Protective Services—Cont'd
Organization, § 6361
Pending complaint file
    Establishment, § 6331
    Information in, § 6335
Performance, investigation, § 6343
Photographs of child, reporting suspected child abuse, § 6314
Plans, local plans, § 6363, 6375
Postmortem investigations, deaths, reporting suspected child abuse, § 6317
Prevention of child abuse, services, § 6365, 6368
Procedures, reporting suspected child abuse, § 6313
Prospective child-care personnel, information relating to, § 6344
Protection
    Child at home or in custody, services, § 6370
    Well-being of child maintained outside home, § 6372
Protective custody, taking child into, § 6369, 6375
    Reporting suspected child abuse, § 6315
Public policy, § 6302
Purchasing services of other agencies, § 6364, 6378
Purpose of law, § 6302
Records, studies of data, § 6342
Registers, statewide central register
    Establishment, § 6331
    Information in, § 6336
Regulations, § 6348
Rehabilitative services for child and family, § 6371
Release of information in confidential reports, § 6340
Removal from home, prevention, § 6373
Reports
    Confidentiality, § 6339
    Coroners, reports to, § 6367
    Deaths, reporting suspected child abuse, § 6317
    Department of Public Welfare
        Continuous availability to receive, § 6366
        Reports to, § 6367
    Founded reports
        Defined, § 6303
        Disposition, § 6338

INDEX

References are to Sections of the Pennsylvania Domestic Relations Code, Pennsylvania Crimes Code, Pennsylvania Judicial Code, Pennsylvania Domestic Relations Court Rules, and Selected Federal Statutes, Court Rules, and Regulations

Child Protective Services—Cont'd
  Indicated reports
    Defined, § 6303
    Disposition, § 6338
    Investigations, § 6368
    Release of information in confidential reports, § 6340
    Reports to Governor and General Assembly, § 6347
    Subject of the report, defined, § 6303
    Suspected child abuse, § 6311 et seq.
      Admission of child to hospital, § 6316
      Deaths, reporting and postmortem investigation, § 6317
      Failure to report, penalty, § 6319
      Immunity from liability, § 6318
      Persons permitted to report, § 6312
      Persons required to report, § 6311
      Photographs and X-rays of child, § 6314
      Procedure, § 6313
      Taking child into protective custody, § 6315
    Unfounded reports
      Defined, § 6303
      Disposition, § 6337
  Responsibilities, § 6362
  Sealing of information, § 6341
  Secretary, defined, § 6303
  Serious bodily injury, defined, confidential information, § 6340
  Services
    Child-care services, defined, § 6303
    Other agencies, purchasing, § 6364
    Prevention and treatment of child abuse, § 6365
    Protection of child at home or in custody, § 6370
    Rehabilitative services for child and family, § 6371
  Sexual abuse, defined, § 6303
  Short title of law, § 6301
  Statewide central register
    Establishment, § 6331
    Information in, § 6336
  Statewide toll-free telephone number, establishment, § 6332
  Studies of data in records, § 6342
  Subject of the report, defined, § 6303

Child Protective Services—Cont'd
  Suspected child abuse, reporting, § 6311 et seq.
  Taking child into protective custody, § 6369
    Reporting suspected child abuse, § 6315
  Telephones, Statewide toll-free telephone number, establishment, § 6332
  Training, § 6383
  Treatment of child abuse, services, § 6365
  Under investigation, defined, § 6303
  Unfounded reports
    Defined, § 6303
    Disposition, § 6337
  X-rays of child, reporting suspected child abuse, § 6314

Child Protective Services Law
  Generally, § 6301 et seq.

Child-Care Services
  Child protective services, prospective child-care personnel, information relating to, § 6344
  Defined, child protective services, § 6303

Child Service Agencies
  Adoption, duties, § 2555

Child Support
  Guidelines, § 4322; Rule 1910.16-1910.16-1
  Payment, Rule 1920.31

Child Support Orders
  Defined
    Interstate family support, § 7101
    Intrastate family support, § 8101

Child Support Program, § 4371 et seq.
  Administration, § 4373
  Agents and agency, designation, § 4372
  Appeal and review, § 4377
  Application of law, § 4372
  Assignment, § 4378
  Child support and establishment of paternity, federal, 42 U.S.C. § 651 et seq.
  Confidential or privileged information, § 4376
  Cooperation, § 4379; § 4380
  Definitions, § 4371
  Disbursements, § 4374
  Electronic funds transfers, § 4374

INDEX

References are to Sections of the Pennsylvania Domestic Relations Code, Pennsylvania Crimes Code, Pennsylvania Judicial Code, Pennsylvania Domestic Relations Court Rules, and Selected Federal Statutes, Court Rules, and Regulations

Child Support Program—Cont'd
Eligibility, § 4380
Fines and penalties, § 4377
Foster homes, reimbursement, § 4374
Garnishment, § 4381
Hearings, § 4380
Incentive payments, § 4373
Intergovernmental cooperation, § 4373
New hire reporting, § 4391 et seq.
Orders, § 4377
Parent locator service, § 4373
Privileges and immunities, § 4377
Records and recordation, § 4375
Registration, § 4376
Rules and regulations, § 4372
Standing, § 4378
Subpoenas, § 4377

Children and Minors
Abused children,
    Access, pending complaint file information, § 6335
    Admission to public or private hospitals, § 6316
    Adoption, termination of parental rights, § 2511 et seq.
    Amendment of child abuse information, § 6341
    At home child, protection services, § 6370
    Audits, child abuse reports, § 6345
    Child protective service, performance investigation, § 6343
    Child Protective Services Law, § 6301 et seq.
    Communications,
        Privileged communications, evidence, § 6381
    Conferences,
        Protective custody, conferring with parent or custodian, § 6315
    Confidential or privileged information,
        Child abuse reports, § 6339
        Evidence § 6381
    Cooperation, state agencies, § 6346
    Crimes and offenses,
        Failure to report child abuse, § 6319, 6346
    Deaths,
        Reporting and post-mortem investigation, § 6317
        Witnesses, reports, § 6381
    Discovery, Rule 1930.5

Children and Minors—Cont'd
Discrimination against persons reporting abuse, actions and proceedings, § 6311
Disposition,
    Complaints, § 6334
    Founded reports, § 6338
    Indicated reports, § 6338
    Unfounded reports, § 6337
Duration of protective custody, § 6315
Education programs, abuse prevention, § 6383
Emergency protective services, § 6375
Evidence, § 6381
    Child abuse reports, § 6338
    Information, § 6341
Failure to confirm oral report, § 6313
Federal Parent Locator Service, 42 U.S.C. § 653
Fines and penalties,
    Failure to report child abuse, § 6319
    Information, the failure to amend or expunge, § 6349
Forms,
    Written reports of abuse, § 6313
Founded reports, disposition, § 6338
Guardian ad litem, § 6382
Hearings
    Detention hearings, protective custody, § 6315, Rule 1920.52
Hospitals, failure to admit child abuse victim, § 6316
In custody child, protection services, § 6370
Indicated reports, disposition, § 6338
Information,
    Prospective child-care personnel, § 6344
Investigations,
    Referrals for investigation, § 6334, 6365
Limitations, toll-free statewide telephone number use, § 6332
Newborn children, § 6316
Notice,
    Protective custody, § 6315
    Protective service, notice to, § 6334

1244

INDEX

References are to Sections of the Pennsylvania Domestic Relations Code, Pennsylvania Crimes Code, Pennsylvania Judicial Code, Pennsylvania Domestic Relations Court Rules, and Selected Federal Statutes, Court Rules, and Regulations

Children and Minors—Cont'd
  Oral reports of abuse, § 6313
  Out of home placement services, § 6365
  Pending complaint file,
    Child abuse reports, § 6331
    Information, § 6335
  Persons required to report suspected abuse, § 6311
  Photograph, § 6314
  Place of detention, protective custody, § 6315
  Postmortem investigations, § 6317
  Prevention, services, § 6365
  Prima facie evidence, § 6381
  Privileges and immunities,
    Reporting child abuse, § 6311, 6318
  Prospective child-care personnel, information, § 6344
  Protective custody, § 6315, 6375
  Rehabilitative services, § 6371
  Release,
    Confidential report information, § 6340
    Statewide central register information, § 6336
  Reports, § 6311 et seq.
    Annual report to governor and general assembly, § 6347
    Persons permitted to report suspected abuse, § 6312
    Persons required to report suspected abuse, § 6311, 6312
    Procedures for reporting, § 6313
    Unavailable persons, court proceedings, § 6381
  Sealing, child abuse information, § 6341
  Services, referrals for, § 6334
  Statewide central register,
    Child abuse, § 6331
    Information, § 6336
  Statewide toll-free telephone number, establishment, § 6332
  Studies, data in child abuse records, § 6342
  Suspected abuse,
    Persons permitted to report, § 6312
    Persons required to report, § 6311
  Taking child into protective custody, § 6369

Children and Minors—Cont'd
  Training programs, abuse prevention, § 6383
  Treatment, services, § 6365
  Unfounded reports, disposition, § 6335, 6337, 6370
  Well being of children maintained outside home, protection, § 6372
  Written reports of abuse, § 6313
  X-rays, § 6314
Acknowledgment of paternity, § 5103
Actions and proceedings,
  Abused children,
    Discrimination actions, persons reporting abuse, § 6311
    Initiation, § 6370
  Age for suing and being sued, § 5101
  Discrimination actions, persons reporting child abuse, § 6311
  Hospitals, failure to admit child abuse victims, § 6316
Adoption, generally, this index
Age,
  Full age attainment, § 5101
Attainment of full age, § 5101
Attorney fees, § 5452
Child abuse. Abused children, generally, ante
Child custody health care or behavioral health practitioners, § 5315
Claim of paternity, § 5103
Compromise and settlement,
  Custody, denial, § 5307
Conferences,
  Protective custody, abused children, conferring with parent or custodian, § 6315
Confidential or privileged information, custody, § 5309, 5429, 5450
Contracts,
  Age for entering into contracts, § 5101
  Contribution among tortfeasors, parental liability for torts of minor, § 5507
  Counselors and counseling, custody, § 5305
Crimes and offenses,
  Child abuse, failure to report, § 6319
  Parental liability for torts of minors, § 5501 et seq.
  Torts of minors, parental liability, § 5501 et seq.

INDEX

References are to Sections of the Pennsylvania Domestic Relations Code, Pennsylvania Crimes Code, Pennsylvania Judicial Code, Pennsylvania Domestic Relations Court Rules, and Selected Federal Statutes, Court Rules, and Regulations

Children and Minors—Cont'd
Custody, § 5301 et seq., 5401 et seq., Rule 1915.1 et seq.
    Compromise and settlement, denial, § 5307
    Death of parent, § 5311
    Definitions, § 5302
    Divorce after pending proceedings, § 5312
    Exemptions, adoption, grandparents and grandchildren, § 5314
    Grandparents and grandchildren, § 5313
    Jurisdiction, § 5401 et seq.
        Child Custody Jurisdiction, generally, this index
Custody status conference, Rule 1930.7
Custody, consolidation of actions, section 4349
Definitions, intrastate family support enforcement, § 8101
Dentists and dentistry, support, § 4326
Discovery, Rule 1930.5
Domicile, § 7201
Emancipation, support of persons, § 4323
Evidence,
    Child abuse proceedings, § 6381
    Presumption of legitimacy, overcoming presumption, § 5104
Failure of hospital to admit child abuse victims, § 6316
Fees, custody, § 5452
Fines and penalties,
    Child abuse,
        Failure to report, § 6319
        Information, the failure to amend or expunge, § 6349
Fingerprinting of children, § 5105
Forms,
    Pleadings, Rule 1930.1
    Written child abuse reports, § 6313
Full age attainment, § 5101
Good faith presumption, child abuse reports, § 6318
Grandparents and grandchildren, custody, § 5313
Guardian and Ward, generally, this index
Guidelines, § 4322
Hearings,
    Protective custody detention hearings, § 6315
    Termination of parental rights, § 2513

Children and Minors—Cont'd
Hospitals,
    Admission of child abuse victims, § 6316
Indemnity, parental liability for torts of minors, § 5507
Injunction,
    Hospitals, failure to admit child abuse victims, § 6316
Investigations and investigators,
    Child abuse victims, postmortem investigations, § 6317
Judgments and decrees,
    Parental liability, torts of minors, § 5504
    Relinquishment of the parental rights, § 2503
Jurisdiction,
    Custody, § 5408
    Personal, § 7201
Legitimacy of children, declaration, § 5102
Marriage,
    Prohibited degrees of consanguinity for marriage, § 1304
    Restrictions on marriage license issuance, § 1304
Medical care and treatment,
    Custody, records, § 5309
Military forces, enlistment, consent, agency receiving custody under parental rights termination decree, § 2521
Modification, custody, § 5423
Monetary limits, parental liability for torts of minors, § 5505
Nonsupport. Support of Persons, generally, this index
Notice,
    Parental rights termination hearings, § 2513
    Protective custody, abused children, § 6315
Oral reports,
    Child abuse reports, § 6313
Parental liability, torts of children, § 5501 et seq.
Parties,
    Parental rights termination, petitions, § 2512
Paternity, generally, this index
Petitions,
    Parental liability for childrens torts, § 5504
    Termination of parental rights, § 2512

INDEX

References are to Sections of the Pennsylvania Domestic Relations Code, Pennsylvania Crimes Code, Pennsylvania Judicial Code, Pennsylvania Domestic Relations Court Rules, and Selected Federal Statutes, Court Rules, and Regulations

Children and Minors—Cont'd
Photographs, abused children, § 6314
Physical examinations, abused children, § 6314
Plans and specifications, custody, orders, implementation, § 5306
Presumptions,
    Child abuse reports, good faith, § 6318
    Legitimacy, overcoming presumption, § 5104
Privileges and immunities,
    Child abuse reports, § 6318
Protective custody,
    Abused children, § 6315
Public policy,
    Child Custody Jurisdiction Act, § 5342
Records and recordation, custody, § 5309
Rehabilitative services,
    Abused children, § 6371
    Child and family, § 6371
Relinquishment, parental rights, § 2501 et seq.
Shared custody, § 5304
Standby guardianship, § 5601
Support generally, this index
Termination, parental rights,
    Attorneys, appointment, § 2313
    Involuntary termination, § 2511 et seq.
    Relinquishment, § 2501 et seq.
    Venue, § 2302
    Voluntary relinquishment, § 2501 et seq.
Torts, parental responsibility, § 5501 et seq.
Uniform child custody jurisdiction. Custody, generally, ante
Venue,
    Termination, parental rights, § 2302
Witnesses,
    Electronic testimony, Rule 1930.3
    Parental rights termination, competency of parents, § 2513
Written reports,
    Child abuse reports, § 6313
X-rays, abused children, § 6314

Children Born Out of Wedlock
Paternity, generally, this index
Support of persons, Rule 1910.15

Civil Contempt
See Contempt

Civil Proceedings
Actions and Proceedings, generally, this index
Civil procedure rules, divorce, Rule 1920.1 et seq.; Rule 1931
    Accounts and accounting, determination of, Rule 1920.33; Rule 1920.75
    Acts of assembly, suspension, Rule 1920.91
    Affidavits,
        Military forces, failure to appear, Rule 1920.46
        Service, waiver, Rule 1920.4
    Answers, Rule 1920.14
    Application of law, Rule 1920.91
    Attorney fees, Rule 1920.31; Rule 1920.52
    Bill of particulars, Rule 1920.21
    Collateral attack on decree, § 3333
    Complaint, Rule 1920.3; Rule 1920.4
        Forms, Rule 1920.12; Rule 1920.72
        Multiple causes of action, Rule 1920.13
    Consent, waiver, notice, entry, judgments and decrees, Rule 1920.72
    Costs, claims, decisions in posttrial relief, Rule 1920.52
    Counselors and counseling, Rule 1920.45
    Counteraffidavits, Rule 1920.72
        Entry of decree, request, Rule 1920.42
    Counterclaim, Rule 1920.15
    Default judgment, Rule 1920.41
    Definitions, Rule 1920.1
    Determination and distribution of property, Rule 1920.33
    Discovery, Rule 1920.22; Rule 1930.5
    Electronic testimony, witnesses, Rule 1930.3
        Testimony outside county, masters, Rule 1920.61
    Failure to appear, military forces, affidavits, Rule 1920.46
    Findings, Masters, reports, Rule 1920.53
    Forms, Rule 1920.71 et seq.
        Complaint, Rule 1920.12
        Counteraffidavits, Rule 1920.72

INDEX

References are to Sections of the Pennsylvania Domestic Relations Code, Pennsylvania Crimes Code, Pennsylvania Judicial Code, Pennsylvania Domestic Relations Court Rules, and Selected Federal Statutes, Court Rules, and Regulations

Civil Proceedings—Cont'd
    Inventories, Rule 1920.75
    Judgments and decrees, Rule 1920.76
    Masters, appointments, Rule 1920.74
    Notice, entry of decree request, Rule 1920.73
    Pleadings, captions, Rule 1930.1
    Hearings, Rule 1920.51 et seq.
        Alternative procedures, masters, Rule 1920.55-1
        De novo requests, Rule 1920.55-3
        Masters and referees, Rule 1920.51 et seq.
    Indigent persons, Rule 1920.62
    Inventories,
        Determination and distribution of property, Rule 1920.33; Rule 1920.75
        Forms, Rule 1920.75
    Joinder,
        Parties, Rule 1920.34
        Related claims, Rule 1920.31 et seq.
    Judgments and decrees, Rule 1920.52
        Entry,
            Request, Rule 1920.73
            Waiver, notice, Rule 1920.72
        Exceptions, Rule 1920.55-2
        Final decree, Rule 1920.42
        Forms, Rule 1920.76
        Hearing de novo, Rule 1920.55-3
        Notice, entry of decree, request, Rule 1920.42
    Mail and mailing, process, service of process, original, Rule 1930.4
    Marital property, hearings, decision in posttrial relief, Rule 1920.52
    Masters and referees, Rule 1920.51 et seq.
        Appeal and review, masters, Rule 1920.55-1 et seq.
        Appointments, Rule 1920.51
            Forms, Rule 1920.74
        Hearings, Rule 1920.53; Rule 1920.54
        Orders, appointments, Rule 1920.74

Civil Proceedings—Cont'd
        Reports, Rule 1920.53
    Military forces, failure to appear, affidavits, Rule 1920.46
    Motions, appointments, masters, forms, Rule 1920.74
    Multiple actions,
        Priorities and preferences, Rule 1920.6
        Supersedeas or stay, Rule 1920.6
    Non pros judgment, Rule 1920.21
    Notice, Rule 1920.51
        Defend and claim rights, forms, Rule 1920.71
        Entry of decree, request, Rule 1920.42; Rule 1920.73
        Hearings, Rule 1920.51
        Judgments and decrees, waiver, Rule 1920.72
        Masters report,
            Exceptions, Rule 1920.55-2
            Hearing de novo, Rule 1920.55-3
        Reports, masters, hearings, Rule 1920.55-2
    Orders, masters, appointments, Rule 1920.74
    Pending actions, Rule 1920.92
    Pleadings, Rule 1920.11 et seq.
        Forms, captions, Rule 1930.1
    Post-trial practice, Rule 1930.2
    Post-trial relief, Rule 1920.52
    Praecipe to transmit record, forms, Rule 1920.73
    Pretrial statements, determination and distribution of property, Rule 1920.33
    Priorities and preferences, actions and proceedings, multiple actions, Rule 1920.6
    Process, service of process, original process, Rule 1930.4
    Property, determination and distribution, Rule 1920.33
    Reconsideration, motions, Rule 1930.2
    Records and recordation, hearings, masters, Rule 1920.55-3
    Reports, masters, Rule 1920.53
        Filing, Rule 1920.55-2
    Setoff and counterclaim, Rule 1920.15
    Severance of actions, Rule 1920.16
    Special relief, Rule 1920.43

INDEX

References are to Sections of the Pennsylvania Domestic Relations Code, Pennsylvania Crimes Code, Pennsylvania Judicial Code, Pennsylvania Domestic Relations Court Rules, and Selected Federal Statutes, Court Rules, and Regulations

Civil Proceedings—Cont'd
  Supersedeas or stay, multiple actions, Rule 1920.6
  Suspension, acts of assembly, Rule 1920.91
  Telecommunications, witnesses, Rule 1930.3
  Venue, Rule 1920.2
  Waiver, notice, judgments and decrees, entry, Rule 1920.72
  Warrant of attorney, Rule 1920.5
  Witnesses,
    Electronic testimony, Pa.R.Civ.P. 1930.3
    Testimony outside county, masters, Rule 1920.61

Clergy
Child abuse, reports, 23 Pa.C.S. § 6311
Confidential or privileged communications, child abuse, 23 Pa.C.S. § 6311
Marriage solemnization, qualifications, 23 Pa.C.S. § 1503
Privileges and immunities, reports, child abuse, 23 Pa.C.S. § 6311

Clerks
Clerk of court, defined, § 102
Defined, § 102
  Adoption, § 2102

Clerks of Court
Defined, § 102

Co-Guardian
Definitions, standby guardianship, 23 Pa.C.S. § 5602

Cohabitation
Agreements, § 3105, 3106

Collaborative Law Process
Short title and scope of chapter, 42 Pa.C.S. § 7401
Definitions, 42 Pa.C.S. § 7402
Beginning the collaborative law process, 42 Pa.C.S. § 7403
Assessment and review, 42 Pa.C.S. § 7404
Collaborative law participation agreement, 42 Pa.C.S. § 7405
Concluding the collaborative attorney, 42 Pa.C.S. § 7406
Disqualification of collaborative attorney, 42 Pa.C.S. § 7407
Disclosure of information, 42 Pa.C.S. § 7408
Confidentiality, 42 Pa.C.S. § 7409
Privilege, 42 Pa.C.S. § 7410
Professional responsibility, 42 Pa.C.S. § 7411

Collateral Attack
Annulment decree, § 3333
Divorce decree, § 3333

Collections
Child support program, § 4373, 4374

Colleges And Universities
Definitions, support, 23 Pa.C.S. § 4327

Collusion
Annulment of marriage, fabricated grounds, § 3309
Divorce proceedings, any fabricated grounds, § 3309
Marriages, divorce defense, abolition, § 3307

Commencement of Proceedings
Custody, partial custody and visitation actions, Rule 1915.3
Divorce or annulment actions, Rule 1920.3
Interstate family support, § 7301
Protection from abuse, § 6106
Protection from Abuse Act actions, Rule 1902
Support, § 4341
  Expedited procedure, § 4342
Support actions, Rule 1910.4
Visitation, Rule 1915.3

Common Pleas Courts
Alimony, Rule 1910.1
Infants, support guidelines, § 4322
Support guidelines, § 4322
Support of persons, Rule 1910.1
  Alternate procedure, support actions, § 4342
  Guidelines, § 4322

Common-Law Marriages
Annulment, § 3303
  Under age parties, grounds for annulment, § 3304
Application of law, § 1103
Void marriages,. § 1103

Commonwealth Agencies
State Agencies, generally, this index

Communications
Confidential communications, defined, protection from abuse, § 6102

Compensation and Salaries
See, also,
  Income, generally, this index
Alimony enforcement, wage attachment, § 3703
Annulment of marriage,

1249

INDEX

References are to Sections of the Pennsylvania Domestic Relations Code, Pennsylvania Crimes Code, Pennsylvania Judicial Code, Pennsylvania Domestic Relations Court Rules, and Selected Federal Statutes, Court Rules, and Regulations

Compensation and Salaries—Cont'd
    Wage attachment, marital property division enforcement, § 3502

Attachment,
    Alimony enforcement, wage attachment, § 3703
    Marital property division enforcement, divorce or annulment proceedings, § 3502

Attorney Fees, generally, this index

Blood tests, reading for paternity purposes, experts, § 5104

Divorce,
    Wage attachments, marital property division enforcement, § 3502

Divorced parties, alimony necessity factor, § 3701

Earnings information, support of persons, Rule 1910.9

Marriage,
    Separate earnings of spouses, rights, § 4104

Mediators, custody Rule 1940.7

Monthly gross income, computation, Rule 1910.16-21

Support, attachment, § 4348

Support, monthly gross income, computation, Rule 1910.16-2

Complaints
Alimony, Rules 1910.4, 1910.5
Child Protective Services, this index
Custody, partial custody and visitation actions, Rules 1915.3, 1915.14, 1915.15
Dismissal, § 3323
Divorce or annulment actions, Rules 1920.3-1920.4, 1920.12, 1920.72
Forms, support of persons, Rule 1910.27
Service, domestic relations matters, Rule 1930.4
Support actions, Rules 1910.5, 1910.26
Visitation, Rules 1915.3, 1915.5
    Form, Rule 1915.15

Compromise and Settlement
Children and minors,
    Custody, denial, § 5307
Support, arrearages, collections, § 4308.1

Computation, Rule 1910.16-1; Rule 1910.16-2
Factors, Rule 1910.16-5
Guidelines, Rule 1910.16-3

Conclusions
Masters, divorce or annulment of marriage actions, Rule 1920.53

Conclusiveness of Judgments and Decrees
Marriages, marital status determination, § 3306

Condonation
Defense abolished, § 3307

Conduct
Child custody jurisdiction, jurisdiction declined by reason of conduct, § 5349

Conference Officers
Defined, common pleas court, Rule 1910.1

Conferences
Contempt petitions, Rule 1910.2; Rule 1910.25-2
Failure or refusal to appear, bench warrants, Rule 1910.13-1; Rule 1910.13-2
Office conference and subsequent proceedings, Rule 1910.11
Orders, Rule 1910.5
    Contempt petitions, Rule 1910.25-2
    Modification, termination, Rule 1910.19
    Officers, recommendations, Rule 1910.12
Summary, contempt petitions, Rule 1910.25-3
Support actions, Rules 1910.11, 1910.12

Confidential or Privileged Information
Address, sex offenses, § 6701 et seq.
Adoption, this index
Battered spouses, shelters, § 5309
Child abuse information, § 6381
Child abuse reports, § 6339
Clergyman, confidential communications to, child abuse, § 6311
Custody of minor children, § 5309
Defined,
    Protection from abuse, § 6102
Marriage licenses issued, records, § 1106
Protection from abuse, § 6116
Support of persons, state agencies, § 4304

Confirmation, Orders, § 7608
Intrastate family support enforcement, § 8414; § 8415

INDEX

References are to Sections of the Pennsylvania Domestic Relations Code, Pennsylvania Crimes Code, Pennsylvania Judicial Code, Pennsylvania Domestic Relations Court Rules, and Selected Federal Statutes, Court Rules, and Regulations

Conflict of Laws
Arrearages, § 7604
Orders, § 7604
Paternity, § 7701

Connivance
Defense abolished, § 3307

Consanguinity
Grounds for annulment, § 3301
Marriage, prohibited degrees of consanguinity for marriage, § 1304
Marriage within degree of, § 1703

Consent Agreements
Domestic violence,
    Contempt, agreement violation, § 6114
    Court approval, § 6108

Consent Certificates
Marriage licenses, filing, § 1309

Consents
Adoption, this index
Counseling, § 3302
Custody, partial custody and visitation actions, Rule 1915.7
Divorce, affidavits, withdrawal, Rule 1920.42
Grounds for divorce, § 3301
Mutual consent divorce, § 3301
Support of children over 18, parents as parties, Rule 1910.3
Waiver, notice, entry, judgments and decrees, Rule 1920.72

Conservators And Conservatorship
Choice of law, long arm jurisdiction, § 7202
Long arm jurisdiction, § 7201

Consignments
Support of persons, § 4349

Consolidation
Support, proceedings, § 4349

Conspiracy
Fabricated grounds for divorce, § 3309

Constructive Trusts
Annulment of marriage, undisclosed assets of parties, § 3505
Divorce, undisclosed assets of parties, § 3505

Construction of Law
Child custody jurisdiction, § 5342
Support, property and contracts, § 4106

Consumer Credit Bureaus
Information to, support, § 4303

Contempt
Alimony arrearages enforcement, § 3703
Annulment of marriage,
    Marital property division enforcement, § 3502
Arrest, protection orders, Rule 1905
Criminal contempt, protection orders, Rule 1905
Custody, award, noncompliance with the order, § 5323
Custody, partial custody and visitation actions, see Rules 1915.12, 1915.14
Divorce,
    Marital property division enforcement, § 3502
Domestic violence,
    Court order or consent agreement violations, § 6114
Examinations, minors or parties, custody or visitation, Rule 1915.8
Petitions, hearings, reports, exceptions, Rule 1910.25-4
    Failure of obligor to appear, § 4344
    Support orders, noncompliance, § 4345
    Visitation or partial custody orders, noncompliance, § 4346
Process, generally, this index
Protection from abuse, violation of order or agreement, § 6114, § 6114.1
Support
Employers, withholding of income, enforcement of support orders, Rule 1910.21
Enforcement of orders, Rule 1910.20
Failure to appear, § 4344
Indigent persons, relatives, § 4603
Noncompliance,
    Support order, § 4345
    Visitation or partial custody order, § 4346
Support actions, Rules 1910.13, 1910.17, 1910.21–1910.22

Contest, Orders, § 7606
Income withholding orders, § 7501.5
Intrastate family support enforcement, § 8412; § 8413
Registration, § 7607
Validity, § 7606

Contestants
Defined, child custody jurisdiction, § 5343

Continuance
Divorce,

INDEX

References are to Sections of the Pennsylvania Domestic Relations Code, Pennsylvania Crimes Code, Pennsylvania Judicial Code, Pennsylvania Domestic Relations Court Rules, and Selected Federal Statutes, Court Rules, and Regulations

Continuance—Cont'd
  Reconciliation, reasonable prospect of reconciliation, § 3301
Domestic violence hearings, § 6107

Contracts
Actions and proceedings,
  Breach of promise to marry actions, § 1902 et seq.
Breach of promise to marry actions, abolition, § 1902
Children and minors,
  Age for entering into contract, § 5101
Custody, denial, § 5307
Divorce
  Construction of law, § 4106
  Parties, effect, § 3105
Marriage, debts
  Contracted before, liability, § 4101
  Contracts for necessaries, proceedings, § 4102
Marriage,
  Cause of action for breach of contract, § 1903
Premarital agreements, § 3106
Protection from abuse, contempt for violation, § 6114

Contributions
Tortious acts of child, contribution of parent from child prohibited, § 5507

Controlled Substances
Chemically Dependent Persons, generally, this index

Conventions And Conferences
Support, office conferences, Rule 1910.11, 1910.12
Support orders, Rule 1910.5

Conviction of Crime
Consideration of when awarding custody, § 5329

Cooperation
Child protective services, agencies, § 6346
Support, state agencies, § 4304

Cooperation with an Investigation
Defined, child protective services, § 6303

Cooperative Exchanges
Pennsylvania Adoption Cooperative Exchange, generally, this index

Copies
Child custody jurisdiction, custody decrees, certified copies, § 5358
Conference officers, reports, Rule 1910.12

Copies—Cont'd
Income and expense information, support of persons, office conference, Rule 1910.11

Coroners
Child abuse, persons required to report, § 6311
Child abuse victims, postmortem investigations, § 6317
Child Protective Services Law, § 6301 et seq.
Investigations,
  Child abuse victims, postmortem investigations, § 6317
Reports,
  Child protective services, reports to corners, § 6367
  Postmortem investigations of child abuse victims, § 6317

Costs
Adoption, investigations, §§ 2535, 2724
Annulment, claims, trial judge decision and post-trial relief, Rule 1920.52
Annulment of marriage,
  Court order, § 3323
  Marital property division enforcement, court award, § 3502
Custody, examinations, Rule 1915.8
Custody or visitation of minors, appointment of attorneys, Rule 1915.11
Divorce, hearing by court, trial judge decision and post-trial relief, Rule 1920.52
Divorce,
  Court order, § 3323
  Jurisdiction, § 3104
Marital property division enforcement, court award, § 3502
  Divorce or annulment actions, Rule 1920.31
  Domestic violence hearings, § 6107
  Guardian and Ward, generally, this index
  Support actions, Rules 1910.4, 1910.26
Mediation, § 3902
Support, § 4351
Visitation, examinations, Rule 1915.8

Counsel Fees
Discovery, Rule 1930.5
Divorce Actions, § 3702, Rule 1920.31

Counseling
Adoption, voluntary relinquishment, § 2505

INDEX

References are to Sections of the Pennsylvania Domestic Relations Code, Pennsylvania Crimes Code, Pennsylvania Judicial Code, Pennsylvania Domestic Relations Court Rules, and Selected Federal Statutes, Court Rules, and Regulations

Counseling—Cont'd
Custody, § 5305
Divorce, § 3302
Divorce or annulment actions, Rule 1920.45

Counselors
Generally, § 3302, Rule 1920.45
Domestic violence counselor-advocate
    Defined, protection from abuse, § 6102
    Protection from abuse, § 6111

Counteraffidavit
Divorce or annulment actions, Rules 1920.42, 1920.72

Counterclaims and Setoff
Custody, partial custody and visitation actions, Rules 1915.5–1915.6
Divorce or annulment actions, Rule 1920.15
Visitation, Rule 1915.5
    Joined parties, Rule 1915.6

Counties
Children and minors,
    Special service agencies, purchasing services, § 6364
Fees,
    Marriage license or declaration fees, § 1105
Forums, marriage forms, uniformity and supply, § 1104
Marriage forms, uniformity and supply, § 1104
Marriage license or declaration fees, § 1105
Protection from abuse, venue, Rule 1901.1
Protection orders registry, § 6109
Purchases,
    Children and youth social service agencies, § 6364
Registration,
    Court orders, domestic violence cases § 6104
Registries,
    Domestic violence orders, placement, § 6109
Transmittal, state share of marriage license or declaration fees, § 1105

Court Orders
Orders, generally, this index

Court Proceedings
Actions and Proceedings, generally, this index

Court Records
Records and Recordation, generally, this index

Courts
Actions and Proceedings, generally, this index
Adoption, jurisdiction, § 2301
Appeal and Review, generally, this index
Child custody jurisdiction
    Assistance, foreign states, § 5361
    Information under oath to be submitted to, § 5350
Clerk, defined, § 102
    Adoption, § 2102
Clerk of court, defined, § 102
Defined, § 102
    Adoption, § 2102
    Children and minors, custody, § 5402
    Indigent persons, support, relatives, § 46 and two
    Protection from abuse, Rule 1901
    Standby guardianship, § 5602
Divorce or annulment actions, court hearings, Rules 1920.32, 1920.51, 1920.52
Judgments and Decrees, generally, this index
Jurisdiction, generally, this index

Credit
Entireties property, support order execution against, § 4364
Payments, interstate family support enforcement, § 7209

Credit Bureaus
Consumer credit bureaus, information to, support, § 4303

Credits
Interstate family support, orders, payments, reconciliation of multiple orders, § 7209
Intrastate family support, payments, orders, issued by more than one tribunal, § 8203
Support orders, execution against entireties property, credit to plaintiff purchaser, § 4364

Crimes and Offenses
Adoption, unauthorized disclosure, § 2910
Application of law,
    Uniform Act on blood test to determine paternity, § 5104

INDEX

References are to Sections of the Pennsylvania Domestic Relations Code, Pennsylvania Crimes Code, Pennsylvania Judicial Code, Pennsylvania Domestic Relations Court Rules, and Selected Federal Statutes, Court Rules, and Regulations

Crimes and Offenses—Cont'd
Arrest, generally, this index
Child abuse, failure to report, § 6319
Child support, failure to pay, 18 U.S.C. § 228
Contempt, generally, this index
Convictions, consideration of when awarding custody, § 5329
Divorce, imprisonment, grounds for divorce, § 3301
Foreign protection orders, violations, private criminal complaints, § 6113.1
Fraud, generally, this index
Newborn children, reports, abandonment, hospitals, § 6506
Perjury, generally, this index
Searches and Seizures, generally, this index
Summary offences,
    Child abuse, failure to report, § 6319
    Support of persons,
        Willful failure to pay, § 4354
Support of persons,
    Willful failure to pay, § 4354
Venue, generally, this index

Criminal Complaints
Private criminal complaints, protection from abuse, violation of order or agreement, § 6113.1

Criminal Proceedings
Tortious acts of children, establishing liability of parent, § 5503

Cruelty
Divorce, life or health endangerment from cruel treatment, grounds for divorce, § 3301

Custody
Generally, § 5301 et seq., 5401 et seq.
Generally, Rules 1915.1-1915.25
Access to records and information, § 5309
Acts of Assembly, Rules 1915.24, 1915.25
Adopted children, exception, § 5314
Agreements, denial of custody, § 5307
Alternate hearing procedures, Rule 1915.4-1
Appeal and review, § 5454
Appearance, § 5430
Appointment of attorney for child, Rule 1915.11

Custody—Cont'd
Arrest, disobedience of order, Rule 1915.14
Attorneys, appointment for minors, Rule 1915.11
Behavioral health practitioners for child, court-appointed, § 5340
Bonds or security, Rule 1915.13
Caption, form, Rule 1915.15
Child abduction prevention, restrictions on, § 5208
Child abuse, consideration of when awarding custody, § 5329.1
Child Custody Jurisdiction, generally, this index
Child Protective Services, generally, this index
Children and minors
    Adopted children, exception, § 5314
    Defined, § 5302
    Removal from jurisdiction, § 5308
    Residing with grandparents, effect, § 5313
    Tortious acts of child, liability of parent not having custody or control of child, § 5508
Commencement of action, Rule 1915.3
Complaint, Rules 1915.3, 1915.15
Consent order, Rule 1915.7
Contempt, Rules 1915.12, 1915.14
Costs
    Appointment of attorney for Child, Rule 1915.14
    Examinations, Rule 1915.8
    Transfer petition and record removal, Rule 1915.2
Counseling, § 5305
Counter-affidavits, relocation of child, § 5337
Counterclaims, Rule 1915.5
Court-appointed child custody healthcare or behavioral health practitioners, § 5315
Custody orders
    Counseling as part of, § 5333
    Modification of existing orders, § 5310
    Plan for implementing, § 5306
    Visitation or partial custody, noncompliance, contempt, § 4346
Custody status conference, Rule 1930.7
Deceased parent, effect, § 5311
Default judgment, Rule 1915.9
Definitions, Rules 1915.1, 1920.1

INDEX

References are to Sections of the Pennsylvania Domestic Relations Code, Pennsylvania Crimes Code, Pennsylvania Judicial Code, Pennsylvania Domestic Relations Court Rules, and Selected Federal Statutes, Court Rules, and Regulations

Custody—Cont'd
Definitions, § 5302
Denial under agreement or plan, § 5307
Discovery, Rule 1915.5, 1930.5
Disobedience of orders, Rules 1915.12, 1915.14
Divorce or annulment actions, Rule 1920.32
Divorced parents, effect, § 5312
Examination, Rules 1915.8, 1915.18
Final Orders, Rule 1915.10
Forms, Rules 1915.15, 1915.16
Full faith and credit, child custody, 28 U.S.C. § 1738A
Grandparents, factors to consider when awarding custody, § 5328
Grandparents, residing with, effect, § 5313
Healthcare practitioners for child, court-appointed, § 5340
Hearing by court, decision and post-trial relief, Rule 1920.52
Information, access to, § 5309
Interrogation of child, Rule 1915.11
Intervention, form, Rule 1915.16
Joinder of parties, Rules 1915.6, 1915.16
Joinder with divorce actions, Rule 1920.32
Judgments and orders
    generally, Rules 1915.3, 1915.10
    consent order, Rule 1915.7
    default judgment, Rule 1915.9
    disobedience of orders, Rules 1915.12, 1915.14
    examinations, Rule 1915.8
    final orders, Rule 1915.10
    forms, Rules 1915.15, 1915.16
Jurisdiction, Rule 1915.5
Jurisdiction, removal of party or child from, § 5308
Legal custody, defined, § 5302
Legal custody, filing for, § 5324
Modification of existing custody orders, § 5310
Notice, form, Rule 1915.16
Office conference, Rule 1915.4-2
Orders of court,
    Appearance, Rules 1915.3, 1915.12
    Consent orders, Rule 1915.7
    Disobedience, Rule 1915.14
        Examination of minor or party, Rule 1915.8
    Examinations, Rule 1915.8
        Form, Rule 1915.18
    Form, Rule 1915.15

Custody—Cont'd
    Examination of minor or party, Rule 1915.18
    Modification, form of petition, Rule 1915.15
Orders. Judgments and orders, supra
Parents
    Deceased parent, effect, § 5311
    Divorce or separation, effect, § 5312
    Tortious acts of child, liability of parent not having custody or control of child, § 5508
Partial custody
    Defined, § 5302
    Hearings,
        Judge, alternative procedures, Rule 1915.4-1
        Officer, Rule 1915.4-2
    Masters, appointment, Rule 1920.51
    Modification, form of petition, Rule 1915.15
    Orders, noncompliance, contempt, § 4346
Parties, joinder, Rule 1915.6
Parties, removal from jurisdiction, § 5308
Petition, disobedience of custody order, Rule 1915.12
Physical and mental examination of persons, Rule 1915.8
Physical custody, defined, § 5302
Physical custody, individuals who may file for, § 5324
Plans
    Denial of custody, § 5307
    Implementing custody order, § 5306
Pleadings
    complaint, Rules 1915.3, 1915.15
    disobedience of custody order, petition, Rule 1915.12
    forms, Rule 1915.15
    responsive pleading by defendant, Rule 1915.5
    transfer of actions, Rule 1915.2
Post-trial relief, Rule 1915.10
Public policy, § 5301
Records, access to, § 5309
Records, interrogation of child, Rule 1915.11
Relocation of child, § 5337
Removal of party or child from jurisdiction, § 5308

INDEX

References are to Sections of the Pennsylvania Domestic Relations Code, Pennsylvania Crimes Code, Pennsylvania Judicial Code, Pennsylvania Domestic Relations Court Rules, and Selected Federal Statutes, Court Rules, and Regulations

Custody—Cont'd
Residing with grandparents, effect, § 5313
Separated parents, effect, § 5312
Service of process, § 1915.12
Service, original process, Rule 1930.4
Shared custody
    Award, § 5304
    Defined, § 5302
Sole custody, award, § 5303
Special relief, Rule 1915.13
Temporary custody, Rule 1915.13
Tortious acts of child, liability of parent not having custody or control of child, § 5508
Transfer of action, Rule 1915.2

Custody—Cont'd
Venue, Rules 1915.2, 1915.5
Visitation
    Defined, § 5302
    Orders, noncompliance, contempt, § 4346

Custody Decrees
Child Custody Jurisdiction, this index

Custody Determination
Defined, child custody jurisdiction, § 5343

Custody Orders
Custody, this index

Custody Proceedings
Defined, child custody jurisdiction, § 5343

—D—

Data
Child protective services, studies of data in records, § 6342

Day Care Centers
Abuse of children, persons required to report, § 6311
Child Protective Services Law, § 6301 et seq.
Registration,
    Self-employed family day care providers, applications, reports, § 6344

De Novo Hearing
Party rights, § 3321

Deadbeat Parents Punishment Act of 1998, 18 U.S.C.§ 228

Death
Child protective services, reporting and postmortem investigation of deaths, § 6317
Custody, deceased parent, effect, § 5311
Divorce, death of either party, effect on alimony, § 3707
Judgments and decrease, § 3323, 3331
Marriage licenses, applications, decree that spouse of applicant is presumed decedent, § 1701
Social security numbers, support obligors, § 4304.1
Standby guardianship, § 5601
Substitution, § 3323

Debts
Divorce, construction of law, § 4106

Debts—Cont'd
Marriage
    Contracts for necessaries, proceedings, § 4102
    Debts contracted before, liability, § 4101

Declaratory Judgments and Decrees
Marriage,
    Marital status determination, § 3306

Decrees
Judgments and Decrees, generally, this index
Arrearages, collections, § 4308.1

Deeds and Conveyances
Annulment of marriage,
    Disposition of property after termination of marriage, § 3504
Divorce,
    Disposition of property after termination of marriage, § 3504
    Entireties property, conveyance to divorced spouse, § 3508
    Entireties property, support order execution against, purchaser or title of validity, § 4361

Default and Default Judgments
Custody, partial custody and visitation actions, Rule 1915.9
Divorce or annulment actions, Rule 1920.41
Support and paternity, § 4342
Visitation, Rule 1915.9
Withholding of income, enforcement of support orders, Rule 1910.21

INDEX

References are to Sections of the Pennsylvania Domestic Relations Code, Pennsylvania Crimes Code, Pennsylvania Judicial Code, Pennsylvania Domestic Relations Court Rules, and Selected Federal Statutes, Court Rules, and Regulations

Defense Of Marriage Act, 28 U.S.C. § 1738C

Defenses
Divorce, § 3307

Definitions
Words and Phrases, generally, this index

Degree of Consanguinity
Marriage within, § 1703
Marriages within prohibited degrees, § 3304

Dental Care
Records, custody of minor children, access, § 5309

Dentists
Child abuse, persons required to report, § 6311
Child Protective Services Law, § 6301 et seq.

Departments
Defined,
    Adoption, § 2551
    Child protective services, § 6303
    Marriage Law, § 1102

Department of Public Welfare
Child Protective Services, this index

Depositions and Discovery
Alimony claims, Rule 1910.9, 1920.22
Annulment of marriage,
    Property of parties, § 3505
Custody, partial custody and visitation actions, Rule 1915.5
Divorce,
    Property of parties, § 3505
Divorce or annulment actions, Rule 1920.22
Earnings information, support of persons, Rule 1910.9
Support actions, Rules 1910.9, 1910.11
Visitation, Rule 1915.5

Desertion
Divorce, grounds, willful and malicious desertion, § 3301

Developmentally Disabled Persons
Mentally Retarded Persons, generally, this index

Disabled Persons
Notice, compliance, Americans with Disabilities Act,
Rules 1910.26, 1915.15, 1915.16

Disclosure
Adoption, unauthorized disclosure, penalty, § 2910
Agreements, § 3105
Arrearages, consumer reporting agencies, § 4303
Child support program, § 4375
Exceptional circumstances, interstate family support enforcement, § 7312
Interstate family support, § 7312
Intrastate family support enforcement, § 8309
Limitations, § 4305
Protection from abuse, addresses, § 6112
Safety of children, interstate family support enforcement, § 7312

Discontinuance
Voluntary agreements for continuing contact, adoption, § 2739

Discovery
Alimony, Rule 1930.5
Custody of minor children, Rule 1915.5
Domestic Relations, Rule 1920.22, Rule 1930.5
Visitation, custody of minor children, Rule 1915.5

Discretion of Court
Adoption,
    Confidential or privileged information, contacting natural parents, § 2905
    Consents, dispensing with those other than adoptee's, § 2713

Diseases
Alcoholics and Intoxicated Persons, generally, this index
Marriage license applicants, statement of freedom from transmittable diseases, § 1302

Disobedience of Orders
Generally, Rules 1910.13, 1915.12, 1915.14

Dissolution
Marital status, divorce, § 3301 et seq.

Distributions
Divorce, property
    Foreign decrees, enforcement, § 3705
    Statement of reasons, § 3506
Marital property, § 3502
Retirement and pensions, allocation, § 3501

INDEX

References are to Sections of the Pennsylvania Domestic Relations Code, Pennsylvania Crimes Code, Pennsylvania Judicial Code, Pennsylvania Domestic Relations Court Rules, and Selected Federal Statutes, Court Rules, and Regulations

District Attorneys
Support matters, duties, § 4306

District Justices (now Magisterial District Judges)
Marriage, qualification to solemnize marriages, § 1503
Protection from abuse, emergency relief, § 6110

Division
Costs, § 3323
Entireties property, division between divorced persons, § 3507
Marital property, equitable division, divorce, § 3502

Divorce
　Generally, § 3101 et seq.
　Generally, Rules 1920.1-1920.92
Abuse, defined, § 3701
Accounts and accounting, determination and distribution of property, Rule 1920.33, 1920.75
Actions and proceedings
　Defendant suffering from mental disorder, § 3308
　Marital status, proceedings to determine, § 3306
Adultery,
　Defense, § 3307
　Grounds for divorce, § 3301
Affidavits,
　Mutual consent to divorce, § 3301
Affidavits, Rules 1920.4, 1920.14, 1920.42, 1920.46, 1920.72
Age,
　Marital property division factor, § 3502
Agreements between parties, effect, § 3105
Alimony, § 3701
　Bar, § 3706
　Death of either party, effect, § 3707
　Defined, § 3103
　Enforcement
　　Arrearages, § 3703
　　Foreign decrees, § 3705
　　Payment, § 3704
Alimony pendente lite, § 3702
　Defined, § 3103
　Enforcement
　　Arrearages, § 3703
　　Foreign decrees, § 3705
　　Payment, § 3704
Alimony, Rules 1920.31, 1920.56

Divorce—Cont'd
Allocation, retirement and pensions, distribution, marital property, § 3501
Allocation of order, Rule 1920.56
Alternative pleading, Rule 1920.13
Annulment
　Decree of court, § 3323
　　Attacks upon decree, limitations, § 3331
　　Opening or vacating decree, § 3332
　　Res judicata and estoppel, § 3333
　Jury trials, § 3322
　Masters, hearings, § 3321
　Void marriages, § 3303
　　Grounds, § 3304
　Voidable marriages, § 3303
　　Grounds, § 3305
Answer, Rules 1920.14-1920.15
Antenuptial agreements, rights determination and disposition, jurisdiction, § 3104
Apart, separate and apart, defined, § 3103
Appearance, § 3309
Applications,
　Jury trial, § 3322
Appointment of master, Rules 1920.51, 1920.74
Appraisals, inventory property of parties, § 3505
Appraisement, Rule 1920.75
Arrearages, alimony, attorney fees, etc., enforcement, § 3703
Attachment,
　Marital property division enforcement, § 3502
　Property being disposed of to defeat obligations, § 3505
　Real or personal property, Rule 1920.43
Attorney fees, § 3502, 3702, 4101, Rules 1920.31, 1920.52
　Court order, § 3323
　Enforcement of arrearages, § 3703
　Jurisdiction, § 3104
　Marital property division enforcement, court award, § 3502
　Posttrial relief, Rule 1920.52
　Pending final disposition, Rule 1920.13
　Waiver, failure to claim, Rule 1920.31

1258

INDEX

References are to Sections of the Pennsylvania Domestic Relations Code, Pennsylvania Crimes Code, Pennsylvania Judicial Code, Pennsylvania Domestic Relations Court Rules, and Selected Federal Statutes, Court Rules, and Regulations

Divorce—Cont'd
Attorneys, Rules 1920.5, 1920.31
Availability of counseling, notice, § 3302
Bar to alimony, § 3706
Barbarous treatment endangering life or health, grounds for divorce, § 3301
Bases of jurisdiction, § 3104
Bequests, marital property status, § 3501
Bifurcation of proceedings, § 3323
Bigamy, grounds for divorce, § 3301
Bill of particulars, Rule 1920.21
Bonds, party leaving jurisdiction, Rule 1920.44
Breakdown in marriage, irretrievable breakdown, grounds for divorce, § 3301
Burden of proof, premarital agreements, § 3106
Children and minors, effect of divorce on custody of children, § 5312
Choices,
    Qualified counseling professionals, unrestricted choice, § 3302
Collateral attack,
    Decree, § 3333
Collusion, § 3309
    Defense abolished, § 3307
Commencement of action, Rule 1920.3
Complaint, Rule 1920.3, 1920.4, 1920.72
    Discontinuance, Rule 1920.17
    Dismissal, § 3323
    Multiple claims, Rule 1920.13
    Withdrawal of complaint, Rule 1920.17
Condonation, defense abolished, § 3307
Conformity to civil action, Rule 1920.1
Connivance, defense abolished § 3307
Consent, mutual consent, grounds for divorce, § 3301
Conspiracy, fabricated grounds for divorce, § 3309
Construction of law, § 3102
    support, property and contracts, § 4106
Constructive trusts, undisclosed assets of parties, § 3505
Contempt,
    Marital property division enforcement, § 3502
Continuance,
    Counseling, § 3302
    Prospect of reconciliation, § 3301

Divorce—Cont'd
Conveyance to divorced spouse, entireties property, § 3508
Costs,
    Award pending final disposition, Rule 1920.13, 1920.52
    Court order, § 3323
    Indigent parties, Rule 1920.62
    Jurisdiction, § 3104
    Marital property division enforcement, court award, § 3502
    Mediation, § 3902
    Waiver, failure to claim, Rule 1920.31
Counseling, § 3302
    Continuance, prospect of reconciliation, court required counseling, § 3301
Rule 1920.45
Counselors, qualified professional counselors, unrestricted choice, § 3302
Counteraffidavit, Rules 1920.42, 1920.72–1920.73
Counterclaims, Rule 1920.15
Court hearings, Rules 1920.51, 1920.52
Cruel treatment endangering life or health, grounds for divorce, § 3301
Custody, effect of divorce on custody of children, § 5312
Custody, joinder of related claims, Rule 1920.32
De novo hearing, party rights, § 3321
Death of party, § 3323(d.1)
    Subsequent attack upon divorce decree, § 3331
Death of either party, effect on alimony, § 3707
Deceased party, substitution, § 3323
Decrees, § 3323
    Effect on property rights, § 3503
        Liens on entireties property, § 3507
    Estoppel, § 3333
    Foreign decrees, enforcement, § 3705
    Limitations on attacks upon decrees, § 3331
    Opening decree, motion, § 3332
    Res judicata, § 3333
    Vacating decree, motion, § 3332
Deeds and conveyances,
    Disposition of property after termination of marriage, § 3504
    Entireties property, conveyance to divorced spouse, § 3508

INDEX

References are to Sections of the Pennsylvania Domestic Relations Code, Pennsylvania Crimes Code, Pennsylvania Judicial Code, Pennsylvania Domestic Relations Court Rules, and Selected Federal Statutes, Court Rules, and Regulations

Divorce—Cont'd
Determination and distribution of property, Rule 1920.33
Default judgment, Rule 1920.41
Defendant suffering from mental disorder, actions, § 3308
Defenses, § 3307
    Enforcement of foreign decrees, § 3705
Definitions, § 3103, Rule 1920.1
    Marital misconduct, alimony, § 3701
    Premarital agreement, § 3106
Denial,
    Marriage not irretrievably broken, court finding, § 3301
Denials, Rule 1920.14
Devises,
    Marital property status, § 3501
Discovery,
Electronic testimony, witnesses, Home 1930.3
    Property of parties, § 3505
    Property, inventory and appraisal, Rule 1920.33
    Rule 1920.22, 1930.5
Dismissal of complaint, § 3323
Disposition of property
    Defeat obligations, § 3505
    Termination of marriage, § 3504
Dissolution, marital status, § 3301 et seq.
Distributions
    Foreign decrees, enforcement, § 3705
    Property, statement of reasons, § 3506
    Related claims, joinder of, Rule 1920.33
Division
    Entireties property between divorced persons, § 3507
    Marital property, equitable division, § 3502
Domicile and residence,
    Parties, prerequisites, § 3104
Earning power increase contributions to other party, marital property division factor, § 3502
Economic circumstances of parties, marital property division factor, § 3502
Educational contributions to other party, marital property division factor, § 3502

Divorce—Cont'd
Effective date, Rule 1920.92
Employability, marital property division factor, § 3502
Enforcement
    Arrearages, alimony, attorney fees, etc., § 3703
    Foreign decrees, § 3705
Entireties property
    Conveyances to divorced spouse, § 3508
    Division between divorced persons, § 3507
    Rights of parties in property sold for support, § 4365
Equitable division of marital property, § 3502
Equity power of court, § 3323
Estate,
    Marital property division factor, § 3502
Estoppel, § 3333
Evidence,
    Burden of proof, premarital agreements, § 31 and six
    New evidence, motion to open or vacate decree, § 3332
    Presumptions,
        Acquired property, marital property status, § 3501
        Continued institutionalization, mental illness or disorder, § 3301
Expenses and expenditures,
    Court order, § 3323
    Enforcement of arrearages, § 3703
Fabricated grounds, collusion, § 3309
Factors,
    Equitable division or marital property, § 3502
Family home,
    Residing in by parties during pendency of action, court award, § 3502
Fault, grounds for divorce, § 3301
Fees, attorneys, § 3702
    Enforcement of arrearages, § 3703
Fees, mediation, § 3902
Fees and expenses, joinder of related claims, Rule 1920.31
Final decree, Rule 1920.42
Findings, masters, reports, Rule 1920.53
Foreign decrees, enforcement, § 3705

INDEX

References are to Sections of the Pennsylvania Domestic Relations Code, Pennsylvania Crimes Code, Pennsylvania Judicial Code, Pennsylvania Domestic Relations Court Rules, and Selected Federal Statutes, Court Rules, and Regulations

Divorce—Cont'd
Foreign forum, subsequent in-state jurisdiction, § 3104
Forms,
Complaint, Rule 1920.12
Counteraffidavits, Rule 1920.72
    Decree, § 3323
    Inventories, Rule 1920.75
    Inventory of property, § 3505
    Judgments and decrees, § 3323, Rule 1920.76
    Masters, appointments, Rule 1920.74
    Pleadings, captions, Rule 1930.1
Forms, Rules 1920.71-1920.76
Fraud,
    Collusion, § 3309
    Decree for procurement by intrinsic fraud, motion to open or vacate, § 3332
    Incumbrances to third parties for inadequate consideration, § 3505
Future capital assets acquisitions opportunities, marital property division factor, § 3502
Future payments, security requirements, insuring compliance with court orders, § 3502
General appearance, § 3309
Gifts,
    Marital property status, § 3501
Grounds for annulment,
    Void marriages, § 3304
    Voidable marriages, § 3305
Grounds for determining jurisdiction, § 3104
Grounds for divorce, § 3301
    Defined, § 3103
Health,
    Endangerment, cruel and barbarous treatment, grounds for divorce, § 3301
    Marital property division factor, § 3502
Health insurance coverage, dependent spouses, court order, § 3702
Hearings,
    Alternative procedures, masters, Rule 1920.55-1
    Cases not requiring hearings, § 3301
    Court hearings, Rules 1920.32, 1920.51, 1920.52

Divorce—Cont'd
    Decrees and orders, Rules 1920.52, 1920.55, 1920.74
    De novo requests, Rule 1920.55-3
    Final decree, Rule 1920.55
    Masters, § 3321
    Masters, Rules 1920.51, 1920.53-1920.55
    Notice, Rules 1920.51, 1920.55
    Objections, master's report, Rule 1920.55
    Related claims, Rule 1920.54
    Reports, Rules 1920.53-1920.55
Homemaker contributions to marital property, marital property division factor, § 3502
Hospitalization insurance coverage, dependent spouses, court order, § 3702
Imprisonment, grounds for divorce, § 3301
Income,
    Amount and sources, a marital property division factor, § 3502
Indigent persons, Rule 1920.62
Indignities,
    Counseling, § 3302
    Intolerable and life burdensome condition, grounds for divorce, § 3301
Injunctions, § 3323
    Disposition of property to defeat obligations, § 3505
Injunctions, special relief, Rule 1920.43
Institutionalization, grounds for divorce, § 3301
Insurance benefits, income source, marital property division factor, § 3502
Interest,
    Court award, interest on unpaid installments, § 3502
Inventories,
    Marital property, § 3505
Inventory, Rule 1920.33, 1920.75
Irretrievable breakdown,
    Counseling, § 3302
    Defined, § 3103
    Grounds for divorce, § 3301
Joinder of parties, Rule 1920.34
Joinder of related claims, Rules 1920.31-1920.33
Judgments, decrees and orders
    Allocation of order, Rule 1920.56
    Appointment of master, Rule 1920.74

INDEX

References are to Sections of the Pennsylvania Domestic Relations Code, Pennsylvania Crimes Code, Pennsylvania Judicial Code, Pennsylvania Domestic Relations Court Rules, and Selected Federal Statutes, Court Rules, and Regulations

Divorce—Cont'd
  Default judgment, Rule 1920.41
  Entry, waiver, notice, Rule 1920.72
  Estoppel, § 3333
  Exceptions, Rule 1920.55-2
  Final decree, Rule 1920.42
  Foreign decrees, enforcement, § 3705
  Forms, Rules 1920.73, 1920.74, 1920.76
  Hearings, Rules 1920.52, 1920.55
  Hearings de novo, Rule 1920.55-3
  Limitations on a tax upon decrees, § 3331
  Notice of intent to request entry of decree, Rules 1920.42, 1920.73
  Opening decree, motion, § 3332
  Report of master, Rule 1920.53 et seq.
  Res judicata, § 3333
  Social Security numbers, § 4304.1
  Vacating decree, motion, § 3332
  Jurisdiction, §§ 3104, 3323
    Lack of jurisdiction, motion to vacate decree, § 3332
  Jury trial, § 3322
  Laches, collateral attack on decree, § 3333
  Length of marriage, marital property division factor, § 3502
  Liabilities of parties, marital property division factor, § 3502
  Liens and incumbrances,
    Marital property, incumbrance to third parties for adequate consideration, void, § 3505
    Security for payments to parties, § 3502
  Life endangerment, cruel and barbarous treatment, grounds for divorce, § 3301
  Life insurance,
    Continued maintenance and beneficiary designations, § 3502
  Limitation of actions,
    Attacks upon divorce decree, § 3331
  Mail and mailing, process, service of process, original, Rule 1930.4
  Malicious desertion, grounds for divorce, § 3301
  Marital property, § 3501 et seq.
    Child custody, division factor, § 3502
    Court powers, equitable distribution issues, § 3502

Divorce—Cont'd
  Defined, § 3501
  Distributions, foreign decrees, enforcement, § 3705
  Equitable distribution,
    Disposition of property to defeat equitable distribution, attachment, § 3505
  Equitable division, § 3502
  Hearings, decision in posttrial relief, Rule 1920.52
  Premarital agreements, burden of proof, § 3106
  Statement of reasons for distribution, § 3506
  Marital status
    Dissolution, § 3301 et seq.
    Proceedings to determine, § 3306
  Masters
    Appointment, Rules 1920.51, 1920.74
    Decrees and orders, Rules 1920.55, 1920.74
    Final decree, Rule 1920.55
    Forms, Rule 1920.74
    Hearings, § 3321, Rules 1920.51, 1920.53-1920.55
    Notice, Rules 1920.51, 1920.55
    Objections, report, Rule 1920.55
    Related claims, hearings, Rule 1920.54
    Reports, Rules 1920.53-1920.55
  Maximum counseling sessions, § 3302
  Mediation, § 3901 et seq.
    Costs, § 3902
    Custody, Rule 1940.1 et seq.
    Evaluations, § 3903
    Fees, § 3902
    Grandfather rights, § 3904
    Guidelines, § 3901
    Rates and charges, § 3902
    Rules and regulations, § 3901
  Medical income source, marital property division factor, § 3502
  Mentally ill persons,
    Commencement of action against mentally ill spouse, § 3308
    Institutionalization, grounds for divorce, § 3301
  Mentally retarded persons, institutionalization, grounds for divorce, § 3301
  Military service, Rule 1920.46
  Modification,
    Agreements between parties, effect, § 3105

INDEX

References are to Sections of the Pennsylvania Domestic Relations Code, Pennsylvania Crimes Code, Pennsylvania Judicial Code, Pennsylvania Domestic Relations Court Rules, and Selected Federal Statutes, Court Rules, and Regulations

Divorce—Cont'd
Mortgages,
    Disposition of property after termination of marriage, § 3504
Motion for appointment of master, Rule 1920.74
Motions,
    Decrees, opening or vacating, § 3332
Multiples causes of action, Rules 1920.6, 1920.13
Mutual consent,
    Counseling, § 3302
    Grounds for divorce, § 3301
Negotiations,
    Property settlement terms, § 3309
Non pros, Rule 1920.21
Notice,
    Counseling availability, § 3302
    Form, Rules 1920.45, 1920.71, 1920.73
    Hearings, Rules 1920.51, 1920.55
    Intent to request entry of decree, Rules 1920.42, 1920.73
    Judgments and decrees, waiver, Rule 1920.72
    Master's report, Rule 1920.55-2
    Reports, masters, hearings, Rule 1920.55-2
Objections, master's report, Rule 1920.55
Obligations, disposition of property to defeat, § 3505
Opening decrees, motion, § 3332
Optional procedure for enforcement of foreign decrees, § 3705
Orders. Judgments, decrees and orders, supra
Parents, effect of divorce on custody of children, § 5312
Partial distribution, marital property, section 35 to
Parties,
    Agreements between, effect, § 3105
    Indigent parties, Rule 1920.62
    Joinder of parties, Rule 1920.34
    Premarital agreements, burden of proof, § 3106
    Security, party leaving jurisdiction, Rule 1920.44
    Substitution for deceased party, § 3323
Partition, rights determination and disposition, jurisdiction, § 3104

Divorce—Cont'd
Payments,
    Future payments, security requirements, insuring compliance with court orders, § 3502
Payments, spousal support, § 3704
Pending actions, Rule 1920.92
Perjury,
    Collusion, § 3309
Personal representative,
    Substitution for deceased party, § 3323
Pleadings, Rules 1920.11 et seq., 1930.1
Postnuptial agreements,
    Marital property status, § 3501
    Rights determination and disposition, jurisdiction, § 3104
Post-trial practice, Rule 1930.2
Post-trial relief, Rule 1920.52
Praecipe to transmit record, Rule 1920.73
Premarital agreements,
    Burden of proof, § 3106
    Marital Property status, § 3501
    Rights determination and disposition, jurisdiction, § 3104
Prenuptial agreements, marital property status, § 3501
Prior marriages, marital property division factor, § 3502
Priority, Rule 1920.6
Procedure
    Decree of court, § 3323
        Attacks upon decrees, limitations, § 3331
        Opening or vacating decrees, § 3332
        Res judicata and estoppel, § 3333
    Hearing by master, § 3321
    Jury trial, § 3322
Procedures for enforcement of foreign decrees, § 3705
Proceedings by indigent parties, Rule 1920.62
Process, service, Rule 1930.4
Professionals, qualified professionals, defined, § 3103
Property, § 3501 et seq.
    Definitions, § 3501
    Discovery, Rule 1920.22
    Disposition of property
        Defeat obligations, § 3505
        Termination of marriage, § 3504

INDEX

References are to Sections of the Pennsylvania Domestic Relations Code, Pennsylvania Crimes Code, Pennsylvania Judicial Code, Pennsylvania Domestic Relations Court Rules, and Selected Federal Statutes, Court Rules, and Regulations

Divorce—Cont'd
  Distributions, statement of reasons, § 3506
  Effect of divorce generally, § 3503
  Entireties property
    Conveyances to divorced spouse, § 3508
    Division between divorced persons, § 3507
    Equitable division, § 3502
    Foreign decrees, enforcement, § 3705
    Inventory and appraisal, Rule 1920.33
    Premarital agreements, burden of proof, § 3106
    Valuation, non-marital property, § 3501
  Marital property
    Defined, § 3501
    Equitable division, § 3502
    Foreign decrees, enforcement, § 3705
    Premarital agreements, burden of proof, § 3106
    Special relief, Rule 1920.43
  Property settlements, jurisdiction, § 3104
  Protection,
    Party interest, temporary court orders, § 3323
  Provocation, defense abolished, § 3307
  Public policy, § 3102
  Qualified professionals,
    Counseling unrestricted choice, § 3302
    Defined, § 3103
  Reconsideration motions, Rule 1930.2
  Reconciliation,
    Reasonable prospect of reconciliation, continuance, § 3301
  Records and recordation, divorce decree recording, effect on liens on entireties property, § 3507
  Recrimination, defense abolished, § 3307
  Related claims, Rules 1920.31-1920.33, 1920.54
  Reports,
    Counseling attendance, § 3302
  Reports, master Rules 1920.53-1920.55-2
  Res judicata, § 3333
  Retirement income source, marital property division factor, § 3502
  Rule to show cause,
    Jury trial application, § 3322

Divorce—Cont'd
  Sales,
    Court ordered sales of property, marital property distribution enforcement, § 3502
    Disposition of property after termination of marriage, § 3504
    Entireties property, division of proceedings, § 3507
  Security, party leaving jurisdiction, Rule 1920.44
  Security requirements,
    Foreign decrees, enforcement, § 3705
    Insuring compliance with court ordered future payments, § 3502
  Seizures of goods, court authorization, marital distribution enforcement, § 3502
  Separate and apart,
    Defined, § 3103
  Separation agreements, rights determination and disposition, jurisdiction, § 3104
  Service of process, Rule 1930.4
  Setoff and counterclaim, Rule 1920.15
  Severance of actions and claims, Rule 1920.16
  Special relief, Rule 1920.43
  Spousal support, § 3702
    Defined, § 3103
    Effect of divorce decree on, Rule 1920.31
    Enforcement of arrearages, § 3703
    Payment, § 3704
  Standard of living, marital property division factor, § 3502
  Statements,
    Reasons for distribution of marital property, § 3506
  Station in life, marital property division factor, § 3502
  Statute of limitations, attacks upon divorce decree, § 3331
  Stays, Rule 1920.6
  Subsequent petition, Rule 1920.15
  Substitution, deceased party, § 3323
  Support, § 3701 et seq.
    Orders, execution against entireties property, rights of divorced persons to sold property, § 4365
    Payment, § 3704
    Spousal support, § 3702
      Defined, § 3103

INDEX

References are to Sections of the Pennsylvania Domestic Relations Code, Pennsylvania Crimes Code, Pennsylvania Judicial Code, Pennsylvania Domestic Relations Court Rules, and Selected Federal Statutes, Court Rules, and Regulations

Divorce—Cont'd
  Enforcement of arrearages, § 3703
  Payment, § 3704
  Support, Rules 1920.31, 1920.56
Telecommunications, witnesses, Rule 1930.3
Termination,
  Disposition of property after termination of marriage, § 3504
  Property rights dependent on marital relationship, § 3503
Testimony outside county, Rule 1920.61
Time,
  Contempt sentences, maximum duration, § 3502
  Desertion duration, ground for divorce, § 3301
  Elapsed time from commencement of action, mutual consent divorce, § 3301
  Institutionalization for mental illness, grounds for divorce, § 3301
  Jury trial application, § 3322
  Limitation of actions, attacks on decrees, § 3331
  Living separate and apart, irretrievably broken marriages, determination, § 3301
Training contributions to other party, marital property division factor, § 3502
Transfers,
  Court ordered property transfers, marital property distribution enforcement, § 3502
Trial, jury trial, § 3322
Trusts and trustees,
  Constructive trusts, undisclosed assets of parties, § 3505
Vacating decrees, motion, § 3332
Value of property set apart to each party, marital property division factor, 23 § 3502
Venue, § 3104
Venue, Rule 1920.2
Veterans benefits, marital property status, § 3501
Visitation rights, jurisdiction, § 3104
Vital statistics information, Rule 1920.46
Vocational skills, marital property division factor, § 3502

Divorce—Cont'd
Void marriages, annulment, § 1702, 3303
  Grounds, § 3304
Voidable marriages, annulment, § 3303
  Grounds, § 3305
Warrant of attorney, Rule 1920.5
Willful desertion, grounds for divorce, § 3301
Witness, testimony outside county, Rule 1920.61
Witnesses, electronic testimony, Rule 1930.3

Divorce Code
Generally, § 3101 et seq.

DNA Testing
Definitions, support of persons, § 4302, 4377
Paternity, § 4343, Rule 1910.15

Dockets
Adoption, entries, § 2906
Custody, transfer of actions, Rule 1915.2
Docketing orders, § 7601, 7602
Support, transfer of entries, Rule 1910.8

Documents
Child custody jurisdiction, preservation for use in other states, § 5362

Domestic and Sexual Violence Victim Address Confidentiality
Generally, § 6701 et seq.
Address Confidentiality Program, § 6703
  Agency use of designated address, § 6707
  Applications, § 6705
  Cancellation of participation, § 6706
  Certification process, § 6705
  Civil immunity, § 6713
  Construction of law, § 6709
  Disclosure of actual address, § 6708
  Emergency disclosure, § 6710
  Expiration of participation, § 6706
  Penalties, § 6711
  Persons eligible to apply, § 6704
  Rules and regulations, § 6712
  Waiver process, § 6709
  Withdrawal of participation, § 67 six

Definitions, § 6702

Domestic Relations
Caption, form, Rule 1930.1
Post-trial practice, Rule 1930.2
Protection from abuse, Rule 1901 et seq.
Reconsideration motions, Rule 1930.2
Testimony, use of telephones, Rule 1930.3

INDEX

References are to Sections of the Pennsylvania Domestic Relations Code, Pennsylvania Crimes Code, Pennsylvania Judicial Code, Pennsylvania Domestic Relations Court Rules, and Selected Federal Statutes, Court Rules, and Regulations

Domestic Relations Code
Generally, § 101 et seq.

Domestic Violence
Generally, § 6101 et seq.
Abuse, defined, § 6102
Actions and proceedings,
    Commencement of actions, § 6106
    Instructions concerning the commencement of proceedings, § 6110
    Procedures, § 6117
    Relief, § 6108
    Remedies, § 6117
Address confidentiality, § 6701 et seq.
Addresses,
    Disclosure propriety, court consideration, § 6112
Adult, defined, § 6102
Advice to plaintiffs, § 6106
Affidavits
    Insufficient funds for fees, commencement of action, § 6106
Amendment of court orders or consent agreements, § 6108
Arraignment, preliminary arraignment, arrested persons, § 6113
Arrest,
    Court order violation, § 6113
Assistance to plaintiffs, § 6106
Attorneys. Right to counsel, generally, post
Certificates and certification,
    Emergency court orders, § 6110
Certified copies, court orders, § 6104
Confidential communications, Defined, § 6102
Confidential or privileged information, § 6116
Consent agreements,
    Contempt, agreement violation, § 6114
    Court approval, § 6108
Contempt,
    Court order or consent agreement violations, § 6114 .1
    Court order or consent agreement violations, § 6113.1, 6114
    Criminal contempt, juvenile delinquents and defendants, § 6114
    Foreign protection order or consent agreement violations, § 6114
Continuance,
    Hearings, § 6107
Costs, § 6107

Domestic Violence—Cont'd
Counselors and counseling,
    Accompaniment of parties to hearings, § 6111
    Confidential or privileged information, § 6116
    Definitions, § 6102
County registry, court order placement in, § 6109
Court orders,
    Arrest for order violation, § 6113
    Contempt, order violation, § 6114
    Emergency orders, § 6110
    Expiration of order, § 6110
    Registration, § 6104
    Service, §§ 6106, 6109
    Temporary orders, § 6107
Death,
    Termination of confidential or privileged information, privilege, § 6116
Definitions, § 6102
Domestic and Sexual Violence Victim Address Confidentiality Act, § 6701 et seq.
Domestic violence counselors/advocates,
    Accompaniment of parties to hearings, § 6111
    Confidential or privileged information, § 6116
    Defined, § 6102
Domestic violence and stalking, federal crimes, 18 U.S.C. § 2261 et seq.
Domestic violence program,
    Defined, § 6102
Double jeopardy,
    Indirect criminal contempt charge hearings, § 6113
Duration of court orders or consent agreements, § 6108
Emergency relief, § 6110
Enforcement, court orders, § 6109
Evidence,
    Registration of court orders, § 6104
Family or household members, defined, § 6102
Fees,
    Credit cards, payment, § 6120
    Filing, petitions, § 6106
    Foreign protection orders, service, § 6113
    Installment payments, § 6120
    Private criminal complaints, protection order violations, § 6113.1

INDEX

References are to Sections of the Pennsylvania Domestic Relations Code, Pennsylvania Crimes Code, Pennsylvania Judicial Code, Pennsylvania Domestic Relations Court Rules, and Selected Federal Statutes, Court Rules, and Regulations

Domestic Violence—Cont'd
Filing fees, affidavit of insufficient funds for, § 6106
Foreign protection orders,
  Civil contempt, violations, § 6114.1
  Definitions, § 6102
  Recognition and enforcement, § 6104, § 6106
  Violations, § 6113.1, § 6114
Former jeopardy,
  Indirect criminal contempt charge hearings, § 6113
Forms,
  Court orders, granting relief, § 6108
  Reports, abuse reports, § 6115
Harassment, protective orders, § 6108
Hearing officers,
  Defined, § 6102
  Emergency relief, granting, § 6110
Hearings, § 6107, Rule 1920.52
  Indirect criminal contempt charges, § 6113
Household, leaving to avoid further abuse, effect, § 6103
Indigency determination, commencement of proceedings, § 6106
Instructions,
  Commencement of proceedings, emergency situations, § 6110
Jurisdiction,
  Indirect criminal contempt charges, violations, protection orders, § 6114
  Protection orders, § 6103
Juvenile delinquents and defendants, § 6114
Local law enforcement agencies, responsibilities, § 6105
Masters for emergency relief, § 6110
Means of service of process, court adoption, § 6106
Minor, defined, § 6102
Mutual protection orders, § 6108
Notice,
  Ramifications of prohibited conduct resumption, court orders, § 6113
Orders,
  Arrest for order violation, § 6113
  Availability, notice, § 6105
  Civil contempt, order violations, § 6114.1
  Contempt, order violation, § 6114
  Coresidency, resumption, effect, § 6108

Domestic Violence—Cont'd
  Emergency orders, § 6110
  Expiration of order, § 6110
  Indirect criminal contempt, § 6114
  Modification, § 6117
  Service, § 6106, § 6109
  Temporary orders, § 6107
Permanent address of plaintiff or minor children, disclosure, § 6112
Petitions,
  Commencement of action, § 6106
  Service, § 6106
Placement, court orders, county registry, § 6109
Police,
  Responsibilities, § 6105
Preliminary arraignment, arrested persons, § 6113
Private criminal complaints, protection order violations, § 6113.1
Privileges and immunities,
  Reporting domestic abuse, § 6115
Procedure following arrest, § 6113
Protection orders, § 6108
  Admissibility, § 6107
  Civil contempt, § 6114.1
  Contempt, order violation, § 6114
  Damages, § 6108
  Ex parte orders, § 6107
  Existence verification, police affecting arrest, § 6113
  Fees, surcharges, § 6106
  Fines and penalties, indirect criminal contempt charges, § 6114
  Harassment, § 6108
  Jurisdiction, § 6103
  Labor and employment, notice, § 6106
  Mutual orders, § 6108
  Police, verification, § 6113
  Right to counsel, indirect criminal contempt charges, § 6114
  Right to jury trial, indirect criminal contempt charges, § 6114
  Stalking, § 6108
  Surcharges, § 6106
  Temporary orders, § 6107
  capital waiver, fees, § 6106
Real estate, title unaffected by court orders or consent agreements, § 6108
Reciprocity, orders, foreign states, § 6104
Registration,
  Court orders, § 6104

INDEX

References are to Sections of the Pennsylvania Domestic Relations Code, Pennsylvania Crimes Code, Pennsylvania Judicial Code, Pennsylvania Domestic Relations Court Rules, and Selected Federal Statutes, Court Rules, and Regulations

Domestic Violence—Cont'd
Relief,
    Emergency relief, § 6110
Reports,
    Abuse, § 6115
Residence, leaving to avoid further abuse, effect, § 6103
Right to counsel,
    Advice to defendants, § 6107
    Contempt trials, § 6114
Right to jury trial, indirect criminal contempt charges, protection orders, § 6114
Searches and seizures,
    Weapons, seizure subsequent to arrest, § 6113
Service of process,
    Commencement of proceedings, § 6106
    Contempt, violations, orders, § 6113.1
    Court orders, § 6109
    Foreign protection orders, fees, § 6113
    Modification, court orders, § 6117
    Original process, Rule 1930.4
Stalking, protective orders, § 6108
Temporary address of plaintiff or minor children, disclosure, § 6112
Temporary court orders, § 6107
Time,
    Contempt sentencing limits, § 6114
    Hearing dates, § 6107
    Protection orders, § 6108
Victims,
    Confidential or privileged information, § 6116
    Defined, § 6102

Domestic Violence—Cont'd
Waiver,
    Confidentiality of communications, § 6116
    Costs, § 6107
    Written, confidentiality privilege, § 6116

Domestic Violence Counselor Advocate
Defined, protection from abuse, § 6102
Protection from abuse, § 6111

Domestic Violence Program
Defined, protection from abuse, § 6102

Domicile and Residence
Annulment of marriage,
    Parties, prerequisites, § 3104
Divorce,
    Parties, prerequisites, § 3104
Domestic abuse, leaving residence to avoid, effect, § 6103
Leaving to avoid domestic abuse, effect, § 6102
Marriage license applications, form requirements, § 1302
Personal jurisdiction, § 7201
Venue, Rule 1910.2

Drugs and Medicine
Parties under influence, grounds for annulment, § 3305

Duress or Coercion
Annulment of marriage, induced marriages, grounds for annulment, § 3305

Duty of Support, Definitions,
Interstate family support, § 7101
Intrastate family support enforcement, § 8101

—E—

Earnings
Compensation and Salaries, generally, this index
Income, generally, this index
Information, Rule 1910.9
Power increase contribution of one party to other, alimony necessity factor, § 3502, § 3701

Earnings Information
Support of persons, Rules 1910.26, 1910.27

Earnings Report
Rule 1910.27

Economic Circumstances
Marital property division factor, divorce or annulment proceedings, § 3502

Education
Child abuse prevention programs, § 6383
Divorced party, contribution of one to other, alimony necessity, § 3701

INDEX

References are to Sections of the Pennsylvania Domestic Relations Code, Pennsylvania Crimes Code, Pennsylvania Judicial Code, Pennsylvania Domestic Relations Court Rules, and Selected Federal Statutes, Court Rules, and Regulations

Education—Cont'd
Educational contribution to other party, marital property division factor, § 3502
Post-high school programs, adult children, expenses, Rule 1910.16-5
Postsecondary education, expenses and expenditures, § 4327

Electronic Testimony
Witnesses, Rule 1930.3

Emancipated Children
Support, § 4323

Emergencies
Domestic violence, emergency relief, § 6110
Marriages,
    Exception to waiting period after license application, § 1303

Emergency Relief
Protection from abuse, minor judiciary, § 6110

Emotional Condition
Divorced parties, alimony necessity factor, § 3701

Employees
Child protective services
    Prospective child-care personnel, information relating to, § 6344
    Violations, penalty, § 6349

Employers
Defined, support, § 4302

Enforcement
Agreements, § 3105
Attachment of wages, § 4348
Child custody jurisdiction, out-of-state custody decree, § 5356
Child medical support, section 4326
Divorce
    Alimony, attorney fees, etc., arrearages, § 3703
    Foreign decrees, § 3705
Law enforcement agencies, protection from abuse, responsibilities, § 6105
Remedies preservation, § 4366
Support, generally, this index

Engagement Ring, § 3501(a)(3)

Entireties Property
Conveyance to divorced spouse, § 3508
Division between divorced persons, § 3507

Entireties Property—Cont'd
Support orders, execution against, § 4361
    Credit to plaintiff purchaser, § 4364
    Other enforcement remedies preserved, § 4366
    Plaintiff's shares of sale proceeds, § 4362
    Rights of divorced persons to sold property, § 4365
    Trustee to distribute, sale proceeds, § 4363

Equitable Division
Discovery, Rule 1930.5
Factors, § 3502
Marital property, divorce, § 3502

Equity
Power of court, § 3323

Escrow
Disputed amounts, overdue support, collection from monetary awards, § 4308.1

Estoppel
Annulment decrees, § 3333
Divorce decrees, § 3333

Evaluations
Children and minors, custody or visitation, Rule 1915.8
Forms, orders, Rule 1915.18

Evidence
Acknowledgments, paternity, Rule 1910.15
Child custody jurisdiction, taking testimony in another state, § 5359
Child protective services, court proceedings, § 6381
Child support guideline application correctness, presumption, § 4322
Custody of minor children, exclusion orders, Rule 1915.8
Disclosure, generally, this index
Domestic violence,
    Registration of court orders, § 6104
Genetic test results, paternity proceedings, § 4343
Marriage,
    Property ownership actions, § 4104
Paternity proceedings,
    Gentic test results, § 4343
    Refusal to submit to blood tests, § 5104
Petition for adoption, hearings, testimony, § 2724

INDEX

References are to Sections of the Pennsylvania Domestic Relations Code, Pennsylvania Crimes Code, Pennsylvania Judicial Code, Pennsylvania Domestic Relations Court Rules, and Selected Federal Statutes, Court Rules, and Regulations

Evidence—Cont'd
Presumptions,
    Child support guideline application correctness, § 4322
    Death of spouse of marriage license applicant, decree, § 1701
    Spousal support guideline application correctness, § 4322
Spousal support guideline application correctness, presumption, § 4322
Support of persons, modification or termination, Rule 1910.19
Visitation, exclusion orders, Rule 1915.8

Examinations
Custody or visitation of minors, Rule 1915.8
Form of order, Rule 1915.18
Marriage licenses
    Oral examination, § 1306
    Syphilis, § 1305

Exceptions
Alimony, contempt petition hearing report Rule 1910.21-5
Masters report, divorce action, Rule 1920.55-2
Partial custody and visitation, report of hearing officer, Rule 1915.4-2
Protection from abuse, Rule 1905
Support,
    Contempt petition hearing report, Rule 1910.21-5
    Office conference, hearings, Rule 1910.12

Exchanges
Pennsylvania Adoption Cooperative Exchange, generally, this index

Exclusive Possession, § 3502

Execution
Enforcement of support orders, Rule 1910.20
Entireties property, support order or execution against, § 4361

Execution—Cont'd
Judgments, decrees or orders, support orders, Rule 1910.20
Judgment for arrearages, Rule 1910.24
Marriage
    Alienation of affections, actions abolished, instruments executed in satisfaction of abolished claims prohibited, § 1905
    Breach of promise to marry, actions abolished, instruments executed in satisfaction of abolished claims prohibited, § 1905
    Debts contracted for necessaries, collection, § 4102
    Divorce, attachment, special relief, Rule 1920.43
Support, this index

Exhibits
Adoption
    Petition for adoption, § 2702
    Reports of intermediaries, § 2534

Expedited Procedure
Support actions, § 4342

Expenses and Expenditures
Adult children, post-secondary education, Rule 1910.16-5
Court order, § 3323
Divorce, § 3702
    Enforcement of arrearages, § 3703
Statements, forms, Rule 1910.27
Support of persons, office conference, verification of child care expenses, Rule 1910.11

Expunge
Defined, child protective services, § 6303

Expungement
Child protective services, information, § 6341

Extradition
Governor, interstate family support enforcement, § 7801

—F—

Family
Custody, generally. Children and Minors, this index
Defined,
    Child-support program, § 4374
    Protection from abuse, § 6302

Family Court Rules
Unified family court rule, Rule 1931

Family Members
Child Protective Services, generally, this index

INDEX

References are to Sections of the Pennsylvania Domestic Relations Code, Pennsylvania Crimes Code, Pennsylvania Judicial Code, Pennsylvania Domestic Relations Court Rules, and Selected Federal Statutes, Court Rules, and Regulations

Family Members—Cont'd
Defined
    Child protective services, § 6303
    Protection from abuse § 6102
Protection from Abuse, generally, this index

Fast Track Appeals
Pa.R.App.P. 102, et seq.

Fault
Divorce, grounds, § 3301

Federal Courts
Judges, marriages, solemnization, § 1503

Federal Parent Locator Service
Children, 42 U.S.C. § 653

Fees
Arrearages, information to consumer credit bureau, § 4303
Child custody jurisdiction, enforcement, § 5450, 5452
Custody, mediation programs, § 3902
Divorce, attorneys, § 3702
    Enforcement of arrearages, § 3703
Interstate family support enforcement, § 7313
Intrastate family support enforcement, § 8313
Marriage, § 1105
Mediation, § 3902
Support, § 4351

Files and Filing
Adoption, reports, intention to adopt, § 2532
Central complaint file. Child Protective Services, this index
Child custody jurisdiction, out-of-state custody decree, § 5356
Marriage licenses, applications and consent certificates, § 1309

Final Judgment or Decree
Divorce or annulment actions, Rule 1920.55

Financial Institutions
Cooperation of financial institutions, § 4304.1
Data collection, § 4304.1

Financial Statements and Reports,
Rule 1910.27; Rule 1910.28
Child support program, § 4375
Cooperation, government agencies and financial institutions, § 4304.1

Financial Statements and Reports—Cont'd
Income and expense statements, forms, Rule 1910.27
Supplemental income statements, Rule 1910.27

Fines and Penalties
Adoption, unauthorized disclosure, § 2910
Arrearages, § 4348
Child protective services
    Failure to report suspected child abuse, § 6319
    Information and personnel violations, § 6349
Child support arrearages, failure to comply, § 4374
Child support program, § 4377
Healthcare providers, acceptance of newborns, failure to report, § 6506
Government agencies and labor organizations, information noncompliance, § 4304.1
Income withholding orders, § 7501.4
Limitations, torts, children and minors, parental liability, § 5505
Protection from abuse, inability to pay, § 6120
Release of information, relinquished firearms, § 6108.5
Subpoenas, noncompliance, § 4305
Support, willful failure to pay support orders, § 4354

Fingerprinting of children, § 5105

Force and Violence
Annulment of marriage, induced marriages, grounds for annulment, § 3305

Foreign Adoption
Foreign adoption registration procedure, Pa.O.C. Rule 15.8

Foreign Countries
Adoption,
    Judgments and decrees, § 2908

Foreign Decrees
Adoption, § 2908
Child Custody Jurisdiction, this index
Divorce, enforcement, § 3705

Foreign Judgments
Children and minors, custody, registration, § 5445, § 5446

Foreign States
Adoption, judgments and decrees, § 2908

INDEX

References are to Sections of the Pennsylvania Domestic Relations Code, Pennsylvania Crimes Code, Pennsylvania Judicial Code, Pennsylvania Domestic Relations Court Rules, and Selected Federal Statutes, Court Rules, and Regulations

Foreign States—Cont'd
Arrest, domestic violence, violation of orders, § 6113
Divorce, foreign decrees, enforcement, § 3705
Domestic violence, arrest, violation of orders, § 6113
Enforcement, cooperation, § 4305
Interstate family support enforcement, § 7101 et seq.
Income withholding orders,
  Employer receipt, § 7501
  Enforcement, § 7502
  Recognition, § 7501
Interstate family support, § 7101 et seq.
Marriage, same-sex marriages, void status, § 1704
Modification of foreign support orders, jurisdiction, § 4352
Nonparties to interstate family support enforcement, § 7304
Notice, orders, modification, § 7614
Paternity acknowledgment, full faith and credit, § 5103
Payments, credit, interstate family support enforcement, § 7209
Priorities and preferences, multiple orders, § 7207

Former Jeopardy
Domestic violence,
  Indirect criminal contempt charge hearings, § 6113

Form or Forms
Accident and health insurance, coverage, Rule 1910.27
Attachment orders, Rule 1910.31
Complaint, Rule 1910.27
Earnings reports, Rule 1910.28
Financial statements and reports, Rule 1910.27
Health insurance coverage information, Rule 1910.27; Rule 1910.28
Income and expense statements, Rule 1910.27
Orders,
  Commencement of action, Rule 1910.27
  Earnings information, Rule 1910.28
  Modification, petitions, Rule 1910.27

Form or Forms—Cont'd
Petitions, modification, Rule 1910.27
Pleadings, captions, Rule 1930.1
Acknowledgement of paternity, support actions, Rule 1910.28
Acknowledgment of paternity forms, § 5103
Adoption, decrees, § 2902
Affidavit, divorce or annulment actions, Rule 1920.72
Annulment of marriage decree, § 3323, Rule 1920.71 et seq.
  Inventory of property, § 3505
Appraisement, divorce or annulment actions, Rule 1920.75
Arrest, bench warrant and request, Rule 1910.13-2
Attachment
  Notice, Rules 1910.29, 1910.30
  Support actions, Rules 1910.29-1910.31
Caption, custody, partial custody and visitation actions, Rule 1915.15
Complaint
  Custody, partial custody and visitation actions, Rule 1915.15
  Divorce or annulment actions, Rule 1920.12, 1920.72
  Support actions, Rule 1910.26
Consent certificates, marriage, form uniformity, § 1104
Contempt petition,
  Custody or visitation of minors, Rule 1915.12
  Support and alimony, Rule 1910.21-1
Custody, partial custody and visitation actions, Rules 1915.15, 1915.16
Divorce,
  Decree, § 3323
  Inventory of property, § 3505
Divorce or annulment actions, Rules 1920.71-1920.76
Domestic relations, caption, Rule 1930.1
Domestic violence,
  Court orders granting relief, § 6108
Genetic tests, paternity, Rule 1930.6
Income and expense statement, Rule 1910.26

INDEX

References are to Sections of the Pennsylvania Domestic Relations Code, Pennsylvania Crimes Code, Pennsylvania Judicial Code, Pennsylvania Domestic Relations Court Rules, and Selected Federal Statutes, Court Rules, and Regulations

Form or Forms—Cont'd
Inventory, divorce actions, Rule 1920.75
Judgments and decrees, § 3323, Rule 1920.76
Laboratories,
    Premarital syphilis examination statements, § 1104
License applications, marriages, form uniformity, § 1104
Marriage, this index
Masters, appointments, Rule 1920.74
Motion for appointment of master, Rule 1920.74
Notice of attachment, Rule 1910.29
Notice to defend and claim rights, Rule 1920.71
Notices, contempt petition, support of persons, Rule 1910.21
Order and notice of joinder; custody proceedings, Rule 1915.6
Order for earnings report and subpoena; support actions, Rule 1910.27
Order of court; custody proceedings, Rule 1915.15
Paternity acknowlegment, Rule 1910.28
Paternity acknowledgment forms, § 5103
Physicians and surgeons,
    Premarital syphilis examination statements, § 1104
Plaintiff's affidavit; divorce action, Rule 1920.73
Pleadings, captions, Rule 1930.1
Praecipe
    transmit record; divorce action Rule 1920.73
Supplemental income statement, Rule 1910.26
Support actions, Rules 1910.26-1910.31
Waiver of trial; paternity issue, Rule 1910.28
Warrant, bench arrest warrant, failure or refusal to appear, hearings or conferences, Rule 1910.13-2

Formula
Support guidelines, Rule 1910.16-3, Rule 1910.16-4

Forum
Child custody jurisdiction, inconvenient forum, § 5348

Foster Care
Child-support program, reimbursement, § 4374
Perspective foster parents, information, standards, § 6344

Founded Reports
Child protective services, disposition, § 6338
Defined, child protective services, § 6303

Fraud
Adoption, consent, § 2711
Annulment of marriage,
    Collusion, § 3309
    Decree procurement by intrinsic fraud, motion to open or vacate, § 3332
    Grounds, § 3305
    Incumbrance of property to third parties for inadequate consideration, § 3505
Divorce,
    Collusion, § 3309
    Decree procurement by intrinsic fraud, motion to open or vacate, § 3332
    Incumbrance of property to third parties for inadequate consideration, § 3505

Full Faith And Credit
Foreign protection orders, protection from abuse, § 6104
Income withholding orders, § 7501.1
Interstate family support enforcement, § 7205
Intrastate family support enforcement, § 8201
Orders, § 7603
Paternity acknowledgment, § 5103
Support, 28 U.S.C. § 1738B

Funds
Transfers, obligors, § 4352

Funeral Directors
Child abuse, persons required to report, § 6311
Child Protective Services Law, § 6301 et seq.

INDEX

References are to Sections of the Pennsylvania Domestic Relations Code, Pennsylvania Crimes Code, Pennsylvania Judicial Code, Pennsylvania Domestic Relations Court Rules, and Selected Federal Statutes, Court Rules, and Regulations

—G—

Garnishment
See, also, Attachment, generally, this index
Child-support program, § 4381
Support, § 4348

General Assembly
Child protective services
Annual reports to, § 6347
Legislative oversight, § 6384

Genetic Tests
Defined, support, § 4302
Paternity actions, § 4343

Gifts
Marital property status, § 3501

Good Faith
Child abuse reports, presumption, § 6318

Goodwill
Valuation, § 3502

Governor
Child protective services, annual reports to, § 6347

Grandparents and Grandchildren
Adoption, custody and visitation, § 5314
Custody, § 5313
Mediation, § 3904
Visitation,
Custody of minor children, § 5311 et seq.

Gross Income
Computation, Rule 1910.16-2

Grounds for Adoption
Involuntary termination, § 2511

Grounds for Annulment
Void marriages, § 3304
Voidable marriages, § 3305

Grounds for Divorce
Defined, divorce, § 3103
Divorce, § 3301
Appointment,
Parental rights termination proceedings, § 2313
Child protective services, court proceedings, guardian ad litem for child, § 6382

Guardian and Ward
Actions and proceedings, parties, Rule 1910.3
Adoption, consent, § 2711
Annulment of marriage,
Guardian consent lacking, underage parties, grounds for annulment, § 3305
Application of the law, standby guardianship, § 5603
Consent, definitions, standby guardianship, § 5602
Forms, standby guardianship, § 5611
Long arm jurisdiction, § 7201
Marriage,
Restrictions on marriage license issuance, § 1304
Minor parents, actions, intrastate family support enforcement, § 8302
Standby guardianship, § 5601
Application of law, § 5603
Bonds, § 5616
Capacity, restoration, parent or guardian, § 5613
Definitions, § 5602
Evidence, presumptions, § 5612
Filing, § 5613
Forms, § 5611
Hearings, § 5612
Jurisdiction, § 5612
Powers and duties, § 5613
Records and recordation, § 5615
Revocation, § 5614

Guidelines
Generally, Rule 1910.16-1 et seq.; Rule 1910.16-2
Child and spousal support, § 4322; Rule 1910.16-3
Child support program, new hire reporting, § 4394
Common pleas, § 4322
Departures, Rule 1910.16-5
Formulas, Rule 1910.16-3; Rule 1910.16-4
Mediation, § 3901
Modification, Rule 1910.16-6
Multiple families, Rule 1910.16-7
Rates and charges, Rule 1910.16-4; Rule 1910.16-3
Substantial change in circumstance, Rule 1910.19
Spousal support, § 4322
Support, Rules 1910.16-1 to 1910.16-5

INDEX

References are to Sections of the Pennsylvania Domestic Relations Code, Pennsylvania Crimes Code, Pennsylvania Judicial Code, Pennsylvania Domestic Relations Court Rules, and Selected Federal Statutes, Court Rules, and Regulations

—H—

Hague Convention
Miscellaneous Federal Domestic Relations Statutes and Regulations, 42 U.S.C. § 11601 et seq.

Health, Department of
Marriage, premarital syphilis examination statements, preparation and furnishing, § 1104

Health and Sanitation
Adoption, healing by spiritual means or prayer, § 2725
Annulment of marriage,
    Marital property division factor, § 3502
Divorce,
    Health endangerment from cruel and barbarous treatment, grounds for divorce, § 3301
    Marital property division factor, § 3502

Health Care Coverage
Defined, mandatory inclusion of child medical support, § 4326

Health Insurance Information
Dependent spouse, § 3701
Forms, Rule 1910.28
Order, Rule 1910.28

Hearing Officers
Attorneys, Rule 1910.12
Defined, common pleas court, Rule 1910.1
Defined, protection from abuse, § 6102
Office conference, Rule 1910.11
Protection from abuse, emergency relief, § 6110

Hearings
Adoption, this index
Alternate procedures, Rule 1920.55-1
After office conference, Rule 1910.12
Alternative hearing procedures, Rule 1910.10
Child custody jurisdiction
    Foreign states, § 5360
    Opportunity to be heard, § 5345
Child support program, § 4380
Contempt petitions, Rule 1910.25-1
Custody, proposed relocation of child, § 5337
Demand after office conference, Rule 1910.11

Hearings—Cont'd
Divorce, master, § 3321, Rule 1920.53 et seq.
Divorce actions, § 3321, Rule 1920.51-1920.54
Entireties property, support order execution against, § 4362
Evidence, notice, Rule 1910.29
Failure or refusal to appear, bench warrants, Rule 1910.13-1; Rule 1910.13-2
Intrastate family support enforcement, contest, orders, § 8412
Jurisdiction, controlling orders, § 7207
Notice, Rule 1920.51
Orders, intrastate family support enforcement, contest, § 8412
Partial custody,
    Hearing officer, Rule 1915.4-2
    Judge, alternative procedures, Rule 1915.4-1
Protection from abuse, § 6107
Support actions, Rules 1910.10-1910.12
Visitation,
    Hearing officer, Rule 1915.4-2
    Judge, alternative procedures, Rule 1915.4-1

History
Medical History Information, generally, this index

Home County
Defined, custody of minor children, Rule 1915.1

Home Evaluations
Child custody or visitation, Rule 1915.8
Form of order, Rule 1915.18

Home State
Defined, child custody jurisdiction, § 5343
Defined, interstate family support, § 7101

Home Studies
Home Studies prior to adoption, § 2530

Homemakers
Contributions to marital property, marital property division factor, divorce or annulment proceedings, § 3502

INDEX

References are to Sections of the Pennsylvania Domestic Relations Code, Pennsylvania Crimes Code, Pennsylvania Judicial Code, Pennsylvania Domestic Relations Court Rules, and Selected Federal Statutes, Court Rules, and Regulations

Homes
Child protective services
   Protecting well-being of child maintained outside home, § 6372
   Protection of child at home or in custody, § 6370

Hospitals
Abandonment, newborn children, § 6501 et seq.
Medical care and treatment, § 6316
Protective custody, § 6315
Abuse of children, persons required to report, § 6311
Adoption, counseling, appointments, § 2505
Child abuse,
   Persons required to report, § 6311
   Victims, admission, § 6316
Child Protective Services Law, § 6301 et seq.
Failure to admit child abuse victims, § 6316
Immunity from liability, reporting suspected child abuse, § 6318
Mentally Retarded Persons, generally, this index
Paternity acknowledgments, duties, § 5103

House of Representatives
General Assembly, generally, this index

Household Members
Family or household members, defined, protection from abuse, § 6102

Husband and Wife
Abuse, protection from abuse, Rule 1901 et seq.
Adoption, consent, § 2711
Battered spouses, shelters, confidential information, § 5309
Confidential or privileged information, Reciprocal enforcement of support, § 4522
Custody, generally. Children and Minors, this index
Custody, children and minors, confidential or privileged information, § 5450
Divorce, generally, this index
Discovery, Rule 1930.5
Forms, pleadings, captions, Rule 1930.1
Indigent persons, support, § 4603
Liability for support, § 4321
Marriage, generally, this index
Pleadings, forms, captions, Rule 1930.1
Protection from Abuse, Rule 1901 et seq.
Same sex marriages, void status, § 1704
Standby guardianship, § 5601

—I—

Identity and Identification
Adopting parents, consents not disclosing, § 2712
Marriage license applicants, § 1301

Illegitimate Children
Children declared to be legitimate, § 5102

Immunites
Privileges and Immunities, generally, this index

Impotency
Annulment of marriage, grounds, § 3305

Impoundment
Adoption, proceedings, § 2905

Imprisonment
Crimes and Offenses, generally, this index
Grounds for divorce, § 3301

Incarceration
Support orders, effect on, § 4352

Income
Annulment of marriage,
   Amount and sources of income, marital property division factor, § 3502
Attachment, support, orders, § 4348, Rule 1910.23
Compensation and Salaries, generally, this index
Computation, Rule 1910.16-2
Defined, support, § 4302
Determination, support guidelines, Rule 1910.16-5
Divorce,
   Amount and sources of income, marital property division factor, § 3502
Divorced parties, income sources, alimony necessity factor, § 3701
Forms, Rule 1910.30

INDEX

References are to Sections of the Pennsylvania Domestic Relations Code, Pennsylvania Crimes Code, Pennsylvania Judicial Code, Pennsylvania Domestic Relations Court Rules, and Selected Federal Statutes, Court Rules, and Regulations

Income—Cont'd
Interstate family support, § 7101
Intrastate family support enforcement, § 8101
Net income, defined, support, § 4302
Reports, Rule 1910.27-1910.28
Statements, forms, Rule 1910.27
Substantial change in circumstances, Rule 1910.19
Support of persons, attachment, § 4302, 4348
Withholding of income, enforcement of support orders, Rule 1910.21

Income and Expense Statement
Form, Rule 1910.26

Income Tax—Federal
Alimony, tax ramifications, alimony necessity factor, § 3701

Income Tax—Local
Alimony, tax ramifications, alimony necessity factor, § 3701
Priorities and preferences, support attachment order, priority over tax withholding, § 4348
Withholding, support attachment order, priority over tax withholding, § 4348

Income Tax—State
Alimony, tax ramifications, alimony necessity factor, § 3701
Refunds,
    Support of persons, intercept program, authorization, § 4307
Withholding, support, attachment, priorities and preferences, § 4348

Income Withholding Orders
Contest, § 7501.5
Definitions,
    Interstate family support, § 7101
    Intrastate family support enforcement, § 8101
Employer receipt, § 7501
Fines and penalties, § 7501.4
Foreign states,
    Employer receipt, § 7501
    Enforcement, § 7502
    Recognition, § 7501
    Privileges and immunities, § 7501.3

Incompetents
Guardian and Ward, generally, this index
Marriage,
    Restrictions on marriage license issuance, § 1304

Incompetents—Cont'd
Mentally Retarded Persons, generally, this index
Standby guardianship, § 5601

Inconvenient Forum
Child custody jurisdiction, § 5348

Indemnity and Indemnification
Juvenile Court procedure, Pa.R.J.C.P. 1100–1800
Tortious acts of child, indemnity of parent from child prohibited, § 5507

Indicated Reports
Child protective services, disposition, § 6338
Defined, child protective services, § 6303

Indigent Persons
Actions and proceedings, relatives, support, § 4605
Contempt, relatives, support, § 4603
Definitions, support, relatives, § 46 and two
Divorce actions, proceedings, Rule 1920.62
Domicile and residence, liens and encumbrances, relatives, support, § 4604
Domestic violence actions, Indigency determination, § 6106
Evidence, § 4605
Exemptions, relatives, support, § 4603, 4604
Husband and wife, support, § 4603
Judgments and decrees, relatives, support, § 4605
Jurisdiction, courts, relatives, support, § 4603
Liens and encumbrances, property, relatives, support, § 4604
Medical care and treatment, relatives, support, § 4603
Notice, hearings, guardian and ward, support, § 4606
Petitions, guardian and ward, support, § 46 and six
Relatives, support, § 4601 et seq.
Support, relatives, § 4601 et seq.

Indignities
Intolerable and burdensome life, grounds for divorce, § 3301

Infants
Children and Minors, generally, this index

INDEX

References are to Sections of the Pennsylvania Domestic Relations Code, Pennsylvania Crimes Code, Pennsylvania Judicial Code, Pennsylvania Domestic Relations Court Rules, and Selected Federal Statutes, Court Rules, and Regulations

Information
Child custody jurisdiction, information under oath to be submitted to court, § 5350
Child Protective Services, this index
Custody, access to, § 5309
Information requests, § 4348
Medical History Information, generally, this index
Prospective adoptive parents, § 6344
Support
    Consumer credit bureaus, information to, § 4303
    Reciprocal enforcement, state information agency, § 4517

Inheritance
Divorced parties, alimony necessity factor, § 3701

Initial Decree
Defined, child custody jurisdiction, § 5343

Injunction
Annulment of marriage,
    Disposition of property to defeat obligations, § 3505
    Proceedings, § 3323
Children and minors, custody, jurisdiction, § 5426
Divorce,
    Disposition of property to defeat obligations, § 3505
    Proceedings, § 3323
Divorce or annulment of marriage action, Rule 1920.43
Hospitals,
    Failure to admit child abuse victims, § 6316
Support orders, Rule 1910.25
Support of persons, special relief, Rule 1910.26

Injuries
Defined, torts of children, § 5501
Serious bodily injury, defined, child protective services, confidential information, § 6340

Innocent Spouse Rule
Income tax, federal, joint returns, 26 C.F.R. § 1.6015-2

Installment Payments
Domestic violence, fines and penalties, fees, § 6120

Institutionalization
Grounds for divorce, § 3301

Instruments
Marriage
    Alienation of affections, actions abolished, instruments executed in satisfaction of abolished claims prohibited, § 1905
    Breach of promise to marry, actions abolished, instruments executed in satisfaction of abolished claims prohibited, § 1905

Insurance
Annulment of marriage,
    Benefits, income source, marital property division factor, § 3502
Child support, mandatory coverage, § 4326
Cooperation, government agencies and financial institutions, support, § 4304.1
Dependent spouses, divorce proceedings, § 3702
Definitions, child medical support, § 4326
Divorce,
    Benefits, income source, marital property division factor, § 3502
    Income sources for divorced parties, alimony necessity factor, § 3701
Forms, support, Rule 1910.27
Health insurance, support of persons, coverage information,
    Form, Rule 1910.26
    Order, Rule 1910.27
Hospital insurance,
    Dependent spouses, divorce proceedings, § 3702
Life insurance,
    Annulment of marriage,
        Continued maintenance and beneficiary designations, § 3502
    Divorce,
        Continued maintenance and beneficiary designations, § 3502
Support,
    Arrearages, collections, § 4308.1
    Guidelines, Rule 1910.16-6
    Mandatory coverage, § 4326

Interception of State Lottery Prize
Child support arrearages, § 4308

INDEX

References are to Sections of the Pennsylvania Domestic Relations Code, Pennsylvania Crimes Code, Pennsylvania Judicial Code, Pennsylvania Domestic Relations Court Rules, and Selected Federal Statutes, Court Rules, and Regulations

Interest
Alimony,
    Unpaid installments, arrearages enforcement, § 3703
Annulment of marriage,
    Court award, interest on unpaid installments, § 3502
Divorce,
    Court award, interest on unpaid installments, § 3502
Foreign divorce decrees, enforcement, § 3705
Support, monthly gross income, computation, Rule 1910.16-2

Interlocutory Order
Support actions; paternity, Rule 1910.5

Intermediaries
Adoption, reports, § 2533
    Exhibits, § 2534
Defined, adoption, § 2102

International Application
Child custody jurisdiction, § 5365

International Child Abduction
Generally, 42 U.S.C. § 11601 et seq.
Appropriations, 42 U.S.C. § 11610
Attorneys, fees, 42 U.S.C. § 11607
Costs, 42 U.S.C. § 11607
Definitions, 42 U.S.C. § 11602, § 11603
District courts, 42 U.S.C. § 11603
Grants, 42 U.S.C. § 11606
Information, 42 U.S.C. § 11606, § 11608
Parent Locator Service, 42 U.S.C. § 11606
Private institutions or organizations, privileges and immunities, 42 U.S.C. § 11606
Remedies for international child abduction, 42 U.S.C. § 11601 et seq.
Rules and regulations, 42 U.S.C. § 11606
Time, 42 U.S.C. § 11603
United States Central Authority, 42 U.S.C. § 11602
Wrongful removal or retention, definitions, 42 U.S.C. § 11603

Interrogation of Child
Custody, partial custody and visitation actions, Rule 1915.11

Interstate Family Support Act
Generally, § 7101 et seq.

Interstate Family Support Enforcement,
Actions and proceedings, § 7301 et seq.

Interstate Family Support Enforcement—Cont'd
Communication between tribunals, § 7317
Confidential or privileged information, § 7316
Discovery, § 7318
Evidence, § 7313; § 7316
Extradition, § 7801
Family immunity, § 7316
Fees, actions and proceedings, § 7313
Jurisdiction, personal jurisdiction, § 7314
Multiple orders, two or more obligees, § 7208
Personal jurisdiction, § 7314
Pleadings, § 7311
Privileges and immunities, § 7314
    Family immunity, § 7316
Responding tribunal, powers and duties, actions and proceedings, § 7305
Self incrimination, § 7316
Service of process, § 7314
Spousal privilege, § 7316
Support enforcement agencies, supervision, § 7308
Witnesses, § 7316

Interstate Rendition, § 7801

Intervention
Children and minors, custody, jurisdiction, § 5425
Custody, partial custody and visitation actions, Rule 1915.6, 1915.16

Intrastate Family Support Enforcement
Application of law, § 8102
Arrearages, § 8411
Contest, orders, § 8412; § 8413
Costs, § 8313
Disclosure, exceptions, § 8309
Discovery, § 8312
Docketing, orders, § 8402
Evidence, § 8311
Exceptions, disclosure, § 8309
Fees, § 8313
Full faith and credit, § 8201
Guardian and ward, minor parents, actions and proceedings, § 8302
Hearings, contest, orders, § 8412
Inappropriate tribunal, § 8305
Initiating tribunal, powers and duties, § 8303
Jurisdiction, common pleas courts, § 8201

1279

INDEX

References are to Sections of the Pennsylvania Domestic Relations Code, Pennsylvania Crimes Code, Pennsylvania Judicial Code, Pennsylvania Domestic Relations Court Rules, and Selected Federal Statutes, Court Rules, and Regulations

Intrastate Family Support Enforcement—Cont'd
Minor parents, guardian and ward, actions and proceedings, § 8302
Multiple orders, § 8202
Nonparentage, defenses, § 8310
Notice, registration, orders, § 8411
Orders,
    Confirmation, § 8414; § 8415
    Contest, § 8412
    Registration, § 8401; § 8402
Paternity, defenses, § 8310
Payments, § 8203
Private counsel, § 8308
Records and recordation, evidence, § 8311
Registration, orders, notice, § 8411
Responding tribunal, powers and duties, § 8304
Support enforcement agencies, powers and duties, § 8306
Transfers, inappropriate tribunal, § 8305
Witnesses, § 8311

Inventories
Annulment of marriage,
    Property inventory of parties, § 3505
Divorce,
    Property inventory of parties, § 3505
Divorce or annulment actions, Rules 1920.33, 1920.75

Investigations and Investigators
Adoption
    Petition for adoption, hearings, § 2724
    Reports of intention to adopt, § 2535
Child Protective Services, this index
Cooperation with an investigation, defined, child protective services, § 6303

Involuntary Termination
Adoption, this index

Irretrievable Breakdown
Defined, divorce, § 3103
Divorce,
    Counseling, § 3302
    Grounds for divorce, § 3301

—J—

Joinder of Actions
Divorce or annulment, Rule 1920.13

Joinder of Parties
Custody, partial custody and visitation actions, Rules 1915.6, 1915.16
Divorce or annulment actions, Rule 1920.34
Related claims, Rule 1920.31 et seq.

Judges
Bankruptcy, marriage, solemnization, § 1503
Marriage, qualification to solemnize marriages, § 1503
Solemnization of marriages, qualification, § 1503

Judgment Dockets
Adoption,
    Decrees, § 2906
    Foreign decrees, § 2908

Judgment By Operation of Law
Defined, support, § 4302

Judgments and Decrees
Abuse, protection from, Rule 1905
Adoption, this index
Alimony enforcement, § 3703

Judgments and Decrees—Cont'd
Allocation, support order, Rules 1910.16, 1920.56
Annulment of Marriage, this index
Arrearages, support actions, § 4352, Rule 1910.24
Collections, § 4308.1
Child custody proceedings,
    Binding effect, § 5353
    Out of state decrees, recognition, § 5354
Custody actions, no default, Rule 1915.9
Custody decrees. Child Custody Jurisdiction, this index
Decree of adoption. Adoption, this index
Decree of termination, effect, adoption, § 2521
Defined, child custody jurisdiction, § 5343
Divorce or annulment of marriage action, Rule 1920.42
    Effect on spousal support order, Rule 1920.31
Final decree, Rules 1920.52, 1920.55
Form, divorce, Rule 1920.76
Masters report, Rules 1920.55-2, 1920.55-3

INDEX

References are to Sections of the Pennsylvania Domestic Relations Code, Pennsylvania Crimes Code, Pennsylvania Judicial Code, Pennsylvania Domestic Relations Court Rules, and Selected Federal Statutes, Court Rules, and Regulations

Judgments and Decrees—Cont'd
Entry, waiver, notice, Rule 1920.72
Enforcement of support orders, Rule 1910.20
Entireties property, support order execution against, § 4361
Estoppel, § 3333
Exceptions, Rule 1920.55-2
Final decree, Rule 1920.42
Foreign Decrees, generally, this index
Initial decree, defined, child custody jurisdiction, § 5343
Judgment by operation of law, defined, support, § 4302
Liens on entireties property, § 3507
Marriage, decree that spouse of applicant is presumed decedent, § 1701
Marriage,
    Debts contracted for necessaries, collection, § 4102
    Loans between spouses, § 4105
Modification decree, defined, child custody jurisdiction, § 5343
Non pros, Rules 1920.21
Opening decree, motion, § 3332
Parental liability, torts of minors, § 5504
Paternity determinations, § 5103
Petition to correct, support, Rule 1910.23-2
Property rights, § 3503
Protection from Abuse Act actions, Rule 1903
Relinquishment, parental rights, § 2503
Res judicata, § 3333
Support actions, Rules 1910.5 et seq.
Support of persons, arrearages, Rules 1910.23-1, 1910.23-2
Support of persons, relinquishment, parental rights, § 2503
Vacating decree, motion, § 3332

Judicial Review
Appeal and Review, generally, this index

Juries
Annulment of marriage proceedings, § 3322
Divorce proceedings, § 3322
Paternity,
    Post-trial relief, Rule 1930.2
Paternity, support of persons, Rule 1910.15
Support of persons, notice of right, Rule 1910.28

Jurisdiction
Adoption
    Court, § 2301
    Venue, § 2302
Child Custody Jurisdiction, generally, this index
Choice of law, long arm jurisdiction, § 7202
Continuing jurisdiction, support orders, § 4352
Crimes and offenses, willful failure to pay, § 4354
Custody, removal of party or child from jurisdiction, § 5308
Custody, partial custody and visitation actions, Rule 1915.5
Divorce, bases, § 3104, § 3323
Domestic violence, protection orders, § 6103
Domicile and residence, personal jurisdiction, § 7201
Foreign states, orders, modification, § 7613
Long arm jurisdiction, paternity establishment and support enforcement, § 4342
Military personnel, § 3104
Motion to vacate decree, § 3332
Nonresidents, long arm jurisdiction, paternity, § 4342
Paternity, § 7701
Personal jurisdiction, nonresidents, § 7201
Protection orders, domestic violence, § 6103
Simultaneous proceedings, interstate family support enforcement, § 7204
Standby guardianship, § 5612
Support
    Support orders, continuing jurisdiction, § 4352, § 5343
    Support actions, Rules 1910.7, 1910.14
Visitation, time of objections, custody of minor children, Rule 1915.5

Jury Trial
Annulment of marriage proceedings, § 3322
Divorce, § 3322
Domestic violence, right to jury trial, § 6114
Paternity,
    Support, Rule 1910.15
Right to jury trial, domestic violence, § 6114

INDEX

References are to Sections of the Pennsylvania Domestic Relations Code, Pennsylvania Crimes Code, Pennsylvania Judicial Code, Pennsylvania Domestic Relations Court Rules, and Selected Federal Statutes, Court Rules, and Regulations

Justices of the Peace
Magisterial District Judges, generally, this index

Juvenile Proceedings
Juvenile Act, 42 Pa.C.S. § 6301 et seq.
Juvenile Court procedure, Pa.R.J.C.P. 1100–1800
Tortious acts of children, establishing liability of parent, § 5503

Juvenile Court Hearing Officer
Appointment, Pa.R. Juv. Ct. Proc., § 1185
Authority, Pa.R. Juv. Ct. Proc., § 1187
Findings and Recommendations, Pa.R. Juv. Ct. Proc., § 1191
Stipulations, Pa. Juv. Ct. Proc., § 1190
Qualification, Pa. Juv. Ct. Proc., § 1182

—L—

Labor Organizations
Cooperation, support, § 4304.1
Definitions, support of persons, § 4302
Fines and penalties, support, information cooperation, § 4304.1

Laboratories
Genetic tests, paternity proceedings, § 4343
Premarital syphilis examination statements, preparation and furnishing, § 1104

Laches
Annulment of marriage,
 Collateral attack on decree, § 3333
Divorce,
 Collateral attack on decree, § 3333

Law
Application of Law, generally, this index
Construction of Law, generally, this index
Judgment by operation of law, defined, support, § 4302
Popular Name Laws, generally, this index
Purpose of law, generally, this index
Scope of law, support, § 4301

Law Enforcement Agencies
Protection from abuse, responsibilities, § 6105

Lawyers
Attorneys, generally, this index

Legal Custody
Defined, custody, § 5302
Defined, minor children, Rule 1915.1

Legal Separation
Divorce, generally, this index

Legislative Oversight
Child protective services, § 6384

Legislature
General Assembly, generally, this index

Legitimate Children
Children declared to be legitimate, § 5102

Liability
Child protective services, reporting suspected child abuse, immunity, § 6318
Liability for Torts of Children, generally, this index
Marriage, debts contracted before, § 4101
Support, § 4321

Liability for Torts of Children
Generally, § 5501 et seq.
Actions and proceedings
 Civil proceedings, establishing liability of parent, § 5504
 Criminal or juvenile proceedings, establishing liability of parent, § 5503
Child, defined, § 5501
Civil proceedings, establishing liability of parent, § 5504
Contribution or indemnity from child prohibited, § 5507
Criminal or juvenile proceedings, establishing liability of parent, § 5503
Custody, liability of parent not having custody or control of child, § 5508
Definitions, § 5501
Double recovery for same injury prohibited, § 5506
Indemnity or contribution from child prohibited, § 5507
Injuries
 Defined, § 5501
 Double recovery for same injury prohibited, § 5506
Monetary limits of liability, § 5505
Parents
 Defined, § 5501
 Liability, § 5502

INDEX

References are to Sections of the Pennsylvania Domestic Relations Code, Pennsylvania Crimes Code, Pennsylvania Judicial Code, Pennsylvania Domestic Relations Court Rules, and Selected Federal Statutes, Court Rules, and Regulations

Liability for Torts of Children—Cont'd
    Civil proceedings, § 5504
    Criminal or juvenile proceedings, § 5503
    Double recovery for same injury prohibited, § 5506
    Indemnity or contribution from child prohibited, § 5507
    Monetary limits of liability, § 5505
    Other liability of parent or child unaffected, § 5509
    Parent not having custody or control of child, § 5508
Person, defined, § 5501
Tortious act, defined § 5501

Licenses and Permits
Defined, marriage, § 1102
Denial or suspension of licenses, § 4355
Marriage, this index
Operating privileges, definitions, support, § 4355
Revocation or suspension,
    Custody, visitation, paternity violations, § 4355
    Support, arrearages, § 4355

Liens and Incumbrances
Arrearages, monetary awards, collections, § 4308.1
Arrears as judgments, § 4352
Child support program, § 4377
Divorce actions, injunctions and special relief, Rule 1920.43
Enforcement of support orders, Rule 1910.20, 1910.22
Entireties property, division between divorced parents, § 3507
Indigent persons, property, relatives, support, priorities and preferences, § 4604

Liens and Incumbrancs—Cont'd
Marital property, § 3505
Overdue support, § 4352
Payments, support, § 4305
Real property liens, § 4352
Security for payment to parties, § 3502

Life Insurance
Continued maintenance and beneficiary designation, § 3502

Limitation
Parental liability for torts of minors, monetary limitation, § 5505

Limitation of Actions
Annulment of marriage, attacks on decrees, § 3331
Arrearages, § 7604
Child abuse report investigations, § 6368
Divorce, attacks on decrees, § 3331
Paternity determinations, § 4343
Support actions, Rule 1910.7

Loans
Divorce, construction of law, § 4106
Married persons, loans between, § 4105

Local Law Enforcement Agencies
Protection from abuse, responsibilities, § 6105

Local Plans
Child protective services, § 6363

Long Arm Procedures
Paternity, establishment, § 4342
Support, enforcement, § 4342, § 7201
Support proceedings, expedited procedure, nonresidents, § 4327

Long Arm Statute
Venue, alimony and support actions, Rule 1910.2

Lotteries
Lottery winnings intercept, support, § 4308

—M—

Magisterial District Judges
Qualifications, solemnization of marriage, § 1503
Retirement and pensions, solemnization of marriage, § 1503

Mail and Mailing
Certified or registered mail,
    Adoption,
        Notice, hearing, § 2721

Mail and Mailing—Cont'd
    Parental rights termination hearing notice, § 2513
Custody orders, notice, 1915.12
Interim orders, Rule 1910.11
Notice, § 4353
Service of process, original, Rule 1930.4
Support of persons, interim order, Rule 1910.11

INDEX

References are to Sections of the Pennsylvania Domestic Relations Code, Pennsylvania Crimes Code, Pennsylvania Judicial Code, Pennsylvania Domestic Relations Court Rules, and Selected Federal Statutes, Court Rules, and Regulations

Malicious Desertion
Divorce, grounds, § 3301

Marital Misconduct
Alimony, defined, § 3701

Marital Property
Defined, divorce, § 3501
Defined, protection from abuse act, Rule 1920.1
Definitions, § 3501
Discovery, Rule 1930.5
Equitable division, divorce, § 3502
Foreign decrees, enforcement, divorce, § 3705
Hearings by court, trial judge decision and post-trial relief, Rule 1920.52
Inventory, divorce actions, Rule 1920.75
Retirement and pensions, allocation, § 3501
Statement of reasons, § 3506

Marital Status
Dissolution, divorce, § 3301 et seq.
Premarital agreements, burden of proof, § 3106
Proceedings to determine, divorce, § 3306

Marriage
Generally, § 1101 et seq.
Absence, spouse of license applicant, death presumption, § 1701
Accord and satisfaction,
    Instruments executed in satisfaction of abolished claims, prohibition, § 1905
Actions and proceedings
    Alienation of affections, actions abolished, § 1901
        Filing or threatening actions prohibited, § 1904
        Instruments executed in satisfaction of abolished claims prohibited, § 1905
        Purpose of law, § 1903
    Breach of promise to marry, actions abolished, § 1902
        Filing or threatening actions prohibited, § 1904
        Instruments executed in satisfaction of abolished claims prohibited, § 1905
        Purpose of law, § 1903
Debts contracted for necessaries, § 4102

Marriage—Cont'd
Marital status determination, § 3306
Property ownership actions, evidence, § 4104
Threats to file prohibited actions, § 1904
Age, license applicants, form requirements, § 1302
Alienation of affections, actions abolished, § 1901
    Filing or threatening actions prohibited, § 1904
    Instruments executed in satisfaction of abolished claims prohibited, § 1905
    Purpose of law, § 1903
Annulment, generally, this index
Appeal and review,
    Marriage license issuance refusal, § 1308
    Serological test physician statement denial, § 1305
Application of law, § 4106
    Common-law marriage, § 1103
Applications, licenses, § 1302
    Decree that spouse of applicant a presumed decedent, § 1701
    Filing, § 1309
Biographical information, license applicants, form requirements, § 1302
Birth places, license applicants, form requirements, § 1302
Breach of promise to marry, actions abolished, § 1902
    Filing or threatening actions prohibited, § 1904
    Instruments executed in satisfaction of abolished claims prohibited, § 1905
    Purpose of law, § 1903
Brothers and sisters, § 1304
    Alienation of affections actions, exception, § 1901
Ceremonies, § 1501 et seq.
    Marriage certificates, form, § 1501
        Ceremonies performed by parties, § 1502
    Persons qualified to solemnize marriages, § 1503
    Returns of marriages, § 1504
Certificates
    Consents, filing, § 1309

INDEX

References are to Sections of the Pennsylvania Domestic Relations Code, Pennsylvania Crimes Code, Pennsylvania Judicial Code, Pennsylvania Domestic Relations Court Rules, and Selected Federal Statutes, Court Rules, and Regulations

Marriage—Cont'd
- Duplicate marriage certificate, signing and returning for recording, § 1504
- Form, § 1501
  - Ceremonies performed by parties, § 1502
  - Right to solemnize own marriage, forms, § 1502
- Children and parents, § 1304
- Common-law marriage, application of law, § 1103
- Compensation
  - Construction of law, divorce, § 4106
  - Right of married persons to separate earnings, § 4104
- Conclusiveness of judgments and decrees, marital status determination § 3306
- Confidential or privileged information,
  - Licenses issued records, § 1106
  - Returns of marriages celebrated, § 1106
  - Serological test statements, § 1305
- Consanguinity,
  - Marriage within prohibited degrees of consanguinity, § 1703
  - Prohibited degrees for marriage, § 1304
- Consent certificates,
  - Filing, § 1309
  - Forms, § 1104
- Construction of law, divorce, § 4106
- Contracts
  - Construction of law, divorce, § 4106
  - Debts contracted before marriage, liability, § 4101
  - Necessaries, proceedings, § 4102
- Cousins, § 1304
- Custody, generally. Children and Minors, this index
- Death, spouse of license applicant, presumption, decree, § 1701
- Debts
  - Contracted before marriage, spousal liability, § 4101
  - Necessaries, debts contracted for, collection, spousal liability, § 4102
- Declaratory judgment actions,
  - Marital status determination, § 3306
- Decree that spouse of license applicant is presumed dead, § 1701

Marriage—Cont'd
- Definitions, § 1102
- Department, defined, § 1102
- Diseases,
  - Transmittable diseases, statement of freedom from, license applicants, § 1302
- District justices, qualification to solemnize marriages, § 1503
- Divorce, generally, this index
- Domestic Relations Code, § 101 et seq.
- Domicile and residence, license applicants, form requirements, § 1302
- Drugs, persons under influence, marriage license issuance restrictions, § 1304
- Duplicate marriage certificates, signing and returning for recording, § 1504
- Duration of marriage license, § 1310
- Earnings, separate earnings, rights, § 4104
- Emergencies
  - Exceptions to waiting period after license application, § 1303
- Evidence,
  - Property ownership actions, § 4104
- Examinations, licenses
  - Oral examination, § 1306
  - Syphilis, § 1305
- Exceptions,
  - Alienation of affections actions, § 1901
  - Waiting period after license application, § 1303
- Executions,
  - Debts contracted from necessaries, collection, § 4102
- Existence of former marriage, marriage during § 1702
- Extraordinary circumstances, exception to waiting period after license application, § 1303
- Fees, § 1105
- Filing,
  - Consent certificates, § 1309
  - License applications, § 1309
- Findings,
  - Death of spouse of license applicant, § 1701
- First marriage, license applicants, form requirements, § 1302

INDEX

References are to Sections of the Pennsylvania Domestic Relations Code, Pennsylvania Crimes Code, Pennsylvania Judicial Code, Pennsylvania Domestic Relations Court Rules, and Selected Federal Statutes, Court Rules, and Regulations

Marriage—Cont'd
Former justices, judges or district justices, qualification to solemnize marriages, § 1503
Former marriage existing, effect of marriage during, § 1702
Forms, § 1104
    Certificates, § 1501
        Ceremonies performed by parties, § 1502
    Future capital assets acquisition opportunity, marital property division factor, divorce or annulment proceedings, § 3502
    License form, § 1310
    License issuance records, § 1106
    Marriage certificates, § 1501, 1502
    Marriage license application, § 1302
    Returns of marriages celebrated, § 1106
    Serological test statement forms, § 1305
    Solemnization of own marriage right certification § 1502
    Uniformity, § 1104
Good faith remarriages, § 1702
Guardian and ward,
    Restrictions on issuance of marriage licenses, § 1304
Identity and identification,
    License applicants, § 1301
Incompetent persons, restrictions on marriage license issuance, § 1304
Issuance of marriage licenses, § 1307
Judges, qualification to solemnize marriages, § 1503
Judgments and decrees,
    Debts contracted for necessaries, collection, § 4102
    Loans between spouses, § 4105
Judicial review, licenses, refusal, § 1308
Justices, qualification to solemnize marriages, § 1503
Laboratories,
    Statements, syphilis examinations, preparation and furnishing, § 1104
Legality of contemplated marriage, oral examination, § 1306
Liability for support, § 4321
Licenses and permits, § 1301 et seq.

Marriage—Cont'd
Alcohol, persons under influence, restrictions on license issuance, § 1304
Appeal and review,
    Refusal to issue license, § 1308
Applications, § 1302
    Decree that spouse of applicant is presumed decedent, § 1701
    Filing, § 1309
    Form, § 1104
Chemically dependent persons, restrictions, § 1304
Consent certificates, filing, § 1309
Defined, § 1102
Drugs, persons under influence, restrictions on license issuance, § 1304
Duration of license, § 1310
Examinations
    Oral examination, § 1306
    Syphilis, § 1305
Fees, § 1105
Forms, §§ 1104, 1310
Identity of applicants, § 1301
Incompetent persons, restrictions on license issuance, § 1304
Issuance, § 1307
    Restrictions, § 1304
Mentally ill persons, restrictions on license issuance, § 1304
Necessity of license, § 1301
Oral examinations, § 1306
Prerequisite to ceremony, § 1503
Records and recordation,
    Licenses issued, § 1106
Refusal, judicial review, § 1308
Relatives, marriage to, § 1304
Required nature of license, § 1101, § 1301
Restrictions on issuance, § 1304
Tests, syphilis, § 1305
Waiting period, § 1303
Loans
    Between married persons, § 4105
    Construction of law, divorce, § 4106
Location of marriage ceremony, § 1301
Maiden names, mothers of license applicants, form requirements, § 1302
Marriage during existence of former marriage, § 1702
Marriage license, defined, § 1102

INDEX

References are to Sections of the Pennsylvania Domestic Relations Code, Pennsylvania Crimes Code, Pennsylvania Judicial Code, Pennsylvania Domestic Relations Court Rules, and Selected Federal Statutes, Court Rules, and Regulations

Marriage—Cont'd
Marriage within degree of consanguinity, § 1703
Mayors, qualification to solemnize marriages, § 1503
Ministers, qualification to solemnize marriages, § 1503
Mortgages,
    Loans between spouses, § 4105
Names, license applicants, form requirements, § 1302
Necessaries, debts contracts for, proceedings, § 4102
Notice,
    Absentee spouse of license applicant, death presumption, § 1701
Oaths and affirmations,
    Oral examination, license applicants, § 1306
Occupations, license applicants, form requirements, § 1302
Oral examinations, license applicants, § 1306
Parents,
    Alienation of affections actions, exception, § 1901
Parents and children, § 1304
Parents of license applicants, required biographical information, § 1302
Parol examinations, license applicants, § 1306
Performance of marriage ceremony, location, § 1301
Permits. Licenses and permits, generally, ante
Physicians and surgeons,
    Statements, preparation and furnishing, syphilis examinations, § 1104
    Syphilis examination and test, § 1305
Place of marriage ceremony, § 1301
Premarital syphilis examination, statement, preparation and furnishing, § 1104
Presumed decedents, decree that spouse of applicant is, § 1701
Priests, qualification to solemnize marriages, § 1503
Prior marriages, oral examination, license applicants, § 1306
Prohibited degrees of consanguinity, § 1304

Marriage—Cont'd
Qualifications, persons solemnizing marriages, § 1503
Rabbis, qualification to solemnize marriages, § 1503
Race, license applicants, form requirements, § 1302
Records and recordation,
    Consent certificates, filing and docketing as public records, § 1309
    Duplicate marriage certificate, signing and returning for recording, § 1504
    License applications, filing and docketing as public records, § 1309
    Licenses issued and celebrations returned, § 1106
    Refusal to issue marriage license, appeal and review, § 1308
Relatives,
    Alienation of affections actions, exception, § 1901
    Prohibited degrees of consanguinity for marriage, § 1304
Remarriage after decree of presumed death, § 1701
Requirement of marriage license, § 1301
Retired justices, judges or district justices, qualification to solemnize marriages, § 1503
Returns, marriages celebrated, records, § 1106
Returns of marriages, § 1504
Right to solemnize own marriage, certification, forms, § 1502
Same sex, § 1704
Second marriage, license applicants, form requirements, § 1302
Senior judges of United States district court or United States district court of appeals, qualifications to solemnize marriage, § 1503
Separate earnings
    Construction of law, divorce, § 4106
    Right of married person to, § 4104
Serological tests for syphilis, § 1305
Sisters,
    Alienation of affections actions, exception, § 1901
Solemnization,
    Parties solemnizing own marriage, § 1504

INDEX

References are to Sections of the Pennsylvania Domestic Relations Code, Pennsylvania Crimes Code, Pennsylvania Judicial Code, Pennsylvania Domestic Relations Court Rules, and Selected Federal Statutes, Court Rules, and Regulations

Marriage—Cont'd
    Persons qualified to solemnize marriage, § 1503
    Right to solemnize own marriage, certification, forms, § 1502
Statistics, § 1106
Status of marriage, determination, proceedings, § 3306
Status of voidable marriages, § 3305
Support of Persons, generally, this index
Syphilis,
    Examinations and tests, § 1305
    Physician and laboratory examinations, statement preparation and furnishing, § 1104
Tests, licenses, syphilis, § 1305
Three day waiting period after license application, § 1303
Time,
    Duration of license, § 1310
    License issuance, § 1307
    Waiting period after license application, § 1303
Transmittable diseases, license applicants, statement of freedom from, § 1302
Unexplained absence, spouse of license applicant, death presumption, § 1701
Uniformity of forms, § 1104
United States court of appeals judges, qualification to solemnize marriages, § 1503
United States district court magistrates, qualification to solemnize marriages, § 1503
Validity period of marriage license, § 1310
Venereal diseases, physician and laboratory examination, statement preparation and furnishing, § 1104
Verified applications for licenses, § 1302
Void marriages, false rumor of death of spouse, § 1702
Void marriages, annulment, § 3303
    Grounds, § 3304
Voidable marriages, annulment, § 3303
    Grounds, § 3305
Waiting period, licenses, § 1303
Written applications for licenses, § 1302

Marriage Ceremonies
Marriage, this index

Marriage Certificates
Form, § 1501
    Ceremonies performed by parties, § 1502

Marriage Law
Generally, § 1101 et seq.

Marriage Licenses
Generally, § 1301, 1302
Defined, marriage, § 1102
Issuance of license, § 1307
Marriage, this index
Restrictions on issuance of license, § 1304
Waiting period, § 1303

Married Persons
Husband and Wife, generally, this index

Masters And Referees
Adverse or pecuniary interest, family law masters, Rule 1920.51
Appeal and review, masters, Rule 1920.55-1 et seq.
Annulment suit,
    Appointment, Rule 1920.51
    Hearings, § 3321, Rule 1920.53 et seq.
Divorce, hearings, § 3321
Divorce actions, Rules 1920.51-1920.55
Forms, Rule 1920.74
Orders, appointments, Rule 1920.74
Reports, Rule 1920.53
Support, appointment, Rule 1920.51

Mayors
Marriage solemnization, qualification, § 1503

Mediation
Generally, Rules 1940.1-1940.8
Application of law, custody, Rule 1940.1, 1940.9
Appointments, mediators, custody, Rule 1940.3
Attorney fees, sanctions, custody, Rule 1940.8
Children and minors, custody, Rule 1940.1 et seq.
Costs, sanctions, custody, Role 1940.8
Custody, Rule 1940.2
Evaluation, § 3903
Existing programs, § 3904
Fees and costs, § 3902
Guidelines, § 3901
Mediation programs, § 3901
Mediators,
    Appointments, custody, Rule 1940.3

INDEX

References are to Sections of the Pennsylvania Domestic Relations Code, Pennsylvania Crimes Code, Pennsylvania Judicial Code, Pennsylvania Domestic Relations Court Rules, and Selected Federal Statutes, Court Rules, and Regulations

Mediation—Cont'd
    Compensation and salaries, custody, Rule 1940.7
    Powers and duties, custody, Rule 1940.5
    Qualifications, custody, Rule 1940.4
Orders, orientation sessions, custody, Rule 1940.3
Orientation sessions, definitions, custody, Rule 1940.2
Review of programs, § 3903
Sanctions, custody, Rule 1940.8
Termination, custody, Rule 1940.6

Medical Benefits
Support of persons,
    Allocation, Rule 1910.16-5
    Office conference, proof of coverage, Rule 1910.11

Medical Care and Treatment
See, also, Health and Sanitation, generally, this index
Accident and health insurance, coverage, forms, Rule 1910.27
Child medical support, requirement, § 4326
Children and minors, custody, records, § 5309
Guidelines, Rule 1910.16-6
Hospitals, generally, this index
Physicians and Surgeons, generally, this index
Support of persons, § 4324

Medical Examiners
Abuse of children, persons required to report, § 6311
Child Protective Services Law, § 6301 et seq.

Medical History Information
Adoption, § 2909
Defined, adoption, § 2102

Medical Income Source
Marital property division factor, § 3502

Medical Records
Child, custody, access to records, § 5309

Medical Support
Inclusion for spouse, § 4324
Mandatory inclusion for child, § 4326

Mental and Physical Examinations
Custody, partial custody and visitation actions, Rule 1915.8

Mental Condition
Divorced parties, alimony necessity factor, § 3701

Mental Disorders
Divorce, defendant suffering from, actions, § 3308

Mentally Ill Persons
See, also, Mentally Retarded Persons, generally, this index
Annulment of marriage,
    Commencement of action against mentally ill spouse, § 3308
    Consent incapability, grounds for annulment, § 3304
Guardian and Ward, generally, this index
Marriage,
    Restrictions on license issuance, § 1304

Mentally Retarded Persons
Annulment of marriage,
    Commencement of action against mentally retarded spouse, § 3308
    Consent incapability, grounds for annulment, § 3304
Divorce,
    Commencement of action against mentally retarded spouse, § 3308
    Institutionalization, grounds for divorce, § 3301
Guardian and Ward, generally, this index
Marriage,
    Restrictions on license issuance, § 1304

Military Forces
Active-duty, marriage, licenses and permits, examinations and examiners § 1306
Affidavits, divorce and annulment of marriage, Rule 1920.46
Annuities, 10 U.S.C. § 1448
Annulment of marriage, Rule 1920.46
Assignments, annuities, 10 U.S.C. § 1450
Attachment, survivor benefit plan, annuities not subject to, 10 U.S.C. § 1450
Child custody proceedings during military deployment, 51 Pa.C.S. § 4109
Children and minors, enlistment, consent, § 2521
Divorce, affidavits, failure to appear, Rule 1920.46

INDEX

References are to Sections of the Pennsylvania Domestic Relations Code, Pennsylvania Crimes Code, Pennsylvania Judicial Code, Pennsylvania Domestic Relations Court Rules, and Selected Federal Statutes, Court Rules, and Regulations

Military Forces—Cont'd
Domestic violence, retirement and pensions, support, 10 U.S.C. § 1408
Enlistment, consent, agency receiving child custody under parental rights termination decree, § 2521
Execution, annuities, 10 U.S.C. § 1450
Failure to appear, divorce, affidavits, Rule 1920.46
Garnishment, exemptions, annuities, 10 U.S.C. § 1450
Insurance, annuities, 10 U.S.C. § 1448
Licenses and permits, marriage, affidavits, § 1306
National Guard, marriage, licenses and permits, waiting period, § 1303
Orders of court, former spouse, elections, 10 U.S.C. § 1448, 1450
Process, annuities, survivor benefit plans, 10 U.S.C. § 1450
Retirement and pensions, 10 U.S.C. § 1408
Support, retirement and pensions, 10 U.S.C. § 1408
Survivor benefit plan, 10 U.S.C. § 1447 et seq.
Termination, annuity payable to beneficiary, 10 U.S.C. § 1450
Waiting period, marriage, licenses and permits, § 1303

Military Service
Divorce or annulment actions, Rule 1920.46

Minor Judiciary
Protection from abuse, emergency relief, § 6110

Minors
Children and Minors, generally, this index

Misdemeanors of the Third Degree
Adoption, unauthorized disclosure, § 2910
Child protective services
  Failure to report suspected child abuse, § 6319
  Information and personnel violations, § 6349

Misrepresentation
Fraud, generally, this index

Modification
Agreements between parties, effect, § 3105

Modification—Cont'd
Child custody jurisdiction, out-of-state custody decree, § 5355
Custody orders, existing orders, § 5310
Defined, child custody jurisdiction, § 5402
Guidelines, Rule 1910.16-6
Orders, Rule 1910.19
  Foreign states, § 7609; § 7611
  Jurisdiction, interstate family support enforcement, § 7205
  Petitions, forms, Rule 1910.27
Postsecondary education, expenses and expenditures, § 4327
Support orders, Rule 1910.19

Modification Decree
Defined, child custody jurisdiction, § 5343

Monetary Limits
Tortious acts of children, liability of parents, § 5505

Mortgages
Annulment of marriage,
  Disposition of property after termination of marriage, § 3504
Divorce,
  Disposition of property after termination of marriage, § 3504
Guidelines, Rule 1910.16-6
Interest, generally, this index
Real property liens, § 4352
Spouses, loans between, security § 4105

Motions
Abuse, protection from, Rule 1905
Annulment of marriage,
  Decrees, opening or vacating, § 3332
Contempt orders, Rule 1910.25-6
Custody, Rule 1915.10
Divorce,
  Decrees, opening or vacating, § 3332
Divorce or annulment actions, appointment of master, Rule 1920.74
Paternity, support of persons, Rule 1910.15
Posttrial motions,
  Alimony, contempt orders, Rule 1910.25-6
  Divorce or annulment of marriage, Rule 1930.2
  Paternity, Rule 1910.15, 1930.2
  Reconsideration, divorce or annulment of marriage, Rule 1930.2
  Support, Rule 1910.16
Reconsideration, domestic relations matters, Rule 1930.2

INDEX

References are to Sections of the Pennsylvania Domestic Relations Code, Pennsylvania Crimes Code, Pennsylvania Judicial Code, Pennsylvania Domestic Relations Court Rules, and Selected Federal Statutes, Court Rules, and Regulations

Motions—Cont'd
Support, guidelines, Rule 1910.16-6
Support of persons,
    Discovery, Rule 1910.12
    Separate listing, Rules 1910.11, 1910.12
Time, filing, domestic relations, Rule 1930.2

Motor Vehicles
Drivers licenses, § 4304.1
Liens and encumbrances, support, overdue obligations, § 4352
Limitations, child support, custody, visitation violations, § 4355

Multiple Matters
Divorce or annulment actions, Rules 1920.6, 1920.13

Municipalities
Support, reciprocal enforcement, remedies if furnishing support, § 4508

Mutual Consent
Divorce,
    Counseling, § 3302
    Grounds for divorce, § 3301

Mutual Consent Divorce
Generally, § 3301

—N—

Names
Adoption,
    Adoptees, § 2904
    Retention of parental names, § 2903
Change of name, 54 Pa.C.S. § 701 et seq.
Divorcing and divorced person may resume prior name, 54 Pa.C.S. § 704
Fingerprints and fingerprinting, § 5105
Informal change, 54 Pa.C.S. § 701
Marriage license applications, form requirement, § 1302
Notice, 54 Pa.C.S. § 701
Orders of court, 54 Pa.C.S. § 702
Petitions, 54 Pa.C.S. § 701
Surviving spouses, 54 Pa.C.S. § 704.1
Waiver, notice, 54 Pa.C.S. § 701
Popular Name Laws, generally, this index

Necessaries
Divorce, construction of law, § 4106
Marriage, debts contracted for necessaries, proceedings, § 4102

Ne Exeat, Writ of
Annulment of marriage, § 3505
Divorce, § 3505

Net Income
Defined, support, § 4302

Newborn Children
Abandoned children, § 6501 et seq.
Immunities, abandonment, hospitals, § 6503, 6507

Newborn Children—Cont'd
Medical care and treatment, abandonment, hospitals, § 6316
Notice, abandonment, hospitals, § 6504, 6505
Privileges and immunities, abandonment, hospitals, § 6503, 6507
Protective custody, abandonment, hospitals, § 6315, 6504
Reports, abandonment, hospitals, § 6505, 6509

No-Fault
Divorce, § 3301

Nonmarital Property Rights
Defined, Protection From Abuse Act, Rule 1920.1

Nonresidents
Child custody jurisdiction, notice and submission to jurisdiction, § 5346, § 5408
Long arm procedures, expedited procedure, commencement of support proceedings, § 4342

Non Pros
Generally, Rules 1920.21.

Nonsupport
Support, generally, this index

Notice
Address, § 4353
Americans with Disabilities Act, compliance, Rules 1910.27, 1915.15, 1915.16
Attachment of income, § 4348, Rule 1910.29

INDEX

References are to Sections of the Pennsylvania Domestic Relations Code, Pennsylvania Crimes Code, Pennsylvania Judicial Code, Pennsylvania Domestic Relations Court Rules, and Selected Federal Statutes, Court Rules, and Regulations

Notice—Cont'd
Attachment orders, judgments and decrees, Rule 1910.30
Automatic adjustments, § 4352
Change of address, parties, Rule 1910.17
Child custody jurisdiction, § 5345
    Persons outside state, § 5346
Child medical support, § 4326
Child support orders, § 4352
Civil contempt, support actions, Rule 1910.21
Counseling availability, § 3302
Custody, form, Rule 1915.12
Custody, partial custody and visitation actions, Rule 1915.16
Defend and claim rights, Rule 1920.71
Delinquent child support obligors, arrearages information, § 4308
Divorce or annulment of marriage, Rule 1920.51
Entry of decree, request, Rule 1920.42
Evidence, hearings, Rule 1910.29
Foreign states, orders, modification, § 7614
Hearing, divorce actions, Rule 1920.51
Hearings, content petitions, Rule 1910.25-3, Rule 1910.25-4
Income withholding orders, § 7501.1
Intrastate family support enforcement, orders, registration, § 8411
Indigent persons,, hearings, support, § 4606
Judgments and arrears, orders, § 4352
Judgments and decrees, waiver, Rule 1920.72
Masters report,
    Exceptions, Rule 1920.55-2

Notice—Cont'd
    Hearing de novo, Rule 1920.55-3
Modification, termination, Rule 1910.19
New hire reporting, child support program, § 4391 et seq.
Newborn children, abandonment, hospitals, § 6504, 6505
noncompliance, child support program, § 4373
Petition for adoption, hearings, § 2721
Registration, orders, intrastate family support enforcement, § 8411
Reports, masters, Rule 1920.55-2
Support actions, attachment, Rules 1910.29, 1910.30
Support enforcement agencies, intrastate family support enforcement, § 8306
Visitation, form, Rule 1915.12
Visitation, joinder of parties, custody of minor children, Rule 1915.6

Notice to Defend
Rule 1920.71

Number or Amount
Support, Rules 1910.16-1 to 1910.16-5

Nurses
Abuse of children, persons required to report, § 6311
Child Protective Services Law, § 6301 et seq.
Practical nurses,
    Abuse of children, persons required to report, § 6311
    Child Protective Services Law, § 6301 et seq.

—O—

Oaths and Affirmations
Adoption,
    Hearings, testimony of adopting parents and adoptee, § 2723
    Intermediaries, reports, § 2533
Child custody jurisdiction, information submitted to court, § 5350

Objections
Divorce or annulment actions, Rule 1920.55
Lanes and encumbrances, enforcement of support orders, Rule 1910.22
Support actions, Rules 1910.12, 1910.30

Obligations
Divorce, disposition of property to defeat, § 3505

Obligees
Definitions,
    Interstate family support, § 7101
    Intrastate family support enforcement, § 8101
    Support, § 4302

Obligors
Definitions,
    Interstate family support, § 7101

INDEX

References are to Sections of the Pennsylvania Domestic Relations Code, Pennsylvania Crimes Code, Pennsylvania Judicial Code, Pennsylvania Domestic Relations Court Rules, and Selected Federal Statutes, Court Rules, and Regulations

Obligors—Cont'd
    Intrastate family support enforcement, § 8101
    Support, § 4302
    Support, failure to appear, contempt, § 4344
    Overdue payments, work activities, § 4352

Offenses
    Crimes and Offenses, generally, this index

Office Conference
    Support actions, Rules 1910.11, 1910.12

Officers
    Hearing officers
        Defined, protection from abuse, § 6102
        Protection from abuse, emergency relief, § 6110
    Support of persons, office conference officers, Rule 1910.11

Opening Decrees
    Motion, § 3332

Operating Privilege
    Denial or suspension of licenses, support, custody or the paternity matters, § 4355

Operation
    Support guidelines, Rule 1910.16-5

Operation of Law
    Judgment by operation of law, defined, support, § 4302

Option or Election
    Divorce or annulment actions, pleadings, Rule 1920.13
    Pleading, alternatives, 1920.13
    Support actions, alternate hearing procedures, Rule 1910.10

Oral Agreements, § 3105

Oral Examinations
    Marriage licenses, § 1306

Order of Support
    Defined, support, § 4302

Orders
    Allocation, Rule 1910.16
    Appeal and review, § 4350
    Appointment of master, Rule 1920.74
    Arrearages,
        Limitations of actions, § 7604
        Specifications, § 4348
    Attachment, income, enforcement, § 4348
    Blood test, paternity determination purposes, § 5104

Orders—Cont'd
    Child custody jurisdiction, appearance, foreign states, § 5360
    Change of circumstances, Rule 1910.17
    Child support program, § 4377
    Commencement of action, forms, Rule 1910.27
    Conferences, Rule 1910.5
        Contempt petitions, Rule 1910.25-2
        Modification, termination, Rule 1910.19
        Officers, recommendations, Rule 1910.12
    Confirmation, § 7608
    Conflict of laws, § 7604
    Contempt, Rule 1910.5; Rule 1910.25-5
    Contest, § 7606
        Income withholding orders, § 7501.5
        Intrastate family support enforcement, § 8412; § 8413
        Registration, § 7607
        Validity, § 7606
    Continuing jurisdiction, § 4352
    Defendants address, change, Rule 1910.17
    Docketing, § 7601; § 7602
    Domestic relations office, payment, § 4325
    Earnings information, form, Rule 1910.28
    Emergency orders, protection from abuse, Rule 1901 et seq.
    Employer receipt, income withholding, § 7501
    Entry of order, entireties property, execution against, § 4361
    Final orders, Rule 1910.11
        Hearing after office conference; Rule 1910.12
        Paternity, Rule 1910.15
    Foreign states,
        Enforcement, § 7502
        Jurisdiction, § 7611
        Modification, § 7609; § 7611
        Recognition, § 7612
    Foreign support orders, § 4352
    Full faith and credit to child custody determinations, 28 U.S.C. § 1738A
    Full faith and credit to child custody determinations, 28 U.S.C. § 1738B
    Genetic tests, paternity, Rule 1910.15
    Hearings, intrastate family support enforcement, contest, § 8412
    Income, attachment, Rule 1910.31
    Income withholding,
        Employer receipt, § 7501
        Employer receipt, § 7501
        Recognition, § 7501

INDEX

References are to Sections of the Pennsylvania Domestic Relations Code, Pennsylvania Crimes Code, Pennsylvania Judicial Code, Pennsylvania Domestic Relations Court Rules, and Selected Federal Statutes, Court Rules, and Regulations

Orders—Cont'd
Interlocutory orders, paternity, Rule 1910.15
Interstate family support enforcement, petitions, § 7401
Intrastate family support enforcement,
    Confirmation, § 8414; § 8415
    Contest, § 8412
    Recognition, § 8202
    Registration, § 8401; § 8402
Jurisdiction, foreign states, § 7611
Limitations of actions, arrearages, § 7604
Mediation, orientation sessions, Rule 1940.3
Modification, Rule 1910.19
    Jurisdiction, interstate family support enforcement, § 7205
    Nonparties to interstate family support enforcement, § 7611
    Petitions, Rule 1910.27
Multiple orders,
    Income withholding orders, § 7501.2
    Interstate family support enforcement, § 7208
    Intrastate family support enforcement, § 8202
Notice, registration, intrastate family support enforcement, § 8411
Office conference recommendation, Rule 1910.11
Paternity, genetic tests, Rule 1910.15
Payments, domestic relations office, § 4325
Postsecondary education, expenses and expenditures, applicability, § 4327
Priorities and preferences, attachment orders, § 4348
Recognition, § 7612
    Foreign states, § 7612

Orders—Cont'd
Interstate family support enforcement, § 7207
Intrastate family support enforcement, § 8202
Registration, § 7601; § 7602
    Confirmation, § 7608
    Contest, § 7606; § 7607
    Effect, § 7603
    Full faith and credit, § 7603
    Modification, foreign states, § 7609; § 7610
    Notice, § 7605
Subsequent proceedings, Rule 1910.18
Supersedeas or stay, § 7607
    Appeal and review, § 4350
Temporary orders, protection from abuse, Rule 1901 et seq.
Termination, Rule 1910.19
Visitation or partial custody, noncompliance, contempt, § 4346
Withholding of income, Rule 1910.21

Organization
Child protective services, § 6361

Overdue Support
Consumer reporting agencies, enforcement of support orders, Rule 1910.20
Definitions, § 4302
    Actions and proceedings, Rule 1910.1
Licenses and permits, § 4377
Liens and incumbrances, enforcement of support orders, Rule 1910.22
Monetary awards, collections, § 4308.1
Reimbursement, child support program, § 4374

Oversight
Legislative oversight, child protective services, § 6384

—P—

Pace
Pennsylvania Adoption Cooperative Exchange, generally, this index

Parents
Adoption, generally, this index
Custody, generally, this index
Defined, adoption, § 2102

Parents—Cont'd
Liability for Torts of Children, this index
Parental consent lacking, underage parties, grounds for annulment, § 3305
Paternity, generally, this index
Persons acting as parent, defined, child custody jurisdiction, § 5343
Support, generally, this index

INDEX

References are to Sections of the Pennsylvania Domestic Relations Code, Pennsylvania Crimes Code, Pennsylvania Judicial Code, Pennsylvania Domestic Relations Court Rules, and Selected Federal Statutes, Court Rules, and Regulations

Parent Coordination
Procedure, Rules 1915.11-1, 1915.22, 1915.23

Partial Custody
Commencement, complaint, Rule 1915.3
Counterclaim, Rule 1915.5
Defined, custody, § 5302
Defined, minor children, Rule 1915.1
Orders, noncompliance, contempt, § 4346
Practice and procedure, Rule 1915.1
Venue, Rule 1915.5

Partial Physical Custody
Award, § 5323
Defined, custody, § 5322
Individuals who may file for, § 5325

Parties
Adoption
    Representation for child, § 2313
    Who may adopt, § 2312
    Who may be adopted, § 2311
Agreements between, § 3105, § 3106
Alimony, Rule 1910.3
Child custody jurisdiction
    Additional, § 5351
    Appearance, § 5352
Custody, removal from jurisdiction, § 5308
Death, § 3323, § 3331
Divorce, agreements, effect, § 3105
Examinations,
    Custody or visitation of minors, Rule 1915.8
    Form of order, Rule 1915.18
Joinder of parties,
    Custody of minor children, Rule 1915.6
    Divorce or annulment of marriage, Rule 1920.34
    Visitation, Rule 1915.6
Support actions, Rule 1910.3

Partition
Determination and disposition, jurisdiction, § 3104

Passports
Applications,
    Children and minors, 22 C.F.R. § 51.27
    Statement under oath, 22 U.S.C. § 213
    Verification, 22 U.S.C. § 213
Children and minors, support, are rewritten his, 42 U.S.C. § 652

Past Due Support
Actions and proceedings, Rule 1910.1
Definitions, § 4302

Paternity
Acknowledgment and claim, § 5103
Acknowledgment, form, Rules 1910.2, 1910.28
Adoption, acknowledgment, certificates and certification, § 5103
Appearance, failure to appear, Rule 1910.15
Assessments, costs, § 4351
Authority for requiring blood tests, § 5104
Birth certificates, § 5103
Birth parents, acknowledgments or affidavits, § 5103
Blood tests to determine, § 5104
Children and minors,
    Paternity determination, § 5102
    Support of persons, § 4343
Child-support program, § 4373
Claim of paternity, § 5103
Compensation and salaries, experts, blood test determinations, § 5104
Costs,
    Assessments, § 4351
    Genetic tests, § 4343
Court orders, blood tests, § 5104
Default judgment, § 4342
Defenses, intrastate family support enforcement, § 8310
Determination of paternity, § 5102
Dismissal and non-suit, Rule 1910.15
Effects, blood test results, § 5104
Electronic testimony, witnesses, Rule 1930.3
Estoppel, actions and proceedings, Rule 1910.15
Evidence,
    Acknowledgments, Rule 1910.15
    Disclosure, § 4342
    Genetic test results, § 4343
    Presumption of legitimacy, overcoming, § 5104, Rule 1910.15
    Refusal to submit to blood tests, § 5104
Experts, compensation, blood test determinations, § 5104
Failure to appear, Rule 1910.15
Forms,
    Acknowledgment of paternity, § 5103
Genetic tests, § 4343, Rule 1910.15, 1930.6
Hearing by court, decision and post-trial relief, Rule 1920.52
Interlocutory orders, Rule 1910.15

INDEX

References are to Sections of the Pennsylvania Domestic Relations Code, Pennsylvania Crimes Code, Pennsylvania Judicial Code, Pennsylvania Domestic Relations Court Rules, and Selected Federal Statutes, Court Rules, and Regulations

Paternity—Cont'd
Intrastate family support enforcement, defenses, § 8310
Jurisdiction, venue, Rule 1910.7
Jury trial,
    Post-trial motions, Rule 1920.52
    Post-trial relief, Rule 1930.2
Long arm jurisdiction, § 7201
Licenses and permits, revocation or suspension, § 4355
Pleadings, forms, captions, Rule 1930.1
Presumptions, Rule 1910.15
Reciprocity, foreign state determinations, § 4343
Refusal to submit to blood tests, evidence, § 5104
Precision, acknowledgment, § 51 and three
Rules, Rule 1930.6
Scope of rights upon acknowledgment of paternity, § 5103
Scope of rights upon claim of paternity, § 5103
Selection of experts, blood test analysis, § 5104
Statute of limitations defense, support of persons, Rule 1910.7
Stipulations, Rule 1910.15
Support, § 4343
Support actions, Rules 1910.7, 1910.15, 1910.28
Time, answer, actions and proceedings, Rule 1910.15
Trial, waiver of right to, Rule 1910.28
Witnesses, § 5103, Rule 1930.3

Payments
Cooperation, financial institutions, § 4304.1
Credit, interstate family support enforcement, § 7209
Domestic relations section of court, payments to, § 3704
Incentive payments, child support program, § 4373
Intrastate family support enforcement, § 8203
Liens and incumbrances, enforcement of support orders, Rule 1910.22
Periodic payment schedules, arrearages, professional or occupational licenses, § 4355
Receipt and disbursement, interstate family support enforcement, § 7319
Revised payment schedules, overdue payments, § 4352

Payments—Cont'd
Support
    Divorce, § 3704
    Orders, § 4325
        Willful failure to pay, § 4354

Penalties
Fines and Penalties, generally, this index

Pending Complaint File
Child protective services
    Establishment, § 6331
    Information in, § 6335

Pending or Pendency of Actions
Alimony, Rules 1920.31, 1920.56
Annulment of marriage, joined of claims, Rule 1920.31
Divorce, joinder of claims, Rule 1920.31
Divorce or annulment actions, Rule 1920.92
Support, Joinder of claims, divorce or annulment of marriage, Rule 1920.31

Pennsylvania Adoption Cooperative Exchange
Generally, § 2551 et seq.
Agencies
    Relative activities unaffected, § 2556
    Responsibilities, § 2555
Application of law, retroactive application, § 2558
Children, registration, § 2553
Definitions, § 2551
Department, defined, § 2551
Establishment, § 2552
PACE, defined, § 2551
Public and private agencies
    Related activities unaffected, § 2556
    Responsibilities, § 2555
Registration of children, § 2553
Regulations, § 2557
Responsibilities, § 2554
    Public and private agencies, § 2555
Retroactive application of law, § 2558
Staff, § 2557

Pensions. See, Retirement and Pensions

Performance
Child protective services, investigation, § 6343
Support, security for attendance or performance, § 4347

INDEX

References are to Sections of the Pennsylvania Domestic Relations Code, Pennsylvania Crimes Code, Pennsylvania Judicial Code, Pennsylvania Domestic Relations Court Rules, and Selected Federal Statutes, Court Rules, and Regulations

Perjury
Annulment of marriage,
   Collusion, § 3309
Divorce,
   Collusion, § 3309

Personal Income Tax
State income tax intercept, support matters, § 4307

Personal Injuries
Collection of overdue support from monetary awards, § 4308.1

Personal Property
Divorce, property rights, § 3501 et seq.
Entireties Property, generally, this index

Persons Acting as Parent
Defined, torts of children, § 5501
Defined, custody or visitation of minors, § 5343, Rule 1915.1
Personal representative, substitution for deceased party, § 3323

Petitions
Civil contempt, alimony and support, Rule 1910.25
Civil contempt, custody, Rule 1915.12
Custody orders, contempt, Rule 1915.12
Entireties property, execution of support order against, § 4362
Interstate family support enforcement, § 7304, § 7311
Involuntary termination, adoption, § 2512
Modification,
   Partial custody or visitation orders, form, Rule 1915.15
   Support orders, form, Rule 1910.27
Orders, interstate family support enforcement, § 7401
Spousal support, divorce proceedings, § 3702
Support of persons, modification, form, Rule 1910.26
Support orders, contempt, Rule 1910.21

Petitions for Adoptions
Adoption, this index

Photographs
Child protective services, reporting suspected child abuse, § 6314

Phrases
Words and Phrases, generally, this index

Physical Custody
Defined
   Child custody jurisdiction, § 5343
   Custody, § 5302
   Custody of minor children, Rule 1915.1

Physical Examinations
Abused children, § 6314
Custody of minor children, Rule 1915.8
Marriage,
   Premarital syphilis examination, statement preparation and furnishing, § 1104
   Syphilis examinations, restrictions on marriage license issuance, § 1304

Physicians and Surgeons
Abuse of children, persons required to report, § 6311
Adoption, medical history information, § 2909
Child Protective Services Law, § 6301 et seq.
Forms,
   Premarital syphilis examination statements, preparation and furnishing, § 1104
Interns,
   Abuse of children, persons required to report, § 6311
   Child Protective Services Law, § 6301 et seq.
Marriage,
   Premarital syphilis examination statements, preparation and furnishing, § 1104
   Syphilis examination and test, § 1305
Medical Care and Treatment, generally, this index

Plans
Child protective services, local plans, § 6363
Custody
   Denial, § 5307
   Orders, plan for implementing, § 5306

Pleadings
Alimony, defendant, Rule 1910.7
Alternatives, Rules 1920.13
Answers,
   Parental liability for torts of minors, § 5504

INDEX

References are to Sections of the Pennsylvania Domestic Relations Code, Pennsylvania Crimes Code, Pennsylvania Judicial Code, Pennsylvania Domestic Relations Court Rules, and Selected Federal Statutes, Court Rules, and Regulations

Pleadings—Cont'd
Caption,
    Domestic relations, actions, form, Rule 1930.1
Continuance, generally, this index
Defendants, Rule 1910.7
Denials, Rules 1920.14
Divorce or annulment actions, Rules 1920.11 et seq.
Forms, Rule 1930.1
Interstate family support enforcement, § 7311
Joinder of claims or causes of action
    divorce or annulment actions, Rules 1920.31-1920.33
Multiple causes of action
    divorce or annulment actions, Rule 1920.13
Protection from abuse, Rule 1905
Support, transfer, Rule 1910.8
Visitation, Rules 1915.2, 1915.5

Police
Domestic violence,
    Court orders, enforcement, § 6109
    Responsibilities, § 6105
Notice, weapons relinquishment, domestic violence, § 6108
Powers and duties, domestic violence cases, § 6105
Reports, domestic violence, incidents, § 6105
Weapons, privileges and immunities, domestic violence, § 6119

Policy
Public Policy, generally, this index

Popular Name Laws
Abuse Law, § 6101 et seq., § 6301 et seq.
Adoption Act, § 2101 et seq.
Child Abuse Law, § 6301 et seq.
Child Custody Law, § 5301 et seq.
Child Protective Services Law, § 6301 et seq.
Divorce Code, § 3101 et seq.
Domestic Relations Code, § 101 et seq.
Domestic and Sexual Violence Victim Address Confidentiality Act, § 6701
Domestic Violence Law, § 6101 et seq.
Interstate Family Support Act, § 7101 et seq.
Intrastate Family Support Enforcement, § 8101 et seq.
Marriage Law, § 1101 et seq.
Newborn Protection Act, § 6501 et seq.
Paternity Law, § 5101 et seq.

Popular Name Laws—Cont'd
Protection from Abuse Act, § 6101 et seq.
Reciprocal Enforcement of Support Law, § 7101 et seq.
Standby Guardianship Act, § 5601
Support Law, § 4301 et seq.
Uniform Act on Blood Test to Determine Paternity, § 5104
Uniform Child Custody Jurisdiction and Enforcement Act, § 5401 et seq.
Uniform Reciprocal Enforcement of Support Act, § 7101 and set

Postmortem Investigations
Child protective services, reporting suspected child abuse, deaths, § 6317

Postnuptial Agreements
Divorce, rights determination and disposition, jurisdiction, § 3104
Marital property status, § 3501

Postnuptial Agreements
Marital property status, § 3501
Rights determination and disposition, jurisdiction, § 3104

Postsecondary Education
Definitions, support, § 4327

Post-Trial Motions
Alimony, contempt orders, Rule 1910.21-7
Child custody orders, Rule 1915.10
Divorce or annulment of marriage, Rules 1920.52, 1930.2
Paternity, Rule 1930.2
    Support of persons, Rule 1910.15
Reconsideration, divorce or annulment of marriage, Rule 1930.2
Support of persons, Rule 1910.16
    Conference officer reports, Rule 1910.12
    Contempt orders, Rule 1910.25-6
    Final orders, Rule 1910.11
    Temporary orders, Rule 1910.11
Time for filing, domestic relations matters, Rule 1930.2

Praecipe
Transmittal of record, divorce or annulment actions, Rule 1920.73

Preferences and Priority
Divorce or annulment actions, Rule 1920.6

Premarital Agreements
Breach of, § 3106
Burden of proof, § 3106
Definitions, § 3106
Marital property status, § 3501

INDEX

References are to Sections of the Pennsylvania Domestic Relations Code, Pennsylvania Crimes Code, Pennsylvania Judicial Code, Pennsylvania Domestic Relations Court Rules, and Selected Federal Statutes, Court Rules, and Regulations

Premarital Agreements—Cont'd
Rights determination and disposition, jurisdiction, § 3104

Prenuptial Agreements
Marital property status, § 3501

Presumed Decedents
Marriage licenses, applications, decree that spouse of applicant is presumed decedent, § 1701

Presumptions
Support award, amount of, Rule 1910.16-1

Prevention
Child protective services, services for prevention and treatment of child abuse, § 6365

Primary Physical Custody
Award, § 5323
Defined, custody, § 5322
Presumption concerning award of, § 5327

Prior Marriages
Marital property division factor, § 3502

Priorities and Preferences
Attachment order, § 4348
Child custody jurisdiction, § 5407
Disbursements, child support program, § 4374
Fees, costs, expenses, § 4351
Liens and incumbrances, overdue support, § 4352
Multiple orders, § 7207
Multiple remedies, intrastate family support enforcement, § 8103
Withholding of income, enforcement of support orders, Rule 1910.21

Private Agencies
Pennsylvania Adoption Cooperative Exchange
  Related activities unaffected, § 2556
  Responsibilities, § 2555

Private Hospitals
Child protective services, reporting suspected child abuse, admission of child to, § 6316

Privileged Information
Confidential or Privileged Information, generally, this index

Privileges and Immunities
Arrearages, monetary awards, collections, § 4308.1
Child protective services, reporting suspected child abuse, immunity from liability, § 6318

Privileges and Immunities—Cont'd
Child support program, § 4377
Family immunity, interstate family support enforcement, § 7316
Garnishment, employers, § 4348
Income withholding, orders, § 7501.3
Interstate family support enforcement, § 7314
Protection from abuse, reporting abuse, § 6115

Procedure
Child protective services, reporting suspected child abuse, § 6313
Divorce, this index
Protection from abuse, § 6117

Proceedings
Actions and Proceedings, generally, this index
Process and Service of Process and Papers
Adoption, notice, § 2721
Custody, partial custody and visitation actions, Rules 1930.4, 1915.12
Divorce or annulment actions, Rules 1930.4, 1920.1
Protection from Abuse Act actions, Rule 1903
Service of process,
  Domestic violence proceedings, § 6106
  Court orders, § 6109
Support actions, Rule 1930.4

Production of Documents
Alimony, financial records, Rule 1920.31
Support, financial records, Rule 1920.31

Professionals
Qualified professional, defined, divorce, § 3103

Programs
Domestic violence program, defined, protection from abuse, § 6102
Promise to Marry
Breach of Promise to Marry, generally, this index

Property.
Construction of law, § 4106
Determination and distribution, Rule 1920.33
Disposition after termination of marriage, § 3504
Disposition to defeat obligations, § 3505

INDEX

References are to Sections of the Pennsylvania Domestic Relations Code, Pennsylvania Crimes Code, Pennsylvania Judicial Code, Pennsylvania Domestic Relations Court Rules, and Selected Federal Statutes, Court Rules, and Regulations

Property—Cont'd
Entireties property,
    Conveyance to divorced spouse, § 3508
    Division between divorce parties, § 3507
Inventory of property, parties, § 3505
Premarital agreements, burden of proof, § 3106
Valuation, nonmarital property, § 3501

Property Rights, § 3501 et seq.
Determination and disposition, jurisdiction, § 3104
Premarital agreements, burden of proof, § 3106

Property Settlements
Jurisdiction, § 3104

Prosecution of Actions
Non pros, Rules 1920.21

Protection
Child protective services
    Protecting well-being of child maintained outside home, § 6372
    Protection of child at home or in custody, § 6370

Protection of Victims of Sexual Violence or Intimidation Act
Generally, 62A01 et seq.
Applicability, 62A18
Arrest for violation of order, 62A12
Civil contempt or modification for violation of order or agreement, 62A15
Commencement of proceedings, 62A05, Rule 1953
Confidentiality, 62A16
Construction, 62A20
Contempt for violation of order, 62A14
Decision, Post-trial relief, Rule 1957
Definitions, 62A03, Rule 1951
Disclosure of addresses, 62A11
Discontinuance or modification, Rule 1958
Emergency relief by minor judiciary, 62A09
Enforcement, Rule 1955
Findings and purpose, 62A02
Forms, Rule 1959
Hearings, 62A06
Inability to pay, 62A19
Private criminal complaints for violation of order or agreement, 62A13
Procedure and other remedies, 62A17, Rule 1956

Protection of Victims of Sexual Violence or Intimidation Act—Cont'd
Relief, 62A07
Responsibilities of law enforcement agencies, 62A04
Service, Rule 1954
Sexual assault counselor, 62A10
Venue, Rule 1952

Protection from Abuse
Generally, § 6101 et seq.
Generally, Rules 1901-1905
Abuse
    Defined, § 6102
    Departure to avoid, effect, § 6103
    Reporting, § 6115
Actions, commencement, Rule 1902
Actions and proceedings, commencement, § 6106
Addresses, disclosure, § 6112
Adult, defined, § 6102
Advocates, domestic violence counselor-advocate, § 6111
    Defined, § 6102
Agencies, local law enforcement agencies, responsibilities, § 6105
Agreements, contempt for violation, § 6114, § 6114.1
Arrest for violation of order, § 6113
Civil contempt, § 6114.1
Commencement of action, Rule 1902
Commencement of proceedings, § 6106
Communications, confidential communications, defined, § 6102
Confidential communications, defined, § 6102
Confidentiality, § 6116
Contempt for violation of order or agreement, § 6114
Counselors, domestic violence counselor-advocate, § 6111
    Defined, § 6102
Decision, Rule 1905
Definitions, Rule 1901
Definitions, § 6102
Departure to avoid abuse, effect, § 6103
Disclosure of addresses, § 6112
Discovery, Rule 1930.5
Domestic violence counselor-advocate, § 6111
    Defined, § 6102
Domestic violence program, defined, § 6102

INDEX

References are to Sections of the Pennsylvania Domestic Relations Code, Pennsylvania Crimes Code, Pennsylvania Judicial Code, Pennsylvania Domestic Relations Court Rules, and Selected Federal Statutes, Court Rules, and Regulations

Protection from Abuse—Cont'd
Emergency relief by minor judiciary, § 6110
Enforcement of order, Rule 1903
Family or household members, defined, § 6102
Fees
    Commencement of proceedings, § 6106
    Inability to pay, § 6120
    Private criminal complaints, violation, § 6113.1
Hearing officers
    Defined, § 6102
    Emergency relief, § 6110
Hearings, § 6107
Households, family or household members, defined, § 6102
Law enforcement agencies, responsibilities, § 6105
Local law enforcement agencies, responsibilities, § 6105
Minor, defined, § 6102
Minor judiciary, emergency relief, § 6110
Officers, hearing officers
    Defined, § 6102
    Emergency relief, § 6110
Orders
    Arrest for violation, § 6113
    Civil contempt for violation, § 6114.1
    Contempt for violation, § 6114
    Full faith and credit, out-of-state orders, § 6118
    Mutual orders of protection, § 6108
    Private criminal complaints for violation, § 6113.1
    Registration, § 6104
    Service, § 6109
    Statewide registry, § 6105
Pleadings, Rule 1904
Post-trial relief, Rule 1905
Private criminal complaints, violation of order or agreement, § 6113.1
Privileges and immunities, reporting abuse, § 6115
Procedure, § 6117
Programs, domestic violence program, defined, § 6102
Registration of order, § 6104
Relief, § 6108
    Emergency relief by minor judiciary, § 6110
Remedies, § 6117
Reporting abuse, § 6115
Service of order, Rule 1930.4

Protection from Abuse—Cont'd
Service of orders, § 6109
Short title of law, § 6101
Venue, Rule 1901.1
Victim, defined, § 6102
Violations
    Agreements, contempt, § 6114, § 6114.1
    Orders
        Arrest, § 6113
        Contempt, § 6114, § 6114.1

Protection from Abuse Act
Generally, § 6101 et seq.

Protective Custody
Child protective services, taking child into, § 6369
    Reporting suspected child abuse, § 6315

Protective Orders
Discovery, Rule 1930.5
Domestic violence, § 6108
    Police verification of order existence, § 6113
Private criminal complaints, violations, § 6113.1
Service of process, Rule 1930.4

Protective Services
Child Protective Services, generally, this index

Prothonotaries
Clerk, defined, § 102
Clerk of court, defined, § 102
Commencing protection from abuse actions, Rule 1902
Court, defined, § 102
Registration,
    Court orders, domestic violence cases, § 6104

Public Agencies
Pennsylvania Adoption Cooperative Exchange
    Related activities unaffected, § 2556
    Responsibilities, § 2555

Public Hospitals
Child protective services, reporting suspected child abuse, admission of child to, § 6316

Public Notice
Notice, generally, this index

Public Policy
Breach of promise to marry actions, abolition, § 1903
Child Custody Jurisdiction Act, § 5342

INDEX

References are to Sections of the Pennsylvania Domestic Relations Code, Pennsylvania Crimes Code, Pennsylvania Judicial Code, Pennsylvania Domestic Relations Court Rules, and Selected Federal Statutes, Court Rules, and Regulations

Public Policy—Cont'd
Child protective services, § 6302
Custody, § 5301
Divorce, § 102, 3102
Marriage, § 1704
Same-sex marriages, § 1704

Public Welfare, Department of
Access,
    Pending complaint file of child abuse reports information, § 6335
Actions and proceedings, joinder, § 4306
Child protective services,
    Performance investigations, § 6343
Child Protective Services Law, § 6301 et seq.
Children, youth and family services office, Pennsylvania adoption cooperative exchange, § 2551 et seq.
Continuous availability, pending compliant file and statewide central register, § 6333
Disposition of child abuse complaints, § 6334
Domestic relations section, powers and duties, § 4305
Income tax refund intercept program, authorization, § 4307
Interstate family support enforcement, § 7310
Limitations, state wide toll-free telephone number use, child abuse, § 6332
Newborn children, abandonment, § 6509
Officers and employees,
    Hiring and regulations, Pennsylvania adoption cooperative exchange staff, § 2557

Public Welfare, Department of—Cont'd
PACE, § 2551 et seq.
Pending complaint file of child abuse reports, § 6331
    Information, § 6335
    Recording complaints, § 6334
Pennsylvania adoption cooperative exchange, § 2551 et seq.
Powers and duties, support enforcement agencies, § 7308
Reports,
    Child protective services reports to department, § 6367
Rules and regulations,
    Child abuse programs, § 6348
    Pennsylvania adoption cooperative exchange implementation, § 2557
Statewide central register of child abuse,
    Establishment, § 6331
    Information, § 6336
Toll-free telephone number, statewide number, child abuse, § 6332

Purchases
Child protective services, purchasing services of other agencies § 6364

Purpose of Law
Child custody jurisdiction, § 5342
Child protective services, § 6302
Marriage
    Alienation of affections, actions abolished, § 1903
    Breach of promise to marry, actions abolished, § 1903

—Q—

Qualifications
Marriage, persons solemnizing, § 1503
Counseling unrestricted choice, § 3302

Qualified Professionals
Defined, divorce, § 3103

—R—

Real Property
Deeds and Conveyances, generally, this index
Divorce, property rights, § 3501 et seq.
Entireties Property, generally, this index
Liens, § 4352

Receivers and Receivership
Appointments, temporary receivers, support, special relief, Rule 1910.26
Support, appointments, temporary receivers, special relief, Rule 1910.26

INDEX

References are to Sections of the Pennsylvania Domestic Relations Code, Pennsylvania Crimes Code, Pennsylvania Judicial Code, Pennsylvania Domestic Relations Court Rules, and Selected Federal Statutes, Court Rules, and Regulations

Reciprocity
Interstate family support enforcement, § 7901
Paternity determinations, foreign states, § 4343

Reconsideration
Divorce or annulment of marriage, motions, Rule 1930.2

Reconciliation
Reasonable prospect of reconciliation, § 3301

Records and Recordation
Adoption, access, § 2905
Child custody jurisdiction, court records, foreign states, request for, § 5363
Custody of minor children, Rule 1915.11
Child protective services, studies of data in records, § 6342
Custody, access, § 5309
Divorce,
    Divorce decree recording, effect on liens on entireties property, § 3507
    Divorce or annulment actions, praecipe to transmit record, Rule 1920.73
Hearings, masters, Rule 1920.55-3
Liens and encumbrances, § 3507
Marriage, § 1106
Orders, child support, program, § 4377
Paternity acknowledgment, videotape, § 5103
Safety procedures, § 4305
Support actions, hearing, Rule 1910.12
Visitation of minor children, Rule 1915.11

Recrimination
Divorce, defense abolition, § 3307

Registering Tribunal
Definitions,
    Interstate family support, § 7101
    Intrastate family support enforcement, § 8101

Registers
Child custody jurisdiction, out-of-state custody decree and proceedings, § 5357
Statewide central register. Child Protective Services, this index

Registration
Child support program, § 4376
Children, Pennsylvania Adoption Cooperative Exchange, § 2553

Registration—Cont'd
Contest, § 7607
Orders, § 7601; § 7602
    Confirmation, § 7608
    Contest, § 7606; § 7607
    Effect, § 7603
    Full faith and credit, § 7603
    Modification, foreign states, § 7609; § 7610
Notice, § 7605
Protection from abuse, orders, § 6104

Regulations
Rules and Regulations, generally, this index

Rehabilitative Services
Child protective services, rehabilitative services for child and family, § 6371

Related Matters
Claims, divorce or annulment actions, Rules 1920.31-1920.33, 1920.54

Relatives
Alienation of affections actions, exception, § 1901
Forms, pleadings, captions, Rule 1930.1
Marriage,
    Prohibited degrees of consanguinity for marriage, § 1304
Protection from Abuse, generally, this index
Witnesses, electronic testimony, Rule 1930.3

Relief
Protection from abuse, § 6108
    Emergency relief by minor judiciary, § 6110
Special relief, Rule 1910.26

Religion
Adoption, § 2725
Custody of minor children, records, access, § 5309

Religious Beliefs
Petition for adoption, hearings, § 2725

Relinquishment
Voluntary relinquishment. Adoption, this index

Remedies and Relief
Children and minors, custody, enforcement, jurisdiction, § 5443
Custody, partial custody and visitation actions, Rule 1915.13
Divorce or annulment actions, Rule 1920.43

INDEX

References are to Sections of the Pennsylvania Domestic Relations Code, Pennsylvania Crimes Code, Pennsylvania Judicial Code, Pennsylvania Domestic Relations Court Rules, and Selected Federal Statutes, Court Rules, and Regulations

Remedies and Relief—Cont'd
Protection from abuse, § 6117
Protection from Abuse Act actions, Rule 1905
Special relief
    custody, partial custody and visitation actions, Rule 1915.13
    divorce or annulment actions, Rule 1920.43
    support actions, Rule 1910.25
Support actions, Rule 1910.25
Support orders, execution against entireties property, other enforcement remedies preserved, § 4366

Reports and Reporting
Adoption, this index
Annulment of marriage, Masters, Rule 1920.53
Arrearages, consumer reporting agencies, § 4303
Child Protective Services, this index
Child-support program, new hire reporting, § 4391 et seq.
Conference officers, Rule 1910.12
Content petitions, Rule 1910.25-4
Counseling, attendance, § 3302
Custody, examinations, Rule 1915.8
Divorce,
    Counseling attendance, § 3302
Divorce or annulment actions, Rules 1920.53-1920.55
Domestic abuse, § 6115
Domestic relations section, § 4353
Earnings report, forms, Rule 1910.28
Findings, Masters, annulment of marriage, divorce, Rule 1920.53
Masters, Rule 1920.53, 1920.55-2
Newborn children, abandonment, hospitals, § 6505, 6509
Protection from abuse, reporting abuse, § 6115
Support, duties, § 4353

Reports and Reporting—Cont'd
Support actions, earnings, Rule 1910.27
Visitation, examinations, custody of minor children, Rule 1915.8

Representation
Adoption, representation for child, § 2313

Res Judicata
Annulment decrees, § 3333
Child custody jurisdiction, decree of court, § 5353
Divorce, decree of court, § 3333

Residence
Domicile and Residence, generally, this index

Retirement and Pensions
Annulment of marriage,
    Income source, marital property division factor, § 3502
Attachment,
    Child-support program, § 4377
    Support, payments, § 4305
Distribution, marital property, § 3501
Divorce,
    Income sources,
        Alimony necessity factor, § 3701
        Marital property division factor, § 3502
Searches and seizures, payments, support, § 4305
Support, monthly gross income, computation, Rule 1910.16-2

Returns
Marriages, § 1504

Review
Appeal and Review, generally, this index

Rules and Regulations
Child protective services, § 6348
Mediation, § 3901
Pennsylvania Adoption Cooperative Exchange, § 2557

—S—

Salaries
Compensation and Salaries, generally, this index

Sales
Court ordered sales of property, marital property distribution enforcement, § 3502

Disposition of property after termination of marriage, § 3504
Entireties property, division of proceedings, § 3507

Same Sex Marriages
Void status, § 1704

INDEX

References are to Sections of the Pennsylvania Domestic Relations Code, Pennsylvania Crimes Code, Pennsylvania Judicial Code, Pennsylvania Domestic Relations Court Rules, and Selected Federal Statutes, Court Rules, and Regulations

Schedules
Guidelines, Rule 1910.16-3

School Nurses
Abused children, persons required to report, § 6311
Child Protective Services Law, § 6301 et seq.

School Officers and Employees
Abuse of children, persons required to report, § 6311
Child Protective Services Law, § 6301 et seq.

Schoolteachers
Abuse of children, persons required to report, § 6311
Child Protective Services Law, § 6301 et seq.

Scope of Law
Support, § 4301

Seals and Sealing
Child protective services, information, § 6341

Searches and Seizures
Alimony enforcement, § 3703
Annulment of marriage,
    Goods seizures, marital property distribution enforcement, § 3502
Divorce,
    Goods seizures, marital property division enforcement, § 3502
Domestic violence arrests, weapons seizure, § 6113

Secretary
Defined, child protective services, § 6303

Security
Alimony, future payments, insuring, arrearages enforcement, § 3703
Annulment of marriage,
    Insuring compliance with court ordered future payments, § 3502
Custody or visitation of minors, Rule 1915.13
Divorce,
    Security requirements, insuring compliance with court ordered future payments, § 3502
Divorce or annulment actions, Rule 1920.44
Support actions, Rule 1910.14

Senate
General Assembly, generally, this index

Separate and Apart
Defined, divorce, § 3103

Separate Earnings
Construction of law, divorce, § 4106
Married persons, right to, § 4104

Separation
Divorce, generally, this index
Parents, effect on custody of children, § 5312

Separation Agreements
Divorce, rights determination and disposition, jurisdiction, § 3104

Serious Bodily Injuries
Defined, child protective services, confidential information, § 6303, § 6340

Serious Mental Disorder
Consent incapability § 3304

Service of Process
Abuse, protection from, Rule 1930.4
Adoption, § 2721
Alimony, Rule 1910.25
Affidavits,
    Divorce and annulment of marriage actions, Rule 1920.4
Annulment of marriage, Rule 1920.4, 1930.4
Attachment orders, support orders, Rule 1910.22
Complaint, divorce actions, Rule 1930.4
Contempt petition, support and alimony, Rule 1910.25
Custody, Rule 1930.4
Divorce, Rule 1920.4 of 1930.4
Domestic relations matters, Rule 1930.4
Domestic violence proceedings, § 6106
Employers, withholding of income, enforcement of support orders, Rule 1910.21
Interstate family support enforcement, § 7314
Longhorn jurisdiction, § 7201
Partial custody, Rule 1930.4
Petition, support and alimony, Rule 1910.25
Protection from abuse,
    Actions for, Rule 1930.4
    Orders, § 6109
Support actions, attachment of wages, salaries and commissions, Rule 1910.22
Visitation, Rule 1915.6, 1915.8, 1930.4

INDEX

References are to Sections of the Pennsylvania Domestic Relations Code, Pennsylvania Crimes Code, Pennsylvania Judicial Code, Pennsylvania Domestic Relations Court Rules, and Selected Federal Statutes, Court Rules, and Regulations

Services
Child Protective Services, generally, this index

Severance of Actions and Claims
Divorce or annulment actions, Rule 1920.16

Sex Trafficking
County Responsibilities, § 5702
Definitions, § 5701
Law Enforcement, § 5703

Sexual Abuse
Defined, child protective services, § 6303

Sexual Violence or Intimidation
See generally, Protection of Victims of Sexual Violence or Intimidation Act, 42 Pa. C.S. § 62A01 et seq., Rule 1251, et seq.
Applicability, 62A18
Arrest for violation of order, 62A12
Civil contempt or modification for violation of order or agreement, 62A15
Commencement of proceedings, 62A05, Rule 1953
Confidentiality, 62A16
Construction, 62A20
Contempt for violation of order, 62A14
Decision, Post-trial relief, Rule 1957
Definitions, 62A03, Rule 1951
Disclosure of addresses, 62A11
Discontinuance or modification, Rule 1958
Emergency relief by minor judiciary, 62A09
Enforcement, Rule 1955
Findings and purpose, 62A02
Forms, Rule 1959
Hearings, 62A06
Inability to pay, 62A19
Private criminal complaints for violation of order or agreement, 62A13
Procedure and other remedies, 62A17, Rule 1956
Relief, 62A07
Responsibilities of law enforcement agencies, 62A04
Service, Rule 1954
Sexual assault counselor, 62A10
Venue, Rule 1952

Shared Custody
Award, § 5304
Defined, custody, § 5302
Defined, minor children, Rule 1915.1

Shared Legal Custody
Access to records and information, § 5336
Award, § 5323
Defined, custody, § 5322

Shared Physical Custody
Award, § 5323
Defined, custody, § 5322

Shelters
Battered spouses, location, confidentiality, § 5309

Sheriffs
Domestic violence petitions or orders, service, § 6106

Short Titles
Adoption Act, § 2101
Child Protective Services Law, § 6301
Divorce Code, § 3101
Domestic Relations Code, § 101
Marriage Law, § 1101
Protection from Abuse Act, § 6101
Uniform Child Custody Jurisdiction and Enforcement Act, § 5401

Social Security
Monthly gross income, computation, Rule 1910.16-2
Numbers, confidential or privileged information, § 4304.1

Social Services
Child Protective Services Law, § 6301 et seq.
Foster homes,
Prospective foster parents, information, § 6344

Social Workers
Child Protective Services Law, § 6301 et seq.

Sole Custody
Award, § 5303

Sole Legal Custody
Access to records and information, § 5336
Award, § 5323
Defined, custody, § 5322

Sole Physical Custody
Award, § 5323
Defined, custody, § 5322
Special Relief, Rule 1920.43

Spousal Support
Defined, divorce, § 3103
Guidelines, § 4322
Interstate family support, § 7101
Intrastate family support enforcement, § 8101
Medical support, § 4324
Support of Persons, generally, this index

INDEX

References are to Sections of the Pennsylvania Domestic Relations Code, Pennsylvania Crimes Code, Pennsylvania Judicial Code, Pennsylvania Domestic Relations Court Rules, and Selected Federal Statutes, Court Rules, and Regulations

Spouses
Husband and Wife, generally, this index

Standard of Living
Alimony, necessity factor, alimony determination, § 3701
Marital property division factor, divorce or annulment proceedings, § 3502

Standby Guardianship Act, § 5601

Staff
Pennsylvania Adoption Cooperative Exchange, § 2557

State Agencies
Cooperation, support, § 4304

State Income Tax Intercept
Support, § 4307

Statements
Divorce, distribution of property, statement of reasons, § 3506
Income and expense statements, form, Rule 1910.27
Supplemental income statements, form, Rule 1910.27
Support actions, income and expenses, Rule 1910.26

Statewide Central Register
Child protective services
   Establishment, § 6331
   Information in, § 6336

Statewide Toll-Free Telephone Number
Child protective services, establishment, § 6332

Station in Life
Marital property division factor, § 3502

Statistics
Adoption,
   Information accumulation and dissemination, registered children, § 2554
Marriage, § 1106

Statutes
Custody, partial custody and visitation actions, suspension, Rules 1915.24, 1915.25
Divorce or annulment actions, suspension, Rule 1920.91
Limitations, statute of, paternity cases, Rule 1910.7
Support actions, suspension, Rules 1910.49, 1910.50

Statutes of Limitation
Limitation of Actions, generally, this index

Stays
Alimony, contempt petition, request for hearing, Rule 1910.21-4
Divorce or annulment actions, Rule 1920.6
Multiple actions, divorce or annulment of marriage, Rule 1920.6
Stay of proceedings, Rule 1910.26
Supersedeas or Stay, this index
Support actions, Rule 1910.24

Studies
Child custody jurisdiction, foreign states, § 5360
Child protective services, studies of data in records, § 6342

Subject of the Report
Defined, child protective services, § 6303

Subpoenas
Court, Failure to Comply, § 5305

Subsequent Matters
Divorce or annulment actions, petition, Rule 1920.15
Support actions, Rules 1910.11, 1910.18

Summary Offenses
Child protective services
   Failure to report suspected child abuse, § 6319
   Information and personnel violations, § 6349
Support, willful failure to pay support orders, § 4354

Supersedeas or Stay
Alimony, contempt petitions, hearings, Rule 1910.25-3
Annulment of marriage, multiple actions, Rule 1920.6
Appeal and review, support of persons, § 4350
Contempt petitions, hearings, Rule 1910.25-3
Divorce, multiple actions, Rule 1920.6
Orders, § 7607
Support of persons, Rule 1910.24

Supplemental Income Statement
Support of persons, Rule 1910.26

Support
Generally, § 4301 et seq.
Generally, Rules 1910.1-1910.50
Accident and health insurance, coverage, forms, Rule 1910.27
Account, definitions, disclosure, cooperation, § 4304.1

INDEX

References are to Sections of the Pennsylvania Domestic Relations Code, Pennsylvania Crimes Code, Pennsylvania Judicial Code, Pennsylvania Domestic Relations Court Rules, and Selected Federal Statutes, Court Rules, and Regulations

Support—Cont'd
Acknowledgement of paternity, Rule 1910.15
Actions and proceedings, § 4341 et seq.
    Alternate procedure, § 4342
    Attendance, interstate families support enforcement, § 7316
    Appeals, effect, § 4350
    Attachment of income, § 4348
    Bonds or security, attendance or performance, § 4347
    Commencement of proceedings, § 4341
        Expedited procedure, § 4342
    Consolidation of proceedings, § 4349
    Costs, § 4351
    Educational expenses, § 4327
    Entireties property, support order execution against, § 4361 et seq.
    Expedited procedure, § 4342
    Fees, § 4351
    Fees, interstate families support enforcement, § 7313
    Interstate families support enforcement, § 7301 et seq.
    Obligors failure to appear, contempt, § 4344
    Paternity, § 4343, 70 71
    Reports, duties, § 4353
    Security for attendance or performance, § 4347
    Simultaneous proceedings, interstate families support enforcement, § 7204
    Support orders, continuing jurisdiction, § 4352
    Transfers, § 4352
Acts of Assembly, Rules 1910.49, 1910.50
Address or employment changes, support order, Rule 1910 .17, §§ 4352-4353
Administration of support matters, § 4305
Adult children, post-high school programs, educational expenses, Rule 1910.16-5
Agencies, state, cooperation, § 4304
Agreement for support, Rule 1910.11
    Postsecondary education, expenses, applicability, § 4327
Alimony, divorce or annulment actions, Rules 1920.31, 1920.56
Allocation, support order, Rules 1910.16, 1920.56

Support—Cont'd
Alternate hearing procedures, Rules 1910.10, 1910.12
Amount of support, Rules 1910.16-1 to 1910.16-5
Annulment of marriage,
    Disposition of property to defeat support obligations, attachment and injunction, § 3505
Answer, contempt petition, Rule 1910.25
Answers, Rule 1910.7
Appeal and review, § 4350, Rule 1910.12
    Paternity, Rule 1910.15
    Subpoenas, § 4305
    Uniform reciprocal enforcement, § 4534
Appeals, effect, § 4350
Appearance
    Contempt, failure of obligor to appear, § 4344
    Security for attendance or performance, § 4347
Arrearages,
    Child medical support, § 4326
    Conflict of laws, § 7604
    Delinquent obligors, names, publication, § 4309
    Disclosure, consumer reporting agencies, § 4303
    Execution of judgment, Rule 1910.24
    Expedited enforcement, 42 U.S.C. § 666
    Fines and penalties, § 4348
    Income tax refund intercept program, § 4307
    Information to consumer credit bureau, § 4303
    Intrastate families support enforcement, § 8411
    Judgments and decrees, § 4352, Rule 1910.24
    Limitations of actions, § 7604
    Monetary awards, collections, § 4308.1
    Periodic payment schedules, professional or occupational licenses, § 4355
    Reports, consumer reporting agencies, § 4303
    State lottery prize interception, § 4308
    Withholding, 42 U.S.C. § 666
Arrearages, Rules 1910.23-1, 1910.23-2
Arrest, disobedience of court order, Rules 1910.13-1, 1910.13-2, 1910.25

INDEX

References are to Sections of the Pennsylvania Domestic Relations Code, Pennsylvania Crimes Code, Pennsylvania Judicial Code, Pennsylvania Domestic Relations Court Rules, and Selected Federal Statutes, Court Rules, and Regulations

Support—Cont'd
Asset information, definitions, disclosure, cooperation, § 4304.1
Assets, substantial change in circumstance, Rule 1910.19
Attachment,
  Child medical support, insurance, § 4348
  Disposition of property to defeat support obligations, divorce or annulment proceedings, § 3505
  Enforcement of support orders, § 4348, Rule 1910.20
  Forms, Rule 1910.31
  Wages and salaries, § 4348
Attachment of income, Rules 1910.22, 1910.29-1910.31
Attendance, security, § 4347
Attorney fees, intrastate families support enforcement, § 8313
Basic Support Obligation, Rule 1910.16-6
Birth related expenses, definitions, child medical support, § 4326
Bonds, defendant leaving jurisdiction, § 4347, Rule 1910.14
Calculation of support obligation, Rule 1910.1604
Child born out of wedlock, Rule 1910.15
Choice of law, uniform reciprocal enforcement of support, § 4507
Change of address, defendant, Rule 1910.17
Child, definition, interstate families support, § 7101
Child medical support, requirements, § 4326
Child support order, definitions, § 7101, § 8101
Civil contempt, Rule 1910.21
Collection of overdue support from monetary awards, § 4308.1
Colleges and universities, expenses and expenditures, § 4327
Commencement of action, Rule 1910.4
Commencement of proceedings, § 4341, Rule 1910.4
  Expedited procedure, § 4342
Compensation or income
  attachment, Rules 1910.22, 1910.29-1910.31
  forms, Rules 1910.29-1910.31
  notice, attachment, Rules 1910.30, 1910.31
  objections, order of attachment, Rule 1910.30

Support—Cont'd
  orders, Rules 1910.26, 1910.27, 1910.30, 1910.31
  report of earnings, Rule 1910.27
  statement of income and expenses, Rule 1910.26
Common pleas, alternate procedure, support actions, § 4342
Compensation and salaries, monthly gross income, computation, Rule 1910.16-2
Complaint,
  District attorneys, § 4306
  Domestic relations section, presentation, § 4305
  Form, Rule 1910.27
Complaint, Rules 1910.5, 1910.26
Complaint, Service, Rule 1930.4
Compromise and settlement, arrearages, collections, § 4308.1
Computation, Rule 1910.16-1, 1910.16-2
  Factors, Rule 1910.16-5
  Guidelines, Rule 1910.16-3
Conferences,
  Contempt petitions, Rules 1910.2, 1910.25.2
  Failure or refusal to appear, bench warrant, Rules 1910.13-1, 1910.13-2
  Office conference and subsequent proceedings, Role 1910.11
  Officers, Rule 1910.1
  Orders of court, Rule 1910.5
  Summary, Rule 1910.11
  Contempt petitions, Rule 1910.25-3
Consolidation of proceedings, § 4349
Construction of law, § 4106
Consumer credit bureaus, information to, § 4303
Contempt
  Employers, withholding of income, enforcement of support orders, Rule 1910.21
  Failure of obligor to appear, § 4344, Rule 1910.25 et seq.
  Noncompliance, support order, § 4345
  Support orders, noncompliance, § 4345
  Visitation or partial custody orders, non-compliance, § 4346
Contempt, Rule 1910.21-1
Continuing jurisdiction, support orders, § 4352

1309

INDEX

References are to Sections of the Pennsylvania Domestic Relations Code, Pennsylvania Crimes Code, Pennsylvania Judicial Code, Pennsylvania Domestic Relations Court Rules, and Selected Federal Statutes, Court Rules, and Regulations

Support—Cont'd
Cooperation, state agencies, § 4304
Copies, support order, Rule 1910.17
Costs, § 4351, § 7313, § 8313
Crimes and offenses,
    Willful failure to pay, § 4354
Custody of minors, consolidation of actions, § 4349
Custody orders, noncompliance, contempt, § 4346
Deadbeat parents, 18 U.S.C. § 228
Default judgment, § 4342
Defendant leaving jurisdiction, Rule 1910.14
Defenses
    Intrastate families support enforcement, paternity, § 8310
    Non-parentage, § 7315, § 8310
Defined, § 4302
Definitions, § 4302
Denial or suspension of licenses, § 4355
Deviation, support guidelines, Rule 1910.16-4
Discovery, Rule 1910.9, 1910.11, 1930.5
Disobedience of court order, Rule 1910.13
Dissolution of attachment, Rule 1910.22
Divorce or annulment actions, Rules 1920.31, 1920.56
Docket entries, transfer, Rule 1910.8
Domestic relations section,
    Duty to report, § 4353
    Powers and duties, § 4305
Earnings information, Rule 1910.9
Education, post secondary education, expenses and expenditures, § 4327
Effective date, support order, Rule 1910.17
Electronic funds transfers, child support program, § 4374
Electronic testimony, witnesses, Rule 1930.3
Emancipated children, § 4323
Employer, defined, § 4302
Employer of defendant, attachment, Rule 1910.22
Enforcement,
    Attachment of wages, § 4348
    Remedies preservation, § 4366
Enforcement, support order, § 4326, § 4348, Rule 1910.20
Entireties property, execution of support order against, § 4361
    Credit to plaintiff purchaser, § 4364
    Other enforcement remedies preserved, § 4366

Support—Cont'd
    Plaintiff's shares of sale proceeds, § 4362
    Rights of divorced persons to sold property, § 4365
    Trustee to distribute sale proceeds, § 4363
Escrows and escrow agents, arrearages, monetary awards, collections, § 4308.1
Exceptions, contempt petition hearing report, Rule 1910.21-5
Execution of support order against entireties property, § 4361
    Credit to plaintiff purchaser, § 4364
    Other enforcement remedies preserved, § 4366
    Plaintiff's shares of sale proceeds, § 4362
    Rights of divorced persons to sold property, § 4365
    Trustee to distribute sale proceeds, § 4363
Execution, judgment for arrearages, Rule 1910.24
Expedited procedure, commencement of proceedings, § 4342
Expenses and expenditures, statements, forms, Rule 1910.27
Extradition, interstate family support enforcement, § 7801
Failure to appear, contempt, § 4344
Federal child support and establishment of paternity, 42 U.S.C. § 651 et seq.
Fees, § 4351
    Arrearages, information to consumer credit bureau, § 4303
Fees and expenses, Rules 1910.4, 1910.26
Financial institutions, cooperation of financial institutions, § 4304.1
Financial statements and reports, Rule 1910.27, 1910.28
Fines and penalties,
    Arrearages, § 4348
Fines and penalties, support orders, willful failure to pay, § 4354
Foreign states,
    Controlling orders, § 7207
    Enforcement, cooperation, § 4305
    Interstate family support, § 7101 et seq.
    Interstate family support enforcement, collections, § 7310

INDEX

References are to Sections of the Pennsylvania Domestic Relations Code, Pennsylvania Crimes Code, Pennsylvania Judicial Code, Pennsylvania Domestic Relations Court Rules, and Selected Federal Statutes, Court Rules, and Regulations

Support—Cont'd
- Modification of foreign support orders, jurisdiction, § 4352
- Nonparties to interstate family support enforcement, § 7304
- Notice, orders, modification, § 7614
- Orders, § 75 of two
- Uniform reciprocal enforcement of support, generally, post
- Foreign support orders, § 4352
- Forms, Rules 1910.26-1910.31
  - Accident and health insurance, coverage, Rule 1910.27
  - Acknowledgment of paternity, Rule 1910.28
  - Attachment orders, Rule 1910.31
  - Complaint, Rule 1910.27
  - Contempt petitions, notice, Rule 1910.21
  - Earnings reports, Rule 1910.28
  - Income and expense statements, Rule 1910.27
  - Health insurance coverage, information, Rule 1910.27, 1910.28
  - Jury trial demand, Rule 1910.28
  - Notice, right to trial, paternity, Rule 1910.28
  - Order
    - Commencement of action, Rule 1910.27
    - Earnings information, Rule 1910.28
- Formula, support guidelines, Rule 1910.16-4
- Fraudulent transfers, obligor funds, § 4352
- Full faith and credit for child support orders, 28 U.S.C. § 1738B
- Garnishment, § 4348
- Gross income, computation, Rule 1910.16-2
- Grids, guidelines, Rule 1910.16-2
- Guidelines, Rule 1910.16-1 et seq.
  - Child and spousal support, § 4322, Rule 1910.16-3
  - Common pleas, § 4322
  - Departures, Rule 1910.16-5
  - Formulas, Rule 1910.16-3, 1910.16-4
  - Modification, Rule 1910.16-6
  - Multiple families, Rule 1910.16-7
  - Rates and charges, Rule 1910.16-3, 1910.16-4
  - Spousal support, § 4322

Support—Cont'd
- Substantial change in circumstance, Rule 1910.19
- Guidelines, amount of support, Rules 1910.16-1 to 1910.16-5
- Health insurance information,
  - Coverage, form, Rule 1910.26
  - Health and accident insurance, guidelines, Rule 1910.16-6
  - Forms, Rule 1910.28
  - Order, Rule 1910.28
- Hearing officers
  - Attorneys, Rule 1910.12
  - Office conference, Rule 1910.11
- Hearings
  - After office conference, Rule 1910.12
  - Alternative hearing procedures, Rules 1910.10, 1910.12
  - Child-support program, § 4380
  - Contempt petitions, Rule 1910.25-1
    - Record hearing, Rule 1910.25-4
  - Demand after office conference, Rule 1910.11
  - Entireties property, support order execution against, plaintiffs share of proceeds, § 4362
  - Failure or refusal to appear, bench warrant, Rules 1910.13-1, 1910.13-2
  - Intrastate family support enforcement, contest, orders, § 8412
  - Jurisdiction, controlling orders, § 7207
  - Notice, Rule 1920.51
  - Orders, intrastate family support enforcement, contests, § 8412
- High Income Cases, Rule 1910.16-3.1
- Home state, definitions, interstate family support, § 7101
- Identity and identification, disclosure, § 4352
- Incarceration, contempt, Rule 1910.25-5
- Income
  - Attachment, § 4348
  - Computation, Rule 1910.16-2
  - Defined, § 4302
  - Forms, Rule 1910.30
  - Order, Rule 1910.31
  - Withholding, § 7501.1 et seq., Rule 1910.21
- Income and expense statement
  - Forms, Rule 1910.26
  - Office conference, Rule 1910.11
- Income tax, refund intercept program, authorization, § 4307

1311

INDEX

References are to Sections of the Pennsylvania Domestic Relations Code, Pennsylvania Crimes Code, Pennsylvania Judicial Code, Pennsylvania Domestic Relations Court Rules, and Selected Federal Statutes, Court Rules, and Regulations

Support—Cont'd
Information to consumer credit bureaus, § 4303
Injunction,
    Disposition of property to defeat support obligations, divorce or annulment proceedings, § 3505
Injunction, special relief, Rule 1910.25
Interstate family support enforcement
    Communication between tribunals, § 7317
    Confidential or privileged information, § 7316
    Discovery, § 7318
    Evidence, § 7313, § 7316
    Extradition, § 7801
    Family community, § 7316
    Fees, actions and proceedings, § 7313
    Jurisdiction, personal jurisdiction, § 7314
    Multiple orders, two or more obligees, § 7208
    Payments, § 7209, § 7319
    Personal jurisdiction, § 7314
    Pleadings, § 7311
    Privileges and immunities, § 7314, § 7316
    Responding tribunal, powers and duties, § 7305
    Self-incrimination, § 7316
    Service of process, § 7314
    Spouse privilege, § 7316
    Support enforcement agencies, supervision, § 7308
    Witnesses, § 7316
Intrastate family support, generally, § 8101 et seq.
    Action by minor parent, § 8302
    Arrearages, § 8411
    Assistance with discovery, § 8312
    Confirmed order, § 8414
    Contest of registration or enforcement, § 8413
    Continuing, exclusive jurisdiction, § 8201
    Costs and fees, § 8313
    Credit for payments, § 8203
    Defenses, § 8310
    Discovery, § 8312
    Duties and powers of responding tribunal, § 8304
    Duties of initiating tribunal, § 8303
    Duties of support enforcement agency, § 8306

Support—Cont'd
    Effect of a confirmed order, § 8415
    Exceptions, § 8309
    Fees, § 8313
    Hearings, contests, § 8412
    Inappropriate tribunal, § 8305
    Multiple orders, § 8202
    Nondisclosure of information in exceptional circumstances, § 8309
    Nonparentage not a defense, § 8310
    Notice of registration of order, § 8411
    Orders, § 8414, 8415
    Eternity, defenses, § 8310 v.
    Private counsel, § 8308
    Procedure to contest validity of registered order, § 8412
    Procedure to register order, § 8402
    Proceedings under this part, § 8301
    Recognition of support orders, § 8202
    Registration of order, § 8401
    Remedies, § 8103
    Scope, § 8102
    Special rules of evidence and procedure, § 8311
    Supervisory duty, § 8307
Joinder, related claims, Rule 1920.31
Judgments
    Arrearages, execution, Rules 1910.24
    Arrears as judgments, § 4352
    Entireties property, support order execution against, § 4361
    Plaintiffs share of proceeds, entireties property, support order execution against, § 4362
    Relinquishment, parental rights, § 2503
Judgments and orders, Rules 1910.5 et seq.
Judgment by operation of law, defined, § 4302
Jurisdiction,
    Continuing jurisdiction, § 4352
    Crimes and offenses, willful failure to pay, § 4354
    Divorce proceedings, § 3104
    Domicile and residence, § 7201
    Issue raised by defendant, Rule 1910.7
    Long arm jurisdiction, § 4342, § 7201
    Modification of child support order of another state, § 7613
    Nonresidents, § 4342
    Paternity, § 7701

INDEX

References are to Sections of the Pennsylvania Domestic Relations Code, Pennsylvania Crimes Code, Pennsylvania Judicial Code, Pennsylvania Domestic Relations Court Rules, and Selected Federal Statutes, Court Rules, and Regulations

Support—Cont'd
- Simultaneous proceedings, interstate family support enforcement, § 7204
- Jurisdiction, support orders, continuing jurisdiction, § 4352
- Jury trial
  - Demand, form, Rule 1910.28
  - Notice of right to, form, Rule 1910.28
- Liability, § 4321
- Licenses, denial or suspension of, § 4355
- Licenses and permits, overdue support, § 4377
- Long arm jurisdiction, § 4342, 7201
- Long arm procedures, expedited procedure, commencement of proceedings, § 4327
- Lien,
  - Arrears as judgments, § 4352
- Lottery winnings intercept, § 4308
- Masters, appointment, Rule 1920.51
- Medical benefits, allocation, Rule 1910.16-5
- Medical care and treatment, § 4324
- Medical support, inclusion, § 4324
- Modification, Rules 1910.17, 1910.19, Rule 1910.16-6, 1910.19
- Motions
  - Discovery, Rule 1910.12
  - Paternity, post trial motion, Rule 1910.15
  - Separate listing, Rule 1910.11
- Multiple families, guidelines, Rule 1910.16-7
- Net income, defined, § 4302
- New hire reporting,
  - Confidentiality, § 4395
  - Definitions, § 4391
  - Employer reporting, § 4392
  - Guidelines, § 4394
  - Penalties, § 4396
  - Use of information, § 4393
- Notice,
  - Attachment of income, § 4348
    - Form, Rule 1910.29
  - Automatic adjustments, § 4352
  - Child medical support, § 4326
  - Decision, objections to income attachment order, Rule 1910.30
  - Hearings, Rule 1910.11
    - Contempt petition, Rules 1910.25-3, 1910.25-4
  - Judgments and arrears, orders, § 4352

Support—Cont'd
- Modification, termination, Rule 1910.19
- Paternity, trial right, form, Rule 1910.28
- Notice, attachment, Rules 1910.29, 1910.30
- Notices
  - Arrearages, execution of judgment, Rule 1910.23
  - Contempt, Rule 1910.21
  - Right to trial, paternity, form, Rule 1910.28
- Objections, Rules 1910.12, 1910.30
- Obligees, definitions, § 4302
  - Interstate family support, § 7101
  - Entrust a family support enforcement, § 8101
- Obligors, failure to appear, contempt, § 4344
  - Definitions, § 4302
- Office conference, Rules 1910.11, 1910.12
- Operating privileges, denial or suspension of, § 4355
- Operation, support guidelines, Rule 1910.16-5
- Orders
  - Allocation, Rules 1910.16, 1920.56
  - Amendments, attachment orders, Rule 1910.22
  - Appeal and review, § 4350
  - Arrearages, specifications, § 4348
  - Attachment,
    - Income, enforcement, § 4348
  - Attachment, Rule 1910.20, 1910.22
    - Form, Rule 1910.29
  - Commencement of action, form, Rule 1910.26
  - Conference officer recommendations, Rule 1910.12
  - Conferences,
    - Appearance, Rule 1910.5
    - Contempt petitions, Rule 1910.21-3
    - Summary recommendations, Rule 1910.11
  - Contempt, Rule 1910.25-5
    - Attachment, employer payments, Rule 1910.22
    - Enforcement, Rule 1910.20
  - Continuing jurisdiction, § 4352
  - Defendants address, change, Rule 1910.17
  - Disobedience, Rule 1910.13

1313

INDEX

References are to Sections of the Pennsylvania Domestic Relations Code, Pennsylvania Crimes Code, Pennsylvania Judicial Code, Pennsylvania Domestic Relations Court Rules, and Selected Federal Statutes, Court Rules, and Regulations

Support—Cont'd
  Domestic relations office, payment, § 4325
  Earnings information, form, Rule 1910.28
  Effective date, Rule 1910.17
  Employment, loss or change, duty to notify, Rule 1910.17
  Enforcement, Rule 1910.20
  Enforcement, attachment of income, § 4348, Rule 1910.20
  Entry of order, entireties property, execution against, § 4361
  Final orders, Rule 1910.11
    Hearing after office conference, Rule 1910.12
    Paternity, Rule 1910.15
  Foreign support orders, § 4352
  Forms, Rule 1910.26
  Health insurance information, Rule 1910.27
  Income, attachment, Role 1910.31
  Income, loss or change, duty to notify, Rule 1910.17
  Income withholding, § 7501, § 7501.1, § 7501.5
  Modification, Rule 1910.19
  Multiple orders, §§ 7501.2, 7208, 8202
  Orders of support, defined, § 4302
  Payment, domestic relations office, § 4325
  Post secondary education, expenses and expenditures, applicability, § 4327
  priorities and preferences, attachment orders, § 4348
  Special relief, Rule 1910.25
  Spousal support, effect of divorce decree on, Rule 1920.31
  Stay of proceedings, Rule 1910.24
  Subsequent proceedings, Rule 1910.18
  Supersedeas or stay, appeal and review, § 4350, § 7607
  Temporary orders, Rules 1910.11, 1910.12
  Termination, Rule 1910.19
  Visitation or partial custody, noncompliance, contempt, § 4346
Orders and judgments, Rules 1910.5 et seq.
Overdue payments, work activities, § 4352
Overdue support from monetary awards, § 4308.1, Rule 1910.22

Support—Cont'd
  Partial custody, orders, noncompliance, contempt, § 4346, Rule 1915.1
  Parties, Rule 1910.3
  Past due support, definitions, § 4302
  Paternity, § 4343
  Paternity, Rules 1910.7, 1910.15, 1910.28
  Payments, support orders, § 4325
    Willful failure to pay, § 4354
  Pendente lite, Rule 1920.56
  Performance, security, § 4347
  Petitions
    Contempt, Rule 1910.25
    Interstate family support enforcement, § 7304, § 7311
    Orders, interstate family support enforcement, § 7401
    Orders, modification or termination, Rule 1910.27
    Spousal support, divorce proceedings, § 3702
    can't temporary orders, interstate family support enforcement, § 7401
  Pleadings
    Generally, Rules 1910.5, 1910.7, 1910.26
    Complaint, Rules 1910.5, 1910.26
    Forms, Rule 1910.26
    Interstate family support enforcement, § 7311
  Post secondary education, expenses and expenditures, § 4327
    No pleading by defendant required, Rule 1910.7
  Post trial motions, Role 1920.52
  Post-trial relief, Rule 1910.16
    Contempt orders, Rule 1910.25-6
    Motions, Rule 1920.52
  Presumption of correctness of amount of award, Rule 1910.16-1, Rule 1910.16-4
  Proceedings, stay, Rule 1910.24
  Proceeding subsequent to order, Rule 1910.18
  Process, transfer of case, Rule 1910.8
  Property, seizure, special relief, Rule 1910.25
  Public welfare department,
    Domestic relations section, powers and duties, § 4305
    Income tax refund intercept program, authorization, § 4307

INDEX

References are to Sections of the Pennsylvania Domestic Relations Code, Pennsylvania Crimes Code, Pennsylvania Judicial Code, Pennsylvania Domestic Relations Court Rules, and Selected Federal Statutes, Court Rules, and Regulations

Support—Cont'd
Reciprocity, § 7901
Recommendations
    Office conference, Rule 1910.11
        Hearing after office conference, Rule 1910.12
Record, hearing, Rule 1910.12
Recreational licenses, denial or suspension of, § 4355
Relatives not living with the client, 55 Pa. Code § 187.21, et seq.
Reports
    Conference officer, Rule 1910.12
    Contempt petition hearings, Rule 1910.25-4
    Domestic relations section, § 4353
    Earnings report, forms, Rule 1910.28
    Employer information, Rule 1910.22
    Hearings after office conference, Rule 1910.12
    Supplemental reports, earnings information, Rule 1910.22
Retirement and pensions, monthly gross income, computation, Rule 1910.16-2
Revised payment schedules, overdue payments, § 4352
Schedules, guidelines, Rule 1910.16-3
Scope of law, § 4301
Security for attendance or performance, § 4347
Security, defendant leaving jurisdiction, Rule 1910.14
Seizure of property, special relief, Rule 1910.25
Separate listing, motion, Rule 1910.11
Service of process, Rule 1930.4
    Attachment of wages, salary and commissions, Rule 1910.22
    Employers, withholding of income, enforcement of support orders, Rule 1910.21
    Interstate family support enforcement, § 7314
    Long arm jurisdiction, § 7201
Social Security, monthly gross income, computation, temporal 1910.16-2
Social Security numbers, confidential or privileged information, § 4304.1
Special relief, Rule 1910.26
Spousal privilege, interstate family support enforcement, § 7316

Support—Cont'd
Spousal support
    Defined, divorce, § 3101
    Divorce, § 3702
        Enforcement of arrearages, § 3703
        Payment, § 3704
        Rule 1920.31
    Medical support, § 4324
Spousal support guidelines, § 4322
Standing, child-support program, § 4378
State agencies, cooperation, § 4304
State income tax intercept, § 4307
State lottery prize, interception, child-support arrearage, § 4308
Statements
    Income and expense statements, form, Rule 1910.26
    Supplemental income statements, form, Rule 1910.26
Statement of income and expenses, Rule 1910.26
Statute of limitations questions, paternity, Rule 1910.7
Stay of proceedings, Rule 1910.26
Subsequent proceedings, Rules 1910.11, 1910.18
Supersedeas or stay, § 4350, Rule 1910.26 a
Supplemental income statement, form, Rule 1910.26
Support enforcement agencies, § 7101, 8101
Support orders
    Continuing jurisdiction, § 4352
    Defined, § 4302
    Execution against entireties property, § 4361
        Credit to plaintiff purchaser, § 4364
        Other enforcement remedies preserved, § 4366
        Plaintiff's shares of sale proceeds, § 4362
        Rights of divorced persons to sold property, § 4365
        Trustee to distribute sale proceeds § 4363
    Noncompliance, contempt, § 4345
    Orders of support, defined, § 4302
    Payment, § 4325
    Reciprocal Enforcement of Support, generally, this index
    Willful failure to pay, § 4354

INDEX

References are to Sections of the Pennsylvania Domestic Relations Code, Pennsylvania Crimes Code, Pennsylvania Judicial Code, Pennsylvania Domestic Relations Court Rules, and Selected Federal Statutes, Court Rules, and Regulations

Support—Cont'd
Suspension, Acts of Assembly, Rules 1910.49, 1910.50
Tax exemptions, dependency text, Rule 1910.16-2
Taxes, state income tax intercept, § 4307
Temporary orders, Rules 1910.11, 1910.12
Termination, support order, Rule 1910.21
Termination of orders, Rule 1910.19
Termination of orders, Rule 1910.19
Title IV-D attorney, § 4306
Transfer of action, Rule 1910.8
Trial
    Paternity, Rule 1910.15
    Jury trial, demand, form, 1910.28
    Notice of right to trial, form, Rule 1910.28
    Waiver, Rule 1910.28
Tuition, guidelines, Rule 1910.16-6
Unemployment compensation
    child support intercept of unemployment compensation, 43 P.S. § 863.1
Uniform interstate family support, generally, § 7101 et seq.
    Action by minor parent, § 7302
    Administrative enforcement of orders, § 7502
    Assistance with discovery, § 7318
    Application of law of this state, § 7303
    Bases for jurisdiction over nonresident, § 7201
    Choice of law, § 7604
    Conditions of rendition, § 7802
    Communications between tribunals, § 7317
    Confirmed order, § 7608
    Contest of registration or enforcement, § 7607
    Continuing, exclusive jurisdiction, § 7205
    Costs and fees, § 7313
    Credit for payments, § 7209
    Duties and powers of responding tribunal, § 7305
    Duties of department, § 7310
    Duties of initiating tribunal, § 7304
    Duties of support enforcement agency, § 7307
    Effect of registration for enforcement, § 7603
    Effect of registration for modification, § 7610

Support—Cont'd
    Enforcement and modification of support order by tribunal having continuing jurisdiction, § 7206
    Grounds for rendition, § 7801
    Inappropriate tribunal, § 7306
    Initiating and responding tribunal of this state, § 7203
    Limited immunity of petitioner, § 7314
    Modification of child support order of another state, § 7611
    Multiple child support orders for two or more obligees, § 7208
    Nondisclosure of information in exceptional circumstances, § 7312
    Nonparentage as defense, § 7315
    Notice of registration of order, § 7605
    Petition to establish support order, § 7401
    Pleadings and accompanying documents, § 7311
    Private counsel, § 7309
    Procedure to contest validity or enforcement of a registered order, § 7606
    Procedure to register child support order of another state for modification, § 7609
    Procedure to register order for enforcement, § 7602
    Procedure when exercising jurisdiction over nonresident, § 7202
    Proceeding to determine parentage, § 7701
    Proceedings under this part, § 7301
    Receipt and disbursement of payments, § 7319
    Recognition of child support orders, § 7207
    Recognition of the income-withholding order of another state, § 7501
    Recognition of order modified in another state, § 7612
    Registration of order for enforcement, § 7601
    Simultaneous proceedings in another state, § 7204
    Special rules of evidence and procedure, § 7316
    Supervisory duty, § 7308
Venue, Rules 1910.2, 1910.7-1910.8

INDEX

References are to Sections of the Pennsylvania Domestic Relations Code, Pennsylvania Crimes Code, Pennsylvania Judicial Code, Pennsylvania Domestic Relations Court Rules, and Selected Federal Statutes, Court Rules, and Regulations

Support—Cont'd
Visitation, orders, noncompliance, contempt, § 4346
Waiver of trial, acknowledgement of paternity, Rule 1910.28
Withholding of income, enforcement of support orders, Role 1910.21 is a
Workers compensation, arrearages, collections, § 4308.1

Syphilis
Marriage licenses
  Examination, § 1305
  Test, § 1305
Marriage restrictions on license issuance, § 1304
Premarital examinations, physician and laboratory statement preparation, § 1104

—T—

Taxes and Taxation
Alimony and separate maintenance payments, 26 U.S.C. § 71; 26 C.F.R. 1.71-1; 26 C.F.R. § 1.71-1T
Alimony payments, 26 U.S.C. § 215; 26 C.F.R. § 1.215.1; 26 C.F.R. § 1.215-1T
Allowance of deductions for personal exemptions, 26 U.S.C. § 151, § 152
State income tax intercept, support matters, § 4307
Tax exemptions, dependency tax, Rule 1910.16-2
Transfers of property between spouses, 26 U.S.C. § 1041; 26 C.F.R. § 1.1041-1T

Telephones
Child protective services, statewide toll-free telephone number, establishment, § 6332

Testimony, domestic relations, Rule 1930.3

Tenancies by the Entireties
Property
  Conveyances to divorced spouse, § 3508
  Division between divorced persons, § 3507
  Support orders, the execution against, § 4361
    Credit to plaintiff purchaser, § 4364
    Other enforcement remedies preserved, § 4366
    Plaintiff's share of sale proceeds, § 4362
    Rights of divorced persons to sold property, § 4365
    Trustee to distribute sale proceeds, § 4363
Terminally ill, § 5601

Terminate
Defined, common pleas court, Rule 1910.1

Termination
Decree of termination, effect, adoption, § 2521
Involuntary termination. Adoption, this index
Orders, withholding of income, Rule 1910.21
Support order, Rule 1910.19
Termination of orders, Rule 1910.19

Testimony
Child custody jurisdiction
  Refusal, § 5450
  Taking in another state, § 5411
Child custody jurisdiction, taking in another state, § 5359
Divorce action, outside the county, Rule 1920.61
Domestic relations, use of telephones, Rule 1930.3
Petition for adoption, hearings, § 2724

Tests and Testing
Marriage licenses, syphilis, § 1305
Paternity, blood tests to determine, § 5104

Threats
Actions and proceedings,
  Marriage, filing prohibited causes of action, § 1904

Time
Contempt, sentence and punishment, § 3502
Custody of minor children, jurisdiction or revenue objection, Rule 1915.5
Limitation of actions, attacks on decrees, § 3331
Limitation of actions, support actions, Rule 1910.7

1317

INDEX

References are to Sections of the Pennsylvania Domestic Relations Code, Pennsylvania Crimes Code, Pennsylvania Judicial Code, Pennsylvania Domestic Relations Court Rules, and Selected Federal Statutes, Court Rules, and Regulations

Time—Cont'd
Living separate and apart, irretrievably broken marriages, determination, § 3301
Notice, actions and proceedings, Rule 1910.6
Post-trial motions,
  Divorce or annulment of marriage, Rule 1930.2
Service,
  Original process, domestic relations matters, Rule 1930.4

Title IV-D Program
Administration, § 4373
Assistance recipients to seek support, § 4378
Central registry, § 4376
Definitions, § 4371
Establishment, § 4372
Garnishment of wages of Commonwealth employees, § 4381
Power to expedite support cases, § 4377
State disbursement unit, § 4374

Title to Property
Entireties property, sale on execution of support order, purchase or title of validity, § 4361

Tortious Acts
Defined, torts of children, § 5501

Torts
Liability for Torts of Children, generally, this index

Training
Child protective services, § 6383

Transfer
Custody of minor children, Rule 1915.2
Intrastate family support enforcement, inappropriate tribunal, § 8305
Support actions, Rule 1910.8
Venue, Rule 1910.2

Treatment
Child protective services, services for prevention and treatment of child abuse, § 6365

Trial
Divorce, jury trial, § 3322
Paternity; support actions, Rule 1910.15
Torts of minors, parental liability, § 5504
Waiver, support actions, Rule 1910.28
Witnesses, generally, this index

Trier of Fact
Defined, common pleas court, Rule 1910.1

Trusts and Trustees
Constructive trusts, undisclosed assets of parties, divorce or annulment proceedings, § 3505
Support of persons,
  Entireties property, support order execution against, proceeds distribution, § 4363

Tuition
Guidelines, Rule 1910.16-6

—U—

Under Investigation
Defined, child protective services, § 6303

Unfounded Reports
Child protective services, disposition, § 6337
Defined, child protective services, § 6303

Unemployment Compensation
Child support intercept of unemployment compensation, 43 P.S. § 863.1

Uniform Act on Blood Test to Determine Paternity
Generally, § 5104

Uniform Acts
Blood tests to determine paternity, § 5104
Child abduction prevention, generally, § 5201 et seq.
Custody, generally. Children and Minors, this index
Uniform Child Custody Jurisdiction and Enforcement Act (UCCJEA)
  Generally, § 5401, et seq.
Uniform interstate family support,
  Generally, § 7101 et seq.

INDEX

References are to Sections of the Pennsylvania Domestic Relations Code, Pennsylvania Crimes Code, Pennsylvania Judicial Code, Pennsylvania Domestic Relations Court Rules, and Selected Federal Statutes, Court Rules, and Regulations

—V—

Vacate
Decrees, motion, § 3332
Defined, common pleas court, Rule 1910.1

Valuation
Nonmarital property, § 3501
Property set apart to each party, marital property division, § 3502

Venue
Abuse, protection, Rule 1901.1
Adoption, § 2302
Alimony, Rule 1910.2
Adoption, § 2302
Annulment of marriage, § 3104
Custody, partial custody and visitation actions, Rules 1915.2, 1915.5
Divorce or annulment actions, Rule 1920.2
Divorce, § 3104
Domicile and residence, alimony, Rule 1910.2
Forum non-conveniens, § 5426, § 5427
Protection from Abuse Act actions, Rule 1901.1
Support actions, Rules 1910.2, 1910.7
Transfers, alimony, Rule 1910.2
Visitation, Rule 1915.2

Veterans Benefits
Marital property status, § 3501

Victims
Defined, protection from abuse, § 6102

Visitation
Appointment of attorney, Rule 1915.11
Arrest, disobedience of court order, Rule 1915.14
Attorneys, appointment for child, Rule 1915.11
Bonds or security, Rule 1915.13
Commencement of action, Rule 1915.3
Complaint, Rule 1915.3
 Form, Rule 1915.15
Consent orders, Rule 1915.7
Contempt, Rule 1915.12
Costs
 Appointment of attorney for child, Rule 1915.11
 Examinations, Rule 1915.8
Counterclaim, Rule 1915.5
Default judgments, Rule 1915.9
Definitions, custody of minor children, § 5302, Rule 1915.1
Discovery, Rules 1915.5, 1930.5

Visitation—Cont'd
Docket entries, transfer of actions, Rule 1915.2
Examinations, Rule 1915.8
Final orders, Rule 1915.10
Forms
 Appearance, order, Rule 1915.15
 Complaint, Rule 1915.15
 Contempt, notice and order to appear, Rule 1915.12
 Intervention of parties, order and notice, Rule 1915.16
 Joinder of party, order and notice, Rule 1915.16
Hearings,
 By court, decision and post-trial relief, Rule 1920.52
 Judge, alternative procedures, Rule 1915.4-1
 Officer, Rule 1915.4-2
Interrogation of child, Rule 1915.11
Intervention, Rule 1915.6
 Order and notice, form, Rule 1915.16
Joinder of parties, Rule 1915.6
 Order and notice, form, Rule 1915.16
Judgments, default, Rule 1915.9
Jurisdiction, time of objections, Rule 1915.5
Masters, appointment, Rule 1920.51
Mental examinations, Rule 1915.8
Noncompliance, contempt, § 4346
Notice and order to appear, contempt, Rule 1915.12
Notices
 Contempt, Rule 1915.12
 Examinations, Rule 1915.8
 Intervention, Rule 1915.6
 Joinder of parties, Rule 1915.6
 Joinder or intervention of parties, form, Rule 1915.16
Orders
 Appearance, Rules 1915.3, 1915.12
 Consent orders, Rule 1915.7
 Contempt, Rule 1915.12
 Defendants appearance, Rule 1915.3
 Disobedience
  Contempt, Rules 1915.12, 1915.14
 Evidence, exclusion, Rule 1915.8
 Examinations, Rule 1915.8

1319

INDEX

References are to Sections of the Pennsylvania Domestic Relations Code, Pennsylvania Crimes Code, Pennsylvania Judicial Code, Pennsylvania Domestic Relations Court Rules, and Selected Federal Statutes, Court Rules, and Regulations

Visitation—Cont'd
  Examinations, Rule 1915.8
  Final orders, Rule 1915.10
  Form, Rule 1915.15
  Joinder or intervention of parties, form, Rule 1915.16
  Support proceedings, Rule 1915.1
  Orders, noncompliance, contempt, support, § 4346
  Petitions, contempt, Rule 1915.12
  Physical examinations, Rule 1915.8
  Pleadings
    Defendants response, Rule 1915.5
    Transfer of actions, Rule 1915.2
  Post-trial relief motions, unavailability, Rule 1915.10
  Process, transfer of actions, Rule 1915.2
  Records, interrogation of child, Rule 1915.11
  Reports, examination, Rule 1915.8
  Service, Rule 1930.4
    Contempt, order to appear, Rule 1915.12
    Joinder of parties, Rule 1915.6
  Special relief, Rule 1915.13
  Support of persons, noncompliance, contempt, § 4346

Visitation—Cont'd
  Transfer of action, Rule 1915.2
  Venue, Rule 1915.2
    Time of objections, Rule 1915.5

Vital Statistics Information
  Divorce or annulment actions, Rule 1920.46
  Licenses and permits,
    Marriage license, defined, § 1102
  Marriage,
    Licenses and returns,
      Records, § 1106

Vocational Skills
  Marital property division factor, divorce and annulment of marriage proceedings, § 3502

Void Marriages
  Annulment, § 3303
    Grounds, § 3304

Voidable Marriages
  Annulment, § 3303
    Grounds, § 3305

Voluntary Relinquishment
  Adoption, this index

—W—

Wages
Compensation and Salaries, generally, this index

Waiting Period
Marriage licenses, § 1303

Waiver
Notice, judgments and decrees, entry, Rule 1920.72
Trial, support actions, Rule 1910.28

Warrant of Attorney
Divorce and annulment actions, Rule 1920.5

Warrants
Bench warrants
  Custody of minor children, Rule 1915.12

Weapons
Actions and proceedings, domestic violence, safekeeping permits, § 6108.3
Arrests, searches and seizures, domestic violence, § 6113

Weapons—Cont'd
Attorney fees, domestic violence, safekeeping permits, § 6108.3
Criminal history record information, § 6107
Dealers, domestic violence, § 6108, § 6108.2
Definitions, domestic violence, protection from abuse, § 6102
Domestic violence, actions and proceedings, § 6108.3, § 6108.4
Fines and penalties, licenses and permits, safekeeping permits, § 6108.3
Forms, domestic violence, temporary relinquishment, Rule 1905
Hearings, domestic violence, temporary relinquishment, modification, § 6108.1
Licenses and permits, actions and proceedings, safekeeping permits, § 6108.3
Modification, domestic violence, temporary relinquishment, 6108.1

INDEX

References are to Sections of the Pennsylvania Domestic Relations Code, Pennsylvania Crimes Code, Pennsylvania Judicial Code, Pennsylvania Domestic Relations Court Rules, and Selected Federal Statutes, Court Rules, and Regulations

Weapons—Cont'd
Petitions, domestic violence, temporary relinquishment, modification, § 6108.1
Privileges and immunities, peace officers, domestic violence, § 6119
Protection orders, domestic violence, temporary relinquishment, forms, Rule 1905
Punitive damages, domestic violence, safekeeping permits, § 6108.3
Relinquishment, protection from abuse, forms, Rule 1905
Returns, temporary relinquishment, domestic violence, § 6108.1
Safekeeping, domestic violence, § 6107, § 6108
Third parties, domestic violence, temporary relinquishment, § 6108.3
Transfers, domestic violence, safekeeping permits, third parties, § 6108.3
Warrants, searches and seizures, domestic violence, § 6121

Wife
Husband and Wife, generally, this index

Willful Desertion
Divorce, grounds, § 3301

Witnesses
Adoption, competency of mother, status of presumptive or putative father as natural father, § 2513
Children and minors,
    Child custody jurisdiction, taking testimony in another state, § 5359 Parental rights termination, competency of parents, § 2513
Divorce or annulment of marriage actions, testimony taken by master, witness outside county, Rule 1920.61
Electronic testimony, Rule 1930.3
Interstate family support enforcement, § 7316
Intrastate family support enforcement, § 8311
Opinion and expert testimony,
    Paternity blood tests, compensation of experts, § 5104
Perjury, generally, this index
Petition for adoption, hearing, § 2724

Words and Phrases
Generally, § 102

Words and Phrases—Cont'd
Abuse, protection from abuse, § 6102
Abuse, protection from abuse, Rules 1901, 1920.1
Adoptee, adoption, § 2102
Adult, protection from abuse, § 6102
Agency, adoption, § 2102
Alimony, divorce, § 3103
Alimony pendente lite, divorce, § 3103
Child
    Custody, § 5302
    Torts of children, § 5501
Child abuse, child protective services, § 6303
Child protective service, § 6303
Child-care services, child protective services, § 6303
Clerk, § 102
    Adoption, § 2102
Clerk of court, § 102
Conference officer, common pleas court, Rule 1910.1
Confidential communications, protection from abuse, § 6102
Contestant, child custody jurisdiction, § 5343
Cooperation with an investigation, child protective services, § 6303
Court, § 102
    Adoption, § 2102
Custody, Rule 1915.1
Custody decree, child custody jurisdiction, § 5343
Custody determination, child custody jurisdiction, § 5343
Custody proceeding, child custody jurisdiction, § 5343
Decree, child custody jurisdiction, § 5343
Department
    Adoption, § 2551
    Child protective services, § 6303
    Marriage, § 1102
    Pennsylvania Adoption Cooperative Exchange, § 2551
Divorce, § 3103
Divorce, Rule 1920.1
Domestic violence counselor-advocate, protection from abuse, § 6102
Domestic violence program, protection from abuse, § 6102
Employer, support, § 4302
Expunge, child protective services, § 6303

INDEX

References are to Sections of the Pennsylvania Domestic Relations Code, Pennsylvania Crimes Code, Pennsylvania Judicial Code, Pennsylvania Domestic Relations Court Rules, and Selected Federal Statutes, Court Rules, and Regulations

Words and Phrases—Cont'd
Family members, child protective services, § 6303
Family or household members, protection from abuse, § 6102
Founded report, child protective services, § 6303
Grounds for divorce, divorce, § 3103
Hearing officer, common pleas court, Rule 1910.1
Hearing officer, protection from abuse, § 6102
Home county, custody, Rule 1915.1
Home state, child custody jurisdiction, § 5343
Income, support, § 4302
Indicated report, child protective services, § 6303
Initial decree, child custody jurisdiction, § 5343
Injury, torts of children, § 5501
Intermediary, adoption, § 2102
Irretrievable breakdown, divorce, § 3103
Judgment by operation of law, support, § 4302
Legal custody, custody, § 5302
Legal custody, minor children, Rule 1915.1
License, marriage, § 1102
Marital property, divorce, § 3501
Marriage license, marriage, § 1102
Medical history information, adoption, § 2102
Minor, protection from abuse, § 6102
Modification decree, child custody jurisdiction, § 5343
Net income, support, § 4302
Order of support, support, § 4302
PACE, Pennsylvania Adoption Cooperative Exchange, § 2551
Parent
    Adoption, § 2102
    Torts of children, § 5501
Partial custody, custody, § 5302

Words and Phrases—Cont'd
Partial custody, Rule 1915.1
Person acting as parent, child custody jurisdiction, § 5343
Person acting as parent, custody or visitation of minors, Rule 1915.1
Person, torts of children, § 5501
Physical custody
    Child custody jurisdiction, § 5343
    Custody, § 5302
    Minor children, Rule 1915.1
Protection from abuse act, Rule 1901, 1920.1
Qualified professionals, divorce, § 3103
Secretary, child protective services, § 6303
Separate and apart, divorce, § 3103
Serious bodily injury, child protective services, confidential information, § 6340
Sexual abuse, child protective services, § 6303
Shared custody, custody, § 5302
Shared custody, Rule 1915.1
Spousal support, divorce, § 3103
Subject of the report, child protective services, § 6303
Support, § 4302
Suspend, common pleas court, Rule 1910.1
Terminate, common pleas court, Rule 1910.1
Tortious act, torts of children, § 5501
Under investigation, child protective services, § 6303
Unfounded report, child protective services, § 6303
Victim, protection from abuse, § 6102
Visitation, custody, § 5302
Visitation, minor children, Rule 1915.1

Workers' Compensation
Collection of overdue support from monetary awards, § 4308.1

—X—

X-Rays
Child protective services, reporting suspected child abuse, § 6314